# THE WOLTERS KLUWER

# BOUVIER
# LAW DICTIONARY

*Compact Edition*

THE WOLTERS KLUWER

# BOUVIER
# LAW DICTIONARY

*Compact Edition*

Stephen Michael Sheppard
*General Editor*

Wolters Kluwer
Law & Business

Published by Wolters Kluwer Law & Business in New York.

Wolters Kluwer Law & Business serves customers worldwide with CCH, Aspen Publishers, and Kluwer Law International products. (www.wolterskluwerlb.com)

To contact Customer Service, e-mail customer.service@wolterskluwer.com, call 1–800–234–1660, fax 1–800–901–9075, or mail correspondence to:

Wolters Kluwer Law & Business
Attn: Order Department
PO Box 990
Frederick, MD 21705

Printed in the United States of America.

1 2 3 4 5 6 7 8 9 0

ISBN 978-0-7355-6852-5

**Library of Congress Cataloging–in–Publication Data**

The Wolters Kluwer Bouvier law dictionary / Stephen Michael Sheppard, general editor. — Compact ed.
    p. cm.
  Based on Bouvier's final text and other classic materials.
  Includes bibliographical references.
  ISBN 978-0-7355-6852-5
  1. Law — United States — Dictionaries.  I. Sheppard, Steve, 1963– II. Bouvier, John, 1787–1851. A law dictionary, adapted to the Constitution and laws of the United States of America, and of the several states of the American union. III. Title: Bouvier law dictionary.
  KF156.W65 2011
  349.7303 — dc23

2011018820

# About Wolters Kluwer Law & Business

Wolters Kluwer Law & Business is a leading global provider of intelligent information and digital solutions for legal and business professionals in key specialty areas, and respected educational resources for professors and law students. Wolters Kluwer Law & Business connects legal and business professionals as well as those in the education market with timely, specialized authoritative content and information–enabled solutions to support success through productivity, accuracy and mobility.

Serving customers worldwide, Wolters Kluwer Law & Business products include those under the Aspen Publishers, CCH, Kluwer Law International, Loislaw, Best Case, ftwilliam. com and MediRegs family of products.

**CCH** products have been a trusted resource since 1913, and are highly regarded resources for legal, securities, antitrust and trade regulation, government contracting, banking, pension, payroll, employment and labor, and healthcare reimbursement and compliance professionals.

**Aspen Publishers** products provide essential information to attorneys, business professionals and law students. Written by preeminent authorities, the product line offers analytical and practical information in a range of specialty practice areas from securities law and intellectual property to mergers and acquisitions and pension/benefits. Aspen's trusted legal education resources provide professors and students with high–quality, up–to–date and effective resources for successful instruction and study in all areas of the law.

**Kluwer Law International** products provide the global business community with reliable international legal information in English. Legal practitioners, corporate counsel and business executives around the world rely on Kluwer Law journals, looseleafs, books, and electronic products for comprehensive information in many areas of international legal practice.

**Loislaw** is a comprehensive online legal research product providing legal content to law firm practitioners of various specializations. Loislaw provides attorneys with the ability to quickly and efficiently find the necessary legal information they need, when and where they need it, by facilitating access to primary law as well as state–specific law, records, forms and treatises.

**Best Case Solutions** is the leading bankruptcy software product to the bankruptcy industry. It provides software and workflow tools to flawlessly streamline petition preparation and the electronic filing process, while timely incorporating ever–changing court requirements.

**ftwilliam.com** offers employee benefits professionals the highest quality plan documents (retirement, welfare and non–qualified) and government forms (5500/PBGC, 1099 and IRS) software at highly competitive prices.

**MediRegs** products provide integrated health care compliance content and software solutions for professionals in healthcare, higher education and life sciences, including professionals in accounting, law and consulting.

Wolters Kluwer Law & Business, a division of Wolters Kluwer, is headquartered in New York. Wolters Kluwer is a market–leading global information services company focused on professionals.

# Contents

**Welcome to the Bouvier Law Dictionary**      **ix**

Caveat Lector      ix

John Bouvier and His Law Dictionary      ix

Scope of the 2011 Editions      ix

**How to Use the Bouvier Law Dictionary Compact Edition**      **xi**

The Order of Words and Phrases      xi
Locating Terms by Topic or Idea      xi
Rules for Alphabetization      xi

The Structure of Entries      xi
Homonym Entries      xi
Cross–References      xi

Occasional Suspension of the Rules      xii

**The Bouvier Law Dictionary Project**      **xiii**

Acknowledgments      xv

---

**The Entries, A–Z      1**

---

First Appendix
**The Declaration of Independence and the United States Constitution      1205**

Second Appendix
**Justices of the United States Supreme Court      1216**

# Welcome to the Bouvier Law Dictionary

The world of law is a world of words. To understand law requires understanding each word and each phrase through which it exists and is employed. More importantly, understanding these words and phrases requires understanding the nuance, variation, complexity, and controversy affecting the meaning of each term in different contexts. The customary tool for this understanding is a law dictionary.

This dictionary is directly based on the first major dictionary of American law, the great dictionary of John Bouvier. In the early 1800's, he defined each term with more than a brief statement, giving a summary followed by a long narrative of the term's meaning in context, based on illustrations chosen from classic and current treatises, statutes, and cases as well as the usage of the lawyers of his time. He drew material from U.S. law as well as English, Scots, French, Spanish, Dutch, German, and other national sources, which were the sources of law that influenced or controlled many questions before the American courts in the early republic.

The Bouvier Law Dictionary is an entirely new book, with new definitions for every term, based on quotations and entries from tens of thousands of new cases, books, and statutes, as well as on Bouvier's final text and other classic materials. The plan follows his patterns, with terms organized both by their relationship in the law and by the alphabet. Moreover, it has longer entries than has become typical of dictionaries, often including discussions of concepts and providing related sub-entries, even when the sub-entry does not happen to start with the same letter as the entry. Thus, this dictionary gives more information about most terms than other modern American law dictionaries, though it may not incorporate every possible term from history or practice.

## Caveat Lector ("Let the Reader Beware")

A legal dictionary is a useful tool, but like all tools it must be used wisely. The Bouvier team has worked for nearly a decade to research, draft, and refine these definitions in order to help the reader understand what each word or phrase means in general and in some context of the role it plays in the law. Many words — in law, as in all speech and writing — vary in their meanings in different contexts. Different fields of law, different jurisdictions, even different sources of law in the same field and venue, may all use terms differently. The statements of the law that are incorporated into these definitions are intended to give light to the meaning of the word or phrase being defined, but they might not be accurate statements of the law in a given jurisdiction.

## John Bouvier and His Law Dictionary

In 1839, John Bouvier wrote and published *A Law Dictionary, Adapted to the Constitution and Laws of the United States of America, and of the Several States of the American Union; with References to the Civil and Other Systems of Foreign Law*. For the next hundred years, the *Bouvier* was the essential legal reference work in the United States. It was the dictionary of Daniel Webster, Abraham Lincoln, and Justice Oliver Wendell Holmes, Jr. It remained important in the twentieth century, being a reference of choice for the likes of Karl Llewellyn, John Henry Wigmore, and E. Allan Farnsworth.

Bouvier was born in France in 1787, immigrating with his family to Philadelphia when he was fifteen. His father died while John was a teenager, and he became apprenticed to a Philadelphia printer, opening his own press in 1808. He ran *The American Telegraph*, a weekly newspaper, and began studying law, becoming a lawyer in 1818 and a judge in 1836. An excellent writer, Bouvier wrote several law books, including the *Institutes of American Law*, but he is best remembered for the book to which he dedicated the remainder of his life — his dictionary.

The first law dictionary written for American lawyers, Bouvier's *Law Dictionary* included many terms from other legal systems, which he believed were necessary for a lawyer to understand and to practice law in the United States. It was encyclopedic, with long entries noting subtle differences in meaning and application, and it cited great numbers of opinions and other authorities, sometimes quoting them at length both to illustrate a term and to encourage readers to examine the original source. John Bouvier collected new material throughout his life, overseeing a second and a third edition. The 1853, or fourth edition, was published after his death, incorporating notes left in his papers.

Bouvier's dictionary was maintained and revised by later editors, including Francis Rawle (1846–1930), Daniel Angell Gleason (1836–1908), and William Edward Baldwin (1883–1966). Many publishers have presented different editions of the work, including the 1880 edition published by Little, Brown, a predecessor company to the Aspen Publishers division of Wolters Kluwer Law & Business. Newly printed copies of earlier editions may be purchased from Lawbook Exchange, a law publisher in Clark, New Jersey, and at www.lawbookexchange.com.

This 2011 edition, under the general editorship of Steve Sheppard, was commenced in 2005.

## Scope of the 2011 Editions

*The Bouvier Law Dictionary* is being published in three editions for 2011: this compact edition, a desk edition, and an electronic edition. The compact edition includes all of the terms, along with their complete definitions, that appear in the other editions, and more than 8,000 entries defining over 10,000 terms. This compares well with the 6,600 terms of John Bouvier's great dictionary. The terms defined are selected because they are essential for the general study and practice of law. Added to these are a few terms to illustrate other ideas and concepts that a well-rounded lawyer should know or might find interesting. For example, this edition includes some essential terms of legal slang, including a number of Yiddish terms often used by lawyers.

The compact edition includes a complete and authoritative transcription of the U.S. Constitution and the Declaration of Independence. It also includes short biographies of every justice of the United States Supreme Court.

> Words are the only tools lawyers have. Just as a skilled carpenter wouldn't drive a nail with a screwdriver, skilled legal writers don't use *fortuitous* when they mean *fortunate*, or *infer* when they mean *imply*.
>
> Bryan A. Garner, *The Word on the Street*, in *Garner on Language and Writing* 215, 218 (ABA 2009) (in homage to Charles Alan Wright).

# A

**a**   The first letter of the modern English alphabet. "A" signifies a variety of functions as a symbol, as a designation of status, and as a word in English and in Latin. It is sometimes invoked by alpha, the word for the first letter in Greek. It is also translated into Alpha (or Alfa) for radio signals and NATO military transmissions, into Adam for some police radio traffic, and into dot, dash in Morse Code.

**a as an abbreviation**   A word commencing in A. When used as the sole letter of an abbreviation, A may stand for the Atlantic Reporter. As a component of other abbreviations, A can stand for any word commencing with that letter, particularly able, abridgment, abstract, academy, accident, account, accountants, accounting, acquired, acts, ad, adjustment, administrator, administrative, admiralty, advanced, advisory, Africa, against, age, agency, agricultural, agriculture, aid, air, Alabama, Alaska, Albany, Alberta, alliance, all, alternative, American, analysis, and, annual, anno, annotated, answer, ante, anti-, appeals, appellant, appellate, appellee, arbitration, Arizona, Arkansas, army, art, arts, asbestos, Asian, association, atomic, attorneys, average, aviation, Australia, authority, and automatic. It may also stand for the initial of the name of an author or case reporter, such as Abbot and Angell. In the transcript of a trial or deposition, "a" designates an answer.

**a as a French word**   After, at, by, for, from, have, to, or in. A may be either a preposition or a verb in Law French. As a preposition, it has a variety of quite different meanings from the Latin: "A la mode" is "after the fashion." "Tenant a volunt" is "tenant at will." "A tort" is "by wrong." "A causa de cy" is "for this reason," and "profit a prendre" is "rights in property from another." A is also the third person form of many verbs, so "il a" is "he has."

**a as a Latin abbreviation**   A vote signalled by the letter a. A was an abbreviation with two senses in Roman law: the sign in the questiones, or criminal tribunals, for absolvo, a vote for acquittal, as opposed to C for condemno. In the comitia, or popular assembly, A was the mark for rejecting new legislation, the sign for antiquo, a vote to leave the old law intact, as opposed to UR for uti rogas, or as you propose, a vote for the new legislation.

**a as a Latin word**   From. A is a form of the Latin preposition ab, which can mean in English from, as well as out of, away from, down from, since, after or other words that describe the derivation of one thing from another, as in a priori (from the cause is derived the result) or a postiori (from the result is derived the cause). Note: the idea of "from" is a bit clunky in these translations, because it often stands in for the reasoning implied in the Latin word "a" in the phrase.

**a as a rating**   Of the highest grade. A is used in a variety of forms for rating the quality of specific products. Many regulatory definitions depend on an alphabetic listing, with A the highest tier. For instance, Grade A beef signals meat from the least mature animal, a cow having a physiological maturity of 9–30 months, as opposed to older animals with coarser meat. Many private ratings also use A as the highest recommendation. For example, bonds are rated by Moody's and other rating services on a three–tier scale, with A bonds the highest quality, and that tier being divided among AAA, AA1, AA2, AA3, A1, A2, A3 (prior to 1996 being A, AA, and AAA), the more letters and the lower the number signal the least risk and highest quality.

*See also:* c, c as a rating.

**a as an English word**   An unspecified one among others. When used as a word, A is an indefinite article, usually meaning one but not a specific one out of a group. It might also mean one of an indeterminate group. The context of the word's use is essential in determining its degree of intended specificity.

**a as criminal label**   A brand for adultery. A was the brand for those found guilty of adultery who were not executed. It is depicted as a cloth letter A worn for life in Nathaniel Hawthorne's novels, which is perhaps not historically accurate. The punishment for adultery in colonial Massachusetts was death, or whipping followed by a requirement to wear an AD for a time.

*See also:* punishment, shaming punishment, scarlet letter.

**a as in hypotheticals**   The first character, or sometimes the second, in the story. When used as the sole letter of an abbreviation, A often stands for a person in the story of a law school hypothetical. In property stories, A is usually the second character, receiving property from O, the owner (as in O to A for life then B.) In most other stories, A is the first character in the plot of the story (as in A enters K with B).

**a coelo usque ad centrum**   *See:* coelum, a coelo usque ad centrum.

**a fortiori**   An argument based on an even stronger argument. A claim a fortiori is one based on another argument or a principle that is so strong as to be unanswerable, or nearly so. Arguments a fortiori are generally offered as a rhetorical flourish in the expectation that no one can stand against them, but they are also vulnerable to the rebuttal that the argument made is not necessarily a conclusion to be derived from the principle that supposedly underlies it.

**a posteriori (a postiori)**  From subsequent understanding. A postiori knowledge arises from observation, measurement, comparison, or testing of the evidence. It is what is known after investigation. Thus, a statement of truth a postiori is roughly equivalent to a statement of what one observes. It is the opposite of a priori, or what is known by reason alone without the use of observation. Statements a postiori are vulnerable to claims that the observations that underly them are faulty or that the reasoning leading from the thing observed to the statement derived is faulty. A posteriori is the accepted modern spelling, although the concept is sometimes written a postiori.
*See also:* a, a priori; prior.

**a prendre**  *See:* profit, profit a prendre (profits a prendre).

**a priori**  From an earlier understanding. A priori knowledge arises from intuition or understanding, prior to investigation. It is what is known before research is conducted. Thus, a statement of a priori truth is equivalent to a hypothesis. It is an assertion from untested assumptions, and the opposite of a postiori. Both terms are statements of legal epistemology.
*See also:* a, a posteriori (a postiori).

**a quo**  From which. A quo signals the starting time or day, especially the beginning of the running of a period, such as a time for filing an appeal or the running of a statute of limitations. That day is generally within the time calculated.
*See also:* ad, ad quem.

**A.A.A. or AAA**  *See:* arbitration, American Arbitration Association (A.A.A. or AAA); agriculture, Agricultural Adjustment Act (A.A.A. or AAA).

**A.A.L.S. or AALS**  *See:* law, law school, Association of American Law Schools (A.A.L.S. or AALS).

**A.B.A. or ABA**  *See:* bar, bar organization, American Bar Association (A.B.A. or ABA).

**A.C.L.U. or ACLU**  *See:* civil rights, civil rights organization, American Civil Liberties Union (A.C.L.U. or ACLU).

**A.C.O. or ACO**  *See:* order, administrative order, administrative compliance order (A.C.O. or ACO).

**A.C.T.L. or ACTL**  *See:* bar, bar organization, American College of Trial Lawyers (A.C.T.L. or ACTL).

**A.D.**  *See:* anno domini (A.D.).

**A.D.A. or ADA**  *See:* disability, personal disability, Americans with Disabilities Act (A.D.A. or ADA).

**A.D.E.A. or ADEA**  *See:* discrimination, Age Discrimination in Employment Act (A.D.E.A. or ADEA).

**A.D.R. or ADR**  *See:* alternative dispute resolution (A.D.R. or ADR).

**A.I.A. or AIA**  *See:* injunction, Anti-Injunction Act (A.I.A. or AIA).

**A.I.D.S. or AIDS**  *See:* Acquired Immune Deficiency Syndrome (A.I.D.S. or AIDS).

**a.k.a. or a/k/a or aka**  *See:* also known as (a.k.a. or a/k/a or aka).

**A.L.I. or ALI**  *See:* reform, law reform, American law Institute (A.L.I. or ALI).

**A.L.J. or ALJ**  *See:* judge, administrative law judge (A.L.J. or ALJ).

**A.L.W.D. Citation Manual or ALWD Citation Manual**  *See:* citation, citation manual, Association of Legal Writing Directors Citation Manual (A.L.W.D. Citation Manual or ALWD Citation Manual).

**A.M.A. or AMA**  *See:* medicine, medical association, American Medical Association (A.M.A. or AMA).

**A.M.E.X. or AMEX**  *See:* security, securities, securities exchange, American Stock Exchange (A.M.E.X. or AMEX).

**A.M.T. or AMT**  *See:* tax, income tax, alternative minimum tax (A.M.T. or AMT).

**A.R.M. or ARM**  *See:* mortgage, adjustable-rate mortgage (A.R.M. or ARM).

**A.T.L.A. or ATLA**  *See:* bar, bar organization, American Trial Lawyers Association (A.T.L.A. or ATLA).

**A.W.O.L. or AWOL**  *See:* absence, absent without leave (A.W.O.L. or AWOL).

**AAJ or Association of Trial Lawyers of America or ATLA**  *See:* bar, bar organization, Association for American Justice (AAJ or Association of Trial Lawyers of America or ATLA).

**ab**  From. The Latin preposition ab, which can mean in English "from" as well as "out of," "away from," "down from," "since," "after," or other words that describe the derivation of one thing from another.
*See also:* trade, international trade, World Trade Organization, standing appellate body (AB).

**ab initio**  From the beginning. To say that something has an aspect ab initio is to say that the aspect has been present in something from the beginning of the relevant time, which is usually since the creation of the thing in question. The statement X is Y ab initio is usually made following a discovery of an effect unknown before, a discovery about X that leads to the conclusion Y. A contract the parties thought was good but that was made for what became known to be an illegal purpose was void ab initio, or void from the start, even if it was only later discovered to be illegal.

*See also:* void (voidability, voidable); ab; initio.

**abandonment (abandon)**  To give up something forever. Abandonment, the act of letting go of any claim of right or potential claim of right in property or other interests, is based on an intent to completely disconnect oneself from someone or something. This intent may be implied from circumstances, as in child abandonment, but it usually must be proven from affirmative acts. Abandonment is sometimes used to describe the condition of having been abandoned.

*See also:* abscondment (abscond or absconding); abandonment, abandonment as non-support; vessel, abandonment of a vessel; dereliction; patent, abandonment of a patent; abandonment, medical abandonment (abandonment of a patient).

**abandonment of a patent**  *See:* patent, abandonment of a patent, express abandonment (formal abandonment); patent, abandonment of a patent, constructive abandonment of a patent (statutory forfeiture or prior public use bar); patent, abandonment of a patent.

**abandonment of a privacy interest**  *See:* interest, privacy interest, abandonment of a privacy interest.

**abandonment of a vessel**  *See:* vessel, abandonment of a vessel.

**abandonment of an equitable servitude**  *See:* servitude, equitable servitude, abandonment of an equitable servitude.

**abandonment of spouse**  *See:* divorce, abandonment of spouse.

**abandonee**  One to whom property is abandoned. An abandonee is the recipient of abandoned property. The term is rarely heard outside of admiralty, which has rules such as salvor's and underwriter's rights dedicating particular interests once abandoned. In general abandonment does not allow an act of will to vest ownership in another person. An act of surrender of property under the common law to the ownership of a particular person is usually a donation or a grant, not an abandonment.

*See also:* salvage.

**abandonment as contract rescission**  Mutual avoidance of a contract by all of the parties to it. Abandonment modifies a contract when the actions or inaction of all parties to the contract indicate they no longer wish to be bound by its terms. The result is to avoid the contract and make it void.

*See also:* breach.

**abandonment as non-support**  Non-performance of a familial or legal duty to support another. Abandonment is the failure to provide the support that is required in a customary or legal relationship between two people. The support required at least includes shelter, food, and health care but may also include the care usually expected in the relationship, such as educational and developmental activities for children, monogamy for spouses, and company for adults. At common law and in equity, abandonment has included an array of criminal and civil penalties. These persist in a variety of forms of action, including actions for criminal abandonment, actions for the loss of parental rights or for the termination of guardianship, and actions for divorce for cause.

*See also:* divorce, abandonment of spouse; abandonment, child abandonment.

**abandonment as renunciation of crime**  Relinquishment of the intent to commit a crime before its commission. Abandonment usually requires a person planning to commit or to assist in a crime to voluntarily exhibit some objective physical manifestation of the lack of intent to commit the crime. In other words, the person who was going to act in a criminal manner must willingly do something that would be interpreted by most people as evidence that person no longer wanted to participate in the criminal activity. If the abandonment of intent is the direct result of actions by the police, the loss of intent will not usually be abandonment.

*See also:* abdication.

**abandonment by debtor**  Offering of property by a debtor for satisfaction of debt. Abandonment of property (usually the collateral for a debt) is sometimes preferable to liquidating the collateral and paying creditors. For example, if the cost of liquidating the collateral would be excessive, or if it would take a considerable amount of time to liquidate the collateral, or if the collateral is worth more in its non-liquidated state, abandonment is more efficient than liquidation. There is no great difference in the word "abandon" as used here and the word "transfer" as used in other contexts.

**abandonment by insured**  Surrender of insured property from the insured to the insurer. Abandonment takes place under an insurance policy, when a claim amounts to a total loss or a constructive total loss, and the assured accepts the insurer's payment in satisfaction of the whole claim, in return for abandonment of the property. In marine insurance, the ship and the cargo are both surrendered.

**abandonment of property**  Giving up property forever. Abandonment of property is the act of relinquishing forever an interest in property, whether the interest is one of ownership, possession, use, claim, or something else. The essential element is one of intent to have nothing to do with the property, rather than intent for something to be done with the property. If, for example, the intent is for the property to go to someone else, it is not abandonment. Intent to abandon might be imputed from certain forms of neglect over a very long period of time, so long as there is no evidence to the contrary.

*See also:* property, found property, abandoned property.

> **abandonment of an easement** An easement holder's conduct demonstrating the easement has been given up forever. Abandonment of an easement occurs when a party has had an easement to use another's property, and the easement holder manifests intent to destroy this interest. Abandonment is usually claimed by the owner of the servient tenement, the land over which the easement runs. It requires proof of both non-use, usually for the length of time needed to prove prescription or adverse possession, as well as other actions or inaction that would support a finding of intentional neglect that amounts to an intent by the easement holder to give up the easement forever. Abandonment of public streets or roads is usually done by the government that maintained them by a decree, which would extinguish any public ways that had not pre-existed the public street or road.

**abandonor** One who has abandoned something or someone. The abandonor is the person who gives up forever something or a relationship with someone. In the context of property, the abandonment is irrevocable, though the abandonor could reclaim the property abandoned with the same license that anyone else could do so. In the context of family law, an abandonor who renounces the abandonment may be entitled to restoration of the familial privileges once lost, although as to a child or adult requiring care the renunciation must be credible and reflect both readiness and ability to resume the familial responsibility, without dispossessing someone who has achieved a greater claim to that responsibility during the abandonment.

**child abandonment** Action or inaction demonstrating a surrender of parental rights. Child abandonment occurs when the action or inaction of a parent toward the parent's child or children indicates that the parent is not carrying out the obligations of parenthood to provide support for the child, from which the law implies the parent's failure of intention to exercise the rights of a parent.

*See also:* abandonment, abandonment as nonsupport; abandonment, criminal abandonment.

**constructive abandonment** Abandonment inferred from circumstances. Constructive abandonment is a condition in which other parties than the owner or claimant are entitled to infer that the owner or claimant has abandoned some property, claim, or defense. Constructive abandonment may arise from long disuse, from conditions that would be a reasonable sign of an intent to abandon, from conduct by the owner or claimant that is inconsistent with ownership or a continued assertion of ownership or intent to possess property or with the prosecution of a claim or defense or interest in maintaining it.

*See also:* patent, abandonment of a patent, constructive abandonment of a patent (statutory forfeiture or prior public use bar).

**criminal abandonment** The failure to support someone whom one has a legal duty to support. Criminal abandonment arises when a parent, guardian, or other legally recognized custodial person fails to provide a child or incompetent adult food, water, shelter, necessary medical care, and, sometimes, financial support. There is usually no requirement that harm follow from the abandonment, because the crime is completed at the time of abandonment.

*See also:* abandonment, child abandonment.

**express abandonment** Abandonment made clear by a statement or an unmistakable act evincing intent. Express abandonment is the abandonment or rejection of any claim, property, or other interest that is accompanied by an act by the abandonor that is either a clear statement of an intent permanently to abandon or by an act that clearly and unmistakably signals such an intent. Express abandonment is required for certain forms of abandonment and has more immediate consequences than implied abandonment owing to the more immediate reasonableness of reliance upon the expression than upon other forms of implied or construed abandonment. Express abandonment is a particular requirement for the government to abandon public lands. Express abandonment of a patent or trademark results in the property abandoned being in the public domain, although abandonment of an application does not. Express abandonment of a claim or defense may estop its revival in a civil action. Express abandonment in admiralty is by a clear and unmistakable act, and it contrasts with inferential abandonment, or abandonment construed from circumstances.

*See also:* patent, abandonment of a patent, express abandonment (formal abandonment).

**medical abandonment (abandonment of a patient)** Premature or improper termination of healthcare. Medical abandonment, or abandonment of a patient, occurs when a professional healthcare provider accepts responsibility for a patient but unilaterally terminates care or treatment while the patient still requires it without ensuring adequate care or treatment will continue. In some circumstances, all that is required by law to ensure further care is notice to the patient that treatment is terminated but should be obtained elsewhere.

*See also:* patient.

**abatement (abate)** Cessation, interruption, or reduction. Abatement describes a form of interference with some process. The term can describe any one of many varying degrees of interference, and the term relates the level of interference to the action that interferes with the underlying process. For instance, abatement of a nuisance ends it or pauses it. Abatement in a judicial proceeding usually stays the action but sometimes results in the action being dismissed. Abatement may result in a change to some degree less than total abolition, often meaning a significant reduction or some process or effect, as with abatement of contamination from pollution.

**abatement in equity**   *See:* equity, equitable defense, abatement in equity.

**abatement of a debt**   *See:* debt, abatement of a debt.

**abatement of a devise**   *See:* devise, abatement of a devise.

**abatement of a legacy**   *See:* legacy, abatement of a legacy.

**abatement of a legal action**   *See:* dismissal, abatement of a legal action.

**abatement of a lien**   *See:* lien, abatement of a lien.

**abatement of a nuisance**   *See:* nuisance, abatement of a nuisance.

**abatement of action**   *See:* plea, plea in abatement (abatement of action).

**abatement of an environmental hazard**   *See:* environment, environmental abatement (abatement of an environmental hazard).

**abatement of rent**   *See:* rent, abatement of rent (rent abatement).

**abatement clause**   Contract clause that reduces payments owed upon satisfaction of a condition. An abatement clause is any provision in a contract that would reduce payments of rents or other money owed in the event a condition is satisfied by the occurrence or non-occurrence of an event. It does not matter whether the clause is labeled or designated as an abatement.

**abatement in equity**   A suspension of an action in equity. The plea of abatement in equity may be brought to stay an action already commenced in equity, pending service on a proper party, after which it may be revived.

**abatement pro rata**   The reduction of value or an obligation according to the ratio of benefit from which it arose. An abatement pro rata is a reduction in the amount of money or value according to the varying levels of benefit one or another person has from the underlying benefit or debt. A tax abatement pro rata is greater for those with higher tax rates. An abatement of a legacy pro rata is greater on those in a single category who have a greater benefit. Abatement pro rata contrasts with abatement by class, in which some are abated before others, or abatement per capita, in which all are abated equally.

**abbreviation**   Shortened version of a word, phrase or document. Abbreviation is usually only thought of as the removal of letters from a word, although more generally it is also used to describe the omission of words from a longer quotation, which is abridgment or redaction. Abbreviation within a word is done either according to an established custom or by either of two means to identify the omitted letters: an apostrophe for letters removed at the start or middle of the word or a period for letters removed at the end, such as int'l for international and ed. for editor. Custom allows abbreviated phrases to be condensed and the space omitted, such as etc. for et cetera. Abbreviation from a quotation of several words is signaled by the use of ellipses at the places of abbreviation.

*See also:* citation, citation manual, Association of Legal Writing Directors Citation Manual (A.L.W.D. Citation Manual or ALWD Citation Manual); citation, citation as summons; citation, citation manual (Bluebook or Uniform System of Citation).

**abdication**   The renunciation of an office or duty. Abdication is the quitting of an office, a term usually reserved for the resignation of a sovereign. It can be said that any holder of an office of great responsibility or for a great time who abandons that office has abdicated its duties.

*See also:* abandonment, abandonment as renunciation of crime.

**abduction**   Criminal restraint or coerced movement of another person. Abduction is causing the restraint or movement of a living person by force, threat, or fraud, when the abductor has no legal privilege to do so. Thus, a police officer's power of arrest or a parent's privilege over a child do not amount to abduction. Abduction does not require that the victim's movement be out of a building; it is sufficient that the person abducted loses the liberty of movement because of the abductor's conduct.

Abduction is both a tort and a crime, as well as an element in the crime of kidnapping. In some jurisdictions, the crime of abduction must be based on force or threat and not on deception. Some jurisdictions have required the force threatened to be of deadly force. Although abduction is now more general in many jurisdictions, in some, the crime of abduction is a still a crime only when the victim is under a specified age, the abduction lacks the consent of the parents (regardless of the consent of the victim), and the purpose of the abduction is to enable marriage or sexual relations.

Note: abduction, in its most general sense, is the carrying away of something. Thus, it is used in medicine to describe the movement of a limb or bone away from a mid-line, pairing, or place of rest. This contrasts with adduction, or the movement of an object toward such a mid-line, pairing, or place of rest.

**child abduction (abduction of a child)**   Carrying away a child by force, fraud, or threat. Abduction of a child is the particular felony of abduction when the victim is under age, usually under the age of eighteen years. Child abduction is often a violation of a court order giving custody of a child to one parent or to a guardian, in which a non-custodial adult transports the child from the control of an adult with legal custody.

*See also:* parent, parental rights, intentional inter-ference with parental rights (causing a minor child to leave or not to return home).

**aberrance (aberrant behavior)** Highly abnormal spontaneous behavior. Aberrance, or aberrant behavior, is apparently unintentional conduct that is highly unusual for the individual who engages in it, such as when a person would not have engaged in some conduct except for unusual circumstances sparking a reflex action that was committed without premeditation or intent. Beyond the context of sentencing, aberrant has a more generalized sense of behavior that is unusual or novel for an individual or for a member of society.
*See also:* behavior.

**aberemurther or eberemoth or eberemors or ebere-murder** *See:* murder, aberemurder (abere-murther or eberemoth or eberemors or ebere–murder).

**abet (abettor or abetter or abbettour)** To encourage a criminal in an act of crime. To abet is an act by one person to instigate or encourage another person to commit crime. It is an element of aiding and abetting, which is conduct generally assisting in other criminal conduct, but abetting refers more to mental, moral, or personal encouragement that shares a common intent with the principal of the crime, rather than to mere technical or physical assistance. Because abetting requires a shared intent that must have been formed prior to the crime, conduct that abets the commission of a crime also usually occurs prior to the criminal activity.

An abettor is a person who abets, that is, who instigates or encourages another person in the commission of a crime. The hallmark of an abettor's criminal liability is in sharing with the principal an intent to commit the crime. In some cases, an abettor can be tried as a principal, while in others, an abettor is only an accessory, and thus subject to a lesser penalty. Note: although the traditional spelling is abettor, the use of an "e" for the "o" is increasingly widespread.
*See also:* inchoate (choate); aiding and abetting (aid and abet).

**abeyance** A delay in proceedings, pending some occurrence. Abeyance is delay in a process or activity while awaiting an event necessary for it to commence or to continue. Thus, a legal action in abeyance pending the decision in a related case is stayed until the second case is resolved.
*See also:* deference (defer); remission (remitter of bail or remitter of debt); plea, criminal plea, plea in abeyance.

    **abeyance of estate** A suspension of ownership. An abeyance of estate is a condition in which an estate has no owner in possession. Abeyance of estate may occur when there is a gap between estates, when because of the way grants were made earlier, there is no person in whom the freehold is vested at a given time. For example, a grant from O to A for life then to the heirs of B would have a gap if A dies before B. B has nothing, only B's heirs, and while B lives no one knows who will be the heirs of B, because they are only estab-lished by law (not by B's will) at B's death. In such a case, the estate would be in abeyance at A's death for as long as B lives. Abeyance of estate is quite rare now, owing to modern rules limiting future contingent interests.

**ABF** *See:* bar, bar organization, American Bar Foundation (ABF).

**abide (abide by or abiding)** To comply. To abide is to accept and conform with a rule or a decision. Abide in this sense echoes the more general sense of biding, abid-ing, or abiding by, of lingering or waiting for some purpose or of suffering some burden. The sense in law is more particular, which is to act or refrain from action as required, as well as to more generally act in a manner consistent with the specific obligation. While abiding is a near synonym for obedience and compliance, the term abiding invokes both a sense of performance over time and a sense that the abiding party endures the obligation rather than prefers it.
*See also:* obedience (disobedience).

**ability (able)** Capacity to function in a specific task. Ability is a sufficient capacity to engage in or complete a relevant task. In the law, it is often a matter of a person having the physical and mental capacity to do something or for a person or a corporation having the availability of sufficient financial and managerial resources to do what is required.
*See also:* capacity, legal capacity.

    **able (able argument or able attorney or able counsel)** Displaying great professional competence. Able, when used to describe an attorney or a legal argu-ment, connotes a level of professionalism that is of notable merit. In this sense, "able" implies perfor-mance beyond the usual meaning of mere ability. David Melinkoff has correctly noted that an "able argument" is a compliment often deployed to console the lawyer who lost it. See David Melinkoff, A Diction-ary of Legal Usage, q.v. (1992). Even so, along with "learned," the adjective "able" is traditionally a term of praise for a lawyer or for an argument.

    **abled** Able–bodied, healthy, and capable. "Abled" depicts a person of ordinary or better health, strength, physical ability, and mental acuity. The term is mainly known through its antonym, disabled, though the more positive abled long preceded the negative var-iant. "Abled" is rare in contemporary speech.

    **financial ability** Assets allowing the fulfillment of a contract. Financial ability is the ability of a party to a contract to pay or finance its contractual commit-ments. Upon entering into a contract, parties are pre-sumed able to support their intention to perform their obligation to the agreement, and one party's failure of a financial ability to perform may make the agreement voidable by the other party. In an option contract, for example, if A offers an option to B, but then B lacks access to enough money to exercise the option during the time it is open, A may then refuse to continue the option without breach.

*presumption of financial ability* A presumption that each party has access to money to perform the contract. If parties enter into a contract presumably they have, or can obtain, the resources — the financial ability — to support their intention to perform their duties under the contract. If, subsequently, a party seeks to avoid its obligations under the bargain by pleading loss of financial ability, that party has the burden of rebutting the presumption that the other party relied on its ability to perform.

**abjuration (to abjure)** Renunciation of a right or claim or interest, particularly citizenship. To abjure is to reject something in a solemn and final manner. Traditionally, abjuration referred to the renunciation under oath of one's allegiance to one's former national sovereign. Abjuration still suggests such a conclusive rejection but it is applied now in a variety of turns of phrase, particularly when an official rejects the duties of office or a judge or legislator rejects an idea as appropriate to the law.

**able** *See:* ability, able (able argument or able attorney or able counsel); ability (able).

**abnormality (abnormal)** Anything that differs from the usual or expected condition. Abnormality is any condition or event that is quite out of the ordinary. In the law what is abnormal may be important as it would put an observer on notice that investigation might reveal further information. In property, an abnormal condition on the land frequently provides inquiry notice of what would be revealed through further investigation. In medicine an abnormality may suggest a medical condition that requires testing to determine the presence of an underlying condition endangering the patient.

**abnormally dangerous activity** *See:* danger, abnormally dangerous activity (inherently dangerous activity or ultra-hazardous activity or ultrahazardous activity).

**abnormally dangerous domestic animal** *See:* animal, abnormally dangerous domestic animal.

**abnormally sensitive plaintiff or glass-jaw plaintiff or eggshell-skull rule or thin-skull rule** *See:* plaintiff, egg-shell plaintiff (abnormally sensitive plaintiff or glass-jaw plaintiff or eggshell-skull rule or thin-skull rule).

**abode (place of abode)** Home or domicile. An abode, or place of abode, is the building, apartment, house, or space where a person lives most of the time and where the person intends to return after leaving it. An abode may be permanent or temporary, as opposed to a domicile, which is presumed to be permanent.

**abolition** The repeal of a legal doctrine or rejection of a social practice. Abolition is the repeal of a law, especially in some manner that rejects the underlying principles reflected in the law. Abolition implies not merely revocation of a law but rejection or annihilation of the rule it contains, such that the rule can never be revived. More generally, abolition is the complete rejection or utter suppression of a social practice. The term in the United States and Great Britain is uniquely associated with the anti-slavery movement, the repeal of the laws supporting slavery, and the freedom of the former slaves.

In common-law pleading, abolition was an amnesty for an accused criminal resulting from the abandonment of a public prosecution.

**abolition of a crime** The repeal or voiding of a law declaring something to be criminal. Abolition may refer to the repeal by a legislature or the declaration by a court that a statute declaring some conduct to be criminal is void.

*See also:* absolution (absolve); clemency.

**abolition of slavery** The prohibition of slavery and repeal of the laws allowing it. Slavery, whether the chattel ownership of a human being or the holding one human being to labor for another without compensation, has occurred throughout history in various places, including the United States of America. Slavery was abolished in the common law of England in the Somersett's Case, 20 State Tr 1, Lofft 1 (1772), and in British law by statute with the Slave Trade Act, 47 Geo III sess. 1 c. 36 (1807) and the Slavery Abolition Act, 3 & 4 Will. IV c. 73 (1833). It was abolished in the United States initially on state-by-state basis, beginning in Pennsylvania in 1780, a process mainly in the Northern states until the military occupation of the South during the American Civil War, according to the Emancipation Proclamation. Slavery was not abolished throughout the United States until the passage of the Thirteenth Amendment in 1865.

*See also:* slavery (slave).

**aboriginal title** *See:* title, aboriginal title.

**aborigine** Native person or indigenous people. Aborigine, translated literally from Latin as from the beginning of the world, refers to the people who descended from the first inhabitants of an area rather than those who later travelled there and claimed the land. The term usually refers to the group who lived in a region at the time it was colonized or claimed by Europeans, as it cannot encompass time immemorial.

**abort** To discontinue some activity prematurely or to prevent an act from occurrence. To abort is to thwart some process or to interrupt the predicate events that would have otherwise resulted in a particular event. The term is derived from the Latin for having disappeared or failed, as well as for the sense of causing the miscarriage of a pregnancy.

*See also:* abortion (abort).

**abortifacient** *See:* abortion, abortifacient.

**abortion (abort)** The termination of a pregnancy other than by live birth of a child. An abortion is any process of ending a pregnancy that does not result in delivery of a child. While the term includes miscarriage and other biological or accidental events, it more often implies an induced abortion, which is an artificial procedure, usually a medical intervention to expel the fetus from the uterus. Abortion is controversial in the United States, and many states have regulated its use in the latter two trimesters of pregnancy. Still, the decision to have an abortion is an aspect of the constitutionally protected right of the mother to privacy. See Roe v. Wade, 410 U.S. 113 (1973) (Blackmun, J.).

*See also:* pregnancy (quick with child or pregnant woman); fetus (fetal, foetus or unborn child); abortion, abortifacient; contraception.

**1. right to privacy** A choice to have an abortion is within the constitutional right to privacy. The decision of a mother to have an abortion is the core element of the privacy right in the abortion process. Other elements of privacy have been recognized, however, in the abortion process, including the physician–patient relationship. The interests of the state in regulation of abortion are predicated on an independent interest in protecting the life, or potential for life, in the fetus. The judicial balance of privacy has thus protected the mother's interest in privacy most when the interest of the state in the fetus is least, that is when it is less developed.

*See also:* privacy, right to privacy (right of privacy or privacy rights); abortion | 3. Roe v. Wade.

**2. free speech** Speech by abortion activists on public sidewalks or streets is protected. The First Amendment grants protection to leafleting, sign displays, and oral communications intended to dissuade a woman considering an abortion. That the messages conveyed by those communications may be offensive to their recipients does not deprive them of constitutional protection. Public sidewalks, streets, and ways are quintessential public forums for free speech and may be used by abortion activists, however, they may not block access to clinics.

**3. Roe v. Wade** The right to choose an abortion is a constitutionally protected aspect of privacy. Roe v. Wade, 410 U.S. 113 (1973) established the federal right of a woman to decide to terminate her pregnancy. The opinion, by Justice Blackmun, declared that such a decision is within scope of the constitutional right to privacy, that the state has an interest in the future child in the fetus, and that the balance between the mother's and the state's interest is in allowing regulation when the fetus is viable. As medical technology then stood, this meant that the state could forbid or regulate abortions in the third trimester, but the state would be limited to regulations required for maternal health in the second trimester and to regulations in the first trimester that did not interfere with the decision made by her and her attending physician.

**4. Planned Parenthood v. Casey** Regulations affecting the right to choose an abortion may not create an undue burden. Planned Parenthood v. Casey, 505 U.S. 833 (1992), affirmed the decision in Roe v. Wade, 410 U.S. 113 (1973), as a matter of stare decisis. The case, two decades after Roe, rejected a clear argument to overturn it after two justices of the Roe's majority had left the Court. A plurality of the Court upheld Roe's basic principles that a woman's right to choose an abortion is a privacy interest protected by due process of law from undue state interference, but it replaced the trimester system with a balancing test. Under the Casey standard, the state may regulate or ban abortion after a fetus becomes viable, though the state may not interfere with an abortion that is medically necessary to protect the life or health of the mother. Otherwise, the state interest in protecting the life of a viable fetus allows regulations that do not amount to an undue burden, which bars a regulation with the purpose or effect of placing a substantial obstacle in the path of a woman seeking an abortion of a nonviable fetus.

**5. Webster v. Reproductive Health Services** States are not required to fund or provide abortions. Webster v. Reproductive Health Services, 492 U.S. 490 (1989) (Rehnquist, C.J.), applied the Court's theory in DeShaney v. Winnebago County Dept. of Social Services, 489 U.S. 189 (1989) (Rehnquist, C.J.) that a right under the due process clause against state deprivation does not confer an affirmative right to state aid in the exercise of the due process right. Thus, the state could forbid state funds and services from being used for the provision of an abortion or abortion counseling.

**6. Stenberg v. Carhart** A state partial–birth abortion ban must allow exceptions for the safety of the mother. Stenberg v. Carhart, 530 U.S. 914 (2000) (Breyer, J.), voided a Missouri state ban on abortion procedures using dilation and evacuation because the ban had no exception for a medically necessary procedure for the life or health of the mother, a consistent requirement in cases since Casey. The state law was similar to a federal law upheld by the court in Gonzales v. Carhart, 550 U.S. 124 (2007) (Kennedy, J.).

*See also:* abortion, partial birth abortion (dilation and evacuation procedure or D&E).

**7. Gonzales v. Carhart** A ban on partial–birth abortion is not an undue burden on a woman's right to choose. Gonzales v. Carhart, 550 U.S. 124 (2007) (Kennedy, J.), upheld a federal ban on abortion procedures using dilation and extraction, even though the federal Partial–Birth Abortion Ban Act of 2003 had no exceptions for the medically required procedure to protect the life or health of the mother. In doing so, the Court, per Justice Kennedy, distinguished its earlier bar of a similar state prohibition in Stenberg v. Carhart, 530 U.S. 914 (2000) (Breyer, J.), noting in the later opinion that the prohibition of one procedure did not pose a substantial obstacle to terminating a pregnancy because alternative procedures were available and relying on Congress's finding that D&E procedures are never necessary for the health and safety of the mother.

*See also:* abortion | 6. Stenberg v. Carhart.

**abortifacient** Anything that can cause an abortion. An abortifacient is any substance or device placed into a woman's body to cause fetal death. Although most abortifacients are manufactured for this purpose, others that pose great risks may be used by women in an attempt to induce an end to a pregnancy.

*See also:* abortion (abort).

**abortion clinic**   A facility where abortions are performed by medical staff. An abortion clinic is a legally operated and regulated facility where a woman can receive medical assistance to terminate a pregnancy. It is sometimes called a Reproductive Health Clinic or a Family Planning Clinic.

*See also:* abortion, blockade of abortion facilities; abortion, Freedom of Access to Clinic Entrances Act (F.A.C.E. or FACE).

**blockade of abortion facilities**   There is no right to blockade a clinic that performs abortions. The abortion clinic blockade was a tactic prominent in the 1980s and 1990s in harassing clinical staff and patients, which was limited by injunction and prosecution. Blockaders have sought to defend their actions as aspects of Free Speech or Freedom of Assembly, but these arguments fail in general for failing to take into account the rights of the people they harass.

*See also:* abortion, Freedom of Access to Clinic Entrances Act (F.A.C.E. or FACE); abortion, abortion clinic.

**Freedom of Access to Clinic Entrances Act**   Blockading a clinic is a federal crime. The Freedom of Access to Clinic Entrances Act, 18 U.S.C. § 248, forbids interference with access to reproductive services.

**criminal abortion**   The once-unlawful act of terminating a pregnancy. The early common law defined abortion as the unlawful killing of a premature baby. This was distinguished from feticide, which was the termination of a pregnancy. Early on, jurisdictions varied in whether to prohibit feticide, though abortion was universally prohibited. Throughout the late nineteenth and twentieth centuries, however, both the common law and statutory provisions seemed to supplant the concept of feticide with abortion, and the old concept of abortion with infanticide. Under this modern definition of abortion, aiding or acting to terminate a fetus was a criminal offense. Criminal abortion included the administration of any procedure or instrument designed to destroy a fetus, as well as any abortifacient medicine or drug. Criminal abortion was abolished in the United States in 1973 with the famous Supreme Court decision in Roe v. Wade.

*See also:* abortion, abortifacient; abortion (abort).

**Freedom of Access to Clinic Entrances Act (F.A.C.E. or FACE)**   Interfering with access to an abortion clinic is a crime. The Freedom of Access to Clinic Entrances Act, 18 U.S.C. § 248(a), recognizes and protects a constitutional right of access by a patient to a clinic providing abortions. The FACE Act creates a federal offense of injuring, intimidating, or interfering with patients or providers at a reproductive health care facility. The statute also creates federal jurisdiction over civil claims arising from, and civil remedies against, actions intended to block access to abortion clinics. The statute excepts from liability parents or guardians who interfere with their own minor child.

*See also:* abortion, blockade of abortion facilities; abortion (abort).

**medically necessary abortion**   A termination of pregnancy to preserve the life or health of the mother. A medically necessary abortion is the best choice, in appropriate medical judgment, to protect the life or health of the mother. Consequently, access to a medically necessary abortion may not be restricted by a state.

**partial birth abortion (dilation and evacuation procedure or D&E)**   An abortion procedure that occurs in part in the birth canal. Partial-birth abortion is a rhetorically laden term used to describe one procedure among many forms of dilation and extraction procedures used in abortion. In this, the fetus is made unviable and then moved into the birth canal for removal.

**regulation of abortion**   Abortion regulations are permitted unless they are an undue burden on the woman. Regulations that make it more difficult for a woman to terminate a pregnancy are constitutionally valid if they serve an appropriate state purpose and if they do not create a substantial obstacle to the woman's decision to have an abortion or to exercise her right to have one, balancing the state interest in the protection of the fetus against her rights through a graduated level of regulation. Prior to the viability of the fetus, the interest of the individual in the control of her own body is higher, and after the fetus becomes viable, it is lower.

*See also:* abortion | 3. Roe v. Wade.

*1. undue burden standard*   Laws cannot be a substantial obstacle to a woman seeking an abortion unless for her health or safety. An undue burden, as established in Planned Parenthood v. Casey, 505 U.S. 833 (1992) (O'Connor, J.), is imposed when a regulation has the purpose or effect of presenting a substantial obstacle to a woman seeking an abortion, if the regulation does not further her health or safety. In order to apply the undue burden standard, then, a court must first determine whether the law was intended to promote the health and safety of the potential patients and whether the law is "necessary" to attain that goal. If the regulation is necessary, it is constitutionally valid; if the regulation is not necessary, it is constitutionally valid only if it does not pose a substantial obstacle.

*See also:* abortion | 4. Planned Parenthood v. Casey.

*2. government funding (Hyde amendment or public funds)*   State or federal funding of abortions may be restricted, but there are limits to the restriction. When government provides funds for medical care, they may be barred from use for abortions by state law. Federal Medicaid funds, which pay states for medical treatment of the poor, were limited from abortions not necessary to save the life of the mother by the Hyde amendment in 1976, an annual rider on the budget that was altered in 1993 to allow funding for abortions of pregnancy resulting from rape or incest. Most states provide Medicaid money under this formula, but a significant minority of states provide state funds from other sources for abortions in other circumstances. Restrictions similar to the Hyde Amendment apply to funds for veterans, American Indians, prisoners, Children's Health Insurance recipients, and others. State constitutions in some states have been read by state courts to forbid such limitations over state actions.

**3. government facility (public facility)** A state medical facility can prohibit the performance of abortions therein. A state medical facility can refuse private physicians and their patients on–site abortions without placing an undue burden on the woman seeking the abortion.

See also: abortion | 5. Webster v. Reproductive Health Services.

**4. abortion counseling** Medical advice on abortion is encouraged but not federally funded. Because it is recommended that a woman give informed consent prior to aborting a pregnancy, the woman must be counseled on the procedure, but federal money cannot be used to support the counseling.

**5. informed consent (abortion counseling)** A state requirement that a woman be told the cost, risk, and alternatives of abortion. A state may require that a woman desiring an abortion be counseled to be informed of all pertinent facts regarding abortion so that she makes an informed choice to choose or not to choose to terminate her pregnancy. What constitutes "pertinent" facts remains controversial, and the requirement is used in many states to attempt to dissuade the woman. This requirement has been held not to be an undue burden, in general, as long as the counseling requirement does not become an undue burden on the woman or compel ideological speech from the attending medical care provider.

**6. parental consent or notification** A state may usually require a parent's notice or consent for a minor's abortion. A requirement for parental notice or consent for minors to receive an abortion must allow a judicial bypass option, allowing the abortion without parental notice or consent if the court finds the minor is sufficiently mature to exercise judgments in such matters and, particularly, to avoid situations in which consent would be inappropriate to be required, such as for an abortion following a case of incest. See Bellotti v. Baird, 443 U.S. 622 (1979) (Powell, J.).

**7. spousal consent or notification** A state cannot require a woman to gain a husband's notice or consent for an abortion. Spousal notification is a state requirement that a woman communicate with her husband regarding her decision to seek an abortion before being allowed access to the procedure. Spousal consent requires the wife gain the husband's consent before the procedure. State laws requiring notice, consent, or both were found unconstitutional in Planned Parenthood of Southeastern Pennsylvania v. Casey, 505 U.S. 833 (1992) (O'Connor, J.).

**8. waiting period** The state may require a short delay after abortion counseling. Although in the 1980s, the Supreme Court held that a waiting period served no constitutional state interest, in Planned Parenthood v. Casey, 505 U.S. 833 (1992) (O'Connor, J.), the Court held that the state has a legitimate interest in protecting unborn children that is served by asking a woman to think about the information she receives about abortion prior to consenting to terminating a pregnancy and, so, prior to undergoing the procedure. Such a waiting period is an undue burden if it poses an appreciable health risk to the woman seeking to terminate her pregnancy.

**9. regulation of medical techniques and facilities** Reproductive health clinics may be regulated as any other clinic is regulated. A clinic providing abortions may be regulated for sanitation, health, safety, and the medical fitness of its procedures, in the same manner as any other clinic providing analogous care. An abortion clinic may not, however, be subject to additional regulations as a clinic that are more burdensome than the regulations of clinics not providing reproductive medical care.

**10. record keeping requirements** A state may require clinics to keep records, but patient rights must be preserved. State regulations requiring a reproductive health clinic to collect and maintain records and to report on procedures are constitutional if the requirements are reasonably directed to the preservation of maternal health and that properly respect a patient's confidentiality and privacy.

**11. prisoners** Prison officials cannot be compelled to provide access to an abortion. Although prison officials are bound to provide medical services to save the life of a prisoner, the prison is not required to provide abortions in other circumstances.

See also: abortion (abort).

**right to choose** A woman's conditional right to terminate her pregnancy. A woman's right to choose is the right of a pregnant woman to choose whether to terminate her pregnancy, and then to choose to do so and have that choice effected with the assistance of licensed medical care providers. The right to choose is an aspect of the right to privacy, though it is subject to distinct limitations that balance the state interest in the life developing within her, that in general allow her the discretion to choose until the fetus reaches a stage of viability and increasingly limited discretion thereafter.

See also: abortion (abort).

**above** Higher, either more senior in a hierarchy of people or earlier in a written text. Above is used in very different senses in legal writing. Most often, it refers to text earlier in a writing than is the reference. To read the reference above or the above–referenced letter means that the reference is earlier in the text than the phrase referring to it. (Usually, these texts could have been better written, but it remains a habit among lawyers.) Above is also used to refer to courts of appeal or courts of last resort, especially in comparison to the courts from which cases are appealed. Thus, one takes up an issue to a higher court, hoping the court above will grant relief on the issue that was denied by the court below.

*See also:* supra; infra.

**above-the-line deduction** *See:* tax, tax deduction, above–the–line deduction (non–itemized deduction).

**abridgement (abridge)** To make shorter in words while preserving the meaning of a text. An abridgment is a text that has been shortened from an earlier, longer text for the sake of brevity alone. An abridged version, or redacted version, should not change the meaning or essence of the ideas set forth in the unabridged text. An abridged text might signal those places in the text where redaction occurred, including the amount of text redacted, or be silent on the subject, so that the reader is not made aware of the removed text in the abridged version.

*See also:* abbreviation; brief, case brief (brief a case).

**abridgment** *See:* lawbook, abridgment.

**abrogation (abrogate)** To repeal or abolish a doctrine of the law. Abrogation was once a term reserved for the most solemn rescission of legal doctrines by express means, but it has become a term for any significant alteration of legal duties. Implied abrogation is more common, perhaps, now than express abrogation, which is to say that abrogation may be more likely a result of the application of a new legal authority leading to the implied demise or an old rule rather than its express repeal or over-ruling.

*See also:* annulment, marital annulment (declaration of invalidity of marriage); repeal; overrule (overruling).

**abrogation of sovereign immunity** *See:* immunity, sovereign immunity, abrogation of sovereign immunity.

**abrogation as loss of authority** Annulment of authority of jurisdiction in an office. Abrogation may represent the annulment of a power in an office or institution. When a power of one office is lost through the grant of that power to another, or through its repeal, the power is abrogated.

*See also:* abrogation (abrogate).

**express abrogation** The announced repeal of a power or doctrine of the law. Express abrogation is a deliberate, expressed action, nearly always in writing, by which a doctrine is repealed or a power is revoked. To say that a statute, a judicial opinion, or a rule or executive order abrogates something implies that the author of the statute, opinion, rule, or order has the constitutional power to do so. It does not, however, require that the abrogation be so clear as not to require interpretation or application to a particular circumstance.

*See also:* expression (explicit or express).

**implied abrogation** The constructive annulment of an existing law. Implied abrogation depicts the extinction of a rule, either from an earlier statute or case opinion, as a result of the logical application of a later rule. It contrasts with express abrogation, which is the deliberate and stated repeal of or amendment to an old statute by a legislature or by the stated overruling of a precedent by a court. Put another way, implied abrogation is the unstated repudiation of the older law because of a logical conflict with a newer law.

**abscondment (abscond or absconding)** To flee or hide to avoid the law. The essence of absconding is to conceal oneself, almost always by fleeing the jurisdiction. Although it sometimes includes things as well, such as stolen property, the term properly means only the person and not the thing, as when one says, the embezzler absconded with the firm's accounts.

*See also:* expatriation (expatriate or expat); fugitive (fugitive from the law or fugitive from justice).

**absence** Being not where one is expected. The condition of not being within the jurisdiction, or in court, or at one's residence, or at one's place of work or study, when one is required or expected to be there. More generally, it is not being where one is sought or supposed to be.

*See also:* appearance; absence, absence without leave (A.W.O.L. or AWOL); absentee.

**absence without leave (A.W.O.L. or AWOL)** Unexcused failure to be present at a military post or duty station. Being AWOL, or absent without leave, is the failure of a member of the military to be at the required place of duty at the time required.

*See also:* absence; missing movement.

**absent deponent** *See:* deposition, deponent, absent deponent.

**absent witness** *See:* witness, absent witness.

**in absentia** Not present. In absentia is a designation for a procedure or action performed while the person it most affects is absent. A person may be adjudged in a civil case in absentia, which is effectively what occurs in a default judgment. A person is not in absentia if that person is represented by an attorney or agent. Thus, criminal trials in which the defendant is not present are not held in absentia, although the physical non–presence of the defendant will affect the defendant's counsel's ability to present the defendant's case.

*See also:* trial, ex parte trial (trial in absentia).

**absentee** A person who is not where that person is expected to be. An absentee is a person, whether a natural or artificial person such as a corporation, not present in a given jurisdiction or location. In some specific usages, an absentee is not in some place in which others have an expectation or right for that person to be. A person may be an absentee for certain purposes though not all, having, for instance, a limited agent or special attorney in a jurisdiction. There is no difference between a person who is absent and an absentee, although conditions in which a person is treated as an absentee vary according to the significance of absence.

For example, a person may be an absentee for a time, such as an absent voter, or a permanent absentee, such as an absentee landlord.

*See also:* employment (employ or employed or employee or employer); witness, absent witness; disability, civil disability, civil death; absent, in absentia; landlord, absentee landlord.

**absentee landlord** *See:* landlord, absentee landlord.

**absolute** Unconditional and unlimited. Any absolute power, interest, right, or idea is one that has no limit in time or degree and no condition that must be satisfied in order to be asserted by its holder. Thus, a fee simple absolute is an ownership interest in land without limitation and that, theoretically, will continue forever. There are many legal interests that are absolute, including absolute guaranty, absolute warranty, absolute right, absolute privilege, absolute immunity, and other forms, each of which being absolute is unconditional. Other forms of interest that are absolute may be immediate, such as an absolute legacy, which vests on the death of the testator, or an absolute priority claim, which must be paid before lesser claims.

**absolute covenant** *See:* covenant, absolute covenant (covenant absolute).

**absolute gift or inter vivos gift** *See:* gift, gift inter vivos (absolute gift or inter vivos gift).

**absolute guaranty** *See:* guaranty, absolute guaranty.

**absolute immunity** *See:* immunity, official immunity, absolute immunity.

**absolute legacy** *See:* legacy, absolute legacy.

**absolute priority rule** *See:* priority, claim priority, absolute priority rule.

**absolute privilege** *See:* privilege, absolute privilege.

**absolute right** *See:* right, absolute right (right absolute).

**absolute veto or silent veto** *See:* veto, pocket veto (absolute veto or silent veto).

**absolution (absolve)** The remission of a punishment or duty. Absolution is an increasingly rare term for being relieved of one's debts or duties, so that one might say one is absolved of a debt. Absolution is closely related to forgiveness, but it differs in that forgiveness is more technically a renunciation of the act giving rise to the duty and absolution a renunciation of the duty. Both senses are, however, included in one another in common usage, as in loan forgiveness. Absolution was once a common term for a criminal acquittal. Both senses derive from the Roman and common-law senses of absolvo.

*See also:* plea, criminal plea, not guilty; acquittal (acquit).

**absorption (absorb)** The process by which one thing becomes an inseparable part of another. Absorption is a physical process in which one substance is integrated into another, such as when a liquid is integrated into a solid, or radiation enters into the cells of an organism, or as in the transmission of ingested alcohol into the bloodstream during digestion. In law, the process of absorption has become a metaphor for a variety of forms of combination, such as corporate mergers and constitutional doctrines, in which one entity survives the combination of two. Absorption in international law describes the integration of one state into another, and in labor law it is the integration of one union into another, in economics and trade it is the integration of the sale of a product into a given market. In banking, finance, transportation, utilities, and some commercial relationships, absorption is the acceptance of a debt or liability, particularly one that had been owed or potentially owed by another party.

**absorption of employees** *See:* employment, absorption of employees.

**absorption rate** *See:* appraisal, absorption rate.

**absorption of real estate** Merger of parcels by common ownership. A dominant estate's absorption of a subservient estate, permissible if the owner of the dominant estate aquires the subservient estate and evidence suggests that merging the two estates into one would be the most beneficial result of the acquisition.

*See also:* easement, merger of estates (merger of easement or merger of tenements); estate, interest, merger of estates.

**delayed absorption defense** A claim that blood alcohol levels result not from over-drinking but from late absorption. Delayed absorption refers to an argument made in some states in rebuttal to evidence of a high blood-alcohol level. The argument is that alcohol may take some time to be absorbed from the stomach into the blood and then expelled into the lungs from which it is measured. This defense is barred in some states as either irrelevant or contrary to public policy.

**absque** Without. Absque is Latin for without, representing the abstract concept of being beyond something, as in damnum absque injuria. The more concrete form would be sine, for not having something.

**absque injuria (absque iniuria)** Without legal injury. Absque injuria is a formula for depicting harms that are too abstract or speculative to be the basis for recovery under the law.
*See also:* sine, sine damno.

**abstention (abstain)** Voluntary restraint, especially as a matter of prudence. To abstain is to refrain from action or participation in some office or event. Abstention is inherently voluntary, yet it suggests that there are principles that would be promoted by inaction.

*See also:* jurisdiction, appellate jurisdiction, Rooker-Feldman doctrine; deference (defer).

**abstention doctrine (doctrine of abstention)** Federal courts should not hear cases better heard in the state courts. The doctrine of abstention reflects the general idea of deference to state courts in certain matters, and it is manifest in a series of specific circumstances under which a federal court's obligation to resolve a controversy brought in a court of proper jurisdiction may be avoided in the interest of the federal recognition of the powers of the states.

*See also:* judge, judicial discretion.

**comity** When abstention is proper, federal respect of state interests trumps a right of access to federal courts. The abstention doctrine is an aspect of federal comity with state courts. Abstention also allows a federal judge to dismiss actions on which the judge would prefer not to rule, or at least would prefer not to rule for the plaintiff or against the defense, until a state court has rendered a judgment.

**Brillhart abstention** A federal court may abstain from declaratory judgment of rights in issue in a state case. Under Brillhart v. Excess Ins. Co. of America, 316 U.S. 491 (1942) (Frankfurter, J.), a federal court may abstain from hearing an action for declaratory judgment, if a proceeding already has been brought in state court that would resolve the same rights in issue between the parties to the later federal declaratory judgment action. This doctrine persists, though Colorado River abstention is more often used in such circumstances.

*See also:* judgment, declaratory judgment (declaratory relief or declaration); abstention, abstention doctrine, Colorado River abstention.

**Burford abstention** Federal courts may refuse to hear a diversity case about complicated state administration. Under Burford v. Sun Oil Co., 319 U.S. 315 (1943) (Black, J.), federal courts may abstain when a case involves complex matters of state law, regulation, or enforcement.

**Colorado River abstention** Federal courts may refuse to hear a diversity case duplicating a pending action in a state court. Under Colorado River Water Conservation District v. United States, 424 U.S. 800 (1976) (Brennan, J.), federal courts may abstain when a case parallels litigation already in the state court, when the two actions raise the same questions of law on the same claims between the parties, and when the case has an additional aspect in which it would be more prudent not to hear the case in the federal court. Often the most important question under Colorado River abstention is which court first assumed jurisdiction, the earlier court being the more appropriate.

**Dombrowski doctrine** Federal courts may enjoin a state prosecution infringing constitutional rights. The Dombrowski doctrine is an exception to Younger abstention, according to which a federal court may enjoin a state criminal court proceeding if the prosecution either is brought in bad faith or has no real hope of success but nevertheless chills the exercise of a constitutional right. Such cases differ from cases in which Younger abstention is usually suggested, in that the usual case suggests that a conviction might violate the Constitution in the event of a successful prosecution, while a Dombrowski case argues that the prosecution itself burdens federally protected rights and was either brought for purpose of burdening these rights or has so little hope of success that federal review of the burden of being prosecuted is appropriate without awaiting a conclusion to the state case.

*See also:* chilling effect (chill); abstention, abstention doctrine, Younger abstention.

**Pullman abstention** Federal courts may refuse to hear a case involving a constitutional question if it can be avoided by a state law question. Under Railroad Commission v. Pullman Co., 312 U.S. 496 (1941) (Frankfurter, J.), federal courts are allowed to abstain from deciding a constitutional question when there is a dispositive question arising under state law, the resolution of which would moot the question of constitutional law.

**Thibodaux abstention** Federal courts may refuse to hear a case that requires a choice of state policy. Under Louisiana Power & Light Co. v. City of Thibodaux, 360 U.S. 25 (1959) (Frankfurter, J.), a federal court may abstain in an action that would require the court to rule on an unclear, ambiguous, undecided issue of state policy. For example, if a federal case requires a decision of whether a county ordinance or municipal ordinance has priority in a state's laws, if the state's law on that matter is unclear, the federal court may abstain from deciding the case that turns on that issue rather than decree on such a matter of state policy from the federal bench. Such matters are very rare.

**Younger abstention** Federal courts will not enjoin a good-faith state criminal trial because a conviction might be unconstitutional. Under Younger v. Harris, 401 U.S. 37 (1971) (Black, J.), federal courts may abstain if a case is filed in federal court complaining of a criminal prosecution ongoing in state court that would, if the state trial results in a conviction, be a constitutional violation. The principle in Younger is that the state courts must have the opportunity to decide the case within the Constitution. Still, Younger abstention is not appropriate if the prosecution appears to be brought in bad faith, or for the purposes of harassment or under a patently unconstitutional law.

*See also:* abstention, abstention doctrine, Burford abstention; abstention, abstention doctrine, Dombrowski doctrine; injunction, Anti-Injunction Act (A.I.A. or AIA).

**abstention in bankruptcy** Actions that incidentally involve a bankruptcy estate may be remanded to state court. Abstention is allowed in bankruptcy court if a claim is brought before the bankruptcy court that rightfully should be heard in the state court.

*See also:* abstention, abstention in bankruptcy, abstention in the interest of justice; abstention, abstention in bankruptcy, mandatory abstention.

**abstention in the interest of justice** A bankruptcy court may abstain when a state hearing would be more just. Abstention in the interest of justice allows a bankruptcy court to abstain in a non-core bankruptcy matter that would be unjust to hear in the federal courts. A court that applies this element of permissive abstention must give some reason why justice would be served by the abstention, but matters similar to those of mandatory abstention would obviously apply, and abstention can be justified for many reasons, including the possibility of receiving fuller, faster resolution in another court, which forum would be more expert with the sources of law involved in the matter, problems of proof in one location or another, and the context in which the matter came before the bankruptcy court.

See also: abstention, abstention in bankruptcy.

**mandatory abstention** Bankruptcy courts must abstain from state cases that are only incidentally in bankruptcy. Mandatory abstention in bankruptcy requires the federal courts to abstain in cases that have been removed from state court into bankruptcy, or that were brought in federal court only under the jurisdiction of a bankruptcy, but that are not really bankruptcy matters. The six elements of mandatory abstention are: (1) a timely motion, (2) a state-law claim or cause of action, (3) not arising from bankruptcy law or a bankruptcy case under Title 11, (4) that is in federal court only owing to some relationship between the case and a bankruptcy, (5) that is in bankruptcy under Title 11, and (6) that is already within the jurisdiction of a state court that can adjudicate the issue in a timely manner.

See also: abstention, abstention in bankruptcy.

**permissive abstention** A bankruptcy court may abstain when a state hearing would favor principles of justice or federalism. Permissive abstention is a bankruptcy doctrine of abstention that is within the discretion of the federal judge to dismiss a non-core action in bankruptcy under Chapter 11 either to serve justice or in the interests of comity with the state courts. Permissive abstention need not be based on both elements; either comity or justice alone is sufficient.

See also: abstention, abstention in bankruptcy.

**abstinence** The blanket avoidance of any conduct, particularly sex, drug use, or alcohol consumption. Abstinence is a form of abstention, but abstinence implies an enduring and unvaried will to abstain rather than refraining from action at one time or another.

**abstract** A summary, or the process of making a summary. An abstract is a condensed version of a longer document. The verb to abstract, which is the process of making an abstract, is pronounced with an emphasis on the second syllable, as opposed to the noun, which emphasizes the first syllable.

See also: procedure, appellate procedure.

**abstract compromis or ad hoc compromis or anticipated compromis or general compromis** See: compromis (abstract compromis or ad hoc compromis or or anticipated compromis or general compromis).

**abstract of record** See: appeal, abstract of record, counter-abstract of record (counter abstract of record or counter-abstract or counter abstract); appeal, abstract of record.

**abstract as general or intangible** A general idea that is not tied to a particular illustration. Abstract concepts are those that are generalized from any given case or circumstance. Most ideas exist at varying levels of abstraction, and one form of argument is to contrast what in an abstract or general level might be the basis of agreement with an illustration in great specificity that might be the source of great disagreement, the question then being how well the example fits the principle. The abstract is often contrasted with the concrete.

Specific doctrines in law turn on the degree to which an idea is abstract or it is concrete or specific. In general, the law will not protect abstractions, at least not in the sense of generalizations. Thus abstract ideas are not subject to patent, and abstract claims may not be pled in a civil action for damages.

**abstract of deed (deed abstract)** A summary of the contents of a deed and its contract for sale. A deed abstract is a summary of a particular deed, including any reservations or exclusions, and often including the conditions and price of an underlying buy-sell agreement for the purchase of the property conveyed by the deed. The abstract of deed can be transcribed into an abstract of title, along with the abstract of other deeds to form a record of the chain of title for the property.

**abstract of judgment** A summary of a judgment recorded in order to enforce it. An abstract of judgment is recorded by a successful plaintiff in court records, usually in a judgment roll. The abstract lists the parties plaintiff as well as the defendant against whom a judgment has been entered, as well as the amount of damages or other relief decreed. Entry of an abstract of judgment related to a specific property puts others on notice of a claim against it, clouding title. Most courts allow a record to be entered by the defendant when the judgment is satisfied.

See also: abstract; title, cloud on title.

**abstract of title (title abstract)** A brief record of each of the deeds in the chain of title to a parcel of land. An abstract of title is a written summary of the deeds and other documents, such as grants, patents, or wills, that describe the chain of title from which the title to an estate rests or is claimed. The abstract should disclose all recorded liens, covenants, easements, and encumbrances on the property as well as any defects of title or wild deeds, if the abstractor learns of them. The abstract is not, however, required to disclose a wild deed or unrecorded interest that is not discovered by a reasonable and prudent title search. An abstract of title should be sufficient for a title examiner to determine the state of title without resort to the deed books or consultation in the record office. An abstract of title might also be required in some actions, such as actions to quiet title or trespass to try title, in which one party might demand it of a claimant to title, according to the procedures of the jurisdiction in which the action is brought.

*See also:* abstract; title, title search (examination of title); deed, wild deed.

**abuse** Improper use or ill treatment. Abuse is to use something contrary to its proper use, particularly as that use is understood according to expectations established through custom. "Abuse" implies a deliberate or intentional corruption of what should be done, and "misuse" implies a negligent or failed effort toward what should be done. Abuse comes from the Latin abutor ("improper use") through abusion ("wrong") in Law French, and it implies wrongfulness in any form. In English, abuse as a verb often modifies a noun, as in alcohol abuse, drug abuse, child abuse, elder abuse, spousal abuse, etc.

**abuse of discretion** *See:* review, standard of review, abuse of discretion; discretion, abuse of discretion, abuse of discretion as standard of review in appeal; discretion, abuse of discretion.

**abuse of discretion as standard in judicial review of administrative decision** *See:* discretion, abuse of discretion as standard in judicial review of administrative decision.

**abuse of discretion as standard of review in appeal** *See:* discretion, abuse of discretion, abuse of discretion as standard of review in appeal.

**abuse of office** *See:* office, abuse of office (abuse of the public trust or abuse of official trust).

**abuse of privilege** *See:* privilege, abuse of privilege (abuse of privileges).

**abuse of process** *See:* process, abuse of process.

**abuse of public or private trust** *See:* trust, abuse of public or private trust.

**abuse of the public trust or abuse of official trust** *See:* office, abuse of office (abuse of the public trust or abuse of official trust).

**abuse as poor treatment** Misuse, neglect, or injury by failing in a moral obligation. Abuse connotes a particular form of misuse, a violation of duty or failure of good conduct that risks or leads to injury. So — drug abuse, child abuse, sexual abuse, spousal abuse, abuse of process, abuse of office — all of these and more represent an obligation that has been corrupted to the harm, or the likely harm, of the offender or someone else. When, as in these illustrations, the abuse is also evidence of a legal liability, it is evidence of a legal obligation, but in most cases that might be thought of as abuse, there is likely to be a socially

recognized non-legal duty that is independent of the legal duty.

*See also:* neglect.

**abuse excuse** A defense or mitigation that a criminal defendant had suffered personal abuse. An abuse excuse is evidence of abuse suffered by the defendant from the victim of the crime, which is sometimes offered as evidence by a defendant in a criminal proceeding, particularly for assault, battery, manslaughter, or homicide. As a defense to the indictment, it very rarely succeeds as a matter of law, although it has the potential to sway juries to find on other grounds that the defendant was either in fear of injury or death and acted from self-defense. In its form as an excuse, however, abuse is also offered as a mitigation in sentencing.

**adult abuse (abuse of adult)** Neglect or abuse by a caregiver or guardian of an adult entrusted to that person's care. Adult abuse occurs when an adult requires another person to care for daily needs or to serve as conservator or guardian to manage financial and other matters, and that person does not perform the duties of care, conservatorship, or guardianship faithfully. Generally a tort as well as a sanctionable violation of the obligations of the conservatorship or guardianship, in cases of physical abuse or life-endangering neglect, adult abuse is a crime in many jurisdictions.

*See also:* abuse, abuse as poor treatment.

**child abuse** Unlawful mistreatment of a child. Child abuse is the physical, mental, or emotional mistreatment of a child. Child abuse may be any of several criminal acts that include infliction of excess pain, assault, sexual abuse, sexual exploitation, neglect, endangerment, or malicious punishment, but need not result in physical injury. Child abuse may be either negligent or intentional, and in most jurisdictions, the higher level of culpability raising the criminal sanctions, but in either case leading to evaluation for a loss of parental rights.

*See also:* abuse, abuse as poor treatment; parent, parental rights.

**domestic abuse** An act or pattern of unjustified physical or mental harm to a member of one's family. Domestic abuse describes a range of behaviors by a person toward one or more members of that person's family, including conduct that creates a persistent form of mental distress but also including all forms and threats of physical abuse, including sexual assault, physical battery, and homicide. Domestic abuse includes the categories of spousal abuse, child abuse, and parental abuse, although the family unit potentially including many members without blood relationships who may have a form of dependency upon the family that includes them within domestic abuse. Domestic abuse is often used to create a coercive or controlling relationship, but this need not be the case, as a controlling or dependent relationship may pre-exist the abusive conduct. In general, physical contact by a parent to discipline a child, such as spanking, or appropriate punishments for misbehavior that induce temporary unhappiness, such as times out or groundings, are not abuse. Likewise, self-defense is not domestic abuse, although the self-defense must be against an imminent threat of injury to oneself or another.

**medical abuse**   Unlawful, intentional, mistreatment of a medical patient. Medical abuse is either the willful mistreatment of a patient during the course of the patient's medical treatment or the willful interference with a medical treatment with the purpose of creating a bad outcome.

*See also:* neglect; abuse, adult abuse (abuse of adult).

**sexual abuse (sex abuse)**   Interference with the sexual organs of one who is underage or who does not desire it. Sexual abuse is contact with the sexual organs of a person who is underage or who does not desire to engage in such activities with the other person. Sexual abuse includes rape as well as less intrusive forms of contact.

*See also:* abuse, child abuse; abuse, adult abuse (abuse of adult).

**abusive discovery**   *See:* discovery, abusive discovery.

**abusive work environment**   *See:* agency, harassment, hostile work environment (abusive work environment).

**abuttals (abut or abutting)**   Adjoining properties and their shared boundary. Property that abuts is property that adjoins by sharing a boundary.

**academic degree**   *See:* degree, academic degree.

**academic freedom**   *See:* university, academic freedom.

**accelerant**   *See:* incendiary (accelerant).

**acceleration (accelerate or accelerated)**   Speeding up, particularly to move a deadline earlier. Acceleration is to do or require some action to be done by an earlier date than initially planned, agreed, or required. To accelerate work is to complete it ahead of the initial date of completion; to accelerate a note is to repay or require its repayment at a date prior to its initial maturity; to accelerate an appeal is to complete the filings according to deadlines shorter than the rules for appellate procedure usually require, to accelerate a remainder is for a future interest to vest in possession prior to its original plan, etc.

*See also:* rent, acceleration of rent (rent acceleration); remainder, contingent remainder, acceleration of the remainder (acceleration of estate or accelerated remainder).

**acceleration of estate or accelerated remainder**   *See:* remainder, contingent remainder, acceleration of the remainder (acceleration of estate or accelerated remainder).

**acceleration of rent**   *See:* rent, acceleration of rent (rent acceleration).

**acceleration clause**   A contract element that an obligation will be performed more quickly if a condition is satisfied or an event occurs. An acceleration clause is a contract clause that provides for a party's conduct, that otherwise may be performed over time or at a time in the future, may be required to be performed earlier, upon a condition in the acceleration clause failing or being satisfied. This clause is often found in loan agreements, in which a debt is to be paid over time or due at some time in the future, though the clause provides the debt may be called for earlier payment when some event occurs. If, for example, an installment debt that would ordinarily be paid over twenty years is secured by an interest on a property by a loan agreement requiring acceleration if the property is used as a security for another debt, and then the borrower allows another lien on the property, the debt may be called and be required to be paid in full. This kind of "or-else" clause may serve as a significant inducement for the party subject to acceleration to observe the contractual obligations that might trigger the acceleration.

**acceptance**

**acceptance as acceptance of an offer**   Agreement to an offer, which can result in the mutual assent necessary to form a contract. An acceptance is a response to an offer that agrees to its terms. The acceptance may be formal or informal, explicit or implied. Once a valid offer is accepted, a contract is usually formed by mutual assent. The common law once required an effective acceptance to match exactly all of the terms of an offer, otherwise mutual assent was not created and no contract could be formed. Under both modern common law and the Uniform Commercial Code, an effective acceptance does not necessarily have to exactly match the terms of the offer to create mutual assent, but the rules and situations in which these exceptions apply are varied and specialized enough so that acceptance still connotes its original, stringent, contractual meaning. A person may accept an offer in any reasonable manner, provided the offeror does not specifically inform the offeree otherwise, some other rule or law does not specify otherwise, and the offeror does not earlier communicate a valid revocation of the offer.

*See also:* silence, silence as acceptance of offer; offer, contract offer, rejection of offer; offer, contract offer.

*1. power of acceptance*   The offeree may accept the offer according to its terms or by any reasonable means in a reasonable time. The offeree — the person or corporate representative to whom the offer is made — has the power of acceptance. The offeree must usually assent to the terms of the offer within a reasonable time and by reasonable means, but within these boundaries the time and form of acceptance are unlimited. The offeror may limit the offeree's power of acceptance by expressly specifying restrictions on the power of acceptance, such as a time by which the offer will expire if it is not accepted, or a particular means by which a valid acceptance must be communicated. When such conditions are specified, the offeree must then reasonably conform to such conditions to create a binding contract.

**2. consequences of acceptance** Agreement to the terms of a bargain. The consequences of acceptance are, generally, that the contract terms are established and both the offer and the acceptance are binding. Even so, one who initially accepted terms or goods may revoke acceptance, if the circumstances in which revocation occurs make the revocation reasonable. These circumstances may involve notice and demand (anticipatory repudiation) or a collateral attempt to find other goods that would satisfy (buyer's duty to cover). One who attempted to perform but learned subsequently that performance did not conform to the contract may remedy the situation, if the means and circumstances make the same reasonable (seller's duty to cure).

**3. duration of power of acceptance** An offer may be taken up in any reasonable time or within any specified time. The duration of power of acceptance — how long an offeree may take to communicate agreement by return to the offeror — is assumed to be that time reasonable under the circumstances. If an offeror desires differently, the offer must expressly specify restrictions on the power of acceptance. The offeree must then conform to those conditions, to create a binding contract.

**4. duration of acceptance** An acceptance is to remain in effect until the contract is performed. The duration of acceptance is the time during which a party can perform on the offered terms and the performance will be considered as an acceptance. Sometimes, the duration is stated in the contract terms offered, but it is usually presumed to be a reasonable amount of time. "Duration of acceptance" as a term is somewhat rare, even if the concept is implied in or the unlabeled term is specified in many offers: even if the term is not stated, neither the offeror nor the offeree have an infinite time to satisfy the other terms.

**5. efficacy** An offeree must actually communicate acceptance to the offeror. An acceptance only creates a valid contract when the offeree tenders an acceptance that communicates to the offeror an agreement with the terms of the offer. Reasonable variations from a requested or typical form of acceptance are sufficient to accept, if the affirmation of the terms of the offer is apparent in the acceptance as communicated.

**6. performance as acceptance** Conduct demonstrating an intent to accept an offer constitutes acceptance. Acceptance may occur not only as a result of an express statement of acceptance but also through conduct by the offeree that expresses willingness to perform in accordance with the offeror's terms. Such performance constitutes acceptance to the offer as made.

**7. promise as acceptance** An offer may be accepted by a promise to perform in response to the offer. Many offers are capable of acceptance by the transmission from the offeree to the offeror of a promise, when the promise is responsive to the conditions of the original offer. Acceptance by a promise occurs when the offeree communicates a promise by which the offeree expresses willingness to perform in accordance with the offeror's terms. The promise must accept the offer without variation or condition.

See also: promise.

**8. acceptance of goods as acceptance of offer (impact of acceptance)** Accepting goods delivered according to an offer is its acceptance. A buyer who accepts goods that either conform to the terms of an offer or are otherwise acceptable according to the terms of the offer is presumed to have accepted the offer.

**9. shipment of goods as acceptance of offer** A merchant offeree's shipment of goods in response to a merchant's offer is an acceptance. If a merchant buyer submits an order to a merchant seller, the seller can informally accept the offer by sending goods that substantially conform to the goods described in the order.

**10. silence as acceptance (failure to respond)** Silence is generally not a valid acceptance. Acceptance by failing to respond is usually not enough of a foundation on which to build the assurance that the parties have mutually agreed to contract terms. Even so, the parties' prior conduct can under some circumstances support a reasonable expectation or objective belief by the offeror that an acceptance may be implied. If a buyer has requested and received the exact same shipment from a seller with the exact same requirement on the same time table for several years, and the seller communicates the offer and information related to the shipment for the following year, or if the buyer accepts the property offered or the benefit of the offer, then the seller may reasonably interpret the buyer's silence as acceptance. Whether the seller is reasonably justified in that presumption or expectation is a matter of fact, depending in part on the knowledge each party has of one another and their behavior toward one another in the prior years.

See also: silence, silence as acceptance of offer.

**battle of the forms (U.C.C. battle of the forms or UCC battle of the forms)** Variation of language between an offer and a would-be acceptance. The battle of the forms arises when there are differences in the boilerplate sent between parties attempting to enter into a contract for a sale. The common–law approach holds that no contract arises unless the terms of the acceptance mirror the terms of the offer. The approach of the Uniform Commercial Code allows a contract to be created even when the standard terms in a boilerplate acceptance conflict with the standard terms of a boilerplate offer, unless the terms in conflict are material or represent an intent to make a counter–offer. If there is no disagreement regarding material terms, under the U.C.C. the contract is deemed to include all of the agreed terms and none of the conflicting terms; the gap–filling rules of the U.C.C. then supply any terms not agreed upon.

**last shot doctrine** The last iteration of a contract's terms prevails. The last shot doctrine, in the battle of the forms, concludes that the terms contained in the last contract form proffered between the parties is the one that establishes the contract terms.

**conditional acceptance** A response to an offer that contains different terms. An invalid acceptance of offered terms pending assent by offeror to additional terms. A conditional acceptance agrees broadly with an offer, but conditions the acceptance upon a particular term that differs from the offer. A conditional acceptance is almost always a counter-offer because the language is too specific to result in acceptance under the generic battle of the forms.

**knockout rule (knock-out rule)** Varying, non-material terms between an offer and proposed acceptance are void. The U.C.C. knockout rule allows the formation of a contract even if the form acceptance sent in response to a form offer has terms that vary from the terms of the offer, the rule knocking out the varying terms as long as the terms are not material to the agreement. Under the knockout rule, the terms in both forms are eliminated from the contract, and the default rules of the U.C.C. are applied to govern the contract instead.

**mailbox rule** An acceptance is made when mailed or irretrievably transmitted. The mailbox rule is a constructive time of acceptance. The rule presumes that any letter given by the offeree to the postal services or sent through another irretrievable communication service was received by the offeror, and the time at which the acceptance binds the offeror is the time of the mailing. The offeror can rebut the presumption of mailing with appropriate evidence, either that the offer was not sent when claimed or that the terms of the offer required a different means of either making or timing its acceptance. The theory that would place the burden of slow communications on the offeror was once popular under an agency theory, but the mailbox rule was the dominant view in the twentieth century. This approach, or a simple pragmatic question of efficiency, might not remain so convincing for the mailbox rule, as communications increase in speed and decrease in expense.

Note, the mailbox rule for contracts is a bit different from the mailbox rule of civil procedure. In contracts, the mailbox rule will apply to an acceptance sent by mail or any other transmission, such as telegram, fax, telex, or potentially electronic mail, as long as the means is ordinarily reasonable for this type of communication and the communication is irretrievable once sent.

*See also:* mail, mailbox rule.

**materially conflicting term** Terms of an acceptance differing from terms in the offer imply rejection of the offer if the term is material. A materially conflicting term in an acceptance is a term in the acceptance that is not logically reconcilable to a term expressed or implied in the offer and that is material to the contract as a whole. An acceptance with a materially conflicting term is not an acceptance but either a counter-offer or an acceptance conditioned on the original offeror's acceptance of the materially conflicting term.

**mirror-image rule (mirror image rule)** Non-commercial offers and acceptances must match exactly to be binding. The mirror-image rule requires that the terms of the acceptance to an offer must duplicate exactly the terms in the offer, otherwise the acceptance is insufficient, and no contract is created. This rule remains the law in most jurisdictions governing contracts that are not subject to the knockout rule of the Uniform Commercial Code or to contracts law that is influenced by it. Thus the mirror-image rule applies to most sales contracts not between merchants and to most contracts not for the sale of goods. It also applies to most international goods contracts, at least to those governed by the United Nations Convention on Contracts for the International Sales of Goods.

*See also:* acceptance, acceptance as acceptance of an offer, varying acceptance (acceptance at variance to an offer); acceptance, acceptance as acceptance of an offer, varying acceptance (acceptance at variance to an offer).

**varying acceptance (acceptance at variance to an offer)** A seeming acceptance that is ineffective owing to differing terms. A varying acceptance, or an acceptance at variance to an offer, is a putative acceptance of an offer. A varying acceptance may be ineffective in jurisdictions and contracts that apply the mirror-image rule, because the acceptance specifies terms that differ from those of the offer. In these jurisdictions, a varying acceptance amounts to a rejection of the offer and to a counter-offer. Agreements subject to the Uniform Commercial Code may be created by a varying offer, as long as the varying terms are not material to the contract.

*See also:* offer, contract offer, rejection of offer; offer, contract offer, counter-offer (counteroffer).

**acceptance of goods** The act of receiving goods and taking ownership of them. Acceptance of goods is the act of receiving goods, retaining them, and taking ownership of them, thus accepting the performance of the seller of the goods as sufficient under the contract both as to their quality and as to their delivery. Unless otherwise specified in the contract or invoice, mere receipt is not the same as acceptance, in part because the recipient must inspect the goods received. Under the Uniform Commercial Code, acceptance is presumed at a reasonable time after receipt unless the buyer acts before then to reject them in some manner that is communicated to the seller.

**revocation of acceptance** Retraction of acceptance when nonconformity of goods was latent or was to be cured but has not been. Revocation of the acceptance of non-conforming goods is allowed when the buyer accepted them in good faith believing them to conform and their non-conformity was not one that the buyer should have known of at the time of acceptance. Revocation is also allowed when acceptance is made in reliance on seller's assurances that the non-conformity will be cured, but the seller does not cure in a reasonable time.

**acceptor** One who accepts something. An acceptor is one who accepts something that is delivered. Generally, the term is used as a rather specific substitute for the offeree or buyer, especially when the acceptor is an agent of the offeree or buyer. Still, a buyer or offeree who accepts a delivery or an instrument is also an acceptor of it.

More technically, the acceptor of a bill of exchange or other negotiable instrument accepts the liability of the bill, note, or draft, and becomes the principal debtor liable for its performance or satisfaction, according to its terms at the time of acceptance.

**acceptor of bill of exchange** One who takes on the obligation of a bill of exchange. The one person or company that agrees to pay a bill of exchange drawn upon that person or company's account.

**access**

**access easement** *See:* easement, access easement (ingress and egress easement).

**access to justice (access to the courts)** The ability to have one's day in court without barriers or favoritism. Access to justice is an ideal that every person with a genuine cause of action should have a right to be heard and the cause redressed in court. Access to justice thus labels a policy that justifies many remedies which, if they were unavailable, might prevent a person from enforcing their rights in court, such as providing an indigent with a trial transcript for a mandatory appeal or with a competent attorney. Access to justice is hostile to the use of doctrines of standing and jurisdiction to prevent some claims from every being heard by a neutral judge.

**access to the courts** *See:* access to justice (access to the courts).

**access as a way to property** A means of reaching a property or way over the lands of another. Access is a route by which a property owner and the owner's guests may transit over public or private land or water to reach the property held. When a means of access is the only practicable access to property, and it is required over a public way or over property of a once-common estate, a right to the public way or a servitude over the private property may exist by necessity. Thus, a particular access might be subject to an easement or be the basis for a servitude or license, but whether a route is an access is a matter

of fact, and whether a right to use such an access as an easement, servitude, or license is a matter of law or equity.

**access as right to institutional benefit** The entitlement to opportunities provided by participation in public or some private institutions. Access is a broad term for the ability of an individual, or sometimes members of a group, to participate in the public sphere. It is usually a matter of participation in a particular institutional setting, as in access to education or access to justice. The term is used in this sense derived by analogy from the law of property.

**handicapped access (disabled access)** The means for a person with a motor disability to enter, use, and leave a building. Handicapped access to certain buildings open to the public is required under a variety of federal and state laws. Buildings open to the public may include apartment buildings and hotels, although not usually private homes. The Fair Housing Act, however, requires adequate handicapped access to multi-family dwellings.

**accession** Obtaining ownership in something. Accession, in general, is the act of acquiring or reaching a position or status, particularly the act of gaining ownership in any form in an asset or property; the act of entering into a position, office, or role; or the act of entering into a treaty, convention, or contract.

**accession as attainment of rank** Achievement, or entry into higher status. Obtaining a higher position, usually after pursuit of the goal, is accession.

**accession as entry into agreement** Entry into a treaty or other agreement among states. Accession is the process of entry into a treaty or contract. Accession also occurs when a person or entity enters, or gains access to, an organization, usually upon meeting certain requirements, and so the term particularly describes the process of a state's entry into an agreement already in force owing to its agreement among other states.

**accession as property improvement** An improvement to property from natural or artificial change. An accession to a parcel is an improvement to the property resulting in an enlargement or a fixture, whether the improvement is created by human action or natural events. So, a tenant's improvement of a road is an accession to the land over which the road runs. The accession is the improvement itself, denominated to express the landlord's right to retain the accession when the lease is terminated and the landlord's reversion becomes possessory. The rule in the common law is still valid in most jurisdictions, that accessions to property that occur during a lease become the property of the landlord at the time of reversion. There are exceptions, however, particularly when a contract for lease specifies to the contrary or when the accession is a trade fixture, an artificial installation made for the purpose of commerce.

**accession as union of properties** The permanent merger of property derived from or united with

**account as statement of fiduciary**  Documentation of finances of an estate or trust. An account by a fiduciary is a record of assets, debts, and disbursements, made from time to time to the beneficiary and to other interested parties. A final accounting is made in the case of a decedent's trustee, administrator, or personal representative of an estate, the account records the assets of the estate, the claims made against it, the settlement of the claims, and the disposition of the assets to the legatees, devisees, beneficiaries, and heirs. A fiduciary can be judicially compelled by the beneficiary or by creditors of the estate to honor the estate's obligations and to render a final accounting.

**account as testimony**  The version of events as told by one person. An account is a narrative of past events, usually by an eyewitness, relating what that witness personally observed. Note: a person recounts, or remembers, an account. Note also: a witness's account may be relayed by a second person, in which case the second person is giving an account of the witness's account.
*See also:* witness, lay witness.

**account current (current account)**  An open account, a statement of debts and obligations owed between two persons. A current account is a recording of obligations that allows transactions between the parties and is updated with each transaction, without a contemplation that the account will be settled or closed on a specific date. "Current account" is often used to describe a form of bank account or a general business outlook for a company or a balance of trade or general economic outlook for a country.

**account receivable (accounts receivable)**  Money billed but not yet collected. Accounts receivable include all of the bills that a business or organization has delivered to its debtors and have not yet been paid, and which the company stating the account has no reason to believe are not likely to be paid. Accounts receivable are represented as a current asset on the balance sheet.
*See also:* receivable.

**account stated**  A statement of an amount certain that is owed by one to another. An account stated is the sum agreed between a debtor and a creditor as the amount that is then owed by the debtor to the creditor to satisfy the debt. Although in passing, a creditor acting alone may claim that an amount demanded is an amount stated, in law the term usually refers to the amount agreed by the debtor and by the creditor.

The account stated is a pleading element for an enforcement action in law for the collection of an agreed debt. In such an action, the plaintiff must "state an account" between the defendant and the plaintiff, which is a statement showing that the defendant agreed to pay the plaintiff a certain amount by a certain time, but failed to do so. The word "account" or the phrase "account stated" should be incorporated into the claim in the complaint.

**accounts payable**  Debt. Accounts payable, the bills a business or organization has not yet paid, is a sum that is represented as a current liability on the business or organization's balance sheet.

**bank account (account in bank)**  A fund deposited into a bank or banking institution, on which a depositor may make demands for payment. Bank accounts are claims — they are actually shares of debt in a common fund, or one of several common funds — held by a bank or banking institution like a credit union or savings and loan. The depositor deposits money into the fund according to a contract entered when the account is opened or altered, with each deposit establishing a claim. The value of the claim will rise over time if the contract specifies that interest will be paid. The contract will specify the forms of withdrawal the depositor may make, which is to say it will specify how the depositor may demand payment from the bank made to the depositor or to third parties the depositor may specify, as when the depositor draws a draft, order, or check on the bank and gives it to someone else. The bank is obligated to honor demands made in accord with the contract, as long as the demand does not exceed the amount of the claim the depositor has against the bank, which is to say as long as the depositor has sufficient funds on deposit in the account to satisfy the claim.
*See also:* trust, Totten trust.

**deposit account**  Account to which the account holder may contribute money. A deposit account is the basic form of personal or business bank account. It is not assured or represented by a certificate of deposit but allows anyone whose name is on the account to add to it.

**joint account**  A bank account held by two or more people or entities as depositors. A joint account in a bank is one in which each depositor has an undivided and equal share of the whole account, which is payable in full to either party at any time. Thus, it operates as if it is a joint interest with a right of survivorship, even though no independent right of survivorship needed to be stated in the opening of the account. In some jurisdictions, joint accounts are separately designated if they are held by two depositors who are husband and wife and the account is held by the entireties. Generally, joint accounts may be held among any number of parties, although they are most common in the management of domestic household accounts.

**mutual account (mutual running account)**  A single, multi-party account in which each party must settle its own charges. A mutual account is a single account held by more than one party, in which each shares access to the account with the others and in which all are liable to the institution holding the account on the single balance. The parties must operate the account with an intent to share the account and according to an express or implied agreement that each will eventually settle or adjust obligations each creates against the account. Note: a mutual account may also be current or running, if it has no time limitations, such as a mutual running account.

*See also:* account, open account.

**open account** An account with a current obligation that may be changed. An open account is an account maintained by an institution for a holder, in which either a credit or a debt exists that may be modified by payments and charges in the future. The term may be used generally for any account in which ongoing transactions are allowed. An open account may have an obligation that is past due and on which payment is required, though this is not usually a defining aspect of the open character of the account.

Open accounts are common among merchants and between merchants and customers. They represent a form of credit extended by the merchant in which both debts and payments made are recorded, and in which further debts and payments are both expected and will be recorded. Interest is sometimes charged on the balance owed at the end of an accounting period, which is added to the balance owed.

**partial account** An incomplete statement of account, particularly to allow partial payment from an estate. A partial account is any incomplete rendering of account. Partial account is often used by an executor, administrator, or personal representative to allow an early disbursement from an estate in probate, when the amounts owed by the estate have been ascertained and assets will clearly exceed amounts to be paid but insufficient time has elapsed to perform all of the functions of the estate.

**accountability (legal accountability)** Legal responsibility for a person's action. Accountability is the legal responsibility for personal action. Accountability may take the forms of liability through agency, partnership, criminal complicity, or otherwise, or it may arise more informally. A parent is accountable for the actions of a young child, and an adult of sound mind is accountable for the adult's own conduct. Some adults lack the capacity to form judgments regarding their conduct and also lack a person to be responsible for them in either a de facto supervision or a conservatorship, and it may be that no one is accountable for their actions.

**accountable officer** *See:* officer, federal officer, accountable officer.

**accountant (accountancy)** A person licensed to monitor and maintain financial transactions of a third party. An accountant is a person trained in the profession of accountancy, who is then licensed to practice it. Informally, any person who maintains financial records or books may be referred to as the accountant of an operation, and such a designation may carry some significance as a matter of reliance, but it does not carry with it the privileges of the profession. Accountancy represents the profession, as well as the processes and the rules, by which an accountant assesses and reports financial information.

*See also:* privilege, evidentiary privilege, accountant–client privilege.

## accounting

**accounting as a remedy (equitable accounting)** A supervised review of assets and liabilities and the disgorgement of funds wrongly held. An accounting is a remedy in equity, in which a third–party auditor of the defendant audits the accounts of the defendant to discern whether the defendant holds money or assets that rightfully belong to the plaintiff, after which the defendant must tender the wrongly held assets to the plaintiff. An accounting requires the tracing of money and goods that result from specific transactions, allowing the determination of allocation of value from one transaction in the fruits of a transaction far down a chain of transaction. An accounting is appropriate when there are grounds to believe that an unjust enrichment, a breach of trust, or an abuse of a bailment, or other wrongdoing has occurred. In such cases, it is particularly useful and appropriate as a remedy if the plaintiff could not have sufficient knowledge of the defendant's conduct to claim an amount owed. Thus, an accounting is appropriate as a remedy for a claim of unjust enrichment, conversion, breach of fiduciary duty, and other claims that might otherwise require the plaintiff to plead a specific amount in damages or injury or to identify property that is wrongly held and subject to forfeiture. An accounting is appropriate for some cases of the infringement of a patent or copyright, to trace the extent of the benefit realized by the infringer. An accounting is also appropriate as a remedy for disputes over common assets, such as the assets of a partnership in dissolution or marriage during divorce. It may be ordered as an ancillary procedure for a partition. In such cases, the equitable nature of an accounting allows the parties to avoid a jury trial in allocating their claims and assets subject to dispute.

An accounting is an equitable remedy, subject to the maxims and defenses of equity, particularly that an accounting is only available when no adequate remedy at law exists. The usual bases for inadequacy of a legal remedy are when there are mutual accounts between plaintiff and defendant, when there is a fiduciary duty of the defendant to render an account to the plaintiff, or when the accounts are held by the defendant and sufficient complexity that otherwise the plaintiff would have no means of knowing the defendant's account of them is accurate.

*See also:* receiver (receivership).

**accrual accounting method (accrual accounting or accrual basis)** Accounting records made at the time rights to income or liability accrues. Accrual-basis accounting records liabilities and assets when they are manifest, not when they are billed or received. Using accrual accounting, if Widgeco receives an order for 100 widgets, it records an asset of that value at the time of the order, not at the time of payment. Likewise, if Widgeco orders 1000 widget knobs, it records the liability at the time of the order, not at the time of the bill or the time of payment. An account that uses accrual-basis accounting for assets must use it for liabilities, and vice versa.

*See also:* expense, accrued expense; accounting, cash-basis accounting method (cash accounting or cash basis).

**cash-basis accounting method (cash accounting or cash basis)** Accounting records made at the time of payment, not the time rights to income or liability accrue. Cash-basis accounting records liabilities and assets when they are paid, not when they are created or billed. Using cash accounting, if Widgeco receives an order for 100 widgets, it waits to record an asset of that value when the payment for it is received, not having recorded it on its books at the time of the order or the time the bill is sent. Likewise, if Widgeco orders 1000 widget knobs, it records the liability at the time the payment is sent, not at the times of the order or the receipt of the bill. An account that uses cash-basis accounting for assets must use it for liabilities, and vice versa.

*See also:* accounting, accrual accounting method (accrual accounting or accrual basis).

**Financial Accounting Standards Board (F.A.S.B. or FASB)** The private, non-profit organization that sets standards for accountancy in the private sector. The FASB is responsible for the creation, organization, and alteration of the Generally Accepted Accounting Principles used in all private accounting in the United States. GAAP standards for governmental accounting are not included within these but are issued by the GASB.

**Generally Accepted Accounting Principles (G.A.A.P. or GAAP)** The rules of accountancy. Generally Accepted Accounting Principles are the rules of engagement for accountants managing the preparation of financial statements, records that lead to corporate statements or tax filings, or any other statement dealing with assets and liabilities on which any person outside of the corporation might rely. GAAP are issued by two bodies, FASB for private accounting and GASB for public accounting.

*See also:* accounting, Financial Accounting Standards Board (F.A.S.B. or FASB).

**Governmental Accounting Standards Board (G.A.S.B. or GASB)** The private, non-profit organization that sets standards for accountancy in the public sector. The GASB is responsible for the creation, organization, and alteration of the Generally Accepted Accounting Principles used in all governmental accounting in the United States. GAAP standards for private accounting are not included within these but are issued by the FASB.

**accreditation** Official approval of professional action. Accreditation is the process by which an individual, entity, or institution is granted official certification to provide certain types of educational, professional, or technical activity or service. The process of accreditation is usually performed by a government agency, a private organization, or a body with experience, knowledge, or vocation in the type of act being accredited; often

under a government license or regulatory delegation to perform the certification. Accrediting agencies and bodies are usually delegated both the power to determine the standards by which accreditation is to be performed and the obligation of inspection and evaluation of the individuals or entities seeking to be given or to retain accreditation.

Most professional activities are subject to accreditation. In many senses there is no difference between the licensure or an individual and the accreditation of an individual, though custom and practice suggest that the one is more often applied to individual and the other more often to institutional qualification. Licensure of an individual to practice law is a form of accreditation, but the accreditation is rarely used in this sense. More often it refers to the process of institutional accreditation, such as the process of accrediting law schools to grant professional degrees as a qualification to practice.

*See also:* law, law school, accredited law school; credential (credentials or credentialling).

**accredited investor** *See:* investor, accredited investor.

**accredited law school** *See:* law, law school, accredited law school.

**accredited representative** *See:* representative, accredited representative.

**accretion** Gradual increase in size, value, number, or mass. Accretion is a process of gradual acquisition of more size or property. Accretion originally was applied to the growth of physical property, as a shoreline grows owing to the deposit of sediment. It also applies to the growth of assets or value in accounts, funds, or assets resulting from appreciation, dividend reinvestment, interest, or other routine increases. Accretion also describes the growth in earnings and wealth that a person is likely to have in the future, which is the measure of future earnings based on the usual conduct of life in the future for a person of a given age, employment, education, and training. Accretion in labor law is the growth of a union or local through the addition of members as a unionized enterprise grows.

**accretion as addition of non-union employees to union** Posting of a once non-union worker to a unionized job. Accretion, as a term of labor law, is a growth of union membership owing to the growth of jobs subject to union control. In most cases, accretion occurs when a person — who has not previously been a member of a union or in a job requiring a union card — is hired into or transferred to a position that requires representation by a union. Such a person joins the union, and that person's membership in the union is accretive.

**accretion as increase of a shore** Building up of sediment deposits near a water line. Accretion is often used to describe the process of the growth of a river bank or shoreline through the gradual deposit of sediment or sand, although it may describe the development of property by windblown dirt or other gradual action such as guano deposition. Accretion is often described as the opposite of erosion, in which land is lost to the action of water, wind, or animal behavior in the reverse of the way it is gained by accretion. Under international law, alteration of a stream or shore through accretion generally moves the borders that are benchmarked by the stream or shore (in contrast to avulsive shifts in which the borders remain static).

*See also:* avulsion; river; boundary.

**accrual (accrue)** Growth or ripening. Accrual is growth in the sense of either increase or ripening. The term is especially common in describing the increased value in an account through the computation of interest or in depicting the ripening of a claim that may then be brought in law or in equity. When a claim has accrued, then, it may be brought into court for redress, and it may not be pursued in court earlier.

*See also:* limitation, limitation of actions, statute of limitations.

**accrual accounting method** *See:* accounting, accrual accounting method (accrual accounting or accrual basis).

**accrual bond** *See:* bond, accrual bond.

**accrued benefit** *See:* benefit, accrued benefit.

**accrued expense** *See:* expense, accrued expense.

**accrued income** *See:* income, accrued income.

**accrued interest** *See:* interest, interest for money, accrued interest.

**accumulation**

**accumulated legacy** *See:* legacy, accumulated legacy.

**accumulated taxable income** *See:* income, accumulated taxable income.

**accusation (accuse or accusatory)** A charge that another person has committed a crime or other serious wrongdoing. As a matter of constitutional law, an accusation is contained in the instrument in which the charges for which a person is arrested are presented to the accused and to the court. Accusations in any such form must be made with sufficient specificity to apprise the accused of what conduct the accused is alleged to have committed and the criminal liability alleged as a result. Such accusations can usually be based only on admissible evidence, although it may be circumstantial. Although it may apply earlier, the right to counsel applies once a formal accusation of a felony has been made.

Accusation generally takes several forms in U.S. criminal procedure. The filing of a police report, the filing of criminal charges, the issuance of an arrest warrant, the making of an arrest, the filing of a criminal information, or the issuance of an indictment are all forms of accusation. Any claim to a police officer that a given person has committed an offense is an accusation, even if it is a claim by one already accused that another person committed the crime. Informally, an accusation is any claim that a

person has committed some wrong, such as a harassment or a violation of workplace safety.

*See also:* recrimination.

**accusatory pleading** *See:* pleading, accusatory pleading.

**accused** A person charged with a criminal act or other misconduct. The accused is the person against whom an accusation is made, particularly of conduct that amounts to a crime. Although an accused may be a criminal defendant, the label is broader, as it applies to any person who has been accused by another of either criminal or civil wrongdoing, and of administrative offenses that may not be brought before a court of law for adjudication. Thus one accused of employment misconduct, such as sexual harassment, is a person accused, even if the conduct is not criminal.

*See also:* defendant, criminal defendant (criminal defense).

**acid rain** *See:* pollution, air pollution, acid rain.

**acknowledged heir** *See:* heir, acknowledged heir.

**acknowledgment (acknowledge)** The verification of a document, identity, or claim. Acknowledgment is, literally, to say that one knows something to be true. An acknowledgment can be the recognition of a signature on a deed as that of the signer, or the deed itself as the true statement of ownership. In the case of a deed, acknowledgment requires a formal statement that usually must be witnessed. Acknowledgment can be of a child as one's own son or daughter, or a debt as one's true liability, or of the receipt of a document or payment, or of any other fact.

The acknowledgment by a person of paternity or maternity of a child is essential in establishing parentage after the death of a supposed parent. In general, a child may prove post-mortem parentage of a parent who acknowledged parentage of the child while the parent was alive, but most jurisdictions create procedural bars to claims of parentage that were not acknowledged during life. Different jurisdictions have differing standards for the conduct required during life to be sufficient as an acknowledgment.

In its strictest sense, acknowledgment is a formal process, usually taking one of two forms. The more common is a written statement acknowledging some fact to be true or some act to have been done (or not done), is signed by the person making it, and in some cases witnessed by a disinterested party or notary. The less common is to make a statement under oath in the presence of a person qualified to administer oaths. All other acts and statements that amount to acknowledgment are informal, whether the informal acknowledgment is a direct statement of the fact acknowledged or a statement or action by which the fact would have been acknowledged by implication. The civil law, such as the Louisiana Code, places significant limits on the acknowledgment of the paternity of a child by any means other than formal acknowledgment.

*See also:* receipt (receive or recipient).

effect of each is at the time in which the effects of both concur, and so the effects of the unilateral actions that amount to a bilateral act is manifest in one event. A two-party contract is a bilateral act.

**external act**  Action visible to others in the doing or the result. External acts are acts that are visible to others. Whether committed by a corporation or an individual, external acts are things done that others may see and may reasonably evaluate for meaning.

**internal act**  An act that is significant within an organization. Internal acts are those in an organization that have meaning only within the organization, although an internal act might have an indirect effect on someone outside the organization; the intended scope of the significance of the act is internal, not external.

**jural act**  Any action that deliberately brings into being a legal obligation, particularly when the action is in a writing. A jural act is one that creates a legal rule or obligation. In particular, jural acts are the decisions reflected in the writings of a contract, of a statute, of a last will and testament, of a trust instrument, or in any other writing that is to create obligations enforceable in law in the future.

**special act (particular act)**  Legislation that does not apply universally in the jurisdiction. Special acts may take many forms, but their hallmark is to have a narrow application by subject matter, beneficiary, or geography so that they do not apply equally to all of the people subject to the laws generally.

**verbal act**  An act committed by words rather than conduct. A verbal act is spoken or written language that has a legal effect on the parties communicating and receiving the message. When a person responds to an offer by saying, "I agree to your terms," an act of mutual assent is created by the words in a verbal act. In the law of evidence, verbal acts are not considered hearsay when they are introduced to prove that an act took place, rather than to prove that any words uttered were true or false.

**acta**  *See:* actus (acta).

**acting**  Temporary holder of a position. Acting is inserted into a title or office to indicate that the person holding the title is substituting for another. The substitute may be required while a permanent holder is sought or while the permanent holder is absent.

**actio**  A pleading or suit; also the duty of an official to carry out a public function or to give a legal order. Actio, the Latin origin of the English word action, represented the performance of a certain range of formal public roles, which for a citizen included seeking redress under the law through the courts or in defending an action, whether criminal or civil. For an official, the actio might be not only an order in the management of a suit but any other official pronouncement required of the office.

*See also:* actus (acta).

**action (actionable or act or acted)**  Anything that is done, which in law is the formal process of seeking relief in court. An action is anything that is done, that is, either a result or the process by which a result is caused, whether by human, mechanical, or natural agency. In law, an action particularly means the means by which the will of the state or the public is exercised, which is usually by a legal proceeding. An action is therefore a civil or criminal proceeding in court.

**action qui tam or qui tam action**  *See:* whistleblower, qui tam (action qui tam or qui tam action).

**action to foreclose mortgage.**  *See:* mortgage, action to foreclose mortgage.

**action to quiet title**  *See:* title, action to quiet title (quiet title).

**action will lie**  *See:* lie (action will lie).

**action as action in court**  A criminal or civil trial. An action may be civil or criminal. A civil action is a lawsuit: one party makes a legal or equitable demand to protect a right or claim a recovery from the other. A criminal action is a prosecution brought by a representative of the government against one or more individuals who are accused of committing a crime.

**action as behavior**  The conduct of a person resulting in some changed circumstance in the physical world. Action is conduct, behavior, or something done. Although action may include willful inaction, such as a deliberate omission of duty, action generally implies affirmative physical conduct. Speech is action. Displaying an image is action. Action is anything that a person does that affects circumstances in the world, no matter how slight, whether the changed circumstance is intended or not.

**civil action**  All actions in law or equity that are not criminal actions. The civil action is the generic term for all lawsuits. In modern federal practice, all forms of action that are not criminal are inherently civil actions. At common law and in some state courts still, civil actions comprise non-criminal actions in law and equity other than those for writs of extraordinary relief, such as habeas corpus or mandamus.

**collusive action**  Claim based on a sham controversy between the parties. A collusive action is a dispute before the courts in which the parties do not have an actual dispute, but one or both of the parties has brought the claim either to obtain a legal precedent for future litigation or for reasons of their own seek a legal answer to a question over which they have no stake between them. Collusive divorce actions were once common prior to the creation of no-fault divorce for irreconcilable differences, though courts often ignored the collusive nature of the action in the interests of expedience. If parties are merely cooperative, or erroneously bring a claim which does not present a ripe controversy, the action is not collusive. Actions to quiet title, actions for declaratory judgment, or other actions seeking a resolution of disputed rights that have yet to be asserted are not collusive.

**criminal action**  An action brought by a government seeking a punishment of the defendant from a public criminal offense. A criminal action is a proceeding in which a defendant is charged with violating a criminal law and then prosecuted by representatives of a government with the end of ascertaining whether there is sufficient evidence of guilt of the defendant and, if so, determining an appropriate punishment. Civil actions are not criminal actions, and various actions having punitive aspects, such as in rem proceedings to forfeit assets connected with a crime or demanded for payment of taxes, or civil actions claiming punitive damages, are not criminal actions. Criminal actions are subject to the procedural requirements of the Fourth, Fifth, Sixth, and Eighth Amendments, generally requiring any loss of property and liberty to be according to the due process of law and particularly requiring speedy trial, representation by counsel, trial by jury in the district of the offense, notice of the accusation, confrontation of witnesses, and compulsory process of favorable witnesses, as well as protections against self-incrimination, double jeopardy, excessive bail or fines or cruel and unusual punishment.

**direct action as claim against insurance company**  A suit against an insurer brought not by the insured but by claimant against the insured. A direct action is a civil action filed against an insurer that could have been brought against an insured person or entity who caused the plaintiff's damages. This form of action is only available in some states, usually pursuant to a direct action statute. In such states, a direct action is usually available even if no finding of liability or judgment has been entered against the insured.

**final agency action**  The final formal exercise of an agency. A final agency action is the last available formal process of decision-making within an agency that would allow the agency any discretion in the outcome of the question or conflict presented. Usually, no judicial review of an agency's action is possible until it is final.

**form of action**  The type of civil action, described by the remedy the plaintiff seeks. The form of action is the category (or, more often, the categories) by which a given civil suit is understood by lawyers and by the court. The form of action dictates the scope of the case—the requirements for pleading by the plaintiff, the defenses available to the defendant, and the scope of potential third-party practice. The form of action will also dictate the jury instructions or required findings by which the action is finally resolved. Modern civil procedure and its concept of notice pleading is less rigid in the evaluation of a case according to the form of action chosen by the plaintiff, but the general scope of the form chosen is still influential in the scope of license a plaintiff may receive in amending or refining a cause once it is filed.

At common law the form of action was limited exclusively to the form of writ sought by the plaintiff, and the forms of writs were circumscribed. Enduring complaints against civil practice under the writ system and the successive systems of forms were that the systems stifled innovation and valued the satisfaction of form above the requirement that the law do justice between the parties. Under the notice pleading standard, there is a nearly infinite number of forms of action, and there are many lists that distinguish among them, just as there are pattern jury instructions and manuals of forms for complaints and defenses, yet new forms of action are invented all the time, and other forms become disused.

**guardianship action**  *See:* guardian, guardianship hearing (competency hearing).

**informal action**  An action by an agency without a formal adversarial proceeding. Informal agency actions describe the broad array of decision-making and enforcement actions done by administrative agencies within the scope of their duties or powers.

**transitory action**  An action that may be brought in any court with jurisdiction over the parties and subject matter. A transitory action is a civil action that may be brought wherever venue is proper over the parties and subject matter, rather than being limited to the single forum of property in dispute, of the locus of the events which led to the action, or of the personal jurisdiction over every party. Most actions that are not in rem are potentially transitory, though the converse term to a transitory action is usually a local action, which may be brought only in one forum.

**actionable (non-actionable)**  Conduct for which an action may be brought. Actionable, at its most general, describes conduct or conditions for which an action may be brought against the actor or party responsible in any court of law or equity, including criminal charges. Conditions that are actionable may include a failure or omission of duty as must as conditions reflecting affirmative or intentional acts.

In defamation the legal designation of "actionable" signals one person's language that is sufficiently damaging to another's reputation and that is not justified by truth or excused as opinion that an action for libel, slander, or defamation may be brought. Language that is not harmful, that is protected speech, that is truthful, or that otherwise may not be the basis of an action is non-actionable.

**activated sludge**  *See:* sludge (activated sludge).

**active**  Engaged in a particular activity, particularly in contrast to something or someone less engaged. Active is an adjective that implies activity, in some contrast to another state of affairs, such as passive, inactive, retired, reactive, or theoretical. An active director, an active trustee, an active reservist all have duties assigned that are greater in their commitment than would be given to mere directors, passive trustees, or inactive reservists. An

**additional perils clause**   *See:* insurance, category of insurance, marine insurance, Inchmaree clause (additional perils clause).

**additive**   Something extra included in another product. An additive, broadly, is any substance mixed into a larger quantity of a different substance, but its more specific meanings are as a chemical or material added to food, drugs, or cosmetics or a chemical added to a fuel or other chemical process. At common law, these additives may be the basis for actions in products liability if they make the product unfit for its intended use, and specific regulations occur in many statutes.

**additur**   An order increasing the amount of damages awarded to a plaintiff. Additur is both the doctrine that authorizes a court to award more monetary relief than a jury awarded, as well as the name of the relief itself. Additur may be granted by the trial judge, usually on motion from the plaintiff, only if the plaintiff has been awarded some relief. It may also be awarded by an appellate court if a motion for additur made below was denied. In all cases, additur is appropriate when damages of a given amount are required as a matter of law given the findings the jurors must have reached to render what verdict they gave, if the jurors awarded a lesser recovery.

*See also:* remittitur.

*federal court and state court*   Additur is available only in some states and not in the federal court. In federal court, additur would amount to a violation of the Seventh Amendment assurance of a civil jury. In federal court the device to raise damages above a jury verdict is for the court to grant a motion for a new trial.

**adduction (adduce)**   To put forward something, particularly evidence in court. Adduction can refer to the physical movement of something toward the front of its location, or the legal denotation of "moving forward." To adduce is to bring forward evidence in court as well as to bring forward arguments that are based on that evidence.

**ademption (adeem)**   The revocation of the legacy written in a will through the later actions of a testator. Ademption is the revocation of a testamentary gift that had been earlier written into a will, caused when a testator creates a will leaving a devise or bequest to another person, after which the testator acts in such a way that makes clear the testator no longer intends for that portion of the will to be carried out. Ademption is implied from the conduct of the testator, usually in one of two forms: ademption by extinction or ademption by satisfaction.

Ademption by extinction results from a testator's inter vivos disposal of the property interest that was to have been transferred post mortem. Thus, if T creates a will that devises Blackacre to T's daughter, but later T sells Blackacre, the devise of Blackacre in the will is adeemed. Sufficient alteration of the property or the ownership interest may be enough to amount to ademption even if the testator continues in its ownership.

Ademption by satisfaction results from the testator's inter vivos transfer of the property given, or a portion of that property, to the legatee or devisee. Thus, if T writes a grant of Blackacre to A into T's will but transfers inter vivos Blackacre to A, then the testamentary gift is adeemed.

Ademption may be whole or partial. A testamentary grant of lands, of which a portion are transferred by the testator while alive, may amount to a partial ademption. In that case, the remainder of the lands persist as a testamentary devise. To determine whether a partial grant adeems the whole or only a part of a grant requires analysis of the post testamentary inter vivos conduct of the testator to determine the testator's intent by the conduct. Some jurisdictions emphasize a change in the nature of the property subject to the gift.

*See also:* revocation (revocability or revocation or revoke).

*general and specific bequests*   Ademption can only affect specific bequests. General bequests are not adeemed.

**adequate**   Sufficient. Adequate, in general, is a standard of sufficiency, that something is enough for its requirement. The term once meant equal, either as equality among things or as equivalent to something else, and so it became more commonly used to mean equal to a requirement or need. Adequacy is a frequent measure in the law, comparing some measure in fact to a measure in law or equity. Adequate relief, for instance, is relief equal to the plaintiff's lawful requirement for relief.

*See also:* class, class action, class, class representative adequate representation; justification (justify or justified or justifiable).

**adequacy of remedy at law**   *See:* equity, equitable defense, adequacy of remedy at law.

**adequate consideration**   *See:* consideration, adequate consideration (inadequate consideration).

**adequate relief**   *See:* relief, adequate relief (inadequate relief).

**adequate warning**   *See:* warning, adequate warning.

**adherence (adhering)**   Attachment and loyalty to a particular authority. Adherence usually implies obedience to a rule or policy. In this sense adherence is a metaphor that has grown so common it has lost most of its metaphorical connotation as akin to adhesiveness. Still, from that idea grew the sense of adherence as alliance or loyalty to a cause, as well as the more common modern sense of willful conformity to the dictates of a law or principle, particularly when the adherer accepts the authority of the law or principle as a binding reason for that conformity.

**adhesive contract**   *See:* contract, specific contracts, adhesive contract (contract of adhesion or adhesion contract).

**adjacent (adjacence)** Near enough to be functionally related. Adjacent property is nearby property. Adjacence is an indeterminate degree of proximity that may include property that actually connects but also includes property sufficiently near to be functionally related. Two parcels separated by a road are adjacent, and even two parcels separated by a third parcel owned by someone else could be adjacent under some conditions, particularly if they are so situated that they can be treated as effectively portions of one operation, such as a single-family estate or a farm or an industrial site.

**adjacent landowner** See: ownership, adjoining owner (adjacent landowner).

**adjective law** See: law, adjective law (adjectival law).

**adjoining (adjoin or adjoinder or adjoiner)** Connected. Adjoining is an adjective that describes a degree of connection between two or more places or things. In general, adjoining has the sense of being joined directly together, by sharing a boundary or by being physically in contact as the sea is to the shore. Adjoining usually has this sense of contiguousness when describing two parcels of land; however, the presence of a road or other way does not bar lands that are separated by it from being considered adjoining, though they touch only constructively and not actually. Likewise, context is essential in determining the scope of connection implied by "adjoined" in a text, particularly in construing a statute: the form of connection need not be a matter of contact but may be a more functional interrelationship with something that is nearby though not physically in contact with its adjoining neighbor. As a matter of usage, a person or thing adjoining something else is the adjoiner, but something smaller attached to something larger is an ajoinder, which is also the process of the attachment.
See also: contiguity (contiguous or abutting).

**adjoining owner** See: ownership, adjoining owner (adjacent landowner).

**adjournment (adjourn)** To stop proceedings or postpone them to a later time. To adjourn is to stop a hearing or meeting. In its traditional sense adjournment implies holding all further work until a future session. A court that "adjourns" ends proceedings for that day but will resume them at a future time. Although the technical sense of adjournment implies that the given proceedings will recommence, common usage has incorporated the sense of "adjournment sine die," or adjournment without a day specified, in which the hearing or meeting adjourned is concluded. Thus an adjournment may often now mean that the proceedings are at an end.
See also: sine, sine die (without day).

**adjudication (adjudicate or adjudicative)** The resolution of a dispute through a formal judgment. An adjudication is the act of judgment, the final determination of a dispute in a court by which a judge resolves the claims the court has heard and enters an order of judgment. In common legal parlance, the term adjudication has come to include all aspects of the trial process that lead to judgment.
See also: hearing, adjudicative hearing (adjudication hearing or adjudicatory hearing).

**adjudication hearing or adjudicatory hearing** See: hearing, adjudicative hearing (adjudication hearing or adjudicatory hearing).

**adjudicative hearing** See: hearing, adjudicative hearing (adjudication hearing or adjudicatory hearing).

**administrative adjudication** Agency process for creation of an administrative order. Administrative adjudication is the process used to formulate an administrative order regarding any subject or hearing within the authority of that agency. Unlike judicial adjudication, agency adjudication rarely employs adversarial proceedings.
See also: review, administrative review; review, judicial review, judicial review of administrative action (administrative judicial review).

**adjustment (adjust)** Alteration, particularly to account for a specific change in circumstance. An adjustment is any change to an established record of performance or guide of performance. Particularly in commercial law, it is the alteration of an account to reflect a change in its status or history.

**adjustable rate or variable rate** See: rate, interest rate, floating rate (adjustable rate or variable rate).

**adjustable-rate mortgage** See: mortgage, adjustable-rate mortgage (A.R.M. or ARM).

**adjusted cost basis** See: basis, adjusted cost basis (adjusted basis or adjusted bases).

**adjusted gross income** See: income, adjusted gross income.

**adjusted net capital gain** See: gain, capital gain, adjusted net capital gain.

**adjustment as claim assessment (adjust)** The ascertainment of the amount that an insured should recover from a loss. An adjustment of an insurance claim is an analysis and valuation of a loss, comparing the loss to the proper allowances and deductions made under the insured's policy, then settling the amount of the payment that the underwriting insurer is obliged to pay out to the insured.
See also: insurance; value (valuation); debt, debt adjustment; gain, capital gain, adjusted net capital gain; income, adjusted gross income; insurance, insurance claim, insurance adjustment; mortgage, adjustable-rate mortgage (A.R.M. or ARM); basis, adjusted cost basis (adjusted basis or adjusted bases); worker, Worker Adjustment and Retraining Notification Act (Warn Act).

**administration (administrator or administer)** The control or direction of anything on behalf of someone else. Administration is now seen as the management of an enterprise, and although modern parlance might pendente lite is appointed to manage an estate and probate a will for the duration of a dispute over the will, usually a contest to the will or a challenge involving the original administrator or executor. The difference between an administrator pendente lite and an administrator ad litem is that the administrator pendente lite is not expected to participate in the litigation, but is merely to conserve the assets of the estate.

See also: administrator, administrator of estate, administrator ad litem.

**ancillary administrator (ancillary administration)** Administrator of property in a jurisdiction other than the general administration. An ancillary administrator is a court–appointed manager to execute bequests in a will when the property of the bequest lies in a jurisdiction other than where the decedent lived and the will is probated. An ancillary administrator's acts are binding in all jurisdictions.

**co-administrator (co-administration or joint administrator)** One of several administrators. A co-administrator is one of several appointed by the court to administer an estate. Although the letters of administration may require consultation, if they do not, each administrator has full powers to act regarding the entire corpus of the estate, subject only to the review by the court with jurisdiction over the estate.

**domiciliary administrator** See: administraton, administration of estate, domiciliary administration (domiciliary administrator).

**foreign administrator** Administrator from another jurisdiction. A foreign administrator is an administrator in a different jurisdiction from the one otherwise under discussion. A foreign administrator may be appointed by a court to oversee any legal action involving a jurisdiction that the foreign administrator is familiar with and that the original administrator or executor is not familiar with. In most cases, the foreign administrator is a domiciliary of the jurisdiction in which the administration must occur.

**general administrator (general administration)** The unconditional administrator of the estate of a decedent. A general administrator is the court–appointed manager of the estate with no conditions as to the duration of the administration or the extent of its jurisdiction. In most cases, a general administration is also a domiciliary administration.

**public administrator (government probate)** Government employee to administer the estate of a decedent. A public administrator is an employee of the city, county, or state whose job is to manage an estate when there is no testament, when there is a testament but no executor has been named, the named executor cannot serve, or no suitable administrator can be appointed to administer the estate.

**special administrator (special administration)** Substitute administrator during conflict. A special administrator is appointed to represent a probate estate or administration, and to manage its assets, when the original executor or administrator is involved in a legal proceeding regarding the will. The administrator must be disinterested not only in the will and estate but also among the competing parties in the contest.

**admiralty** Law relating to the seas, maritime commerce, or navigation. Admiralty is a broad body of law governing the transport of goods and passengers by water, the purchase and charter of vessels, the hiring and maintenance of officers and crew, the transportation of people and goods, the navigation of vessels, and the insurance of vessels, people, and cargo.

See also: court, court of admiralty (admiralty court).

**Admiralty Clause** See: constitution, U.S. Constitution, clauses, Admiralty Clause.

**admiralty court** See: court, court of admiralty (admiralty court).

**admiralty jurisdiction** See: jurisdiction, admiralty jurisdiction.

**maritime nexus** A tort in admiralty must be related to maritime activity. Maritime nexus is an essential test to determine jurisdiction in admiralty for a tort, which is satisfied if the plaintiff demonstrates both that the incident giving rise to the action had a potentially disruptive impact on maritime commerce and that the general character of the activity giving rise to the incident shows a substantial relationship to traditional maritime activity.

**admissibility (admissible)** The fitness of any piece of evidence or testimony for its introduction into court in a given cause of action. Admissibility is the appropriateness of introducing each piece of evidence or testimony under the rules of evidence. Admissible evidence under the Federal Rules of Evidence includes all testimony or tangible evidence that has any tendency to demonstrate any fact relevant to the case, if the evidence is relevant to the facts in issue and not barred by any laws or rules reflecting broader policies of evidence. Whether evidence is admissible is always a question of law, committed to the sound discretion of the trial judge.

Evidence is not automatically admitted because it is admissible, and a party does not have a right to the admission of all admissible evidence. Otherwise admissible evidence may be barred from use at trial, if the judge finds the evidence wasteful, redundant, confusing, or posing a danger of prejudice to either party that would outweigh its probative value.

**conditional admissibility** Allowance of evidence upon the condition that later evidence will prove its admissibility. Conditional admissibility is granted by the court when evidence is proffered under conditions in which it is not admissible, although later argument or evidence would make it admissible.

The court's admission is, if not later revisited, generally presumed to have allowed the evidence. A conditional admission is similar to taking a ruling on admission under advisement, although a conditional admission still allows introduction of the evidence into the record at the time the ruling is made. In the event a condition is not satisfied later in the trial, the opposing side may move, or the court may order, the evidence stricken from the record.

**curative admissibility** Evidence that would be barred but for actions by an opponent. Curative admissibility allows the introduction of evidence that one party would be usually barred from introducing, but that party is allowed to introduce because an opposing party has wrongly introduced other, inadmissible evidence on the same point, and the curative evidence has a reasonable potential to rebut the impression created by the other party's inadmissible evidence.

**inadmissibility (inadmissibility)** Evidence that is not fit for introduction in a given action. Inadmissibility of evidence arises either from a general prohibition, such as the bar on parol evidence to contradict a written and executed contract or from the application of the rules of evidence in a specific cause, such as a determination by the court that a crime scene photograph is more prejudicial to the defendant than probative of who caused the harms depicted in the scene.

**limited admissibility** Evidence admitted for a single purpose or not for a single purpose must be used in that manner. Limited admission is the practice of admitting evidence only for a specific purpose and not for another purpose. Evidence introduced only to show knowledge of a technique that violates the law might not, for instance, be used to show presence at a crime scene.

**admission** Allowed to enter or to be accepted. As seen in the senses of admission below, as a form of statement of the truth, as an allowance of evidence, as an entry to an event, association, institution, or building, the common elements are allowance of physical activity and acceptance of ideas.

**admission against interest or declaration against interest** See: hearsay, hearsay exception, hearsay exception declarant is unavailable, statement against interest (admission against interest or declaration against interest).

**admission by party-opponent** See: hearsay, hearsay exclusion, admission by party-opponent.

**admission by reciprocity** See: bar, admission to the bar, admission by reciprocity.

**admission of a fact** See: evidence, admission of a fact.

**admission pro hac vice** See: bar, admission to the bar, admission pro hac vice (admission pro hoc vice).

**admission to the bar** See: bar, admission to the bar.

## evidentiary admission

**admission as concession of a fact** To admit a statement or accept another's statement as true. An admission, as a matter of procedure and of evidence, is a statement of fact made in a pleading, as testimony in open court, or otherwise on the record in a legal or regulatory proceeding, to which a party may be bound by the party's opponent in later proceedings. Admissions are often requested during discovery in a pre-trial request for admission, and a party's failure to admit to facts then known to the party is an abuse of discovery warranting later sanctions. Pursuant to the federal rules of evidence, an admission is not hearsay when the admission is against the interests of the declarant, the declarant is a party to the lawsuit, and the admission is proffered by the declarant's party-opponent. An admission of guilt in a criminal procedure amounts to a confession.

**agreed admissions (agreed statement of facts)** Admissions submitted by both parties to the court. Agreed admissions are offered by parties on each side of a legal dispute, thus admitting certain facts reciprocally, which avoids the time and expense of proving these facts in the case in chief on either side. Lists of agreed admissions are often required by local rules to be offered at or near the pre-trial conference as part of an agreed statement of facts.

**admission against penal interest (penal interest)** Statements that expose the declarant to criminal liability. An admission against penal interest is a declaration or an adopted admission that amounts to a confession by the declarant or adopter of liability for some crime. An admission against penal interest falls within an exception to the hearsay rule for statements against interest, but the federal rule requires the statement to have other indicia of its reliability, and the Confrontation Clause may require that such statements have been made in conditions of cross-examination.

See also: hearsay, hearsay exception, hearsay exception declarant is unavailable, statement against interest (admission against interest or declaration against interest); penal (penal law).

**extrajudicial admission (evidential admission)** An out-of-court statement by a party entered into evidence. An extrajudicial admission is a statement made out of court or claimed to have been made out of court. It is a more common name for an evidential admission. Unlike admissions made in the pre-trial procedure or during the trial, an extrajudicial admission is not made on the record and usually requires further examination by the court to determine its admissibility, as well as evaluation by the finder of fact to determine its sufficiency as proof of a contested issue of fact.

**implied admission** Admission construed from silence or conduct following the statement of another. An implied admission occurs when a party involved in a case has acted in such a way that an observer may infer an admission of wrong-doing from the conduct. Telling a false alibi, fleeing the scene of a crime or a jurisdiction, giving inconsistent statements, and other similar conduct that is unlikely by one not guilty of a crime, or in the civil context can best be explained by a given set of facts, may be construed as an implied admission of the facts. Note: an implied admission is not an admission in the sense of the rules of civil and criminal procedure.

**adoptive admission**    Admission construed from agreement or silence following the statement of another. An adoptive admission occurs in one of two ways: either, a party hears a statement by another person and agrees with it, or the party hears a statement that would usually invoke a response but does not respond, and that silence is construed as an agreement with the statement. The latter case is also termed a tacit admission and is now a form of adoptive admission, although it raises obvious questions of context and weight in considering the meaning of the silence. In most cases, adoptive admissions are used to bring evidence that a criminal defendant has agreed with a statement suggesting the defendant was guilty. Such evidence is not barred as involuntary self-incrimination under the Fifth Amendment, because the admission is said to have been voluntary. Although there is a great deal of confusion among adoptive admission, implied admission, and tacit admission, and as the Brown case below illustrates, courts have long muddled these terms, they are really quite different: adoptive admission requires a statement by another person to be the cause of agreement or silence in conditions that an innocent defendant would be expected to object. An implied admission is an admission of wrong-doing implied from the defendant's conduct, such as flight from the scene or telling a false story. These extra-judicial admissions are not admissions in the sense of the rules of civil and criminal procedure.

**tacit admission (admission by silence)** Adoptive admission construed from silence following the statement of another. A tacit admission is a form of adoptive admission. It occurs when a party greets with silence a statement that would have prompted objection if the statement were not true. This may be taken as evidence of agreement with the statement as a tacit admission. Care must be taken that such an extrajudicial admission is not treated as an admission in the sense of procedural rules or introduced as if it were a confession in a criminal case. A tacit admission cannot be treated as evidence of guilt in a manner that would impair the right to silence under the Fifth Amendment, which does not allow a silence from a refusal to testify as evidence of guilt. Griffin v. California, 380 U.S. 609 (1965).

There is also a grave risk that silence is implied as admission when there are many stronger reasons to explain the silence, such as an assertion of the right to counsel. Even so, courts have held that the jury may hear evidence from a tacit admission, though such evidence can only be reliable as long as there is evidence that the conditions in which the silence that met the statement was indeed fully voluntary by a criminal defendant.

**request for admissions**    A list of alleged facts sent from one party to another seeking the other party to admit their truth. A request for admissions is a list of statements sent from one party to the opposing party before a trial. The party receiving the list must either deny the truth of the statements, or they will be deemed admitted. A party who proves that the other party should have admitted to a requested admission is entitled to sanctions.

**admonition (admonishment or admonish)**    A warning that a responsibility or requirement may not be met. An admonition is a reprimand, a warning given by someone in authority that a person is not acting according to guidelines or expectations. Judges frequently find themselves admonishing lawyers, although the technique may also be applied to witnesses, parties, spectators, jurors, and court personnel.
*See also:* reprimand.

**adoption (adopt)**

**adoption as endorsement**    A merger of the argument or ideas of another into one's own statement. Adoption is the rhetorical device of taking up another argument or statement as one's own at the time. When a judge accepts the report of a magistrate, a sentencing officer, child protective services officer, or other court officer, as the opinion of the court, the report is adopted. Thus a state can adopt a uniform law, a nation can adopt a convention, or a company can adopt a marketing plan.
*See also:* incorporation, incorporation by reference.

**adoption as taking into family**    The act of assuming the parental obligations over a minor as a matter of law. Adoption is the process by which an adult becomes the legal parent of a child who was not the parent's child continuously from birth. The new legal parent assumes parental rights, responsibilities, and obligations for the child, and the child becomes the legal heir of the parent with the same priority as if the child was the natural progeny of the parent. Approval for an adoption is made by a court, usually based upon a study of the fitness of the applicant by adoption counselors with a state agency, which considers whether or not the prospective guardian is suitable for a particular child and whether the adoptive home would serve the best interests of the child. There is usually an abbreviated procedure when the would-be parent is a relative or step-parent of the child. Adoption is not the same as guardianship; a child who is a ward subject to a guardian does not become the heir at law of the guardian in the manner that an adopted child becomes the heir of an adoptive parent. (A ward can receive a devise or bequest from a guardian, however, just as an adoptive child can from an adoptive parent.) Even so, both a guardian of a child and a parent of a child have the same responsibilities for care and maintenance of the child or ward.

*homosexuality* Homosexuality has been a consideration in some states affecting fitness to adopt. Although homosexuality has been a disqualifying factor in adoption fitness reviews, the end of the legal prohibition on adult, consensual sexual acts as well as the allowance of same–sex marriage have supported criticism of this practice.

**adoptive admission** *See:* admission, evidentiary admission, implied admission, adoptive admission.

**ADR** *See:* security, securities, American Depositary Receipt (ADR).

**adult** A person who has reached the age of majority and is of full legal age under the law. An adult is a person who has reached the age of majority, of independence from parents and guardians. At the common law, this occurred when a person reached the age of twenty-one, at which time the person was treated as an adult for all purposes. A minor could be relieved of minority by court order and treated as an adult for certain purposes prior to that age. In the 1970s many states lowered the age of majority, in keeping with the Twenty-Sixth Amendment's mandate of the vote at the age of eighteen. Even so, most states continue an obligation of child support until the age of twenty-one, and the age at which childhood ends and adulthood begins may vary for other purposes. State legislatures have set various ages, but a common age at which a person may marry without parental consent is eighteen, marry with parental consent is between twelve and seventeen, may have sex without violating the law is sixteen if the partner is also sixteen, may carry a weapon is fourteen, may drive a car is fifteen, may hold employment is fifteen, may purchase alcohol is twenty–one. Federal law allows voting at eighteen and military enlistment at eighteen.

*See also:* age (of age); maturity (mature or matures).

**adult abuse** *See:* abuse, adult abuse (abuse of adult).

**age of consent** The minimum age at which the law recognizes consent to sex or to marriage. The age of consent is the age in years at which a person is deemed old enough according to the law of a given jurisdiction to consent to engage in sexual activity or to consent to a contract for marriage. This age for each purpose varies among states. In general, states determine the age of consent to marriage to be slightly higher than the age at which a person may consent to sexual activity, though a person may marry younger with the consent of a parent. Age for marriage ranges from twelve to seventeen, but when consent is required by a person without consent also being given by a parent, the age ranges from eighteen to twenty–one. Most states make

exceptions for younger marriage if the woman is pregnant. The range of ages of consent to sexual relations is less varied, on average being sixteen, if the partner is within the same age range, or eighteen if not. Note: the capacity to consent is, in many cases, independent of the age of consent. A mentally infirm person may lack capacity regardless of age, and certain persons, such as those who are incarcerated or, in some jurisdictions, students, as a matter of law, may lack capacity to consent to the advances of those in authority.

*See also:* adult; minority, minor, contributing to the delinquency of a minor (corruption of a minor).

**age of majority (legal age)** The age of legal adulthood for most purposes in a jurisdiction. The age of majority is the legal age at which a person is no longer considered a minor but considered an adult. At common law the age of majority was twenty–one, though it has been modified by constitutional amendment for voting and by statute for many purposes in the states. The age, for most purposes, ranges from seventeen to twenty–one, though eighteen is now a presumptive age of majority for the entry into contracts and other purposes in many states. For certain purposes, particularly for marriage, the age of majority may be as young as fourteen, and for other purposes, such as for the maintenance of trusts or for child support, minority may be considered to persist until twenty–four. When an event is specified to occur at a person's age of majority in a will, trust, or contract, if the intent of the maker of the instrument can be ascertained, that may trump the general age of the jurisdiction. There is no difference for most practical purposes between age of majority and legal age and full age.

*See also:* adult, full age (legal age); disability (legal disability); minority, minor; juvenile.

**consenting adult** Adults who capably and voluntarily engage in a practice. A consenting adult is a person over the age of consent who voluntarily participates in some activity. A consenting adult who engages in acts protected by the constitutional right of privacy with no one else or with only other consenting adults is immune from prosecution.

**full age (legal age)** Twenty–one or the age of majority. Full age is a traditional term at law for the age of twenty–one years, the customary designation of the entry of adulthood. Depending upon the context in which the term is applied, the term may be a synonym for the age of majority, which has been lowered in most jurisdictions.

*See also:* child, non–age (not of age); adult, age of majority (legal age).

**adulteration (adulterate or adulterant)** Contamination or combination with an improper material. Adulteration is any process by which an otherwise pure substance becomes mixed with something that degrades it. Adulteration is usually the deliberate mixing of a dangerous or undesirable substance into another substance, particularly when inclusion of the adulterating substance is forbidden by law from the adulterated substance, at least as that substance is labeled. Though adulteration is most often discussed in human consumer products, such as food, drugs, and cosmetics, many substances may be adulterated, such as fuel (Americans tend to speak of fuel contamination and the English tend to speak of fuel adulteration). Adulteration can be either intentional, as when an adulterant is used to reduce manufacturing costs, or accidental, as when insects or vermin fall into food or through a process of natural decay.

*See also:* dilution, dilutant.

**food adulteration (adulterated food or impure food or unwholesome food)** The addition of material to food that is forbidden by law. The adulteration of food is the combination of food with any additive that is not legally allowed in a particular food intended for consumption by humans or animals, or the creation or storage of food in any manner that renders it unfit for consumption by its intended consumers. Adulterated food is also impure food.

*See also:* adulteration (adulterate or adulterant).

## adultery (adulterer or alterous) Sex between a
married person and anyone not that person's spouse. Adultery is an act of sex, nearly always requiring intercourse, when one partner is married and the other is not that partner's spouse. Although adultery remains a crime under the statutes of several states, it is rarely prosecuted outside of courts martial, which consider adultery by members of the service to be an offense against good order. More commonly, adultery is grounds for an action for divorce for cause, when one is sought rather than a divorce based on irreconcilable differences. Adultery can still be brought in rare circumstances as a tort action by the innocent spouse against the interloper, but not in a state that has done away with that cause of action for adultery or the action for criminal conversation, unless the action is based on consequences of the adulterous affair, such as fathering children. More likely, however, such actions are brought, when they can be, as actions for alienation of affection. There is no significant difference between adultery and criminal conversation. The interloper may assert a defense of lack of knowledge or intent as to the married party's status, and lack of intent is a defense by any party if the act was not voluntary by that party.

*See also:* fornication; conversation, criminal conversation; conversation, criminal conversation; marriage (marital).

## advance (advancement) Anything moved forward
in time, space, or status. An advance is the change to anything that is increased, improved, or moved forward in relationship to its former position or other similar things. A person may advance, or be advanced, by promotion from one position or station of employment to one that is higher, and thus that person has been given advancement. Any conduct that has a pattern of progress from beginning to end may advance, just as it

may retreat or suffer setbacks. Thus, a civil action may advance by its movement from pleadings to discovery to pre-trial, to trial, to judgment, to appeal, or to recovery, or to settlement. More generally, an improvement to a device or an increase in human knowledge is an advancement.

There are many forms of advancement of obligations or interests. Advancement of an inheritance or bequest is its settlement by inter vivos gift to the heir or legatee. When advancement is used without further qualification, or used in its primary legal sense, it is an advancement against an inheritance or bequest.

Advancement of a payment is its transfer prior to a date due, and so a pay advance is a payment by an employer to an employee of pay from a later paycheck, which is deducted from the pay when it would be later paid to the employee. However, advancement of a date of payment due is its requirement before an earlier stated date.

Note: advance is now both a noun and a verb. With rare exceptions, there is no significance between advance in its noun form and advancement.

*See also:* death, living will (advance directive); inheritance, advancement.

**advance directive** *See:* death, living will (advance directive).

**advanced notice of proposed rulemaking** *See:* rulemaking, public notice of proposed rule (advanced notice of proposed rulemaking).

**advancement** *See:* inheritance, advancement.

**advancing prostitution** *See:* prostitution, promoting prostitution (advancing prostitution).

## adversary (adversarial) One who is opposed to
another. Adversaries oppose one another. In the legal context, the adversaries are to be the attorneys, as well as the parties, and while the contest between the parties is of the greater significance, it is the contest between the attorneys that is the inevitable professional focus. Adversarial depicts any situation in which the people involved are adversaries, particularly a trial in which the parties dispute the facts and law.

*See also:* party, party to a contract.

**adversarial negotiation** *See:* negotiation, adversarial negotiation (assertive negotiation or hardball tactics or hard-ball tactics).

**adversarial system** *See:* law, legal system, adversarial system (adversary system).

## adverse (adversity) Opposed or contrary to one's
interests. Adversity is opposition to one's interests or success in any way, and anything adverse manifests that adversity.

*See also:* authority, legal authority, adverse authority.

**adversarial negotiation** *See:* negotiation, adversarial negotiation (assertive negotiation or hardball tactics or hard-ball tactics).

**adversarial system**   *See:* law, legal system, adversarial system (adversary system).

**adverse authority**   *See:* authority, legal authority, adverse authority.

**adverse employment action or adverse job action or job action**   *See:* employment, employment action (adverse employment action or adverse job action or job action).

**adverse party**   *See:* party, party to an action, adverse party.

**adverse possession**   *See:* possession, adverse possession.

**adverse possession of mineral rights**   *See:* possession, adverse possession, adverse possession of mineral rights (mineral rights adversely possessed).

**adverse ruling**   A decision by the court against the interests of one party in an action or trial. An adverse ruling is a matter of perspective. Nearly every ruling favors one party and disfavors another, no matter how sound the law and the facts underpinning the ruling. From the perspective of any party, an adverse ruling is one the party loses.

**adversity**   *See:* adverse (adversity).

**adversity of possession**   *See:* possession, adverse possession, hostile possession (adversity of possession).

**advertisement (ad)**   A notice intended to inform the public of events, investments, products, services, or similar matters. An advertisement is a notice in any medium distributed to the public that depicts anything that the advertiser desires the public to know. In particular, ads are used to promote goods for purchase and services for hire. Such an ad is presumptively not an offer that can be accepted to form a contract, but if the ad is made by a merchant with the intent to serve as an offer or with sufficient specificity that a reasonable purchaser might consider it an offer, the advertiser might be bound to the terms of the ad by an attempt at acceptance. Other forms of advertisement include legal notices, which are considered notice to all the world.
  *See also:* publication; offer, contract offer; sale (exchange or sale); deceit, false advertising; offer, contract offer | 3. advertisement as offer.

**Advice and Consent Clause**   *See:* constitution, U.S. Constitution, clauses, Advice and Consent Clause.

**advice of counsel**   *See:* lawyer, legal advice (advice of counsel).

**advice of counsel defense**   *See:* lawyer, legal advice, advice of counsel defense.

**advisement**   Consideration for later decision. When someone takes something under advisement, the person is thinking about it. When a court "takes this matter under advisement," the judge is holding the matter, usually a motion, for consideration in the light of the remainder of the hearing or trial, often for the purpose of evaluating the prudence of the motion in the light of the poster of the action as a whole, or, sometimes to determine the validity of the motion in the light of further evidence or argument or to examine the matter in private or, very rarely, to engage in research or conference with law clerks or (especially in appellate courts) other judges.
  *See also:* arbitration, advisory arbitration; jury, advisory jury; opinion, judicial opinion, advisory opinion; opinion, judicial opinion, advisory opinion declaratory judgment and advisory opinion.

**advisory arbitration**   *See:* arbitration, advisory arbitration.

**advisory jury**   *See:* jury, advisory jury.

**advisory opinion**   *See:* opinion, judicial opinion, advisory opinion declaratory judgment and advisory opinion; opinion, judicial opinion, advisory opinion.

**advocacy**   The presentation of the best argument in law or equity that the facts underlying an argument will allow. Advocacy, literally, is to give voice to an argument or concern, and legal advocacy is the representation of the interests of a client before the institutions of law.

  **zealous advocacy (zealous advocate)**   An attorney must represent each client to the fullest extent under the law. Zealous advocacy requires representation to the attorney's fullest abilities without violating the rules of professional responsibility. It requires not only presenting each argument required by a client to every institution in which that client has business but also framing each argument in the strongest terms of the law that benefit the client while remaining faithful to the facts and to the law itself. Zealous advocacy may be better understood at its limits than at its center. For instance, an attorney is required to prosecute the client's interest but may not file or appeal frivolous cases. An attorney is required to engage vigorously in the adversary system, but may not attack the credibility or the ethics of the opposing party or judge without great and legitimate cause. An attorney is required to examine witnesses and persuade the fact finder to an outcome favoring the client, but the attorney must always do so in good faith that at least some evidence supports the attorney's position. Zealous advocacy is a requirement of the oaths required by attorneys admitted to the bar, and this passionate commitment to the service of the client's interest under law is essential to the success of the adversary system of justice.

**advocate**

  **advocate as attorney**   A lawyer specially qualified to practice in an ecclesiastical or civil court. Advocate is a rank of attorney in many legal systems, but informally it may refer to any lawyer arguing a cause, or indeed to

**alien office**   Any office for the registration of foreign travelers. The alien office is, in many countries, the office for the issuance of passports and visas, or the office for the registration of resident aliens within a given district.

**alienage**   The condition of being an alien. Alienage is the status of being an alien. Alienage is a suspect classification as a matter of equal protection, and laws that burden only aliens as a group must satisfy a review of strict scrutiny. It has been suggested that there are, however, two forms of alienage, one of permanent residence, and one of temporary residence, and for at least some purposes, a law that discriminates against temporary resident aliens is to be evaluated not on strict scrutiny but to determine that it has a rational basis.

**documentation of alien**   Proof of legal presence in the country. Documentation is required of any alien to accept employment in the United States, and an employer who hires an alien without appropriate documentation, even if the alien is lawfully present in the country, may violate the Immigration and Nationality Act. Documentation includes proof of both the individual's identity and status, which may be by passport or photo-bearing alien card or by a combination of proofs of identification and employment eligibility.

**illegal alien (illegal immigrant or illegal worker or unauthorized alien)**   One who has entered a country without complying with its rules of immigration and travel. An illegal alien is a subject or citizen of a foreign state who enters or remains in another country without lawful permission to do so, particularly with an intent to stay. In the United States, illegal immigration is believed to provide more immigration than legal immigration. Illegal immigrants are subject to fine and deportation, and their employers are subject to civil fines of $100 to $1000 per undocumented employee. Even so, the children of illegal immigrants who are born in the United States become citizens at birth, and a variety of rights that apply to all persons in the United States protect illegal immigrants as well.

**resident alien**   An alien legally residing within the state. A resident alien is a person whose domicile lies in a country where that person is not a citizen. In the United States, a resident alien is an alien who was admitted to the United States with a right of permanent residence, colloquially referred to as a "green card." In most circumstances, a resident alien must demonstrate a continuous residence for five years in order to petition for naturalization. For the purposes of taxation, resident aliens include any alien who has a substantial presence in the United States, regardless of the alien's visa status.

**undocumented alien (undocumented worker)**   A person lacking proof of lawful residence or employability. An undocumented alien is any alien without documentation to prove the alien is present in the country with a lawful or unlawful status. The phrases "undocumented alien" and "undocumented worker" are often used euphemistically to refer to illegal aliens, even though many undocumented workers and aliens are lawfully present in a workplace or a country, but they lack the documentation required to prove that status. In either sense, undocumented aliens are protected under the Fair Labor Standards Act and are assured basic protections of due process of law.

**alienability (alienable or alienate or aliene)**   Capable of being disowned or transferred. Alienability is the capacity of a property, chattel, incorporeal estate, or parcel of real property to be donated or sold by its owner to another. One may alienate any property that is alienable. Alienability is a condition of ownership, but ownership does not require unfettered discretion to alienate. Property held by the entireties is alienable only with the consent of both owners. Life tenants and others who hold less than a fee simple absolute may alienate only so much of the property as they hold and no more. A life tenant may usually alienate a life estate, but cannot alienate the reversion — or remainder — estates that are held by others.

Models of the social contract associated with Thomas Hobbes and Robert Filmer presumed that rights are alienable and, once transferred from the citizens to the leader, may never be regained. These ideas were rejected with a model of inalienable rights associated with John Locke, Thomas Jefferson, and the Declaration of Independence.

**alienability of property (alienable or alienate)**   The capacity of property to be conveyed by its owner to another. Alienability is the nature of a property interest that makes it possible for it to be transferred to another person or entity. Alienability is nearly synonymous with transferability. Not all property is alienable, and many assets, powers, and obligations are not property in the strict sense and are so not alienable, such as the right to vote.

*rules favoring alienability*   Under the common law, rules evolved from the feudal restraints on land that restricted lands to family succession and allowed a tenant to transfer a fee only with the approval of an overlord to allow a fee holder to alienate lands as an aspect of ownership. Though some of these rules were quite technical responses to earlier technicalities, the sum of their effects is to make the sale and transfer of land easier, which requires greater restrictions on a landowner's ability to tie lands up in the future. The two most significant forms of these are rules that bar some restraints on alienation and rules that require any ambiguity in a grant to be construed in favor of alienability.

As a result, a reservation of condition on grant of land so that the land cannot be alienated is presumed void. A grant to an unknown grantee who will not be known for two generations fails under the rule against perpetuities. The grant of life estate with a remainder in the heirs of the grantee is read as a grant in fee simple absolute, although this rule is no longer the case in most jurisdictions. A grant of an estate that might expire prior to contingent remainder is void under the doctrine of the destructibility of contingent remainders. And estates given for a term of years or as an estate for years that last longer than fifty years (or some other number) are subject to reconstruction under the law against remoteness.

*See also:* perpetuity, Rule Against Perpetuities (RAP or Rule Against Remoteness); Shelley's Case (Rule in Shelley's Case); title, doctrine of worthier title (doctrine of reversions).

**inalienability (unalienable or inalienable)** Incapable of being transferred from one who possesses or owns it to another. Inalienability, or unalienability, is a condition of property that is vested in such a manner that it cannot be alienated; there is no means by which it can be transferred to another person. Many interests are inalienable by the design at the time they are created, such as the benefit to the trust over the res of a spendthrift trust. Other interests are inalienable in that an attempt to alienate the interest will destroy it, such as a share in a joint tenancy. Theoretically, certain liberties or capacities are now considered inalienable, such as liberty.

One of the great arguments of liberty was between Thomas Hobbes and John Locke, which turned on the question of the inalienability of natural rights and liberties. Hobbes believed that individuals had alienated their natural liberty to the monarch in a social contract, and Locke argued that certain aspects of liberty are inalienable. Jefferson and the other drafters of the Declaration of Independence adopted Locke's view of liberty, which is why rights in the Declaration are inalienable. Although Bouvier made some sense of a difference between inalienable and unalienable, there is no significant difference between them.

**restraint on alienation** A condition limiting an owner from alienating the thing owned. A restraint on alienation is any condition, covenant, lease, deed, or other limitation that prevents or unreasonably restricts an owner from transferring ownership in property to another. There are three customary forms: disabling restraint, forfeiture restraint, and promissory restraint. A disabling restraint bars the grantee from the power to transfer the interest to another, declaring any attempt to do so void. A forfeiture restraint does not void the grantee's power to transfer the property but limits it so that any attempt by the grantee to transfer cuts short the grantee's interest and transfers the property to a third party designated by the grantor. A promissory restraint depends on a promise by the grantee made to the grantor at or before the grant as a condition or covenant of the grant that the grantee will never to transfer the interest to another. The general rule, which applies to all three forms, is that restraints on alienation to a grant in fee simple are void. Restraints on alienation in a lease, however, may be valid, and in certain rare circumstances, some promissory restraints on a fee may be upheld.

*See also:* perpetuity, Rule Against Perpetuities (RAP or Rule Against Remoteness).

**alienated premises clause** *See:* insurance, category of insurance, property insurance, alienated premises clause (alienation clause).

## alienation

**alienation as alienation of property (alienate)** Voluntary conveyance of property. Alienation occurs when the owner of a property gives, donates, or sells the property, voluntarily intending to transfer title, possession, or both. The primary element of alienation is the loss of ownership as a result of some action by the alienor. Although some recent writers describe any loss of ownership as alienation — as through adverse possession, prescription, or condemnation — the common law usually distinguishes alienation from loss of ownership by the actions of the alienee. Though alienation may occur by devise at death, the term is usually now used largely to describe inter vivos transfers (transfers done while the alienor is alive). Alienation is both the power to alienate property and the action of doing so. The power of alienation is favored in law, and restraints on alienation are upheld only if the restraint is in the public interest. Not all transfers of interest amount to alienation. Transferring interests short of ownership, such as limited tenancies, might not amount to alienation. Some interests cannot be alienated. In general (and unless the power of alienation is surrendered by contract or by a reasonable and lawful restraint), any estate can be alienated, whether it is vested or contingent, possessory, non-possessory, present, or future. The alienation is effective at the time of transfer, even if the interest is non-possessory at that time.

**alienation as mental state of separation** Estrangement and detachment from a person, a culture, or society as a whole. Alienation is a sense of non-belonging, particularly in a circumstance or place one finds unfamiliar, disconnected, or unwelcoming. Alienation usually refers to the sense of disconnection with society, as found in existentialism as chararacterized by Jean-Paul Sarte, as well as the sociological writings of Emile Durkheim. It can also refer in forensic psychiatry to the study of mental illness or abnormality caused by this detachment, with an emphasis on aberrant behavior that violates criminal law.

**alienation clause** *See:* insurance, category of insurance, property insurance, alienated premises clause (alienation clause).

**alienation of affections** The tort of encouraging one spouse to lose affection for the other spouse. Alienation of affection is a common-law tort that may be brought in some states against a third party who distracts one spouse from the marriage. It is a civil action, the elements of which are: (1) the existence of a marriage with love and affection between the spouses (2) followed by the alienation of that love and affection, which is to say that one spouse's affection for other is diminished or destroyed, (3) because of (4) the acts of the defendant, (5) which if proven were done with malice or intent may give rise to punitive damages.

common-law or statutory right to make or have made such a statement, without being required to take an oath and without cross-examination. The court, however, may question the defendant during the allocution, although the defendant's right to silence will allow the defendant not to answer. The defendant's right to allocution is not unlimited, though, and the court may curtail an allocution if the defendant is irrelevant, unreasonable, or abusive. The defendant may waive allocution. In proceedings in which a victim or victim's representative may make a statement prior to trial, that statement is also termed an allocution.

**allonge**   An endorsement appended to commercial paper. An allonge is a piece of paper added to a bill of exchange or other commercial paper on which an endorsement to the bill or paper is made.

**allotment**   Amount or portion to be distributed. An allotment is a distribution as a portion, a share of what is partitioned. It is roughly the same as an allocation, the difference being that an allocation is made by the designer with a greater degree of discretion.

An allotment in land is a portion of land held by an individual owner from a larger tract held for a common purpose. There are many illustrations, such as property ownerships in certain tribal reservations for non-resident tribal members and allotments in community gardens.

From this sense, the quotas allocated for the production of agricultural goods under various farm bills and earlier agricultural regulations are also known as allotments.

*See also:* allocation (allocate or allocated).

**allowance (allow)**   To approve or permit. Allowance is the process of approval, and in the sense of payment it is what is approved to be paid. To allow an action is to approve of it or grant permission that it be done.

*See also:* permit (permitted); bankruptcy, bankruptcy claim, allowed claim.

**allowed claim**   *See:* bankruptcy, bankruptcy claim, allowed claim.

**alluvion (alluvium or alluvial shift)**   Gradual change in the land around a moving body of water. Alluvion is the small amount of earth or debris deposited on a shore or bank by moving water that adds up over time to change the boundary of the water. Alluvium, or alluvial material or alluvial deposits, are the matter that has been or will be deposited in such a manner. Under the common law and international law, river banks and shorelines altered by alluvial shifts are generally considered to alter any boundaries that depend on them, increasing the property of the owner or state. Civil law grants increased property on alluvial lands to the state, but it is usually not an increase in the lands of the private property holder.

*See also:* river.

**ally**   *See:* international, international alliance (ally).

**also known as (A.K.A. or a/k/a or AKA)**   Designation of alias. Also known as, in the form of words or its abbreviations, is an introduction to an alias. Indictments, orders, subpoenas, and other legal instruments often list aliases prefaced by this designation in order to ensure notice to the person described as well as to others.

**alter ego**   An entity that is effectively the same entity as another that is seemingly distinct. An alter ego is a person or legal entity that is so intertwined with another that the two can reasonably be considered one entity. A court may find jurisdiction or liability for an alter ego that applies to an entity that might otherwise have been immune or able to avoid it. For example, a corporate identity has the legal consequence of limiting the liability of those persons who legitimately do business on the corporation's behalf; however, if an individual uses the corporate entity as an alter ego, the corporate limitations on liability will be disregarded for that individual.

**alter-ego rule**   *See:* veil, corporate veil, alter-ego rule (instrumentality rule).

**alteration (alter)**   Any change, especially a change to a document that is unilateral or fraudulent. An alteration is a change, and in law it refers to a change of obligations or a change of the writing in a document. An alteration of an instrument may be material or immaterial, in which case the alteration must be done by those with authority initially to create the instrument, with the consent of all of the parties to it. A change to correct a mere scrivener's error is immaterial, but a change affecting a term material to a contract, a description of land, the size of a bequest, or any other integral part of the instrument is material. In either case, an alteration that is made by a person who is a party to an instrument or contract with multiple parties, who unilaterally changes the terms to that person's advantage and without the consent of the other parties commits a fraudulent alteration, and the alteration will be deemed void. Note: not every change to an instrument or contract is an alteration; only those that are made by the parties or their successors in interest amounts to alteration.

**altered check**   *See:* check, raised check (altered check).

**material alteration**   An alteration to a material term in an instrument. A material alteration is a change of a term in an instrument, such as a contract, lease, deed, covenant, will, or other writing that reflects interests of one or more parties, which changes one of the interests conveyed, transferred, or created in the instrument.

**alternative (alternate)**   One option among several or more. An alternative is a choice from a variety of possible choices. Pleading in the alternative is, however, a device for presenting several options in sequence; if one fails then the next is presented.

*See also:* election (elective); contract, specific contracts, alternative contract; performance, contract performance, alternative performance; pleading, alternative pleading (pleading in the alternative or pled in the alternative); liability, product liability, strict product liability, reasonable alternative design; promise, alternative promises; remainder, alternative remainder; name, alias.

**alternative contract** *See:* contract, specific contracts, alternative contract.

**alternative minimum tax** *See:* tax, income tax, alternative minimum tax (A.M.T. or AMT).

**alternative performance** *See:* performance, contract performance, alternative performance.

**alternative pleading** *See:* pleading, alternative pleading (pleading in the alternative or pled in the alternative).

**alternative promises** *See:* promise, alternative promises.

**alternative remainder** *See:* remainder, alternative remainder.

**alternative dispute resolution (A.D.R. or ADR)** Means to resolve a controversy without resort to judicial process. Alternative dispute resolution uses a neutral facilitator to moderate a non–adversarial discussion intended to craft a mutually satisfactory solution to the dispute at hand. ADR includes mediation, or a voluntary negotiation of the dispute, and arbitration, a binding hearing by a third party who decides between competing arguments.

> **multi-step dispute resolution clause** ADR agreement clause requiring procedures prior to arbitration. A multi-step dispute resolution clause modifies an arbitration or other ADR clause, requiring that a party with a grievance first take designated steps to present and resolve the grievance, usually within the organization that employs the party, prior to arbitration or mediation. If the aggrieved party does not find a remedy through these procedures, the clause usually then allows for arbitration of the claim, rather than litigation.

**amalgamation** The merger of multiple entities into one. Amalgamation is the combination or unity that occurs when two or more separate elements combine.

**amanuensis** A scribe who transcribes dictation. An amanuensis is a person, or increasingly a machine, that writes what a person dictates.
*See also:* scrivener.

**amatory tort or Heart Balm Act** *See:* tort, dignitary tort, heart balm tort (amatory tort or Heart Balm Act).

**ambassador (ambassadress)** A senior diplomat who represents a foreign nation in the host nation. An ambassador is the chief permanent representative of one country to another, stationed in the capital of a host country. Ambassadors, along with the embassy staff, represent the diplomatic mission of their home country and are accorded diplomatic immunity. Ambassadorial immunity is extended further to the family of an ambassador while it is in the host country. In the United States, ambassadors are appointed by the President, with the advice and consent of the Senate. An ambassador takes up that office upon the presentation and acceptance of credentials. Note: the older styles of formal English altered the suffix for a lady with an ambassadorial rank to be addressed as ambassadress; this is no longer done in many states, and care should be taken to contact the office of protocol or the embassy of that state if a doubt arises as to the style preferred by that diplomat.

**ambiguity (ambiguous or ambiguousness)** Availability of more than one meaning. Ambiguity is the potential in a text or in speech to have more than one sense. Ambiguity is probably inherent in all language, and so it is a matter of degree. As a legal matter, a text will be considered ambiguous to the extent that a reader can reasonably interpret one meaning but a different reader could reasonably interpret a different meaning from the same words. Patent ambiguity is obvious from the words alone, but latent ambiguity arises from the application of the words in context. Once a text is found to be legally ambiguous, a variety of tools of interpretation become available that are not generally used for an unambiguous text. Ambiguous contracts, wills, and trust instruments are interpreted according to parol evidence that might otherwise be excluded. Rules of interpretation specially apply to ambiguous instruments: ambiguous insurance contracts, for instance, are read in the light more favorable to the insured. Ambiguous statutes are read in the light less likely to cause constitutional conflict, more likely to accomplish the general aims of the legislature in enacting the statute, and with some deference to the interpretations of an agency tasked with its performance. Ambiguous criminal statutes are read with lenity.
*See also:* contract, contract interpretation, contract ambiguity (ambiguous contract); gharar.

> **ambiguous contract** *See:* contract, contract interpretation, contract ambiguity (ambiguous contract).

**ambit** The boundaries around a place or an idea. Ambit depicts the boundaries of a place or, metaphorically, anything at all. The ambit of a word is the edges of the scope of its meaning. The ambit of a statute is the extent of its application. The ambit of a court is its jurisdiction. These metaphorical senses are very popular among contemporary legal writers, but historically were less central to the meaning of the word than the word's geographic sense. Note, ambit is a collective noun that implies all of the boundaries encompassing the thing being described, as to any one concept, statute, or place, there is only an ambit, not ambits.

**ambulance chaser** *See:* lawyer, ambulance chaser.

**ambulatory** Capable of movement or alteration. Ambulatory means that a thing is movable. An ambulatory document is not yet fixed or final and, therefore, it may be modified or revoked. The term also has some legal significance when assessing the standard of care for persons whose ability to move has been compromised by injury or illness.

**ambush**   To assault a person by a planned, surprise attack. Ambush is a means of carrying out a sudden premeditated assault without warning to the victim. It is treated in the law both as evidence of premeditation for the crime of assault, or battery, or homicide that follows, as well as an aggravating circumstance in sentencing for such crimes.

Ambush also describes any procedural tactic in a criminal or civil action by which one party gains an advantage through surprise. Ambush is discouraged in the rules and law governing procedure and evidence.

*See also:* lurking (lurk); lying, lying in wait.

**amelioration (ameliorate or ameliorative)**   To ease, to improve. Amelioration is anything done to minimize or diminish a burden, harm, or damage, whether the hardship was caused by human action, nature, or the law itself. Mitigation of damages is an ameliorative act, as is cover in the event of a breach. Ameliorative statutes diminish a penalty from what was once required.

*See also:* waste, doctrine of waste, ameliorative waste (meliorating waste or ameliorating waste).

**amelioration doctrine**   A statute reducing a criminal penalty applies to pending cases but does not alter sentences rendered. The amelioration doctrine determines the effect of a statute that lowers the penalty to which a person who commits a particular crime is subject. Unless there is evidence of legislative intent to the contrary, the lesser punishment is applied to future cases as well as to pending cases, regardless of whether the criminal act was allegedly committed before the ameliorative statute was passed. The amelioration doctrine does not disturb cases in which a sentence has already been pronounced.

**ameliorative waste**   *See:* waste, doctrine of waste, ameliorative waste (meliorating waste or ameliorating waste).

**amenability (amenable)**   Availability. Amenability is availability, and one who is amenable to suit in a given jurisdiction is available for process there.

*See also:* subject.

**amendment (amend)**   An addition, alteration or other change to an existing document or statement. Anything amended is altered. Statements, indictments, pleadings, contracts, regulations, legislative bills, statutes, even constitutions, all may be amended. Amendment may be as simple as writing an addendum or it may require a formal process of adoption and approval, but the hallmark of amendment is that it follows either the same process of adoption as the original text or statement or that it follow a procedure specified by the same authority according to which the original took its form.

*See also:* legislation, amendment to a bill; legislation, amendment from the floor (floor amendment); pleading, amendment of pleading (amended pleading or amendment to a pleading); pleading, amended pleading; judgment, amendment of judgment (motion to alter judgment or motion to amend judgment); rider.

**amended answer**   *See:* answer, answer as pleading, amended answer.

**amendment of judgment**   *See:* judgment, amendment of judgment (motion to alter judgment or motion to amend judgment).

**amendment of pleading**   *See:* pleading, amendment of pleading (amended pleading or amendment to a pleading).

**amendment proposed**   *See:* constitution, U.S. Constitution, amendment proposed, Equal Rights Amendment (ERA or E.R.A.).

**amendment to a bill**   *See:* legislation, amendment to a bill.

**amendment to a statute**   *See:* legislation, amendment to a statute.

**amendment to a pleading**   An alteration to a pleading already filed, presenting new arguments or withdrawing old arguments. Amendment is a correction to a pleading already filed. Each amended pleading is actually a new pleading filed with the court that adopts by reference the earlier pleading and modifies the arguments or statements made in the earlier pleading. The rules governing amendments are usually specific to the pleadings involved, and there are differing rules for the amendment of complaints, answers, indictments, and discovery. Amendment of a pleading is usually allowed once as a matter of right within twenty days of filing or until a response to the pleading is filed, or it is allowed by consent of the opposing party in the action or by leave of the court. Not all changes to a pleading are amendments; a pleading filed to alter an earlier pleading solely to reflect events after the initial filing of the pleading is a supplemental pleading.

*See also:* pleading, amended pleading; answer, answer as pleading, amended answer; pleading, supplemental pleading.

**relation back (relation back doctrine)**   The raising of new matter in an amended pleading, as if the new matter was raised at the time of the first pleading. The doctrine of relation back is a means of considering amendments to have truly amended an earlier pleading, relating back to the first pleading as a matter of time. In some instances, this may allow a procedural move that might otherwise be time-barred under a statute of limitations or other procedural limit.

**amends**

**amends as offer of satisfaction**   A remedy volunteered by a wrongdoer. Amends is a specific form of satisfaction, given either in anticipation of rehabilitation or as a bar to a further action. As a bar to an action, amends is now usually pursued either as a defense of accord and satisfaction or through an offer of judgment. Amends is still not uncommon as a remedy given by a wrongdoer to an injured party or to a government which is not required by a court as a judgment, but which must be completed before a wrongdoer may be rehabilitated in some way. Thus, an official or a lawyer who has been otherwise punished might still be expected to make amends to a victim, to the bar, or to the government before being relieved of some disability as a result of the wrongdoing.

**amercement (amerciament)**  A very old punishment of money for a minor crime. Amercement, which was spelled various ways, was a manner and a form of punishment used in medieval common-law courts in the manner that today a fine of money might be used. There was once a distinction between being required to pay an amercement or to pay a fine, though that difference changed over time and eventually meant little, after which the practices merged into the modern criminal fine. Originally, a fine was for more serious crimes, and amercements were allowed in lesser tribunals with no power to fine. Amercements were varied in amount and took into account the extent of the harm done rather than being categorically assessed. To amerce someone was to assess the penalty, just as "to fine" someone is to assess that penalty. A person amerced was under a judgment of amercement.

See also: fine.

**American**

**American Arbitration Association**  See: arbitration, American Arbitration Association (A.A.A. or AAA).

**American Bar Association**  See: bar, bar organization, American Bar Association (A.B.A. or ABA).

**American Bar Foundation**  See: bar, bar organization, American Bar Foundation (ABF).

**American Civil Liberties Union**  See: civil rights, civil rights organization, American Civil Liberties Union (A.C.L.U. or ACLU).

**American College of Trial Lawyers**  See: bar, bar organization, American College of Trial Lawyers (A.C.T.L. or ACTL).

**American Depositary Receipt**  See: security, securities, American Depositary Receipt (ADR).

**American Inns of Court**  See: bar, bar organization, American Inns of Court.

**American Law Institute**  See: reform, law reform, American Law Institute (A.L.I. or ALI); bar, bar organization, American Law Institute.

**American Medical Association**  See: medicine, medical association, American Medical Association (A.M.A. or AMA).

**American Rule**  See: fee, fee for services, attorney's fees, fee shifting, American Rule (common-law rule).

**American rule of leasehold**  See: lease, leasehold, American rule of leasehold.

**American Stock Exchange**  See: security, securities, securities exchange, American Stock Exchange, little board; security, securities, securities exchange, American Stock Exchange (A.M.E.X. or AMEX).

**American Trial Lawyers Association**  See: bar, bar organization, American Trial Lawyers Association (A.T.L.A. or ATLA).

**Americans with Disabilities Act**  See: disability, personal disability, Americans with Disabilities Act (A.D.A. or ADA).

**amicus (amici)**  A "friend" who seeks to be heard in a controversy but who is not a party. An amicus is a friend, or someone acting in a friendly manner or rendering important services. As amicus curiae, such a person or entity may seek to be heard in the adjudication despite not being a party to it because the friend has some particular expertise or interest that the court might wish to hear represented in its deliberations. The plural of amicus is amici.

**amicus brief**  See: brief, amicus brief (amicus curiae brief).

**amicus curiae (friend of the court)**  A nonparty with an interest or expertise in a case who informs the court on a matter of law or of fact. An amicus curiae is a friend of the court, one who is not a party to a case but volunteers to inform the judge on a matter of law or of fact. (It is quite rare that an amicus appears before a jury.) The brief that the amicus supplies may ultimately favor one party's position over the other's, so long as the overall thrust of the brief is informative rather than adversarial. An amicus curiae does not participate by right but only by permission, or leave of the court, usually granted upon motion and order. A court may consult any person or entity as an amicus curiae, although it is now the custom for such consultations to be made a part of the record, and in criminal cases a failure of such consultation to be open to the defendant may violate the confrontation clause. Amici differ from parties as they have no interest directly affected by the outcome of the proceedings, and they differ from most witnesses because the amicus volunteers to be present.

An amicus curiae may also apply to the court to appear in favor of a minor who is party to the proceedings, regardless whether the amicus and the minor are related.

See also: court; lawyer; brief, amicus brief (amicus curiae brief).

**amnesty**   Act of oblivion from a government given to one who committed a criminal act. Amnesty is a particular form of abandonment of criminal liability, which is taken by the state to free a person or group who committed a criminal act from disability or further risk of prosecution as a result of the crime. An act of amnesty is neither forgiveness nor exoneration but a legal fiction that the acts never occurred. Amnesty is usually granted by a head of state, and it is an inherent aspect of executive power. In some countries it may be granted by legislation or judicial decree. Amnesty has a legal effect similar to a pardon, though the rationale of a pardon includes a sense of forgiveness or absolution that amnesty lacks. Amnesty is often conditional, in that its award depends on the individual or members of a group given it returning to duty or renouncing some conduct within a given time.

*See also:* reprieve; commutation (commutative or commute).

**amortization (amortize)**   To extinguish a debt or an asset through reduction over time. Amortization is, literally, the killing off of an asset or debt by slow reduction over time until its extinction. It is a tool of accounting as well as of law. Typically, a debt is amortizable when the principal and interest are made payable through installment payments over a period of time, and it is amortized once the last payment is made. The value of an asset may be amortized by depreciating it in increments over time until the book value of the asset is zero. This is possible in accounting the value of an investment in property, even if the market value of the property increases over the same period. Once a debt secured by a lien on a property is fully amortized, the security interest is void.

*See also:* funds, sinking fund; depreciation; loan, amortized loan.

**amortization of a land use**   *See:* taking, regulatory taking, amortization of a land use.

**amortized debt method of interest**   *See:* interest, interest for money, add-on interest, declining balance (amortized debt method of interest).

**amortized loan**   *See:* loan, amortized loan.

**amount in controversy**   *See:* jurisdiction, diversity jurisdiction, amount in controversy.

**amphibole**   *See:* fallacy, amphibole (deliberate ambiguity).

**anadromous fish**   *See:* fish, anadromous fish (anadromous stocks of fish).

**analogy**   A comparison between two cases to extract principles in common. Analogy is a process of comparison, by which any two situations or ideas are related to one another. Analogy is inherent in metaphors, similes, allegories, parables, and maxims, in which a sense is expressed that the proper result before is the proper result later. In legal reasoning, analogy is used in the synthesis of cases, to apply the lessons of one case in the circumstances of another. Legal reasoning employs analogy very frequently, especially in determining the fitness of a precedent as an authority in a later case. In applying a precedent to an argument, a strong analogy is one in which the salient facts of one case are very similar to the salient facts of the second case, which gives rise to an inference that the outcome of the first case should be copied in the second case. A weak analogy has fewer similar facts or more salient facts of considerable difference, and as a result there is less apparent reason to reach the same outcome in the later case.

*See also:* precedent, all fours.

**analogical reasoning**   *See:* reason, analogical reasoning; argument, analogical reasoning.

**analysis**   A very careful study based on a process of examination without prejudged conclusions. Analysis is a generic term for a wide range of processes of examination of any argument, idea, practice, or thing. Among the characteristics forms of analysis share are these: the use of a process of examination rather than an ad hoc consideration; the study of anything by its components as well as by the whole; the examination of causes that lead to the thing studied as well as results that come from it; the context of the thing, including comparisons to similar and dissimilar things; the testing of ideas about the thing as hypotheses rather than conclusions.

**conceptual analysis**   Studying of one thing by the construction and examination of constituent concepts. Conceptual analysis is the evaluation of any idea as the intersection among larger concepts. The idea being evaluated is the bit of overlap among the constituents, each of which is a larger concept than the idea itself.

**analytical jurisprudence**   *See:* jurisprudence, analytical jurisprudence.

**anarchy (criminal anarchy or anarchist)**   A society without governance or a state. Anarchy is a social system without government, law, or leaders in office above others. Considered a utopian model in political philosophy, anarchy, or anarchism, is viewed with dread by most observers who believe it inevitably leads to a breakdown of social order and an increase in violence and danger. An anarchist is one who subscribes to or promotes anarchy as a way of life. Anarchy, less strictly, is a metaphor for any confused or disorganized state of affairs.

Criminal anarchy is an act by one person that incites another immediately to disobey the law or the lawful authority of the state in a manner that presents a clear and present danger to the safety of others or the order of the state, in violation of a valid statute or ordinance and not in a manner that amounts only to constitutionally protected speech. Such statutes may label the conduct sedition, incitement, or criminal anarchy.

*See also:* syndicalism; sedition.

**anathema**   A thing or idea so reviled, it is and should be shunned. Anathema was once a punishment of the ecclesiastical courts for violations of canon law, in which the defendant was exiled from the church and its members. That meaning is now obsolete, but the word retains its sense of condemnation, and something that is anathema is so insulting to a person, group, or institution that it should be avoided at all costs.

**anatomical gift**   See: gift, anatomical gift, Organ Procurement and Transportation Network (OPTN); gift, anatomical gift.

**ancestor**   See: descent, ancestor (ascendant).

**ancestry (ancestral)**   Lineage, including ethnic characteristics and cultural traditions. Ancestry is the category created by one's ancestors. Discrimination based on a person's cultural and ethnic ancestry is forbidden by the Fifteenth Amendment to the United States Constitution. No law may be used as an instrument for generating prejudice and hostility against persons whose ancestry is made plain by ethnic characteristics or adherence to cultural traditions.

**anchorage or moor or unmooring**   See: mooring (anchorage or moor or unmooring).

**anchoring effect**   See: effect, anchoring effect.

**ancient**   Very old. Ancient is a generic term for anything or anyone that is very old or the nature of being very old. Ancient is relative, along the lines of young, old, ancient. When describing people, an ancient is an ancestor, living or dead. When considering history, ancient is any time prior to the medieval period. When considering local artifacts, ancient may merely mean old within common memory.
   *See also:* light, ancient lights (easement for light and air).

   **ancient document**   See: evidence, authentication, ancient document (ancient writing).

   **ancient documents**   See: hearsay, hearsay exception, hearsay allowed regardless of witness availability, ancient documents.

   **ancient lights**   See: light, ancient lights (easement for light and air).

   **ancient writing**   See: evidence, authentication, ancient document (ancient writing).

**ancillary**   Supplemental to something else. Anything ancillary is incidental or peripheral to another thing. The term comes from the Latin for servant, in the sense that the ancillary activity serves a primary activity.
   *See also:* administrator, administrator of estate, ancillary administrator (ancillary administration); claim, claim for relief, ancillary claim (ancillary suit); jurisdiction, ancillary jurisdiction; relief, ancillary relief; derivative.

**ancillary administration**   See: administrator, administrator of estate, ancillary administrator (ancillary administration); administration, administration of estate, ancillary administration.

**ancillary claim**   See: claim, claim for relief, ancillary claim (ancillary suit).

**ancillary jurisdiction**   See: jurisdiction, ancillary jurisdiction.

**ancillary relief**   See: relief, ancillary relief.

**ancillary suit**   See: claim, claim for relief, ancillary claim (ancillary suit).

**and**   Plus. "And" is a conjunction that has an inherent ambiguity in its use, sometimes meaning no more than what follows is in a list with what precedes it, and sometimes aggregating what follows into a whole with what precedes it. These senses are the additional sense and the conjunctive sense of the word; in this way, "the clerk requires A, B, and C," may mean that the clerk requires one of the three or that the clerk requires all three at once. Further, the structure of a sentence preceding a list may imply that a conjunction in the list in either sense merely distinguishes the elements of the list that are alternative or conditional; in this way, "the clerk will occasionally require A, B, and C, but sometimes only D" whichever way one interprets the "and," D might substitute for all three, only one, or be an independent requirement. Only context can prove which interpretation of "and" was meant, but the difference is often critical in law. As a matter of drafting, this ambiguity can be diminished through more explanation. Thus, there is much more guidance in this: "For most filings, the clerk requires every applicant to perform A, as well as to perform B, and also to perform C. In the case of an emergency filing only, the clerk will dispense with the requirements of A and B and C, and will only require D."
   *See also:* or.

   **and his heirs**   See: fee, estate in fee, fee simple absolute, and his heirs (and her heirs or and their heirs).

**Anders brief**   See: counsellor, counsel, withdrawal of counsel, Anders brief.

**androgyne or hermaphroditic or intersex or intersexual or transgender**   See: hermaphrodite (androgyne or hermaphroditic or intersex or intersexual or transgender).

**animal**   A multicellular organism of the kingdom Animalia. An animal is a multicellular organism that is classified by biologists into the kingdom Animalia. It is heterotropic, or capable of digesting organic food through an internal organ, and it creates progeny by means of some sort of sexual reproduction. When "animal" is used in legal drafting, it usually means all animals other than human beings. Still, according to context, statutory and regulatory use of the word animal have sometimes meant only mammals, or mammals and birds, or any animals other than fish or insects. Even so, given the presumption that "animal" without any other qualification is read broadly, interpreting such limitations in the absence of a statutory definition requires context. Animals are differentiated under the law in many ways, particularly by whether they are domesticated or wild; whether they are farm animals or otherwise raised for food, fiber, or other commercial products; whether they are endangered, threatened or potentially threatened with extinction.

*See also:* religion, freedom of religion, free exercise of religion | 5. sacrifice of animals; pest; right, animal rights; sacrifice; trafficking, trafficking animals or plants (animal trafficking or plant trafficking).

**animal cruelty**   *See:* cruelty, animal cruelty.

**animal nuisance**   *See:* nuisance, animal nuisance.

**animal rights**   *See:* right, animal rights, speciesism; right, animal rights.

**animal trafficking or plant trafficking**   *See:* trafficking, trafficking animals or plants (animal trafficking or plant trafficking).

**abnormally dangerous domestic animal**   An animal so dangerous its owner will be strictly liable for any harm it causes. Abnormally dangerous domestic animals are those that are not customarily kept in confinement because they pose an unusual risk of human injury. Thus the keeping as pets of venomous snakes and other wild animals, particularly carnivores known to attack people, usually gives rise to strict liability. Even so, such animals may be kept in a special environment subject to control by specialists, such as a zoo, in which case injuries they cause will be usually subject to a standard of negligence.

**companion animal**   An animal bred and used as a companion to humans. A companion animal is a pet, an animal that has been successfully bred to reduce its wild characteristics, in order that it may benefit, and live in close proximity to, humans.

**domesticated animal**   An animal bred for human use. A domesticated animal is an animal that has been bred as a species or tamed as an individual to reduce its wild tendencies, allowing the animal to be kept in proximity to humans without the animal returning to its wild state. Unless the context suggests otherwise, "domesticated animals" in a statute or regulation includes both pets and farm animals, as well as other service animals. However, in some contexts, a provision regarding domesticated animals will not apply to an animal that is a member of a species usually considered domesticated but that is itself feral and untamed.

*See also:* domitae naturae; agriculture, domestication.

**exotic animal**   An animal rare or oddly employed in a given locale. An exotic animal is an animal that is not natural to the geographic area it is found in, or that is employed in such a way as to be unnatural to common human interaction with that species.

**farm animal**   An animal bred and kept for production of facilitation of agriculture. An animal bred and kept solely for the production of food, food products; the commercial production of animals or animal products; or the facilitation of agriculture generally. Depending upon context, a farm animal (like a rooster) need not be on a farm to be considered a farm animal, and some animals on farms (like dogs or cats) may be considered a farm animal though in another context they would not.

**nuisance animal**   A wild animal that is liable to injure property or health. A nuisance animal is an animal whose natural behavior or characteristics tend to damage human health or human property or to displace other animal species or harm natural environments. A nuisance animal may be an invasive species or a single animal that is dislocated from its natural habitat. A wild animal in a human environment, such as a bear in a suburb, is a nuisance animal. Note: one may easily confuse a nuisance animal with an animal nuisance, and the terms are sometimes used interchangeably. The difference is that the nuisance animal is a wild animal that threatens either human activity or natural populations as a result of its natural activities out of captivity, while an animal nuisance is a nuisance caused by an animal captive or under the care of a human being. Only context or some indication of the intent of the drafter or speaker may distinguish which is meant, or whether both might be meant, by a usage.

**police animal**   A dog, horse, or other animal trained to assist the police. Police animal is the generic term for a police dog, police horse, or other animal that is trained and deployed in the service of a police department. Purposefully hurting a police animal, or plotting to do so, is a crime.

*See also:* dog, sniffer dog (cadaver dog or detection dog).

**service animal (seeing-eye dog)**   An animal trained to perform a service for humans. A service animal is specially trained and employed by a person for assistance with a human task. An important group of service animals are service animals assisting with daily tasks, particularly when used by a disabled person to compensate for the disability, as in the case of seeing-eye dogs for the blind. Service animals as a group include dogs trained for other tasks, such as cadaver dogs and other sniffer dogs, and animals of other species, such as birds and porpoises. Note: companion animals represent a different category of animal, those used for company and diversion but not necessarily trained to perform tasks different from pets in general. A service animal may be a companion animal and vice versa, but this does not alter their distinct forms of assistance.

*See also:* dog, sniffer dog (cadaver dog or detection dog).

**wild animal**  An undomesticated animal. Wild animals are animals that are not or cannot be domesticated, including animals that are hybrids of domesticated and wild animals. Wild animals generally require some special force or restraint to be kept in proximity to humans. The common law ascertained whether a animal is wild by its being ferae naturae or having animus revertendi. A person who keeps a wild animal that injures another is usually strictly liable for the damages it causes.

*See also:* ferae, ferae naturae.

**animo revertendi**  *See:* animus, animus revertendi (animo revertendi).

**animus**  Intent in general, or particular ill will. Animus is an intent. Any sentient being can have an animus, and it is unnecessary that animus be an articulable idea of what one plans to do. Animals can have an animus, just as people do, and in this light the sense is stronger of animus being as much instinct as intentionality, and it is expressed as "impulse." On the other hand, animus is seen also as the rational and soulful aspect of human action, and in this sense, animus is better translated as "will" as in a mental forcefulness. In various legal writing, intent is also synonymous with motive and purpose.

Animus has long been confused with animosity, or ill will, and through such misuse has acquired that sense. Thus, a discriminatory animus is an ill will toward an individual or a group on the basis of some characteristic.

*See also:* mens.

**animus furandi (furandi animus)**  The intent to steal. Animus furandi is the Latin tag for the knowledge and intent to take wrongful possession, the mental state needed to commit larceny or theft. The taking itself must occur with this animus, or with an immediate will to convert the possession to the taker's possession at a moment the taker knew the item taken to be the possession of another.

*See also:* theft; thief; larceny (larcenous).

**animus revertendi (animo revertendi)**  The intent or will to return. Animus revertendi is the impulse to return. It is the central means for determining many aspects of ownership and identity, such as whether a wild animal has become domesticated, whether an expatriate remains a citizen, whether an owner has abandoned property, or whether the property has become severed by accident such as in a shipwreck. The instinct to return, or the will or intent to do so, preserves the link between the animal and owner, the citizen and state, or the ship and owner.

**animus testandi**  The intention to make a testament or will. Animus testandi is the intent of the testator to make a last will and testament. Indeed, the phrase expresses the very nature of the person's will, from which the word "will" is derived as the label for the instrument created. The intention must be very specific, an intent not only to give away property at death but also an intent to do so through the specific terms of the instrument being created.

**annex**  Something an extension of something else. An annex is an item that is attached to or associated with a more prominent or significant item. It is synonymous with appendix in a writing or extension in a building or subdivision. Annex is also used in the verb form to describe the action of making such a connection.

*See also:* mediation, court-annexed mediation; administrator, administrator of estate, administrator cum testamento annexo.

**annexation**  Addition of lands to a political jurisdiction. Annexation, in general, is the combination of two formerly independent things into one. Annexation is the process by which a fixture becomes part and parcel with the land on which it is affixed. The term is informally used as to individual parcels of land to refer to combination of two parcels into common ownership such that they are given a new common description and treated as one.

Most notably in contemporary practice, annexation is the process of enlargement of a political unit, or jurisdiction, especially when a municipality moves its boundaries to encompass new lands. The process of municipal annexation is usually set by state law, but when it has implications for voting districts, in some states, it may be subject to review by the federal government under the Voting Rights Act.

*See also:* fixture.

**anno domini (A.D.)**  In the year of our Lord. A.D. designates a year in the Christian calendar, the calendar that has become the default calendar in the commercial world. As an abbreviation of anno domini it is more correctly written before the number, such as A.D. 1918, not 1918 A.D. (though B.C. or B.C.E. are written following the number of the year). The abbreviation is not properly used in government communications in the United States, and its use grows increasingly rare.

*See also:* year.

**annotation as notation (anno. or ann. or annotated)**  Editorial enlargement of a legal text by the inclusion of notes to law and scholarship. Annotation is the inclusion with a particular text — such as a statute, judicial opinion, or treatise section — of various notes from cases, statutes, treatises, articles, and the like. Cross-references, notes to later and earlier laws, scholarly criticism, application notes, and other discussion of the text in issue is frequently included. Many codes are annotated, such as the United States Code (U.S.C.), which is annotated by two competing services, the United States Code Annotated (U.S.C.A.) and the United States Code Service (U.S.C.S.); although the basic text of the code is the same among all three series, the additional materials vary somewhat among the latter two, which are privately printed. Annotation is a modern term for what was earlier known as glossation, and so the annotations are sometimes called a gloss.

**annual**  *See:* year, annual.

**annual exclusion**  *See:* tax, gift tax, annual exclusion.

**annual percentage rate**   *See:* interest, interest for money, annual percentage rate (APR).

**annuity**   Financial instrument that pays out over time at specific intervals. An annuity is a fixed allowance or income received, usually upon an investment of time, money, or capital, which is paid out for a specified period, sometimes a lifetime. Annuities allow a person to accumulate tax–deferred funds for retirement and then, if desired, receive a guaranteed income payable for life, or specified period of time. Annuities are offered by insurance companies and sold by licensed agents. A person or entity who owes another a large amount of money will often opt to pay them an annuity, or through smaller quantities over a long period of time on a spec-ified schedule. Large damage awards are often tendered to individuals through the defendant's purchase of an annuity to the benefit of the plaintiff.
*See also:* pension.

**annulment**

**marital annulment (declaration of invalidity of marriage)**   Declaration that a marriage is void ab initio. Annulment is the voiding of an act, treating it as if it never occurred. The annulment of a marriage is a declaration that a marriage was invalid, or void from its inception, and is to be treated as if it never occurred, except that property jointly held is to be divided as if there is a divorce and a child born or adopted between the marriage and annulment is the child of both members of the couple. Grounds for annulment include legal incapacity (including youth), mental incapacity (whether permanent or temporary), impo-tence, an existing marriage, procurement of the marriage by fraud or coercion, a failure in the solem-nization of a wedding, or that the marriage otherwise violated the law. Annulment is sought by a party from a court, although the party seeking annulment may be a putative spouse or another person acting in the interests of the putative spouse.
*See also:* marriage (marital); nullification.

**post-mortem annulment**   An annulment follow-ing the death of one or both putative spouses. A post–mortem annulment is an annulment requested or declared following the death of one or both puta-tive spouses. An annulment in some states may be granted if the proceedings for annulment were com-menced prior to death, and in a few states, a proceed-ing may be brought by an interested party after the death of one of the putative spouses, if the basis for the annulment was lack of mental capacity by the decedent to enter the marriage.
*See also:* post, post mortem.

**anonymous (anonymity)**   Without a name. Some-one or something anonymous lacks a name or identifi-cation, whether the identity is of a person, a thing, or a creator or owner of a thing. An anonymous work is one with an unidentified creator or author. An author sometimes remains anonymous because his or her work advances an unpopular viewpoint, but the rationale is usually irrelevant to the fact of anonymity. Anonymity is no defense to defamation or copyright infringement; if the identity of an anonymous author or creator is ascertained, the author or creator may be held to defend an action for the work.
*See also:* name.

**answer**   A reply to a question or an assertion. An answer is a response, particularly to a question. An answer can be any response to an action or statement, when the response is intended as a reaction to the action, statement, or question. Most importantly in pleading, an answer is the pleading containing a response to a claim in a complaint. During the taking of testimony, an answer is the second part of a colloquy intended to develop evidence from a witness or an argument from a party.
*See also:* pleading, responsive pleading.

**answer as pleading**   The first pleading of a defendant. An answer responds to a plaintiff's initial pleadings. It contains denials, rebuttals, and additional allega-tions. If the answer contains counter–claims or cross–claims, by custom and according to many local rules, the pleading must be labeled to indicate them.
*See also:* nihil, nihil dicit (nihil dicit judgment).

**amended answer**   An answer that has been revised and moved for filing. An amended answer is subject to the usual rules of an amended pleading, in that it usually may be made within a specified number of days or prior to a response, or made with the opponent's consent or leave of the court. Still, when an answer raises affirmative defenses or counterclaims, it may be treated with greater scrutiny by the court in allowing leave to amend the answer, in the same way that the court would exercise greater care in allowing the amend-ment of a complaint.

**evasive answer**   An insufficient response to a dis-covery request or a question in trial. An evasive answer is one that seeks to avoid answering the question that was asked. An evasive answer usually seems useful but actually is unresponsive. A party during discovery or by a witness while under oath makes an evasive answer at the risk of sanctions.

**sham answer (false answer or sham)**   A factually untrue response to a pleading or question. A sham or false answer is an answer that is untrue and mis-leading. In pleadings, it is subject to both a motion to strike and to sanctions, including dismissal of an action. In sworn testimony it is subject to sanctions, as well as to prosecution for perjury. When made in discussions with police or other state investigators or in a criminal proceeding, it may be the basis for pros-ecution for obstruction of justice.
*See also:* sham.

**ante**   Before, at some time prior or earlier in a text. Ante means before. In legal drafting, it generally refers to a part of the text before the reference. Ante sometimes is used in English as an independent adjective, but more often it appears as a prefix to another Latinate word, such as antebellum or antemeridian. It appears in Latin phrases of continuing vitality, when it usually follows the noun, as in status quo ante.

*See also:* post.

**ante-nuptial agreement or prenuptial agreement or prenup or pre-nuptial agreement or pre-nuptial contract or prenuptial contract or marriage settlement** *See:* marriage, premarital agreement (ante-nuptial agreement or prenuptial agreement or prenup or pre-nuptial agreement or pre-nuptial contract or pre-nuptial contract or marriage settlement).

**ante-nuptial or pre-nuptial or post-nuptial or post-nuptial** *See:* nuptial, post nuptial (ante-nuptial or pre-nuptial or post-nuptial or postnuptial).

**ante as stakes** The stakes, based on an investment before the negotiation or game begins. Ante represents the stakes one has in a process or game. Ante is a metaphor taken from the payment made before a poker game commences, which can be increased by other players who "up the ante," increasing the stakes in the game. Ante refers to the initial bid, bet, or offer in a negotiation. To up the ante is to increase that initial demand, requiring more from the other party, usually without offering more in return.

**antecedent** Occurring prior to something else. Antecedent is the condition of going before, whether in time or in order of appearance as in a text. A clause of a contract that is written in the text of the contract before another clause is antecedent to the later clause, just as a grandparent is antecedent to a grandchild. Antecedent is a near synonym to precedent, but antecedent can be used to indicate order or time without suggesting the legal authority, customary hierarchy, or logical significance that are often implied by precedence.

**antedate** To precede another event in time. Antedate is now generally used to describe chronological relationships. It was once used, and occasionally is still used, to describe the inscription of a date that is passed at the time of the inscription on an instrument, a practice now called "backdating" more often than antedating.

*See also:* date, backdate (antedate).

**anthropology of law** *See:* law, anthropology of law (legal anthropology).

**anti** Opposing. Anti- is usually a prefix to a word, such as antibacterial, denoting a substance that harms bacteria. In compound words less accepted by use, the prefix may be hyphenated, as in anti-war. The word used alone, as a noun, suggests people who are opposed to something, such as anti-development property owners. The collective noun, "antis," refers to any opposition group or its members, defined by their opposition to some policy or activity.

*See also:* ante; pollution, degradation (anti-degradation or non-degradation or antidegradation or

nondegradation); injunction, Anti-Injunction act (A.I.A. or AIA); miscegenation (anti-miscegenation law); retaliation, anti-retaliation law; pro.

**anti-competitive conduct or anticompetitiveness** *See:* competition, anticompetitive conduct (anticompetitive conduct or anticompetitiveness).

**anti-degradation or non-degradation or antidegradation or nondegradation** *See:* pollution, degradation (anti-degradation or non-degradation or antidegradation or nondegradation).

**anti-dumping duties** *See:* trade, international trade, anti-dumping laws (anti-dumping duties).

**anti-dumping laws** *See:* trade, international trade, anti-dumping laws (anti-dumping duties).

**Anti-Injunction Act** *See:* injunction, Anti-Injunction Act (A.I.A. or AIA).

**anti-injunction bill** *See:* union, labor union, labor laws, anti-injunction bill (Norris-Laguardia Act).

**anti-lapse statute** *See:* will, last will and testament, antilapse statute.

**anti-miscegenation law** *See:* miscegenation (anti-miscegenation law).

**anti-recidivist law or three strikes law** *See:* recidivism, three-strikes law (anti-recidivist law or three strikes law).

**anti-retaliation law** *See:* retaliation, anti-retaliation law.

**anti-retaliation provision** *See:* civil rights, Civil Rights Act, Civil Rights Act of 1964, Title VII, anti-retaliation provision.

**anticipation (anticipate or anticipatory)** Conduct that occurs prior to the time an expected event occurs. Anticipation has a general connotation of waiting for something, but anticipation at common law is an action made prematurely or before its expected time. There are a variety of specific meanings for anticipation in the law: an action made "in anticipation" is an action made with particular knowledge that signals an intent, such as a gift made in anticipation of death or a trust created in anticipation of the birth of a child. Anticipation in patent and other claims to sole rights signals an earlier patent or claim that is the same in its essentials as a later application for a patent or claim. Anticipation as a matter of causation — particularly in contract, tort, and criminal law — is an expectation of particular result that is believed likely to follow from a particular plan, cause, or chain of causation.

*See also:* breach, breach of contract, anticipatory breach; repudiation, anticipatory repudiation.

**anticipatory breach** *See:* breach, breach of contract, anticipatory breach.

**anticipatory repudiation** *See:* repudiation, anticipatory repudiation insolvency as anticipatory repudiation; repudiation, anticipatory repudiation.

**antinomy**   A contradiction. Antinomy is a contradiction, whether of two statements in a single text or among several laws or decisions.
*See also:* contradiction (contradict).

**antitrust law**   Legislation designed to ensure free trade and competition in the market. Antitrust law consists of common–law principles and legislation that works to prevent agreements and practices that amount to a monopoly or anti–competitive behavior, particularly regulating potential mergers and acquisitions and investigating business practices to protect a free market. The common law was hostile to monopolies, and early anti–monopoly law in the United States was largely a matter for the state courts. Federal antitrust law arose in the late 1800s as a way to combat trusts and monopolies, beginning with the Interstate Commerce Act of 1887 and the Sherman Anti–Trust Act of 1890. The nineteenth-century basis for antitrust law was to inhibit corporations and combinations from harming public morals through corrupting dependencies; the contemporary basis is to ensure fair price competition in a free market.

**Sherman Antitrust Act (Sherman Act)**   The federal law that makes a crime of acts in restraint of trade. The Sherman Antitrust Act of 1890, 26 Stat. 209, codified at 15 U.S.C. § 1, et seq. (2007), declares any actions that restrain trade or commerce a criminal violation of federal law. The most essential forms of crime under this law are illegal trusts, or combinations of businesses, which use a variety of contracts (which may be unwritten) to fix the prices of goods and services to the detriment of suppliers or customers. The original theories underlying antitrust manifest in the act were based on the harm done to the individuals whose livelihoods were captive to such industries as shipping, manufacture, and mining, whose monopolies created a servility among those dependent upon them. This theory has in later decades been supplemented by a view of antitrust as a means of protecting competition in the market in order to ensure low consumer prices.
*See also:* monopoly (monopolize or monopolizer or monopolist).

**parallel conduct (parallel behavior)**   Businesses acting similarly in their pricing or influence in a shared market. Parallel conduct is the similar conduct of businesses, merchants, or other selling or buying in the market, that has a cumulative effect in sum on the market. Parallel conduct is indicative of anti–competitive behavior but not conclusive evidence of an agreement in restraint of trade.

**rule of reason (reason in antitrust)**   Unreasonable restraints of trade are forbidden, not size or monopoly per se. The rule of reason in antitrust law bars only those business combinations or contracts among suppliers and recipients that unreasonably restrain trade; thus size alone or monopolistic power alone are not illegal. The rule of reason applies a totality of the circumstances test for violations of section one of the Sherman Act.
*See also:* interpretation, statutory interpretation, rule of reason in interpretation.

**APA**   *See:* law, administrative law, Administrative Procedure Act (APA).

**APO or A.P.O. or penalty order**   *See:* order, administrative order, administrative penalty order (APO or A.P.O. or penalty order).

**apparent**   Obvious. Something apparent is something that can be be observed, or it is at least understood from what can be observed. There are many specific designations of something apparent in the law: an apparent defect is a defect that is either obvious or should be known from what is obvious, thus distinguishing it from a concealed defect. An apparent argument is the argument that is made, as opposed to a hidden agenda behind the argument. The division, however, between apparent and concealed is one of degree and not a perfect divorce between the two. Courts must act according to apparent evidence, and, as the maxim goes, what does not appear does not exist.
*See also:* easement, apparent easement; heir, heir apparent (apparent heir or heir presumptive or presumptive heir).

**apparent agent**   *See:* agent, apparent agent (implied agent).

**apparent easement**   *See:* easement, apparent easement.

**apparent heir or heir presumptive or presumptive heir**   *See:* heir, heir apparent (apparent heir or heir presumptive or presumptive heir).

**appeal (appealable or appellate)**   The review in one tribunal of the proceedings and decisions of another, either as to law or fact, or both. An appeal is a direct review of a decision by a legal official by a different body with the legal authority to alter or reverse the initial decision. Appeal is not the only means of reviewing an official decision. There are collateral means of review, such as habeas corpus and certiorari from state to federal courts. Appeal is, however, a direct means by which the legal system allows immediate review of decisions and correction of errors. Appeals most famously occur in courts, when a party losing an issue in a lower court requests review and reversal of that issue by a higher court, but there are also appeals within agencies and appeals from agencies to courts. To exercise its authority, a court must have appellate jurisdiction over the court or agency rendering the initial decision as well as have subject matter jurisdiction over the issue under review. Appeals are subject to standards of review, which vary according to the forum and the issues presented. In general, matters of substantive law are reviewed de novo, matters of procedure are reviewed with deference to the discretion of the tribunal below, and findings of fact are reviewed with great deference, particularly if the findings are made by a jury. Any aspect of an appeal is appellate. Any matter subject to appeal is appealable. Appeal is sought by the appellant and resisted by the appellee. Thus, when an appeal is granted, the decision favors the appellant, and the decision below is reversed. When an appeal is denied, the appellee has won the appeal, and the decision below is upheld.

*See also:* jurisdiction, appellate jurisdiction; procedure, appellate procedure; review, appellate review; decision, appealable decision; bond, supersedeas bond; review, standard of review; error, writ of error (restricted appeal); review.

**appealable decision** *See:* order, court order, appealable order (appealable decision); decision, appealable decision.

**appeal bond** *See:* bond, appeal bond (cost bond).

**abstract of record** A brief recount of the pertinent information from a trial court. The abstract of record is a summary of the record from the trial court, including the essential pleadings and evidence, and a summary of the events at trial or hearings that are the basis of the appeal. The appellant is responsible for filing the abstract of record.

**counter-abstract of record (counter abstract of record or counter-abstract or counter abstract)** An additional abstract of record prepared by the appellee. A counter-abstract is sometimes submitted in an appeal by the respondent (or the appellee), particularly when the abstract of record submitted by the petitioner (or the appellant) omits material that the respondent believes will be essential to the appellate court's review of the judgment below, or the respondent believes it will place the respondent's argument in a better light on appeal.

*See also:* abstract.

**cross-appeal** An appeal of an issue raised by the appellee. A cross-appeal is the appellate equivalent of a counter-claim, by which the appellee raises an issue that is distinct from the issues raised by the appellant when the appeal was first brought. In a cross-appeal, the appellee's issue must arise from the record below in the same procedural conditions as did the appellant's. The issue raised on cross-appeal must have been raised but lost (to the appellee's detriment) and preserved in the record of the court below, or it must be a matter of continuing concern, such as jurisdiction.

**direct appeal** An appeal to the court with appellate jurisdiction over a tribunal. A direct appeal, in general, is an appeal of any final order in a trial court to a court with appellate jurisdiction over the trial court. A direct appeal contrasts with collateral appeal, which is an interlocutory review, and collateral review, which is often conducted by a court without appellate jurisdiction over the court entering the challenged order. Under some court rules, a direct appeal labels a rare form of appeal allowed by leave of the highest court of a jurisdiction without intermediate review by a court of appeals.

**frivolous appeal** A request for review of a case in which no reviewable error exists. A frivolous appeal is an appeal of an order, when there is no reasonable basis for the appeal. Most courts have a rule allowing sanctions for the filing of frivolous appeals, although the courts are often quite lenient in the application of such rules.

**interlocutory appeal** Appeal of an order in a case that has not reached its conclusion in the trial court. Interlocutory appeal is an appeal of any order in a trial court other than the final order — it is an appeal of a decision made during the pleading, discovery, or trial stages of an action before a final decision granting or denying relief in the case. Most interlocutory appeals are taken only with leave of the courts, usually requiring both a certification of the issue for interlocutory appeal by the trial court and an acceptance of the appeal by the appellate court. There are a very few cases in which an interlocutory appeal may be made as of right; for instance in federal courts, there is a right to interlocutory appeal from an order denying arbitration, under 9 U.S.C. §16, and there are some appeals as of right from bankruptcy under 11 U.S.C. §362(a). Discretionary appeals in the federal system are only allowed of an order (1) that finally determines claims of right separable from, and collateral to, rights asserted in the action (2) that are too important to be denied review and too independent of the cause itself to require that appellate consideration be deferred until the whole case is adjudicated.

**in media res** In the middle of the proceedings. Any event in media res occurs during the course of some activity or proceeding. Thus, a motion made during a trial is made in media res. An appeal in media res is an interlocutory appeal. It is not essential that the act be at the mid-point of the period of the activity to be in media res; the activity need merely be ongoing at the time.

**notice of appeal** A lower court filing noting the appeal of an order. A notice of appeal is a pleading made in a trial court or, in some cases, an intermediate court of appeal, giving notice that an order in that court is appealed to another court. The notice must name the parties to the appeal; note the order, judgment, or other decision appealed; and record the court to which the appeal is taken. A notice of appeal must usually be filed within thirty days of the entry of the order appealed.

**post-conviction relief (postconviction relief)** The review of the constitutionality or justice of a conviction other than by direct appeal. Post-conviction relief is any procedure that allows the review of the constitutionality or the justice of a conviction other than through the usual review of a conviction by direct appeal. Post-conviction relief describes all collateral attacks on a conviction, such as through petitions for habeas corpus, as well as specific state procedures for the presentation of newly discovered evidence of innocence or other matters for review of the conviction.

**appearance** Presenting oneself in court. An appearance is a physical or constructive presence in court, by which a party acknowledges an action pending there and the court's jurisdiction over the matter and that party. Any filing or act in court will amount to an appearance. Although no longer used in federal court, some states allow an appearance that does not amount to an acceptance of jurisdiction, allowing a defendant complaining that the court lacks jurisdiction either over a dispute or over the defendant to make a special or limited appearance to raise that argument. A general appearance need not be made by a special pleading or hearing. In the plaintiff's case, appearance is usually accomplished by filing the complaint, just as in the defendant's case it is usually accomplished by filing the answer. Appearance may be either in person or through counsel.

*See also:* court.

**appearance bond** *See:* bond, bail bond (appearance bond); bail, bail bond (appearance bond).

**appearance docket** *See:* docket, appearance docket.

**general appearance** Appearance without limitation in the matter before the court. A general appearance is one in which parties submit themselves to the court's authority for decision of issues that are unspecified related to the matter filed before the court. This kind of submission may be contrasted by the kind in which a party appears for a restricted reason only, such as to oppose the court's jurisdiction without submitting to it. A party who enters a general appearance voluntarily accepts the court's jurisdiction by doing so, and that party is barred from later attacking a judgment or other order on the basis of a failure of jurisdiction.

**initial appearance (presentment for initial appearance)** The first appearance of the accused before a magistrate or judge. An initial appearance is designed to inform someone accused of a crime what the charges are and to ensure that the accused is aware of the accused's rights in the legal process. In the federal system and most states, the initial appearance is separate from the arraignment, and the accused does not enter a plea at the initial appearance. There is no significant difference between a limited and a special appearance, although the rules of some courts employ only one term or the other. This proceeding is sometimes referred to as a presentment, which is a truncated form of presentment for initial appearance, the action of the officers responsible for the arrestee's detention bringing the prisoner before the court for the intial appearance.

**limited appearance** Appearance to contest jurisdiction. A limited appearance is one in which a defendant or intervenor comes before a court for the sole purpose of arguing that the court lacks jurisdiction in a pending case. By doing so, the appearant does not concede jurisdiction, and the court will usually rule on the question of jurisdiction before requiring other unrelated participation in the case by that party. Limited appearances are made in the federal courts by leave of the court, although the limited appearance is now less common in federal practice than is a motion to dismiss to accomplish the same purpose. There is no significant difference between a limited and a special appearance, although the rules of some courts employ only one term or the other.

**non-appearance (nonappearance or failure to appear)** Failure to be in court when expected. Non-appearance is any failure of a party, witness, or attorney to be present in court on the date and at the time that the person is ordered to do so. Non-appearance may be the basis for default in a civil proceeding, for contempt of court, or for a warrant for the crime of failure to appear in a criminal proceeding.

**failure to appear (bail-jumping or bail jumping or jump bail)** A defendant's absence from a criminal proceeding. Failure to appear is a crime committed when a defendant who has been issued a summons in a criminal case does not attend court on the stated date and time. Late arrival may be excused, and the decision to issue a warrant for the arrest of a non-appearing defendant rests with the trial judge or magistrate. A failure to appear for a hearing or trial for which bail had been posted will result in a forfeiture of the bail, unless the defendant or the defendant's bond holder can demonstrate that there was good cause for the failure to appear.

*See also:* failure (fail).

**special appearance** Appearance to contest jurisdiction. A special appearance is one in which a defendant or intervenor comes before a court for the sole purpose of arguing that the court lacks jurisdiction in a pending case. By doing so, the appearant does not concede jurisdiction, and the court will usually rule on the question of jurisdiction before requiring other unrelated participation in the case by that party. Limited appearances are made in the federal courts by leave of the court, although the limited appearance is now less common in federal practice than is a motion to dismiss, used to accomplish the same purpose. There is no significant difference between a limited and a special appearance, although the rules of some courts employ only one term or the other.

**substitution of parties** The replacement of one party to an action by a different party with the same interests. Substitution of parties is the termination of the appearance of a party in favor of the entry or appearance by another with the same or similar interests as the party who withdrew. In general, substitution is warranted by a transfer of interest from the party to a successor, by the death of a party, or by incapacity of a party. The mere appearance of one entity will usually not suffice for the appearance required of another. A substitute for a requested, advised, or mandatory appearance in court will only be sufficient if the substitute has identical interests and an identical method and reason for protecting those interests.

*See also:* substitution (substitute).

**telephone appearance**  Presence in court via telecommunication technology. Telephone appearance is appearance at a hearing or trial by telephone rather than in person. It is usually allowed by the court when a party, lawyer, or very rarely a witness cannot physically appear but is amenable to participation in a court proceeding. Telephone appearance is not a form of appearance in the general procedural sense of accepting jurisdiction.

**appel**  De novo review by a French court. Appel is a general review of a lower decision by a cour d'appel, including a review of both law and fact, both of which are considered de novo.

**appellant**  The losing party requesting correction of administrative or lower-court error. The appellant is the party requesting that a superior court review the decision of an administrative agency or lower court. In cases in which the review of a lower court is made pursuant to a writ of certiorari, this party is the petitioner, and in cases brought on a writ of error, this party is the plaintiff in error, regardless of whether the party was the plaintiff at trial or not.

*See also:* appeal (appealable or appellate).

**appellate**  *See:* appeal.

**appellate court or court of appeals or intermediate court**  *See:* court, U.S. court, court of appeal (appellate court or court of appeals or intermediate court).

**appellate jurisdiction**  *See:* jurisdiction, appellate jurisdiction, Rooker–Feldman Doctrine; jurisdiction, appellate jurisdiction.

**appellate procedure**  *See:* procedure, appellate procedure.

**appellate record**  *See:* record, appellate record, defective record; record, appellate record (trial record or record on appeal).

**appellate review**  *See:* review, appellate review.

**appellee**  A winning party below, who must defend that decision on appeal. An appellee is a party who opposes the appellant's appeal of a lower court decision to an appellate court. In cases in which the review of a lower court is made pursuant to a writ of certiorari, this party is the respondent, and in cases brought on a writ of error, this party is the defendant in error, regardless of whether the party was the defendant at trial or not.

*See also:* appeal (appealable or appellate).

**appointee**  One who is chosen for a particular position. An appointee is a person chosen for a certain position. Although one remains an appointee for certain purposes forever, the word connotes the status between appointment and commencement of office, or when an additional requirement must be met before

commencement of office before that requirement is met. For instance, a presidential appointee to a judgeship may await confirmation, or having been confirmed be awaiting investiture. Having been invested, a judge may be described as an appointee of the president whose nomination led to the judgeship, but it is not appropriate to describe the judge merely as an appointee.

*See also:* appointment (appoint).

**appointment (appoint)**  The selection of whom to hold an office, or a property. Appointment in the governmental sense is the process of selecting and investing a person in an office. Appointments are made according to a lawful power to make the appointment. In the constitutional structure of American governments, this is usually an executive function, but for certain purposes may be made by officers of the legislative or judicial branches. Appointment may require further legislative or judicial actions to ratify or approve the selected person for office. Appointments are, however, more often made in a private domain, as when an executor is appointed by a judge following nomination by the testator in the language of a will.

As a matter of property, appointment is the designation of who shall hold a given parcel of lands, when the person making the appointment (the owner or the donee of the power of appointment) has the authority to invest the lands in the person or entity appointed.

*See also:* nomination (nominate).

**recess appointment (vacancy appointment)**  A temporary Presidential appointment without Senatorial confirmation. A recess appointment is an executive appointment made while a legislature is in recess. The President of the United States may appoint officers, judges, and ambassadors during a recess of the Senate without advice and consent, although such an appointment is temporary and must expire at the conclusion of the present session of Congress.

**Appointments Clauses**  *See:* constitution, U.S. Constitution, clauses, Appointments Clauses (Recess Appointments Clause).

**apportionment**

**apportionment as allocation of voters (reapportionment or re-apportionment)**  Drawing boundaries or allocating representation in a legislature or other election. Reapportionment is the redistribution of representation for a legislative body, usually based on recent population changes that have been recently recorded in a census. Such measures must comport with the U.S. Constitution, not only the Fourteenth Amendment's requirement of equal protection of the laws but also the specific amendments that affect access to the ballot, such as the Fourteenth Amendment's requirement of proportional representation for house seats and, most significantly, the Fifteenth Amendment's stricture, "The right of citizens of the United States to vote shall not be denied or abridged by the United States or by any State on account of race, color, or previous condition of servitude." In certain states and counties, reapportionment is subject to pre–clearance under the Voting Rights Act.

**apportionment of rents or payments**  Division and distribution of property once held as a whole among several holders. Apportionment is an allocation and division of an asset that is subject to a contract, such as rent, so that a risk in the transaction that becomes manifest is born between the two parties. There are conditions in which no apportionment is required, such as a landlord's eviction of a tenant from lease for a period of years, in which case, the tenant would owe no more rents.
*See also:* liability, apportionment of liability.

**apportionment of liability**  *See:* liability, apportionment of liability, market–share liability; liability, apportionment of liability.

**appraisal (appraisement)**  Valuation of property. An appraisal is the determination of the fair market value of a piece of property. The most common formulation of fair market value is what a reasonable purchaser would pay at arm's length in cash at the time of the valuation. Appraisals are required as a condition precedent to many transactions, notably insurance contracts and mortgages. Appraisals are also required prior to the sale of assets in most probated estates.
*See also:* value (valuation).

**absorption rate**  The speed at which property sells in a given market. The absorption rate of property sales is the average speed at which parcels are sold, or are likely to be sold in a given market at a given time, at market prices. The absorption rate is one condition of the appraisal of the value of commercial or investment real estate. Note: the absorption rate for property has nothing to do with absorption of parcels of property on into another.
*See also:* appraisal (appraisement); absorption, absorption of real estate.

**insurance appraisal**  Valuation of the cost that would be required to replace an insured item. An insurance appraisal is an appraisal specifically required to enter or continue an insurance policy or to settle a claim, in which property is appraised to determine its replacement value.

**appraiser**  One who ascertains the value of property. An appraiser is a person who is appointed by an appropriate authority to appraise the value of a given asset or assets. More generally, an appraiser is someone qualified to perform such appraisals. Frequently, appraisers are specialists in a particular field, and an appraisal of a particular genre of property, such as a gem or a gas field, ordinarily requires an appraisal by someone qualified through experience or training to make such appraisals. Bonded appraisers carry insurance against professional errors, and certified appraisers are members of professional associations.

*See also:* insurer, insurance personnel, insurance appraiser.

**apprehension**

**apprehension as anticipation (apprehend)**  Fear of a future occurrence. Apprehension is a dread of something likely to happen. Apprehension is an element of assault, in which case it is both a knowledge of events from which one might base a belief one will be battered or otherwise harmed, as well as a reasonable belief that harm is likely to follow. It is important to understand, though, that the common–law understanding of apprehension is closer to fear or instinct, and it would be unwise to demand articulable statements of knowledge of events that move as swiftly as those of assault. Apprehension may be presumed from circumstances, awareness of those circumstances, and reaction to those circumstances.

**apprehension as arrest (apprehend)**  Capture or possession. Apprehension is taking someone or something into one's control or custody. Apprehension implies an element of physicality, implied from the earlier senses of the word as grasping hold, as in collaring the suspect, but the element of physical contact is not required in the United States. Apprehension as a matter of usage does vary somewhat from the broader idea of arrest, in that the sense of apprehension is of a person sought prior to the capture, particularly someone for whom a warrant has been issued or who has fled from an attempted arrest already.

**apprenticeship (apprentice)**  A period of training for a person learning a craft or trade, supervised by a skilled practitioner. Apprenticeships are periods of onthe–job instruction for an apprentice, by whatever name. Apprenticeships can be formal or informal. Formal apprenticeships are usually governed by contracts with a union or trade group or master in a field. They allow the apprentice to work for a set period of time at a lower pay rate in return for providing the apprentice with training that meets some standard of skill. Informal apprenticeships are merely at–will employment arrangements in which an unskilled worker is expected to acquire skills while on the job. An apprentice is a trainee who is entitled to the full protection of the law from various forms of discrimination.

**apprisal (apprise)**  To become informed of a fact or learned in a subject. Apprisal is the state of knowledge, and to apprise a person of some fact is to inform the person of it. Apprise, in law, is used to depict the process of making oneself informed. A lawyer and litigant have an obligation to remain apprised of the condition of litigation while it proceeds in the courts. Apprise has grown into the reflexive of the older form of keeping another apprised, and apprise now also signifies the process of one person's informing another, particularly when a police officer apprises a suspect of the suspect's constitutional rights by reading a Miranda card to the suspect. Note: apprise is sometimes confused with appraise, which is the evaluation of a thing rather than merely the knowledge of it.

*See also:* appraisal (appraisement).

### appropriation

**appropriation of likeness** *See:* privacy, invasion of privacy, appropriation of likeness.

**appropriation of name** *See:* privacy, invasion of privacy, appropriation of name.

**Appropriations Clause** *See:* constitution, U.S. Constitution, clauses, Appropriations Clause.

**appropriation as allocation of a debt** Designated payment of a money owed to a creditor. Appropriation is the payment of money to a creditor and the designation of that money toward a particular debt the creditor holds. The debtor has the power to appropriate the payment to one or another account, unless that power has been surrendered by contract. In the absence of a surrender under the terms of a contract or the debtor's appropriation, the creditor also has that power. If neither party has surrendered the power under contract nor exercised that power, the law appropriates payments among several debts held by a single creditor with preference for debts. That priority is, first, to a debt that the debtor is under a duty to a third person to pay immediately; second, to overdue interest rather than principal and to an unsecured or precarious debt rather than to one that is secured or certain of payment; third, to the earliest matured debt; and fourth, ratably among debts of the same maturity.

**appropriation as allocation of funds (appropriate)** To set aside public money for a specific purpose. Appropriation is the process of legislative authorization for the expenditure of public funds. A process of appropriation is required for federal expenditure in Article I, Section 9, and the expenditure of federal moneys in a manner that is not appropriate is unconstitutional.

*See also:* misappropriation (misappropriate).

**appurtenance (appurtenant)** An accessory to something more significant. An appurtenance is an appendage, a distinct element that is still a component of and subordinate to something else. Appurtenances of a parcel of real property include all of the rights incident to owning the land, including the right to possess attachments such as buildings, the right to use easements that are transferred with the property (as opposed to easements in gross, which remained the property of the grantor unless specifically transferred).

*See also:* covenant, real covenant, appurtenant covenant (covenant appurtenant); easement, appurtenant easement (easement appurtenant).

**appurtenant covenant** *See:* covenant, real covenant, appurtenant covenant (covenant appurtenant).

**appurtenant easement** *See:* easement, appurtenant easement (easement appurtenant).

**APR** *See:* interest, interest for money, annual percentage rate (APR).

**aqua (aquae)** Water. Aqua is Latin for water, and the term occurs in numerous maxims concerning water, whether surface waters such as oceans, rivers, and lakes or subsurface waters. The English terms aquatic and aqueous are derived from it.

**aquaculture** The farming of fresh and saltwater organisms. Aquaculture is farm fishing, the farming of either fresh and saltwater plants or animals for harvesting, sale, and consumption. Seawater aquaculture has gained particular attention in recent years, and the national aquaculture policy is directed specifically to marine farming. Still, the term also includes pond farming and fish hatchery management, practices that antedate the use of the term by some years. Aquaculture facilities that are not well managed pose a significant potential for the generation of harmful wastes, both from animal waste and unconsumed inputs.

**aquifer** A natural underground water source. An aquifer is an underground formation of rock and soil through which groundwater is stored and moves. Aquifers are the source of water for wells. Depending upon the geology of the particular aquifer, most can be easily contaminated by the seepage of sewage as well as leachate from landfills or mining. Urbanization and well-fed irrigation tends to drain aquifers, both by consuming water from the aquifer faster than it would naturally recharge and by increasing the quantity of impermeable surfaces, like structures and parking lots, resulting in rainwater running off into artificial aqueducts and into streams rather than being absorbed into the ground.

**arable land** *See:* land, arable land (erable land or errable land).

**arbiter** *See:* arbitrator (arbiter).

**arbitrability** *See:* arbitration, arbitrability (arbitrable or inarbitrable or non-arbitrable).

**arbitrage (arbitrageur or arbitrager)** Trading by nearly simultaneous purchases and sales of assets that realizes a profit. Arbitrage is a process of trading among various markets for assets or securities that exploits the difference between prices for the same asset in different markets. Arbitrage usually involves the nearly simultaneous purchase and resale of a security in order to exploit the imbalance in price between two or more markets. The investor profits from the discounted purchase for the asset in one market (in which the asset is bought) by immediately reselling the asset in a different market at a higher price.

**arbitral award** *See:* arbitration, arbitral award, foreign arbitral award; arbitration, arbitral award (arbitrament).

**arbitrament** *See:* arbitration, arbitral award (arbitrament); arbitration (arbitrament).

**arbitrariness (arbitrary)** Decisions depending on the will of the official rather than the facts and the law. An arbitrary action is the result of the will of an individual, rather than the reasonable or reasoned application of the law to a given array of facts. Every act of discretion, however, is not arbitrary; the law requires officials to act within boundaries circumscribed by law, yet even within these boundaries to apply general principles of law and the foundational notions of justice to the facts as they are established as a matter of record. An official who acts as the facts might be thought to be, in disregard of the evidence, or who acts as the laws might be, in disregard of the archives of the law, acts arbitrarily. Although one more often encounters the question of arbitrariness now as a standard of review for judicial actions, historically, the greatest concern has been arbitrary action by the executive, followed by concern for arbitrary legislation. As American law in the twenty-first century has come to include more equitable functions, the question of arbitrariness has arisen anew, in part because chancellors hold such broad discretion they have been accused of being arbitrary, but the more frequent complaint is by those who disagree with a decision and cloak their disagreement with charges of judicial activism and arbitrariness.

*See also:* review, standard of review, arbitrary and capricious.

**arbitrary and capricious** *See:* review, standard of review, arbitrary and capricious.

**arbitrary detention** *See:* detention, arbitrary detention.

**arbitration (arbitrament)** A method by which disputes are decided out of court. Arbitration is a non-judicial consideration of a dispute that both sides agree will result in a final decision on the merits of the dispute. The parties to the arbitration submit the dispute to an arbitrator, or panel of arbitrators, for review, hearing, and adjudication in a binding decision. In some respects arbitration is similar to litigation; for example, both sides present arguments and evidence, including witnesses, to a neutral decision-maker. An arbitrator may apply any evidentiary rules and substantive law that appears fair or is required in the arbitral procedure, which can be much broader than what is allowed as the basis for decision by a court. Arbitration is an abbreviated, efficient means of resolving disputes, the outcome of which contractually has the force of a mandatory, binding determination. Courts that subsequently review the proceedings on appeal have only a limited role; the general rule now is that they must defer to arbitration findings. If, however, consent to arbitration proceedings has been extracted between parties of substantially unequal bargaining strength, such as in a standardized form contract required of a consumer, the arbitration clause may be unenforceable.

*See also:* arbitrator (arbiter); accord, accord and satisfaction | 6. arbitration; arbitration, arbitration clause; mediation.

**advisory arbitration** Non-binding arbitration Advisory arbitration is a form of fact-finding review between the parties. It is not binding arbitration, in that neither party must adhere to the arbitrator's decision. Rather, it allows each party to test the strength of their argument in the light of the contested evidence.

**American Arbitration Association (A.A.A. or AAA)** An organization designed to facilitate the use of arbitration to resolve disputes. The AAA is a national body for providing both rules for arbitration and a body of experienced arbitrators.

**arbitrability (arbitrable or inarbitrable or non-arbitrable)** The condition of a dispute that may be resolved by arbitration. Arbitrability is the availability of binding arbitration to resolve a given dispute between or among specific parties. Arbitrability must arise as a matter of the consent of the parties to submit to the resolution of their claims and defenses by arbitration. This consent may be manifest prior to the recognition of the parties that they have a dispute, from an arbitration agreement or arbitration clause in a more general agreement made before the dispute arises. Consent to arbitrate may also be manifest by an agreement by the parties made following their recognition of the dispute, by which the parties consent to submit the dispute to arbitration.

Whether a dispute is arbitrable may be itself arbitrable. An agreement to arbitrate may designate such questions for arbitration. Even so, a party who challenges the arbitrability of an arbitration agreement or the designation of the issue of arbitrability to be arbitrated may refuse to submit to arbitration and seek judicial review of a challenge to the validity of that clause or designation, even if the agreement as a whole is not subject to litigation.

**arbitral award (arbitrament)** A final decision by an arbitrator. An arbitral award is a decision by an arbitrator. Parties who might sue in a private cause of action in court may elect to submit their claims and arguments to arbitration, and the award of relief to one side or the other by an arbitrator or panel of arbitrators is an arbitral award. If the parties had negotiated the arbitral agreement or arbitration clause in a larger contract, or if the arbitration is required as a matter of law, not only is the arbitral award likely to be enforced in a court of law, but any attempt by either of the parties to litigate the same issue is likely to be dismissed.

**foreign arbitral award** An arbitral award rendered abroad from a commercial dispute with a foreign citizen. A foreign arbitral award is any award from an arbitration held out of the country in which it must be enforced. Within the confines of the New York Convention on the Recognition and Enforcement of Foreign Arbitral Awards, the award subject to local legal process has more constraints: the arbitration must have arisen from a commercial dispute in which one party is a non-citizen or in which the dispute is over foreign property.

**Arbitration Act (Federal Arbitration Act or F.A.A. or FAA)** Arbitation in matters of admiralty and interstate commerce may be enforced in federal and state courts. The Federal Arbitration Act of 1925 allows judicial enforcement of valid arbitration agreements in disputes otherwise in federal courts, and it preempts state laws that would forbid enforcement of arbitral awards. The act reversed the common–law prohibition on the enforcement of arbitration clauses in court. The act does not create any presumptions of validity of an arbitration clause, which remains only as enforceable as would another contract or contract clause, nor does it create a federal cause of action in a situation that would not otherwise be within federal jurisdiction.

**arbitration clause** A provision in a contract requiring non–judicial resolution of disputes. An arbitration clause amounts to a distinct agreement between the parties to a contract that the parties will refrain from litigation in the event a disagreement arises under the contract and that the parties will accept and be bound by arbitration. An arbitration clause is both an element of a contract in which it occurs and an agreement to arbitrate, although the consideration by one party to accept the arbitration clause may be inextricable from the consideration of the underlying agreement as a whole.

Arbitration clauses are subject to judicial review just as any other contract clause subject to a dispute, although only as to their enforceability. The clause is enforceable if the parties both freely and knowingly agreed to the clause. On the other hand, the clause may be unconscionable and unenforceable if it was extracted by a party of substantially greater bargaining strength, or one party was unaware of its presence in a boilerplate contract or had no opportunity to negotiate it, as is often the case where consumers are involved.

**final–offer arbitration** Arbitration in which each side offers a settlement and one is selected. In final–offer arbitration, each party submits an offer that would seem to resolve the dispute between them under the law. The arbitrator selects whichever of the parties' potential solutions would more likely resolve the conflict equitably and justly. Unlike arbitration generally, this form allows the parties to retain at least potential influence over the resolution. The selection of a final offer may be something of a game: if one party is convinced it should win under the facts and the law, it may offer nothing, but if it believes it might lose, it can offer a compromise solution.

**grievance arbitration (rights arbitration)** Arbitration to interpret an existing collective bargaining agreement. Grievance arbitration is a form of labor arbitration, which is used in disputes between an employer and a union about what performance is required under an existing collective–bargaining agreement or other employment agreement. It is the same as rights arbitration.

**high–low abitration** Arbitration that limits the range of damages that might be awarded at trial. High–low arbitration is an agreement between the parties to a lawsuit to reduce or inflate the amount to be paid according to a predetermined scale by which the award of damages will be assessed. The effect is to limit the losses that might be incurred by either side by capping the amount of the plaintiff's recovery but ensuring that some payment will be made. In some instances, the trial verdict needs then only to be on liability in general, the amount of damages having then been agreed in advance. In others, the court will find an amount of damages, but the actual payment will be translated into a predetermined schedule.

**interests arbitration** Arbitration to negotiate a new collective bargaining agreement. Interest arbitration is a process by which the parties arbitrate the interests each has that must be integrated into an agreement, after which an agreement is drafted. It is the essential process in an arbitrated negotiation to create a new collective bargaining agreement.

**mini–trial** Informal proceedings for hearing business disputes. A mini–trial is a form of arbitration in which representatives of two parties who disagree on the facts or their significance present their cases to a group including executives of the parties with the power to settle the dispute, as well as to a neutral expert who can predict the outcome of the dispute if the dispute is resolved in court. The executives hear the presentations and then are expected to negotiate a resolution, with the prediction of the neutral party for guidance.

*See also:* arbitration (arbitrament).

**ouster doctrine** Arbitration clauses are disfavored limits on court jurisdiction. The ouster doctrine disfavors arbitration requirements arising from arbitration contracts and clauses because the agreement to arbitrate being made prior to the parties' knowledge of the suit results in the improper ouster of judicial jurisdiction. That view has been less prominent since the passage of the Federal Arbitration Act but persists in states that follow the common–law view on arbitration.

**arbitrator (arbiter)** The decision–maker in out–of–court proceedings. An arbitrator is the adjudicator who resolves the dispute in contractually agreed–to, out–of–court proceedings. An arbitrator might serve on a panel of arbitration.

*See also:* arbitration (arbitrament).

**archives (archival or archive or archivist)** Officially kept historical records concerning a nation or state. Archives in the legal sense include records as well as the places of storage of official records of the courts and other public bodies. Thus, a law library is a form of archive.

**are or centiare or deciare**   *See:* land, measure of land, hectare (are or centiare or deciare).

**Areopagus**   *See:* court, Greek court, Areopagus (Court of the Areopagus or Areiopagos).

**arguendo**   Assuming a proposition for the sake of argument. Arguendo implies that an assertion is hypothetical, that it is being offered for the sake of an argument. A statement arguendo might, or it might not, reflect the position that the speaker intends to stake out and defend. It is a thrust in rhetoric designed to see what sort of parries it might evoke. Arguendo is also a formal term of rhetoric that is increasingly unknown, and its use might appear affected to some species of lawyers.

**argument**   Analysis, in which the law is applied to the facts to advocate for a given result. Argument is both the process of giving reasons to believe that some idea is true, or at least probably true, and the label for the reason or reasons that are given. The processes of argument were once taught as rhetoric, which now, however, is rarely studied. Current legal education incorporates it as an element of legal advocacy or legal writing. The essential argument in a judicial opinion is still sometimes described as the ratio decidendi, the reasoning for the decision.
   *See also:* therefore (therefor); lawyer.

**argument at trial**   *See:* trial, argument at trial (trial argument).

**argument list or index of authorities**   *See:* brief, table of authorities (argument list or index of authorities).

**analogical reasoning**   The process of reasoning by comparison, particularly in the application of precedents to later situations. Analogical reasoning seeks to compare two or more things by assessing the degree to which they are different or alike. Identifying significant factual similarities between things may justify treating them the same. In law, this is seen in the assessment of the degree to which a precedent resolved a similar problem and to what extent it should be repeated in the later case. The enterprise of analogical reasoning seeks not exact identities, but only those resemblances that are material to the decision whether comparable circumstances ought to invoke application of the same legal principles or policies. Analogy does not allow evaluation of the rightness or wrongness of the earlier decision; it only allows a comparison of one thing to another.
   *See also:* reason, analogical reasoning.

**deductive reasoning**   Determining something specific from general ideas. Deductive reasoning uses broad premises to determine the answer to a more specific question. For example, if it is proven that all fish live in the water, it may be deduced that a particular breed of fish lives in the water. Another example is the deduction that it snowed last night when there was no snow on the ground at five p.m. and the ground was covered in snow at three o'clock

the next morning. The understood generalization there is that snow would cover the ground only if it had fallen from the sky.

**golden-rule argument (victim's shoes argument)**   The argument to a jury to imagine themselves suffering the harm allegedly caused in a case. The golden-rule argument is an old favorite of prosecutors and plaintiff's lawyers, asking jurors to think of themselves suffering as the lawyer claims there was suffering. This argument is meant to inflame the jury and to ignore the questions of both whether such suffering did occur and, if so, whether the defendant indeed caused it. Thus, it is improper in most jurisdictions and may amount to both attorney misconduct and to reversible error, if it is allowed by the court.

**inductive reasoning**   Drawing a general conclusion from several specific facts. Inductive reasoning uses many particular instances to determine the answer to a broad question. For example, if it is proven that one million species of fish live in the water, and no species of fish has been found living out of the water, it may be induced that all fish will live in the water. Another example is the induction that American corporations will never go completely paperless, drawn from the many instances of people printing out memoranda they receive via e-mail.

**legal argument**   An argument derived in whole or part from legal sources. A legal argument is a series of statements based, at least in part, on the sources of law, which leads to a statement of what the rules of law require, forbid, or allow. A legal argument must proceed from sources of law, applied according to custom, logic, and reason, to argue that the law requires a given conclusion. In the case of a specific legal argument, the argument proceeds from facts to determine the legal sources that seem to apply in assessing those facts to reach a given conclusion. In all cases, a well-made legal argument considers alternative cases to the case proposed and demonstrates either the falsity of the alternatives or the preference for the chosen case, or both. In many instances concerning facts, it cannot fully be established what did occur or what did not occur. In such cases (among others) the argument must be a matter of degree: what is more or less likely between alternatives or most likely among them all.
   A legal argument may be general and universal, applying broadly and to all persons in a category of cases, or it may be specific and concrete, applying in the light of specific facts.
   Legal arguments made in the general sense are based on the interaction of rules derived from sources of law, often focusing on whether a particular statement of a rule is law, such as whether the Eighth Amendment applies to limit state officials from cruel and unusual punishments. Such an argument can be made and defended regardless of any state and regardless of whether an in individual is an official — or a state official — in a given case.

Legal arguments in the specific sense are dependent on the sufficiency of facts as a measure of a legal requirement. They are more often made concretely, in the manner of whether a particular set of facts (or more often particular series of inferences derived from evidence) support a given requirement of the law that would be applied to a given person or entity. In such cases, the answer to a given question depends on whether the facts that may be established are sufficient to satisfy a standard of law. In the example above, if the Eighth Amendment applies to the act of a state official, whether it applies to the actions of a particular individual will turn on whether the actions of that individual amount to a punishment as a matter of fact.

*See also:* reason (reasons or reasoning).

**CRAC (conclusion rule application conclusion or conclusion rule analysis conclusion or C.R.A.C.)** An outline for the analysis of a legal issue, beginning with the conclusion. "Conclusion, Rule, Application, Conclusion" is a convention of organization that is helpful in a legal argument that seeks to persuade the reader to a given conclusion. The process begins by announcing the conclusion. Next the governing legal rule is set forth. Following are illustrations of the legal rule's application to the particular fact situation under decision. The conclusion is then re-stated.

**IRAC (issue rule application conclusion or issue rule analysis conclusion or I.R.A.C.)** An outline for the analysis of a legal issue, beginning with the issue. "Issue, Rule, Analysis, Conclusion" is a convention helpful in presenting a legal argument. The process begins by announcing the issue, in a concise statement that melds the legal rule with the material facts of the case under decision, in a manner that strongly points to the outcome advocated. Next the governing legal rule is set forth. Following are illustrations of the legal rule's application to the particular fact situation under decision. The conclusion is then stated.

**modus ponens (modus ponendo ponens)** Accepting one thing leads to another, and then asserting the one thing as proof of the other. Modus ponens is a deductive argument that asserts a cause between two statements, then asserts the first statement to prove the second. This can be seen in several ways, including these three: (1) It follows from P being true that Q is true. P is true, therefore logically Q must be true, too. (2) Any person who exceeds the speed limit without good cause has violated the speed law. Steve has exceeded the speed limit without good cause, therefore he has violated the speed law. (3) If one exceeds the speed limit without good cause, then one violates the speed law. Steve has exceeded the speed limit and has no good cause, therefore he has violated the speed law. For these arguments to be true, the premises must be true; if one is not true the argument is not proven.

The modus ponens argument is one of the most basic forms of legal analysis. A. A legal standard applied to a type of fact specified in the standard would lead to a result as a matter of law. B. This is the fact. C. This legal standard applied to this fact requires this result as a matter of law.

**modus tollens (modus tollendo ponens)** Deductive argument using the formula if X is untrue then so must be Y. Modus pollens is use of logic to disprove a point such as: If a child arrives home after a designated time, that child should be grounded. Your daughter arrived home before the scheduled time, so she should not be grounded. Modus tollens is a deductive argument that asserts a cause between two statements, then asserts the failure of the second statement to prove the failure of the first. This can be seen in several ways, including these three: (1) It follows from P being true that Q is true. Q is not true, therefore logically P must be not true either. (2) Any person who exceeds the speed limit without good cause has violated the speed law. Steve has not violated the speed law, therefore he has not exceeded the speed limit without good cause. (3) If one exceeds the speed limit without good cause, then one violates the speed law. Steve has not violated the speed law, therefore he has not exceeded the speed limit without good cause. If one can disprove this argument for every possibility, one can prove the contrary.

**Morton's Fork** Arguing alternative causes for one effect, any of which cause an opponent's loss. Morton's Fork, named for a fifteenth-century tax-collecting Chancellor of Henry VII, is the rhetorical trope of offering two alternative explanations for an opponent's position, although the opponent will lose the argument if either is correct. There are several approaches to argument, however, that fall under this label. Morton's original approach was merely to vary his reasons for paying the tax (actually a quasi-tax known as a benevolence), by offering two different arguments, one for the thrifty and one for the profligate. The more modern argument has one rather than two opponents, and seeks to bind the opponent to either of two narratives, either being sufficient to condemn the opponent. The opponent's responses must be either to reject both narratives and offer a third or to demonstrate that the apparent condemnation of one or both arguments on offer is false, and the narratives do not lead to liability as suggested.

**oral argument** The dialogue of attorneys with the bench disputing legal questions. An oral argument is any argument made by the lawyer by speech in court. Although much oral argument amounts to a speech by the attorney to the bench, oral argument is more helpfully a dialogue between the attorney and the judge or judges to develop ideas essential to the application of the laws to the questions then before them. Oral argument takes place in many places throughout pre-trial, trial, and appeal. In general, the lawyer for the movant, plaintiff, or appellant speaks first and last, as that party who has the burden of persuasion.

**syllogism (false syllogism)**  Argument to prove a conclusion from two reasons. A syllogism asserts two premises from which a conclusion may be proved. The major premise is a statement describing a category. The minor premise is a statement that the object in discussion is in the category, so the conclusion is that the object is as described. So, this is a major premise: all trout are fish. This is a minor premise: all fish live in water. This is the conclusion: therefore, all trout live in water. For a syllogism to be true, both premises must be true and accurately related to one another. A false syllogism has a false premise or false relationship between premises. A false premise is this: penguins are birds. All birds can fly. Therefore, penguins can fly. But it was not true that all birds can fly, so the conclusion is not proven. Likewise, a false relationship is one that does not necessitate the relationship implied by the premises: Penguins are birds. Some birds eat worms. Therefore penguins eat worms. Clearly not proven because the relationship between the two premises is inexact.

**argumentativeness  (argumentative)**  Needless verbal combativeness, particularly with a witness. To be argumentative is to engage in unneeded dispute. Argumentative objections lack merit, even if they might be technically accurate, when they are raised for the purpose of needless annoyance of the opponent or disturbance of the court. Argumentative pleadings raise challenges, complaints, claims, or disputes that are not true or provable, or are not relevant to what genuine legal disputes are really between the parties.
*See also:* instruction, jury instruction, argumentative instruction.

**argumentum ad hominem**  *See:* fallacy, ad hominem (argumentum ad hominem).

**aristocracy**  *See:* government, forms of government, aristocracy.

**arm**  *See:* arms, arms as weaponry (arm).

**arm or arms**  *See:* gun, firearm (arm or arms).

**armed conflict**  *See:* war, armed conflict.

**armed forces**  The combined military services of a nation or political entity. Armed forces is the generic term for the military organizations and personnel of a nation or political entity, as well as any para–military or mercenary forces under national or political control or authority.

> **United States Armed Forces**  The United States Armed Forces comprise the Army, Navy, Air Force, Marine Corps, and Coast Guard.

**armed robbery**  *See:* robbery, armed robbery.

**armistice**  A lasting suspension of military hostilities. An armistice is a cessation of military operations between two combatant groups. Although not meant to be a permanent peace, it is more than a truce, which is a temporary cessation of hostilities, and an armistice is usually in contemplation of a final termination of hostilities. For example, military actions in World War I ended with an armistice, which was succeeded by the Treaty of Versailles. Even so, the armistice halting combat in the Korean Conflict of the 1950s has yet to result in a peace treaty.
*See also:* war (warfare).

**arms**

> **arms as weaponry (arm)**  An instrument used for either attack or defense. Arms refers to weapons, particularly tools customarily used to fight or hurt people. Personal weapons include firearms, knives, swords, clubs, and other light weapons that can be carried on the person, but arms includes heavy weapons used by a military force on land, sea, or air. Arms may also have a metaphorical quality, as in a spear or shield in legal argument.

**Army Clause**  *See:* constitution, U.S. Constitution, clauses, Army Clause.

**arraignment**  The proceeding in which one accused of a crime enters a plea in response to the accusations. The arraignment is that part of the criminal proceeding during which the defendant is called to the bar and formally presented with accusations from an indictment or other initial criminal pleading, which recites the actions of which the defendant is accused and the crimes to which the defendant must plead. The defendant will then plead either guilty, not guilty, or nolo contendere. In some cases the plea will be conditioned, as in a plea of not guilty by reason of insanity. Though most arraignments are made in person, the defendant may waive personal appearance in federal court and in many state courts for certain offenses. The arraignment usually includes a judicial review of the suspect's detention, receipt and recording an entry of the plea in the record, and the setting of future proceedings in the case.
*See also:* arrest; plea, criminal plea; trial, fair trial (rights of criminal defendants).

**Arranda–Bruton error or Bruton rule**  *See:* confession, Bruton error (Arranda–Bruton error or Bruton rule).

**array or identification parade or line up or line-up or photo array or show up or showup or show-up**  *See:* identification, identification procedure, police lineup (array or identification parade or line up or line–up or photo array or show up or showup or show–up).

**array or jury pool or venire panel**  *See:* jury, jury selection, jury panel (array or jury pool or venire panel).

**arrearage (arrear or arrears or in arrears)** A balance past due. Arrearage, money still owed after the due date has passed, is more commonly described as arrears or, less often, money in arrear.

**arrest** The physical or authoritative restraint of a person. An arrest is a compelled stop, and to arrest someone is to deprive them of their liberty of movement. When made by an agent of the government, an arrest is a seizure of the person under the Fourth Amendment. In most instances, an arrest is accomplished either by a person's physical restraint or a result of a person's reasonable belief that the person is not free to leave, based upon the conduct of a governmental agent. An arrest may be made pursuant to a warrant, but it may also be made based on a police agent's inherent authority to make an arrest. Indeed any person may make an arrest, but if the arrest is not proved to be a valid restraint of a person who has violated the law, private individuals may be liable for wrongful arrest or for kidnapping.

*See also:* search, search and seizure; detainer.

*arrest as a civil matter* Detention or compulsion to bring someone before a court in a civil proceeding. Arrest, though usually a prelude to a criminal proceeding, may be used in a very few jurisdictions to compel participation in any civil process. Arrests can be performed both by police officers and by private citizens, although an arrest that is not according to law may amount to unlawful arrest or kidnapping.

**arrest of judgment** *See:* judgment, arrest of judgment.

**arrest record** *See:* record, arrest record, Sandoval hearing; record, arrest record (criminal history record or rap sheet).

**arrest warrant** *See:* warrant, arrest warrant.

**citizen's arrest** The act of a private citizen taking another person into custody. Citizen's arrest, or private arrest, is the arrest of someone for committing a crime that is not made by a police officer or governmental agent. The power to make such arrests is a limited authority conferred by the state to private citizens to arrest another person, and it is usually limited to instances in which an arresting citizen witnesses a felony or a breach of the peace by the arrestee.

**custodial arrest** *See:* custody, penal custody, custodial arrest.

**false arrest** Detention of a person absent probable cause. A false arrest is the tort of detention of a person when the person detaining lacks a valid arrest warrant or probable cause that the person has committed a specific criminal act. The tort action for false arrest may allow recovery in damages against a private party or a police officer, though the police officer is usually entitled to immunity from such claims.

**malicious arrest** Invalidly taking a person into police custody for problems with the individual unrelated to criminal activity. Malicious arrest is a false arrest performed for reasons personal to the arresting individual, rather than for an actual law-enforcing function. The arrest must be targeted toward a particular individual to be considered an act of malice.

The tort of malicious arrest, in some jurisdictions a form of false imprisonment, is an intentional tort for which punitive damages are available and in others is the same as the tort of false arrest, for which damages are limited to compensatory damages absent a showing of recklessness, bad faith, wanton disregard for duty, or a deliberate intent to harm the arrestee. Malicious arrest by a state agent is also a violation of one's civil rights under the Fifth Amendment and subject to habeas release or injunction, as well as an action under 42 U.S.C. § 1983.

False imprisonment is also a private tort akin to kidnapping, in which one person is detained by another against the will of the first, regardless of whether the detaining person is a public officer or not, as long as the detaining person has no lawful privilege to do so. The tort is an intentional tort and is subject to compensatory and punitive damages.

**pretextual arrest (pretextual stop)** The detention of a person for a motive other than the one specified. A pretextual arrest is an arrest by a police officer who suspects that an individual is involved in a criminal offense, but lacks the probable cause to detain the suspect for that offense, and chooses instead to arrest the suspect for a different offense, even if under other circumstances the officer would not have done so. In general, as long as the officer had the authority to arrest the suspect for the offense charged, then the detention is lawful, and any evidence that later develops relating to the major offense is not barred by reason of the arrest alone.

*See also:* pretext (pretextual).

**resisting arrest** Taking action to avoid arrest or police custody. Resisting arrest is a crime of preventing a police officer from lawfully carrying out the arrest of the resisting person, who was being arrested for a different offense. A person resists arrest when the person knows that the person is lawfully being taken into police custody and affirmatively acts in a manner that would interfere with that custody. If the person resists an official or other person who is not acting according to law, whether attempting an arrest that is invalid or by using excessive force, an action in self-defense is not resisting arrest.

**unlawful arrest (wrongful arrest)** An arrest without warrant, probable cause, or valid exigency. An unlawful arrest is an arrest made by a police official without lawful authority to arrest the person detained. Under the U.S. and state constitutions, an arrest must be based on an arrest warrant, sufficient probable cause known to the officer at the time of the arrest, or an exigent circumstance such as the minimal detention required to make a lawful search. An otherwise lawful arrest may become unlawful, particularly if the detention that results from the arrest extends for a time unreasonably longer than its justification, or if excessive force or objectively unreasonable means are employed.

A person subject to unlawful arrest is entitled to release unless a valid arrest or detention is later made, and such release may be accomplished through a proceeding for habeas corpus. Certain evidence gathered only as a result of an unlawful arrest may be barred from use in a subsequent criminal proceeding against the person unlawfully arrested. In some circumstances in which the arresting official knew or should have known the arrest was unlawful, the person arrested may bring an action for the tort of false arrest, as well as an action for the vindication of federally protected civil rights.

*See also:* civil rights, civil rights enforcement action, Bivens action; civil rights, civil rights enforcement action, 1983 action; habeas corpus (great writ); search, exclusionary rule, fruit of the poisonous tree.

**right to resist unlawful arrest**   The privilege to resist an unlawful detention by the police. In general, there is no longer a right to use reasonable force to resist an unlawful arrest by an identified police officer, acting within the scope of the officer's authority. Such a right to resist arrest was a privilege of the common law, and it persists in many cases against attempts at arrest by private citizens. Likewise, it underpins the continuing right to use reasonable and non-deadly force to resist entry to the police to one's property without a valid warrant or probable cause. When, however, a person attempts to use force to avoid an arrest the person believes to be unlawful, the person may be committing an obstruction of justice.

**warrantless arrest**   A valid arrest made without an arrest warrant. A warrantless arrest is an arrest made without an arrest warrant. Warrantless arrests are only valid if the circumstances of the arrest place it in a recognized exception to the warrant requirement, such as arresting officer's belief that there is probable cause the arrestee has committed a crime and there is an exigency that does not permit the time to acquire a warrant.

**arrestee**   A person arrested. An arrestee is a person who has been arrested and has been neither convicted nor acquitted. A person remains an arrestee following an arrest regardless of whether the person is kept under arrest or in custody. Thus an arrestee may be released after having been arrested, whether on bail, personal recognizance, or under no terms of release at all.

In Scots law, an arrestee is a person whose property has been arrested by a regular arrestment.

*See also:* arrestment.

**arrestment**   A form of third-party attachment in Scots Law. An arrestment is a form of attachment by a creditor of a debtor's property or money in the hands of a third party, in order to secure it for the satisfaction of the debt, which is used in Scots law.

**Arrowsmith Doctrine**   *See:* Gain, Arrowsmith Doctrine.

**arson**   Wrongful destruction of property through fire or explosion. Arson is the burning of any building or property of another, or the burning of one's own property for criminal or fraudulent purposes. Common–law arson was the burning of another's house or outhouse within the curtilage. Burning required the actual charring of some part of the real property. Unlike the common law, habitation of a dwelling need no longer be proved under most arson statutes. Arson of any building in interstate commerce, which includes rental buildings, is a federal offense under 18 U.S.C. § 844(i).

*See also:* murder, felony murder arson.

## Article

**Article 1**   *See:* constitution, U.S. Constitution, Article 1 (Article I or Article One or the Legislative Article).

**Article 2**   *See:* United Nations, United Nations Charter, article 2(4) of the UN Charter; constitution, U.S. Constitution, Article 2 (Article II or article two or the executive article).

**Article 2 of the UCC**   *See:* contracts, uniform commercial code, Article 2 of the UCC (UCC Article Two).

**Article 3**   *See:* constitution, U.S. Constitution, Article 3 (Article III or Article Three or the Judicial Article).

**Article 3 of the UCC**   *See:* contracts, Uniform Commercial Code, Article 3 of the UCC (UCC Article Three).

**Article 4**   *See:* constitution, U.S. Constitution, Article 4 (Article IV or Article Four or States Article).

**Article 5**   *See:* constitution, U.S. Constitution, Article 5 (Article V or Article Five or Amending Article).

**Article 51 of the UN Charter**   *See:* United Nations, United Nations Charter, Article 51 of the UN Charter.

**Article 6**   *See:* constitution, U.S. Constitution, Article 6 (Article VI or Article Six or Obligations, Supremacy and Oaths Article).

**Article 7**   *See:* constitution, U.S. Constitution, Article 7 (Article VII or Article Seven or Ratification Article).

**Article 9 of the UCC**   *See:* contracts, Uniform Commercial Code, Article 9 of the UCC (UCC Article Nine).

**Article I Court or Article One Court or Legislative Court**   *See:* court, U.S. court, Article I Tribunal (Article I Court or Article One Court or Legislative Court).

**Article I or Article One or the Legislative Article**   *See:* constitution, U.S. Constitution, Article 1 (Article I or Article One or the Legislative Article).

**Article I tribunal**   *See:* court, U.S. court, Article I tribunal (Article I court or Article One court or legislative court).

**Article II or Article Two or the Executive Article** *See:* constitution, U.S. Constitution, Article 2 (Article II or Article Two or the Executive Article).

**Article II court or Article Two court** *See:* court, U.S. court, Article II tribunal (Article II court or Article Two court).

**Article II judge** *See:* judge, Article II judge.

**Article II tribunal** *See:* court, U.S. court, Article II tribunal (Article II court or Article Two court).

**Article III court** *See:* court, U.S. court, Article III court.

**Article III judge** *See:* judge, Article III judge.

**Article III or Article Three or the Judicial Article** *See:* constitution, U.S. Constitution, Article 3 (Article III or Article Three or the Judicial Article).

**Article IV or Article Four or States Article** *See:* constitution, U.S. Constitution, Article 4 (Article IV or Article Four or States Article).

**Article V or Article Five or Amending Article** *See:* constitution, U.S. Constitution, Article 5 (Article V or Article Five or Amending Article).

**Article VI or Article Six or Obligations Article** *See:* constitution, U.S. Constitution, Article 6 (Article VI or Article Six or Obligations, Supremacy and Oaths Article).

**Article VII or Article Seven or Ratification Article** *See:* constitution, U.S. Constitution, Article 7 (Article VII or Article Seven or Ratification Article).

**Articles of Confederation** *See:* constitution, Articles of Confederation.

**articles of impeachment** *See:* impeachment, impeachment of official, articles of impeachment.

**articles of incorporation or articles of association or certificate of incorporation** *See:* corporation, charter (articles of incorporation or articles of association or certificate of incorporation).

**articles of partnership** *See:* partnership, partnership agreement (articles of partnership).

**articles of war** *See:* military, military law, articles of war.

**articulo mortis or causa mortis or death-bed declaration or dying declaration** *See:* death, contemplation of death (articulo mortis or causa mortis or deathbed declaration or dying declaration).

**artificial** Made by humans. Artificial is something done by artifice, which is to say done by human activity. Artificial usually contrasts with natural, in that an artificial material or state of affairs results from human activity and the natural does not.
  *See also:* person, artificial person (legal personality); water, water rights artificial use.

**artificial person** *See:* person, artificial person (legal personality).

**as**

**as applied** *See:* challenge, constitutional challenge, as applied (as-applied).

**as-is (as is)** A disclaimer of warranty for any latent defect or from any representation. The label "as-is" signifies that its buyer will be obtaining it in its present condition, with no guaranty or warranty of its reliability. Goods sold as is may arrive with a wide range of flaws or defects, and property sold as is may have a variety of defects of title or limitations of use, in neither case providing a recourse to the seller. Goods sold as is subject to the UCC's article two trump other statutory or implied warranties. Even so, claims that a product not subject to the UCC is sold as is cannot usually trump a statutory warranty of merchantability or a dangerous defect known to the seller but not disclosed to the buyer.

**as of right** *See:* right, legal right, by right (as of right).

**asbestos** A fire-retardant but cancer-causing mineral, once used in many products. Asbestos is a fibrous mineral, which is mined from the ground and found mostly with vermiculite deposits, once commonly used by manufacturers and builders because of its resistance to heat and its utility as an insulator. Studies have linked the inhalation of asbestos fibers with illnesses such as mesothelioma and asbestosis, which has led to the banning of such material in many countries worldwide. There are two general types of asbestos, amphibole and chrysotile. There are six specific types of minerals: the one chrysotile, a serpentine mineral with long and flexible fibers; and five amphibole with relatively brittle crystalline fibers, actinolite asbestos, tremolite asbestos, anthophyllite asbestos, crocidolite asbestos, and amosite asbestos. Some studies show that amphibole fibers stay in the lungs longer than chrysotile, and this tendency may account for their increased toxicity. Regardless of the mineral, asbestos generally poses a greater danger to human health when it is friable, or crumbly, as opposed to in sheets or moulds.

**non-friable asbestos (friable asbestos)** Asbestos that does not easily crumble or break. Non-friable asbestos is hard and generally retains its integrity under normal pressure, so that materials made from it do not easily crumble and release small particles of asbestos. This is critical because friable asbestos materials that do break easily can send asbestos particulate into the air and create health hazards for anyone who inhales them. Non-friable asbestos materials usually contain some hardening agent, such as cement or asphalt, which prevent the asbestos fibers and particles from easily breaking away. These types of materials are generally only hazardous if they are structurally compromised or weakened.

**asbestosis**   A chronic inflammation of lung tissue resulting from asbestos exposure. Asbestosis is the scarring of lung tissue as a result of inhaling asbestos fibers. It causes shortness of breath and in its most severe cases, can lead to respiratory failure. People who have had extensive exposure to asbestos are at a severe risk of developing the illness. Amphibole type asbestos tends to have more harmful effects because it stays in the lungs longer as a result of its longer fiber. There is no known treatment for the disease.

**ascendant**   *See:* descent, ancestor (ascendant).

**ascertainable damages**   *See:* damages, classes of damages, measurable damages (ascertainable damages).

**Ashwander rules**   *See:* justiciability, Ashwander rules.

**asmakhta**   A Biblical authority for a principle, but not its source. Asmakhta is, literally, a prop. A Biblical passage cited as support for a legal principle, although the passage is not really considered to be its source, the passage serves as a mnemonic.

**aspiration (aspire or aspirational)**   Goal, hope, or dream for the future. An aspiration is something intended for the future, particularly a goal that manifests the performance of moral obligations, which is generally presented to be later attained by unspecified means. When reduced to language, an aspiration may be a direction or a guideline, but it is not usually a directly enforceable standard for performance. Statutory language that is strictly aspirational is not enforceable, yet the mere fact that a statute incorporates aspirational goals or is written in broad and aspirational terms does not mean that it is only aspirational, particularly if an agency is delegated the responsibility of creating regulations that pursue the manifestation of that aspiration. In contracts, statutes, wills, and other instruments, aspirational language may be used as a means of establishing the intent of the drafters in interpretation of an instrument.
   *See also:* interpretation, statutory interpretation (construction of a statute or statutory construction); contract, contract interpretation (contract construction); hortatory.

**asportation**   The unlawful carrying away of a person or property. Asportation is the carrying away of the object of a crime from the scene of the crime, although the slightest movement is usually sufficient to prove asportation, so long as the movement was with the intent to finally remove the property from the control of its owner or the person from that person's full liberty of movement. Asportation is a defining element of theft, robbery, larceny and burglary, and in the case of burglary, asportation is sufficient to demonstrate the use of force. Asportation of a person is an element of kidnapping.
   *See also:* larceny (larcenous).

**assailant**   One who assaults another. An assailant in both the common law and general legal usage is one who commits an assault, by any means. Thus a person who commits the crime or tort of assault is an assailant.

**assassination (assassin)**   Premeditated murder, particularly for political reasons or for hire. Assassination is the crime of premeditated murder, particularly when it is committed for political reasons. At common law, assassination was predominately a murder committed by an assassin, which is to say death by a hired killer. The sense of assassination as a death perpetrated for political or even social ends is derived from the older sense of hired murder, as such killers have been so often employed to such ends. There is no exception in the law of war to the criminal prohibition on assassination other than death in a combat zone.
   *See also:* police, police organizations, Secret Service.

**assault**   An unlawful act that places a person in reasonable apprehension of an imminent battery. An "assault" is an action that is intended to cause another person a harmful or offensive contact or an intended action that puts another person in apprehension of such contact. In some jurisdictions, assault is committed even if the intent is just to scare or intimidate the person. Assault is an intentional tort, a violation of the private duty of care toward others, and a claim for assault may seek both compensatory and punitive damages. Assault is also a crime, sometimes designated as "assault," as in federal criminal law that applies at sea, and sometimes as a component or aspect of "assault and battery."
   *See also:* tort, dignitary tort; battery, battery as tort; mayhem (maim).

**aggravated assault**   An assault that could result in serious bodily harm or that is otherwise heinous. Aggravated assault is an assault but in a form of particular wrongfulness. Commonly, it is an assault that could lead to death or serious bodily harm. Assault with a deadly weapon is inherently an aggravated assault. It may also include assault on police officers or in resistance to lawful authority, or an assault made in a particularly shocking or brutal manner or for particularly heartless or cruel reasons.

**attempted assault**   An attempt to threaten a person with battery. Attempted assault is an attempt to threaten a person with an immediate fear of a battery or personal harm. An attempt to commit an assault is, in many jurisdictions, not recognized as a crime because assault consists of an attempt to commit an offensive or harmful contact, and one cannot attempt an attempt.

**sexual assault (indecent assault)**   A sexual act with a person who is underage, who does not consent to the act, or who cannot consent. Sexual assault is the performance by a person of a sexual act with another person who does not or cannot consent to the act. The inability to consent can be a legal inability, such as being under the age of consent, or a physical inability, such as lack of consciousness or mental acuity.

In many jurisdictions, various forms of sexual assault have replaced the common-law criminal categories of rape.

Sexual assault in most jurisdictions includes several categories of offense of varying levels of severity or culpability. Different states employ differing definitions and categorical distinctions, usually either according to whether force is used or threatened, the form and severity of any force employed, the nature of a relationship or trust that is abused, other means used to negate a lack of consent, and extent of harm to the victim. States that increase the severity of sexual assault according to its resulting harms include pregnancy as well as injury or great bodily harm to the victim. States that require proof of force place a greater burden of proof on the prosecution and the victim, while states that rely only on the absence of consent allow a wider category of prosecutions.

*See also:* rape, rape as sexual assault, criminal sexual conduct (sexual conduct); rape.

**transferred intent** An intent to harm one person is intentional even when the intended act harms someone else instead. Transferred intent is an intent motivated by some action that was meant to cause one result but that in fact causes a different result, and the law treats the intention to cause the first result as sufficient to make the different result intentional. This is significant when a person intends to harm one person but accidentally harms another person instead. The intent to harm the first is transferred from the intended victim to the actual victim. As a result, missing an intended victim is no defense to an action by an unintended victim.

**assent** Agreement with previous conduct. Assent is agreement, particularly to a contract that has been negotiated previously. Assent can be manifested expressly by words or through implication from conduct.

There is little difference today between assent and consent in this context, but some distinction persists that the difference of "by one's will," which is the essence of assent, and "through one's will," which is consent. At common law, assent was the term required of executors to an act on behalf of an estate, but this distinction is now obsolete.

*See also:* agreement.

**mutual assent** Agreement by all parties to the same understanding of the undertakings to be performed in a contract. Mutual assent, the essence of an enforceable contract, occurs when both parties can be seen to have intended a bargain that is understandable according to terms common to both parties' intent, the parties have expressed these terms in a manner understandable to both, and they have expressed to each other acceptance of the same understanding of the common terms.

*See also:* contract, agreement, meeting of the minds (manifestation of mutual assent).

**assertive negotiation or hardball tactics or hardball tactics** *See:* negotiation, adversarial negotiation (assertive negotiation or hardball tactics or hard-ball tactics).

**assessment (assess)** Evaluation, as of value or fitness for a task, or to set an amount owed. An assessment is a form of evaluation of a person, thing, or situation, for some specific purpose, such as its improvement conformity with some standard. In law, assessment may take a variety of forms in this sense, such as an environmental assessment of a major federal project, a student skills assessment, under the Americans with Disability Act, a mine safety assessment, and so on. The more customary meaning, though, is the valuation of property and determination of the applicable rate to set a tax or a fee that is owed, such as a property tax, sewer fee, utility rate, or other contingent valuation and cost. In this sense, assessment of damages or costs is the allocation of damages or costs to one or more defendants once a plaintiff has proved an action and established grounds for such relief.

*See also:* appraisal (appraisement).

**assessment of damages or computation of damages or measure of damages** *See:* damages, calculation of damages (assessment of damages or computation of damages or measure of damages).

**asset** Something of value. An asset is any property that has a value, usually assessed by its convertability into money or its equivalent. Assets may be tangible, such as real property, personal property, cash, or anything else with a physical existence. Assets also may be intangible, such as accounts receivable, claims at law, or shares of stock or bonds. The significance of an asset in law is slightly different from the meaning of asset in business and accounting, in which an asset is the future potential for revenue from a past transaction, and the potential benefit need not be realized through a legally enforceable means.

*See also:* derivative, financial derivative.

**asset protection trust** *See:* trust, spendthrift trust (asset protection trust).

**after-acquired asset** Something of value obtained following a significant date. After-acquired assets are assets that a person gains later than the time the person incurs an obligation or grants a security interest. One can give a security interest in after-acquired property, so that the property is subject to the lien or other interest at the time it is acquired. This idea is now encompassed in the U.C.C. in the term "new value."

**capital asset** Property with a useful life of more than a year. A capital asset is property that has a useful life of greater than one year and that is held not for sale or resale but for use or consumption by the taxpayer. Capital assets do not include intellectual property created by the taxpayer, or other specified categories of property, that are either exempted from tax or taxed not as capital.

*See also:* loss, capital loss.

**intangible asset** Property with value but no concrete existence. An intangible asset is property without physical substance, such as good will, a bond, or a share of stock in a company. Even when a share is represented by a certificate, the certificate is but a symbol of the ownership and not the thing that is owned itself.

**tangible asset** A fixed or current asset with a readily ascertained value. A tangible asset is a distinct category of asset in accounting, including only such fixed assets and cash assets that are on hand and readily marketable, or are currently receivable.

## assets

**current assets** Assets intended to be converted quickly into cash or consumed. Current assets are assets that are cash, cash equivalents, or inventory or materials that are normally converted into cash or are usually consumed either within one year or within the normal operating cycle of the business.

**net assets (net asset value or net current assets)** The value of current assets minus current liabilities. Net assets refers to the functional value of all assets once that value is reduced to reflect current debts. There are several ways of computing net assets, including book value, reproduction cost, going-concern value, and liquidation value.

## assignment

**assignment as assignment of rights and duties** The delegation of rights and duties to another. Assignment is the transfer of a right, duty, or interest conferred by a contract, held in property, conferred by agency, or in any other way held by law, to another party. An assignment is not valid unless it is accepted by the assignee, although in most instances in which the assignment is a delegation of rights, acceptance may be presumed. Although at common law, most interests are freely assignable, an interest that is inalienable may not be assigned. Some duties under contracts may be assigned only with the consent of the other parties to the contracts, and some obligations of agents and fiduciaries may only be assigned with the consent of the principal of the agent or the beneficiary of the fiduciary.
See also: rights, legal right, assignable right (non-assignable right); lease, assignable lease (non-assignable lease or unassignable lease).

**assignment as succession to property (assign)** Conveyance of property interest. Assignment is any transfer of property, whether it is real property, personal property, intellectual property, or other intangible goods. Assignment includes all of the benefits and uses, as well as duties and obligations, held by the transferor.
See also: succession (successor or predecessor).

**assign** See: contract, assignment of contract (assign); assignment, assignment as succession to property (assign); assignee, assign (assigns).

**assignable lease** See: lease, assignable lease (non-assignable lease or unassignable lease).

**assignable right** See: rights, legal right, assignable right (non-assignable right).

**assigned counsel** See: counselor, assigned counsel (court-appointed counsel).

**assignee** One who assumes the duties and privileges of another. An assignee is a person or entity to whom an assignment is made. Accepting an assignment places the assignee completely in the role of the assignor, accepting both the rights and benefits as well as the duties and obligations that had been the assignor's. Still, a beneficiary to whom the assignor owed a duty can compel performance by the assignee but might still be able to compel performance from the assignor unless the beneficiary had consented to the assignment.

**assign (assigns)** An assignee or a potential assignee. An assign is a person or entity to whom an interest is assigned. When a grant, contract, deed or other instrument designates a party's assigns, these include all persons or entities to whom an interest may be transferred in the future. Such a designation is used to limit (or prove the absence of a limit on) the interest of the present holder and to transfer the interest to all later recipients with the same limitation on the interest. Only later, when property has been transferred, are some assigns the actual transferees.

**assignment for the benefit of creditors** See: creditor, assignment for the benefit of creditors.

**assignment of contract** See: contract, assignment of contract prohibition of assignment; contract, assignment of contract (assign).

**assignment of error** See: error, assignment of error (assignment of errors).

**assignment of errors** See: error, assignment of error (assignment of errors).

**assignment of lease** See: lease, assignment of lease.

**assimilative crime** See: crime, assimilative crime.

**Assimilative Crimes Act** See: reservation, tribal reservation, Assimilative Crimes Act.

**assistance (assist or assisted)** Help provided to someone else or something else. Assistance is any form of aid, comfort, or service. Assistance can take any form including the payments of money; provision of goods; support by food, clothing, and shelter; or merely the provision of information.
See also: birth, assisted birth; family, family planning, assisted reproduction; law, law school, legal pedagogy, Computer Assisted Legal Instruction (C.A.L.I. or CALI); suicide, assisted suicide (aiding a suicide).

**assisted birth** See: birth, assisted birth.

**assisted reproduction** *See:* family, family planning, assisted reproduction, gestational surrogacy (surrogate mother); family, family planning, assisted reproduction.

**assisted suicide** *See:* suicide, assisted suicide (aiding a suicide).

**assize or assizes** *See:* court, English court, Court of Assize (assize or assizes).

**associate** *See:* lawyer, law firm, lawyers, associate, summer associate (summer clerk); lawyer, law firm, lawyers, associate; association (associate).

**associate judge** *See:* judge, associate judge (associate justice).

**associate justice** *See:* judge, associate judge (associate justice).

**association (associate)** A group of people working to some common purpose. An association is a collection of people collaborating to meet a common goal. Associations may be incorporated under the laws of a jurisdiction, or they may be unincorporated. Note: the verb, associate, is sometimes used to convey the more general activity of meeting with at least one other person for any purpose. The noun, associate, is a person or entity who is a member or constituent of the association.

*See also:* corporation (corporate or incorporate); cooperative, agricultural cooperative (cooperative association); association, freedom of association; trade, trade association; club.

**Association for American Justice** *See:* bar, bar organization, Association for American Justice (AAJ or Association of Trial Lawyers of America or ATLA).

**Association of American Law Schools** *See:* law, law school, Association of American Law Schools (A.A.L.S. or AALS).

**Association of Legal Writing Directors Citation Manual** *See:* citation, citation manual, Association of Legal Writing Directors Citation Manual (A.L.W.D. Citation Manual or ALWD Citation Manual).

**freedom of association** The right of individuals to associate to further their personal beliefs. Freedom of association is the right to associate with whom one chooses, either for private interaction or for public expression.

*1. strict scrutiny* A burden on the right of association is subject to strict scrutiny.

*2. illegal groups* Mere membership in a group whose members perform illegal actions cannot be a crime. The individual member must perform an illegal act or, at least, know of a purpose of the organization to engage in illegal acts. Even so, abetting criminal acts through financial or other material support of an organization that funds such acts may be a crime. Membership in a criminal organization was a basis

for indictment in international law at the International Military Tribunal in Nuremburg in 1945. *See also:* terrorism, material support.

*3. compulsory disclosure* Compulsory disclosure of membership in an organization burdens the freedom of association. An organization may be required by a court or police official to disclose its membership, or a particular member's identity, only if there is a showing of sufficient state interest to do so, and only if the disclosure required is narrowly tailored to that interest.

*4. loyalty oaths* Public employees may be required to take an oath of loyalty to the U.S. Constitution or to a state constitution as a condition of employment, without violating their freedom of association. Loyalty oaths that otherwise burden the freedom of speech, freedom of conscience, or freedom of association may not be required by the state or the United States. *See also:* oath, loyalty oath.

**associational standing** *See:* standing in court, third-party standing, associational standing (organizational standing).

**assumpsit** An action to recover a wrongful enrichment sounding in contract or tort. Assumpsit is a common-law action to recover damages for another party's failure to perform a duty recognized in the law. It is also called restitution in law. Although the action of assumpsit is an early action in equity from which arose much of the modern law of contract and remedies, assumpsit continues as a cause of action in law that parallels the action in equity for unjust enrichment. So an action at law in assumpsit will lie for the return of consideration when a contract is avoided or rescinded, for the return of stolen property, for the return of a bailment to the bailor, and similar actions to recover in law a benefit held only at the wrongful expense of another. *See also:* non, non assumpsit.

**indebitatus assumpsit (numquam indebitatus)** An obsolete action to enforce a promise to pay a debt. Indebitatus assumpsit was once a common form of action for assumpsit, and a core form of the assumpsit action, brought by a plaintiff claiming that a debt existed that was owed by the defendant, for which an implied promise was made based on separate consideration, and the debt not being paid the action would lie for the promise. The plea of numquam indebitatus that is, there is no debt, was the plea in answer or abatement of the action.

**assumption of mortgage** *See:* mortgage, assumption of mortgage.

**assumption of risk** *See:* risk, assumption of risk, knowledge of risk (knowing assumption); defense, specific defense, assumption of risk.

**assurances (further assurances or adequate assurance of performance)** A promise that performance will occur in the future. Assurances, including further assurances or adequate assurance of performance, are an independent promise that a prior promise will be fulfilled. Assurances may be made for any purpose, but they give rise to an independent basis for reliance, such that a failure to perform the promise following assurance may be considered both a failure of the promise and a cause of action for reliance on the assurance. Further assurances are a promise made after a contract and a demand for assurance, that the contract will be performed. Note: the assurances in the covenant of further assurances are also an independent promise made to carry out a prior promise, although these are specific to the execution of new instruments in support of a deed.

*See also:* covenant, covenant of title, covenant of further assurances (warranty of further assurances).

**demand for assurances**  A call for reassurance that performance will occur despite conditions giving rise to insecurity. A demand for assurances is a request for an additional promise that obligations under an existing contract will be met. Under the Uniform Commercial Code, a demand for assurances may be made when one party to a contract has a reasonable basis to believe that the other party may not meet its contractual obligations. Reasonable grounds for demand include the other party's repudiation of the contract, assignment of its interests in the contract, or business-related circumstances affecting the party's ability to perform. A demand for assurances should be in writing and will excuse further performance of the demandant until assurances are made. If the demand is not answered satisfactorily, demandant may treat the contract as breached and seek other avenues to mitigate damages.

**assured**  Whom an insurance policy designates as the party it protects. The assured on a policy is the person or entity designated as the party whose interests are insured against the losses or perils depicted in the policy. In most policies and general usage there is little difference between denominating a party as an insured or as an assured. Some polices have one insured, the party who enters the policy and is responsible for the payment of its premium, but may have many assureds, the specific parties whose conduct, property, or liability is within the scope of coverage.

*See also:* insured.

**asylum**  A refuge that is immune from being invaded upon by the government. An asylum is a place of refuge, where those who are being pursued by a government may be free from that pursuit. Although there is no asylum in the United States for those sought to answer for lawful judicial process, the United States does offer asylum to refugees from other states seeking safety from persecution in their own country.

*See also:* immunity; refouler (non-refoulement or refoulement); refugee (asylum seeker).

**asylum seeker**  *See:* refugee (asylum seeker).

**at**

**at large**  *See:* large (at large).

**at law**  Anything related to the process of the common law, rather than that of equity. The phrase "at law" is used to point out that a thing is to be done according to the course of the common law; it is distinguished from a proceeding in equity. Thus attorneys may be attorneys at law, counselors in equity, or both. This distinction being less common than it once was, the phrase is increasingly generic in describing anything having to do with the practice of law.

*See also:* law.

**at will**  *See:* will, at will.

**at-will employment**  *See:* employment, at-will employment (at-will employee or at-will employer).

**at-will tenancy**  *See:* lease, leasehold, tenancy, tenancy at will (at-will tenancy).

**atheist (atheism or atheistic)**  A person who does not believe in any deity. An atheist believes that no god exists. Some atheists cite a lack of empirical evidence proving a divine existence to support this conclusion.

**ATON**  *See:* navigation, aid to navigation (ATON).

**attaché**  A mid-level diplomatic official with a particular portfolio or specialty. The attaché is a specialist connected with a diplomatic staff, usually delegated to the embassy by another department of the sending government. The military attaché, for instance, is a military officer seconded by the defense department or war ministry to the state department or foreign ministry for posting to the particular country.

*See also:* diplomat, attaché (attaché).

**attachment (pretrial attachment or pre-trial attachment)**  Taking of the defendant's property to satisfy a judgment. Attachment is a means by which a successful plaintiff who has received a judgment may enforce the judgment by asking the to court order a sheriff to seize property for sale in order to pay the amount owed. Attachment is not available over property immune from claims or attachment, such as property subject to a homestead immunity.

Pre-trial attachment allows a plaintiff seeking to recover a debt to have property of the defendant seized before or during trial and held in trust, pending the outcome of the trial, to ensure payment if the plaintiff is awarded a judgment against the defendant. Attachment requires the plaintiff to post a bond, payable to the defendant if the plaintiff loses, and because attachment amounts to a taking of a property interest, it must be done according to the due process of law.

*See also:* lien, attachment lien.

**attachment bond**  *See:* bond, attachment bond.

**attachment lien**  *See:* lien, attachment lien.

**attainder**

**attainder of treason**  The punishment for treason. Attainder of treason is the lawful punishment for which a person convicted of treason is liable, which currently can involve death, prison, monetary fines, or bar from holding office. Attainder of treason is patently allowed in the U.S. Constitution, even though bills of attainder are forbidden, which has confused observers who assume that attainder means the same thing in each clause. Attainder, however, is not restricted to a bill of attainder, and in the common law attainder referred to any punishment at all but with a particular emphasis on the forfeiture of property that might have passed to one's children. Thus, attainder of treason in the United States is whatever punishment for treason as Congress may set, but these punishments are restricted to penalties upon the traitor and not to the traitor's children.

**bill of attainder**   A legislative act that inflicts punishment without a judicial trial. A bill of attainder is any finding of guilt or decree of punishment for wrongdoing upon an individual or specific group made by a legislature. Impeachment is not a bill of attainder. Bills of attainder are forbidden under the U.S. Constitution from both Congress and any state legislature.

*separation of powers*   The prohibitions on bills of attainder are one tool for ensuring separation of powers. Legislatures in the American constitutional system may make laws but they cannot enforce them. That function, particularly the determination that the conduct of an individual violates a law, is reserved solely for the judiciary. An effort by a legislature to usurp that role, through any means other than through the discipline of its own membership or the impeachment of officials for malfeasance, is very likely to violate one or the other of the bill of attainder clauses.

*punishment defined*   Punishment in a bill of attainder is not determined by a label in the legislative act. Rather, it is measured by the legislative intent and context in which the act is passed. A legislative act with an intent or effect of enacting a punishment against an individual, a specified group of people, or a readily identified group of people for conduct already committed or being committed amounts to a punishment regardless of the name of the enactment.

**attainment zone**   *See:* pollution, air pollution, National Ambient Air Quality Standards, attainment zone.

**attempt**   Effort by which one endeavors to cause a specific result. An attempt is an effort to achieve some object, something actually done and not merely contemplated toward achieving a goal. In criminal law, an attempt is the act of criminal attempt.

**attempted assault**   *See:* assault, attempted assault.

**attempted battery**   *See:* battery, attempted battery.

**criminal attempt**   The crime of preparing or attempting to commit a crime. Criminal attempt is an attempt to do anything that would be a crime if done. Criminal attempt requires both an intent to do the unlawful thing and an overt act that is somehow related to its accomplishment. Because most defendants charged with criminal attempt do not actually commit the crime, the crime of attempt is committed when a crime is frustrated, such as by arrest or other circumstance. A jurisdiction may define a separate offense of an attempt to commit a specific crime, such as attempted murder, but in the absence of such a definition, the general bar on attempts would still create a crime of attempt to commit murder.

*See also:* offense, inchoate offense attempt.

**impossibility of attempt (impossible attempt)**   An attempt is not criminal if the ultimate crime was impossible. Impossibility of attempt is a defense to criminal attempt that is available in limited circumstances, particularly if the attempt was legally impossible or inherently impossible. Criminal intent is not a crime if the the crime intended breaks no law, and criminal intent is inherently impossible if it is attempted by means that could not succeed under any circumstances. Mere factual impossibility, such as an attempt at murder that failed because of a jammed gun or the intervention of the police, is not a defense. The distinctions between factual, legal, and inherent possibility are not clear, and there is considerable variation among jurisdictions in what amounts to an effective defense. The Model Penal Code has abrogated the defense and so jettisoned the distinction between legal and factual impossibility in many states, yet some defenses of inherent possibility persist as applications of the doctrine of legality.

**indispensable element test**   Attempt requires the capability of committing each element of the intended crime. The indispensable element test is a defining element of the crime of attempt to commit a crime, which is employed by some jurisdictions to determine the attempt to be complete when the accused became capable of carrying out each element of a plan to commit the intended crime. In other words, once the accused had taken every step necessary to carry out the crime though the accused still had not executed the crime itself, the crime of attempt was complete.

More generally, any test may require an indispensable element, which is to say that some critical condition must be satisfied in order for the test to be passed.

**last-proximate-act test**   A discredited test for attempt as an act that can lead to a crime. The last-proximate-act test is a distinct formula for determining when a person has committed an attempt to commit a crime, by which the attempt is complete when the person has performed the last action that could be foreseeably required before the commission of the crime. Most courts, and the Model Penal Code, have rejected this standard.

**probable-desistance test**   The defendant's acts must demonstrate unequivocally intent to commit the crime. The probable-desistance test, also called the equivocality test, assesses whether the acts of a defendant made in furtherance of a planned crime have reached a stage that demonstrates there would be no further equivocation regarding the commission of the crime. Conduct is sufficient to amount to an attempt if the actor has reached a point in planning or execution suggesting it is unlikely that the actor will voluntarily desis from completing the course of action toward the crime. The test measures the proof not only of a charge that the defendant had been attempting the crime, but also the defense that the defendant had or was about to abandon the crime following some steps toward its planning or commission.

**attenuation doctrine** *See:* search, exclusionary rule, exception to the exclusionary rule, attenuation doctrine.

**attestation (attest)** Witness to another's action. To attest means to witness to another's act and to subscribe to it as a witness. Many attestations are made by notaries public, but any competent adult may properly attest to a signature, oath, or other act of legal consequence.
*See also:* witness, attesting witness (subscribing witness).

**attesting witness** *See:* witness, attesting witness (subscribing witness).

**Atticus Finch** *See:* Finch (Atticus Finch).

**attorn** *See:* attornment (attorn).

**attorney (attorney at law or attorney-at-law or attorneys at law)** One who is licensed to practice law on behalf of another person. An attorney, by which one nearly always means an attorney at law, is an officer of the court who represents another person before it. To become an attorney, one must become a lawyer, having been certified to have sufficient character and fitness to practice law as a fiduciary for others, completed legal education sufficient to take a bar examination, obtained a score on that exam sufficient to be admitted to the state's bar, and taken an oath of admission to that bar. Attorneys are subject at all times to the discipline of their profession and the courts that have licensed them to practice.

The term "attorney" includes both attorneys at law and attorneys in fact, the attorney in fact being the designation for an agent, who need not be a lawyer. This usage is rare except in a letter or instrument of appointment of the agent, and unless the context of a usage clearly suggests that the term attorney means an attorney in fact, it nearly certainly means an attorney at law.
*See also:* representation, legal representation (representation by counsel); lawyer; trust, client trust account (lawyer's trust account).

**attorney-client privilege** *See:* privilege, evidentiary privilege, attorney-client.

**attorney discipline** *See:* lawyer, lawyer discipline (attorney discipline).

**attorney fees** *See:* fees, attorney fees, Equal Access to Justice Act (E.A.J.A. or EAJA).

**attorney misconduct** *See:* misconduct, attorney misconduct (lawyer misconduct).

**attorney number or bar number** *See:* bar, bar card (attorney number or bar number).

**attorney oath** *See:* oath, oath of attorney (attorney oath).

**attorney-witness** *See:* witness, attorney-witness (lawyer-witness).

**attorney's fee** *See:* fee, fee for services, attorney's fee.

**attorney general** The chief law enforcement officer of the state or nation. The attorney general is the executive officer responsible in each jurisdiction for the administration of justice, including the direction or support of criminal prosecutions, the defense of the state in civil actions, the maintenance of civil actions in the name of the state, and advising the chief executive and legislature on matters arising under the constitution and laws. There is a separate attorney general for the U.S. and for each state.

The United States Attorney General is appointed by the President with the advice and consent of the Senate, is a member of the cabinet and is the head of the U.S. Department of Justice, as well as coordinating the work of the United States Attorneys. State attorneys general are either elected or appointed according to the constitution of each state.

**attorney in fact** A person acting as the agent of another. An attorney in fact is an agent who is empowered to act on behalf of a principal. Although an attorney in fact might be an attorney at law, there is no implication that this is so owing to the agency alone. An attorney in fact owes a fiduciary duty to the principal in carrying out the agency.

**power of attorney** An appointment of a person to act as one's agent. A power of attorney is an instrument in writing through which a person appoints another to act as an agent, as well as the authority conferred upon the agent by that writing. The person who executes the power of attorney is the principal and the person empowered by it is the agent. The power of attorney is either general and unlimited or special and limited to particular tasks. In most jurisdictions, a power of attorney must specifically state in writing that it empowers the agent to transfer or receive title in land on behalf of the principal, and it must separately state that it empowers the agent to make a gift of property of the principal, or it is ineffective for these purposes. A power of attorney may be witnessed or notarized, and some states require such an authentication for the agency to be effective for many transactions.

**durable power of attorney** A power of attorney valid during the principal's incapacity. A durable power of attorney is a power of attorney that explicitly declares that the agency it creates will persist in the event the principal becomes incapacitated or disabled. In the ordinary agency, the principal has the power to terminate the agency, but if the principal becomes incapacitated, this power is lost, so a durable power of attorney may not be terminated in that way, although it may terminate if a time limitation is defined in the power of attorney. An agency created with a durable power of attorney may, in some jurisdictions, be competent to make decisions regarding medical care, although express authority or instructions are required for an agent with durable power of attorney to make end–of–life care decisions.

**general power of attorney (general agent)** An agency without limitation to specific tasks. A general power of attorney is an agency created without limitation to perform only specific tasks or functions on behalf of the principal. The person or entity holding a general power of attorney is a general agent. Even so, in most jurisdictions, a general power of attorney must expressly state an authority to perform certain specialized tasks, such as transfer property, initiate litigation, make gifts, and make end–of–life decisions.

**medical power of attorney** *See:* death, living will (advance directive).

**panel attorney (court-appointed attorney)** Private lawyer working as or for a public defender. A panel attorney is an attorney who practices law in the private sector but represents a criminal defendant, usually for a minor stipend paid by the state. Criminal courts once commonly maintained lists of attorneys practicing within the jurisdiction to whom cases were assigned to represent indigent defendants. Following the rise of public defenders' offices, panel attorneys are still used when a public defender is not available, owing to staff shortages, conflicts, or other limitations.

**attornment (attorn)** Agreement to be bound, or agree to be bound. Attorn, in its most specific sense, is the agreement of a person leasing property to continue to be bound by a lease when someone else becomes the landlord. The word attorn still most frequently refers to this type of agreement, and it was used for some years in the UCC to describe a bailee's recognition of a duty to a substitute bailor. More metaphorically, it now refers to one's assent to be bound to any duty and as a verb has come loosely to mean agreeing to be bound to perform an obligation.

**attractive nuisance** *See:* nuisance, attractive nuisance (turntable doctrine).

**attribution of income** *See:* income, attribution of income.

**attrition**

**attrition as diminishing return** Reduced profits from increased costs. Attrition, a common pattern of profit and loss seen during times of inflation, is frequently attributed to higher production costs.

**attrition as reduction in staff or membership** Natural, gradual decline in the number of employees or attendees. Attrition is the loss of employees from a company as a result of their own volition or as a result of an unavoidable natural event (i.e., health reasons or death). If the employer requests or demands the employee leave or the employee is forced to leave because of a situation involving the company, this is not attrition.

**auction** Sale of goods through a bidding process. At auction, members of the general public are invited to make offers for the purchase of property. The property can be real or personal. The offers, called bids, are usually given orally to an auctioneer in the presence of all other potential purchasers. When the bidding ceases, the auctioneer ends the sale, and the highest bidder obtains the property for the offered price regardless of its actual market value. The law generally requires an auctioneer take measures to ensure that there are no artificial attempts to inflate the final purchase price. Auction is used as both the noun and the verb to describe the sale.

*See also:* puffer, puffer in an auction; sale, conditions of sale.

**auction bid** *See:* bid, auction bid.

**audience**

**captive audience** Required attendance of a meeting or event. A captive audience is created in a workplace or school when a student or employee has no real choice but to attend, either because of work obligations, instructions from supervisors, or customary expectations. Speech in meetings or events with captive audiences may be regulated in a more restrictive manner than might otherwise be allowed. School events may restrict speech that would amount to religious speech. Workplace events are barred by labor laws from speech by union or management related to an election to be held within twenty–four hours.

**audit (auditor)** Financial review of an individual, business, or governmental unit. Audit is both the process and the result of examining the records and documents of a person, company, or governmental unit to determine whether all applicable laws have been complied with in the management of money or in other activities. Audits can be conducted by the IRS, accounting firms, or internal audit committees. Audit can also be used in the verb form as the actual conducting of an audit. An auditor is one who conducts an audit, or the chief among those who do so. The term auditor, or listener, like the term audit, to listen, is an echo of the medieval practice before literacy among the wealthy was common, of the auditors listening to the accounts read to them by scriveners, payers, and payees.

**audit trail** Documentation of an audit's procedure. An audit trail is the documentation, either on paper or in electronic media, of the specific events and records reviewed during an audit, so that the manner in which the audit was performed may be examined as a part of a subsequent audit or compliance review by the federal or state agencies.

**tax audit (examination of tax return)**  An audit of a tax filing and its underlying records. A tax audit, or an examination of a return, includes any form of examination by the officials of a tax authority to review the validity of a tax filing or tax status, as well as the records of the taxpayer, to determine the accuracy and completeness of the information reported, the accuracy of the tax liability computed, the validity of any claims made and sufficiency of any taxes paid. An initial level of computerized examination is made of all federal returns, and some returns are subject to further examination by administrative auditors, which may lead to taxpayer interviews, records reviews, an audit letter, hearing and appeal.

**audita querela (writ of audita querela)**  Petition to revise an order because the law has changed. Audita querela is a writ allowing either appeal of an order or a new review of an order. Under the common law, a petition for a writ of audita querela could be brought either to reform a judgment in a civil proceeding or to reform or set aside a criminal conviction or sentence (although the federal rules of civil procedure and the rules of most states have abolished the writ in civil actions).

Although a judgment debtor under the common law could seek relief in audita querela based on newly discovered evidence, and in extraordinary circumstances it might still be sought on that basis, in general other rules now govern review based on newly discovered evidence. The writ now is much more likely to be sought on the basis of a change in the law with retroactive application that affects the validity of the order. Audita querela assumes or asserts that the court has made a valid ruling based on the law as it stood at the time, but the law has since changed.

*See also:* remedy, extraordinary remedy (extraordinary relief); remedy, post–conviction remedy.

**aula regis**  *See:* curia, curia regis (aula regis).

**Aulus Agerius or Numerius Negidiusor Seius or Stichus**  *See:* name, fictitious name, Titius (Aulus Agerius or Numerius Negidiusor Seius or Stichus).

**auter**  *See:* autre (auter).

**auter droit or en autre droit**  *See:* standing in court, third–party standing, autre droit (auter droit or en autre droit).

**authentic act**  *See:* act, authentic act.

**authentication of evidence**  *See:* evidence, authentication of evidence (voir dire of evidence).

**authenticity (authentic)**  Original or authoritative aspect of a text or other evidence. Authenticity is the property of acceptability that comes of either being the original or the legal equivalent of the original.

*See also:* evidence (evidentiary); act, authentic act; evidence, authentication of evidence (voir dire of evidence).

**author of legislation**  *See:* legislation, author of legislation.

**authority**  A person or institution with power over a person, or the power itself. Authority is the relationship between one person and another, or between one person and an institution, so that the first person will act according to the rule of the other person or the institution. The key to the first person's action is not agreement with the particular rule but a more fundamental acceptance of the rules announced by the other person or the institution as the reason to act. Authority provides a reason for acting according to the rule, not an independent assessment of the merits of the rule or the action. According to legal positivism, when the authority is the authority of law, a person follows the law because the person believes the law should be followed, not because acting according to any given rule of law is better than acting some other way. A naturalist view of authority would be more contingent on the substance of the law, and a person follows the law because the person believes it is good to do so because following the law generally leads to better conduct overall when assessed against a fundamental moral framework.

*scope of authority*  The scope of authority is the limit of the powers of the authority of some official or agent. Actions that are within the scope may be committed according to the powers of that office, and actions beyond it are ultra vires.

**actual authority**  Power clearly granted by one entity to another. Actual authority is the core scope of an agency, the forms of conduct that the principal clearly intends the agent is to perform on the principal's behalf when the agency is created. Actual authority may be created by an express declaration of agency, such as by a power of attorney or by direct instruction, or it may be created by inference, when the principal acts in such a manner that an effective agency is created by the principal's actions. Not all actions that imply an expectation of another's conduct to the benefit of the actor give rise to actual authority, however. For example, the creation of a bailment does not create an agency in the bailee but only a narrower obligation to preserve and return the bailment.

**authority as agency**  The power of one person to act on behalf of another. Authority is the essence of agency, whether the agent is called a representative, an officer, an attorney, or something else. The person with authority might act for another person or for a corporation or government. Actions taken by someone for another person without the authority to represent that person are usually void. The authority might be granted by the person or entity represented or, in rare cases such as a conservatorship, guardianship, or representation of a decedent's estate, the authority may be conferred by a court. The authority to perform certain tasks, such as to enter into contracts for the sale of land, usually must be demonstrated in writing.

**authority as sources of the law**   The precedents, statutes, and writings that support a legal argument. Authority in legal argument is sum of sources of law that bear upon an assertion of what the law is in a given situation. Different legal systems at different times have different hierarchies of authority. In the twenty-first–century United States, arguments based on the text of a statute have a stronger influence over a wider arena of questions than might have been the case in 1790, while the precedents of English law are, on some topics, now less influential. Likewise, the influence of treatises as authority is greater in Germany than in the United States. The scope of American authority acceptable in legal argument has included a wider range of social data than once it did, thanks to the use of social science data by Louis Brandeis, in Muller v. Oregon, 208 U.S. 412 (1908).

**authority of office**   Powers that are inherent in holding a certain post. Authority of office is sum of the powers inherent in a given office. For instance, Commander in Chief of the United States Army is a power that is reserved for the President of the United States, therefore Commander in Chief of the United States Army is a power of the President of the United States by authority of office. Every office has a scope of authority, and there are rarely clear lines that perfectly assess its edge, though there are certain tasks clearly within that authority and certain tasks clearly outside of it. The nature of separation of powers and the American concept of the rule of law depend upon limited authority in every office in order to ensure a division of labor in the legal system.

**constituted authorities (duly constituted authority)** An official who holds office according to a grant of power. The constituted authorities is a label both for the particular powers delegated or authorized by the constituents through a constitution but also the officials who are vested with these powers. The phrase is unfortunately often used because of its high-flown sound, the adjective and its adverb "duly" not being intended with specificity but merely as emphasis. Yet, the idea of constituted authority was once a clearly distinguishing notion from its opposite, a constituting authority. In that juxtaposition, the constituting authority conferred powers upon the constituted authority.

**constructive authority (implied authority)**   Authority that is not granted expressly, but can reasonably be inferred from the situation. Constructive authority is authority that one may reasonably believe a person has with which to carry out a particular task or to give a particular instruction, either as a holder of an office or as an agent for another.

**incidental authority**   Powers implied in the authorization of other powers. Incidental authority is any authority of a public or private agent, company, or agency that is not expressly granted but that is implied in the express grant of other authority. Incidental authority is not unlimited, and it can usually be quite difficult to determine the exact limit of what is implied in any express grant of power. Presumptions arise for assessing claims of implied authority, such as in the scope of agency a presumption against an implied power to sell or transfer realty without an express or general power to do so in the agent, or such as in the scope of government a presumption against a power that would intrude upon the traditional powers granted to another arm of the government or upon the liberties of the individual.

**adverse authority**   Law in opposition to the position of the party presenting the case. Adverse authority is law, usually case law, that presents an argument contrary to that being made by the party using the case. Often, a party will use adverse authority to distinguish the issue at hand from that authority, but a party should disclose adverse authority in the interests of fairness and professional ethics.

**persuasive authority**   Non-binding legal precedent. Persuasive authority is non-binding authority to which a judge or authority is not obliged to defer, but may choose to rely on, in order to arrive at a decision in a case. Persuasive authority would include law from other jurisdictions, statements in treatises or other lawbooks.

**public authority**   The power to prescribe the rules governing some conduct. Public authority is a power held in the nation state, or in a state of the union or other sovereign, that allows some people to regulate the conduct of others by virtue of legal office. Public authority may be exercised directly, as when a majority of a legislature passes a law, or delegated, as when an agency is created to promulgate regulations implementing a law or to enforce the law through the exercise of official discretion.
   *See also:* public.

**authorization (authorize)**   Advance approval. To authorize is to permit or give permission to do an action or to give power to the one authorized to perform a task. The U.S. Constitution, for instance, authorizes the different branches of government to undertake courses of action that are exclusive to its branch.
   *See also:* union, labor union, union organization, decertification; union, labor union, labor organization, authorization card.

**authorization**   *See:* ijazah (authorization).

**authorization card**   *See:* union, labor union, labor organization, authorization card.

**autocracy**   *See:* government, forms of government, autocracy (dictatorship or monocracy).

**automatic disclosure**   *See:* disclosure, discovery disclosure, automatic disclosure (mandatory disclosure).

**automatic stay** *See:* stay, automatic stay; bankruptcy, automatic stay.

**automatism** *See:* mens, mens rea, automatism.

**automobile** Motorized, or otherwise self-propelled, vehicle. An automobile, in its most generic sense, is a motor vehicle, any form of self-propelled vehicle. As a matter of transportation law, automobiles are distinct from trucks and specialized motor vehicles, a self-propelled, four-wheeled vehicle intended for use on roads, and designed primarily for the carriage of the driver or driver and passengers.

The federal Clean Air Act defines an automobile as a vehicle with four wheels that is propelled by fuel (or by alternative fuel) and manufactured primarily for use on public streets, roads, and highways (and not on a rail line). Most importantly for the purposes of the automobile air emissions regulation, an automobile is generally not more than 6,000 pounds in gross vehicle weight. Under some circumstances, though, a vehicle meeting other requirements may be considered an automobile under the Clean Air Act if it is up to 8,500 or even 10,000 pounds of gross vehicle weight.

*See also:* accident, vehicular accident (automobile accident or car accident); pollution, air pollution, emission, motor vehicle emission standards; insurance, category of insurance, automobile insurance; guest, automobile guest; search, warrantless search, automobile exception (vehicle exception); warrant, search warrant, automobile exception; vehicle (motor vehicle); homicide, vehicular homicide.

**automobile accident or car accident** *See:* accident, vehicular accident (automobile accident or car accident).

**automobile exception** *See:* warrant, search warrant, automobile exception; search, warrantless search, automobile exception (vehicle exception).

**automobile guest** *See:* guest, automobile guest.

**automobile insurance** *See:* insurance, category of insurance, automobile insurance, no–fault insurance; insurance, category of insurance, automobile insurance.

**automobile product liability** *See:* liability, product liability, automobile product liability (automotive product liability).

**autonomic law** *See:* law, autonomic law.

**autonomy** Self-governance. Autonomy is the practical ability and legal power of an entity to engage in self-government. In an international political sense it refers to a group of people being able to engage in self governance. In a government sense it refers to a government entity able to engage in its own activities without interference from other entities or branches of government.

*See also:* law, autonomic law.

**autopsy (necropsy)** The forensic examination of a corpse. An autopsy is an examination conducted by a doctor—usually a licensed pathologist, medical examiner, or coroner—on a corpse. The purpose in most cases is to determine a cause of death, though inquiries are often made concerning other evidence related to identification of the body, matters of public health, and to evidence that may aid in a criminal investigation of the conditions or environment of the body of the deceased during life, at the time immediately prior to death, or after death. There is no real difference between an autopsy and a post–mortem examination. The term autopsy is sometimes used to describe the post–mortem medical examination of animals or even plants, though the preferred term for such an examination of beings that are not human is necropsy.

*See also:* exhumation (exhume or disinter); coroner (medical examiner or pathologist or forensic pathologist or medical legal investigator or MLI); corpse (cadaver or dead body).

**autre (auter)** Other. Autre is a French pronoun commonly used in Law French phrases to mean other, another, or, sometimes, different, such as per autre vie, for the life of another person. It is sometimes spelled auter, with no difference in meaning.

**autre droit** *See:* standing in court, third–party standing, autre droit (auter droit or en autre droit).

**autrefois** Another time, usually a prior time. Autrefois is a French term for "another time." In U.S. practice, it is nearly always an earlier time, used especially in the terms related to double jeopardy arising from an earlier prosecution arising from the same facts—autrefois convict for an earlier conviction and autrefois acquit for an earlier acquittal.

**availment (avail)** Benefit, use, or shelter. Availment is any profit, benefit, use, or shelter. One may accordingly avail oneself of any beneficial opportunity. In a jurisdictional sense, availment describes a litigant's purposeful acceptance of the benefits and protections of a particular jurisdiction's law, which is then sufficient to establish minimum contacts in that area that would subject it to jurisdiction. To avail oneself of a benefit implies one accepts the duties it implies.

**avdp** *See:* weight, avoirdupois (avdp).

**averah (aveira)** A sin. Averah is a transgression of the law.

**averment (aver)** A claim made to substantiate a statement as true, whether or not under oath. An averment is a statement that is intended to demonstrate the truth or sufficiency of another statement, so that, for instance, the averment supports the claim of breach of duty and demand for damages in a complaint. Indeed, statements of fact in a complaint, answer, or indictment are averments. General averments are broad assertions of the facts underlying a case, and particular averments are specific claims of facts in support of a case. Averments are made under oath or in a pleading but may be made on one's best belief and need not be based on personal observation; they are subject to later proof. The more technical senses of averment are now generally lost and there is now little difference between an averment and an allegation.

*See also:* denial (denied or deny); allegation (allege or alleged).

**avizandum** Judicial decision to be rendered at another time. An avizandum is a judgment in Scots law deferred to a later time, akin to the practice in the United States of a judge taking a ruling under advisement.

**avocat** A lawyer licensed in France, Quebec, or other French-influenced legal systems. Avocat specifically refers to an attorney who is licensed to practice law in France or French Canada and who also is allowed to actively participate in trials. One who has a legal education, or even a license to practice, but is not qualified to appear in court would not be an avocat but would be a notary in some instances, an avoué in others, or more generally a maître.

*See also:* lawyer.

**avoidance (avoid or avoidable)** Evasion or contradiction. Avoidance can be a physical act of evasion, such as swerving a car to avoid a collision, or a rhetorical tactic, such as skipping over a sensitive topic in conversation. As a matter of motion or trial practice, avoidance is an aspect of "confession and avoidance," which admits a premise but disputes a conclusion. Confession and avoidance is the basis for most affirmative defenses, in which the defendant argues that the facts asserted may be true, but that there can be no liability because of the defense, as well as many motions of summary judgment, in that the movant declares the parties agree on the facts but that the non-movant is wrong as a matter of law.

*See also:* cost, best cost avoider (most efficient cost avoider); fiduciary, fiduciary duty, duty to avoid conflicts of interest; confession, confession and avoidance.

**avoidable consequences** *See:* damages, calculation of damages, mitigation of damages (avoidable consequences).

**avoidable preference** *See:* bankruptcy, preference, avoidable preference, Deprizio Doctrine; bankruptcy, preference, avoidable preference.

**avoidance or renunciation** *See:* contract, specific contracts, voidable contract, disaffirmance (avoidance or renunciation).

**avoirdupois** *See:* weight, avoirdupois (avdp).

**avon** Intentional sin. Avon is a sin committed intentionally or deliberately in Jewish law.

**avowal**

**avowal action** *See:* paternity, avowal action.

**avowal as statement (avow or avowant or avowed)** An attestation or oath that a statement is true. An avowal is a statement made under oath or attestation of the truth of an asserted fact and justification under law. To avow is thus to solemnly commit to the truth of some statement or otherwise to promise a declaration represents the truth, as well as the legitimacy or justification of some matter as a matter of law. The term originally meant to confess or disclose information that the avowant held formerly as a secret, and that sense is still incorporated in some usages.

**avowtry (avowterer)** An old term for adultery. Avowtry was both a condition of adultery and the common-law crime of adultery. The crime was committed by an avowterer, who as a man (married or unmarried) who committed a sexual act with a married woman. The condition of avowtry applied to a woman who persisted in an adulterous affair after discovery, and it voided her dowry. Note: avowtry is very different from avowry, which was a declaration in replevin.

*See also:* adultery (adulterer or alterous).

**avulsion** A sudden change in the banks or course of riparian waters. Avulsion is a sudden change of a watercourse, particularly the addition or removal of land, most often from the banks of a river or other running body of water. Such an immediate change may have effects on boundary lines between properties, or on a much larger scale, between nation-states, but the general rule is that boundaries do not change owing to avulsive shifts of rivers, banks, or shores.

*See also:* river; island; boundary; accretion, accretion as increase of a shore.

**axiom (axiomatic)** A proposition that is so well accepted it can be taken for granted. An axiom is a statement that is considered to be self-evident and does not need any additional proof in order to prove it. Legal axioms consist of any established principles within the legal field, such as the ability for parties to freely enter into contract with one another or actual harm being required for negligence. Any self-evident statement is axiomatic, but legal axioms are accepted principles in law, a legal axiom is a maxim.

*See also:* contract, contract interpretation negotiated terms vs. standard terms.

**ayatollah** An honorific title for a religious leader in Shia society. Ayatollah literally means a sign of God. This title is conferred onto leading Shia clerics after many years of study. Ayatollahs are capable of handing down religious edicts from sources of Islamic law.

*See also:* Imam.

**azharah ('azharah)** An express statement of prohibition in the Torah. Azharah is a warning. In order to impose criminal penalties, the Torah must contain a statement prohibiting the act in question (the azharah) as well as a statement specifying the penalty. If either prohibition or penalty is missing, no punishment can be imposed, though the act remains forbidden. Azharah can also mean enlightenment, and so care of the context of the phrase is essential.

# B

**b**   The second letter of the modern English alphabet. "B" signifies a variety of functions as a symbol and as a designation of status. It is sometimes invoked by beta, the word for the second letter in Greek. It is translated into Bravo for radio signals and NATO military transmissions, into Boy for some police radio traffic, and into dash, dot, dot, dot in Morse Code.

**b as a rating**   Of the penultimate quality and ranking. B is used in a variety of forms for rating the quality of specific products. Many regulatory definitions depend on an alphabetic listing, with A the highest tier, and B the tier below it. For instance, Grade B beef signals meat from the more but not the most mature animal, a cow having a physiological maturity of thirty to forty–two months, as opposed to older animals with coarser meat or younger animals with preferable meat. Many private ratings also use "C" as the lowest recommendation among those recommendations the agency is willing to make. For example, bonds are rated by Moody's and other rating services on a three–tier scale, with A bonds the highest quality, and that tier being divided among Baa1, Baa2, Baa3, Ba1, Ba1, Ba3, B1, B2, B3 (prior to 1996 being Ba1, Ba, B1, and B), the more letters that are incorporated the less risk and the higher the quality of the debt instrument.

*See also:* a, a as a rating; c, c as a rating; c, c as a rating; c, c as a rating.

**b as an abbreviation**   A word commencing in b. The letter B following a name may stand for Baron, as a judge in the Court of Exchequer. As a component of other abbreviations, b or B can stand for any word commencing with that letter, particularly bachelor, baccalaureus, Bahamas, bail, balance, Baltimore, banco, bancus, bank, banking, bankruptcy, bar, barrister, Baylor, before, bench, Berkeley, Bermuda, bill, biographical, black board, bond, bonum, book, Boston, Brigham, British, Brooklyn, brought, budget, Buffalo, bulletin, bureau, and business. B may also stand for the initial of the name of an author or case reporter, such as Bacon, Bailey, Ball, Banning, Barron, Benloe, Best, Bingham, Bishop, Black, Bracton, Browne, Brooke, Buchanan, Burns, Burrow, and Busbee.

**b as in hypotheticals**   The second character in the story. When used as the sole letter of an abbreviation, B often stands for a person, the second character in the story of a law school hypothetical.

**b and e**   *See:* breaking and entering (b and e).

**B.F.O.Q. or BFOQ**   *See:* discrimination, employment discrimination, bona fide occupational qualification (B.F.O.Q. or BFOQ).

**b/l**   *See:* bill, bill of lading (b/l).

**Baby Doe**   *See:* name, fictitious name, Baby Doe (Baby M).

**baby lawyer**   *See:* lawyer, newbie (baby lawyer, greenhorn).

**Baby M**   *See:* name, fictitious name, Baby Doe (Baby M).

**bachelor of laws**   *See:* degree, academic degree, law degree, bachelor of laws (LL.B. or LLB).

**back pay**   *See:* pay, back pay (backpay).

**back-loaded payment**   *See:* payment, back-loaded payment.

**backdate**   *See:* date, backdate (antedate).

**backpay**   *See:* pay, back pay (backpay).

**bad debts**   *See:* debt, bad debts.

**bad-faith**   *See:* faith, bad-faith (mala fides).

**bad faith bargaining**   *See:* bargain, surface bargaining (bad faith bargaining).

**bad faith denial**   *See:* insurance, insurance claim, denial of claim, bad faith denial (denial in bad faith or wrongful refusal or tortious denial of benefits).

**bad-faith breach**   *See:* breach, breach of contract, bad-faith breach (tortious breach of contract).

**bad-man concept of law**   *See:* law, theories of law, ontology of law, bad-man concept of law (bad man theory).

**bad Samaritan**   *See:* samaritan, bad Samaritan.

**badge**   A symbol of status, often worn on a person's clothing. A badge is an insignia that may be worn by persons to indicate their rank or position. For instance, police officers often wear badges on their shirts so as to indicate to the general public that they are law enforcement officers, and a police officer's display of an authentic badge is usually sufficient to identify the officer for the purposes of establishing liability for resistance to arrest. In other contexts, workers who enter secure premises may be required to show or wear an identification badge in order to gain access. Identification badges in the workplace usually remain the property of the employer, which may demand their surrender if an employee leaves that employment. Generically, the term "badge" may refer to anything that indicates some designation, achievement, or status. Metaphorically, "badge" refers to anything that is a symbol or proof of something else, such as a large house being a badge of wealth.

*See also:* slavery, badge of slavery.

**badger game**   *See:* extortion, badger game.

**bail**   Surety given as a pledge that a person will appear in court. Bail is a deposit of money, or an interest in property, deposited with the court and liable to forfeiture if the person for whom it is deposited does not appear at the time of a specified hearing. Bail is the surety bond posted by a charged criminal suspect to ensure the suspect does not flee the jurisdiction or fail to appear in court at the time appointed. As surety, bail allows the criminal suspect to remain in the custody of the person posting bail instead of in criminal detention, pending further proceedings in the suspect's case. Bail can also, and once did, label the person who acted as the surety, or the person whose promise the court accepts (often not the person who has to appear).

*See also:* surety (suretyship).

**bail bond (appearance bond)**   A bond purchased from a private source to secure bail. A bail bond is a security posted by a third party as the surety that an accused criminal will appear in court at a hearing, trial, or other specified date. Customarily, the defendant or others on behalf of the defendant pay 10 percent of the value of the bond to the bond dealer, customarily still called a "bail bondsman." The bondsman posts a bond in the full amount, guaranteeing 100 percent of the bond. If the defendant appears, the bondsman owes the court nothing (or is refunded the whole bond). If the defendant fails to appear, the bond may be forfeit, and the bondsman must pay the whole amount of the bail to the court. The bondsman may attempt to recover the lost funds from the defendant or other sureties, but such efforts rarely succeed. Thus, if Abner is arrested, and the court allows bail at $50,000, Abner and his family may ask Bob the bondsman for a bail bond, for which they pay a non-refundable $5,000 (sometimes more but rarely less) and undertake a conditional promissory note for the remaining $45,000. Bob posts the $50,000 note with the court, forfeit if Abner fails to appear on the first day of the next month for a hearing. Abner is released into the custody of Bob. If Abner appears, Bob is given his entire $50,000 note back. If Abner doesn't appear, Bob's note is forfeit.

**bail jumping (bail jumper or jumping bail or jump bail)**   Refusing to return as requested after release prior to incarceration or hearing. Bail jumping is the crime of failure to appear at the time and place specified as the condition of release, when a person had been arrested and was awaiting a hearing or trial but was released subject to bail. Bail jumping is the same offense as a willful failure to appear.

**bail-jumping or bail jumping or jump bail**   *See:* appearance, non-appearance, failure to appear (bail-jumping or bail jumping or jump bail).

**personal recognizance (personal recognizance bond or release on recognizance or ROR or R.O.R.)**   A pledge of honor to return for a hearing or trial. A personal recognizance bond, which gives rise to a release on recognizance, is the release of a criminal defendant according to a pledge recorded in court of the defendant's good faith, rather than a surety of money, that the defendant will appear at a hearing or trial or such places and times as are designated in the pledge. Thus a release on personal recognizance has the same obligation of appearance as a release on bail, but there is no payment of money or potential obligation to a bail bondsman.

*See also:* recognizance.

**bailee**   *See:* bailment, bailee (bailiff).

**bailer**   *See:* bailment, bailor (bailer).

**bailiff**   Officer of the court who ensures safety and compliance with judicial orders. A bailiff is a law enforcement officer responsible for maintaining order in court. In the United States, bailiffs are often deputy sheriffs, municipal police officers, or members of the Federal Marshal's Service. The bailiff's duties usually include courthouse security, enforcement of the judge's orders, seeing to the needs of the jurors, and the guard and transfer of prisoners.

*See also:* bailment, bailee (bailiff); tipstaff.

**bailiwick (baliva)**   A sheriff's jurisdiction, or a particular arena of expertise. A bailiwick, technically, is the physical jurisdiction of a sheriff, or, perhaps, any other law enforcement officer. The term is more often encountered, however, as a metaphor representing the particular focus of a person's or institution's expertise or commitments.

*See also:* bailiff.

**bailment**   A chattel possessed by one person but owned by another to whom it must be redelivered. A bailment is a legal relationship between the owner of personal property and another who possesses the property but must return it. A bailment arises when the property is delivered in a manner that conveys mere possession rather than ownership of the property, and the other receives it in circumstances that would ordinarily require return of the property in the future. The bailment describes the property as well as the relationship. The owner is the bailor and the possessor is the bailee. Depending upon the form or circumstances of the bailment, the bailee may be obligated to act for the benefit of the bailor as trustee over the property.

See also: bailment, bailee (bailiff); bailment, bailor (bailer); pawn; deposit.

**bailee (bailiff)**   One who accepts temporary custody of another's chattels. A bailee holds a bailment until its restoration to the bailor. In other words, the bailee temporarily receives property from its owner, usually to the benefit of the owner, and holds the property for a specified purpose without obtaining any rights to ownership. For example, a bailee may be a dry-cleaner who possesses another's clothes to launder and return them, a mechanic who possesses another's automobile to repair and return it, or a warehouse that possesses another's goods to store them. The term bailiff has been used historically as a synonym for bailee; although bailiff is more often used to describe a court officer, that officer might indeed act as a bailee in the sense of a temporary custodian of property deposited into court.

**bailor (bailer)**   The true owner of chattels delivered into bailment. A bailor owns personal property and conveys that property to the bailee who will hold the property until its restoration to the bailor. The bailor may specify a purpose toward which the property is to be used that may be a condition of its acceptance by the bailee, and the bailor is entitled at least to the benefit of a duty of good faith from the bailee. Some bailments give rise to a trust in the bailment, with the bailor as the beneficiary of the trust.

**constructive bailment (involuntary bailment)**   Bailment arising by operation of law or equity out of circumstances. A constructive bailment, or involuntary bailment, results from one party's possession of another's chattel that is acquired by the first party through legal means but not from conditions expressed by the parties at or before the delivery and acceptance of a chattel. Thus a constructive, or involuntary, bailment arises not from mutual consent of the bailor and bailee but through circumstances in which the law construes one party's possession of property owned by another to amount to a bailment, even if neither party had intended one to arise. Practically any delivery of property not intended to vest ownership in the recipient creates a constructive bailment (though this statement must be understood not to include all manner of transfers, because not all amount to a delivery; abandonment is not delivery, for example). It usually arises when through accident or emergency, property comes into the possession of one who does not have title to it. The status of constructive bailment requires a comparative analysis of the strength of the claims to title by the possessor and

by the allegedly rightful owner, not merely an error in acquisition.

When a constructive bailment is found in property the bailee would not have accepted as a bailment, or when an involuntary bailee incurs expenses to the benefit of the bailor or the ultimate recipient, the bailor or the recipient may have a duty to compensate the bailee. The bailee must maintain and return the bailment (or allow its collection). A failure of the bailee to return the property gives rise to an action for conversion, which is subject to the usual limitations periods for intentional torts. Following the lapse of that period, in the absence of such an action, involuntary bailments are subject to prescription, allowing title to ripen in the bailee. Note: there is no essential difference between an involuntary bailment and a constructive bailment.

**involuntary bailment**   See also: bailment, constructive bailment (involuntary bailment).

**bait and switch**   See: fraud, bait and switch.

**balance**   The amount of money owed by a debtor. The balance is the amount owed from a customer to a merchant or other creditor. This is usually reflected in bills, invoices, or statements with a "balance due," although the balance due is only that portion of the balance that is to be paid at the time of the invoice. A balance may be carried on terms of credit that require its payment in installments. The word "balance" alone implies a debt, but the balance may also be stated as a "credit balance," in which the customer is owed money by a merchant, which may be applied to future debts or demanded by the customer.

See also: finances, financial statement.

**balance of trade**   See: trade, international trade, balance of trade (trade balance).

**balance sheet**   A statement of assets, liabilities, and owner's equity. A balance sheet is the foundational record for every corporation's assets and liabilities. The traditional merchant's balance sheet recorded the debits and credits for each customer, as well as the sum of debits and credits to produce a balance for the merchant overall. Revenues and expenses do not appear distinctly on the balance sheet but are on the income statement.

In an age of electronic records, similar statements are often created from records stored according to various schemes in databases. In the United States, corporations are generally required to maintain and publish balance sheets according to Generally Accepted Accounting Principles.

**balancing test**   Judicial decision–making based on a compromise among competing interests. The balancing test is a generic description of any judicial decision–making process that weighs the goals of various competing interests and seeks a decision that satisfies each goal as much as possible. Judicially created balancing tests are common throughout the law. Some commentators complain that balancing tests allow courts too much discretion, inviting rulings based on bias or whim, diminishing predictability and encouraging inconsistency. Even so, balancing tests are essential to the development of rules in novel situations and to the application of two or more inconsistent rules of policies in a given dispute.

**baliva**   *See:* bailiwick (baliva).

**ballistics**   The science of projectiles. Ballistics is the science of the physical property of projectiles, especially bullets. The term applies to both the study of the motion of projectiles and the forensic examination of bullets and shell casings for evidentiary purposes. Forensic ballistics is often used as direct evidence to determine the type of weapon, or even the particular weapon, used in a crime.
*See also:* forensics (forensic science).

**balloon payment**   *See:* payment, balloon payment.

**ballot**   The record of a vote or the process of collecting and recording votes. A ballot is an instrument used to record the choice of a voter in an election. Ballots have evolved with time and technology, once being little balls placed in one side or another of a box, then becoming written scripts on which marks were made or marks were punched, and now being electronic records. Although ballots are most famously used in elections for public offices, they are also used in votes in private and corporate settings. The term ballot also refers generically to the entire process of an election, and the ballot box is the container into which ballots are placed, in which they are to be kept secure during an election until the box is opened by an authorized official for counting, after which the ballots are again secured until the time for recounting or challenges has passed.
*See also:* election (elective); vote (voting); president, President of the United States of America, Electoral College (Presidential Elector).

**black ball**   To exclude a person from an association. To black ball is to cast a negative vote against or associating an individual into membership in a club or into a position of employment. More generally, it is to disparage someone's reputation for the purpose of unseating that person from some position. The casting of ballots by marbles or small balls is quite old, which is, indeed, the origin of the word ballot. In ball-and-box voting systems, a single negative vote, signified by a black ball as opposed to a white, rejects an applicant from membership or preferment. In others, some higher level of dissatisfaction must be shown.

**butterfly ballot**   A punch-card ballot with candidates' names printed on both sides of the punch holes. The butterfly ballot is a device used to guide voters in punch-card voting or, occasionally, in paper-ballot marking. The ballot has cards printed with candidates' names, one or more cards on each side of a vertical trough between the cards in which holes are designated for each printed name. The voter

indicates by punching or marking in the hole that corresponds to the name or ballot issue on one of the cards. Infamously used in Florida during the 2000 presidential election, critics claimed the ballot was confusing because a voter could have indicated a box that did not correspond to the voter's preferred candidate.

**chad**   A paper chip that falls from a voter's punch-marked paper ballot. A chad is a tiny rectangle perforated into a punch-hole ballot, which is designed to separate from the ballot when a voter punches the corresponding hole representing the candidate for whom the vote is cast. Chads came to prominence in the 2000 U.S. presidential election, particularly in the state of Florida, where many paper ballots were used. Election workers had great difficulty in ascertaining the choices that voters had made due to the different variations in the ballots from which the chads that they encountered were imperfectly removed — dimpled chads, pregnant chads, hanging chads, etc. Note: though there has been a concerted effort to promote chad as a plural noun, it is still more commonly made plural by the addition of an "s."

**ban**   A prohibition. A ban is a formal command or edict prohibiting the doing of anything.
*See also:* bandit; edict.

**bandit**   An armed robber. Bandit is a legally non-specific word for a dangerous criminal, usually an armed robber. Although "bandit" is derived from one under a ban, or therefore one who has been outlawed, it has acquired a more specific sense in the United States, particularly associated with gang members who held up stages and trains. It is now used more generally for robbers or burglars who harm or threaten their victims or witnesses. Banditry is the commission of an act or acts that are associated with bandits.

**banishment (banish)**   An order to leave a jurisdiction and not to return. Banishment is an order, either as a punishment or as a condition of probation to leave a jurisdiction for a specified period of time or for life. As a metaphor, banishment is any restriction of a person from one place or to another place, or the extinction of any idea.

**bank**

**bank account**   *See:* account, bank account (account in bank).

**bank bill**   *See:* note, bank note (bank bill).

**bank deposit**   *See:* deposit, bank deposit.

**bank draft**   *See:* draft, draft as negotiable instrument, bank draft, overdraft (overdraw or overdrawn); draft, draft as negotiable instrument, bank draft.

**bank note**   *See:* note, bank note (bank bill).

**bank as financial corporation** An institution holding, investing, lending, and accounting for money. Banks are corporations that accept deposits of money, provide loans of money and other services, such as extending credit for its borrowing customers and issuing negotiable instruments evidencing debt agreements. In general terms, a bank may be a private bank, a national bank, or a credit union; likewise, a bank may be primarily a commercial bank, investment bank, or retail bank. Each is subject to state or federal charter and regulations. To bank is the verb describing the business conducted with a bank. Metaphorically, to bank is a synonym for to rely.

*See also:* finances, financial institution.

**bank as shore (riverbank or banks)** The shore of a river or body of water. A bank is any slope of ground, as in an embankment. At the edges of rivers or other waters the banks are that part of the riverbed that rises up to meet the adjoining land, forming the boundary of the water. The bank may be used as a matter of local custom as a boundary of property ownership or of jurisdiction or of sovereignty. The banks may also be the basis for measurement of a boundary elsewhere, such as the mid-point between them. "Banks" is, incidentally, used in the plural for the boundary on one side of a river as well as for both sides. This convention confuses some people, and bank in the singular is now acceptable for one side alone.

*See also:* river; shore (shoreline).

**central bank** A bank with a monopoly over a national currency. A central bank is a bank or other institution that lends money to the nation in which it is granted a monopoly over the supply of money into the economy, having the effect, in most large economies, of a high degree of control over interest rates and the value of the currency. In the United States, the Federal Reserve Banks operate as the central bank. Note: The U.S. Mint and the Bureau of Engraving and Printing, both in the Department of the Treasury, physically create money; the federal reserve stores it as physical and intellectual property and lends it to the Treasury and to commercial banks.

*See also:* bank, Federal Reserve System (Federal Reserve Bank).

**collecting bank** Bank that collects a negotiable instrument and presents it to the payor bank. A collecting bank is any bank that received a negotiable instrument and transfers it to another bank for ultimate payment. A collecting bank may be any bank except the payor bank; so a collecting bank may be a depositary bank or a presenting bank, depending on the transfers of a given instrument.

**commercial bank** Institution that takes deposits and makes commercial loans. A commercial bank is a financial institution that, as defining aspects of its business, takes deposits and makes commercial loans. A commercial bank may provide a variety of additional banking, trust, retail, and advising services to private and commercial clients.

**credit union** Financial institution owned and operated in part by its depositors. A credit union is a nonprofit bank owned by its depositors, for all purposes of commercial law indistinguishable from other commercial banks. Credit unions were authorized by federal law in 1934 under the Federal Credit Union Act, 48 Sta. 1216, and are still chartered and regulated independently of other banks. Federal credit unions are chartered by the National Credit Union Administration, and state credit unions are chartered by the appropriate state agency or board in their respective states.

**depositary bank (depository bank)** The first bank to which a negotiable instrument is presented. A depositary bank is the first financial institution that accepts a negotiable instrument, even if the bank is also the payor bank (unless the instrument is immediately paid at the counter). There is no difference in meaning when depositary is spelled with an "o" or an "a" in its penultimate syllable.

*See also:* depositary (depository or repository).

**failed bank (bank failure or bank seizure or bank takeover)** A bank that cannot meet its obligations from its assets. A failed bank is a banking institution or corporation that does not have sufficient assets, particularly deposits, to meet the obligations of its depositors and creditors. A failed bank is usually closed by its insurer. In the United States the insurer is usually the Federal Deposit Insurance Corporation, which pays depositors to the level of their insurance and acts as the receiver of the bank, settling its debts and selling on or restructuring its assets. Note: although the failure of the bank occurs when its accounts are no longer sufficient and not when it is later declared closed, writers for the FDIC and others may mean the failure of the bank to be its closure or takeover. The context is essential to discern meaning if the distinction is material in a given usage.

**Federal Deposit Insurance Corporation (F.D.I.C. or FDIC)** Federal agency that insures bank deposits. The Federal Deposit Insurance Corporation, or FDIC, is a federal agency that supervises financial institutions, sets bank standards and regulations for federally insured banks, insures individual deposits, and manages receiverships, in order to maintain the stability and public confidence in the United States financial system. Most banks in the United States participate in the FDIC insurance program. The FDIC has specific guidelines for various account types in order to determine the level of insurance coverage. For instance, in 2010, single accounts were insured against bank defaults, up to $250,000.

**deposit insurance** Guarantee that deposits will be repaid if lost due to a bank failure. Deposit insurance is a limited guarantee to a depositor with a qualified deposit in a bank with deposit insurance that value lost owing to a failure of the bank will be assured. The limit requires payment to a certain limit per depositor per institution.

**federal funds rate**   Interest rate for overnight loans between banks. The federal funds rate is the rate at which banks loan money overnight to other banks. The federal funds rate is determined by taking the weighted average of the rates on overnight federal funds transactions among members of the federal reserve system.

**Federal Home Loan Bank (FHLB)**   Government-sponsored enterprise providing mortgage funding. The Federal Home Loan Bank system is a government-sponsored enterprise created to provide a stable source of funds for residential mortgages. The mission of the Federal Home Loan Banks is to support member institutions' residential mortgage and economic development lending activities. Lenders eligible for Federal Home Loan Bank membership include savings banks, savings and loan associations, cooperative banks, commercial banks, credit unions, and insurance companies that are active in housing finance. In 2011, the system had twelve Federal Home Loan Banks and over 8,100 member financial institutions.

**Federal Home Loan Mortgage Corporation (Freddie Mac)**   Quasi-federal corporation engaged in the secondary mortgage market. The Federal Home Loan Mortgage Corporation (Freddie Mac) is a congressionally chartered, stockholder-owned corporation whose main purpose is to provide liquidity to the secondary mortgage market.

**Federal National Mortgage Association (Fannie Mae)**   Quasi-federal entity providing a market for residential mortgages. The Federal National Mortgage Association (Fannie Mae) is a congressionally chartered, stockholder-owned corporation that was developed to provide a secondary market for the resale of residential mortgages.

**Federal Reserve System (Federal Reserve Bank)**   The central bank of the United States. The Federal Reserve System is the central bank of the United States. An independent agency of the federal government, it conducts monetary policy, maintains the stability of financial markets, and provides services to financial institutions and government agencies. It is also responsible for the regulation of the United States money supply and the determination of rates of interest for certain federal loans into the banking system. The system is sometimes described as if it is a bank, though it is not. Rather it is a system of twelve regional reserve banks, each subject to a governor and its own nine-member board of directors. The twelve governors comprise the Federal Open Market Committee, which sets standards for credit and money supply. The system as a whole is managed by a seven-member Board of Governors, each of whom is a presidential appointee to a fourteen-year term.

**intermediary bank**   Bank to which an item is transferred but not depositary or payor bank. An intermediary bank is a financial institution to which an item is transferred in course of collection except the depository or payor bank.

**payor bank (drawee bank)**   The bank on whose account a draft is drawn. The payor bank is the drawee bank, the bank on which a draft or other negotiable instrument is drawn, which ultimately must honor or dishonor the draft. That is to say, the payor bank holds the bank account on which a check is drawn, which is where the check is ultimately presented for payment, and which must pay the check or dishonor it.

**presenting bank**   A bank that presents a negotiable instrument to the drawee bank. A presenting bank presents an instrument to the bank against which the instrument is drawn.

**trust company**   Financial institution authorized to hold property for the benefit of others. A trust company is a bank that is chartered with a particular recognition of its purpose of acting as a trustee, holding property for the benefit of others. This purpose will generally require particular expertise in asset management including investment acumen. More generically, a trust company can be any corporation that is doing business primarily as a trustee, regulated as a bank but not managing deposits or providing other banking services.

**bankruptcy (bankrupt)**   Process for an overextended debtor to manage debts under court protection. Bankruptcy is a system through which a debtor may discharge or diminish debt, according to schemes that vary according to the relative ability of the individual or entity to continue as a going concern even with such assistance. Bankruptcy proceedings are authorized by the U.S. Constitution and created solely by federal statute and rules, particularly the Bankruptcy Code, under which three main chapters provide procedures. Liquidation, under Chapter 7, requires the bankrupt to surrender control and ownership over most of its assets to a trustee, who sells them (sometimes including going businesses as a single asset) and divides the proceeds among creditors. Reorganization, under Chapter 11, allows the debtor to dispose of assets, forgive debts, engage in mergers, or other plans for the acquisition of new capital. Adjustment, under Chapter 13, requires a plan for the payment of debts by the debtor, which is approved by the creditors and the court.

Although bankruptcy is a federal matter, federal courts have interpreted the federal Bankruptcy Code to modify, not supplant, relevant state statutes. Thus, while a debtor must seek bankruptcy protection in federal court, state law may control certain issues such as which of the debtor's possessions may be liquidated; a common exception is the debtor's homestead.

Note: a debtor who takes advantage of bankruptcy protections is a bankrupt. In common usage, "bankrupt" may represent any economic state in which a person, state, or entity is without liquid assets, regardless of debts. Metaphorically, it may mean any idea or position without value or merit.

**automatic stay**   *See:* stay, automatic stay.

**bankruptcy as financial status (bankrupt)** Incapable of repaying one's debts. In common usage, a debtor is bankrupt, or in a state of bankruptcy, when the individual or institution no longer has the financial ability to repay creditors or maintain operations. In this sense, bankruptcy does not depend upon resort to the protection of bankruptcy procedures. Colloquially, a bankrupt refers to one who has no money.

**bankruptcy claim**

**allowed claim** A valid claim against assets in a bankruptcy proceeding. An allowed claim is a claim filed by a creditor in a bankruptcy proceeding that either had no objections filed against it by an interested party or is upheld after an objection following review by the court.

**priority claim** A claim to be satisfied before other claims are paid. A priority claim in bankruptcy is a claim that is given precedence of satisfaction ahead of other claims. A bankruptcy plan may have several levels of priority. Priority of bankruptcy claims relates to payments of claims in general and is distinct from the priority of claims in property that is subject to security interests.
*See also:* priority; priority, claim priority, absolute priority rule.

**unsecured claim** A claim made on an unsecured debt. An unsecured claim is a claim that is not a secured claim as defined under the bankruptcy code, primarily any claim on a debt that has not been secured through a valid lien in any property in which the bankruptcy estate has an interest. Unsecured claims are satisfied from property a debtor liquidates only after the satisfaction of secured claims.

**Bankruptcy Code** The statutes governing the procedures of and access to bankruptcy protection. The Bankruptcy Code, 11 U.S.C. § 1 et seq., sets forth the forms and practices of bankruptcy in the United States. The Code establishes six forms of bankruptcy proceeding: Chapter 7, Liquidation; Chapter 9, Adjustment of Debts of a Municipality; Chapter 11, Reorganization; Chapter 12, Adjustment of Debts of a Farmer or Fisherman; Chapter 13, Adjustment of Debts of an Individual; and Chapter 15, Ancillary and Cross-Border Cases.

**bankruptcy estate (bankrupt estate)** All of the assets of the person declaring bankruptcy that may be used to satisfy creditors. The bankruptcy estate is the sum of all of the bankrupt's assets, including property that has not been fully realized, such as pending inheritances, actions in litigation, or stock options or tax or other benefits owed but not distributed, if they are accrued to the debtor within 180 days of filing. Excepted from the estate are those assets that are excluded by statute, particularly assets held only as trustee for others, assets in spendthrift trusts to the benefit of the bankrupt (though payments made or to be made from them during the time of the bankruptcy are in), and the assets in retirement plans, and assets that cannot be claimed by creditors under state law, such as a homestead property that is protected up to a limit set by state law.

**diminution of estate doctrine** A bankrupt's transfer to one creditor so that others of the same class cannot recover as well. A diminution of estate occurs when a transfer to one creditor diminishes directly or indirectly the fund from which other creditors of the same class as the transferee creditor might recover payment on the debts owed them by the transferor. Where a person owns property, but has used it as security against a form of credit, the creditor has an interest in the property. If the owner wishes to convey the property to another, courts apply the diminution of estate doctrine to determine whether the creditor's interest should prevent the conveyance.

**bankruptcy plan** A list of steps the bankrupt will take to manage its debts. A plan is required in all bankruptcies other than Chapter 7 liquidations, and the negotiation between the debtor or trustee and creditors and its approval by the court are the heart of bankruptcy procedure. The plan is a detailed analysis of the reorganization or adjustments, which amounts to a contract between the debtor and creditors, which must conform to the Bankruptcy Code, and which must be approved by the court.

**bankruptcy protection** The privileges a bankrupt receives through bankruptcy procedures. Bankruptcy protection consists of measures open to a person, organization, or business unable to pay debts owed to creditors through proceedings in a federal bankruptcy court. The most important forms of protection are the single action to establish the amounts of debts and to structure their management, the finality of a plan that would diminish the amount owed in return for assurances of payment, and the finality of discharge of the debts upon discharge from bankruptcy.

**Bankruptcy Rules** The Federal Rules of Bankruptcy Procedure. The Bankruptcy Rules are national rules of bankruptcy procedure, drafted by the Advisory Committee on Bankruptcy Rules, promulgated by the U.S. Supreme Court, and published as an appendix to Title 11 of the U.S. Code. The rules are augmented by local rules for the bankruptcy court in every federal judicial district.

**Chapter 7 filing (Chapter Seven filing)** Petition to discharge debt through liquidation of assets. A Chapter 7 filing is entered by a debtor who, under a means test required by the Bankruptcy Abuse Prevention and Consumer Protection Act of 2005, does not possess enough assets to satisfy outstanding debts. A Bankruptcy Trustee takes possession of the eligible assets of the debtor's estate, excluding exempt property such as a homestead, and then sells the assets and apportions the proceeds of the sales among creditors. If no non-exempt assets are available, the filing is a "no–asset case," an unsecured creditor may receive nothing but find the debt discharged.

*See also:* bankruptcy, discharge in bankruptcy.

**Chapter 9 filing (Chapter Nine filing)**   A petition of a municipality to adjust its debts. A Chapter 9 bankruptcy filing allows a municipality seeks debt adjustment, in a manner similar to Chapter 13 for individuals. Before the municipality can seek the protection offered by a Chapter 9 filing, the municipality must be authorized to declare bankruptcy either by state law or by an authorized state official, and, usually, it must make a good faith effort to obtain an agreement with its creditors.

**Chapter 11 filing (Reorganization in Bankruptcy or Chapter Eleven filing)**   A petition to reorganize a commercial enterprise and its contractual obligations. A Chapter 11 filing is a declaration of bankruptcy in which a debtor continues in business but restructures assets, obligations, and debts in a court–approved plan. The defining characteristic of a Chapter 11 filing is the asset reorganization that transforms a debtor into a debtor–in–possession. With a few exceptions, this requires the debtor to behave as a trustee to the benefit of the creditors of the bankruptcy estate. The debtor–in–possession is then afforded the protections and benefits offered at law to the trustee of an estate but is also burdened by the fiduciary responsibilities mandated for trustees. Though Chapter 11 bankruptcy protects businesses, it is also available to individuals whose debts are eligible for restructuring rather than requiring liquidation.

*See also:* debt, debtor in possession.

**cram down (cramdown or cram–down)**   Approval of a debt reorganization over the objection of a creditor. A cram down is a process of Chapter 11 debt reorganization over the objection of a creditor or class of creditors. When the creditor is made no worse off by a fair cram–down reorganization plan than the creditor would be if the debtor were in liquidation, the interests of the creditor may be sacrificed in favor of superior creditors. A cram down must provide the creditor with a lien securing the claim and with a promise of future property distributions (such as deferred cash payments), the total value of the distributions at the time of the effective date of the plan being not less than the allowed amount of such claim. The plan is figuratively "crammed down the throat" of the unhappy creditor. The phrase is sometimes written as one word, but the better usages are to hyphenate the words when they are a preceding adjective or to leave them as two words when they are a noun.

**Chapter 12 filing (Chapter Twelve filing)**   A petition by a family farmer or fisherman to adjust debts in bankruptcy. A Chapter 12 filing is a declaration of bankruptcy by a family farmer or fisherman to adjust debts under specific rules applicable to the forms of loans and creditors likely to be affected by the bankruptcy of such enterprises. Chapter 12 filings are available only to individuals operating a qualifying family farm or commercial fishing service that generates annual income. A Chapter 12 bankrupt becomes a debtor–in–possession, retaining active management powers over the estate as the trustee of the estate, with certain statutorily defined proceeds from the estate going toward the repayment of creditors. Among other protections, a Chapter 12 filing limits the accrual of interest against any property used in the qualifying enterprise, as long as that property is not sold.

**Chapter 13 filing (Chapter Thirteen filing)**   A petition by an individual to adjust debts in bankruptcy. A Chapter 13 filing is a declaration of bankruptcy by an individual to adjust debts rather than to enter liquidation. Chapter 13 bankruptcy requires the greatest possible recoveries for creditors that leaves the debtor with sufficient assets for basic needs. Chapter 13 considers the debtor's future earning capacity as well as present assets in structuring a plan that requires periodic payments to compensate unsecured creditors with an ultimate amount not less than the creditors would have received if the bankrupt had filed under Chapter 7, but not more than the bankrupt is able to pay, based upon his current salary and living expenses.

**discharge in bankruptcy**   A release from further liability for certain debts following bankruptcy. A discharge is a release from further liability for the debts that had been subject to a bankruptcy proceeding.

**gap period**   Time of the bankruptcy from the petition to the order of relief. The gap period is the time from the filing of a petition for involuntary bankruptcy and the order of relief.

**involuntary bankruptcy**   A bankruptcy proceeding filed by someone not the debtor. An involuntary bankruptcy is a proceeding for the bankruptcy of a debtor under Chapter 7 or Chapter 11, in which the creditor or creditors of a debtor initiate the proceeding without the debtor's consent. Certain forms of debtor cannot be brought involuntarily into a bankruptcy court, particularly farmers, non–profit associations, banks, credit unions, savings and loans, and insurance corporations, or brokers under Chapter 11 or railroads under Chapter 7. A partnership may be brought into Chapter 7, either by its creditors or by a group of partners less than the whole partnership. Involuntary bankruptcy may only be filed if the debtor is in arrears on undisputed debts for at least $10,000 or is under the management of a custodian for 120 days.

**joint bankruptcy**   A single petition in bankruptcy filed by two married persons. A joint bankruptcy is filed under Section 302 of the U.S. Bankruptcy Code by lawfully married couples, essentially creating two bankruptcy cases administered together to save time and court costs. A joint filing of bankruptcy does not automatically combine the two debtors' estates.

**preference (prefer)**   The debtor's favor of one creditor over others. A preference, in law, is the assignment of an interest in one's property or assets to one creditor that is not made available to all creditors. Under U.S.

law generally, such preferences are freely allowed as long as the debtor is solvent, but such preferences made after a debtor becomes insolvent or is in contemplation of bankruptcy are either void under state law, construed as a general assignment to the benefit of all creditors under state law, or made voidable by a trustee in bankruptcy.

**avoidable preference** Untimely transfer of assets to favor one creditor over another. An avoidable preference is any payment on an existing debt that had been made by a bankrupt within ninety days before the bankrupt filed for bankruptcy, that was made while the soon-to-be bankrupt was in fact insolvent but that placed the creditor whom the soon-to-be bankrupt had paid in a better position than the creditor would have been if there had been no payment and the creditor had been paid only a share of the debt payable from the assets in liquidation. An avoidable preference is a preference because the debtor gave a preference, or a more lucrative deal to one creditor than to others, and it is avoidable because it can be overturned later in bankruptcy. On the bankruptcy trustee's proof of the avoidability of a transaction, the transaction is rescinded and the assets conveyed in it are returned from the creditor to whom it was paid, back into the corpus of the estate.

**Deprizio doctrine** A debtor's payments in the year before bankruptcy may be revoked. The Deprizio doctrine grants a trustee or debtor-in-possession the right to revoke a payment made to an outside creditor if the payment was made less than a year before the initial bankruptcy filing, if such revocation will benefit an inside creditor.

**suggestion of bankruptcy** A notice of bankruptcy filed in a pending civil suit. A suggestion of bankruptcy is a notice filed in an ongoing civil suit, usually a debt collection action that is stayed by filing of a petition in bankruptcy. The suggestion gives notice to the court and to the parties of the bankruptcy filing, as well as notice of the federal stay on the pending matters.

**trustee in bankruptcy (bankruptcy trustee)** An individual appointed by a judge to manage the bankrupt estate. A bankruptcy trustee is appointed by the bankruptcy judge to undertake certain duties in managing a bankrupt estate. A competent party with no interest in the estate of the bankrupt, or in a claimaint against the estate, or in a potential claimant of the estate, who has not served as an examiner of the estate may be appointed by the court as a bankruptcy trustee, unless the matter is one in which the United States Trustee must be appointed. A trustee may be appointed in a Chapter 11 case or Chapter 2 case and substitute for the debtor in possession as the party in any pending action, proceeding, or matter. The liquidation of an estate under Chapter 7 contemplates the appointment of a trustee.

A trustee is obligated to operate the estate so as to minimize losses, assert claims on the estate's behalf including the collection of accounts receivable and debts owed, including engaging in litigation to recover assets properly within the estate, whether those assets are in the possession of the bankrupt or another. The trustee must liquidate the assets of the estate as required by the court, and give periodic reports to the court or to creditors on the status of the estate and its liquidation. The bankruptcy trustee must evaluate claims against the estate and defend the estate against invalid claims. A trustee of an institution with medical patients is particularly obligated to ensure the health and care of those patients including their relocation if necessary.

The bankruptcy trustee represents the estate in the bankruptcy proceedings and may argue for or against various dispositions of the assets and various resolutions of the bankruptcy. The bankruptcy trustee is empowered to manage the estate's assets for the benefit of the bankrupt and the entire set of all creditors, and that management may not favor a single class of creditors.

# bar

**bar as lawyer's domain** An area for lawyers behind a physical barrier in the courtroom. The bar is the physical barrier separating the public from the officers of the court, including lawyers, clerks, bailiffs, and reporters. The area between the bar and the bench is the particular area for lawyers to stand and argue, although the convention in the United States is to allow parties to sit within the bar at counsel's table.

*See also:* lawyer.

**bar as prohibition** Any obstacle to the achievement of a given end. A bar, like a barrier, is a prohibition by law or equity of any action or conduct. A statute of limitations bars a late action at law (and laches bars a late action in equity), lack of sufficient age bars matrimony, public policy bars the enforcement of an unconscionable contract, and an easement may bar construction on property subject to a way.

**bar (the bar)** The whole body of lawyers. The bar is the aggregative term for all of the lawyers in a jurisdiction, or all of the lawyers there are. In these senses, it is often capitalized in order to distinguish it from other similar terms, such as that for a saloon. Used generically, the term does not indicate a bar association or its members, unless membership in such an association is a sine qua non for practice in that jurisdiction.

**admission to the bar** The requirements for a license to practice law in a jurisdiction. Admission to the bar is the process by which an individual is recognized as a lawyer entitled to practice law in a jurisdiction. Admission includes a series of steps required to become licensed to practice law, as required by the courts, the bar, and sometimes the legislature of each state. In most U.S. jurisdictions, these steps include completion of a law degree, proof of good moral character and fitness to practice law, passage of a bar examination, motion by an admitted member of the bar, and the taking of an oath. The requirements of licensure are intended to ensure the public is represented by competent and scrupulous attorneys. Admission is not required to practice law — an individual may act on his or her own behalf, including appearing in trial without counsel — but it is a requirement for a person to act as an attorney at law on behalf of another.

See also: oath, oath of attorney (attorney oath); degree, academic degree, law degree, juris doctor (J.D. or JD).

**admission by reciprocity**   Admission of an attorney from another jurisdiction by reciprocal arrangement. Admission by reciprocity allows admission of an attorney from one jurisdiction in another pursuant to an agreement between the bars of the two jurisdictions allowing members of the bar from each jurisdiction to be admitted to practice in the other jurisdiction without taking an additional bar exam. Admission by reciprocity usually requires proof of competency, residency, and admissibility of lawyers from the jurisdiction in the other jurisdiction. Most states also require an incoming attorney to reside in the new jurisdiction for a period of time.

See also: reciprocity (reciprocal).

**admission pro hac vice (admission pro hoc vice)**
Admission of a foreign attorney to be heard in one matter. Admission pro hac vice is the judicial allowance of an attorney, not licensed in a given jurisdiction, to represent a client in that jurisdiction in a particular case. Generally an attorney must be licensed in another jurisdiction and be associated with an attorney admitted to practice in the admitting jurisdiction. Local rules and judicial instruction may require more information, but admission usually requires a motion for admission, accompanied by a certificate of good standing from the bar of the attorney's usual state of practice. Most states limit the frequency an attorney may appear in the state pro hac, rather than becoming admitted in the state. The phrase is spelled now both "hac" and "hoc," owing apparently to the pronunciation of hac as near to hock, but hac is the customary and grammatically correct form. (Both hac and hoc are derived in Latin from hic; hac is the ablative, and hoc is the nominative or accusative.)

See also: pro, pro hac vice.

**bar exam (bar examination)**   A written test given to applicants to practice law. A bar examination is required to be admitted to practice law in almost every state. It is intended to test the knowledge of a candidate of the rules of law and the ability to apply those rules to specific situations in a professional and ethical manner. The exam is administered in each jurisdiction by state bar examiners, pursuant to the requirements established by the legislature, bar, or state supreme court. Different states test differently, and bar

exams often incorporate multiple choice and essay questions over various disciplines of the law, including general legal competency and professional responsibility. Scores on some multi-state exams administered by the National Conference of Bar Examiners — the Multistate Bar Exam (MBE), the Multistate Performance Test (MPT), the Multistate Essay Exam (MEE), and the Multistate Professional Responsibility Exam (MPRE) — may be incorporated into licensure and examination processes.

**character and fitness**   High ability and reliability required of a lawyer. Proof of good character and fitness to practice law is required of any applicant to be admitted to practice in most jurisdictions. This requirement is to protect both clients and the court from unscrupulous, unlearned, lazy, or foolish lawyers. As with other licensing criteria, a state's bar normally determines whether a person's character and fitness are sufficient for the practice of law. When making this determination, many criteria are evaluated, including the references of the candidate's teachers and employers, the candidate's credit history, police records, and personal history involving dishonest or otherwise bad acts. Generally, no single act prohibits a person from being admitted to the bar, but the dishonesty, illegality, frequency, number, and date of such acts may result in the rejection of an applicant as unfit.

**diploma privilege (diplomate privilege)**   Admission to the bar without examination. The diploma privilege is a statutory doctrine that allows graduates of accredited law schools to be admitted to a state's bar without the need for an examination. This doctrine has been largely abolished in the United States.

See also: privilege.

**Multistate Bar Examination (M.B.E. or MBE)**   A nationwide bar examination used in most states. The Multistate Bar Examination is, in 2011, an examination of 200 multiple-choice questions in contracts, torts, constitutional law, criminal law, evidence, and real property. The MBE is one of four multistate examinations created by the National Conference of Bar Examiners, and it is presently used in all American jurisdictions except for Louisiana, Washington, and Puerto Rico.

**Multistate Essay Exam (M.E.E. or MEE)**   A nationwide essay test incorporated in many bar examinations. The Multistate Essay Exam is, in 2011, a collection of thirty-minute essay questions arising from: Agency and Partnership, Commercial Paper (Negotiable Instruments), Conflict of Laws, Corporations and Limited Liability Companies, Decedent's Estates, Family Law, Federal Civil Procedure, Sales, Secured Transactions, and Trusts and Future Interests. It is required in slightly less than half of U.S. jurisdictions.

**Multistate Performance Test (M.P.T. or MPT)** A test in problem solving required in some bar examinations. The Multistate Performance Test is a problem–solving exercise created by the National Conference of Bar Examiners to assess a candidate's ability to assess facts from a realistic situation and apply legal materials to those facts, using careful reasoning. In 2011, a majority of U.S. jurisdictions required this test.

**Multistate Professional Responsibility Exam (M.P.R.E. or MPRE)** A nationwide examination of professional standards of attorney's conduct. The Multistate Professional Responsibility Exam, in 2011, comprised sixty multiple–choice questions given in a two–hour and five minute period, testing knowledge and understanding of the rules of ethics in the legal profession. It is required in nearly every jurisdiction.

**oath of attorney** *See:* oath, oath of attorney (attorney oath).

**state residence requirement** A requirement that a person reside in a state for a minimum time before admission to the bar. Residence for at least a brief time is required in some states to be admitted to practice. In 1985, the U.S. Supreme Court held that the vocation of law is necessary for the national economy and thus protected under the privileges and immunities clause, and a lengthy residence requirement unduly burdened this privilege. Requirements of three to six months' residence have been held constitutional when they relate to investigating an incoming attorney's character and fitness, but such requirements are becoming less common.

**bar card (attorney number or bar number)** A card issued by the bar identifying the bearer as an attorney. The bar card is a pocket–sized proof of an active license to practice law. The bar card usually displays the attorney's bar number (sometimes called an attorney number), which is required on pleadings in most jurisdictions.

**bar organization**

**American Bar Association (A.B.A. or ABA)** The leading national organization of attorneys in the United States. The American Bar Association is a voluntary association of lawyers in the United States and around the world, founded in 1878 to promote the development of the law and the Bar. In 2011, the ABA had over 400,000 members and was headquartered in Chicago, Illinois. The ABA is led by a president, board of governors, and house of delegates. The ABA is the agency that accredits law schools throughout the United States, and many jurisdictions admit to the bar only graduates from an ABA accredited law school. The ABA sponsors various philanthropic organizations, promulgates codes of professional conduct (many of which are adopted by state bars), opines on legal issues, and reviews judicial nominees. The ABA publishes the American Bar Association Journal monthly.

**American Bar Foundation (ABF)** A non–profit national interdisciplinary legal research institute. The American Bar Foundation was founded in 1952 as a research foundation to provide objective and empirical research from the various social sciences that would benefit lawyers, law professors, and other legal scholars.

**American College of Trial Lawyers (A.C.T.L. or ACTL)** Group of trial lawyers in United States and Canada. The American College of Trial Lawyers is a selective association of trial lawyers in the United States and Canada. Founded in 1950, the college is dedicated to maintaining and improving the standards of trial practice, the administration of justice and the ethics of the profession.

**American Inns of Court** Association of judges, lawyers, law students, and law professors. American Inns of Court is an association of local inns, each with judges and lawyers, and often with law teachers and students, which meet monthly to improve the skills, professionalism, and ethics of the bench and bar.

**American Law Institute** *See:* reform, law reform, American Law Institute (A.L.I. or ALI).

**American Trial Lawyers Association (A.T.L.A. or ATLA)** A professional organization of U.S. trial lawyers. The American Trial Lawyers Association is an organization of litigators representing civil plaintiffs and criminal defendants, its members being selected through special invitation. ATLA publishes The American Trial Lawyer.

**Association for American Justice (A.A.J. or AAJ or Association of Trial Lawyers of America or A.T.L.A. or ATLA)** A large professional organization of U.S. trial lawyers. The Association for American Justice is an organization of litigators, particularly concerned with the representation of plaintiffs in civil actions. In 2011, the AAJ, formerly the Association of Trial Lawyers of America, had over 50,000 members and published Trial magazine and the Law Reporter.

**Federal Bar Association (F.B.A. or FBA)** A private association of lawyers practicing in federal courts. The Federal Bar Association is the primary voluntary organization for private and governmental lawyers and judges practicing and sitting in federal courts within the United States. Founded in 1920, the FBA had 16,000 members and eighty chapters in 2011. The FBA lobbies Congress on behalf of judicial independence, better court conditions, and issues such as access to justice. The FBA publishes The Federal Lawyer.

**International Association of Defense Counsel (I.A.D.C. or IADC)** A professional organization of U.S. corporate and insurance defense lawyers. The International Association of Defense Counsel is an organization of corporate and insurance defense lawyers, its members being selected through special invitation. IADC publishes The Defense Counsel Journal.

**specialty bar associations**  Association of lawyers who specialize in a particular field of practice. A specialty bar is a voluntary association of lawyers who specialize in a particular field of law, such as the Association of Interstate Trucking Lawyers of America or the American Immigration Lawyers Association. As with bar associations in general, a specialty bar association engages in law reform, which may amount to lobbying, and promotes the interests of its member lawyers.

**state bar association**  Professional organization of attorneys in a given state. A state's bar or bar association is a professional organization comprising attorneys practicing in or associated with a single state. Some associations are integrated, in that licensure to practice law requires membership, and others are voluntary. State bar associations hold various events, fundraisers, continuing legal education courses, and networking opportunities for the attorneys within their specific state. State bar associations can also issue sanctions and suspend or take away an attorney's license due to misconduct.

**continuing legal education (C.L.E. or CLE)**  Courses for attorneys to maintain and increase professional competence. Continuing legal education is coursework intended for members of the practicing bar, which provides exposure to a nearly unlimited array of courses that are intended to improve the skill and professionalism of each member of the bar, including basic concepts of legal practice and substantive areas of practice; current developments in the law, including new rules, new laws, and current controversies in the law; practical advice on law-office management, client development, and professional management issues; the ethics of law and professional responsibility. Most states or bars require licensed attorneys to complete several courses of CLE each year as a condition of continued licensure.

**integrated bar (unified bar)**  A bar that all lawyers must join to be licensed to practice in a state. An integrated bar requires membership as a condition for the practice of law in its jurisdiction. A slight majority of states in the United States have integrated bars.

**Baraita'**  A teaching of early rabbis that is not in the Mishnah. The Baraita' are Jewish teachings of the Tannaim not integrated into the Mishnah; they are very influential sources of understanding in Jewish law.
*See also:* Torah, Mishneh Torah.

**bargain (bargaining)**  An agreement to exchange promises, goods, money, or conduct. A bargain is an exchange of goods, money, or services between two or more parties, in which each side receives value. A bargain is usually the result of negotiation, which may be presumed to have occurred from most exchanges, in that each party enters the exchange voluntarily accepting the value offered by the other party, even if the terms of the exchange are not subject to specific offers and counteroffers. A bargain is the first step of two in the making of a contract, the second being the expression of the bargain in words or conduct that render it enforceable as a matter of law. Though the two steps are often accomplished simultaneously, when they are distinct in time, it is quite possible for the bargain never to result in an agreement. The term bargain is also a synonym for the negotiations that lead to, or might lead to, such an exchange, and colloquially, a bargain refers to an acquisition at a particularly favorable price.

**bargain and sale deed**  *See:* deed, bargain and sale deed (bargain–and–sale deed).

**bargain test of consideration**  *See:* consideration, bargain test of consideration (bargain theory of consideration).

**bargaining impasse**  *See:* union, labor union, collective bargaining, bargaining impasse.

**bargaining order**  *See:* union, labor union, union organization, bargaining order.

**bargaining unit**  *See:* union, labor union, collective bargaining, bargaining unit.

**coordinated bargaining**  Collaboration of parties during a negotiation. Coordinated bargaining occurs when the negotiators share information and collaborate in reaching a deal; it does not imply that the negotiation is not conducted at arms' length, and it is presumptively lawful.

**good faith bargaining**  A genuine attempt to reach an agreement. Good faith bargaining involves two or more parties, all of whom are sincerely attempting to discuss their areas of conflict and determine methods by which those conflicts can be resolved. Bargaining in good faith is not required by law in every instance of negotiation, although it is required in most conditions subject to judicial or administrative oversight, such as bankruptcy and collective bargaining. Moreover, the entry of a party into bargaining that is not in good faith an attempt to reach a bargain may give rise to a claim of detrimental reliance or of fraud by the other party, akin to the civilian action for culpa in contrahendo.
*See also:* reliance, detrimental reliance; culpa, culpa in contrahendo (c in c).

**pattern bargaining**  Negotiating for terms from other agreements. Pattern bargaining uses other bargaining agreements from similar earlier negotiations as a template for present negotiation.

**surface bargaining (bad faith bargaining)**  Negotiating with a motive other than to reach an agreement. Surface bargaining occurs when a negotiator is acting for the sake of appearances rather than out of a good-faith intent to resolve differences and reach a deal.
*See also:* faith, bad faith (mala fides).

**barge**   A flat–bottomed boat used to transport goods. A barge is, most often, a flat–bottomed boat of around 195 feet long with a beam of 35 feet, particularly used to transport goods along rivers and canals. Barges may be self–propelled, although the great number are not and only move when pushed or towed. Barges are often assembled into "tows" of great extent, which are propelled and navigated by tugboats. There are other forms of vessels described by the term "barge," including an officers' boat carried on military vessels, and there are many forms of barge in the commercial sense, including lighters and scows, but most barges are defined by the cargo for which they are configured.

**baron**   A husband, a judge, or a noble. Baron is still seen in old cases to denote a husband, just as feme denoted a wife. In other contexts, the term baron may represent one of the Barons of the Exchequer, a judicial office that existed in Scotland until 1856 and in England until 1880, or it may represent a title of peerage in England or of nobility from a European state.

   **baron covert**   *See:* coverture (baron covert).

**barratry (barrator)**   Offense of encouraging litigation by others for one's own gain. Barratry is the crime of engendering civil litigation by enticing a person to bring a civil suit, if the barrator has no personal relationship to the action but will realize some gain through inducing the lawsuit. Individuals guilty of barratry can be punished for a misdemeanor; penalties include revoking licenses to practice law or another profession. Corporations are subject to a fine of not more than $10,000 and, if they are foreign, mandatory revocation of their authority to do business within the state. Any person who gives money or services to a barrator for committing barratry is also guilty of barratry. Thus, if a lawyer were to pay a fee to a runner or an ambulance chaser who recruits accident victims in an emergency room to sue the drivers who hit them, the runner would be a barrator, and both the runner and the lawyer would be guilty of barratry. Barratry in the federal courts is punished, though rarely. In some jurisdictions, barratry is of wider scope, including both bribery of a judge, the exploitation and sale of public offices, and other offenses to the administration of justice.
   *See also:* champerty (champertous); maintenance, maintenance in litigation.

**barrel**   A unit of measure for volume. The barrel is a unit of measure that varies according to the system of measure in which it is used. For oil as measured in the United States, a barrel is forty–two gallons. Barrels for wine and beer are smaller. The "steel barrel" of colloquial usage is a steel drum, usually of fifty–five gallons.

**barring of entail**   *See:* fee, estate in fee, fee tail, bar of entail (barring of entail).

**barrister**   *See:* lawyer, barrister.

**barter**   Payments made by trade. Barter is a transaction in which goods or services, instead of money, are traded as payment for other goods or services.
   *See also:* swap (swap agreement).

**base**

   **base estate**   *See:* tenure, feudal tenure, base estate (base fee).

   **base fee**   *See:* tenure, feudal tenure, base estate (base fee).

   **base pay**   *See:* pay, base pay.

   **base as inferior**   Lowly, or fundamental. Base, in the common law, is a description of a person, thing, or practice, to describe it as inferior in quality or significance. In older writings, when used to describe an estate in land, a base estate was the least important in the structure of estates, usually a serfdom. This sense is now less common, and care must be taken to distinguish this once–customary legal sense from some contemporary use in which base is confused with "basic" or fundamental, in which case the base estate would be the fee simple (which, of course, is a high estate). Thus base pay is a person's fundamental or essential pay, not counting bonuses, benefits, and the like. It might be quite superior pay but is fundamental.
   *See also:* pay, base pay.

**baseless objection or frivolous objection**   *See:* objection, vexatious objection (baseless objection or frivolous objection).

**basic good**   *See:* good, basic good (primary good or fundamental good).

**basic intent**   *See:* intent, general intent (basic intent).

**basic norm**   *See:* norm, basic norm (grundnorm).

**basis**   The value of an investment property. Basis is the value of a property, whether the value is used to determine equity or assets for the purpose of tax assessment or for use as collateral or sale. Basis also refers to the means by which the value is determined, according to its cost, or with adjustments for increases or decreases in value, or on some other basis.

   **adjusted cost basis (adjusted basis or adjusted bases)**   The full cost of an asset, including expenses and maintenance but reduced by subsidies. The adjusted cost basis for an asset is the amount of the original cost basis (including purchase price paid, taxes, transportation costs, and fees), which has been adjusted by the addition of the costs of improvements, fees, and expenses associated with the asset's maintenance and sale (including commissions and taxes the seller pays and transportation costs borne by the seller) and also adjusted by the reduction for subsidies or tax benefits, losses from theft or damage, losses from deprecation, amortization, or depletion, or other unusual losses to value.

**basis point (BP or BPS)** .01 percent. A basis point depicts numerical value of one one–hundredth (1/100) of one percent, or .0001 of the whole value. Basis points are used to denominate and calculate, among other things, interest rates, bond yields, and the future values of investment instruments.

**bastardy (bastard)** Illegitimacy of a child. Bastardy is an increasingly obsolete term for the condition of being conceived or born of parents who were not lawfully married at the time. Bastardy was once a limitation on a variety of legal powers, such as the power of a parent to recover for the wrongful death of a child. Such limitations are now subject to strict scrutiny under the Equal Protection Clause, and effectively, there is no difference under the law between an acknowledged child born out of wedlock and one within it. The term is abusive and is usually an insult when directed at a male.

**Bates numbering** *See:* numbering, Bates numbering.

**Bates stamp** *See:* stamp, Bates stamp; date, Bates stamp.

**BATNA** *See:* negotiation, best alternative to a negotiated agreement (BATNA).

**Batson challenge** *See:* jury, jury selection, juror challenge, peremptory challenge, Batson challenge (racial challenge or gender challenge or Batson motion).

**battel or judicial duel or trial by combat or wager of battle** *See:* trial, trial by battle (battel or judicial duel or trial by combat or wager of battle).

**battered woman syndrome** *See:* defense, self defense, battered–woman syndrome (battered woman syndrome).

**battery (batter)** To hit heavily or repeatedly. In general, to batter is to beat a person or an object, particularly to beat until great damage is done, the sense of battering.
*See also:* tort, dignitary tort; mayhem (maim).

**attempted battery** Conduct that would have been a battery had it not been thwarted. The crime of attempted battery is one in which there is no actual touching, just the intent and effort to do so. The punch swung or the pistol fired are attempted batteries if they miss the person at which they were aimed. Attempted battery is not in itself a tort, although it amounts to assault if, and only if, the intended victim becomes aware of the attack during the attempt and believes the battery will occur.

**battery as tort** Unconsented physical contact with the body of a person. Battery is the tort of intentionally touching another person without permission, causing either harm or offense. Touching in this sense may amount to a slight brush or a walloping punch, but

the defining element is that the touching is unwanted and either offensive or harmful.

*1. contact* Any contact, be its damage ever so slight, is sufficient to plead battery.

*2. indirect contact* Contact amounting to battery may be caused by the defendant. The requirements for a battery may be satisfied through indirect contact, as long as the defendant sets in motion the events that ultimately produce the end result of contact with the plaintiff. The limit to such indirect causation has long been debated, and it is treated, to an extent, as the limit of proximate cause.

*3. touching* Touching and contact with a person are synonymous.

*4. intentionality* Battery must be intentional. In determining whether a contact was intentional, the trier of fact must determine whether the defendant either had the purpose of causing the contact that occurred or had known with substantial certainty that some such contact would occur as a result of intended conduct. The intent requirement can therefore be satisfied by transferred intent, in which the defendant intended to cause a battery to one person but misses and harms another.

*5. offensiveness* The harm of a contact may be reasonable offense. The test for an offensive contact that is a battery is one of a reasonable person standard. Would a reasonable person, looking objectively at the contact, or in the same position as the plaintiff, be offended by the contact that had occurred? This test is designed so that the hypersensitive person who subjectively feels offended cannot then substantiate a claim for battery.

**criminal battery** Unlawful harm to the body of another person. Battery is the unlawful use of force against any part of the body of another person, which results in either injury or an offensive touching. The circumstances of the battery are significant in determining legislative designations of culpability. At common law the degree to which the battery represented a depraved impulse, and legislatively the role of the victim, increase the severity of the criminal offense.
*See also:* mayhem (maim).

**aggravated battery** A very serious battery. Aggravated battery is a battery of particular danger or harm to the victim or to society. A battery that results in particularly serious injury, or that employed a weapon (or instrument that could be used as a weapon), or that was brought against a person of special trust or dependence, may all be treated as aggravated batteries. Aggravated battery, in most jurisdictions, is either a misdemeanor or a felony depending upon the severity of injury, the official character of the victim, or other circumstances.

**simple battery** Unarmed but intentional infliction of mild bodily harm. Simple battery is the infliction of mild bodily harm without the aid of a dangerous weapon, with the specific intent to do so, and without the victim's willing consent. Battery, referred to alone, is usually meant as simple battery, though battery is in fact a larger category of offenses in most jurisdictions. Even so, in most jurisdictions, simple battery is usually a misdemeanor, though it may be charged as a felony if committed against an official, child, or other victim of a classification that is subject to greater than average protection under the statute.

**medical battery (healing arts battery)** An unconsented medical procedure. Medical battery is a physical contact with a patient by a medical care provider through a medical procedure, often surgery, that was not disclosed to and consented by the patient. Informed patient consent to a procedure is a defense to an action for harms resulting from its non-negligent performance.

**sexual battery (criminal sexual battery or CSC)** Non-consensual physical contact involving the sexual organs of either party. Sexual battery is a crime of non-consensual contact with the sexual organs of the victim or contact causing the victim to have such contact with the sexual organs of the perpetrator. The failure of consent may result from force, a threat of force, or an implied threat of force, or it may result from contact with a person underage or mentally infirm who cannot consent. Sexual battery is similar to rape, yet in most jurisdictions, battery requires only a touching and not proof of penetration.

**battle of the forms** *See:* acceptance, acceptance as acceptance of an offer, battle of the forms (U.C.C. battle of the forms or UCC battle of the forms).

**bawdy-house or bordello or house of ill fame or house of ill repute or house of prostitution** *See:* prostitution, brothel (bawdy-house or bordello or house of ill fame or house of ill repute or house of prostitution).

**Baxt (Bi-Baxt)** Fortune or fate. Baxt, encompassing the notions of luck or fate, most closely resembles the Americanized notion of Buddhist karma. The term usually refers to good luck or good karma while Bi-Baxt refers to bad luck or bad karma.

**bay** A large body of water with land on three sides. A bay is an area of a sea that reaches into the adjoining land with significant breadth and area to be thought larger than a mere cove or harbor. Bays present interesting questions of the maritime borders of the landward states, which often claim the whole bay as territorial sea. The basic principle is that a bay twenty-four miles or less across at its mouth is internal waters, but a larger body of water has international waters beyond the twelve-mile band of territorial sea that rings shores of the bay.

**be on the lookout** *See:* search, manhunt, be on the lookout (all-points bulletin or bolo or APB).

**bearer** The person in possession of a negotiable instrument or other thing. The bearer is the possessor, and the bearer of a negotiable instrument is entitled to payment on the instrument if the instrument is made payable to bearer, to the order of bearer, to cash, or if the instrument has no designated payee at all.
*See also:* instrument, negotiable instrument, order instrument (payable to order or pay to the order of).

**bearer bond** *See:* bond, bearer bond.

**bearer instrument** *See:* instrument, negotiable instrument, bearer instrument (payable to bearer).

**beauty pageant** A potential client's search for an attorney or law firm. The beauty pageant is but one of many ironic labels for the search process to find a new attorney or firm or other professional service. Large cases may provoke a litigant's hiring a law firm to hold the beauty pageant to hire additional law firms.

**Beck rights** *See:* union, labor union, union dues, Beck rights.

**begging the question or to beg the question** *See:* fallacy, petitio principii (begging the question or to beg the question).

**behavior** Manner and conduct. Behavior describes both the manner of activity in a relevant time and the general manner in which a person engages in private and public conduct.
*See also:* aberrance (aberrant behavior).

**bein adam la-chavero** *See:* ben adam la-havero (bein adam la-chavero).

**bein adam la-makom or adam la-makom** *See:* mitzvot bein adam la-makom (bein adam la-makom or adam la-makom).

**belief of impending death** *See:* hearsay, hearsay exception, exception only when declarant is unavailable, belief of impending death (dying declaration).

**bellum (bello)** War. Bellum is the state of war between two nations or states.
*See also:* status, status quo.

**below-the-line deduction** *See:* tax, tax deduction, itemized deduction (below-the-line deduction); tax, tax deduction, below-the-line deduction.

**ben adam la-havero (bein adam la-chavero)** Divine laws governing relations between one person and another. The ben adam l'chavero are commandments that apply between two people in Jewish law. Transliterated from the Hebrew for "between you and another person," the phrase is written variously in English, including bein Adam la havero.

**bench** The judge's seat, the judge, or the judiciary as a whole. The bench is the physical location of the judge in the courtroom and, by extension, the label for the power of a judge or the collective of the judiciary. Presumably, in the dawn of Norman English law, judges sat on a bench (or banc) so that more than one could be seated together in a tribunal. In short order, the bench represented a court with multiple judges, such as the Court of King's Bench, as opposed to courts with a sole judge. In time, the term has expanded to include not only the place of the judge in the physical courtroom but the office of a judgeship, and the judiciary as a whole. Indeed, in the contemporary U.S., the bench of a courtroom now refers not to the judges' chairs but to the judge's desk or desk and dias.

*See also:* court; warrant, bench warrant; trial, bench trial; opinion, judicial opinion, bench opinion.

**bench conference or side-bar or sidebar conference** *See:* trial, argument at trial, side bar (bench conference or side-bar or sidebar conference).

**bench memorandum** *See:* brief, bench memorandum (bench memo or bench brief).

**bench opinion** *See:* opinion, judicial opinion, bench opinion.

**bench trial** *See:* trial, bench trial.

**bench warrant** *See:* warrant, bench warrant.

**en banc (en banc sitting or sitting en banc)** The whole bench. En banc is law French persisting in English, which means literally before the bench. In early writing in French or incompletely translated from French, to be en banc is merely to be before a given court, such as King's Bench. In contemporary usage, the term implies not a bench alone but the whole bench.

Thus, today a hearing or action en banc is one heard by all of the judges of a given court. This implies a hearing only by those judges on active service in the court, and in a few courts, a review en banc may be held by a limited number of even those judges. In most instances a review en banc is taken of a decision rendered by a panel of judges drawn from a larger court, the whole of which hears the review.

**hot bench (cold bench or hot court or cold court)** A well-prepared judge who asks questions of the lawyers. The hot bench holds judges well-prepared on the issues and record before the court, who ask questions of the counsel before them in order to explore fully the issues and their implications for the law. A cold bench holds judges who are passive and listen through the lawyers' arguments without meaningful dialogue.

**benchmark tampering** *See:* survey, removal of survey mark (benchmark tampering).

**beneficial** *See:* benefit (beneficial).

**beneficial owner** *See:* ownership, beneficial ownership (beneficial owner).

**beneficial use** *See:* use, use of property, beneficial use.

**beneficiary** One who is entitled to a benefit. A beneficiary is anyone who is to receive a benefit from the actions of another person. Although there is an implication of gratuitousness in the concept of benefit, this is misleading, as the benefit is often the result of purchase, effort, or creation by the beneficiary, as when the settlor of a trust creates a trust of which the settlor is in fact the beneficiary.

*See also:* promisee.

**contingent beneficiary** A beneficiary whose benefit only vests upon a condition. A contingent beneficiary is any beneficiary whose benefit may only be received following the failure or satisfaction of a condition precedent that is inherent or expressed in the creation of the benefit. Contingent beneficiaries can be created in any circumstance in which there is a beneficiary, but they are usually created in a trust instrument or an insurance policy. The contingent beneficiary of a trust is treated in the same manner as the holder of a contingent remainder or an executory interest, in that the benefit only becomes vested if the condition is satisfied within a time frame that is usually fixed at the death of the settlor or a prior beneficiary. Yet the contingent beneficiary of an insurance policy is more akin to an alternate beneficiary, and that benefit vests when the prior beneficiary dies or is unable to receive the benefit, even if this occurs after the assured's death.

**insurance beneficiary** A third party who receives the proceeds of an insurance policy. A beneficiary is a person selected by an insured whom the insurance company pays on a claim, rather than paying the insured. This is particularly necessary for life insurance, for which payments are made to beneficiaries designated by the insured while alive.

**residuary beneficiary (residual beneficiary)** Recipient of a trust interests left over after other gifts. A residuary beneficiary receives what interests remain in a trust after the specific and general grants of benefit have been allocated, if any remain unallocated. A residuary beneficiary is, relative to a trust, in a similar position to the residuary legatee in a will. Perhaps because residuary beneficiary seems to combine elements of a testamentary beneficiary and residuary legatee, lawyers and judges will use these terms interchangeably, even though the residuary legatee, properly so called, is not a recipient of a direct legal interest under a will but receives an equitable interest in the benefit.

**testamentary beneficiary** Person or entity receiving a gift via a will. A beneficiary is a human being or entity named in a will to receive an interest from the decedent's estate.

**third-party beneficiary** One who derives a benefit from another's contract. A third-party beneficiary of a contract receives a benefit by agreement of the parties to the contract, even though the third-party beneficiary is not a party. A contract may be created for the purpose of benefiting the third-party beneficiary, or the benefit may be ancillary to a different contractual purpose. Generally, a third-party beneficiary has the same rights to enforce the contract as would the principal contracting parties, although not the same responsibilities: though a third-party beneficiary may sue for breach of contract, the third-party beneficiary cannot breach the contract.

**trust beneficiary**   The recipient of the benefits of a trust. A beneficiary is a person or entity for whose benefit the trustee owns and manages the assets of the trust. A beneficiary may not also be a trustee, although a settlor may create a trust of which the settlor is a beneficiary.

**benefit (beneficial)**   A gain in property, profit, opportunity, or interest. A benefit is any good thing that results from any activity, such as the benefit of the bargain. A benefit is often compared to a burden, particularly as the benefit is one that is conferred by law, as in the taking of private property for public use, in which case the public use is a public benefit. Administrative and statutory analyses have adopted a utiliarian approach to the examination of the validity of laws that burden interests protected by law, which is to ensure that the burdens are clearly outweighed by public benefits.
*See also:*  balance, balancing test; burden.

**benefit of clergy**   *See:*  clergy, benefit of clergy.

**benefit of the bargain damages**   *See:*  damages, contract damages, expectation damages (benefit of the bargain damages); damages, contract damages, benefit of the bargain damages (benefit-of-the-bargain).

**benefit of the covenant**   *See:*  covenant, real covenant, benefit of the covenant.

**benefit of the easement**   *See:*  easement, benefit of the easement.

**accrued benefit**   Retirement funds to which an employee has become entitled. Accrued benefits are an account payable at the time of retirement, funded to the level accrued during employment. The most common accrued benefits are paid into pension plans and 401(k) accounts.

**death benefit (death benefits)**   Payment made to a survivor on the death of a worker or insured. A death benefit is a payment made to surviving spouses and children following the death of a member of certain benefit plans, such as Social Security, the Longshore Harborworkers Compensation Act, and state workers' compensation programs. Death benefits also describe the insurance benefit established by a life insurance policy, under which any beneficiary may be designated in the policy, without regard to family relationship, although private insurance benefits may or may not be intended to be included in the term when it is used in contracts or statutes.

**employee benefit**   *See:*  employment, employee benefit plan.

**retention of benefits**   Keeping a benefit from a contract that is not performed. Retention of benefits under a contract occurs where one party keeps a contractual benefit received from the other while not performing its side of the bargain.

  *equitable estoppel*   One who retains the benefit is estopped from denying the contract. Equitable estoppel of the denial of a benefit retention requires that a party who has accepted some of the benefits of a contract must admit to the existence of the contract and is barred from acts inconsistent with its terms.
*See also:*  estoppel, equitable estoppel.

**benefit-of-the-bargain**   *See:*  damages, contract damages, benefit of the bargain damages (benefit-of-the-bargain).

**benign discrimination**   *See:*  discrimination, racial discrimination, benign discrimination (benign use of racial classifications).

**bent (bent of mind)**   Corrupt. Bent has a host of meanings in general, most of which are derived from its core meaning as having an angle, such something straight being altered into an angle or a person leaning from the waist. In law, a person's bent, or bent of mind, is a proclivity, aptitude, interest, or intent in moving toward a given goal. Note: in England, to describe a person as bent is to suggest the person is corrupt, particularly that the person takes bribes for official favors; it may also describe a person's sexual interests.

**bequest (bequeath)**   A testamentary gift. A bequest is any testamentary gift of personal property. The distinction among bequest, legacy, and devise has, however, been greatly weakened in the twentieth century. In the common law, a bequest was personal property, and the word bequest was used in describing the gift given and legacy of the gift received. In neither case was real property given, which was described as a devise. Contemporary legislation has tended to follow the lead of the model uniform statutes in employing devise for both real and personal testamentary gifts.

**demonstrative bequest**   A testamentary gift of a certain amount of money, for services or from a specific fund. A demonstrative bequest is a testamentary gift of a designated amount of money to a particular legatee. Although some jurisdictions require that the testator specify in the will a given account, or source, or asset from which a demonstrative bequest must be paid, other courts have ignored this requirement when there is evidence that the bequest is intended as a post-mortem payment for services provided to the testator. Demonstrative gifts are protected from ademption in the same degree as specific legacies.

**general bequest**   A gift from general estate funds and assets. A general bequest is a testamentary gift of a share or interest in an estate of of a specified, monetary amount to be paid out of an estate's general funds. The defining feature of the general bequest is that the bequest is general and not of a discrete and described asset or specific unit of property to be given to the legatee.

**lapsed bequest (lapsed legacy or lapse of devise or lapse of legacy)** Testamentary gift to someone who predeceases the testator. A lapsed bequest, lapsed devise, or lapsed legacy, is a grant in a will to a recipient who dies before the testator. When such a gift lapses, the well written testament will provide for an alternative devisee or alternative legatee, or provide further instructions. In the absence of any such evidence of the testator's intent, the common law would void the gift, although most states have now passed an anti-lapse statute. The result is a variety of possible outcomes. In some jurisdictions the property will pass to the estate of the deceased, and then be treated in the estate of the grantee either as an inheritance subject to the rules for intestacy or as an after-acquired asset to be distributed according to the recipient's will, according to the law of the jurisdiction. In others, the devise or legacy is void and considered an asset of the testator, to be treated either as an inheritance subject to the rules for intestacy or as an after-acquired asset to be distributed according to the recipient's will, according to the law of the jurisdiction.

*See also:* legacy, void legacy.

**specific bequest (specific legacy or special legacy)** Gift of a particular chattel that is designated in the will to a specific legatee. A specific bequest is specific when the recipient is clearly identified by name and the portion or asset of the estate to be received is also clearly identified. Specific bequests are commonly used to distribute specific chattels — especially heirlooms — to specific individuals identified by the testator.

*See also:* legatee, specific legatee; special.

**Bernstein letter** *See:* state, act of state doctrine, Bernstein letter.

**Berry rule** *See:* criminal, criminal appeal, Berry rule.

**best alternative to a negotiated agreement** *See:* negotiation, best alternative to a negotiated agreement (BATNA).

**best cost avoider** *See:* cost, best cost avoider (most efficient cost avoider).

**best efforts** *See:* performance, contract performance, best efforts.

**best interests of the child** *See:* child, child custody, best interests of the child.

**best price rule** *See:* takeover, tender offer, best price rule.

**best-evidence rule** *See:* evidence, documentary evidence, best-evidence rule.

**bestiality** Any sexual act between a person and an animal. Bestiality is any sexual conduct performed by a person with a non-human animal. Bestiality is a crime in most U.S. jurisdictions, defined within sodomy or related statutes. Many jurisdictions include bestiality among images that are defined as obsenity. Bestiality charges are most likely to arise as components of a complaint in divorce proceedings.

*See also:* buggery (bugger or buggerer); sodomy (sodomize or sodomite).

**bestowal (bestow)** To give a benefit, power, or authority. Bestowal is a rather poetic term depicting the grant of an authority, benefit, or power, usually with some implied obligations or limitations. To bestow can, however, describe the simple act of giving a gift.

**bet (betting or bettor or numbers)** Entry of a wager. To bet is to place a wager, or to place a stake of some property in a game of chance or a prediction of an outcome. Many bets are placed legally. In many instances, however, placing a bet is illegal, either because it is placed in a jurisdiction in which gambling is a criminal act or because it is placed in a jurisdiction in which it is allowed but not placed through an authorized and regulated service. Betting by players of sports in a game they will play is universally prohibited by both sports contracts and state laws.

*See also:* gaming (gambling or gamble); wager.

**bet din (beth din)** A rabbinic court. The bet din is an ecclesiastical tribunal judged by rabbis.

**beta coefficient** *See:* risk, beta coefficient.

**betterment (betterments)** A permanent improvement. A betterment is a permanent improvement to realty, particularly the construction of a building or an increase in the size of an existing structure. Betterments are a more narrow category of improvements, because improvements may be of temporary benefit and need not increase the value of the property. A betterment, however, must be more than routine repair of customary maintenance and must add value to the property.

*See also:* repair, repairs (subsequent remedial measure).

**beyond a reasonable doubt** *See:* proof, burden of proof, beyond a reasonable doubt (proof beyond a reasonable doubt).

**beyond cavil** *See:* cavil (beyond cavil).

**Bi-Baxt** *See:* Baxt (Bi-Baxt).

**bias** Preference before analysis that sways personal judgment. Bias is any degree of prejudgment or reliance on prior assumptions in examining evidence or making a decision. Bias may arise from broad prejudices or stereotypes, and the courts have recognized particular dangers from laws influenced by bias by demanding more justification of laws that reflect old biases, which is strict scrutiny of laws burdening a suspect class. Even so, countless forms of dangerous bias persist in law, such as racial profiling. Yet all forms of presumption are also forms of bias: A presumption in favor of finding acts by an administrative agency to be lawful may be in error in a given case as might any other decision influenced by bias rather than evidence alone.

*See also:* justice; prejudice.

**pecuniary bias**  A prejudice in favor of one's financial interests. Pecuniary bias describes a conflict of interest arising from investments, employment, or financial opportunities that favor one party or cause in a proceeding. Pecuniary bias might be direct, such as a suit against one's employer, or indirect, such as a hope to write a book that would sell better given a particularly dramatic outcome in a case.

**bicameral legislature**  *See:* legislature, bicameral legislature (bicameralism).

**bid (bidder)**  An offer to enter a contract, especially in a competition or open market. A bid is an offer made by a bidder in a setting in which the offer is compared to other offers, particularly in an auction, a contract up for bids, or a publicly traded market. Differing rules govern each setting to determine the rights of a bidder. In the case of a public auction without reserve, the bid may be seen as a contingent acceptance of an open offer. In the case of a contract up for bids, the form of invitation to bid will usually reserve the right to accept no bids, which may be implied in any event. In the case of a publicly traded market, a bid is made to the world and may be accepted by anyone in the market.

*See also:* auction; offer, contract offer; bid, auction bid; bid, auction bid; bid, auction bid.

**auction bid**  An offer to purchase made in an auction. A bid is a bidder's commitment to pay a specific price for the thing on offer in an auction. The effect of a bid as a predicate to a contract varies according to the form of auction. In an absolute auction or auction without reserve, the opening of bids is an offer and each bid is an acceptance contingent upon remaining the highest bid, becoming binding upon the hammer, or close of bidding. In an auction with reserve, the auctioneer or owner reserves the right not to conclude the sale unless specified conditions are met, which is usually a minimum upset price or reserve price but which also may be qualifications of bidders or of other aspects of the bid. A bid is then an offer, which is accepted at the fall of the hammer or close of the auction. In either case, the bid is considered withdrawn either when a higher bid is placed or if the bidder acts to withdraw it before the hammer by means in accord with the auction's rules.

**bid solicitation (invitation to bid or request for proposals or RFP)**  A call for submission of offers to enter into a contract. A bid solicitation is issued by an entity that seeks to enter a contract to sell or purchase goods or services and invites potential contractors to bid on the contract or to propose an offer to sell, purchase, or perform. The invitation or request may be quite detailed in the conditions that must be met by a bidder or proposer, and it may require a test for qualification to enter a bid or proposal. Neither the solicitation nor the bid creates a contract, although the bidder may be held to the terms of a bid if the bid is accepted without having been validly withdrawn prior to acceptance.

**contractor bid (contractor)**  An offer to perform construction at a price certain. A contractor's bid is an offer to perform work that has been advertised for bids. The contractor's bid is subject to review and comparison to other bids not only for price but for the details of the work to be performed, the time of its completion, the contractor's experience and reputation. The bid does not create the contract, although the contracting bidder may be held to the terms of the bid if the bid is accepted.

**firm bid**  An offer that is an unusually reliable offer or is temporarily irrevocable. A firm bid is a bid of particular reliability in its price offered and in the bidder's willingness to perform the contract if accepted. In securities, it is an offer to purchase or sell a security at the market amount that prevails at the moment of acceptance. As a contractor's bid, the firm bid is an offer that is unambiguous, ascertainable, definite, and with a price computable on its face. A bid for work or a sale made according to bidding under the "firm bid rule" is akin to a firm offer, a bid that becomes irrevocable for a stated period of time, while the bid is being entertained and compared with other bids.

**open bid**  A bid that may be lowered before acceptance. Open bids are bids that are subject to revision prior to acceptance or the close of a contract bidding period. Governments and general contractors often rely upon open bids to find suppliers for various goods and services. In an open bid, the customer invites any and all suppliers of the desired goods and services to submit a quotation based upon specifications put forward by the customer. The bid may be modified or revoked any time prior to the close of the bidding period, when the customer accepts the lowest qualified bid. The open-bid system or process is therefore public among the bidders, as opposed to a closed-bid or sealed-bid system, in which the bids of each bidder are kept secret from other bidders.

**sealed bid (sealed-bid process or sealed-bid system or closed bid or closed-bid process)**  An unalterable offer that is kept secret from other bidders. In a sealed-bid process, the customer invites any and all parties to submit a confidential bid. The bid is then irrevocable and unalterable, and the details of the bid remain unknown until after the close of the bidding period. The customer, then, unseals and opens all the bids simultaneously, accepting the lowest qualified bid.

**Bid'ah**   Acts meant in worship that depart from approved precedent. Bid'ah refers to innovations in matters of faith and worship, a problematic concept because the practice of forms of worship not explicitly sanctioned by Muhammad is unorthodox. Bid'ah is thus a contentious term. Bid'ah in 'Ibadaat or acts of worship is haram in Islam, which accepts a view that Allah completed his religion in Islam, and no new form of worship is necessary. Sectarian groups will often accuse rivals of Bid'ah as a means to show the superiority of their point of view, and the criminality of the opponents' point of view.

**bien-fonds**   Real estate. Bien-fonds is French, in the old code meaning real estate. Note: the term bien fonde is used for well founded, in the sense of a decision that is well reasoned from the law.

**biennial**   At intervals of two years. A biennial event occurs every other year. A biennial legislature meets every two years. Elections for the U.S. House of Representatives are biennial.

**bifurcated trial**   See: trial, bifurcated trial (bifurcation or bifurcate or bifurcated).

**big board**   See: security, securities, securities exchange, big board.

**bigamy**   See: marriage, polygamy, bigamy (bigamous).

**bilateral act**   See: act, bilateral act.

**bilateral contract**   See: contract, specific contracts, bilateral contract.

**bill**   A formal writing. A bill is a medieval term for a writing of a formal or public character, and in that sense it persists in many legal phrases. It is apparently a corruption based on the pronunciation of the Latin "bulla," for an amulet that became a seal, and thus referred to any writing that was worthy of a seal, and on the French "bille" for list, evolving not only into bull as in Papal Bull but into bill as in Bill of Rights, bill in chancery, the legislative bill, and the bill on account.
   See also: legislation, bill, senate bill (S.B. or SB); legislation, bill, markup of a bill; legislation, bill, house bill (H.B. or HB).

**bill of attainder**   See: attainder, bill of attainder.

**Bill of Attainder clauses**   See: constitution, U.S. Constitution, clauses, Bill of Attainder clauses.

**bill of certiorari**   See: certiorari, bill of certiorari (writ of certiorari in equity).

**bill of credit**   Money based on the general credit of the state. Bills of Credit, promissory notes intended for exchange in the same way as money, are forbidden to states under Article I, Section 10 of the U.S. Constitution.

**bill of discovery**   See: discovery, bill of discovery.

**bill of indictment**   See: indictment, bill of indictment.

**bill of particulars**   See: indictment, bill of particulars.

**bill quia timet or writ quia timet**   See: quia, quia timet (bill quia timet or writ quia timet).

**bill as legislation**   A draft law. A bill is a writing by a member or a committee submitted for consideration by a legislature, and then to the executive for approval to become law.
   See also: attainder, bill of attainder; legislation, bill, senate bill (S.B. or SB); legislation, omnibus legislation (omnibus bill).

   **engrossed bill**   A bill that has passed one house of a legislature. An engrossed bill is printed in the form by which it finally passes one house of a legislature and is presented to the other house for consideration.
      See also: engrossment (engross or engrossed or ingross or ingrossed or ingrossment or blue-backed).

   **enrolled bill**   A bill that has been passed by both houses of a legislature. An enrolled bill is a bill that has passed the legislature and is printed in its final form in which it is to be presented to the chief executive for signature. If signed, the bill will become law with the language in which it is enrolled.
      See also: presentment.

   **revenue bill**   Legislation that levies taxes or fees as revenue. A revenue bill has the purpose of raising revenues for the government and creates or raises a tax in order to do so. Under the Origination Clause of the U.S. Constitution, all revenue bills must be first passed by the House of Representatives.

**bill as obligation of debt**   Representation of debt owed to the sender. A bill is a written statement of a debt that is owing, although the term also refers to the underlying debt itself. Usually, the bill lists the amount to be paid and the entity to which it must be paid. Some bills contain other information, such as how the obligation was incurred and who is responsible for payment. Initially, the bill was either issued or, more commonly, signed or initialed by the debtor, but this practice is now rare.

**bill as pleading**   Initial pleading in a court of equity. The bill in equity is the initial pleading in chancery practice. In the federal courts and most state courts, the bill in equity has been supplanted by use of a complaint that puts the party on notice of the facts underlying the general cause. In those jurisdictions that persist in relying on the bill of equity, a bill is a complaint in writing addressed to the chancellor, containing the names of the parties to the suit, both complainant and defendant, a statement of the facts on which the complainant relies, and the allegation which he makes, with an averment that the acts that the party has complained of are contrary to equity, and a prayer for relief and proper process.

*See also:* quia, quia timet (bill quia timet or writ quia timet); certiorari, bill of certiorari (writ of certiorari in equity); discovery, bill of discovery.

**bill of exchange** A document that can be exchanged for money. A bill of exchange is an instrument that purports to stand in lieu of payment by directing a third party to issue actual payment upon receipt of the bill. Though the term is now relegated to certain legal technicalities and antiquated case law, the bill of exchange has largely been superseded by the draft, particularly the check, and by statements of accounts payable.
*See also:* instrument, negotiable instrument.

**bill of lading (b/l)** An instrument by a carrier acknowledging the possession of goods and terms of transport. A bill of lading is a written instrument signed by a carrier or an agent, such as a truck driver or ship's master, that inventories goods received for transport and states the terms under which they are shipped, usually including their destination and estimated time of delivery to a stated recipient or place. The bill of lading is assignable and, in a form that is slightly analogous to title, the bill represents an ownership interest in the goods, which is held by the possessor of the bill.

**COGSA provision (paramount provision)** Any clause in the bill of lading implied or required by the Carriage of Goods by Sea Act. COGSA provisions are implied in every bill of lading under the Carriage of Goods by Sea Act, 46 U.S.C. § 1304, unless the shipper and carrier expressly contract the provisions away.

**Pomerene bill of lading** A bill of lading negotiable in several jurisdictions. A Pomerene bill of lading is a bill of lading that satisfies the Pomerene Act, 49 U.S.C. § 80101, which applies to bills of lading issued by common carriers for the transport of goods within Washington, D.C., within U.S. territories, within states (even if transported through another state or a foreign country), and from a U.S. state to a foreign country. The act indicates the requirements which must be met for a bill of lading to be negotiable.

**bill of rights** *See:* right, bill of rights; constitution, U.S. Constitution.

**Bill of Rights of 1689** *See:* rights, bill of rights, English Bill of Rights (Bill of Rights of 1689).

**bill of sale** A document listing goods or services sold from one party to another. A bill of sale is a document listing the goods or services sold from a seller to a purchaser and the consideration paid, and to be executed it must bear the signatures of the seller and the purchaser, which are usually witnessed by a notary public. The bill of sale acts as a writing to satisfy the Statute of Frauds, as a proof of transfer of ownership, and as a security in the property tranfered.

**billa vera or no bill or no true bill or not found or ignoramus** *See:* indictment, true bill indictment (billa vera or no bill or no true bill or not found or ignoramus).

**billable hour** *See:* fee, fee for services, attorney's fee, billable hour (billable time or billables or hourly fee).

**billing error** *See:* credit, consumer credit, billing error.

**billion gallons per day** *See:* gallon, million gallons per day, billion gallons per day (M.G.D. or MGD, B.G.D. or BGD).

**bind (binding or bound)** To become obligated under the law. To be bound is to be subject to an obligation that is enforceable in law or in equity. A binding contract is therefore an enforceable contract, and a trustee who is bound by the trust instrument must follow its dictates or be held to account in a court of equity. Bind and being bound were once reserved for more serious contracts, such as those made by indenture, and these terms are usually invoked with a sense of moral significance beyond the legal notion of enforceability.
*See also:* obligation (oblige or obligator or obligee or obligor); effect (effective).

**binder policy** *See:* insurance, insurance policy, binder policy.

**binding precedent** *See:* precedent, binding precedent.

**binding promise** *See:* promise, binding promise.

**bound over (bind over or bound over)** Judicial commitment of a person to appear at a hearing or trial. To bind a person is to commit that person to do something, and in the case of binding someone to a hearing or a trial, it is to order that person to appear at the place and time indicated. A person bound over for trial may be held in custody, may be released on bail or bond, or may be released on personal recognizance. A defendant is usually bound over for trial at a preliminary hearing, and the commitment to appear must be on the specific charges upon which the defendant is to be tried.

**biodegradability (biodegradable)** The degree and speed with which a chemical or object will decompose into its elements. Biodegradability is the speed and manner in which an object or chemical decomposes, or degrades into its component substances, particularly inert matter. Biodegradability is a debatable term, sometimes used in marketing products to make them appear environmentally safe, though such claims ignore the long time required for genuine biodegredation.

**biodiversity** The variety of plants and animals in an ecosystem or biosphere. Biodiversity is the variety of different species found in a given area, which is a measure of the status of an ecosystem. Biodiversity is essential for a variety of functions in a given system, not the least being the ability of plant and animal species to respond to changes in the environment.

**biological father** *See:* family, father, natural father (biological father).

**biosolid** Fertilizer produced from sewerage sludge. Biosolids are waste organics and sediment that are a product of waste water treatment and may be applied to land as fertilizer, or stored in landfills. If too much is land-applied, the runoff can create non-point source pollution in streams, lakes, and oceans.

**biotechnology** Altering the chemical or biological structures of animals or plants. Biotechnology is the direct alteration of the chemical or biological constituents of a plant or animal in order to alter its characteristics. Biotechnology includes genetic engineering as well as the use of proteins, enzymes, and chemicals to alter the processes of the animal or plant, to create characteristics that are economically beneficial. Biotechnology also includes more conventional techniques, such as selective breeding, cross-pollination, and hybridization. Modern techniques now enable scientists to move genes (and therefore desirable traits) in ways they could not before — and with greater ease and precision.

*See also:* gene, genetically modified organism (living modified organism or G.M.O. or GMO or L.M.O. or LMO); technology.

    **stem cell** Generic, immature cells that may grow into any form of cell in the human body. Stem cells may turn into any given specialized cell of the many different cell types in the body, such as a muscle cell, a red blood cell, or a brain cell. They appear to repair various systems in the body, and they can theoretically divide without limit, to replenish other cells as long as the person or animal lives; stem cells present significant potential for new medical therapies. Although the technology of stem-cell research is rapidly changing with new research, stem cells are currently derived from bone marrow, embryos, or biomatter generated at birth. The use of embryonic stem cells is a matter of great controversy because of the relationship to abortion.

**birth** The independence of a newborn from a mother. Birth is production of a living baby from a pregnant mother. Although all animals give birth, the term is particularly used for the live birth of mammals, especially humans. Birth may be by unassisted (or natural) or assisted, by such means as Caesarean section or induced labor. Birth is considered to be accomplished once the child is alive and fully outside the mother's body, whether or not the umbilical cord remains attached. At common law, the intentional causing of death to a foetus or unborn child was not murder until the moment of birth. Some jurisdictions have instituted various statutory offenses of foeticide and fetal injury.

*See also:* life; fetus, feticide (foeticide).

**assisted birth** Birth with the aid of drugs or medical procedures. Assisted birth is a birth with any assistance to the birth through the use of artificial manipulation, drugs, or medical procedures, including Caesarean section and induced labor.

**birth control** *See:* family, family planning, birth control.

**birth defect** A medical abnormality present at birth. Birth defects are abnormalities that occur to newborn babies, and can be of a physical or mental nature. While such defects can occur through natural processes, such as hereditary reasons or complications arising from pregnancy, they can also occur through artificial means, such as exposure to environmental agents or toxic substances during pregnancy or complications during delivery and birth.

**Caesarean section (C-section)** Birth through surgery. A Caesarean section is the surgical removal of a baby through the mother's abdominal wall rather than natural force through the birth canal. Although the process is ancient, this complicated procedure will usually be performed only if the health of the mother or child requires it. There is now no difference in the law between a birth by Caeserean section and a birth through any other means.

*See also:* birth.

**gestation period** The period of time for a pregnancy. A gestation period is the length of time required for a fetus to grow from zygote to delivery, in a human mother, or in any other animal that reproduces through live birth. The gestation period for humans is, of course, roughly nine months. As a general rule among mammals, the smaller the animal the shorter the gestation period, though marsupials have an even shorter period owing to their additional care of their young. A whale may require nearly two years, while an opossum needs less than two weeks.

**wrongful birth (wrongful life)** Medical malpractice claim related to a child's birth. Wrongful birth actions are usually actions by a child's parents against doctors or hospitals for medical malpractice, either for a medical error in procedures that resulted in the birth (such as a negligent sterilization) and which resulted in birth defects in their child (such as an improper delivery), or for a failure to provide accurate information that the parents would have relied on to abort the pregnancy to avoid the birth of a disabled child (such as failing to inform the parents of the presence of Down syndrome). These three theories have been allowed in most jurisdictions, although statutes in some states have limited recoveries to the costs of medical care, pain and suffering, and the additional costs of care for an impaired child.

*See also:* pregnancy, wrongful pregnancy (wrongful conception).

**bite (biter)** An assault employing the assailant's teeth. A bite is an assault by a person or an animal, in which the assailant strikes the victim with the assailant's teeth or, in the case of animals without teeth, fangs, jaws, or mandibles. The teeth need not be the living natural teeth of the assailant, but the teeth must be in the assailant's mouth at the time. Bite marks or wounds are often used as evidence of an assault, not only providing identification of the biter but also evidence from location and degree of severity as a tool for determining the relevant events. An expert in bite-mark evidence is a forensic odontologist.

**Bivens action**   *See:* civil rights, civil rights enforcement action, Bivens action.

**black ball**   *See:* ballot, black ball.

**black letter law**   *See:* law, black letter law (blackletter law or hornbook law).

**black market**   *See:* market, black market (underground economy or underground market).

**black or Afro-American or Negro**   *See:* race, race as social category, African American (black or Afro-American or Negro).

**black-robe disease**   *See:* judge, black-robe disease.

**Blackacre (Whiteacre or Redacre or Greenacre)** A hypothetical parcel of land. Blackacre is a generic parcel of land. It has been bought, sold, devised, subdivided, zoned, condemned, leased, developed, prescribed, and ransomed for centuries in law schools. It is still used in legal writing, particularly in judicial opinions and treatises, to describe any generic land. When a hypothetical requires additional, separate parcels, as when an easement might be appurtenant, custom decrees the use of other colors — Whiteacre, Redacre, Greenacre, and Blueacre being popular.
   *See also:* title, root of title.

**blacklist (blacklisting or enemies list)**   A list of people who are condemned for real or imagined transgressions. A blacklist is both a list and a process of denunciation of individuals or activities for some offense against the presumed order. Blacklists of union members, especially organizers and strikers, were popular among union-busting companies in the nineteenth century. Blacklists of communists were compiled by federal and state agencies in the 1940s and 1950s, and do-not-fly lists in the 2000s have been characterized as blacklists.
   *See also:* ballot, black ball.

**blackmail**   *See:* extortion, blackmail (criminal coercion).

**blank**   *See:* form, blank.

**blanket bond**   *See:* bond, fidelity bond (blanket bond).

**blanket insurance**   *See:* insurance, category of insurance, property insurance, blanket insurance (blanket policy).

**blasphemy (blaspheme or blasphemous)**   The mockery of God or a religious obligation. Blasphemy in U.S. criminal law was the crime of speech knowingly considered offensive to God, Jesus Christ, or the Holy Spirit, or otherwise speech condemned under the dictates of the Christian faith. The various justifications for the crime included, initially, its religious prohibition and then, later, that blasphemy was a willful attempt to lessen the confidence of others in a divine being. Statutes enshrining this crime have been struck down as violations of the Establishment Clause of the First Amendment and of state constitutions, although they remain on the statute books. Blasphemy by various labels remains an offense in most systems of religious law. Further, blasphemous speech may be considered offensive so as to amount to fighting words or, when not directed at a public figure, profanity or obscenity.

**blight**   A widespread disease or cause that destroys crops. Blight is both a particular class of pathogenic infections of crops that cause browning and death and a description of any condition that leads a crop to fail, and metaphorically, any cause of ruin or decay.

**urban blight**   Economically depressed and physically substandard areas of urban housing. Urban blight describes areas of cities that suffer from the decay of buildings, low levels of employment and economic opportunity, and a high rate of crime. It is characterized by property abandonment, high crime, disproportionate amounts of people below the poverty line, and otherwise unaesthetically pleasing landscape. A designation of an area as blighted by a municipal zoning or planning agency will justify the use of eminent domain to foster redevelopment. There have been criticisms of such urban redevelopment plans as being insensitive to local culture, overly favorable to corporate industry, and contrary to property rights, notwithstanding that cities have used such plans to replace crack houses with new housing, parks, and shopping areas.

**blindness (blind)**   The physical inability to see. A blind person cannot see better than 20/200 through either eye, while wearing eyeglasses. The designation of 20/200 under the Snellen scale means that a person twenty feet from a series of letters cannot read them unless they are the size that a person with normal eyesight could read at a distance of two hundred feet. Blindness is a basis for relief through Social Security, and it is a disability that requires accommodation in qualified employment under the Americans with Disability Act and many state laws.

**blind pig**   *See:* pig, blind pig, blind pig as bar; pig, blind pig (blind hog).

**blind pig as bar**   *See:* pig, blind pig, blind pig as bar.

**blind plea**   *See:* plea, criminal plea, blind plea (plead blind).

**blind trust**   *See:* trust, blind trust (business trust).

**bloc**   A group united by a shared characteristic. A bloc is a group of individuals, countries, or corporations united by a shared interest, belief, or identity. Blocs are often formed within legislatures to coordinate voting among legislators of similar views, and blocs describe groups of shareholders allied toward a particular end in a shareholders' vote in a corporation. Racial bloc voting in public elections may affect analysis of electoral boundaries under the Voting Rights Act. Corporations may share information within a bloc as a means of lobbying or seeking a governmental objective only within the limits of antitrust regulations on market coordination.

**blockade**   Military investment of a place to prevent access to it. A blockade is a an isolation of a port, region, town, or country, by military force, allowing communication into the blockaded area only with the permission of the blockading force. A blockade was considered an act of war before the U.N. Charter, and it is still considered a use of military force under or an act of aggression.

**blockade of abortion facilities**   *See:* abortion, blockade of abortion facilities, Freedom of Access to Clinic Entrances Act; abortion, blockade of abortion facilities.

**blockbusting (block-busting)**   Inducing the sale of property by asserting that minorities are moving into the area. Blockbusting is used by buyers of residential property seeking a lower price to give the property owner the impression that individuals of another race are moving near to the owner's propety and that the ingress of other races will have an undesirable effect on the owner. The buyer will then make an offer without solicitation, hoping the owner will sell quickly and at a lower price before the property becomes devalued. The buyer will then sell the property at a higher price.

**blood**   Kinship. Blood describes a line of descent from common ancestors, and blood relationships are the basis for degrees of consanguinity in determining descent to heirs.

**blood alcohol level (blood alchohol content or B.A.C. or BAC)**   A measure of alcohol in a person's body. Blood alcohol level is the ratio of alcohol to blood, as measured by a clinical examination of a sample of blood or urine or by an analysis of a breath exhaled. Although many commercial breathalizers have been admitted as evidence for determining blood alcohol levels, there is still skepticism as to their accuracy, and blood analysis performed by accepted procedures in a qualified laboratory is a more reliable indicator of alcohol presence and concentration.
*See also:* sobriety, field sobriety test.

**blood quantum**   Degree of descent from a full member of a tribe or indigenous group. Blood quantum is used to determine eligibility in a federally recognized tribe, and it has been applied also to determine who is a native Hawaiian. Generally, if one grandparent was a full-blooded member of a tribe, the grandchild is as well. All other claims to membership vary from tribe to tribe, often with many exceptions.

**Blue Book or Uniform System of Citation**   *See:* citation, citation manual (Blue Book or Uniform System of Citation).

**blue law**   *See:* sabbath, blue law (Sunday law or Sunday closing law).

**blue pencil rule**   *See:* covenant, real covenant, restrictive covenant, blue pencil rule (blue pencil test).

**blue-sky law**   *See:* security, securities, securities fraud, blue-sky law.

**board of directors**   *See:* corporation, director, board of directors (corporate board or board).

**boat or ship**   *See:* vessel (boat or ship).

**boc**   A charter describing a grant of land and its privileges or a book of charters. The boc is the forerunner of the modern deed, a written memorial of a grant of lands that enumerates the scope of the land and the privileges that are conveyed with it. A collection of bocs is also a boc, which is likely the origin of the English word "book."
*See also:* charter, charter as deed; deed.

**BOCB**   *See:* buyer, buyer in ordinary course of business (BOCB).

**body (corpus or corporal or bodily)**   The physical form taken by a human being or animal. The body is the physical organism of a human being or an animal. It incorporates a network of systems of organs comprising a variety of tissues, cells, fluids, and chemicals. In some senses, to refer to the body of an animal is to refer to its trunk, or torso and abdomen, rather than to an appendage such as an arm or finger.

In law, the body may refer to the living and thinking person, to the body of the living person, or to a dead body. Corpus, Latin for "body," is used in many instances for the same meaning.

Metaphorically, a body may refer to any complete assemblage of related materials, such as a body of research or a body of writings. Body is also used to speak of a single association, such as a body politic or a legislative body. In the same manner as "body" may refer to the trunk as opposed to the whole, the term metaphorically is sometimes used to refer only to the central aspects of anything with ancillary parts, such as the body of a text (without regard to notes or amendments), or a body of troops (without regard to sentries or outriders).
*See also:* person (personality); corpus.

**bodily harm**   *See:* injury, bodily injury (bodily harm).

**bodily heir**   *See:* heir, bodily heir (heir of the body).

**bodily intrusion**   *See:* search, bodily search, bodily intrusion; rape, rape as sexual assault, bodily intrusion (penetration or physical penetration).

**bodily search**   *See:* search, bodily search.

**body part (body tissue or organ tissue or tissue)**   An organ, tissue, or component of the body. A body part is a component of the body that has either an integral nature to it, such as an eye or other organ; a commonality among cells, such as a tissue sample; or a geographic proximity so that the components are interconnected. Under the anatomical gift act, a part is specifically an eye, organ, or tissue sample.

> **ownership of body parts**   Body parts excised from the body are owned by their recipient. Body parts in the living body are the property of the person whose body it is, yet the ownership interest is limited in that parts may be given away as donations but, in most cases, not sold. Body parts removed from the body are a possession and may also be treated as property, either as abandoned property when no contract or gift agreement governs their disposition, or as the property of a donee if the donor grants ownership at or before their removal. Body parts are subject to transactions and protected by laws against theft and conversion.

**boilerplate**   Generic language in a legal instrument. Boilerplate is any language in a contract or other instrument that purports to define the rights and duties of the parties but that lacks any specific application to the situation in which it is employed. Absent any evidence a clause in boilerplate language was negotiated between the parties, the clause in boilerplate is presumed to be interpreted and construed against the interests of one who offers it.

*See also:* contract, contract formation, form contract, boilerplate contract.

> **boilerplate contract**   *See:* contract, contract formation, form contract, boilerplate contract unconscionability; contract, contract formation, form contract, boilerplate contract.

**bona (bonos or bonum or bonus)**   Good or goods. Bonus is a Latin word meaning "good" and in the plural "goods." As a word unto itself, it is rare now in these senses of legal drafting, but for the English sense of the word as "bonus," for something additional. Bonus has considerable use in various phrases, including technical terms used in property and contract law, such as nulla bona ("no goods"), bona vacantia ("vacant goods"), or bona notabilia ("notable goods"); and in criminal, international, and constitutional law, such as contra bonos mores ("against public policy"). It is also a component of the common English idiom "bona fide," which literally translates as "good faith."

*See also:* property; bona, bona fide (bona fides).

> **bona fide (bona fides)**   Genuine. Bona fide, literally translated as "good faith," describes a situation that is as it is represented to be. A person who has a good faith belief has no reason to believe otherwise, in particular no notice of a claim contrary to that belief. To describe an offer, an agent, or a statement as bona fide offer, a bona fide representative, or a bona fide statement is to assert that each is accurate, that there was no intent by the offeror, the principal or agent, or the speaker to deceive, and that none of the three had any information that should have put them on notice that their statements or actions were not as they seem.

Bona fides, which is not so much the genuine Latin as the Latin phrase with an English plural, refers to a person's credentials or a proof of identity or experience.

*See also:* offer, contract offer, bona fide offer; bona (bonos or bonum or bonus); faith, good faith (bona fide); holder, bona fide holder for value (holder in good faith); purchaser, bona fide purchaser (bona fide purchaser for value or B.F.P. or B.F.P.V. or BFP or BFPV).

> **bona fide error in judgment or good faith error in judgment**   *See:* mistake, honest mistake (bona fide error in judgment or good faith error in judgment).

> **bona fide holder for value**   *See:* holder, bona fide holder for value (holder in good faith).

> **bona fide occupational qualification**   *See:* discrimination, employment discrimination, bona fide occupational qualification (B.F.O.Q. or BFOQ).

> **bona fide offer**   *See:* offer, contract offer, bona fide offer.

> **bona fide purchaser for value or B.F.P. or B.F.P.V. or BFP or BFPV**   *See:* purchaser, bona fide purchaser (bona fide purchaser for value or B.F.P. or B.F.P.V. or BFP or BFPV).

## bond

> **bond as assurance**   An assurance purchased to guarantee conduct or performance. A bond is a monetary assurance purchased by someone with an obligation from a third party, that guarantees the obligor will fulfill the obligation or the money of the assurance will be paid to the obligee. Where an obligation is particularly tenuous or may require unexpected funds, the contracting parties may require a bond to be secured in trust, usually for a set amount of money to cover the unforeseen costs or damages.

> **bond as debt security**   Instrument expressing a promise to pay money at a future date. A bond is an instrument by which an obligor, who can be a person, a company, a government, or other legal entity, demonstrates the promise to pay the obligee a specified amount of money at a fixed future date. Bonds expressing a debt incorporate their terms of repayment into the amount to be repaid when the bond matures. Bonds are traded on public markets, and bonds may be the underlying principle for derivatives.
>
> *See also:* obligation (oblige or obligator or obligee or obligor).

> **bond as interpersonal relation**   A sense of comfort, trust, and friendship. A bond is an especially trusting or emotionally intimate relationship between two people.

**bond coupon** *See:* coupon, coupon bond (bond coupon).

**accrual bond** Bond for which full repayment is made at maturity. An accrual bond is one in which the face value of the bond and the interest over the life of the bond is paid at maturity. Thus, interest is not paid on an ongoing or initial basis.

*See also:* deposit, certificate of deposit (CD or C.D.).

**appeal bond (cost bond)** Assurance that court costs of an appeal will be paid. An appeal bond is a financial guaranty posted by the appellant to pay costs that may arise as a result of appealing the case. If the subject matter of the action invokes a rule shifting the attorney's fees, the anticipated fees of the appellee's attorneys in defending the appeal are included in the coverage of the bond. The appeal bond does not, however, include an amount for the delay of enforcement of a judgment, which is the purpose of a supersedeas bond.

**attachment bond** A bond posted against the value of property subject to attachment. An attachment bond is a security deposited into court for the value of the property sought under an attachment order or writ. An attachment bond is usually required of the plaintiff who seeks attachment of property as a pre-trial security to ensure payment of a final judgment in the plaintiff's favor, the bond being a security to reimburse the defendant in the event the plaintiff loses and the attachment was unnecessary. A defendant may also post an attachment bond in lieu of allowing attachment of the defendant's property or to secure the return of property already attached by the plaintiff.

**bail bond (appearance bond)** *See:* bail, bail bond (appearance bond).

**bearer bond** Bond payable to whomever possesses it. Bearer bonds are presumptively owned by whomever possesses them. They are blank as to owner and are paid on the presentation of coupons by the bearer.

**bond indenture** An agreement between a bond-issuer and a bondholder. A bond indenture is a formal agreement between the issuer and holder of a bond, detailing the rights and responsibilities of each party in connection with the issuance of the bond.

*See also:* indenture.

**bond retirement** Repayment of a bond's face value. When a bond is retired, the bond issuer pays the face value of the bond to the investor then holding the bond. Bonds may only be retired in accordance to the bond's security contract or applicable law. Retirement may occur at or before the date of maturity, although at issuance, retirement is anticipated at the date of maturity. An issuer's decision to retire a bond before it matures has two important consequences. First, the issuer saves money because he is no longer paying interest on the bond to the investor (as he would normally do until the bond matured). In parallel, the investor loses all the future interest the bond would have paid had the issuer not retired the bond. The classic motivation behind bond retirement prior to maturity is a reduction in interest rates which makes it profitable for an issuer to retire all his bonds, then reissue those bonds at the current, lower interest rate. In this way, early bond retirement may be viewed as a refinancing tool.

**convertible bond** A bond exchangeable for company stock. A bond is convertible if the investor may convert the bond into shares of common stock of the bond issuer's company. Thus, only businesses trading in stock may issue convertible bonds. Convertible bonds are often an attractive fund-raising tool for issuers. First, because a convertible bond may be exchanged for company stock, the issuer often pays less interest to the investor on the bond. Second, issuing convertible bonds may side-step the conventional wisdom that when a company trading in stock issues normal (that is, non-convertible) bonds, that act signals that the company's stock is overvalued (which may lead to a decrease in the stock's trading price). Convertible bonds are also attractive to investors. Although a convertible bond often yields less interest than a normal bond, a convertible bond allows the investor to exchange his bond for common stock often at a premium over the stock's market price. As a result, the convertible bond is usually sold at a higher price than a non-convertible bond. Convertible bonds are almost always redeemable by the issuer on demand.

**coupon bond (bond coupon)** Bearer bond redeemable in increments, paid on coupons cut from the bond. Coupon bonds are bonds payable to the bearer, which have detachable substitutes, or coupons, that may be removed and presented for payment of interest owed at intervals. Coupon bonds, used primarily for their expedient transfer methods, can be negotiated by anyone holding the bond, or a coupon detached from the bond.

**debenture (debenture bond or debenture note)** Bond reflecting corporate debt unsecured by collateral. Debentures are long-term unsecured debt given to a named owner, nearly always by a business corporation, the loan being secured only by the good faith of the business and a claim on its potential revenue, rather than by a security interest in a designated surety or security interest.

**fidelity bond (blanket bond)** An insurance contract assuring against an employee's potential deceit. A fidelity bond is a form of insurance that contractually indemnifies the bondholder, usually a corporation such as a bank, against losses sustained as a result of dishonest behavior on the corporation's employees or agents.

**forthcoming bond (delivery bond or discharging bond or dissolution bond)** Money posted as an assurance of delivery of property. A forthcoming bond insures that specific property that is subject to forfeiture following litigation, such as property subject to a security interest that has been called on a debt, will be delivered to a sheriff or other court officer when it is demanded to satisfy a judgment or execution of a judgment. A forthcoming bond may be requested from a creditor whenever a debtor holds property that might be subject to pretrial attachment or replevin, the debtor prefers to continue to possess the property during the litigation, and the creditor accepts the bond in lieu of seizure of the assets. A sheriff's notice the property subject to the bond is to be sold on a given day is presumptively sufficient to give notice to render the property or forfeit the bond in compensation for any losses suffered by the creditor.

**general obligation bond (full-faith-and-credit bond)** The security created from a loan to a government. A general obligation bond is a debt instrument representing a monetary obligation insured by a government's taxing power. A entity may lend money to a government, usually a city or other municipality, via a general obligation bond because repayment is guaranteed by the government's taxing power. In addition, many general obligation bonds are insured, often by a monoline insurance agency whose sole business is to issue insurance on the payment of general obligation bonds. The bond is usually transferable on the securities market.

**government position bond (official bond)** Financial assurance posted to assure a public officer will carry out official obligations. A government position bond is a financial guaranty that a public officer will perform the office competently and in good faith. Most such bonds are purchased from underwriters for periods of three years. In the event of a default in performance in the office, the bond issuer will make good to the government entity those losses suffered as a result of the wrongdoing by the official or the fiduciary. In many cases, the express terms of the bond require prosecution of the official in order to require indemnity. For some officials, such as a county treasurer, the law or the government executive may require both a position bond and a fiduciary bond. In some jurisdictions, there is no distinction between the bond required of a public official and the bond required of a court-supervised fiduciary.

**guaranty bond** A surety entered in guaranty of performance by a principal. A guaranty bond is any money placed in trust by a third party to be used in the event that an obligor fails to make a scheduled or required payment or otherwise to perform an obligation of payment or service.

**immigration delivery bond (immigration bond)** An appearance bond for aliens awaiting an immigration hearing or departure. An immigration delivery bond is a guaranty that an alien will either appear at an immigration hearing or will voluntarily depart from the United States.

**interim bond** Specific type of bail bond paid to avoid the procedures of booking at the police station. An interim bond is a monetary obligation to ensure the appearance of the accused at criminal proceedings. In some jurisdictions, a person accused of a minor, non-violent crime is offered the opportunity to post an interim bond with the arresting officer prior to formal arrest in order to ensure the appearance of the accused at criminal trial.

**judicial bond** Money posted under the direction of a court. A judicial bond is a financial commitment paid into court on the direction of a judge. At its broadest application, there are many forms of judicial bond arising from rules and routine orders, including appeal bonds, appearance bonds, attachment bonds, bail bonds, recognizance bonds, and the like. The term is more narrowly used for to require an assurance by a party before the court that the party will perform some obligation that is more particular conduct than is routine.

**junk bond (high-yield bond or high-yield debt obligation)** Debt security issued by an entity with a high risk of default. High-yield bonds are debt securities like other corporate bonds, yet they offer a higher yield because they are issued by an entity that has a risk of defaulting on the scheduled payments required on the bonds that is much higher than the usual investment-grade entity.

**liability bond** Money deposited as a financial assurance against damages. A liability bond is a monetary obligation created to cover any possible damages caused in a given activity, much like an insurance policy. A liability bond usually involves a one-time payment of money into a trust that can be returned to the obligor if no harm is caused. It is a common device used for self-insurance, such when a company has a legal obligation to provide driver's insurance but prefers to self-insure rather than to pay an insurance premium to a third-party provider.

**maintenance bond** A guaranty of a promise that a building or goods will be maintained. A maintenance bond is a monetary obligation that guarantees an underlying performance obligation to maintain goods or structures for a specified period of time.

**municipal bond (muni)** Tax-exempt bonds issued by non-federal government entities. Municipal bonds, or "munis," are debt instruments issued by city, county, state, and other governmental entities, as well as enterprises with a public purpose, such as utilities, universities, and hospitals. The critical difference to investors between municipal and non-municipal bonds is that income from municipal bonds is exempt from federal taxes and often from state and local taxes. Because of this tax exemption, municipal bonds usually offer lower interest rates to investors than other bonds but still remain attractive because differences in interest rates are negated by the bonds' tax status. This allows municipalities to fund projects for less cost.

**option tender bond (option bond or OTB or multimaturity bond or put bond or put option bond)** Bond that provides it can be satisfied before the maturity date. An option tender bond is a debt instrument security that entitles the obligee to a tender of the amount of the bond before the maturity date. An obligor is bound by the terms of the bond; therefore, the obligor must satisfy the bond amount upon request by obligee.

**payment bond** A guaranty that workers and vendors will be paid. A payment bond is a financial guaranty from a surety that a contractor will timely pay subcontractors, suppliers and vendors, and laborers who provide goods or services to the contractor in a construction contract. Although the bond ensures payments to laborers and suppliers, the fundamental beneficiary of the bond is the owner of the structure under construction, as the bond will ensure that the contractor's failure to pay will not result in materialmen's liens or other claims on the structure.

**peace bond (bond to keep the peace or surety of the peace)** Money posted by one under a court order to desist from an activity. A peace bond is a monetary assurance posted by a person subject to a court order that the person will abide by the dictates of the order. Peace bonds operate as conditional fines, sought by motion by someone who can demonstrate a reason to fear being the victim of unlawful conduct by another person. If the court finds cause to believe the threat is well founded, the court may order the respondent to comply with a series of limitations of conduct, such as maintaining a distance from the movant, and to post a bond with the court that is forfeit to the movant if the respondent violates the terms of the order.

*See also:* order, court order, restraining order.

**performance bond** *See:* bond, surety bond (performance bond).

**replevin bond (claim-property bond or redelivery bond)** Guaranty posted by a plaintiff as a condition of replevin of the defendant's property. A replevin bond is a financial assurance required of a plaintiff seeking replevin of a defendant's property, which will compensate the defendant for lost use of the property or harm or loss incurred while in the possession of the plaintiff, if the plaintiff is not successful in the suit for which the property was subject to replevin. If the property replevined is not returned on the day of judgment in the replevin action, the principal of the bond (the plaintiff of the replevin action) becomes liable and the surety of the bond is therefore also liable.

*See also:* replevin (writ of replevin or replevy or repleviable).

**replevy bond** Guaranty posted by a defendant to retain possession of property that is subject to replevin. A replevy bond is a finanacial assurance required of the defendant who seeks to keep property subject to replevin by the plaintiff, which will compensate the plaintiff for loss of use of the property or harm or loss incurred while the property remains in the possession of the defendant, if the plaintiff is successful in the suit for which the property was subject to replevin.

**revenue bond (improvement bond)** Debt security issued by a public entity to build some structure, paid from its revenues. Revenue bonds finance improvements to public property, often to build bridges or roads. The name is derived from a repayment structure requiring that any payments made on the bond will come from funds generated by the fees required for use of the structure.

**savings bond (government bond or government security)** Interest-earning debt instrument issued by the United States government. A savings bond is acknowledgment of a contract between the purchaser of the savings bond and the federal government. The amount on the face of the bond is the amount that will be owed to the registrant named by the purchaser after the period of time indicated on the bond. The bond generates interest at an amount that is specified at the time of issuance, although some savings bonds now have variable rates. Savings bonds may not be redeemed in less than one year.

**supersedeas bond** A bond posted to stay enforcement of a judgment. A supersedeas bond is posted when a person requests that the judgment of the lower court not be enforced while the appeal is heard. It is a guaranty that the appealing party will pay the judgment, or the costs of the appeal, if the appeal is lost. A supersedeas bond differs from an appeal bond, both of which may be required of an appellant who moves to stay enforcement of a judgment pending appeal, but a supersedeas bond assures payment for money that may be owed as a result of the merits of the underlying judgment and stay of its execution, whereas an appeal bond assures payment of money that may become owed as a result of litigating an appeal. In other words, an appellant's supersedeas bond is retrospective to compensate a successful appellee for losses from the delay in payment of a judgment, but an appeal bond is prospective, to compensate a successful appellee for costs incurred in the appeal.

*See also:* bond, appeal bond (cost bond); supersedeas (stay pending appeal).

**surety bond (performance bond)** A sum of money posted to assure that a duty is performed. A surety bond is a financial guaranty of obligations that are specified under a bond agreement, in which an obligee requires a bond and is the beneficiary of the bond, which assures the conduct of the principal and which is issued by a surety company or other third party. There is a great variety of surety bonds. Note: there is no essential difference between a surety bond and a performance bond.

**zero coupon bond** Debt security instrument accruing all interest, which is paid upon maturity. A zero-coupon bond is a security that accrues undistributed interest that is paid, along with principal, to the bondholder at the date of maturity.

**bondage**

> **bondage as slavery** The condition of being held in slavery. Bondage is another term for slavery, which is illegal in the United States under the Thirteenth Amendment.
> *See also:* slavery (slave).

**bonos or bonum or bonus** *See:* bona (bonos or bonum or bonus).

**bonus** A gratuity or premium. A bonus is something given, either as a gift or addition or in excess of a regular stipulation. Bonuses are routinely employed in construction contracts as incentives for early completion and high quality. An employee bonus is a form of compensation in excess of regular salary, often made a part of an employment agreement that will calculate a bonus as a percentage of the employer's profits to create an incentive for greater productivity among the workforces as a whole.

**book** Record. Book, as a noun, refers to something that has been documented. Book, as a verb, refers to the act of documenting something, in which sense it has myriad specialized forms, as in the processing of an arrestee, the entry of a party into a contract, or the recording of a transaction.
> *See also:* value, book value (net asset value).

> **book value** *See:* value, book value (net asset value).

**book as bound composition** A writing on pages bound between covers or its electronic equivalent. The book is the most fundamental tool for the storage and transmission of written information in human history. Books have existed in many forms, including sculptures and scrolls, but the dominant form in Western culture from the medieval to the present is a writing that is inscribed or printed on sheets of paper (or sometimes vellum, parchment, or other media) that are bound between covers. The advent of electronic books has altered this definition, but it remains a useful basis for analogy to electronic texts of a form that either originates or emulates a printed book.

**book as business record (books)** Records of transactions, debts, and assets of a business. The books are the financial records of a business, and they take a multitude of forms. Most importantly, the books include the record of accounts. While once maintained in hand-written ledgers, "books" is now a bit euphemistic, given that these accounts have become nearly universally electronic records.

**book as criminal process** The formal intake and processing of a person arrested by the police. Booking is the process of formally recording the arrest of a criminal suspect into the state records. Booking may include the identification of the suspect, recording of distinguishing characteristics, photography, and fingerprinting.

**book-land (charter land)** Feudal lands held according to deed in return for rents and services. Book-land was another term in feudal law for land held by free socage.
> *See also:* tenure, feudal tenure, socage, free and common socage.

**bookie (make book)** One who takes and pays illegal wagers. A bookie is a person who runs or fronts a gambling enterprise. A bookie may take wagers, set odds, determine payouts, and manage the finances of a group of bettors. To make book is to accept, or sometimes to place, such wagers on a given event, such as a fight, game, or race.

**boot** Taxable consideration in a nontaxable transaction. A boot is anything that is supplemental to a transaction or to more core or focused activity. The term is an echo of the old "bote" in the common law, which was a category of the many rights incidental to an interest in land. Its most common modern usage is that portion of a non-taxable transaction that is taxable. It includes many incidental properties, particularly assets acquired in a corporate combination other than those that were the subject of the bargain.
> *See also:* bote.

**bootleg** Materials that are unlawful to possess or transport. Something bootleg is something that must be smuggled to avoid its detection by legal authorities. Bootleg property may be illegal per se, such as prohibited drugs, or it may be illegal in a particular context, such as alcohol that has not been given a tax stamp. Media that is reproduced in violation of its copyright is bootleg.

**bootstrap doctrine** Jurisdiction is not contested after an action is concluded. The bootstrap doctrine bars an attack on a court's jurisdiction over any case, if that attack is brought not as a defense or direct appeal but as a collateral attack. The doctrine arises in response to the power of the courts to act within their jurisdiction when deciding any matter is within their jurisdiction, which can lead to jurisdiction over a matter solely on the basis of a court's jurisdiction to determine it lacks jurisdiction over the matter. There are many non-doctrinal uses of the bootstrap with which one pulls oneself up: any act by a plaintiff to demonstrate jurisdiction over a defendant is prone to a charge of bootstrapping.

**booty** Personal property captured on land in war. The doctrine of booty, in which soldiers and a combatant state may keep private and public property captured in war, is obsolete.
> *See also:* prize, prize as captured vessel (prize vessel or law of prize).

**bordello** *See:* prostitution, brothel (bawdy-house or bordello or house of ill fame or house of ill repute or house of prostitution).

**border (frontier)** The edge dividing states, municipalities, or other jurisdictions. A border is the end of one territory and the beginning of another, in a line surrounding every state or jurisdiction, over which are either other states or jurisdictions or international waters. Borders are the geographical limits of a state's sovereignty and the physical limits of the applications of many of the state's laws.

**Bork (to Bork)** Rejecting a judicial nominee because of the nominee's philosophy. To Bork a nomination for a judicial office is to thwart the nomination by voicing concerns over a nominee's judicial temperament or philosophy. The term originated with President Ronald Reagan's nomination of Judge Robert Bork, a judge on the U.S. Court of Appeals for the District of Columbia, to the U.S. Supreme Court in 1986. Judge Bork was considered by many critics to be too extreme in his opinions to serve as a high court judge, especially when contrasted with Justice Lewis Powell, whom he would have replaced. On October 23, 1987, his nomination failed in the U.S. Senate by a 58–42 vote.

**bote** A privilege incidental to something else, or a compensation for a wrong. Bote is a medieval term for a privilege arising from a particular circumstance. Most notably, the bote was the measure of damages or restitution for a wrong done: man bote was the equivalent of damages for wrongful death. Other forms of bote were particular privileges of a tenant to take an amount of lumber from a lord's woods for specific uses, such as house–bote.
*See also:* deodand.

> **man bote (manbote or man-bote)** Blood money paid to recompense a homicide. Man bote was money, or often chattels or property, given by a person who committed homicide or that person's family to the survivors of the victim, as a form of restitution. Once the man bote was accepted no further punishment was ordinarily sought, either by the family or by the sheriff.
> *See also:* restitution, criminal restitution (victim compensation).

**bouche de la loi** *See:* metaphor, metaphor of law, mouth of the law (bouche de la loi).

**Boulwarism** *See:* union, labor union, collective bargaining, Boulwarism.

**bound** A limit, or the act of restraint. Bound has several meanings as a noun, a verb, and an adjective. As a noun, it can be a boundary or other limitation on a thing or an action. As an adjective, it is used to describe something that has been connected or attached to another thing. As a verb cognate, it refers to the action of surrounding something, usually the subject of such a verb is the boundary. A bound defines the limits beyond which that thing does not extend, and to bound a thing is to delimit it by the surrounds. Thus a mountain range may be the visible bound of a territory, and bound the country all around. In property disputes, visible bounds may be provided by a fence, a road, or even a ditch;

however, the invisible bounds of decency delimit the realm of unreasonability. But in the end, all are bound by the law of the land, with the Supreme Court, placed by Congress, on watch of the surround.

> **bound over** *See:* bind, bound over (bind over or bound over).

**boundary** The separation between two adjoining properties. A boundary is a natural or artificial line marking the line between two pieces of land.

> **agreed-boundary doctrine** Boundary disputes once settled are settled for all time. Under the agreed-boundary doctrine, a disputed boundary between landowners can be settled, and subsequent successors to those parties can be bound to such an agreement.

> **boundary line** A line designating a boundary. A boundary line is a boundary defined by a line described either according to existing lines, such as roads or rivers, or between specific points that are designated, either by custom or in an instrument. When the line runs between designated points, the line need not be completely straight, because it can run from one to another call or mark, employing many calls or marks. A turning point is a call or a mark that is not one terminus of a line. The line is presumed to run exactly straight between the two nearest calls or marks.
> *See also:* survey (surveyor or surveying).

> **building line (set back)** Building may occur inside a line within lot boundaries. A building line is a line established by law or regulation beyond which a building may not extend. Cities and towns may promulgate legislation, or subdivisions may impose restrictive covenants, defining the minimum distance between the frontage to a street and the house or building to be built upon the land. This is often referred to as a "set back." Such restriction may also cover the distance between side and back property lines and the building line. Although there may be exceptions for temporary or uninhabited structures, the building line defines the area on a property where a structure may be built.

> **call** A boundary landmark in a real property survey. A call is an object used as a reference point in a land survey to designate boundaries. A call can fall into one of several categories: natural monuments, artificial monuments, adjoining boundaries, compass directions, distances, indications of areas, and place names.

> **meander line** A fictional line defining the natural curves of a navigable body of water. A meander line is a surveyor's and cartographer's estimate of the shoreline at its average location along the water's edge. The boundary may be fixed in relation to the meander line, but the meander line is a measure of the land and that water's edge, and if the boundary happens to be set at the meander line, then it becomes also the boundary, but it is not usually the boundary itself.

**thalweg (thalweg doctrine or rule of the thalweg)** The most navigable track in a watercourse. The thalweg is the line in a river, fjord, or other watercourse that represents its most navigable channel. Although the thalweg is presumably the deepest channel, the movement of currents and requirements of navigation may vary, and the thalweg is usually established through a combination of soundings and of evidence of the practice of pilots and captains familiar with the waters, the premise being that the downstream traffic will occupy the thalweg. A thalweg is not fixed in one location but is likely to move as the watercourse changes over time.

The rule of the thalweg is a means of demarcating an exact boundary between two U.S. states or two international states that are generally divided by a watercourse. The jurisdiction of each runs to the thalweg. There are several exceptions, one being if by local custom or treaty another boundary is accepted, one being if the rule would work considerable hardship to one state and principles of division ex aequo et bono would reach a more measured result, one being a principle affecting a migratory island, which moves the boundary as the island moves across the thalweg by accretion yet leaves the boundary if the island moves across the thalweg by avulsion.

*See also:* avulsion; accretion.

**bounded rationality** *See:* rationality, bounded rationality.

**bounds** *See:* metes and bounds (butts and bounds).

**bounty hunter** One who locates fugitives and delivers them to custody. A bounty hunter pursues defendants in criminal causes, escapees, and others who either jumped bail, missed a court appearance or are wanted by the police. Bounty hunters are usually paid by bail bondsmen but may freelance to collect rewards offered by public authorities. The arrest authority of a bounty hunter is usually limited to that of an agent of the bail bondsman, although it may be no more than that of a citizen.

**boutique law firm** *See:* lawyer, law firm, boutique law firm.

**bovine spongiform encephalopathy (BSE or mad cow disease)** Mad cow disease. Caused by a prion, bovine spongiform encephalopathy is a communciable disease transmitted by ingestion of beef products, especially nervous tissues.

**boycott** A refusal to trade with an entity to coerce it to change a policy. A boycott is any cessation of trade, commerce, or some other activity as an act of protest against a policy or action. Boycotts may be spontaneous acts among individuals affected by some policy or contract, but they are as often organized by a union or an association or a state. The purpose of a boycott is to create an economic hardship that affects the company, state, or people engaged in the targeted policy of action. U.S.

boycotts have included the boycotts of employers engaged in unfair labor practices, of businesses and transportation lines that refuse to give equal service on the basis of race, and of consumer goods produced by companies with environmentally harmful practices. Boycotts may be international, as in the boycott of the 1980 Olympics to protest the Soviet invasion of Afghanistan. The term, both noun and verb, is derived from Capt. Charles C. Boycott, a nineteenth–century Irish land agent whose fields went unharvested after he refused to adjust the rents of tenant farmers. Boycotts now differ from strikes, in that a strike is a refusal to work, while a boycott is a refusal to trade. When the trade is trade in services, as is the case among contractors or consulting professionals, the withdrawal of services to the entity they serve may have effects similar to a strike but is still a boycott.

*See also:* union, labor union, labor dispute, labor strike (walkout).

**consumer boycott** Abstention from the purchase of products as a protest of some practice. A consumer boycott is a protest of a policy, pursuit or practice of another party effected by voluntarily ceasing an activity from which that other party derives economic benefit. A consumer boycott involves a group of people deciding not to purchase a product or line of products, or not to shop at a specific location. The goal of the consumer boycott is to raise public awareness of the offending policies or activities and thereby, create coercive economic pressure upon the company to change those policies or practices.

**labor boycott** Boycott of goods or services of an employer to gain better working or contract conditions. A labor boycott is employees' refusal to buy goods or patronize the services of an employer in an effort to coerce the employer to improve contract or working conditions or otherwise to alter its business practices. A labor boycott is lawful if its primary purpose is to improve conditions for laborers. However, the boycott may be unlawful if its purpose it to punish or cause irreparable injury.

**secondary boycott** Boycott of one entity to coerce a different entity. A secondary boycott is the boycott of one entity in order to bring economic pressure upon another, which may be a supplier or market for the goods or services of the entity boycotted. Secondary boycott is sometimes used to describe what more narrowly is a sympathetic boycott, in which a boycott is started by a group of consumers or workers against one company, and then additional companies, additional consumer groups, or other unions initiate a second, sympathetic boycott of the same company.

**BP or BPS** *See:* basis, basis point (BP or BPS).

**Brady Act** *See:* gun, gun control, Brady Act (Brady Bill).

**Brady material** *See:* exculpation, exculpatory evidence, Brady material (Brady evidence).

**brain death** *See:* death, moment of death, brain death, higher brain death; death, moment of death, brain death (brain life).

**brain life** *See:* life, brain life; death, moment of death, brain death (brain life).

**brand (branding)** A mark, especially a mark burned into the skin. The brand, burned into human skin, has been employed as a punishment from antiquity to the colonial experience in America. Branding is forbidden as a punishment for crimes in the United States under the Eighth Amendment, and it is forbidden as a punishment under international law. Metaphorically, branding also includes the concept of labeling a person as a criminal to be shunned or shamed, which is not inherently unconstitutional and is one aspect of criminal identification statutes, such as Megan's Law.

Brands are, of course, also used as an identification of property, particularly to mark the ownership of cattle. From this sense arises the brand as a means of identifying the maker, distributor, or seller of merchandise.

*See also:* sex, sex offender, Megan's Law (sex offender registration or sex offender registry).

**brand as commercial label (brand name)** A trademark or service mark used to identify the source of good or provider of a service. A brand is a sign, symbol, word or phrase that is created and employed to identify the maker, distributor, seller, or provider of goods or services. A brand is a trademark on goods or a service mark for services provided, and in either sense if subject to protection as intellectual property.

*See also:* trademark; trademark, mark, service mark (servicemark).

**Brandeis brief** *See:* brief, Brandeis brief.

**breach** The breaking of a duty. A breach is a violation of any obligation or duty, whether it is specific to the individual, such as a breach of contract, or it is general, such as a breach of the peace. Breach is both noun and verb, and it is a near synonym with break or violation in many of these senses.

*See also:* abandonment, abandonment as contract rescission; dereliction, dereliction of duty.

**breach of promise of marriage** *See:* marriage, promise of marriage, breach of promise of marriage (breach of promise to marry).

**breach of promise to marry** *See:* marriage, promise of marriage, breach of promise of marriage (breach of promise to marry).

**breach of the peace** *See:* peace, disturbing the peace (breach of the peace).

**breach of warranty** *See:* warranty, breach of warranty.

**breach of contract (breach of covenant or breach of warranty)** Failure to perform an obligation required under a contract. A breach of contract is the failure to fulfill an obligation arising from a contract, whether the obligation arises from a written or an oral agreement, whether the obligation was expressed in clear language, was implied from the circumstances of the agreement and the conduct of the parties, or arose through operation of the law or equity as a result of the relations between the parties to the contract. Breach may result from a party's failure to perform an obligation, from an act that is contrary to an obligation, from the performance of an act that the party is obligated not to perform, by interfering with the other party's performance of its obligations, or by repudiating the agreement or an obligation within it. A breach usually gives rise to obligations by the breaching party and rights in the non-breaching party, but not every breach gives rise to a cause of action to enforce the contract. Material breaches, which is to say, violations of obligations that are of some degree of importance within the contract, may be the basis for enforcement, but only if the plaintiff can demonstrate that there was a valid contract, that it was indeed breached, and that some harm or has been or will be suffered by the non-breaching party or a third-party beneficiary contemplated under the contract. Even still, the breaching party might be able to prove a justification for the breach or an excuse from performance, and so diminish its liability. The question of whether a contract has been breached is usually a question of fact.

*discovery of breach* A buyer has a only a reasonable time to discover and object to nonconformity. Discovery of breach in the sale of goods under the U.C.C. must occur within a reasonable time after the receipt of contracted-for goods or services, so a buyer must inspect all purchases as soon as possible. Under the common law, a breach of contract is actionable from the time the discovery takes place or should reasonably have taken place.

**anticipatory breach** Words or conduct rejecting performance before the time of performance. Anticipatory breach is an act or statement by one party to a contract that demonstrates to the other party that the first party will not perform obligations under the contract at the time required. Anticipatory breach thus amounts to a repudiation of the whole contract. For the non-breaching party to prove it is owed a remedy because the other party has indeed breached, the non-breaching party must prove the breaching party refused to perform its obligation, that the refusal was made through positive statements or actions that signaled the breaching party absolutely or unconditionally would not or could not perform its duty.

*See also:* assurances (further assurances or adequate assurance of performance); repudiation, anticipatory repudiation.

**bad-faith breach (tortious breach of contract)** A breach of a contract that amounts to a tort. A bad-faith breach of contract is a breach of contract that has no justification, excuse, or reasonable basis. In many jurisdictions, bad-faith breach is a particular tort, in others it is a form of tortious breach, and in others, neither action is recognized. Either bad-faith breach or tortious breach amount to a breach with no justification, and so a justification is a defense to the action in tort. Yet a justification must arise from more than the preference of the breaching party to keep the benefit of the bargain, as that benefit is ordinarily lost by breach. Commonly, actions for a breach of contract in bad faith are brought against insurance companies for the wrongful denial of claims made under an insurance policy, but there are other factual environments in which bad faith breach arises, including any breach that involves deliberate, dishonest conduct or that manifests a malicious intent toward the non-breaching party or a third party, or that is born of a desire to oppress or harm others through the breach. Conduct that constitutes negligence or bad judgment is not bad faith, so long as the party has made an effort to observe reasonable commercial standards of fair dealing. The burden of proving bad faith is on the party against which the power had been exercised.

**efficient breach**   A breach that is economically worthwhile to the breaching party. An efficient breach is a breach of contract that gives rise to a right to a remedy by the non-breaching party, but that occurs in economic circumstances in which the breaching party is financially better off by breaching and paying damages or some other remedy than it would be if it performed. The efficiency of a breach is legally irrelevant, except in so far as it might disprove a claim for breach in bad faith or that it might suggest that damages or restitution are more appropriate remedies in a circumstance than would be specific performance. Still, some commentators promote the concept of the efficient breach, both as a means of assessment of the economic or social desirability of a breach and as an argument for moderation in remedies for such a breach.

**excused breach (excuse of performance or excuse of condition)**   The waiver of the duty to perform. An excused breach is a failure to perform a duty under a contract, or a condition of such performance, when that duty is excused through a change of condition, particularly by the other party's own breach of the contract. When the other party's conduct makes impossible or unnecessary a party's performance, it is excused.

*See also:* excuse (excusable or excused).

**material breach (immaterial breach)**   Breach of an obligation that is essential to the whole contract. Material breach is a breach of an obligation under a contract, when the performance of that obligation is a very important, or defining element of the agreement between the parties. Put another way, the breach must be of an obligation the hoped-for performance of which had been a reason that led the non-breaching party to enter into the agreement or which is essential for the purposes for which the non-breaching party entered it. The

failure to perform must be so irreparable and substantial that it destroys the value of the contract for the non-breaching party.

A material breach by one party immediately excuses further performance by the other parties to a contract. Following a material breach, an action for breach and damages will lie if the non-breaching party has suffered any damage.

In contrast, a breach that is not reasonably likely to affect the purpose of the contract or harm the non-breaching party is immaterial or non-material. An immaterial breach does not excuse further performance by the non-breaching party, though it may justify a demand for further assurances.

**partial breach**   Partial breach does not excuse the non-breaching party from performance. A partial breach is one that fails completely to honor promises, but does so in a manner that still preserves the overall value of a contract.

**threat to breach**   A warning that one party will not perform. A threat to breach is not necessarily unreasonable, provided circumstances exist to excuse further performance.

**total breach**   A failure to perform that destroys the value of the contract to the other party. A total breach is a failure by one party to honor its promises in a contract, amounting in sum to an eradication of the value of the contract to the non-breaching party. A total breach is a material breach in which the non-breaching party is justified in terminating that party's own performance and repudiating the contract. In contrast, a partial breach, which may be material, is not so comprehensive in comparison to the value of the performance overall that the remaining performance by the breaching party is sufficient part performance to bar either non-performance or repudiation by the non-breaching party.

*See also:* breach, breach of contract, anticipatory breach.

## breach of duty

**breach of fiduciary duty**   *See:* fiduciary, fiduciary duty.

**duty of care**   *See:* care, duty of care.

**tortious breach of duty**   Any failure to perform a duty implied by the law, that causes harm to another. A breach of a duty is tortious if the duty arises from any general obligation in law that is recognized by the legislature or the courts as a duty rather than a specific obligation voluntarily undertaken by the parties to a contract. The three basic duties in tort are not to intentionally cause harm to others, not to harm others through negligence, and not to allow harm to others through very dangerous activities.

## breathalyzer (breath tester or alcohol detector)

A machine that determines blood alcohol content from expelled breath. The breathalyzer is both a trade name and a generic term for an instrument used by law enforcement officers quickly to assess the blood alcohol content of a person, usually in order to assess whether to detain that person as inebriated beyond the legal limit, either in public or behind the wheel of a vehicle. A record of the result of a breathalyzer test is admissible in court, although the training of the technician who uses the machine, the method by which it was used, and the maintenance and effectiveness of the machine are material to the evaluation of such evidence. Breathalyzers are manufactured by various companies, and some are considered less reliable than others; none are currently thought as accurate as a blood alcohol analysis performed by a qualified forensic laboratory.

**ignition interlock device (IID or I.I.D.)** A breathalyzer required to start a car. An ignition interlock device is a form of alcohol measurement device installed in a car, which requires the driver to test the alcohol saturation of the driver's breath in order to start the car or, at random intervals, to continue to drive it. Courts may order installation of an IID as a form of punishment for a conviction for DUI or DWI.

**brevia** *See:* writ (brevia).

**bribery (bribe)** Giving gifts to influence another's action in office or employment. Bribery is the promise or gift of money or other benefits to any person in order to influence the behavior of a person in a matter that affects a public office, position of trust, or employment. Although the common-law offense of bribery was generally restricted to attempts to influence a person in a position of public trust, such as a judge or a legislator, the position of public trust may be transient. Bribing voters in an election is bribery as well as voter fraud, and bribing jurors is bribery as well as subornation. Bribery now includes the subornation of the duty of loyalty of an employee, and the offer of gifts or promises to an officer or employee of a company for any action that is a corrupt practice, that is illegal, or that amounts to commercial bribery.

**hush money** A bribe to buy a person's silence or inaction. Hush money is a specific type of bribe, given to someone to keep them from prosecuting, testifying or otherwise relaying information that might be damaging to the entity giving the bribe.

**bricolage (bricoleur)** A theory using all the evidence available, whether or not it fits together. Bricolage describes any description or theory that flows from all of the available evidence, regardless of how consistent or contradictory the evidence is or the imprecision it causes in the description or theory. The term bricolage is borrowed from anthropology to describe several approaches to legal theory, which are closely related to pragmatism and that reject the boundaries of more formal concepts and theories. A person who creates a bricolage is a bricoleur.

**bridge loan** *See:* loan, bridge loan.

**brief** A written argument of the facts, law, and policy presented to a court. A brief is a legal argument submitted in writing to a court considering a motion or other decision pending in a case before it. The brief is an integral part of trial practice, and briefs are submitted to support most dispositive motions, as well as motions in limine, motions regarding jury instructions, and questions on which the court invited particular legal research. Briefs are required by both sides in nearly all appeals. In both trial and appellate briefing, there is usually a local rule that supplements a general rule of procedure, which cumulatively set forth the requirements for contents, page limits, printing standards, and cover color. The pattern of briefing is generally for the movant or appellant to file a brief, then for the opponent to the motion or the appellee to file a response, then for the movant or appellant to file a reply. In most instances, non-parties with an interest in a case attempt to influence its outcome through briefs as amici curiae.

**amicus brief (amicus curiae brief)** *See:* amicus curiae (friend of the court).

**bench memorandum (bench memo or bench brief)** A clerk's brief on the legal issues of a case written for a judge. A bench memorandum, or bench brief, is a summary of the issues in a pending case, including the issues as raised by the parties, the legal arguments and evidence underlying those issues, issues not raised by the parties, and additional legal research. Although some judges prepare a bench brief for the judge's own use, bench briefs are more often prepared by a judge's law clerk for that judge's use, by the clerks of one judge for consideration by other judges, or by the staff attorney for a court for the use of judges assigned to hear a case. A bench brief is often used by a judge to prepare for a hearing or trial, prior to the hearing of an appeal, or prior to the drafting or promulgation of an opinion. The content and structure of bench memoranda vary widely among judges. A similar brief is often written by students managing law school moot court programs in order to assist judges in preparing for mock trials and oral arguments.

**Brandeis Brief** A brief using social science data to prove a fact of legal significance. The first Brandeis Brief was written by Louis Brandeis and Josephine Goldmark, defending a state statute restricting the hours of employment for women, in Muller v. Oregon, 208 U.S. 412 (1908). The brief depicted hundreds of studies by social scientists to demonstrate the discrimination and health risks that were the focus of the Oregon law. The term now refers to a legal argument based on social science, although it is less appropriately used to describe any very long brief.

**case brief (brief a case)** Outlined notes made while studying a judicial opinion. A case brief is a summary of the elements of the judicial opinions in a case, usually prepared by students studying the case as a requirement for a law course. The brief is a list of core elements from the case, such as the facts, disposition at trial, issue presented, analysis, conclusion, ruling, dissenting analyses, and disposition on remand. Various teachers and writers have preferred categories, and not all apply in every case. In general, students new to the study of law write long and careful briefs and learn much about the case through that process, but within a few weeks their fears abate, their briefs shrink, and the process fails. The most important role of the brief is not to isolate a rule of law but to understand the process by which the case arose and reached a decision, so that the student can apply a similar analysis to similar facts in the future.

*See also:* law, law school, legal pedagogy, case method (casebook method or Socratic method).

**letter brief**   Written legal argument submitted as a letter to court and opposing counsel. A letter brief is a very short legal argument presented not as a formal brief but as correspondence to the court, copied to the other counsel of record. Letter briefs are often used to suggest to a court changes in the law following an argument but prior to the disposition of the matter argued.

**memorandum brief**   The brief in a trial court. A memorandum brief is a consolidation of two synonymous terms — brief as well as memorandum of arguments and authorities — both represent the same form of written legal argument, and the memorandum brief is a common label.

**table of authorities (argument list or index of authorities)**   The authorities presented in a legal argument. The table of authorities, or sometimes the table of cases, in a brief lists all of the sources of law being argued in the brief, along with their citations from the books in which they were published and, increasingly, the databases in which they are stored for on-line access. This was once known as the argument list.

*See also:* authority, authority as agency.

**trial brief**   A pre-trial outline of a party's legal arguments. A trial brief is a document prepared by an attorney detailing the arguments to be advanced in the either a civil or criminal trial. Trial briefs are required in nearly all federal court proceedings, and in some contested administrative proceedings, but they are not required in many state trial proceedings. The brief will generally include a statement of the case, which is a recitation of the facts of the case along with the most salient evidence that demonstrates those facts, followed by detailed legal arguments of the issues affecting liability that apply and a table of authorities that support those arguments. Trial briefs are usually submitted in advance of trial, often required by local rules to be served on the court and opposing counsel before the pre-trial conference.

**brig**   A jail or prison in the sea services. A brig is a naval jail or prison, either a restricted area aboard ship or on a naval base used for the detention of those under charge or on punishment detail, under the jurisdiction of the U.S. Navy, the U.S. Marine Corps, or the U.S. Coast Guard. Most brigs in the navy are staffed by Marine guards. This use of the term is distinct from the two-masted square-rigged sailing ship of the same name,

although the use of brigs as prison hulks may explain the term's penal origin.

**bright-line rule (bright line rule or bright line test or binary test)**   A legal standard requiring satisfaction or failure of a condition. A bright-line rule is a standard for deciding a legal issue based upon the apparently unambiguous satisfaction or failure of satisfaction of a condition. An example of such a rule is the age requirement for being a member of Congress set out in Article 1, Section 2, Clause 2 of the U.S. Constitution, which requires that a person first attain the age of twenty-five to be seated in the House of Representatives. Some courts are so keen to avoid the appearance of discretion by adopting a bright-line rule, that the label is sometimes (and unfortunately) applied to complex rules that depend on the satisfaction of more than a condition that admits to many degrees of satisfaction, or to a rule that depends on the satisfaction of several conditions. Bright-line rules are often contrasted with balancing tests, yet often a seeming bright line requires considerable balancing of competing interests or frailties of evidence either to determine whether ambiguous or uncertain facts satisfy a condition or to determine the facts that would satisfy a seemingly clear but in fact ambiguous condition. There is no difference between a bright-line rule, a bright-line test, a bright-line standard, or a bright line (in this context).

**Brillhart abstention**   *See:* abstention, abstention doctrine, Brillhart abstention.

### broadcasting

**equal time rule (equal-time rule)**   Broadcasters of a political candidate must give equal time to an opponent. The Equal Time Rule, part of the Communications Act of 1934 and partially codified at 47 U.S.C. § 315 (2010), requires any broadcaster that offers a political candidate time on air to give equal time to any opposing candidate who requests it. Exceptions to the rule include documentaries, on-the-spot news events, bona fide interviews, and scheduled newscasts. The broadcast of debates does not give rise to the equal-time rule because they are news events. The rule was instituted to prevent broadcasters from possessing undue influence over the course of elections. Its emphasis on access by candidates to broadcasters differs from the now-obsolete fairness doctrine, which required honest, equitable and balanced presentation of matters of public importance.

**fairness doctrine**   A former FCC rule requiring unbiased presentation of controversial public affairs. The fairness doctrine was an FCC rule that required licensed broadcasters to present controversial matters in the public interest without bias but in a manner that is honest, equitable and balanced. It was abolished in 1987.

*See also:* broadcasting, equal time rule (equal-time rule).

**Brocard** A maxim stated in Latin. A Brocard is a maxim, particularly a Latinate maxim used in canon or civil law. The term is derived from Bishop Burchard, an eleventh–century German canonist. It is better to capitalize the first letter.
*See also:* maxim.

**broken windows policing** *See:* police, policing, broken windows policing (quality of life policing or neighborhood order policing).

**broker (brokerage)** Intermediary between a buyer and seller. A broker serves as a conduit of information and consideration between a buyer and a seller, often facilitating negotiations between the parties contemplating a contract for goods or services. Thus brokers arrange a variety of transactions, and different brokers negotiate the purchase or trading of insurance, loans, realty, shipping, securities, and merchandise, and commodities. A broker rarely takes the objects sold into possession, that being the role of an escrow agent, delivery agent, or factor. A broker is usually an individual, but a law firm, brokerage, bank, or other institution may act as a broker for certain purposes. A broker may be an agent for one, both, or neither party. As a commercial broker, or public broker, the broker is merely an agent for the principal represented and not a fiduciary. When the brokering relationship requires advice from the broker to the principal, upon which the principal is likely to rely, or must rely, the broker becomes a fiduciary.

**securities broker (registered broker or stock broker or initiating broker or future commodities merchant)** A person buying and selling securities on behalf of others. A stock broker is a person in the business of buying and selling corporate equity stocks for clients other than the broker's employer. Securities brokers buy and sell a wider range of securities that are publicly listed and traded on public exchanges, and sometimes securities that are privately held. Securities brokers who are registered include two primary forms of broker, an introducing broker (IB) and a Futures Commission merchant (FCM); a single trade is likely placed by the principal (or the client) with the IB, who forwards the trade to the FCM to be transacted on a trading floor.
*See also:* share, share as stock.

**brothel** *See:* prostitution, brothel (bawdy–house or bordello or house of ill fame or house of ill repute or house of prostitution).

**brother** *See:* family, sibling, brother (sister).

**brother-in-law or sister in law or sister-in-law** *See:* family, sibling, brother in law (brother–in–law or sister in law or sister-in-law).

**browse-wrap agreement** *See:* contract, specific contracts, clickwrap agreement (browse–wrap agreement).

**brush name or nom de pinceau or nom de plume or pen name** *See:* name, alias, pseudonym (brush name or nom de pinceau or nom de plume or pen name).

**brutality (brutal)** The use of excessive physical force or the causing of excessive damage. Brutality is the inhumane, base, or uncivilized treatment of another person, usually by the use of excessive physical force or the infliction of pain or mental stress, but generally by the treatment of a person in a manner that denies the dignity of either the brute or the victim.
*See also:* police, police brutality; police, police brutality (excessive force by police).

**police brutality** *See:* police, police brutality.

**Bruton error** *See:* confession, Bruton error (Arranda-Bruton error or Bruton rule).

**BSE or mad cow disease** *See:* bovine spongiform encephalopathy (BSE or mad cow disease).

**bubkus (bupkus)** Nothing, or a mere token.

**buccal swab** *See:* deoxyribonucleic acid, buccal swab.

**budget** A detailed accounting of anticipated revenue and expenditures. A budget is a plan of the income and expense for a given time into the future, allocating funds for particular expenses and setting priorities for their expenditure. It typically includes an accounting of all funds reasonably expected to be earned or generated, and an accounting of all expenditures that are authorized to draw upon those funds.

**Budget of the United States Government** The federal budget. The Budget of the United States Government is the formal name for the budget for all agencies of the United States that is proposed by the President for enactment by the Congress to fund programs in the fiscal year following it.
More generally, the federal budget is the sum of legislation passed by the Congress to fund federal projects for a given year. The budget is enacted according to a pattern derived in part from the Constitution, in part from statute and executive order, and in part from custom. The President proposes a budget to the House of Representatives. The House introduces a form of the budget as an appropriations bill and passes it with whatever amendments are agreed in the House. The Senate takes it up and amends it, and the two versions are reconciled and passed then by both houses. The President must sign the budget as a whole and lacks the ability to refuse spending on specific items.
*See also:* reconciliation, congressional reconciliation (reconciliation bill or reconciliation instruction or reconciliation process).

**budget resolution** A non–binding plan for federal taxes and spending. A federal budget resolution is a non–binding concurrent resolution that establishes a plan for revenues and spending several years into the future, according to which additional bills are drafted as spending and revenue legislation that are enacted as law.

**buffer**   Empty or unused land or space around a sensitive area. A buffer is an area around a critical bit of geography, or between two areas, in which no use or activity is allowed that would affect the critical use of the protected areas. A buffer may be required around or between farmland to thwart the intermingling of unwanted seeds or fertilizers.

**bug or wire or hidden microphone**   *See:* surveillance, electronic surveillance, covert listening device (bug or wire or hidden microphone).

**buggery (bugger or buggerer)**   Deviant sexual activity. At the common law, buggery was the crime of any sexual act between a person and an animal. It was later expanded to include any sexual contact considered unnatural or illegal, but most often meant homosexual sex. Buggery is now nearly synonymous with sodomy, whether committed by people of different or the same genders, although sodomy has been recurrently defined to include acts by mouth that are generally not included in buggery, and buggery includes acts with animals that might or might not be included in sodomy. Private acts of buggery between consenting adults are constitutionally protected, yet other acts of buggery remain criminal. A bugger or buggerer is a person who engages in buggery.
   *See also:* sodomy (sodomize or sodomitel).

**building line**   *See:* boundary, building line (set back).

**bulk goods**   *See:* goods, bulk goods (bulk of goods).

**bulk sale**   *See:* sale, bulk sale.

**bunco scheme**   *See:* fraud, confidence game, bunco scheme (bunco man or bunco men).

**bundle of rights metaphor**   *See:* property, bundle of rights metaphor (bundle of sticks).

**bundling (bundled discount)**   The sale of multiple products in a single bundle for purchase. Bundling is the practice of selling a variety of separate products in a single unit or bundle. Bundling has become a common practice in the sale of computer software. A bundled discount occurs when a firm sells a bundle of goods for a lower price in sum than the seller charges for the goods sold individually.

**buoy**   A marker in a body of water. A buoy is any marker or small platform that floats upon the surface of a body of water, anchored to the lakebed, riverbottom, or seabed. The most common buoys are aids to navigation that mark navigational channels, provide markers for the direction of navigation, and warn of hazards to navigation. As part of the lateral system of navigation, navigational buoys are divided into nun buoys and can buoys: the nun being tapered at the top, colored red, and given odd numbers, the cans being square at the top, colored green, and given even numbers. As a vessel enters a harbor from the sea, it is to keep the cans to port and the nuns to starboard. Moving or damaging a navigation buoy is a violation of federal law. Other buoys include mooring buoys, weather observation buoys, and private buoys such as salvage buoys and buoys marking aquacultural areas.

**bupkus**   *See:* bubkus (bupkus).

**burden**   Obligation or limitation of action or use, a cost. A burden, the metaphorical notion of a weight to be carried, is the description of any cost, obligation, or limitation in legal analysis. It is the opposite of a benefit. The burden under a statute is the cost, effort, and lost opportunities of compliance with it. The burden under a contract is the cost of performance. Burdens, however, exist in the absence of statutes and laws as well, as one must bear the burden of the nuisances of neighbors and the loss of freedom from monopolies, as well as the burdens of parenthood, of homeownership, employer responsibility for employees, and so on. Law and economics and administrative law attempt to monetize burdens, using the valuations of choice to compare the costs of regulatory alternatives. Constitutional law attempts a more rhetorical balance, in comparing the burdens on commerce to the benefits sought as a legislative purpose. Evidence and trial practice have an array of varying levels of burden, all upon the party who would prove a point either in legal argument or as a fact.
   *See also:* balance, balancing test; benefit (beneficial); easement, burden of the easement; proof, burden of proof | burden of persuasion and burden of production and burden of proof; onus.

**burden of going forward**   *See:* proof, burden of production (burden of going forward).

**burden of persuasion**   *See:* proof, burden of persuasion.

**burden of production**   *See:* proof, burden of production (burden of going forward).

**burden of proof**   *See:* proof, burden of proof, scintilla of evidence; proof, burden of proof, preponderance of the evidence; proof, burden of proof, modicum of evidence (some evidence or any evidence or no evidence); proof, burden of proof, manifest weight of the evidence; proof, burden of proof, irrefragable proof (irrefutable proof); proof, burden of proof, clear and positive proof; proof, burden of proof, clear and convincing evidence (proof by clear and convincing evidence); proof, burden of proof, beyond a reasonable doubt (proof beyond a reasonable doubt); proof, burden of proof | burden of persuasion and burden of production and burden of proof; proof, burden of proof (standard of proof).

**burden of the covenant**   *See:* covenant, real covenant, burden of the covenant (running of the burden).

**burden of the easement** *See:* easement, burden of the easement.

**Bureau of Alcohol** *See:* police, police organizations, Bureau of Alcohol, Tobacco, Firearms, and Explosives.

**Bureau of Land Management** *See:* land, public lands, U.S. Department of Interior, Bureau of Land Management.

**bureaucracy (bureaucrat)** The structure of personnel within the divisions of government. Bureaucracy is the system of personnel, regulations, and customs that performs and governs the actions of a large organization or the offices of the government. A bureaucracy involves divisions of labor among persons and offices and a well-organized hierarchy. A bureaucrat is a professional within a bureaucracy. Both bureaucrat and bureaucracy are recurrently used as terms of abuse of government officials, although a bureaucracy is essential to the successful implementation of government policy in a large citizenry.
*See also:* government, forms of government, bureaucracy.

**Burford abstention** *See:* abstention, abstention doctrine, Burford abstention.

**Burger court** *See:* court, U.S. court, U.S. Supreme Court, Burger court.

**burglary (burglar or burgle or burglarize or burglarious or burglariously)** Illegally entering a building to commit a felony. Burglary is the felony of trespassing in a building that is normally occupied by people with the intent to commit a theft or other felony therein. At the common law, burglary was the breaking and entering of the dwelling of another at night with the intent to commit a felony within that dwelling. Contrary to the common association of burglary with theft, burglary has always included such entries with the intent to commit other felonies, including the intent to murder, kidnap, assault, rape, menace, etc. Statutory modifications and judicial interpretations have broadened the scope of burglary and created a variety of categories within it. There are many variations among jurisdictions on the formula of burglary, differing in the definition of the building, whether the building need be occupied, whether the offense must be committed at night, why the entry is wrongful, and the purpose of the entry. A burglary is the act of a burglar; to burgle or burglarize is to engage in that act; to do something as a part of a burglary is to be burglarious or to act burglariously.
*See also:* stealing (steal or stolen); thief; robber; robbery (rob).
*common law* Breaking and entering into a dwelling at night to commit a felony. At the common law, burglary was the illegal breaking and entering into a dwelling house during the hours of darkness with the intent to commit a felony in the house. At the common law, hours of darkness required a dimunition in the ability of a person to see and recognize another. The intent to commit any felony while in the dwelling was sufficient for the commission of the crime.

**burglariously (burglarious)** A pleading requirement in some jurisdictions for a charge of burglary. "Burglariously" is a technical term that was necessary at common law to satisfy the requirements of an indictment of burglary. Some jurisdictions still require this term to be used in the indictment, though many modern jurisdictions have moved away from this requirement as long as all of the elements of a crime have been satisfied.

**cat burglar (second-story man)** One who uses stealth or cover of darkness to enter into buildings to commit theft. Cat burglars are burglars who use stealth or cover of night to enter into buildings to commit theft. Because of the dexterity required to climb walls, the term is often applied to burglars who enter through elevated windows or doors, likewise the term, second-story man.

**burial rights** *See:* sepulchre, right of sepulchre (burial rights).

**burqa or burqua or burka or niqab or purdah** *See:* veil (burqa or burqua or burka or niqab or purdah).

**bursting-bubble theory** *See:* presumption, bursting-bubble theory (Thayerian rule).

**business** Any enterprise creating employment, service, or profit. Business, in most senses of law, is any operation of buying, selling, manufacture, or service conducted for profit. In a larger sense business signifies any operation intended to persist over time in which a person or a group of people pool and utilize their labor, expertise, and resources to achieve a goal or set of goals. Business is only loosely a synonym for a corporation, because business is done by individuals yet the business is the enterprise or activity and the corporation is the entity that performs it. Colloquially, "business" has many senses, particularly a reference to one's private affairs and a reference to mechanical or biological processes, as in "the business end of a gun" (the barrel) or "the business end of a horse" (the rear).
*See also:* hearsay, hearsay exception, hearsay allowed regardless of witness availability, business record (regularly conducted activity or business-records).

**business accommodation** *See:* accommodation, business accommodation.

**business acquisition** *See:* acquisition, corporate acquisition (business acquisition).

**business combination** *See:* combination, business combination.

**business court** *See:* court, business court.

**business enterprise** An entity engaged in business. A business enterprise is any entity, whether it is an individual, a corporation, an unincorporated association, or, in some instances, an arm of a government, that is continuously engaged in commercial activity, especially buying and selling goods, assets, or services.

**minority business enterprise** A business enterprise that is majority-owned by members of a racial minority. A minority business enterprise is any business enterprise that is owned, or at least a 51% stake of it is owned, by U.S. citizens who are African American, Latino, Asian, American Indians, Eskimos, or Aleutian Islanders. Certain grants and contracts are reserved for competition from minority business enterprises.

**business expense** *See:* expense, business expense.

**business franchise** *See:* franchise, business franchise (franchise agreement).

**business guest** *See:* invitee (business guest).

**business hours** *See:* time, hour, business hours (close of business or COB).

**business income tax** *See:* tax, business income tax (business privilege tax).

**business judgment rule** Corporate directors must act for the corporation in good faith. The business judgment rule is a barrier to liability for decision made by the directors of corporations, in which the wisdom of a judgment is not to be second-guessed by a court, and the director will not be liable for mistaken decisions, as long as each director acted with due care, undivided loyalty to the company, and in good faith, assumes that corporate directors act on an informed basis and in good faith when taking actions on behalf of the corporation.

**business method patent** *See:* patent, business method patent (business model patent).

**business model patent** *See:* patent, business method patent (business model patent).

**business necessity test** Balancing test to determine whether discriminatory hiring practice is defensible. Business necessity is a defense to a claim of discriminatory hiring or promotion requirements of a private employer that creates a burden or benefit that falls with statistically significant disproportion on one gender or race. The defense can justify the requirement if there is no evidence of a deliberate use for a discriminatory purpose and the failure to use the requirement would significantly decrease the status of the company, interfere with the company's legitimate business, or endanger the company's employees.

**business privilege tax** *See:* tax, business income tax (business privilege tax).

**business purpose doctrine (business-purpose)** Activities must be related to business to qualify for preferential tax treatment. The business purpose doctrine was first articulated in Gregory v. Helvering, 293 U.S. 465 (1935), which held that transactions with no purpose in furthering the goals of the business other than reducing tax liability would not be recognized as business expenses as a matter of tax law.

**business record** *See:* record, business record; hearsay, hearsay exception, hearsay allowed regardless of witness availability, business record (regularly conducted activity or business-records).

**business trust** *See:* trust, blind trust (business trust).

**place of business** A place where the work of a business is done. A place of business is a fixed place where the tasks are performed that are associated with the business of a person or entity. Places of business include a place of commerce in which transactions between the individual or entity are performed, a place of service where services to the public are provided, a place of administration where managerial or support work is performed to facilitate business elsewhere, including warehouses or stores for inventory or supplies. An entity may have more than one place of business, indeed many more, though only one will be its principal place of business. Not every place a person or entity conducts business is a place of business, and spaces not under the control of the individual or entity, such as a bank or auction house controlled by others do not become the place of business of a person who goes to such a place to engage in a transaction. A vehicle may be a place of business, although by custom a place of business is in one location, and for some purposes depending on both the rationale of the legal designation and the facts, a vehicle would be a place of business. A range of law affects places of business, not the least being zoning laws, employment laws, health and safety laws, liquor laws, tax laws, and the rules of civil procedure.

**principal place of business (corporate domicile)** Where the officers of a business control it. The principal place of business of an entity is the place where the officers of that entity ordinarily perform the tasks that direct, control, and coordinate the entity's activities. Metaphorically, the principal place of business is the entity's nerve center or its heart. It will usually be the place where the entity maintains its headquarters, unless the headquarters is not the actual center of direction, control, and coordination.

A corporation may be served process at its principal place of business, and the forum in which it is located has jurisdiction over it. More specifically, a corporation's principal place of business is a forum for its citizenship as a matter of federal diversity jurisdiction. Under 28 U.S.C. § 1332(c)(1), a corporation is a citizen of the state in which it is incorporated and also of the state in which it has its principal place of business. Note: there is no difference between a corporation's domicile and its principal place of business. *See also:* forum.

**bust (busted)** An arrest, or to be observed committing a wrongful act. A bust is a slang term with a variety of meanings. In police slang it is a common term for a criminal arrest, particularly an arrest on the basis of drug possession or other street crimes. More generally, to be busted depicts any person being observed in the commission of an illegal, incriminating, or embarrassing act; it is also used to depict one person physically assaulting another person or shooting another person with a firearm (an act for which there are many other slang terms, such as "pop" or "crack"). A bust may also depict a party, particularly with many people in attendance, or raucous behavior. (Its more customary meanings are the human torso or a sculpture of a head and torso.)

*See also:* arrest.

**but-for causation**   *See:* causation, but–for causation (but–for cause and but–for test).

**butterfly ballot**   *See:* ballot, butterfly ballot.

**butts and bounds**   *See:* metes and bounds (butts and bounds).

**buy**

**buy–in (buy in)**   An investment that allows future investments or activity. A buy–in is any initial investment or an investment for the purpose of later activity. The term's meaning varies in specific contexts. In contracts, buying–in is offering a discount to establish a business relationship to provide goods or services, with the expectation that the value of discount will be recovered in increased prices under that contract or subsequent contracts during the relationship. In securities, a buy–in is authorization to a broker to acquire securities to cover a short position. In some auctions or foreclosure sales, a buy–in is equivalent to a buy–back, in which the original owner acquires the property on offer. In partnerships, a buy–in is an investment in a partnership made by an outside party in order to gain equity in the partnership.

**buy–sell agreement**   *See:* sale, land sale, buy–sell agreement (buy/sell agreement).

**buyer (buy)**   The one who receives the property or service in a contract. A buyer is the party in a sale who purchases goods or services from a seller; the buyer receives (or the buyer's designee receives) some ownership interest in the goods or some benefit from the servicer, in return for money or other valuable consideration provided by the buyer. The buyer need not acquire the goods at the time of purchase but merely enter into a contract to acquire them at a later date. To buy refers to the action or conduct of a buyer.

*See also:* seller (sell); purchaser.

**buyer in ordinary course of business (BOCB)**   A good-faith buyer who purchases goods from an ordinary business. A buyer in ordinary course of business is a purchaser who buys goods from a seller who appears to be in a regular business and who has no reason to believe that the sale would affect the ownership rights or security interests of a third party. Certain transactions inherently put a buyer on notice of such a potential interest, such as a purchase from a pawnbroker. A buyer in ordinary course may be for cash or for property, for credit or not, and on secured or unsecured credit. The buyer in ordinary course takes goods that had been held by the seller subject to a security interest to the benefit of a third party, but the third party loses the security interest in the goods following the transfer to the buyer in ordinary course of business.

*See also:* ordinariness (ordinary as routine or ordinarily).

**buying on margin**   *See:* margin, buying on margin, margin call (maintenance call); margin, buying on margin.

**buyout**   The acquisition of all of the seller's interests. A buyout is the complete acquisition of an interest, the trade by one party of all of the rights and interests in an enterprise or employment or activity to an entity for money, value, or rights, sometimes including rights or ownership interests in the entity that buys the party out. Thus a contract buyout is the purchase of an assignment or cancellation of all of the interests of the party under the contract, an employment buyout is purchase of a surrender of all tenure and claims to past, present, and future compensation and benefits, and a corporate buyout is the purchase of all value and all relationships of the former corporation.

**leveraged buyout (LBO)**   The purchase of a firm using borrowed funds. A leveraged buyout is an acquisition of a firm, when firm's capital stock or assets are purchased with borrowed money, causing the company after the acquisition to be burdened with the new debt, which is usually secured by the company's assets.

**management buyout (MBO)**   Acquisition of a company from its owners by its managers. A management buyout is an acquisition of a company by a group of existing managers within the company, who acquire capital or arrange sufficient debt to leverage the purchase of the company from existing shareholders or owners.

**by right**   *See:* right, legal right, by right (as of right).

**by–law (bylaw)**   The rules that govern the ordinary businesses of an association. By–laws, or rules of governance, for a voluntary association form a contract binding on all of the members of the association for as long as they continue in their membership. Many organizations and associations have a charter or constitution providing for basic powers and structures as well as for the creation of by–laws setting forth rules for business and routine activities, and other associations and organizations have only by–laws. By–laws determine the name and purpose of the association, designate officers and their duties, provide for the election of officers, the conduct of meetings, the duties of members, and the manner of adoption and amendment of the by–laws.

*See also:* corporation, corporate by–laws (bylaw or by–law).

**bystander**   One nearby, particularly a person nearby an injury to a family member. A bystander to an event is a person nearby when it occurs who has no part in instigating the event. Bystanders may, however, be deeply affected by an event, being physically or emotionally injured by it or choosing to assist or interfere in it. A bystander to a tort may recover injuries suffered by the bystander, either physical injuries suffered as a result of the event itself or damages for mental distress if the bystander witnesses a harm to a family member provoking a sense of shock in the bystander. As a matter of usage, a bystander to a given event does not lose that standing by giving aid to someone harmed by it afterward, at which point the bystander may be considered a good Samaritan. Given the general uninvolvement inherent in bystanding, the term "innocent bystander" is redundant.

# C

**c**   The third letter of the modern English alphabet. "C" signifies a variety of functions as a symbol and as a designation of status. It is sometimes invoked by gamma, the word for the third letter in Greek. In medieval manuscripts and in early printed sources, "c" sometimes represents "t." It is translated into Charlie for radio signals and NATO military transmissions, into Charles for some police radio traffic, and into dash, dot, dash, dot in Morse Code.

*See also:* carbon (c ).

**C corporation**   *See:* corporation, corporations, C corporation.

**c as a Latin abbreviation**   A Latin word commencing in c. C is frequently an abbreviation for the Codex Justinianus, or the Code of Justinian. It was an abbreviation in Roman law, the sign for condemno, a vote for conviction in the questiones (or criminal tribunals) as opposed to A for absolvo.

**c as a rating**   Of the lowest acceptable ranking. C is used in a variety of forms for rating the quality of specific products. Many regulatory definitions depend on an alphabetic listing, with A the highest tier, and C either being the lowest or being the mediocre. For instance, Grade C beef signals meat from the least mature animal, a cow having a physiological maturity of forty-two to seventy-two months, as opposed to older animals with coarser meat and to younger animals with preferable meat. The USDA, however, has two lower categories, a D and an E tier, for animals of seventy-two and ninety-six months respectively, so the sense of C in this example is of middling maturity, not the least mature. Many private ratings also use "c" as the lowest recommendation among those recommendations the agency is willing to make. For example, bonds are rated by Moody's and other rating services on a three-tier scale, with A bonds the highest quality, and that tier being divided among Caa, Ca, C (prior to 1996 being the same), the more letters "a" that are incorporated the less risk and higher quality.

*See also:* a, a as a rating.

**c as a Roman numeral**   Latin symbol for one hundred (100). C is one hundred when used as a numeral. In the Roman system of numeralization, the addition of a C to the right of another Roman numeral adds 100 to the numerical value. The addition of a C to the left of another Roman numeral subtracts 100 from the numerical value.

**c as an abbreviation**   A word commencing in c. When used as the sole letter of an abbreviation, C may stand for circa, for the Latin about, referring to a likely date for an event. Also in dating, it may be a regnal year for Charles (Caro.) and it may stand for circuit (as in court), civil, contre (vs. in French), court, chapter (as in a statute or a book), century (as in 18th c.), or college. In a circle or sometimes otherwise, it refers to copyright. In Shepardization, it means criticized. As a component of other abbreviations, C can stand for any word commencing with that letter, particularly those above and Calcutta, calendar, California, Canada, Canadian, canal, case, cases, Catholic, central, chamber, Chancellor, Chancery, charter, chartered, Chicago, chief, China, Chinese, church, clean, clerk, coast, code, codex, Colorado, Columbia, comment, commerce, committee, common, Commonwealth, comprehensive, conference, Congress, Connecticut, conservative, constitution, convict, corporation, corpus, cost, council, county, credit, criminal, crown, cumulative, current, customs, and cyclopedia. It may also stand for the initial of the name of an author or case reporter, such as Cameron, Caines, Clarke, Cohen, or Cushing.

**c as copyright symbol ©**   The symbol of a copyright over the matter on which it appears. The copyright symbol used in the copyright notice in a perceptible copy of a copyrighted work is a C in a circle: ©. The copyright symbol in HTML is ©. In Java Script and XML it is ©. In Java Script and XSL it is ©.

*See also:* trademark, trademark symbol, r as trademark symbol ®.

**c as in hypotheticals**   The third character in the story. C often stands for a person, the third character in the story of a law school hypothetical. It might also stand for a corporation, and increasingly it may stand for a contract, although K is traditionally used for contracts to distinguish it from the character C.

**C-section**   *See:* birth, Caesarean section (C-section).

**C in C**   *See:* culpa, culpa in contrahendo (C in C).

**C.A.A. or CAA**   *See:* pollution, air pollution, Clean Air Act (C.A.A. or CAA).

**C.A.F.E. standards or cafe standards**   *See:* carbon, corporate average fuel economy standards (C.A.F.E. standards or CAFE standards).

**C.A.F.O. or CAFO** *See:* farm, concentrated animal feed operation (C.A.F.O. or CAFO).

**C.A.L.I. or CALI** *See:* law, law school, legal pedagogy, Computer Assisted Legal Instruction (C.A.L.I. or CALI).

**C.A.L.R. or CALR** *See:* research, legal research, Computer Assisted Legal Research (C.A.L.R. or CALR).

**C.B.A. or CBA** *See:* union, labor union, collective bargaining, collective bargaining agreement (C.B.A. or CBA).

**C.C.P.A. or CCPA** *See:* credit, consumer credit, Consumer Credit Protection Act (C.C.P.A. or CCPA).

**C.F.R. or CFR** *See:* regulation, Code of Federal Regulations (C.F.R. or CFR).

**C.G.L. or CGL** *See:* insurance, category of insurance, liability insurance, commercial general liability (C.G.L. or CGL).

**C.I.F. or CIF** *See:* shipping, shipping term, incoterm, cost of insurance and freight (C.I.F. or CIF).

**C.I.T.E.S. or CITES** *See:* species, endangered species, Convention on the International Trade in Endangered Species (C.I.T.E.S. or CITES).

**C.L. or CL** *See:* law, civil law (C.L. or CL).

**C.L.E. or CLE** *See:* bar, continuing legal education (C.L.E. or CLE).

**C.L.S. or CLS** *See:* jurisprudence, critical legal studies (C.L.S. or CLS).

**C.N. or CN or Napoleonic Code** *See:* France, French law, Code Napoleon (C.N. or CN or Napoleonic Code).

**C.O.B.R.A.** *See:* employment, employee benefit plan, health insurance plan, COBRA (C.O.B.R.A.).

**C.O.D.** *See:* shipping, shipping term, cash on delivery (C.O.D.).

**C.R.I.T. or CRT or CRIT** *See:* race, race as social construct, cross-race identification theory (C.R.I.T. or CRT or CRIT).

**ca.** *See:* circa (ca.).

**ca. res.** *See:* capias, capias ad respondendum (ca. res.).

**cabinet** A board of official advisers, usually in government. A cabinet consists of the officers who act as a single body to conduct administrative business and give advice to a chief executive. The title "cabinet" is usually reserved for governmental entities, most famously the Cabinet of the President, which by custom includes all of the secretaries of departments and by executive order includes certain White House officers and heads of other agencies. The text of the Constitution establishes only the role of principal officers and accords no particular authority to the Cabinet as an entity, although under the Twenty–Fifth Amendment, a majority of the principal officers of the departments and the Vice President may determine the President has somehow been rendered unfit to carry on in office, and the succession to the Presidency descends through the Cabinet members.

**cadaver dog or detection dog** *See:* dog, sniffer dog (cadaver dog or detection dog).

**cadaver or dead body** *See:* corpse (cadaver or dead body).

**cadi or kadi** *See:* qadi (cadi or kadi).

**Caesarean section** *See:* birth, Caesarean section (C–section).

**cafeteria plan** *See:* employment, employee benefit plan, cafeteria plan.

**calculation of damages** *See:* damages, calculation of damages (assessment of damages or computation of damages or measure of damages).

**calendar** The system for organizing time by years, months, and days. The calendar is a system or device for determining and evidencing the organization of the year. The calendar in Western nations commences, following the Gregorian reforms of the Roman calendar, on January 1 and is of 365 days (366 every fourth year). This calendar has been adopted by most nations for purposes of commerce and governance, including China and India, although each retains customary calendars that commence the new year on lunar or solar events. The Julian calendar, which begins its year on September 1, is still used in the Orthodox Church worldwide. Likewise, the Islamic calendar in Muslim states other than Iran, the Hebrew calendar in Israel, the Persian calendar in Iran and Afghanistan, the Buddhist calendar in Thailand, the Ethiopian calendar, and others are still used locally, although usually with some measure of integration to the Western calendar. Some businesses use a fiscal calendar, which adjusts the months to assign a fixed number of weeks per month. The most common of these is promoted by the International Standards Organization, or ISO, which starts every week on a Monday, the first week of the year being whichever week contains January fourth in the western calendar.
*See also:* session.

**court calendar** The schedule of a court's vacations and sessions, including trials and hearings. The court calendar documents the dates of court sessions and vacations, and for each session records docket calls, motion days, hearings, and trials as they are scheduled. To schedule a motion for hearing, a pre-trial conference, or a trial is to calendar it. Calendaring a case for trial is often done long before the trial itself, and the trial date from the calendar will govern the schedule of its preparation, such as the pre-trial conference and the drafting of jury instructions.

**off calendar** Postponed. If a case is off calendar, or put off the calendar, it has been removed from the court's schedule pending further action. Putting a case off the calendar is not a judgment on the case, final or otherwise.

**tickler calendar** A calendar that warns of looming deadlines. A tickler calendar is a system of reminders of upcoming tasks, organized so that every required filing or activity will be performed prior to or on its deadline. Tickler systems were managed by hand, written into paper calendars so that every open file's upcoming deadlines were given warning with sufficient time to meet them. Although the repository of the tickler is now likely to be automated, the system is only as effective as the entries initially made in it and the follow through given to its warnings.

**Caliph (Khalif or Caliphate or Khilafa)** The earthly regent of the Prophet Muhammad and pan-national leader of all the faithful. The Caliph is the worldly leader of all Muslim states. The word is an Anglicized version of the Arabic term Khalif, which literally means vice-regent or representative. The word is derived from kh la fa — to succeed. In Sunni Islam, the Khalif was seen as the successor of the Prophet in terms of his temporal political leadership, though not, of course, as prophet. The Caliph rules the Caliphate, an Anglicization of the Arabic Khilafa which refers to an Islamic state, to which all Islamic rulers are subordinate. There is not a Caliph at the present, which many observers suggest is one reason for the disarray among increasingly national variants of Islamic law.

**call** See: boundary, call.

**call option** See: option, securities option, call option (option call or call).

**call-in pay** See: pay, call-in pay.

**calumny (calumniate or calumniator or calumnious or calumniation)** A false accusation of criminal conduct. Calumniation is, technically, the act of accusing another of having committed a crime, when the accuser knows the other to be innocent. In Louisiana, a calumnious statement against a decedent may be the basis for the disinheritance of the calumniator. In common usage, however, calumniation more loosely suggests slanderous, libelous, or defamatory assertions, without the sense that the asserted conduct was itself unlawful.

**Calvo (Carlos Calvo)** A nineteenth-century Argentine diplomat and legal philosopher. Carlos Calvo (1824–1906) is best known for publishing Derecho Internacional Teórico y Práctico de Europa y America (1863), from which is derived from the Calvo Doctrine and for whom the Calvo Clause is named.

**Calvo Clause** A treaty, law, or contract clause that commits disputes to a national court. The Calvo Clause describes both specific provisions in the national laws of many countries as well as clauses in private contracts requiring disputes to be heard in the national courts of the nation in which (or with which) the contract is made. The Calvo Doctrine and the Calvo Clause are easily confused, but they are quite different. The Calvo Doctrine requires each state to treat aliens as it treats its nationals, a principle that has not yet been wholly recognized as international law. Calvo Clauses are matters of domestic law in each state and of private contracts, and they are not in themselves a principle intended to be a rule of international law.

See also: Calvo, Calvo Doctrine.

**Calvo Doctrine** States should treat aliens as they treat their subjects and may not use debts to justify invasion. The Calvo Doctrine is an argument for the restraint of states in their relations with others, particularly in requiring a state to treat aliens under the law in the same manner as it treats its nationals and in barring a state from using force to collect debts or enforce financial obligations by other states. This doctrine has specific effects in a variety of legal questions, particularly in the right to own property. A product of the great Argentine international law scholar Carlos Calvo's theory of state equality (first argued in 1868), it was particularly significant in the relationship between Latin American states and the United States, in a balance that has been most tested by expropriations of the property of aliens. Applying the Calvo approach to alien forfeitures, a state must treat aliens as it would treat its own subjects, no worse but no better, compensating an alien only to the extent that it would compensate its own nationals for damages suffered by the expropriation of property. If under a state's laws its nationals are entitled to no compensation for expropriated property, an alien likewise would have no right to compensation. So much of the Calvo Doctrine as related to debts was restated by Argentine foreign minister Luis Maria Drago in 1902, and it is sometimes known by that name.

See also: Calvo, Calvo Clause; intervention, Drago Doctrine.

**camera** Chamber. Camera is Latin for chamber, or room. Usually, the term stands for a judicial chambers, which is to say the judge's office. Several courts incorporate the word into their name, notably the Court of Star Chamber, or Camera Stellata, which met in a room of Westminster Palace with stars painted on its ceiling.

See also: court, English court, Star Chamber (Court of Star Chamber); chamber, judicial chambers (judge's chamber or judicial chamber).

**Camera Stellata** The Court of Star Chamber. Camera Stellata is Latin for chamber of stars, or as it is now well-known, the Star Chamber, and it refers to the Court of Star Chamber.

*See also:* court, English court, Star Chamber (Court of Star Chamber).

**in camera** *See:* in, in camera.

**Camp Delta or Camp X-Ray** *See:* prison, military prison, Guantanamo Bay (Camp Delta or Camp X-Ray).

**can** Able but not required. The verb can implies the potential to do something, either as a matter of ability or of discretion, but it does not imply a requirement of action.

**can as fire** To terminate the employment of an employee or contractor. "To can" is a colloquial reference for removing someone from a position of employment or service.

**canal** A water-filled trench that connects two larger bodies of water. A canal is a trench designed to contain and utilize water to create a navigable passage for boats or ships across land dividing two bodies of water. Canals such as the Panama Canal, which links the Atlantic and Pacific Oceans, and the Suez Canal, which links the Mediterranean Sea and the Red Sea, are international straits through which the states controlling the watercourse may not interfere with innocent passage.

**canary in the coal mine** *See:* species, indicator species (canary in the coal mine).

**canary or stool pigeon or pigeon** *See:* informant, snitch (canary or stool pigeon or pigeon).

**cancellation (cancel)** The voiding or destruction of an instrument or legal relationship. Cancellation, traditionally, is an act performed upon a written instrument in order to render it no longer negotiable, usually by crossing out its terms, marking "cancelled" upon it, tearing the paper, or punching holes in the paper. From this sense has arisen the term's general meaning as a renunciation of an obligation, particularly under a negotiable instrument, a contract, a will, a deed, or other instrument of obligation.

Cancellation specifically connotes the declaration by one party to a contract that has been breached by another party that the now-breached contract is considered by the non-breaching party to be terminated. Cancellation thus preserves the canceling, non-breaching party's rights but signals to other parties that it will perform nothing more under the contract.

Cancellation of a last will and testament is its renunciation or voiding by the testator. No other party may cancel a will.

*See also:* revocation (revocability or revocation or revoke).

**cancellation as a remedy (equitable cancellation)** The declaration an instrument is void as of that time. Cancellation is a remedy in equity by which an instrument is declared to be void and, usually, to

be rendered up or to be given by any holder of the instrument to its maker. Cancellation is similar to rescission, although with a distinction. The cancellation of an instrument or obligation is treated as occurring at the time of the cancellation and does not require the undoing of any act already carried out under instrument or in pursuance of the obligation. On the other hand, rescission requires restoration of the position of any party affected by an obligation or instrument to their position ex ante, to be restored to a place as if the instrument or obligation had never been made, so any act already carried out would be reversed, if possible.

*See also:* rescission, equitable rescission.

**cancer** Disease of uncontrolled cell division. Cancer, whether in humans or animals, is a condition in which cells in the body mutate and divide irregularly and excessively. A cancerous cell can spread the abnormality by causing nearby tissue cells to become cancerous or by moving through the circulatory or lymphatic systems. Cancer is often fatal. Some people are genetically predisposed to cancerous mutations, but even people with no predisposition to the disorder may contract cancer, sometimes as a result of exposure to carcinogenic agents.

**cancer cluster** A location with an unusually high incidence of cancer. A cancer cluster is a geographical relationship among instances of cancer in a discrete location that exceeds the statistical likelihood of cancer for the region surrounding the location. The existence of a cancer cluster is not, in itself, proof of an environmental hazard, though environmental hazards may cause cancer clusters. The concentration of cancer cases in a locale might be caused by one or more environmental hazards, by a genetic predisposition among members of a population, or be merely a statistical anamoly without any particular cause.

**cancer risk assessment** Determining the increase of cancer risk caused by a single factor. A cancer risk assessment is an investigative process by which epidemiologists, oncologists, and other experts determine the increase in risk of cancer inducement for a human, a population, or a region as a result of the exposure of a particular substance.

**carcinogen (carcinogenicity)** Any chemical agent or other substance that may cause cancer. A carcinogen is any substance which is known to contribute to the appearance of cancer within the human body. Carcinogenicity is the likelihood of a substance causing or contributing to the development of cancer in an individual or population of organisms exposed to it. Carcinogenicity is usually measured as either a potential to cause or not cause or as a ratio of reaction over time multiplied by the load or quantity of exposure.

**mesothelioma** A cancer of the membranes of internal organs, associated with asbestos exposure. Mesothelioma is a form of cancer that forms in the mesothelium, the membrane that covers many of the internal organs. It is a form of cancer particularly associated with exposure to asbestos; three–quarters of known cases of mesothelioma are among those with a history of asbestos exposure.

**candidate**   A person put forward for an office. A candidate is anyone who aspires to or is recruited for an office, position, or employment. The term implies an aspect of selection or qualification that must be completed in order for the candidate to succeed. Candidates for election to public office must, therefore, be elected by the voters of their constituency. Candidates, once identified, are rightly considered in the light of their potential obligations if the candidacy is successful; thus a candidate for judicial office is held to account to some of the canons of judicial ethics. The term evolved in classical Rome from the white robes worn by candidates for office, from which also comes the term candid.

**cannibalism (cannibal)**   The consumption of a human being by a fellow human being. Cannibalism is the act of consuming the flesh of another person. Though the eating of human flesh has occurred in societies throughout human history, it has been universally condemned as morally repugnant. Although widely thought to be a crime, cannibalism, or any eating of a corpse, was not in itself a crime under the common law or, more importantly, admiralty law, although it might be considered the criminal abuse of a corpse. Because most acts of cannibalism are preceded by the murder of the victim, the cannibal is usually indicted for homicide, as was the notorious case of Jeffrey Dahmer, a serial killer, in 1991. Only Idaho has expressly made cannibalism a crime.

*See also:* corpse (cadaver or dead body).

**canon**   A fundamental principle. Canon is an ancient word for a decree with the force of law, and it remains a term of art in the law for a basic rule invoking a comprehensive obligation, particularly one that arises axiomatically from the nature of things. The designation of a rule in law as a canon once was intended to distinguish an ecclesiastical rule from the laws of princes and legislatures, but in the last few centuries, the term canon in the secular law signals the rule it invokes as being both important and a principle that is to be applied to a given situation according to its purpose rather than with technical exceptions. Thus, the laws of the Christian churches remain canon law, but the principles of interpretation are canons of construction, and important rules of professional ethics are sometimes labeled canons. Payments made by tenants to ecclesiastical landlords were sometimes called the Canon, which was eventually applied to describe a species of quit-rent owed to secular landlords as well. Canon has numerous non–legal meanings, all of them being something subject to a rule, such as the church officer or the musical form, and not the least being the designation of fundamental texts in a body of literature.

*See also:* canon, canon law (ecclesiastical law); interpretation, statutory interpretation, canon of construction; lawyer, lawyer discipline, disciplinary rules, canons of ethics (code of professional responsibility).

**canon of construction**   *See:* interpretation, statutory interpretation, canon of construction.

**canon law (ecclesiastical law)**   Once the laws of the Christian church, now the laws of the various churches. Canon law is the body of law developed in the Christian church from Roman law to govern disputes both in the church and among the people and princes who were bound to it. Its origins are in the councils and episcopal proclamations of the third century, and it grew into its greatest flower in the middle ages, particularly with the writings of Gratian around 1140 and the reforms of Gregory in 1234. Further refinements, enlargements through new legislation and glosses on old texts, continued especially through the Council of Trent in 1545, the codification of Pius X in 1918, and the revision of John XXIII in 1963. Though canon law ceased to be a papal matter in 1571, it continued to have force in England under royal decree until 1857, since when it has been used to varying degrees within the various branches of the Christian church. In the United States, canon law is largely the project of the Roman Catholic Church, although protestant denominations, especially the Episcopal Church, retain large portions of canon law as the rule of the church.

*canon law and Roman law (ecclesia vivit lege romana)*   Canon law was largely derived from Roman law. Later imperial canon law was largely derived from Roman law. This reliance was quite natural, given that Roman law was largely organized in a manner already compatible with Christianity as a Roman state religion: Constantine chaired the Council of Nicea in 325 CE, and the Corpus Juris of Justinian was promulgated two centuries later, from 529 to 534. Thus the Codex contained regulations of religion from a Christian perspective, but more importantly, the organization of imperial Roman law had matured during the first engagements of the Christian church with laws. After the demise of the Eastern empire, canon law necessarily took on a life of its own, and the sources to which canonists looked to inspire the organization and method of their legal system were usually Roman, and usually later Roman–law materials. This process was greatly accelerated with the thirteenth–century revival of Eastern Roman law in Ravenna, Bologna, and Paris.

*See also:* note (notes).

**canonist**   One learned in canon law. A canonist is a specialist in canon law, particularly a glossator or, later, an author of canon law texts.

**Codex Juris Canonici (Code of Canon Law)**   The primary source of canon law for the contemporary church. The Code of Canon Law remains the foundation for the regulation of ecclesiastical affairs in the Roman church. The current edition of the code was adopted in 1983, revising the code promulgated in 1917 as a synthesis of the texts and codes then in force. The Code is subject to amendment by papal rescript. Though the official text is in Latin, the vernacular languages are employed for most purposes.

**Corpus Juris Canonici**  The later collections of canon laws. The Corpus Juris Canonici was developed from the Decretals of Gratian in the twelfth century, which were modified by order of Gregory IX and Boniface VII in the thirteenth century, and the last major component was added by John XXII, Clement C in the fourteenth. The work was made more orderly during the pontificate of Pius V in the sixteenth century, who assembled the Correctores Romani, a great collection of canon scholars, whose work was first published in 1582 and was the primary source of canon law until World War I, when the Codex Iuris Canonici succeeded it. The Corpus Juris Canonici is usually referred to by book, title, and chapter (or liber, titulus, et caput). The various titles are summarized in rubrics that generally had the force of law.

*See also:* canon, canon law (ecclesiastical law).

**decretals (Decretals of Gratian or decretum gratiani)**  Papal letters resolving disputes. Decretals are canon–law decisions of the early medieval popes written in letters. A decretum is a pontifical decision, that is a decision by the Pope, and an epistola decretalis is a letter containing such a decision. Any given decretum was not, and indeed is not, a source of general law but a decision in a given case brought before the Pope and given consideration. There are earlier decretals and later decretals than those collected in the famous collections of decretrals in the Decretals of Gratian around 1150, which he glossed with annotations, and eventually in the Corpus Juris Canonici in 1580, which became a primary source for the Codex Juris Canonici, which is the Code of Canon Law. Note that a decretal is still used to refer to something related to a judicial decree, and as a noun refers to a particular judgment in chancery.

*See also:* decree, decretal.

**canons of ethics**  *See:* lawyer, lawyer discipline, disciplinary rules, canons of ethics (code of professional responsibility).

## canvass

**canvass as campaign**  Solicitation of a community. A canvass is any solicitation through a population, seeking some form of assistance. A canvass may seek information, agreement with an idea, political commitment to support a candidate or cause, or financial support.

**cap and trade**  *See:* pollution, cap and trade, emissions trading; pollution, cap and trade, emissions cap; pollution, cap and trade.

**capable of repetition yet evading review**  *See:* justiciability, mootness, capable of repetition yet evading review.

**capacity**  The ability to hold or possess, including things and ideas. Capacity is the physical and mental ability to contain things and ideas and to do things. The term, originating in the Latin idea of what the lungs can hold, became the metaphorical basis for the lawful ability of a person to enter into an inheritance, and thus to exercise other powers at law. Capacity persists in English both as a reference to the volume a container may hold, and thus to the measure of a cable, pipe, or other facility for storage, and as a reference for the ability of a person to be lawfully vested with powers to act in a manner of significance under the law.

*See also:* sui, sui juris (non sui juris).

**capacity diminished or diminished capacity**  *See:* responsibility, diminished responsibility (capacity diminished or diminished capacity).

**capacity to consent**  *See:* consent, capacity to consent.

**capacity as agent (representative capacity)**  The significance of an act for another and not on the actor's behalf. Capacity as an agent is the form for an agent acting not for the agent's personal benefit or purpose but only for the benefit or on behalf of another person or entity, the agent's principal. In this sense, an action by a person may give rise to liability or opportunity for the principal and not for the agent. Further, an action brought against the agent in this capacity is not one in which the agent is personally liable.

*See also:* agent, actual agency.

**capacity as power of office**  The extent of the discretion to act within the scope of one's office. Capacity is the extent of the powers and duties of an office, job, or position of employment. Actions by an agent in the capacity of the agent may be attributed to a principal, but actions by an agent beyond the agent's capacity generally cannot be. Likewise, insurance policies that insure for acts within the scope of employment or official capacity do not insure against claims that arise from acts committed beyond that capacity. The scope of capacity is usually a question both of fact and of law. In the case of public officials, capacity may be coextensive with powers.

**criminal capacity**  The ability to understand and control one's actions. Criminal capacity is the general term for a criminal defendant's ability to form a certain state of mind or motive, understand or evaluate the defendant's own actions, or control them. It is the sufficient mental ability to form the guilty mind that is specified as the mens rea, as well as the ability to acquire the knowledge and intent required to meet the definitions of criminal conduct. Though in many instances, a person who lacks criminal capacity lacks legal capacity generally, the tests and forms of assessment for each tend to differ.

*See also:* mind (sound mind or unsound mind).

**diminished capacity**  A reduced mental state in the commission of a crime. Diminished capacity is a lack of ability to form the requisite knowledge or intent to commit a crime, of a person who otherwise is legally sane. Intoxication, abuse, trauma, disease, mental disability, and other physical or mental interference with knowledge or intent may cause diminished capacity, although a lack of personal responsibility does not. Diminished capacity is usually raised as an affirmative defense to a criminal charge, asserting the defendant has a mental disease or defect that does not amount to legal insanity but that still prevented the defendant from forming the specific intent to commit a criminal act. The effect of the defense varies according to its basis for assertion as well as varying among jurisdictions: in some it is a complete defense against some crimes; in others it is a basis for a reduced charge, and in yet others, it is a mitigation of sentence.

**incapacity to commit a crime (lack of criminal capacity or M'Naghten rule)** The inability or irresponsibility to tell right from wrong in the commission of a crime. Incapacity is an excuse to a crime, based on a defendant's inability to discern the nature of the act, to be responsible for the act, or to discern the wrongdoing inherent in an act. Incapacity may arise as a matter of age or as a matter of mental inability to form the knowledge required of capacity. Capacity is an element of criminal definition, and, once a suggestion is made that a defendant lacks capacity, the state must prove capacity. Therefore, incapacity need not be proven by the defense, but capacity must be proven by the prosecutor in the face of a claim of incapacity. The standard of the wrongfulness that is the test of the defendant's understanding is an objective, social concept of wrongdoing, not a subjective or personal understanding held by the defendant. The test is named for Lord Chief Justice Tindall's opinion in M'Naghten's case [1843] HL J16.

**mental defect as incapacity (idiocy or imbecility or idiot or imbecile or idiotic)** A mental disease or defect preventing the awareness required for criminal responsibility. A mental defect is a condition caused by a disease or defective aspect of the brain as a result of which of a person lacks the awareness required to form an understanding of the criminality of the person's own conduct or to conform that person's own conduct to the requirements of the law. The standard of mental defectiveness is a modern substitute for earlier standards of idiocy, in which a person lacked nearly all intellectual ability, and of imbecility, which was less severe than idiocy. The practical effect of both standards was to operate as an excuse from criminal liability, and for most purposes, each was merged into the M'Naghten test. That test has been refined into the standard of excuse for mental defect or for mental deficiency.

**youth as incapacity (infancy)** An infant or immature minor lacks criminal capacity. Youth is a basis for incapacity to commit a crime. A child under seven years of age is immune from criminal indictment, and a child from seven to seventeen is evaluated to determine whether the child has the capacity requisite. Even so, youthful lack of capacity is not a defense to a juvenile delinquency hearing.

*See also:* offender, youthful offender (juvenile offender or juvy).

**earning capacity** Potential for future income. Earning capacity is the amount of money that a person is reasonably likely to earn in a specified period of time, an assessment that is often used in calculating awards of damages in civil suits or awards of alimony or child support in divorce cases. In most cases, earning capacity is not based on a rigid actuarial formula; courts instead calculate an individual's earning capacity by taking into account various personal factors, including present and past income, age, health, education, training, and previous employment history. In workers' compensation and other statutory computations, however, a computation for earning capacity is specified in the statute; in some cases earning capacity is nothing more than lost wages, in which an estimate of time lost and to be lost is multiplied by an hourly wage already earned.

**individual capacity (personal capacity)** A defendant sued as a private person, not as an agent. Individual capacity designates an individual party in an action brought against the person not as an agent of the government but as a private individual for personal claims not arising from actions within the scope of office. The defendant is only liable for actions committed outside the scope of the agency that otherwise defined the plaintiff's relationship with the defendant. A claim brought against a person in the person's official and individual capacities encompasses both theories of liability.

**legal capacity** Mental and legal qualification to contract or make wills, deeds, or otherwise alter one's legal and equitable interests. Capacity is a measure of the ability, qualification, and competence of an individual, association, corporation, or government to perform civil acts, such as enter into a contract or transfer property. Capacity of the individual may be limited by insufficient age, by insufficient mental ability, or by a lawful disability as a result of a criminal conviction. Every adult is presumed to have the capacity to manage their legal affairs, to consent to acts that otherwise would invade one's privacy, to enter into contracts, and to freely alienate property owned by that adult. Capacity is not considered developed until adulthood, usually at the age of majority. Capacity may be diminished or lost, though, either by temporary impairment, such as by drunkenness, illness, or duress, or by permanent disability, such as senile dementia or court order. Capacity of an artificial person must be affirmatively created by the operation of law through constitutional powers in the case of government, or through statutory powers conferred through charter and executed according to appropriate means in the case of corporations.

*See also:* age (of age); mens, mens rea | capacity and mens rea; mens, mens rea | criminal incapacity | intoxication.

### incapacity (lack of contractual capacity or lack of capacity)

Lack of full age, independence, or reason. Incapacity is the lack of legal capacity to enter a contract. Minority, or a lack of control over one's affairs such that either a conservator has been appointed or the other party to a contract should have known the party lacks awareness of the legal significance of the act, amount to a lack of capacity. Legal disabilities created as a result of a criminal conviction do not, ordinarily, affect capacity to contract. A contract made by one who lacks capacity is not void but is voidable, and it may be ratified either by the formerly disabled party following the lifting of the disability or by one empowered to act on that person's behalf, such as a conservator or guardian.

*See also:* sui, sui juris (non sui juris).

### non compos mentis (non compotes mentis or non compos)

Legal incapacity. Non compos mentis, Latin for "not of sound mind," is a customary label for all forms of legal incapacity other than youth, whether the incapacity arises from a condition that is permanent or temporary. At common law, a person non compos mentis (or non compotes mentis) was either then an idiot, or afflicted with insufficient mental ability to engage in most daily tasks, or a lunatic, a person subject to delusions or other forms of mental illness, although all conditions that prevent a person from understanding the practical or moral significance of the person's actions amount to a person's being non compos mentis. The legal significance mirrors a general usage, in which to refer to someone as "non compos" is to suggest that they are mentally incapacitated and not to be held morally responsible for what the person does or says.

### non sui juris

Without legal capacity, and immune from suit. Non sui juris is a customary designation for someone or something without the capacity to sue or be sued. This status once resulted from a person's minority, but it is more often found in contemporary usage because an entity is sued, which is either immune from suit or which is not the property entity but a department or component of a larger entity, the smaller entity having no legal personality.

### marital capacity

A person's role in a marriage as a matter of law. Marital capacity as it is generally written refers to the relationship of a person to a marriage and rights in the marriage and marital property, as established under the law of a particular jurisdiction. If one spouse is sued only to extinguish spousal interests in property owned by the other spouse, which is sought to satisfy a claim against the other spouse, the first spouse is present in a marital capacity.

### mental capacity

The ability to assess, reason, and recall. Mental capacity is the ability to learn, think, and remember. It is a general term that is often used in law to coordinate specific ideas of legal capacity, mens rea, or volition. It is rarely used in itself except to determine the extent of a person's injury or disability. Even so, mental capacity is sometimes used as a synonym for legal capacity, particularly in determining whether a person has the capacity to enter a contract or to create a will.

### cognitive test

An assessment of a person's ability to learn and to recall information. A cognitive test is an assessment given to a person whose mental capacity is in issue to determine the degree to which the person is functionally capable of perceiving and accepting information from sources in the test, of reasoning from those sources to some degree, and of recalling that information. Cognitive tests may be based on an objective scale of human performance or on a relative scale, in which the test subject's performance is compared to the average skills of a younger or older person in school.

### official capacity (representative capacity as defendant)

A defendant sued as an agent, not as a private person. Official capacity is a designation for an individual party, nearly always a defendant, to distinguish the claim against the person as one brought against him or her in a representative capacity as an agent, employee, or officer of a government or, according to context in a representative capacity for a corporation. The defendant is only liable for actions committed within the scope of the agency that otherwise defined the plaintiff's relationship with the defendant.

### testamentary capacity

Sufficient awareness and understanding to make a will. Testamentary capacity is a measure of an adult's mental competence to perform a binding testamentary act, especially to execute a Last Will and Testament. Capacity is presumed in all adults, and the burden is upon a person who would demonstrate an act is made without capacity to prove lack of capacity as a matter of fact. Capacity requires that a testator understand the legal effects of the act to be committed, the extent of the testator's property, the identities of people who would be the natural objects of the testator's affections (family members whether or not they are devised a thing in the will), the significance of the dispositions that are the will, and be able to express by signature or mark the intent that these dispositions occur. These five elements are variously organized in judicial and statutory tests for competence. Proof of incompetence depends on proof of an absence of understanding for one or more of these elements at the time of the testamentary act. While often pled as if it were part and parcel with testamentary capacity, whether a will was the product of undue influence is a distinct question, although the plea is more likely to succeed if there is proof of a weakened mind that is more amenable to influence.

**insane delusion**  A person believing irrational things pertinent to a will lacks capacity to make one. An insane delusion is a belief that is of a nature that no rational person would believe it, and that arises without reasonable foundation and cannot be disbelieved despite evidence to the contrary. A person with an insane delusion that is relevant to the person's estate, heirs, or legatees is normally lacking in testamentary capacity, though a will may be reformed to omit only such clauses as were affected by the delusion.

**capias**  A writ of arrest. Capias is a category of writ ordering peace officers to seize and deliver the person named in the writ to the court that issued it. In some U.S. jurisdictions a capias is used instead of an arrest warrant.

The most common types of capias writs are capias ad respondendum and capias ad satisfaciendum. When the term capias is used without these qualifications in a criminal hearing, it is usually an abbreviation of capias ad respondendum, which is a form for the arrest of a person charged with a misdemeanor or with non-appearance at a hearing. (In Texas, the preferred writ in this circumstance may be the capias pro fine.) A capias ad respondendum in a civil proceeding was once used as a basis for securing personal jurisdiction over the defendant, though this writ has been replaced by modern service of process. The capia ad satisfaciendum, or ca. sa., was an arrest of a defendant who is held in order to allow a plaintiff who has received a civil judgment to execute the judgment.

See also: warrant, arrest warrant; capias, capias ad respondendum (ca. res.); capias, capias ad satisfaciendum.

**capias ad respondendum (ca. res.)**  A predecessor to service of process. A capias ad respondendum is a customary form of service of process by a sheriff or similar officer. The writ is still used in some jurisdictions as a writ of arrest in a criminal proceeding. In civil actions, it was once used as a summons of the defendant, ordering the sheriff or other officer to serve notice on a defendant of a pending civil action and to hold the defendant in custody to answer the action, though the defendant could post a bond for release. In most instances, to speak of capias is to speak of capias ad respondendum.

See also: bail.

**capias ad satisfaciendum**  A writ to arrest a defendant and secure execution of a judgment. A writ of capias ad satisfaciendum at common law was a writ for execution of judgment, in which the court directed the sheriff or other officer to place a defendant under arrest and to be detained until a civil judgment is satisfied. In the few jurisdictions that still use this writ, it is similar to a contempt order requiring satisfaction of judgment from a defendant who has not complied with prior orders or lawful demands for payment on a judgment.

**capita (caput or capite or capitum)**  A person, or the head. Caput is a Latin term both for head and for person, and its plural is capita. Thus, it is often an element in phrases such as per capita, for "by heads" or "per person," and it is a root for aspects of words such as capital for the head or top of anything. In the system of distribution for estates intestate, a distribution allocates an equal share to each person in a class or category.

See also: succession (successor or predecessor).

**capital**  Of the highest form. The varied meanings of "capital" all relate to its origins in an Indo-European term for head. The capital of a state or nation is its place of government. (Or, intriguingly, a capital is a seat of government.) A capital offense is one serious enough to warrant the punishment of death. In finance, capital refers to the basis of investment, as opposed to the interest that the investment accrues, and more generally it refers to wealth that may be traded.

**capital asset**  See: asset, capital asset.

**capital asset pricing model**  See: security, securities, securities valuation, capital asset pricing model (CAPM).

**capital expenditure**  See: expense, capital expenditure.

**capital gain**  See: gain, capital gain, net capital gain; gain, capital gain, adjusted net capital gain; gain, capital gain.

**capital-gains tax**  See: tax, capital-gains tax.

**capital improvement**  See: improvement, improvement to land, capital improvement.

**capital loss**  See: loss, capital loss.

**capital murder**  See: murder, capital murder.

**capital offense**  See: crime, capital offense (capital crime).

**capital outlay**  See: expense, capital outlay.

**capital punishment**  See: punishment, death penalty (capital punishment, execution).

**capital as seat of government**  Center of governance. The capital of a nation or a state is the designated physical location of the sovereign operations of the state, particularly its legislature, official office of its chief executive, and the chambers of its highest court. National capitals are the site of foreign embassies. Certain functions are required under some state constitutions only to be performed within its capital, and if the function is performed elsewhere it is of no effect.

**capital crime (capital offense)**  A crime punishable by death. A capital crime is a crime that may be punishable by death, regardless of whether in a given case the death penalty is sought or imposed. The early common law considered all felonies to be capital crimes.

*See also:* crime, capital offense (capital crime); punishment, death penalty (capital punishment, execution); execution, execution of a sentence of death (execution).

**non-capital crime (noncapital crime)** Crime ineligible for the death penalty. Non-capital crimes are crimes for which the death penalty is not available as a punishment, either as a matter of statute or as a matter of indictment.

**commercial capital** Assets that can be liquidated. Capital refers to expendable assets, primarily assets that are routinely converted into other forms of wealth, including money, securities, real and personal property, and, under some circumstances, obligations that may be transferred. Though a literal rendering of capital could encompass nearly all property, the term ranges from capital that is intended to mean liquid assets to a "capital asset" that is intended to be held for a period of a year or more. Capital is subject to a nearly infinite number of categories, including the source from which the capital is raised, such as capital raised from debts such as bonds (debt capital) and capital raised from the issuance of equity such as shares of stock (equity capital). Capital is also categorized by the purposes to which it is allocated or assigned, such as capital held as a hedge against risks (risk capital) or capital intended for a particular form of investment (venture capital). Capital may be less a category of assets than a measure of accounting, such as working capital, which is the difference between the assets and liabilities of an enterprise.

*See also:* tax, capital–gains tax; asset, capital asset; security, securities, securities valuation, capital asset pricing model (CAPM); loss, capital loss; expense, capital outlay.

**mezzanine capital (mezzanine equity or mezzanine loan or mezzanine debt or mezzanine financing or mezzanine investment fund)** Capital raised from debt following existing debt. Mezzanine capital is a form of capital derived from debt that is in the middle between other priorities of debt, below existing capital obligations and above commercial or short-term obligations. Mezzanine capital may be raised through the issuance of new equity or debt or both. If mezzanine equity is issued, it is likely to be preferred stock without voting rights, and if mezzanine debt is issued it is likely to be unsecured, or if it is secured, it amounts to something like a second mortgage. The whole of a mezzanine package is likely to be placed with a private lender or equity group, and repaid through a combination of payments in cash, in kind, and in equity, probably by warrants in the first instance. Mezzanine capital is typically more expensive than the sale or senior debt or the issuance of common stock, and it is used primarily for leveraged buyouts and for real estate development.

*See also:* buyout, corporate buyout, leveraged buyout (LBO).

**recapitalization (recapitalize)** Raising capital through sales of assets, equity, or debt. Recapitalization may include a variety of acts by a corporation or other business entity to increase its liquid capital, whether or not these acts lead to levels of capital that meet or exceed earlier levels. The most common means of recapitalization are the sale of assets, the issuance and offering of new equity, and the sale of debt. These acts may or may not be conducted with independent buyers, and the recapitalization may amount to no more than the shuffling of assets on the books of the one entity, or among the entity and other, integrated entities.

**venture capital (VC or risk capital or start-up capital)** Capital provided to a new commercial venture. Venture capital, generally, is any investment in a young enterprise intended both to assist the new commercial venture in developing its business into profitability and to yield high returns to the initial investors in a small venture with a high growth potential. Venture capital, more specifically, is a particular form of investment by a venture capital firm that provides an investment but also provides expertise in the development, marketing, and sale of the product of the young venture, realizing a significant profit from the relationship when the company is sufficiently mature for the investors to be repaid by the larger, sound entity.

**capitalism** The protection of private property and market commerce under the rule of law. Capitalism is an economic system based on private ownership of wealth and the means of the production of wealth production in society. Individuals are free to pursue their own interests, constrained only by the market forces of supply and demand. Capitalism does not preclude governmental regulation of markets, although regulation is limited to the assurance of honesty and security in transactions and the assurance of civic functions the market will not sufficiently perform. At its extreme, capitalism rejects public ownership of goods other than those needed to maintain a minimal state.

**capitation** Any measure that is paid or priced person by person. A capitation is any payment or obligation that is assessed per capita, or for every person in a relevant population. A capitation payment is thus a payment made for every person in a group or status, whether the payment is made once or recurrently. For example, a payment to hospitals by a medical insurer, assessed for every person insured, is a capitation payment, and the amount of the payment is the capitation rate.

In election law, a capitation is a poll tax, or a direct tax levied on every person, or adult or member of a class of person. States may collect capitations, although they are forbidden from the U.S. government and may not be a basis for the right to vote in any U.S. election. (Though it is not clear whether an income tax is a capitation, under the Sixteenth Amendment's allowance of a personal income tax, if it is a capitation, it is an exception to the Twenty–Fourth Amendment's prohibition on any capitation as a precondition to vote in a federal election. No state may enact a capitation or poll tax without violating the Equal Protection Clause.)

*See also:* tax (taxation); tax, poll tax (head tax or capitation tax); constitution, U.S. Constitution, Amendment 24 (Amendment XXIV or Twenty–Fourth Amendment).

**CAPM** *See:* security, securities, securities valuation, capital asset pricing model (CAPM).

**capriciousness (capricious or capriciously or caprice)** Unjustifiable. Capriciousness is the quality of an action or decision that lacks a foundation that makes any sense. Capriciousness is usually one half of deferential standard of review that would uphold a decision that is not arbitrary and capricious. To an extent, caprice is an emphasis on arbitrariness, yet capriciousness emphasizes the aspect of the decision being both personally rather than officially made and that it is unjustified in its making. Thus, a decision that lacks a reasonable foundation based on at least some form of evidence as applied to an appropriate policy, rule, or legal standard is capricious. An official decision taken for strictly personal reasons that do not equate to public reasons of an official justification is capricious as an official act.

*See also:* arbitrariness (arbitrary); review, standard of review, arbitrary and capricious.

**captain** Leader. A captain is a leader. Captain has many variant meanings in military law, maritime and admiralty law, corporate law, health law, tort law, and the law of agency. The term derives from head, and represents the leader, or head, of a group.

**captain of a vessel** *See:* ship, captain of a vessel, master; ship, captain of a vessel (sea captain or ship captain).

**captain of the ship doctrine** *See:* malpractice, medical malpractice, captain of the ship doctrine (doctrine of the captain of the ship).

**caption** The initial heading of a pleading or official document. The caption is now mainly the heading of a pleading, warrant, or document. In federal civil pleadings, the caption includes the court's name, a title incorporating the names of the parties or nature of the cause, a file number assigned by the court, and a designation of the form of the pleading (complaint; answer to a complaint; answer to a counterclaim designated as a counterclaim; answer to a crossclaim; third–party complaint; answer to a third–party complaint; or a reply to an answer).

Caption is still sometimes used to describe the statements of jurisdiction, although that usage is somewhat rare. The term in this sense is in the old "Certificate of Caption." Caption in that sense was equivalent to arrest, a sense that the word much longer retained in Scots law as the name of a warrant for the seizure of goods.

*See also:* arrest; warrant, arrest warrant; pleading.

**captive audience** *See:* audience, captive audience.

**capture (law of capture)** The act of creating new dominion over anything taken from a free or wild state. The capture of anything, or anyone, is to take it into one's custody, to acquire power over it so that it is captive to the will of the captor. Capture includes many practical senses that are specific to the taking control of physical entities such as wild animals, or people, or liquids and gasses, as well as metaphorical senses that invoke a similar process over ideas and images.

The law of capture allows wild animals and natural resources to be owned by the first captor. In some cases, as in a common pool of oil or water, this rule conflicts with older notions of property ownership, because it allows a person owning one parcel to draw oil or water from a common pool, extracting at least some oil or water from the portion of the pool under another's parcel.

*See also:* animal, wild animal, ferae naturae.

*natural resources* The law of capture applies to subterranean liquids and gas. Gas and liquid below the surface of the land are treated in a manner not unlike a wild animal in most jurisdictions, which apply a law of capture to give ownership to whomever can successfully extract them from a place the owner has a privilege to do so.

**captive** Anyone or anything that is not at liberty but is subject to the constraint of a person. A captive is someone or something (like an animal) that has been taken from its liberty. Captives do not lose their civil rights by virtue of their captivity. A captive taken on a battlefield may be a prisoner of war, a status that persists through all successive and continuous captivity.

**captor** One who captures a person or property. A captor, during an armed conflict, is one who has taken property from an enemy, or who has captured the person of an enemy. The captor of property may legally keep that seized property only in accordance with the laws controlling belligerents' rights, which in most cases forbid the taking of private property or the private retention of public property. More generally, a captor is anyone who captures a person, which may give rise to a claim for kidnapping, false imprisonment when the capture is not done in accordance with the law of arrest, or who captures an animal, which is lawful depending upon the property interests involved.

**capture as military seizure** Seizure of property or person as an act of war. Capture occurs when a person is taken prisoner or when a place or property is taken under control or into custody by combatants of a hostile military force. Capture is governed by the Uniform Code of Military Justice and by the laws of war.

**capture as taking an animal** A person's taking control of a wild animal. Capture occurs when a person exercises dominion, or purposefully controls, a wild animal and prevents it from escape. Generally, a captured animal is the property of its captor. The American common-law rule of capture is associated with, and was famously held in, the 1805 fox-hunting case Pierson v. Post, 3 Cai. R. 175, 2 Am. Dec. 264 (N.Y. 1805).

**rule of capture**   What a well can capture is owned by the well's owner. The rule of capture is an American common-law rule that entitles absolute ownership of a natural resource through seizure with intent to reduce to possession. The rule originally evolved around disputes over the seizure of wild animals, but has been applied by modern courts to subsurface natural resources. By way of illustration, a court might apply the law of capture to a dispute over oil drilling by saying that the party who extracted the oil is its owner, even if the subsurface oil reservoir sits under multiple properties. This common law rule has been modified in many jurisdictions to protect public policy interests; water rights, for example, are generally not subject to the rule of capture. Many jurisdictions with significant oil or gas deposits have also modified the law of capture to enforce their specific policy goals.

There are less prominent rules and maxims under the rubric of capture or the rule of capture. In some, an ability to control some property or rights allows the taking of possession or title in other property or rights. In others, the effect of one legal condition implies an additional condition.

**caput or capite or capitum**   *See:* capita (caput or capite or capitum).

**carbon (C)**   The sixth element of the chemical table. Carbon (C) is the fundamental element in all organic compounds, thus being essential to life on Earth. Carbon is also essential to many fuels, producing atmospheric carbon, most forms of which form pollutant chemicals as well as greenhouse gases. One form of pollution regulation is therefore a tax on carbon consumption, or carbon tax, which might be surcharged on the purchase of petroleum, coal, natural gas, or other carbon fuels.

*See also:* pollution, air pollution, criteria pollutants, carbon monoxide (CO).

**carbon copy**   *See:* copy, carbon copy.

**carbon credit (emission reduction unit or E.R.U. or ERU or certified emission reduction credit or C.E.R. or CER)**   Unit of carbon credited for reduced carbon production from a baseline in a carbon-trading scheme. Carbon credits are tradable commodities that are assigned to a carbon emitter in return for reduced or unused carbon production under the cap-and-trade system instituted following the ratification of the Kyoto Protocol.

**carbon dioxide (CO$_2$)**   An odorless, colorless gas formed of two oxygen atoms and one carbon atom. Carbon dioxide exists as a gas in the earth's atmosphere. It is produced by animal respiration and absorbed by plants during photosynthesis. CO$_2$ is a greenhouse gas, which means that it allows sunlight into the Earth's atmosphere but diminishes the escape of heat from the earth's atmosphere.

**carbon footprint**   Measurement of carbon produced by an entity or activity. A carbon footprint is a metaphor for the carbon consumed and released by a process, activity, or entity. Although a variety of means have been developed for isolating a formula for computing the extent of the carbon footprint, as of 2011, there is not yet a legally universal definition of carbon footprint that would, for instance, determine what forms of predicate activities count in the carbon footprint of a given action, or what value to give the varying role of carbon released in forms other than air emissions, or what function is played in offsets by tree plantings or sequestrations in computing the footprint itself as a gross or net datum.

**carbon monoxide (CO)**   An odorless, colorless gas in automobile exhausts. Carbon monoxide is produced when a carbon-based fuel, such as wood, coal, oil or propane is burned for energy but there is not enough oxygen to form a complete carbon dioxide molecule. CO is an asphyxiant as well as a toxic gas that causes the bloodstream of living animals, including humans, to stop transporting oxygen to the tissues.

**carbon tax**   A fee for acquiring or consuming carbon-based fuels. Carbon tax is an umbrella term for a variety of taxes and fees that create a financial penalty for the generation of carbon-based emissions, by taxing the consumption of carbon fuels that generate such emissions. To an extent, fuel taxes are carbon taxes.

**chlorofluorocarbon (CFC or hydrochlorofluorocarbon or HCFC)**   A compound of carbon, fluorine, and chlorine. A chlorofluorocarbon, or CFC is any of the great number of compounds formed of carbon, fluorine, and chlorine, especially volatile compounds based on methane and ethane that are harmful to the ozone layer or that are strong greenhouse gases, or both. Common examples include freon and halon. They are volatile organic compounds (VOCs) and greenhouse gases (GHGs). Hydrochlorofluorocarbons, or HCFCs, are similar compounds including hydrogen atoms, which destroy ozone and are being phased out in favor of hydrofluorocarbons, or HFCs, which are not known to harm ozone, though they are greenhouse gases and are likely to become more heavily regulated.

*See also:* ozone.

**corporate average fuel economy standards (C.A.F.E. standards or CAFE standards)**   Vehicle fuel efficiency standards. CAFE standards set a federal minimum average fuel efficiency for a manufacturer's truck fleet or passenger car fleet. Standards for car fuel consumption are set under the Energy Policy and Conservation Act.

**carcinogen** *See:* cancer, carcinogen (carcinogenicity).

**card check election** *See:* union, labor union, labor organization, card check election.

**care** Responsibility. Care is a responsibility in the performance of one's tasks. In vernacular English, "care" is a broad term, which initially meant a sorrow or grief but also a sense of being charged with a duty particularly to perform a task or to protect others. An ordinary duty of care is thus what one is customarily expected to do in performing the tasks one undertakes, with an understanding that one is always charged with some responsibility for those affected by one's actions. There are many distinct senses of care, with corresponding differences in responsibility and liability. The care of others whom a medical, ecclesiastical, or other professional might treat is both a more focused duty and one dependent on professional skills and standards. The care of a child or a dependent adult is a comprehensive obligation of food, shelter, and comfort. In the law, these are often reduced to levels of a duty of care, expressed in a range from the highest degree of care, to a fiduciary level of care, to reasonable care, to the slightest degree of care, to no responsibility to care.

*See also:* negligence, standard of care; care, duty of care, reasonable care.

**carelessness (careless)** Behaving without sufficient care under the circumstances. Carelessness is the condition of acting carelessly, which is the condition of any person who does anything with less than a responsible level of care, or whose attention to a given matter or the person's surroundings is less than a responsible level of care. Inattention, a failure to consider the consequences of a given action or occurrence, behavior without regard for the risk of harm the behavior poses to people or property, indulgence or intemperance, partiality or self-interest, knowing injustice, cruelty, or falsehood are each sometimes the hallmark of carelessness. Carelessness has varying degrees as a matter of criminal and civil liability; carelessness is more similar to simple negligence when it is used as a standard of civil liability, but it is more like gross or knowingly reckless disregard for the harms one might cause when used as a standard of criminal liability. In both cases, however, whether particular conduct is careless depends on the context in which the conduct occurs. When there is an established custom among those who engage in the conduct in question, that custom may establish a pattern of safe or reasonable behavior against which the conduct in question can be measured. The inherent or apparent dangerousness of conduct, the preparation or knowledge of the actor, and the degree to which the vulnerability or reliance of the parties injured may all affect carelessness.

**duty of care** The degree of responsibility arising from any circumstance or relationship. Duty of care is the specific obligation or level of responsibility that applies in every situation from one person or entity toward another person or entity. The general duty of care is one of reasonable conduct toward others, but there are both heightened and diminished duties, such as the higher level of responsibility of a fiduciary or the diminished level of a property owner toward a trespasser. The duty of care, however, is best understood within a context defined by a potential breach, such as the duty of care owed by a landlord to a tenant or the duty to a tenant's guest to provide accesses safe from structural dangers. Thus, a railroad may owe very different duties to a passenger with a ticket or a hobo riding the rails on the same train.

*See also:* breach, breach of duty, breach of fiduciary duty; breach, breach of duty, duty of care; negligence, standard of care.

**common duty** A duty shared by more than one party. A common duty is a duty that is independently assigned to more than one person. A person holding a common duty in concert with another person or persons has an obligation to perform the duty that is not abated until the duty is in fact finally performed, whether by that person, another who holds the common duty as well or, in some circumstances, by a third party with no duty. The common duty may arise from the owner's obligations of property co-owned, or from a contract in which a duty of one party is apportioned or shared, or from a responsibility of one party to secure the performance of another, to the benefit of a third, such as in a case of respondeat superior.

**common-law duty of landholder** A duty of one in possession of land to ensure the safety of another on the land. A common-law duty is any duty that arises under the common law. The common-law duty of a landholder is the particular duty of care that one who owns or possesses land has to another party who is on the land to maintain the land reasonably and with due care to the potential harms the land might pose to those who enter it.

This common-law duty famously varied according to the status by which the other party is present. An invitee, or one present for commercial purposes, receives the highest duty of care, in that the landholder must take affirmative measures to ensure safe conditions. A licensee, or one present merely for social purposes, must be reasonably assured of the absence of dangerous conditions. A trespasser is owed a duty of no unreasonable dangers, a duty often not much different from the duty owed a licensee. The common-law duty has been abrogated by statute or by decision in many jurisdictions to erase the distinction between invitee and licensee and to act as a reasonable person in maintaining property in a reasonably safe condition in view of all the circumstances, including the likelihood of injury to others who enter the land, the potential seriousness of such injuries, and the burden on the respective parties of avoiding the risk.

*See also:* trespasser, duty to trespassers; invitee (business guest); licensee, licensee by invitation (licensee by permission); negligence (negligent).

**reasonable care** The conduct of a reasonably prudent person in the circumstances. Reasonable care is the scope of behavior that an objective observer would accept as appropriate under the circumstances in question for a person of reasonableness and prudence, without unusual levels of skill or confidence.

**careless interference with traffic** *See:* traffic, careless interference with traffic.

**cargo** Goods carried on a vessel, plane, train, or vehicle. Cargo is the matter shipped aboard any transport vessel. In admiralty, it is what is carried aboard a ship, other than the material and stores belonging to the ship and crew. Generally, cargo refers only to goods and freight, but it may also refer to passengers. Cargo may be bulk, break bulk, project or heavy-lift, vehicular, or container, and it may be dry or liquid. Bulk cargo is poured directly into the tanks or holds of the transport vessel, such as salt, coal, or grain. Break bulk cargo is loaded onto pallets or stored in boxes such as tea chests that are stowed in the holds or on deck. Project cargo, also called heavy-lift cargo, are large objects that are hoisted intact into or onto the transport vessel. Vehicular cargo, especially automobiles, are loaded usually by driving into the hold or cargo deck of the transport unit. Container cargo is loaded in advance into intermodal transport units, or shipping containers, and loaded as a single unit per container. Oil, petroleum distillates, and liquified gas are all forms of liquid cargo. Cargo on a vessel or in interstate or international transportation is listed on a cargo manifest.
*See also:* ship.

**cargo manifest** *See:* manifest, cargo manifest.

**supercargo** A representative of the cargo owner aboard a vessel. The supercargo is the agent of the cargo owner, aboard a vessel to supervise the management of the cargo during a voyage. As agent of the cargo owner, the supercargo has the authority to sell or purchase or receive cargo during the voyage. Though the term is still used in this particular sense, it is more generally used to describe a person who is aboard a vessel for no particular reason.

**carnal knowledge** *See:* knowledge, carnal knowledge (carnally knew).

**Carolingian law** *See:* feud, feudalism, Carolingian law (Salic law).

**carrier (private carrier)** A business that transports people or goods, though not the public. A private carrier is a business that transports people or goods but does not hold itself out to the public as offering that service. A private carrier is not a common carrier. The classic example of a private carrier is a furniture store that does transport sold furniture to a buyer's home, though the furniture store does not offer its transportation services to the public. A private carrier owes only a duty of reasonable care to its customers, as contrasted with a common carrier that owes a duty of heightened care.
*See also:* carrier, common carrier.

**carrier of disease (vector)** Anything that physically distributes the pathogens of disease. A carrier is anything, but particularly a person or animal, that carries a bacterium, parasite, spore, virus, or other biological matter that causes infection or infestation of a disease in another. Carriers and potential carriers may be regulated in the police power of the state.
*See also:* police, police power (powers of police).

**common carrier** A business that transports people or goods, offering these services to the public. A common carrier is a business that offers transportation of the people or its goods to the public for a fee. A common carrier owes a heightened duty of care to its passengers above mere reasonableness, although jurisdictions define this heightened standard differently. A common carrier owes the "highest" duty of care to its passengers consistent with the practical running of the transportation. For example, according to the Restatement of Torts, a common carrier owes a duty of reasonable care to its passengers, but additionally it must provide aid to those passengers if they become sick or injured. Common carriers often carry goods at prices set forth in tariffs, or general rate schedules, filed with regulators.

**insurance carrier** *See:* insurer (insurance carrier or insurance company).

**carta** *See:* charta (carta).

**carte blanche** The total, discretionary authority to act. Carte blanche, or a blank check, means an unlimited discretionary authority to act. At common law, however, the term referred to a signature of a principal, on white letter paper, with sufficient space above the signature for an authorized agent to add text. A principal who signed carte blanche was bound to whatever text his agent wrote above the signature.
*See also:* form, blank.

**cartel** A group of businesses engaged in the restraint of trade. A cartel is a group of businesses that fixes prices and markets for trade in products, especially to avoid competition among one another and to create an advantage in competing with others. Although one purpose of a cartel may be to fix prices higher than the market, cartels in restraint of trade are illegal, regardless of their effect on price.

**carve-out (carveout)** An omission from a rule, property, or plan. "Carve-out" is a slang term for a reservation, an exception, or an omission. A right reserved from a general grant of ownership may be described as a carve-out. Carve-outs often appear in immunity agreements offered by prosecutors, creating an exception from a broad grant of immunity for some particular conduct or some contingency, in which case the contractor would not be immune.

Carve-outs have particular significance in accounting for assets subject to regulation. A carve-out of taxable assets is to take a portion of income from an income-producing asset. A carve-out from a liquidation plan would be a portion of the entity being liquidated that would be retained by the owner.

## case

**case**  *See:* trespass, trespass on the case (case).

**Case and Controversy Clause**  *See:* constitution, U.S. Constitution, clauses, Case and Controversy Clause.

**case as argument (theory of the case)**  A litigant's claims or defenses and their support. A case is any argument, and when applied to a lawsuit, the case is shorthand for the litigant's theory of the case, in which each litigant assesses the facts underlying specific legal claims, in the light of the legal authority for those claims to apply to the facts to support a result.

*See also:* prima, prima facie, prima facie case; precedent, case of first impression.

**case as dispute in court**  Contest formally initiated in a court of law or equity. A case is a civil or criminal matter filed for ultimate disposition in court, whether or not it reaches a disposition by the court or is settled or dismissed beforehand. In law schools, appellate case reports are often referred to as if they are the case, rather than a report of opinions on appeal in the case. Note: in the sense of an action in court, there is no difference between a case and a cause.

*See also:* suit (lawsuit); cause, cause as dispute in court; law, law school, legal pedagogy, case method (casebook method or socratic method); case, caseload (case load).

**case as trespass on the case**  *See:* trespass, trespass on the case (case).

**case at bar (instant case or case at issue)**  The matter or issue before the court The phrase "at bar" refers to the particular matter, action, or issue before the court or, literally, at the bar of the court. The phrase has the same significance as the "case sub judice," the "issue sub judice," the relatively inoffensive "case at issue" and, most regrettably, "the instant case." The "case at bar" is one of this variety of stock phrases used by lawyers and judges in lieu of saying "the issue at hand," "the issue here," or something more specific.

*See also:* sub, sub judice.

**case brief**  *See:* brief, case brief (brief a case).

**case in chief**  The initial evidence and argument for relief in court. The case in chief is the presentation of the evidence and the argument in support of a litigant's position regarding the facts and the law underlying a civil claim, a criminal charge, or a defense. The case in chief does not include evidence that is intended to rebut the case in chief of the other litigants.

If the plaintiff presents the case in chief and, at its close, the case in chief is clearly insufficient for relief to be granted to the plaintiff, the court is to dismiss the case. Likewise, if a prosecution's case in chief is insufficient to support the charge or indictment against the defendant, the charge or indictment is to be dismissed, and a defendant's insufficient case in chief in support of a defense requires the defense be dismissed or stricken.

On appeal or reconsideration, the court must consider all of the evidence in the record to uphold an order dismissing a claim, charge, or defense, including evidence offered beyond the case in chief.

*See also:* dismissal (dismiss).

**case law**  *See:* law, case law (caselaw or decisional law).

**case method**  *See:* law, law school, legal pedagogy, case method (casebook method or Socratic method).

**case of first impression**  *See:* precedent, case of first impression.

**case reports**  *See:* reports, case reports, nominative reports (nominate reports or named reports); reports, case reports, headnote; reports, case reports (reporter or rpts. or rptr.).

**case reports or case reporter or report**  *See:* lawbook, reporter (case reports or case reporter or report).

**casebook**  *See:* lawbook, casebook.

**casebook method or Socratic method**  *See:* law, law school, legal pedagogy, case method (casebook method or Socratic method).

**caseload (case load)**  The number of cases assigned to a person, firm, or court. Caseload is the ratio of work over time for a lawyer, law firm, administrator, agency, police officer, police agency, judge, or court. Caseload is a function of the number of active files, each arising from a specific cause of action or case for investigation, as defined for each purpose of analysis, that number being counted for a specific time. The higher the caseload, the greater the stress on those to whom they are assigned, the slower their management, and the greater the likelihood of negligence in their management.

## cash

**cash accounting or cash basis**  *See:* accounting, cash-basis accounting method (cash accounting or cash basis).

**cash-basis accounting method**  *See:* accounting, cash-basis accounting method (cash accounting or cash basis).

**cash on delivery**  *See:* shipping, shipping term, cash on delivery (C.O.D.).

**cash equivalency** The value of a thing in dollars. Cash equivalency is the translation in value of a thing into currency value, such as the marketable value of stocks and bonds on hand in dollars. The term is sometimes used to represent the value required in cash equivalents to meet a cash requirement, although this use may be confused with the more general meaning.

**cash equivalent (cash equivalency)** An investment asset with a value to which it may be converted in cash. A cash equivalent is an investment, such as a stock, bond, certificate of deposit, or other instrument reflecting equity or debt that is mature or near maturity and may be converted to cash. Cash equivalents may be treated like cash in balance sheets. When a cash possession requirement may be satisfied by possession of cash equivalents, the requirements, rather confusingly, may be called a cash equivalency requirement.

**cassation** French appeal on a legal question. Cassation is the highest level of review in the courts of France, considering questions of pure law arising from disputes in the courts below.
*See also:* reprieve.

**casting vote** *See:* vote, parlimentary vote, casting vote (deciding vote or tie–breaking vote).

**castle doctrine** *See:* defense, self defense, castle doctrine.

**castration** The removal of testes or ovaries from a person or animal. Castration is the removal of a person's or animal's testes or ovaries. Historically, it most often refers to the physical removal of a mature adult's testicles or the whole of the genitalia. Current methods include not only physical removal but also the chemical, genetic, or neurological interference with reproduction so that a person or animal cannot reproduce. Castration is a criminal act when done maliciously against another, and at common law, the crime of castration was punishable by retaliatory castration. The crime of castration is now punished by fine and imprisonment. Some jurisdictions punish serial sex offenders with physical or chemical castration, or offer a reduced sentence to sex offenders who voluntarily submit to such procedures. As a punishment, castration is constitutionally suspect as cruel and unusual punishment, although its voluntary use has been upheld. In all cases, the alteration of the hormonal levels in the body is likely to have effects beyond the loss of reproductive capacity. As to animals, castration is also referred to as neutering, altering, and gelding. As to humans, in males it is also known as orchiectomy or orchidectomy. As a metaphor in legal slang, castration refers to the weakening of a person's authority or influence, an argument, or a case.

**casual ejector** *See:* ejectment, casual ejector.

**casualty (casualty loss)** The damage or loss of personal property. A casualty is a person's loss or damage of personal property, not related to business or profit, that results from fire, storm, shipwreck, theft, natural occurrence, negligence, or other casualty. Casualty losses are the basis for a personal deduction in federal taxes, and they are the basis for casualty claims under private insurance policies of indemnity.

**casus** Cause. Casus, the Latin word for a result of a given cause or an event that results from it, is the basis for many maxims and tags, either as the cause of an event or the purpose of a law or contract.
*See also:* war, law of war, casus belli.

**casus belli** *See:* war, law of war, casus belli.

**cat burglar** *See:* burglary, cat burglar (second–story man); burglary, cat burglar (second–story man).

**catadromous fish** *See:* fish, catadromous fish (catadromous stocks of fish).

**catchall exception** *See:* hearsay, hearsay exception, residual exception (catchall exception).

**categorical exclusion** *See:* environment, National Environmental Policy Act, environmental assessment, categorical exclusion.

**categorical imperative** *See:* ethics, categorical imperative (reciprocity or the Golden Rule).

**categorical taking** *See:* taking, regulatory taking, categorical taking (denial of economically viable use or wipe out of use).

**category of insurance** *See:* insurance, category of insurance.

**caucus** A group of like–minded people who confer or deliberate. A caucus, generally, is any small group of people with a common interest who debate or confer in order to reach a position that will be taken in a larger setting. Often, it depicts a group of politicians who determine a position to which they hope to sway a larger group. Thus, a caucus frequently describes legislators from a given area or those devoted to a particular cause. Caucuses are also meetings of party members who select nominees to represent a political party in a general election. Caucus has become a verb as well as a noun, according to which individuals caucus. To say "caucus together" is redundant.

**caucus as in negotiation (separate caucus)** A group on one side of a negotiation or dispute. A caucus, as a term of negotiation, is the group of parties, counsel, or assistants on one side during a mediation, arbitration, or other proceeding for negotiation or dispute resolution. The mediator or negotiator will often keep the parties physically separated into their caucuses and carry information and offers between them. Mediation in such a format is therefore known as caucus mediation. Caucus mediation may be used as a tool between sessions of joint mediation. A person, particularly an attorney, who serves as a mediator or arbitrator is subject to a duty to both parties and, in most instances, cannot be a member of a caucus.

**causa**   Latin term meaning cause. Causa is a Latin term meaning "cause," both in the sense of "case" and in the sense of a practical reason for an occurrence or action. Causa has various slang terms in the U.S. from other Romance languages; in Spanish it means "cause," and is often used to refer to political or progressive causes, and in pidgin Italian it means "because."

**causa mortis**   Caused by a belief in impending death. Causa mortis describes any action based in a belief that the actor is about to die. Not all acts done prior to death are done causa mortis, nor does survival negate the fact that actions were made causa mortis. Rather, everything done with a subjective belief that the actor is about to die from some particular cause is done causa mortis, and — if the actor does survive — may be repudiated unless others have acted sufficiently in reliance to give rise to estoppel. A gift causa mortis requires the gift to be made in anticipation of impending death, with donative intent, with delivery and with acceptance while the donor lives. These last two requirements distinguish a gift causa mortis from a testamentary gift, because the gift causa mortis must be made and accepted while the donor lives.

See also: causa; in, in extremis; death, contemplation of death (articulo mortis or causa mortis or deathbed declaration or dying declaration).

**causation (cause or causality)**   The processes that lead from any event to any result. Causation is the relationship between two events, one producing the other. There are few concepts more important to the law in determining the basis for liability for harm, which generally is limited to those people or entities responsible for what caused the harm. This limitation can be quite difficult to describe, much less to determine as the extent of legal responsibility. A person who steals produce from a store causes the loss to store, but is there also a legal cause by someone else who wagered with the thief to cause the theft, or by the store owner if the produce was left unguarded on the street, or is there a legal cause for the parent of the thief, or would the legal cause vary if the thief is twelve, or forty? To what extent does a supervening cause absolve the creator of a prior but thwarted cause? The law has evolved a variety of labels for the forms and degrees of causation that are the basis of liability. In general, these are both matters of law, in which some forms of cause are legally cognizable and some are not, as well as of fact, in which some forms of cause are possible but must actually influence events or motivate conduct. Causation is easily confused with intent, which is quite different; one might cause a result one has no intent to cause, just as one might intend a result, which one does not cause (even if some other

cause brings about the result). Causation is the process that leads from cause to result; causality is a quality of being a cause, which is slightly different from causal, which is the aspect of causing something. For example, one might say that the bump caused the lamp to fall, so the bump was causal in its fall; the cause of the lamp's fall was the bump. The causation of the lamp's fall was the relationship between the bump and the lamp, and the causality in the bump was the point of contact, direction, and degree of force in it.

*cause*   The force, idea, statement, or event of causation. A cause is the specific element that initiates any causation. It may be an action by a person or company, a natural phenomenon, an idea or belief, or anything spoken or any communication received. A cause may be an act or an omission of conduct. Because causation is so complex, many events or acts are causes of nearly every given result, just as most results have many, many causes.

See also: causation, but-for causation (but-for cause and but-for test); causation, actual cause (cause in fact or factual case or producing cause); causation, concurrent causes; causation, dependent cause; causation, multiple causes; causation, mediate cause; causation, remote cause; causation, sole cause; causation, superseding cause (superceding cause).

**act of God or act of nature**   See: God, act of God (act of nature or actus dei or casus fortuitus or force of nature or fortuitous event).

**actual cause (cause in fact or factual case or producing cause)**   Any necessary cause, or a significant cause of a result. An actual cause is any cause that leads as a matter of fact to a given result. There is no inherent reason why actual cause would be limited to immediate causes, although a principle of reasonableness is usually implied so that causes that are too remote and less significant in the assessment of a result than many other causes are generally not considered actual causes. Without this implied limit, there is no difference between an actual cause and a necessary cause or a but-for cause.

**but-for causation (but-for cause and but-for test)**   A necessary cause. But-for causation is an easily remembered phrase for a necessary cause, in that if this cause had not happened, then this result could not have followed. In other words but for this cause, this effect could not have occurred. There are, however, a nearly limitless number of but-for causes.

**chain of causation**   Successive events proceeding from a cause or leading to a result. A chain of causation is a sequence of events that proceed in causal steps from a particular cause or that led from cause to cause to a particular result. A useful if misleading metaphor is a chain of falling dominoes (which is misleading in its appearance of inevitability). A chain of causation describes the relationship between one cause and a distantly caused event, or between one result and a distantly originating cause. To the degree a particular chain of causation is foreseeable or the cause is unreasonably dangerous, a person who sets in motion a chain of causation may be responsible for harmful results produced by an event at the end of several successive causes, each set in motion by a succeeding cause from the person's initial act.

**concurrent causes**  Causes close in time that combine to produce a single result. Concurrent causes are distinct events that coordinate to produce a single result. A plaintiff may assert concurrent causation as a theory to prove harm when defendant's act was not the sole cause of the plaintiff's injury, but was a substantial factor with some other cause in producing the harm. When two defendants have each acted concurrently to produce a harm, the plaintiff must only prove that the injury was the substantial result of each act, for which the defendants are then jointly liable. Either defendant may avoid liability by proving the other defendant was the sole proximate cause of plaintiff's injury. This shift of the burden of proof reflects defendants' access to the evidence related to the cause of the plaintiff's injury than does the plaintiff, which is better than the plaintiff's likely access to such evidence. Concurrent causes of a loss to someone insured by a policy that would exclude one cause would not prevent the assured from a valid claim under the policy for full payment owing to the loss by a non-excluded concurrent cause. Concurrent causes are effectively multiple causes, and there is little benefit in trying to distinguish them (the difference that "concurrent causes" implies that the causal events or occur at roughly the same time, while multiple causes might not be concurrent is hardly borne out in the cases, in which concurrent causes are as likely to be concurrent in the manifestation of their effects as in the causal events).

**dependent cause**  An act in a chain of causation that does not break the chain. A dependent cause is a middle cause in a chain of causation, one that is caused by one thing and that causes another, as result of which the result eventually occurs. A dependent cause does not break the chain of causation, nor does it limit the responsibility of a party who initiated some earlier cause in the chain. This failure to break the chain results either because the dependent cause was itself caused by the relevant prior cause, or because the cause was a foreseeable result at the time of the relevant prior cause and would not have come into existence without it.

**force majeure**  See: force, force majeure.

**general causation (causability or causality)**  The potential for a material or event to cause a result. General causation is the degree to which a substance, activity, or event has the potential to cause a result, especially to bring about a particular harm or a harmful condition in person. Thus, whether exposure to a given chemical may cause a particular disease is a question of general causation. An affirmative answer is necessary but not sufficient to determine whether a given person's disease was caused by exposure to that chemical.

**immediate cause**  The last event or action that led to a result. The immediate cause is the last cause, the cause that is manifest just prior to the result, regardless of what causes might have led to the immediate cause. The actor whose action produces an immediate cause is liable for its harmful results unless the action is not a breach of duty, is justified, or is excused. Although it is tempting to limit liability or responsibility only to immediate causes, the law does not do so for several reasons: in practice isolating what in fact is the immediate cause is often quite complicated, and the immediate cause might have been an inevitable result of a preceding cause that was more clearly the product of negligence or wrongdoing.

**independent cause (new and independent cause)**  A cause unrelated to another cause related to the same result. An independent cause is an actual cause that is distinct from and not caused by another cause. An independent cause breaks a chain of causation if the independent cause is so significant in producing the result that the earlier cause becomes so remote from the result that there is no longer a causal connection between the earlier cause and the result, even if the earlier cause would have caused the result had the independent cause not occurred. An independent clause is also an intervening cause.

*See also:* sine, sine qua non.

**intermediate cause**  A foreseeable, dependent cause in a chain of causation. An intermediate cause is any event or condition brought about by an earlier cause, from which point the intermediate cause was foreseeable, and through which the earlier cause acts to create a later result.

**intervening cause**  A cause in fact that disrupts a chain of causation. An intervening cause is any act, event or omission that interferes with a chain of causation, causing in fact a particular result that would likely have resulted from other causes but for the intervention of the intervening cause. It is not necessary that an intervening cause be a sole cause or even a final or proximate cause (the Ohio result below notwithstanding, because an intervening cause may itself be subject to a later intervening cause). What defines an intervention is its interruption of the chain of events from one putative cause, not that it is a final cause of the result. This is the difference between an intervening cause and a superseding cause, in that the superseding cause fully interposes and terminates the causal effect of the prior cause. This distinction between intervening and superseding causes is, however, rarely maintained by lawyers and judges, and intervening cause is often used to describe a superseding cause.

**mediate cause**  A cause that is not the immediate cause of a result. A mediate cause is any cause in fact that is not the immediate or direct cause of a result. A mediate cause may be the significant originating cause of a chain or causation or it might be a dependent cause in a chain of causation.

**multiple causes**  A variety of causes for a single result. An injury may be said to have multiple causes when more than one cause or chain of causation is necessary to produce a result. Multiple causes may be the basis for a reduction in the degree of responsibility for the entity or person responsible for one cause. Multiple causes might also be concurrent causes, although there is less of an implication that the multiple causes occurred in the same time frame. Thus, multiple causes amount to distinct occurrences leading to a result, while concurrent causes amount, usually to a single occurrence.

*See also:* causation, concurrent causes.

**proximate cause (direct cause or efficient cause or jural cause or legal cause)**  A cause near enough to a result to be legally responsible for it. A proximate cause is a cause that is sufficient among all possible or examined causes to be considered at least one responsible cause for a particular result, according to the analysis of facts required by law. Proximate cause is better understood by its purpose than by its conflicting tests: proximacy — or nearness — establishes the extent of liability for harms caused as a result of given causes. Even so, many tests or formulae are used, including the popular but–for test, in which a result would not have occurred but for the cause under consideration without a significant intervening cause. Other tests include the significant–factor test, the direct–cause test, and the substantial–and–close test, among others.

Any person responsible for a proximate cause is responsible for its results. Establishing proximate cause is a matter of fact, although it usually requires the satisfaction of three pleading elements: the act of the defendant was a factual cause of the plaintiff's harm; the harm of the plaintiff was a natural, probable, or foreseeable result of the defendant's act, and no later intervening cause was more responsible. More than one cause may be a proximate cause without any one being an intervening cause that would limit the causative nature of the others, if each is a substantial cause of the resulting harm. To prove proximate causation does not, of course, prove liability, as the plaintiff must also prove the defendant's act was in violation of a duty of care or some other legal obligation. There are many variant terms for proximate cause; the term in the Restatements is usually "legal cause," and Justice Cardozo was prone to the term jural cause, but there is no great difference among these terms.

*See also:* negligence, last clear chance (last–clear-chance doctrine).

**regulatory causation**  Chain of causation from a governmental allowance to the harm allowed. Regulatory causation depicts a chain of causation from the act of a legislature, agency, or office of government to the harm realized as a result of the acts of public or private agents that would not have been allowed but for the act of the government. Thus, when an agency permits some conduct, it is the regulatory cause for the harms

that are the direct result of conduct within the scope permitted.

**remote cause**  A cause that is much less significant than others in a result. A remote cause is an actual cause that is a minor influence upon a result when compared to other causes that are much more influential in bringing about the event or occurrence under consideration. Remote causes are often predicate to a more direct or proximate cause. Although remote causes usually are causes from which a given result is not foreseeable or reasonably likely to be anticipated, unforeseeability and unanticipatability are not essential for a cause to be remote, particularly given the contingent nature of causality when evaluated from a cause looking into the future.

*See also:* remote (remoteness or remotely).

**sole cause**  The only legal cause for a particular result. Sole cause is a finding of fact that only one cause is legally responsible for a given result, and thus any other causes are not responsible for it. Thus, one of several co–defendants sued by a plaintiff alleging that each defendant has concurrently caused the plaintiff's injury might argue that there the act of a different defendant was the sole cause of the plaintiff's injury. In situations of comparative fault, the defense may also attempt to show that the plaintiff's own conduct was the sole cause of the plaintiff's injury. If there is any other cause in fact, there is not a sole cause, which therefore requires proof that the result under consideration had no other cause in fact than the sole cause under consideration.

**specific causation**  Proof of a harm to the plaintiff by a process of general causation. Specific causation is the result in a particular instance that flows from a condition or potential of general causation. Specific causation is required in many jurisdictions in products liability, negligence, or other actions in which a plaintiff argues a medical condition is the result of exposure to a chemical, condition, or device or is the result of some activity. Proving such cases may require not only general causation, proof that the exposure or activity could cause the plaintiff's condition, but also specific causation, that in this particular case it did cause that condition. The difficulty of proof of specific causation is mitigated to a degree by the ability of the finder of fact to find proof of specific causation from statistical evidence, as long as there is a chain of causation between the conduct of a defendant and the events directly affecting the plaintiff.

**substantial cause (substantial factor)**  A proximate multiple or concurrent cause. A substantial cause is a multiple cause or concurrent cause that is a legally meaningful cause of the result. Like proximate cause, substantiality is better understood by its purpose than its analyses: if a cause is sufficient among others to be seen as a substantial cause for a result, then legal responsibility for the result will attach to the agent of that cause.

**superseding cause (superceding cause)**  A cause in fact that breaks a chain of causation. A superseding cause is a cause that interrupts a chain of causation from one event to a potential resulting event. It is not necessary that a superseding cause be a sole cause or even a final or proximate cause; what defines a supercession is its interruption of the chain of events from one putative cause, not that it is a final cause of the result. Note: there is no real difference between a superceding cause and an intervening cause. Also, there is no difference between supercede and supersede; the spelling with the "c" is merely an older variant.

## cause

**cause as dispute in court**  Contest formally initiated in a court of law or equity. A case is a civil or criminal matter filed for ultimate disposition in court, whether or not it reaches a disposition by the court or is settled or dismissed beforehand. There is no difference between this sense of cause and case in this sense.

*See also:* case, case as dispute in court.

**cause of action**  The factual and legal bases for a claimant's civil action. The cause of action is the combination of facts and legal claims that are proven by those facts that give rise to a private action for relief in law or in equity.

*See also:* suit (lawsuit).

**causing a minor child to leave or not to return home**  *See:* parent, parental rights, intentional interference with parental rights (causing a minor child to leave or not to return home).

**probable cause**  The reasonable basis for suspicion of a crime or evidence of a crime. Probable cause is the whole set of facts and conditions that form a reasonable basis for a reasonable police officer to suspect a crime has been committed, a person has committed it, or there is evidence of it in a given place at a given time. In the absence of an indictment, the police or prosecution must demonstrate to a judge the bases of their probable cause to believe a specific crime was (or is being or about to be) committed by a given person or entity in order for the judge to issue an arrest warrant. Likewise, the police or prosecution must demonstrate to a judge the bases of their probable cause to believe in a specific crime's commission and the location of evidence of that crime in order for the judge to issue a search warrant for the place and evidence believed to be there. Probable cause may also be the basis for an unwarranted arrest and a reasonable, unwarranted search.

The evidence required to demonstrate probable cause is greater than a potential, a hunch, or a suspicion. It must be based on observation of witnesses or the evaluation of tangible evidence that rationally supports a reasonable conclusion regarding the crime, suspect or evidence. Each case depends on its own evidence in its own circumstances, yet the decisions must be based not only on evidence but on an articulable rationale derived from evidence.

The basis for probable cause need not be so certain as proof beyond a reasonable doubt, but it must be sufficiently compelling as to justify government agents in depriving a party of privacy, property, or liberty.

*See also:* arrest; warrant, arrest warrant; arrest, warrantless arrest; search, warrantless search; warrant, search warrant; probable.

**Darden hearing (informant tip suppression hearing)**  A hearing to evaluate an informant's tip as probable cause. A Darden hearing, following New York v. Darden, 313 N.E.2d 49, 52 (N.Y. 1974), is an in camera, ex parte proceeding between the prosecution and the court to determine the reliability of a confidential informant's tip to the police and its sufficiency of that tip as the basis of probable cause for a search or an arrest.

**fellow–officer rule (fellow officer rule or collective knowledge doctrine)**  A police officer's probable cause may arise from the knowledge of other officers. The fellow–officer rule empowers a police officer to make a lawful arrest or search based on probable cause, even though the officer's knowledge forming probable cause does not arise from the officer's personal observations or knowledge, if the officer relies on the knowledge of another officer, or all of the knowledge of a group of officers, and the whole content of the knowledge held by either the other officer or the group would be sufficient to support probable cause.

**cautionary jury instruction**  *See:* instruction, jury instruction, cautionary jury instruction (prophylactic instruction).

**caveat**  A warning. Caveat, in its most basic sense, is Latin for "let each person beware" and is intended to put the audience to some statement on notice of some problem. In most legal contexts, it asks the audience to be alert to specific problems or liabilities to an enterprise or to be aware of certain exceptions to a statement. It has specific meanings in procedure, by which the caveat is a motion for delay, in title work, by which it warns of an unrecorded interest, and in probate, by which it was once a common pleading to initiate a will contest. All three senses are now much less common than they once were, the usage being taken over generally by the sense of caveat emptor.

*See also:* probate, will contest, caveat to the probate of a will (caveator).

**caveat to the probate of a will**  *See:* probate, will contest, caveat to the probate of a will (caveator).

**caveat actor**  Let who does beware the risks in what one does. Caveat actor is a broad maxim that reflects the more specific doctrines of assumption of risk and implied liability: anyone involved in an activity should be on alert for potential dangers or harms inherent in their chosen pursuit.

**caveat emptor**   Let the buyer beware. Caveat emptor is a maxim placing the risk in acquisition upon the purchaser rather than the seller, which at the common law placed on the buyer the responsibility of inspection of goods or lands as well as of determining the seller had title to what was sold. This maxim has been considerably restricted to bar claims against defects or nonconformity that the buyer could reasonably have discovered on inspection when the buyer had an opportunity to inspect and there was no fraud or concealment of the defect or nonconforming aspect.

**caveat venditor (caveat vendor)**   Let the seller beware. Caveat venditor is a maxim in which the seller is liable for defects or nonconformities in goods sold, particularly by holding vendors liable for known and undisclosed latent defects and by implying warranties as a matter of law. The most essential are that buildings are constructed under an implied warranty of good workmanship, leases are given subject to an implied warranty of habitability, and goods are sold subject to implied warranties of title, or merchantability, and of fitness for a particular use.

**caveator**   *See:* probate, will contest, caveat to the probate of a will (caveator).

**cavil (beyond cavil)**   A false or trivial argument. A cavil, technically, is a false argument, by which an unsupportable conclusion is supposed to be proved from fair premises. In common usage, a cavil has become any overly subtle or trivial argument, and in both senses "cavil" alone is now a bit rare. That said, the term is quite popular with lawyers and judges who claim that some point is so well established or accepted that it is now "beyond cavil," which is to say that the point is not to be questioned.

**CBA**   *See:* value, cost–benefit analysis (CBA).

**CCE**   *See:* trafficking, drug trafficking, continuing criminal enterprise (CCE).

**CD or C.D.**   *See:* deposit, certificate of deposit (CD or C.D.).

**CDS**   *See:* credit, credit default swap (CDS).

**ce (ca)**   This, that, or the other thing. Ce (or ca, depending on its case) is a French definite pronoun frequently used in Law French maxims. It is both singular and plural.

**cede**   To grant. To cede is to grant, either in the sense of transfer or gift, as in cession, or as in the sense of concede or accept, as in ceding a point of argument.
   *See also:* transfer.

**celebrant**   One who celebrates. A celebrant, broadly, is any participant in a celebration, particularly a religious festival. More technically, it is the principal officiating in an ecclesiastical service or, in a marriage, it is another term for the officiant of record.

**cell**   A unit in a larger whole. A cell is a small living quarters, at first a small dependent monastery or hermit's hut, then an apartment or lodging in a larger building, from which come the cell of a monk or a prisoner. From this sense, the word acquired its meaning in biology of a unit of component organization in a larger organism. Cell also metaphorically refers to any unit or faction of a larger group, particularly a local group in a political organization.

**prison cell (jail cell)**   Living quarters for the inmate of a prison or jail. A cell is a single room in a detention facility. Each cell is designed for a particular capacity according to its use. The capacity for a cell for overnight detention is limited by the sleeping accommodations provided for each person assigned and adequate sanitary facilities for the group as a whole, although an overcrowded cell alone may not give rise to cruel or unusual punishment.

**Celotex standard**   *See:* judgment, summary judgment, Celotex standard.

**cemetery or mausoleum**   *See:* sepulchre (cemetery or mausoleum).

**censure**   Official criticism. Censure is an official statement of reprimand, particularly one given to a person in an office of trust or confidence who has violated the obligations of that office.

**census**   A counting of a population. A census is any enumeration of the inhabitants of any given population. Most famously in the United States, the Constitution requires a decennial census, or a count taken every ten years, of every person living in the United States. There are, however, many forms of census, including the enumeration of the patients in a hospital or the animals or plants of a particular species on a particular tract of land.

**center of the earth to the roof of the sky**   *See:* property, real property, cujus est solum ejus est usque ad coelum (center of the earth to the roof of the sky).

**central bank**   *See:* bank, central bank.

**central case**   *See:* meaning, core meaning (central case).

**ceremonial deism**   *See:* religion, freedom of religion, establishment of religion, ceremonial deism.

**ceremonial marriage**   *See:* marriage, ceremonial marriage (solemnized marriage).

**cert. or writ of certiorari**   *See:* certiorari (cert. or writ of certiorari).

**certainty (certain)**  The highest degree to which a belief can be assured. Certainty is a mental state in which a person is convinced that some belief the person holds is correct, without reservations or doubts. How certainty comes about in the mind has been argued among philosophers and medical observers for centuries, largely between two views — that certainty results from the operation of reason and is an act of intellect or that it operates from the operation of emotion and sympathy and is an act of personality. Both positions have merit, and different circumstances may be better described by one approach or the other in varying degrees. Although certainty is long understood to have limitations, some social scientists now believe that a sense of certainty can pose risks to the person who holds it, as it creates a strong inhibition to evaluating new evidence that contradicts the belief about which the holder is certain. Certainty was once the standard of proof in criminal cases, which was lowered to become the standard of proof beyond a reasonable doubt. Certainty in a text or standard of conduct denotes the absence of ambiguity, even a single viable interpretation.

*See also:* damages, contract damages, certainty of damages; proof, burden of proof (standard of proof).

**certainty of damages**  *See:* damages, contract damages, certainty of damages.

**certificate**  Official documentation of procedure, occurrence, or fact. A certificate is a writing that certifies that some act has occurred, standard has been achieved, or procedure has been completed. Certificates are traditionally issued under seal, although that practice has been replaced by signature for most purposes, and many electronic certificates have replaced the seal with a security code. Because of its authenticity through its creation by a particular officer, a certificate can serve as proof of the facts it asserts. Certificates are used for many purposes, not the least being certificates of service, which are appended to all pleadings and notices that must be served on other parties in litigation.

*See also:* deposit, certificate of deposit (CD or C.D.); service, service of process, certificate of service.

**certificate of deposit**  *See:* deposit, certificate of deposit (CD or C.D.).

**certificate of good faith**  *See:* discovery, certificate of good faith.

**certificate of service**  *See:* service, service of process, certificate of service.

**certification bar**  *See:* union, labor union, labor organization, certification bar.

**certification of a question of law**  A court's submission of a question of state law to that state's high court. The certification of a question of law is made from federal courts to state courts when the consideration of a case properly in the federal court requires resolution of a matter of state law, and the federal court considers the state law to be unclear on the matter. The state's laws must allow such certification. The court usually certifies the question in an order setting out the facts of the case, the legal posture under which it is before the court, and the specific question or questions that the court hopes will be answered by the court to which it is certified. Although it is possible for one state court to certify an issue to another, this procedure is usually employed by U.S. courts of appeal certifying questions to state supreme courts.

**certified mediator**  *See:* mediator, certified mediator.

**certiorari (cert. or writ of certiorari)**  A high court's discretionary review of an action by a lower court or agency. The writ of certiorari is an order by a high court to a lower court or to an agency, requiring the lower court or agency to "inform" the high court on some matter, usually by transmitting its files to the court for review. Certiorari is similar to an appeal in establishing the jurisdiction of the higher court over the parties to the action below. Even so, unlike most forms of appeal, there is no right to certiorari that a petitioner might claim, but certiorari is a matter in the discretion of the reviewing court. (Appeal was once more common than certiorari in the U.S. Supreme Court, certiorari becoming the basis for most of the Court's docket in 1925.)

In the U.S. Supreme Court, a petition may be made for the review of a final decision in a state court or of a federal court of appeals, the petitioner setting forth the grounds for review, and the respondent arguing against review. Certiorari is described by Rule 10, which makes certiorari more likely if there is a conflict between a decision of the court under review and another court of appeals or state supreme court on an important matter of federal law. Certiorari is not generally used merely to correct errors by a lower court. If four justices agree to grant certiorari, the writ of certiorari is issued to the court below.

Because certiorari results from a petition, the party who seeks review is the petitioner, and the other party is the respondent, even if the other party does not oppose review. A case heard on certiorari is usually restricted in scope to the specific issues on which the court orders argument in its order granting certiorari.

*See also:* review; appeal (appealable or appellate).

**bill of certiorari (writ of certiorari in equity)**  A pleading seeking review in equity of an administrative order. A bill of certiorari, or in some jurisdictions a writ of certiorari, may be sought in a court of equity for review of an administrative order by a governmental agency subject to the court's jurisdiction. As skill in equity pleading has declined, the bill has become rare. Although this proceeding is theoretically available in the general jurisdiction of federal courts under the All Writs Act, such actions are more often brought as declaratory judgment actions or actions for an injunction.

**certworthy (cert worthy or cert-worthy)**  An issue or case likely to be heard by the Supreme Court.

Certworthy issues are those that fall squarely into the categories that are likely to garner the votes of four justices to review a case on certiorari. Issues in which a federal statute has been declared unconstitutional, in which there is a split among the circuits, or in which a serious conflict between the state and federal governments are particularly certworthy. In the years during which the U.S. Supreme Court was led by Chief Justices Burger and Rehnquist, a miscarriage of justice in an individual case became uncertworthy.

**petition for a writ of certiorari**  A pleading seeking a writ of certiorari. A petition for a writ of certiorari may be filed seeking review of a final decision in a state court or a U.S. Court of Appeals within ninety days of the decision. The petition must conform to the rules, setting out the petitioner's grounds for review of the decision below, including why those grounds are certworthy.
*See also:* petition.

**rule of four**  At least four justices must vote to grant certiorari. The rule of four is the informal name for the custom on the United States Supreme Court by which certiorari is granted on a petition for which four justices vote to grant the writ.

**cessante ratione legis, cessat et ipsa lex**  When a law's reason ends, so should the law. Cessante ratione legis, cessat et ipsa lex, is a maxim of the common law meaning, "when the reason of the law ceases, the law itself ceases." As with many maxims, its significance includes more than one application. It signals the change of a legal obligation dependent on specific facts, so that if the facts change the obligation changes. It may also signal a reason to change the obligation of law if the basis for that obligation changes.

**cession**

**Indian cession**  Lands ceded by an Indian tribe or nation to the United States. An Indian cession is the transfer of lands from a tribe or nation, which controlled the lands at that time, to the United States. Cession refers to the lands as well as to the documents by which the cession was recorded and to the process. Ceded lands were then usually granted by the United States to inviduals or corporations by grant or land patent.

**cestui**  The person. Cestui is Law French for "he." It is integral to a variety of phrases to refer to a person and has no gender significance in modern law.
*See also:* trust, cestui que trust; use, doctrine of uses, cestui que use.

**cestui que trust**  *See:* trust, cestui que trust.

**cestui que use**  *See:* use, doctrine of uses, cestui que use.

**cf.**  *See:* citation, citation signal, confer (cf.).

**CFC or hydrochlorofluorocarbon or HCFC**  *See:* carbon, chlorofluorocarbon (CFC or hydrochlorofluorocarbon or HCFC).

**chad**  *See:* ballot, chad.

**chain**

**chain conspiracy**  *See:* conspiracy, chain conspiracy.

**chain gang**  *See:* incarceration, imprisonment, hard labor (chain gang).

**chain of causation**  *See:* causation, chain of causation.

**chain of custody**  *See:* evidence, custody of evidence, chain of custody.

**chain of title**  *See:* title, chain of title, chain of title in land; title, chain of title, chain of title in intellectual property.

**challenge**  An objection, accusation, or exception to some course of conduct. In law, a challenge is an accusation, an argument that must overcome a presumption or another argument that is already established. So the word in law has both the more general connotation of a difficult task and the specific legal connotation of an objection or claim that must be argued. Challenge is therefore the term for a variety of motions that would bar someone or something from participation in a trial. Most often, it refers to a claim that a potential juror should not be seated, although this particular sense of challenge is now more formal and less contested than it once was, owing to the allowance of peremptory challenges. Challenge is also the term for an objection to the introduction of a particular piece of evidence or testimony in trial. More generally, it may refer to any invitation to argument or to any counter-argument.
*See also:* challenge, constitutional challenge, facial challenge (challenge on its face or unconstitutional per se); challenge, constitutional challenge, as applied (as-applied); jury, jury selection, juror challenge, challenge for cause; jury, jury selection, juror challenge, peremptory challenge, Batson challenge (racial challenge or gender challenge or Batson motion); jury, jury selection, jury challenge, challenge to panel; jury, jury selection, juror challenge (jury challenge).

**challenge for cause**  *See:* jury, jury selection, juror challenge, challenge for cause.

**challenge to panel**  *See:* jury, jury selection, jury challenge, challenge to panel.

**Constitutional challenge**

**challenge as applied (as-applied)**  Claim that a law as applied in the specific situation violates the Constitution. A challenge as applied made to a state constitution, or a state or federal statute, precedent, rule, policy, or other law, claims that the challenged law is unconstitutional as it is applied in a given situation that has given rise to the challenge.

Challenge of a law as applied may, for instance, be based on a charge that a facially neutral regulation is being applied to bar the exercise of constitutional right, or that it creates an unjustified burden on a class under equal protection, or that it violates the plaintiff's right to due process of law.

**facial challenge (challenge on its face or unconstitutional per se)**   Claim that a law inherently violates the constitution. A facial challenge to a state constitution, or a state or federal statute, precedent, rule, policy, or other law, claims that the challenged law is unconstitutional owing to a flaw that is inescapable in its ordinary application as it is applied in a given situation that has given rise to the challenge. It is to say that the law is unconstitutional on its face: the constitutional failing is apparent in the text, and there is no reasonable interpretation of the text that can save it. The law, regardless of how it is applied, will, for instance, bar the exercise of constitutional right, or that it creates an unjustified burden on a class under equal protection, or that it violates the plaintiff's right to due process of law.

**chamber**   A room or, metaphorically, the body of people who meet in a given room. A chamber is a room, particularly the office of a judge or the debating hall of a legislative assembly. In the legislative sense, the term has come to be used to refer to the people who meet there. Thus, the U.S. Senate is sometimes referred to as the upper chamber. Note: the term comes from the Latin for "vaulted ceiling," the manner in which stonework was once commonly arranged to make a ceiling for an inner room.
*See also:* camera.

**judicial chambers (judge's chamber or judicial chamber)**   The rooms assigned for a judge's use in a courthouse. The judge's chambers includes all of the rooms assigned for the use of a judge in a courthouse. Depending on the design of the courthouse, this may be a simple office used by several judges, or it may be a rather grand suite with many offices for the judge and judge's staff, a conference room, and a library. When a judge requires a meeting in chambers, it is understood to designate either a conference room or an office customarily used for this purpose. The judge may hold conferences in chambers, or in camera, on the record (with a transcript prepared by a court reporter) or off the record.

**lower chamber**   The more popular body in a bicameral legislature. The lower chamber is a designation for the lesser division of an organization of several divisions. Most commonly, it refers to the larger of the two houses of a legislature or the Congress, being lower in that the members have less influence because of their greater numbers required for a given vote, even if there are certain privileges accorded to it that are denied the upper chamber. The U.S. House of Representatives is the lower chamber of the Congress. The

lower chamber may also designate a court within a court, which hears matters that are subject to review by other courts within that court.

**upper chamber**   The less popular body in a bicameral legislature. The upper chamber is a designation for the senior division of an organization of several divisions. Most commonly, it refers to the smaller of the two houses of a legislature or the Congress, being above in that the members have greater influence because of the fewer numbers required for a given vote, and also in that some legislation by routine is sent from the lower to the upper for final approval. The U.S. Senate is the upper chamber of the Congress. The upper chamber may also designate a court within a court, which hears matters on review from other courts within that court.

**champerty (champertous)**   An investment in a civil suit by a meddler. Champerty is the purchasing of a share in a lawsuit by someone with no real connection to the subject matter of the suit or to its parties or counsel. An agreement by someone not connected to a case to underwrite it by giving money or value in return for a fee or a share in a judgment is champertous, and in most jurisdictions it is void. Thus money given to support an action by someone with a bona fide interest in the case owing to its subject matter or to the parties is not champertous. An attorney's advancing expenses or time to support a case, in return for later reimbursement or payment, is not champerty.
*See also:* maintenance, maintenance in litigation.

**champertor**   One who engages in champerty. A champertor is the lawyer or other party who purchases an interest in an action that the champertor would otherwise have no interest in. An attorney carrying forward an action on a contingency fee or other deferred compensation for services rendered and risk accepted is not a champertor.
*See also:* champerty (champertous); lawyer.

**champion**   A person who fights for another. A champion is a person who fights in the place of, or on behalf of the honor, of another person. Lawyers are sometimes poetically represented as the champions of their clients.

**chance**   The result of random or unlikely circumstances. Chance is the unpredictability of a given occurrence. Chance is a synonym for fortune or misfortune, in that it represents a randomness of at least one condition that causes an event. Thus, games of chance invariably have a winner, yet at least some degree of randomness of condition or unpredictability affect each player so that none may be certain they will win. Chance does not need to be unforeseeable, and many chance occurrences are the result of a combination of events that is foreseeable but still sufficiently random in the combination to be uncertain or unpredictable that it will indeed occur. Harm that occurs by chance cannot be intended, and intended harm does not occur by chance. Thus, harm by chance is usually an accident and not the basis of criminal or civil liability unless there was an act of strict liability that was a proximate cause of the harm.

**chance verdict**   *See:* verdict, verdict by lot (chance verdict).

**chancellor**   Judicial officer in equity. The chancellor is an officer appointed to preside over a court of equity. In the United States, jurisdictions that retain a bench divided between law and equity are likely to have judges of law and chancellors in equity. A chancellor usually presides over a chancery court. There are other judicial officers in equity, including masters and vice chancellors in the United States. A chancellor originally acted as the chief administrative or secretarial assistant to a monarch, presiding over the chancery or administrative agency. These roles persist in both judicial and administrative contexts. In the United Kingdom, the Lord Chancellor is Keeper of the Great Seal, not only the highest judicial officer in England and Wales, presiding over the Chancery Division of the Supreme Court, but also the member of the government responsible for the management of the courts and the prime minister's policies regarding justice, sitting as Speaker of the House of Lords. In canon law, the chancellor is the vicar-general of the bishop and the law officer who presides on matters of ecclesiastical law arising in the diocese. Chancellors also preside as the chief administrator under a president or king, as administrators such as the Chancellor of the Exchequer in the United Kingdom, as the leader of some universities, as the foreperson of a jury under Scots law, and other roles in which the traditional leader of an activity is responsible for acts of discretion and management.
   *See also:* master, master in chancery; judge, chancellor; judge, English judge, Lord Chancellor (Lord High Chancellor or Lord Keeper of the Great Seal).
   *discretion of the chancellor*   The chancellor's discretion is very great. The discretion of a chancellor to ascertain the facts of a dispute is, effectively, that of a jury, subject to reversal on appeal only for such clearly arbitrary or unreasonable findings that no reasonable chancellor could have reached such conclusions from the evidence in the record. The discretion of the chancellor to do equity is likewise quite broad, as great in scope as the needs of equity to secure a remedy for all rights denied and profitable misdeeds that are properly before it. It is well to remember that a judge of a court of both equity and of law, such as a U.S. District Judge, enjoys this discretion when sitting in equity, just as does a chancellor.
   *See also:* discretion.

**chancellor as head of a university**   The head of a university or school, subject to other authority. A chancellor is the titular head of many universities. In the United States, it is the title for the chief operating officer in charge or a university or campus of a university, often holding this title to denote the office's subordination to a system-wide university president. In some cases, as in the U.K., the office is generally honorary, and although the office is technically responsible to a council or to a visitor, or to the

monarch, the office is generally a ceremonial post with no superior authority and all practical obligations performed by a vice chancellor.

**chancellor of a diocese**   An ecclesiastical judge and administrator. A chancellor is a judge and administrator within a diocese, appointed by its bishop to act as an adviser on canon law to the bishop, as an administrator over diocesan and parish-diocesan relationships, and as judge in matters of canon law.

**Chancellor of the Exchequer**   The minister of finance of the United Kingdom. The Chancellor of the Exchequer is an administrative position that has had a variety of judicial functions over the centuries but does not now. The Chancellor of the Exchequer is, today, the head of the British Treasury, a cabinet minister selected by the Prime Minister to set financial policy for the government.

**chancery (chancery court)**   A court of equity. Chancery, or chancery court, is a court of particular jurisdiction set by statute and custom that specializes in equity and is presided over by a chancellor. As of 2011, Delaware, Mississippi, and Tennessee retain chancery courts distinct from the courts of general jurisdiction. New Jersey has a General Equity Division of its Superior Courts, and Arkansas has Circuit Courts with Chancery Dockets. U.S. district courts have the powers of chancery courts. Several courts of specialized jurisdiction are successors to chancery courts, particularly family courts and probate courts.

**change**

**change of name**   *See:* name, change of name (corporate name change or personal name change).

**change of neighborhood or change in the neighborhood**   *See:* covenant, real covenant, change-in-the-neighborhood doctrine (change of neighborhood or change in the neighorhood).

**change of venue**   *See:* venue, change of venue.

**change order**   Instruction to alter the product or work in an ongoing contract. A change order is an instruction from the buyer or owner to the contractor to alter the scope of work, the product required, or other aspects of the project that was subject to a contract. Change orders on a construction contract may result from changes to the plans for the structures being built, such as substitutions of material, changes in design, changes in deadlines, and the like. Change orders are usually contemplated in the underlying contract, and the order will alter (usually increasing) the cost of the work required, according to the terms of the contract and the nature of the change. Most contracts require change orders to be in writing, but some oral instructions may none the less be valid change orders.

**change-in-the-neighborhood doctrine**   *See:* covenant, real covenant, change-in-the-neighborhood doctrine (change of neighborhood or change in the neighorhood).

**changes to a deposition**  *See:* deposition, changes to a deposition.

**chaplain**  A religious leader appointed to serve an institutional role. A chaplain is a member of a religion's clergy appointed to serve the private and ceremonial religious needs of an institution. Chaplains serve in the military and both houses of the Congress. Chaplains may also acts as religious advisers or confessors to individuals, in both personal and public capacities. Although public funds may support the chaplains of public institutions, the activities of those chaplains may not violate the Separation Clause of the First Amendment.

**Chapter 7 filing**  *See:* bankruptcy, Chapter 7 filing (Chapter Seven filing).

**Chapter 9 filing**  *See:* bankruptcy, Chapter 9 filing (Chapter Nine filing).

**Chapter 11 filing**  *See:* bankruptcy, Chapter 11 filing, cram down (cramdown or cram-down); bankruptcy, Chapter 11 filing (reorganization in bankruptcy or Chapter Eleven filing).

**Chapter 12 filing**  *See:* bankruptcy, Chapter 12 filing (Chapter Twelve filing).

**Chapter 13 filing**  *See:* bankruptcy, Chapter 13 filing (Chapter Thirteen filing).

**character**  A person's disposition to act according to a given virtue or not. Character is a broad description of the tendency — or unlikelihood — of an individual to act with trustworthiness, honesty, courage, or some other particular virtue. Character is sometimes confused with reputation, which is in fact the belief of others in someone's character.
*See also:* evidence, character evidence; witness, character witness.

**character and fitness**  *See:* bar, admission to the bar, character and fitness.

**character evidence**  *See:* evidence, character evidence.

**character witness**  *See:* witness, character witness.

**charge**  A burden or assignment, particularly a criminal accusation or a financial liability. A charge is a burden or a load, an assignment or accusation. In criminal law, the charge is a formal accusation of allegations of criminal liability, but it is also an instruction to a civil or criminal jury. As a verb, it may refer to either of those actions. In financial transactions, a charge is an expression of a debt, particularly one that is to be carried on credit prior to payment.

**charge as criminal charge**  A formal accusation that one has committed a specific crime. A charge is a formal accusation of criminal liability. As a matter of due process of law, a person arrested has a right to be informed of the charge for which the arrest is made. The charges may originate with an arrest owing to probable cause, or to any charging instrument. The government may amend the charges against a criminal defendant, moving to add charges prior to trial or to diminish or dismiss charges prior to judgment.

**charging instrument**  A document listing charges for which a suspect is liable for arrest. The charging instrument is the formal record of charges issued against a criminal suspect. In the state courts it may be an indictment, an information, or a criminal complaint. The federal courts are bound by the Fifth Amendment to require all criminal charges in felony cases to be made by indictment by the grand jury, although a misdemeanor may be charged by an information filed by a U.S. Attorney.
*See also:* information, information as criminal information; complaint, criminal complaint.

**holding charge**  An arrest on a pretext while more serious charges are investigated. A holding charge is a basis for the arrest of a person suspected of a serious crime that is under investigation and unready to be the basis for a charge or arrest. Holding charges may also be used to harass suspects or witnesses. There are serious concerns over the use of holding charges when the charge for which the arrest is made is trumped up solely for the purpose of temporary detention. Still, when the suspect or witness is genuinely believed by the police and prosecutors to have committed acts that amount to the conduct charged and that conduct amounts to a valid crime, there is no reason not to employ a holding charge pending the development of further evidence or preparation of further charges.

**charge as expense (charges)**  Something one must pay; or the process of incurring such debt. Charge, in the financial world, refers to a debt someone has incurred. Often, this debt was incurred by a purchase on credit, but it can also be incurred in other ways. Charge is also seen as the verb of the action leading to the expense. There are a host of specialized charges, categorized not only by the basis for the charge, such as a late charge or restocking charge, but the manner in which they are presented, such as an undisclosed charge.

**charge as obligation**  Duty to pay funds, provide support, or perform some task. Charge, in the meaning of duty or obligation, has a wide range of meanings, such as an assigned task or responsibility, the duty to assign a task or responsibility, a weight or burden to be carried or imposed on another, or the duty to care for another. Most often in law, a charge is an obligation to pay funds or to provide support. A parent is charged with the care and support of a child. A debtor is charged with the repayment of the debt. A surety is charges with paying a debt if the debtor does not. A sheriff is charged with managing the law enforcement of a county. In all cases, a charge ends with a discharge.

**charge bargain**  *See:* plea, criminal plea, plea bargain, charge bargain.

**charge conference**  *See:* instruction, jury instruction, jury instruction conference (charge conference).

**charge off (charge-off or chargeoff)**  Writing off a debt as a loss. To charge off a debt owed or an account receivable is to consider the asset no longer likely to be paid to write off the asset from the books. By removing it as an asset, it is recorded as a loss, and so it accrues a tax benefit.

**charge on the land**  *See:* land, charge on the land (charge upon the land).

**charge to the jury or to charge the jury or jury charge or instruction to the jury**  *See:* instruction, jury instruction (charge to the jury or to charge the jury or jury charge or instruction to the jury).

**charging order**  *See:* judgment, judgment creditor, charging order.

**charging party**  *See:* party, charging party.

**party to be charged**  *See:* signature, party to be charged.

**charity**  Kind action toward others. Charity, or the Golden Rule that each one of us has an obligation to treat others as one would hope to be treated, is the most basic duty of moral behavior. The obligation of charity is ancient and exists in nearly every religious and moral system of thought. It applies to all forms of conduct, to acts done and not done, toward everyone. As such, it underlies many moral and legal duties, particularly the duties of officials toward citizens. Charity is most often considered in the law as a contribution of money or services to an enterprise engaged in the relief of poor people. Charitable deductions, however, are allowed for several varieties of money and goods given to authorized non-profit organizations as defined by I.R.C. § 501(c)(3).

*See also:* ethics, categorical imperative (reciprocity or the Golden Rule).

**charitable contribution (charitable deduction)**  A gift of money or property to a government-recognized charity. A charitable contribution is a gift of cash, a financial instrument, or property made to an organization qualified by a state or by the I.R.S. as a charitable enterprise. The organizations that may receive charitable contributions include eligible donees that have qualified as non-profit charities, as well as governments, churches, religious organizations, and public charities with receipts less than $5,000 per year.

A charitable contribution is the basis for a charitable deduction on the income taxes of the donor. The donor may not receive services or things of value in return for the amount of the contribution in the amount that would be the basis for a deduction in tax liability.

**charitable corporation**  A corporation operating for the benefit of society. A charitable corporation is an organization that is incorporated under state or federal law and that is devoted to a charitable purpose or purposes according to its charter.

**charitable immunity**  *See:* immunity, civil immunity, charitable immunity.

**charitable organization**  Any entity devoted to the betterment of society, whether it is incorporated or not. A charitable organization is any group of people, whether or not it is a corporation, that is devoted to the support of causes that are in the public interest, especially for the improvement of the lives of others. Although Section 501(c)(3) of the tax code lists charitable purposes as only one of several purposes that organizations may have under this section, casual description of all entities that are recognized by the IRS as exempt under subsection (3) has caused all of them to be described as charitable organizations.

**charitable purpose**  A corporate purpose to assist the poor or to improve society. Charitable purpose is one of the purposes for a non-profit corporation exempt from taxation under section 501(c)(3). It is the most general of the purposes, and indeed the other purposes listed within the section are specific forms of charitable endeavor. The hallmark of a charitable purpose is the assistance of others with no tangible benefit to those rendering aid to individuals in need or to society as a whole.

**charitable remainder trust**  *See:* trust, charitable remainder trust (unitrust or charitable remainder unitrust or CRUT).

**charitable trust**  *See:* trust, charitable trust; charity, charitable trust.

**charitable use**  *See:* use, use of property, charitable use (pious use).

**charity as a virtue**  Acting toward others as you would have them act unto you. Charity is the tool for evaluating justice that threads most through different societies and different theories. It implies a rational application of the Golden Rule: Do unto others as you would have them do unto you. In one way or another, this rule is the basis for most theories and concepts of substantive justice. It can be applied to law by asking, is the argument a given lawyer or official advances an argument they believe should be applied to them as well?

**charity care**  Free medical services. Charity care is hospital care or other medical services provided to an indigent patient without charge.

**charlatan**  An imposter or fraud. A charlatan is a confidence trickster who presents either himself or some scheme or product in a manner that is intended to persuade others that the person or thing presented has merits or value that are, in fact, not there. Useless or dangerous patent medicines were sold by charlatans, and false doctors and other impersonators of professions are charlatans. The regrettable lawyer who makes an argument or denies a claim when the argument or denial are contrary to the facts may be labeled a charlatan.

**charta (carta)** A written paper or letter, and so a charter or deed. Charta was originally a sheet on which one could write, whether of vellum, parchment, or paper. The word also applied to letters in correspondence but was early applied to writings of deeds and contracts, from which was derived charter.

*See also:* charter, charter as fundamental document; constitution, English constitution, Magna Carta (Magna Charta or Great Charter).

**charter**

**charter land** *See:* book–land (charter land).

**charter of incorporation (corporate charter or articles of incorporation)** *See:* corporation, charter (articles of incorporation or articles of association or certificate of incorporation).

**Charter of the United Nations** *See:* United Nations, United Nations Charter (Charter of the United Nations).

**charter as charter of a vessel** Any lease for the use of a ship or vessel. A charter is any contract for the use of a ship that remains the property of another. Though charter is a general term for the leasing of a vessel or a portion of a vessel, the term is more specifically a short hand for the written affreightment contract under admiralty law that is more properly called a charter–party. Charter–party itself is a much older and more general term for a charter written in two forms on one parchment, like an indenture.

Charters include contracts for the transport of people or freight. A charter may include the hire of a vessel, a specific vessel, or vessel and captain, or vessel, captain and crew and the provision of all services and supplies for a voyage or for a period of time.

There are many forms of charter. A time charter is a charter for the use of a vessel for any lawful purpose for a specified time. A demise charter, or a bareboat charter, is type of time charter in which the charterer hires the captain and crew, assuming all of the owner's liability and obligations of maintenance. A voyage charter is a hire of the vessel, master, and crew, for a single trip from one point to another, in which the owner usually provides supplies.

**charter as deed** A record of a land transaction. A charter, when it is a grant of ownership in lands is form of deed issued by a sovereign. A charter may be conditioned or unconditional.

*See also:* patent, land patent.

**charter as fundamental document** A grant of authorities or liberties. A charter is a document that acts as a fundamental principle or power for an organization, whether a government or a corporation. Thus charters are the initial grant of powers to private corporation, municipal corporations, and sometimes to individuals or to all of the people. In the last case, a charter may operate as a grant of powers or rights to one group and a denial to officials of the power to interfere with the grant.

**charter as hired transportation** The hire of a car, bus, train, or other transport, with driver and crew. A charter, as in a charter bus or charter train, is a transportation service for people that is offered to the public for hire. Most states license charter services, requiring insurance, testing of personnel, and regular safety inspections. Charters may be of a car, bus, airplane, or any other mode of transport, including both the vehicle and crew. There are more technical aspects of maritime charters under admiralty law, but charters in the non-admiralty sense are usually equivalent to a gross charter under admiralty law.

**charter-party (ship charter)** A contract for the lease of a ship to carry freight. A charter-party is a contract of affreightment by which a ship is let in whole or in part. A charter-party is often referred to merely as a "charter," and a shipping charter for the shipment of goods by sea is usually a charter-party. The term arises from the former practice of engrossing both texts of a contract for shipping or for the lease of the vessel onto a single piece of parchment, rather in the same manner as an indenture. The charter-party has implied undertakings by both charterer and shipowner, not the least being that the charterer will not intentionally endanger the ship.

**Chase court** *See:* court, U.S. court, U.S. Supreme Court, Chase court.

**chase**

**chase as of animal** The pursuit of a wild animal. Chase was once the process of acquiring property in a wild animal. It is now seen as generally ineffective in law and it acquires no rights until the animal is occupied, by being either either killed or captured or, in certain instances, marked.

*See also:* animal, wild animal, ferae naturae; ferae, ferae naturae.

**chastity (chaste or unchaste)** Abstinence from sexual conduct outside of marriage. Chastity is the condition of refraining from any sexual activities with any person other than one's lawful spouse. Although historically, the imbalances between genders have made chastity predominately a standard for the behavior of women, both men and women can be chaste or unchaste. The term chastity is sometimes employed when the concept of virginity is meant, although virginity excludes all sexual activity with any other person at all times past and present, a condition that is also chaste for those who are not married. Chastity is still found in some statutes and cases arising from actions and prosecutions for seduction, alienation of affection, child abuse, and other sexual offenses. Although evidence regarding chastity or unchastity is barred by rape shield laws, in jurisdictions without them or actions outside their scope, evidence of unchastity may be germane to determine whether alienation of affection or seduction occurred. An imputation of unchastity may be defamation per se or slander per se.

**chattel**  Any property that is tangible but neither land nor a part of lands, usually goods. A chattel is anything that may be owned that is physically tangible but that is not a parcel of land or anything that is part of a parcel of land. Chattels are personalty, or things owned by the person, and so money is not a chattel, because it is not owned in this sense. Not all forms of personal property are chattels, however, because chattels do not include intangible personal property, such as a security or a chose in action. Chattels include both personal and real chattels, and the word chattel, or the phrase personal property, encompasses both. Personal chattels are all chattels other than real chattels, including such predictable things as clothes, art, books, furniture, jewelry, a car, a pencil, and so on. Real chattels are personalty that has significance owing to its relationship to real property, such as the physical instrument of a deed or, more commonly as a leasehold or estate less than a freehold in land. Chattels of either form may be held in co-tenancies. The word chattel comes from the Latin and French terms for cattle, which is a useful means of understanding its concept: to own the cattle is not the same as to own the field. At common law, chattels were not subject to freeholds, but five forms of estate could be held in chattels: an estate for years, an estate from year to year, an estate at will, an estate on sufferance, and an estate elegit (which no longer exists, but was created when a judgment creditor held the property under the appropriate writ).

*See also:* property, personal property, tangible personal property; trespass, trespass to chattel; property, personal property (personalty).

**chattels subject to adverse possession**  *See:* possession, adverse possession, chattels subject to adverse possession (personalty adversely possessed).

**chattel paper**  A written record of a debt that records a security for that debt in goods. Chattel paper is the class of instruments that both form a record of a debt and describe a security interest in specific goods that secure that debt. Chattel papers include leases of goods, car notes, documents expressing liens in goods, and other instruments, particularly promissory notes that are transferable statements of debt and security that assert an ownership interest in the possessor of the note. Most written records of consumer credit transactions that result in a security interest record that interest by chattel paper. Purchasers of a chattel paper, by giving additional value over the debt that is secured, acquire an interest in the paper that is senior to earlier holders.

**electronic chattel paper**  A unique electronic record that is treated as a chattel paper. An electronic chattel paper is an electronic record of a chattel paper, created and stored in such a manner that only one copy of the record exists in a form at any one time, and the holder of that record is considered to possess the electronic paper in a manner like that of the possessor of a tangible chattel paper.

**personal chattel (chattel personal)**  Tangible personal property. Personal chattels are such objects or interests that a person may own. Personal chattels do not include things that cannot be owned, like people or money. They do include intangible interests, such as intellectual property or a right of action. The ownership interest may be partial, such as a tenancy in common or a joint ownership, as when two people both have title to one car.

**personal effects**  Personal chattels that are closely associated with their owner. Personal effects are personal chattels that are routinely used by the person in daily activities, especially objects carried on the person, such as clothes, wallet, jewelry, or a watch, and objects used daily or routinely, such as toiletries and clothing; papers, books, and records; privately owned tools of a trade or hobby, such as an artist's paints or a writer's computer. The meaning of personal effects will vary according to context: the personal effects left by a decedents' will is a broader category than is the personal effects inventoried at a police booking. Unless the context of a will suggests otherwise, a car is usually not considered within one's personal effects.

**real chattel (chattel real)**  Any personal interest in a parcel of land, or any interest related to a parcel of land. Real chattels include two quite different forms of property. One is the tangible object that relates to an interest in land, such as a deed box. The other is an interest in lands that is less than the whole estate or freehold of a parcel, which is held as personal property; in other words a lease, future interest, or present value of a possessory interest limited by a future interest. These forms of interest in land are both personal and real (just as a lease is both a matter of property and contract). That real chattels are personal is significant in including them in lists of personal property or on lists of real property, although they are not, for this reason, subject to taxation as both realty and as personalty.

**recapture of chattel (self-help)**  Acting on one's own to take back chattels wrongfully taken by another. Self-help, or the recapture of a chattel, is the lawful use of one's own initiative, without a court order, to take possession of a chattel that is lawfully one's own from a person who has taken it without a lawful claim to possess it. It is most commonly used to take back an item that has been stolen, such as a snatched purse or shoplifted goods. Self-help must be attempted only after the chattel has been at least briefly under the other person's control. In some jurisdictions it must be accomplished without force or violence, although in more jurisdictions, a reasonable and moderate amount of non-deadly force may be threatened or used to gain access to the chattel from someone's person or property.

See also: self, self help (self-help); repossession (repo or repossess).

**cheat** An act of fraud or deceit. A cheat is both the person who engages in cheating and the act of doing so. To cheat is to gain an unfair advantage, and when doing so amounts to an act of fraud, deceit, or unjust enrichment, it may give rise to a criminal charge or civil action. Thus, cheating in a school examination may not be criminally sanctioned, but cheating in a professional examination may be. Cheating at cards for money is both an act of fraud and an act of unjust enrichment, and cheating on one's tax returns is tax fraud.

**check (cheque)** A written order to a bank from an account holder, to disburse a sum of money to order or to the entity named in the writing. A check is a bill of exchange, usually a negotiable instrument, that orders a bank to deliver on demand a specified denomination of funds to the person or entity named in the instrument, or to order (as in to "cash"). A check is drawn by a drawer and is made payable to the payee. The regulation of the movement of a check from the moment it is drawn until the last payment is made through all of the participating banking institutions is generally under Sections Three and Four of the Uniform Commercial Code. Money orders or other instruments that perform this function are in fact checks. The term check comes from the same route as the check in chess, in which the movement of something is stopped or controlled: the early check was a paper in which a portion was removed as a tally or receipt.

See also: instrument, negotiable instrument.

**check kiting** See: kiting, check kiting (kiting checks or check fraud or paper hanging); fraud, check kiting (check fraud or paper hanging).

**check with insufficient funds (N.S.F. or NSF or NSF check or hot check or bad check or bounced check)** A check drawn on an account containing less money than the value of the instrument when it is presented. An NSF check is a check presented to a bank when the drawer does not have money in the account against which the check is drawn equal to or greater than the value of the check. The check will then be dishonored and returned to the individual, merchant, bank or other entity that presented it for payment, a process colloquially known as bouncing, and a check that is so returned to the person or entity who first accepted it is known as a "bounced check." When there is evidence that the drawer knowingly or intentionally presented the check without sufficient funds, the drawer is committing an act of fraud, which is prosecuted in many jurisdictions under a "hot check" law.

See also: draft, draft as negotiable instrument, bank draft, overdraft (overdraw or overdrawn).

**raised check (altered check)** A check drawn but then increased in its value. A raised check is any check or order that is written for one value and then changed (or, its value is "raised") to require payment for a higher value than than the value for which it was originally written. When this is done deliberately by the maker of the check, the maker is liable for its increased value, although the drawee bank may still refuse to honor the instrument. If the check was not deliberately altered by the maker, the instrument is materially altered and void under UCC §3–407(1)(c). A holder in due course of the raised check may present it in its original amount and is entitled to payment of the original amount. UCC §3–407(3).

**stale check (stale-dated check)** A check that has become voidable through age. A stale check is one that has become sufficiently old that a bank may refuse to honor it. At common law, there was no mandatory time limit, although UCC §4–404 sets a limit of six months on checks that are not certified. Banks may set a limit on the age of checks the bank will honor according to the agreement with their depositors, and makers of checks may set such limits through language of limitation on the face of the instrument. Such particular time limits vary widely, but they are usually from three months to a year. A check that is stale but not void under an agreement or a limitation written on the instrument puts the bank on notice that it might not be valid, but without more, the bank is not under a duty to investigate the check before honoring.

**third-party check** A check presented for payment to an assignee of the original payee. A third-party check is written by a drawer made payable to a payee, who then endorses the check and assigns its payment to a third entity, who presents the check at a bank for payment. The payment of a debt by the debtor's presentation of a check written by another party to the debtor that the debtor has assigned to the payment of the creditor is a conditional payment, made final only upon the check being honored by the issuing bank. A third-party check may be held in due course, if its recipient accepts it in good faith and without notice of a security interest in it. If a check is presented and honored, the payment is effective, but if it is dishonored the check represents an independent promise to the creditor to pay that amount.

**checkoff** See: union, labor union, union dues, check-off; tax, checkoff.

**checkpoint stop** See: stop, police stop, checkpoint stop, sobriety checkpoint; stop, police stop, checkpoint stop.

**checks and balances**  *See:* constitution, U.S. Constitution, ideals, separation of powers, checks and balances.

**chemical solution**  *See:* solution, chemical solution (chemical suspension).

**cheque**  *See:* check (cheque).

**Chevron deference**  *See:* agency, agency as government authority, Chevron deference (Chevron standard of review or Chevron rule).

**chicken game**  *See:* game, game theory, chicken game (hawk–dove game or snowdrift).

**chief**  The head person. A chief is the person who is first among any group of which the person is chief. A chief justice, chief minister, chief magistrate, chief of police, etc., are each the person who is above the other justices, ministers, magistrates, police officers, etc. A chief may or may not be the direct or actual supervisor of the others. Although the term originated as a description of a person, it may refers to inanimate objects, particularly arguments, as the principal or most significant among others.

> **chief judge**  *See:* judge, chief judge.

> **chief justice**  *See:* judge, justice, chief justice.

**child (children)**  A person's son or daughter, or anyone below the age of majority. A child is any person who does not have full legal capacity owing to young age. A child is considered in law to lack the capacity to enter contracts, commit crimes, or to hold positions of trust or responsibility. Fixing the age at which childhood ends and adulthood begins is notoriously difficult and varies with different purposes. More information on these various limits is provided here in the definition for adult.

A child of a parent is the son or daughter or the legally adopted son or daughter of the parent. As of 2011, there is no distinction in the law between the relationship to a parent of a child born as a result of medical assistance in delivery or fertilization and of a child who is not. It is likely, and preferable, that a child born of a father or mother through post-mortem fertilization should be called a child of that father or mother, whatever legal limits there might be to claims upon the father's or mother's estates made on the behalf of the child.

*See also:* abandonment, child abandonment; abduction, child abduction (abduction of a child); abuse, child abuse; child, child endangerment; fetus (fetal, foetus or unborn child); guardian, guardianship of children; molestation, child molestation (molestation of a child or child molester); neglect, child neglect; negligence, child negligence (negligent entrustment of child or negligent entrustment to a child); pornography, child pornography; rape, rape as sexual assault, rape of a child (child rape or carnal knowledge of a juvenile); tax, tax credit, child tax credit (child-and-dependent-care tax credit); tax, income tax, unearned income of minor children (kiddie tax).

**child abandonment**  *See:* abandonment, child abandonment.

**child abduction**  *See:* abduction, child abduction (abduction of a child).

**child abuse**  *See:* abuse, child abuse.

**child abuse syndrome**  *See:* rape, rape trauma syndrome (child abuse syndrome).

**child and dependent care expenses credit**  *See:* tax, income tax, tax credit, child and dependent care expenses credit (child care credit).

**child care credit**  *See:* tax, income tax, tax credit, child and dependent care expenses credit (child care credit).

**Child Citizenship Act**  *See:* citizenship, naturalized citizen, Child Citizenship Act.

**child labor**  *See:* labor, child labor.

**child molestation**  *See:* molestation, child molestation (molestation of a child or child molester).

**child neglect**  *See:* neglect, child neglect.

**child negligence**  *See:* negligence, child negligence (negligent entrustment of child or negligent entrustment to a child).

**child pornography**  *See:* pornography, child pornography.

**child rape or carnal knowledge of a juvenile**  *See:* rape, rape as sexual assault, rape of a child (child rape or carnal knowledge of a juvenile).

**child tax credit**  *See:* tax, tax credit, child tax credit (child-and-dependent-care tax credit).

**child-and-dependent-care tax credit**  *See:* tax, tax credit, child tax credit (child-and-dependent-care tax credit).

**child custody**  The legal obligation or physical authority to care, nurture, and protect a child. Child custody is an adult's authority and practical obligation to care for a minor child. Child custody may be physical custody, in which the parent shelters and supervises the child, or it may be legal custody, which may or may not be physically proximate to the child on a continuous basis. Custody may be lost by court order if there is a finding of neglect or abuse. Custody may also be lost as a result of the dissolution of a marriage between a child's parents, when custody may be awarded to one parent and not to the other. When child custody is awarded jointly to both parents although they live apart, the parent with whom the child lives has physical custody while the other has legal custody. When custody is awarded only to one parent, that parent is the custodial parent and the other is the non-custodial parent. The award of custody in all situations is to be made according to a standard of the best interests of the child, not on the basis of parental desires alone.

The visitation rights of a non-custodial parent as they are designated in a custody or visitation order are not in themselves a right of custody, although they are an enforceable parental right.

*See also:* parent, parental rights, intentional interference with parental rights (causing a minor child to leave or not to return home).

**best interests of the child**  The available conditions of greatest safety, nurture, and growth for a child. The best interests of the child is the touchstone for all decisions of custody, change of custody, visitation, child management plan approval, or other judicial orders affecting the disposition of responsibility for a child. There is no perfect balance of interests, and every case requires careful examination of all of the evidence in context, but the best interests of the child would seek to ensure that, under the circumstances available, any order must be made that is the most likely to promote love and affection between the child and others; to ensure a capable, moral, healthy guardian, who will encourage contact with the other parent; with the means and desire to shelter, feed, clothe, care for, educate, and support the child; to provide a stable environment for as long as possible, and free from abuse or violence; and to reflect the child's preference.

**child custody hearing**  A hearing following divorce, to award custody of a child to one or both parents. A child custody hearing is held following a divorce in cases in which the divorcing parents cannot agree on a plan of custody for their children, or when the court seeks confidence in such a plan presented. Custody is to be awarded in the manner that is in the best interest of the child. With the exception of custody hearings over Indian children, which are governed by the Indian Child Welfare Act of 1978 (partially codified as 25 U.S.C. § 1901 et seq.), custody disputes are exclusively in the jurisdiction of state courts.

**child dependency hearing (parental rights hearing)**  Hearing on whether a child is to be returned to parents or placed in custody. A child dependency hearing is a proceeding that follows a hearing that has determined a child has been the victim of abuse or neglect. The dependency hearing determines whether the child will remain in the home of the parents or guardians or that custody of the child will be awarded to the state.

**disposition hearing**  Hearing to determine whether a child in custody may return to the child's family. A disposition hearing is a post-custody hearing brought by a parent who has lost custody as a result of neglect or abuse, or as a result of a finding of delinquency, in which the parent seeks to have custody of the child restored.

**joint custody (divided custody or shared custody)**  The sharing of one child's custody between two parents living apart. Joint custody is an arrangement of parental rights in which both parents share parental rights. There are two species of joint custody: joint legal custody and joint physical custody. Joint legal custody is practiced in all American jurisdictions and is essentially an investiture of pertinent legal rights and responsibilities in both parents. Most jurisdictions presume that joint legal custody is in the best interests of the child, though that presumption may be rebutted by sufficient evidence of a parent who seeks sole custody or by the state. Joint physical custody is practiced in a minority of jurisdictions and entails a division of physical housing and maintenance responsibilities over the child that differs from sole custody with visitation rights.

**physical custody**  Custody of the person of the child. Physical custody by a parent includes the obligation to house, feed, clothe, educate, and care for a child on a routine basis, as well as the exercise of decision-making authority over a child with respect to the child's well-being and physical maintenance. Physical custody implies legal custody unless it has been expressly assigned to the other parent or a third-party guardian.

**sole custody**  Grant to one parent of all parental rights over a child. Sole custody is the custody of a child by one parent alone. Sole custody may be awarded as sole legal custody, sole physical custody, or both. Sole legal custody entails an assignment to one parent of all legal rights and duties pertaining to the child, while sole physical custody mandates that the child live exclusively with one parent.

**visitation rights (visitation order)**  The right of a non-custodial parent to interact with a child. Visitation rights are the authority to visit, or be visited by, a child in the custody of another person. Visitation rights are commonly awarded to a non-custodial parent, establishing frequency, times, and conditions of visitation with the child in another parent's custody. Visitation may be awarded to grandparents and others if the court awarding visitation believes such an order is in the best interests of the child.

**child endangerment**  Placing a minor in a situation of harm or likely harm. Child endangerment is the criminal infliction of harm, or the criminal increasing of risk of harm, upon a minor. The harm may be physical, mental, or emotional, and it need not come about by physical contact. Actual endangerment need not be proved to sustain a charge of child endangerment; the defendant's knowledge of the danger of the child's environment (such as leaving the child in an environment used for the sale of illegal drugs) may be sufficient, if the defendant placed the child in that environment.

**child protective service (child support service or child youth and family services)** State agency responsible for the protection and well-being of children. Child protective services is the state agency responsible for the protection, care, and rehabilitation of children. The agency investigates claims of child abuse or neglect, acts (in some jurisdictions) as prosecutor or plaintiff in securing their custody from abusive or negligent guardians, oversees the foster-child program and acts as the legal guardian of foster children, placing them with foster parents. There are many variations on the name of the agency fulfilling this role among the states.

**child rearing (childrearing)** Child birth or adoption, nurture and support. Child rearing is the upbringing, education, and socialization of a child. The goal of child rearing is to prepare the child to engage in a productive and meaningful life within society. Generally, child rearing is an individual obligation on each parent or guardian, although the task is usually shared among members of a family. The right to have and rear children is a fundamental right under the Constitutions of the United States and most states, although this right does not extend so far as to limit access to healthcare or basic welfare or to control the content of education.

**child support** Funds owed by a parent to support a child in another person's custody. Child support includes all obligations that a court orders a non-custodial parent to provide to a person with custody of the parent's child. Usually, this amounts to a periodic payment of money to assist a custodial parent or legal guardian with the child's direct expenses, such as food, clothing, and education, as well as indirect expenses such as housing, utilities, and transportation. It may also include the direct payment of insurance, school tuition and fees, and other expenses. The right of child support is the child's, not the custodial adult's, and the duty to collect such support and to provide to the child persists in the custodial adult until it is terminated by court order.

**three-pony rule** Children of wealthy families require full support but not overindulgence. The three-pony rule is a metaphor for the balance required in setting an appropriate requirement of child support for the non-custodial parent of a child one of whose parents is of significant means. The child be assured enough support that the child has not only the necessities of life but also access to the benefits of a child of means, but the court should not require support that amounts to over-indulgence, the rule being that three ponies is enough for one kid. The metaphor has no application for children from households of middle-income families or parents of more modest means.

**dead-born child (still born child)** A child who is not delivered alive. A dead-born child is a child separated from the mother, who never has life independent of the mother. A dead-born child not considered an heir or a member of a class of legatees or devisees, and a will granting an interest to "a child" is not affected by the birth.

**foster child** A child who is a ward of the state and entrusted to a non-relative for care. A foster child is a child who has become the responsibility of the state, and whom the state entrusts to an adult for care and supervision, who is unrelated to the child by blood or other legal ties. A state agency is generally charged with the care or oversight of such a child and becomes the legal guardian, charged with deciding who shall be responsible for the care and upbringing of the child on behalf of the state. The foster parents are usually paid by the state. The term may also be applied though it is less accurate, to any adopted child, particularly when the adoptive parent is not a family member but regardless of whether the child was once a ward of the state. In some regions of the United States, this process may happen informally when a parent dies or voluntarily and unofficially surrenders care of a child to another adult, and such children may be casually described as foster children.

*See also:* parent, foster parent.

**illegitimate child (legitimate child or nonmarital child or bastard or legitimacy or illegitimacy)** A child born outside a lawful marriage. An illegitimate child is neither born nor conceived by parents during a lawful marriage to one another. A child conceived during an adulterous relationship during a marriage is therefore illegitimate, as is one who was conceived and born before marriage. Though illegitimate children were once denied inheritance by law (although they could take an interest devised or bequeathed by will), such denials violate the modern understanding of the equal protection of the laws, which allows all children proven to have been conceived by a parent equal treatment without regard to the parent's marital state. State or federal laws that create a burden on the basis of illegitimacy are unconstitutional unless the law can survive strict scrutiny, which seems logically unlikely ever to occur, with the exception of proof of paternity.

Birth during marriage establishes a presumption in favor of paternity by the mother's husband, a presumption that is not allowed for illegitimate children, who must either be acknowledged by the father or prove paternity during the allowed time to do so in the relevant jurisdiction. This concept is otherwise largely obsolete. An illegitimate child was once commonly called a bastard child, regardless of gender, though this term has long held a pejorative meaning and it is now rarely used in law, nor is the condition of illegitimacy still politely or appropriately referred to as bastardy.

The remaining functions of legitimacy in legal usage are found in cases that seek to establish or refute a claim of paternity and to determine who is a legal heir. These considerations do not turn upon whether a child was born during a marriage but whether in fact the person is the child of another individual. The law might be well served by the obsolescence of the term.

*See also:* bastardy (bastard).

**Mansfield Rule**   A married parent's claim of illegitimacy is barred after a child's birth. Lord Mansfield's Rule bars the introduction in an action to determine parentage, of a statement made after a child's birth by a husband or wife who were married at the time the mother gave birth to the child, that either is not the child's parent. In the light of contemporary understandings of parentage and the utility of biological evidence, this rule is now rarely upheld and has been repealed by legislation in some jurisdictions. Note, there is also a Lord Mansfield's rule regarding challenges to a verdict.

**incorrigible child**   A child whose bad behavior justifies state supervision. An incorrigible child is any child who habitually breaks reasonable rules placed upon him by the child's parent or guardian, to the extent that the child is not deemed capable of properly functioning within the bounds of civilized society. A child who has been deemed incorrigible by a court of competent jurisdiction may be subject to extraordinary state supervision.

**non-age (not of age)**   Younger than the age required for a given task. A person not of age is a child or, within a given context, is younger than an age requirement. Thus, a ten-year-old is not of age for marriage.
*See also:* adult, full age (legal age).

**chilling effect (chill)**   An inhibition that discourages any conduct. A chilling effect is a condition in which a party is inhibited from some conduct because of an action, threatened action, or condition — in which case the threat, act, or condition is said to chill the conduct. Chilling effects are usually alleged when a law, regulation, or enforcement action by a government official or an employer appears likely to scare citizens or workers into abandoning or avoiding the exercise of their lawful rights. A chilling effect can be a burden — even a prior restraint — on the exercise of those rights that is sufficient to justify an injunction against the chilling action, threat, or condition.

## Chinese law

**Ming Code**   The Chinese code of laws adopted in 1367. The Ming Code was a law reform of the Ming Dynasty, an important classical source of Chinese law that influenced the development of early modern law in Asia.

**Tang Code**   The Tang Code of Perpetual Splendor, the legal code of the Tang Dynasty in China, issued in 624 CE, and integrating Confucian principles into older Chinese laws. The 500 sections of the code were issued in twelve volumes, organized by Tang minister Fan Xuanling. The criminal sections of the code enshrine a sophisticated system of criminal responsibility and lenity.

**Chinese wall**   *See:* conflict, conflict of interest, Chinese wall (ethical wall).

**chlorofluorocarbon**   *See:* carbon, chlorofluorocarbon (CFC or hydrochlorofluorocarbon or HCFC).

**choate**   *See:* inchoate (choate).

**choice (choose)**   Selection of one from among two or more options. Choice is the determination of which one of a number of options one prefers. Choice therefore requires the existence of options. Choice refers not only to the process of choosing, but also to each of the options available, to the collective of options available, and to the finally selected option. Choice has acquired a particular meaning in the political and legal arguments over abortion, in which choice refers to the availability to a pregnant mother of the option to seek and receive an abortion.
*See also:* election (elective); abortion (abort).

**choice of law (choice of governing law or choice-of-law rules or choice of laws)**   The rules of which laws to apply in a given dispute from among the laws of several possible jurisdictions. Choice of law depicts several things. Primarily, it is the analysis by a court of which substantive law to apply in a dispute before that court when the circumstances of the case suggest that the laws of the forum are not the only laws that might govern the dispute. This analysis is performed according to the choice-of-law rules of that court. According to those rules, the court (which has proper jurisdiction over the dispute) might choose to apply the law of another jurisdiction. Secondarily, choice of law is an abbreviated label for the choice of law clause, the attempt by one or more parties to a contract to specify in the contract which law should govern interpretation or disputes arising under the contract. Such statement by the parties is also called "express choice of law." Choice of law might have both connotations when an arbitration contract is reached, in which parties to a dispute submit that dispute for arbitration, having negotiated the substantive law that the arbitration panel or arbitrator should apply. Choice of law governs only substantive law, and the law of the forum as to procedure, evidence, and other technical matters is unaffected.

**choice of law clause (choice-of-law clause)**   A contract clause designating the law for a later dispute. A choice of law clause is a contract provision by which the parties specify that a particular body of law, often the law of a particular state or jurisdiction, will govern any dispute arising from or related to the contract between the parties. Such clauses may favor sophisticated parties who have a better understanding of the conduct that a particular jurisdiction requires and surprise unsophisticated consumers, who may find themselves surprised by law that differs from that of the jurisdiction in which they generally transact business. Note: a choice of law clause differs from a forum selection clause, which specifies where a dispute will be heard, not what law should apply.

**Erie Doctrine** A federal court in diversity jurisdiction should apply state substantive law. Under the Erie Doctrine, named for Erie Railroad Co. v. Tompkins, 304 U.S. 64 (1938) (Brandeis, J.), a federal court that has jurisdiction over a proceeding because of diversity of citizenship must apply state law to resolve the substantive issues arising in the case. In most cases, choice of law rules will result in the state law applied being the law of the state in which the federal court sits. Procedural matters are governed by federal law. The policy underlying the doctrine is to reduce the changes in substantive outcome that might arise from an action being heard in the state court or the federal court in the same place.

*law of the state* The substantive rules of obligation and liability in state law. Under the Erie Doctrine, a federal court is required to apply state law when hearing diversity cases. In determining what that state law is, the court will look to statutory provisions and decisions of that state's appellate courts or lower courts, or to the writings of scholars who have studied an issue within a state's laws. Federal courts may certify a question of law to a state supreme court.

*limitation of actions* State statutes of limitations apply in federal diversity actions. Under the outcome-determinative test, although a statute of limitations is technically a procedural law, the application of a state statute of limitations could dramatically affect the outcome of the case in that it determines whether the case even has an outcome; thus the state law is applied.

*procedural law and substantive law* Federal rules of procedure and evidence but state substantive law apply in diversity cases. Under the Erie Doctrine, federal courts hearing claims based on diversity of citizenship are required to apply state substantive law and federal procedural law. Whether a particular provision is substantive or procedural is a matter of law to be determined by the court through inquiry into the scope of the federal procedural law, and the nature of any conflicts with parallel state law, that would result in the preemptive operation of federal law.

**Klaxon Doctrine (Erie-Klaxon Doctrine or Erie-and-Klaxon Doctrine)** Federal courts apply the choice of law rules of the state in which they sit. The Klaxon Doctrine, named for Klaxon Co. v. Stentor Electric Manufacturing Co., 313 U.S. 487, (1941) (Reed, J.), which was derived from the Erie Doctrine, states that conflicts-of-law questions will be considered as substantive law questions. Thus a federal court sitting in diversity applies state rules of conflicts of laws rather than an independent body of federal conflicts law.

**outcome-determinative test** The federal court in diversity should apply state law if it would require a different outcome from federal law. The outcome determinative test is used by federal courts exercising diversity jurisdiction to determine whether an issue is "substantive" to determine whether an issue is "substantive"

under the Erie Doctrine, so that state law applies, rather than procedural, in which case federal law would apply. If the application of the state rule would have a significant effect on the outcome of the litigation that would differ from the federal rule, then in the interest of fairness to the litigants, the state rule should be deemed substantive and be applied.

**interest-analysis technique** Choice of law of the jurisdiction with the strongest interest in a dispute. Interest analysis is a choice-of-law test to determine the substantive law that should apply in a given dispute, by assessing the reasons why a state or other jurisdiction would have a stronger or weaker interest in the dispute. Several factors may be taken into account in an interest analysis, such as the citizenship of the parties, location where a substantial portion of the events surrounding the dispute took place, and location of the evidence or witnesses. The law of the state that has the strongest interest should be applied.

**lex domicilii** *See:* lex, lex domicilii.

**lex fori** *See:* lex, lex fori.

**lex loci (lex situs or lex rei sitae or lex loci delicti or etc.)** *See:* lex, lex loci (lex loci delecti or lex loci contractus or lex loci rei sitae or lex situs).

**lex patriae** *See:* lex, lex patriae.

**proper law** The law that applies to a dispute according to choice of law rules. The proper law is the law of any jurisdiction that a court determines governs the substantive legal questions of a dispute before it. The proper substantive law might be the law of that forum or of another jurisdiction. The proper procedural law is always the law of the forum, or lex fori.

**Rules of Decision Act** Statute requiring the federal courts to apply state law in matters arising under state law. The Rules of Decision Act, codified at 28 U.S.C. §1652, requires that the federal courts look to state law in adjudication cases with the following exceptions: 1. where the case involves a right created by a federal statute, treaty or the Constitution; 2. where the case involves a right created under federal common law; and 3. where there is a federal interest.

**forms of choice**

**devil's bargain** A self-serving choice that is inevitably contrary to the interests of the person who chooses it. A devil's bargain describes any choice for an attractive but self-defeating goal. Many choices amount to a preference for short-term benefits at the expense of long-term success, either because the consumption of the goods chosen destroys the chance of continued opportunity, or because the selection destroys a more important opportunity. The devil's bargain is a constant risk in plea bargaining.

**Hobson's choice**   An apparent choice that is no choice, having only one option. A Hobson's choice is, effectively, no choice at all. A Hobson's choice is a choice that is offered in a manner that seems to allow selection among several alternatives but is in fact only one option. Hobson's choice is sometimes confused with the devil's bargain, a choice among two evils.

See also: choice, devil's bargain.

**tragic choice**   A choice among two or more morally undesirable options. Tragic choices are policy choices that must be made between options that are both highly undesirable. In hypotheticals, each choice usually reflects a distinct moral priority from the other.

**chokehold**   See: police, police brutality, chokehold (choke-hold or choke hold or sleeper hold).

**choose**   See: choice (choose).

**chop shop**   A garage used by car thieves to dismantle vehicles for their parts. A chop shop is a garage or other similar location used by car thieves in order to disassemble vehicles and then sell them for parts. This not only allows thieves to potentially bring in more illicit revenue, since parts sold individually may be worth more than the entire car itself, but also makes the recovery of such a vehicle extremely difficult for the police because the vehicle is now in several pieces, many of which are not distinguishable from other car parts.

**chose**   A thing. Chose is the French word for "thing" in the same vein that "res" is the word in Latin, at their most general, both meaning the noun representing the property in which some interest exists or ownership or right is claimed. Chose is a bit more specific, in that it refers only to chattels, or personal property, either that can be possessed (whether tangible or intangible, like a chose in action) or that can be performed. The plural is choses.

**chose in action (thing in action or chose en action or chose in suspense)**   A right to proceed on a claim in court and to receive its remedy if there is one. A chose in action is the right an individual or group brings a claim before a court. A chose in action exists once the claim exists, not when a complaint or bill is filed. A chose in action is an intangible form of personal property, and in most but not all instances, a chose in action is transferable to a different person or group. The chose in action has value, even if that value is somewhat speculative. Choses in action originated in equity, where third-party standing was easier to achieve. The assignment of a chose in action is now available in many claims at law, as well as in equity, particularly any on a claim that itself may be assigned, such as most claims for payment on a debt. The chose persists only as long as the claim is valid and unsatisfied, but the chose terminates if the claim expires, such as a claim that has not been filed but that has been barred under the statute of limitations, or if it is satisfied, either by judgment or compromise and

settlement. Note: there is no difference between a chose in action, a thing in action, a chose en action, and a claim upon which an action may be brought. Article 9 of the Uniform Commercial Code defines general intangible personal property to include "things in action," though the term is much older than the Code. A chose in suspense is also a chose in action: both terms differ from the chose in possession, in which the claimant enjoys actual or constructive possession of the property in issue.

**chose jugée**   The thing already adjudged. Chose jugée, or more fully, l'autorité de la chose jugée, is the principle roughly equivalent to res judicata in the common law.

**Choshen Mishpat (Hoshen Mishpat)**   The largest of four volumes of Jewish civil law. The Choshen Mishpat is a component of the basic civil law of Judaism, dealing with the rules of sale and procedure, but also reaching many dimensions of personal life and obligation. It is part of the Arbaah Turim (and subsequently of the Shulhan Arukh and many other halakhic works, which follow the same pattern) that deals with civil law as a whole.

**Christian Science**   See: church, churches in signal case law, Christian Science.

**chronic**   Recurring or persistent. A chronic condition is one that does not abate under ordinary conditions but persists. Chronic, high levels of air pollution, for instance, have a cumulative effect that contributes to diseases such as asthma and lung cancer.

**chthonic law**   See: jurisprudence, chthonic law.

**chukim chukkim**   See: hukim (chukim chukkim).

**church**   An institution primarily for the practice of religion, especially a form of Christianity. A church describes a society of persons that belongs to a given religion as well as the building and grounds that are used by that society for its practice in one place or another. Although "church" is a generic term in the United States, according to which it may refer to churches, cathedrals, temples, mosques, or any place of public worship by a society of any form of religion, the term is particularly used to describe societies in the Christian religion and structures used for Christian worship. Within that framework, the governance of the church may act in a manner like that of non-profit corporations, such that the structure of the church determines the rights and interests of the various constituent institutions and individuals. This allocation of authority and rights is especially important in determining the ownership of property and assets held by the church, as well as the extent of its status as taxable or non-taxable under federal and state laws.

A person who makes an individual contribution to a church is eligible to deduct that contribution from that person's federal income tax, within certain limits and under certain circumstances. For this purpose, a church must in fact be a religious organization and its primary identity must arise from the association of individuals who periodically meet together in an association to practice or express their religion.

*See also:* religion; ecclesiastic.

**church bombing** *See:* religion, place of worship, damage to a place of worship (church bombing).

**church autonomy doctrine** Judicial abstention from review over disputes of church doctrine. The church autonomy doctrine is a constitutional and prudential rule by which courts will not hear litigation based on a dispute of church faith, doctrine, means of governance, and other internal matters that are inherently within the discretion of the ecclesiastical corporation. The doctrine is not unlimited, however, and does not bar inquiries beyond matters of faith internal to the church, such as whether an institution is in fact a church, the nature of its structure, the lawful application of a legitimate structure to reach a decision affecting the rights or interests of its members, the nature of certain hiring or job actions governed by law, and the acquisition, use, control or disposal of property. Such matters are within the usual realms of the law, governed by rules, for instance, of agency, employment, non-profit corporations, property, or taxation.

*See also:* polity.

**churches in signal case law**

**Christian Science** A Christian church that strongly promotes spiritual healing. Members of the Church of Christ, Scientist, are also referred to as adherents of Christian Science. Members sometimes refuse medical treatment for serious illness, relying on prayer and moral regeneration instead. Competent adults are accorded a right to do this for themselves, but not for their children.

**Jehovah's Witness** A member of a particular Christian church that rejects the taking of oaths. Jehovah's Witnesses are members of a Christian church practicing acceptance of the entire Biblical text as the literal word of God. In the practice of their faith, members of this church have refused to salute national flags, take oaths or pledges, or accept certain medical practices, particularly blood transfusions. Their rights to do so as the exercise of freedom of religion have been often upheld in the courts.

**churning** *See:* security, securities, securities fraud, churning.

**chutzpah** Absurdly bold. Chutzpah is a Yiddish slang term popular among lawyers depicting a particularly brash form of courage; it is said to be derived from the term for the exercise of outlandish testicular fortitude.

*See also:* Yiddish.

**chutzpah doctrine** Do not seek relief for a problem that you caused. The chutzpah doctrine is a maxim of modern U.S. jurisprudence, which extends the equitable notions of clean hands and legal doctrines such

as coming to the nuisance to a more general bar to a remedy sought to cure a problem that the party seeking it knowingly caused. The doctrine was coined in Marks v. Commissioner of Internal Revenue, 947 F.2d 983, 986 (D.C. Cir. 1991), when fugitives from justice argued against a tax judgment on the basis of a lack of notice. As of 2011, it has not been expressly adopted but in a few courts, although its allure has been recognized by many.

**CIPA or C.I.P.A.** *See:* information, classified information, Classified Information Procedures Act (CIPA or C.I.P.A.).

**circa (ca.)** Around a given time. Circa indicates an approximate period of time, particularly some time past, used especially when the exact date is not known. The most common abbreviations for "circa" are "c." or "ca."

**circuit**

**circuit court** *See:* court, U.S. court, U.S. Court of Appeals (circuit court); court, circuit court, federal circuit court; court, circuit court (riding the circuit).

**circuit justice** *See:* judge, justice, circuit justice.

**circuit law** *See:* court, U.S. court, U.S. Court of Appeals, law of the circuit (circuit law).

**circularity**

**circular argument or circulus in demonstrando or circularity** *See:* fallacy, tautology (circular argument or circulus in demonstrando or circularity).

**circular priority** *See:* lien, circularity of liens (circular priority).

**circularity of liens** *See:* lien, circularity of liens (circular priority).

**circumlocution (circumlocutionist)** A roundabout statement or speech. A circumlocution is a wordy, complex, or euphemistic way of presenting a point yet still avoiding it somehow. It may be used to mislead or deceive. Circumlocution is usually frowned upon among good lawyers.

**circumstance (circumstances)** Any of the haphazard or intended elements that may be relevant in understanding an event. A circumstance is any fact or condition that in any way describes or influences a fact. A circumstance in trial is not what proves a particular fact but the fact itself. Once the fact of some circumstance is established to some degree, the legal significance of the circumstance may be asserted. Some circumstances, such as knowledge, danger, or opportunity or intent, may affect criminal or civil liability. Some circumstances, such as mitigating or aggravating circumstances or the possibility of mitigating losses, may affect not only liability but also punishment or damages.

Circumstance has a non-legal meaning that is sometimes confused with its legal meaning, in its sense as the social or economic position of a given individual or family.

This is as much the point as circumstances generally in the concept of a change in circumstance in family law.

**aggravating circumstance (aggravating factors)** Any fact or condition that makes a situation worse. An aggravating circumstance is a fact or condition that makes a situation worse than it would be otherwise. Particularly in criminal procedure, it is a circumstance that would require a particular person's actions in committing a crime to be seen as worse than they would be without that circumstance. Aggravating circumstances thus justify a harsher punishment than would otherwise be appropriate. Aggravating circumstances include evidence of prior conviction; whether a death was caused in commission of another crime; heinous, cruel or depraved behavior; pecuniary gain; vulnerability of the victim; and degree of premeditation. Aggravating circumstances are most important in capital murder cases. Courts in capital cases may consider mandatory aggravating circumstances, which are set by statute, and permissive aggravating circumstances, which are selected by the sentencing authority, in assessing the degree of culpability of the defendant for the purposes of imposing the most appropriate sentence.

*See also:* circumstance, mitigating circumstance (mitigating factors).

**exigent circumstance** *See:* search, warrantless search, exigent circumstances.

**extraordinary circumstances** Circumstances that are rare and extreme when compared to likely circumstances. Extraordinary circumstances are events or conditions so different from the circumstances that one would reasonably expect, that the circumstances justify unusual treatment under the law. In particular, extraordinary circumstances justify the revision of a court order, a contract, a treaty, or other instrument, in order to reflect a change in circumstances from those anticipated in the future as it was predictable at the time of the original order, contract, treaty or other instrument. The policy against such revisions being fairly strong, the nature of such extraordinary circumstances must usually be clearly demonstrable and also sufficiently distinct as to have been beyond the changes that could be reasonably foreseen at the time of the initial order.

*See also:* ordinariness, extraordinariness (extraordinary or extraordinarily); circumstance, aggravating circumstance (aggravating factors); circumstance, mitigating circumstance (mitigating factors).

**fundamental change in circumstances** The extreme circumstances required to terminate a treaty. A fundamental change in circumstances justifies a state's withdrawal from a treaty if the circumstance was unforeseeable at the time of the treaty's negotiation, signature, or ratification; if the circumstance affects a fundamental purpose of the treaty; the circumstance relates to a reason for the parties to enter the treaty; the circumstance significantly alters the obligations of a state under the treaty; and the changed obligations would still be required to be performed by the state if it did not withdraw.

**mitigating circumstance (mitigating factors)** Any fact or condition that makes a situation better. A mitigating circumstance is a fact or condition that makes a situation better than it would be otherwise. Particularly in criminal procedure, it is a circumstance that would require a particular person's actions in committing a crime to be seen as better than they would be without that circumstance. Mitigating circumstance thus justify a lighter punishment than would otherwise be appropriate. A mitigating circumstance does not support the degree of absolute leniency extended to a defendant in cases of excuse, privilege, affirmative defense, immunity or mistake of fact. Mitigating circumstances include reduced mental capacity, duress, slight participation in the criminal enterprise, the participation of others, mental or emotional issues, and consent. Mitigating circumstances are most important in capital murder cases, in which mandatory mitigating circumstances, which are set by statute, and permissive mitigating circumstances, which are considered at the discretion of the sentencing authority, may reduce the apparent degree of culpability of the defendant and justify a sentence less than death.

*See also:* circumstance, aggravating circumstance (aggravating factors).

**surrounding circumstances** Context. The surrounding circumstances comprise the total context of a particular fact or occurrence, especially indirect evidence that might tend to explain a given fact or occurrence. The surrounding circumstances provide extrinsic evidence from which a trier of fact can more clearly determine the facts of a case. In contract law, surrounding circumstances may be barred by the parol evidence rule, unless used to show that the contract is fully integrated or to provide interpretation of the contract. In criminal law, the surrounding circumstances may determine the level of culpability that applies to a given act.

**totality of the circumstances (totality of the circumstances test)** Assessment of all known and relevant information. The totality of the circumstances is an examination of a given act or event in the light of all known and conceivable circumstances, excluding nothing and giving no one fact, action, or condition a controlling influence upon the assessment. Totality of the circumstances is a condition for the evaluation of evidence, more of an assessment of proof than a burden of proof. Totality of the circumstances is used to assess the reasonableness of an officer's suspicion a crime has occurred, and it is used in many other assessments of administrative decisions, such as the appropriateness of an electoral map.

*See also:* totality.

**circumstantial evidence** *See:* evidence, circumstantial evidence.

**circumstantial incrimination** *See:* incrimination, incriminating circumstance (circumstantial incrimination).

**CISG** *See:* contracts, contract for the sale of goods, United Nations Convention on Contracts for the International Sale of Goods (CISG).

# citation

**citation as summons** A command to appear before a court to answer a minor criminal charge. A citation is an administrative order or a judicial writ ordering a person to appear in a specific court at the time and date specified to answer the charge in the citation. The citation includes both an accusation and summons, and failure to appear result in a penalty independent of the infraction charged in the citation. Citations may be written by law enforcement personnel and immediately delivered to the defendant, such as a citation given for a traffic violation.

*See also:* summons (summon or summoned); abbreviation; order, citation order (citations order).

**legal citation (cite)** A reference to a specific source in an argument or legal discussion. A legal citation, often abbreviated to a "cite" is a reference providing sufficient information to locate materials from which a statement is quoted or suggested, or in which some material relevant to the argument being made can be found. Citation is a general term and may refer to any such reference. Legal citation has, however, two meanings. The first is any reference to an earlier source in the legal materials, such as to say that some matter was dealt with by Chief Justice Marshall in Marbury or is an obligation of the courts under the Civil Rights Act of 1871. The second is the technical citation to authority in a given text or source of law, such as to Marbury v. Madison, 5 U.S. (1 Cranch) 137 (1803), or such as to 28 U.S.C. §1983 (2011). These technical forms of reference are usually what is meant by legal citations. Within legal citations that occur in legal materials, some may be to sources of law and some may be to the record in a given proceeding, citing, for instance, to evidence that is argued to support a finding of fact. Citations to sources of law tend to follow formulaic abbreviations in order to facilitate easy location of the material in a law library or legal database.

*See also:* citation, legal citation, citation of authorities.

**citation manual (Bluebook or Uniform System of Citation)** Citation guide used in the United States, famous for its blue cover. The Bluebook: A Uniform System of Citation was developed and is updated by the Harvard Law Review, Columbia Law Review, University of Pennsylvania Law Review, and the Yale Law Review, and provides information on how to properly cite to legal sources of information. *See also:* abbreviation.

**Association of Legal Writing Directors Citation Manual (A.L.W.D. Citation Manual or ALWD Citation Manual)** A simplified guide to legal-citation form. The ALWD Citation Manual is a practical guide that is intended to simplify and clarify legal citation form. It is an alternative to the authoritative but densely complicated system established in the Bluebook. The Bluebook is published by editors of law reviews. The Manual, published by the Association of Legal Writing Directors, is written by a group of professors who preside over the teaching of legal research and writing in law schools. *See also:* abbreviation.

**citation of authorities** Reference to a source of law. A citation of authorities is a reference to the text of a case, law, statute or other source of law that is used in an argument to locate the source of a quotation or an idea or an example that is a reference in the argument. Authorities here refers to legal authorities, invariably a written work of law, generally constitutional provisions, statutes and treaties, regulations, judicial opinions, and scholarly writings. Generally, citations to the record or to other factual bases of argument are not treated as the citation of authorities. Citations should help an argument, not lard it up with spurious or duplicative authority, and lawyers are often cautioned against over-citation.

**citation signals**

**accord** A signal that sources following it agree with sources preceding it. Accord signals a citation to a reference that agrees with the statements that preceded the citation in the text. It is more specific than the signals "see" and "see also," which merely suggest a relationship to the statements. It suggests a more direct parallel to the ideas presented and a stronger degree of agreement than does "cf." or "confer." Yet accord does not suggest mere repetition as does "see, i.e.," and "to wit" or illustration, as does "see e.g." and "videlicet" or "viz."

*See also:* citation, citation signal, confer (cf.).

**confer (cf.)** Compare, or the following sources agree though perhaps only broadly so. Cf. is a citation signal for compare. It is derived from an abbreviation based on the Latin word "confer" meaning to "compare" or "consult." In legal writing, "cf." often invites a reader to compare the source that follows to the argument of the author or to a preceding source. The comparison per "cf." does not signal except through context whether the sources or arguments compared will be apparently compatible with or contrary to one another.

**contra** Authority that follows contradicts the authority or argument preceding. Contra signals authority counter to the point or authority that precedes the signal. *See also:* contra.

**e.g.** For example. E.g. as a citation signal represents one of many authorities for a given point. It is especially helpful to use such a formulation to avoid long and duplicative string cites. *See also:* videlicet (viz.); exempli gratia (e.g. or eg).

**following pages (ff. or et seq.)** And those pages following. FF. is an abbreviation for folios, which stands for "as well as the pages following." The abbreviation signals reader to look to a particular page of a citation as well as those pages following for the source of the cited information. It is derived from the Latin habit of making plural an abbreviating letter by doubling the letter. Here, the letter "f." had stood for folio, or page from a sheet, and its doubling to "ff." signaled the reference to being over several folio pages. "Et seq." is an abbreviation for "et sequens" or "and what follows," whether in that form or several others, such as et sequentes or et sequentia.

*See also:* et, et sequentia (et sequens or et sequentes or et sequitur or et seq. or et seqq.).

**id. or ibid.** Read the previous citation in this place. Both id. and ibid. have the same significance in legal citation, although the practice of using id. is preferred as a matter of custom and the tyranny of the legal citation manuals.

*See also:* idem (id.).

**i.e.** That is. Although i.e. can be used to introduce a citation, if the citation is well chosen, its use is probably unnecessary, and the cite can be placed in the note or the text without such a prefatory signal.

**infra and supra** *See:* infra; supra.

**q.v.** *See:* quod, quod vide (q.v.).

**see** The authority that follows the signal supports the general point just made. See as a signal indicates that the authority that follows the word is a general source for the point being made. The point may indeed be derived from this source.

**see also** A further reference related to the point made in the prior reference cited. See also signals additional authority for a proposition discussed in a reference cited immediately before this signal. The decision to insert a "see also" signal may indicate that the material cited subsequently is more general, follows a variety of approaches, is redundant, or is less essential than the material first cited.

**citationized (citationizer)** Awkward neologism for annotated statutes. Citationized and its related annotation service, seems to be used only in Oklahoma. The Citationizer, a related tool for annotating statutes and aggregating case law, has to date been employed only in recent experiments with on-line access to public legal materials by the wild and woolly courts of New Mexico, Oklahoma, and Wyoming.

**cite-checking (shepardizing or key-citing)** Comparing a reference to its source. Cite-checking is the generic process of comparing a citation to a reference in a particular writing to that reference to ensure that the citation is accurate and the reference is sound, such as a statute not having been repealed or altered, or an opinion not having been overturned on appeal or reversed in later proceedings, Westlaw uses key-citing for this process on-line. LEXIS–NEXIS has acquired the series Shepard's Citators, which are now on-line, and which are consulted as Shepardizing.

**cititis (overcitation)** The overuse of citation in legal writing. Cititis is the term coined by Karl Llewellyn for the indiscriminate use of citation in legal writing. The plague continues.

**legal citology** The study of the citations in legal writings. Legal citology is the examination of patterns and practice in the use of citations by legal writers. Examples include the examination of the writings of a jurist to determine the sources the jurist cites as a means of estimating the influences on the jurist's thought or the sources the jurist wishes to promote, as well as the search through cases, articles, treatises, and annotations to examine the influence of a given source of law or writer.

**parallel citation** The location of an identical reference in an additional source. A parallel citation is a citation to a single reference that is found in more than one source, by listing two or more of the sources for the same reference. Because case law, statutes, and other legal authorities are often published by several publishers, the same material may be found in several texts. For example, Supreme Court cases may be found in the United States Reports (U.S.), the Supreme Court Reports, Lawyer's Edition (L. Ed.), or in the Supreme Court Reporter (S. Ct.). Since any particular case may be found in each set of books, a case may have two possible citations. Either the official citation, or the citation to the source the author actually used, should be listed first, and the parallel cite gives the location of the same quote or material in the "parallel" source. To an extent, the need for parallel citation has been eclipsed by computer-assisted legal research.

**parenthetical (parentheticals)** A cite's short depiction of a case's holding or relevance. A parenthetical is a brief recitation of the holding of a case or the particular relevance a case has to the proposition in the text for which the case is cited. The recitation is included in the citation between parentheses at the conclusion of the cite, following the date or the judge, if the judge is noted. Parentheticals are useful but should not be used if the information that would be provided in the parenthetical either is so obvious from the context that the information in the parenthetical is redundant or is so obscure or cumulative as to be of little or no value to a reader.

**pinpoint citation (pinpoint cite)** The citation to an exact page in a source. A pinpoint citation gives the exact location, usually the page number but sometimes the number of a line, paragraph, or section, from which a quotation or other exact reference is derived. For example, the hypothetical citation 100 U.S. 75, 101 is a pinpoint citation to page 101, which should be the exact page upon which the authority cited is found, in an opinion that commenced on page 75.

*See also:* passim.

**citizen**   A person with the full rights and privileges of membership in a state. A citizen of the United States is a person who is either a natural born citizen whether by virtue of a citizen-parent or by birth on U.S. soil, or a naturalized citizen by virtue of residence, qualification, and oath according to law, or by adoption as a child by U.S. citizens. A person may be a citizen but not be eligible to vote, because children are disenfranchised citizens, as are convicted felons, according to the law of many states.

*See also:* jus, jus as right of citizenship, jus sanguinis; jus, jus as right of citizenship, jus soli; naturalization; constitution, U.S. Constitution, clauses, Citizenship Clause (Naturalization Clause).

*citizen and national and subject*   A citizen is a full member in a democracy, republic, or nation-state that confers that title as a matter of law on its members. Many states do not, because the structure of the state does not depend on a citizenry. Thus monarchies may not have citizens but have subjects. For example, a full member of the United Kingdom is a subject, that is a person who owes allegiance to the monarch of the kingdom. A further distinction is made between citizens and nationals. Nationals include both citizens and others who owe allegiance for life to the nation-state. In the United States, nationals include both citizens and members of the U.S. armed forces who are not citizens.

*See also:* nationality (national); subject, subject as national.

*District of Columbia*   Residents of the federal district are under the direct jurisdiction of the federal government. Unlike citizens of the several states of the United States of America, citizens of the District of Columbia are directly subject to the jurisdiction of the federal government. The District of Columbia is a unique entity, belonging to no state, and housing the seat of the national government. Residents of the District pay taxes and are subject to the same duties as citizens of the several states, but are not eligible for all of the same rights. In particular, citizens of the District have no voting rights for federal offices. Instead, residents of Washington, D.C. are subject to the direct legislative control of the Congress, whose membership they have no power to elect. The District of Columbia Home Rule Act, P.L. 93-198; 87 Stat. 777; D.C. Code §1-201 (1973) established a mayor and thirteen-member council to establish local laws and provide municipal services, although this government is subject to congressional oversight.

*United States of America*   A citizen of the U.S. and of a state by birth or by naturalization. A citizen of the United States of America is a member of that country who has attained all the rights and incurred all the duties of citizenship either through naturalization or by birth. The United States allows citizenship by birth through either jus soliis, by being born on U.S. soil, or jus sanguinis, by being born the child of a citizen. A U.S. citizen is inherently also a citizen of the state in which the citizen maintains the citizen's principal residence (including the District of Columbia, although there citizens may not have full rights to vote in federal elections).

**citizen suit (taxpayer action or taxpayer suit)**   An action brought by a private citizen in vindication of a public interest. The citizen suit is a civil action brought against a private entity or a public agency to secure compliance with the law on a matter of public importance. Some citizen suits are specifically authorized by federal statutes, such as an action under the Ports and Harbors Act or under Title VII; others are saved from pre-emption or extinction by citizen suit savings provisions, such as the Clean Air Act's allowance of citizen enforcements of common-law interests, and others are common-law actions that have not been affected by statutes, such as actions qui tam. The private citizen may also sometimes seek equitable relief from state and federal agencies that violate statutory or constitutional requirements or who fail to fulfill their obligations in implementing legislation. The private attorney general theory describes these actions.

**private attorney general theory**   The allowance of attorney's fees to those who bring a private action to enforce a public right. The private attorney general theory is a policy according to which a private citizen who commences a lawsuit to vindicate a public interest should be able to recoup attorney fees. It has generally been applied in federal causes of action by legislation, particularly for the enforcement of civil rights. Some states allow such recoveries as a matter of state constitutional or common law. This is an exception to the American Rule prohibiting the recovery of attorney fees.

**citizenship**   The status of membership in a state according to the laws of that state. Citizenship is a status conferred upon all residents of a nation or state who meet criteria in the laws of that nation or state. The citizen is thereby entitled to certain rights and incurs certain responsibilities. Such rights include protection of that jurisdiction's laws and the right to bring actions in that state's courts. Such duties might include payment of taxes or military service and the responsibility to answer charges or actions in that state's courts. In its broadest sense, citizenship is the same as nationality and includes the relationship of an individual to the state in a monarchy, even though the individual in a monarchy is properly called a subject rather than a citizen. In the United States, citizenship is a matter of federal law, established either by birth or naturalization. Citizenship by birth results from birth either to a citizen parent or on U.S. soil.

*See also:* nationality (national); naturalization.

*domicile and citizenship*   A domicile is where one maintains one's primary residence, and citizenship is where one's legal obligations are determined. Citizenship may be based on domicile, although this is usually only done in the sense of citizenship of one state or another within the United States and not as between sovereign nation–states. Domicile is not always dispositive in either case. Internationally, a person may have multiple nationalities and but one domicile. Further, one may establish a domicile away from one's country of citizenship without renouncing one's citizenship. Within the United States, one might have a temporary domicile and retain sufficient interests and contacts to retain a permanent citizenship elsewhere.

*See also:* domicile (domicil or domiciliary).

*residence and citizenship* The place at which one lives. Residence is merely a place in which one lives for a time, which may or may not be intended as permanent. Residence without an intent to establish a primary residence does not in itself establish citizenship, although residence may be a requirement for naturalization.

**corporate citizenship** Corporate citizenship is in the jurisdictions of incorporation and the principal place of business. Corporate citizenship is a legal relationship between the corporation as artificial person and the jurisdictions in which it is treated as having citizenship. A corporation is a citizen of the jurisdiction in which it is chartered, and it is also a citizen of the jurisdiction in which it has its principal place of business.

*partnership* A partnership is a citizen of every jurisdiction in which a partner is a citizen. Put another way, the citizenship of a partnership is in every jurisdiction a partner has citizenship.

**natural-born citizen (natural born citizen)** A child born in the United States or born a child of a citizen. A natural-born citizen is a person who is a citizen at birth, which is the case if the person is born in the United States and subject to its jurisdiction, or (regardless of the place of birth) is the child or one or both parents who are citizens at the time of the child's birth.

*See also:* native.

**naturalized citizen (naturalization)** Any person who was born an alien but becomes a citizen later in life. A naturalized citizen is any person who becomes a citizen through the procedures established by Congress to confer citizenship on a non–citizen. To apply for naturalization, most adults must be permanent residents for five years, although spouses of U.S. citizens must be permanent residents for three years, and members of the U.S. armed forces may apply after one year of service. All applicants must show good moral character, a knowledge of English and civics, and an attachment to the U.S. Constitution.

*See also:* naturalization; oath, oath of allegiance (naturalization oath).

**Child Citizenship Act** A foreign child lawfully entering the U.S. to be adopted becomes a citizen on final adoption by a U.S. citizen. The Child Citizenship Act of 2000, 8 U.S.C. §§ 1431–33 (2008), allows a foreign child who is adopted by a U.S. citizen to become a citizen when the child is present in the U.S. and the adoption if made final.

**citizen's arrest** *See:* arrest, citizen's arrest.

**city** A urban area significant for its size, authority, or history. A city is a municipal corporation organized under state law and defined as a city by state law and its charter. The definition of city varies from state to state, but they are usually defined by population or by the satisfaction of various conditions to perform certain services. A city is considered a part of the state for federal purposes, and the U.S. Constitution binds city officials.

*See also:* municipality (municipal corporation).

**civil** Social in general, but non–criminal in U.S. law or based on Roman law. Civil has many meanings in law, nearly all arising from the role of the citizen (civis) in the civic sphere of ancient Greece and Rome. Thus, the civil law is neo-Roman law, or the law of the states of continental Europe and those states that follow them. In the U.S., a civil action or any civil matter is not criminal. As a general matter, a civil proceeding is also one that is neither ecclesiastical or natural, so a civil marriage ceremony is not a church wedding and civil death is not natural death.

*See also:* action, civil action; arrest | arrest as a civil matter; conspiracy, civil conspiracy; contempt of court | civil contempt vs. criminal contempt; court, civil court; disability, civil disability, civil death; disability, civil disability (civil disabilities); forfeiture, civil forfeiture; immunity, civil immunity; law, civil law (C.L. or CL); liability, civil liability; civil rights, civil rights organization, American Civil Liberties Union (A.C.L.U. or ACLU); marriage, civil marriage (secular marriage); marriage, civil union (domestic partnership); obedience, civil disobedience; disorder, civil disorder; penalty, civil penalty (civil sanction).

**civil action** *See:* action, civil action.

**Civil Code of Louisiana** *See:* law, civil law, Civil Code of Louisiana.

**civil commitment** *See:* commitment, civil commitment, voluntary commitment; commitment, civil commitment, involuntary commitment (mandatory commitment).

**civil conspiracy** *See:* conspiracy, civil conspiracy.

**civil court** *See:* court, civil court.

**civil death** *See:* disability, civil disability, civil death, civiliter mortuus; disability, civil disability, civil death.

**civil disabilities** *See:* disability, civil disability (civil disabilities).

**civil disobedience** *See:* obedience, civil disobedience.

**civil disorder** *See:* disorder, civil disorder.

**civil forfeiture** *See:* forfeiture, civil forfeiture, innocent owner; forfeiture, civil forfeiture | double jeopardy; forfeiture, civil forfeiture.

**civil Gideon** *See:* counselor, right to counsel, right to civil counsel (civil Gideon).

**civil immunity** immunity, civil immunity.

**civil law**   *See:* law, civil law, Civil Code of Louisiana; law, civil law (C.L. or CL).

**civil liability**   *See:* liability, civil liability.

**civil liberties**   *See:* civil rights (civil liberties).

**civil marriage**   *See:* marriage, civil marriage (secular marriage).

**civil penalty**   *See:* penalty, civil penalty (civil sanction).

**civil procedure**   *See:* procedure, civil procedure.

**civil rights (civil liberties)**   The rights and freedoms accorded free individuals in the state. Civil rights are the whole of the rights and liberties that are provided by law to any person who is required to obey the laws and is not under a punishment by law for a criminal act. More broadly, civil rights may refer to the rights to protection, dignity, and liberty that any person might have good reason to expect from the state. In the first sense, civil rights are the rights established in the federal and state constitutions and laws that are available to all to assert as claims against their limitation by officials. In the second sense, they are the customary arguments for the rights of the individual, as made in the Declaration of Independence and important political statements, such as those of Thomas Jefferson, Abraham Lincoln, Franklin Roosevelt, and Martin Luther King, Jr. Perhaps the most fundamental civil rights from either perspective are the rights to due process of law and to equal protection of the laws, to free speech, religion, and privacy, and to political participation, such as the right of suffrage, or voting. Many states extend these principles to include rights to education, and many countries extend them to include the basic necessities of life.

**civil rights act (civil rights law)**   A statute enshrining a specific assurance of civil rights. The civil rights acts are a series of statutes passed by Congress under its powers to enforce the Reconstruction Amendments and the Commerce Clause. They include the Civil Rights Act of 1866, extending citizenship to freed slaves, the Civil Rights Act of 1871 (the Ku Klux Klan Act), providing a civil cause of action for the deprivation of civil rights by anyone acting under color of state law, the Civil Rights Act of 1875, barring discrimination in public accommodations, the Civil Rights Act of 1957, which created the Civil Rights Commission, the Civil Rights Act of 1960, federalizing election monitoring, the Civil Rights Act of 1964, barring discrimination based on race, color, religion, sex, and national origin by federal and state governments or in restaurants and hotels in interstate commerce, the Civil Rights Act of 1968 (the Fair Housing Act), barring discrimination in renting or selling housing, and the Civil Rights Act of 1991, ensuring workers can bring claims for workplace discrimination. State civil rights acts provide similar and farther reaching protections under state law.

*1. private conduct*   Private conduct involves the actions of an individual or privately held business entity that are not encouraged or regulated by any governmental policy and whose conduct or enterprise is not related to any government interest. Private conduct may be an expression of a person's values, religious beliefs, cultural backgrounds, and other expressions of the mind or soul upon which reasonable men may differ. The freedom to hold such beliefs and to engage in such conduct is protected and the Fourteenth Amendment provides no shield against private conduct even if it is discriminatory. Even so, private conduct that burdens a federal right to engage freely in commerce, or to hold housing, or any other basis of federal jurisdiction, such as the use of federal moneys, may be regulated.

*2. public accommodations*   Public accommodations are barred from discrimination in their access or services by the Civil Rights Act of 1964, even if they are privately owned. A private enterprise which invites in the public to use its facilities and whose operations affect commerce. Public accommodations include inns, hotels, restaurants, theaters, laundromats, grocery stores, and other such facilities where people expect access.

**Civil Rights Act of 1866 (Section 1981)**   Equal rights are secured under the law to all persons regardless of race or color. The Civil Rights Act of 1866 was the first of the Reconstruction Acts, designed to protect freedman following the Civil War. All citizens are ensured equal rights regardless of color, race, or nation of origin, to the protections of contract, property, evidence, and judicial procedure. Anyone who denied these rights to former slaves commited a misdemeanor, and upon conviction faced a fine or imprisonment.

*See also:* race, race as social category; law, color of law.

**Civil Rights Act of 1871 (Ku Klux Klan Act)**   The deprivation of rights under color of state law is a crime and also the basis of a civil action. The Civil Rights Act of 1871 established a civil and a criminal remedy to enforce federally protected civil rights against any person who would deprive another of those rights acting under color of state law.

*See also:* civil rights, civil rights enforcement action, 1983 action; color (colorable or colour or colourable); Ku Klux Klan.

**Civil Rights Act of 1875**   Public accommodations shall not be denied according to race. The Civil Rights Act of 1875 was one of the last Reconstruction Acts, declaring a federal prohibition on the refusal of service in a public accommodation on the basis of race. The act's application to conduct by private citizens was struck down in the Civil Rights Cases, 109 U.S. 3 (1993), which limited the act only to conduct by state officials or other state actors.

**Civil Rights Act of 1957**   No person shall be kept from voting by threats or violence. The Civil Rights Act of 1957 barred the use of threats or violence to intimidate or bar anyone from voting in a federal election. It also established the Commission on Civil Rights and created an Assistant Attorney General, impliedly for the purpose of enforcing civil rights.

**Civil Rights Act of 1960** The U.S. may inspect federal elections and challenge them in court. The Civil Rights Act of 1960 established federal poll watchers in the U.S. Department of Justice, required officials to retain voting and voter registration records, and gave the U.S. Attorney General express authority to sue in federal court to uphold voting laws and to restore voters wrongly struck or barred from the voting rolls.

**Civil Rights Act of 1964** Discrimination in public services by race, color, religion, sex, or national origin is barred, even from private actors. The Civil Rights Act of 1964, P.L. 82–352, 78 Stat. 241, forbade discrimination on the basis of race, color, sex, religion, or national origin. Title I provided for access to voting, barring literacy tests and other obstacles to the ballot. Title II barred discrimination in places of public accommodations such as hotels, cinemas, and restaurants affecting interstate commerce, on the ground of race, color, religion, or national origin. Title III required the desegregation of public institutions. Title IV provided specific requirements and assistance for the desegregation of public schools. Title V enlarged the powers of the Civil Rights Commission. Title VI barred discrimination in federally funded programs. Title VII barred discrimination in employment on the basis of race, color, religion, sex, or national origin, and it created the Equal Employment Opportunity Commission. Title VIII required the collection of voting statistics by race. Title IX provided that the Attorney General may intervene in civil rights enforcement actions. Title X created the Department of Commerce Community Relations Service.

*Commerce Clause* The Civil Rights Act of 1964 was enacted under Congress's Powers over interstate commerce. The Interstate Commerce Clause of the United States Constitution grants the Congress the power to regulate commerce among the several states, which was the basis asserted by Congress for the Civil Rights Act, primarily to avoid consideration of the Act by the Senate Judiciary Committee, which under Senate rules would have reviewed a statute based on the Fourteenth Amendment, and which was stacked with Senators like Mississippi's James Eastland, who were hostile to the Act.

**Title VI (Title Six)** No federally funded programs may bar access on the basis of race, color, or national origin. Title VI of the Civil Rights Act of 1964 prohibits discrimination in federally funded programs. This section applies only to incidents of intentional discrimination on the basis of race, color, or national origin. Even so, the discriminatory intent may still be implied from proof of a discriminatory effect having a disparate impact upon members of a listed group.

**Title VII (Title Seven)** Federal statute prohibiting discrimination in employment Title VII of the Civil Rights Act of 1964 prohibits discrimination in any aspect of employment. An employer is prevented from discrimination in hiring, promotion, transfer, or firing on the basis of race, color, sex, religion or national origin. Title VII requires the exhaustion of other remedies, such as in-house grievance procedures, as well as administrative procedures, prior to the filing of a civil law suit.

*See also:* discrimination; discrimination, employment discrimination.

**Anti-Retaliation Provision** Employers may not punish workers who exercise their Title VII rights. The Anti-Retaliation Provision of Title VII, section 703(a) of the Civil Rights Act of 1964, codified at 42 U.S.C. §2003(a), bars employers from discriminating against employees who have challenged an employment condition or practice as a violation of Title VII, regardless of whether the challenge is informal or legal. A plaintiff must usually prove an adverse action by an employer was in some way a response to the plaintiff's activities protected by law. In some conditions, the employer will be held responsible for adverse actions by employees who create a hostile work environment for the person engaging in protected conduct, if the employer knows of the hostile environment and does not act to abate it.

**Civil Rights Act of 1968 (Fair Housing Act)** *See:* housing, Fair Housing Act (F.H.A. or FHA).

**Civil Rights Act of 1991** Title VII allows employees to recover damages for employment discrimination, proved by disparate impact. The Civil Rights Act of 1991 was passed to ensure employees could sue for discrimination in violation of Title VII, despite attempts by the Supreme Court to limit such actions. Price Waterhouse v. Hopkins, 490 U.S. 228 (1989), shifting the burden of proof of the employer's practices to the employee, Wards Cove Packing Co. v. Atonio, 490 U.S. 642 (1989), limiting evidence of disparate impact, Martin v. Wilks, 490 U.S. 755 (1989), allowing nonparties to challenge late a decree of discrimination, and Patterson v. McLean Credit Union, 491 U.S. 164 (1989), barring damages for racial harassment, were all limited or abrogated by the act.

**conspiracy to interfere with civil rights (Section 1985)** Anyone who conspires to interfere with the civil rights of another or to hinder their protection is liable for the damages of that conspiracy. A conspiracy to interfere with civil rights is a crime under federal law, and it gives rise to a civil action for damages from any person harmed as a result of it.

**neglect of duty (Section 1986)**   An official is liable for harms from civil rights violations the official allows. Section 1986, a portion of the Ku Klux Klan Act, creates a civil cause of action for damages suffered by anyone harmed as a result of the violation of their civil rights, that may be brought against any person with a duty to prevent such harms who failed to prevent them even though that person had knowledge of a conspiracy to inflict them.

**prevailing party**   A party who obtains final relief in an action under a Civil Rights Act. The prevailing party is the party substantially successful on at least some final aspect of a civil rights enforcement action. The success need not mean every claim is won but at least some aspect of the behavior of the other party or the legal relationship between the parties must be altered as a result of the case. A prevailing party may be either a plaintiff or a defendant, although the prevailing defendant must not merely win the judgment but further demonstrate that the plaintiff's claim was brought in bad faith, or was clearly groundless or malicious.

*See also:* prevail (prevailing party).

**state actor (governmental actor)**   Any official of the state or anyone acting under color of state authority when abridging a civil right. A state actor, or in the federal context a governmental actor, is any person who harms another person in a manner that infringes on the other person's civil rights, when the person doing the harm is an official of the government, is acting under orders from such an official, is carrying out a duty or power created by the government, is funded by the government, or is acting sufficiently in concert with state officials as to be in any manner an agent of the officials. Actions under Section 1983 may be brought against any person acting "under color of state law," which limits causes of action to state actors. The state actor requirement is an extension of the state action requirement imposed on the Fourteenth Amendment in the Civil Rights Cases, 109 U.S. 3 (1883).

**Title IX (Title Nine or Title 9 or Patsy T. Mink Equal Opportunity in Education Act )**   Women shall have the same federal educational funding opportunities as men. Title IX established in 1972 a principle of equitable access by both genders to federally funded educational programs. Although it applies to all educational programs, including ancillary programs such as housing, Title IX is best known for its regulatory interpretation by the federal Department of Education, which has particularly applied Title IX to sports programs, requiring equitable funding for women to play intramural and intercollegiate sports when men's programs are funded. It does not apply to gender-specific social programs, such as fraternities or sororities. Many states have extended these requirements to all education, not only federally funded programs.

**Voting Rights Act**   States may not create barriers to voting that discriminate on race or a surrogate for race. The National Voting Rights Act of 1965, codified at 42 U.S.C. §1971, et seq., bars states from property qualifications, literacy tests, and gerrymandering designed to deny Blacks access to the polls or effective representation through elections.

**civil rights enforcement action**   *See:* fee, fee for services, attorney's fee, fee shifting, civil rights enforcement action.

**1983 Action**   A person whose federal rights are harmed by a state actor may recover damages for resulting injuries. A 1983 Action is a civil claim brought under the Civil Rights Act of 1871, for damages or for a declaration or an injunction against violating a declaration, against any person acting under color of state law to violate any federally recognized right or privilege.

*See also:* Ku Klux Klan; civil rights, Civil Rights Act, Civil Rights Act of 1871 (Ku Klux Klan Act); law, color of law.

**Bivens action**   A federal civil action against a federal official for the violation of constitutional rights. A Bivens action is a claim against an individual federal official for that person's actions in depriving the plaintiff of a federal constitutional right. The name arises from the 1971 case in which the cause of action was first recognized in the Supreme Court, Bivens v. Six Unknown Named Agents, 403 U.S. 388 (1971). Bivens actions are not available if an adequate administrative or state tort remedy is available, nor can a Bivens claim generally be brought against anyone who is not employed by the government of the United States. Bivens actions are a federal parallel to 1983 actions against state officials.

*See also:* tort, Federal Tort Claims Act (F.T.C.A. or FTCA); civil rights, civil rights enforcement action, 1983 Action.

**civil rights attorney's fees**   The prevailing party in a civil rights case may recover attorney's fees from the other party. The Civil Rights Attorney's Fees Act of 1976, 42 U.S.C. §1988 (2011), established the power of a court to award attorney's fees as a part of the costs of a civil rights action, from the actions listed in the statute and its various amendments. The court has the discretion to award fees to the prevailing party: to the plaintiff if the plaintiff substantially prevails on any element of its claims, and to a defendant if the defendant prevails on its defense and only if the plaintiff's case was frivolous or clearly unfounded.

*See also:* fee, fee for services, attorney's fees; fee, fee for services, attorney's fee, fee shifting, lodestar amount (lode-star or lodestar method); fee, fee for services, attorney's fee, fee shifting, Equal Access to Justice Act (EAJA or E.A.J.A.).

**civil rights organization (civil rights workers or civil rights lawyers)** An organization seeking legal or political protection of civil rights. Civil rights organizations take many forms, each attempting to influence public officials and the citizenry on the importance of the recognition and protection of civil rights. Some civil rights organizations have emphasized education through social action, and others have emphasized litigation.

**American Civil Liberties Union (A.C.L.U. or ACLU)** Organization that litigates constitutional civil liberties. The American Civil Liberties Union is a national organization whose stated purpose is to ensure civil liberties inherent in the United States and state constitutions. The organization frequently defends the free speech rights of others, even when they engage in conduct or espouse opinions contrary to the personal views of the organization's members or officers.

**National Association for the Advancement of Colored People (N.A.A.C.P. or NAACP)** An organization that promotes civil rights, particularly through litigation. The National Association for the Advancement of Colored People, or NAACP, was founded in 1909 to organize citizens to suppress lynching and to seek to establish equality under the law for African Americans. The NAACP and the NAACP Legal Defense Fund took the leading role in crafting the litigation strategy that ended de jure segregation and carried much of the most significant litigation of the Civil Rights Movement in the twentieth century. It remains an active organization in supporting civil rights in society, politics, and litigation.

**NAACP Legal Defense Fund (LDF)** The litigation and education foundation created from the NAACP. The NAACP Legal Defense and Education Fund, Inc., or LDF, was the separately incorporated non-profit arm of the NAACP, created by Thurgood Marshall to litigate civil rights actions with separate liability from the NAACP as a whole. The LDF is a leading organization that continues to bring litigation to promote civil rights and social justice.

**Southern Poverty Law Center (SPLC)** A civil rights organization that litigates against institutional and organizational bigotry. The Southern Poverty Law Center monitors the activities of domestic terrorists and organizations that encourage hate and violence, and litigates claims against such organizations on behalf of their victims and to deprive the organizations of resources. The SPLC also supports education programs for diversity.

**civil sanction** *See:* penalty, civil penalty (civil sanction).

**civil service** The career civilian employees of a government. The U.S. Civil Service includes all employees of the federal government who are not elected, not appointed to serve at the pleasure of the President, and who are not in the military services or foreign service. Civil service positions are historically to be protected from political interference in their selection and promotion. Following the enactment of the Pendleton Civil Service Reform Act of 1883, the civil service was regulated by the Civil Service Commission, which was replaced by the Civil Service Reform Act of 1978, Pub.L. 95–454, 92 Stat. 1111 (October 13, 1978) by the Office of Personnel Management and the Merit Systems Protection Board.

**Hatch Act** Civil servants, once barred from politics, may now engage in political speech. The Hatch Act of 1939, codified at 5 U.S.C. § 7321 (2008), initially barred federal civil servants from political activities, thus discouraging politicians from patronage in attempting to fill civil service positions. It has been amended to allow many employees to engage in most forms of political activity, though some restrictions remain.

**civil theft** *See:* conversion, tortious conversion (civil theft).

**civil union** *See:* marriage, civil union (domestic partnership).

**civilian**

**civilian as not military** From a military perspective, anything not military. A civilian is a person who is not a member of a uniformed armed force, not subject to the direct or general orders of military commands, and not required or privileged to wear a military uniform. For the purposes of the law of war, a civilian is presumptively a non–combatant, although not all non–combatants are civilians (the wounded, military doctors, military chaplains, and others are military non–combatants). Civilians are generally not subject to the jurisdiction of military courts, although sufficient integration with the actions of a military unit may rebut this presumption. More generically, a civilian is any person not in a uniformed service, such as the police.

**civilian as of civil law** Anything related to the civil law of Rome, Europe, Louisiana, or to its theory. A civilian is a person who practices, writes, or otherwise employs the civil law. As an adjective, civilian in this sense refers to any person, text, idea, country, or other aspect of any manifestation of the civil law.

**civiliter mortuus** *See:* disability, civil disability, civil death, civiliter mortuus.

**civility** Respect for the dignity of others, regardless of circumstances. Civility is the moral and professional duty of every attorney toward each person whom the attorney affects, to respect that person's dignity, regardless of disagreement and regardless of the person's apparent faults or conduct. Civility is an essential aspect of professionalism, and the obligation to respect the dignity of each other person is particularly essential in the profession in the treatment of other lawyers. The duty of civility is an aspect of the duty of charity, to treat all people in the manner that a rational person would desire to be treated. Civility does not require a person to ignore the faults of others or the harms they create, but to treat the person who would cause such problems with care and regard, while requiring the person to correct the faults that have been made, mitigating the harms caused and minimizing the dangers of the future. An attorney's duty of civility is not, therefore, derived from the performance of others of their duties, but on each person's duty to society and to the profession.

*See also:* charity, charity as a virtue; profession, professionalism; empathy.

**civitas**   The conditions of citizenship.

**claim**   A demand for satisfaction for a loss or harm, or an argument. A claim is any assertion of an interest that must be satisfied according to law by a payment of money or the transfer of property. A claim may be asserted from one party against another as a private matter, or it may be the basis of a civil action. To be valid in law, a claim must make an assertion for which relief can be granted. One may assert ownership of a property, either real or personal, or one may assert the suffering of damages for a breach of a right or duty owed. A claim may also be made to counter one made by the opposing party, such as in a counterclaim, or one made by a co-party as in a cross-claim. In such an instance, one might also claim a defense. But all these claims require proof and the burden is on the claimant to so provide. More generally, a claim is an assertion, an argument that something is the case.

**claim and delivery**   *See:* repossession, claim and delivery.

**claim for relief**   *See:* relief, claim for relief.

**claim of right**   *See:* possession, adverse possession, claim of right.

**claim of right or colour of right**   *See:* right, legal right, color of right (claim of right or colour of right).

**claim preclusion**   *See:* res, res judicata, claim preclusion.

**claim priority**   *See:* priority, claim priority, super priority; priority, claim priority, absolute priority rule; priority, claim priority (priority of claims).

**aggregate claims (aggregation of claims or aggregated claim)**   Multiple claims in one suit. The aggregation of claims is the bundling of several claims into one claim, when each underlying claim might have been brought as a separate action by the plaintiff against the defendant. Claims may also be aggregated if they are brought by different plaintiffs who hold an undivided common interest, such as a wrongful death estate or co-tenants, all with claims arising from the common interest against the same defendant. If the aggregated claims

in sum are greater than a jurisdictional amount, such as the amount required to enter a federal court in diversity, the aggregated claim may be brought in the federal court, even if neither claim would have been allowed by itself. Aggregation may be accomplished in the initial pleading or through subsequent joinder.

**ancillary claim (ancillary suit)**   A state claim allowed in federal court owing to its relationship to a federal claim. An ancillary claim is a claim that has no basis for the jurisdiction of the federal court on its own merits, but because it is factually and logically dependent on a separate claim that is properly in the federal court, it will be heard in the same federal cause of action. Thus a claim lacking either a federal question or the basis for diversity may be heard in federal court as a claim in a case in which a federal question or other basis of federal jurisdiction is present. If, however, the federal case is dismissed for some reason, then the ancillary claim is likewise dismissed.

*See also:* jurisdiction, ancillary jurisdiction.

**counterclaim**   A claim made by a defendant against a plaintiff. A counterclaim is a claim made against any opposing party that is raised after the original claim of the plaintiff has been filed. Such claims may be made by a defendant against a plaintiff or by a plaintiff against a subsequently joined defendant who has brought a counterclaim against the plaintiff. Counterclaims are governed by Rule 13 of the Federal Rules of Civil Procedure or related state rules. Counterclaims are compulsory or permissive. Compulsory counterclaims arise from the same occurrence or transactions as the subject matter of the original claim, and a failure to plead a compulsory counterclaim results in waiver of the claim. Permissive counterclaims are unrelated to the subject matter of the original claim and constitute any other claims one party may have against the other at the time. Failure to plead permissive counterclaims will not result in waiver.

*See also:* sue (countersue).

*default*   A default on a counterclaim is the failure to answer the counterclaim. The defendant may be granted a default judgment for the plaintiff's failure to file a timely answer to a counterclaim.

*See also:* judgment, default judgment.

*supplemental jurisdiction*   A federal court may allow a state-law counterclaim to a federal action as a matter within the supplemental jurisdiction of the court.

*third parties*   A defendant may bring a claim against a third party. In other words, a defendant may initiate a claim against a person or entity not already in the suit as plaintiff or co-defendant, in which case the defendant is the third-party plaintiff. (The defendant/third-party plaintiff must do all that is required to bring the claim, not only meeting all the obligations of establishing jurisdiction over the third-party defendant but demonstrating the new claim is sufficiently related to the ongoing case to bring the new claims in the same action.) The third-party defendant must file an answer to the claims against it, just as a regular defendant must. The third-party defendant may also assert counterclaims against the defendant/third-party plaintiff just as the defendant/third-party plaintiff could against the original plaintiff.

**compulsory counterclaim**  A counterclaim arising from the same occurrence from which the plaintiff's claim arose. A compulsory counterclaim must be raised in the suit in which a claim arising from the same transaction or events has been brought against the potential counterclaimant. If, for example, a plaintiff sues a defendant for non-performance on a contract, and if the defendant believes the plaintiff owes the defendant money on the same contract, the defendant's failure to raise the counterclaim for the money owed during an action on the plaintiff's claim for non-performance is likely to waive the claim for the money owed.

*Failure to plead*  Compulsory counterclaims must be raised in the first responsive pleading; otherwise they will be deemed waived and may not be raised again, even in a separate proceeding.

**counterclaimant (counterdemandant)**  One who brings a counterclaim. A counterclaimant is the party who raises a counterclaim. The counterclaimant is often the defendant in the suit as a whole, a status that does not change with the filing of a counterclaim.

**permissive counterclaim**  A counterclaim that does not arise from the same occurrence as the original claim. A permissive counterclaim does not arise out of the original transaction or occurrence that constitutes the subject matter of the plaintiff's original claim. A permissive counterclaim may be joined at the discretion of the court. Failure to state a permissive claim does not constitute waiver of the claim, and, therefore, it may be raised later in a separate proceeding.

*See also:* claim, counterclaim, compulsory counterclaim; claim, counterclaim, compulsory counterclaim | failure to plead; claim, counterclaim, compulsory counterclaim.

**crossclaim (cross-claim)**  A claim by a defendant against a defendant or a plaintiff against a plaintiff. A crossclaim is a claim made by one party against a co-party in an an action. A crossclaim may be brought by a plaintiff against another plaintiff or by a defendant against another defendant. A cross-claim must usually arise from the same transaction or occurrence that is the subject matter of the original action. For example, a claim by one defendant to another defendant in the same action for indemnity against the plaintiff's claim brought against the first defendant is a cross-claim. The crossclaimant may be referred to as the cross-plaintiff, and party against whom the crossclaim is sought is the cross-defendant.

**dormant claim (long-dormant claim)**  A claim that might have been filed but has not. A dormant claim is a claim that has not been filed, even though the conditions giving rise to the claim are past and the period in which one would expect such a claim to be brought has commenced or expired. A long-dormant claim arose sufficiently long ago that others either lack notice of its existence or have a right to rely on its non-pursuit, so that its pursuit becomes a question of limitations of any action based upon that claim. Laches or limitations usually bar long-dormant claims.

**insurance claim**  *See:* insurance, insurance claim.

**liquidated claim**  A claim for which the amount owed can be readily ascertained. A liquidated claim is any claim in which the value of the claim is easily ascertained to a sum certain. The most common forms of claims for liquidated damages are those in which the amount is specified in advance by contract, in which the claim is for a debt the amount of which is undisputed, or in which the claim is for a judgment that has already been rendered for a specific amount. In general, interest is owed by the debtor to the creditor on liquidated claims from the time that both the money is owed and the amount is readily ascertainable.

*See also:* damages, contract damages, liquidated damages (liquidation of damages); sum (sum certain).

**non-claim (nonclaim)**  A failure to present a claim in the time allowed. Non-claim is the failure to present a claim during a period designated for the presentation of claims of its particular form. In particular, non-claim describes a claim against the estate of a decedent that is not presented during the period of probate set aside and given notice for the presentation of such claims. Non-claims are barred.

**proof of claim**  A creditor's written statement making a claim in bankruptcy. A proof of claim is a written notice of a claim that is filed in a bankruptcy proceeding according to the form specified in the bankruptcy rules, with documents substantiating the claim itself and, if available, the perfection of the claim. A proof of claim establishes a prima facie case that the claim is valid and owed by the debtor.

**property claim**  An assertion of a right to title in or to the possession or use of some property. A property claim is an assertion that some property in the possession or occupation of another should be surrendered to the ownership, possession, or use of the claimant. Property claims may arise from a claim of ownership, whether by title or prescription, or from a claim of right to possess or to use, such as under a bailment, license, easement, or lease.

*See also:* possession, adverse possession, claim of right.

**ownership claim**  A claim to ownership by right of title or prescription. An ownership claim is an assertion of an ownership interest in some property, whether the ownership is based on title acquired by grant or by adverse possession or pre-scription through possession over sufficient time that all other claims to ownership are now cut off by limitation of actions.

**secured claim**  A claim secured by a lien on property. A secured claim is a creditor's claim that is secured by a lien on property held by the debtor. In bankruptcy, a secured claim is secured by a lien on any property in which the bankruptcy estate has an interest, or which is subject to a setoff from a mutual debt owed by the creditor to the bankrupt debtor.
*See also:* debt, secured debt.

**unsecured claim**  A claim made on an unsecured debt. An unsecured claim is a claim that is not a secured claim as defined under the bankruptcy code, primarily any claim on a debt that has not been secured through a valid lien in any property in which the bankruptcy estate has an interest. Unsecured claims are satisfied from property a debtor liquidates only after the satisfaction of secured claims.

**stale claim**  A claim barred by the passage of time. A stale claim is a claim arising from a debt, an event, or a transaction so distant in the past that an allowance of an action upon the claim would be unjust, and so it is barred either by a statute of limitations, a statute of repose, or a doctrine such as laches.
*See also:* limitation, limitation of action (limitations of actions).

**surrender of claim (release)**  Agreement to accept a settlement of a claim in exchange for its discharge. A surrender of claim by agreement is a form of release of the claim.
*See also:* release.

**tax claim**  A claim related to the payment of taxes. A tax claim represents any claim for moneys owed in the collection of taxes, usually being a claim by the government for taxes owed but sometimes being a claim by a taxpayer for a refund of taxes wrongfully collected or paid. Tax claims may be brought for the payment or refund of any form of tax, whether it is an income tax, property tax, excise tax, sales tax, convenience tax, etc.

**claim of right**  A business asset treated as owned property under this claim is considered gross income for the year of receipt. Under the claim of right doctrine, any money or property a business receives and treats as its own without restriction as to the disposition of the property must be included as part of the gross income for the year of receipt. The cash or other property must consti-tute income for the business under its method of accounting, and the business must have un-restricted control over the use and disposition of the cash or other property received. If for some reason the taxpayer must restore a substantial part of the money or property claimed of right, then she may deduct the restoration.

**claim-property bond or redelivery bond**  *See:* bond, replevin bond (claim-property bond or redelivery bond).

**claims-made policy**  *See:* insurance, insurance policy, claims-made policy.

**clan**  A large group of kin within a tribe. A clan is a group of people united by common descent, often from a common ancestor. The clan forms a kinship-based intermediate subgroup between the family and the larger tribal unit.

**clandestine**  Secret. Anything clandestine is done by stealth, presumptively for improper or illegal reasons. Undercover and intelligence-gathering institutions and operations are clandestine services owing to their secrecy.

**clandestine crime (clandestine offense)**  A con-cealed crime. A clandestine crime is something done in secrecy, or at least beyond public notice.

**class**  Any group of people or things that share a common aspect, place in an organization, or burden by law. A class is any group of people, ideas, actions, or things defined by a common aspect of identity, whether the definition occurs by grant, action, law, or social order. In general, a class of people is created by social, economic, cultural, or functional similarities that mark its members as distinct from other people in their society. In general, a class of things, such as animals, rocks, or stationery, is designated according to shared attributes when compared to other things. Actions, ideas, and other taxonomic forms are all capable of being organized into classes.

Class is used very frequently in law to describe both categories of people, such as the members of each cate-gory created by a given law, and categories of things, such as categories of criminal offense. Class has particular meaning in describing plaintiffs in a class action.

Nearly every law creates a class or refers by express language or logical operation to a class that exists by conduct or social identity: statutes may define farmers who grow chickens as a class, or those who grow over 100,000 chickens at a time as a different class. A person making over $250,000 in taxable income may be in an economic class that is identified by regulation, just as a person who is a female is in a genetic and social class that may be an element of a legal definition. Classes are cre-ated by private conduct, as when a group is harmed by some conduct and forms a class to bring a class action. Classes are created by private action under the law as well, as in the creation of a class of legatees by will or a class of shareholders by stock issuance.

Class is used in law to designate a single group isolated from the rest of a given population of thing, as well as categories of relative merit or danger. Categories are designated by class of felony or misdemeanor, of land-fills, of heirs at different levels of consanguinity, of equi-ties, and so forth.

*See also:* descent (descender); equality, equal protection of the laws, classification (class).

**class gift** *See:* gift, class gift, divide–and–pay–over rule; gift, class gift.

**class of descendants** *See:* descent, descendant, class of descendants.

**class action** An action with many plaintiffs joined into a class as a single plaintiff. A class action is a claim brought by a representative plaintiff on behalf of a number of individuals, who are certified as a class and whose claims are represented by the class representative and a single legal team, although members may retain individual counsel. A class is to be "certified" by the court if the members of the class must meet the four requirements of numerosity, commonality, typicality, and adequacy. Therefore the class must be sufficiently numerous, usually fifty or more. Each member's claim must raise a question of law or fact common to all of the others. The party to be the named representative of the class must also meet certain requirements, must raise a claim typical of the class, and be able to represent the class fairly and adequately.

*See also:* joinder, joinder of offenses (joinder of defendants or prejudicial joinder); union, mass action theory.

*class action and mass action* A class action is created by motion of the plaintiffs, but a mass action is created by motion of the defendant. A mass action involves a large number of individual claims, such as a large number of people injured in a single incident. Such incidents may be instantaneous, such as in mass automobile accidents, or continuous, as in toxic tort cases stemming from exposure to a single source of pollution.

*See also:* class, class action, mass action.

**appeal of class action** Both a class representative and an unnamed member may appeal an order in a class action. Parties to a class action may seek appellate review at various points during the litigation, including interlocutory review of class certification, appointment of class counsel, and certain other procedural issues. Because judgments in a class action bind all class members, a question then arises as to the appellate rights of unnamed members of the class. The courts have allowed unnamed class members to appeal settlements if they intervene in order to so appeal, hence becoming named parties to the action.

**death knell doctrine** An interlocutory order in a class action may be appealed if it would bar further litigation. The death knell doctrine is designed to protect unnamed class members in a class action. The doctrine provides protection when a class representative declines to appeal an order dismissing the class action, thereby leaving the class without a representative. If the plaintiff would still have sufficient inducement to continue the suit regardless of the order, then the order is not appealable, but if the probability of further litigation is very low owing to the effect of the order, then the order will be appealable.

**class certification** Judicial order establishing a class. Class certification is an authorization by the court that a class has indeed met the requirements necessary to maintain a class action under Federal Rule of Civil Procedure 23 or its state equivalent. The four criteria under the rule are: First, the members of class are so numerous that a single non–class action created by joinder of all of the claimants who would be the members, in which each party would be separately represented, is impracticable. Second, that at least some substantive (not just procedural) questions of law, or some questions of fact are in common among every claim by each potential member of the class. Third, the representative parties who have claims or have defenses that are typical of the claims or defenses of the members of the proposed class. Fourth, there is sufficient evidence before the court that the representative parties will fairly and adequately protect the interests of members of the class who are not personally represented by counsel in the action.

*notice* Each member of a class must be given actual or constructive notice of a pending class action. Notice in class actions is necessary to afford absent and unnamed class members the right to exercise their option under Rule 23(b)(3) to opt out of the suit and pursue their own litigation. Notice is also necessary to inform class members of any award to which they may be entitled. The notice requirement is met if the notice is reasonably tailored to inform potential class members of a suit or in the case of notice of settlement, reasonably understandable as to the terms of the settlement and the class members' options thereunder.

*adequate representation* The class representative must adequately represent the interests of each member of the class. If no class representative can adequately represent the interests of each and all of the members of the class, the court must consider either the creation of sub-classes that can be adequately represented or, as a last resort, dissolving the class by revoking the class certification.

**limited–fund rationale** A basis for class actions when the plaintiffs' claims exceed the defendants' assets. The limited fund rationale for class actions allows recovery to all claimants even when a settlement or award is insufficient to cover fully all the claims of all the participating class members. For the rationale to apply, the total aggregated liquidated claims must exceed the total available funds, the whole of the inadequate fund must be devoted to the claims, and the distribution of the funds must be made equitably among all claimants.

**numerosity** Being of a sufficient number. Numerosity is the standard of sufficient numbers to satisfy some numerical criterion. In class actions, numerosity is satisfied when the parties allegedly injured by the conduct attributed to the defendant are sufficiently numerous that the action is better pursued by a class action than by individual actions.

**opt in** A plaintiff's choice to join a class. An opt-in class action structure requires each potential plaintiff to give notice to the court, usually through the counsel of the representative, that the plaintiff has elected to be a member of the class. A federal court will allow a class certification in which class members must opt in only when the class is formed under Federal Rule of Civil Procedure 23(b)(3), not under Rule 23(b)(1) or (2).

*See also:* option, opt in.

**opt out** A potential plaintiff's choice not to enter a class action. To opt out, in the context of a class action, is a potential plaintiff's signal to the court that that party will not join the class, and so will not be present in the action. A court will allow class members to opt out only when the class is formed under Federal Rule of Civil Procedure 23(b)(3), not under Rule 23(b)(1) or (2). Members of a class formed as a matter of efficency under 23(b)(3) must be sent notice of their ability to be independently represented in the class or to opt out of the class and to bring an independent action. Generally, "opt out" forms are sent out to class members along with the notice of the pending suit. The courts will specify the time period in which a class member must elect to "opt out." If the court does not receive notice before that date, then the ability to opt out is usually forfeit.

*See also:* option, opt out.

**partial certification** Approval of a class only for particular issues but not all in a given case or cases. Partial certification is approval by the court to proceed in a class action suit on part of the class representative's claims in a class action suit. A class action may be partially certified, for instance as to a factual aspect of the claim for liability but not liability in every case, or if the class is certified as to liability, it might not be certified as to remedy.

**hybrid class action** A class action from which class members may opt out. A hybrid class action is a class action recognized under Federal Rule of Civil Procedure 23(b)(3), in which potential plaintiffs may opt out of the class and elect not to be bound by the outcome of the case. The outcome is then binding upon the class representatives and all who choose to join in the class. Those who

opt out may bring a separate action. The term is still used, although it is no longer a separate designation under Rule 23.

**mass action** A single action created by the defendant or the court from a group of single actions. A group of 100 or more individual plaintiffs seeking to have a single trial on common issues may be treated as a single class, as if they had filed their suit as a class action. This treatment may allow a defendant to remove a case filed in state court to federal court, unless all of the plaintiffs are from the forum state or contiguous states and the action both arises from an act in the forum state and is governed by that state's laws and not federal law.

*See also:* class, class action; union, mass action theory.

**mass tort class action** A class action seeking tort compensation for a process or event that gives rise to a great number of injuries. A class action may be brought for a mass tort, caused either by a single event, such as an explosion or chemical spill, or by a product or process, such as the use of a chemical or health device.

*See also:* tort, mass tort (mass accident).

**settlement of class action (Girsh factors)** A court may only approve a class-action settlement fair to all involved. A settlement of a class action is inherently one negotiated among counsel for the class representatives and the defendants, but it is subject to court approval on grounds that require the settlement to conform not only to the law and rules governing class actions and the underlying substantive claims but also that protect the interests of the class members and others with claims who are not in the class. A test for the sufficiency of a settlement of a class action used in many jurisdictions was articulated by Judge Garth of the Third Circuit, requiring the court to inquire into the difficulty of the litigation to be avoided, effect on the class, lessons from discovery, likelihood of liability being proved, likelihood of damages being proved, effects on the class of trial, effects on the defendants of a greater judgment, reasonableness of the settlement fund in the light of the plaintiff's best case, and reasonableness of the settlement fund in the light of the defendant's best case. See Girsh v. Jepson, 521 F.2d 1 156 (3d Cir. 1975).

**spurious class action** An action intended to invite more plaintiffs to join. A spurious class action is an action brought by one or more plaintiffs with the intent of adding more plaintiffs through a process of permissive joinder or intervention. Under the pre-1966 form of Federal Rule of Civil Procedure 23, actions in federal court could be brought denominated as spurious class actions, though this is no longer the case. The term persists informally but is increasingly rare.

*See also:* spurious.

**subclass**  A division in a class to represent a position distinct from the rest of the class. A subclass is a division within the class of plaintiffs in a class action. A subclass may be created by judicial order, as needed to represent potentially opposed or varying claims held by different members of the class or to allow differing views of the proof as seen by members of the class, providing independent attorneys to represent the arguments of each subclass. A class may be subdivided on motion of either party or by the court acting on its own motion.

**class of descendants (testamentary class)**  A category of heirs to a decedent's estate specified by familial relationship. A class of descendants is a group of relatives named as devisees or legatees in a will or described as a category by an intestate succession statute, who will receive an allocation of the estate and divide it equally among the members of the class. The class is defined by label rather than by the names of the beneficiaries, whether the label is "my children" or "the heirs of the body of Fred" or "all my descendents then living." A class is open so long as the conditions by which one can join the class are still possible, and it is closed when it is no longer possible to satisfy those conditions: in the example of "the heirs of the body of Fred" the class is open so long as he lives, and it is closed when Fred has been dead nine months.

**class gift rule (rule of convenience)**  A class remains open until its logical close or the testator's death. The class gift rule requires that the class to which a testamentary gift is made remains open until either the testator dies or an inescapable and nonreplicable condition defining the class has ended. Thus, a grant "to the children of Mildred alive at her death" creates a class that is closed at the death of Mildred. It is easy to mistake an inescapable and nonreplicable condition of the class. A testamentary grant merely "to the children of Mildred" would not necessarily close at Mildred's death; if Mildred predeceases the testator, the class is then closed to new members but not finally defined until the death of the testator.

*See also:* remainder, remainder subject to open.

**class subject to open**  A class that is not finally ascertained. Anything subject to open is not yet closed. This term is usually applied to a class to whom a gift is made, which is defined in such a manner that the membership in the class was not perfectly known when the gift was planned, such as when a will is drafted, but will be known when the gift must vest, such as at the testator's time of death or the death of a life tenant in the case of a class given a remainder of a life estate. As common law, a class subject to open that was not finally ascertained prior to the running of the time for the Rule Against Perpetuities could violate the rule, but most jurisdictions have modified the rule to allow interpretation to close the class rather than void it and destroy grants to those class members who are already identified.

*See also:* remainder, remainder subject to open.

**legal classification (governmental classification)**  The division by law of people, facts, or rules into categories. Legal classification describes the process of dividing people, places, things, acts, or ideas into categories, and legal classifications are the resulting classes of people, places and so on that are created. Categories may be discerned by analysis, not only by looking to the express statements of legislation or orders but also by considering the operation of the law. Categories are essential, for instance, in understanding the system of estates in land or in considering the duties of a landowner to someone upon the land.

One form of classification is made, or an existing classification is employed and its significance is enhanced, in every statute or order: by declaring, for instance, some action may be done, must be done, or must not be done, the statute or order makes a category of all the conduct that may be considered that action. Many categories place an individual person in a group to be allowed or barred from some action or regulated in some way, and to some degree a person may choose the category by which the person will be treated by legal officials, such as the categories of citizen and non-citizen or married or single tax filers.

Personal and group classifications in legislation that turn on characteristics that have been considered according to custom to be immutable, such as gender, parentage, or nationality, are subject to greater scrutiny under constitutional law. At the greatest constitutional level of scrutiny are the suspect classifications: race, religion, and national origin. At an intermediate level of constitutional scrutiny are quasi-suspect classifications: gender and legitimacy of birth. Legislation or other laws relying on non-suspect classifications are examined with a presumption of validity.

Additional classifications are designated by statute, often called protected classes or protected classifications. These classes include suspect classes as well as others, and these are given protection against discrimination by employers and private parties on the basis of class membership.

*See also:* discrimination; scrutiny, standards of scrutiny.

**class of one**  A class created by law of just one person or entity. A class of one is a category of treatment created by legislation or executive order by creating a unique burden or benefit in the law that applies to only one person or entity. A burden on a class, even though it is of one member, that differs from burdens or benefits on all others must be justified by a rational relationship to a legitimate state purpose, or it will appear to be an unjustified use of arbitrary discretion. This review of discretion need not imply that all acts of discretion are arbitrary or subject to review as arbitrary, but the discretion must be exercised in some demonstrably legitimate manner.

**discrete and insular class**   *See:* minority, minority group, discrete and insular minority.

**non-suspect class (nonsuspect class or ordinary class)**   Any class burdened by law that is not suspect or quasi-suspect. A non-suspect class is a class created by the definition of a group of people in a statute, regulation, order, or other law, who are a legal class but not a suspect class, because the definition does not rely upon a concept of race, color, gender, or other grounds that would make the class at least quasi-suspect. Nearly every law affecting a group defines or adopts a definition of the group as a non-suspect class. Laws burdening a non-suspect class are evaluated to determine that there is a rational relationship between the burden on the class as defined and a legitimate state interest or a legitimate governmental purpose.

**protected class**   Any class protected by law from discrimination against its members. A protected class is a group of people that is defined by law according to some characteristic and that is given specific protection against discriminatory action by others, including the government, employers, unions, and the providers of public accommodation or housing. Classes that are constitutionally protected by strict or intermediate scrutiny are inherently protected groups, to be burdened by government discrimination only under limited circumstances. These groups are likewise protected against private discrimination under civil rights acts such as 42 U.S.C. § 1981 or § 1983.

All other classes that are protected are protected by statute, usually against public and private discrimination, according to the nature of the statutory protection. Under Title VII, groups by race, color, religion, sex, or national origin are protected classes. Advanced age defines a protected class under the Age Discrimination in Employment Act. Disability defines a protected class (of many subclasses) under the Rehabilitation Act and Americans with Disabilities Act. Other acts create protected classifications for limited purposes for veterans, members of the armed forces reserve, and union members. Some states now designate a protected class for homosexuals.

*See also:* discrimination.

**quasi-suspect classification (quasi-suspect class)**
Gender, illegitimacy, and sometimes alienage and gender preference when employed by law to define a class. A quasi-suspect class is a class of people that is recognized by the U.S. Supreme Court as the focus of a statute regulation, order, or other law, who are not a suspect class but which has still historically faced discrimination as a matter of law and which is at least to some degree a discrete and insular minority that has been excluded from the legislative process. Laws burdening a non-suspect class are subject to intermediate scrutiny, violating the requirements of equal protection if the burden is intended for an invidious purpose or if it

cannot be justified because the law in fact serves an important governmental objective, and the burden is substantially related to achievement of that objective.

Many attempts to include other groups within the scope of quasi-suspect classification have failed, at least failed to alter the interpretation of the U.S. Constitution, including efforts to include groups defined by their members being homosexual, aged, poor, obese, sex offenders, disabled, prior felons, speakers of other languages, and members of specific national groups of immigrants. This effort is distinct from the actions of legislators, such as the designation by Congress of protected classes that are not quasi-suspect classes, such as the aged or the disabled.

As a matter of state constitutional law, some of these groups have been designated as quasi-suspect class. For example, in 2008, homosexuals were designated a quasi-suspect class in Connecticut.

*See also:* interest, state interest, substantial state interest; scrutiny, standards of scrutiny, intermediate scrutiny.

**suspect classification (suspect class)**   Race, color, ethnicity, national origin, or religion when employed by law to define a class. A suspect class is a class of people that is recognized by the Supreme Court as the focus of a statute, regulation, order, or other law, who have historically faced discrimination as a matter of law and that are perceived to be a minority of a defined population that has been excluded from the legislative process. Laws burdening a suspect class are subject to strict scrutiny, violating the requirements of equal protection if the burden is intended for an invidious purpose or if it cannot be justified because the law in fact serves a compelling governmental purpose, and the law is narrowly tailored to achievement of that purpose.

*See also:* scrutiny, standards of scrutiny, strict scrutiny.

**classes of damages**   *See:* damages, classes of damages, classes of damages.

**classification**   *See:* equality, equal protection of the laws, classification (class).

**classification of offenses**   *See:* offense, classification of offenses (graded offense or classified offense).

**classified evidence**   *See:* evidence, classified evidence.

**classified information**   *See:* information, classified information, Classified Information Procedures Act (CIPA or C.I.P.A.); information, classified information.

**Classified Information Procedures Act**   *See:* information, classified information, Classified Information Procedures Act (CIPA or C.I.P.A.).

**clause** A single provision in a longer portion of a document, such as a contract provision. A clause is a component statement in a legal document, such as a constitution, treaty, statute, regulation, contract, will, trust, license, appointment, etc. The clause is the least component in which a coherent statement of duty, obligation, or information is provided. It might be a component of a sentence, a sentence unto itself, a group of sentences, a paragraph, or even a series of paragraphs, yet the clause has only one subject matter. There are many clauses known by name in constitutional law, such as the Due Process Clauses, or that are nominated with great frequency in private instruments such as a forum selection clause or a time-is-of-the-essence clause. In certain form documents, especially insurance contracts and commercial paper, clauses acquire a consistency that allows adjudication of meaning of a clause in one instance to apply to the interpretation of the same clause in a different instrument in a later situation.

*See also:* abatement, abatement clause; acceleration, acceleration clause; ad, ad damnum (ad damnum clause); choice, choice of law, choice of law clause (choice-of-law clause); severability of statute, savings clause (saving clause); legislation, savings clause; clause, omnibus clause; insurance, insurance policy, no action clause; alternative dispute resolution, multi-step dispute resolution clause; merger, merger clause (integration clause); ipso, ipso facto, ipso facto clause; forum, forum selection clause; risk, force-majeure clause; insurance, insurance beneficiary, facility of payment clause; insurance, insurance coverage, multiple insurance coverage, escape clause (other insurance clause); price, escalating price (laddering or escalator clause); security, security interest, due-on-sale clause; liability | cognovit; arbitration, arbitration clause.

**execution clause (self-executing)** The clause by which the signatories of an instrument execute the instrument. An execution clause specifies a condition that must be satisfied upon which the whole instrument comes into effect. The most common form is the signature clause, by which a contract, deed, will, or other instrument is executed once it is signed by the maker of the instrument or by the contracting parties and any witnesses who are specified.

*See also:* execution (executable or execute or executed or executory).

**introductory clause** A statement of purpose or preamble. An introductory clause is a general statement of the purpose for which an instrument has been drafted. Courts may look on such clauses as surplusage, but such a clause may be helpful in discerning the intention of the drafter when analyzing other clauses.

*See also:* hortatory; surplus, surplusage as irrelevant language.

**omnibus clause** A clause embracing broad conditions not specifically enumerated. An omnibus clause is a catch-all provision that applies to a variety of unspecified miscellaneous items or eventualities that were not inventoried in other clauses in an instrument, such as a statute or a contract. Many contracts contain such clauses to ensure that all the agreed upon terms are included in the contract. The prayer for general and unspecified relief at the close of a complaint is a specialized form of an omnibus clause.

*See also:* omnibus.

**clauses** *See:* constitution, U.S. Constitution, clauses; contract, contract clauses.

## clean

**Clean Air Act** *See:* Pollution, air pollution, Clean Air Act (C.A.A. or CAA).

**Clean Up Doctrine** *See:* jurisdiction, equitable jurisdiction, Clean-Up Doctrine (Clean Up Doctrine).

**Clean Water Act** *See:* pollution, water pollution, Clean Water Act (CWA).

**Clean-Hands Doctrine** *See:* equity, equitable defense, Unclean Hands Doctrine (Clean-Hands Doctrine).

## clear

**clear and convincing evidence** *See:* proof, burden of proof, clear and convincing evidence (proof by clear and convincing evidence).

**clear and positive proof** *See:* proof, burden of proof, clear and positive proof.

**clear and present danger test** *See:* speech, freedom of speech, clear and present danger test (offensive words).

**clear error** *See:* review, standards of review, clear error; error, clear error (clearly erroneous or manifest error or obvious error or plain error or clearly wrong).

**clear title or merchantable title** *See:* title, marketable title (clear title or merchantable title).

**clearcutting** *See:* timber, clearcutting.

**clearly erroneous** *See:* review, standard of review, clearly erroneous.

**clemency** An executive or administrative order reducing the sentence of a crime. Clemency is an act of mercy afforded another. Clemency in its more general forms at law refers to a reduction or commutation of a sentence, an offer of probation, or immunity from prosecution. As a matter of federal criminal procedure, an Order of Clemency is issued only by the President, commuting the sentence of a person convicted of a federal crime. Governors with the power to pardon usually also have the power of clemency.

*See also:* commutation (commutative or commute); execution, execution of a sentence of death (execution).

**clergy (member of the clergy or cleric or clergyman)** A ministering officer of an organized religion. The clergy are the group, and a member of the clergy (or cleric) is an individual, who are authorized by a religious organization to minister to the religious needs of its membership. Clergy in various faiths take many titles, such as apostle, minister, deacon, priest, rabbi, imam, preacher, leader, shaman, prophet, bishop, cardinal, sheikh, pope, patriarch, hieromonk, cantor, stake leader, monk, deacon, mohel, rector, vicar, or presbyters. The distinguishing feature is that each office is one that is ordained or called to a role that is eligible to administer to the members of the religion. A reference in law to clergy includes all such offices, even if the religion's doctrine, such as some interpretations the rabbinate in Judaism, does not define them as clergy. Not all religious offices are clerical; lay offices such as warden, vestrymen, committee member, or treasurer are not within the clergy.

*See also:* church.

**benefit of clergy**  An exemption for clerics from the regular criminal courts. Benefit of clergy was an exemption for churchmen from capital punishment and, in most cases, from prosecution for felonies in the regular criminal courts, such defendants being transferred to canon law (or later civil law) courts, or given more lenient sentences. Henry II of England exempted members of holy orders from prosecution in his courts in 1172, following his penance for the death of Archbishop Becket. Owing both to the status of medieval university students as taking low orders and to the presumption that those who could read had been students, benefit of clergy was extended to the literate in 1351. Although there were always a few exemptions, such as treason, the list of exemptions grew beginning in 1512, and after a variety of modifications it was abolished in 1827. Benefit of clergy was abolished in the courts of the United States in 1790, but it was allowed in some state courts until the 1850s. One who had been allowed benefit of clergy was often branded on the thumb as a reference for later attempts to do so.

*See also:* lay, laity.

**clerical privilege or minister's privilege**  *See:* privilege, evidentiary privilege, priest–penitent privilege (clerical privilege or minister's privilege).

**clerk**  One who keeps records. A clerk is any person who maintains or creates records. The term means both a lesser official who works in an office in a support role, such as a law clerk or office clerk, as well as an important public official who is an official keeper of records, such as a clerk of court, county clerk, or city clerk. Note: "clerk" is pronounced to rhyme with "perk" in the United States but with "park" in the United Kingdom.

**clerk as cleric**  Any member of the clergy.

**clerk of court**  An official who keeps the records of the court. The clerk of the court is an official charged with the responsibility of keeping the records and accounts of the court. The office of clerk receives all court filing including pleadings, motions, documents and orders. The clerk often has ministerial functions far beyond the management of the court's records, including providing court staff and managing the summoning of the venire for jury service. For this reason, in some jurisdictions, the clerk of court also manages voter registration and the voter rolls, although that task has increasingly been given to specialized election commissions and officials. The clerk of the court is likely to be assisted by a chief deputy clerk and a large number of deputy clerks or assistant clerks. The professional and kindly treatment of the clerk of the court and the deputies is essential to the successful practice of law.

**prothonotary (pronotary)**  The clerk of court in certain jurisdictions. A prothonotary or pronotary, is the title for the clerk of the court and keeper of records, a term still much in use in Pennsylvania.

**clerkship**  Internship in a professional office. A clerkship is an internship or apprenticeship designed to provide the clerk with practical experience in the practice of a profession. Completion of a clerkship may be required for certification in some professions. In the legal profession, a clerkship may involve assisting a practicing attorney or judge in the performance of their duties. Some jurisdictions require completion of a clerkship for a designated period of time before being admitted to the bar. In medicine, clerkships cover both the theory and practice of specific areas of medicine, and are also required for certification as a doctor.

**law clerk (student intern or internship or clerkship)**  An attorney or law graduate who assists a judge, or a student who assists a judge or lawyer. A judicial law clerk acts as an assistant to the judge. The law clerk is often an attorney licensed to practice law but may be an unlicensed law graduate. The duties of a clerk as determined by the judge for which the clerk works, or for the judges if the clerk assists more than one. The clerk may perform duties in managing the flow of motions and trials but is more likely to conduct research, find authorities, and aid in examining the theories upon which an attorney's arguments are presented in court. Some law clerks draft opinions in whole for the judge's review and signature. Judicial opinions often reflect considerable unacknowledged assistance of the law clerk.

Some law firms and judges denominate law students who assist them as "law clerks," and such work is usually referred to as "clerking." Even so, the increasingly common practice now is to describe law students in a summer employment position in a firm as "summer associates," to describe students working in law firms at other times as "interns" or just as "law students," and to describe law students in a judge's chambers as "student interns" or "student clerks." Interns may be present in the firm or the chambers not for compensation but for academic credit based on both the experience acquired and some related research or report based on that experience.

*See also:* lawyer, law firm, lawyers, associate, summer associate (summer clerk).

**OSCAR**  A web site for federal law clerks' applications. OSCAR is the Online System for

Clerkship Application and Review, a central, online clearinghouse for clerkship applications and references for applicants to become a law clerk with a federal judge.

**clickwrap agreement**  *See:* contract, specific contracts, clickwrap agreement (browse–wrap agreement).

**client**  A person who relies on the professional services of another. The client of an attorney is the person or entity represented and advised by the attorney. A client relationship commences for an attorney with an agreement, with the performance of services in reliance on a request for representation, or with a statement of representation on which the client relies. An attorney owes a client a duty of zealous representation, balanced by the obligation to serve justice and act as an officer of the court. An attorney has an obligation to keep the confidence of a client, limited only by rare exceptions in the public interest. An attorney has an obligation to keep the client informed of matters related to the client's interest, to inform the client of the law related to the client's affairs, and to defer to the client's decisions, although the attorney has no obligation to the client to perform or refrain from any act contrary to the highest standards of professional responsibility and to the law. In the case of government attorneys, the client is the government and the state or nation, and not a supervisor, political party, or administrative division of it. The client was, in classical Rome, a plebian or citizen subject to the patronage of a patrician.

*See also:* privilege, evidentiary privilege, attorney-client privilege; advocacy, zealous advocacy (zealous advocate).

**client trust account**  *See:* trust, client trust account (lawyer's trust account).

**clinic**  An office for the diagnosis and treatment of members of the public, usually of health or law. A health clinic is a medical facility where health care workers provide diagnostic services and medical care. A legal clinic is an office providing pro bono or subsidized legal services to members of the public who qualify for its services, usually owing to poverty or special needs. Many legal clinics are within a teaching institution such as a law school, in which attorneys and faculty members train and supervise law students, who provide legal services to the public.

**clinical legal education**  Legal education through supervised practice. Clinical legal education is a process of instruction and supervised practice by students. The clinical legal studies movement emerged in the 1960s, emphasizing "law in action" and advocating legal clinics designed to teach basic lawyering skills. Most law schools now provide a clinical legal experience, in which faculty train students who certify to practice within certain limits and under the faculty's supervision.

**student lawyer rules**  Law students in clinics may provide certain legal services. Student lawyer rules

in the rules of court in many states allow students to perform certain duties, following a certification process and acting under a supervisor, that would otherwise violate the standards prohibiting the unauthorized practice of law. The scope of the duties a student may legally perform varies. Some states allow students only to perform as a paralegal, while others permit a student to represent an indigent client in criminal proceedings.

**supervising attorney**  An attorney who supervises law students in a clinic. A supervising attorney is a member of the bar who supervises law students in a legal clinic. Often the supervising attorney is a member of the faculty of the law school housing the clinic. The supervising attorney is responsible for assigning students various legal tasks, supervising their efforts and teaching them related skills, and, ultimately, is responsible for the quality of their work.

**clone**  *See:* gene, genetically modified organism, clone.

## close (closing)

**close corporation**  *See:* corporation, corporations, close corporation (closely held corporation).

**close of business or COB**  *See:* time, hour, business hours (close of business or COB).

**close as property**  Any property or structure. The close has evolved in meaning from lands enclosed by fences or buildings to any interest in lands. The close is used still to describe a building or lands that have been entered when describing a trespass, although this rather confusing holdover from the writ of trespass quare clausum fregit is less helpful in drafting than a clear identification of the location and nature of the lands or buildings entered.

**closed shop**  *See:* union, labor union, shop, closed shop (union shop).

**closely held corporation**  *See:* corporation, corporations, close corporation (closely held corporation).

**closing**  *See:* sale, land sale, closing and settlement (closing).

**closing and settlement**  *See:* sale, land sale, closing and settlement (closing).

**closing argument**  *See:* trial, argument at trial, closing argument (summation or closing statement at trial).

**closing instructions or instructions at end of trial or final charge to the jury**  *See:* instruction, jury instruction, final jury instruction (closing instructions or instructions at end of trial or final charge to the jury).

**closing statement of purchase**  *See:* purchase, closing statement of purchase.

**cloture** Closing, or the end of a debate. A motion for cloture is a motion to end a debate. In the United States Senate, with its longstanding tradition for unlimited debate, filibustering was often employed in order to prevent the passage of certain pieces of legislation, and in order to cease debating, a supermajority vote of sixty senators was needed in order to end debate.

*See also:* filibuster.

**cloud on title** *See:* title, cloud on title.

**club** An association. A club is a private association, which is not inherently incorporated or a partnership. A club may be incorporated, and many are as not-for-profit corporations. The members of a club may be liable in contract and tort only for their own actions, although if the club adopts a criminal purpose, continued knowing membership may make a member an accessory. The right to form or join a club is an aspect of the freedom of association, but a club may be regulated, even as to its membership, to achieve a compelling governmental purpose, such as ending invidious discrimination, as long as the regulation does not burden the ability of the members to advocate a viewpoint or to form a private association for that purpose.

*See also:* association (associate).

**clue** Evidence that may answer a question under investigation. A clue is a datum found during an investigation, or a datum that suggests an event has occurred, from which an investigation may be initiated. Once the results of an investigation are prepared for a hearing or a trial, such data are usually considered not as clues but as evidence. Even so, the specific data considered in different stages of an investigation may be material in hearings to determine their later admissibility, as well as the admissibility of other evidence. Therefore, what information, or clues, had been collected by an officer prior to a decision to stop a suspect or to engage in a search may be essential in determining whether the stop or search were lawful and constitutional.

**CO** *See:* pollution, air pollution, criteria pollutants, carbon monoxide (CO); carbon, carbon monoxide (CO).

**CO or conscientious objection** *See:* conscience, conscientious objector (CO or conscientious objection).

**co-** Prefix indicating joint participation. "Co-" appears before a word to show that more than one person is involved in the denoted activity.

*See also:* joint; administrator, administrator of estate, co-administrator (co-administration or joint administrator); conspiracy, conspirator (coconspirator or co-conspirator); defendant, codefendant (co-defendant); cohabitation (co-habitation); commingling (comingling or co-mingling); cooperative, cooperative enterprise (co-op or cooperative association); partner, copartner (co-partner); tenancy, co-tenancy (cotenant or co-tenant or cotenancy); venture, joint venture (co-venturer or coventurer); party, party to an action, co-party (co-parties or coparty); plaintiff, co-plaintiff (coplaintiff);

principal, co-principals (coprincipal); cooperative, residential cooperative (co-operative tenancy or co-operative ownership or coop or co-op).

**co-administration or joint administrator** *See:* administrator, administrator of estate, co-administrator (co-administration or joint administrator).

**co-administrator** *See:* administrator, administrator of estate, co-administrator (co-administration or joint administrator).

**co-conspirator** *See:* conspiracy, conspirator (co-conspirator or co-conspirator).

**co-defendant** *See:* defendant, codefendant (co-defendant).

**co-habitation** *See:* cohabitation (co-habitation).

**co-habitation contract** *See:* cohabitation, cohabitation contract (co-habitation contract).

**co-inventor or joint invention** *See:* inventor, joint inventor (co-inventor or joint invention).

**co-op or cooperative association** *See:* cooperative, cooperative enterprise (co-op or cooperative association).

**co-operative tenancy or co-operative ownership or coop or co-op** *See:* cooperative, residential cooperative (co-operative tenancy or co-operative ownership or coop or co-op).

**co-owner or co-tenant** *See:* ownership, concurrent ownership (co-owner or co-tenant).

**co-partner** *See:* partner, copartner (co-partner).

**co-party** *See:* party, party to an action, co-party (co-parties or coparty).

**co-plaintiff** *See:* plaintiff, co-plaintiff (coplaintiff).

**co-principals** *See:* principal, co-principals (coprincipal).

**co-signature** *See:* indorsement, co-signature (co-signer or cosign or cosigner).

**co-signer or cosign or cosigner** *See:* indorsement, co-signature (co-signer or cosign or cosigner).

**co-tenancy** *See:* tenancy, co-tenancy (cotenant or co-tenant or cotenancy).

**co-trustees** *See:* trustee, joint trustees (co-trustees).

**co-venturer or coventurer** *See:* venture, joint venture (co-venturer or coventurer).

**Co.** *See:* company, company as commercial organization (co.).

**CO$_2$** *See:* carbon, carbon dioxide (CO$_2$).

**coalition bargaining** *See:* union, labor union, collective bargaining, coalition bargaining.

**Coase Theorem** The more economically beneficial result should always prevail. The Coase Theorem asserts that liability rules do not determine what people do, but the values they put on competing forms of conduct do. In the language of law and economics, when bargaining costs are zero, the initial assignment of legal entitlements does not affect the efficiency of the resulting allocation of resources. This result favors polluters and other intrusive uses of property, as it assumes there is no benefit to a claim based on prior ownership of the land or virtue that is not monetized. Or, at least it assumes there are no benefits beyond what would be bargained to protect the use of the land itself.

*See also:* economy, law and economics; nuisance, sic utere tuo ut alienum non laedas.

## coast

**Coast Guard (USCG)** Federal sea–going law–enforcement military service. The United States Coast Guard is a military service whose officers and petty officers have the powers to enforce federal laws at sea, in U.S. ports, and on the federal waters of the United States. The peculiar circumstances of criminal investigation and the enforcement of laws at sea have allowed the Coast Guard a unique exemption from the requirement of search warrants or probable cause to search when searching vessels or persons aboard. The Coast Guard is specifically tasked with enforcement of maritime laws (including the regulations of vessels and crew and the maintenance of aids to navigation), environmental laws, the law of the sea, federal criminal laws, and port security, as well as with military operations. The USCG is an agency within the Department of Homeland Security, unless it is transferred to the Department of the Navy, which may be done in times of war (though the Coast Guard provides support for Navy activities at other times as well). Founded on August 4, 1791, as the Revenue Cutter Service in the Treasury Department, the Coast Guard is the oldest continuously active naval or military service of the United States.

**coast line (coastline or baseline)** The place where the land is bound by the sea. The coast line is an thin strip of land that comes in direct contact with the sea. The coast line is usually measured from the mean low water mark, which is the edge of the marine waters.

*See also:* boundary.

**coastal zone** Seaward and landward areas adjacent to the coast. Coastal zones are the confluence of the land and the sea. They are therefore rich in biodiversity. They often include estuaries, which act as filters for pollutants that would otherwise wash into the ocean from the land. Coastal zones are also delicate areas because they can be easily contaminated by draining or the contribution of nutrients from over-fertilization of the watershed. The coastal waters (including lands therein and thereunder) and the adjacent shore lands (including the waters therein and thereunder), strongly influence each other. Coastal waters near the shorelines of several coastal states include islands, transitional and intertidal areas, salt marshes, wetlands, and beaches. The zone extends, in Great Lakes waters, to the international boundary between the United States and Canada, and in other areas, it runs seaward to the outer limit of the U.S. territorial sea.

**Coastal Zone Management Act (CZMA)** Legislation preserving coastal zones without eliminating economic development. The Coastal Zone Management Act 1972, codified at 16 U.S.C. §§ 1451–1465 (CZMA) empowers NOAA's Office of Ocean and Coastal Resource Management (OCRM) to regulate development in coastal regions to provide for management of the nation's coastal resources, including the Great Lakes, and to balance economic development with environmental conservation.

**COBRA** *See:* employment, employee benefit plan, health insurance plan, COBRA (C.O.B.R.A.).

**cocaine** *See:* drug, controlled substance, cocaine, crack cocaine.

**coconspirator or co-conspirator** *See:* conspiracy, conspirator (coconspirator or co-conspirator).

**code (codification or codify)** A topically organized collection of statutes, laws, or rules. A code is a publication of statutes or, less commonly, of rules, organized into a coherent and analytical whole. The verb form of the integration of rules into a code is to codify. There are many codes of statutes, rules, and regulations, though not all are called a code, such as the Federal Rules of Evidence, which is — in essence — a code. A rule or statute in a code is to be read in the context of the code as a whole.

The concept of a code as an organization of statutes enacted at various times long predates the Roman Empire, but it is often associated with the Codex of the Corpus Juris of Justinian. Though most U.S. states have a code in which statutes are topically arranged, the Civil Code of Louisiana is still largely based on the French Code Napoleon.

*See also:* penal, penal code.

**Code Napoleon** *See:* France, French Law, Code Napoleon (C.N. or CN or Napoleonic Code).

**Code of Canon Law** *See:* canon, canon law, Codex Juris Canonici (Code of Canon Law).

**Code of Federal Regulations** *See:* regulation, Code of Federal Regulations (C.F.R. or CFR).

**Code of Hammurabi** *See:* Sumerian Law, Code of Hammurabi.

**Code of Professional Responsibility** *See:* lawyer, lawyer discipline, disciplinary rules, Canons of Ethics (Code of Professional Responsibility).

**code pleading** *See:* pleading, pleading theories, code pleading (fact pleading).

**Field Code** The earliest code of civil procedure in the U.S. The Field Code, more properly called the

New York Code of Procedure of 1848, is more often called by the named of its author, David Dudley Field. It was the first comprehensive code of civil procedure in American law. The Code framed a single set of procedural rules for the application of both law and equity in the courts. The effect was to both simplify the forms of action and the forms of pleadings from the old writ system, as well as to minimize the differences between equity pleading and common-law pleading, which in turn diminished the danger of error in the use of procedures and pleadings.

**codefendant** *See:* defendant, codefendant (co-defendant).

**codex** A code of laws. Codex is an ancient label for a book, particularly a roll or volume. From this sense it has long stood in law for a collection of parts gathered together and organized into a whole, as in the Codex Justiniani. Code is derived from this.

**codicil** *See:* will, last will and testament, codicil.

**codification or codify** *See:* code (codification or codify).

**coelum (coeli)** The heavens. Coelum, in the legal sense, refers to the skies above a parcel of land. Coeli and coelo are plural forms of coelum.
*See also:* property, real property, cujus est solum ejus est usque ad coelum (center of the earth to the roof of the sky).

**a coelo usque ad centrum** From the ceiling of the heavens to the center of the Earth. A traditional description of the ownership of land, including rights to air and to minerals. It is now a bit obsolete in the face of technology, because modern doctrines of property give no ownership that would impede very high overflights nor limit some types of mineral exploitation, such as by lateral drilling into a common pool.
*See also:* mineral; oil, fingerprint of the oil (oil fingerprinting).

**coercion** Influence, compulsion, or restraint that diminishes free will. Coercion is any force, threat, harm, compulsion, restraint, or influence intended to diminish the free will of an individual and to cause them to do or to refrain from doing anything. Coercion is the basis for the crime of criminal coercion, which is a form of blackmail. Coercion is also an excuse for a criminal act procured by another through coercion, and it makes voidable by the coerced party any contract that was entered as a result of coercion. Likewise, a treaty adopted by a state under coercion from another state, or by an agent personally coerced to enter it, is voidable by the state that was the victim of the coercion.
*See also:* intimidation (intimidate or indimidating or intimidated); necessity; extortion, blackmail (criminal coercion).

**coerced confession** *See:* confession, coerced confession (involuntary confession).

**cognate (cognation)** The relationship among members of a family or closely related ideas. Cognates are related things. The word cognation is now rare in the common law, although civilian lawyers still use the term for the family relationship, as between a parent and child. Cognates in a more general sense are both words formed from a common root and offenses defined from similar elements of the criminal act. In civilian and Scots law, a cognate relationship is derived only from a maternal relationship and not from a paternal line.

**cognate offense** *See:* offense, cognate offense.

**cognitive test** *See:* capacity, mental capacity, cognitive test.

**cognizance (cognisance or cognisant or cognizant)**

**cognizable (cognisable)** Legally significant. Anything cognizable is knowable or identifiable. From its context in legal usage, the thing that is cognizable is usually a question within a particular scope of a legal rule or jurisdiction. Thus, to say that a fact is cognizable under a law means that it has a particular meaning under it, that the fact is juridically significant; it is essentially a metaphor that the law recognizes the fact. For a court to take cognizance over a given action or issue, is to assert jurisdiction over it; the term is generally not used to describe jurisdiction over a person or party.
*See also:* recognizance.

**cognizance as authority (cognisance)** Jurisdiction or authority. Cognizance is the result of taking notice and asserting jurisdiction as a result. To have cognizance over a matter is to have authority to adjudicate it.
*See also:* recognizance.

**cognizance as awareness** Knowledge. Cognizance, in its most general use, refers to having sufficient knowledge to understand or recognize something perceived.

**cognovit (cognovit actionem clause or cognovit clause or cognovit note)** A defendant's confession of liability. A cognovit is a form available under the common law to confess judgment, or to confess a particular degree of liability, allowing the plaintiff a judgment and execution in a particular amount designated in the cognovit note. A cognovit entered after the running of the statute of limitations on a debt does not toll or relate back, and an action on the debt would not be revived. Cognovits integrated into consumer credit instruments, which once were common, are now unenforceable. There is no essential difference between confession of judgment and cognovit.
*See also:* confession; judgment, confession of judgment.

**COGSA provision** *See:* bill, bill of lading, COGSA provision (paramount provision).

**cohabitation (co-habitation)** Two adults living together in the manner of a married couple. Cohabitation is the joint maintenance of one household between two adults who treat one another as spouses. While quite a few married people do cohabitate, the term is usually applied to an unmarried couple, whose cohabitation has most of the attributes of marital life, including sexual activity, although without the solemnity of matrimony or an effort to satisfy the requirements of common–law marriage. In jurisdictions that have or do recognize common–law marriage, notorious cohabitation for a sufficient period of time is its essential requirement.

*See also:* marriage, consummation of marriage; marriage, common–law marriage.

**cohabitation contract (co-habitation contract)** An agreement between people living together, but not married, to distribute their property. A cohabitation contract is a legally binding and enforceable agreement entered between two people who are cohabiting, governing their property and interests. A common form of cohabitation agreement agrees to a schedule for the distribution of property at death or separation, as well as to other significant legal rights that would occur or attach by operation of law if the two parties were married to one another. People not related or married to each other may agree to distribute their property to each other, or to others, by operation of private agreement.

**coif** A soft cloth hat once worn by senior lawyers and judges. The coif is a skullcap once worn in England as a mark of distinction at the bar. It is the symbol of an academic legal honors society in the United States, the Order of the Coif. Note: the word is pronounce "koyf," not "kwoff."

*See also:* serjeant (serjeant at law or serjeant–counter); law, law school, order of the coif.

**Coinage Clause** *See:* constitution, U.S. Constitution, clauses, Coinage Clause.

**coinsurance** *See:* insurance, coinsurance.

**cold bench or hot court or cold court** *See:* bench, hot bench (cold bench or hot court or cold court).

**collaborative negotiation** *See:* negotiation, collaborative negotiation (accommodation in negotiation).

**collateral** Related to something else. Collateral designates a relationship between two persons, things, or promises. Though the term implies a parallel relationship, such as between collateral relatives (who are siblings) the term more fully describes a relationship between a secondary or ancillary to a primary person, thing, or promise. Thus, the direct ancestor is a parent, and a collateral ancestor is an uncle or an aunt.

There are many examples in the law. A collateral action is not a direct appeal but a secondary action in court challenging the result in a primary action.

A security interest is a commitment that becomes significant only in the default of another commitment.

**collateral action** *See:* res, res judicata, collateral attack on a judgment (collateral action).

**collateral agreement** *See:* contract, collateral contract (collateral agreement); agreement, collateral agreement.

**collateral attack on a judgment** *See:* judgment, review of judgment, collateral attack; res, res judicata, collateral attack on a judgment (collateral action).

**collateral consanguinity** *See:* consanguinity, collateral consanguinity.

**collateral contract** *See:* contract, collateral contract (collateral agreement).

**collateral descendant** *See:* descent, descendant, collateral descendant.

**collateral descendent or collateral kinsmen or collateral line or collateral relative or collaterals** *See:* heir, collateral heir (collateral descendent or collateral kinsmen or collateral line or collateral relative or collaterals).

**collateral estoppel** *See:* res, res judicata, collateral estoppel; estoppel, collateral estoppel.

**collateral heir** *See:* heir, collateral heir (collateral descendent or collateral kinsmen or collateral line or collateral relative or collaterals).

**collateral issue rule** *See:* impeachment, impeachment of witness, collateral issue rule.

**collateral negligence** *See:* negligence, collateral negligence.

**collateral proceeding** *See:* proceeding, collateral proceeding.

**collateral security** *See:* security, security interest, collateral security.

**after-acquired collateral (after-acquired property)** Security for a loan acquired post-loan processing. After-acquired collateral is collateral for a loan that is obtained after the contract has been made for the loan. The contract must specify that it will create a security interest in some specific form in defined property that might later accrue to or be acquired by the creditor. After-acquired collateral for security interests created under Article 9 of the UCC are governed by Section 9–204, which limits security in after-acquired consumer goods to those acquired by the debtor within ten days of the secured party's giving of value to the debtor.

**collateral as security** Security for an obligation. Collateral is something of comparable value held in trust by a creditor as assurance that a debt will be paid. Collateral can be money, chattel property, an interest in real property, investment securities, or anything else of merchantable value, but in nearly all instances the creditor has discretion to accept the collateral in kind and in amount. Once a debt is repaid according to its terms, the creditor is obligated to return the collateral to the debtor.

*See also:* ancillary; comparability (comparable).

**cross-collateral (cross-collateralization)** An agreement creating a security interest in more than the contracted-for goods. Cross-collateral is a security interest that is created by a grant of security in goods other than those purchased and subject as ordinary collateral for their finance. Cross-collateralization is used to provide additional security against a default on a given debt, but it is subject to the essential limit on the exercise of a security interest that the secured party may not take more value than the value of the secured debt. If, for instance, a merchant has sold a refrigerator to a purchaser, and the purchaser then finances a television, a security interest then given by the purchaser in the refrigerator as a security or additional security for financing the television is by cross-collateral. Cross-collateralization may be made of later-acquired goods. When cross-collateralization over goods not otherwise subject to purchase or negotiation occurs at a time before or after the financed goods are purchased or their terms negotiated, the clause or agreement requiring the cross-collateralization may be be void as unconscionable or adhesive unless it is clearly disclosed and its effects are understood by the party who purportedly grants the security interest.

**collateral-order doctrine** *See:* order, court order, appealable order, collateral-order doctrine.

**collateral-source rule** *See:* damages, tort damages, collateral-source rule.

**collateralized debt obligation** *See:* security, securities, collateralized debt obligation, mortgage-backed security; security, securities, collateralized debt obligation (collateralized loan obligation or CLO or CDO).

**collateralized loan obligation or CLO or CDO** *See:* security, securities, collateralized debt obligation (collateralized loan obligation or CLO or CDO).

**collation** *See:* hotchpot (collation).

**collecting bank** *See:* bank, collecting bank.

**collective bargaining** *See:* labor union, collective bargaining.

**collective bargaining agreement** *See:* union, labor union, collective bargaining, collective bargaining agreement (C.B.A. CBA).

**collective entity doctrine** *See:* incrimination, self-incrimination, collective entity doctrine.

**college** *See:* university, college.

**collision (collide)** Two or more people or objects coming into physical contact with one another. A collision is the event of colliding and the movement of the force from the contact of each entity through the other.

**collision regulations (COLREGS)** *See:* navigation, collision regulations (COLREGS or navigation rules).

**collision between vessels** Physical contact between two vessels when one has way on, that is, when one is in motion.

**colloquium** *See:* defamation, colloquium.

**colloquy (colloquium or plea colloquy)** A conference conducted through dialogue. A colloquy, generally, is a conversation among two or more people that has the sense of pursuing some idea or truth through dialogue. A judge will employ a colloquy with a criminal defendant to ask questions of the defendant prior to the defendant's waiver of a right or entry of a plea. The purpose of the colloquy is to determine that predicates to the waiver or entry are satisfied and to create a record. Thus, questions are asked in waiving a right, such as to a jury trial to ensure that the defendant acts knowingly and voluntarily in waiving that right. In the case of a plea entry, questions are asked to test the veracity and voluntariness of the defendant's statements and to test the defendant's acceptance of responsibility, sincerity of remorse, or other personal attributes that might affect the ability of the court to accept the plea or to order a sentence.

*See also:* slander (slanderer); defamation, colloquium; plea, criminal plea.

**collusion (collude or collusive)** A partnership to commit fraud. Collusion is any act by one person with another that is intended to lead toward a fraudulent action. Collusion particularly suggests that a person is dishonest or disloyal while dealing with another, as when an agent colludes with another to enter a contract contrary to the principal's interests. It does not matter whether the fraud intended to result from collusion is itself a crime or tort or whether it is an abuse of process, such as a false filing in court between parties who are not truly adverse to one another; any legal act that is the result of collusion is presumptively void.

*See also:* action, collusive action.

**collusive action** *See:* action, collusive action.

**collusive joinder** *See:* joinder, joinder of parties, collusive joinder (improper joinder or manufactured joinder).

**color (colorable or colour or colourable)** What is apparent is prima facie correct or justified. Color, in law, is a metaphor for the appearance of presumptive legality and truth in an action or argument. Thus a colorable claim is one that has a bona fide appearance of legality, whether it ultimately proves to be correct or not. Thus, color of title is a claim of ownership based on a title, an act under color of state law is an act authorized by state law, and a colorable claim is a claim that is apparently valid under the facts and the law. Color in these senses suggests that the assertion is presumptively true, although it might not be found true on closer analysis. Color — whether express color or implied color — once had a more formal significance in pleadings under the writ system in which color was sometimes more of a pretext than a good-faith expectation of the law, but this sense is now largely obsolete.

*See also:* right, legal right, color of right (claim of right or colour of right).

**color of law**   *See:* law, color of law.

**color of office**   *See:* office, color of office.

**color of right**   *See:* right, legal right, color of right (claim of right or colour of right).

**color of title**   *See:* title, color of title.

**colored**   Once a label for African Americans, now a broad measure of colorism. "Colored" described African Americans during the nineteenth century and the Jim Crow era in the South. Voter rolls in some states were divided, with some books bound in white and marked "White" and others bound in green and marked "Colored." Water fountains and entrances in courthouses were segregated for use, denominated "colored" or "white."

**colorism**   Discrimination based on skin color. Colorism is discrimination based on pigmented skin color, whether the discrimination is based on a concept of color alone, based on a concept of race for which color is a surrogate indicator, or based on no concept but an unarticulated preference that is acted upon knowingly or with demonstrable and statistically significant frequency. Discrimination on the basis of color is forbidden under the Fifteenth Amendment, 24 U.S.C. § 1981, and Title VII.

*See also:* civil rights, Civil Rights Act, Civil Rights Act of 1866 (Section 1981).

**gang colors**   Insignia representing a criminal gang. Gang colors are symbols of criminal gangs, worn or carried by members and associates, ranging widely in form, from complex pseudo-heraldry painted or stitched onto jackets to mere strips of cloth or stripes of paint in colors associated with a gang.

**Colorado River abstention**   *See:* abstention, abstention doctrine, Colorado River abstention.

**COLREGS or navigation rules**   *See:* navigation, collision regulations (COLREGS or navigation rules).

**com.**   *See:* company, investment company (com.).

**combatant**   A person who fights. A combatant, generally, is a person who fights, and the common law defined fighting as mutual combat. Metaphorically, any person or entity engaged in a serious competition may be said to be combatants.

The law of war and military law are more focused in the use of combatant. For the purposes of personnel assignment, certain billets are combatant assignments owing to their training for combat and the expectation that the unit and the servicemember will be in combat. For the purposes of the Foreign Tort Claims Act, combatant includes a person engaged in combat operations during a period of hostilities.

In the early twenty-first century, the U.S. briefly employed a distinction between combatants who were enemy combatants and unlawful enemy combatants, though both groups were combatants. This distinction, which was highly controversial and apparently intended to allow the detention of unlawful combatants outside of the protections of the Geneva Conventions, was enacted into U.S. statutes by the Military Commissions Act of 2006, but reliance on the distinction may have been abandoned by the president in 2009.

**enemy combatant**   A individual combatant of the enemy. An enemy combatant is a person who acts as a combatant against the military forces of the United States, either under the orders of an enemy state or in substantial aid of an enemy state. It is possible for citizens of the United States to be enemy combatants.

An enemy combatant who is captured is subject to treatment under the protocols established by international law, particularly in the Geneva Conventions of 1949.

*See also:* enemy.

**non-combatant (noncombatant)**   A person barred from, and immune from, combat. A non-combatant is a person who is unqualified as a combatant during an armed conflict. It is a violation of the law of war to deliberately act to kill or harm a non-combatant. Non-combatants include civilians who happen to live or be near a theater of combat and perform no work of a military character. Members of the military are sometimes non-combatants, if the military personnel are assigned and acting in a role that is traditionally unarmed, including medical personnel, clergy, and support staff, as well as prisoners not seeking to escape and the wounded not seeking to engage in combat.

**unlawful combatant (unlawful enemy combatant)**   A combatant accused of violating the law. An unlawful combatant, generally, is a member of a combatant force who violates the laws of war, the local criminal law, or the regulations of the occupying power. Such a person is not saved from prosecution for such illegal conduct by the status of being prisoner of war.

The Military Commissions Act of 2006 defined all persons who engaged in combat or provided support to the enemies of the United States to be unlawful combatants if they are not lawful combatants. A lawful combatant is one who is a member of the regular military forces of an enemy state, member of a militia of the enemy state or a member of the military of an enemy government that is not recognized by the United States.

An example that was essential to the passage of the 2006 Act is the treatment of enemy combatants in the Afghan operations from 2001 to 20011. Members of al

Qaeda and the Taliban were defined to be unlawful combatants, despite more general attributes that might accord with the definition. The act's definition is highly controversial and may no longer reflect the U.S. executive position on the designation of combatants.

**combination**   A union made from different things. A combination is any joining of once-independent entities into a new whole, as in the creation of a new machine from myriad parts. The term once had a quite negative implication in law, particularly used for conspiracies or business collectives in violation of the law or public policy, but this sense of combination is now rarely used. More commonly, a combination depicts a business merger, acquisition, management contract, or other means of integration that is not presumed to be unlawful or harmful to the market. A combination in intellectual property is the integration of things earlier created so that a new thing is created, which is patentable.

*See also:* conspiracy (conspire).

**business combination**   Any integration of corporations. Business combination is the most general term for all forms of integration of two corporations. The term includes merger, acquisition, direct investment, consolidation, joint management plans or agreements, controlling stock acquisitions, or other means by which the independence of one or both corporations is significantly diminished or any control is passed from one to the other or to an intermediary.

**combined sewer overflow**   *See:* sewerage, combined sewer overflow (sanitary sewer overflow or CSO or SSO).

**come**

**come-to-Jesus meeting**   A meeting in which a person must face a difficult decision or idea. The come-to-Jesus meeting, a term in popular use, refers to a meeting where a person must finally decide whether to do or not do something that has been delayed. In the slang of legal practice it tends to be a meeting between a lawyer and a client, in which the lawyer sets out the case against the client and advises a settlement or, if the client is a defendant in a criminal case, a plea bargain. There are many variations, and prosecutors sometimes have come-to-Jesus sessions with defense lawyers.

**comes now**   A customary preface to a motion or pleading. "Comes now the plaintiff" (or whichever party has drafted the pleading or made the motion or response) is a customary formality that has long been used to identify the party at the outset of a motion, pleading, or argument. The significance of the verb is that the party approaches the court, bringing an issue for the court's consideration. The court's usage is similar, "this matter comes before the court on motion of the plaintiff" (or whichever party filed the motion). Some critics of such language find it empty

and ceremonial, but it does little harm to understanding and has many defenders.

**coming to the nuisance**   *See:* nuisance, coming to the nuisance.

**comingled funds**   *See:* funds, comingled funds (commingling of funds).

**comingling or co-mingling**   *See:* commingling (comingling or co-mingling).

**comity**   An act of accommodation or courtesy. Comity generally refers to any gesture of good will among equals. In particular it refers to an act by one state or sovereign made for the convenience of another, though not under a legal obligation to do so, even though a reciprocal benefit might be implied by the doing.

*See also:* jurisdiction, appellate jurisdiction, Rooker-Feldman Doctrine; deference (defer).

**Comity Clause**   *See:* constitution, U.S. Constitution, clauses, Privileges and Immunities Clause (Comity Clause).

**judicial comity (federal-state comity or interstate comity or international comity)**   Judges in coordinate jurisdictions will not hear matters more suited to be heard elsewhere. Comity is a prudential requirement that a court not hear a matter that is either already being heard in a court in another jurisdiction or is so closely related to that jurisdiction that it would be improper to hear the cause. Comity takes many forms, in particular comity between federal and state courts, comity among courts in different states, and comity with the courts of foreign nations. Most commonly, federal courts applying comity, would not hear habeas cases or collateral attacks on criminal prosecutions until the state courts had completed the trial, appeal, and state collateral review processes. This role of comity has now been codified for some purposes in the Antiterrorism and Effective Death Penalty Act of 1996, 28 U.S.C. § 2244. Because comity otherwise is prudential, its considerations may be less significant in a given cause, particularly if the prudent court is aware of evidence that the plaintiff cannot have the cause fairly heard in the other jurisdiction.

*See also:* federalism, doctrine of our federalism; jurisdiction, appellate jurisdiction, Rooker-Feldman Doctrine.

**command theory of law**   *See:* jurisprudence, legal positivism, command theory of law.

**commentary**   *See:* lawbook, treatise (commentary).

**commerce (commercial)**   Producing, storing, buying, selling, trading, and even destroying goods and services. Commerce is any single bit of the activity that amounts in sum to the economy. The definition of commerce has been the object of great controversy, because of its defining role in the powers of Congress in the

Commerce Clause, and the powers of Congress related to commerce have expanded as the legal understanding of commerce has expanded. The most limited, and antiquated, notion of commerce is the interchange of one product for another or for money. This sense is captured by Dr. Johnson in his great dictionary, when he defined commerce as intercourse, by which he meant the pattern of interchange. The most expansive meaning includes all forms of human endeavor, including work and nonwork, production and non-production, ownership and non-ownership, that affect the economic life of humanity. Between these extremes lies the contemporary notion of commerce in the United States.

Commerce is the creation, sale, purchase, exchange, or transfer of any commodity for another commodity — with a commodity now understood to include any thing or any service that has the potential to be traded for another thing, service, or money. The regulation of commerce may have a scope broader than this.

*See also:* bank, commercial bank; immunity, sovereign immunity, foreign sovereign immunity, commercial-activity exception; law, commercial law; lease, commercial lease; loan, commercial loan; reasonable, commercially reasonable (commercial reasonableness); speech, commercial speech; trade.

**Commerce Clause** *See:* constitution, U.S. Constitution, clauses, Commerce Clause.

**e-commerce** Business transacted over the Internet. E-commerce is business conducted between two parties through predominantly or exclusively by means of electronic communication through the Internet. E-commerce includes the buying and selling of goods and services, as well as the placement and consumption of advertisements and marketing. Transactions through e-commerce are essentially the same as transactions through more traditional means, including the same protections and responsibilities afforded through statutory or common law mechanisms, including any applicable section of the Uniform Commercial Code or the Restatement (Second) of Contracts. E-commerce is a method of doing business rather than a type of business done; as a result, almost all transactions could theoretically be carried out through e-commercial means.

*See also:* signature, digital signature.

### regulation of commerce

**commerce with Indian tribes** The Congressional regulation of Indian affairs. Commerce with Indian tribes is one of the fields that Congress is tasked to regulate in the Commerce Clause. In fact, the regulation of trade among or between the tribes and the United States is a small component of the broader powers assumed under this power to regulate Indian affairs.

**dormant commerce power** A state may not unduly burden foreign or interstate commerce. The dormant commerce power is a federal power implied in the Constitution both by the structure of the Commerce Clauses and by the structure of powers allocated to the central and state governments. Though the framers considered the problem of unexercised federal power over commerce, the label of the power being dormant, or asleep, when Congress has not exercised it was raised by Chief Justice Marshall in Gibbons v. Ogden, 22 U.S. 1, 189 (1824). The power is sometimes ascribed to Congress, but it is actually a power of the courts to review and strike down a state law regulating commerce, either because the the state law burdens interstate commerce to the benefit of intrastate commerce or because the state law intrudes too deeply into the potential for national regulation.

The dormant commerce power takes several distinct forms. States may not create barriers to entry into intrastate markets that deny an equal and fair opportunity to businesses in other states to enter the market of each state. States are barred from regulation that unduly burdens interstate commerce by creating regulations that fall unfairly upon foreign business that operate in the state. States are barred from discriminating against a foreign entity in their regulations and taxes or benefiting local businesses in any manner that amounts to economic protection of the local business, unless the law in fact promotes an important state purpose and there is no less burdensome means to promote it. States may, however, burden interstate commerce as needed when the burden is only incidental, or a secondary effect, of a law properly regulating activity in the state, though such burdens are unconstitutional unless they are clearly less than their benefit to appropriate state interests. Note: the dormant commerce power does not apply to a conflict between a state regulation and a federal statute; that would more likely be a question of preemption.

**Complete Auto Test (four-factor test)** A state may fairly tax interstate commerce. The complete auto test assesses the constitutional fairness of a state tax on a foreign company with an activity within the state, allowing the tax as an acceptable burden on interstate commerce if the tax is applied to an activity with a substantial nexus with the taxing state, if the tax is fairly apportioned between domestic and foreign entities, if the tax does not discriminate against interstate commerce, and if the tax is fairly related to the services provided by the state. The test was announced in Complete Auto Transit, Inc. v. Brady, 430 U.S. 274, 279 (1977), by Justice Blackmun, overruling the holding of Spector Motor Service v. O'Connor, 340 U.S. 602 (1951), barring states from taxing interstate activities. Under Complete Auto, interstate commerce "must be made to pay its way," or to pay its fair share of the tax burden. 430 U.S. at 281.

*See also:* tax, business income tax (business privilege tax).

**Cooley Doctrine** States may incidentally burden interstate commerce. The Cooley Doctrine was an early determination of the porous boundary between state and federal regulation of intrastate commerce, holding that a state regulation of interstate activity is valid if, first, there is no incompatible Congressional regulation, second, the regulation is intended to govern local matters and only incidentally affects interstate activity, and third, does not create an undue burden on interstate activities. The doctrine, developed in and after Cooley v. Board of Wardens, 53 U.S. (12 How.) 299 (1851), has been refined and generally supplanted by the Pike test, following Pike v. Bruce Church, Inc., 397 U.S. 137 (1970) (Stewart, J.).

*See also:* commerce, regulation of commerce, dormant commerce power, Pike test (balancing test).

**dormant foreign commerce clause**  States are limited from regulation burdening foreign commerce. The dormant foreign commerce power, which is also sometimes called the dormant foreign commerce clause, bars states from regulation that unduly burdens foreign commerce, the power of the Congress to regulate foreign commerce, or the power of the executive over foreign affairs. It is an interpretation of the foreign commerce clause that parallels the similar interpretation of the interstate commerce clause, although preemption includes not only preemptive acts by Congress but also preemptive acts of the President. State laws that implicate foreign affairs evaluated similarly to those that burden interstate commerce, though the interest of the executive is more readily favored in cases of state intrusion.

**Pike test (balancing test)**  A non–discriminating state law may not create a burden on interstate commerce clearly exceeding its local benefit. The Pike test, from Pike v. Bruce Church, Inc., 397 U.S. 137 (1970) (Stewart, J.), is the balancing test of dormant commerce, used when there is no evidence that a state's legislature intended to harm interstate commerce, and when the structure of the state law regulates both in-state and out-of-state commercial entities alike, and when the statute is intended to promote a legitimate local public interest. In that case, the statute is presumably valid, and it will be upheld unless the sum of the burdens on interstate commerce created by the law clearly outweighs the sum of benefits to legitimate local interests. The Pike test refined and replaced the Cooley Doctrine.

*See also:* interest, state interest, legimate state interest (legitimate governmental purpose).

**interstate commerce**  The regulation of domestic economic activity. The power of Congress to regulate interstate commerce, established in the Commerce Clause, includes the power to regulate buying and selling across state lines, transportation of goods between states, intrastate channels of interstate commerce, instrumentalities of interstate commerce, intrastate commerce necessary to effectively regulate interstate markets, and in effect, the whole of the national economy as well as any constituent element. This power is sometimes seen as much greater in extent than was originally contemplated, and so some core aspects of intrastate commerce that have a particularly moral aspect, such as the regulation of prostitution or other vice laws, may be reserved to the states for regulation.

*See also:* kidnapping, federal kidnapping (federal kidnapping charge).

**aggregation doctrine**  Many acts of local commerce effect interstate commerce. The aggregation doctrine extends Congress' authority to regulate interstate commerce, because sufficiently large numbers of local transactions aggregate into a national and interstate affect that is substantial enough to subject the sum to the regulation of interstate commerce. The most famous case standing for this doctrine is Wickard v. Filburn, 317 U.S. 111 (1942), which allowed national wheat quotas to limit a farmer's production of wheat for his own use owing to the affect on wheat prices of farmers across the country producing their own wheat and thus affecting national price and supply.

*See also:* commerce, regulation of commerce, interstate commerce, cumulative effect theory.

**cumulative effect theory**  The cumulative effects of intrastate commerce affect interstate commerce. The cumulative effects theory allows Congress to regulate local activities, if the sum of such local activities nationwide has a substantial cumulative effect on interstate commerce. In essence, there is little difference between the cumulative effects theory and the aggregation doctrine: acts in the aggregate have a cumulative effect that must be substantial in their effect on interstate commerce.

*See also:* commerce, regulation of commerce, interstate commerce, aggregation doctrine.

**Interstate Commerce Act**  Interstate carriers shall not favor some shippers over others. The Interstate Commerce Act of 1887, 24 Stat. 379, codified at 49 U.S.C. § 301 (2007), forbids railroads and shippers in interstate commerce from a variety of unfair practices in setting prices and conditions of shipment. The act established the Interstate Commerce Commission, which enacted further regulations to govern the safety and economics of the interstate shipment of goods and people. The Commission was integrated into other bureaucracies in 1995, but many of its regulations are still in force.

**Interstate Commerce Commission (ICC or I.C.C.)**  An historically important federal agency regulating interstate transportation and commerce. The Interstate Commerce Commission, or ICC, was one of the earliest federal regulatory agencies, established in 1887 to regulate interstate commerce. It was abolished in 1995 and its tasks are now carried out by the Surface Transportation Board and other agencies in the Department of Transportation.

**intrastate commerce**   Commerce of a local character occuring solely within one state. Intrastate commerce is commerce strictly within a single state. As a practical matter, little commercial activity has no effect at all outside a locality, and the limit once posed by intrastate commerce on interstate commerce has been reduced to very little. The primary limit on interstate commerce is no longer intrastate commerce but an intrusion into the customary arenas of state regulation.

## commerce (commercial)

**commercial-activity exception**   *See:* immunity, sovereign immunity, foreign sovereign immunity, commercial-activity exception.

**commercial bank**   *See:* bank, commercial bank.

**commercial capital**   capital, commercial capital.

**commercial covenant**   *See:* covenant, real covenant, covenant in gross (commercial covenant).

**commercial easement**   *See:* easement, easement in gross (commercial easement).

**commercial general liability**   *See:* insurance, category of insurance, liability insurance, commercial general liability (C.G.L. CGL).

**commercial law**   *See:* law, commercial law.

**commercial lease**   *See:* lease, commercial lease.

**commercial loan**   *See:* loan, commercial loan.

**commercial reasonableness**   *See:* reasonable, commercially reasonable (commercial reasonableness).

**commercial speech**   *See:* speech, commercial speech.

**commercially reasonable**   *See:* reasonable, commercially reasonable (commercial reasonableness).

**commercial paper**   Negotiable short-term debt instruments issued by commercial entities and unsecured by collateral. Commercial paper is a class of negotiable instrument representing an obligation to pay a certain value under a particular circumstance. It is a means for a corporation to borrow small amounts of money without the efforts of issuing a bond. The debt arising from that obligation is usually priced at a discount based on the interest rates prevailing at the time of issuance. Promissory notes, certificates of deposit, bills of exchange, bills of lading, orders for delivery of goods, and express orders are all forms of commercial paper. Although their terms vary, commercial paper is rarely denominated above $100,000 or have a maturity date longer than 270 days, because instruments that mature later must be registered with the U.S. Securities and Exchange Commission. The instrument may be issued by a commercial entity like a bank or a brokerage, but its terms, including its amount, are likely assigned by the maker, the person who signs the instrument or undertakes to ensure its payment. Commercial paper is regulated in every jurisdiction of the U.S. under article three of that jurisdiction's version of the Uniform Commercial Code.

*See also:* instrument, negotiable instrument.

**commingling (comingling or co-mingling)**   Integrating once-separate assets into one account or stock. Commingling is the combination of assets, whether money or goods, so that no obvious distinction persists between the assets based on their source. Commingling gives rise to a presumption that the assets have acquired the character of the account or stock in which they result, although claims upon the assets prior to their commingling may persist as against the resulting account or stock. Commingling may have a variety of consequences depending upon its context. Commingling of the assets of shareholders with the assets of the corporations is a basis for a claimant against the corporation to pierce the corporate veil. Commingling of the assets of a trust with the assets of a trustee may be a violation of the trustee's fiduciary obligations to the beneficiary. Commingling the assets of a client with the assets of an attorney may violate the attorney's duty to the client.

**commingled goods**   *See:* goods, commingled goods.

**commingling of funds**   *See:* funds, comingled funds (commingling of funds).

**commission (commissioner)**   A public agency, especially one tasked with oversight of others or drafting of policy. A commission is a public agency that is delegated the responsibility of developing regulations and public policy to implement broad legislative goals. The commission is often led by a commissioner or a small group of commissioners, and the term may refer to the holders of such commissions alone or to the entire agency including its sometimes quite sizable staff. Commissions are frequently created for the purpose of overseeing other agencies and private entities to ensure compliance with such statutes and regulations. Examples include the Federal Communications Commission, the Federal Trade Commission, the New York State Public Service Commission, the Arizona State Boxing Commission, and the San Francisco Police Commission.

**commission as fee**   A portion of a transaction retained as compensation. A commission is a fee retained, or sometimes paid, to a trustee, realtor, broker, auctioneer, seller, or other agent as compensation for the services rendered in the performance of some affair, such as a sale. The amount is either determined in advance by a specific agreement or is an amount governed by the practice of such agents in a given locale.

*See also:* rake, rake as commission (rake off or take or vigorish or vig).

**commission as office**  An appointment to office, or the instrument declaring such an appointment. A commission is an appointment in which a specific person is commissioned as a specific officer of the government.

**commission of office**  The document that is evidence of an appointment to office. A commission is an instrument issued by the government under seal and by an authorized signator, granted to a person appointed to office that describes the nature of the office and the powers associated with it.

**commissive waste**  *See:* waste, doctrine of waste, commissive waste (voluntary waste).

## commitment (commit)

**commit crime or commit a crime**  *See:* crime, commission of crime (commit crime or commit a crime).

**commitment order**  *See:* custody, commitment order.

**involuntary commitment (mandatory commitment)**  The entry of a person to supervision in a mental hospital or police facility against that person's will. Involuntary commitment is the court-ordered placement of a person with a mental illness into a mental hospital, mental clinic, or in some cases a jail or penitentiary because the person's illness or incapacity is found to create a danger of harm to the self or to others. Involuntary commitment proceedings take a person's liberty at the request of the state and are judicial matters that must meet the standards of at least minimal due process.
*See also:* guardian, guardianship hearing (competency hearing); competency (competence or competent or incompetence or incompetency or incompetent).

**voluntary commitment**  The entry of a person to supervision in a mental hospital or police facility at that person's request. Voluntary commitment is the entry of a person to a mental health facility at that person's own request. In general, admission on a voluntary basis to a supervised mental health environment is a matter of contract, and it is usually not subject to due process. There is some difficulty in determining the voluntariness of a commitment if the person lacks capacity, which may necessitate a hearing to determine capacity or to appoint a guardian. When a person is voluntarily committed, after which a member of staff determines that the person poses a danger to the patient or to others, a refusal to discharge requires a hearing subject to due process.
*See also:* capacity.

**commodification**  *See:* value, commodification (monetization or dollarization).

**commodity**  A tangible, fungible good that is traded or for which futures are traded. A commodity is any good that is supplied without distinction as to one unit or another, at least within standard categories of quality and quantity. Bulk goods, whether refined, such as gasoline, or unrefined, such as Texas intermediate crude oil, are inherently commodities. The price for a commodity is usually established through trades in public exchanges. A contract for the provision of a commodity is considered fulfilled by the delivery of the quantity of the goods specified of a suitable quality, without regard to one or another lot of the goods. Agricultural commodities are defined by statute for the regulation of trading, particularly in futures, and include a host of plant and animal products, but not onions.
*See:* Chicago Mercantile Exch. v. Tieken, 178 F. Supp. 779, 782–83 (N.D. Ill. 1959) about the onions.
*See also:* fungibility (fungible).

**Commodity Futures Trading Commission**  *See:* security, securities, securities regulation, Commodity Futures Trading Commission.

## common

**common article**  *See:* war, law of war, Geneva Conventions, common article.

**common authority rule**  *See:* search, permission to search, common–authority rule (common authority rule).

**common bench or banco communis or bancus communis**  *See:* court, English court, court of common pleas (common bench or banco communis or bancus communis).

**common carrier**  *See:* carrier, common carrier.

**common defense**  *See:* constitution, U.S. Constitution, ideals, common defense.

**common design rule**  *See:* conspiracy, common design rule.

**common duty**  *See:* care, duty of care, common duty.

**common easement**  *See:* easement, common easement.

**common knowledge**  *See:* knowledge, common knowledge (public knowledge).

**common law**  *See:* law, common law (lex communis).

**common-law copyright**  *See:* copyright, common-law copyright.

**common-law crime**  *See:* crime, common-law crime.

**common-law duty of landholder**  *See:* care, duty of care, common-law duty of landholder.

**common-law lawyer or admiralty lawyer or canon lawyer or civilian lawyer**  *See:* lawyer, common-law lawyer (common lawyer or admiralty lawyer or canon lawyer or civilian lawyer).

**common-law marriage**  *See:* marriage, common-law marriage.

**common-law rule** *See:* fee, fee for services, attorney's fees, fee shifting, American rule (common law rule); law, common law, common-law rule.

**common nucleus of facts** *See:* jurisdiction, supplemental jurisdiction, common nucleus of facts (common question).

**common question** *See:* jurisdiction, supplemental jurisdiction, common nucleus of facts (common question).

**common recovery** *See:* recovery, common recovery (common vouchee or recoverer).

**common scheme evidence** *See:* crime, signature crime (common scheme evidence).

**common seal** *See:* seal, corporate seal (common seal).

**common share** *See:* share, share as stock, common stock (common share).

**common stock** *See:* share, share as stock, common stock (common share).

**common vouchee or recoverer** *See:* recovery, common recovery (common vouchee or recoverer).

**commonwealth** A community of free people or states. A commonwealth is an association of people or states in whom the welfare of each is pursued in common by all. Four states of the United States denominate themselves as commonwealths rather than as states—Kentucky, Massachusetts, Pennsylvania, Virginia—and the U.S. territories of Puerto Rico and the Northern Mariana Islands. There is no difference under the U.S. Constitution between a state and a commonwealth or a territory and a commonwealth. In an international context, the term Commonwealth, alone, usually refers to British institutions, initially referring to the United Kingdom, then to the members of the British Commonwealth, now to the Commonwealth of Nations. The alliance of states formerly in the Soviet Union is the Commonwealth of Independent States. Various nation-states, notably Australia, are also commonwealths.
*See also:* state.

**communism** *See:* government, forms of government, communism.

**communitarianism** Law and justice arise from values shared in a community. Communitarianism is theoretical response to theories of justice based on radical individualism, which presumed that an individual could hold values and make choices unencumbered by the values and choices of others, particularly the people of preceding generations. Communitarian recognition of shared values leads to a higher priority for certain public goods and actions, such as education and culture.

**community property** *See:* marriage, marital property, community property.

**community standards of obscenity** *See:* obscenity, Miller test, contemporary community standards of obscenity (community standards of obscenity).

**commutation (commutative or commute)** A reduction in sentence. A commutation is a substitution of sentences, the new sentence being less severe than a sentence earlier pronounced following a conviction for a crime. A commutation may be granted by a judicial, executive, or administrative authority according to a constitutional or statutory grant of authority. A commutation does not remove any disability created by the conviction. Commutations may be conditional, forfeit if the conditions are not satisfied, in which case the original sentence is restored.
*See also:* clemency.

**commutative contract** *See:* contract, specific contracts, commutative contract.

**commutative justice** *See:* justice, commutative justice.

**compact** An agreement. A compact is an agreement, whether a contract among private parties or an agreement among states or a treaty among nations. A compact among states is an interstate compact and may only be entered by them with the consent of Congress. A compact among nation-states is a treaty and governed according to the law of treaties.

**Compact Clause** *See:* constitution, U.S. Constitution, clauses, Compact Clause (Interstate Compact Clause).

**companion animal** *See:* animal, companion animal.

**company**

**company as commercial organization (co.)** An association organized under the laws of a state to carry on a legitimate business. A company is a business enterprise, nearly always a corporation organized as a business corporation or corporation for profit, although the term "company" is not restricted to such an organization and could depict a business owned as a partnership or a sole proprietorship. Customarily, company still refers to large enterprises in manufacture, shipping, finance, or commerce. When used in a corporate name, the word (whether it is whole or abbreviated) is a part of the name and not a designation of legal form.
*See also:* corporation (corporate or incorporate); firm; club.

**company as companions** A group, or the presence of others. Company refers to everyone in a group with a common association or purpose. Thus, companions are members of a company. Mere proximity is insufficient, and affinity is not required, but some knowingly shared enterprise, no matter how vague or informal, is required.

**holding company**  A company whose purpose is to control another company. A holding company is a company that is organized primarily for the purpose of exercising control over another company or companies. This control may be achieved through the direct ownership of a closely held corporation or through a controlling interest in publicly traded stocks.

**investment company**  A company that issues or invests securities or similar investments. An investment company is a company that has a principal business of issuing public securities on behalf of other firms, or that manages securities or similar investments as its business.

**joint-stock company (joint stock bank or joint stock company)**  A hybrid business organization, a partnership in a trust. A joint-stock company is a partnership in which partners have shares on a pro-rata basis depending on their contributions to the company, and only those with the powers of a director may make decisions binding the whole. Rather than file incorporation documents, the partners commit their assets to a trust with the partners as trustees and the company as as the beneficiary. No partner is able then to remove the committed assets from the trust, but each partner may sell that partner's owership interest subject to trust. As partners in a company, each trustee is entitled to a portion of the value of the company as a beneficiary of the trust.

**limited liability company (L.L.C. or LLC)**  Business entity that combines elements of partnership and corporation. A limited liability company is a type of business recognized as a separate legal entity apart from the owners of the company. Members are admitted in a manner similar to a partnership, but the extent of liability is limited to corporate assets. An LLC offers the tax advantages of a partnership but the limit of liability of a corporation.
*See also:* corporation, corporations, limited liability corporation.

**title company**  *See:* title, title company (title plant).

**comparability (comparable)**  Roughly equivalent. Comparability in nearly every legal usage is a measure of two things, finding them to perform the same function or otherwise to have the same value or nearly the same value. Two comparable regulations require essentially the same conduct, albeit perhaps by different people or in different situations. A comparable price for two items would be roughly the same price. Comparable lots of land are similarly situated in location, of roughly similar size with structures of similar use, size, and condition.
*See also:* discrimination, employment discrimination, comparable worth.

**comparable worth**  *See:* discrimination, employment discrimination, comparable worth.

**comparative**  Anything that compares various causes, effects, or methodologies, studied by a consistent method. Comparative signals a comparison. The law employs countless forms of comparative analysis, the most essential in the common law being to compare the facts of a precedent to the later facts of a situation that might or might not be governed by the rule from the earlier case, depending on the degree of similarity between the new facts and the old that is discerned by their comparison.

Comparative analysis in law is often a task of comparing the rules of different legal systems, determining not only the differences in conduct allowed or forbidden but also the procedures and concepts by which criminal and civil liability are created by substantive law and assessed in particular cases. This comparison may occur between different jurisdictions in the same country, such as comparing the law of one U.S. state to another, or among states, or among different legal systems, including among different legal systems existing at different times.
*See also:* liability, comparative liability (comparative fault or comparative responsibility); negligence, comparative negligence.

**comparative fault or comparative responsibility**  *See:* liability, comparative liability (comparative fault or comparative responsibility).

**comparative law**  *See:* law, comparative law.

**comparative liability**  *See:* liability, comparative liability (comparative fault or comparative responsibility).

**comparative negligence**  *See:* negligence, comparative negligence.

**comparative rectitude**  *See:* divorce, grounds for divorce, comparative rectitude.

**compass**  To consider. To compass a crime was to imagine it, which was once considered the first step toward committing it.

**compel or compulsory**  *See:* compulsion (compel or compulsory).

**compelling governmental purpose**  *See:* interest, state interest, compelling state interest (compelling governmental purpose).

**compelling state interest**  *See:* interest, state interest, compelling state interest (compelling governmental purpose).

**compensation (compensable or compensate or compensatory)**  Reimbursement for work done, damages suffered, or property surrendered. Compensation connotes a replacement for something lost or given. In the most common form, compensation is the wage, money, or value paid for services provided, as in wages for employment. Compensation also occurs in sales, as the value in money, goods, or services compensating the other party for its consideration, such that in this sense consideration is also compensation. Compensation is the basis for damages suffered by a breach of a legal duty. In this sense, if something is compensable it can be ascertained through some means of determining with some certainty its value, either the value lost or the value required for it to be replaced. Ascertaining compensation may amount to a market comparison of the rate for a given form of labor for time spent; or it may be the appraisal of market value for a chattel or real property. Situations involving pain and suffering or personal loss may require a more subjective assessment, such as the value of a lost limb or pet or family member.

*See also:* remuneration (remunerative); employment, unemployment, unemployment compensation (unemployment benefits or unemployment insurance).

**compensation protection or assured compensation or parachute payment**  *See:* officer, corporate officer, executive officer, executive compensation, golden parachute (compensation protection or assured compensation or parachute payment).

**employment compensation**  Payment for services rendered. Employment compensation is wages paid to an employee. Compensation is either present or deferred, although the same work may generate both forms of compensation. When the compensation is rendered from term to term by the employer, or on behalf of the employer, following the work performed, it is present compensation, and state law ordinarily requires the payment of present compensation at regular intervals, each fortnight or each month, unless the employee accepts a written contract with other provisions, although a pro rata amount must be paid if the employment ends before the end of a term or begins later than the start of a term. Present compensation is vested in the employee once the work is performed. Deferred compensation, including bonuses, may be contingent on conditions subsequent to its performance, such as employment continuing until the bonus is vested or paid.

*See also:* pay (paycheck); officer, corporate officer, executive officer, executive compensation; employment (employ or employed or employee or employer); risk, assumption of risk (assumption of the risk).

**deferred compensation**  Compensation accrued but not to be paid out until a later year. Deferred compensation is compensation earned in a given year, and the rights to the compensation are conferred in that year, but the compensation itself is not paid to the employee until a later year. Deferred compensation may be held by the employer, disbursed to a trust or annuity or other third party but must remain beyond the control of the employee or it becomes taxable compensation in the year it is accrued. Otherwise, deferred compensation is taxable for the year in which it is disbursed to the employee. A bonus or other year-end payment is not deferred compensation.

**just compensation**  The level of payment required of the state for taking private property for a public use. Just compensation is required by the Fifth Amendment for all private property taken for a public use. It forms the basis for all payments made for adverse possession or condemnation of property or interests by the state or federal government. The formula for setting a valuation of a property interest is objective: what a reasonable buyer would pay in cash to a reasonable seller of such property at the time appointed. The value is not to include the change of value caused by the public use that led to the taking, whether the property would be more or less commercially valuable, but the value should include any reasonable expenses above the market value that would in fact be incurred by the owner, such as interest, the amortized value of lost rents, or moving expenses necessitated by the taking.

**compensatory damages**  *See:* damages, classes of damages, compensatory damages; compensation, compensatory damages.

**competency (competence or competent or incompetence or incompetency or incompetent)**  Mental and physical ability sufficient for a given purpose. Competence is a measure of human ability that varies according to the inquiry in which competence is relevant. Competence to hold public office, to make a will, competence to stand trial for a criminal matter, and competence to be executed all turn on distinct measures. Some of these are measures of character, knowledge, and skill, as for the competence to practice law. There is, however, a baseline of awareness of one's identity, one's condition, one's surroundings, and the identity of others that is fundamental to all forms of competence, and without which one is inherently incompetent for all purposes in law. Beyond this level of competence, the question required by law is whether the person is competent to understand what is being done and to perform the tasks required with understanding of their significance and sufficient skill to accomplish them.

*See also:* ethics, legal ethics, competence.

**competency hearing**  *See:* guardian, guardianship hearing (competency hearing).

**competency to stand trial**  A defendant who can understand and assist the defense is competent for trial. Competency to stand trial is a measure of the defendant's awareness and mental abilities, in that the defendant must be aware of the nature and potential consequences of the proceedings in which the defendant is involved and also to be capable of assisting in the defense of the case. Competency to stand trial is distinct from insanity generally and a claim of lack of competency at the time of the commission of an alleged criminal act. A defendant not capable of one or the other is incompetent to stand trial or to enter a plea of guilt, as a matter of due process of law.

**competent evidence**  *See:* evidence, competent evidence.

**competent witness**  *See:* witness, competent witness (incompetent witness).

**competition**  The pursuit with others of a common goal to be achieved by some but not all. Competition is the contest among two or more parties who strive to achieve a purpose or prize that is not open to all. Competition takes a host of forms, such as in sport and in politics. In a commercial sense competitors seek the acquisition of business — seeking to provide or acquire services or goods at the greatest volume, profit, or particular form in a given market — while other commercial enterprises seek the same business from the same potential buyers or sellers.

**competing presumptions**  *See:* presumption, conflicting presumptions (competing presumptions).

**competitive equilibrium**  *See:* equilibrium, competitive equilibrium.

**anticompetitive conduct (anti-competitive conduct or anticompetitiveness)**  Conduct intended to or causing a reduction in competition. Anticompetitive conduct includes all actions that allow, or are intended to allow, the actor to control the price of a good in the market or to exclude competition from it. Absent evidence of intent, it can be hard to distinguish unusually successful competitiveness with anticompetitiveness: some increases in market share are both reasonable and fairly the result of a highly competitive product or business model, and some actions that would be anticompetitive to exclude monopolistically others from a particular market, such as through a monopoly over materials subject to a patent or copyright, are allowed as a matter of law and public policy. Even so, anticompetitive conduct that is unreasonable or unfair or committed with the intent of acquiring a monopoly or other unfair advantage in the market may violate state anticompetition laws as well as the Sherman Anti-Trust Act or the competition laws of other nations. Anticompetitive conduct in such forms is contrary to public policy because it diminishes the independence and dignity of economically limited suppliers and limits the freedom of choice and of contract of consumers.

**competition law**  Antitrust law. Competition law is the term for the regulation of business to ensure adequate competition in the United Kingdom, the European Union, and most of the world. In the United States this arena of law is called antitrust law.

**horizontal competition**  Competition among different distributors of similar goods to the same buyers. Horizontal competition occurs when several distributors of similar goods compete to provide those goods to the same buyers. More generally, it refers to any competitive or seemingly competitive activity among entities who are not superior to one another but are roughly equal in their legal ability and organizational authority.

*See also:* agreement, horizontal agreement; price, price fixing, horizontal price fixing.

**perfect competition**  Market equilibrium of revenues with costs and profits. Perfect competition is an economic term for the market when a number of firms are producing competing goods and the market for the goods is sufficient to consume them at a price that is equivalent to the costs and profits, or put another way in which marginal costs equal marginal revenues. No firm in a situation of perfect competition may set the price of its goods. The closer a market is to having perfect competition, the better is that market. The term is popular among scholars of anti-trust, but as of 2011, it is not commonly used by the courts.

**complaint**  The pleading that commences a civil action. A complaint is the first pleading in most civil suits. The complaint is filed by the plaintiff, or by any party raising a claim for which a remedy is sought from the court. The complaint must allege the court's jurisdiction over the plaintiff's claim, in most jurisdictions allege sufficient facts to put the defendant on notice of the allegations of fact and claims of law and equity that are being brought, and ask for the relief the plaintiff seeks. There are civil suits that commence with other pleadings, although these pleadings are usually contingent on a complaint being filed. Actions in equity may commence with a petition, and actions in admiralty with a libel.

*See also:* plaint; trial, bifurcated trial (bifurcation or bifurcate or bifurcated); relief, prayer for relief.

**criminal complaint**  A judicial order charging a suspect with specific crimes. A criminal complaint is a court-issued document charging an individual with the commission of a crime or crimes. Procedures vary among jurisdictions, and while an application for a complaint is usually presented to the court, it is often presented to the prosecutor in the first instance, who determines whether to present it to the court. Complaints are usually initiated by an application for a complaint, along with an affidavit by the complainant, sometimes titled an affidavit of probable cause. The judge reviews the statements made in the application and affidavit, sometimes in a hearing with notice to the defendant. In all cases if the judge is satisfied there is sufficient probable cause that the person named in the complaint has committed the specified crimes, the judge will sign and issue the complaint. In some jurisdictions, the complaint amounts to an arrest warrant; in others the judge will issue a compatible warrant. There are varying usages, and in some jurisdictions, the complaint is consolidated with its application. Standing to file an application for a complaint is usually limited by statute to a prosecutor, police officer, victim, or person who witnesses the criminal activity. The affidavit accompanying the petition must disclose the basis of the knowledge of the affiant.

**cross-complaint (cross action)** A new cause filed by the defendant against the plaintiff or a third party in an ongoing case. A cross complaint is filed by a defendant in an ongoing civil action, alleging a distinct and independent cause of action against either the plaintiff or a third party. A proper cross-complaint creates two simultaneous actions pending in the same court between the same parties, in the latter of which the defendant in the original action becomes the plaintiff who must allege facts in the cross complaint that are sufficient to maintain the action and seek a specified remedy.

**verified complaint** A complaint alleging facts that are attested to be true. A verified complaint is a complaint, counterclaim, or other pleading raising a claim in a civil cause of action, to which the plaintiff or claimant party has attached or incorporated a statement specifically attesting to the truth of the allegations of fact made in the complaint, and the party has signed the statement under oath or similar affirmation, subject both to sanction under the rules of court and the law of perjury. A verified complaint is a specific requirement for certain causes of action. In most jurisdictions, an attorney may verify a complaint as the agent of the party, although in some instances, only the party's verification is sufficient, and in others both the party and the attorney must verify the complaint.

*See also:* verification (verify).

**well-pleaded complaint** The jurisdiction of a cause is ascertained from the statements of the complaint. The well-pleaded complaint if not a different form of a complaint but a doctrine for the evaluation of jurisdiction to determine whether the facts alleged are sufficient to sustain the jurisdiction of the court in which the complaint is filed. Thus, in federal court, a complaint filed in its diversity jurisdiction must be sufficient to ascertain the sufficiency of the claim and diversity of the parties, and a complaint filed in its federal-question jurisdiction must be sufficient to ascertain the nature of the question and the federal doctrines under which it arises.

## completeness (complete or completely)

**complete diversity** *See:* jurisdiction, diversity jurisdiction, complete diversity.

**completed gift** *See:* gift, completed gift.

**completely integrated contract** *See:* contract, contract interpretation, integrated contract (completely integrated contract).

**compliance (comply)** Conformity to the requirements of the law. Compliance is the sum of behavior of a person or entity that conforms to all of the requirements of the laws for all behavior by that person or entity. Compliance is a broader concept than obedience, in that obedience is knowing acquiescence to the law. Compliance includes both knowing obedience and performance of the acts that are legally required without regard to their requirement under the law. Even so, compliance, particularly with a scheme of regulation, usually requires knowing the specific regulation of the law and deliberate steps to conform behavior to the legal requirements. In some industries, compliance requires oversight over so many regulated activities that perfect compliance is rarely attained, creating inherent regulatory risk and corporate liability.

*See also:* observance (observe as of a duty).

**compliance monitoring** Ongoing self-audit of performance compared to regulatory requirements. Compliance monitoring is a system of audits performed regularly by a regulated enterprise to ensure compliance with laws and regulations. Federal and state agencies are rarely funded sufficiently to enforce fully many of the regulations and laws for which they have enforcement responsibility, and so such agencies usually rely on the regulated enterprise to collect and maintain records of behavior to assess compliance after the fact. The agencies also provide incentives, primarily reduced penalties, for self-reported incidents of non-compliance.

**substantial compliance** Conformity with essential if not all requirements. Substantial compliance is, like substantial performance, the performance with the essential lawful obligations in some regard. In contracts, substantial compliance is the same as substantial performance. In pleading and the performance of a court order, substantial compliance is compliance with the essential elements of the rule or order, which may or may not be sufficient compliance to excuse any other neglect. As to matters of regulation, substantial compliance may be sufficient to avoid fines for deliberate or intentional neglect or violation.

*See also:* performance, substantial performance.

**composite work** *See:* work, copyrightable work, composite work.

**compounding (compound)** Creating using multiple parts, increasing by external additions. Compounding is the act of adding something or combining something. In law, it is often used to describe the cumulation of crimes from different aspects of a single action. For instance, a convicted felon in possession of a firearm who robs a bank, particularly in adding offense to offense in a series of actions that violate the criminal law, each step then compounding the offense. In this sense the offer of an accused felon to buy off the felon's accuser is a form of compounding the offense. From this early understanding of compounding an offense has come the idea of compound criminal offense.

Compound, as an adjective, usually means consisting of many parts, or added onto itself. Compound, as a noun, is the result of such an activity. It usually refers to a combination of materials forming an aggregate, as in a chemical compound or several buildings arranged to form a single complex. There are many terms, such as compound interest, in which the term represents both the act and the result of compounding.

*See also:* interest, interest for money, compound interest.

**compound a felony or compounding an offense** *See:* compounding, compounding an offense (compound a felony or compounding an offense).

**compound interest** *See:* interest, interest for money, compound interest.

**compounding an offense (compound a felony or compounding an offense)** A private settlement of a criminal action. Compounding an offense is the crime of a private settlement of a criminal prosecution by the victim. The victim who accepts money on behalf of the accused or otherwise agrees not to assist in a prosecution for any personal benefit commits a crime by doing so. A person who accepts such a deal may be convicted of compounding, whether the state ultimately prosecutes the original accused or not. Compounding at common law was a misdemeanor, but it is now punished under most state statutes as a felony.
*See also:* collusion (collude or collusive).

**Comprehensive Environmental Response Compensation and Liability Act or C.E.R.C.L.A. or CERCLA** *See:* pollution, superfund (Comprehensive Environmental Response Compensation and Liability Act or C.E.R.C.L.A. or CERCLA).

**compromis (abstract compromis or ad hoc compromis or anticipated compromis or general compromis)** Agreement, particularly the agreed statement of a dispute in arbitration. Compromis is a French term for an agreement, particularly an agreement to participate in an arbitration. A compromis prepared for one dispute or issue is an ad hoc compromis, but a compromis prepared in anticipation of the arbitration of a class of issues or body of claims is an abstract compromis, general compromis, or anticipated compromis.

Compromis is used routinely to label the agreed statement of facts and legal issues that are presented for arbitration by the parties, whether to an arbitral panel or to certain international tribunals, such as the International Court of Justice. Compromis is therefore the label used to state the case presented to the advocates in the Jessup International Moot Court.

**compromise** Settlement of a dispute by all parties yielding their claims. A compromise is an agreement by which an argument, dispute, or disagreement is resolved as a result of the opposing parties each moderating their claims in return for the moderation of their opponents. Compromise is particularly important in the settlement of a lawsuit, in which the litigants agree to terms sufficient for all to agree to satisfy pending claims, vacate an action, or to close an action through an agreed settlement. Many more claims and liabilities are settled by compromise without litigation. In most instances, the essence of compromise is that both sides receive less than the whole benefit they might receive in litigation or dispute, but surrender that part which is lost in return for certainty of an outcome and for a speedier resolution, as well, perhaps, for a more amicable settlement than

might result from the determined pursuit of the full claim.

**compromise verdict** *See:* verdict, compromise verdict (jury pardon or jury mercy).

**offer of compromise** An offer to compromise a claim or settle a case. An offer of compromise is an offer made to settle a pending claim or legal action. It includes an offer of anything of value — including the surrender or reduction of a claim, payments of money or transfers of property or of rights — presented by one side to another in a dispute, whether it has been filed or not, as an inducement to settle the claims related to it. In a criminal action or criminal investigation, an offer of a plea may be considered an offer of compromise.

**comptroller** Financial officer responsible for audits. A comptroller is a financial officer within an organization, who is particularly responsible for controlling accounts and monitoring expenditures essentially maintaining an ongoing audit of the organization. The position sometimes held by the chief accountant in the organization, has a narrower scope of office than that normally associated with the Chief Financial Officer or Treasurer, positions to which a comptroller is likely to report.

**compulsion (compel or compulsory)** Forcible inducement to action. Compulsion is the inducement of a person or entity to act through coercive means that effectively reduce the choices available to the person or entity to a choice to act as compelled or to face a negative consequence. Coercion by lawful authority to compel a person to carry out an obligation does not void that obligation, but other forms of personal compulsion that lead to private conduct may make that conduct voidable. Compulsion may result from acts of nature, such as a vessel's compelled entry to port during a storm, a form of compulsion that is excused under the doctrine of force majeure.
*See also:* claim, counterclaim, compulsory counterclaim; claim, counterclaim, compulsory counterclaim | failure to plead; association, freedom of association | 3. compulsory disclosure; insurance, compulsory insurance; joinder, joinder of parties, compulsory joinder; dismissal, nonsuit, compulsory nonsuit.

**compulsory counterclaim** *See:* claim, counterclaim, compulsory counterclaim | failure to plead; claim, counterclaim, compulsory counterclaim.

**compulsory insurance** *See:* insurance, compulsory insurance.

**compulsory joinder** *See:* joinder, joinder of parties, compulsory joinder, feasibility; joinder, joinder of parties, compulsory joinder.

**compulsory joinder rule** *See:* joinder of offenses, compulsory joinder rule (compulsory joinder statute or compulsory joinder of offenses).

**compulsory nonsuit** *See:* dismissal, nonsuit, compulsory nonsuit.

**Compulsory Process Clause** *See:* constitution, U.S. Constitution, clauses, Compulsory Process Clause.

**compurgation (compurgator)** The purging of an accusation through combat or oath. Compurgation was a medieval form of defending oneself against criminal charges, either through wager of battle or through the taking of oaths supported by oath-helpers, or compurgators. Both forms of proof are now obsolete.
*See also:* trial, trial by battle (battle or judicial duel or trial by combat or wager of battle); oath.

**computer**

**computer-assisted legal instruction** *See:* law, law school, legal pedagogy, computer-assisted legal instruction (C.A.L.I. or CALI).

**computer-assisted legal research** *See:* research, legal research, computer-assisted legal research (C.A.L.R. or CALR).

**computer crime** Crime in which a computer is a tool or venue of criminal conduct. Computer crime is a growing category of offense, in which a criminal act, usually analogous to theft, fraud, trespass, or vandalism, is committed with the aid of a computer. In particular, such crimes include unauthorized access to a computer system, or hacking, as well as phishing, the fraudulent acquisition of information through electronic mail.

**Comstock law** *See:* obscenity, Comstock law.

**concealment (conceal)** The suppression, disguise, or misrepresentation of a fact. Concealment is any action or inaction that prevents another person from the knowledge of a given fact. Concealment may be subtle, as Blackstone suggested, being no more than the employment of speech or actions naturally calculated to lull the suspicions of a careful person, inducing the person to forego additional inquiry into a matter upon which the other party has information. The legal significance of concealment varies according to context. Concealment may be a crime in itself, or it may be an element of a fraudulent act or transaction, or it may give rise to a voidable contract or an equitable claim related to knowing concealment of latent defects in property. Yet not all concealment is actionable. When there is no duty to provide information, particularly when one party to a contract or sale has no information not readily available to the other, or there is no legal duty to disclose defects, and the party knows of no latent defects, or the information concealed is of no public value, concealment may give rise to neither civil nor criminal liability.
*See also:* latency (latent); patency (patent).

**concealed weapon** *See:* weapon, concealed weapon.

**fraudulent concealment** Harm caused by concealment of a fact that one has a duty to disclose. Fraudulent concealment is a tort that may be brought by a person or entity to whom the defendant owes a duty of disclosure of all material facts, which the defendant does not disclose, because the defendant intends to deceive or defraud the plaintiff through the concealment, and following the concealment the plaintiff takes some action in justifiable reliance on the information then available, including the information or lack of information provided by the defendant, as a result of which the plaintiff suffers damages. The degree to which the concealed information is a sole cause of the plaintiff's action is the subject of some mild debate, but the essential question is whether the plaintiff would not have done what was done, or would have acted differently, had the defendant not engaged in concealment.

**concentrated animal feed operation** *See:* farm, concentrated animal feed operation (C.A.F.O. or CAFO).

**conceptual analysis** *See:* analysis, conceptual analysis.

**concern**

**public concern** Matter of rational interest to the public. Public concern is a standard for evaluating the content of speech, by assessing whether the speech raises a matter of significance not to the speaker alone but to the public at large in a matter that appears to the speaker to require investigation or reform.
*See also:* public.

**touch and concern** Having an effect on land and its use. Touch and concern is a measure of the relationship of a covenant or easement to the servient tenement, or the land burdened by the interest created or recognized in the covenant or easement. The interest touches and concerns the land if the interest alters what would otherwise be the legal or equitable abilities of any of the parties to use the land in issue.

**concert-of-action rule** *See:* conspiracy, concert-of-action rule (Wharton's rule).

**conciliation (conciliatory)** Process of informal investigation and resolution of a dispute. In general, conciliation is a process by which one party gains the good will and trust of the other. As a matter of alternative dispute resolution, it is a process of engagement between aggrieved parties including investigation of the issues raised in a dispute and negotiations intended to resolve the dispute that arose from them, the process is often facilitated, and the conciliator is more of an investigator than would be an arbitrator or mediator. Conciliation is more often used in employment, labor, and family law contexts than in others, though it is a useful means of alternative dispute resolution generally.
*See also:* alternative dispute resolution (A.D.R. or ADR).

**conciliation agreement** An out-of-court settlement between a wronged employee, the employer, and the

EEOC. A conciliation agreement is a settlement to an employment discrimination complaint reached out of court among the employee, the employer, and the Equal Employment Opportunity Commission.

**conclusion**   The end of an argument or process. A conclusion is an end. In a properly made logical argument, a conclusion from a given proposition being proved is a statement that inevitably follows and is not subject to further debate. Thus a conclusion is sometimes a fact that cannot be denied owing to the record or admission of another fact. A conclusion is also the end of a process or inquiry, following which further action is foreclosed.

*See also:* estoppel (estop or estopped).

**conclusion of law**   *See:* ruling, conclusion of law (legal conclusion).

**conclusion rule application conclusion or conclusion rule analysis conclusion or C.R.A.C.**   *See:* argument, legal argument, CRAC (conclusion rule application conclusion or conclusion rule analysis conclusion or C.R.A.C.).

**conclusive presumption**   *See:* presumption, rebuttable presumption, irrebuttable presumption (conclusive presumption).

**conclusory**   A conclusion drawn from insufficient evidence. A conclusory statement is an unproven statement, a claim that is not sufficiently derived from the available evidence of the facts or the law.

**concomitance (concomitant or concomitantly)** A necessary relatedness. Concomitance is a relationship between two things that are related in such a manner that one makes necessary the other or gives it definition. Something concomitant with something else is closely related to it, one being a likely or a necessary outcome or aspect of the other. Thus a cause and an effect are concomitant of one another, as are two close associates, like Mutt and Jeff.

**concurrence (concurrent or concurring)**   Simultaneity and compatibility. Concurrence is an attribute of one thing with another that requires them to fit together and occur at the same time. In this sense, concurrence includes two vessels running alongside one another on concurrent courses, two jurisdictions that exercise concurrent jurisdiction over the same event, two houses of a legislature agreeing over one bill, or two judges who concur in one and other's opinion. In each case, the enterprises are separate and distinct but their operations occur without interference. This separateness, however, may be constructive rather than practical, as two penal sentences served concurrently are served at the same time by the same person in the same place.

**concurrent causes**   *See:* causation, concurrent causes.

**concurrent conditions**   *See:* condition, concurrent conditions (mutual conditions).

**concurrent covenant**   *See:* covenant, concurrent covenant.

**concurrent jurisdiction**   *See:* jurisdiction, concurrent jurisdiction.

**concurrent ownership**   *See:* ownership, concurrent ownership, ownership in indivision; ownership, concurrent ownership (co-owner or co-tenant).

**concurrent power**   *See:* power, concurrent power.

**concurrent representation or multiple representation**
*See:* representation, legal representation, joint representation (concurrent representation or multiple representation).

**condemnation (condemn)**   A final, authoritative declaration that someone or something is unfit. Condemnation is both the process of accusation and the ruling issued upon someone or something as wrongful, unfit, or corrupt. To condemn thus means both to accuse and to sentence a person for some crime or offense. To condemn a building or other thing is to declare it unfit for use.

Note: condemnation of a person is sometimes confused with an order of death, owing to the use of the longer phrase, condemned to die, but condemnation is the term by which any sentence is imposed. Though the term is usually employed only for severe sentences, it is not only a sentence of death.

*See also:* taking, regulatory taking (inverse condemnation or regulatory takings); escheat.

**condemnation as censure**   Stern rebuke or criticism, usually in a public manner. Condemnation is a form of punishment through public criticism, particularly from an authority or group of which the person or entity condemned is a member. The intent is not only to create shame in the person condemned but also to harm the person's standing in the eyes of other members and the public at large.

**condemnation as conviction**   The act of finding one guilty of criminal offense. A condemnation is a conviction for which a person shall be punished. Condemnation does not, as a matter of legal usage, suggest by itself that a person has been condemned to suffer death, although the term has acquired this loose meaning in popular culture.

**condemnation of a hazardous structure**   Declaration of unfitness. A condemnation order is a designation that a structure is dangerous and should be evacuated until it is repaired or destroyed. Procedures for the condemnation of buildings vary among jurisdictions, and some orders authorize the municipality or other jurisdiction that seeks or issues the order to destroy the building. A condemnation required owing to the hazards of a structure or its risk to health and safety differs from condemnation when a government takes title for a public use, and no compensation to the property owner is required. Even so, unless an emergency requires immediate action to protect the lives or property of others, a condemnation order issued without satisfying the notice requirements of due process of law is constitutionally infirm.

**condemnation through eminent domain** A forced acquisition of real property through a government power. Condemnation is the procedure for taking title to property through eminent domain. Condemned property is transferred to the state, which must give just compensation to the owner in return.

**quick condemnation (quick-take proceeding)** Condemnation by payment prior to a hearing. A quick condemnation is a proceeding allowed by statute in some jurisdictions and to the federal government, in which the condemnor can acquire property it reasonably determines is needed before the completion of formal condemnation proceedings. A quick condemnation results in payment by the condemnor of the valuation of the property pending the actual valuation award by the court.

**condemnee** The owner whose property interest is condemned. The condemnee is the party whose property is acquired by the condemnor. There may be several condemnees for a single property, as all interests owned in the property, including rights of way, servitudes, covenants, co-tenancies, and future interests must be condemned.

**condemnor** The entity that seeks property through condemnation. A condemnor may be the government of the United States, the government of a state, a subdivision of a state, or a public entity, such as a utility, on which a state has delegated the power of eminent domain for certain purposes.

**condition (unconditional or conditional or defeasance)** An action or event that is a prerequisite to a legal action. A condition is any requirement that must be met or not met in order for the legal action or obligation that is modified by the condition to commence or to end. A condition may be written either as a condition precedent, structured so that it must be satisfied for an action to commence or continue, or as a condition subsequent, structured so that if the condition is satisfied, the action ends or is void. It is not a requirement that a condition depend on actions or events in the future, and conditions depending on the continued performance of a duty or existence of a condition are enforceable. Conditions are used in innumerable ways to structure relationships in contracts, wills, trusts, or other instruments or relationships.

A condition in a contract may be written so that it must be satisfied for the contract to come into force, or it may be a requirement by a party to determine what amounts to full performance. Frequently the performance of one party is subject to conditions precedent, sometimes including conditions beyond the control of either party and sometimes including conditions under the control of the other party.

An estate may be subject to condition either in its vesting or in its retention. A condition may be used in a will to determine which of several devisees will take, or in a trust to determine when the trust will be dissolved. Conditions may amount to terms, as in a lease in which an at-will tenancy may be conditioned on the performance of certain services by the tenant or by the landlord.

The same condition may be drafted in a variety of logical forms: affirmative (if X occurs) or negative (if the logical opposite of X fails); continuous (as long as X continues) or initial (if X occurs) or terminal (if ever X fails).

Any offer, claim, agreement, or other statement that lacks an express or implied condition is unconditional, and to state that an offer is unconditional is generally to disclaim any implied conditions. Even so, warranties and conditions implied by law may not be disclaimed by a general statement of unconditionality but must usually be specifically disclaimed.

*See also:* acceptance, acceptance as acceptance of an offer, conditional acceptance; admissibility, conditional admissibility; covenant, conditional covenant; delivery, delivery of possession, conditional delivery; devise, conditional devise; gift, conditional gift; intent, conditional intent; legacy, conditional legacy (contingent legacy); limitation, conditional limitation; privilege, conditional privilege; promise, conditional promise; purpose, conditional purpose; release, custodial release, conditional release; taking, regulatory taking, conditional use; zoning, conditional zoning.

**conditional acceptance** *See:* acceptance, acceptance as acceptance of an offer, conditional acceptance.

**conditional admissibility** *See:* admissibility, conditional admissibility.

**conditional covenant** *See:* covenant, conditional covenant.

**conditional delivery** *See:* delivery, delivery of possession, conditional delivery.

**conditional devise** *See:* devise, conditional devise.

**conditional gift** *See:* gift, conditional gift.

**conditional intent** *See:* intent, conditional intent.

**conditional legacy** *See:* legacy, conditional legacy (contingent legacy).

**conditional limitation** *See:* limitation, conditional limitation.

**conditional plea** *See:* plea, criminal plea, conditional plea.

**conditional privilege** *See:* privilege, conditional privilege.

**conditional promise** *See:* promise, conditional promise.

**conditional purpose** *See:* purpose, conditional purpose.

**conditional release** *See:* release, custodial release, conditional release.

**conditional signature** *See:* signature, conditional signature.

**conditional use**   *See:* use, use of property, conditional use; taking, regulatory taking, conditional use.

**conditional use permit or special permit zoning or special use permit**   *See:* zoning, special use zoning (conditional use permit or special permit zoning or special use permit).

**conditional zoning**   *See:* zoning, conditional zoning, incentive zoning; zoning, conditional zoning.

**conditions of sale**   *See:* sale, conditions of sale.

**condition as status**   One's state of mind and body, or social and economic standing. A person's condition may mean a variety of attributes. In the common law, condition meant the particular class and marital status of an individual, as well as the broader notion of one's economic and social opportunities, though this use is less common. More commonly today, it reflects a person's state of mind and body, such as being injured, exhausted, drunk, or alert. Thus a person in critical condition is badly injured or gravely ill, while a person in top condition is particularly fit.
   *See also:* status.

**concurrent conditions (mutual conditions)**   Conditions that must be satisfied more or less simultaneously. Concurrent conditions are conditions that must be performed or satisfied at or near the same time. This is particularly true when each party to a contract has obligations that are mutually dependent, that is the performance by each is a condition that must be satisfied in order to require the performance of the other.
   *See also:* mutuality (mutual); obligation, mutuality of obligation; concurrence (concurrent or concurring).

**condition precedent**   A condition that must occur prior to the ripening of an interest, right, or claim. A condition precedent is any event upon which a right, claim or other legal or equitable interest depends. Most commonly, a condition precedent is an event at which the vesting of a property interest occurs. If the condition never occurs (or does not occur before a specified time), the condition fails, and the property interest does not vest. Most conditions are conditions precedent. The rarer forms of condition are the condition subsequent, which occurs after an event to terminate a right, claim, or interest, or contemporary conditions, which occur simultaneously. When no time is specified, context will usually determine which among the three is intended, but a "condition" may be presumed to be a condition precedent.

**condition subsequent (subsequent condition)**   A condition that may occur following the vesting of an interest, right, or claim to alter or destroy it. A condition subsequent is any event upon which a right, claim, or other legal or equitable interest may be altered after it has come into being or vested. Most commonly, a condition subsequent is an event at which a vested property interest is destroyed or transferred. If the condition never occurs (or does not occur before a specified time), the condition

fails, and the property interest continues to vest in holder. Because most conditions are conditions precedent, unless context makes clear that a condition is a condition subsequent, the term "condition" alone may be presumed to be a condition precedent rather than a condition subsequent.
   *See also:* fee, estate in fee, fee simple subject to condition subsequent (F.S.S.C.S. or FSSCS).

**constructive condition**   A condition implied in an instrument by law or equity. An instrument may have a condition implied by judicial construction, particularly when the logical or fair application of the instrument would imply such a condition.

**express condition**   A condition expressly stated in a contract or other instrument. An express condition is a statement that applies to a contract, will, or other instrument and is expressly stated either in writing for a written instrument or in discussion between the parties in an oral agreement. That is, an express condition is an element of the contract or instrument that clearly manifests the will of the maker or makers, and it is not implied or construed. An express condition is usually strictly enforced, and thus, if it is ambiguous, it is treated as a constructive condition. In many jurisdictions, the rule of strict enforcement of express conditions is limited further to apply only when the condition is material.
   *See also:* expression (explicit or express).

**failure of condition**   The failure of an event to occur that is a condition upon a right or obligation. Failure of condition describes any circumstance in which a condition must be satisfied before an obligation is created or must be exercised. The most common failure of condition in contracts is the failure of one party to perform its promise under the contract, which is a condition precedent to the other party's performance. Failure of condition in a lease, deed, will, gift, or other grant is the non-occurrence of an event by a specified time (or, depending on how the clause is drafted, by the occurence of an event or a non-event) according to which a property interest is created, terminated, or transferred.
   *See also:* failure (fail).

**implied condition**   Requirement not expressly stated but obviously intended by the parties. An implied condition is a condition not expressed in an agreement or instrument but inferred later from the circumstances at the time the instrument or agreement was created or from default rules. Thus, under the UCC, price, delivery, quality, indeed every term but quantity may be implied in a contract. At its broadest, the meaning of implied condition includes constructive condition, which would otherwise be a condition created through the interpretation of express conditions or through the operation of law.

**negative condition**   Requirement that a party refrain from some conduct. A negative condition is a condition dependent upon the stated event or action not taking place. If the event or action occurs, the condition fails.

**supervening condition (supervene)**   An event beyond the control of the parties. A supervening condition is an event or occurrence that cannot be caused or prevented by the parties to a contract, but its occurrence may alter the parties' obligations none the less. Storms, disasters, wars, acts of the government, and other forms of force majeure are supervening conditions.

## condominium

**condominium as jurisdiction (condominia)**   A territory subject to more than one power or jurisdiction. A condominium is any territory that is subject to the authority of more than one sovereign. This arrangement is typically a solution to problems of demarcation or management of a frontier and was once a means of colonial administration. The term is a corruption of co–dominium.

*See also:* dominium.

**condominium as property (condo or condos)**   A single unit of ownership within a larger property. A condominium is an arrangement of ownership of a building or other property development, which is divided into physically distinct units within the larger whole, so that each owner holds one or more units as a separate owner. A building of units that might otherwise be leased that is arranged so the units may be sold is a condominium, as is each unit that is sold.

In some jurisdictions, a condominium implies no more ownership of the building than ownership of the unit, although the condominium ownership is usually contingent upon a maintenance fee for the building as a whole. In other jurisdictions, the ownership of a condominium also implies co-ownership in all common property in the larger building or development, an arrangement that is also called a cooperative or coop. Statutory names aside, a condominium may be owned within a building that is either wholly owned by a building owner or that is wholly owned by a cooperative. Note: in Latin, the plural is condominia, but condominium has passed into English, and condominiums is more commonly used.

*See also:* cooperative, residential cooperative (co-operative tenancy or co-operative ownership or coop or co-op).

## confederacy

**confederacy as among states**   An alliance. A confederacy is both an agreement and the group of states that enter the agreement forming an alliance. The term was applied historically to compacts among U.S. states, although it may still describe agreements among nation-states.

**confederacy as conspiracy**   A conspiracy. A confederacy is a conspiracy, which is the sense in which a criminal confederate acts as an accomplice or conspirator.

*See also:* conspiracy (conspire).

**confederation (federation)**   A federal state, or an association of entities. A confederation is a government created from a group of formerly autonomous governments. There is no essential difference between a federation and a confederation, although there is a slight sense of greater integration of the parts into the whole in the use of confederation. The Confederate States of America chose this noun to emphasize the difference between its view of the federal relationship and that of the United States of America.

*See also:* e, e pluribus unum; federation.

**confer**   *See:* citation, citation signal, confer (cf.).

**confession**   A person's voluntary declaration of the commission of a criminal act. A confession is a statement of one's own wrong doing. In the context of criminal law, it is a statement by a person who has committed acts that amount to a crime, made to another person and describing or acknowledging the acts that were done. A confession is inherently limited to a statement of facts and to personal conduct; the legal implications of this conduct are an element of a plea. For a confession to be admitted into evidence or otherwise be the basis or an action in a criminal cause, it must be made only by a person with the capacity to take such a grave responsibility. A confession of a given act may be express, or it may be implied, the implied confession being made in statements or actions regarding other acts or events from which the implication may be properly drawn. It must be made knowingly and voluntarily, and it must be truthful, although its truth may be presumed as long as the confession is obtained without improper influence or persuasion or without any extraneous cause to doubt its veracity, and of course, the presumed truth of a confession is rebutted by facts known or established to the contrary. Still, there is an ever-present danger of false confession, and it is the responsibility of the defendant's counsel, the prosecution, the police, and the court to ensure that a false confession is not presented to the court as evidence.

*cat-out-of-the-bag theory*   The effect of having once confessed. A person who confesses under circumstances in which the confession is inadmissible or otherwise unusable is under a continuing mental burden as a result of that confession despite its disutility by the police. Knowing that others know of the confession, the person who confessed is under greater pressure to do so again.

**confession of judgment**   *See:* judgment, confession of judgment.

**Bruton error (Arranda-Bruton error or Bruton rule)**   Mistaken allowance of a co-defendant's extrajudicial confession to implicate the non-confessing co-defendant. The Bruton error is a violation of the Bruton rule: the extrajudicial confession of one co-defendant may not be admitted in a joint trial. The allowance of such a confession so that it implicates the non-confessing co-defendant is a Bruton error, because it denies the non-confessing defendant the right to cross-examine the confessing defendant. The error may be harmless, if a sufficient curative action may be taken or if there is otherwise ample evidence against a defendant to convict.

**coerced confession (involuntary confession)** Admission of guilt made following coercive treatment. A coerced confession is a confession to criminal conduct that is made following a period of treatment in which the person confessing had been coerced, by conditions of confinement or treatment, by the use or threat of physical violence, or with illegal threats toward others than the person confessing, such as a family member. Coerced confessions are inherently inadmissible in a court of law. Further, the conduct that coerces such confessions not only violates the Due Process Clause of the Constitution but is likely a criminal act in itself.

**confession and avoidance** Admitting a factual premise but denying the legal conclusion asserted. Confession and avoidance is a plea that admits the facts asserted as true but submits either new facts or a difference of legal argument. Confession and avoidance underlies both affirmative defenses and motions for summary judgment, in which the facts are not challenged but the legal significance of the facts offered by the non-movant is rejected.
*See also:* avoidance (avoid or avoidable).

**corpus delicti rule (corroboration rule)** A confession must be corroborated with independent evidence. The corpus delicti rule, also called the corroboration rule, requires the state to produce evidence to corroborate a defendant's confession or statement of responsibility for a crime, sufficient to demonstrate to the reasonable satisfaction of the court that the crime occurred and was committed by the defendant. The requirement is a common-law requirement that may be refined by statute.
*See also:* death.

**naked confession** Confession unaccompanied by any incriminating or corroborating evidence. A naked confession is not corroborated by independent proof that the statements made in the confession are true. A naked confession made in a court of record may be the basis of the acceptance of a plea, although the judge accepting the plea must be confident of the voluntariness and truth of the confession. A naked confession made out of court must be verified by some evidence to serve as the basis of a plea.

**successive confession** A second confession to an action or crime already confessed. A successive confession is a confession made following an earlier confession, particularly when the first confession is inadmissible as evidence owing to a constitutional or procedural fault. A successive confession is sometimes sought as a cure for the fault, but the second confession may be no more admissible than the first, unless the constitutional or procedural flaw of the first is abated to an extent that the person confessing is in a position essentially similar to the position the person would be if the constitutional or procedural failure had not occurred.

*See also:* counselor, right to counsel; incrimination, self-incrimination (privilege against self-incrimination or right to silence).

**voluntary confession (voluntariness of a confession)** An uncoerced confession freely given. A voluntary confession is a person's incriminating statement that is made without any coercion (including prolonged detention), not made following any abuse or coercion or threat of abuse or coercion, made with the person's knowledge that the person is not required to make the statement, and made by someone of age and capacity to appreciate that such statements may have significance for the person's criminal liability. A confession must be voluntary to be admitted into evidence against a person in any criminal trial as a matter of due process of law, and in any federal trial as a matter of statute. Not all voluntary confessions are admissible. A confession by a person in custody that is given after an unreasonable delay in presenting the person before a judge is still inadmissible even if it is otherwise voluntary.

**Jackson-Denno hearing** A hearing to assess the voluntariness of a confession to a crime. A Jackson-Denno hearing is a hearing before the trial judge or magistrate with jurisdiction over a criminal cause, to determine if a confession by the defendant was freely and voluntarily given. Based on Jackson v. Denno, 378 U.S. 368 (1964), the hearing is not a federal requirement unless there is some reason known to the prosecution or entered on the record by the defense to challenge the confession's voluntariness, although such a hearing is required in many states when a confession is entered into evidence or into a court docket. The hearing usually requires a statement of the defendant and a colloquy between the defendant and the judge; it is often merged into a hearing on a motion to accept a plea.
*See also:* colloquy (colloquium or plea colloquy); voluntariness (voluntary or volunteer).

**confidence game** *See:* fraud, confidence game.

**confidentiality (confidential)** The maintenance of information in secrecy. Confidentiality is a condition of the management of information, by which individuals with access to the information are forbidden from allowing the information to become public, and so others who seek the information from them must be denied access to it. Confidentiality may be a designation of administrative law, military law or regulation, diplomatic regulation and custom, or a private matter that is recognized by the courts as a matter of public policy. Some forms of confidentiality are sufficiently significant as a matter of public policy that information that is confidential for these reasons is not discoverable or admissible in court for as long as the confidentiality is reasonably maintained.

An evidentiary privilege allows information protected as confidential to be immune from discovery or compelled disclosure. A privilege, however, requires that all information subject to a privilege be confidential both at the time the information was provided to the person in a position of trust and later. The dissemination of such information beyond the agents of the person in trust for the reasonable purposes for which it was provided destroys the confidence and so destroys the privilege.

*See also:* confidentiality, all–or–nothing rule; fides (fide).

**all-or-nothing rule**   Once confidentiality is waived it cannot be restored. The "all or nothing" rule of evidentiary privilege is a limit on the privilege such that any disclosure of confidential information, other than within the limits of in camera review or other uses within the scope of the privilege, waives the privilege, and the information once protected is no longer privileged from use. There are exceptions to this rule, most importantly in that material subject to confidentiality for reasons of public policy or security is not necessarily subject to wider dissemination owing to a single breach. The all–or–nothing rule in prison censorship is quite distinct and does not apply to the evidentiary privilege.

**confinement after acquittal on grounds of insanity**   *See:* detention, preventive detention (confinement after acquittal on grounds of insanity).

**confirmation of contract**   *See:* contract, confirmation of contract, written confirmation of oral agreement; contract, confirmation of contract.

**confirmation of the charters**   *See:* constitution, English constitution, confirmation of the charters (confirmatio chartorum).

**confiscation (confiscate)**   The seizure of forfeit goods by an agent of the government. Confiscation is the action of a government, through its officials, taking possession of property that is held by an individual in violation of the law. The property may be confiscated because it is contraband, owing to its illegality per se, such as child pornography, or illegality under the circumstances, such as moneys not allowed to be held by prisoners or controlled substances not permitted to be held by someone without a proper permit. Property may be confiscated though legal in itself but seized as a matter of public policy, as when property is taken for payment of taxes owed or as a matter of condemnation. In general, in the United States, the confiscation is used to describe state and federal action only over contraband, and forfeiture or condemnation is used for other forms of seizure; condemnation is, however, used to describe the taking of private property for a public use or for its value to the treasury, even when the private owner is not paid proper compensation.

*See also:* seizure (seize); forfeiture.

**conflict**   A disagreement or opposition between ideas, individuals, or entities. A conflict is a fight, any situation in which people find themselves in opposition to one another or in a situation in which two ideas or entities are at odds. Conflict does not, by definition require resolution in a given manner. Conflict may result in a continuing tension, in a resolution in favor of one side of the dispute or another, or in a reconciliation or compromise. A conflict among jurisdictions, for instance may result in the courts of one jurisdiction hearing a cause, in both accepting concurrent jurisdiction, or in neither hearing the cause.

**conflict of laws**   *See:* law, conflict of laws.

**conflict of interest**   Any division of loyalties owed to different entities by the same person or firm. A conflict of interest arises when one person, firm, or other entity owes a duty of loyalty to two different entities whose interests may require different decisions or actions. A public official may have a conflict of interest by having employment or property that is regulated by an entity or office in which the official has influence. A corporate officer or employee may have a conflict of interest owing to a relationship with a corporation that competes, supplies, or purchases from that corporation. An attorney may have a conflict of interests owing to the representation of two clients whose legal requirements require direct opposition, conflicting arguments, or even conflicting advice, or an attorney may have a conflict when a client's interest vary from the attorney's own financial or legal interests. Genuine adversity of interests is not required to create a conflict of interest, as mere inference that the representation of a client's interest is in conflict is sufficient. A conflict of interest may be tolerated in many but not all circumstances among attorneys, when it is disclosed to the parties involved, its implications are known to those parties, and the parties knowingly and intentionally agree to the representation none the less. In most fiduciary relationships and public offices, no conflict of interest is allowed.

*See also:* fiduciary, fiduciary duty, duty to avoid conflicts of interest; ethics, legal ethics | 2. conflict of interest; representation, legal representation, joint representation (concurrent representation or multiple representation); interest; representation, legal representation, successive representation.

**Chinese Wall (ethical wall)**   A barrier between those entitled to possess information and those forbidden to use it. A Chinese Wall is a protocol that prevents a person or group who is barred from using certain information from communicating with those in the same or a related organization who have that information. In a law firm, a Chinese Wall may be a policy that precludes an attorney in the firm who has a conflict of interest with a client from participating in any matter or receiving any information regarding that client; such resolutions of a potential or actual conflict must be disclosed and accepted by both affected clients, but they are still perilous.

*See also:* wall.

**conflict out**   Withdrawing as counsel to one party owing to a conflict of interest. To be conflicted out is to opt out of the representation of one client owing to a conflict of interest arising from the present or past representation of a party with a conflicting position or claim. The presumption in such situations is that counsel should decline to represent the later client and continue to represent the earlier.

**Garcia hearing**  A hearing on a criminal defense attorney's conflict of interest. A Garcia hearing is a judicial evaluation of the extent of an attorney's conflicts of interest in representing a criminal defendant, including a determination of whether the defendant knowingly and freely waived any conflicts that are found to exist. See United States v. Garcia, 517 F.2d 272, 277 (5th Cir. 1975) (Gewin, J.).

**representation of multiple parties**  *See:* representation, legal representation, joint representation (concurrent representation or multiple representation); representation, legal representation, successive representation.

**self-dealing (self dealing)**  The use of a fiduciary position for one's own benefit. Self-dealing is a broad term including all acts by a person in an office of trust — including a government official, corporate officer or director, trustee, attorney, or other fiduciary — who uses that position of trust in a manner that benefits the officer rather than those for whom the office is intended to benefit. Self-dealing includes not only the appropriation of assets subject to the officer's control but also the use of the office's influence.

More narrowly, self-dealing describes a contract, sale, exchange, or lease between a non-profit corporation or trust and a person disqualified from engaging in such arrangements as too closely related to the corporation or trust. A non-profit corporation or trust that engages in self-dealing loses its tax exemption.

*See also:* conflict, conflict of interest.

**conflicts of laws (private international law)**  The rules of law to determine which jurisdiction's laws apply to a given matter. Conflicts of laws rules determine what law from among more than one possible jurisdiction applies in a given situation. The first question of conflicts analysis is to determine which jurisdiction is the appropriate forum in which to consider all other questions. Once a court has accepted jurisdiction, question raised and essential to resolve the action must be analyzed to divide the procedural questions of law from the substantive questions of law. The forum court then applies local rules for the choice of law to determine, if the rules vary, which jurisdiction's law governs each question before applying those rules to adjudicate the dispute. In general, the procedural questions of law are resolved according to the rules of law that apply in the jurisdiction of the forum court. The substantive questions are resolved according to the conflicts rules as they apply to the facts of that action and the pleadings and other legal actions taken already by the parties.

**conflicting presumptions**  *See:* presumption, conflicting presumptions (competing presumptions).

**confrontation**  Challenge to opposing evidence and witnesses. Confrontation is the constitutional right of a person accused of a crime to be present to see and cross-examine adverse witnesses and to challenge evidence against the accused's case. The right of direct confrontation with an adverse witness is not now thought to be unlimited, but it can only be overcome when other means of ensuring the testimony would be sufficiently reliable are available or when the protection of the witness is of paramount importance and other means are available of testing the credibility of the witness. The purposes of confrontation are not only to benefit the accused but to serve justice by ensuring the reliability of evidence in criminal proceedings.

*See also:* witness; trial, fair trial (rights of criminal defendants).

**Confrontation Clause**  *See:* constitution, U.S. Constitution, clauses, Confrontation Clause.

**conglomerate**  *See:* corporation, corporations, conglomerate.

**Congress**  The legislative branch of the United States, or any other assembly. The Congress is the Senate and the House of Representatives, which together hold the legislative power of the United States. The word congress more generally means any assembly of persons, especially one held for political reasons, such as a political party congress, yet in the law of the United States, its meaning is more likely to be the United States legislature.

**congress as between individuals**  Sex. Congress is sometimes used to describe intercourse.

*See also:* sex, sexual act (sexual conduct or sex act).

**Congressional Emoluments Clause or Ineligibility Clause**  *See:* constitution, U.S. Constitution, clauses, Emoluments Clause (Congressional Emoluments Clause or Ineligibility Clause).

**congressional frank or frank privilege**  *See:* frank (congressional frank or frank privilege).

**congressional immunity**  *See:* immunity, official immunity, legislative immunity (congressional immunity).

**congressional preemption or express preemption or implied preemption**  *See:* preemption, constitutional preemption, federal preemption of state law (congressional preemption or express preemption or implied preemption).

**congressional reconciliation**  *See:* reconciliation, congressional reconciliation (reconciliation bill or reconciliation instruction or reconciliation process).

**congressional resolution**  *See:* resolution, congressional resolution, joint resolution; resolution, congressional resolution.

**Congressional Budget Office** An agency reporting to Congress to estimate federal revenues and budget costs. The Congressional Budget Office, or CBO, is an Article II agency answerable to Congress established in 1974 to provide members of Congress with non-partisan projections of the future revenues and costs of the federal government, particularly estimating the costs associated with spending approved by the budget or enacted into law through spending legislation.

**congressional district** The geographical region within one state from which a member of the House of Representatives is elected. A congressional district is a geographical region within a single state from which a Representative is elected. It also refers to the people living within that region, who elect its Representative. The legislature in each state is empowered to draw the boundaries for each district in its state, each of which make a good–faith effort to achieve the most nearly practicable equality of population among the districts in the state, although de minimis, unavoidable variations in population are allowed for limited purposes. Election district lines are subject to review, and challenge under the Voter Rights Act and Equal Protection Clause if they dilute the voting power of individuals in a racial minority.

**delegate** A non–voting territorial representative in the U.S. House of Representatives. A delegate in the U.S. House of Representatives is a member from a territory, with all of the powers of membership except of voting on legislation.

**Government Accountability Office (G.A.O. or GAO)** Congressional agency that monitors federal funds and government services. The Government Accountability Office is an Article II agency, answerable to Congress, that monitors and investigates the expenditures of money and the performance of statutory obligations by government offices and agencies. GAO reports are issued at the request of Congress, by public law mandate, and under the authority of the Comptroller General. The GAO was initially established in 1921 as the General Accounting Office, the name that persisted until it was renamed in 2004.

**Member of Congress (congressman or congress-woman or congressperson or M.C.)** A member of the House of Representatives, or the Senate. Member of Congress, when used generically in the United States, describes a member of either house of the Congress. When used as a title, however, it refers only to those in the House of Representatives. As a result, members of the House sometimes use the abbreviation "M.C." following their names as a designation of this title. Former members of the House are usually referred to as a member of the particular number of the Congress in which they served, so that, for instance, a member in 2008 was a Member of the 100th Congress.

**senatorial courtesy** Senators of the President's party influence appointments of officials in their states. Senatorial courtesy is a customary process of consultation between the White House, cabinet offices, and members of the U.S. Senate, by which the senior senator of the President's party in each state recommends the appointee to vacant offices that the President has the power to appoint in that state, subject to the advice and consent of the Senate. As the Senate could balk at an appointment for any reason at all, this process ensures that the person nominated by the President will be sponsored by the senator most likely to be heard regarding the vacant office. When no senator is of the President's party, the White House staff or appropriate federal department is likely to recommend a nominee. Most federal judges and U.S. Attorneys are appointed as a result of senatorial courtesy.

**conjecture** A well–made guess. A conjecture is a statement of what might be true, made without sufficient evidence in support of the statement to make probable that the statement is correct.
*See also:* evidence (evidentiary).

**conjugal (conjugacy)** Marital, especially suggesting the physical relationship between spouses. Conjugal refers to any aspect of the relationship between spouses. Conjugal partnerships under the civil law are the legal entity created between married people. Conjugal rights include consortium, the rights of intimate association expressed in sexual relations between spouses. Conjugal visits by spouses to inmates in custody allow sufficient privacy to exercise such rights. Note: though conjugacy is the noun form of the word, and conjugal is the adjective, the term is so rarely used as a noun that it is here considered mainly as an adjective.
*See also:* right, legal right, conjugal rights (marital right); prisoner, conjugal visit (overnight familial visit).

**conjugal rights** *See:* right, legal right, conjugal rights (marital right).

**conjugal visit** *See:* prisoner, conjugal visit (overnight familial visit).

**conjunctive (disjunctive)** Terms that are written to express a close relationship. A conjunctive expression is one in which all of its elements are treated as a whole or in a particular and close relationship. A list of elements in a statute, each of which must be satisfied to establish an interest is conjunctive. The opposite is a disjunctive expression, in which the elements are distinguished or set apart from one another. Even though "and" in a list suggests conjunction, though "but not" in a list suggests disjunction, no perfect formula or reliance on word choice is sufficient to prove that a clause, sentence, or phrase is conjunctive or disjunctive; only careful contextual analysis can do so.

**conquest** The acquisition of territory by military victory and occupation. The doctrine of conquest allowed a state to acquire territory through the military defeat of a people and occupation of its lands. The conquered lands and people could be either incorporated into the conquering state or kept as a vassal state. Following World War II, acquisition of lands through conquest has been rejected as a legitimate means of state expansion. The term conquest designates both the means of acquisition and the thing acquired.

**consanguinity**  Blood relationship between family members. Consanguinity at common law described only relationships by blood or by genetic descent from a common ancestor. Consanguinity describes the specific relationship between two individuals of the same family, and it also describes the whole of the relationships among or affecting all individuals descending from a common ancestor. It is the specific description of all the branches of a family tree. A table of consanguinity depicts any potential decedent, surrounded by various levels of relationship within any level, by law, all relatives living at the time of the decedent's death are heirs of that same level, sharing equally in their inheritance from the decedent, before any heir of the next level would take anything by inheritance. The term has been generally enlarged through usage, statutory change, and constitutional interpretation to include not only family relationships of blood (including relationships created by birth), but also relationships of affinity (including relationships created by law through marriage and adoption). Different jurisdictions may have varying laws describing not only the classification establishing degrees within which each member of a family is of the same relation to an individual within it but also the table of consanguinity in that jurisdiction maps that specifies the degrees and relationships that succeed in classifications to an inheritance, such that an inheritance would vest in the members of the highest classification in which an heir survives, excluding any heirs in more remote classifications.

*See also:* kin (kindred); affinity; incest (incestuous or incestuousness); descent, statute of descent.

**collateral consanguinity**  The familial relationships between siblings or cousins. Collateral consanguinity describes all family members who have a common ancestor but who are not descended directly from one another. Cousins (including aunts and uncles) and siblings have collateral consanguinity.

**degree of consanguinity**  The relational distance among members of a family. A degree of consanguinity is a measure of the levels of family between one person and another. The particular family members in the same degree of consanguinity varies according to the law in that jurisdiction. At common law, a parent or child is in the same degree of consanguinity relative to one another. A third cousin is in the same degree of consanguinity to all third cousins of the same remove and to second cousins of one less remove.

**lineal consanguinity**  The family relationships among ancestors and descendants. Lineal consanguinity describes all family members who are descended from or who are ancestors to one another. Parents and children, grandparents and grandchildren, etc., have lineal consanguinity.

**conscience**  The capacity to distinguish right from wrong. Conscience is the mental ability to understand the moral obligations of oneself or others. Although the existence and nature of conscience is widely agreed, its causes and development, as well as the particular dictates of conscience, are subject to much debate. To some degree conscience appears to be innate, developing as a person matures from a child to an adult, a developed conscience being a hallmark of maturity. To some degree the requirements of conscience appear to vary according to the moral ecology in which the person lives.

**conscience of the court**  *See:* court, conscience of the court.

**conscientious objector (CO or conscientious objection)**  One who rejects a public duty on moral or religious grounds. A conscientious objector, in its broad form, is a person who objects to performing a duty because the person believes that the performance itself or some consequence of its performance, violates the person's ethics or religion. In its more particular form, a conscientious objector is someone who refuses to participate in military service or in the registration for military service on such grounds.

**conscionability (conscionable or unconscionability or unconscionable)**  Fair, just, and reasonable. Conscionability is the fairness and reasonableness of any action or state of affairs. Whatever is conscionable is equitable and fair among those affected by it. Something that is unconscionable is unjust, unfair, or unreasonable.

**conscious avoidance or willful ignorance or deliberate ignorance**  *See:* knowledge, constructive knowledge, willful blindness (conscious avoidance or willful ignorance or deliberate ignorance).

**consent**  Agreement to something proposed. Consent is the knowing and intentional act of acceptance or agreement to a proposition. Consent may be manifest in words, which is express consent, or by conduct (including silence in rare and appropriate circumstances), which is implied consent. Consent implies the ability to form consent, including sufficient age, physical and mental ability, and information, and an act that might otherwise amount to consent that lacks any of these preconditions is invalid. A person relying in good faith on an act of apparent consent that does lack such a precondition, whose good faith is based on having no reason to know or suspect such a lack, may be entitled to rely on the apparent consent. Consent is a defense to a tort or to certain crimes, in that the party who is injured or harmed by otherwise criminal or tortious conduct may consent to the conduct.

*See also:* assent; agreement; decree, consent decree (final consent decree or interlocutory consent decree); search, warrantless search, consent search (consented search); exculpation, exculpatory clause.

**age of consent**  *See:* adult, age of consent.

**consent decree**  *See:* decree, consent decree (final consent decree or interlocutory consent decree).

**consent jurisdiction**  *See:* jurisdiction, in personam jurisdiction, voluntary jurisdiction (consent jurisdiction).

**consent search**  *See:* search, warrantless search, consent search (consented search).

**consented search**  *See:* search, warrantless search, consent search (consented search).

**consenting adult**  *See:* adult, consenting adult.

**capacity to consent**  The age, mental ability and legal status to form consent. Capacity to consent is the sum of the physical and mental abilities to form consent with the conditions logically required to consent to a given proposition. Thus a child may not consent to a contract, nor may one person consent to something on behalf of another unless that person has a valid agency that would allow the consent to bind the other.

**express consent**  Stated permission or acceptance of a proposal. Express consent is a statement, whether spoken or written, by which permission is given for something to occur or by which a proposition is accepted.
   *See also:* expression (explicit or express).

**implied consent**  Consent implied from the circumstances or by law. Implied consent is consent that is given without its deliberate expression by the consenting party. Consent may be implied from conduct, when a person's actions would reasonably lead an observer to believe the action amounts to a statement of consent; when a police officer asks to enter a dwelling and the adult occupant opens the door and silently stands aside, the officer may imply consent to enter from the conduct. Consent may be implied, actually construed, as a matter of law, as when implied consent statutes imply consent to search a driver from the operation of a motor vehicle or the request for a driver's license.

**informed consent**  Consent given with appropriate knowledge. Informed consent is consent that is given after the person giving consent has learned all of the information that would be reasonably required for the basis of a reasonable decision. In many instances, for an institution or professional to prove that the decision-maker was sufficiently informed over a matter to give informed consent, the institution or professional will provide the information requisite to making such a decision in an informed way, but the provision of this information is not a legal requirement to receive informed consent unless a custom, statute, or regulation requires it.
   An attorney has an obligation to provide a client with adequate information and explanation of a proposed course of action and its alternatives for the client to know of the material risks of each before consenting to a proposal. By definition, professionals and fiduciaries have similar obligations to their clients and to those with a reasonable right to rely on their advice before consenting to some conduct. This is particularly true of health care professionals.

**informed consent to a medical procedure**  Assent to a medical treatment after learning of its potential effects. Informed consent to a medical procedure, or any form of informed consent prior to the receipt of medical care, indicates that a person has requested or agreed to a course of care involving medical procedures after having understood the procedure's effects, risks, and alternatives. Although informed consent is in fact a subjective question of a patient's understanding, it is more often assessed by an objective measure of the information that is provided to the patient or the patient's representative to ensure consent to a medical procedure is based on sufficient information to be informed, as well as the express consent of the patient or the representative to the procedure following review of that information. The measures of what amounts to sufficiency of the information varies among jurisdictions, but in general it is a clear explanation of what is to be done and what the reasonably likely outcomes might be, including the risks of harm that might follow and including the alternative procedures that might be available. The information should be provided in a manner that is likely to be understood by the specific patient or representative in as timely a manner as circumstances reasonably allow before consent must be given. The failure to provide sufficient information to a patient before performing a medical procedure may amount to a breach of the physician's duty of care to the patient.

**consequence**

**consequential damages**  *See:* damages, classes of damages, consequential damages.

**consequential loss**  *See:* loss, consequential loss.

**consequentialism or teleological**  *See:* jurisprudence, teleology (consequentialism or teleological).

**conservation easement**  *See:* easement, conservation easement.

**conservatism**  *See:* jurisprudence, conservatism.

**conservatorship (conservator)**  A guardian for a person mentally in incapable of self-management. A guardian appointed by a court as the legal representative of an adult during that person's life, upon a finding by the court that the person represented lacks the mental capacity to manage that person's legal and financial affairs. A person subject to a conservatorship lacks capacity as a matter of law to enter a contract, that being the province for that person of the conservator.

**consideration**  A bargain essential to create a binding contract; the exchange of some act or thing which motivates the parties to contract with each other. Consideration is any promise, payment, service, or thing that could be given by one party of the contract under its terms to compensate the other party for their actions under the contract. Consideration is an essential aspect of an enforceable contract. Many forms of consideration are valid consideration, although an act already performed or a service usually done gratuitously lack the benefit of the bargain from the other party and are insufficient. In general, parties are free to contract for whatever greater or lesser consideration they choose, and mere imbalance between the value of the consideration by one party and the value by the other does not amount to insufficient consideration.

*detriment as consideration*  Consideration may be any legal action to one's detriment. Consideration may be forgoing something the party has power or ability to do.

**adequate consideration (inadequate consideration)**  Consideration sufficient in form and quantity to bind the other party to the contract. Adequate consideration is a matter of legal sufficiency in determining that the detriment accepted by the promissor or the benefit given to the promissee is sufficient to bind the promissee to the terms of the contract. A recitation in a written contract that the consideration is adequate is not conclusive of the matter, although a consideration of any reasonable value may be considered adequate for the purpose of determining a valid contract exists. Even so, in most circumstances, the consideration from both parties must have at least rough parity or give rise to an evaluation of the other circumstances affecting the creation of the contract to discern fraud, abuse of a fiduciary position, etc. A sufficiently great imbalance in value, or the failure of any meaningful consideration by one side of the contract, amounts to a failure of consideration and a void contract.

**bargain test of consideration (bargain theory of consideration)**  A thing that is bargained for is adequate consideration. The bargain test of consideration measures a promise, goods, property, service, or payment as sufficient if it was the other party genuinely bargained to receive. The bargain test supplants other views of consideration that require rough economic parity between the benefit to one party and the benefit to the other in order for either benefit to be adequate consideration. The bargain test thus provides that what is offered by one side is sufficient to amount to consideration that would bind the other party if it is what the other party sought to receive through the bargain. The bargain test is, like any theory of consideration, limited in its role in determining that a bargain is enforceable as a contract by other doctrines, such as capacity, adhesion, and unconscionablility.

*See also:* capacity, legal capacity; contract, specific contracts, adhesive contract (contract of adhesion or adhesion contract).

**illegal consideration**  Illegal or wrongful acts may not be consideration. Illegal consideration is any act, forbearance, or promise that is offered by one party to a purported contract that would be illegal or contrary to public policy to perform. If the court will not enforce a promise made because the promise is against the law or because the court's enforcement would violate sound public policy, then no enforceable contract can be made, and the other party to the contract cannot require it to be performed.

**preexisting duty rule (pre-existing duty rule)**  A duty that existed before a bargain is not its consideration. The pre-existing duty rule bars one party from using as consideration in a contract any duty that the party was already bound to perform before entering the contract. In other words, a contract to do what one already has to do by law is no contract. There are many exceptions, not the least being that of settlement agreements: a contract to settle a disputed duty is enforceable, even though one side claims the duty pre-existed the settlement agreement, in that the side who must then perform the duty is offering to settle its dispute as further consideration.

**reciprocal dealing**  The use of a purchase as consideration for a sale. Reciprocal dealing is a practice by which a seller contracts to provide goods or services to a buyer, and at the same time or in the same transaction also agrees to buy goods or services from the buyer, and each of the promises to buy form all or part of the consideration for selling. In other words, A agrees to buy green widgets from B, if B will buy blue widgets from A; after which, B's sale of green widgets is treated as an inducement for A to sell blue widgets.

**sham consideration**  Consideration that does not really exist. Sham consideration is no consideration, or consideration that might appear to exist but that does not in fact, or consideration that is so patently less valuable or beneficial to the party to receive it as to suggest that the agreement does not reflect a genuine bargain but either a fraud or collusion. Sometimes a pre-existing duty is considered a sham consideration.

**surrender of claim**  The transfer or destruction of a valid claim in law or equity is consideration.

**valuable consideration**  Consideration of sufficient value to amount to bind the receiving party to the contract. Valuable consideration is sufficient consideration, which is to say that whatever is the consideration is sufficient in kind and in quantity to satisfy the rule requiring consideration of each party in order to bind the other to the agreement.

**consignment**  The delivery of something to another without assigning all ownership in it. Consignment is the transfer of goods into the care of another, particularly for shipment, storage, sale, or other purposes, usually while retaining an interest in the goods. Unless other legal obligations intervene, consignment creates a bailment in the consignee, with bailor's interest remaining in the consignor (although this effect does not, of course, follow from consignment of goods by a carrier or other consignee to their owner).

*See also:* bailment.

**consignee**   The recipient of a consignment. A consignee is one to whom a consignment is made.

**consignor**   One who makes a consignment. The consignor is the person who consigns some property to the care of another person. A consignor may be an agent of another, such as a shipping agent for an owner of the goods shipped.

## consolidation

**consolidation of actions**   A single trial of several actions with a common issue of fact. Consolidation is the aggregation of several (sometimes many) civil actions into a single trial, whether that trial determines all questions of fact and liability or only one or a few issues in common among the actions consolidated. A judge has the discretion to order consolidation of actions that present the same issue of fact or issue of law or both. Consolidation is appropriate if it will save time but not jeopardize the ability of each part to present fully unique aspects of its case, in other words if the consolidation will save more time and expense than it costs. Actions may be consolidated only for certain purposes, including consolidation for procedural questions or for the determination of certain questions of law, transferring or separating the actions for the determination of questions that are sufficiently specific to each action as to be more efficiently or appropriately considered alone.

**joint trial**   The trial of separate criminal cases in one proceeding. Criminal actions may be consolidated for trial, for pretrial hearings, for one phase or issue of a trial, or for sentencing only. A joint trial in federal criminal procedure is the trial together of separate cases brought under separate indictments, the trial proceeding as if the charges had been brought in one indictment against all the defendants. A joint trial is presumed to be appropriate if all of the defendants could have been joined in a single indictment or information and if a joint trial will not impair a fair trial for any defendant. A defendant in such a situation bears the burden of demonstrating a more likely acquittal in a separate trial.

**consortium**   Connection through a specific relationship. Consortium is the activity and benefit of a relationship, nearly always in law between two spouses, although informally it may apply to any two individuals. There are many forms of consortium as a matter of the history and logic of the term, yet marital consortium is nearly always intended by modern usage. Consortium is the basis for "consorting" which usually has a more sinister connotation.

**consorting**   To visit or participate in activities with another. A person consorting with another is engaging in some form of commerce, conspiracy, or other joint activity with the other. Consorting has a particular significance of unsavory conduct, as in consorting with the enemy, which is a basis for treason, consorting with prostitutes, which is to patronize them, consorting with criminals, which is (often) to act as an accomplice for them.

**loss of consortium**   The lost opportunity for marital love, support, and sex. Loss of consortium is the customary depiction of a spouse's injury when the other spouse dies or is injured such that the physical relationship of the marriage is destroyed. Lost consortium is considered a discrete basis of damages that is not speculative but to be given a reasonable value. Lost consortium is distinct from the support a spouse might have received from the other spouse's wages or income, although that amount is sometimes included within the term along with the other benefits of spousal support.

**conspiracy (conspire)**   Collaborating with another to commit a crime. Conspiracy is a crime committed when two or more people plan or work together to do anything that is itself a crime. It does not matter whether the crime itself is ever performed or attempted. Nor does it matter if one participant has no intention to commit the crime; as long as the participant plans or works with at least one other person in support of the supposed future criminal act, that participant is conspiring to commit the crime.

**conspiracy to interfere with civil rights**   *See:* civil rights, Civil Rights Act, conspiracy to interfere with civil rights (Section 1985).

**chain conspiracy**   A series of conspiracies in a common purpose. A chain conspiracy is a series of conspiracies, with each conspiracy connected to the one just prior and just following but no other relationship to the entire chain. Unlike a wheel conspiracy, a chain conspiracy does not have a central organization. A conspirator in one link of the chain is a conspirator in the whole chain as long the the individual has knowledge of the relationship of the link to another venture.

**civil conspiracy**   A private cause of action for conspiracy to commit a crime or tort. A civil conspiracy is a collaboration of two or more persons or entities to commit either something criminal, tortious, or both, or to do something lawful by unlawful means, and as a result of their resulting action, the plaintiff suffers damages. The plaintiff then has an action for the underlying wrong as well as for civil conspiracy.

**common–design rule**   Culpability assigned to all members of a group engaged in criminal activity together. The common–design rule treats each conspirator as equally responsible for the actions of all of the conspirators who are engaged in a common criminal design or agreement.

**concert-of-action rule (Wharton's rule)** A crime requiring several people does not give rise to conspiracy by the same people when they plan and commit it. Wharton's rule is a judicial presumption against the prosecution for conspiracy of a principal acting with another principal to commit the single crime they plan together. Thus, under this rule, a moonshiner's illegal sale of untaxed whiskey is a crime requiring two people — the buyer and the seller — and they are not conspirators but principals. Wharton's rule applies the essential idea that the conspiracy to commit a crime and the crime that is the object of the conspiracy are merged into a single criminal act at the time of the commission of the crime. As long as the parties are necessary to the commission of the crime, they are not also conspiring by planning the crime they planned to commit. There are many exceptions, however, though the most signal limitation is that the planning of a crime between a principal and an accomplice who is not essential to the crime does not violate Wharton's rule. (So, a driver for the moonshiner could conspire with the moonshiner, because the driver is not essential to the crime.) Likewise, the rule does not apply to a series of illegal transactions or crimes. And the rule may be trumped by legislative abrogation. See F. Wharton, Criminal Law (1932).

**conspirator (coconspirator or co-conspirator)** One who conspires with another to commit a crime. A conspirator is a member of a conspiracy. Two members of the same conspiracy are co-conspirators with one another.

**Pinkerton rule (Pinkerton doctrine or Pinkerton instruction)** A conspirator is liable for the acts of all co-conspirators. The Pinkerton rule establishes criminal liability for each member of a conspiracy for the acts of co-conspirators committed during the member's participation in the conspiracy, as long as the act for which the member is to be liable is related to the object of the conspiracy and (in most jurisdictions) was a reasonably foreseeable consequence of the conspiracy or its contemplated actions. The Pinkerton rule is the basis for an analogous rule of civil liability. See Pinkerton v. United States, 328 U.S. 640, 646–647 (1946) (Douglas, J.).

**seditious conspiracy** A conspiracy against the authority of the government. Seditious conspiracy includes any conspiracy against the authority of the government of the United States, including any conspiracy to bring about its overthrow by force, war against it, the opposition of its authority, or the use of force to seize government property or to delay the enforcement or operation of any law.

**unindicted co-conspirator** A person who conspired with a defendant but is not named in that defendant's indictment. An unindicted co-conspirator is a conspirator, whose identity is known or unknown to the grand jury, but who is not identified by name as a conspirator in the indictment of another person in the same conspiracy.

**wheel conspiracy (rimless wheel conspiracy)** A series of conspiracies with each one connected to a central conspiracy. A wheel conspiracy is an organization of conspiracies, in which a coordinating individual or group conspires independently with a series of other individuals or groups, keeping each separate from the other. Wheel conspiracies lead to questions of prosecutorial discretion regarding the efficacy of arresting the small-time operators in the spokes, as well as evidentiary questions of the magnitude of the conspiracy, such as whether a conspirator in one group may be charged with conspiring not with the coordinator but with the other groups. Absent evidence of actual or constructive knowledge of the plans or actions of the other groups on the spokes, prosecutions of members of a single spoke are usually limited to its own planning and to its contacts with the hub. Constructive knowledge is sufficient for a conspirator in one spoke of the wheel to be a conspirator in the whole wheel, if the individual has knowledge of the relationship of the spoke to another venture.

**constable** An officer of county law enforcement specially tasked with service of process. The constable is a law enforcement officer, directly elected in some jurisdictions, often tasked with maintaining the peace, carrying out court orders, serving tax notices and service of process, assisting a coroner or sheriff, transporting evidence, and transporting prisoners.

**constituent**

**constituent as one represented in government** A person represented by someone else, particularly in government. A constituent is a person who is represented by another person. In government, a constituent is the person whom a legislator, especially, or any elected official represents in office.
*See also:* vote, voter (elector); citizen; client.

**constitute** Sufficient under some standard to create a legal fact. To constitute, as a legal usage, now means to satisfy a legal standard, in the sense that certain evidence may demonstrate the satisfaction of a legal category of fact, such as a particular act constituting a crime. In this the usage evokes an older usage for "constitute" in the sense of authorizing a legal office or status. This particular usage is rather confusing and now should be avoided when possible, except in the most formal of cases, such as in the constitution of a tribunal.

**constituted authorities** *See:* authority, constituted authorities (duly constituted authority).

**constitution** The fundamental laws of a state, governing the actions of officials and the making and execution of laws. A constitution is the organization of a government, literally the creation of what constitutes the state. Like a contract, a constitution may be written or unwritten. In most instances now, a constitution is reflected in a document, such as the U.S. Constitution of 1789 as amended, but the constitution is more than the document, such as the modern understanding of federalism, which bears only a token resemblance to the depiction in the text. In a real sense, the constitution of every government is essentially the customs and expectations shared by officials and the governed, often based on a document, according to which officials act and limit the scope of others' actions with the support of different officials and the people who are governed by them. Constitutions therefore depend on the commitment of officials and of the people to be sustained, regardless of the language in constitutional texts.

*See also:* law, constitutional law.

**Constitution Day and Citizenship Day** *See:* day, Constitution Day and Citizenship Day.

**constitutional challenge** *See:* challenge, constitutional challenge, facial challenge (challenge on its face or unconstitutional per se); challenge, constitutional challenge, as applied (as-applied).

**constitutional court** *See:* court, constitutional court.

**constitutional law** *See:* law, constitutional law.

**constitutional preemption** *See:* preemption, constitutional preemption.

**constitutional right** *See:* right, constitutional right.

**Articles of Confederation** The interstate compact regulating the United States from 1781 to 1789. The Articles of Confederation was an instrument proposed in 1777 and ratified in 1789 as the constitution for the central government among the thirteen states. The Articles were informally used prior to ratification, setting forth the powers of the Congress and the roles of the states, but the weak central government lacked the ability to manage defense and foreign relations. The Articles were replaced by the U.S. Constitution upon its ratification in 1789.

**bill of rights (bills of rights)** Limitations on government power, enshrining rights for individuals. A bill of rights is a series of limitations on the power of government officials as a matter of the constitution of government. The rights of the individuals subject to that government result from the lack of authority of the officials to contravene them. There are many bills of rights. The most famous, perhaps, is the U.S. Bill of Rights, which were twelve amendments proposed in 1791, of which ten were ratified that year, but there are many others, including bills of rights in the constitutions of the various states of the United States, and the instrument on which the Bill of Rights is modeled, the English Bill of Rights of 1689, 1 Will. & Mar. sess. 2, c.2. Questions persist of whether a bill or rights creates rights or only recognizes rights that are inherent in either the nature of humankind or the justifications of government.

**constitutionality (constitutional)** Consonance with the constitution. Constitutional, in general, is a status of any statute, law or treaty, or of any executive or administrative action, or any judicial order or action, being in agreement with the constitution of the

government in which it is done or made. Constitutions, in general, bind the actions of every official of the government, and every action is either constitutional or void.

**declaration of rights** A statement of the rights of the individual. A declaration of rights is a statement, usually in a constitution, constitutional amendment, or similar fundamental document that is not easily changed, of a specific set of rights held by the individual, within the scope of which the government and its officials may not interfere or, depending upon context within the scope of which the government and its officials must act to secure the benefits of the rights for those who hold them. There is no inherent difference between a declaration or rights and a bill of rights, the difference being the custom of a given jurisdiction.

**Confirmation of the Charters (Confirmatio Chartorum)** The recognition of Magna Carta as law. The Confirmation of the Charters, or Confirmatio Chartorum, is a statute passed in 1297, finally establishing the principles of Magna Carta and subsequent enactments as the law of the realm. Its most significant provisions included the assertion, agreed by Edward I, that future taxes would be passed only with the consent of Parliament.

*See also:* constitution, English Constitution, Magna Carta (Magna Charta or Great Charter).

**English Bill of Rights** *See:* rights, bill of rights, English Bill of Rights (Bill of Rights of 1689).

**Magna Carta (Magna Charta or Great Charter)** The great early medieval declaration of English law. Magna Carta is an English constitutional instrument that required the monarch of England to recognize and abide by the law and the institutions of law. In part a restatement of many obligations in the coronation of oaths of King John and Henry I, the charter followed a period of increasing conflict between the crown, the church, the nobility, and the country, resulting in open rebellion. The first version of Magna Carta, also called the Articles of the Barons, was signed by John on June 10, 1215, under pressure from the nobility, who had more or less captured him at Runnymede, a meadow along the River Thames near Windsor Castle. The enrolled copy filed in Chancery in July 1215 is Magna Carta. John repudiated the charter as soon as he was free of the barons, leading to a civil war, during which John died of illness, leaving his young son Henry III, whose regent reissued Magna Charta in October 1216, with some changes, supplemented in 1217 by the Charter of the Forest, and re-issued by Henry himself in a shorter form when he came of age in 1225. This form became law with the Confirmatio Cartorum issued by Henry III's son, Edward I, in 1297. Magna Charta was the predicate for numerous later constitutional settlements, most notably in the early modern era, the Petition of Right of 1628, the English Bill of Rights, and the U.S. Bill of Rights. Carta is often written "charta," and both words are pronounced with a hard "c." Literally, the term means great charter or, more simply, large paper.

*See also:* magna (magnum or magnus); constitution.

**Petition of Right of 1628**   The King may not raise taxes but through Parliament, may not imprison but by law, nor quarter troops in homes in peace. The Petition of Right of 1628 was an instrument adopted by Parliament and assented by Charles I, which influenced both the English Bill of Rights and was a direct model for the U.S. Bill of Rights. Drafted largely by the aging former chief justice, Sir Edward Coke, it sought to settle arguments between the commons and Charles I, particularly seeking him to end the practices of requiring knights to loan the crown money as an alternative to tax, or imprisoning those who did not pay it, as well as other incidents of arrest and detention without lawful warrants. Charles did not honor the letter or spirit of the Petition, a factor that helped precipitate the English Civil War.

*See also:* petition, Petition of Right; constitution, U.S. Constitution, Bill of Rights.

**state constitution**   The constitution of each state or commonwealth in the United States. State constitution is the generic term for the constitution of each of the now-fifty states and commonwealths that are the United States of America. Each constitution performs the same function, which is to establish the government of the state, delimiting certain functions among various offices, setting forth the procedures for the creation, change, and application of law, and declaring certain rights and powers of the people. State constitutions for new states are valid only once Congress has passed an enabling act allowing a state to do so. State constitutions tend to be quite long and detail a variety of state agencies that are further defined by statutes. State constitutions may not conflict with the Constitution of the United States owing to the Supremacy Clause, though they may provide more extensive rights to the people of the state against the state than would the federal constitution.

**U.S. Constitution (United States Constitution)**   The fundamental law of the United States of America. The United States Constitution is the highest law in the United States. The term depicts the text of the instrument by that name ratified in 1789 and amended from time to time, as well as the customs that have been accepted by the three branches of government, the states, and the people as the means by which the government and laws function.

**Article 1 (Article I or Article One or the Legislative Article)**   The first Article establishes and empowers the Congress. The Legislative Article provides for the creation of the Congress of a Senate and a House of Representatives; sets the qualifications and means of election for both, providing two senators per state and a proportion of representatives per state based on population; provides for election under state law as determined by the Congress and requires an annual assembly; makes each chamber judge of its own affairs; provides for public compensation, privilege of office, and limitation from conflicting offices; sets procedures for enacting laws; delegates specific powers and such further powers as are necessary and proper for their exercise, limits the Congress from certain actions; and limits states from actions barred by or given to the Congress.

*See also:* congress.

**Article 2 (Article II or Article Two or the Executive Article)**   The second Article establishes and empowers the President and executive branch. The Executive Article provides for the office of the President of the United States, election by the Electoral College, a Vice President to serve if the Presidency is vacated, undiminished compensation, the oath of office, powers as commander in chief, of foreign affairs and appointment, have powers of Congressional recommendation and adjournment, a requirement to follow the laws, and for impeachment.

**Article 3 (Article III or Article Three or the Judicial Article)**   The third Article establishes and empowers the judicial branch. The Judicial Article provides for the creation of the Supreme Court and such inferior courts as Congress shall create; provides for the selection of judges with tenure for life, establishes the extent of federal judicial powers over federal cases and controversies, provides for original jurisdiction in the U.S. Supreme Court, criminal jury trials, limits on the crime of treason and abolishes attainder.

*See also:* immunity, sovereign immunity, state sovereign immunity (eleventh amendment immunity); court, supreme court; judge, judicial branch.

**Article 4 (Article IV or Article Four or States Article)**   The fourth Article requires states to respect the laws of other states, and it provides for the creation of new states. Article Four provides that states shall give full faith and credit to the acts and judgments of other states, that states shall grant to the citizens of other states the privileges and immunities given to their own, that states shall extradite criminal suspects to one another, that Congress shall regulate territories and create new states with the consent of states affected by each creation, and that the federal government shall assure a republican form of government in each state.

*See also:* government, forms of government, republic.

**Article 5 (Article V or Article Five or Amending Article)**   The fifth Article specifies the process for amendment of the Constitution. Article V specifies that the Constitution may be amended by a two-thirds vote in both houses of Congress and ratification by three-fourths of the states, or by Convention.

*See also:* amendment (amend).

**Article 6 (Article VI or Article Six or Supremacy and Oaths Article)**  The sixth Article requires national coordination of the federal debt, federal laws, and state and federal offices. According to Article IV, national debts are assumed, national laws are supreme, both federal and state officials must support the Constitution, though no religious test may ever be applied.

*See also:* oath.

**Article 7 (Article VII or Article Seven or Ratification Article)**  The seventh Article set the process of ratification. Article VII required nine states for ratification, each doing so in a state ratifying convention.

**amendment**  A formal alteration of the Constitutional text ratified in 1789. There have been twenty-seven amendments to the U.S. Constitution, of which eleven were proposed in the Bill of Rights. Amendments take place only according to one of the procedures required in article five: either a bill from both houses of Congress passed by two-thirds of each house and ratified by three-fourths of the states, or a petition for a convention from two-thirds of the states leads to a convention that adopts amendments ratified by three-fourths of the states. Thus far, all amendments have begun in Congress rather than in convention. Amendment aside, all other changes to the constitution are customary.

**Amendment 1 (Amendment I or First Amendment)**  Congress may not establish a religion or prohibit free exercise of religion, free speech, free press, free assembly, or the right to petition. The First Amendment provides: "Congress shall make no law respecting an establishment of religion, or prohibiting the free exercise thereof or abridging the freedom of speech, or of the press or the right of the people peaceably to assemble, and to petition the Government for a redress of grievances." U.S. Const. amend. I (1791). All of these obligations have been applied to the states through incorporation into the Due Process Clause of the Fourteenth Amendment.

*See also:* speech; press (member of the press); petition, right to petition; religion, freedom of religion, virginia statute for religious freedom.

**Freedom of Association**  *See:* association, Freedom of Association.

**Freedom of Religion**  *See:* religion, Freedom of Religion.

**Freedom of Speech**  *See:* speech, Freedom of Speech (right of free speech or liberty of speech).

**Freedom of the Press**  *See:* press (member of the press); press, freedom of the press (liberty of the press).

**Amendment 2 (Amendment II or Right to Bear Arms or Second Amendment)**  The right of the people to keep and bear arms. The Second Amendment provides: "A well regulated Militia, being necessary to the security of a free State, the right of the people to keep and bear Arms, shall not be infringed." U.S. Const. amend. II (1791). In 2008, the amendment was interpreted to confer an individual right, and in 2010, the amendment was incorporated into the Due Process Clause of the Fourteenth Amendment.

*See also:* arms, arms as weaponry (arm).

**Amendment 3 (Amendment III or Third Amendment)**  House owners shall not quarter troops in peace, or but by law in war. The Third Amendment provides: "No Soldier shall, in time of peace be quartered in any house, without the consent of the Owner, nor in time of war, but in a manner to be prescribed by law." U.S. Const. amend. III (1791).

**Amendment 4 (Amendment IV or Fourth Amendment)**  Search and seizure may not be unreasonable, and warrants must be based on probable cause, proved and specific. The Fourth Amendment provides: "The right of the people to be secure in their persons, houses, papers, and effects, against unreasonable searches and seizures, shall not be violated, and no Warrants shall issue, but upon probable cause, supported by Oath or affirmation, and particularly describing the place to be searched, and the persons or things to be seized." U.S. Const. amend. IV.

*See also:* search, search and seizure; seizure (seize).

**Amendment 5 (Amendment V or Fifth Amendment)**  The rights to a federal Grand Jury, to avoid double jeopardy, against self-incrimination, to due process of law, and to compensation for taken private property are secured to each person. The Fifth Amendment provides: "No person shall be held to answer for a capital, or otherwise infamous crime, unless on a presentment or indictment of a Grand Jury, except in cases arising in the land or naval forces, or in the Militia, when in actual service in time of War or public danger; nor shall any person be subject for the same offence to be twice put in jeopardy of life or limb; nor shall be compelled in any criminal case to be a witness against himself, nor be deprived of life, liberty, or property, without due process of law; nor shall private property be taken for public use, without just compensation." U.S. Const. amend. V (1791). The provisions of the Fifth Amendment, with the exception of the Grand Jury clause, have been incorporated into the Due Process Clause of the Fourteenth Amendment and bind the states.

*See also:* Miranda rule (Miranda warning or Miranda rights); jury, grand jury; due process of law.

**Amendment 6 (Amendment VI or Sixth Amendment)**  The rights to a speedy trial, to a public trial, to a local jury trial, in a court of law, to formal charges, present and confront witnesses, and to the assistance of counsel is secured for each person accused of a crime. The Sixth Amendment provides:

"In all criminal prosecutions, the accused shall enjoy the right to a speedy and public trial, by an impartial jury of the State and district wherein the crime shall have been committed, which district shall have been previously ascertained by law, and to be informed of the nature and cause of the accusation; to be confronted with the witnesses against him; to have compulsory process for obtaining witnesses in his favor, and to have the Assistance of Counsel for his defence." U.S. Const. amend VI (1791). The provisions of the Sixth Amendment have each been incorporated into the Due Process Clause of the Fourteenth Amendment and bind the states.

*See also:* Miranda rule (Miranda warning or Miranda rights).

**Amendment 7 (Amendment VII or Seventh Amendment)** The right to a jury trial is secured to federal civil litigants. The Seventh Amendment provides: "In Suits at common law, where the value in controversy shall exceed twenty dollars, the right of trial by jury shall be preserved, and no fact tried by a jury, shall be otherwise re-examined in any Court of the United States, than according to the rules of the common law." U.S. Const. amend VII (1791). The provisions of the Seventh Amendment have not been incorporated into the Due Process Clause of the Fourteenth Amendment and do not bind the states.

*See also:* jury (juror).

**Amendment 8 (Amendment VIII or Eighth Amendment)** A person accused of a federal crime may not be exposed to cruel and unusual punishment, excessive fines, nor excessive bail. The Eighth Amendment provides: "Excessive bail shall not be required, nor excessive fines imposed, nor cruel and unusual punishments inflicted." U.S. Const. amend. VIII (1791). The cruel and unusual punishment clause has been incorporated into the Due Process Clause of the Fourteenth Amendment and binds the states, although a question remains as to the excessive bails clause. This clause has also been raised as the basis for limits on civil awards of punitive damages.

**Amendment 9 (Amendment IX or Ninth Amendment)** The enumerated rights in the constitution are not all the rights there are. The Ninth Amendment provides: "The enumeration in the Constitution, of certain rights, shall not be construed to deny or disparage others retained by the people." U.S. Const. amend. IX (1791). The Ninth Amendment has not been incorporated into the Due Process Clause, largely because its logical structure causes it to limit the scope of the powers of the central government. Even so, the Ninth Amendment is a strong element in the "penumbra of rights" that is collectively described as a right to privacy.

**Amendment 10 (Amendment X or Tenth Amendment)** The states reserve all rights not expressly granted to the federal government. The Tenth Amendment provides: "The powers not delegated to the United States by the Constitution, nor prohibited by it to the States, are reserved to the States respectively, or to the people." U.S. Const. amend. X (1791).

*See also:* sovereignty, state sovereignty.

**Amendment 11 (Amendment XI or Eleventh Amendment)** Each state is immune from federal suit unless Congress or the state allows it. The Eleventh Amendment provides: "The Judicial power of the United States shall not be construed to extend to any suit in law or equity, commenced or prosecuted against one of the United States by Citizens of another State, or by Citizens or Subjects of any Foreign State." U.S. Const. amend. XI (1795). The amendment overruled an allowance of such a suit in Chisholm v. Georgia, 2 U.S. 419 (2 Dall.) (1793). The prohibition on suits by a foreign citizen against states in federal court was extended to bar suits against a state by its own citizen in Hans v. Louisiana, 134 U.S. 1 (1890), an extension that remains controversial. Congress may abrogate this immunity.

*See also:* sovereignty, state sovereignty; immunity, sovereign immunity, state sovereign immunity (Eleventh Amendment Immunity).

**Amendment 12 (Amendment XII or Twelfth Amendment)** Electoral college procedures. The Twelfth Amendment provides: "The Electors shall meet in their respective states and vote by ballot for President and Vice-President, one of whom, at least, shall not be an inhabitant of the same state with themselves; they shall name in their ballots the person voted for as President, and in distinct ballots the person voted for as Vice-President, and they shall make distinct lists of all persons voted for as President, and of all persons voted for as Vice-President, and of the number of votes for each, which lists they shall sign and certify, and transmit sealed to the seat of the government of the United States, directed to the President of the Senate; the President of the Senate shall, in the presence of the Senate and House of Representatives, open all the certificates and the votes shall then be counted; The person having the greatest number of votes for President, shall be the President, if such number be a majority of the whole number of Electors appointed; and if no person have such majority, then from the persons having the highest numbers not exceeding three on the list of those voted for as President, the House of Representatives shall choose immediately, by ballot, the President. But in choosing the President, the votes shall be taken by states, the representation from each state having one vote; a quorum for this purpose shall consist of a member or members from two-thirds of the states, and a majority of all the states shall be necessary to a choice. [And if the House of Representatives shall not choose a President whenever the right of choice shall devolve upon them, before the fourth day of March next following, then the Vice-President shall act as President, as in case of the death or other constitutional disability of the President.] The person having the greatest number of votes as Vice-President, shall be the Vice-President, if such number be a majority of the whole number of Electors appointed, and if no person have a majority, then from the two highest numbers on the list, the Senate shall choose the Vice-President; a quorum for the purpose shall consist of two-thirds of the whole number of Senators, and a majority of the whole number shall be necessary to a choice. But no person constitutionally ineligible to the office of President shall be eligible to that of Vice-President of the United States." U.S. Const. amend. XII (1804). The bracketed text was superseded by the Twentieth Amendment.

**Amendment 13 (Amendment XIII or Thirteenth Amendment)** Slavery is abolished in the United States. The Thirteenth Amendment provides: "Neither slavery nor involuntary servitude, except as a punishment for crime whereof the party shall have been duly convicted, shall exist within the United States, or any place subject to their jurisdiction." U.S. Const. amend. XIII (1865).

*See also:* slavery, involuntary servitude, peonage (debt bondage); Reconstruction, Reconstruction amendments; emancipation; abolition; slavery, forced labor; slavery (slave).

**Amendment 14 (Amendment XIV or Fourteenth Amendment)** Citizens of the U.S. are citizens of states, which shall ensure to each the rights to due process of law and equal protection of the laws, and a state that denies suffrage to some of its citizens shall lose seats in Congress. The Fourteenth Amendment provides: "1. All persons born or naturalized in the United States, and subject to the jurisdiction thereof, are citizens of the United States and of the State wherein they reside. No State shall make or enforce any law which shall abridge the privileges or immunities of citizens of the United States; nor shall any State deprive any person of life, liberty, or property, without due process of law; nor deny to any person within its jurisdiction the equal protection of the laws. 2. Representatives shall be apportioned among the several States according to their respective numbers, counting the whole number of persons in each State, excluding Indians not taxed. But when the right to vote at any election for the choice of electors for President and Vice-President of the United States, Representatives in Congress, the Executive and Judicial officers of a State, or the members of the Legislature thereof, is denied to any of the male inhabitants of such State, [being twenty-one years of age], and citizens of the United States, or in any way abridged, except for participation in rebellion, or other crime, the basis of representation therein shall be reduced in the proportion which the number of such male citizens shall bear to the whole number of male citizens twenty-one years of age in such State. 3. No

person shall be a Senator or Representative in Congress, or elector of President and Vice-President, or hold any office, civil or military, under the United States, or under any State, who, having previously taken an oath, as a member of Congress, or as an officer of the United States, or as a member of any State legislature, or as an executive or judicial officer of any State, to support the Constitution of the United States, shall have engaged in insurrection or rebellion against the same, or given aid or comfort to the enemies thereof. But Congress may by a vote of two-thirds of each House, remove such disability. 4. The validity of the public debt of the United States, authorized by law, including debts incurred for payment of pensions and bounties for services in suppressing insurrection or rebellion, shall not be questioned. But neither the United States nor any State shall assume or pay any debt or obligation incurred in aid of insurrection or rebellion against the United States, or any claim for the loss or emancipation of any slave; but all such debts, obligations and claims shall be held illegal and void." U.S. Const. amend. XIV (1868). Bracketed text superseded by the Twenty-Sixth Amendment.

*See also:* Reconstruction, Reconstruction amendments.

**Amendment 15 (Amendment XV or Fifteenth Amendment)** Voting rights are secured to all citizens regardless of race, color or previous conditions of servitude. The Fifteenth Amendment provides: "1. The right of citizens of the United States to vote shall not be denied or abridged by the United States or by any State on account of race, color, or previous condition of servitude. 2. The Congress shall have power to enforce this article by appropriate legislation." U.S. Const. amend. XV (1870).

*See also:* Reconstruction, Reconstruction amendments.

**Amendment 16 (Amendment XVI or Sixteenth Amendment)** The United States has an income tax. The Sixteenth Amendment provides: "The Congress shall have power to lay and collect taxes on incomes, from whatever source derived, without apportionment among the several States, and without regard to any census or enumeration." U.S. Const. amend. XVI (1913).

*See also:* tax (taxation).

**Amendment 17 (Amendment XVII or Seventeenth Amendment)** Senators shall be elected by popular vote. The Seventeenth Amendment provides: "The Senate of the United States shall be composed of two Senators from each State, elected by the people thereof, for six years; and each Senator shall have one vote. The electors in each State shall have the qualifications requisite for electors of the most numerous branch of the State legislatures. When vacancies happen in the representation of any State in the Senate, the executive authority of such State shall issue writs of election to fill such vacancies: Provided, That the legislature of any State may empower the executive thereof to make temporary appointments until the people fill the vacancies by election as the legislature may direct. This amendment shall not be so construed as to affect the election or term of any Senator chosen before it becomes valid as part of the Constitution." U.S. Const. amend. XVII (1913).

**Amendment 18 (Amendment XVIII or Eighteenth Amendment)** The prohibition of alcohol, which would be repealed by the Twenty-First Amendment. The Eighteenth Amendment provides: "Section 1. After one year from the ratification of this article the manufacture, sale, or transportation of intoxicating liquors within, the importation thereof into, or the exportation thereof from the United States and all territory subject to the jurisdiction thereof for beverage purposes is hereby prohibited. Section 2. The Congress and the several States shall have concurrent power to enforce this article by appropriate legislation. Section 3. This article shall be inoperative unless it shall have been ratified as an amendment to the Constitution by the legislatures of the several States, as provided in the Constitution, within seven years from the date of the submission hereof to the States by the Congress." U.S. Const. amend. XVIII (1919).
*See also:* prohibition, prohibition of alcohol.

**Amendment 19 (Amendment XIX or Nineteenth Amendment or Women's Suffrage Amendment)** The right to vote is secured for women. The Nineteenth Amendment provides: "The right of citizens of the United States to vote shall not be denied or abridged by the United States or by any State on account of sex. Congress shall have power to enforce this article by appropriate legislation." U.S. Const. amend. XIX (1920).
*See also:* vote, suffrage (suffragette).

**Amendment 20 (Amendment XX or Twentieth Amendment)** Dates for terms of office are set, and the succession for a dead president elect is determined. The Twentieth Amendment provides: "1. The terms of the President and the Vice President shall end at noon on the 20th day of January, and the terms of Senators and Representatives at noon on the 3d day of January, of the years in which such terms would have ended if this article had not been ratified; and the terms of their successors shall then begin. 2. The Congress shall assemble at least once in every year, and such meeting shall begin at noon on the 3d day of January, unless they shall by law appoint a different day. 3. If, at the time fixed for the beginning of the term of the President, the President elect shall have died, the Vice President elect shall become President. If a President shall not have been chosen before the time fixed for the beginning of his term, or if the President elect shall have failed to qualify, then the Vice President elect shall act as President until a President shall have qualified; and the Congress may by law provide for the case wherein neither a President elect nor a Vice

President shall have qualified, declaring who shall then act as President, or the manner in which one who is to act shall be selected, and such person shall act accordingly until a President or Vice President shall have qualified. 4. The Congress may by law provide for the case of the death of any of the persons from whom the House of Representatives may choose a President whenever the right of choice shall have devolved upon them, and for the case of the death of any of the persons from whom the Senate may choose a Vice President whenever the right of choice shall have devolved upon them. 5. Sections 1 and 2 shall take effect on the 15th day of October following the ratification of this article. 6. This article shall be inoperative unless it shall have been ratified as an amendment to the Constitution by the legislatures of three-fourths of the several States within seven years from the date of its submission." U.S. Const. amend. XX (1933).

**Amendment 21 (Amendment XXI or Twenty-First Amendment)** Prohibition is repealed. The Twenty-First Amendment provides: "1. The eighteenth article of amendment to the Constitution of the United States is hereby repealed. 2. The transportation or importation into any State, Territory, or Possession of the United States for delivery or use therein of intoxicating liquors, in violation of the laws thereof, is hereby prohibited. 3. This article shall be inoperative unless it shall have been ratified as an amendment to the Constitution by conventions in the several States, as provided in the Constitution, within seven years from the date of the submission hereof to the States by the Congress." U.S. Const. amend. XXI (1933). Note: the repeal of federal prohibition left prohibition intact in each state until repealed by each state for its own territory. This gave each state considerable power to regulate and tax alcohol that would ordinarily be denied it under the Commerce Clause.
*See also:* Prohibition, prohibition of alcohol; repeal.

**Amendment 22 (Amendment XXII or Twenty-Second Amendment)** A President may only be elected to two terms. The Twenty-Second Amendment provides: "1. No person shall be elected to the office of the President more than twice, and no person who has held the office of President, or acted as President, for more than two years of a term to which some other person was elected President shall be elected to the office of President more than once. But this Article shall not apply to any person holding the office of President when this Article was proposed by Congress, and shall not prevent any person who may be holding the office of President, or acting as President, during the term within which this Article becomes operative from holding the office of President or acting as President during the remainder of such term. 2. This article shall be inoperative unless it shall have been ratified as an amendment to the Constitution by the legislatures of three-fourths of the several States within seven years from the date of its submission to the States by the Congress." U.S. Const. amend. XXII (1951).

See also: president; term, term of office, term limit.

**Amendment 23 (Amendment XXIII or Twenty-Third Amendment)** Citizens in Washington, D.C. may vote for President. The Twenty-Third Amendment provides: "1. The District constituting the seat of Government of the United States shall appoint in such manner as Congress may direct: A number of electors of President and Vice President equal to the whole number of Senators and Representatives in Congress to which the District would be entitled if it were a State, but in no event more than the least populous State; they shall be in addition to those appointed by the States, but they shall be considered, for the purposes of the election of President and Vice President, to be electors appointed by a State; and they shall meet in the District and perform such duties as provided by the twelfth article of amendment. 2. The Congress shall have power to enforce this article by appropriate legislation." U.S. Const. amend. XXIII (1961).

**Amendment 24 (Amendment XXIV or Twenty-Fourth Amendment)** The poll tax is abolished. The Twenty-Fourth Amendment provides: "1. The right of citizens of the United States to vote in any primary or other election for President or Vice President, for electors for President or Vice President, or for Senator or Representative in Congress, shall not be denied or abridged by the United States or any State by reason of failure to pay poll tax or other tax. 2. The Congress shall have power to enforce this article by appropriate legislation." U.S. Const. amend. XXIV (1964).

See also: tax, poll tax (head tax or capitation tax).

**Amendment 25 (Amendment XXV or Twenty-Fifth Amendment)** Presidential succession is established. The Twenty-Fifth Amendment provides: "1. In case of the removal of the President from office or of his death or resignation, the Vice President shall become President. 2. Whenever there is a vacancy in the office of the Vice President, the President shall nominate a Vice President who shall take office upon confirmation by a majority vote of both Houses of Congress. 3. Whenever the President transmits to the President pro tempore of the Senate and the Speaker of the House of Representatives his written declaration that he is unable to discharge the powers and duties of his office, and until he transmits to them a written declaration to the contrary, such powers and duties shall be discharged by the Vice President as Acting President. 4. Whenever the Vice President and a majority of either the principal officers of the executive departments or of such other body as Congress may by law provide, transmit to the President pro tempore of the Senate and the Speaker of the House of Representatives their written declaration that the President is unable to discharge the powers and

duties of his office, the Vice President shall immediately assume the powers and duties of the office as Acting President. Thereafter, when the President transmits to the President pro tempore of the Senate and the Speaker of the House of Representatives his written declaration that no inability exists, he shall resume the powers and duties of his office unless the Vice President and a majority of either the principal officers of the executive department or of such other body as Congress may by law provide, transmit within four days to the President pro tempore of the Senate and the Speaker of the House of Representatives their written declaration that the President is unable to discharge the powers and duties of his office. Thereupon Congress shall decide the issue, assembling within forty-eight hours for that purpose if not in session. If the Congress, within twenty-one days after receipt of the latter written declaration, or, if Congress is not in session, within twenty-one days after Congress is required to assemble, determines by two-thirds vote of both Houses that the President is unable to discharge the powers and duties of his office, the Vice President shall continue to discharge the same as Acting President; otherwise, the President shall resume the powers and duties of his office." U.S. Const. amend. XXV (1967).

**Amendment 26 (Amendment XXVI or Twenty-Sixth Amendment)** Citizens may vote at the age of eighteen. The Twenty-Sixth Amendment provides: "1. The right of citizens of the United States, who are eighteen years of age or older, to vote shall not be denied or abridged by the United States or by any State on account of age. 2. The Congress shall have power to enforce this article by appropriate legislation." U.S. Const. amend XXVI (1971).

**Amendment 27 (Amendment XXVII or Twenty-Seventh Amendment)** Congressional pay changes take effect in the next Congress. The Twenty-Seventh Amendment provides: "No law, varying the compensation for the services of the Senators and Representatives, shall take effect, until an election of representatives shall have intervened." U.S. Const. amend. XXVII (1992). This amendment was originally proposed in the Bill of Rights as its second article, but it was not ratified until 1992.

**Equal Rights Amendment (ERA or E.R.A.)** A proposed amendment assuring equal rights by gender. The Equal Rights Amendment, proposed in 1923, was adopted by Congress in 1971 but failed to receive the ratification of three-fourths of the state within seven years. It provides:

Section 1. Equality of rights under the law shall not be denied or abridged by the United States or by any State on account of sex.

Section 2. The Congress shall have the power to enforce, by appropriate legislation, the provisions of this article.

Section 3. This amendment shall take effect two years after the date of ratification.

**Bill of Rights**  The first ten amendments to the U.S. Constitution to be ratified. The Bill of Rights is the collective label for the first ten amendments to be ratified, as well as the term for the document in which the first twelve amendments were proposed. These twelve amendments were proposed by the First Congress to the states, on September 25, 1789. The states ratified the third through the twelfth amendments proposed, which were then renumbered: what is now the First Amendment was originally the third amendment of the Bill of Rights. (Of the two omitted, one, setting a number of constituents for each congressional seat, was never ratified, and two, limiting pay raises for Congress, passed in 1992 as the Twenty-Seventh Amendment). The Bill of Rights, modeled after the English Bill of Rights, Petition of Right, and Magna Carta, was intended to limit the potential of tyranny by either the Congress or the Executive. The passage of amendments of some form to that purpose had been an express or implied condition for the ratification of the Constitution by several states.

**incorporation of rights**  The Due Process Clause of the Fourteenth Amendment incorporates some substantive rights from the first ten amendments. Incorporation of rights is the doctrine that applies certain individual rights in the Bill of Rights to apply to the states my implication through the Due Process Clause of the Fourteenth Amendment. Although there are predicate cases, the first clear application of the process of incorporation was in Gitlow v. New York, 268 U.S. 652 (1925), binding the states to the First Amendment.

**incorporated rights**  The individual rights of the first ten amendments that bind the states. These provisions and doctrines of the Bill of Rights have been, or have not been, incorporated in the Due Process Clause and bind the states:

Amendment 1. Establishment of Religion. Incorporated. See Everson v. Board of Education, 330 U.S. 1 (1947).

Amendment 1. Free Exercise of Religion. Incorporated. See Cantwell v. Connecticut, 310 U.S. 296 (1940); Hamilton v. Regents of the Univ. of California, 293 U.S. 245 (1934).

Amendment 1. Freedom of Speech. Incorporated. See Gitlow v. New York, 268 U.S. 652 (1925).

Amendment 1. Freedom of the Press. Incorporated. See Near v. Minnesota, 283 U.S. 697 (1931).

Amendment 1. Right of Assembly. Incorporated. See DeJonge v. Oregon, 299 U.S. 353 (1937).

Amendment 1. Right to Petition the Government. Incorporated. See Edwards v. South Carolina, 372 U.S. 229 (1963); DeJonge v. Oregon, 299 U.S. 353 (1937).

Amendment 2. Keep and Bear Arms Clause. Incorporated. See McDonald v. Chicago, 556 U.S. ___, 130 S.Ct. 3020 (June 28, 2010). This amendment was held to create an individual right and apply to the District of Columbia in D.C. v. Heller, 554 U.S. ___, 128 S. Ct. 2783 (2008).

Amendment 3. Quartering of Soldiers. Not incorporated. But see Engblom v. Carey, 522 F. Supp. 57, 67–68 (S.D.N.Y. 1981), rev'd on other grounds, 677 F.2d 957 (2d Cir. 1982).

Amendment 4. Unreasonable Search and Seizure. Incorporated. See Mapp v. Ohio, 367 U.S. 643 (1961); Wolf v. Colorado, 338 U.S. 25 (1949).

Amendment 4. Unreasonable Search and Seizure — Exclusionary Rule. Incorporated. See Mapp v. Ohio, 367 U.S. 643 (1961).

Amendment 4. Unreasonable Search and Seizure — Unreasonableness tests for warrantless search. Incorporated. See Ker v. California, 374 U.S. 23 (1963).

Amendment 4. Warrant Clause. Incorporated. See Aguilar v. Texas, 378 U.S. 108 (1964).

Amendment 5. Grand Jury Clause. Not incorporated. See Hurtado v. California, 110 U.S. 516 (1884).

Amendment 5. Double Jeopardy. Incorporated. See Benton v. Maryland, 395 U.S. 784 (1969).

Amendment 5. Compelled Self-Incrimination. Incorporated. See Malloy v. Hogan, 378 U.S. 1 (1964).

Amendment 5. Compelled Self-Incrimination — Warning Before Interrogation. Incorporated. See Miranda v. Arizona, 384 U.S. 436 (1966).

Amendment 5. Due Process Clause. Not incorporated. The Fifth Amendment Due Process Clause applies only to the federal government; the Due Process Clause of the Fourteenth Amendment applies to the states.

Amendment 5. Takings Clause (Just Compensation). Incorporated. See Chicago, Burlington & Quincy Railroad Co. v. City of Chicago, 166 U.S. 226 (1897).

Amendment 6. Right to a Speedy Trial. Incorporated. See Klopfer v. North Carolina, 386 U.S. 213 (1967).

Amendment 6. Right to a Public Trial. Incorporated. See In re Oliver, 333 U.S. 257 (1948).

Amendment 6. Right to an Impartial Jury at Trial. Incorporated. See Duncan v. Louisiana, 391 U.S. 145 (1968); Parker v. Gladden, 385 U.S. 363 (1966).

Amendment 6. Right to an Impartial Jury at Trial — Trial of a Minor. Not incorporated. See McKeiver v. Pennsylvania, 403 U.S. 528 (1971).

Amendment 6. Right to Notice of Accusations. Incorporated. See In re Oliver, 333 U.S. 257 (1948).

Amendment 6. Right to Confront Witnesses. Incorporated. See Pointer v. Texas, 380 U.S. 400 (1965).

Amendment 6. Right to Compulsory Process. Incorporated. See Washington v. Texas, 388 U.S. 14 (1967).

Amendment 6. Right to the Assistance of Counsel in Felony Cases. Incorporated. See Gideon v. Wainwright, 372 U.S. 335 (1963).

Amendment 6. Right to the Assistance of Counsel in Capital Cases. Incorporated. See Powell v. Alabama, 287 U.S. 45 (1932).

Amendment 7. Right to Civil Jury. Not incorporated. See Curtis v. Loether, 415 U.S. 189 (1974).

Amendment 8. Excessive Bail and Fines Clauses. Incorporated, probably. See Murphy v. Hunt, 455 U.S. 478 (1982); Baze v. Rees, 128 S. Ct. 1520, 1529 (2008).

Amendment 8. Cruel and Unusual Punishments Clause. Incorporated. See Robinson v. California, 370 U.S. 660 (1962).

Amendment 9. Unenumerated Rights. Not directly incorporated, but an element of the right to privacy.

Amendment 10. Reservation of Rights to States or to the People. Not incorporated.

The following rights are incorporated, in that they arise from the Bill of Rights and they bind the states through the Due Process Clause of the Fourteenth Amendment, although these rights do not arise from a particular clause or even a single amendment:

Right of Expressive Association (speech and assembly). See Boy Scouts of America v. Dale, 530 U.S. 640 (2000).

Right to Privacy (penumbra of rights in First, Third, Fourth, Fifth, and Ninth Amendments). See Griswold v. Connecticut, 381 U.S. 479 (1965).

**selective incorporation**   The process of incorporating individual rights into the Fourteenth Amendment, clause by clause, from the Bill of Rights. Selective incorporation recognizes individual guarantees of the federal Bill of Rights into the Due Process Clause of the Fourteenth Amendment, doing so piecemeal. Thus some amendments bind the states as well as the federal government, but they do so clause by clause, and not all clauses have been incorporated.

**total incorporation**   The claim that all of the individual rights of the first ten amendments are incorporated into the Due Process Clause. The doctrine of total incorporation, promoted by Justice Hugo Black but yet to be accepted by a majority of the Supreme Court, would bind the states to recognize all of the individual rights that must be recognized by the federal government under the Bill of Rights, through their wholesale incorporation into the Due Process Clause of the Fourteenth Amendment.

### clauses

**1808 Clause**   Slavery could be prohibited only after 1808. The 1808 Clause provides: "The Migration or Importation of such Persons as any of the States now existing shall think proper to admit, shall not be prohibited by the Congress prior to the Year one thousand eight hundred and eight, but a tax or duty may be imposed on such Importation, not exceeding ten dollars for each Person." U.S. Const. art. I, §9, cl. 1 (1789). The 1808 clause was one of the many compromises in the drafting process related to slavery and regionalism. Despite being rendered moot by its own terms after 1808, the 1808 clause was one proof for abolitionists and progressives that the Constitution of 1789 was corrupted by an acceptance of slavery as a matter of constitutional law. The abolition of slavery in the Thirteenth Amendment finally answered the questions the clause implied.

**Admiralty Clause**   The federal courts shall hear admiralty and maritime cases. The Admiralty Clause provides: "The judicial Power shall extend . . . to all Cases of admiralty and maritime Jurisdiction." U.S. Const. art. III §2, cl. 1 (1789). U.S. admiralty law is usually federal common law, although Congress may override a judicial determination.

**Advice and Consent Clause**   The President's appointments of Ambassadors, Judges, and principal officers, shall be with the approval of the Senate. The Advice and Consent Clause provides: "He shall have Power, by and with the Advice and Consent of the Senate, to make Treaties, provided two thirds of the Senators present concur; and he shall nominate, and by and with the Advice and Consent of the Senate, shall appoint Ambassadors, other public Ministers and Consuls, Judges of the Supreme Court, and all other Officers of the United States, whose Appointments are not herein otherwise provided for, and which shall be established by Law: but the Congress may by Law vest the Appointment of such inferior Officers, as they think proper, in the President alone, in the Courts of Law, or in the Heads of Departments." U.S. Const. art. II §2, cl. 2 (1789). The Senate must give advice and consent to treaties by a two-thirds majority of those present, but the ratio for advice and consent to appointments is not specified, and by custom and rule is by majority vote, although such a vote is subject to other rules, which may require cloture, or three-fifths, to overcome a filibuster.

*See also:* officer, federal officer, inferior officer.

**Appointments Clauses (Recess Appointments Clause)**   The President shall appoint principal officers with the advice and consent of the Senate, but other officers shall be appointed as required by law. The Appointments Clause provides: "He [the President] shall have Power, by and with the Advice and Consent of the Senate, to make Treaties, provided two thirds of the Senators present concur; and he shall nominate, and by and with the Advice and Consent of the Senate, shall appoint Ambassadors, other public

Ministers and Consuls, Judges of the Supreme Court, and all other Officers of the United States, whose Appointments are not herein otherwise provided for, and which shall be established by Law: but the Congress may by Law vest the Appointment of such inferior Officers, as they think proper, in the President alone, in the Courts of Law, or in the Heads of Departments. The President shall have Power to fill up all Vacancies that may happen during the Recess of the Senate, by granting Commissions which shall expire at the End of their next Session." U.S. Const. art. II § 2 (1789). Clause two is the Recess Appointments Clause. This clause provides three means of appointments. The first, for principal officers, ambassadors, and judges, requires the advice and consent of the Senate, which is given by a majority of the Senators voting. The second, for inferior officers, is given to the discretion of the President, which may be delegated to other executives as provided by law. The third, for any appointees, is a temporary appointment by the President, which is not subject to advice and consent but which expires at the end of the Congressional session.

*See also:* appointment (appoint); appointment, recess appointment (vacancy appointment).

**Appropriations Clause** Congress must appropriate all funds and designate the manner in which they are to be spent. The Appropriations Clause provides: "No money shall be drawn from the treasury, but in consequence of appropriations made by law." U.S. Const. art. I § 9, cl. 7 (1789).

*See also:* spending, spending power (power of the purse).

**Army Clause** The Congress may provide for an Army. The Army Clause provides: "The Congress shall have Power ... To raise and support Armies, but no Appropriation of Money to that Use shall be for a longer Term than two Years . . . ." U.S. Const. art. I § 8, cl. 12 (1789).

**Bill of Attainder Clauses** Congress and the state legislatures are each barred from bills of attainder. The Bill of Attainder Clauses provide: "No Bill of Attainder ... shall be passed . . . ." and "No State shall ... pass any Bill of Attainder . . . ." U.S. Const. art. I §§ 9–10 (1789).

*See also:* attainder, bill of attainder.

**Case and Controversy Clause** The judicial power extends to cases and to controversies as enumerated. The Case and Controversy Clause provides: "The judicial Power shall extend to all Cases, in Law and Equity, arising under this Constitution, the Laws of the United States, and Treaties made, or which shall be made, under their Authority — to all Cases affecting Ambassadors, other public Ministers and Consuls — to all Cases of admiralty and maritime Jurisdiction — to Controversies to which the United States shall be a Party — to Controversies between two or more States — between a State and Citizens of another State — between Citizens of different States — between Citizens of the same State claiming Lands under Grants of different States, and between a State, or the Citizens thereof, and foreign States, Citizens or Subjects." U.S. Const. art. III, cl. 1 (1789). Cases as listed in this clause are defined by the federal sources of the substantive law that govern them. Controversies as listed in this clause are defined by the federal interest in the parties to the action.

**Citizenship Clause (Naturalization Clause)** All persons born or naturalized in the United States are citizens of the United States and of their state of residence. The Citizenship Clause provides: "All persons born or naturalized in the United States, and subject to the jurisdiction thereof, are citizens of the United States and of the state wherein they reside. No state shall make or enforce any law which shall abridge the privileges or immunities of citizens of the United States." U.S. Const. amend. XIV § 1 (1868).

*See also:* citizen; naturalization.

**Coinage Clause** Congress may create, regulate, and fix the standards of money. The Coinage Clause provides: "The Congress shall have power . . . To coin money, regulate the value thereof, and of foreign coin, and fix the standard of weights and measures." U.S. Const. art. I, § 8, cl. 5 (1791).

*See also:* money.

**Commerce Clause** Congress has the power to regulate commerce for the whole nation. The Commerce Clause provides: "The Congress shall have Power To regulate Commerce with foreign Nations, and among the several States, and with the Indian Tribes;" U.S. Const. art I § 8, cl. 3 (1789). The Commerce Clause includes the three clauses of the Foreign Commerce Clause, the Interstate Commerce Clause, and the Indian Commerce Clause.

*See also:* commerce (commercial).

**Dormant Commerce Clause (Negative Commerce Clause)** The doctrine of the dormant commerce power. The dormant Commerce Clause is not actually a clause at all but an interpretation of the Commerce Clauses. Also called the negative Commerce Clause, it is a judicial doctrine reserving certain regulations of (mainly) interstate commerce but also foreign commerce from state regulation. More properly, it is known as the dormant commerce power, where it is here more fully defined.

*See also:* commerce, regulation of commerce, dormant commerce power.

**Foreign Commerce Clause** Congress may regulate commerce with foreign nations. The Foreign Commerce Clause provides: "The Congress shall have Power ... To regulate Commerce with foreign Nations . . . ." U.S.

Const. art. I, § 8, cl. 1(3) (1789). The foreign commerce clause allows Congressional action, which in turn allows executive action. The executive power over foreign affairs is independent but may be broadened by grants of authority by Congress.

**Indian Commerce Clause** Congress shall regulate Indian affairs. The Indian Commerce Clause provides: "The Congress shall have Power . . . To regulate Commerce . . . with the Indian Tribes." U.S. Const. art. I, § 8, cl. 3 (1789).

*See also:* commerce, regulation of commerce, commerce with Indian tribes.

**Interstate Commerce Clause** Congress may regulate anything affecting commerce between states. The Interstate Commerce Clause provides: "The Congress shall have Power . . . To regulate Commerce . . . and among the several States . . . ." U.S. Const. art. I, § 8, cl. 3 (1789). This clause has served as the basis for much of the Congress's regulation in the United States, and a reference only to "the Commerce Clause" is nearly always to the Interstate Commerce Clause. The scope of the "commerce power" of Congress is controversial, including not only people, goods, and services directly in commerce but also the means for their transportation, and activities affecting that transportation or commerce, as well as the effects of activities not in themselves but in the aggregate of all such activities. The result is that it is now widely accepted that Congress may regulate practically all matters that affect the economy in the United States that do not intrude on the powers of the states to control state officials and that do not violate the specific limits of power expressed in the text or implied from the recognition of individual freedoms or liberties.

*See also:* commerce, regulation of commerce, interstate commerce; commerce, regulation of commerce, interstate commerce.

**Compact Clause (Interstate Compact Clause)** No State shall enter into an interstate organization or an international alliance. The Compact Clause provides: "No State shall, without the Consent of Congress . . . enter into any Agreement or Compact with another State, or with a foreign Power, or engage in War, unless actually invaded, or in such imminent Danger as will not admit of delay." U.S. Const. art. I, § 10 (1791).

*See also:* compact.

**Compulsory Process Clause** The accused has the right to compulsory process for gathering witnesses. The Compulsory Process Clause provides: "In all criminal prosecutions, the accused shall enjoy the right . . . to have compulsory process for obtaining witnesses in his favor." U.S. Const. amend. VI (1791).

*See also:* service, service of process.

**Confrontation Clause** The accused has the right to confront the government's witnesses. The Confrontation Clause provides: "In all criminal prosecutions, the accused shall enjoy the right . . . to be confronted with the witnesses against him." U.S. Const. amend. VI (1791).

*See also:* confrontation; testimony, testimonial statement.

**Contracts Clause (Impairment of Contracts Clause)** A state may not unduly impair an obligation arising under a lawful contract between private parties. The Contracts Clause provides: "No State shall . . . pass any . . . Law impairing the Obligation of Contracts." U.S. Const. art. I, § 10, cl. 1 (1789). This clause does not limit the Congress or the federal government but limits the states alone from unreasonably or unnecessarily interfering with contracts.

**Copyright Clause (Copyright and Patent Clause or Patent and Copyright Clause or Intellectual Property Clause or Progressive Clause)** Congress may grant authors and inventors the exclusive rights to their writings and discoveries. The Copyright Clause provides: "The Congress shall have Power To . . . promote the Progress of Science and useful Arts, by securing for limited Times to Authors and Inventors the exclusive Right to their respective Writings and Discoveries." U.S. Const. art. I, § 8, cl. 8.

*See also:* patent.

**Cruel and Unusual Punishment Clause** Neither the United States nor a state may inflict a cruel or unusual punishment for a crime. The Cruel and Unusual Punishment Clause provides: "[N]or cruel and unusual punishments inflicted." U.S. Const. amend. VIII (1792). This provision has been made binding on the states through incorporation into the Due Process Clause of the Fourteenth Amendment. See Robinson v. California, 370 U.S. 660 (1962). The language of the clause is derived from the English Bill of Rights of 1689.

*See also:* punishment, cruel and unusual punishment, proportionality review; punishment (punish); punishment, cruel and unusual punishment.

**Declaration of War Clause (War Clause)** Congress declares war. The Declaration of War Clause provides: "The Congress shall have Power . . . To declare War." U.S. Const. art. 1, § 8, cl. 11 (1787).

**Disposing Clause** Congress has the power to dispose or regulate all U.S. territory and property. The Disposing Clause provides: "The Congress shall have power to dispose of and make all needful rules and regulations respecting the territory or other property belonging to the United States." U.S. Const. art. IV, §3, cl. 2 (1789).

**Diversity of Citizenship Clause**  Federal courts shall have jurisdiction over cases arising between citizens of different states. The Diversity of Citizenship Clause provides, in part: "The judicial Power shall extend to all Cases, in Law and Equity . . . between Citizens of different States." U.S. Const. art. III, §2, cl. 1 (1789).

**Double Jeopardy Clause**  No person can be tried twice by the same sovereign for the same offense. The Double Jeopardy Clause provides, in part: "[N]or shall any person be subject for the same offense to be twice put in jeopardy of life or limb." U.S. Const. amend. V (1791).

*See also:* jeopardy, double jeopardy.

**Due Process Clauses**  No agent of the government may subject any person to the loss of life, liberty, or property without due process of law. The Due Process Clause of the Fifth Amendment provides: "No person shall . . . be deprived of life, liberty, or property, without due process of law." U.S. Const. amend. V, cl. 4 (1791).

The Due Process Clause of the Fourteenth Amendment provides: "No State shall . . . deny to any person life, liberty, or property, without due process of law;" U.S. Const. amend. V, cl. 1 (1868).

The Fifth Amendment Due Process Clause binds the federal government, and the Fourteenth Amendment Due Process Clause binds the state governments. The Fifth Amendment Due Process Clause has been interpreted to require equal protection of the laws from the federal government as well.

*See also:* taking (takings or taking of private property without just compensation).

**Elections Clause (Election Clause)**  The states regulate Congressional elections, subject to Congressional limits. The Elections Clause provides: "The Times, Places and Manner of holding Elections for Senators and Representatives, shall be prescribed in each State by the Legislature thereof; but the Congress may at any time by Law make or alter such Regulations, except as to the Places of chusing Senators." U.S. Const. art. I §4, cl. 1 (1789). The significance of the last clause has been altered by the Seventeenth Amendment.

**Emoluments Clause (Congressional Emoluments Clause or Ineligibility Clause)**  Members of Congress may not create or fund offices to which they shall be appointed. The Congressional Emoluments Clause provides: "No Senator or Representative shall, during the Time for which he was elected, be appointed to any civil Office under the Authority of the United States, which shall have been created, or the Emoluments whereof shall have been encreased during such time; and no Person holding any Office under the United States, shall be a Member of either House during his Continuance in Office." U.S. Const. art. I §6, cl. 2 (1789). The Congressional Emoluments Clause is also known as the Ineligibility Clause. Note: there are two clauses known by custom as the Emoluments Clause. The other is also known as the Foreign Emoluments Clause.

*See also:* emolument; constitution, U.S. Constitution, clauses, Emoluments Clause (Foreign Emoluments Clause).

**Emoluments Clause (Foreign Emoluments Clause)**  No federal officer may accept a gift from a foreign state without Congressional approval. The Foreign Emoluments Clause provides: "No Person holding any Office of Profit or Trust under [the United States], shall, without the Consent of the Congress, accept of any present, Emolument, Office, or Title, of any kind whatever, from any King, Prince, or foreign State." U.S. Const. art. I, §9, cl. 8 (1789). Note: two clauses are known by custom as the Emoluments Clause, the other being Article One, Section Six, which is also known as the Congressional Emoluments Clause or the Ineligibility Clause.

*See also:* emolument; constitution, U.S. Constitution, clauses, Emoluments Clause (Congressional Emoluments Clause or Ineligibility Clause).

**Enabling Clauses**  Congress or the state legislatures are empowered to effect the powers in amendments. The Enabling Clauses provide:

Congress shall have power to enforce this article by appropriate legislation. U.S. Const. amend. XIII (1865).

The Congress shall have the power to enforce, by appropriate legislation, the provisions of this article. U.S. Const. amend. XIV (1868).

The Congress shall have the power to enforce this article by appropriate legislation. U.S. Const. amend. XV (1870).

The Congress and the several States shall have concurrent power to enforce this article by appropriate legislation. U.S. Const. amend. XVIII (1919).

Congress shall have power to enforce this article by appropriate legislation. U.S. Const. amend. XIX (1920).

The Congress shall have power to enforce this article by appropriate legislation. U.S. Const. amend. XXIII (1961).

The Congress shall have power to enforce this article by appropriate legislation. U.S. Const. amend. XXIV (1964).

The Congress shall have power to enforce this article by appropriate legislation. U.S. Const. amend. XXVI (1971).

Impliedly, Congress was granted the power to enable all of the legal requirements of the Constitution of 1791, and Article I, Section 8, is properly thought of as an enumeration of powers and not as an enabling clause.

**Enclave Clause**  Congress alone enacts legislation over the federal district and federal property. The Enclave Clause provides: "To exercise exclusive Legislation in all Cases whatsoever, over such District (not exceeding ten Miles square) as may, by Cession of particular States, and the acceptance of Congress, become the Seat of the Government of the United States, and to exercise like Authority over all Places purchased by the Consent of the Legislature of the State in which the Same shall be, for the Erection of Forts, Magazines, Arsenals, Dock-Yards, and other needful Buildings." U.S. Const. art. I, § 8, cl. 17 (1789).

**Equal Protection Clause**  No person within the jurisdiction of the United States shall be denied the equal protection of its laws. The Equal Protection Clause of the Fourteenth Amendment provides: "No State shall . . . deny to any person within its jurisdiction the equal protection of the laws." U.S. Const. amend. XIV, cl. 1. The guarantee of equal protection of the laws requires the assessment of all categories created by laws that assign a burden or a benefit to one group but not to another. The courts apply an historical test, in that burdens that fall on groups that have been the basis of great discrimination in the present or the past require the greatest level of governmental justification. The principle of equal protection has been read into the Due Process Clause of the Fifth Amendment to bind the federal government to a similar constraint.

*See also:* equality (equal); equality, equal protection of the law.

**Establishment Clause**  The government may not establish a religion in the United States. The Establishment Clause provides: "Congress shall make no law respecting an establishment of religion . . ." U.S. Const. amend. I (1791).

*See also:* religion, freedom of religion.

**Ex Post Facto Clause**  Federal and State governments may not pass retroactive laws. The Ex Post Facto Clauses provide: "No . . . ex post facto Law shall be passed . . . ." "No state shall . . . pass any . . . ex post facto law." U.S. Const. art. I, §§ 9–10 (1789).

*See also:* attainder, bill of attainder; retroactivity (retroactive effect); ex, ex post facto (ex post facto law).

**Exceptions and Regulations Clause (Exceptions Clause or Regulations Clause)**  Congress may create exceptions to the Supreme Court's appellate jurisdiction. The Exceptions and Regulations Clause provides: "[In all cases affecting ambassadors, other public ministers and consuls, and those in which a state shall be party, the Supreme Court shall have original jurisdiction.] In all the other cases before mentioned, the Supreme Court shall have appellate jurisdiction, both as to law and fact, with such exceptions, and under such regulations as the Congress shall make." U.S. Const. art. III, § 2, cl. 2 (1789).

**Excessive Fines Clause**  A court can not impose an excessive fine on a guilty party. The Excessive Fines Clause provides: "[N]or excessive fines imposed." U.S. Const. amend. VIII (1792).

**Export Clause**  States may only regulate exports when necessary for inspection, and any proceeds go to the federal government. The Export Clause provides: "No state shall, without the consent of the Congress, lay any imposts or duties on imports or exports, except what may be absolutely necessary for executing its inspection laws: and the net produce of all duties and imposts, laid by any state on imports or exports, shall be for the use of the treasury of the United States; and all such laws shall be subject to the revision and control of the Congress." U.S. Const. art. I, § 10, cl. 2 (1789). This clause does not bar regular property or inventory taxes on property that is intended for export. Also called the Import–Export Clause, it is usually quoted as a limit on the powers of the states at this length. It is also quoted at greater length when considering the powers of Congress.

*See also:* exportation (export); constitution, U.S. Constitution, clauses, Import–Export Clause.

**Extradition Clause (Interstate Rendition Clause)**  States must extradite any person accused of a crime upon the demand of another state. The Extradition Clause provides: "A person charged in any state with treason, felony, or other crime, who shall flee from justice, and be found in another state, shall on demand of the executive authority of the state from which he fled, be delivered up, to be removed to the state having jurisdiction of the crime." U.S. Const. art. IV, § 2 (1789).

*See also:* extradition.

**Faithful Execution Clause (Faithfully Executed Clause)**  The President must faithfully execute the laws. The Faithfully Executed Clause provides: "He [the President] . . . shall take Care that the Laws be faithfully executed." U.S. Const. art. II, § 3 (1789).

*See also:* execution (executable or execute or executed or executory).

**Foreign Gifts Clause (Foreign Gifts and Titles Clause)**  No federal official may accept a gift or title from a foreign power without the consent of the Congress. The Emoluments Clause provides: "[N]o Person holding any Office of Profit or Trust under them, shall, without the Consent of the Congress, accept of any present, Emolument, Office, or Title, of any kind whatever, from any King, Prince or foreign State." U.S.

Const. art. I § 9. "Them" here refers to the United States.

*See also:* emolument.

**Free Exercise Clause**  Congress may not hinder the free exercise of religion. The Free Exercise Clause provides: "Congress shall make no law [respecting an establishment of religion, or] . . . prohibiting the free exercise thereof;" U.S. Const. amend. I (1791).

[The bracketed text is the Establishment Clause, included here to clarify the meaning of "thereof."]

*See also:* religion, freedom of religion.

**Full Faith and Credit Clause**  Each state must honor the the laws of other states that do not expressly conflict with their own. The Full Faith and Credit Clause provides: "Full Faith and Credit shall be given in each State to the public Acts, Records, and judicial Proceedings of every other State. And the Congress may by general Laws prescribe the Manner in which such Acts, Records and Proceedings shall be proved, and the Effect thereof." U.S. Const. art. IV, § 1 (1789).

**General Welfare Clause**  Congress has broad powers to provide for the general welfare of Americans. The General Welfare Clause provides: "The Congress shall have Power . . . to provide for the . . . general Welfare of the United States." U.S. Const. art. I § 8, cl. 1 (1792).

*See also:* welfare (general welfare or public welfare).

**Grand Jury Clause**  Every federal felony prosecution must commence in the grand jury. The Grand Jury Clause provides: "No person shall be held to answer for a capital, or otherwise infamous crime, unless on a presentment or indictment of a Grand Jury, except in cases arising in the land or naval forces, or in the Militia, when in actual service in time of War or public danger;" U.S. Const. amend. V (1791). The Grand Jury Clause has not been incorporated into the Due Process Clause of the Fourteenth Amendment, and so it remains binding on the United States but not upon the several states. Likewise, a grand jury is not required prior to a court martial unless Congress provides for such a procedure or an analogous process. Although the Fifth Amendment requires a federal grand jury, it does not decree particular procedures for it, which have traditionally been left to the discretion of the prosecutor, with only limited supervision by the courts.

*See also:* jury, grand jury.

**Habeas Corpus Clause**  Each person is entitled to challenge the basis of the person's confinement by the government. The Habeas Corpus Clause provides: "The Privilege of the Writ of Habeas Corpus shall not be suspended, unless when in Cases of Rebellion or Invasion the public

Safety may require it." U.S. Const. art. I, § 9, cl. 2 (1789).

*See also:* suspension (suspend).

**Impeachment Clause**  Both houses of Congress must act to remove a person from office. The Impeachment Clause provides: "The President, Vice President and all civil officers of the United States, shall be removed from office on impeachment for, and conviction of, treason, bribery, or other high crimes and mis-demeanors."

The mechanisms of impeachment are set forth in Article Two: "The House of Representatives . . . shall have the sole power of impeachment." U.S. Const. art. I, § 2, cl. 5.

"The Senate shall have the sole power to try all impeachments. When sitting for that purpose, they shall be on oath or affirmation. When the President of the United States is tried, the Chief Justice shall preside: And no person shall be convicted without the concurrence of two thirds of the members present. Judgment in cases of impeachment shall not extend further than to removal from office, and disqualification to hold and enjoy any office of honor, trust or profit under the United States: but the party convicted shall nevertheless be liable and subject to indictment, trial, judgment and punishment, according to law." U.S. Const. art. II, § 3 cl. 5-6.

*See also:* impeachment, impeachment of official.

**Import-Export Clause**  International tariffs are in the federal legislative jurisdiction. The Import-Export Clause provides: "No State shall, without the Consent of the Congress, lay any Imposts or Duties on Imports or Exports, except what may be absolutely necessary for executing it's inspection Laws: and the net Produce of all Duties and Imposts, laid by any State on Imports or Exports, shall be for the Use of the Treasury of the United States; and all such Laws shall be subject to the Revision and Controul of the Congress." U.S. Const. art. I, § 10, cl. 2 (1789). Though this text is also the export clause, in its context relating to the powers of Congress rather than the states, it is usually given its fuller quotation.

*See also:* constitution, U.S. Constitution, clauses, Export Clause.

**Jury Clause (Impartial Jury Clause or Criminal Jury Clause)**  Every adult accused of a serious crime shall be tried by an impartial jury. The Jury Clause of the Sixth Amendment provides: "In all criminal prosecutions, the accused shall enjoy the right to a speedy and public trial, by an impartial jury of the State and district wherein the crime shall have been committed, which district shall have been previously ascertained by law," U.S. Const. amend. VI (1791). The Jury Clause was incorporated into the Due Process Clause of the Fourteenth Amendment in Duncan v. Louisiana, 391 U.S. 145 (1968), and so it remains binding on the United States as well as the several states. Note: the clause does not state a requirement of "trial by one's peers." Note also: there is a Jury Clause in the Seventh Amendment providing for a civil jury in federal court.

*See also:* trial, jury trial (trial by jury).

**Liberty Clause** A state may not burden a liberty interest but by due process of law. The Liberty Clause provides: "nor shall any State deprive any person of ... liberty ... without due process of law." U.S. Const. amend. XIV (1868). Interests protected by the liberty clause are liberty interests, and are either fundamental and protected by strict scrutiny, or not.

*See also:* liberty; due process of law, liberty interest.

**Marque and Reprisal Clauses** Only Congress may commission privateers. There are two Marque and Reprisal Clauses, which provide: "The Congress shall have the Power To ... grant Letters of Marque and Reprisal ..." U.S. Const. art. I, § 8, cl. 10 (1789), and: "No State shall ... grant Letters of Marque and Reprisal ..." U.S. Const. art. I, § 10, cl. 1 (1789).

*See also:* privateer; marque and reprisal.

**Militia Clauses** Congress determines the means by which the President calls out the militia. The Militia Clauses provide: "The Congress shall have Power ... To provide for calling forth the Militia to execute the Laws of the Union, suppress Insurrections and repel Invasions; To provide for organizing, arming, and disciplining, the Militia, and for governing such Part of them as may be employed in the Service of the United States, reserving to the States respectively, the Appointment of the Officers, and the Authority of training the Militia according to the discipline prescribed by Congress ..." U.S. Const. art. I, § 8, cl. 15–16 (1789).

*See also:* militia.

**Natural-Born Citizen Clause** The President must have been a citizen from birth. The Natural-Born Citizen Clause provides: "No Person except a natural born Citizen, or a Citizen of the United States, at the time of the Adoption of this Constitution, shall be eligible to the Office of President, ..." U.S. Const. art. II, § 1 (1787).

*See also:* citizen, natural-born citizen (natural born citizen); qualification, qualification as requirement.

**Navy Clause (Naval Clause)** Congress may create and maintain the Navy. The Navy Clause provides: "The Congress shall have Power to ... provide and maintain a Navy ..." U.S. Const. art. I, § 8, cl. 13 (1789).

**Necessary and Proper Clause (Elastic Clause or Basket Clause or Coefficient Clause or Sweeping Clause)** Congress may pass unspecified laws to achieve specified powers. The

Necessary and Proper Clause provides: "The Congress shall have power to ... make all laws which shall be necessary and proper for carrying into execution the foregoing powers, and all other powers vested by this Constitution in the government of the United States, or in any department or officer thereof." U.S. Const. art. I, § 8, cl. 18 (1789). This clause has been interpreted to provide a scope of congressional power greater than the powers enumerated, which is exercised when Congress deems it necessary to do so in aid of the enumerated powers.

*See also:* proper.

**Oath or Affirmation Clause (Oath Clause or Affirmation Clause or Oath of Office Clause)** All state and federal officers must swear or affirm to be bound by the U.S. Constitution. The Affirmation Clause provides: "The Senators and Representatives before mentioned, and the Members of the several State Legislatures, and all executive and judicial Officers, both of the United States and of the several States, shall be bound by Oath or Affirmation, to support this Constitution; ..." U.S. Const. art. VI, cl. 3 (1789).

*See also:* affirmation, affirmation as quasi-oath (affirm); oath.

**Origination Clause** Revenue bills must start in the House of Representatives. The Origination Clause provides: "All Bills for raising Revenue shall originate in the House of Representatives; but the Senate may propose or concur with Amendments as on other Bills." U.S. Const. art. I, § 7, cl. 1 (1791).

*See also:* bill, bill as legislation, revenue bill.

**Pardon Clause** The President may pardon or commute the sentence of federal criminals. The Pardon Clause provides: "and he shall have Power to grant Reprieves and Pardons for Offences against the United States, except in Cases of Impeachment." U.S. Const. art. II, § 2 (1789).

*See also:* clemency; commutation (commutative or commute).

**Petition Clause** Any citizen may petition the federal government to redress a grievance. The Petition Clause provides: "Congress shall make no law ... abridging ... the right of the people ... to petition the Government for a redress of grievances." U.S. Const. amend. I (1789).

*See also:* petition, right to petition.

**Post Offices Clause (Post Road Clause)** The federal government will create a national mail service. The Post Offices Clause provides: "The Congress shall have Power ... To establish Post Offices and post Roads; ..." U.S. Const., art. 1, § 8, cl. 7 (1787).

**Privileges and Immunities Clause (Comity Clause)** Citizens of each state have equal rights in all states. The Privileges and Immunities

Clause provides: "The Citizens of each State shall be entitled to all Privileges and Immunities of Citizens in the several States." U.S. Const. art. IV, § 2, cl. 1 (1789).

*See also:* privilege; privilege, privileges and immunities.

**Property Clause (Needful Rules Clause)** Federal lands are subject to federal law. The Property Clause provide: "The Congress shall have power to dispose of and make all needful rules and regulations respecting the territory or other property belonging to the United States; and nothing in this Constitution shall be so construed as to prejudice any claims of the United States, or of any particular State." U.S. Const., art. IV, § 3, cl. 2. Federal property is therefore subject to federal law rather than state law, unless Congress provides to the contrary.

*See also:* land, federal land (federal lands or U.S. government property).

**Regulation of Forces Clause (Military Regulation Clause)** Congress creates military law. The Military Regulation Clause provides: "Congress shall have Power . . . To make Rules for the Government and Regulation of the land and naval Forces . . . U.S. Const. art. I, § 8, cl. 11 (1789).

*See also:* military, military law, articles of war; military, military law; war, law of war (law of armed conflict or LOW or LOAC).

**Religious Test Clause** No U.S. or state official must espouse a religion. The Religious Test Clause provides: "[N]o religious test shall ever be required as a qualification to any office, or public trust under the United States." U.S. Const. art. 6, § 3 (1789).

*See also:* qualification, qualification as requirement.

**Republican Form of Government Clause (Guarantee Clause)** Congress must maintain unity of and Republican governance of the individual states. The Guarantee Clause provides: "The United States shall guarantee to every State in this Union a Republican Form of Government, and shall protect each of them against Invasion; and on Application of the Legislature, or of the Executive (when the Legislature cannot be convened) against domestic Violence." U.S. Const. art. IV, § 4 (1789).

*See also:* government, forms of government, republic.

**Self-Incrimination Clause** The Fifth Amendment proscribes forcing a defendant to testify or otherwise confess statements admitting illegal activity. The Fifth Amendment provides: "[N]or shall be compelled in any criminal case to be a witness against himself." U.S. Const. amend. V (1791).

*See also:* privilege; confession; incrimination, self-incrimination (privilege against self-incrimination or right to silence); search, exclusionary rule; incrimination, self-incrimination, collective entity doctrine.

**Speech or Debate Clause (Speech and Debate Clause or Speech Clause)** Statements made during congressional speech and debate are privileged speech. The Speech or Debate Clause provides: "The Senators and Representatives . . . shall in all Cases, except Treason, Felony and Breach of the Peace, be privileged from Arrest; . . . and for any Speech or Debate in either House, they shall not be questioned in any other Place." U.S. Const. art. I, § 6, cl. 1 (1789).

*See also:* immunity, official immunity, legislative immunity (congressional immunity).

**Statehood Clause** Congress creates new states, with the consent of each state whose boundary is affected. The Statehood Clause provides: "New States may be admitted by the Congress into this Union; but no new State shall be formed or erected within the Jurisdiction of any other State; nor any State be formed by the Junction of two or more States, or Parts of States, without the Consent of the Legislatures of the States concerned as well as of the Congress." U.S. Const. art. 4, § 3 (1787).

*See also:* sovereignty, state sovereignty, equal footing doctrine (equal–footing doctrine).

**Statement and Accounts Clause** The Federal accounts must be published. The Statement and Accounts Clause provides: "[A] regular statement and account of receipts and expenditures of all public money shall be published from time to time." U.S. Const. art. I, § 9, cl. 7 (1789).

**Supremacy Clause** Federal law takes precedence over state laws. The Supremacy Clause provides: "This Constitution, and the Laws of the United States which shall be made in Pursuance thereof; and all Treaties made, or which shall be made, under the Authority of the United States, shall be the supreme Law of the Land; and the Judges in every State shall be bound thereby, any Thing in the Constitution or Laws of any State to the Contrary notwithstanding." U.S. Const. art. VI, cl. 2 (1789).

*See also:* supremacy (supreme).

**Suspension Clause** The right to habeas shall not be suspended but during rebellion or invasion. The Suspension Clause provides: "The privilege of the writ of habeas corpus shall not be suspended, unless when in cases of rebellion or invasion the public safety may require it." U.S. Const., art. I, § 9, cl. 2.

**Takings Clause** The Fifth Amendment prohibits public use of private property without just compensation. The Fifth Amendment provides in part: "Nor shall private property be taken for public use, without just compensation." U.S. Const. amend. V (1791). The obligations in this clause have been applied to the states through incorporation into the Due Process Clause of the Fourteenth Amendment. See Chicago, Burlington & Quincy Railroad Co. v. City of Chicago, 166 U.S. 226 (1897) (Harlan, J.).

See also: taking (takings or taking of private property without just compensation); lease, leasehold, leasehold interest.

**Titles of Nobility Clauses**  Neither the United States nor any state grants titles of nobility. The Titles of Nobility Clauses provide: "No Title of Nobility shall be granted by the United States: . . ." and "No State shall . . . grant any Title of Nobility." U.S. Const. art. I § 9, cl. 8, art. I, § 10, cl. 1 (1789).

See also: title, title as form of address (Mr. or Ms. or Miss or Mrs. or Hon. or Excellency).

**Treason Clauses**  Treason is narrowly defined and requires two witnesses to one act or a confession in court. The Treason Clauses provide: "Treason against the United States, shall consist only in levying War against them, or in adhering to their Enemies, giving them Aid and Comfort. No Person shall be convicted of Treason unless on the Testimony of two Witnesses to the same overt Act, or on Confession in open Court. The Congress shall have power to declare the Punishment of Treason, but no Attainder of Treason shall work Corruption of Blood, or Forfeiture except during the Life of the Person attainted." The Treason Clauses apply only to prosecutions for treason and not to other crimes, such as subversion or sedition, even though such crimes are treasonous. U.S. Const. art. III, § 3 (1789).

See also: treason (traitor).

**Treaty Clause**  The President may enter treaties, subject to Senate approval. The Treaty Clause provides: "He shall have Power, by and with the Advice and Consent of the Senate, to make Treaties, provided two thirds of the Senators present concur . . . ." U.S. Const. art. II, cl. 2 (1789).

See also: treaty, ratification of treaty (treaty ratification).

**Veto Clause**  The President may veto a bill, but the Congress may override the veto. The Veto Clause provides: "If he approve he shall sign it, but if not he shall return it, with his Objections to that House in which it shall have originated, who shall enter the Objections at large on their Journal, and proceed to reconsider it. If after such Reconsideration two thirds of that House shall agree to pass the Bill, it shall be sent, together with the Objections, to the other House, by which it shall likewise be reconsidered, and if approved by two thirds of that House, it shall become a Law. But in all such Cases the Votes of both Houses shall be determined by Yeas and Nays, and the Names of the Persons voting for and against the Bill shall be entered on the Journal of each House respectively." Note: the text does not use the word 'veto.'" U.S. Const. art. 1, § 7 (1787).

See also: veto.

**constitutional remedy**  A remedy, based in a court's equitable discretion, for a violation of a state or federal constitution. Constitutional remedies arise from the judicial powers of the Constitution, invested in the federal courts by Article III and in the state courts by state constitutions and the operation of the Supremacy Clause. In both cases, the power to craft a remedy for a breach of the Constitution is inherently equitable, except for the rare case in which a remedy is specified in a constitutional text. Often, a constitutional remedy will take the form of an injunction, prohibiting or requiring a government action.

See also: equity, equitable remedy (equitable relief).

**Framers**  The participants in the debates and drafting of the constitution. The Framers of the Constitution include all of the fifty-five people who directly participated in debates, drafting, and voting on the text of the constitution. The term is most often employed to mean the members of the Constitutional Convention in 1787; however, it is often used more loosely, to include those who were instrumental in the ratification process as well. John Jay, for example, did not attend the convention but authored five articles published in The Federalist Papers. Indeed, at its broadest, The Framers include not only the convention members and drafters of the Constitution of 1787 but also the drafters and promoters of the Bill of Rights. "Framers" is also employed to describe the drafters, backers, and debaters of particular amendments to the Constitution, and in this sense, there is a more limited sense in which there are Framers of the Bill of Rights, as well as, say, the Framers of the Fourteenth Amendment.

signers (signatories)  The thirty-nine members of the Constitutional Convention who signed the Constitutional text. Those members who signed the text were:

Connecticut: William Samuel Johnson, Roger Sherman

Delaware: George Read, Gunning Bedford, Jr., John Dickinson, Richard Bassett, Jacob Broom

Georgia: William Few, Abraham Baldwin

Maryland: James McHenry, Daniel of St. Thomas Jenifer, Daniel Carroll

Massachusetts: Nathaniel Gorham, Rufus King

New Hampshire: John Langdon, Nicholas Gilman

New Jersey: William Livingston, David Brearly, William Paterson, Jonathan Dayton

New York: Alexander Hamilton

North Carolina: William Blount, Richard Dobbs Spaight, Hugh Williamson

Pennsylvania: Benjamin Franklin, Thomas Mifflin, Robert Morris, George Clymer, Thomas Fitzsimons, Jared Ingersoll, James Wilson, Gouverneur Morris

South Carolina: John Rutledge, Charles Cotesworth Pinckney, Charles Pinckney, Pierce Butler

Rhode Island: none

Virginia: John Blair, James Madison Jr., George Washington

### constitutional ideals

**common defense**  The military defense of the nation. The common defense is a constitutional ideal that is given effect by the organization of a military by the Congress, which is commanded by the President as commander in chief.

**created equal**  The recognition of an equal dignity in every person. The phrase "We hold these truths to be self-evident, that all men are created equal . . ." is in the Declaration of Independence, not in a ratified constitutional text. It is, however, a predicate to the Equal Protection Clause of the Fourteenth Amendment and the equal protection prong of the Due Process Clause of the Fifth Amendment.

*See also:* equality (equal).

**federalism**  The division of governmental powers between a central government and state governments. Federalism, in the American legal system, is the division of powers between a central government and the various state governments. There are two, distinct arguments for federalism, the first being that a division of authority operates to diminish the likelihood of tyranny. The states would check the executive, particularly through the selection of the President and the members of the Congress, and the federal government would check the states, initially through the assurance of a Republican form of government, and then latterly through enforcement of the Thirteenth, Fourteenth, and Fifteenth Amendments. Federalism also allows a compromise between a need for variations in laws and politics at a local level and a need for national uniformity of policies and for a national assurance of certain services, such as a common defense and common economic policy. This balance is reflected in the reserved powers of the states and the delegated powers of the central government. Though the balance has tilted toward the central government over time, particularly following the amendments passed after the Civil War, states of the United States still retain considerable autonomy over their laws.

*See also:* federalism; sovereignty, state sovereignty; supremacy (supreme).

**pursuit of happiness**  The individual search for rational personal fulfillment. The concept or an "unalienable right" to "the pursuit of happiness" was written into the opening paragraph of the Declaration of Independence. It is not in the text of the U.S. Constitution. The concept has, however, exerted a significant influence on later readings of the Constitution. It is almost certainly mistaken to read the idea of happiness here as a mere synonym for property and anachronistic to read it as a defense of the chase of personal pleasure. Thomas Jefferson more likely intended it to be read as a right to the pursuit of personal pleasure within the boundaries of the public good.

**separation of powers**  The division of the legislative, judicial and executive powers. Separation of powers is the division of the powers of the state into three competing structures of government, a Congress holding all legislative power, a President holding all executive power, and a Supreme Court and lesser courts holding all judicial power. The idea is that the competition for authority among the three groups will discourage any one entity from supremacy, or tyranny. This idea depends upon checks and balances being actively employed by each branch to monitor the excesses of the other two.

**checks and balances**  The allocation of powers among the branches of government to ensure that none become so powerful as to threaten the liberty of the individual. Checks and balances describes the specific allocation of authority that is in sum the separation of powers. Ideally, according to this allocation, the officials of each branch to correct excesses of the officials of the other branches, balancing the authority of government. Although the phrase is usually now meant to describe only allocations of powers among the three branches of the federal government, as used in the eighteenth century, the phrase included the division of authorities among the states and the central government as well.

*See also:* spending, spending power (power of the purse).

**coordinate branch**  Each of the three branches of government. The three branches are each said to be a coordinate branch, in that no one can govern without coordinating its authority with the other two. For a member of one branch to describe another as coordinate is to emphasize their relative equality of authority.

**intent of the Framers (Framers' intent)**  A best guess of what the Framers had in mind when they wrote a portion of the text. The intent of the Framers is a modern statement about the expectations of the Framers when a text was written into the Constitution. Divining the intent of the Framers is an exercise in historicism, in which a limited array of texts written by Framers or about Framers at the time of the drafting are considered and a particular idea of what the Framers must have been thinking is identified.

**interstate compact (interstate agreement)** An agreement between states approved by Congress. An interstate compact is any contract or agreement between two or more states of the United States, which is allowed only upon the assent of the Congress.

**unconstitutional** Contrary to the constitution. Any action of an official, any rule or regulation, any statute, any court mandate or order that is not authorized by the constitution of the jurisdiction in which it occurs is unconstitutional. Unconstitutional actions or laws may thus occur when an act is beyond scope of the powers of office as it is created by or under the constitution. Or, it may occur when an action or law particularly violates a requirement or a prohibition in the constitution.

**construction or interpret or construe** *See:* interpretation (construction or interpret or construe).

**constructive** Any term or obligation arising from interpretation. Anything that is constructive in law or equity is read into the text or the situation. Constructive presence, constructive notice, a constructive right, a constructive condition, etc., are all implied by operation of law or equity from circumstances.

*See also:* possession, adverse possession, constructive adverse possession; condition, constructive condition; delivery, delivery of possession, constructive delivery (constructive–receipt doctrine); discharge, employment discharge, constructive discharge; eviction, constructive eviction; fraud, constructive fraud; larceny, constructive larceny; possession, constructive possession; take, constructive taking (constructively take); trust, constructive trust.

**constructive abandonment** *See:* abandonment, constructive abandonment.

**constructive abandonment of a patent** *See:* patent, abandonment of a patent, constructive abandonment of a patent (statutory forfeiture or prior public use bar).

**constructive adverse possession** *See:* possession, adverse possession, constructive adverse possession.

**constructive authority** *See:* authority, constructive authority (implied authority).

**constructive bailment** *See:* bailment, constructive bailment (involuntary bailment).

**constructive condition** *See:* condition, constructive condition.

**constructive delivery** *See:* delivery, delivery of possession, constructive delivery (constructive-receipt doctrine).

**constructive discharge** *See:* discharge, employment discharge, constructive discharge.

**constructive eviction** *See:* eviction, constructive eviction.

**constructive fraud** *See:* fraud, constructive fraud.

**constructive intent** *See:* intent, constructive intent (presumed intent).

**constructive knowledge** *See:* knowledge, constructive knowledge (presumed knowledge, presumptive knowledge).

**constructive larceny** *See:* larceny, constructive larceny.

**constructive notice** *See:* notice, constructive notice (record notice).

**constructive possession** *See:* possession, constructive possession.

**constructive-receipt doctrine** *See:* delivery, delivery of possession, constructive delivery (constructive-receipt doctrine).

**constructively take** *See:* take, constructive taking (constructively take).

**constructive taking** *See:* take, constructive taking (constructively take).

**constructive trust** *See:* trust, constructive trust.

**constructive unlawful possession** *See:* possession, constructive possession, constructive unlawful possession (accessorial possession).

**consul** Diplomatic agent performing commercial, economic and social functions. A consul is any consular officer who is appointed by a state to provide consular services in another state, including the management of passports and visas, facilitation in the movement of contracts, deeds, documents, and service in litigation, assistance with trade and commercial development and the maintenance of amicable ties between the two states. A state may have several consular officers in another state, each with a consular district and staff. The term may refer in some contexts only to the consul–general or to a consul holding that title, but in other usages include a vice–consul general or consular staff. Consuls enjoy limited immunity from interference in their duties by local law enforcement, though it is by no means as extensive as diplomatic immunity.

*See also:* ambassador (ambassadress); diplomat, consul.

**consular immunity** The immunity of a consul and the consulate from process. Consuls are entitled to immunity from civil process related to any act of consular business and criminal immunity from local process, except for grave crimes. Consular premises, correspondence, and files are inviolable and immune to search or seizure.

*See also:* diplomat, diplomatic immunity.

**consulate (consular post or consular premises)** The offices or building housing a consul's office. A consulate is an office or building in a receiving state housing a consul, consular staff, or consular archives. Consulates may fly the flag and display the coat of arms of the receiving state. Consulates are immune from search and seizure of documents related to the specific work of the consul as a diplomatic agent, and consulates are exempt from taxation by the receiving state.

**consumable**  Goods that will be destroyed or valueless after normal use. Consumables are goods that are consumed through use, or that through storage or use become so valueless that there is no capital in them sufficient for them to be subject to depreciation.

**consumer**  The ultimate intended user of a good or service. The consumer is the person or entity that is the ultimate intended user of a product or service, regardless of whether the consumer purchased the product or service. Thus, the person or entity purchasing or acquiring a product for use is a consumer, as is a person or entity given a product or purchasing it from someone who has already used it. A consumer may be a business or merchant that sells services or goods to consumers, but it is still a consumer as to the products and services it uses in its business. In the context of the UCC, however, a consumer is presumed to be an individual who intends to use the goods in a domestic setting.

*See also:* boycott, consumer boycott; credit, consumer credit, Consumer Credit Protection Act (C.C.P.A. or CCPA); debt, consumer debt; fraud, consumer fraud.

**consumer boycott**  *See:* boycott, consumer boycott.

**consumer credit**  *See:* credit, consumer credit, Consumer Credit Protection Act (C.C.P.A. or CCPA); credit, consumer credit, billing error.

**Consumer Credit Protection Act**  *See:* credit, consumer credit, Consumer Credit Protection Act (C.C.P.A. or CCPA).

**consumer debt**  *See:* debt, consumer debt.

**consumer expectation test**  *See:* liability, product liability, product defect, consumer expectation test.

**consumer fraud**  *See:* fraud, consumer fraud.

**consumer picket**  *See:* picket, consumer picket.

**Consumer Price Index**  *See:* price, Consumer Price Index (CPI).

**consumer warranty or manufacturer's warranty**  *See:* warranty, sales warranty, warranty of merchantability (consumer warranty or manufacturer's warranty).

**end user**  The ultimate consumer. The end user is the person or entity that is the final buyer of a product or service, who purchases or acquires it for use, consumption, or retention, without a purpose of resale or transfer.

**consummation (consummate)**  Completion. Consummation is the completion of any act or process. The consummation of a contract negotiation is the entry of the parties into the contract, but the consummation of the contract is the final performance by the later performing party. The word is now most often used in the context of a marriage, which is consummated by the spouses through an act of intercourse following the wedding ceremony.

**consummation of marriage**  *See:* marriage, consummation of marriage.

**contaminant (contaminate)**  Any matter that corrupts or pollutes the substance it contacts. A contaminant is a substance that is present in a material or in the air, water, or soil and that causes a harmful reaction in the material or the environmental matrix. A contaminate may be chemical, biological, nuclear, or even photonic; the defining aspect of the contaminate is that it contaminates the specific environment in which it occurs. Like a poison in food or dust in a clean room, the contaminant might not contaminate a different substance or environment.

**contaminate release**  *See:* release, contaminate release, deliberate release; release, contaminate release (release of contaminate).

**contamination**  Overload of a contaminant in a single environment. Contamination is the effect when a contaminant (whether it is a chemical or a biological agent) is present in a substance or in the environment in a sufficient quantity to render the substance unfit for use or the environment a risk to human health or its own stability. Generally the quantity that results in contamination is an amount of the substance that is too great a quantity or load to be assimilated or to decay through natural processes in a relevant time frame.

**contemnor**  *See:* contempt of court, contemnor.

**contemplation of death**  *See:* death, contemplation of death (articulo mortis or causa mortis or death-bed declaration or dying declaration).

**contemporaneous agreement**  *See:* agreement, contemporaneous agreement.

**contemporary community standards of obscenity**  *See:* obscenity, Miller test, contemporary community standards of obscenity (community standards of obscenity).

**contempt of court**  Willful disregard for the authority and decorum of a court. Contempt of court is conduct that interrupts the order of court or that evinces disrespect for the administration of justice by the court. Disobedience of a court order, or any conduct that seeks to embarrass, impede or obstruct the function of the courts constitutes contempt. Contempt may be either civil or criminal, though either may result in sanctions including fines or imprisonment.

*See also:* subpoena.

*civil contempt vs. criminal contempt* Contempt of court is civil if the purpose and structure of the remedy is to encourage compliance with the court's order. It is criminal if the purpose is more inherently punitive in nature or the structure of the order is finite regardless of any compliance by the contemnor.

**contemnor** A person who acts in contempt of court. A contemnor is any person who engages in conduct in contempt of court. It is not necessary for a person to be held in contempt of court to be a contemnor.

**contempt proceeding** A hearing on civil contempt or a trial on criminal contempt. A contempt proceeding is a consideration of whether a person or entity shall be held in contempt of court. A civil contempt hearing may be a summary proceeding before the court, although some notice that is reasonable in the circumstances is usually required, and a finding of civil contempt cannot amount to a criminal penalty but only a penalty tailored to require compliance with an order of the court. A criminal contempt hearing must comply with the requirements of due process for a criminal proceeding, and it may result in a criminal punishment.

**direct contempt** An act of contempt made in court and in the presence of the judge. A direct contempt is an action by any person, whether a party, attorney, witness, observer, or official that interferes with the court's interest in maintaining order and the authority of the court and that is committed in court during a hearing, trial, or other proceeding.

**indirect contempt** An act of contempt of court occurring out of court. An indirect contempt is an action by any person that interferes with the order and authority of the court, such as the willful refusal of a party, a witness, or an attorney to attend court under an order to do so, or a failure to obey an order of the court such as the performance of an act or making of a payment in remedy.

**contiguity (contiguous or abutting)** Touching or interconnected. Contiguity is immediate proximity. Two parcels of property are contiguous when they share a common boundary, even if that boundary is only at a corner.

*See also:* adjacent (adjacence).

**contiguous zone** *See:* sea, Law of the Sea, national waters, contiguous zone (customs zone or customs enforcement zone).

**continental shelf** *See:* sea, Law of the Sea, national waters, continental shelf (outer continental shelf).

**contingency (contingent)** Something that might or might not occur. A contingency is an event that might or might not take place in the future, according to which a given consequence may follow. A contingency is thus akin to a condition subsequent, in that if event A occurs then B, which was authorized in advance, may or will also occur.

*See also:* liability, contingent liability; beneficiary, contingent beneficiary; fee, fee for services, attorney's fee, contingency fee (contingent fee); remainder, contingent remainder; limitation, conditional limitation.

**contingency fee** *See:* fee, fee for services, attorney's fee, contingency fee (contingent fee).

**contingent beneficiary** *See:* beneficiary, contingent beneficiary.

**contingent claim** *See:* debt, contingent claim.

**contingent estate or estate upon condition** *See:* estate, interest, estate on condition (contingent estate or estate upon condition).

**contingent fee** *See:* fee, fee for services, attorney's fee, contingency fee (contingent fee).

**contingent legacy** *See:* legacy, conditional legacy (contingent legacy).

**contingent liability** *See:* liability, contingent liability.

**contingent remainder** *See:* remainder, contingent remainder.

**continuance (continue)** A delay in a proceeding. A continuance is an order putting off a hearing, argument, trial, or other proceeding in a legal action. A continuance may be granted by the court sua sponte or on motion by one of the parties. Although the court is required to ensure a speedy criminal trial and the management of a civil action without undue delay, the court in its discretion may order a continuance to ensure fairness to a criminal defendant, ensure sufficient notice or time for a party to prepare or attend, to allow the attendance of parties or witnesses, or other reasonable grounds. Generally, as a matter of professional courtesy, counsel will not object to the first motion of an opponent for a continuance in a given action.

**continuing**

**continuing crime** *See:* crime, continuous crime (continuing crime).

**continuing criminal enterprise** *See:* trafficking, drug trafficking, continuing criminal enterprise (CCE).

**continuing damages** *See:* damages, classes of damages, continuing damages.

**continuing legal education** *See:* bar, continuing legal education (C.L.E. or CLE).

**continuing objection** *See:* objection, continuing objection (durable objection or running objection or standing objection).

**continuing offense** *See:* offense, continuing offense.

**continuing trespass doctrine** *See:* larceny, continuing trespass doctrine.

**continuing violation** *See:* harassment, continuing violation.

**continuing violation doctrine** *See:* limitation, limitation of actions, statute of limitations, tolling, continuing violation doctrine.

## continuity (continual or continuation or continuing or continuous)
Without ceasing or alteration. Continuity is the aspect of any activity or existence to persist without a significant interruption or change. Continuity of an activity is not lost by occasional or recurrent hiatus in the activity, if the hiatus is routine, brief, or occasioned only by a superior force for the time the force is effective, and if the hiatus is begun with an expectation of the activity's resumption.

There are many standards in law that require continuity, such as the standards for continuous occupation of land to acquire adverse possession or continuous notorious cohabitation to establish common–law marriage, or continuous occupation to sustain a claim of sovereignty. In all these cases, continuity may be considered unbroken despite minor and customary interruptions of activity, but continuity might have been broken by even a brief interruption caused by another party claiming a right contrary to the party seeking later to prove continuous action.

*See also:* bar, continuing legal education (C.L.E. or CLE); damages, classes of damages, continuing damages; discrimination, employment discrimination, doctrine of continuing violation; harassment, continuing violation; objection, continuing objection (durable objection or running objection or standing objection); offense, continuing offense; possession, adverse possession, continuous possession; possession, adverse possession, continuous possession, seasonal possession; crime, continuous crime (continuing crime); easement, continuous easement; easement, discontinuous easement (discontinuing easement or intermittent easement or noncontinuous easement); prescription, prescription of property | continuous-adverse-use principle.

**continuous crime** *See:* crime, continuous crime (continuing crime).

**continuous easement** *See:* easement, continuous easement.

**continuous possession** *See:* possession, adverse possession, continuous possession, seasonal possession; possession, adverse possession, continuous possession.

**continuous-treatment doctrine** *See:* limitation, limitation of actions, statute of limitations, tolling, continuous-treatment doctrine.

## contortion

**contortion as interpretation (contorted logic)** Complicated and counter-intuitive interpretation. A contortion is an interpretation that requires a series of related arguments from the evidence, each argument asserted as if it is required to sustain the next argument and logically relate it from the evidence to the conclusion, which is often a conclusion that is contrary to ordinary expectations of the meaning of the evidence. Contortion is not distortion, and a contortive argument is not necessarily untrue; it is just complicated and, usually, surprising. The truth or falsity of the contorted argument depends on the strength of each step of the argument as well as the overall result.

**contorts (con-torts)** A course combining the doctrines of contracts and torts. Contorts is a course offered sometimes in law schools, based on Grant Gilmore's observation that the obligations of contracts and the obligations of torts are better taught in a single class in law school. The result is not entirely unlike the civil law class in obligations. Contorts is not to be confused with the student's abbreviation for a course in constitutional torts.

**contra** Opposing. Contra is a Law Latin term that is used both in drafting and in citation to refer to something that is opposed to the statement or reference that preceded the word. It is both an element of phrases, such as contra bonos mores, or against good morals, and the root of words in English, such as contradict, or to speak against some proposition. Preceding a citation, it suggests the cite is contrary authority to the preceding cite.

*See also:* citation, citation signal, contra; pro.

**contra non valentum** *See:* possession, adverse possession, contra non valentum (contra non valentem).

**contra proferentem** *See:* contract, contract interpretation, contract ambiguity, contra proferentem (against the drafter).

**contraband** Anything illegal to possess. Contraband is anything that is possessed, traded, or carried in violation of the law. Anything smuggled is contraband. An object may be contraband because its possession is forbidden owing to its very nature, such as child pornography, to its possession by one not authorized to possess it, such as a controlled pharmaceutical, or to its failure to be taxed or certified according to law, such as untaxed whiskey.

*See also:* smuggling (smuggle or smuggler).

**contraception** The prevention of birth by interfering with sexual reproduction. Contraception is a form of birth control used within a heterosexual adult sexual relationship or affecting a sexual act between such partners through any artificial means to prevent the female partner from becoming pregnant or developing a foetus. The most common forms involve a device that creates a barrier between the sperm and the egg, such as a condom, diaphragm, or cervical cap. Other forms interfere with the production of sperm or eggs, either physically, such as a vasectomy for men or tubal ligation for women, or through the use of hormones, such as synthetic progestogen, or "the Pill." Emergency contraception, or a "morning after pill," such as Mifeprex, may be used after sex. There is great controversy as to whether abortion is or is not considered contraception, but when used as a matter of law, the term contraception presumptively does not include abortion or abortive measures for use later than emergency contraception.

*See also:* family, family planning, birth control; abortion (abort).

**contract (k)**  A contract is an enforceable agreement, or the legal obligations stemming from an agreement. A contract is an arrangement between two or more competent parties who intentionally and voluntarily exchange money, promise, or thing of value in return for money, promise, or thing of value, none of which is for a purpose against the law or public policy. A unjustified or unexcused failure to perform a material obligation created in a contract will give rise to an action in law by the party injured by the non–performance. "K" is frequently the abbreviation for contract.

*See also:* k; term, contract term.

**contract between spouses**  *See:* marriage, marital agreement (contract between spouses).

**contract covenant**  *See:* covenant, contract covenant.

**contract damages**  *See:* damages, contract damages.

**contract deposit**  *See:* deposit, contract deposit.

**contract for deed**  *See:* mortgage, land contract (contract for deed).

**contract for the sale of goods**  *See:* contracts, contract for the sale of goods, United Nations Convention on Contracts for the International Sale of Goods (CISG).

**contract interpretation**  *See:* contracts, contract interpretation.

**contract–market differential**  *See:* damages, contract damages, contract–market differential.

**contract offer**  *See:* offer, contract offer.

**contract performance**  *See:* performance, contract performance, alternative performance.

**contract term**  *See:* term, contract term.

**acceptance**  *See:* acceptance, acceptance as acceptance of an offer.

**agreement**  Concurrence in contract terms, which can be expressly communicated between the parties or implied by their conduct. An agreement is the bargain formed by the parties. Agreement usually arises from an acceptance of an offer, either by express agreement or such statements or conduct that is reasonably implied as acceptance, based on the parties' past conduct or dealings with one another. In general, an agreement is synonymous with a contract that reflects it.

*See also:* agreement.

**agreement to agree**  A preliminary agreement to form a later contract. Agreements to agree sometimes occur prior to a contract, but they are usually unenforceable, as they are merely inchoate acts that have not yet reached fruition. They may, however, create obligations to negotiate in good faith or otherwise create a context for detrimental reliance in the event the later contract is not entered.

**meeting of the minds (manifestation of mutual assent)**  Agreement among the parties to the essential terms of a contract. The meeting of the minds is a metaphor for the mutual agreement of the various parties to a contract to its essential terms, including a shared understanding of what each term entails. Meeting of the minds does not require proof of each party's subjective understanding of the terms but objective evidence of a common agreement, which in the case of a written contract is to be found in the writing itself. In the case of an oral agreement, evidence of a mutual understanding requires evidence that at one time or another the parties held a mutual understanding, but this too is manifest in words and behavior, not in evidence of mental states. The doctrine once required evidence of the thoughts of the contracting parties, but unless the doctrine is understood as wholly unrelated to a mental state, it is generally considered obsolete, having been replaced by other evidence of contract formation by objective manifestations of mutual assent through signature on a writing, through performance and, above all, through commitments of consideration in a bargain.

**assignment of contract (assign)**  Conveyance of the rights and duties in a contract to a third party. The assignment of a contract is the transfer by one party to a contract of all of the obligations and privileges the party holds in the agreement to a third party. The assignment is complete as between assignor and assignee, but the other contracting party retains the right of satisfaction against the assignor until it manifests acceptance of the assignment, when the other contracting party's sole right of satisfaction is against the assignee.

*prohibition of assignment*  A contract may provide that it may not be assigned. Prohibition of assignment exists when a contract contains a clause providing that the rights and duties created by it may not be assigned by one, both, or any parties to it. Prohibition of assignments may be qualified, barring assignment without prior consent, or absolute. Absolute prohibitions are, however, subject to amendment of the contract by the parties. A contract for the provision of certain services may be unassignable by operation of law, regardless of the express terms of the contract, in which case no clause allowing assignment will be valid.

**collateral contracts (collateral agreements)**  An independent agreement related to another agreement. A collateral contract is an agreement that exists alongside and is connected with another agreement, in which case each contract is collateral to the other. One collateral contract may provide terms or conditions affecting or essential to the other. Either is likely to be essential in interpreting the other.

*See also:* contract, specific contracts, reciprocal contract (mutual agreement).

**confirmation of contract**   An acknowledgment of an existing contract and acceptance of its terms. A confirmation of a contract is a form of ratification, made after the contract has been entered. A confirmation may be a condition subsequent to the obligations to perform some or all obligations under a contract, as when a contract must be confirmed or ratified by a vote of a corporate board or by the assent of a principal when the contract is entered by an agent.

**written confirmation of oral agreement**   A writing that confirms an agreement orally made. A written confirmation of an oral agreement operates as an acceptance of the terms offered by the party not confirming. A written confirmation by one party will not serve as a writing that would bind the other party under the statute of frauds, though it may serve as evidence of the agreement between both parties regardless of the statute of frauds.

**contract bar**   A limitation in time on contract re-negotiations. A contract bar is an express clause in a contract that provides when a limited time during which the agreement, its terms, or its process may be challenged or be renegotiated. After that time, the contract must be honored until its expiration. Contract bars are common in employment contracts and in union agreements.

*fraud*   Fraud can be the basis for voiding a contract. Fraud by one party in the negotiation or execution of a contract makes the contract voidable by the other party, regardless of a contract bar.

**contract formation (formation of contract)**   The creation of an agreement to which each party is bound by law. Contract formation is the process by which two or more parties enter a contractual relationship. Formation occurs through conduct of each of the parties that gives evidence of the intent of each to both perform an obligation under the contract and to accept the performance of the other parties. Over time, the law has required various tests to determine whether a contract has been formed. The common law required some contracts to be written in a document signed under seal. Later, contracts could be formed only when there was evidence of a meeting of the minds or that the contracting parties shared and assented to a common understanding of the obligations required under the agreement. The current understanding seeks objective evidence of mutual promises, usually proven by evidence of offer and acceptance, that are adequate consideration for the other promises. Such evidence may, however, arise solely from the conduct of the parties, and a contract may be inferred from conduct that is only reasonably interpreted as evidence of such mutual promises implied by the parties through their actions. Some other requirements

persist for certain contracts, particularly that specific contracts under the Statute of Frauds, such as for the sale of an interest in land, must have been signed by the party to be bound to them.

Formation requires certain conditions precedent, particularly that each of the parties has the capacity to enter a contract and the purpose of the contract is lawful and in accord with public policy. Formation does not include the conduct of parties before or after, and so negotiations prior to formation are not part of formation, although they influence it. Thus, if prior to the acts of formation, both parties engage in a mistake, or one party commits fraud, duress, or illegal conduct, the later acts that might otherwise amount to formation do not do so as a matter of law.

**contract implied in law**   *See:* contract, contract formation, quasi contract (contract implied in law or implied–in–law–contract or quasi-contract or quasi contractus).

**express contract**   A communicated agreement between the parties. An express contract is an agreement made deliberately through communications between the parties, whether the communications are oral or written. The term is used to contrast an agreement with a contract implied in law, sometimes called a quasi–contract.

*See also:* expression (explicit or express).

**form contract**   A standardized contract containing non–negotiable terms. A form contract is a contract on pre–printed papers, in which the names of the parties and other details are inserted into a form in which all of the other terms are drafted by the form provider and, generally, not subject to negotiation by either party at the time of entry.

**boilerplate contract**   A form contract using stock language without negotiation. A boilerplate contract is a contract employing already drafted form language to establish a host of terms binding the parties, leaving only a very few terms to be inserted by the parties to the particular contract. Such contracts are often stitched together from a variety of boilerplate clauses. Boilerplate contracts are used to establish rights and duties in transactions that tend to be of a repetitive character, such as leases, realty transfers, insurance agreements, and sales. Such repetition is efficient, because it saves drafting labor and serves the values of expectation and stability. When a clause is interpreted in one dispute by a court to have a particular meaning, that interpretation is available to other courts in determining the meaning of the same clause in other contracts. (This has the benefit for a contracting industry, such as insurance companies, of retaining language under which it wins and redrafting language under which it loses.) In a contract, boilerplate is often held to be unenforceable because it is present in error, or the product of mutual mistake, etc., but it is not presumed void as a matter of law. When used in contracts between parties of unequal sophistication and bargaining strength, boilerplate may be a factor in a clause's unconscionability, owing to the absence of meaningful negotiation and the imbalance of power in the drafter's favor.

*See also:* merger, merger clause (integration clause).

**unconscionability** Boilerplate contracts are unconscionable if boilerplate language creates an unfair and undisclosed advantage for the party that drafts or presents the form. The mere fact that the unconscionable act is in a form, or that it is widely used, is no rebuttal to a defense against enforcement of the contract as being unconscionable. As a matter of fact, most courts would consider the fact a clause was in boilerplate evidence of its not being the subject of negotiation or of clear disclosure.

**illusory contract** A contract that is unenforceable for failure of consideration. An illusory contact is an agreement where the only consideration given by one or both parties is insufficiently valuable to form an enforceable contract, as when the consideration offered by one party is an unperformable or unenforceable promise or is of very little value compared to the consideration offered by the other party.

*See also:* consideration.

**implied contract (inferred contract or contract implied in fact)** A contract arising from the conduct of the parties, and later recognized by law or equity. An implied contract arises between two parties whose mutual conduct, particularly mutual reliance, suggests that the parties have each in fact silently agreed to a contract through actions by each that create an expectation in the other of further performance, which may be treated by either as if a contract had been expressly created. A court will examine the conduct of the parties, particularly communications between the parties, the past relations between the parties, the conduct of each and the knowledge by the other of that conduct and may imply a contract to perform further conduct in accord with reasonable expectations that arose from the situation.

**quasi contract (contract implied in law or implied-in-law-contract or quasi-contract or quasi contractus)** Resitutionary obligation implied by law or equity. A contract implied in law or, in its older form, a quasi-contract, is not a contract but an obligation implied by law from circumstances in which a person or entity acts unilaterally to create a binding obligation toward another. A wide variety of conduct creates such obligations in various circumstances, including any conduct that encourages detrimental reliance, any conduct in which one person places him- or herself in a position of agency for another, or the voluntary assumption of certain roles created in law or equity that imply an obligation to others. Most such contracts are implied in law as a formula for restitution when some conduct by the plaintiff or someone acting on behalf of the plaintiff confers a benefit on the defendant who benefits in fact from it and accepts and retains the benefit under circumstances that would be inequitable to do so without compensating the plaintiff.

*See also:* restitution (writ of restitution); unjust enrichment; reliance, detrimental reliance.

**statute of frauds** *See:* fraud, statute of frauds.

**contract interpretation (contract construction)** The depiction of the terms of a contract and their application to answer specific questions. Interpretation of a contract is the process of answering a question from a contract as a whole and its particular terms in the context in which it was made and the requirements of the law. Interpretation may require little analysis to determine whether the contract requires some obligation or not, and whether that obligation has been or must be performed. But when the terms are in any way ambiguous, either in their making or in their application to facts related to the contract's performance, more analysis is required. There is no significant difference between contract interpretation and contract construction.

*negotiated terms vs. standard terms* A negotiated term controls a standard term. When there are terms in an agreement, some of which were negotiated by the parties and others of which were standard of boilerplate, any apparent conflict between the terms must be resolved in favor of enforcing the negotiated terms.

**contract ambiguity (ambiguous contract)** A term or contract susceptible to more than one meaning. Ambiguity in contract arises when more than one reasonable interpretation or meaning is possible in the depiction of a term of a contract or in the depiction of the contract as a whole. Ambiguity in the statement, also called patent ambiguity, may arise because of error or incompleteness in the expression of the contract, varied potential meanings of the language as drafted or employed, failure to include certain language, or because the meaning of words varies according to the context in which they are employed. Ambiguity in effect, also called latent ambiguity, may arise because the terms of the contract are confusing or provide alternative courses of action when an attempt is made to apply them in the actual circumstances surrounding the facts of performance. A court engaged in the interpretation of a contract may make a specific finding that a clause or term is ambiguous, which is a signal that the court will engage in further interpretation to discover an unstated meaning of the contract or to determine the obligations of the parties in a manner not clearly stated in the text.

*See also:* ambiguity (ambiguous or ambiguousness).

**contra proferentem (against the drafter)** An ambiguous clause is read against the interest of its drafter. Under the doctrine of contra proferentem, a clause in a contract susceptible to several meanings will be given the meaning most favorable to the non–drafting party, particularly when the the non–drafting party had a distinct disadvantage or the drafting party had a distinct advantage from the clause. The doctrine may not apply, however, when the parties to a contract are each sophisticated negotiating parties with equivalent bargaining power.

*See also:* insurance, insurance policy (insurance contract or insurance agreement).

**latent ambiguity** An ambiguity that arises from events or circumstances. A latent ambiguity arises in contract interpretation when a term, despite its apparently clear and unambiguous text or statement, becomes ambiguous owing to external facts in the application or performance of the particular agreement.

*See also:* contract, contract interpretation, contract ambiguity (ambiguous contract); latency (latent).

**patent ambiguity** A contract whose stated terms are ambiguous. Patent ambiguity in a contract is ambiguity that is apparent from the reading of the text or the evidence of an oral agreement, without any additional question of ambiguity arising from the facts surrounding performance or practice. A finding of patent ambiguity is sometimes said to require that the ambiguity to be obvious, gross, or glaring, but the more useful tests (1) whether the contract's language, when read by a reasonable observer, has only one meaning for every material term and (2) to the extent it does not, whether it is patently ambiguous. An offer containing a patently ambiguous term puts the offeree to a duty to inquire as to the meaning of the term, and the offeree may be bound to the less favorable interpretation of the term through lack of inquiry.

*See also:* ambiguity (ambiguous or ambiguousness); contract, contract interpretation, contract ambiguity, latent ambiguity.

**ejusdem generis** *See:* interpretation, ejusdem generis.

**four corners rule** The purpose of a contract must be gleaned from its entirety rather than a part. The four corners rule requires the purpose of a contract, the intention of the parties in entering it, be discerned from an examination of the entire text, even to each of the "four corners" of the paper upon which it is written, and not to a single clause or few components. When interpreting a contract according to this doctrine, the court will look at the whole agreement between the parties, even if it is contained in several memorials, oral agreements, emails, or documents.

The four corners doctrine still does not resort to parol or extrinsic evidence.

**gap-filler** A provision to be read into a contract that has left an essential term unstated. Gap-fillers are contract terms judicially imposed when an agreement is silent in their regard, has left the terms indefinite, or has omitted them. The terms may be implied from the parties' course of dealing (a sequence of previous conduct between the parties), UCC § 1–205(1), their courses of performance (the contract specifies repeated occasions to perform), UCC § 2–208(1), or the usage in the trade (a common practice in the specific business), UCC § 1–205(2). Gaps may also be filled by presumptions from statutes or common law or by the ascertaining of a reasonable term. A contract may be upheld with gap-fillers implied into the contract, even if it would be unenforceable without them.

*See also:* performance, contract performance, course of performance.

**integrated contract (completely integrated contract)** Written contract purporting to include all of its terms. An integrated contract is a written contract that contains all of its terms, and no other terms are to be implied or construed through interpretation. An integrated contract may or may not include a clause declaring it to be an integrated, or fully integrated, contract. Regardless, the mere statement in a contract that it is integrated is insufficient to prove that all of the material terms are actually present therein, but if the contract is indeed comprehensive, and there is no evidence to demonstrate that it is incomplete or erroneous, and it contains clauses that are sufficient in scope, purpose, and specificity to answer all of the relevant questions that arise under the contract that it would reasonably appear to be complete, there is no need to interpret or construe additional terms.

**objective theory of contracts** Contract is interpreted by reasonable meaning to observer. The objective theory of contracts holds that a contract is to be interpreted by its outward manifestations, rather than by what one or all of the parties had privately in mind that it ought to say. Such terms or language that was employed in the making of the contract, whether written or oral, must be understood by what a reasonable person acting in a reasonable manner would have meant by those terms of language.

*See also:* objective (objective standard or objectivity).

**parol contract (oral contract or verbal contract)** A contract that is unwritten, in whole or in part. A parol contract is an unwritten contract, a valid agreement made by its parties verbally rather than in writing. Thus, a parol contract must satisfy the usual requirements of a valid agreement—including competence of the parties, consideration, and valid purpose. The terms of a valid parol contract must not, however, violate the statute of frauds, which does require a writing for certain promises to be enforced.

Note: a contract is parol if any of its terms are inherently proven only by parol evidence. Thus a partially written contract is also a parol contract, because it must rely on parol evidence for its essential terms.

*See also:* parol.

**plain meaning (objective interpretation of contracts)** Interpretation of the text with the least possible inference or external knowledge. Interpretation according to plain meaning of a contract is interpretation of the words, sentences, and paragraphs in the agreement with the least inference and art possible. The "plain" meaning of a term must require, in legal interpretation, that a term include the specialized meaning of it in law, rather than only the common usage of words among speakers in the general population.

Plain-meaning interpretation bars the use of implications of intent or purpose to determine the obligations of the contracting parties; it bars the use of legal presumptions and default constructions of texts, as well, of course, of parol evidence and extrinsic evidence of purpose. That said, some of these tools of interpretation are required by law, interpretative method notwithstanding. Thus, plain meaning cannot bar evidence of fraud in the inducement, and in many courts it cannot bar evidence of mutual mistake.

*See also:* interpretation (construction or interpret or construe); interpretation, plain meaning (plain language rule).

**sanctity of contract** Valid contracts are presumed to be enforced. When possible, a court will interpret a contract to have been formed and to be enforceable. A bad bargain is enforceable as long as it is a valid bargain.

**severance (doctrine of severance or severability of clauses or blue pencil rule)** Contracts may be modified by excising unenforceable clauses. Severance is the interpretation and reformation of a contract by considering void a clause or clauses that are illegal, unconscionable or in any way unenforceable in an otherwise valid contract. The court may rescind any such terms, if excising them will allow the parties still to act according to valid underlying purposes of the contract. The term has a variety of variants, all of the same purpose, including the informal "blue pencil rule."

*See also:* statute, severability of statute (severance of statute); reform, reformation of a writing

(reformation of contract or reformation of an instrument).

**subjective theory of contract** A contract depends on the parties' actual intent. The subjective theory of contract is the residual influence of the early understanding of the doctrine of meeting of the minds. It is now nearly obsolete in determining questions of contract formation, although it has a continuing utility in contract interpretation through the use of parol evidence when it is allowed.

**contract right (contractual right)** A right created by a contract and enforceable in law. A contractual right is a right that is created as a result of an agreement between parties to a contract, which provides each party with rights and duties toward one another that would otherwise not exist but for the contract, and that are are enforceable as a matter of law. A contract right includes implied and incidental rights that the parties would reasonably be understood to have undertaken, such as rights to enforcement of expressed rights. The essential example of a contractual right is the right to the performance of the other party. An example of an implied contractual right is the right to recover damages if one party fails to perform a promise in a valid contract (assuming that no such right is expressed in the agreement).

*See also:* right; right, legal right.

**contractor (contract worker)** One who enters into a contract to perform work independently and not as an employee. A contractor, generally, is any party to a contract. In the context of work and employment, a contractor is any person or entity providing services or performing work, according to a contract for those services or work rather than an employee of the person or entity that receives the services or completed work. The contractor receives payment for the work performed rather than wages. A contractor is responsible for performing the work according to the expectations of the contract but otherwise is independent in determining the time, personnel, and place of the work to be performed.

**contractor bid** *See:* bid, contractor bid (contractor).

**independent contractor** A self-employed person providing services or goods not as an employee. An independent contractor is a person who provides work to a person or entity not as an employee subject to the management of the person or entity but as a freelance, answerable only for the results of the contract. If the recipient of the services or goods does not control what the worker does and how the worker does his or her job, does not manage the business aspects of the worker's expenses and benefits, or have a contract for employment or benefits, the worker is likely to be an independent contractor.

**sub-contractor (subcontractor)** A contractor hired to work for another contractor. A sub-contractor is any person or entity contracted by a contractor to perform work on the primary contract for a job or services to another. The contractor is responsible to the sub-contractor and to the buyer for the payment of each sub-contractor as well as for the quality and delivery of all work performed on the contract, whether by the contractor's employees or the sub-contractor's. Sub-contractors work in many fields, but the use of sub-contractors is particularly common in construction. Construction projects require a wide array of skilled artisans, such as electricians, carpenters, and plumbers, to build a structure. A general contractor, which has the contract with a buyer to build a structure, enters into individual contracts with the individuals or entities providing each specialized service the general contractor does not provide as part of the general contract. These subcontractor practitioners agree to work on the basis of contracts entered-into with the general contractor, which may or may not be subject to the approval of the buyer.

## contract clauses

**choice of law clause** *See:* choice, choice of law, choice of law clause (choice-of-law clause).

**forum selection clause** *See:* forum, forum selection clause.

**most favored nation clause (me too clause or most favored nation clause)** One party's promise to use the most favorable terms given to third parties. A most favored nations clause is a contract clause in which one party offers the other a term that may vary if the offering party extends a more generous term to any third party in the future, who would be otherwise in a similar position to the offeree. Thus, labor, sales, pricing agreements and terms, I.P. licenses, and other agreements between a consumer of services or goods and a provider or a provider of services and goods and a consumer may incorporate a clause, often regarding pricing or compensation, ensuring preferential treatment to one or another or both, if the terms are varied for others in the future. The clause is sometimes described as a "me, too" clause, in that the offeree is assured of the terms given to other similar offerees in the future.

*See also:* nation, most favored nation.

**discharge of a contract** The extinction of an obligation under a contract. Discharge of a contract is the fulfillment or annulment of all of a party's obligations under it, through performance or through some other means such as payment, extinction of the obligation through impossibility or the performance of another, or through some other means by which the party has no more obligations that persist.

**divisibility of contract (divisible contract)** Contract with incremental consideration by both parties. The divisibility of a contract is the ability of the consideration of each party to the contract to be isolated into components that can be apportioned, allowing the consideration tendered by partial performance to be applied correspondingly to only a part of the consideration of the other party. This means is particularly useful in assessing damages in the event of breach following partial performance.

**liberty of contract (impairment of contract or freedom of contract or obligations of contract)** The state may not interfere with the rights lawfully established by a contract. Liberty of contract limits a government from unduly impairing an obligation arising under a lawful contract between private parties. Although the protection of the freedom of contract between employers and employees was once the basis for the invalidity of wage and hour laws, there is very little contracted between individuals that may not be regulated by a state or federal law.

*three-part test* To determine whether a state law has violated the Contracts Clause, the Court asks, first, whether the law is a substantial impairment, second, whether there is a significant and legitimate public purpose for the law, and third, whether the burdens of the law are reasonable and appropriate to that public purpose.

*See:* U.S. Const. art. I, § 10, cl. 1.

*See also:* constitution, U.S. Constitution, clauses, Contracts Clause (Impairment of Contracts Clause).

## specific contracts

**accessory contract** A contract made to assure the performance of another contract. An accessory contract is any contract that ensures the performance of obligations under another contract. A common form of accessory contract is the ratification, a second contract by which the parties ratify and adopt the obligations of an earlier contract. The parties to the accessory contract may be the same as, or different from, the first contracting parties. Other forms include various forms of guaranty, including suretyship, indemnity, pledge, and warranty. In all cases, when the underlying contract is performed or its debt is paid, the accessory obligation is discharged.

**adhesive contract (contract of adhesion or adhesion contract)** Agreement that allows one party no bargaining power. An adhesion contract is an agreement by which one party is given no right to negotiate any of the terms of the contract, which is often a standardized form. An adhesion contract is offered by one party who gives no rights of negotiation or bargaining power to the other party, who must "take it or leave it." Adhesion contracts are interpreted with any ambiguity in the meaning or application of terms read to the benefit of the non-drafting party. Terms that alter the rights of the non-drafting party in any manner not directly connected to the essential purpose of the contract must be clearly indicated and may still be unenforceable as lacking consent or consideration, or otherwise being unconscionable.

**aleatory contract**   Contract subject to contingent performance. An aleatory contract conditions the requirement for the performance of at least one of the parties upon the occurrence of some specified event in the future. If the event specified in the contract does not occur, or does not occur within a specified time, then there is no obligation on the party whose performance was conditional to perform under the contract. Most insurance contracts are aleatory, in that the insurer usually has no obligation to perform contract unless it is given notice of an occurrence or a claim.

*See also:* contingency (contingent).

**alternative contract**   Agreement providing for two or more ways for one party to perform. An alternative contract is an agreement between parties that provides at least two ways in which one party may perform that party's obligations under the agreement. Alternative contracts may be contingent, providing that if a specified event occurs then performance shall be carried out in one manner, and if that specified event does not occur then performance shall be carried out in another manner.

*See also:* promise, alternative promises.

**bilateral contract**   Agreement founded on mutual promises to act in the future. A bilateral contract is an agreement that obligates both parties to do something in the future to fulfill the obligations of the agreement. For example, if a buyer enters into an agreement with a seller by which the seller will ship X widgets to the buyer on certain date, and the buyer will pay Y price upon receipt, both parties must act in the future to fulfill the obligations of the agreement.

**clickwrap agreement (browse-wrap agreement)**   An agreement offered by a website and accepted by a visitor by a mouse click. A clickwrap agreement is a contract term or condition of use found on an Internet website, to which a visitor must consent in order to gain access to the content of the site. The user consents to the term or condition by clicking on a dialog box that says "I Agree" or "I Accept" or something similar. Often the consumer cannot proceed with the online transaction until after agreeing to the term or condition. Sometimes the terms are numerous and may require scrolling down a page before clicking the button to assent to the terms. Clickwrap agreements are considered writings as they can be printed or stored. Though a clickwrap agreement may be valid, it is inherently a boilerplate agreement, which terms are not subject to negotiation.

*See also:* contract, contract formation, form contract, boilerplate contract.

**commutative contract**   An exchange of equivalent things. A commutative contract is one in which the parties give and receive equivalent things. The subject of the promise is equivalent to the promised consideration.

**contract for employment (employment contract)**   Agreement specifying terms of employment. An employment contract is an agreement between employee and employer specifying the terms of the employment. Provisions often included in employment contracts are the work to be performed, the duration of the employment, and compensation arrangement. An employment contract may be written or oral, and if written, it may specify the grounds for which an employee may be fired. An employment contract may have a variety of terms implied by law, including a minimum wage, minimum benefits, and limitations on discrimination on forbidden grounds.

*See also:* employment (employ or employed or employee or employer).

**contract for sale of goods**   A contract between a merchant to sell and another to buy goods. A contract for the sale of goods between a merchant and a merchant or between a merchant and a consumer that would have the merchant sell goods to the buyer. Such an agreement is governed by the Uniform Commercial Code if it is between parties in the United States or by the United Nations Convention on Contracts for the International Sale of Goods otherwise.

**contract for sale of land**   A purchase agreement for land. A contract for the sale of land is simply an agreement to buy and to sell a parcel of land. The contract must be clear as to the location of the land and the quantity of the land sold, which may be depicted by metes and bounds or by a unique address. Contracts for the sale of land are subject to the statute of frauds and so must be evidenced by a writing signed by the party to be bound.

**destination contract**   Agreement specifying particular location for delivery. A destination contract specifies that the performance of one party is not complete until goods or objects to be transferred under the contract are in fact delivered to a specified location. The delivery to the specified location in a destination contract is a condition precedent to the performance of the buyer, allowing the buyer to rescind the transaction if the goods are not delivered to the location on time. In the absence of instructions to the contrary, a contract is presumed not to be a destination contract but a shipment contract.

*See also:* contract, specific contracts, shipment contract.

**executed contract**   A contract that has been fully performed. Executed contract has two significantly different meanings. In its more technical sense, an executed contract is an agreement according to which all parties have fulfilled their obligations.

In this sense, an executed contract may be either written or oral. The opposite form to an executed contract is an executory contract, in which some of the terms are still yet to be performed or fulfilled.

In a less technical but more commonly used sense, lawyers speak of an executed contract to mean a fully completed writing, in the sense that the instrument that reflects the contract is executed rather than the underlying agreement. In this sense, the contract is executed when the execution clause is complete, usually by signature of the parties or their representatives and witnesses if there are any.

**executory contract**   A contract that has not been fully performed. An executory contract has been entered but not fully performed, because at least some essential obligation remains to be performed by at least one of the parties.

**forward contract (spot contract)**   A contract specifying performance in the future. A forward contract is an agreement by which at least one party agrees to perform in the future, particularly to deliver goods or services at a particular time in the future for a price determined in the present. Many transactions are committed by forward contracts, particularly agreements to buy or sell property, to buy or sell commodities, to exchange currency, and to buy or sell investment assets. A forward contract is similar to a futures contract, but unlike a futures contract is ineligible for trading on an exchange, usually because the assets subject to the contract are not represented in a standardized form. The contrast to a forward contract is a spot contract, by which the sale occurs nearly immediately.

*See also:* contract, specific contracts, futures contract.

**futures contract**   Promise for commercial dealings with specific merchandise at a specified future date. A futures contract is an agreement to buy or to sell a commodity at a fixed price on a date certain. The contract is itself transferable and marketable until the date it is honored. The contract is made at the time it is entered, although its performance is another contract to be made on the specified date in the future. Futures contracts are traded and, as traded investment vehicles, subject to regulation. The ability to buy and sell futures contracts on an exchange is an essential difference between them and forward contracts.

*See also:* contract, specific contracts, forward contract (spot contract).

**gratuitous contract (contract of benevolence)**   Contract where consideration is emotional. A gratuitous contract is a contract based on a promise that has no financial benefit to the promisor and no consideration from the other party. Gratuitous contracts are not enforceable as contracts, although in extraordinary circumstances, in which the promisor is aware of reliance or encourages reliance, the gratuitous contract might be the basis of enforcement through detrimental reliance.

*See also:* reliance, detrimental reliance.

**illegal contract**   Contract with a purpose or obligation contrary to law. An illegal contract is an instrument or arrangement that has the trappings of a contract but that has either an illegal purpose or a stipulation that would require conduct that is illegal or is contrary to public policy. A agreement to commit a crime is inherently an illegal contract (as well as conspiracy), and a contract that requires activity in violation of health and safety laws is also an illegal contract. Courts will not enforce an illegal contract. As a matter of law, an illegal contract is impossible and does not exist, though the parties might behave as if it does.

*severability (divisibility)*   Principle that courts will excise offending clauses and retain the rest. Severability permits courts to salvage such elements of a contract that are reasonable and legal, while jettisoning illegal elements as unenforceable.

**installment contract (installment plan or intallment purchase or installment sale)**   Agreement providing for incremental delivery of payment or goods. An installment contract is an agreement that provides for the incremental delivery of payments or of goods, each delivery of which is separately accepted. Regardless of whether the contract states it is one or a number of contracts, under the UCC, an installment contract is a single contract, regardless of the number of payments or deliveries. Installment contracts are used in many purchases of goods and equipment and for many finance and credit transactions, especially installment credit arrangements such as mortgages.

**nude contract (nudum pactum)**   A contract unsupported by consideration. A nude contract lacks adequate consideration by one party. It amounts to a gift from the party providing consideration to the party who does not. Nude contracts are unenforceable in law.

The phrase in English, nude contract, is a translation of nudum pactum, itself abbreviated from the maxim nudum pactum ex quo non oritur actio, the court will not hear an action on a naked contract.

*See also:* pactum, nudum pactum.

**nugatory contract**   A contract that is worthless at least to one party. A nugatory contract is one that has nothing but trivial value, at least to one party. Though nugatory contracts are usually one-sided, the term might embrace a contract that has no real value to any party to it.

*See also:* nugatory.

**option contract**   A offer that cannot be revoked for a specified time or until a specified event. An option contract is a contract to keep open an offer for a time or until a condition fails or is satisfied. An option contract is distinct from the contract that would result of the option is exercised, and so the option contract requires consideration independent of the contract offered. Even so, in the event the offeree accepts the option, the option contract may be structured so that the consideration to create the option contract may be merged into and a component of the consideration of the final contract.

*See also:* offer, contract offer, irrevocable offer (firm offer); share, share as stock, stock option (warrant for stock or stock warrant or securities option or share option); perpetuity, rule against perpetuities | option to purchase land.

**option contract to purchase land**   An option to buy an interest in land. An option contract to acquire an interest in land is valid in the law, although like other options, it must be subject to valid consideration. A land purchase option was, at common law, subject to the statute of frauds and so required to be in writing and signed by the party to be charged with the writing. More recent case law in some jurisdictions requires only that the exercise of the option be in writing but allows the enforcement of the option even if the option itself does not satisfy the statute.

*rule against perpetuities and options*   An option contract to purchase land is subject to the rule against perpetuities. If the option may work so that the effect of the option is to vest an interest, that is to say create a vested interest through the exercise of the option, in a period longer than the lives in being and twenty-one years, the option violates the rule. Thus, to violate the rule, an option must be held by a corporation or be transferable among individuals.

*See also:* perpetuity, rule against perpetuities (rap or rule against remoteness).

**personal services contract (personal service)**   A contract requiring performance by a named individual. A personal services contract is a contract for the performance of a service by a named individual, who is either the promisor or the principal for an agent who enters the contract on behalf of the individual. Work by artists, musicians, artisans, and professionals is often contracted by personal services contracts.

**reciprocal contract (mutual agreement)**   A contract in which both parties are to perform an obligation. A reciprocal contract is a contract in which both parties have consented to an obligation to perform some duty. Most contracts are reciprocal. In the civil law, reciprocal contracts are divided between perfectly reciprocal contracts and imperfectly reciprocal, the difference being that the imperfectly reciprocal contract incorporates affirmative duties by only one party and negative duties by the other. In the common law, unless required to distinguish a contract form a unilateral contract or a naked contract, to describe a contract as a reciprocal contract may be a mere redundancy.

**recorded contract (unrecorded contract)**   The final version of a contract expressed in a record. A recorded contract is a contract for the sale of goods expressed in a written or electronic record that is intended by the parties to be the final expression of their agreement. Under the amendments of the Uniform Commercial Code promulgated in 2003, the rules applied to a written contract for the sale of goods were enlarged to include agreements expressed by a record, whether the record is in writing or electronic. An unrecorded agreement may still be valid under the U.C.C., being proved by evidence from the conduct of the parties, by proof of offer and acceptance, or by proof of confirmation of the agreement in a record. Note: a recorded contract should not be confused with a recorded lien or debt, which are not merely claims expressed in a record but are are claims recorded in an official registry.

*See also:* fraud, statute of frauds, writing (memorandum or note).

**severable contract**   One agreement that may be broken into several distinct, enforceable contracts. A severable contract comprises several elements, each of which can stand independently as an enforceable contract, independent of the others. Severable contracts are often used in agreements requiring multiple shipments of goods. In these cases, each shipment is paid for at time of delivery and is treated as subject to a single fully functioning agreement amidst an all-encompassing agreement.

**shipment contract**   Agreement requiring seller to deliver goods by carrier. A shipment contract is a contract for the sale of goods by which the seller is to deliver the goods by carrier, usually specifying the carrier, and the risk of loss is transferred to the buyer at the time the goods are delivered by the seller to the carrier. Unless a contract specifies to the contrary, contracts are presumed to be shipment contracts.

*See also:* contract, specific contracts, destination contract.

**shrinkwrap agreement (shrink wrap contract)**   License terms that are impliedly accepted by opening a package. A shrinkwrap agreement is a contract to grant a license subject to specific terms, which are printed on a part of the wrapper on the package that is to be used subject to the license. Opening the package is implied acceptance of the terms, which often are given general notice on the package and printed in fuller form inside the box. Shrinkwrap agreements developed in an effort to control the use of software, and they are still commonly found on software packages. As software is increasingly downloaded or accessed other than through the acquisition of boxes of media on discs, shrinkwrap agreements are used less often than clickwrap agreements. At least some of these licenses are unenforceable as contracts because the buyer is under no obligation to read the agreement prior to purchase.

*See also:* contract, specific contracts, clickwrap agreement (browse–wrap agreement).

**supply contract**  A contract by a seller to supply goods or services to a buyer on an ongoing basis. A supply contract is an agreement by a seller to supply goods to a buyer for a period of time. The supply contract may specify a definite quantity to be delivered at given times, may specify an indefinite quantity, or may be an output contract or a requirements contract.

**output contract (outputs contract)**  Contract obligating the seller to sell all units produced to the buyer. An output contract creates an obligation between a buyer and seller obligating the seller to deliver to the buyer all goods of a particular kind that the seller produces during the period of the contract, and it obligates the buyer to accept the goods and pay for them. The seller has an implied obligation of best efforts in most jurisdictions, but otherwise, the parties bear the burden of both unusually high and unusually low production. Output contracts are often used in commodities production, such as agribusiness and fuel.

*See also:* performance, contract performance, best efforts.

**requirements contract**  Contract obligating the seller to sell all units required by the buyer. A requirement contract provides that a buyer agrees to buy and a seller agrees to sell all of the specified goods to the buyer that the buyer shall require during the life of the contract. A requirements contract ensures the seller a source of revenue and the buyer a source of goods throughout the duration of the contract.

*See also:* performance, contract performance, best efforts.

**take–or–pay clause**  A commitment to take possession of the goods or pay nonetheless. A take or pay clause is a covenant in certain supply contracts, in which a buyer agrees to purchase a set amount of the product supplied, whether the buyer can take possession of it or not. Take–or–pay clauses are particularly used in the supply contracts for the supply of natural gas, by which a buyer promises a producer to take or to pay for a specified quantity of gas for a given time, usually at a price agreed in the original contract. A take–or–pay contract with a fixed, agreed price is a form of futures contract, although gas contracts are not regulated in the manner of agricultural futures.

**unilateral contract**  A contract formed by the offeree's performance. A unilateral contract is an agreement under which the contract is formed by the acceptance of the offeree in the form of the offeree's performance. Many employment contracts are unilateral contracts, in which the terms of the employer's offer are accepted by the work performed by the employee, which then binds the employer to the terms of the offer as a contract governing the time the employment is performed.

**void contract**  A seeming contract irrevocably flawed at its creation. A void contract is an arrangement that appears to be a contract but is not, owing to an infirmity that cannot be ignored or remedied, and thus the arrangement will not bind either party. A putative contract may be void either because the essentials for the formation of the contract were never met or because it is contrary to law or public policy. In the first instance, the failure to form the contract must be of a form that one party cannot cure the failure to allow the contract to be performed (as when a party was under the age of capacity but ratified the contract when of age), or the contract is merely voidable and not void.

*See also:* void (voidability, voidable).

**voidable contract**  A contract with a defect in formation that can be cured. A voidable contract is an agreement that has a flaw in its formation that could result in the contract being void, but the flaw may be cured by some conduct by one of the parties. In practice, the contract is likely to be treated as valid until it is avoided by the party who could cure the defect and opts not to do so. Thus a contract entered into by a person lacking the mental capacity to enter a contract, who was known to the other party to be infirm and under a conservatorship, might be treated by both parties as valid until renounced by the conservator. In such a case, the contract would be avoided, or in some jurisdictions rescinded, and anything done or transferred could be subject to restitution. Likewise, a contract between a minor and another might be treated as valid until the minor or a guardian renounces it, although the minor could indeed cure the defect by ratification after reaching the age of majority.

*See also:* title, voidable title.

**disaffirmance (avoidance or renunciation)**  The rejection of a voidable contract by the innocent party. An act of disaffirmance is an act by one who enters a voidable contract who repudiates the contract. Disaffirmance may be by declaration or by conduct. If by conduct it may be concluded by returning any benefit received under it. Declaration requires only the communication of an intent to disaffirm to the other party, although declaration may require the return of a benefit if one had been received. A minor, for instance, may disaffirm either while still under minority or reasonably soon after reaching majority or through the actions of a guardian or legal representative. A corporation may disaffirm an agreement entered by an officer with a conflict of interest known to the other party to the contract. In some jurisdictions, a contract entered by a minor is not inherently subject to disaffirmance but may be disaffirmed only if it is unreasonable. There is no practical difference between a renunciation, avoidance, or disaffirmance by the innocent party to a voidable contract.

**ratification of a contract**   The confirmation of a once-voidable contract. Ratification is the process of confirming a contract that had been voidable, curing the infirmity in the formation of the contract and agreeing to be bound to its terms. Ratification is only effective when done by the party who otherwise could void or disafirm the contract.

**spot contract**   *See:* contract, specific contracts, forward contract (spot contract).

**subcontract**   Agreement made by one party to a contract with a third-party for completion of the original contract. A sub contract is made by one party to a primary contract to engage work or secure lands or goods in order to satisfy obligations under the primary contract.

**contractarianism**   *See:* social contract (contractarianism).

**Contracts Clause**   *See:* constitution, U.S. Constitution, clauses, Contracts Clause (Impairment of Contracts Clause).

**contracts law**

**United Nations Convention on Contracts for the International Sale of Goods (CISG)**   Treaty over international contracts to buy and sell goods. The UN Convention on Contracts for the Sale of Goods, applicable in most major commercial states (though not, in 2011 in the UK) governs most international contracts to buy and sell goods. Unlike the UCC, the CISG is concerned mainly with contract formation, performance, and breach, rather than with security interests, commercial paper, and other concomitant aspects of a commercial transaction. One of its greatest differences in contract formation is the CISG not requiring a writing in circumstances the UCC would. The CISG relies inherently on bilateral contracts of definite terms, relying on offer and acceptance to form a contract and providing for damages based on foreseeability in the event of breach.

**Uniform Commercial Code (UCC or U.C.C.)**   A uniform law governing sales and commercial transactions. The Uniform Commercial Code is a uniform law, created under the auspices of the National Conference of Commissioners on Uniform State Laws and the American Law Institute, by a committee chaired by ALI director Judge Herbert F. Goodrich, with much of the drafting done by Karl Llewellyn. It was promulgated in 1952 and has been adopted in whole or in large

part in every state and local jurisdiction. The UCC is constantly subject to revision, and it now has eleven titles: Article 1 is general provisions. Article 2 regulates sales. Article 2A regulates leases. Article 3 regulates negotiable instruments. Article 4 regulates bank deposits. Article 4A regulates funds transfers. Article 5 regulates letters of credit. Article 6 regulates sales and transfers in bulk. Article 7 regulates instruments of title like bills of lading. Article 8 regulates investment securities. Article 9 regulates secured transactions. Article 2 was revised in 2003, but it had not been adopted as of 2008, and neither version of Article 2 is used in Louisiana.

*comments*   Explanatory text following each section of the UCC. The comments following each of the black–letter sections of the UCC include elaboration, explanation, and illustrations of the principles in the black letter. While officially less authoritative than the black letter, in part because the comments are meant to amplify the black–letter text rather than to replace them, the comments are often more useful in resolving a particular question under the section.

*general principles of law and equity*   The common law and equity persist when the code does not contradict. General principles of law and equity are recognized in the UCC as the background legal rules. To the degree that the UCC does not contradict principles laid down by the courts, those principles remain in force augmenting the rules of the UCC. This provision operates in its way as a reminder that statutes in the United States are said to trump judicial expressions of state law that are not interpretations of the constitutions, but the statutes are not to be so widely interpreted as to alter or abolish the common law or equity without a clear legislative intent to do so.

**Article 2 of the UCC (UCC Article Two)**   Article 2 regulates sales. Article 2 defines and describes the sale of goods between a merchant and another or between and among merchants. Article 2 does not apply to the sale of real property or interests that are not goods, nor does it apply to the sale of realty. The UCC does not entirely displace the common law of contract as it would otherwise apply to a contract for the sale of goods, and in any question that is not expressly governed by a code provision, the common law applies.

**Article 3 of the UCC (UCC Article Three)**   Article 3 regulates negotiable instruments. Article 3 of the UCC defines and provides for the regulation of negotiable instruments as the UCC defines them. Article 3 limits negotiable instruments to an instrument, usually though not necessarily commercial paper, on which is an unconditional promise or order to pay value to a person or entity that is payable to bearer or to order when it is issued or possessed by a holder, that is payable on demand or after a time certain, and that incorporates no extraneous promise or instruction (though three forms of instruction or promise incidental to payment are allowed). Article three thus regulates checks, drafts, orders, certificates of deposit, promissory notes, among other instruments. Article 3 does not reach all instruments that are negotiable, however, because letters of credit are regulated under Article 5; warehouse receipts, bills of lading, and transferable documents of title are regulated under Article 7; and investment securities are regulated under Article 8.

*See also:* instrument, negotiable instrument.

**Article 9 of the UCC (UCC Article Nine)**  Article 9 regulates secured transactions. Article 9 defines and describes a security interest in personal property or chattels, particularly arising in a secured transaction other than a mortgage. It does not regulate security interests arising by law otherwise, such as liens created by tax debts or by operation of law such as materialmen's liens or judgment liens.

*See also:* transaction, secured transaction (security agreement); lien (lienholder).

**contradiction (contradict)**  Disagreement between two statements on the same subject. A contradiction is a conflict between two statements or sources of information as to the same subject or point. Contradiction in a contract or other instrument is a form of ambiguity. Contradiction in testimony or between witnesses testifying to the same question requires the finder of fact to determine which, if either, of the opposing statements is more likely to be true. Contradiction may suggest error or perjury in a witness, but it does not do so inevitably. In the ordinary course of human observation and memory, some contradiction is not only likely but potentially a source of evidence of the veracity of the witness.

**contrat**  A bilateral agreement under French law. Contrat, contract in French, is a valid contract as long as it is bilateral. French law does not, however, require mutuality of consideration in a bilateral contract.

**contravention (contravene)**  Infraction or violation of any rule. A contravention, or an action in contravention, is a violation of a rule, law or order, or of a contract, corporate by-law or other source of private law. The term in U.S. law is broader than a breach of the criminal law alone, including both infractions of private law and civil regulations as well as official violations of a treaty or the constitution. Although contravention in a criminal context may suggest a minor violation, contravention in American legal usage generally suggests a violation of a more serious law.

**contravention as petty offense**  A minor offense in some jurisdictions. A contravention is a minor offense punished by a fine ordered by the executive rather than a harsher punishment by the judiciary. The term is used in France and other states.

**contributing to the delinquency of a minor**  *See:* minority, minor, contributing to the delinquency of a minor (corruption of a minor).

**contribution**  Indemnification. Contribution is the debt, demand, or process for reimbursement when several parties are responsible for a debt, and one party pays the whole debt, or more than its share; the overpaying party is entitled to contribution from each of the other debtors of the amount it paid over its rightful share.

**contributory negligence**  *See:* negligence, contributory negligence.

**control of corporation**  *See:* corporation, control of corporation (corporate control).

**control technology**  *See:* technology, control technology (pollution control technology).

**controlled substance**  *See:* drug, controlled substance.

**convalescent home**  *See:* nursing, nursing home (convalescent home).

**conversation**

**criminal conversation**  A tort claim for adultery against the interloper. Criminal conversation is a euphemism for adultery, and it represents a private cause of action brought by the non-adulterous spouse against the third-party who had sexual relations with the adulterous spouse. Criminal conversation differs from alienation of affections, in that criminal conversation requires the adultery to be consummated between the defendant and the adulterous spouse; alienation of affections requires only that the defendant have acted to persuade one spouse to leave or reject the other.

*See also:* tort, dignitary tort, heart balm tort (amatory tort or Heart Balm Act).

**conversion**  Alteration of one thing into another. A conversion is any transformation of something's character, meaning, or identity. Thus assets may be traded for other assets, for instance, converting money into land. Some forms of conversion, such as a conversion of ownership or a conversion of the function of a thing from a legal function to an illegal function, have significant legal implications.

**conversion rate for currency exchange (rate of exchange or exchange rate or security exchange)**  The ratio between the value of one currency and another. The conversion rate for currency is the value that once currency will purchase in a different currency, for instance the ratio between the value of the U.S. dollar and the Euro. The conversion should be specified in a contract to a particular ratio or the conversion given to buyers or sellers of one currency at a given trading exchange at a time certain or closing on a certain date.

**tortious conversion (civil theft)** Unlawful acquisition of or interference with a chattel. Conversion is the possession of or dominion over the chattel property of another, without permission and with the intent to dispossess the rightful owner of title to it, at least for a time. Mere interference with the owner's use of property can be conversion, so long as the interference is sufficient to amount to a loss of control by the owner so that it would be reasonable to demand payment for the interference.

Many forms of conduct may amount to conversion, which is the result when the conduct of one party so interferes with the dominion over chattel instead of dominion by its true owner or lawful possessor. The simplest form of conduct is to take the property from the owner, but other forms of conduct by another are also conversion owing to their interference with dominion. Conduct that results in the destruction of the property, or a fraud that results in the loss of the property, or the unlawful detention of property once lawfully held (even while it remains in the owner's possession), or a delivery of goods into the control of another, are all forms of conversion.

*See also:* maleficium.

**conversion of intangibles** The conversion of personal but intangible property. Conversion of intangibles is the tortious conversion of the incorporeal personal property of another person. This usually occurs by the taking, destruction, or wrongful retention of documents that represent the property, such as bonds, notes, or other instruments that represent intangible rights, including a right to receive money in an amount certain or certainly ascertained.

*See also:* property, forms of property, incorporeal property (intangible property or intangibles); property, forms of property, incorporeal property (intangible property or intangibles).

**convertible bond** *See:* bond, convertible bond.

**conveyance (convey)** The transfer and assignment to another of any right or interest. A conveyance is a transfer and assignment of one party's interest to another. Conveyance implies more than a transfer made by mere delivery; it implies that the transferor has assigned the transferor's interests in the property delivered, wholly devolving onto the transferee the transferor's former rights and interests in the property subject to delivery. Conveyance is thus usually made through delivery of a formal writing such as by a deed. The verb form, to convey, has a wider range of meanings, including a less rigid connotation that includes transfer of title by delivery, especially as to the transfer of title in a chattel or intangible, but not a fuller assignment of interests.

*See also:* deed; deed, warranty deed.

**fraudulent conveyance** A debtor's transfer of property to another to avoid its loss to a creditor. A fraudulent conveyance is one person's transfer of property to another for the purpose of preventing that property from being used to settle debts owed to someone else. An action to set aside a fraudulent conveyance is usually brought by the creditor, although it might be brought by others, such as a bankruptcy trustee. Generally, the creditor must prove that the debtor either transferred the money or property specifically to avoid the creditor's claim, or that the debtor did so merely without receiving appropriate consideration in return. An action to set aside a fraudulent conveyance may sound in equity or law. A statutory cause of action is provided in the Uniform Fraudulent Transfer Act.

**mesne conveyance** An ownership after one grant but before another. A mesne conveyance is an historical ownership of a property that follows one grant relevant to the issue at hand but comes prior to another grant. Thus, if there is a grant of Blackacre from O to A and his heirs, followed by a grant from A to B and her heirs, followed by a grant from B to C and her heirs, followed by a grant from C to P and her heirs, then A and B and C each held a mesne conveyance as between O and P.

*See also:* mesne.

**conviction** A judgment of guilt rendered against a criminal defendant in a competent court. A conviction is a finding of guilt. The conviction may be rendered against a defendant based on a jury verdict of guilt, a bench trial, or a confession accepted by the court. Although the term once applied to civil or criminal verdicts against a defendant, it is now rare to hear it other than in a criminal context. The origin of a conviction is in the early jury verdict: the jury was convinced, or held a conviction, of the defendant's guilt.

*See also:* condemnation (condemn); jury (juror).

**convict** A person convicted of a serious crime. A person is a convict if the person has been convicted of a crime, whether or not the conviction was based on a jury verdict, a bench trial, or a confession.

**ex-con** A person who has been a convict or jail prisoner. Ex-con has numerous slang connotations, most obviously for a person who has been committed to a penitentiary as a convict but more generically for anyone convicted of a serious crime.

**wrongful conviction** A judgment of guilt against a defendant who is in fact innocent of the crime. Wrongful conviction is the conviction of an innocent defendant. Wrongful conviction works an incalculable injustice to the person convicted, destroying a life owing to an error by the state. Perhaps as dangerous, a wrongful conviction ensures that the person responsible for a crime that was committed is very nearly immune from further investigation or prosecution.

**Cooley doctrine** *See:* commerce, regulation of commerce, dormant commerce power, Cooley doctrine.

**cooling off period**  *See:* wait, waiting period (cooling off period); union, labor union, labor dispute, cooling–off period.

**cooperative**

**cooperative federalism**  *See:* federalism, cooperative federalism.

**agricultural cooperative (cooperative association)** Farmers cooperating in processing, shipping, selling, or marketing farm produce. A Cooperative Association is an organization of farmers created to process, prepare for market, ship, or market the farm products of members of the association.

**cooperative enterprise (co-op or cooperative association)**  Business owned by its patrons. A cooperative is a company that is owed by the people who benefit from the company's property, services, or goods. Common forms include agricultural co-ops, electric co-ops, and housing co-ops.

**residential cooperative (co-operative tenancy or co-operative ownership or coop or co-op)** A residential organization owned by its tenants. A residential cooperative is a single enterprise owning property in the name of its tenants. Most residential cooperatives own a single residential enterprise, such as an apartment building, in which each unit is individually owned, and each unit-owner is an owner of the whole enterprise. A cooperative is usually governed by a cooperative board, which acts as a governing body to approve purchases, sales, and other transfers, dues or assessments, and building regulations.

The legal description of the ownership of a single unit within a co-operative may vary from jurisdiction to jurisdiction, but it is technically a condominium. This is a bit confusing, because the practical difference between most co-op apartments and condo apartments is that the condo apartment is often in a building owned by a landlord (usually a holding company or investment company), while a co-op apartment is thought to be in a building owned by the tenants. This is true enough, yet the particular form of ownership of both units is the same; it is a condominium ownership interest.

*See also:* cooperative, cooperative enterprise (co-op or cooperative association); condominium, condiminum as property (condo or condos).

**coordinate branch**  *See:* constitution, U.S. Constitution, ideals, separation of powers, coordinate branch.

**coordinated bargaining**  *See:* bargain, coordinated bargaining.

**coparceny or co-parcener or coparceners or parcenary**  *See:* heir, parcener (coparceny or co-parcener or coparceners or parcenary).

**copartner**  *See:* partner, copartner (co-partner).

**coplaintiff**  *See:* plaintiff, co-plaintiff (coplaintiff).

**coprincipal**  *See:* principal, co-principals (coprincipal).

**copy**  Anything that substantially reproduces the form or concept of something else. A copy is a duplicate, at least to some degree, of something done or made before the copy. There are various standards that apply to a copy in different contexts. A copy of a photo or document must be a true copy of the best available evidence to be introduced into court.

Copy has particular significance in intellectual property, in which the holder of a copyright or a patent has a monopoly over the production of copies made from the original. A copy of a copyrighted text or patented design may be made in a different medium from the original, being a copy so long as most viewers would perceive the copy to manifest the idea of the original. A copy of a document is a copy for some purposes if it merely restates language or images from the original, but for others the copy must be nearly exact as to the prose or to the image of the original document. An authoritative copy of a document that has no material flaws in its reproduction of the original is a true copy. Such a copy of an object is a replica. Note: copy is both a verb and a noun.

**carbon copy**  Exact replica. A carbon copy is a metaphor for an exact duplicate. The term arose from the use of a sheet of carbon paper to duplicate a page typed on a typewriter, a blank sheet behind the carbon page imprinting the letters as they were struck on the original page. With the advent of photocopiers and word processors, this practice has become rare in developed countries, and the term now refers to older records made in this manner and to anything duplicated so well that it is a facsimile of its original.

**copyhold**  *See:* tenure, feudal tenure, copyhold.

**copyright**  The interest of a creator in a physical work of art, space, sound, or literature. Copyright is an interest granted by law to the author of each original work that is fixed in a tangible medium of expression, whether that expression is published or unpublished. There is some argument over whether the interest is a form of property or a privilege to exclude others' use. Copyright protects original authored works, including literary, dramatic, musical, and artistic works, such as poetry, novels, movies, songs, computer software, and architecture. Copyright does not protect facts, ideas, systems, or methods of operation, although it may protect the way these things are expressed, and at least some protection for some forms of idea, system, or method is available in patent. Copyright extends no farther than its lawful extent, which does not include the inherent power of others to fair use or free expression regarding copyrighted matter.

The power to regulate copyright is dedicated to Congress by the Patent and Copyright Clause of the Constitution. The U.S. approach continued the English notion of a statutory copyright since the Statute of Anne, or the Copyright Act 1709, 8 Anne c. 19, which recognized copyright as a personal right of an author, over which the author held a transferable monopoly for fourteen years from its first publication. The first Congress enacted the first federal Copyright Act in 1790, providing protection for a fourteen-year term that could be renewed once and extending copyright to mechanical reproductions of music. The terms of copyright protection have been successively increased, in 1831, 1901, 1962, 1976, and 1998, after which the copyright terms for new works are the lesser of ninety-five years from publication by a corporation or, for a work by a living person for the life of the last surviving author plus seventy years. Copyright law are codified in the U.S. Code in title 17.

Certain state-law recognitions of copyright persisted as common-law copyright until the copyright act of 1978, after which most state copyright claims are preempted.

International law protects copyright, and the regime of copyright recognition and protection is managed in part by the World Intellectual Property Organization, in part by the World Trade Organization according to its Agreement on Trade-related Aspects of Intellectual Property Rights, and in part by treaties and other arrangements between states.

*See also:* intellectual property (I.P. or IP).

**Copyright and Patent Clause or Patent and Copyright Clause or Intellectual Property Clause or Progressive Clause**   *See:* constitution, U.S. Constitution, clauses, Copyright Clause (Copyright and Patent Clause or Patent and Copyright Clause or Intellectual Property Clause or Progressive Clause).

**Copyright Clause**   *See:* constitution, U.S. Constitution, clauses, Copyright Clause (Copyright and Patent Clause or Patent and Copyright Clause or Intellectual Property Clause or Progressive Clause).

**copyright deposit**   *See:* deposit, copyright deposit.

**copyrightable work**   *See:* work, copyrightable work, work for hire (work made for hire); work, copyrightable work, composite work; work, copyrightable work.

**copyright owner**   One who owns rights protected by the copyright laws. A copyright owner is a person or entity entitled to the protection of the copyright laws against infringement of the copyright on written work, image or object, sound recording, or videographic recording. A copyright in a work is initially owned by its author, although the legal author of a work made for hire may be the employer or contractor of the creator in fact. The creator in fact is, however, presumed to be the author. Copyright ownership may be joint, just as there may be joint authors. Copyright ownership is transferable by assignment as well as by license or lease, although in jurisdictions that recognize the moral rights of an author as an aspect of copyright, the moral rights may not be alienated. (The United States recognizes moral rights only in visual works and allows waiver of those rights.)

An owner of any interest in a copyright may register that interest with the copyright office, and only an owner is entitled to make a valid registration. Even so, registration is not required to create or to protect a copyright, though it is essential in order to pursue some remedies. Thus, a copyright owner is not required to register the copyright.

Note: the owner of an object subject to copyright is not, for that reason, the copyright owner. The owner of a copy of copyrighted matter has the power to sell or transfer that copy, and to display it, without the permission of the copyright holder, unless the transfer of the object to the owner of the copy, or a prior owner of the copy, was contingent on waiving these rights.

**common-law copyright**   State protection of copyrights, now mainly interests in certain visual images. Common-law copyright is the copyright law of the states that persisted in domains that were not subject to a federal copyright statute. One of the essential purposes of copyright under the common law was to protect the privacy interests of the creators of texts, to allow their control of publication by others. For much of the twentieth century, state law protected copyrights in sound recordings and images as well as in unpublished writings, none of which were yet subject to federal protection. Congress has abolished the bulk of common-law copyright with amendments to the copyright act in 1972 and 1978, with certain limited exceptions for images created from live performances. State common-law protection, however, persists for those common law rights that were created before January 1, 1978, that have yet to lapse.

**fair use**   A limit on copyright to allow the fair use of an expression. Fair use is a limitation on copyright, allowing a person other than the copyright holder to quote from a copyrighted work. Congress has created a vague definition of fair use, which depends on the sum of four factors: the form of use, including whether the use is for profit, the nature of the copyrighted work, the significance of the quote to the work quoted, and the effect of the quote in diminishing the value of the quoted work to the copyright owner. Fair use, by definition, does not require the permission of the copyright holder. There is some ambiguity in whether the claim of a copyright extends to matter that is fair use; some courts have read fair use as a defense to a claim for the use of copyrighted matter, but the better description is that the copyright holder has no claim for fair use, as fair use is beyond the scope of the copyright.

**infringement of copyright (copyright piracy or copyright infringement)**   The unlawful copying of material under a copyright held by another. Copyright infringement is the unlawful copying of material that is subject to a copyright held by a person other than the copier, or any other interference with the copyright owner's exclusive right to reproduce or distribute copies, to prepare a derivative work, or to publicly perform, display, or broadcast the specific works. A claim of infringement requires the plaintiff to prove that the plaintiff is the holder of an interest in a copyright, whether by initial creation or by assignment or license. The plaintiff must also prove that the use complained of is an unlawful copy of the original elements of the work under copyright and not merely a use of ideas within it.

Infringement requires that the work copied be subject to copyright, and there is no infringement in copying a work in the public domain. Not all copying of copyrighted works amounts to infringement. Copying that is not unlawful includes fair use.

*See also:* copyright, fair use; piracy, piracy of copyright or patent (software piracy or anti–piracy).

**substantial similarity**   A sufficient correlation of ideas and expression for a later work to infringe an earlier work. Substantial similarity is the essential test for copyright infringement between two works, in which the author of a later work is accused of infringing on the copyright in the earlier work. Substantial similarity is demonstrated when both intrinsic and extrinsic evidence demonstrate that both the general idea and significant elements of the expression of those ideas are present in the later work.

**coram**   Before the court. Coram, literally, translates as "before" or "in the presence of." In writs, owing to the significance of its use by a judge to reflect an action by the court, whether by that judge or by a predecessor, it customarily means "in this court."

**coram nobis (coram vobis)**   A writ allowing a court to correct its own error. A writ of error coram nobis is a procedure for a court to reopen an old judgment and to review and correct it for a mistake or infirmity. Coram nobis must be brought before the court that entered the original order rather than a court of appeal or a court that might hear collateral review, and it must be brought in a timely fashion. Coram nobis is available in the federal courts under the All Writs Act but is only available for review by a federal court of an order it has entered. Note: there is no contemporary distinction between a writ of coram nobis and a writ of coram vobis other than the cosmetic difference that some writs were once initiated with language "before us" and others "before you" during the review. Coram nobis is now the preferred term.

*See also:* appeal (appealable or appellate); error, writ of error (restricted appeal); remedy, post–conviction remedy.

**core meaning**   *See:* meaning, core meaning (central case).

**coroner (medical examiner or pathologist or forensic pathologist or medical legal investigator or MLI)**   The county officer charged with investigation of all questionable deaths. The coroner in the United States is an official whose principal duty is to investigate the potential cause of death of each person in a county whose death is under circumstances giving rise to a suspicion of homicide. Coroners often perform or supervise the performance of autopsies, and in some jurisdictions still hold inquests to present evidence to a coroner's

jury to assess the likelihood of death by natural or man-made causes. Coroners also serve in many jurisdictions as an interim replacement for the sheriff when required. The office of coroner is a medieval position, once the principal crown officer in a county, hence the name. Some states have retitled the office to be a medical examiner.

*See also:* laboratory, crime laboratory (forensics lab or crime lab or police lab or police crime lab).

**coroner's verdict**   *See:* verdict, coroner's verdict.

**inquest of the coroner (coroner's inquest)**   A coroner's formal review of the evidence related to the cause of a death. An inquest is an examination of the evidence related to a person's death, held by a jury of laypersons summoned by the coroner or a deputy coroner who conducts the inquest to determine the cause of death. The inquest usually hears forensic evidence from an autopsy and, perhaps, from the scene of the discovery of the decedent's body, as well as testimony from witnesses. The jury is to vote to determine a cause of death, and though its findings are not conclusive in a court of law, a finding of homicide will usually precipitate a police investigation of the apparent crime. The customary size of a coroner's jury is of six members, and although procedures vary, in most jurisdictions, the sheriff summons the jury on request of the coroner, following procedures used to empanel other juries by summoning people from the voter rolls.

*See also:* jury (juror); inquest.

**corpora delecti**   *See:* corpus, corpus delecti (corpora delecti).

**corporal**

**corporal as bodily**   Relating to the human body. Anything corporal is done with, to, or regarding the body.

*See also:* body (corpus).

**corporal punishment**   *See:* punishment, corporal punishment (paddling or spanking or torture).

**corporate**   *See:* corporation (corporate or incorporate)

**corporate acquisition**   *See:* acquisition, corporate acquisition (business acquisition).

**corporate alias**   *See:* name, alias, corporate alias (d/b/a or f/d/b/a or a/k/a or trade name).

**corporate average fuel economy standards**   *See:* carbon, corporate average fuel economy standards (C.A.F.E. standards or CAFE standards).

**corporate board or board**   *See:* corporation, director, board of directors (corporate board or board).

**corporate buyout**   *See:* buyout, corporate buyout, leveraged buyout (LBO).

**corporate by-laws**   *See:* corporation, corporate by-laws (bylaw or by-law).

**corporate campaign**  *See:* union, labor union, labor dispute, corporate campaign.

**corporate charter or articles of incorporation**  *See:* charter, charter of incorporation (corporate charter or articles of incorporation).

**corporate citizenship**  *See:* citizenship, corporate citizenship.

**corporate control**  *See:* corporation, control of corporation (corporate control).

**corporate deposition**  *See:* deposition, Rule 30(b) (6) deposition (corporate deposition).

**corporate director**  *See:* corporation, director (corporate director).

**corporate domicile**  *See:* business, place of business, principal place of business (corporate domicile).

**corporate incorporation**  *See:* incorporation, corporate incorporation (promoter or incorporator).

**corporate insider or inside information**  *See:* insider (corporate insider or inside information).

**corporate merger**  *See:* merger, corporate merger.

**corporate name change or personal name change**  *See:* name, change of name (corporate name change or personal name change).

**corporate officer**  *See:* officer, corporate officer.

**corporate opportunity doctrine**  *See:* corporation, corporate opportunity doctrine.

**corporate reorganization**  *See:* reorganization, corporate reorganization.

**corporate seal**  *See:* seal, corporate seal (common seal).

**corporate speech**  *See:* speech, freedom of speech, corporate speech.

**corporate takeover**  *See:* takeover, corporate takeover, poison pill.

**corporate trustee**  *See:* trustee, corporate trustee.

**corporate veil**  *See:* veil, corporate veil (piercing the corporate veil or pierce the corporate veil).

**corporation (corporate or incorporate)**  A group of people chartered by a government to act as a single legal person with liability for its acts limited to its assets. A corporation is a group of individual people, who receive a charter from a state or national government, entitling them to act as a single legal entity, which can carry out most legal functions but which has a liability limited to the assets of the corporation rather than a liability that extends, except in very rare instances, to the assets of the individuals. Corporations may take many forms, but every corporation is a creature of statute, limited in its powers to those allowed by statute in the jurisdiction in which it is incorporated and further limited to the powers and purposes in the charter granted to it by the government of that jurisdiction. Corporations are sometimes referred to as artificial persons, having constitutional rights in some degree like those held by a natural person, yet to the degree these privileges are rights of the corporation rather than the collective rights of its individual members, these privileges are always subject to the limits of statute and charter. A corporation is subject to tax as an independent entity, although the structure of the corporation will alter the regulatory and tax liability of the corporation. Non-profit corporations may be exempt from taxation, and corporations of limited scope, structure, or purpose may have special obligations for state or federal tax, particularly the S corporation and the sole proprietorship.

*See also:* shareholder (stockholder); charter, charter of incorporation (corporate charter or articles of incorporation); company, company as commercial organization (co.); person, artificial person (legal personality); syndicate (syndication).

**charter (articles of incorporation or articles of association or certificate of incorporation)**  The decree from a state establishing the powers and identity of a corporation. A charter of incorporation is a document issued by a government office, usually a state secretary of state or similar office, that confers upon a corporation its powers and sets forth its purposes. A charter may be changed by a corporation only with the consent of the issuing government. Other than the usage employed in various statutes, there is no effective difference between "corporate charter," or a "certificate of incorporation," either of which will incorporate by reference or enroll the "articles of incorporation" or "articles of association." In each case, the instrument issued by the state may be brief, incorporating by reference or as an attachment the articles presented by the corporation's incorporators and approved by the state, or it may incorporate them in whole.

**control of corporation (corporate control)**  Ownership of more than 49.9 percent of the shares of stock. Control of a corporation is the same as a control of a majority of the voting shares in the corporation, or 50 percent or more of the voting shares. Operational or working control may be had by control of less, if the shares that are controlled are sufficient with proxies and other devices to determine the outcome of matters voted on by the shareholders.

**corporate by-laws (bylaw or by-law)**  Private rules for the internal government of an organization. By-laws are an organization's administrative rules that govern how it operates and makes decisions. A corporation's by-laws are usually adopted, altered, or amended by the board of directors, unless this power is reserved to the shareholders in the articles of incorporation. The corporate by-laws delineate the responsibilities, powers, and procedures of corporate boards and offices. In no instance can by-laws provide a power to a corporate official or agent that is greater than the powers of the corporation under the laws of the jurisdiction in which it is incorporated or greater than the powers conferred under the corporation's articles of incorporation or charter.

**corporate opportunity doctrine** A corporate official who personally controls any relevant business opportunity must allow the corporation first refusal of the opportunity. The corporate opportunity doctrine requires disclosure by a corporate officer or director of an opportunity to engage in business along the same lines as the corporation engages in. The corporation must be afforded the chance to engage in the opportunity, amounting to a right of first refusal for the corporation. If the corporation fails to take advantage of the disclosed opportunity, the corporate official may take advantage of the opportunity personally or through another business venture unrelated to the corporation. This may apply to a member of a corporate board of directors to preclude that member from investing in companies competing with the company the director serves, unless the company renounces the interest or expectancy involved. A similar but distinct doctrine applies to a partner with an opportunity distinct from that of the partnership.

## corporations

**C corporation** Business entity taxed distinctly from its owners. A C corporation is a business entity that is treated as a completely separate entity from its owner for all purposes, particularly liability and taxation. The income of a C corporation is taxed as it was received by the corporation rather than the owners. When a C corporation distributes money to its owners, each owner is liable for personal tax on the money received. Most stock corporations are C corporations.

**close corporation (closely held corporation)** A corporation whose ownership shares are not publicly traded. A close corporation is an incorporated entity that has no public trading in its ownership shares on a securities market, although shares of ownership may be privately traded as provided by the corporation's charter and by-laws. The rules for ownership, including rules for trading, are determined by the corporations law of the jurisdiction in which the entity is incorporated. In many cases, the duties of day-to-day management of a close corporation are performed by shareholders. Individual shareholders of a close corporation may have an unequal number of shares, resulting in majority and minority shareholders.

**conglomerate** A single corporation formed of other corporations. A conglomerate is a corporation containing multiple corporations. Commonly, there is a parent company and a host of subsidiaries that are integrated to various extents in their management and activities. The parent company may be no more than a holding company, and the subsidiaries only loosely integrated, if at all, into a single corporate regime. The term is derived from geology, in which a conglomerate is a whole formed of many parts cemented into a heterogeneous whole.

**parent corporation** Business entity that forms another business entity and retains ownership in the new entity. A parent corporation is a corporation that creates or acquires another business entity, retaining ownership or control in the new entity, which is the subsidiary corporation.

**subsidiary corporation** Business entity wholly owned or controlled by another corporation. A subsidiary corporation is a corporation that is wholly owned or controlled by another corporation, which is the parent corporation. A parent corporation may create or acquire a subsidiary to enter a distinct line of business, to do business in a new jurisdiction, to allow internal competition, or as a legacy of other business combinations. Goods transferred from the parent to a subsidiary, between subsidiaries, or from a subsidiary to a parent must be accounted using a transfer pricing scheme.

**domestic corporation** Business entity formed within the United States. A domestic corporation is a business entity that is created or organized under the laws of the United States or any state within the United States or the District of Columbia, when referred to within that jurisdiction. That is, a corporation is domestic in a location if it is created or organized under the law of the jurisdiction governing that location.

**dummy corporation** Business entity formed solely to execute an illegal transaction. A dummy corporation is a business entity formed for no purpose other than to serve as a conduit for illegal transactions. Dummy corporations, which often have no business purpose beyond facilitating one transaction, are not illegal per se, but there are very few transactions through dummy corporations that are not essentially fraudulent.

**foreign corporation (alien corporation)** Corporation formed outside the state or nation in question. A foreign corporation is a business entity formed or existing under the laws of any state, other than than the state in which a matter arises. That is a corporation is foreign to a location if it is created or organized under the law of a jurisdiction other than the jurisdiction governing that location. In Arkansas, a corporation incorporated in the State of Missouri and another incorporated in the Republic of Ireland would both be foreign corporations. Both an out-of-state corporation and an international corporation are also alien corporations, although the term is more often employed for the international corporation.

**limited liability corporation** Corporation whose owners' liability is limited to the value of their investments. A limited liability corporation is chartered so that the legal extent of the liability of each owner is the value of that owner's shares in the corporation. Personal assets of individual owners beyond those shares or their value, may not be the basis for execution of judgment or otherwise taken to pay the obligations of the corporation.

**nonprofit corporation (non-profit corporation or not-for-profit corporation)** Corporation formed for a purpose other than generating a profit. A non-profit corporation is a corporation formed for a purpose public, civic, social, religious, charitable or other purpose that is not to generate profit. Non-profit corporations may enjoy exemption from state and federal taxes, although the corporation must be recognized by the Internal Revenue Service as a non-profit corporation under Rule 501 to qualify for exemption of taxes from the federal government and from most states. Charitable corporations are inherently non-profit, but they must be organized under the non-profit corporation statute and qualify for tax exemption to be treated as tax exempt. Non-profit corporations are recognized for purposes other than charitable purposes.

*See also:* charity, charitable corporation; charity, charitable purpose.

**charitable corporation** Company operating for a charitable purpose. A charitable corporation operates not for the benefit of the corporation, its owners, officers, or employees, but for the benefit of a completely external group of people. Charitable corporations may engage in commerce, but the proceeds of commerce must wholly benefit the charitable purpose of the corporation.

Most charitable organizations are organized as not-for-profit corporations according to state law. Charitable corporations qualify to be recognized by the Internal Revenue Service as not for profit, thus exempting their income from taxation and allowing gifts from others to be eligible as charitable tax deductions. Still, the charity must file for this recognition, and most charities must file returns with the IRS to maintain their status.

**director (corporate director)** A person who has a seat on the board of directors. A director is a person who has a seat on a corporation's board of directors. A director is a fiduciary to that corporation and is responsible for voting in the best interests of the corporation, according to the articles of incorporation and bylaws of the corporation. Each director is individually responsible to the corporation for all actions of the board, even for some actions only ratified by the board when proposed by corporate officers or board committees on which the director does not serve. Directors are generally responsible for establishing broad policies and objectives, selecting, reviewing, and removing the chief executive and other senior officers, approving the budget and overall use of finances, and accounting to the shareholders and to other stakeholders for the corporation generally.

There are a variety of roles for which directors are chosen: the usual board includes both inside directors, who are corporate officers, and outside directors, who are not employees or officers of the corporation.

**board of directors (corporate board or board)** The collective of the directors responsible for the affairs of an organization. The board of directors of an organization is a group of people who are vested with active management powers over all of the affairs of the organization. Though many types of organizations have boards of directors, it is the usual authority for the management and oversight of a business corporation, whose members are either designated from the officers or elected by the shareholders. A corporation may choose to title its board by a variety of names, including board of control and board of trustees, though a board of trustees is usually appointed only for a non-profit corporation or corporate trust. Normally, the board of directors of a corporation delegates a significant amount of its oversight responsibilities to the executive officers of the corporation, who are led by the chief executive officer and are answerable to the board, as the board is the penultimate corporate authority (the shareholders as a body comprise the ultimate corporate authority). Shareholders with a large interest in a corporation generally take a position on the board as a part of the oversight of their own investment; this is not always the case, however, and sometimes a majority shareholder has no official position within the company itself.

**member (corporator)** An owner of a corporation. The members of a corporation are those with an ownership interest, whether they are shareholders of a class giving ownership or members of a closely held corporation without shares.

*See also:* shareholder (stockholder); member.

**professional corporation (P.C. or PC)** Business entity formed to provide professional services to clients. A professional corporation is a business entity that is organized for the purpose of providing professional services to clients. Professional corporations are often structured to provide a corporate form for a sole practitioner or group of professionals in the law, medicine, architecture, or other professions with members who are themselves individually licensed and responsible to a licensing authority for their conduct.

**public corporation (public authority or government corporation or public-benefit corporation)** Business entity formed by the state to serve the public interest. A public corporation is a business entity formed by a state for a purpose that serves the public interest. Public corporations may be owned by the state, may be created by the state but have no further public ownership, or be a hybrid in form. Public corporations may be independent in their funding or be supported by public funds. And, public corporations may be governed by managers who derive their authority from the State or by managers appointed by an independent board. A host of different names are used for such entities, including public authority, public-benefit corporation, and government corporation, as well as specific forms of corporation such as port authority, but there is little conformity among states between a given structure and a given classification. Although it is possible for a state by statute to allow for the creation of a public corporation for profit, most are created as inherently non-profit or organized under the state's non-profit corporations law. Note: the term "public corporation" is also used loosely to represent a corporation that is publicly traded, as opposed to a close corporation. Context is essential to distinguish these usages.

*See also:* public.

**public-service corporation** Business entity formed to serve the public interest through the provision of services. A public-service corporation is a business entity formed for the purpose of serving the public interest whom, as a result of their relationship with the public, has the authority to exercise certain rights not available to the general public. Many public service corporations are specifically chartered by legislative act, though most are privately organized under state statutes as for-profit corporations. Most states regulate the activities of public service corporations through an oversight commission or board. The most common example of a public-service corporation is a utility company, which has the power of eminent domain to acquire easements and lands in fee in order to establish and service distribution lines.

**quasi-corporation** A county or other de facto state or municipal corporation. A quasi-corporation is a de facto municipal or state corporation, treated as if it is organized under state law to be a separate corporation though it has not been so established. The term is also loosely used to describe business entities that resemble corporations, such as joint-stock companies, but this usage is not to be encouraged.

**registered corporation** A corporation that files securities reports with the SEC. A registered corporation is a corporation whose securites are registered with the U.S. Securities and Exchange Commission in accordance with the Securities Act of 1933. Registered corporations include both domestic and foreign corporations that are registered in a given jurisdiction. Filings made by registered corporations are available from the EDGAR public database on the Internet.

**shell corporation** Business entity formed to execute a legal transaction. A shell corporation is a business entity formed only for the purpose of executing a transaction. Shell corporations are generally capitalized with funds from a sole investor or a parent corporation's stock. They are often used as a strategic tax planning vehicle, although they may be used for the legally questionable purpose of obscuring the real party in interest in a transaction. For example, in a merger companies will often create a shell corporation for one party to the merger to merge into so that the target corporation will become a wholly owned subsidiary of the parent corporation. This facilitates the need to isolate the assets and liabilities of the target corporation rather than intermingling them with the parent corporation's assets and liabilities.

**small-business corporation (S corporation)** Corporation taxed like a group of sole proprietorships. An S corporation is an incorporated business entity that operates like a C corporation, but its organization allows its taxes to be calculated for the corporation as a whole but paid by individual shareholders pro rata by their stake in the company, rather than by the company, so that the tax liability for each equity stakeholder is more like a sole proprietorship rather than like a traditional stock corporation. Among other requirements to qualify as an S corporation, the corporation may not have more than one class of stock and may not be a member of an affiliated group of corporations. S corporations are commonly used in small ventures because owners can offset income through the use of corporate losses.

**corporator** *See:* corporation, member (corporator).

**corporeal (incorporeal)** Having a physical substance that can be felt and touched, as opposed to having no mass at all. Corporeal, from the Latin "corpus," meaning body, describes something tangible. Incorporeal things are intangible items with no physical mass.

**corporeal ownership** *See:* ownership, corporeal ownership (incorporeal ownership).

**corporeal possession** *See:* possession, corporeal possession (incorporeal possession).

**corporeal property** *See:* property, forms of property, corporeal property (tangible property).

**corpse (cadaver or dead body)** A dead body. A corpse, generally, is the body of a dead person or animal. An animal corpse is owned by whomever owned a domestic animal, whomever has killed a wild animal and taken possession of it, or whomever is the property owner of an unclaimed wild animal. The greater difficulty in the law is the significance of the corpse of a human being. Although a corpse is not the property of anyone, in some jurisdictions there may be a quasi-property right in the next of kin allowing them to control its disposition. The right to authorize internment, as well as autopsies of a corpse, is vested in public officials and the next of kin, and in some jurisdictions, an executor or administrator of the decedent's estate. A corpse is the responsibility of those who have possession of it, and the abuse of a corpse is a crime. The power to authorize the harvesting of bodily organs or tissue for medical use varies from state to state, with some states presuming the consent of drivers, with others allowing an organ donor's notification, and in all allowing hospitals to follow the instructions made by the decedent while competent to give them before death. Note: there is no essential difference between a corpse and a cadaver; both mean a dead body.

*See also:* property, property right, quasi–property right; cannibalism (cannibal); sepulchre, right of sepulchre (burial rights); exhumation (exhume or disinter); autopsy (necropsy).

**interference with a corpse (desecration of a venerated object)** Taking or harming a dead body without a license to do so. Interference with a corpse is any movement or removal of a corpse, removal of a portion of the body or clothing or property present on a corpse or interference with the interment, cremation, or burial of a corpse before during or after its completion without a license to do so by the next of kin, estate of the decedent, or the state. Interference with a corpse is both an independent tort and, in some instances, the underlying action for deliberate or negligent infliction of emotional distress. In most instances, interference with a corpse is a misdemeanor, although removal from a grave or other burial or interment chamber may amount to a felony or either theft or grave robbery.

**corpus** A body, whether of a person, polity, or ideas. Corpus is a Latin word that signifies body, used both literally, as in the body of a person, and — more often — metaphorically, as the collection of ideas, texts, parts, or components of a whole, as in the body of the civil law. The assets of an estate or a trust are sometimes referred to as a corpus.

*See also:* body (corpus); confession, corpus delicti rule (corroboration rule); canon, canon law, corpus juris canonici; Roman law, corpus juris civilis.

**corpus delicti rule** *See:* confession, corpus delicti rule (corroboration rule).

**corpus juris canonici** *See:* canon, canon law, corpus juris canonici.

**corpus juris civilis** *See:* Roman law, corpus juris civilis, Institutes of Justinian (Justinian's Institutes); Roman law, corpus juris civilis.

**corpus delicti (corpora delecti)** The essence of the crime, which is to be proved. The corpus delicti is the essence of the crime, which is to say the essential allegations of a crime having been committed and that the defendant was legally responsible for the crime. The corpus delicti should be proved at trial by the evidence in the case and the prosecution's argument. In the event the defendant confesses, the prosecution may use the same evidence to corroborate the confession. Note, the body referred to by corpus is not the corpse of a homicide victim but the body of evidence and allegation required to plead and prove the crime. In a homicide case, overwhelming circumstantial evidence in the absence of a victim's remains may indeed be sufficient to amount to a corpus delicti. Note: the plural is corpora delecti.

*See also:* confession, corpus delicti rule (corroboration rule).

**correction** *See:* justice, corrective justice (correction).

**corrective justice** *See:* justice, corrective justice (correction).

**correlative** Mutually dependent or defining. Correlative things are interdependent things: the one is essential to the other, for existence or at least for definition. A joint tenancy is correlative with another joint tenancy, as are co–mortgages, spousal rights, etc. Some interests that are defined according to other interests and vice versa are correlative, such as a future interest and its preceding interest, like a fee simple determinable and a possibility of reverter.

*See also:* right, Hohfeldian right (Hohfeldian duty).

**correlative rights** *See:* right, property right, correlative rights.

**corroboration (corroborating evidence or corroborating witness)** Evidence that strengthens the persuasiveness of something else. Corroboration is a strengthening that comes from accumulation or agreement, particularly when one piece of evidence suggests a fact, and a different piece of evidence suggests the same fact, each piece corroborates the other. Corroboration differs from cumulation, in that corroborating evidence arises from a different source from the corroborated evidence to support the same conclusion; at least one form of cumulative evidence is no more than multiple iterations of evidence of the same form or from the same source (although corroborative evidence becomes cumulative once its conclusion is well established, and further corroboration for the conclusion will not be practically distinct from the evidence already presented).

Certain forms of evidence must be corroborated in order to be presented in court, or if used to prove certain crimes must have been corroborated to support the indictment and conviction. At common law, for instance, the testimony of a victim of certain crimes required corroboration, as did the testimony of an accomplice as the basis of conviction for a co–accomplice. Under the Constitution's Treason Clause, no person may be convicted of treason without the corroborating witnesses who will testify to the same overt act of treason.

**corroboration rule** *See:* confession, corpus delicti rule (corroboration rule).

**corrosive substance** *See:* hazard, hazardous substance, corrosive substance (corrosive chemical or corrosive material).

**corruption** The abuse of any legal power. Corruption is, in general, the degradation of something once pure, noble, or correct. In law, it is the failure to use a legal power in the manner and for the purpose it was invested in its holder. In the sense of degraded interest, it was once used to describe the effects of attainder on a convict's children, who could not take titles or property owing to the corruption of blood. This doctrine is now obsolete in Western law.

**corruption of a minor** *See:* minority, minor, contributing to the delinquency of a minor (corruption of a minor).

**corruption of office** Any official act inconsistent with the duty of office or the rights of others. The use of a public office for private gain, or a corporate office for personal advantage, is inherently corrupt. The use of governmental powers to advance a political party rather than the government itself is corrupt. The use of an office of trust to gain money for oneself or one's allies is corrupt. The failure to exercise fiduciary powers to the benefit of those for whom the powers exist, whether the beneficiary of a trust or the citizenry who look to office, is corrupt. Corruption may result from many causes other than greed alone, including not only coercion by others but also indolence, incompetence, and ignorance.

*See also:* office.

**Foreign Corrupt Practices Act (FCPA)** No agent of a U.S. concern may bribe or give a kickback to a foreign official. The Foreign Corrupt Practices Act forbids agents of U.S. corporations to pay money or give gifts to the agents of a foreign government in order to induce the agent or another to secure an improper advantage for the U.S. corporation.

*See also:* kickback; racketeering (racket).

**silver or lead (plato o plomo)** Accept a bribe or die. Silver or lead is a catchphrase for the enticement to corruption of officials by a combination of threats and bribes.

**cost** A required expenditure in money or value for whatever is sought or required. Cost is the payment associated with any given endeavor, whether for an acquisition of property or services or for participation in an activity, such as litigation or education. As considered by law, cost, or costs, is usually measured in money, although from an economic point of view, cost is measured by anything that is valued by the person who must expend (or forgo) it.

*See also:* fee, fee for services, attorney's fees.

**cost-benefit analysis** *See:* value, cost-benefit analysis (CBA).

**cost bond** *See:* bond, appeal bond (cost bond).

**cost of completion** *See:* damages, contract damages, cost of completion.

**cost of insurance and freight** *See:* shipping, shipping term, incoterm, cost of insurance and freight (C.I.F. or CIF).

**cost of performance** *See:* performance, cost of performance.

**best cost avoider (most efficient cost avoider)** Whoever can best and most cheaply minimize risks. A best cost avoider, which is to say the most efficient cost avoider, is the person or entity who can most efficiently take effective precautions to minimize the risks and cost of any endeavor or transaction.

**opportunity cost** What is forgone when a choice is made. An opportunity cost is the value of an option that one might have pursued but did not, owing to a choice to pursue another option.

**replacement cost** The cost of actual replacement of property. Replacement cost is the present value of the replacement of property lost or damaged with new property of identical form and quality, or at least with property as similar as possible in form and quality and capable of use in the same manner as the property lost if an exact replacement is impossible.

**transaction cost** A cost in making an agreement; not the cost to perform it. A transaction cost is an economic term for the costs involved in reaching a given transaction, which is to say all of the costs to the parties to the transaction other than the costs of its actual performance. There are innumerable forms of transaction cost, but the largest categories are information costs, bargaining costs, and enforcement costs.

Information costs include the cost of locating a party with whom to engage in a transaction (which is sometimes called a search cost), and acquiring sufficient information to engage in a reasoned negotiation, including information regarding competitive prices. Bargaining costs include the actual cost of negotiation including the costs of inducing a bargain other than the expense required in it, and including the costs of reaching a decision to accept a deal once it is negotiated. Enforcement costs include insurance, observation, inspection, and negotiation as performance occurs, as well as the costs of any potential delay in performance, litigation to secure performance, or other expenses to either ensure performance by one's own entity or by the other party.

**cotenant or co-tenant or cotenancy** *See:* tenancy, co-tenancy (cotenant or co-tenant or cotenancy).

**Council of Europe** *See:* Europe, Council of Europe.

**counselor (counsellor)** An attorney at law. A counselor, generally, is an advisor. In law, a counsellor is an officer of the court, who is empowered to represent others before the court, and who is licensed to give legal advice and serve public and private clients in the interests of justice. Other than through customary usage in a jurisdiction or office, there is no difference in the meaning of counsellor or counselor.

*See also:* lawyer.

**counselor-patient privilege** *See:* privilege, evidentiary privilege, counselor-patient privilege (psychotherapist privilege or therapist-patient privilege or psychiatrist privilege).

**assigned counsel (court-appointed counsel)** A court-appointed attorney for a client. Assigned counsel is counsel appointed by the court to represent a criminal defendant. The Sixth Amendment provides for court-appointed counsel for an indigent defendant. Although such appointments are compensated, very begrudgingly, by most states or the federal government, the court has the customary power to request that any attorney licensed by it serve as appointed counsel, as long as they have the requisite skills to serve.

**counsel** Advice, and the lawyer who provides it. Counsel has a several related meanings, all derived from the general understanding of counsel as advice. (Thus, to keep one's counsel is to advise no one but oneself.) A counsel, or conseller, is a lawyer, often referred to in given advisory role, such as "counsel for the plaintiff" or "counsel for the defense" or private counsel or public counsel. The advice given by counsel is also often called the counsel of the attorney. The right to counsel is a mixture of the right to the attorney and the right to the attorney's services and advice. Though it can be made plural as counsels, counsel is more properly a collective noun, and a judge often asks, "are counsel ready to proceed?"

> **Queen's Counsel (King's Counsel or Q.C. or K.C.)** A designation for a distinguished, senior barrister. A Queen's Counsel is a barrister designated by letters patent as one of the queen's counsel learned in the law. The designation is one of particular trust and confidence and signals a member of the bar senior in dignity and precedence. A Q.C. (or K.C. if a king sits on the throne) is uniquely entitled to wear a gown of silk.
>
> *See also:* coif; serjeant (serjeant at law or serjeant–counter).

**general counsel** The chief legal officer of a corporation or agency. The general counsel is the chief attorney for a corporation, government agency or other entity. The general counsel is responsible for advising the corporate officers on all legal matters, though in many corporations, a general counsel is assisted by other lawyers under the counsel's supervision as well as by outside lawyers associated to assist the corporation in various matters, particularly with litigation or matters in jurisdictions foreign to the entity's principal place of business.

**in-house counsel** An attorney who is employed full time by an entity. An in-house counsel is an attorney who works within a corporation, partnership, or other entity, to provide it legal counsel and representation. In-house counsel often coordinate the work of outside counsel, many of whom are local counsel in various affairs far from the headquarters of the entity. Usually, the chief in-house counsel is the general counsel.

**right to counsel** The right to the effective legal counsel in a criminal proceeding. Right to counsel is assured by the Sixth Amendment, which has been incorporated into the Due Process Clause of the Fourteenth Amendment, as well as state constitutions, so that every criminal defendant who faces a potential loss of liberty has access to an attorney who provides effective assistance of counsel at each stage of the criminal process. Right to counsel applies whether the defendant can afford to hire a lawyer or not, in

which case the court will appoint a lawyer without charge to the defendant.

**effective assistance of counsel** The minimum standard of care of an attorney for a criminal defendant. Effective assistance of counsel is both a constitutional requirement to ensure the right to counsel and a standard of care according to which the representation the accused receives is sufficient if the accused is convicted. Effective assistance requires the attorney to exercise reasonable professional judgment, to take such steps as a reasonable attorney would take to prepare for trial, to reasonably represent the defendant's interests at trial and in post-trial proceedings, and to do so without a conflict of interest. An attorney's lapse in providing assistance does not render the representation ineffective unless either the failure was reasonably probable to have affected the outcome of the proceedings or the failure was so patent and likely to prejudice the outcome that it isn't worth a hearing to determine that prejudice occurred.

*See also:* trial, fair trial (rights of criminal defendants).

**ineffective assistance of counsel (defective performance)** Legal representation below an objective standard of reasonableness. Ineffective assistance of counsel is both a standard of inadequate performance for a lawyer in a criminal representation and a failure of due process of law for the criminal defendant. A person who has suffered a punishment in a criminal proceeding to which there is a right to counsel but who received ineffective assistance is ordinarily entitled to a new proceeding with adequate representation, as long as there is a reasonable probability that the result might have been different if the person had received adequate legal assistance. Further, a criminal defendant who is not advised by the defendant's attorney of the direct consequences of a sentence, including its effect on the defendant's immigration status, is not provided effective counsel by that attorney (though the attorney's failure to describe every collateral consequence of a charge does not necessarily amount to ineffective assistance).

> **Strickland test** A defendant's lawyer must meet an objective standard of competence, or if not the incompetence was likely to alter the outcome. A claim for federal relief from a criminal conviction, which is based on a claim of ineffective assistance of counsel to the defendant at trial must meet the two-part test of Strickland v. Washington, 466 U.S. 668 (1984). The defense counsel must have failed to reach an objective standard of performance, and there must be a reasonable probability that, had the attorney been competent, the result would have been materially different.

**right to civil counsel (civil Gideon)** A right to counsel in certain civil and administrative matters. The right to civil counsel is a right extended by statute in some states to indigents who have either been brought to court or to an administrative tribunal or who have a reasonable basis for a civil action but cannot afford counsel to protect their rights. The movement to recognize such rights is particularly focused on providing counsel to parents in custody deprivation hearings. The right is known also as the "civil Gideon" right from the recognition of a right to counsel in criminal cases in Gideon v. Wainwright, 372 U.S. 335 (1963) (Black, J.).

See also: counselor, assigned counsel (court-appointed counsel).

**special counsel** See: prosecutor, special counsel.

**waiver of counsel (waiver of right to counsel)** A criminal defendant's refusal of counsel at any stage in the criminal process. A waiver of counsel by a person subject to interrogation or who has been charged with a crime is a statement that is made by a person with full capacity, that is knowing and voluntary, and that clearly and unequivocally rejects representation or assistance by an attorney at law during the pending proceedings. A waiver of counsel may be withdrawn, although the withdrawal of the waiver is only prospective and does not affect the validity of any otherwise lawful process that took place following the waiver and up to the moment of the withdrawal of the waiver. A court should be reluctant to find a defendant has waived a right to counsel, preferring to hear an express waiver. Even so an implied waiver occurs if, after a person has been given Miranda warnings and has clearly demonstrated understanding the person has a right to counsel, the person deliberately, voluntarily, and intentionally speaks with a person known to be a police official of material that reasonably involves the matters of representation.

**withdrawal of counsel** The termination of representation by a lawyer during a legal action. Withdrawal of counsel is the process of an attorney's removal from the representation of a client then before a court in either a criminal or a civil proceeding. Withdrawal is allowed only by leave of the court.

> **Anders brief** A brief by federal appointed counsel justifying withdrawal from a frivolous criminal defense. An Anders brief is required, following Anders v. California, 386 U.S. 738 (1967), for an attorney serving by appointment as counsel to a criminal appellant, allowing withdrawal after the attorney advises the court the defense is frivolous and filling a brief that inventories any possible argument of merit for appeal.

**count**

**count as a cause of action** A single, distinct allegation in a complaint or indictment. A count is a declaration or allegation of a cause of action. A suit may contain several causes of action; each distinct cause constitutes a single count. A count in a civil complaint represents a distinct theory of the case and a particular basis for a remedy. Several counts in a civil action may be brought in the alternative, in that if one theory or another is proved a single remedy suffices both. A count in a criminal charge or indictment represents a distinct allegation of a crime, and the defendant may be sentenced on that count alone and on other counts as well. A count and a charge in this sense are the same in many jurisdictions.

See also: cause, cause as dispute in court.

**counter**

> **counter abstract of record or counter-abstract or counter abstract** See: appeal, abstract of record, counter-abstract of record (counter abstract of record or counter-abstract or counter abstract).

> **counterclaim** See: claim, counterclaim, permissive counterclaim; claim, counterclaim, counterclaimant (counterdemandant); claim, counterclaim, compulsory counterclaim | failure to plead; claim, counterclaim, compulsory counterclaim; claim, counterclaim | third parties; claim, counterclaim | supplemental jurisdiction; claim, counterclaim | default; claim, counterclaim.

> **counterclaimant** See: claim, counterclaim, counterclaimant (counterdemandant).

> **counterdemandant** See: claim, counterclaim, counterclaimant (counterdemandant).

> **countermajoritarian difficulty** See: review, judicial review, countermajoritarian difficulty.

> **counter-offer** See: offer, contract offer, counter-offer (counteroffer).

> **counterpromise** See: promise, counterpromise.

> **countersign** See: signature, countersignature (countersign).

> **countersue** See: sue (countersue).

**counterfeiting (counterfeit or counterfeitor or counterfeitable)** The forgery of money, documents, or other things of value. Counterfeiting is the fraudulent duplication of anything of value. The counterfeiting of money is the creation of any facsimile or duplicate or a coin, note, or currency. Counterfeiting includes the duplication of official seals, instruments, stamps, checks, or other paper representing value, as well as products and goods.

See also: currency.

**county** A regional division of a state. A county in the United States is an administrative department of a state. The U.S. practice was adopted from England, in which the realm was divided into counties for administration and defense, each county subject to the jurisdiction of a sheriff. In the U.S., each state determines under its constitution and statutes the powers, responsibilities, and governmental structure for its counties.

See also: shire; state.

**county court** *See:* court, U.S. state court, county court (quorum court).

**parish** A county in Louisiana or a district within a church. A parish is the equivalent of a county in the state of Louisiana. In the church, it was both a single church's congregation and the region from within which the people formed the congregation. The parish thus had an ecclesiastical jurisdiction, which was useful for civil government as well.

> **police jury** The legislative body of a Louisiana parish. The police jury is an elected assembly of varying size that legislates and administers parish functions in most Louisiana parishes. In some parishes, these functions are performed by a commission or council, which divide executive from legislative functions, but as of 2011, this remains less common in the state.

**coupon** A bearer instrument proving payment owed for an increment of a bond or other debt instrument. A coupon is an increment of a debt service, which were once physical portions of a debt instrument that were cut off and presented for payment on or after the date the coupon payment was owing. Once the date had passed, the coupon represented a claim on the bond issuer or other maker of the debt instrument. In cases of coupon bonds, but in others depending on the terms of the coupon, the coupon became a bearer instrument in and of itself. This whole practice is now increasingly rare, having been replaced largely by electronic records and transfers of funds.
*See also:* bond, coupon bond (bond coupon).

> **coupon bond (bond coupon)** Negotiable instrument including the large original document and several detachable substitutes.
> *See also:* bond, coupon bond (bond coupon).

**courier (diplomatic courier)** A person or service that carries messages for others. A courier is a carrier of letters or other papers. Diplomatic couriers are entitled to immunity from the inspection of items under diplomatic seal or in the diplomatic pouch.

**course**

> **course of business (course of trade)** Routine actions in the conduct of the affairs of a company or business. The course of business, or the course of trade, describes the customary actions followed in carrying out the daily tasks of an office, business, or corporation. Reference to the course of business allows presumptions to establish certain actions as likely having taken place when no evidence to the contrary is available.

> **course of employment** *See:* liability, vicarious liability, course of employment (scope of employment).

> **course of performance** *See:* performance, contract performance, course of performance.

**course of ship** The movements of a vessel from one place to another. The course of a ship refers either to the anticipated track the ship will travel that is marked and plotted on a nautical chart or navigational computer in advance of its movement, or to the actual course navigated by the vessel through the waters.

**course of the voyage** The anticipated route from one port to another. The course of voyage is an anticipated or customary route from one port to the next, on which parties have a right to rely when entering a shipping agreement or charter. It does not necessarily describe the course actually plotted or navigated by the vessel.

**of course** Done in the usual order of the proceedings. Anything of course is done according to the rules or the established custom and protocol. Something of course in a trial is generally not required to be moved or petitioned, though if a motion or petition is required, it will presumptively be granted.

**court** An office vested with the judicial power of a state. A court is a legal office of a government vested with the power to adjudicate disputes, to issue orders to officials and to citizens requiring them to comply with laws and its orders, and to order remedies for public or private failings to conform to the laws.

The term court is quite broad, including the place and its officials. The legal meaning of "court" devolved from the courts of kings, who heard disputes and rendered judgments, into specialized offices exercising state power to apply the law to particular matters.

Courts in the United States include trial and appellate courts, courts of general jurisdiction and courts of limited jurisdiction, courts of law and courts of equity, as well as specialized courts created for a particular category of case or dispute. Not all entities of government that are named a court are primarily judicial in function or power: certain states employ the term court for legislative bodies, such as general court or quorum court, and administrative courts exercise a ministerial function of hearing or reviewing claims or citations as a matter of executive power, subject to judicial oversight.
*See also:* tribunal.

**court-annexed mediation** *See:* mediation, court-annexed mediation.

**court-appointed attorney** *See:* attorney, panel attorney (court-appointed attorney).

**court-appointed counsel** *See:* counselor, assigned counsel (court-appointed counsel).

**court calendar** *See:* calendar, court calendar, calendar call; calendar, court calendar.

**court fee** *See:* fee, fee for services, court fee, jury fee; fee, fee for services, court fee, filing fee; fee, fee for services, court fee, docket fee.

**court of equity** *See:* equity, court of equity.

**court order** *See:* order, court order, scheduling order; order, court order, restraining order; order, court order, interlocutory orders (interlocutory decision); order, court order, ex parte order; order, court order, appealable order, collateral–order doctrine; order, court order, appealable order (appealable decision); order, court order.

**court–packing plan** *See:* pack, court–packing plan (judiciary reorganization bill of 1937 or switch in time that saved nine).

**court records** *See:* record, court records, public access to court electronic records (P.A.C.E.R. or PACER).

**court reporter** *See:* reporter, court reporter.

**court rule** *See:* rule, rule of court (court rule).

**court term** *See:* term, court term (session of court).

**administrative court** Article II court for appeal of administrative decisions. An administrative court is located in an agency or department of the executive branch and has exclusive and limited jurisdiction over disputes appealed from administrators in that agency or department. The administrative court deals with disputes between individuals and the government agency as well as with review of administrative decisions affecting the individual alone. In nearly all instances, a claimant must exhaust appeals through the administrative process before seeking review of the claim in the Article III courts.
*See also:* law, administrative law.

**business court** Tribunal with jurisdiction over commercial and corporate claims. A business court is organized in some states to hear complicated matters arising over business organization and finance, shareholder claims, and related matters, including commercial disputes. Chancery courts and courts of general jurisdiction hear such matters in other states. In some jurisdictions that have business courts, assignment of a matter in a court of general jurisdiction to a business court is optional with the parties.

**circuit court (riding the circuit)** A court with jurisdiction over a region within a state or nation. A circuit court is a court that includes several jurisdictions or locales within it. In the common law, the circuit referred to a court with no permanent seat, but with a judge that "rides the circuit" or travels among locales within its jurisdiction. Judges riding the circuit would sometimes carry their lawbooks in their saddle bags. Today, state circuit courts tend to be trial courts of general jurisdiction, and federal circuit courts are courts of appeal. In each case, there is likely to be a geographic domain subject to its jurisdiction.
*See also:* court, circuit court, federal circuit court; court, English court, justices in Eyre (Eire).

**Federal Circuit Court** The U.S. Court of Appeals for the Federal Circuit, or any U.S. Court of Appeals.

**civil court** A court for civil actions. The civil courts provide a forum for the resolution of disputes not brought as a criminal proceeding. A particular court, such as state courts of general jurisdiction, may be empowered to hear both civil and criminal causes, but when hearing a non–criminal matter, the court is a civil court.

**conscience of the court** The moral values of law and justice. The conscience of the court is the understanding of justice and of the propriety of the judgeship that would require action or a restraint from action as an aspect of moral duty in the service of the law. Although the responsibility for applying such an understanding rests with each judge individually, that vesting of discretion does not mean that there is no external basis for the assessment of its exercise. Every assessment must give great deference to the individual judge making the assessment, because only the person holding the judgeship has the responsibility of action at the moment, yet such deference is not unlimited, and failures to incorporate reasonably available information into the assessment of the conscientious decision are but one way in which the conscience might fail to do justice such that—despite such deference—the decision must be criticized or reversed.
*See also:* discretion.

**constitutional court** A court expressly created in a constitution, or a court to which constitutional questions are referred. In the United States, a constitutional court is a court specifically enumerated in the constitution organizing a government, and a constitutional court may not be abolished by the legislature or executive. In the United States, only the Supreme Court is generally thought to be a constitutional court, though there may be a constitutional requirement that inferior federal courts exist. State constitutions vary in the courts that are constitutional, although most require a highest court, an intermediate appellate court and a system of trial courts, vesting the legislature with the power to create as needed new courts that are not constitutional courts.

A constitutional court in its more international sense is a court given specific competence to determine a constitutional question, particularly to exercise judicial review over executive, administrative or legislative acts. This function is performed in the United States by the U.S. Supreme Court and, for matters affecting state constitutions, by the highest courts in their states. In both cases, however, inferior courts have constitutional powers to interpret the Constitution.

**court crier (court cryer)** The person who calls court. The court crier opens and closes a session of court. The crier uses a method specified by court rules, which was adopted by judicial order or was continued from long–standing custom. In most trial courts, the cry is performed by a bailiff, sheriff's deputy, police officer, or marshal. In most appellate courts, it is performed by a clerk.
*See also:* bailiff; court, court cry, oyez.

**oyez** Hear ye. Oyez is the cry used by custom to commence a court session in the United States Supreme Court and in other courts. The whole cry is "Oyez, oyez, oyez. The Honorable, Chief Justice and the Associate Justices of the Supreme Court of the United States. All persons having business before this honorable Court are admonished to draw nigh and give their attention, for the Court is now sitting. God save the United States and this honorable Court." The term is derived from "oyer" and pronounced in the wonderful way in which Law French is corrupted to sound a bit like "Oh, yes."

*See also:* oyer.

**court of admiralty (admiralty court)**   A court with jurisdiction in admiralty or maritime law. An admiralty court in the United States is the United States District Courts, and the courts hearing appeals in such causes. In England and Wales, Admiralty is now heard by the Admiralty Judge and other authorized judges on the Court of the Queen's Bench Division of the High Court.

**court of equity (chancery court)**   A court that may grant equitable remedies. Courts of equity include both courts specifically created to act only in equity, such as chancery courts, and courts given authority to act in law and in equity, such as the U.S. District Courts. Courts of equity apply the principles of equity and such rules of equity pleading as persist with the rules of civil procedure and evidence in equitable actions.

**court of general jurisdiction**   Trial court with presumptive subject matter jurisdiction over all civil and criminal disputes that may be heard in the state. A court of general jurisdiction is empowered to hear all cases in the first instance of civil and criminal jurisdiction that are not dedicated exclusively to a court of limited jurisdiction.

**court of last resort**   Tribunal from which there is no appeal. A court of last resort, in general, is the court in a legal system beyond which there is no appeal or standing institution by which to overturn a decision. The U.S. Supreme Court is the court of last resort for the United States federal system. The New York Court of Appeals, the California Supreme Court, and the Massachusetts Supreme Judicial Court are all courts of last resort in their respective jurisdictions. Courts of last resort are not without institutional means of reversal, as there are rarely used means of reversal by constitutional amendment or, occasionally, by legislative action, and the court itself is usually capable of reversing earlier decisions. As to certain cases, however, the court of last resort might well not be the highest court, because appellate jurisdiction is limited to a lower court, such as a court of criminal appeals. Thus, when review of a state decision by a federal court is limited to review of decisions by the court of last resort, the limitation is understood not to require a decision by the highest court in the state but the highest court that must hear appeals of the given decision.

**court of law**   A court of record that applies the rules of law. A court of law is a court of record described usually in this way to distinguish it from other courts, such as administrative courts or court of equity, that do not apply the law generally but employ specialized rules of decision.

**court of limited jurisdiction**   Court of record dedicated to hear specialized subject matter or claims. A court of limited jurisdiction is a court of record, which is limited to hear certain actions by subject matter or the value of the claims before it. Small claims court, probate court, and magistrate's court are courts of limited jurisdiction.

*See also:* safe, safe harbor.

**family court**   Court of record with jurisdiction over affairs of children and families. A family court is a specialized court organized in most states, with exclusive jurisdiction over matters dealing with children, including adoption, custody, maintenance, neglect, abuse, and abandonment, and with matters of marriage, including divorce, property settlement, and the enforcement of awards.

**surrogate's court**   A family and probate court. A surrogate's court is a court of limited jurisdiction hearing, in most instances, matters affecting probate and decedent's estates, as well as matters of adoptions and wards of the court. The judge presiding over a surrogate's court is a called the Surrogate, and other judges of the court are Depute Surrogates.

**(F.I.S.A. Court or FISA Court)**   A special federal court reviewing motions to allow electronic surveillance. The FISA Court was established under the Foreign Intelligence Surveillance Act, 92 Stat. 1783, to issue warrants for domestic surveillance of suspected foreign intelligence agents. Following the USA Patriot Act of 2001, 115 Stat. 272, the court was expanded from seven to eleven judges. In 2002, the court held that the FBI had not sufficiently acted to minimize the likelihood information gathered for intelligence would be used for criminal law enforcement, though what procedural changes may have followed this holding remain classified as of 2010. The court's decisions may be appealed to the Foreign Intelligence Surveillance Court of Review.

**housing court**   A municipal court that hears housing violations. A housing court is a court established in several larger cities, to hear criminal and civil matters arising from violations of housing, building, fire, zoning, health, waste collection, sidewalk and agricultural and air pollution codes. Some housing courts also hear civil disputes between landlord and tenant.

**juvenile court (juvenile proceeding)**   A court with jurisdiction over child custody, care, and offenses. A juvenile court is a court of limited jurisdiction that hears children in need of services (CHINS), care and protection petitions, adoption, guardianship, termination of parental rights proceedings, delinquency, adult contribution to delinquency, and youthful offender cases.

The criminal–law jurisdiction varies, and courts in various states hear charges against offenders older than six or seven and under the age of eighteen years, though a few states limit jurisdiction to fifteen years or younger, and some determine the jurisdiction on a case-by-case basis. Conduct that is attributed to a minor that would be a crime if committed by an adult is usually not treated as a criminal offense in a juvenile court but as an instance of juvenile delinquency.

The juvenile court has wide discretion in dealing not only with issues of delinquency but also issues of parental fitness, adult abuse, and other issues related to the care, conduct, and status of a child. It can order detention in an eligible facility within the jurisdiction, can alter parental rights, or order new living arrangements.

**probate court**   Court hearing matters of guardianships, wills, estates and trusts. A probate court is a court established to hear actions and petitions arising from wills, estates, and guardianships, and trusts. Probate courts supervise the administration of estates and review probate filings, the satisfaction of creditors, and the distribution of estate assets to devisees, legatees, beneficiaries, and heirs. In some jurisdictions, the probate court acts also as the family court.

*See also:* probate.

**court of original jurisdiction**   Court in which a particular cause is first filed. A court of original jurisdiction is the court that is appropriate for the initiation of a given cause of action.

*See also:* original (originality); safe, safe harbor.

**court of record**   A court in which proceedings are recorded and binding as law. A court of record is a court created as a court of record, required to maintain records of its proceedings for the purposes of review and for the purposes of binding the parties to actions in that court to the matter recorded. All courts with criminal jurisdiction are inherently courts of record unless they are legislatively created not as courts of record, as are certain justice courts. To be a court of record, the court must be given a specific jurisdiction and be provided with a judge or justice, an obligation to maintain records, and a seal or a clerk whose authentication functions as a seal.

*See also:* record, of record.

**court recorder**   One who records a hearing or trial in court. A court recorder is a clerk of court licensed professional who audiophonically records a court session, filing it with the clerk of court or with the court reporter. Note: a Recorder's Court is a court of limited jurisdiction, and the Recorder, or judge of that court, is not a court recorder.

**domestic court (domestic tribunal)**   A national court. A domestic court, in international law, is a court with powers under the laws of a single nation-state, whether that court is a national court or a state court.

**drug court**   A court that hears trials for drug offenses and can order discretionary remedies. A drug court is a court organized at the state trial court level, either as

an independent court or as a special jurisdiction of the regular criminal court, to hear trials and motions in the prosecution of a drug offense. The drug courts have varying scopes of jurisdiction and discretion in remedies, but all have a greater discretion than a typical criminal tribunal to order remedial supervision and education.

**staffing meeting**   A status hearing for the review of a drug court case. At a staffing meeting, the drug court judge presides over a meeting of a prosecutor, a certified counselor of the court, probation officers, counsel, and other staff to assess the medical, social, and legal records of a criminal defendant or drug court candidate to determine whether the candidate will be accepted into the jurisdiction of the drug court, or what changes of treatments or other orders should be entered.

### English courts

**Court of Assize (Assize or Assizes)**   A medieval English court that preceded the circuit courts. The assizes were circuit courts distributed throughout the country that sat with juries four times yearly to hear criminal causes and certain private actions dealing primarily with claims to lands and estates.

**Court of Common Pleas (Common Bench or Banco Communis or Bancus Communis)**   The royal court for civil actions, from which came much of the common law. The Court of Common Pleas existed from the thirteenth century until 1880, with jurisdiction over civil actions between private litigants, cases involving royal interests being kept for the Court of King's Bench and the Exchequer, which acquired concurrent jurisdictions over many areas of the private common law, but common pleas retained sole jurisdiction over matters of property. Many of the most significant doctrines of the common law, particularly in the law of property, originated in the Court of Common Pleas.

**Court of King's Bench (Queen's Bench)**   The supervisory court of the common law. The Court of King's Bench, known as the Court of Queen's Bench when a queen is monarch, was the senior common-law court from the 1300's until its abolition in 1875, when it was merged into the High Court. The Court of Common Pleas was established earlier as a distinct court, but King's Bench remained an element of the coram rege for a century longer, eventually being recognized as a separate institution, with original and appellate criminal jurisdiction, the power of habeas corpus, appellate civil jurisdiction, which was often used for matters of particular relationship to the crown, and supervisory powers asserted through prerogative writs.

**Justices in Eyre (Eire)**   The early Norman courts of the circuit justices. The Court of the Justices in Eyre was the first court of the itinerant judges in Norman England. Justices went on Eyre were members of the royal Aula Regis, who were sent to travel the kingdom holding courts, once every seven years from 1176 until Magna Carta. After Magna Carta, they held court annually and the courts were gradually replaced by the courts of Assizes, which performed this function by the end of the 1200s, though the Eyre of the Forest continued for many years.

*See also:* court, circuit court (riding the circuit); court, English court, court of assize (assize or assizes).

**nisi prius court**    A local trial in lieu of a trial in London. A trial nisi prius, or the nisi prius court, was held in the locality in which a dispute arose, essentially by delegation from the court in Westminster. The name is from the writ by which the trial was ordered, to be held unless there is an earlier trial of the action in the court issuing the writ. This system worked well for actions that were dedicated by Magna Carta and later statutes to be heard in London but which would be more convenient to the parties to be held in their own locale.

**Star Chamber (Court of Star Chamber)**    A prerogative court to try matters of state and those affecting the powerful. The Court of Star Chamber was a court from 1487 to 1641, comprising privy councilors, the chief justices, and several bishops, who sat without a jury to hear cases of official corruption, crimes against justice, trade disputes, and some misdemeanors, property offenses, and, over time, defamation. The court followed a procedure specific to it, including examination under oath, the use of witnesses, and a poll of the judges. Although torture was not allowed in Star Chamber proceedings, the proceedings were held in secret. As England moved toward its Civil War in the 1600s, the Court of Star Chamber acquired a dreadful reputation as a court of unbridled discretion that used torture and abused legal process to persecute royal enemies. Star Chamber remains a metaphor for a powerful, secret, and dangerous court.

**terms of court**    The four terms of court of the English Court of Appeal. The four terms of court in England, effectively one for late autumn, one for winter, one for spring, and one for early summer, defined the legal calendar of England, as well as the academic calendar of some universities and other institutions, for centuries. The English courts ended this calendar in 1873, though it has been revived, with four terms: Michaelmas Term from October to December, Hilary Term from January to April, Easter Term in May, and Trinity Term in June and July.

*See also:* term, court term (session of court).

**Easter Term**    The English court term in early spring. Easter Term is usually a short term, in April or May. It is, of course, named for the Feast of Easter, which is a movable feast, held in the Western Church in March or April.

**Hilary Term**    The English court term in late winter. Hilary Term is a long term, usually running from early January through April, depending on the date of Easter, which sets the start of the next term. It is named for the feast of St. Hilary of Poitiers, a feast day of the Western Church on January 13 or 14, which also nicely preceded Plough Monday, the day on which laborers were once ritually to return to work after Christmas, which is still near to the first day of court.

**Michaelmas Term**    The English court term in late autumn. Michaelmas Term is the first term of the court year, now running from early October to mid–December. It is named for the Feast of Saint Michael the Archangel, which in the Western Church is on September 29.

**Trinity Term**    The English court term in late spring. Trinity Term is the last term of the court year, usually running from early June to late July, though its start depends in part on the end of the Easter Term that precedes it. It is named for the Feast of the Trinity, which is a movable feast in May or June in the Western Church, determined as the Sunday following Pentecost, or eight weeks after Easter Day.

**full court (en banc court)**    A court with all of its judges present. A full court is a court in which all of the judges assigned to it are present for an argument. This is also known as a sitting of the bench en banc.

*See also:* bench, en banc (en banc sitting or sitting en banc).

### Greek courts

**Areopagus (court of the Areopagus or Areiopagos)**    The highest criminal court of ancient Athens. The Areopagus is a hill in Athens on which met the most powerful Athenian law court, other than assembly and the senate but with certain jurisdiction beyond theirs. More fully called the Council of the Areopagus, the court pre–existed the democracy, which it served as the highest criminal court, although it also held legislative and administrative authority from time to time throughout Athenian history. The Areopagites were responsible for education of the young, and this court condemned Socrates to death. Its members for life were those former archons who were adjudged not to have been incompetent or corrupt during office.

**human rights tribunal**    *See:* right, human right, human rights tribunal.

**inherent power of the court**    What a court can do. Courts have inherent powers that are essential to their performance of the broad authority vested in every court of law or equity. Among these powers are the power to carry out the judicial functions of the law. Thus, a court has an inherent power to hear disputes properly before it; it has an inherent power to discipline lawyers practicing before it and litigants lawfully before it; it has an inherent power to enforce its orders, and it has an inherent power to secure the physical safety and environment of the court itself.

**international court**  Any court or tribunal established among states or by an international organization. An international court is a court or a tribunal that is created by the action of an international organization through the actions or agreement of more than one state, to hear causes under international law or under particular rules of decision specific to that court. Examples include the International Court of Justice, the Permanent Court of International Justice, the International Criminal Court, and the International Military Tribunals. International courts have no monopoly in the application of international law, and a domestic court, that is to say a national court, is likely to hear disputes in which international law supplies the rules of decision.

    **ad hoc tribunal**  An international court created for a particular cause or cases. An ad hoc tribunal is an international court created to hear causes arising from a particular area or as a result of a particular crisis. The most prominent examples, the International Court for the Former Yugoslovia and the International Court for Rwanda, were created by United Nations Security Council resolutions.

    *See also:* ad, ad hoc.

    **hybrid court**  A court both international and domestic in origin, judicial personnel, or purpose. A hybrid court in international law is a court created by state, by a group of states, by an international organization, or by some combination of state and organization, to hear disputes and criminal causes arising from an area or conflict. Hybrid courts were established in Kosovo (1999), in East Timor (2000), and in Sierra Leone (2002).

    *See also:* hybrid.

**International Court of Justice (I.C.J. or ICJ)**  The principal judicial body of the United Nations. The International Court of Justice, or ICJ, is the court of the United Nations, and the statute creating the ICJ is an element of the United Nations Charter. Fifteen judges sit on the court, elected by the Security Council and the General Assembly to nine-year terms. The ICJ sits in the Peace Palace in The Hague, in the Netherlands.

    Only states may appear in the ICJ, although certain matters may be referred to the ICJ by the Security Council. A state may opt to accept ICJ jurisdiction at the request of any state that is a member of the ICJ, or a state may reserve the right to appear or abstain from the ICJ's jurisdiction. Decisions of the ICJ are considered a significant source of international law but are binding only upon the parties to the action then before the court.

**International Criminal Court (I.C.C. or ICC)**  An international tribunal to try serious crimes under international law. The International Criminal Court is a permanent court that takes jurisdiction over accusations of genocide, crimes against humanity, and war crimes, when no nation-state with proper authority over the accused will investigate the allegations in good faith. The Court sits in The Hague and was established in 2002 with the coming into force of the 1998 Rome Statute of the International Criminal Court. As of 2010, over one hundred countries have ratified the treaty and joined the court.

    **International Military Tribunal, Far East (I.M.T.F.E. or IMTFE or Tokyo War Crimes Trials or Tokyo Trials)**  The international court in Japan from 1946 to 1948. The International Military Tribunal, Far East, tried twenty-eight leaders of Imperial Japan for crimes against peace, war crimes, crimes against humanity, and conspiracy. These trials were followed by national trials, held in the various countries. Although four former prime ministers were tried, Emperor Hirohito was not tried. The twenty-five defendants whose case reached judgment were convicted, of whom seven were executed and the rest imprisoned. In the judgments, Judge Pal of India dissented as to the findings of guilt. Japan accepted the legitimacy of the trials in 1951.

    **International Military Tribunal, Nuremberg (Nuremburg Trials or I.M.T. or I.M.T.N. or IMT or IMTN)**  The international court in Germany from 1945 to 1946. The International Military Tribunal, Nuremberg, tried twenty-four leaders of Nazi Germany and six German organizations for crimes against peace, war crimes, crimes against humanity, and conspiracy. These trials were followed by trials of the Nuremberg Military Tribunals, from 1946 to 1949, held in the various areas of allied control, the U.S. trials being of 185 defendants, of whom 142 were found guilty, France and particularly Great Britain holding many more, and both France and the USSR holding further trials of Germans accused of war crimes in their respective countries. The Nuremberg trials were hardly the first trials for crimes of war, though they were the first international criminal trials and the first trials to hold individuals accountable for criminal acts by states.

    **Permanent Court of International Justice (P.C.I.J. or PCIJ)**  The predecessor court to the International Court of Justice. The Permanent Court of International Justice, or PCIJ, was the first international court of general jurisdiction among modern states, the international arbitral tribunal created by the Covenant of the League of Nations after World War I. The PCIJ sat from 1922 to 1946, deciding twenty-nine contentious inter-state cases and issuing twenty-seven advisory opinions. Its rulings remain an important source of international law.

**kangaroo court**  A bad or unjust court, or a mock court outside the law. A kangaroo court is, usually, not a court at all but a popular and informal gathering to praise or abuse others. When the term is applied to a court of law, it suggests a wholesale failure of procedure or decorum such that justice is unlikely to have been done. Though the phrase might seem Australian, it was certainly coined in the United States before the American Civil War, describing the hopping of judges riding circuit from place to place, dispensing law from a saddlebag.

**moot court**   *See:* simulation, moot court.

**open court (public court)**   A court proceeding open to the public. Open court is a court in session that is open to the public. A person attending, participating, or observing open court is subject to abide by the rules and decorum of the courtroom. Further, a court in open session may be closed to certain persons, such as witnesses yet to be called when the rule requiring the sequestration of witnesses has been invoked. There is no presumption from a court being in public or open session that the proceedings may be photographed, videographed or transmitted, such records being made only by leave of the court.

*See also:* witness, sequestration of witness (rule or or the rule or separation of witnesses).

**out of court (out-of-court)**   Anything not of record in a judicial proceeding. In most instances, out of court describes any statement, action, or status made or done that was not on the record in a judicial proceeding. For instance, an out of court settlement is likely to be negotiated in the physical space of a courthouse or even a courtroom, but the negotiations are not made on a court record. Even though the settlement may be filed with the court — such as when the parties agree in the settlement to enter a motion to dismiss or for entry of judgment — the settlement itself is considered made out of court. So, too, if witness makes a statement in the bathroom of the courthouse during recess in a trial, that statement is made out of court for the purposes of the analysis of hearsay. Note: Statements and actions made out of the hearing of the jury are not necessarily out of court. Side-bar discussions, in camera proceedings, and other matters of record may happen during a jury proceeding in the jury's absence and not be made out of court.

More generally, "out of court" means a physical separation from the court and courtroom activities, as when an attorney is out of court or bills for out-of-court work.

**oyer and terminer**   A criminal trial court formerly in England and America. The court of oyer and terminer was a court held by a judge sitting alone when on the circuit holding a court of assize. The judge held several commissions to summon various courts, one being of assize and nisi prius, the others being oyer and terminer, and general gaol delivery. The commission of oyer and terminer, or the court of hearing and disposition, could hear indictments brought before the judge. The phrase, oyer and terminer, is law French for "hear" and "determine"; thus the court was a court of hearings and decisions.

*See also:* oyer.

**supreme court**   A court with jurisdiction over others. A supreme court, in most jurisdictions, is a court with appellate authority over all other courts, the highest judicial authority of the jurisdiction. Owing to variations in custom, this usage is not universal, and the court may be a lower court in some systems, as in New York, where the supreme court includes both the state trial courts and intermediate appellate division.

**trial court (court of first instance)**   A court that hears civil or criminal trials. A trial court is any court empowered to hear trials, which is usually to say the first court of record to hear a given matter and render judgment in it, as opposed to the appeals court.

**Article I tribunal (Article I court or Article One court or legislative court)**   Court created by Congress, without life–tenured judges. Article I courts describe courts created by Congress without the independence granted to Article III courts of life tenure and undiminishable salary. U.S. Bankruptcy Courts and the offices of U.S. Magistrate–Judges are Article I courts. The term is used informally and, confusingly, many Article I courts are actually within the Article III court processes: the judges of Article I courts are usually appointed by Article III judges; the appeal from Article I courts is to Article III courts, and the jurisdiction of Article I courts is usually concomitant with Article III courts. An exception is the U.S. Tax Court, which is an Article I court with national jurisdiction.

**Article II tribunal (Article II court or Article Two court)**   Agency tribunal making or reviewing administrative decisions. An Article II court is a court within the executive branch, either an administrative court or military court created under authority delegated to the President by Congress. Article II courts in most government departments are actually administrative boards, either hearing claims or citations or reviewing lower decisions by officials within the same agency. Immigration Courts, administrative law courts, and the Tax Court are Article II courts. Judges on all of these tribunals are Article II judges, employees of the executive branch, and there is considerable question of the degree of independence such judges may have.

**Article III court**   A court organized under Article III of the U.S. Constitution. Article III courts are the Supreme Court of the United States and such inferior courts as Congress authorizes under Article III under the U.S. Constitution. Article III judges are appointed by the President with the advice and consent of the Senate and serve for life or until resignation or impeachment. The administration of Article III courts is both inherent in each court and subject to the management of the Judicial Conference of the United States. Their powers extend to all judicial powers of the United States, including all cases or controversies committed to the federal courts, as well as within the jurisdiction determined for the courts by the U.S. Congress.

**court of appeal (appellate court or court of appeals or intermediate court)** A court of errors and review, subject to a higher court. A court of appeals, in most instances is a court of error and appeal, to which one who is convicted of a crime or against whom a judgment is rendered in a trial court may appeal for review of the judgment below, seeking a reversal for errors of law or mistakes in the use of the evidence or procedure. In this sense, courts of appeals are usually intermediate, subject to further review by a high court. The term, court of appeal, however, may be assigned either to an intermediate court, as is the case of the United States Courts of Appeal or to a high court, as is the case of the New York Court of Appeals. A court of general jurisdiction may be vested with the authority of a court of appeals, in hearing appeals from courts of limited jurisdiction or administrative tribunals.

See also: appeal (appealable or appellate); review, standard of review; appellant; appellee.

**Court of Appeals for Veterans Claims (Court of Veterans Appeals or CAVC)** Court hearing appeals of veterans' claims to benefits. The Court of Appeals for Veterans Claims is a specialized federal court of record organized under Article I, with jurisdiction limited to the appeal of claims for benefits by veterans of the U.S. Armed Forces that have been finally decided by the Board of Veterans' Appeals. The court was previously the United States Court of Veterans Appeals. It is within the Department of Veterans Affairs but is independent, with seven judges appointed by the President to fifteen-year terms.

**court of criminal appeals (state criminal appellate court)** A state court for the review of criminal matters. A court of criminal appeals is a state appellate court for the appellate review of interlocutory orders, convictions, sentences, and, sometimes, collateral matters arising from criminal trials or convictions. Note: the military appeals process incorporates a court of criminal appeals for the review of sentences of courts martial. Context is essential to distinguish which court is intended by a given usage.

**court-martial (court martial or courts martial)** A court of military officers in a service branch of the United States military. The court martial is a military court, authorized by the Uniform Code of Military Justice, and proceeding according to the Manual for Courts Martial: United States. Courts martial have jurisdiction over all military personnel, each court martial being created by its branch of the service to hear charges against its own members for violations of the UCMJ and the law of war.

See also: military, military law.

**U.S. Court of Appeals for the Armed Forces** An Article I court with appellate review of courts martial. The United States Court of Appeals for the Armed Forces is an independent court established by Congress within the Executive Branch, whose judges serve fifteen-year-terms and decide all appeals from courts-martial within any branch of the United States military services.

**federal court** A court of law of the United States. A federal court is any court organized under the authority of the United States Constitution. As the term is ordinarily used, it refers to courts of general and appellate jurisdiction under Article III, the U.S. district courts, courts of appeal, and Supreme Court. Even so, the term includes Article I courts, such as the Tax Court, and only the context of the term's use will determine its intended scope.

**justice court** A state court of limited jurisdiction, usually not a court of record. Justice courts are the courts of justices of the peace or justice court judges, state courts of limited jurisdiction, which varies somewhat from state to state. Most hear minor criminal matters, particularly traffic citations, as well as small civil claims. Proceedings in most justice courts are not of record, the judgment being the only record of proceedings before them.

**municipal court** A court organized within a city, village, or township. A municipal court is a court organized within a particular municipality, with jurisdiction over offenses under municipal ordinances and such petty state offenses as are dedicated to it by state statute. Municipal courts also often maintain a small claims division for civil matters, and some have an appellate function for administrative matters arising under municipal government.

**small-claims court** A local court for legal resolution of small-value claims. Small-claims courts are state or municipal courts of limited jurisdiction with authority to hear claims for small amounts of money, whose court costs and legal fees might otherwise be greater than the amount in controversy. Although some jurisdictions denominate a court as a "small-claims court" the term is often applied informally to justice courts, county courts, and municipal courts with civil jurisdictions distinct from the state court of general jurisdiction for that geographic district. Small-claims courts so called, or other courts in their small-claims capacities, often employ simplified rules for service, evidence, hearings, and enforcements of judgment, with appeal to the court of general jurisdiction.

**state court** A court organized under a state's constitution. A state court is a court organized by a state, including for most purposes the District of Columbia's courts as organized under Congressional authority.

**county court (quorum court)** Tribunal with jurisdiction over the political subdivision it sits in. A county court is a state court with jurisdiction over the county in which it sits. In many states, it is a strictly judicial function, with county judges hearing causes within statutorily set civil and criminal jurisdiction. In other states, the county court, also known as a quorum court, is a legislative body for the county, its members being justices of the peace or county court judges, whose jurisdiction is otherwise limited to the single-judge court.

*See also:* county, parish, police jury.

**Tax Court (U.S. Tax Court)**  A specialized trial court for appeals from the Commissioner of Internal Revenue. The United States Tax Court is an administrative court that hears appeals brought by taxpayers from a finding of a tax deficiency by the Commissioner of Internal Revenue. In the event of a finding of deficiency, the taxpayer may pay the amount and then sue for its return in the taxpayer's U.S. District Court or the U.S. Court of Federal Claims, but if the taxpayer chooses not to pay the claim is heard by the Tax Court. Appeals from the Tax Court are to the Circuit Court of Appeal with jurisdiction over the taxpayer. Tax Court is an Article I court, created as a successor to the Board of Tax Appeals.

*See also:* tax (taxation).

**U.S. Court of Appeals (circuit court)**  One of the federal intermediate appellate courts. The United States Courts of Appeals are divided into circuits by geography and, for a few courts, subject matter. Appeals are brought to these courts from the U.S. district courts and from U.S. agencies. Owing to the rarity of review in the U.S. Supreme Court, in practice, review by these courts is the final review for nearly all federal cases.

*See also:* court, circuit court (riding the circuit).

**law of the circuit (circuit law)**  The law derived from the precedents of a single circuit court of the U.S. Court of Appeals. The law of the circuit is a customary understanding of federal law describing the particular rules derived from the precedents of one of the federal courts of appeals. Because the appellate authority of each circuit specially applies to all lower federal courts that must appeal to it, the decisions of, say, the Fifth Circuit establish the federal law in Louisiana, Mississippi, and Texas. Once a panel of a court of appeals has determined a particular rule of law in a case before it, later panels sitting on other cases are expected to abide by the earlier case as precedent or to overturn the earlier case only under such circumstances as would warrant the over-ruling of precedent. In such cases, it is usual to take the question to the whole court in a rehearing en banc for resolution. When there is a conflict among the circuits, it is expected that the lower courts will follow the law of the circuit in which they are located, although this is a custom not always followed.

**U.S. District Court**  A United States trial court of general jurisdiction. The United States District Courts are the primary trial courts of the United States. The district court is not the only trial court, however, as particular matters may originate in the United States Supreme Court, courts martial, in the federal agencies, and in specialized courts constituted for limited purposes, such as the Court of International Trade and the U.S. Court of Federal Claims. The U.S. District Court is a court of law, of equity, and of admiralty, with a power given by statute of appellate review over certain matters from bankruptcy courts, magistrate judges, and federal agencies. Most matters in district court are heard by one judge, although certain matters regarding voter district reapportionment or civil rights enforcement are heard by a panel of three judges. As of 2011, there are ninety-four federal judicial districts. Most districts are divided into geographic divisions for easier administration and judicial assignment.

**U.S. Supreme Court (SCOTUS)**  The court of last resort for federal issues in the United States. The United States Supreme Court is a constitutional court established by Article Three of the Constitution and serving as the court of last resort in the federal system. The Chief Justice of the United States presides over the court, which for most purposes sits en banc, with all active judges who have not recused themselves present for argument and decision.

The Court hears nearly all cases in a process of review of a lower federal court or state's highest court that is commenced through certiorari, leaving the court with the discretion to hear or not to hear cases for which review is petitioned. The few cases heard by the Court in its original jurisdiction are usually heard first by a special master, who receives and reviews evidence to prepare a report and recommendation for the Court's review.

In the first decade of the twenty-first century, journalists and lawyers have abbreviated the Court into SCOTUS, an acronym resonant with POTUS, an acronym for the President.

**Burger Court**  The U.S. Supreme Court from 1969 to 1986. The Burger Court is an informal reference to the U.S. Supreme Court during Warren E. Burger's seventeen-year service as Chief Justice, hearing such landmark cases such as United States v. Nixon, 418 U.S. 683 (1974); Roe v. Wade, 410 U.S. 113 (1973); and Lemon v. Kurtzman, 403 U.S. 602 (1971).

**Chase Court**  The U.S. Supreme Court from 1864 to 1873. The Chase Court is an informal reference to the U.S. Supreme Court during Salmon P. Chase's nine years of service as Chief Justice. Chase appointed John Rock to argue before the Court, the first African American to do so, but the most famous events during his tenure were the early Reconstruction cases and the impeachment of Andrew Johnson.

**Ellsworth Court**   The U.S. Supreme Court from 1796 to 1800. The Ellsworth Court is an informal reference to the U.S. Supreme Court during Oliver Ellsworth's five-year service as Chief Justice, which was notable as Ellsworth spent two years of it in France settling the quasi-war. This era for the Court is rarely discussed.

**Four Horsemen**   Justices Van Devanter, McReynolds, Sutherland, and Butler. The Four Horsemen were justices of the U.S. Supreme Court who publicly opposed progressive legislation in the states and by President Franklin Roosevelt during the New Deal. Willis Van Devanter, Jame McReynolds, George Sutherland, and Pierce Butler became famous for their opposition to reform legislation, particularly wage and hour laws. Recent research suggests, however, that these justices supported progressive causes in less famous cases.

**Fuller Court**   The U.S. Supreme Court from 1888 to 1910. The Fuller Court is an informal reference to the U.S. Supreme Court during Melville Fuller's twenty-two-year service as Chief Justice, during which the Court decided Plessy v. Ferguson, 163 U.S. 537 (1896), United States v. E.C. Knight, 156 U.S. 1 (1895), Lochner v. New York, 198 U.S. 45 (1905), and other rejections of Reconstruction and progressive legislation.

**Hughes Court (New Deal Court)**   The U.S. Supreme Court from 1930 to 1941. The Hughes Court is an informal reference to the U.S. Supreme Court during the eleven-year service of Charles Evans Hughes as Chief Justice, during which the Court initially rejected and then allowed the constitutionality of New Deal legislation and state progressive legislation, particularly in NLRB v. Jones & Laughlin Steel Corp. 301 U.S. 1 (1937). This was a period of growing recognitions of civil liberties, as in Near v. Minnesota, 283 U.S. 697 (1931), which barred prior restraint of the press.

**Jay Court**   The U.S. Supreme Court from 1789 to 1795. The Jay Court is an informal reference to the earliest years of the U.S. Supreme Court, during John Jay's six-year service as Chief Justice, during which the Court flirted with judicial review in Calder v. Bull, 3 U.S. (3 Dall.) 386 (1798), and Chisholm v. Georgia, 2 U.S. (2 Dall.) 419 (1793), which led to the Eleventh Amendment.

**Lochner Court**   The U.S. Supreme Court at the end of the nineteenth century. The Lochner Court is a label for the U.S. Supreme Court in the time of Lochner v. New York, 198 U.S. 45 (1905), but the term more particularly describes the Court's perceived hostility to progressive social legislation by Congress or the state legislatures, manifest in a number of decisions before and after.

*See also:* Lochnerism.

**Marshall Court**   The U.S. Supreme Court from 1801 to 1835. The Marshall Court is an informal reference to the U.S. Supreme Court during John Marshall's tenure as Chief Justice, hearing such landmark cases such as Marbury v. Madison, 5 U.S. (1 Cranch) 137 (1803); Dartmouth College v. Woodward, 17 U.S. (4 Wheat.) 518 (1819); MuCulloch v. Maryland, 17 U.S. (4 Wheat.) 316 (1819); and Gibbons v. Ogden, 22 U.S. (6 Wheat.) 1 (1824).

**Rehnquist Court**   The U.S. Supreme Court from 1986 to 2005. The Rehnquist Court is an informal reference to the U.S. Supreme Court during William Rehnquist's nineteen-year tenure as Chief Justice. The Court is known for its division between justices seeking limited rights and regulations and those seeking to maintain the scope of New Deal regulation and Warren-Court rights.

**Roberts Court**   The U.S. Supreme Court since 2005. The Roberts Court is an informal reference to the U.S. Supreme Court during John Roberts' chief justiceship, which continues at the time of the publication of this edition, it began in 2005.

**Rutledge Court**   The U.S. Supreme Court in the autumn of 1795. The Rutledge Court is an informal reference to the U.S. Supreme Court during John Rutledge's five-month tenure as Chief Justice. It is very rarely mentioned.

**Stone Court**   The U.S. Supreme Court from 1941 to 1946. The Stone Court is an informal reference to the U.S. Supreme Court during Harlan Fiske Stone's five-year service as Chief Justice, which was essentially the Court during World War II, which heard such cases as Ex parte Quirin, 317 U.S. 1 (1942), Korematsu v. United States, 323 U.S. 214 (1944), In re Yamashita, 327 U.S. 1 (1946), and the Rosenberg appeal.

**Taft Court**   The U.S. Supreme Court from 1921 to 1930. The Taft Court is an informal reference to the U.S. Supreme Court during William Howard Taft's nine-year service as Chief Justice, during which the present Supreme Court Building was created, the number of cases the Court heard was lessened, and the hold of Lochner-era cases continued to be undermined by dissents criticizing their rationale, as in Adkins v. Children's Hospital, 261 U.S. 525 (1923).

**Taney Court**   The U.S. Supreme Court from 1836 to 1864. The Taney Court is an informal reference to the U.S. Supreme Court during Roger B. Taney's three decades as Chief Justice, which was largely marked by a retreat from the Marshall Court's nationalism, with the exception of the Dred Scott case, 60 U.S. (19 How.) 393 (1857), and the cases of the Civil War, including the great habeas case, Ex parte Merryman, 17 F. Cas. 144 (1861).

**Vinson Court** The U.S. Supreme Court from 1946 to 1953. The Vinson Court is an informal reference to the U.S. Supreme Court during Frederick Moore Vinson's seven-year service as Chief Justice, during which the Court grappled with the demobilization from World War II, the issues of the Korean War and the start of the Cold War, as well as the growing concern for the imperial presidency as illustrated by the very divisive Youngstown Sheet & Tube Co. v. Sawyer, 343 U.S. 579 (1952).

**Waite Court** The U.S. Supreme Court from 1874 to 1888. The Waite Court is an informal reference to the U.S. Supreme Court during Morrison R. Waite's fourteen-year tenure as Chief Justice, during which the Court began to dismantle the reforms of Reconstruction, notoriously ruling that private discrimination was not a matter for federal regulation in the Civil Rights Cases, 109 U.S. 3 (1883).

**Warren Court** The U.S. Supreme Court from 1953 to 1969. The Warren Court is an informal reference to the U.S. Supreme Court during Earl Warren's sixteen-year tenure as Chief Justice. Landmark cases from this time include Reynolds v. Sims, 377 U.S. 533 (1964); Baker v. Carr, 369 U.S. 186 (1962); Brown v. Bd. of Educ., 347 U.S. 483 (1954); and Miranda v. Arizona, 384 U.S. 436 (1966). The court was known for the the end of de jure segregation and the protection of individual rights against limits from either state or federal government.

**White Court** The U.S. Supreme Court from 1910 to 1921. The White Court is an informal reference to the U.S. Supreme Court during Edward Douglass White's ten-year term as Chief Justice. The period was marked by subtly growing success for labor cases, including Wilson v. New, 243 U.S. 332 (1917), and for upholding the Adamson Act of 1916, which fixed minimum wages and maximum hours for railroad workers.

**courtesy** *See:* spouse, surviving spouse's interest, curtesy (courtesy).

## courthouse

**multi-door courthouse (multidoor courthouse)** Different cases fare differently with different types of ADR. The multi-door courthouse is a metaphor in alternative dispute resolution, which emphasizes the different results that may attend a given dispute, according to which door it enters the courthouse, in other words, according to the form of dispute resolution with which it is pursued.

**covenant** A solemn promise. A covenant is a promise of a particularly solemn nature, made in such a manner as to communicate its enduring character and the highest commitment that the promise will be fulfilled. A covenant is not inherently enforceable by the covenantee but may become so owing to circumstances in which it is an aspect of a contract. Covenant as a term may depict not only a promise in a contract but a contract itself, or a treaty or other solemn agreement. Covenants in land, real covenants, are promises affecting the use of property, some of which bind all subsequent holders of the property.

*See also:* servitude; servitude, equitable servitude, abandonment of an equitable servitude.

**covenant for quiet enjoyment** *See:* lease, lease covenant, covenant for quiet enjoyment.

**covenant marriage** *See:* marriage, covenant marriage.

**covenant of habitability** *See:* lease, lease covenant, covenant of habitability.

**covenant of repair** *See:* repair (covenant of repair).

**absolute covenant (covenant absolute)** An unconditional promise. An absolute covenant is a promise that is unrestricted or without condition that the covenantor will perform the promised action, regardless of cost or inconvenience. Implied, even within an absolute covenant, is that the covenantor might not perform the covenant at the request of the covenantee or the covenantee's successors in toto.

**concurrent covenant** Covenant conditioned on a reciprocal covenant. A concurrent covenant is one of two or more covenants that are entered at the same time as other mutual promises among the covenantors. The covenants are each dependent on the other's performance, and so each must be performed at the same time. In other words, concurrent covenants are promises made at the same time to be performed at the same time.

**conditional covenant** Covenant dependent upon occurrence or nonoccurence of event. A conditional covenant is a covenant that is subject to a condition. In the event the condition is failed or satisfied, depending on the covenant's language, the promise made under the covenant is either void or required to be performed at that time.

**contract covenant** A distinct promise expressed or implied in a contract. A covenant within a contract is a personal commitment to carry out a given duty under the contract or to ensure that it is performed. Covenants may be present in a contract either by expression or implication.

**implied covenant** A promise unexpressed but still necessary to the promises expressed. An implied covenant is a promise by one party to a contract that is not expressed but must be implied, or the purposes of the contract would be frustrated.

**implied covenant of good faith and fair dealing** Every contract implies a duty not to harm the other party's ability to receive its due or perform its duty. The implied covenant of good faith and fair dealing in every contract is a commitment read into the contract as a matter of law that each party must, in the formation and performance of its obligations under the contract, deal without fraud or deceit toward the other party and do nothing that unreasonably interferes with the other party's ability to receive its benefit under the contract or that unreasonably interferes with the other party's performance of its duties under the contract.

**non-competition covenant (non-competition clause or non-compete clause)** A promise not to compete with the promissee's business. A covenant not to compete, or a non-compete clause or a non-competition agreement, is a contractual obligation not to do something that competes with the business of the other contracting party. A promise not to compete may be required by an employer in an employment contract, stipulating that the employee will not work for a competing interest during or after employment with the employer. The clause sometimes becomes effective when an employee leaves the company, restricting the now-former-employee from direct competition with the company in a manner that would allow the employee to unreasonably benefit from the employees knowledge of business contacts gained while employed, to the employer's detriment. Such promises are also common in agreements to license a product or publish a book, in which the licensor or author promises not to sell competing products to other entities without prior permission. Indeed, covenants not to compete are routine in a variety of service contracts or contracts for products. Yet if a covenant not to compete is used routinely in such a manner as to create a monopoly or restrain trade, it may be anticompetitive under the antitrust laws.

Covenants not to compete are usually enforceable by specific performance or injunction, and damages may be available for breach. Even so, a covenant not to compete has an implied limitation in time and geography following severance from employment. If the clause is so broad as effectively to bar the employee from the employee's trade or profession, the clause is unreasonable and contrary to public policy. The measure of reasonableness is usually that a clause must be limited by time, type of work, contacts with prior contacts, and geography to a reasonable protection of the former employer that does not amount to an unreasonable burden on the former employee or the public.

*See also:* competition.

**covenant not to sue** Release of a cause of action as to a single potential defendant. A covenant not to sue is a promise made by a person or entity with a cause of action to forebear from bringing a suit against the party liable for the claim. The covenant may be perpetual or only for a time, and if it is not specified, a covenant not to sue presumptively is perpetual. A covenant entered into as a part or as a result of a settlement agreement if an action has already been filed is usually filed with the court. A covenant not to sue is not a general release, applying only to the party named, the covenantee.

**covenant of title (deed warranty or title covenant)** Any of the six covenants generally included in a warranty deed or an additional covenant from grantor to grantee. A covenant of title is any of the customary six covenants of a warranty deed: the covenant of seisin, the covenant of the right to convey, the covenant against encumbrances, the covenant of warranty, the covenant of quiet enjoyment, and the covenant of further assurances. Warranty deeds are defined by their inclusion of these six covenants, and in many states they are implied by the term "warranty deed" regardless of their expression in the text of the deed. Special warranty deeds do not covenant against breaches based on claims of a defect in title prior to the grantor's title, but general warranty deeds warrant against all breaches regardless of their origin during or before the grantor's possession.

**covenant against encumbrances (warranty against encumbrances)** Express promise that there are no clouds on title or competing claims. The covenant against encumbrances is a present covenant in the warranty deed, although it could be entered as a sole covenant. The promise of the covenantor is that there are no encumbrances on the property, which is to say that there are no claims from others to own or occupy the land. A covenant against encumbrances, like all covenants of title, may be either special or general, the general covenant warranting against encumbrances that would have arisen prior to the covenantor's ownership as well as those that would have arisen during that ownership.

*See also:* encumbrance (encumberance or incumbrance).

**covenant of further assurances (warranty of further assurances)** Express promise to execute any necessary documents to ensure the conveyance is completed. The covenant of further assurances is a future covenant in the warranty deed, although it could be entered as a sole covenant. The promise of the covenantor is that the covenantor will execute any additional documents that may be needed in the future to perfect the title which the original deed purports to convey.

*See also:* assurances (further assurances or adequate assurance of performance).

**covenant of quiet enjoyment (covenant for quiet enjoyment or warranty of quiet enjoyment or general warranty)** Express promise that there are no claimants to title with a superior claim to the grantor's. The covenant of quiet enjoyment is a future covenant in the warranty deed, although it could be entered as a sole covenant. The promise of the covenantor is the covenantor will defend an action brought against the covenantee or, in most jurisdictions, the covenantee's assigns through subsequent grants of the land, in the event a claimant brings an action against the grantee (or assign), claiming a superior title. It should be noted that the understanding of "quiet enjoyment" in the sense of a deed covenant is a much more restrictive than its meaning as a covenant for quiet enjoyment in a lease. A breach of the covenant of quiet enjoyment is established if there is a successful eviction by one with a title found to be superior to the covenantor's, or a judicial decree of title in another that would have the same effect if it is enforced.

*See also:* lease, lease covenant, covenant for quiet enjoyment; eviction (evict).

**covenant of right to convey (covenant for title)** Express promise that the covenantor has the legal authority to complete the conveyance of the land. The covenant of right to convey is a present covenant in the warranty deed, although it could be entered as a sole covenant. The promise of the covenantor is that the covenantor, who is the grantor of the deed, has legal and equitable title to the land and the power to convey it to the covenantee, who is the grantee of the land. The covenant is breached, if it is breached, at the moment of the conveyance, if the covenantor lacked title or authority to convey the property; actual eviction is not required to prove breach, merely the proof that the covenantor lacked title. Analytically, there is no difference between the right to convey and the right to seisin; a breach of one is a breach of both. The distinction in language and the persistence of the two covenants is a matter of custom more than logic.

**covenant of seisin (covenant for title)** Express promise that the covenantor has title in the land of the quality and quantity conveyed to the covenantee. The covenant of seisin is a present covenant in the warranty deed, although it could be entered as a sole covenant. The promise of the covenantor is that the covenantor, the grantor of the deed and of the lands it describes, holds title to the lands in the quality and quantity described in the deed. If indeed the covenantor does not own those lands at the time of entering the covenant (the time of delivery of the deed), then the covenant is broken, and the covenantee has an action against the covenantor for damages.

There is no difference among the covenant of seisin, the covenant of title, and the covenant for title, and there is no analytical difference between the covenant of seisin and the covenant of right to convey. The covenant of seisin promises only that the covenantor holds the title by quality to be conveyed. If the grant is of a grantor's interest by fee simple subject to a condition subsequent, then the covenant is for seisin in the land to that extent, as fee simple subject to a condition subsequent and no more or less of an estate is covenanted. The covenant is personal and does not run with the land.

The covenant is breached, if it is breached, at the time of the conveyance. An action may be brought by the covenantee from that moment until the limitations on such an action have run, without a need to prove the grantee was dispossessed.

*See also:* seisin (seizin or seisin in law or seised of seized of).

**covenant of warranty** Express promise to indemnify against future claimants with paramount claims to title. The covenant of warranty is a future covenant in the warranty deed, although it could be entered as a sole covenant. The promise of the covenantor is that the covenantor will compensate the covenantee and the covenantee's assigns for losses suffered from a valid claim to the land, if that claim is based on an enforceable interest in the land that existed or was bound to exist at the time of the covenant. Because the warranty is good only against successful claims, it amounts to an assurance like an indemnity against loss of title rather than a promise to defend title. The covenantee, the grantee of the lands, has a claim against the covenantor, the grantor of the lands, only once the grantee has been actually or constructively evicted by a successful claimant with paramount title to that conveyed by the grantor. Thus, the covenant of warranty cannot be invoked by a grantee who took an interest described in the deed as a life estate if the holder of the reversion claims title at the end of the measuring life. The warranty extends to defense against encumbrances under the covenant against encumbrances, and a grantee who must suffer a claim to an easement, tax lien, or covenant on the land that attached prior to the deed may claim against the covenantor under the covenant of warranty.

*See also:* warranty.

**future covenant** Any of the three covenants for future actions in a warranty deed. Future covenants refer to any of the covenants of a general warranty deed to perform actions following the conveyance of the property. These are the covenants of warranty, quiet enjoyment, and further assurances. A grantor's action or inaction cannot violate a future covenant until after the deed has been delivered and the grantee has taken possession of the property. Thus, the statute of limitation on a future covenant does not run on a breach of a future covenant until the time that a demand is made upon a grantor to perform a task that has been covenanted and the grantor fails to do so.

**present covenant** Three promises of present title in a warranty deed. A present covenant, also called a covenant of title, is one of the three present covenants of a warranty deed: the covenant of seisin, the covenant of right to convey, and the covenant against encumbrances, each of which is an assurance of the quality of title at the time of the conveyance. These covenants are broken, if they are broken, at the time the deed is conveyed. A grantee's claim for breach of any of these is good immediately after the conveyance and at any time until the statute of limitations has run, without proof of a claim or hostile action by a third party being made against the grantee. On the other hand, if a claim is made against the grantee by a third party asserting a claim of title contrary to the covenants of title, and the grantee successfully defends the claim on the merits, the grantor has not violated the covenants, and the grantee has no claim against the grantor for these covenants.

*See also:* deed, deed covenant.

**special covenant against encumbrances** Warrants against third–party in the property created by the grantor. A special covenant against encumbrances warrants only against claims against the property created to the benefit of third parties during the ownership of the covenantor.

**express covenant** A covenant stated in writing. An express covenant is a covenant stated in writing, whether in an instrument that performs no other function or as a clause within a deed, lease, sale agreement, contract, or other instrument.

*See also:* expression (explicit or express).

**implied negative covenant** Any rights that are not expressly surrendered as a promise are reserved. An implied negative covenant is not a covenant in an instrument but a doctrine limiting the covenants made in an instrument to those that are stated expressly. The implied negative covenant describes the reservation of all rights that are not promised to be assigned or abrogated by the instrument. It exemplifies the legal policy that if a person makes an explicit promise to allow one or more enumerated things, the promissor did not intend to promise anything else. Despite the policy, a person may not rely on the implied negative covenant quietly to reserve rights for future use that will be exercised in a manner inconsistent with the covenants that are expressed. Action on such implied rights would amount to a violation of the expressed covenants.

**real covenant (covenant in land or covenant real)** A dedication of an interest in the property to the benefit of an individual or the holder of another property. A real covenant is a promise by a landholder to do, to refrain, or to allow something to be done on a given parcel. A covenant must be created in writing, either as a specific instrument or in a deed. Real covenants are affirmative or negative, either requiring the covenantor to do something or to refrain from doing something.

Real covenants may be granted to a person or entity, which are commercial covenants or covenants in gross. Yet the more common appurtenant covenant is granted to another landholder, in a manner that attaches the benefit of the covenant to the land of the landholder, allowing the benefit also to run with the land, or to be held by owners who succeed the recipient of the covenant. Regardless of whether the real covenant is commercial or appurtenant, its burdens run with the land, binding successive landholders to the land burdened by the covenant, which is to say that once a landholder has entered a real covenant, unless the covenant includes a clause

terminating it in the future, it applies to the land regardless of who later acquires it. A real covenant can be acquired back from the holder of its benefit, by grant, purchase, or prescription.

*See also:* servitude, equitable servitude (reciprocal negative easement).

*covenant and easement* An easement is the right to the use of another's land, whether it is created by grant or prescription. A covenant is a grant by a landowner of an interest in land, which might or might not include the grantee's use of the land. A covenant can create an easement, although it need not, but an easement cannot create a covenant.

*covenant and equitable servitude* Covenants arise from a specific grant of or retention of an interest in the form of a covenant. Equitable servitudes arise through the operation of equity under the circumstances of the development of uses of property and surrounding lands. Thus an equitable servitude may create the same interests that a covenant would make, but the equitable servitude was not written as a covenant is written. Instead the equitable servitude is implied by the courts from circumstances.

**affirmative covenant** An agreement to perform a duty that benefits the land or the grantor. An affirmative covenant is a covenant by which the covenantor promises to do something on the land, such as making a specific improvement, like a fence. It contrasts with the more common negative covenant, in which the covenantor promises not to do something, such as not building a wall or gate over a way.

**appurtenant covenant (covenant appurtenant)** A covenant related to the use of occupation of the land. An appurtenant covenant is a covenant whose promise is related to the ownership, use, or occupancy of the land on the parcel of land to which it relates.

**benefit of the covenant** The advantage from a covenant to the covenantee or the covenantee's lands. The benefit of the covenant is the advantage gained by the promise made, whether the covenant confers an easement, protects a view, assures a water supply, or gives another benefit, which is assured to the covenantee or to the land owned by the covenantee. The benefit will run with the land, that is benefit subsequent owners of the covenantee's lands, if it was intended to do so by the initial parties and the subsequent covenantees are in privity of possession with one another.

**burden of the covenant (running of the burden)** The obligation to perform a real covenant. The burden is the obligation of a covenant, which in a negative covenant is the obligation not to interfere with the acts allowed under the covenant to the holder of the property to which the benefit is assigned and which in an affirmative covenant is the obligation to perform such acts as are specified. A burden will run with the land, or bind successors to the owner of the land who first accepts the burden, if the parties initially intend it to run, and if the burden is in writing, the burden touches and concerns the land, and the successor owner has privity with the predecessor owner.

*See also:* run, run with the land (running with the land).

**change-in-the-neighborhood doctrine (change of neighborhood or change in the neighorhood)** Covenant lapses through change of surrounding land use. The change-in-the-neighborhood doctrine allows a court to equitably reform or rescind a covenant if the uses of the surrounding lands or property relevant to the parcel subject to the covenant have changed in their character or use sufficiently that the purposes of the covenant are no longer meaningfully capable of being fulfilled.

**covenant in gross (commercial covenant)** A real covenant that does not run with the land. A covenant in gross is a real covenant that does not run with the land but is a personal or commercial relationship between the covenantor and the covenantee. A covenant in gross is assignable, but it is not inherently assigned owing to the transfer of property once held by either party to the covenant.

**restrictive covenant** Covenant limiting the use of the land. Restrictive covenants are real covenants creating limitations on the use of the land, which are often intended to maintain the property to a certain character of use. Although any real covenant with a restriction on use is a restrictive covenant, most of these covenants in the United States are used as a means of private land use regulation, in which structures are limited to a range of purpose, size, and appearance, with limitations or obligations of maintenance, and with limitations on occupancy or alienation, among other use restrictions. Restrictive covenants are often mutual covenants, making them mutually restrictive covenants, each binding the others in a neighborhood.

**blue-pencil rule (blue pencil test)** The judicial deletion of unreasonable terms to save a covenant. The blue-pencil rule permits a court to interpret covenants from the standpoint of objective reasonableness. The blue-pencil rule is similar in principle to the severability or divisibility rule, by which an overall contract may be preserved even if portions of it must be stricken as invalid. Applying the blue-pencil rule, if unreasonable language in a clause or provision can be elided, and the intent of the covenant can then be given effect in a reasonable manner, the covenant may be upheld as edited.

**racial covenant (racially restrictive covenant)** A covenant limiting future ownership on the basis of race. Racial covenants are a form of restrictive covenant that limit to whom an owner may sell or grant an interest in property, on the basis of the recipient's race. A racial

covenant is unenforceable in law as a violation of equal protection of the laws.

**covenantee** One who benefits from a covenant. A covenantee is the beneficiary of a covenant, often the recipient of the covenant from the covenantor. A covenantee of a covenant stands as does a promisee of a promise.

**covenantor** One who is bound by a covenant. The covenantor is the maker of a covenant. Successors in interest to the covenantor may be bound to the covenant, although they lack the intent needed by the covenantor to establish the covenant.

**covenants of title** *See:* title, covenants of title.

**Coventry Act** *See:* mayhem, Coventry Act.

**cover** The buyer's purchase of substitute goods in mitigation of damages from the seller's breach. Cover is the purchase of substitute goods to cover the absence of goods that were contracted for sale by the buyer but not timely delivered owing to the seller's breach of the contract. In most instances, a buyer must take reasonable steps to cover rather than to merely rest on the right of recovery under the contract without making any attempt to mitigate damages.

*See also:* resale (resell or right to resell); damages, contract damages, mitigation of damages; damages, contract damages, cover.

**coverage or cover or covered claim** *See:* insurance, insurance coverage (coverage or cover or covered claim).

**covert listening device** *See:* surveillance, electronic surveillance, covert listening device (bug or wire or hidden microphone).

**covert**

**covert mission (covert operation or covert means or secret mission or black operations or black ops)** A police, military, intelligence-gathering, or investigative action that is not publicly acknowledged by the state or other sponsor. A covert mission is any mission that is not acknowledged by the government that sponsors it, or whose participants are under orders either to remain undetected or to remain unattributed to its state sponsor. State actions by covert means are still subject to the principle of state. responsibility. Corporate actions that are unacknowledged may give rise not only to liability in the event the action violates a criminal law or a private right, but may give rise to further liability under RICO or as a conspiracy.

*See also:* overt.

**coverture (baron covert)** A wife's interest in marital assets. Coverture is used in the current law of the United States as a general term for the interests of a wife in the assets of a marriage, whether they are divided at divorce or death. The term in the common law had a broader sense, as the status of a woman in marriage. This sense, which implied the wife's role under the protection of her husband, with the further implication that she had not independent power to contract or hold property, has long been obsolete. The common–law condition is implied by the use of covert in covert de baron, baron covert, and femme covert.

*See also:* feme (feme covert or baron and feme or feme sole).

**cowboy lawyer or Rambo lawyer** *See:* lawyer, junkyard dog lawyer (cowboy lawyer or Rambo lawyer).

**CPI** *See:* price, Consumer Price Index (CPI).

**CRAC** *See:* argument, legal argument, CRAC (conclusion rule application conclusion or conclusion rule analysis conclusion or C.R.A.C.).

**crack cocaine** *See:* drug, controlled substance, cocaine, crack cocaine.

**crack house or meth house** *See:* nuisance, public nuisance, drug house (crack house or meth house).

**cram down** *See:* bankruptcy, Chapter 11 filing, cram down (cramdown or cram–down).

**cramdown or cram-down** *See:* bankruptcy, Chapter 11 filing, cram down (cramdown or cram–down).

**crashworthiness doctrine** *See:* liability, product liability, automobile product liability, crashworthiness doctrine.

**created equal** *See:* constitution, U.S. Constitution, ideals, created equal.

**creatio ex nihilo** *See:* ex, ex nihilo (creatio ex nihilo).

**creature of statute** *See:* statute, creature of statute.

**creche** *See:* religion, freedom of religion, creche.

**credential (credentials or credentialling)** Qualification or the evidence of being qualified. A credential, generally, is the basis for someone giving credence, and specifically it is the basis for the qualification of a person or entity to engage in some profession or task. Credentials are the proof of a credential, such as the badge and identification card of a police officer or the bar card of an attorney. A credentialing authority, such as a court or a state bar, is responsible for determining that a credential is awarded only to a candidate that has fully satisfied an appropriate range of criteria to enjoy the privileges of the credential. A credential may be forfeit if its holder does not maintain it through required retraining and actions consonant with its award. Credential in a medical facility is permission to perform there the medical services of the category for which a physician or other professional is credentialled.

*See also:* accreditation.

**credibility** Believability. Credibility is the potential a person, testimony, statement, claim, or other argument has to be believed. Credibility is, to an extent, a matter of the correlation of evidence with other evidence. Yet in human affairs, some people enjoy a reputation for veracity or dishonesty; some people have committed acts of dishonesty in the past; and some people appear to be more credible than others owing to personal appearance, voice, and manner. The law of evidence allows such aspects of reputation, past acts, or human appearance to be considered as indicators of credibility in a particular matter in dispute, although the reliability of such indicators is not certain. The credibility of evidence is presumed in the law to be best weighed by the jury or judge as finder of fact, rather than on a record alone.

*See also:* discredit.

**credible witness** *See:* witness, credible witness.

**credit** One's ability to borrow from lenders. Credit, in general, is the sense in which one has established the trust of confidence of others, as when one person credits another's story. In accounting a credit is an asset. In commercial law, and usually in legal usage, credit refers to the ability of a person or entity to borrow money, particularly from established lenders such as banks, the lender trusting that the money will be repaid. Credit may also refer to the terms under which credit is in fact extended, including the amount lent, at a given rate of interest, with particular collateral presented or subject to a security interest, for a given period of time. In either sense, a letter of credit is a statement of the availability of money by the issuing bank on behalf of the creditor, whether the bank has issued the letter of credit in return for payment or as a loan in itself to the creditor.

*See also:* loan (lending or lend).

**credit union** *See:* bank, credit union.

**credit bureau (credit-reporting bureau or credit agency)** An organization that collects and sells credit histories. A credit bureau is an organization that collects and archives the individual debts and history of repayment on the debts of corporations and individuals. Some companies collect far more information, including age, lifestyle, location, family, and medical risk factors. The bureau acts on various information, generating from these archives a score of the credit–worthiness of each person or corporation with such an archive. This score is provided for a fee by the bureau to those who might or might not extend credit to individuals or corporations in these archives. Such reports were once available to anyone who asked but are now sold to only qualified extenders of credit or to those for whom the would–be debtor has executed a release. As of 2011, there are three widely employed credit bureaus: Equifax, Experian, and TransUnion.

**billing error**   Mistaken charge or credit report. A billing error is a report of a credit charge made in error, whether owing to a mistake by the creditor or the credit bureau.

**Consumer Credit Protection Act (C.C.P.A. or CCPA)**   Federal regulation of credit providers, debt collectors, and credit bureaus. Consumer Credit Protection Act is a broad federal statute, codified at 15 U.S.C. §§ 1601–1693 and 18 U.S.C. §§ 891–896, encompassing a number of specific acts to regulate the gathering of information regarding credit, the advertisement of credit, the lending of money under credit arrangements, certain aspects of debt collection, and fairness in credit provision. Component acts include the Consumer Credit Protection Act or Truth in Lending Act, the Fair Credit Billing Act, the Fair Credit Reporting Act, the Equal Credit Opportunity Act, the Fair Debt Collection Practices Act, the Electronic Fund Transfer Act, and Truth in Lending (Regulation Z).

**credit default swap (CDS)**   Insurance agreement assuring against default in a debt–collateralized equity. A credit default swap is an insurance agreement underwriting against a default in a collateralized debt obligation, or other equity instrument backed by a debt.

*See also:* security, securities, collateralized debt obligation (collateralized loan obligation or CLO or CDO); swap (swap agreement).

**credit freeze**   A refusal of further credit by a creditor to a debtor. A credit freeze is, in the first instance, a refusal to extend credit to an entity, even if the credit had earlier been promised. A credit freeze is often accompanied by a demand for payment on outstanding debts. Banks or other lenders who employ a credit freeze risk violation of outstanding contracts to provide credit.

**creditworthiness (creditworthy)**   Indicators of a debtor's likely repayment of a debt. Creditworthiness is the sum of all of the information that a lender or credit bureau accumulates regarding a borrower's likely ability and willingness to repay a debt, often summarized as a credit score.

**Equal Credit Opportunity Act (E.C.O.A. or ECOA)**   Credit providers may not withhold credit on forbidden grounds. The Equal Credit Opportunity Act, partially codified at 15 U.S.C. § 1691 et seq., prevents creditors from discriminating against applicants on the basis of race, color, marital status, national origin, religion, sex, age (as long as the person can lawfully contract in the jurisdiction), reliance on public assistance, or use of a right under the Consumer Credit Protection Act.

**letter of credit (LC or L.C.)**   An irrevocable promise to pay funds on demand. A letter of credit is a communication from one party to another that assures

payment of (or up to) a specific amount that will be made upon a given event in the future. Usually this takes the form of a bank or other financial institution issuing a document on behalf of the buyer of goods, after which the letter is transmitted to the bank of the seller of goods, and the seller is notified of the bank's receipt, which will serve as the basis of payment to the seller once the bank receives confirmation of the receipt of the goods by the buyer. The letter of credit is honored once the specified documents are presented or events occur, at which time the honoring institution pays the seller (or other honoree) and makes a demand against the issuer for payment on the credit, and the issuing bank transfers the funds from the account of the buyer or from funds the buyer had deposited to secure the letter of credit at the outset. Letters of credit are regulated in the United States by the laws enacted in each state under article 5 of the Uniform Commercial Code.

*See also:* contracts, Uniform Commercial Code (UCC or U.C.C.).

**line of credit**   *See:* loan, open–end loan.

**creditor**   One to whom payment or performance is owed. A creditor is a person or entity that has a right to require payment or performance in fulfillment of an obligation, whether it arises under contract or otherwise. Creditors have as their assets the debts owed by debtors. There are many divisions among creditors, and in the event of a debtor's bankruptcy or default and receivership, certain creditors are given priority over others. These priorities vary in their satisfaction from assets generally or from assets subject to security interests. Secured creditors will ordinarily have priority over others in money realized from assets in which the creditor has perfected a security interest. Thus creditors who have established liens on assets are paid first from those assets, including tax liens, mortgage liens, and liens by vendors, landlords, wage earners, or other statutorily prioritized creditors. More general debts are then satisfied in priority, usually first paying money proved to be owed for child support, then to judgment creditors, who have a judicial decree for the debt owed; the claims of mortgage holders without liens, and then unsecured debts, which are usually paid pro rata.

**assignment for the benefit of creditors**   Alternative to bankruptcy for insolvent debtors. Assignment for the benefit of creditors is, essentially, an informal bankruptcy process. The debtor must liquidate all but what is statutorily exempt and put it into a trust naming any outstanding creditors as pro rata beneficiaries of the trust. Because it is informal, court costs can be avoided and bankruptcy does not become part of the debtor's credit history. However, because it is informal, neither the debtor nor the creditor has the protections of the court. A creditor may not receive an amount comparable to the debt owed, and a debtor may have to liquidate assets which could have been exempted by a bankruptcy court.

**creditor's bill**  Suit in equity to force payment of debt. A creditor's bill is an equitable remedy sought usually as a last resort when all remedies in law have failed, but the debtor has been unjustly enriched and the creditor has been unduly burdened with the loss. The remedies in restitution that are available are of a wider range than damages alone.

**tableau of distribution**  A list of creditors. A tableau of distribution is a table of distributions to be made to creditors either by an insolvent or by the estate for a decedent.

**crime**  An offense against a public criminal law. A crime is any conduct that violates the criminal law, including felonies, misdemeanors, and criminal citations. Though the common law established crimes, including a variety of categories of behavior that were said to violate the king's peace, the law of the United States no longer recognizes common law crimes as crime but requires that crimes be condemned by statute. The statutes of a state define crimes in that state, and the statutes of the United States define federal crimes. Behavior that is considered a crime must be behavior forbidden by statute, and a crime is not defined by an arrest or conviction for conduct that is not condemned as a crime according to a statute. Statutes declaring certain behavior criminal must accord with the constitutions governing their enacting legislature. Thus, criminal prohibitions must satisfy due process of law, particularly by being clear as to what behavior is forbidden, must satisfy equal protection of the law, particularly by not creating an irrational or undue burden on a single classification of person, and by conforming to the prohibition on ex post facto laws, by being enacted before the behavior of a person charged. In most instances the behavior that is made criminal is defined by the combination of an action with a given state of mind in committing the action.

*See also:* flagrante delicto (in flagrante delicto or red handed); penal (penal law); penal, penal code; delict (quasi–delict or delictual).

**assimilative crime**  *See:* reservation, tribal reservation, assimilative crimes act.

**crime against humanity**  *See:* war, law of war, war crime, crime against humanity.

**crime against nature**  *See:* sodomy, crime against nature (unnatural act).

**crime-fraud exception**  *See:* privilege, evidentiary privilege, attorney–client privilege, crime–fraud exception.

**crime laboratory**  *See:* laboratory, crime laboratory (forensics lab or crime lab or police lab or police crime lab).

**crime of passion**  *See:* manslaughter, crime of passion (heat of passion or sudden passion).

**capital offense (capital crime)**  Crime for which the punishment may be death. A capital offense, or a capital crime, is an offense for which the statutes of

the jurisdiction in which it is tried allow a punishment of death by execution, if those statutes are constitutional. A person commits a capital offense by committing an act that violates a criminal prohibition punishable by death, even if the person is neither indicted with such a liability or sentenced to death.

**commission of crime (commit crime or commit a crime)**  A guilty act that violates the criminal law. The commission of a crime is the action, including the act itself and the mental state required, that together violate a prohibition of the criminal law. In this sense, a commission includes acts of commission or affirmative acts that violate the law, and acts of omission, or negative acts that violate the law,

**common-law crime**  Conduct that is a crime according to the common law rather than a statute. A common–law crime is an act that is subject to criminal prosecution and punishment according to custom and the precedents of the common law. Common–law crimes have been abolished in the United States in favor of statutory definition.

**computer crime**  *See:* computer, computer crime.

**continuous crime (continuing crime)**  A criminal act following a previous criminal act which is essentially an extension of the first. A continuing crime is a single action over a period of time or a series of actions that would be sufficient in themselves to constitute separate criminal offenses but that are so compressed in time, place, singleness of purpose, and continuity of action as to constitute a single transaction.

**crime of omission**  Failure to perform or comply with a lawful duty. A crime of omission is a criminal act caused by failing to do what is required by law. Three examples are the failure to report criminal conduct for which one has a responsibility to report, thus making the non–reporter an accessory to the crime; the unexcused failure to file an income tax return; and the criminal failure to care for a child in one's custody. A crime of omission takes place in the jurisdiction in which the duty was required.

**criminal act**  Conduct punishable as a crime. A criminal act is either an act or an omission committed with the requisite mindset that violates the criminal law. Under the model penal code, and in most jurisdictions, the criminal act requires a criminal act, or actus reus, and a prohibited state of mind, the mens rea. "Criminal act" is sometimes said in lieu of actus reus, in which case, it depicts the conduct alone and not the mental state with which it is committed.

*See also:* actus, actus reus; mens, mens rea (mental state).

**federal crime**  Criminal activity prohibited by federal statute. A federal crime is a crime under the laws of the United States. The same act may be subject to the concurrent jurisdiction of state law, and indeed both the United States and a state or states may independently prosecute and punish the same act, if different aspects of it are an offense under each jurisdiction. Federal crimes must be made criminal by an Act of Congress, which must be within Congress's powers under the Constitution. Most federal crimes are codified under title 18 of the United States Code, though military crimes are also federal crimes and are codified in the Uniform Code of Military Justice, are in title 10.

**fruits of a crime (loot or swag or fruit of the crime)** The rewards of a criminal act. The fruits of the crime are objects or money taken during the criminal act or as a result of it, or any value realized from the criminal conduct, directly or indirectly. Possession of the fruits of the crime is evidence of commission, and an expectation to share in the fruits of a crime is evidence of participation in it. Fruits of the crime are forfeit in addition to a fine or other punishment.

*See also:* forfeiture, criminal forfeiture; deodand.

**hate crime (hate-motivated crime)** A crime motivated by bigotry. A hate crime is a criminal act in which the race, religion, or other classification of the victim was an element in the motivation for the commission of the act. The effect of a hate crime is generally to increase the penalty from the penalty that would ordinarily be applied to the crime if it was committed for other reasons; it may also be used to identify crimes of special interest for the allocation of police resources in investigation.

**high crime (high crimes)** Crime for which an official may be impeached. A high crime is a crime of sufficient seriousness that it may form the basis for the impeachment of a legal official. It is clear from Article II § 4 that "high crimes" includes treason and bribery, but otherwise, the ambits of the crimes that are or are not high crimes is uncertain. More generally, high crime is equivalent to a felony or a serious offense under the criminal law.

**infamous crime** Shameful conduct that violates the criminal law. An infamous crime is a crime that has been designated a crime of great shame. At various times, the term has been used specifically to designate sodomy, felonies generally, crimes of moral turpitude, and high crimes eligible for impeachment. In nineteenth English law, the infamous crime was restricted to buggery, or sodomy with a human or animal, and with the repeal of this law in 1916 the term lost any technical meaning in England. The term in the United States is now most often synonymous with felony, or any crime punishable by death or imprisonment for a year or more. Still, the significance of the term varies widely among jurisdictions.

**signature crime (common scheme evidence)** Illegal behavior characteristic of a particular criminal. A signature crime is a crime that is so similar in a high number of factors to other crimes known to be committed by a single individual that a reasonable inference may be drawn that the same person who committed the other crimes committed this one. In other words, a signature crime so clearly manifests the unique modus operandi of one individual that it is reasonable to conclude that only that one person committed the crime. Police, prosecutors, and judges should be skeptical of overly relying on a signature crime theory as evidence of guilt, owing to the risks not only of coincidence and copycats but also of deliberate duplication to misdirect suspicion.

*See also:* signature; modus, modus operandi (signature facts or MO or M.O.).

**status crime** Law making a crime of being a member of a specific group. A status crime is a crime that a person commits by being a person in a particular status, such as a member of a gang, a member of a terrorist organization, a drug addict, or a homeless person. A traditional status crime is that of vagrancy, which as sometimes applied effectively creates a criminal status of homelessness. The more common form of status crime is to define one element of a crime as membership in a group or a classification of citizen. If the group is organized for a criminal purpose, such as a criminal gang, such definitions do not violate the constitution. Yet if the group is not organized according to an inherently illegal purpose, such crimes may interfere with the freedoms of association, assembly, or speech. Defining a crime by status raises serious questions both of equal protection of the law and of due process of law.

*See also:* status; vagrant (vagrancy).

**victimless crime** Criminal conduct that does not harm another party. A victimless crime is a criminal act that does not harm another person or the interests of another person, or, by some definitions, create an unreasonable risk of such harms. The consumption of illegal drugs is the most commonly claimed form of victimless crime. Many crimes may appear harmless but create a harm, albeit diffuse and affecting all of the members of the state, such as bribery. From a perspective of the justification of criminal law that suggests its purpose is to prevent harm, the prohibition of victimless crimes is not a justified use of state power.

*See also:* harm (harmdoer or harmful).

**violent crime** Any crime that causes or risks injury or death to the victim. A violent crime is any crime committed with a dangerous weapon or that is committed in circumstances that result in or risk the injury or death of an intended victim or bystander. "Violent crime" is also a collective noun, including all such acts in a place or during a particular time.

**white-collar crime (white collar crime)** A non-violent crime of fraud or theft by a white-collar employee. White-collar crime includes the criminal actions of officers and employees of corporations or institutions who steal or defraud their employers or clients, including all forms of illegal financial activity in which the criminal exploits access to corporate, governmental, or professional office or employment to facilitate commission of the crime. A non-violent crime committed on the job is usually considered committed by a white–collar criminal if the offender is a person of high social or economic standing. The term is derived from the white shirt collars once customary to men's professional shirts.

### crimen

**crimen falsi (falsi crimen)** A crime demonstrating dishonesty or false statement. Crimen falsi is a common–law category of crimes, derived from the civilian crime of fraud, but being much broader and including all crimes that demonstrate that a person who could commit such acts is willing to act falsely or betray a trust. Crimen falsi extends to all crimes involving forgery, fraud, conversion, receiving stolen goods, or acts that interfere with a fair accounting of business or with the honest administration of justice generally. A person convicted of a crime of crimen falsi is barred in most jurisdictions from holding public office or other positions of public trust, including sometimes from the practice of law. Evidence of a conviction of crimen falsi is admissible for the impeachment of a witness under federal rule 609, even after ten years, unless the person convicted was pardoned or rehabilitated or the sentence was annulled.

Crimen falsi is also the civil–law crime of fraud, including forgery, counterfeiting, and perjury or false oaths.

*See also:* forgery.

### criminal (criminality or criminalization or decriminalization)
A person convicted of a crime or anything related to crime. A criminal is a person who commits a crime, particularly a person who commits a crime and is convicted of it. Criminal also refers to a crime or criminal behavior in any way. Criminality is a measurement of something illegal, and criminalization is the act or process of making something illegal. Decriminalization is the act or process of making something that was once illegal legal.

*See also:* wrong, wrongdoer (wrong–doer).

**criminal abandonment** *See:* abandonment, criminal abandonment.

**criminal abortion** *See:* abortion, criminal abortion.

**criminal act** *See:* crime, criminal act.

**criminal action** *See:* action, criminal action.

**criminal anarchy or anarchist** *See:* anarchy (criminal anarchy or anarchist).

**criminal at large** *See:* large, criminal at large (escapee at large or suspect at large).

**criminal attempt** *See:* attempt, criminal attempt, probable–desistance test; attempt, criminal attempt, last–proximate–act test; attempt, criminal attempt, indispensable element test; attempt, criminal attempt, imposssibility of attempt (impossible attempt); attempt, criminal attempt.

**criminal battery** *See:* battery, criminal battery.

**criminal capacity** *See:* capacity, criminal capacity.

**criminal coercion** *See:* extortion, blackmail (criminal coercion).

**criminal complaint** *See:* complaint, criminal complaint.

**criminal conversation** *See:* conversation, criminal conversation.

**criminal defamation** *See:* libel, criminal libel (criminal defamation).

**criminal defendant** *See:* defendant, criminal defendant (criminal defense).

**criminal defense** *See:* defendant, criminal defendant (criminal defense).

**criminal facilitation** *See:* facilitation, criminal facilitation (facilitate).

**criminal forfeiture** *See:* forfeiture, criminal forfeiture.

**criminal history record or rap sheet** *See:* record, arrest record (criminal history record or rap sheet).

**criminal homicide** *See:* homicide, criminal homicide (culpable homicide or felonious homicide).

**criminal immunity** *See:* immunity, criminal immunity.

**criminal jurisdiction** *See:* jurisdiction, criminal jurisdiction, Ker–Frisbie doctrine; jurisdiction, criminal jurisdiction.

**criminal law** *See:* law, criminal law.

**criminal libel** *See:* libel, criminal libel (criminal defamation).

**criminal mischief** *See:* mischief, criminal mischief (malicious mischief).

**criminal plea** *See:* plea, criminal plea.

**criminal possession** *See:* possession, unlawful possession (criminal possession).

**criminal principal** *See:* principal, criminal principal, principal in the first degree; principal, criminal principal.

**criminal procedure** *See:* procedure, criminal procedure.

**criminal restitution** *See:* restitution, criminal restitution (victim compensation).

**criminal sexual battery or CSC** *See:* battery, sexual battery (criminal sexual battery or CSC).

**criminal sexual conduct** *See:* rape, rape as sexual assault, criminal sexual conduct (sexual conduct).

**criminal strict liability** *See:* liability, strict liability, criminal strict liability (offense of strict liability).

**criminal syndicate** *See:* syndicate, criminal syndicate.

**criminal trial and new trial**

**Berry rule**   The standard of review for motions for a new criminal trial. The Berry rule is the standard of review applied to a criminal defendant's post-conviction motion for a new trial based on newly discovered evidence. The Berry rule is a four-part element test: if the defendant's evidence is innocently discovered, is newly discovered, is material, and probably would result in the defendant's acquittal, the court will order a new trial. Although the Federal Rules of Criminal Procedure control how and when a defendant must file a motion for a new trial, the Berry rule controls how the court reviews such motions. It should be noted that the Berry rule creates a very high burden for the defendant.

**criminal conduct**   Behavior prohibited by criminal law. Criminal conduct is the commission of an act or acts with the requisite state of mind, that make the actor liable for criminal prosecution, regardless of whether such prosecution takes place.

**criminology**   The study of crime. Criminology is the study of crime and all of its facets, particularly the causes of criminal behavior, the means of detection and investigation of particular crimes, and the social means of diminishing the likelihood of criminal activity. Criminology is an inherently interdisciplinary field, incorporating biology, anthropology, medicine, psychology, and sociology with law. Although some approaches to criminology would include the determination of what conduct or conditions should or should not be considered criminal, that question is usually considered the domain of criminal law and criminal theory.
*See also:* alienist; penology; law, criminal law; penal (penal law).

**criteria pollutant**   *See:* pollution, air pollution, criteria pollutant.

**critical habitat**   *See:* species, endangered species, endangered species act, critical habitat.

**critical legal studies**   *See:* jurisprudence, critical legal studies (C.L.S. or CLS).

**critical race theory**   *See:* jurisprudence, critical race theory (critical-race theory or C.R.T. or CRT).

**crits**   *See:* jurisprudence, critical legal studies, crits.

**cross**   Any intersection or turn about. To cross, in general, is either to intersect or exchange. In a hearing or trial, cross is an abbreviation for "cross-examine" or "cross-examination."
*See also:* appeal, cross-appeal; claim, crossclaim (cross-claim); claim, counterclaim; collateral, cross-collateral (cross-collateralization); complaint, cross-complaint (cross action); remainder, cross remainder (cross-remainder); race, race as social construct, cross-race identification theory (C.R.I.T. or CRT or CRIT); offer, contract offer, cross-offer; motion, cross motion (cross-motion).

**cross action**   *See:* complaint, cross-complaint (cross action).

**cross-appeal**   *See:* appeal, cross-appeal.

**cross as signature**   *See:* signature, X as signature (cross as signature).

**cross-claim**   *See:* claim, crossclaim (cross-claim).

**cross-collateral**   *See:* collateral, cross-collateral (cross-collateralization).

**cross-collateralization**   *See:* collateral, cross-collateral (cross-collateralization).

**cross-complaint**   *See:* complaint, cross-complaint (cross action).

**cross examination or cross ex or cross-ex or cross-question**   *See:* examination, examination of a witness, cross-examination (cross examination or cross ex or cross-ex or cross-question).

**cross motion**   *See:* motion, cross motion (cross-motion).

**cross-offer**   *See:* offer, contract offer, cross-offer.

**cross-race identification theory**   *See:* race, race as social construct, cross-race identification theory (C.R.I.T. or CRT or CRIT).

**cross remainder**   *See:* remainder, cross remainder (cross-remainder).

**crown**   The monarch, or the monarch's hat. The crown is usually used in legal writing to refer to the monarch, or the office of the king or queen then reigning. A crown possession is then a terrority that is subject to the sovereignty of the monarch.

**cruel and unusual punishment**   *See:* punishment, cruel and unusual punishment, proportionality review; punishment, Cruel and Unusual Punishment.

**Cruel and Unusual Punishment Clause**   *See:* constitution, U.S. Constitution, clauses, Cruel and Unusual Punishment Clause.

**cruel treatment or extreme cruelty**   *See:* cruelty, legal cruelty (cruel treatment or extreme cruelty).

**cruelty**   Causing pain or unhappiness for no justifiable reason. Cruelty is the mistreatment of a person or animal — especially a child, pet, prisoner, or otherwise someone or something under one's care — by causing physical or mental distress without a very good cause to do so. Cruelty may result from a deliberate action or from neglect or error.

**animal cruelty**   Causing unnecessary suffering to an animal. Animal cruelty is the negligent or intentional subjection of an animal to needless suffering, including by failure to shelter, feed, or give water to the animal when it is under one's control.

**legal cruelty (cruel treatment or extreme cruelty)**
Cruelty to a level is intolerable within a family. Legal cruelty is a level of mistreatment that justifies divorce for cause or loss of parental rights. There are various formulations from state to state, although it is not clear in the case law that a comparatively higher or lower standard is intended in given states from their neighbors, the touchstone in all being a state of intolerability, which would appear to be measured best by a present sense for well-founded fear or disgust likely to persist in the future. In general, a single cruel act, particularly by neglect or other than by physical abuse, lacks the extremity required, although an act of physical abuse, an act that genuinely threatens the life of the victim, or a pattern of recurrent threats, physical harm to others in a manner that frightens the victim, coupled with alcohol or drug abuse or other acts that allow a diminished responsibility by the abuser, or with acts or statements by the abuser intended to create a state of fear or anxiety in the victim amount to cruelty.

**mental cruelty** Cruel acts that causes anguish or other mental harm. Mental cruelty is a form of harm without a very good cause, which need not include physical harm, but its result is a harmful emotional state such as fear, self-doubt, anxiety, embarrassment, remorse, grief, or sadness, or a harmful effect on one's reason or memory, such as dissociation, diminished rational capacity or recollection. These results need not be extreme to be cruel, and evidence of them may be adduced from the behavior of the abuser.

**CSI effect** *See:* forensics, CSI effect (CSI syndrome).

**cujus est solum ejus est usque ad coelum** *See:* property, real property, cujus est solum ejus est usque ad coelum (center of the earth to the roof of the sky).

**culpa** Fault. Culpa, a Roman law term for fault or blameworthiness, is still used in a variety of legal phrases, most significantly as the root of culpability.
*See also:* fault; culpability (culpable); meus, mea culpa.

**culpa in contrahendo (C in C)** Wrongdoing during a negotiation. Culpa in contrahendo is a civilian concept for negotiation in bad faith, or for wrongdoing during a negotiation that harms the other party. There is no perfect analog in the common law, although certain actions that amount to C in C would also be actionable under theories of detrimental reliance, unjust enrichment, or fraud. The doctrine is recognized in Louisiana and Puerto Rico.
*See also:* reliance, detrimental reliance; inducement, fraud in the inducement.

**culpability (culpable)** Legal responsibility for a crime. Culpability is a generic term for responsibility, and for the various mental states according to which one is responsible, for a criminal act, usually intentionality, knowledge, recklessness, criminal negligence, or strict liability.
*See also:* culpa.

**culpable** *See:* culpability (culpable).

**culpable homicide or felonious homicide** *See:* homicide, criminal homicide (culpable homicide or felonious homicide).

**culpable negligence** *See:* negligence, gross negligence (culpable negligence).

**cum** With. Cum is a preposition for "with."

**cumulative** The heap of all of the relevant things. Anything cumulative is, like a cumulus cloud, heaped all together. Though cumulative is not in itself perjorative, cumulativeness does not so much suggest an effort at completeness as it implies the effects of piling on. Thus, cumulative evidence is inherently duplicative and potentially confusing. Cumulative acts are then either all of the acts of a given set of actors or the additional acts that follow an earlier act, either way the cummulative effect of the acts is the effect when all considered at once.
*See also:* error, cumulative effect doctrine (cumulative error doctrine or doctrine of cumulative error); evidence, cumulative evidence.

**cumulative effect doctrine** *See:* error, cumulative effect doctrine (cumulative error doctrine or doctrine of cumulative error).

**cumulative effect theory** *See:* commerce, regulation of commerce, interstate commerce, cumulative effect theory.

**cumulative error doctrine or doctrine of cumulative error** *See:* error, cumulative effect doctrine (cumulative error doctrine or doctrine of cumulative error).

**cumulative evidence** *See:* evidence, cumulative evidence.

**cunwu gonkai** Making public village affairs. Cunwu gonkai is transparency in the management and accounts of Chinese village operations.

**curable error** *See:* error, curable error (incurable error).

**curative admissibility** *See:* admissibility, curative admissibility.

**curative-admissibility doctrine** *See:* evidence, curative-admissibility doctrine.

**curative instruction** *See:* instruction, jury instruction, curative instruction.

**curative law** *See:* law, remedial law (curative law).

**curator** A conservator. A curator is a conservator, one appointed as agent and manager of a person lacking the competence to manage financial affairs.
*See also:* conservatorship (conservator).

**curator of the estate**   A manager of the estate prior to the appointment of a permanent executor or personal representative. A curator is a temporary manager of the estate of a decedent, appointed to conserve the assets of the estate pending the appointment of an executor or personal representative.
*See also:* executor (executrix).

**cure**   To take care of a person, thing, or situation that has been harmed in some way. Cure, generally, is the process by which a person or entity cares for a person, property, or state of affairs that has been harmed or impaired in some manner, as a result of which the impairment is alleviated or resolved. Cure is both a noun and a verb.

**cure and maintenance**   *See:* seaman, maintenance of a seaman (cure and maintenance).

**cure as mitigation of damages**   A seller's timely replacement for non-conforming goods. Cure is the remedy of a seller for a defect in goods provided to the buyer by substituting goods that conform to the requirement of the contract. Cure is available as a remedy at the seller's option in the event the buyer rejects goods and the seller can cure before the time of delivery. The seller has a right to cure prior to the time of delivery and may cure with the buyer's permission thereafter, mitigating damages.

**cure of default**   *See:* default, cure of default (curing default).

**curia**

**curia regis (aula regis)**   A medieval English royal court. The curia regis was a medieval English court, in which the king and his counselors answered petitions and dispensed justice. During the period this court existed, roughly from the Norman Conquest in 1066 to the end of the thirteenth century, the delegation of certain questions to specialists in the king's retinue led to the creation of the justiciars and soon to permanent law courts, as well as to the development of Parliament, which had become customary by the middle 1200s and in roughly its modern form by the later 1300s.
*See also:* rex (regina or regis or regnal).

**currency**   The money authorized in a given state as its legal tender. Currency is the money authorized by the national government as the legal tender of the state and the basis for the valuation of all goods and services and for the payment of debts under the law. Not all money is manifest in the physical form of currency, although the money is authorized for its creation and exists from the time of its creation, whether or not it is represented in currency. The unauthorized duplication of currency is counterfeiting.

The currency of the United States is the dollar, manifest in all of its printed and coined multiples and divisions.
*See also:* note, bank note (bank bill); counterfeiting (counterfeit or counterfeitor or counterfeitable); money.

**current account**   *See:* account, account current (current account).

**current assets**   *See:* assets, current assets.

**curtesy**   *See:* spouse, surviving spouse's interest, curtesy (courtesy).

**curtilage**   The yards enclosed around a house. A curtilage is the space comprising the yards and other lands around a house. The extent of the curtilage is imprecise, but it is a reasonable space around a house in which a reasonable person would have an expectation of privacy. Determining that extent for a given lot will vary according to the nature of the enclosures erected on the land, the use made by residents of the spaces, the proximity to the house and to outbuildings, and the actual expanse involved. Police officers are barred from actual searches of the curtilage without a warrant or probable cause, although observations made in the curtilage through ordinary observation may be considered observations in plain view.
*See also:* search, warrantless search, plain view (plain-view doctrine).

**custodial arrest**   *See:* custody, penal custody, custodial arrest; arrest, custodial arrest.

**custodial interrogation**   *See:* interrogation, custodial interrogation; custody, penal custody, custodial interrogation.

**custodial release**   *See:* release, custodial release, conditional release; release, custodial release (discharge or release from custody).

**custodian of property**   *See:* custody, custodian of property.

**custody**   The duty of care and possession of a person or thing. Custody is the status of being a custodian, a person or institution that is responsible for the possession and care of a person or a thing. Since Roman law, this term has included jailors and attendants as well as bailees. Custody now includes child custody, or the right of a guardian or parent to shelter and care for a child.
*See also:* habeas corpus | custody.

**child custody**   *See:* child, child custody..

**custody of evidence**   *See:* evidence, custody of evidence, chain of custody; evidence, custody of evidence (evidence locker).

**commitment order**   An order placing an individual into the custody of another, including a prison, an asylum, or a home. A commitment order is an order placing an individual under the custody of another individual or an institution. Commission to custody now follows an order of imprisonment as a result of a criminal conviction. Commitment, in the form of civil commitment is employed in the award of custody of a person with significant mental health needs to an individual or institution if the person is committed to the care of a mental health institution. Debtors are no longer committed to custody.

**custodian of property**  A person responsible for the care of property. A custodian of property is a person who must maintain the physical integrity and security of the property, including any care of maintenance ordinarily required to keep the property from degrading in form or value, and who must produce or transfer the property to its rightful owner or lawful user. A bailee is inherently a custodian of property. A person who holds a testator's will is the custodian of the will, and if the custodian knows of the will and its significance has a legal obligation to protect the instrument from harm and to produce it on the death of the testator.

**custody as posession in trust**  Possession of a thing in trust for another. Custody of property means the care and possession of a thing on behalf of someone else, or occasionally the public itself. In this sense, custody is distinct from ownership of the item, since one can have ownership without custody and another can have custody without ownership; rather it creates a form of trust by which the object is held until required by its owner or held for the benefit of the owner. In many instances regarding chattels, the notion of custody in trust is more easily managed as a bailment.
*See also:* bailment.

**legal custody**  Authority to enter or avoid a child's legal commitments. Legal custody by a parent is the power to make decisions about a child's assets, maintenance, and healthcare. In some cases a parent may be awarded physical custody, while another parent, or a guardian, guardian ad litem, or conservator is awarded legal custody.

**penal custody**  Detention by lawful authority for punishment or housing pending a hearing related to a criminal matter. Custody in a penal sense is the involuntary detention of a person either as punishment for a crime, or as a means of managing a person accused of a crime or who is a material witness to a crime and whose voluntary presence or security cannot be otherwise assured.

**penal custody (physical custody)**  The physical detention of an individual in a jail or prison. Physical custody, or penal custody, is the physical management of a prisoner in a place of detention.

**custodial arrest**  Arrest with the intent to detain the arrestee for further proceedings. A custodial arrest is an arrest in which a person is brought into custody, which allows searches of the person incidental to the custody that would not otherwise be reasonable under the Fourth Amendment, but which also create obligations of release or charge.
*See also:* arrest, custodial arrest; arrest, custodial arrest.

**custodial interrogation**  *See:* interrogation, custodial interrogation.

**protective custody of a prisoner**  The segregation of prisoner for the prisoner's safety. Protective custody, as a matter of penal custody, is a form of incarceration that isolates a prisoner from the general prison population. This isolation is carried out in order to effectuate the prisoner's safety, upon the reasonable belief of the prison staff that the prisoner would be in inordinate danger in the general population.

**witness security (witness protection)**  Supervision or incarceration of a witness. Protective custody, as a matter of non-penal custody, is a form of incarceration or restricted and supervised movement, in which a person is kept in custody not as a punishment but for the person's protection or to ensure the person's availability for trial or for a hearing. This form of custody is used for witnesses to a crime both before and after trials related to the crime, as well as others before or during a trial whose safety is threatened as a result of their participation in the criminal justice system. Thus a witness to a crime may be ordered into protective custody. The primary form of witness security in the U.S. is the Witness Security Program of the Department of Justice.

Protective custody may be voluntary or involuntary, and involuntary custody may be required only on a court order. In most state laws, a person may be ordered to protective custody after being declared a material witness, and if the custody is involuntary, it is usually limited to a renewable period of time, sometimes to no more than fourteen days.
*See also:* witness, witness security program (Witness Protection Program or Witness Protection Act).

**custom (customary)**  A practice that has acquired the force of law. Custom is a practice in a relevant community that is of sufficient form, time, and pervasiveness that it has given rise to an expectation that members of the community ought to engage in the practice, and has thus acquired the force of law.

Although not often referred to as custom by name, the common law very often incorporates custom as the source of law, both in its justifications of law and in its rules of liability and proof. The very nature of the development of precedent and later reliance upon it is a specialized form of judicial custom. Tort standards include concepts that are customary by other names when it incorporates industry standards and when it looks to the "reasonable person" standard for a duty of care. Likewise, the past practices of the parties form a part of the understanding of contracts and thus a standard of presumptive liability. Many aspects of property interest turn upon custom, not the least being the interests established by prescription through longterm usage and the standards of usage created by land use. Even criminal law and evidence rely on custom in that the jury must assess reasonableness and ordinary expectations of behavior in determining such questions as the state of mind of a defendant or the credibility of a witness.

Custom is an essential and recognized source of law in international law, such as the customary basis for the compliance with treaties.

Proving custom can be a difficult business. Customs are not established by uniformity of practice, as there will usually be some deviance from law, regardless of its source. Customs are proven when their proof is required by evidence of a sufficient level of conforming behavior by a salient group in the relevant community, who behave as if such behavior is an obligation, over time and to the present or recent past.

In this, it is important to note the difference between custom and precedent. As a basis of liability and obligation, custom in law is a current practice, one that is presently the expectation of a salient group in whatever community is relevant to the question. This is what is meant by custom as lex loci. Precedent is evidence of past custom, which may be sufficient to establish a presumption of contemporary currency of the same custom, but it is insufficient in itself without more. On the other hand, mere violations of custom in the recent past are insufficient to demonstrate that the custom is not still vital but in fact breached, giving rise to liability for the deviant behavior.

*See also:* urf; time; law, customary law; minhag (minhagim); pattern and practice.

**customary easement** *See:* easement, easement by custom (customary easement).

**customary international law** *See:* international law, customary international law.

**customary law** *See:* law, customary law.

**custom and usage** A practice or understanding in a government office that has informal authority equivalent to a formal regulation. Custom and usage is one definition of state law as considered in 42 U.S.C. § 1983, in which the informal or unstated practices of state officials, particularly of law enforcement officers, may influence the expected or allowed conduct of the officials, in a manner like a formal ordinance, statute, rule or regulation. Thus a person whose federally protected rights are infringed as a result of a person acting under color of a state custom or usage, has a cause of action, even though the person was injured because "that's how things are" rather than "that's the rule."

**international custom** A practice that has become a legal obligation. Custom is the most ancient and fundamental source of international law, describing the practices of states that are sufficiently widespread and of a form as to give rise to an expectation by other states that each state has an obligation to act according to that practice. Custom may be reflected in treaties but need not be stated in a treaty to bind the behavior of states. Significant customs include the obligation to obey treaties, to respect the dignity of diplomats, and, in the contemporary world, to use force only in self-defense or to maintain the peace as directed by the Security Council. That such customs are reflected in treaties is evidence of the custom but not the source

of the custom: that lies in the behavior and expectations of states.

**jus cogens (erga omnes obligationes or peremptory norms)** A universal norm in customary international law. Jus cogens is the set of norms in customary international law that are universally recognized and accepted by the international community. Deviations from the jus cogens are not permitted unless they are superseded by a subsequent change in the jus cogens. The principles of jus cogens are also known as obligations erga omnes partes.

**opinio juris (opinio juris sive necessitatis)** The understanding of customary law. Opinio juris is an abbreviation for opinio juris sive necessitatis, Latin for "understood to be the law, or a requirement," which is one of the two elements for the determination that a practice has become a binding custom in international law. Opinio juris is the understanding apparent in the sources of law or in the actions and statements of national officials that a widespread or universal practice has achieved such an expectation or reliance among states that the states have become bound to support the practice and to follow it as a matter of customary law.

**customs**

**customs duty** A tax on imported goods. Customs refers to any tax payable upon goods and merchandise imported or exported. The customs duty on any given shipment is the amount owed in tax.

**U.S. Customs and Border Protection** The U.S. border-security agency that oversees international transit, imports, and exports. The U.S. Customs and Border Protection is an agency within the Department of Homeland Security charged with monitoring all imports and exports for violations of U.S. trade law, preventing the entrance of terrorists into the country, and collecting import duties. It is the successor organization to the U.S. Customs Service, which was merged in March 2003 with parts of the Immigration and Naturalization Service and the Department of Agriculture.

**U.S. Immigration and Customs Enforcement (I.C.E. or ICE)** The U.S. agency overseeing immigration and inland customs enforcement. The U.S. Immigration and Customs Enforcement agency manages immigration in the United States and has particular intelligence and enforcement powers related to customs enforcement. ICE agents in the Office of Detention and Removal Operations are particularly tasked with the arrest and deportation of undocumented aliens present in the United States.

**customs zone or customs enforcement zone** *See:* sea, Law of the Sea, national waters, contiguous zone (customs zone or customs enforcement zone).

**CWA** *See:* pollution, water pollution, clean water act (CWA).

**cy**  This, or the thing here. Cy is a law French pronoun for this, or this thing here. The word is pronounced "see" though it is now commonly mispronounced "sigh."

**cy pres**  Close in meaning. Cy pres is a doctrine for the reformation of documents, by which a grant or clause that is impossible or impracticable to perform may be reformed to the next best interpretation that would carry out the grantor's, settlor's, or testator's intent. If, a testator's original intent that the estate, in part or in whole, should be used for a charitable purpose is frustrated, a court by cy pres may approve a similar charitable beneficiary, whose receipt of the gift would achieve as nearly as possible the same ends as the testator's purpose. The intent, however, must be ascertained by the court as closely and specifically as possible, and a mere substitution of charities that would not obtain the testator's purpose would be insufficient. As a matter of policy it is presumed that the charitable intent should be honored even if the specific gift could not. Note: the term, from Law French, translates roughly as "near to this." It is most appropriately pronounced "see pray," though it is commonly pronounced "sigh pray," in either case with the emphasis on the second word.

  **doctrine of approximation**  A reformed grant should reflect the grantor's intent as nearly as possible. Cy pres is both a doctrine and a formula for the reformation of a grant, such as a provisions in a will, gift instrument or trust instrument, that is impracticable or impossible to perform, to allow the original language to be reformed to a new purpose or function as near as possible to the original purpose. Thus, when a donor makes a donation in trust for charitable purposes, equity presumes that the donated property shall forever be devoted to that purpose. However, if a time comes when the original objective is no longer possible to achieve, the court may apply the doctrine of cy pres — or approximation — and allow the donated property to be used for a purpose "as near as possible" to the original, rather than allowing the charitable trust to fail. The signal question is the degree to which the new purpose is near to the original purpose, which is a fact-intensive inquiry. A grant to a town hospital may be best understood as supporting a particular institution, as providing hospital care for the poor, hospital care for the town, health care for the town, public health in general, or something else. The best evidence of the donor's intent is required to determine what level of specificity should govern a choice among such options. Such decisions are, historically, made by a court and not by a trustee or beneficiary. Note: though in some jurisdictions, cy pres was limited to the construction of charitable gifts, by and large there is now no analytically significant difference between cy pres and approximation. Rather some materials use one term, some the other, and some both.

**czar (czarina or czarowitz or tsar or tsarina or tsarowitz)**  The head of an agency or program. The Czar, or Tsar, was the monarch of Russia. Czarina (Tsarina) was the title of his wife, or the ruler, should the ruler have been a woman. Czarowitz (Tsarowitz) was the title of their eldest son; akin to a prince. The term is used for the head of an agency, particularly one with extraordinary powers of discretion, such as an Energy Czar, Drug Czar, Intelligence Czar, etc. Even so, such officials are, of course, bound by the constitution, statutes, and regulations, as well as their oaths of office, in their roles.

  **Drug Czar (drug lord)**  Drug gang leader, or the chief drugs enforcement officer. Drug Czar has two distinct and contradictory meanings. In common parlance, it is the leader of a network manufacturing, importing, or selling illegal drugs. When used with specificity, it is the Director of the Office of National Drug Control Policy.

**CZMA**  See: coast, Coastal Zone Management Act (CZMA).

> Such is the character of human language, that no word conveys to the mind, in all situations, one single definite idea; and nothing is more common than to use words in a figurative sense.
>
> McCulloch v. Maryland, 17 U.S. (Wheat.) 316, 366 (1819) (Marshall, C.J.).

# D

**d**  The fourth letter of the modern English alphabet. "D" signifies a variety of functions as a symbol and as a designation of status. It is sometimes invoked by Delta, the word for the fourth letter in Greek. It is translated into delta for radio signals and NATO military transmissions, into David for some police radio traffic, and into dash, dot, dot in Morse Code.

**d as a Latin abbreviation**  The Digest, or a vote to condemn. "D" is the abbreviation for the Digesta Justiniani, or Digest of Justinian. It was also an abbreviation in Roman law, the sign for damno, a vote for comdenmation in the comitia, or courts of popular assembly, as opposed to "L" for libero freedom and "NL" for non liquet for a case that is unclear to the voter.
　　*See also:*  non, non liquet (NL).

**d as a Roman numeral**  Latin symbol for 500. D is 500 when used as a numeral. In the Roman system of numeralization, placement of a D to the right of another Roman numeral adds 500 to the numerical value. The placement of a D to the left of another Roman numeral subtracts 500 from the numerical value. If a dash is placed above it, the abbreviation represents 5,000.

**d as an abbreviation**  A word commencing in d. When used as the sole letter of an abbreviation, D often stands for the defendant, especially in law school hypotheticals. It may also stand for date, de, debitum, debt, deceased, degree, died, digest, dismissed, distinguished, district, docket, and doctor. As a component of other abbreviations, D can stand for any word commencing with that letter, particularly those above and daily, Dakota, data, day, dead, death, debit, declaration, decoration, descent, defender, defense, Delaware, delivered, delivery, Denmark, Denver, department, deputy, descriptive, Dickinson, disaster, discount, distribution, divinity, division, divorce, dominion, drawer, driving, and drug. It may also stand for the initial of the name of an author or case reporter, such as Dallas, Davison, Dowling, and Dunlop.

**d as in hypotheticals**  The defendant, or the fourth character. D often stands for the defendant, whether in a civil or criminal proceeding, or it might refer to any person who is the fourth character in the story of a law school hypothetical. D may also represent a devisee, or it may sometimes stand for a daughter. Traditionally, when D is used for the defendant, it is invoked with a Greek delta, a triangle, Δ.

**D.E.A. or DEA**  *See:*  police, police organization, Drug Enforcement Administration (D.E.A. or DEA).

**D.F.R. or DFR**  *See:*  fiduciary, fiduciary duty, duty of fair representation (D.F.R. or DFR).

**D.N.A. or DNA**  *See:*  deoxyribonucleic acid (D.N.A. or DNA).

**D.U.I. or DUI or operating a vehicle under the influence or O.V.U.I. or OVUI**  *See:*  driving, driving under the influence (D.U.I. or DUI or operating a vehicle under the influence or O.V.U.I. or OVUI).

**D.W.O.P. or DWOP or neglect of prosecution**  *See:*  dismissal, grounds for dismissal, dismissal for want of prosecution (D.W.O.P. or DWOP or neglect of prosecution).

**d/b/a or f/d/b/a or a/k/a or trade name**  *See:*  name, alias, corporate alias (d/b/a or f/d/b/a or a/k/a or trade name).

**Dairy Queen rule**  *See:*  equity, equitable procedure, jury, Dairy Queen rule.

**damage (harm or loss)**  Loss to a person or property. Damage is the measurable loss or injury occurring to a person or a person's property or interests. The fact of damage is independent of the agency of its cause or the degree of intent or negligence related to that agency. Damage caused by another person may be compensable under law, while damage not the result of a human agency is generally not compensable except by a contract of risk assurance, such as by insurance. Certain unlawful acts that produce no damage may still be minimally compensable under law, such as most intentional torts; such "damage" is referred to as "nominal damage." A person who negligently causes damage may be liable for the cost of "making whole" the damaged person or property, while a person who recklessly or intentionally causes damage may be liable for a penalty above the cost of making whole.

**damage deposit**  *See:*  deposit, security deposit (damage deposit).

**damage to a place of worship**  *See:*  religion, place of worship, damage to a place of worship (church bombing).

**damages**  A remedy in money for an injury to one's person, property, or rights. Damages are a form of recovery in law awarded to a person who has sustained an injury to person, property, or rights, from the defendant whose actions led to this injury. The basic purpose of damages is compensatory, to restore a party injured through a violation of a legal duty to the position the party would have been in without the injury, although other purposes are punitive, to punish outrageous conduct, and nominal, to recognize the occurence of an injury or of a breach of duty.

The plaintiff must prove the extent of the injury in order to recover damages in most civil actions, although certain causes of actions allow proof of damages to be presumed, as in the case of tort per se. Damages may not be speculative or hypothetical, in that the plaintiff must give proof of the calculation of the injury or loss, but this does not bar the proof of future damages, which may be estimated.

*See also:* relief; remedy (remediable or remedied or remedies); equity, equitable remedy (equitable relief); relief, monetary relief.

*damages and restitution* Damages are paid by a person who has been unjustly enriched at the expense of another, but restitution is remedy in equity or in law in which a person is returned to the original position before loss or injury, or to the position that person would have been in had the breach not occurred. Although damages are always paid in money, and restitution may be paid in money, an award of money in restitution is not an award of damages. Damages (other than punitives) are calculated by what is required to make whole the plaintiff. Restitution is calculated according to what gains the defendant accrued as a result of wrongdoing.

**calculation of damages (assessment of damages or computation of damages or measure of damages)** The process by which a court determines the amount of money that should be awarded to a successful plaintiff. Calculation of damages is the computation of the money that should be awarded for damage, harm, or injury that the plaintiff proves the plaintiff did or is likely to suffer, as well as, if there are to be punitive damages, the appropriate amount of money to be required as a suitable punishment of the defendant. The determination of the standards of law or equity to apply in a given case is a matter for the court to determine as a matter of law. The calculation of the damages by applying these standards to the facts established in the record is a matter of fact, committed to the jury or to the court if the judge sits as a trier of fact as well as of law. Note: there is little difference now among the meanings of assessment, computation, or measure of damages.

*Interest* Damages from past claims are usually entitled to interest. Interest is usually calculated as a portion of damages by calculating the value of the actual damages suffered at the time the claim was due and owed, either as a contract claim or as a tort claim on which a demand was properly made, and then adding an amount equal to the prevailing consumer lending interest rate for that period.

*See also:* damages, calculation of damages (assessment of damages or computation of damages or measure of damages); interest, interest for money; damages, classes of damages, future damages.

**aggravation of damages** Damage after the breach of duty giving rise to the claim. Aggravation of damages are additional damages claimed for events that followed the event from which the claim arose, either as a natural consequence of the defendant's initial breach of duty or as a result of further actions by the defendant that were tied in logic and time to the initial breach. Aggravation of damages is a means of determining the extent of compensatory damages owed, and although the terms are often confused, aggravated damages are different, being the additional damages pled for some outrageous aspect of the defendant's conduct.

*See also:* damages, calculation of damages (assessment of damages or computation of damages or measure of damages); aggravation (aggravated or aggravating); damages, classes of damages, aggravated damages.

**discount for present value (inflation factor)** Inflation is factored into the present value of awards of damages for future losses. A discount for present value is applied to awards of damages for future losses for which the defendant is already responsible. The discount recognizes that the effect of inflation means that a dollar paid today will be worth more than the dollar would be if it was paid in ten years. When calculating the present value of future damages, any present award must account for inflation's effect on the award over time. This is usually done by adding to the value an estimate of average market rates of interest over time, discounting it by the average expected rate of inflation for the same time. There are more specialized formulae for damages suffered in investment losses that consider inflation when inflation is an aspect of the investment already.

*See also:* damages, calculation of damages (assessment of damages or computation of damages or measure of damages).

**double recovery** Payment twice for the same injury. Double recovery is the forbidden collection of payment in full, from two or more sources of payment as a matter of obligation, for an amount greater than the damage suffered. Double recovery does not depend on whether one payment is made as a result of the litigation of a claim, voluntary payment under a contract or as a liability, or payment following an administrative claim. Payment from a collateral source, however, does not amount to a double recovery.

**excessive damages** Damages greater than are allowed by law. Excessive damages are damages that are greater than those the law requires or allows for a given theory of recovery in any cause of action. Compensatory damages may not be based on a theory of damage not recognized in law nor, for any allowed theory, can they exceed a reasonable computation. Punitive, exemplary, multiple, and nominal damages are allowed only when the law allows them and may not exceed an amount reasonably calculated to achieve the policies underlying these ends. Even so, most defendants claim that damages awarded are excessive no matter how fairly or scrupulously calculated, and zeal to ensure that the law does not exact an excess should not limit a fair recovery or diminish a responsible penalty.

**mitigation of damages (avoidable consequences)** A plaintiff must take reasonable steps to avoid further damage. Mitigation of damages, or the doctrine of avoidable consequences, is a doctrine of remedies that requires a plaintiff to take reasonable steps to avoid making the damage the plaintiff suffered any greater than need be. Without diminishing the responsibility of the defendant, the plaintiff may neither act unreasonably to increase the damage suffered nor avoid the reasonable steps a responsible party would take to keep a harm from growing worse. Under the doctrine of avoidable consequences, a plaintiff whose action or inaction aggravated the harm caused by the defendant will not receive full compensation for the harm; the damages will be mitigated to the extent the plaintiff was at fault for the damages.

*See also:* damages, calculation of damages (assessment of damages or computation of damages or measure of damages); damages, contract damages, mitigation of damages.

**setoff (offset or right of setoff or set-off)** The reduction of damages for an amount already paid. Setoff is a defense according to which the defendant is given credit in the calculation of damages owed to the plaintiff. The credit arises in one of two situations: If the defendant or an agent has already given the plaintiff money or value, the amount of money or value given that reduced the damage suffered by the plaintiff is deducted from the damages owed by the defendant, or if the plaintiff validly owes money to the defendant, regardless of whether the debt arises from a breach of contract, a tort, or otherwise, the amount of the debt owed by the plaintiff to the defendant is set off against the damages that would be otherwise owed by the defendant to the plaintiff. Setoff, sometimes called the right to setoff, is an application of the rule forbidding double recovery. The right of setoff may be constrained by a contract and usually does not apply in a case of indemnification by an insurance company.

*See also:* equity, equitable pleading, equitable recoupment; setoff (offset).

**treble damages (double damages or double or multiple damages or trebles)** Statutory enhancement of a compensatory award. Treble or double damages are statutorily allowable enhancements of an award for compensatory damages. Damage enhancements provide a means of deterrence for the type of conduct covered in the statutes. Legislatures may create multiple-damage awards as a means of deterring unlawful conduct or punishing

conduct it finds contrary to public policy. As with punitive damages, however, treble damages should not be required or allowed to a jury for punishing conduct owing to its harm to others, such a motive of punishment amounting either to an invasion of criminal procedure or the takings clause.

*See also:* damages, calculation of damages (assessment of damages or computation of damages or measure of damages).

**wrongdoer rule** The defendant bears the burden of a failure to prove damages if the right is proved but the amount is uncertain. The wrongdoer rule in pleading and remedies shifts the burden of a failure to prove the amount of damages with certainty from the plaintiff to the defendant, when the facts otherwise proved by the plaintiff demonstrate that the existence of damage is certain, and the only uncertainty is as to a specific value or amount.

**classes of damages** The categories of damages. Damages are classified in many ways, primarily as nominal, compensatory, and punitive. Some theorists distinguish restitutionary recoveries from damages entirely, and others would consider it a form of punitive damages. Within these categories are many formulations for the calculation of damages, chiefly within compensatory damages. Compensatory damages include damages for past, present, and future damages, each with a variety of formulae for computation. Different theories of the case sometimes require different theories of damages. A single action may include many different claims from across the classes of damages. Although the plaintiff should never be awarded damages that cumulate so as to give a double recovery for any loss, various theories may be cumulated to allow recoveries for different aspects of a single loss. Moreover, alternative theories of damages for the same loss may be initially sought in the alternative.

**actual damages** Damages that compensate the plaintiff for actual losses. Actual damages reimburse the plaintiff for the damage actually suffered as a result of the defendant's breach of duty. The usual description is that actual damages make whole the plaintiff, or leave the plaintiff in no worse condition following the defendant's injury to the person, property, economic interest, or rights than the plaintiff would have been in otherwise. Actual damages include, among other things, property damage, lost profits, the value of destroyed or stolen goods, medical expenses, lost wages, the value of physical pain and mental suffering, lost financial support of a spouse, and lost consortium. Actual damages include both general and special damages, if the special damages were actually suffered or are reasonably certain actually to be suffered, such as consequential damages, although all such special damages must be separately pled. Actual damages may be prospective as well as retrospective. Actual damages are not punitive, and no aspect of an award of actual damages should be based on the intent to punish the defendant for wrongful conduct or to make an example of the defendant to others. In general usage, no essential difference is intended between actual damages and compensatory damages, although some statutes and the case law of some jurisdictions favor one over the other. That said, in some contexts compensatory damages include liquidated damages and could include nominal damages, and in such contexts neither would be equivalent to the actual damages that would otherwise be calculated.

*See also:* damages, classes of damages, compensatory damages.

**aggravated damages**   Damages for outrageousness in the defendant's conduct. Aggravated damages are a form of damage not based on monetary loss to the plaintiff but on the outrage provoked by the defendant's conduct in causing the plaintiff's injury with intent, knowledge of the breach of duty, or gross negligence. It is akin to punitive damages, but more limited in scope. Aggravated damages are usually not allowed in causes of action in which punitive damages are barred, such as a suit against a physician in Illinois. Note: aggravated damages are related but not the same as aggravation of damages.

*See also:* aggravation (aggravated or aggravating).

**compensatory damages**   Damages that compensate the plaintiff for actual losses. Compensatory damages reimburse the plaintiff for the damage actually suffered as a result of the defendant's breach of duty. The usual description is that compensatory damages make whole the plaintiff, or leave the plaintiff in no worse condition following the defendant's injury to the person, property, economic interest, or rights than the plaintiff would have been in otherwise. Compensatory damages include, among other things, property damage, lost profits, the value of destroyed or stolen goods, medical expenses, lost wages, the value of physical pain and mental suffering, lost financial support of a spouse, and lost consortium. Compensatory damages may be prospective as well as retrospective. Compensatory damages include both general and special damages, if the special damages are compensatory in nature, such as consequential damages, although all such special damages must be separately pled. Compensatory theory underlies other forms of damage, including nominal damages, but compensatory damages are not punitive, and no aspect of an award of compensatory damages should be based on the intent to punish the defendant for wrongful conduct or to make an example of the defendant to others. In general usage, no essential difference is intended between actual damages and compensatory damages, although some statutes and the case law of some jurisdictions favor one over the other. That said, compensatory damages, in some contexts, include liquidated damages, and in such contexts liquidated damages need not be equivalent to the actual damages that would otherwise be calculated.

*See also:* damages, classes of damages, actual damages.

**consequential damages**   Secondary damages arising from the plaintiff's injury. Consequential damages are damages owed for harm that follows naturally, but not directly, from the defendant's conduct. For example, a breach of contract might result not only in the loss of profits that would have been realized from the contracted work but also in a loss of other business to the plaintiff, who was unable to accept a different contract as a result of the lost profits. Consequential damages may be limited in some jurisdictions for claims in contract to those damages contemplated by the parties at the time the contract was made; no similar limitations apply in tort. Consequential damages are pleaded separately, as a form of special damages.

*See also:* damages, contract damages, lost profits; foreseeability (foreseeable); loss, consequential loss.

**continuing damages**   Damages that persist from the original injury. Continuing damages are compensation for harm that persists over time. Continuing damages may result either from continuing conduct or from the persistent effects of concluded conduct. This difference affects limitations of actions. An action for continuing damages from concluded conduct must be brought within the limitations period that runs from the time the conduct concludes. Thus, for example, if the plaintiff falls and then suffers a persistent pain, the plaintiff might claim continuing damages, but the action must be brought within the limitations period from the fall. An action for continuing damages from continuing conduct may be brought at any time during the conduct or within the limitations period from the conduct's conclusion, though in some jurisdictions damages would only be calculated for the limitations period prior to the action's being brought.

**future damages**   Damages awarded for harm not yet suffered from a past injury. Future damages are damages awarded in the present for harms that the plaintiff is certain to suffer in the future, which were caused by an event in the past for which the defendant is liable. Future damages may be estimated, but the estimate may not be speculative. Rather, it must be based on economic, medical, and actuarial likelihoods of specific forms of damage that will have specific estimated costs, that will persist for a specific estimated time. The final calculation of costs to the plaintiff is discounted for inflation.

*See also:* damages, classes of damages, consequential damages.

**general damages (presumed damages)**   Damages presumed from a breach of duty that need not be specifically proven. General damages are the value of the injury or harm from a breach of duty that is presumed to have been suffered by the plaintiff as a result of the wrongful act or breach of contract by the defendant. The existence of general damages in the event a particular wrong is proved is so common that there is no need to plead their amount or elements of cause, though a plea for relief is still required.

When a plaintiff proves the elements of certain torts, particularly constitutional torts, intentional torts, and dignitary torts, the law presumes that an injury has occurred to the victim, and the finder of fact is allowed to assess the damage as the value of the harm suffered by the plaintiff, without detailed proof of its forms or amounts. Following the proof of elements, the defendant may attempt to prove that in fact the plaintiff suffered no damage. General damages are not always available for a cause of action in tort and are only to be pled in actions in which they are allowed.

General damages in a breach of contract for the sale of goods are the same as the difference in market value from the date delivery would have occurred and the value when goods were secured.

**hedonic damages (loss of enjoyment of life)**
Damages arising from lost quality of life. Hedonic damages are damages for personal injury resulting from a discernible loss of enjoyment of life. Hedonic damages are usually ascertained by the inability of the plaintiff to perform activities that are generally considered to lack monetary value but are nevertheless important to the quality of life, particularly when the plaintiff performed such activities prior to the injury giving rise to the action. Hedonic damages are distinct from pain and suffering.
*See also:* life, quality of life; hedonism.

**measurable damages (ascertainable damages)**
Damages based on evidence of past, present, or future damage. Measurable damages are those that can be established with specificity, meaning that there is sufficient evidence as to have confidence that an amount of money does in fact reasonably represent a genuine loss to the plaintiff. Measurable damages may include estimates based on rough or inexact data, such as market comparisons, earnings estimates, and statistical likelihoods, but cannot include speculation with no basis in fact.

**nominal damages**  Award of a token amount for damages. Nominal damages are a trivial amount awarded to recognize a breach of a duty owed by the defendant to the plaintiff, rather than as a measure of recompense for loss or detriment sustained. Nominal damages provide vindication to a plaintiff for the loss of a right in a situation in which a precise calculation of actual damages is impossible or in which the damages would be so trivial as to be beside the point, and general damages are either not sought or are not available for the cause of action. Federal courts may award nominal damages in actions properly before them when state tort law would award nominal damages, including federal civil rights actions.

**non-economic damages**  Losses assessed not from the value of property or commerce. Non-economic damages are damages that are measured not by calculating the lost value of a commercial or employment opportunity or the value of property but by ascertaining the value of something personal to the plaintiff, such as pain and suffering, emotional distress, or a lost hedonic capacity to engage in a life project. Punitive or exemplary damages are also sometimes included in the term.

**punitive damages (exemplary damages or punis or punitives)**  Civil damages that punish the defendant for wrongful conduct. Punitive damages are civil damages awarded in a tort action as a means of punishing the wrongful conduct of the defendant. In general, punitive damages are awarded only in cases in which a plaintiff has first proven tortious conduct leading to harm and been awarded compensatory damages, or at least (in some jurisdictions) nominal damages. The tort may arise out of a breach of contract, but an ordinary breach of contract does not give rise to a claim for punitive damages. In claiming an injury, the plaintiff may allege that the defendant's conduct was wanton, willful, and deliberate, with the knowledge that it would violate either the plaintiff's rights or public policy. If the jury finds these allegations proven, the jury may award damages, in some jurisdictions basing them in part on the defendant's assets in order to account for the significance of an award as a punishment to the defendant.

In some jurisdictions punitive damages are labeled exemplary damages, but despite the fact that different formulae are used, there is little difference in the results that is owing to the difference in label.

*due process considerations*  The U.S. Constitution limits awards of punitive damages. Due process of law restricts state and federal assessment of damages in two situations: punitive damages are awarded in an amount that are so grossly excessive of the government's legitimate interest in punishment and deterrence that they are arbitrary, and punitive damages awarded to punish the defendant for harming individuals who are not party to the action in which the remedy is sought.
*See also:* due process of law.

**special damages**  Damages that must be specifically pled. Special damages are actual damages that arise as the legal and natural consequence of an injury but are not general damages and are not implied by law, and so these damages must be specifically and particularly stated in the pleadings as independent bases for damages. Special damages must, in contracts, be foreseeable, but their occurrence is a contingent result of the particular injury, rather than an inescapable result of any breach under the contract. There is little difference between consequential damages and special damages, though actions for breach of contract are more likely to plead consequential damages, and actions for tort are more likely to plead special damages.

*See also:* special; damages, classes of damages, consequential damages.

**contract damages**  Money to compensate for losses caused by another's breach of contract. Contract damages are solely compensatory or restitutionary, although punitive damages may be awarded for an independent tort that arises in relation to a contract or breach of contract.

*See also:* remedy (remediable or remedied or remedies).

*contract price as limit to damages*  Contract damages in the event of a breach may be limited to the contract price if the parties agree to such a limitation as a material term of the contract and if the limitation is reasonable.

**certainty of damages**  Compensatory damages must be based on a clear statement of losses in certain amounts. Certainty of damages is a requirement of compensatory damages. This is not to say that the damages, especially for pain and suffering, emotional distress, or future damages, may not be based on estimates or comparative and analogous reasoning. Indeed, a future contingency may be calculated and the risk of the contingency used to discount or enhance an award, but the assessment cannot be hypothetical or speculative.

*See also:* damages, contract damages, lost profits.

**contract-market differential**  The difference between the initial price of the contract and the later price in the market. The contract–market differential is a measure of damages that applies when the plaintiff is a buyer who has been been unable to cover adequately and seeks money damages instead of substitute goods.

*See also:* damages, contract damages, cover.

**cost of completion**  The cash amount required to finish the contracted-for project. The cost of completion is the actual amount required to restore or rectify a project under a contract that has been improperly constructed or supplied owing to a breach in performance by a builder or supplier. The cost is assessed according to the actual cost of correction, restoration, or completion at the time it is to be done rather than at the time of breach.

**cover**  A buyer's substitution of goods for those a seller failed to deliver. Cover is the acquisition by a buyer of replacement goods when a seller fails to deliver, breaching a contract to provide the same form of goods. Cover must be made in a timely, good faith effort to obtain a substitute for the goods specified in a contract. Any increase in the cost of the cover over the contract price may be recovered as damages, as well as incidental expenses incurred in the acquisition less any incidental expenses saved as a result of the breach.

*See also:* damages, contract damages, contract-market differential.

**damages for breach of warranty**  The difference between the value of goods as delivered and as warranted. Damages for breach of warranty are determined by ascertaining the difference between the value of the non–conforming goods at the time of delivery and the value they would have had if they had been as warranted.

**expectation damages (benefit of the bargain damages)**  The expected return from the bargain, had it been completed. Expectation damages are measured by the result, especially the profit, that the plaintiff would have realized if the contract had been performed as the plaintiff had expected it to be, the relevant expectation being at the time of entry into the contract. In other words, the injured party is entitled to the benefit of the bargain that party actually expected to receive at the time of entry into the bargain, as long as that expectation was reasonable in light of the contract as a whole.

**economic waste**  Expectation damages are not awarded when they would be much more than the loss of reasonable value. The doctrine of economic waste is a limitation on the general principle of damages that a party injured by another's breach should be awarded damages sufficient to realize the benefits that party had reasonably expected under the contract. The doctrine states that if the amount of such damages would be significantly more than the additional benefit in value to the injured party, then the damages beyond the economic benefit would amount to waste and the damages should be limited to the loss in value received as a result of the breach.

**foreseeable damages**  Damages that were understood as a potential consequence of breach. Foreseeable damages are those that either were understood in fact by the parties at the time of entry into the contract as a potential consequence of a breach of the contract or would have been understood by a reasonable and prudent party to have potentially resulted from the natural and usual course of events that might stem from the breach of a duty or contract. The latter description is also considered reasonably foreseeable damages. Unless the parties contract otherwise, contract damages are usually limited to reasonably foreseeable damages.

**Hadley v. Baxendale Rule**  Contract damages are only recoverable for a loss from breach reasonably foreseeable or actually foreseen by the defendant. The Rule of Hadley v. Baxendale, 9 Ex. 341, 156 Eng. Rep. 145 (1854), is sometimes stated as two rules and sometimes as one. As two rules, they are: First, a plaintiff may only recover damages that are the natural result of the defendant's breach. Second, the plaintiff may only recover damages from such losses as both parties might reasonably have expected at the time they entered the contract to have resulted later from a breach. As a single rule, it is: A plaintiff may only recover damages that were the natural consequence of the breach that the defendant should reasonably have expected to follow from it.

**incidental damages** Damages for lost expenses that supplemented the primary task. Incidental damages are damages to compensate for lost expenses incurred from duties that are ancillary to the primary tasks that were compensated by damages. Thus, if a buyer rejects non-conforming goods and is therefore entitled to compensatory damages for the lost expectation from the receipt of conforming goods, the buyer may also recover incidental damages for storing, inspecting, and returning the goods to the seller.

*See also:* incident, incident as incidental.

**liquidated damages (liquidation of damages)** An amount agreed upon beforehand to be paid in damages in the event of a breach. Liquidated damages are the specific amounts of damages which the parties predetermine will satisfy claims arising under their contract, in the event of a breach by one party or the other. In order to be upheld by the court, the amount of liquidated damages must be reasonable in the light of either the harm anticipated when the contract was entered or the actual harm later realized. If it should appear that the amount of liquidated damages is excessive and merely a pretext for punitive measures in case of breach, the liquidated damages agreement is void, and damages must be assessed from proof. Fundamentally, the law of contracts disapproves penalty clauses, although it applauds fair and reasonable allocations of risk.

*See also:* liquidation, liquidation of a claim (debt liquidation).

**loss-of-bargain rule (loss of bargain rule)** The difference between a contract price and the market price. The loss of bargain affords a measure of damages for a breach of warranty that is measured by the difference between the contract price for the goods or property and the market price as it stood at the time of contemplated performance. Loss of bargain is not exactly the same as benefit of the bargain: Loss of bargain is a measure of difference from the market, while benefit of the bargain is a measure of the actual profits that would have been realized, which might be more or less than the market difference.

**loss-volume** A loss incapable of mitigation caused by the repudiation or breach of a contract. Loss-volume damages are those incurred through the repudiation or breach of a contract involving benefits the plaintiff could have received had the original contract been performed, but now are unattainable due to that repudiation or breach. For example, if a client repudiates a contract to make a sign for his or her business, the sign company will be unable to sell the sign to any one else, and so will be unable to mitigate damages. Loss-volume damages also include those incurred due to the loss of another contract caused by the repudiation of the first. In such a case, a plaintiff will have to show the capacity to make the additional profit and that he or she would have done so absent the defendant's repudiation or breach.

*See also:* damages, contract damages, contract-market differential.

**lost profits** Profits lost to the plaintiff because of the defendant's breach. Lost profits are net income that the plaintiff would have realized if the defendant had performed under a contract, but which the plaintiff could not realize because the defendant did not perform. Lost profits are not always available as damages because they are limited to profits that were reasonably foreseeable by the defendant at the time of the contract as dependent upon the defendant's performance. Lost profits must be pled as special damages, and they must be demonstrable to a reasonable likelihood that the goods or services the plaintiff would have sold would have been purchased, that an essential reason the goods or services could not be sold was the defendant's breach, and the costs and income from the goods or services that would in fact have been realized can be ascertained without speculation.

*See also:* damages, classes of damages, consequential damages; damages, contract damages, certainty of damages.

**mitigation of damages** Efforts by the plaintiff to avoid damage that need not be suffered from the defendant's breach. The duty to take reasonable steps in mitigation of damages is an implied duty in contracts as well as a doctrine of remedies. Buyers are required to act independently to remediate a seller's breach — rather than merely rest on their contract rights without making any attempt to mitigate damages.

*See also:* cover.

**penalty clause** A contract clause setting damages disproportionately greater than a likely loss. A penalty clause in a contract purports to stipulate the damages to be paid by one party to the other in the event of a breach of contract or other non-performance that is disproportionate to the damage that the party to be paid is likely to suffer. A penalty clause works to punish non-performance rather than to compensate for unavoidable losses suffered as a result of the non-performance. Some penalty clauses are written as liquidated damage clauses, but the amount assessed is too great against the likely potential loss from the breach to represent actual liquidation of potential compensatory damages. Whether a clause is written with one party's intent to punish breach or the amount of damages is overstated as an error, a penalty clause is presumptively unenforceable.

*See also:* damages, contract damages, liquidated damages (liquidation of damages).

**quantum meruit (quantum valebant)** Damages for unpaid services that are determined by the market rate. Quantum meruit literally means "as much as is deserved" and is a formula for damages when the buyer of a person's services breaches a contract, but the amount to be paid for the the services was never fully determined or was unambiguously ascertained. In a case in which a contract is either implied or express but is lacking a clear level of compensation, the damages against the buyer are determined by quantum meruit, the value of the goods or services, of the quality received, in the market in which they were provided. The same formula is applied for the sale of goods as for services, though the label for what the goods deserve is "quantum valebant." Note: quantum meruit is often confused with restitution, the difference being that quantum meruit is the market value of the services provided and restitution is their value to the defendant, which may differ.

*See also:* restitution (writ of restitution).

**reliance damages** The plaintiff's harm from relying on defendant in the false hope of the defendant's performance. Reliance damages recoup the damage suffered by the plaintiff because the plaintiff expended funds or material, made commitments, or made other investments because the plaintiff relied on the defendant's promise to act, the defendant did not make good on the promise, and thus the plaintiff's actions were wasted.

**extraordinary damages (extraordinary remedy)** Damages other than compensatory damages. Extraordinary damages describe all forms of damage based on a theory of punishment or discouragement of like conduct, including punitive damages, exemplary damages, multiple damages, and aggravated damages.

*See also:* ordinariness, extraordinariness (extraordinary or extraordinarily).

**loss-of-chance doctrine (lost chance)** The value of a lost opportunity for care, recovery, or survival. Loss of chance is a measure of damages for medical malpractice that ascertains the value of a patient's lost, delayed, or reduced chance of recovery or survival that resulted from the wrongdoing of the healthcare provider.

**diminution damages (lost value in real property)** The difference in property value following the breach of duty. Diminution damages, or the lost value in real property, is the difference in the value of property caused by tortious interference with the property, by a governmental taking of property through physical occupation, or by a breach of contract in certain circumstances. Diminution damages are measured as the difference between the fair market value prior to the breach and the value following the breach. Despite the term "diminution," the difference following a breach in rare instances may be an increase in value, for which no damages are to be awarded.

**pain and suffering (p&s)** The physical pain and emotional suffering that follow from bodily injury. Pain and suffering are the measures of the direct and indirect harms felt by a person suffering from bodily injury. Pain refers to physical pain or the neural agony caused by the injury or its consequential treatment. Suffering refers to the emotional loss, depression, malaise, or sorrow that is the indirect result of the injury and its other consequences, such as the disappointment or sorrow that follows the loss of activities or the inconvenience or anger that follows economic disruption. Different jurisdictions allow different formulae for describing pain and suffering, with some allowing for computation of harm per diem and others requiring a single assessment over time. Some jurisdictions include hedonic damages as an element of pain and suffering, while others require them to be separately pled and proven. Damages for pain and suffering in a wrongful death case may be computed for the suffering of the decedent prior to death, though in various jurisdictions survivors are entitled to separate claims, including the value of their lost enjoyment of the decedent's company, support, and, in the case of a spouse or legally cognizable partner, loss of consortium.

*See also:* hedonism.

*per diem* Per diem calculations of pain and suffering allow a jury to consider the value of plaintiff's pain and suffering for a single day and then to multiply it over the number of days it has persisted or will persist. Some jurisdictions do not allow such an argument to be made to the jury, though it is allowed now in most jurisdictions.
*See also:* per, per diem.

**proof of damages** Evidence to substantiate the damage the plaintiff allegedly suffered. Proof of damages is a distinct presentation of evidence to demonstrate the harm the plaintiff suffered as a result of the conduct for which the defendant is responsible. Damages must be proved with reasonable certainty rather than by speculation, although well grounded estimates are suitable, particularly when evidence is required for future damages, which is harm or expenses yet to be suffered. Unless damages were incidentally proved in the case for liability, a failure to present proof of damages in a civil action for which damages are sought may bar the award of any damages.

**tort damages** Compensatory and punitive damages. Damages in tort allow both for the compensation of actual loss suffered by the plaintiff as a result of the defendant's breach of duty and for the punishment of the defendant for deliberate and wrongful conduct.

**collateral-source rule**  A tortfeasor's debt is not reduced by another's payment to the victim. The collateral source rule bars a tortfeasor from attempting to reduce damages owed to the plaintiff because the victim has received payments of benefits from a third party unconnected with the tortfeasor. Thus, a driver who injures a pedestrian may not reduce the driver's liability because the pedestrian's insurance pays the pedestrian's medical bills (although the language of the insurance contract may allow the pedestrian's insurer to recover from the driver). On the other hand, a payment by the driver's insurer to the pedestrian would not trigger the collateral-source rule, thus the pedestrian's claim for damages against the driver would be reduced by the amount of the driver's insurer's payments. A collateral source is any third party not acting to benefit the tortfeasor and need not be an insurer.

*See also:* damages, calculation of damages (assessment of damages or computation of damages or measure of damages); damages, calculation of damages, double recovery.

**economic loss rule (economic-loss rule)**  Bar against compensatory tort damages for financial loss. The economic loss rule restricts compensatory damages in tort to damages arising from physical harm, rather than financial loss, caused by a tort. The rule does not apply to intentional torts or business torts, but seems to arise mainly in product liability cases. There are a great many exceptions to the rule, and its rationale, which is a pretty dubious affair, would appear to be an attempted substitution for the more traditional rule of limiting damages to those proximately caused by the defendant's breach of a general duty.

*See also:* injury, economic injury; damages, calculation of damages (assessment of damages or computation of damages or measure of damages).

**daminozide**  *See:* alar (daminozide).

**damnum**  Injury, or damages. Damnum translates into a variety of words for harm or injury to one's person or interests. The common law term includes injuries that are compensable in law.

**damnum absque injuria (damnum sine injuria)**  Injury for which no action lies at law. Damnum absque injuria is a harm for which no remedy will be granted in law. The customary basis for this description is that the harm occurred through no one's breach of duty. It is also used when the harm is acceptable as a matter of public policy or because no claim may be brought as a matter of standing, immunity, or other doctrines of procedure. The term is sometimes written as damnum

sine . . . in various formulations, paraphrasing Justinian's Fourth Institute, paragraph 9.

*See also:* injuria, injuria absque damno (injuria absque damnum).

**danger**  Exposure to a risk of substantial harm. Danger is the existence of, potential for, or threat of, substantial harm. Every person has a duty to guard others against a danger from conditions under the person's control. In other words, one has a duty to protect others from foreseeable and unreasonable risks posed by one's actions or conditions for which one has a responsibility.

Some activities are abnormally dangerous by their very nature, such as handling explosives. Abnormally dangerous activities may give rise to strict liability if they cause injury to innocent bystanders. Still, a person who voluntarily engages in an abnormally dangerous activity, like a boxer in a boxing match, is likely to have assumed the risk of injury in the activity itself.

**abnormally dangerous activity (inherently dangerous activity or ultra-hazardous activity or ultrahazardous activity)**  Activity of unusual risk even when performed with care. Abnormally dangerous activity is conduct that is so dangerous by its very nature that its participants should be responsible for all of the harms the conduct causes. The destruction of buildings, the use of high explosives, the use of especially hazardous materials, and the keeping of unusually dangerous animals are typical of acts giving rise to strict liability under this doctrine. Whether an activity is abnormally dangerous is a question of law, not of fact. In order to determine whether an activity is abnormally dangerous, courts will consider the following factors: the existence of a high degree of risk of harm, the likelihood that any resulting harm will be great, the inability to eliminate the danger with reasonable care, the extent to which the activity is not commonly practiced, the inappropriateness of the activity for where it is conducted, and the activity's value to the community weighed against the danger. The distinct tort theory of abnormally dangerous activity was promulgated in Rylands v. Fletcher, [1] LR 3 HL 330 (1868). The Restatement Second of Torts subsequently adopted the ultra-hazardous test from Rylands, later revised to the current abnormally dangerous activity language.

**latent danger (hidden danger)**  A danger that is not apparent to an ordinary observer. A latent danger is a danger or condition that poses a risk of harm to a person but which, owing to some condition or circumstance, is hidden from the person at risk. A latent danger may be made patent through warning signs and signals that are clear, visible, and reasonably likely to give timely notice of the danger. Note: the word latent is pronounced with a long "a" and a stress on the first syllable.

**patent danger (obvious danger)**  A danger that is apparent to an ordinary observer. A patent danger is a danger or condition that poses a risk of harm to a person, and that risk is apparent from the circumstances or appearance of the device, property, or condition that poses the danger or is obvious from the activity that gives rise to it. The measure of appearence is whether the risk would be apparent to a reasonably prudent person, not the individual who encountered the dangerous condition. A latent danger may be made patent through warning signs and signals that are clear, visible, and reasonably likely to give timely notice of the danger. Note: the word patent, in this context, is not pronounced as it is a patent for an invention but pronounced with a long "a" and a stress on the first syllable.

**dangerous dog**   *See:* dog, dangerous dog (dog bite or one bite rule).

**dangerous instrumentality**   *See:* instrumentality, dangerous instrumentality.

**dangerous product or unreasonably dangerous product**   *See:* liability, product liability, strict product liability, unavoidably unsafe product (dangerous product or unreasonably dangerous product).

**Darden hearing**   *See:* cause, probable cause, Darden hearing (informant tip suppression hearing).

**date rape**   *See:* rape, rape as sexual assault, date rape (acquaintance rape).

**date**

**backdate (antedate)**   To date a document earlier than when it is made. To backdate an instrument is to assign a date to it that is earlier than the date on which the instrument is made, whether by signature or otherwise. The effect of backdating is to create the impression that the instrument was made at a time earlier than it is in fact made, which may be acceptable in a replacement instrument, but care must be taken that the instrument does not give rise to fraud. The backdating of some instruments may void the instrument.

**Bates stamp**   *See:* stamp, Bates stamp.

**post date (post-date or postdate)**   To date a document later than when it was made. To post date an instrument is to assign a date to it, whether by signature or otherwise, that is later than the date on which the instrument was made. The effect of post dating is to delay the effective operation of the instrument from the date it was made until the date that is assigned. The post-dating of some instruments may void the instrument.

**dative executor or executor dativus**   *See:* executor, dative testamentary executor (dative executor or executor dativus).

**Daubert test**   *See:* witness, expert witness, Daubert test.

**daughter in law**   *See:* family, child, daughter in law (daughter-in-law).

**day**   A customary period of twenty-four hours. A day is a division of time consisting of twenty-four hours from midnight to the following midnight in any given place. (Minor fluctuations in the minutes of a day sometimes legislated because of astronomical corrections to the calendar are ignored.) Days are understood by custom to be ordered and named by days of the week and numbered by days of the month, although they can be counted from any event forward or backward. When a number of days is specified in a time frame for a short period, the number is reduced by non-working days, which are included in periods of twelve days or more. The first day of a period of days is not counted, and the period concludes either at midnight or the close of the relevant business on the last day.

**Constitution Day and Citizenship Day**   September 17, a day of remembrance and commemoration of the Constitution. Constitution Day, which is also Citizenship Day, is a federally designated day for reflection on the meaning of the U.S. Constitution and its ideals. September 17, the anniversary of the signing of the Constitution of 1787, is set aside by federal statute and by statute in many states for this purpose. Educational institutions receiving federal funds are required to observe Constitution Day within a week of its anniversary.

**law day (lage dayum)**   Any day when a legal obligation is due. Law day, in the early common law, was a day of open court when motions or hearings could be brought before the court for disposition. In the United States, the term is used in some courts as a date for hearings or trials, in some states scheduled twice per month. In some jurisdictions it is merged with or replaced by motion day.

In many jurisdictions, law day is the date designated in a private agreement for the parties, or one party, to perform a legal obligation. The date to close a land sale agreement, the date to pay the debt secured by a mortgage, the date to pay a creditor or one of several creditors, are each designated as a law day. A failure to perform the obligation on law day is a default of the obligation.

*See also:* sale, sale closing; day, motion day.

**Law Day USA**   May 1, a day of remembrance and commemoration of the law. Law Day is a federally designated day for reflection on the ideals of justice and the benefits of the rule of law, set aside for May 1 by federal statute and by statute in many states.

**motion day**   A day in the court calendar for the hearing of motions. Motion day, in many jurisdictions, is a day in the trial court calendar for the oral argument of motions in actions then pending before the court. Motion days are usually set by local rule for one day per week, with the argument on each motion taken in the order of the attorney's appearance that day. Motion days in federal court are governed by Rule 78. Longer hearings for more complicated motions are usually scheduled on days other than motion day, and very brief matters may be heard on other days according to the discretion of the judge.

In some jurisdictions, law day and motion day are merged in the court calendar.

*See also:* motion (movant or move); day, law day (lage dayum).

**de**  Of. De is a Latin preposition that can mean in English "of," as well as "from this place," "made from these components," or "regarding."

**de facto classification**  *See:* equality, equal protectionl of the laws, classification, de facto classification.

**de facto taking**  *See:* taking, de facto taking (inverse condemnation).

**de jure classification**  *See:* equality, equal protection of the laws, classification, de jure classification.

**de micromis party**  *See:* pollution, superfund, de micromis party.

**de minimus non curat lex**  *See:* lex, lex non curat de minimis (de minimus non curat lex).

**de novo**  *See:* review, standards of review, de novo.

**de novo review**  *See:* review, standard of review, appeal de novo (de novo review).

**de donis (statute de donis conditionalibus)**  The birth of the perpetuity. The statute de donis was a chapter in the Statutes of Westminster of 1285, which re-established the fee tail in England by making the disentailment of land in fee very difficult to do. This allowed noble families the better to tie their estates to their children, increasing the power of the family at the expense of the crown. Among other effects, the statute enshrined primogeniture, or inheritance by the first male child.

*See also:* perpetuity, perpetuity in land (perpetuities); feud, feudalism (feudal law).

**de facto**  In fact. De facto means that whatever is asserted is a matter of fact and thus is true because of events and circumstances rather than solely by legal decree. There are many data established differently de jure and de facto. Speed limits, boundaries, and rights may all exist according to decree as a matter of law but the legal significance of the decrees is much less than the behavior of officials and citizens, who recognize quite different speed limits, boundaries, or rights de facto.

*See also:* de, de jure; ipso, ipso facto; facto.

**de injuria**  Of his own wrongdoing. De injuria was the label for a standard phrase in pleading, representing the idea of an intentional, unexcused, and unjustified harm.

**de jure**  By law. De jure in contemporary usage nearly always means "as a matter of law." The term is Latin for either "by right" or "by law," although the differences in meaning are usually clear from the context in which the phrase is used. When an owner enters a property de jure, this is by right or by right of ownership (though this usage is now rather rare). When a statute creates a discriminatory burden de jure, this is by law or in the express language of the statute. De jure in this sense is usually juxtaposed with de facto, meaning "in fact."

*See also:* de, de facto.

**de minimis**  Trivial. De minimis is a Latin term for "of the least." De minimis refers to a thing which is of minimal and inconsequential effect, such as harmless error in a trial court decision, or of a nominal quantity, such as de minimis costs. In general, anything de minimis is not actionable or punishable in the law; in most jurisdictions, a de minimis violation is a defense to a charge of violation of a criminal law, and a de minimus breach or harm is a defense to a claim in contract or tort

*See also:* nominal; party, party to an action, nominal party.

**de novo**  To look at an issue as if from the start. De novo, Latin for "anew" or "from the first," refers to an appellate standard of review that requires the court to look at an issue afresh, without deference to the lower court's decision. An appeal de novo is a complete consideration of all of the issues, facts, and law in the case without regard for the findings made by the court that had previously heard the case.

*See also:* plenary, plenary review; trial, trial de novo.

**de-oraita**  *See:* mide-oraita (de-oraita).

**de-rabanan or de-rabbanan**  *See:* mide-rabanan (de-rabanan or de-rabbanan).

**dead hand**  *See:* perpetuity, rule against perpetuities, dead hand (the dead hand).

**dead-born child**  *See:* child, dead-born child (still born child).

**deadly force**  *See:* force, physical force, deadly force.

**death**  The end of life. Death is the cessation of life, either through natural means or human causation. The death of a person engaged in litigation is communicated to the court and to the parties through the filing of a Suggestion of Death.

*See also:* disability, civil disability, civil death; death, suggestion of death; demise; life.

**death benefit**  *See:* employment, employee benefit plan, death benefit; benefit, death benefit (death benefits).

**death knell doctrine**  *See:* class, class action, appeal of class action, death knell doctrine.

**death penalty**  *See:* punishment, death penalty, lethal injection; punishment, death penalty (capital punishment, execution).

**death sentence**  *See:* sentence, death sentence.

**death tax**  *See:* tax, death tax, inheritance tax; tax, death tax, estate tax, generation-skipping transfer tax (skip person or GST); tax, death tax, estate tax; tax, death tax.

**death warrant**  *See:* warrant, death warrant.

**contemplation of death (articulo mortis or causa mortis or death-bed declaration or dying declaration)** Thoughts on one's deathbed. Contemplation of death is one's own belief that one will die very soon from a cause that has already occurred. A statement or action made in contemplation of death, or articulo causa mortis, is a statement or action made when a person genuinely believes that death is imminent. Because the law presumes these circumstances to be unusual, statements made in these conditions are treated as having a high degree of reliability, thus being given exceptional treatment under the laws of evidence. Gifts causa mortis are valid if they are otherwise complete, though the gift may ordinarily be repudiated by the grantor if the grantor recovers and desires to void the gift.
*See also:* in, in extremis.

**death row**  Prison area housing inmates sentenced to death. Death row encompasses the cells and prisoner common areas in a prison that house inmates who have been sentenced to death.

**Do Not Resuscitate Orders (DNR Orders or D.N.R. Order)**  An advance directive that a patient not be revived. A Do Not Resuscitate Order is an advance directive made by a patient or qualified representative that a patient who suffers heart failure or another potentially fatal occurrence not be revived through certain means or by any means.
*See also:* death, living will (advance directive).

**living will (advance directive)**  A written declaration of health care decisions made in advance of incapacity. A living will is a writing that provides instructions regarding the declarant's health care decisions in advance of incapacity. Living wills, also known as advance directives, may take many forms. A proxy directive designates a health care representative and gives that representative a power of attorney to make health care decisions on behalf of the declarant. An instruction directive instructs either a representative, a health care provider, or both, of the declarant's wishes for forms of treatment. An advance directive specifies whether or not to attempt resuscitation or when to terminate life sustaining medical care. The primary difference between a living will or an advance directive and a medical power of attorney is that the living will or advance directive may be effective, whether or not the proxy directive is included or can be honored by the proxy, but the power of attorney depends on the designated agency to be available to act as attorney in fact. Hospitals and physicians may take such a document as clear and convincing evidence of a patient's wishes, and operations that would otherwise require consent may amount to medical battery.
*See also:* death, right to die; death, do not resuscitate orders (DNR orders or D.N.R. order).

**moment of death**  The time at which life ceases. The moment of death is the time at which the biological processes that constitute life — the respiratory and circulatory systems, among others — cease to function, leading to a permanent shutdown of the brain. The legal standard for defining the moment of death can differ from jurisdiction to jurisdiction.

**brain death (brain life)**  The irreversible cessation of control activity in the brain. Brain death is the measure of human death by the complete and irreversible cessation of function, or control activity, in the brain, often measured not directly but by the brain's inability to control the involuntary activity of other organs. Other criteria for death exist in medicine, but brain death may be the sole criterion in cases in which a person's respiration and circulation are being kept artificially functional.
Brain life is not the precise opposite of brain death. A person whose brain functions are discernable, particularly through consciousness or the management of other bodily functions but also through measurement of neural activity, demonstrates brain life.

**higher brain death**  The cessation of the cerebral functions of the brain. Higher brain death is the complete and irreversible cessation of the cerebral functions of the brain, without loss of the brain stem function. Higher brain death does not result in the loss of automatic and reflexive physical activities such as breathing, circulation, and reflex reactions. Some advocates of the use of higher brain death as the standard for the moment of death hold that cognition is the essence of what it is to be human, and, therefore, if this cerebral capacity is permanently lost, the patient should be considered dead.

**heart-lung death**  The irreversible stopping of the heart and lungs. Heart-lung death is the measure of human death by the complete and irreversible cessation of pulmonary and respiratory functions. In most cases, heart-lung death precedes brain death, because the loss of heart function prevents oxygen from reaching the brain and results in the cessation of brain activity.

**Uniform Determination of Death Act**  Law defining death as the irreversible loss of circulatory, respiratory, or mental functions. The Uniform Determination of Death Act is a model law drafted by the American Medical Association and the American Bar Association. The act defines death as either the irreversible cessation of heart and lung function or the irreversible cessation of all brain function, including that of the brain stem. All fifty states have adopted this model law in some form.

**presumption of death**  A constructive determination of death based on disappearance. A presumption of death arises when a person has been missing from all known domiciles, following diligent inquiry that has yielded no information or suggestion of the person's activities or presence alive for a period of seven years or more. Statutes in some jurisdictions have lessened this time requirement under certain circumstances.

**right to die** The patient's right to refuse treatment, causing death. The right to die is invoked in several contexts, most importantly for the claim that an individual has the right to use a living will or to control treatment to end life. The term is asserted in many cases to prevent state or medical interference with a claim of the patient or a patient's representative, and the argument is strongest in circumstances following unconsciousness that appears permanent. This remains a controversial idea, generally but tentatively accepted in such circumstances by the U.S. Supreme Court in the Cruzan case. The term "right to die" is also used, with less acceptance in the law, for a putative right to accept or assist in an assisted suicide.

*See also:* suicide, assisted suicide (aiding a suicide); death, living will (advance directive).

**simultaneous death**

**Uniform Simultaneous Death Acts** Law construing simultaneous death to be predecession for the purposes of the vesting of interests and rights. The Uniform Simultaneous Death Act is a model law adopted by many states that allows for a legal determination that one person predeceased another if that person failed to survive the other by 120 hours. Under this construction, insurance proceeds that might have lapsed are paid to the survivor's beneficiaries, heirs at law are established in closer levels of consanguinity, and devises and legacies in wills vest and descend that otherwise would have skipped members of families.

**suggestion of death** A filing informing the court of the death of a party. A suggestion of death is a statement filed with the court in a civil action that informs the court of the death of a party and identifies a successor to the estate who may be substituted for the decedent.

*See also:* death.

**vegetative state (persistent vegetative state or PVS)** The irreversible loss of cognitive and behavioral function. A person in a vegetative state has no cognitive functions, including consciousness and behavioral responses. Autonomic functions are performed, but there is no expectation that the person will regain functions requiring the cerebral cortex.

**wrongful death** The death of a person caused by another's wrongdoing, giving rise to a tort action for damages. Wrongful death is the death of a person as a result of the tortious conduct of another person or legal entity. A wrongful death action is a civil action for damages brought by the victim's survivors, regardless of a criminal proceeding that might or might not be brought against the defendant. Wrongful death actions are statutory exceptions to the general rule that personal actions do not persist after the death of the person harmed, and statutes determine not only the scope of the class of plaintiffs but also the bases of liability and the scope of remedies available.

*See also:* distress, emotional distress, negligent infliction of emotional distress (N.I.E.D. or NIED).

**wrongful death beneficiaries (wrongful death estate)** The group of statutory plaintiffs in a wrongful death action. The beneficiaries of a wrongful death action are designated by statute in each jurisdiction, and usually include the decedent's parents, spouse, children, and next of kin who were alive at the time of the decedent's death. In some jurisdictions, any of these people may initiate an action, and the proceeds are divided among the statutory beneficiaries. In other jurisdictions, the decedent's executor brings the action and the proceeds are distributed either to the statutory beneficiaries or as an asset of the probate estate, whichever is designated in the statute. In jurisdictions in which the group of beneficiaries differs in membership from the heirs or the probate beneficiaries, the group as a whole is the wrongful death estate (as opposed to the probate estate).

*See also:* executor (executrix); legatee.

**debar or disbar** *See:* lawyer, lawyer discipline, sanctions, disbarment (debar or disbar).

**debenture** *See:* bond, debenture (debenture bond or debenture note).

**debenture bond or debenture note** *See:* bond, debenture (debenture bond or debenture note).

**debt (debtor or creditor)** An obligation to pay money to another. A debt is a lawful duty of one person to pay money to another. A debt from one person, the debtor, to another, the creditor, gives rise to a claim by the creditor against the debtor, which, in the event of default, may be asserted in court to demand payment. A debt may be structured into a series of periodic payments, with interest or debt service allocated among the periods, or a debt may be an amount owed and to be paid within a single time frame.

A debt that is merely a debt that is owed, but a debt in arrears is one that is behind in a schedule of payments such that the debtor owes the amount of several periodic payments. A debt in default is a debt that has fallen so far in arrears that the creditor is justified in calling the whole debt and seeking payment from sureties or through seizure of any property by which the debt is secured.

In the early common law, debt was an action for the recovery of losses sustained when the defendant did not fulfill an obligation toward the plaintiff. Its primary distinction was a duty owed but not performed, which led to the defendant's damage. Debt contrasted with trespass, which was the writ for recovery for damage from an affirmative act that was forbidden. Debt, rather, was the writ for recovery for damage from the failure to commit an affirmative act that was required. Thus, in different traditions of Christian prayer, the Latin "debita" is translated sometimes into debt and sometimes into trespass.

In a colloquial, non-legal sense, a debt is any form of obligation, particularly a moral obligation by a person to reciprocate a benefit received from another person in the past. Such obligations may be enforceable in law as the bases of estoppel, unjust enrichment, or quasi–contract, but they are generally not a basis for an action in debt.

**debt bondage**   *See:* slavery, involuntary servitude, peonage (debt bondage).

**debt liquidation**   *See:* liquidation, liquidation of a claim (debt liquidation).

**abatement of a debt**   The reduction in amount of the money that is owed on an otherwise unchanged debt. Abatement is the act of a creditor reducing the amount a debtor owes for the prompt payment of the debt.
   *See also:* mitigation (mitigate or mitigating).

**account debtor**   The party responsible for repayment of money owed by another entity. An account debtor assumes, or is assigned, the duty to meet the financial obligations of a designated person or entity.

**bad debts**   Debts that are unlikely to be paid and cannot be collected. Bad debts are either debts that the borrower lacks the funds or capital to pay, or they are overdue payables that a business cannot expect to recover from the borrower. Debts that would cost the creditor more to collect than the debt is worth are bad debts.

**consumer debt**   A debt for a personal, family, or household purpose. Consumer debt is debt incurred for purposes not connected to a business or profits. Consumer debts are accrued the purposes of acquiring or paying debts or taxes on the food, shelter, transportation, support, education, and consumption by the debtor or the debtor's family that one would reasonably be expected to incur for daily or personal expenses. Consumer debt includes debts for luxury goods acquired for non–commercial reasons, although luxury goods and the debt to acquire them are subject to distinct treatment in the bankruptcy estate. Chapter seven bankruptcy filings that are primarily for consumer debt that amount to abuse of bankruptcy relief may be dismissed or converted to a bankruptcy under Chapters 11 or 13.

**contingent claim**   An obligation that depends on a future occurrence. A contingent claim is an obligation that becomes owed only upon the occurrence in the future of a specified event. For instance, one who co–signs a loan for another's benefit is legally required to retire the loan, but only in the event that the other party to the loan is unable to retire the loan.
   *See also:* contingency (contingent).

**debt adjustment**   A re–valuation of a debt. A debt adjustment occurs when an obligation is changed to reflect new circumstances. In a bankruptcy proceeding, a debt is usually lessened to reflect the obligor's inability to pay. Otherwise, however, debt adjustments are inherently made by the creditor.

**debt ratio**   The percentage of all capital represents debt. The debt ratio is the ratio of debt to the whole of a person's or entity's capital. Thus, a debt ratio of 25% means that the holder's capital amounts to 75%

equity and 25% debt. This is different from the debt–to–equity ratio, which is the ratio of debt to equity, rather than overall capital. Thus, as long as debt, equity, and capital are defined the same way both times, a debt–to–equity ratio of 25% amounts to a debt ratio of 20%.

**debt–to–equity ratio**   The percentage of an entity's equity that equals its debt. The debt–to–equity ratio is the ratio of a person's or entity's debt to its equity, representing how much debt a firm has for every dollar of equity. A debt–to–equity ratio of 25% would mean that for every hundred dollars of equity, there is twenty–five dollars of debt outstanding. Investors and creditors employ the ratio to assess the strength of a firm's balance sheet: the lower the ratio, the stronger the firm.

**debt service**   The total amount owed in a period or for a debt, including principal and interest. The debt service is the amount owed on a debt, whether expressed as the sum of all payments to be made over the life of the debt or as the amount of a single payment to be made for each period in which a payment is due. Thus, debt service may be spoken of as the debt service on a note, bond, or other debt, meaning the amount of principal and interest in total. Or, it may be referred to as the monthly, quarterly, or annual debt service, meaning the sum of the payments, for both interest and principal, to be made in the specified periods.

**debtee–debtor**   The amount owed for a benefit received. A debt is an obligation to pay a specified sum of money at a specified time in the future, due by certain and express agreement. Debts are traditionally dispensed with through payment, but can also be discharged through other methods, such as rescission or a statute of limitations. When a debtor owes debts to several different creditors, there may be a hierarchical structure as to which creditors will have their claims satisfied first.

**secured debt**   A debt backed by a security interest in the debtor's property. A secured debt is a debt in any amount that is subject to a security agreement or other means by which a security interest in collateral is available to the creditor if the debtor defaults. In the event of bankruptcy, the collateral must be used first to satisfy debts it secures before it may be used to satisfy the debtor's unsecured debts.

**unsecured debt**   Debt that is not secured by a security interest in collateral. Unsecured debt is any type of debt not backed by collateral. Common unsecured debts include credit card bills, personal loans, and medical bills.

**unliquidated debt (unliquidated claim)**   A debt in an amount that is not known. An unliquidated debt, or unliquidated claim, is a claim arising though the value in cash that would reasonably satisfy the claim is unknown or is uncertain. As a practical matter, the unliquidated nature of a claim is only material when the merit or value of the claim is in dispute.

## debtor

**debtor's rights**  *See:* repossession, debtor's rights.

**debtors' exemption (exempt assets)**  Assets that a bankrupt debtor exempt from the bankruptcy estate. A debtors' exemption refers to specific assets that a debtor in bankruptcy may exempt from the bankruptcy estate, thus denying creditors access to these assets as a source of payment for debts. Exempt assets are those required basic necessities of life for the debtor, usually the homestead and personal effects at a minimum. The Bankruptcy Code provides a federal list of exemptions, or a debtor may opt to claim the exemptions available under state law, which is limited only by certain limits on the state homestead exemption. The policy of the rule is to protect at least a minimum amount of assets for a debtor in bankruptcy so that the debtor does not become a public charge after the bankruptcy proceedings have concluded. A debtor may convert non-exempt property into exempt property before filing a petition in bankruptcy, as long as the conversion does not have the badges of fraud, such as assets covertly moved or hidden within exempt property.

*See also:* homestead.

**debtor in possession**  A bankrupt debtor under Chapter 11. The debtor-in-possession is a Chapter 11 bankrupt debtor, who retains possession of the property in the bankruptcy estate while the bankruptcy proceeds, but with limitations on the disposal of interests or assets in the estate that are the same as if a trustee had been appointed over the estate. The bankrupt debtor has a distinct legal personality from the debtor-in-possession, in that the bankrupt debtor may enter into new agreements that do not affect the property subject to the bankruptcy estate even during the bankruptcy process.

*See also:* bankruptcy, Chapter 11 filing (reorganization in bankruptcy or Chapter Eleven filing).

**decedent**  A person who has died. A decedent is a human being who has died, and whose interests or actions are the subject of an action, will, or other legal inquiry. The decedent's estate is then all of the property interests owned by the decedent at the moment of death.

**deceit (deceive or deception)**  A knowing misrepresentation of a fact or circumstance, intended to mislead another person. Deceit is an intentional use of words, silence, or actions that is intended to cause another person to believe something that is not the truth. Deceit is a crime, a basis for the avoidance of a contract, and a violation of professional ethics for attorneys, as well as an element of the tort of fraudulent misrepresentation. Deceit is an element of fraud, the difference between the two being that deceit is conduct that intends to mislead another person, and the deceitful act is completed whether or not the observer or hearer falls for the deception, while fraud requires that the person believe the deception and act on the false information. In other words, deceit is in the attempt to defraud, whether the fraudulent result occurs or not. Crimes of deceit are thus any crimes in which the defendant committed an act of deceit in the commission of the offense, although certain crimes, such as false imprisonment by deceit, incorporate deceit into the definition of the crime.

**deceptive practices**  Harmful business deception in breach of a duty. Engaging in a deceptive practice, or an unfair and deceptive practice, is an intentional tort caused by a person or entity engaged in business that issues a statement or causes some act that is intended or likely to mislead a customer, competitor, or supplier to suffer a financial loss or loss of a business opportunity. Though this description might appear to include most business practices, those within the scope of the tort include immoral, unethical, or unscrupulous methods that are intended to mislead or deceive another party in a business transaction, such that this deception causes damages to the victim.

*See also:* torts, economic tort.

**rascality test**  A test for conduct unusually unfair in a field of commerce. The rascality test determines whether conduct in trade or a transaction is unfair if it is the conduct of a rascal, a person whose actions, in the words of Judge Kass of the Massachusetts Court of Appeals "would raise an eyebrow of someone inured to the rough and tumble of the world of commerce." This test, now used in New Hampshire, evaluates the conduct of the party in the light of the considerations of the transaction, who the parties are, what their relevant skills and knowledge were, the nature of the putatively unfair conduct, and the likely harm of such conduct to the other party. Massachusetts itself focuses now on fewer but broader issues — the nature of challenged conduct and the purpose and effect of that conduct. Note: the rascality test is used to evaluate a claim of unfairness not brought under a more specific standard of deceptive practice.

**false advertising**  The false or misleading promotion of a product or service for sale. False advertising is the publication of advertising for a product or service that is either false as a matter of fact or that is sufficiently misleading that it is likely to deceive or confuse customers in some manner that benefits the maker or advertiser of the product or service. False advertising is actionable under federal law by the Lanham Act, 15 U.S.C. § 43(a)(1)(B) (2011), although statements that cannot be proved true or false and statements so bald or general as to be mere puffery are not within the scope of this prohibition.

**puffery (puff or puffing)**  Inflated claims regarding a product or service for sale. Puffery, or the puff, are statements made by sellers that no reasonable person would rely upon in assessing the quality or utility of a product or service. Such statements do not amount to the basis of warranty, and the eventual failure of a product or service to live up to puffed-up claims is not usually a basis for an action of express warranty. Still, not every statement made during a sales pitch will be excused as puff, so that seemingly informational statements regarding a product's fitness that could not be otherwise assessed by a buyer may be relied on by the buyer as aspects of the warranty of fitness. "Puffing" is the spewing of puffery.

*See also:* deceit, false advertising.

**decertification** *See:* union, labor union, union organization, decertification.

**deciding vote or tie-breaking vote** *See:* vote, parlimentary vote, casting vote (deciding vote or tie-breaking vote).

**decisionism** *See:* jurisprudence, decisionism (dezisionismus).

**declarant** A person who has made a declaration. A declarant is a person who makes a statement, particularly a statement offered into evidence during a judicial proceeding. The statement is nearly always a written or spoken assertion, although the declarant can make a statement by bodily actions, silence, or inaction, as long as the conduct can reasonably be interpreted as a positive assertion.

*See also:* statement; hearsay; hearsay, declarant.

**declaration** A statement that makes clear some matter, particularly rights or obligations. A declaration is a statement that provides specificity in fact regarding any matter that would otherwise be less clear. Many statements are in fact declarations for certain purposes, though a declaration, whether spoken or written, is generally made in some manner that demonstrates a deliberateness or seriousness in its making that is out of the ordinary, and the statement is considered a declaration owing to the circumstances in which it is made and the subject of its words.

In law, many specific forms of declaration are made. A condominium declaration is a formal depiction or statement of obligations among condominium holders in a condominium property development. A variety of types of statement that may be admissible in evidence despite other rules are allowed when the statement amounts to a select form of declaration made in circumstances of likely veracity, such as a dying declaration or declaration against penal interest. A declaration may be used to label predicate statements in a contract. In common-law pleading, a declaration was an instrument that served the function of the modern complaint.

**declaration of invalidity of marriage** *See:* annulment, marital annulment (declaration of invalidity of marriage).

**declaration of rights** *See:* constitution, declaration of rights.

**declaration of war** *See:* war, declaration of war.

**Declaration of War Clause** *See:* constitution, U.S. Constitution, clauses, Declaration of War Clause (War Clause).

**declaratory judgment** *See:* judgment, declaratory judgment (declaratory relief or declaration).

**declaratory relief** *See:* relief, declaratory relief.

**declaratory theory of law** *See:* law, declaratory theory of law.

**declination (declination letter)** A statement declining to do something, particularly to prosecute the recipient. A declination is a statement declining to do or to accept something. There are several declinations with distinct significance in the law. An insurer's declination is a denial of a claim. A party nominee's declination is a rejection of the nomination or the placement of the nominee's name on the ballot.

A prosecutor's declination is a statement that the recipient shall not be prosecuted for the exact offense in the jurisdiction mentioned, although a prosecutorial declination letter is impliedly subject to the later discovery of evidence independent of the cooperation of the recipient. A statement of immunity is generally a broader statement that is more enforceable as a matter of reliance than is a declination letter, although a court may enforce a declination letter to its terms if a recipient fully cooperated with government officials following its receipt.

*See also:* immunity, criminal immunity.

**declining balance** *See:* interest, interest for money, add-on interest, declining balance (amortized debt method of interest).

**decree** A declaration of law. A decree is a declaration made by an official according to a power granted to the official under the law. Decree is derived from the Latin decretum, and from that word, which is still essential in canon law, decree was often reserved for edicts by a pope, king, or executive. Decree was then more commonly used to describe a final order in a case arising in fields of law that owed particular debts to civil or canon law—mainly equity and admiralty in the United States—while a final order under the common law was referred to as a judgment or mandate. This distinction is fading but persists most in jurisdictions that retain a divided bench of chancellors and judges. Owing to these judicial customs, certain orders remain likely to be labeled as a decree rather than a judgment, even if the order is issued by a court of law, such as orders in family law like a divorce decree, decree of child custody, and property settlement decree.

**consent decree (final consent decree or interlocutory consent decree)** A judicial decree based on the consent of the parties in a civil or criminal action. A consent decree is a court order that results from a voluntary agreement entered into between the parties. Consent decrees can be ordered in civil actions as well as criminal trials, and represent the parties' consent that the court should decide the dispute in a particular manner. An interlocutory consent decree is entered during the proceeding or trial, and although the decree binds the parties for the issues it concerns, an interlocutory decree does not preclude all of the disputed issues. A final consent decree decides all of the disputed issues and is binding in future litigation. Either decree can be appealed, and, like a contract, will be upheld unless the appellant demonstrates that the decree is invalid owing to mutual mistake, misrepresentation, coercion, or other doctrines of avoidance. A consent decree differs from a private settlement agreement in that the settlement agreement is between the parties alone, and although the court may approve the agreement and as a result enter a consent decree, the agreement is distinct.

**decretal**   Related to a decree or a component of a decree. Decretal is an adjectival form of the term "decree," as well as a noun referring to a particular form of decree such as a medieval papal order by letter or a final judgment in Scots law. In its contemporary usage in American law, decretal usually refers either to a component of a decree, an effect of a decree, or an aspect of a decree.

**decretals**   *See:* canon, canon law, decretals (Decretals of Gratian or decretum gratiani).

**dedication**   The grant of a license, easement, or fee in land for public benefit. Dedication describes the transfer of a property interest to the use of the general public or for a charitable purpose, whether the property in fee is retained by a private owner, acquired by a public entity, or had been owned by the public entity but sequestered. Thus, a dedication may result in a transfer of title, in the creation of an easement held by a government, or in the creation of a license or easement to benefit the public or a charitable entity.
   *See also:* easement.

**deductible**

**deductible as insurance claim offset**   A value below which an insurer will not pay a claim. A deductible is the value that an insured must accept as the insured's responsibility for a loss prior to making a claim on an insurance policy for the insurer to pay the value of a loss in excess of the deductible. Thus the deductible is the maximum amount of money, agreed upon by the parties to the insurance contract, that must be paid by the insured before the insurer indemnifies for the remainder of the loss (up to the claim or policy limit, a maximum amount of total indemnity, which is also agreed in the policy).

**deduction from taxable income**   *See:* tax, tax deduction (deduction from taxable income).

**deductive reasoning**   *See:* reason, deductive reasoning; argument, deductive reasoning.

**deed**   A document by which an interest in property is conveyed. A deed is a writing that memorializes the transfer of an interest in property, usually real property, from one party to another. The delivery and acceptance of a deed satisfies the requirement that a gift or sale of property be delivered in order for the gift or sale to be final because delivery of the deed represents the delivery

of the immovable parcel of land. As such, transferring the deed is considered constructive delivery of the realty. At common law, the term "deed" was used more broadly to include a variety of instruments, including contracts under seal, indentures, and other forms of service agreements, but such uses are now rare.
   *See also:* conveyance (convey); survey (surveyor or surveying).

**deed abstract**   *See:* abstract, abstract of deed (deed abstract).

**deed merger or merger of deed and contract**   *See:* merger, merger of deed and contract (deed merger or merger of deed and contract).

**deed of trust**   *See:* mortgage, deed of trust.

**deed warranty or title covenant**   *See:* covenant, covenant of title (deed warranty or title covenant).

**bargain and sale deed (bargain-and-sale deed)**   A deed transferring property without covenants or warranties. A bargain and sale deed conveys property without covenants or warranty, dictating that the property is accepted as is. To that extent there is little difference between a bargain and sale deed and a quitclaim deed. The difference arises in that the bargain and sale deed is often filed to place others on notice of a sale prior to closing, and following conveyance a warranty deed will be recorded.

**habendum clause (tenendum clause or habendum et tenendum clause)**   The written power to have and to hold property in fee simple. The habendum clause, or the habendum et tenendum, is a recital beginning in English, "to have and to hold," followed by the exact nature of the estate created by the grantor in the grantee by deed. This clause should list conditions, reservations, and limitations on the fee, such as an executory interest, reversion, or remainder. If the clause is present with no condition, it is proof of fee simple.
   *See also:* fee, estate in fee, fee simple absolute (FSA or F.S.A.).

**quitclaim deed**   A deed with no warranty of title. A quitclaim deed conveys whatever title the grantor has to the grantee and, as such, contains no warranties. A quitclaim deed does not ensure the buyer or recipient that the grantor has any interest to transfer, or that the transfer of interests is valid or otherwise successful. A quitclaim deed is often used to quiet title by deeding a claim to demonstrate the claim is extinguished. It is also used in situations when prior title is unclear or in doubt.
   *See also:* deed, warranty deed.

**stranger to the deed**   A third party to a deed. A stranger to the deed is a party who is neither the grantor nor the grantee of the property. Under the common law, an easement cannot be reserved to a third party. A minority of U.S. jurisdictions, however, do allow a reservation or a dedication of an easement to a stranger, but in others the easement must be granted prior to the transfer of the deed, or it will be of no effect. An easement on the land that is not disclosed amounts to a cloud on the title.

*See also:* easement; easement, reservation of easement (reserved easement).

**warranty deed** A deed containing six warranties assuring the title it conveys. A warranty deed is an instrument of conveyance in which the grantor makes six forms of covenants to the grantee that relate to the quality of the title being conveyed. A warranty deed incorporates both present and future covenants. The present covenants are those of seisin, the right to convey and against encumbrances. The future covenants are those of warranty, future enjoyment, and further assurances. The present covenants, if breached, become actionable from the time of the conveyance, but the future covenants are actionable only from the time when a claim is made or their breach becomes known to the grantee for as long as the grantee holds the title. In a general warranty deed, the covenants apply retrospectively to the entire life of the property and are not limited to the time the grantor has owned it. A special warranty deed contains all six covenants, but they are restricted only to the claims arising from actions during the grantor's ownership.

*See also:* conveyance (convey); deed, quitclaim deed.

**special warranty deed** A deed warranting only against encumbrances created by the grantor. A special warranty deed includes covenants assuring against claims that arise from only the grantor's ownership of the property and not that of previous owners.

**wild deed** An unrecorded, misfiled, or fraudulent deed. A wild deed is a deed that causes a cloud on title, for one of several reasons. Most commonly, the deed was an otherwise valid transfer of an interest in property but was not properly recorded. Further, it may be a deed by a grantor whose interest arose by some means that was not properly recorded, so that the grantor is not found by searching the grantor/grantee index. In some instances, the wild deed is simply a fraudulent deed, one created by a party who had no interest to grant, or a putative deed created by a party with only a contested interest that is later found not to be valid. In any case, the wild deed represents a claim to the land that is not apparently in the chain of title and cannot readily be ascertained in a title search.

**deep pocket (deep pockets)** The wealthy party to an action. The deep pocket is a well-funded party or potential party to an action. A plaintiff with deep pockets may maintain an expensive lawsuit. A defendant with deep pockets is able to satisfy a large judgment but has more resources to defend the suit.

**defamation** Injury to one's reputation caused by another's false communication. Defamation is a false communication that damages a person's reputation. At the common law, defamation, originating in the action for libel, slander, or scandal, required that the defendant publicize a statement about the plaintiff that was of a defamatory nature to a third party. Publication required a communication in a form that was understandable to a person other than the plaintiff. A statement was considered defamatory if it exposed the plaintiff to "public scorn, hatred, contempt or ridicule," thereby lowering the plaintiff in the community's esteem or tending to cause others to avoid the plaintiff. Finally, persons who heard the defamatory statement must have understood or believed it to refer to the plaintiff. In the early common law, truth was not an inherent defense,

In most jurisdictions, this formula has been simplified so that defamation requires the defendant to communicate an untrue statement to third parties that in fact harms the plaintiff's feelings, business interests, professional standing, or other measurable interest, and the defendant acted either in negligent or intentional disregard of the truth to the contrary of the statement. Truth is a defense, and the defendant's evidence of the truth of the statement usually gives rise to a question of fact for the jury. Various privileges may give rise to a defense as well, particularly a First Amendment privilege to speak about public figures, which may be lost under a showing of actual malice by the speaker, or a deliberate indifference of knowing disregard of the truth. Prior permission or assent to publication by the defendant is also a defense that may be offered by the plaintiff, but usually only if the permission was given to the plaintiff or an agent rather than to the world. Punitive or exemplary damages are only available if the statement was made with knowledge of its falsity or intent to damage the plaintiff, and in some jurisdictions, are unavailable unless a demand for retraction was tendered on behalf of the plaintiff to the defendant and not honored.

*See also:* slander (slanderer).

*falsity* Statements must be false in order to make a claim of defamation. A modern defamation suit stands on the proposition that a person's false statements injured the victim's reputation. However, a defendant may contend as an affirmative defense that the statements made were in fact true. If the defense of truth is proven, there is no defamation.

*opinion* A stated opinion that has no claim to be fact is not defamatory. A statement of opinion, even if published to a third party and damaging to the plaintiff's reputation, will not be actionable as defamation. If the plaintiff cannot show that the alleged defamatory statement was one of fact, or of mixed opinion and fact, then the suit will be dismissed for failure to state a claim. Thus, an affirmative defense to defamation is that the statement made was purely a representation of the defendant's opinion. When pleadings are filed in a defamation suit on a motion to dismiss, the court will consider whether the statement could be proved true or false by a preponderance of the evidence. If the court determines that the statement cannot be found true or false, then the statement is one of opinion and cannot be defamatory.

**colloquium** In a defamation action, the allegation satisfying the publication requirement. A colloquium is the element in a defamation action alleging that a statement concerning the plaintiff was transmitted by the defendant to a third party. The publication requirement of a suit in defamation is satisfied if colloquium is properly proved.

**defamation of a private figure**  Defamation not protected by standards ensuring free speech. Defamation of a private figure can be pled as a tort claim under state law without the constitutional limit required by the First Amendment when the victim is a public figure. A private figure is defined as every person who is not a public figure, the latter of which have found notoriety through fame, office, or injection of oneself into a public matter or controversy. When the plaintiff in a defamation suit is a private figure, the ordinary pleading standards for defamation apply.

**defamation of a public figure**  Defamation of a public figure requires actual malice. The defamation of a public figure may be the subject of a state law claim for defamation if both the ordinary requirements of defamation against a private figure are met and the plaintiff can prove that the defendant acted with actual malice under the standards of New York Times v. Sullivan, 376 U.S. 254 (1964). A public figure is typically an individual who has achieved such fame or notoriety that the person is a public figure for any purpose. Still, an individual can, owing to the individual's interjection into a question of current public significance, also be a public figure for a limited purpose related to the defamation.

*See also:* public; malice, actual malice.

**limited-purpose public figure**  A person in the public eye only for a particular matter. A limited-purpose public figure is a person who is not generally in the public eye owing to fame or to office but who has garnered public attention as a result of participating in a particular event or issue, as a result of which the person is a public figure on matters relating to that event or issue. A person who is a limited-purpose public figure may not bring a defamation claim for alleged defamation on the matter of the person's notoriety without meeting the constitutional standard of actual malice, but the same person may bring a defamation action for statements not related to the same subject matter and need meet only the usual state standards of pleading.

**defamation per quod (double entendre)**  A statement that only potentially defames its victim. Defamation per quod signifies a statement that becomes defamatory only with interpretation to ascertain a secondary meaning that is reasonably derived from the statement but that is not the same as its more obvious meaning. Defamation per quod is the same as innuendo or insult by double entendre, a statement with an inherently double meaning. In order to determine whether the speaker is liable, the analysis usually turns upon the objective likelihood that the defamatory meaning would be the meaning understood by those to whom the statement was published. A defense to defamation per quod is that the speaker

made a good-faith mistake and did not intend the secondary, potentially defamatory meaning.

*See also:* libel, libel per quod; slander, slander per quod.

**defamation per se**  A statement that unquestionably defames its victim. Defamation per se is a statement that is defamatory on its face, a statement that is clearly injurious to the person who is the object of the statement. At the common law, the primary form of defamation per se is a statement that a person has committed a crime, particularly a crime of moral turpitude, a statement that a person has an infectious disease that would lead to isolation from society, or a statement directed against the competence, fitness, or trustworthiness of an individual related to that individuals' employment or profession.

**foreign defamation judgment**  A remedy granted in an action for defamation outside the United States. A foreign defamation judgment is a final judgment that is awarded in a court that is foreign to the United States, in an action or a other proceeding for defamation, libel, slander, or a similar claim alleging that forms of speech are false, have caused damage to reputation or emotional distress, have presented any person in a false light, or have resulted in criticism, dishonor, or condemnation of any person. A foreign defamation judgment is not to be enforced or recognized in a state or federal court in the United States unless one of two conditions is proved by the party who seeks its recognition or enforcement. The moving party may enforce the judgment by proving that the foreign determination afforded the defendant at least as much protection for the freedom of speech and of the press as is available under U.S. law and the law of the state in which enforcement or recognition is sought. The moving party may also enforce the judgment by proving that, regardless of the protections for speech and the press afforded by the foreign jurisdiction in general, the defendant would have been found liable or guilty of defamation in the jurisdiction in which its recognition or enforcement is sought.

*See also:* judgment, enforcement of judgment, Uniform Enforcement of Foreign Judgments Act (UEFJA).

**publication of a defamatory statement**  Communication of a defamatory statement to a third party. Publication of a defamatory statement—whether it is libel, slander, or defamation without regard to media—is the communication of the statement to a third party. Defamation is not actionable if it is only communicated to the person who would be defamed.

*See also:* publication.

**default**  A clear failure to perform an obligation. Default is the non-performance of a duty, whether the duty arises under a contract, a rule of court, or a general duty. Default is used mainly to describe a failure to perform a specific duty, which is undertaken voluntarily or knowingly, such as the payment of funds under a loan agreement, the performance of duties in civil or criminal proceedings, or the performance of duty under a contract. Minor flaws in performance or failure to perform inessential obligations related to a material obligation are not the bases of default, which is used to describe a complete breach of the obligation.

Default in the context of court proceedings means a failure to perform an obligation required, typically the failure of the defendant to answer the complaint or, occasionally, the failure of the plaintiff to prosecute the cause. A default judgment for the plaintiff is entered if the defendant defaults by failing to answer the complaint.

*See also:* judgment, default judgment.

**breach and default**   A default is a breach of a material term of a contract of such magnitude that the non-breaching party may void the whole contract.

**cure of default (curing default)**   Making good on the obligation defaulted. To cure a default is to make good on the obligation that was not performed as well as any subsequent harm caused by the initial failure of performance. The effect of a cure is to restore the non-defaulting party to the condition in which that party should have been situated but for the defaulting conduct. Thus, if a debt is owed and not paid and so defaulted and a foreclosure commenced against the collateral, the debtor could cure by paying the debt and reimbursing the creditor for the expenses associated with the initiation of the foreclosure. When a default is technical or procedural, curing the default may require performance of tasks specified in the same rules or procedures that were not observed, giving rise to the default. Thus a contract might contain provisions for conduct that must be performed or lead to default of the contract, yet the same provisions may specify remedial conduct that may be performed to cure the default.

**defeasibility (defeasible or indefeasibility or indefeasible or indefeasibly)**   The destructability of a legal interest when a contingency occurs. Defeasibility is the capacity of an interest or right to be destroyed, undone, or annulled. Its opposite, indefeasibility, is the indestructability of such a right or interest within any relevant time period.

A defeasible interest in land may be destroyed if a contingent event, by which the interest is defined, occurs. Thus a fee simple determinable is defeasible because the condition precedent on which the fee depends may end, thus ending the fee. Defeasibility is not the same as transferability, and a fee simple determinable may be alienated without destroying the fee for the reason of alienation alone.

Defeasibility implies a contingency and not a certainty. Certain interests are not considered defeasible because their defeat is certain, such as a life estate, which will inevitably be destroyed at the end of the life of the life tenant. Indefeasibility is usually a matter of logic or definition under the law. A fee simple absolute is indefeasible by definition: it may technically last forever. That the fee simple determinable may be converted into a defeasible fee and a contingent future

interest does not change the fee simple absolute's fundamental character as indefeasible in itself.

*See also:* fee, estate in fee, fee simple subject to condition subsequent (F.S.S.C.S. or FSSCS); fee, estate in fee, fee simple subject to executory limitation (fee simple subject to an exectuory interest or F.S.S.E.I. or FSSEI or FSSEL); limitation, limitation of estate.

**defeasible estate**   *See:* estate, interest, defeasible estate (estate subject to defeasance or destructible fee or determinable estate or base fee or qualified fee).

**defeasible remainder**   *See:* remainder, defeasible remainder, vested remainder subject to complete defeasance; remainder, defeasible remainder, indefeasibly vested remainder; remainder, defeasible remainder (remainder subject to defeasance).

**defect (defective or defectiveness)**   A flaw that reduces the value, appearance, performance, or reliability of anything or anyone. A defect is an imperfection, incompleteness, or error in some person, thing, process, or action that diminishes the merit or value of whatever or whomever in which it occurs. A defect in a thing, such as a building or product, may be latent (non-obvious after a reasonable inspection) or patent (obvious on reasonable inspection).

Something defective has a material defect. The mere presence of a defect in a thing, no matter how slight, does not generally make the thing defective. How significant a defect must be in order to render the product, place, or other thing defective varies, but in general, a defective thing has a defect that impairs its value or prevents its safe or proper use. Thus, for example, defective workmanship in a repair or construction is workmanship that is insufficiently performed for the material built to be used as anticipated, or that increases the cost of maintenance or diminishes the value of the resulting work beyond the reasonable expectations the recipient of the work had a right to expect.

**defect in parties**   *See:* party, party to an action, defect of parties (defect in parties).

**defect, birth defect**   *See:* birth, birth defect.

**defect as legal inadequacy**   A failure in an instrument or act to satisfy the relevant legal standard. A legal defect is the absence of something required by law for an instrument or action. For instance, a complaint must state the action in terms that comport with the trial court's rules for jurisdiction and venue; failure to do so is a legal defect in the document. A defect can be either curable or fatal. If the defect is curable, the document or process can be corrected, with the result that it will have the intended legal effect. If it is fatal, the document or process is seriously or substantively defective, and thus cannot be made legally effective.

*See also:* cure, cure as mitigation of damages.

**defective deed**   *See:* title, recordation of title, recordation of defective instrument (defective deed).

**defective design**   *See:* product, defective product, design defect (defective design).

**defective manufacture**  *See:* product, defective product, manufacturing defect (defective manufacture).

**defective performance**  *See:* counselor, right to counsel, ineffective assistance of counsel (defective performance).

**defective product**  *See:* product, defective product; liability, product liability, product defect (defective product).

**defective record**  *See:* record, appellate record, defective record.

**defendant**  The person against whom a civil action or criminal charge is brought. The defendant is the party who is sued by the plaintiff or prosecuted by the government. *See also:* plaintiff; prosecution (prosecute).

**defendant capacity**  *See:* capacity, defendant capacity, official capacity (representative capacity as defendant); capacity, defendant capacity, marital capacity; capacity, defendant capacity, individual capacity (personal capacity).

**defendant in error**  *See:* error, writ of error, plaintiff in error (defendant in error).

**codefendant (co-defendant)**  One of several defendants in the same action. A codefendant is one among several defendants in the same action, either because they are each served as defendants in the same civil action or because they are charged or tried together for the same (or related) criminal offenses.
*See also:* party, party to a contract.

**criminal defendant (criminal defense)**  One against whom an adversary criminal process has been initiated. A criminal defendant is a person or entity against whom an adversary criminal procedure has been initiated, whether by information, indictment, arrest, or any other initial process. A criminal defendant is entitled to independent counsel at all critical stages of the proceedings, including interrogation once a judicial process has been initiated. There is no difference in a criminal proceeding between the accused and the defendant. Note: statements of the defendant are different from statements of the defense, which are made by counsel for the defense unless the defendant is pro se.
*See also:* prosecution (prosecute); accused.

**third-party defendant**  A defendant brought into a civil action by another defendant. A third-party defendant is a party who is not initially sued by the plaintiff but who is brought into the case by the original defendant as a party who may also be responsible for paying any damages that may be found to have been suffered by the plaintiff.

**defenestration (defenestrate)**  The complete rejection of an argument or a person. Defenestration is the complete dismissal of an argument or doctrine. It may also mean a rejection of a person either socially, politically, or rhetorically. The term is an allusion to the word's historical meaning for throwing a person or thing out of a window.

**defense**

**Defense of Marriage Act**  *See:* marriage, Defense of Marriage Act (DOMA or D.O.M.A.).

**defense as in a pleading**  A denial of the truth or validity of a civil complaint or criminal charge. A defense in an answer, pleading, or argument is an assertion that the grounds on which the plaintiff or prosecutor alleges the defendant is liable are incorrect or unavailable under the law. A defense may be a general defense, such as a general denial, which amounts only to an assertion that what the plaintiff says is sufficiently untrue, or unactionable in that the plaintiff cannot prove the case. Some defenses may be of a form that must be specially pleaded and, once raised, must be refuted by the plaintiff. Another kind of defense is an affirmative defense, for which the defendant may have to provide sufficient evidence to assert, after which the plaintiff must refute it to win a judgment.

**affirmative defense (plea in avoidance)**  A defense that does not stem from a contradiction of the plaintiff's statement of facts. An affirmative defense is a ground for dismissal of an action or claim that does not depend on the facts raised in the complaint but on a new assertion of facts or law that would bar the remedy sought by the plaintiff. An affirmative defense must be separately pled in an answer, amended answer, or other responsive pleading, or it is waived. Examples of affirmative defenses include the barring of a claim because the statute of limitations has run, because of a plaintiff's failure to exhaust administrative remedies, or, in equity, because a plaintiff comes before the court with unclean hands.

**dilatory defense**  A defense asserted for no other purpose but delay. A dilatory defense is one raised solely, or at least primarily, for the purpose of creating delay or additional expense for the movant.
*See also:* dilatory.

**derivative defense**  A defense that challenges an element of the claim made. A derivative defense is a defense to a civil claim or criminal charge that rejects a particular fact essential to the allegations made against the defendant. Examples of derivative defenses include arguments that the defendant did not do, or know, or intend, or understand what is alleged or necessary to prove what is alleged.
*See also:* mens, mens rea (mental state); actus, actus reus.

**excuse (excusable or excused)**

**malicious defense**  The deliberate pleading of a meritless defense to an action. Malicious defense is the tort of raising a defense to a civil action in which the defendant has actual knowledge or calculated indifference at the time the defense is raised that either the defendant is not entitled to prevail on the defense or that the facts relevant to the plaintiff's claim make the defendant liable for the remedy sought. A defense raised solely to vex the plaintiff or to delay paying a lawful claim, or that must succeed only by reliance on perjured testimony or false evidence is malicious. Upon proving malicious defense, the plaintiff against whom the defense was alleged is entitled to the same damages as are recoverable in a malicious prosecution claim.

*See also:* process, abuse of process.

### specific defenses

**assumption of risk** *See:* risk, assumption of risk (assumption of the risk).

**entrapment (inducement)** *See:* entrapment.

**equitable defense** *See:* equity, equitable defense.

**excuse** *See:* excuse (excusable or excused)

**justification** *See:* justification (justify or justified or justifiable).

**last clear chance** *See:* negligence, last clear chance (last-clear-chance doctrine).

**self-defense (self defense or defense of others or defense of property)** The use of force justified by defending oneself or another from injury. Self-defense is a justification for threat, assault, battery or killing raised by a defendant in criminal law or tort. The defendant must have been under a good faith belief that the defendant's own person, or another person whom the defendant sought to rescue, was in peril of injury caused by the person whom the defendant threatened, assaulted, battered, or killed. In most jurisdictions the belief must have been based on objectively reasonable indications of an actual threat, and the defendant must have used force that was proportional to the harm intended by the injured person.

**Battered-Woman Syndrome (Battered Woman Syndrome)** A defense that past abuse excuses a later act by the victim. Battered-Woman Syndrome is a defense raised in criminal or civil actions for battery, murder, wrongful death or similar offenses, in which the defendant woman argues that the attack on which the claim or charge is based resulted from past acts of abuse by the object of her attack. Battered-Woman Syndrome has several variations, but the core principle resembles a form of mental incapacitation: a woman who is in an abusive relationship becomes emotionally subjugated and sees a violent act as the only means of self-protection, protection of a child or other person, or ending the subjugation. Battered-Woman Syndrome is not the same as the justification of self-defense in general, as the syndrome is a fact-specific excuse that is usually raised when a woman is accused of battery, murder, assault, or similar offenses against a male relative, spouse, or partner whom she alleges had abused her.

**castle doctrine** A person attacked at home can use deadly force in self-defense. The castle doctrine allows a person in that person's own home to use deadly force in self-defense with no duty of retreat. In jurisdictions that require retreat, if one is available, before using deadly force in self-defense, the requirement of retreat does not apply in one's home, which one is entitled to defend, as Sir Edward Coke said, like one's castle. Thus the castle doctrine is an exception to the limitation (in some jurisdictions) on the defense of self-defense.

*See also:* defense, self-defense, retreat (duty to retreat or retreat rule or rule of retreat).

**imperfect self-defense (imperfect self defense)** Homicide defense of self-defense based on a good faith mistake. Imperfect self-defense is a defense to homicide that allows evidence of a good faith mistake to negate the mental state required for homicide, typically malice, and reduce the charge from murder or first-degree homicide to voluntary manslaughter. It is therefore not an absolute defense but a mitigation based on a failure to have the requisite mens rea for first-degree murder. Thus a defendant who kills another person in the actual, but unreasonable and false, belief that the defendant is in imminent mortal danger from the victim cannot defeat the charge utterly, as if the death were justified, but may have the charge reduced as partially excused. Imperfect self-defense must be raised by the defendant, and its proof turns on the actual belief by the defendant that the defendant was in fact in danger, that the danger was imminent and life threatening, and that only the use of force in self-defense at that moment would avert the danger. The unreasonableness of the belief is not unlimited; imperfect self-defense is neither an alternate plea for insanity nor an excuse for vengeful or political crimes. Imperfect self-defense may be raised in some jurisdictions on the basis of rescue or third-party self defense, if the defendant believed in good faith that a person whom the defendant was attempting to rescue was in danger in the same conditions of danger required to assert the defense of the self. Note: not all jurisdictions recognize imperfect self-defense. Imperfect self-defense is allowed in some jurisdictions, particularly those that require an objectively reasonable basis, rather than a good faith mistake, for self-defense.

*See also:* defense, self defense (self-defense or defense of others or defense of property).

**retreat (duty to retreat or retreat rule or rule of retreat)** The duty to evade personal danger before using force against it. Retreat under the law means to remove oneself from peril or danger. At common law, a person who is threatened with force has a general duty to retreat before using force in self-defense, as long as the person threatened can do so without danger of bodily harm or death. Some jurisdictions have repealed this rule by statute, but even those that have not have imposed significant limitations on the rule. For example, one does not have a duty to retreat in one's own home or business, even if the attack is by another inhabitant of the home. Additionally, one need not retreat beyond a reasonable distance in the face of deadly force, and if the assault continues to be pressed, the victim is not required to retreat further. The duty to retreat is related to, but distinct from, the duty to use only such force as is proportional to the threat and sufficient to end it, because self-defense justifies only such force as is necessary to end the danger to the initial victim; it does not license the victim to kill the assailant unnecessarily.

*See also:* defense, self defense, castle doctrine.

**third-party guilt (empty chair defense or fellow servant rule or hypothetical person defense or SODDI defense)** Criminal defense based on the accusation of an unknown party. Third-party guilt is a specific criminal defense that admits that a crime occurred but denies that it was committed by the defendant. Therefore, it is a claim that the crime must have been committed by a person or persons unknown or a hypothetical person. There are many labels for this defense, including SODDI, or "some other dude did it," when no specific third party is accused by the defense. When the defense claims that a specific person perpetrated the crime, the defense is TODDI, or That Other Dude Did It. These assertions are necessarily variations on an alibi defense.

Evidence in support of such defenses is not always admissible. In many jurisdictions the defense must present facts not only that are inconsistent with the guilt of the accused but also that raise at least a reasonable inference of innocence for the accused.

**three wicked sisters (wicked sisters of the common law or unholy trinity)** Common-law bars to recovery for injured workers. The three wicked sisters of the common law were assumption of risk, the fellow servant rule, and contributory negligence. These defenses ensured that workers injured on the job were highly unlikely to have an action against their employer for damages or injunction against unsafe working conditions.

*See also:* defense, specific defense, assumption of risk; defense, specific defense, third-party guilt (empty chair defense or fellow servant rule or hypothetical person defense or SODDI defense); contributory negligence; risk, assumption of risk (assumption of the risk).

**national defense** The military security of the United States. The national defense is a statutory term that reflects the constitutional premise of providing for the common defense, referring to the broadest military defense of the United States in its territory, citizens, and possessions.

**deference (defer)** To yield to someone or something else, at least for a time. Deference is an act of restraint by a person or entity with the authority or power to act but who chooses not to do so in order to abide the result of another's action, or at least to await the completion of the other's action to determine whether or not to act. Deference in the law is essential to the functioning of the legal system, in which a single legal determination depends on a division of labor, so that a legal official tasked with one component of a decision must defer to other officials in their respective tasks. The allure of deference in allowing the official to evade responsibility for a decision or action committed to the office, however, endangers the legal system at least as much as the risk of failures of deference. The proper limit of deference may be the same as the proper scope of discretion, but deference, inherently, must fall within the scope of discretion: an official may only defer when the official has the power to act. As such, deference does not ultimately foreclose the possibility of action, as the deferring official retains an obligation to act if the official to which deference is given fails to act or acts unlawfully in some manner.

Deference, in general, is appropriate by one official or entity toward another, when the law creating their offices delegates a particular task or expertise to one and not the other. Courts defer to one another in this way, as well as to legislatures and executives, and legislatures and executives defer to one another and to the courts. This is both the essence of separation of powers and the basis of a reasonable division of labor among the creation, execution, and interpretation of law — recognizing that such categories are never perfect.

Courts in the United States defer routinely to one another, so that trial courts defer to courts of appeal and supreme courts on matters of the interpretation of law, and appellate courts defer to trial courts on matters of trial discretion, such as the admission or significance of evidence. Judges defer to juries on matters found by the jury as fact, and juries defer to judges on matters of law. In addition, federal courts defer to Congress on matters of legislative authority and to agencies, which are created by legislation, to execute and interpret the legislative matters committed to that agency. Both executives and legislatures defer to courts on constitutional matters and on matters in which courts have a customary expertise or commitment, such as their own rules.

*See also:* abeyance; comity; abstention (abstain).

**defer as delay** To delay or postpone. To defer a payment or obligation is to extend the time within which it is to be made or performed. Deference in this sense does not alter the person or entity responsible for making the payment or performing the obligation.

**deferred compensation or deferred revenue**
*See:* compensation, employment compensation, deferred compensation; income, deferred income (deferred compensation or deferred revenue).

**deferred income** *See:* income, deferred income (deferred compensation or deferred revenue).

**deficiency (deficiency suit)** The amount owed on a debt after the collateral securing the debt has been sold. A deficiency is the amount that remains due on a debt that has been subject to the collection or forfeiture of collateral that secured the debt, which has been sold and the net proceeds have been applied to the earlier value of the debt. A deficiency action, or deficiency suit, is an action to collect on the amount that remains.

**deficiency judgment** *See:* judgment, deficiency judgment.

**definite failure of issue** *See:* issue, issue as child, failure of issue, definite failure of issue.

**definition** The assignment of ideas or concepts to a word or phrase. Definition is both the result and the process of interpreting the ideas or concepts that are represented by a given term (usually a word or phrase). These ideas or concepts give meaning to the term that represents them. Definition in law is a process of inventorying the ideas or concepts that might be signified by a given word or phrase according either to the assignment of that significance by the act of a legal institution or as a matter of custom or usage.

In some instances, such as the assignment in a statute of a meaning to a word or phrase used in that statute, the authority of the statutory drafters and the legislature that enacts it is presumed to be very strong, though textual evidence of mistake or confusion may rebut such a presumption. Yet it is quite rare for a term to have a single meaning, and although the limited understanding that might allow a sole definition to be applied in a statute is possible in some circumstances, it is more often the case that a term has both a variety of subtly different, but related, meanings as well as a number of homonyms that are different words in the same form, and only context allows selection among them.

Definition is inevitably a process of engagement by the reader of a term or by its hearer, in which the person encountering the term must ascertain its meaning through interpretation, sometimes from context alone, sometimes by custom, and sometimes from the declaration of the author or speaker.

*See also:* ex, ex vi termini.

**degradation** *See:* pollution, degradation (anti-degradation or non-degradation or antidegradation or nondegradation).

**degree**

**degree of consanguinity** *See:* consanguinity, degree of consanguinity.

**academic degree** A title awarded to a student on the completion of study. An academic degree is a title and recognition of distinction awarded by an institution of higher learning. The great majority of academic degrees are earned degrees while the others are honorary degrees (or degrees awarded honoris causa), given to an individual in recognition of unusual scholarship, achievement, or service.

The earned academic degree is a title awarded by a school or university to an individual student for the completion of a course of study with sufficient distinction to merit the award. Academic degrees in the U.S. are subject to indirect regulation by the U.S. Department of Education and the various states, which allow accreditation agencies to determine the sufficiency of the degree programs of schools and universities, authorizing the award of degrees including diplomas, certificates, associates' degrees, bachelors' degrees, masters' degrees, professional degrees, and doctorates. A student must ordinarily be in an approved course of study toward a degree at an accredited institution in order to qualify for federal student financial aid.

**law degree** A professional degree in law and one of the qualifications to practice law. A law degree is any of the several academic degrees in law, including the Bachelor of Laws, Juris Doctor, Master of Laws, and Doctor of the Science of Law, most of which are recognized by the legal profession as an element of qualification to practice law. In some jurisdictions, a person must obtain a law degree — usually the LL.B. or J.D. — from an accredited school of law in order to qualify to petition for admission to practice law. In other jurisdictions, a law degree is not required so long as the person passes the bar examination, presumably after apprenticing with an attorney or judge. A law degree, however, is generally not sufficient on its own to allow a person to practice law; one must pass the bar examination offered, except in Wisconsin, which allows students who graduate from an accredited law school within the state to practice law without taking the bar exam through the "diploma privilege."

**Bachelor of Laws (LL.B. or LLB)** The first university degree in law. The Bachelor of Laws is the first degree in law, awarded by law schools, colleges, and universities for legal study. In the United States, it has been largely superseded by the Juris Doctor, which is the functional equivalent. Both represent the completion of the basic course of study, which is now three years, presumably following the completion of an undergraduate degree. The LL.B. is, however, the much older degree, having been awarded in medieval universities. The degree is abbreviated based on its Latin translation, Legum Baccalaureus. As the degree initially represented the successful study of both canon and civil law, the word law was made plural, done by doubling the "L." In some countries, such as Canada and South

Africa, the use of the plural form of law indicates study of common law and civil law. In some degree programs, the degree is in the singular: Bachelor of Law, abbreviated B.L. or L.B.

**Doctor of Laws (LL.D. or LLD)** A doctoral degree in law, usually given as an honor. The Doctor of Laws is, in the United States, an honorific degree bestowed both to legal scholars and to benefactors, leaders, jurists, and public servants whom a college or university determines deserve a solemn honor at their commencement. A few medieval universities bestowed an LL.D. in recognition of scholarship in law of an unusually high order, and the title is still used for this purpose in some European institutions.

**Juris Doctor (J.D. or JD)** The initial professional degree in law in the United States. The Juris Doctor is the initial degree awarded in most law schools in the United States. It is the successor to, and in most instances the equivalent of, the Bachelor of Laws. The Juris Doctor usually requires three years of study, which in most cases is not commenced until the completion of an undergraduate degree in any field. The J.D. was an American creation around the turn of the twentieth century, initially consisting of studies following an undergraduate course, or a longer period of study than that required for the LL.B., and coupled with a research requirement demanding some degree of specialization. With the conversion of the LL.B. course to an exclusively graduate J.D. course, the graduate, scholarly, and specializing functions of the early J.D. courses of study have evolved into the LL.M. and (quite rarely) the J.S.D. courses.

**Master of Laws (LL.M. or LLM)** The first graduate degree in law. The Master of Laws is a degree requiring coursework and research beyond the initial law degree, in most cases for one year, culminating in a research thesis or dissertation. The title is translated from Legum Magister, from which is derived the translation "law," which long ago implied a particular arena of legal study from the medieval courses civil and canon law. To master both domains of law required the plural form in the medieval manner of repeating a letter to demonstrate that it is plural continues here, and legum, the plural of lex, is abbreviated with the doubled l, or as ll. Though it is rare that the LL.M. candidate today study canon or civil law, the use of the plural persists. There are a wide variety of courses in specialized arenas of law, as well as courses in the general study of law as determined by the LL.M. candidate.

**degrees of murder** *See:* murder, degrees of murder, third-degree murder (murder in the third degree or murder-three or murder-3); murder, degrees of murder, second-degree murder (murder in the second degree or murder-two or murder-2); murder, degrees of murder, first-degree murder (murder in the first degree or murder-one or murder-1).

**delay** A pause in some process during which nothing relevant to it happens. Delay is a halt in some process or activity for a period of time of any duration, so long as the process or activity is presumed to recommence. Delay may be essential, as when a time for response to a pleading is incorporated into the rules of procedure or when a period of discovery is extended to allow industrious efforts made in good faith to complete the location and analysis of evidence. Unreasonable or dilatory delay is, however, an abuse of process in procedure. In contracts, when time is of the essence in the contract, a delay for any reason presumptively amounts to breach.
*See also:* dilatory.

**delayed absorption defense** *See:* absorption, delayed absorption defense.

### delegation (delegable or delegate or delegatee or delegator)
The referral of rights and duties to a third party. In contract law, the delegation of duties is the process of giving a third party the power to act as an agent for the original contracting party. The delegation of these duties normally does not eliminate any liability on the part of the principal; the principal remains legally responsible for the actions of the delegate that are within the scope of the delegated duties. Not all responsibilities are delegable; some responsibilities — such as casting a vote in a federal election — may not be exercised by anyone other than the person with that responsibility. Thus, the usage of delegation is this: a delegator delegates delegable powers and duties to a delegate.

**delegate** *See:* congress, delegate.

**delegation doctrine (non-delegation doctrine or non-delegation doctrine)** A legislature may delegate regulatory powers to enforce a statute but not legislative powers to set policy. The delegation doctrine both describes and limits the extent to which a legislature may empower the executive branch. A legislature can delegate power to the executive branch to execute the laws the legislature enacts, but it cannot delegate its fundamental power of legislation, which is non-delegable. Thus, if the legislature delegated powers of such breadth and discretion that the executive must engage in the equivalent of legislation to carry out its duty under the legislation, this delegation, and its enacting legislation, would be considered void as a violation of the limits on the legislature's powers. This doctrine can be applied quite unpredictably, but it signals the degree to which a legislature may properly delegate the power to make rules to carry into detailed effect the reasonable broad goals enacted into legislation.

**non-delegable duty (nondelegable duty)** A responsibility that cannot be contracted away or referred to a third party. A non-delegable duty is one that cannot be transferred to another party. Most such duties arise from a particular responsibility that is personal to its holder, such as a relationship between the holder and another person or the state. In this sense, a non-delegable duty is akin to an inalienable right.

**delegitimation**   *See:* jurisprudence, critical legal studies, delegitimation.

**deliberate ambiguity**   *See:* fallacy, amphibole (deliberate ambiguity).

**deliberate indifference**   *See:* indifference, deliberate indifference.

**deliberate release**   *See:* release, contaminate release, deliberate release.

**delict (quasi-delict or delictual)**   A deliberate act in breach of duty that causes harm to another. A delict is a wrong, akin to a tort, in which a person or entity commits an intentional act in violation of a general duty, which is a duty that does not arise from a contract or fiduciary relationship, causing injury to another. In such a case, the victim has a cause of action against the performer of the delict. A delict may be private or public, and there is some degree of overlap between minor criminal offenses and public delicts. The doctrines of tort in the common law are, to an extent, derived from the law of delict.

Many legal systems, notably Scots law, recognize an action for quasi-delict, in which the duty is breached through negligence rather than an intentional act.

A delict in international law is a wrong done by one state, or agents for whom it is responsible, to another state, other than by a violation of a treaty.

*See also:* wrong (wrongfulness or wrondoing or wrongful); tort (tortious); crime.

**délict**   A civil wrong that can be punished as a crime under French law. Délict is a civil wrong in French law, akin to a tort in the common law. Like tort law, a single act may be the basis for a criminal prosecution as well as a private cause of action. Délict is derived from delict in Roman law.

**delinquency (delinquent)**   Someone who fails in a duty. Delinquency is the state of failing in a duty, and a delinquent is an offender, a person failing to do or not to do what is required by law. Thus, a criminal is a delinquent, and a payment or promise not performed when due is delinquent. The term is used for an individual who has not performed some duty, particularly in reporting for conscription or in violating criminal laws as a youthful offender.

**delinquent loan**   *See:* loan, delinquent loan.

**juvenile delinquent (delinquent child or juvenile delinquency)**   A child who violates the law. A delinquent child (or a juvenile delinquent) is a child who commits an unlawful act, particularly the violation of a criminal law. The delinquent is variously defined as a minor, a child, an adolescent, any person old enough to have some degree of responsibility but still not having reached the age of majority, or a child between specific ages, such as a child between seven and seventeen. A delinquent child is not usually subject to criminal punishment but given guidance, treatment, or rehabilitation through the juvenile justice system, with the hope of encouraging the child to lead a more productive and law-abiding life.

*See also:* offender, youthful offender (juvenile offender or Juvy).

**person in need of supervision (PINS or CHINS or JINS)**   A child so prone to wrongdoing as to require state supervision. A person in need of supervision, or a PINS, is a minor of less than eighteen years, who is unwilling or unable to be controlled or responsible under the supervision of a parent or lawful guardian, a condition described as being incorrigible, ungovernable, or habitually disobedient. In some states, an offense related to minor drug possession or prostitution by a minor will also satisfy the PINS designation. The term in some jurisdictions is child in need of supervision (CHINS) or juvenile in need of supervision (JINS). A person in need of supervision need not have committed an offense, but the person's conduct has become known to the child welfare officers, police, or schools as indicative of a requirement of supervision. A minor adjudged a person in need of supervision may be placed in foster care, in an institution for children, or under the supervision of the childen's parole or child services system but not removed from the child's home.

The term "delinquent" has become widespread owing to its use in the Interstate Compact for Juveniles. The compact details the management of children on probation or parole who have run away from their jurisdiction, notes who in the finding jurisdiction is to return such juveniles and, as required by this agreement, who in the home jurisdiction is to accept the return of such juveniles when they are sent.

**delivery**   The transmission of a thing from one person or condition into another. Delivery, broadly, means to move something freely or into freedom, and in this sense we still associate delivery with deliverance, the sense in which a person is freed from bondage or captivity and the sense in which a child is born. The association in old law French of what was freely dispensed with the clothes a servant was given by a lord or master meant that the term livery acquired a sense of symbols of ownership that is still associated with the livery of a herald or of a jockey, and it is in this sense that livery of seisin denoted the ceremony of symbolic transfer of possession of an estate. From all this comes the modern sense in which delivery is most encountered, as delivery of possession.

*See also:* receipt (receive or recipient); gift, gift inter vivos (absolute gift or inter vivos gift); seisin, livery of seisin; delivery, delivery of possession; livery; transfer; tradition.

**delivery bond or discharging bond or dissolution bond** *See:* bond, forthcoming bond (delivery bond or discharging bond or dissolution bond).

**delivery of a child** *See:* child, delivery of a child.

**delivery of possession** The act of handing over possession of a property from one person to another. Delivery is the action by which the possession of a thing is transmitted from one person into the power and possession of another. The act may be actual or constructive: actual delivery is possible only when the thing is sufficiently portable to be literally handed from one person to the other. If not, as in the case of intangible goods, real property, or immensely large items, the delivery may be symbolic (as in the transfer of a deed, a key, or a clot of dirt). Transfer may be direct (immediate) to the transferee or indirect (mediate) through an escrow or by attornment. Delivery transfers possession, but is not in itself proof of transfer of ownership. However, when a contract pre-exists delivery so that the contract is performed by delivery, delivery then causes a transfer of ownership.

A usage note of interest: deliver is unrelated to deliberate, which looks and sounds similar. Delivery arises from the law French livrer for hand over or dispense, which in turn was derived from liberare or setting free; while deliberate arises from librare or libra for balance or scale on which arguments are measured, at least metaphorically.

*See also:* livery; delivery.

**actual delivery** The physical transfer of an item, intending in good faith to transfer its possession. Actual delivery is the physical transfer of an item from one person to another, with the intent of transferring ownership to the person who receives it, or on whose behalf it is received. Actual delivery is presumed to be the method of delivery under a contract for the sale of goods unless another means of delivery is specified.

*See also:* delivery, delivery of possession, constructive delivery (constructive-receipt doctrine); delivery, delivery of possession, delivery of gift; delivery, delivery of possession, symbolic delivery.

**manual tradition** Delivery by hand. Manual tradition is a customary term for actual delivery by hand of a chattel, deed, service of process, or other item. Customarily, manual tradition requires delivery from the hand of the deliverer to the hand of the deliveree.

**conditional delivery** Delivery that is not complete until the occurrence of an event other than physical transfer. A conditional delivery is a physical transfer of property that is not intended to transfer possession until a separate event has occurred, usually after the fact. Thus a physical transfer made in advance of the sale of the property transferred is a conditional delivery that only becomes final when the sale is concluded.

**constructive delivery (constructive-receipt doctrine)** Delivery completed by the conduct of the transferor and the transferee. Constructive delivery occurs in the absence of either actual delivery or symbolic delivery and when the parties act as if delivery has occurred. Thus, if a buyer and seller of a load of widgets treat the widgets as if they were delivered to the seller, even though they are still on the seller's lot and no other symbolic transfer has taken place, the widgets are constructively delivered to the buyer, though they are still not in the buyer's actual possession.

*See also:* delivery, delivery of possession, actual delivery; possession, constructive possession, constructive possession in property.

**delivery of deed** The transfer of a deed and ownership in the land the deed describes. Delivery of a deed is the physical transfer of a deed to land with the intent to transfer the ownership of the land. As land cannot be physically delivered, a deed is used to symbolize the transfer when the deed actually changes from the hands of the conveyor to the recipient and there is evidence that the conveyor intended to convey the land, the deed has been delivered. A new deed is usually created for the purpose of each delivery; it is not expected that the grantor will physically hand over the deed the grantor once received. The deed may be delivered into the keeping of an attorney or agent, and delivery will still be considered complete.

**delivery of gift** The irrevocable transfer of possession from donor to donee. Delivery of a gift is an actual or symbolic delivery that is uncontingent and irrevocable, made by acts that signal an intent by the donor to divest ownership. The gift is effective, and ownership transferred, when the delivery occurs with sufficient intent and without rejection by the donee. Delivery in most jurisdictions implies acceptance unless the donee acts affirmatively to reject the delivery.

*See also:* delivery, delivery of possession, actual delivery.

**symbolic delivery** A physical transfer of something signifying the property transferred. Symbolic delivery involves the transfer of an instrument or object that symbolizes the property being delivered, whether the property is real, a chattel, or intangible. A deed may symbolize title to the land it describes, while a key may symbolize the door to a building on the land (and so the total estate of the land and the building). Similarly, a car key may symbolize the car, or a safe deposit key may symbolize the safe deposit box contents that it accesses.

The use of a symbol for delivery requires intent that the transfer of the symbol in fact amount to delivery of possession or ownership of the property symbolized.

*See also:* delivery, delivery of possession, actual delivery.

***constructive delivery and symbolic delivery*** Symbolic delivery differs from constructive delivery, although neither constructive delivery nor symbolic delivery is actual delivery. Symbolic delivery is the transfer of some object or symbol in lieu of physically transferring the property conveyed. Constructive delivery may or may not have such a symbol, its hallmark being the behavior of the parties as if the delivery had occurred.

**demand for assurances**   *See:* assurances, demand for assurances.

**demesne**   A person's own property or estate. Demesne includes the whole of one's property in lands, or such of a parcel or tract as is under one's control. It is the Law French term from which "domain" is derived.

*See also:* domain.

**demise**   Death. Demise is a term used in legal drafting to refer to someone's death. Demise of land thus followed the death of a landholder, as land was for that reason transferred to the now–dead landholder's successor, either an heir, remainderman, reversioner, devisee, or other party who took at death. Thus, the term is still used loosely to refer to any conveyance of land.

*See also:* death.

**democracy**   *See:* government, forms of government, democracy.

**demonstrative bequest**   *See:* bequest, demonstrative bequest.

**demonstrative evidence**   *See:* evidence, demonstrative evidence.

**demonstrative legacy**   *See:* legacy, demonstrative legacy.

**demurrer**   A defense pleading contesting only the legal merits of the case. A demurrer is a defense pleading that admits to the facts of the complaint but objects to the plaintiff's legal conclusions and claims drawn from them. The demurrer is the pleading that seeks confession and avoidance. The federal rules and analogous state rules have replaced the demurrer with the motion to dismiss under Rule 12(b)(6).

*See also:* denial (denied or deny); motion, dispositive motion, | Rule 12(b)(6) (failure to state a claim upon which relief can be granted).

**demystification**   *See:* jurisprudence, critical legal studies, demystification.

**Den Haag**   *See:* Hague (the Hague, Den Haag).

**denial (denied or deny)**   The rejection or negation of a request or claim, or the refusal to provide something required. Denial is the act of saying no. Denial in trial practice is the act of rejecting an assertion, an argument, or a petition, motion or request. An attorney's denial in pleading is the rejection of an assertion made by the opposing party. A judge's denial of a motion or petition is the refusal to grant the order that was sought. Denial may also be the deprivation of some requirement, as in the denial of food to a dependent person.

*See also:* demurrers.

**denial in bad faith or wrongful refusal or tortious denial of benefits**   *See:* insurance, insurance claim, denial of claim, bad faith denial (denial in bad faith or wrongful refusal or tortious denial of benefits).

**denial of claim**   *See:* insurance, insurance claim, denial of claim, wrongful denial of benefits; insurance, insurance claim, denial of claim, bad faith denial (denial in bad faith or wrongful refusal or tortious denial of benefits); insurance, insurance claim, denial of insurance claim (denial of claim).

**denial of economically viable use or wipe out of use**   *See:* taking, regulatory taking, categorical taking (denial of economically viable use or wipe out of use).

**denial of insurance claim**   *See:* insurance, insurance claim, denial of insurance claim (denial of claim).

**denial as contradiction**   The rejection in pleading of an assertion made by a party opponent. A denial is a statement contradicting the statement made by another party in a pleading. In particular, a denial is a response by the defendant to an averment or claim made by the plaintiff in the complaint and operates as a defense to the claims made by or based on the averment or claim.

**denial as deprivation**   The failure to provide what is necessary. Denial may be a failure to provide, as when a court fails to provide due process of law, a parent fails to provide food, shelter, or care to a child, a doctor fails to provide medical care, or a captor fails to provide food, shelter, and safety to a captive. Denial in such circumstance does not require a request to be articulated. Instead, the duty to provide the good — and would–be recipient's need for it — are sufficiently obvious that the failure to provide is a denial, whether it is a deliberate refusal or a negligent omission.

**denial as mental state**   A contradictory state of disbelief of a known truth. Denial can refer to a mental state of conscious rejection of information one knows to be true.

**deodand**   The instrument of crime which is forfeit to the sovereign. The deodand was the name once given to the instrument of murder or the tools employed in a serious crime. The deodand was forfeit to the sovereign and was to be employed in appropriate and wholesome tasks. The concept of the forfeiture of the deodand is still perpetuated in forfeiture proceedings brought by the government to seize the instruments of criminal activity.

*See also:* forfeiture.

**deontological duty**   *See:* duty, deontological duty.

**deontology**   *See:* jurisprudence, deontology (deontic or deontologically).

**deoxyribonucleic acid (D.N.A. or DNA)**   Nucleic acid that is unique to each person's genetic identity. Deoxyribonucleic acid, or DNA, contains genetic instructions that are critical to the growth and function of every living organism on Earth. DNA is unique to each person's genetic identity, shared only by identical twins, thus allowing both the identification of cells and tissue samples as belonging to a specific individual as well as the mapping of family relationships.

> **buccal swab**   A common means of acquiring DNA evidence from the mouth of a witness or suspect. A buccal swab is a speedy, convenient, and minimally invasive method of acquiring body fluids for the purpose of the assessment of the donor's DNA. The swab is taken by rubbing a sterile cotton swab in the cheeks of the donor's mouth.

**dependency exemption**   *See:* tax, tax exemption, dependency exemption.

**dependent (lawful dependent or legal dependent)**   A person relying on another's support. A dependent is a person who depends on another person for support, particularly financial support, but also in some cases for different forms of support in daily life, such as for food, clothing, shelter, love, companionship, or nurture. A dependent may be any person who is infirm, whether through youth, age, or incapacity, and supported by another.

Certain relationships of dependency arise, whether or not they are between close family members, that may affect legal relationships, such as the making of a will or a contract. A fiduciary relationship is created when a person places unusual trust, confidence or reliance on another in a position of superior knowledge, skill, or authority, such as a lawyer or a priest. Such a relationship requires the fiduciary to exercise loyalty, skill, and care.

As a matter of tax computation, a dependent is a relative, usually, but not always, a child under the age of nineteen or a child who is a student under the age of twenty-four who depends on a parent for financial support, and for whom the parent may claim a tax deduction.

*See also:* tax, tax credit, child tax credit (child-and-dependent-care tax credit).

**dependent cause**   *See:* causation, dependent cause.

**dependent promises**   *See:* promise, dependent promises (mutual promise or mutually dependent promise).

**depletion**   The diminution of a resource in a parcel of land. Depletion the reduction of any particular resource found in the land. The removal of oil, gas, or other minerals depletes the stock of such resources in the tract from which they are taken. Soil that is degraded through agriculture is likewise depleted when its capacity for the support of specific crops is diminished, even if that capacity could be renewed through natural activity or the use of inputs such as fertilizer or minerals. Likewise, property with old-growth trees is depleted of them when they are harvested, even if new trees are planted, because the new trees cannot renew the lost old growth.

*See also:* waste.

**deponent**   *See:* deposition, deponent, absent deponent; deposition, deponent.

**deportation (deportability)**   The ejection of a non-citizen from a state. Deportation is the involuntary removal of a non-citizen from the deporting country. Deportation may be to any country, although it is usually to the country of the deportee's nationality. Deportation in the United States follows a civil proceeding brought before an immigration judge, who may order the deportation if a non-citizen is deportable. If the person is an alien and either present in the United States without valid authority to have entered and to remain or has committed a criminal offense of deportable type, that individual can be deported.

*See also:* deportation, DHS detainer (immigration detainer or notice of action).

> **DHS detainer (immigration detainer or notice of action)**   An immigration notice to release a detainee to ICE. An immigration detainer, usually described as a detainer, is a Department of Homeland Security form labeled a Notice of Action. It is delivered to a state or federal law enforcement agency, both giving notice to that agency that the Department of Homeland Security seeks to take custody of an alien in that agency's custody and requesting notice from the custodial agency prior to the alien's release, so that the Department can take custody and hold the alien for a hearing and possible deportation.
>
> *See also:* deportation (deportability).

**depose**   *See:* deposition, deposition as removal from office (depose); deposition (depose).

**deposit**   Goods or money kept as a bailment or credit until required. A deposit is a temporary grant of money or property to another who will hold it until it is reclaimed or until the depositor releases it to become the property of another. A deposit into bailment is the transfer of the bailed property from the bailor to the bailee. A deposit into a bank account is not, however, a bailment, because a bank deposit amounts to a claim for the contractual value of the amount deposited over time. Not all deposits into a bank are bank deposits, though, and a deposit into a bank holding box is a more traditional bailment, or special deposit, in that the property must be returned in a specific form.

*See also:* money, earnest money; bailment.

**deposit insurance**   *See:* bank, Federal Deposit Insurance Corporation, deposit insurance.

**bank deposit**   A transfer of money to a bank creating a claim by the depositor. A bank deposit is a deposit of money by a depositor into a bank, according to an existing contract between the bank and the depositor that determines the terms under which the account will be maintained. Deposits are added to the balance in the account, the sum of which amounts to a debt by the bank to the depositor, who is its creditor. Demands may be made on that debt according to the terms of the contract. Bank deposits of funds into an account are presumed to be general deposits.

**certificate of deposit (CD or C.D.)**   Written acknowledgment of receipt of money and a repayment obligation. A certificate of deposit is a written acknowledgment of the receipt of money deposited into a banking institution, along with an obligation to repay it, usually given by a banker to a depositor. The certificate might state the rate of interest to be paid over a period of maturity in the certificate, or it might have variable terms or more complicated features. A certificate of deposit may be treated as a security, although it is subject to federal depositor insurance protection in federally insured banking institutions, which in 2011 insured CDs of up to $250,000 in value. Because the interest rate paid on a certificate of deposit is typically under five percent, a CD is generally considered a conservative investment.

*See also:* bond, accrual bond.

**contract deposit**   *See:* money, earnest money.

**copyright deposit**   A copy of a recording or printed matter necessary to register a copyright. A copyright deposit is a recording or a copy of the best edition of printed material that is to be registered in the U.S. Copyright Office. A copyright deposit and registration is required to bring an action for infringement in U.S. courts.

**deposit account**   *See:* account, deposit account.

**deposit into court (deposit in court)**   A payment to the court clerk as a surety against costs or claims. A deposit into court is a payment made to a court, usually to the office of the clerk of the court, and is often required as a security from the plaintiff against costs that are likely to be assessed. Either a deposit into court or a bond is usually required before an application for a pre-judgment remedy will be granted, to serve as a basis for the compensation of the defendant in the event the defendant prevails. Payment into court may also be required from the defendant if there is a showing by the plaintiff that the defendant is likely to remove assets from the jurisdiction to avoid a judgment. A deposit into court may not be effective unless it is required by a court order or a statute.

**general deposit**   A deposit that is to be repaid in kind or by value. A general deposit is a deposit that is to be repaid in kind, rather than by the return of the specific chattel deposited. A deposit into a bank or into a common pool of resources is a general deposit, as the depositor has no expectation of the return of the specific funds or goods but does have a claim to the funds in the bank or the goods in the pool.

**patent deposit**   A deposit of a biological sample of a patented substance. A patent deposit is a deposit of a biological sample, such as a bacterium or synthetically produced cell line, into a public depository as a means of enabling the public to access it. Making this deposit satisfies a requirement for obtaining a patent for the substance.

**security deposit (damage deposit)**   A payment to secure a contract performance. A security deposit is a deposit of money or property to secure performance of a covenant or duty by a party to a contract. A common security deposit is the payment of money by a tenant to a landlord (or into escrow for the landlord) under a rental agreement in order to secure the tenant's future performance of the obligations under the lease, particularly the obligation not to commit waste and the obligation to complete the term of the lease. A landlord who enters at the conclusion of the lease by a tenant who did not commit waste but left the premises tenantable and undiminished except for ordinary wear and tear must refund the security deposit in full.

A damage deposit is a form of security deposit, held only as a security against waste caused by unusual damage to the premises or furnishings.

**special deposit**   A deposit of an object that is to be returned intact. A special deposit is a deposit of money or property that is not to be commingled with other funds or property by the bailee but to be held and returned to the depositor in the form in which it was deposited.

**depositary (depository or repository)**   A place in which, or a person with which, something is deposited or kept. Depositary, depository, and repository are synonyms in one sense, each meaning a place or institution into which something, such as money or valuables, is deposited. There are, however, differences in emphasis in this sense as well as unique meanings attached to each word.

A depositary tends to be an individual who accepts a deposit, a bailee without reward. Even so, a bank may be a depositary, and other institutions create or accept depositary interests, such as an American depositary share or receipt.

A depository is typically an institution or place, though this is not always the case. A depository institution is an entity, like a bank, savings and loan, or credit union, that accepts deposits and is regulated to ensure the security of claims made against the deposits. A bank that is a depository bank may also be a depositary bank, as there is no apparent difference in meaning.

A repository is a term for a place of internment of a body or the ashes of a cremated body. In international law, a repository refers to an office in which the official texts of treaties, ratifications, exceptions, or other diplomatic correspondence are housed. While a depository emphasizes the act of deposition, the repository emphasizes the security of the deposited thing's repose.

*See also:* security, securities, American depositary receipt (ADR); bank, depositary bank (depository bank).

**depositary bank** *See:* bank, depositary bank (depository bank).

**deposition (depose)** Out-of-court testimony of a witness transcribed. A deposition is the testimony of a witness, given out of court but under oath, subject to cross-examination, and memorialized in an official transcript recorded by an authorized court reporter. Depositions are available for use in court as evidence of a witness's testimony, although the content of a deposition is not necessarily admissible. Depositions are ordinarily used in lieu of live testimony in trial when a witness is unavailable to testify, but portions of depositions may be introduced for impeachment and other purposes when a witness who gave the deposition is on the stand at trial.

*See also:* testimony (testify); office, removal from office.

*admissibility (use at trial)* In general, a deposition is inadmissible at trial because the witness who gave the deposition is expected to testify to whatever evidence is in the deposition. Even so, the deposition may be admitted by either party if it is used to impeach or counter an impeachment of the witness's testimony. Moreover, depositions are available for use when a witness is unavailable for trial and the testimony is necessary to prevent a failure of justice. Such a necessity implies that the evidence is sufficiently material to either party's case that it might affect its outcome, and the content of the evidence cannot be attested to by another source of equivalent reliability.

*oath* A deposition is taken only after the deponent has sworn an oath or affirmation. A deponent must swear or affirm to the truthfulness of the testimony to be given in the deposition, just as the deponent would do if the testimony were given on the witness stand in court. The oath is usually administered to the witness by the court reporter. As with other oaths, the oath of a deponent may be dispensed with if the deponent affirms the truth of the statements to be made according to an appropriate formulaic statement required by the person administering the affirmation.

*written questions* Federal Rule of Civil Procedure 31 provides that depositions may be based on written questions provided to the witness in advance. This process allows for judicial review of the scope of questions prior to the deposition as well as a more careful and rehearsed response by the witness.

*See also:* interrogatory (interrogatories or propounded interrogatories).

**changes to a deposition** A witness may change a deposition prior to signing it. A change to a deposition may be made by a witness for any reason prior to signing the deposition. After signing it, however, changes may only be made within thirty days by submitting to the officer conducting the deposition, usually a court

reporter, a list with a statement of the change or each of the changes to be made, with reasons for each change. The officer then appends the list to the deposition. The court need not accept the errata, and the reasons must be not only provided but also sufficient to allow the changes into the record, otherwise, as several courts have noted, the deposition becomes a "take-home examination."

*See also:* erratum (errata or errata list or errata sheet).

**deponent** A person who gives testimony at a deposition. A deponent is one who testifies under oath at a deposition, or from whom a deposition is sought.

*See also:* witness.

**absent deponent** One who does not appear for a deposition. An absent deponent is a person who is summoned to a deposition but fails to appear at the appointed place and at the time.

**deposition as removal from office (depose)** To remove a person from office. To depose a person from office means to remove that individual from office involuntarily. Deposition can also be used in the context of causing a person to resign, provided the resignation is coerced and not voluntary.

**in perpetuam rei memoriam** A written deposition taken to memorialize testimony. An examination in perpetuam rei memoriam (Latin for "for the pepetual remembrance of a thing") was taken according to the common law, in equity, or in anticipation of an action and under orders of a court of equity or commissioners, of a person whose age or infirmity supported a concern that the evidence must be recorded or be unavailable at trial.

**Rule 30(b)(6) deposition (corporate deposition)** The deposition of a representative of a corporation or similar entity. A Rule 30(b)(6) deposition is a deposition of a representative of a corporation, government agency, or other entity, who is responding on behalf of the entity. The notice or subpoena must give reasonable particularity as to the subjects and actions about which the witness will be questioned, and the entity is required to send an officer or agent capable of answering such questions, if such a person exists within the entity.

**depository bank** *See:* bank, depositary bank (depository bank).

**depository or repository** *See:* depositary (depository or repository).

**depraved indifference** *See:* indifference, extreme indifference (depraved indifference).

**depraved-heart murder or depraved-mind murder** *See:* murder, extreme-indifference murder (depraved-heart murder or depraved-mind murder).

**depravity**   A deficiency of moral sensibility. Depravity is a lack of conscience, a disinterest in doing what is morally right or lawfully due, or in not avoiding a moral wrong or the breach of a duty. A depraved person is unfit of a position required by law or in equity to fulfill a moral or fiduciary duty. Thus a parent or guardian is inherently unfit to care for a child, and a depraved person is unfit to serve as a fiduciary or in a position of trust.

Depravity is related to lack of capacity but distinct as a matter of definition: a person may be depraved though a person is able to discern right from wrong or of discerning duty from breach. A person who lacks legal capacity is not generally said to be depraved, because the person lacks the capacity that is misused through depravity. Yet a person who lacks capacity is also barred for that reason from the same roles as a person depraved would be. Even so, when a rule would bar a person from a role as parent, guardian, trustee, fiduciary or the like on the one basis, the other basis may often be presumed to be included.

*See also:* murder, extreme–indifference murder (depraved–heart murder or depraved–mind murder).

**depreciation**   An asset's loss of value relative to the asset's useful life. Depreciation is the reduction in the value of an asset, calculated over the useful life anticipated for the asset at the time of its acquisition. Reasons that an asset or property depreciates include wear and tear, age, deterioration, and obsolescence. Both tangible and intangible assets can depreciate.

For income tax purposes, depreciation is recorded as a deductible non–cash expense. The higher the depreciation allowance deducted in a given year, the lower the taxable income and cash disbursements in the form of income tax.

*See also:* amortization (amortize); tax, tax deduction (deduction from taxable income); depreciation, functional depreciation.

> **functional depreciation**   An asset's decline in value owing to obsolescence. Functional depreciation occurs when an asset becomes obsolete or useless owing to changing conditions, business practices, or markets. Functional depreciation is independent of the physical condition, prior use, or continued usability of the asset.
>
> *See also:* depreciation.

**Deprizio doctrine**   *See:* bankruptcy, preference, avoidable preference, Deprizio doctrine.

**deputy**   An assistant to an officer, who has the delegated powers of that office. A deputy is any assistant appointed by an officer to carry out the duties of that office, with the exception of decisions requiring personal discretion that may not be delegated by custom or law. For instance, a deputy sheriff may exercise the sheriff's powers of law enforcement but usually lacks the administrative responsibility for the office unless one or another of these responsibilities is specifically deputed to the individual.

*See also:* sheriff.

**derelict (derelicto)**   Abandoned and neglected. A derelict is any abandoned property, meaning that the owner has relinquished possession, either voluntarily or by necessity, with no intent to reacquire the property. The use of the term to describe real and chattel property is now less common than it once was. This sense, which was once restricted to the civil law, entered the language of common lawyers from admiralty, being the technical reference for ships and other sea vessels that have been abandoned by their captain and crew or owner as a matter of admiralty law. Note: derelict is both a noun and an adjective. As a noun, it usually refers to a vessel or chattel; it ordinarily applied only as an adjective to realty.

In the common law, derelict lands refer to lands cast up by the sea through accretion or avulsion. Accreted lands, those that are slowly deposited, are the property of the landholder adjoining them. Avulsive lands, those that have been suddenly deposited, are considered the property of the government.

From these technical senses derelict has acquired a general sense that is sometimes found in legal usage, of property that is neglected sufficiently to appear as if it is abandoned.

*See also:* dereliction; ship, wreck, derelict vessel.

> **derelict vessel**   *See:* ship, wreck, derelict vessel.

> **derelict as outcast person**   A person who is not well integrated into society. A derelict is an individual who is not integrated into society in a manner appropriate to the person's age. The term, used in this context in a manner like its use to describe a derelict vessel, is often associated with a person who abandons others or has been abandoned by others, and it incorporates a suggestion that the person no longer has a reasonable measure of self–control. In most contexts, it is a term laden with harsh judgment and dismissiveness, although it may also be a term used to elicit sympathy.

**dereliction**   The abandonment of a thing, person, or obligation. Dereliction is the act of abandonment of a vessel, personal property, person, or personal responsibility. It is most often used for the abandonment of a vessel on the high seas by its captain and crew or at a mooring by its owner. A derelict vessel is subject to salvage. Dereliction of personal property is its abandonment to the public, such that any person who finds it may keep it. From this definition comes the phrase "dereliction of duty," which means failing to perform an obligation to such an extent that it is tantamount to the official abandonment of the office. In each sense, dereliction may be either willful or negligent; whether dereliction occurs is determined by the result.

*See also:* derelict (derelicto).

> **dereliction of duty**   Failure to perform a duty. Dereliction of duty, or to be derelict in one's duties, is the failure to perform a duty without excuse or justification for the non–performance.
>
> *See also:* breach.

**derivative**   Anything that arises as a consequence of something else. A derivative is anything that is derived from something else, that is, anything that is a result from a particular source and so the derivative gains at least some defining part of its character from the character of the source. There are many derivative relationships in the law, of which these are just illustration: A shareholder's derivative suit is derived from the corporation's right to bring the suit, and both the nature of the cause of action and the shareholder's standing are derived from the potential claim the corporation might have made. Derivative title is the nature of the title of a grantee or successor in interest, which being derived from a prior title can never be greater in form than the prior title. A derivative work is a work that is based on an earlier work, such as a sequel to a book. Derivative evidence is evidence gathered from information acquired from earlier evidence, and if the earlier evidence was inadmissible because it was acquired unconstitutionally, the later evidence is likely also to be inadmissible. A derivative offense is an offense, the criminality of which is dependent on the criminality of another offense, such as receiving stolen property, which is an offense only because of the earlier theft. A derivative as a financial instrument refers to a security that has some interest in another security.

*See also:* ancillary; shareholder, shareholder litigation, shareholder derivative suit.

**derivative defense**   *See:* defense, defense in pleading, general defense, derivative defense.

**derivative entrapment**   *See:* entrapment, derivative entrapment (third-party entrapment).

**financial derivative**   A financial instrument that derives its value from underlying assets or instruments. A financial derivative is an instrument, the value of which is based on the value of associated underlying assets or instruments. A derivative has no inherent value, but as the market affects the underlying value, the value of the derivative correspondingly increases or decreases. The most common examples of derivatives are futures, options, and exchanges. Examples of underlying assets or instruments are commodities, securities, loans, interest rates, exchange rates, and even other derivatives.

*See also:* asset; speculation (speculate or speculator or speculative).

**derogation (derogate)**   An alteration of prior law. Derogation occurs when there is a conflict between a prior law and a subsequent legal action, after which the effect or scope of the earlier law is reduced, though some aspects of the earlier law persist. Derogation is a change of the law, with the later rule replacing some aspects of the earlier rule. For example, a statute in derogation of the common law supplants the common law rule with the statutory rule, though the common law persists in every regard except for the common law that was directly in conflict with the statute. Note: a complete rejection of the whole scope of an earlier law is not derogation but is abrogation. Note also: derogation is sometime used to mean mere contradiction or violation; though this is not strictly accurate, the use is so common that care must be taken to recognize the drafter's intent.

**descent (descender)**   The intestate succession of a decedent's property among heirs established by law. Descent is both the process by which an heir takes property at the death of a decedent and the order of succession in which heirs are identified and their interests are ranked and divided. Descent does not take place when all of a decedent's property is disposed of according to a valid will, although the possibility of descent often remains for any interests that were not wholly disposed of by testamentary disposition.

**ancestor (ascendant)**   A parent or any forebearer of a parent. Ancestors are those persons who have preceded one another in direct descent, such as parents, grandparents, great-grandparents, and so on. Descent from a particular ancestor is the basis for many forms of identity in later generations, particularly for membership under tribal law in American Indian tribes and associations such as those for the decedents of American colonists or revolutionaries.

In its most generic sense, "ancestor" may be invoked to represent not just the direct line of predecessors of a person or family but the prior generations of a people, nation, or all of humanity. The term may also represent the basic facts of a person's lineage, and as such is often a euphemism for identity based on race or other social constructs. From a legal standpoint, there is no difference between an ancestor and an ascendant.

**descendant**   A child, grandchild, or further grandchild to any degree. A descendant is a child or that child's child, and so on, from the ancestor in question. All of the children, grandchildren, and great-grandchildren to every generation from one person are that person's descendants.

**class of descendants**   A category of family members defined by description. A class of descendants is a group that is defined by a label or definition, such as "my children" or "our children." Each label includes the noun or nouns and all of the terms that are reasonably read to define or further elaborate on the application of the label to determine who is and who is not within the classification. Thus, a grant from O to "my children" would be read more broadly than a grant to "my children alive at the time of my death" but is distinct from "my children alive and their children" or "my children, but if any child shall have died before me, leaving a surviving child or children, whether by birth or adoption, then equally to that child or those children who are then living in the place of my child." The last grant of the preceding sentence clearly provides both a more careful description of the class and alternative instructions for the management of gifts.

**collateral descendant**  *See:* heir, collateral heir (collateral descendent or collateral kinsmen or collateral line or collateral relative or collaterals).

**lineal descendant (direct descendant or lineals)**  A blood relative who is of direct issue. Lineal descendants, such as children and grandchildren, descend from one another from one generation to the next. Lineals are listed in a stack along the same vertical axis in the table of consanguinity or the family tree. There is no difference between a direct descendant and a lineal descendant.

*See also:* family, father; family, mother.

**line**  The line of descent from parent to child to grandchild, and so on. The line is the sequence of persons who have descended from a common ancestor, placed in the order of their birth.

**matrilineal descendant (patrilineal descendent)**  A descendant from a mother, or a mother's mother, and so on. A matrilineal descendant is a child of a given mother or in a line from mother to daughter to the present child. Matrilineal descent is a common means of ascertaining nationality or membership in a tribe or people.

In contrast, patrilineal descent is determined from father to son to the present child. Note: a matrilineal descendant may be either male or female, though only a female may be a matrilineal ancestor. Similarly, while a patrilineal descendant may be either male or female, only a male may be a patrilineal ancestor.

*See also:* partus sequitur ventrem.

**statute of descent**  A statute specifying the order of a decedent's heirs. A statute of descent is legislation, adopted in every state, that determines the means and order by which property descends to heirs as a matter of law in the absence of a valid will or a will that completely disposes of the decedent's property. Statutes of descent in different jurisdictions assign differing formulae for distributions among a single class of heirs as well as different definitions of priority among the ancestors, siblings, and descendants of the decedent.

*See also:* heir, haeres (heres or haeredes proximi or natus or legitimus or remotiores or factus); consanguinity.

**desecration (desecrate)**  An injury to something that people venerate. Desecration, generally, is an injury to something held sacred. In law it is either the physical damage, pollution, or improper use of a place or thing with which people, or a group of people, have an emotional bond similar to that which a religious devotee would ascribe to a sacred space or object. Thus, injury to or ill use of a corpse, a churchyard, and a national flag have all been depicted as desecration.

Attempts to make the desecration of such objects criminal failed when desecration was described in vague terms, like contemptuous treatment or disrespect, and efforts to define improper use have not been successful in the criminal context. When desecration is more closely defined by specific actions, such as littering on a grave or the writing of graffiti in a church, however, such problems diminish. Civil claims for desecration may be brought as breach of contract against funeral homes and cemeteries or as trespass generally.

*See also:* sacrilege; robbery, grave robbing (grave robbery).

**desecration of a venerated object**  *See:* corpse, interference with a corpse (desecration of a venerated object).

**desegregation**  *See:* segregation, desegregation (integration).

**desertion (desert or deserter)**  Abandonment of a duty or the people to whom the duty is owed. Desertion occurs when a person responsible for the performance of the duty stops performing it with no intent to continue to perform or ever return to it.

**military desertion**  Absence from duty without leave and with no intent to return. Desertion is an absence of a member of a military service from a post of duty without leave and with the intention not to return.

**design defect**  *See:* product, defective product, design defect (defective design).

**designation**  The assignment by reference of an interest in an instrument. A designation is a specific assignment of some interest in an instrument creating a gift or grant to a specific recipient, whether the recipient is named or only described. A designation may occur in many instruments, such as a devise, bequest, or legacy in a will; a benefit in an insurance policy; or a receipt of a payment in a contract, to a particular recipient, whether or not the recipient is named. Designation is more common, and most narrowly construed, in a will. In all cases, the recipient must be uniquely identified by the words of the assignment in the context of their creation, in order for the designation to be valid.

**designated public forum**  *See:* speech, freedom of speech, forum, public forum, designated public forum.

**despot (despotism)**  An absolute ruler. A despot is a tyrannical ruler, who exercises supreme, unchallenged control over some dominion. Despots consolidate power in themselves, generally refuse to tolerate any dissent, and use their power to benefit themselves rather than their subjects.

*See also:* government, forms of government, fascism.

**destination contract**  *See:* contract, specific contracts, destination contract.

**destroyed will**  *See:* will, last will and testament, lost will (destroyed will).

**destructibility rule** *See:* remainder, contingent remainder, rule of the destructibility of contingent remainders (destructibility rule).

**destructible trust** *See:* trust, destructible trust (indestructible trust).

**destruction** Complete ruin. Destruction is the general term for the disorganization or breaking apart of a thing, person, capacity, place, or organization, rendering its use impossible or ending its existence as a whole. The term usually implies a sudden or violent act, but as this is not an element of its meaning, destruction can be gradual or orderly. Destruction is perhaps best understood as the antonym of construction.

*See also:* goods | 1. destruction of identified goods; weapon, weapon of mass destruction (WMD).

**desuetude** The obsolescence of a law through non-enforcement. Desuetude is a form of obsolescence marked particularly by neglect or disuse of a thing. In law, desuetude may be used to describe a law, especially a criminal prohibition, that has been long unenforced. In Scots law, desuetude is a doctrine of abandonment of a statute that has been unenforced for a long time. In the United States, a similar argument can made that a statute or other prohibition has been abandoned when there has been an utter lack of enforcement of the statute or prohibition for a significant period of time, during which the statute or prohibition is widely known to be violated and the violations are ignored. Thus, the argument goes, a revival of the prohibition would lack notice or rationale, and prosecuting an individual under the statute or prohibition could amount to a violation of due process of law. That said, while this argument is often made, it very rarely succeeds.

*See also:* time.

**detainer** The involuntary detention of a person, or the temporary seizure of property. Detainer is the act of holding a person involuntarily or of withholding property from its owner without consent. Once it has complied with constitutional and statutory requirements, the government can lawfully detain a person or property for a period of time without committing false imprisonment or giving rise to an action for habeas corpus, though the person may have legal recourse against the party that effectuated the action if the detention or seizure is unlawful. Technically, a person is detained but goods are distrained, though this distinction is less common now.

*See also:* seizure (seize); arrest.

**detention (detain or detainee)** Keeping a person or thing in custody so that he, she, or it cannot be removed without permission. Detention is the act of keeping something or someone from movement. Detention in law occurs in many contexts: natural, as is the result of storm or injury; voluntary, as is the result of civil commitment; involuntary and civil, as is the result of an attachment; and involuntary and police or

criminal, as is the case in pre-trial custody. Detention of a person without legal authority, however, is kidnapping, giving rise to both criminal and civil liability. A detainee may challenge the lawfulness of the detention by a public official by filing a petition for habeas corpus.

*See also:* embezzlement; prisoner (inmate).

**arbitrary detention** A detention that is not justified under the law. An arbitrary detention is the detention by police of any person without a legally sufficient basis for the detainment. Arbitrary detention gives rise to an action for habeas corpus as well as a constitutional tort under the Fourth Amendment, and, if prolonged, is a violation of international law actionable under the Alien Tort Claims Act.

**pretrial detention** The detention of a criminal defendant before trial. Pretrial detention is the maintenance of a criminal defendant in detention prior to trial on one or more of several independent grounds: the defendant has been denied bail because the court found the defendant posed a danger to others or a risk of flight; the defendant could not afford bail; or bail was granted but revoked.

**preventive detention (confinement after acquittal on grounds of insanity)** The incarceration of an unusually dangerous detainee for an indefinite period of time. Preventive detention occurs when a person who is found to pose an unusual risk of harm to others is held in custody until the basis for the danger posed is thought to have abated. The detention must result from either a criminal hearing or a civil hearing with safeguards to ensure that the detention does not have punitive goals. In some jurisdictions, confinement in a manner equal to preventive detention is required of a person accused of a violent crime who is acquitted on the basis of insanity. The preventive detention of aliens pending deportation is limited to a reasonable period of time.

**prolonged detention** A detention that lasts longer than is justified. A prolonged detention is the detention by police of any person for a period of time that unreasonably exceeds the justification for the detainment. An unduly prolonged detention gives rise to a claim for release through habeas corpus as well as forming the basis for an action in tort under the Fourth Amendment. A prolonged and arbitrary detention is actionable under the Alien Tort Claims Act.

**determinability (determinable)** Able to be destroyed. Anything that is determinable is something that may be determined, which, in the case of a legal interest, is something contingent that is destroyed if the contingency is satisfied. For instance, a fee simple determinable ends if its contingency fails.

**deterrence** Inhibiting someone from committing some act or form of act. Deterrence is the function of law to restrain each person from conduct that violates the law. Deterrence is thus a reason for officials to set punishments or penalties at a level that is believed to be sufficient to cause such restraint. Deterrence is thought to require greater criminal penalties for repeat offenders, as repeat offenders are more likely to commit a crime yet again. Likewise, it justifies greater penalties in tort for knowing and willful acts.

**deterrence theory**   The law should discourage people from doing harm or wrong. Deterrence theory is a justification for laws, particularly in criminal law and torts, that the law should discourage people from doing wrong, however wrong is defined. The conduct to be deterred is a matter of great debate, the leading categories being conduct that is thought to be immoral, wrongful, harmful, or economically inefficient, but the idea that law can deter people from some conduct is common to all of these arguments. In European and American jurisprudence, deterrence is usually seen as the opposing doctrine to retributivism or corrective justice, which is not, of course, the only non–deterrent theory, others including the theories of rehabilitation and reintegration, which receive greater emphasis in other systems.

*See also:* retribution.

**general deterrence**   The deterrence of people in general from committing a wrong. General deterrence is the use of the threat of legal punishment not to punish the wrongdoer but to use the wrongdoer as an example to discourage others from similar conduct. General deterrence is thus a basis for setting punishments, including punitive damages, as well as determining the sentencing of a criminal or awarding punitive damages against a tortfeasor. This is the basis for two great cliches of prosecutorial rhetoric, plaintiff's closing arguments, and legal journalism, that a sentence "sends a message," proving that "crime does not pay."

**specific deterrence (personal deterrence)**   The deterrence of one wrongdoer from repeating the wrong. Specific deterrence is the discouragement of an individual criminal or tortfeasor from repeating the type of wrong that the wrongdoer is known to have done. As a matter of policy, a criminal sentence or punitive civil judgment ought to be of sufficient severity to ensure specific deterrence, and specific deterrence is a more important goal of criminal justice than is general deterrence.

*See also:* deterrence, general deterrence.

**deterrent punishment**   *See:* punishment, deterrent punishment (exemplary punishment or deterrent theory or exemplary theory).

**detinue**   An action to recover personal property wrongly held by another. Detinue is a remedy and a common–law form of action for the recovery of personal property either owned by the plaintiff or to which the plaintiff has a right of immediate possession that is held in the possession of another person without a legal right to do so, although the other person acquired possession in a lawful manner. A bailee who refuses to return a bailment lawfully established and concluded but for the return of the property is liable for detinue

for its return. In many jurisdictions, including England, detinue has been abolished, and in most U.S. jurisdictions, replevin or claim and recovery are now used instead. In some jurisdictions, detinue persists as either a common–law or statutory action.

*See also:* trover; replevin (writ of replevin or replevy or repleviable).

**detrimental reliance**   *See:* reliance, detrimental reliance.

**deus**   God. Deus means God Almighty in nearly every legal usage encountered. Even so, in classical Latin, and in some poetic uses in later legal Latin, it may stand for a particularly noble form of human lord or hero.

### development

**developer**   The creator of a housing or commercial development. A developer is an entity or person that buys or acquires rights to create buildings, landscape, and infrastructure for any land use other than for the developer's sole enjoyment. Developers create a variety of kinds of developments, from shopping centers, suburban neighborhoods, and office blocks to parks and natural habitats. Developers organize financing, ensure regulatory compliance, and develop marketing and sales for the development, and are involved in the designing, constructing, and the hiring of architects, engineers, and contractors to build the actual structures.

**development of land (develop)**   The preparation and use of land for an economic purpose. Development is the use of land for human purposes, especially to generate wealth through any means other than extraction or severance. Development may include acquisition as well as the preparation and use of land for the construction or location of buildings or amenities upon it, usually increasing the density of human activity upon it.

**developmental disability**   *See:* disability, personal disability, developmental disability.

**deviance (deviancy or deviant)**   Varying from the required or the customary. Deviance is a variation from what is expected or required, and in the law it describes either any departure by a citizen from a lawful duty, particularly the commission of a criminal act or an act against public morals, or any departure by an official from the boundaries of discretion or the customary exercise of discretion associated with that office. Deviance is particularly associated with sexual conduct that violates the law.

**devil's bargain**   *See:* choice, devil's bargain.

**devise (devisable or devisee or deviser or devisor)**   A bequest of real or other property by will. A devise, in its most technical sense in the common law, is a grant of real property through a last will and testament. In contemporary legal usage following the

Uniform Probate Code, however, it is proper to speak of any bequest by a last will and testament as a devise. Thus the act of leaving property to someone in a will is also called devising the property. The devisor is the testator, and the devisee is the recipient. Lands or other property capable of being devised are thus subject to devisement, and so are devisable.

*See also:* inheritance (inherit).

*devise and legacy* At common law a devise is of realty, and a legacy is of personalty; under the UPC, a devise may be of either. A will governed by the common law uses the term devise to represent a testamentary gift of real property and the term legacy to represent a gift of chattels, intangibles, and other personal property. The Uniform Probate Code has done away with this distinction, using devise to mean a testamentary disposition of either real or personal property.

*See also:* legacy, abatement of a legacy.

*order of devises* Estate assets are applied first to specific devises, then to general devises, then to residual devises.

*See also:* devise, specific devise; devise, general devise.

**abatement of a devise** Reduction of a devise to pay the debts on a specific or more important devise. An abatement of a devise is the action of an executor in taking all, or part, of a gift of a lower-priority devise or devises in a will in order to fulfill devises that are higher in the hierarchy. An abatement of a devise is effectively the same as an abatement of a legacy.

*See also:* legacy, abatement of a legacy.

**conditional devise** A devise that becomes effective if a prior condition is met. A conditional devise is a devise that depends for its full vesting in the devisee upon the satisfaction of a condition that might or might not occur. The same effect is given to a conditional devise as is given to a conditional legacy.

*See also:* legacy, conditional legacy (contingent legacy).

**executory devise** An executory interest created by testamentary disposition. An executory devise is a grant by testamentary disposition of a future interest in the devisee that will become possessory upon the occurence of a specified, contingent event. Executory devises, like all executory interests, are subject to the rule against perpetuities and must vest or fail within twenty-one years of a life in being at the time of the making of the will.

*See also:* interest, executory interest (E.I. or EI or executory bequest).

**general devise** A gift to be paid out of the general estate. A general devise, or a devise that is general, is a devise specified in a will that may be satisfied by money or any thing of value, rather than by the transfer of a specified and unique item or fund.

*See also:* devise | order of devises.

**specific devise** The devise of a unique property that is specially designated in a will. A specific devise, or a devise that is specific, is a grant to a specific devisee of property or an asset that is distinct from the testator's

assets generally and can be clearly identified. The grant need not be perfect in its description but must be sufficiently clear that there is no ambiguity as which of the estate's assets is meant.

*See also:* devise | order of devises.

**dezisionismus** *See:* jurisprudence, decisionism (dezisionismus).

**dhimmi (zhimmi)** A non-Muslim in a country subject to Islamic government. A dhimmi is a non-Muslim in a country governed by classical Islamic law and who was allowed to retain the dhimmi's religion, subject to a tax, known as Jizya, and several limitations. The practice has its roots in the Constitution of Medina, which was signed by the Prophet and dealt with the Arab and Jewish tribes of Medina. Dhimmis pay the jizya or serve in the military, which exempts them from the jizya, and are entitled to the protection of the state. The term and its doctrine are now controversial and a focus for arguments over the potential imperialism of Islam.

**DHS detainer** *See:* deportation, DHS detainer (immigration detainer or notice of action).

**dian** A form of deposit as security for a loan in Chinese law. A dian is a contractual relation between a debtor and creditor, whereby the debtor transfers property to the creditor for a specified time or until the underlying debt is repaid.

**diberah Torah ki-leshon bene Adam (diberah Torah bilshon benei Adam)** Some questions in the Torah arise from frailties in human language. Diberah Torah ki-leshon bene Adam, translated as "the Torah speaks in human language," is a tool of rabbinic interpretation that allows reconciliation among seemingly contradictory passages. Ordinarily, every aspect of the Torah — even spelling peculiarities — is taken to be significant, but occasionally such interpretation is rejected on the grounds of Diberah Torah ki-leshon bene Adam.

**dictation (dictate)** Speech intended for transcription. Dictation is the speech by one person that is to be recorded in writing word for word by another person or transcribed by a machine.

**dictatorship or monocracy** *See:* government, forms of government, autocracy (dictatorship or monocracy).

**dicto simpliciter** *See:* fallacy, dicto simpliciter.

**dictum** *See:* opinion, judicial opinion, dictum (obiter dictum or dicta).

**gratis dictum** A volunteered statement. Gratis dictum is a statement volunteered by the speaker and is thus unsolicited by another person or by the circumstances. A confession is sometimes described as gratis dictum, but this is only true if the confessing party has volunteered the statement without its being solicited by others.

**difference principle**   *See:* justice, Rawlsian justice, difference principle (second principle of justice).

**digital phonorecord delivery**   *See:* phonorecord (digital phonorecord delivery).

**digital signature**   *See:* signature, digital signature.

**dignitary tort**   *See:* tort, dignitary tort, heart balm tort (amatory tort or Heart Balm Act); tort, dignitary tort.

**dilapidation**   *See:* nuisance.

**dilation and evacuation procedure or d&e**   *See:* abortion, partial birth abortion (dilation and evacuation procedure or d&e).

**dilatory**   Done for the purpose of delay. Anything dilatory is done for the purpose of consuming time. Dilatory actions are causes of actions brought or defended solely for the purpose of delaying the performance of a legal obligation. Dilatory motions are intended to slow the cause of action. In the modern practice of law, dilatory practice by attorneys may serve not only to waste the time of the court and opponent but also to increase the movant's fees. A reasonable delay required to gather evidence, prepare a case, or assemble staff or witnesses is not dilatory.
*See also:* delay; defense, defense in pleading, dilatory defense; ethics, legal ethics | 3. dilatory tactics.

**dilatory defense**   *See:* defense, defense in pleading, dilatory defense.

**diligence**   The use of effort and care in performing one's duties. Diligence, the opposite of negligence, is the high level of care and attention required to do one's duty with thoroughness.
*See also:* negligence (negligent).

**due diligence**   The customary investigation and care required in the circumstances. Due diligence is a level of inquiry and care that includes responding to known dangers, determining unknown but reasonably predictable dangers, assessing such dangers, and taking reasonable steps to cure the potential for harm each danger poses. In civil law systems, due diligence is a general duty, akin to the reasonable care requirement in common law jurisdictions. In common law systems, however, due diligence is either a particular duty or a general duty that arises in particular circumstances, such as the duty of a professional or a fiduciary to investigate matters prior to rendering an opinion or taking some action. A party who fails to discover information that would have been found had the party timely exercised a duty of due diligence may be treated as if it had such information from the time it would have been discovered.

*See also:* fiduciary, fiduciary duty, duty to investigate; fiduciary, fiduciary duty; notice; inquiry, notice inquiry, red flag.

**dilution (dilute or diluted)**   Weakening the proportion of something by adding something else. Dilution is the process of reducing the share or proportion of a substance, a group within a larger population, or the significance of an action or condition by the introduction of another substance, group, action, or condition.

Dilution is also used to describe the effect of diluting a precursor substance. Thus, if the number of a company's outstanding shares is enlarged, the earlier shares each represent a share of ownership of the company that is diminished by the proportion of the new shares; the issuance of new shares dilutes the voting power and ownership benefits of the old shares.

Finally, a dilution of a substance in a chemical solution arises from the addition of other chemicals to the original solution.
*See also:* trademark, dilution of trademark (trademark dilution).

**dilution of trademark**   *See:* trademark, dilution of trademark (trademark dilution).

**dilutant**   An additive that reduces the proportion of the substance to which it is added. A dilutant is any substance that, when added to another substance, diminishes the ratio of the initial substance to the resulting mixture. It is common practice in the illegal drug trade to dilute a controlled substance prior to sale, often many times, each time diluting the actual ratio of the drug present in the substance sold. For the purposes of establishing criminal conduct, the size or weight of a controlled substance illegally sold is not reduced by the portion of the substance that amounts from the addition of dilutants
*See also:* adulteration (adulterate or adulterant).

**diminished capacity**   *See:* capacity, criminal capacity, diminished capacity.

**diminished responsibility**   *See:* responsibility, diminished responsibility (capacity diminished or diminished capacity).

**diminution damages**   *See:* damages, measure of damages, diminution damages (lost value in real property).

**diminution of estate doctrine**   *See:* bankruptcy, bankruptcy estate, diminution of estate doctrine.

**din**   *See:* kal va–homer (din).

**dina de–malkhuta dina (dina dmalchuta dina)**   The law of the state is binding upon Jews. Dina de–malkhuta dina, or "the law of the state is the law" indicates that (for most purposes) the enactments of the state are binding upon observant Jews in that state as a matter of Jewish law.

**diploma privilege** *See:* bar, admission to the bar, diploma privilege (diplomate privilege).

**diplomat (diplomatic agent)** A public officer of one state who serves its affairs in a foreign state. A diplomat is a public officer who has been commissioned by a government to conduct its affairs in a foreign country. Diplomats enjoy a particular rank among members of a state's diplomatic or foreign service. They are stationed either in domestic offices or at embassies, consulates, or ministries, from which they manage the affairs of their home country, representatives of the receiving state, and individuals and entities of various nationalities. Diplomats are extended certain privileges by their receiving state, such as immunity from prosecution and taxation.

> **consul** *See:* consul.

> **diplomate privilege** *See:* bar, admission to the bar, diploma privilege (diplomate privilege).

> **diplomatic courier** *See:* courier (diplomatic courier).

> **diplomatic immunity** *See:* immunity, diplomatic immunity.

> **attaché (attache)** A person attached to a diplomatic staff for a specific purpose. An attaché is a person attached to a diplomatic mission for a specific function not usually performed by the diplomatic personnel, but within the scope of the mission as a whole. For instance, military attachés and cultural attachés provide military and cultural information to the ambassador and serve as conduits of information from and to the host country. Attachés are considered diplomatic personnel.

> **diplomacy** The art and protocol of interstate relations. Diplomacy includes all of the lawful means by which officials representing states seek to manage their relations.
> *See also:* protocol.

> **diplomatic bag (diplomatic pouch)** Any device for the transit of goods or correspondence between a state and its embassies. The diplomatic bag, or the diplomatic pouch, is any mailbag, chest, container, or other device for shipment that is sent by a representative of the government of a state to its diplomatic staff in another state (or vice versa), is labeled as the diplomatic bag or diplomatic goods, and is immune from delay, search, or duty. If the bag is used for the importation of contraband into the receiving state, however, the sending state has violated the international laws of diplomacy.

> **diplomatic immunity** The immunity of a foreign diplomatic agent from criminal and civil process. Diplomatic immunity is a form of sovereign immunity recognized in customary international law and treaty. A diplomat is immune from arrest or subpoena and may not be served in a civil suit, searched, or asked to give evidence in the state to which the diplomat is appointed to represent the diplomat's sending state. The sending state may, however, waive immunity

on behalf of the diplomat or carry out such investigations or process itself.
> *See also:* consul, consular immunity.

> **diplomatic precedence (diplomatic rank or diplomatic staff)** Diplomatic protocol recognizing higher office and longer tenure. An order of precedence is used in diplomatic and state functions to place those in rank according to the seniority of office and length of tenure, which for ambassadors is measured by time of appointment to the receiving state. The order is: Head of State, Deputy Head of State, Head of Government, Deputy Head of Government, Minister of State or Secretary of State, Ambassador Extraordinary and Plenipotentiary, Ministers Plenipotentiary, Ministers, Chargé d'Affaires ad hoc or pro tempore, Chargé d'Affaires ad interim, Minister–Counselors, Counselors (or Senior Secretaries in the absence of Counselors), Army, Naval and Air Attachés, Civilian Attachés, First Secretaries, Second Secretaries, Assistant Army, Naval and Air Attachés Civilian Assistant, Attachés, Third Secretaries and Assistant Attachés.
> *See also:* primary (primarily).

> **full powers** *See:* treaty, full powers.

> **recall (letter of recall)** A notice sent to a receiving state that a diplomat has been called home. The recall of a diplomat is an act by the diplomat's home state that either expressly or impliedly requires the diplomat to leave the state to which the diplomat was accredited. A recall may be permanent or temporary. A recall may be the result of a suspension in diplomatic representation between the two states, or it may be a matter of the personnel alone.
> A letter of recall is the notice from a sending state to a receiving state that an ambassador or other minister has been recalled from the receiving state.

>> **persona non grata** A state's label rejecting a person as the diplomatic agent of another state. Persona non grata, Latin for a person out of favor, is a designation given by the receiving state of a diplomat or other person from a sending state, whom the receiving state considers to be unacceptable in the role for which they are present. The sending state must either recall the person or give the person a new role to which the receiving state is amenable.
>> *See also:* persona non grata (persona non grata letter).

## direct (directed)

**direct action** *See:* shareholder, shareholder litigation, direct action; action, direct action, direct action as claim against insurance company.

**direct action as claim against insurance company** *See:* action, direct action, direct action as claim against insurance company.

**direct appeal** *See:* appeal, direct appeal.

**direct cause or efficient cause or jural cause or legal cause** *See:* causation, proximate cause (direct cause or efficient cause or jural cause or legal cause).

**direct contempt**  *See:* contempt of court, direct contempt.

**direct democracy in the jury**  *See:* jury, direct democracy in the jury.

**direct descendant or lineals**  *See:* descent, descendant, lineal descendant (direct descendant or lineals).

**direct evidence**  *See:* evidence, direct evidence, smoking gun; evidence, direct evidence (indirect evidence).

**direct examination**  *See:* examination, examination of a witness, direct examination.

**direct loss**  *See:* loss, direct loss.

**directed verdict**  *See:* verdict, directed verdict; verdict, directed verdict.

**director**  *See:* corporation, director, board of directors (corporate board or board); corporation, director (corporate director).

**dirty**  An act, a person, or a thing that is illegal or corrupt. Dirty colloquially describes anything done improperly, especially that an activity is illegal, a person is corrupt, or some assets have been obtained through illegal means.

**disability (legal disability)**  A person's lack of capacity to do anything enforceable by law. A legal disability is any barrier arising from a personal condition that prevents a person from establishing legal capacity. A legal capacity may be general, barring any action of significance in the law, or be specific to a particular legal action, such as voting. An act or omission that would otherwise alter the legal interests of a person under a general legal disability is of no effect. A person under a general disability can neither act as a matter of law nor consent to or agree to the act or offer of another. Thus, a person under a general disability cannot enter into a contract, cannot make a will, and cannot create a power of attorney, although a guardian or conservator may be appointed to do so by a court of appropriate jurisdiction. Likewise, a person under a general disability is not liable to the usual obligations to defend interests in court, and so claims arising from lands held by a person in disability are tolled until the disability is alleviated; land may not, for instance, be adversely possessed against a minor. The two contemporary general legal disabilities are minority (or being younger than the age of consent or adulthood required for a given purpose) and mental disability (or a lack of sufficient awareness or intellect to give free and informed consent, whether the lack arises from advanced age or otherwise).

Most specific disabilities arise by operation of law, such as the loss of suffrage by a convicted felon; or disability caused by a failure of capacity granted by law, such as the failure of a non-citizen to qualify for registration to vote. The common law once recognized many more disabilities, including disabilities based on race, gender, marital status, conditions of servitude, illiteracy, lack of property, or failure to pay taxes.

*See also:* party, party to a contract; adult, age of majority (legal age); disability, civil disability (civil disabilities).

**disability accomodation**  *See:* accomodation, reasonable accommodation (disability accomodation).

**disability discrimination**  *See:* discrimination, disability discrimination.

**disability insurance**  *See:* insurance, category of insurance, disability insurance.

**civil disability (civil disabilities)**  The loss of a civil right as a consequence of committing a crime. A civil disability is the loss of a civil right by either judicial decree or legislative decree, or as a statutory function ancillary to a finding of guilt for certain crimes. Thus, a person convicted of one of a category of felonies may be barred from voting, holding office, carrying a weapon, qualifying to practice law or other professions, or occupying a position of trust, or punished with such other disabilities as the legislature or court decrees. The requirements as applied to certain felons, such as sex offenders, that such individuals cannot live near schools are not generally considered civil disabilities but are only conditions of release. The difference between a civil disability and a condition of release is largely one of customary depiction, yet in general, civil disabilities are more often directed to participation in civic life, particularly by voting or holding office.

Civil disabilities may be restored in most jurisdictions by a court order or pardon.

*See also:* disability (legal disability).

**civil death**  The treatment of a prisoner as one who is legally dead. Traditionally, civil death was the complete disability of a prisoner under the law and included barring the prisoner from suit and from the defense of suits, stripping the prisoner of all legal powers and interests, including suffrage, office, and civil rights, and distributing the prisoner's property to heirs or devisees as if the prisoner had died. Civil death is now considered a violation of due process of law in the United States, although other disabilities and declarations of incapacity persist.

*See also:* death.

**civiliter mortuus**  Civil death. Civiliter mortuus was once the designation of a decree or status of civil death.

**individualized education plan (IEP)**  A written plan for the education of a disabled student. An individualized education program is a written statement for a child with a disability that is developed and later managed in a meeting of an IEP team made up of the child's parents or guardians, teachers, counselors, and therapists. The IEP must include the student's present achievement and performance, specific goals for future attainment, specific services and plans to be employed by the parties designated to employ them, and benchmarks for future attainment of those goals.

**Individuals with Disabilities Education Act (IDEA)**
Federal law ensuring educational services for disabled students. The Individuals with Disabilities Education Act (IDEA), codified in 20 U.S.C. §1400, provides for free appropriate public education for disabled students. In employs a plan unique to each child to meet the learning needs of the child within the least restrictive environment and to prepare each student for more education, employment, and an independent life.

**major life activity**   Actions that are reasonably essential in the daily life of a person in modern society. A major life activity is an action that is of central importance to most people's daily lives, regardless of whether the action is one performed in public or in private and whether or not the action is essential to employment. Examples of major life activities are breathing, eating, drinking, sleeping, seeing, hearing, listening, sitting, walking, standing, lifting, bending, speaking, communicating, associating with others, working, reading, learning, concentrating, and writing. Courts are divided about driving, such that while driving long distances is not considered a major life activity, driving within a limited area may well be so central to life in certain jurisdictions that it constitutes a major life activity. In contrast, the participation in specific acts that are of significant concern to an individual, but which are not fundamental to daily life, such as participating in sports or a hobby, are not major life activities.

Although some activities have been determined to be major life activities as a matter of law, determining what is a daily life activity is generally a question of fact. Under the Americans with Disabilities Act, a person whose ability to engage in a major life activity is substantially impaired is considered disabled.

**personal disability (handicap or mental disability or physical disability)**   A physical or mental impairment that limits a major life activity of an individual. While a disability generally refers to any physical or mental impairment, a disability cognizable by law must be sufficiently severe that it substantially limits the impaired person from one or more major life activities. In this sense, there is little distinction between a disability and a handicap, other than specific usages in varying statutes. Although most considerations of disability do not include durational requirements, a disability under the Social Security Act requires the disability to persist for a year or more.

*affirmative action*   Affirmative action, in the context of employing disabled individuals, refers to the duty of an employer to alter workspaces and labor methods or to create new methods to allow a qualified person with a disability to perform the necessary functions of a particular job.

Note: as a matter of both political and legal rhetoric, some commentators and attorneys recurrently argue that affirmative action requires an employer must accept an unreasonable burden or must disadvantage non-disabled employees. Such arguments are counter to the law, which requires only reasonable accommodation and does not require burdens to other employees.

**Americans with Disabilities Act (A.D.A. or ADA)**
Civil rights legislation outlawing discrimination against disabled persons. The Americans with Disabilities Act, codified at 42 U.S.C. §12101 (2008), ensures that individuals with physical and mental disabilities are allowed equal access to jobs, buildings, roads, and services through reasonable accommodation of their personal disability.

**developmental disability**   A mental or physical condition beginning in childhood that impedes the development of ordinary activities or skills. A developmental disability is a chronic condition that results from a mental or physical impairment originating in childhood or adolescence, and impedes major life activities, such as communicating, mobility, learning, and independent living.

**disabled individual (disabled person)**   A person impaired physically or mentally. A disabled individual has a physical or mental disability that significantly alters that person's daily life, such as requiring new or unusual strategies to bathe, cook meals, buy groceries, or perform the movements or activities of employment.

**employment capacity**   The ability to perform a task required of a particular job. Employment capacity is a physical or mental ability to carry out a task or perform a duty required in a particular employment or job. A person whose disability prevents or diminishes the person's ability to perform reasonably and well that task or duty, to the point that the person cannot physically or mentally tolerate doing so but for brief periods of time without an unreasonable accommodation is disabled from that employment.

*See also:* employment (employ or employed or employee or employer).

**permanent disability (temporary disability)**   The unabating inability to perform gainful employment. Permanent disability is an assessment that the condition causing the disability will never abate, and the disability, of whatever degree (partial or total), will persist indefinitely.

Temporary disability is an assessment that the condition or the effects of the injury causing the disability will abate, and thus relief is only required for a time. Temporary disability may be determined from the nature of an injury or a condition, and many benefit plans provide a set period of relief for temporary disability following certain forms of injury.

Either permanent or temporary disability may be total or partial.

**total disability (partial disability)** The inability to perform gainful employment. Total disability is a measure of personal disability and is used, among other things, to assess a person's eligibility for disability benefits under public or private insurance plans. Because of variations between insurance plans, there is no single definition, but two competing theories exist, one focusing on the disability to perform one's own occupation and the other on the disability to perform any occupation at all. In federal law, whether or not an individual has a total disability turns on that person's ability to perform any occupation.

The measure of disability is whether the claimant can tolerate the conditions of the work environment and perform the tasks required to sustain the employment. A claimant is totally disabled from an occupation by a condition if, as a result of the condition, the claimant can perform the tasks required only for a brief period of time or can perform so few of the required tasks that the claimant could not be hired or retained in a position in that occupation.

Partial disability is a disability that is not so comprehensive as to prevent any employment in the occupation but is sufficiently limiting so that the claimant is limited in the tasks that can be performed such that the opportunity for successful employment or preferment in that employment will be limited. Partial disability is usually assessed as a percentage of ability, so, for example, a person might be assessed as 25 percent disabled.

Either total or partial disability may be permanent or temporary.

**disabled access** *See:* access, handicapped access (disabled access).

**disabled individual** *See:* disability, personal disability, disabled individual (disabled person).

**disabled person** *See:* disability, personal disability, disabled individual (disabled person).

**disaffirmance** *See:* contract, specific contracts, voidable contract, disaffirmance (avoidance or renunciation).

**disaster relief or poor relief** *See:* relief, relief as public assistance (disaster relief or poor relief).

**disbarment** *See:* lawyer, lawyer discipline, sanctions, disbarment (debar disbar).

**discharge** A release from duty or confinement. Discharge is a release from some restraint or obligation. A discharge of a person is a release from care, confinement, contract, debt, or duty—such as the discharge of a patient from a hospital or a debtor from a debt. In the case of debt and duty, a discharge from such obligations is based on their performance rather than on relief for other reasons. An object may also be discharged, meaning that it is released from some source or restraint, as in the discharge of a bullet from a rifle or cargo from a ship's hold.

*See also:* release, custodial release (discharge or release from custody).

**discharge in bankruptcy** *See:* bankruptcy, discharge in bankruptcy.

**discharge of a contract** *See:* contract, discharge of a contract.

**discharge of firearm** *See:* firearm, discharge of firearm.

**discharge of the jury** *See:* jury, discharge of the jury.

**discharge or release from custody** *See:* release, custodial release (discharge or release from custody).

**discharge or wastewater** *See:* effluent (discharge or wastewater).

**discharge as emission** The release of any substance into the environment. In environmental law, a discharge is the emission of a substance into the environment, whether the release is a solid or liquid released into a water body, a gas or particulate released into the air, or a solid, liquid or gas released into the ground. Discharge refers both to the act of release and to the materials released.

*See also:* release, contaminate release (release of contaminate).

**discharge from custody** To be released from custody. To discharge someone from custody is to release that person from confinement upon the completion of a sentence or upon an order of release before the completion of a sentence.

**discharge of a jury** *See:* jury, discharge of the jury.

**discharge of contract** *See:* contract, discharge of a contract.

**discharge of debt** *See:* bankruptcy, discharge in bankruptcy.

**employment discharge (discharge from employment or firing)** An employer's removal of an employee from the employee's job. An employment discharge is the removal of an employee from the office or position the employee held; it is the termination of an employee's performance of a job. The term implies the expulsion of the employee from participation in any employment by the employer. Discharge is done wholly by the employer; it is involuntary for the employee, although an employee's election of one form of discharge over another remains a discharge. Discharge can therefore be either overt or constructive.

*See also:* employment (employ or employed or employee or employer).

**constructive discharge** An employee's resignation compelled by the employer's severe or unreasonable conduct. A constructive discharge occurs when an employee resigns because of the employer's creation or allowance of circumstances in the employment that are so severe or unreasonable that no reasonable person in the employee's position would remain in the employment. Such circumstances may also arise from the behavior of co-workers (and in some cases customers or vendors), if the behavior is known to the employer, particularly to a supervisor, and negligently or deliberately tolerated. Constructive discharge may result from a hostile workplace environment, which, if the hostility is based on race, gender or other unlawful bases of workplace discrimination, may result in an unlawful discharge.

**just cause**  A fair and reasonable basis for the discharge of an employee. Just cause, in general, is a reasonable and sufficient basis for some action. When the phrase is used in law, a just cause is sufficient for the action that results that no liability will attach to the action based on that reason.

Just cause in the discharge of an employee is a basis for the decision that arises from a demonstrable and reasonable assessment of the employee's conduct as being sufficiently contrary to the interests of the employer that a competent, disinterested person acting in good faith in the place of the employer, after evaluating the performance record and conduct of the employee in the context of the employee's duties and the employer's expectations and support, would consider the discharge to be reasonable and based on sufficient cause.

**retaliatory discharge**  Firing an employee for exercising a right or performing a duty protected by law. Retaliatory discharge is the discharge of an employee as a result of an action by the employee that is protected from retaliation as a matter of public policy. An employee at common law who fulfills a legal duty, who refuses to participate in an unlawful or wrongful act, or who exercises a right allowed under law engages in protected activity. Retaliation for complaints to supervisors or the appropriate public authorities of unlawful activity in the workplace, for suit against an employer, for claiming lawfully allowed benefits, or other acts protected by public policy gives rise to an action at common law, as well as statutory causes of action in many jurisdictions.

*See also:* retaliation, employment retaliation.

**wrongful discharge**  Firing an employee for reasons forbidden by law or contrary to public policy. Wrongful discharge is the termination of employment on grounds or under circumstances that violate a statute or public policy, such as for refusing to violate the law, or on a basis that itself violates the law, such an as action that discriminates on the basis of race, gender, or other forbidden bases of employment discrimination. Even when an employee is terminable at the will of the employer, if the employee is fired for reasons that contravene public policy, the termination is a wrongful discharge, the at-will status notwithstanding.

**military discharge**  The final severance of a member from a military service. A military discharge is a certificate or release from active duty sent to a person enlisted in a military service, following the termination of the terms of enlistment, the order of a court martial, or as prescribed by the secretary with jurisdiction over that service.

**disciplinary rule**  *See:* lawyer, lawyer discipline, disciplinary rule.

**disciplinary rules**  *See:* lawyer, lawyer discipline, disciplinary rules, rules of professional conduct; lawyer, lawyer discipline, disciplinary rules, oath as basis of discipline; lawyer, lawyer discipline, disciplinary rules, canons of ethics (code of professional responsibility).

**disclaimer**  A statement renouncing an interest or duty. A disclaimer is a statement abandoning or rejecting an interest, claim, or duty. When the disclaimer is a rejection of an interest of the speaker's, such as of an interest in realty or a claim that might be brought in law, the disclaimer operates to void or abandon the interest or any claim upon it, as long as the interest is not inalienable. When a disclaimer is of a duty, its effect will depend upon whether the duty may be disclaimed as a matter of law or equity. Such a disclaimer is often made, through a contract clause, notice, label, or utterance that places limitations on the acceptance of responsibility or duty of the maker of the statement. Disclaimers are a more particular form of notice, and a notice statement in general may amount to an implied disclaimer either by disclosing patent defects or dangers or by attempting to place the reader or hearer in a position of responsibility for whatever risks follow that is superior to the responsibility of the maker of the statement. Many disclaimers, particularly disclaimers of warranty, are contrary to law and void.

*See also:* notice; warranty.

**disclaimer of warranty**  *See:* warranty, disclaimer of warranty.

**disclaimer as refusal to accept estate**  A refusal to accept ownership. A disclaimer, particularly a disclaimer of an estate, is a refusal to accept a grant of property, whether through inheritance, devise, gift, or sale. A disclaimer of estate is a refusal to accept an interest in realty, and such a disclaimer must be in writing to assure title in others, although an unwritten disclaimer may become binding through detrimental reliance or prescription. More generally, a disclaimer may operate as the renunciation of a gift, devise, or legacy, whether of realty or other legal or equitable interests.

*See also:* refusal (refuse).

**disclosure**  A release of information. A disclosure is the dissemination of information that had previously been kept from public knowledge. In many cases, statutes or rules require certain information to be disclosed in order to promote the free flow of information necessary for legal process, good government, or the education and safety of the public. For instance, packaged foods that are sold in U.S. supermarkets are required to have nutrition labels that disclose the food's ingredients, and the terms of credit arrangements must be disclosed to borrowers.

**disclosure statement** Any statement of information required by law or not otherwise readily known. A disclosure statement is a statement that provides information which otherwise would not readily be available to the audience to which the statement is made and to which the disclosing party will be held accountable. Disclosure statements are required in many contexts, including statements of ownership made by defendants in a federal criminal proceeding and in statements of liability in federally regulated credit transactions.

**automatic disclosure (mandatory disclosure)** A disclosure of evidence required without request or motion. Automatic disclosure is the requirement that evidence be disclosed to an opponent within the period for discovery prior to trial, whether or not the opponent seeks it by motion or request.

**initial disclosure** A party's required provision of basic information to the opposing party. Initial disclosure is the mandated disclosure of required information by one party to the other, usually within thirty days of entry into the action and without waiting for a discovery request. Generally, under Federal Rule of Civil Procedure 26(a) (and many states' rules that parallel the federal rules), a litigant must immediately provide to the opposing party the names and addresses of all known people who are likely to possess discoverable information and the general subject under which that information falls; a list of all documents and tangibles that the litigant may use to establish its claims or defenses; a computation of any damages the litigant claims; and any insurance contract that is at issue in the action. Although initial discovery is required in most actions, some are exempt, the most common of which are administrative proceedings and actions brought by incarcerated, pro se litigants. A party that learns of information that alters its initial disclosure is required to relay to its opponent the new information.

**pretrial disclosure** A disclosure made before trial. A pretrial disclosure is any disclosure made before trial, whether it is an initial disclosure or subsequent disclosure required by the rules, a disclosure made in response to discovery, or a voluntary disclosure.

**supplemental disclosure** An amendment to an initial disclosure. A supplemental disclosure is an addition or correction to an initial disclosure or an expert witness's report. Any initial disclosure required under the rules must be supplemented in a timely manner by a written supplemental disclosure when the disclosing party learns that the information initially disclosed was either incorrect or incomplete at the time of the initial disclosure or that the underlying information has changed, making the information in the initial disclosure incomplete or inaccurate. A party's failure to make a reasonable effort in good faith to stay informed of such information cannot excuse a failure to make a supplemental disclosure when circumstances require it. A failure to make supplemental disclosures will be punished by sanctions in the same manner as a failure to make an initial disclosure.

**duty to disclose (duty of disclosure)** A duty to notify another of particular information. A duty to disclose information arises when a person should reasonably know that that individual is in possession of information that would affect a decision or act of another, that a failure to disclose the information is reasonably likely to harm the other person in the decision or action, and that there is a relationship between the two parties, such as privity of estate or of contract, a professional arrangement as between a lawyer, broker, or doctor and a client, or a reliance as between the ultimate consumer of goods and its manufacturer.

**non-disclosure (nondisclosure)** The failure to disclose something known or within one's control. Non-disclosure is any failure to disclose information or evidence known to the relevant party or within that party's control. Non-disclosure of information may be a requirement, as under laws or regulations regulating classified information or an agreement to keep information secure, or as a matter of a professional obligation, such as the confidentially of communications to a lawyer or a priest.

Non-disclosure when there is a requirement of disclosure may be a tort, a crime, or the basis for avoiding or rescinding a contract or of its breach. In the context of discovery, non-disclosure of properly requested or legally required information may give rise to sanctions.

**discontinuance (discontinue or discontinuous)** A voluntary halt to some conduct, that might be renewed. A discontinuance is the failure to continue in some pursuit. In general, any action may be discontinued, and the term at its broadest meaning includes actions that cease for any reason, whether temporarily, permanently, or for an indefinite but potentially infinite time. Yet, in law, a discontinuance implies a voluntary cessation of an action that might be later commenced again. Cessation in this sense must occur as a result of the will of the person or entity whose continuance would otherwise persist; it cannot be required by order. In civil procedure, a discontinuance is a voluntary termination of a civil action, with the potential that it might be revived.

In the common law, a discontinuance was an interference with an estate held in fee tail, which was distinct from an ouster of the holder in tail. This usage is now obsolete.

**discontinuous easement** *See:* easement, discontinuous easement (discontinuing easement or intermittent easement or noncontinuous easement).

**discount** A reduction in the asking price. A discount is a reduction from the asking price in the price demanded by the seller from the buyer, either at the time of the sale or at the time of the demand for payment. To describe a product or service as being discount is to say that it is at a comparative bargain.

To discount a note or other commercial paper is to offer to sell or to agree to buy the paper at a price below its face value.

*See also:* rebate.

**discount for present value** *See:* damages, calculation of damages, discount for present value (inflation factor).

**discovery (discoverable)** The process through which attorneys acquire evidence in a case prior to trial. Discovery describes the process by which attorneys learn of the evidence known or held by other parties before trial. Discovery encompasses practically everything an attorney may or must do under the rules of civil or criminal procedure to acquire evidence before trial, although it usually does not refer to the acquisition of evidence from the party the attorney represents, from a non-party who cooperates with that attorney, or from the attorney's investigations that do not require the cooperation of other parties or the court.

Discovery can be divided into many categories, such as documentary, testimonial, and physical discovery, but the more significant divisions are generally between discovery that is mandated for disclosure without motion, discovery that is required upon motion, and discovery that is privileged from disclosure.

Discovery is not the same as admission into the record of a court or hearing, and evidence that is discoverable might or might not be admissible, but any evidence that is arguably admissible is inherently discoverable.

*See also:* interrogatory (interrogatories or propounded interrogatories).

**discovery abuse** *See:* ethics, legal ethics, discovery abuse.

**discovery disclosure** *See:* disclosure, discovery disclosure, supplemental disclosure; disclosure, discovery disclosure, pretrial disclosure; disclosure, discovery disclosure, initial disclosure; disclosure, discovery disclosure, automatic disclosure (mandatory disclosure).

**discovery immunity** *See:* immunity, discovery immunity, work–product immunity | attorney–client privilege and work product; immunity, discovery immunity, work–product immunity (work product immunity or work–product rule or work product privilege); immunity, discovery immunity.

**discovery rule** *See:* limitation, limitation of actions, statute of limitations, tolling, discovery rule.

**discovery sanction** *See:* sanction, discovery sanction.

**abusive discovery** Motions, requests, or production in discovery to inconvenience or delay one's opponent. Abusive discovery is discovery for the purpose of causing expense, difficulty, or embarrassment to one's opponent without a reasonable likelihood of identifying evidence that might prove a claim or defense or demonstrate the reliability or unreliability of other evidence. Abusive discovery can take many forms, from the filing of extraneous motions, requests for production, depositions, and questions or demands, to the production of unnecessary documents, physical evidence, answers, and testimony, any of which is intended to cause a burden to the other side. Discovery for the purpose of securing information required for the development of a case is not abusive, however, and a claim that appropriate discovery is abusive is itself an abuse.

**administrative discovery** Discovery during an administrative process. Administrative discovery is the discovery of evidence made by either the government or a private party during the discovery phase of an administrative proceeding. Searches, reports, statements, and disclosures required by statutes, regulations, or administrative orders during an administrative process may ordinarily become part of the record, although they must be entered into the record before or during a hearing. All such material may ordinarily be introduced if it is otherwise admissible in a subsequent civil or criminal action.

**bill of discovery** An equitable proceeding with discovery as its remedy. A bill of discovery is a proceeding in a court's equitable jurisdiction, the remedy sought being the discovery of evidence that may be used in a separate proceeding.

**certificate of good faith** A certificate stating that the movant has complied in good faith with the rules. A certificate of good faith is a certificate made by counsel that the attorney has acted in good faith to comply with the rules of procedure in negotiating with opposing counsel. This certificate is required of a party who seeks to compel discovery or to have a protective order; in both cases the attorney may not seek relief from the court without first having attempted in good faith to resolve the discovery dispute through consultation with opposing counsel.

**discovery as invention** An invention or improvement to any thing. A discovery is an invention of a new thing or an improvement to a thing that already existed. The discovery must not have been known before in order to be eligible for patent.

*See also:* invention.

**discovery immunity (discovery privilege)** Discovery may be limited if it is privileged against disclosure or barred if it poses an undue burden on a party or another. Discovery immunity limits a party from seeking discovery of information that would violate a privilege against disclosure that is recognized by rule, statute, or common law. Information that is not inherently privileged may be barred from discovery if it would be a burden upon the person producing it and qualify for a protective order under Federal Rule of Civil Procedure 26(c) or a state equivalent.

*See also:* privilege.

**request to inspect property**  A request to enter or inspect property for discovery. A request to inspect property is a discovery request that requires the receiving party to permit access to real property or chattel property which are possessed or controlled by the party on whom the request is served. The request may be made only to interested parties and must fall within the general scope of permissible discovery requests. The request may be contained within a subpoena and may be subject to an Order to Compel. In jurisdictions with liberal discovery doctrines, the purpose and scope underlying the demand of entry may be broad.

**protective order**  A court order barring certain discovery. A protective order in discovery is a court order barring inquiry by one or all parties into certain matters, limiting inquiry into specified matters, requiring certain information to be kept confidential, specifying the time and place of discovery or of disclosures, forbidding certain forms of discovery by one or all parties, or forbidding all disclosure or discovery. Under Federal Rule of Civil Procedure 26, a motion for a protective order must contain a declaration that the party has unsuccessfully sought in good faith an agreement from the parties regarding the matters in the motion. The court may enter a protective order for good cause, including the protection of a party or other person from annoyance, embarrassment, oppression, or undue burden or expense.

*See also:* motion, motion for protective order.

**document discovery**  The discovery of records or papers. Document discovery is the inspection or duplication by one party of written materials, particularly documents in the control of another party, sought through a production request pursuant to Federal Rule of Civil Procedure 34, or documents in the control of a witness that are produced as a result of a subpoena duces tecum. Although documents are referred to in Rule 34A(1)(a) as distinct from electronic records, a document that is stored in an electronic storage device is included in a request for documents.

**official record**  *See:* record, official record.

**request for production (production request or request to produce or inspect documents)**  A motion seeking documents from another party. A request for production is a discovery motion served on a party that lists documents or papers to be produced for duplication by the requesting party. A request for production must list documents with great specificity or by category. It may require the responding party to translate the documents into English, and it includes documents whether they are written on paper or stored electronically.

**request for admissions**  *See:* admission, request for admissions.

**scope of discovery**  The limits to the content and form of information that may be gathered during discovery. The scope of discovery is the extent to which a party may employ that party's allowance to seek information from other parties and third parties in preparation for a civil or criminal action. In general, a party to a civil action may seek non-privileged matter that is relevant to any party's claim or defense, even if it would be inadmissible at trial, so long as the discovery appears reasonably calculated to lead to admissible evidence. Privileged information, such as communications subject to a valid attorney–client privilege, is outside the scope of discovery.

A court will enforce a party's right to collect information within the scope of discovery, but material that would be unfair to seek from a party or material that inherently confuses the issues before the court might be outside the scope of discovery. The scope of discovery is usually more expansive in equity, admiralty, and state courts than it is in federal court.

*See also:* evidence, admissibility (admissible).

**mental examination**  An examination of the witness by an appropriate mental health professional. A mental examination is an examination by a psychiatrist, psychologist, certified parapsychologist, or licensed mental health professional who is both competent to examine the witness's purported condition that is relevant to the controversy and without a bias in the case, and who then provides a report of the examination — including the observation or tests performed, their results, and the examiner's conclusions — to counsel. The examination should be performed by a specialist appropriate to the question presented by the witness's claimed infirmity, using medically accepted procedures for the examination. Bias may arise from many causes, for example, if the examiner is regularly employed or seeks employment by one of the real parties in interest.

**physical examination**  An examination of the witness by an appropriate medical professional. A physical examination is a medical examination by a physician or other medical professional who is both competent to examine the witness's purported condition that is relevant to the controversy and without a bias in the case, who then provides a report of the examination — including the observation or tests performed, their results, and the examiner's conclusions — to counsel. The examination should be performed by a specialist appropriate to the question presented by the claimed infirmity of the witness and using medically accepted procedures for the examination. Bias may arise from many causes, particularly if the examiner is regularly employed or seeks employment by one of the real parties in interest.

**witness statement**  Any statements written, spoken, or adopted by a witness. A witness statement is any statement written or spoken and recorded by the witness, or any statement written or transcribed for the witness and later adopted by signature or other form of assent. Witness statements are inherently discoverable unless they are privileged.

**discredit** To diminish the apparent credibility of a witness or evidence. To discredit is to diminish the reliance that others should place on a person or evidence. To discredit a witness is to give reasons why the witness may lack capacity, ability, knowledge, or truthfulness. If the witness is a fact witness, attempts to discredit may suggest the witness erred in the observation or the recollection of the events recalled in testimony. If the witness is an expert, attempts may suggest that the witness observed the wrong data, employed the wrong methodology, or reached improper conclusions. In both cases, evidence of bias or interest in the result may serve to discredit testimony.

*See also:* credibility.

**discrete and insular class** *See:* class, legal classification, discrete and insular class.

**discrete and insular minority** *See:* minority, minority group, discrete and insular minority.

**discretion** Judgment, often on the part of a magistrate or judge. Discretion is the judgment of a person making a decision, as well as the scope of office or responsibility within which the person is responsible for making such a decision. To act with discretion is not to act on a whim. Discretion requires the person acting to consider all of the evidence that might be relevant to the decision, all of the possible decisions that might be made in a circumstance, the reasons for deciding in one or another manner, and then to seek an outcome that will best fit with the purposes for which the person has the discretion to make such a decision.

*See also:* indeterminacy, legal indeterminacy; judge, judicial discretion; power, plenary power; jurisprudence, mechanistic jurisprudence; office; obedience (disobedience).

**abuse of discretion** An unreasonable or unjustified act by a judge or official. Abuse of discretion takes many forms, but in every instance it is an act or decision by a judge or other official that is made within the scope of office but that is not appropriate in the light of the facts upon which the decision could be based or upon the laws, policies, or justice that should be promoted by the decision. Appellate courts and other review tribunals will overturn decisions only if they find that the trial judge or official subject to review committed an abuse of discretion. Usually, a decision will only be reversed on appeal if the decision was a clear or gross abuse of the official's discretion, based on whimsy, contrary to the evidence in the record, or tainted by a failure of knowledge, effort, or care.

**abuse of discretion as standard in judicial review of administrative decision** Burden of persuasion requiring a showing of a clearly erroneous or illogical decision by an administrative agency. Abuse of discretion is a highly deferential burden of persuasion that is applied to the review of a decision of fact by an administrative agency working within its Congressionally or legislatively authorized powers.

*See also:* review, standard of review; review, standard of review, abuse of discretion; review, standard of review, arbitrary and capricious; review, standard of review, clearly erroneous.

**abuse of discretion as standard of review in appeal** A standard of review that is highly deferential to the decision of the lower court. Abuse of discretion presumes the validity of the lower court's decision, reversing that decision only if the appellant can demonstrate that the judge below abused the court's discretion, such as by acting for reasons of personal interest or motive, by failing to account for relevant evidence before the court, by failing to apply the appropriate rules of law, by relying on inappropriate bases of judgment, or by acting without any apparent reason at all. The standards of review for abuse of discretion and determinations that are arbitrary and capricious are similar, each being more associated with a particular area of legal review, but abuse of discretion is probably the broader category.

**judicial discretion (discretion of the court or sound discretion)** The independent authority of the judge. Judicial discretion is the authority of the judge to decide questions which are properly submitted according to the rules of evidence and law and within a scope of decision in which the individual must assess the evidence, interpret the rules of law, and make a decision that is not clearly required by the rules, the evidence, or any authority, and for which the judge alone is responsible. That the decision is committed to this discretion does not mean the judge has unbounded liberty in making it, as the decision, like all acts of office, must still be grounded in the judge's best efforts to carry out the oath and duties of the office to the benefit of the law and the people.

*See also:* oath.

**discretionary act** *See:* immunity, official immunity, discretionary act.

**discretionary review** *See:* review, discretionary review.

**discrimination** Perceiving or treating people, or things, differently from one another. Discrimination, in general, is the act of perceiving difference, particularly among people or among things that are apparently similar. Discrimination in the law is the division of individuals or things into categories and providing for different treatment of the people or the things in one category from the treatment of those in another. The law creates many such categories, discriminating between hazardous materials and hazardous wastes and allowing employers and other private parties to act in a manner that defines many more categories with a discriminating significance in law, such as the different treatment of a secured creditor compared to a non-secured creditor. Some of these acts of legal discrimination violate constitutional or statutory standards that govern either official conduct, such as the equal protection clause, due process clause, or commerce clause; or private conduct, such as Title VII.

The history of the United States is riddled with long periods of discrimination on the basis of gender and race, and the effects of this discrimination are still apparent both in the residual effects of laws that did discriminate and those that have been enacted to end discrimination. Discrimination between individuals on the basis of race, color, gender, nationality, parentage, age and handicap were all once required by law in various manners, but each is now generally forbidden by constitution and statute. A legal requirement of discrimination is called de jure discrimination, while a factual effect of discrimination not required by law but by social pressure or individual choice is de facto discrimination.

Discrimination can be difficult to prove, in part because motivations of any type can be difficult to prove. Few people now desire to be thought of as discriminating on the basis of race or gender or similar categories, yet many people act from discriminatory impulses and rationales. Whether a person has in fact acted in a manner that is discriminatory is a question of fact, but two of its more useful means of proof are whether the person would have behaved differently toward a person of a different gender, race, or other circumstance; from this test comes the idea of actual comparison. The first form of comparison is based on intent: disparate impact assesses whether a person or entity in fact treated similar people of different races, genders, or other characteristics in significantly different ways. The second form is based on effect: disparate impact assesses whether a person or entity created policies or rules that placed a greater burden on members of a race or gender or other characteristic, but that had no previously identified non-discriminatory purpose to justify it.

*See also:* recruit, recruiting on campus (Solomon amendment); stereotype (gender stereotype or racial stereotype or stereotypical); segregation (racial segregation or segregation by gender); job, job applicant (employment applicant).

**segregation and desegregation** *See:* segregation (racial segregation or segregation by gender).

**age discrimination** Prejudicial treatment of a person based on advanced age. Age discrimination is the prejudicial treatment of a person due to that individual's advancing age. In the workplace, age discrimination of persons aged forty and over violates the Age Discrimination in Employment Act, codified at 29 U.S.C. § 621, et seq. (2008).

**Age Discrimination in Employment Act (A.D.E.A. or ADEA)** Employers and unions may not discriminate against older workers. The Age Discrimination in Employment Act of 1967, Pub. L. No. 90–202, 81 Stat. 602 (Dec. 15, 1967), codified at 29 U.S.C. § 621, et seq.

(2008), protects older workers from discrimination in hiring, promotion, pay, and other aspects of employment, when the discrimination occurs by employers (with twenty or more employees), employment agencies, or unions who favor younger workers over an employee who is forty years of age or older. Even so, age may be used as a basis for job selection or promotion, when it represents a bona fide occupational qualification (BFOQ) reasonably necessary to the normal operation of the particular business, where the differentiation is based on reasonable factors other than age, or when required by law in a foreign country.

**disability discrimination** Discrimination based on disability. Disability discrimination is any unreasonable discrimination exercised toward a disabled person, through either disparate treatment or the failure to accommodate. Disparate treatment is discrimination against an otherwise qualified individual because of a handicap, and failure to accommodate is the refusal of an employer to make reasonable, requested accommodations to allow the employee to perform assigned work despite the employee's documented physical or mental disability.

**discriminatory animus** *See:* animus.

**discriminatory purpose (discriminatory intent or purposeful discrimination)** An intent to disadvantage one group when crafting a rule, policy, or procedure in the law or elsewhere. Discriminatory purpose is an intent to confer an advantage on one group or to deny that advantage to other groups within a population. The discriminatory purpose to encourage vote dilution in creating an electoral district or ballot law is one that would create electoral opportunities for the election of a member of one race and deny it to others, assuming racially biased voting behavior. Discriminatory purpose in employment policies means to create a rule or policy that would have the intended result of fostering an advantage for one race, gender, age, or other class, or that would deny that advantage to other classes. In both cases, it is immaterial that such a purpose is not apparent in the rule, policy, boundaries, or law, if the standard was created with the intent that it have this result.

**employment discrimination** Any discrimination that is barred by law in the workplace. Employment discrimination is any prohibited discrimination that occurs within the work environment as it specifically relates to the plaintiff's occupation. Such discrimination can occur with respect to assignments, benefits, compensation, hiring, promoting, termination, terms of employment, transfers, or work environment. Employment discrimination is barred by both state and federal law, though many state laws bar discrimination on grounds that are more extensive than those imposed by federal law.

*See also:* employment (employ or employed or employee or employer); employment, employment action (adverse employment action or adverse job action or job action).

**bona fide occupational qualification (B.F.O.Q. or BFOQ)** A valid reason for an employment rule or hiring criterion. A bona fide occupational qualification is a requirement for a person to perform a specific job, which an employer must demand of a successful employee assigned that job. In the event an employee argues that a job qualification is discriminatory, the employer may claim that the requirement is a bona fide occupational qualification as a defense against the claim.

*See also:* stereotype (gender stereotype or racial stereotype or stereotypical).

**comparable worth** Equivalent pay for equivalent, though different, work. Comparable worth is a theory of compensation that attempts to equalize away the effects that have been perceived between the jobs and careers that have been more traditionally held by men compared to those held by women. In general, jobs that are typically performed by women are paid much less than those typically performed by men. Comparable worth would attach a premium to the compensation of such jobs to value them as if they were, in general, equivalent to a similar trade or employment held more often by males.

**disparate impact** Apparently neutral behavior that has a discriminatory effect. Disparate impact is a discriminatory effect of an employment policy, despite the lack of apparent evidence that the policy was created with a discriminatory purpose.

**disparate treatment** Intentionally discriminatory treatment in employment. Disparate treatment in employment occurs when an employee is subject to a burden from an action or policy in employment, either as a result of a discriminatory intent or a policy or decision with a disparate impact that has no legitimate and non-discriminatory rationale.

**doctrine of continuing violation** Discrimination or harassment arising from repetitious conduct. A continuing violation is a pattern of conduct that, over time, amounts to employment discrimination or harassment. An element of the discriminatory or harassing nature is the repetition or persistence of behavior, such that a reasonable person in the plaintiff's position might not have considered the initial instances of the conduct to be actionable but over time the conduct became injurious. A continuing violation may be brought after the 300-day limitations period for discrimination or harassment claims would have run from the initial conduct, as an equitable exception to the limitation and based on the initial lack of an apparent claim.

*See also:* limitation, limitation of actions, statute of limitations, tolling, continuing violation doctrine.

**Kolstad defense** Employers who make good faith attempts to comply with Title VII are immune from punitive damages under it. The Kolstad defense, from Kolstad v. American Dental Association., 527 U.S. 526 (1999), provides that an employer who employs a manager who has been found guilty of employment discrimination is not liable for punitive damages for employment discrimination if the employer made a good faith effort to comply with Title VII.

**prima facie case of discrimination** Evidence sufficient to require an employer to demonstrate a neutral reason for an adverse job action. A prima facie case of employment discrimination under Title VII is established when an employee proves (i) the employee belongs to a protected minority; (ii) that the employee applied and was qualified for a job for which the employer was seeking applicants; (iii) that despite the employee's qualifications the employee was rejected; and (iv) that, after the employee's rejection, the position remained open and the employer continued to seek applicants from persons with the employee's qualifications, or less.

*See also:* prima, prima facie, prima facie case.

**religious discrimination** Discrimination on the basis of religious affiliation or belief. Religious discrimination is discrimination, whether by intent or effect, against an employee's religious affiliation or identity or its related beliefs or practices. Discriminatory effects are common when workers of a non-minority faith enter a workplace, such as when work rules that accommodate the religious calendars or daily observances of majority religion workers fail to accommodate the calendars or observances of minority religion workers, despite the fact that a reasonable accommodation is available.

**systemic discrimination** Discrimination in the policies or practices of an employer. Systemic discrimination consists of employment policies or practices that differentiate or perpetuate an existing sense of difference between employees on the basis of group identity, not through a single act but through policies, customs, or practices that subtly or distinctly remind employees of their status as members of one group or another.

**invidious discrimination** Any distinction drawn in a population for inappropriate reasons. Invidious discrimination is the creation or perpetuation of a burden on one individual or group, particularly if the motivation for the creation of that burden is ill-will toward the individual or group or a desire to harm one for the benefit of another.

**national origin discrimination** Discrimination in law or employment on the basis of a person's nation of birth or ancestry. National origin discrimination is discriminatory treatment in law, employment, or the exercise of any legal right, on the basis of an individual's nation of origin or the nation of origin of the individual's ancestors, or because an individual has the physical, cultural, or linguistic characteristics that the discriminating person or entity believes is identifiable by national origin.

**pretextual reason (pretextual justification)**  A sham reason disguising a different purpose for a policy, law, or action. A pretextual reason is a legitimate reason offered to cloak the real, and improper, reasons for a decision, policy, or law. An employment policy, a challenge to a juror, a voter qualification, or any other action of legal consequence may be motivated by the desire to discriminate on the basis of race or another improper purpose, and that motive may be disguised through the suggestion that the action is actually intended to affect a different and legitimate purpose. A court given any reason to suspect that a justification for any act of legal significance is mere pretext is obligated to assess the justification closely through collateral evidence of the genuine motivation for the act.

*See also:* pretext (pretextual).

**racial discrimination**  Discrimination against a person or group because of race, ethnicity, or origin. Racial discrimination includes any form of discrimination based on race, including ethnicity, color, and national origin. The meaning of race has changed dramatically over the last century and a half, but under the specific laws that forbid discrimination based on race, race is either defined or understood, and in the case of the former, it is defined according to color, nationality, heritage, or family descent. Any law that allows a burden or benefit to be allocated on the basis of race is presumed to be discriminatory on its face and is upheld only if it passes strict scrutiny. Unjustified racial discrimination is barred in employment, education, the provision of services to the public, housing, and voting.

**benign discrimination (benign use of racial classifications)**  Laws that use racial designations to assist victims of past discrimination. Benign discrimination is the discrimination in laws, whether passed by Congress or other legislatures, designed to compensate victims of past governmental or societal discrimination. Judicial review of laws employing benign discrimination is by intermediate review rather than strict scrutiny.

**sex discrimination (gender discrimination)**  Unfair treatment based on actual or perceived gender. Sex discrimination is treatment based on actual or perceived gender that is less favorable to members of one gender than to another. When manifest in a law or exercised by a government agent, sex discrimination may violate the equal protection clause. When committed without sufficient justification by an employer, it amounts to employment discrimination.

**sexual orientation discrimination**  Discrimination on the basis of perceived sexual orientation. Discrimination on the basis of sexual orientation is treatment of persons with actual or perceived sexual orientation that is less favorable than the treatment offered to others with a different sexual orientation. In most instances it is a denial of a right, privilege, or opportunity to a person who is or who is perceived to be homosexual on the basis of the person's orientation or on the basis of the gender of the person's partner. In many jurisdictions, discrimination in employment on the basis of sexual orientation violates laws against discrimination on the basis of sexual orientation or on the basis of gender. Discrimination against an individual based on perceived orientation is usually sufficient to state a cause of action, the actual orientation of the plaintiff notwithstanding.

**discriminatory harassment**  *See:* harassment, discriminatory harassment.

**discriminatory price**  *See:* price, discriminatory price (discriminatory pricing).

**disentailment**  *See:* fee, estate in fee, fee tail, entail, disentailment.

**disgorgement of a fee**  *See:* fee, fee for services, attorney's fee, disgorgement of a fee.

**dishonor**  *See:* instrument, negotiable instrument, honor of a negotiable instrument, dishonor.

**disinherison**  *See:* inheritance, distinheritance, disinherison (disherison).

**disinheritance**  *See:* inheritance, disinheritance (disheritor disinherit).

**disinter**  *See:* internment (disinter or inter).

**disinterested witness**  *See:* witness, disinterested witness (interested witness).

**disjoinder**  *See:* joinder, disjoinder.

**disjunctive**  *See:* conjunctive (disjunctive).

**dismissal (dismiss)**  The rejection of a complaint, claim, indictment, or charge. A dismissal is a determination by the judge of a trial court that a complaint or indictment, or a particular count of the complaint or indictment, is to be removed from the court without further hearing. A dismissal may be with prejudice, in which case the dismissal acts as a final decision forever barring the claims made, or it may be without prejudice, in which case the claims can be refiled in a corrected form, as long as they would not be otherwise barred by a doctrine of limitations.

*See also:* dismissal, abatement of a legal action; case, case in chief.

*mootness*  An action on a moot claim will be dismissed.

**abatement of a legal action**  Dismissal or suspension of a case. Abatement is a suspension of proceedings as a matter of right and usually results in the dismissal of an action at law. At the common law, an action that was abated was dismissed, often as a result of a mistake in the form of action, and would have to be refiled in order to be revived. Many contemporary statutory actions and pleas, such as a motion to arbitrate, however, act to abate the action in a manner that allows its revival within the same case. In its most technical sense, abatement is usually required by law or under court rules, and motions to abate an action are to be granted as a matter of right, not of judicial discretion, if the pleading for the abatement is well made.

*See also:* dismissal (dismiss).

**discontinuance**   A withdrawal by the plaintiff prior to trial, ending an action. A discontinuance is the interruption of civil proceedings by the plaintiff in a manner like nonsuit or voluntary dismissal, in which the plaintiff serves notice of discontinuance to the court and other parties, after which the action is removed from the docket if no other plaintiff remains. Discontinuance is allowed as a matter of right prior to the defendant's answer or by order afterward. Like a nonsuit, it may toll a statute of limitation.

Discontinuance may be treated like a voluntary dismissal, in the sense that it does not operate as a judgment on the merits, although the effect of the plaintiff's taking two voluntary discontinuances may bar further claims in that jurisdiction, if allowing a third action would work a hardship on the defendant. In jurisdictions that allow both nonsuit and discontinuance, the discontinuance may be allowed prior to trial and the nonsuit after trial but prior to judgment.

*See also:* dismissal, nonsuit.

**dismissal with prejudice (dismissal without prejudice)**   The dismissal of an action that may not be refiled. A dismissal with prejudice is the final dismissal of an action, with res adjudicata attaching to the judgment so that the plaintiff may not bring an action on the same facts against the same defendants in any court.

A dismissal without prejudice is a dismissal that is final only as to that filing, meaning that the claim may be refiled in the same or a different court with jurisdiction over the matter, as long as limitations do not bar the later filing.

**grounds for dismissal**

**failure of service**   *See:* service, service of process.

**forum non conveniens**   *See:* jurisdiction, forum non conveniens (transfer to a more convenient forum).

**limitation of action**   *See:* limitation, limitation of action (limitations of actions).

**res judicata**   *See:* res, res judicata (res adjudicata).

**satisfaction**   *See:* accord, accord and satisfaction.

**spoliation of evidence**   *See:* spoliation, spoliation of evidence | dismissal.

**standing**   *See:* standing in court.

**dismissal for want of prosecution (D.W.O.P. or DWOP or neglect of prosecution)**   Dismissal for a plaintiff's neglect of a suit. Want of prosecution, or neglect of prosecution, is a basis in federal court for dismissal of a civil action for failure to follow the rules or an order. In many state courts,

want of prosecution is basis for dismissal or nonsuit for a failure to prosecute or for inexcusable neglect. Usually, the dismissal for failure to prosecute is made without prejudice, although such a dismissal does not toll limitations as might a nonsuit.

*See also:* dismissal, nonsuit.

**failure to comply with order or rules**   A plaintiff may be dismissed for failure to comply with the rules or a court order. A failure to comply with an order or a rule is the basis for dismissal under Federal Rule 41 and its state analogues. The nature of the rule allows dismissal for both failures to comply with court rules or orders at any stage of the action, including the failure to join parties, amend a complaint, enter into a pre-trial order, and appear for trial. Under the federal rules, the motion for dismissal for the failure to comply with a rule or order can only be made by a defendant in order to dismiss a claim and not by a plaintiff to dismiss a defense, although some state rules allow such motions by either party.

**failure to state a claim upon which relief can be granted (Rule 12(b)(6) motion or 12(b)(6))**   Facts giving rise to no claim in law or equity that can support an action. A failure to state a claim upon which relief can be granted is the insufficiency of a complaint or other initial pleading because, as a matter of law or equity that may be applied in that court, the claim cannot be the basis for a remedy. Because a complaint must present the facts to support a claim for a remedy under the law, an action cannot be dismissed if any plausible interpretation of the facts as presented would support any claim for relief. Even if the facts alleged in the complaint are provable and true, unless the facts demonstrate the defendant is liable in a manner the law will grant the plaintiff a remedy, the complaint should be dismissed under this rule.

The defendant's motion or assertion in a responsive pleading that the complaint fails to state a claim is governed by Rule 12(b)(6), which is further developed in Rule 12(d), which specifies that a motion based on matter outside the pleadings, if such matter is accepted by the court, is no longer a motion for dismissal but a motion for summary judgment, subject to the standards of Rule 56.

**Twombly test (Twombly standard)**   The facts of the complaint must state a claim that is plausible on its face. The Twombly test, from Bell Atlantic Corp. v. Twombly, 550 U.S. 544 (2007), requires a motion to dismiss for failure to state a claim to be denied if a complaint and the pleadings associated with it in the record allege facts that are sufficient to state a claim for relief that is plausible on its face. If the facts alleged are merely conceivable (or inconcievable) but not plausible, the motion should be granted. As of 2010, it is not clear that the Twombly standard persists, or whether it was overturned by Ashcroft v. Iqbal, 556 U.S. —, 129 S.Ct. 1937 (2009).

*See also:* pleading, pleading theories, notice pleading, plausible on its face (Twombly standard or Iqbal test or facial plausibility).

**lack of jurisdiction**  A complaint can be dismissed for lack of jurisdiction. Lack of jurisdiction is a basis for dismissal of a civil action under Federal Rule 12 and its state analogues. A defendant must move to dismiss for lack of subject matter jurisdiction or personal jurisdiction, improper venue, improper process, or improper service of process. If the defendant does not move to dismiss on these grounds in the Answer or other responsive pleading, or in its first motion in the court, the failure of jurisdiction is waived, and the action continues. However, if the court lacks subject matter jurisdiction, the failure of the defendant to raise an objection is immaterial. Lack of subject matter jurisdiction is always a ground for dismissal, whenever it is properly raised by a party or by the court sua sponte.

*See also:* jurisdiction (legislative jurisdiction or executive jurisdiction or judicial jurisdiction).

**involuntary dismissal**  A dismissal of an action not made at the plaintiff's request. An involuntary dismissal is a dismissal by a court other than at the plaintiff's request, usually because the plaintiff has concluded discovery or trial and cannot prove the action as filed or because of a failure to comply with court rules or a court order. Although involuntary dismissal is sometimes used to describe any dismissal opposed by the plaintiff under Rule 12, only Rule 41(b) motions are called involuntary dismissals in the text of the federal rules. An involuntary dismissal ordered under Rule 12 or Rule 41, that is not based on jurisdiction, failure of process, joinder, or venue, is both an adjudication on the merits and an appealable order.

*See also:* dismissal, voluntary dismissal.

**nonsuit**  Dismissal of the plaintiff's case for failure of proof or prosecution. Nonsuit is a judgment dismissing the plaintiff's case, either on the plaintiff's own motion or on the motion of the defendant, for the plaintiff's failure either to plead a legally sufficient case or to prosecute timely the steps of the civil action. In the Federal Rules, the nonsuit has been replaced by dismissal under rules 12 and 41. Voluntary nonsuit is usually without prejudice, unless it is the result of a settlement or a de facto retreat before loss.

*See also:* dismissal, discontinuance.

**compulsory nonsuit**  A nonsuit granted on motion from the defense on the legal merits. A compulsory nonsuit results from a defendant's motion for involuntary nonsuit based on the plaintiff's failure to state a legally sufficient case. It is a state motion for nonsuit akin to a Federal 12(b)(6) motion for dismissal for failure to state a claim. The difference between a compulsory and an involuntary nonsuit is that the involuntary nonsuit is a result of unilateral action of the plaintiff in the face of otherwise certain defeat, while compulsory nonsuit results from a motion by the defendant.

*See also:* dismissal, nonsuit, involuntary nonsuit.

**involuntary nonsuit**  A nonsuit taken once the plaintiff's loss is inevitable. An involuntary nonsuit is a nonsuit made by the plaintiff following either an adversary ruling that has made it certain that the plaintiff will suffer an involuntary dismissal or a hostile judgment, or the defendant's motion on grounds for which judgment would be final. The difference between an involuntary and a compulsory nonsuit is that the compulsory nonsuit is a result of a motion by the defendant rather than by unilateral action of the plaintiff.

**voluntary dismissal**  A dismissal by motion of or agreed to by the plaintiff. A voluntary dismissal is the termination of an action on the motion of the plaintiff, either acting alone or in agreement with the defense; it is the federal equivalent of a voluntary nonsuit. A voluntary dismissal may be taken by the plaintiff by right prior to the defendant's first pleading in the case if all parties stipulate to a dismissal. Voluntary dismissals after the defendant has entered to which the defendant does not stipulate the dismissal are made by court order. A voluntary dismissal does not extinguish a counterclaim filed before the dismissal. Voluntary dismissals are presumptively without prejudice and do not operate to bar a further filing, but this presumption fails if there was a previous voluntary dismissal or if the motion, stipulation, or court order specifies that the dismissal is with prejudice. A voluntary dismissal without prejudice cannot be appealed.

**disobedience**  *See:* obedience (disobedience).

**disorder**

**civil disorder**  A disturbance to the public caused by a group of people. A civil disorder, in the common law, is a public disturbance caused by three or more persons acting together in a manner that endangers others, threatens to harm property, or which results in such injury or damage. Civil disorder has also been used to describe the conditions of neighborhoods in which the elements of civil order, including general obedience to the law, respect for property, and the reasonable maintenance of property, are absent or inhibited.

*See also:* riot.

**disorderly conduct (disorderly person)**  Conduct that disturbs the peace. Disorderly conduct, like breach of the peace, is a general term that encompasses a great many criminal actions in violation of the peace and order of a community, although it is not without limits. The once-common means of defining the offense by its harm to the community or violation of order did not provide sufficient notice of what conduct was criminal, leaving police with too great a discretion to define the crime on the curbside and eventually leading the courts to void such laws as unconstitutionally vague in violation of due process of law. More modern definitions of disorderly conduct require acts of willful conduct, with lists that vary from jurisdiction to jurisdiction, but which usually include fighting, making loud and unusual noise that affects others, making public threats or obscene speech, blocking public roads or walks, disturbing public events, wrongly filing police or fire reports, damaging public or private property, etc. Most states distinguish conduct that is disorderly or a breach of the peace from disturbances in general, which must take place in a public road, space, or property. Most such offenses are misdemeanors.

A disorderly person is a person who commits disorderly conduct. Note, though, that to term a place a "disorderly house" is usually to indicate its use as a place for commercial sex.

*See also:* peace, disturbing the peace (breach of the peace).

**disparagement (disparaging goods or disparaging title or trade libel)** Criticism of goods or merchandise. Disparagement, or trade libel, is the tortious description of the goods or merchandise of a producer or seller, such that the criticism is untrue or misleading, or is a statement not based on reliable scientific data, and, under the common law, though not in statutory causes of action for agricultural disparagement, discourages consumers from buying the particular goods. Disparagement is also a tort when a person falsely claims a person or entity lacks title to land or other property.

*See also:* libel, food libel.

**disparate impact** *See:* discrimination, employment discrimination, disparate impact.

**disparate treatment** *See:* discrimination, employment discrimination, disparate treatment.

**dispensation (dispensatio)** A relaxation of the law to allow a deviation from a legal requirement. A dispensation is an allowance for a person to dispense with obedience to a lawful requirement. A dispensation is an exception from a general law that is allowed only to a particular individual and does not form the basis for an exception from compliance with the same law by other people. Dispensations are usually associated with canon law, but several forms of U.S. law amount to the exercise of a dispensing power, such as the granting of a variance from a zoning law or the allowance of a waiver from compliance with a law by an administrative agency. By definition, dispensation is a legislative prerogative that may be delegated, thus it differs from the granting of pardons or clemency by an executive.

A dispensation in private law also exists, in which a grantor retains a power to dispense with a requirement of land use, and its exercise may also be called a dispensation.

**displacement** Removal as a result of some outside force. Displacement, in general, is the removal of an object or person from its position as a result of some force or motive other than in the thing or person removed.

In admiralty, displacement is the mass of the vessel, represented by the weight of the water that the vessel displaces. Even though the displacement is calculated, it represents the water being forced from the volume of the vessel.

A person may be displaced from office, from a position of employment, from housing, or from a home or state. A person who loses a house owing to eminent domain is a displaced person, as is a refugee who flees a natural disaster or combat zone.

A law that is replaced by a law from a more authoritative source is displaced.

**displaced person** A person who has been forced from home. A displaced person is a person who has been required to leave the person's domicile by some superior force. In U.S. law, a displaced person is one who has been ejected from a home taken by eminent domain by a state or the United States, such persons including the owner of the condemned property and all of its lawful occupants, who are entitled to relocation assistance in some circumstances. More generally, a displaced person is one who has fled an area distressed by a natural disaster or similar event and is no longer able to return to that person's former domicile. In international law, a displaced person is a person who has left a home or hometown to seek shelter from combat or a natural disaster, such a person being "internally displaced" if the person is housed or seeking housing within the person's native state, or "internationally displaced" if the person is housed or seeking housing outside the person's native state.

*See also:* refugee (asylum seeker).

**displacement from a building** The removal of owners or tenants from a building. Displacement from a building is the forced removal of owners or tenants from a building, whether the building is used for housing, commerce, or some other purpose, by an order of ejectment or condemnation by a public agency. Displacement in this sense differs from ordinary eviction, which is usually brought by a person with superior title against an occupant, such as a landlord against a holdover tenant or an owner against a trespasser. Although an order of eviction may be a part of the process of displacement, a person displaced from housing, and in many instances a business or entity displaced from a building, is entitled to compensation.

More generally, displacement arises when a person moves from a housing area for any reason, including economic and social changes affecting the person's housing, neighborhood, or city.

*See also:* eviction (evict).

**statutory displacement of the common law** The replacement of a common law doctrine by a statute. Displacement of the common law occurs when a legislature adopts a statute or code that fully regulates a particular subject of commerce or private life, or a claim or basis of liability that had been subject to doctrines and precedent of the common law. Common law principles or claims are not inherently displaced because legislation is passed affecting a claim; the statute must either expressly abrogate the common law or provide a requirement, regulation, rule, claim, defense, or remedy that conflicts with the common law. A conflict is determined either if a regulation, rule, or claim established in the statute differs from the common law and is declared in the statute to be exclusive or if it is found by a court to have been intended to be or constructively required to be exclusive. A statutory defense to a common law cause of action, in most cases, amounts to displacement. Still, there is a presumption in favor of finding that the common law has not been displaced, following the maxim of statutory construction that a statute in derogation of the common law is to be strictly construed. Thus, if a common law principle or rule can be construed to complement or supplement a statutory requirement and the statute does not expressly displace the common law, the common law principle or rule is probably not displaced.

Note: there are may forms of displacement of law, which occurs whenever a law from one source is replaced by a law from another source. Preemption of state law by federal law is a form of displacement, but it is more common to use displacement in law to describe the substitution of common law by statutory law, and to use preemption to describe the substitution of state law by federal law.

*See also:* preemption, constitutional preemption, federal preemption of state law (congressional preemption or express preemption or implied preemption).

**disposable income**   *See:* income, disposable income.

**disposess proceeding**   *See:* eviction, summary eviction (disposess proceeding).

**Disposing Clause**   *See:* constitution, U.S. Constitution, clauses, Disposing Clause.

**disposition (dispose)**   The transfer or allocation of property to another. A disposition is the transfer or allocation of property by one person to another; it may also refer to the actual document or instrument which effectuates such a transfer. Dispositions most often arise in a will, in which transfers of property are made between the testator and the recipients.

**disposition hearing**   *See:* child, child custody, disposition hearing.

**disposition without trial**   *See:* trial, disposition without trial.

**dispositive fact**   *See:* fact, dispositive fact.

**dispositive motion**   *See:* motion, dispositive motion, | Rule 12(b)(6) (failure to state a claim upon which relief can be granted); motion, dispositive motion, motion to dismiss; motion, dispositive motion.

**dispossession**   To involuntarily lose possession of a property interest. Dispossession is the loss of a property caused by another person's action to take possession from the person dispossessed. Usually, dispossession refers to chattels, although it may also refer to the taking of possession without ownership of real property, as in a lease; or to a dispossession as a step toward claiming title through adverse possession. Technically a person who would be dispossessed of an ownership in real property is disseized.

**disproportional or proportional or proportionate**   *See:* proportionality (disproportional or proportional or proportionate).

**disproportionate burden**   *See:* scrutiny, standards of scrutiny, disproportionate burden.

**dispute**   An argument. A dispute is a quarrel or controversy between two or more parties. It exists when there is a genuine issue of material fact or an issue as to the application of law to the facts of a particular case. To dispute refers to the participation in the dispute, as well as to offer a specific argument put forward in the dispute.

**dispute settlement body**   *See:* trade, international trade, World Trade Organization, dispute settlement body (DSB).

**disqualification (disqualify)**   The removal for cause of counsel, judge, juror, or other officer from participation in an action or in office. Disqualification is the process for the removal of a judge, opposing counsel, juror, or other officer from participation in a judicial proceeding for any reason. Disqualification of a judge or juror is usually based upon an interest in the cause of action or a demonstrable bias or inability to hear the cause without prejudice. Disqualification of an opposing counsel may be based on lack of expertise or performance in the case, but it is usually based either on a conflict of interest either because the attorney cannot adequately represent the attorney's own client or because the attorney had earlier represented the party now opposing the attorney's client, and the judge finds that disqualification is necessary to ensure justice is done between the parties.

A disqualification in a single action is not a disqualification from holding office. A disqualification per se is a prohibition on a person's performing or holding a given office. So, for instance, a convicted felon may be disqualified from holding a given office, and without a pardon or other rehabilitation, the disqualification is permanent.

*See also:* office, removal from office.

**disqualification of juror or disqualified juror**   *See:* jury, jury selection, juror disqualification (disqualification of juror or disqualified juror).

**disseisin**   The taking of ownership in realty. Disseisin was the ouster or taking of real property from the person who held seisin, or freehold ownership in it, through any claim to a superior title or any adverse interest. This includes wrongful disseisin, an entry onto the land that interferes with the true owner's possession, with the intent to take title by prescription; it also includes ouster of the true owner under a claim of superior title.

*See also:* dispossession.

**novel disseisin** A writ for a feudal tenant to recover land. Novel disseisin was the writ by which a tenant in the feudal system — whether a tenant in fee simple, fee tail, or for a term of life — could be awarded new seisin in the lands from which he had been barred by the unlawul occupation of another party. The writ allowed both the return of seisin and damages.

**dissent** A disagreement with something said or done. Dissent is a person's disagreement, either express or implied, with a statement made or action taken by another. Dissent is the antonym of assent.

*See also:* opinion, judicial opinion, dissenting opinion (dissent).

**dissenting opinion** *See:* opinion, judicial opinion, dissenting opinion (dissent).

**dissolution of marriage** *See:* divorce (dissolution of marriage).

**dissolution of partnership** *See:* partnership, dissolution of partnership (to dissolve a partnership).

**disinheritance** *See:* inheritance, disinheritance, disinherison (disherison).

**distress** A severe condition of stress or strain. Distress is a condition in which some adversity or challenging condition has led to stress or strain. In various contexts, distress is a condition of unusual risk or harm. For example, distress of a vessel describes a ship in peril of sinking or suffering damage to the vessel, its personnel, and/or cargo. Distress of a chattel suggests its loss or harm. Distress of a person suggests an individual who is in trouble, sickness, or pain. Financial distress is used to describe a lack of capital for current needs.

At common law, the distress of property is the seizure of property subject to some claim, particularly following a default on a mortgage secured by the property or default on a lease for failure to pay rents. The distress, or distraint, was a common-law action for recovery of property as well as the means of self-help, and though the term is rarely used in these technical senses, distressed property remains a legal description of mortgaged land subject to foreclosure or chattels subject to repossession.

**distress as self help (distrain)** A claim against property for recovery or payment of a debt. Distress is an obsolete form of self-help for the recovery of goods wrongfully held by another or of goods held by a debtor in arrears, or for a landlord to seize chattels in payment of unpaid rents. The object of the seizure of goods other than those wrongfully held was, in theory, to force the debtor or obligor to appear in court in a distress proceeding to order the payment of the amounts due. This proceeding has generally been replaced by attachment, garnishment, replevin, and the enforcement of liens. Property subject to distress was said to be distrained.

*See also:* self, self help (self-help).

**emotional distress** Mental suffering or anxiety as an emotional response to some event or condition. Emotional distress is mental suffering that arises from the effects or memory of a particular event, occurrence, pattern of events, or condition. Emotional distress can usually be discerned from its symptoms of anxiety, depression, loss of ability to perform certain tasks, or physical illness. Severe emotional distress is unendurable emotional distress, distress of a form that a reasonable person would consider to be more than a person ought to be expected to bear. In some jurisdictions, severe emotion distress is such distress that its mental or physical symptoms ought to be diagnosed and treated by a licensed physician or mental health professional.

**intentional infliction of emotional distress (I.I.E.D. or IIED or outrage)** Emotional distress purposefully caused by another person. Intentional infliction of emotional distress is the tort of deliberately acting to cause another person to suffer from emotional harm. The elements of the tort are presented in varying formulae in different jurisdictions, but in general, if the defendant intentionally or recklessly engages in extreme and outrageous conduct that causes emotional distress to another, then the defendant is liable for the emotional distress and, if bodily harm to the victim results from it, for such bodily harm. People other than the initial victim may also recover, including witnesses and family members, although non-family witnesses are usually limited from recovering damages for harms that do not result from bodily injury.

*freedom of speech* A claim for intentional infliction of emotional distress may not be brought by a public figure or a public official under circumstances in which libel would be constitutionally barred.
*See also:* malice, actual malice.

*impact* The impact rule, which applies in many jurisdictions in order to limit claims for negligent infliction of emotional distress, is not required when there is evidence that the defendant intended the defendant's conduct to cause the emotional distress or related injury to the plaintiff.
*See also:* distress, emotional distress, negligent infliction of emotional distress, impact rule.

**negligent infliction of emotional distress (N.I.E.D. or NIED)** Emotional distress caused by the negligence of another person. Negligent infliction of emotional distress is the tort of committing negligent action that causes mental or emotional harm (such as fright or anxiety) that is not directly brought about by a physical injury. In order to prove NIED, the plaintiff must show that the defendant breached a duty of due care owed to the plaintiff, and the breach caused the plaintiff's emotional injury. Physical injury to the plaintiff may result as well, but it is not a necessary element of the tort. NIED is recognized in only a few jurisdictions in the United States, although most will recognize pain and suffering, including emotional distress, in an action for negligence.

*See also:* outrage; death, wrongful death.

**impact rule** Bodily contact allows recovery for pain and suffering by a victim or witness to an accident. The impact rule traditionally limited recovery for mental pain and suffering in a claim for negligent infliction of emotional distress to plaintiffs who had been physically touched by some matter associated with the negligent act, such as a plaintiff being hit by the defendant's car, or a witness to an accident being hit with a victim's blood. This rule has been rejected in most states and is followed in fewer than a dozen U.S. jurisdictions, most of which have moderated its effect both by creating a variety of exceptions, such as an allowance for witnesses of an injury to a member of the witness's family to recover, and by allowing recovery when the proof demonstrates mental pain and suffering that resulted in physical symptoms apparent soon after the negligent act.

**zone-of-danger rule** The distress of a person in a zone of danger is actionable. The zone of danger is a geographical area near an accident or incident causing injury, within which a person would be in danger of the same injury. Under the zone-of-danger rule, which is applied in some jurisdictions to claims of negligent infliction of emotional distress in lieu of the impact rule, the only parties who may bring an action against the party causing such an injury brought not for physical harm but for infliction of emotional distress are those persons who were within the zone of danger. A mere bystander in no risk of injury would be barred from bringing a claim.

**mental distress** Any mental condition that would normally require treatment or cause physical illness. Mental distress, in general, is any anguish or emotional stress that interferes with the ordinary activities of a person's daily life. In many legal claims, mental distress is only a basis for recovery when it is considered serious mental distress, meaning any form of mental illness or psychiatric condition that involves some temporary, substantial incapacity or mental illness or condition that would normally require psychiatric treatment; it is also a mental condition that causes a physical or bodily illness.

# distress

**distribution**

**distribution of estate (distribute or distributor)** The allocation of the property of an intestate decedent to the heirs. Distribution is the determination of which heirs at law are entitled to shares of property from the estate of an individual who died intestate, followed by the liquidation of the estate and the allocation of a proper share to each heir according to the distribution.

**distribution in kind** A distribution of property rather than of money. A distribution in kind is the transfer of property, rather than of money, to an heir. The value of the property distributed is deducted from the heir's share of the whole value of the estate, and any difference is made up in money. Any overage in value is usually recompensed pro rata to the other heirs.

**per capita** Shares in an estate are allocated equally to each person. Per capita is a term for measurement or assessment of the share of an estate according to each person to whom shares shall go, each receiving the same value of share. The distribution of an estate among heirs per capita, with each heir of the same class receiving an equal portion of the whole, contrasts with a distribution per stirpes, in which each heir receives a portion of a share allocated by stock, so that a person of one status may receive more than a person of another.

*See also:* per, per capita.

**per capita with representation (modified per stirpes)** Shares in an estate are allocated according to relationships in the family but then equally per person. A distribution that is per capita with representation occurs when a decedent has living heirs in one level of consanguinity but was predeceased by another person who would have been an heir of that level, and the predeceased person has living heirs. The heirs of the predeceased kin are also heirs of the decedent but they do not receive a portion equal to the more direct heirs. If the state provides for distribution per capita with representation, the unequal heirs are entitled to a per capita distribution of the portion that would have gone to the relative who predeceased the decedent. For example, imagine Agnes dies in a jurisdiction with representation per capita (having been predeceased by Bob her husband and by her parents) having had children Charlie, Don, and Edna, but Charlie had predeceased Agnes, too. Charlie has two children, Filbert and Gina, who are both alive at Agnes's death, and who will each take one-half of the share of the estate of Agnes that would have gone to Charlie.

**per stirpes (in stirpes or rule of representation)** Shares in an estate are allocated by roles in the family. Per stirpes, which is Latin for "by stock," is the formula for the allocation of a distribution from a decedent's estate according to the family relationships the various distributees have to the decedent. Distribution per stirpes contrasts with per capita, in which each of the distributees would receive an equal share of the distribution, regardless of familial descent. The difference is easily illustrated: Assume A dies, having had children B and C, with B having predeceased A and leaving children D and E, and A's interests to go to all of his children and grandchildren alive at his death. A per capita distribution would give C, D, and E each one third. A per stirpes distribution would give C one-half, D one-quarter, and E one-quarter. Distribution per stirpes is also distribution according to the rule of representation.

**distributive justice**   *See:* justice, distributive justice.

**district**   A geographic division of a state into separate jurisdictional districts. A district is a division mapped across the land, within which a court, office or administration is allocated duties. In this manner, national, state, and municipal courts, offices, and administrations are distributed, each with a unique jurisdiction in a single district with every area subject to the jurisdiction of one court, office, or administration. The United States courts of general jurisdiction are divided into districts within each state. Congressional districts are likewise divided in each state.

**disturbing the peace**   *See:* peace, disturbing the peace (breach of the peace).

**divano (diwano)**   Romani alternative dispute resolution. A divano is an informal negotiation procedure practiced by the Romani culture, in which all of the parties involved in a dispute participate in a discussion with a neutral third-party in order to facilitate a settlement.

**diversion (pretrial diversion or pre-trial diversion)**   The use of therapeutic rehabilitation as an alternative to criminal prosecution. Diversion is the channeling of a criminal defendant into a program for rehabilitation or treatment of a condition that is the underlying cause of the defendant's criminal conduct in lieu of prosecution for a crime the defendant allegedly committed and upon the agreement of the prosecutor. In particular, diversion helps defendants who are addicted to drugs or alcohol or who commit a crime while under the influence, although other forms of rehabilitation can also be employed. Diversion requires completion of the prescribed treatment, which usually includes the performance of additional compliance, and a diverted defendant who does not complete treatment and comply with these requirements can be subject to a reinstated prosecution. In the case of a completed diversion, however, the record of the criminal arrest may be expunged.

*See also:* court, drug court.

**diversity jurisdiction**   *See:* jurisdiction, diversity jurisdiction (diversity of citizenship).

**diversity of citizenship**   *See:* jurisdiction, diversity jurisdiction (diversity of citizenship).

**Diversity of Citizenship Clause**   *See:* constitution, U.S. Constitution, clauses, Diversity of Citizenship Clause.

**divestiture (divest or divestment or divesture)**   The alienation of a right, office, or ownership. Divestiture

describes the process of shedding one's claim or interest in a legal ownership, right, interest, or office. The word was used originally to depict the removal of one's clothes, or vestments. In legal drafting there is no significant difference intended between divestiture, divesture, and divestment, although there is a connotation that divestment is wholly voluntary while divestiture and divesture are involuntary.

Divestiture is the opposite of investiture.

**divide-and-pay-over rule**   *See:* gift, class gift, divide-and-pay-over rule.

**divided custody or shared custody**   *See:* child, child custody, joint custody (divided custody or shared custody).

**dividend**   A portion of profits or a payment. A dividend is a portion of the principal or profits from some thing or activity, divided among its owners. The most common form is a stock dividend, a payment from profits realized by a corporation and divided so as to pay a portion for each share of stock. More generally, a dividend represents any share in a payment distributed among a group of payees.

**dividend income**   *See:* income, dividend income.

**dividends-received deduction**   *See:* tax, tax deduction, dividends-received deduction.

**divisible contract**   *See:* contract, divisibility of contract (divisible contract).

**divisible harm**   *See:* harm, divisible harm (divisible injury or divisible harms).

**division of property**   *See:* divorce, division of property, equitable distribution.

**divorce (dissolution of marriage)**   The judicial termination of a marriage. A divorce is a judgment by the state that dissolves a marriage, terminating the legal relationship between the spouses. Physical separation of the spouses cannot, by itself, amount to a divorce. Divorce must be granted during the lives of both spouses and is only available to two people who were married as a matter of law. There is no difference between a divorce and a dissolution of marriage. The older forms of divorce a vinculo matrimonii are what is now known as divorce, and divorce a menso et thoro is now generally a decree of separation.

**abandonment of spouse**   The departure of one spouse from the other, intending never to return. Abandonment is a physical separation between spouses, initiated by the abandoning spouse with the intent never to return to the abandoned spouse. Abandonment for a year in some jurisdictions, three in others, is sufficient grounds to grant a divorce to the abandoned spouse.

*See also:* abandonment, abandonment as non-support.

**equitable distribution**  The equitable division of marital assets following divorce. Equitable distribution is the allocation of property between former spouses according to equity and with a presumption of equality that is modified based each spouse's relative contribution to or waste of the marital assets, the age of each spouse, the length of the marriage, each spouse's likely future income and liability, and the need for housing in the event of child custody. Equitable distribution, like all property divisions at divorce, does not take into account obligations of alimony or child support.

**divorce a mensa et thoro (mensa et thoro or divorce from bed and board)**  Permanent legal separation but not a full divorce. Divorce a mensa et thoro, customarily translated as "divorce from bed and board," is the common–law term for the permanent separation of a still–married couple. A couple who has been divorced from bed and board are still married as a matter of law and are barred from marrying again, and their property interests and obligations of financial support remain the same, but there is no obligation or expectation that the couple will live together.

Mensa, originally the Latin for "food on the table," by the Middle Ages had come to mean "all of one's goods." Thoro, from thorus (or torus), is the conjugal bed of a married couple.

*See also:* divorce, separation (marital separation or legal separation or judicial separation).

**grounds for divorce**  The bases for a divorce awarded for cause. Grounds for divorce vary from jurisdiction to jurisdiction and include all grounds for awarding a judgment of divorce to a party. At common law, divorce was granted only for cause, which initially consisted of adultery, cruelty, or desertion for a period of time. Later cause came to include irreconcilable differences, though this was usually a statutory change. Modern grounds for divorce include impotence, bigamy, adultery, abandonment or desertion for a year or more, outrageous conduct or cruelty toward the other spouse (including assault or attempted homicide), incarceration for a statutory period of time during the marriage (usually one to three years, or more), conviction of a felony, habitual drunkenness or alcohol abuse, or the infection of the other spouse with a sexually transmitted disease. Note: when the terms "grounds" or "cause" are used, the speaker usually means grounds for divorce arising from fault. Grounds are rarely intended to include the dissolution of the marriage on the basis of irreconcilable differences or irreconcilable breakdown, which are grounds for divorce nonetheless.

**comparative rectitude**  Judgment for the lesser fault in a divorce for cause. Comparative rectitude, a doctrine used only in the increasingly rare cases of divorce for cause, required a divorce to be awarded as a judgment to the spouse less at fault in a divorce for cause from a marriage in which both spouses committed some wrongdoing.

**irreconcilable differences divorce (I.D. or ID or I.D. divorce or irretrievable breakdown of the marriage or I.B.M. or IBM or IBM divorce or no–fault divorce)**  A divorce granted in law when a marriage has ended in fact. Irreconcilable differences refers to the cause of an irretrievable breakdown of a marriage, and one, either, or both standards are the basis for divorce in most states absent a showing of traditional grounds of fault by one party or another. Thus, divorce on the grounds of irreconcilable differences or an irretrievable breakdown is colloquially described as no–fault divorce.

Attempts to further define which differences between the spouses are irreconcilable usually turn on the subjective understanding of the parties, such that in order to meet the standard for an ID divorce, both spouses must believe that the differences between them cannot be reconciled. In most jurisdictions, a waiting period is required between the filling and the hearing of a divorce on these grounds, and in many states an ID divorce will not be granted unless there has been a prior physical separation, whether or not the separation occurred under a decree of separation.

*community property*  In states recognizing community property, each spouse takes one–half of the community's assets at divorce and retains his or her individual property.

*See also:* marriage, marital property, community property.

**separation (marital separation or legal separation or judicial separation)**  Spouses who live apart but are still married. A separation, or marital separation, is the agreement or decree that the two spouses will live apart from one another while remaining married. A separation may occur informally, by a separation agreement, or by a separation decree (or judicial order of separation), and the rights of the parties vary according both to the form of the separation and the laws in the jurisdiction in which they are domiciled. The primary difference between a separation and a divorce is that in a separation, the legal relationship between the separated spouses as married people persists, allowing spousal interests in one another's property at death, a spousal privilege for testimony in actions not brought by the other spouse, and tax filings as spouses.

*See also:* divorce (dissolution of marriage); divorce, divorce a mensa et thoro (mensa et thoro or divorce from bed and board).

**living separate and apart**  A couple with no sexual relationship. The standard for living separate and apart varies between jurisdictions, but its hallmark is that the two parties involved do not engage in sexual activity with one another. Some jurisdictions require each party to live in a separate residence, while others allow segregated quarters within a single residence.

*See also:* divorce, divorce a mensa et thoro (mensa et thoro or divorce from bed and board).

**diwano**   *See:* divano (diwano).

**DNR order or D.N.R. order**   *See:* death, do not resuscitate orders (DNR orders or D.N.R. order).

**do justice though the heavens may fall**   *See:* justice, fiat justitia ruat coelum (do justice though the heavens may fall).

**docket**   The court's calendar of judicial proceedings. A docket is the court's record of scheduled proceedings for both the court as a whole and for each case pending before it. The docket is usually maintained by the clerk of court. Most courts maintain one docket for the court overall as well as a separate criminal docket and civil docket, which are each organized to ensure both fair priority among cases and balance between the two dockets in the allocation of court resources. Recently, these records have been maintained electronically in systems like PACER, the docket access system for federal courts.
*See also:* record, court records, public access to court electronic records (P.A.C.E.R. or PACER).

**docket fee**   *See:* fee, fee for services, court fee, docket fee.

**appearance docket**   The record of parties, counsel, pleadings, and orders in each case. The appearance docket is the court record of parties, counsel who appear for parties, motions, and orders filed in each case before the court. In many courts, this is also called the case docket. To docket a motion, notice, or order is to file it on the appearance docket. In nearly every instance, anything that is docketed is to be served on the parties.

**docket call**   The calling of pending cases for a review of their status and entry of appropriate orders. A docket call is the calling of pending cases in a given trial court, generally at the beginning of a term of the court, for the purposes of setting a trial date, granting a continuation, entering a default judgment, or making any other required disposition.

**doctor**

**Doctor of Laws**   *See:* degree, academic degree, law degree, Doctor of Laws (LL.D. or LLD).

**Doctor of the Science of Law**   *See:* law, law degree, Doctor of the Science of Law (Doctor of Juridical Science or J.S.D. JSD or S.J.D. SJD).

**doctor-patient privilege**   *See:* privilege, evidentiary privilege, doctor-patient privilege (physician-patient privilege or patient-physician privilege).

**Doctor of Medicine (Dr. or M.D. or physician)**   A person licensed to practice medicine. A Doctor of Medicine is a person who has been conferred a degree in medicine from an accredited medical school and who has been licensed to practice medicine within a jurisdiction by the appropriate licensing agency.

Although an M.D. is a particular degree representing a specific course of medical training, a person may be a medical doctor after obtaining a professional degree as a doctor in various medical fields, including osteopathy, dentistry, surgery, and optometry, as long as the person is licensed by the appropriate agency in the jurisdiction and does not exceed the scope of that license.
*See also:* physician.

**quack**   An unskilled medical practitioner. A quack is either a medical doctor without genuine medical knowledge or skills or a person who fraudulently creates the impression of being a doctor despite not having completed the training and licensure required and is thus engaged in the unauthorized practice of medicine.

**doctoring**   Alteration or tampering. To doctor a thing is to change it. Thus, to doctor evidence is to tamper with it, like changing a document or other piece of evidence in order to create support for an assertion of fact, regardless of whether the assertion is true or false.

**doctrine**

**doctrine of abstention**   *See:* abstention, abstention doctrine (doctrine of abstention).

**doctrine of approximation**   *See:* cy pres, doctrine of approximation.

**doctrine of continuing violation**   *See:* discrimination, employment discrimination, doctrine of continuing violation.

**doctrine of our federalism**   *See:* federalism, doctrine of our federalism.

**doctrine of precedent**   *See:* precedent (doctrine of precedent).

**doctrine of reversions**   *See:* title, doctrine of worthier title (doctrine of reversions).

**doctrine of severance or severability of clauses or blue pencil rule**   *See:* contracts, contract interpretation, severance (doctrine of severance or severability of clauses or blue pencil rule).

**doctrine of the captain of the ship**   *See:* malpractice, medical malpractice, captain of the ship doctrine (doctrine of the captain of the ship).

**doctrine of uses**   *See:* use, doctrine of uses, statute of uses; use, doctrine of uses, cestui que use; use, doctrine of uses (equitable use or beneficial use).

**doctrine of waste**   *See:* waste, doctrine of waste (property waste).

**doctrine of worthier title**   *See:* title, doctrine of worthier title, inter vivos branch of the doctrine of worthier title; title, doctrine of worthier title (doctrine of reversions).

## document

**document discovery** *See:* discovery, document discovery, official record; discovery, document discovery.

**document draft** *See:* draft, draft of a document (document draft).

**documentary draft** *See:* draft, draft as negotiable instrument, documentary draft.

**documentary evidence** *See:* evidence, documentary evidence, best-evidence rule; evidence, documen-tary evidence.

**documentation of alien** *See:* alien, documentation of alien.

**documents affecting an interest in property** *See:* hearsay, hearsay exception, hearsay allowed regardless of witness availability, documents affecting an interest in property.

**dog** The domesticated canine. Dog, in a legal rule, includes all dogs, whether they are pets or not, unless the term is further modified such as sniffer dog, guard dog, companion dog, or domesticated dog. Dog does not presumably include wild, undomesticated dogs. Dogs are owned by humans, and the owner of a dog is liable for the injuries it causes if the dog has been maintained negligently or used maliciously. A dog that is a hazard to the public safety may be forfeit from the owner.

**seeing eye dog** *See:* animal, service animal (seeing eye dog).

**dangerous dog (dog bite or one bite rule)** A dog that has demonstrated its dangerousness. A dangerous dog is a dog that has bitten, attacked, or menaced a person or domesticated animal without provocation. The first instance of this behavior puts the dog's owner on notice of the animal's dangerousness, and the owner may then be strictly liable for any subsequent injuries the dog causes, especially for dog bites to people or other animals. Though this standard is sometimes called the one–bite rule, this label is misleading because the dog need not have bitten in order to be considered dangerous; merely showing a dangerous propensity is sufficient. Some jurisdictions regulate dangerous dogs, requiring they be registered and controlled.

**dog fighting** Causing a dog to fight another dog. Dog fighting is the creation of a situation in which a dog is likely to fight another dog for any reason other than the bona fide protection of a person, property, or the dog itself. When dog fighting is done intentionally or knowingly, it is a crime. Knowingly allowing a dog that one owns or for which one has any responsibility to fight with another dog and failing to take reasonable steps to intervene is prima facie evidence of dog fighting.
*See also:* cruelty, animal cruelty.

**dog won't hunt** A response to a mistaken or foolish proposition. "That dog won't hunt" is a common epigrammatic response to a statement that the listener believes is false or impossible.

**sniffer dog (cadaver dog or detection dog)** A dog trained to detect people or chemicals by smell. A sniffer dog, or a cadaver dog or detection dog, is a dog trained in search or surveillance by the detection of odor. Sniffer dogs are routinely used in searches for contraband, and an alert by a trained sniffer dog is probable cause to believe that the person, space, or container indicated by the dog contains the contraband the dog is trained to detect. A cadaver dog is specially trained to smell out a dead body or part of a dead body. Other specialized dogs include drug–detection dogs, accelerant–detection dogs, bomb–sniffing dogs, and the venerable tracker. If evidence from the dog is to be introduced in court, a proper foundation—including the dog's training, mission record, number of successes and failures on task, and handler record—is essential to establish the dog's credibility and qualification. Such detail is usually not required to rely on a dog's evidence to establish probable cause for a warrant.
*See also:* alert, alert by sniffer dog; smell (odor).

**watchdog (guard dog)** A dog trained or kept as a guardian of property. A watchdog is a dog kept for security, particularly for the purpose of alerting the owner to an intruder or discouraging a person from entering. The owner of a property is entitled to keep a watchdog, to the degree the dog is analogous to devices that are allowed for the protection of property, such as alarms, locks, and automatically closing doors, though the dog cannot pose the kind of unreasonable danger analogous to using a loaded spring gun to protect property.

**dogma** A belief that is widely held as true beyond question. Dogma is a customary idea of what is true, held to be so authoritative by most members, or the elite members, of a community, that doubt and disagreement with the idea is considered improper behavior by others.

**DOHSA** *See:* death, wrongful death, Death on the High Seas Act (DOHSA).

**DOMA or D.O.M.A.** *See:* marriage, Defense of Marriage Act (DOMA or D.O.M.A.).

**domain** Property subject to the control of an owner or a state. A domain is the whole of the lands, people, and powers that are subject to the control of either an individual or a state. In the sense of dominion, domain is the right of control itself rather than the thing controlled, although this nicety was rarely used in Bouvier's time and is now likely obsolete. Generally, "to survey one's domain" is to observe one's property in lands.

In the sense of domain as property subject to one's exclusive control, the term is used as a figure of speech to mean an exclusive authority or jurisdiction. Thus, some task or question in an office that is the domain of one clerk is within the scope of that clerk's duties. This usage includes any category that is subject to the control of a particular person, institution, or rule, such as the domain of equity, the domain of the district court, and the domain of expert testimony. In this sense, domain might or might not mean that the person or entity has sole power over some matter, an idea more similar to that of province; this intent is more clearly signaled by stating something is within one's exclusive domain.

*See also:* demesne; province.

**eminent domain** *See:* condemnation, condemnation through eminent domain.

**internet domain (domain name or internet address)** The word-based address corresponding to a computer identity on the internet. An internet domain name is part of a uniform resource locator, or URL, which uses words and figures in lieu of numbers to designate a unique address for a computer connected to the internet. Domain names, as of 2010, were approved internationally by a non-profit global corporation, The Internet Corporation for Assigned Names and Numbers.

*See also:* internet (web or world wide web).

**public domain** The property of the state or of the people. Public domain, in general, is anything that is held in common among the members of the public and may not be owned or controlled by a single entity or owner, other than the United States, for the benefit of the people. This form of property ownership is especially important in its contemporary usage in intellectual property law, as material that might be subject to patent, copyright, or trademark that is in the public domain remains free to be used by all.

Intellectual property in the public domain includes all property that cannot be subject to copyright, patent, or trademark, whether it is public because of its nature, such as an idea (as opposed to the particular form of its expression), or because it is material created by the U.S. government, or is public through operation of the law, such as materials older than copyright or other protection persists. Matter that was once subject to such regulation, the term of which has since expired, is in the public domain, and once material has entered the public domain, it cannot be removed from it.

**Dombrowski doctrine** *See:* abstention, abstention doctrine, Dombrowski doctrine.

**dome (doom)** A judgment or decree in Anglo-Saxon law. In Anglo-Saxon law, a doom was an order, whether a judgment in a case or a decree made in general, issued in the name of the king.

**domestic**

**domestic abuse** *See:* abuse, domestic abuse.

**domestic corporation** *See:* corporation, corporations, domestic corporation.

**domestic court** *See:* court, domestic court (domestic tribunal).

**domestic partnership** *See:* marriage, civil union (domestic partnership).

**domestic terrorism** *See:* terrorism, domestic terrorism.

**domestic tribunal** *See:* court, domestic court (domestic tribunal).

**domesticated animal** *See:* animal, domesticated animal.

**domestication** *See:* agriculture, domestication.

**domicile (domicil or domiciliary)** A person's primary residence. A domicile is a person's primary residence, the headquarters from which a person has no intention of permanent departure. A domicile differs from a residence or habitation in that a person or entity can have only one domicile.

Domicile in the United States is not essential to citizenship, although domicile is required in most instances for a person to be naturalized. Domicile within a particular state is essential for ascertaining citizenship in that state of the United States. Further, domicile establishes an important relationship between an individual and a state in international law, which may justify an assertion of citizenship by the domiciliary state and another state in which the person resides or has interests.

*See also:* lex, lex domicilii; residence (residency or reside).

**domiciliary administration** *See:* administraton, administration of estate, domiciliary administration (domiciliary administrator).

**domiciliary administrator** *See:* administraton, administration of estate, domiciliary administration (domiciliary administrator).

**dominant estate** *See:* easement, dominant estate (dominant tenement).

**dominant tenement** *See:* tenement, dominant tenement; easement, dominant estate (dominant tenement).

**dominion** Control, most often over property. Dominion is the control inherent in ownership, most often of property, including the power to use it or dispose of it at will.

**dominium** Dominion, ownership, or control. Dominum, in the private sense, means ownership, and in the public sense, means sovereignty. It is the origin of many terms in the law, including dominion and condominium.

*See also:* condominium, condominium as jurisdiction (condominia).

**domitae naturae** Domesticated animals. Domitae naturae are animals suited for living with human beings. The owner of a domesticated animal has a property interest in it and may protect that interest in conversion, trespass, and other common law or statutory actions, but the owner is also responsible to others for any unreasonable damage that the animal causes.

*See also:* ferae, ferae naturae; animal, domesticated animal.

**donation (donate or donee or donor)** A gift. A donation is a transfer of property to another with no exchange of value, pecuniary or otherwise, to the transferor. The donation is effective and irrevocable when a donor knowingly and intending to give the gift forever and without condition delivers the property or a symbol of the property to the donee, and the donee accepts it. A donation is a gift, and it is often done for charitable purposes. To perform such an act is to donate. The recipient of a donation is a donee; the entity making the conveyance is a donor.

*See also:* gift (gift over or give).

**donatio mortis causa** *See:* gift, gift causa mortis.

**doom** *See:* dome (doom).

**door in the face** *See:* negotiation, negotiation technique, rejection–then–retreat tactic (door in the face).

**dormant claim** *See:* claim, dormant claim (long-dormant claim).

**Dormant Commerce Clause** *See:* constitution, U.S. Constitution, clauses, Commerce Clause, Dormant Commerce Clause (Negative Commerce Clause).

**dormant commerce power** *See:* commerce, regulation of commerce, dormant commerce power.

**Dormant Foreign Commerce Clause** *See:* commerce, regulation of commerce, dormant commerce power, Dormant Foreign Commerce Clause.

**dossier** A file. A dossier is a collection or bunch of papers, most often used to describe all of the papers collected about a person, such as a personnel or investigative file. A dossier may be physical or electronic, in a single location or in several.

**double**

**double criminality** *See:* extradition, double criminality (dual criminality).

**double damages or double or multiple damages or trebles** *See:* damages, calculation of damages, treble damages (double damages or double or multiple damages or trebles).

**double effect test** *See:* wrong, double–effect test (double effect test).

**double entendre** *See:* defamation, defamation per quod (double entendre).

**double hearsay or totem pole hearsay** *See:* hearsay, hearsay within hearsay (double hearsay or totem pole hearsay).

**double hull** *See:* hull, double hull.

**double indemnity** *See:* indemnity, double indemnity (double indemnity clause).

**double indemnity clause** *See:* indemnity, double indemnity (double indemnity clause).

**double Irish** *See:* tax, tax shelter, Dutch sandwich (double Irish).

**double jeopardy** *See:* jeopardy, double jeopardy, former jeopardy; jeopardy, double jeopardy, dual-sovereignty doctrine; jeopardy, double jeopardy.

**Double Jeopardy Clause** *See:* constitution, U.S. Constitution, clauses, Double Jeopardy Clause.

**double nexus test** *See:* taking, regulatory taking, conditional use, double–nexus analysis (double nexus test).

**double recovery** *See:* damages, calculation of damages, double recovery.

**double-breasted operation** *See:* union, labor union, shop, double–breasted operation.

**double-effect test** *See:* wrong, double–effect test (double effect test).

**double-nexus analysis** *See:* taking, regulatory taking, conditional use, double–nexus analysis (double nexus test).

**doubt** The cause of any degree of uncertainty on a given issue. A doubt is any idea or condition that interferes with a person's sense of certainty regarding an issue, question, fact, or observation. As used in law, there is some appropriate circularity: a doubt may exist owing to a person's lack of certainty; and a person's doubt prevents that person's certainty. Thus a person who is uncertain has doubt, a doubt, or doubts. Doubt is a condition, while a doubt is a specific reason which one might attribute as the cause of the condition. Whether a person can articulate, name, or describe a doubt does not determine whether the doubt exists: its existence as to a given matter is proved if a person is not certain about it.

**reasonable doubt** *See:* proof, burden of proof, beyond a reasonable doubt (proof beyond a reasonable doubt).

**dower** *See:* spouse, surviving spouse's interest, dower.

**down payment** *See:* payment, down payment.

**dowress** *See:* spouse, surviving spouse's interest, dower, dowress.

**dowry** Property given by or for one spouse to the other at marriage. Dowry is marriage goods, the estates and possessions brought to the marriage by one spouse and given to the other. Traditionally, in many western countries, a sufficient dowry was required by the groom from the family of the bride in order for the marriage to proceed. Though now rare in England and the United States, the custom of dowry remains prevalent in many cultures but varies as to whether it is expected from the bride or the groom.

Dowry may also be conditional, in that it is to be paid only in the event of a divorce, although courts in the U.S. are reluctant to enforce such dowry agreements if the amount involved might serve as an inducement to divorce. Dowry is not to be confused with dower, which is the common-law origin of the statutory elective share.

*See also:* spouse, surviving spouse's interest, elective share.

**Dr. or M.D. or physician** *See:* doctor, Doctor of Medicine (Dr. or M.D. or physician).

**draft (draught)** To draw. To draft, or draught, is to draw, and this is the common factor between draft animals (which pull the plow), drafts as negotiable instruments (which are drawn on account), drafts of beer (which are drawn from its cask), architectural drafts, the draft of a written document (both of which are drawn on paper), and the draft of civilians for military service (who are drawn up in lists). Note: there is no difference in the pronunciation of the two spellings.

**draft as negotiable instrument** A check drawn by a bank rather than by a payor. A draft is a instrument drawn by a bank or other party, at the request of a payor, and to the benefit of a payee designated by the payor, that is drawn against funds tendered by the payor to that institution or party or tendered to a third party on its behalf, authorizing the payee to present it for payment to be covered by the tendered funds. A cashier's check is an example of a draft.

**bank draft** A check. A bank draft is an instruction to a bank to provide funds from an account in payment on the instruction. In other words, the drawer issues a draft to the payee that may be presented to the drawee institution for payment. The draft may be presented to anyone whose name appears on the draft who presents the draft to any bank, for presentation to the bank on which the draft is drawn for payment. The formal name for the instrument informally known as a check, the bank draft is a type of bill of exchange.
*See also:* instrument.

**overdraft (overdraw or overdrawn)** A draw on a bank account greater than its balance. An overdraft is a check or draw made against a bank account that is greater than the balance funds available in the account, including both the balance on hand pending claims for paper presented and fees then owed. An overdraft may be honored or not honored by the bank against which the draft is drawn. An overdraft that is honored amounts to a debt owed by the depositor to the bank holding the overdrawn account.

Banks offer "overdraft protection" for accounts, a form of advance insurance according to which the bank honors a check that would create an overdraft, charging a fee to do so for each check it honors on overdraft, as well as charging interest on the balance of the overdraft for as long as it persists.

*See also:* check, check with insufficient funds (N.S.F. or NSF or NSF check or hot check or bad check or bounced check).

**documentary draft** A draft that is only honored after the drawee inspects its attached instruments. A documentary draft is a negotiable instrument, a draft that is to be presented to the drawee or a drawee's bank, along with previously designated documents, instructions, or securities, after which the drawee or the drawee's bank is to forward the draft with other, corresponding instruments to the drawer or the drawer's bank, at which time the drawer will verify that the corresponding instruments are in order and instruct the drawer's bank to honor the draft or to return the draft unpaid.

**sight draft** A draft that is honored upon presentation. A sight draft includes any draft or bill of exchange that is payable on demand, and it is often the instrument used for payment against a letter of credit. Money is to be paid by the drawee bank. Although the language is payable at sight, many sight drafts require payment within a time certain from presentment.

**draft of a document (document draft)** One version of a document. A draft of a document is one version of it, as the writer or writers of the document develop a text from a first draft to a final draft. To say that a document is a draft suggests that it is not the final version, which is rarely called a draft but rather gets its name from the form of document that is being created: the letter, pleading, manuscript, etc.

To designate a document as a draft, however, does not excuse its technical defects. A draft document that is to be read by others ought to be proofread for the convenience of the reader as well as the efficiency of its development in later drafts. A draft other than a final draft is expected to be incomplete as to its structure, development of ideas, and argument, but not to its form. Even so, proofreading and editing are usually more intensive in later drafts than in earlier drafts of a single document.

Draft is both a verb and a noun, meaning the task of drafting and the draft that results.

**Drago doctrine** *See:* intervention, Drago doctrine.

**Dram-Shop Act** *See:* intoxication, Dram-Shop Act (Dram-Shop Rule or Dram Shop Rule).

**draught** *See:* draft (draught).

**draw and quarter**   *See:* punishment, draw and quarter (quartering or to be drawn and quartered).

**draw straws or draw lots**   *See:* lot, drawing lots (draw straws or draw lots).

**drawee bank**   *See:* bank, payor bank (drawee bank).

**drawing lots**   *See:* lot, drawing lots (draw straws or draw lots).

**dredge**   To remove silt and soil below a body of water, or the solids thus removed. To dredge is to remove silt and soil underlying a river, channel, or other body of water. A dredge is a vessel used for that purpose, and the dredge that results is the solid matter that is removed in the process. Dredging in many waterways is an environmentally disruptive process that destroys animal and plant habitats, although it may be essential for the passage of vessels.

**drek**   A worthless thing. Drek is a very disapproving and harsh term for something of no value at all. Literally, it is Yiddish for "crap."

**drift net**   *See:* net, drift net.

**driver**   *See:* driving (driver).

**driver license**   *See:* license, driver license (driver's license).

**driving (driver)**   Operating a vehicle or vessel. Driving is the act of controlling the motions, speed, or direction of a moving vehicle or vessel; or of being responsible for the control of the vehicle or vessel while it is under way. It is not possible to drive a vehicle that is parked or a vessel that is moored or at anchor. It is possible, however, to drive a vehicle that is standing or stopped or to drive a vessel underway but not making way.

**driving while black**   *See:* profile, racial profiling, driving while black (DWB).

**driving under the influence (D.U.I. or DUI or operating a vehicle under the influence or O.V.U.I. or OVUI)**   Driving under the influence of alcohol or drugs. Driving under the influence, or DUI, is the operation of a motor vehicle, aircraft, or watercraft while lacking ordinary physical or mental control as a result of the consumption of alcohol or drugs. A blood alcohol content at or above .08 is sufficient to establish a person's intoxication in most jurisdictions. Some jurisdictions distinguish DUI per se, which occurs when a driver has a blood alcohol content at .10 or above, from DUI by impairment, which occurs at .08 or above.

Some jurisdictions have enacted the statutory offense of DUI as a lesser offense compared to driving while intoxicated (DWI). Contemporary practice among states, however, is to combine the offenses into DUI and define it as driving with a blood alcohol level at .08 or above or driving while the influence of the intoxicant impairs the ability to drive by slowing or diminishing reactions, judgment, thought, conduct, or movement.

*See also:* driving, driving while intoxicated (operating a vehicle while intoxicated or driving while impaired or D.W.I. or DWI); sobriety (sober).

**driving while intoxicated (operating a vehicle while intoxicated or driving while impaired or D.W.I. or DWI)**   Driving while intoxicated from alcohol or drugs. Driving while intoxicated, or DWI, is the operation of a motor vehicle, aircraft, or watercraft while lacking ordinary physical or mental control as a result of the consumption of alcohol or drugs. A blood alcohol content at or above .08 is sufficient to establish a person's intoxication in most jurisdictions. Some states have amended their statutes to rename this offense driving under the influence.

Note: the variations among states of labels between DWI, DUI, OWI, and OUI is confusing. Some states, such as New York, denominate operation of a vehicle with greater impairment, in 2010 with a blood alcohol level above .08 as DWI, while designating a lesser level of impairment as DUI. Some jurisdictions use either DUI or DWI as the designation for offenses at any level, with different punishments for more severe offenses. Some jurisdictions label the offense using the term operating rather than driving, thus making clearer the offense applies to the operation of a vehicle even if the skill of driving is not in evidence or to apply to the operation of certain forms of machinery.

*See also:* driving, driving under the influence (D.U.I. or DUI or operating a vehicle under the influence or O.V.U.I. or OVUI); sobriety (sober); intoxication (drunkenness or alcoholic impairment).

**hit and run**   A collision from which the person at fault flees. A hit and run is an auto accident from which the driver of the vehicle that causes the incident fails to stop at the scene in order to be identified and give reasonable aid, and instead leaves the scene of the accident. A driver who engages in a hit and run commits an offense that is distinct from the accident itself. Note: in order to be a hit and run driver, the driver must have been aware that an accident did in fact occur.

*See also:* care, duty of care, common duty.

**joyriding**   The criminal borrowing of a vehicle. Joyriding is the taking of another person's automobile without that person's consent and with no intent to permanently deprive the owner of the vehicle. Joyriding is recognized as an offense in most, but not all, jurisdictions and is usually a lesser-included offense of auto theft. Thus, a conviction for joyriding precludes a conviction under a more serious auto theft crime for the same conduct.

*See also:* bailment.

**droit**   A customary right. Droit is the French term for the law in the sense of what is right, or the grand principles of the law. In French there are several distinct terms for justice, including justice, jus, and équité.

In both English Law French and French Law, droit is closer to the sense of law than to laws in the Fourteenth

Amendment: droit is the overall sense of law invoked by due process of law, and loi is more like the sense of specific laws in equal protection of the laws.

*See also:* loi.

**droit de seigneur or droit de cuissage or right of first night**   *See:* jus, jus primae nocte (droit de seigneur or droit de cuissage or right of first night).

**drug (drugs)**   A chemical that alters the human or animal body in which it is introduced. Drugs are chemical substances other than food that alter the mood, behavior, or functions of the body or an organ of the body of a person or animal. In law, drugs are often designated, particularly on a list of drugs subject to regulation. Note: drug is both a noun and a verb. To drug someone is to administer a drug to another person. A person whose abilities are impaired as a result of a drug is drugged.

**drug courier indicators**   *See:* profile, drug courier profile (drug courier indicators).

**drug courier profile**   *See:* profile, drug courier profile (drug courier indicators).

**drug court**   *See:* court, drug court, staffing meeting; court, drug court.

**drug czar**   *See:* czar, drug czar (drug lord).

**Drug Enforcement Administration**   *See:* police, police organization, Drug Enforcement Administration (D.E.A. DEA).

**drug house**   *See:* nuisance, public nuisance, drug house (crack house or meth house).

**drug lord**   *See:* czar, drug czar (drug lord).

**drug trafficking**   *See:* trafficking, drug trafficking, continuing criminal enterprise (CCE); trafficking, drug trafficking.

**controlled substance**   A drug, the usage or possession of which is regulated in the United States. A controlled substance is any drug or other substance, particularly the precurser materials from which drugs are made, that is placed on a schedule of controlled substances owing to its likelihood of abuse, addiction, and either its lack of a bona fide medical use or its risk of diversion from bona fide medical uses.

*See also:* trafficking, drug trafficking, continuing criminal enterprise (CCE).

**crack cocaine**   Cocaine mixed with baking soda. Crack cocaine, or crack, is an illegal drug created by combining more expensive cocaine with baking soda to form a rock that can be easily and inexpensively made, sold, or bought and then smoked to cause the effects of a stimulant.

**drug schedule (schedule I or schedule II or schedule III or schedule IV or schedule V)**   Drug classifications based on a drug's potential for medical use or personal abuse. The five drug schedules of the Controlled Substances Act place drugs under different regimes of legal enforcement and create different penalties for possession without a license or prescription, according to currently accepted medical uses and the potential for personal abuse of the drug.

Schedule I drugs, such as heroin, are unsafe, lack any accepted medical use, and have a high potential for abuse. Schedule II drugs, such as methadone, have a severely restricted medical use but a high potential for abuse and addiction. Schedule III drugs, such as amphetamines, have an accepted medical use with moderate potential for abuse and addiction. Schedule IV drugs and schedule V drugs, such as barbitol and dilute codeine, have accepted medical uses with successively lower potential for abuse and addiction.

**drug paraphernalia**   An item that could be employed in the use of a controlled substance. Drug paraphernalia is any tool or device that may be used for the preparation or consumption of a controlled substance. Possession of drug paraphernalia with the intent to use it for such a purpose is a misdemeanor in most jurisdictions.

**drug test**   A test of tissue, fluids, or breath to detect drugs in the body. A drug test is a sample and analysis of a substance such as blood, urine, saliva, breath, or tissue from a person's body, taken for the purpose of determining if pharmaceuticals, particularly controlled substances, are present in the body. Some drug tests are used to determine not only the presence of specific drugs but also their concentration. Note: though drug testing may include breath testing, the terms are often used distinctly owing to the predominate use of breath testing to detect the presence of alcohol.

**drunkenness or alcoholic impairment**   *See:* intoxication (drunkenness or alcoholic impairment).

**DSB**   *See:* trade, international trade, World Trade Organization, dispute settlement body (DSB).

**dual criminality**   *See:* extradition, double criminality (dual criminality).

**dual motive**   *See:* motive, dual motive.

**dual-sovereignty doctrine**   *See:* jeopardy, double jeopardy, dual-sovereignty doctrine.

**due**   What a person owes or is owed, as a matter of debt or justice. What is due means what ought to be done, given, paid, or ensured to another. Due has several different senses. What is due is often an amount of money owed, or an obligation required at the time that it is required, which is the time it is due. More generally, what is due is the respect for all of the rights and interests a person may lawfully and morally assert.

In its first sense, "due" may describe nearly all aspects of a debt or other obligation; what is due, when it is due, where it is due, to whom it is due, and from whom it is due. In all of these instances, "due" is used with the sense of something owed but adds an element of immediacy, such that a penalty or additional obligation is likely in the event that an obligation not performed as due that does not apply for the more mediate "owed." Once something owed is due, it is subject to immediate demand.

In its second sense, a person's "due" is what the person may reasonably demand from others, from the state, or from the law. In this sense, ensuring a person what the person is due has been a nearly universal foundation of legal duty and of justice.

*See also:* owing (owe or owed or owes); justice, commutative justice.

**due course of law** *See:* due process of law, due course of law.

**due diligence** *See:* diligence, due diligence.

**Due Process Clauses** *See:* constitution, U.S. Constitution, clauses, Due Process Clauses.

**due process of law** Constitutional rights in life, liberty and property interests that cannot be burdened without due cause or appropriate procedures. Due process of law is a fundamental aspect of the law, including not only the process by which law must be created and applied but also the scope within which certain laws must be made and enforced and beyond which laws ought to leave individuals to their own liberty. Thus, due process of law includes both a procedural aspect and a substantive aspect.

No burden or obligation can be created in law unless it is established according to the rules of law for the creation of new laws, nor can any burden or liability be enforced against anyone except by the methods appropriately created for such enforcement. Certain conduct and interests substantively cannot be limited by law unless the limit is justified by a compelling governmental interest that is narrowly pursued. No conduct and interests in one's life, liberty, or property can be burdened without appropriate procedures. Due process of law also incorporates a requirement of equal treatment under the law, and in the absence of such a requirement, as in the Fifth Amendment, equal protection of the laws is implied as a matter of due process.

*See also:* law, law of the land (lex terrae); enforcement, law enforcement, selective enforcement; equality, equal protection of the law; property, interest in property (property interest).

*administrative actions (Eldredge test or Matthews v. Eldredge Test)* A procedure used by an administrative agency will be upheld as a matter of due process of law if it meets the tests of Matthews v. Eldredge, 424 U.S. 319 (1976): A private interest must be affected by the administrative action; the procedures used must pose a discernible risk of an erroneous deprivation of that private interest; there must be a probable value to additional or substitute procedural safeguards in diminishing that risk; and the value of the proposed procedural safeguard must be greater than the government's interest in the existing process, including the difference in cost and administrative burdens the proposed new process would require.

*two-tier standard of review* Burdens on interests that are fundamental, meaning those that are components of a concept of ordered liberty, are subject to strict scrutiny. Burdens on interests that are not fundamental are subject only to rational-basis reviews.

**due course of law** Due process of law. Due course of law is a state doctrine equivalent of due process of law.

**liberty interest** The interest in engaging in the conduct of one's choosing. A liberty interest is any form of conduct, action, or even inaction, that reflects in any way a customary understanding of what a person ought to be free to do, so that a law burdening that interest must be justified as a matter of due process of law. Those liberty interests that are truly fundamental to the national sense of customary allowance or ordered liberty may only be limited if the limitation satisfies strict scrutiny.

**life interest** The interest in keeping one's life. A life interest is an interest in one's own life that may not be taken by the state or the United States without due process of law.

**ordered liberty** The historical test for substantive due process. The concept of ordered liberty was suggested by Justice Cardozo as the way of defining those rights that are subject to the substantive protections of due process of law. It has remained the measure of rights, particularly for determining which elements of the Bill of Rights should be incorporated in the Due Process Clause of the Fourteenth Amendment. It has, however, also served as a tool for the interpretation of liberty interests in the Due Process Clause, such that conduct as is implicit in the nature of ordered liberty is sufficiently fundamental to require strict scrutiny of any law that burdens it. See Palko v. State of Connecticut, 302 U.S. 319, 324–25 (1937) (Cardozo, J.).

*See also:* right, constitutional right, fundamental constitutional right (fundamental right).

**procedural due process** Notice and the opportunity to be heard by an impartial tribunal before suffering a burden under law. Procedural due process is a constitutional guaranty to each individual, that the individual will not suffer a burden by an unfair procedure under the law, in that no burden will be created that does not first require liability of the burden and then an opportunity to be heard and to object to an impartial decision-maker before the burden is exacted. The rules of procedural due process are not usually thought of as limiting legislative action, which is considered to employ sufficient procedure inherently, but the distinctions otherwise between substantive and procedural process in governmental action are imprecise. Any process that adjudicates a particular individual's right or interest or that creates a rule regulating a particular activity or conduct is subject to procedural due process. The greater the particularity of a legal process, the more certain that procedural due process is required of it.

*See also:* notice, fair notice doctrine; vagueness, vagueness doctrine (void for vagueness doctrine).

**Parratt-Hudson doctrine** A state deprivation of a right contrary to its process may be remedied by a later hearing. The Parratt-Hudson doctrine is a defense to a claim that a state agent violated a right to procedural due process by depriving the plaintiff of an interest in violation of established rules or procedures. The defense allows the state to remedy the constitutional harm of failing to provide a pre-deprivation hearing by providing a sufficient post-deprivation hearing that is capable of remedying a wrongful deprivation. The doctrine emerged in Parratt v. Taylor, 451 U.S. 527 (1981) and Hudson v. Palmer, 468 U.S. 517 (1984), although it was limited in Zinermon v. Burch, 494 U.S. 113 (1990) to allow a claim if the state agent was given broad discretion and little guidance in performing the actions that amounted to the deprivation.

**property interest** One's interest in the ownership, possession, and use of property. A property interest is an interest in one's property, labor, or reasonably expected entitlements that may not be taken by a state or the United States without due process of law. A property interest for the purposes of due process differs from a property interest for the purposes of the taking clause, in that the due process clause protects a wider range of property interests, particularly in relation to employment.

**substantive due process** The protection of fundamental individual rights as due process of law. Substantive due process is a doctrine arising from the Due Process Clauses of the Fifth and Fourteenth Amendments that assures to each person that no law will burden an individual right or exceed a limit on the government, if that right or limit is essential to the idea of ordered liberty, unless the law has an exceptionally strong justification and burdens the right or exceeds the limit as slightly as possible to satisfy that justification.

**due-on-sale clause** *See:* security, security interest, due-on-sale clause.

**duly constituted authority** *See:* authority, constituted authorities (duly constituted authority).

**dummy corporation** *See:* corporation, corporations, dummy corporation.

**dump truck** A criminal defense counsel who pleads out every case. Dump truck is a metaphor for a criminal defense attorney, especially a public defender, who convinces all of the defender's clients to plead guilty.

**dumping of patients** *See:* patient, dumping of patients (patient dumping).

**Dunaway hearing or Franks hearing or Huntley hearing or Mapp hearing** *See:* search, exclusionary rule, suppression hearing (Dunaway hearing or Franks hearing or Huntley hearing or Mapp hearing).

**durable lease** *See:* lease, durable lease.

**durable objection or running objection or standing objection** *See:* objection, continuing objection (durable objection or running objection or standing objection).

**durable power of attorney** *See:* attorney, attorney in fact, power of attorney, durable power of attorney.

**duress** An unlawful threat that limits the victim's independence of judgment or action. Duress is any improper threat or condition, such as coercion, that limits a person's ability to think or act independently. Not every threat gives rise to duress, however, so that a threat not to do business, if the threatening party is free to avoid such business under the circumstances, is not the basis of duress.

The presence of duress destroys the independence required of the party subject to duress to freely enter a contract. Thus, a contract formed while one party is under duress related to the contract is voidable by that party at a later date when the conditions causing duress have abated.

*See also:* coercion.

**dust in the eyes** A distraction or a small injury. Dust in the eyes is an evocative simile that refers to a minor physical injury, after which other damages may be ascertained. Another, older, use of the phrase is to describe a distracting legal argument that is intended to prevent a judge or jury from attending to the fundamental questions of a case.

**Dutch sandwich** *See:* tax, tax shelter, Dutch sandwich (double Irish).

**duties (tarriff duty)** Taxes levied upon persons or things. Duties are a form of taxation imposed by the state upon persons or things. Duties can encompass all taxes in the broadest sense of the word. More often, however, it is used to describe customs which are imposed on imported goods. Duty in this sense is the same as duties.

**duty** Conduct required by law, custom, morality, or personal commitment. Duty is the requirement to perform some conduct. The scope of duty varies from the performance of a single task to the performance of all of the responsibilities of an office. A duty to do something for another person or entity often creates a right in the other that the duty be performed, and a breach of such a duty gives rise to a cause of action for violation of the right. There are, however, duties in law, such as the duties of most public officials, that do not give rise to rights that are actionable at law.

Duties in law include obligations that arise from sources other than law, and many of these moral duties are enforceable as legal duties. Indeed, most legal duties are also moral duties, such as the moral duty not to take the life of another person without good cause, which is the legal duty not to commit murder, or the moral duty not to harm another by trick, which is the legal duty not to commit fraud.

The enforcement of moral duties in law, however, reaches deeper, particularly in the enforcement of duties that once were said to be equitable duties. Equitable duties are enforced in jurisdictions that have a separate court of equity but are otherwise matters of general jurisdiction. A duty under a contract may be enforced at law, as in the award of damages for breach, or in equity, as in the award of specific performance. A general duty, such as the duty to take reasonable steps to avoid harm to others, may be enforced retrospectively, by the award of damages for maintenance of a private nuisance, or in equity, by an injunction to prevent the noxious use of the property causing the nuisance. Equity will enforce the duty of a fiduciary, such as a trustee, both those duties that are clearly established by law, such as the stated duties in the trust instrument, and those established by custom or that ought to be apparent as a matter of reasonableness. The legal duty of a parent to care for a child includes a variety of customary moral obligations that are not reducible to a set of legal rules.

Yet some duties are strictly moral duties and are not enforced under law, at least not against all persons. In the United States, for instance, the law does not impose a duty on a healthy swimmer to rescue a nearby drowning child. The law would, however, impose a duty on a lifeguard to rescue the child drowning in the lifeguard's jurisdiction. The moral assumption in either circumstance would require each—the lifeguard and the healthy swimmer—to do the right thing and rescue the child. Likewise, a person who promises seriously to do something, which the promisee dearly hopes will occur, undertakes a moral duty to carry out the promise but faces a legal duty only if there was a valid contract, detrimental reliance, or something similar. When there is a valid contract or detrimental reliance, the law will enforce the moral duty with the legal duty, but otherwise the enforcement of the moral duty is left to the promissor, the promissee, or others who know of the promise.

In most instances, duty is defined by the purposes and reasons for the conduct required. The whole of most forms of duty is not defined by liability for enforcement, and the scope of most forms of duty cannot be perfectly defined. The duty of a fiduciary to exercise good faith cannot be inventoried or delineated, nor can the duty of a police officer or other public official. Doctors, teachers, parents, bankers, executors, corporate directors, judges, and crossing guards all have duties that cannot be reduced to a list of tasks or understood by their liability in law. At the margins, a breach of these duties may be punished or rectified by the law, yet in most instances, a breach of such duties is not subject to a legal remedy, being enforced instead by personal conscience, public opinion, or employer selection.

A duty may be breached by a failure to perform, an error in performance, or an excess or abuse of the authority by which the duty is invested.

The difference between a duty and another form of obligation is one of degree. Duty is usually the term of greater seriousness, suggesting a responsibility that is less easily dispensed with by means other than performance.

*See also:* obligation (oblige or obligator or obligee or obligor); justice, commutative justice; office.

**duty of care**   *See:* care, duty of care, reasonable care; care, duty of care, common-law duty of landholder; care, duty of care, common duty; care, duty of care; breach, breach of duty, duty of care.

**duty of disclosure**   *See:* disclosure, duty to disclose (duty of disclosure).

**duty of fair representation**   *See:* fiduciary, fiduciary duty, duty of fair representation (D.F.R. or DFR).

**duty of good faith**   *See:* fiduciary, fiduciary duty, duty of good faith.

**duty of knowledge or skill**   *See:* fiduciary, fiduciary duty, duty of knowledge or skill.

**duty of loyalty**   *See:* fiduciary, fiduciary duty, duty of loyalty.

**duty of prudent investment**   *See:* fiduciary, fiduciary duty, duty of prudent investment.

**duty to avoid conflicts of interest**   *See:* fiduciary, fiduciary duty, duty to avoid conflicts of interest.

**duty to disclose**   *See:* disclosure, duty to disclose (duty of disclosure).

**duty to investigate**   *See:* fiduciary, fiduciary duty, duty to investigate.

**duty to obey the law or obligation to obey the law**   *See:* obedience, moral duty to obey the law (duty to obey the law or obligation to obey the law).

**duty to provide security**   *See:* lease, duty to provide security.

**duty to rescue**   *See:* rescue, duty to rescue.

**duty to retreat or retreat rule or rule of retreat**   *See:* defense, self-defense, retreat (duty to retreat or retreat rule or rule of retreat).

**duty to trespassers**   *See:* trespasser, duty to trespassers.

**duty to warn**   *See:* warning, duty to warn.

**deontological duty**   A duty based on right and wrong, rather than what would be a good result. Particularly associated with Aristotle and Immanuel Kant, deontological duties are obligations to do the right thing because it is right, even if there will be unpleasant consequences. This contrasts with utility, which assesses conduct solely by its consequences.

**duty to treat**   The duty of hospitals to provide emergency care to those in need. The duty to treat exists in most jurisdictions and imposes upon hospitals that provide emergency medical care an obligation to provide care to all individuals who present themselves at the hospital, regardless of the patient's ability to pay. The obligation has been imposed by statute, regulation, and as a matter of common law and usually extends only to emergency stabilization or screening services.

**general duty (duty of reasonable care)**  A duty owed not to an individual but to all comers in a given situation. A general duty is a duty a person or entity owes to all who one might injure through a failure to use reasonable care in the particular circumstances in which the person or entity is at any given time. In most instances, an unexcused or unjustified breach of a general duty that results in harm to another is negligence, giving rise to a civil action for compensation for the harm.

Reasonable care varies with the circumstances so that a situation that would ordinarily give rise to a heightened standard of care, attention, or caution alters the duty accordingly. Thus a store owner's general duty to customers and employees requires additional conduct to meet the definition of reasonable care than would be required of the owner of an empty warehouse to a trespasser. The general duty is not without limits of reasonableness on complaints for breach, and a breach of duty arising from an honest error of judgment will not, in some jurisdictions, give rise to a claim for damages.

**DWB**  *See:* profile, racial profiling, driving while black (DWB).

**dwelling (dwelling house)**  A building in which a person lives. A dwelling is a building that is inhabited by at least one person on an ongoing basis. A dwelling might be designed or built for the purpose of human shelter, or it might have been intended for another purpose but used for this one. A building is a dwelling, even if only a small portion of its space is used for that purpose (although some housing codes consider a building a dwelling only if it is used for no unrelated purpose). A dwelling house is a place in which rooms are rented, each for the purpose of serving as a dwelling.

**dying declaration**  *See:* hearsay, hearsay exception, exception only when declarant is unavailable, belief of impending death (dying declaration).

**dynamite charge**  *See:* instruction, jury instruction, additional instruction, Allen charge (dynamite charge).

> A word is not a crystal, transparent and unchanged, it is the skin of a living thought and may vary greatly in color and content according to the circumstances and the time in which it is used.
>
> Towne v. Eisner, 245 U.S. 418, 425 (1918) (Holmes, J.).

# E

**e**   The fifth letter of the modern English alphabet. "E" signifies a variety of functions as a symbol, as a designation of status, and as a letter in Latin. It is sometimes invoked by epsilon, the word for the fourth letter in Greek. It is translated into "Echo" for radio signals and NATO military transmissions, into "Edward" for some police radio traffic, and into dot in Morse Code.

**e & o**   See: insurance, category of insurance, errors and omissions insurance (e&o) (professional services insurance or lawyer.

**e as a French word**   And. E is found in some Law French phrases as a contraction of "et" for "and."

**e as a Latin word**   From. E is a form of the Latin ex, for "out of" or "from."
See also: ex.

**e as an abbreviation**   A word commencing in E. When used as the sole letter of an abbreviation, E often stands for east or equity. It may also stand for Earl, Easter, ecclesiastical, economic, edition, editor, electronic, employee, employment, encyclopedia, England, equal, error, Europe, exchequer, executive, experimental, and export. It may also stand for the initial of the name of an author or case reporter, such as Eaton, Ebersole, Eden, Edgar, Edward, Ellis, and Estee.

**e converso**   On the contrary. E converso is a Latin phrase meaning from the contrary perspective or "on the other hand." It has fallen into disuse, as its idiomatic translation has become more commonplace.

**e pluribus unum**   From many, one. "E pluribus unum" is a Latin phrase that translates as "from many, one," a slogan of unity taken from a poem once attributed to the Latin poet Virgil. It is emblazoned in the scroll held in the eagle's beak on the obverse of the Great Seal of the United States. Originally in the seal to represent the union of a single nation from its constituent states, various authors have extolled it as a sign of America as the home to peoples of many nations, a culture of many cultures, even an idea of many ideas.

**e-commerce**   See: commerce, e-commerce.

**e-mail**   See: mail, electronic mail (e-mail).

**e-passport**   See: passport (e-passport).

**E.A.J.A. or EAJA**   See: fee, fee for services, attorney's fee, fee shifting, Equal Access To Justice Act (E.A.J.A. or EAJA).

**E.B.E. or EBE**   See: entrapment, entrapment by estoppel (E.B.E or EBE).

**E.C. or EC**   See: Europe, European Community (E.C. or EC).

**E.C.O.A. or ECOA**   See: credit, Equal Credit Opportunity Act (E.C.O.A. or ECOA).

**E.D.P. or EDP**   See: person, emotionally disturbed person (E.D.P. or EDP).

**E.E.O.C. or EEOC**   See: employment, Equal Employment Opportunity Commission (E.E.O.C. or EEOC).

**E.E.Z. or EEZ**   See: Sea, Law of the Sea, National Waters, Exclusive Economic Zone (E.E.Z. or EEZ).

**E.F.T. or EFT**   See: funds, electronic funds transfer (E.F.T. or EFT).

**e.g.**   See: citation, citation signal, e.g.; exempli gratia (e.g. or eg).

**E.I. or EI or executory bequest**   See: interest, executory interest (E.I. or EI or executory bequest).

**E.I.S. or EIS**   See: environment, National Environmental Policy Act (N.E.P.A. or NEPA), environmental impact statement (E.I.S. or EIS).

**E.I.T.C. or EITC**   See: tax, income tax, tax credit, earned income tax credit (E.I.T.C. or EITC).

**E.M.T.A.L.A. or EMTALA or Patient Dumping Act**
See: medicine, emergency medicine, Emergency Medical Treatment And Labor Act (E.M.T.A.L.A. or EMTALA or Patient Dumping Act).

**E.O. or EO or Ex. Ord.**   See: order, executive order (E.O. or EO or Ex. Ord.).

**E.P.A. or EPA**   See: environment, Environmental Protection Agency (E.P.A. or EPA).

**E.P.S. or EPS**   See: share, share as stock, shareholder value, earnings per share (E.P.S. or EPS).

**E.R.A. or ERA**   See: constitution, U.S. Constitution, amendment proposed, Equal Rights Amendment (E.R.A. or ERA).

**E.R.I.S.A. or ERISA**  *See:* employment, employee benefit plan, retirement plan, Employee Retirement Income Security Act (E.R.I.S.A. or ERISA).

**E.S.A. or ESA**  *See:* species, endangered species, Endangered Species Act (E.S.A. or ESA).

**E.S.O.P. or ESOP**  *See:* employment, employee benefit plan, employee stock ownership plan (E.S.O.P. or ESOP).

**E.T.F. or ETF**  *See:* security, securities, exchange traded fund (E.T.F. or ETF).

**E.U. or EU**  *See:* Europe, European Union (E.U. or EU).

**E.A. or EA**  *See:* environment, National Environmental Policy Act, environmental assessment (E.A. or EA).

**ear witness**  *See:* witness, earwitness (ear witness).

**earnings (earn or earned)**  Compensation from employment, or revenue generated by business activities. Earnings are the income of an individual or revenue of a corporation. For an individual, earnings are all income received for services provided by the individual to an employer, client, or contracting party, whether they are defined as wages, salaries, commissions, bonuses, pension payments or retirement pay. For a business entity, earnings include income generated by business activities, the gross income of the company as it is reported to shareholders or owners.

> **earned income**  *See:* income, earned income, taxation and tax law.

> **earned income tax credit**  *See:* tax, income tax, tax credit, earned income tax credit (E.I.T.C. or EITC).

> **earnest money**  *See:* money, earnest money.

> **earning capacity**  *See:* capacity, earning capacity.

> **earnings per share**  *See:* share, share as stock, shareholder value, earnings per share (EPS).

**earwigging (earwig)**  Ex parte communications with a judge. Earwigging is any improper communication between a lawyer and a judge in a manner in which the lawyer's opposing counsel may not know of the communication or respond timely to what is communicated. Earwigging is particularly troubling when it is initiated by the lawyer in an effort to gain an advantage in a case through the presentation of information that would ordinarily not be admissible or reliable. Earwigging or attempted earwigging is punishable by the courts under court rules as well as the inherent power of the courts over their counsel.
*See also:* ex, ex parte, ex parte communication; ex, ex parte.

**earwitness**  *See:* witness, earwitness (ear witness).

**easement**  A privilege allowing the limited use of another's lands. An easement is a limited privilege to use lands that are not owned by the privilege holder. It is a privilege for a specific, limited use of another's land that is vested in the owner of the easement, with a duty concurrently vested in the owner of the property upon which the easement sits not to interfere with the lawful use of the easement.

Easements take two forms: appurtenant and in gross. Appurtenant easements are held by whomever owns the parcel of land to which the benefit of the easement is attached, and the easement is said to run with the land, benefiting each successive owner of that parcel. Easements in gross are held by the person or entity without regard to any land the person or entity owns. In all cases, an easement creates a servient estate (or tenement), which describes the land over which the easement runs. Appurtenant easements create a dominant estate, which is the land whose owner holds the liberty to use the easement by virtue of the ownership. Easements in gross do not have a dominant estate.

Easements may be established by grant, reservation, implication, necessity, or prescription. A grant is a deliberate creation and transfer of an easement from the owner of the servient tenement to the new owner of the easement. A reservation is a creation of an easement and retention of the easement when the owner of the servient tenement grants the land of that tenement in fee to another person. Implication is an equitable or legal allowance of an easement over lands once held in a common parcel, and which thus require a way for access. Necessity is an equitable allowance of an easement over once–commonly–owned land in order to allow access over some lands to reach land that otherwise would not have access. A prescription is the creation of an easement through non–permissive use over an amount of time at least as long as the statute of limitations for trespass in that jurisdiction.

Easements at the common law were principally to allow a right of way (or the right of passage across the servient estate), to allow access to water, air, light, support in the ground, and to erect party walls and common fences. Easements today, however, allow nearly any use of another's land, as long as the use can be specified by a grant and the owner of the easement is not the same party as the owner of the servient estate, or, if the easement is appurtenant, the two estates are not owned by the same person or entity. Easements may take many forms, including a right to place a structure, crops, or objects, or to remove resources, such as by fishing, but their primary form is as a right of way for access to the dominant tenement. An easement that purports to use the whole of the servient estate, to the exclusion of its owner, is not an easement but a fee or leasehold.
*See also:* dedication; servitude, equitable servitude (reciprocal negative easement); servitude; easement, merger of estates (merger of easement or merger of tenements); deed, stranger to the deed.

> **easements and covenants**  *See:* covenant, real covenant | covenant and easement.

> **revocation**  An easement created by grant or license may be revoked according to its terms, whether express or implied. If the easement is for a term of years (that is, for any specified time or until any specified date) the

easement is revoked at the end of the term. If the grant or license is not renewed, and if the use for which the easement was created is not terminated, but despite both of these conditions the owner of the dominant tenement takes no action to assert the rights of the tenement, a court may consider the time at which the the holder of the servient tenement or other holder of the easement commences inchoate prescription of the easement to be the time of expiry. Even so, in most jurisdictions, prescription may only be found if the easement holder acted under color of right, which in those jurisdictions may be thwarted if the user believed the use to be only a matter of a license that persists.

**access easement (ingress and egress easement)** The right to cross the land of another. An access easement is one which allows an individual to cross the land of the servient estate to gain access to something on the other side, usually the dominant estate. At common law, and in many jurisdictions today, an access easement is an easement of "ingress and egress." One function of an access easement is to limit the scope of an easement from what would otherwise be an unrestricted way: the way in access easement is limited to traffic originating or concluding in the dominant estate, while traffic over the servient estate through the dominant estate and onward, with no particular engagement on the dominant estate, would not be within its scope.

**affirmative easement** The right to enter the servient estate to do something. An affirmative easement gives the owner of the easement a right to enter the servient estate to carry out some purpose, such as travel on a way or to erect a common fence. At common law, all easements were affirmative, negative easements being impossible (a rule giving rise to the restrictive covenant).

**apparent easement** An easement that can be deduced from physical evidence. An apparent easement is revealed, or can be deduced, from an inspection of the property. Evidence can include tire tracks, worn trails in the grass, a gate gap in a fence or hedge, or a road.

**appurtenant easement (easement appurtenant)** An easement held by the owner of the dominant estate and running with the land. An appurtenant easement is an easement that runs with the dominant estate, that is owned by whomever owns the dominant estate, and that holds the benefit to the use of the land in the servient estate. More generally, an appurtenant easement is an easement in one parcel that is enjoyed by the owner of another, nearby parcel.

When the dominant estate is transferred to a new owner, the easement is transferred with it, and the old owner of the dominant estate ceases to have an easement over the servient estate. Likewise, when the servient estate is transferred, the duty to suffer the easement is transferred to the new owner. If, however, the dominant and servient estates of an appurtenant easement are held by the same owner, then the easement is merged and destroyed. A new

easement could be created if the owner transferred one property or the other, but the new easement would have to be created as if an easement had never existed.

**benefit of the easement** The right to use the easement. The benefit is the right to use an easement, held by the owner of the dominant tenement for an appurtenant easement, of the easement itself for an easement in gross, or as a member of the public for a public way.

**burden of the easement** The duty to allow use of the easement by the owner of the servient estate. The burden of the easement is the duty and any ancillary responsibilities of the owner of the servient estate to allow those with a right to use the easement to do so. The burden for an easement creating a way to travel over an estate requires providing reasonable access. This does not, for instance, forbid the erection of a gate, but it would require the gate to be opened for passage by the easement holder.

**common easement** An easement that is owned by more than one party. A common easement is an easement which is deeded to multiple owners. Common easements are often created in subdivisions, where the owners of many different tracts are each granted an appurtenant easement in a common area. A common easement is by definition non-exclusive, although not all non-exclusive easements are common, as there must be others with the privilege to use the non-exclusive easement.

Holders of a common easement have a duty not to interfere with the use of other holders in the easement.

**conservation easement** An easement designed to protect the environment. A conservation easement is a limitation on the use and development of lands owned by a governmental agency or charitable organization, that thereby may prohibit the owner of the property from engaging in certain activities on the land or require certain practices on the land that would protect the environment.

**continuous easement** The right to use another's land that may not be limited, even for brief periods of time. A continuous easement imposes a constant burden on the servient tenement that may not be halted even briefly without violating the easement. Access to water, light, and air is continuous, in contrast to an easement establishing a right of way, which cannot practicably be in use at all times. A test for a continuous easement is whether the easement permanently alters the character and nature of the property on which it is placed. Any type of easement can be a continuous easement if it carries with it a permanent alteration to the character of the property.

**discontinuous easement (discontinuing easement or intermittent easement or noncontinuous easement)** An easement used from time to time. A discontinuous easement is one that by its nature is not in continuous use by the easement owner. These are easements that require entry onto the servient estate rather than, as with continuous easements, allow for the enjoyment of the benefits of the servient estate from the dominant estate. Thus, a right of way or a right to take water are non–continuous easements.

**dominant estate (dominant tenement)**  Land benefited by an appurtenant easement. A dominant estate is the parcel of land that is benefited by an easement which runs with the land and is sometimes referred to as the dominant tenement. There is no great difference between the two terms, although the more contemporary use of "estate" emphasizes the property interest as a whole, while the use of "tenement" emphasizes the nature of the tenure in the land.

**easement by custom (customary easement)**  A public easement established by custom. An easement by custom is an easement established by longtime use by members of the public over private land. It is a form of prescription, though not by an individual or landholder but by the public as a group. Customary easements are most likely to be found at a point of access to a waterway or beach or to reach a public park or similar space.

**easement by estoppel**  An easement arising from promissory estoppel. An easement by estoppel arises from one party's reasonable reliance upon another's permission to use property, when the relying party changes position in reliance on the permission. The recognition and enforcement of an easement by estoppel is an inherently equitable remedy.

**easement by implication (implied easement)**  An easement implied from the use of one property to benefit another by a common owner. An easement by implication is an appurtenant easement between two tracts of land arising from their treatment when the two tracts were owned by a single owner, during which the use of one tract was sufficiently necessary to the use and enjoyment of the other tract, such that a purchaser of the other tract would reasonably assume that an easement to continue the use of the first tract is implied in the sale of the other tract. When one of the two tracts is sold, unless there is evidence to the contrary, an implication arises that an easement will persist over the tract that was necessary to use the other tract, the first tract being servient to the other, the dominant estate, for the necessary purpose. For example, if O owns Blackacre and Whiteacre, and O builds a house on each but a well on only Blackacre, which is plumbed to give water to Whiteacre (which is Whiteacre's only source of water), when O sells Whiteacre, in the absence of a clear rejection of an easement by the parties, a court will likely hold an easement arose by implication over Blackacre that the owner of Whiteacre has an easement to take water from the well of Blackacre.

Easements by implication may be implied in law or in fact. Implication by law holds that the easement exists even if the circumstances do not require it. Implication by fact holds that the easement exists primarily as a function of the facts, and a change in circumstances may destroy the easement.

**easement by necessity (implied easement of absolute necessity)**  An easement granted to access a road from a landlocked tract. An easement by necessity is created when two tracts that were once owned by a single person or entity are divided in ownership, and an easement over one tract is reasonably necessary for access to the other tract. At common law, an easement of necessity was granted only when it was absolutely necessary for the use and enjoyment of the dominant land, although some jurisdictions have allowed necessity as a matter of reasonable necessity, though not merely of convenience. Easements by necessity arise as a matter of implication but are not the same as implied easements, in that an easement of necessity need not have been in use at the time the dominant and servient estates were severed from one another, while an implied easement must have been in use at the time of severance.

*See also:* land, landlocked, landlocked as innaccessible by land (land–locked).

**easement for light and air**  *See:* light, ancient lights (easement for light and air).

**easement in gross (commercial easement)**  An easement owned by a person or entity and not tied to a dominant estate. An easement in gross, also called a commercial easement, is held by an individual or entity, usually by grant or prescription, but not by virtue of ownership of a benefited parcel of land. Easements in gross do not run with the land and are subject to certain rules and restrictions dependent upon the jurisdiction in which the easement lies. An easement in gross is subject to the terms of its creation in scope, time, and alienability, but unless it is by a grant that specifies otherwise, an easement in gross for commercial purposes may be freely alienated, devised, or inherited. Easements in gross for personal use are presumably devisable and heritable, and while their inter vivos alienability was once somewhat disfavored, without evidence to the contrary, they are probably alienable.

*See also:* in, in gross.

**easement of prior use (easement by prior use or easement from prior use)**  An implied easement observable at the time of conveyance. An easement of prior use is a form of implied easement, in which the owner of a tract of land conveys part of the tract, and an apparent easement is contained on the conveyed parcel that is not expressly reserved or renounced in the conveyance. This varies from an easement by necessity or an easement by implication, in that there is no requirement of need or reasonable need to find an easement of prior use.

**equitable easement**  An easement established over several tracts severed from a common tract. Equitable easements arise through operation of equity rather than through legally enforceable doctrines, grants, reservations or prescription. Equity may imply an easement as a remedy in an action unrelated to an express easement or other legal easement, including easements by estoppel and easements required to avoid unjust enrichment. Most often, equity implies an easement when a single tract is subdivided, with each component subject to a deed restriction or covenant containing a restriction on use, and such restrictions in some way depend on reciprocity in the other lots being similarly restricted. Unless there is manifest evidence that the original creator of the restrictions did not intend all of the lots to carry such restrictions, and unless a later grantee of an unrestricted lot relied on the absence of such a restriction and had a good faith reason to be unaware of the restrictions on the neighboring lots, then the lots remaining that were held by the creator at that time will be equitably subject to an easement similar in restriction and scope to the restriction written into the deeds or covenants.

**express easement**   An easement conveyed in writing. An express easement is clearly written on an instrument of conveyance, such as a deed or grant, issued by the owner of the servient tenement.
*See also:* expression (explicit or express).

**inchoate easement (inchoate prescriptive easement or inchoate prescriptive rights)**   One's use of another's land that may ripen into a prescriptive easement. An inchoate easement is a means of describing the interest of one whose use of another's land may, if all other requirements are met over time, ripen into a prescriptive easement. This is the interest that one user transfers to another user to tack. An inchoate easement may, however, be said not to exist at all in the law, as it establishes no rights or privileges and cannot be owned until it ceases to exist by ripening into a permanent easement.
*See also:* inchoate (choate).

**light and air easement (air and light easement or air easement or light easement or view easement)**   A privilege to unobstructed light and air. An easement of light and air prohibits the owner of the servient estate from doing anything on the land that would materially alter the flow of light and air onto the dominant estate. Jurisdictions differ in how an easement of light and air is created; some have held that it must be through an express grant, and others have held that it may be implied. An easement of light and air operates as does a restrictive covenant, prohibiting certain types of construction on the burdened estate.

**merger of estates (merger of easement or merger of tenements)**   Common ownership of easement and servient estate, destroying the easement. A merger of a servient estate with the ownership interest of the easement extinguishes the easement. An easement requires a distinction between its holder and the ownership of the land, which is usually by the division of ownership between the dominant and the servient estates, each with separate ownership rights. When the property is conveyed in such a way that one person takes both estates, or the holder of an easement in gross holds title to the servient land, then merger occurs, and the easement is dissolved. In the event of a common easement or a joint tenancy in

which one of several owners of either the easement of the servient estate is the same, merger does not occur owing to the difference in ownership that persists for the other easement holders.
*See also:* easement; merger.

**negative easement**   The restriction of the servient estate from specific uses. A negative easement is the privilege of a non-owner of an estate to restrain the owner of the estate from doing something with or on the land. Though there are implied negative obligations upon the owner of a servient estate burdened by an affirmative easement, such that the servient estate owner cannot interfere with the lawful use of the easement, a negative easement differs from such obligations because there is no affirmative right in the easement owner other than to enforce the negative easement and enjoy its benefit from afar.

**prescriptive easement**   An easement acquired through use alone. A prescriptive easement is an easement acquired in a manner similar to that in which an estate in fee is acquired by adverse possession (though an easement is incorporeal and cannot be possessed). Formulae vary from jurisdiction to jurisdiction, but a prescriptive easement arises from the use of another's lands in a manner that is actual, open, hostile to the landowner's right to exclude, and unceasing or uninterrupted for the period of time prescribed by statute for prescription, which is usually the same as that for adverse possession, or (if such a time is not set specifically) the time in which the landowner might bring an action for ejectment or for trespass (usually between seven and twenty-one years). Some jurisdictions require a claim of right, though some do not. Exclusivity is often on the list, but this must be understood, as is continuous, within the context of the use; in general both require that there is not an interruption of the reasonably expected pattern of use, particularly by a legal action or practical interference by the landowner.
*See also:* prescription, prescription of property (prescriptible).

**tacking**   The computation of time, including successors in interest. Tacking, relative to the prescription of an easement, is the ability of a person who uses an easement adversely to another to take advantage of the timer the predecessor in interest also used the same easement adversely to another, so that the time of the earlier and later user are added together when determining whether the period for prescription has run. Tacking occurs when there is a transfer of interest between either the owner of the servient land to a successor or the user of the inchoate easement in the land to a successor user, so long as either transfer occurs before the adverse use ripens into a prescribed easement. Tacking of the time against the landowner and a successor requires there be privity of estate between them, although there can be tacking after tacking among more than two parties. Further, tacking may occur, but the time for prescription will still be tolled if the subsequent landowner is a minor or otherwise lacks capacity. Tacking of the time by the user requires there to be some relationship between the initial user and subsequent user as to amount to something like privity, such as privity of estate of what would be the dominant estate.

*See also:* possession, adverse possession, tacking.

**public easement**   An easement for use by the public rather than a specific easement holder alone. A public easement is an easement held by the public, rather than an individual, entity, or specified group. Public easements are created by prescription or by dedication by the landholder. Usually the state controls the easement, although a member of the public may have standing to enforce an easement as against a private landholder burdened by the easement.

*See also:* public.

**reservation of easement (reserved easement)**   An easement retained by the grantor in lands otherwise transferred in fee to another. A reservation of an easement is the creation of an easement by the grantor of the estate over which the easement runs, at the time the grantor transfers the estate in fee to the grantee. The easement is reserved, which is to say that the grantor creates the easement by not granting it to the grantee of the estate as a whole (other than the easement). A reservation may be to the benefit of a parcel of land that continues to be owned by the grantor, or it may be a personal easement to the benefit of the grantor and the grantor's assigns.

*See also:* deed, stranger to the deed.

**running with the land**   *See:* run, run with the land (running with the land).

**servient estate (servient tenement)**   Land subject to an easement for use by others than its owner. A servient estate is a tract of land that has the burden of an easement. The owner of the servient tenement has a duty to the easement holder not to interfere with the proper and lawful use of the land within the scope of the easement.

*See also:* servient.

**solar easement**   An easement for access to sunlight for use in power generation. A solar easement is a new form of light and air easement that forbids the burdened estate from allowing new foliage or construction to obstruct a solar energy collecting device on the dominant estate. Solar easements may be created by grant or estoppel, but they are more often created by statute in order to encourage the development and usage of solar energy systems in powering residences and businesses. Like all light and air easements, a solar easement is fundamentally negative, in that the primary powers and rights entrusted to the owner of the dominant estate are prohibitive powers that can be exercised upon the servient estate; but unlike many light and air easements, solar easements can also prohibit the planting of any shrubbery that would cause shade to fall onto the solar panels.

Few states have enacted statutes creating solar easements, but the tendency thus far is revealing. In California, while a solar easement is an appurtenant right, rather than an easement in gross, it is not restricted solely to adjoining lands; instead, it is legitimately applicable to any neighboring land, adjoining or not, that interferes with a person's ability to use solar power.

**Easter term**   *See:* court, English court, terms of court, Easter term.

**eavesdrop (eavesdropper, eavesdropping)**   To listen to the conversations of others. Eavesdropping is the deliberate listening to the private conversation of other people for the purpose of spreading the information thus gained to others. The offense of open-air eavesdropping is no longer a crime in most jurisdictions, although it has been succeeded by new statutes that prohibit eavesdropping, or unlawful eavesdropping, by the unconsented use of a listening or recording device, as well as the transmission of information learned through the use of such devices to another person. Traditional eavesdropping now may be an element of the different offense of stalking, or it may give rise to a private tort for invasion of privacy, or it may amount to a search when performed by the police.

The term originated from the practice of would-be blackmailers and slanderers who waited by the eaves of a building to listen through windows to the conversations of those inside. In modern usage, eavesdropping includes more than obtaining auditory access to verbal conversations; it also includes spying on someone's communications by electronic means, particularly through listening devices and wiretaps, correspondence, electronic or physical, and obtaining records of telephone conversations. Eavesdropping is normally a tortious and criminal act when undertaken by a private citizen, but modern cases have granted governmental authorities increasing power to eavesdrop in the interests of preventing crime or ensuring national security. Such observations, when unwarranted, are sometimes regarded as legitimate exceptions to the Fourth Amendment, depending upon various factors, but the general prohibition against unwarranted searches remains in force.

**unlawful eavesdropping**   The use of a listening device to overhear a confidential discussion. Unlawful eavesdropping is the intentional use of a wiretap, bug, or other listening or recording device to overhear or record a conversation or communication, when all of the parties recorded or overheard have not consented to the use, contrary to the law of that place.

**ecclesiastic**   A member of the clergy. An ecclesiastic is a person recognized within a religion as entitled to respect for holding religious office. In the Christian church, ecclesiastic includes any person who has taken holy orders.

*See also:* church.

**ecclesiastical law**   *See:* canon, canon law (ecclesiastical law).

**ecology (ecologist)** The study of relationships between organisms within a natural environment. Ecology is the study of the relationships between living organisms and their environment, the science that examines the impact of life on an environment and on other life. An ecology is thus the whole network of such relationships in a given area. Ecologists are people engaged in the study of ecology.

**economics**

    **economic analysis of rulemaking** *See:* order, executive order, Executive Order 12866 (economic analysis of rulemaking).

    **economic efficiency** *See:* efficiency, economic efficiency.

    **economic injury** *See:* injury, economic injury.

    **economic life** *See:* value, economic life.

    **economic loss rule** *See:* damages, tort damages, economic loss rule (economic–loss rule).

    **economic rent** *See:* rent, economic rent, rent seeking (rent seeker or rent–seeking); rent, economic rent (rentiers).

    **economic tort** *See:* torts, economic tort.

    **economic waste** *See:* waste, economic waste; damages, contract damages, expectation damages, economic waste.

    **economic-loss rule** *See:* damages, tort damages, economic loss rule (economic–loss rule).

    **economy (economic or economics or oeconomic or oeconomy)** The sum of all systems of value in a given time and place. An economy is the collection of interdependent commercial and monetary systems for a specified region. The combination of these systems is both microscopic and macroscopic in nature, accounting for both the purchase of a package of gum and the merger of two multinational corporations. In short, an area's economy is the sum of all commercial transactions that have occurred in that area within a specified time.

    **law and economics** The study of law and justice through economic theory. Law and economics is the study of the legal regulation of human activity by evaluating the effects of law on human behavior through economic assumptions and analyses. Law and economics is a descendant of utilitarianism, although the highest goals of law and economics are not the maximization of utility but the greatest efficiency and wealth.

**ecosystem** A system consisting of the environment and the biological community that inhabits it. An ecosystem is a system of hydrologic, meterologic, terrestrial oceanographic, and human systems containing the biological community and the surrounding environment. Within an ecosystem, organisms interact with one other and the environment, and changing or interfering with variables or factors can have significant effects on the rest of the system. Ecologists somewhat artificially define each ecosystem in order to study these relationships and to determine how best to preserve them.

**EDGAR** *See:* security, securities, securities regulation, Securities and Exchange Commission, EDGAR.

**edict** A public law or command of law. An edict is a law or command that has been proclaimed in the public spaces or published to be read throughout the land, usually by (or in the name of) the sovereign or enacted through the legislative body. The edicts of Roman emperors were new laws made through imperial decree alone, which were also called constitutiones principum.

**effect (effective)** The result of a cause, particularly a law or legal order. An effect is an event or condition in the world that has a cause. The consequences of laws, the changes in the behavior of individuals, and the significance of things or events are a result of their definition under the law. Effects are also of great consideration in considering criminal and civil liability for actions that in some degree are their cause, as well as evidence that would demonstrate the causation leading to a given effect.
*See also:* bind (binding or bound); judgment, final judgment.

    **anchoring effect** An influence on a party that is not otherwise relevant to the dispute. An anchoring effect is the influence on a party to a dispute that arises from an idea, event, person or other reference point that has little or nothing to do with the dispute at hand. Anchoring effects may greatly hinder negotiations with such a party to resolve the dispute because the considerations or offers of other parties are unlikely to alter the perception of the anchored party.

    **effective assistance of counsel** *See:* counselor, right to counsel, effective assistance of counsel.

    **effective tax rate** *See:* tax, tax rate, effective tax rate.

**effects** The property owned by an individual. Effects represents all of the relevant property of an individual. When it appears in a will, the term must be interpreted by both its occurence in phrases and by other evidence of intent, but personal effects generally represents the testator's personal chattels for daily use, while worldly effects generally represents all of the testator's property, real, chattel, or incorporeal. A prisoner's personal effects are those objects impounded at the time of arrest or incarceration to be returned (if possession is lawful) upon release.

**efficacy (efficacious or efficaciousness)** Effectiveness. Efficacy is the power to bring about the effect that something is intended to produce. Efficacy is often confused with efficiency, but the difference is that efficacy is the potential of a plan or operation to succeed,

371

while efficiency is the ease or ratio of resources required for it to do so.

*See also:* efficiency (efficient).

**legal efficacy**   *See:* forgery, legal efficacy.

**efficiency (efficient)**   The degree to which resources are best used and least wasted in any process. Efficiency is a measure of the resources required to produce the result sought. It is a measure both of waste and the effectiveness of the allocation of resources. As a measure of economy, efficiency is a state of allocation in which value is maximized across all transactions. As a measure of the work or production of an individual, it is a measure of the quality and quantity of the work that person performs in a given time, relative to other workers. As a measure of a machine, it is a measure of how well the machine operates either in comparison to its ideal performance or to its consumption of input resources. As a measure of a system of human performance, such as education, healthcare, or government, it is the distribution and overall receipt of the intended benefit relative to the resources allocated to the system as a whole.

*See also:* efficacy (efficacious or efficaciousness).

**allocative efficiency**   The production of the greatest number of goods at the lowest cost. Allocative efficiency is the production of the greatest amount of goods at the lowest cost and is achieved when the total value of the gains accruing from a policy decision are greater than the total losses.

**economic efficiency**   A waste-elimination ideal for businesses. Economic efficiency is a mathematically-derived business ideal that seeks to eliminate waste and refine resource allocation in order to maximize revenue generation. It is often a putative justification for breaches of contractual obligations, but it is rarely held to be so significant as to absolve all liability incurred by the breach. It is also a common ground for pleading damages in a tort action, usually invoked along these lines: "Defendant's actions have damaged the economic efficiency of my business operation, resulting in $n of lost profits."

**Kaldor-Hicks efficiency (Kaldor-Hicks criterion or Kaldor-Hicks test)**   A transaction that makes both parties better off in sum, even if one is less well off. Kaldor–Hicks efficiency justifies a transaction in which one party is sufficiently better off because that party's gain is greater than the burden on the other party. The difficulty from most perspectives is that the transaction is economically efficient even if the burdened party is not compensated. The Kaldor-Hicks criterion is used in some cases to argue that a transaction is justified even if it is not willed by both parties but is an externality that is transferred to a recipient who does not voluntarily accept it. This criterion is used by some to justify pollution and other activities on economic grounds, which observers from other perspectives would consider immoral or unjustifiable.

**Pareto optimality (Pareto efficiency or Pareto superiority)**   An equilibrium in which any trade would result in less overall wealth. A Pareto optimal situation is a state of affairs in which any transaction will lead to an overall loss of wealth, and change that benefits one party must cause another party to lose more than the first one gains. Pareto optimality is the theoretical outcome from a series of transactions that are Pareto efficient, or Pareto superior, in which each of the parties are better off through the transaction, unlike Kaldor-Hicks efficiency, in which only one party need be better off than the other is worse off.

**Pigovian efficiency**   Each enterprise must bear the cost of the externalities it creates. Pigovian efficiency requires that the market include otherwise externalized social costs in the costs of production and — ultimately — in the cost of goods produced. Under this approach, when such costs are not internalized, the law may require compensation to the public from the enterprise that does not bear the cost of the externalities it creates. Thus, from this perspective, a polluter must pay for the cost of its pollution.

*See also:* economy, law and economics.

**efficient breach**   *See:* breach, breach of contract, efficient breach.

**effluent (discharge or wastewater)**   Liquids discharged onto land or into a body of water. Effluent is any water or liquid that flows from a source. In most instances in the law, it is water that has been contaminated with waste, primarily organic waste. The term encompasses all water that has been contaminated in this manner, including wastewater that has been chemically treated to reduce its contamination. The storage and control of effluent is typically a problem associated with sewage or wastewater processing. In order to remove the waste, several steps must be taken, including filtering out suspended particulate, neutralizing chemicals, killing microorganisms, managing temperature, and ensuring appropriate oxygenation.

**EFT**   *See:* funds, electronic funds transfer (EFT).

**egg-shell plaintiff**   *See:* plaintiff, egg-shell plaintiff (abnormally sensitive plaintiff or glass-jaw plaintiff or eggshell-skull rule or thin skull rule).

**egregious**   Unusual or extreme, especially unusually bad. Egregious means remarkable or extraordinary (whether good or bad) but is used so often to modify words like "harm" or "wrongdoing" that it has acquired guilt by association and is now used by legal writers and speakers to mean remarkably bad or awful.

**egress (ingress or regress)**   Exiting, or the right to exit a property. Egress is the right to exit from a property. It is usually paired with "ingress" in describing easement rights and rights in a common area in a lease, and — sometimes still — with "regress," the right to return to the property from afar.

**Eire**   *See:* court, English court, justices in Eyre (Eire).

**EIS**   *See:* environment, national environmental policy act (NEPA), environmental impact statement (EIS).

**ejectment (eject or ejection)**   A civil action to recover land from one in possession of it. Ejectment is a common law cause of action to expel a defendant from a parcel of land by reason of the plaintiff's superior claim to title. In contemporary proceedings, the only pleading requirements are that the plaintiff assert that the defendant is in possession of a certain tract and that the plaintiff has paramount title over the defendant's claim to title, upon which the plaintiff is entitled to a judgment of ejectment and to quiet title, and to damages for the plaintiff's dispossession.

At common law, ejectment was predicated upon one or two fictitious leases one of which was offered to the plaintiff by the defendant, an actual entry by the plaintiff, and the plaintiff's ouster by the defendant, with the defendant relying solely upon the superiority of the claim to the land. This series of procedural hurdles is remarkable when compared to the modern incarnation of the action.

*See also:* trespass, trespass for mesne profits.

*eviction*   A proceeding for eviction is often synonymous with an action for ejectment. Courts and lawyers often use the terms interchangeably, although technically an ejectment is a cause of action, while an order of eviction is a remedy. As housing codes have merged the two terms, in many jurisdictions there is little or no difference between them.

**ejusdem generis**   *See:* interpretation, ejusdem generis; contract, contract interpretation, ejusdem generis.

**elastic clause or basket clause or coefficient clause or sweeping clause**   *See:* constitution, U.S. Constitution, clauses, Necessary and Proper Clause (Elastic Clause or Basket Clause or Coefficient Clause or Sweeping Clause).

**elder law**   The arenas of law of particular interest to elderly clients. Elder law is an area of legal practice concerned with the particular legal questions of an older clientele, especially in regard to personal and financial planning, health management, and probate and estate planning. In some jurisdictions, notably Florida, elder law is an area of professional specialization and certification.

**election (elective)**   A choice. An election is a choice between several mutually exclusive options. The term refers to the democratic function of an election both as a means of collectively selecting a person to fill an office or post and voting for matters of public commitment, such as legislation by referendum.

Election also describes the selection by a person who has the right to choose of one of several incompatible interests under the law, for instance, the election of a debtor to pay a debt immediately or over installments, the election of a plaintiff to seek only one of several alternative remedies, or the election of a surviving spouse to take an inheritance assured by law or to take the devise left by the decedent spouse by will. In each case, once the election is made and signaled by some act, it is binding on the elector.

*See also:* nomination (nominate).

**Election Clause**   *See:* constitution, U.S. Constitution, clauses, Elections Clause (Election Clause).

**election of performance**   *See:* performance, election of performance.

**election of plaintiff or election of actions or several-remedies rule**   *See:* remedies, election of remedies (election of plaintiff or election of actions or several-remedies rule).

**election of remedies**   *See:* remedies, election of remedies (election of plaintiff or election of actions or several-remedies rule).

**election recall or recall election or recall referendum**   *See:* recall, representative recall (election recall or recall election or recall referendum).

**elective franchise**   *See:* franchise, elective franchise.

**elective share**   *See:* spouse, surviving spouse's interest, elective share.

**election of a devise (election of a legacy)**   The choice of a devisee either to accept or reject a devise in a will. The election of a devise is a choice between one of two or more potential distributions from a decedent's estate. The most common is to make a choice that a devisee must make between on the one hand accepting a bequest, legacy, or devise in a will and thus give up other rights in the estate under law, or on the other hand rejecting the bequest, legacy, or devise in order to exercise those rights under law. Thus, a former spouse must either elect to accept a distribution under the decedent spouse's will or to exercise the elective share but cannot do both.

There are other forms of election of a devise. For example, a devisee may accept a devise under the will that is conditioned upon some performance or duty, leaving the devisee the option to elect to perform the duty or to forfeit the devise. If, for instance, T devises a large tract of land to A on the condition that A give to B a small tract of land already A owns, then A can either accept T's land and give away the small tract or keep the small tract and so reject T's devise. A cannot keep both T's large tract and the small tract.

**election contest**   A challenge to an election vote tally or the means of election. An election contest is an administrative or legal dispute over the outcome of an election. It may take several forms, including a recount, a challenge to the qualifications of voters, a challenge to the means of disqualifying voters, allegations of unconstitutional barriers to voting, claims of disqualifying conduct by a candidate, and claims against the qualifications or eligibility of the winning candidate. States provide administrative procedures for hearing election contests, for which there is judicial review, while allegations of violations of federally protected rights in voting are subject to federal review.

**election district (election precinct)** A geographical area in which all votes are counted together. An election district, or precinct, is a geographical area demarcated by statute or ordinance, within which a poll or polls are established for counting the votes of all those within the district and reporting the results as a unit. The drawing of boundaries for election districts in certain states is subject to oversight under Section 5 of the Voting Rights Act.

**election fraud** The use of money, threats, or trickery to interfere with an election for office. Election fraud includes any action that is intended to interfere with the independent vote of each qualified voter for the qualified candidate the voter prefers. Fraud includes the use of trickery, bribery, threats or violence, or any artifice that would usurp some aspect of the electoral process. A person convicted of election fraud is often barred by statute from subsequently holding a legal office or a position of trust.

**elector** *See:* vote, voter (elector).

**Electoral College** *See:* president, President of the United States of America, Electoral College (presidential elector).

**electronic chattel paper** *See:* chattel, chattel paper, electronic chattel paper.

**electronic funds transfer** *See:* funds, electronic funds transfer (EFT).

**electronic mail** *See:* mail, electronic mail (e-mail).

**electronic surveillance** *See:* surveillance, electronic surveillance.

**eleemosynary** Charitable. Eleemosynary is a traditional designation for a charitable enterprise, or one who is supported by donations to do good works.

**Eleventh Amendment immunity** *See:* immunity, sovereign immunity, state sovereign immunity (Eleventh Amendment immunity).

**eligibility (eligible or ineligible or ineligibility)** The capacity to be given a position or to enter a status. One who is eligible for a position or status is one with the capacity to accept it or be selected for it. Criteria of eligibility are set both by law and by circumstance. For example, eligibility for election to federal office is specified in the Constitution, with limits on citizenship, age, and, for Congress, residence. Eligibility for certain benefits of employment depends on criteria established by statute and the corresponding employment contract. A person who is not eligible is ineligible.

**Ellerth/Farragher defense** *See:* agency, harassment, hostile work environment, Ellerth–Faragher defense (Ellerth/Farragher defense).

**Ellsworth Court** *See:* court, U.S. court, U.S. Supreme Court, Ellsworth Court.

**eloquence** The art of speaking and writing well. Eloquence is the art of persuasive writing and speech. In order for a legal argument to be eloquent, it should be written clearly with sufficient detail to allow for precision but without redundancy. The facts should be presented fairly, the law must be presented honestly, and the significance of the matter at hand should be made clear to the reader or listener without histrionics or ill will toward one's opponent. Every statement should have art enough to be memorable but not so much as to obscure the law or the facts in issue.

**emancipation** The liberation of someone formerly under another's authority. Emancipation is liberation from another's ownership, control, or authority. The emancipation of slaves in the United States was required by the Thirteenth Amendment. Since then, the term is most often used to describe the time when a minor child reaches the age of majority and is free both of parental control and to participate in civil society. Emancipation may also occur by judicial decree when a child is relieved of minority by order of the court, by marriage, by leaving school or home, by military enlistment, by criminal conviction as an adult, or by cohabitation without parental consent.
*See also:* manumission.

**emancipation of a minor** *See:* minor, minority, emancipation of a minor (relief from the disabilities of minority or emancipated minor).

**embargo** A prohibition against the movement of vessels or goods from or to some place. An embargo is a declaration prohibiting certain transport or trade with a particular country, port, or place. A state's declaration of an embargo is not itself a use of force, though it may be a threat to use force under the United Nations Charter. A voluntary embargo of a state's own goods to prevent them being transported from the state or to a given state does not implicate the United Nations Charter but may violate both bilateral trade agreements and the General Agreement on Tariffs and Trade. An embargo, particularly of arms shipments, may be required by the United Nations Security Council. Prominent recent examples are the Arab oil embargos of 1967 and 1973, and the U.S. embargo of Cuba, authorized by the Foreign Assistance Act of 1961.

**embezzlement** The taking of property entrusted to the taker by another person. Embezzlement is the unlawful retention or disposition of property or money over which one has lawful supervision or access. The act of embezzlement occurs when the property or money is secreted, transferred, removed, or treated in a manner that would divert it from its ordinary use or management to the control of the embezzler or another; such actions would be equivalent to those at common law that would constitute at least an action for conversion.

*See also:* peculation (peculate or peculative); stealing (steal or stolen); detention (detain or detainee); robbery (rob).

**embracery** *See:* jury, embracery (tampering with the jury or embracer or jury tampering or juror bribery).

**embryo** *See:* zygote, embryo, pre-embryo (preembryo); zygote, embryo.

**emergency** *See:* necessity, emergency.

**emergency medicine** *See:* medicine, emergency medicine, Emergency Medical Treatment and Labor Act (E.M.T.A.L.A. or EMTALA or Patient Dumping Act).

**emigration** *See:* immigration, emigrant (emigration).

**eminent domain** *See:* condemnation, condemnation through eminent domain.

**emissary** Ambassador. An emissary was once a provocateur, but today it is more likely a title for an ambassador.

**emission** *See:* pollution, air pollution, emission, motor vehicle emission standards, tailpipe emissions (exhaust); pollution, air pollution, emission, motor vehicle emission standards; pollution, air pollution, emission (emit).

**emission (emit or bodily emission)** Any substance emitted from a body, machine, or storage device. An emission is a discharge, usually of a fluid or gas, from any body or place. In criminal law, an emission often refers to the release of blood, semen, urine, or other fluids from the body. In environmental law, emission refers to the release of gasses and liquids into the environment from a facility, plant, vehicle, vessel, or any other device for the storage or use of a liquid or gas. Note: emission is a noun and a verb, though the active form of the verb is emit.

**emission reduction unit or E.R.U. or ERU or certified emission reduction credit or C.E.R. or CER** *See:* carbon, carbon credit (emission reduction unit or E.R.U. or ERU or certified emission reduction credit or C.E.R. or CER).

**emissions cap** *See:* pollution, cap and trade, emissions cap.

**emissions trading** *See:* pollution, cap and trade, emissions trading.

**emolument** The pay and benefits of a public office. An emolument is any profit, benefit or gain that results from some service or effort, often the payment in return

for the performance of a service or employment. By the fifteenth century, the term had acquired the implication of a benefit or profit that was expected to be received from an office or employment, though today the term takes many forms, including honors and intangible benefits like knowledge, respect, and fame. In the Emoluments Clause of the Constitution, however, it seems to be specifically related to money or value, because it is distinguished from other honors and titles.

**Emoluments Clause** *See:* constitution, U.S. Constitution, clauses, Emoluments Clause (Foreign Emoluments Clause); constitution, U.S. Constitution, clauses, Emoluments Clause (Congressional Emoluments Clause or Ineligibility Clause).

**emotional distress** *See:* distress, emotional distress.

**empathy** One person's perception of how another person understands the world. Empathy is a form of knowledge about other people, specifically the sense by which one person knows how and what another person understands about the world in general or any fact or situation or idea in particular. Empathy allows one person to understand the motivations, emotions, and knowledge of another, as well as that person's ignorance, confusion, and mistakes. Empathy allows a person to see the world as another sees it.

Empathy may be encouraged by the person seeking to understand the other, or it may be encouraged by the other seeking to be understood. In this sense, empathy is a rhetorical device in which a lawyer or other advocate encourages a listener to identify with the lawyer or with the lawyer's client, seeing the world through the other's eyes.

Empathy is essential to the moral assessment of another person's actions. One person's judgment of another that is wholly lacking in empathy for the other is not likely to accurately assess the other person's mental state, motivations, purposes, circumstances, or condition. A decision regarding the law based on a lack of empathy would, under most theories of justice, meet the requirements of justice only accidentally. Empathy is also essential to effective rule-making, as it is the basis for predicting forms of behavior, understanding what will follow the enactment of the rule, and the degree to which that behavior and understanding will lead to conformity to the rule and greater trust in the law. Empathy among groups in society is essential for a successful and peaceful constitutional democracy among a pluralistic community.

Note: empathy is easily confused with emotion or mercy. Empathy is itself neither of these, although empathy requires an understanding of the other person's emotions, and it may be a precondition to most acts of mercy. Neither is empathy the same as sympathy.

**employee misconduct** *See:* unemployment, unemployment compensation, employee misconduct (misconduct by employee).

**employment (employ or employed or employee or employer)** A job that mandates specific duties and how they are to be performed. An employment is a job or office held by an individual that mandates the performance of certain duties for which wages or a salary are awarded. Employment is of an employee, and while the term is used to describe the hiring of a contractor, this is not in the technical sense of employment as a matter of law but the general sense of employment as the use of services.

The scope of employment obligations are often dictated by contract, either written or oral, and may be defined by a common contract of general terms of employment for all employees of a single employer. Each state defines employment under state law, but the definition for federal taxation purposes is essential for distinguishing obligations to employees from obligations to independent contractors for most purposes, such that employment is a job in which both what is done and how it will be done are controlled by the employer.

Employment is regulated by state and by federal law, and these vary according to the size of the employer and jurisdiction but generally include include wage and hour restrictions, age limitations barring child labor, laws against employment discrimination, the provision of safe working conditions, access to collective bargaining, pension guarantees, and payroll tax requirements.

*See also:* compensation, employment compensation; contract, specific contracts, contract for employment (employment contract); discharge, employment discharge (discharge from employment or firing); discrimination, employment discrimination; job.

**employment applicant** *See:* job, job applicant (employment applicant).

**employment capacity** *See:* disability, personal disability, employment capacity.

**employment compensation** *See:* compensation, employment compensation, deferred compensation; compensation, employment compensation.

**employment contract** *See:* contract, specific contracts, contract for employment (employment contract).

**employment discharge** *See:* discharge, employment discharge (discharge from employment or firing).

**employment discrimination** *See:* discrimination, employment discrimination.

**employment retaliation** *See:* retaliation, employment retaliation.

**absorption of employees** The practice of preserving labor rights when integrating personnel of merged companies. Absorption occurs when employees, collective bargaining units, or collective bargaining agreements between two companies that have combined into one are integrated, and aspects of the labor relations of the company that is being subsumed are integrated directly into the resulting company.

**at-will employment (at-will employee or at-will employer)** Employment that may end at any time. At-will employment is employment that may be ended by either the employer or the employee without notice, at any time and for any reason not forbidden by law as discriminatory. Tenured employees and employees for a term are not employed at will. Note: the hyphen is used when the phrase is used as an adjective prior to the noun but not when it follows the noun. Thus, one would write at-will employee or employment at-will or at-will-employment doctrine.

**employee** One who works under the control of an employer. An employee is a worker employed by an employer. Most importantly, the employee is assigned duties by the employer and controlled in how those duties are to be carried out. States define who is an employee under state law, but federal law determines not only tax liability and reporting responsibility for employers but also other federal employment obligations. Most employees are common-law employees, whose status depends on the worker's behavior, financial independence, and form of the relationship. If the company has the right to control what the worker does; how the worker does the job; when, how, and how much the worker is paid for wages; the worker's expenses, and benefits; and the content of the employment contract and employment benefits, the worker is a common-law employee. Some employees are designated by statute, such as delivery drivers, insurance agents, home piece-workers, and traveling sales personnel.

**employee benefit plan** Payments and services other than wages in exchange for employment. Benefits are the collective term for a variety of payments and services made to or on behalf of an employee, some of which are mandated by law and some of which are voluntary. Those that are required of many employers and many workers are the payment of worker's compensation insurance, government health insurance (Medicaid), and government retirement insurance (Social Security). Those that may provided without a legal obligation include health, life, and disability insurance payment contributions; retirement plan contributions; dependent care programs (such as nurseries); and work-related educational assistance. The provision of specific benefits is often specified in an employment contract or collective bargaining agreement.

**cafeteria plan** Employee benefits not subject to taxation. A cafeteria plan gives an employee the option to have some benefits paid directly from the employee's paycheck prior to the calculation of income tax. These benefits typically include daycare, insurance, and prescription drug costs.

**death benefit** *See:* benefit, death benefit (death benefits).

**employee stock ownership plan (E.S.O.P. or ESOP)** A company-issued stock benefit plan. An employee stock ownership plan (ESOP) is an individual account plan in which qualifying employees of a company earn or have the ability to purchase shares of stock in the company by which they are employed.

**fringe benefit** Employment compensation other than wages. Fringe benefits are employment benefits that exceed the scope of wages. Fringe benefits are generally treated as employee compensation for the purpose of accounting and labor costs, but the most common examples are either exempt from income tax or deferred.

*Coordination of Benefits* A coordination of benefits provision is a clause in an insurance policy that determines in what order benefits will be paid in the event of multiple insurance policies covering the same risk. COB provisions are common in group health plans.

**COBRA (C.O.B.R.A.)** Short-term health insurance available after leaving health-insured employment. The Consolidated Omnibus Budget Reconciliation Act of 1985 (COBRA), amended ERISA to provide employees of covered employers (and the dependents of such employees) the right to a continuation of group health insurance held as an employee for eighteen months or, under some circumstances, for thirty-six months. To exercise this right, the employee must have been a member of a qualified group plan; have a qualifying event, such as termination of employment or employed spouse's qualification for Medicare that would (but for COBRA) terminate all medical insurance coverage; have filed a notice with the plan within sixty days of notice of eligibility; and then assume responsibility for all payments for the insurance, including the former employer's contribution, up to 102 percent of the plan's premium for the former employee.

**health maintenance organization (H.M.O. or HMO or managed care organization)** A private health insurer that contracts with health providers to serve its members. A health maintenance organization, or HMO, is an organization that enrolls participants, often by agreement with an employer to enroll its employees, into a group health care plan that provides only specified medical services that are provided by health care professionals and institutions that are under contract with the organization to provide such services at pre-arranged rates for reimbursement.

**Employee Retirement Income Security Act (E.R.I.S.A. or ERISA)** A federal statute regulating private employee retirement and health insurance funds. ERISA, the Employee Retirement Income Security Act of 1974, partially codified at 29 U.S.C. § 1001, et seq., is a federal law that regulates benefit plans created by employers to provide for employee retirement and health insurance. ERISA requires employers to act as fiduciaries for their employees in managing such plans, creating federal liability for the failure to provide employees with accurate information or appropriate management.

*See also:* pension, individual retirement account (I.R.A. or IRA); pension; retirement, retirement plan, qualified retirement plan.

**Family and Medical Leave Act (F.M.L.A. or FMLA)** A federal act providing employees leave for family or personal needs. The Family and Medical Leave Act is a federal statute that requires employers to provide up to twelve weeks of unpaid leave in any twelve-month period for the birth or adoption of children, the care of children or other family members, or for an employee's own illness. To be eligible for FMLA leave, the worker must have been employed by the employer for at least twelve months and have at least 1,250 hours of service within the twelve-months preceding the leave. Further, the FMLA applies only to employers that employ least fifty employees within a seventy-five mile radius of the employee's worksite.

**public employee** Any non-elected employee of a government. A public employee is any person who is employed by any governmental entity except for elected officials and independent contractors who perform services for the government. Public employment is sometimes within the civil service of the government and regulated according to the rules governing that service. Public employees are usually held to a standard of conduct that places them in the role of a quasi-fiduciary.

**employment action (adverse employment action or adverse job action or job action)** A change or denial of change to a worker's condition of employment. An employment action is any action or the denial of a requested or authorized action made by a supervisor or superior that affects the pay, status, title, location, duties, or condition of employment accorded to a worker or employee. Although both beneficial and adverse employment actions exist, when the term "employment action" is used alone, it generally refers to an adverse employment action, one in which the employee is or would be adversely affected by the decision. Adversity need not involve a loss of pay or the loss of an increase in pay but can also include a change of circumstance that the employee would be understood by the supervisor or superior not to welcome. An adverse employment action that follows a discriminatory act by a supervisor is a violation of laws against discrimination in the workplace. Further, an employment action against a person believed to be a labor organizer may violate the protections of labor organizers.

The term "job action" is effectively the same as an employment action, when used to mean an act of the action as labor action; discrimination, employment discrimination.

**Equal Employment Opportunity Commission (E.E.O.C. or EEOC)** A federal agency that enforces anti-discrimination laws in employment. The Equal Employment Opportunity Commission is an independent federal agency tasked with eliminating employment discrimination and workplace harassment. It is a regulatory board that articulates the limits of potentially illicit workplace behavior and is often the first administrative board to hear an employment law dispute. It is headed by five commissioners who serve alternating four-year terms and oversee a large staff.

**unemployment (unemployed)** Lacking work for compensation. Unemployment, in general, means to be without work. As used in the law, it is usually refers to someone who would prefer to be, or ordinarily is, in the workforce, and thus describes the state of a person who is ordinarily employed being without employment for compensation. A person who is unemployed is presumed to be ready, able, and willing to work but is unable to do so.

**underemployment (under-employed)** A person working less than the person is qualified to work. Underemployment describes the situation of a person who is employed in a trade or at a level that is significantly lower in terms of responsibility or pay than a person with the same skill, work record, and other qualifications would ordinarily take. Voluntary underemployment by a person with an obligation of child support or other non-dischargeable debt is a basis for refusing to alter the obligation, which otherwise might be reduced owing to a reduction in income.

**unemployment compensation (unemployment benefits or unemployment insurance)** Money paid for a period by the state to residents who seek but cannot find work. Unemployment compensation or unemployment benefits are payments made for a time to individuals who have been fired or laid off without cause on the employee's part, to provide income while the former employee seeks new employment. The benefits are paid from funds collected from employers under state unemployment tax acts (SUTAs) and augmented by state and federal revenues. Most employers receive a federal tax credit for a portion of their SUTA payments.

**empty chair defense or fellow servant rule or hypothetical person defense or SODDI defense** *See:* defense, specific defense, third–party guilt (empty chair defense or fellow servant rule or hypothetical person defense or SODDI defense).

**en** In, or within. En is a French preposition that translates as in, within, or inside. It is a frequent element in French maxims.

**en banc** *See:* bench, en banc (en banc sitting or sitting en banc).

**en banc court** *See:* court, full court (en banc court).

**en banc sitting or sitting en banc** *See:* bench, en banc (en banc sitting or sitting en banc).

**Enabling Clauses** *See:* constitution, U.S. Constitution, clauses, Enabling Clauses.

**Enclave Clause** *See:* constitution, U.S. Constitution, clauses, Enclave Clause.

**encroachment** The unlawful possession of a portion of another's property. Encroachment is the unlawful possession of the property of another. As the term implies, it is usually partial, and an encroachment is often a possession or continuous form of use, such as a fence, building or road, that could ripen into an easement by prescription if allowed to remain without ejectment.

*encumbrance and encroachment* Encroachments, like encumbrances, may cloud the marketability of the property's title and thereby reduce its value. The difference between the two is that an encroachment is a physical occupation without lawful rights or license to be on the land, while an ecumbrance is a lawful interest creating a right in the land, such as an easement, covenant, mortgage, or lien.

**encumbrance (encumbrance or incumbrance)** A legal burden on an estate that diminishes its value or marketability. An encumbrance is a burden or charge upon an estate that is attached to the estate and diminishes its value, for example, a mortgage or lien against the land. Easements, covenants, and servitudes are usually considered encumbrances, although in certain circumstances in which they enhance the value of the property and do not limit the owner's rights or use, they might be held not to be encumbrances. There is no practical difference between the term when spelled with an initial i or e; encumbrance or incumbrance are the same except for slightly different patterns in chains of case precedents and selections by statutory drafters.

**end justifies the means** *See:* means, ends justify the means (end justifies the means).

**end user** *See:* consumer, end user.

**endangered species** *See:* Endangered Species Act (E.S.A. or ESA); species, endangered species, Convention on the International Trade in Endangered Species (C.I.T.E.S. CITES); species, endangered species.

**endnote** A note at the end of the document or chapter. An endnote is a note providing commentary on the text or a reference of authority for it that is printed at the end of the document or book, or at the end of a section or chapter. There is no difference in significance between an endnote, a footnote, or a marginal note.

*See also:* footnote; margin, marginal note (note in the margin).

**endorsement** *See:* indorsement (endorsement, endorse, indorse).

**endorsement test** *See:* religion, freedom of religion, establishment of religion, endorsement test.

**endowment (endow)** A gift to fund future operations, or the fund itself. An endowment is a provision for the support of the future operations of a charitable enterprise, such as a hospital or school. As a result, an endowment is both the granting of an unusual gift and the repository of such gifts. The term is derived from the word dower, as in the bestowal of dower to a wife, but in this context is now obsolete. The verb to endow means to generically bestow a gift for the recipient's support.

*See also:* gift (gift over or give).

**ends** *See:* means (ends).

**enemy** A state at war with another, its people, and its military. An enemy, as a matter of international law, is the state with which another state is engaged in a declared state of war or armed combat in fact. The citizens or subjects of that state are alien enemies and are themselves enemies, as are each member of the military forces of the enemy state. Enemy has a broad definition when construing the offense of giving relief or support to the enemy, though it is narrowly construed to include only organized military units of the enemy as an element of the crime of misconduct in the face of the enemy.

Note: the colloquial use of "enemy" to describe any opponent in a civilian context, such as a market competitor, has no real legal significance.

*See also:* alien, alien enemy (Alien Enemies Act); combatant, enemy combatant.

**enemy combatant** *See:* combatant, enemy combatant.

**enforcement** The power and obligation of officials to ensure behavior conforming to the rules of the law. Generally, enforcement is the application of a rule in order to ensure that those bound by it behave in conformity with it. In law, enforcement is the execution or application of the rules of law to a particular case. The power of enforcement, like the power of legislation, is a defining element of sovereignty, or the powers of a state.

**enforcement jurisdiction** *See:* jurisdiction, enforcement jurisdiction.

**enforcement of judgment** *See:* judgment, enforcement of judgment, Uniform Enforcement of Foreign Judgments Act (UEFJA); judgment, enforcement of judgment, satisfaction of judgment; judgment, enforcement of judgment, judgment roll; judgment, enforcement of judgment, judgment debtor; judgment, enforcement of judgment, judgment creditor; judgment, enforcement of judgment (execution of judgment).

**law enforcement** The individuals and institutions that enforce laws, particularly criminal law. Law enforcement comprises the organizations established by governments to ensure that the laws, particularly the criminal law, are obeyed and enforced; institutions for the recruitment and training of police officers; the coordination of intelligence and data regarding criminal activity; the prevention of crime and support of community order through community policing and support; the management of officers and agents in the suppression of potential criminal activity; the detection of criminal activity and the identification of its perpetrators; and the collection of evidence and presentation of such evidence to the courts for appropriate punishment, all under the laws. Law enforcement organizations in the United States exist at every level of government, including counties and parishes, villages, townships, towns, and cities, and include regional and special authorities, such as park police, and federal police authorities, such as the Federal Bureau of Investigation and the U.S. Coast Guard. Special military legal authorities, including the military police, shore patrol, provost marshals, and investigation and intelligence services, maintain jurisdiction over military personnel. Law enforcement agencies include administrative agencies with officers that are otherwise tasked with the enforcement of specific laws, such as game wardens and immigration agents. Every law enforcement agency, officer, and agent is, however, responsible for conformity to statutes and regulations specific to the agency as well as statutes and constitutional limitations regarding both the powers of the state and the rights of the individual.

**selective enforcement** Tortiously or criminally unjust application of a law. Selective enforcement is the inequitable application of the law in a manner that unduly favors or burdens one private party as against another, or as one person or group as against the general population. In general, selective enforcement is neither a defense to a criminal action nor a basis for a civil claim by the person who is subject to selective enforcement, because the person against whom enforcement is brought is, in fact, in violation of the law that is being enforced. Selective enforcement is not the same as false accusation or conviction of the innocent; rather, the crux of selective enforcement is that the focus of the enforcement or the pattern of enforcement is unfair or a burden for some among a larger population of lawbreakers.

Selective enforcement may occasionally be a sufficient basis for a criminal defense or for a civil or criminal action against the person responsible for the selective enforcement, if the purpose of the enforcement is itself unlawful or unconstitutional. Thus a claim of selective enforcement must be based not only on a demonstration of selective treatment of the claimant that differs from the treatment of others known or reasonably knowable to the enforcing authority but also a demonstration that the motivation for the enforcement against the claimaint is for a constitutionally impermissible purpose, such as personal malice or bad faith by the enforcing officer or an officer of the enforcing authority, or the inhibition or punishment for the claimant's exercise of constitutionally protected rights, or the claimant's membership in a suspect class. Selective enforcement on such grounds, among other concerns, amounts to a violation of due process of the law.

*See also:* due process of law.

**English Bill of Rights**  *See:* rights, bill of rights, English Bill of Rights (Bill of Rights of 1689); constitution, English Constitution, English Bill of Rights.

**English Constitution**  *See:* constitution, English Constitution.

**English court**  *See:* court, English court.

**English judge**  *See:* judge, English judge, master of the rolls; judge, English judge, lord chancellor (lord high chancellor or lord keeper of the great seal).

**English rule**  *See:* fee, fee for services, attorney's fees, fee shifting, English rule.

**English rule of leasehold**  *See:* lease, leasehold, English rule of leasehold.

**engrossment (engross or engrossed or ingross or ingrossed or ingrossment or blue-backed)**  To prepare a document in its final form. Engrossment, literally to place in large letters, is the process of creating a final copy of a document, the copy that will be executed and serve as the final, official instrument. Contracts, wills, deeds, trust instruments, and legislation are often executed with a final engrossment. In many instances, this will result in the final instrument being printed and bound or sometimes affixed to a blue backing sheet with any signatures to be placed or seals to be affixed on the engrossed copy. An engrossment of a contract upon the minutes of a corporation is done either by the inscription of the contract by its complete language into the minutes or by a physical insertion of the contract into the minute book. There is no difference between engrossment and ingrossment in this context.

> **engrossed bill**  *See:* bill, bill as legislation, engrossed bill.

**enhanced interrogation**  *See:* interrogation, enhanced interrogation (extraordinary interrogation techniques).

**enjoin**  *See:* injunction, enjoin (enjoined).

**enlargement of time**  *See:* time, extension of time (enlargement of time).

**enquête de police**  *See:* police, enquête de police.

**enrolled bill**  *See:* bill, bill as legislation, enrolled bill.

**ensign**  *See:* flag (ensign).

**entail**  *See:* fee, estate in fee, fee tail, entail (entailment); fee, estate in fee, fee tail, entail, disentailment.

**enter**  *See:* entry (enter).

**enterprise value**  *See:* value, enterprise value.

**entire use**  *See:* use, use of property, entire use.

**entirety or tenancy by the entirety or tenants by the entireties**  *See:* tenancy, co-tenancy, tenancy by the entireties (entirety or tenancy by the entirety or tenants by the entireties).

**entity (legal entity)**  A person, association, or corporation with legal rights and obligations. A legal entity is an individual body with legal rights and obligations. The entity may consist of a single person or be an aggregate of multiple people. An entity may be a government or an autonomous division of a government, such as a municipal corporation, or it may be a corporation, partnership, or, in some jurisdictions, an unincorporated association.

> **entity representation**  *See:* representation, legal representation, entity representation (organizational client).

> **entity theory of partnership**  *See:* partnership, theory of partnership, entity theory of partnership.

**entrapment**  An affirmative defense alleging police persuasion to commit a crime. Entrapment is an affirmative defense alleging that the conception and planning of a crime was by a police officer or agent, and that the official inducement of the defendant was so substantial as to eliminate the defendant's criminal liability. The government may rebut an entrapment defense by proving that the defendant had been predisposed to commit such an offense as the one charged following government inducement. Whether entrapment has occurred is a question of fact, and if successfully proven is a sufficient basis for an acquittal.

*See also:* defense, specific pleading, entrapment (inducement).

> **derivative entrapment (third-party entrapment)**  Entrapment via a third party. Derivative entrapment is a rarely allowed affirmative defense to a criminal charge, being a form of entrapment in which the defendant argues inducement to participate in a criminal activity by government conduct or statements that were relayed to the defendant through a third party. Derivative entrapment is distinct from vicarious entrapment, in which the defendant is recruited to participate in the crime by someone who is entrapped, in which case the defendant has no defense because the defendant chose to engage in the crime without any lure by the government. Derivative entrapment is particularly applicable when the government targets the defendant and acts through agents or third parties in a deliberate effort to coax the defendant into committing a crime. If the agent or third party is unaware of the government impetus to recruit the defendant, some jurisdictions will allow the defense as derivative or third-party entrapment and others will bar it as vicarious entrapment.
> 
> *See also:* entrapment.

> **entrapment by estoppel (EBE or E.B.E.)**  Conduct that has been reasonably endorsed as legal by an official cannot be prosecuted. Entrapment by estoppel

is an affirmative defense to a criminal charge, in which the defendant asserts that the defendant would not have committed the alleged conduct except that the defendant in fact relied reasonably and in good faith on an authorized government official who informed the defendant in advance of the conduct that the conduct would be legal, but the government official was actually wrong and the conduct was illegal. This test has many qualifications, the most significant being actual reliance, so that but for the approving advice the defendant would not have engaged in the conduct, and reasonableness, such that the advice provided must have been of such a form, authority, and conclusion that a reasonable law-abiding person would have accepted the information as correct and not have been on notice to inquire further.

*See also:* lawyer, legal advice, advice of counsel defense.

**Sherman-Sorrells doctrine (subjective approach)** Entrapment occurs only when the defendant lacked a predisposition to the crime. The Sherman-Sorrells doctrine is a definition of entrapment based on a subjective assessment of the defendant's mindset before the introduction of the government agent. The subjective assessment focuses on whether the criminal conduct was induced by a government agent and whether the accused lacked a predisposition to commit the conduct. The defendant must have been induced to the degree that the defendant had no criminal intent until the government agent suggested that the defendant commit the criminal act. Only a minority of states apply an objective test for entrapment, known as the the Roberts-Frankfurter Doctrine after the dissenters in Sorrells v. United States and Sherman v. United States, respectively.

**entry (enter)** To place in or on. Entry has many meanings in the law, but their common element is the placement of something or someone, including oneself, in or on a location. Thus making an entry in book-keeping means to place an entry on an accounts sheet or ledger book, an entry into a dwelling is the placing of oneself in the house, an entry onto the land means to take possession of the property, and to enter an appearance is to record an attorney's participation on the appearance docket, just as to enter an order is to record it on the case docket.

**entry in a legislative journal** *See:* legislation, legislative history, journal entry (entry in a legislative journal).

**entry onto the land** *See:* land, entry onto the land.

**entry of judgment**

**forcible entry** An entry to property by force. Forcible entry is a violent entry onto property, or an entry accompanied by such force or threat of force as to be accomplished despite resistance, and for most usages, there is no difference between the entry being legally justified or not. Commonly, forcible entry describes an entry to property made with force or a threat of force under the authority of law, such as by a police officer acting under a warrant or with probable cause to believe a crime is in progress.

This sense of forcible entry differs from its meaning in the common law. Originally, forcible entry referred to an entry by force without the authority of law, such as a trespass vi et armis or as a self-help eviction. Such meanings persist in tort.

Both senses of the word are now to be found in the opinions, and care must be taken to distinguish which usage is intended. Still, careful drafting would not consider lawful entry to be forcible entry.

*See also:* trespass, trespass vi et armis.

**right of entry (R.O.E. or ROE or right of re-entry or power of termination)** A future interest empowering the grantor to retake property if a specified event occurs. A right of entry is a future interest retained by the grantor through the grantor's creation of a fee simple subject to a condition subsequent. If the condition subsequent occurs, the grantor (or the grantor's successors) may exercise the right of entry to enter the land and dispossess the grantee (or the grantee's successors). A right of entry is also known as a power of termination, since the grantee's interest in the property is extinguished when the grantor "re-enters" the property. A right of entry is vested in the grantor at the time of its creation and thus is not subject to the rule against perpetuities, though it may be cut off by a recording statute or similar law.

*See also:* reversion, reverter, possibility of reverter (possibility of a reverter); fee, estate in fee; fee simple subject to condition subsequent (F.S.S.C.S. or FSSCS); interest, future interest.

**enumerated right** *See:* right, enumerated right; right, constitutional right, enumerated right.

**enure** *See:* inure (enure).

**environment (environmental)** The sum of all resources in an area. An environment is the sum of natural and artificial conditions and resources in a given area. The natural environment encompasses air, water, earth, and the biological organisms in an area, other than humans. The artificial environment comprises all of the components of an environment altered or constructed by human activity. Environments, both natural and artificial, are often defined generally in terms of their effect on humans—for example, a discriminatory environment as opposed to a neutral or friendly one. Environment is defined by scale, ranging from planetary environment to components such as the atmosphere or oceans, to locales of varying scope, to individual ecosystems on a microscopic scale. Environment is also used to describe the social environment in which one person exists among others.

*See also:* pollution; harassment, sexual harassment; jurisprudence, natural law (jure naturae or lex naturale).

**environmental abatement (abatement of an environmental hazard)** The reduction or elimination of an environmental hazard. Environmental abatement is the process of reducing chemical contamination in waters, air, land, or buildings. Abatement does not imply total elimination but suggests a decrease in the pollutant to a level that is established by regulation or determined through chemical assessment to be safe for the use for which the contaminated property is generally employed.

**environmental audit** Assessment of practices to diminish risks of harm and ensure compliance with environmental law. An environmental audit assesses an entity's observance of permits, regulations, and other standards of environmental management, including insurance policies and standards of best practice. Such audits are usually performed by an independent party, but many entities incorporate internal compliance procedures with external reviews. An effective audit will not only ensure compliance with the law but also minimize risk and waste.

**environmental citizen suit** A private civil action for enforcing environmental quality. An environmental citizen suit is a private civil action for environmental protection and is usually brought under a citizen suit provision of an environmental protection statute, either to enforce the statute or to bring common-law claims preserved by the statute or to bring both forms of claim to stop an activity that may harm the environment or to recover for injuries from such harms.

**environmental justice** Ensuring a safe and healthy environment for all. Environmental justice is an argument for social justice that seeks to reverse or to mitigate the dangers arising from the custom of locating human activities that generate high levels of pollution or risk contamination or injury near cities or neighborhoods of poor or disenfranchised people.

**environmental law** Laws that limit the environmental harm of human activity. Environmental law is the body of laws that require the assessment of the impact on the natural and human environments caused by human activity and, sometimes, by natural activity, as well as the regulation of conduct with negative environmental impacts, typically by regulating, modifying, or prohibiting certain activities understood to be causes of the prohibited impact.

Environmental laws include the causes of action that arise from environmental harms to private interests, such as nuisance, trespass, negligence, assault, and product liability. Environmental laws also include local, state, national, and international regulatory schemes for the limitation of harm to the environment through the production, use, and disposal of toxic substances, the alteration of natural environments, the restriction of emissions into the air or water, the regulation of wastes, and the management of resources and extractions.

**Environmental Protection Agency (E.P.A. or EPA)** The federal agency primarily charged with safeguarding the environment. The United States Environmental Protection Agency is a federal agency charged with instituting and maintaining active efforts to improve the environment and ameliorate the harmful effects of human activity upon it. It is the agency tasked with the management of and regulations under the Clean Air Act, the Clean Water Act, the Resource Conservation Act, and Superfund, among others. Other agencies, like the Food and Drug Administration, the Department of Agriculture, the U.S. Coast Guard, the Nuclear Regulatory Commission, and the Department of Energy have various roles in the control of substances and activities that pose environmental risk.

**National Environmental Policy Act (N.E.P.A. or NEPA)** Federal agencies must weigh the environmental harm of every major federal action. The National Environmental Policy Act of 1969 was enacted on January 1, 1970 and requires federal agencies to consider environmental concerns when planning every major federal activity, legislation, and regulation. It obligates agencies to study and assess the potential environmental impacts of government activity, including compliance with other statutes, such as the Endangered Species Act and the Clean Water Act, and to seek less harmful means of achieving governmental goals. If the agency determines that the action is a major federal action that significantly affects the quality of the human environment, then a full report, an environmental impact statement, is required. The act also created the Council on Environmental Quality.

**environmental impact statement (E.I.S or EIS)** Final assessment of the environmental impacts of a major federal project. An environmental impact statement is a report required under NEPA to analyze the environmental impacts of a major federal project or other agency activity. An EIS must describe each environmental impact in detail, consider available alternatives to the proposed action, and list commitments of resources already made. The Council on Environmental Quality oversees the completion of an EIS and its compliance with NEPA, although judicial review under the Administrative Procedure Act is also available.

*Administrative Procedure Act (A.P.A. or APA)* The National Environmental Policy Act (N.E.P.A. or NEPA), like nearly all acts that deal with agency regulations, is subject to the requirements of the Administrative Procedure Act. Complaints can be brought under APA to enforce failures by an agency to perform its administrative functions under NEPA, particularly in regards to the agency's requirements that it manage the project at hand, study the potential harms of the project, disclose them, and consider alternatives to the project, pursuing the least harmful alternative to accomplish the required objective.

**environmental assessment (E.A. or EA)** Initial assessment of the environmental impact of a major federal project. An environmental assessment is either an agency's assessment or a major federal project that provides the basis for the agency's determination to prepare or avoid an environmental impact statement. By completing an EA and appropriately finding no significant impact, the agency complies with NEPA. Courts will generally scrutinize environmental assessments made by agencies that determine that an EIS is not required.

> **categorical exclusion** An action for which no NEPA review is required. A categorical exclusion under NEPA is a group of actions that, either individually or cumulatively, would not significantly affect the environment and thus do not require an environmental assessment or environmental impact statement in accordance with NEPA. The determination of what is a categorical exclusion often becomes litigated because it will establish the amount of procedural steps a federal agency will need to take prior to instituting an agency action.

> **finding of no significant impact (F.O.N.S.I. or FONSI)** A finding that no environmental impact statement is required. A finding of no significant impact (FONSI) is an agency's decision that, based on an environmental assessment, a proposed action will have no significant impact on the environment and thus does not require the preparation of an environmental impact statement.

**hard-look doctrine** An agency must take a hard look at the effects of an action, even an approved one. The hard-look doctrine is a requirement that an agency make a careful and heightened examination of the environmental harms that may be caused by a federal action, whether the agency has prepared an environmental assessment (EA), determined that an exclusion makes unnecessary an EA, or completed an environmental impact statement (EIS) that failed to account for the newly discovered harm. A hard look requires the agency to ensure it and all participating agencies were considering all the relevant facts, listening to diverse viewpoints from affected interests, consistently obeying their own regulations, and explaining their decisions as a reasoned exercise of the agency's discretion in each specific case. If the information collected demonstrates that a major federal action will affect the quality of the human environment to a significant extent not already considered, an EIS or supplemental EIS is needed.

**major federal project (major federal action)** A federal policy, plan, project, or program of sufficient scale to warrant NEPA review. A major federal action, or a major federal project, is a project of sufficient scale that it is likely to have a significant effect on the quality of the human environment, so that its lead agency should comply with the assessment provisions of the National Environmental Policy Act. No definitive scale of funding, prospective environmental damage, or geographic coverage defines the word major, but any significant project is intended by Congress to be included. Agency attempts to evade the appearance of a major federal action by "over-tiering" or breaking a project into small components to evade NEPA review violate the intent and letter of the act.

**environmental justice** *See:* justice, environmental justice.

**environmental mitigation** *See:* mitigation, environmental mitigation, mitigation bank; mitigation, environmental mitigation.

**environmental risk assessment** *See:* risk, risk assessment, environmental risk assessment.

**envoy** *See:* diplomat, envoy.

**epidemiological evidence** *See:* proof, forms of proof, epidemiological proof (epidemiological evidence); evidence, epidemiological evidence.

**epistemology of law** *See:* law, theories of law, epistemology of law.

**equal**

> **equal access rule** *See:* possession, constructive possession, equal access rule (equal-access rule).

> **Equal Access to Justice Act** *See:* fees, attorney fees, Equal Access to Justice Act (E.A.J.A. or EAJA); fee, fee for services, attorney's fee, fee shifting, Equal Access to Justice Act (EAJA or E.A.J.A.).

> **Equal Credit Opportunity Act** *See:* credit, Equal Credit Opportunity Act (E.C.O.A. or ECOA).

> **Equal Employment Opportunity Commission** *See:* employment, Equal Employment Opportunity Commission (E.E.O.C. or EEOC).

> **equal footing doctrine** *See:* sovereignty, state sovereignty, equal footing doctrine (equal-footing doctrine).

> **equal justice under law** *See:* equality, equal justice under the law (equal justice under law).

> **equal justice under the law** *See:* equality, equal justice under the law (equal justice under law).

> **equal pay** *See:* pay, equal pay (fair pay).

> **Equal Protection Clause** *See:* constitution, U.S. Constitution, clauses, Equal Protection Clause.

> **equal protection of the law** *See:* equality, equal protection of the law.

> **equal protection of the laws** *See:* equality, equal protection of the laws, Hunter doctrine; equality, equal protection of the laws, governmental interest; equality, equal protection of the laws, classification, de jure classification; equality, equal protection of the laws, classification, de facto classification; equality,

equal protection of the laws | appointed counsel during appeals; equality, equal protection of the laws, classification (class).

**Equal Rights Amendment**  *See:* constitution, U.S. Constitution, amendment proposed, Equal Rights Amendment (ERA or E.R.A.).

**equal time rule**  *See:* broadcasting, equal time rule (equal-time rule).

**equality (equal)**  Each possessing the same rights and duties as the other. Equality is the most fundamental requirement of the law, to treat each person before the law in the same manner. This sense of equality is buttressed by due process of law, which ensures that there is not equality of deprivation but equal access to the fair enforcement and adjudication of rational and reasonable laws. Legal equality cannot cure all social and economic inequality, but it can serve as an ideal for policies that affect social and economic inequalities, by promoting standards of equal dignity, equal access to public resources, and equal opportunity in the enjoyment of public goods, especially education, and in the development of the private ability to exercise individual liberty.

Equality is an essential tool in the crafting of remedies, and it is measured in a variety of forms, including but not limited to monetary equivalence.

**affirmative action**  Any program of educational or occupational opportunities for members of a minority group subject to discrimination. Affirmative action is the use of recruitment, incentives, and preferences in hiring and advancement to promote members of historically disadvantaged groups in education, the workplace, and the award of government contracts. Affirmative action was instituted to remedy the effects of generations of discrimination in education, employment, and commercial opportunities, particularly on the bases of race and of gender. Affirmative action in education has largely been supplanted by diversity policies that eschew quotas or target enrollments but seek diversity as a part of wider policies to benefit the student community as a whole.

Some policies by state institutions implementing affirmative action amount to reverse discrimination and are unconstitutional. Even so, affirmative action may be both constitutional in itself and in a particular remedial context.

*See also:* discrimination.

**equal justice under the law (equal justice under law)**  Equality as a measure of justice. Equal justice under the law is the broad principle that equality is a requirement of justice, the sense according to which all people are created equal. "Equal Justice Under Law" is inscribed on the entablature of the Supreme Court building in Washington, D.C.

*See also:* justice.

**equal protection of the law**  Each law should treat similarly situated individuals in a similar manner. Equal protection of the law is one manifestation of the ancient principle of equal justice under the law

and is required in the U.S. Constitution by states under the Fourteenth Amendment's equal protection clause and by the national government under the Fifth Amendment's due process clause. Equal protection requires each law, whether it is a statute, regulation, order, or application of custom, to treat similarly situated people in a similar way.

Equal-protection analysis thus questions how people are classified as similar or different in their situations, requiring that all such classifications be rational and that the allocations of benefits and burdens be appropriate for the purpose the government seeks to achieve through the law. When classifications are used as a means of excluding a group from the political process or from social interaction generally, laws that discriminate against such people must be justified by stronger rationales.

*See also:* due process of law.

**classification (class)**  A segment of the population with differing rights or duties under the law. A classification determines the membership in a class, a subdivision of a jurisdiction's population that is under a burden, given a benefit, or otherwise treated distinctly from others under the law. The creation of such classes is intrinsic to the nature of legislative enactments: those who are liable as felons are a different class from those who are not. Classes that are classified by law to turn upon a non-legal classification, such as gender, skin color, or parentage, are different from classes based solely on conduct. Classifications that have been the basis for historical discrimination are of particular concern under the Equal Protection Clause, which protects classes from undue discriminatory treatment under the law.

*Appointed counsel during appeals*  Appointed counsel on appeal is a personal right guaranteed by the Equal Protection Clause of the Fourteenth Amendment. Appointed counsel on appeal is a Sixth Amendment right at the trial level but evaporates at the conclusion of trial. The right to appointed counsel for appellate review, according to the Supreme Court in Douglas v. California, 372 U.S. 353 (1963), emanates from the Fourteenth Amendment's guarantee of equal protection. Prior to this decision, the right to counsel on appeal was subject to restriction and recission by state law.

**de facto classification**  *See:* de, de facto.

**Hunter doctrine**  A procedure may not be required to enact legislation only when it would favor a protected class. The Hunter doctrine, from Hunter v. Erickson, 393 U.S. 385 (1969), bars political or procedural requirements that are necessary to enact legislation that would benefit a protected class, but that had not been required prior to a particular piece of legislation that would do so or that appears intended to make difficult the passage of such legislation.

**equality before the law (equality under the law)**  All are alike in their submission to the law. Equality before the law, also called equality under the law, is a philosophical concept expressing the idea that all people are to be treated equally by the law, with no special rights or deference given to any particular individual or group. The idea arose in the U.S. and France in their post-revolutionary periods, over-throwing more ancient notions of divine monarchy and natural aristocracy.

**separate-but-equal doctrine (separate but equal)**
The former doctrine of de jure segregation. The sepa-rate-but-equal-doctrine justified legally enforced segregation by race, and sometimes by gender. The doctrine held that segregation laws were consti-tutional as long as separate facilities were essentially equal. As a matter of fact, such facilities were rarely equal in size, scope, or funding, and, more pertinently, the existence of segregation meant that true equality was effectively impossible. While the term predates the case, it was made famous in Plessy v. Ferguson, 163 U.S. 537, 551 (1896), in which the Court held that separating train passengers on the basis of race did not violate the Fourteenth Amendment. The doctrine was a rejected in Brown v. Board of Education, 347 U.S. 483 (1954). Beginning with Brown, the Supreme Court dis-mantled, piece by piece, the legal justifications for sep-arate-but-equal laws all over the country. Today, "separate but equal" is a matter of great historical — but no current — legal significance.

*See also:* reconstruction, reconstruction as an American era.

**equilibrium (equilibria)**   Balance. Equilibrium is the degree to which various elements of a kinetic system are equally distributed. Equilibrium is achieved when the distribution is relatively equal and stable. The plural form is equilibria.

**competitive equilibrium**   A stable balance between fluctuating economic forces. Competitive equilibrium, which is rare, is achieved when supply and demand for a given commodity in a given market achieve a balance, or homeostasis. Usually, the balance is upset because one of the two things increases or decreases.

**Nash equilibrium**   *See:* game, game theory, Nash equilibrium.

**reflective equilibrium**   The assessment of a theory through comparison to instinctive understandings of a proper result. Reflective equilibrium is a tool in the philosophy of John Rawls for the assessment of a theory of justice, and perhaps for all theories regard-ing judgment, by which the theory is described and applied to a given problem, after which the results of the application are compared to our pre-existing instincts of good judgment or, in his case, to justice. The theory is refined and applied again, then refined and applied again as often as need be until the theory reflects our instincts.

**equity (equitable)**   A power in the legal system to craft special remedies in appropriate disputes, or the prudence that should govern such remedies. Equity, in general, is the use of rightness, fairness, and equality to adjudicate a dispute. In the legal system, equity is both the determination of a legal dispute through general principles of right and the use of these principles to pre-vent overly strict applications of general laws in specific circumstances. In England and the United States, these principles are available in litigation affecting specific subject matters or seeking particular remedies. In some jurisdictions, separate courts of equity persist. England maintained separate courts of equity, and many jurisdic-tions in the United States have had a separate equity bench, although only a few states retain them. Most courts of general jurisdiction, like the United States District Courts are courts of equity as well as law. As of 2011, only the states of Delaware, Mississippi, and Ten-nessee maintained a separate court of chancery. These courts have jurisdiction in particular matters customar-ily in equity, such as the the enforcement of a trust or a fiduciary duty, determination of the validity of a will, family law, trusts, matters of specific performance, resti-tution, injunction, and extraordinary relief. Equitable remedies in constitutional cases gave U.S. district courts in the twentieth century broad latitude to issue injunc-tions to remedy constitutional torts.

Equity relies less on precedent and more on principle, and equity jurisprudence, now an arcane but still vital art, has broader principles for standing and for relief than are available in law, governed by flexible principles of decision, especially maxims.

Equity is derived from the law Latin "aequitas," and it is referred to as a decision ex aequo et bono in both civil and international law.

*See also:* fiduciary, fiduciary duty; performance, specific performance | equitable principles; ex, ex aequo et bono.

**equitable accounting**   *See:* accounting, accounting as a remedy (equitable accounting).

**equitable cancellation**   *See:* cancellation, cancella-tion as a remedy (equitable cancellation).

**equitable conversion**   *See:* sale, land sale, equitable conversion (equitable owner).

**equitable distribution**   *See:* divorce, division of property, equitable distribution.

**equitable easement**   *See:* easement, equitable ease-ment.

**equitable estoppel**   *See:* estoppel, equitable estop-pel, judicial estoppel; estoppel, equitable estoppel.

**equitable foreclosure**   *See:* foreclosure, equitable foreclosure.

**equitable interest**   *See:* equity, equitable value, equitable interest.

**equitable jurisdiction**   *See:* jurisdiction, equitable jurisdiction (equity jurisdiction).

**equitable maxim**   *See:* maxim, equitable maxim.

**equitable owner**   *See:* sale, land sale, equitable con-version (equitable owner).

**equitable partition**   *See:* partition, equitable partition.

**equitable remedy**   *See:* equitable remedy (equitable relief).

**equitable rescission**   *See:* rescission, equitable rescission.

**equitable right of redemption**   *See:* mortgage, rights of redemption of mortgage, equitable right of redemption.

**equitable servitude**   *See:* equitable servitude (reciprocal negative easement).

**equitable subordination or subordination agreement**   *See:* subordination (equitable subordination or subordination agreement).

**equitable title**   *See:* title, equitable title.

**equitable use or beneficial use**   *See:* use, doctrine of uses (equitable use or beneficial use).

**equitable waste**   *See:* waste, doctrine of waste, equitable waste.

**equitable defense**   A defense to an action in equity or in a court's equitable jurisdiction. Equitable defenses are defenses that are valid in equity but not necessarily in law. Most equitable defenses are maxims, defensive principles that guide the court in exercising equitable power, such as "one who comes before equity must come with clean hands" or "equity aids the vigilant and not those who slumber on their rights." Equitable defenses are available in a court of general jurisdiction when the plaintiff seeks a remedy that is primarily equitable, such as an injunction.

  **abatement in equity**   *See:* abatement, abatement in equity.

  **adequacy of remedy at law**   Equity will not aid a plaintiff who may be made whole by a remedy at law. The adequacy of a remedy at law is an affirmative defense in equity, by which a defendant claims the legal remedies that are available to the a plaintiff are sufficient, in and of themselves, to rectify any harm allegedly suffered. If the remedy at law is adequate, no equitable remedy can be had. To show the inadequacy of legal remedies, the person seeking equity must show that an injury cognizable in equity cannot be remedied in law or that a harm will be suffered in the future that no legal remedy could prevent.

  *See also:* equity, equitable remedy (equitable relief).

  **estoppel**   *See:* estoppel (estop or estopped).

  **laches**   *See:* limitation, limitation of actions, laches.

  **unclean hands doctrine (clean-hands doctrine)**   A wrongdoer is not entitled to equitable relief. Unclean hands is a short hand for the maxim, "one who comes before equity must come with clean hands," which is to say that a plaintiff cannot seek relief in equity for the defendant's misdeeds when the plaintiff has done the same or worse.

The misdeeds must, however, be related to the cause of action. The doctrine is sometimes conflated with a separate maxim, "he who seeks equity must do equity," which requires the performance of an affirmative duty, while the clean hands maxim requires restraint from wrongdoing.

  *See also:* in, in pari delicto (in par delicto).

**equitable pleading**

  **equitable recoupment**   A counterclaim brought later than it could be filed as a claim. Equitable recoupment allows a party to revive a claim in equity that would be barred under law by the statute of limitations, under the circumstances of the recoupment claim being brought essentially as a counterclaim that is related to a different claim brought against the party seeking recoupment. It is designed to avoid situations in which injustice would occur were the statute of limitations to be applied to prevent an offset of a claim that still goes forward. Recoupment may be had against a governmental civil claim as well as a private cause of action.

  *See also:* limitation, limitation of actions, statute of limitations; damages, calculation of damages, setoff (offset or right of setoff or set-off).

  **jury in equity**   Equity is a matter for a judge or chancellor, not a jury. A jury in equity is very rare and, when empaneled, is not the final arbiter of fact, as it was and still is in a trial at law. Chancery courts may convene an advisory jury but retain the duty to decide questions of fact, although in certain jurisdictions, a jury is uniquely tasked to prove a will in a contest to a will. In cases involving purely equitable questions, no right to a jury trial exists under the United States Constitution, but even if the thrust of a case is equitable, the right to a jury still attaches to questions of law.

  **Dairy Queen rule**   A jury may hear legal issues in a federal equity case. The Dairy Queen rule, from Dairy Queen, Inc. v. Wood, 369 U.S. 469 (1962), applies the federal right to a civil jury to hear issues of law in an otherwise equitable federal case. Legal issues may be segregated and submitted to a jury for findings of fact, even if the case sounds predominately in equity. An exception for cases of racial sensitivity may persist, in which the court will find facts arising from legal issues.

  *See also:* jury (juror).

**equitable remedy (equitable relief)**   Injunction, specific performance, restitution, or other remedies exclusive to equity. Equitable remedies, in general, are in personam orders requiring the defendant to do equity to the plaintiff. Equity does not employ legal remedies unless there are ancillary legal claims in a predominately equitable cause, thus damages are rarely given in equity. A court in equity has an obligation to fashion such a remedy as is required to do justice according to the peculiar facts before it.

The most common form of equitable remedy is the injunction. Other forms include specific performance, accounting, rescission, division, declaratory relief, estoppel, subrogation, rectification, a constructive trust, an equitable lien, and equitable restitution. Equity may also employ the prerogative writs, such as mandamus and prohibition.

*See also:* relief; equity, equitable defense, adequacy of remedy at law; damages.

**injunction** *See.* injunction (injunctive relief)

**lis pendens** *See:* lien, lis pendens.

**sequestration** *See:* sequestration (sequester).

**specific performance** *See:* performance, specific performance.

**equitable value**

**equitable interest** An interest that is protected in equity rather than by law. An equitable interest is a form of property or claim that is enforceable in equity even if it does not exist as a matter of the common law. The most common form of equitable interest is the interest of a beneficiary in a trust, and though the beneficiary has no ownership of the trust, the beneficiary does have an interest that can be enforced in equity in the management of the trust by the trustee. The mortgage equity of redemption is another form of equitable interest, although it is usually protected by statute as well.

*See also:* title, equitable title.

**equity of redemption (mortgage equity or property equity)** The value of a property minus the amount owed on its mortgage. Equity of redemption, often referred to merely as "equity" or the "equity in one's property," refers to the value of the right of a mortgagor in the property that has been mortgaged, since the mortgagor is the beneficiary who uses the property while the mortgagee is the bank or other financing entity or an assignee. Thus, the amount of the mortgagor's equity is the difference in the value of the underlying property and the encumbrances upon it in mortgages and liens. In the event of a default by the mortgagor and a foreclosure sale by the mortgagee, the mortgagee may retain only the amount owed on the debt underlying the mortgage, plus expenses. The remaining amount would be held in trust by the mortgagee and available to the mortgagor, if need be, by an action in equity to redeem that amount. A mortgagor cannot, even by contract, waive or surrender an equity of redemption.

*See also:* mortgage; mortgage, rights of redemption of mortgage, equitable right of redemption.

**negative equity (under water or underwater)** The value by which a debt exceeds the value of property that secures it. Negative equity is the difference between the outstanding amount of a secured debt and the value of some property that secures the debt, when the amount of the debt is greater than the value of the property.

When a debt is secured by a mortgage, deed of trust, or other security in real property exceeds its appraised resale value, the negative equity that results colloquially describes the property as "under water."

*See also:* mortgage; sale, short sale, short sale of mortgaged property.

**latent equity** Undiscovered property interest of a third-party to a conveyance. Latent equity refers to an equitable, unrecorded interest in property. In a race-notice jurisdiction, bona fide purchasers and mortgagees take title free of latent equities, unless the bona fide purchaser had actual or constructive notice of the latent equity, in which case the equity interest survives.

**sweat equity** Value given to a property or business through non-monetary contribution. Sweat equity is an informal term referring to an ownership stake or value created in property obtained through actual work rather than a monetary contribution or purchase. Sweat equity is common when one party has a business idea but lacks funds, and another party enters by making a monetary contribution. In this situation, the non-contributing party earns equity by actually laboring for the business.

**erable land or errable land** *See:* land, arable land (erable land or errable land).

**erga omnes obligationes or peremptory norms** *See:* custom, international custom, jus cogens (erga omnes obligationes or peremptory norms).

**Erie doctrine** *See:* choice, choice of law, Erie doctrine.

**Erie-Klaxon doctrine or Erie-and-Klaxon doctrine** *See:* choice, choice of law, Klaxon doctrine (Erie-Klaxon doctrine or Erie-and-Klaxon doctrine).

**erosion (erode)** A gradual reduction or degradation of anything. Erosion is a process by which any thing is diminished over time, particularly through an action of physical or intellectual conflict with competing forces. There are many illustrations common in legal usage. Soil is eroded from the surface of the land by rain, wind, and surface water. Shores are eroded by waves, wind, and water pressure. Mountains are eroded by wind and rain, and stone is eroded particularly by acid rain. From these physical senses of the word comes the rhetorical notion that rules or principles of law are eroded by exceptions and limitations.

**erosion as decrease of a shore (riparian erosion or littoral erosion)** The natural removal of matter from the edge of a body of water. Erosion is a natural process by which waters remove matter from the lands that border them. As the process continues, the shore retreats inland from the body of water, and the water surface increases.

Erosion is caused by a variety of effects of water on the soil and vegetation on the shore, including the friction and pressure of water moving past, the energy of waves, and the erosion of rain and runoff. Erosion may be caused or exacerbated by human activity, including the removal of vegetation, such as the felling of trees from riverbanks, and the destruction of buffering land masses, such as the draining of marshlands. Note: erosion of a watercourse is riparian erosion, and erosion of a seashore is littoral erosion. The opposite effect of erosion is accretion. Sudden erosion is avulsive.

*See also:* avulsion; accretion, accretion as increase of a shore.

**erotica or porn or porno**   *See:* pornography (erotica or porn or porno).

**erratum (errata or errata list or errata sheet)**   An error. An erratum is an error. The plural, errata, is often used to label a list of errors. An errata list or sheet is often included in a book and is intended to be incorporated into the reading of the text. In better libraries, errata are sometimes noted in the text by hand.

In depositions, errata may be noted by the deponent following review of the transcript, and an errata sheet filed with the deposition, although the original transcript will remain the official record. A quote from a text or deposition that includes original text modified by errata should incorporate the changes, although the fact of the change may be noted with the citation.

*See also:* deposition, changes to a deposition.

**erroneous judgment**   *See:* judgment, erroneous judgment.

**error**   A deviation from the truth about a fact or from the law in crafting a ruling. Errors take many forms, but in the law they are errors either of fact or of law. An error of fact is a mistake in judgment or a deviation from truth when considering the evidence in establishing a matter of fact. An error of law is a mistake, omission, or deviation from a legal standard in ruling on a matter of law, whether substantive or procedural.

Judges and lawyers both err. It is usually the responsibility of the party burdened by an error to object to the error and request a remedy to diminish the burden, either judicial reconsideration, a curative instruction, a mistrial, or a reversal on appeal. The reversibility of an error depends on the influence it has or might have on a verdict or judgment. Types of errors include clerical errors, harmless errors, manifest errors, procedural errors or reversible errors.

*See also:* error, evidentiary error.

**assignment of error (assignment of errors)**   Designation of trial errors as the basis for appeal. Assignment of error is the process, as well as the pleading, on appeal by which an appellant alleges errors in the record of a trial. The errors assigned may be procedural, or they may be assertions of errors in a conclusion of law, or errors in the interpretation of evidence, or in making findings of fact.

An assignment of error must be made with specificity, being definite, certain, and affirmatively shown and designated in the record. An assignment of error equating to a mere assertion without demonstration in the record and support from argument and legal authorities may be deemed waived and will not be considered on appeal unless the error is obvious and clearly prejudicial.

**clear error (clearly erroneous or manifest error or obvious error or plain error or clearly wrong)**   A mistake by a court or agency that is so wrong as to be beyond dispute. Clear error (and all its variants in legal language) describe a mistake of law, procedure, or evidence, that is sufficiently apparent that there can be little or no doubt that the deciding court or administrative agency made a mistake. The differences between the various phrases expressing clear error matter, because each one is used in different contexts and case law. Even so, the primary inquiry in each case is whether the effect of the mistake, for one reason or another, requires reversal.

All of these phrases express the level of certainty in the conclusion that an error in judgment was made that is required in order to reverse the decision based on that judgment. Conversely, these phrases express the level of deference that a reviewing court must give to a decision of the court below, so that the lower decision will not be disturbed unless there is the required level of confidence both that an error occurred and that the error was harmful, in that it might have affected the outcome in the court below. "Clear error" and "clearly erroneous" are terms of art used in the review by a court of another court's rulings. Manifest error, plain error, clearly wrong, obvious error and other variations are not necessarily terms of art in this way but may be used in a variety of administrative and appellate reviews.

**cumulative effect doctrine (cumulative error doctrine or doctrine of cumulative error)**   Multiple harmless errors may, in sum, require reversal. The cumulative effect doctrine provides that a number of harmless errors create harm. Even though each error might not have affected the verdict or judgment, at some point enough errors have a cumulative effect in which it is impossible to have confidence that justice was done. If the sum of the errors is reasonably likely to have affected a civil verdict or might reasonably have led to a different criminal outcome, then the verdict and judgment should be reversed, and a new trial should be held.

**curable error (incurable error)**   An error in a trial that can be cured by an instruction to the jury. A curable error is an error made by a lawyer, judge, or witness in trial that violates the law but is so insignificant that the effects can be reversed by a curative instruction to the jury. A motion is required for such an instruction, and an appeal will only lie either if the instruction is not given or if it is given but an objection persists that the error is not curable in fact.

An incurable error is one that is so prejudicial to one party or the other that no instruction is likely to allow a verdict that is not influenced by the mistake. A mistrial should result from an incurable error.

**evidentiary error**  The mistaken admission or prohibition of evidence at trial. An evidentiary error is a ruling by the trial court that mistakenly admits, excludes, or otherwise interprets an item in evidence. If one of the party's substantial rights are affected, particularly if the decision was reasonably likely to alter the outcome or judgment, the error is reversible.
*See also:* error.

**harmless error (error in vacuo)**  A trial error that neither affects the outcome nor burdens an important right. A harmless error is an error that neither burdened a significant right of one of the litigants nor had a reasonable likelihood of affecting the outcome of the trial. Courts of appeals effectively divide all errors into reversible errors or harmless errors, the difference being that a harmless error is not a basis for the reversal of a verdict or judgment. Even so, errors that are harmless when analyzed individually may have a cumulative effect that casts doubt on the judgment and require a rehearing or reversal. Thus, a court should not presume that the errors that assisted one party were offset by errors that assisted the other, as such a collection of errors could raise more doubts about the judgment. A harmless error is occasionally called an error in vacuo, or an error by itself, suggesting that the error has no significance in context.

**preservation of error**  Error must be preserved for plain error to be argued on appeal. Preservation of error is the means of objection to a suspected error at trial and is essential in asking for a correction from the trial judge as well as to ensure a record of the argument of error for use in reconsideration or appeal.
*See also:* exception, exception as record of objection.

**procedural error**  An error of procedure. A procedural error is an error of procedure, rather than of substance, in the drafting and filing of pleadings, in the management of parties, in the process of discovery, in the motions before, during, and after trial, in the processing of evidence, and in the preparation, filing, and argument of appeals, in the recovery of costs or fees, and in the execution of a judgment. Most procedural errors can be cured by amendment or motion, if the error is acted upon quickly by the attorney who makes it, before any harm is done by reliance by opposing counsel. Procedural errors that are not corrected may be excused by the court in the interests of efficiency or in the event the burden on opposing counsel or the court is minimal. Even so, procedural errors that burden opposing counsel, that are unfair, that cause delay or inefficiency for the court or third parties, or — most unforgivably — that are deliberate, may be the basis for adverse rulings or sanctions.
*See also:* error.

**reversible error (prejudicial error)**  An error that burdens a substantial right of the appellant or might have affected the outcome of the trial. A reversible error is an error that prejudiced the party appealing the verdict, either by unjustifiably burdening a substantial right of that party or by creating an effect that was reasonably likely to affect the verdict or judgment in the case. A reversible error is not, in itself, a basis for reversal, as the error must have been the basis for a timely objection or motion in the trial court to give the trial court an opportunity to reconsider or to cure the error. But if the error has been properly preserved for review on appeal, the appellate court should reverse the verdict or judgment below when it finds a reversible error was committed.
*See also:* mistrial; error; error, cumulative effect doctrine (cumulative error doctrine or doctrine of cumulative error).

**scrivener's error**  A mistake in drafting or transcription. A scrivener's error, which goes by many names, is an accidental or unintended error in the drafting or transcription of a document, including legislation, contracts, wills, trusts, verdicts, court orders, and anything that can be written. A scrivener's error cannot be presumed but must be established by comparison of the error to the actual intent of the drafter or drafters. While scrivener's errors can ordinarily be corrected by a substituted document, if this is impossible, as with legislation or a jury verdict, legal officials should interpret the writing as if the mistake had not been made.

**structural error**  A trial error so serious that the conviction must be set aside in collateral review. A structural error is an error in a criminal proceeding that is so serious that the conviction must be set aside in collateral review, even if there is no evidence of harm or prejudice to the defendant's case. This form of error is no longer accepted in federal review, following Chapman v. California, 386 U.S. 18 (1967), which found that procedural errors in violation of the Constitution can be considered harmless.

**writ of error (restricted appeal)**  Appellate review of an error of law when appeal is unavailable. A writ of error is a pleading by which a party who has been in some way aggrieved by a decision of a court of law but who is not entitled to a direct appeal may seek review of specified claims of error in the decision. A writ of error may be employed to review a decision by a clerk or court of limited jurisdiction in a court of general jurisdiction, or a decision by a trial court or appellate court by the next higher court. It is now rare, though it is used in some jurisdictions for collateral order claims. Note: in Texas the writ of error has been replaced by the restricted appeal.
*See also:* coram, coram nobis (coram vobis); appeal (appealable or appellate).

**plaintiff in error (defendant in error)**  The party who appeals a decision, claiming error. A plaintiff in error was once the common term for the party now usually labeled the appellant. The term is still used in some state appellate courts that review cases by writ of error. The plaintiff in error is the party who brings a complaint in error or writ of error as the basis for an appellate review of a decision made by a court of inferior jurisdiction to the court in which error is sought. A plaintiff in error (effectively the appellant) is opposed by the defendant in error (effectively the appellee).

See also: appellant; appellee; error, writ of error (restricted appeal).

**errors and omissions insurance**  See: insurance, category of insurance, errors and omissions insurance (e & o) (professional services insurance or lawyer.

**escalating price**  See: price, escalating price (laddering or escalator clause).

**escape**

**escape clause**  See: insurance, insurance coverage, multiple insurance coverage, escape clause (other insurance clause).

**escape warrant**  See: warrant, escape warrant (fugitive warrant).

**prisoner escape (escape from custody)**  The illegal freedom of a person subject to prison, jail, or police custody. Escape is any deliverance of a prisoner in jail, prison, or police custody into freedom to which the prisoner is not lawfully entitled, whether the deliverance is brought about by the prisoner or by someone else.

**escapee at large or suspect at large**  See: large, criminal at large (escapee at large or suspect at large).

**escheat**  The reversion of uninherited or abandoned property to the state. Escheat is the transfer of property to the state when it has no owner. Land escheats upon the intestate death of its title holder when there are no heirs alive to take it. Land and chattels also escheat when they are abandoned. All other actions in which the state would take title are either condemnation or forfeiture proceedings.

See also: property, found property (finds or law of finds or law of finders); condemnation (condemn); forfeiture.

**escrow**  A delivery of something to a third party to hold until a condition is fulfilled to deliver to the transferee. Escrow is a conditional delivery of any thing — such as money, an instrument, deed, or property — to a third party who is not an agent of the transferor or the transferee, who holds the deposited thing in escrow until a condition is fulfilled and then transfers the thing to the transferee. Because the delivery is conditional, it is not accepted by the transferee and final until the second delivery, the delivery from the escrow agent to the transferee. The thing in escrow is usually not subject to recall unless the condition fails to occur within a time established before the first delivery from the transferor to the escrow agent. The escrow agent is usually entitled to a fee

for the service of holding the escrow account, which is often paid by both of the parties to the transaction; fees in most jurisdictions are not regulated and may vary widely.

**escuage**  See: tenure, feudal tenure, military tenure, knight's service (escuage).

**espionage**  Spying. Espionage is the crime of attempting to gain information from an organization or state and to transfer it to another organization or state. The act of industrial espionage, which is an independent crime in many jurisdictions and can be treated both as theft and as conversion, is to transfer such information from one company to another without a license to do so.

**esse or covenant for a thing in esse**  See: in, in esse (esse or covenant for a thing in esse).

**essential nexus**  See: taking, essential nexus.

**essential reliance**  See: reliance, essential reliance.

**essentialism**  Considering a person or thing as representative of a category. Essentialism is the consideration of anything according to the group within which it is defined, and it has been applied, particularly in critical scholarship, to describe the use of racial and gender stereotypes, such as considering all women to be the same. It is mainly used as a term of abuse and criticism.

**essoin**  An excuse offered for a delay in appearance. An essoin was once the label for an excuse that a party bound to be in court on a particular day offered for not being there. In the common law, it was also a name for the first day of term, when writs were returned. Essoin is a corruption from the law French from the Latin exordium, or the beginning of a speech or project.

See also: continuance (continue).

**establishment (establish or disestablish or disestablishment)**  Creation or authorization of an operation or institution. Establishment is the action of creating or recognizing, in law or in fact, any institution, office, place, or person, so that the person or thing established has an authority and certain privileges that are recognized by others.

Disestablishment is the action of terminating or removing such recognition, whether in fact or in law. Disestablishmentarianism describes the movements that seek specifically to end the establishment of a church as the established religion of a state. Antidisestablishmentarianism is a counter-movement that seeks to maintain an established church, such as the Church of England or the Church of Scotland.

**Establishment Clause**  See: constitution, U.S. Constitution, clauses, Establishment Clause.

**establishment of religion**  See: religion, freedom of religion, establishment of religion (separation of church and state).

**estate** An interest in land, the land itself, or the condition of wealth or status. Estate has several, related meanings. At its core in law, it is the particular interest one has when one owns real property – the fee, the freehold, the non-freehold, and the future interest are various categories of estate in land. The system of estates, in this sense, is the sum of all present and future interests, freehold and non-freehold, that one may hold in land. Estate also represents a single holding of land, particularly a tract of customary significance, such as the lands associated with a manor house. Further, estate signals the whole of the property an individual possesses, and after death, the estate is the property the decedent leaves to heirs, devisees, and creditors. The use of the term to mean the social status of an individual is now less common, but it is still encountered in literature, as is the customary designation of the estates of France into the church, the nobles, and the commons, to which Carlyle attributed Burke's claim that the press were a "fourth estate."

**bankruptcy estate** *See:* bankruptcy, bankruptcy estate (bankrupt estate).

**estate as measure of worth** The sum of all of one's wealth and possessions, minus one's debts. Estate can refer to the value of real and personal property owned by a specific group or individual, deducting that which is owed to others, particularly at the time of death.

**estate in fee** *See:* fee, estate in fee.

**estate tax** *See:* tax, death tax, estate tax.

**estate planning** Planning the distribution of a client's assets at death. Estate planning is the provision by lawyers of information and choices to their clients to allow the clients to form and carry out their wishes for passing assets in an orderly and efficient manner to designated beneficiaries without paying more tax than necessary. Estate planning includes the drafting of wills, creation of trusts, establishing powers of attorney, careful uses of inter vivos transfers, a variety of asset management duties, and the calculation of potential taxes according to various plans.

**freehold estate** An interest in lands with title of ownership. A freehold estate is an estate in lands or real property that has title, even if the title is limited in time to a present possessory estate. All freehold estates are considered property interests. A freehold is alienable, although it may be only alienated subject to any condition according to which it was created, such as a life estate being sold to last only so long as the original life tenant lives. The hallmark of a freehold estate is that it is an ownership interest in land that has no fixed time for destruction, as does a lease (or at least the legal fiction of a lease). Effectively, all forms of fee simple and the life estate are freeholds.

**future interest** *See:* interest, future interest.

**executory interest** *See:* interest, executory interest (E.I. or EI or executory bequest).

**remainder** *See:* remainder.

**reversion** *See:* reversion.

**right of entry** *See:* entry, right of entry (R.O.E. or ROE or right of re-entry or power of termination).

**interest**

**defeasible estate (estate subject to defeasance or destructible fee or determinable estate or base fee or qualified fee)** An estate that may be destroyed owing to a condition. A defeasible estate is an estate in land transferred to its owner and accepted, subject to a condition that may divest the owner of possession and pass to the holder of a future interest. The condition may written to divest the owner if the condition is fulfilled by an event occurring in the future or failing to occur by a given time in the future, or it may be fulfilled if a condition that is ongoing at the time the owner accepts the land ceases to be fulfilled. Defeasible estates are always subject to some form of future interest, either in the grantor (and the grantor's successors), as some form of a reversionary interest, or in one or more grantees (and their successors in interest), as remainders or executory interests. In the absence of an expression in one manner or another, the law implies a reversionary interest.

**estate on condition (contingent estate or estate upon condition)** An interest in property dependent upon a condition to vest or be defeated. An estate on condition is an interest in property that is dependent upon an express or implied occurrence or non-occurrence prior to vesting or occupation. Contingent estates usually refer to future interests, such as an executory interest, although the term can also be used to describe an estate that may be lost on condition, such as the fee simple subject to a condition subsequent.
*See also:* interest.

**life estate (life interest)** A freehold interest in property until the death of the holder. A life estate is a freehold interest in property, the duration of which is determined by the life of the person holding the interest, who is the life tenant. If the duration is measured by the life of someone other than the tenant, the estate is a life estate pur autre vie. In either event, the estate is inherently limited in time and must be followed either by a reversion or a remainder.
*See also:* interest; tenant, life tenant; remainder.

**life estate pur autre vie** An estate measured by a life other than the tenant's. A life estate pur autre vie is a tenancy that lasts only so long as the life of a person who is not the tenant in possession. Thus, if Blackacre is granted from "O to A for my life" then A has a life estate pur autre vie measured by O's life, and O has a reversion.
*See also:* interest.

**merger of estates** A common ownership of several estates in one property creates a fee. Merger of estates occurs when one person owns several related present possessory or future interests in the same property, operating in the same way that merger through common ownership combines both a servient estate and the easements over it. When a surface owner acquires the mineral rights to the same tract, the mineral rights are no longer severed but merged. Likewise, when a life tenant acquires the reversion following the life tenancy, and there are no other future or co-interests, the life tenant and reversion are merged into a fee simple absolute.

See also: interest.

**non-possessory interest (nonpossessory interest)** An interest in property other than the right of possession in fact. A non-possessory interest in an estate is an interest that establishes ownership or a claim of ownership, benefit, or use in a property without a right of possession. Examples include future interests, easements, and the benefits of a trust. All are enforceable in law or in equity, though none are possessory.

**present possessory interest (possessory estate or present estate)** An ownership interest in some property allowing possession in fact at the time. A present possessory interest is an interest in property that, as a matter of law, allows possession at the moment in question. As an estate, a present possessory estate creates a freehold, an ownership interest in land, that entitles the owner to possession of the estate from the time of the conveyance to the new owner. All forms of fee simple, fee tail, and the life estates are present possessory estates. There is no difference between a present possessory estate and a present possessory interest in an estate. One of the essential aspects of a present possessory interest is its contrast with a future interest. Not all present interests are possessory: present interests include both freehold estates, which are estates in title and possession, and non-freehold estates, which are estates in possession but not title, such as a leasehold.

See also: estate, future interest; interest.

**separate estate** Property owned only by one spouse in a marriage or one partner in a partnership. A separate estate describes the property that is distinctly owned by a person who might presumably only hold such property as a share in a partnership or marriage. Thus, the property that is distinctly owned by one spouse and is separate from marital property or community property is separate property as to marriage. Likewise, property owned by one partner and maintained separately from the property of the partnership is separate property as to the partnership.

**taxable estate** Assets owned at death or recently transferred that are subject to tax. The taxable estate includes the gross estate, which is all assets and interests in property that belonged to the decedent at the time of death, as well as the value of all gifts made less than three years prior to death that exceed the limit on non-taxable gifts, from which all deductions (such as the maritable deduction, charitable deduction, mortgage deduction, and administration expenses) are made according to the tax code. State estate tax rates are independent of federal estate tax rates, and state definitions of the taxable estate may also vary. In 2011, federal estate tax was owed only on taxable estates and qualified gifts over $.5 million.

**estimated tax** See: tax, income tax, estimated tax.

**estoppel (estop or estopped)** A prohibition against a present assertion contrary to past conduct. Estoppel bars a party from alleging or denying a fact, or asserting a right or defense, that contradicts a former position the party has taken in a pleading, testimony, or statement out of court. Estoppel generally applies when one party makes a statement that induces others to act in reliance on it, others do rely on it to their detriment, after which the party making the statement attempts to assert some fact or defense contrary to the statement that would disadvantage the relying party, and so the party attempting to make the assertion is estopped from doing so. Estoppel was originally a doctrine of equity but is available at law.

**collateral estoppel** See: res, res judicata, collateral estoppel.

**equitable estoppel** A party may not alter conduct the party knows induced reliance by another, who would be harmed by the change. Equitable estoppel is a prohibition enforced in equity against a party whose conduct was an inducement to another party reasonably to rely on it to the other party's detriment, such that the other party would be harmed if the conduct were to end or change, and the merits between the parties support an order estopping the first party from altering or ending its conduct.

The nature of the conduct that may give rise to estoppel is nearly limitless, though the conduct must be lawful; unlawful conduct will not be estopped. The conduct may be an act or a failure to act, as when a party refrains from enforcing its interests or appears to have impliedly waived its rights.

Only conduct by the party to be estopped (or that party's agent) gives rise to estoppel. This may be difficult to discern, as when, for instance, A owns Blackacre, and B builds a road over Blackacre. Much later, A objects to the road and seeks to eject B. Though A may appear to have engaged in no conduct, A refrained from objecting to the road's construction, which is sufficient conduct to find that A is estopped from seeking to eject B.

The conduct of the party to be estopped must in some manner induce reliance by the other party upon it. Inducement need not have been intended or overt but the effect of the conduct as an inducement must be apparent to an observer. At the least, the other party must have known of the conduct by the party to be estopped, and the other party's conduct must have been a reasonable response to or result of the conduct by the party to be estopped.

The other party must in fact rely on the conduct by the party to be estopped, and that reliance must involve some detriment, such as a change of economic position, expenditure or commitment of capital, or forgoing a similar business opportunity.

The reliance must be made in good faith and be reasonable. A reliance on conduct known to the relying party not to be intended for reliance cannot be the basis for estoppel.

The nature of the relying party's conduct in reliance and the conduct of the party to be estopped, in light of all of the relevant circumstances, must be such that the court determines in the balance of the equities sustains the request for estoppel.

**judicial estoppel** Estoppel of a party in one action from contradicting that party's claims in another. Judicial estoppel is a form of equitable estoppel intended to protect the integrity of the courts by preventing a party who asserts a claim in one legal proceeding from relying on a claim that is inconsistent with it in a later proceeding. Though a court may raise judicial estoppel sua sponte, most claims of estoppel are raised by the party who seeks to hold an opposing party accountable for inconsistent positions. Equity and the standards of equitable pleading must be satisfied for a litigant to raise such a claim, and it should be granted against a a party raising a position that is challenged when that party's position in a cause is clearly inconsistent with its position in a prior case; when the party taking the challenged position has succeeded in persuading a court in another action to accept its position in that other court when that position would create the perception that either the first or the second court was misled as to a matter of fact by the party; and when the party espousing the challenged position would gain an unfair advantage or impose an unfair detriment on an opposing party if its later position were accepted.

**promissory estoppel** Estopping a party from denying a contract entered or a promise made. Promissory estoppel bars a promisor from withdrawing or disclaiming a promise when the promisee has already reasonably relied upon the promise to change a position. Promissory estoppel is thus the remedy for a party who claims detrimental reliance on a promise, and it may bar a party to a contract from asserting that no valid contract exists owing to a lack of consideration.

*See also:* reliance, detrimental reliance.

***Estoppel and statute of frauds*** Promissory estoppel may rebut a defense based on the statute of frauds and applies even to promises that fall within the statute. When there is evidence of a promise, other than in writing, and proof of reasonable reliance, the statute of frauds is no bar to an action based on estoppel, particularly when a party induces a second party to forgo a signed writing with the promise that such a writing is not needed, and injustice may only be avoided by enforcement of that promise through estoppel.

*See also:* easement, easement by estoppel.

**estray** A stray animal with no known owner. Estrays are animals found at large, the owner of which is not apparent or cannot be identified with reasonable effort. Estrays become public property.

**et** And. Et means "and." Et is not the only conjunction or means of forming a combination among nouns in Latin, which often turns nouns into a conjunctive form.

**et alia (et al.)** And the others. Et alia means "and the other people," a phrase that usually follows a person or several people serving as examples or leaders of a group, to represent the remainder of the group.

*See also:* et, et cetera (et caetera or etc.); inter, inter alia.

**et cetera (et caetera or etc.)** And others like that. Et cetera, nearly always used in its abbreviated form of "etc.," means "and the others," referring to others of a kind already described. It is used to follow lists, series, or narrations of events, to depict further unnamed events, people, or things that would follow in the pattern already established. Etc. differs from et al. both in the form of its abbreviation and the significance for people to whom it may refer. Etc. is more indeterminate, while et al. refers to members of a particular group.

*See also:* et, et alia (et al.); inter, inter alia.

**et sequentia (et sequens or et sequentes or et sequitur or et seq. or et seqq.)** And the following. Et seq. denotes a series of items, often statutory provisions, that continue from the item cited just prior to the abbreviation. Et seq. is an abbreviation representing several phrases derived from the Latin verb sequor, to follow. They vary in their grammatical structure by number and case, et sequitur being singular (for the one thing following, or "and it follows") and et sequentes or et sequentia being plural (for the several things following). Other variants are et sequens (the following), et sequente (in what follows). All of these can be abbreviated et seq., but by convention any plural form is made by doubling the final letter, as et seqq. The plural form is only needed for a variety of lists or sequences, not for several provisions, items, or names in a single series or list.

**et ux.** *See:* uxor, et uxor (et ux.).

**ETF or E.T.F.** *See:* security, securities, exchange traded fund (ETF or E.T.F.).

**ethical duty of candor** *See:* ethics, legal ethics, obligation to disclose adverse authority (ethical duty of candor).

**ethical wall** *See:* conflict, conflict of interest, Chinese wall (ethical wall).

**ethics (ethical)** The duties a good person ought to perform. Ethics is the sum of what a good person would do either in general or in a specific situation. It is thus also the study of personal duties and what each person ought to do. It is closely related to morality, and as defined by some, there is no difference between the two ideas. The main difference, however, is that ethics is the study of each person's duties while morality is the study of the duties that people owe to one another.

The study of ethics and the theories that have developed from ethics are closely related to law, forming the basis not only for many laws governing individual conduct but also the duties of attorneys and officials in carrying out their oaths of office and, perhaps most importantly, are at the core of the arguments for justice as it is to be applied by each official.

*See also:* justice; morality (moral).

**categorical imperative (reciprocity or the Golden Rule)** An act is just if the motive for it could logically be followed by everybody without any contradictions. The categorical imperative is a test of ethical conduct invented by the German philosopher Immanuel Kant, who said that every act is based on a maxim, which modern lawyers would think of as motive, and if the act is right to do, the maxim can be made into a universal law, so that if everyone acted from this motive then their conduct would be rational and good and not cause a logical contradiction; in such a case, the act is ethical. Thus, everyone could act from charity because if everyone helped others, people would be helped, but everyone cannot steal because if everyone stole there would be nothing unstolen to steal.

Kant's imperative is a clever statement of reciprocity, a variation of the Golden Rule: do unto others as you would have them do unto you. It is also the central idea of charity.

*See also:* charity.

**legal ethics** The professional obligations of a lawyer, including those codified by rule. Legal ethics is a body of rules and standards of conduct that the legal culture imposes on its members. Ethical standards arise, as does their authority over the attorney, from the oath of the attorney, the inherent power of the courts to discipline lawyers before the bench, the culture of the profession, and the standards of liability for fiduciaries and professionals. Moreover, each state has codified legal ethics into canons or rules, although these are not the extent of the ethics required of an attorney. Even so, under the rules, legal ethics usually require attorneys to avoid conflicts of interest; to practice with diligence; to avoid frivolous, false, fraudulent, or harassing behavior; to zealously represent their clients; and generally to avoid the appearance of impropriety. A violation of legal ethics subjects the professional to sanctions from the professional bar and from the courts. The violation of a rule or canon of legal ethics does not, by itself, give rise to tort liability. Such a violation is, however, evidence of a breach of duty in an action for fiduciary liability or professional negligence.

*1. false testimony* A lawyer may not knowingly use perjured testimony or false evidence.

*See also:* perjury (perjure).

*2. conflict of interest* An attorney should not represent a client if the attorney has truly divided loyalties between that client and another.

*See also:* conflict, conflict of interest.

*3. dilatory tactics* Dilatory tactics is the use of procedural rules for the purpose of dragging out, stalling, or delaying a legal matter and include filings, motions, or inaction for the purpose of delay. Though all too common in practice, dilatory motions are unprofessional.

*See also:* dilatory.

*4. sexual relations* Sexual relations between a lawyer and client are barred under current standards, unless they were having a consensual sexual relationship when the client–lawyer relationship commenced.

**competence** A lawyer should have the knowledge and commitment necessary to represent each client. Competence, for a lawyer, requires a sufficient knowledge of the law, the requisite skill in investigating the client's circumstances and evaluating the client's liabilities and needs, and the thoroughness and preparation that are reasonably necessary for the representation of the client. Good will and best wishes are no substitute for genuine knowledge, skill, care, tenacity and prudence guided by the law.

*See also:* competency (competence or competent or incompetence or incompetency or incompetent).

**discovery abuse** A lawyer may not abuse discovery. Discovery abuse is the violation or misuse of, or failure to perform, one of the many state or federal rules of discovery. Improper uses of discovery include harassment, delay, or needless increase in the cost of litigation, such as by seeking evidence far beyond the proper scope of discovery in a matter. The abuse most harmful to justice is the obstruction of another party's access to evidence, particularly by hiding, altering, or destroying evidence or deliberately omitting evidence sought in the midst of an otherwise apparently conforming production of evidence. Discovery abuse may result in sanctions against an attorney, client, or both.

*See also:* sanction, discovery sanction.

**frivolous claim** A claim not well grounded in the facts or the law. A frivolous claim is a demand or an action brought against a party by an attorney that is either not well grounded in fact or well justified in law, even when accounting for the possible evolution of the law.

**frivolous defense** A defense not well grounded in the facts or the law. A frivolous defense is a defense raised against a claim or action that is not well grounded in the facts that are known or should be known to the defendant to which the plaintiff has a right of access or discovery that is likely reasonably to be employed, or that is not well grounded in law, even when accounting for possible evolution of the law. A defense raised solely to increase the delay of a plaintiff's recovery or the cost of a plaintiff's action is frivolous.

**malpractice** *See:* malpractice, legal malpractice.

**obligation to disclose adverse authority (ethical duty of candor)** A duty to disclose authority adverse to the attorney's argument. The obligation to disclose adverse authority requires an attorney making an argument under the law to disclose authority of which the attorney is aware that is contrary to the argument being made. This obligation arises not only from the various codes of professional responsibility but also from the attorney's oath and obligations to uphold the law, and to do otherwise amounts to a fraud upon the court, a needless risk to the client, and a violation of the attorney's oath and the rules of court. Courts may enforce this obligation through regulations, such as Rule 11, or through their inherent powers to discipline lawyers who are licensed to appear before them.

*See also:* sanction, litigation sanction, Rule Eleven (Rule 11); bar, admission to the bar, oath of attorney.

**unethical conduct** Conduct that violates a professional expectation, law, rule, or oath. Unethical conduct by an attorney is conduct that is worthy of censure by members of the legal profession and includes any act in violation of a widely held professional expectation, a law, a rule of the bar, or the oath of the attorney. Each lawyer and judge has a responsibility to report any unethical conduct observed to the disciplinary committee of the bar with jurisdiction over that lawyer.

## Euclidean zoning *See:* zoning, Euclidean zoning.

## Europe

**Council of Europe** The political organization of Europe. The Council of Europe is the political council that coordinates legal, social, educational, and political stability among all the states of Europe, particularly through the institutions of the Committee of Ministers, the Parliamentary Assembly, the secretariat, and the European Court of Human Rights. Larger than the European Union, the Council of Europe is less integrated than the EU into national policy.

*See also:* rights, human right, Human Rights Tribunal, European Court of Human Rights.

**euro** Unit of currency used by most member countries in Europe. The Euro is the official unit of currency used by a majority of the states of Europe, including states in and out of the European Union. (As of 2011, these are Austria, Belgium, Cyprus, Finland, France, Germany, Greece, Ireland, Italy, Luxembourg, Malta, the Netherlands, Portugal, Slovakia, Slovenia, and Spain, as well as Monaco, San Marino, Vatican City, Montenegro, and Kosovo.) The Eurozone comprises the EU member states that use the Euro; other states use it through unilateral adoption or arrangement with the European Central Bank (ECB). The Euro was meant to facilitate and ease currency transactions within the European Union by creating a single currency that could be used in all member countries.

**European Community (E.C. or EC)** The core economic and regulatory institution of the European Union. The European Community is one of three pillars of the European Union, which was created from the Community created by the Maastricht Treaty of 1993. The Community is the institutional home, still of certain core institutions of the EU, including the European Commission, the European Parliament, and the Council of Ministers. The EC creates regulations with an element of supranationalism, in that it helps govern and formulate social and economic policy for the member states of the EU.

**European Court of Human Rights** *See:* rights, human right, human rights tribunal, european court of human rights.

**European Union (E.U. or EU)** A political and economic union comprised of most states on the European continent. The European Union (EU) was formally established by the Maastricht Treaty of 1993, but has its roots in previous economic communities formed by several European states, such as the European Economic Community (EEC) and the European Coal and Steel Community. As of 2011, the EU consists of 27 member states: Austria, Belgium, Bulgaria, Cyprus, the Czech Republic, Denmark, Estonia, Finland, France, Germany, Greece, Hungary, Ireland, Italy, Latvia, Lithuania, Luxembourg, Malta, the Netherlands, Poland, Portugal, Romania, Slovakia, Slovenia, Spain, Sweden, and the United Kingdom. The organization was established to ensure peace and prosperity in Europe by ensuring that goods, capital, persons and services could freely move about within the various member countries, thereby becoming a single market. The EU currently maintains common trade and economic policies, and it generates roughly 30% of the gross world product. Many of its member states have adopted the euro as their currency.

**euthanasia** The deliberate ending of a person's life for medical reasons. Euthanasia, generally means a gentle and easy death, but in nearly every sense in the law it indicates the deliberate and painless taking of the life of someone or something by medical means. Euthanasia is usually spoken of regarding people who are terminally ill and in pain or lacking dignity, as well as injured or ill animals. The codes of the medical associations generally prohibit euthanasia, although this is a question of great controversy and nuance.

**eutrophication** The increase of plant life in a body of water. Eutrophcation is a process of increasing levels of plant life, which in some instances causes the conversion of a lake to a marsh but in other instances leads to an algae bloom and decomposition, which can lead to hypoxia and the death of animals living in the water. Eutrophication is increased by the presence of phosphorous and other runoff from human activity.

*See also:* hypoxia.

**evasive answer** *See:* answer, evasive answer.

**Even ha-Ezer**   Jewish rules of family law. Even ha-Ezer was written by Rabbi Jacob ben Asher in the 1300s and has become part of the the great component of the Halakhic code, or Shulhan Arukh, known as the Tur or the Arbaah Turim. The Even ha-Ezer deals with marriage, divorce, and other family matters.

**eviction (evict)**   To deprive a person of physical possession of land or other realty. Eviction is a judicial process for the removal of a person from occupation of real property when that person has no legal privilege to occupy it. By virtue of the right to exclude, a landowner or a tenant may evict those wrongfully possessing the land to their detriment; however, neither may resort to self-help. Eviction can be either actual or constructive, partial or total. The elements a plaintiff must satisfy to bring a cause of action for eviction vary from jurisdiction to jurisdiction, while a lessor's wrongful eviction of a lessee will give rise in most jurisdictions to an action for breach of the covenant of quiet enjoyment, regardless of whether the eviction is constructive or actual.

*See also:* displacement, displacement from a building; covenant, covenant of title, covenant of quiet enjoyment (covenant for quiet enjoyment or warranty of quiet enjoyment or general warranty); eviction | self-help.

*self-help*   Self-help, when referring to an eviction, includes any action taken outside of the legal system whereby a person, usually a landowner or landlord, seeks to recover possession of land from the current occupant. The law generally discourages self-help, and its use exposes the actor to liability for harm done to the evicted person or chattels. Self-help may be allowed if the landowner has the right to repossess the property, causes no harm to the tenant or the tenant's chattels, and accomplishes the repossession without breaching the peace.

*See also:* trespasser, duty to trespassers; eviction (evict).

**actual eviction**   The actual dispossession of a tenant by the landlord. Actual eviction is the physical deprivation of the tenant to access to all or part of the premises leased through the deliberate act of the landlord, whether the landlord accomplishes the deprivation through self-help or by court order of ejectment or eviction.

**constructive eviction**   An eviction construed from interference with the tenant's use of the premises. Constructive eviction occurs when the premises are substantially unavailable to the tenant as they were promised by the landlord in the lease. An interference with the tenant's use caused by a person with title superior to the landlord or by the landlord or an agent amounts to constructive eviction. More commonly, constructive eviction occurs when the landlord does not maintain the premises of a leasehold in a condition that allows them to be reasonably used for the purpose for which they are rented. A constructive eviction may be governed by statute or ordinance in a given jurisdiction, but usually the tenant must elect to void the lease and vacate the premises or to abate the rent and remain in possession.

*See also:* lease, lease covenant, covenant for quiet enjoyment.

**partial eviction**   Eviction from a portion of the premises leased. Partial eviction is an eviction of the tenant from less than all of the premises under lease. Partial eviction may be actual or constructive. If, for instance, the landlord locks the tenant out from one room of an apartment that was rented in whole (including the now-locked room), the landlord has engaged in an actual, partial eviction. If, however, the conditions of the apartment are such that the same room is unfit for use, owing perhaps to a broken window or leaking roof, the landlord has allowed a constructive, partial eviction. In most jurisdictions, a partial eviction allows an abatement of rents equal to the percentage of the leased premises from which the tenant was evicted that lasts as long as the partial eviction lasts.

**retaliatory eviction**   The eviction of a tenant for exercising a right against the landlord. A retaliatory eviction is a termination of a lease or the eviction of a tenant following a timely, good-faith complaint by the tenant that the landlord is in violation of a housing code, building code, or health code; has breached a covenant such as the implied covenant of habitability; or has failed to maintain the premises so as to amount to a constructive eviction, provided that the tenant is not in default on payment of rents or otherwise in material breach of the lease. Retaliatory evictions are forbidden in most jurisdictions.

*See also:* retaliation (retaliate or retaliatory).

**summary eviction (dispossess proceeding)**   A statutory proceeding for the quick eviction of a non-paying tenant. Summary eviction refers to a statutory proceeding available in most jurisdictions, in which a landlord seeks to evict a tenant with a minimum of time and process. Generally, the statutory schemes allows a landlord to file an affidavit, citing that the tenant's failure to pay rent amounts to a breach of the lease, that is to be served on the tenant. After a brief time for service, if there is no answer by the tenant, the court will then issue a warrant or order of eviction. The tenant may file a counter-affidavit alleging that rent has been paid in a timely manner and request a trial on the facts. In order for the tenant to remain on the premises during the time before trial, most jurisdiction require the tenant to post bond in an amount equaling the landlord's potential recovery. If the landlord prevails, the bond is forfeit and the tenant evicted.

Under some statutes, notably in New Jersey, the statutory procedure for summary eviction is conducted in a dispossess proceeding.

**evidence (evidentiary)**   Any thing or statement that might prove the truth of the fact at issue. Evidence is that which demonstrates, makes clear, or proves the truth of the fact at issue. In the common-law system, evidence is evaluated by the trier of fact, which may be a jury or a judge. Evidence falls into many categories based on form, reliability, and intended use. Relevant evidence tends to prove a fact at ultimate issue in a judicial proceeding. Direct evidence establishes the truth of a fact at issue, and does not arise from any inferences, while indirect evidence does. Primary or "best" evidence is the actual instrument that, by its existence, proves the terms of a contract, deed, will, or other instrument; whereas secondary evidence is everything else.

*See also:* fact; proof (provable or prove).

**evidence from torture** *See:* torture, evidence from torture.

**admissibility (admissible)** Evidence qualified to be introduced at trial or in a hearing. Admissible evidence is evidence that is qualified to be received into the judicial or administrative record, usually at a trial or hearing. Evidence must be relevant and not disqualified under any applicable rule, statute, or constitutional doctrine.

*See also:* discovery, scope of discovery.

**exclusionary hearing** *See:* search, exclusionary rule, suppression hearing (Dunaway hearing or Franks hearing or Huntley hearing or Mapp hearing).

**admission of a fact** *See:* admission, admission as concession of a fact.

**authentication of evidence (voir dire of evidence)** Verification of the source, or validity of an exhibit. Authentication is the process of assuring that an exhibit proposed for admission is accurate and what it appears to be. In most instances, a person who collected or is competent to testify to the origin and content of the evidence provides a foundation for the court to determine that the evidence is authentic. Authentication may be established by any party with actual knowledge regarding the evidence. Thus, a photographer may authenticate a photograph the photographer took, as might a person who was a subject in the photo. Records may be authenticated by certification by a proper officer, through attestation, that the record is in due form. Even so, the authentication of some evidence in criminal matters may also require proof of the chain of custody, which must be provided by proper custodians.

*See also:* voir dire.

**ancient document (ancient writing)** An authentic document of twenty years or more. An ancient writing is a document that has existed for twenty years or more, which may be admitted into evidence without regard to any statement it may contain that would be hearsay in another document. An ancient writing is to be authenticated according to Federal Rule of Evidence 901(b)(8), according to which the document should be in a position that creates no suspicion concerning the document's authenticity; in a place where, if the document is authentic, it would likely be; have been in existence twenty years or more at the time it is offered.

**character evidence** Evidence of a person's reputation. Character evidence is evidence of a person's reputation among that person's acquaintances or within a community in which the person is known, particularly as to a person's reputation for a virtue, vice, or other trait of human conduct, such as a propensity for violence or peacefulness and mendacity or truthfulness. At common law, the introduction of a person's character was controlled by the general rules of admissibility, such as whether the witness's character was sufficiently probative to a particular issue. Under the federal rules, evidence of a person's reputation for truthfulness is always admissible if the person is a witness, but evidence of a person's reputation is not admissible if that evidence is offered to prove the person committed any particular act consonant with that reputation. A criminal defendant, however, may introduce character evidence to disprove an allegation of conduct at odds with the defendant's character, in which case the prosecutor may offer character evidence only to rebut the defendant's character evidence offered for this reason.

**circumstantial evidence** Evidence of one fact that implies another. Circumstantial evidence is evidence that is not direct evidence to prove a fact in issue but the proof of one fact that, once established, makes more likely the proof of a different fact. Circumstantial evidence alone may be sufficient to establish liability in a civil case or guilt in a criminal trial, but the evidence must still be sufficient to meet the burden of proof. In federal court, a jury may draw any reasonable inference it wishes from circumstantial evidence. In many state jurisdictions, however, the jury in a criminal case may only draw reasonable inferences from circumstantial evidence when those inferences are irreconcilable with any other reasonable theory of an accused's innocence.

**classified evidence** *See:* information, classified information, Classified Information Procedures Act (CIPA or C.I.P.A.).

**competent evidence** Admissible evidence. Competent evidence is evidence that is admissible in a given action. It is not only relevant but also suitable to be qualified under the rules and laws governing evidence of its form. (Thus, evidence that might have been admissible but for a bar in a given action as a violation of a constitutional right is not competent evidence.) This somewhat archaic term has largely been supplanted by the concepts of admissibility and relevance.

**cumulative evidence** Redundant evidence. Cumulative evidence is evidence that is sufficiently similar to other, already admitted items of evidence that prove the very point for which the new evidence is offered. Evidence that is merely cumulative is unnecessary and, by definition, it cannot help the trier of fact. Federal Rule of Evidence 403 bars needless presentation of cumulative evidence.

**curative-admissibility doctrine** A judge may allow inadmissible evidence to cure a wrongful admission of evidence by the other party. The curative-admissibility doctrine gives the judge discretion to cure the harm from the wrongful introduction of inadmissible evidence by one party by allowing the other party to introduce different, inadmissible evidence to counter the harm done by the first wrongful admission. It is one of the two forms of opening the door to evidence (the other being specific-contradiction impeachment of a witness).

**custody of evidence (evidence locker)** The sole physical control of a piece of evidence. Custody of evidence is the control of access to evidence, particularly when evidence is seized and held, either by a police department, in a law firm, or in a bank or place of escrow. Proof of custody requires not only proof of the procedures for storage, access, and security that would demonstrate control and a monopoly of access to the evidence during the time of its custody but also proof of the identities of all of the individual custodians.

**chain of custody** A record of the transfers of custody of a single piece of evidence. A chain of custody is a sequential record of possession or supervision for a particular piece of evidence. When an object is determined to be physical evidence, those having direct physical possession of that object from the time of the determination are obligated to sign and record the duration and nature of their possession of the evidence, so as to provide an indisputable paper trail for those who have interacted with the evidence in question.

**demonstrative evidence** Evidence to explain or illustrate other evidence already admitted. Demonstrative evidence explains or illustrates other evidence that is already in the record. Demonstrative evidence includes images such as photographs, enlargements, replicas, and video that may be used to illustrate evidence regarding a fact to the trier of fact. Demonstrative evidence is often introduced to explain the testimony of an expert witness. The standard for admitting demonstrative evidence is the same as for the admission of direct or indirect evidence, although, as with expert testimony, there may be a greater concern that the evidence might invade the province of the jury to determine the validity or value of the evidence already introduced.

**direct evidence (indirect evidence)** Evidence that proves a fact without any interpretation. Direct evidence includes all evidence that directly states a claim or a fact. For example, eyewitness testimony or observation of an event is direct evidence that the event occurred.

Indirect evidence is evidence that demonstrates a fact only through interpretation, in that the fact must be inferred from an analysis of the evidence or it must be understood from an implication within the evidence. Any fact presumed from another fact is indirect. Note: circumstantial evidence is a form of indirect evidence.

*See also:* evidence, circumstantial evidence.

**smoking gun** A single piece of very convincing evidence. A smoking gun is a metaphor for a piece of evidence that is very highly probative of a given fact in issue, particularly of the guilt of a person for a crime, but potentially of knowledge, responsibility, causation, or any other disputed fact. The metaphor, of course, is taken from the idea that a person found holding a smoking gun near a gunshot victim is a logical suspect in assessing who might have shot the victim. Yet, smoking-gun evidence, like all evidence, must be considered carefully in the light of its context to ensure that what appears to be the case really is.

**documentary evidence** Documents, records, papers, or writings that contain relevant information. Documentary evidence includes any evidence in a document, regardless of whether the document is manifest on paper or stored in another form, such as a computer file.

**best-evidence rule** The original of a text or image should be used, if possible. The best-evidence rule requires that an original of a writing, photo, recording, or similar object be admitted to prove its contents. A substitute or duplicate of the original will only be allowed either if the original is not available or after a diligent effort to produce it has failed. For example, if the literal terms of a contact are in dispute, the best evidence to prove the contents is the original copy of the contract itself. At common law, only the original could be introduced, but in modern practice, the best-evidence rule has been considerably relaxed this standard. The Federal Rules of Evidence allow several exceptions to the best-evidence rule, including that a duplicate of the instrument "is admissible so long as there is no genuine question raised as to the authenticity of the original."

**epidemiological evidence** Evidence of a statistical likelihood of the cause of an illness. Epidemiological evidence is any evidence, usually in the form of studies or statistical analysis, that shows some degree of statistical likelihood that a particular condition or illness is the result of a particular cause.

**evidentiary error** *See:* error, evidentiary error.

**exhibit (exhibit list)** A piece of physical or documentary evidence. An exhibit is a paper, writing, or object marked as evidence, submitted to the court, established as admissible through a process of voir dire (which may be waived by opposing counsel through a failure to object to its admission), ordered entered into the record by the court, and recorded by the clerk on an exhibit's list. In most jurisdictions, each party is to list proposed exhibits in filings prior to pre-trial motions and the pre-trial conference.

**extrinsic evidence** Evidence that sheds light on a matter from a source other than the matter itself. Extrinsic evidence is all evidence relating to some fact or question that arises indirectly, such as the meaning of a witness's statement when the meaning is not inferred from the statement but developed through other witnesses or by cross-examination of the witness, evidence of the cause of a car crash taken from tire marks rather than eyewitness accounts, evidence used in one trial that was developed in a different trial, or evidence of the meaning of a writing other than the writing itself.

A common form of extrinsic evidence is evidence of the meaning of a document, such as a will, a contract, a patent, or even legislation, other than the words of the document itself. Extrinsic evidence therefore includes not only statements by the negotiators, signers, and drafters of a document but also physical evidence from the media on which it was drafted and other evidence that might describe its history. Legislative history is extrinsic evidence of legislation. Expert evidence of the meaning of a device or procedure is extrinsic to a patent. Extrinsic evidence includes parol evidence, which is subject to the parol evidence rule in contracts, in which such evidence is generally not admissible to change or contradict the meaning of a contract but is allowed to resolve an ambiguity or to demonstrate mutual mistake, fraud, incapacity, later alteration or amendment, or other bases of avoidance or alteration of a contract that cannot be discerned from the text.

**Federal Rules of Evidence (F.R.E. or FRE)**  The code prescribing the use of evidence in federal courts. The Federal Rules of Evidence establish the rules for the admission and use of evidence in federal district and bankruptcy courts. The rules are very influential in state courts and have been adopted with few alterations in most jurisdictions. The rules were initially promulgated by Congress in 1975, after a decade of study and debate and incorporating many long-standing customs and rules, as well as implementing a variety of reforms. The Supreme Court has the power to amend the rules without passing the amendments through Congress. The rules vary in their specificity, being sometimes more detailed, as in the rules of hearsay, than others, as in the case of privileges.

**illegally obtained evidence (unlawfully obtained evidence)**  Evidence obtained in violation of the law. Illegally obtained evidence includes any evidence obtained in violation of the Constitution of the United States or a state constitution to which the person is subject, of a criminal law, a rule of evidence, or — in some cases — a principle of private wrong in tort. The customary approach in the United States is to allow illegally obtained evidence into court, as long as the evidence is sufficiently authenticated and otherwise eligible under the applicable rules of evidence. This approach is limited in criminal cases by the exclusionary rule and the doctrine of the fruit of the poisonous tree, such that material taken by officers or agents of the state in violation of the Fourth Amendment is barred. Certain evidence taken unlawfully, particularly through unauthorized wire tapping, is excluded by law. Other material that is acquired unlawfully (such as material stolen by an independent third party and voluntarily surrendered

to the police or to a fourth party) may not be barred. Even so, the decision to admit evidence rests with the discretion of the trial court, and a reasonable belief that a party engaged in criminal or tortious conduct may be sufficient for a court to bar the use of the evidence as a discovery sanction or as an application of the rules of evidence or the inherent powers of the court.

*See also:* search, exclusionary rule.

**intrinsic evidence**  Evidence inherent in a matter or document. Intrinsic evidence is evidence that arises directly from the matter in question and is thus the most essential evidence as to any question of fact. The text of a document is intrinsic to the meaning of a document. The statement made by a a witness is intrinsic to whether the statement was perjured. Intrinsic evidence is, however, wider in scope than the sole object or moment in question, such that there is more intrinsic evidence in a homicide than the murder weapon alone, and its scope varies according to the question. In all cases, intrinsic evidence includes every source of fact that is essential to the legally significant question before the court. Intrinsic evidence in a patent dispute includes not only the patent but also the claims made, the specification underlying the patent grant, and the prosecution history. Intrinsic evidence in a property dispute would include not only the more recent deed but also all of the instruments recorded, and instruments, such as a will or contract, essential to the deed. Unless there is suspicion of fraud or forgery, intrinsic evidence is generally considered more reliable than extrinsic evidence.

*See also:* evidence, extrinsic evidence.

**material evidence**  Evidence that may prove an essential fact. Material evidence is all evidence that is likely to influence the finder of fact toward a particular finding of a fact essential to the outcome of a trial or hearing. To label evidence as material is to claim that it is more than just relevant and to suggest that its exclusion would amount to irreparable harm to the proceeding.

*See also:* fact, material fact.

**modicum of evidence**  *See:* proof, burden of proof, modicum of evidence (some evidence or any evidence or no evidence).

**multiple evidence**  Evidence that may be admitted for one purpose but not another. Multiple evidence is evidence that is admissible to prove one fact at issue but is not admissible to prove another fact at issue in the same proceeding. A curative instruction is usually required, but multiple evidence must always be reviewed to determine that its probative value for the admissible purpose outweighs the potential for prejudice in its inadmissible uses.

**newly discovered evidence**  Evidence previously not known to the party or counsel who proffers it. Newly discovered evidence is evidence that was not previously known to exist by either the party or the counsel representing the party who seeks to admit the evidence. Knowledge by the opposing party of the evidence's existence does not generally bar the consideration of evidence as newly discovered. Even so, a party may not offer newly discovered evidence after the time for introduction of evidence unless the party offering it did in fact make a good faith, timely, and reasonably diligent effort to discover all relevant evidence including evidence of the offered form. Newly discovered evidence may ordinarily be admitted at trial at the discretion of the trial court, which may take additional steps to ensure fairness to the non-admitting party.

Newly discovered evidence is also a basis for a motion for a new civil trial or a motion for relief from judgment or an order in a civil action. As of 2010, a motion for new trial based on newly discovered evidence must be made within ten, or sometimes twenty, days and for relief of judgment must be made within a reasonable time but less than one year.

Newly discovered evidence may be the basis for a new trial or a resentencing in a criminal proceeding.

**opinion evidence**   Witness testimony of an opinion. Opinion evidence is a witness's belief regarding some fact in issue. Opinion evidence is either lay or expert, though "opinion evidence" usually refers to lay testimony, and "expert opinion" or "expert testimony" refer to testimony by an expert. Generally, lay opinion evidence is admissible if it is rationally based upon the perception of the witness, and also helpful for a clear understanding of the witness's testimony or the determination of a fact in issue. For example, a lay witness may testify to a person's smell, speech, and walk and also offer an opinion that the person was drunk.

Common-law courts were reluctant to admit lay opinion testimony, although that rule has softened in contemporary procedure. Expert opinion must meet the standards of expert testimony.

*See also:* witness, expert (expert witness); opinion.

**parol evidence (parol evidence rule or parol-evidence rule)**   Extrinsic evidence may not contradict a contract but can explain ambiguous terms. Parol evidence is extrinsic evidence used to interpret a written contract (and only a written contract). Parol evidence is usually testimony of the recollection of a party, negotiator, or drafter of the contract, although it may also include records or statements made prior to or during the contract's drafting.

The parol evidence rule is a common-law rule of evidence that has been codified in many jurisdictions to bar the use of parol evidence to interpret a contract if the evidence is introduced to contradict the meaning of the contract or the primary obligations created by the contract. The rule does not, however, bar the use of parol evidence to interpret and apply written terms in the contract that are ambiguous or incomplete or were omitted from the writing, or that demonstrate a scrivener's error, mistake, fraud, deception, or other bases for avoiding the contract or annulling the writing as a whole.

Parol, in this sense is derived from the French word "parole," meaning word or speech, which is the comon link to the term parole from jail or prison, in which the prisoner gives the prisoner's word to return.

*See also:* evidence, extrinsic evidence.

*inapplicability to subsequent agreements or modifications*   The parol evidence rule does not prohibit extrinsic evidence of agreements or modifications made to a written contract after its final signing. This limit, however, does not apply to parol evidence offered to prove or contradict the subsequent agreements or modifications.

**presumptive evidence (presumption)**   Evidence proving enough of a fact for the trier of fact to presume it is true. Presumptive evidence includes all evidence that would establish a presumption. The evidence is not conclusive of the matter in itself, and it may be rebutted by the opposing party through the introduction of further evidence. In the absence of a rebuttal, the trier of fact is justified in finding the presumed fact to be proved as a matter of law, though such a finding is not required, as the finder must still find that the presumption is established by the appropriate burden of proof.

*See also:* presumption.

**prima facie evidence**   Evidence sufficient to win an action if not rebutted. Prima facie evidence is a quantity of admissible evidence that is sufficient to support a party's claims of law and win a judgment in an action or a claim, if no rebuttal is offered to the evidence. Prima facie evidence is a form of presumptive evidence.

*See also:* prima, prima facie; prima, prima facie, prima facie case.

**probative evidence**   Evidence that might prove a material fact for which it is offered. Probative evidence is any evidence that might prove a claimed material fact. That probative evidence tends to prove a contested fact distinguishes it from relevant evidence, which tends either to prove or to disprove a fact in issue, although the fact in issue to be proven by probative evidence may be that something did not occur. Not all probative evidence is admissible. Under the Federal Rules of Evidence and many states rules, evidence may not be admitted if its probative value is substantially outweighed by the danger of unfair prejudice that might arise from the jury's exposure to the evidence.

**rebuttal evidence (rebutting evidence)**   Evidence used to contradict already-admitted evidence. Rebuttal evidence is introduced to further explain, counteract, or disprove evidence and inferences drawn from evidence that has already been introduced and admitted. Rebuttal evidence usually refers to evidence offered by a plaintiff in response to a defendant's case-in-chief. In some circumstances, a party may not be permitted to offer rebuttal evidence if the party should have offered that evidence during the party's own case-in-chief.

*See also:* rebuttal (rebut or rebuttable or rebutter).

**relevant evidence (relevance)** Evidence that might assist in the finding of a fact of consequence in an action. Relevant evidence, under the federal rules, is all evidence having any tendency to make the existence of any fact that is material to the determination of the proceeding more probable or less probable than it would be without the evidence. Relevance does not depend on whether the finder of fact relies upon the evidence but on the potential of the evidence to assist the finder of fact in deciding a given question of fact more one way than another.

*See also:* relevance (relevancy or relevant).

**irrelevant evidence (irrelevance)** Evidence that cannot assist in the finding of a fact of consequence in an action. Irrelevant evidence is evidence that has no likelihood of assisting a trier of fact in ascertaining any fact in issue in an action. The admission of irrelevant evidence is not, in itself, a reversible error, unless the irrelevant evidence was prejudicial to the case of the party who loses the judgment in the action, was confusing to the finder of fact, or the irrelevant evidence may reasonably be thought in any manner to have affected the outcome of the case.

**some evidence** *See:* proof, burden of proof, modicum of evidence (some evidence or any evidence or no evidence).

**spoliation of evidence** *See:* spoliation, spoliation of evidence.

**substantial evidence** Enough evidence to support an argument, though it might not win. Substantial evidence is evidence that is sufficient to raise an issue and, perhaps, to determine it. Substantial evidence for a conclusion is enough evidence so that a reasonable person could reach the conclusion reached, but not so much that another reasonable person might not disagree. This is very nearly the lowest level of scrutiny for a review of another's decision, second only to the standard for abuse of discretion, and it is likely the easiest standard by which an error of fact will be upheld in a substantive rule. For example, the review of administrative orders and of other determinations that are given a wide measure of discretion is whether the order or determination is supported by substantial evidence.

**totality of the evidence** All of the evidence considered. The totality of the evidence is a manner of weighing the evidence by considering all of the evidence without regard to the degree to which one or another statement or exhibit supports or contradicts a given allegation but considering, in sum, whether the allegation is more or less proved. Although the totality of the evidence is an apparent measure of scope and method, it is used by many courts as a burden of proof to assess the level of confidence that something established is possible, though not necessarily more likely than not. The totality of the evidence is also used to compare rebuttal evidence or to assess the sufficiency of evidence

following a prima facie case used to establish evidence of a claim or presumption.

*See also:* totality.

**evidential admission** *See:* admission, evidentiary admission, extrajudicial admission (evidential admission).

**evidentiary admission** *See:* admission, evidentiary admission.

**evidentiary error** *See:* evidence, evidentiary error; error, evidentiary error.

**evidentiary privilege** *See:* privilege, evidentiary privilege.

**ex** From, or former. Ex is a latin word that expresses a variety of English prepositions, including "from," "of," "out of," "for," and "because of." In a modern colloquial sense, it also means "former" or "formerly." Ex is usually found as an element of a phrase or as a prefix.

*See also:* e, e as a latin word; ex, ex parte; ex, ex tempore.

**ex parte application** *See:* motion, ex parte motion (ex parte application).

**ex parte motion** *See:* motion, ex parte motion (ex parte application).

**ex parte order** *See:* order, court order, ex parte order.

**ex parte trial** *See:* trial, ex parte trial (trial in absentia).

**Ex Post Facto Clause** *See:* constitution, U.S. Constitution, clauses, Ex Post Facto Clause.

**ex post facto law** *See:* law, ex post facto law.

**ex rel.** *See:* ex relatione (ex rel.).

**ex relatione (ex rel.)** On behalf of. Ex rel. is an abbreviation for ex relatione, meaning "on the relation of," which is a common form for pleading cases brought by one party on the information of a different party, who is called the relator. This form is often used for actions brought by a state on the information of a private party. For instance, "State ex rel. Smith v. Jones" is an action by the State against Jones, brought as a result of the complaint of Smith.

*See also:* relator (relatrix).

**ex aequo et bono** In equity and good conscience. Ex aequo et bono is a standard of care in which fairness, equal treatment and responsibility of duty are the essential principles of a decision. It is the standard of equitable adjudication under international law.

*See also:* equity (equitable).

**ex ante** Before the event. Ex ante describes a time before the event in discussion. A value ex ante was the value before a relevant event. A rationale ex ante was the reasoning that was made, or at least that was possible, based on information available before an event.

*See also:* rationale, rationale ex ante.

**ex cathedra** An official decree, rather than a personal statement. Ex cathedra is a canon law term that describes a statement made by the Pope of Rome in the discharge of his office as Pontiff, in defining a doctrine regarding faith or morals to be held by the universal church. Thus, when the Pope issues a pronouncement specifically intended as an authoritative statement, it is ex cathedra. Ex cathedra literally means "from the chair," and it long described official pronouncements of bishops from the episcopal throne. More generally, the term describes any statements made by a person acting in an official capacity and exercising some authority.

**ex nihilo (creatio ex nihilo)** Out of nothing. Ex nihilo means "from nothing." It is usually a part of a phrase meaning to invent from nothing, either inveint ex nihilo, create ex nihilo, or creatio ex nihilo, all of which echo the idea of absolute creation, that the universe was created from a great void of emptiness.

**ex officio** By virtue of office. Ex officio denotes a task to be performed or office that is held by virtue of the holding of another office. The duties of each office are ex officio. The Vice President of the United States presides over the United States Senate ex officio. A person who is a member of a body ex officio might or might not have all the duties of a member of the body, and some ex officio members of committees and assemblies have a limited privilege to vote.

*See also:* office; pro, pro tempore (pro tem); officer; official.

**ex parte** Of one party. Ex parte describes any procedure performed by or for one party alone, whether or not other parties might be interested in the procedure. An ex parte hearing is a hearing in which only one party is present or represented. Although there are exceptions (especially for emergencies or when one party cannot be located), in general, ex parte hearings or proceedings may not be held without adequate and reasonable notice to opposing parties, after which they may proceed according to the rules of the court.

*See also:* order, court order, ex parte order; ex; disclosure; earwigging (earwig); motion, ex parte motion (ex parte application); trial, ex parte trial (trial in absentia).

**ex parte communication** A communication by one party to the court. An ex parte communication is any communication to the court by one party rather than all. This includes communication from a party or counsel for a party in an action with the judge presiding in that case, a communication that does not follow the procedures for communication with an official empowered to decide an adversarial matter under the law, a communication by an attorney with a witness known or likely to be a witness for the opposing party, a communication with a party opponent without notice to that party's counsel, a communication between the judge and the jury without counsel present, and others. As the hallmark of an ex parte communication is a failure to give notice to counsel, the term also includes communications between the judge and jury that may affect the jury's verdict when counsel are not apprised of the communication. Ex parte communications are generally forbidden, both by court or agency rules and by rules of professional responsibility.

*See also:* earwigging (earwig).

**ex post facto (ex post facto law)** Made after the fact. Anything ex post facto is created after the event, and an ex post facto law is a law passed after the event to which the law is being applied occurred. Many powers in law operate ex post facto, in which case they have a retroactive effect. The doctrine barring laws ex post facto applies to the creation of new criminal prohibitions, which would make criminal conduct that — when it was committed — was not criminal. The ex post facto prohibition also applies to changes in the law that would make more severe the punishment or easier the conviction than it was at the time the act was committed. Thus, a law that first makes an act a crime, that increases the severity of a crime, that increases the punishment for a crime, or that allows new forms of evidence (or bars old forms of evidence) in a criminal trial may not be applied at the trial for an offense alleged to arise from events prior to the passage of the law. Retroactive laws affecting civil matters face no such prohibition, although they may amount to an interference with contract, a violation of due process, a taking, or some other prohibited conduct.

**ex tempore** Unpremeditated. Ex tempore, meaning "from the time," refers to something done on the spot, such as a speech, decision, appointment, or action to be performed at the time it is requested and with no preparation. Ex tempore may also suggest a thing done temporarily or for a brief time, although this usage is now rare.

*See also:* temporary; ex.

**ex vi termini** As a matter of definition. Ex vi termini is a Latin tag that literally means "from the force of the word," and is used to describe an inescapable result of the definition of a legal requirement, obligation, or power. Thus, to say that a lease is not full ownership or that a debt is liable to be paid is to make a statement about a lease or a debt ex vi termini, or as a matter of their definition.

*See also:* definition; interpretation (construction or interpret or construe).

**ex-con** *See:* conviction, convict, ex-con.

**examination (exam or examine or examined)** To test or investigate a person or object. Examination is a process of evaluation, the testing of something or someone though investigation and inquiry. Thus, to examine a witness is to put questions to the witness that develop in the light of the witness's answers. Examination of a document is to ask about its clerical sufficiency or actual authenticity by comparison to standards or with the use of physical comparisons. To examine a candidate for the bar or for a degree in a course of study is to question the candidate and assess the candidate's answers against a standard of knowledge and skills.

**examination of a suspect**  *See:* interrogation (examination of a suspect).

**examination of tax return**  *See:* audit, tax audit (examination of tax return).

**examination of title**  *See:* title, title search (examination of title).

**examination of a witness**  The interrogation of a witness. The examination of a witness is the putting of questions to the witness while the witness is under oath or affirmation and subject to a penalty for perjury. Examination often implies direct examination, being the initial examination of the witness by the first attorney, on whose client's behalf the witness is first called to the stand, however, the examination of a witness in sum includes both direct and cross-examination, as well as subesquent questions on redirect examination, recross examination, and so forth. The scope of examination is inherently limited in subsequent phases to further consideration of matters first raised on direct examination or to matters that would affect the witness's credibility.

**cross-examination (cross examination or cross ex or cross-ex or cross-question)**  A witness's second interrogation by counsel. Cross-examination is the first examination of a witness by the party who did not initially have the witness called to testify. The scope of the cross-examination is limited to matters that were developed in the direct examination and matters affecting the reliability of the witness's testimony, such that the cross-examiner may test the impressions that would have arisen from the witness's first testimony. Other matters upon which the witness might testify are not foreclosed by this limit, as the party who did not initially call the witness could call the witness for further direct testimony, which in turn would elicit another round of cross-examination by the attorney (the same attorney who had carried on direct examination in the first testimony engages in cross-examination when the other attorney calls the witness). Cross-examination does not inherently allow the use of leading questions, but leading questions are allowed if the witness is hostile to the party whose attorney is engaged in the cross-examination.

**direct examination**  A witness's first interrogation by counsel. Direct examination is the first questioning of a witness in a hearing, trial, deposition, or other proceeding. Most witnesses on direct examination are friendly to the party whose lawyer has requested that the court call the witness to testify, and so leading questions are usually barred on direct examination. If counsel has called a hostile witness, however, leading questions are allowed even on direct examination.

**recross examination (re-cross or recross-examination)**  The fourth examination of a witness by counsel. Recross examination is the second interrogation of a witness by the counsel opposing the counsel who requested that the witness be called to testify. The scope of recross examination is limited to the inquiries of the earlier examination. The attorney on recross is usually allowed to ask leading questions.

**redirect examination (re-examination or re-direct examination)**  A witness's third interrogation by counsel. Redirect examination is the interrogation of a witness following cross-examination. The scope of the questions on redirect includes not only those matters raised on direct examination but also all matters raised on cross-examination as well. The purpose of redirect may be to rehabilitate a witness after cross-examination, to emphasize testimony raised on direct examination and obscured during cross-examination, or to clarify a matter that was confused during cross-examination. The same rules on leading questions for direct examination apply for redirect.

**medical examination**

**independent medical examination (IME)**  A physical or mental examination by an independent medical professional. An independent medical examination, often called an IME, is an examination of a party or person whose medical condition is relevant to a dispute, by a doctor, specialist, or other examiner qualified for the examination required and who is not associated with any of the parties in the dispute. In civil actions, Rule 35 of the Federal Rules and most state rules provide for a medical examination, which is presumed by most courts to be an independent medical examination, at the expense of the party moving for the exam. As a matter of the logic of the situation, the examiner might be paid by one of the parties and still be independent, particularly in a personal injury matter when an examination of the plaintiff is sought by the defense and paid for by the defense or in a criminal matter when an examiner may be paid by the state. That being said, an employee of one of the parties, such as a prison doctor, or a person who either has been routinely receiving such assignments and pay from one party or has hopes to receive more from one party, may lack the independence required to perform an IME. In such a case, the other party should logically be able to challenge either the initial appointment of that examiner or the final report, seeking a genuinely independent assessment of the report or a new examination by a genuinely independent examiner.

**exception**

**exception for public safety to Miranda**  *See:* Miranda rule, public-safety exception (exception for public safety to Miranda).

**exception to hearsay**   *See:* hearsay, hearsay exception (exception to hearsay).

**exception to the exclusion**   *See:* insurance, insurance policy, policy exclusion, exception to the exclusion.

**exception to the exclusionary rule**   *See:* search, exclusionary rule, exception to the exclusionary rule.

**exception as record of objection**   A recorded objection. An exception is a disagreement with a statement or ruling made on the record of an administrative tribunal, trial, deposition, or in response to a ruling, as by a report and recommendation of a magistrate. A properly made exception memorializes an objection to some act or decision, so that the objection's basis, the court's ruling, and the continuing objection of counsel are available to the court for reconsideration and to the objecting counsel as a basis for appeal.
   *See also:* objection (object or objectionable).

**Exceptions and Regulations Clause**   *See:* constitution, U.S. Constitution, clauses, Exceptions and Regulations Clause (Exceptions Clause or Regulations Clause).

**excess (excessive or excessiveness)**   More than reasonable or necessary. Excess is an expression of degree relating to any quantity, whether it is of things or of an attribute of human action, depicting it as greater than required or desirable. Something present in excess or done to excess is excessive. In law, many measures of quantity or degree are limited to something not excessive.
   Thus, excessive force, excessive damages, excessive delay, and excessive discounts are all presumptively unlawful.

**excessive damages**   *See:* damages, calculation of damages, excessive damages.

**Excessive Fines Clause**   *See:* constitution, U.S. Constitution, clauses, Excessive Fines Clause.

**excessive force**   *See:* force, physical force, excessive force.

**excessive force by police**   *See:* police, police brutality (excessive force by police).

**excessive pricing**   *See:* price, excessive pricing (gouging or price gouging).

**excessively low pricing**   *See:* price, predatory pricing (excessively low pricing).

**exchange or sale**   *See:* sale (exchange or sale).

**exchange-traded fund**   *See:* security, securities, exchange-traded fund (E.T.F. or ETF).

**excise**   A sales or use tax. Excise is a charge by the state upon goods that are manufactured, used, or sold. A sales tax and a use tax are forms of excise tax. Historically, excise referred to inland taxes on domestic goods, while customs referred to tax at the port on imported goods.
   *See also:* tax, sales tax (sales and use tax).

**excited utterance**   *See:* hearsay, hearsay exception, hearsay allowed regardless of witness availability, excited utterance (spontaneous declaration or spontaneous exclamation).

**exclusion (exclude)**   The refusal or prohibition of inclusion. Exclusion is to place something outside or to restrain it from coming inside of a place or category. Thus, an owner's power to exclude others from a property is the power to keep them out of it, the exclusion of evidence is to keep it from the trial, and an insurance exclusion keeps a claim outside the scope of the coverage.
   *See also:* use, use of property, exclusive use; search, exclusionary rule.

**exclusion of juror or excused juror or excluded juror**   *See:* jury, jury selection, excuse of juror (exclusion of juror or excused juror or excluded juror).

**exclusionary hearing**   *See:* evidence, admissibility, exclusionary hearing.

**exclusionary rule**   *See:* search, exclusionary rule.

**exclusive**   Having the sole right or privilege. An exclusive right or privilege is a right or a privilege that empowers the holder to exclude all others from its exercise. It is the essence of a patent, a monopoly, or absolute ownership, being the power to control the use or doing of the thing patented, monopolized, or owned. As a matter of public policy, it is rare that exclusivity is absolute, as the power to exclude other citizens does not imply the power to exclude an official, such as an officer serving a warrant.

**exclusive economic zone**   *See:* sea, law of the sea, national waters, exclusive economic zone (EEZ).

**exclusive possession**   *See:* possession, adverse possession, exclusive possession.

**exclusive use**   *See:* use, use of property, exclusive use | trademark; use, use of property, exclusive use.

**exculpation (exculpate or exculpatory)**   Relief from blame. Exculpation is proof that someone is not worthy of blame, whether in general or for a particular crime or allegation. The acquittal of a criminal defendant is formal exculpation as a matter of law, yet the exculpatory evidence that proved the defendant's innocence was the source of the exculpation. Evidence tending to increase the probability of facts that will relieve a person of liability is referred to as "exculpatory." Contracts may include "exculpatory clauses" that purport to hold a party harmless from certain forms of liability.
   *See also:* exoneration (exonerate); exculpation, exculpatory clause; acquittal (acquit); exculpation, exculpatory evidence, Brady material (Brady evidence); exculpation, exculpatory evidence, Jencks material (Jencks act or Jencks evidence or Jencks statement); inculpation (inculpate or inculpatory).

**exculpatory clause** Contract provision of forbearance from suit. An exculpatory clause is a contract provision by which one party expressly agrees not to hold the other party liable for some past or future conduct. An exculpatory clause cannot be ambiguous, cannot purport to bar litigation for intentional, willful, or criminal acts, and cannot otherwise be enforced if it is contrary to public policy. Courts strictly construe exculpatory clauses against the party seeking exculpation.

*See also:* exculpation (exculpate or exculpatory); risk, assumption of risk, express assumption of risk.

**exculpatory evidence**

**Brady material (Brady evidence)** Evidence known to the government that favors a criminal defendant. Brady material includes all evidence that might cast a reasonable doubt as to a criminal defendant's guilt, that is known to or in the possession of the government. Following Brady v. Maryland, 373 U.S. 83 (1963), the government, whether the police or the prosecutor, has a duty to disclose such evidence to the accused upon demand. On appeal or motion for retrial, the defendant is entitled to relief for a Brady violation if the defendant can show that evidence existed that was favorable to the defendant's case, either because it is exculpatory or because it could have been used to impeach a government witness or evidence; that the evidence was suppressed by the government, whether willfully or inadvertently; and that the defendant's defense was prejudiced by the suppression.

*See also:* exculpation, exculpatory evidence, Giglio material (Giglio evidence); exculpation (exculpate or exculpatory).

**Giglio material (Giglio evidence)** Evidence of false testimony. Giglio material is evidence of false testimony in a criminal proceeding that has a reasonable probability of affecting the judgment of the jury. Giglio evidence is a form of Brady evidence and the government must produce such evidence as part of a demand for Brady evidence. Moreover, the prosecution's failure to disclose evidence of perjury to the defendant and to the court is both a violation of the defendant's right to due process of law and a violation of the prosecutor's personal obligations to the court and to the bar.

*See also:* exculpation, exculpatory evidence, Brady material (Brady evidence); perjury (perjure).

**Jencks material (Jencks act or Jencks evidence or Jencks statement)** Relevant, prior written witness statements held by the government. Jencks material includes all written statements by a witness that are in the possession of the United States and that relate to the subject matter of a witness's testimony. A defendant may move for the government to disclose Jencks material from any witness after a witness has testified.

*See also:* exculpation (exculpate or exculpatory).

**excuse (excusable or excused)** A circumstance relieving a wrongdoer from punishment. An excuse is a reason alleged for doing something that, but for that reason, is wrongful and deserves punishment. Excuse is considered a basis for reducing responsibility for the consequences of an action, not because the action was not wrongful but because the excusing circumstance interfered with the competent, accurate, and independent knowledge and action that are the hallmarks of responsibility for which one is liable in criminal or tort law. A valid excuse, if proven, is a basis for acquittal or for mitigation of punishment for a criminal act, or a basis for barring punitive damages and, sometimes, for reducing or barring compensatory damages in a civil action for tort. Excuses include mistake, duress, superior orders, insanity (or lack of criminal capacity)

*See also:* breach, breach of contract, excused breach (excuse of performance or excuse of condition); jury, jury selection, excuse of juror (exclusion of juror or excused juror or excluded juror).

**excusable homicide** *See:* homicide, excusable homicide.

**excuse** *See:* defense, defense in pleading, specific defense, excuse.

**excuse of juror** *See:* jury, jury selection, excuse of juror (exclusion of juror or excused juror or excluded juror).

**excuse of performance or excuse of condition** *See:* breach, breach of contract, excused breach (excuse of performance or excuse of condition).

**excused breach** *See:* breach, breach of contract, excused breach (excuse of performance or excuse of condition).

**executed contract** *See:* contract, specific contracts, executed contract.

**execution (executable or execute or executed or executory)** The accomplishment of a plan or the satisfaction of an order or requirement. Execution is the doing of something, especially by following a plan, order, requirement, or rule. Until a task is accomplished or a requirement satisfied the task or requirement is executory. When they are done, they are executed. Thus a contract that is entered but not fulfilled is executory, but when the performances of the parties are concluded, the contract is executed.

**execution clause** *See:* clause, execution clause (self-executing).

**execution of judgment** *See:* judgment, execution of judgment, judgment-proof party (judgment proof); judgment, enforcement of judgment (execution of judgment).

**execution of a sentence of death (execution)** Causing the death of a criminal convict according to a sentence of death. Execution of judgment according to a sentence of death is an instance of capital punishment. It is usually abbreviated and referred to as simply an "execution." Executions are only performed in a limited number of U.S. jurisdictions and in a minority of countries in the world, notably in China. As of 2011, execution in the United States may be performed in federal prisons, both military and civilian, and in thirty-seven states, most notably Texas, performed usually by lethal injection, though it also may be by electric chair, gas chamber, hanging, or firing squad.

*See also:* clemency; punishment, death penalty (capital punishment, execution); capital, capital crime (capital offense); execution, execution of a sentence of death, executioner.

**executioner** The person who carries out a sentence of death. An executioner is a person employed by a state or national government to put a criminal to death according to the criminal's sentence. In England, the executioner was appointed by the High Sheriff. In the United States, the role is usually performed by personnel of the state department of corrections or the Federal Bureau of Prisons. Executions in the military are performed as directed by the commander of the facility holding the condemned member of service.

*See also:* execution, execution of a sentence of death (execution).

**self-executing** Any instrument that is enforceable without further action. A self-executing instrument is any instrument that is sufficient on its face to determine what obligations are imposed as a result of its underlying commitment, so that no further instrument must be drafted or act taken in order for the instrument to take effect and be enforced. Thus a constitutional provision that applies without further legislation, a contract that makes certain obligations binding without requiring performance or other conduct by one party or the other, a treaty that is effective as law without local implementing laws are all self-executing.

*See also:* treaty, self-executing treaty (non–self-executing treaty).

**executive** *See:* management, executive.

**executive branch of government** The branch that causes the laws to be carried out. The executive branch is established by Article Two of the Constitution, vesting the executive power in the President and officers who serve under the president to execute or carry out the laws and to ensure they are obeyed. The executive has no inherent lawmaking capacity but only such powers as are conferred by the Constitution or delegated by the Congress to the executive branch.

**executive compensation** *See:* officer, corporate officer, executive officer, executive compensation, perquisite (perk or perks); officer, corporate officer, executive officer, executive compensation, golden parachute (compensation protection or assured compensation or parachute payment); officer, corporate officer, executive officer, executive compensation.

**executive jurisdiction** *See:* jurisdiction, executive jurisdiction.

**Executive Office of the President** *See:* President, White House (Executive Office of the President).

**executive officer** *See:* officer, corporate officer, executive officer.

**executive order** *See:* order, executive order, Executive Order 12866 (economic analysis of rulemaking); order, executive order, Executive Order 10988; order, executive order (E.O. or EO or Ex. Ord.).

**executive privilege** *See:* privilege, evidentiary privilege, executive privilege.

**executor (executrix)** Court appointed manager of the probate of a will and the testator's estate. An executor is a person named by the testator to manage the affairs of the testator's estate and the distribution of the assets of the estate, and who is appointed by the court to do so. The appointment is effected by the issuance of letters testamentary to the executor. Mere nomination of a person to serve by the testator in the will is insufficient, owing to the potential unwillingness or incapacity to serve. In most jurisdictions the executor must be a citizen of the state in which the probate of the will is held. Executors are sometimes family members or other individuals who were close to the testator, or sometimes they are companies who commonly serve in a fiduciary capacity, such as a trust company. Executors are commonly represented by counsel who prepare court filings, manage claims, and defend the estate if needed. The executor is entitled to a fee from the estate, set by statute, as well as to the estate's payment for a bond, required in most jurisdictions unless expressly waived by the testator in the will, to insure the executor against claims and the estate against losses.

An executrix is a woman serving in such a capacity, although this term is now obsolete, and a person of either gender in this role is usually referred to as the executor. Note: in jurisdictions that have adopted the less poetic Uniform Probate Code, a person acting as what would have been the executor (or the administrator for that matter) is now graced with the title "personal representative."

*See also:* representative, personal representative; administrator, administrator of estate (administratrix or administrator for the estate); death, wrongful death, wrongful death beneficiaries (wrongful death estate); probate.

*administrator, curator, executor, and personal representative* There is no difference in the powers or obligations of executors, administrators, curators, or personal representatives. Customarily, individuals nominated by a testator and approved by a court to probate a will are executors, because their job is to execute the will. Individuals selected by the court to manage an intestate estate, on the other hand, are administrators as they administer the law. The Uniform Probate Code ignores this distinction, using the term "personal representative" in both cases. A curator has the same duties as an executor or administrator but exercises them only on a temporary basis, being appointed to protect the estate until such time as letters testamentary or letters of administration are issued.

**dative testamentary executor (dative executor or executor dativus)** A civil-law executor appointed after the death of the original executor. A dative testamentary executor is chosen by the court to administer an estate if the executor dies while the probate estate remains open. This form of executor seems to be used exclusively in proceedings governed by the civil law, as in Louisiana.

**executor de son tort** An unauthorized executor. An executor de son tort is not, in fact, an executor, but someone who claims to be the executor of a will and assumes the role despite no evidence of such appointment.

**joint executor** One of several executors with equal authority over an estate. A joint exectuor is one of several executors appointed to probate an estate, usually owing to the testator's nomination of two or more people to serve jointly as executors. Each joint executor is an agent of the other joint executor(s) because frequently the testator's intention is that they will work together, so that if one executor makes a decision it is presumed to have been made by the other(s) as well.

**special executor** An executor charged with a component of a testator's estate. A special executor is appointed to manage only a portion of the estate or to manage interests under the will for a limited time or in a defined location. Frequently, a person appointed for this role will be denominated as a special administrator, though both terms are used, and Iowa, for example, appoints special executors.

**testamentary executor (executor testamentarius)** The executor named by the testator in the will. An executor testamentarius is named in the testament by the testator as the person to serve as executor of the decedent's estate. A testamentary executor must still be appointed by a judge with jurisdiction over wills and given letters testamentary, according to which the executor may act for the estate.
*See also:* probate, letters testamentary (letters of administration).

**executory** Not completely executed. Anything executory is started and not yet finished, or in the process of being completed but remains uncompleted. An executory contract is not fully performed. An executory trust is not yet in full effect. An executory devise is not yet vested. In each instance, some condition must be satisfied or some act yet performed in order for the legal action to be executed.

**executory accord** *See:* accord, accord and satisfaction, executory accord.

**executory contract** *See:* contract, specific contracts, executory contract.

**executory devise** *See:* devise, executory devise.

**executory interest** *See:* interest, executory interest (E.I. or EI or executory bequest).

**executrix** *See:* executor (executrix).

**exemplary damages or punis or punitives** *See:* damages, classes of damages, punitive damages (exemplary damages or punis or punitives).

**exemplary punishment or deterrent theory or exemplary theory** *See:* punishment, deterrent punishment (exemplary punishment or deterrent theory or exemplary theory).

**exempli gratia (e.g. or eg)** For example. E.g. is the abbreviation of exempli gratia, which is Latin for "for the sake of example." It is used to introduce an illustration or example of a point. Note: the difference between i.e. and e.g. is that e.g. introduces examples that illustrate, but do not define, the point being made. The implication is that e.g. precedes examples chosen from a greater number, any of which might illustrate the preceding clause. In most cases, i.e. is more definitive.
*See also:* videlicet (viz.).

**exemption (exempt)**

**debtors' exemption** *See:* debtor, debtors' exemption (exempt assets).

**exempt assets** *See:* debtor, debtors' exemption (exempt assets).

**exempt income** *See:* income, exempt income.

**exemptions from garnishment** *See:* garnishment, exemptions from garnishment.

**exhaust** *See:* pollution, air pollution, emission, motor vehicle emission standards, tailpipe emissions (exhaust).

**exhaustion (exhaust)** To be emptied, completed, expelled, or worn out. Exhaustion in the law means to complete some task, whether it is done satisfactorily or not. Thus, to exhaust a time limit is to wait until the time is past; to exhaust an issue is to argue it until no argument is reasonably likely to be useful; and to exhaust appeals is to seek all available appeals and to receive a ruling on each, regardless of its outcome.

Exhaust in the mechanical and environmental contexts is the material expelled from a machine or process, particularly gases and liquids expelled into the environment.

**exhaustion of remedies** All required process has been tried but failed. Exhaustion of remedies is a doctrine of review and appeal that requires that all preliminary opportunities for relief be attempted with no success before the current petition for review or appeal is filed. Rules requiring the exhaustion of remedies may require private or informal attempts, and in a sense, rules requiring mediation or arbitration prior to an action are a form of exhaustion requirement. Most rules requiring exhaustion of remedies, however, mandate the use of a formal, if private, procedure, as with an employment claim against an employer or union; or the pursuit of administrative procedures for review or administrative appeal, as with the review of an administrative decision; or the pursuit of state procedures for federal review of a state decision, as with the review of a habeas corpus petition.

> **right to sue letter**  A agency's notice to a private litigant that it may pursue a claim. A right to sue letter is a notice provided by a government agency to a private litigant stating that the agency has determined that the government's interest will not be impeded by the recipient's claim, and thus the recipient may bring a private cause of action. Most right to sue letters are issued following an investigation of the recipient's complaint, which may be subject to administrative citation or litigation and must be lodged with the agency before the complainant may bring an independent cause of action. In most cases, the agency issues the right to sue letter when determining that the agency will not pursue the charge itself.

**exhibit**  *See:* evidence, exhibit (exhibit list).

**exhumation (exhume or disinter)**  The removal of a dead body from the grave. Exhumation, usually accomplished by an order of exhumation, is the removal of a dead body from a grave or other place of repose. Exhumation is necessary for performing post-mortem autopsies, which may be required for criminal investigations or for the determination of lineage or descent.
*See also:* corpse (cadaver or dead body).

**exigency (exigencies or exigent)**  Emergency. Exigency has several distinct senses, both of which depict a circumstance that requires action without delay. In its primary (and older) sense, exigency is an urgent condition requiring immediate action. This urgent sense of exigence is still very important in law as the sense in which an exigent circumstance is an exception to the warrant requirement for searches. In this sense, an exigent condition is immediate and compelling, and not merely important or difficult. The term comes from the medieval Latin exigentia, or urgency. An exigent condition in this sense may justify or excuse an official who omits a legal or procedural requirement in carrying out an official task. This allowance is only available in circumstances in which the official might reasonably believe that whatever permission, approval, or form might have been sought would be granted, but the present emergency would make such procedures moot.

Exigency has a second, distinct sense, as a condition that must be overcome to achieve some goal. This sense gives rise to a third, in which something exigent is the means of overcoming the condition interfering with attaining a goal, and in this sense exigence might not even be intended to suggest that some exigent action is the only means of overcoming such a condition. This sense of exigency is unlikely to have anything urgent about it. In this sense, the exigency of a situation is just the requirements of some task, such as the exigency of feeding a prisoner.

It is easy to confuse these various senses of the word, but it is essential to distinguish them. Exigency in the first sense, which excuses procedural defects, can be confused with exigency in the second, which ought not to be the basis for altering procedures or excusing a failure of any procedural safeguard. Erosion of procedural safeguards from such confusion is apparent in the use of the term, as exigencies are more and more suggested that turn out to be mere obligations or inconveniences, rather than a genuinely urgent demands for action.
*See also:* search, warrantless search, exigent circumstances.

> **exigent circumstance**  *See:* circumstance, exigent circumstance.

> **exigent circumstances**  *See:* search, warrantless search, exigent circumstances.

**exoneration (exonerate)**  The relief from a burden or duty. Exoneration is the act of discharging a burden or a duty from a person or entity that was formerly bound by it. Exoneration of a debt is the debt's satisfaction through payment or by its rescission. Exoneration of a liability may be accomplished as a result of a court order, as when the defendant escapes a burden either through affirmative argument or through the plaintiff's (or the government's) failure to meet its burden of proof. It can also occur through operation of law. Exoneration does not necessarily mean that a person is innocent or had no legal obligation; rather, it means only that the government has failed to present evidence sufficient to convict or that the obligation will go unenforced because of other issues, such as technicalities like a limitation of the action as moot or out of time.
*See also:* exculpation (exculpate or exculpatory).

**exotic animal**  *See:* animal, exotic animal.

**exotic species**  *See:* species, alien species (exotic species).

**expatriate or expat**  *See:* expatriation (expatriate or expat).

**expectation damages**  *See:* damages, contract damages, expectation damages, economic waste; damages, contract damages, expectation damages (benefit of the bargain damages).

**expectation of privacy**  *See:* privacy, right to privacy, expectation of privacy; privacy, expectation of privacy | garbage.

**expenditure**  *See:* expense (expenditure).

**expense (expenditure)**  A payment made or owed to another. An expense is the outflow of money in exchange for a good or service. There are several technical senses of expense that are closely related. An expense (in accounting) is a transaction involving an outflow or using up of an asset or an incurrence of a liability. An expense (in taxation) is an item subtracted from a person's or business's gross income to determine their taxable income.

**accrued expense** An expense subtracted from income but not yet paid. An accrued expense is an expense that an entity has subtracted from income but has yet to pay. Accrued expenses are used only when a business uses the accrual method of accounting, as opposed to the cash method of accounting.
*See also:* accounting, accrual accounting method (accrual accounting or accrual basis).

**all-events test** An expense is incurred when its liability is final and of a definite amount. The all-events test is used to determine when an expense is to be regarded as incurred as a matter of federal income taxation. To satisfy the all events test the liability must be final and definite in amount, fixed and absolute, and unconditional.

**business expense** A cost incurred to carry on a trade or business. A business expense is an expenditure that is made primarily for the benefit of the trade or business on behalf of which the expense is incurred. Under the Internal Revenue Code, a business expense can be deducted from the taxable income of the going concern, provided that the expense is ordinary, reasonable, paid or incurred within the taxable year, and paid in the course of carrying on a trade or business activity.

**ordinary and necessary expenses** Customary business outlays deductible under IRC 162(a). Ordinary and necessary expenses are expenses deductible against an entity's income that fall within the purview of IRC 162(a) as "necessary," meaning appropriate and helpful in the development of the taxpayer's business, and "ordinary," meaning that they occur regularly (as opposed to a capital expenditure).
*See also:* overhead.

**capital expenditure** Payment to obtain or increase the value of a long-term asset. A capital expenditure is any amount paid out for new buildings or for permanent improvements or betterments made to increase the value of any capital asset.

**capital outlay** The value, in cash, required for the acquisition of a capital asset. A capital outlay is the unfinanced portion of a transaction to purchase land or permanent improvements, or the money in cash required to effectuate it. For example, a $100,000 land purchase that is financed by a third party for 80% of its price requires a $20,000 capital outlay.

**extraordinary expense** A rare, non-recurring expense. An extraordinary expense is an unusual expense that is unanticipated and non-recurring, such as a charge for restructuring through a reduction in force.

*See also:* ordinariness, extraordinariness (extraordinary or extraordinarily).

**personal expense** An outlay benefiting the taxpayer individually. A personal expense is an expenditure that serves to benefit the taxpayer solely in an individual capacity. There are countless forms of personal expense, which is effectively every expense that is neither a business expense or a family expense. The mere fact that an expense is a personal expense does not forbid the expense from being deductible.

**expert (expertise)** One with extraordinary knowledge, skill, or experience in a given field. An expert is a person with unusually great knowledge, skill, or experience with a given task or body of knowledge. Professional expertise gives rise to a reliance interest in those who contract with an expert, and a person who advertises his or her expertise or allows others to hold out that expertise for reliance will be held to a standard of care relative to similar experts, rather than the standard of care of a layperson. The same is true of a professional claiming expertise in an arcane area of the profession, such as a lawyer claiming expertise in a particular specialty.
*See also:* witness, expert (expert witness).

**expert witness** *See:* witness, expert witness, Daubert test; witness, expert (expert witness).

**explicit or express** *See:* expression (explicit or express).

**exploitation** Unfair or irrational use. Exploitation is the taking of an unfair or unreasonable advantage of a person, resource, thing, or circumstance.

**exportation (export)** To send forth anything, particularly from one country to another. Exportation means, literally, to send out anything from one's ports, but in law it refers to the sending of goods, services, or people from one country to another. Goods sent in this manner are often subject to customs and tariffs, although goods intended for export are often immune from local excise taxes.

**Export Clause** *See:* constitution, U.S. Constitution, clauses, Export Clause.

**Schedule B Number (Schedule B System)** An inventory of goods commonly imported and subject to tariff. The Schedule B system is maintained by the U.S. Census Bureau for the classification of products commonly manufactured in and exported from the United States. All products are classified on Schedule B according to the international system for the harmonization of tariffs. Many Schedule B numbers correspond with the HTS numbers used for tracking imports, and exporters are usually required to list both on shipping documents.

**express** *See:* expression (explicit or express).

**express abandonment** *See:* patent, abandonment of a patent, express abandonment (formal abandonment); abandonment, express abandonment.

**express abrogation** *See:* abrogation, express abrogation.

**express agency** *See:* agent, express agency.

**express assumption of risk** *See:* risk, assumption of risk, express assumption of risk.

**express condition** *See:* condition, express condition.

**express consent** *See:* consent, express consent.

**express contract** *See:* contract, contract formation, express contract.

**express covenant** *See:* covenant, express covenant.

**express easement** *See:* easement, express easement.

**express malice** *See:* malice, express malice.

**express repeal** *See:* repeal, express repeal.

**express waiver** *See:* waiver, express waiver.

**expressio unius est exclusio alterius** *See:* interpretation, expressio unius est exclusio alterius (expressio unius exclusio alterius est).

**expression (explicit or express)** A clear statement. Expression is a statement making known or explaining an idea, fact, obligation, or other thing, whether the expression is oral or written. Within a relevant context, expression usually supersedes implication, which is to say that the language of a statute, or contract, or other instrument, is usually preferable to what may be implied from it, although evidence of intent or purpose may be helpful in interpreting the meaning of the language itself. Note: there is little difference in the adjectives "express" or "explicit" as references to a particular expression, though explicit suggests the plainest and clearest form of expression possible.

*See also:* abrogation, express abrogation; agent, express agency; condition, express condition; consent, express consent; contract, contract formation, express contract; covenant, express covenant; easement, express easement; malice, express malice; repeal, express repeal; risk, assumption of risk, express assumption of risk; waiver, express waiver.

**freedom of expression** The communication of ideas through speech, conduct, or images is protected, but not without limits. Freedom of expression is sometimes used as a synonym for the freedom of speech, but the freedom of expression is more than a mere restatement of the freedom of speech. Freedom of expression emphasizes constitutional protection for expressive speech, as well as expressive conduct, incorporating within this freedom a liberty to engage in forms of conduct in which an idea is expressed even though it is not stated in words. Freedom of expression thus includes the right to receive information as well as the right to express ideas in ways other than traditional speech, both "expressive speech" and conduct that communicates a message to others. Wearing a patch or an arm band, nude dancing, playing music, and other actions that communicate an idea, even a very simple banal idea, are within the protection of the freedom of expression. Even so, conduct that is expressive but that is illegal for reasons without regard to the content of the speech expressed may be regulated.

*See also:* speech, expressive conduct.

**flag desecration** *See:* flag, flag desecration (flag burning).

**expressive conduct** *See:* speech, expressive conduct.

**expropriation or expropriate or nationalize** *See:* nationalization, nationalization of property (expropriation or expropriate or nationalize).

**expungement (record expungement)** Erasure or removal, particularly from a record. Expungement means to wipe something out or to take it off a page, whether it is a person from a list, an entry from a record, or a memory from the mind. In law, it is often used to describe the official deletion of a record, such as the removal of an entry of arrest from a record of the arrests in a jurisdiction. Actions to expunge the record of a criminal charge or arrest may be formal and require a showing of error, or they may be informal, committed to the discretion of the court or other official.

*See also:* record, arrest record (criminal history record or rap sheet).

**extension of time** *See:* time, extension of time (enlargement of time).

**external act** *See:* act, external act.

**externality (negative externality or positive externality)** Any benefit or burden shifted from its creator to another. An externality is a benefit or burden that is not fully realized within the entity that makes it but is shifted in whole or in part to the economic environment beyond.

A negative externality is a cost that is not internalized, an externalized burden that a person or entity creates but does not bear, instead shifting the burden to others. Pollution is a classic externality, as a company that generates smoke as part of its plant operations effectively stores the particles and gasses of its smoke in the rivers, land, houses and people downwind, without compensating anyone for the storage.

A positive externality is a benefit that is not internalized, an externalized benefit that a person or entity creates but does not realize, instead shifting the benefit to others. Employee trading is a classic positive externality, in which an entity's payroll benefits merchants in the community around the entity's operations, without being compensated by the merchants for their increased trade.

*See also:* free, free rider (freeloader or freerider).

**extortion**   The use of threats or the abuse of office to obtain property. Extortion is the crime of using fear, force or a threat of force in order to gain another's property, interest, or benefit, even though the victim consents to the transfer. Extortion is a separate offense but also considered larceny or theft.

The victim's consent is no defense to extortion, having been procured by violence or threat. At common law extortion was a property offense in which a public official took money or property under the pretense of entitlement to the property by virtue of the office. Such abuse of office still amounts to extortion, but by judicial interpretation and by statute the term now includes a gain through threats.

*See also:* larceny (larcenous); theft.

**badger game**   Enticing a victim to immoral conduct then used for extortion. A badger game is a type of extortion involving a victim, a confidence man, and his confederate. Although a badger game changes in form and substance to fit the extortion's particular purpose, the shakedown generally involves the con man enticing the victim to engage in an embarrassing or immoral act, such as adultery or scandalous sex, with the confederate. After the victim performs or attempts to perform the act with the confederate, the con man informs the victim that his illicit act will be made public unless the victim complies with the con man's demands.

**blackmail (criminal coercion)**   Unlawful force, fear, or threats used to spur another to conduct. Blackmail is the criminal employment of force, fear, or threats against a person or entity in order to acquire something of value. It is immaterial that the threat, or even an act designed to create fear, might be legal in and of itself; coupled with the intent to acquire something of value from the victim, the act is blackmail. Blackmail is an informal term for extortion, or as the Model Penal Code defines it, theft by extortion, although extortion at common law was committed by a public official, while blackmail can be committed by anyone. Some jurisdictions have more particularly defined conduct amounting to common-law blackmail as criminal coercion.

**extortionate credit transaction or loan shark**   *See:* loan, loansharking (extortionate credit transaction or loan shark).

**extra-terrestrial**   *See:* alien, alien as extraterrestrial (extra-terrestrial).

**extradition**   The transfer of a fugitive to another state or country for trial. Extradition is the process by which a country or state sends a person who is in custody to another jurisdiction in which the person is accused of a crime, so the person may be may be tried there. International extradition may be ad hoc, upon a particular request from the requesting country to the sending country, or it may be pursuant to an extradition treaty by which each state consents to such requests in advance, at least with regard to certain offenses. Many countries will not extradite a person to face a criminal charge for conduct that is not illegal in that country or to face a penalty not allowed under that country's law. Thus, countries without capitol punishment will not usually extradite a person who might be sentenced to death without an assurance that capital punishment will not be sought in that case.

**Extradition Clause**   *See:* constitution, U.S. Constitution, clauses, Extradition Clause (Interstate Rendition Clause).

**extradition warrant**   *See:* warrant, extradition warrant (rendition warrant).

**double criminality (dual criminality)**   Extradition is available only for acts criminal in both states. The principle of double criminality requires that an offense for which a person is to be extradited is a criminal offense in both the requesting and the sending state; it is generally a requirement of extradition.

**specialty**   A state may only try a person for crimes for which he was extradited or crimes committed after extradition. The principle of specialty is mandatory in many extradition agreements, requiring that a person extradited be tried in the requisitioning state only for those crimes that were the specific basis for the request for extradition and for crimes that are alleged to have occurred after extradition.

*See also:* special.

**extrahazardous**   *See:* hazard, extrahazardous (more than ordinarily hazardous).

**extrajudicial admission**   *See:* admission, evidentiary admission, extrajudicial admission (evidential admission).

**extraordinariness**   *See:* ordinariness, extraordinariness (extraordinary or extraordinarily).

**extraordinary circumstances**   *See:* circumstance, extraordinary circumstances.

**extraordinary damages**   *See:* damages, forms of damages, extraordinary damages (extraordinary remedy).

**extraordinary expense**   *See:* expense, extraordinary expense.

**extraordinary interrogation techniques**   *See:* interrogation, enhanced interrogation (extraordinary interrogation techniques).

**extraordinary remedy**   *See:* remedy, extraordinary remedy (extraordinary relief); damages, forms of damages, extraordinary damages (extraordinary remedy).

**extraordinary rendition**   *See:* rendition, extraordinary rendition (irregular rendition).

**extraordinary repair**  *See:* repair, extraordinary repair.

**extraterritorial jurisdiction**  *See:* jurisdiction, extraterritorial jurisdiction.

**extraterritoriality**  An effect of a law beyond its jurisdiction of origin. Extraterritoriality is the application of laws to people, entities, lands, environment, or activities beyond the borders of the state that promulgates the laws. There is a general presumption against an extraterritorial effect of a law. Although extraterritorial application of a state's laws to its own citizens or subjects is appropriate, application to persons subject to other states who are not in the jurisdiction of the legislating state may be seen by a different state in which such legislation is asserted to be a challenge to its sovereignty. The extraterritorial effect of a given law may be limited by the language of statutes; the operation of constitutional law, particularly the Due Process Clause; or judicial prudence, particularly through comity, the national law of other states, or international law, any of which may justify other states in failing to give effect to a state's assertion of extraterritorial authority.

See also: sovereign (sovereignty).

**extreme indifference**  *See:* indifference, extreme indifference (depraved indifference).

**extreme–indifference murder**  *See:* murder, extreme-indifference murder (depraved–heart murder or depraved mind murder).

**extrinsic evidence**  *See:* evidence, extrinsic evidence.

**eye witness**  *See:* witness, eyewitness (eye witness).

**eyes of the law**  *See:* metaphor, metaphor of law, eyes of the law (in the eye of the law).

# F

**f**  The sixth letter of the modern English alphabet. "F" signifies a variety of functions as a symbol and as a designation of status. It is translated into "Foxtrot" for radio signals and NATO military transmissions, into "Frank" for some police radio traffic, and into dot, dot, dash, dot in Morse Code. In early modern printing, particularly in the English colonies of the eighteenth century, a character like an f was used, which was the German s, an elongated form of the s used in various places, such as in the first s to emphasize the double "s." Thus, in the Declaration of Independence, the word Congress appears at a quick glance to read Congrefs. This is in fact Congress, and it was pronounced with an 's' not an 'fs' at its end.

**f as an abbreviation**  A word commencing in F. When used as the sole letter of an abbreviation, F often stands for footnote and federal, particularly the federal case reporter, with F. as the first series, F.2d as the second and F.3d as the third. It may also stand for faculty, fair, family, field, finance, Florida, followed, food, foreign, forum, free, French, and full. It may also stand for the name of an author or case reporter, such as Fairchild, Fairfield, Fanton, Fitzherbert, Fonblanque, Foord, Fox, and Fraser.

**f as criminal label**  A brand for conviction under benefit of clergy. The letter F branded on the skin of the face was used to mark those who had been convicted of a felony under benefit of clergy, which would suggest they lived when they would otherwise have died. It was also used to mark those guilty of falsity and frays (or fighting), if the punishment was for a second offense (the first offense having cost the fighter his outer ears).
*See also:* t, t as criminal label.

**F.A.C.E. or FACE**  *See:* abortion, Freedom of Access to Clinic Entrances Act (F.A.C.E. or FACE).

**F.A.S. or FAS**  *See:* shipping, shipping term, incoterm, free alongside ship (F.A.S. or FAS).

**F.A.S.B. or FASB**  *See:* accounting, Financial Accounting Standards Board (F.A.S.B. or FASB).

**F.B.A. or FBA**  *See:* bar, bar organization, Federal Bar Association (F.B.A. or FBA).

**F.B.I. or FBI**  *See:* police, police organizations, Federal Bureau of Investigation (F.B.I. or FBI).

**F.C.P.A. or FCPA**  *See:* corruption, Foreign Corrupt Practices Act (F.C.P.A. or FCPA).

**F.D.I.C. or FDIC**  *See:* bank, Federal Deposit Insurance Corporation (F.D.I.C. or FDIC).

**F.H.A. or FHA**  *See:* housing, Fair Housing Act (F.H.A. FHA).

**F.H.L.B. or FHLB**  *See:* bank, Federal Home Loan Bank (F.H.L.B. or FHLB).

**F.I.C.A. tax or FICA tax**  *See:* tax, payroll tax, Federal Insurance Contributions Act (F.I.C.A. Tax or FICA Tax).

**F.I.F.R.A. or FIFRA**  *See:* pesticide, Federal Insecticide, Fungicide, and Rodenticide Act (F.I.F.R.A. or FIFRA).

**F.I.P. or FIP or S.I.P. or SIP**  *See:* pollution, air pollution, clean air act, implementation plan (F.I.P. or FIP or S.I.P. or SIP).

**F.I.S.A. court or FISA court**  *See:* court, court of limited jurisdiction, Foreign Intelligence Surveillance Court, (F.I.S.A. court or FISA court).

**f.k.a. or fka or f/k/a**  *See:* formerly known as (FKA or fka or f/k/a).

**F.L.S.A. or FLSA or minimum wage or wage and hours law**  *See:* labor, Fair Labor Standards Act (F.L.S.A. or FLSA or minimum wage or wage and hours law).

**F.M.C.S. or FMCS**  *See:* mediator, Federal Mediation and Conciliation Service (F.M.C.S. or FMCS).

**F.M.L.A. or FMLA**  *See:* employment, employee benefit, Family And Medical Leave Act (F.M.L.A. or FMLA).

**F.M.V. or FMV**  *See:* value, market value, fair market value (F.M.V. or FMV).

**F.O.B. or FOB**  *See:* shipping, shipping term, incoterm, free on board (F.O.B. or FOB); shipping, shipping term, freight on board (F.O.B. or FOB).

**F.O.I.A. or FOIA or foiable**  *See:* information, Freedom of Information Act (F.O.I.A. or FOIA or foiable).

**F.O.N.S.I. or FONSI**  *See:* environment, National Environmental Policy Act, environmental assessment, finding of no significant impact (F.O.N.S.I. or FONSI).

**F.R.E. or FRE**  *See:* evidence, Federal Rules of Evidence (F.R.E. or FRE).

**F.S.A. or FSA**  *See:* fee, estate in fee, fee simple absolute (F.S.A. or FSA).

**F.S.D. or FSD**   *See:* fee, estate in fee, fee simple determinable (F.S.D. or FSD).

**F.S.S.C.S. or FSSCS**   *See:* fee, estate in fee, fee simple subject to condition subsequent (F.S.S.C.S. or FSSCS).

**F.T.C.A. or FTCA**   *See:* tort, Federal Tort Claims Act (F.T.C.A. or FTCA).

**F.W.P.C.A. FWPCA**   *See:* pollution, water pollution, Federal Water Pollution Control Act (F.W.P.C.A. FWPCA).

**F.Y. or FY**   *See:* year, fiscal year (F.Y. or FY).

**fa (lu)**   Law, especially the law applied by legal institutions in Chinese law. Fa means law in Mandarin and is roughly equivalent to the amalgam of customary and positive law, as opposed to virtue or propriety. Fa-chih is the legal system, a rule derived from the legal system, or legality in general. Fa ch'uan is the whole set of laws and is closest to the concept of law as in due process of law.
   *See also:* li (li ki).

**fabrication (fabricate or fabricated or fabricated testimony)**   Invention or creation, whether of an authentic or false product. Fabrication denotes invention as well as creation, and so a thing fabricated is anything made or made up. Fabrication can mean invention or construction, entitling its inventor or its creator to rights or interests in the thing, including ownership or a lien pending compensation if it is owned by another. Yet it can also mean a lie or forgery, which expose those who rely on it to risk, and its maker to liability and punishment.

**face**   The surface, or the part most visible of any one or thing. The face is a legal metaphor, drawn from the face of the human being, for the visible part of anything, which is the first encountered, inspected, or contested. The law uses "face" in many contexts, some metaphorical, such as "in the the face of the evidence" for a matter seemingly unsupported by the evidence, and some ranging from slightly to fully literal, such as "face-to-face confrontation of witnesses" for the cross-exmination of a live witness in court, or "on the face of the pleadings" for a more literal reference to the actual text of the pleadings, but even this contrasts with its similar "error on face of the evidence," which is a metaphor for an error that amounts to injustice.

   **face of the pleadings**   *See:* pleading, face of the pleadings.

   **facial challenge**   *See:* challenge, constitutional challenge, facial challenge (challenge on its face or unconstitutional per se).

**facilitation**

   **criminal facilitation (facilitate)**   Assistance, particularly to a crime. Facilitation, in general, is to assist in making something happen or occur, and in this sense it is an element of many offenses. Criminal facilitation is the knowing act of providing a person or entity with a component of the means or opportunity to commit a crime. Criminal facilitation requires more than mere conspiracy, such as an actual attempt or success by the other's criminal efforts. The knowledge requisite for criminal facilitation need not extend to the whole of the planned crime, but it must include a belief that the person or entity that receives the aid will probably commit an act that is a crime.

**facility of payment clause**   *See:* insurance, insurance beneficiary, facility of payment clause.

**facsimile (fax)**   A paper image transmitted and printed by the recipient. A facsimile, nearly always termed a "fax," is a particular form of photocopy and transmission over a phone or data line from a sender to a recipient, who stores or prints the image. Most jurisdictions hold that a facsimile is admissible evidence when a photocopy would be similarly admissible. A facsimile transmission may be used to give proper notice of a motion or pleading (though not service of process) to parties in litigation.
   *See also:* filing (file).

**fact**   Anything that is or was true in the world. A fact is any aspect of accurate knowledge of what is true — what is actually the case about anything, anyone, anywhere, anytime, as it is or was in actual existence. A fact can be simple and unlikely to be analyzed according to component facts, or complicated and comprising many other facts. A fact is not limited to what is tangible, visible, or in any way the object of human senses or laboratory measurement. Facts include ideas and beliefs, at least in so far as they were thought and believed. Thoughts, intentions, and unarticulated fancies of the mind are facts in and of themselves, whether they are correct statements about facts in the world. In this sense, a state of mind is a fact, one of particular importance in establishing elements such as intent, disregard, or mens rea.
   The law distinguishes facts, which are events and conditions in the world regulated by law, from the law itself. Although the existence of law is itself a fact, proof of the law is usually not considered a proof of a fact, in part to avoid confusion, though the law of foreign jurisdictions is sometimes treated as a matter of fact. Facts are determined in the legal system solely through the consideration of evidence that may be admitted in court to be evaluated by a trier of fact. In common-law jurisdictions, the trier of fact is usually a jury, though it may be a judge in some circumstances. In actions under the civil law (with the exception of the U.S. jury in criminal cases), the trier of fact is always a judge, or a panel of judges.
   *See also:* fact, legal fact; evidence (evidentiary); notice, judicial notice (judicially noticed fact).

   **fact pleading**   *See:* pleading, pleading theories, code pleading (fact pleading).

   **dispositive fact**   A fact that controls the outcome in a dispute under the law. A dispositive fact is one that directs, controls, or disposes of the answer in a question raised by law in a given dispute. If a dispositive fact is found in a given dispute, then the dispute must have a particular outcome under the law.

**finding of fact (findings of fact or conclusion of fact or factual conclusion)**   A ruling of facts derived from evidence. A finding of fact is a judicial ruling in the form of a statement of conclusions derived from evidence. More generally, findings of fact is a statement of the facts that are explained by the evidence, along with conclusions that are not evidence in themselves but that are inferred or deduced from the evidence that is. In argument, conclusions are a summary with which a party seeks to persuade a finder of fact to adopt one theory of the case as proven. As a statement by a judge or magistrate, it is a summary of the facts as found by a court following a review of the evidence.

*See also:* finding; ruling, finding of fact (fact finding or fact finder or finder of fact).

**historical fact**   A fact established as having occurred in the past. An historical fact is a fact established from evidence of past events and is not a fact found from legal analysis or legal interpretation. An historical fact found by a state court is presumed to be correct by a federal court on collateral review, as in a habeas proceeding, which distinguishes an historical fact from other facts, especially a mixed question of fact and of law.

In most contemporary senses, "historical fact" is a redundancy, as it amounts to an emphasis of a fact that is found only from the evidence, the fact being a statement of what occurred at some time past that was relevant to the legal issues later before the court. Other than the current status of persons or property, pure findings of fact, that is, every finding that is not a mixed issue of law and fact that is found by a court, is a finding of an historical fact. There is little or no difference between a pure fact and an historical fact or, for that matter, the synonyms employed for historical fact, such as basic fact or primary fact.

The nineteenth-century sense of historical fact was a fact of general or public notoriety that was likely to be beyond argument. Historical facts were particularly susceptible to judicial notice or proof by reputation, which could be established by ancient records.

An additional sense of historical fact has become apparent in recent years, in which judges attempt to divide questions of fact appropriate for jury determination from questions of fact appropriate for judicial determination. In this dichotomy, an historical fact is a fact the jury may find, though other facts are for the judge. There is reason to believe that this division is unjustified, and that it is a ruse by which questions that are otherwise dedicated to the jury are wrongly denied a jury determination, particularly when a constitutional right to a jury trial is at issue.

*See also:* notice, judicial notice (judicially noticed fact).

**inferential fact (inference of fact)**   Factual conclusions indirectly derived from the evidence. An inferential fact is a fact that is established indirectly and is found by the finder of fact by inference from the evidence that supports some other finding of fact. Thus, for example, if there is evidence that A hit B and also evidence that B had, moments earlier, uttered a convincing threat to A, an inference may be established that A hit B because of the threat, even if there is no testimony or other direct evidence of causation. A finding of an inferential fact is a finding of fact.

**juridical fact**   Conditions or events that produce legal effects. A juridical fact is a fact that, by its being true, has an effect in law. The facts in the record of a case that has been decided are juridical facts related to the scope of its decision. The fact of a person's possession of land, a deed having been recorded, or a person walking a trail are all juridical facts. An opinion handed down in a case is a juridical fact, as is a statute being passed, signed, and engrossed.

**legal fact**   A fact that leads to a particular conclusion of law. A legal fact is a fact that must be ascertained in order to determine a related question of law. In some instances, a pleading standard or rule of law employ the term in a more exacting sense nearer to judicial fact, as a fact that must be found to be established by the court, which is so central to a legal dispute that a determination of the fact necessarily determines the legal issue.

*See also:* fact; fiction, legal fiction (fiction of law).

**material fact**   A fact that might alter the outcome of a dispute. A material fact is a fact that is important in some way to a given situation that is at issue. At law, the use of materiality to distinguish one fact that matters from facts that don't is common. Thus a material fact is a fact that has a reasonable potential to affect the the outcome of a legal dispute, to alter a person's decision in deciding to do or not to do something, or to alter in some discernable way a person's understanding or belief regarding another fact in issue.

*See also:* evidence, material evidence.

**genuine issue of material fact**   An argument with competing evidence concerning a fact essential to a claim or defense. A genuine issue of material fact is a bona fide argument between conflicting interpretations of the evidence related to a contested fact that could be found for either party based on the evidence available. The conflict must arise from evidence in the record, and it must relate to a fact that is material to one or more theories of the case. In other words, a genuine issue of material fact would suggest that from the available record, the court could reasonably make different findings related to a fact, which could alter the validity of a party's claim or defense, depending on which finding is made. Any doubts on the potential findings are to be resolved in favor of the party who has not sought judgment. The phrase is a test of pleadings, particularly as to whether, in light of the evidence then in the record read most favorably to the non-moving party, summary judgment is appropriate because there are no contested facts that would require a trial to determine the facts; the action can be resolved by a ruling on each contested claim of the meaning of the law or the application to the uncontested material facts.

**probative fact**   A fact that serves to prove an element of a claim or defense. A probative fact is a fact that tends to prove an essential element of the cause of action. Probative is derived from the old French for "prove." Probative facts were once distinguished from "ultimate" facts, facts that were actual elements of the claim, such as those that would prove there was a breach of duty or suggested that the contract was formed. By comparison, probative facts were the component facts that were needed to prove an ultimate fact, such as what the defendant was charged with doing or whether the plaintiff actually signed the contract. This distinction is now rare, and probative facts are now considered all of the facts essential to prove an argument according to a standard of law or principle of equity.

**ultimate fact**   A fact established through inference or in light of the law. The term "ultimate fact" has two distinct meanings. The first is the same as a mixed fact, or a fact that supports both an issue of law and fact, such that the finder of fact determines both the facts and their legal significance from the evidence in an ultimate (or final) determination of the facts. The second meaning is similar but distinct because it refers to a fact determined by inference from other facts already established. In this sense, an ultimate fact is a fact as determined by the court from a combination of direct observations of evidence and inferences drawn from those observations.

Although judges separate facts into primary and ultimate facts, the distinction must be seen as one of degree, to which the finder of fact relies on observation or inference rather than an actual division of thought between one and the other. Indeed, even a primary fact derived from observation of direct testimony or tangible evidence requires some interpretation, such as to establish the confidence with which the testimony is accurate, complete, and truthful, or the tangible evidence is authentic, reliable, and salient.

**facto**   The fact. Facto is Latin for fact, whether as an act or event or as an assertion that something is the case, such as a chattel exists, or it is in a person's possession. Many facts are established from evidence, either as a specific point in fact or as the concept of fact, meaning the state of events and conditions that have been historically obtained in the world. De facto, for instance, has many nuanced meanings, most of which are as socially constructed as they are physically essential: some things are matters of fact as much because they are seen as fact as because the are inescapably that way, and facto may embrace any point on that continuum. Still, in law, matters of fact are often so designated to contrast them with matters of law.

*See also:* ipso, ipso facto; de, de facto; ex, ex post facto (ex post facto law).

**factor**

**factor as agent or auditor**   An agent. The factor was a commercial agent in English and American law in the nineteenth century, but the term in this sense is no longer as widely used in the United States, though it is still common in statutes. In Scots law the factor is either a bailiff or a form of trustee. In some U.S. jurisdictions, a factor was one who was subject to garnishment.

**factor as component of reason**   A single cause or reason, an element in a larger scheme. A factor in legal writing is usually a single reason among several to carry out a particular action or a single consideration in a larger evaluation. The term apparently entered legal analysis from mathematics, a subject in which a factor usually means an element of a ratio or statistic.

**factum (fraud in the factum)**   The deed or the thing done. Factum usually represents a thing done or made. Factum, like facto, is a form of "facio" and may be used in the same way to represent a fact, as in factum probendum or facto juridicum, which mean a fact to be proven or a fact found by the judge. Though less common in usage now, fraud in the factum describes a forgery or a counterfeit writing, with factum referring to making of the instrument.

*See also:* forgery.

**failure (fail)**   The non-performance of any task, or the non-satisfaction of a condition or requirement. A failure is the final non-performance — or non-occurrence — of something that was required, planned, or commenced. Time is essential for failure, such that something that is not finished or is yet to be commenced does not make the thing a failure. Rather, failure occurs at a time when the occurrence or performance is past due and still not done. In commercial law, a failure is a stoppage of payment or the fact of non-payment when an instrument is presented. In contracts, a failure of condition means that a condition is not fulfilled at a time specified or at a time when it must reasonably have been performed for the performer to not be in breach. In property, failure of issue occurs when the last heir dies without a child.

*See also:* appearance, non-appearance, failure to appear (bail-jumping or bail jumping or jump bail); condition, failure of condition; legacy, failed legacy; market, market failure; issue, issue as child, failure of issue; inference | failure to introduce.

**failed bank**   *See:* bank, failed bank (bank failure or bank seizure or bank takeover).

**failed legacy**   *See:* legacy, failed legacy.

**failure of condition**   *See:* condition, failure of condition.

**failure of issue**   *See:* issue, issue as child, failure of issue, indefinite failure of issue; issue, issue as child, failure of issue, definite failure of issue; issue, issue as child, failure of issue; fee, estate in fee, fee tail, failure of issue.

**failure of service**   See: dismissal, grounds for dismissal, failure of service.

**failure to appear**   See: appearance, non-appearance, failure to appear (bail-jumping or bail jumping or jump bail).

**failure to comply with order or rules**   See: dismissal, grounds for dismissal, failure to comply with order or rules.

**failure to file return**   See: tax, tax crime, failure to file return.

**failure to state a claim upon which relief can be granted**   See: dismissal, grounds for dismissal, failure to state a claim upon which relief can be granted, Twombly test (Twombly standard); dismissal, grounds for dismissal, failure to state a claim upon which relief can be granted (Rule 12(b)(6) motion or 12(b)(6)).

**failure to warn**   See: liability, product liability, product defect, failure to warn (marketing defect).

## fairness (fair)

**fair hearing**   See: hearing, fair hearing.

**Fair Housing Act**   See: housing, Fair Housing Act (F.H.A. FHA); civil rights, Civil Rights Act, Civil Rights Act of 1968 (Fair Housing Act).

**Fair Labor Standards Act**   See: labor, Fair Labor Standards Act (F.L.S.A. or FLSA or minimum wage or wage and hours law).

**fair market value**   See: value, market value, fair market value (FMV).

**fair notice doctrine**   See: notice, fair notice doctrine.

**fair pay**   See: pay, equal pay (fair pay).

**fair play and substantial justice**   See: jurisdiction, in personam jurisdiction, minimum contacts, fair play and substantial justice.

**fair share of union dues**   See: union, labor union, union dues, fair share of union dues.

**fair trial**   See: trial, fair trial (rights of criminal defendants).

**fair use**   See: copyright, fair use.

**fair warning**   See: warning, fair warning.

**fairness doctrine**   See: broadcasting, fairness doctrine.

**faith**   Honesty, care, and loyalty. Faith, in general, signifies confidence in something not fully known, from belief in religion to more mundane bases of hope or loyalty, as for sports teams. In law, faith holds a particular meaning within that broader concept and is more apparent in the word faithfulness, as the idea that a person exhibits faith toward others with honesty, full disclosure, great care, and loyalty. Thus, a witness faithfully reporting events demonstrates honesty and candor and a police officer claiming to act with a good faith belief asserts that the officer really did believe what is said, without reservation and without contrary beliefs of motives. Faith requires confidence in an action because of its source, the form of authority in acts of faith arising from the actor rather than the reasons for the act, which is its sense in "full faith and credit" as well as in the sense of merit others may have in a person acting in good faith. Faith is derived from the Latin fides, by way of the French feal, from which several synonyms for faith, such as fealty, fiduciary, and bona fide can be traced.
*See also:* bona, bona fide (bona fides); fiduciary.

**bad faith (mala fides)**   Lacking in honesty or care for the other. Bad faith is a failure of good faith. An act in bad faith is an act by one person or entity that affects another, failing to accord a reasonable duty of care toward the other, unjustifiably harming the other's interests by an act of a quality or form that would not occur if the person or entity had acted with good faith. An act in bad faith need not be fraudulent or utterly dishonest. Rather, it is sufficient that an act that harms the other be careless, negligent, insufficiently researched, or made without the bona fide legal and equitable interests of the other taken sufficiently into account. Bad faith is a translation from mala fides, which is sometimes used to express the same idea.
*See also:* bargain, surface bargaining (bad faith bargaining); insurance, insurance claim, denial of claim, bad faith denial (denial in bad faith or wrongful refusal or tortious denial of benefits).

**good faith (bona fide)**   The honest and fair pursuit of one's stated and reasonable purposes. Good faith is sincerity, a measure to assess one's own conduct and the conduct of others. Good faith is subjective, measuring what one knows, rather than entirely determining what one should reasonably believe under the circumstances. Yet, the subjective aspect of good faith has an objective limit in that contradictions between knowledge and the purpose for which one acquires or employs knowledge may bar good faith. That is, willful ignorance, or deliberate naivete, or intentionally ambiguous motives cannot be held or asserted in good faith. Good faith, the descendant from the Roman concepts of bona fides and fides publica, is one of the oldest ideas in the law.
*See also:* discovery, certificate of good faith; fiduciary, fiduciary duty, duty of good faith; holder, bona fide holder for value (holder in good faith).

**Faithful Execution Clause**   See: constitution, U.S. Constitution, clauses, Faithful Execution Clause (Faithfully Executed Clause).

**fallacy**   An error in reasoning. Fallacy is an error in the reasoning of an argument, as well as the collective noun for all such errors. Fallacy takes many forms, but the essential ones are logical, in that certain relationships among ideas may look to be complete and prove a point, but they do not, or social, in that certain claims about human behavior in the world may seem comprehensive and accurate but are not.

*See also:* fallacy, ad hominem (argumentum ad hominem).

**ad hominem (argumentum ad hominem)**   An argument directed not against a statement but against the person who made it. An ad hominem argument is a rhetorical fallacy that argues the falsity of a statement solely because of the person making it. Ad hominem arguement is character assassination in lieu of reason. The use of ad hominem argument is a symptom of an unprofessional lawyer. A lawyer violates professional courtesy and ethics by asserting that a point or claim in issue must be wrong because of the lawyer who made it. When such an argument is directed against a judge, it is contempt of court. The Latin tag means "against the person."

*See also:* fallacy; fallacy, ad verecundiam.

**ad ignorantiam**   An appeal to ignorance as proof of a fact. The fallacy ad ignorantiam is the improper assertion that a claim is false because it has not been proved. The fallacy also depicts an assertion that a claim is true because its rejection has not been proved. Thus to argue that X is not the law because X has not been proved to be the law is an appeal to ignorance. Unlike many of the other logical fallacies, the ad ignorantiam argument has been fully embraced by the law, embodied in the principle that a person is innocent until proven guilty.

**ad misericordiam**   An improper appeal to pity in attempting to prove a fact. The ad misericordiam fallacy is the improper appeal to the listener's pity. The fallacy is not in seeking an emotional support from a listener for a given argument but in seeking to prove a fact by imploring a hearer to agree with a claim, without regard to the evidence for or against it.

**ad verecundiam**   An improper appeal to existing authority. A fallacy ad verecundiam is an improper appeal to the established authority of either a person or an institution. The basis of this appeal may be a human reluctance to challenge authority, convention, or power, though such reluctance cannot establish the truth of a statement, from one source or another, any more than a willingness to reject a statement based on its source can prove the lack of truth of that statement, as in an ad hominem argument.

*See also:* fallacy, ad hominem (argumentum ad hominem); ipse, ipse dixit.

**amphibole (deliberate ambiguity)**   An improper ambiguity. An amphibole is the deliberate use of an improper ambiguity in a statement that, when read, may lead to different or even opposing interpretations of the proper meaning of the statement. The use of amphibole arises when the writer or speaker interjects vagueness to lure a listener's or reader's agreement to one of several meanings, knowing that no one meaning is assured for later listeners or readers. Thus a movant might seek agreement to a vague motion from several people, intending each to interpret it in a manner each would find favorable though one might in fact strongly oppose what another who supports the motion believes the motion to do.

*See also:* ambiguity (ambiguous or ambiguousness).

**dicto simpliciter**   The improper application of a general rule. The fallacy of accident, or a dicto simpliciter ad dictum secundum quid, is an improper application of a general rule to a specific situation without acknowledging the qualifications or exceptions to the general rule that apply to the situation.

*See also:* simpliciter.

**fallacy of composition**   The improper attribution of individual traits to the group to which the individual belongs. The fallacy of composition is a linguistic fallacy that improperly attributes to the group a characteristic of an individual in the group.

**fallacy of division**   The improper attribution of group traits to an individual in the group. The fallacy of division is a linguistic fallacy improperly attributing a trait of a group to an individual within that group. This is the traditional use of this fallacy in rhetoric. In law, the label is also used to describe attributes of parts of some action or project, and thus avoiding describing the nature of the whole action or project.

*See also:* pleading, special pleading.

**false dichotomy (false binarism)**   The improper assumption that there are two (or only two) choices. A false dichotomy is a rhetorical fallacy that assumes that the choice at hand must be between two options and only two options, such as: good or bad, illegal or legal, constitutional or unconstitutional. The difficulty with this thinking is that the answers to most questions are actually a matter of degree. Thus, the common law employs a reasonableness standard, which is a question of whether something is more or less reasonable. The civilian system, on the other hand, is more likely to employ the concept of right or wrong, and to do so in a binary sense, so that either a duty exists or it does not or an act is according to right or not. A dichotomy itself is not a fallacy, and it is often referred to by its term after Aristotle: the law of excluded middle.

**ignoratio elenchi (skirting the issue or straw argument)**   Arguing all but the central or difficult elements of one's argument. The fallacy ignoratio elenchi is to ignore the issue in dispute or to omit the parts of an argument that would be difficult to refute or explain. This often occurs when a lawyer skips the most recently made argument and refutes a different argument, an act that is often called arguing against a strawman or making a straw argument. The lawyer selects an argument that is more easily won and claims to have defeated it, leaving the much stronger argument against the lawyer's position unanswered. This is frustrating for the opponent and to the court, and it is unprofessional conduct from the lawyer. Note: the strawman in the sense of argument is very different from the straw or strawman of property, which is still fictitious but serves the function of actually holding the property, if briefly, in a fictitious two-party transaction.

*See also:* straw (strawman or straw man or straw person).

**naturalistic fallacy**   The improper appeal to the properties of things that are good. The naturalistic fallacy is an improper argument for the moral goodness of a thing because the thing possesses properties of other things that are good.

**non sequitur**   The conclusion does not follow the premise. From the Latin "it does not follow," a non sequitur is a fallacy of logic where the proposed conclusion does not follow the given premise. In other words, the reasons for an argument are insufficient to support the conclusion that is offered from them. For instance, to say that Sam likes dogs, so he will like my dog is a non sequitur, because the mere fact that Sam likes dogs cannot establish that Sam will like a given dog. Still, if it were true that Sam likes all dogs, then it would be true that Sam likes my dog. Note: in more general conversation, a non sequitur is merely a new topic interjected without a clear relationship to the preceding topics. These two ideas are related but not to be confused with one another.

*See also:* non, non sequitur.

**Parmenides' fallacy**   The improper comparison of one time to another. Parmenides' fallacy is the comparison of the past to the present or the present to the future to determine whether the change in a historical, social, economic, or political condition has made the later age preferable, as in, "Are we better off now than before the Federal Reserve?" The error is to compare the times before and after the change of condition, rather than to compare the effects at the same time with the change of condition, comparing the life of the times with a counterfactual life of the times that would otherwise have been. Otherwise, the effect of other changes of conditions is too great to ascertain the influence of the condition in question. Thus, it is better to ask, "Would we be better off without the Federal Reserve?" which is a different question. This fallacy is sometimes called Parmenides' Fallacy, for the pre–Socratic philosopher who claimed there is no change, though several distinct fallacies are attributed to him.

**petitio principii (begging the question or to beg the question)**   The improper assumption of the truth of a conclusion. The petitio principii fallacy assumes the truth of the conclusion advanced by the premise. The conclusion, in essence is offered as a justification for the premise, rather than the other way around. This is also known as begging the question or accepting the truth of the answer as proof of the question. Circular reasoning is the application of the petitio principii

fallacy to multiple connected conclusions, in which the conclusion must be true for proof of the conclusion.

**post hoc ergo propter hoc**   The improper attribution of causation based on order of occurrence. The post hoc ergo propter hoc fallacy is the improper attribution of causation for an event to a preceding event, based solely on the fact that the one preceded the other. Rather, causation requires proof that the prior event in some manner led to the later event, not just that it happened first.

**red herring**   The improper introduction of an irrelevant topic. A red herring is the improper introduction of a different topic of debate to distract or preempt the original discussion. In legal education, a red herring is a fact or point introduced into a hypothetical question for no reason essential to an analysis of the question but to test a student's ability to focus on only the relevant facts.

**reductio ad absurdam**   The confusion of an absurd conclusion with a false premise. Reductio ad absurdam is a logical fallacy in which, first, a premise is claimed to lead to a conclusion that appears absurd or false, and second, as the conclusion is absurd, the premise is claimed to be absurd or false. The fallacy is in the assumption that the conclusion being absurd proves the absurdity of the premise. The argument often ends with the claim that, the premise being proved false, its opposite must be true. Of course, this argument is illogical because, like the non sequitur, the absurdity of one conclusion asserted from a premise does not prove it is the only or best conclusion drawn from the premise. Nor could proving a conclusion false prove that a premise is false. Despite its common use as a fallacy, reductio ad absurdam is used occasionally to prove a contradictory premise and is most often used this way in mathamatical proofs and tightly controlled logical syllogisms.

**slippery slope (thin edge of the wedge or camel's nose argument)**   An argument that unlimited consequences will follow a decision. The slippery slope is the most common description of an argument that a given decision by a judge or other official risks unlimited and disastrous consequences, particularly if the decision is in any way novel or varies from established precedent. The metaphor is that once one starts falling down a slippery slope, one can hardly stop until reaching the bottom. Similarly, once one allows the nose of the camel under (or into) the tent, the rest of the camel will follow, and once one allows the thin edge of the wedge, the whole wedge will enter. These are all fallacies, in that whatever principle is threatened by an absurd consequence is reason enough to limit the precedential effect of the first decision so that it does not support such a consequence.

*See also:* parade of horribles.

**straw argument (man of straw argument)**   A rebuttal to an argument that was not made. A straw argument is an argument made against a position that no opponent has taken. The traditional term was man-of-straw argument, implying that the person who made the rebuttal would rather oppose a strawman than a live human opponent.

A straw argument may be made in order to create the appearance of justification by creating a false appearance of a rebuttal of the falsification of the argument. More often, the straw argument is used to recharacterize, or mischaracterize, the argument an opponent is making, so that a weaker argument than the opponent's is vigrously opposed, creating the impression that the opponent really mounted the weaker argument (and not the stronger one the opponent did make) and that one has actually rebutted one's opponent when one has not.

*See also:* fallacy, ignoratio elenchi (skirting the issue or straw argument); straw (strawman or straw man or straw person).

**tautology (circular argument or circulus in demonstrando or circularity)**   An argument that attempts to prove itself. A tautology is an argument with a conclusion that restates its premise, such as, "This is criminal because it is wrong, and it is wrong because it is criminal." Any argument that assumes its conclusion contains some form of this mistake. This does not mean that all tautologies are false, as some are merely descriptions or definitions, but the statement of a definition does not prove, by itself, the truth of the definition. A circular argument differs from a catch-22, or other situations in which the a person's choice is among only bad options or options that lead to the same end. These may seem circular but are not fallacies.

*See also:* choice, Hobson's choice; argument, Morton's fork.

## false

**false advertising**   *See:* deceit, false advertising, puffery (puff or puffing); deceit, false advertising.

**false answer or sham**   *See:* answer, sham answer (false answer or sham).

**false arrest**   *See:* arrest, false arrest.

**false binarism**   *See:* fallacy, false dichotomy (false binarism).

**False Claims Act**   *See:* fraud, False Claims Act (Lincoln's law).

**false dichotomy**   *See:* fallacy, false dichotomy (false binarism).

**false imprisonment**   *See:* incarceration, imprisonment, false imprisonment.

**false light**   *See:* privacy, invasion of privacy, false light; libel, false light.

**false plea**   *See:* plea, criminal plea, false plea (take the fall).

**false pretense or larceny by false pretense or larceny by false promise or larceny by fraud or larceny by fraudulent scheme**   *See:* larceny, larceny by trick (false pretense or larceny by false pretense or larceny by false promise or larceny by fraud or larceny by fraudulent scheme).

**false representation**   *See:* representation, false representation.

**false statement**   *See:* statement, false statement.

**false syllogism**   *See:* argument, syllogism (false syllogism).

**falsehood**   A statement made with knowledge that it is contrary to the truth. A falsehood is a wilful act or declaration that is made with the knowledge that the act or declaration is contrary to the truth. A falsehood can be committed by actions intended to convey an idea that the actor knows to be untrue, though it may be more commonly performed by statements that declare or imply statements about the world that are not true. Visual images that depict ideas that are untrue are also falsehoods. A falsehood is not, in itself, a crime or violation of a duty, and falsehoods are essential to many forms of art, such as the writing of fiction.

A falsehood does becomes unlawful in any context in which the falsehood violates a general or special duty. This happens when the false speaker or actor has promised to tell the truth, as when a witness is under oath; when others may rely on the falsehood as if it is true, as in the negotiation of a contract; or when a person has a duty to act truthfully that does not arise from a particular promise, as by a fiduciary in actions affecting a beneficiary.

*See also:* hearsay.

**falsi crimen**   *See:* crimen, crimen falsi (falsi crimen).

**family (household)**   A small unit of people, usually related to one another by blood, adoption, or marriage. The family is a group of people who are related by birth, adoption, legal guardianship, or marriage and who are interconnected in their responsibilities and their financial, social, and emotional commitments in such a manner that they are customarily treated as a family, whether its members live together in a common dwelling or apart. For some purposes in law, particularly related to zoning and housing law as it is defined in some jurisdictions, a family may include one or more members who are not related by blood, adoption, or marriage, but who treat others in the unit and are treated in the unit in the same manner as those who are so related to one another.

The family is an important unit for purposes of regulation because parents have responsibilities to provide for their children with shelter, food, care, education, and other necessities of daily life. In each of these regulatory arenas, the term "family" is likely to be defined by statute or regulation, yet there is a constitutional liberty interest embodied in each person to decide to create a family, which may only be limited with appropriate levels of care under the constitution.

The family is an important measure of housing density, and for the purpose of federal fair housing law, a family includes a single individual. The family differs from a household, which need not have the same financial, emotional, and social interconnection or parental responsibilities, although a family may also be a household.

**Family and Medical Leave Act** *See:* employment, employee benefit, Family and Medical Leave Act (F.M.L.A. or FMLA).

**family court** *See:* court, court of limited jurisdiction, family court, surrogate's court; court, court of limited jurisdiction, family court.

**family history** *See:* hearsay, hearsay exception, exception only when declarant is unavailable, family history (personal history).

**family partnership** *See:* partnership, family partnership.

**family planning**

**assisted reproduction** Any medical assistance to make a successful pregnancy more likely. Assisted reproduction encompasses a range of medical treatments used to increase the likelihood of human pregnancy. Assisted reproduction includes treatment of both partners, including treatments ranging from the management of diet, environment, and hormones to artificial insemination and in–vitro fertilization, to surrogate pregnancy.
*See also:* in, in vitro; zygote.

**gestational surrogacy (surrogate mother)** The reproduction by one woman of a child for another. Gestational surrogacy is the process by which one woman conceives, carries, and births the child of another woman or for another person to whom she will give the child after birth for care, apart from herself.
*See also:* parent, surrogate parent.

**birth control** Any means of preventing pregnancy. Birth control encompasses a host of strategies by which people engaged in close relationships attempt to reduce the likelihood of pregnancy, including abstinence, sterilization, the use of medicines after the fact, the prior use of oral or implanted pharmaceutical contraceptives, the use of physical contraception through barriers in or on the genitalia, and the use of various behaviors designed to prevent insemination during a period of a woman's fertility.

The decision to use birth control was recognized as an aspect of privacy in Griswold v. Connecticut, 381 U.S. 479 (1965).
*See also:* privacy; contraception.

**father** A male parent. A father is a male who is the direct biological ancestor of a child, or, alternatively, a male who has been adjudicated as bearing an equivalent relationship to a child, usually a minor. This adjudication can take the form of a decree of adoption or legal recognition in a paternity action. The law presumes that the husband of a woman at any point during the period between the likely conception and birth of a child to the woman is the child's father. A father, more generally, is a man who has fathered at least one child, or who has served in the role of father to a minor child.
*See also:* descent, descendant, lineal descendant (direct descendant or lineals); parent.

**father in law (father-in-law)** The father of one's spouse. Father in law describes the relationship of between any person and the father of his spouse. As a matter of usage, there seems to be no difference made between a father in law who is a biological, adopted, or step father in this role — all are fathers in law, which is reasonable as there would be no difference to the relationship in intestacy. Fathers in law are not heirs at law and do not inherit from intestate estates, although they may, of course, be devisees or legatees under a will, which is why the term is one of affinity and not legal relationship.

**legal father** The father of record. A legal father is usually the man married to the biological mother of a child at the child's birth, unless this man's name does not appear on the birth certificate or if there is a court finding that this man is not the father of the child.

**natural father (biological father)** A man who conceived a child with its mother. A natural father, also known as a biological father, generally, is a man who conceived a child with the mother of the child, the paternity of whom has been established. In some jurisdictions, a man who is proved medically to be the natural father of a child but who has not been legally acknowledged or behaved in such a manner as to be the presumed father establishes standing in matters relative to the child, particularly child custody. Some state statutes allow proof of natural fatherhood by vaious means and according to multiple definitions, as a result of which more than one person might be potentially a natural father, although such statutes also establish a priority so that a child has only one natural father as a matter of law.

**presumed father (presumed paternity)** A man married to the mother at the time of her child's birth. A presumed father is defined by state law and refers, generally, to a man who receives an infant child into his home, who supports and treats a child as a parent would be expected to treat a child, or who openly holds out the child as his natural child. Specifically, a man married to the mother of a child within a defined period of time prior to or after the birth of a child is a presumed father. If a presumed father dies without renouncing paternity, in most jurisdictions, the child will be treated as a child and heir. A presumed father can rebut the presumption, in part by renunciation but more certainly by submitting to comparative medical tests for paternity.

*See also:* presumption.

**putative father**   A person believed to be the father of a child. A putative father is person reputed to be the biological father of a given child, but not yet to have been adjudged the father by a court with proper jurisdiction or found to have been married to the child's mother at the time of conception or birth.

**head of household (head of the household)**   The person responsible for supporting others in a household. The head of household is a designation of the adult who is most responsible for the economic support and the organization of a household or family. At common law, this role was presumed in a family to be the role of the husband and father. Contemporary usage, however, relies on functional definitions, in which a head of household is the person on whom others in the household or family depend for financial support and moral authority, and who has accepted an obligation to provide for them.

The designation of head of household as a matter of personal federal income tax is used to distinguish the filing status from married and other single filers. In this context, a head of household is unmarried but pays for more than half of the expenses of maintaining a home, and either has an adult parent who is a dependent or has another dependent who lives in the home more than half the year. This filing status entitles filers to a lower tax rate and higher standard deduction than if they filed as single taxpayers.

**mother**   A female parent. A mother is a female who is the direct biological ancestor of a child or who has been decreed by court order to stand in such a relationship to a child, usually a minor. A mother, more generally, is a woman who has given birth to at least one child or who has served in the role of mother to a minor child.

*See also:* parent; descent, descendant, lineal descendant (direct descendant or lineals).

**mother in law (mother-in-law)**   The mother of one's spouse. Mother in law describes the relationship between any person and the mother of that person's spouse. As a matter of usage, there seems to be no difference made between a mother in law who is a biological, adopted, or a stepmother, as all of these are mothers in law, which is reasonable as there would be no difference to the relationship in intestacy. Mothers in law are not heirs at law and do not inherit from intestate estates, although they may, of course, be devisees or legatees under a will, which is why the term is one of affinity and not legal relationship.

**Fannie Mae**   *See:* bank, Federal National Mortgage Association (Fannie Mae).

**faqih (fuqaha)**   A jurist whose pronouncement is a source of law. A Faqih is, literally, the possessor of Fiqh. Commonly, it refers to an Islamic religious scholar who is a trained jurist or a master of the Fiqh. Such scholars issue fatawa, or edicts. The fuqaha are both a specific group of such scholars or a region as a whole.

**fard**   Obligations of the person and obligations of the community, in Islamic law. Fard, one of the hukm shari'a (or shari'a injunction), means obligatory, the commission of which is rewardable, the omission of which is a sin. Fard takes two forms, fard al-'ayn, or individual obligations such as prayers, and fard kifayyah, or communal obligations, such as jihad. Fard is thought to be synonymous with wajib, in all but the Hanafi school.

*See also:* wajib.

**farm (farmer or farming)**   Land used for agriculture. A farm is a single holding of land, including all or parts of a tract or tracts, a portion of which is used for agricultural cultivation. The farm once customarily included a house, outbuildings, yard, gardens, orchards, and fields, all of which were implied by the term "farm" in the deed, but whether the term holds such an implication (including a house, for instance) depends on the intent of the grantor. The term farm is derived from the medieval annual rents or tax, which were called the farm, paid by an agricultural tenant to the lord of the manor, though farms also included municipal taxes.

**farm animal**   *See:* animal, farm animal.

**concentrated animal feed operation (C.A.F.O. or CAFO)**   A high-density animal production facility. A concentrated animal feed operation is an integral part of the industrialized agricultural system, in which hundreds or thousands of livestock are raised and kept in very close quarters on a facility or lot on which crops are not grown, for a period of at least forty five days in a given year. These operations generate high-volume waste that is prone to runoff and overflow, which may increase the nutrification of waterways. CAFOs often employ distinct production techniques and levels of medication higher than other animal production operations. They are regulated both for their waste management and their food production.

**fascism**   *See:* government, forms of government, fascism.

**fasiq**   A sinful or morally corrupt Muslim. A fasiq is a person who is sinful and corrupted, particularly a Muslim who has transgressed in a very serious and obstinate way.

**fatawa**   *See:* fatwa (fatawa).

**father**   *See:* family, father.

**father in law**   *See:* family, father, father in law (father-in-law).

**fatwa (fatawa)** A judgment made according to Islamic law. A fatwa is a decree or judgment passed by a mufti that determines an obligation according to shari'a.

*See also:* mufti.

**fault** Legal responsibility for harm or damages. Fault is both a determination in law of who is legally responsible for the consequences of a legal wrong and a statement about the factual world that a particular harm, damage, breach of contract, or failure of duty was caused in some degree by a given person or entity. Every such harm, damages, etc., is subject to fault analysis in determining the percentage of causation that can be attributed to each actor or condition that total 100% of the fault for the event.

Liability depends on the legal responsibility for fault, not on fault as a matter of historical fact. Still, fault as a matter of historical fact has some influence, though not necessarily a controlling influence, on the determination of legal fault. Thus, in tort claims, strict liability assesses fault to the person or entity that is strictly liable, as someone injured through a failure of a strict duty may hold the strictly liable party wholly at fault as a matter of law, regardless of any distribution of fault as a matter of fact. On the other hand, the doctrine of contributory negligence once placed all legal fault on the person injured if the person injured was even slightly at fault as a matter of fact. Most United States jurisdictions, however, now allow a fault to be compared and allocated, so that legal fault more strongly correlates to a determination of fault in fact.

*See also:* liability, comparative liability (comparative fault or comparative responsibility); liability (liable); liability, strict liability; culpa.

**fax** *See:* facsimile (fax).

**fear** An apprehension of harm or loss in the future. Fear is a sense of dread, the belief or sense of a danger approaching physically or in time. Fear is an element of many torts and crimes, such as assault, and is a critical element in many definitions of terrorism, which often incorporate the intent to create a fear of harm, particularly through a fear of future acts of terrorism.

**feasance** The performance of any action. Feasance means performance, and although feasance is rarely found on its own, it is the essence of several cognates for corruption (malfeasance), error (misfeasance), or failure (nonfeasance) in the performance of an action. Malfeasance, wrongful performance, is an act or conduct that is not allowed under the law. Misfeasance is an act that is allowed under the law but that is not performed according to the allowed or required criteria and, as a result of the nonconformity, some harm occurs. Nonfeasance is the failure to do what one is required to do. All three terms imply a failure of duty that gives rise to some form of liability, particularly when performed by a person in public office, corporate office, or another fiduciary position. The element of intent in malfeasance makes it the most serious breach of duty, and it is often a crime as well as a basis for impeachment or removal from office.

**malfeasance (mal feasance or mal-feasance)** Wrongful or unjust conduct. Malfeasance, in general, is a term for an act of wrongdoing or unjust action but is often reserved to depict a serious breach of obligation, an unjust performance of an office or a putative duty that is not justified (or even condoned) by the law governing that office or performance, such as an abuse of office or a position of trust. An act of malfeasance must be knowing and deliberate, otherwise, it would be misfeasance. Malfeasance is often employed with a deliberately broad degree of discretion in its application that need not make the term vague, but that recognizes that forms of wrongdoing are likely to be more numerous than description would encompass.

*See also:* feasance.

**misfeasance (mis-feasance)** Error in the performance of a duty. Misfeasance, or improper performance, is an act or conduct that is generally allowed (or even required) under the law, but which, in the case at hand, was not performed according to the allowed or required criteria, and as a result of the error causes harm. Misfeasance, in short, is the bungling of an obligation to the injury of another person.

*See also:* feasance.

**nonfeasance (non-feasance or non feasance)** The failure to do what one is required to do. Nonfeasance is a failure of duty, particularly by one who holds a public office or position of trust, such as a police officer or a fiduciary, to act or to perform a task that a reasonable person with such a duty would have performed.

*See also:* feasance.

**feasibility** *See:* joinder, joinder of parties, compulsory joinder, feasibility.

**federal** Relating to the U.S. government or any other government of states. Federal refers to a federation, and in the context of the United States, it refers to the government of the United States as well as to its particular agencies. The federal district refers to the District of Columbia, and federal courts are the courts of the United States. Federal refers also to the relationship of the central government to the states, as in the federal balance of authority. Federal may also refer to any national system comprising a central government and state governments, and many nations operate on a federal basis, notably the Federal Republic of Germany.

**Federal Arbitration Act or F.A.A. or FAA** *See:* arbitration, Arbitration Act (Federal Arbitration Act or F.A.A. or FAA).

**Federal Bar Association** *See:* bar, bar organization, Federal Bar Association (F.B.A. or FBA).

**Federal Bureau of Investigation** *See:* police, police organizations, Federal Bureau of Investigation (F.B.I. or FBI).

**federal circuit court** *See:* court, circuit court, federal circuit court.

**federal common law**   *See:* law, common law, federal common law.

**federal court**   *See:* court, U.S. court, federal court.

**federal crime**   *See:* crime, federal crime.

**Federal Deposit Insurance Corporation**   *See:* bank, Federal Deposit Insurance Corporation, deposit insurance; bank, Federal Deposit Insurance Corporation (F.D.I.C. or FDIC).

**federal funds rate**   *See:* bank, federal funds rate.

**Federal Home Loan Bank**   *See:* bank, Federal Home Loan Bank (FHLB).

**Federal Home Loan Mortgage Corporation**   *See:* bank, Federal Home Loan Mortgage Corporation (freddie mac).

**Federal Insurance Contibutions Act**   *See:* social security, Federal Insurance Contibutions Act (FICA).

**Federal Insurance Contributions Act**   *See:* tax, payroll tax, Federal Insurance Contibutions Act (F.I.C.A. tax or FICA tax).

**federal jurisdiction**   *See:* jurisdiction, federal jurisdiction.

**federal kidnapping**   *See:* kidnapping, federal kidnapping (federal kidnapping charge).

**federal land**   *See:* land, federal land (federal lands or U.S. government property).

**federal lands or U.S. government property**   *See:* land, federal land (federal lands or U.S. government property).

**federal law**   *See:* law, federal law.

**Federal Maritime Commission**   *See:* maritime, Federal Maritime Commission.

**Federal Mediation and Conciliation Service**   *See:* mediator, Federal Mediation and Conciliation Service (F.M.C.S. or FMCS).

**Federal National Mortgage Association**   *See:* mortgage, Federal National Mortgage Association (Fannie Mae or F.N.M.A. or FNMA); bank, Federal National Mortgage Association (Fannie Mae).

**federal officer**   *See:* officer, federal officer, principal officer; officer, federal officer, inferior officer; officer, federal officer, accountable officer.

**federal preemption of state law**   *See:* preemption, constitutional preemption, federal preemption of state law (congressional preemption or express preemption or implied preemption).

**federal question jurisdiction**   *See:* jurisdiction, federal-question jurisdiction (federal question jurisdiction).

**Federal Register**   *See:* regulation, Federal Register.

**Federal Reserve bank**   *See:* bank, Federal Reserve system (Federal Reserve bank).

**Federal Reserve system**   *See:* bank, Federal Reserve system (Federal Reserve bank).

**Federal Rules of Evidence**   *See:* evidence, Federal Rules of Evidence (F.R.E. or FRE).

**Federal Tort Claims Act**   *See:* tort, Federal Tort Claims Act (F.T.C.A. or FTCA).

**Federal Water Pollution Control Act**   *See:* pollution, water pollution, Federal Water Pollution Control Act (F.W.P.C.A. FWPCA).

**federal-question jurisdiction**   *See:* jurisdiction, federal-question jurisdiction (federal question jurisdiction).

**federal-state comity or interstate comity or international comity**   *See:* comity, judicial comity (federal-state comity or interstate comity or international comity).

**federalism**   A government divided between central and state authorities. Federalism is a form of government in which the power to make, execute, and adjudicate the law is divided between a central government and one or more state governments. The state governments have a degree of autonomy regarding local matters, and the central government has autonomy regarding collective affairs, with each having authority over matters of both local and collective significance.
   *See also:* government, forms of government, federalism; sovereignty, state sovereignty; constitution, U.S. Constitution, ideals, federalism.

**cooperative federalism**   The federal government's method of sharing responsibility with states for their separate governmental problems. Cooperative federalism is the process by which the federal government shares responsibility with the states for the states' own particular needs and problems by offering them a choice either of regulating certain activities according to federal standards or of having state law pre-empted by federal regulation.

**doctrine of "Our Federalism"**   A reference to the belief that the federal government should allow the states to run their own governments without its interference "Our Federalism" refers to Justice Black's analysis stating that the entire country functions better when the federal government acknowledges the states, as separate governments, and abstains from interfering in the states' running of their respective governments.
   *See also:* jurisdiction, appellate jurisdiction, Rooker-Feldman doctrine.

**federally recognized tribe**   *See:* tribe, recognized tribe (federally recognized tribe).

**federation**   *See:* confederation (federation).

**feudalism**   *See:* feud, fedualism.

**fee**  Property or money given in return for services. Fee is a broad term that includes both a perpetual interest in lands and money owed in return for services. These two ideas have a common origin in the feudal nature of land-holdings, in which lands were held in return for services rendered to the king or lord from whom they were held. Feudal England did not distinguish between the idea of a right to the use of land and the idea of a quid pro quo for service, as both were aspects of the fee in land. By the later middle ages, the idea of value for service stood on its own, although the concept that the use of lands depended upon some services persisted. In contemporary usage, the services required to hold a land by fee have become obsolete, but the idea of rendering value for services has grown more robust, so a fee is now ownership of lands without regard to services, or a fee is value charged or given in return for actual services. The term is derived from the feoh, old English for property, especially cattle and probably comes from fieu in old French for property granted for services, and fedum in medieval Latin, along with fehu–od, Frankish for payment, fihu in Gothic, and vieh in old German.

**fee patent**  *See:* patent, land patent, fee patent.

**estate in fee**  An ownership interest in land that may exist forever. The fee is the basic unit of ownership in land, the estate that may continue forever and is transferred from owner to owner. To designate an ownership interest as a fee, usually as a fee simple but sometimes a fee tail or otherwise, means that the fee is alienable and heritable and thus may be transferred during the life of the owner and inherited at death, or a fee owned by a corporation may be transferred to successors in interest. To label an estate as a fee does not mean that it cannot be destroyed, but that the ability of the land to be owned will not be destroyed, even if by its terms the right to own the fee terminates in one person and commences in another, as in a present estate followed by a future interest. There are many forms of fee, although every fee is a present possessory interest, but many are subject to limitation or divestment by the holders of future interests. The term "fee" is derived from feodum or feud.

*See also:* feud, feudalism (feudal law); feud (feod or fief or feodum or feudum).

**fee simple absolute (FSA or F.S.A.)**  Alienable and heritable ownership that is unlimited in the future. A fee simple absolute is the most extensive possible ownership interest in land. The fee is without condition or limitation, and the owner may alienate the land, use it in any lawful manner, and dispose of it by will or inheritance at death. The estate will descend to heirs or be given to legatees, and in theory goes into the future forever. A grant of a fee simple without a condition or limitation by someone who holds a fee simple absolute is presumed to be a grant in fee simple absolute. Thus, a grant of Blackacre by "O to A and her heirs" creates a fee simple absolute and no future interests.

*See also:* title, relativity of title.

**"and his heirs" ("and her heirs" or "and their heirs")**  A phrase that signals a grant in fee simple absolute. A grant to the grantee "and his heirs," "and her heirs," "and their heirs," or "heirs and assigns" signals that the grant is made in fee simple absolute. The legal implication is that the transfer of property is without any condition that would automatically cut off any heirs. No interest is reserved to the grantor, and no interest is created in heirs, children, or anyone other than the grantee by this language. Likewise, a recipient of property transferred using this phrase is not obliged, later, to transfer the property to the recipient's descendants. A grant made to the grantee and the grantee's heirs creates no interest at that time or in the future in the grantee's heirs, as the grantee's heirs cannot then be ascertained. The grant creates only a possibility that the estate will descend to the heirs on the death intestate of the grantee if the land is not otherwise disposed of.

**fee simple conditional**  The predecessor of the fee tail. The fee simple conditional was an estate conveyed to a grantee by the words, "to A and the heirs of his body." The purpose was to give the land to the grantee and his descendants, generation after generation. If the grantee cut off the inheritance rights of the grantee's issue, the estate would revert to the grantor. However, Medieval courts did not interpret the conveyance as desired by the barons, leading to the statutory creation of the fee tail.

**fee simple determinable (F.S.D. or FSD)**  A fee simple that expires when a condition precedent becomes no longer true. A fee simple determinable is a fee that was structured by its creator to give ownership to the grantee and the to grantee's successors for as long as a stated condition is satisfied. When the condition is violated, the estate comes to an end, and the future interest retained by the grantor, which is called the possibility of reverter, become possessory. Thus, a grant of Blackacre from "O to A and her heirs, for as long as Blackacre is used to support a school" is a fee simple determinable in A, with a possibility of reverter in O (that passes to O's legal successors). A fee simple determinable may last indefinitely, but if the condition fails, in this case, if the property is no longer used to support a school, then the future interest become possessory, and O or O's heirs or legatees may enter Blackacre.

*See also:* defeasibility (defeasible or indefeasibility or indefeasible or indefeasibly).

*rule against perpetuities*  Future interests retained by the grantor, such as a possibility of reverter following a fee simple determinable, are not subject to the rule against perpetuities. Rather, they are deemed to be vested as soon as they arise.

*See also:* perpetuity, rule against perpetuities (RAP or rule against remoteness).

**fee simple subject to condition subsequent (F.S.S.C.S. or FSSCS)**  A fee simple that may be cut short to the benefit of the grantor upon the occurrence of a pre-established condition. A fee simple subject to condition subsequent is a fee simple that vests in its grantee, who may hold the estate forever, but if a condition stipulated by the grantor at the time of the grant later occurs, the grantor has the right to enter the land and retake it. A fee simple subject to condition subsequent is therefore not automatically terminated when the condition subsequent occurs. Rather, the grantor or grantor's successor in interest may elect to exercise the right of entry. A fee simple subject to condition subsequent is created by a conveyance of a fee simple followed by language providing that the fee simple may be divested by the transferor if a specified event happens. Thus, a grant of Blackacre from "O to A and her heirs, but if ever the land shall be used to raise llamas, O shall have the right to re-enter" creates a fee simple subject to a condition subsequent in A and a right of entry (or power of termination) in O.

*See also:* entry, right of entry (R.O.E. or ROE or right of re-entry or power of termination); defeasibility (defeasible or indefeasibility or indefeasible or indefeasibly).

*fee simple subject to executory limitation and fee simple subject to a condition subsequent* The difference between these two defeasible fees is that the fee simple subject to an executory limitation must be followed by an exectutory interest in a grantee, while a fee simple subject to a condition subsequent must be followed by a right of entry or other similar future interest retained by the grantor.

**fee simple subject to executory limitation (fee simple subject to an exectuory interest or F.S.S.E.I. or FSSEI or FSSEL)** A fee simple that may be lost to another grantee if a condition is fulfilled. A fee simple subject to an executory limitation is a fee that may go on forever or be transferred to another grantee if a condition specified at the time of the grantor is satisfied, either by the occurrence of a condition subsequent or by the non-occurrence of a condition precedent, at which time the title and right of possession of the holder will be cut off and the grant will pass to the grantee, or grantees, who holds an executory interest. There is no difference between a fee simple subject to an executory interest and a fee simple subject to an executory limitation. The executory limitation refers to the defined ending of the present interest, and the executory interest refers to the interest that will follow that ending.

There are several differences between a fee simple subject to an executory limitation and both the fee simple subject to a condition subsequent and the fee simple determinable. While the fee simple subject to a condition subsequent and the fee simple determinable are limited by a future interest in the grantor, the fee simple subject to an executory limitation is limited by an interest in a third-party grantee.

Furthermore, the fee simple subject to an executory limitation does not depend on whether the condition is true or not true during the fee holder's occupation of the land. Thus, a grant of Blackacre from "O to A and her heirs but if ever the land shall be used to raise llamas, then to B and her heirs" creates a fee simple subject to an executory limitation in A and an executory interest in B.

The structure of a fee simple subject to an executory limitation can look like a remainder, but the FSEL differs by having a contingency that makes the future interest an executory interest, which is subject to the rule against perpetuities while a remainder is not. Thus, a grant of Blackacre by "O to A and her heirs, but if A dies without issue surviving her, to B and her heirs" gives A a fee simple subject to an executory limitation (or subject to divestment by B's executory interest) and B an executory interest that becomes possessory only by divesting A. O has kept nothing.

*See also:* interest, executory interest (E.I. or EI or executory bequest); defeasibility (defeasible or indefeasibility or indefeasible or indefeasibly); fee, estate in fee, fee simple determinable (F.S.D. or FSD).

**fee tail** An estate that descends to a grantee's surviving lineal descendants, expiring when the last one is dead. A fee tail is an estate in land that is restricted to the ownership of the grantee and the grantee's children and their children, down the line of descent until there are no children, which is a condition known as failure of issue. At the failure of issue, the estate is terminated and a reversion in the grantor becomes possessory, unless the grantor has designated a remainder instead. A fee tail is signaled by a conveyance to the grantee and the heirs of the body. Thus, a grant of Blackacre from "O to A and the heirs of her body" creates only a fee tail in A, creates nothing in A's heirs and nothing in the children of A at that time, and creates a reversion in O. (O could have given the interest away to a third party as a remainder but did not in this illustration.) At A's death, property descends to A's children in fee tail, and at the last death of the last of A's children, it descends again to the children of that child, and so on. Yet if A dies with no surviving child, or if any child dies with no surviving child, then there is a failure of issue, and the property reverts to O.

A fee tail was once difficult to break, and a variety of devices, including fine and recovery were used to convert the estate to something that could be sold or granted for longer than the life of the present tenant. Modern law allows the land to be disentailed by an inter vivos conveyance in fee simple absolute.

Some jurisdictions have abolished fee tail by statute. In such jurisdictions, a grant of a fee tail, made either in name or as a grant to the heirs of the body, is interpreted as creating a life estate in the grantee and a remainder in the grantee's children.

*See also:* issue, issue as child, failure of issue; tail; remainder.

**"and the heirs of the body"** A phrase that signals a grant in fee tail. A grant to the grantee "and the heirs of his body," "and the heirs of her body," or "and the heirs of their bodies" signals that the grant is made in fee tail. The legal implication is that the interest in the grantee or grantees is a fee tail, and a reversion is created in the grantor. No interest is created in the heirs or issue of the grantee at that time, and, indeed, at that time, the identity of the heirs of the grantee cannot be known. The use of the language "and the heirs of the body" is evidence of the intent to create a fee tail, and other language in the grant suggesting an intent other than to create a fee tail would create an ambiguity that must be resolved using ordinary means of document interpretation.

**bar of entail (barring of entail)** Any operation that converts a fee tail to another estate. The bar of an entail is any operation, whether by law or conveyance, that converts ownership in fee tail to another ownership, usually a fee simple. Many American jurisdictions have adopted statutes automatically converting all estates in fee tail to estates in fee simple or life estates, and other states have enacted procedural regulations by which an owner in fee tail may convert the ownership to fee simple, usually through a straw conveyance. The process of the bar of entailment is centuries old, having once included the use of common recovery and the action for fine, but these became unnecessary once a tenant in tail could disentail by inter vivos alienation.

*See also:* fee, estate in fee, fee tail, entail, disentailment; straw (strawman or straw man or straw person).

**disentailment** Avoiding or destroying a fee tail. Disentailment is the conversion of a fee tail to another form of estate, either a fee simple or life estate, or some other interest that is no longer entailed. If an estate in tail is conveyed, any attempt to circumvent, eliminate, or change the nature of that estate is an attempt to disentail the estate. In contemporary practice, an inter vivos transfer of an estate tail amounts to disentailment, though a confiscation or condemnation of the present possessory interest does not.

*See also:* fee, estate in fee, fee tail, bar of entail (barring of entail).

**entail (entailment)** An estate of successive life tenancies usually passed by issue. An entail is a present interest in a fee tail, which amounts to a life estate in the tenant and a remainder in the tenant's children who are alive at the tenant's death. To entail property is to convey it in fee tail.

**failure of issue** *See:* issue, issue as child, failure of issue.

**fee for services**

**attorney's fees** A payment made to an attorney for services performed. Attorney's fees include both the payment of one's own attorneys and, occasionally, the payment of an opponent's attorneys following the opponent's success in court. The general rule in the United States is that one pays one's own lawyers, and these payments include fees for a great range of legal and support services. Most lawyers arrange all matters regarding fees in a written representation agreement, but attorneys may also collect reasonable fees, even if they were not specified, under an oral agreement of representation. Certain instances allow fee-shifting, or the payment of the winner's lawyers and expenses by the losing parties, such as civil rights cases and contract actions in which the parties agreed to fee shifting as a matter of the contract under dispute, if the contract and fee-shifting provision are found to be valid.

*See also:* cost.

**billable hour (billable time or billables or hourly fee)** A block of time for which a lawyer may charge a client. A billable hour is a component of time that a lawyer may charge to a client. The hour is computed in increments, varying from firm to firm, of as low as one-tenth of an hour. In some firms, an hour is discounted to fifty minutes to allow for necessary distractions. If work is done during that increment, the lawyer may bill the whole of the increment to the client. The whole time spent in providing certain services, such as travel, may be billed even when the legal work performed for the client is minimal. Clients have noted the questionable nature of some billing practices and negotiated specific practices in billing hours as well as negotiating rates. There is considerable evidence that the practice of billing by the hour has created an incentive for some firms to behave in a manner not fully consistent with the best representation of the client.

*See also:* time.

**contingency fee (contingent fee)** A fee based on a percentage of the recovery if an action is successful. A contingent fee, or a fee on contingency, is a fee that is owed by the client to the lawyer only if the lawyer is successful in representing the client by recovering damages or some other award, from a defendant, an insurer, or a third party. In many contingent fee arrangements, the attorney keeps one-third of the value of the award, transferring to the client the remaining two-thirds. Contingent fees are common in the United States among plaintiffs' counsel, but they are rare in defense and in other countries, many of which forbid them.

The contingent fee is often criticized by the defense bar as encouraging plaintiffs to bring frivolous cases, but it may actually discourage them, as the plaintiff's lawyer recovers nothing from a lost case. The contingent fee is also criticized because it reduces the recovery of a meritorious claim, such that a person who loses a leg would recover only two-thirds of the compensation awarded for the leg. Yet the response here is that, but for the lawyer bearing the risk and paying the costs, the one-legged plaintiff probably would not have had the means to seek any recovery at all. For many poor people, a lawyer on a contingent basis is essential for their access to the court. In the end, the contingent fee is a natural response to a system of civil litigation, particularly in tort, that follows the American rule, in which all clients must pay for their own lawyers.

**disgorgement of a fee**   An attorney's fees are repaid to the client or paid to a third party. Disgorgement of an attorney's fee is the transfer of money received as fees either back to the client or to another party. Disgorgement may be required as a sanction in response to a failure of duty by the lawyer to the client, or it may be a remedy for breach in the representation agreement or for a billing error. A mere order of an attorney to pay money that is not related to the acceptance of a particular fee from a particular client is not disgorgement, nor is an order that a client pay money as a result of paying an attorney's fee. In most instances, disgorgement results in the repayment of the fee to the client who paid it. In some instances, the fee is disgorged to a third party, often to a charitable enterprise in some public service related to the form of wrong done that gave rise to the disgorgement.

**fee sharing**   The sharing of fees among lawyers. Fee sharing is the allocation of fees received for a single representation among several lawyers. Fee sharing is appropriate when one lawyer refers a case to another, when one lawyer associates another on a matter in order to gain access to the others' expertise or, sometimes, availability to ensure timely action for the client. Fee sharing outside of the partnership distribution is not, though, ordinarily appropriate when a lawyer provides no service for a client at all. Fee sharing among lawyers is acceptable, but ethical rules generally prohibit the sharing of fees in any form that resembles profit-sharing or partnership with non-lawyers.

**fee shifting**   The payment of the winner's attorney's fees by the losing party in an action in court. In a fee-shifting case, the winning party is given an award from the losing party to compensate the winning party for that party's attorney's fees in the case. Fee shifting is rare in the U.S., usually occurring in an action with a statutory provision that allows fee shifting in that type of case, such as a civil rights enforcement action,

a consumer protection action, a case of employment discrimination, an environmental defense action, or a case subject to a state fee-shifting law. Fees may also shift according to a valid contractual provision when the contract is disputed. Fee shifting for all or part of the representation of a case is also available as a sanction for the misconduct of an attorney or a client. State laws allowing fee-shifting abound, sometimes in large arenas of litigation. For example, in Arkansas, all actions for the enforcement of contracts allow fee shifting. In most actions the decision to grant an order allowing recovery of attorneys fees rests with the discretion of the trial court.

**American rule (common-law rule)**   Each party in a dispute pays its own attorneys' fees. The American rule describes the practice in most U.S. civil cases in which each side pays its own lawyers. This custom may be abrogated by statute, and the rule does not apply if there is contempt or any other serious violation of the rule or court order, if there is bad faith by one side, if there is a common fund, or if there is a substantial benefit to the public from the litigation. The rule is sometimes referred to as the common-law rule because the rule is subordinate to a statutory rebuttal.

**English rule**   The losing party pays the attorneys' fees of the winner at the court's discretion. The English rule of attorney fee allocation provides that the losing party in many categories of litigation pay the attorneys' fees of the winning party as one element of costs. It is a default rule of fee shifting in civil litigation. The rule is called the English rule in the U.S. and not in England. Indeed, it is not actually English but is the approach taken in most of Europe. In most legal systems that have a default rule allowing fee shifting, there are exceptions, the most important being that the loser will not be required to pay the successful party's attorney's fees unless the court in its discretion believes such payment is just.

**Equal Access to Justice Act (EAJA or E.A.J.A.)**   Successful plaintiffs may recover their attorney's fees in claims against the U.S. government. The Equal Access to Justice Act (EAJA), 28 U.S.C. § 2412(b) (2008), is a fee-shifting statute that allows a successful claimant against the government to recover attorneys' fees, costs, and certain expenses, including the fees of experts. Award under the act is in the discretion of the court, but unlike actions subject to Section 1988, most claims under the EAJA will fail if officials who denied the claim initially were substantially justified in their decisions or actions, especially if there was a clear and reasonable basis in law for the denying the claim, regardless of whether that basis is ultimately upheld by the agencies or the courts.

**Hyde Amendment**   Successful criminal defendants may recover attorneys' fees if their federal prosecution is vexatious, frivolous, or in bad faith. The Hyde Amendment, Pub. L. No. 105–119, Section 617, 111 Stat. 2440, 2519 (1997), allows federal criminal defendants who suffer a "vexatious" or "frivolous" prosecution, or a prosecution brought "in bad faith" to recover legal fees for their representation. For reasons beyond public knowledge, the amendment has never been placed clearly in the U.S. Code, the codifiers being content to add it as a note at the end of 18 U.S.C. §3006A (2008). Note: there are several laws known for Congressman Henry Hyde; this one is different from the one about abortion funding.

See also: abortion, regulation of abortion | 2. government funding (hyde amendment or public funds).

**lodestar amount (lode-star or lodestar method)**   The reasonable rate for an attorney of a given skill in a given market in a given form of action. A lodestar amount is the fee that a reasonable attorney would expect to be paid in a particular legal market for a particular type of work and is usually an hourly rate. In considering the amount that a prevailing party is owed for attorney's fees in a case in which the court determines fee shifting is appropriate, the court will usually determine a lodestar amount, which represents a calculation of the usual fee for an attorney in such a case in that forum, as well as the quality of the work performed, the difficulty of the work, the experience or skill of the attorney, the result, the extent to which the work would bar other representation, the degree of risk of compensation under which the lawyer took the representation, and the novelty in the representation. This yields an hourly rate, or lodestar, that will be due to the lawyers in that case, and then that amount will be multiplied by the approved hours worked to determine a total bill.

**fixed fee**   The provision of specified legal services in return for an agreed–upon sum of money. A fixed fee representation is one in which the particular tasks and representation to be performed by the attorney and a set price for these services is agreed upon in advance. A fixed fee representation may include a variety of stages in which difference steps of a case or transaction have defined fees, and an arrangement is specified regarding when and by whom those steps will be authorized.

**retainer fee (retainer or on retainer)**   A fee paid in advance of services rendered by an attorney. A retainer is a fee paid by a client to an attorney both as an advance against future bills and as consideration for a client representation agreement before services are performed. Attorneys are generally not allowed to keep a retainer, other than a nominal amount, if services are never performed. One function of a retainer by the client is to ensure that the client is entitled to the attorney's duty of loyalty, so that the attorney would have a conflict of interest if an opponent sought the attorney's counsel. An attorney who is on retainer has accepted such a retainer. It is not correct, however, to refer to such an attorney as a retainer, as the word applied to a person implies a personal servant.

**reasonable attorney's fees**   A fee for legal services that is reasonable under the circumstances. A reasonable attorney's fee is measured by the work performed, the difficulty of the work, the experience and reputation of the attorney(s), the market for their services otherwise, and the efforts actually entailed. It is not measured by the bill presented, although such a bill is not irrelevant.

**court fee**

**docket fee**   A fee for filing a pleading or paper in a court record. A docket fee is a fee that is authorized in some jurisdictions to be charged by the clerk of court for each document filed in the docket of a case. Some docket fees are applied only in particular circumstances, such as the preparation of the docket for appeal. Docket fees, as with other court fees, may be waived for pleadings in forma pauperis.

**filing fee**   A fee for the initiation of a civil suit. A filing fee is a fee that is charged in many jurisdictions for the initial filing in a civil action in order to open a docket for that case. The term is more generally used for any fee required for the filing of a paper in court, including the fee for recording a deed, a will, or a judgment, or for docketing pleadings, transcripts, or other filings of record.

See also: filing (file).

**jury fee**   A fee for the services of a jury. A jury fee is a reimbursement to the court of the expenses for jury service by members of a venire that is assessed by the clerk of court in some jurisdictions against the party in a civil action who demands a jury trial.

**financing fee**

**origination fee**   The fee charged by a lender to initiate a loan. An origination fee is a surcharge on a loan that many financial institutions assess at the time of issuance of a loan, in addition to fees for services provided to the borrower, such as surveys and the costs of closing, and to the interest charged for the loan itself. The origination fee is usually calculated as a percentage of the total amount of the loan.

**monetary fee** A payment required for a particular service. A fee is a payment in money that is made by a person or entity that seeks or receives a service, particularly from a financial office or bank, a professional or professional enterprise, from a school or educational institution, or from a government. Fee may function both as personal compensation and as reimbursement or income to an institution.

**fellow officer rule or collective knowledge doctrine** *See:* cause, probable cause, fellow–officer rule (fellow officer rule or collective knowledge doctrine).

**felo de se** *See:* suicide (felo de se).

**felony (felon or felonious)** A crime punishable by death or imprisonment for at least one year. Felony is the highest classification of criminal offenses, which are generally divided into felonies, misdemeanors, and infractions. In states with criminal statutes based on the Model Penal Code, an offense must both be designated as a felony in the statute and carry with it a penalty exceeding one year of imprisonment. At common law, felony included specific crimes that were punishable by attainder or death, and although this designation eventually included crimes with lesser punishments, it was usually reserved for the most serious offenses — murder, mayhem, rape, larceny, robbery, burglary, and arson. In some jurisdictions, "high misdemeanor" is still used to describe offenses that are felonies elsewhere, such as treason, arson, misue of office, and receiving stolen goods.

A person convicted of a felony is a "felon." As a consequence of conviction, felons in most U.S. jurisdictions lose certain rights, such as the rights to vote, own firearms, and hold public office.

**felony class (felony classification)** A category of felony based on the seriousness of the crime. A felony class, or classification of felony, is a category drawn by statute between various forms of felony in order to distinguish more serious offenses that are subject to more significant penalties.

**felony-murder rule** *See:* murder, felony murder (felony–murder rule).

**female circumcision** *See:* mutilation, genital mutilation (female circumcision).

**feme¯ (feme covert or baron and feme or feme sole)** A woman. Feme, or femme, was a term in law French that persisted in the American common law into the twentieth century. Written with an article, "la feme," the term denoted the wife, and written "femele," it denoted girls.

Special terms for women of a particular status were used in the common law, all based on the law French "feme." Thus a feme sole is an unmarried woman, or solo woman, and a feme covert is a married woman because she was subject to coverture or the limitations of marriage, which would make her immune from certain suits. "Baron and feme" designated husband and wife. A feme sole trader was a married woman who acted for herself in commerce and so was liable to suit as would be an unmarried woman.

**feminism** Priority for the equality of women and recognition of women's values. Feminism describes an historical social movement as well as a legal and political perspective that demands equality of opportunity and treatment for women while also recognizing and integrating the values and priorities of women when they differ from those of men.

*See also:* jurisprudence, feminist jurisprudence (feminist legal theory).

**feod or fief or feodum or feudum** *See:* feud (feod or fief or feodum or feudum).

**ferae (ferus)** Feral. Ferae is the Latin adjective from the noun ferus, or wild thing. Anything ferae is wild and untamed.

**ferae naturae** Of a wild nature. Ferae naturae is a wild nature. It depicts animals that are of a species that is usually wild and untamed. The measure of an animal that is ferae naturae is that it is not sufficiently domesticated to return to captivity of its own will. Thus, an animal that is from a species generally wild can be tamed, losing its disposition ferae naturae by acquiring an animus revertendi. Once that has occurred, property in the animal persists whether it is on the owner's property or not. Until that time, property in the wild animal only persists as long as it is a captive or when it is killed.

*See also:* animal, wild animal, ferae naturae; capture (law of capture); domitae naturae; game, game animal.

**mineral ferae naturae** Ownership in pooled or migratory mineral interests requires capture. The mineral ferae naturae is a metaphorical description of oil, gas, water, and other extractable and migratory mineral interests in property that likens them to wild animals and so limits the otherwise absolute ownership in them that might be afforded to the land owner in whose property they occur. The doctrine of minerals ferae naturae supports the rule of capture, by which ownership is held in whomever can extract and control the resource, even if it is ultimately extracted from a pool in another's land.

*See also:* capture, rule of capture.

**fertile octogenarian** *See:* perpetutity, rule against perpetuity, what–might–happen test, fertile octogenarian.

**ferus** *See:* ferae (ferus).

**fetters or legcuffs or leg irons or shackling** *See:* restraint, physical restraint, shackles (fetters or legcuffs or leg irons or shackling).

**fetus (fetal, foetus, or unborn child)** A developing human prior to birth. Fetus, foetus, and unborn child are terms for a developing human prior to birth. Among the three, fetus is the most widely used term among members of the medical community. "Unborn child" is the term used for the same purpose that is preferred by opponents of abortion or a right to abortion.

*See also:* abortion (abort); uterus (utero or in utero).

**feticide (foeticide)**  Deliberately causing the death of a viable human fetus other than by medical abortion. Feticide is the intentional, knowing or reckless termination of pregnancy or causing of injury to a fetus, resulting in the death of an otherwise viable human fetus. Feticide may be criminalized specifically by statute or by virtue of precedent defining the term "human being" or "person" in a murder statute as including a fetus or unborn child who may become viable outside and independent of the mother. An abortion conducted according to lawfully prescribed procedures by a licensed medical practitioner is not a feticide.

*See also:* abortion (abort).

**feud (feod or fief or feodum or feudum)**  Ancient terms for the fee in land. The feud is a predecessor to the later term, fee, meaning an estate in land. Feud is the root of feudalism, the medieval legal and social structure based upon the relationships between the feudal lords and their tenants. Although feud is derived from the medieval Latin feodum for estate, that term is not itself derived from Latin but more likely from the Frankish term for cattle or payment.

*See also:* fee, estate in fee.

**feudal service**  *See:* service, feudal service (tenant services).

**feudal tenure**  *See:* tenure, feudal tenure (feudalism or feudal system).

**feud as cycle of revenge**  A series of reprisals between parties. A feud is a cycle of bad acts between two parties or two groups, in which each acts to harm the other, each justifying new harmful acts according to prior harm caused by the other.

*See also:* reprisal.

**feudal incidents**  Obligations of a feudal tenant to a lord. Incidents included all of the duties a feudal tenant owed to a lord, including homage, or obedience; wardship, or the control of lands while a tenant is a minor; marriage, or the right of approval or refusal of a given spouse for a tenant; aids, or customary gifts; and relief, or a tax paid by the tenant for the entrance into the tenancy.

*See also:* ownership, incidents of ownership; incident, incident as incidental.

**feudalism (feudal law)**  The medieval social, political, and legal hierarchy. Feudalism was a strictly organized system of land that was allocated by grants from the monarch to tenants in chief, who would then grant smaller parcels of land to tenants, who might in turn grant to subtenants a tenure in land, each in return for loyalty and services rendered to the grantor, with both grantees and grantors continuing the relationship, sometimes for many generations. Everyone, save the king, was subservient to someone who was lord over those lands and who was accorded a variety of rights and privileges in addition to the services to be rendered by the tenants. The feud was the fee, the basis of the tenancy.

The feudal law was organized to both ensure the balance of the feudal bargain between king and tenant and to ascertain the obligations of each to one another in the land and services that were the means of the balance and exchange. Feudal law emphasized peace, order, the status of each feudal office and tenancy, and respect for the obligations of property holdings.

*See also:* fee, estate in fee; tenure, feudal tenure (feudalism or feudal system).

**Carolingian law (Salic law)**  The law of the medieval Franks. The Carolingians were the Frankish kings descended from Charles Martel, whose son, Pepin the Short, established a dynasty that replaced the Merovingians in 751, and whose son Charlemagne (741–814) consolidated the first great empire in northern Europe after the fall of Rome. The Franks occupied much of what is now Germany, France, and Belgium.

The Carolingian laws depended on the scabini, the newly created class of professional legal experts, and their essential precepts were the Salic laws, which were created in the very early 500s and refined in the Lex Ripuaria of about 630 and the Lex Saxonum of 798 and 802 CE. The Salic laws were the basis of much of the core of feudal land law, particularly the agnatic succession, which required lands to descend from a holder to the first male successor, rather than to a female, thus favoring primogeniture and doing much to develop the feudal estate. The empire was divided in the late ninth century, but the influence of its legal system pervaded Europe, including Normandy, from where William invaded England a century and a half later.

**subinfeudation**  The creation of a lesser estate by the holder of a greater estate. Subinfeudation was the feudal means in law by which a tenant effectively subdivided a tenancy, creating the portion of the old tenancy as an inferior tenancy subject to the tenant's superiority. Because the tenants held their estates from the crown or from a tenant in chief and were usually lords themselves, the result was usually the creation by a lord of an estate held by a more minor tenant, subject to all of the requirements of the lord's tenancy plus whatever additional incidents the lord upon which the lord chose to condition the fee. Subinfeudation by a mesne lord might be barred by that lord's tenant in chief or by any other lord from whom an intervening lord held the tenancy. Although the term is often used to describe the actions of mesne lords or lesser lords, the process of subinfeudation was common among tenants-in-chief. The monarch did not engage in subinfeudation but in the grant of a fee which, by definition, was a tenancy in chief. In the early middle ages, the holder of a tenancy, however created, could not alienate the tenancy without the permission of the lord from whom the tenancy was held.

See also: landlord, mesne lord.

**FF. or et seq.**  See: citation, citation signal, following pages (FF. or et seq.).

**fi fa or fi. fa.**  See: writ, fieri facias (fi fa or fi. fa.).

**fiat**  An order or command. Fiat is a Latin phrase meaning "so be it," that is still used to describe a command or judgment that must be obeyed. To use the word fiat implies a high degree of discretion on the part of the entity that issues the command, and to describe rule by fiat is to imply a criticism that the mandate may not be based on underlying rules or principles.

**fiat justitia ruat coelum**  See: justice, fiat justitia ruat coelum (do justice though the heavens may fall).

**fiction (fictitious)**  Anything pretended or invented but presented as true. Fiction, in the law, is essentially as it is in literature, an invention or artifice presented as if it might be true, though with the intention by its inventor or creator that those who rely on it treat it simultaneously as if it were true while knowing that it is not.

**legal fiction (fiction of law)**  A fiction invented for the convenience of the law. A legal fiction is a statement about some event or occurrence that is not true as a matter of historical fact but that is accepted as true for the convenience of administering a legal rule in a given context or for the broader policies underlying the law. Legal fictions may be express or implied and once accepted by the court, the fact that the fiction is untrue is not grounds for overturning the decision because the effect is one of policy rather than fact. In the nineteenth century, Sir Henry Maine observed that the greatest of legal fictions is the notion that the law does not change over time.

See also: fact, legal fact.

**fictitious name**  See: name, fictitious name, titius (aulus agerius or numerius negidiusor seius or stichus); name, fictitious name, John Doe (Richard Roe or Jane Doe); name, fictitious name, Baby Doe (Baby M); name, fictitious name.

**fidelity bond**  See: bond, fidelity bond (blanket bond).

**fides (fide)**  Faith. Fides is the element of faith in "good faith" or bona fides. Its root is the same as is the root for fiduciary and fidelity.

See also: purchaser, bona fide purchaser (bona fide purchaser for value or B.F.P. or B.F.P.V. or BFP or BFPV); affidavit; fiduciary; bona, bona fide (bona fides); confidentiality (confidential).

**fiduciary**  A person in whom another reposes special confidence and reliance. A fiduciary is a person with a responsibility that requires a higher level of care by the person and trust by others than the usual commercial or social relationship. A fiduciary must put the interests of the person or entity relying upon the fiduciary above the fiduciary's own interests, and a fiduciary usually has an affirmative duty to act for those relying on the good faith of the fiduciary, rather than merely a duty not to act negligently: fiduciaries must have or acquire sufficient knowledge and skill to carry out the office in good faith, must act affirmatively to avoid waste or loss in managing assets, and must act to inform the other in many circumstances. Certain positions inherently require fiduciary duties, particularly a trustee to a beneficiary, an accountant to a client, a doctor to a patient, a lawyer to a client, a corporate officer to a shareholder, an investment manager to a client, etc. Fiduciary duties do not admit to easy definition or limitation, and their enforcement is occasionally a matter of contract or fraud but more often a matter for equity. Famously, the term fiduciary is derived from "fides" or faith, marking both the faith others must have in the fiduciary and the good faith owed to them.

See also: influence; faith; jurisdiction, equitable jurisdiction | fiduciary; fides (fide).

**fiduciary law**  See: trustee, fiduciary law, successor trustee.

**fiduciary duty**  The heightened duties of care owed by a fiduciary to the principal. Fiduciary duty encompasses a range of obligations that a fiduciary owes to the person or entity who relies on the fiduciary. The duty is both general, in that the fiduciary must exercise good faith, placing the interests of the principal above the fiduciary's interests, and specific, in that the fiduciary has a duty of loyalty to avoid conflicts of interest, to use the fiduciary's best efforts, and to avoid misrepresentation.

Most actions for breach of a fiduciary duty require clear and convincing evidence of a violation of this heightened expectation of trust. The recognition and enforcement of a fiduciary duty is a matter of equity jurisdiction, and even in courts of general jurisdiction such matters are subject to equitable pleading standards, including equitable principles of standing, and to equitable remedies.

See also: diligence, due diligence; equity (equitable).

**duty of fair representation (D.F.R. or DFR)**  A fiduciary for a group may not treat individual members preferentially. The duty of fair representation requires that an agent for a group of people — such as multiple beneficiaries of the same trust, members of a union, or members of a class of shareholders — may not discriminate in the treatment of the individual members of that group.

**duty of good faith**  A fiduciary must be honest and use best efforts on behalf of the principal. The fiduciary duty of good faith requires a fiduciary to act with honesty and to use best efforts in all that is said and done for or on behalf of the principal. The duty also implies it's a prohibition against its rejection: a fiduciary may not act in bad faith, or with deliberate falsity, with an intent to harm, or in betrayal of the principal's interests.

**duty of knowledge or skill**   A fiduciary has a duty to exercise at least reasonable knowledge and skill. The fiduciary duty of knowledge or of skill varies according to the circumstance. A fiduciary is usually charged with a duty to exercise reasonable care, knowledge, and skill. If, however, a fiduciary relationship is based upon a confidential relationship in which the principal's reason for reliance on the fiduciary is either a claim by the fiduciary or a reasonable expectation by the principal that the fiduciary has extraordinary knowledge or skill, then the fiduciary has an obligation to act according to that higher standard, according to what a reasonable person among persons with such high levels of skill would do. Thus a company or firm with unusual expertise that offers confidential services based on that expertise, such as a law firm, accountancy firm, engineering firm, management consultancy or other entity that provides more than a mere commercial transaction, will be held to the standard of care appropriate to protect the reliance of the principal on such a specialized fiduciary.

**duty of loyalty**   A fiduciary has a duty to act in the best interests of the principal. A duty of loyalty is the obligation of a fiduciary created by the nature of the relationship between parties. The precise obligation required varies, depending on the nature of the relationship, but can generally be described as the "undivided and unselfish" duty to act in the best interests of the principal.

**duty of prudent investment**   A trustee must invest the res with prudence. The duty of prudent investment requires a trustee, or other bailee charged with a res in trust that should be or can be committed for the financial gain of the beneficiaries, to manage the corpus by making prudent investments. The trustee must act reasonably even though the trustee bears no personal risk of loss. In some jurisdictions, the duty is discharged relative to the whole res, so that the duty is measured over time according to the whole average or pattern of transactions, not as to every single transaction, although every transaction must still be made in good faith and to the intended benefit of the beneficiary.

**duty to avoid conflicts of interest**   A duty to act with undivided loyalty. The duty to avoid conflicts of interest is a fundamental aspect of a fiduciary's role. The fiduciary's obligation of good faith requires that the fiduciary not diminish that good faith through competing commitments that would divert the fiduciary from the time, focus, and interest in the singular benefit of the particular beneficiary, rather than balancing that benefit against the benefit of others to whom the fiduciary might otherwise have given assistance. This duty is not absolute, and a minor conflict may be managed if the fiduciary discloses the potential of conflict to the parties whose interests or needs are potential rivals for the fiduciary's attention and advice, if the nature and scope of the potential rivalry are disclosed to both, if each has a meaningful and informed option to discontinue the fiduciary relationship or to accept it with the conflict, and if each does. Even so, some conflicts are too severe to be waived, and some beneficiaries of a conflicted fiduciary lack the capacity to sufficiently understand the conflict and waive it.

See also: conflict, conflict of interest.

**duty to investigate**   A responsibility that requires the obligee to reasonably investigate. The duty to investigate is a responsibility arising out of a special relationship between parties that requires a fiduciary to reasonably investigate matters affecting the beneficiary if the fiduciary learns of anything that would make a reasonably prudent person suspicious that further information is required to serve the beneficiary's interests. In the context of attorneys, this obligation is a critical element of effective assistance of counsel, particularly when an attorney represents a client with a potential or active matter in litigation. What must be investigated and the amount of investigation considered reasonable will vary based on the relationship and the circumstances. The term "due diligence" is sometimes used synonymously in this context

See also: diligence, due diligence.

**Field code**   See: code, Field code.

**field sobriety test**   See: sobriety, field sobriety test.

**fieri (in fieri)**   Execution. Fieri is execution, usually as encountered in the writ of execution, the fieri facias. In fieri denotes the ongoing process of execution that has not been perfected or completed. A record in fieri may be amended.

See also: writ, fieri facias (fi fa or fi. fa.).

**fieri facias**   See: writ, fieri facias (fi fa or fi. fa.).

**fighting words**   See: speech, fighting words.

**filibuster**   A speech made as a tactical delay to block legislation. A filibuster is a speech without end, a delay tactic used by United States Senators in order to block or delay passage of certain legislation. A filibuster may be made by one member of a chamber alone or, in some circumstances, by several members in succession. In the United States Senate, legislation may not proceed to a vote on a matter subject to filibuster until a motion for cloture is passed, which requires an affirmative three-fifths vote. Put another way, when the minority party wants to delay legislation that would more than likely pass if brought to a vote, the minority party speaks on the Senate floor indefinitely, until the majority party either withdraws the legislation or some other agreement is reached.

See also: cloture.

**filing (file)**   The deposit of an instrument in an office to keep it as a record. A filing is the delivery and receipt for deposit of any document in a public office that receives such documents, records their existence in a catalog, and stores them for later reference or processing. In many, though not all instances, the filing of such a document creates a public record of the document. The procedures that must be met to file a document vary according to the nature of the document and the rules of the office. Some offices once required hand delivery of certain documents, but now most offices also accept delivery by messenger service, or by U.S. or official mails. Increasingly, filings may be by fax, by electronic mail, and by submission of forms by electronic interface through the internet. A presentation of a document by a means or in a form that does not conform to the public rules of the office may require the clerk or agent who receives the document to reject it. Even if a document is accepted and recorded, under the law, the filling may not have been effective if later events make clear that the document was not in its proper form or if certain conditions that must have been met for filing had not in fact been met, and the attempt to file the document, though it was accepted, may be treated as a nullity. A great number of documents are filed in courts and in public agencies, not the least being court pleadings and documents of record in litigation, tax returns, corporate filings with state and federal offices, and records of vital statistics such as birth certificates and death certificates.

The etymology of the filing of records is of some interest and formed the core of the 1853 definition. The practice of the law courts in London was to collect the writs, receipts, and filings in a given action by piercing each record with a long needle and pulling a string through the parchment or paper, so that all of the records for each case were in order of their receipt on the string. The string was a file (a name that might itself have arisen from the needle) but the ordering all of the papers on the file became known as the file as well, so that any column of papers, and then any organized array of papers, became the file. The term file now includes purely electronic organizations of data. It is unclear which came first, the file of papers (when they are in a line on a string) or the file of people (when they are in a line one behind another), though both seem to have emerged in the late sixteenth century in England.

*See also:* fee, fee for services, court fee, filing fee; facsimile (fax).

**filing fee**   *See:* fee, fee for services, court fee, filing fee.

**fill**   *See:* water, wetlands, fill.

**finality (final)**   The end of the matter. Finality is the element of an action, appeal, endeavor, or anything at all that puts an end to it. In procedure, something final contrasts with something interlocutory or intermediate. A final order is the last order of a court, and from it an appeal may be taken, in most cases as of right, while an interlocutory order is an order in the midst of the process and usually an appeal can be taken only by permission.

**final agency action**   *See:* action, final agency action.

**final consent decree or interlocutory consent decree**   *See:* decree, consent decree (final consent decree or interlocutory consent decree).

**final judgment**   *See:* judgment, final judgment.

**final jury instruction**   *See:* instruction, jury instruction, final jury instruction (closing instructions or instructions at end of trial or final charge to the jury).

**final order**   *See:* order, final order, final order rule; order, final order.

**final order rule**   *See:* order, final order, final order rule.

**final–offer arbitration**   *See:* arbitration, final–offer arbitration.

## finances

**Financial Accounting Standards Board**   *See:* accounting, Financial Accounting Standards Board (F.A.S.B. or FASB).

**financial derivative**   *See:* derivative, financial derivative.

**Financial Industry Regulatory Authority**   *See:* security, securities, securities regulation, Financial Industry Regulatory Authority (FINRA or NASD).

**financing fee**   *See:* fee, fee for services, financing fee, origination fee.

**financial institution**   An entity involved in financial activities. A financial institution is any entity whose primary activity is engaging in financial transactions. A bank is a financial institution.

*See also:* bank, bank as financial corporation.

**financial statement**   A document showing the assets, obligations, and fiscal position of a person or business. A financial statement is a document that discloses the financial position of a person or entity as a going concern. Financial statements take a variety of forms, most commonly a balance sheet, income statement, and cash flow statement. Financial statements are the primary medium of disclosure of assets and debts for public and private companies.

**financier**   Anyone engaged in the lending and management of money. A financier is a person or financial institution that engages in the lending and management of money. The term is commonly used to describe principal officers or managers of organizations that participate in commercial lending transactions and investment banking.

**financial ability**   *See:* ability, financial ability | presumption of financial ability; ability, financial ability.

**Finch (Atticus Finch)**   A lawyer who defends the unjustly accused. Atticus Finch is the lawyer in Harper Lee's 1960 novel, To Kill a Mockingbird, played by Gregory Peck in the 1962 movie. Practicing law in a depression–era small town in Alabama, Finch is appointed to represent an African American, Tom Robinson, who is falsely accused of the rape of a white woman. Finch does so with great ability, demonstrating to the reader Tom's innocence, though Lee's fictional jury, like real Alabama juries in similar cases of the twentieth century, wrongfully convicts him, patently because of his race.

Finch has proved an enduring model of the morally upright lawyer who takes an unpopular client and does his best. Although Finch has been criticized as insufficiently critical of a racist system, these criticisms have not been widely accepted, and the character remains a metaphor of the good lawyer whose sense of right and wrong trumps both personal interest and communal pressures.

*See also:* Mason (Perry Mason); metaphor.

**find (finder or finders)**　Personal property that once was lost, mislaid, or abandoned but now found. A find is a chattel, some personal property, that is located by one person after it has been lost by another. The person who finds the object is its finder. The law of finders generally allows the finder to keep the find as against all claimants except the person who lost the object or the true owner if the person who lost it was someone else. A finder is obligated to take reasonable steps to identify the true owner but is entitled to a fee or deposit from the true owner at the time the owner recovers the object.

*See also:* property, found property (finds or law of finds or law of finders).

**finding**　A determination of a fact as a matter of institutional record. A finding is a determination by a court, legislature, or other body, of some matter of fact. A finding is particularly important as the factual predicate to a policy or judgment.

*See also:* fact, finding of fact (findings of fact or conclusion of fact or factual conclusion).

**finding of fact**　*See:* ruling, finding of fact (fact finding or fact finder or finder of fact); fact, finding of fact (findings of fact or conclusion of fact or factual conclusion).

**finding of no significant impact**　*See:* environment, National Environmental Policy Act, environmental assessment, finding of no significant impact (F.O.N.S.I. or FONSI).

**finds or law of finds or law of finders**　*See:* property, found property (finds or law of finds or law of finders).

**fine**　An amount of money assessed as a punishment. A fine, in contemporary usage, nearly always represents a sum of money assessed by a court or administrator as a penalty for an infraction of a law or regulation. In the English common law, a fine was a price paid to commence a leasehold and was also the term for a type of conveyance, but both of these usages are now rare in the United States. The term is derived from fin or finis,

the end, because the fine is determined at the end of the proceeding.

*See also:* penalty (penalize or penalized or penalizing); sentence.

**fine as penalty**　Money assessed as a punishment. A fine is a punitive assessment of money intended to punish illegal acts or conditions, or to coerce the recipient to perform a legally obligated action or to maintain a legally required condition. The purpose of the assessment is essential to determine its character as a fine.

*See also:* penalty (penalize or penalized or penalizing).

**fingerprint**　The pattern of ridges on the skin of fingertips, or the marks made by them on objects. A fingerprint is the pattern unique to each individual that is formed on the skin of nearly all human fingers and made by tiny ridges in the skin, through which perspiration is left like a barely visible stamp on objects touched or handled. Fingerprints are used to identify a person who has touched an object by comparing the patterns of the print on the object to a record of a print made by the person's fingers. A latent fingerprint is a fingerprint that is only made visible through a technique such as exposure to chemicals or a particulate that reacts to or adheres to the excretions of the print.

**fingerprint of the oil**　*See:* oil, fingerprint of the oil (oil fingerprinting).

**Finnisian goods**　*See:* good, underived good (Finnisian goods).

**FINRA or NASD**　*See:* security, securities, securities regulation, Financial Industry Regulatory Authority (FINRA or NASD).

**fiqh**　*See:* sharia, fiqh, usul al-fiqh (usul al'fiqh, usool al-fiqh); sharia, fiqh.

**firearm**

**discharge of firearm**　The release of ammunition from a weapon. To discharge a weapon is to fire it, whether or not there is a human agency involved or the human involved intended to do so. In the case of a firearm, a discharge may include the discharge of blank ammunition as well as ammunition fitted with a projectile.

**firearms**　*See:* police, police organizations, Bureau of Alcohol, Tobacco, Firearms, and Explosives.

**firefighter's rule**　*See:* rescue, professional rescuer doctrine (firefighter's rule).

**firm**　Any entity formed by incorporation or partnership. A firm is the entity created by a partnership, corporation, or any other business association. In law, a firm usually means a law firm, a partnership among attorneys at law.

**firm bid**    *See:* bid, firm bid.

**firm offer**    *See:* offer, contract offer, irrevocable offer (firm offer); offer, contract offer, firm offer.

**first appearance or preliminary examination**
*See:* hearing, preliminary hearing (first appearance or preliminary examination).

**first principle of justice**    *See:* justice, Rawlsian justice, principle of right (first principle of justice).

**first refusal**    *See:* preemption, right of preemption, first refusal (right of first refusal).

**first-degree felony murder**    *See:* murder, felony murder, first-degree felony murder.

**first-degree murder**    *See:* murder, degrees of murder, first-degree murder (murder in the first degree or murder-one or murder-1).

**fiscal year**    *See:* year, fiscal year (FY).

**fish**    Scaly, cold-blooded aquatic animals with fins. Fish are well-known animals living in inland waters and in the seas. The ownership of fish depends on the manner in which they occur. A fish raised on a farm is considered the property of the farmer, as would be the case of any domesticated animal. A fish raised in a sea-bed fishery is treated in the same manner unless it is released into the sea. A fish in the sea or a river or lake is considered to be ferae naturae, and no property is acquired in it from presence alone by a littoral or riparian owner unless the entirety of the body of water is owned.

The fish of the sea, like all marine resources, are subject to national control under international law. A littoral state has absolute control over the fish and fisheries in its territorial sea, its contiguous zone, and its exclusive economic zone. The state has an exclusive right over bottom-dwelling fish on its continental shelf up to 350 miles from the shore. States may have exclusive control over certain fisheries as against other states under bilateral or multi-lateral treaties for the management of those fisheries.

**anadromous fish (anadromous stocks of fish)**    Fish born in fresh water but living mainly at sea. Anadromous fish live most of their lives at sea but travel up rivers to fresh water to spawn, and so the young are also born in fresh water. Such fish are subject to U.S. regulation at sea by the NOAA National Marine Fisheries Service, though they are regulated in inland waters by the U.S. Fish and Wildlife Service and the various riparian states. Salmon, eel, and shad are anadromous.

**catadromous fish (catadromous stocks of fish)**    Fish that live mainly in fresh water but spawn at sea. Catadromous fish live most of their lives in rivers and streams but travel down rivers to the sea to spawn, and so the young are also born at sea. Many eels are catadromous.

**fishing expedition**    A process intended not to prove existing claims but to discover new claims. A fishing expedition is a civil action, criminal interrogation, arrest, or other legal process based on an allegation that is commenced with the purpose not of proving that allegation but of discovering yet-unknown evidence that would support further allegations. A fishing expedition is not inherently unethical, as long as the initial allegation is supported by sufficient evidence and the initial legal process is itself valid.

**highly migratory fish (highly migratory stocks of fish)**    Fish that cover vast areas of the sea. Highly migratory fish are fish that travel great distances in the sea. Tuna, mackerel, sailfish, swordfish, dolphin, sauries, and ocean sharks are listed as highly migratory fish. Cetaceans, though mammals, are subject to similar regulation under the law of the sea.

**fishing or hunt or fish**    *See:* hunting (fishing or hunt or fish).

**fitness (unfit)**    Suitable, worthy, or prepared for some task. Fitness is a measure of the appropriateness of a person, entity, or procedure in performing any role or task. Thus, a person is fit for given employment when that person has the skills and manner required to perform the job, such as a person qualified as a teacher or fit to teach. Similarly, a person is a fit parent when the person has the skills, will, and resources to provide the support the child requires. Someone fit to stand trial is both mentally and physically capable of participating in the trial and aiding in the defense.

Anything or anyone unfit either lacks an essential aspect of fitness or has some condition that bars fitness, such as a food unfit for human consumption, or an apartment that is unfit for human habitation.

*See also:* bar, admission to the bar, character and fitness; parent, fitness of parent (parental fitness).

**fitness of parent**    *See:* parent, fitness of parent (parental fitness).

**fixed fee**    *See:* fee, fee for services, attorney's fee, fixed fee.

**fixed-price contract**    A contract establishing the amount of compensation in advance of, and in case of, breach.

**fixture**    Personal property that is regarded as part of the land. A fixture is a chattel that has been so annexed to the land that it is regarded as part of the land and belongs to the person owning the land. If an object is attached to the land, is of such a nature that it is treated as an aspect of the land, and was intended to be an element of the land, it is a fixture. When land is sold, fixtures on it are presumed to be transferred with the land unless they are specifically reserved. Likewise, when land is surrendered by a tenant to a landlord, any fixtures installed by the tenant may be removed, and any damage done by the removal should be repaired, or the fixtures may be abandoned with the return of the property.

**trade fixture** Objects used in business that are attached to realty. A trade fixture is any fixture that is affixed to the premises of real property but that is done so only for a purpose related to the the the performance of some business or trade. A trade fixture need not be a machine, specialized tool, or furnishing unique to the trade or business, though such specialized fixtures are presumptively trade fixtures unless the user is not engaged in their related trades. Although fixtures generally are surrendered to the landlord at the termination of the lease, the terms of many leases allow the tenant to remove trade fixtures, which remain the property of the tenant rather than become party of the landlord's reversion.

**fka or fka or f/k/a** *See:* formerly known as (FKA or fka or f/k/a).

**flag (ensign)** A symbol as of cloth, particularly the symbol of a nation or institution. A flag is a large cloth symbol, usually displayed or waved from a pole or rope, or the depiction based on such a symbol. A flag is commonly used to identify an institution, such as a nation, state, or military unit, although a flag may symbolize anything.

To flag, generally, is either to identify something according to a flag, as when a vessel is flagged and so identified with the nation under which it is registered, or to attract the attention of others as if one waves a flag. To flag has other meanings less germane to law, not the least being to droop as does a flag without wind.

**flag of convenience** *See:* vessel, flag vessel, flag of convenience.

**flag state** *See:* state, flag state.

**flag state or flag ship** *See:* vessel, flag vessel (flag state or flag ship).

**flag vessel** *See:* vessel, flag vessel, flag of convenience; vessel, flag vessel (flag state or flag ship).

**flag desecration (flag burning)** The misuse or destruction of a flag. Flag desecration is the misuse or destruction of a flag. In the United States, flag desecration, or flag burning, refers to the desecrating or burning of the flag of the United States or other nation as a statement intended to protest or shock. Though such acts are intended to provoke outrage, the Supreme Court of the United States ruled in Texas v. Johnson, 491 U.S. 397 (1989), that flag burning is a protected form of speech under the First Amendment. Laws that prohibit disrespect or contempt for the flag of the United States, a state of the union, or a foreign state may be unconstitutional, either as a prior restraint of speech or for vagueness in violation of due process of law.

**Flag of the United States of America** The standard of the United States of America. The Flag of the United States of America consists of thirteen horizontal stripes, alternating in red and white, and a canton of blue containing fifty white stars, one for each state, aligned in proportional, horizontal rows. The designer of the flag is unknown and is perhaps attributable to Betsy Ross or Francis Hopkinson, but the basic design was adopted by the Continental Congress in the Flag Act of 1777. Although the Flag's dimensions and appearance have been altered by amendment and executive order since 1777, especially to increase the number and specify the pattern of stars with the addition of new states, the basic structure of the Flag has remained constant since 1818, when the number of stripes was fixed at thirteen. Federal law provides the manner in which the Flag should be displayed and maintained.

**flagrante delicto (in flagrante delicto or red handed)** Being caught in the commission of a wrongful act. In flagrante delicto is Latin for "in the heat of the crime," and describes catching a person in the act of doing some wrong. It is synonymous with the phrase "being caught red-handed."

*See also:* crime; prima, prima facie, prima facie case.

**flammable substance** *See:* hazard, hazardous substance, flammable substance (inflammable substance or combustible material).

**flat tax** *See:* tax, tax rate, flat tax.

**floatables** *See:* sewerage, floatable (floatables).

**floating rate** *See:* rate, interest rate, floating rate (adjustable rate or variable rate).

**floating zone** *See:* zoning, floating zone.

**floor amendment** *See:* legislation, amendment from the floor (floor amendment).

**flotsam** *See:* salvage, flotsam.

**FMV** *See:* value, market value, fair market value (FMV).

**focal species** *See:* species, focal species.

**foeticide** *See:* fetus, feticide (foeticide).

**foetus or unborn child** *See:* fetus (fetal, foetus or unborn child).

**following pages** *See:* citation, citation signal, following pages (FF. or et seq.).

**food (food product)** Anything eaten or absorbed for nutrition. Food includes any substance that is eaten or absorbed by a plant or animal as a source of nutrients for the functions of life. As a matter of regulation, food is usually divided into food for humans and food for all other animals. Plant food is usually distinctly labeled and regulated.

**food adulteration**   *See:* adulteration, food adulteration (adulterated food or impure food or unwholesome food).

**food libel**   *See:* libel, food libel.

**food recall or product recall**   *See:* recall, recall of product (food recall or product recall).

**food law**   The law affecting food. Food law includes statutes, regulations, treaties, and caselaw that affect the materials and substances that are used in the agricultural production, harvesting, transportation, processing, packaging, labelling, storage, use, and waste of food, and to all measures which may have a direct or indirect impact on food safety.

**organic food**   Food grown without chemicals or hormones. Organic food is a category of standards and designations of food that is derived from animals and plants cultivated without most pesticides or chemical inputs and without certain genetic or hormonal treatments or modifications, and, sometimes, without certain forms of processing or refinement. The use of organic as a label for food is subject to a variety of standards according to the type of food.

**footnote**   A note to a text at the bottom of a page. A footnote is an annotation to a text at the bottom of its page. Footnotes may be used for many purposes, primarily in legal drafting being used for citation to authority from which the text is derived but also being used to illuminate, extend, or criticize the point being made in the text near the note or to locate that point in the existing literature, even when that literature was not directly a source for the point being made. Footnotes are usually preferred by Western readers to endnotes or marginal notes. There is a dangerous propensity of academic legal editors to require more footnotes than the reader can possibly tolerate, but used well, footnotes are an elegant assistance to the reader.

*See also:* note, footnote; scrutiny, standards of scrutiny, strict scrutiny, footnote four (footnote four or the footnote); endnote; margin, marginal note (note in the margin).

**footnote four or the footnote**   *See:* scrutiny, standards of scrutiny, strict scrutiny, footnote four (footnote four or the footnote).

**forbearance**   A delay by which a creditor waits for payment after it is due. A forbearance, in general, is any refusal to do what one otherwise has a right to do. As to debts, a forebearance is a formal delay by a creditor in the collection of a debt owed by a debtor, which once made by the creditor is enforceable by the debtor. The creditor may not attempt to collect the debt during a period of forbearance, although the creditor may charge and collect interest that accumulates during that period.

**forbidden inference**   *See:* inference, forbidden inference.

**force (forcible)**   Physical strength or violence. In physics, force is power in motion. In law, force refers to physical strength or violence, whether caused by weapons, machines, or the use of the human body. A person may use whatever force is reasonably necessary for self defense or the defense of others, but most jurisdictions prohibit the use of deadly force to protect mere property. Likewise, police officers are authorized to use reasonable force to achieve the lawful goals of law enforcement. A law that forbids the use of force in some situation, as in the recruitment of or discouragement from joining a labor union, may imply a prohibition on the threat of force to achieve the same ends. The use and threat of force are inherently coercive, and a contract or other private interest procured by force or by threat of force are inherently voidable after the fact by the victim.

The use of force is a defining element of some crimes, such as battery, and the threat of force may be a defining element of some crimes, such as second–degree robbery.

**force and effect**   *See:* effect, force and effect.

**force of law**   *See:* law, force of law.

**force-majeure clause**   *See:* risk, force–majeure clause.

**forced heir**   *See:* heir, forced heir (statutory heir).

**forced labor**   *See:* slavery, forced labor.

**forcible entry**   *See:* entry, forcible entry.

**deadly force**   Force that is likely to cause death. Deadly force is force of a type and magnitude that is likely to cause death or serious bodily harm. Private citizens may use deadly force to defend themselves or others when they reasonably believe themselves or the people they are protecting to be in danger of serious bodily harm or death. Outside of the home, private citizens may use deadly force absent a reasonably safe avenue of retreat. Police officers are usually restricted in their use of deadly force to similar circumstances, owing to constitutional interests that prevent the taking of life without due process of law.

*use of to make arrest*   A police officer may use deadly force to stop or apprehend a suspect, but only if the officer has probable cause to believe and does in good faith believe that the suspect poses an imminent threat of serious bodily harm to the officer or others. Officers may not use deadly force to apprehend nonviolent suspects.

**excessive force**   Much more force than is required to achieve a lawful goal. Excessive force is the use of an objectively unreasonable level of force or violence to perform a lawful act or achieve a lawful goal. This standard may vary somewhat when the force is applied by a private person with less training than a public officer, but the standard is effectively the same. The use of force, particularly deadly force, is limited to situations of self–defense, rescue, and the protection of the public from danger. The use of force in a manner that objectively exceeds what is reasonably required to achieve these goals exceeds the scope of the privilege to use force. When excessive force is used by public officials, especially the police, that use violates the Fourth Amendment of the U.S. Constitution. Note, however, that an overwhelming threat of force need not be excessive force, if the threat is used to diminish the likelihood of resistance to lawful authority (and so make less likely the use of force itself) and if the force actually employed is carefully measured in its use so as to be reasonably proportionate to the actual threat.

*See also:* force (forcible); police, police brutality.

**force majeure** An act of God. Force majeure, French for greater force, describes any event that is unexpected by all parties, not caused by any party, and affects the relationship between them, limits the ability of either to perform a duty, or requires one to intrude on a privilege of the other. Contracting parties may use a "force majeure clause" to indicate that a party owes no liability to the other in the event force majeure makes performance impossible. Force majeure may require acts of necessity to save lives or property. In most contexts, an act of God is also force majeure, although force majeure includes not only natural events but also acts by a human agency, such as war or labor unrest, that are usually not within the scope of acts of God.

*See also:* God, act of God (act of nature or actus dei or or casus fortuitus or force of nature or fortuitous event); vis, vis major; illegality, supervening illegality.

**foreclosure** A proceeding by a creditor to take title of property that secures a debt. A foreclosure is a judicial proceeding in which a mortgagee (the creditor) gains a court-ordered judgment terminating the mortgagor's (the lender's) possession of the property subject to a debt, usually a mortgage, and by which the mortgagor's equitable right of redemption to the property is barred or foreclosed forever. Foreclosure occurs when the mortgagee seeks it after the mortgagor defaults by not making the required payments against the debt secured by the mortgage on the land. Foreclosure terminates the mortgagor's ownership and transfers it to the mortgagee, although the mortgagee must either sell the property or deduct the value of the property from the outstanding debt, tendering to the mortgagor the remainder of any value of the property in excess of the amount of the debt and expenses.

*See also:* mortgage; sheriff, sheriff's sale (foreclosure sale or courthouse auction).

**foreclosure sale or courthouse auction** *See:* sheriff, sheriff's sale (foreclosure sale or courthouse auction).

**equitable foreclosure** A foreclosure in which the mortgagor retains possession until the sale of the property. An equitable foreclosure is the modern day proceeding in which a mortgagee obtains a court-ordered judgment to terminate the right of redemption in a property on which a mortgagor has failed to make payments. The property is then sold through a proceeding so as to satisfy the mortgagor's debt against the mortgagee. This is a change from the traditional foreclosure process, in which the mortgagee would simply take possession of the property after the mortgagor had defaulted, and the mortgagor might have to seek relief in equity for the return of any equity of redemption retained by the mortgagee.

**judicial foreclosure** Proceeding for foreclosure heard and approved in court. Judicial foreclosure is a process for the foreclosure of property securing a debt that has entered default, in which the lender determines all parties with an interest in the property and files a pleading in court seeking a foreclosure and lis pendens with service to all parties, after which the court hears the motion, and, if it determines that there is a valid debt that is in default entitling the lender to foreclose, grants the lender a judgment ordering foreclosure and sale, after which there is a possibility of the creditor's redemption and a further hearing to determine whether a deficiency judgment is required. This process is required in some jurisdictions whether property is held subject to mortgage or to a deed of trust, though in others it may be side-stepped by non-judicial foreclosure on a deed of trust or by other non-judicial means to avoid the strict process of foreclosure.

**non-judicial foreclosure (nonjudicial foreclosure)** A trustee's direct sale of mortgaged property. Non-judicial foreclosure is the most common process for the foreclosure of mortgaged land in the contemporary United States, because it is the process mortgagors (borrowers) agree to in the granting of a deed of trust to the mortgagee (lender). That is to say that in most jurisdictions, few borrowers provide a traditional mortgage interest to a lender to secure their loan, but rather that the lender more often takes a deed of trust, which incorporates terms for non-judicial foreclosure less burdensome on the creditor than the process of foreclosure on a traditional mortgage. In the event of a default, the mortgagee already holds the property under the deed of trust and enters the land according to its terms without resorting to a foreclosure action and sheriff's sale. The property on which the underlying loan is made is then sold by the trustee, and any value realized by the sale that is greater than the outstanding loan balance and expenses of the non-judicial foreclosure and sale is returned to the borrower.

*See also:* mortgage, deed of trust; mortgage | deed of trust.

**foreigner (foreign)** A person or thing from a foreign country. Foreign, generally, means strange or unusual. Anything or anyone foreign is from a foreign place, either a foreign state or country. Thus, a person or thing that is carried from its native state or country to another becomes foreign. Foreign goods are imports. Foreign persons are aliens. In practice, foreign within the United States refers to both international and out-of-state acts or parties.

**foreign administrator** *See:* administrator, administrator of estate, foreign administrator.

**foreign arbitral award**   *See:* arbitration, arbitral award, foreign arbitral award.

**Foreign Commerce Clause**   *See:* constitution, U.S. Constitution, clauses, Commerce Clause, Foreign Commerce Clause.

**foreign corporation**   *See:* corporation, corporations, foreign corporation (alien corporation).

**Foreign Corrupt Practices Act**   *See:* corruption, Foreign Corrupt Practices Act (FCPA).

**foreign defamation judgment**   *See:* defamation, foreign defamation judgment.

**Foreign Emoluments Clause**   *See:* constitution, U.S. Constitution, clauses, Emoluments Clause (Foreign Emoluments Clause).

**Foreign Gifts and Titles Clause**   *See:* constitution, U.S. Constitution, clauses, Foreign Gifts Clause (Foreign Gifts and Titles Clause).

**Foreign Gifts Clause**   *See:* constitution, U.S. Constitution, clauses, Foreign Gifts Clause (Foreign Gifts and Titles Clause).

**foreign intelligence surveillance court**   *See:* court, court of limited jurisdiction, foreign intelligence surveillance court (F.I.S.A. court or FISA court).

**foreign sovereign immunity**   *See:* immunity, sovereign immunity, foreign sovereign immunity.

**foreman**   *See:* jury, foreperson (foreman).

**forensics (forensic science)**   The scientific analysis of physical evidence. Forensics is the analysis of evidence in a court of law, and forensic science is the use of scientific analysis to evaluate physical evidence that may be used in a judicial proceeding. Forensic science is most often associated with criminal investigations to determine the conditions of a crime scene or the evaluation of other physical evidence to compare identifying evidence with materials or individual people. Popular crime and punishment TV shows have increased public interest in forensic science, leading to an increase in both general awareness of and expectations that forensic evidence will be collected and used in courts.
*See also:* laboratory, crime laboratory (forensics lab or crime lab or police lab or police crime lab).

**forensics lab or crime lab or police lab or police crime lab**   *See:* laboratory, crime laboratory (forensics lab or crime lab or police lab or police crime lab).

**CSI effect (CSI syndrome)**   Unreasonable or high juror expectations for forensic evidence. The CSI effect is a belief by jurors and the public that evidence from forensic collection and analysis is, or should be, reliable and comprehensive. The effect arises from television series that depict intensive investigations of crimes using comprehensive forensic evaluations, particularly CSI: Crime Scene Investigation, which began broadcasting in the year 2000. As of 2011, the CSI effect was not yet well studied or documented and concern for the influence it may exert on jurors varies, ranging from unrealistic expectations by jurors regarding the effectiveness of forensic evidence to a potential for over-reliance on such evidence when it is presented. At its extreme, such concern arises from a fear that jurors will expect scientific evidence, such as DNA evidence, in a case in which it is irrelevant or unneeded and consider the absence of such evidence as somehow meaningful.

**foreperson**   *See:* jury, foreperson (foreman).

**foreseeability (foreseeable)**   The likelihood of anticipating a future harm from a present danger. Forseeability is the degree to which a risk of some harm was likely to be known in advance of the harm being realized in fact. Foreseeability is also the extent to which a reasonable person of ordinary intelligence would have perceived at a relevant time before a harm occurs from some condition that a particular risk of that particular harm did indeed exist. In other words, a reasonable person in the same situation would have anticipated the harm would occur. Although the courts routinely inquire after a harm whether the danger that caused the harm was foreseeable, the inquiry should not be one of hindsight but should be whether a person in the situation in which the harm might have been avoided would reasonably have been likely to ascertain the dangers then posed by the circumstances.
*See also:* damages, classes of damages, consequential damages.

**foreseeable damages**   *See:* damages, contract damages, foreseeable damages, Hadley v. Baxendale rule; damages, contract damages, foreseeable damages.

**Palsgraf rule**   Liability in negligence arises from the foreseeability of harm. The Palsgraf rule grounds liability for negligent acts not on the defendant's creation of the proximate cause of the plaintiff's injury but on the foreseeability of the injury to the plaintiff by someone in the defendant's position, such that if the defendant should reasonably have foreseen that injury would result from the action then the defendant was negligent in committing the action.
The rule arises from Judge Benjamin Cardozo's opinion in Palsgraf v. Long Island Railroad Co., 162 N.E. 99 (N.Y. 1928), in which the railroad guards jostled Mrs. Helen Palsgraff when helping her board the train, as a result of which she dropped a package she held, which contained fireworks that ignited when they hit the rail, leading to the falling of a railroad scale, which injured Mrs. Palsgraff. Cardozo rejected the proximate cause analysis of the dissent in the case and found the injury unforeseeable by the railroad's guards, overturning a jury award in Mrs. Palsgraff's favor.

**unforeseeability (unforseen)**   A very low likelihood of anticipating a future harm from a present danger. Unforeseeability is a condition in which a reasonable observer in a given situation would be unlikely to anticipate a particular outcome in that situation or a particular consequence or result from an apparent cause. Usually, a person is not responsible for unforeseen consequences of that person's actions, unless the consequence was reasonably foreseeable, or unless the person has a heightened duty or standard of care, according to which the consequence would be foreseeable. Thus, a layperson might reasonably not foresee a danger in the construction or maintenance of a bridge, even if an engineer would be reasonably expected to do so.

*See also:* foreseeability (foreseeable).

**foreshore or littoral rights or litorral interests**
*See:* shore, littoral area (foreshore or littoral rights or litorral interests).

**forfeiture**   The loss of a right owing to wrongdoing or a breach of a public or private duty. A forfeiture is the loss, with no compensation, of interests in property or some other right, occurring as punishment for an illegal act or as a consequence of the default of an obligation. The kind of obligation could be a general obligation, such as a duty in tort, an obligation arising under contract, or an obligation arising under special rules of law, for example, the rules of civil procedure. A forfeiture is limited to a loss of rights held by the forfeiting party and may not include the demand of an affirmative duty such as the payment of a fine or damages nor the loss of the rights of a party not in default or subject to punishment.

A forfeiture may be criminal or civil. A criminal forfeiture occurs in conjunction with a criminal conviction and is an element of the criminal sentence or ancillary to a criminal judgment. A civil forfeiture may be effected, regardless of any criminal conviction, if there is sufficient evidence that the crime occurred and a claim may be made either against the property itself or the forfeiting party for assets acquired or maintained through the conduct giving rise to the forfeiture.

*See also:* deodand.

**forfeiture by wrongdoing**   *See:* hearsay, hearsay exception, exception only when declarant is unavailable, forfeiture by wrongdoing.

**civil forfeiture**   An in rem action by the government to seize the tools or proceeds of a crime. Civil forfeiture describes a variety of federal and state proceedings, usually judicial but sometimes administrative, for the seizure of assets that have been used to commit a crime or are proceeds from criminal activity. Unlike criminal proceedings, these actions are brought against the objects, usually without any regard to whether the present owner is guilty of a crime. Federal forfeiture laws, however, allow an innocent owner to offer a defense to such actions. The burden of proof in a civil forfeiture rests on the government, although an innocent owner must prove that the owner is indeed innocent by a preponderance of the evidence.

**double jeopardy**   Civil forfeitures under federal law are considered to be private causes of action brought by the government and not a penalty affecting due process or double jeopardy. See Hudson v. United States, 522 U.S. 93, 98–100 (1997). Even so, under some state constitutions, civil forfeiture is considered a penalty for the purpose of double jeopardy. See, e.g., N.M. v. Nunez, 129 N.M. 63, 2 P.3d 264 (1999).

**innocent owner**   An owner of property used in a crime or acquired from its proceeds but not liable for its forfeiture. An innocent owner owns property that has been sought in civil forfeiture but has a defense because the owner either did not know of the conduct giving rise to the forfeiture or, upon learning of the conduct giving rise to the forfeiture, did all that reasonably could be expected under the circumstances to end the use of the property in a manner related to the forfeitable conduct.

**criminal forfeiture**   The seizure of assets employed in or acquired by criminal activity as part of a criminal judgment. Criminal forfeiture is an in personam procedure commenced by a government that adjudges property held by a person accused of a crime, to have been used in a crime, or to be acquired from proceeds of the crime. Although the forfeiture requires proof of the relationship of the assets to a criminal act by the owner, it does not require conviction of the owner. A successful forfeiture results in the government that brought the action being awarded title and possession of the property sought, which the government may allocate to specific agencies for use or for sale.

**forgery**   A fraudulent making of a writing. A forgery is any fraudulent making of a writing or portion of a writing or electronic writing in order to interfere with another person's right in the writing or in order to cause another person to rely on the writing as if it were genuine. A common example of a forgery is the re-creation of a signature of another person to create the appearance or impression that the other person has given consent to a particular action or authorized a given instrument. Indeed, procuring a person's actual signature by fraud is the fraudulent creation of a writing and amounts, also, to forgery. Forgeries that are sufficiently proven can negate a contract, a will, or an instrument filed in court, and the person who commits a forgery commits a crime, which is usually a felony.

*See also:* factum (fraud in the factum).

**legal efficacy**   Appearance sufficient to give a genuine instrument legal effect. Legal efficacy is a test of liability for the forgery of an instrument, such that the forger is liable for the crime of forgery only if the unauthorized writing, if it were genuine, would make the instrument valid. Thus, the false instrument is efficacious unless its invalidity is discovered.

**form**   A rubric copied repeatedly to create a legal document or pleading. A form is a model of the language to be used generally for a particular legal matter, whether it is a contract, a will, a pleading, a motion, or any other instrument. The use of forms has served to ease the drafting process, especially for new lawyers, and help create consistent drafting standards for many legal documents, to the point where many state bars create "form books" that consist of many standard forms for common drafting tasks within the legal profession. The specific details of a given transaction or situation are written into the appropriate gaps in language, and any language that is inappropriate to a given situation is omitted and any additional language required in the case is inserted before the instrument is made final for ratification, signature, transmittal, or filing. Some forms are pre–printed or, now, electronically managed, but the concept of the form includes all sorts of pre–existing component language assembled into a new legal instrument.

The form, therefore, when juxtaposed to substance, is the particular language with which a pleading, contract, or instrument is made, as opposed to its purpose, intent, and the essence of its factual and legal claims.

**form contract** *See:* contract, contract formation, form contract, boilerplate contract | unconscionability; contract, contract formation, form contract, boilerplate contract; contract, contract formation, form contract.

**form I-9** *See:* immigration, immigration form, form I–9 (I–9 form).

**form of action** *See:* action, form of action.

**blank** A space in a document or form for the later insertion of information. A blank is a place in a text for the addition of details specific to the use of the text for a particular purpose, such as the places for the entry of the particulars regarding the parties or their claims in a form pleading. The blank may be a line, box, space between words or punctuation, or other place on a page or text, or it may be a data entry space or field for a database or other electronic record. In either case, the blank is at one time created by a person or entity who drafts or modifies a text to make it usable for more than one use, and when the text is later copied for a specific use, the form is completed by the insertion of the specific details into the blank.

As a matter of copyright, under the blank forms rule, a text or form that is composed of blanks is not subject to copyright, unless copyrightable text is sufficiently integrated into the text or form to have an explanatory value.

**formal abandonment** *See:* patent, abandonment of a patent, express abandonment (formal abandonment).

**formal rulemaking** *See:* rulemaking, formal rulemaking.

**formalist** *See:* jurisprudence, legal formalism (formalist).

**former jeopardy** *See:* jeopardy, double jeopardy, former jeopardy.

**former testimony** *See:* hearsay, hearsay exception, exception only when declarant is unavailable, former testimony.

**formerly known as (f.k.a. or fka or f/k/a)** The designation of the previous name for a person or entity. "Formerly known as" is a predicate to a person or entity's now–obsolete name, when the present name is changed or is unknown. The abbreviation f/k/a is common in pleadings, especially to give notice of a prior name for individuals or corporations that have adopted a new name.

**fornication** Extramarital sex. Fornication is the crime sexual intercourse with a person who is not one's spouse. Although the offense has been repealed by statute in many jurisdictions, it persists as an offense in many parts of the United States, although its definition is often limited only to behavior that is open and notorious, which is not to say the acts of the participants must be done in public but that they must be known of in the community, usually meaning the participants are living together. Prosecution for fornication with no other charge is rare, but it is not uncommon to tack on a charge of fornication with other charges. A prosecution for fornication that is not part of a commercial transaction or an act of prostitution between consenting adults in private is almost surely in violation of the contemporary standards of constitutional privacy.

*See also:* sex, sexual act (sexual conduct or sex act).

**forthcoming bond** *See:* bond, forthcoming bond (delivery bond or discharging bond or dissolution bond).

**forum** The jurisdiction and institution in which a dispute is heard. The forum is both the jurisdiction and the court or other tribunal in which a dispute may be heard. To designate a forum to hear a dispute is to designate a particular body that will hear the dispute, or any dispute that might arise, but the designation also creates a presumption that the dispute will be determined by the law or rules that are routinely applied in that forum. Broadly, the concept of forum includes both specific jurisdictions and courts as well as panels that might be called by an arbitral association or body.

Forum also depicts any place in which public speech occurs, which is or may be of special interest in determining whether laws violate the freedom of speech, several forms of which are examined in greater detail in the entry under speech.

*See also:* speech, freedom of speech, forum, public forum, limited public forum; speech, freedom of speech, forum, public forum, designated public forum; speech, freedom of speech, forum, public forum (traditional public forum); speech, freedom of speech, forum, non-public forum (nonpublic forum); situs; speech, feedom of speech, forum.

*venue and forum* Although many use the terms venue and forum interchangeably to describe a proper location within a jurisdiction to hear a case, the terms have different meanings. A forum is a court or the jurisdiction of a court, while the venue is the geographical location within the forum where the court physically sits.

**forum non conveniens** *See:* jurisdiction, forum non conveniens (transfer to a more convenient forum).

**forum conveniens** A convenient forum. The forum conveniens is either the only court having jurisdiction over a matter or the court least burdensome to the parties from among several eligible courts to hear an action. By definition, a court that rightly hears an action is a forum conveniens.

**forum selection clause** A contract clause that specifies the forum in which potential claims are to be adjudicated. A forum selection clause is a provision in a contract by which the parties agree that any disputes that arise between them related to the contract must be litigated in a particular forum, according to the convenience of one or both parties. In a manner similar to a choice of law clause, identification of a particular forum may serve the value of predictability by clarifying sophisticated parties' common understanding of the convenience, or inconvenience, they can expect if they pursue the litigation. If there is no other choice of law clause, a forum selection clause may also serve as evidence that the parties intended the agreement to be governed by the law of the forum selected. Forum selection clauses are not inherently enforceable, and if the clause is adhesive, particularly if it is not fully disclosed to a party who lacks the sophistication or power to negotiate the clause, a court may find the clause unenforceable.

**prorogation clause (prorogated jurisdiction)** A forum selection clause applied in another court. A prorogation clause is a forum selection clause as seen through the lens of another forum. The term comes from Scots law and allows contracting parties to select a forum that is not unreasonable for either party and to designate it as the forum for any disputes arising from the contract. If a party brings suit on the contract in another forum, as to that forum, the enforcement of the forum selection clause requires dismissal, or deferral (the effect of either being really to postpone the dispute). Thus, the court that gives effect to the clause does so by dismissing it from its docket, which — presuming the dispute is brought in the selected forum — only prorogues the dispute rather than finally dismissing it.

**forum shopping** Selection among several jurisdictions of the most favorable to a party. Forum shopping is the practice by both plaintiffs and defendants of seeking to bring a claim or transfer an action to the forum the litigant believes is the most likely to favor its own argument. Such favoritism might be perceived because of objective differences in the law of the forum, such as a longer or shorter period of limitations or more or less favorable rules governing the plaintiff's standing. It might also arise from the attorneys' perception of hostility or favoritism toward a type of claim or party by the bench or the jury pool in a given forum.

Forum shopping is only possible among jurisdictions in which the shopping party can establish jurisdiction over the other party. A plaintiff shops to file a complaint for a forum among the venues in which the plaintiff may establish personal and subject-matter jurisdiction over the defendant. A defendant shops to remove, transfer, or file a new action against a plaintiff in a jurisdiction in which the defendant may establish personal and subject-matter jurisdiction over the plaintiff. Despite the potential for a defendant to forum shop, however, the law presumes the right of a plaintiff to bring a cause in the forum of the plaintiff's choosing, and the defendant may usually only select a forum by a pre-emptive filing of an action, such as a declaratory judgment action, or by remand or transfer of an action under circumstances allowing such transitions under the rules, or by opening a second action under circumstances that would not require the second action's dismissal.

**neutral forum** A forum that has no advantage for any party to a dispute. A neutral forum offers no advantage or convenience to one party or another in a dispute, nor is it believed in good faith to benefit any party to a forum selection contract clause that is intended to provide a neutral forum in the event of a dispute.

**forward contract** *See:* contract, specific contracts, forward contract (spot contract).

**foster** To encourage. To foster is to support, nurture, and encourage something or someone.

**foster child** *See:* child, foster child.

**foster parent** *See:* parent, foster parent.

**foster care (foster family or foster placement)** Court-ordered care for a child outside of the family home. Foster care is the long-term, court-ordered supervision of a minor by public authorities, whether in a public institution or under the supervision of a private citizen as a foster parent. If a court determines that the best interests of the minor so require, the court may rule that state or county social services take custody of the child from the parents, parent with custody, or guardian, and transfer the minor to a facility operated by the state or county. The minor remains in the custody of the state until the minor may be placed in a licensed private home, until the minor is emancipated, or until the custody of the parent or guardian is restored by court order.

**found property** *See:* property, found property (finds or law of finds or law of finders).

**foundation (lay a foundation or laying a foundation or foundation for evidence)** To establish facts essential to the admission of specific evidence. The foundation of a legal argument is evidence or argument that establishes a point necessary in order to achieve something else. In contemporary usage, a foundation is usually an evidentiary showing required before introducing certain evidence that would otherwise be inadmissible, such as evidence introduced solely to impeach a witness. More generally (though less common now), a lawyer must lay a foundation to prove that any relief is justified in the case of a motion, order, or judgment, and particularly in an ex parte action.

**four corners rule**   *See:* contract, contract interpretation, four corners rule.

**Four Horsemen**   *See:* court, U.S. court, U.S. Supreme Court, Four Horsemen.

**four unities**   *See:* tenancy, co-tenancy, joint tenancy, unities, four unities (TITS).

**four-factor test**   *See:* commerce, regulation of commerce, interstate commerce, dormant commerce power, complete auto test (four-factor test).

**fraction (fractional)**   A portion, or anything less than a whole unit. A fraction is a part of anything, whether it is a share in ownership of a whole thing or a portion of a thing that is subdivided. A fraction may be any portion of the unit, including an undesignated percentage. A share of stock, ownership in land, ownership of rights in land such as mineral rights, and other things may be owned by each of several people as a fractional interest, either as co-owners (as in the tenancy in common) or as owners of a portion segregated from the unit (as in the fractional share of stock).
*See also:* share, share as stock, fractional share.

**fractional share**   *See:* share, share as stock, fractional share.

**framers**   *See:* constitution, U.S. Constitution, framers | signers (signatories); constitution, U.S. Constitution, framers.

**framers' intent**   *See:* constitution, U.S. Constitution, intent of the framers (framers' intent).

**France**

**Code Napoleon (C.N. or CN or Napoleonic Code)**   The code of France of 1804. The Code Napoléon, or more properly, the Code Civil des Français, organized French customary law into three categories echoing Roman law: status of the person, property, and the acquisition of property. The code was very influential in Louisiana, and its influence can still be discerned in much of the Louisiana Code.

**franchise (affranchise or enfranchisement or disenfranchisement)**   To be free, or to be freed. Enfranchisement is the entry of an individual as a full member in political society, the hallmark of which in the United States is the right to vote in elections for public office. Disenfranchisement means to be banished or stripped of such membership and, in the U.S., to lose one's right to vote. In the corporate setting, enfranchisement means to be given voting rights.

**business franchise (franchise agreement)**   A license to engage in business under the trademark or name of the grantor. A franchise is a license granted by the owner of a trademark or tradename to another to engage in business in a certain area under the franchisor's name or employing the franchisor's products, according to which the franchisor may exert a significant degree of control or influence over the franchisee's method of operation, and for which the franchisee pays a fee to the franchisor. Many businesses are arranged as franchises, common examples being fast food restaurants like McDonald's and Subway.

**elective franchise**   The right to vote. Franchise means the right to vote, usually in the context of elections to public office, though it may also be in the context of other elections, including the right to vote in a private association, as a shareholder or a director of a corporation, or as a member of a public body, such as a legislature or commission.

**frank (congressional frank or frank privilege)**   Free services, especially free passage, postage, or rent. Frank generally signifies something unburdened, candid, or free from restraint or cost. In law, it now usually refers to a privilege to do something without a fee, such as to ride on a railroad or, in the case of members of Congress, to send mail at the public's expense.

**frankalmoign**   *See:* tenure, feudal tenure, frankalmoign (religious tenure).

**franklin**   *See:* freeholder (franklin).

**fratricide**   *See:* homicide, parricide, fratricide.

**fraud (fraudulent or defraud)**   A trick to induce another to act to the other's harm for one's own benefit. Fraud includes any act intended to deceive another person or to encourage the other person to do anything that the actor believes will be to the other's harm but to the benefit of the actor or a third party. Fraud encompasses a wide range of conduct that conceals the true facts of a situation or creates a false impression upon which the actor seeks a victim to rely to the victim's harm. The two broad forms of fraud are the knowing misrepresentation of facts and the intentional concealment of a material fact in order to create a false impression, either done with the intent to induce another person to rely on the facts or impression to the harm of the other person and the advantage of the actor or a confederate of the actor.

Actual fraud occurs when the actor makes an affirmative statement of misrepresentation or does anything that is an act of deception. Constructive fraud occurs when the actor merely conceals a fact or is silent regarding it when the actor knows the victim is preparing to act to the victim's detriment while relying on the actor's silence. Both forms of fraud are criminal and sufficient to void a contract, although proof of intent to harm, or at least cause a loss to, the defendant is essential under either form. Another alternative for the victim is seek restitution or bring an action in tort.

Not every falsehood, however, is fraud, even when a falsehood made by a speaker who intends the hearer to rely upon it. A statement that is too outlandish to be reasonably believed, one that requires illegal conduct in order to rely upon it, or one that is too general to be the basis for specific reliance may not be fraudulent.

Thus, statements made in jest or as a parody that would not be the basis of any reasonable action, statements made as part of a criminal enterprise toward co-conspirators, and statements made as mere advertising puffery have been found not to be fraud as a basis for civil recovery. Further, not every omission can be fraud, and no liability can accrue when the actor has no duty to disclose or to speak and any reliance on silence by another person would be unreasonable.

**fraud in the factum**   See: factum (fraud in the factum).

**fraud in the inducement**   See: inducement, fraud in the inducement.

**fraudulent misrepresentation**   See: representation, misrepresentation, intentional misrepresentation (fraudulent misrepresentation).

**fraudulent concealment**   See: concealment, fraudulent concealment.

**fraudulent conveyance**   See: conveyance, fraudulent conveyance, uniform fraudulent conveyances act (U.F.C.A. or UFCA).

**fraudulent joinder**   See: joinder, joinder of parties, fraudulent joinder.

**actual fraud**   A fraud committed by a deliberate misstatement. Actual fraud is a false statement about a fact that the actor knows to be false or is reckless as to its falsity, made by an actor to a victim with the intent to deceive the victim and upon which the victim relies and thus suffers a harm or loss. Actual fraud is a crime, as well as a tort and a basis for compensation or restitution, rescission of a contract, and punitive damages in tort.
See also: fraud, consumer fraud.

**bait and switch**   The false advertisement of one product to elicit the purchase of another. The bait and switch is a form of false advertising in which a seller advertises an attractive product to bait a customer to come to the seller, all the while intending to substitute a less desirable product for the customer to purchase. The switched product invariably has a higher purchase price, an increased profit for the seller, or a less marketable characteristic than the product advertised. A bait and switch differs from a "loss-leader" sale, in which the seller specifically informs the customer that a limited number of units of a product are for sale at a discount. Bait and switch advertising is the basis for an action of common-law fraud, as well as for unjust enrichment and sometimes breach of contract. Many jurisdictions provide statutory remedies for loss as a result of this practice.

**check kiting (check fraud or paper hanging)**   See: kiting, check kiting (kiting checks or check fraud or paper hanging).

**confidence game (scam or swindle or swindling or con game or con artist or con man)**   A plan of activity intended to defraud a victim. A confidence game, or a swindle, is a form of fraud by which a victim is presented a false story or invented circumstance that is created to trick the victim into providing money, property, or information owned or in the possession or control of the victim to the teller of the story or a confederate. It does not matter whether the victim was a victim identified prior to the commission of the swindle or a bystander lured into it during its commission. Some confidence games follow patterns that are so recurrent that the pattern is known by a customary name. Confidence games are prosecuted under various titles in different jurisdictions, not only as fraud, swindling, theft, or theft by trick but also as specific offenses by name, such as "three card monte."
See also: racketeering (racket).

**bunco scheme (bunco man or bunco men)**   A scam to steal money from an unsuspecting target. Bunco schemes are frauds with such colorful names as the Pidgeon Drop, Bank Examiner, or the Jamaica Switch, whereby the actor uses false confidence, slight of hand, fictional stories or some combination of all of these to take money or other valuables from an unsuspecting target. Bunco schemes may be treated either as fraud or larceny by trick.

**Ponzi scheme (Ponzi game)**   Investment scheme with returns for early investors paid from later investments. A Ponzi scheme is an investment arrangement whereby returns to investors are financed through the acquisition of new investors, rather than on the success of an underlying business venture.

**constructive fraud**   An act or silence creating a false impression to another's detriment. A constructive fraud is committed when the actor has a duty toward the victim arising from their relationship that is violated when the actor either makes a deceptive statement regarding a fact or remains silent or lacks candor, creating a false impression regarding a fact material to the future conduct of the victim, the victim relies on the false impression, and the victim suffers a loss or injury to the advantage of the actor or to one whom the actor prefers or assists by the injury to the victim. Constructive fraud is both sufficient to avoid a contract and to give rise to an action for unjust enrichment, restitution, or tort. If there is evidence of criminal intent, constructive fraud is a crime.

**consumer fraud**   A deliberate misrepresentation on which a business intends for consumers to rely. Consumer fraud is a form of misrepresentation committed by a seller against a buyer or a group of buyers, to whom a business deliberately misrepresents any thing with the intent that a consumer will rely on the misrepresentation, resulting in harm or loss to at least some consumer who does so. Consumer fraud is barred by statute and, unlike common-law fraud, in most jurisdictions is complete at the time of a deliberate misrepresentation or the commission of a deceitful practice. An action for consumer fraud does not require proof of reliance on the misrepresentation by or deception of a consumer. Consumer fraud committed by a seller involved with interstate commerce is regulated by the Federal Trade Commission.

*See also:* fraud, actual fraud; security, securities, securities fraud (Rule 10b-5).

**False Claims Act (Lincoln's law)**   The prohibition of a fraudulent claim from government payment. The False Claims Act (FCA) prohibits claims against the government that are not owed in law and in fact, creating both civil and criminal liability for the claimant. The False Claims Act reaches claims arising under entitlements programs, such as Social Security and Medicaid, employment benefits, such as civil service pay and veteran's benefits, services and purchase contracts, tort claims, and property claims, or any claim for payment or for a debt that might result in payment. A claim will violate the act if it is a seemingly valid claim based on an unlawful or illegal contract, or if the claim is not accurately representative of a claim incurred in fact, as long as the claim is presented with knowledge that the claim is not in fact accurate. Amendments to the FCA in 2009 and 2010 make clear that the failure to repay an overpayment made from the U.S. government or from an agency funded by it, so that the recipient accepted or retained funds it was reckless not to know it was not entitled to receive amounts to a false claim.

The False Claims Act may be enforced by the United States through either a criminal or a civil suit. It may also be enforced by a private citizen through a qui tam action, filed initially under seal with notice to the federal government to allow the federal government to intervene in the action.

*See also:* whistleblower, qui tam (action qui tam or qui tam action).

**intent to defraud**   A person's purpose in tricking or deceiving another person. Intent to defraud is the mental state one has while acting with the intention to induce, by deceit or trickery, a victim to rely upon the deception or the trick. The act of committing a fraud is complete at the time of the trick or deceitful act or statement, whether or not the victim in fact relies upon it. Thus, not all acts that are fraudulent are criminal, and an act that amounts to fraud owing to a mistake made in good faith or that is based on a permission or license later revoked is not fraudulent as a matter of criminal law, although it may be fraud sufficient for the victim to avoid a contract or seek compensation. Evidence of good intention may be introduced by a defendant to rebut an argument by the prosecutor that a potentially fraudulent action was performed with an intent to defraud.

**mail fraud**   The use of the mail to carry out a fraudulent plan. Mail fraud includes any fraudulent scheme to defraud another of money or property by means of false or fraudulent pretenses, representations, or promises that in any manner use the mails to carry out the scheme.

**Medicare fraud (upcoding)**   Deliberately billing Medicare for services not needed or unperformed. Medicare fraud is the intentional filing of a claim for reimbursement from Medicare funds, which the filer (or the person for whom the filing is made) knows is a request for reimbursement for a procedure or treatment that was not performed, was performed below the standard for which reimbursement is requested, or was unnecessary but performed at least in part for the purpose of generating the bill for reimbursement. Medicare fraud is prosecuted as fraud, often under the wire fraud statute, 18 U.S.C. § 1343, mail fraud statute, 18 U.S.C. § 1341, or the False Claims Act, 18 U.S.C. § 287. Medicare fraud may amount to fraud or to Medicaid fraud under state law.

*See also:* fraud, mail fraud.

**Statute of Frauds**   The law requiring certain contracts to be in writing. The Statute of Frauds requires certain classes of contracts to be reflected in a writing. The particular categories vary from jurisdiction to jurisdiction but generally include a contract in which one of the parties is an executor or administrator for an absent party; a contract involving a surety, or payment of the debts of another; a contract of marriage; a contract for an interest in land; a contract for the sale or purchase of property valued at over $500; a contract for a service valued in excess of $5,000; a contract, the performance of which is contemplated to take longer than one year; and a contract involving securities. The Statute of Frauds originated in England in 1677, passed as An act for Prevention of Frauds and Perjuries, 29 Car. II., c.3, and applied only to contracts for land, marriage, or the payment of another's debts, or for a contract the performance of which would take longer than a year. The statute's name reflected its purpose, which is to avoid instances of perjury and fraudulent claims in contractual relationships.

The reliance on a signed writing as a basis for protection against fraud may be diminishin. The UNCISG, which governs most international contracts, does not rely on writings. Moreover, the manner by which fraud may be carried out differs considerably between the parchment writings of Restoration England and the age of electronic writings. Even so, the requirement is still significant in the United States.

*See also:* fraud, statute of frauds | signature requirement.

*signature requirement*   The signature requirement ensures that a writing memorializing a contract subject to the Statute of Frauds is unenforceable unless the defendant, the party to be bound, has signed the writing. For purposes of the UCC and the Statute of Frauds, a signature can be any intentional mark made or adopted by the party against whom enforcement is sought. Thus, the party or an authorized agent is considered to have signed the written document so long as the mark or symbol was made with the intent to authenticate the contract.

*See also:* fraud, statute of frauds.

**full performance doctrine**   Full performance is an exception to the Statute of Frauds. The full performance doctrine is an exception to the Statute of Frauds, which will not bar the enforcement of an unwritten contract to which it otherwise applies, if the other party has fully performed its obligations under the contract. Full performance by one party may demonstrate the existence of the contract, unless there is evidence of fraud or mistake in the performance. Full performance of material terms by both parties is sufficient to require enforcement regardless of the statute.

**partial performance doctrine (part performance doctrine)**  Part performance may bind the other party to an oral contract, despite the Statute of Frauds. The doctrine of partial performance is an exception to the Statute of Frauds, an agreement that would otherwise be subject to the statute, but no writing signed by the seller can be produced, may nevertheless be enforced if the purchaser has partly performed the agreement and the if also seller has accepted the partial performance. This exception is a form of evidence that the agreement exists that a court in equity may accept in lieu of the writing. Note: full performance and partial performance are similar as exceptions to the statute, but they differ in that partial performance is an exception only if the other party accepts the performance, while full performance is an exception once it is complete, regardless of whether the other party accepts it.

**performance in more than one year**  A promise that takes more than a year to perform is subject to the Statute of Frauds. Performance requiring more than one year is a condition according to which an agreement becomes subject to the Statute of Frauds. The contract must either be expressly agreed to require more than a year or be effectively impossible to perform in less than one year in order to be subject to the statute. A contract that might or might not be performed in that time would not ordinarily fall under the statute just because the performance ends up taking longer.

**writing (memorandum or note)**  Any writing that memorializes the contract's essential terms. A writing is anything in or on which the essential terms of a contract are written and on which the party to be bound has placed a signature. The language may be in any form, so long as there are words handwritten, printed, or typed onto any reasonably durable surface such that a record is made, and the writing is sufficient to memorialize the essential terms of the agreement, in the case of goods being the quantity, and for land, the price and address. No title or particular form is required to satisfy the writing requirement of the statute of frauds, except that the writing must be signed by the person who is to be bound to it.
See also: writing (write or written); signature.

**Freddie Mac**  See: Bank, Federal Home Loan Mortgage Corporation (Freddie Mac).

**free**

**free alongside ship**  See: shipping, shipping term, incoterm, free alongside ship (F.A.S. or FAS).

**free and common socage**  See: tenure, feudal tenure, socage, free and common socage.

**free cash flow**  See: value, free cash flow.

**Free Exercise Clause**  See: constitution, U.S. Constitution, clauses, Free Exercise Clause.

**free exercise of religion**  See: religion, freedom of religion, free exercise of religion.

**free on board**  See: shipping, shipping term, incoterm, free on board (F.O.B. or FOB).

**free passage**  See: passage, free passage (innocent passage over land).

**free rider (freeloader or freerider)**  Someone who takes advantage of the investments or efforts of others. A free rider is an expression enshrined in its metaphorical origin, the fare-skipper who rides the subway or bus without having paid the fare, thus taking advantage of the service that is paid for and supported by others. There are many forms of free riders, including both a large corporation that generates pollution that is borne by others who grow sick from their pollution and a worker whose pay rises owing to the negotiation of other workers for higher pay.
See also: externality (negative externality or positive externality).

**freedom**  The right to do what one chooses to do. Freedom, the state of being free, is the power to do what one chooses, without a master or restraints created by law. Freedom, like liberty, implies a responsibility that is a natural constraint to act with due regard of others and the good of all; freedom is not license. As freedom is usually understood today, it is synonymous with liberty, but as a matter of historical context, freedom is best understood by its most historically significant antithesis — slavery — as opposed to tyranny, which is the traditional antithesis of liberty.

**Freedom of Access to Clinic Entrances Act**  See: abortion, Freedom of Access to Clinic Entrances Act (F.A.C.E. or FACE); abortion, blockade of abortion facilities, Freedom of Access to Clinic Entrances Act.

**freedom of association**  See: constitution, U.S. Constitution, Amendment 1, freedom of association; association, freedom of association.

**freedom of expression**  See: expression, freedom of expression | flag desecration; expression, freedom of expression.

**freedom of information**  See: information, freedom of information.

**Freedom of Information Act**  See: information, Freedom of Information Act (F.O.I.A. or FOIA or foiable).

**freedom of religion**  See: religion, freedom of religion; constitution, U.S. Constitution, Amendment 1, freedom of religion.

**freedom of speech**  *See:* speech, freedom of speech (right of free speech or liberty of speech); constitution, U.S. Constitution, Amendment 1, freedom of speech.

**freedom of testation**  *See:* testation (freedom of testation).

**freedom of the press**  *See:* press, freedom of the press (liberty of the press); constitution, U.S. Constitution, Amendment 1, freedom of the press.

**freedom of the seas**  *See:* sea, law of the sea, international waters, high seas (freedom of the seas).

**freehold estate**  *See:* estate, freehold estate, non-freehold estate; estate, freehold estate.

**freeholder (franklin)**  A property ower A freeholder is a property owner. In the common law, a freeholder was a person who owned a freehold, rather than a manor (which would place one in the gentry) or a copyhold (which would tie one to the land as a peasant). The freeholder was thus a free person but not of the gentry. In the United States, the designation of freeholder became synonymous with any rights holders qualified by property ownership, including voting before the property qualification was abolished. A freeholder thus is now a property owner or, metaphorically, a citizen. Note: a franklin was another term for a common-law freeholder.
  *See also:* vote, voter (elector).

**freeze out**  *See:* shareholder, freeze out (squeeze out or squeeze-out or freeze-out ).

**freight on board**  *See:* shipping, shipping term, freight on board (F.O.B. or FOB).

## French

**Law French**  A French dialect in which English law was written until 1650. Law French is an Anglo–French Creole dialect that was used for the argument of cases; the education of young lawyers; the writing of statutes, writs, records, and law books; and the decisions of cases in England for four centuries. Adopted in English law several hundred years after the conquest, French was the language of the royal court and became a professional language used in speech and writing from the mid 1200s until the mid 1400s, its oral use becoming less common except for formal recitations of pleadings. It continued in legal writing until the seventeenth century, Sir Edward Coke's 1620 Institutes being the first major legal text in English, and the Act of 1650 requiring lawbooks and report from then on to be in English. Still, the first Law French dictionaries appeared only in 1702, and many terms still in use originate in Law French. Note, although capitalized in headings and to commence a sentence, it is probably more common to write "law French," though "Law French" is used, too.

  *See also:* jargon, legal jargon (legalese or legalism); latin, law latin.

**fresh suit**  *See:* pursuit, hot pursuit, hot pursuit (fresh suit).

**friable**  Crumbly. A friable material is one that is capable of being easily broken or crumbled into a powder. The Environmental Protection Agency has promulgated regulations that deal with friable asbestos–containing materials.

**friend of the court**  *See:* amicus curiae (friend of the court).

**fringe benefit**  *See:* employment, employee benefit plan, fringe benefit.

**frisk**  *See:* search, bodily search, frisk (pat down or pat–down search).

**frivolous appeal**  *See:* appeal, frivolous appeal.

**frivolous claim**  *See:* ethics, legal ethics, frivolous claim.

**frivolous defense**  *See:* ethics, legal ethics, frivolous defense.

**frolic**  A personal act performed by an employee on company time. A frolic is an act by an employee at a time the employee is otherwise considered to be in the scope of employment but which is itself the personal business of the employee and not related to the employee's job. To label an act a frolic suggests that the employee is not merely engaging in the minor personal business any reasonable employee might conduct briefly or necessarily throughout a day, but is engaging in longer periods of time to consume or divert additional resources of the employer for personal gain or gratification. Frolics most often occur when an employee conducts wholly personal business while in the place of employment or when an employee is absent from the place of employment during a time of employment. Injuries sustained during a frolic are outside the scope of employment, and an employer is not liable for injuries or damage caused by the employee's frolic.

**frontier**  *See:* border (frontier).

**fruit of the poisonous tree**  *See:* search, exclusionary rule, fruit of the poisonous tree.

**fruits of a crime**  *See:* crime, fruits of a crime (loot or swag or fruit of the crime).

**frustration (frustrated party)**  Interference that prevents intended conduct. Frustration is any interference with the plans of one person or entity by the conduct of another person or entity, or by circumstances beyond the control of the planner, such as bad weather or shipwreck, that prevent the planner from carrying out the plan.

**frustration of purpose**  A change of circumstance that defeats the purpose of the contract. Frustration of purpose occurs when a express or implied assumption was made by one party to a contract, and circumstances not caused by that party unexpectedly alter the assumption so that the purpose that party had in entering the contract becomes unattainable through the performance of the contract. Although a contract may specify otherwise, in the absence of a statement to the contrary, frustration of purpose is an appropriate basis for discharging further duties from all parties to the contract, although in such a situation, the party not seeking the contract to be discharged will be entitled to compensation for any losses suffered through any performance that has already been completed.

**fugitive (fugitive from the law or fugitive from justice)**  A person seeking to avoid arrest by law enforcement officials. A fugitive is a person who is wanted by law enforcement officers and who is attempting to elude capture. A fugitive under federal law is either in flight from federal custody or arrest or is a fugitive under state law who crosses state lines.

**fugitive warrant**  *See:* warrant, escape warrant (fugitive warrant).

**fugitive resources**  Resources in their natural state that may move from place to place. Fugitive resources, such as surface and groundwater, wild animals, oil and natural gas, are inherently mobile and are not subject to the dominion and individual proprietorship of any person over them. When they escape, they are restored to their wild and unowned state.

**full**

**full age**  *See:* adult, full age (legal age).

**full and final release**  *See:* release, release in full (full and final release).

**full court**  *See:* court, full court (en banc court).

**Full Faith and Credit Clause**  *See:* constitution, U.S. Constitution, clauses, Full Faith and Credit Clause.

**full performance doctrine**  *See:* fraud, statute of frauds, full performance doctrine.

**full powers**  *See:* treaty, full powers; diplomat, full powers.

**full-faith-and-credit bond**  *See:* bond, general obligation bond (full-faith-and-credit bond).

**Fuller Court**  *See:* court, U.S. court, U.S. Supreme Court, Fuller Court.

**functional depreciation**  *See:* depreciation, functional depreciation.

**functional equivalence**  *See:* environment, National Environmental Policy Act (NEPA), functional equivalence.

**functional utility**  *See:* utility, functional utility.

**fundamental (non-fundamental)**  Essential, whether as logically necessary or historically critical. Fundamental represents an aspect of anything that it at its core, literally, the base on which a whole idea, institution, or enterprise is built. A fundamental law is a basic law essential to understanding a legal system. A fundamental principle is a basic principle that should be manifest in a system or obeyed by its participants before other non–fundamental principles or rules.

**fundamental change in circumstances**  *See:* circumstance, fundamental change in circumstances.

**fundamental constitutional right**  *See:* right, constitutional right, fundamental constitutional right (fundamental right).

**fundamental law**  *See:* law, fundamental law.

**fundamental right**  *See:* right, constitutional right, fundamental constitutional right (fundamental right).

**funds**

**comingled funds (commingling of funds)**  Money or property in a single account that should be maintained separately. Comingled funds include any money or other forms of value that might be kept in separate accounts and that ought to be segregated for the purposes of accountability, but that are instead kept in a common account so that the origin, identity, or ownership of particular assets in the account cannot be easily determined.
*See also:* trust, client trust account (lawyer's trust account).

**electronic funds transfer (EFT)**  A transfer of funds from one account to another by electronic instruction alone. An electronic funds transfer is a transfer initiated through an electronic terminal, telephone, computer, or magnetic tape that authorizes a financial institution to debit one account and to credit another. Electronic funds transfers are becoming a very common medium of payment, often performed by credit and debit cards but also often used in lieu of standing orders or payment plans and for interbank transfers.

**general fund (general revenue fund)**  A government account that holds public funds. A general fund is a governmental account that holds public money and from which appropriations are generally paid. In contrast, most states hold numerous special funds that are established to collect moneys from certain sources and to fund specified activities.

**hedge fund**  A private investment fund not registered as an investment company. A hedge fund is a private investment fund or pool that invests and trades in a variety of investment vehicles such as commodities, stocks, bonds, and currencies, with a particular function of hedging against specific losses caused by market activity. At least until 2010, hedge funds were not registered as investment companies but relied on securities law exemptions to bypass registration requirements, though this exemption was considered likely to end that year.

**revolving fund**   Renewable credit extended over a defined period. A revolving fund is an authorization of financing that the debtor may demand at will up to a specified amount, after which the debtor will repay amounts borrowed, and against which the debtor may continue to borrow up to the amount authorized, as long as payments are made routinely on outstanding debt.

**sinking fund**   A fund set aside to satisfy a debt. A sinking fund is an account that makes payments of interest and principal on a debt until the debt is retired. The fund is structured to accumulate only the value required ultimately to satisfy the debt, after which the fund is dissolved. A sinking fund that supports a variety of debts may be created to manage all of them and to incorporate new debts, and thus is not intended to be retired but to retire individual debts. The value of taxes pledged to a governmental unit's sinking fund or of money held in a sinking fund — though not securities held in it — is usually counted against any ceiling on indebtedness allowed to that unit. Note: although the greater number of sinking funds are created for the repayment of public debt, sinking funds may be created to ensure payment of any long-term debt, including private debt or corporate debt.

**fungibility (fungible)**   Property of goods or securities that are indistinguishable from one unit to the next. Fungibility is a characteristic of goods or securities that are valued by number, weight, or measure, with an assumption that there is no difference in quality or value between one or the other. For example, a certain weight and composition of crude oil, like "light, sweet crude," is fungible, and one barrel of light, sweet crude will be valued at the same price as another barrel of light, sweet crude at the same moment, other market conditions being equal. Fungibility results either from trade usage,

inherent qualities of the good or security, or the assumption of the parties to a contract with respect to the goods or securities traded.

*See also:* commodity; oil (petroleum); quality (qualitative).

**fungible commodity**   *See:* goods, fungible goods (fungible commodity).

**fungible goods**   *See:* goods, fungible goods (fungible commodity).

**fungicide**   A material that inhibits or destroys a fungus. Fungicides are chemicals that inhibit the growth or destroy active growths of a fungus. The use of fungicide is regulated in a manner similar to the use of insecticide.

*See also:* pesticide, Federal Insecticide, Fungicide, and Rodenticide Act (FIFRA or F.I.F.R.A.).

**fuqaha**   *See:* faqih (fuqaha).

**furandi animus**   *See:* animus, animus furandi (furandi animus).

**further assurances or adequate assurance of performance**   *See:* assurances (further assurances or adequate assurance of performance).

**future**

**future covenant**   *See:* covenant, covenant of title, future covenant.

**future damages**   *See:* damages, classes of damages, future damages.

**future interest**   *See:* property, interest in property, future interest; interest, future interest.

**future performance**   *See:* performance, future performance.

**future value**   *See:* value, present value (future value).

**futures contract**   *See:* contract, specific contracts, futures contract.

**FY**   *See:* year, fiscal year (FY).

Words in themselves may be harmless,
while accent and manner may make them deadly.

West Virginia v. Kerns, 47 W.V. 266, 269 (1899) (Dent, J.).

# G

**g**   The seventh letter of the modern English alphabet. "G" signifies a variety of functions as a symbol. In terms inherited by the common law from Law French, "g" was sometimes used for the sound of "w," as in gage for wage. G is translated into "Golf" for radio signals and NATO military transmissions, into "George" for some police radio traffic, and into dash, dash, dot in Morse Code.

**g as an abbreviation**   A word commencing in G. When used as the sole letter of an abbreviation, G often stands for government. It may also stand for gas, gavel, general, George, Georgia, German, gift, grand, granted, great, and guaranteed. It may also stand for the initial of the name of an author or case reporter, such as Gale, Gill, Godefroi, Goldsmith, Gould, Graham and Guthrie.

**G.A.A.P. or GAAP**   *See:* accounting, generally accepted accounting principles (G.A.A.P. or GAAP).

**G.A.O. or GAO**   *See:* congress, Government Accountability Office (G.A.O. or GAO).

**G.A.S.B. or GASB**   *See:* accounting, Governmental Standards Accounting Board (G.A.S.B. or GASB).

**G.I.N.A.**   *See:* gene, Genetic Information Non–Discrimination Act (GINA, or G.I.N.A.).

**gabel**   *See:* gavel (gabel).

**Gacaca court**   *See:* rights, human right, human rights tribunal, truth and reconciliation commission, Gacaca court.

**gag order**   *See:* speech, regulation of speech, gag order.

**gain**   Profit. Gain is the profit made on a sale or from the retention of an investment. Gain is calculated by finding the difference between the adjusted basis of an asset and the amount realized on the disposition or current appraisal of the same asset.
*See also:* profit (profits).

**Arrowsmith doctrine**   Prior transactions may be examined in an audit of a later transaction. The Arrowsmith doctrine states that a characterization of a transaction for purposes of tax accounting may require examination of prior, related transactions. The doctrine stems from the United States Supreme Court case, Arrowsmith *v. Comissioner*, 344 U.S. 6 (1952) (Black, J.).

**capital gain**   Profit realized from the sale of a capital asset. Capital gain is the amount of profit that is realized on the sale of a capital asset. Profit is the gain, the excess of the price realized over the cost basis of acquisition or creation of the capital asset. There is no negative capital gain, but a capital asset that is liquidated at a deficiency is a capital loss. In other words, if an asset, such as a stock, realty, a building, or any other investment is sold or valued for more than was paid to acquire it and maintain it, there is a capital gain, but if it is sold or valued for less than the cost of its acquisition and maintenance, there is a capital loss. Capital gains are taxed differently if the asset has been held for one year or less, which are short–term gains, or more than one year, which are long–term gains. Long–term capital gains receive preferential tax rates when compared to ordinary income.
*See also:* asset, capital asset; loss, capital loss; profit (profits).

**adjusted net capital gain**   Net capital gain minus any unrecaptured gains. Adjusted net capital gain is the sum of all sales of capital assets, taking into account sale price and basis, reduced by the sum of unrecaptured gain under IRC § 1250 and 28 percent rate gain, plus qualified dividend income.

**net capital gain**   The amount by which long–term capital gains exceeds short–term capital losses. Net capital gain for a given year is the amount that, in that year, a taxpayer's long–term capital gains at the end of that tax year outweigh the taxpayer's short–term capital losses for that year.

**ordinary gain**   Profit from sale of an ordinary asset, rather than a capital asset. Ordinary gain is the profit from the sale, disposition, or appraisal of a non–capital asset. Thus, the sale of produce or other assets that are not capital assets, at a rate that is greater than the cost of inputs, production, and expenses, is ordinary gain. In 2011, ordinary gain was taxed at ordinary income rates, which were less favorable from a tax perspective than capital gain because, for most people, capital gain rates were lower than most ordinary income tax rates.

**recognized gain (Section 1231 gain or gain under Section 1231)**   Gain from the sale of an asset measured by its sale price minus its adjusted cost basis. Recognized gain is the gain realized on the sale of an asset, determined by the sale price, from which the adjusted cost basis is deducted. A taxpayer will pay taxes on the recognized gain from a sale of an asset, with the amount of the recognized gain being taxed according to the tax classification of the asset.
*See also:* income, ordinary income.

**gaje** *See:* gajikano (gaji, gajo, gaje, gajikane).

**Gallagher Agreement** *See:* settlement, Mary Carter Agreement (Gallagher Agreement).

**gallon**

**Million gallons per day (or M.G.D. or MGD or B.G.D. or BGD)** A measure of water flow. Million gallons per day, or millions of gallons per day, is the measure of the flow of water, particularly of industrial water consumption or discharge into rivers, lakes, and streams. MGD is an average of the flow over a relevant period of time, usually a moving average over a window of time.

**gallows** Structure on which criminals condemned to die by hanging are executed. The gallows is a structure designed for execution by hanging, with a post for a rope or strap to be attached to the neck of the condemned person and a trap door that is opened to cause the condemned person to drop and to break the neck, causing death. The horror of the gallows has given rise to its use as a metaphor both for the death penalty generally and for anything that causes dread or fear, especially at the hands of state officials.

**gambling or gamble** *See:* gaming (gambling or gamble).

**game** Any form of contest played according to rules. A game is a contest played according to rules. The contest can be of one person alone, seeking to perform with greater skill or luck, or it can be among several people, or between teams of people, or among larger aggregates, such as corporations or states. Games have long served as a source of entertainment, leisure, and development, but the idea of the game and the psychology of game playing pervades many aspects of life, including education, commerce, art, science, international affairs, and war. Although the game as a concept is often dismissed as a child's amusement, games, like play, remain a powerful metaphor for the most serious of adult work, not the least in understanding a resort to rules to guide appropriate action. Law, particularly in the making of deals and in the resolution of disputes, has strong aspects of game play.

**game animal** Wild mammal, bird, or fish. Game animal, under the common law, includes all wild animals and birds, particularly those which are liable to be hunted, as well as fish (though not usually shellfish). Statutes in various states have a more restricted definition, such as limiting game not to include non-indigenous species, endangered species, or young animals. These definitions are generally used in wildlife management regulation though not necessarily affecting property interests or other defining elements of game subject to capture or taking in the wild.

*See also:* ferae, ferae naturae.

**game law** Regulations on the hunting and management of wild animals. Game law includes the regulation of hunting, of the use of animals and animal products, and of wildlife management. In some states, fisheries regulation is a component of game law, and only context or the definitions within the regulation will distinguish whether a game law applies also to fish, though a game regulation presumably applies to birds and reptiles and of course to mammals.

**game theory** Models of human action and decision that may be tested through practice. Game theory is a form of modeling human behavior to predict how people will behave under certain circumstances. Developed largely in economics, game theory is somewhat akin to the philosophical hypothetical and to legal moot courts, and indeed many games and many game solutions originate in philosophy and in law. The primary difference is that game theorists often develop and assess solutions to specific games by asking groups of people to participate in a structured application of the game to assess patterns in the various outcomes reached. Game theory thus allows the test of various assumptions about human values and preferences, as well as decision-making in particular circumstances, such as circumstances of limited information.

**chicken game (hawk-dove game or snowdrift)** A choice between conflict and coordination. The game of chicken is an anti-coordination game, in which two parties in competition are given an option to oppose one another or avoid a conflict. The potential benefit if one chooses a conflict and the other avoids, and the null result if both avoid, are much less damaging in all than the disaster that will occur if both choose the conflict.

**Nash equilibrium** A state of play when no player would gain by changing strategy. A Nash equilibrium is a concept of game resolution, in which the competitors in a game have each chosen the best strategy for personal benefit in the light of all of the other strategies of the other players. This usually requires each to select a mutually beneficial strategy. Nash equilibrium does not specify the most efficient outcome for all or the greatest value to any, only the most balanced resolution with complete knowledge. Mathematician John Nash first stated the solution.

**prisoner's dilemma** Information failure leads to coordination failure. The prisoner's dilemma is a game in which two people have been arrested for a crime and held in separate rooms; the only evidence would be testimony from one or both of the prisoners. Both prisoners are told that if both of them testify, they will each serve five years in prison; if neither of them testify, they will each serve six months in prison; if one testifies and the other remains silent, the defector will go free, and the silent prisoner will serve ten years. If they can coordinate, they would obviously choose to remain silent and both serve six months in prison. However, in a situation where asked to simply trust one another, many people in the game have acted from the fear that the other person will defect, and they elect to testify. The game is famous among economists and philosophers, with many variations, particularly in whether the game is repeated, which allow punishments for past betrayals. The game was invented in 1950 by RAND researchers Merill Flood and Melving Dresher but named and refined by mathematician Albert Tucker.

**race to the bottom (race for the bottom)**   Competition among rule systems sacrifices long-term welfare for short-term gain. The race to the bottom began in law as Louis Brandeis's descriptions of states attempting to lure business by competing with taxes and regulations that favored business but risked long-term hazard and expense. In game theory, the race to the bottom describes the common resolution of the prisoner's dilemma, in which game players sacrifice potential good outcomes requiring cooperation for bad outcomes derived from competitive advantage. People engaged in a race to the bottom choose to pursue short-term personal gains even at the expense of greater long-term losses and collective losses.

**stag hunt (trust dilemma or assurance game)**   A risk to self-preservation outweighs trust in cooperation. The stag hunt game is a study of choice between a risk of self-preservation and trust required for social cooperation, in which each player is told a group of people may hunt deer or rabbits; if everyone chooses to hunt deer, they must work together as a group, and the entire group will be fed well, but if anyone chooses to hunt rabbit, only the people hunting rabbit will be fed, and they will be fed marginally well. The obvious choice is for everyone to hunt deer, but the fear of starving if anyone else were to hunt rabbit causes people to lean toward hunting for rabbit, thus sabotaging the greater good of hunting deer. The problem was probably created by Rousseau.

**zero-sum game**   Success for one person must come at the cost of another. In a zero-sum game, the sum of wins and losses among all players is constant, so for one party to win, another necessarily loses. Zero-sum games often create a false impression that any help to one person must be a hindrance to others. In bargaining and in economic modeling, zero-sum suggests that there is a fixed or diminishing allocation of resources and so any improved position of one bargainer must result in a lesser allocation to the other. In most negotiating contexts, a zero-sum model represents a failure of imagination in examining adequately the conditions of the negotiation or game to consider moves that benefit both or all parties, as well as those that increase resources overall.

**gaming (gambling or gamble)**   A contract to enter a game of skill or chance that one might win or lose. Gaming is the same as gambling: an agreement between two or more people or a person and an entity by which they agree that they shall play a game with certain rules at cards, dice, or another contrivance, and that each might be a loser in the game. At common law, such games were generally legal, treated as contracts between the parties. Today, almost every jurisdiction has laws defining and either prohibiting, regulating, or allowing gaming, and it is rare that a jurisdiction allows risking value on absolutely any outcome. Other activities that fit the definition of gaming are excluded now from gaming by custom, rule, or statute. For instance, financial investments are not gaming, nor are insurance contracts. *See also:* wager.

**Indian gaming**   Gambling on tribal lands. Indian gaming includes all gambling operations that are authorized on tribal lands, regardless of whether such gambling is permitted or prohibited elsewhere in the state. The tribes' powers to authorize gambling is independent of the states, although it is regulated by the Indian Gaming Regulatory Act, 25 U.S.C. §2701, et seq., which requires tribal-state compacts for casinos and allows tribes to manage bingo, card games, and similar gaming without state coordination, although all Indian gaming is subject to oversight by the National Indian Gaming Commission.

**lottery (gift enterprise or raffle)**   A game in which one purchases a chance to win a prize. A lottery is a scheme by which a prize is given by chance to a player who gives consideration to play, the sum of such consideration not only underwriting the prize and costs of the scheme but also providing its sponsor with income from the players. The term "lottery" was once relatively generic but is now limited usually to games managed by a state monopoly in many states, most of which are used to raise revenues for the state budget or state programs. Though there are many variations, the most well known form is a game in which players purchase a ticket bearing a numbered sequence, and a prize is awarded to holders of tickets bearing a sequence drawn at random from a wheel or other random-number-generating device. Other forms of lottery are defined variously, usually a raffle or a gift enterprise, in which players acquire a chance to win some property or service rather than money. Bingo, keno, and other games of chance, including the use of slot machine or electronic games, are usually separately regulated. Running an unlicensed lottery or engaging in a rigged lottery are criminal offenses.

Lottery is also a generic term for a distribution of a scarce resource by random distribution throughout a population. In this sense, a lottery is merely a program to allocate a scarce resource that employs an equal chance among competitors, as in the Diversity Immigrant Visa Program, which is effectively a lottery, or a housing lottery to allocate scarce housing among eligible students.

**running the numbers (numbers running)** Illegal gambling on a professional scale. Numbers running is the management of bets, markers, plays, and other obligations and transfers associated with illegal gambling.

**gang** A peer group that socializes its members to commit criminal acts. A gang is a peer group that develops a particular identity and that is used by older members to socialize new members to accept a degree of group identity as a matter of personal identity. To this extent, a gang is a club or any other successful social organization, but the gang that is of interest to the law incorporates into this socialization a value in the conduct of criminal activity, encouraging its members to violate the law in the interests of the gang or for personal recognition within the gang. Gangs are the primary vehicle in the United States for the distribution of illegal drugs, and gang competition is a continuing source of violence.

*See also:* recruit (gang recruitment or recruiting); loitering, gang loitering; racketeering, organized crime.

**gang colors** *See:* color, gang colors.

**gang loitering** *See:* loitering, gang loitering.

**gang recruitment or recruiting** *See:* recruit (gang recruitment or recruiting).

**gaol** *See:* jail (gaol).

**gaoler** *See:* jail, jailer (gaoler).

**gap** A void between things or rules, especially a situation that is ambiguous in law. A gap describes the space between two discrete things, such as objects or periods of time. Legal theorists use gap, following H.L.A. Hart's idea that law has an open texture, to describe areas of human activity not regulated by law, owing to ambiguities in the descriptions of what is forbidden or allowed.

*See also:* rules, open texture of rules; indeterminacy, legal indeterminacy; lawfulness (lawful or unlawfulness or unlawful).

**gap-filler** *See:* contract, contract interpretation, gap-filler.

**gap period** *See:* bankruptcy, gap period.

**lacuna (lacunae)** Something missing in a text or narrative. A lacuna is a hole, usually a logical gap in a text, such as a statute, jury instruction, contract, in which a word, phrase, or idea is omitted that an informed reader would know should be there or that the writer or speaker intended to be. Thus a requirement logically required in a statute for the other requirements to be coherent that was omitted from its drafting is a lacuna. A jury instruction that would help the jury interpret the evidence before them that was not given is a lacuna; a term required or useful in a contract that is omitted is a lacuna. Lacunae are sometimes logical or functional omissions but they may also be physical omissions in that a portion of the text was not printed or written, or a page or portion of it is lost or destroyed. A story may have lacunae, gaps in its telling, just as evidence may.

**garbage** *See:* trash (garbage).

**Garcia hearing** *See:* conflict, conflict of interest, Garcia hearing.

**garnishment (garnish or garnishee)** Process to collect a judgment debtor's money or property held by a third party. Garnishment is a method by which a judgment creditor (who is the successful claimaint in a suit) may acquire property of the judgment debtor (who lost a judgment in that suit) that is not held by the debtor but by a third party, such as an employer, bank, bailee, or other person or entity with property or obligations to the benefit of the debtor. The judgment creditor becomes a plaintiff in a new action for garnishment, serving a summons of garnishment on the third-party entity from whom the plaintiff seeks the assets, who is the garnishee. The summons or an attached affidavit sets forth the date and court of the judgment against the judgment debtor, the amount owed in sum, and the amount or property held by the garnishee to be surrendered to the plaintiff. The plaintiff must also serve a notice of garnishment on the defendant who may answer and contest (or traverse) the plaintiff's claim. If the court finds the plaintiff is entitled to garnishment, the garnishee will allow the plaintiff to garnish the defendant's assets or property in the defendant's control. Certain assets and claims are exempt from garnishment, though ordinary wages are not.

*See also:* judgment, enforcement of judgment, judgment creditor; judgment, enforcement of judgment, judgment debtor.

**exemptions from garnishment** A plaintiff may not garnish exempt categories of property. Exemptions from garnishment vary somewhat from jurisdiction to jurisdiction but usually include the defendant's homestead and furnishings (to a given value), tools of a trade, government benefits and relief payments, insurance proceeds on a claim, wrongful death payments, a car, and income from a minor child.

**GATT** *See:* trade, international trade, General Agreement on Tariffs and Trade (GATT).

**gavel (gabel)** A tax or payment made to one's superior. Gavel is law French for a tax of any form, whether it is a tax, rent, or tribute, paid in money or goods.

Note: the mallet used by a judge or meeting chair is also a gavel, presumably owing to the gavel's ancient use in auctions over good lost to unpaid taxes.

**gavelkind** *See:* tenure, feudal tenure, gavelkind.

**Gemara** Later written components of the Talmud. The Gemara, or additions, are the interpretations of the

Mishnah by Jewish scholars, collected after 200 C.E. The Mishnah and the Gemara together make up the Talmud. Though the Mishnah is common to all Talmudic traditions, there are two forms of Gemara, which distinguish the Babylonian Talmud from the Jerusalem Talmud.

**gender (sex as identity)** The degree to which a person, animal, or thing is male or female. Gender, describes whether someone or something has characteristics more typical of males or more typical of females. The common law admitted only to two genders as a matter of legal rights, although there was recognition that some individuals were hermaphroditic.

English is unusual among European languages in having few nouns other than for animals that are gendered, and the law once divided many private offices between terms of a male and female holder, such as executor and executrix. When the masculine form was used (as in king), it usually encompassed obligations toward, by, or of a female official (such as the queen). Contemporary usage rarely distinguishes between the gender of terms, employing either one or the other word without much regard to the apparent gender of the officer holder so that there are now female executors, or creating a neologism, such as personal representative. As a matter of identity, there is no difference between sex and gender.

*See also:* hermaphrodite (androgyne or hermaphroditic or intersex or intersexual or transgender); sex; sexuality.

**gender discrimination** *See:* discrimination, sex discrimination (gender discrimination).

**gender stereotype or racial stereotype or stereotypical** *See:* stereotype (gender stereotype or racial stereotype or stereotypical).

**gene (genetic)** A unit of heredity in organisms. A gene is an element of the cells of every organism that lives or has lived on Earth, that provides all of the information about the organism that makes it specific and unique, and that is associated with the inheritance of all aspects and traits of one organism in its progeny. Each person's genetic structure amounts to information in that person's genes, which control every quantified aspect of human identity from appearance to health. Genes may be affected by disease or environment, both interfering with the health of the individual and the inheritance of that individual's children. Genetic therapy, on the other hand, may allow alteration of genetic information in a variety of ways to alter characteristics, including capacities for health and disease resistance.

*See also:* deoxyribonucleic acid.

**Genetic Information Non-Discrimination Act (GINA or G.I.N.A.)** Draft legislation to protect genetic privacy. The Genetic Non-Discrimination Act is a draft federal statute that would, if enacted, bar health insurers and employers from using an applicant's genetic information as a basis for refusing coverage or employment.

**genetically modified organism (living modified organism or G.M.O. or GMO or L.M.O. or LMO)** Plant that has been altered through implanted genetic information. A genetically modified organism is a plant or animal that has been altered by the introduction or alteration of information in its genetic code. Most GMOs are created plants for easier or more efficient cultivation to increase the food supply at lower cost through resistance to pesticides, disease, or parasites such as insects. Some applications of genetic modification only slightly differ from the process of selective breeding and other modern forms of cultivation, but great skepticism persists over the long–term implications of the transfers of genetic information between animal and plant species, as well as any risks to human health from food created through such means.

*See also:* biotechnology; gene (genetic).

**clone** Reproduction of an animal or plant by artificially duplicating its genes. Clones are exact replicas of an organism, fabricated by duplicating the exact genetic material taken from that organism. The artificial process is highly controversial because it carries with it the risk of unforeseeable and unintended consequences and because it alters the powers of humans over themselves and the natural world.

**general**

**general administration** *See:* administrator, administrator of estate, general administrator (general administration).

**general agency** *See:* agent, general agency.

**general agent** *See:* attorney, attorney in fact, power of attorney, general power of attorney (general agent).

**General Agreement on Tariffs and Trade** *See:* trade, international trade, General Agreement on Tariffs and Trade (GATT).

**general appearance** *See:* jurisdiction, in personam jurisdiction, voluntary jurisdiction, general appearance; appearance, general appearance.

**general average** *See:* liability, joint liability, general average.

**general bequest** *See:* bequest, general bequest.

**general causation** *See:* causation, general causation (causability or causality).

**general counsel** *See:* counselor, general counsel.

**general damages** *See:* damages, classes of damages, general damages (presumed damages).

**general defense** *See:* defense, defense in pleading, general defense, derivative defense.

**general deposit**   *See:* deposit, general deposit.

**general deterrence**   *See:* deterrence, general deterrence.

**general devise**   *See:* devise, general devise.

**general duty**   *See:* duty, general duty (duty of reasonable care).

**general fund**   *See:* funds, general fund (general revenue fund).

**general intent**   *See:* intent, general intent (basic intent).

**general jurisdiction**   *See:* jurisdiction, general jurisdiction.

**general law**   *See:* law, general law.

**general legacy**   *See:* legacy, general legacy.

**general legatee**   *See:* legatee, general legatee.

**general malice**   *See:* malice, general malice (universal malice).

**general obligation bond**   *See:* bond, general obligation bond (full–faith–and–credit bond).

**general partnership**   *See:* partnership, general partnership (general partner).

**general power of appointment**   *See:* power, power of appointment (general power of appointment).

**general power of attorney**   *See:* attorney, attorney in fact, power of attorney, general power of attorney (general agent).

**general revenue fund**   *See:* funds, general fund (general revenue fund).

**general verdict**   *See:* verdict, general verdict, general–verdict rule; verdict, general verdict.

**general warrant**   *See:* warrant, general warrant, writ of assistance (Paxton's Case); warrant, general warrant.

**general warranty**   *See:* warranty, general warranty (general warranty of property).

**General Welfare Clause**   *See:* constitution, U.S. Constitution, clauses, General Welfare Clause.

**general welfare or public welfare**   *See:* welfare (general welfare or public welfare).

**general–verdict rule**   *See:* verdict, general verdict, general–verdict rule.

**generally accepted accounting principles**   *See:* accounting, generally accepted accounting principles (G.A.A.P. or GAAP).

**generation–skipping transfer tax**   *See:* tax, death tax, estate tax, generation–skipping transfer tax (skip person or GST).

**generic**   Typical. Generic connotes something that is representative of its genus, or its type. Generic goods are goods typical of their category, and not sold according to a particular brand. Generic terms are not so specific as to be eligible for copyright or trademark protection: Kleenex may be copyrighted or trademarked, but tissue cannot be.

**generic mark**   *See:* trademark, mark, generic mark, genericide (proprietary eponym); trademark, mark, generic mark (genericism).

**genericide**   *See:* trademark, mark, generic mark, genericide (proprietary eponym).

**genericism**   *See:* trademark, mark, generic mark (genericism).

**genetically modified organism**   *See:* organism, genetically modified organism.

**Geneva conventions**   *See:* war, law of war, Geneva conventions.

**genital mutilation**   *See:* mutilation, genital mutilation (female circumcision).

**genocide**   *See:* war, law of war, war crime, genocide.

**gentrification**   Transition of low–value land use to high–value land use. Gentrification is a process of the conversion of low–value lands in an urban area to high–value uses, particularly the move from low-income housing to high–income housing. Gentrification increases land values and property tax revenues, but it also creates instability and the involuntary displacement of former residents and tenants. Municipalities may properly use their zoning and land use rules either to encourage or to discourage gentrification, or both in different areas, according to the needs of the municipality as properly determined by municipal officials.

**genuineness (genuine)**   Authenticity, the object or person being truly as presented. Anything genuine is wholly as it appears to be, particularly as to its source and its nature. Often it is easier to determine genuineness by rejecting its opposite: something genuine is no forgery or counterfeit or false claim or fabrication or lie or deceit, or anyone or anything put forward in a manner to create a false impression.

**genuine issue of material fact**   *See:* issue, issue before the court, genuine issue of material fact; fact, material fact, genuine issue of material fact.

**germaneness (germane)**   Closely related to the purpose or topic under consideration. Germaneness is a reasonable relationship between a new topic, idea, argument, or claim and the prior subject of interest. For one thing to be germane to another implies that they arise from the same stock or family. In general, germaneness in law requires that an amendment to a bill or a counterclaim filed in a suit be related to the subject matter of the initial legislation or the claim initially filed.

**gerrymandering (gerrymander)**  The artful mapping of voting districts to dilute or to concentrate voting blocs. Gerrymandering is the process of dividing political units in ways that deliberately create advantages for incumbents or their political allies, by placing voters based on their predicted behavior at the polls in districts that dilute the vote of some voters and consolidate the votes of others. Gerrymandered districts were once used to dilute the votes of racial minorities, and such districts are now considered violations of the Voter Rights Act and the Fifteenth Amendment.

Political gerrymanders, however, continue to be considered acceptable under the federal constitution, although they distort democracy to the benefit of incumbent officials, exacerbate political differences in the polity, and lead to frequent and confusing movements of political boundaries. The Supreme Court, per Chief Justice Rehnquist in the heavily criticized decision of Vieth v. Jubelirer, 541 U.S. 267 (2004), held that the use of gerrymandering by a political party controlling a state legislature to favor its own members in congressional races does not violate the constitution. The term derives from the name of a governor of Massachusetts, Elbridge Gerry, who, in the early nineteenth century, signed into law a districting plan created by Jeffersonian Democrats that had one district shaped like a salamander.

**Gesetz**  The specific rules of German law. Gesetz describes the specific laws that govern individual obligations and duties, sometimes in German legal theory equated with the positive law or the statutory law in the code. Gesetz is equivalent to the laws in the United States, rather than to the law in its grandest sense. Gesetz is often contrasted with recht, the more principled sense of law as right. Gesetz is more like loi in French law or legge in Italian.
*See also:* law, comparative law; recht.

**gestation period**  *See:* birth, gestation period.

**gestational surrogacy**  *See:* family, family planning, assisted reproduction, gestational surrogacy (surrogate mother).

**Gezerah Shavah**  An inference drawn from one Biblical passage to another based on similar wording. Gezerah Shavah is a principle in Jewish law of interpretation to be used in understanding ambiguous or unclear words or phrases in the midrash: if the unclear word or halakha is used elsewhere in a text in which its meaning is clear, then that other understanding may be used to interpret the unclear word or halakha. The principle is similar but more subtle than the common law tool of interpretation in pari materia.

**gharar**  Ambiguity, particularly in an agreement. Gharar is ambiguity or the existence of an ambiguous provision in a contract, which renders the contract void in Shariiah.
*See also:* ambiguity (ambiguous or ambiguousness).

**GHG or G.H.G.**  *See:* pollution, air pollution, greenhouse gas (GHG or G.H.G.).

**gift (gift over or give)**  A conveyance of property without any obligation to do so. A gift is a voluntary conveyance, a transfer of property or an interest in property that is not required of the giver by the receipt of a promise of consideration or by any other duty to transfer it. In order for a gift to be valid and irrevocable by the giver, not only must the giver have an intent to transfer ownership forever to the recipient but also the gift must be delivered to the recipient and accepted by the recipient.

Both the giver's intent and the recipient's acceptance may, in some circumstances, be presumed. Intent may be presumed by the giver's actions, as long as the giver makes no action or statement that is contrary to that intent. Acceptance by the recipient may be presumed from the effective delivery of the property, whether delivery is by actual or constructive delivery.

Note: the verb for making a gift is sometimes "gift" or "gift over," usages that were once common but now rare. The use of "give" or "donate" is much less confusing for the same purpose.
*See also:* donation (donate or donee or donor); offer; endowment (endow).

**gift enterprise or raffle**  *See:* gaming, lottery (gift enterprise or raffle).

**gift tax**  *See:* tax, gift tax, annual exclusion; tax, gift tax.

**anatomical gift**  A donation of a post-mortem human body or body part. An anatomical gift is the donation of a human body or part of a body after death, given to an institution for medicine, education, or research for the purpose of transplantation, therapy, research, or education. States regulate these transfers to ensure that the donor's consent is truly given for a body part to be donated, and that the transfer is not done in exchange for payment or any type of consideration, as that is considered be contrary to public policy.

**class gift**  A bequest or a devise to class rather than to named individuals. Class gifts are bequests, legacies, or devises made to a testamentary class rather than to an individual or to a list of individuals. A class may be a class of descendants or a class defined by other means. Grants such as "to my nephews" or "to the students at the time of my death who were most recently enrolled in Professor Norvell's classes" grant an interest to all of the nephews or to all of the professor's students, who are then presumed to share and share alike in the respective grants. The language describing the class should be sufficiently definite that those who are included in the class are definitely ascertainable. A gift to a group of unascertainable beings is invalid.

**divide-and-pay-over rule**  A class gift is contingent if is not a direct gift to the class but an order to a trustee. The divide-and-pay-over rule is used to determine whether a gift to a class immediately vests or the gift is contingent on an event before vesting. If the language of the grant is to the members of a class, then it is considered immediately to vest, even if its transfer will be delayed until after a condition is satisfied. But if the language of the grant is an instruction to a trustee to pay the members of the class when the condition is satisfied, the gift is considered contingent, vesting only at the time of the condition's satisfaction.

**completed gift**  A gift without remaining conditions, that is final and irrevocable. A completed gift is a donation in which the donor parts finally and forever with dominion and control of the property. No condition may remain unsatisfied or contingent, and delivery must be finally effected. A donor has no power in the law to revoke or reverse a completed gift; although as a practical matter, a donor may request a donee to give back the gift, the donee has no enforceable obligation in law to do so that arises from the gift alone.

**conditional gift**  A gift that is contingent upon a future occurrence. A conditional gift is a voluntary conveyance of any property that is made with an intent to transfer possession, and yet title and ownership are not transferred until a condition is satisfied or a period has passed without a condition being satisfied. Even if physical delivery occurs prior to the satisfaction of the condition, the delivery is not effective until after the condition is satisfied. Upon the satisfaction of the condition, the title is transferred, and a second delivery is not required. However, if the condition fails or is otherwise unsatisfied, title does not pass and the donor is entitled to the property's repossession.

**gift causa mortis**  A gift made in contemplation of the giver's impending death. A gift causa mortis is an inter vivos gift made at a time the giver believes that the giver will soon die. A gift causa mortis is presumed valid, although some are nullified owing to the donors incidental lack of capacity. A gift causa mortis, is not irrevocable until the death of the donor or a reasonable time after the gift. If the donor recovers, the gift is revoked automatically, although, of course, the giver may renounce the revocation or make the gift anew should the giver choose to do so.

*See also:* gift, gift inter vivos (absolute gift or inter vivos gift).

**gift inter vivos (absolute gift or inter vivos gift)**  A gift given while the giver lives. A gift inter vivos is a gift made during the donor's life. This is distinct, obviously, from a bequest or devise in a will that becomes effective only at death. It is also distinct from a gift causa mortis, which is made in the donor's belief that the donor will soon die. A gift inter vivos is irrevocable upon an intended, completed grant that is delivered and accepted.

*See also:* gift, gift causa mortis; delivery; inter, inter vivos.

**promise to make a gift**  A would-be donor's statement that a gift will be made in the future. A promise to make a gift is presumptively an unenforceable promise. If, however, the promise is an element of an otherwise valid contract or if there is promissory estoppel arising from detrimental reliance, then the promise may not be retracted but is binding on the promissor.

**split gift**  Gift made by either spouse treated as made half from each spouse. A split gift is a gift to a person or entity from a husband and wife that is presumed to have been given half from the husband and half from the wife, and treated as if that is so for tax purposes, even if it was funded entirely by one spouse alone or made from property solely in the ownership or control of the one spouse. Split gifts are advantageous in calculating the individual limits on gift and estate tax exemptions and credits.

**taxable gift**  A transfer of property for less than its full value. A taxable gift is defined distinctly from a gift in general, being any transfer of property for less than an adequate and full consideration, or for less than a reasonable approximation of its market value. The amount by which the value of the gift is less than the value received by the giver is the taxable value of the gift.

Note: the IRC defines "taxable gifts" distinctly from taxable gift. Taxable gifts are the amount of gifts made in a calendar year, less certain deductions.

**gift to a minor (Uniform Gifts to Minors Act or U.G.M.A. or UGMA or Uniform Transfers to Minors Act or U.T.M.A.)**  A gift to a child of a future interest in land may come within the annual exclusion from gift tax. A grant to a minor is subject to the annual exclusion from gift tax, but the annual exclusion does not ordinarily apply to gifts of a future interest in property; if the gift is of a future interest in land to a minor, however, the gift is subject to the exclusion after all, and so it may be exempt from tax up to the amount of the exclusion. Qualifying gifts must be managed so that the property and income is expendable for the benefit of the minor, so that the property and income therefrom pass to the minor once the minor reaches the age of twenty-one, and so that if the minor dies before reaching twenty-one years of age, then the property and income must be included in the minor's estate.

**Giglio evidence**  *See:* exculpation, exculpatory evidence, Giglio material (Giglio evidence).

**GINA**  *See:* gene, Genetic Information Non-Discrimination Act (GINA or G.I.N.A.).

**Girsh factors**  *See:* class, class action, settlement of class action (Girsh factors).

**glass ceiling**  A customary barrier limiting women and members of some races from employment promotion. The glass ceiling is a metaphorical label for a custom or practice that bars women or people identified by race from promotions past one or another step on a corporate ladder.

**glebe (glebe land or glebe-lands)** Lands owned by a church. Glebe is land that is owned by a church. Though it is often now written "glebe lands" for the ease of readers no longer used to the term, this usage is a bit redundant, as glebe means a particular form of land.

**gloss (glossation or glossator)** Commentary on an older text. Gloss is a later commentary upon an earlier text, usually printed in the notes and introduction to a later edition of the text. Coke on Littleton is Coke's gloss on Littleton's earlier book. In a way, every annotated edition of a text or a code is a form of gloss, and to annotate a code or text is the act of glossation.

Usually, to speak in general of glossators or glosses is to speak of medieval canon texts, the most famous of which is the twelfth-century Decretum of Gratian, which provided then contemporary commentary on a collection of earlier canon materials.

*See also:* footnote; law, black letter law (blackletter law or hornbook law); canon, canon law, decretals (decretals of gratian or decretum gratiani).

**God (supreme being or creator)** The divine creator of all human-kind. God is the subject of an unlimited number of descriptions or beliefs. When "God" is written or said in the law of the United States, however, it usually represents one or more of the monotheistic concepts of God, either brought to the United States by immigrants from Christian Europe or developed along similar lines. The two major divisions among these concepts are whether God acts in history after the creation (the primary difference between deism — God set up the universe and now it goes on its own — and theism — God set up the universe but continues to intervene), and whether God created only good or is also the creator of evil. These divisions are often argued among theologians, and though they may have little practical effect in the law, legal usage does appear sometimes to favor one or another concept. For example, some usages of God in the law appear theistic, such as the assumption underpinning the idea of an "act of God" or invocations for God's intercession at the start of a session of Court or of a legislature. On the other hand, many aspects of the founding of the country appear deistic, such as the recognition of a "creator" who is "nature's God" in the Declaration of Independence. This sense of God is perpetuated in the symbols associated with "ceremonial deism," or at least in that analysis of them.

In some contexts, the term "God" might embrace a broader notion of a "Supreme Being," which would include many additional concepts of the divine, including forms of polytheism that suggest a unity among Gods or a superiority of a God, or a still broader definition that might include a concept that accepts immortal beings of supernatural powers, or a concept of a divine aspect of the Earth, or of natural forces, or of humanity itself.

The federal Constitution, particularly in the Free Exercise clause of the First Amendment and in the state constitutions, protects individuals and groups from persecution based on their beliefs regarding God. The restriction of citizenship, office, or any other public good on the basis of a belief or rejection of a belief in God is likely to violate several strictures of the U.S. Constitution, including the Free Exercise Clause and Establishment Clause, the Due Process Clause, the Equal Protection Clause, and the Religious Test Clause, as well as provisions in most state constitutions.

*See also:* church; religion; religion, freedom of religion; religion, freedom of religion, establishment of religion, ceremonial deism.

**act of God (act of nature or actus dei or or casus fortuitus or force of nature or fortuitous event )** A cause of damage or interference without human fault. Act of God describes any storm, wind, earthquake, meteorite strike, falling limb, or other occurrence not precipitated by a human agency, which causes damage, injury, delay, or some other harm. Unless a contract specifies otherwise, performance under a contract is not excused when the performance is prevented by an Act of God, for instance a flood that renders a factory unusable. Even so, neither party is generally responsible to the other for damages suffered directly as a result not of delay but of harm caused by an Act of God. Act of God is synonymous with Act of Nature, both of which are also forms of force majeure, but force majeure is a broader concept than the other two, because force majeure includes acts caused by human agency, such as strikes, riots, or wars.

*See also:* force, force majeure.

**image of God (imago dei)** Each person is created equal. That mankind is made in the image of God is an article of faith for Jewish, Christian, and Islamic belief. The concept both justified and labeled an important argument among Christians in Europe and America in the seventeenth to nineteenth centuries, which rejected the claims to a divine right of kings or of nobility to rule, as well as to a theological defense of slavery, because all people are made in the image of God. This argument is central to the statement of the Declaration of Independence in 1776, that all people "are created equal, that they are endowed by their Creator with certain inalienable rights . . ."

*See also:* equality (equal).

**in God we trust** The national motto of the United States. "In God we trust" is the motto of the United States. It has been found not to violate the Establishment Clause of the First Amendment.

**going-concern value** *See:* value, going-concern value (value as a going concern).

**golden parachute** *See:* officer, corporate officer, executive officer, executive compensation, golden parachute (compensation protection or assured compensation or parachute payment).

**Golden-Rule argument** *See:* argument, Golden–Rule argument (victim's shoes argument).

**good** Something sufficient to be acceptable for a purpose or preferred over its alternatives. Good, in law, is an adjective that represents a standard of suitability or appropriateness for a given purpose or preference. Good faith, good workmanship, good cause, good land, good water, are all standards by which some action or thing is assessed and found sufficient for the purposes of assessment.

A good, the noun, in law is much rarer than its plural form of goods, which are salable things, or merchandise.

In jurisprudence and moral or political philosophy, the good is a common term for those things sought on the basis of preference, convenience, or as a resource. This sense of the good is often contrasted with a sense of the right, which depicts those things sought on the basis of moral or ethical duty.

**good behavior** *See:* sentence, reduction of sentence, good behavior (good time).

**good faith** *See:* faith, good faith (bona fide).

**good faith bargaining** *See:* bargain, good faith bargaining.

**good faith exception or good-faith exception or Leon exception or reasonable error exception** *See:* search, exclusionary rule, good–faith exception (good faith exception or Leon exception or reasonable error exception).

**good samaritan law or good samaritan doctrine** *See:* samaritan, good samaritan statute (good samaritan law or good samaritan doctrine).

**good time** *See:* time, good time; sentence, reduction of sentence, good behavior (good time).

**goodwill or corporate goodwill** *See:* good will (goodwill or corporate goodwill).

**basic good (primary good or fundamental good)** The few conditions that are essential to a well–led life. Basic goods are the most important forms of the good, the projects that are essential to the well–led life or even to life itself. There are many formulations of the fundamental goods, and certain labels are associated with certain methods of ascertaining the good and lists of goods, often differing because the authors' larger theories vary in the manner in which the goods are used. Thus, for instance, Finnis argues strongly for a traditional concept of basic goods, which we identify through a direct and underived understanding, of life, knowledge, play, aesthetics, sociability, practical reasonableness, and religion. Rawls defines a similar but particular form of good that performs a less central role in his theory, in which he describes the primary social goods, goods that every rational person needs to be free and equal with others in society, including political rights, freedom of movement and occupation, the powers and prerogatives of public office, wealth, and the social bases of self–respect.

**underived good (Finnisian goods)** An inherently moral and good trait or state of being. An underived good is an aspect of existence that, simply because of its own characteristics, is moral and worthy of attainment by humans. John Finnis is largely responsible for the modern theory of underived goods, basing his work on the scholastic thought of Thomas Aquinas. Finnis identifies seven of these goods in his treatise Natural Law and Natural Rights: life, knowledge, play, aesthetic experience, sociability, practical reasonableness and religion.

**goods** Anything of value that is movable, identifiable and salable. Goods are tangible, identifiable, and movable property that may be bought and sold. Although goods can be bought or sold for any price, as the object of a contract they are assumed to have a minimum objective value. The terms goods almost always refers to personal property, since real property is practically immovable at the time of sale. In general, the term is not used in a manner that includes commercial paper or negotiable instruments, and in the Uniform Commercial Code, goods does not include money. Even so, for certain purposes when the term is defined between parties and in the civil law of some states, goods may include not only such commercial paper but also securities and cash.

*See also:* merchandise (wares).

*1. destruction of identified goods* When goods that are specified in a contract are lost prior to their delivery to the buyer, through no fault of the buyer, the buyer may elect to avoid or amend the contract.

*See also:* destruction.

*2. disposition of rejected goods* The manner in which a buyer disposes of rejected goods. Disposition of rejected goods occurs after the buyer receives goods pursuant to a contract but rejects them as non–conforming to the terms of the contract, when the buyer either stores the goods for the seller to collect, reships the goods to the seller, or resells them.

**bulk goods (bulk of goods)** Goods sold by volume rather than by unit. Bulk goods are goods sold by volume rather than by a count of the units sold. Bulk goods are usually transported in bulk, loaded by conveyor or pipe into train cars or ship's holds. A bulk of goods is the quantity of bulk goods in a particular lot, shipment, or storage facility.

**commingled goods** Goods combined and so losing their specific identity. Commingled goods are goods that are physically united or intermixed with other goods to the point that their identity is lost in a product or mass. A common example of commingled goods is the combination of grains from different farms into a single grain elevator: once the elevator operator has combined several farmers' crops in one elevator, the goods from a single farmer cannot be distinguished from those of another.

**fungible goods (fungible commodity)** Interchangeable goods. Fungible goods are goods of which no unit has uniquely identifying characteristics, each unit or quantity of a given good being sufficiently indistinguishable from the next any unit that — by nature or by usage of the trade or by contract — each unit is treated as equivalent to any other unit of the same quantity.

*See also:* fungibility (fungible).

**non-conforming goods (nonconforming goods)**
Goods that are not as described under the contract for their purchase. Non-conforming goods are goods that have been contracted for purchase and delivered to the buyer, but that are not substantially equivalent to the description of the goods in the contract. Generally, a buyer may accept or reject in whole or part non-conforming goods. Rejection does not mean the buyer may not take the goods into the buyer's possession. Rather, "rejection" is a term of art that means the buyer makes a decision to repudiate the non-conforming goods under the terms of the contract within a reasonable amount of time after delivery, and then to seasonably notify the seller. It is also possible for a buyer to revoke acceptance of non-conforming goods if the buyer was wrongly induced to accept the non-conforming goods, or the seller promised to cure the nonconformity and failed to do so. A seller of rejected, non-conforming goods is in breach of contract, and the buyer is entitled to damages, both for non-delivery of the goods and and damage suffered from an insufficient "cover," that is, any good-faith and reasonable cost of contracting for substitute goods.

*See also:* goods.

**rejection of goods** A buyer's refusal to accept or retain delivered goods. Rejection of goods is the refusal by the buyer of goods to accept delivery or to retain goods that have been delivered. Rejection is not effective until buyer has notified the seller of the election to reject the goods. Rejection, whether a rejection of delivery or a decision made soon after delivery, differs from a revocation of acceptance, mainly in the time that elapses from the effected delivery.

**stolen goods (stolen property)** Chattels or other property that have been stolen. Stolen goods, or stolen property, are the objects of a theft, larceny, or other property crime. The goods have the character of stolen goods from the moment they have been the object of the crime until such time as either the true owner has recovered them, or the statute of limitations has run upon their receipt. In some jurisdictions, the goods cease to have the character of stolen goods under the doctrine of market overt, if they are bought by a bona fide purchaser for value in a public sale. The possession of stolen property is a crime, and knowingly receiving stolen property without an intent to restore it to its owner is a distinct crime in most jurisdictions.

*See also:* theft.

**receiver of stolen goods (receiving stolen property)** A person who knowingly accepts stolen goods from another. A receiver of stolen goods is a person or entity who has taken possession of stolen property, who either knows or (in some jurisdictions) reasonably should have known that the property was stolen, and who took possession for reasons other than to restore the property to its lawful owner. A receiver of stolen goods is not the same person as the thief and is not an accomplice to the original theft by virtue of the receipt. In other words, the crimes of theft and receiving stolen goods are mutually exclusive. Thus, a pawnbroker who deals in stolen goods but does not assist in the actual theft is merely a "fence" and liable as a receiver, but a pawnbroker who aids in the commission of the theft is an accomplice and liable for the theft itself.

**goodwill (good will or corporate goodwill)**
Intangible benefits of an entity's reputation and relationships. Goodwill is an intangible value assigned a dollar amount by a corporations executives and accountants to represent the premium over assets and debts that a company is said to be worth in the marketplace. Goodwill is, roughly, the difference between the value of the net assets of a company (the gross assets less its debts) and the market value of the company as a whole, for instance, as measured by the capitalization of its stock or by its purchase price at the time of its acquisition by another company.

**gouging or price gouging** *See:* price, excessive pricing (gouging or price gouging).

**government** The organization of rules, offices, and powers of the state. Government is the whole organization that governs the state, not only its personnel but their duties, organization, powers and limits. There are many forms of government, differing chiefly in how decisions of governance are made and executed and by whom. The allocation of powers and obligations of a government is its constitution.

*See also:* constitution.

**Government Accountability Office** *See:* Congress, Government Accountability Office (G.A.O. or GAO).

**government agent or federal agent** *See:* police, police agent (government agent or federal agent).

**government bond or government security** *See:* bond, savings bond (government bond or government security).

**government-issued identification** *See:* identification, evidence, government-issued identification.

**government position bond** *See:* bond, government position bond (official bond).

**government probate** *See:* administrator, administrator of estate, public administrator (government probate).

**governmental actor** *See:* civil rights, civil rights act, state actor (governmental actor).

**governmental actor or state actor** *See:* state, U.S. state, state action (governmental actor or state actor).

**governmental classification**  *See:* class, legal classification (governmental classification).

**governmental interest**  *See:* equality, equal protection of the laws, governmental interest.

**governmental interest or governmental purpose** *See:* interest, state interest (governmental interest or govermental purpose).

**Governmental Standards Accounting Board**  *See:* accounting, Governmental Standards Accounting Board (G.A.S.B. or GASB).

### forms of government

**aristocracy**  Rule by an hereditary elite. An aristocracy is a form of government in which a small class of people controls the government, participation in which is a right of the members of that class inherited from their parents and passed on to their children. The non–governing classes remain always subordinate to the governing class.

**autocracy (dictatorship or monocracy)**  Rule by a decider with limitless authority. An autocracy is a government with a single ruler unlimited by the law administered effectively by other persons — a state ruled by one person who makes all decisions in the state. More accurately, an autocrat is claimed to make all decisions; an autocrat often relies on others in order to maintain control, such as support from nobles or the military so as to keep power.
*See also:* government, forms of government, monarchy (kingdom or monarch); government, forms of government, fascism.

**bureaucracy**  Rule by administrative officials. Bureaucracy, as a form of government, is the control of the state by a network of officials in offices, each managing specialized arenas of social life, and the officials replacing themselves with more officials. Bureaucracy — as a form of government — presumes that there is no meaningful authority over the officials from the people, a legislature, a monarch, or an executive. In this it differs from bureaucracy as an aspect of government, in which the officials are subordinate and responsive to the legal obligations defined by others.
*See also:* bureaucracy (bureaucrat).

**communism**  Rule by an egalitarian proletariat. Communism, in its ideal form, is not a government but a self–ruling society that is controlled for and by an egalitarian, classless collective of laborers. Regardless of the ideal form, communist governments that have been formed in practice, most notably the U.S.S.R., have usually been bureaucratic oligarchies.

**democracy**  Rule of, by, and for the people. Democracy is the form of government according to which the sovereign power of the state is held inalienably and in common among all of the people of the state in a body. Pure democracy is an ideal form, in which all decisions of the state are made by a majority of all of the people in it. Direct democracy more often refers to the creation or application of laws by the actual decision of the people as a whole, which is usually represented by a majority of voters or by a representative group, such as a jury. The most important corollary to this principle is that all officials are subordinate to the will of the people as a whole, not merely to a majority, and officials hold their offices in trust to the benefit of each member of the whole body. More, no group of officials or any one official may lay claim to sovereignty because it cannot be transferred.

**fascism**  Rule of a society for the good of the state. Fascism is a form of government in which all private and social commitments are organized to support a state engaged in a constant struggle against enemies of the state, both external and internal. Encouraged to accept both a national myth and a philosophy of grievance against state enemies, every individual is limited to the liberty essential to engage in a heroic struggle for the state, directed by unquestioned state leaders. The governments of Germany and Italy during World War II were fascist, and a common element of fascism in history is the corruption of not only history and language but also liberty, such as a statist defense of liberty or the defense of constitutionalism through an unfettered executive. The basis of law is the decision of the state leader; once the decider acts, the law is altered to justify and to support the action.
*See also:* jurisprudence, decisionism (dezisionismus); government, forms of government, tyranny (tyrant); despot (despotism).

**federalism**  *See:* federalism.

**kleptocracy**  Rule by thieves. A kleptocracy is a government in which the officials are thieves. Although not an ideal type of government, it arises if the holders of office take office in order to use its authority for their personal ends, or, after taking their offices, they use them to benefit themselves and their political or personal allies rather than to the benefit of the governed.
*See also:* corruption, corruption of office.

**matriarchy (matriarchate or gynocracy)**  Rule by women. A matriarchy is a form of government in which all of the ruling elite, or at least all essential government officials, are women. A more general term for matriarchate is gynocracy, the difference being that a matriarchate would privilege women who are older or have been mothers; the gynocracy is less hierarchical. Anthropologists believe that some early cultures were gynocratic, and the gynocracy is an ideal argued by certain feminist theorists in order to juxtapose the conflicts and failures of phallocracies.
*See also:* jurisprudence, feminist jurisprudence (feminist legal theory).

**mixed government**  A hybrid government combining several forms of organization. Mixed government combines several forms of governmental structure, such as an oligarchic federation, bureaucratic republic, or a communist dictatorship.

*See also:* hybrid.

**monarchy (kingdom or monarch)**  Rule by an hereditary monarch. Monarchy, in its ideal form, is a government ruled by a single individual, who is a child of the former ruler. Monarchies are distinct from autocracies or tyrannies as a matter of custom, in that a monarch agrees to serve the people ruled and exercises the powers of state in the interest of subjects rather than for personal gain. In practice, monarchy in the modern world tends to be a constitutional monarchy, in which the monarch retains certain prerogatives and customary powers that are never tested by use, while governance is managed by a representative government and a bureaucracy. A monarchy may be titled a kingdom, which it usually retains as its name even while ruled by a queen, as in the United Kingdom.

*See also:* people, sovereign people; government, forms of government, monarchy, queen.

**king**  The monarch who is male. The King is the male head of state in a monarchy. A host of offices are defined by the monarch, and are defined the King's when a king reigns and the Queen's when a queen reigns. The wife of the king may be made queen. For the chronology of the kings and queens of England since the Conquest, see regnal year.

*See also:* government, forms of government, monarchy, queen; year, regnal year.

**queen**  The monarch who is female. The Queen is the female head of state in a monarchy. A host of offices are defined by the monarch, being defined as the King's when a king reigns and the Queen's when a queen reigns. The husband of a queen may be designated king or as prince, particularly prince consort. A queen who is crowned only as the wife of a ruling king is a queen consort, as opposed to a queen regnant, who is monarch. For the chronology of the kings and queens of England since the Conquest, see regnal year.

*See also:* year, regnal year; government, forms of government, monarchy (kingdom or monarch); government, forms of government, monarchy, king.

**ochlocracy (majority rule or mobocracy or mob rule)**  Rule by the will of the majority without obligations of principle or reason. Ochlocracy is a traditional term for mob rule, or rule by the majority when no principle or reason restrains passion and self-interest. Majority rule, without constitutional limit, is ochlocracy.

**oligarchy**  Rule by a small group of elites. Oligarchy is government by a few citizens, who use the power of the state for whatever ends they choose. The government of a state by a council of military officers is a military oligarchy.

**patriarchy (patriachate or phallocracy)**  Rule by men, particularly when the state subordinates women. Patriarchy is government by men, and to use the term implies a hierarchy of men over women and powerful older men over other, younger or powerless men. Patriarchy is a basis for the criticism of the state, particularly when men use the power of the state to marginalize women and issues important to women, and use means of state power that to engage in conflict and other masculine enterprise at the expense of a nurturing community.

*See also:* jurisprudence, feminist jurisprudence (feminist legal theory); misogyny (misogynist).

**plutocracy (timocracy)**  Rule by the wealthy. Plutocracy is government controlled by those with the greatest wealth in society. Plutocracy is closely related to timocracy, or rule by those owning property. In its more extreme forms, plutocracy amounts to an oligarchy of the wealthy. In its more moderate form, it is a requirement of some quantum of property to participate in government. Solon's reforms in ancient Athens instituted timocracy to bring stability to the polis. A common argument in American electoral politics is that the influence of wealthy individuals and corporations over elected officials corrupts the republic into a plutocracy.

**republic**  Rule based on the will of the people. A republic is a government in which the people select representatives whose power is limited to use for the common benefit of all of the people in the state. Any state with a representative form of government, in which the leaders of the state are elected by the populace, may be loosely considered a republic, yet the core understanding of the term require both a meaningful choice of officials from among qualified candidates as well as a means of ensuring the officials exercise their power for the public good.

**republicanism**  Rule promoting law, individual liberty, and civic virtues. Republicanism is a theory of the state that requires a democratically elected but divided government under law, which encourages liberty balanced by basic civic virtues among its people. The theory is derived from the political philosophy of classical Rome and of early modern Europe, such as the writings of Machiavelli about Livy. Note: republicanism is, at most, only vaguely related to a republican political party.

**theocracy (theocratic)**  Rule according to a religious code. Theocracy is either a government based directly on religious principles, or a government controlled by leaders of a church or religious movement. Most such governments are overt in their claims to enforce the will of God as law, sometimes directly and sometimes as understood through an existing legal system. Colonial Massachusetts and late–twentieth–century Iran were theocratic states. A government enforcing religious principals on the basis of religion alone but with a secular veneer is a crypto–theocracy.

*See also:* God (supreme being or creator).

**tyranny (tyrant)**   Rule by one person, who is unfettered by law. Tyranny is rule of a state by a tyrant, a chief executive who is capable of practically any act in the name of the state without regard to the limits of authority in a balanced legal system. The tyrant may use unlimited discretion over the power of the state both to sustain the tyrant's security in office and, presumably, to further the tyrant's interests at the expense of the interests of the individuals in the state.

*See also:* government, forms of government, fascism.

**goy (goyim or goyishe)**   Anyone not Jewish. Goy is the term in Hebrew and in Yiddish for "Gentile," or not Jewish. A person or a nation may be a goy, and several of them are goyim. Anything realted to or done in the manner that a goy would do it is goyishe.

**grace period**   *See:* period, grace period.

**grade**   A measure of rank or quality. A grade is a comparative measure of quality or achievement or status, which vary according to context. For instance, a class grade is an evaluation of performance and achievement; a pay grade is a designation of status and compensation; a grade of food is a designation of quality and content.

> **graded offense or classified offense**   *See:* offense, classification of offenses (graded offense or classified offense).

**grand (graund)**   Large. Grand, in English, means not only important or impressive but also having a certain bigness relative to other, similar things. Thus in law, grand usually means that it is larger than something else that is similar, though it may also mean that it is more important. Grand larceny is both, but the grand jury is simply bigger.

*See also:* petit.

> **grand jury**   *See:* jury, grand jury.

> **grand larceny**   *See:* larceny, grand larceny.

> **grand–jury witness**   *See:* witness, grand–jury witness.

**grandfathering (grandfather clause)**   Exception of a current practice from a new prohibition. Grandfathering is the exception from a new law, whether a statute, rule, or other requirement, that allows practices at the time of the new law to persist even though the practices do not conform to the new law. This caveat might be expressed in the new law or inferred later.

When a grandfather provision is written into a law or recognized later, the non–conforming activity is allowed without the new prohibition, but the allowance is rarely permanent. The allowance might be for a specific period, for a reasonable period, of for as long as its current practitioner engages in it (but the right to engage in the practice is not transferable or revivable once the current practitioner ceases). Grandfather clauses are particularly common in laws that affect contract rights or property rights in order to avoid takings or interference with contracts.

**grantee**   The party who receives property from the grantor. A grantee is the party who receives property, or an interest in property, that was not owned by the grantee immediately prior to the receipt. It does not matter whether the property is sold or given as a gift; in either case the person who receives it is as the new owner is the grantee. A grantee may be dead, in which case the property either is held by the grantee's estate during probate or administration or descends to testamentary assigns or heirs at law (though the property may be subject to tax as if it were granted to the assigns or heirs by the dead grantee).

*See also:* grantor; title, title search, grantor–grantee index (grantor grantee index).

**grantor**   The party who grants property to the grantee. A grantor is the party who owns property, or an interest in property, and confers that property onto another. It does not matter whether the property is sold or given as a gift; in either case the person who had it but surrendered it to the new owner is the grantor. A grantor is always living at the time of the delivery of the granted property. A grant implies a grant inter vivos, or while the grantor lives. A grant that is not effected while a grantor lives is void. The means of grant after death is through a testamentary disposition — a devise or legacy in a Will, in which case, the grantor is the estate of the decedent.

*See also:* title, title search, grantor–grantee index (grantor grantee index).

> **grantor grantee or grantor–grantee index**   *See:* title, title search, grantor–grantee index (grantor grantee index).

**gratis**   Freely done or given. Gratis describes anything done or given without a claim or reward or a claim upon consideration. Anything offered gratis is offered without charge.

*See also:* promise, gratuitous promise.

> **gratis dictum**   *See:* dictum, gratis dictum.

**gratuitousness (gratuitous)**   Lacking necessity, or even justification. Gratuitousness represents several forms of unnecessity. Its meanings range from the noble to the scurrilous. In its noble form, a gratuitous act is charitable, the giving of property or time to others, gratis, without thought of compensation. In its scurrilous form, a gratuitous act is completely without justification or reason, such as a gratuitous insult, made without provocation, justification, or excuse.

**gratuitous agent**   *See:* agent, gratuitous agent.

**gratuitous contract**   *See:* contract, specific contracts, gratuitous contract (contract of benevolence).

**gratuitous promise**   *See:* promise, gratuitous promise.

**graund**   *See:* grand (graund).

**gravamen**   The harm or injury done that gave rise to a claim or prosecution. Gravamen is an ancient term for accusation, and its use persists as the basis of a claim against someone, which is used to compare judgments after the fact. Two judgments or verdicts of the same gravamen arise from the one incident or conduct for which, under one theory or another, the defendant was found liable or convicted.

**grave robbery**   *See:* robbery, grave robbing (grave robbery).

**great writ**   *See:* habeas corpus (great writ).

**Greek court**   *See:* court, Greek court, Areopagus (court of the Areopagus or Areiopagos).

**green card**   *See:* immigration, green card (permanent resident card).

**greenbelt (greenspace)**   A space of forests or fields in or around an urban area. A greenbelt is a zone of agricultural or undeveloped planted lands around an urban area, which is preserved both for its benefits in air quality and to maintain a sense of aesthetics or integrity in the community as a matter of land use. Greenspace includes any parkland, forest, or agricultural space within the urban geography used for the same purpose.

**greenhorn**   *See:* lawyer, newbie (baby lawyer, greenhorn).

**greenhouse gas**   *See:* pollution, air pollution, greenhouse gas (GHG or G.H.G.).

**Greensboro Truth and Reconciliation Commission**   *See:* rights, human right, human rights tribunal, truth and reconciliation commission, Greensboro Truth and Reconciliation Commission.

**grievance**   A complaint, or the harm of which one might complain. A grievance is both a harm suffered without a just cause and the complaint made for redress for it. In employment, particularly in employment subject to a collective bargaining agreement, a grievance is a complaint that initiates a procedure for review of the grievance that was suffered, which may or may not give rise to specific relief for the aggrieved worker. In any context in which a person is harmed by another person, particularly by an employer, an administrator, or an official, particular customs and usages in that context

determine whether grievance is to be used to depict the harm or the claim made upon it or both.

**grievance arbitration**   *See:* arbitration, grievance arbitration (rights arbitration).

**gross**   The fullest extent. Gross, as an adjective, is large, or more particularly, full. Thus, gross regarding a quantity is the full amount without any adjustment to the amount for any purpose. Thus, a gross income is the whole income prior to adjusting it for credits, exemptions, or deductions; Gross weight is the whole weight without accounting for containers; gross income is not reduced by costs of inventory, overhead, or expenses.

"Gross" when modifying an obligation or a liability means the fullest extent of that obligation or liability. Thus, gross negligence is the greatest degree of negligence, likewise, gross indecency is indecency of the most offensive extent.

*See also:* negligence, gross negligence (culpable negligence).

**gross as a quantity**   Twelve dozen. A gross is 144 of anything, usually a packaged as a dozen packages of a dozen units each.

**gross income**   *See:* income, gross income.

**gross margin**   *See:* margin, gross margin (net margin).

**gross misdemeanor**   *See:* misdemeanor, gross misdemeanor.

**gross negligence**   *See:* negligence, gross negligence (culpable negligence).

**gross profit**   *See:* profit, gross profit (gross profits or gross loss).

**gross profits or gross loss**   *See:* profit, gross profit (gross profits or gross loss).

**gross sexual imposition**   *See:* rape, gross sexual imposition.

**ground lease**   *See:* lease, ground lease.

**grounds**   The rationale for an argument, claim, or decision. The grounds for an argument or a claim or decision is the set of reasons and the reasoning on which it rests.

**grounds for dismissal**   *See:* dismissal, grounds for dismissal.

**grounds for divorce**   *See:* divorce, grounds for divorce, comparative rectitude; divorce, grounds for divorce.

**groundwater**   *See:* water, groundwater, runoff; water, groundwater.

**group insurance**   *See:* insurance, group insurance.

**group libel**   *See:* libel, group libel.

**grundnorm**   *See:* norm, basic norm (grundnorm).

**Guantanamo Bay**   *See:* prison, military prison, Guantanamo Bay (Camp Delta or Camp X-Ray).

**guarantee**   *See:* guaranty, guarantee.

**Guarantee Clause**   *See:* constitution, U.S. Constitution, clauses, Republican Form of Government Clause (Guarantee Clause).

**guarantor**   *See:* guaranty, guarantor.

**guaranty**   Assurance of the future payment of another's debt. A guaranty is a promise made to a creditor that the creditor will receive payment on a debt from the guarantor in the event a debtor does not make good on the debt. A guaranty is thus made among three parties, and it assures that performance will take place by the principal debtor when it is required, after which the creditor, who is the guarantee, may make a claim for performance from the guarantor. A guaranty may be a promise enforceable as a contract for which consideration is given to the guarantor, or it may be a promise made binding by the reliance of the guarantee in advancing credit to the debtor. A guaranty is not actionable, and it may not be the basis of a claim by the guarantee against the guarantor until a breach of contract or failure of performance by the debtor.

A guaranty may take many forms, and a contract that calls itself a guaranty may not be a guaranty in this sense. Thus, a loan agreement that is co-signed may amount to a guaranty of the co-signer as guarantor to the loan-making institution, even though the loan agreement does not specify that role by name. Likewise, a promise by the debtor to guaranty the debtor's own obligation is not a guaranty, nor, usually, is a promise by a third party to pay a debt already owing.

Guaranty is often written with a double "e" in lieu of a y, to stand for the contract and not standing only for the promisor. Context is essential to know which is meant: the promisor or the promise. The variation in typography for the promise makes no difference in the legal significance of the term representing it.

*guaranty and insurance and letter of credit and surety and warranty*   All are forms of assurance that something will be done. A guaranty, insurance policy, letter of credit, surety, or warranty are each forms of assurance that something will be done or that some amount will be paid when due. Often they are used loosely and interchangeably; particularly guaranty, warranty, and surety are often used with no distinction intended. Their differences are subtle but, depending upon the context in which the terms are used, these differences may be quite important in determining the obligations created.

A guaranty is a promise between a guarantor and a guarantee that another party will perform in the future for the guarantee. A loan guaranty, for instance, is a promise of one person (the guarantor) to pay back a loan entered by another person (the debtor), from the person to whom the guaranty is made (the creditor and guarantee) if but only if the debtor does not pay in the future. Insurance, or indemnity, is a contract between the insurer and the insured, for the insurer to indemnify the insured for an actual loss or liability the insured suffers in the event the debtor fails to pay the creditor. Insurance may be contracted by the creditor, the debtor, or a third party, but only if the contract requires the insurer to pay the creditor is the insurance contract a guaranty. Insurance may in fact be used to underwrite a guaranty to the creditor, as in a guaranty bond. A letter of credit is a promise by the issuer to pay money directly and on appropriate demand. It does not depend on another party's prior failure to perform any obligation. A surety is a contract to pay the debt of another, made directly between the surety and the creditor, and it does not depend on non-performance by the debtor, for the creditor to make a claim against the surety (though satisfaction of the debt by the debtor will extinguish the surety contract as well). A warranty is usually a promise between the debtor and the creditor to make good some defect in a condition that should already have been fulfilled. Note: there are other forms of warranty.

**guaranty bond**   *See:* bond, guaranty bond.

**absolute guaranty**   A guaranty that is not conditioned on a claim being made to the debtor. An absolute guaranty is an unconditional guaranty by the guarantor to pay the creditor the specified debt at the time of its maturity, in the event the principal does not pay the debt, but without requiring a demand upon the debtor or a judgment by the creditor, or any other condition. Note: the term "absolute" was once applied to any conditional guaranty once its conditions were satisfied, but this sense is now rare.

*See also:* guaranty.

**guarantee**   A person to whom a guaranty is made. Guarantee is, technically, the creditor to whom a guaranty is made. Guarantee is also an alternative spelling of guaranty, the promise itself (especially the promise to pay the debts of another person), and only context will indicate which is meant.

**guarantor**   Whoever makes a guaranty. A guarantor is any person or entity who promises to pay a loan if the principal does not. A guarantor is subject to the terms of a loan only to the extent the principal is. A guarantor provides an assurance that another party will pay a debt, but this assurance differs from the assurance provided by a surety: a surety is primarily and directly liable for a debt, and a creditor may pursue a surety for payment without regard to the payments of the debtor. A guarantor is only liable if the debtor defaults on the debt. Many states have laws regulating differently the interests of sureties and guarantors.

If a creditor relieves the principle from the obligation to pay, or takes any action that places the guarantor in a worse position, then the guarantor is also relieved from the obligation to pay. If the principal satisfies the loan, the guaranty is extinguished. On the other hand, if the principal fails to satisfy the loan when due, the creditor must ordinarily pursue the principal first and failing to achieve satisfaction of the debt, pursue the guarantor.

*See also:* surety (suretyship).

**guard dog**   *See:* dog, watchdog (guard dog).

**guardian (guardianship)**   Person responsible for the care and affairs of another person. A person who is appointed by a court as a fiduciary to care for the person and legal affairs of another, who is called the ward. The guardian of a child is an adult appointed to act as the lawful authority, provider, and caretaker for the child, as well as the trustee of any property the child has and the legal representative for all purposes in which the child has legal affairs. A guardian may also be appointed for an adult who lacks the capacity to manage daily affairs in life as well as the capacity to manage financial or legal matters. Guardianship may be plenary, or general, or may be specific in scope. There are more limited forms of fiduciary than a guardianship, however, particularly the trustee, the agent, and the conservator or curator.

*See also:* trustee; conservatorship (conservator); family, father.

*conservator and trustee and guardian*   All are fiduciaries who manage the affairs of another. There are considerable differences between a conservator, a trustee, and a guardian. A guardian is responsible for the care of the person of the ward, as well as for all of the ward's legal affairs and the management of all of the ward's property, but the guardian has a responsibility of care that may exceed use of the ward's assets alone. A conservator is responsible only for legal and financial decisions on behalf of the ward. The conservator does not care for or physically manage the daily affairs of the ward. The trustee manages only such assets as the trustee owns for the benefit of the beneficiary and has no other obligations to the beneficiary than to manage the res of the trust and to otherwise carry out the instructions of the settlor of the trust.

*guardianship action*   *See:* action, guardianship action.

**guardian ad litem (special guardian)**   Person appointed by a court to represent the interests of a ward throughout an action before that court. A guardian ad litem is appointed to represent the legal interests of a person in an action then pending in the court in which the guardian is appointed. Depending on the jurisdiction, an eligible guardian may be required to be a member of the bar or, at least, to have reached the age of majority, as well as to be physically, mentally, and legally capable of fulfilling the duties of guardianship. A guardian ad litem is often appointed to represent a child's interest in a dispute regarding custody or alleged abuse of that child, when a parent would not be able to represent the interests of the child without a conflict of interest, or the interests of an orphaned child in the probate of the estate of the child's last surviving parent. A guardian ad litem may also be appointed for a person lacking capacity who is brought into litigation.

*See also:* special; ad, ad litem.

**next friend**   An agent other than a guardian for an incompetent person in an action. A next friend is a person competent to appear in court who stands for a party who is not competent to do so, owing to youth, to a lack of mental capacity, or to a legal disability. A next friend is not a guardian ad litem, as the next friend is a volunteer and not a court appointee. The next friend recognized by a court may, however, make decisions regarding a case that would ordinarily be taken by the real party in interest (who lacks the power to make such decisions). A next friend may generally not appear pro se but must act through counsel.

*See also:* competency (competence or competent or incompetence or incompetency or incompetent).

**guardianship hearing (competency hearing)**   A hearing on a person's capacity and the appointment of a guardian. A guardianship hearing determines whether a person is legally incapacitated, or incompetent. If the court finds the person before it lacking in capacity and in need of a guardian, the court will appoint someone to be the person's legal guardian. A guardianship hearing is usually initiated by any interested party filing a guardianship petition. A person may not seek the appointment of a guardian in the manner that a settlor may select a trustee, or even as a testator nominates an exectutor. Even so, the wishes of the ward are taken into account if the ward is of age and has an independent voice with which to express a preference.

**guardianship of children**   Guardians are responsible for all aspect's of a child's development. A guardian of a child is responsible for ensuring every aspect of the child's physical care, shelter, clothing, and health; education; spiritual, emotional, and moral growth; and upbringing. A guardian might or might not be a custodial guardian, but the guardian's obligations persist even if the guardian lacks custody of the child.

**guest**   A person present on the lands of another, as either an invitee or licensee. Anyone using the property of another with the owner's permission. The standard of care that a landowner owes to a guest is not determined by the guest's status as guest alone. Following the common law, the standard of care owed by the landowner varies according to whether the guest is present for business or commercial reasons, in which case the guest is a business guest or invitee, or whether the guest is a social guest, in which case the guest is a licensee (regardless of whether the guest is invited). The standard of care owed to an invitee is higher than that of a licensee.

A guest of a hotel, motel, or other public accommodation is subject to specific rules, established by statute in each jurisdiction.

*See also:* land, liability to other on the land, guest; land, liability to other on the land, licensee.

**automobile guest** A passenger in a car with a driver. An automobile guest is a passenger in an automobile, present at the invitation of the driver or owner of the vehicle. A guest may be a paying guest, such as a taxi passenger, or a non–paying guest, such as a family member or carpool member. The guest in an automobile may have certain duties while riding as a passenger in the vehicle of another, and in some jurisdictions, a failure of those duties may be both actionable in itself and a bar to recovery for injuries caused by the driver. A guest may be required to protest against the negligence or recklessness of the driver, and if the driver continues to persist with such behavior, there may be a duty upon the guest to leave the vehicle if there is an opportunity to do so.

See also: automobile.

**guilt (guilty)** A legal determination of criminal responsibility. Guilt, in law, is the effect of a judicial determination that an individual or entity has violated the criminal law. Liability to be found guilty is not the same as guilt, and a person who commits an act that in fact violates the criminal law is culpable for the crime but not legally guilty of it until a court of appropriate jurisdiction pronounces guilt. A jury verdict of guilt or a plea of guilt are insufficient in themselves to establish guilt as a matter of law, which does not attach until the verdict or plea is accepted by a court as the basis for a judgment of conviction. Likewise, if the judgment is vacated, either by the trial court on reconsideration or as a result of an appeal, the effect is as if the defendant was never guilty at all. The same effect results from a pardon for the crime of which a person has been found guilty.

Guilt, in the sense of a mental state, may be an important element of the evidence of a crime, which might increase the likelihood of conviction, or the remorse that a defendant might show, which might be a mitigating factor in sentencing. Otherwise, psychological guilt is not an element in guilt at law.

See also: insanity, not guilty by reason of insanity; plea, criminal plea, not guilty; verdict, not guilty ( verdict of not guilty or not–guilty verdict); trial, bifurcated trial, guilt phase trial (liability phase trial).

**guilt phase trial** See: trial, bifurcated trial, guilt phase trial (liability phase trial).

**guilty but insane or GBMI or G.B.M.I.** See: plea, criminal plea, guilty but mentally ill (guilty but insane or GBMI or G.B.M.I.).

**guilty but mentally ill** See: plea, criminal plea, guilty but mentally ill (guilty but insane or GBMI or G.B.M.I.).

**guilty plea** See: plea, plea, criminal plea, guilty plea.

**guilty verdict or verdict of guilt** See: verdict, guilty (guilty verdict or verdict of guilt).

**in pari delicto (in par delicto)** See: in, in pari delicto (in par delicto).

**gun** A weapon that expels a projectile through a barrel. A gun is a device that expels a projectile through a barrel or tube. A gun need not be designed or intended as a weapon; some (like the nail gun) are intended for peaceful use, but most guns are designed for use as a weapon. A gun may propel the projectile by any means, such as a chemical explosion, a release of air, or pulse of magnetism. The great majority of modern guns use some form of chemical charge that explodes, causing a gas to expel the projectile. The term "gun," in general, includes all classes of these weapons, including artillery, although context is essential to determine whether the term is employed to mean a small arm, a weapon that may be carried by one person.

Firearms are inherently guns, and a statute or law that uses one term might well be synonymous with the other, although context is essential to determine that this is a correct interpretation of the statute or law. Laws regulating the use of guns and their ammunition are not uncommon, both as to the type of gun, the manner of its use, and the place of its carriage.

Arms, within the meaning of the Second Amendment, probably includes all forms of guns, although the limitations on restrictions of the carriage and use of such guns are quite controversial.

**firearm (arm or arms)** A weapon a single person may carry that fires a projectile. A firearm, in most statutes and regulations, is a gun that may be carried and fired by one person and that employs a chemical explosion to propel its projectile. In the absence of context or language to the contrary, "firearm" is likely to be synonymous with "gun" to mean only such small arms — rifles, pistols, shotguns, machine guns, and the like — that may be carried and operated by one person. As a matter of federal law, firearm includes both the whole and the parts of a firearm and any destructive explosive devices intended for use as a weapon.

As a matter of the Second Amendment, "arms" refers to all instruments that constitute bearable arms, even those that were not in existence at the time of founding. The right to bear such firearms is an individual right, though it is still subject to reasonable restriction and regulation.

Note: Some few jurisdictions consider devices that propel a projectile by air or mechanical energy, such as BB guns and air rifles, to be firearms within their general statutes, though such devices are regulated in most jurisdictions specifically rather than regulating the devices of children and adolescents with the weapons of adults.

See also: weapon.

**gun control** Regulation of any ownership or use of a firearm. Gun control is the regulation of the possession, ownership, sale, purchase, carriage, or use of a firearm, including the forms of weapon and ammunition that are lawful, the places or conditions in which they may be used, and by whom. The Second Amendment bars a state from forbidding the private possession of all forms of arms by all individuals in a state or city; however, reasonable regulations intended to control crime or the hazards of gun use are non unconstitutional.

Gun control in the United States is a highly contested issue. Those seeking regulations of firearms argue a concern to abate the frequent accidents and terrible acts of violence using firearms. Those seeking to prevent such regulation argue that firearms are essential for personal protection and individual autonomy, and they claim gun ownership is part of a republican tradition in the United States. The history of gun ownership in the United States, and the original purposes of the Second Amendment are themselves subject to great debate.

*See also:* constitution, U.S. Constitution, Amendment 2 (Amendment II or right to bear arms or Second Amendment).

**Brady Act (Brady Bill)**   Handgun buyers must pass a nationwide background check. The Brady Act, more fully the Brady Handgun Violence Prevention Act of 1993, codified at 18 U.S.C. § 921, et seq. (2011), prohibits a firearms dealer's sale of a handgun to any private purchaser without first checking the National Instant Check System (NICS), a national registry created by the Brady Act, which affirms or rejects the buyer under the criteria of the National Gun Control Act of 1968, codified at 18 U.S.C. § 921, et seq. (2011), particularly forbidding a sale to a fugitive, convicted felon, or domestic abuser. The act is named for James Brady, the White House Press Secretary who was injured during the attempted assassination of Ronald Reagan in 1981.

**spring gun (trap gun or man trap)**   A firearm rigged to shoot trespassers on a property. A spring gun is a firearm that is fixed to some platform, such as a wall, floor, or furniture, with a spring and a line running to the trigger, the idea being that a person entering the property on which there is a spring gun will pull the line and be shot by the weapon. There is no real difference between a spring gun and a trap gun. The same legal prohibition applies to a man trap or other device in which a trespasser is liable to be seriously injured or killed by a device intended to deter trespassers.

> Law and obedience to law are facts confirmed every day to us all in our experience of life. If the result of a definition is to make them seem to be illusions, so much the worse for the definition; we must enlarge it till it is broad enough to answer to realities.
>
> Benjamin N. Cardozo, *The Nature of the Judicial Process* 127 (Yale University Press 1921).

# H

**h**   The eighth letter of the modern English alphabet. "H" signifies a variety of functions as a symbol. It is translated into "hotel" for radio signals and NATO military transmissions, into "Henry" for some police radio traffic, and into dot, dot, dot, dot in Morse Code.

**h as an abbreviation**   A word commencing in H. When used as the first word of an abbreviation, H often stands for habeas, half, harmonized, Harvard, Hawaii, health, Hebrew, Henry (as in the King), herald's, hic, high, highest, home, homosexual, house, House (as in Congress), and human. As a title, it may stand for Hers, Highness, His, or Honorable. It may also stand for the initial of an author or case reporter, such as, Hale, Hall, Handy, Hansard, Hare, Harris, Harrison, Hartley, Hay, Hayes, Hazelton, Hazlitt, Henry, Hilary, Hill, Hopwood, Howard, and Hunter.

Selecting the proper article to precede the abbreviation "h" is tricky. The pronunciations of the letter h being what they are, the form of the article preceding a word starting in h will vary according to whether the h or the succeeding vowel is pronounced more prominently: a home but an honor. In either case, the abbreviation is likely to be preceded by "an" rather than "a."

**h as in hypotheticals**   Holder, or husband. H often stands for the holder of a commercial paper in the story of a law school hypothetical. When the designation is HDC it is holder in due course. In property, or other hypotheticals not drawn from commercial law, h is likely to represent husband.

**H.B. or HB**   *See:* legislation, bill, house bill (H.B. or HB).

**H.D.C. or HDC**   *See:* holder, holder in due course (H.D.C. or HDC).

**H.I.V. or HIV**   *See:* virus, human immunodeficiency virus (H.I.V. or HIV).

**H.M.O. or HMO or managed care organization**
*See:* employment, employee benefit plan, health insurance plan, health maintenance organization (H.M.O. or HMO or managed care organization).

**habeas corpus (great writ)**   A review of the lawfulness of any person's custody or restraint by a government official. Habeas corpus is a process of judicial review of any person's detention, whether by formal custody, incarceration, or continuing restraint, by an official or agent of the government of a state or the federal government. The term "habeas corpus" is Latin for produce the body, the order in the writ issued according to the common law to the person who held the petitioner in detention. The proceeding is initiated by a petition, or application filed by the detainee, who is the petitioner even if the pleading is prepared by others on behalf of the detainee, to a court of law with jurisdiction over the person who has detained the petitioner, that person being the respondent.

Both state and federal courts have jurisdiction to issue a writ of habeas corpus for individuals in custody under their laws or the authority of their respective governments. In both cases, a petitioner must first exhaust other remedies and alternative means of review. Thus, a person arrested for a crime that person believes is unconstitutional must challenge the constitutionality of the criminal definition in the trial proceeding and then complete an appeal process before raising the issue through a petition for a writ of habeas corpus. Likewise, a person held in custody by state officials is required to seek habeas from a state court first and complete that review before seeking habeas in federal court.

A petition, or application, is served on the respondent, who must either prove the person is not detained by the respondent or the respondent's agents or must prove the custody is not in violation of the Constitution or the laws or treaties of the United States or, in state court, of the constitution and laws of that state or the United States. Depending on the claims made by the petitioner, the court may review the respondent's authority to hold the petitioner, the evidence and procedures by which the petitioner came into the respondent's control, the sufficiency of the evidence against the petitioner, and claims of unconstitutional process that may have led the petitioner to be arrested, detained, or convicted. A finding by the court that the detention is unlawful usually leads to an order to the respondent that the petitioner be released.

The right of review of custody by habeas corpus is a fundamental constitutional right. It is a bulwark of individual liberty, having been used in England since at least the fourteenth century to free people who were held by local lords or church courts without legal authority or without having complied with the requirements of the law, and the courts have jealously guarded this prerogative. A 1772 petition for habeas corpus by James Somersett led to the end of slavery in England. Habeas corpus is protected in the U.S. Constitution from interference, being allowed suspension only if "in cases of rebellion or invasion, the public safety may require it," a condition that has only been met during the American Civil War.

Habeas corpus is available to anyone held by officials of an American government, even military agents, although it is not available for a battlefield detention during actual hostilities.

*See also:* corpus, habeas corpus; war, war powers.

*custody* Habeas is only available to a person in custody or otherwise detained. A habeas petitioner must in fact be held involuntarily by state or federal authorities at the time of the petition. The petition must allege custody as well as a specific, unconstitutional aspect of that custody. "Custody" in this context must be involuntary and ongoing. Custody includes detention or arrest that is has been been the subject of an indictment, information, or charge as well as detention or custody pursuant to an indictment, information, or charge. If, however, the petition is based on custody as a result of a sentence following a conviction for a crime, the person convicted cannot seek habeas corpus for relief from a sentence if the sentence has already expired, even the petitioner is still in custody because the sentence was later lengthened or the petitioner was sentenced for other offenses.

**Habeas Corpus Clause**   *See:* constitution, U.S. Constitution, clauses, Habeas Corpus Clause.

**procedural-default doctrine**   Federal habeas is barred when state habeas is denied for failure to meet a clear procedural requirement. The procedural-default doctrine bars the grant of habeas corpus by a federal court if a state court has already refused to consider a petitioner's federal claims, on the sole basis of a failure by the prisoner to meet a state procedural requirement. For the procedural-default doctrine to serve as a defense by the state to federal review, the state rule must have been clear, consistently applied in prior cases, and well established at the time of the petitioner's claimed default.

**habendum clause**   *See:* deed, habendum clause (tenendum clause or habendum et tenendum clause).

**habere**   To have. Habere is the Latin verb meaning generally to have or to possess, and it is the root of habendum, which is an essential word in most deeds, the have in "to have and to hold." At common law, a writ of habere facias possessionem was issued if the court determined that a buyer of real property was unable to take possession because of a holdover tenant; the writ of habere facias empowered a sheriff to evict the holdover tenant and put the bona fide purchaser in possession of the land in question.

**habendum (habendum et tenendum)**   *See:* deed, habendum clause (tenendum clause or habendum et tenendum clause).

**habit (habitual or habitually)**   An action or condition arising from repetition. A habit is a reflexive action of the body or mind by an individual, which is learned from frequent repetition of the same act. To suggest that something is done by habit is to suggest it is done without particular thought but as a matter of personal routine. Evidence that a particular action is a habit of a given individual is usually admissible to prove conduct in conformity with that habit.

**habitability (warranty of habitability or implied covenant of habitability)**   Promise that a residential property is suitable for living. The covenant of habitability takes two forms, one that applies to leased premises and one that applies to purchases.

As to leases, the covenant of habitability is a promise by a landlord to a residential tenant that the premises leased will be fit for human habitation throughout the period of the lease. A covenant may be express or implied. The covenant is breached if the conditions of the premises become unfit for human habitation, either by being unsafe, unhealthy, or physically or environmentally hazardous. In many jurisdictions, the requirements for the physical condition of living quarters in a housing code may serve as the presumptive conditions that satisfy the covenant, even though the code is enforced through an action by the state or the tenant that is independent of an enforcement of the covenant. A failure of the premises to meet these conditions may result in either a partial or a total constructive eviction. In many jurisdictions, the remedies of the tenant of withholding rent or of repairing a faulty condition and deducting the price of the rent is predicated on the covenant. There is no difference between a warranty of habitability in a residential lease and a covenant of habitability in a residential lease.

As to purchases, in many jurisdictions, an implied warranty of habitability is implied in the sale of residential buildings, creating an action against the contractor or builder for faults in design or construction that make the home unsafe or otherwise unfit for use as a dwelling in whole or in part. Such an action must usually be brought in a reasonable time, or a time set by statute. Not all jurisdictions recognize this warranty, and some of those that do limit its action to the initial purchaser of the dwelling. Moreover, some jurisdictions limit the action to new dwellings and to contractors, while others allow the action for previously built dwellings and against the vendor.

**habitat**   The ecology in which a species may survive, or a local ecosystem. Habitat has several related meanings. It comprises the biophysical requirements for the survival of an animal or plant: the natural conditions in which a particular species may survive and reproduce. It is also the specific area in which an animal or plant is found, including the interrelated natural systems, plants, and animals, whose integration define the localized ecosystem in which the animal or plant lives. Habitat can be defined in physical terms, such as acreage, or may be defined in terms of the biological and geographical features it encompasses. A habitat is critical to an endangered species if it contains features essential to the short-term survival of a species, such that environmental management is necessary to protect the species dependent on that habitat. Destruction of the critical habitat of an endangered species violates the Endangered Species Act.

*See also:* ecosystem; environment (environmental); species, endangered species.

**riparian habitat**   An ecology near a river or stream affected by the watercourse. A riparian habitat is a habitat adjoining or near a river or stream that is affected by the proximity of the watercourse to the plant and animal species that are present.

**habitation**   The right to dwell in a house or abode. Habitation is the lawful right to reside in a dwelling, although contemporary usage has condensed what was once a place of habitation to the mere term, habitation, so that there is now little difference between the place and the right to live there.

*See also:* dwelling (dwelling house); homestead.

**place of habitation**   Living, or a place where someone lives. Habitation is the act of living, especially living in a given locale. The distinction between the act and its place is nearly lost in modern English, and when used as a noun there is no real difference in most legal usage between a habitation and a dwelling.

**hadd (hudud)**   Serious crimes requiring severe punishment in Islamic law. Hadd, or in plural hudud, is a separation between two things according to Lisan al-'Arab. The hudud are more generally the limits set by Allah, such as laws of diet, dress, and social interaction. More specifically, the hudud are seven serious crimes whose punishment is prescribed by Allah. Human judges, who might be emotionally aroused by the commission of such crimes, do not determine their punishment. The crimes are apostasy, adultery, defamation, theft, brigandry, rebellion, and the drinking of alcohol. The sentences required are death for apostasy, adultery, brigandry, and rebellion; amputation for theft; and lashes for defamation and drinking. In contrast to hudud, which have severe mandatory sentences, ta'zir crimes are left to the judge's discretion in setting punishment. The burden of proof for hudud is very high, and convictions are rare.

**hadith**   *See:* shari'a, sources, hadith (ahadith).

**Hadley v. Baxendale Rule**   *See:* damages, contract damages, foreseeable damages, Hadley v. Baxendale Rule.

**haeres**   *See:* heir, haeres (heres or haeredes proximi or natus or legitimus or remotiores or factus).

**Hague (The Hague, Den Haag)**   The seat of the International Court of Justice. The Hague (Den Haag in Dutch) is the third largest city in the Netherlands and the de facto seat of government, though not actually its capital. Numerous treaties have been negotiated in The Hague, and it is the site of several institutions associated with international law, including the International Court of Justice, the International Criminal Court, Europol, and

several International Criminal Tribunals. A general reference to The Hague is usually a reference to one of the international tribunals, usually the International Court of Justice. Note: in English, the "t" of the article is capitalized when referring to the city, although not when Hague is used as an adjective or modifier (unless the article "the" is a part of the formal title of the noun). Thus, the Hague courts meet in the Hague and enforce the Hague Convention.

**Hague Conventions**   *See:* war, law of war, Hague Conventions (Hague Convention).

**Hague Academy of International Law**   Global institute for research and teaching in international law. The Hague Academy of International Law is an institute for research and teaching in international law, created in 1923 with funding from the Carnegie Foundation and located at the Peace Palace in The Hague.

**Haig–Simons income**   *See:* income, Haig–Simons income.

**halaal**   *See:* halal (halaal).

**halakhah (halakha)**   Jewish legal practices. Halakha is both the law of the Jewish people and the legal determination of a given question.

**halal (halaal)**   What is permitted in Islamic law. Halal is the general statement of what is allowed, what is permitted according to shari'a. Halal is similar in meaning to Mubah, but it is more general, encompassing a wide varieties of license. Food that is permitted to be eaten by a Muslim is specifically halal. Halal is the opposite of haram.

*See also:* kashrut.

**hale into court (hale to court or hail into court)**   To drag someone into a court proceeding. To hale someone into court is to draw them into a legal proceeding, either as a criminal or civil defendant or, less commonly, as a witness or other party. The sense of hale in this customary phrase is that of hale like hauling or dragging, such as haling (or hauling) a rope. This sense of hale being less common in general, hale is sometimes confused with its homonym for greeting or calling, and so the phrase is sometimes wrongly spelled "hail" into court.

*See also:* summons (summon or summoned).

**half**   One equal share of two shares in the whole. A half is one of two equal portions of a whole property. To specify that one of two people have a half interest in property, without more, is usually to have one-half of the whole interest, not a discrete portion that is 50 percent of the portions when assembled.

*See also:* moiety (moieties).

**Hand formula**   *See:* negligence, Hand formula (Learned Hand test or Hand rule).

**hand uplifted or raised hand** *See:* oath, uplifted hand (hand uplifted or raised hand).

**handcuffs** *See:* restraint, physical restraint, handcuff (handcuffs).

**handicap or mental disability or physical disability** *See:* disability, personal disability (handicap or mental disability or physical disability).

**handicapped access** *See:* access, handicapped access (disabled access).

**hanging judge** *See:* judge, hanging judge.

**hanging paragraph** *See:* cram down, hanging paragraph.

**haraam (haram)** Forbidden. Haraam is a category of prohibited acts; as one of the five hukm shari', to commit haraam is a sin, and to avoid haraam is to be rewarded. Anything done or used in violation of the law becomes itself haraam, and any place where certain people may not go, whether believers or others, is haraam to them. Haraam is the opposite of halal.
*See also:* makruh.

**harassment** The intentional offense or annoyance of another. Harassment is conduct or communications to or about an individual, whether done anonymously or not, that is intended to inconvenience, alarm, or offend the victim.
*See also:* stalking (stalk or stalker); jus, jus primae nocte (droit de seigneur or droit de cuissage or right of first night); agency, harassment, hostile work environment, Ellerth–Faragher defense (Ellerth/Farragher defense); agency, harassment, hostile work environment (abusive work environment).

  **continuing violation** *See:* discrimination, employment discrimination, doctrine of continuing violation; limitation, limitation of actions, statute of limitations, tolling, continuing violation doctrine.

  **discriminatory harassment** Harassment in an employment setting that amounts to unlawful discrimination. Discriminatory harassment is a harassing act or pattern of harassing conduct by one or more people toward one or more members of a group protected from employment discrimination under the U.S. Constitution, Title VII of the Civil Rights Act, or state law. In general, discriminatory harassment is divided into claims based on quid pro quo harassment and hostile work environment. It also includes harassment that is in retaliation for efforts to counter or complain of unlawful harassment, whether the retaliation is against a member of a protected class or someone else who associates with such members or attempts to counter harassment or advocate for the interests of one or more members of a protected class.

  **quid pro quo harassment** Harassment that must be tolerated to avoid harm in one's employment or to receive a benefit in one's employment. Quid pro quo harassment is harassment of an employee by a supervisor or manager with influence or authority over the employee or the employee's workplace, which is made in such a context that the employee must tolerate the harassment in order to receive a beneficial, tangible employment action or to avoid a detrimental, tangible employment action. The nexus between the toleration of the harassment and the employment action must be demonstrated by a tangible action that follows the refusal to accept or tolerate the harassment, either because the promised positive action, for which the employee would otherwise have been qualified, is refused or (much more often) because a negative action occurs. The nexus need not have been stated expressly; whether it was present prior to the tangible employment action is a matter of fact to be determined by the finder of fact from the evidence.
  *See also:* quid, quid pro quo.

  **sexual harassment** Unwelcome conduct of a sexual nature that interferes with its recipient's work or academic environment. Sexual harassment is any act or course of conduct or communication that is unwelcome by the person toward which it is directed, that is of a sexual nature — including advances, requests for sexual favors, contact with the body of either person — and that has the purpose or effect of unreasonably interfering with an individual's work by creating an intimidating, hostile, or offensive work or academic environment.
  *See also:* environment (environmental).

**harbor** A sheltered anchorage for ships. A harbor is any place where ships may ride at anchor in safety. Harbors may be natural or artificial. The term harbor has a broad metaphorical sense, in being any form of haven or shelter.
*See also:* safe, safe harbor.

**harboring (to harbor)** Hiding a person or thing from custody or capture. Harboring is the act of knowingly concealing a person or property in order to protect it from discovery, capture, arrest, or seizure. Any act that provides a location for use by a fugitive, including the provision of food or shelter or any help in avoiding detection and apprehension, is harboring a fugitive.

**hard labor** *See:* incarceration, imprisonment, hard labor (chain gang).

**hard-look doctrine** *See:* environment, national environmental policy act, hard-look doctrine.

**harm (harmdoer or harmful)** Any injury done to a person, entity, or property. Harm includes every form of injury that may be done to a person, entity or property, and any kind of loss that may be suffered. Harm to property is not limited to obvious or tangible damage, and harm can include anything done to a property that materially reduces the value of the property. Similarly, harm to persons is not limited to physical injury;

depending upon the applicable law, it can include mental anguish and emotional harm. Economically, harm may include a host of events that limit choice or increase inefficiency.

There are a great number of terms that are nearly interchangeable for harm in its sense in law. Evil, mischief, injury, hurt, damage, loss, pain each result in a particular form of harm. In a sense, harm is the most generic of all such forms of negative aspect of conduct, event, or thing, or condition.

Harm is both a noun and a verb. For a harmdoer to cause someone harm is to harm that person, the harmful result of which is a harm itself.

Harm, as the action of causing harm, includes both those actions that directly cause harm and those that do so indirectly, or as Blackstone said, both mediately and immediately. Thus, a person who causes another person to harm a third has harmed the third person.

See also: damage (harm or loss).

**divisible harm (divisible injury or divisible harms)** Injuries apportionable between two or more defendants. Divisible harms are injuries resulting from the tortious action of two or more parties, each of whom may be held liable only for the amount of the injury that party caused. If either the plaintiff's own negligence or an innocent source (such as an Act of God) causes a portion of a divisible harm, no defendant should be held liable for the damage caused by that source.

See also: liability, comparative liability (comparative fault or comparative responsibility).

**harm principle** The law must allow liberty to do anything but harm another person. The harm principle allows the only justification for legal intervention in private acts to be the prevention of one person from harming another person. The harm principle is controversial both in its limits to harms to people and in the many measures of what harm may be the harm that justifies state intervention.

**irreparable harm** See: injury, irreparable injury (irreparable harm).

**harmless error** See: error, harmless error (error in vacuo).

**harmonized tariff system** See: tariff, tariff as tax, harmonized tariff system (tariff system of the United States or TSUS or HTS).

**Hatch Act** See: civil service, Hatch Act.

**hate crime** See: crime, hate crime (hate-motivated crime).

**hate speech** See: speech, freedom of speech, hate speech (intimidation).

**hatra-ah** The caution given to a person about to commit a crime in Islamic law. Hatra-ah is a warning that must be given to a criminal and received in the presence of two valid witnesses in order to prove that the criminal acted with the requisite intent to be punished for a serious crime.

**hawk–dove game or snowdrift** See: game, game theory, chicken game (hawk–dove game or snowdrift).

**hazard (hazardous)** Anything posing a risk of immediate injury or loss. A hazard is an object or a condition that creates a likelihood that an injury will occur to a person, vessel, building, or anything else. The nature of a hazard is to be in such a location or condition that an injury will certainly result if only a very few additional conditions occur.

**extrahazardous (more than ordinarily hazardous)** A danger that requires unusual vigilance or repair. An extrahazardous condition, or a condition that is more than ordinarily hazardous, is a recognized or apparent hazard that requires more diligence to minimize or avoid the dangers it poses than is usual in daily life, but that is not so dangerous as to require strict liability for all injuries that result. When a condition of some road or way or place is such that accidents or injuries result there, or when it substantially resembles such a place elsewhere, a person or entity responsible for it has a heightened duty to minimize the danger, although it may not be so clear that the responsible person or entity is responsible for every accident that then might occur.

**hazardous substance (hazardous material or hazmat or Haz. Mat.)** Any substance posing a risk to human health, especially if it is flammable, toxic, corrosive, or explosive. A hazardous substance is a substance that poses a danger to human health through exposure by proximity, inhalation, ingestion, or absorption. Hazardous substances under state and federal law vary in definition, the primary definition being that under the Federal Hazardous Substances Act, that requires labeling of hazardous substances that are flammable, toxic, corrosive, or explosive. The FHSA, however, does not include pesticides, food, tobacco, drugs, or fuels, which are separately regulated, and many of which are hazardous. Various agencies, however, employ different definitions according to the scope of their statutory duties. The U.S. Occupational Safety and Health Administration (OSHA) includes materials that pose a danger to workers, including any substance or chemical that poses a "health hazard" or "physical hazard," including: chemicals which are carcinogens, toxic agents, irritants, corrosives, sensitizers; agents which act on the hematopoietic system; agents which damage the lungs, skin, eyes, or mucous membranes; chemicals which are combustible, explosive, flammable, oxidizers, pyrophorics, unstable–reactive or water–reactive; and chemicals which in the course of normal handling, use, or storage may produce or release dusts, gases, fumes, vapors, mists or smoke that have any of these characteristics. See 29 CFR § 1910.1200 (2010). The U.S. Environmental Protection Agency defines hazardous materials as chemicals or substances that can cause harm to people, plants, or animals when released by spilling, leaking, pumping, pouring, emitting, emptying, discharging, injecting, escaping, leaching, dumping or disposing into the environment. Its list of hazardous and extremely hazardous materials includes OSHA hazardous materials. See 40 CFR Pt. 355 (2010). The U.S. Department of Transportation defines a hazardous material as any item or chemical that is a risk to public safety or the environment when being transported or moved. See 49 CFR Pt. 105 (2010), and various industry-specific codes. The U.S. Nuclear Regulatory Commission regulates "special nuclear source" or by-product materials or radioactive substances. See 10 CFR Pt. 20 (2010).

Hazardous substances as a matter of tort include a wide range of materials that pose a risk of injury when used in a foreseeable manner, including electrical, chemical, mechanical, optical, and other risks. Hazardous substances as a matter of contract, particularly insurance contracts, include only what is specified in the contract, although the specification may be by description, by reference to lists maintained by private or public agencies, or by incorporation by reference of particular inventories or lists of the assured or the insurer.

**corrosive substance (corrosive chemical or corrosive material)** Any substance that destroys living animal tissue on contact. A corrosive substance is a hazardous substance because it causes the cellular structure of living human or animal tissue to lose its organization as cellular tissue on contact. The substance causes the tissue to break down or dissolve. Note: corrosive substances under the federal hazardous materials statutes include some corrosive chemicals but not all. A chemical may have a corrosive effect on other materials but not be corrosive on human tissue.

**flammable substance (inflammable substance or combustible material)** A substance that burns in ordinary conditions. Flammability is the potential of a solid, liquid, or gas to burn, or rapidly oxidize and release heat. Flammability is graduated by statute among substances that are "extremely flammable," "flammable," and "combustible." The regulatory definitions of these grades generated by the Consumer Product Safety Commission depend on the flashpoint temperature of the substance (and pressure if it is a contained gas): extremely flammable materials have a flashpoint at or below twenty degrees Fahrenheit; flammable materials have a flashpoint above twenty degrees and below one hundred degrees; combustible materials have a flashpoint at or above one hundred degrees up to and including one hundred and fifty degrees. Note: inflammable means "flammable" as well as "not flammable." This is confusing and potentially deadly. It is better not to use inflammable at all and to use "flammable" and either "not flammable" or "nonflammable."

*See also:* sanction (sanctions).

**moral hazard** *See:* morality, moral hazard.

**occupational hazard** A danger associated with a particular job or occupation. An occupational hazard is a danger that is associated with the tasks or workplace of a particular job or occupation. Workplace employers are required by state and federal laws to perform specific actions and to incorporate specific safety designs for particular work environments, and an employer is liable to an employee if the employee is injured owing to the negligent allowance by the employer of an occupational hazard.

**hazardous waste** *See:* waste, waste material, hazardous waste, toxic waste; waste, waste material, hazardous waste, hazardous waste manifest; waste, waste material, hazardous waste.

## head

**head of government** *See:* state, head of state (head of government).

**head of household** *See:* family, head of household (head of the household).

**head of state** *See:* state, head of state (head of government).

**head tax or capitation tax** *See:* tax, poll tax (head tax or capitation tax).

**headnote** *See:* reports, case reports, headnote; note, headnote.

**healing arts** *See:* medicine (healing arts).

**health** The quality of function of the mind and the organs of the body. Health is the degree to which the parts of the living body and mind function well. Health includes both mental health and physical health. As a measure, one may be in good or poor health, though an unqualified statement that one is healthy is a statement implying a lack of illness or injury. Health is a measure of not only the human being but also all living organisms and, metaphorically, any system. Thus, one speaks of the health not only of an animal or a plant but of an ecosystem, or of the oceans, or of the banking system. A healthy system in such a sense is one in which each organ, or component is itself sound and functioning as it ought to do, and the relationships among the organs of the system are, as Bouvier said, concordant, or agreeable.

**health information** *See:* record, medical records (health information).

**health insurance** *See:* insurance, category of insurance, health insurance.

**health insurance plan** *See:* employment, employee benefit plan, health insurance plan, health maintenance organization (H.M.O. or HMO or managed care organization); employment, employee benefit plan, health insurance plan, COBRA (C.O.B.R.A.);

employment, employee benefit plan, health insurance plan | coordination of benefits.

**health maintenance organization** *See:* employment, employee benefit plan, health insurance plan, health maintenance organization (H.M.O. or HMO or managed care organization).

**health care**  The range of medical services and policies encouraging long and healthy life. Health care is a range of medical services and policies, including traditional medical services provided to a patient by doctors, nurses, and hospitals but ranging through an array of services to provide an array of ancillary forms of skilled care, to promote knowledge and tools for diagnostic and treatment capability, to minimize environmental health risks, and to finance these services through public and private means.

*See also:* Medicaid; Medicare.

**Health Insurance Portability and Accountability Act (HIPAA or Kennedy-Kassebaum Act)**  Federal standards for privacy and security of health-care information. The Health Insurance Portability and Accountability Act of 1996 (HIPAA) establishes standards for the privacy and security of health-care information, creates standards for electronic data interchange of health information, and makes health care coverage more portable when individuals change employers. HIPAA allows disclosures of medical records other than by patient permission in limited circumstances, including the protection of public health, compliance with judicial orders, and certain governmental purposes. HIPAA, Pub. L. No. 104-191, 110 Stat. 1936, is codified throughout titles 18, 26, 29, and 42 of the U.S. Code.

*See also:* privacy, medical privacy | Health Insurance Portablility and Accountability Act.

**Patient Protection and Affordable Care Act (Affordable Case Act or Obamacare or PPACA)**  A federal regulation of health-care economics requiring most persons to have health insurance. The Patient Protection and Affordable Care Act is a comprehensive federal regulation of health care and health insurance passed in 2010. Pub.L. 111-148, 124 Stat. 119 (2010). It affects many arenas of health care and medical insurance, as well as criminal law regarding false claims and fraud, providing both a subsidy for the poor to receive insurance and an incentive system to encourage preventive medicine. Its most controversial requirement is the Minimum Essential Coverage Provision, a federal tax on nearly every individual who does not receive insurance through an employer, from a third party, or by personal acquisition of health-care coverage. As of 2011, the constitutionality of this provision (which is sometimes called, misleadingly, the individual mandate) was much debated, with lower federal courts divided on whether the mandate was in the scope of the necessary and proper regulation of interstate commerce. The view of most academics is that the

purchase of health care or refusal to do so is a federally regulable economic decision. Note: owing to the strong association between the bill and the presidential administration of Barack Obama, the statute has acquired the slang label of Obamacare, a term used initially by opponents of the law and increasingly embraced by its defenders.

**Surgeon General**  The chief of the U.S. Public Health Service. The U.S. Surgeon General leads the U.S. Public Health Service and is responsible for leading educational, advocacy, and policy strategies related to the protection and improvement of public health in the United States. As do other members of the USPHS, the Surgeon General holds a rank in the commissioned corps of the service, equivalent to a rank in the U.S. Navy, usually that of a vice admiral.

**public health**  The science and regulation of the conditions required for health. Public health includes the study and implementation of the conditions required to protect and improve health among individuals in communities, states, and the world by means of preventative medicine, health education, communicable disease control, and the application of the social and sanitary sciences. Public health is the most fundamental arena of traditional state police powers, and it has been accepted as an appropriate basis for federal regulation as a matter of interstate commerce and treaty powers. Property taken as required to effect public health is not subject to takings analysis.

*See also:* police, police power (powers of police); public.

**hearing**  Proceeding at which a party will be heard. A hearing is the argument of any question of law, fact, or both, before a person or panel that hears arguments or evidence on the question and determines an answer that is binding on those who argued it. A hearing may be an adjudication of a whole dispute on its merits in an administrative setting, though the term is rarely used for a hearing on the merits in a court of law. A hearing in court is usually a consideration or a preliminary question or a dispute over a matter of procedure or evidence; the final adjudication of the substance of a dispute is done in trial.

*due process in a hearing*  A hearing in which a person's life, liberty, or property interests are in issue must satisfy the requirements of due process of law. A hearing, to be constitutionally valid as a matter of due process, must meet certain minimum criteria. The hearing must be before an unbiased adjudicator with the power to act or not to act as a result of the evidence presented at the trial. The hearing must follow notice to all the parties adequate for them to prepare. The hearing must be held so that all of the parties may present evidence essential to its outcome, to hear the evidence of others against them, and to be able to argue the reasons why the decision should favor themselves. The hearing should result in a decision based on reasons derived from the evidence and standards of law, which should be subject to review by an impartial appellate body.

Hearings not subject to due process may still require notice, an opportunity to be heard, an impartial judge, and review, which are essential to administrative justice.

**adjudicative hearing (adjudication hearing or adjudicatory hearing)** An administrative hearing on the merits of a petition or complaint. An adjudicative hearing is a final review on the merits of a substantive issue pending before an administrative tribunal, whether in an agency or department or in a judicial hearing that does not amount to a full trial. The rules governing various procedures in various forums may use one or another of the otherwise synonymous phrases among adjudication hearing, adjudicatory hearing, or adjudicative hearing, but other than those specified by rules there is little difference: each is a hearing to adjudicate the claim, petition, charge, or matter before it. A common distinction, however, is that an adjudicative hearing may determine the substance of a matter, with a second hearing to determine a disposition, thus allowing administrative personnel to complete additional research and reporting between the adjudication and disposition, as well as to allow pre-disposition negotiation between the parties involved who then understand the liabilities in issue. Thus, an adjudicatory hearing may determine a child to be a delinquent, and a disposition hearing will determine whether the child will be placed in one or another environment or program.

**administrative hearing** A hearing within an executive agency to adjudicate a claim or dispute. An administrative hearing is a hearing held not by a court but by an executive agency of the government. An administrative hearing is held according to statutes and regulations of the government of which the agency is part. In most instances, an administrative hearing is either an initial determination of someone's rights, duties, privileges, or immunities, or it is an administrative appeal from an initial determination made by an officer of the agency. In either case, the hearing must comply with both the administrative procedures that govern the agency as well as with such requirement of due process of law as attach owing to the liberty or property interests at stake for the citizen before the hearing.

**fair hearing** A hearing that satisfies the requirements of due process.

**judicial hearing** A hearing before a judge. A judicial hearing is a hearing before a judge. A judicial hearing differs from a trial, even a bench trial, because the subject of the hearing is not the evaluation of the evidence and arguments on the final merits of a case but upon a more limited question requiring a more limited ruling. A judicial hearing differs from an administrative hearing, in that it is before an independent member of the judiciary, rather than an agency employee.

**motion hearing** A judicial hearing on the merits of a party's motion. A judicial proceeding hearing an argument on the merits of a motion pending before a court. Motion hearings may be pre-trial, post-trial, or post-judgment, or during a trial. A motion hearing held during a jury trial on the matter in which the motion is lodged is usually held out of the presence of the jury, either informally as a side bar conference or in chambers, or, if witnesses are to be called, with the jury excused from the courtroom. Depending on the complexity of the dispute, the court may schedule the hearing sua sponte, or the moving party may request the hearing. The hearing will usually result in a dispositive order on the motion or motions in question, although a motion hearing might or might not be reported and held on the record.

**prehearing conference** A meeting to ascertain evidence and arguments and promote settlement before a hearing. A prehearing conference is a meeting between the opponents preparing for a hearing, which serves much the same functions as a pretrial conference: the parties list their witnesses, evidence, and arguments, and attempt to settle the matter prior to the hearing.

*See also:* pretrial, pretrial conference (pretrial memorandum or pre-trial conference).

**preliminary hearing (first appearance or preliminary examination)** A pretrial hearing to determine whether probable cause exists to hold a defendant for trial on a criminal charge. A preliminary hearing is a pre-trial proceeding required in most states and the federal criminal system for any person arrested for a felony when the defendant is not yet indicted by a grand jury (or waives indictment). The preliminary hearing must be held soon after charge or arrest, usually within twenty days, or ten days after the initial appearance if in custody.

The primary function of the preliminary hearing is for the judge, or magistrate-judge, to hear evidence to determine whether sufficient evidence exists to find probable cause both that the offense charged was committed and that the defendant committed it. The defendant is allowed to cross-examine prosecution witnesses and may produce evidence. The court in a preliminary hearing may also decide issues of admissibility in anticipation of trial, and set the amount of the defendant's bail if bail is required. Note: various jurisdictions have different procedures for the preliminary hearing, some incorporating processes that in others are done in arraignment or other hearings; in general, there is no difference between such a hearing whether it is denominated a preliminary hearing, preliminary examination, or first appearance.

*See also:* arraignment.

**rehearing** A second consideration of evidence or argument of a matter heard once already. A rehearing is a second hearing on a matter for which a first hearing has been held. A rehearing might be employed by the court to cure a procedural defect in an initial hearing, to hear newly discovered evidence, to hear extended argument on a matter of law or fact, or for any other purpose deemed sufficient by a court prior to reaching a decision in the matter before it.

Rehearing differs from retrial in that a rehearing implies a new hearing with new argument, limited in scope to those matters designated by the court, rather than a new trial on all of the issues. Rehearing differs from reconsideration, in that reconsideration is more often a matter of motion following a decision of the court, while rehearing may be ordered prior to a decision.

**hearsay**   A statement that is not testimony, offered in court to prove the point of the statement. Hearsay, in general, is any statement made out of court (or, if made in court, not made as testimony under oath in the time and place the statement is used) that is introduced in court to prove the "truth of the matter asserted" by the maker of the statement. In other words, the statement is being used to prove that what was said is true. Such statements are generally not allowed in evidence for various reasons including questions of reliability of the speaker, the potential for error in the statement that cannot be explored at trial, and because the person making the statement is not available for further examination or cross-examination. A statement may be hearsay whether it is said aloud or written in any form.

Only out-of-court statements introduced to prove that what was said in the statement is true are hearsay. Statements that are introduced for other reasons are not. Thus, a statement is not hearsay even if it is reported by a witness who overheard the statement shared between a party and another person if the statement is introduced to prove that the party knew the other person, although it might be hearsay if the statement was introduced to prove that what the party told the other person was true. The danger, however, that such statements may be interpreted as proving the truth of the matter asserted make such uses vulnerable to objection owing to their potential misuse. The potential for such misuse is sometimes curable by an instruction to the jury, but often it is not completely curable because the jurors may still believe the statement is evidence of what was reportedly said.

Further, not all out-of-court statements introduced in court to prove their point are hearsay. Some prior statements by witnesses and some admissions by a party opponent are excluded from the definition of hearsay.

In addition, there are thirty exceptions to the bar on hearsay, which allow hearsay statements to be entered into evidence. These include a general exception allowing probative, trustworthy, best-available evidence that serves the interest of justice.

Hearsay statements that are entered in evidence against a defendant in a criminal trial are subject to further limitations under the Confrontation Clause. This constitutional limit requires a hearsay statement that is allowed for use in a testimonial capacity to be admitted only if it was made made in conditions that allowed for a meaningful confrontation of the declarant, such as cross-examination.

*See also:* declarant; evidence (evidentiary); confrontation; falsehood.

**declarant**   The person who made an out-of-court statement. The declarant is the speaker who made a statement out of court that later becomes subject to analysis for hearsay in order to determine the admissibility of the statement.

*See also:* declarant.

**hearsay exception (exception to hearsay)**   Hearsay statements that are admissible in court. A hearsay exception is one of thirty categories of hearsay that is admissible even though the statement meets the definition of hearsay and would otherwise be barred from use at trial. Each category reflects a policy judgment that the normal risks of the unreliability of hearsay are outweighed by some indicia of reliability that increases the inherent reliability or probative value of such evidence. Note: The exceptions apply only to statements that are hearsay; exclusions from hearsay are distinct and not subject to exception, because excluded statements are not barred as hearsay anyway.

Some exceptions apply only if the declarant is not available to testify in the matter in which the statement is to be proffered for admission.

Exceptions that apply whether or not the declarant is available to testify include a statement of present sense impression; of excited utterance; of then-existing condition; a statement made for medical diagnosis or treatment; a recorded recollection; a record of regularly conducted activity; a lack of record in records of regularly conducted activity; a public record or report, or a lack thereof; a record of vital statistics; a record of family data of a religious organization; a certification of a marriage, baptism, or similar ceremony; a family record; a document affecting an interest in property or a statement therein; information from an ancient document; a market report or commercial publication; a learned treatise; a statement regarding reputation concerning personal or family history, boundaries, or general history; a statement of reputation as to character; a final judgment of previous conviction; a judgment as proof of personal, family, or general history, or boundaries.

Exceptions that apply only when the declarant is not available to testify include: some statements given in former testimony, statements made under a belief of impending death, a statement made against the declarant's interest, a statement of personal or family history, and a statement made by a witness whom the other party had wrongly kept from the hearing.

A residual exception allows hearsay even if no other exception will allow it. If other circumstantial guarantees of trustworthiness of the evidence are offered to prove the material fact at issue in the statement, and if the statement is more probative than other evidence reasonably available to the proponent, and if both the spirit of the rules and the requirements of justice would be best served by admission, then the evidence should be heard.

Note: In a criminal trial, the allowance of hearsay by an exception is no assurance of the statement's final admissibility. A statement otherwise admissible that is a testimonial statement that, if introduced would violate the Confrontation Clause, is still barred.

*See also:* hearsay, hearsay exclusion.

**exception only when declarant is unavailable (unavailability)** Hearsay statements that are only admissible if the declarant is unavailable to testify on that issue. A hearsay exception only when the declarant is unavailable is limited to use when the declarant cannot or will not testify as to the particular subject matter of the hearsay statement.

Unavailability is a term of art under the Federal Rules of Evidence, turning upon the ultimate failure of the declarant to testify on the specific subject matter of the hearsay. A declarant who is unavailable is exempt from testimony on that subject under a privilege, refuses to testify regardless of an order, claims a lack of memory, is physically or mentally unable to testify, is dead, or is absent.

**belief of impending death (dying declaration)** A statement by a declarant who believes that he or she is about to die. The statement made under belief of impending death is a statement made by the declarant at a moment when the declarant truly believes that the declarant's death is very soon to occur and inevitable. The measure of such statements is whether the declarant believes that death is likely, not whether it in fact occurs, and the hearsay dying declaration is still admissible for a declarant who recovers, just as it is in the event the declarant was not in fact in mortal danger.

Such statements are admissible hearsay when the declarant is unavailable to testify. Under the federal rules, however, the use of such statements usually is limited only to the cause or circumstances the declarant believes have brought about the defendant's impending death. The rationale for admitting such statements is that a declarant is thought to have little or no reason to make false statements on the deathbed.

*See also:* causa, causa mortis; in, in extremis.

**family history (personal history)** A statement of certain facts about one's own history or a matter of family history. A statement of personal history is a statement by a declarant regarding the declarant's own birth, parentage, marriage, or similarly personal and significant history, and a statement of family history is a statement regarding a member of the declarant's family regarding a similar subject. A statement of personal history or a statement of family history may be admitted regardless of hearsay, if the declarant is unavailable to testify. A statement of personal or family history is admissible even if the declarant had no means of acquiring the information directly. A statement of family history, however, may require evidence that the declarant was sufficiently intimate with the branch of the family or the person about whom the statement is made as to be likely to have accurate information about the subject matter of the statement.

**forfeiture by wrongdoing** A statement of a witness unavailable to testify owing to the opposing party's wrongdoing. Forfeiture by wrongdoing is an aspect of hearsay that allows the use of hearsay in any proceeding in which the party against whom the evidence is proffered acted wrongly, as a result of which the declarant is unavailable as a witness on that matter. At common law, a defendant in a murder trial could not bar statements made by the victim, on the assumption that the defendant's conduct caused the victim's unavailability as a witness. In the light of the Confrontation Clause, however, the forfeiture by wrongdoing exception only applies if the defendant causes the witness to be unavailable through an act that was intended to prevent that witness from testifying. A wrongful act, even a murder, made without this intention does not waive the defendant's Sixth Amendment right to confront and cross-examine the witness. This limitation does not apply in civil matters. The rationale behind this rule should be abundantly clear: the objecting party should not be allowed to weaken the strength of his opposing party's case by preventing witnesses who would have otherwise taken the stand in support from appearing in court. Such a practice, if endorsed, would allow for any party to do the same and would cast doubt on the legitimacy of the court and the final ruling.

**former testimony** A statement made under oath in an earlier proceeding against the same or a similar party. Former testimony is a statement made as a witness at a hearing or deposition other than the hearing or deposition in which the former testimony is offered, and if two conditions are met. First the declarant must have been under oath and subject to cross-examination at the time of the earlier statement. Second, the party then allowed the cross-examination must either have been the same party who intends to introduce the old testimony in the later proceeding or have been another party that was either a predecessor in interest to the current party or so similar that the party opposing the witness had the same motive and opportunity to develop or confront the testimony through questioning the witness. Such statements are admissible hearsay when the declarant is unavailable to testify.

**statement against interest (admission against interest or declaration against interest)** A statement so contrary to the declarant's interests that it is likely to be true. A statement against interest is a statement that is so contrary to the declarant's legal or financial interests that no reasonable person would make such a statement unless it were true. Such statements are admissible hearsay when the declarant is unavailable to testify. The rules of evidence provide extensive illustrations of forms of interest against which a statement may be made, including the declarant's pecuniary interest, proprietary interest, a statement that would expose the declarant to civil liability or to criminal liability, or generally any statement contrary to a meaningful interest of the declarant, such that a reasonable person in the declarant's position would not have made it unless it was actually true. A statement must be made intentionally and knowingly to be an admission, and so a statement is only an admission against interest if the declarant knows that the statement is contrary to an interest of the declarant at the time the statement is made.

*See also:* admission.

### hearsay allowed regardless of witness availability

**ancient documents**  A statement in an authentic document twenty years old or older. Ancient documents are documents of proven (or unquestioned) authenticity that are at least twenty years old.

The form of proof required to demonstrate a document's authenticity depends on the nature of the document. Documents that have been held in an archive, library, or similar institution may be authenticated by a statement from the official housing the document that the document is as presented. Some documents may require validation by appropriate experts, but some documents may also be self-authenticating. Documents are authenticated under Federal Rule of Evidence 901 by evidence that is sufficient to support a finding that the matter in question is what its proponent claims it to be. Specifically in Rule 901(b)(8), the document should be a condition that creates no suspicion concerning the document's authenticity; in a place where, if the document is authentic, it would likely be; and have been in existence twenty years or more at the time it is offered. Statements in an authentic ancient document are not barred as hearsay.

*See also:* evidence, authentication, ancient document (ancient writing).

**business record (regularly conducted activity or business-records)**  A statement made in a record kept as a matter of routine by a business. A business record is any record that is created or kept as a matter of the normal course of business. Authenticated business records are allowed in evidence, and statements made within a business record that was created and kept as a matter of the routine of the entity conducting that business are admissible under the business-records exception to the hearsay rule.

*See also:* record, medical records (health information).

**documents affecting an interest in property**  Deed, grant, letter, will, or other document that might affect a property interest. A document affecting an interest in property includes deeds, patents, wills, letters, or any other instruments, documents, or records that purport to establish or affect an interest in property. Such documents are admissible and statements in them are admissible despite being hearsay, unless the persons or entities whose interest are purportedly established in the document have not behaved or acted in a manner consistent with the statements in the document.

*See also:* book, book as business record (books).

**excited utterance (spontaneous declaration or spontaneous exclamation)**  An unthinking statement made at a moment of great surprise and stress. An excited utterance is a statement made during or immediately after the declarant is surprised by a startling event or condition, while the declarant is under the stress of excitement caused by the event or condition. Excited utterances are admissible evidence despite both the hearsay rule and the Confrontation Clause, because they are only admissible when the circumstances of the statement are sufficient to demonstrate that the statement was an unthinking, unplanned reaction to events. To introduce an excited utterance, the proponent must demonstrate that the statement was made during or following a startling event or condition, that the statement was made while the declarant was under the stress of excitement caused by the event or condition, and the statement relates to the startling event or condition. The emotional state of excitement or stress of excitement may take many forms, but it must be sufficient that a reasonable person would be sufficiently attentive to the event or condition in itself that collateral issues, such as fault, responsibility, or reputation would not be then material. The manner in which the excitement is caused may be direct, as when the declarant is a participant in the event or a witness to it, or indirect, as when the declarant learns of the event later. By definition, a statement may be an excited utterance and not perfectly contemporaneous with the event, but it must be made while the emotional state caused by the event or condition persists. Many, though not all, statements that are excited utterance are also forms of statement or present sense impression.

**judgment of previous conviction**  A final judgment of guilt in a criminal action for a felony. A judgment of previous conviction is a record of a final judgment of guilt in a felony criminal proceeding, as long as the defendant was liable for death or imprisonment of more than a year, regardless of the sentence imposed. The judgment may have been entered either following trial or the entry of a plea other than a plea of no contest or nolo contendere. A judgment of previous conviction is admissible hearsay to prove any fact essential to sustain the judgment, as long as it is used only to prove a fact essential to the judgment in a proceeding against the person initially accused and adjudged or, if the judgment is used in a proceeding against someone other than the initial accused, if it is used only for the purpose of impeachment of credibility as a witness. A judgment of previous conviction is admissible while an appeal of that judgment is pending, though the judgment is not admissible if it is vacated or reversed, even if proceedings persist in that cause.

See also: conviction.

**learned treatise** A statement in a publication of scholarly authority. A learned treatise includes any published scholarly authority, whether in a book or treatise per se or in an article, report, pamphlet, or other publication in a scholarly discipline. Statements in a learned treatise are admissible hearsay when relied upon by an expert witness.

The hallmark of a learned treatise is a publication that is written by a professional in the subject field of the publication, whose reputation depends upon the publication's accuracy. Statements in a learned treatise are admissible, but the treatise itself is not to be treated as an exhibit. The proponent of a statement from a learned treatise must demonstrate that the publication is reliable, whether by expert testimony, by stipulation, by testimony, or by judicial notice. The rationale for admitting such statements into evidence is that they are usually indicative of trustworthiness, as they have been written by people with special training and education within those fields and have not been written for the specific purpose of influencing the litigation at hand. Note: publication need not be in a physically printed binding, but electronic publication in a manner consistent with scholarly publication in that discipline at the time is sufficient.

See also: witness, expert (expert witness).

**medical statement (medical treatment or medical complaint)** A statement of medical history or condition made while seeking or receiving diagnosis or treatment. A medical statement is any statement regarding a personal medical or health condition or personal medical history, including past or present symptoms, pain or other symptoms, sensations, or general information related to an injury, illness, or other health difficulty, that is made by the declarant for the purpose receiving medical diagnosis or treatment and is at least reasonably pertinent to the condition or injury or its diagnosis or treatment. A medical statement may be made by a patient or, if circumstances establish a high degree of reliability in the statement, by a person responsible for a patient, such as a parent. A medical statement may be admissible if it is made to a medical professional, to an emergency responder, or to any person whose assistance with a medical emergency might reasonably be considered essential for emergency treatment or care. Medical statements are usually admitted because of their trustworthiness, as they are most often made by a doctor to a patient while having conversations concerning a medical condition. The statements made must be reasonably pertinent to treatment and diagnosis; thus, accusations of blame or liability made by a doctor are almost always excluded from this exception.

**present sense impression** A narrative of an event or condition made while the declarant observes it or immediately after. A statement of present sense impression describes or explains an event or condition made while the declarant actually observes or perceives the event or condition, or it is made immediately afterwards. These statements are admissible hearsay because when made while witnessing the event or in its immediate aftermath, the possibility of deception or untruth on the part of the declarant is greatly diminished, and also the veracity of the statement, because made immediately, is likely to provide an accurate testimonial account of the event. Many, though not all, statements that are statement of present sense impression are also statements made as an excited utterance or are statements of present condition, but the use of these statements are set out as distinct exceptions, subject to different limitations of use.

**public record (public records or public reports)** A report or record by a public official or office that is required to be made by law. A public record is any record, report, statement, or other compilation of data, in any form, that is created by a public officer or agency that either sets forth the activities of that office or agency, or sets forth any matter the officer or agency is required by law to observe or report or that sets forth the factual findings or determination resulting from an investigation by that office or agency. Public records are admissible hearsay within certain limits. In a criminal case, for example, no public record is admissible under the public records exception to hearsay if the record reports a matter observed by police officers or other law enforcement personnel. Note also that in civil actions or in any proceedings against the government in a criminal case, a public record is admissible hearsay only if the factual findings resulting from an investigation made pursuant to authority granted by law do not rely on sources of information or result from other circumstances that indicate a lack of trustworthiness. The public records exception exists because these records are generally considered to be trustworthy since they are usually generated by public servants as part of their duties associated with a public service, and they are often essential for a witness to recollect the specific events relative to a report.

*See also:* public.

**record of religious organization**  A statement regarding personal or family history kept as a regular record by a religious organization. A statement of a religious organization is a statement by a church, temple, mosque, or other institution, that is kept in a regularly maintained record of family or personal history, including a statement of birth, death, marriage, legitimacy, family relationship, or burial.

*See also:* statistic, vital statistics.

**recorded recollection (past recollection recorded)**  A contemporaneous record used to refresh a later insufficient recollection of the events recorded. A recorded recollection is a statement, memorandum, notes, or other record made by a witness, or made by another and adopted by the witness, of the witness's memory of a then-past event, which is made for any purpose but that was made or adopted by the witness when the witness still had a fresh and clear memory of the events recollected and that was apparently perceived then by the witness to reflect correctly the knowledge of the witness of the event. A recorded recollection may be read into evidence without regard to hearsay, from which it is an exception, even if the declarant is available, if the witness at the time of its use has insufficient recollection to testify fully and accurately. A recorded recollection may be read into the record but not used as an exhibit unless offered by the party adverse to the witness who recorded the recollection.

*See also:* recollection (recollect).

**regularly conducted activity**  *See:* hearsay, hearsay exception, hearsay allowed regardless of witness availability, business record (regularly conducted activity or business-records).

**reputation**  A community's opinion of a person or entity. Reputation is an opinion that is widely held by members in a community, as to any fact or any evaluation of a person, institution, or any thing. A jury is not barred from learning of a matter of reputation, if that reputation is relevant to an issue before it. Evidence of reputation must be derived from members of the community in which reputation would be expected to arise as a matter of personal observation and association among those holding the opinion.

Generally, reputation of character may never be used to prove a disputed fact of human action on the basis of conformity to reputation. Even so, reputation may be used as evidence to prove a disputed fact, even of human action, as to matters of personal history, family history, general history, and property boundaries, interests, and uses. It is also relevant and sometimes allowable to prove the likelihood (or unlikelihood) of a witness's telling the truth.

*See also:* reputation; opinion.

**reputation as to character**  Opinion as to a person's good or bad reputation among people in a group. Reputation as to character is a cumulative opinion about a person's good or bad character, not the opinion that the witness actually holds about that person. Reputation as to character is general, and it does not usually include a reputation for specific conduct, but reputation for more general traits, such as for trustworthiness or untrustworthiness, for honesty or deceitfulness, for craftsmanship or poor work, for imagination, or chastity, or fairness, or any other trait of character — or its absence or opposite. Federal Rule of Evidence 803(21) allows admission of reputation of a person among either a community or a group of associates, which would allow evidence of reputation within a geographic community as well as among a community of interest, such as business associates. Reputation of character is admissible despite its potential otherwise as hearsay.

The circumstances in which reputation for character are admissible vary widely, particularly in criminal cases. Often character evidence that is not admissible in a prosecution's case in chief may be admitted to rebut claims made by the defense. Otherwise, character evidence regarding a criminal defendant or victim is admissible only according to Rule 404, and character evidence regarding a witness is allowed under Rule 608. Rule 404 allows the accused to introduce evidence of a trait of character of either the accused or the victim (subject to Rule 412), after which the prosecution may rebut it. Rule 608 allows opinion or reputation for untruthfulness to be raised by the party hostile to the witness, after which the party in support of the witness may give evidence of opinion or reputation for truthfulness.

*See also:* witness, character witness; reputation.

**then-existing condition (state-of-mind exception)**  A statement made concerning a personal condition at the time. A statement of a then-existing condition is a statement made that describes the declarant's state of mind, emotion, sensation, or physical condition, as of that moment. Such statements are admissible hearsay, in a manner similar to other present sense impressions, but with particular limitations that do not allow a statement of mental condition including a belief or a memory. The rationale for the introduction of such statements into evidence is that, like present sense impressions, they are generally accurate reflections of a person's own state of mind or physical condition, as opposed to statements made by other witnesses of the person's condition.

**vital statistics** Public record of births, deaths, and marriages. A record of vital statistics is a public record, created by a government official relating to the marriages, births, deaths and fetal deaths in a jurisdiction over a given time. Records of vital statistics are admissible hearsay under Federal Rule of Evidence 803(9) without the limits of more general public records and reports allowed under Rule 803(8). The exception for vital statistics includes not only the actual records, but also the official reports that are compiled and generated from those records.

See also: hearsay, hearsay exception, hearsay allowed regardless of witness availability, vital statistics.

**residual exception (catchall exception)** Hearsay that is sufficiently reliable that it should be admitted in the interests of justice. The residual exception, or catchall exception, to the hearsay rule allows the admission of hearsay statements that do not fall under the exceptions covered under Rules 803 and 804 that, nevertheless, possess similar circumstantial guarantees of trustworthiness that are equivalent to those of the categorical exceptions. Hearsay that is admissable under this exception must be offered as evidence of a material fact, be more probative than other evidence that can be procured through reasonable efforts, and serve the purposes of the rules of evidence and interests of justice. Hearsay statements proffered under this exception may only be admitted after reasonable advance notice to the opposing party of the statement and such evidence as would be required to evaluate the proffer under the rules.

**hearsay exclusion** Statements excluded from hearsay by definition. A hearsay exclusion is a statement that is not made in testimony at the trial or hearing in which it is used but that is not considered hearsay by definition in the rules, and therefore is inherently admissible in evidence. There are two forms of hearsay exclusion, a prior statement by a witness and an admission by a party-opponent.

Note: A hearsay exclusion operates differently but to the same result as a hearsay exception: in both cases, evidence falling into the definition is admissible in court, subject to the limitations of other rules.

**admission by party-opponent** An admission made or adopted by a party, its agent, or its co-conspirator. An admission by a party-opponent includes any statement introduced by one party to an action, and the statement was made by, adopted by, or legally attributable to the opposing party. There is no difference, for purposes of admissibility, whether the statement is made by the party or an agent or a co-conspirator, as long as the agent acts in the scope of agency or the co-conspirator acts during the course and in furtherance of the conspiracy. The party offering the statement need offer no additional requirements of indicia of reliability, because the party-opponent is present and can rebut such statements if necessary. An admission by a party-opponent is excluded from hearsay and is admissible without regard to having been made other than in testimony in the proceeding or hearing at hand.

See also: admission.

**prior statement by witness** An earlier statement by a witness who later testifies in a trial or hearing. A prior statement by a witness is any statement made by a witness prior to giving testimony in in a trial or hearing. Two forms of prior statement are excluded from hearsay, which may be used in three ways under Rule 801. First, statements made in a prior proceeding under oath and subject to cross-examination may be used to impeach or contradict a witness's later inconsistent testimony. Second, a statement made not under oath or in proceeding may be used, either to give evidence in support of testimony attacked as altered or to give evidence related to the identity of a witness identified after first perceiving the person.

**prior consistent statement** A prior statement by a witness that agrees with later testimony. A prior consistent statement by a witness is any statement once made by a witness in any place or manner who testifies at a later trial or hearing and is at the later trial or hearing subject to cross-examination regarding the earlier statement, which is offered to rebut an express or implied charge against the declarant of recent fabrication or improper influence or motive. The earlier statement is not hearsay under the federal rule, and is admissible under Federal Rule of Evidence 801(d)(1)(B) if it is offered for these purposes. Unlike the use of the prior inconsistent statement under Rule 801(d)(1)(A), the prior consistent statement need not be one taken under oath. However, its limitation is that it can only be entered for purposes of rehabilitating a witness.

**prior inconsistent statement** A prior statement by a witness that does not agree with later testimony. A prior inconsistent statement by a witness is a statement in an earlier proceeding that contradicts a statement made in a later proceeding, in which the prior statement may be introduced. To qualify for admission and not be hearsay, the earlier statement by the witness must have been made under oath and subject to cross examination and liable for perjury, and the later statement must be made at a trial or hearing or other proceeding in which the witness is under oath and subject to cross-examination. The earlier statement is not hearsay under the federal rule, and is admissible under Federal Rule of Evidence 801(d)(1)(A) if the earlier statement is in fact inconsistent with the later testimony, and, of course, if the earlier statement was made under oath in a proceeding where the witness was subject to the penalty of perjury and was subject to cross examination. The statement does not have to be wholly inconsistent with later testimony; if the two are in tension with one another or conflict in some meaningful way, then Rule 801(d)(1)(A) allows for its use.

**hearsay within hearsay (double hearsay or totem pole hearsay)** A hearsay statement containing yet another hearsay statement. Hearsay within hearsay occurs when a hearsay statement offered for admission into evidence contains one or more hearsay statements. Hearsay within hearsay is admissible under Federal Rule of Evidence 805 if any exception to the hearsay bar would admit the containing statement and the statement contained within. Different exceptions may be used to admit the containing statement from the exceptions allowing admission of the contained statement. Certain hearsay exceptions, such as the business records exception, embrace the idea of hearsay within hearsay and thus do not require reference to Rule 805. Nevertheless, such statements can still be excluded if a trial judge feels that their admission into evidence would be more prejudicial than probative.

**statement (hearsay statement)** Words or gestures made, written, or spoken. A statement, as a matter of hearsay, is any form of communication made out of court that may be proffered in court as evidence of a person's assertion or intended assertion as to some fact or evidence.

*See also:* statement.

**heart balm tort** *See:* tort, dignitary tort, heart balm tort (amatory tort or heart balm act).

**heart–lung death** *See:* death, moment of death, heart–lung death.

**heat of passion or sudden passion** *See:* manslaughter, crime of passion (heat of passion or sudden passion).

**heckler's veto** *See:* speech, freedom of speech, heckler's veto.

**hectare** *See:* land, measure of land, hectare (are or centiare or deciare).

**hedge fund** *See:* funds, hedge fund.

**hedonism** The cultivation of happiness as the highest good. Hedonism is both the philosophy that considers pleasure, or happiness, the highest good available for human pursuit and the manner of behavior that seeks out pleasure or satisfaction and avoids pain or discomfort.

*See also:* life, quality of life; damages, classes of damages, hedonic damages (loss of enjoyment of life); value, hedonic valuation.

**hedonic damages** *See:* damages, classes of damages, hedonic damages (loss of enjoyment of life).

**hedonic valuation** *See:* value, hedonic valuation.

**heeding presumption** *See:* label, warning label, heeding presumption.

**heir (heiress)** A family member entitled to an intestate inheritance. An heir is a person who is designated by the laws of a given state as eligible under some circumstances to take a share of the estate of a decedent who dies intestate or who does not dispose of all assets by a valid will. Heirs are designated by statute, and ordered in levels according to the degree of kinship from the decedent, the levels customarily being the levels of consanguinity. Various statutes determine differing formulae for the division of an estate among heirs, though all allow for more distant heirs to be cut off from inheritance when closer heirs survive to inherit.

An heir of an heir is also an heir. Given that an inheritance descends by blood, a descendant heir is heir to everything to which the ancestor is heir.

The term "heir" is both masculine and feminine, although owing to its obsolete meaning as only a male, the term "heiress" is a female heir. This distinction, and the term, is now nearly obsolete as a term of law, although it persists in popular usage, often to mean any female who succeeds to a family fortune, which means that the successor is likely to be a devisee, legatee, or beneficiary.

*devisee or legatee and heir (heir by devise)* Heir is sometimes meant to include those who take by will and not by law. Heir means, most specifically, only a person designated by law as a possible recipient of an estate intestate. Those who take by the gift of a testator by will are not heirs by reason of the gift, but are devisees if they take an interest in realty or legatees if they take an interest in chattels. Even so, in some wills, and in some other odd contexts, the word "heir" is intended to include those who take by will. In such circumstances, the intent of the testator of a will would govern, as it would if a statute used the term in this manner.

*See also:* legatee | devisee and legatee.

**acknowledged heir** An heir recognized by the decedent by acts or designation while alive. An acknowledged heir is an heir by virtue of acknowledged paternity. More generally, the term "acknowledged heir" may represent the heirs known at death or disappearance in a lengthy or delayed estate administration.

**afterborn heir** *See:* posthumous heir.

**bodily heir (heir of the body)** A child or grandchild of the decedent. A bodily heir, or an heir of the body, is a lineal descendant of the decedent, which is to say all issue, or more plainly each child, grandchild, or any successor grandchild. As with lineal heirs generally, an intent of the grantor to use this antiquated term to disfavor adopted children should be proven by clear evidence to rebut the judicial policy of treating all lawful children with equality.

Heirs of the body enjoy a particular place in the law owing to the descent of property held in fee tail only through heirs of the body.

*See also:* fee, estate in fee, fee tail.

**collateral heir (collateral descendent or collateral kinsmen or collateral line or collateral relative or collaterals)**   A blood relative not of direct issue. Collateral descendants, such as siblings, cousins, aunts, and uncles, share a common relative in an earlier generation but are not parent to child or grandparent to grandchild to one another. They are in the various branches at angles or alongside one another in the table of consanguinity, or the family tree.

**forced heir (statutory heir)**   An heir who cannot be disinherited without cause. A forced heir is a person who under civil law cannot be barred from the legitime, or lawful portion of another's estate, without a sufficient cause to allow disinherison, such as neglect of the parent.

**haeres (heres or haeredes proximi or natus or legitimus or remotiores or factus)**   Heir. Haeres, or heres, is Latin for heir or successor. Although today an heir is technically a person who will inherit all or a portion of a decedent's intestate estate, at common law, the category of haeres included the haeres factus, who would now be considered a devisee or legatee. The intestate heir of contemporary usage was the haeres natus or haeres legitimus. Other forms of haeres were haeredes proximi–children or descendants, which contrasted with haeredes remotiores, who were kin other than children or descendants. An haeres factus was an heir by testament, which was distinct from the haeres natus, the heir who takes an interest by law.

*See also:* descent, statute of descent; succession (successor or predecessor).

**heir apparent (apparent heir or heir presumptive or presumptive heir)**   A person who will be an heir of another, if the other dies first. An heir apparent is a person who has an indefeasible right to an inheritance, provided that the person survives the would-be decedent. The status is indefeasible because the conditions of heirship are determined by statute, not according to a last will and testament, and they are not alienable (though of course the proceeds of an inheritance are alienable).

Technically, an heir presumptive is an heir apparent whose inheritance would be barred if another child were born to the would–decedent or an intervening family member. This distinction, however, is rarely applied, and usually a person described as an heir presumptive is an heir apparent.

Note: every person who is an heir apparent of another person is in the opposite position to them as well: if A is an heir apparent of B, then B is an heir apparent of A.

**heir of the blood (lineal heir)**   An heir by being a direct descendant or a direct ancestor. An heir of the blood, which is the same as a lineal heir, is an heir who is either a direct ancestor or a direct descendant of the decedent, as opposed to a collateral or spousal heirs. In other words, heirs of the blood would include a parent, grandparent, child, or grandchild, but not a cousin or spouse. The term heir of the blood includes heir of the body. These distinctions are now quite rare.

**heir of the body**   The lineal descendants of a decedent. An heir of the body is a lineal descendant of the decedent. At common law, heir of the body excluded all children who were not direct descendants by breeding and birth; adoptive children were excluded. In the rare instance such a term is still used in a will, the intent of the testator that such an exclusion is intended must be exceedingly clear to overcome the public policy of treating all children of an ancestor with equality.

**laughing heir**   A distant relative who inherits from a decedent not personally known. A laughing heir is a person who inherits from a decedent who is so distantly related that the heir knew little or nothing of the decedent's existence and suffers no bereavement or remorse at the death of the heir's benefactor. The same term is used, loosely, to describe a remote devisee or legatee who receives a bequest as the result of the operation of the will of the celebrated long-lost relative.

**parcener (coparceny or co-parcener or coparceners or parcenary)**   An heir who is one of the children of a decedent. A parcener is an heir by virtue of being one of several surviving children of the decedent. At common law, parceners, or co-pareners, were daughters, but this limitation in language has not persisted in the United States. Any children who are heirs at the moment of a decedent's death, to all of whom any property goes with unity of title, interest, and possession are coparceners.

An estate that descends by law to more than one child of the decedent descends to each as a co-parcener of the other, and the co-parceners have a particular form of co-tenancy. A co-parcener is a sibling of other co-parceners. At common law, the parcenary interest was distinct from any other co-tenancy, in the middle between a joint tenancy and a tenancy in common. Co-parceners were considered to each have an undivided joint interest but to have no right of survivorship, so the land descended from the co-parcener and was alienable. The language of parcenary interests persists in statutes of partition but otherwise is quite rare.

*See also:* tenancy, co-tenancy (cotenant or co-tenant or cotenancy).

**posthumous heir (afterborn child or posthumous child or quasi-posthumous child or afterborn heir)**   A child born after a parent dies. An afterborn heir is, traditionally, a child born after the death of the child's father. A child born following the death of a mother during childbirth was usually considered born while she lived. With the development of surrogate mothers, an afterborn heir can now be born following the death of a mother. With the development of genetic storage, children can be conceived following the death of one or both parents, which is the problem of post–mortem conception.

A child conceived following the death of one parent is considered the heir of both if they were married at the one parent's death and there is evidence of the dead parent's consent while alive to the conception, although this rule may be subject to increased litigation in the twenty–first century. As of 2011 the legal status of an after–conceived child as an heir of the child's genetic parents, if both parents were dead prior to conception, is uncertain in most states, though it is likely that there would be no legal right of inheritance by the child to the genetic parents, though there would be such a right from the birth parents.

*See also:* heir, afterborn heir.

**pretermitted heir (pretermitted child)**  A descendant unintentionally omitted from a will. A pretermitted heir is a descendant unintentionally omitted from a will, usually a child born or adopted after the testator drafted a will, which was not later amended to reflect the child's birth or adoption. A grant of a legacy or a devise written into the will to named children or grandchildren made before the birth or adoption of another is usually reformed to include the other under pretermitted child statutes or judicial doctrines of interpretation, designed to prevent injustice to a descendant from occurring when the testator does not maintain the will according to evolving circumstance. Most jurisdictions would reform all testamentary gifts, including trusts, to account for and include a pretermitted heir.

**heirloom (heir loom)**  A chattel passed down to a descendant from an ancestor. An heirloom is a chattel that is held by a descendant and that once belonged to an ancestor. Such evocative property as a portrait, bed, bible, jeweled ring, or lock of hair may be an heirloom, as may more mundane objects, such as a doorknob, hairbrush, or dog leash. An heirloom was originally part and parcel of an estate, including both chattels essential to the estate and chattels of customary significance to the family, and once the status of an heirloom was established, under the common law it then descended by inheritance to the heir or heirs at law and could not be transferred by will.

Heirlooms now may be acquired by inheritance, in transfer by will, by inter vivos donation, or in some contexts that do not effectively disturb a continuity of familial association, through reacquisition from a third party, because the means of transmission less defines the heirloom than the sentimental or historical significance to the descendant that the heirloom had been a possession of the ancestor. An heirloom need not be the result of a unique craft but must have been owned or used by an ancestor and have a symbolic value to the descendant distinct and unaffected by any market value. Heirlooms include chattels that lack a unique significance to the descendant but that are essential or parcel to realty or other property once belonging to an ancestor.

Heirlooms are exempt from forfeiture for a general debt under the asset forfeiture rules of some jurisdictions. Though there is no limit to the number of objects or value of property that may be considered heirlooms in the possession of one descendant, asset forfeiture shelters may limit the overall value or number of heirlooms that may be claimed.

*See also:* chattel.

**held**  *See:* hold (holding, held).

**Her Honor or His Honor or Their Honors or Hizzoner**  *See:* honor, Your Honor (Her Honor or His Honor or their Honors or Hizzoner).

**herbicide**  Chemicals that kill plant life. Herbicides are chemicals that destroy plants. Although there are naturally occurring herbicides, the terms is nearly always used in law to describe artificial chemicals used to control plant growth, particularly to inhibit unwanted plants in agricultural land. The use of herbicides is subject to environmental regulation or other laws in order to prevent contamination of other plants and animals and to avoid accidental runoff into streams and other bodies of water. There are many examples: Agent Orange was an herbicide used by the U.S. military in the Vietnam War, and Roundup© is popular in an age when certain crop plants may be bioengineered to resist it.

**hereditament (hereditaments)**  Anything of a form that can be inherited. An hereditament is an interest that the law can recognize as a property interest subject to inheritance. In this sense, inheritance is the transfer of a property interest at death as a matter of law and not by devise or legacy transferred after death by a will (even though, obviously, hereditaments may be transferred by will and often are so transferred). A person's hereditaments are the sum of all of that person's property interests that will survive the person's death. The hereditaments that are related to a particular property, particularly real estate, are the sum of all of its divisible interests. Hereditaments are divided into corporeal and incorporeal, which is property manifest in tangible terms and the rights and interests that are derived from such tangible property.

> **incorporeal hereditament**  An intangible right or interest that is derived from tangible property. An incorporeal hereditament may label any intangible interest in a tangible property, whether real or chattel. Thus, an easement, or a profit, or a vested future interest are all incorporeal herediitaments. The term was once much more robust, including a great number of powers and interests, but most of these forms of property are now obsolete.

**heres or haeredes proximi or natus or legitimus or remotiores or factus**  *See:* heir, haeres (heres or haeredes proximi or natus or legitimus or remotiores or factus).

**heresy (heretic)**　An act or statement in violation of church doctrine. Heresy includes any speech or action that violates the dogma, or religious teachings and doctrine, particularly error in any belief required by the Christian church. A heretic is a person who commits heresy. In many ecclesiastical courts, heresy can be committed by thought alone, either by having thoughts contrary to dogma or by not actively and fully embracing each element of dogma. Common law, since Sir Edward Coke's time, has not allowed prosecution for thoughts that were not spoken. Heresy cannot be a crime in the United States owing to the constitutional prohibition of an established church, or in Europe, owing to the protections of freedom of religion under the European Convention on Human Rights.

"Heretic" has acquired a metaphorical significance as anyone who does not accept an established convention. Note: do not confuse heresy with hearsay.

*See also:* dogma; religion, freedom of religion, establishment of religion (separation of church and state).

**heritability (inheritability)**　The eligibility of specific property to be inherited, or sometimes left by will. Heritability is the capacity of some property to be given by descent from an owner to an heir. Heritability is easily confused with inheritability, but unlike many words with an in- prefix, inheritability is not an antonym. Rather it is a synonym that once meant the same as heritability. In contemporary usage, heritability tends to refer to the capacity of property to be inherited through intestate succession, while inheritability includes not only property that can be inherited intestate but also property that can be granted by a testamentary gift. This ambiguity is rarely significant in practice, as the question usually arises in situations in which the nature of the potential transfer of property is already established as either testate or intestate, and the question rarely turns on the label but on the nature of the property itself.

**hermaphrodite (androgyne or hermaphroditic or intersex or intersexual or transgender)**　A person with both male and female aspects of the body. A hermaphrodite is a living creature that is both male and female, although in law the term is used primarily to describe a human with physical characteristics of both, particularly a person with some development of the sexual organs of both genders.

The common law, following canon and Roman precedents, treated a hermaphrodite as either male or female, according to the gender that appeared to an observer to be the predominate sex in the person. Given the advantages in property law accorded to the male, this likely created a strong inclination to find all hermaphrodites to be male, although a male-designated hermaphrodite could not then lawfully marry a male.

Contemporary medicine recognizes mental, physical, and artificial bases for hermaphrodism. A person may be born with physical characteristics of both genders. A person may have emotional or psychological identity with the gender other than that of the person's reproductive capacity. An incompletely transgendered person may be changed by chemical and surgical means to have some of the characteristics of a new gender.

The legal significance of gender identity remains important in many jurisdictions, and in legal circumstances in which the law requires a gendered identity of male or of female, the contemporary approach is effectively to allow a hermaphodite to select one of the other identity, although some form of estoppel then applies to the selection. In cases of confinement such as military training or incarceration, the hermaphrodite may be reasonably isolated by officials from others of the selected gender. Note: Bouvier stated categorically that hermaphrodites do not exist among humans, which is both contrary to the long-standing common law and medical experience.

**hermeneutics**　Interpretation, particularly according to a particular frame of reference. Hermeneutics, generally, is the interpretation of communication. In law, it usually means the interpretation of a law or a legal text in the light of a particular tradition, sometimes manifest in an idea or goal, reading words or clauses in the text as signs that signify some aspect of that tradition. In its simplest forms, it is like interpreting the language of a statute according to an independently ascertained legislative purpose by reading each word, phrase, sentence, and paragraph in the manner that would be most consonant with that purpose.

*See also:* midot (middot).

**hiatus**　A lengthy pause or recess. A hiatus is a break or pause from activity. Through usage, a hiatus has often been considered the same as a lengthy hiatus, and so to use the term suggests a more than slight period of time given the circumstance.

**hidden danger**　*See:* danger, latent danger (hidden danger).

**hierarchy**　The structure of power in an organization. A hierarchy is the order by which some offices or persons have authority (whether by rule or in practice) over others in an organization (whether formal or informal). A hierarchy implies that some people or institutions in an organization have the power to cause others to act according to the powerful one's design.

*See also:* law, law school, hierarchy of legal education.

**hierarchy of legal education**　*See:* law, law school, hierarchy of legal education.

**hierarchy of norms**　*See:* norm, hierarchy of norms.

**needs theory (hierarchy of human needs)**　Motivations are ranked by their priority. The hierarchy of needs is a theory of Abraham Maslow that argues humans have a series of innate needs, which are understood and pursued in a hierarchical fashion. Physiological needs, the requirements of air, food, water, and sexual expression must be satisfied first. Next are needs for safety, whether physical bodily safety or security for physical needs through health, finance, and employment. Then are social needs of love, friendship, and attachment, such as for family. Then are concerns for self-esteem and, finally, self-actualization, or the fullest development of one's talents. Though the theory is interesting, more recent sociological evidence suggests that all of these levels may be pursued simultaneously, even among those with the greatest risk to their most basic needs.

## high

**high crime**   *See:* crime, high crime (high crimes).

**high seas**   *See:* sea, law of the sea, international waters, high seas (freedom of the seas).

**high water mark**   *See:* shoreline, high water mark (mean high water mark or MHW).

**high-low abitration**   *See:* arbitration, high-low abitration.

**high-yield bond or high-yield debt obligation**   *See:* bond, junk bond (high-yield bond or high-yield debt obligation).

**high-yield security**   *See:* security, securities, high-yield security (junk bond).

**higher brain death**   *See:* death, moment of death, brain death, higher brain death.

**highest and best use**   *See:* use, use of property, highest and best use.

**highly migratory fish**   *See:* fish, highly migratory fish (highly migratory stocks of fish).

**highly migratory stocks of fish**   *See:* fish, highly migratory fish (highly migratory stocks of fish).

**hijab**   The headscarf worn by Muslim women. The hijab is derived from h j b, to cover, and is the traditional head covering of an observant Muslimah — female Muslim. The wearing of the hijab in public is fard or obligatory in all schools of Islam. Traditionally, all Muslims are required to cover the aurah of the body, men and women alike, though not as as symbol of the faith, like the personal decision to wear a cross, but as an act of faith like the Jewish male obligation to wear the yarmulke, or skullcap.
*See also:* veil (burqa or burqua or burka or niqab or purdah).

**hijacking (hijack or hijacker)**   The commandeering of a vehicle, ship, plane, or craft. Hijacking is the seizure of control of any means of transportation, including a car, truck, ship, plane, or other craft for the use of a private person without an ownership or lawful allowance to control it. Hijacking is a form of larceny, and if the vehicle or craft is populated, hijacking may also amount to kidnapping, although it is also separately a crime. The hijacking of an aircraft is referred to as "air piracy" in U.S. statutes.
*See also:* piracy (pirate or piratical or piratically); piracy, air piracy (aircraft piracy or skyjacking).

**Hilary term**   *See:* court, English Court, terms of court, Hilary term.

**Hill-Burton funds**   *See:* health, health care, Hill-Burton Act (Hill-Burton funds).

**hindrance (hinder)**   Any obstruction of a person's conduct or movement. A hindrance is any action or object that makes difficult or impossible a person's travel, activity, assertion of a right or interest, use of property, performance of a contract, or any other action or legal benefit. Hindrance is often expressed as part of the customary phrase "without let or hindrance," which is today a bit redundant, but that reflects the medieval understanding of let as a restraint caused by a physical or inanimate barrier, while hindrance was caused by human agency.
*See also:* impediment (impediments).

**HIPAA or Kennedy-Kassebaum Act**   *See:* health, health care, Health Insurance Portability and Accountability Act (HIPAA or Kennedy-Kassebaum Act).

**hire**   To contract for the use of labor or property. To hire is to enter a contract for the use of someone's labor in return for some compensation. A thing may be hired, as when an object is leased or rented, though it is less common in the United States than in the United Kingdom for hire to describe the use of a bailment.
So in the U.S., to engage a person as an employee is to hire that person, but so is an engagement of a contractor to perform services for a short time. In the U.K., hire is as likely to suggest what in the U.S. is a rental service, such as the hiring of a bicycle or formal clothes.
The common basis for the hiring of a person and of a bailment is in the origin of the term; in the early common law, the hire was the payment given for any form of service, including the use of a chattel. This idea became associated with the commencement of a relationship subject to hire, which became the hire of the person or property, which now, at least in the U.S., includes the person. Thus, a new hire is a newly hired person.

**hiring hall**   A place or system for employment referrals. A hiring hall is a specific place, or sometimes a system, used as a clearing house for matching workers to jobs according to skill and seniority. Most hiring halls are controlled by union locals for the purpose of matching available union members to positions in union employment. In such cases, the employer and the union will have a collective bargaining agreement establishing the union as the sole provider of employees for the employer. When workers are needed, the employer will contact the hiring hall, and the hiring hall will supply the requested workers. For example, a contractor that needed electricians or carpenters for a job would request the type and number of workers needed from the hiring hall, which would assign them as required under the bargaining agreement.

**history (historic)** The study or narrative of past events. History, in general, is not only the study of society, culture, and events in the past but also the particular narrative of events and context that preceded any event. The history of a given event may, however, be one or both of two quite different things. A history of a given event is both the context and the specific events that preceded that event and the particular recital or recitals of those facts that are recorded and presented as true about it. Thus the legislative history of a statute is, on the one hand, all of the events and context that preceded and may have affected the drafting of the bill or bills that became the statute, as well as the events and context that surround the decisions of various officials as the bill moved through the legislative process. On the other hand, a legislative history may be a brief rendering of the official records of the bill as it moved through amendments, perhaps along with an official report generated by a committee and a record of votes for and against its passage.

Lawyers and judges are constantly engaging in a form of historical analysis, by referring to the archive of legal materials written in the past and placing them in a context for use in the future. Even so, there is great skepticism that lawyers are equipped to use most historical archives in a manner that develops an accurate understanding of the events they depict.

*See also:* legislation, legislative history.

**historic district** *See:* zoning, historic district.

**historical fact** *See:* fact, historical fact.

**historical jurisprudence** *See:* jurisprudence, historical jurisprudence.

**hit and run** *See:* driving, hit and run.

**hoax** A false report or fabrication of an event. A hoax is an act intended to trick a person or the public into believing that a fabricated event or occurrence is true. A hoax may be an element in a confidence game or fraud.

When a hoax is of an event or condition that would cause alarm or danger, such as a false bomb threat, the hoax may amount to a criminal threat or violate specific criminal prohibitions against hoax devices, hoax warnings, or hoax threats.

In general legal and popular writing, a hoax may represent anything that is deceptive, whether intentional or not. Indeed, the term appears to be a corruption of hocus or hocus pocus, as the term of art for a conjurer.

**hoax device** Anything made to look like a device that causes destruction or harm. A hoax device is any item that is made to look like an inciendary device or bomb. The making and usage of such a device can carry with it penalties just as strict as those for persons who make actual incendiaries or bombs.

**Hobson's choice** *See:* choice, Hobson's choice.

**hoc** Object or purpose. Hoc is a Latin term of many roles that may be an object, purpose, activity, or thing, and it has many other translations into English. Hoc is usually best defined as an element of a colloquial phrase, as in ad hoc or post hoc, for to the present case or after the fact.

*See also:* ad, ad hoc; post, post hoc.

**Hohfeldian right** *See:* right, Hohfeldian right (Hohfeldian duty).

**hoist by your own petard** *See:* petard (hoist by your own petard).

**hold (holding or held)** To be in control of any thing. To hold has many different meanings in the law, including possessing, ruling, requiring, and retaining. The relations among these senses trace back to Old English and Saxon words haldan and healdan, meaning keeping and watching over, from which we still have the sense of "holdup" and "behold." Into these senses have gone the Latin idea of habendum for having, so that the term "hold" means to possess as well. Thus, the sense of hold varies according to context: in property, to hold is to possess; in evidence and constitutional law, to hold is to bear a right or privilege; in contracts, parties are held to an obligation; in procedural contexts, to hold hearing or trial is to watch over it and to conduct it, and a holding is the ruling that controls the dispute in a matter.

**holding as possession (holdings)** Anything owned or possessed. A holding is a possession, particularly an asset or property. One's holdings are all of one's possessions, but holdings may often refer to either a particular asset, such as "real estate holdings" as well as to the share one has in a larger assets, such as "a thirty percent holding in the corporation."

**holding period (long-term holding period or short-term holding period)** Length of time an asset is owned. Holding period refers to the length of time an entity owns an asset. The holding period of an asset determines whether it is subject to long-term capital gains rates, which tend to be more favorable than short-term rates, which have historically been the same as the rate on ordinary income. In 2011, the short-term holding period was one year or less, and the long-term holding period was more than one year.

**holding as ruling on a matter of law** The controlling rule or principle in a judicial opinion. The holding of an opinion is the statement of the rule or principle of law that is most essential to the mandate of the case. An opinion in a given case may have several holdings that are independent of one another or several that are logically necessary to one another. Isolating the holding can sometimes be difficult, and the statement by the judge, magistrate, or justice authoring the opinion that a given passage is the holding, or is what is held that day, is suggestive but not controlling on later interpretations of that opinion.

**hold-over or holding over or holdover tenant**
*See:* tenant, tenant as lessee, holdover tenant (hold–over or holding over or holdover tenant).

**holder**  One who holds something, which is usually a negotiable instrument. A holder, in general, is anyone who holds anything. In the law, the term "holder," when it is not otherwise modified, nearly always refers to the holder of a negotiable instrument.

Under the Uniform Commercial Code, a holder is a holder for one of three reasons: 1) the holder is the person who is in possession of a negotiable instrument, and the instrument is either made payable to "bearer" or the instrument is made payable to the person who is holding it, who is identified by name; 2) the holder is the person in possession of a negotiable, tangible document of title, and the goods in which the document expresses title are either listed as deliverable to "bearer" or listed as deliverable to the order of the person who is holding it, who is the person in possession of the document; or 3) the holder is the person in control of a negotiable electronic document of title.

*See also:* instrument, negotiable instrument.

**bona fide holder for value (holder in good faith)**
Holder of a negotiable instrument free of any equitable claims. A bona fide holder is a holder of a negotiable instrument, who has accepted the instrument before its due date, and who has given value for it or accepted it as collateral security, and who takes it without notice of a defense existing against it in the hands of the person from whom it was received. A bona fide holder for value is given shelter in equity, which is to say that the doctrines of equity will allow this holder to take possession of the instrument without any equitable defenses to honoring it. As a practical matter, most jurisdictions now use the holder in due course standard of the Uniform Commercial Code for the same function.

*See also:* purchaser, bona fide purchaser (bona fide purchaser for value or B.F.P. or B.F.P.V. or BFP or BFPV).

**holder in due course (H.D.C. or HDC)**  Buyer of a negotiable instrument, who had no notice of a defect in its title. A holder in due course is a holder of a negotiable instrument who bought the instrument in good faith with no knowledge of an infirmity in the instrument or a defect in the title of the person negotiating it. The holder in due course acquires title free from all defenses and claims that might allow the maker or payor of the instrument to avoid honoring it. In order to establish that one is a holder in due course, one must establish each element of the Uniform Commercial Code definition: that one is a holder, that the instrument is a negotiable instrument, that the holder took it for value, that the holder took the instrument in good faith, and that the holder took the instrument without notice that it is overdue or has been dishonored or of any defense against or claim to it on the part of another.

The holder in due course (HDC) is the term used in the UCC as adopted in most states, and it is generally the successor label for the bona fide purchaser for value (BFPV) for negotiable instruments, which most jurisdictions continue to use for purchasers of chattels and, in some instances, is still used for negotiable instrument. The differences between an HDC and a BFPV as to negotiable instruments are slight, turning mainly on the variations in statutory adoptions from state to state. The primary differences as to negotiable instruments is the effect of precedents under the UCC versus the precedents of courts applying the traditional limits of equitable defenses.

**holding charge**  *See:* charge, charge as criminal charge, holding charge.

**holding company**  *See:* company, holding company.

**holdout**  One of a community of who will not act with the rest. A holdout is anyone who will not participate in a group activity. A holdout juror refuses to join in the verdict of the majority. A holdout seller refuses to sell when others with related property sell. A holdout bidder delays bidding until other bidders have done so.

The term holdouts may represents a variety of distinct motives. Some holdouts seek to prevent a deal the rest of the community seeks. Some seek independence from the deal, and others seek simply a more lucrative deal. In the last instance, a holdout may delay a sale, not to sabotage the sale or remain aloof from it, but to reap a premium available to the last transaction essential to an enterprise. This sort of bargaining is common in negotiations, whether for a contract or in legislative negotiation.

**holdover tenant**  *See:* tenant, tenant as lessee, hold-over tenant (hold–over or holding over or holdover tenant).

**holograph (holographic)**  Anything written by hand. Any document or instrument that has been written by hand, rather being typed, printed, or electronically drafted. The term is most often used to refer to a holographic will.

*See also:* manuscript.

**holographic will**  *See:* will, last will and testament, holographic will (holograph).

**Holy Office of the Inquisition**  *See:* inquisition, Holy Office of the Inquisition (Holy Inquisition or Holy Office).

**homage**  Obedience to an authority. Homage was the the primary feudal incident, the feudal obligation by a vassal to obey the lord with authority over the vassal, as established by feudal tenure: whoever was a tenant of the lord owed the lord homage. Moreover, a vassal who owed homage to a lord owed homage to that lord's superior, the vassal's overlord. Homage implied the vassal would give not only obedience but also specific services that might vary according to the relationship; it also implied protection of the vassal by the lord. The obedience was not subject to whimsical demands, however, and its most important form was in the avoidance of conduct that would injure the lord or the lord's interest.

Homage in contemporary legal usage persists as a word for obedience, particularly unthinking devotion to a principle or rule.

**home**  *See:* house (home).

**home-equity loan**  *See:* loan, home-equity loan.

**homeowner**  *See:* insurance, category of insurance, liability insurance, homeowner.

**home rule**  *See:* municipality, home rule.

**intimacies of the home (intimacy in the home)** Activity and space in the home with a constitutionally protected expectation of privacy. The intimacies of the home depict the ordinary scope of the activities of daily life of individuals in their dwellings. As between consenting adults, this includes a great deal that is not controversial but extends also to non-commercial sexual activity, without regard to the gender of partners or the purpose of the activity. The intimacies of the home are not limited to non-commercial activity but extend to the purchase of goods related to such intimacy. A search of the home is also an invasion of the intimacy of the home, and there is an inherent expectation of privacy by a resident in a home. Further, the intimacy of the home is recognized as an arena in which the right of privacy is strong, and a law that regulates conduct within it must be well justified. In the light of Lawrence v. Texas, 539 U.S. 558 (2003), there is some question of the level of justification required of a law burdening the intimacy of the home, some observers arguing for a compelling state interest, and others requiring something more like intermediate scrutiny to seek an important governmental interest.

*See also:* privacy.

**homestead**  The place of one's home, which is exempt from most creditors' liens. The homestead is one's place at which one has one's primary home. In most instances, the homestead is exempt from seizure to satisfy general debts of its owner. The homestead is defined according to state law, and the implications of what property is in a homestead or not is critical to defining rights of a debtor and of creditors as well as of spouses and, often, of tax liabilities.

Most state definitions allow the homestead to be the dwelling, its land, and outbuildings. The dwelling may, however, be a condominium, a boat, a mobile home, or any other place that is in fact the primary dwelling place of the person whose homestead it is. Homesteads are generally dwellings owned in fee, though the exemption may also apply to chattels naturally in the homestead, in which case the homestead may apply also to leased premises and to cooperatives. (Most jurisdictions allow chattels only up to a particular value, which is often low owing to a failure to amend the law despite the effects of inflation.)

Some jurisdictions have a state-wide limit to a defined homestead in land or value. Some limit the size of a homestead variably, allowing less land for an urban homestead and more for a rural or agricultural homestead.

The homestead exempts the property of both a debtor and the debtor's spouse, although it does not exempt an interest by one homesteading owner in common from the liens on the other share of the property owned by a non-homesteading co-owner.

*See also:* debtor, debtors' exemption (exempt assets); residence (residency or reside).

**homestead exemption**  The limitation on the collection of judgments or some taxes from a homestead. A homestead exemption is the limitation of a homestead from the collection of debts, satisfaction of judgments, or claims in bankruptcy. In some states, it also creates an exemption for realty taxes, which are not collected at all, or collected only above an exempt value on the homestead property.

A homestead usually does not exempt all debts from security in the homestead nor all debts from execution against it. A loan to purchase, a mortgage, a deed of trust, a materialman's lien, and a tax lien are usually excluded by state law from the homestead exemption. Thus, a mortgage entered in order to buy the homestead may still be defaulted upon and the homestead securing the loan taken by the mortgagee.

Bankruptcy law leaves the definition not only of the homestead but also of the homestead exemption to state law for the purposes of computing the assets of a bankruptcy estate. Even so, certain claims that may be brought by a spouse may be allowed in bankruptcy against the debtor's homestead as a matter of federal bankruptcy law, regardless of their exemption in the state law of the homestead.

Many states require that a homestead be declared by the filing of a declaration of homestead or a declaration of estate of homestead with a state or county office. A failure to make such a filing in a state that requires it may forfeit the protection of the homestead exemption.

**probate homestead**  The right of a surviving spouse and children to remain on the decedent spouse or parent's homestead without claims. A probate homestead is a right, usually created by state constitution, that allows the surviving spouse and minor or unmarried children to live on a decedent's homestead for life, exempt from execution or forced sale by creditors of the decedent. Jurisdictions vary as to the probate homestead coming into effect automatically on the death of the homestead owner with a surviving spouse or child or being recognized only on motion or application. Probate homestead is usually available in states that do not recognize dower or the elective share. The area of land, the duration, the holders of the right, and the maximum dollar amount of the homestead exemption vary from state to state, usually mirroring the homestead exemption.

*See also:* probate, probate of a will.

**statutory homestead** The homestead to which the homestead exemption applies by state law. The statutory homestead is both the homestead as defined in state law and the exemption of that homestead from satisfaction of the claims of creditors. To claim a homestead right, a debtor must ordinarily show that the property is owned and occupied by the debtor as a primary residence. The area of land, the duration, the holders of the right, and the maximum dollar amount of the homestead exemption are matters of individual state provision. It may differ for those living in town or in the country.

**homicide** Causing the end of the life of another human being. Homicide is the act by which one person causes the death of a person. In general, homicide is a broad term, including not only suicide but also the justifiable acts of killing another person, whether the death is brought about in a manner or for reasons that violate the law or in a manner or for reasons that do not violate the law.

As a matter of law, though, homicide is invariably restricted to the taking of the life of another human being without a lawful basis or a justification for doing so. In this sense, the taking of the life of another according to the law by a police officer in the line of duty, or according to the law of war and military regulations by a soldier on a battlefield, is not homicide. Although there are variations according to the statutes and case law of different jurisdictions, there is little difference between various forms of criminal homicide and various degrees of murder.

*See also:* death, wrongful death; manslaughter (manslaughterer); murder, felony murder, first–degree felony murder.

**criminal homicide (culpable homicide or felonious homicide)** An unjustified homicide. Causing the death of another human being, without a justification in law to do so or excuse from its penalty. In most instances in contemporary usage, criminal homicide is the same as murder. In a civil context, a criminal homicide may be treated as a wrongful death.

*See also:* murder, degrees of murder, first–degree murder (murder in the first degree or murder–one or murder–1).

**excusable homicide** The killing of a human being by reasonable mistake or accident. Excusable homicide is the accidental or mistaken killing of a human being while performing an otherwise lawful act. Thus an excusable homicide occurs by accident, misfortune, or mistake during the course of any lawful act by lawful means, performed with the usual and ordinary caution, and without any unlawful intent, or upon any sudden provocation or combat, without any dangerous weapon being used and not done in a cruel or unusual manner. A common excusable homicide is the accidental killing of an aggressor while acting in self defense. Even if the intentional use of deadly force was not justifiable given the circumstances, the accidental killing is excusable if the self defender acted lawfully and by lawful means.

*See also:* excuse (excusable or excused); homicide, justifiable homicide (justified homicide or lawful homicide).

**fratricide** Causing the death of one's own brother or sister. Fratricide is the homicide of one's brother or sister. The term does not create a separate offense but describes one form of the act of homicide or, more commonly, murder or manslaughter.

In military slang, fratricide is the killing of a fellow soldier or sailor by a member of the same military service or unit.

**innocent homicide** Homicide that cannot be the basis of a criminal conviction. Innocent homicide is the causing of the death of a person under circumstances by which the death is either justified or excused. Justifiable homicide and excusable homicide are different, but neither results in criminal liability.

*See also:* homicide, excusable homicide; homicide, justifiable homicide (justified homicide or lawful homicide).

**involuntary homicide** Vehicular homicide or involuntary manslaughter. Involuntary homicide is a form of unintentional homicide, which is akin to either negligent homicide, involuntary manslaughter, or vehicular homicide in most U.S. jurisdictions. Involuntary homicide is still the label for negligent homicide in many civil law jurisdictions.

*See also:* homicide, vehicular homicide.

**justifiable homicide (justified homicide or lawful homicide)** The taking of a human life that is justified by law. Justifiable homicide is the killing of a human being under circumstances of justification, that is circumstances that either require or allow the killing with no liability. Justifications of homicide include self-defense from mortal danger and the defense of another then in mortal danger. It is also justified when done by a judge or other in obedience to the law, such as a soldier on a battlefield operating within the scope of lawful orders or the action of an executioner carrying out a death warrant. A police officer's use of deadly force resulting in a homicide is justified if the use of force was required or allowed under the law of the jurisdiction governing that officer and the federal requirements of due process.

**matricide** Causing the death of one's own mother. Matricide is the homicide of one's mother. Although the common law created more serious categories of offense for matricide, contemporary law considers such elements of homicide as potentially aggravating factors in sentencing for homicide or murder.

*See also:* parricide.

**negligent homicide** Causing the death of another person through negligence. Negligent homicide is the crime of causing the death of another through negligent conduct. Negligent homicide is a category of homicide in the Model Penal Code, which distinguishes negligent homicide from manslaughter on the basis of the defendant's awareness of the risks of the defendant's behavior. If the defendant places another person at risk of death without the defendant's knowing that the defendant's conduct places the other in a substantial and unjustifiable risk of death, the defendant acts negligently, and a death that results is negligent homicide. On the other hand, if the defendant had done the same thing, aware of the risk it posed for another person but doing so nonetheless, the defendant acts recklessly, and the death that results is manslaughter. In states that do not follow the Model Penal Code, there may be more overlap between the offenses, particularly if the state recognizes both negligent homicide and involuntary manslaughter, which turn on even finer distinctions of mens rea.

*See also:* murder, degrees of murder, second degree murder (murder in the second degree or murder-two or murder-2); manslaughter (manslaughterer).

**patricide**  Causing the death of one's own father. Patricide is the homicide of one's father. Although the common law created more serious categories of offense for patricide (patricide being a basis for petit treason), contemporary law considers such elements of homicide as potentially aggravating factors in sentencing for homicide or murder. Regicide is sometimes metaphorically called patricide.

*See also:* parricide.

**regicide (tyrannicide)**  Causing the death of a monarch. Regicide is the crime of causing the death of a king, queen, or other monarch entitled to rule a state. In England, to speak of regicides usually invokes the members of the Parliamentary court who signed the death warrant of Charles I, and in France the revolutionaries who executed Louis XVI. Regicide is both homicide and treason. Regicide is sometimes metaphorically called parricide. Michael Walzer has distinguished regicide into two forms of political act: the first is the murder of the monarch, leaving intact the monarchy and its prestige to be filled by a successor; the second is the murder of the monarch and the cultural destruction or abandonment of the monarchy. Only the second makes unlikely the ultimate punishment of the regicides.

Tryannicide is causing the death of a tyrant, and the defense of a charge of regicide is usually that the monarch had become a tyrant, an enemy of the people, and forfeited the right of monarchy.

*See also:* rex (regina or regis or regnal).

**vehicular homicide**  Causing the death of a person through the unlawful operation of a motor vehicle. Vehicular homicide is causing the death of a person as a result of the operation of a motor vehicle in any unlawful manner. States that designate degrees of vehicular homicide usually specify specific traffic violations of particular danger, such as driving under the influence of alcohol or drugs, reckless driving, driving at an excessive speed, maneuvering to avoid police interception, or passing a parked school bus as elements of the first-degree vehicular homicide,

relegating other offenses either to vehicular manslaughter or to second degree vehicular homicide.

*See also:* vehicle (motor vehicle).

**homo**  A reference to all mankind, or to a particular person, or to a man. Homo is Latin for "man" in nearly all of the senses in which man is used in contemporary English, particularly to mean all of humanity or a particular person or, least often, a male as opposed to a female human being. Note: slang usage of this term refers to a homosexual person, in a manner that is usually intended as an insult.

**hominem**  *See:* fallacy, ad hominem (argumentum ad hominem).

**homologation (homologate or homologated)**  The confirmation of a decision made by a notary, executor, or other official. Homologation is a process in the civil law, particularly in Louisiana, by which a court of justice adopts, confirms, and orders the execution of a ruling made by a quasi-judicial official, such as a notary, trustee, executor, or receiver. The official will create a plan, as when a notary delineates the partition of property, which does not become final until it has been homologated by a court with jurisdiction over the matter.

*See also:* probation.

**homosexuality (homosexual or gay or queer or lesbian or bi-sexual or LGBT)**  Sexual attraction to a person of one's own gender. Homosexuality is attraction with sexual interest by any person to persons of the same sex. Acts of sexual activity between people of the same gender are homosexual acts, and a person who either has such an attraction or engages in such acts as a significant means of sexual expression is a homosexual. Although animals other than humans may engage in homosexual acts, the use of homosexuality and homosexual in legal materials is generally restricted to human beings. The terms "gay" and "queer" are often used in the same manners that homosexual is used.

Among some communities, the use of homosexuality to describe conduct by women is not acceptable, and "lesbian" is preferred for women who are attracted to other women. A person who engages in sexual acts or is attracted equally to persons of the same gender or other gender is considered bisexual. The law frequently fails to reflect these distinctions, and the use of homosexual in a statute or opinion may include each of these categories.

*See also:* hermaphrodite (androgyne or hermaphroditic or intersex or intersexual or transgender); jurisprudence, queer legal theory.

**honesty**  To treat others with honor and to speak the truth. Honesty is the treatment of other people by giving to each what is due to each, ensuring that the right thing is done, and the truth is spoken. Honesty in communication is more than merely avoiding a falsehood in speech or a document; it is ensuring that what is said is, as the oath says, "the truth, the whole truth, and nothing but the truth." Yet honesty includes actions as well as words, and it is an essential and often mandatory deportment of officials and those in the legal profession.

*See also:* justice.

**honest mistake** *See:* mistake, honest mistake (bona fide error in judgment or good faith error in judgment).

## honor

**honor of a negotiable instrument** *See:* instrument, negotiable instrument, honor of a negotiable instrument, dishonor; instrument, negotiable instrument, honor of a negotiable instrument.

**Your Honor (Her Honor or His Honor or Their Honors or Hizzoner)** An honorific title used when addressing judges in the United States. Your Honor is a courteous form of address used when speaking or writing to judges in the United States. Repeated failure to properly address the judge may be more than a breach of decorum and may result in a contempt of court charge. Once a judge steps down from the bench, use of the honorific is no longer to be encouraged by the judge, but it is still frequently done as a matter of respect, particularly if the judge does not return to the practice of law. Hizzoner, or "His Honor," is never used directly in speech to a judge or in reference to a judge except in jest.

**honorarium (honoraria)** Money given as a reward for services voluntarily rendered. An honorarium is a gift of money given in recognition of a service already rendered or to be voluntarily performed. Although an honorarium is not described as a fee or a wage, an honorarium must be reported as income and is taxable as income. The promise of an honorarium may be enforceable if it is an inducement to perform a voluntary service that is then performed. The plural form is honoraria.

**horizontal** Entities of similar authority or sequence in a hierarchy or series. A horizontal organization is one in which no unit holds authority over others. States are sometimes said to be vertically organized toward their subjects, and citizens are horizontally organized toward one another.

**horizontal agreement** *See:* agreement, horizontal agreement.

**horizontal competition** *See:* competition, horizontal competition.

**horizontal price fixing** *See:* price, price fixing, horizontal price fixing.

**horizontal privity of estate** *See:* privity, privity of estate, horizontal privity of estate.

**hornbook** *See:* lawbook, hornbook.

**hornbook method** *See:* law, law school, legal pedagogy, lecture method (hornbook method).

**hortatory** Language that is not binding or mandatory. Hortatory language is encouraging or guiding but not mandatory; it does not give rise to duties that may be enforced at law or in equity (which is a circularity). Hortatory language may, however, be a useful guide to the interpretation of other language in an instrument as a means of ascertaining the purpose or intent of the drafter either in language that creates legally or equitably enforceable obligations or in the instrument as a whole.

*See also:* surplus, surplusage as irrelevant language.

**hoshen mishpat** *See:* choshen mishpat (hoshen mishpat).

**hospital** A facility for the daily provision of acute medical care by physicians. A hospital is a institution that provides daily care by physicians of the acute medical conditions of patients. There is considerable overlap among certain forms of clinic and the concept of a hospital, but in most jurisdictions, hospitals are particularly subject to state regulation and oversight, requiring a state certificate of need to be established and subject to a variety of credentials and inspections.

*See also:* health, health care.

**hostage (hostages)** A person captured and held to secure the conduct of another person or entity. A hostage is a person held by a captor, who confines the the hostage, holding the liberty and safety of the hostage as a security in exchange for particular conduct by a third party. A hostage may be held merely for ransom or for the performance of some act, such as an act of state by the government of the hostage's home state or another government. Though in contemporary usage hostages are held against their will, under the classical law of war, hostages were exchanged between states as the security of each state's performance of treaties. To take a hostage against the hostage's will is both kidnapping and a potential war crime.

**hostility (hostile)** The treatment of another as an enemy. Hostility is the treatment by one party of another as its enemy or opponent, particularly by competing without compromise to control a single thing. Hostility is thus both a condition of open or covert warfare between two or more states as well as a condition of opposition between two or more private parties. Even so, hostility is possible between one party and another, when the conduct and intent of hostility are present only by one party.

Hostilities depict the events as well as the period of time during which war persists between states.

*See also:* war (warfare).

**hostile possession** *See:* possession, adverse possession, hostile possession (adversity of possession).

**hostile witness** *See:* witness, hostile witness.

**hostile work environment** *See:* agency, harassment, hostile work environment, Ellerth–Faragher defense (Ellerth/Farragher defense); agency, harassment, hostile work environment (abusive work environment).

## hot

**hot bench**  *See:* bench, hot bench (cold bench or hot court or cold court).

**hot pursuit**  *See:* pursuit, hot pursuit, hot pursuit (fresh suit).

**hot pursuit exception**  *See:* warrant, search warrant, hot pursuit exception.

**hotchpot (collation)**  Mixing property together for the purposes of dividing it equally. A hotchpot is a blending and mixing together of the property of different persons for the purposes of dividing it equally and reallocating it among those who are entitled to it. In practice, hotchpot is usually a means of considering inter vivos gifts to heirs in a distribution of an intestate estate to ensure equality of distribution, in that the heirs who received a qualifying gift ahead of the decedent's death allow it to be factored into the estate in order to receive such additional shares as comes from the hotchpot rather than the inter vivos gifts alone.

**hour**  *See:* time, hour, business hours (close of business or COB).

**house (home)**  A building for human habitation, usually for one or two families. A house is a building intended to shelter a particular human activity. In general, the term house, without any other qualification, is a building created to be a long-term dwelling for humans, usually for one family though sometimes for more. House loses this connotation when it is a component of, say, lighthouse, workhouse, outhouse, or smokehouse.

When a "house" is devised in a will or otherwise donated, a rebuttable presumption arises that the house includes the lands it occupies as well as outbuildings and other appurtenances.

In most instances in property and land use regulation, a house is presumed to be a single-family residence. Zoning laws, however, tend to be specific in defining houses authorized for construction in a given zone as single family, two-family, or more. By definition, a house may represent either a multiple family residence or, in some surviving uses from earlier conventions, a single apartment or residential area within a multiple-family residence.

Though the formal distinction between house and home is that a house is a structure and a home is the community of people within it, in most documents and grants of property, no distinction is intended between them. Indeed, according to context, house may mean a community, such as a banking, legislative, or educational institution.

*See also:* zoning (land-use zone); domicile (domicil or domiciliary) | home.

**house bill**  *See:* legislation, bill, house bill (H.B. or HB).

**house as legislative chamber**  One chamber of a legislature, usually the more populous. A house represents a single body in a legislature, usually the House of Representatives, or sometimes the assembly or otherwise the larger chamber of a bicameral legislature. References are sometimes made, however, to either legislative body as a its own house.

**household**  *See:* family (household).

## housing

**Fair Housing Act (F.H.A. or FHA)**  Legislation barring discrimination in the sale or rental of most housing. The Fair Housing Act, initially passed in 1968 and amended in 1974 and 1988, bars discrimination on the basis of race, color, religion, sex, familial status, national origin, and as amended, from limitations on the basis of physical handicap. The act applies to advertisements and the process of sale and rental of housing as well as the willingness to sell or rent a dwelling. The act does not apply to individuals selling their own houses without an agent or to individuals letting rooms in a house in which they live, renting to four or fewer families.

**household employment tax**  *See:* tax, payroll tax, household employment tax (nanny tax).

**housing court**  *See:* court, court of limited jurisdiction, housing court.

**public housing**  Housing owned by the government and leased to private parties. Public housing is governmental housing, which is made available by lease, sometimes at no rent, to individuals and families. Public housing is often regulated housing, in which the lease incorporates regulations for use and conduct by tenants, their invitees and licensees. Public housing is essentially housing for the poor.

**public housing authority**  Agency charged with providing low-income housing. A public housing authority is an agency of a state or municipal government charged with providing affordable housing for low-income persons.

**publicly assisted housing**  Housing financed by loans guaranteed by the government. Publicly assisted housing refers to any home the acquisition of which is financed by a loan guaranteed by the government.

**hovel**  A very small and substandard house. The term "hovel" was once used to depict a storage shed, but it is now nearly always used to describe a house of mean estate, inhabited by a poor person out of necessity.

**hudud**  *See:* hadd (hudud).

**hue and cry**  A summons for citizens to join in catching a felon. The hue and cry was the means by which a posse was formed in medieval England to chase and attempt to capture a person suspected of committing a crime. The image of the hue and cry as a shouted demand for adult men to come to the aid of the sheriff is partially accurate, although the hue and cry was also performed by proclamation and the posting of signs. Hue and cry allowed a citizen to seize another without fear or reprisal, but it was also a duty that was to be performed by all citizens, to report a known felony, to report the discovery of a dead body, to attempt to arrest a fleeing felon, and to join a posse when a call of hue and cry was raised.

*See also:* posse; posse, posse comitatus (sheriff).

**Hughes Court** *See:* court, U.S. court, U.S. Supreme Court, Hughes Court (new deal court).

**hukim (chukim chukkim)** Jewish laws based on authority rather than reason. The hukim are commandments that have their authority from their pronouncement alone, rather than owing to some rational reason that can be given for them, as opposed to mishpatim (and in some systems, eduyot).

*See also:* mishpatim.

**hukm (akham)** A command or prohibition issued by Islamic jurists or derived from a divine command. Hukm is, literally, a relationship between two points, like cause and effect. In Islamic law, it depicts any law or edict, especially a rule articulated by the ijma' from a divine command. Akham is the plural form of hukm.

**hull** The frame or body of a vessel. A hull is the frame or body of a ship or boat, including the entire portion that is submerged and that continues up to the main deck. The hull excludes the superstructure, cranes, stacks, and masts. The design of the hull is essential for the seaworthiness of any vessel.

**Hull formula** *See:* nationalization, nationalization of property, Hull formula.

**double hull** A doubled outer wall of a ship. A double hull is a hull within a hull, a double wall surrounding the body of the ship, with a void of about ten feet between the two bulkheads. The double hull makes a breach less likely in a collision and is required of new oil tankers and preferred for large vessels operating in areas of likely collision with ice or undersea obstacles.

**human immunodeficiency virus** *See:* virus, human immunodeficiency virus (H.I.V. or HIV ).

**human rights** *See:* right, human right (human rights).

**human rights tribunal** *See:* right, human right, human rights tribunal; court, human rights tribunal.

**human trafficking** *See:* trafficking, human trafficking.

**human will** *See:* will (human will).

**humankind or man** *See:* mankind (humankind or man).

**hundred** A local division of a county. The hundred was a division of a county that was initially composed of one hundred households, within which the heads of the household were collectively responsible for the detection and prevention of crimes as well as the raising of certain taxes and performance of other duties. A court of the hundred (or hundred gemote) heard minor cases that were not within the jurisdiction of the county court. The hundred is a forerunner of the later U.S. county beat or ward, and the court of the hundred was succeed by the justice of the peace.

*See also:* judge, justice of the peace (j.p. or jp or justice court judge).

**hung jury or deadlocked jury** *See:* verdict, no verdict (hung jury or deadlocked jury).

**Hunter doctrine** *See:* equality, equal protection of the laws, Hunter doctrine.

**hunting (fishing or hunt or fish)** Chasing, stalking, trapping, or taking a wild animal. Hunting includes all of the acts associated with pursuing or taking wild animals, other than fish. (Fishing is generally considered a distinct activity, though it is indeed the hunting of fish.) Hunting is regulated in every state and on federal lands by the game laws that govern that jurisdiction.

*See also:* game, game animal; game, game animal, game law.

**husband** *See:* family, spouse, husband.

**husband–wife immunity or interspousal immunity** *See:* immunity, spousal immunity (husband–wife immunity or interspousal immunity).

**hush money** *See:* bribery, hush money.

**hybrid** Combination. A hybrid is anything that has attributes of several things. For example, hybrid plants or animals are interbred between two species, and a hybrid vehicle employs more than one source of power for its propulsion. Thus, a hybrid cause of action or hybrid suit combines independent causes of action against different parties into a single action that shares sufficient elements of a common claim to move forward as one cause.

**hybrid class action** *See:* class, class action, hybrid class action.

**hybrid comparative negligence** *See:* negligence, comparative negligence, modified comparative negligence (hybrid comparative negligence).

**hybrid court** *See:* court, international court, hybrid court.

**Hyde Amendment** *See:* fee, fee for services, attorney's fee, fee shifting, Hyde Amendment.

**hydrocarbon lease or oil lease or gas lease** *See:* lease, mineral lease (hydrocarbon lease or oil lease or gas lease).

**hydrology** The study of the movements of water in and on the Earth. Hydrology is both the science and process of water movement as it makes its way through the water cycle from precipitation to eventual evaporation, particularly studying its movements over and through land, and in various bodies of water.

**hypnosis (hypnotism or hypnotic or trance or mesmerism or braidism)** A sleep-like state of altered mental awareness created by suggestion or monotony. Hypnosis is a mental state created by a combination of suggestion and monotony that is akin to sleep but that differs from naturally induced sleep by allowing the person hypnotized to hear and respond to statements and suggestions.

A person in a state of hypnosis is hypnotized, or in an hypnotic state or, as it is now less commonly said, an hypnotic trance. The hypnotist employs a trustworthy voice and repetitive suggestion, occasionally with other aids that create a monotonous effect to hypnotize another person.

**hypnotically induced testimony** *See:* testimony, hypnotically induced testimony (hypnotic testimony or post-hypnotic testimony).

**hypothecation (hypothec)** The pledge of an asset as collateral for a debt. Hypothecation is a form of pawning or pledging an asset as collateral for debt. The asset may be restricted to particular forms, such as immovables in the civil law, including negotiable instruments. Hypothecation includes a pledge of assets to settle an existing debt as well as the acceptance of a form of lien on assets to secure a new debt. Hypothecation may describe both the contractual establishment of the interest, like a lien, as well as the actual transfer of the property hypothecated.

**hypothetical (hypo)** A story or question put forward for the sake of argument. A hypothetical is a question, story, or statement based on an hypothesis, a claim advanced for the sake of an argument to test the significance of the argument, not advanced because the person advancing it actually believes in the truth or falsity of the question, the story, or the statement. A hypothetical, or a hypo, is more fully described as a hypothetical question or hypothetical story.

In law school, a great deal of classroom work is designed to imagine the function or failure of a rule or principle in a novel factual environment, and stories invented to discuss this imagined use of the rule or principle are hypotheticals. Hypotheticals are used as the basis for law school exams and bar exams, and they are often used to test a point or to prove a claim in legal argument.

*See also:* Blackacre (Whiteacre or Redacre or Greenacre); widget.

**hypothetical question** *See:* question, hypothetical question.

**hypoxia (hypoxic zone or dead zone)** A condition of oxygen deprivation, especially in a body of water. Hypoxia is a condition of oxygen depletion, and it is the effect in waters that have been contaminated by excessive decomposition of plant life, which displace dissolved oxygen in the water, thus killing animals in the waters. Hypoxic zones, or dead zones, will not support fish or large animals in water. Many international waters, such as the Gulf of Mexico, have large hypoxic zones. In 2008, the Gulf of Mexico's hypoxic zone was roughly the size of Massachusetts.

*See also:* eutrophication.

> Words being symbols, they do not speak without a gloss.
>
> Rochin v. California, 342 U.S. 165 (1952) (Frankfurter, J.)

# I

**i**   The ninth letter of the modern English alphabet. "I" signifies a variety of functions as a symbol, such as the mark for "incomplete." It is translated into India for radio signals and NATO military transmissions, into Ida for some police radio traffic, and into dot, dot in Morse Code.

**i as a Roman numeral**   Latin symbol for one (1). I is one when used as a numeral. In the Roman system of numeralization, the addition of an one to the right of another Roman numeral adds one to the numerical value. The addition of an one to the left of another Roman numeral subtracts one from the numerical value.

**i as an abbreviation**   A word commencing in I. When used as the first letter of an abbreviation, I often stands for international. It may also stand for id, Idaho, Illinois, immediate, immigration, impeachment, in, income, independent, index, Indian, Indiana, industrial, information, institute, inter-, interior, Iowa, Ireland, Irish, and Italian. As a reporter, it may stand for India.

**I-9 Form**   *See:* immigration, immigration form, Form I-9 (I-9 Form).

**I.A.D.C. or IADC**   *See:* bar, bar organization, International Association of Defense Counsel (I.A.D.C. or IADC).

**I.C.C. or ICC**   *See:* court, international court, International Criminal Court (I.C.C. or ICC).

**I.C.E. or ICE**   *See:* customs, U.S. Immigration and Customs Enforcement (I.C.E. or ICE).

**I.C.J. or ICJ**   *See:* court, international court, International Court of Justice (I.C.J. or ICJ).

**I.D. or ID or I.D. divorce or irretrievable breakdown of the marriage or I.B.M. or IBM or IBM divorce or no-fault divorce**   *See:* divorce, irreconcilable differences divorce (I.D. or ID or I.D. divorce or irretrievable breakdown of the marriage or I.B.M. or IBM or IBM divorce or no-fault divorce).

**i.e.**   *See:* id est (i.e.); citation, citation signal, i.e.

**I.F.P. or IFP**   *See:* indigency, in forma pauperis (I.F.P. or IFP).

**I.I.E.D. or IIED or outrage**   *See:* distress, emotional distress, intentional infliction of emotional distress (I.I.E.D. or IIED or Outrage).

**I.L.C. or ILC**   *See:* international law, International Law Commission (I.L.C. or ILC).

**I.P. or IP**   *See:* intellectual property (I.P. or IP).

**I.R.A. or IRA**   *See:* pension, individual retirement account (I.R.A. or IRA).

**I.R.B. or IRB**   *See:* revenue, internal revenue, Internal Revenue Bulletin (I.R.B. or IRB).

**I.R.B.s IRBs**   *See:* institution, institutional review boards (I.R.B.s IRBs).

**I.R.S. or IRS**   *See:* revenue, internal revenue, Internal Revenue Service (I.R.S. or IRS).

**ibidem (ibid.)**   In the same place as the prior source cited. Ibidem signals a repetition of the citation just given. Ibidem, literally means "in the same place" in Latin. In legal citation, ibidem is generally not used, but the closely related "idem," for "the same" is used, which is why we have "id." rather than "ibid." in modern legal citation.
   *See also:* idem (id.); loco citato (loc. cit.); quod, quod vide (q.v.).

**id.**   *See:* idem (id.).

**id est (i.e.)**   That is. Id est, which is nearly always abbreviated "i.e.", is Latin for "that is" or, more fully, "that is to say." I.e. signals that what follows is a defining illustration of the point that preceded it. It is easy to confuse i.e. with e.g. E.g., or exempli gratia, translates more literally as "for the sake of example" and may represent any illustrations of the point made before. Although this is not a perfect distinction and there are many illustrations that overlap, i.e. should be thought of as providing a definitive example or list, which are essential to the point being made. In contrast, e.g. should be thought of as providing samples or examples that might have been chosen otherwise with no loss of meaning to the reader.
   *See also:* videlicet (viz.).

**IDEA**   *See:* disability, education of children with disabilities, Individuals with Disabilities Education Act (IDEA).

**ideal**   The best possible form of an idea. An ideal is the most perfected manifestation possible of anything. In classical philosophy, following Plato, everything that has a form, which includes everything that can be named or described, has an ideal form that does not exist on Earth but does exist. The notion in contemporary philosphy of the central case is a revision of the ideal.

The most important ideals to law are the best forms of law, the goals for human and political behavior that the officials of law ought to pursue. Ideals in this form are central to the philosophy of natural law, as well as to critical models of constitutional law, such as Edwin Corwin's higher law background of the constitution and Ronald Dworkin's model for the best interpretation of the law.

**ideal type**   The best practical illustration of a form or idea. An ideal type is an example that best illustrates the idea it exemplifies. The concept of the ideal type is quite old, but the term has a particular meaning used in legal sociology developed by Max Weber.

**ideals**   *See:* constitution, U.S. Constitution, ideals.

**idem (id.)**   The source is the same as the preceding source. Idem signals a repetition of the citation just given before it. Idem is abbreviated "id." or at the start of a note or cite as "Id." Though small differences in nuance developed more as a result of nineteenth- and twentieth-century custom and usage among different scholarly communities, there is little real difference other than citation conventions used in different disciplines between ibid. (from ibidem) and id. (from idem). Lawyers tend to use id. more, and scholars in other fields tend to use ibid. Few readers are tolerant of the hosts of footnotes with an "id.," each tracking the citation of the note before it until the diligent reader must turn back over pages of repetitious and uninformative notes to find the source of the idea in the text. Yet generations of law review editors put them in.

*See also:* loco citato (loc. cit.); ibidem (ibid.).

**idem sonans**   An excuse for misspellings that sound like the word intended. Idem sonans, literally meaning "sounds the same," is a doctrine of interpretation that allows a misspelled word to have the same legal effect that the word would have had if it had been spelled correctly, provided that the variations in spelling have the same sounds when read aloud. Idem sonans thus creates a duty to investigate based on notice inquiry in matters of title search or service of process or other investigative responsibility. Even so, if the spelling of a word with precision is material to the legal issue, then idem sonans usually does not apply.

*See also:* misnomer (misnomer rule).

**identification (identity or identify or I.D. or ID)**   A statement, document, or process relating a person's name or identity. Identification, generally, is the relationship of an identity to a person or thing. In law, identification is usually the means by which the identity of a person is determined by name. This may occur through the person's statement of a name or a name and other identifying information such as the address of the person's residence. Such a statement obviously does not amount to proof of identification. A person has no general constitutional right that would excuse a failure to identify oneself to a lawful police authority upon a reasonable and lawful demand for identification.

A document of identification, such as an authentic government-issued identification, may serve both to establish and to prove a person's identity.

Identification in other contexts, such as when a person refuses to provide identification or when a person is found incapacitated or dead, may be a matter of forensic examination.

**government-issued identification**   Proof of a person's identity that is issued by a government. Government-issued identification is any personal identification card, badge, papers, or device that is issued to the holder by the government. Common forms include a driver's license, a passport, a Social Security card, travel papers issued by a government, and a voter's registration card. Some forms are quite specialized, such as a military identification card, military travel orders, a police officer's identification card, or a security pass card for a government installation.

**identity fraud**   *See:* theft, identity theft (identity fraud).

**identity or identify or I.D. or ID**   *See:* identification (identity or identify or I.D. or ID).

**identity theft**   *See:* theft, identity theft, skimmer device; theft, identity theft (identity fraud).

**identification procedure**   A means to ascertain who did something or was in a given location at given time. An identification procedure is a means by which a specific person is identified as the person of interest in a criminal investigation. The most common form of identification procedure is forensic, in which physical evidence of a person is correlated to the physical and genetic traits that make likely a single person as the source of that evidence. More popular in crime drama and still essential to many investigations is an identification procedure in which a witness is asked to identify a person observed from a lineup, from a book of photographs or computer file of images, or through recognition at a hearing or trial. The method of procedure must be one in which there is no likelihood of the procedure itself suggesting a selection by the witness.

**Neil standard**   Minimal process required to justify the identification of the defendant in trial by a witness. The Neil standard is a five-prong test to measure the validity of a witness identification, following the standards in Neil v. Biggers, 409 U.S. 188 (1972), which must be met in order for a witness's identification of a defendant to be admitted in a criminal trial. The five elements of the test are that the the witness had a sufficient chance to view the actual offender during the crime, that the witness had a sufficient degree of attention to that observation to form an impression of identity, that the accuracy of the witness's description prior to the identification was sufficient, that the witness had sufficient certainty during the confrontation, and that there was not too long a time between the crime and the confrontation with the person later identified.

**police lineup (array or identification parade or line up or line-up or photo array or show up or showup or show-up)** A line of people from which a witness is asked to identify a person once seen. A police lineup is used by the police or other authority to identify a suspect or person of interest in the involvement of a crime, either from a group of live people or from a group of photographs or images. A witness may be asked to recollect and identify the already apprehended suspect from amongst other persons with similar physical features and characteristics. The successful identification by a witness of the correct suspect can then be used as evidence against the accused at trial.

A police lineup must be done properly so as to not be overly suggestive toward one particular individual. There must be others similar to the suspect within the lineup. The suspect must not be dressed in a way that stands apart from the others. The police must also not say or do anything to lead the witness to pick one particular person over the others.

*See also:* race, race as social construct, cross-race identification theory (C.R.I.T. or CRT or CRIT).

**Wade hearing** A hearing to review the constitutionality an identification procedure. A Wade hearing is a suppression hearing to review the admissibility of the out-of-court identification of a defendant by a witness, in order to ensure the reasonableness of police conduct and a lack of a taint of suggestiveness. A Wade hearing is not automatic but must be made on motion of the defense, although it may be required by the court sua sponte. The hearing should ascertain the reasonableness of police conduct, especially whether the identification was made without suggestiveness by others to the witness, and if so, whether the witness had an independent source from which to make in-court identification.

**idiocy or imbecility or idiot or imbecile or idiotic** *See:* capacity, criminal capacity, incapacity to commit a crime, mental defect as incapacity (idiocy or imbecility or idiot or imbecile or idiotic).

**IEP** *See:* disability, education of children with disabilities, individualized education plan (IEP).

**ignition interlock device** *See:* breathalyzer, ignition interlock device (IID or I.I.D.).

**ignominy (ignominious or ignominiously)** Public disgrace. Ignominy is a state of public dishonor, particularly as a result of immoral conduct or a gross breach of duty.

**ignoramus** A rejection of a bill of indictment by the grand jury. Ignoramus, Latin for "we do not know," is a notation of the grand jury, once used to indicate the rejection of a bill for indictment. Although the term persists in a few state constitutions, it is now effectively obsolete, being replaced by the notations, "no true bill" or "dismissed" or the like.

The unfortunate use of the term for a person who either knows nothing of a specific event or is of diminished mental capacity is not a legal designation.

**ignorance** The absence of knowledge. Ignorance in common usage is the lack of knowledge, whether in general or of a given point or fact. Ignorance is closely related to mistake or error, and ignorance may be essential to error, but ignorance is generally treated as a separate mental state: error is a claim made contrary to a statement that is the truth; mistake is a claim unintentionally contrary to the truth; and ignorance is an absence of a sense of the truth. All of these categories are quite fuzzy and overlapping, and each presumes that there is a truth of the matter to be known, which might not be so.

As a failure of knowledge, evidence of ignorance can be quite elusive. A person's inability to articulate an idea is no proof of ignorance of it. Likewise, a person's proximity to evidence for a fact is no proof of actual knowledge of the evidence or of that fact.

In law, ignorance depends not only on an absence of actual knowledge, but an absence of constructive knowledge. That is, ignorance as a legal concept is only available when no duty of knowledge exists that would be breached by an absence of knowledge. Thus, each person is charged to know the law (at least in most instances), and so actual ignorance of a legal obligation is no defense to a charge under that law. Likewise, events that give rise to constructive or inquiry notice prevent ignorance of a fact from being recognized in law, so the recordation of a deed or the presence of a chemical discharge pipe would prevent a buyer of the deeded land with the pipe from claiming ignorance of the deed or of the prior existence of chemicals, regardless of what the buyer knows or fails to know. Imputed knowledge, such as knowledge held by an agent, may bar a claim of ignorance by a principal or corporation. A duty of good faith investigation, of best efforts, of due diligence, of a fiduciary responsibility, or other similar affirmative duty to gain knowledge may prevent ignorance from being legally significant.

*See also:* knowledge (know or knowing or knowingly).

**ignorance of fact** A failure to know of something that one has no duty to have known. Ignorance of fact is a failure to know something that had an effect on one's legal duties or liabilities. Ignorance of fact may arise either from a mistake of fact, in which one believes something that is not in fact true, or in which one has utterly no idea about the fact in issue. Ignorance of fact is not relevant to the law if one has a duty to discover the fact and fails to make a reasonable and good faith attempt to do so. Ignorance of fact is a component both of mistake of fact, as that would be part and parcel of mutual mistake in the formation of a contract, and of a defense to a criminal charge in which knowledge is an element of the crime.

**ignorance of law (ignorance of the law)** The failure to know of a legal duty or liability for specific conduct. Ignorance of the law is the failure of a person or all responsible parties in an entity to know of a legal duty to engage in some conduct or a legal liability for engaging in some conduct. Famously, ignorance of the law is not generally a defense in a criminal action, nor is it a defense in tort. On the other hand, ignorance of the law may be the basis for a mutual mistake underlying a contract.

Ignorance of law is, however, a defense available in a narrow category of criminal actions, in which the defendant is accused of engaging in conduct knowing the conduct to be illegal, or engaging in it willfully or purposefully to violate the law. In these cases, knowledge of the law is an element of the offense, and the prosecutor must prove the defendant's knowledge. Though the defense may argue ignorance of the law in prosecutions for offenses such as these, ignorance of the law is not an affirmative defense that must be pled by the defendant.

Some jurisdictions allow ignorance of the law in any matter in which the legal prohibition is not obvious or based on a clear moral precept but arises only as a result of regulatory prohibition. The line between malum in se, for which ignorance is no defense, and mala prohibita, for which ignorance may be a defense, can be a bit indeterminate.

*See also:* mistake, mistake of law; malum, malum in se (mala in se).

**ignorantia juris non excusat (ignorance maxim)** Ignorance of the law is no excuse. Ignorantia juris non excusat is the Latin tag for the ignorance maxim in criminal law. The maxim is, as are most maxims, subject to exception and interpretation, the sum of which are generally now considered not according to the maxim but according to the relevant law governing ignorance of law in that context.

*See also:* ignorance, ignorance of law (ignorance of the law).

**moral wrong theory (moral-wrong doctrine)** Ignorance cannot excuse breach of laws barring morally wrong conduct. Moral wrong theory limits the defenses of ignorance to criminal prohibitions and the absence of a mens rea in the commission of the actus reas to conduct that is malum prohibitum; such defenses are no bar to prosecution of conduct that is malum in se. In other words, criminal conduct that is morally wrong cannot be the basis for the defense of ignorance, because the very immorality of the conduct prohibited placed the potential offender on notice that legal officials could punish anyone who committed it.

*See also:* malum, malum in se (mala in se).

**voluntary ignorance (willful ignorance)** Ignorance of a fact despite sufficient notice of it or a duty to investigate it. Voluntary ignorance, or willful ignorance, is ignorance in fact that cannot be acknowledged in law as the basis for an excuse or mental state. Three situations account for most situations of voluntary ignorance. A person is given information and chooses to disregard it, which is usually willful ignorance. A person is under a duty to discover information but fails to perform the duty, which is usually voluntary ignorance. A person is given sufficient notice of information by indirect evidence such that only genuine negligence or an act or will would have prevented the person's understanding of the fact, in which case the situation may be one of willful or voluntary ignorance. Although the difference between willful or voluntary ignorance might be useful in rare instances of competing claims of ignorance — such as in balancing the equities between two parties, both of whom seek to be excused from some constructive, implied, or imputed knowledge — in most instances, there is no difference in the law, and neither is a basis for excuse from the knowledge not held by the party.

**ignoratio elenchi** *See:* fallacy, ignoratio elenchi (skirting the issue or straw argument).

**IID or I.I.D.** *See:* breathalyzer, ignition interlock device (IID or I.I.D.).

**ijazah (authorization)** A signal that a student is proficient to teach on a text or area of study. An ijazah is a sign, usually a certificate, that an Islamic teacher gives to a student to demonstrate the student's proficiency in the study of a text or an area of law and the student's allowance to teach on that subject. The term is from Ja wa za — to endorse, approve, or validate. Ijazah are central to Islamic education as the link in the chain for the transmission of knowledge in a line of teaching unbroken from the Prophet. Classically, the role of the ijazah is to protect the religion from corrupt teaching. Many contemporary leaders of radical groups have not participated in this tradition.

**ijma** *See:* shari'a, sources, ijma.

**ijtihad** An Islamic legal opinion outside the scope of the express requirements of the Quran and the Sunna. Ijtihad, literally "effort," is the legal interpretation derived by a jurist from recognized principles on an issue not explicitly addressed in the Quran and Sunna, from all of which the jurist must work to ascertain a statement of the right thing to do in response to a such a question.

**ill** Wrongly, badly, inadvisedly, or just plain foolishly. Ill is a prefix or adverb modifying practically any word in legal practice, the implication of all being that the thing described should not have been done or that the thing is corrupted, dangerous, or unsuitable for its purpose. As with "well," when ill is used as an adverb, it is usually not hyphenated: "An ill reasoned argument does not save a pleading ill founded in fact."

*See also:* harm (harmdoer or harmful); wrong (wrongfulness or wrondoing or wrongful).

**ill fame** *See:* prostitution, ill fame.

**illegality (illegal)** Unlawfulness. Illegality is the aspect of any conduct or act that is forbidden by any law from whatever source. Illegality may be limited by context to include only such conduct or action that violates a criminal prohibition, but the more usual sense is that illegality includes all conduct in violation of public law. In other words, illegal conduct violates a duty of administrative law, criminal law, constitutional law, international law, maritime law, and any other law that would be enforced by an official or in the name of the people or the government, but it does not include conduct actionable only in contracts or tort or any other category of private law that is enforced only by a party injured by it.

*See also:* legal (legality); lawfulness (lawful or unlawfulness or unlawful).

**illegal alien** *See:* alien, illegal alien (illegal immigrant or illegal worker or unauthorized alien).

**illegal consideration** *See:* consideration, illegal consideration.

**illegal contract** *See:* contract, specific contracts, illegal contract | severability (divisibility); contract, specific contracts, illegal contract.

**illegal immigrant or illegal worker or unauthorized alien** *See:* alien, illegal alien (illegal immigrant or illegal worker or unauthorized alien).

**illegally obtained evidence** *See:* evidence, illegally obtained evidence (unlawfully obtained evidence).

**supervening illegality** A change of law prohibiting conduct required under a contract. Supervening illegality is a form of force majeure, in which conduct that was legal at the time it was required during the formation of a contract becomes illegal, whether as a result of new legislation or a change in the interpretation of existing law. Performance of the obligation is therefore excused and, if the conduct is material to the contract, the contract may be rescinded.

*See also:* force, force majeure.

**illegitimate child** *See:* child, illegitimate child (legitimate child or nonmarital child or bastard or legitimacy or illegitimacy).

**illegitimus** Unlawful. Illegitimus is Latin for illegal or forbidden. It is the antonym in Latin of legitimus. Note: Illegitimus (or illegitimi) is not Latin for illegitimate in the sense of parentage.

*See also:* legitimus.

**illegitimi non carborundum** Don't let the bastards get you down. "Illegitimi Non Carborundum" is popular motto in mock Latin that is seemingly beloved of a certain stripe of lawyer, who universally accepts it as meaning, literally, "Don't let the bastards grind you down." Actually, it was invented in the twentieth century and means nothing sensible in Latin at all. If one must say such things, a more appropriate formulation is "Nunquam filii canis sinam vincere."

**illicit** *See:* licit, illicit.

**illicit sexual activity** *See:* rape, statutory rape, illicit sexual activity.

**illiteracy (illiterate)** The inability to read a text in any language. Illiteracy is the condition of lacking the skills of reading a text and of comprehending its meaning. A person who is illiterate cannot comprehend the meaning of a written will, contract, or other instrument unless it is read aloud.

**illusion** Something that appears to be other than it truly is. Illusion is the effect of a person's perceiving an object or state of affairs and reaching a conclusion that is not an accurate description of the object or state of affairs as it is in fact. Whether a misperception amounts to an illusion is a matter of degree, but if a reasonable person might base an idea, decision, or action on the condition apparent, but the idea, decision, or action would have been different had the true condition been known, the misperception is an illusion. An illusion may be deliberately caused by a person, or it may be an accident. Illusion in the nineteenth century was a clinical term used to describe mental illness resulting in any form of false perception.

**illusory** The characteristic of deceptiveness. Illusory refers to illusion, and language in the law that creates the appearance of a duty, or an immunity, or protection that will not in fact be realized creates an illusion of such benefits. Thus, to describe as illusory a law or contract, or an element of a law or contract, is to claim it is at least deceptive, or ineffective or meaningless.

**illusory contract** *See:* contract, contract formation, illusory contract.

**illusory promise** *See:* promise, illusory promise.

**image of God** *See:* God, image of God (imago dei).

**imago dei** *See:* God, image of God (imago dei).

**imam** The religious leader of a Sunni Muslim community. An imam is the prayer leader or otherwise the religious leader of a community of Muslims. Imam literally means to be in front. Imams in America take on a role similar to ministers and priests, in that they are expected to take care of all the ceremonial needs of the community, as well as provide counseling to community members. Imams may or may not exercise political leadership in the community as well.

*See also:* mullah.

**IME** *See:* examination, medical examination, independent medical examination (IME).

**immaterial breach** *See:* breach, breach of contract, material breach (immaterial breach).

**immaterial issue** *See:* issue, issue before the court, material issue (immaterial issue).

**immediate appearance**  *See:* search, warrantless search, plain view, immediate appearance (immediately apparent).

**immediate cause**  *See:* causation, immediate cause.

**immediate possession**  *See:* possession, immediate possession.

**immediately apparent**  *See:* search, warrantless search, plain view, immediate appearance (immediately apparent).

**immemorial possession**  *See:* possession, immemorial possession.

**immigration (immigrant)**  The permanent movement of a person into one country from another. Immigration is the movement of a person, or a group of people into one country from another. The process by which a person who has immigrated to a country achieves citizenship is naturalization. In the United States, immigration and naturalization are regulated by Congress, and the implementation of immigration law is committed mainly to the Department of Homeland Security.

**immigration bond**  *See:* bond, immigration delivery bond (immigration bond).

**immigration delivery bond**  *See:* bond, immigration delivery bond (immigration bond).

**immigration detainer or notice of action**  *See:* deportation, DHS detainer (immigration detainer or notice of action).

**Alien and Sedition Acts (Smith Act)**  Four 1798 U.S. statutes regulating aliens, speech, and press. The Alien and Sedition Acts are four statutes that were passed by the federalist-controlled Congress in 1798: The Naturalization Act, Act of June 18, 1798, ch. 54, 1 Stat. 566. The Alien Friends Act, Act of June 25, 1798, ch. 58, 1 Stat. 570. The Alien Enemies Act, Act of July 6, 1798, ch. 66, 1 Stat. 577. The Sedition Act, Act of July 14, 1798, ch. 74, 1 Stat. 596. Collectively, they were intended to increase the regulation of resident aliens and to protect the political party then in office from criticism. The Sedition Act expired in 1801 following nineteen prosecutions which were considered unconstitutional by many at the time. All of those convicted were pardoned by Thomas Jefferson. Nonetheless, its intent persists in the Smith Act, or Alien Registration Act or 1940, codified at 18 U.S.C. § 2385. The regulation of aliens and the process of naturalization continue in later laws. The Alien Enemies law was reenacted last in 1918 in substantially the same language as in 1798, and it remains in force as of 2011.

*See also:* sedition.

**emigrant (emigration)**  A person who leaves from a country to reside permanently in another. An emigrant is a person who has left one country to live permanently elsewhere. The concept of emigration is obviously relative to the country under discussion. A person who is an immigrant in one state is,

unless the person was previously stateless, an emigrant from another. Emigration is regulated in many countries, which require exit visas for citizens or subjects prior to departure. Likewise, countries vary considerably in the rights afforded to emigrants, ranging from the abrogation of home citizenship to continued participation in elections and other privileges.

**green card (permanent resident card)**  The identification issued by the United States of a permanent resident alien. A green card is a permanent resident's card, Form I-551 issued by the Bureau of Citizenship and Immigration Services, a bureau of the U.S. Department of Homeland Security. Its current form is not actually colored green, although the version of Form I-151 employed from 1951 until 1977 was green. The green card serves as authorization for its holder to take up residence and employment within the United States, and a resident holding a green card and meeting other requirements will eventually qualify to apply for United States citizenship.

**Immigration and Naturalization Service (INS)**  Former federal agency charged with overseeing United States immigration. The United States Immigration and Naturalization Service was formerly a part of the United States Department of Justice and was charged with overseeing United States immigration policy. With the creation of the Department of Homeland Security, INS ceased to exist on March 1, 2003, its functions thereafter being performed by the U.S. Citizenship and Immigration Services.

**immigration court**  Article I tribunal for the appeal of immigration orders. An immigration court is an administrative tribunal in the Department of Justice that hears appeals of administrative decisions made in the Department of Homeland Security. Immigration courts are staffed by immigration judges, who are Article I judges, and from whom an appeal lies to the Board of Immigration Appeals, from which judicial review is available in the United States Circuit Court. Immigration Courts sit without juries, although the basic requirements of due process of law must be ensured in every action before them.

**Form I-9 (I-9 Form)**  Required proof of eligibility to work in the U.S. Department of Homeland Security. Form I-9 requires proof of citizenship or valid status as a resident alien or alien allowed to work in the United States. The form must be completed and signed by the employee who provides the employer with two different forms of proof of identity and proof of employment authorization, which must be examined by the employer, who attests to the apparent authenticity of the proof provided. Every employer must require every employee properly to complete a Form I-9, the employer filing the information with the U.S. Citizenship and Immigration Services to verify eligibility and retaining the form.

**immorality (immoral)**  Conduct that is unreasonable in violating community or general norms of behavior.

Immorality is the violation of a moral standard. In general immorality is not in itself a violation of the law. Even so, many legal standards reflect a moral norm, whether a general moral norm like the universal moral condemnation of the murder of a human being, or a community moral norm, like the hours when noise may be made outside without causing a nuisance.

Immorality is often a term in an employment contract, providing that an employee is subject to dismissal for immoral acts. In some instances immorality is defined by standards of the criminal law, to include criminal acts involving moral turpitude. In others, the standard of immorality is one of offense to community standards or, in the case of teachers, failing to present an appropriate model of behavior to children. These standards are often a euphemism for a prohibition on sexual relations with students, with children, or with adults in an improper manner, such as with prostitutes or in public, or the improper possession of pornographic materials. Broader ranges of conduct include offenses or incidents involving the consumption of drugs or alcohol, acts that violate the criminal law, or that amount to a violation of a quasi-fiduciary or fiduciary role. In employment at will, a failure to define immorality is irrelevant, and because an employer may terminate an employee without cause, the vagueness of a stated cause is immaterial. Even so, a false statement that an employee is terminated for immoral behavior amounts to defamation. In a position in which an employee may only be terminated for cause, the most essential element of immorality is that the employee was on notice of what amounts to immoral conduct before any allegation of immorality is made.

**immovables or movable property or movables**
See: property, immovable property (immovables or movable property or movables).

**immunity**   A privilege from the performance of any duty that would otherwise be required. Immunity, in the law, is the legal allowance of an individual or entity to avoid the performance of a duty that would be required except for the immunity. A person may be immune from a legal requirement of service, such as military service or jury service, or be immune from service of process or compelled testimony. In certain instances, a prohibition or disenfranchisement operates as a basis of immunity, as in a jurisdiction that bars convicted felons from voting operates also to create an immunity from service on a jury.

**civil immunity**   Immunity from civil suit. Civil immunity is immunity from suit and from process in a suit for a private cause of action. Civil immunity does not arise from immunity from criminal process, and circumstances that lead to immunity from prosecution for a crime need not suggest immunity from civil process. Civil immunity may arise from constitutional, statutory, or judicial limitations on actions against individuals holding particular offices, such as government officials, or upon individuals who perform certain actions, such as a good Samaritan. Civil immunity may be absolute, qualified, or limited only to actions done in a good faith belief in their lawfulness.

**charitable immunity**   Immunity of a charitable entity from suits for negligence. Charitable immunity is a form of immunity from civil actions for tort, particularly for claims arising from the negligent actions of the officers or employees of a charity. The immunity was absolute in the common law, and it remains so in a few jurisdictions, although the more common rule now is to retain immunity for simple negligence but to waive it for gross negligence and all intentional torts. Charitable immunity does not extend to actions for harm to the charity itself, nor to claims for equitable relief.

**parental immunity**   Immunity of a parent from civil actions brought by the parent's child. Parental immunity bars tort claims from a minor and dependent child of the parent for negligence. Thus a parent is generally immune from suit, whether brought by the child, by the other parent, or by a third party, for damages for negligence, even negligence resulting in wrongful death. Parental immunity does not, however, extend to actions for damages resulting from intentional torts or actions that demonstrate a depraved mind, nor does parental immunity bar criminal actions, actions related to custody or property, or a direct action against an insurer.

Some jurisdictions have abandoned parental immunity, subject to various exceptions. Still, in some jurisdictions, the principle of reciprocation requires that a child be immune from suit by a parent, the parent's injuries from the child's negligent acts.

**criminal immunity**   Immunity from prosecution for a crime. Criminal immunity is immunity from prosecution for a crime, which commonly occurs in one of the following three scenarios. First, a person may have a status, for example as a head of state, making that person generally immune from criminal process. Second, a person may have received a pardon for the acts alleged or a grant of immunity by the executive, for example witness immunity. Third, a person may enjoy immunity as the result of the operation of law owing to the running of the statute of limitations on the acts underlying the crime, the effect of double jeopardy as a result of an acquittal, or the absence of criminality for the acts alleged.

See also: declination (declination letter); immunity, witness immunity.

**diplomatic immunity**   See: diplomat, diplomatic immunity.

**consular immunity**   See: consul, consular immunity.

**discovery immunity**   See: discovery (discoverable).

**work-product immunity (work product immunity or work-product rule or work product privilege)**   Qualified immunity from discovery of the writings of a lawyer in preparation for litigation. Work product immunity is a qualified immunity from discovery, usually barring the production of documents or other tangible writings, if the discovery seeks material created by an attorney or a member of the attorney's staff or trial team in anticipation of litigation. The immunity is not absolute. A court may order discovery of material if the material is not privileged and the party seeking the material can demonstrate that it cannot reasonably acquire the material or substantially similar material without significant hardship and the material is necessary to a fair presentation of the seeking party's case or, as required under the federal rules, the party seeking discovery must demonstrate substantial need of the materials in the preparation of his or her case and that he or she is unable without undue hardship to obtain the substantial equivalent of the materials by other means.

Even if the party seeking such material can prove these preconditions, the party may not receive material that would violate the attorney–client privilege or other privileges of the party (as opposed to the party's counsel). Thus, work–product materials that would disclose the client's statements, impressions, or opinions are excluded from any exception to the immunity.

The work–product rule, generally, cannot bar a former client from seeing documents prepared in the client's service. Nor does the rule apply in later litigation against that client. The rule generally does not apply in later litigation, although it may if the litigation is against the same litigants or litigants in substantially the same role as those in the litigation for which the work was first produced.

*See also:* privilege.

***attorney-client privilege and work product*** The scope and function of attorney client privilege differ from that of work–product immunity. Work–product immunity is related but different from attorney–client privilege. Work–product immunity applies only to materials prepared in anticipation of litigation or trial, and bars their discovery unless the party seeking them can show a substantial need, i.e., the party is unable without undue hardship to otherwise obtain the substantial equivalent of the materials sought. Work product might include materials that are communicated between attorney and client, but it is largely not derived from such communications but from the labor of the attorney and the attorney's staff. Attorney-client privilege includes all professionally oriented communication between the attorney and the client and is absolutely privileged, regardless of substantial need. Both the immunity and the privilege may be waived by the client, but the lawyer may waive work–product immunity.

**intergovernmental immunity (intergovernmental immunities)** The barriers of federalism that limit each government from obligating the others. Intergovernmental immunities limit the central government

from creating obligations upon the states — whether by regulating state officials, exposing the state to federal suit, or creating tax liability — and limit the state government from creating similar obligations upon other states of the central government.

*See also:* federalism.

**official immunity**

**absolute immunity** Immunity from criminal or civil process, without exception. Absolute immunity is immunity from all causes of action that might be brought against an individual. Absolute immunity is exceedingly rare, usually limited to the exceptional cases of certain heads of state within their jurisdiction. Absolute immunity in its perfect sense would place a person above the law.

Thus, when it is used in most instances, absolute immunity means immunity from certain forms of process, without exception for all acts within a particular scope of conduct and for a particular time. Thus, in the U.S. absolute immunity may bar only civil suits but not criminal liability for acts committed by certain officials, such as police officers, judges, and executives.

*See also:* immunity; immunity, sovereign immunity.

**discretionary act** Any action within an official's responsibility that requires indepedent judgment. Discretionary acts are the acts of an official within the scope of office that require the official to exercise independence of thought and responsibility of judgment. Officials and the governments that employ them are usually immune from suit for discretionary acts by officials. The boundaries of discretion, however, are also the boundaries of immunity, and for instance, an official lacks the ability under law to exercise official discretion to commit or order an illegal act, and no immunity applies to an official's act that violates the criminal law or exceeds the scope of the official's office. A corporate officer who acts beyond the scope of discretion acts ultra vires.

**judicial immunity** Immunity of a judge from civil actions for all acts made in the scope of office. Judicial immunity is an absolute civil immunity from claims for damages for all acts or omissions within the scope of office. Judicial immunity is no bar to actions in the scope of office related to the performance of office, such as an action for a writ of mandamus or prohibition, nor does it bar a criminal action for abuse of office or other misconduct.

**legislative immunity (congressional immunity)** Legislator's civil immunity for acts done in the preparation of legislation. Legislative immunity, or Congressional immunity, is an immunity from private suit for acts committed in the process of preparing, submitting, and discussing legislation. Thus, a statement made by a member of Congress or a report made by an aide to that member cannot be the basis, for instance, of a claim in slander. States determine the scope of the immunity against state claims that will be extended to state legislators, which is usually a matter of state constitutional law. Federal Congressional immunity is an extension of the Speech and Debate Clause.

*See also:* privilege, evidentiary privilege, legislative privilege.

**ministerial act** Any action within an official's non-discretionary routine. Ministerial acts are the acts of an official within the scope of office that do not require the official to exercise independence of thought or responsibility of judgment. The official carrying out a ministerial role is usually doing so as a matter of routine. Officials and the governments that employ them enjoy only qualified immunity from suit for harm done by ministerial acts of officials.

**presidential immunity** The limited immunity from civil and criminal claims against the President of the United States. Presidential immunity is immunity afforded to the President of the United States from civil or criminal process for official actions committed while in office. This immunity is absolute for civil actions for damages from official conduct. The president is not immune while in office from process from personal actions committed prior to inauguration. For criminal acts committed while in office while the president is in office, the only legal remedy is impeachment by the House of Representatives and trial by the United States Senate, after which the former president may be indicted for criminal acts that formed the basis of the impeachment.

**qualified immunity** Official immunity that is lost if the official violates the clearly established rights of another. Qualified immunity is an immunity from civil suit extended to police officers, administrators, and other public officials who are alleged to have violated the rights of a person while the official was performing a discretionary function of office, if the official's conduct does not violate a clearly established statutory or constitutional right that would have been known to a reasonable person. To assert qualified immunity, the official must demonstrate either that the facts alleged by the plaintiff, when taken in the light most favorable to the plaintiff, do not amount to a violation of a right protected by the constitution or statute. Or, if a right might have been violated, the official must demonstrate that the right was not so clearly established that the law had not put the official on notice regarding the right so as to make a reasonable person in the official's position aware that his or her conduct would clearly be unlawful.

**sovereign immunity** The immunity of a state from involuntary appearance in a court of law. Sovereign immunity is the immunity of a state from appearing to answer any charge or any demand in a court of law, unless the state voluntarily does so. Sovereign immunity is a vestigial doctrine that persists from the time when a nation's monarch was personally immune from all judicial process, both in that nation's courts and in the courts of other nations. This was a matter both of comity and practicality. The doctrine persists in international law as a matter of comity and owing to the preference of most governments to manage private claims against foreign states as a matter of diplomacy.

*See also:* tort, Federal Tort Claims Act (F.T.C.A. or FTCA).

**abrogation of sovereign immunity** The limitation of a state's sovereign immunity. The abrogation of sovereign immunity is a process by which a state loses its immunity from process in a court of law. Abrogation of sovereign immunity usually arises from the state's action through legislation amounting to a standing, voluntary waiver of immunity from civil process, either in allowing actions in a limited category of cases, such as intentional torts, or more broadly allowing suits in all cases or all but a few excepted categories of case.

In the United States, the Congress of the United States may abrogate the immunity of the individual states as to a specific matter within Congressional powers derived from the Reconstruction Amendments, especially section five of the Fourteenth Amendment.

As a matter of international law, abrogation may result from the state's accession into a treaty or other supranational document waiving immunity from process in certain tribunals or a given forum, such as the International Court of Justice. Waiver of sovereign immunity in a given action does not amount to abrogation of the immunity generally.

Scholars and jurists have argued that abrogation may also arise from forfeiture, when the conduct of state officials toward the subjects of that state or toward other states so contravenes the fundamental purposes for the recognition of the state that, effectively, as a matter of law the state no longer exists.

*See also:* tort, Federal Tort Claims Act (F.T.C.A. or FTCA); abrogation (abrogate).

**foreign sovereign immunity** The immunity of a foreign state from process in a domestic court. Foreign sovereign immunity is the bar to actions in a domestic court against a foreign state or government. In the United States, foreign sovereign immunity bars civil actions against a foreign state in both state courts and federal courts. Foreign sovereign immunity does not apply in a given matter if the foreign state waives its immunity, whether expressly or impliedly by voluntarily appearing within the court for any purpose related to an action other than to challenge jurisdiction. Further, foreign sovereign immunity does not extend to actions in violation of the laws of nations or to specific acts for which the Congress has abrogated sovereign immunity.

**commercial-activity exception** Exception to foreign sovereign immunity for state activities of a commercial nature. The commercial–activity exception to foreign sovereign immunity provides an avenue to sue a foreign state in a domestic court if the action is based upon a commercial activity carried on in the United States by the foreign state, or is based on an act performed in the United States in connection with a commercial activity of the foreign state elsewhere, or is based on an act outside the territory of the United States in connection with a commercial activity of the foreign state elsewhere and that act causes direct effect in the United States. A plaintiff need only show that one of these conditions is met for the commercial activities exception to apply.

The commercial activities doctrine applies also the sovereignty of the United States and to the sovereignty of individual states, in that either form of government that enters the marketplace and throws off the cloak of sovereignty is no longer immune from its actions. Such entry must be clear and distinct from the regular commercial activities needed in support of governmental activities, as a result of which the state is in the market like any private actor.

**Tate letter** U.S. policy announcement restricting foreign sovereign immunity. The Tate letter was issued by the Acting Legal Advisor to the State Department, Jack B. Tate, on May 19, 1952, reprinted in 26 Dept. State Bull. 984, 984 (1952), announcing the U.S. policy of restrictive sovereign immunity, and abandoning the previous adherence to absolute sovereign immunity as a matter of executive police. The theory of restrictive sovereign immunity was later reflected in the Foreign Sovereign Immunities Act, 28 U.S.C. §§ 1330, 1332, 1441, 1602–1611 (2006). Sometimes, letters of executive interest in a single case are referred to as Tate letters, particularly when the question before a court is whether a claim of immunity asserted by a state should be recognized. When such letters are asserted in a case involving act of state as opposed to sovereign immunity, they are Bernstein letters. Even so, such letters are, as of 2011, not usually issued.

**state sovereign immunity (Eleventh Amendment immunity)** The immunity of a state from suit in federal court. State sovereign immunity bars all actions against a state in federal court, unless the specific form of action is allowed by the Constitution or a valid act of Congress. Actions are not barred if the state waives its immunity, if the action is for equitable relief from a violation of the Constitution itself, or if it is an action for which Congress has abrogated state immunity, particularly actions under statutes passed under Congress's authority under section five of the Fourteenth Amendment. Actions brought against a state by other states are not barred, although they are committed to the original jurisdiction of the U.S. Supreme Court.

The doctrine of sovereign immunity was initially rejected by the Court, in Chisholm v. Georgia, 2 U.S. (2 Dall.) 419 (1793), in which an action was allowed against Georgia by a South Carolinian seeking payment for war supplies. John Jay and a majority of the court allowed the claim. Thereafter, Congress proposed and the states ratified the Eleventh Amendment, which bars only claims against a state in federal court by a person in another state or country.

A century after ratification of the Amendment, the Supreme Court first announced that the Constitution bars claims against a state by its own citizen, in Hans v. Louisiana, 134 U.S. 1 (1890). A continuing argument persists that neither the Eleventh Amendment nor any other power but the Court's own precedents following Hans justifies this doctrine beyond the amendment's limit on claims against a state in a federal court's diversity jurisdiction.

*See also:* sovereignty, state sovereignty; federalism, doctrine of our federalism.

*1. exceptions* Immunity may be waived by state, abrogated by Congress, or relaxed in an action only for equitable relief for ongoing federal claims.

*2. cities and counties* State immunity does not bar actions against local governments. Civil actions may be brought in federal court against city and county officials and agencies without contravening the Eleventh Amendment. However, if the agency defendant is in fact a branch of the state government itself, such as a state water management district or local state office, immunity may apply.

**spousal immunity (husband–wife immunity or interspousal immunity)** An obsolete doctrine barring a spouse from recovery in tort from the other spouse. Spousal immunity forbids one spouse to sue the other spouse in tort. The theories underlying the immunity were once that tort was impossible between spouses (an idea that turned in part on the concept of the wife as property of the husband) and now that there are policies of discouraging actions that would interfere with family harmony and of discouraging potentially collusive actions. Spousal immunity is now abolished in most U.S. jurisdictions, and limited in the remaining jurisdictions to actions that clearly implicate one of the underlying policies, i.e., actions that do not implicate family harmony or collusion are usually not barred. Note: spousal immunity sometimes describes the immunity of one spouse from process compelling testimony against the other spouse in a deposition, hearing, or trial. Customarily, this immunity is not labeled as spousal immunity; the privilege not to testify is usually termed the spousal privilege.

*See also:* privilege, spousal privilege (marital privilege or husband–and–wife privilege).

**witness immunity** Immunity from prosecution granted to a witness in return for testimony. Witness immunity is immunity from criminal prosecution granted to a witness by a prosecutor in return for the witness's waiver of the privilege against self-incrimination and for the witness's subsequent testimony, nearly always in furtherance of the prosecution of someone other than the witness. Witness immunity may be absolute, exonerating the witness from all prosecutions for past offense, although such immunity is exceedingly rare. More commonly it is limited to transactional or use immunity.

**informal immunity (pocket immunity)**  A promise of immunity from a prosecutor not made of record in a court. Informal immunity is a pledge by an individual prosecutor that a witness will not be prosecuted on the basis of the testimony the witness might give. Informal immunity may give rise to a form of estoppel, but it in most cases, informal immunity is not recognized in court to bar a later prosecution against the witness brought by another prosecutor, particularly not a prosecution brought in another jurisdiction.

**testimonial immunity**  Immunity of a witness from a civil action based on testimony given in trial. Testimonial immunity is a bar to civil actions against a witness in a criminal or a civil action, if the civil action is brought for damages arising from the testimony given in court. In some jurisdictions, testimonial immunity is limited to actions arising from claims of injury based on false testimony or defamation. Testimonial immunity is no bar, however, to claims against a party for abuse of process nor to criminal actions for perjury.

**transactional immunity**  Immunity from prosecution for a crime of which evidence is given by a witness. Transactional immunity is an assurance of immunity given by a prosecutor to a witness that bars prosecution for any crime related to the subject matter about which the the witness testifies or produces tangible evidence. Transactional immunity does not inherently bar use of the evidence provided by the witness in a different prosecution arising from different subject matter.

**use immunity**  A bar against prosecutorial use of evidence provided by a witness. Use immunity is an assurance given by a prosecutor to a witness that bars the use of the evidence provided from any use in any prosecution against that witness, either in a pending criminal action or in any later proceedings. In a way, use immunity is a misleading term, as the witness is not made immune from prosecution but given a privilege against the use of the evidence. Because a violation of use immunity would violate the Fifth Amendment stricture against self-incrimination, the assurance of use immunity by a prosecutor in one jurisdiction is generally a bar against its use by prosecutors elsewhere.

**impact rule**  *See:* distress, emotional distress, negligent infliction of emotional distress, impact rule.

**impairment (impaired)**  The diminished ability to perform a function or task. Impairment is a reduced capacity of a person or a thing to do something that would otherwise be within the abilities of the person or thing to do. To impair something or someone is to make it or the person worse in some manner, to make the person less capable of performing a function or to interfere with or diminish the capacity of the person to act. Thus to drive or operate a vehicle or vessel while impaired is to do so while lacking the capacity ordinarily required, owing either to the presence of alcohol or drugs in the body or to a lack of sleep or other physical or mental condition. A person who is substantially impaired in a major life activity is disabled as a matter of federal law. A contract that is impaired is either limited in its scope or in the ability of one party or the other to enforce its obligations.

**impairment of contract or freedom of contract or obligations of contract**  *See:* contract, liberty of contract (impairment of contract or freedom of contract or obligations of contract).

**Impairment of Contracts Clause**  *See:* constitution, U.S. Constitution, clauses, Contracts Clause (Impairment of Contracts Clause).

**impanel a jury**  *See:* jury, impanel a jury (seat the jury or select the jury or jury return or return of a jury).

**impartiality (impartial or partiality or partial)**  Fair-mindedness and equality in the consideration and treatment of each person among all. Impartiality is the quality of lacking a bias or prejudice that would favor or disfavor a person, interest, group, or cause. It is the opposite of partiality, or a bias toward someone or something that would influence one's judgment to prefer an outcome that favors the preferred result. A judge has a duty to be impartial toward all parties before the court, as does each juror. A legislator and administrator have a duty to be impartial toward all parties subject to the laws they create. A lawyer serving the needs of a client is not bound to be impartial but may be partial toward the client's interests, though such partiality may not justify a violation of the law or the attorney's responsibility as an officer of the law and of the courts.

An impartial judge or juror not only have no direct interest in the case but approach it with an open mind, without a preconception of liability or immunity, guilt or innocence. A judge who knows the outcome before hearing the case is not impartial. This is true whether in trial or on appeal. Partiality is picking the winner on a basis other than according to the facts, the law, and the principles of justice.

**Impartial Jury Clause or Criminal Jury Clause**  *See:* constitution, U.S. Constitution, clauses, jury clause (Impartial Jury Clause or Criminal Jury Clause).

**impeachment (impeach)**  Accusation. Impeachment has several closely related senses, which amount to a process of accusation. The word seems to have arisen from both the Law French empechemont for hindrance or fetters and from a similar but unrelated Law Latin word for accusation, impetere. By the eighteenth century, the term had developed both to denote the accusation of a public officer of unfitness or wrongdoing and to challenge testimony or other evidence, particularly through the accusation of a witness.

**Impeachment Clause** *See:* constitution, U.S. Constitution, clauses, Impeachment Clause.

**impeachment of waste** *See:* waste, doctrine of waste, impeachment of waste.

**impeachment of official** An accusation against an official that the official should be removed from office. Impeachment is the accusation against an officer of government, that for some specified reason the officer is not fit to continue in office and should be removed. An impeachment is not itself an order of removal or of conviction. Such orders follow a trial upon the impeachment, which is usually held by another body. Under the Impeachment Clause of the United States Constitution, only the U.S. House of Representatives may impeach a judge or executive officer, and upon a finding of impeachment, the U.S. Senate must try the impeachment sitting as a court over which the Chief Justice of the United States presides. Judgment may be for acquittal, or if two–thirds vote in favor, for removal and also for disqualification from office. A person impeached and removed is then liable for prosecution for any offense for which the person was impeached.

**Articles of Impeachment** The instrument of accusation issued in an impeachment. Articles of Impeachment constitute a single instrument issued from the impeaching body to the trying body following an impeachment, setting forth the particulars for which an official was impeached. It is the constitutional equivalent of an indictment.

**impeachment of witness** Any challenge to the credibility of a witness. Impeachment of a witness is the challenge to a witness's testimony by an attorney whose client's argument or evidence is less persuasive as a result of the witness's evidence. Impeachment is the usual purpose of cross–examination.

Impeachment may take several forms, the simplest being the questioning of the witness in a manner that casts doubt in the minds of observers that the witness was accurately relating the events the witness has related in testimony. Impeachment may involve presentation of prior testimony by the witness to demonstrate inconsistent statements or a lack of ability either to perceive or recall the events related. Impeachment may also involve the presentation of evidence that the witness has a reason to lie or has a history of untruthfulness. The rules of evidence limit certain evidence, including the use of past criminal conduct by the witness, if the crime was a felony or a crime of dishonesty, if the crime was not committed while a minor, is not pending appeal, was not pardoned, and is not more prejudicial than probative. The religious beliefs or non–belief may not be used as a basis of impeachment of a witness in the United States.

**collateral issue rule** A witness may not be impeached with evidence otherwise irrelevant to a case. The collateral issue rule prohibits the impeachment of a witness's testimony with extrinsic evidence that is only relevant as a tool of impeachment and otherwise would have no relevance in the case at all. The essence of the collateral issue rule is its limit on extrinsic evidence, or evidence that would otherwise not be introduced into the case because it is not relevant to any of the factual issues needed to resolve the legal issues presented. Compare these hypotheticals: on the one hand, if Witness A testifies to seeing the defendant in possession of contraband at a given time and place (for which possession the defendant is charged). Witness B then is called to testify that the defendant was elsewhere at that time. Witness B's testimony impeaching Witness A's testimony is acceptable without violating the collateral issue rule: the contradictory evidence of Witness B is relevant to the defendant's alibi and is not extrinsic to the claims of the case. On the other hand, Witness B testifies that the defendant likes boating, which is not relevant to the contraband possession trial. Witness C then is called to testify that the defendant hates boating. C's proposed evidence is extrinsic and collateral, and so it is barred under the rule. The maxim of the collateral issue rule is that evidence is not relevant merely to contradict a fact that can be contradicted. Evidence that contradicts testimony on an issue is only relevant if the issue itself is relevant.

**impediment (impediments)** A legal barrier to entry into a contract, or to its performance. An impediment is a hindrance or disability that prohibits a person or entity from entering into a contract. At common law, an impediment was strictly a disability barring a person as a matter of law from entering any contract, as does youth, or barring a person from entering into a specific contract, as a person's marriage bar the person from entering a second marriage. Legal usage has grown less disciplined, however, and the term sometimes includes a sense from its more general, non–legal usage, to include impediments to performance rather than only impediments to the creation of the contract. Interpretation of the use of the term in context is essential to determine in which sense the word is intended.

**impediment to marriage** *See:* marriage, impediment to marriage.

**imperfection or perfect or imperfect** *See:* perfection (imperfection or perfect or imperfect).

**imperfect self-defense** *See:* defense, self-defense, imperfect self defense (imperfect self-defense).

**imperfect title** *See:* title, perfection of title (imperfect title).

**impertinence (impertinent)** Irrelevance. Impertinence describes the use of argument or evidence that is irrelevant and distracting from the issues raised in a case. Despite this technical sense in its origin, to be impertinent has become more associated with silliness or inappropriateness than with a deliberate test of the bounds of relevance, and only context can distinguish the sense in which the word is used.

**impertinent matter in a pleading**  *See:* pleading, impertinent matter in a pleading.

**impleader (third-party practice or third party practice)**  The process for a civil defendant to bring in another defendant. Impleader is the process by which a defendant in a civil action brings in a new party as a defendant as well. The defendant files a third-party complaint against the new party, who is the third-party defendant. The rules of some jurisdictions allow impleader by a plaintiff, although the plaintiff usually prefers to file a complaint or an amended complaint against a new defendant.

Note: do not confuse impleader with intervention or interpleader. Impleader is the initiation of suit by a defendant against a new defendant, who is usually present involuntarily. Intervention is the voluntary entry of a new plaintiff or defendant into an ongoing suit. Interpleader is the means by which a party who might have liability to multiple parties sues them all or counterclaims against all seeking a single remedy. Although impleader is closely related to joinder, and indeed is a form of joinder, the latter is usually performed by the plaintiff and impleader by the defendant, following slightly differing procedures. Although impleader is a form of joinder, the term joinder is more often used to describe a party's bringing into an action a party with an adverse interest, rather than the specific tool of a defendant's impleading another defendant.

*See also:* joinder, joinder of claims; intervention (intervene or intervenor).

**implementation plan**  *See:* pollution, air pollution, Clean Air Act, implementation plan (F.I.P. or FIP or S.I.P. or SIP).

**implication (implicate, implied)**  Something expressed indirectly. An implication is a fact or conclusion that is an indirect result of what is said or done. Thus, an implication may be a sub-text in a statement or text, a meaning that is implied by an author to be "read between the lines" of the text by the reader. An implication may also be a fact or conclusion that is unstated, not overtly done, but is a logical requirement of what is stated or done. Thus, to accept an office implies that one will perform the duties of office.

An implication that creates a legal duty will only bind the holder of that duty if the person is put sufficiently on notice of the duty, which is established if, for instance, the duty is a logical necessity arising form the persons' own conduct. Note: imply is often confused with infer. An inference is a conclusion drawn from evidence by a reader or hearer; implication is a conclusion suggested by an author or speaker.

**implied abrogation**  *See:* abrogation, implied abrogation.

**implied acquittal**  *See:* acquittal, acquittal by implication (implied acquittal).

**implied admission**  *See:* admission, evidentiary admission, implied admission.

**implied agent**  *See:* agent, apparent agent (implied agent).

**implied assumption of risk**  *See:* risk, assumption of risk, implied assumption of risk.

**implied authority**  *See:* authority, constructive authority (implied authority).

**implied condition**  *See:* condition, implied condition.

**implied consent**  *See:* consent, implied consent.

**implied contract**  *See:* contract, contract formation, implied contract (inferred contract or contract implied in fact).

**implied covenant**  *See:* covenant, contract covenant, implied covenant.

**implied covenant of good faith and fair dealing**  *See:* covenant, contract covenant, implied covenant of good faith and fair dealing.

**implied easement**  *See:* implication, easement by implication (implied easement); easement, easement by implication (implied easement).

**implied easement of absolute necessity**  *See:* easement, easement by necessity (implied easement of absolute necessity).

**implied in law**  *See:* contract, contract formation, quasi contract (contract implied in law or implied-in-law contract or quasi-contract or quasi contractus).

**implied malice**  *See:* malice, implied malice.

**implied negative covenant**  *See:* covenant, implied negative covenant.

**implied notice**  *See:* notice, implied notice.

**implied power**  *See:* power, implied power.

**implied promise**  *See:* promise, implied promise.

**implied repeal**  *See:* repeal, implied repeal (repeal by implication).

**implied trust**  *See:* trust, implied trust.

**implied waiver**  *See:* waiver, implied waiver.

**implied warranty**  *See:* implication, implied warranty.

**import (imports or imported)**  Goods brought into the state from states abroad. Imports are goods manufactured or assembled in another state and brought into a state for sale or possession. A tax on imports is a tariff, customs duty, or impost. The United States and many other states require most imports to be labeled with their country of origin.

**Import-Export Clause** *See:* constitution, U.S. Constitution, clauses, Import–Export Clause.

**important governmental objective** *See:* interest, state interest, important governmental objective.

**importunity (importuning)** To solicit a person's conduct, especially through bribery or harassment. Importunity is a solicitation of a person's action or endorsement. Although importuning may be legal, it is often used to describe solicitation that is either accompanied by an illegal act or corrupting influence or is for an illegal purpose or end.

**importuning a juror** The solicitation of a juror's vote. The importunity of a juror is the attempt to influence a juror's vote by any person not a member of the jury or in open court on the record of an action or in the grand jury room while in session. Importunity of these forms may amount to embracery and be a criminal offense. Importunity by other jurors, by counsel, or witnesses during a proceeding is no more than the attempt to influence the juror's vote by appeal to evidence, passion, or sympathy.

**impossibility** A condition in which an action or event cannot physically or lawfully take place. Impossibility in law has several forms, the obvious being something that cannot physically occur but the second being something that cannot lawfully occur. In either case, a party that had intended, agreed, or been tasked to do something impossible is usually excused from the duty of doing so, although an alternative duty may arise as a result.

**impossibility of performance** Performance of a duty is excused when a change of circumstance renders it impossible. Impossibility of performance of a duty under a contract, will, or trust is a defense for a claim of breach for non-performance of that duty. If the performance of the duty became impossible owing to unforeseen but changed circumstance, the performance is excused. A contract that required performance of a duty that was impossible ab initio is almost certainly based on a mutual mistake and may be rescinded. A will or trust based upon it will require reformation. In any case, impossibility would be an affirmative defense to a claim of breach of duty or be a basis for an affirmative claim of equitable relief. In some jurisdictions, impossibility of performance requires proof that a party attempted alternative means of performance that proved to be either impossible or substantially different from the performance contemplated by the parties in the making of the contract.

*impossiblity and impracticability and frustration* Impossibility of performance is one of three affirmative defenses against breach of contract for non-performance arising from an unforeseen material change in circumstances. Impossibility of performance requires that the performance be effectively not possible to carry out. Impracticability of performance requires that the performance be possible, but only with dramatically increased and unforeseen

difficulty, and a significantly increased cost of performance may amount to impracticability. Frustration of purpose requires that the performance be possible but the reason for the performance has become moot or irrelevant to the interests of the party who would benefit from performance.

**impossible attempt** *See:* attempt, criminal attempt, imposssibility of attempt (impossible attempt).

**impossibility of attempt** *See:* attempt, criminal attempt, imposssibility of attempt (impossible attempt).

**impost** A tax on imports. An impost is a tax placed on goods imported into the country. No state may place an impost on goods from other states.

Note: a tax on imports is usually referred to as an impost in the constitutional text, as a tariff in nineteenth-century tax law, and as customs in contemporary usage.

**impost or customs duty or import fee or rate tariff** *See:* tariff (impost or customs duty or import fee or rate tariff).

**impoundment (impound or impounded or pound)** The holding of property in the custody of the government. Impoundment, in general, is the control of property in a given place, such as the impoundment of waters behind a dam. In law, it usually is the custodial management of property, which is held by a government officer, usually by a police agency. Property or money may be impounded as evidence, as a property that poses a significant danger or potential danger to the public, as goods subject to dispute in ownership, as goods held as security for bail or for satisfaction of a putative debt being litigated, or for the good of a person in preventative detention.

**impracticability (impracticable)** Requiring unreasonable effort. Impracticability is a condition in which a task or duty could possibly be performed but only with extraordinary and unreasonable effort. When a duty under a contract to perform is accepted with a particular expectation for the difficulty and cost of performance, and then unforeseen circumstances increase the difficulty or cost to the point of impracticability, then even though the performance is still possible, the doctrine of impracticability will allow a party with the duty to perform to avoid the duty, unless other circumstances or the language of the contract would prevent it. If the duty was material to the contract, the duty-holder's decision to discharge the responsibility to render the duty may amount to rescission of the contract.

*See also:* impossibility.

**imprimatur** A symbol of approval. The imprimatur, literally a stamp onto the page, was the designation of a book as licensed for publication. The imprimatur was given under canon law to texts that complied with dogma. Imprimatur was issued in England during the regulation of printing there, especially during the rule of Charles I and the archbishopric of William Laud, a period from about 1625 to 1640. Printing had been regulated since Henry VIII; earlier regulation had been primarily by licenses and monopolies to print at all or to print certain subjects or forms of matter, as well as proclamations or prosecutions after the fact. The imprimatur was briefly revived during the Restoration.

Imprimatur in contemporary usage (other than in canon law) is now used as a metaphor indicating approval or endorsement to be implied from circumstance. Thus, a criminal act that is committed with the knowledge of or in front of police officers with jurisdiction over that crime who inexplicably fail to intervene may be said to have occurred with the imprimatur of police sanction.

Imprimatur is particularly of concern when religious activities are carried on in government-owned facilities, which might, for reasons of the location alone, create the impression that the government has given its assent to the activities, including whatever speech occurs there.

**imprisonment**   *See:* incarceration, imprisonment.

**improper joinder or manufactured joinder**   *See:* joinder, joinder of parties, collusive joinder (improper joinder or manufactured joinder).

**improper party**   *See:* party, party to an action, proper party (improper party).

**improper venue**   *See:* venue, improper venue | improper venue and forum non conveniens; venue, improper venue.

**improvement**

**improved land**   *See:* land, improved land (unimproved land).

**improvement bond**   *See:* bond, revenue bond (improvement bond).

**improvement to land (improvements)**   Any permanent change to land that increases its value. An improvement to land is any form of alteration to the land that is intended to be and likely to be permanent that improves the value of the land and makes it possible to use the land in a manner that was not possible before. Permanent buildings and other structures are improvements, and an enlargement of an existing building would be an improvement, although a renovation or repair of an existing structure is not. Other examples include the addition of foundations, drives, walks, fences, utility services, and other engineering structures; the planting of gardens or grading or other alteration of topography as landscape design; the building of docks, weirs, boatslips, dams, and other benefits to riparian property; the drilling of an oil or gas well, the construction of a mill run, a wind turbine, or any other permanent installation for the extraction of natural resources; and the installation of barns, water wells, irrigation systems, or other permanent agricultural facilities. The installation of usually temporary structures, such as a billboard or any fixture that is inherently temporary, like a portable shed, is not an improvement.

An improvement is transferred when the land is transferred. The value of improvements is an element of the value of the property as a whole, and tax valuations of property are usually increased when improvements are made.

**capital improvement**   Improvements that are likely to last for many years and improve the property value. Capital improvements are improvements to the land that add to the value of the property in a manner that will last for at least several years, such as permanent structures and higher value, permanent installations.

**imprudent or prudent**   *See:* prudence (imprudent or prudent).

**imputation (impute or imputed or imputative)**
The attribution to another person of any form of responsibility for some action, condition, or thing. Imputation is the charging of a person with knowledge, liability, duty, or any other form of responsibility regardless of whether that person has acted to seek or to accept that responsibility. Most forms of constructive knowledge of responsibility as a result of an agency are manifest in a specific instance by the knowledge or the responsibility being imputed upon the person held to account for the knowledge of the action.

Note: to impute is not the same as to infer, which is much less specific. Imputation is a claim that a person has some knowledge, duty, etc., and although the claim might be inferred from some circumstance, the inference is the process by which the observer reaches an understanding, and imputation is the process by which the person claims responsibility for another from that knowledge.

**imputed contributory negligence**   *See:* imputation, imputed contributory negligence.

**imputed income**   *See:* imputation, imputed income.

**imputed knowledge**   *See:* knowledge, constructive knowledge, imputed knowledge.

**imputed notice**   *See:* notice, imputed notice.

**IMTFE or Tokyo war crimes trials or Tokyo trials**
*See:* court, international court, international military tribunal, International Military tribunal, Far East (IMTFE or Tokyo war crimes trials or Tokyo trials).

**in**   A statement of close relationship between two things. In is a versatile word in English that may be difficult to isolate in meaning in a given phrase or use, but that generally expresses a close relationship between one thing and another, whether that relationship is one of inclusion or integration, geographical proximity, form or kind, condition, perception, or other relationships. The word existed in Latin and Law French, as well as Old Norse and Old English, and it has acquired a very long list of uses as a matter of custom.

As a matter of legal interpretation, *in* within a text is usually only meaningful within a context. In some cases, the meaning of "in" is a matter of contrast, such as "not out," "not near" or "not on." If *in* is used as a preposition, the meaning must depend on what is in what, such as "printed in trade dress," "participated in the conspiracy," "payment in cash," "appearing in court," "made in Norway," or "delivery in June." There are technical phrases, such as "in gross" or "in lieu" that have a relatively fixed meaning, usually from Latin or French, though some are in English, such as "in God we trust."

**in as a Latin preposition**   A preposition that express location or movement according to context. In, as a Latin preposition, gathers its meaning from the context of the word it modifies. In the varying contexts of space, time, motion, and relationship, it has a variety of meanings, among them: in, within, on, among, during, under, in the case of, toward, and by.

**in absentia**   *See:* absent, in absentia.

**in camera**   In Chambers. In camera describes any activity that takes place in the privacy of the judge's chambers. By extension, the phrase describes a discussion, argument, or activity that occurs as a matter of official conduct but not in public. Motions argued in camera or other matters might be made a matter of record or not according to the decisions of the judge. Conferences among judges of a panel or appellate court are private and similarly off the record, but these are held usually in a conference room rather than one judge's chambers and ordinarily are not described as in camera. Review of sensitive evidence to determine whether it is subject to a privilege or otherwise admissible, including the interview of witnesses whose identity is kept from the public, is often done by a judge in camera.
*See also:* chamber, judicial chambers (judge's chamber or judicial chamber).

**in esse (esse or covenant for a thing in esse)**   Existing in fact and not merely as a potential. In esse describes a thing that is done or exists, as opposed to something potential. Anything that has happened or is happening is in esse, and in many contexts to be in esse is the same as to be vested rather than contingent, to be ongoing rather than actionable, or to be commenced rather than contemplated, yet in all cases in which no permanent structure or property results, not to be fully concluded. A person is in esse if the person has been born and still lives. A criminal prosecution is in esse if the charge has been served on the defendant or an indictment has been issued and the criminal action that follows has not reached a final judgment.
In property the distinction between a thing in esse and in posse particularly arises when there is doubt over whether a structure had been built or existed at the time a covenant regarding it is made. Under the common law, a property covenant to perform a duty that relates to a thing in esse is presumed to bind not only the specific covenantors but also to run with the land to bind future property holders, unless the covenantors expressly limit the covenant

from binding their heirs and assigns by express language. Whether the object of the covenant exists at the time or is still yet to exist is the defining question of whether it is in esse. A duty to repair a dock that exists is a duty toward an object in esse, not in posse, even though the materials and repairs themselves are in posse, because the dock yet exists.

**in extremis**   Near to death. A person in extremis is at the end of life, or the person thinks the end of life is very near. A person who creates a will or gives while in extremis acts in causa mortis, whether or not the person recovers. If the person does recover, a gift causa mortis may be rescinded, even if it is accepted, and a last will and testament, of course, may always be renounced or substituted.
*See also:* will, last will and testament, nuncupative will (oral will or noncupative will).

**in fieri**   *See:* fieri (in fieri).

**in flagrante delicto or red handed**   *See:* flagrante delicto (in flagrante delicto or red handed).

**in forma pauperis**   *See:* indigency, in forma pauperis (I.F.P. or IFP).

**In God We Trust**   *See:* God, In God We Trust.

**in gross**   At large. In gross literally means "at large," or untied to a particular parcel or place. A person in gross is a person of no fixed abode. An easement in gross is held by any owner, not necessarily the owner of a particular parcel of land.
*See also:* servitude; easement, easement in gross (commercial easement).

**in haec verba (in haec verbo)**   By the particular words. In haec verba is a Latin phrase that introduces a particular text or language in issue, or that refers to a recitation of the text or language. A requirement that a text or statement, such as the text of a will or a contract or a libel or an obscene printing or a recitation of things said, be pled in haec verba is a requirement to quote the language of the text or statement exactly, especially in a complaint or a pleading.

**in kind**   *See:* kind, in kind.

**in lieu**   In the place of something else. In lieu signals that one thing or person has been substituted for another thing or person.

**in limine**   At the beginning. In limine is, literally, at the threshold, or at the start of some process. Thus a motion in limine is a motion made at the opening of the trial. In reality, motions in limine are often made immediately before the trial commences.
*See also:* motion, motion in limine.

**in loco parentis**   *See:* parent, in loco parentis.

**in media res**   *See:* appeal, interlocutory appeal, in media res.

**in mortua manu**   *See:* mortmain, in mortua manu.

**in pais or pays**   *See:* pais (in pais or pays).

**in pari delicto (in par delicto)** Of equal guilt. In pari delicto, or of equal guilt, is a bar to recovery by a plaintiff for losses caused in fact by the plaintiff's deliberate wrongdoing. It is a legal doctrine that reflects the equitable defense of clean hands.

**in pari materia** *See:* interpretation, in pari materia (pari materia).

**in perpetuam** *See:* perpetuity, in perpetuam (perpetuam).

**in perpetuam rei memoriam** *See:* deposition, in perpetuam rei memoriam.

**in perpetuity** *See:* perpetual (in perpetuity).

**in personam** Against the person. In personam is Latin for upon the person, and an action in personam is an action brought against the defendant (whether a person or an entity) rather than against property. An order that is in personam must be performed by the party against whom it is issued, or that party may be in contempt of court. In contrast, an order in rem may be carried out by a sheriff or by the plaintiff; a defendant need not answer or comply with it.

*See also:* personal; in, in rem.

**in personam jurisdiction** *See:* jurisdiction, in personam jurisdiction (personal jurisdiction).

**in posse (posse or covenant for a thing in posse)** Potential but unrealized and not in existence. In posse describes a thing that might be done but that has not yet been done, particularly a structure that might be built but that has not been built. Under the common law, a property covenant to perform a duty that relates to a thing in posse is limited to the specific covenantors and does not run with the land to bind future property holders, unless the covenantors agree to bind their heirs and assigns by express language. Whether the object of the covenant exists at the time or is still yet to exist is the defining question of whether it is in posse. A duty to repair a dock that exists is a duty toward an object in esse, not in posse, even though the materials and repairs themselves are in posse, because the dock yet exists.

*See also:* in, in esse (esse or covenant for a thing in esse); posse.

**in propria persona or in Pro. Per.** *See:* pro, pro se (in propria persona or in Pro. Per.).

**in re** *See:* re (in re).

**in rem** Against the thing. In rem, which literally means upon the thing, is a basis of jurisdiction over property. This technical term of jurisdiction or remedies is used to designate proceedings or actions instituted against the thing, as opposed to proceedings or actions against a person (whether a natural person or an entity), which are in personam. Rem is derived from res, which means thing in Latin.

There are two forms of actions in rem. True, or "pure," actions in rem determine ownership over property as against everyone in the world, such as an action to quiet title in real property. Quasi in rem actions are brought against a known owner or possessor to establish rights between the plaintiff and the defendant, such as a lien foreclosure. However, it is not always fair to commence an action in rem, and the Due Process clauses of the U.S. Constitution and many state constitutions may forbid some actions or require personal service of process, following the doctrine of Pennoyer v. Neff, 95 U.S. 714 (1877). Although this requirement has been largely supplanted by the minimum contacts test for quasi in rem jurisdiction, following International Shoe Co. v. Washington, 326 U.S. 310 (1945), it has not affected much of pure in rem jurisdiction. Shaffer v. Heitner, 433 U.S. 186 (1977). Occasionally, in rem jurisdiction may exist concurrently over a single property in both federal and state court, particularly over treasure trove, in which case federal in rem jurisdiction is not limited by the Eleventh Amendment. See California v. Deep Sea Research, 523 U.S. 491 (1998). It may be difficult to establish the situs of the res for actions against intellectual property, such as an internet domain name. See Thomas R. Lee, In Rem Jurisdiction in Cyberspace, 75 Wash. L. Rev. 97 (2000).

Forfeiture proceedings to seize property used in a crime or forfeit to the government for non-payment of taxes are in rem. See 28 U.S.C. § 1395. And, admiralty proceedings affecting an ownership interest in a vessel or cargo are inherently in rem.

*See also:* in, in personam; jurisdiction, in rem jurisdiction; res.

**in rem jurisdiction** *See:* jurisdiction, in rem jurisdiction, quasi in rem jurisdiction; jurisdiction, in rem jurisdiction.

**quasi in rem** *See:* jurisdiction, in rem jurisdiction, quasi in rem jurisdiction.

**in situ** In place. In situ, literally in its original location, refers to anything physical or metaphorical considered in its initial condition or location. The initiality of this condition or location is a matter of context. Thus, oil may be in situ before it is pumped from a well. Or, it may be in situ in a seller's tank farm prior to a contract for purchase. Or, it may be under a sheriff's lien awaiting a suit over its ownership. The originality of the location depends on the context in which the oil was relevant to the discussion. In general, however, a natural resource in situ has not been extracted from its original location on or in the Earth.

A court in situ is in its primary courthouse.

*See also:* locus, locus in quo.

**in stirpes or rule of representation** *See:* distribution, distribution of estate, per stirpes (in stirpes or rule of representation).

**in the eye of the law** *See:* metaphor, metaphor of law, eyes of the law (in the eye of the law).

**in the margin** *See:* margin (in the margin).

**in terrorem (in terrorem clause or no contest clause)** By threat. In terrorem is, literally, by the use of threats or fear, and it refers to clauses that create great penalties to coerce various forms of behavior, most notably the in terrorem clause sometimes written into a will, which includes a threat of the loss of a devise or of all interests against a beneficiary under the will who challenges it seeking a greater share from it.

**in toto**   In its entirety. In toto means in all, or in the whole. It represents the sum of all of the components, elements, values, or other things that are potentially considered in an analysis. A document or pleading read in toto is read completely and without omission, considering each element within the context of the whole, rather than reading each element in isolation from the others.

**in transitu**   In transit. In transit is a designation for goods during shipment and until delivery.

**in vacuo**   Out of context. In vacuo means, literally, in a vacuum, but the term is a metaphor that means something exists or is considered as a specific idea, without regard to its context, historical development, or future implications.

**in vitro**   Performed outside a living organism. In vitro means, literally, under glass. Its most common uses in law are to describe a procedure done in a laboratory environment, which is particularly the case for the creation of anything grown, altered, initiated, or sustained in a laboratory and then implanted in a living organism.

An in vitro fertilization is the implantation of a zygote into a woman's womb, the zygote having been created in a laboratory.

*See also:* zygote.

**in witness whereof**   *See:* signature, in witness whereof.

**in-house counsel**   *See:* counselor, in-house counsel.

## inaction

**legislative inaction (legislative re-enactment)**   The view that a legislature ratifies a judicial decision by inaction or re-enactment. Legislative inaction is a signal employed by some judges to demonstrate that a judicial interpretation of a statute, or a decision otherwise subject to legislative revision, has been effectively ratified by the legislature because the legislature has not seen fit to pass a new statute or amend the old one to reverse the effect of the judicial decision. Given the inordinate complexities in setting the agendas of legislatures, this signal is, in most instances, misleading.

**inadequate consideration**   *See:* consideration, adequate consideration (inadequate consideration).

**inadequate relief**   *See:* relief, adequate relief (inadequate relief).

**inadequate verdict**   *See:* verdict, inadequate verdict.

**inadmissibility**   *See:* admissibility, inadmissibility (inadmissibility).

**inadvertent act or unintended act**   *See:* mens, mens rea, unintentional act (inadvertent act or unintended act).

**inalienability**   *See:* alienability, inalienability (unalienable or inalienable).

**inalienable rights or unalienable right or unalienable rights**   *See:* right, inalienable right (inalienable rights or unalienable right or unalienable rights).

**incapacity**   *See:* capacity, legal capacity, incapacity (lack of contractual capacity or lack of capacity).

**incapacity to commit a crime**   *See:* capacity, criminal capacity, incapacity to commit a crime (lack of criminal capacity or M'Naghten rule).

## incarceration

**imprisonment**   The confinement or restraint of a person. Imprisonment is the confinement of a person by another such that most of the activities of daily life are controlled or prohibited, particularly the freedom of movement. Imprisonment is presumably involuntary, and a person who voluntarily pleads guilty in the knowledge a sentence of imprisonment will follow is not considered voluntarily incarcerated or imprisoned. Not all involuntary confinements are imprisonment, however, and school attendance is not imprisonment, regardless of legal requirements of children to attend.

Imprisonment is lawful or unlawful, lawful imprisonment being the result of a sentence by a court of law. Unlawful imprisonment is both a crime and a tort of false imprisonment.

**imprisonment as criminal punishment**   Service of a sentence requiring detention in a prison or jail for a period of time. Imprisonment is the confinement of a person to prison or jail. Despite its broader senses, in law, usage of imprisonment is generally restricted to mean detention as a sentence for a period of time greater than a year following a determination of guilt for a crime, and it is usually reserved for such a detention when served in a prison facility rather than a local jail. Other forms of incarceration prior to sentence or trial are usually referred to as detention or as jail.

*See also:* sentence.

**false imprisonment**   The deprivation of the liberty of another person without a lawful privilege to do so. False imprisonment is both a crime and separately a private tort akin to kidnapping, in which one person is detained by another against the will of the first, regardless of whether the detaining person is a public officer or not, as long as the detaining person has no lawful privilege or statutory authority to do so in the situation of the detention. The tort is an intentional tort and is subject to compensatory and punitive damages. When a police officer or other government agent with a power of arrest commits a false imprisonment, the tort may also be one of malicious arrest, although otherwise the torts of false imprisonment and false arrest are distinct.

*See also:* arrest, malicious arrest; arrest, false arrest.

**hard labor (chain gang)**  A punishment of work for the benefit of the state or county. Hard labor is a punishment to which a person convicted of a crime may be sentenced or to which in some jurisdictions a person convicted and sentenced to prison may be assigned, in which the person performs labor for the benefit of the state or the county of a form equivalent to the labor required by a free person in full employment. In some states, hard labor is an alternative to incarceration, awarded to a prisoner in a trusty status so that the prisoner performs the work out of the jail or prison.

Hard labor is not, as depictions in popular movies would have it, punishment labor, such as breaking rocks with mallets. Hard labor may, however, be work in agricultural or other manual labor, or it may be work in a prison industry. Labor that is excessive or dangerous in its physical demands so that it poses a serious risk to the health of the convict violates the limits of cruel and unusual punishment.

Work on the chain gang is one means of hard labor, in which a convict performs manual work near roadways while chained to other convicts. Serious concerns for the safety of convicts chained together near a motorway have forced many states to abandon the practice in favor of simple work teams in bright clothing, or to follow more rigorous rules to ensure convict health and safety.

**life imprisonment (life sentence or life)**  A sentence of imprisonment until death. Life imprisonment is a sentence that may be imposed following a judgment of conviction for specific crimes in which the defendant is committed to be held in prison until death. Some sentences are specific in allowing a possibility of parole, or early release allowed on a showing of reformed behavior. Some sentences are specific in forbidding any possibility of parole, and some are issued under statutes or in penal systems that have no option of parole. In the case of a person sentenced to life imprisonment who is either ineligible for parole or never granted parole, that person shall live out the remainder of the person's life in prison. As a matter of constitutional law, when a jury considers the sentence of a person who has been convicted of committing a crime that makes the defendant eligible for a sentence of death, the jury must have the option of a life sentence instead.

**life without parole (LWOP or L.W.O.P.)**  A sentence of imprisonment until death, for which no parole will be granted. Life without parole is a a specific sentence in many jurisdictions, which a person is sentenced to serve the remainder of the person's life in prison during which there will be no possibility of release on parole. As of 1984, federal offenders are no longer eligible for parole, and so a life sentence in a U.S. court for a federal offense is inherently a sentence of life without parole.

**solitary confinement (solitary imprisonment or solitary incarceration or isolation cell)**  The segregation of a prisoner from all other prisoners. Solitary confinement is the isolation of a prisoner from other prisoners, usually for a period of time as a punishment for an infraction of the regulations of the detention facility, but in some cases as a condition of incarceration. Solitary confinement can be controversial, and its use for long periods without reasonable cause has been argued to amount to cruel and unusual punishment.

**prolonged incarceration (prolonged detention)**  Confinement of a prisoner or detainee for a time longer than that allowed or required by law. Prolonged incarceration is physical confinement of a prisoner or detainee beyond what is allowed by law. Prolonged incarceration is the basis for a petition for a writ of habeas corpus, which should be granted for a prisoner who is unjustifiably incarcerated after the term of a sentence is expired. It is also available to a prisoner who is held without process for a time period longer than that allowed by procedural due process. For a given crime or offense, there is not necessarily an identifiable time beyond which an individual has a valid prolonged incarceration claim. However, the Supreme Court has recognized that the lapse of a certain amount of time is an element in assessing the existence of a constitutional encroachment.

**incendiary (accelerant)**  The potential to cause a fire. An incendiary is a person or substance that causes or encourages the spread of a fire. Accelerants are incendiary chemicals. When used to cause a fire for the purpose of causing harm to a persons or property, the use of an incendiary is arson, and the possession of incendiaries for this purpose is a crime in most jurisdictions.

An incendiary device is a machine, tool, weapon, or any other thing that uses chemicals or energy to cause a fire.

Incendiary is also a metaphor for speech or action that incites others to any activity.

*See also:* speech, inflammatory speech (incendiary speech).

**incendiary speech**  *See:* speech, inflammatory speech (incendiary speech).

**incentive**  Offer, gift, or promise made to encourage behavior from the recipient. An incentive is any thing or promise offered by one party to another to encourage a behavior in the other. Many incentives are neither rare nor unique for a given transaction; a given level of pay is an incentive to an employee to accept or remain in a position, and a given price is an incentive both to a buyer and to a seller to sell something. In many instances, though, the incentive offer or incentive pay is made specifically to an individual and not others, in an effort to create a sense of loyalty to the employer or contacting party.

**incentive zoning**  *See:* zoning, conditional zoning, incentive zoning.

**perverse incentive**  Incentive that encourages behavior contrary to its purpose. A perverse incentive creates an unintended and undesired consequence, particularly when a condition, rule, offer, or other form of incentive induces behavior that reverses, contradicts, or interferes with the policy, goal, or purpose for which the incentive was created. There are many illustrations of perverse incentives, such as a bounty system that pays people to report their own legal infractions, which leads to more infractions.

**incest (incestuous or incestuousness)**  The crime of sexual intercourse between members of one family. Incest is a sexual relationship between a parent and child, between siblings, or first cousins regardless of generation. When one person engages in sexual acts with another, knowing that the other person is sufficiently closely related, the person with such knowledge (of both of them if they both know) commits the crime of incest. The extent of the relationships forbidden varies somewhat from state to state.

Consent is no defense to the criminal charge of incest. When marriage is attempted or solemnized between individuals within such a relationship, the marriage is void, and subject either to annulment or divorce. In such case, ignorance of the relationship at the time of the marriage is no defense in an action for annulment or divorce. In most jurisdictions, incest does not depend on blood lineage but is committed even if the relationship exists as a matter of law owing to an adoption or marriage. Various theories underlie incest law, including arguments for genetic health of a child who may result, for genetic health of the species as a whole, for limiting the dangers of imbalances of power within the family that would expose women to a risk of abuse, for violations of a fiduciary duty within the family, and a naturalist argument that such relations are contrary to human dignity or right. A libertarian argument exists that would allow such relations between consenting adults if there is no risk of a resulting birth.

*See also:* marriage (marital).

**Inchmaree clause**  *See:* insurance, category of insurance, marine insurance, Inchmaree clause (additional perils clause).

**inchoate (choate)**  Started but not finished. Anything inchoate has been initiated in some manner but not finally completed. There are many inchoate interests in the law. An inchoate claim is a claim for a legal remedy that may be filed for relief in court but has not been filed.

Inchoate dower is an interest that is potential in a living spouse's property, but not subject yet to claim. An inchoate contract is executory and not executed, and an inchoate crime is a crime that has been planned or attempted, but not committed (even if the inchoate crime is a distinct and separate crime).

Unlike many similar words, inchoate is not formed by adding a negative prefix to an affirmative body of the word. Choate is derived from inchoate, which itself was derived from the Latin incohare, which means to begin, itself derived from in cohum for the leash of the ox yoke. The odd result is the contemporary use of choate for an executed, completed, perfected, or final interest.

*See also:* abet (abettor or abetter or abbettour); easement, inchoate easement (inchoate prescriptive easement or inchoate prescriptive rights); offense, inchoate offense.

**inchoate easement**  *See:* easement, inchoate easement (inchoate prescriptive easement or inchoate prescriptive rights).

**inchoate offense**  *See:* offense, inchoate offense | attempt; offense, inchoate offense.

**incident**

**incident**  *See:* occurrence (incident).

**incident as incidental**  Collateral or incidental. Incidental is an adjective referring to an event or legal obligation that exists collaterally with another. An incidental event or obligation bears no strong causal relationship to the primary event. Rather, an incidental event or obligation relates to the first event by happenstance; although the two occur at around the same time, the incidental event is peripheral and subordinate to the first.

*See also:* damages, contract damages, incidental damages; ownership, incidents of ownership; feud, feudal incidents.

**incident to arrest**  *See:* search, incident to arrest, protective sweep; search, incident to arrest (search incident to arrest).

**incidental authority**  *See:* authority, incidental authority.

**incidental damages**  *See:* damages, contract damages, incidental damages.

**incidents of ownership**  *See:* ownership, incidents of ownership.

**incitement (incite or incited or inciter or incitee)**  The motivation of another person to action. Incitement is the influence by one person on another to do something that would not be done except for this influence. One person's incitement of another to carry out an act of violence or some other crime usually makes the inciter an accessory or accomplice of the incitee who becomes the principal of the act or crime.

An incitement through public speech may take many forms, some of which are protected by the First Amendment's freedom of speech. Even so, if a public speech succeeds in inciting three or more members of the audience to commit a riot or immediate criminal or violent acts, or if a public speech attempts to incite members of the audience to riot or to commit immediate criminal or violent acts and clearly produces a present and immediate danger that the audience will do so, then the speech is an incitement to riot, and the inciter may be be enjoined or arrested.

**incitement to riot**   *See:* riot, incitement to riot.

**inclusiveness**   *See:* scrutiny, standards of scrutiny, inclusiveness (overinclusiveness or underinclusiveness).

**income**   Gain in wealth realized from one's labor, property, commerce, or investment. Income is any accession to wealth from whatever source derived. Although a gift is not, in itself, usually considered income, once a gift is received any wealth generated from it is considered income.
*See also:* tax, income tax.

*tips (gratuity or tip)*   Gratuity in recognition of a service performed. A tip is a sum or money presented by a customer to a service provider as a gift in recognition of some service performed. The customer determines whether a tip is to be given and its amount, and generally the customer has the right to determine who shall be the recipient of the gratuity. In the absence of an agreement to the contrary between the recipient and a third party, a tip becomes the property of the person in recognition of whose service it is presented by the customer. A tip is included in earned income for tax purposes.

**capital gain**   *See:* gain, capital gain.

**income tax**   *See:* tax, income tax.

**salary**   *See:* salary.

**accrued income**   Income earned but yet to be paid. Accrued income is any accession to wealth from whatever source derived in which the recipient has completed all of the requirements necessary to earn the income, but payment has not been received. For accrual-based taxpayers, any accrued income is taxed to the recipient of the income at the time all necessary elements required to receive the income have transpired. In contrast, for cash-based taxpayers, any accrued income is taxed to the recipient of the income at the time of payment.

**accumulated taxable income**   Income retained in excess of the needs of a business. Accumulated taxable income is the amount of income retained in a given year beyond the amount required for the reasonable needs of a business. This amount is subject to a penalty rate of taxation.

**aggregate income**   The sum of income from all sources in a given year for the filing taxpayer unit. Aggregate income refers to the sum of income that is added to other income for tax purposes. The most common example of aggregate income is the number that results when a husband and wife's income are added together to determine their tax liability.

**attribution of income**   Assignment of potential income or a portion of income to calculate taxes or other liabilities. Attribution of income occurs when a payment or asset, or a potential payment or asset, is calculated as a part of a person's income or assets without regard to whether that person claims it. Attribution occurs in order to prevent fraud by one who would prefer to claim diminished assets, for instance, as the basis of a tax liability or responsibility for alimony. It also occurs when one has a duty to pay another based on income and seeks to diminish that duty by voluntarily accepting lower pay or by wasting assets.

**deferred income (deferred compensation or deferred revenue)**   The right to receive a payment at some time after the right accrues. Deferred income, whether it is personal compensation or corporate revenue, is income to which one acquires an entitlement at one time for payment at a later time, usually in later years or accounting periods.

**disposable income**   Income left to spend or invest after expenses are paid. Disposable income is discretionary income, the amount of money received as income in a given period that remains after all of the bills—the necessary or contracted expenses—are paid. Disposable income is computed as part of a determination of a borrower's creditworthiness, and it is a factor in determining both the amounts of settlements in divorce property distributions and in designing a bankruptcy schedule or plan.

**dividend income**   Income paid to a business owner as a distribution of business earnings. Dividend income is income paid to business owners out of the earnings of the business. In stock corporations, for example, dividends are declared and paid on a per share basis to all stockholders, usually on a quarterly basis.

**earned income, taxation and tax law**   Total amount of commissions, wages or salary received in a relevant time period. Earned income is the total amount of commissions, wages or salary received by a person or entity.

**exempt income**   Income that is not taxable. Exempt income is income received by a taxpayer but that is not subject to income taxation. Common examples of exempt income are interest from tax-exempt bonds and most death benefits paid from life insurance policies.

**gross income**   All income received in any form. Gross income refers to all income from whatever source derived, although certain forms of money received by that taxpayer that are not considered income may still be excluded, such as gifts below the taxable threshold. Gross income, minus deductions, is taxable income.

**adjusted gross income**   Gross income less all deductions. Adjusted gross income is a taxpayer's gross income minus all of a taxpayer's valid deductions for the same period of time.

**Haig-Simons income**   Increase in the value of stored assets and the market value of assets consumed. The Haig–Simons definition of income provides that income is the sum of (1) the market value of rights exercised in consumption during the period, and (2) the increase in the value of the store of property rights, or wealth, between the beginning and the end of the period.

**income statement (profit and loss statement or p and l)**   Financial disclosure depicting the profit and loss for a business over a given time. An income statement is a financial disclosure that provides the profit and loss calculations for a given business over a specific time, usually a fiscal year. The income statement identifies revenues, direct costs to produce those revenues, such as cost of goods sold, or cost of sales, and the expenses necessary to support the operation, both direct and indirect, in the form of general administrative and selling expenses. Public companies are required to produce income statements on a periodic basis for purposes of disclosure. Private companies usually must provide income statements for lending purposes but not for the general public.

**net income**   Gross income minus all lawful deductions. Net income is the remainder of gross income from which all applicable deductions, including taxes paid, have been subtracted.

**ordinary income**   Gain realized from anything but a sale realizing capital gain. Ordinary income is any gain a taxpayer realizes from activities, such as compensation, including salaries, wages, tips, honoraria, partnership shares, and the like, or from the sale or exchange of property, if that property is depreciable property or otherwise not a capital asset nor 1231(b) property. Ordinary income is taxed at the ordinary income rates, which are typically higher than income from the sale or exchange of a capital asset.

*See also:* gain, recognized gain (Section 1231 gain or gain under Section 1231).

**passive income (passive activity)**   Income from business activity in which the taxpayer presumably is not directly active. Passive income is income derived through the operation of an activity that is not a business activity or in which the expectation is that the income recipient would passively receive revenues or returns. Rents, royalties, dividends, and pension receipts are usually passive income.

**non-passive income**   Income from an activity in which the taxpayer materially participated. Non-passive income is any accession to wealth that is derived from an activity in which the taxpayer materially participates. Non-passive income generally comes from a person's main form of employment, such as wages or a salary received for services rendered to an employer.

**taxable income**   Amount of income subject to taxation. Taxable income means the amount of income subject to taxation after all deductions are taken.

*See also:* tax, income tax.

**unearned income**   All income received that is not earned through compensated activity. Unearned income is all income that is not earned through labor or services subject to any form of compensation. Unearned income is usually payment without regard to any services currently performed, although it may include income contractually obligated from prior employment. Common forms of unearned income include dividend income from corporations, rental income, and Social Security benefits.

**incommensurability   (incommensurable)**   The incapacity of a thing to be compared with or valued relative to another thing. Incommensurability applies to certain ideas and things that cannot be compared with or translated into others. Heirlooms and other objects of emotional value are effectively incommensurable. When there is no common denominator to value ideas or things across cultural valuations or that have personal or emotional significance, no tool (such as monetization) can realistically be used to compare, rank, or value them. There are seeming aspects of incommensurability, in which two measures seem too different to compare them, but relative magnitude and context will allow various forms of comparison, as in the balance of economic cost to social value.

**incommunicado**   Uncommunicative. Incommunicado connotes the inability or unwillingness to communicate with others. A prisoner held incommunicado is not allowed communication with others. In general, a person who imprisons another in any manner in a facility or who holds a person (other than a prisoner of war) incommunicado violates that person's civil rights by denying that prisoner access to legal counsel.

**incompetence**

**incompetence as lack of authority**   A lack of jurisdiction over a matter or a party. Incompetence, for a court or tribunal, is the absence of competence in the sense of jurisdiction or authority to hear a cause. Incompetence usually occurs because a given matter is properly in another court already or because the court lacks subject matter or personal jurisdiction in the matter before it.

**incompetent   witness**   *See:* witness,   competent witness (incompetent witness).

**incontestability clause**   *See:* insurance, incontestability clause (incontestible).

**incorporation**

**incorporated rights**   *See:* constitution, U.S. Constitution, bill of rights, incorporation of rights, incorporated rights.

**incorporation of rights**   *See:* constitution, U.S. Constitution, Bill of Rights, incorporation of rights.

**corporate incorporation (promoter or incorporator)**   The process of the formation and recognition of a corporation. Incorporation is, in the corporate sense, the creation of a corporation by organizing initial members or owners, selecting an initial board, adopting a charter and by-laws, and seeking and then receiving a registration or a charter from the government under which the corporation is organized. The person who performs the labor required for incorporation is a promoter, and the acts made by a promoter on behalf of the unincorporated entity that becomes the corporation are then ratified by the corporation through the action of its directors once they are formed. The person who signs the filing of the the certificate of incorporation is the incorporator. The promoter may or may not also be the incorporator.

*See also:* corporation (corporate or incorporate).

**incorporation by reference** Treatment of one text as if it is integrated into another text. Incorporation by reference is the means by which one text can be drafted to refer to another text that is then treated as a result of the reference as if it were entirely written into and integrated into the first text. Thus, if an employment contract incorporates by reference an employee handbook as terms of employment, the employment contract incorporates every term from the handbook into the contract as if it had been been written into the contract. Such forms of incorporation allow changes in the incorporated text to alter the meaning of the incorporating text. When this process of indirect alteration works to unfairly alter the terms of a contract, the incorporated changes may prove unenforceable.

**incorporationism** The idea that law enshrines moral concepts from extra-legal sources. Incorporationism is the idea that specific laws incorporate moral obligations, which arise or exist without regard to the legal recognition of the moral duty. In other words, laws such as criminal laws that prohibit conduct that is malum in se, such as murder, incorporate a moral duty not to murder.

**incorporeal** *See:* corporeal (incorporeal).

**incorporeal hereditament** *See:* hereditament, incorporeal hereditament.

**incorporeal ownership** *See:* ownership, corporeal ownership (incorporeal ownership).

**incorporeal possession** *See:* possession, corporeal possession (incorporeal possession).

**incorporeal property** *See:* property, forms of property, incorporeal property (intangible property or intangibles).

**incorrigibility (incorrigible)** Lacking the ability to be corrected. Incorrigibility is the absence of correctability, the ability to reform or to be rehabilitated. A person who will not end a habit or practice of wrongdoing is incorrigible. Many jurisdictions presume incorrigibility from recidivism, in the assumption that a person who commits an offense again is beyond reformation. Thus,

in some jurisdictions, a repeat offender is, by definition, incorrigible.

As a factual matter, however, the assumption that recidivism proves incorrigibility is often false. Although an incorrigible person might well be a recidivist, there is no reason to believe in a particular case that a recidivist is inherently incorrigible. Although a person's repetition of a particular form of wrongful conduct is evidence of incorrigibility, only repetition of the wrongdoing following genuine, reasonable, and individually tailored efforts to encourage the person to reform demonstrates incorrigibility. Further, a person who is incorrigible as an adolescent or young adult may reform in maturity.

*See also:* recidivism (recidivist); punishment, rehabilitative punishment (reformation of criminals).

**incorrigible child** *See:* child, incorrigible child.

**incoterm** *See:* shipping, shipping term, incoterm, free on board (F.O.B. or FOB); shipping, shipping term, incoterm, free alongside ship (F.A.S. or FAS); shipping, shipping term, incoterm, cost of insurance and freight (C.I.F. or CIF); shipping, shipping term, incoterm (shipping term).

**increment (incremental or incrementally or incrementalism or checkerboard statutes)** Done by small steps. An increment is a component among others in a larger project or activity. To act incrementally is to carry out a plan or a change through a series of small measures rather than by one large project. Though an increment is often thought of as an increase, incremental decrease occurs as well, in the manner that a large estate may be sold off a few acres at a time.

The common law is usually pictured as developing incrementally, making very slight adjustments to its rules and principles by applying precedent that is subtly altered as circumstances and culture changes. This depiction of legal change contrasts with the actions of legislation, which is seen as the tool of more dramatic change in the requirements of laws. In truth, both judicial articulation of precedent and legislation are capable of—and engage in—both comprehensive and incremental change. Ronald Dworkin has referred to legislation that regulates a particular domain of conduct through increments, leaving certain acts unregulated while others are regulated as a checkerboard approach, which is contrary to the principle of legal integrity.

**incrimination (incriminate or incriminating)** Demonstrating or suggesting one is responsible for a criminal act. Incrimination is the attribute of a statement or evidence to suggest that a person or entity has committed an act that amounts to a crime. The term was once a synonym for the accusation of a crime by another person, even the prosecutor's charging of a defendant with a crime. Contemporary usage has expanded the sense of incrimination to include self-incrimination and incrimination by the evidence, as well as incrimination through the statements of witnesses and purported co-conspirators. In all of these senses, incrimination may be direct, such as a statement or other sign that seems clearly to demonstrate a particular person or entity committed a particular act, or it may be indirect, indicating that someone with a certain attribute or characteristic did so. Incrimination is not a finding of guilt.

*See also:* statement, incriminating statement; inculpation (inculpate or inculpatory).

**incriminating statement** *See:* statement, incriminating statement.

**incriminating circumstance (circumstantial incrimination)** A fact or condition that contributes to a suspicion of criminal behavior. An incriminating circumstance is any of the details surrounding a fact or occurrence that raise a suspicion of criminal conduct. Although one incriminating circumstance might be sufficient to justify a suspicion of wrongdoing, it is as likely that a series or aggregation of incriminating circumstances (especially when there are no contrary explanations or exculpatory evidence) gives rise to a suspicion or to a conviction that a person has committed a crime.

**self-incrimination (privilege against self-incrimination or right to silence)** A statement that suggests the speaker has committed a crime. Self-incrimination is any act or statement by an individual or the representative of an entity that tends to demonstrate the speaker or entity has committed a criminal act. Self-incrimination may occur intentionally, as in a confession, or it may occur unintentionally as in a statement made that would tend to prove motive or opportunity to commit a crime, though the person making the statement is unaware of that tendency at the time of making the statement.

The Fifth Amendment recognizes a privilege against self-incrimination that allows a person in custody or in court to remain silent and offer no statement or testimony, and no inference of guilt may be raised as a result of the silence. More, the privilege allows a person in custody or subject to police interview or interrogation to terminate the questioning.

The Fifth Amendment privilege against involuntary testimony that would lead to self-incrimination includes a privilege against performing conduct or speech other than testimony that would tend to incriminate the performer or speaker, but this privilege does not prevent all self-incrimination from being heard in court. A person may offer testimony voluntarily that is self-incriminating. Further, incriminating conduct that is observed and recorded by others may be brought into court if done so within the bounds of the rules of evidence.

**collective entity doctrine** A corporation has no privilege against self-incrimination. The collective entity doctrine precludes a corporation from asserting a privilege against self-incrimination. Thus corporate records must be produced in response to a subpoena, and corporate officials may be compelled to testify regarding corporate wrongdoing (though not under risk of personal criminal liability). The collective entity doctrine applies to any corporation regardless of its form or size.

**link in chain (link-in-chain principle)** Self-incrimination includes evidence that could lead to identity. The link–in–chain principle includes within the privilege against self-incrimination evidence that would give rise to a person's identity as the perpetrator of a criminal act. If a statement sought would be a link in a chain of evidence that would lead to the incrimination of the person providing the statement, the statement may be withheld as within the scope of the privilege.

**inculpation (inculpate or inculpatory)** Demonstrating culpability. Inculpation is demonstration of culpability, or legal responsibility for a given act, especially a crime. Inculpation is similar to incrimination, in that both represent a form of responsibility; the difference is that inculpation refers to responsibility for the wrongful conduct, and incrimination emphasizes more the aspect of criminal liability for that conduct. That difference, however, is now rarely observed, if ever it was much followed, and the two terms are now near synonyms. Inculpatory evidence is evidence that points toward a person's guilt in performing some act; its opposite is exculpatory evidence, which points toward a person's innocence of it.

*See also:* exculpation (exculpate or exculpatory); incrimination (incriminate or incriminating).

**incumbent (incumbency)** The present holder of an office or position. An incumbent is the person presently in office or holding a position or role. Incumbency is the sum of benefits and significance that a person derives from office. The power of incumbency is the incumbent's authority to use the fact of holding office as a means toward any end, sometimes to improve the law and better the lives of others, but the term is more often encountered within an allegation that an incumbent uses that authority to make removal from office more difficult, to make a greater claim for benefits in the office, and to increase its authority.

**incurable error** *See:* error, curable error (incurable error).

**indebitatus assumpsit** *See:* assumpsit, indebitatus assumpsit (numquam debitatus).

**indebtedness** The state of owing a debt. Indebtedness is the condition of owing money or services to another. Indebtedness arises when a debt is created, and indebtedness implies that one or another debt is owed. To be indebted to another does not suggest that a person or entity has greater debts than assets or that a debt is currently in default or owing.

*See also:* debt.

**indecency** Conduct or speech contrary to traditional morals. Indecency is the contravention of the traditional morals of a community or, in a national broadcast, the limits of decency in the national culture. Indecency includes both acts and speech. Speech or acts may be indecent owing to both the forum of their presentation and their audience as well as to their content. In general, subjects or references involving an act of sex, of the excretion of bodily wastes, of violence against people or animals, and the deliberate abuse of venerated objects or places may be indecent. Mild references to such subjects are likely to be indecent in some venues, before some audiences, and in some contexts but not all. References to such subjects could, however, be made in such a deliberate and provocative manner as to be indecent per se.

As a matter of free speech, the mere fact that a particular message is considered to be indecent does not give it any less First Amendment protection, unless it is also obscene. By protecting speech despite its indecency, the constitution protects minority viewpoints that are disliked by the majority, allowing art, individuality, and challenge to the status quo.

Indecency in broadcasts regulated by the federal government is held to the regulatory standard governing broadcast licensure. This standard forbids indecent speech or reference in certain times or in broadcasts to general audiences, even if the indecent reference is out of context and fleeting.

**indecent exposure (public indecency)** Exposure of the genitals or sexual conduct in public. Indecent exposure is the state crime of intentionally exposing one's genitals in public in a manner that offends or is reckless as to its likelihood of offending another person. Nudity, the commission of sexual acts, and the fondling of the parts of another's body in a sexualized manner in public or in the company of minors may amount to indecent exposure. The specific formulations of the conduct forbidden vary. Some jurisdictions forbid the same conduct as public indecency.

**indecent speech** Language or material that is patently offensive for the medium in which it is communicated. Indecent speech includes any language or image that is communicated in any forum or by any means, that is patently shocking or offensive according to the standards of the community in which it is communicated. In most contexts, indecent speech that is not obscene is protected under the First Amendment, and it may only be regulated in furtherance of a compelling governmental interest that is pursued by the regulation using the most narrowly tailored means. In the case of broadcast media, however, which are highly regulated by the government in return for access to the commons of the transmission spectrum, indecent speech is subject to more stringent regulation, and speech that is patently offensive as measured by contemporary community standards for the medium, particularly depiction of sexual or excretory activities and organs is banned from broadcast at times of the day when there is a reasonable risk that children may be in the audience, presently from 6 am to 10 pm.

See also: obscenity (obscene); speech, freedom of speech | 2. indecency v. obscenity.

**indecent assault** See: assault, sexual assault (indecent assault).

**indefeasibly vested remainder** See: remainder, defeasible remainder, indefeasibly vested remainder.

**indefiniteness (indefinite)** Not defined. Indefiniteness is a lack of definition or specificity. Examples abound in the law. An indefinite time is a time without a specific start or, more often, a specific end. Indefinite duties are duties that are not specified by others but left to the duty-holder to determine. Indefinite damages are damages that are not specified in a given amount.

**indefinite failure of issue** See: issue, issue as child, failure of issue, indefinite failure of issue.

**indefinite partnership** See: partnership, partnership, dissolution of partnership, partnership at will (indefinite partnership).

**indemnity (indemnification or indemnify or indemnitor or indemitee)** Compensation for loss to prevent damage resulting from the loss. Indemnity is a payment made by an indemnitor to an indemnitee compensating the indemnitee for any loss suffered as the result of an accident, incident, or event that would cause the indemnitee a loss were it not for the indemnity. In its broadest forms, indemnity includes any compensation for a loss. Usually, however, indemnity implies a payment made under an agreement in which one party agrees to make good a loss by another, and a common form of indemnity is an insurance policy claim payment.

An indemnity agreement is a contract by which the indemnitor promises to hold the indemnitee harmless from loss or damage of some kind specified in the agreement, irrespective of the liability of any third person for that loss or damage. An indemnity agreement, such as an insurance policy, may, however, have additional clauses, such as a subrogation clause, that allow the indemnitor to pursue relief against a liable third party.

Indemnity differs from surety in that there are only two parties to most indemnity agreements (the indemnitor and the indemnitee); surety has three (the debtor, the creditor, and the surety assuring the debtor's duty to the creditor).

See also: insurance; surety (suretyship).

**double indemnity (double indemnity clause)** An indemnity agreement that pays twice its value. Double indemnity is an obligation to pay two times the value of an indemnity insurance policy when a claim arises under certain circumstances. A double indemnity clause in a life insurance policy is a promise to pay twice the value of indemnity for the insured's life, if the insured dies in an accident rather than by suicide, homicide, or natural causes.

**indemnitee (indemnitor)** The person to be paid in the event of indemnification. An indemnitee is the party entitled to receive a payment of indemnity from the indemnitor.

**indenture** A particularly formal contract or deed. An indenture is a contract of particular duration or significance, which takes its name from the practice, which began in medieval England and persisted into the twentieth century, of writing a contract in duplicate onto one large piece of parchment, then cutting the parchment in a uniquely jagged line that could later demonstrate each was the copy of the other. The line indented each copy, thus each is an indenture. Indentures were used for conveyances of land as well as for contracts for services of seven years. Thus, indentured servants were placed for service under an indentured contract. A less expensive form did not make both sides identical, but rendered one as the counterpart, or summary and receipt, of the full agreement.

Indenture persists in a few forms. Indenture is still used for for certain contracts for apprenticeship in the U.S., though under more closely regulated conditions. More commonly the term is used for a bond indenture, which is an indentured trust created to delineate the various interests created when bonds are issued or employed in a corporate financing arrangement, to create a range of particular assurances for the bonds, or different categories of bond, for the life of the bonds issued.

*See also:* bond, bond indenture.

### independence (independent)

**independent cause** *See:* causation, independent cause (new and independent cause).

**independent contractor** *See:* contractor, independent contractor.

**independent counsel** *See:* prosecutor, independent counsel.

**independent medical examination** *See:* examination, medical examination, independent medical examination (IME).

**independent promises** *See:* promise, independent promises.

**independent source** *See:* search, exclusionary rule, exception to the exclusionary rule, independent-source doctrine (independent source).

**independent-source doctrine** *See:* search, exclusionary rule, exception to the exclusionary rule, independent-source doctrine (independent source).

**indestructible trust** *See:* trust, destructible trust (indestructible trust).

**indeterminacy (indeterminate)** Lacking specific designation of a thing or idea invoked. Indeterminacy is a lack of determinacy, an omission of some specification or detail that would — if it were provided — make a particular reference unique, specific, or ascertained.

Indeterminacy may result from the impossibility of determinacy in a given situation (such as the origin of life) or from an omission in the composition of some statement (such as the quality of the goods purchased).

**legal indeterminacy** Lack of specificity in legal rules that allows judges or officials to act from personal whim. Legal indeterminacy is an argument that the law is so indeterminate that its standards are so inherently vague, that the rules of law are irrelevant to the actual decisions of officials, who may and do act instead from personal will based on prejudice, bias, or whim. Some variant of this argument has recurred for centuries, such as when John Selden made a similar complaint about equity. It was strongly argued by Jerome Frank in Law and the Modern Mind. It has been widely accepted that the primary question is to what degree the rules of law can dictate outcomes to specific questions, compared to the opposite question, which is to what degree those outcomes depend on the discretion of officials. H.L.A. Hart argues that some measure of indeterminacy is essential to law but that the discretion of officials in its use is bounded.

*See also:* discretion.

**index offense** *See:* offense, index offense.

**Indian** Indigenous people of the United States, or a person from India, or from the Indies. Indian indicates several distinct nationalities. In the United States, Indian usually refers to American Indian, either the whole of the tribes, nations, and peoples who were the inhabitants of North America before the advent of Europeans, or a specific unit of membership within that group. Indians who were (or whose ancestors were) native to the United States are also referred to as Native Americans or American Indians, although reference to specific tribal membership is to be preferred in general. Indian also refers to people who are in, from, or descended from the nation of India or from the Caribbean islands known still as the the Indies.

*See also:* tribe.

**Indian cession** *See:* cession, Indian cession.

**Indian Commerce Clause** *See:* constitution, U.S. Constitution, clauses, Commerce Clause, Indian Commerce Clause.

**Indian gaming** *See:* gaming, Indian gaming.

**Indian reservation** *See:* reservation, tribal reservation (Indian reservation).

**Indian country** Reservation lands. Indian country refers to all lands within the recognized reservations of American Indian tribes recognized by the federal government. Indian country is within the boundaries of states but not subject to state jurisdiction.

**Indian or Native American Indian (Native American or American Indian)** A descendant of the inhabitants of the North America before European immigration. Indian as a reference to American Indians is synonymous with Native American and with Native Peoples. Indian as a collective noun is usually less helpful and less descriptive than a reference to the tribe, people, or nation the reference implicates.

American Indians are citizens of the United States. An Indian on a reservation is subject to the laws of the tribe that governs it, as well as the United States Constitution. Indians not on the reservation are subject to and protected by state law, the United States law, and the U.S. Constitution.

**indications of death** *See:* death, indications of death, rigor mortis.

**indicator species** *See:* species, indicator species (canary in the coal mine).

**indicia** Marks or evidence. Indicia are marks or signs indicating some other significance. Indicia may be physical and literal, as are the markings on a crate, or they may be metaphorical or behavioral, as the symptoms of an illness. Marks or signs are indicia owing to their signifying something else, even if the significance is for the purpose of classication of the things indicated by the marks into categories. In a word, indicia indicate.

**indictment (indict)** Accusation of a grand jury upon finding probable cause that the defendant committed the crime charged. An indictment is a formal, written accusation against a person or persons or entity, authorized by the vote of at least a majority of a properly summoned grand jury, which must have found that there was sufficient evidence to amount to probable cause that the indictees had committed the crimes of which the indictment accuses them. Indictments presented to the grand jury by a prosecutor are either returned "True Bill" if they are approved or "No Bill" if they are not, or they are not returned at all. The foreperson of the jury signs the indictment in the event it is returned. If a record is not available for a returned bill, or if there is irregularity in its marking, the error must be timely raised by the defendant on motion or by the prosecutor or the court. In the event there is a good faith question regarding the issuance of an indictment, a court hearing may consider evidence from the prosecutor or, in unusual circumstances, by the foreperson of the grand jury.

The Fifth Amendment requires a grand jury to indict any person who would be prosecuted for a felony in the federal courts. Even so, there is no federal right to a grand jury hearing or indictment in the state courts, and roughly half the states do not use the indictment, relying instead on a prosecutor to present a criminal information that is considered for its sufficiency after the arrest. *See also:* jury, grand jury; information, information as criminal information.

**bill of indictment** The written form of an indictment. A bill of indictment is the written statement of accusation presented to a grand jury and returned to the court endorsed a true bill, and then served upon the defendant. The bill of indictment has been replaced in some jurisdictions by an instrument termed the indictment.

**bill of particulars** A written clarification and elaboration of an indictment or information. A bill of particulars is a statement providing specific details of the offense charged against a defendant that elaborates on the allegations of the charging instrument. The defendant may move for a bill of particulars from the prosecution, in the federal system by right until ten days after arraignment or by leave of the court at any time thereafter. Seeking a bill of particulars in a criminal case is roughly equivalent to moving for a more definite statement in a civil action.

*See also:* pleading, motion for more definite statement.

**true bill indictment (billa vera or no bill or no true bill or not found or ignoramus)** The mark of assent of the grand jury to a bill of indictment. "True Bill" is written or stamped on a bill of indictment and signed by the foreperson after a grand jury has voted to assent to the indictment. If the grand jury votes not to bring forward the proposed indictment, the bill of indictment is endorsed "Dismissed," "Not Found," "No Bill," "No True Bill." The designations "ignoramus," or "we know not" are now very rarely used.

*See also:* ignoramus.

**indifference** Apathy toward a condition or the result of an act. Indifference is a mental state in which a person has no significant preference or interest in a given condition or the potential result of a particular action. Indifference in the law reflects a lack of care regarding a harm that takes place or a duty that should be performed, regardless of whether the harm in fact occurs or the duty is carried out. Indifference may result in negligence or a breach of duty, although it is also a mental state that may make a given action a crime or an intentional tort.

*See also:* murder, extreme–indifference murder (depraved–heart murder or depraved mind murder).

**deliberate indifference** An omission of duty arising from something known or obvious. Deliberate indifference is indifference that appears so patent to an observer that the person must either have known of, or exerted some thought to remain unknowing of, the condition to which the person acted indifferently. Deliberate indifference arises in circumstances in which the person knows of a condition and is responsible for the likely consequences of that condition, as well as circumstances in which the person knows in fact of those consequences and does not mitigate or prevent harm from them.

**extreme indifference (depraved indifference)** Indifference to the risk of extreme harm from one's action. Extreme indifference, or depraved indifference, is indifference to the risk of death, injury, or destruction that is a foreseeable result of one's actions. Depraved or extreme indifference depicts a risk of unusual magnitude or an act of particular immorality or brutality, not merely an act intending to cause a particular harm made without regard to whether it will succeed.

See also: murder, extreme–indifference murder (depraved–heart murder or depraved mind murder); murder, extreme–indifference murder (depraved–heart murder or depraved mind murder).

**indigency (indigent)**  Poverty. Indigency is a person's lack of sufficient wealth or financial means to satisfy a particular requirement. In the law, indigence is ordinarily measured by whether a person has sufficient financial resources to retain legal counsel. A person who lacks the funds to hire an attorney to represent that person in a given matter is indigent. In the case of a criminal action in which counsel is constitutionally required, an indigent defendant must be provided counsel by court appointment. Indigent litigants may be excused from paying for certain costs and fees in court filings, which are brought in forma pauperis.

In other settings, indigency is a qualifying legal characteristic for the provision of a variety of services without charge or at a reduced rate, not the least being medical care from certain hospitals.

**in forma pauperis (I.F.P. or IFP)**  An indigent litigant's status allowing the waiver of court filing fees and costs. In forma pauperis means, literally, appearing as a pauper. An in forma pauperis litigant must petition to be granted this status by the court, filing an affidavit with the petition in which the litigant asserts a lack of funds required to pay court fees. Although an indigent litigant may appear in forma pauperis and also qualify for court–appointed counsel in a criminal action, the two designations are distinct and independent, and the qualifications for one relief do not assure the other. Further, a designation of a person in forma pauperis in one court does not act as a designation generally, and a litigant must ordinarily seek new designation in each court in which the litigant appears.

See also: privilege, abuse of privilege (abuse of privileges); pauper.

**indirect contempt**  See: contempt of court, indirect contempt.

**indirect evidence**  See: evidence, direct evidence (indirect evidence).

**indirect trespass**  See: trespass, indirect trespass.

**indispensable element test**  See: attempt, criminal attempt, indispensable element test.

**indispensable party**  See: party, party to an action, indispensable party.

**individual capacity**  See: capacity, defendant capacity, individual capacity (personal capacity).

**individual retirement account**  See: pension, individual retirement account (I.R.A. or IRA).

**individualized education plan**  See: disability, education of children with disabilities, individualized education plan (IEP).

**Individuals with Disabilities Education Act**  See: disability, education of children with disabilities, Individuals with Disabilities Education Act (IDEA).

**individuation of laws**  See: law, individuation of laws.

**indorsement (endorsement, indorse)**  To write one's name as an authentication or transfer of an interest. Indorsement is, literally, to write on the back of an instrument. The term now generally signifies a writing anywhere on a negotiable instrument, contract, receipt, or other document, indicating that the indorser has received the document as presumably valid and authentic.

If the indorser indorses the instrument to another, the indorser effectively puts the indorsee into the indorser's place, giving the indorsee the right to receive whatever benefit in the instrument that might have been realized by the indorser. A common example is a third party check. A drafts a check to B. B indorses the check to C. C may then present the check to a bank by cashing it there, by which the bank will draw funds from A's bank to the benefit of C's account.

See also: recourse, without recourse (sans recours or with recourse); signature, countersignature (countersign).

**co-signature (co-signer or cosign or cosigner)**  A second person's indorsement that amounts to a guaranty of the first's duty. A cosignature is an indorsement by a second party of an agreement, note, surety, or other instrument that has already been signed by one party, by which the second party accepts a liability under the instrument to perform the obligations of a first party in the event the one party defaults on them.

See also: loan, recourse loan; signature.

**inducement (induce)**  Any incentive for a party to commit a given action or a disincentive to refrain from it. An inducement is anything that influences a person or entity to act in a given manner. Inducements include all manner of profit, gain, or reward that might be realized from the action or if not from the action from another source in order to persuade the party to commit the action. Many inducements are integral to a contract, such as pay and benefits offered to a prospective employee. Others are collateral to the transaction itself, such as a bounty paid by a government to a hunter to hunt an overstocked animal, a reward paid for the return of a lost object, or a finder's fee given to a broker for arranging a new contractual relationship. An inducement may be legal, such as a commitment to sell all of one's output in an outputs contract, or illegal, such as an agreement to accept a given bid in return for a bribe. Inducement may be based on persuasion alone without a promise of money or tangible goods, as in a sales agent's persuasion of a person to enter a contract or a conspirator's luring of a co–conspirator into a criminal enterprise.

*See also:* entrapment.

**fraud in the inducement**   A fraud by one party in the process of negotiating a contract. Fraud in the inducement is a basis for avoiding a contract, in which the party that would avoid performance demonstrates that the other party committed fraud in the negotiation of the contract, by deliberately misstating a material fact or by creating a false impression, on which the avoiding party relied in entering into the contract. A contract procured by the fraud of one party is voidable by the other party but is not inherently void; the party who committed the fraud is neither entitled to profit nor to avoid responsibility created by its misdeed.

*See also:* culpa, culpa in contrahendo (c in c).

**induced reliance**   *See:* reliance, unbargained–for reliance (induced reliance).

**inductive reasoning**   *See:* reason, inductive reasoning; argument, inductive reasoning.

**ineffective assistance of counsel**   *See:* counselor, right to counsel, ineffective assistance of counsel, Strickland test; counselor, right to counsel, ineffective assistance of counsel (defective performance).

**inevitable discovery**   *See:* search, exclusionary rule, exception to the exclusionary rule, inevitable-discovery doctrine (inevitable discovery).

**infamy (infamous)**   The state of dishonor. Infamy is a status in the common law, brought about by the commission of specific crimes that in contemporary usage have a significance not unlike crimen falsi, or crimes of moral turpitude as well as crimes of breach of trust or office. A person who was infamous was barred from taking oaths, thus barring the person from serving as a witness, from serving as a juror, or from holding office.

Infamia, or disgrace, was a significant concept in Roman law, attaching as a matter of fact when one had a reputation of doing disgraceful things and as a matter of law when one was adjudged of doing them.

When used as a euphemism to describe a particular crime, infamy was until recently a shorthand for the crime of sodomy, the infamous crime.

**infamous crime**   *See:* crime, infamous crime.

**infancy (infant)**   Youth too immature for practical responsibility over oneself or one's conduct. Infancy, at the common law, was the same as minority, in that anyone lacking the full capacity of a mature adult was an infant. Contemporary legal usage has largely abandoned this sense of infant, instead differentiating minors from infants in a manner more like general usage: a minor is anyone not an adult, but an infant is a child who as a result of youth lacks the mental capacity for any form of personal responsibility. A minor may therefore be an infant or a juvenile.

A parent or guardian is particularly obligated to supervise an infant to guard the infant from risks of harm and to ensure that basic needs are met. An infant is not responsible for acts committed that, by an adult would be criminal or tortious, although a supervising adult may have third–party liability for such acts. Infants lack the ability to enter contracts or to hold positions of trust or responsibility, or to make informed decisions regarding health care or to consent to acts requiring consent.

*See also:* major; juvenile.

**infancy**   *See:* capacity, criminal capacity, incapacity to commit a crime, youth as incapacity (infancy).

**infanticide**   Causing the death of an infant. Infanticide is the killing of an infant. Any person who causes the death of a child, from any moment following the child's live birth to the time at which the child becomes capable of independence in living and responsibility, commits infanticide. Abortion is not infanticide by definition; abortion takes place prior to the completion of a live birth.

**inference (infer)**   A conclusion drawn by a reader from a text or an observer from circumstances. An inference is a conclusion drawn from reasons or evidence. In reading a text, a reader draws inferences from the words of the text; the reader infers the meaning of the text from the evidence of the words of the document. In considering evidence, a finder of fact infers the meaning of evidence, reaching decisions including not only the inferences drawn from the evidence but also the level of confidence that the finder of fact has that those inferences are accurate and either supported by the evidence specifically or in sum, or at least that the inferences are not contradicted by the evidence.

Note: inference is often confused with imply. Inference is a conclusion drawn from evidence by a reader or hearer; implication is a conclusion suggested by an author or speaker.

*See also:* judgment, summary judgment, reasonable-inference rule (reasonable inference).

**inference of fact**   *See:* fact, inferential fact (inference of fact).

**forbidden inference**   An assumption that a person acted from proof of similar past acts. The forbidden inference is an inference that a person committed an act derived from evidence that the person had committed similar acts in the past. In criminal cases, evidence may not be introduced to demonstrate past acts if the evidence suggests a likelihood that a juror will make the forbidden inference. Argument expressly or impliedly raising the forbidden inference is — of course — forbidden, and if the court allows such argument from a prosecutor, the argument usually amounts to reversible error. Even so, certain evidence of past bad acts is admissible, particularly to prove the identity of a person who performed a task similar to the past acts.

*See also:* modus, modus operandi (signature facts or MO or M.O.).

**inference-on-inference rule (inference on an inference or inference upon inference)** An inference from an inference may be argued if each inference may be argued. The inference–on–inference rule once forbade argument for a factual conclusion inferred from a source that is itself inferred from other sources. That understanding of the rule is now accepted in a few jurisdictions, having been largely rejected, though the rule is now quoted for the opposite conclusion, allowing inference upon inference from the evidence, but only if each inference in the chain of inferences is sufficiently demonstrated by its own reasoning and by relevant evidence and only if the conclusion that is reached is not independently forbidden as a matter of law or implausible as a matter of fact or logic. Each inference must independently meet the level of certainty required in that forum, or it may not be argued, nor may any further inference may be drawn from it.

The inference–on–inference rule applies to the analysis of facts. When applied to the standards of law to determine the extent of legal liability in a given situation or legal power in a different situation, the rule is more heavily circumscribed in that the conclusion derived from several levels of inference from a legal standard must not conflict that standard or with others.

**inferential fact** *See:* fact, inferential fact (inference of fact).

**inferiority (inferior)** A person, office, or institution subordinate to another. Inferiority, literally being below or underneath, is a condition in a hierarchy in which there are others above. An inferior officer is subordinate to a principal officer or superior officer. An inferior tribunal is subordinate to a superior tribunal or supreme tribunal.

A person who considered an inferior in the common law was a person of a legal class below others, such as a villein, or relative to a peer, a commoner.

**inferior officer** *See:* officer, federal officer, inferior officer.

**inferred contract or contract implied in fact** *See:* contract, contract formation, implied contract (inferred contract or contract implied in fact).

**infinitum** *See:* ad, ad infinitum.

**infirmity (infirm)** Weakness or ill health. Infirmity, in its literal sense, is any aspect of the body or mind that is feeble or weak, whether because of illness, injury, a lack of development, or decay owing to age. Metaphorically, infirmity may be said to afflict anything, and so an infirm opinion is one that is weak of feeble for some reason, either its use of the law, its account of the facts, or its reasoning.

**inflammable substance or combustible material** *See:* hazard, hazardous substance, flammable substance (inflammable substance or combustible material).

**inflammatory speech** *See:* speech, inflammatory speech (incendiary speech).

**inflation factor** *See:* damages, calculation of damages, discount for present value (inflation factor).

**influence** The power to affect the thoughts or actions of others. Influence in the law is the role that a person, a text, an institution, or any other thing has as a source of reasons for thought or action for others. An influential person is one who has a form of authority, being a person to whom others listen and are inclined to agree with because of who the person is rather than just what the person says. An influential text is one that is consulted, quoted, or emulated, the ideas of which are accepted by readers and followed by them.

Influence is, in this sense, a metaphor derived from its older use to depict the movement of liquids, including the influence that caused liquids to flow in certain ways, and thus to describe other physical forces, especially the gravitational influence of one celestial body on another. Thus, influence among human affairs is like the influence of the sun on the planets.

The fact of a person's influence over others creates a moral obligation upon the influential person that is sometimes recognized in law; a benefit procured through the use of undue influence is usually an unjust enrichment and subject to restitution. This is especially true when a fiduciary relationship arises with the influential person in a fiduciary capacity to others.

*See also:* unjust enrichment; fiduciary.

**informality** The failure to observe the formal requirements of procedure. Informality is the lack of conformity to formal requirements in pleading, filing, service, hearing attendance, and decorum overall. In court proceedings, informality may be excused only so long as the lack of formality does not prejudice the opposing party (assuming that party is not similarly informal).

**informal action** *See:* action, informal action.

**informal immunity** *See:* immunity, witness immunity, informal immunity (pocket immunity).

**informal probate** *See:* probate, informal probate.

**informal rulemaking** *See:* rulemaking, informal rulemaking.

**informant** *See:* police, police agent, informant (informer or confidential informant or CI or canary or pigeon or rat or snitch or stool pigeon).

**informant tip suppression hearing** *See:* cause, probable cause, Darden hearing (informant tip suppression hearing).

**agent provocateur (agents provocateurs)** A police agent or informant who provokes a crime. An agent provocateur is a police officer or informant who actively encourages a person or group to engage in a crime. The crime resulting may be considered the result of entrapment. Agents provocateurs have historically been placed by the state in social movements, such as labor organizations and civil rights organizations not only to encourage criminal acts for the purpose of later prosecution but also to provoke a diminished public support for the movement.

Note: agent provocateur is French, not English, pronounced more like "ah jaunt prohvohkahtuer"

**snitch (canary or stool pigeon or pigeon)** A person who informs the police of the details of a crime. A snitch, or canary or a stool pigeon or a pigeon, is a person who gives information to the police that incriminates another person in a crime, particularly when the person is a confederate of the other person, or even a principal in a crime or a related crime, and the person trades the information incriminating a former confederate for immunity or lenience. Although there are variations, such terms as these are usually employed regardless of the truth of the information provided or the informant's motive for providing it.

## information

**classified information** Information classified for control by the government. Classified information is information that is in the control of the government. It is usually designated Top Secret, Secret, or Confidential, because an official has concluded that the dissemination of the information could damage the national security of the United States. Classified information is to be controlled so that no one receives such information without both a security clearance appropriate to the level the information is designated for control and a need to know the specific information to be released. Any person who knowingly releases classified information related to intelligence to an unauthorized person commits a felony. There are other designations for the control of government information, notably For Official Use Only, but such information is not classified. Classified information is exempt from disclosure under the Freedom of Information Act, and it is subject to subpoena as evidence only under the controls of the bench under the Classified Information Procedures Act. Information that is not classified but nonetheless includes any information related to national defense is subject to a separate capitol crime for release to any person who may communicate it to a foreign government.

**Classified Information Procedures Act (CIPA or C.I.P.A.)** Classified information may be barred, used, or controlled, by the court. The Classified Information Procedures Act allows both criminal defendants and the United States to present evidence that includes classified information. The act gives the court the power to hear motions by the United States to use substitutes or bar such evidence, after which the court may dismiss charges or the case as needed to do justice.

**freedom of information** The freedom of the citizen to be informed of government actions and information. Freedom of information is the right of access to information held by the government. Although there are certain powers one might have owing to contract or litigation to gain information held by private parties, there generally is no broad freedom of information in the private sphere. The U.S. Constitution provides no express guaranty of freedom of information, but it gives no power to the federal government to retain information at the expense of the governed. Freedom of information is secured either by statute, as in the case of the Freedom of Information Act, or as an aspect of other, recognized rights, such as the rights of due process, of criminal procedure, of habeas corpus, and of free speech. Even so, a freedom of information may be recognized as one of those blessings of liberty that is an unenumerated right under the Ninth Amendment, an aspect of the Republican Form of Government, or an aspect of the due process of law that is essential to ordered liberty.

**sunshine law** *See:* sunshine law (open meetings law).

**Freedom of Information Act (F.O.I.A. or FOIA or foiable)** A federal or state statute requiring government agencies to release information on request. A Freedom of Information Act is a statute that requires the dissemination of information held by government agencies, through regular publication of such information or by the release of such information upon request. The statutes are usually known by the acronym FOIA, though many state acts have other titles. The most well known FOIA is the federal act, passed initially in 1966 and amended several times since, most importantly in the post–Watergate Privacy Act of 1974. The federal FOIA, codified at 5 U.S.C. § 552, establishes presumptive access to federal information upon request by any member of the public for inspection and copying, although it also excepts nine categories of information from such access.

The nine categories of government information exempt from federal FOIA disclosure are: (1) Anything related to national security or foreign policy specifically ordered secret under an Executive Order. (2) Internal personnel rules and practices of an agency. (3) Information specifically exempted from disclosure by statute. (4) Trade secrets and commercial or financial information obtained from a person and privileged or confidential. (5) Letters or memoranda that would be barred from discovery in litigation. (6) Files related to agency personnel that would constitute a clearly unwarranted invasion of personal privacy. (7) Law enforcement records if their production could reasonably be expected to interfere with enforcement proceedings, to deprive a person of a right to a fair trial or an impartial adjudication, to constitute an unwarranted invasion of personal privacy, to disclose the identity of a confidential source of that or another agency, to disclose techniques and procedures for law enforcement investigations or prosecutions, to disclose law enforcement methods and so risk circumvention of the law, or to endanger the life or physical safety of any individual. (8) Records from the examination, operating, or condition reports of financial institutions. (9) Geological and geophysical information and data, including maps, concerning wells. There is a continuous tension in every exemption over whether the agency holding such information abuses this exemption to withhold information that is in fact accessible under the statute.

Although the word is unlovely, any information that is accessible under a Freedom of Information Act is "foiable," or "FOIAable," which sounds quite like "foible."

See also: press, freedom of the press (liberty of the press).

**information as criminal information**  A formal statement charging that a person or entity committed a specified crime. An information is a pleading filed by an official in a criminal action that charges the defendant with a crime. In some jurisdictions, the criminal complaint or the accusation is used for the same purpose as an information. An information is similar in content to an indictment, but an information is issued by a prosecutor or law enforcement officer with the court rather than by action of the grand jury. A person arrested under an information must be first examined in a preliminary hearing, in which the case against the arrestee is presented before a judge who must determine whether there is sufficient evidence to hold the arrestee for trial. Thus, the essential differences between the information and the indictment involve when and by whom is a review of the evidence undertaken to determine if there is probable cause to believe the defendant has committed the crime to be charged. The indictment is based on a hearing by the grand jury before the arrest, and the information is reviewed in a hearing before the judge after it.

The Fifth Amendment precludes the use of an information to charge a person with a capital crime, which must be based on a grand jury's indictment.

See also: indictment (indict); charge, charge as criminal charge, charging instrument.

**informed consent to a medical procedure**  See: consent, informed consent to a medical procedure.

**informer or confidential informant or CI or canary or pigeon or rat or snitch or stool pigeon** See: police, police agent, informant (informer or confidential informant or CI or canary or pigeon or rat or snitch or stool pigeon).

**infraction**  The breach of a rule or law. An infraction is a violation of a rule or law. It is to break the law. Infraction, in the legal sense, is derived from its literal meaning of causing a fracture, as in breaking a piece of glass.

**infringement (infringe or infringing)**  A violation of the limits of a law, a right, or an interest. An infringement is any intrusion upon a boundary established by law. A neighbor's infringing structure is a structure built on one's property, and an infringement of a patent is the duplication of the patented process or device without a license to do so. An official who usurps the authority of another office infringes upon it. Thus any action by an official or private party that violates the limits of a lawful right or interest held by another is an infringement.

See also: infraction.

**infringement of copyright**  See: copyright, infringement of copyright (copyright piracy or copyright infringement).

**infringement of patent**  See: patent, infringement of patent (patent infringement or infringer).

**infringement of trademark**  See: trademark, infringement of trademark, palming off (reverse palming off); trademark, infringement of trademark (trademark infringement).

**ingress and egress easement**  See: easement, access easement (ingress and egress easement).

**ingress or regress**  See: egress (ingress or regress).

**inhabitant**  A resident of one place with an intent to remain there. An inhabitant is a person who inhabits a particular domicile, jurisdiction, state, or nation. An inhabitant must not be a transient but a person who not only does reside but intends to persist in residing in that place. A person does not cease to be an inhabitant of that person's habitation by temporary absence of travel, and even an extended absence does not change the person's inhabitance as long as the person considers the habitation as the person's home and intends to return there.

**inherence (inherent, inhering)**  Any aspect of a person, place, law, or idea that results of its very existence. Inherence is the nature of a thing, what is essential of it. Any attribute or aspect of a thing, whether a person, an idea, a law or anything else, is inherent if it is true without reference to proof from some external source or derivation.

The rights to life, liberty, property, and the pursuit of happiness are inherent in the individual and are not conferred by the state.

An inherent authority of a court or office is an authority held in the office by its very definition, not because that authority is conferred from somewhere or someone else. Thus, the judicial power of the courts is inherent in the court, but the specific jurisdiction of one court or another to hear certain matters is conferred upon those courts by constitutional or statutory grants of jurisdiction.

An inherent authority, power, or right is not reducible by the act of others, nor is it alienable by the act of its holders.

**inherent power of the court**  See: court, inherent power of the court.

**inherent vice**  See: product, defective product, latent product defect (inherent vice).

**inherently dangerous activity or ultra-hazardous activity or ultrahazardous activity** See: danger, abnormally dangerous activity (inherently dangerous activity or ultra-hazardous activity or ultrahazardous activity).

**inheritability**   *See:* heritability (inheritability).

**inheritance (inherit)**   The property an heir would receive from a decedent's estate in the absence of a valid will. An inheritance is what, by law, a surviving family member would receive through a distribution of an intestate's estate, if a decedent were to die with no valid last will and testament. If a decedent dies testate, a grant by will or property to a devisee or legatee under the will who is also an heir at law is also termed an inheritance if it is the same property or share that the devisee or legatee would have inherited had there been no will.

Few testators are aware of either technical meaning of the term "inheritance," and anything conveyed from the estate of a decedent to an heir or to a legatee is called, as a matter of popular usage, an inheritance. Thus, if a testator employs the term inheritance in a will, care must be taken to ensure that the term is intended in one sense or the other.

*See also:* devise (devisable or devisee or deviser or devisor); legacy (legatee or legator).

**inheritance tax**   *See:* tax, death tax, inheritance tax.

**advancement**   A gift inter vivos that is deducted from an heir's share of an inheritance. An advancement is a gift made to a person who is a prospective heir of the donor and that is intended to serve as the donee's inheritance in lieu of the inheritance after death, or to serve as some portion of it instead of the whole. In some jurisdictions, an advancement may be made against a devise or legacy under a last will and testament, although at common law, a will was not affected by an advancement unless it operated to remove a specific bequest.

The court may have difficulty in ascertaining whether an inter vivos gift is intended by the donor and later decedent to have been, at the time of the gift, an advancement. There are many reasons a person might have for making a substantial gift to one or another potential heir, and construing intent at the time from testimony after the donor's death is a difficult business. Yet if the evidence demonstrates the intent of the donor to make the gift as an advancement, then the share of the donee's interest in the intestate estate, or if the advancement is under a will then in demonstrative, residual, or general legacy is reduced by that amount. If the value of the advancement is equal to or greater than the shares of other similarly situated heirs or legatees, then the heir receiving the advancement receives nothing more from the intestate estate or from that legacy. An advancement does not interfere with specific bequests unless the advancement is of the funds or property bequeathed.

**disinheritance (disheritor or disinherit)**   The act of depriving an heir of an inheritance. Disinheritance includes any action that interferes with the inheritance that an heir would otherwise have received.

Technically, disinheritance only occurs when a legal heir's inheritance is barred, usually through the drafting or alteration of a will so that the would-be decedent gives the inheritance as a legacy or devise to someone else. (A legal heir's inheritance may also be barred through other means, such as the birth of a child that would cut off the inheritance that might have occurred for a more distant relative, yet such acts are rarely taken for the purpose of disinheritance.)

More generally, the popular usage of "disinheritance" depicts that alteration of a will to strike out the devise or bequest that had been there for one beneficiary and leaving that property to someone else. Only careful analysis of context will determine which sense of "disinheritance" is intended by the testator if such a word is used.

Disinheritance cannot disturb dower or curtesy, and the modern probate law of many states make the disinheritance of a spouse a practical impossibility, conferring upon the surviving spouse an elective share that would take precedence over a will. Disinheritance cannot effect community property or property held by the entireties. Under the civil law of succession, particularly in Louisiana, a forced heir, or a child who is disabled or under the age of twenty-four, has a protected interest that cannot be disinherited.

**disinherison (disherison)**   The disinheritance for cause of a forced heir. Disinherison is the civil law concept of disinheritance of a forced heir from the legitime, or the barring of a statutory heir, usually a child, from the legally required inheritance owing to a lawful cause. Though this concept has long been the law of Louisiana, the restrictions on disinherison were accidentally abolished by the legislature in 1999, effective in 2001.

*See also:* heir, forced heir (statutory heir).

**inhumanity (inhuman)**   Conduct that causes harms of a form or extent beyond civilized justifications. Inhumanity is a condition of mind or conduct that is more associated with the brutal or savage animal than with a civilized human being. Specifically, inhuman conduct is any conduct that inflicts destruction, abuse, pain, or hardship that is not justified by the need to engage in such conduct to avert worse suffering. In all cases, inhuman conduct describes abuse for its own sake, or for the sake of revenge or reprisal or threat to others.

**iniquity (iniquitous)**   Contrary to justice and equity. Iniquity is the rejection of equity. Though the term has acquired a broader connotation of a moral general sense of evil, iniquity technically represents the failure of the duty to behave toward others with justice, charity, and equity. Iniquity is the special province of slothful or corrupt lawyers or legal officials.

**initial appearance**   *See:* appearance, initial appearance (presentment for initial appearance).

**initial disclosure**   *See:* disclosure, discovery disclosure, initial disclosure.

**initial public offering**   *See:* share, share as stock, offering, public offering, initial public offering (IPO or I.P.O.); offering, initial public offering.

**initiative (intiated law or initiated act or initiated amendment or direct legislation)**   A law initiated by popular petition rather than draft statute or constitution amendment. An initiative is a means by which a law may be proposed outside of the usual legislative process, usually by a petition. Although most initiatives lead to a referendum, which is a popular vote by which a law is enacted or defeated, the initiative is itself a separate process, and many states allow a bill to be proposed to the legislature by initiative, the legislature then voting or failing to enact the initiated law. Both initiative and referendum are sometimes referred to as direct legislation.

**initio**   The beginning. Initio is Latin for the verb to begin, and standing alone, it is translated sometimes into English as a noun — the beginning.

**iniuria**   *See:* injuria (iniuria).

**injunction**   *See:* equity, equitable remedy, injunction.

**injunction (injunctive relief)**   A judicial order to a person or entity to do or to refrain from any act. An injunction is a remedy granted by a court of equity or a court of general jurisdiction, including equity, that orders the party who receives it to perform some act or to refrain from performing some act. The injunction is a flexible remedy, and the act required may be simple or complex, to be performed immediately or over time, subject to the ongoing and direct supervision of the court or merely subject later to contempt if it is not performed.

A valid injunction must be specific as to the party or parties bound to it, who must have been properly before the court through service prior to the injunction. It must state with reasonable specificity the acts or act that are required or restrained. Under the federal rules, the order must also state the reasons for its issuance.

Unless specified as a legal remedy by statute, an injunction is an equitable remedy, and whether it issues from a court of equity or a court of general jurisdiction, the requirement of equitable pleading must be satisfied. A party seeking an injunction must not only satisfy the requirements of pleading to survive equitable defenses, but the injunction will be appropriate only if the judge believes that the balance of the equities favor its issue.

Most remedies for violations of the Constitution of the United States or of a given state are injunctive.

**Anti-Injunction Act (A.I.A. or AIA)**   A federal court may not enjoin a parallel state action. The Anti-Injunction Act, codified at 28 U.S.C. § 2283, bars federal courts from enjoining an action in state court on the sole ground of similarity between the state action and a pending federal action. Even so, the AIA does not bar injunctions against state actions on matters in certain exceptional cases. The federal court may enjoin a state proceeding if the injunction is necessary to aid in the federal court's jurisdiction, if it is necessary to protect or effectuate its judgments, if it is to stay a matter removed to a federal court, if the injunction is an appropriate remedy to an action specifically enacted by federal statute, such as injunctions sought under 42 U.S.C. § 1983, if the federal injunction of the state proceeding is required to prevent a violation of a federally protected right. Note: the Anti-Injunction Act is not the only federal defenses to an injunction. Other statutes, such as the Norris-LaGuardia Act, 29 U.S.C. § 101 may apply, as might the equitable defenses to injunctive relief.

*See also:* abstention, abstention doctrine, Younger abstention.

**enjoin (enjoined)**   To command or require, particularly by order of injunction. To enjoin a person is to command the person, and to enjoin an activity is to forbid or require it. A court enjoins someone through various orders, most importantly by an injunction. "Injunction" is related to the verb through a common derivation from the Latin injungo, with enjoin derived from the Law French enjoindre.

**permanent injunction**   An injunction without end. A permanent injunction is an injunction that specifies no termination for its mandate. A permanent injunction may be later rescinded or vacated, or it may be rendered unenforceable if it is violated and no subsequent attempt is timely made for its enforcement. Otherwise, the effects of the injunction will persist as long as the individual or entity who is enjoined shall live, and in some instances, the effect will persist for a successor in interest. In most instances, a permanent injunction is the final order in an action that seeks an injunction. For that reason, the permanent injunction differs from a preliminary injunction, which may not be required but for a specified time or until the action reaches a judgment.

**preliminary injunction (P.I. or PI)**   An injunction given as a pre-trial remedy. A preliminary injunction is an injunction awarded before trial in order to prevent harm that the plaintiff might suffer if the defendant is not required to do something or to perform some action, or not to do something that is the object of the plaintiff's claims. The object of a preliminary injunction must be related to the basis for a claim for permanent relief. To seek a preliminary injunction, the plaintiff must seek final equitable relief, either the same injunction made permanent or similar relief arising in equity and not just in law. (In other words, in a suit for damages as a final remedy, a plaintiff may not seek a preliminary injunction to preserve a fund for such damages, although the plaintiff can seek other pre-trial remedies, such as a pre-trial attachment or lien.) Unlike a temporary restraining order, or TRO, a PI requires a hearing with notice to the defendant allowing the defendant a reasonable opportunity to oppose the injunction.

Thus, a plaintiff must demonstrate at the time of the motion for preliminary injunction that the plaintiff has given timely notice of the motion to the defendant, that the plaintiff has a reasonable likelihood of success on the claims in the suit related to the injunction, that the plaintiff seeks permanent equitable relief, and that the plaintiff will suffer irremediable harm if an injunction is not granted immediately.

**temporary restraining order (T.R.O. or TRO)** An injunction that may be issued without notice or a full hearing that expires quickly unless renewed. A temporary restraining order, or TRO, is a form of injunction that is available in a situation that is so urgent that the plaintiff convinces the court the plaintiff may suffer irreparable harm without an immediate order enjoining the defendant from some imminent action. The urgency is so great that there is no time to assure service of process and a full hearing with the defendant represented. The TRO may be issued ex parte, but if it is to be done so, the plaintiff must have attempted in good faith to serve process and give notice of any hearing but failed to achieve it. In the federal courts, a TRO granted without notice or representation at the motion hearing must expire within ten days of issuance, although it may be extended for cause or be superseded by a preliminary injunction.

Many states have less stringent requirements on the TRO, treating it more as an ex parte preliminary injunction.

*See also:* order, court order, restraining order.

**injuria (iniuria)** Unlawful act. Injuria is Latin for an act or harm that is of a form and cause that are acknowledged by the law. It is conduct or action that may be enjoined or rectified, as well as conduct that may deserve punishment.

*See also:* injuria, injuria absque damno (injuria absque damnum).

**injuria absque damno (injuria absque damnum)** Violation of duty without damage. Injuria absque damno, or wrongdoing without harm, describes a breach of duty that does not give rise to significant harms. The term is a defense to an action, arguing that there are no damages sufficient to sustain a cause of action. Regardless of any breach of duty there may have been, no action can be brought without legally significant damages for this sort of cause of action. The term is similar to the de minimis maxim, that the law does not deal with trifles. In both forms, these defenses are the logical opposite of the defense of damnum absque injuria, or harm without wrongdoing.

*See also:* injuria (iniuria); lex, lex non curat de minimis (de minimus non curat lex); damnum, damnum absque injuria (damnum sine injuria).

**injury (injurious)** Damage. Injury is a broad term for the damaging results of a harmful action. Injury may be suffered to one's body, mind, reputation, economic opportunities, or property. Injury implies the result of a particular act or condition with an external cause, rather than an inherent or endemic aspect of life.

Injury is usually defined with some specificity in the coverage clauses of insurance policies. Injury in that sense is not injury in general, but merely a covered injury.

**aggravation of injury** The worsening of an injury by conduct that occurs following the initial injury. The aggravation of an injury is a worsening of a condition, or the exacerbation of an injury, as a result of an act or event that follows and is distinct from the cause of the initial injury. If the defendant is not responsible for the act or event that aggravates the injury, the defendant is not liable for the cost of treatment or damages resulting from the aggravation or worsened condition. The rationale for this limitation of the defendant's liability is that the the aggravation breaks the causal connection between the defendant's tortious conduct and the plaintiff's subsequent aggravated injuries. A trier of fact must determine whether a plaintiff's injuries were in fact aggravated, or whether they are subsequent injuries that came as a result of the defendant's conduct.

**bodily injury (bodily harm)** Physical harm to the person, no matter how slight. Bodily injury, or as it is often written in statutes — bodily harm — is an element of many a crime or tort. Bodily harm is physical harm to the body of a natural person that is sustained as a result of the contact or touching of another. The conduct may be intentional, reckless or negligent, but as long as the victim involuntarily sustains some physical injury to his person, no matter how slight, the element of bodily harm is met. The harm need not be offensive, and indeed it may even have been initially consented to, as in the case of negligent medical treatment. Bodily harm may be classified as to severity, as in grievous or great bodily harm, serious enough to cause permanent or protracted loss of function or permanent disfigurement.

*See also:* rape, rape as sexual assault, bodily intrusion (penetration or physical penetration).

**economic injury** An economic loss sustained as the result of the conduct of another person or entity. An economic injury is a damage that occurs that is manifest solely as a lost revenue, increased expense, or lost economic opportunity. When economic injuries are the basis of a complaint for breach of duty, those injuries cannot be speculative, and evidence must be presented that clearly establishes a loss; it must also be proved that but for the conduct of the defendant, the purported economic injury would not have occurred. Economic injury in tort is usually barred as a basis for compensatory damages by the economic loss rule.

**irreparable injury (irreparable harm)** An injury that cannot be made whole by the payment of damages Irreparable injury is a term of art for an injury for which there is no adequate remedy at law, one that is more fit for injunction than damages. An injury may be irreparable because absent an injunction, the injury will persist. Likewise, an injury may be irreparable because once it occurs, there will be no way perfectly to restore the status quo ante, or because the injury will amount to a breach of trust or other fiduciary duty or will provoke pain and suffering that cannot be fully compensated through the payments of money.

**legal injury**  An injury that is actionable at law. A legal injury is an injury that is subject to redress at law. An injury for which no legal action exists is not a legal injury.

See also: limitation, limitation of actions, statute of limitations, legal injury rule (legal–injury rule).

**personal injury (P.I. or PI)**  An injury of the mind or the body of a natural person. A personal injury is the actual or presumed injury suffered by a real person, rather than an artificial person, such as a corporation. Personal injury includes physical injury, pain, and bodily injury, as well as mental and emotional suffering. A personal injury may arise from a variety of conditions, not all of which are physically traumatic, such as wrongful imprisonment and the tort of assault. Not every injury suffered by a natural person is a personal injury, however, and an injury to property alone is not a personal injury, even if the property is owned by one person.

Note: a claim for personal injury includes not only the expenses for treatment but also lost wages and compensation for the suffering of personal injury.

**pre-conception injury (preconception injury)**  An injury to a parent that affects a later-conceived child. A pre-conception injury is an injury suffered by a parent—usually, though not necessarily, the mother—that caused harm to a later-conceived child.

**prenatal injury**  An injury to a fetus other than by appropriate medical care. A prenatal injury is an injury to a fetus, whether the injury results from conduct by the pregnant mother, by conditions affecting the mother before or during pregnancy, or by injury to the pregnant woman that results in injury to the fetus. Conduct that is not within the appropriate confines of informed consent and prudent medical care that injures or affects the health of a fetus may be actionable if either the conduct occurs after the fetus becomes viable or, notwithstanding whether the conduct occurred before or after viability, the child was later born alive.

**injustice**  See: justice, injustice (unjust).

**manifest injustice**  A failure of legal process in a given case that results in a clearly unacceptable ruling. Manifest injustice in a judicial decision or in the outcome of a legal dispute is a fundamental flaw in the court's decision that would lead to a result that is both inequitable and contrary to applicable policy.

**inmate**  A prisoner, or one who dwells in the dwelling of another. An inmate, in contemporary usage, is a person who has been incarcerated. The term was more general in the language of the common law, meaning a person who resided in a house owned by another person (not the inmate's spouse). From this sense arose the modern understanding of an inmate who is a resident in a building owned by the state: an inmate is a person confined under a sentence to a jail, prison, prison farm, or increasingly even to detention in the inmate's own home.

See also: prisoner (inmate).

**inner morality of law**  See: morality, inner morality of law.

**innocence (innocent)**  The absence of guilt as a matter of fact. Innocence is a matter of fact that a person did not commit a given crime or any crime. Innocence is not a verdict, and a verdict that a defendant is not guilty does not amount to a finding of innocence, but to a finding that the jury or judge was not sufficiently convinced by the prosecutor of the defendant's guilt. Likewise, a person who is innocent may be found guilty as a matter of law, although the person's innocence persists because it is a matter of fact not of law; the judgment of guilt is a legal liability, not an alteration of history. Even so, a person found guilty of a crime will be treated by the institutions of law as if the person is guilty and not innocent.

The law presumes that every person is innocent of all criminal behavior and requires that each person be found not guilty and freed from confinement or detention unless the state can prove guilt beyond a reasonable doubt.

See also: guilt (guilty).

**actual innocence**  Innocence in fact, by which the defendant did not do what is claimed. Actual innocence is real innocence; the failure of the defendant to have done the crimes charged.

Actual innocence describes a claim of innocence made on appeal or in a suit for collateral relief from a criminal sentence, such as a petition for habeas corpus, when the convict makes a claim of innocence that is purportedly made in good faith, and there is some evidence that the convict did not in fact commit the crime that was the basis of the sentence. In general, an argument for actual innocence is not alone sufficient to grant habeas or other relief, although it is essential as an element in granting relief on the basis of some forms of procedural defect in the trial or on the basis of a miscarriage of justice.

**legal innocence (legal insufficiency)**  Innocence in law, in which the defendant's conduct did not violate the technical limits of law. Legal innocence results from the conduct of the defendant not fully satisfying the specific requirements of the criminal law under which the defendant is charged. It is innocence because some element of the crime was not met, though other elements may have been. Legal innocence is often conflated with legal insufficiency, or the failure of the evidence to be sufficient to prove actual guilt (despite a verdict of guilt having been reached).

Legal innocence is rarely a label applied to an argument by the defendant or habeas plaintiff. Rather, it is usually a characterization made to a claim for relief applied by the prosecutor or government or by the court. A claim of legal innocence is given less weight than actual innocence in most arguments during a collateral review of a conviction or sentence, particularly in a claim of manifest injustice or an argument to be relieved of the statute of limitations for constitutional challenges to a conviction. On direct appeal, however, clear evidence of legal innocence ought to be sufficient for reversal of a conviction.

**presumption of innocence**   The requirement that the government prove every element of a criminal action. The presumption of innocence establishes the burden of persuasion in criminal cases: the prosecutor must prove each element of the criminal charge, or the defendant must be acquitted. Like all presumptions, sufficient evidence can rebut the presumption, but lacking sufficient evidence (in criminal cases, proof beyond a reasonable doubt) the effect of the presumption stands.

It is clear error in a criminal cause for the jury not to be instructed on the defendant's presumption of innocence or on the state's burden of persuasion in such a manner as to have the same effect.

**innocent agent**   *See:* agent, innocent agent.

**innocent homicide**   *See:* homicide, innocent homicide.

**innocent owner**   *See:* forfeiture, civil forfeiture, innocent owner.

**innocent party**   *See:* party, innocent party.

**innocent passage**   *See:* passage, innocent passage (innocent passage at sea).

**innocent passage at sea**   *See:* passage, innocent passage (innocent passage at sea).

**innocent passage over land**   *See:* passage, free passage (innocent passage over land).

**innuendo**   A suggestive remark. Innuendo, in contemporary legal usage, is a claim in some actions for employment discrimination as well as for defamation and other dignitary torts in which the defendant is said to have made an assertion indirectly, as in a sly reference that hearers would understand maligns the plaintiff, even though no overt statement regarding the plaintiff's character was made.

This aspect of innuendo is derived from its older, technical meaning in writing as the part of speech that introduced a phrase illustrating or explaining a word or phrase before. "To wit," "that is to say," and "in other words" would have been innuendo. That sense gave rise to innuendo's meaning the word that would be later explained or illustrated. From that stylistic usage grew the rhetorical sense of a word or phrase containing hidden meaning.

*See also:* libel, libel per quod; slander, slander per quod.

**inquest**   An official inquiry. An inquest is a formal hearing to investigate specific matters required by law or order to be investigated. Inquests, in general, are held by either officials or a panel of jurors. In a sense, a grand jury hearing is an inquest.

The coroner's inquest is the most common form of inquest, and when "inquest" is used alone, it ordinarily refers to an inquiry into the cause of death of a person who died, particularly under circumstances that might be the basis for suspicion of murder.

*See also:* coroner, inquest of the coroner (coroner's inquest).

**inquest of the coroner**   *See:* coroner, inquest of the coroner (coroner's inquest).

**inquiry**

**inquiry notice**   *See:* notice, inquiry notice.

**red flag**   Anything that would alert a reasonable person of a problem. A red flag is a metaphor for any information or condition that would give warning to a person of reasonable care and prudence in a given situation that some condition exists that could cause harm, injury, loss, or at least peril. The term follows from the customary use of red flags physically to signal danger, particularly on railroads, in construction, in the military, on roads, and at sea. In law, a red flag rule is a rule imposing certain investigations or prophylactic steps upon the discovery of a condition.

*See also:* diligence, due diligence.

**inquisition (inquisitor or inquisitorial)**   Examination of evidence by the same person or body who is to rule in a hearing. An inquisition is a hearing or trial in which the examination of facts and development of evidence is by the person or group who will reach the decision, such as a judge, magistrate, jury, sheriff, coroner, or other officer. This method of hearing contrasts with the adversary proceeding in which the examination of facts and evidence is performed by counsel for the opposing sides of a case. The grand jury is an inquistorial device, and the inquistorial method is employed in many civil-law legal systems.

**Holy Office of the Inquisition (Holy Inquisition or Holy Office)**   An ecclesiastical tribunal empowered to prosecute heresy among clerics and laypeople. The inquisition was a tribunal of the Catholic Church dedicated to the detection, reform, and punishment of heresy. The inquisition took a variety of forms, many of them responsive to the church in particular states, from the twelfth century until 1908, when the name was changed and functions somewhat altered. Its successor at the present time is the Congregation for the Doctrine of the Faith in Rome.

**inquisitorial legal system**   *See:* law, legal system, inquisitorial legal system.

**INS**   *See:* immigration, Immigration and Naturalization Service (INS).

**insanity (insane or sanity or sane)**   The lack of reason and reasonableness in thought or action. Insanity is a category depicting a variety of conditions that result in a person's thoughts or actions being unreasonable or abnormal, such that the person engages in thought or conduct that is persistently abnormal or demonstrates a lack of judgment to make sound decisions, that disturbs the peace of society, or that poses a danger to the person or others.

An insane person is neither inherently excused from criminal liability nor barred from making valid instruments such contracts or wills. The test for each purpose of law is whether the person's mental defect prevents the person from forming the mental state required for liability in the first instance or responsible conduct in the second.

Sanity is sometimes defined as the capacity to function with sound understanding of the world around oneself, with reason and reasonable judgment and action. Sanity is occasionally defined as the opposite of insanity: a person who is not insane is sane. This binary definition is factually misleading, and yet it has proved useful to legal officials who must determine that someone has or lacks sufficient capacity at a given moment to be held accountable for the person's actions then. The presumption that each person is sane requires that whomever would prove insanity do so with evidence of insanity at whatever moment is relevant to the pending legal issue.

**insane delusion**   *See:* capacity, testamentary capacity, insane delusion.

**insane impulse or policeman at the elbow test**   *See:* insanity, irresistible impulse (insane impulse or policeman at the elbow test).

**irresistible impulse (insane impulse or policeman at the elbow test)**   A sudden and overwhelming passion acted on without reason or thought. Irresistible impulse is a defense to a criminal charge, claiming excuse as a result of the diminished capacity of the defendant brought on by a sudden urge that could not be contained by self control or rational judgment. Irresistible impulse is related but different from insanity, in that there is no claim made that the defendant was not otherwise of sound mind.

One test for irresistible impulse is the "policeman at the elbow" test, by which the finder of fact considers whether the defendant would have committed the act while knowing the defendant was being observed by the police: the defense seems proved if the defendant would have done it anyway. If the defendant would not have been deterred at that moment, but would have been under ordinary circumstances, then that defendant is thought to have acted under an impulse the defendant could not resist. On the other hand, a failure of this test does not prove an absence of irresistible impulse.

The defense is not available in all jurisdictions. California, for instance, abolished it by statute in 2002.

*See also:* responsibility, diminished responsibility (capacity diminished or diminished capacity).

**lunatic**   A person lacking capacity to manage affairs or commit a crime. A lunatic is a person who lacks capacity owing to a temporary or recurring disability, and during a period of incapacity is not responsible for actions the person commits. The term is now somewhat discredited and growing rare in legal usage.

**temporary insanity**   A loss of sanity that is restored with time. Temporary insanity is a condition that arises and abates in a person otherwise sane. Temporary insanity is not a plea in criminal law, but an aspect of the plea of incapacity in the basis of mental defect or insanity, in which the defense explains how a defendant who is sane at the time of trial was not sane at the time of the offense. Likewise, a claim of temporary insanity may be raised in a will contest to suggest a person who was otherwise lucid lacked the mental capacity to enter a will at the time a will was signed.

### insider (corporate insider or inside information)
Someone with knowledge available only to those in a special corporate relationship. A corporate insider is a person with special knowledge of the corporation. There are several levels of definition. For the purpose of trading reports, an insider of a corporation is a director, officer, key employee or owner of more than ten percent of the corporation. Trades by insiders must be disclosed to the public and to regulators. A broader definition of insider applies to the bar against acting on information not available to the public in trading equity or debt issued by or related to the corporation. In that sense, an insider includes any person employed by a corporation, or a contractor or a fiduciary of the corporation, who, in that capacity, acquires knowledge of the corporation and its activities that is not available to the general public. Another person who acts on inside information, knowing it to have originated as inside information still unknown to the general public, commits an offense under the securities laws.

**insider trading**   Trading a security while possessing material information about it unknown to the public. Insider trading occurs when an individual trades in securities of a public company while possessing information concerning the public company that is material to the value of the security and not known to the public. Insider trading is a crime as well as a violation of rules governing dealers and traders regulated by the Securities Exchange Commission (SEC).

### insidiousness (insidious)   Trickiness or deceptiveness.
Insidiousness is a particular type of deceptiveness that is associated with hidden plots or tricks. Writers often confuse invidious with insidious. Someone insidious is dangerously tricky, often because the person poses some unknown danger. Someone invidious is the object of jealousy, mistrust, or ill will.

*See also:* invidiousness (invidious).

### insolvency (solvency or insolvent or solvent)
The inability to pay one's debts or meet one's obligations. Insolvency results when a person or entity has more debts owed than assets to pay them and can not meet its ongoing obligations to others. Technically, insolvency occurs when the insolvent person or entity has liabilities greater than the fair market value of assets available.

Insolvency is used in bankruptcy calculations as well as cancellation of debt income calculations. A party to a contract that proclaims itself insolvent or is found to be insolvent by another party may be required to give further assurances of performance as well as ordered by a court to give specific performance.

Solvency is, conversely, the ability to pay one's bills and meet one's financial obligations.

## inspection

**inspection and regulatory search** *See:* search, warrantless search, administrative search.

**inspector** An officer tasked with the examination of something. An inspector is an examiner, an official tasked with the review of something, either for approval or for investigation to determine that what is reviewed accords with regulations or the law. Thus, inspector is often used as a police office, an inspector being charged with investigation of suspected criminal activity. Inspector may designate an official charged with examining goods or facilities, as in customs inspectors or building inspectors. Inspector may also designate an official charged with administrative oversight and conformity, as in many government agencies and military services.

**inspector general** Officer who investigates wrongdoing throughout an organization. An inspector general is an independent officer in a government department or agency who is tasked with certain annual audits, regular oversight, and ad hoc review of programs and official performance to ensure that the department or agency performs its lawful obligations and to ensure that any illegal activity is discovered and corrected. An inspector general is usually authorized to initiate civil and criminal investigations as well as administrative review.

**installment (instalment)** A component or portion of something larger. An installment is any portion of a larger whole. In the law the significance of an installment is to represent a partial performance of an obligation. Usually, an installment is a payment made on a regular basis against a long-term debt. Each payment represents partial payment of the debt, until all of the payments are made and the debt is excused. The performance of other contract obligations may occur in installments, such as in the shipment of goods of the construction of projects. The completion of each installment amounts to partial performance of the contract as a whole.

**installment contract** *See:* contract, specific contracts, installment contract (installment plan or intallment purchase or installment sale).

**installment loan** *See:* loan, installment loan.

**instant case or case at issue** *See:* case, case at bar (instant case or case at issue).

**institute** *See:* lawbook, institute.

**Institutes of Justinian** *See:* Roman law, corpus juris civilis, Institutes of Justinian (Justinian's Institutes).

## instruction

**jury instruction (charge to the jury or to charge the jury or jury charge or instruction to the jury)** Judicial directive to the jurors regarding the law or the requirements of service in the case. A jury instruction is given by the judge to the members of the jury to explain what is happening in the court, to explain the law, to explain certain aspects of the evidence, and to assist the jurors in understanding their duties in reaching a verdict. Some instructions are given at the start of a trial, others during the trial, and some at the close of the trial, which customarily include instructions regarding the law that the jurors are to apply to their understanding of the evidence they perceived during the trial in order to reach a verdict. Other instructions may be given by the judge during the jurors's deliberations.

Some instructions are given as part of the jury selection, or voir dire. Other instructions, particularly curative instructions regarding evidence and instructions regarding juror conduct, are given during the trial itself.

The parties are ordinarily required to submit a draft of instructions to the court in advance of the trial, and the judge will ordinarily inform the parties of the closing instructions the judge has selected to give, allowing the parties to object to the instructions, to negotiate what instructions will be used, and to make their record of objections for appeal, if needed. All of this is done out of the hearing of the jury.

Other than the particular customs of various jurisdictions, there is no difference between a jury instruction and a charge to the jury.

*See also:* trial, jury trial (trial by jury).

**additional instruction** An instruction given following closing instructions. An additional instruction is an instruction given by the judge to the jury following the closing or final instructions. Additional instructions are usually the judge's answer to a specific question submitted by a juror or by the foreperson, seeking a clarification of a closing instruction or further information regarding some point of law or the evidence. Additional instructions are to be given on the record following communication with counsel, who are to be given an opportunity to object before the instruction is given. Additional instructions are often given in writing by the judge for communication through the bailiff to the jury room.

**Allen charge (dynamite charge)** An instruction imploring a deadlocked jury to reach a decision. An Allen charge, which was allowed in Allen v. United States, 164 U.S. 492, 501–502 (1896), is an additional instruction given by the court to the jury after the jury has initially been instructed, instructing the jurors to continue to pursue agreement, even if the jury reports that it is potentially not going to reach a unanimous verdict. The charge usually incorporates an exhortation to the jury to keep deliberating in an attempt to reach a decision. In it the judge asks jurors favoring both sides to reevaluate their positions to be sure they have not overlooked any piece of evidence; informs the jury that regardless of the charge, they still have a right to fail to come to an agreement; and reminds the jurors that in a criminal trial, the burden of proving guilt resides with the government. The decision to give such an instruction is in the discretion of the trial judge. An Allen charge is not needed in a case in which a unanimous verdict is not required. The instruction is sometimes called a dynamite charge, owing to its ability to blast a verdict from a jury.

**argumentative instruction**  A jury instruction that seeks to sway the jury in its verdict. An argumentative instruction is a jury instruction that attempts to invade the province of the jury as the sole trier of fact, by placing emphasis on a particular fact, theory, claim, or defense in an apparent effort to sway the jury toward one verdict or another. An argumentative instruction with which the jury's verdict agrees is a reversible error.

**cautionary jury instruction (prophylactic instruction)**  An instruction to the jury regarding a possible mistake or misunderstanding in the trial. A cautionary instruction regarding a trial is a charge by the judge to the jurors to ensure that some aspect of the trial, some evidence introduced, testimony made, action involving a party or other personnel does not influence the jurors in an inappropriate way or encourage a mistaken or false impression. The most common cautionary instructions are that certain evidence is to be considered for a specified purpose and no others. An instruction that no inference may be given to a criminal defendant's failure to testify is cautionary. A prophylactic instruction is the same as a cautionary instruction.

**curative instruction**  An instruction to remedy an error in trial. A curative instruction is given to jurors by a judge during the trial following a mistake in procedure or in the management of evidence, in which the jury is told that the mistaken action, the evidence perceived, or the testimony heard is to be disregarded and forgotten or is to be used only for a limited purpose. Some mistakes or evidentiary errors are too grave to be cured by instruction, in which case — if the mistake or error is sufficiently grave and material that it might alter the outcome of the trial — the judge is required to order a mistrial.

**final jury instruction (closing instructions or instructions at end of trial or final charge to the jury)**  Instructions given to the jury at the close of the evidence. Final jury instructions are given to the jury after the close of the evidence. Final

instructions, or the final charge of the jury, are often required prior to the attorneys' closing arguments. The instructions often include a series of standard instructions regarding the role of the jury, the manner of voting for a verdict, the burden of proof, the admonition that the arguments of counsel are neither evidence nor a basis for a verdict, and the standards of law that are to be applied by the jury in order for it to determine the verdict in the case. The instructions are customarily given orally and in open court to the jurors. Written instructions were once barred from the jury room, but are now usually given in most jurisdictions upon the request of the jury.

**jury instruction conference (charge conference)**  A meeting among counsel and the court to review jury instructions before they are given. A jury instruction conference, or a charge conference, is a conference on the record in which the court and counsel for the parties consider proposed jury instructions, allowing counsel to object to proposed instruction and to negotiate alternatives. The instruction conference may be part of a pre-trial conference or held separately and, in some jurisdictions, is held only on motion of a party or the court. A failure to object to a jury instruction, which must be timely made, is usually a waiver of an objection to that instruction and thus a bar to appeal on the grounds of an error of law based upon it.

**model instruction (pattern instruction or standard instruction or suggested instruction or uniform instruction)**  A jury instruction promulgated by a court or bar for repetitive use. A model jury instruction, also called a pattern instruction or a standard instruction, is an instruction taken from a book or set of instructions that has been drafted and adopted by a jurisdiction's courts, by the bar of that jurisdiction, or by some other group. Model instructions usually set forth the legal standards to be applied in actions with given claims and given defenses, and the court in a particular case must modify the instruction to fit the circumstances of the claim or the defense raised in that case. Model instructions often are written with blanks to be filled in for this purpose. Model instructions are often promulgated in separate books of civil instructions and of criminal instructions.

Model instructions are most often used during jury selection and in the jury's final instructions prior to closing argument. Model instructions are usually supplemented with special instructions.

**ostrich instruction (conscious avoidance)**  A jury may find that deliberate ignorance is a form of knowledge. The ostrich instruction, or the conscious avoidance instruction, is a instruction from the judge to the jury allowing jurors to impute knowledge to a party from evidence demonstrating the party acted deliberately to avoid the knowledge of which the defendant is charged. The term comes from the myth that an ostrich will bury its head in the sand at the onset of danger.

*See also:* knowledge, constructive knowledge, willful blindness (conscious avoidance or willful ignorance or deliberate ignorance).

**peremptory instruction (mandatory instruction)** An instruction to give a particular verdict if a particular fact is found. A peremptory instruction, also called a mandatory instruction, instructs the jurors to reach a particular verdict if they find that particular question of fact in a given way based on the evidence. Peremptory instructions may not require the jurors to find the facts as suggested, but if they do so find the facts, the instructions require a given verdict. The jurors, however, may choose not to render that verdict regardless of the instruction to do so.

*See also:* peremptory (peremptorily); jury, jury selection, juror challenge, peremptory challenge.

**sentencing instruction** An instruction to a jury in a criminal trial on how to assess a sentence. A sentencing instruction in a criminal trial is given to a jury at the close of the evidence. In most trials, the sentencing instruction will be contingent upon the finding of guilt on one or more of the counts charged. If the trial is a bifurcated trial with a guilt phase and a sentencing phase, the sentencing instructions follow the close of evidence in the sentencing phase.

*See also:* sentence.

**single-juror instruction (unanimity instruction)** An instruction that every juror must independently agree with the verdict. A single juror instruction is a form of the voting instruction. In cases in which jurors must reach a unanimous verdict, particularly in criminal cases, the court may instruct the jury not only that it must reach unanimity in its verdict but also may not reach a verdict if a single juror dissents from it.

*See also:* jury | agreement and unanimity.

**instrument** The document in which any legal arrangement is reduced to writing. An instrument is a document, or an electronic document, that serves as a memorial of the legal ordering of affairs that it represents. A contract, gift, trust, agency relationship, lease, and many other legal relationships may be created by conduct but memorialized in an instrument by which the relationship is given detail. Some legal relationships cannot exist unless they are committed into an instrument, such as a deed, a last will and testament, or a negotiable instrument. The laws of some jurisdictions allow an instrument to exist in an electronic form, whether stored, displayed, or transmitted, with protocols for signing the instrument and for ensuring the instrument's security from destruction or alteration. Such an allowance is not, as of 2011, universal in the United States, and some instruments must be committed in physical form to paper, parchment, or some other writing media.

**instrument of ratification** *See:* treaty, ratification of a treaty, instrument of ratification.

**negotiable instrument** An instrument recording a promise or order to pay money to the bearer or promisee. A negotiable instrument is one of several forms of commercial paper that allow the transfer of money by recording a promise or order to pay money, either to the bearer of the paper or to the promisee whose name is recorded on the paper. A check is the most common form of negotiable instrument, but the category includes a variety of other instruments, including promissory notes and bills of exchange (of which checks are the primary example). The hallmarks of a negotiable instrument are that it is an instrument (whether in paper or electronic form) that includes a promise or an order to pay a fixed sum of money, that is payable on demand from the time it is issued or received by a holder until the lapse of a definite time, and that requires nothing more from the payee bearer or order promissee than to present the instrument to a payor.

The Uniform Commercial Code governs negotiable instruments in the various states of the United States. In other jurisdictions, the law of negotiable instruments reaches also to instruments that are separately regulated under the UCC, especially mortgages (in UCC Article 3 apart from negotiable instruments), letters of credit (UCC Article 5), bills of lading (UCC Article 7), and stocks and bonds (in UCC Article 8).

*See also:* check (cheque); bill, bill of exchange; instrument, negotiable instrument, order instrument (payable to order or pay to the order of).

**bearer instrument (payable to bearer)** A negotiable instrument to be paid to anyone presenting it. A bearer instrument is any commercial paper that is endorsed "payable to bearer" or "payable to the order of bearer" or payable to "cash," which amount to an instruction that the instrument is to be honored by payment to any person who presents it for payment. The negotiation of the instrument for payment requires delivery.

*See also:* bearer; instrument, negotiable instrument, order instrument (payable to order or pay to the order of).

**honor of a negotiable instrument** Payment on a negotiable instrument presented to the payor, the drawee, or a third party. To honor a negotiable instrument is to perform the instruction on the instrument, which varies somewhat according to the form of the instrument. For a bill of exchange, such as a check, to honor it is to accept the check and to pay the amount ordered or required to be paid.

**dishonor** A refusal to honor an instrument presented for payment or settlement. Dishonor is the refusal to honor an instrument. A bank or other institution may elect to dishonor an instrument presented by the appropriate party (the bearer of a bearer instrument, the drawee of a an order, or a holder in due course) if the institution has a defense to the honoring of the instrument. Defenses are either real, such as fraud or forgery, or personal, such as insolvency of the holder of the account on which the instrument is drawn. The bank must give timely notice of dishonor to the party who presents it.

If an instrument is honored within the time allowed in its jurisdiction, and the institution becomes aware of a defense that would have allowed it to dishonor the instrument, the instrument may be dishonored and the presenter may be issued a charge back for the amount of the instrument. Wrongful dishonor gives rise to a claim not only for the value of the instrument but also for damages suffered as a result of the wrongful dishonor.

**order instrument (payable to order or pay to the order of)** A negotiable instrument endorsed "pay to the order of." An order is an instruction written on an instrument that makes that instrument payable to the person or entity noted. A typical order is "pay to the order of" a named payee or to bearer. The presence of this order in writing on the instrument has the effect of making the instrument a negotiable instrument. Use of one or the other of the words "order" or "bearer" are essential to the negotiability of an instrument (at least of all instruments other than checks), and small variations of wording do not alter the effect as long as the intent is to make the instrument payable to order. An order to pay that does not specify the payee is payable to the bearer. The instruction must be written at the time the instrument is first issued or at the time its first a holder takes possession of it.

*See also:* bearer; instrument, negotiable instrument.

**presentment of a negotiable instrument (presentation of a check)** The demand to pay an instrument. Presentment is the formal presentation of a negotiable instrument made with the demand of a person who is entitled to enforce a negotiable instrument to the bank or entity on which it is drawn, requiring the bank or entity to honor the instrument and pay its value. The instrument must be indorsed, and presentment must be made according to the terms of the instrument itself. The bank or entity may return an instrument without dishonoring it if either condition is not fulfilled. If the instrument meets both conditions and is not paid on the day of its presentment (or the day following), the instrument is dishonored.

*See also:* presentment.

**instrumentality** A means by which something is accomplished. An instrumentality is the means by which something is achieved or performed. There are several distinct meanings in law, the oldest of which is effectively the same as tools or machinery; the devices by which things are done.

From this sense, the instrumentality of a truck, bridge, road, canal, ship, dock, warehouse, airport, or any other means for the transportation or shipment of goods is an instrumentality of commerce, and usually therefore an instrumentality of interstate commerce, thus allowing federal regulation under the Commerce Clause.

An instrumentality of a corporation is an office, contractor, or other entity or person who is engaged in activities on its behalf. Likewise, an instrumentality of a state is any enterprise or person who is acting either under the direction of that state or by arrangement with the state to perform functions on its behalf.

**instrumentality rule** *See:* veil, corporate veil, alter-ego rule (instrumentality rule).

**dangerous instrumentality** A condition of some property that poses unusual danger to others. A dangerous instrumentality is any condition of land or a chattel that poses an unusual risk of harm or danger. As a matter of tort, a dangerous instrumentality is likely to require that the danger not be apparent, and the heightened duty of care of the person responsible for a dangerous instrumentality includes not only the obligations to maintain the instrumentality in such a manner as to minimize its risk to others, such as in keeping children away from it, but also to warn others of its existence.

Some things are inherently dangerous, such as a stick of dynamite or a firearm, and such things are sometimes labeled inherently dangerous. The use of an inherently dangerous instrumentality in the commission of a crime may be the basis for an increased sentence.

Other things are only dangerous in a particular context or under certain conditions, though in such a context or condition, they are dangerous instrumentalities. Caselaw varies among jurisdictions as to whether specific hazards, notoriously varying concerning swimming pools and waters, are or are not dangerous instrumentalities as a matter of law. In general, though, whether a particular instrumentality is dangerous is a question of fact.

**insurance** Contract by which an insurer promises to pay an indemnity or benefit after a specified event, in return for a premium paid by the insured. Insurance is a contractual relationship under which an insured pays a premium of money to an insurer, and the insurer promises either to indemnify the insured for losses the insured suffers from certain specified contingencies or perils (as in a health insurance policy, an auto policy, homeowner's policy or commercial general liability policy), or to pay to a named beneficiary of the policy a specified amount or determinable benefit in connection with ascertained risk contingencies (as in a life insurance policy), or to act as a surety in the event the insured becomes liable to a third party (as in the liability coverage of an auto policy, a homeowner's policy, or a commercial general liability policy), or otherwise to assure against a specified risk. The contract of insurance is manifest in the insurance policy.

The fundamental purpose of insurance is to provide risk management through contract. The insured pays a premium to the insurer. The premium charged by the insurer is set an amount that is (or at least is supposed to be) statistically likely to be an amount of money that is marginally less than the average of all claims and benefits made against policies like the contract in question. The insurer can allocate the risk among a great number of similar contracts, collecting premiums from all, out of which a pool is created from which payments are made to some in response to claims. The pool itself may be additionally insured through reinsurance, which pools risk among pools held by various insurers.

The system of insurance still has risks inherent in it, which are only somewhat moderated by regulation. As long as the premiums are set to an appropriate price for risk, there is good faith by both the insureds and the insurer, and no catastrophe befalls the system by which a host of claims are made faster than the pool can absorb them, since the insurance pool is capable of paying the indemnity or benefit required for each claim made. The regulation of insurance in the United States, with the exception of pension funds governed by ERISA and a few other similar statutes, is largely done by the various states.

*See also:* indemnity (indemnification or indemnify or indemnitor or indemitee).

**insurable interest**   *See:* interest, insurable interest.

**insurance adjuster**   *See:* insurer, insurance personnel, insurance adjuster.

**insurance agent**   *See:* insurer, insurance personnel, insurance agent.

**insurance appraisal**   *See:* appraisal, insurance appraisal.

**insurance appraiser**   *See:* insurer, insurance personnel, insurance appraiser.

**insurance beneficiary**   *See:* beneficiary, insurance beneficiary.

**insurance broker**   *See:* insurer, insurance personnel, insurance broker.

**insurance carrier or insurance company**   *See:* insurer (insurance carrier or insurance company).

**insurance claim**   *See:* claim, insurance claim.

**insurance loss**   *See:* loss, insurance loss, known loss (known-loss rule); loss, insurance loss (loss insured).

**insurance personnel**   *See:* insurer, insurance personnel, insurance broker; insurer, insurance personnel, insurance appraiser; insurer, insurance personnel, insurance agent; insurer, insurance personnel, insurance adjuster.

**insurance premium**   *See:* premium, insurance premium.

**insurance trust**   *See:* trust, insurance trust.

**category of insurance**

**automobile insurance**   Insurance covering damage to one's vehicle and liability coverage for damage or injury to others. Automobile insurance is usually both property and liability insurance for damage or loss related to an automobile, particularly a collision or theft involving the automobile. Policy coverage is usually based on collision or incident, and coverage usually does not extend to ordinary maintenance or wear to the automobile. Most states require automobile insurance of drivers licensed in that state.

**no-fault insurance**   An insurance scheme in which risks and claims are assessed without regard to fault. No-fault insurance is a scheme of insurance in which fault is immaterial to a claim or its indemnity. No-fault insurance is a form of first-party insurance, as each assured is indemnified by its own insurer. The most common form of no-fault insurance is automobile insurance, in which the insureds pay into a common risk pool, from which claims of damage by each insured and claims of indemnity to non-members is paid. Twelve states have either optional or compulsory no-fault auto insurance as of 2011. No-fault policies are frequently bundled with underinsured or uninsured motorist coverage.

**disability insurance**   Insurance covering expenses and lost of income due to a disability. Disability insurance protects the income of the insured from loss due to disability. A disability is defined as the inability to engage in a physical or mental impairment that substantially limits one or more of the major life activities of the insured.

**errors and omissions insurance (E&O) (professional services insurance or lawyer**   Insurance with coverage against damage from errors or omissions in rendering professional services. Errors and omissions insurance provides coverage for a professional against damages suffered by others as a result of the professional's performance of services or provision of advice to a client or to another with a right to rely on it. A common example of errors and omissions insurance is the policy of a lawyer against claims for malpractice. E&O policies are often supplemental to a comprehensive general liability insurance policy.

*See also:* malpractice.

**health insurance**   Insurance against medical expenses. Health insurance is medical insurance, insurance covering the expenses for medical care incurred by the assured, not only in the event of an illness or accident but also for preventive medicine. Health insurance has many forms, including policies with coverage specifically for hospitalization or minor treatments.

The insurer of a health insurance plan may be a private insurance company, a public/private entity such as Blue Cross Blue Shield, an ERISA plan managed by an employer (often in collaboration with an insurance company), or a government entity, such as Medicare and Medicaid. Various plans are structured to assure medical services in different ways, some specifying a facility or staff that provides covered treatment, many requiring an assured to participate in a health management organization, but others allowing the assured to select any available health care provider.

**liability insurance (third-party insurance)** Insurance against claims brought against the insured by a third party. Liability insurance provides coverage for specified categories of claims brought against the policyholder by a third party. The most common coverage is for claims bought by third parties who claim to have been injured as a result of the negligence of one of the assureds under the policy. Liability insurance is also commonly called "third-party" insurance.

Liability policies usually provide an indemnity clause, by which the insurer promises to pay a valid claim, as well as a defense clause, by which the insurer promises to defend an action against an assured arising from a covered claim, and a subrogation clause, in which the assured agrees to assign to the insurer rights of action arising that the assured might otherwise bring related to a covered claim that is paid by the insurer.

**commercial general liability (C.G.L. or CGL)** Insurance for liability and property risks for commercial business operations. Commercial general liability insurance provides coverage to business and commercial entities for specified categories of claim arising from injury to property and from liability for claims brought against an assured by a third party. The most common forms of liability coverage are for bodily injury, non-bodily personal injury (such as libel), and advertising injury, whether the claim arises form conduct of the entity or an employee. CGL policies are sometimes called business liability policies.

**homeowner's policy** Insurance for damage to property of, or liability from, a home. Homeowner's insurance is the primary form of property and liability for non-commercial property owners who have a residence on the property. The coverage of homeowner's policies varies but usually include coverage for damage to property, furnishings, and personal property in a home caused by fire, theft, storm, lightning and accident, including losing objects of value, as well as liability to guests on the premises and, in some rare instances, off of the premises.

**life insurance** Insurance that pays a benefit at the death of the assured. Life insurance is insurance under which the insurer pays a beneficiary or beneficiaries a specific amount of money upon the death of the assured. Life insurance may be issued to assure the life of someone other than the insured, as when a corporation insures the life of an officer. Life insurance is one of the oldest forms of commercial insurance, dating back to at least seventeenth-century England. Policies vary in the structure of premiums and benefits, and three forms of life insurance sold in the United States

today include term life insurance, whole life insurance, and universal life insurance.

**term life insurance (term assurance)** Insurance providing a specified death benefit during the term the policy is in force. Term life insurance provides for a specified death benefit for the term of the policy, which is usually on a year-to-year basis and dependent on payment of premiums to the insurer during each term. Typically, term life insurance is "guaranteed renewable," meaning that the insured has the option of deciding whether to continue paying premiums and thereby keeping the policy in force, and "natural premium," meaning that the premiums increase with advancing age according to the increased chance of death. Level term life insurance has an assurance that premiums will not increase annually but in longer increments, usually in five- or ten-year steps. Term insurance builds no cash value, as do whole or universal life insurance.

**universal life insurance** Life insurance with adjustable premiums and benefits. Universal life insurance has a risk component and a savings component and pays a specified benefit at the death of the assured. Each periodic premium is allocated by the insurer between a cost of insurance charge and a cash remainder, on which the insurer will pay interest. Universal life allows for changes in terms over the life of the policy, allowing the insured to adjust both premium payment amounts and the death benefit.

**whole life insurance (straight life insurance or ordinary life insurance)** Life insurance with a death benefit and savings element. Whole life insurance provides a fixed death benefit with a savings component, which are structured so that premiums remain constant over the projected course of the policy. In whole life insurance, the premiums paid in the early years of the policy exceed what is necessary to provide the term life insurance benefit, so the policy builds up a reserve that is applied to the term life insurance benefit later in life. If the policy is canceled early, the insured may recover some of the reserve, the amount recoverable being the "surrender value" of the policy.

**marine insurance** Insurance providing indemnity for loss or damage to a vessel, personnel, or cargo. Marine insurance covers loss to the assured and indemnity for claims against the assured by third parties resulting from the operation of a vessel, or damages suffered by its crew, passengers, or cargo. Policy coverage by marine insurance policies varies greatly, depending upon the issuance to cover a voyage, period of time, the vessel generally, or the cargo. In the United States, the construction and enforcement of marine insurance policies is ordinarily a matter of state and not federal law, regardless of the forum in which an action arises.

**Inchmaree clause (additional perils clause)** Marine insurance coverage for specified risks to the vessel. An Inchmaree clause is a rider or specific coverage provision that specifies coverage for perils beyond the ordinary perils of the sea, which are listed in the clause and usually include coverage for damage caused by boiler, shaft, or other mechanical failures, by latent defects in the ship's equipment or machinery, or by faults or errors in the navigation or management of the ship. Exclusions and exceptions adding or removing risks are common. The clause was introduced after the 1887 case arising from the loss of the Inchmaree in which "all other perils" was construed not to include such risks, Thames & Mersey Marine Insurance Co. v. Hamilton, Fraser & Co., 12 App. Cas. 484 (H.L. 1887).

**mortgage insurance (mortgage indemnity guaranty)** Insurance against default by the borrower under a mortgage loan. Mortgage insurance is insurance procured by a mortgage lender against losses by the lender that might be incurred in the event of the default, death, or disability of the borrower under the mortgage loan. Mortgage insurance is typically required when a borrower has less than twenty percent equity in the mortgaged asset. The premium for mortgage insurance is often always prepaid by the borrower at the time of the issuance of the policy, usually at a rate equal to 1.75 percent of the amount of the loan if it is insured by a public agency or a rate up to 6 percent through private insurers. Not all mortgage insurance is prepaid by the borrower, however, and policies vary between borrower-paid private mortgage insurance, or BPMI, and lender-paid private mortgage insurance, or LPMI, for which the premium is often incorporated into the interest charged to the borrower by the lender.

**property insurance** Insurance covering damage to the property of the assured. Property insurance provides coverage for damage suffered to the property of the assured. Although automobile policies are a form of property insurance, the term "property insurance" usually means coverage for damage to buildings, their contents and goods caused by fire, earthquake, lightning, wind, and water. Policies vary considerably in the risks covered, and most property policies do not cover damage from flood. Many common forms of property insurance are now consolidated with liability insurance, such as homeowner's insurance and commercial general liability insurance.

Property insurance is the oldest form of commercial insurance, dating back to marine insurance sold in the late Middle Ages. From marine insurance, property insurance spread inland, first covering goods destined for a sea voyage against the possibility of fire in the warehouse, then spreading to cover buildings and their contents against fire, more broadly. The property insurance market in the United States expanded rapidly in the mid-nineteenth century, although the market suffered from periodic insolvencies until insurers recognized the importance of diversifying geographically, and state insurance regulators improved their ability to identify and prevent financial weakness.

**alienated premises clause (alienation clause)** Exclusion of coverage for damage to property following its alienation by the assured. An alienated premises clause limits coverage of a property policy to property under the ownership or control of the assured at the time of an occurence. Even in occurrence-based insurance policies, the alienation clause bars coverage for an occurrence affecting the property after it is alienated.

**coinsurance** The division of risk between insurer and insured or among several insurers. Coinsurance refers to the division of a single risk among more than one party, in the United States, meaning a risk shared between the insurer and the insured. A common form of coinsurance are the deductible amount in property policies and automobile policies and the patient co-payment or "co-pay" amount in health and pharmaceutical policies. Other forms include clauses in policies that increase the required deductible or self-insurance of the policy-holder if the holder under-reports the risk of loss or value of insured property.

In international and maritime insurance, coinsurance refers to a form of reinsurance, in which a single risk is placed among several insurers, which bundle the risk through joint underwriting of a policy managed by a lead office, or ceding company.

*See also:* insurance, reinsurance (re-insurance or reinsure).

**compulsory insurance** Insurance required by law. Compulsory insurance is required by law of individuals or entities engaged in particular activities. Common examples include automobile liability insurance and worker's compensation insurance.

**group insurance** Insurance procured by a single entity to cover each member of a group of individuals. Group insurance is provided by an insurer to members of a group at the direction of a central entity. Group insurance is often offered through a company as the central entity administering the policy on behalf of an insurer for its employees who are the insureds. The insureds are the members of the group, and the central entity is treated as an agent of the insurer in administering the policy. The individuals are usually not provided a copy of the master policy but only a certificate of insurance.

**incontestability clause (incontestible)** Clause limiting insurer's defenses after the policy has been in force a certain time. An incontestability clause in an insurance contract puts a time limit on the insurer to cancel a policy or to challenge the validity of a statement made on an application by the insured. A basis for the rejection of a claim, which would also be a defense to a suit brought to enforce the contract and require payment of a claim, that is based upon a misstatement by the insured on the application or on a condition to entry into the contract, is barred once the time in an incontestability clause has run, thus making the policy incontestable by the insurer on the specified grounds.

**facility of payment clause** Clause allowing insurer to pay proceeds to non-policyholder. A facility of payment clause in an insurance policy is an appointment by the insured directing the the insurer to pay the proceeds of the policy to a designated beneficiary. A facility of payment clause is common in life insurance policies, allowing payment directly to beneficiaries rather than to the decedent's estate.

**insurance claim** An assured's application for benefits under an insurance contract. An insurance claim is a claim to be paid benefits, submitted by or on behalf of a person or entity insured under an insurance policy or contract, asserting that some condition in the contract has been satisfied and requesting the insurer to pay a benefit that is due upon the satisfaction of that condition. The insured, the beneficiary, or a representative of either, such as the executor of an estate, presents the claim. The insurance company will then have the claim assessed and either honor it and pay out the benefit or deny it. A claim made in bad faith may amount to fraud, but a denial made in bad faith may give rise to a distinct cause of action for bad faith denial of an insurance claim.

*See also:* insurance, insurance claim, denial of claim, bad faith denial (denial in bad faith or wrongful refusal or tortious denial of benefits).

**denial of insurance claim (denial of claim)** An insurer's failure to pay or defend after a claim is made on a policy. A denial of an insurance claim is an insurer's failure to pay a benefit or indemnity or to defend an action against an assured or to provide another benefit expressly provided in a policy when a claim is presented by an assured. A denial of an insurance claim may be valid if the claim does not conform to the policy, particularly by being outside the scope of coverage or by being filed later than the policy allows. Even so, in most jurisdictions, a denial of insurance is unreasonable, despite being valid, if it is made only following an unreasonable delay or made with no explanation of the basis for denial. A denial that is not made for a reason justified by the express terms of the policy is a wrongful denial, and if it is made knowing that there is no reason for denial, it is made in bad faith.

**bad faith denial (denial in bad faith or wrongful refusal or tortious denial of benefits)** The tort of denying a valid insurance claim for indemnity or defense. Bad faith denial of an insurance claim is a tort under state law committed by an insurer through conduct related to the denial of a valid claim for benefits, whether for payment of indemnity or for defense or other assured services. Various jurisdictions label the tort wrongful denial or tortious denial. Cases present two essential theories for a claim of bad faith denial, although they often have overlapping factual circumstances. In general, a denial that has no arguable basis under the plan or policy is a denial in bad faith. The other primary theory is that the bad faith is a tort independent of a breach of the contract. The two approaches, however, do seem to be satisfied with similar evidence, in that the requirement of independence seems provable if there is evidence that the denial was made by agents or officers of the insurer who knew of no arguable or reasonable basis for the denial at the time. Likewise, evidence that the denial was made for reasons unconnected to the validity or invalidity of the claim but for an unrelated purpose, such as to harm the claimant or generically as a business decision to benefit the insurer, would also amount to bad faith. On the other hand, a denial that is improper, but that is at least based in good faith on a reasonable or arguable basis, is a wrongful denial rather than a bad faith denial.

A plaintiff who proves bad faith denial may recover not only compensatory damages but also punitive or exemplary damages.

*See also:* insurance, insurance claim.

**wrongful denial of benefits** The contract action for denial of an insurance claim owed payment under a policy. Wrongful denial of benefits is a breach of contract under an insurance policy, committed by an insurer that denies a claim that is valid under the insurance policy or plan under which it is made. The action may be brought only in contract, as long as there is an arguable or reasonable basis for the insurer to have denied the claim. A plaintiff, usually an assured, a beneficiary, an insured, or a plan representative, may seek compensatory damages and, in most cases, interest and attorney's fees. No punitive or exemplary damages are usually available for wrongful denial, as they might be for bad faith denial.

ERISA allows a specific claim for wrongful denial of benefits in U.S. district court, which is limited to recovery by participants to the amount that should have been distributed and attorney's fees, or by the plan to the amount that should have been distributed, attorney's fees, interest, and "such other legal or equitable relief as the court deems appropriate."

**insurance adjustment** The sum of money the insurance company is willing to pay a claimant. An insurance adjustment states the value an insurance company places on a claim, taking into consideration the money owed to the claimant and the value of avoiding legal proceedings.

**subrogation (subrogation clause)**  Assignment of a claim or action in return for indemnity. Subrogation is the means by which an indemnitor assumes the rights of an indemnitee against the party whose damage to or claims against the indemnitee gave rise to the indemnity. Subrogation may arise as a matter of a subrogation clause, as in an insurance policy or other contract, or it may arise as an equitable remedy to prevent unjust enrichment of the indemnitee. In its most common form, subrogation allows an insurance company to "stand in the shoes" of its assured to collect from the tortfeasor whose harm to the assured caused the insurer to indemnify the assured. Because the insurer stands in the shoes of the assured, subrogation usually provides the insurer the same but no greater rights against the tortfeasor than the assured as plaintiff would have had.

See also: subrogation.

**total loss (total)**  Property damage so great the insurer pays the whole value of a property policy. A total loss is a loss claimed under a property insurance policy in which the damage to the insured property is sufficiently great in value or kind that the insurer may elect to pay the full amount of the insured value of the property. A total loss is defined in the policy. Most often a total loss results when the cost of repair or replacement is greater than the market value of the property, although it also occurs when the insured property becomes so damaged that it loses its specific character and is so disintegrated that the property can no longer be designated as the structure which was insured. A total loss can occur regardless of whether some parts of the insured property remain usable. In a marine policy or automobile policy, a total loss usually results in a transfer by abandonment of the property to the insurer; in a property policy, a total loss usually results in a liquidated demand for the full value of the policy but the property is not abandoned to the insurer.

**insurance coverage (coverage or cover or covered claim)**  The specific or general risks or contingencies that give rise to claims under an insurance policy. Insurance coverage is the scope of the risks that are assured in a policy, or the whole of the potential claims that the insured or other parties might make against the insurer on the basis of a given policy. If a particular risk is covered, and the risk becomes manifest through an occurrence, the insurer must pay a claim for damage suffered. The extent of coverage is the extent of the risk assumed by the insurer. Put another way, the extent of the coverage is the whole set of possible claims that may be honored, limited by the value of the coverage as a whole.

Coverage in a given category of policy varies greatly according to the structure of the policy: coverage is described, but from what is described certain risks may be excluded, but from what is excluded, certain risks may be excepted. Further, additional coverage may be provided in riders or amendments or additional coverage, each of which may be subject to their own exclusions or exceptions. Some riders or additional coverage may insure against risks that were excluded in the primary coverage. The premium is assessed as a function of the measure of all of the risks in the coverage.

**escape clause (other insurance clause)**  Insurance clause avoiding insurer liability when other insurance may cover a claim. An escape clause is language in an insurance policy that purports to absolve the insurer from liability in the event the insured has "other insurance" that covers the event that occurred spurring liability. Courts construe escape clauses very narrowly and distinguish the duty to pay claims from the duty to defend as affected by such clauses.

**pro rata clause**  Provision limiting liability to an insurer's respective share of risk. A pro rata clause in an insurance policy limits the liability of the insurer to its respective share of any loss relative to other coverage of the assured with other insurers. Pro rata clauses are particularly common in large insurance policies that must be spread between multiple companies in order to provide the requisite loss coverage. In these situations, one insurance company will only be liable for the amount of the loss they agreed to participate in based on the happening of a certain event.

**stop-loss insurance**  Insurance of a self-insurance fund against a very large loss. Stop-loss insurance is coverage for a self-insurance plan that provides indemnity against unexpectedly high losses resulting from claims against the self-insurance pool or fund. As a result, stop-loss insurance often has a very high deductible, or a high threshold for self-insurance.

**insurance policy (insurance contract or insurance agreement)**  A contract providing insurance from an insurer to an insured. An insurance policy is a written contract between an insurer and the insured, by which the insurer promises to indemnify the insured for any losses suffered by the insured within the scope of coverage of the policy if the insured makes a timely claim to the insurer, and for which the insured pays a premium or enters a security for the payments of the premium over the life of the policy. Insurance policies are interpreted contra proferentem, and all ambiguities in interpretation are to be resolved against the insurer.

See also: contract, contract interpretation, contract ambiguity, contra proferentem (against the drafter).

**binder policy**  Provisional insurance in force during the establishment of a formal policy. A binder is an insurance policy that provides temporary protection for the insured until the insurer makes final the insured's formal policy.

**no action clause**   Provision limiting liability of an insurer until a final judgment against an assured is given. A no action clause in an insurance agreement allows an insurer to avoid payment on a claim for indemnity to an assured unless and until there is a final judgment imposing liability. A no action clause is usually limited to the duty to pay claims, and unless the language of the policy is clear, does not affect a duty to defend if such a duty is otherwise within the scope of the policy.

**policy exclusion**   A limitation of certain risks from the scope of coverage of a policy. A policy exclusion is a qualification from coverage specified by the coverage provisions of the insurance policy, such that the risks specified in the exclusion are outside the scope of coverage, notwithstanding the language of the coverage clauses. In an ambiguous case, an exclusion is to be narrowly construed.

*See also:* exclusion (exclude).

**exception to the exclusion**   An assurance of certain risks that are otherwise limited from coverage in the policy. An exception to a policy exclusion is a qualification from excluded coverage, so that the excepted claims or risks are covered under the policy, notwithstanding the language of the exclusion clauses. In an ambiguous case, an exclusion is to be broadly construed.

**policy limit**   The monetary extent of the policy's coverage. The policy limit is the full value that the insurer may be called upon by the insured to expend in payment, judgment, or settlement of claims made under the policy. Unless specifically expressed in the contract, the policy limit is not affected by expenses for the legal defense of, or in making claims related to, the insured.

*See also:* deductible, deductible as insurance claim offset.

**policy rider**   A policy amendment. A policy rider is a provision that is added to an insurance policy that either limits or expands the coverage or benefits provided under the policy. A rider is often a standard form amendment assuring a specific risk that is not usually within the scope of a form policy, such as a homeowner's policy or comprehensive general liability (CGL) policy.

**paid-up insurance**   Insurance policy for which all premiums have been paid. Paid-up insurance is an insurance policy in which all required premiums have been paid, either through payment at the time the policy is entered, as is the case for most mortgage insurance, or through periodic payments until the risk pool for the policy is fully funded. Under the terms of some life insurance policies, the insured then stops making payments. Under others, an insured may elect then to stop payment or to continue payment to increase the value or benefit of the policy. Under others, the insured is

expected to continue making payments to increase the value or benefit.

**McCarran-Ferguson Act**   The business of insurance is subject not to federal but to state regulation. The McCarran-Ferguson Act, codified at 15 U.S.C. § 1011, was passed in 1945, preserving to each state the power of regulation over insurance issued in that state. The act effectively overturned the U.S. Supreme Court's opinion in U.S. v. South-Eastern Underwriters, 322 U.S. 533 (1944), holding that the insurance business is a matter of interstate commerce and so regulable by the Congress. Even so, the Court's opinion would allow Congress to repeal McCarran-Ferguson or to impliedly repeal it by regulation.

**reinsurance (re-insurance or reinsure)**   Insurance taken by an insurer to insure itself against claims. Reinsurance is a means of spreading risk held by a single, primary insurer into a larger pool of insurance, in which the primary insurer purchases insurance from a re-insurer against claims made by the insureds of the primary insurer, thereby transferring risk to the reinsurance. In the event of claims that meet the definitions that trigger the reinsurance policy, the reinsurer indemnifies the primary insurer.

The primary insurer is also called the original insurer, the ceding insurer or ceding company, or the cedant. The reinsurer is also called the assuming company. Reinsurance is sometimes termed "coinsurance," particularly if the reinsurer receives a proportion of the premium equivalent to a share of the risk.

*See also:* insurance, coinsurance.

**self insurance**   *See:* risk, risk retention (risk retention group).

**insured (assured)**   Person or entity that procures insurance. An insured is a person or entity that procures a policy of insurance. The insured accepts the duty to pay the premium and also to represent to the insurer in good faith all of the facts and circumstances surrounding the insurance contract so that both parties may make an informed decision about the amount and value of the risk at stake. The insured is not necessarily the assured of a property or indemnity policy, and the insured is rarely a beneficiary of a life policy. The insured must, however, have an insurable interest in property subject to insurance and a sufficient relationship with the assured to justify a life insurance policy for another person to satisfy the requirements of public policy. In general, when a court speaks of an insured, however, there is little or no difference between the insured and an assured.

*See also:* assured.

**additional insured**   A party assured other than the primary insured party. An additional insured is a party who is assured under an insurance policy without being the primary insured party. In many instances, the additional insured is named in the policy. Even so, an additional insured is also a party for whom assurance arises either by reference in the policy, such as a member of a family, or by an agreement by the named insured to add the name of the additional insured.

**named insured** The person or entity named as the insured in the policy. A named insured is a person or entity whose name appears in the insurance policy. The named insureds may not be the only insured parties, there being the possibility of additional insureds.

**insurer (insurance carrier or insurance company)**
An insurance provider. An insurer is either a self-insurer or an insurance carrier. A self-insurer maintains a risk pool that it manages for itself in order to satisfy claims made against it or to make good its own losses. A carrier is a provider of insurance that issues or underwrites insurance policies for others. A carrier may be an insurance company, a public insurance fund, or a compensation carrier, which underwrites policies of worker's compensation insurance. Insurers, including self-insurers of employee risks, are regulated by the states in which they are headquartered and in which they issue insurance policies.

**insurance adjuster** Insurer's representative who places an initial value on a pending claim. An insurance adjuster is an employee or contractor of the insurer who evaluates a claim for indemnity to assess the value of a loss, the risks and potential liabilities contingent on it, and sets an initial valuation of the valid claim that is owed. An adjuster is allowed to consider the risks and costs of litigation but is to act on the value of the claim as determined by the policy language under which the claim is brought and the available evidence related to the loss. An independent adjuster is a contractor who performs adjustment for one or more insurers, and an independent adjuster owes a duty of care in each claim to the insurer whose claim is adjusted.

**insurance agent** One who sells insurance to assureds for an insurer. An insurance agent acts on behalf of an insurance company to procure customers, to negotiate polices, and to enter insurance contracts. Insurance agents are either exclusive, representing a single carrier, or they are non-exclusive, having an arrangement with several carriers for whom they place polices. Agents are considered agents of the insurer and not of the insured. Agents in most states must pass certifying exams in order to engage in the placement of insurance policies.

**insurance appraiser** An appraiser specializing in the appraisal of insurance losses. An insurance appraiser specializes in valuing the cost of repair or replacement of goods, such as a car that has been damaged in a wreck, or estimates the costs of recovery following property losses.

*See also:* appraiser.

**insurance broker** One who arranges insurance for others from various insurers. An insurance broker is an intermediary between those seeking insurance and various insurance companies. A broker differs from an insurance agent, in that the agent acts for one insurer as its agent, while a broker is independent of the several insurers with and for whom it negotiates. A broker may therefore function as an agent of the insured rather than the insurer.

Note: In other insurance organizations in England, notably in Lloyd's, a broker may be an agent of the insurer.

*See also:* insurer, insurers, Lloyd's of London (Lloyd's Policy); broker (brokerage).

**Lloyd's of London (Lloyd's Policy)** A market of syndicates of insurance brokers sharing common offices and services. Lloyd's, or Lloyd's of London, is a market for insurance that has grown from the placement of maritime insurance contracts among underwriters and factors in the coffee house of Edward Lloyd in London. Lloyd's is a complex institution, housing a network of syndicates, partnerships, and companies that engage in the placement of insurance policies and that manages several common services. An insurance policy placed with a Lloyd's broker or service company, who places a policy through one or more managing agents among a number of syndicates or corporate groups and individuals, allocated the risk of the policy and the rights to premiums from it among them.

*See also:* insurer, insurance personnel, insurance broker.

**title company** *See:* title, title company (title plant).

**insurgency (insurgent)** A group seeking to overturn an established government or order. An insurgency is a group or movement that seeks to remove an established government or order, and an insurgent is a member of such a group. Although older cases distinguished among a recognized movement of independence, an unrecognized insurgent movement considered favorably by foreign states, and a disfavored rebellion, this distinction seems to have been lost in contemporary usage, and an insurgent and a rebel seem to be fully equated. Metaphorically, any person seeking to change an established organization, such as a stockholder seeking to overthrow the board of corporate directors, is also described as an insurgent.

**insurrection** A domestic attempt of revolution. Insurrection is a rebellion of the citizens or subjects of a country against its government, in an attempt through violence or force of arms to supplant the lawfully constituted government with another.

Article One, section eight of the Constitution provides Congress with the power "[t]o provide for calling for the Militia to execute the Laws of the Union or to suppress Insurrections or repel Invasions." Accordingly, the Insurrection Act of 1807 as amended has accorded the president the authority to call out the militia or national guard of a state faced with insurrection or interference with federal law when the governor or legislature of a state requests this be done. Further, section three of the Fourteenth Amendment bars officers of the United States or any state who take part in insurrection or rebellion from holding civil office unless Congress removes their disability.

*See also:* treason (traitor).

**intangible asset**  *See:* asset, intangible asset.

**intangible property or intangibles**  *See:* property, forms of property, incorporeal property (intangible property or intangibles).

**integrated bar**  *See:* bar, integrated bar (unified bar).

**integrated contract**  *See:* contract, contract interpretation, integrated contract (completely integrated contract).

**integration**  *See:* segregation, desegregation (integration).

**integration clause**  *See:* merger, merger clause (integration clause).

**intellectual property (I.P. or IP)**  Protection under the law for interests in creations and inventions. Intellectual property is the whole set of intangible rights that authors, inventors, and other creators have in the items they write, invent, or create. To have intellectual property in a thing is to have an effective monopoly on its use, such that the property rights holder may enjoin or recover from others who infringe on the rights through unfair duplication or wrongful use. Intellectual property in anything is usually limited in time, although the lengths of time and manner of calculation vary dramatically among and within the categories.

Intellectual property is usually divided among three categories: copyright, patent, and trademark. In the United States, each is the province of federal regulation, as well as the common law. There is also a growing field of international law regulating intellectual property both as a field of international agreements unto itself and as an aspect of the regulation of trade.

*See also:* copyright; patent; trademark.

**intended-use doctrine**  *See:* use, use of property, intended-use doctrine; liability, product liability, intended-use doctrine, unintended use; liability, product liability, intended-use doctrine.

**intent (intention, intentionally)**  The desire to achieve a specific goal. Intent is the motivation of a person to achieve a particular result or purpose through some action. The great majority of acts of legal significance must be accomplished with the intent to perform that act. A last will and testament, for example, is not valid unless the testator signs the will with the intent that the instrument be the testator's last will and testament. Intent therefore requires capacity and knowledge, at least in some degree, of what is intended, as in this example in which the testator must have the ability to know as well as some idea of what a

last will and testament is and what effects it will have under the law.

Intent can also be a communal affair, or be considered to be the intention of a group, as in the idea that a legislature can have intent or a corporate entity can have intent. Intent by a legislature is usually in contrast to purpose, which is broader and represents a more abstract policy than does legislative intent, which more often represents specific results intended by an act or statute.

Intention in the sense it is used in torts and criminal law may be much less deliberative and less of a question of prior consideration to an action than it is consideration at the moment of an action. Such inquiries usually commence with an act and attempt to reconstruct the intent related to it; a process often performed in two steps.

The first inquiry is whether an action was intended or not intended at all, whether something was done with the intent to achieve the result that occurred (or a substantially similar or related result) or was done by accident or misfortune. If the act was intended, then the question turns on whether the result was intended, whether something happened that altered the result in a relevant manner from the intended result. If the actor's goal had been substantially the same or similar to the result that occurred, then the actor intended the result. Thus in considering whether a person who threw a rock and killed another has committed murder, the question of intent is critical: if the person intended the death of the other, the act is in one range of homicide, but if the person intended the rock to land harmlessly in a lake, the act is in a range of manslaughter.

In the absence of reliable evidence of intent, intent may be presumed from certain actions.

*See also:* purpose; will (human will); motive.

**intent of the drafter**  *See:* interpretation, intent of the drafter, originalism (original intent); interpretation, intent of the drafter.

**intent of the framers**  *See:* constitution, U.S. Constitution, intent of the framers (framers' intent).

**intent to defraud**  *See:* fraud, intent to defraud.

**conditional intent**  Intent to achieve a result only if a condition is satisfied. Conditional intent is an intent to achieve a particular goal through some conduct, but the goal will be desired only in the event an independent condition is satisfied. The intent would be defeated if the condition remains unsatisfied.

**constructive intent (presumed intent)**  Intent to commit an action presumed from the action itself. Constructive intent is the presumption of a person's intent that is inferred after the fact from sole evidence of the act the person committed. For example, if a person removes money from another's bank account, constructive intent supports a finding that the person intended to remove the money from that account.

The law often allows constructive intent to serve when no evidence of intent is available, or when the only evidence available — testimony of a wrongdoer whose intent is in issue — appears to the finder of fact to be self-serving and contradicted by more compelling evidence. Thus, intent may be inferred from conduct alone. Such an inference is questionable in many cases, and commentators have long suggested the more apparently deliberate the conduct, the greater the likelihood that the conduct is intended. The resolution is often to refuse to allow constructive intent alone but to allow circumstantial evidence of intent from facts surrounding the act, thus establishing proof of the intent not from the act alone but from its circumstances. This is circumstantial proof of intent rather than constructive intent.

*See also:* constructive.

**general intent (basic intent)**   The intent to carry out a given action. General intent is an intent to do something, regardless of any specific intent to cause a consequence of the something done. General intent is usually contrasted with a lack of intent; the conduct was either intended or accidental or unthinking. Evidence of any more specific level of intention — deliberate, conscious, purposeful, or premeditated — would also demonstrate the less specific level of general intent.

**legislative intent (statutory intent)**   The result intended by the legislature in enacting a given statute. Legislative intent is the specific end sought to be made law by the enactment of a statute or other legislative instrument. Divining the intent of the legislature, a corporate body of many individuals with varying capacities or knowledge and skill in the law, who may or may not have had a focused attention or understanding of a given piece of legislation, is a difficult business.

Legislative intent is derived from a host of sources of intent, including formal statements issued by organs of the enacting legislative groups as to their intention; evidence of broad and related purposes associated with the act; historical evidence of the problems that led to the formation of an intention; including earlier incarnations of a writing associated with the act and their alterations; and the contemporaneous statements of people who were particularly essential relative to the action within the group (although we tend to be mistrustful of later statements less potentially influenced by the need to influence the group and more to influence later perception of the intended act). Even so, there is some skepticism that a single intention of a group of people is a coherent idea, and it might be easier in some sense to accept a broader purpose or goal than an animating intent to achieve it. Some interpreters believe that it is so hard to divine a single intention from the aggregation of so many people's actions that the effort must always be forbidden and that only the resulting text may be evidence of intent.

In ascertaining legislative intent, formal statements prepared by the committees responsible for passage usually have great weight, as do statements made at the time of the introduction of bills. Statements made during debates on the floor and in committee hearings, and statements made during hearings, usually are accorded less weight. Signing statements by the executive are rarely given much significance as a basis for understanding the intent of the legislative branch.

**specific intent**   The intent to cause a consequence of an action. Specific intent is the motivation to commit an act not merely for the act's sake but for the purpose of causing a particular result from the act. For example, if an archer shoots an arrow at a rock, intending the ricochet to hit Smith and wound him, the archer has the general intent to shoot at the rock but the specific intent to wound Smith.

**transferred intent**   An intent to commit one offense or harm that causes another instead. Transferred intent is an intent to cause one result by an action that causes a different result. In any analysis of a particular action to determine whether it breached a duty in tort or violated a prohibition in the criminal law, the defendant would have a defense to a claim if the claim requires intent, if the defendant had not intended to cause the result that occurred. However, the defense would fail if the defendant acted to cause an act that was similar or wrongful in a manner similar to the action that occurred. Intent is sufficient for the second wrongful act if the defendant had intended to cause a first wrongful action that resulted in the second action being manifest. Thus, if an archer attempts to shoot an arrow at Smith but hits Jones, the archer's intent is sufficient for the archer's injury of Jones to have been intentional.

On the other hand, transferred intent does not bar other defenses, and a justification sufficient for the first action would also justify the second action under either a doctrine of justification or excuse. If the archer was acting in self-defense in shooting at Smith, either the justification would be sufficient for the shot or an excuse would be allowed for the error in an action for shooting Jones.

*See also:* transfer.

**intentional infliction of emotional distress**   *See:* distress, emotional distress, intentional infliction of emotional distress | impact; distress, emotional distress, intentional infliction of emotional distress | freedom of speech; distress, emotional distress, intentional infliction of emotional distress (I.I.E.D. or IIED or outrage).

**intentional interference with parental rights**   *See:* parent, parental rights, intentional interference with parental rights (causing a minor child to leave or not to return home).

**intentional misrepresentation**   *See:* representation, misrepresentation, intentional misrepresentation (fraudulent misrepresentation).

**intentional tort**   *See:* tort, intentional tort.

**inter**   Between or among, or in the midst of something. Inter is the Latin preposition for a relationship between or among different things, times, places, people. Translated in a relationship among things or people it means between or among. Translated in a relationship among times or lives, it means while or during. In English, it is usually found as a prefix, as in interstate, which is between two or more states.

*See also:* intra.

**inter alia**   Among other things. Inter alia is Latin for "among other things." It is used to introduce an illustrative example or to provide a detail regarding the matter preceding it in the text.

*See also:* et, et alia (et al.); et, et cetera (et caetera or etc.).

**inter vivos**   While alive. Inter vivos is Latin for "in the midst of life," or "while alive." Anything done by a living person is done inter vivos. A gift inter vivos is effective while alive, though a grant post mortem, or after death, can only be effected through a trust or by devise or legacy in a valid will under such circumstances that the grant may be carried out by an executor or administrator. As Bouvier points out, a grant of a fee in land inter vivos does have an unusual custom of being made to the grantee and to the grantee's heirs. Note: a grant made causa mortis is still a grant made inter vivos.

*See also:* title, doctrine of worthier title, inter vivos branch of the doctrine of worthier title; gift, gift inter vivos (absolute gift or inter vivos gift); post, post mortem; causa, causa mortis.

**inter vivos branch of the doctrine of worthier title**
*See:* title, doctrine of worthier title, inter vivos branch of the doctrine of worthier title.

**inter vivos trust**   *See:* trust, inter vivos trust, revocable trust (irrevocable trust); trust, inter vivos trust (living trust).

**interest**   A benefit to be gained or a loss to be suffered according to some action or condition. Interest is a relationship between a person or entity and any person, entity, or thing — including a piece of property, corporation, contract, cause in law, trust, estate of a decedent, partner, family member, or a subsidiary corporation, or even a criminal enterprise, or an election campaign. One may have an interest in anything. The relationship then expressed by the legal sense of "interest" is one in which the person has a gain that might be realized or a loss that might be suffered according to an action or condition that affects the the thing.

An interest may be, but need not be, financial, and the law will recognize interests in family relationships, memberships without a cash value in an association, and other private interests without monetary value, as well as public interests, such as an interest in one's exercise of liberty through travel, speech, religious exercise, education, and civic participation.

Interests are essential to many standards in law. Conflict of interest assesses whether the interest or a person or entity is sufficiently contrary to the interests of a client that the client cannot be fairly or wholly represented. Interests in the object of litigation are essential to determine a sufficient relationship that the object of litigation will be fully represented and done without frivolousness by a stranger to the matter. An interest in a cause may affect a witness's credibility and be required to be disclosed in a trial.

Various forms of interest are essential to litigation, such as challenging the enforceability of a contract, to enforcing a fiduciary duty, to challenging a public action; these are the basis of considerable strains of case-law in each jurisdiction. Such rules assessing interests vary, however, according to whether the interest is considered in equity or in the law alone.

Equity defines interest broadly, and the law defines it narrowly. The law requires an interest to be either financial or a demonstrable interest recognized in law, such as an interest of a family member in the flourishing of another member of the same family. Equity considers a variety of forms of harm that might be suffered in defining an interest in avoiding such harms, including the avoidance of the unjust enrichment of another, the bases of restitution, or the interest in an association or personal investments of time and effort, most of which would not be cognizable as the basis for an interest in law.

*See also:* conflict, conflict of interest; standing in court; estate, interest, present possessory interest (possessory estate or present estate); estate, interest, non-possessory interest (nonpossessory interest); estate, interest, merger of estates; estate, interest, life estate pur autre vie; estate, interest, life estate (life interest); estate, interest, estate on condition (contingent estate or estate upon condition); estate, interest, defeasible estate (estate subject to defeasance or destructible fee or determinable estate or base fee or qualified fee).

**interest in property**   *See:* property, interest in property, terminable interest; property, interest in property, future interest; property, interest in property (property interest).

**interest on client trust account**   *See:* trust, client trust account, interest on client trust account (interest on lawyer's trust account or IOLTA).

**interest rate**   *See:* rate, interest rate, rate lock (ratelock); rate, interest rate, prime rate; rate, interest rate, floating rate (adjustable rate or variable rate); rate, interest rate (rate of interest).

**executory interest (E.I. or EI or executory bequest)**
A grantee's future interest that divests the present possessor upon the satisfaction of a condition. An executory interest is a future interest in property that might or might not become possessory in a grantee. Like all future interests, the executory interest is one of two or more interests created at the same time by a grantor, the present possessory interest, which will eventually come to an end, and the future interest, which would then become possessory and change its name.

An executory interest must (by definition) be given to a grantee. The defining elements of an executory interest require that the grantor gives the interest to a grantee in a form that will later cut short a present interest in a fee simple subject to an executory limitation, if, and when, a contingent event takes place. Thus, a grant of Blackacre from "O to A and her heirs but if ever the land shall be used to raise llamas, then to B and her heirs" creates a fee simple subject to an executory limitation in A and an executory interest in B. O has kept nothing. An executory interest is not a vested interest for the purposes of the rule against perpetuities.

*See also:* devise, executory devise; fee, estate in fee, fee simple subject to executory limitation (fee simple subject to an exectuory interest or F.S.S.E.I. or FSSEI or FSSEL).

**remainder and executory interest**   A remainder follows a life estate, fee tail, or tenancy, and an executory interest may cut short anything. A remainder is the future interest in a grantee that follows the defined end of a prior estate. A life estate naturally ends at the death of the life tenant, and a grant that had been made to a grantee that becomes possessory after the life tenant's death must be a remainder. In contrast, an executory interest becomes possessory by some event that might take place, if it ever takes place, at a time that cannot be known at the time of the grant. If this interest is given to a grantee (rather than reserved to the grantor), it is an executory interest. Such interests that are reserved to the grantor are the possibility of reverter or right of entry.

**rule against perpetuities**   Executory interests must vest or fail within twenty-one years after death of last person alive when created. The rule against perpetuities provides that executory interests must vest or fail within twenty-one years of a life in being at the time of the making of the will.

*See also:* perpetuity, rule against perpetuities (rap or rule against remoteness).

**shifting executory interest**   An executory interest that ends one grantee's possession in favor of another grantee. A shifting executory interest is an executory interest that ends a prior interest in another grantee (rather than ending the possession of the grantor). Thus, a grant of Blackacre from "O to A and her heirs but if ever the land shall be used to raise llamas, then to B and her heirs" creates a fee simple subject to an executory limitation in A and an executory interest in B. This executory interest is a shifting interest because grantee B would divest A, who is also a grantee. There is little difference in law between a springing and shifting interest, but professors like students to know these things.

**springing executory interest**   An executory interest that ends the grantor's possession in favor of a grantee. A springing executory interest is an executory interest that ends a prior interest in the grantor (rather than ending the possession of an intermediate grantee). Thus, a grant of Blackacre from "O to A and her heirs if ever the land shall be used to raise llamas" creates a fee simple subject to an executory limitation in O and an executory interest in A. This executory interest is a springing interest because grantee A would divest grantor O, and there is no other grantee. There is little difference in law between a springing and shifting interest, but professors like students to know these things.

**future interest**   A right to possession in the future. A future interest is an ownership interest in property that is owned in the present but has only a right of future possession and no right of present possession. It is created when the ownership of a piece of property is divided between ownership in the present and ownership in the future. The future interest or interests thus created may be transferred at the time of creation, even though they do not include an immediate right of possession. A future interest will or might become a present possessory interest, but only after something happens to make it possessory, such as the death the holder of a prior interest that terminated on the death of its holder.

Future interest is a legal term of art. Its primary forms in modern practice are three that are retained by the grantor and two given to grantees. Those future interests that are retained by the grantor at the time that the future interests are divided from prior interests include reversion, possibility of reverter, and right of entry (which may sometimes be the very similar power of termination). Those given to a grantee at the time the interests are divided from the prior interests are the remainder and the executory interest.

All future interests, are created at the same time as a prior interest by a common grantor. For example, the executory interest is one of two or more interests created at the same time by a grantor: the present possessory interest, which will eventually come to an end and be followed by the future interest, which would then become possessory and also then change its name.

*See also:* entry, right of entry (R.O.E. or ROE or right of re-entry or power of termination); remainder; reversion; reversion, reverter, possibility of reverter.

**insurable interest**   A party's interest in a thing allowing the party to insure it. An insurable interest is a relationship with specific property from which one will derive financial advantage from its preservation, or would suffer financial loss from its destruction. The interest may be somewhat indirect, but the interest must be sufficient that the insurance contract does not amount to speculation or mere gambling. Thus, one may not enter into a life insurance policy on a stranger but may do so for oneself, a family member, or an employee.

**interest for money**   The profit a lender receives on a loan. Interest for money is the profit taken by a lender from a borrower who is required not only to repay the principal amount of the loan but also to pay an additional amount equal to a portion of the amount borrowed, the additional amount being the interest, and the size of the portion over time being the rate of interest. Interest is a matter of contract in most instances, but it will be implied as owed by a person or entity who owes money to another over time, for instance owing to an unpaid claim upon which a plaintiff receives a judgment against a defendant. Thus pre-judgment interest is interest required by a court for the defendant to pay on the claim, computed from the time the claim accrued until the claim is adjudged as owed; post-judgment interest accrues from the time of the judgment until the moment the debt is actually paid.

*See also:* usury (usurious).

**accrued interest**   Interest accumulated over some period. Accrued interest is the amount of interest that an instrument has earned in some relevant time, usually since the last payment out, the last recapitalization of interest, or from the beginning of the accumulation.

**declining balance (amortized debt method of interest)**   Interest paid only on the principal remaining owed in each payment. Declining balance interest is a method of calculating interest to be paid in each installment on a debt by multiplying the interest rate against the amount of the unpaid principal remaining at the time of the payment, thus allowing a declining payment of interest with every payment. This method is usually contrasted with the straight-line method. In most circumstances, the straight-line interest method generates the payment of more interest on an installment debt than does the declining balance method when used for debts of the same interest rate over the same number of payments.

*See also:* interest, interest for money, straight-line method interest (add-on or precomputed interest or straight-line interest or rule of 78s).

**annual percentage rate (APR)**   The rate of interest that a borrower will pay on a loan over a given year. The annual percentage rate (APR) is a measure of the total cost of credit to a consumer, calculated as an annual percentage of the amount of credit granted for the whole term of a loan. There are a variety of means of calculating APR, some of which vary according to the terms of the loan (for instance whether interest is simple or compound) and some of which require the inclusion of fees associated with a loan and some of which do not. APR compares loans rates in increments of one year, whether the loan is for a year, for a lesser period, or a longer period. Using a simple formula, a loan with no fees for one month (and to be paid at the end of that month) with a total interest payment of 10 percent has an APR of 120 percent. Incorporating fees, a loan with a 2 percent origination fee for five years and an annual interest rate of 5 percent has an APR of 5.819 percent.

*See also:* usury (usurious).

**compound interest**   Interest computed to include interest upon the interest owed. Compound interest is the sum of both the interest owed on a loan and the interest on the interest owed on the loan. The expense of compound interest is a function of the interest rate and the frequency at which the interest is compounded; interest compounded daily generates a higher interest rate over time than interest compounded monthly. There are a variety of formulae for the computation of compound interest. The effective rate of interest is the amount of interest charged with the effect of compounding factored in for the a given year.

**straight-line method interest (add-on or pre-computed interest or straight-line interest or rule of 78s)**   Interest on the full amount of the original principal divided among all payments. Straight-line interest is a method of calculating interest to be paid in each installment on a debt by multiplying the interest rate against the full amount of the original principal. Interest payments are then determined by dividing the principal plus interest by the number of total payments to be made. This method is usually contrasted with the declining balance method. In most circumstances, the straight-line interest method generates the payment of more interest on an installment debt than does the declining balance method when used for debts of the same interest rate over the same number of payments.

*See also:* interest, interest for money, add-on interest, declining balance (amortized debt method of interest).

**privacy interest**   *See:* privacy.

**abandonment of a privacy interest**   Conduct that police may think indicates a person has rejected an expectation of privacy in specific property. Abandonment of a privacy interest occurs when a person, who would have had a reasonable expectation of privacy in some object, such as a briefcase, a parcel, or a container, acts in such a way that a reasonable observer would believe in that context that the person had no expectation of privacy in the parcel or object. No one statement is enough for a police officer or investigator to reach this conclusion, and arguments made by a suspect that the object is not to be searched may be sufficient to preclude a belief the object was abandoned.

*See also:* search, search and seizure.

**state interest (governmental interest or govermental purpose)**   The reason for a government to regulate or litigate any issue. A state or governmental interest is a reason for a government to act in some particular affair. A state interest valid under the constitution of the state or of the United States is essential to every statute, executive action, and judicial order. An action for which no state interest can be discerned, or for which only an invalid interest or purpose can be discerned is unconstitutional, and officials acting under the authority of such actions act unconstitutionally.

Determining the state interests or governmental interests in a particular statute or project can be complex, and in general the courts have not sought historical accuracy but to determine whether a reasonable interest can be assigned for the legislation's enactment or the action taken, demanding greater care only when the statute or action infringes on a constitutionally protected interest or appears to burden a protected class as a matter of equal protection of the laws.

As a matter of understanding the law and applying it, the historical interest of the state in enacting a statute is essential in determining the legislative intent of that statute, just as it would be to ascertain the administrative purpose of an order.

*See also:* scrutiny, standards of scrutiny.

**compelling state interest (compelling governmental purpose)**  A reason for governance more compelling than the protection of individual rights. A compelling state interest (or compelling governmental purpose) is an interest of the government of such magnitude that it justifies at least the limited infringement of constitutionally protected rights of the individual. A compelling state interest is required for a statute or executive act to satisfy review under strict constitutional scrutiny.

There can be no exhaustive list of compelling interests, but they include the protection of other, conflicting constitutional rights, the remedy of past violations of constitutional rights (including the dismantling of the effects of de jure racial segregation), the enforcement of a direct constitutional requirement upon one of the branches of government, the protection of scarce natural resources from destruction, and the protection against a demonstrable and immediate threat to national security interests.

*See also:* scrutiny, standards of scrutiny, strict scrutiny.

**important governmental objective**  A reason for governance sufficiently compelling to justify a burden in the law greater on one gender than the other or an indirect burden on constitutional rights. An important governmental objective is an interest of the government of such magnitude that it justifies a burden on one gender or another—or a burden on any other quasi-suspect class—despite the requirement that such burdens do not violate equal protection of the laws as a matter of intermediate scrutiny. It is also sufficient to justify regulations that burden constitutionally protected interests or individual rights that are incidentally limited.

**legitimate state interest (legitimate governmental purpose)**  A constitutionally valid reason for governance sufficient to justify a statute or order that infringes upon no constitutional right and burdens no suspect or quasi-suspect class. A legitimate state interest is an interest of the government that is allowed by the government's constitution and that is of sufficient merit that a statute or order based upon it is not arbitrary or unreasonable. A legitimate state interest is required for a statute or order to satisfy examination under constitutional rational basis review. A legitimate state interest is insufficient to justify a statute or executive act that burdens a suspect or quasi-suspect class or infringes on a constitutionally protected right.

*See also:* scrutiny, standards of scrutiny, rational-basis review (rational relationship test).

**substantial state interest**  A reason for governance sufficiently compelling to justify the incidental infringement of constitutional liberties.

A substantial state interest is an interest of the government of such magnitude that it justifies at least the incidental infringement of constitutionally protected rights of the individual to liberty from regulation as a requirement for the government to achieve an end that does not otherwise limit constitutional rights. A substantial state interest is much like an important governmental objective, in being of greater constitutional significance than a legitimate interest but less than a compelling interest, and a substantial state interest is used in some cases dealing with quasi-suspect classes. It is not clear that a substantial state interest and an important governmental objective are synonymous. Examples of a substantial interest include the control of crime and the sufficient regulation of a commodities market to prevent its collapse.

*See also:* class, legal classification, quasi-suspect classification (quasi-suspect class).

**interest-analysis technique**  *See:* choice, choice of law, interest-analysis technique.

**interested party**  *See:* party, interested party.

**interested witness**  *See:* witness, interested witness; witness, disinterested witness (interested witness).

**interests arbitration**  *See:* arbitration, interests arbitration.

**interference**  Disturbance. Interference includes a variety of forms of intermeddling conduct that intrudes upon a person, interrupts or strains a relationship, or hinders an activity. Interference in general may be knowing or unknowing, negligent or deliberate. In specific contexts of criminal or civil liability, however, more specific mental states are required, and the form of interference may be quite specific to the liability. An interference with a right includes any act that makes the conduct protected by that right more difficult to perform. Interference with a relationship need not occur directly but may be indirect, as in interference with custodial relations, with a prospective business advantage, or with a right of contract, in each of which interference may occur through unwitting third parties. Interference is also an antiquated term for a physical assault on a person, including sexual assault.

**interference with a corpse**  *See:* corpse, interference with a corpse (desecration of a venerated object).

**tortious interference with contract (interference with a right of contract)**  A stranger's deliberate interference with one party's contract performance, to the harm of another party. Interference with a contract is a tort committed by a person or entity not a party to the contract, by which that party knowingly and intentionally induces a party to a valid and ongoing contract not to perform a material duty under the contract, to the damage of another party to the contract. In the usual example, A and B have a contract, and C induces B to breach it, to the harm of A. A may sue C in tort for interference (and may also sue B in contract for breach).

A party who is injured by tortious interference may bring an action against the interfering third party in tort, even if the injured party would not have been able to bring any action for breach of contract. For example, suppose A and B have a contract for A to provide services to B for a year. C knows of the contract and deliberately induces A to stop providing services to B but to provide them to E. As a result of C's actions, A breaches the contract with B (regardless of what then B does for E). B has an action in contract for breach against A but also has an action in tort for interference against C. (Even if B then provides services to E, there is no information here that E induced A's conduct, so B has no action against E.)

**intergovernmental immunities**  *See:* immunity, intergovernmental immunity (intergovernmental immunities).

**interim**  Between terms. Interim is a temporary gap between periods. An interim official holds office during the absence of a permanent occupant or between permanent appointments to that office, as in interim dean, interim chair, interim director.

**interim bond**  *See:* bond, interim bond.

**interim trustee**  *See:* trustee, interim trustee (temporary trustee or trustee ad litem or trustee pro tem).

**interlocutory**  In the midst of the action. Anything interlocutory is done during the process of an action at any time between the commencement and final judgment or order. An interlocutory order is an order entered during the jurisdiction of the court over an action, and a final order would terminate that jurisdiction over at least some party or some claim in an action.

**interlocutory appeal**  *See:* appeal, interlocutory appeal, in media res; appeal, interlocutory appeal.

**interlocutory decision**  *See:* order, court order, interlocutory orders (interlocutory decision).

**interlocutory judgment**  *See:* judgment, interlocutory judgment.

**interlocutory orders**  *See:* order, court order, interlocutory orders (interlocutory decision).

**intermeddler (officious intermeddler or volunteer or stranger)**  One who who confers an unsolicited benefit upon another. An intermeddler is a person or entity who confers a benefit, either by money or by granting a right or other action, upon a recipient who has not acted in any manner to solicit or seek out the benefit, and the person conferring the benefit has no legal or moral obligation (such as a parent for a child or a spouse for a spouse or partner for a partner) to do so. In such cases, the recipient is under no legal or equitable obligation to make restitution for the benefit, and the uncompensated retention of the benefit is not unjust enrichment.

*See also:* stranger; restitution (writ of restitution); unjust enrichment.

**intermediary**  *See:* mediator (intermediary).

**intermediary bank**  *See:* bank, intermediary bank.

## intermediate

**intermediate cause**  *See:* causation, intermediate cause.

**intermediate scrutiny**  *See:* scrutiny, standards of scrutiny, intermediate scrutiny.

**intermediate theory or lien theory or title theory**  *See:* mortgage, mortgage theory (intermediate theory or lien theory or title theory).

**intermediation**  *See:* mediation, intermediation (intermediator or intermediatory).

**intermediator or intermediatory**  *See:* mediation, intermediation (intermediator or intermediatory).

## internal

**internal act**  *See:* act, internal act.

**internal revenue**  *See:* revenue, internal revenue, Internal Revenue Service (I.R.S. or IRS); revenue, internal revenue, Internal Revenue Code (Tax Code or IRC); revenue, internal revenue, Internal Revenue Bulletin (I.R.B. or IRB).

**Internal Revenue Bulletin**  *See:* revenue, internal revenue, Internal Revenue Bulletin (I.R.B. or IRB).

**Internal Revenue Code**  *See:* revenue, internal revenue, Internal Revenue Code (Tax Code or IRC).

**Internal Revenue Service**  *See:* revenue, internal revenue, Internal Revenue Service (I.R.S. or IRS).

## international

**International Association of Defense Counsel**  *See:* bar, bar organization, International Association of Defense Counsel (IADC).

**international court**  *See:* court, international court.

**International Court of Justice**  *See:* court, international court, International Court of Justice (I.C.J. or ICJ).

**International Criminal Court**  *See:* court, international court, International Criminal Court (I.C.C. or ICC).

**International Criminal Police Organization**  *See:* police, police organization, International Criminal Police Organization (Interpol).

**international custom**  *See:* custom, international custom, opinio juris (opinio juris sive necessitatis); custom, international custom, jus cogens (erga omnes obligationes or peremptory norms); custom, international custom.

**international league**  *See:* league (international league).

**international military tribunal**  *See:* court, international court, international military tribunal.

**international parental kidnapping** *See:* kidnapping, parental kidnapping (international parental kidnapping).

**international strait** *See:* sea, law of the sea, international waters, international strait (international waterway).

**international terrorism** *See:* terrorism, international terrorism.

**international trade** *See:* trade, international trade.

**International Trade Commission** *See:* trade, international trade, international trade commission.

**international waters** *See:* sea, law of the sea, international waters, international strait (international waterway); sea, law of the sea, international waters, high seas (freedom of the seas).

**international waterway** *See:* sea, law of the sea, international waters, international strait (international waterway).

**international alliance (ally)** An agreement between two or more states. An alliance is treaty or an agreement between or among states. It may consist of solely economic arrangements, or can consist of military ones, where the two powers agree to come to the defense and aid of the other in the event of an attack.

**international law (law of nations or public international law)** The law between nation-states regulating people and goods and the states themselves. International law is the law of states, in the sense of nation-state. It includes the treaties, customs, national laws, and legal principles that regulate the affairs of states, including their participation and regulation of international activity and, sometimes, the activity within a single state. International law is created by the conduct of the officials of states when the conduct is performed in such a manner that the officials of other states would expect such conduct to be a duty in the future, by the actions of international bodies representing states, as well by the evolution of basic notions of law arising from specialized sources of international law and general sources of law agreed across the world. Most international law is enforced in national courts and by the officials of states in the regulation of their own citizens. Most international executive activity is coordinated by states individually or through the United Nations, as in the work of the High Commissioner for Refugees.

In rare instances, one or more states seek to compel other states to comply with international law, which takes place usually through diplomacy or through resort to mediating or arbitrating states or institutions. In the rarest instances, states resort to dispute settlement through the international institutions such as the World Trade Organization or the International Court of Justice, or to law enforcement through international tribunals such as the International Criminal Court.

International law is sometimes divided among public international law and other fields, such as international trade or international transactions. In this sense, public international law is the law governing states and state officials, particularly concerned with the questions of the sources of law and the limits of state conduct under the law. Note: there is no difference between public international law and the law of nations. Note also: private international law is a term used by civil lawyers for what common lawyers consider conflict of laws.

*See also:* public; jus, jus gentium; law.

**customary international law** Practices of states that amount to obligations of future behavior. Customary international law is the law among states arising from the patterns of behavior among states that other states recognize gives rise to expectations and reliance, from which a law is recognized. Customary international law includes the most fundamental notions of international law, such as the custom that treaties shall be honored by their parties. Customary international law also includes countless individual forms of state behavior that have been accepted as required by the officials of other states, such as the custom that non-militarized fishing boats are not to be taken during wartime. Custom may or may not be reflected in treaties, but treaties may incorporate custom, and custom may arise from treaties.

*See also:* sea, law of the sea (sea laws); treaty.

**International Law Commission (I.L.C. or ILC)** Commission of the United Nations charged to develop international law. The International Law Commission was formed in 1948, and its mandate is the progressive development and codification of international law, in accordance with article 13(1)(a) of the Charter of the United Nations. It consists of 34 members who are deemed to be of "recognized competence in international law." The ILC has been responsible for the crafting of influential reports and treaties that have greatly increased the portion of international law reflected in positive law.

**internecine** Mutually destructive. Internecine depicts combat or violence for its own sake; a destructiveness sought by each side of a conflict against the other that is its own justification, regardless of spurious rationale.

**internet (web or world wide web)** A global network of computer networks. The internet is an international network of computers and computer networks that allows the transfer of data, text, images, and video placed on the internet by a user in one place to be accessed by an unrelated and uncoordinated user in nearly any other place on Earth. The internet is an instrumentality of interstate and international commerce, as well as the result of the federal and state governments' participation in and regulation of the market, yet the policy of the Congress has been to encourage growth of the internet with the least regulation possible in order to foster commerce, speech, and civic participation.

Commerce on the internet is regulable as commerce elsewhere, although difficulty attends determining the jurisdiction in which an internet company exists or an internet contract is made. In general, courts and regulators have found an internet business to be located where the personnel for the business are located as well as where servers for the service are located and where inventory is maintained.

*See also:* mail, electronic mail (e-mail).

**internet domain** *See:* domain, internet domain (domain name or internet address).

**interpleader (interplead or interpled)** A determination of liability to the unknown one of several claimants. Interpleader is a procedure in a civil action by which a party confronted by several claimants for a single remedy may require the competing claimants to prove whose claim is good, if any, to avoid having to pay multiple claims when only one is owed or to satisfy several competing judgments when only one may be honored. Interpleader may be brought as a plaintiff or as a defendant. An interpleading plaintiff may bring an action for interpleader against all claimants, and an interpleading defendant may either interplead other parties or join additional parties. In either case, the liable party may only use interpleader to avoid multiple liablity for a single debt or claim, not liability independently owed separately to each party for different debts or claims.

In some jurisdictions, the interpleading party may only bring an action, counterclaim, or crossclaim for interpleader if it first confesses liability that is owed. In most jurisdictions, an interpleading party (other than the government) is required to post a bond in the amount that might be required eventually to pay to the successful claimant, if the interpleading party either confesses liability or is later found liable for the claim.

*1. deposit into court* The interpleading party may be required to deposit a bond into court for the value of the judgment for which it has accepted liability. This is a pleading requirement in some jurisdictions, and it is required at the discretion of the court in others.

*2. restraint under 28 U.S.C. § 2361* Parties subject to interpleader are restrained from seeking other related remedies. In the federal statute governing interpleader in U.S., though not state courts, the court may issue a restraining order against any suit arising from the same subject matter as the claims subject to interpleader.

**INTERPOL** *See:* police, police organization, International Criminal Police Organization (INTERPOL).

**interpolation (interpolate or interpolated)** Insertion. An interpolation is an insertion of matter into an existing text, image, or recording, with the particular sense that the insertion is not easily detected. For instance, a later edition of a book may include interpolations, which would be new text integrated into the text of the prior edition in such a manner that a reader of only the new text would be unaware of the original and the added prose. Interpolation may occur in spoken narrative or in performance as well as in any regime of data or information.

**interposition (interpose)** An obsolete claim that state sovereignty may intervene between a federal law and a state's people. Interposition, in general, is an action by which a person or institution interposes itself into a larger process, particularly if it intrudes between a cause and an effect. In the law, it was a label once used from time to time to describe the power asserted on behalf of the states either to follow a state construction of federal constitutional law that was contrary to a federal pronouncement or to prefer a state remedy or law over the federal remedy or law, regardless of the idea of the supremacy of the federal constitution and laws. Whatever merit the idea had was greatly diminished in Justice Story's opinion in Martin v. Hunter's Lessee, 14 U.S. 304 (1813), and finally disposed of with the military defeat of the Confederate armies, yet it still arises from time to time.

**interpretation (construction or interpret or construe)** The process of giving meaning to a words, signs, or images. Interpretation is the process by which a person gives meaning for a current purpose to anything that person encounters, particularly to texts, statements, signs, or images. Interpretation is required by every reader, listener, or viewer to make sense of what is perceived. Put another way, reading is interpreting; listening is interpreting; observing is interpreting.

In the law, interpretation is the process of discerning a meaning and an application to some relevant question from any kind of text or statement. Interpretation is required to apply a statute, case opinion, contract, will, trust instrument, letter, or a statement in evidence to any situation or question. Although this application tends to occur through perception of the text from which the reader takes a meaning the reader believes is plausible, argument among readers over the meaning of seemingly clear texts is so common that there is a strong observation to be made that texts are inherently ambiguous. That is, in part, because words are inherently ambiguous, even when used with care and with proper allocation of their technical meaning. Interpretation is thus a matter of degrees of confidence: each reader's interpretation is less likely to be correct or incorrect as to be more accurate or less accurate.

In general, the judicial order of interpretation in the contemporary United States is first, that the reader is to interpret a text according to the meaning of the words they employ. Second, in the event there is ambiguity in that interpretation, which occurs when the text is susceptible to more than one plausible interpretation, the reader is to interpret the text according to the specific intent that the drafter of the text sought the text to achieve, using the extrinsic evidence available. The third step is for the reader to apply the tools of interpretation, including the interpretative canon, such as Bouvier lists in the derivation for this entry (in the desk edition). The fourth step is for the reader to consider the fundamental purpose the drafter had in creating the text, particularly the legislative policy if the text is a statute, to identify a broad goal that would guide any interpretation by favoring outcomes that would support that goal.

An alternative approach for the modern interpreter is to attempt to understand the language of the text in its historical context and surrounding contemporary legal framework, giving the text an interpretation that fits best with its language, context, and current integration into contemporary law. This approach would not necessarily favor one of the three approaches over the others but would rely on whichever is the most supported by the facts and so appears to the interpreter to be the most likely to yield the reading that produces the greatest authority in the law.

*See also:* designation; definition; diberah torah ki-leshon bene adam (diberah torah bilshon benei adam); interpretation, statutory interpretation (construction of a statute or statutory construction); ex, ex vi termini.

**interpretative rule**  *See:* rule, interpretative rule.

**ejusdem generis**  Generic terms following a list must be interpreted within the context of the list. Ejusdem generis is a Latin term meaning "of the same kind." It is used as a rule of construction in interpreting vague or expansive terms that follow an enumerated list, and its application limits non–enumerated terms to be included within the guidelines operating upon the list only if the non–enumerated term is substantially similar to an item on the list.

**expressio unius est exclusio alterius (expressio unius exclusio alterius est)**  The omission of an item from a list is presumed to exclude it. Expressio unius ut exclusio alterius, or "the expression of one thing is the exclusion of another," is a maxim of interpretation applied to statutes, contracts, and other instruments, in which a list that omits something is presumed to have been written deliberately to exclude it. Such a maxim should not, generally, be given priority over clear evidence of a scrivener's error or of an intent by the drafter to the contrary.

**in pari materia (pari materia)**  On the same matter. In pari materia is a tool of interpretation that requires related texts to be read together. Thus, several statutes on the same subject should be read collectively in order to interpret the application of each to the subject.

**intent of the drafter**  *See:* intent, legislative intent (statutory intent).

**originalism (original intent)**  Interpretation of a text by its understanding at the time of its creation. Originalism, or interpretation according to original intent, is the interpretation of a text according to the beliefs later interpreters suppose that the drafter had at the time of the drafting, either of the meaning of the specific language chosen or of the purpose of the instrument created, or both. Many people believe that the U.S. Constitution of 1787 should be interpreted according to the original intent of the drafters. This has several meanings; one of the most common is to interpret the specific language of a clause according to the understanding that a hypothetical member of the Constitutional Convention might have had of it. It might also apply to an understanding of the purpose of some article or clause or to the whole instrument. Originalism is a controversial doctrine, both in the manner in which it might be applied and in the balance it might have with other methods of interpretation.

**Ockham's razor**  The simplest explanation is the most likely. Ockham's razor is technically stated, "plurality ought not be posited unnecessarily," which is to say that the argument with the least steps is best. The maxim of interpretation and analysis is attributed to William of Ockham, an English monk who died in 1349, although the idea is far older.

**plain meaning (plain language rule)**  Meaning of the language as it would be understood when written. The plain meaning of a text is the meaning given by a later reader of a text according to a reasonable understanding of the meaning of the text in the time and place it is written. Plain meaning does not prohibit the reading of terms of art within the context in which they would have been employed, but it does limit interpretation from a broader attempt to construe the text in the light of the drafter's purpose or intent.

*See also:* interpretation, strict construction.

**statutory interpretation (construction of a statute or statutory construction)**  The process of relating a statute to a particular issue or question. Statutory interpretation, like interpretation generally, is the process of giving meaning in a particular context to the language of a statute. The common law and statutes themselves have given rise to both customs of interpretation and canons by which words and ideas are construed in the process of interpretation. The many choices to be made in methods of interpretation, and indeed whether interpretation even takes place or should take place, is sometimes quite controversial. Still, the general customs of interpretation as they are usually promoted in the early twentieth century are these. The first priority is to consider the plain language of the statute. If the language of the statute has such a shared meaning among the lawyers and judges and all are confident that the meaning they derive from the language would be widely shared, then they are unlikely to do more to interpret the statute. Second, the statute is parsed to consider its application to a question, and again if one application seems widely accepted, all is well. But, if there is a division of opinion, such that there are two or more reasonable applications, then the statute is considered ambiguous and further interpretation is required. That explores the purpose of the statute as understood by its legislators, the intent they might have had in selecting the words of the statute while drafting, the problem the statute was thought to solve, the fit with other statutes and other areas of the law, and the fit of the statute's apparent or possible requirements with the practices of other jurisdictions or the evolving standards of decency or moral notions of the purpose of the state, such as the promotion of freedom of the individual.

**canon of construction**  A principle or rule used in interpretation. A canon of construction is one among many rules adopted by the courts to interpret statutes. Many evolved in the English common law, some borrowed from the interpretation of grants, wills, and contracts. Each canon originated in an interpretation of a text in a given context but was treated as having more general application by later courts or scholars. Canons are often expressed as maxims.

**legislative history** *See:* legislation, legislative history.

**legislative purpose** The broad goals that a statute is intended to achieve. The legislative purpose is the change in society or government that the drafters of a statute hope to effect by the statute. The purpose is the goal of reform embodied in the words of the statute, the concept that the words are to represent in sum. Legislative purpose is sometimes the same as legislative intent, although the phrases are sometimes distinguished when intent refers to the legislator's intended significance of a word or phrase, and purpose refers to the legislator's expectation of the effect of the statute.

*See also:* mischief (mischevious); intent, legislative intent (statutory intent).

**Yick Wo case (Yick Wo rule or Yick Wo doctrine)** A statute must be examined for its purpose and effect, not merely its facial statements. In Yick Wo v. Hopkins, 118 U.S. 356 (1886), a facially neutral regulation of clothes cleaners in San Francisco burdened wooden shops owned by Chinese cleaners but not the brick shops owned by white Americans. The Court looked to the statute's purpose and effects rather than its facial neutrality. Yick Wo stands for several propositions, not the least being an unlawful purpose or effect of a statute is not saved by neutral language. The case is also cited as the basis for the doctrine that official discrimination between persons in similar circumstances, material to their rights, must be justified, the predicate for all equal protection jurisprudence.

**rule of reason in interpretation** A later, reasoned interpretation of a statute in its contemporary context. The rule of reason in statutory interpretation is a rule of interpretation that requires the purpose of a text to be given priority over words that seem contrary to it, though the purpose must be understood from the words and both should be used as well and as thoroughly as possible. The rule of reason is neither strict nor liberal in assessing the scope of a text.

**strict construction** Reading a text to apply to the fewest possible situations. Strict construction, or narrow construction, is the interpretation of a text that gives it the narrowest, least application, or least effect. Thus, under the common law, a statute in derogation of the common law was to be strictly construed, or interpreted to apply only to the cases in which it most clearly and obviously applied, and any ambiguous cases were to be found outside the statute's scope. This sense of strict interpretation did not turn any less on the statute's purpose than on its language.

As commonly used in contemporary interpretation, strict construction is based on the text rather than the purpose. In this sense, it is the reliance on the choice of words by the drafters in the belief that the simplest possible understanding of every word will yield the best understanding of the text as a whole. Strict construction relies on plain meaning at the expense of the likely intent or purpose of the drafter, and it is reluctant to find ambiguity or error. An unmoderated interpretative philosophy of strict construction from this perspective will enforce a view of a law, contract, or testamentary will that is absurd or illogical.

**interpreter** A translator of languages. An interpreter is person that translates speech from one language into another. A criminal defendant who does not speak English in a court in the United States is entitled to the assistance of an interpreter throughout the proceedings. An interpreter may be used for witnesses who lack a sufficient ability in English to assist the court. Most states now employ a system of interpreter certification in order to certify the competence and to train interpreters for these purposes.

An interpreter who assists an attorney in relations with a client or witness is within the scope of attorney-client privilege regarding communications with the client and attorney work product for communications with others.

**interregnum** A time between monarchies. An interregnum occurs between the death of one monarch and the installation of a successor. In England, interregnum was usually avoided with the custom of a successive monarch being treated as monarch prior to coronation. The period in England from 1649 to 1660 is often referred to as the Interregnum, the Commonwealth filling the gap between the death of Charles I and the restoration of Charles II. The term, metaphorically, refers to any interruption in governance.

**interrogation (examination of a suspect)** The process of questioning a person suspected of a crime. Interrogation is the process of inquiry by which police or other law enforcement personnel seek information from a person suspected of a crime. Interrogation is distinct from interview, in that the police seek not merely information in general from the suspect, but also statements from the suspect that are either directly or indirectly incriminating of the suspect in a crime. Interrogation may involve direct questions or other action designed ultimately to elicit such an incrimination. Interrogation is subject to the due process of law, including a right to counsel, and the requirements of a Miranda warning attach at the commencement of every interrogation in which a suspect has not already adequately waived such rights.

**custodial interrogation** Interrogation of a person in the custody of law enforcement officials. Custodial interrogation is interrogation following a person's arrest or custody, whether the interrogation occurs in a police car, office, jail, or prison, or the interrogation occurs elsewhere. The hallmark of custodial interrogation is that the person knows that the person is in custody and has no freedom to leave. During custodial interrogation, the stakes of interrogation are higher than when a person is free to go, and any statement made in custody during interrogation is presumed to be coerced under the Fifth Amendment. Thus, an interrogated person's waiver of a right to counsel must be voluntary, clear, express, and unequivocal, and be communicated by some method other than by simply answering questions or otherwise complying with the requests or orders of the police.

*See also:* Miranda rule (Miranda warning or Miranda rights).

**enhanced interrogation (extraordinary interrogation techniques)** Abuse during interrogation. Enhanced interrogation is a euphemism for abuse during a custodial interrogation for the purpose of gaining information from the victim. Coined by Gestapo interrogators in 1937, the term was revived in 2003 by interrogators of the U.S. Department of Defense, Central Intelligence Agency, and their contractors. Although in 2011, the use of enhanced interrogation was still defended as lawful, it has been the subject of strong declarations of illegality under U.S. laws against torture and under international law.

*See also:* ordinariness, extraordinariness (extraordinary or extraordinarily).

**interrogatory (interrogatories or propounded interrogatories)** A written question submitted by one party to another for answer during discovery. An interrogatory is a written question, usually one of a series of such questions, submitted by one party to another during the discovery phase of a civil action. Although some states allow for broader discovery, the federal rules allow only twenty-five questions and subquestions to be submitted to a party without leave of the court. The purpose of an interrogatory is the discovery of information related to the factual and legal background of the case then at hand, and while interrogatories, like all discovery, may exceed the scope of admissible testimony, some relationship to the allegations of the case or to the development of further evidence is required.

A party served with interrogatories must answer them under oath, signed and in writing, within thirty days of service. Each and every interrogatory must be fully and separately completed. A party may object to answering an interrogatory that seeks information beyond the scope of the rules or that is privileged. An answer that is genuinely not known to the party and cannot be discovered by a reasonable good faith inquiry may be answered as not known. That said, an interrogatory to a corporation or other entity must be answered by an officer or agent who can furnish the information available.

The abuse of discovery is all too common in U.S. law, and interrogatories are especially notorious for it. An attorney who seeks irrelevant information or propounds interrogatories merely to annoy an opponent or increase the costs of litigation or, more often, out of sheer repetition and lack of imagination, contributes to the expense and harassment of litigation. It is for these reasons that interrogatories and their answers must be signed, exposing both attorney and client to sanctions in the event the interrogatories are used in a manner amounting to abuse. Interrogatories submitted to a party to inconvenience or to embarrass a party or for reasons with no bona fide relationship to the filing party's case are abusive; besides the submitting party's liability for sanctions, the party served need not answer abusive interrogatories.

*See also:* discovery, interrogatory, deposition | written questions.

**special interrogatory (jury interrogatory)** A question of fact submitted to the jury for a verdict other than the general verdict. A special interrogatory, or jury interrogatory, is a question addressed to the jury, in which the jury is asked to make a specific finding regarding a fact in dispute. The questions submitted in this manner should be few, should be brief and clear, and should be answerable with a brief answer. The answer to this question is a special verdict, and it is distinct from the general verdict.

*See also:* special; verdict, special verdict.

**interstate** Affecting more than one state. Interstate depicts anything that affects, contacts, travels in or otherwise associates two states or more. Interstate waters flow among states, interstate transportation carries goods or people from one state into another, and so on. Interstate commerce, famously a basis for federal regulation of economic activity in the national market, includes goods, services, and transport moving between the states, the means of such transport, and such activities that affect any commerce in multiple states.

In international law, interstate is effectively international; the states implied are not states of a single nation but the sovereign states themselves.

**interstate agreement** *See:* constitution, U.S. Constitution, interstate compact (interstate agreement).

**interstate commerce** *See:* commerce, regulation of commerce, interstate commerce.

**Interstate Commerce Act** *See:* commerce, regulation of commerce, interstate commerce, Interstate Commerce Act.

**Interstate Commerce Clause** *See:* constitution, U.S. Constitution, clauses, Commerce Clause, Interstate Commerce Clause.

**Interstate Commerce Commission** *See:* commerce, regulation of commerce, interstate commerce, Interstate Commerce Commission (ICC or I.C.C.).

**interstate compact** *See:* constitution, U.S. Constitution, interstate compact (interstate agreement).

**Interstate Compact Clause** *See:* constitution, U.S. Constitution, clauses, Compact Clause (Interstate Compact Clause).

**interstate pollution** *See:* pollution, interstate pollution, trail smelter arbitration; pollution, interstate pollution.

**Interstate Rendition Clause** *See:* constitution, U.S. Constitution, clauses, Extradition Clause (Interstate Rendition Clause).

**Interstate Transportation** *See:* prostitution, Mann Act (Interstate Transportation).

**intervention (intervene or intervenor)** A third party's entry into an established civil action. Intervention, in a civil action, is the entry by a new party into an ongoing action when the new party enters not as a result of suit or service by a plaintiff or defendant already present in the action. The intervenor must have either a legal or equitable interest that may be affected by a judgment in the action then pending or a claim or defense that has a question of fact or law in common with the action then pending. If the intervenor claims to have an interest in the case, intervention is of right, otherwise the intervention is by leave of the court.

The intervenor joins the case either as a plaintiff or a defendant, in either case by serving a timely motion to intervene on the existing parties, the motion setting out the claim or the defense the intervenor seeks to present in the action, as well as the bases for the intervenor's argument that intervention is proper.

*See also:* joinder, joinder of parties.

**intervening cause** *See:* causation, intervening cause.

### intervention as between states

**Drago doctrine** A state may not attack another state to collect a debt. The Drago doctrine rejected the notion that a colonial power could intervene in an American state or occupy its territory in response to that state's unpaid public debt. This doctrine preceded the U.N. Charter, which is consonant with this view.

*See also:* Calvo, Calvo doctrine.

**intervenor** The party who intervenes or seeks to intervene. An intervenor is the party who moves to intervene in an existing civil action, whether or not intervention is granted. An intervenor is often designated by the predominate nature of the intervention as presenting a claim or a defense. An intervenor presenting a claim, even against the existing plaintiff, may be referred to as the Plaintiff-Intervenor. An intervenor raising a defense, even against a counterclaim raised by a defendant, may be referred to as the Defendant-Intervenor. The labels are not merely formal, identifying the association of the arguments raised with the arguments of the other parties, but also substantive, for the party will be bound by the decision in that regard.

**intervention as of right** An intervention to protect a direct interest in the pending civil action. An intervention as of right is an intervention in a civil action by a third party with a significant interest at stake in the action, though the party was not initially a defendant or plaintiff the party has a right to be present in the case. To intervene as of right, an intervenor must allege a specific and substantial legal or equitable interest that is related to the property or transaction that is the subject of the action, that a judgment in the action may harm the intervenor's interests in it, that the motion is timely in relation to the development of the action, and that the parties already before the court may not represent adequately the intervenor's interests. If the court determines that the intervenor has proven these elements of the motion to intervene, the intervenor has a right to the intervention. Intevention by right is also accorded to any party who is conferred a right to intervene in such a matter by statute.

**permissive intervention** Intervention by an intervenor who shares a question of law or fact with the parties already present. Permissive intervention is a matter for the discretion of the trial court and may be allowed for a party who does not assert a substantial legal or equitable interest in the property or transaction that gave rise to the case, but who nonetheless has an interest in a question of fact or of law then pending. Permissive intervention is also allowed to a government agency in actions arising under its rules or statutes, as well as to litigants specifically empowered by statute to intervene in an action of the kind pending.

**intestacy (intestatable or intestate or intestation or testacy)** Status of a decedent without a valid will. Intestacy is the status of an individual who has died without executing a valid last will and testament. A person may die intestate because the person dies not having made a last will and testament or if the person in fact had made a will, at the time of the person's death the will is lost, unknown, invalid, or otherwise incapable of probate. The rules for the distribution of the property of an intestate are the rules of inheritance, which are also called the rules of intestate succession and are determined by statute in every jurisdiction. As a matter of usage, a person who dies testate is thus someone who dies leaving a valid will. It may be noted, however, that the rules of intestate succession govern all assets of a testate decedent that are not properly or fully disposed of by the will's instructions.

**intestate death** Dying without a will. Intestate death refers to the situation when an individual dies without executing a valid will during the individual's lifetime.

**intiated law or initiated act or initiated amendment or direct legislation** *See:* initiative (intiated law or initiated act or initiated amendment or direct legislation).

**intimacies of the home** *See:* home, intimacies of the home (intimacy in the home).

**intimidation (intimidate or intimidating or intimidated)** A threat used to coerce another to action or inaction. Intimidation is a form of coercion in which the intimidating person employs direct or indirect communication to induce fear in a person or group in order to cause the person or group to do something or refrain from doing something. A contract procured by intimidation would be procured through coercion and voidable by the person coerced. When intimidation is used to coerce a person to commit a criminal act, the intimidation may be the basis for a defense of reduced responsibility or, in an extreme case, a defense of a lack of capacity. Intimidation is an element of a number of criminal offenses, such as extortion. Intimidation in its general sense is, literally, the encouragement of timidity.

*See also:* coercion; speech, freedom of speech, hate speech (intimidation).

**intoxication (drunkenness or alcoholic impairment)** A state of altered mental or physical ability caused by the consumption of alcohol or chemicals. Intoxication is a state of the mind or body that is altered in some manner owing either to the presence of alcohol in the blood resulting from its ingestion or the presence of a chemical medicine or other drug or toxin that is placed in the body through ingestion, inhalation, absorption, or injection. Intoxication is the effect of drinking a sufficient quantity of alcohol in wine, beer, or spirits. A sufficiently pronounced state of intoxication is drunkenness, which is established in the common law when one's ability to reason, to assess and control one's actions, or to physically control one's actions is impaired below an objectively normal ability, regardless of the opinion of the person impaired. Intoxication is also the effect of chemical alterations to bodily functions, as well as to mood, intellect, sensory perception, awareness, and other mental states caused by drug consumption, whether the drug is lawfully prescribed or illegally used, as well as by the consumption of nonpharmaceutical chemicals.

Intoxication may impair an individual sufficiently that the individual is incompetent to enter a contract, to execute a last will and testament, to settle a trust, or to make any other legally binding act. Intoxication diminishes a person's ability to make reasonable judgment and to tell right from wrong, and yet voluntary intoxication is not a defense affecting criminal responsibility. Various jurisdictions have particular tests to determine when intoxication amounts to public intoxication, but the general test is when an intoxicated person becomes a nuisance to others or a presents a danger to the person or to others. Most jurisdictions are more specific as to the level of intoxication that amounts to driving while intoxicated, which is usually benchmarked to a blood alcohol level for alcohol and a functional test for drug use. Some statutes and other writings in law refer to intoxication solely to mean impairment from alcohol, and some statutes refer to intoxication to mean impairment from alcohol or from drugs, and further some statutes consider intoxication to include glue sniffing and the consumption of other non-medical chemicals. Only context or textual interpretation can establish the boundaries of the cause of intoxication that apply in a given case.

*See also:* sobriety (sober).

**dram-shop act (dram-shop rule or dram shop rule)** Liability of one serving alcohol for the acts of those served. A dram shop is a bar or saloon. Dram-shop liability is the liability for the injuries to another caused by an intoxicated customer to whom a bar or restaurant had negligently served alcohol. In most jurisdictions dram-shop liability is not strict liability, but a negligence standard for a service of alcohol either to a minor or to a person whom the server knows or should reasonably know is already intoxicated, usually a standard of visible or clear intoxication. In other jurisdictions, a dram shop that provides alcohol to a person who becomes intoxicated is at least comparatively liable for that person's harms to others, even if the person became intoxicated by consuming alcohol procured elsewhere.

The dram-shop act of most jurisdictions requires alcohol to be provided by an employee of a commercial enterprise. Other jurisdictions include liability for non-commercial or private service within the same statute, or judicially construe similar liability to apply to social hosts.

**public intoxication (public drunkenness)** Intoxication in a public place. Public intoxication is the offense or misdemeanor of being intoxicated and appearing to be intoxicated in a public place. The nature of the public place is often left undefined in the statute but includes streets, parks, public property, and the private property of others if the offender is not a guest there. (Even though bars and saloons are public places, patrons inside the bar are considered invitees of the establishment).

Public intoxication was once a primary offense in every jurisdiction, in that police were encouraged to arrest offenders on this basis alone. The modern trend is to consider public intoxication a secondary offense, citing a drunken person for public intoxication only in cases in which the person is creating a nuisance or other offense. This policy allows the police more easily to ensure care and shelter to intoxicated individuals rather than merely punishing them. There is no difference between public intoxication and public drunkenness other than the conditions that one jurisdiction or another might express in its statutes or ordinances for the offense.

*See also:* public.

**intra** Within. Intra is Latin for "within." It is most commonly used in English as a prefix, as in intrastate, which is wholly within a state.

*See also:* inter.

**intra vires** Within the scope of power or authority. Intra vires is a Latin term designating an action as within the powers of whomever commits it. An act of an agent intra vires is within the scope of agency.

Intra vires contrasts with ultra vires, or outside the scope of one's authority.
*See also:* ultra vires.

**intracorporate immunity**  *See:* conspiracy, intra-corporate immunity.

**intrastate commerce**  *See:* commerce, regulation of commerce, intrastate commerce.

**intrinsic evidence**  *See:* evidence, intrinsic evidence.

**introductory clause**  *See:* clause, introductory clause.

**intrusion upon solitude**  *See:* privacy, invasion of privacy, intrusion upon solitude (intrusion upon seclusion).

**inure (enure)**  To have a particular effect. Inure is to have a particular effect or result. The term is frequently used to express to whose benefit some thing is done. Although the phrase is often written "inure to the benefit of x," inure does not imply a benefit, and it is possible for a detriment to inure as well. There is no difference in meaning between inure and enure.

**invalidity or invalid or invalidation or valid or validation or validate**  *See:* validity (invalidity or invalid or invalidation or valid or validation or validate).

**invasion of privacy**  *See:* privacy, invasion of privacy.

**invention**  Any thing that is first created or discovered by a person. An invention is either a thing, including a living thing, or a process that is first discovered or created by a human being, who is its inventor. An invention may be a change or an improvement upon an earlier thing, but the change must be sufficient to so alter the earlier thing that the invention is novel. The invention itself is in the mental effort of creation as manifest in its conception, description, and design; the actual fabrication of the invention is secondary.

The right to control of the intellectual property an inventor has in an invention is secured through a patent.
*See also:* patent.

**inventor**  The first person to create an invention. An inventor is the person responsible for the creation of or advance in an invention. The inventor need not fabricate the thing or process in order to have created it but must be the person who first forms a clear, definite understanding of the thing or process that is invented, and this understanding must be manifest in some form of writing, plan, or model that is sufficiently complete that the invention could be fabricated by a person of ordinary skills in the relevant field with no further research or experimentation. Several inventors may work jointly to invent one thing.
*See also:* invention.

**joint inventor (co-inventor or joint invention)**  One who creates an invention with another. A joint inventor is a person who works with another to collaboratively create an invention. Several inventors may work jointly to invent one object or process. If each contributes in some significant manner to conception or invention, and each inventor contributes to joint arrival at a definite and permanent idea of the invention as it will be used in practice, they are each joint inventors. A joint invention is an invention created by joint inventors through a process of joint invention.

**inventory**  A written list of items of property, or the property itself. Inventory is the sum of property, particularly the goods on hand of a commercial enterprise. It is also the list of that property, as well as the process of counting, listing, and reconciling the counts with the list of the property. Inventories are taken in a variety of circumstances for a variety of reasons. A list of inventory is taken routinely for every business not only to determine the value of its assets, but also to allow for planning in acquisition and supply chain management.

The inventory of a commercial enterprise is subject to a property tax in most jurisdictions, and like most property, its acquisition and its depreciation are business expenses that are usually tax deductions from business income tax.

There are many examples of inventory. An inventory is taken of the assets, realty, and chattels of a decedent in order to transfer or liquidate the inventory. An inventory is also made when property subject to trust is conveyed to a new trustee, and when it is transferred or audited. An inventory is made of personal possessions impounded at the time of an arrest and assignment of the arrestee to jail.
*See also:* search, inventory search.

**inventory search**  *See:* search, inventory search.

**lower-of-cost-or-market method**  Accounting valuation of assets at the lower of cost or present market value. Lower-of-cost-or-market method is a measure used for the valuation of assets in inventory, marking the value at the lower of the actual cost of the asset or its value in the current market.

**mark to market (mark-to-market rule)**  Accounting procedure requiring valuation of assets by present market value. Mark to market is an accounting procedure for valuing non-investment securities and futures contracts. Applying mark-to-market valuation, a security is valued at the market price at the time of each inventory, but a futures contract is valued at the value of the security at the end of the taxable year. Thus, the book value of an asset retained from one inventory period to the next varies according to changes in its market value from the time of the first inventory to the second. For futures contracts, losses and gains are accounted as forty percent short-term capital gains and sixty percent long-term capital gains.

**inverse condemnation or regulatory takings**  *See:* taking, regulatory taking (inverse condemnation or regulatory takings).

## investigation (investigative or investigatory)

**investigative detention**   *See:* stop, police stop, investigative detention (stop and frisk or Terry stop); detention, investigative detention.

**investigative grand jury**   *See:* jury, grand jury, investigative grand jury (investigatory grand jury).

**investigative stop or traffic stop**   *See:* stop, police stop (investigative stop or traffic stop).

**investment (invest)**   The management of an asset to create greater value in the future. Investment is the management of an asset or capital to create greater value that may be returned to the investor in the future. The hallmark of an investment is that wealth or property that might be consumed in the present is managed in some manner that is expected to generate income or grow in value over time.

There are countless examples. The purchase of land in the anticipation of its growth in value is investment, as well as the improvement or development of land in the hope that the land will become more valuable than the cost of development. The purchase of shares in a corporation in the anticipation of the corporation's payments of dividends to shareholders and, potentially, of the share's growth in value is an investment. Likewise is the purchase of bonds in anticipation of the payments to be received, as well, potentially, as the growth in value of the bond. Investment includes the deposit of money into interest-bearing accounts or funds, as well as the acquisition of raw materials or future contracts regarding raw materials, in the anticipation, potentially, of the growth in value of the materials.

**investment company**   *See:* company, investment company (com.).

**investment security**   *See:* security, securities, investment security.

## investor

**accredited investor**   Person who meets certain financial criteria. An accredited investor is defined by the Securities and Exchange Commission as an individual or financial business entity that has met the criterion necessary to conduct investment transactions on a large scale.

**invidiousness (invidious)**   A motivation of ill will or jealousy. Invidiousness is an inappropriate motivation in doing something, particularly in creating a burden on or discriminating against a group. Invidiousness is, in effect, the urge to harm someone or something out of jealousy, envy, unpopularity of the victim, or sheer ill will by the abuser.

*See also:* insidiousness (insidious); ill.

**invidious discrimination**   *See:* discrimination, invidious discrimination.

**inviolability (inviolable or inviolate)**   Unable to be violated or harmed. Inviolability is a condition of a law or rule and of a person or embassy. In the sense of an inviolate law or rule (or inviolable law or rule), inviolability connotes an emphasis against a breach of the rule; there can be no lessening of the law's force. In the sense of the person or embassy, inviolability forbids any personal violation or intrusion, in the sense that both the ambassador and ambassadorial staff and the embassy or mission premises are immune from legal process and are to be protected by the host state from interference. Inviolability is no assurance that a rule or person will not be violated as a matter of fact. However, when such violations occur, inviolability requires a swift remedy, and the violation cannot serve as a precedent for further violation.

**invitation (invite or invited)**   A landowner's expression of desire that a person enter the land for a trade or commercial purpose. An invitation, in general usage, is an expression of desire that the invitee should participate in some practice or event that is managed, hosted, or on the property of the invitor. In the law of property, an invitation is the condition by which a person on the land is justified in believing that the landowner desires the invitee to enter the land for the purpose of commercial activity, trade, or business. The invitation lasts so long as required for the reasonable performance of the commerce, trade or business. An invitation thus expires when the transaction for which it is issues is concluded; however, it also may be rescinded at any time by the landowner.

**invitation to bid or request for proposals or RFP**   *See:* bid, bid solicitation (invitation to bid or request for proposals or RFP).

**invitee (business guest)**   A person invited onto land for a business-related purpose. An invitee is a person on the land of another who is present as a result of an invitation by the owner or possessor for a purpose related to business, as opposed to a purpose utterly unrelated to the owner's business or property, such as a social purpose. The invitation may be express or implied, although implication may not be later inferred if an invitation to a particular invitee had been earlier refused or withdrawn. A person who enters private land made open to all members of the public, such as a commercial property used for retail sales that is apparently accessible to all, is an invitee.

A landowner owes a duty to the invitee to exercise ordinary care in the maintenance of the property, in particular to keep the premises and approaches safe from conditions that are foreseeably likely to injure anyone on the land. This task requires a higher duty of care than that required toward licensees or trespassers.

*See also:* land, liability to other on the land, invitee; licensee; trespasser; invitation (invite or invited).

**invocation (invoke)**   A request for aid from some authority or power. An invocation is a prayer, in the general sense, used in both law and religion, the pursuit of some form of relief according to the authority or power that is invoked by the person who pursues it. There are several, distinct forms of invocation in the law.

Most well known are public invocations, which are statements seeking guidance and goodness for members of a public gathering. Many courts immersed in the difficulties of evaluating the religious implications of an invocation in a public school have asserted that all invocations are religious, which most are generally considered to be. An invocation may indeed be a religious prayer, seeking wisdom or help from God, but an invocation can also be secular, seeking wisdom from nature, eternal verities, or the collective or inherited understanding of humanity.

The invocation of a constitutional right is a statement by a citizen that the citizen expects that right to be honored by an official. Such invocations have been narrowly interpreted. It has been declared that a suspect in a criminal investigation must clearly request counsel to invoke a Sixth Amendment right to counsel, which is not, in at least some circumstances, also an invocation of other rights, such as a Fifth Amendment privilege against self-incrimination.

Invocations take a variety of forms in trial and legal argument. For example, the invocation of a legal authority, such as a precedent, is the assertion that the authority governs some question or dispute. The invocation of a presumption in an administrative or judicial proceeding is created by offering certain proof. The "invocation of the rule" can serve as a request for sequestration.

**invoke the rule (the rule in trial)**   To request or order sequestration of witnesses. To "invoke the rule" in trial is to request the judge to sequester the witnesses other than the parties.
*See also:* witness, sequestration of witness (rule or or the rule or separation of witnesses).

**invoice**   A written account of goods sold or shipped or of services provided. An invoice is an account of services provided or of goods that are sold or shipped (or to be shipped) from a seller to an agent, buyer, or other recipient. In either case, an invoice to both a detailed statement of the form in which value is provided to its recipient from the provider. As a practical matter, many entities employ an invoice as a demand for payment.

In itself, the invoice is a detailed statement of the nature, quantity, and cost or price of the things or services invoiced. As for goods, the invoice usually lists the date of shipment and the address to which they are, to be, or have been shipped. As for services, the invoice usually lists the form of services provided where, by whom provided, and by whom received. An invoice may also include terms of purchase, payment, or shipment, and although the invoice is not itself a contract, the expression in an invoice of terms of a contract for the sale of goods may be deemed accepted by the invoicer unless timely objected to by the invoicee.

**involuntary**   *See:* voluntary, involuntary.

**involuntary bailment**   *See:* bailment, involuntary bailment; bailment, constructive bailment (involuntary bailment).

**involuntary bankruptcy**   *See:* bankruptcy, involuntary bankruptcy.

**involuntary commitment**   *See:* commitment, civil commitment, involuntary commitment (mandatory commitment).

**involuntary confession**   *See:* confession, coerced confession (involuntary confession).

**involuntary dismissal**   *See:* dismissal, involuntary dismissal.

**involuntary homicide**   *See:* homicide, involuntary homicide.

**involuntary intoxication**   *See:* intoxication, involuntary intoxication.

**involuntary manslaughter**   *See:* manslaughter, involuntary manslaughter.

**involuntary murder**   *See:* murder, involuntary murder.

**involuntary nonsuit**   *See:* dismissal, nonsuit, involuntary nonsuit.

**involuntary servitude**   *See:* slavery, involuntary servitude, peonage (debt bondage); slavery, involuntary servitude; servitude, involuntary servitude.

**IPO or I.P.O.**   *See:* share, share as stock, offering, public offering, initial public offering (IPO or I.P.O.).

**ipse**   The person in question. Ipse is a Latin pronoun that emphasizes the person who does whatever is stated in the verb that follows or precedes it.

**ipse dixit**   A conclusion stated without rationale or proof. Ipse dixit, Latin for "he said it," is a label for a statement offered as if it settles some question, even though no evidence, rationale, or justification is offered in its support. Ipse dixit is often an implied assertion of authority in the speaker, that is implying that what the speaker says is true because of the authority of the speaker. As to matters of fact in the world, such a resort to authority is the fallacy ad verecundiam, although as to matters of formal authority, as in a military command, such a resort to authority the statement may be valid ipse dixit.
*See also:* fallacy, ad verecundiam.

**ipso**

**ipso facto**   For this reason alone. Ipso facto is Latin for "for this reason," or "for this fact alone." Ipso facto usually introduces a conclusion that is a necessary corollary to a given fact. The first fact being established, ipso facto, the conclusion is also established.
*See also:* de, de facto; facto.

**ipso facto clause** Clause that purports to void a contract if a party becomes insolvent. An ipso facto clause in an agreement claims to void the agreement if a specified party, usually a debtor in the agreement, files for bankruptcy. In general, such clauses are not contrary to public policy, though they are upheld only in extraordinary circumstances.

**ipso jure** By operation of law. Ipso jure represents any condition or obligation that exists or is true because of the operation of law. Anything that is declared to be true or to exist as a result the operation of law is ipso jure. Something ispo jure does not depend on a judgment by a court or litigation to be true; it is true because circumstances required by law for it to be true have been satisfied.

**IRAC** *See:* argument, legal argument, IRAC (issue rule application conclusion or issue rule analysis conclusion or I.R.A.C.).

**irrebuttable presumption** *See:* presumption, rebuttable presumption, irrebuttable presumption (conclusive presumption).

**irreconcilable differences divorce** *See:* divorce, irreconcilable differences divorce (I.D. or ID or I.D. divorce or irretrievable breakdown of the marriage or I.B.M. or IBM or IBM divorce or no-fault divorce).

**irrefragable proof** *See:* proof, burden of proof, irrefragable proof (irrefutable proof).

**irrefutable proof** *See:* proof, burden of proof, irrefragable proof (irrefutable proof).

**irregular rendition** *See:* rendition, extraordinary rendition (irregular rendition).

**irrelevance** *See:* evidence, relevant evidence, irrelevant evidence (irrelevance).

**irreparable harm** *See:* injury, irreparable injury (irreparable harm); harm, irreparable harm.

**irresistible impulse** *See:* insanity, irresistible impulse (insane impulse or policeman at the elbow test).

**irrevocability** *See:* revocation, irrevocability (irrevocable).

**irrevocable** *See:* revocation, irrevocability (irrevocable).

**irrevocable offer** *See:* offer, contract offer, irrevocable offer (firm offer).

**irrevocable trust** *See:* trust, inter vivos trust, revocable trust (irrevocable trust).

**is** The present of "to be," at the time or at all times. Is, the third person, present tense of "to be," stands for the state of affairs at a given time. The word therefore has an ambiguous temporal element: it may refer to the limited time in which the statement is made or to the whole of time before and after the statement. This sort of temporal ambiguity is common in verb forms. It gave rise to the most famous legal definition of the 1990s, whether "is" is what is or what was and will be. The question was never really resolved.

**is-ought or ought/is** *See:* ought, ought and is (is-ought or ought/is).

**Islam** The Muslim faith. Islam comes from the root s-l-m, which means both submission and peace. It refers to the faith of Muslims and the surrender to Allah. It is the imperative form of the word.

**island** Natural, habitable land surrounded by water. An island is an area of land that is surrounded by water but that is above the water despite the water's usual rise and fall. An island may be in a river, lake, or the sea. The definition of an island in a nation's territorial waters is a matter of the law of that jurisdiction, and most states define artificial islands made of dirt, stone, and other natural material as an island. An artificial island such as an oil rig, light station, or other structure is usually not defined as an island.

Under international law, an island must be naturally formed, though it may be subject to artificial protection or enlargement. Natural formation includes the operation of tectonic pressure and movement, volcanic eruption, erosion and accretion, siltation, and biological activity, such as the development of guano deposits, and root massing in siltation. As a matter of international law, rocks incapable of human habitation or economic life are not islands.

Islands have seas and zones of their own, which may extend or create a national interest in the ocean. An island owned by a state occurring within a continental state's territorial sea would have the effect of creating an extended territorial sea, but if the island were independent or owned by another state, the territorial sea of the continental state would be limited by the territorial sea and zones of the island.

**ism** A slang label for a prejudice. An ism is a type of discrimination, the term being derived from the suffix attached to the collective noun promoted by the discriminatory thought, such as specieism, nationalism, or racism.

**issue (issuance)** Anything sent forth or handed down, the process of doing so, or a question subject to debate. An issue is something sent out from its origin. Thus, the issue of a person is that person's child. The issue of a court proceeding is the resolution of the questions pending before it (though in practice, the issue presented for resolution has become known as the issue itself). The issue of a piece of commercial paper, a financial security, or other instrument, or of a book or periodical such as a newspaper, or of a child, is the process as well as the result, and so a paper is issued, is subject to issuance, and is an issue.

**issue pleading**   *See:* pleading, pleading theories, issue pleading.

**issue preclusion**   *See:* res, res judicata, issue preclusion.

**issue rule application conclusion or issue rule analysis conclusion or I.R.A.C.**   *See:* argument, legal argument, IRAC (issue rule application conclusion or issue rule analysis conclusion or I.R.A.C.).

**issuability (issuable)**   Capable of being made subject to issue. Issuability is the capacity of anything to be issued or to be brought forward as an issue.

**issue as child**   A child born from or conceived by a given person, and all successive children from that child. Issue includes all of the children born of a given person and all of the children born from them, and so on. Although issue is often used in a sense that implies or specifies it to mean only the first generation — in other words only the child or children who are actually born of or conceived by the person — presumptively the term means all of the grandchildren, etc. Courts have been inclined to interpret issue to include adoptive children unless there is strong evidence of an intent of the testator, settlor, or other drafter employing the term to the contrary. Likewise, to grant an interest to a person's "issue" does not bar children born through artificial means from the genetic matter of that person from a gift from that person by grant or by testamentary disposition, although some means of determining the intent of the drafter would be required to determine the scope of the term in such a case.

> **failure of issue**   The death of a person survived by no living children or their descendants. Failure of issue is a person's death without a surviving child, grandchild, or other direct descendant. In the event of a failure of issue, a grant to the person that is then to descend to issue is cut off. In most instances, the will, trust instrument, or other instrument that creates a grant in tail specifies what is to occur in the event of a failure of issue, either assigning a remainder to subsequent grantee or retaining a reversion of the grant to the successors of the original grantor. When no subsequent grantee is specified, as in the case of a fee tail with no remainder, the grant implies a reversion to the initial grantor.
> *See also:* failure (fail); fee, estate in fee, fee tail; remainder; reversion.

> **definite failure of issue**   A failure of issue that must occur at the time of a specified event. A definite failure of issue is a condition upon when a failure of issue must occur, usually at the time of the death of the first grantee or devisee. If the issue had not failed by the time that the failure must be definite, then the condition of failure of issue is destroyed. Thus, if a grant thought to be a fee tail is conditioned on a definite failure of issue by the death of the last surviving child of the

grantee, if the last surviving child dies and issue has not then failed, because there is a surviving child of a prior grantee, the fee tail is converted to a fee simple. In general, a grant conditioned on a definite failure of issue is a conditional grant rather than a fee tail.

> **indefinite failure of issue**   A failure of issue that may occur without a limit by time or occurrence. An indefinite failure of issue is a failure of issue that may happen at any time in the future, which is not limited to occurring within a given time or prior to a specific event.

**issue before the court (question before the court or contested issue or disputed issue or issue in dispute)**   A question that must be resolved from the evidence or the law to resolve a dispute in court. An issue is a point of dispute or a question that is material to an action that is argued between the parties and adjudged by the court or by the jury. The identity of issues is essential for procedural allocation of the resolution of the issues, and each issue is designated according to whether the given issue is a matter of fact to be found from evidence by the trier of facts, a matter of law to be found from analysis and interpretation of the archive of legal materials, or a mixed matter requiring the application of law to the evidence.

The identity of issues has evolved greatly over the last two centuries. Judges have spent great energy in creating legal issues that reduce the scope of the questions that may be decided by disputed facts, which have resulted in a more restricted role for the jury in the legal process. For a judge to define an issue as an issue of law is to deny the questions under that issue to the jury. When an issue cannot be resolved using evidence presented by the parties, the issue must logically present either a question of fact or a mixed question, and the definition of the question as one of law risks denying constitutional rights and customary expectations that the matter is one for the jury.

*See also:* pleading, pleading theories, issue pleading; question.

> **issue of fact (question of fact or factual issue)**   A question regarding past events. An issue of fact is a dispute between the parties in which each party asserts a version of actions or events in the past that differs from the other in some material way. The purposes in considering the issue are to resolve the difference and to determine from the evidence which of the competing claims of what happened in the past is demonstrably true. An issue of fact may only be resolved according to admissible evidence. Issues of fact are determined by the trier of fact, which in many cases is a jury. Issues of fact found at trial, particularly by a jury, are given considerable deference on appeal, being disturbed only if there is evidence of wrongdoing or mistake in the legal instructions or if the jury reaches such an absurd result that no reasonable juror could have done so.
> *See also:* fact.

**issue of law (question of law or legal issue)** An issue in without a significant dispute of the facts. An issue of law is a question solely of what are the legal obligations of one or more of the parties to an action. A legal issue is independent of any factual issue, and the outcome of a legal issue depends solely upon the determination of the state of law as interpreted from sources in the legal archive. Issues of law are for the sole determination of the court, and they are not submitted to a jury. Further, issues of law are reviewed de novo on appeal with no deference to the decision made in the court below.

**issue on appeal (question presented for review)** The question to be reviewed by an appellate court. An issue on appeal is a particular issue, whether an issue of fact, an issue of law, or a mixed issue of fact and law, that is the subject of the appeal. The appellant raises issues on appeal, although the appellee may raise further issues on cross-appeal, or in some instances in rebuttal. Under the rules of some appellate courts, particularly in state supreme courts, issues are presented in the petition to hear the appeal, or in the case of the U.S. Supreme Court the petition for certiorari, and its responses. The court grants review only as to specific issues, which might or might not be those the parties raised. In appellate courts of error, an error raised is the same as an issue on appeal.

An issue raised on appeal must have been fairly and properly raised and preserved in the court below. A failure to preserve an issue at trial or in an intermediate appeals court waives that issue, barring its appeal further. In many jurisdictions, a motion to reconsider must be filed raising the issue subject to appeal, before an appeal can be taken on that issue, or it is waived.

The standard of review for each issue will vary, with deference being given to the trial court on matters of discretion over motions and to the finder of fact on factual issues. Issues of law on appeal will be heard with no deference to the lower court.

See also: issue, issue before the court, issue of law (question of law or legal issue); issue, issue before the court, issue of fact (question of fact or factual issue).

**material issue (immaterial issue)** An issue related to a case before the court. A material issue is an issue that may be raised in a civil or criminal action in court because it is relevant and lawful for resolution of the action. Whether the issue has been properly or timely raised cannot affect its materiality. An issue that is not relevant to an action or that is barred by law from being heard in the action is not material to it, which is called an immaterial issue. Material issues may be issues of law, fact, or mixed. Immaterial issues are either irrelevant to the action before the court or not lawfully appropriate to resolve the issues that properly are before it.

**mixed issue of fact and law (mixed question or issue of law and fact)** An issue in which both the facts and the law are in dispute. An issue of fact and law, or a mixed issue, is an issue before the court in which resolution of the one issue requires the court both to consider disputed evidence to determine factual matters and to consider disputed legal authority to determine the legal obligations of the parties. The legal matter must be resolved to determine the factual matter, and the factual matter must be resolved to determine the legal matter.

A mixed issue may be resolved at trial by one of three schemes. It may be divided into component issues so that the component issues of law may be resolved independently of the component issues of fact, or it may be submitted to the jury as a question of fact presented in the alternative, or it may be submitted to the jury with appropriate legal instructions to find a given legal result in the event the jury finds a given fact as one or another party has argued it.

See also: issue, issue before the court, issue of law (question of law or legal issue); issue, issue before the court, issue of fact (question of fact or factual issue).

**tender of issue** Formal presentation of an issue in court. The tender of an issue is the raising of a question of fact, law, or a mixture of fact and law to be resolved by the court in an action. An issue that has been tendered may be submitted to a jury with proper instructions or, in the event of a matter heard without a jury, to the court. To tender an issue does not, alone, assure that it must be addressed, as the opposing party or the court may object to a given issue on any ground.

**joinder of issue** The agreed focus of each party in an action to contest specific issues of fact and of law. The joinder of issue in an action is the effect prior to trial at which the parties focus their issue or issues so that each specific claim of law and of fact are the subject of argument and proof. As a practical matter, this focus usually develops during the exchange of pleadings and through discovery, having been completed by the time of a pre-trial conference or the submission of jury instructions.

**istihsan** The preference for a new rule over an old rule. Istihsan is a means in Islamic law of developing a new rule from authority, which is to be preferred to an older rule. Although istihsan has been likened to equity, this analogy is less apt than one in which a new constitutional principle is derived from the text and substituted for a principle that had been earlier derived from the same text. The principle is employed heavily by the Hanafi school of Sunni jurisprudence.

**itemized deduction** See: tax, tax deduction, itemized deduction (below-the-line deduction).

**itinerancy (itinerant)** Prone to travel. Itinerancy is travel, and—as it more often is used—an itinerant or an itinerant person is a person who travels or journeys from one place to the next. Itinerant judges were therefore traveling judges, or as it became known, judges who rode the circuit. An itinerant person, or an itinerant, is a traveler.

**iure** *See:* jus, jure (iure).

**ius** *See:* jus (ius).

**ius commune** *See:* jus, jus commune (ius commune).

> [T]his society has a peculiar cant and jargon of their own,
> that no other mortal can understand, and wherein
> all their laws are written . . .
>
> Jonathan Swift, *Gulliver's Travels* (1726), in 8 *The Prose Works of JonathanSwift*,
> D.D. 261 (Temple Scott, ed.) (George Bell, 1899).

# J

**j**   The tenth letter of the modern English alphabet. "J" signifies a variety of functions as a symbol. It is translated into Juliett (or Juliet) for radio signals and NATO military transmissions, into John for some police radio traffic, and into dot, dash, dash, dash in Morse Code. J was not a letter in classical or medieval Latin, the sound becoming common before the letter was invented, probably during the time of early European printing. Its first use in English was derived from French, and some senses of i shifted to j between 1580 and the 1630s.

**j as an abbreviation**   A word commencing in J. When preceding or following a name, J. usually stands for Judge or Justice. When used as the sole letter of an abbreviation, J often stands for Journal. It may also stand for Japan, Japanese, joint, judgment, judicial, judiciary, juncta, juris, jurisprudence, jurist, justice, and Justinian. It may also stand for the initial of the name of an author or case reporter, such as Jacob, James, John, Johnson, and Jones.

**J.A.G. or JAG or TJAG or judge advocate**
*See:* judge, judge advocate general (J.A.G. or JAG or TJAG or judge advocate).

**J.D. or JD**   *See:* degree, academic degree, law degree, Juris Doctor (J.D. or JD).

**J.N.O.V. or JNOV or judgment as a matter of law or JML or JMOL or judgment non obstante veredicto**
*See:* judgment, judgment notwithstanding the verdict (J.N.O.V. or JNOV or judgment as a matter of law or JML or JMOL or judgment non obstante veredicto).

**J.P. or JP or justice court judge**   *See:* judge, justice of the peace (J.P. or JP or justice court judge).

**Jackson-Denno hearing**   *See:* confession, Jackson-Denno hearing.

**jail (gaol)**   A place for the confinement of prisoners. A jail is a building, or portion of a building, used to confine prisoners, especially in local jurisdictions. A person initially detained on suspicion of a crime, a person who has been charged awaiting trial, or a person held under a protective order might all be detained in a jail without having been sentenced to a term of confinement as a criminal sentence. Even so, jails are a primary means of incarceration for criminals convicted of crimes in a community, although longer term inmates are likely to be transferred to prisons. Although there are many exceptions, a jail tends to be under the jurisdiction of a county or municipality, and a prison tends to be under state or federal jurisdiction. Note: gaol and jail are pronounced the same.

**jail cell**   *See:* cell, prison cell (jail cell).

**jailer (gaoler)**   The keeper of a jail. A jailer is a person who has custody over a jail and of the prisoners within it. The jailer, often a deputy sheriff in the U.S., is responsible under the law for the health, safety, and security of every person in custody or on the premises otherwise. The early English and American spelling, as gaoler, was pronounced as the modern jailer.

**jargon**   Phrases and terms with a special meaning for a specific group. Jargon is any language that is developed by and employed by a particular community among a broader community of speakers of a language. Every profession has some form of jargon, and most communities develop a particular argot that may amount to a jargon.

**legal jargon (legalese or legalism)**   Language exclusive to the legal profession. Legal jargon are words and phrases that are exclusively used by lawyers and judges or, even more confusingly to the non-lawyer, words used in the law that have a meaning quite different from their meaning in general usage. Judges and legislative drafters are the source of most jargon.

As with all specialized languages in a profession, legal jargon affords some benefits and some detriments to the law. Used well, jargon allows a greater degree of specificity and economy of language, and the risks of the poor use of jargon are probably not greater than the risks of the poor use of general language anyway. Even so, jargon creates an impediment to lay understanding of the law, increasing the likelihood of mistake even for the unusual person who seeks to understand a legal obligation and perform it.

Legalese is an especially convoluted form of legal jargon that is unnecessicarily complex or opaque. A legalism is a particular word or phrase that has meaning only in the context of legal jargon.

*See also:* French, law French; Latin, Law Latin.

**Jay Court**   *See:* court, U.S. court, U.S. Supreme Court, Jay Court.

**jaywalking**   *See:* pedestrian,   pedestrian   offense (jaywalking).

**Jehovah's Witness**   *See:* church, church, Jehovah's Witnesses.

**Jencks Act or Jencks evidence or Jencks statement**   *See:* exculpation, exculpatory evidence, Jencks material (Jencks Act or Jencks evidence or Jencks statement).

**Jencks material**   *See:* exculpation, exculpatory evidence, Jencks material (Jencks Act or Jencks evidence or Jencks statement).

**jeopardy**   A danger of some harm, especially of criminal punishment. Jeopardy is any risk of loss. In criminal law, jeopardy is the particular risk of criminal liability created at the moment of the commencement of a prosecution.

**double jeopardy**   A risk of a second trial for an offense of which one has been already tried. Double jeopardy is a second trial for an offense of which one has been already acquitted or convicted. The term originates in the common law, as the object of a prohibition against a person's being tried twice for the same criminal offense. The Constitution declares that no person "for the same offense, be twice put in jeopardy of life and limb." The effect of this constitutional privilege is not only to prevent a retrial once either a jury verdict or final judgment of acquittal in a criminal action has been entered or a finding of guilt and final order of punishment has been mandated but also to prevent appeal by the prosecution of a final judgment based on the evidence.

Double jeopardy arises most often owing either to "same offense" considerations, in which two or more statutes prohibit the same conduct and are brought as separate charges for the same action rather than alternative or lesser included offense charges or to "unit of prosecution" issues, which involve the number of violations from the same statute a prosecutor can charge the defendant based on one sequence of events.

Double jeopardy does not bar prosecution for the same conduct by different sovereigns for offenses against each from the same conduct, nor does criminal double jeopardy affect civil liability. Although an appeal by the state of an acquittal is rare, double jeopardy does not bar an appeal of a criminal acquittal on procedural grounds of other bases that would not result in a retrial of an issue on which the defendant has been found not guilty. A civil suit by a private party is not barred, even though it arises from conduct for which a defendant has been acquitted of a criminal action arising from it. Likewise, a civil judgment for the defense for some conduct would not preclude a prosecution against the defendant for a criminal charge based on the same conduct.

*See also:* joinder of offenses, compulsory joinder rule (compulsory joinder statute or compulsory

joinder of offenses); non, non bis in idem (ne bis in idem); res, res judicata, collateral estoppel.

**dual-sovereignty doctrine**   Two states may prosecute the same defendant for the same offense. The doctrine of dual sovereignty allows more than one government to prosecute a defendant for the same conduct, so long as each has valid jurisdiction over the offense, without violating the Double Jeopardy Clause of the Fifth Amendment. Thus, both the United States and a state may prosecute a single defendant for the same conduct. So may two or more states or an Indian tribe and another government. The dual–sovereignty clause does not, however, allow multiple prosecutions by different departments of the same government; a federal criminal action may not be brought for the conduct for which a single defendant has been subject to a court–martial, nor may a county and a state bring separate prosecutions for the same conduct.

**former jeopardy**   The first trial of which the second trial is forbidden. Former jeopardy is the condition of having been tried for a particular act and, therefore, is also the basis of a motion to dismiss a subsequent indictment, information, or trial on the basis of double jeopardy.

**jetsam**   *See:* salvage, jetsam (jettison).

**jettison**   *See:* salvage, jetsam (jettison).

**jihad**   A personal struggle for one's conscience or a military conflict. Jihad is struggle, or perseverance. Traditionally, it does not mean holy war, although it has been corrupted to that meaning among non–scholars. War is haram in Islam. Defense of the faith is required, though, and this may take a physical form, if need be, when it may only be in defense of the Faith of Islam itself, and not a country, land, region, culture, or any other worldly thing. From the Arabic root j-h-d, which means to struggle or persevere.

**Jim Crow law (race laws)**   The laws of racial segregation. Jim Crow laws were the statutes, municipal ordinances, and case decisions that created and enforced de jure segregation and reinforced de facto segregation of Americans based on the construction of race, which persisted from the end of Reconstruction to the end of the Civil Rights Movement. Jim Crow laws were prominent in southern states, but there was no lack of similar laws in northern and western states, as well as federal laws. Jim Crow laws were constitutional under the federal constitutional doctrines of state sovereign immunity and of separate but equal treatment, complying with the notion of equal protection of the laws enshrined in Plessy v. Ferguson, 163 U.S. 537 (1896), although their dismantling commenced as early as World War I, with such cases as Buchanan v. Warley 245 U.S. 60 (1917), outlawing the legal segregation of housing. The end of Jim Crow came with the rejection of the Plessy doctrine in Brown v. Board of Education, 347 U.S. 483 (1954) and the passage of the federal civil rights and voting rights acts in the 1960s.

*See also:* equality, separate–but–equal doctrine (separate but equal); immunity, sovereign immunity, state sovereign immunity (eleventh amendment immunity); slavery, badge of slavery; marginalization (marginalized group); tax, poll tax (head tax or capitation tax); lynching (lynch, lynch–law).

**job**   Work for another with monetary gain, whether lawful or criminal. A job is an informal term for a particular employment, whether as an employee or as a contractor. It is a formal term for many types of contracted work. A job also refers to a specific task or role given to an otherwise more generally employed worker. A job for fabrication, such as manufacture or printing, or for sale, is a specific contract for the delivery of goods of a particular form, quantity, and quality of material. "Job lot" thus refers to a discreet stock of the material.

*See also:* employment (employ or employed or employee or employer).

**job as compensated work**   Activity regularly performed for compensation. A trade, occupation, employment, profession for which one is compensated.

**job action as employment action**   *See:* employment, employment action (adverse employment action or adverse job action or job action).

**job action as labor action**   A self–help measure by employees or a union. A job action is a means by which a union brings pressure on an employer to concede a matter in negotiation between the management and the workers of a plant, employer, or industry. Job actions primarily include strikes, slowdowns, sick–outs, work–to–rule plans, picketing, and other similar activities. Job actions may be legal or protected by contract or labor regulation, or they may be illegal depending upon who commits them and whether or not the job action violates a regulation or court order.

*See also:* employment, employment action (adverse employment action or adverse job action or job action).

**job applicant (employment applicant)**   A person who applies for a job. A job applicant is a person who seeks in good faith to be offered a job, whether a part–time or full–time position, as a contractor or an employee, and who takes the steps required by an employer in order to be considered for a position of employment. Federal law forbids most employers from discriminating against or among job applicants on the basis of the federally restricted characteristics of race, color, religion, sex, national origin, age (if the applicant is over 40), and disability. State laws may extend similar prohibitions to discrimination, such as the bar in New York to discrimination on the basis of age, race, creed, color, national origin, sexual orientation, military status, sex, disability, predisposing genetic characteristics, or marital status.

*See also:* discrimination.

**job applicant pool**   The people available in a given region qualified and available to apply for a job. A job applicant pool is a statistical estimate of the people who are capable and available to apply for a given job in the geographical region in which the hire is to be made or applications are to be taken. The job applicant pool is a benchmark for the assessment of discriminatory practices in hiring and promotion.

**job–relatedness (work–related or employment related)**   Related to the performance of one's job. Job–relatedness describes the scope of a relationship between a worker or applicant for a work position and the performance of the tasks of the work. Job–related tests must have a relationship to the successful performance of a job to be used for the selection or promotion of worker in a manner that is not discriminatory. Job–relatedness, measured by both assigned duties and tasks reasonably related to the performance of assigned duties, is the measure of the scope of workers' compensation insurance. An injury that is job–related is covered under most plans. An injury that is not job–related is not covered.

**jobber**   A supplier in a commercial supply chain. A jobber buys goods or commodities and resells them, usually in job lots.

**John**   *See:* prostitution, John.

**John Doe**   *See:* name, fictitious name, John Doe (Richard Roe or Jane Doe).

**John Doe warrant**   *See:* warrant, John Doe warrant.

**joinder**

   **joinder of issue**   *See:* issue, joinder of issue.

   **joinder of offenses**

      **compulsory joinder rule (compulsory joinder statute or compulsory joinder of offenses)**   All offenses to be charged from the same conduct must be tried in one action. The compulsory joinder rule as a matter of criminal procedure requires that of all of the charges that may be brought by a single sovereign against a particular defendant that are based on a single act or from the same conduct or transaction be presented for trial in a single action. Those charges, including lesser included offenses or ancillary charges or tack–on offenses that are not brought in the first action, may be barred by speedy trial rules, but in most jurisdictions they are barred by a statute or court rule requiring compulsory joinder of offenses. The federal courts have no compulsory joinder rule, although the speedy trial rule applies to later offenses that might have been charged at the time of the first charge.

      *See also:* jeopardy, double jeopardy.

   **disjoinder**   The separation of a joined action. Disjoinder is the division of a joined action into two or more separate actions. Disjoinder is not a term particularly limited to civil or criminal actions but used in either context, albeit rarely. Disjoinder, a noun, is more often referred to by the verb to sever.

**joinder of actions** The collection into one action of various causes between the same litigants. Joinder of actions, in general, is the collection of various causes for relief among the same groups of litigants or the same criminal defendant into a single cause of action.

As a matter of civil procedure, joinder of claims may be accomplished through many means, not least by the designation of all of the actions a plaintiff might have into a single complaint or by the designation of all defenses and counterclaims by a defendant against the plaintiff into the pleadings of the same action. The technical pleading requirements of Bouvier's day, which segregated actions by form of claim or recovery, have been largely repealed, allowing pleading in the alternative in a single complaint as well as a host of other means to consolidate actions.

As a matter of criminal procedure, joinder of claims is allowed as long as each charge could have been brought separately. The old rules of indictment have given way to multiple–count indictments incorporating contingent charges and charges for lesser included offenses.

**joinder of claims** The gathering of several claims among common parties into one action. Joinder of claims is the collection of more than one claim or counterclaim with another between two or more parties in a single action. In the federal rules of civil procedure, joinder of claims is encouraged under Federal Rule of Civil Procedure 18.

Joinder of claims generally refers to the joining of claims which would, if each existed in the absence of the other, be heard in a different forum. Thus, the use of pendent or ancillary jurisdiction to join a state claim with a federal claim, like the use of the clean-up doctrine in equity to hear an additional legal claim, allows the joinder of claims that would ordinarily be heard in different courts. Joinder in an action with more than two parties does not require that every claim or cross–claim be directed against all other parties.

Joinder allows claims to be joined in the alternative as well as contingently, so that one claim may not be valid if another claim succeeds.

**joinder of offenses (joinder of defendants or prejudicial joinder)** Aggregation of criminal charges into a single action. Joinder of offenses, or "joinder" when used in a criminal action, is either the listing of separate counts against a single defendant or the listing of counts against separate defendants in a single criminal action. Joinder of offenses against a single defendant is proper if the charges arise from a single transaction, occurrence or action, have a similar character or victim, or are part of a common scheme, plan, or enterprise. Joinder of offenses against multiple defendants in a single action is proper if each defendant participated in a scheme, plan, or enterprise common to all of the others. The joinder of several defendants does not require that each be charged exactly as the others.

**joinder of parties** The addition of a plaintiff or defendant after the complaint is filed. Joinder of parties is the means by which a litigant in a pending civil action brings an additional party into that litigation. Joinder may be performed by either the plaintiff or the defendant. Certain parties are necessary to the litigation and a failure to join these parties to an action may require its dismissal. Other parties may be joined for the efficiency or convenience of the parties. Joinder is initiated by a party, and a party may claim the absence of a party who must be present for the court either to hear fully the claims in the action or to give an adequate remedy may either join the other party or complain to the court of the other party's failure to do so. In the event a present party fails to join a required party to the action, and the joinder is not feasible for jurisdictional reasons, the court may dismiss the action, although dismissal is usually not appropriate if the plaintiff would have no other forum available in which to bring the action.

Note that joinder is an act to bring a third party into an action initiated by an existing party in that action. Intervention is an act to join an action by a party not already present in that action. Impleader is the specific form of joinder of parties used by a defendant to join a third party as a co–defendant. Of course, parties may be joined by a plaintiff initially by filling the complaint against multiple defendants, which is done through service and not through motion.

*See also:* intervention (intervene or intervenor).

*jurisdiction* In order to be properly joined, a person or entity who would be joined must either be subject to the jurisdiction in which an action is pending or waive its objections to jurisdiction. The joining of a necessary party may alter the diversity of the parties altering the scope of federal jurisdiction in the case. Even so, a party joined on spurious grounds merely for the purpose of establishing or defeating jurisdiction in an action must be dismissed.

*required party or indispensable party or necessary party* A required party is a party in whose absence the court cannot accord complete relief among existing parties. As a matter of custom, a required party who must be joined is considered a necessary party if that party feasibly can be joined under Rule 19(a) but called an indispensible party if that party cannot be feasibly joined under 19(a) and relief must be considered under Rule 19(b).

*See also:* party, party to an action, indispensable party; party, party to an action, necessary party.

**collusive joinder (improper joinder or manufactured joinder)** The joinder of a party only to create federal diversity jurisdiction Collusive joinder is the joinder of a party who does not have a bona fide interest in the case in order to create diversity of citizenship among the parties so that the case can be removed from state court to federal court. The collusion usually occurs through an attempt to assign an interest or claim or to create an agency, representation, or fiduciary role to a person located in a convenient jurisdiction. This assignment may take place during the action or at any time prior, though the assignment might have been a bona fide decision made without regard to litigation, an appearance of collusion arises with evidence that the assignment or creation of the role for the party was made at least in contemplation of the potential for litigation. The party seeking to remove must prove that diversity jurisdiction is proper at all times when it may become an issue in federal court, and if there is a suggestion a joinder is collusive or otherwise improper, the district court must be satisfied that diversity is fully and properly established, or it must remand the action to state court.

*See also:* collusion (collude or collusive).

**compulsory joinder** The obligation of a current party to join a required party to the action. Compulsory joinder is the joinder of a necessary party to an action, or the action will be dismissed if the plaintiff does not join the party to the action. Joinder may be compelled, by order of the court if necessary, when a party is absent from an action and any one of three conditions is satisfied: if the court cannot award complete relief to the parties already before the court without the party; if the missing party claims an interest that requires that party's presence to protect that interest; or if the failure to bring the party into the action would expose one of the parties in the action to multiple or potentially inconsistent liabilities.

> **feasibility** Capable of being haled into court through joinder. Feasibility is a requirement for joinder of a necessary party under Federal Rule of Civil Procedure 19(a), which designates a party whose joinder is feasible if the party is subject to service of process and the party's joinder would not destroy the court's jurisdiction over the subject matter already established.

**fraudulent joinder** The joinder of a party only to defeat federal diversity jurisdiction. Fraudulent joinder is the joinder of a party who does not have a bona fide interest in the case in order to defeat diversity of citizenship among the parties so that the case cannot be removed from state court to federal court or, if the case was first brought in federal court, to seek a remand. When a court determines that a non-diverse party has been fraudulently joined, the action remains in federal court without remand, and the fraudulently-joined party is either dismissed from the action or remains without regard to citizenship.

The fraudulent nature of a fraudulent joinder is established functionally: if the purportedly fraudulently-joined party is a defendant, the joinder is fraudulent if the plaintiff has no valid cause of action against that defendant. Likewise, if the purportedly fraudulently-joined party is a plaintiff, the joinder is fraudulent if the joined plaintiff has no

valid claim to make against the defendants. In either case, the fraudulent joinder will fail if a non-joining party proves actual fraud or collusion either in the filing of the joinder or in actions that created relationships that would be predicate to the filing of joinder, and these actions were made in contemplation of the likelihood of litigation. The party seeking to file an action in diversity, to remove or to avoid remand must prove that diversity jurisdiction is proper at all times when it may become an issue in federal court. If there is a suggestion a joinder is collusive or otherwise improper, the district court must be satisfied that diversity is fully and properly established, or it must remand the action to state court.

**permissive joinder** Joinder allowed to aggregate all of the claims with common issues of fact and law. Permissive joinder is the assertion of claims against different parties in the same action (whether the joinder is made by motion or in the initial complaint). Permissive joinder requires that all of the claims in the action arise from the same transaction or occurrence or condition and that each claim has some issues of law or fact in common with the others.

**misjoinder** A joinder of a party, a claim, or an offense made in error. A misjoinder is a joinder that is wrongfully made, or a joinder that becomes wrongful under the rules or statutes owing to a change in circumstance. Misjoinder may occur through an error in process or by the joining of an improper claim or an unrelated party. The remedy for misjoinder will vary according to its cause, but remedies include severance of actions, bifurcation of a single action, dismissal or a claim or charge, dismissal of a party, or the dismissal of an action, information, or indictment.

**non-joinder (nonjoinder)** The failure to join a party, claim, or offense. Non-joinder may refer to any failure to join a party, claim, or offense, although it is most often employed to describe a plaintiff's failure to join a party in a civil action. If the party is a required party, the defendant or the court may move to compel joinder, or for dismissal if the party is necessary or indispensable and not joined.

**joint** United into a common bond or unit. Joint depicts an especially unified collaboration. In the law, a joint arrangement usually arises from or requires that the parties have a more integrated obligation toward one another than the usual arrangement of that type. Thus a joint tenancy has a greater requirement of unity between the co-tenants than does a tenancy in common, a joint action places the co-plaintiffs in a more collaborative relationship than separate actions, and joint tortfeasors collaboratively bring about a common harm.

> **joint account** *See:* account, joint account.

> **joint and mutual will** *See:* will, last will and testament, joint and mutual will (mutual will).

**joint and several liability**  *See:* liability, joint and several liability.

**joint bankruptcy**  *See:* bankruptcy, joint bankruptcy.

**joint custody**  *See:* child, child custody, joint custody (divided custody or shared custody).

**joint-defense privilege**  *See:* privilege, evidentiary privilege, attorney-client privilege, joint-defense privilege.

**joint executor**  *See:* executor, joint executor.

**joint inventor**  *See:* inventor, joint inventor (co-inventor or joint invention).

**joint liability**  *See:* liability, joint liability, York–Antwerp rules; liability, joint liability, general average; liability, joint liability.

**joint representation**  *See:* representation, legal representation, joint representation (concurrent representation or multiple representation).

**joint resolution**  *See:* resolution, congressional resolution, joint resolution.

**joint return**  *See:* tax, tax filing, tax filing status, married filling jointly (joint return).

**joint stock bank or joint stock company**  *See:* company, joint-stock company (joint stock bank or joint stock company).

**joint-stock company**  *See:* company, joint-stock company (joint stock bank or joint stock company).

**joint tenancy**  *See:* tenancy, co–tenancy, joint tenancy, unities, four unities (tits); tenancy, co–tenancy, joint tenancy, per my et per tout (per tout); tenancy, co–tenancy, joint tenancy | right of survivorship; tenancy, co–tenancy, joint tenancy (joint tenants or joint estate).

**joint tenants or joint estate**  *See:* tenancy, co-tenancy, joint tenancy (joint tenants or joint estate).

**joint tortfeasor**  *See:* tortfeasor, joint tortfeasor (active tortfeasor or passive tortfeasor or concurrent tortfeasor).

**joint trial**  *See:* consolidation, consolidation of actions, joint trial.

**joint trustees**  *See:* trustee, joint trustees (co-trustees).

**joint venture**  *See:* venture, joint venture (co-venturer or coventurer).

**JOTP or JOP**  *See:* judgment, judgment on the pleadings (JOTP or JOP).

**journal entry**  *See:* legislation, legislative history, journal entry (entry in a legislative journal).

**joyriding**  *See:* driving, joyriding.

**Judaism**  The faith of the Jewish people. Judaism is the monotheistic religion of the Jewish people, whose practices and beliefs are recorded in the Torah, or Tanakh, the five books of Moses. The practice of Judaism is based on the 613 commandments of the Torah, as elaborated and understood through interpretations in the Mishnah and the Talmud. There is a close relationship among Judaism, Christianity, and Islam, all of which share some aspects of a common tradition of monotheism and respect for a revered text as the source of the law of the faithful.

**judex**  The judge, or the office of the judge. Judex is Latin for a judge, or the power or office of the judge.
*See also:* judge (judicial).

**judge (judicial)**  A public officer appointed to decide questions of law in dispute. A judge is, broadly, any person who occupies a legal office that is dedicated to the application of the law to particular questions of fact and to the pronouncement of a judgment or order as a result of that application. Within a given legal system, there may be many titles for judges, and some individuals will perform the role of a judge but be titled justice, justice of the peace, or magistrate.

Within every advanced legal system, judges act with discretion within particular boundaries. Some of these boundaries are substantive, such as the range of permissible understanding of the texts of contracts, statutes, precedents, and other sources of law. Some are jurisdictional, in which only certain matters may be raised before a judge, limited by geography, subject matter, and the scope of the powers of the court. Some boundaries are functional, in that judges of courts of limited jurisdiction, judges of courts of general jurisdiction, and judges of appeal each are given particular and distinct authority to hear matters of differing types, even if the various matters might arise in the same cause of action.
*See also:* judge, black-robe disease; shenpanyuan; judex.

**judge as witness**  *See:* witness, judge as witness.

**activist judge**  A judge willing to depart from the strictest reading of precedent, statute, or text. Activist judge is a term of criticism applied to judges who appear (to the critic) to have relied on personal preference or broad policy to reach a decision that is contrary to statutes or case precedents. As with many such terms, activism is in the eye of the beholder: judges applying policy favored by the speaker are courageous strict constructionists restoring essential values of the law, while judges applying policy disliked by the speaker are activist judges putting preference ahead of precedent.

**administrative law judge (A.L.J. or ALJ)**  An administrative officer who acts as a judge to review appeals or hear claims in an agency. An administrative law judge is an executive official in an administrative agency, appointed to hear specific citations and complaints filed under that agency's regulations, as well as appeals of order or decisions made within the agency. Although these judges are not members of the judicial branch, they are accorded greater autonomy and wider discretion than other agency personnel.

**Article II judge** A judge who holds office in executive agency rather than a court of law. An Article II judge is a judge whose appointment is completely at the behest of the executive and whose authority is limited to a scope of Presidential authority. Article II judges are usually administrative law judges, immigration judges, or judges otherwise appointed to serve within an executive agency as defined by Article II of the U.S. Constitution. The term is also used to describe a recess appointment of a judge, who is not subject in the federal system to the advice and consent of the Senate until the next Senate term. Some states have the equivalent of Article II judges, for judges who are responsible to the governor of that state.

**Article III judge** A judge in the judicial branch of government. An Article III judge is a judge whose office is assigned to the judicial branch, and whose appointment to the judgeship, in the federal system is nominated by the President with the advice and consent of the Senate. The term is also used in some states, particularly those with the courts and judicial power described in the third article of the state constitution.

**associate judge (associate justice)** A judge or justice who does not ordinarily preside over the court when in session. An associate judge or justice does not preside in court when it is in session. Although Justices of the U.S. Supreme Court other than the Chief Justice of the United States are customarily referred to as associate justices, that term does not appear in the U.S. Constitution, but justice does. The term is used as a matter of the constitutional or statutory text in some states.

**black-robe disease** Arrogance in a judge. Black-robe disease is a slang term for a judge who flaunts judicial power and dominates proceedings at the expense of the dispensation of justice.
*See also:* judge (judicial).

**chancellor** A judicial officer in equity. A chancellor is a judicial officer in equity. Though few states retain the office of Chancellor, the powers in equity of a judge in a court of general jurisdiction are often referred to a the powers of the chancellor.
*See also:* chancellor.

**chief judge** The judge who presides over the court and its administration. The chief judge presides at hearings of the court when the judge is present, but the role that distinguishes a chief judge from other judges of the same court is that the chief judge is responsible for the administration of the court. Although certain tasks may be outside the scope of the chief judge's authority (given, for instance, to the clerk of court or to the sheriff or marshal for administration), the chief judge is responsible for all administration related to the performance of the court otherwise, including the delicate task of leadership among the other judges. In most courts, a chief judge is assigned by custom according to seniority among the judges available when there is a vacancy. The Chief Judge of the State of New York is that state's highest judicial position.

**Lord Chancellor (Lord High Chancellor or Lord Keeper of the Great Seal)** The chief judicial officer of England and the highest source of equity. The Lord Chancellor is the highest judicial officer in England and Wales and, as the Secretary of State for Justice, the member of the British government responsible for the management of the courts and the prime minister's policies regarding justice. The Chancellor was once the sole final judge of matters in equity, but following the reforms of 2005, the Lord Chancellor presides over the Chancery Division of the Supreme Court. The Lord Chancellor is Keeper of the Great Seal, the device that signals the assent of the monarch to all writs, orders, and letters patent.

**Master of the Rolls** A judge of the Court of Appeal and President of the Civil Division. The Master of the Rolls in the contemporary English judiciary is the presiding judge of the civil division of the Court of Appeal for England and Wales. By custom, the position is second in the English judiciary to the Lord Chief Justice and third behind the Lord Chancellor. Historically, this office was an appellate judge of equity, serving as the deputy of the Lord Chancellor.

**hanging judge** A judge reputed to inflict the severest possible sentence in a criminal action. A hanging judge is a judge who is more inclined to sentence a convicted criminal defendant to the most severe possible punishment allowed by statute. Such a judge is less likely to show mercy or consider mitigating circumstances in proscribing punishment. The presence of this type of judge presiding over one's case may lead to defense counsel requesting either a recusal or alternate venue.

**judge advocate general (J.A.G. or JAG or TJAG or judge advocate)** A military law officer. The judge advocates general are military officers in the Army, Navy, and Air Force, who advise the heads of the military services on matters of law, especially military law, international law, and the law of war, and criminal and civilian law that affect the military or its members. Officers who work in this capacity in each service are members of the judge advocate general's corp, and the chief of the corps for each service is the Judge Advocate General, or TJAG. General in this usage means generality not rank, and the TJAG of the Navy is usually a vice admiral.

A judge advocate general is distinct from the officer presiding at a court martial. The judge presiding at a court martial may or may not be a member of the JAG corps, depending upon whom the officer summoning the court martial appoints. JAG officers will support a court martial by providing counsel for both sides as well as support for the bench.

**judge shopping**   An attempt to place a matter before a sympathetic judge. Judge shopping is the practice of lawyers and police to place matters for judicial action before a judge who is perceived to favor the matter or the type of litigant represented by the judge shopper. Judge shopping is akin to forum shopping but usually restricted to seeking to be heard by one of the several judges within the forum in which jurisdiction over the matter involved is clear.

**judgeship**   The office of a judge. The judgeship is the office of a judge, the position in the legal and constitutional structure that brings both specific authority and responsibility as well as inherent duties and powers. The most important of these obligations are to hear disputes properly before the court in an impartial manner, to assess the facts and the law with knowledge and skill, and in good faith to render opinions and judgments that are fair, accurate, trustworthy, and in keeping with the best traditions of the law.

**judicial activism**   *See:* judge, activist judge.

**judicial branch**   A branch of government consisting of judges and the court system. The judicial branch of a government is the branch of government including the courts system, including the judiciary itself, the courts, clerk's offices, bailiffs and marshals, and such ancillary offices as are required to exercise the judicial power of the government. In the United States government, the judicial branch is made up of one Supreme Court and such lower courts as Congress creates, all of which are invested with the judicial power of the United States according to Article III of the Constitution.

In a system of government divided among three branches by separation of powers, the judiciary is uniquely tasked with interpretation of the laws. The legislative branch creating laws, the executive branch carrying them out, the judicial branch is required to determine how to apply laws in specific questions when there is disagreement between officials of other branches, between private citizens, or between officials and citizens. This division of authority is essential, for instance, in the functioning of criminal law, by which the legislature must define a crime, the executive investigate a person for committing an act that amounts to a crime, but the judicial branch must determine that there is sufficient evidence to warrant arrest and then to be adjudged guilty of committing it. Though every branch is obligated to interpret its own constitutional obligations and limitations, the final determination of the constitutionality of actions by the Congress or by the President is usually a matter for the federal courts.

**judicial discretion**   The judge's power to act within the boundaries of the law. Judicial discretion is the authority given to a judge to determine the best answer to a question within a framework established by law and according to the evidence available. Discretion is a personal judgment that is informed by knowledge and observation, and although a judge may give reasons for an act of discretion, the reasons offered are less essential that the act itself in determining whether the act was within or beyond the scope of the judge's discretion. Discretion of a judge is sometimes seen as greater or lesser depending upon the judge's action, so that trial judge's decision to grant or deny a motion regarding evidence or courtroom management is given great weight, allowing both greater discretion to the judge and requiring greater deference to that decision by later judges than, say, an interpretation of a statute by that same trial judge.

*See also:* discretion.

**judicial economy**   Reducing the court's case load. Judicial economy is the goal of many judges: to reduce the number of cases pending in court by reducing the number of cases brought and by simplifying those that are filed. Judicial economy, carefully pursued, is in the interests of the bench, the public, and the litigants, by reducing the costs and burdens of litigation. Procedural devices such as simplified pleading, joinder of claims or parties, class actions, and tightly enforced calendars are tools of this pursuit. Even so, judicial economy is a dangerous concept when invoked to close the courthouse door to claims that merit relief in law or equity.

**juge d'instruction**   An investigating magistrate. The juge d'instruction is an independent judge, a magistrate with the powers to investigate any suspected criminal activity, including the powers of search, remand, and interrogation, and to bring charges without requiring the permission of the French executive (as would be the case for an ordinary prosecutor). The juge d'instruction is distinctly charged with examining all of the available evidence to discover both evidence of guilt and evidence that might exonerate any suspect of a crime.

**justice (justiceship)**   A title for a judge. A justice is a judge holding a judgeship that by custom, statute, or constitutional designation is accorded this title. The great number of justiceships are on courts denominated a supreme court or a justice court, which are the highest and the lowest courts in many judicial hierarchies. This custom is not uniform, however, as the New York courts demonstrate by placing their supreme courts as trial courts presided over by justices, and their court of appeals being a court of last resort, so that the Chief Judge of the State of New York takes precedence before all justices on that state's benches.

**chief justice**   The presiding officer of a supreme court. The chief justice is the justice who presides over a supreme court. The Chief Justice of the United States, as well as the chief justices or state chief judges, are also charged with overseeing the administration of the courts in their respective jurisdictions.

**circuit justice** The justice assigned to hear motions from a given appellate circuit. The circuit justice is a member of the U.S. Supreme Court who is assigned to hear single-justice motions from each circuit. There are more circuits than justices, and some justices are circuit justice to more than one circuit.

**justice of the peace (J.P. or JP or justice court judge)** A public officer presiding over a local court of limited jurisdiction. A justice of the peace presides over the court of a justice of the peace, which in many jurisdictions have been succeeded by a justice court. A justice of the peace in many jurisdictions need not be a qualified lawyer but is elected or appointed and then given minimal training in the laws that apply in that court. Justices of the peace are limited in jurisdiction to a precinct within a county, in criminal subject matter to the hearing of misdemeanors and to the issuance of process including search warrants, and in civil matters to small claims. As a public officer, justices of the peace in most jurisdictions have the power to solemnize a marriage.

Many states have replaced justice of the peace with justice court judges, sometimes with increased requirements of qualification and expanded subject matter jurisdiction. Most matters may be appealed from a justice of the peace to a state circuit court, where they are reviewed de novo.

**lay judge** A judge who is not required to be trained as a lawyer. A lay judge is a judge occupying a judgeship that is not usually filled by an attorney or person otherwise learned in the law. The office of justice of the peace is by custom an office of a lay judge. Jurors are sometimes called lay judges, although this usage is increasingly rare. Lay judges are routinely seated in a three-judge court in a civilian legal system, in which the lay judge has particular responsibility for the finding of facts; such lay judges are usually trained for the role albeit not through qualification for the practice of law.

**magistrate** A judge with limited jurisdiction but administrative authority. A magistrate is a judge given limited jurisdiction, particularly jurisdiction over the procedural or technical proceedings in a criminal investigation or criminal proceeding prior to trial, who also has certain administrative jurisdiction, such as jurisdiction over complaints from prisoners or paupers.

In its broader usage, magistrate may mean any person holding a public office whose authority includes the exercise of the power of the state or the magistracy. In this example, the chief executive is sometimes called the chief magistrate, although this usage has grown uncommon as the term has become more closely associated with the exercise of judicial power rather than executive power.

**magistrate–judge (magistrate judge)** A judicial officer in an office of limited authority. A United States Magistrate–Judge is the holder of a magistrate judgeship, a judicial office with specific and limited duties in support of a court of general jurisdiction. United States magistrates may hear a variety of motions, try minor cases that do not require the summoning of a jury, act by appointment in the absence of a judge over certain matters, assist in the trial of a case otherwise supervised by a judge, and hear certain matters on which the magistrate rules by report and recommendation to the U.S. District Judge.

The magistrate–judge is particularly responsible for reviewing motions in criminal causes, including petitions for search warrants and arrest warrants based on probable cause. In this role, the magistrate's obligation to remain neutral and detached in reviewing and ruling on the motion or petition is an essential role in the justice system.

*See also:* magister; master, special master.

**senior judge (senior status or judge on senior status)** A judge with long service and a reduced caseload. A judge on senior status is a judge who has served for a required number of years to qualify for such status, and who requests it, after which the judge usually assigned a reduced case-load. Federal judges are authorized to take senior status in lieu of retirement, for which a judge is eligible after fifteen years on the federal bench and after reaching age sixty-five. A senior judge maintains a docket of between twenty-five and one hundred percent of the usual docket for a judge of that court. Both senior judges and retired judges retain the pay of an active judge.

**judge's chamber or judicial chamber** *See:* chamber, judicial chambers (judge's chamber or judicial chamber).

**judgment** A decree ruling on a matter, imposing a sentence, or granting a remedy. A judgment is the order ruling to grant or deny relief in any matter pending before a court. A judgment may be partial or complete, preliminary or final, summary or following a trial. In each instance, the judgment is the order that decrees what official action must follow the determination of the questions of law and fact raised in the action before the court. There are countless examples of forms of judgment. A judgment might dismiss a party or a claim or an action. A judgment might require pretrial relief or order final relief to a successful plaintiff.

The defining aspect of a judgment is that it decrees the grant or denial of some relief sought by a party before the court. An opinion of the court on a matter of law contended between the parties might include the language of a judgment, by which the court orders the parties to do or refrain from some thing, or a judgment may be made by a separate instrument or by an oral ruling from the bench or in chambers, as long as the ruling is on the record of the action. The label upon the instrument issued is not controlling, and a judgment may be issued in an order, opinion, decree, writ, or other judicial pronouncement. A judgment is inherently appealable, whether or not an appeal of the judgment is taken by a party dissatisfied with it.

**judgment lien**   *See:* lien, judgment lien.

**judgment nisi or common order**   *See:* order, order nisi (judgment nisi or common order).

**judgment of previous conviction**   *See:* hearsay, hearsay exception, hearsay allowed regardless of witness availability, judgment of previous conviction.

**amendment of judgment (motion to alter judgment or motion to amend judgment)**   The substitution of a changed judgment for an earlier judgment in an action. Amendment of judgment is a determination by the court that issues a judgment to alter its terms, whether to award judgment to the benefit of a different party, alter the terms or amount of an award, or otherwise to correct a mistake that the court determines was made in the judgment initially filed in the action. Amendment may occur on the court's own motion, on the motion of a party (which is required in the federal rules to be made within 10 days of its entry), or at the direction of a court with appellate jurisdiction over the court that first entered the judgment.

**arrest of judgment**   A judge's refusal to enter judgment or a stay of a judgment once entered. Arrest of judgment is a bar to the entry or enforcement of judgment entered by the judge in a case in which judgment might otherwise appear to be due. Arrest of judgment operates either to prevent its entry if the judgment has not been entered on the judgment rolls, or if it has been, to stay its enforcement.

Arrest of judgment used to be common in civil actions, where it has generally been replaced with a stay of judgment (which amounts to the same thing). Arrest of judgment is still common practice in criminal procedure, particularly if the defendant can demonstrate a defect in the indictment or information or other failure of procedure. Some courts allow arrest of judgment on the basis of insufficient evidence to support a conviction. Arrest of judgment is specified to be available to the defendant under the rules of criminal procedure, though a court may in its discretion enter it on the motion of any party or sua sponte.

**confession of judgment**   The agreement of a defendant to pay the claim filed. A confession of judgment is a petition, statement, or motion filed by the defendant, counter-defendant, or any other party in a civil action against whom a claim has been pled, accepting judgment against itself in the amount and form of remedy that has been claimed against it and (in most jurisdictions) accepting the validity or justice of the claim filed, after which the clerk of the court shall enter judgment against the party who confessed judgment. If judgment is not confessed by the party in person but by an attorney, either a power of attorney or warrant of attorney with a specific grant of power to confess judgment is usually required to be filed with the petition. A confession of judgment amounts to a waiver of any error in the action, and there is no appeal following a confession of judgment. Confession of judgment is similar to cognovit.

*See also:* cognovit (cognovit actionem clause or cognovit clause or cognovit note).

**declaratory judgment (declaratory relief or declaration)**   A declaration of rights, status, or obligation under law or equity. A declaratory judgment is a judicial order declaring the rights or claims of parties who have a real dispute that they cannot resolve without a judicial assessment of their arguments of fact or law, yet the dispute is not brought for a specific remedy. A declaratory judgment may not be sought to re-open questions once settled between the parties in a prior action or settlement of a prior action. Nor may a declaratory judgment be sought in a collusive proceeding in which the parties have no adverse interests. A declaratory judgment may, however, be the basis for a later enforcement of the rights or duties declared by it.

*See also:* opinion, judicial opinion, advisory opinion.

**default judgment**   Judgment entered upon the failure of a defendant to answer a complaint. A default judgment is entered in a civil action in response to a party's failure to perform those acts required to defend or to promote its cause. Most often, default judgment is entered against a defendant because the defendant fails to answer a complaint. The plaintiff seeking default against a non-answering defendant must establish in a court hearing that the defendant has been served with the summons and complaint, that the defendant has not appeared or answered, that the defendant is not known to be a minor or an incompetent person or in the military and subject to protection under the Soldiers and Sailors Relief Act of 1940, or if the defendant has appeared in the action that the defendant was provided with notice of the application for default judgment at least three days prior to the hearing set on the motion.

Default judgment may be entered by the court as a sanction for misconduct by a party. If either party causes an inexcusable burden upon the other through dilatory tactics, by a failure to provide discovery, or by burdensome or unneeded demands, or if a party fails in a significant and inexcusable fashion to appear at hearings, to file responses to motions, or to answer summonses, or if a party otherwise acts in a manner that constructively forfeits the court's protections in the action, then the court has the discretion to enter judgment against the party in default of its duties.

*See also:* nihil, nihil dicit (nihil dicit judgment); default; default, cure of default (curing default).

**deficiency judgment** Judgment for a debt remaining after a judicial sale intended to satisfy it. A deficiency judgment is a judgment entered at the close of a judicial sale in which a debtor's property has been auctioned to pay a debt, usually to pay a debt on which a judgment has already been rendered by the court. If the value received by the court following the sale is less than the amount previously adjudged as owed by the debtor to the creditor, the court will enter a deficiency judgment allowing further enforcement by the creditor against the debtor until the debt is paid in full or otherwise exhausted.

**enforcement of judgment (execution of judgment)** Any self-help, executive action, or judicial decree sought to enforce a judgment. Enforcement of judgment includes all of the means by which a plaintiff who has been successful in an action may enforce the judgment against a defendant if the defendant does not timely comply with the judgment in all respects. Enforcement of judgment is the same, in most instances, as execution of judgment.

The means and tools available for enforcement vary according to the nature of judgment. Self-help is lawful in some jurisdictions, as long as there is no breach of the peace. Otherwise, an order for the specific means of enforcement sought must usually be separately moved and argued. Such a motion may be made only on an enrolled judgment. Enforcing a judgment in the jurisdiction in which it is rendered may be done based on the enrollment of that judgment by the court. In all other jurisdictions in which enforcement will be sought, the judgment must be separately enrolled. Motions for an order of attachment and sale, lien, and garnishment are common means of enforcement, and in unusual cases, injunction and contempt of court will lie. Once a judgment is satisfied in full, it may no longer be enforced.

*See also:* sheriff, sheriff's sale (foreclosure sale or courthouse auction); scire, scire facias.

**judgment creditor** A creditor whose claim is manifest in the judgment of a court. A judgment creditor is a person or entity with a right to collect on a judgment rendered against the debtor, who was a party to the action from which the judgment against the debtor arose. A judgment creditor may execute the judgment, but if the judgment debtor files bankruptcy, the effect of the judgment gives no greater priority to the judgment creditor than the underlying status of the debt, with no priority over creditors with secured interests.

*See also:* judgment, enforcement of judgment, judgment debtor.

**judgment debtor** A debtor whose debt is manifest in the judgment of a court. A judgment debtor is a person or entity against whom a judgment has been entered by a court, requiring the payment of a debt. A judgment debtor who does not timely pay the debt subject to judgment is liable for contempt of court.

*See also:* judgment, enforcement of judgment, judgment creditor.

**judgment roll** A court record of judgments recorded pending execution. The judgment roll is a record of judgments entered against defendants in the jurisdiction, which establishes a lien against the property of the defendant until the judgment is satisfied, at which time the judgment is stricken from the roll.

*See also:* lien (lienholder).

**satisfaction of judgment** A record that a judgment has been fulfilled. Satisfaction of judgment is a record entry in a court docket made by a successful party who is awarded a judgment, in which that party declares that the other party has satisfied the obligations specified in the judgment. The filing of a satisfaction of judgment ends the case and terminates the court's jurisdiction over the parties, unless some order has previously been entered to the contrary. Satisfaction of judgment terminates the accrual of interest on the judgment.

Satisfaction of judgment must be entered by the party in whose favor judgment was entered, and it may only be entered upon a proper judgment then valid against the party who is said to have satisfied it, and only upon some evidence of actual satisfaction, even if such evidence is only the declaration of the other party.

**Uniform Enforcement of Foreign Judgments Act (UEFJA)** A uniform law establishing the procedures to enforce the court judgments of other states. The Uniform Enforcement of Foreign Judgments Act is a uniform law that established the procedure for the recognition and enforcement in a signatory state of a judgment issued in another state. As of 2008, 47 U.S. jurisdictions have adopted the act. Since the enforcement of judgments issued in other states is required under the Full Faith and Credit Clause of the U.S. Constitution, the UEFJA's primary role is procedural.

*See also:* defamation, foreign defamation judgment.

**erroneous judgment** *See:* review, standard of review, clearly erroneous.

**final judgment** The judgment that concludes a civil action. A final judgment disposes of all issues, claims, and defenses in a pending civil action, leaving no jurisdiction for the court except to enforce the judgment. An appeal may be taken from a final judgment.

*See also:* effect (effective).

**interlocutory judgment** A judgment entered prior to a final judgment. An interlocutory judgment is an order disposing of a claim, party, charge, defense, or procedural question in an action but that does not conclude the entire action. An interlocutory judgment, like any interlocutory order, may be appealed with leave of the court.

**charging order** An order diverting a partner's income from a partnership to the partner's judgment creditor. A charging order is a remedy available to a judgment creditor to require payment from a partnership of money that is owed to a partner. A charging order is to a partner's share payments what an order of garnishment is to an employee's paycheck.

**judgment non prosequitur (non pros)** *See:* nolle, nolle prosequi (nolle pros. or null pros. or non prosequitur or non pros.).

**judgment notwithstanding the verdict (J.N.O.V. or JNOV or judgment as a matter of law or JML or JMOL or judgment non obstante veredicto)** A judgment entered by the judge that contradicts the verdict of the jury. A judgment notwithstanding the verdict, which is still abbreviated JNOV, may be entered by a judge following a jury verdict in a case in which the judge believes that the evidence was so insufficient to support the verdict that a reasonable jury would not have a legally sufficient evidentiary basis to reach the verdict rendered by the jury. In effect, to grant a JNOV, the judge overrules the jury and enters judgment against the party whom the jury had voted to give relief. A JNOV may be entered for the case as a whole or on one or more issues within the case.

A judgment notwithstanding the verdict may usually be entertained by the judge only if the party who seeks it had earlier moved for a directed verdict, at the close of the evidence in the case.

The federal rules in force as of 2008 allow a motion for judgment as a matter of law at any time before the case is submitted to the jury. If the motion is denied, the motion may be renewed following a jury verdict, and the court may grant the motion rendering judgment for the movant without regard to the jury's verdict against the movant. At that time, the court should also conditionally rule on whether a new trial will be held if the motion is later vacated or reversed.

There is no difference between a judgment as a matter of law that is rendered after a jury verdict to the contrary, a judgment notwithstanding the verdict, and a judgment non obstante veredicto. These motions are, however, customarily used in civil matters. In a criminal matter, the court may acquit a defendant by a motion to acquit made or renewed following a verdict of guilt, but the court may not convict a defendant following a verdict of acquittal.

*See also:* acquittal (acquit); non, non obstante.

**judgment on the merits** A judgment entered following a consideration of the questions of law and fact. A judgment on the merits is a judgment following a trial or motions in which the questions of law and fact upon which the issues of the case are joined were reviewed and a judgment upon the claims and defenses is entered. A judgment on the merits operates as a final judgment for res judicata and collateral estoppel. It contrasts with a judgment dismissing an action on procedural or jurisdictional grounds.

*See also:* res, res judicata (res adjudicata).

**judgment on the pleadings (JOTP or JOP)** A judgment based on the pleadings alone and without need of further evidence. A judgment on the pleadings is a judgment entered on the basis of legal questions in the claims and defenses presented. Under Federal Rule of Civil Procedure 12(c), judgment on the pleadings may be sought by either party after the time for all responsive pleadings has passed and early enough not to delay the trial calendar. The judge may enter judgment for either party if no question of fact is in dispute that would bar a decision on the basis of the law alone, or if judgment will lie for one party if such questions as are in dispute are considered in the light most favorable to the party not being awarded judgment. Judgment on the pleadings may be granted on procedural grounds under Rule 12, or for the legal sufficiency of the complaint under 12(b)(6), although a motion for judgment on the pleadings is distinct from a Rule 12 motion to dismiss. If information is presented to the court that arises outside of the pleadings, the court may treat the judgment as summary judgment under Rule 56.

**judgment-proof party (judgment proof)** A party who cannot pay a judgment if one is rendered against it. A judgment-proof party is a party to an action (or a potential party) against whom no execution of judgment will be possible, either as a practical matter or as a legal result. A party with no assets or income with which to satisfy a judgment simply cannot do so. A party that is not personally amenable to suit and has no assets that may be the basis for jurisdiction, or that has already entered into a settlement or against which a judgment on the matter has been entered, is technically proof against judgment.

**money judgment** A judgment to be satisfied by the payment of money. A money judgment is a judgment that requires the payment of money to the plaintiff as all or part of the remedy. An award of damages, restitution, specific performance to transfer funds or make payments, or an injunction to pay money are all money judgments. A judgment ordering compensation for attorneys' fees is not, for that purpose alone, a money judgment.

**offer of judgment** An offer to settle prior to trial. An offer of judgment is a formal offer to settle a claim, made by the defendant against that claim to the plaintiff, which must offer terms of settlement including costs and be served on the opposing party at least ten days prior to a scheduled trial. If an offer of settlement is accepted, the parties may file the notice and acceptance, and the clerk will enter judgment accordingly. If the offer is not accepted, and if the party who received the offer does not receive a more favorable outcome than the offer, that party is liable for all court costs incurred after the offer, even if that party otherwise prevails.

**relief from judgment** The stay or dissolution of a judgment. Relief from judgment includes several forms of relief, including a stay of execution of judgment, a reduction of an award, an order vacating or setting aside a judgment, or an order substituting, clarifying, modifying, or correcting a judgment. A court has the inherent power to grant relief from judgment for good cause, whether the cause is presented on motion or discovered by the court, although when a case is on appeal, any such relief requires the assent of the appellate court with jurisdiction over the cause.

A party under the burden of a judgment may seek relief from a final order on any grounds that justify relief, so long as the motion is timely. In the federal courts, a motion must ordinarily be brought within a year, but in state courts, the time for such motions may be much shorter. The filing of a motion for relief from judgment does not, as a result of the filing, stay the execution of judgment.

The filing of a motion for relief from judgment may stay the running of the time for the filing of an appeal in the federal system when such motions are made (i) for judgment under Rule 50(b); (ii) to amend or make additional factual findings under Rule 52(b), whether or not granting the motion would alter the judgment; (iii) for attorneys' fees under Rule 54 if the district court extends the time to appeal under Rule 58; (iv) to alter or amend the judgment under Rule 59; (v) for a new trial under Rule 59; or (vi) for relief under Rule 60 if the motion is filed no later than ten days after the judgment is entered, according to Federal Rule of Appellate Procedure 4(a).

*See also:* remedy, extraordinary remedy (extraordinary relief).

**collateral attack**   A new action that would alter or void the judgment of an earlier action. Collateral attack on a judgment is a separate cause of action brought to challenge the legality or sufficiency of a judgment rendered in an earlier action. In the vast majority of cases, it is a civil action seeking to set aside a criminal conviction, usually through a petition for a writ of habeas corpus.

Collateral attack differs from direct appeal, which is a review by an appellate court of the proceedings of the first judgment. Collateral attack is usually made through a separate suit against an officer of the government responsible for executing the judgment of the first action, such as an action for habeas corpus or an action for mandamus or for an injunction against a deprivation of a constitutional right.

**summary judgment**   Judgment as a matter of law sought by motion before trial when no facts are in issue. Summary judgment is a specialized motion for judgment as a matter of law, sought by any party to an action when the issues in dispute may be determined without regard to any genuine dispute over a material fact. The facts must either be agreed or such dispute as remains is either over immaterial facts or sufficiently determinable that the court may render judgment considering any questions of fact as if they are resolved in the manner that most favors the non-moving party (or, in the event of cross-motions for judgment, in the manner that favors the party which will lose the judgment). If the court determines that the claims and defenses can be resolved through

application of the law to the issues that remain, the court should give a legal opinion on those issues and render judgment. If, however, genuine issues of material fact remain between the parties, the court should deny the motions on all claims or defenses affected by the remaining issues of fact. The court may grant partial summary judgment regarding any claims or issues that are severable from the rest of the action and that can be ruled on without regard to a genuine issue of material fact.

**Celotex standard**   Summary judgment should strike all claims not supported by evidence. The standard in Celotex Corp. v. Catrett, 477 U.S. 317 (1986), allows a federal trial court to enter judgment against a claim or defense if the party who has pled that claim or defense fails to make a showing of evidence sufficient to establish the existence of an element essential to that party's case, and on which that party will bear the burden of proof at trial. This standard means that an argument for which no evidence is adduced at all, or for which no evidence contradicts the other party's evidence on that argument, is ripe for summary judgment. Although Celotex emphasizes Federal Rule 56's generous standard for summary judgment, care is required to ensure that the use of summary judgment does not impinge on the right to a civil jury trial, which is required if one is demanded in a federal case at law, if there is any genuine issue of fact.

**Morgan Rule of civil procedure**   Summary judgment denials must be appealed on issues of law alone. The Morgan Rule in civil procedure limits appeals of the denial of a motion for summary judgment to allow only appeals of those denials based on the law alone; a denial based on the presence of genuine questions of material fact is not an appealable order.

**partial summary judgment**   An order granting summary judgment as to one theory, claim, defense, or party, among several. A partial summary judgment is a judgment ruling on some, but not all, of the claims and defenses pending in an action before the court. As long as a genuine issue of material fact persists as to some issues or claims or defenses among some parties, a summary judgment (even if it is not denominated as partial) is only a partial summary judgment.

**reasonable-inference rule (reasonable inference)** Inferences in legal judgment must favor the party against whom judgment is given. The reasonable-inference rule determines the scope of interpretation of the evidence in favor of a party against whom has been sought summary judgment or judgment as a matter of law, so that no judgment should be entered if a reasonable inference from the evidence would support the party's case. The implication of the rule is that all inferences when considering the evidence before the court in a motion for judgment must be drawn to favor the non-moving party, or in the event both parties have moved for judgment, all inferences from evidence must be considered in the light most favorable to the side against whom judgment would be rendered. If all of the pending questions of fact may be resolved by such inferences favoring a party, yet judgment would still lie against that party, there is no issue of fact that would bar judgment.

See also: inference (infer).

**take-nothing judgment** Judgment rendered for the defendant. A take-nothing judgment is a judgment for the defendant, in which the court rules the plaintiff shall "take nothing."

**judicature** The role and functions of the judiciary of a given court or in general. Judicature is the broadest sense of the role and duties of the judge. It is also the particular role of a judge, which persists over time in a given jurisdiction as the office is occupied by successive individuals and even as the name or location alters. Thus, when two courts are consolidated into one, the judicature of each persists over all of the prior actions in the two courts in the actions as heard in the resulting court.

**judicial** See: judge (judicial).

**judicial activism** See: judge, activist judge.

**judicial bond** See: bond, judicial bond.

**judicial branch** See: judge, judicial branch.

**judicial chambers** See: chamber, judicial chambers (judge's chamber or judicial chamber).

**judicial comity** See: comity, judicial comity (federal-state comity or interstate comity or international comity).

**judicial discretion** See: judge, judicial discretion; discretion, judicial discretion (discretion of the court or sound discretion).

**judicial economy** See: judge, judicial economy.

**judicial estoppel** See: estoppel, equitable estoppel, judicial estoppel.

**judicial foreclosure** See: foreclosure, judicial foreclosure.

**judicial hearing** See: hearing, judicial hearing.

**judicial immunity** See: immunity, official immunity, judicial immunity.

**judicial lien** See: lien, judicial lien.

**judicial notice** See: notice, judicial notice (judicially noticed fact).

**judicial opinion** See: opinion, judicial opinion.

**judicial restraint** See: judge, judicial activism (judicial restraint).

**judicial review** See: review, judicial review.

**judicial review of administrative action** See: review, judicial review, judicial review of administrative action (administrative judicial review).

**judicially noticed fact** See: notice, judicial notice (judicially noticed fact).

**judiciary** All of the judges and their powers. The judiciary is both the abstract sense of the judge as a source of power and decision and the specific collective of individuals appointed to every judgeship. Rhetorically, the judiciary is usually invoked as a champion of the constitutional order and of individual rights, with a duty invested in each member and in the whole to guard against abuse, tyranny, and injustice, and to do so through the principled application of constitutions, laws, statutes, the the customs of the common law and the principles of equity.

**Judiciary Reorganization Bill of 1937 or switch in time that saved nine** See: pack, court-packing plan (Judiciary Reorganization Bill of 1937 or switch in time that saved nine).

**juge d'instruction** See: judge, juge d'instruction.

**junior partner** See: partner, junior partner.

**junk bond** See: security, securities, high-yield security (junk bond); bond, junk bond (high-yield bond or high-yield debt obligation).

**junkyard dog lawyer** See: lawyer, junkyard dog lawyer (cowboy lawyer or rambo lawyer).

**jural (jural relations)** Legal, or related to the law or to rights the law protects. Jural, in American legal usage, is a synonym for legal, in the sense of something created by the law. In this sense, it is most often used for jural entity or jural personality, such as possessed by a corporation.

Jural, in Roman law and in most every other legal system, depicts the legal personality of every person or entity: jural relations are the rights and duties that result from the legal conception of the person.

**jural act** See: act, jural act.

**jure** See: jus, jure (iure).

**jure naturae or lex naturale** See: jurisprudence, natural law (jure naturae or lex naturale).

**juridical (juridically)** Legal, particularly relating to anything done in or by a court. Juridical is a poetic term for legal, such as a juridical person or entity, which is quite the same as a legal person or entity. Juridically signifies anything done with particular observance of the requirements of the law, and in this sense, it signifies anything done according to the practices, procedure, customs of a court or courts in general.

**juridical fact** See: fact, juridical fact.

**juris** See: jus, (juris or jure or ius).

**juris civilis or ius civile or iuris civilis** See: jus, jus civile (juris civilis or ius civile or iuris civilis).

**juris doctor** *See:* degree, academic degree, law degree, juris doctor (J.D. JD).

**jurisdiction (legislative jurisdiction or executive jurisdiction or judicial jurisdiction)** The power of a government, court, or official over a given matter, person, or place. Jurisdiction is the inherent power of a nation-state, a state of the union, a local government, an Indian tribe or other government to legislate or regulate any matter. It is also the power conferred by the relevant constitution and statutes upon a court or an officer lawfully to assert authority over a person or a subject matter or a place. In both senses, jurisdiction takes three essential forms.

Legislative jurisdiction is the power to regulate a given form of activity, all activity in a given place, or all activity by a given person. Enforcement jurisdiction (sometimes called executive jurisdiction) is the authority to exercise that power in fact through oversight, investigation, or arrest. Judicial jurisdiction (sometimes called penal jurisdiction as well as enforcement jurisdiction) includes not only the authority of officials to bring a matter before a court but also the authority of courts to adjudicate an action involving a given person or matter. There are many forms of jurisdiction that incorporate several aspects of the three forms of legislative, enforcement, and judicial jurisdiction, such as regulatory or administrative jurisdiction delegated by a legislature to an administrative agency, which may be thought of as incorporating all three forms of jurisdiction: the agency makes rules, engages in oversight of regulated entities, and enforces the rules when an entity is thought to have violated them.

The scope of jurisdiction may vary according to the form of process by which it is enforced. Most importantly, the scope of jurisdiction varies among criminal jurisdiction, regulatory jurisdiction, and civil jurisdiction.

Jurisdiction allows the court or an officer to order anyone subject to the law to comply with the law and a specific lawful order or to be penalized for not doing so under the law. Jurisdiction may be exclusive or concurrent, that is held by one authority alone or shared. Jurisdiction may be general or limited, that is presumed to extend to all people and matters or limited to certain subjects or actions. Certain people or entities may be immune from jurisdiction, such as the head of state of a foreign power.

There are many forms of judicial jurisdiction in the United States. A court of general jurisdiction is usually limited to a specific geography, and the court is presumed to have jurisdiction over all persons and legal issues that arise in that area. Courts have jurisdiction only to act in matters properly before them and upon parties properly before the court. Other courts have limited jurisdiction, either owing to limit to a specialized subject matter, limitations based on the parties to the action, or because the court is limited to hearing cases on appeal from other courts.

*See also:* dismissal, grounds for dismissal, lack of jurisdiction.

**jurisdiction as place** The physical extent of the power of a state, court, or official. A jurisdiction is a place, the physical area in which a nation-state or government, a court, an agency, or an official is presumed to have exclusive authority to legislate and enforce the law. As a general matter, a jurisdiction is either a political entity, such as a nation-state, state of the union, municipality, or a district, such as a judicial district.

The scope of a court's jurisdiction, in the sense of its authority, often depends on the geography of its jurisdiction. The authority of jurisdiction over many disputes and claims extends to those arising within a given geography.

*See also:* venue; forum.

**admiralty jurisdiction** Authority over disputes arising from navigation or maritime commerce. Admiralty jurisdiction in the United States is committed to the U.S. district courts in their admiralty jurisdiction and to the state courts at the election of the plaintiff unless the defendant removes the action to federal court. All matters arising from disputes regarding maritime contracts, torts, mariners, and property — including the ownership of vessels, cargo and shipwrecks — are in admiralty.

**ancillary jurisdiction** Federal supplemental jurisdiction of a state counterclaim related to a federal claim. Ancillary jurisdiction allows a court to rule on a claim that is not ordinarily within its jurisdiction because the claim is sufficiently related to another claim that is before the court and properly in its jurisdiction.

Though the ancillary jurisdiction has other applications, it is usually applied to that aspect of supplemental jurisdiction by which a federal court may hear a state claim raised by the defense, usually as a counterclaim, based on facts related to the the the same transaction or common nucleus of fact from which the plaintiff's claim arose that was the basis of the plaintiff's federal claim. Ancillary jurisdiction has been essentially merged into supplemental jurisdiction by 28 U.S.C. § 1367 (2008).

**appellate jurisdiction** The jurisdiction to hear an appeal of decision by a lower court. Appellate jurisdiction is the power to hear an appeal of a decision made by another court. Appellate jurisdiction is generally determined by statute, either in the state system by the state legislature or in the federal system by Congress.

*See also:* jurisdiction (legislative jurisdiction or executive jurisdiction or judicial jurisdiction).

**Rooker-Feldman doctrine** Only the U.S. Supreme Court has direct federal review of a state court's decision. The Rooker-Feldman doctrine is a rule of appellate procedure enunciated by the United States Supreme Court in two cases, Rooker v. Fidelity Trust Co., 263 U.S. 413 (1923), and District of Columbia Court of Appeals v. Feldman, 460 U.S. 462 (1983), holding that no federal court other than the Supreme Court has subject matter jurisdiction to sit in direct review of a state court decision, unless Congress enacts legislation that specifically authorizes such a review. Attempts to secure review of a state court order by filing a later action in a U.S. district court are usually barred by a lack of jurisdiction under this doctrine.

*See also:* comity; federalism, doctrine of our federalism; abstention (abstain).

**concurrent jurisdiction** The jurisdiction of two governments or courts over the same place, person, or matter. Concurrent jurisdiction is multiple jurisdiction, the jurisdiction of more than one court, state, or agency over a single matter, person, or place. As with jurisdiction generally, concurrent jurisdiction refers to the power to regulate, the act of execution or policing, and the hearing of an action arising from it. Thus, several regulatory agencies may have concurrent jurisdiction to regulate one activity. Several governments may have concurrent regulation over one criminal act, or several courts may have concurrent jurisdiction over one action. In the United States, concurrent judicial jurisdiction is particularly common owing to the number of causes of action that may be either state or federal (or both) according to the parties and subject matter.

**condominium** *See:* condominium, condominium as jurisdiction (condominia).

**criminal jurisdiction** The power to declare an act a crime and to prosecute a person for its commission. Criminal jurisdiction is both a form of legislative jurisdiction, by which a government has the authority to declare particular conduct to be a crime, and a form of enforcement jurisdiction, by which the agents of that government have the power to arrest a person for such conduct and the courts of that government have the power to try and to order punishment for it. Criminal jurisdiction is customarily based on the location of the conduct, the location of the harm that occurs or is intended to occur as a result of the conduct, the nationality of the person who engages in it, the nationality of a person or entity harmed by it, and the nature of the conduct itself. The criminal jurisdiction of a nation–state may thus extend to actions by its citizens, to acts that occur within its territory, to acts that harm its citizens, to acts that harm the government itself, and to acts that — by their very nature — are likely to harm the government of the state or to harm the interests of all humankind. Examples of the last two categories include counterfeiting the nation's currency and slave trafficking.

In the United States, individual states have criminal jurisdiction limited in the same manner as a nation state. In many U.S. states, legislative criminal jurisdiction of local governments is often limited to crimes defined under local ordinance, major crimes being defined by the state. Even so, local law enforcement officials are usually empowered with criminal law enforcement powers to enforce state laws and to present those accused of their violation to state courts.

The criminal jurisdiction of Indian tribes and nations is complex. In general, it extends to some acts on tribal land and to some acts committed by one Indian against another.

**Ker–Frisbie doctrine** Improper police conduct does not defeat the jurisdiction of a tribunal. The Ker–Frisbie doctrine bars the defendant in a criminal case from asserting as a defense to a criminal charge any illegality of the means by which the defendant is brought into or found within the territory of the court's jurisdiction. The doctrine arose in Frisbie v. Collins, 342 U.S. 519 (1952) and Ker v. Illinois, 119 U.S. 436 (1886), the Frisbie case applying in interstate jurisdiction the doctrine in U.S. international jurisdiction from Ker. Thus, a defendant who is illegally kidnapped by police officers in one jurisdiction and illegally transported to another may not raise the kidnapping or transportation as a defense to the jurisdiction of the court in the second jurisdiction or to the charges the defendant faces, generally. The defendant may bring a civil action against the officers for the kidnapping, and the authorities in the first jurisdiction may bring a criminal charge for kidnapping against the police officers, but neither affects the prosecution against the defendant in the second jurisdiction.

**diversity jurisdiction (diversity of citizenship)** Federal jurisdiction over claims between citizens of different jurisdictions. Diversity jurisdiction is jurisdiction in the federal courts arising from the diversity of citizenship of the plaintiffs from the citizenship of the defendants, in that the two parties (or groups of parties) are citizens of different states of the union, citizens of different nation–states, or a foreign nation-state. Diversity jurisdiction is a basis of federal jurisdiction according to the controversies listed in the Case and Controversies clause of the U.S. Constitution, as well as the designation of jurisdiction by statute, according to which diversity jurisdiction may only be brought if the amount in controversy exceeds a statutory minimum.

*See also:* removal, removal to federal court (removal jurisdiction).

**amount in controversy** The amount that may be required to satisfy the plaintiff's appropriate demands. The amount in controversy is the value of the case as stated in the plaintiff's complaint, provided the demands for remedy are not patently unlawful, unreasonable, or depicted by any party in a manner that inflates the amount for the purpose of establishing jurisdiction. The amount in controversy is a jurisdictional element in many state courts, as well as in federal courts hearing a cause in its diversity jurisdiction. The amount in controversy may also be required in pleading some non-jurisdictional elements of a case, such as eligibility for interpleader. Further, the amount in controversy is an element in the court's discretion in determining the allowance of the scope of discovery, the commitment of judicial resources, and the degree of oversight that is required in a case.

As of 2009, the amount in controversy required for diversity jurisdiction in federal court was $75,000.

**complete diversity**  No plaintiff and no defendant are citizens of the same state. Complete diversity describes a relationship between all of the plaintiffs and all of the defendants in which no defendant is a citizen of the same state as any plaintiff. Although diversity jurisdiction usually requires complete diversity, a violation of complete diversity caused only by the joining of a non-diverse party as a result of supplemental jurisdiction may not defeat diversity jurisdiction that is otherwise established.

**enforcement jurisdiction**  *See:* jurisdiction (legislative jurisdiction or executive jurisdiction or judicial jurisdiction).

**equitable jurisdiction (equity jurisdiction)**  Equitable jurisdiction is broader than law but does not include legal jurisdiction. Equitable jurisdiction results from both statutory grants of jurisdiction and the customary applications of maxims of equity, particularly that "equity will suffer no harm to be done without a remedy," which is limited by "equity follows the law." Thus a court in equity will hear and grant relief to a plaintiff with a cognizable interest in jeopardy who would otherwise be barred from the jurisdiction of a court of law, although it will not find jurisdiction generally if the law would provide a sufficient remedy. A useful metaphor is that equity provides a moat of jurisdiction around the law: that which the law will fully hear is not equitable, but equity will protect interests the law will not recognize and compel individuals to do equity when the law would not have jurisdiction to do so.

*equity acts in personam*  Equitable jurisdiction depends on in personam jurisdiction. The court in equity has such jurisdiction as the court acquires through its grant of statutory jurisdiction and through its prudential allowance of the use of that grant. The traditional basis of equitable jurisdiction is in personam, and so when equity has jurisdiction over a person or entity, it has jurisdiction to hear claims in equity against that person or entity. The effect of this maxim is also to determine interest in property at the moment through orders binding the party, which do not attach to the property. That said, if a court of equity, or a court of general jurisdiction hearing an action in equity, is conferred jurisdiction in rem, and by that jurisdiction the court acquires authority over a claim, the court may still hear the claim if jurisdiction can otherwise be had over the party.

*fiduciary*  Equity has inherent authority over the enforcement of a fiduciary duty. A fiduciary duty may be determined and enforced in equity, even if no contract or other basis for liability exists in law. This is one of the most ancient bases of equity, and it is the basis for a variety of modern corporate claims.

*partnership*  Equity has inherent jurisdiction over matters involving a partnership. Partnerships involve an inherently fiduciary relationship between and among the partners, and equity has traditionally determined the rights and interests of partners as well as the dissolution of partnerships and partition of partnership assets. If a jurisdiction by statute confers certain authority regarding a partnership to a court of general jurisdiction, unless the statute expressly extinguishes the court's equitable powers, the court hears such actions in an equitable capacity.

*remedy*  Equity will hear a valid claim that cannot be satisfied by a legal remedy. A claim in law or in equity that cannot be adequately remedied by a remedy at law, such as damages, but that can be remedied in equity, as through an injunction is, for the reason of the remedy alone, within the scope of equitable jurisdiction. Thus, many constitutional claims that do not seek a money judgment but seek a remedy through injunction are equitable claims.

*standing*  Equitable standing may be based on a legal or an equitable interest. Standing in equity is based on an interest cognizable in equity, which may be a legal interest that is subject to a harm or injury for which there is not a sufficient remedy at law, or an equitable interest that is either not cognizable at law or is not sufficiently remediable at law.

**clean-up doctrine (clean up doctrine)**  An action in equity may include incidental claims at law. The clean-up doctrine requires a court of equity with jurisdiction over an equitable action to hear claims at law that are related to the equitable action. Rather like supplemental jurisdiction in federal court, the clean-up doctrine allows the chancery court, or a court of general jurisdiction in equity, with an equitable action properly before it to hear all of the claims, counter-claims, and defenses necessary to do justice among the parties to the action, regardless of whether each is equitable.

**executive jurisdiction**  *See:* jurisdiction (legislative jurisdiction or executive jurisdiction or judicial jurisdiction).

**extraterritorial jurisdiction**  Jurisdiction over a person, claim, or property beyond the border of the state or court. Extra-territorial jurisdiction is the assertion of any form of jurisdiction over a person, an event or claim, or property that is outside the physical jurisdiction of the state or the court asserting the jurisdiction. Extraterritorial jurisdiction is allowed under international law, as long as a sufficient relationship exists between the state asserting the jurisdiction and either the person or the claim upon which jurisdiction is based. A claim that a defendant is a national of a state, has harmed a national of a state, has committed a crime on the soil of the state, or has committed a crime with an effect on the soil of a state, has committed an offense against the sovereign power of the state itself, or has committed an act considered a crime of universal jurisdiction is sufficient to establish extra-territorial jurisdiction for most purposes of national criminal law under international law. An action involving a contract in the territory or under the territory's laws, a delict or tort that affects a national or took place in the territory, a matter affecting rights secured under a state's laws (such as marital interests) or a matter affecting property in the territory as usually sufficient for the assertion of extraterritorial jurisdiction in civil matters.

**federal jurisdiction** The scope of authority given to the federal courts by Congress. Federal jurisdiction is the sum of the specific categories of jurisdiction that are within the scope of federal judicial power under Article III of the Constitution that Congress has conferred upon the courts by statute. Federal jurisdiction may be exclusive, in that no state court has jurisdiction over the same matter, or concurrent, in which a state court or a federal court may hear the matter.

Federal jurisdiction includes all federal cases and controversies inventoried in the Constitution, including federal-question jurisdiction, or cases arising under federal law, and diversity jurisdiction, or controversies between citizens of two different states; as well as cases affecting ambassadors and cases arising under admiralty or maritime law, and controversies to which the United States is a party, to which a state is a party against citizens of a another state, or involving a foreign state or foreign parties. By far, the greatest number of cases of federal jurisdiction are cases to which the United States is a party, owing to federal criminal cases. The largest categories of federal civil actions are diversity cases and cases arising under federal laws.

Federal jurisdiction must be pled by the party who seeks to bring a civil action into a federal court. The statutory basis of jurisdiction must be identified, and the complaint must allege sufficient facts as to support the claim of jurisdiction pled.

See also: constitution, U.S. Constitution, clauses, case and controversy clause.

**federal-question jurisdiction (federal question jurisdiction)** Jurisdiction in actions arising under the U.S. Constitution, laws, or treaties. Federal-question jurisdiction provides jurisdiction in the federal courts for all actions in which a claim or defense is based upon or arises under the Constitution, statutes, regulations, treaties or customary international law of the United States. Jurisdiction arising from a federal question is broadly construed, and there is a policy of both the encouragement of such cases to be filed in federal courts rather than state courts and to allow removal of such cases from state courts.

See also: removal, removal to federal court (removal jurisdiction).

**forum non conveniens (transfer to a more convenient forum)** A court whose selection is inconvenient to a defendant. Forum non conveniens (Latin for "inconvenient forum") is a doctrine that allows a party to request a court to exercise its discretion and decline to accept jurisdiction in a case if the convenience to the parties and the interests of justice would be better served if the action were heard in a different forum. A

party may move for dismissal on the grounds of forum non conveniens, and in deciding whether to grant such a motion the court will give some deference to the plaintiff's choice of forum, weighed against whether an alternative forum exits in which the defendant is amenable to service and a remedy is available, the location of evidence and convenience of witnesses, and the relative difficulty of judicial supervision of the action.

See also: forum, forum conveniens.

**general jurisdiction** See: court, court of general jurisdiction.

**in personam jurisdiction (personal jurisdiction)** A court's jurisdiction over a person or entity. In personam jurisdiction is personal jurisdiction, the authority of the court over the person of an individual or entity that allows the court to order that person to appear and to comply with an order or remedy. In personam jurisdiction may be based upon physical presence in a jurisdiction, a legal presence in the jurisdiction such as domicile or legal residence, an action committed within the jurisdiction by which jurisdiction is established before the party leaves (such as a crime or the injury of another), an action that has a criminal or harmful effect in the jurisdiction, or a commercial presence of such contacts that are at least minimal and that do not offend the traditional notions of fair play and substantial justice to hale a party with such contacts into court in the forum.

In personam jurisdiction over a party is sufficient for a court to adjudicate the rights and interests of that party, including the determination of claims and defenses in property. In personam jurisdiction is often contrasted with in rem jurisdiction, by which a court has jurisdiction over property and may determine the rights of parties as they may relate to that property. Yet the potential of jurisdiction over all parties interested in some property by asserting jurisdiction over the property does not preclude jurisdiction over the parties in personam. In this way, for example, the property rights of parties to a divorce may be determined as a result of the in personam jurisdiction over the parties, without regard to jurisdiction over all of the property otherwise.

See also: jurisdiction, in rem jurisdiction; in, in personam.

*due process of law* Jurisdiction over a foreign party must be fairly based on contacts with the forum. Due process of law under the U.S. Constitution requires any attempt to establish personal jurisdiction over a non-resident defendant to meet the basic requirements of fairness, including at least a substantial connection between the defendant and the forum jurisdiction, demonstrated by at least minimum contacts between the defendant and the forum that were purposefully directed toward the specific forum by the defendant.

**long-arm statute (long-arm jurisdiction)** A statute asserting jurisdiction over a non-resident. A long-arm statute vests the courts of a state with jurisdiction over non-residents of the state for certain purposes. These purposes and their definitions vary from state to state, but they generally include committing a crime or tort within the state (even if only its results or effects occur within the state and the acts that cause them were performed elsewhere), conducting business in the state, holds property within the state, or has family matters situated in the state. Owing to the jurisdiction being predicated upon claims, a well-founded assertion that the defendant committed acts amounting to these requirements is sufficient to establish jurisdiction under the statute. The exercise of jurisdiction under the statute, however, must comport with the requirements of due process of law in the United States, and if service is to be effected or the action is to be enforced in another country, the jurisdiction must be compatible with international law.

**minimum contacts**  The least contact between a defendant and forum that supports jurisdiction. Minimum contacts describes the factual basis of a deliberate conduct of a potential foreign defendant to the forum asserting jurisdiction over that defendant that is the least degree of involvement in the forum state that would be fair as the basis for jurisdiction. There is no perfect formula for the nature or quanta of such contacts, but the contacts must demonstrate a knowing and purposive relationship to the forum. Illustrative acts include the appointment of a local agent for process, the employment of personnel in the forum, maintenance of inventory or performance of manufacture or processing in the forum, execution of contracts in the forum, recurring visits to the forum by personnel employed by the defendant, a significant value or portion of sales made directly from the defendant into the forum, and the deliberate placement of advertisement or marketing in the forum (as opposed to an incidental presence of such material owing to a national or regional promotional campaign).

    **fair play and substantial justice**  The constitutional requirement of fair jurisdiction over a stranger to the forum. Fair play and substantial justice is the test of the constitutional limits of the exercise of extraterritorial in personam jurisdiction. If the person who would be haled into court from outside of the jurisdiction has a deliberate relationship with activities, property, commerce, or other persons in the forum, the relationship would provide sufficient contacts that the person would not be unfairly haled into court there. Without these minimum contacts, the attempt of the forum to exercise jurisdiction is unfair and offends basic notions of justice.
    *See also:* hale into court (hale to court or hail into court).

**voluntary jurisdiction (consent jurisdiction)**  A defendant may voluntarily accept jurisdiction.

Voluntary jurisdiction is jurisdiction accepted by a defendant regardless of other immunities from jurisdiction the defendant might assert. The defendant consents to the jurisdiction rather than requiring it to be proved, or regardless of its potential for proof. Voluntary jurisdiction may arise from the defendant's express waiver of immunity or express acceptance of jurisdiction, from its failure to assert immunity or failure of adequate service of process, or from its presence otherwise before the court, such as through a filing it had otherwise made as a plaintiff in the same forum during roughly the same period of time.

    **general appearance**  An appearance by the defendant for all purposes in answer to suit. A general appearance is the appearance of a defendant in court in answer to the action brought against it. The general appearance amounts to acceptance of the court's jurisdiction over the defendant.

    **special appearance (limited appearance)**  An appearance solely to contest jurisdiction, service or a preliminary matter. A limited appearance is the appearance of a defendant for the specific purpose of contesting the jurisdiction of the court over the defendant, or for the specific purpose of moving to dismiss for ineffective service of process, or for any other preliminary matter, without accepting the jurisdiction of the court over the defendant. A limited appearance allows counsel for the defendant to appear as the attorney for the defendant within the jurisdiction of the forum without waiving jurisdictional defenses.
    *See also:* special.

**in rem jurisdiction**  Jurisdiction over the thing that is contested in the action. In rem jurisdiction is the power of the courts to determine the ownership and interests in property located within the territory of the court's jurisdiction. Thus, an action against the property is within the court's in rem jurisdiction, affecting all persons who might have an interest in the property, whether each person is otherwise amenable to the court's jurisdiction or not.

**quasi in rem jurisdiction**  An action against a person's property in order to acquire jurisdiction over the person. A quasi in rem action allows a court to gain personal jurisdiction over an absent party that has an interest in property within the jurisdiction even though the court otherwise could not attain personal jurisdiction over that person. This duality of jurisdiction has given rise to concerns for the due process of law, rather like the due process concerns of long-arm statutes: a court is ordinarily limited to its territorial jurisdiction for process against defendants in quasi in rem actions. More specifically, an action quasi in rem is an action initiated by in personam service even though the effect of the action is to determine the rights to some property. Thus, although a quasi in rem action is not brought as an in rem action, it is as if it is an in rem action, and certain jurisdictional aspects of the case will be treated as if it is in rem, not just as in personam.

*See also:* quasi; in, in rem.

**judicial jurisdiction** *See:* jurisdiction (legislative jurisdiction or executive jurisdiction or judicial jurisdiction).

**legislative jurisdiction** *See:* jurisdiction (legislative jurisdiction or executive jurisdiction or judicial jurisdiction).

**limited jurisdiction** Jurisdiction of a court restricted by subject matter, process, value of claims, or limits in criminal sentence. Limited jurisdiction is the extent of jurisdiction of a court, that is assigned to hear civil matters of a specified subject matter (or set of subjects), among specific classes of parties, or of a set range in value; or to hear criminal matters of a specified range of offenses or potential punishments. The term is most often used for specialized courts—such as family courts and probate courts—and courts assigned causes of great number but small value—such as justice courts, municipal courts, night courts. Limited jurisdiction contrasts with general jurisdiction, the jurisdiction of a court without such limits (although the existence of a court of limited jurisdiction, such as a probate court, may deprive a court of general jurisdiction of jurisdiction over probate matters). Though it is not common to speak of them as courts of limited jurisdiction, federal courts are courts of limited jurisdiction, as are courts of appeal.

*See also:* court, court of limited jurisdiction.

**original jurisdiction** Jurisdiction over the first instance of proceedings in an action. Original jurisdiction over an action is jurisdiction of the court in which the first pleading of that action is properly filed. Famously, the original jurisdiction of the U.S. Supreme Court is limited to actions affecting ambassadors, ministers and consuls and actions between states. The original jurisdiction of state courts of general jurisdiction is presumably the original jurisdiction for all actions that may be brought in a given state, except for those specifically assigned to the jurisdiction of courts of limited jurisdiction.

**pendent jurisdiction** Federal supplemental jurisdiction from facts in common with a federal claim. Pendent jurisdiction is the specific authority of a federal court to hear a state claim arising from a common nucleus of fact from which a federal action is brought. Pendent jurisdiction has been merged with ancillary jurisdiction into supplementary jurisdiction, under 28 U.S.C. § 1367 (2008). The plaintiff asserted all pendent claims in the complaint, and the district court had the discretion to allow jurisdiction for so long as the court deemed the pendent claims were more beneficial to justice to be heard in the same forum as the federal claims.

**pendent-party jurisdiction** Supplemental jurisdiction over a state party related to a federal claim. Pendent-party jurisdiction is jurisdiction that may be asserted against a party who otherwise would not be subject to federal jurisdiction, but whose claim or defense arises from a common nucleus of fact with a claim that is validly in federal court owing either to its subject matter or the diversity of parties. Pendent-party jurisdiction is now considered a form of supplemental jurisdiction.

*See also:* jurisdiction, supplemental jurisdiction.

**personal jurisdiction** *See:* jurisdiction, in personam jurisdiction (personal jurisdiction).

**subject matter jurisdiction** Jurisdiction established over an action based on the legal issues it raises. Subject matter jurisdiction arises from the questions of law asserted in a claim or defense in an action. If a remedy sought, or a basis for that remedy or for its denial, depends upon an analysis of the laws of a specified subject, jurisdiction based on that subject matter is established. For example, federal-question jurisdiction is subject matter jurisdiction based on a claim or defense that requires the application of the U.S. Constitution, statutes, treaties, regulations, or precedents, and such state law as is required is less essential to the issues of the case. Admiralty jurisdiction is inherently based on the subject matter of disputes affecting the vessels, crew, or cargo or maritime commerce. In the Case or Controversies Clause of the Constitution, the forms of case that are listed are all bases of subject-matter jurisdiction.

*See also:* safe, safe harbor.

**supplemental jurisdiction** Federal jurisdiction over state claims arising from the basis of a federal claim. Supplemental jurisdiction is the basis for federal jurisdiction over state claims that are so related to claims in an action that may properly be brought within the original jurisdiction of a federal court that they form part of the same case or controversy as the federal action. Supplemental jurisdiction, codified in 1990, consolidated ancillary jurisdiction, pendent-claim jurisdiction, and pendent-party jurisdiction.

**common nucleus of facts (common question)** Evidence in common between two or more claims or defenses. A common nucleus of facts is one element of the determination of a sufficient relationship between a state claim and a federal claim for the state claim to be heard in a federal court along with the federal claim. The most essential test is whether there are significant elements of proof, particular forms of evidence, that are appropriately submitted by the parties to establish either the sufficiency of the the plaintiff's or defendant's assertions related to one claim that are also to be appropriately submitted by the parties to establish the sufficient of the assertions in the other claim.

**territorial jurisdiction** The jurisdiction of a state or a court throughout its geographic domain. Territorial jurisdiction is the authority to legislate or hear civil or criminal actions related to people, events, and property occurring on or affecting a specific territory of the Earth, delimited by the boundaries of the state or the territorial grant of jurisdiction to a specific court.

**one-hundred mile bulge**  Federal process may be served in the district or for one hundred miles around it. The hundred–mile bulge is the hundred miles beyond the borders of the territorial boundaries of the district of a United States District Court, within which service from that court may be lawfully effected.

**tribal jurisdiction**  The jurisdiction of the courts of an Indian tribe. The jurisdiction of the tribal courts over a particular person or claim is a federal question, determined in part by tribal law and in part by federal law, which in general establish tribal jurisdiction over Indian lands, tribal membership, domestic relations among tribal members, criminal acts on tribal lands, and certain consented activities with non–tribal members.

**want of jurisdiction (lack of jurisdiction or beyond the jurisdiction)**  A failure to establish jurisdiction. Want of jurisdiction is a failure to have jurisdiction over an action or a party. Want of jurisdiction may arise owing to a failure of the court to have authority over a person, place, or subject matter or to a failure of an officer or a party to perform the technical requirements to establish jurisdiction in a particular action.

**jurisdictional plea**  *See:* plea, jurisdictional plea.

**jurisprude**  A legal scholar or theorist. A jurisprude is a person of unusual learning in the law, particularly a student of legal philosophy. It may be used as a term of humor or derision for an overly analytical lawyer.

**jurisprudence (legal philosophy or legal theory or legal science)**  The study of law and justice to describe better what they are and ought to be. Jurisprudence has many senses, but two are particularly common. In the broader sense, jurisprudence is a synonym for the study and practice of law. In the narrower sense, jurisprudence is the study of the philosophy of law.

In the sense of legal philosophy, jurisprudence is the study of four things through innumerable methodologies: what the law is, what the law ought to be, what justice is, and what justice ought to be. This might seem a bit redundant, but it is not.

Law is different from justice, law being whatever the law is and justice being an ideal of what law should be from certain perspectives. The problem of describing something and prescribing it are also different: saying what something observed actually is (and improving one's methods of observation and description) is not the same as saying what it ought to be. Even justice is not the same as describing what law ought to be, because although there might be some overlap, one can think of many ways of imagining the perfect law, or legal system, that would not be based upon traditional concepts of justice.

The sense of the philosophy of law that underpins Bouvier's definition is the idea of legal science, in which the law was to be constantly refined in order better to understand its underlying truths, in a sense not unlike refining the understanding of chemistry to understand better the chemical properties of the elements and compounds. This idea of law as a human investigation of a natural phenomenon is no longer fashionable, and law is now seen much more to be an invention or creation of human officials. Even so, many views of justice and some influential views of law continue to be based on arguments of natural or inherent formation and definition of what law should be or what law inherently would be.

*See also:* law.

**analytical jurisprudence**  The study of law through the language of concepts, frameworks, and justifications in the law. Analytical jurisprudence is the descriptive study of law, with an emphasis on the specific significance of its language and operation as a structure of authority and will, based largely on H.L.A. Hart's restoration of the tools of Jeremy Bentham and importation of the ideas of Ludwig Wittgenstein into jurisprudence. From Bentham came the close analysis of harm and causation, and from Wittgenstein the analysis of language. Yet another strain from Bentham through John Austin, Albert Venn Dicey, and Thomas Erskine Holland which studied positive law as a something like the study of grammar, which like jurisprudence, is an analysis of actions and rules.

*See also:* jurisprudence, legal positivism (positivism).

**chthonic law**  Law based on an indigenous tradition of norms. Chthonic law is traditional law, particularly law originating in an oral tradition that is integrated into cultural patterns of obligation. In many cultures it embraces the whole of the religious, traditional, and tribal elements of the norms that are enforced by social structures, including a legal system.

*See also:* canon, canon law (ecclesiastical law).

**conservatism**  Just law is based on tradition and legitimate authority. Conservatism in law draws from many philosophical and social movements, but representing three distinct groups of ideas: law should promote certain traditional values in society; law should promote the autonomy of the individual and the market free from state interference; and the substance of law should be limited to the results of certain traditional institutional statements of law and methods of legal action. The earliest of these views is the Enlightenment idea of individual freedom from state interference, which is now also called classical liberalism, associated with writers like Immanuel Kant and John Locke. The view that the law should conserve social norms that have been endorsed by a community's traditions and moral elite and is indeed a defining aspect of the community is associated with the writings of Edmund Burke. The view that the law should be based on legitimating institutional claims, limited to traditional statements made by such institutions with their authority is associated with writers such as Thomas Cooley and Antonin Scalia.

**critical legal studies (C.L.S. or CLS)** The criticism of liberalism and formalism through demystification and delegitimation. Critical legal studies, or CLS, was a radical assault on the traditional views of law and modern liberal theories of the state, which developed in the late 1960s and peaked in the 1980s. Reviving the most radical claims of legal realism, CLS writers applied tools from Marxist political science, structural sociology and French literary theory to argue that the law is merely a power structure to protect elites and to burden and marginalize the poor and other groups. CLS provoked a backlash of conservative theory and fostered new liberal theory in Feminist Jurisprudence and Race Critical Theory.

See also: jurisprudence, legal realism.

**crits** Professors and lawyers engaged in critical legal studies. Crits were a spectacular intellectual force in the legal academy in the 1980s and into the 1990s. Their early numbers were led by young teachers, particularly Roberto Unger, Duncan Kennedy, Mark Kelman, David Kairys, and Mark Tushnet. They were followed by a second generation even younger, like Pierre Schlagg, though others of the second wave broke away into Race Critical Studies and Feminist Jurisprudence.

**delegitimation** Rebutting traditional justifications of the law. Delegitimation or, as it is often written, delegitimization, is the process of trashing writ large, demonstrating the failure of law to end injustice and calling for an end to law that perpetuates social injustice.

**demystification** Debunking traditional justifications of law. Demystification was the process of mapping writ large. Demystification demonstrates the actions of legal officials, particularly when judges decide questions of law, are not a mystical process of rules and reasoning. Rather demystification depicts official decisions as political acts that promote a particular distribution of social, political, and economic power.

**mapping** Analyzing the law to demonstrate its fundamental contradictions. Mapping, or analyzing the contradictions of law, is the initial step in trashing.

**trashing** Exposing internal contradictions in law's claims to justification. Trashing has evolved from a neo-Dadaist exercise in locating the contradictions in law, liberal theory, compromise, and implementation into a post-structuralist attempt to contrast the ideals of law and its manifestation, particularly in its failure to protect the poor. In both, it has strongly followed the tools of deconstructionism in literary theory, though in the second, it has imported more tools from structural and post-structural sociology.

**Critical Race Theory (Critical-Race Theory or C.R.T. or CRT)** Understanding law and legal institutions with race as a defining aspect of both. Critical Race Theory is an outgrowth of the Civil Rights Movement and Critical Legal Studies, asserting that U.S. law is based on racial distinctions, many of which were created by the law, that law perpetuates a power structure privileging some racial identities and cultures over others, and that genuine equality and justice cannot occur in law until this structure is recognized and its inequities remedied by giving power to the previously disadvantaged.

**decisionism (dezisionismus)** A decision is valid based on its origin not on its content. Decisionism is a doctrine for the justification of laws, orders, and rules, that determines their validity not according to the justice, morality, or ethics of their substance but according to the fact that the law, order, or rule is made by the appropriate authority. Thus, whatever the appropriate authority does is inherently and inarguably valid and deserving of obedience. Decisionism has a long lineage but is best known now through the theories of Carl Schmitt, by which it is closely associated with fascism. Decisionism is also, however, an element of all theories justifying laws by source alone, including those based on discourse or reference to the democratic will.

See also: government, forms of government, fascism.

**deontology (deontic or deontologically)** Duty as the basis for all action. Deontology is the study of morals and conduct based on the deontos, or duty, that requires certain conduct, or ideas, or actions. Rights theory is a deontological approach, requiring a respect for individual rights despite sometimes undesirable outcomes. To interpret anything deontologically is to consider what duties or obligations arise in a situation first, and then to consider how they are to be carried out and then to examine the consequences. The opposing theoretical approach is teleology, which seeks to promote just ends rather than just means. Despite many efforts to defend teleology from deontology, and vice versa, it is possible to create a variety of hybrids between them, such as pragmatism.

**feminist jurisprudence (feminist legal theory)** The criticism of law as a male–dominated activity and its reform. Feminist jurisprudence is a critical vision of law that attacks its gendered methods and rules, which reflect masculine assumptions of everything from the best means to resolve disputes to the best customs in society. Feminist jurisprudence is a constructive theory, arguing for alternatives based on a feminist perspective, particularly seeking to reform areas of law of significance for women, such as family law, employment law, and crimes against women. Feminist jurisprudence also has a constructive theory of legal methodology, seeking to bring nurturing and communitarian models of law to bear in legal analysis and legal systems.

**historical jurisprudence** The study of law as an historical artifact. Historical jurisprudence is a particular branch of legal philosophy associated with certain continental legal philosophers from the nineteenth and early twentieth centuries, such as von Savigny and Genet. The general premise of historical jurisprudence was that law resulted from the personality of the people of a nation: the fundamental ideas and particular variations in the laws of a country reflected the national character and its historical development.

**legal formalism (formalist)**  The rules of law have a definite form and significance. Legal formalism is an approach to jurisprudence akin to positivism, that emphasizes the nature of the rules of the law, contending that each rule has a form that meets certain criteria and that officials have an obligation to understand and act according to such rules. As a matter of emphasis, legal formalists are often concerned with the manner and degree to which judges follow rules, regardless of whether the rules arise from prior decisions or from legislative action.

*See also:* jurisprudence, legal positivism (positivism).

**legal pluralism**  A single normative system may include many competing norms. Legal pluralism is a model of norms in legal philosophy that describes a normative system like the law as the sum of a variety of obligations arising from different justifications, which also allows a variety of justifications to support a given obligation, even if the justifications are theoretically incompatible. It is a pragragmatic approach to norms and to law that recognizes the persusasive limits of a single approach to the law. Rawls's idea of overlapping consensus is a form of legal pluralism.

**legal positivism (positivism)**  Law is only what is recognized by officials as the rules of law. Legal positivism is the study of law as a system of rules created from rules that are inherent aspects of a state. The legal system is effectively the sum of laws, which are the union of secondary rules — the rules according to which laws are created (or recognized), are applied to given situations (or adjudicated), and are changed — and primary rules — the rules that govern the daily affairs of citizens. At its core, legal positivism rejects the idea that law is recognized or created by morality or justice, contending instead that while law may reflect morality or an idea of justice, what makes it law is the action of the creation of laws according to rules for their creation.

*See also:* law, legal system; jurisprudence, analytical jurisprudence.

**command theory of law**  Law is a command from the sovereign to the subject, enforced by a threat of punishment. The command theory of law is a recurrent model of law, based on the idea that the law is a set of orders for people to do or to refrain from certain things. It is incomplete in many ways, but mainly in that many laws affecting private conduct do not take this form and in that it does not describe many laws affecting the conduct of officials.

**primary rule**  *See:* rule, legal rule, primary rule.

**secondary rule**  *See:* rule, legal rule, secondary rule.

**separability thesis**  The idea that law and morals are separate. The separability thesis distinguishes law from morals and other normative systems. Law, according to the separability thesis, is what is created as law according to rules of law for making laws. Morality may provide a source for the standard selected by law for a given rule of law but is not itself the law. Indeed, proponents of the separability thesis argue that there is no essential relationship between morality and law; law may be immoral and still be law.

*See also:* jurisprudence, natural law (jure naturae or lex naturale).

**legal realism**  Law is not rules alone but includes what officials do with them. Legal realism is a method for understanding the law that focuses on how officials act and why they act as they do in order to understand and improve the legal system. Though no two realists agree on what realism means, most believe the law results from some balance between the role of earlier created rules, social and historical facts, and the social and intellectual backgrounds of the officials. Legal realism was closely associated with progressive critiques of law in the early twentieth century, and its successor movements include critical legal scholarship, legal nihilism, feminist legal theory, and critical race scholarship. Responsive movements include a reinvigorated school of legal positivism and natural law theory, as well as a synthesis between several aspects of realism and formalism that became legal process.

*See also:* jurisprudence, critical legal studies (C.L.S. or CLS); rule, legal rule, rule–scepticism (rule skepticism).

**legal semiotics (semiotics)**  Law is composed of signs. Semiotics generally is the the study of symbols as the expression of language and ideas, and in law it is the idea that rules and commands are expressed in signs that reflect underlying significance of legal obligation, opportunity, liability, and so forth. The principal argument of legal semiotics is that laws are signs, and signs are relationships between particular signifiers (like the language of a statute or a judge's robe or a stop sign) and particular signifieds (like a liability if one fails to do something or the physical arrest of a person by a police officer). A given signified may be semiotically related to many signs, and vice versa, and the form of the relationship may have many contingent elements that increase or decrease the sign's explanatory value.

*See also:* symbol (symbolic); semantics.

**legal voluntarism**  Law may enshrine any demands upon the subject, without limits. Voluntarism is a metaphysical claim that ethics are driven by the will more than by reason. In some ways it is a natural theory, being ascribed to the nature of humankind in creation, but it justifies a positivist model of law. It has many complicated and abstract arguments, and it has recurred in significance through many eras, not the least being in the writings of the medieval scholastics, Immanuel Kant, David Hume, Friedrich Neitzche, and the pragmatists.

**liberalism (liberal)** The citizens should be free from state interference. The theory of liberalism has many facets, but the oldest is the classical view that the individual should be free of state interference, to pursue rational projects of the individual's own choosing. Modern forms of liberalism require the state to provide institutions to allow each person to pursue such projects, including an assurance of equal opportunity in or treatment by society, a foundation of education, material health and safety, and the means to subsist.

**libertarian legal theory (libertarianism or libertarian jurisprudence)** Law must ensure individuals and property from others' harm and from regulation. Libertarian legal theory is a critique of law that seeks the least intrusive degree of state involvement in the affairs of the individual. Libertarian jurisprudence argues for rights against state intrusion into private choices and action, for laws that punish directly harmful conduct, and for a tax system that is the least possible to ensure defense from foreign attack and the basic assurance of police protection from harm to the individual and from harm to property. All other private goods and public goods will be provided by the operation of the market and private choice.

*See also:* state, minimal state.

**mechanistic jurisprudence** The overly rigid or unthinking application of rules. Mechanistic jurisprudence is not a school of jurisprudence but the label for a straw argument that the rules of law could be applied with machine–like precision, requiring no interpretation or human judgment in their application. Mechanistic jurisprudence labels a legal system with no discretion for the individual official. Legal realists, who argued for wide arenas of discretion, labeled arguments for legal science, for formalism and for positivism arguments as mechanistic, which were largely unfair characterizations of these positions. Later arguments against interpretation, judicial activism, and the development of precedent do, however, smack of a mechanistic element in them.

*See also:* discretion.

**natural law (jure naturae or lex naturale)** Law must enshrine natural principles of reason and justice. Natural law is a broad term including many different approaches to law, some intended to describe and some intended to criticize. The most essential strains have been arguments in law's defense and arguments for law reform. The most enduring natural arguments may not be those that suggest there is a natural legal answer to all questions but those that claim there is a common core of legal rules justified either by reason or by the universal needs of the human being in community. Natural law has been argued as the basis for several fundamental tests for law, including the inherent right of self-defense, the principles of liberty and of equality, and of the obligation of the state to promote the virtues or underived goods of every citizen.

*See also:* jurisprudence, legal positivism, separability thesis; right, natural right; malum, malum in se (mala in se); environment (environmental).

**normativism (legal normativism)** Law is best understood as a type of norm. Legal normativism posits that the legal system is an arrangement of normative ideas that have particular sources, some of which are institutional and some of which are not, and that the legal system operates within — and succeeds or fails in — an environment that includes many other normative systems. So, law is created and enforced in a society that includes manners, religion, and institutions (such as the military, or media, or sports) that create and inculcate norms. All of these norms are used by people when they imagine what their obligations are in various situations, and so it is easier to understand how and why people obey (or do not obey) the law, by seeing the law in this broader normative environment.

**paternalism (paternalist law)** Laws are enacted for the good of the person they regulate. Legal paternalism is a justification of law because the law will improve the life of the person or facilitate the person's pursuit of virtue, good projects, or opportunities. The term is derived from the idea of the state as like a parent, enacting laws to educate the citizenry and to enforce duties owed not only by each person to others but also by each person to the self. Paternalism is generally used in modern liberal theory to criticize police laws regulating health, safety, welfare and morals.

*See also:* parens patriae.

**perfectionism (legal perfectionism)** Law should encourage each person to live the best possible life. Legal perfectionism is a justification of laws according to which a law may be enacted to encourage each person (or at least some people) to pursue a view of the good, not just for those individuals' own sake, but for the good of all. The idea of the state as the arbiter of civic virtue is a classical notion. Aristotle argued that the state should use laws to identify and encourage civic morals in each person, which is justification for the state. Though legal perfectionism can be dismissed as about taste or marginal behavior, legal perfectionism is capable of justifying essential laws, such as the prohibition of murder, because all good persons would reject murder, and that is good not only for the would–be murderer, but for everyone. This approach is controversial, as it requires a debate of the content of the good, or the right, which is the basis for the prohibition or requirement of law. And it is difficult, in that the law must be clear in its strictures to demonstrate the moral notion that is promoted or discouraged through law. Yet it allows laws which encourage good behavior even if the behavior is unpopular or economically inefficient.

**positivism** *See:* jurisprudence, legal positivism.

**postmodern legal theory (pomo)** An eclectic approach to description and criticism. Postmodern legal theory, or pomo law, is a response to formalism and positivism and related schools as well as to critical legal studies, feminist jurisprudence, and critical race theory. Pomo theories are less doctrinaire and more inclusive of competing views, leading many to dismiss this approach, though others see it as a restoration of bricolage.

**pragmatism (legal pragmatism)** Law is what law appears to be; it ought to be what seems best. Legal pragmatism is an eclectic and counter–theoretical theory that measures thought by the degree to which it leads to action, and otherwise it accepts that things are as they are and that things should be as they should be, an acceptance that does not depend on philosophical foundations. This particularly American approach to legal epistemology and justice allows criticism of the law and description of the law from nearly all perspectives, evaluating them according to their apparent accuracy and benefit to society.

Pragmatism is often inaccurately presented as if it lacks theory, but the more accurate description would be that it does not privilege theory above observation or other forms of knowledge. Certainly, it does not lack technique. One consequence of pragmatism is that one can be better or worse at pragmatism to the degree to which one bases decisions on the most robust set of evidence reasonably available, making choices among the greatest array of possible alternatives that may be reasonably developed. In other words, one must base a legal decision on the greatest array of evidence practically available and make the decision in the best possible manner, selecting among all manners of making decisions available. There is no preliminary rejection of any evidence, or any means of making decisions (whether ends or means).

The quintessential American approach to decision-making, pragmatism is not an excuse for laziness or short cuts, though it does require action, and all investigation or analysis is appropriate that may alter action. Any research or pondering of the question for its own sake rather than to do something with its result is a waste of time, but even this does not mean theory is useless, only that it is an instrument to guide later decision and action.

**queer legal theory** The criticism of law from a perspective of non–heterosexuality. Queer legal theory is a criticism of law based on resistance to latent heterosexist assumptions in the creation and enforcement of legal norms. Building on critical legal studies and feminist legal theory, queer legal theory challenges assumptions that turn on identity, such as the definitions of marriage, spouse, and family in the common law, which depend on gendered definitions and expectations, as well as the legal construction of gender itself. This school of thought also tends to address transgender issues.

*See also:* marriage, same-sex marriage (same sex marriage or gay marriage or marriage by homosexuals); hermaphrodite (androgyne or hermaphroditic or intersex or intersexual or transgender).

**sociological jurisprudence (sociology of law)** The study of law as a social fact. Sociological jurisprudence is the study of law as a system in human society and the influence of systems of human society upon the law, using tools that have been developed for the study of people in community by sociologists. It includes a variety of approaches that study the law as the object of human activity in communities through the tools of sociology. It includes studying the behavior of people subject to law, particularly questions of obedience and deviance, as well as the behavior of lawyers and officials as communities or subcultures in themselves. Sociological jurisprudence is largely a descriptive endeavor. The primary difference between sociological jurisprudence and the sociology of law is who writes it: sociology of law is generally written by sociologists, and sociological jurisprudence is generally written by lawyers. Perhaps the most influential sociologists to study law were Max Weber, Talcott Parson, and C. Wright Mills; and the most influential American lawyers to study sociology have been Roscoe Pound and Karl Llewellyn.

**teleology (consequentialism or teleological)** The ends as justifications of the means. Teleology, now more often called consequentialism, is the study of morals and conduct based on the telos, or end that arises from the conduct, idea or action. Utilitarianism and law and economics are telelological approaches to moral assessment. To interpret anything teleologically is to consider it according to its potential results as opposed to its form, rationale, or premises. The opposing theoretical approach is deontology, which emphasizes the right means of action over the ends that result.

*See also:* jurisprudence, deontology (deontic or deontologically).

**utilitarianism** Laws should promote the greatest good for the most people. Utilitarianism is a consequentialist theory of justice in which the primary assessment of law is whether the law, all things considered, creates the greatest good possible. Utilitarianism sums the good (or, happiness or pleasure) of everyone involved, and requires a theory for understanding what is happiness, or the good, or pleasure, or whatever is measured. Different theorists prefer different measures, comparing happiness or pleasure, or the good, as offset by unhappiness, or evil, or pain, or harm. Harm caused by the law is a factor in all approaches, however, and a common understanding of utility, which is the balance of pain and pleasure, is whether the happiness created by the law, minus the harms caused by its creation and enforcement, outweigh the harms the law would diminish and prevent, minus the happiness lost to the people who had enjoyed the harmful acts now forbidden. Utilitarians debate the proper means for the measurement of happiness and harm, as well as the comparison of seemingly incommensurable values, and there are questions of whether happiness in harmful acts should count and whether there ought to be limits according to minimal satisfactions for individuals, and many other details of the theory, but the theory underlies much of later consequential-ist and economic thought.

**jurist (juristic)** A particularly influential and able judge, scholar, or lawyer. A jurist is a person whose skill in the law has acquired an authority such that the person's arguments and writings are a source of law in themselves.

**juror** *See:* jury (juror).

**juror challenge** *See:* jury, jury selection, juror challenge (jury challenge).

**juror disqualification** *See:* jury, jury selection, juror disqualification (disqualification of juror or disqualified juror).

**juror misconduct** *See:* jury, juror misconduct.

**juror number** *See:* jury, juror number.

**jury (juror)** A group of laypeople under oath who hear evidence and adjudge its significance in law. The jury is a group of citizens who hear evidence and decide based upon it which outcome of some factual contro-versy is best supported by the evidence presented. In the United States the members of a jury are usually drawn from those citizens who are registered to vote, who are summoned by a state or federal official to serve for a brief time on a panel with other jurors. Jurors hear specific matters arising in law, about which they will listen to evidence and assess it, reaching a decision jointly, after which legal officials will issue various legal judgments and orders based upon their decision.

There are several forms of jury. When the term is used with no modification, "jury" nearly always refers to a petit jury or trial jury, which has from six to twelve mem-bers, plus alternates. The petit jury sits in criminal and civil actions, hearing witnesses and reviewing tangible evidence in a trial, and after being instructed by the judge on the legal structure of questions to be answered from the evidence, debate among themselves until reaching an agreed answer to the questions presented, presenting this answer in the form of a verdict.

The grand jury is larger, often twenty or more, who hear evidence from a prosecutor of suspected criminal conduct on the part of individuals whom the prosecutor wishes to indict for specific offenses. The grand jurors vote to indict the suspect or not to do so.

Other, more specialized juries are summoned from time to time, such as a coroner's jury.

*See also:* pais (in pais or pays); equity, equitable pro-cedure, jury, dairy queen rule; lay (layperson or layman or laymen); verdict.

*agreement and unanimity* A criminal jury in most states must reach a unanimous verdict, but this is not always true, and the U.S. Supreme Court has allowed convictions based on a supermajority (such as ten to two), although due process requires at least some assur-ance that the jury may not too easily find guilt as a result of its voting structure. However, the sentence of death must be by a unanimous vote.

A jury hearing evidence in a civil action need not reach a unanimous verdict, and some states allow a lesser agreement in some or all civil actions.

The rules of grand jury voting vary from state to state, but many require that a grand jury must usually assent to an indictment by at least a three–fourths vote.

**jury clause** *See:* constitution, U.S. Constitution, clauses, jury clause (impartial jury clause or criminal jury clause).

**jury fee** *See:* fee, fee for services, court fee, jury fee.

**jury in equity** *See:* equity, equitable procedure, jury in equity.

**jury instruction** *See:* instruction, jury instruction (charge to the jury or to charge the jury or jury charge or instruction to the jury); interrogatory, jury instruc-tion, special interrogatory (jury interrogatory).

**jury instruction conference** *See:* instruction, jury instruction, jury instruction conference (charge conference).

**jury interrogatory** *See:* interrogatory, jury instruc-tion, special interrogatory (jury interrogatory).

**jury pardon or jury mercy** *See:* verdict, compromise verdict (jury pardon or jury mercy).

**jury poll** *See:* poll, jury poll.

**jury trial** *See:* trial, jury trial (trial by jury).

**advisory jury** A jury whose verdict is not authorita-tive but only instructive. An advisory jury hears evidence and renders an opinion regarding its signif-icance and the degree to which facts are proved, but the judge is not required to defer to the jury's deter-mination of the significance of the evidence of the proof of facts, or, particularly, of the appropriate criminal sentence or civil judgment allowed under the law.

**direct democracy in the jury** Leaving judgments of law to a jury is an aspect of democratic government. The jury requires claims of criminality raised by state officials to be accepted by citizens representing the people as a whole, as well as providing private liti-gants a means of resorting to a democratic judgment on the merits of private claims and defenses that have been brought to law for public resolution. In these capacities, the jury serves as a check on the powers of the state to prevent state officials from asserting authority over the people that is not acceptable to the people as a whole.

**discharge of the jury** The dismissal of a jury. The dis-charge of a jury is the formal conclusion of a jury's service from a trial in which the jury was sworn and charged.

**embracery (tampering with the jury or embracer or jury tampering or juror bribery)** Attempting to influence a juror. Embracery is the crime of an unlaw-ful attempt to corrupt or influence a juror, regardless of whether the attempt succeeds. Embracery may take place in a civil or criminal action, concerning a juror in the grand or petit jury. Embracery may occur through offers of gifts or bribes as well as by threats or hostile acts toward the juror or others. Embracery raises a presumption of misconduct in the trial that should be the basis of a mistrial. Embracery, jury tampering, and misconduct regarding the jury are crimes, usually misdemeanors, committed both by the person attempting to influence or influencing the juror and, in the event of a juror accepting a bribe or gift of value, they are felonies by both the embracer and by the juror. Some jurisdictions recognize a tort of embracery that may be brought by a party in a civil action who is injured as a result of the unlawful interference with the juror.

*See also:* tampering (tamper).

**foreperson (foreman)**  The person who chairs the jury. A foreperson is a member of a grand jury or a petit jury, who is elected by the members of the jury to chair deliberations, coordinate communications with the judge, and who completes the jury verdict form (if there is one), who tenders the verdict to the judge, and who often is requested to read the verdict in court.

**grand jury**  A large jury which investigates crimes and indicts defendants in felony cases. The grand jury is a jury of laypersons, who examine evidence to determine whether the evidence suggests probable cause to believe a person or entity accused of a crime has indeed committed it. If so, it authorizes an indictment against the defendant, which is the basis for arrest and trial before a different jury that determines guilt. Sometimes the grand jury is strictly summoned to investigate a crime, but usually, it is summoned to consider bills of indictment, which its foreperson endorses to allow indictment or not. A refusal by a grand jury to issue an indictment does not amount to an acquittal, and jeopardy does not attach, so a prosecutor who fails in the first attempt at indictment is free to seek indictment from a later grand jury. A prosecutor usually controls the agenda and evidence before the grand jury, and the prosecutor is under no duty to put on evidence contrary to the state's case against a given defendant. Even so, a grand jury may investigate what a sufficient number of members chooses to investigate, and in many jurisdictions, the grand jury may petition and be provided police investigators to pursue inquiries of the jury's choice. The hearings of a grand jury are secret, and the unauthorized disclosure of testimony or evidence from a grand jury hearing is an offense.

*See also:* indictment (indict).

**investigative grand jury (investigatory grand jury)**  A grand jury that investigates misdeeds of its choosing. An investigative grand jury is a grand jury that is expressly charged with the investigation of matters of public interest that may amount to criminal conduct, abuse of office, or dereliction of office, or that may amount to any serious crimes of which it is aware. A grand jury that is not specifically charged to make such investigations may, in most jurisdictions, do so on its own authority anyway, requesting investigative assistance, summoning and subpoenaing witnesses, and issuing indictments on its own information. Investigative grand juries without any definite charge are now rare.

**presentment of the grand jury**  A grand jury report of potential crimes. The presentment of the grand jury is an instrument issued by the investigating grand jury to the court, by which the jury gives notice of criminal acts that its members believe have occurred in its jurisdiction. Though the presentment of the grand jury was established in the twelfth century, it is still in use in some U.S. jurisdictions, now being limited to use by an investigating grand jury. The presentment differs from an information or indictment in that the jurors themselves initiate the charge in the presentment.

Note: the presentment of the grand jury is fundamentally different from a modern presentment to the grand jury. The modern presentment to the grand jury is the presentation of a case, indictment, or evidence to the grand jury for its action.

*See also:* presentment; indictment, true bill indictment.

**impanel a jury (seat the jury or select the jury or jury return or return of a jury)**  To select members of the jury from the venire and to administer the oath to each juror. To impanel the jury is to create it, which is done at the conclusion of voir dire by the naming of the jurors and by their each taking the oath as a juror. (In some jurisdictions the oath is administered to all members of the venire and is not repeated.)

**juror misconduct**  Activity prohibited of a member of the jury. Juror misconduct includes any activity by a juror that is prohibited by the court's instructions to the jury, that is barred by statute or the Constitution, or that otherwise would prejudice the parties to the action heard by the jury on which the juror serves from receiving a fair and impartial hearing. Examples of juror misconduct include communicating with litigants or their counsel outside of trial, revealing information to other non-jury members, performing outside research in order to reach their verdict, or engaging in tactics designed to pressure other jurors into voting for one verdict over another. Jurors are warned of these types of activities before trial starts, and are told that depending on the severity of the violation, they may be removed for failure to comply with the rules. Extreme misconduct, such as receiving money or a promise of opportunity or value in return for a vote, is a criminal offense.

**juror number**  An identifying number assigned to a member of the venire or of the jury. Juror numbers as identification tools are used for purposes of anonymity, both in the selection process, and then once the jury has been seated, during the course of trial. Numbers are used to protect the identities of those who end up serving, so that there are no repercussions from possibly ruling one way or another. Juror numbers are also used for organization purposes, in order to help litigants more easily identify people in the jury box. In many courts, the number of the juror is the number of the seat in which the juror first sits in the jury box.

**jury box**   The area for the seating of jurors. The jury box is a portion of the courtroom in which the jury is seated while present in the courtroom while the court is in session. By custom, the area has a seat for each juror and alternate juror, and all of the seats are segregated from the rest of the courtroom by a rail or a low wall. The jury box should be located in such a manner that the jurors have a clear and direct view of the forward edge of the witness stand, of the judge, and of the attorney's podium. While the jury is seated, it is usually forbidden for anyone but a juror, other than the bailiff, to approach the box without leave of the court.

**jury deliberations**   Discussions amongst jurors after the parties rest at trial in order to reach a verdict. Jury deliberations occur after the conclusion of a trial, once both the prosecution and the defense have rested and the judge has instructed the jury, and the jury has retired from the courtroom. Deliberations occur until a jury has reached a verdict or has determined that it cannot find sufficient agreement to reach a verdict according to its instructions.

**jury nullification (jury lenity or jury annulment or jury pardon power or jury mercy-dispensing power)**   A jury's power to acquit or return a lesser verdict even if the prosecution has met all burdens. Jury nullification is one of several labels for the inherent power of the jury to render its verdict according to conscience, even if to do so, jurors must reject the legal conclusions that are logically required from the evidence before them. A jury hearing a criminal case has the power to acquit the defendant, even if the evidence is overwhelming and unrebuttable that the defendant committed the act for which the the defendant is charged, if the jury is unwilling in good conscience to abide by the instructions to do convict in such circumstances. The same power allows a jury to convict a defendant of a lesser included offense even though the jury accepts the validity of evidence demonstrating the defendant committed a more serious offense. Jurors are rarely instructed on this power, but it is error to instruct the jury that exercising this power would violate the jurors' oaths. A juror does not violate the juror's oath by acquitting a defendant or giving a lesser verdict from mercy or sympathy or even the rejection of a law as immoral or unconstitutional. Such a verdict does violate the juror's oath if the acquittal or lesser verdict was motivated by the juror's interest in one or another party in the case case, by a prejudice against a party or other form of prejudgment, by an acceptance of a bribe or the hope doing so, or by acting for reasons that violate the principles of due process of law or equal protection of the laws.
*See also:* nullification.

**jury poll**   A survey of the vote of each juror after a verdict has been given. A jury poll is a survey of individual jurors to ensure that the verdict reported by the foreperson represents accurately the vote of each juror. A poll in a criminal jury must be taken if a party requests it or if the judge has reason to question the jury's verdict. A poll may be taken in a civil action at the discretion of the judge. If the poll reveals that the verdict does not represent the individual judgment of all of the jurors (or a majority if allowed in that action), the judge may either return the jury to its deliberations or declare a mistrial. If there is a jury poll, the judgment on a verdict is not entered until after the poll is taken.

**jury selection (voir dire of the jury)**   The process of summoning, questioning, challenging, and seating members of a jury. Jury selection includes the entire process of the creation of a particular jury, from the determination of the population from which potential jurors shall be summoned to the final seating of a panel and their alternates. In most cases, jurors are summoned by court order in a random process from names and addresses on the voter rolls in the district in which the court will sit. Those who answer the summons are the jury pool, from which often a smaller group, the venire, is selected for consideration for seating in particular trial. These prospective jurors, or venire persons, are then questioned as to their history and personal philosophy regarding the pending action, the parties and their counsel, and its subject matter. Attorneys may challenge potential jurors from the jury, either for cause or without cause, and the court may strike jurors whom it believes would be biased, disruptive, or unfair. A panel is then selected, usually of the number required plus one or more alternates. The panel is called, the jurors move into the jury box, and take an oath to serve as a juror.

**excuse of juror (exclusion of juror or excused juror or excluded juror)**   The court may, in its discretion, excuse a juror from service for any lawful reason. A person summoned for jury service, a member of a jury pool, or a member of a jury may be excused (or excluded) from service by the judge for any reason that does not violate the law or the constitution. Individuals may be excused in the discretion of the court upon a showing by the potential juror that service would cause an extraordinary hardship. In the federal system, the failure to seat a person based on challenge or upon a potential for bias, disruption, or the violation of secrecy amounts to excuse or to exclusion.

In some jurisdictions potential jurors are excused or disqualified as a matter of statute or custom owing to their occupations, such as religious leaders, including priests, rabbis, imams, or ministers; doctors; police officers or firefighters; judges or lawyers; and those in the military on active duty. Besides excuse or exclusion, some members of the jury pool may be disqualified, although there is considerable overlap in the grounds within one court for excuse of for disqualification. There is general difference in usage between excuse from exclusion, although excuse usually arises from reasons considered beyond the potential juror's control.

*See also:* excuse (excusable or excused); jury, jury selection, juror disqualification (disqualification of juror or disqualified juror).

**juror challenge (jury challenge)** The contesting of one about to serve on a jury. Juror challenges can be made by a party, pursuant to the jurisdiction's rules of criminal procedure. These challenges can be made based on an actual cause, for instance, a prospective juror having a conflict of interest with one of the parties involved in the case, or without cause, also known as a peremptory challenge. Each party is allotted a certain number of these challenges that they can use to strike potential jurors off a jury.

**challenge for cause** A motion to exclude a potential juror for a stated reason. A juror challenge for cause is a challenge to the seating of a specific venire member, based on any of a number of legitimate reasons, such as a potential conflict of interest between the juror and a party in the case, indicia of a particular bias against a party or a party's argument that the juror could not overcome to perform the office, the juror's poor health, or alternate obligations that will occur during the trial and distract the juror's attention or require the juror to be later excused. Challenging a juror for cause does not count against either side's number of peremptory challenges, and the issue can be raised by both the litigating parties and the judge in the case.

**peremptory challenge** A motion to exclude a potential juror for no stated reason. A peremptory challenge is a challenge to prevent any potential juror from selection to a jury, for which the challenging party need give no cause. In most jurisdictions, each party to the action has a limited number of peremptory challenges, which is usually greater in a capital case or a case of unusual complexity or notoriety. Although each party is limited to the same number of peremptory challenges as the other, the court may also strike venire members on its own motion, and each side has an unlimited number of challenges for cause. If there is an insufficient number of jurors to seat a full jury following the use of challenges, a new pool may be summoned. A peremptory challenge may not be used to strike a juror or jurors solely on the basis of race or gender without violating both the rights of the jurors and the other litigants and the constitutional assurances of due process of law.

*See also:* peremptory (peremptorily).

**Batson challenge (racial challenge or gender challenge or Batson motion)** An objection to a jury from which jurors were struck on the basis of race or gender. A Batson challenge is a motion objecting to a party's challenge to the seating of one or more members of the jury pool that was made on the basis of a juror's race, in an attempt to constitute a jury with a particular racial mix or bias in violation of the rule in Batson v. Kentucky, 476 U.S. 79 (1986). Later cases have extended the scope of the Batson challenge to include a challenge to a juror on the basis of gender. The other party may object to the peremptory challenge of a juror, and the objecting party must make a prima facie case that the challenge was based on the gender or race of the potential juror. The challenged party must then articulate a race–neutral or gender–neutral basis for the challenge, but in any case the judge must deny the challenge if there is evidence of purposeful discrimination against a juror on the basis of race or gender. The denial of such an objection is essential to protect the parties and the obligation of the courts to ensure a fair and impartial jury. Note: though the term is usually said as "Batson challenge," this usage can be a bit confusing, as it is sometimes used to describe the peremptory challenge or challenges made by the party who would exclude someone from the jury and sometimes used to describe the objection of the other party, who argues that such challenges violate the Batson doctrines. The term is best used to describe a challenge to a jury list composed with jurors struck on potentially unconstitutional grounds.

**juror disqualification (disqualification of juror or disqualified juror)** The removal of a venire member or a juror for bias or good cause. Juror disqualification occurs when a judge determines the juror cannot perform the office of juror for lack of proper age, lack of U.S. citizenship, lack of a local residence, for a legal disability from service (such as a record of a felony conviction), for a lack of mental capacity, for the inability to read or write, or, upon a determination by the court, the person is incapable of unbiased service or service that does not disrupt the proceedings.

*See also:* jury, jury selection, excuse of juror (exclusion of juror or excused juror or excluded juror).

**challenge to panel** A motion to discharge a whole jury. A challenge to a jury pool is a motion, nearly always in a criminal case, in which the defendant seeks to discharge the jury that is seated for the action and commence a new jury selection. A challenge must be based upon a claim raised in good faith that the process of selection was incurably flawed and in material violation of the statutes or rules governing the process of jury selection.

**jury packing (jury fixing)** The selection of jurors with a prior sympathy to one cause in an action. To "pack the jury" is to select jurors whom a lawyer believes will eventually side with that lawyer's cause when it comes time to decide the verdict. Packing the jury is a prohibited practice and can subject a lawyer to disciplinary action and possibly worse. If any person attempts to influence a juror or to bribe or seek commitments from a person who may be summoned to serve on a jury or a member of a venire or panel, this is jury fixing and is the crime of embracery.

**jury panel (array or jury pool or venire panel)** The group of people summoned to, and reporting for, jury duty. A jury panel consists of citizens who are called up to serve on a jury, and each person is a prospective jury member. A jury panel is supposed to roughly represent the area from which it is drawn, though it is not required to be perfectly proportionate.

**jury summons** A court order requiring a person to appear for jury duty. A jury summons is an order of the court mailed by the clerk of the court or similar official to prospective jurors who have been randomly selected for service. Answering a jury summons is mandatory in most jurisdictions, and the failure to appear at the required time and place hearing without just cause is a misdemeanor offense, though it may also be treated as a criminal contempt of court.

*See also:* contempt of court.

**jury wheel** Contraption used to determine who is called up for jury selection. A jury wheel is a device that was once widely used for jury selection. While its use is now rare, its metaphorical significance persists as a means of juror selection in a manner like a lottery. The wheel physically contains either slips cut from the lists of eligible jurors, taken either from a list of registered voters within a particular jurisdiction, or alternatively, a list of licensed drivers. Jury wheels are supposed to represent the populations in which they serve, to ensure that those who are called for duty and eventually do serve are randomly summoned but still roughly reflective of the population in which they sit.

**mock jury (shadow jury)** A private group that emulates the decision-making of a trial jury. A mock jury is a jury of volunteers in a mock trial or other non-binding, extra-legal activity designed to demonstrate the trial system, recreate a trial scene, practice the presentation of evidence or trial tactics, or evaluate a hypothetical or historical case. Sometimes these functions are also performed for academic reasons in the manner of a shadow jury.

A shadow jury is employed by lawyers to evaluate a case just as a real jury does. The members are selected in a manner to approximate the social background of the jurors on the actual panel and exposed to different litigation techniques by the lawyers, so as to determine what is effective in swaying opinion one way or another. The lawyers then alter their tactics in the trial in response to the feedback received.

**petit jury (trial jury)** The jury empaneled in a trial. The petit jury, or trial jury, is the finder of facts in the trial of a civil or criminal action that, for any reason, is not heard only by a magistrate, judge, or panel of judges. The petit jury is so called because it is smaller than the grand jury. Members of a petit jury are not judges, and though an attorney may be called as a citizen, the members of the jury are selected from a venire of citizens randomly summoned from the jurisdiction.

The customary trial jury in the United States had twelve members, though since 1970 the number has been allowed to vary, particularly in civil trials. A typical criminal petit jury is now six, though some are of nine or twelve, though a jury of six must act unanimously. (Many jurisdictions allow a jury to act less than unanimously.) The federal civil jury is now six, and many states have moved to this number as well.

The right to trial by a petit jury is considered fundamental to the American system of laws, and in the federal system the criminal jury trial is ensured in U.S. courts and state courts by the Sixth Amendment, and the civil jury is ensured in U.S. courts by the Seventh Amendment. Each state must determine what rights to a jury in a civil action it will extend, though a jury trial is a matter of right in most states for most serious actions not in equity.

*See also:* jury, grand jury; petit.

**province of the jury** The exclusive power of the jury to assess facts independently of other influences. The province of the jury is the scope of the jury's authority to act as the sole finder of facts in a trial in which a jury is empaneled, or in a cause of action in which any party is entitled to a jury. A judicial order that takes the determination of facts from a jury is inherently disfavored under the common law, and it may be an unconstitutional deprivation of a party's right to a jury under the Sixth Amendment in a criminal action and under the Seventh Amendment in a federal civil action. Expert evidence or jury instructions are barred if either would operate as a conclusion regarding questions of fact that are to be presented to the jury.

*See also:* equity, equitable procedure, jury in equity.

**right to trial by jury (right to a jury)** The right to a jury in all serious criminal actions and in federal civil actions. The right to trial by jury is a constitutional right ensured both to a criminal defendant charged with a serious crime and to a civil litigant in federal court and in many state courts. The right to a criminal jury is established in the Sixth Amendment, not only as to guilt or innocence but as to the determination of any fact that may affect a sentence or penal liability, in any action for which the defendant may potentially be sentenced to detention for six months or more. The right to a civil jury is established in the Seventh Amendment, preserving the right to the jury in legal actions as they existed in 1791, which, among other actions, did not provide for juries in equity or admiralty.

**sequestration of the jury (sequestered jury)** The isolation of members of a criminal jury during trial. Sequestration is the order of a judge requiring the jurors (and usually any alternates impaneled) to be kept from contact with other persons during the course of a trial. In general, juries are not sequestered, but sequestration is ordered in some cases in which there is a reasonable likelihood of juror influence by the media or by other persons, if there is a chance of jury tampering, or if there is a chance of injury to a juror.

*See also:* sequestration (sequester); custody, protective custody, witness security (witness protection).

**jus (juris or jure or ius)** Law in the grand sense, or a right protected by law. Jus is the Latin term that compares to lex for the law as opposed to one of the laws. Jus may represent either law in its general and idealized sense, as it does in "due process of law" and from which jus is the root of the word, justice. Or, it may represent a particular right that is to be protected by law, as in jus sanguinis, the right of citizenship on the basis of the blood inheritance from one's parents. The genitive case, or possessive case, of jus is juris. Thus, juris is the form of jus that represents "of law" in modifying another noun. Both jus and juris are sometimes written with an "i" for the "j" owing to the medieval creation of the "j," which is not found in classical Latin.

**jus ad bellum** *See:* war, law of war, jus ad bellum.

**jus cogens** *See:* custom, international custom, jus cogens (erga omnes obligationes or peremptory norms).

**jus in bello** *See:* war, law of war, jus in bello.

**jus tertii or vendor standing or agency standing** *See:* standing in court, third–party standing (jus tertii or vendor standing or agency standing).

**jure (iure)** Right, or the law. Jure is a form of jus, and in most senses it represents either the law in some broad sense or a right that is to be protected by law. Unmodified or not modifying a noun, jure may mean either law or justice.

*See also:* de, de jure.

**jus as right of citizenship**

**jus sanguinis** Citizenship established by parentage. Jus sanguinis, literally "law of the blood," is the lineal basis of citizenship or nationality, established for a child in different states' legal systems either by birth from one or both parents who are citizens of a state at the time of the child's birth. In the United States, section one of the Fourteenth Amendment establishes jus soli as one basis for citizenship, throughout the nation, but jus sanguinis is established in U.S. law by statute.

**jus soli** Citizenship established by the location of birth. Jus soli is basis of citizenship, established for a child from the location of the child's birth in the territory of the nation–state in which citizenship is thus established. Jus soli differs from jus sanguinis, and the citizenship of the parents is irrelevant to the citizenship of a child established by jus soli. Note: many sources imagine that jus soli is translated as law of the soil. It might seem more appropriate to consider the translation to have originated from the law of the king's dominion.

In the United States, the right of citizenship to be acquired by jus soli is established in section one of the Fourteenth Amendment. That provides "all persons born . . . in the United States and subject to the jurisdiction thereof, are citizens of the United States and of the State wherein they reside."

*See also:* ratione, ratione soli; jus, jus as right of citizenship, jus sanguinis.

**jus ad rem** The law of the thing. Jus ad rem describes interests that can be acquired in property, particularly through use or occupation that have not ripened by prescription or the running of sufficient time to amount to title. Inchoate rights or other contingent rights thus established are jus ad rem, which may be sufficient to trump the claims of some but not all claimants to the same thing. Thus an inchoate right by an occupant might be good against a trespasser but not the true owner.

**jus civile (juris civilis or ius civile or iuris civilis)** The law governing the private affairs among Romans. Jus civilis was the detailed private law binding among Romans. It is often contrasted to the jus gentium, which applied among or with other members of peoples, and with jus naturale, which was neither limited in its effects to Romans nor created by the specific acts of Roman officials.

**jus commune (ius commune)** A concept of the law as a unified system of laws across nation–states. The ius commune, or common law, was developed in medieval Europe and provided a pan–national source of laws, built from a rediscovered understanding of Roman law and canon law, in an echo of the Roman ius gentium and ius naturale. The ius commune persists as not only a basis for the criticism of national laws but as a model for integrated supranational legal systems.

*See also:* jurisprudence, chthonic law; canon, canon law (ecclesiastical law).

**jus fetialis (jus feciale or ius fetiales)** The law of war. Jus fetiale, which was corrupted into jus feciale in the middle ages, is the law of war and national obligation, which was once committed to a special college of fetiales, the priest–lawyers who arbitrated causes to determine whether a grievance amounted to a cassus belli or basis for war.

*See also:* war, law of war (law of armed conflict or LOW or LOAC).

**jus gentium** The law of nations, or the law of peoples. Jus gentium, in Roman law, was the law that bound both Romans and non–Romans. Its use, therefore, was of particular importance in governing commercial transactions dealing with trade in and out of Roman dominions. From this it grew in scope to include the laws governing a variety of international transactions and remains a synonym of international law.

*See also:* international law (law of nations or public international law).

**jus primae nocte (droit de seigneur or droit de cuissage or right of first night)**  The mythical right of a lord to take peasant women on their wedding nights. The right of the first night, or jus primae nocte, is a story that persists under several labels, according to which one of the feudal incidents of a manor was the right of the lord of the manor to take the virginity of a peasant woman on the night of her marriage. The story is almost certainly a fantasy that arose over a confusion of the rights of the lord of the manor to require permission or approval for marriages by a peasant off of the manor. Regardless of its likely false past, the concept has been reborn in many ways, not the least in sexual harassment by supervisors of their employees.

*See also:* harassment.

**just**   *See:* justice, just (unjust).

**just cause**   *See:* discharge, employment discharge, just cause.

**just compensation**   *See:* compensation, just compensation.

**justice**   Fairness, goodness, and rightness in the law. Justice is the most essential tool for the criticism of the law to ensure that the requirements of the law and the manner in which it is created and enforced are in the best senses in the interests of the governed. There are many definitions of justice, and many formulae for discerning justice or applying it to law.

Bouvier quoted first the once-famous statement from Sandars's translation of Justinian's Institutes: "the constant and perpetual disposition to render every man his due," but what was once rendered "to give everyone his due" could have been translated as "to give to each the greatest right that they are allowed." And, a fair reading of justice is the constant obligation to ensure that what duties are required to fulfill each person's rights or privileges are fully rendered.

Justice may be analyzed in many ways, but its main divisions in contemporary jurisprudence have been along two axes: the objects of justice and the sources or duties of justice. To this may be added a third: who must do justice.

The objects of justice, traditionally, were individuals (or in the case of international law individual states). Justice as understood by Justinian and Bouvier was either done or not done to each person. The concepts of justice in most religious texts, and in the basic works of natural law, such as those of Augustine, Aquinas, Grotius, and Kant, are predominately concerned with justice to individuals. In the case of the justice of the king, or of GOD, there was an abstract notion of justice toward the whole people of the dominion as well. In the nineteenth century, concepts of justice as seen by the likes of Herbert Spencer, Jeremy Bentham, and the utilitarians, justice became a social or collective measure, summed across numbers of people, albeit for quite different reasons. This idea of social justice rather than individual justice as the highest concept of justice has persisted in many liberal models of justice in the later twentieth century.

The sources of justice have been argued for centuries. The earliest claims are that justice is demanded by divine command. Justice is also said to be a natural duty, required by the nature of creation or the obvious morality of it. Some of the most sophisticated arguments of the seventeenth and eighteenth centuries and later are contractarian, that people surrender freedom in return for justice. This argument has been developed in the twentieth century by Mackie, Rawls and others into a view of a social contract made not (as the seventeenth century contracts of Hobbes and Locke) between the people and a sovereign, but rather among the people themselves. Some naturalist or utilitarian arguments are based on reason or morality, or an underived understanding of what is good and right in the world. To these arguments may be added a concept of duty derived from oaths and the express and implied promises made by officials in accepting their roles of authority over others.

Who is bound to do justice, classically, was twofold: the most common object of discussion of justice was universal, each person in private and public relations was expected to do justice to all others as one of the personal virtues. There were specific claims of the obligation of monarchs, of GOD, of judges, and other officials to do justice to the people who depended upon them, claims often made in the same breath of a proof that the monarch or divinity was in fact quite just or that the judge or official was not. In the contemporary age, the obligation of justice has become bureaucratized and made social, and it is now depicted as an obligation of the government or, as in Rawls's theory, of society overall. Another approach is to restore the personal obligation of justice within the bureaucratic model, an approach integral to some modern investigations of unjust states, such as the International Military Tribunal at Nuremburg, in which individuals were held personally accountable for violations of the duty of justice in their offices by, for instance, conspiring to commit crimes against humanity. On a more mundane scale, every official in every legal system, including jurors and voters, may be seen to have an obligation of justice toward each person affected by their actions empowered by law.

*See also:* judge, justice, circuit justice; judge, justice, chief justice; judge, justice (justiceship); equality, equal justice under the law (equal justice under law); ethics (ethical); morality (moral).

**justice court**   *See:* court, U.S. court, justice court.

**justice of the peace**   *See:* judge, justice of the peace (J.P. or JP or justice court judge).

**commutative justice**   The justice of fair exchange. Commutative justice is the basis for two separate senses of justice: one between individuals and one among all of the people in society. Between individuals, commutative justice is the ideal balance of ensuring that all contracts are fair and fairly enforced, without unjust enrichment or deliberate breach, so that each person is fairly rewarded for their efforts and their reasonable bargains. Among the individuals of society, commutative justice is an ideal system of compensation so that all workers are compensated according to the real or meaningful value of their contributions to society. Thus, not only firefighters, teachers, and police officers, but also stock traders and bankers, would be compensated according to the merits of their contributions, not according to what the market or politics demands.

*See also:* duty; due.

**corrective justice (correction)**   Justice based on fair compensation for harms done. Corrective justice is an aspect of both public law and private law. Most theories of restitution, damages (other than punitive damages) and even mitigation are manifestations of corrective justice in the private sphere. Corrective justice is also an influential basis for some theories of criminal punishment. The goal of corrective justice is the balance between fully rectifying the harm suffered by the misdeeds of another, and not creating unjust enrichment through the rectification.

**distributive justice**   Justice as the fair distribution of wealth and other goods among all individuals. Distributive justice has several distinct senses, but each involve the distribution of honor, wealth, or goods among members of a society. In its classical sense, distributive justice required that wealth and opportunity be allocated to each person according to merit, and the basis of merit was understood to be a contested idea that would be argued among different interested groups, but the distribution still required a justification of merit in some form. In its modern sense, distributive justice requires the distribution of wealth, goods, and opportunity with equality to all. In one of the leading formulations, by John Rawls, distributive justice would require that the least well off are supported, and the most well off are justified in their fortune by their support of the least well off.

*See also:* justice, Rawlsian justice, difference principle (second principle of justice).

**environmental justice**   *See:* environment, environmental justice.

**fiat justitia ruat coelum (do justice though the heavens may fall)**   Justice must be done no matter how unpopular it may be. Fiat justitia ruat coelum, Latin for "do justice, though the heavens may fall," was a maxim made famous in the common law by the Lord Mansfield, in his refusal to accept the condition of slavery in the common law, in Sommersett's Case in 1772, and in 1788 in the case of the rabble–rousing Parliamentarian John Wilkes. In both instances the opinion would be, he believed, unpopular with powerful men but required under the law. The phrase stands still as a maxim for the obligation of the court to do what is right, though it is deeply unpopular.

**injustice (unjust)**   The failure to ensure justice for an individual, group, or state. Injustice is both the absence of justice and the affirmative wrong in the abuse of neglect to use the power of the law. Injustice occurs as a matter of fact, as a matter of means, and as a matter of ends. Injustice in fact occurs when a person who is innocent is accused or convicted of a crime, or a person who has done no wrong suffers a judgment, regardless of how fair or careful the legal requirements or process that resulted in the wrongful accusation, conviction, or judgment. Injustice in means is the creation or enforcement of laws without regard for the effect of the law on each person, so that the burdens of the legal system fall negligently upon many people, as when officials favor the needs of a political party over the needs of all, or expedience is preferred to justice in each case. Injustice in ends occurs when legal officials employ the law for any end but for the benefit of each person subject to it, when they ignore the dangers to anyone that law should guard against, or when the law itself favors some over others.

Injustice is usually perceived differently from justice, and it serves as a useful means, in practice, for the pursuit of justice. Practically, the most just answer to any question is likely to be the answer that is the least unjust.

Note: unjust is the adjectival form for the noun, injustice.

**just (unjust)**   Lawful, fair, good, and right. Just is a depiction of justice, and an action done by law that comports with the requirements of justice is itself just. An action done by law, or done contrary to the law, that does not meet the requirements of justice is unjust.

The most significant bases of justice—fairness, goodness, and rightness—must be applied to the consideration of the application of a law to each person affected by it, and not merely in the aggregate in order to determine its justness.

**justice as judicial officer**   *See:* judge (judicial); judge, justice (justiceship).

**obstruction of justice**   *See:* obstruction, obstruction of justice.

**Rawlsian justice**   Justice as fairness based on the right before the good. Rawlsian justice is a model of social justice created by John Rawls, according to which society should be organized to be fair, securing the rights of individuals first and the best distribution of goods second. Laws should be written and judged as just or unjust according to how well the laws promote those goals in that order.

**difference principle (second principle of justice)**   Wealth and social goods should be allocated to benefit those who receive the least. The difference principle is Rawls's second principle of justice, that wealth and social goods should be distributed in society so that those who receive the greatest share do so because they will use that larger share in such a way that those with the least share will be better off than they could have been if those with the large shares had less.

*See also:* justice, distributive justice.

**original position**   A thought experiment to construct a fair model of justice. The original position is Rawls's famous hypothetical in which hypothetical players would negotiate all of the allocations of rights and goods in a just world, after they are placed behind a veil of ignorance, so that they will not know their ultimate lot in life, what they would be or want or desire, beyond a few basic goods, and whether they would be rich or powerful, or poor or disenfranchised. Rawls's view was that players in such circumstances would necessarily select principles of social justice that would assure liberty first and then a just distribution of economic and social resources.

*See also:* original (originality).

**principle of right (first principle of justice)**   Each person should have the greatest liberty compatible with others' liberty. The principle of rights is Rawls's first principle of justice, that each person has an equal right to the most extensive basic liberty that would be compatible with a similar liberty for others. Rawls based this idea on a Lockean ideas of rights, which are themselves an extension of the common-law maxim of nuisance, sic utere tuo ut non alienam laedas, use your property only so far as to not harm that of others.

**veil of ignorance**   A tool to ensure disinterested rationality in choosing a fair model of justice. The veil of ignorance is an aspect of John Rawls's original position, in which the players bargaining for a social structure do not know anything about their preference for one or another view of the good in life, except for a thin theory of the good in which all would want the same things, such as food, shelter, and comfort. Further, the players would not know whether they would be wealthy, powerful, skilled, smart, pretty, sociable, or lack all of these benefits in society.

**retributive justice (retributivism)**   Justice based on punishment equal to the wrong a person has done. Retributive justice is based on the penalty of wrongfulness. Punishment conceived of retributively is a response to the intentionality of the harms created by a person, not merely their harmful effects. Retribution is not mere revenge, as it is sometimes depicted, but a response intended to restore a violation of moral duty by exacting a penalty equal to the breach of the duty. Thus, proportionality is an essential justification of retributive punishment as well as limit on the extent of punishment that can be justified.

*See also:* punishment, retributive punishment; retaliation, lex talionis; retribution.

**justices in Eyre**   *See:* court, English Court, justices in Eyre (Eire).

**justiceship**   *See:* judge, justice (justiceship).

**justiciability (justiciable or non-justiciable or non-justiciability or unjusticiable or prudential rules)**   The prudential fitness of a case to be heard by a court. Justiciability is the aspect of every dispute underlying an action that demonstrates to a judge with jurisdiction to hear the action that it is an appropriate use of judicial power to do so. In the eighteenth century, justiciability was adopted into the common law from civil law and understood as a power of jurisdiction that might or might not be exercised by national courts over international questions. It has evolved as a basis for the courts' discretion to hear or not to hear specific causes of action. In essence, it is the set of principles determining when a court will consent to hear a case over which it has jurisdiction.

Presumptively, a court will hear any action between two parties with an interest at issue over which the court has jurisdiction; while jurisdiction must be pled the circumstances of justiciability are generally presumed from the claims and defenses filed. Justiciability is usually raised as a defense or raised sua sponte by the court.

Thus an argument over justiciability usually arises as an argument that a cause before the court is non-justiciable, and that argument is usually based on a specific argument. These arguments are: lack of standing by the plaintiff to bring the claim filed, untimeliness in that the issue is either unripe or moot, political question in that the claim requires the court to adjudge an issue committed to another branch of government, or (and this is quite rare) a general lack of justiciability because the court does not want to grant the relief requested or rule on the issues presented for reasons of prudence.

Justiciability per se, the idea that the courts should only act when the judge considers it prudent to do so, is distinct from the other prudential grounds of justiciability writ large, in that justiciability per se is an exercise of pure discretion by the court as opposed to an interpretation of some aspect of the case or controversy clause or other constitutional commitments. To dismiss a case as unjusticiable is to deny the plaintiff relief, and to do so effectively leaves in place whatever state of affairs led to the claims, which may well have been a state of affairs deeply challenging to the constitutional or social order. To withdraw a court from such affairs preserves the court from certain types of criticism and evades the difficulties of reaching a decision, articulating a basis for that decision, crafting a remedy, and enforcing it. Yet, such a withdrawal also risks the surrender of judicial authority to enforce the constitution and to protect individual rights.

Justiciability includes not only justiciability per se but a variety of doctrines that arise, mainly, as a part of the courts' interpretation of their own powers, thus also being described in general as prudential rules. Standing is a matter of both justiciability and, often, of remedy, and it is often considered a doctrine distinct from the prudential rules.

*See also:* standing in court.

**Ashwander rules** Seven rules of the justiciability of claims that a statute violates the U.S. Constitution. The Ashwander rules are seven rules for the justiciability of claims seeking judicial review of federal laws, collected and announced by Justice Brandeis, concurring in Ashwander v. Tennessee Valley Authority, 297 U.S. 288 (1936). These rules require a justiciable constitutional challenge to a statute to: arise in an adversarial proceeding, be timely, be tied to the facts before the court, be inescapably necessary to decide the case, be brought by a plaintiff with an injury to personal or property interests from the operation of the statute, who has not benefited from the statute voluntarily, and there is no constitutional interpretation of the statute available.

**mootness** Being of no practical effect in the world. Mootness is the condition of a dispute or a claim that renders it immune from effect by any order by a court of law. Most commonly, mootness arises because some fact in the world that would once have been affected by a court order has altered, so the order no longer would affect that fact. For instance, if a landowner seeks to protect a landmark from demolition through injunction, but the landmark falls over of its own accord and the demotion order is vacated, an injunction could no longer alter the dispute, and so the dispute over the demolition of the landmark is moot.

Certain disputes arise over facts that are inherently short-lived, altering before a final court order could affect them. A claim arising from such facts may be saved from mootness by an exception to the general rule of mootness, because a claim from such facts is capable of repetition but evading review. This exception allowed the legality of abortions, election procedures, and other time-limited events to be considered, which otherwise would have been routinely mooted and not subject to judicial scrutiny.

**capable of repetition yet evading review** A repeating claim that is routinely mooted despite routine harm. Capable of repetition yet evading review is the formula for an exception to the prudential doctrine of mootness, in which a claim of a constitutional harm is made moot owing to facts that are likely to repeat and bar a similar claim in the future (or that is made moot owing to facts that have made prior claims moot already) may be heard because the recurring cause of mootness may mean that such claims are never heard and relief is never given. The doctrine has at times been limited only to those claims in which the plaintiff before the court can demonstrate that there is a likely repetition of the claim by the same plaintiff, though such a severe restriction leads at times to a controversial closing of the courthouse door.

**public interest exception** A matter otherwise moot may be heard in the public interest. The public interest exception to mootness allows a court to hear an issue that is of great public interest to be heard though it might otherwise be moot. Issues that fall within the exception vary in scope, but they include questions as to the validity of a governmental proceeding or decision. This exception is the larger description of the exception to mootness for cases that are likely to recur and affect other parties in the future yet still evade review.

*See also:* public; justiciability, mootness, capable of repetition yet evading review.

**non-justiciable (nonjusticiable)** A case in which the plaintiff's claims are not justiciable. Non-justiciability is the effect in any claim in which the plaintiff lacks standing, the claim is unripe, the claim is moot, the claim presents a political question, or the claim is otherwise found not to be prudent as a matter of justiciability per se.

**political question** An issue unfit for the courts but committed to another branch of the government. A political question is an issue arising in an action that is not properly a question for courts of law but is a question for the political branches of government. A party who raises a defense to an action that it raises a political question must demonstrate that the issue satisfies three elements: it raises a constitutional question that is committed in the clear text of the Constitution to either the Congress or the President, that is not susceptible to a clear order by a court that could be thought likely to be enforceable, and that would be likely to lead to a continuing argument in the other branches that is not finally settled by the Court's order. To some degree, however, political question is also a purer form of justiciability, in which the Court may hear, and has heard, cases that meet these criteria if it chooses in its discretion to do so.

**ripeness (unripeness or ripe or unripe claim)** The timeliness of a claim for relief. Ripeness is the aspect of a plaintiff's claim for relief that would make a judgment timely and useful, rather than too early or too late. If the plaintiff has suffered or is in imminent danger of suffering an injury or harm as a result of the conduct of the defendant, then there is a ripe, or live, case or controversy. An unripe claim is a claim that might arise but that is not so certain to arise that injury is imminent. Thus, ripeness is the opposite of mootness, with the distinct sense that a cause is unripe until an injury is imminent or manifest, when it becomes ripe, and it remains ripe until the injury is abated and any damages are resolved, cured, or irrelevant, after which the cause becomes moot. A ripe case may still be unjusticiable if the plaintiff lacks standing or the claim is otherwise of a political question or non-justiciable.

**unripeness (prematurity or unripe of premature)** The untimeliness of a claim for relief that is not yet owed. Unripeness, or prematurity, is a condition of a claim that has not yet matured to a point in which a remedy is available that would cure an injury or prevent an imminent injury. The mere potential that an injury might occur leaves a claim for the possibility of the injury unripe. This is not to say that a person who is about to be harmed has no ripe claim; only that the harm must be imminent and reasonably certain to occur.

**justification (justify or justified or justifiable)** A good legal reason for an exception from a general obligation. A justification is a good and legal reason for a person to do something that, if done in other circumstances, would violate a legal obligation. A justification acts not just to negate the duty or prohibition to the contrary but to supersede such duties or prohibitions entirely, making right the otherwise wrong conduct. Justifications such as self-defense, rescue (or defense of another), and necessity mean that otherwise prohibited conduct such as assault or trespass are allowed as a matter of law. Of course, justifications are not unlimited, and self-defense against an assailant is only justified to the extent the acts committed are genuinely in self-defense; hitting a gunman or taking the gun would be justified, but taking the gunman's wallet would not be. Justifications are often confused with excuses, which are not general allowances by law for all conduct of a type considered rightful acts to do, but rather specific alleviations from punishment or liability for a wrongful act committed in a limited circumstance when criminal or civil liability would not accomplish its ordinary goals. Thus, self-defense is a justification; mistake is an excuse. This distinction is not perfect, and there is a continuing argument over whether an act from duress or from reasonable mistake should be thought justified or excused.

Justifications are both private and public. Conduct such as arrest or trespass that is ordinarily the basis for liability is justified if carried out under a valid warrant of arrest or search and seizure.

**justifiable homicide** *See:* homicide, justifiable homicide (justified homicide or lawful homicide).

**justifiable reliance or reasonable reliance or rely** *See:* reliance (justifiable reliance or reasonable reliance or rely).

**overlapping consensus** A single idea accepted from many philosophical perspectives. As described by the philosopher John Rawls, an overlapping consensus arises when citizens, who otherwise differ in their moral, philosophical and religious beliefs, are able to endorse the basic political structure of society for various reasons, which each finds morally persuasive but none of which are derived from wholly religious or non-rational grounds.

**Justinian's institutes** *See:* Roman law, corpus juris civilis, institutes of Justinian (Justinian's institutes).

**juvenile** An older child or adolescent. A juvenile is a person who is younger than an adult but older than an infant requiring constant supervision, which is to say usually a person between six and eighteen years of age. Different jurisdictions have slightly varying standards for the presumption of responsibility at specific ages, but a determination that a person is a juvenile will ordinarily limit the degree of criminal responsibility and the power to enter into legal obligations. For example, the Supreme Court has held that the imposition of the death sentence on juveniles violates the Eighth Amendment's prohibition on cruel and unusual punishment.

*See also:* major; adult, age of majority (legal age).

**juvenile court** *See:* court, court of limited jurisdiction, juvenile court (juvenile proceeding).

**juvenile delinquent** *See:* delinquent, juvenile delinquent, person in need of supervision (PINS or CHINS or JINS); delinquent, juvenile delinquent (delinquent child or juvenile delinquency).

**juvenile offender or juvy** *See:* offender, youthful offender (juvenile offender or juvy).

**juvenile proceeding** *See:* court, court of limited jurisdiction, juvenile court (juvenile proceeding).

> The usage of writers and speakers in particular departments
> of learning or branches of business undoubtedly often diverts
> the meaning of words and phrases from that which they
> import in their common and ordinary use; and the law
> not unfrequently thus assigns a peculiar signification to
> words, when they are found in legal treatises, or
> availed of for legal purposes.
>
> Jones v. Robbins, 8 Gray 329 (Mass. 1857) (Shaw, J.).

# K

**k**   The eleventh letter of the modern English alphabet. "K" signifies a variety of functions as a symbol. It is translated into Kilo for radio signals and NATO military transmissions, into King for some police radio traffic, and into dash, dot, dash in Morse Code.
*See also:* contract (k).

**k as an abbreviation**   A word commencing with k. When used as the sole letter of an abbreviation, K often stands for Kansas, Kentucky, Kenya, Kilom King, King's, and Korean. As an abbreviation of a title, it may stand for Knight. As a numeric abbreviation, K is used to represent a thousand, as in 10K for 10,000. It may also stand for the initial of the name of an author or case reporter, such as Kames, Kay, Keane, Kerford, Key, Keyes, Knapp, Knox, and Kotze.

**k as in hypotheticals**   Contract. K often stands for a contract, especially a written contract, in law school hypothetical stories. (It may also stand for the doctrine of contract as a whole.) K in this case is probably a Greek kappa, rather than the English letter k, but its use distinguishes the symbol for the contract from C if C represents the third character in the hypo.

**kal va-homer (din)**   A Jewish legal ruling based on an inference a fortiori. Kal va-homer is a form of interpretation in which a principle may be derived from a case and a case derived from a principle, in a manner not unlike casuistry.

**Kaldor-Hicks efficiency**   *See:* efficiency, Kaldor-Hicks efficiency (Kaldor–Hicks criterion or Kaldor–Hicks test).

**kangaroo court**   *See:* court, kangaroo court.

**kashrut**   The kosher dietary laws of Judaism. Kashrut are the kosher dietary laws, as defined in the Torah and elaborated in the Talmud. The kashrut symbol on a packaged food indicates that the food has been approved by a rabbi or kashrut board to be suitable to eat in a kosher kitchen after its wrapping or packaging is removed there. Food that is not kashrut is treif.
*See also:* kosher.

**keel-haul (keelhaul or keelhauling)**   To drag a sailor bodily under the ship as a punishment. Keelhauling was the practice of corporal punishment for severe infractions of naval discipline, inflicted by passing the sailor's body under the keel of the ship. The sentence is popularly described in literature but was never apparently used in the U.S. Navy, and it was rarely used in the Royal Navy after the seventeenth century.

**keelhaul or keelhauling**   *See:* keel-haul (keelhaul or keelhauling).

**Ker-Frisbie Doctrine**   *See:* jurisdiction, criminal jurisdiction, Ker-Frisbie doctrine.

**key**   Instrument or code for opening or shutting a lock. A key is the device that opens or shuts a lock. The delivery of a key is symbolic of the delivery of the property it unlocks, as long as the delivery is made in a context in which it is intended as delivery of the property it unlocks, and physical delivery of that property would be impracticable. The conversion of a key amounts to a conversion of the thing unlocked.
*See also:* quay (key); delivery, delivery of possession, symbolic delivery; conversion.

**keystone species**   *See:* species, keystone species.

**khalif or caliphate or khilafa**   *See:* caliph (khalif or caliphate or khilafa).

**khulu'a**   *See:* talaq (khulu'a).

**kickback**   A bribe to induce an agent to enter a contract for another. A kickback is the payment money or something of value returned to the agent of a principal, corporation, or government, in return for a contract with the principal, corporation or government. A kickback is sometimes described as a finder's fee, placement fee, gift, or commission, but unlike such legitimate payments paid by the agent's employer or principal, these are paid to the agent by the contracting outside party.
*See also:* corruption, Foreign Corrupt Practices Act (FCPA).

**kiddie tax**   *See:* tax, income tax, unearned income of minor children (kiddie tax).

**kidnapping (kidnapper or kidnap)**   The abduction or restraint of a person without consent or lawful authority. Kidnapping is the crime of taking or holding any person without that person's consent or a lawful power to do so. An abduction for the purpose of fraud or ransom is a serious felony. Abduction alone, however, is usually a felony or serious misdemeanor. Restraint alone that is not coupled with abduction or transport of the victim is kidnapping in some jurisdiction and the crime of false imprisonment in others. The civil tort of wrongful imprisonment is committed under circumstances that amount to the crime of kidnapping.

Not all takings of a person are kidnapping or abduction. A parent may take control of a child, a person may take custody of a relative who requires restraint, or a police officer make a lawful arrest, because these are bases of lawful authority for each of these acts.

*See also:* ransom; abduction.

**federal kidnapping (federal kidnapping charge)** Transporting a kidnap victim over state lines or federal territory. A federal kidnapping is a kidnapping that is within federal jurisdiction under the Federal Kidnapping Act. An abduction affects federal jurisdiction if the victim is transported across state lines, or if the kidnapper travels in instate or foreign commerce or uses an instrumentality of interstate commerce in committing the offense. Further, the act applies to abduction subject to federal jurisdiction over maritime, admiralty, or aircraft, or because the victim is a foreign official, protected person or guest, or a public officer. If the kidnapping results in the death of the victim, the offender may be sentenced to death or to life in prison; otherwise the offender may be sentenced to prison for a term of years or for life.

**parental kidnapping (international parental kidnapping)** Interference with a parent's visitation or custody by another parent or guardian. Parental kidnapping is the concealment, abduction, or transportation of a child by a parent or guardian of that child, in order to prevent another parent or guardian from visitation, custody, or any other exercise of parental rights. Parental kidnapping is a crime in most jurisdictions, and it is also a contempt of court in the court in which a custody order was issued. Parental kidnapping in which a child is transported from the United States or detained in another country is international kidnapping, which is a federal offense.

*See also:* child, child custody.

**kin (kindred)** One's family. The kindred of any person include ancestors, or ascendents; children and grandchildren and so on, or descendents; siblings, cousins, aunts, uncles, nieces, and nephews, or collaterals. The term is sometimes used to describe a clan, which is a group of related families.

At common law, kindred were related by blood, and so family members by marriage or adoption were not included in the term. Contemporary usage of kin parallels the sense of family, so that kin includes all persons related as a matter of law. Indeed, the poetic term "kindred spirit" has allowed the original metaphorical sense of being like one's family to supplant the familial limit, so that for many speakers, kindred means merely a companionable sensibility and outlook on life. "Kith and kin" is an antiquated phrase meaning friends and family.

*See also:* family (household).

**next of kin** The closest members of one's family. The next of kin are the members of one's immediate family. As a matter of law, the term is limited to those people living who are the closest blood relatives to the person in question. Closeness is determined by the appropriate table of consanguinity as reflected in the intestacy laws of the jurisdiction.

As a matter of custom the term is employed in a context to include a spouse and not only relatives by blood. Most forms or requirements that specify a designation of next of kin include a spouse within the group, either by including the spouse as kin or listing the spouse with the kin.

**kind**

**in kind** Property in its physical form, or property similar to property in issue. In kind refers to specific property, either the property itself in issue or similar property of the same form, quality, and value as the property in issue. Thus, a distribution in kind is a distribution of the property itself, and not a liquidation and distribution of proceeds. A partition in kind is a division of property into lots, rather than its liquidation and the allocation of its proceeds to its common owners. Yet payment in kind implies payment in property or assets, particularly in the commodity transferred under a contract, and such property need not be the exact property otherwise contemplated, but it may be similar property of an equal quality and value per unit.

**king** *See:* government, forms of government, monarchy, king.

**kingdom or monarch** *See:* government, forms of government, monarchy (kingdom or monarch).

**king's counsel or Q.C. or K.C.** *See:* counsel, queen's counsel (king's counsel or Q.C. or K.C.).

**kiting**

**check kiting (kiting checks or check fraud or paper hanging)** Uttering a bad check from one account to cover a bad check from another. Kiting checks occurs when one person with access to multiple accounts takes advantage of the delay in processing checks by depositing bad checks from one account into the other accounts. The check which has been deposited increases the funds which appear to be available in the account until it is discovered that the check never cleared. Many financial institutions now institute a waiting period before checks deposited into an account can be withdrawn.

**Klaxon doctrine** *See:* choice, choice of law, Klaxon doctrine (Erie-Klaxon doctrine or Erie-and-Klaxon doctrine).

**kleptocracy**   *See:* government, forms of government, kleptocracy.

**kleptomaniac (kleptomania)**   A person with a pathological compulsion to steal. Kleptomania is a psychological disorder in which a person has a compulsion to steal that is beyond the person's will to resist. Although there are few cases in which the defense has been successful, it is possible that kleptomania may be a defense to a criminal charge for theft or larceny because the taking of the property would not have been willful or deliberate. Regardless, evidence of kleptomania may require counseling or observation as a condition of release. Kleptomania is not a disability in disability law.
    *See also:* larceny (larcenous); robbery (rob); stealing (steal or stolen).

**knight's service**   *See:* tenure, feudal tenure, military tenure, knight's service (escuage).

**knight's tenure**   *See:* tenure, feudal tenure, military tenure, knight's tenure, shield money (scutage).

**knock-and-announce rule**   *See:* search, knock-and-announce rule, useless-gesture exception; search, knock-and-announce rule.

**knockout rule (knock-out rule)**   *See:* acceptance, acceptance as acceptance of an offer, knockout rule (knock-out rule).

**knowledge (know or knowing or knowingly)**   An awareness of anything. In general, knowledge is the conscious possession of information or understanding, usually acquired by observation, experience, study, invention, or description by others. In legal contexts, knowledge usually amounts to a person's exposure to some item of information that is specific to an action or enterprise and which alters one's duties. Knowledge may alter one's duty of care toward others, as in the knowledge of a defective good or defect in property, which might give rise to a duty of disclosure or warning, or one's knowledge of another's intentions or actions, which might give rise to promissory estoppel. In this sense, to act knowingly is an element of the mens reas required for the commission of certain crimes; one cannot be punished for certain offenses unless one had information essential to the crime.
    The law will often imply a duty to acquire knowledge, such as a duty to investigate or the duty to be informed required of a police officer or a private fiduciary, or a liability that attaches to some conduct whether one acquires it knowingly or otherwise, such as the liability of a property owner who acquires property with hazardous chemical wastes.
    Knowledge in the law usually increases one's duties, creating an incentive for a person to evade knowledge, or to allege ignorance, despite having actual knowledge or having a duty to acquire knowledge that was avoided. Thus knowledge as a matter of law has an objective quality, in that a person will be considered by law to have knowledge in circumstances that give rise to a reasonable expectation that a person in those circumstances would have acquired such knowledge. This consideration occurs usually through constructive knowledge or presumed knowledge. Thus, knowledge by a corporation includes knowledge held by all of the members and employees of the corporation, as well as knowledge in its records.
    Knowledge might but need not be a matter of perfect awareness by an individual, and knowledge may amount to inferences from something of which a person is aware. Perhaps most essentially in law, knowledge does not require a perfect expression, either of the sources or reasons of the knowledge or a description of what is known. Many conclusions are required in the law, such as a knowledge or belief in a person's trustworthiness or guilt, that cannot be reduced further than a conclusion but are considered knowledge nonetheless.

**know by these presents**   *See:* presents (know by these presents).

**know or knowing or knowingly**   *See:* knowledge (know or knowing or knowingly).

**knowing assumption**   *See:* risk, assumption of risk, knowledge of risk (knowing assumption).

**knowing disregard for the truth**   *See:* recklessness, reckless disregard for the truth (knowing disregard for the truth).

**knowledge of risk**   *See:* risk, assumption of risk, knowledge of risk (knowing assumption).

**actual knowledge**   Conscious awareness of specific information. Actual knowledge is personal, conscious awareness of something, rather than awareness that may only become conscious through further inference, analysis, or observation. Actual knowledge is "real knowledge" information that the person knowing understands that the person knows it.

**carnal knowledge (carnally knew)**   An act of sexual intercourse. Carnal knowledge is a euphemistic term in criminal law and military law for any act of sexual congress, although it is most often used to refer to intercourse with a victim of rape or with someone under the age of consent. Carnal knowledge literally means knowledge of the body, yet the term implies in law knowledge in the sense of sexual relations with the body of another person. Unless specified otherwise in a given statute, carnal knowledge does not require completed intercourse, referring to any contacts between various parts of the bodies of the participants when the contacts are for the purposes of sexual gratification or interest.

**common knowledge (public knowledge)**   Information known and undisputed among members of a community. Common knowledge is a measure of the dispersion of information among members of a community or society. If information is widely known among people strangers to the person or event to which the information pertains, and if it is generally accepted as true without dispute, it is common knowledge or public knowledge. A court may accept an idea as proven on the basis of common knowledge as a matter of judicial notice. Still, that some idea is understood as a matter of common knowledge or public knowledge does not ensure or prove the truth of the idea, although it may demonstrate a condition required for an act or condition in law, such as notoriety of possession or a couple holding themselves out as married.

*See also:* notice, judicial notice (judicially noticed fact).

**constructive knowledge (presumed knowledge, presumptive knowledge)** Information a person is presumed to have acquired from circumstance. Constructive knowledge is information that a person is presumed to have acquired from some other information. This may happen because the person has a duty to make certain inquiries or investigations about some information in general. It may also arise because the person learns of some other information and has a duty to investigate the significance of the other information, and if the person had made a reasonable investigation would have actually gained the knowledge the law will construe the person to have. For example, a person must investigate the title recorded to land in order to know the valid title holder of the property, and so the law construes that person's knowledge of a properly recorded deed whether the person investigated the records or not. Or, if a person is buying a property and discovers an old pile of rusted chemical buckets, the law would presume the person would engage in a reasonable investigation to determine whether the property was contaminated with the chemicals, and the person will be construed to know there may have been chemicals dumped there. Thus a person may not employ willful ignorance to find refuge in the law from a responsibility or duty that would arise from information deliberately or negligently avoided. The law treats the person as having the knowledge a reasonable person would have had, even if the person in question lacks the information as actual knowledge.

*See also:* knowledge (know or knowing or knowingly).

**imputed knowledge** A principal's knowledge construed from an agent's knowledge. Imputed knowledge is a form of constructive knowledge, in which the knowledge of an agent is considered to be the knowledge of the principal, either as a matter of the duties of the special agent and principal or as a matter of public policy or of general liability for a supervisory agent. Imputed knowledge arises in either of two circumstances. First, information regarding a fact is imputed to the entity employing the agent if the scope of the agency of the agent includes responsibility for either the acquisition or transmission to others of information related to this fact. Second, if the agent is a person tasked with general responsibility of any form for the management or policy-making or supervision of the department or component of the entity in which the fact arises or has significance, the knowledge of the agent is imputed to the whole entity.

**reason to know** A basis for reasonable inquiry, inference, or knowledge. A reason to know some information is any basis for constructive knowledge of that information. A reason to know a particular fact arises from one of two situations. In the first, one fact is known to the person in question, from which a reasonable inference of a second fact would have been drawn by a reasonable person. In the second, the known fact would have provoked a reasonable person to investigate further, or it would have provoked a reasonable person with the duty of the person in question to investigate further.

**willful blindness (conscious avoidance or willful ignorance or deliberate ignorance)** Knowledge construed from voluntary ignorance or a failure of duty. Willful blindness is a basis for constructive knowledge arising from a person's failure to learn what would otherwise be known in a circumstance when there was a duty to learn such knowledge or when the circumstances were such that only a person who sought ignorance would remain unaware of the knowledge. Blindness in this sense is a metaphor, unrelated to the physical loss of sight. Willful blindness arises usually when a person claims to be unaware of an illegal characteristic of something in the person's possession or in membership of an entity, such as a government or a corporation or partnership.

In the case of possession, the standard of willful blindness is fact–intensive and amounts to something near negligence: would a reasonable person suspect there is contraband in the thing a person comes to possess? If so, a person in possession of a thing may be construed to know its criminal aspects.

In the case of membership in an entity, the standard depends on a reasonable understanding of one's duties or responsibilities in the entity, the standard of constructive knowledge arising in a manner either like simple negligence or from an affirmative duty of care. The duty is most extensive for a supervisor, arising from a position of responsibility: would a reasonable supervisor exercising reasonable diligence and oversight through reasonable, diligent, and properly instructed subordinates have failed to learn of the improper activity? Yet an employee or subordinate is also liable to be held to a constructive knowledge of information of which the person is willfully blind, particularly if the information arises from the scope of the individual's duties or if the person has actual knowledge of conditions that would cause an ordinarily reasonable person to believe in a likelihood of wrongdoing but the person ignores such conditions. Note: there is no real difference among willful ignorance, deliberate blindness, or any other combinations of these terms.

In securities law, the standard for willful blindness is that of conscious avoidance. A corporate officer is liable for knowledge of wrongdoing that was consciously avoided. A jury may infer a defendant knew of a particular fact if the defendant is aware of other circumstances that gave a high probability of the existence of the particular fact, unless the defendant actually held a belief that the fact did not then exist or could not be true.

*See also:* instruction, jury instruction, ostrich instruction (conscious avoidance); blindness (blind).

**known-loss rule**   *See:* loss, insurance loss, known loss (known-loss rule).

**Kolstad defense**   *See:* discrimination, employment discrimination, Kolstad defense.

**kosher**   Sanctioned for use according to Orthodox Judaism. Kosher generally refers to all that is done in a rightful manner, anything done in a manner sanctioned by law and custom. Kosher in Jewish law is most often used to describe the foods, technique, and implements to be used in preparing a meal according to the dietary laws of kashrut. Foods that are advertised as being kosher but that are not are deceptively advertised, and their sale may be a criminal offense, as well as a private tort of fraud.

*See also:* kashrut.

**kris (Kris-Romani)**   Romani tribunal. A kris is a hearing to resolve a dispute or complaint among Romani, at which at least one member of the Gypsy's society presides and elicits the stories of several witnesses. The witnesses must speak in Romani about the events which led to the kris, which may lead to the resolution of a dispute that arose from them.

**krisnitorya (krisnitori)**   Romani elders who function as a judiciary. The krisnitorya are selected from among the respected men of Romani to live with the accused in a hearing and to listen to the entire hearing in order to make a decision at the close of the case. When they render a decision, it is immediately effective. The krisnitorya are empowered to require a fine, a corporal punishment, or a designation of the defendant as marime, or the banishment of someone found unclean.

*See also:* marime.

**Ku Klux Klan**   A white supremacist organization. The Ku Klux Klan is a criminal organization that advocates racial separation and the supremacy of white Christian people over everyone else. Founded in 1866 by former Confederate soldiers, the Klan is a semi-secret society, which uses robes and hoods to hide the identity of its members. Members of the Klan have committed lyching, and other acts of domestic terrorism, including arson, bombings, murder, and extortion to deny African Americans and others of their civil rights. Although the Klan remains active in the United States, successor groups have grown larger, such as the militia movement, the Aryan Nation, and other sponsors of racial and religious hatred, many encouraged by conservative media and politicians.

Specifically to combat the Klan, Congress enacted the Civil Rights Act of 1871, also known as the Ku Klux Klan Act, 42 U.S.C § 1985, designates a conspiracy to deprive a person of a federal right as both a federal crime and the basis for civil suit.

*See also:* civil rights, civil rights enforcement action, 1983 Action; civil rights, Civil Rights Act, Civil Rights Act of 1871 (Ku Klux Klan Act).

**Ku Klux Klan Act**   *See:* civil rights, Civil Rights Act, Civil Rights Act of 1871 (Ku Klux Klan Act).

> Deduction without definition of terms is a game of
> cop and robber: you can have anything you catch.
>
> Karl Llewellyn, *The Bramble Bush* 79 (4th ed.) (Oxford University Press, 2009).

# L

**l**   The twelfth letter of the modern English alphabet. "L" signifies a variety of functions as a symbol. It is translated into Lima for radio signals and NATO military transmissions, into Lincoln for some police radio traffic, and into dot, dash, dot, dot in Morse Code.

**l as a Latin abbreviation**   Acquit. L was an an abbreviation in Roman law, the sign for libero, a vote to free the accused, cast in the comitia, or courts of popular assembly, as opposed to D for damno, freedom, and NL for non liquet, for a case that is unclear to the voter. *See also:* non, non liquet (NL).

**l as a roman numeral**   Latin symbol for fifty (50). L is fifty when used as a numeral. In the Roman system of numeralization, the addition of an L to the right of another Roman numeral adds 50 to the numerical value. The addition of an L to the left of another Roman numeral subtracts 50 from the numerical value.

**l as an abbreviation**   A word commencing in l. As used in Shepard's citation system, l stands for a court's refusal to extend a prior judicial decision beyond the precise factual issue involved in that prior case. When preceding a name, L often stands for Lord, as in the English title for members of its bench. When used as the sole letter of an abbreviation, l often stands for law. It may also stand for labor, landlord, Laotion, lawyer, legal, leges (latin for law), legislative, letter, liber (latin for free, not slave), library, licensing, limited, local, locus, Louisiana, and lower. It may also stand for the initial of an author or case reporter, such as Lalor, Lambard, Lane, Langdell, Lansing, Lawson, Leake, Leigh, Leigh, Lely, Lewin, Lewis, Lloyd, and Ludlow.

**l as in hypotheticals**   The Landlord. L often stands for the landlord in the story of a law school hypothetical. Traditionally, when l is used for the landlord, it is invoked with a Greek lambda.

**L.J. or LJ or law journal or review or l. rev. or LR**
*See:* review, law review (L.J. or LJ or law journal or review or l. rev. or LR).

**L.L.C. or LLC**   *See:* company, limited–liability company (L.L.C. or LLC).

**L.S.**   *See:* locus, locus sigilli (L.S.).

**lab**   *See:* laboratory (lab).

**label**   The text or symbol printed on an object or package. A label is any text, symbols, or identifying marks placed on a package or a product, whether by direct inscription or by writing the information on a paper or card that is affixed to it. A label may perform a variety of functions, including (at least) identifying a shipper and a recipient; identifying contents; identifying a country of fabrication or origination; listing component contents, including the nutritional value of a food; listing chemical, biolological, or radiological hazards; providing warnings of hazards from use or misuse; or marketing and advertising. A number of labels are required on containers in shipment, particularly those in international transit to allow for speedy inventory and clearance through customs. The trade in counterfeit labels affecting assets of intellectual property is a distinct crime. The placement of false labels for trade or consumer goods, or the failure to place required labels for hazardous goods when stored or in transit may amount to the violations of a variety of regulations of such goods, such the offense of misbranding, as well as amounting to fraud if others rely on the incorrect labeling of the goods.

The very idea of the label is somewhat evoked by its origin as the cloth, parchment, leather, or paper strip that was threaded through slots in a charter or instrument, to hang away from it and allow the seal of the maker or signator to be affixed. The label was the connection between the instrument and the sign of the maker who gave the instrument significance.

Label may, of course, be used in other, rhetorical senses, both as a metaphor for metaphor and as an form of stereotype or designation of a person, place, activity, or thing.
*See also:* trademark, trade dress.

**warning label**   A label warning of a hazard inherent in a thing or contingent on its use. A warning label is a label affixed, displayed, or packaged with a substance or device that is intended to provide to a person near the substance or device, or consuming the substance, or using the device with notice of dangers inherent in the thing or that might occur according to the manner in which the thing is used, consumed, stored, transported, or proximate with various substances. A warning label must be both sufficient to express the warning adequately and compelling in appearance to attract reasonable notice from the likely user or other person to be warned.

**heeding presumption**   Presumption that a person would have heeded a warning on a dangerous product. The heeding presumption is applied in product liability cases when a product is claimed to be defective or dangerous owing to a failure to warn the consumer or properly label the product. The presumption is allowed that the consumer would have followed an adequate warning had one been provided. The manufacturer or other defendant may rebut the presumption only through evidence that such a warning would not have been heeded by the plaintiff, or by the average consumer.

See also: label; liability, product liability (products liability).

**labor**   The work a person does, or the whole of the workers and their work. Labor has several distinct senses in the law. In the oldest sense, labor is the work or effort that a person exerted in order to accomplish any task, especially for an employer. In the eighteenth century, the term came also to describe the aggregate of such work performed by the workers as a collective, and in the nineteenth century, the term came to refer to the collective of workers themselves. When labor organizations and unions became common, labor became, and remains, a colloquial phrase for the members of unions and similarly placed workers, the antonym being management.

**labor boycott**   See: boycott, labor boycott.

**labor dispute**   See: union, labor union, labor dispute.

**labor law**   See: union, labor union, labor law.

**Labor-Management Relations Act**   See: union, labor union, labor law, Labor-Management Relations Act (Taft–Hartley Act).

**labor mediation**   See: mediation, labor mediation.

**labor organization**   See: union, labor union (labor organization).

**labor picket**   See: union, labor union, labor dispute, labor picket (stranger picketing).

**labor strike**   See: union, labor union, labor dispute, labor strike (walkout).

**labor union**   See: union, labor union (labor organization).

**child labor**   Unrelated employees under age 16, or 18 in a hazardous environment. Child labor is the employment of children other than the employer's own children or wards, in any employment under the age of 16, or in manufacture, mining, or a hazardous environment under the age of 18. No employer engaged in interstate commerce may employ child labor, and the shipment of goods made by child labor is a crime.

**Fair Labor Standards Act (F.L.S.A. or FLSA or minimum wage or wage and hours law)**   The source of federal wage and hour laws. The Fair Labor Standards Act of 1938, 52 Stat. 1060, ch. 676 (June 25, 1938), established a national minimum wage and hour law, outlawed oppressive child labor, and established a work week by hours, after which employees are entitled to

overtime, paid at "time and a half," or 150 percent of their usual pay. In 1938, the national minimum wage was 25 cents per hour, rising over seven years to 40 cents. As of 2011, the wage is $7.25. States are allowed to set a higher minimum wage without conflict with the FLSA wage.

**labor market (labor pool)**   The pool of available workers qualified for a job, in a locale or nationwide. A labor market is both the whole population of the workers who are available and capable of performing a specific type of work in a given area and the spectrum of work available for a workers in that area. In general, a labor market is a local affair, the area involved being the geography that may be covered daily by a worker travelling by reasonable means from home to work, although in context the labor market may represent regional or national markets.

Representations regarding the existence of a labor market of a particular size of a particular skill level in a given area may be a material element of a contract. Further, comparisons to the demographics of a labor market are routinely used for comparisons of hiring practices to determine the disparate impact of recruitment and hiring practices. The availability of a particular form of employment that may be accessible to an injured worker within the labor market in which the person lives or formerly worked is essential to determine disability, and it is often relevant to separation benefits and unemployment insurance payments.

**Occupational Safety and Health Act (OSHA)**   The national workplace safety and health standards. The Occupational Safety and Health Act of 1970, 84 Stat. 1590 (Dec. 29, 1970), created federal standards for workplace safety and worker health, and created the Occupational Safety and Health Administration in the Department of Labor to create national regulations, require employer records of safety compliance and violations, and perform inspections of workplaces to ensure compliance.

**laboratory (lab)**   A professional facility for the creation or evaluation of data. A laboratory is a facility for the creation of information of scientific or engineering interest, including the evaluation of such data using protocols developed using professional means from scientific or engineering foundations. The name of a laboratory is not controlling, but it is a result of its function.

**crime laboratory (forensics lab or crime lab or police lab or police crime lab)**   A laboratory specializing in forensic science to evaluate potential evidence. A crime laboratory is a laboratory that specializes in the analysis of evidence and potential evidence using the tools of the forensic sciences. Crime labs often perform examinations of materials to determine the identification of individuals through biological remains and physical evidence, to determine the content or composition or age of materials, and to manage data accumulated from such examinations, such as fingerprint libraries, bullet libraries, DNA libraries, etc. Most states operate a crime laboratory, as do the Federal Bureau of Investigation and other law enforcement agencies. Private corporations and universities also operate crime laboratories. Crime labs are accredited by The American Society of Crime Laboratory Directors/Laboratory Accreditation Board, or ASCLD/LAB.

*See also:* coroner (medical examiner or pathologist or forensic pathologist or medical legal investigator or mli); forensics (forensic science).

**Underwriters Laboratories (UL)**  A private entity that sets product standards for safety and use. Underwriters Laboratories, or UL, is a private, nonprofit corporation with a global network of laboratories and facilities that evaluate, test, and write standards and specifications for safe products to meet specific consumer and industrial uses. UL tests products to determine whether the product meets its standards, in which case the manufacturer may mark the product with a "UL". Many building, manufacture, and inspection codes require the use of UL-designated components.

**laborer**  A worker whose tasks are primarily physical in their performance. A laborer has several senses that must be disinguished by context. In its most traditional sense a laborer is a manual worker, performing mainly muscular or manual efforts, rather than mainly intellectual, commercial, artisan, or managerial efforts. In a more specific sense in the construction trades, a laborer is a particular rank worker who performs unskilled or semi-skilled work, assisting various skilled workers. In a broader sense, a laborer is synonymous with any worker or employee, although this sense is rare in legal writing.

**laches**  *See:* limitation, limitation of actions, laches; equity, equitable defense, laches.

**lack of contractual capacity or lack of capacity**  *See:* capacity, legal capacity, incapacity (lack of contractual capacity or lack of capacity).

**lack of criminal capacity or M'Naghten rule**  *See:* capacity, criminal capacity, incapacity to commit a crime (lack of criminal capacity or M'Naghten rule).

**lack of jurisdiction**  *See:* dismissal, grounds for dismissal, lack of jurisdiction.

**lack of jurisdiction or beyond the jurisdiction**  *See:* jurisdiction, want of jurisdiction (lack of jurisdiction or beyond the jurisdiction).

**lacuna**  *See:* gap, lacuna (lacunae).

**laddering or escalator clause**  *See:* price, escalating price (laddering or escalator clause).

**lady or lordship or or ladyship or lordships**  *See:* lord (lady or lordship or or ladyship or lordships).

**lagan**  *See:* salvage, ligan (lagan).

**lage dayum**  *See:* day, law day (lage dayum).

**laissez-faire**  Non-intervention in the affairs of others. Laissez-faire, a French term figuratively meaning "let them alone" (though it more literally translates as "let them do"), is a slogan and maxim for non-intervention in the affairs of others, particularly non-intervention by the state in the affairs of individuals and merchants in the market. There is recurrent controversy over the best balance of regulation and freedom in capitalist democracy, and laissez-faire represents, in most instances, the argument for the least regulation. In broader usage, laissez-faire may represent a live-and-let-live allowance for the conduct of others, regardless of the seeming wisdom of what others do.

**laity**  *See:* lay, laity.

**lame duck**  *See:* office, lame duck (lame-duck term or lame-duck congress).

**land (lands)**  The uppermost surface of the Earth. Land includes ground, soil, earth, wetlands, and smaller bodies of water. Though there are both subterranean lands and undersea lands, the term usually refers to surface lands not fully submerged by the sea or other bodies of water. Lands include the structures on or in them, as long as the structure has a reasonable degree of permanence, and so to transfer lands includes the transfer of a a shed, a cottage, a factory, or a castle built on them.

At common law, lands were said to extend from the center of the Earth to the roof of the sky. Contemporary law includes in land control over the air above and sub-soils below, including the mineral interests under the land, yet this control is now circumscribed by modern doctrines allowing the transit of airplanes at high altitude and the loss of minerals in a common pool to the rule of capture.

The ownership of lands includes the ownership of the produce of the land, including the crops grown and harvested, wildlife, woods, and minerals taken or not, as well as riparian interests in streams that cross or border the land. Most of these elements of the land can be severed from the whole and transferred to a person other than the owner of the lands. Once that severance has happened, ownership of the land no longer includes ownership of whatever interest or estate has been severed.

Lands are owned according to their estate, and lands may be divided into ownership of present and future estates (as with a life estate and remainder), as well as between the right of possession and the right of ownership (as with a lease), and among several owners at once (as with a tenancy in common).

*See also:* ratione, ratione soli; ownership, landowner.

**land contract**  *See:* mortgage, land contract (contract for deed); contracts, specific contracts, land contract.

**land mark**  *See:* landmark (land mark).

**land patent**   *See:* patent, land patent, fee patent; patent, land patent.

**land sale**   *See:* sale, land sale (sale of land or sale of lands or sale of property or real estate transaction).

**land trust**   *See:* trust, land trust.

**land use**   *See:* zoning, land use.

**allocation of land**   Determination of the use of each portion of public lands. Allocation of land is a land management decision in which the manager must determine how to use land to satisfy a prioritized list of uses. This decision is made by balancing long and short term production and harvesting goals with current environmental pressures. Allocation of land decisions are synonymous with historical crop rotation determinations.

**arable land (erable land or errable land)**   Land suitable for farming crops. Arable land is capable of agriculture, particularly for the use of row crops. It is land that is cleared of trees and debris, and is capable of being plowed.

**charge on the land (charge upon the land)**   An obligation amounting to a lien on a parcel of land. A charge on the land is an obligation by the landowner that effectively creates a lien on a designated parcel as security for the obligation. Charges on the land were traditionally contingent grants by a prior holder, such as "O to A provided he support B," but a charge is now any claim for payment made upon the holder of lands that would require proof to refute the claim. Charges on the land are a cloud on title.

**entry onto the land**   The taking possession of lands by the legal owner, or a temporary presence. Entry onto land has two distinct senses. In its contemporary form, it is merely a temporary presence on land, which may be committed by an owner, a licensee, invitee, or trespasser.

In its more formal sense, entry onto the land is lawful claim of a landowner to possession of the property. It was once a prerequisite to certain actions to establish title, but it is not used merely to describe an owner's taking possession of lands. It is distinct from the more general form of entry, which may be by a guest, invitee, or trespasser, and which usually implies an entry to a structure than to the land itself.

**federal land (federal lands or U.S. government property)**   Land owned or controlled by the United States government. Federal lands are lands owned by the United States government or controlled by the United States government or a federal agency under lease or otherwise and managed according to federal law. Military installations, U.S. Post Offices, national forests, national parks, federal highways, U.S. embassies abroad, are all examples of federal lands. Federal lands are subject to federal law under the needful rules clause.

**improved land (unimproved land)**   Lands on which permanent improvements have increased value. Improved land is land on which improvements have been made. The mere act of clearing land is generally not considered improvement, and indeed at the common law was likely to be considered waste. Improved land must have permanent fixtures that enhance value over time, and although these are usually buildings, the construction of sufficient other improvements so that the land has some specific uses other than as unimproved land will do. Improved land is often treated distinctly from unimproved land in the law, such as the Interstate Land Sales Act, 15 U.S.C. §1703, which exempts improved land on which there are buildings from its restrictions.

*See also:* improvement, improvement to land (improvements).

**land use (land use regulation)**   The ways in which land can be used, and its regulation. Land use is the generic term for all uses for which lands may be developed or maintained. It is also a broad arena for the study of property law and regulation. Land use regulation includes not only private means, such as the use of contracts and grants of easement and covenants by which large subdivisions and developments may be regulated, but also public means, such as zoning, urban planning and dedication, public works and parks, building and use codes, utility regulation, environmental design, and road regulation.

**landlocked as inaccessible to water**   The lack of a shore or harbor accessible from specific lands. Landlocked, relative to waters, is the lack of a reasonably accessible facility to use a body of water for navigation and commerce. Context is essential in the use of such a term, and a small frontage, large enough to place a dinghy in the water or to run a water pipe, may be sufficient access for a residential lot to have sufficient water access that it is not landlocked. Yet a nation-state or state of the union would still be considered landlocked unless it has a port, harbor, or river such that it can manage its commercial and military access to the seas.

**landlocked as inaccessible by land (land-locked)**   Property with no way or road connecting it to a public way or road. Landlocked, relative to lands and not waters, is the lack of a reasonably accessible way or road that connects a parcel of land to a public way or road. A parcel completely surrounded by lands owned by others, with no easement or way of the surrounding lands, is landlocked. If a parcel is severed from a common parcel, and by the severance becomes landlocked, an easement by necessity is construed in the law, unless the grant of the landlocked parcel expressly and clearly bars the creation of such an easement. Even so, if a habitation is on a landlocked parcel, an easement may be required as a matter of the jurisdiction's police powers for emergency access by state vehicles.

*See also:* easement, easement by necessity (implied easement of absolute necessity).

**liability to other on the land** The duty of care of a landholder to a person present upon the land. The liability of an owner to another person on the owner's land depends upon how the other person comes to be on the land. The standard of care due to another person on one's lands depends on whether the person is an invitee, a licensee, or a trespasser.

**guest** *See:* guest.

**invitee** *See:* invitee (business guest).

**licensee** *See:* licensee.

**trespasser** *See:* trespasser.

**measures of land**

**acre** A common square measure of lands in the U.S. An acre is 43,560 square feet, 4,047 square meters, or 4,840 square yards of land. It is slightly less than the size of an American football field, an American football field being 1.32 acres (soccer pitches being this size or larger). There are two standards for the acre: the U.S. survey acre and the international acre, which is very slightly less and of no practical difference for most land calculations. An acre is a measure of total land surface area and does not imply any particular shape.

**hectare (are or centiare or deciare)** Ten thousand square meters of land. A hectare is the metric unit for the basic measure of lands, equal to ten thousand square meters of land, also called centiares in some legal systems. The hectare is divided into 10 deciares or into 100 ares. A hectare is roughly equal to four-tenths of an acre.

**public lands (land on public domain or sovereign lands)** Land owned or controlled by a government. Public lands can refer to one of several categories of lands. In its broadest sense, public lands include all lands owned by the United States, individual states of the union, and their agencies and subdivisions. More commonly, however, a designation of public lands includes only such government lands as are subject to general laws and managed for public purposes but may be sold or acquired the better to promote those purposes. In this sense, "public domain lands" are similar. Sovereign lands and federal lands include a variety of more specifically dedicated lands, which are subject to specific laws rather than general laws. Some writers refer to federal lands as public lands without this distinction, however, which is confusing; only careful examination of the context of such writings can distinguish which is meant.

*See also:* land, federal land (federal lands or U.S. government property).

**public domain land** Unimproved land owned by the government. Public domain land is unimproved land owned by the government, practically all of it acquired during cessions of land to the United States from other sovereigns and never granted to corporations, states, or private landholder by patent. Public domain lands include the seabed beyond the territorial sea subject to state control but within U.S. jurisdiction on the continental shelf. Public domain land may be granted, sold, or leased, and interests in it may be leased or used, subject to the regulation of Congress. Proceeds from the management of these public domain lands are paid to the United States Treasury. There are recurrent inquiries into the royalties paid for mining and other uses and extractions on public domain lands.

**Bureau of Land Management** Government agency responsible for public lands. The Bureau of Land Management, a bureau within United States Department of Interior, manages designated federal public lands, which amounted to 258 million acres in 2011. The bureau is a successor to the interior requirements of the Land Ordinance of 1785 and manages federal lands for to encourage their health, diversity, and productivity, for the use and enjoyment of present and future citizens.

**school trust land (sixteenth section land)** Lands in most states held in trust to support public schools. School trust land is real property owned by the state or a local government for the purpose of supporting and benefiting the schools of that state. Most such lands were granted to the state by the federal government, following the pattern started with the Northwest Ordinance, which committed the 16th section of every township for this purpose. Some states succeeded in frittering away these grants by selling them and wasting the money on trivial projects, but many states still maintain a portion of their public education budget from the income generated through leases of this realty.

**landfill**

**municipal solid waste landfill (M.S.W.L.F. or MSWLF)** Landfill operated by or for a municipality for household wastes. A municipal solid waste landfill that is owned by a municipality or operated for one, that receives only household wastes and other nonhazardous wastes. MSWLFs are subject to a specific rate regime in most jurisdictions, which is distinct from privately operated landfills. Landfills are permitted under a regime that seeks source reduction first, recycling, second, and disposal, whether in landfill or furnaces, last. The landfill is, to an extent, the analog for solid waste of the publicly-owned water treatment facility.

*See also:* waste, waste material, solid waste.

**landholder** An owner of the land. A landholder is usually an owner but in some limited contexts may also be a tenant or other party with a right to hold the land. A landholder is free to alienate the land, to sell or grant the interest the landholder holds to another person. At common law, a landholder was a tenant-in-chief, though the term was and still is rarely used in law, a more precise term being preferred, such as owner or landowner.

**landlord (lessor)** One who rents a property to another, holding the reversion. The landlord is the owner of property rented to a tenant. By definition, all property under lease has a landlord and a tenant, who are also called the lessor and lessee. A landlord has all of the rights of a reversion-holder in the property, as well as all of the lawful rights created by the lease. Thus, the landlord has a common-law right of repossession at the termination of the lease and a right that the property not be subject to waste by the tenant, as well as rights under the contract, which usually include a right to receive rents and such other provisions as the two agree. A landlord has a duty to provide premises without a superior claimant to possession, and in most of the United States, to provide them suitable for use in the manner contemplated by parties on entering the lease.

In the event a tenant assigns a lease, the new tenant substitutes for the prior tenant, but in the event the tenant subleases to a sub-tenant, the sub-tenant behaves toward the tenant as if they are tenant and landlord, but the preferred usage is not to alter the titles and retain the identities of landlord, tenant, and sub-tenant. (Or, lessor, lessee, and sub-lessee.)

As to real property, there is no real difference between landlord and tenant and lessor or lessee of the terms, though as a matter of usage, the pairing of landlord and tenant emphasizes somewhat the aspects of the leasehold arising from property law, and the more general pairing of lessor and lessee tends to emphasize the contractual nature of the lease. In all events, it is best not to vary in a single text from the reliance on one pair, to draft a lease with landlord and with tenant throughout rather than to mix and match.

*See also:* lease; rent.

**absentee landlord** An rental property owner who rarely sees the property. An absentee landlord is a a lessor of property who is only rarely, if ever, present on the property itself, managing both tenant relations and maintenance at a distance or through agents. Many absentee landlords hold the property solely as an investment and are considered unlikely to make reasonable and necessary expenditures for maintenance and repairs. In most jurisdictions, an absentee landlord who does not contractually accept a duty to repair premises that are injured after a tenant takes possession and who does not perceive the injury to the premises is not bound to repair them absent a statutory or regulatory duty to do so. Further, a landlord without notice of a nuisance or other danger on the premises is not liable to neighbors or others injured by the action of a tenant. Although not present in the jurisdiction personally, a corporation or individual landlord is constructively present owing both to ownership of the property and the contractual right of occupancy.

*See also:* absentee.

**landlord-tenant relationship** The rights and duties of the tenant and the landlord. The landlord-tenant relationship commences either when a tenant occupies the property of another or when a lease agreement that has been entered comes into force. The landlord-tenant relationship is in privity of estate and, if it is subject to a lease agreement, privity of contract. The whole set of obligations of each to the other depend upon the nature of the tenancy, whether it is by sufferance, at will, for a term of years, or periodic, as well as the terms of any lease agreement between them.

*See also:* tenant, tenant as lessee.

**mesne lord** An intermediate landlord. A mesne lord was an intermediate landlord, who held tenancies below but still owed obligations to another landlord above. Mesne lords were usually, though not always, members of the petty nobility.

*See also:* feud, feudalism, subinfeudation; tenant, tenant of the desmesne (tenant in desmesne).

**landmark (land mark)** Anything of enduring prominence. A landmark was, initially, a pile of stones or a monument erected to denote a boundary between two properties or states, and the term retains a related sense as a reference point in surveying. The term is also a customary description of points on land used in the navigation of vessels near coasts. Its metaphorical sense, however, is to represent prominence that persists over time (or is expected to persist into the future), as in a landmark property, landmark opinion, or other landmark event. As a landmark property, the property is of sufficient historic, cultural, or aesthetic significance that the government may order land use restrictions on the alteration of the property. As a landmark opinion or event, the opinion or event is thought to rise above other opinions or events in history owing to its significance, usually because it is thought to have changed the course of events in some unusually significant way.

**landmark case** *See:* precedent, landmark case (leading case or landmark opinion or landmark decision).

**landmark property** A building or site designated for preservation as a landmark. A landmark as a matter of land use is a building that is designated according to federal, state, or municipal law, usually by local ordinance as a landmark building or structure or property. Buildings or structures designated as landmarks are usually subject to regulation and administrative approval before any substantial change can be made to their function or appearance. Designation criteria vary but usually include a combination of age, historical significance, special character or aesthetic interest or value as part of the development, heritage, or the cultural characteristics of the city, state, or nation.

**landmine** *See:* mine, military mine, landmine.

**landowner** *See:* ownership, landowner.

**laojiao** Re-education through labor. Laojiao is a sentence from petty crimes and political offenses in the law of modern China.

**lapse** The failure of a right, duty, or interest from time or changed circumstance. Lapse is the termination of a right, interest, duty, or obligation as a result of the passage of time, a failure or satisfaction of condition, or a change in circumstance. Many interests lapse if they are not exercised or preserved in time. For example, an offer may lapse if it is not accepted or rejected in a reasonable time or by the time specified in the offer's terms. A cause of action may lapse if it is not brought within the time of limitations, and a claim under a contract for insurance may lapse if no claim is presented to the insurer in the time specified in the contract. Lapse may also occur through a change in circumstance that moots an interest that was created; so a specific devise or legacy written into a will may lapse if the devisee or legatee dies before the testator's death or before a condition would be satisfied necessary to take the gift. Other changes of condition are related to time, as when any contract or obligation requiring periodic payments or performance lapses at some time following a cessation of payments or performance. The effect of a lapse is either to destroy the interest or transfer the interest from a claimant to those against whom a claim would be made, in a process like merger, though in practice there is little difference between the two theories.

**lapsed bequest** *See:* bequest, lapsed bequest (lapsed legacy or lapse of devise or lapse of legacy).

**lapsed legacy or lapse of devise or lapse of legacy** *See:* bequest, lapsed bequest (lapsed legacy or lapse of devise or lapse of legacy).

**larceny (larcenous)** The intentional and unjustified taking of another person's personal property Larceny is the basic crime of stealing. That is, it is the act of taking the goods, car, weapon, animal, negotiable instrument, or other form of personal property from a person, without lawful authority (such as an attachment order), without violence or its threat (which would be robbery or burglary), and without an abuse of trust or permission (which would be embezzlement). A prosecution for larceny requires proof the defendant knowingly removed (or carried away) the personal property of another person from that person's control or property with the intent of depriving the owner of its possession by retaining the goods or transferring them to another. Larceny by trick or false pretenses specifically includes in larceny an owner's being tricked to carry away or give away the property stolen.

Most jurisdictions do not have a crime of larceny per se but the felony of grand larceny and the misdemeanor or petit larceny (sometimes in a variety of degrees), which are distinguished from one another by either the nature of the object taken or by its apparent value. Some jurisdictions have merged larceny into the criminal prohibition of theft, which is the approach of the Model Penal Code.

*See also:* theft; stealing (steal or stolen); kleptomaniac (kleptomania); robbery (rob).

**aggravated larceny** Larceny accompanied by violence or stealth. Aggravated larceny is possible by combining the offense of larceny with the general rules of aggravation of a criminal offense, usually by the commission of the crime with violence, or with a weapon, or with threats of violence to achieve the criminal purpose. In most jurisdictions, aggravated larceny is better understood and more properly charged as either robbery, for violent larceny, or burglary, for larceny of a house at night. Larceny is, therefore, often a lesser included offense for a charge of robbery or burglary.

**constructive larceny** Receiving stolen goods. Constructive larceny is larceny presumed as a matter of law from the voluntary receipt of goods or other property that one knows or should know is the fruit of a larceny, when one has no lawful authority to receive it or intent to return it to its owner or to a lawful recipient.

**continuing trespass doctrine** Larceny persists for so long as the property is in the thief's possession. The continuing trespass doctrine extends the time of a theft or larceny until the thief disposes of the stolen property. This doctrine has the effects both of extending the period of limitations under which an act of larceny may be charged and of including accessories after the fact as principals in the performance of the original crime.

**grand larceny** A serious deprivation of another's property. Grand larceny is the unlawful deprivation of another person of goods of specified kind, of a specified value, or by a specified means that amount to a felony. The statute usually designates goods above a specific value (in 2011 between $100 and $1,000), or goods of a particular kind, including an automobile, a firearm, a farm animal, a dog, a credit card, drug precursor chemicals, or an identification card, among other specified objects of larceny. Larceny by removing property from the owner's person, such as pickpocketing, is grand larceny in most jurisdictions, as well as a distinct offense. Grand larceny is treated as theft in the third degree in Model Penal Code jurisdictions.

**larceny by trick (false pretense or larceny by false pretense or larceny by false promise or larceny by fraud or larceny by fraudulent scheme)** Depriving another of property by deception. Larceny by trick is an act or scheme through which the thief acquires control of the victim's property through some trick or deception. Larceny by trick occurs whether the thief, the victim, or a third party transfers control or possession of the property into the control of the thief. It does not matter whether the deception is by means of a false promise or a fraudulent scheme or some other confidence game or trick, the fundamental question being only that the thief intends to acquire or divert to another person some property (which may be money) of the victim without a lawful basis for doing so, and the thief does so.

**petty larceny (petit larceny or small larceny)** Larceny that is not grand larceny. Petty larceny is the unlawful taking of property that is not defined as the object of grand larceny. petty larceny, or petit larceny, is a misdemeanor. Thus, property of less than an amount assigned in a jurisdiction as the basis for grand larceny, that is not of a form of property that amounts to grand larceny, such as a car or a firearm, is the object of petit larceny. Petit larceny is also known as small larceny.

*See also:* petit.

**simple larceny** Larceny without violence. Simple larceny is larceny without an aggravating factor, which is usually larceny without violence.

**large (at large)** Unrestricted. Large, in the legal sense, represents someone or something unconfined, unrestrained, unsupervised, and generally at liberty. Thus, an animal at large is either not in confinement or not under the supervision of a minder but free to roam (even if it becomes stuck elsewhere than its owner's pen by its own volition). A legislator or other official elected at large is elected from throughout the relevant jurisdiction over which the whole legislature has authority, without limitation to a particular district. A statute at large is not a statute limited in its scope to a particular individual or entity as is a private law. A person at large is free of constraint or supervision and free to travel without permission or condition.

**criminal at large (escapee at large or suspect at large)** A person not in police custody or supervision. To be at large, such as a criminal at large, or any other person at large, is to lack physical restraint or supervision by a police officer, parole officer, prison official, or other police institution or official. That a person is not in custody does not demonstrate the person is at large, as a person subject to supervision through routine checks or to limited movement under judicial order or an order of conditional release is not at large as long as the person complies with the order.

**lasciviousness (lascivious or lasciviously)** Likely to or intended to encourage thoughts related to sexual conduct. Lasciviousness is the quality of speech, images, conduct, music, or any other form of conduct or communication that encourages the recipient of the communication to think of sex. Lasciviousness may be intended or unintended by the person creating the communication, and although it has an undeniably subjective element, the very assertion that some communication or conduct is lascivious is to claim that the communication or conduct objectively would encourage thoughts of sexual behavior by those who are exposed to the communication or conduct. Note: lasciviousness is, usually, more general and abstract than lewdness, and it is more provocative than mere sexiness. Further, there is some confusion of the word lascivious related to the abuse or exploitation of children, in that the creation or distribution of an image of a child that is lascivious or is intended for use in a lascivious manner is a crime. This does not mean that lasciviousness is limited to images or actions involving a child.

*See also:* lewdness (lewd); obscenity (obscene).

**last clear chance** *See:* negligence, last clear chance (last–clear–chance doctrine); defense, specific defense, last clear chance.

**last-clear-chance doctrine** *See:* negligence, last clear chance (last–clear–chance doctrine).

**last-proximate-act test** *See:* attempt, criminal attempt, last-proximate-act test.

**last resort** *See:* resort (last resort).

**last shot doctrine** *See:* acceptance, acceptance as acceptance of an offer, battle of the forms, last shot doctrine.

**last will and testament** *See:* will, last will and testament (testament).

**latency (latent)** A quality or condition that is not reasonably apparent by inspection alone. Latency is a quality of anything that is hidden from reasonable observation or inspection, either known only to someone especially familiar with the thing or known to no one at all. Thus an object with a latent strength or failing would not be perceived by most observers or inspectors accurately. A latent defect of a product is a defect that is not reasonably discoverable by a buyer or consumer. A latent defect in a title or instrument is an ambiguity or irrationality that is not apparent in the text but discoverable only with additional information or context. Latent (the hidden) is often contrasted with patent (the apparent).

*See also:* product, defective product, latent product defect (inherent vice); patency (patent); contract, contract interpretation, contract ambiguity, latent ambiguity; equity, equitable value, latent equity; title, title defect, latent defect of title.

**latent ambiguity** *See:* contract, contract interpretation, contract ambiguity, latent ambiguity.

**latent danger** *See:* danger, latent danger (hidden danger).

**latent defect of title** *See:* title, title defect, latent defect of title.

**latent equity** *See:* equity, equitable value, latent equity.

**latent product defect** *See:* product, defective product, latent product defect (inherent vice).

**lateral support** *See:* support, support of land, lateral support.

## Latin

**law Latin** Latin phrases in contemporary legal usage. Law Latin is an element of legal usage in the United States and throughout the common-law and civilian legal communities. Certain phrases, such as habeas corpus, are part of the custom and lore of the law, and their use provides an efficiency that is an element of a professional language. Even so, the use of some phrases that have become obsolete through disuse or confusing through misuse, should be discouraged and performed only with care, precision, and such clarity of surrounding prose as to make the sense clear to readers of English.

Law Latin is not today a full language, in that there is not a population of competent speakers who would likely choose to converse for long in any meaningful sense using only the tools of law Latin. Nor does law Latin incorporate the complete vocabulary, syntax, and context of classical or medieval Latin. Rather it has become more of an assortment of words and phrases, incorporating classical terms, medieval terms, and neologisms, which are integrated into the vernacular of the language native to each jurisdiction. Note: the "l" in "law" is not capitalized in the term, though of course it might be if the term initiates a sentence or occurs in a title.

*See also:* French, law French; jargon.

**laughing heir** *See:* heir, laughing heir.

**laundering of monetary instruments** *See:* money, laundering of monetary instruments (money laundering or money launderer).

**law** The system of laws in a state or community that follow certain basic forms. Law means many different things: the whole idea of the law; the system of laws in a given state; the sum of the laws in force at a given time and place; a statement in a statute, regulation, book, or case opinion; the practice of law by lawyers and judges; or the requirement to do or not do something because of the law.

Law in its grandest sense means an ideal of law that is a system of rules followed by officials and by those subject to law in their daily lives, which are fair and just. In this, law is made by public actions divided among officials to ensure fairness and care. The law is made and enforced for the benefit of the subject and not the officials. It protects the subjects from one another and from official abuse or neglect. The law is fairly, impartially, and consistently enforced with wise and equitable interpretation and application in specific cases. That sense of the ideal of law is sometimes called the rule of law or law in the sense of due process of law, in both senses incorporating ideas of just procedures and just substance into the understanding of what law is.

Another meaning of law is in what it does. The laws authorize the actions of state officials, guide the conduct of those subject to state power, justify punishment and privileges from the state, and ensure the liberties of those subject to state authority. On the other hand, law also perpetuates power relationships in society, defines citizenship and allocates its privileges, determines what actions are criminal, gives rights of action to enforce by private means, affects and structures the economy, and defines and orders the movement of property.

One way to define law is as an act of human agency. A law is a specific rule created or recognized by the officials of the legal system of a state to regulate certain actions of the persons and entities in that state, as well as the officials themselves. From this idea, the law is the whole of such rules, as well as the system itself and certain fundamental ideas of how such systems and rules ought to function and what they ought to do. (There are, also, rules that function between and among states that are recognized by the officials of the states, too, a subject explored further as international law.)

Law is also seen as a process for the political control of individuals through the use of the force or violence of the state. In this, the laws are to be obeyed or the individual who fails to do so will be punished. The law is therefore the basis of social order. In this role, law both reflects the identity people have of the individual and of the nation governed by such laws. Even so, there are many laws that are not enforced by force (or enforced at all), and the effectiveness of many laws that are the basis for official enforcement may not depend on enforcement as much as on compliance or compatible behavior without enforcement.

Law in the sense it is usually understood — that related to the practice of law by officials, lawyers, and those who seek the assistance of the law over commerce, property, or liberty — refers to the law in a given place and time. In this practical sense, there is great confusion over where law comes from, or where one finds law.

The law is inherited from past custom: traditions established by prior generations and made anew within each generation, as if the law is "new corn grown from old fields." Laws are written by means established in the past — in constitutions, statutes, case opinions, rules and regulations, ordinances, treatises, and the like — but it is a mistake to believe that the law as written is sufficient to articulate any given rule of law: most of the time, there is too much writing, with too many variations and conflicts within and among the writings, but at the same time, specific cases arise on which no writing is perfectly apt because the case had not arisen just that way before. The law is therefore applied and interpreted in the light of the past understanding of the law and using practices of lawyers and judges that have evolved over time.

The rules are written in the law, but the written law cannot, by itself, be the basis for official action or citizen compliance. Rather, the written law must be applied or interpreted into a form that can affect people's lives. For example, a criminal statute may prohibit certain conduct, but a prosecutor must evaluate a citizen's action to decide whether it is equivalent to the prohibited conduct, and the judge and jury must agree that the person should be punished according to the written law. In its practical sense, the law is a combination of a written archive of legal materials created by officials over time, along with a continuing but changing interpretation in the legal culture that manages it.

There is another sense of law, one more abstract (sometimes called pure law or general law), over which lawyers and philosophers have long argued. Law in this sense includes the elements that define the law (as opposed to other types of power or command or basis for behavior).

One approach to this abstract sense of law is based on a model of rules created or enforced as an element of the state. These rules are justified by an historical act by which a group takes (or are given) power over the state and thus have the power to govern arbitrarily or to do so by law. When the state is subject to law, that power is exercised by this initial group or its successors in the making and enforcement of laws. These laws are the constitutional and administrative laws of the state, and using the methods and powers in these laws, the same officials create other laws that regulate the conduct of the people governed by the state, such as the criminal law and private law. This approach is associated with legal positivism.

Another approach to this abstract sense is based on a model of law as including ideals of the just rule of law that guide the practical, specific rules of law in any legal system. This model is argued by many people to be a form of law and not only a concept of justice. In this intermediate sense are basic principles that tend to make sense as rules of humans in community or that tend to mark what is best in human or official action. People talk in this sense when talking of natural law (sometimes), of just law, of due process of law, and it is the sense of law that translates from jus (as opposed to lex), particularly from jus commune or jus gentium. The difference between this sense of law and the idea of justice is slight, but in general, this argument assumes that the law of a state incorporates this sense of just law within it, rather than, like justice, being a criticism applied to laws form an external source.

There are many other understandings of law in its general sense, some understandings relying more on political and social definitions—such as describing the law as a tool for maintaining the powerful in their power or describing the law as a means of restraining the weak from interfering with the strong. Some understandings depend entirely on the conduct of officials and ignore the effect of the archive of the writings of law. Other understandings depend entirely on the written law but ignore the varied outcomes that might have appeared to be required by the archive and that can only have been selected as a result of the behavior of officials. Other understandings depend on the effect on the citizenry or upon the interests of those with relative wealth to describe law as a cause. Debating among the strengths and weaknesses of these understandings and others is the province of jurisprudence.

Besides these very general meanings of law, law is used in daily practice as a marker to distinguish among types of information. In this usage, a question before a court might be a question of law or a question of fact or a mixed question of law and of fact. Or, a matter might be one of law rather than equity (though, at some level of abstraction, both law and equity are included in "the law"). Or, a question might be a matter of law or of policy or a matter of law or of politics.

Law in its broadest sense includes all of the principles, rules, and guides of action in the physical and metaphysical world as experienced or imagined by humankind. People talk in this sense when speaking of the laws of physics, or of mathematics. In this sense, people speak of law sometimes to include rules of human behavior when speaking of divine law, of natural law and of behavioral laws.

*See also:* law, written law (lex scripta); international law (law of nations or public international law).

**law as a system of rules**   *See:* rule, legal rule (law as a system of rules).

**law and economics**   *See:* economy, law and economics.

**law clerk**   *See:* clerk, law clerk, oscar; clerk, law clerk (student intern or internship or clerkship).

**law day**   *See:* day, law day, Law Day USA; day, law day (lage dayum).

**law degree**   *See:* degree, academic degree, law degree.

**law enforcement**   *See:* enforcement, law enforcement, selective enforcement; enforcement, law enforcement.

**law enforcement officer or peace officer**   *See:* police, police officer (law enforcement officer or peace officer).

**law firm**   *See:* lawyer, law firm.

**law French**   *See:* French, law French.

**law Latin**   *See:* Latin, law Latin.

**law merchant**   *See:* merchant, law merchant (lex mercatoria).

**law of armed conflict or LOW or LOAC**   *See:* war, law of war (law of armed conflict or LOW or LOAC).

**law of capture**   *See:* capture (law of capture).

**law of nations or public international law**   *See:* international law (law of nations or public international law).

**law of the case**   *See:* res, res judicata, law of the case.

**law of the circuit**   *See:* court, U.S. court, U.S. court of appeals, law of the circuit (circuit law).

**law of the market**   *See:* market (law of the market).

**law of the sea**   *See:* sea, law of the sea (sea laws).

**law of war**   *See:* law of war (law of armed conflict or LOW or LOAC).

**law partner**   *See:* lawyer, law firm, lawyers, law partner.

**law reform**   *See:* reform, law reform.

**law review** *See:* review, law review (L.J. or LJ or law journal or review or l. rev. or LR).

**adjective law (adjectival law)** The procedures and practice of the law, not its substance. Adjective law is the law that modifies the substance of the law — in other words, the procedures and methods by which law is applied and created. Thus, the rules of criminal procedure and criminal procedure, local rules of court, customs of attorneys and judges, and even the rules of procedure and customs of legislatures, administrative and police agencies, and the executives are adjective law. This term was once more common than it is now.

**administrative law** The law of regulations, rules, orders, and other actions by a government's executive. Administrative law is the regulation of regulation. It includes the procedures, obligations, and limitations placed on the executive, not only by the legislature, by the chief executive, and by higher levels of bureaucracy in an agency, but also by the constitutional limits of legislative delegation of powers to the agency. Administrative law in its broadest sense therefore includes elements of constitutional law as well as elements of the substantive laws of many substantive areas regulated by administrative agencies. Yet in its narrower sense, administrative law is the particular set of statutes and regulations according to which every agency creates and applies the law within the agency's discretion.

In the United States, the most essential statute of administrative law is the Administrative Procedures Act of 1946, 5 U.S.C. 500, et seq., which is similar to the state Model Administrative Procedures Act. The APA requires agencies to engage in an open process of rule-making, by which every agency provides drafts of regulations to the public for comment, and then receives comments and engages with their substance before promulgating the regulation. The APA requires regulations to be publicly available, and uniform standards be adopted for their application and adjudication. The APA establishes judicial review of regulations in general and in their application, although in most cases judicial review may only follow the exhaustion of administrative remedies.

*See also:* regulation (regulate or reg.).

**administrative conference** The body that creates rules of administrative procedure. The Administrative Council creates rules governing administrative procedure, which apply throughout the executive branch.

**Administrative Procedure Act (APA)** Regulations that operate as laws require prior notice and comment. The Administrative Procedures Act (APA), 5 U.S.C. § 553 (2008), sets procedural requirements for nearly all government agency rule making, except for purely the creation of rules binding only agency personnel and contracts and certain rules affecting the military and foreign affairs. Under the APA, all proposed rules must be subject to notice to the public, mainly by being published in the Federal Register, and must be open to public comment before they may be made final.

*See also:* regulation (regulate or reg.).

**anthropology of law (legal anthropology)** The study of law applying analytical tools of anthropology. The anthropology of law is the study of legal systems within their social and cultural contexts. It views law as inseparable from the people who act in and are subject to it, as influenced by language, history, culture, and tradition. Legal anthropology examines both the subcultures of lawyers and legal officials and the cultural integration of laws with other normative systems in the societies in which the law is examined.

**autonomic law** Laws of voluntary associations, similar to law in the state. Autonomic law describes the rules of organizations and associations, when those rules create norms that affect the lives of their members in a manner similar to the norms created by the legal system of a state. Autonomic laws apply only to those who are members of the certain institution governed by the laws. The rules of churches, unions, the laws and customs of Gypsies, the rules of sports leagues, and other similar sets of rules are autonomic.

**case law (caselaw of decisional law)** The law enunciated in the opinions of judges deciding cases. Case law is the sum of law expressed by judges when ruling on the questions of law before the courts in specific cases. Case law is the basis of common-law research and analysis.

**black letter law (blackletter law or hornbook law)** The basic principles of a subject in the law. Black letter law is a metaphor for the essential principles and rules of the law in each subject area of legal practice or study. It is synonymous with hornbook law, the principles that might be listed in a student summary of a field, though black letter law is inherently more sophisticated and, thorough-going, and potentially arcane. The term comes from the practice of medieval scriveners and early modern publishers of printing the core text of a glossed law book in bold print, with the notes glossing the core text in fine print.

*See also:* gloss (glossation or glossator).

**civil law (C.L. or CL)** The laws of states that enact legislation in the Roman style. Civil law is the broad name for the tradition encompassing the legal systems of France, Germany, Spain, Louisiana, and other states that follow the Roman model for legislation and legal development. It is a mistake to think that the civilian system depends wholly on legislation; judicial and scholarly development is essential for the application of the codes in a given context, but in each system legislation performs an essential role, and the description of a legal issue commences with a requirement of the code of laws in that jurisdiction.

*See also:* civil.

**Civil Code of Louisiana** The codified laws of Louisiana, governing private law disputes. The Louisiana Civil Code governs private law matters in Louisiana. To a large extent modeled upon the Code Napoleon of France, the Louisiana Code was enacted in 1808 and has been routinely amended ever since.

**color of law** The appearance that some act is allowed or required by law. Color of law is the apparent authorization by law of some action that would be otherwise forbidden. The formula for liability of a person as a state actor when the person violates the rights of another is that the violating person acts under color of state law; this formula is satisfied by the performance of an action that is allowed by the statutes, ordinances, caselaw, or executive policies, of a state or its subdivision.

*See also:* civil rights, civil rights enforcement action, 1983 action; office, color of office.

**commercial law** The law regulating of transactions among businesses and banks. Commercial law is a broad field of law governing the transactions and disputes that arise among businesses that buy and sell goods and the banks and other institutions that facilitate such transactions. Commercial law is a bit of a hybrid field in the United States, which overlaps with the law of contracts, banking, and shipping, as well as fiduciary law, property, and remedies. Specific areas of law affecting commerce, such as the creation and regulation of corporations or the taxation of transactions, are by custom not considered commercial law. Unlike many countries, disputes arising under commercial law in the United States are heard in the regular courts with jurisdiction over civil matters.

The bulk of commercial law in the United States is state law, much of it governed by state adoptions of the Uniform Commercial Code. The U.C.C.'s titles are often considered the scope of U.S. commercial law: sales, leases, negotiable instruments, bank deposits, fund transfers, letters of credit, bulk transfers and sales, documents of title such as bills of lading, investment securities, and secured transactions. Even so, many additional state laws regulate commercial conduct as do federal regulations of interstate commerce, in matters as diverse as labeling laws, product safety, employee civil rights, workplace safety, and environmental protection. International transactions are potentially governed by international law as well, particularly treaties such as the United Nations Convention on Contracts for the International Sale of Goods.

**common law (lex communis)** The law arising from judicial decisions in practical cases. The common law is the generic name for the legal system of the United States and the other legal systems built roughly from English models. It is often described as merely judge-made law, but the reality of the integration of legislation, precedent, and current argument and policy into judicial opinion is much more subtle and complex. The hallmarks of the common law are these: Legislation is an important source of law, but it is not the only source of law. The judicial application of laws in specific cases is an important source of later law. The laws are common to all of the people in a jurisdiction, with general rules that apply to everyone who might find themselves in a given situation. The law reflects the customs, habits, and expectations of the people it governs. The law is a predictive enterprise, not a retrospective skill, as much a matter of procedure as substance, and only a person skilled in the culture of procedural application and of substantive interpretation is likely to be fairly accurate in explaining a legal question.

Readers in the twenty-first century may find certain elements of this list surprising, owing to rhetoric in the late twentieth century that depicts much common-law methodology as "judicial activism" but the understanding of Bouvier's in 1853 is nearer to the U.S. tradition from the founding until the 1970s, that the common law is derived by judges from precedent reflecting the practice of the people. Certain of those precedents were reflected in legislation, others in judicial opinions, and still others in shared experience, but a result of law that created an obligation that did not fit with the evolving customs of society would have been criticized as a poor precedent and not followed, while a result of law that reflected such evolving customs would be seen as good authority for later decisions.

The term, the common law, and much of its method, is broadly taken from the English methods of law, particularly as they were understood during the colonial experience, a period marked by the legal writers from Sir Edward Coke to Sir William Blackstone. Yet, the influence of the common law as an international system in which American courts relied on opinions from other common-law countries was common until the mid-twentieth century.

The common law is, and always has been, a combination of writings and understandings that cannot be fully written. It is the combination of an archive of law and a culture of its practice. Although all legal systems share these two aspects, the common law has long recognized that a portion of its law is in the lex non scripta, the unwritten law.

*See also:* burglary | common law; law, common law, common-law rule; copyright, common-law copyright; lawyer, common-law lawyer (common lawyer or admiralty lawyer or canon lawyer or civilian lawyer); marriage, common-law marriage.

**common-law rule** A rule or principle of law developed by courts. A common-law rule is a rule that originated in the common-law system, either in England through a synthesis of judicial opinions (or a synthesis of judicial opinions and statutes), or in the United States through a synthesis of judicial opinions and treatises. A statute may restate a common-law rule, and indeed many statutes are intended to clarify or simplify common-law rules, although the statute is then applied according to common law methods of statutory interpretation.

**federal common law** Rules of decision originating in the federal courts. The federal common law is the body of law created by courts, usually U.S. courts but oftimes also state courts, that develop rules for decisions on questions arising under federal law as described in Article III or, put another way, that answer questions before the courts arising in federal question cases. Federal common law also describes interpretations of federal statutes and rules, as well as ruling on matters of laws arising initially from federal statutes or rules but for which no statute or rule provides a basis for decision.

In Erie Railroad Co. v. Tompkins, 304 U.S. 64 (1938), Justice Brandeis noted that there is no general, federal common law, which is a bit misleading, in that there are so many specific arenas of federal common law that certain general principles can be found among them. Still, the adage is correct in that general principles of the common law providing rules of decision for most causes of action in U.S. courts under diversity jurisdiction are the product of state courts interpreting state common law.

The federal common law is limited by the Constitution just as a statute would be, particularly by the substantive and procedural limits of the Due Process Clause of the Fifth Amendment.

*See also:* choice, choice of law, Erie doctrine.

**reception of the common law** *See:* reception, reception of the common law (reception statutes).

**comparative law** The study of law by comparing different legal systems. Comparative law is both a method of legal analysis and a body of scholarship developed by that method, of considering any given question of law from two or more perspectives drawn from different legal systems and cultures. Comparative law is very old, and it is inherent among the legal systems of nations that are closely engaged with other legal systems, such as the later Roman law and canon law, or state and federal law, or the laws of states that frequently trade goods between one another. Comparative law may be between the legal systems of different states, or between the legal systems of different times, between a legal system integrated into a state and one that is not, between different bodies of law and procedure in the same state and time, or any other comparative division.

The technique is to describe and assess the similarities and differences between different approaches to the regulation of the same issue in the different systems. Why, for instance, would one jurisdiction make an act criminal but another jurisdiction make is legal? What benefit is there from one jurisdiction to allow punitive damages and another not? Why would one system employ a civil jury and the other use a three-person bench instead? Through such questions, comparative law not only allows a clearer understanding of both legal systems examined but also provides a foundation for the criticism and improvement of both systems from a foundation of principles and justification that result from those understandings.

Comparative law in the United States was both routine and deeply integrated into the practice of American lawyers in the eighteenth and nineteenth centuries, as befits the law of a nation of immigrants. Bouvier's 1853 edition contains thousands of references to civilian texts to explain common-law terms and hundreds of entries of civilian terms, as well as many terms from other legal systems. This early and consistent integration is unsurprising, given the reliance of U.S. law on English and Scots law for much of its initial public law, on French and English legal theory for much of its constitution, on Dutch and then German law for much of its commercial law, and on civilian principles for much of its probate and tort law. Only with the great mass of American law generated in the twentieth century did the citation by judges of foreign courts diminish (although the continued borrowing of foreign ideas by scholars of the uniform laws and restatements more than made up the difference), and the academic study of comparative law became a discipline distinct from other fields of law. In the twenty-first century, globalization in the practice of law has increased pressure on U.S. law schools to increase the integration of comparative techniques in most fields of legal study, and indeed globalization has led to increased practice by U.S. lawyers both in multiple national jurisdictions and in supranational venues, such as before the WTO and international arbitral bodies.

**constitutional law** The laws by which officials hold office, make laws, and carry them out. Constitutional law is the body of laws according to which the customs and laws of a state are manifest through the selection and installation of officials; the distribution of power among them in means suitable to withstand inevitable struggles for more power; the creation of new laws and recognition or rejection of old laws; the creation, implementation, and enforcement of laws; and the determination of limitations on each of these actions, both to contain the powers of officials and to provide some liberties to the citizens. Constitutional law may be seen as an alloy of ideas created in the past, manifest in certain settlements following power struggles among citizens or officials, and of actions by officials in the present as they engage in similar struggles.

In the United States, constitutional law is largely the product of the federal courts, particularly the U.S. Supreme Court, although certain resolutions of questions and disputes have originated with the legislation of Congress, with the actions and statements of Presidents, with the laws the states, and with social facts and events, such as the reality of slavery, the American Civil War, and the post-bellum Reconstruction of the South. The recurrent questions of constitutional law in the United States tend to be the extent of powers of the federal government and the states to regulate human affairs, the powers and limitations of the U.S. Courts, the President, and the Congress, and the liberty of the individual from interference by officials of the state or federal governments.

The text of constitutional instruments is a central source of authority for the structure of a constitution in most legal systems. Indeed, the text of a constitution may be so identified with a state's constitutional law that for a speaker to refer to its constitution is intended by that speaker to refer to the text of its constitution then in force.

In the United States, a written constitution adopted in 1787, ratified and provided just twenty–seven amendments in the next two centuries, has been the basis for most constitutional law. Yet that text cannot answer most questions without interpretation, and certain customary ideas were either lodged there by their drafters or found there by their readers despite the drafters' failure to express these ideas by words in the text. Separation of powers, federalism, sovereignty, judicial review, executive prerogative, and other essential concepts of U.S. Constitutional law are matters of interpretation rather than textual statement. In other legal systems, constitutional texts are more or less direct in their statements of the structure and legal limits of governance. The British constitution is famously, though inaccurately, said to be unwritten, though its constitutional instruments are as old as Magna Carta, which was adopted in 1215.

*See also:* constitution.

**criminal law**   The law of crime and its punishment. Criminal law is the broad term for the laws that apply in any jurisdiction to define certain conduct or conditions as a crime, so that a crime is – by definition – conduct or condition in violation of the definitions of the criminal law. Criminal law includes punishments within its definitions, such that the crime is defined in part by the punishment for which a person or entity committing that crime may be liable. Although criminal law was initially derived from the common law of England, the constitutional and criminal law of the United States, both federal and state, require the definition of a crime according to statute. Though at its broadest conception, criminal law may include the procedures of a criminal investigation and trial, those areas are now generally considered matters of criminal procedure.

*See also:* penal (penal law).

**customary law**   Conduct so routine and expected that the law enforces the expectation. Customary law is the legal enforcement of customs among the members of the community bound by a legal system. Thus, customary law in a given state is the legal enforcement of customs that evolve among the people that form the community of that state; customary law in international law is the legal enforcement of customs that evolve among the representatives of states that form the international community.

Customary law has long been recognized as the heart of the common law, which looked to social customs as the primary source of common–law rules. Indeed, by enshrining standards such as reasonable

foreseeability in contract, and the expectation of a reasonable person in tort, custom remains an integral part of many core ideas in the U.S. common law.

Specific rules adopted by courts and legislatures reflect customary understanding from social practice that are adapted into the principles of legal rules, such as the limits on the disinheritance of a spouse, the obligations of a parent to support a child, or the duty of a fiduciary to a beneficiary. There is a relationship between these two families of normative structures, and as such customary practices change, so have rules changed, and sometimes as rules change so have customs.

*See also:* custom (customary).

**declaratory theory of law**   Judges pronounce pre-existing, if previously unarticulated, law. The declaratory theory of law describes the method of the common law as the judicial ascertainment of a pre-existing rule, rather than the creation or invention of a new rule. Regardless of how new or unusual the statement may be, the judge merely declares what was already the law rather than making new law.

There are several bases for the declaratory theory. One is that it rests on the "brooding ominipresence of the law" in Holmes's phrase, some spirit of the law rooted in a perfectly right answer that may arise from a perfect understanding of existing legal sources, like the young Ronald Dworkin's Hercules might find the one right answer to every case.

The other basis rests on an integration of the process of the common law with social custom— the moral and social patterns of expectation arising from human interaction—this understanding that the law takes its rules from the norms of social practice underlies the mature Dworkin's Hercules in Law's Empire (1986).

**ex post facto law**   *See:* ex, ex post facto (ex post facto law).

**federal law**   The law of the United States of America. Federal law is the law of the United States of America, including all law that originates in the U.S. Constitution, the statutes of Congress, the treaties to which the United States is a member, the customary international law, the decisions of federal courts, the regulations of the executive agencies elaborating on powers delegated by the Congress, and the lawful and constitutional orders of officials of the executive branch. There is a broader sense of federal law, including not only the law of the United States but also the laws of the various states, but this genuinely federal construct of federal law is rare.

**force of law**   A condition by which a statement of the law is considered to bind officials and subjects. The force of law is a condition that an official statement, such as legislation, regulations, rulings, precedents, or other sources of law, acquire once they are promulgated and considered effective as a source of liability that would bind individuals or entities to do what the statement requires.

**fundamental law**   The most basic law. Fundamental law describes those laws that are the foundation for other laws in a legal system. In the law of the United States this usually implies the U.S. Constitution, sometimes just a few core elements of it such as the principles of separation of powers based on distributed powers limits on the executive, legislative, and judicial powers to the powers granted to each branch; federalism based on the supremacy of federal law but the continued independence of the states, due process of law and equal protection of the laws, and the protection of individual rights against official interference.

Fundamental law in a more general sense implies different notions according to an observer's philosophical perspective. For example: To a positivist, a fundamental law would be a grundnorm, an ultimate rule of recognition, or at least an essential secondary rule. To a natural law theorist, a fundamental law would be a natural principle of law that reflects either the need to ensure and promote a basic underived good for the people or an essential virtue. To a utilitarian, the fundamental law is the principle of utility, that all laws should do more good than harm, or cause more happiness than pain among the members of the populace. To an historian, the fundamental law would be several things, likely the customs and stated laws that define the constitutional allocations of role in the legal system, particularly the most evocative and symbolic of those laws giving rise to settlements of constitutional conflicts.

**general law**   A statute of general purpose or the unspecialized law. As a matter of legislation, a general law is a statute that is passed by a legislature to regulate the conduct of all persons similarly situated throughout its jurisdiction. Although practice varies among jurisdictions, general laws are usually distinct from private bills, budgets, and resolutions.

As a matter of legal practice, general law is the same as the substance of a general practice, the law writ large without specialization. Thus as a matter of administration, general law is likely to mean all matters other than the specialized focus of an agency.

As a matter of jurisprudence, a general law is a law that applies without limitation to all persons in a given place, as opposed to a special law that would apply to some and not others.

**individuation of laws**   Defining the scope of each specific law. Individuation generally is the sorting out of each unique entity from a population or mass. The individuation of law is the description of a specific law.

The problem of individuation in law is seen in part in the question of how best to define a law and its scope, whether to think of each statute, regulation, or common-law principle as a real law or to think of the sum of sources of law that yield an answer to a given question. In other words, what is the best way to describe a law by the section and name of a statute or by what a person must do to comply with it, including all of the later statutes and interpretations that apply.

**Doctor of the Science of Law (Doctor of Juridical Science or J.S.D. or JSD or S.J.D. or SJD)**   The earned doctorate in law. The degree Doctor of the Science of Law is composed and abbreviated several ways in the United States, but it represents the earned doctorate and terminal academic degree in legal study.

**law of the land (lex terrae)**   The laws validly in force in a place. The law of the land is the collective term for any law or all laws that are in force in a given jurisdiction at a given time. Thus, the constitution, statutes, principles arising from caselaw, administrative regulations, and international laws adapted to local law are all the law of the land. In older usages, the law of the land represents the common law, particularly the common law as it might be put before a jury. From this sense, the law of the land connotes specific elements of procedural requirements on all of its substance, in a sense resonant with the rule of law and with due process of law.

*See also:* law, rule of law; due process of law.

**law school (legal education)**   The three-year graduate program which prepares most attorneys to commence practice. Law school, in the United States, is an institution offering a course of study in the law that results in a degree that would be a qualification to be examined to enter the profession of law in most U.S. jurisdictions. A law school consists of a faculty of attorneys or scholars and students who generally already hold at least one university degree and who are to take the equivalent of three years of full-time study to complete their course.

The first year is typically devoted to learning the basic skills of ascertaining principles and rules that may be applied in factual situations, from reading legal materials, notably from the opinions of judges in cases before appellate courts but also from statutes, regulations, constitutions, scholarly treatises and articles, and reference works. For hundreds of years, students have attempted to evade this work through the use of commercial outlines and study aids, with mixed success.

The typical U.S. law school requires some courses of study—such as criminal law, property law, tort law, civil procedure, constitutional law, and professional responsibility (or legal ethics), as well as a course in research and writing for lawyers. Schools then provide an array of elective coursework in a great number of specialized fields of practice and a number of aspects of the history, philosophy, and policy of law and its related disciplines. Most law schools provide opportunities for students to develop and practice skills under faculty supervision through participation in clinics and externships in legal practice environments.

Law schools in the United States are either nationally accredited, accredited regionally or by a state agency, or unaccredited. As of 2010, there are 200 accredited schools, whose students are qualified upon graduation to apply for the bar examination in any state. Other schools may provide some measure of legal education, but their students may take the bar exam only in the few states that do not require an accredited degree. Note: in general, there is no difference among schools denominated College of Law, School of Law, or Law School.

See also: rhetoric; bar, admission to the bar, bar exam (bar examination).

**accredited law school**  A law school certified so that its graduates may join the bar. An accredited law school is a school or college of law that has been inspected and received a certification from an accrediting agency that the educational and professional content of its degree programs is sufficient for its students to join the bar of its jurisdiction. A few states accredit schools within their state for this purpose, but most states accept the accreditation of the agency authorized to accredit professional law school programs by the U.S. Department of Education, which is, and has long been, the American Bar Association. Graduation from an accredited law school is generally sufficient, with proof of character and fitness, to sit for the bar exam in any jurisdiction.

See also: accreditation.

**Association of American Law Schools (A.A.L.S. or AALS)**  An association of law schools in the United States. The Association of American Law Schools is an association of law schools that promotes the improvement of legal education and the legal profession. Most, though not all, accredited law schools in the United States and Canada are members of the AALS. Membership is conferred by the association upon accredited schools that have offered five years of instruction and successfully graduated at least three classes of law students and that have met the association's standards of core values, student admissions, non-discrimination and affirmative action, faculty quality and governance, curriculum and instruction, library resources, facilities, and finances.

**hierarchy of legal education**  There is a range of greater and lesser prestige among law schools. The hierarchy of legal education is an observation made by Duncan Kennedy that legal education promotes unconstructive hierarchies among law schools, among law students, and among law firms, and lawyers.

See also: hierarchy.

**Law School Admissions Test or LSAT**  A standardized national evaluation for law school applicants. The Law School Admissions Test is the pre-admission evaluatory tool used by nearly every law school in the United States as an element in the process of admissions. The function of the test is to combine a variety of questions testing various domains of skill and knowledge to assess the statistical likelihood of performance of the applicant in first-year law school end-of-course examinations.

Most law schools use a combination of LSAT scores, undergraduate and graduate grade point average, and life experience in selecting applicants whom they will admit.

**case method (casebook method or Socratic method)**  The study of law through the reading and discussion of cases. The case method is a customary means of instruction in law school, in which the students of a class are assigned to read carefully a case or cases on a given topic prior to class, and the professor uses questions to various students in the group as a means of developing an inquiry into the facts and context from which arose the dispute, the legal doctrines that were in issue, the means by which the judges of the court understood those doctrines and applied them to the facts and context, and the sufficiency of the result as a matter of law and justice.

The case method has been controversial since its adoption in the late nineteenth century. The goals of case-method instruction are to teach a process of legal analysis, a means of understanding rules and doctrines as dynamic rather than static, and to keep the students engaged in a participative and active learning experience. These goals are not always achieved, and law professors often fall back on a quiz technique of asking the student to spot the issue, recite the facts and holding, and then to move on. Even when the case method is done well, marginal students have complained for a century that they would rather be passively taught static rules they can memorize with little effort and with no public risks if they miss the points of the readings. Thus a tension persists between the use of dialogue and monologue in law-school classes. One result of this tension is that in the early twenty-first century many courses in the first year are taught through dialogue, but many upper-class courses are taught either through monologue or discussion that is less didactic, less focused on topics or conclusion that have been predetermined by the teacher.

See also: brief, case brief (brief a case); lawbook, casebook.

**Computer Assisted Legal Instruction (C.A.L.I. or CALI)**  A group promoting computer assisted self-education in the law. CALI is an association, as well as the product the association develops, to allow students to use computer platforms to test and develop their understanding of concepts, rules, and principles in their applications to specific situations. CALI encourages the development of software and courseware to be shared among law schools and other legal institutions.

See also: research, legal research, computer assisted legal research (C.A.L.R. or CALR).

**lecture method (hornbook method)**  Teaching through the recitation of rules of law, narrating examples. The lecture method is the generic term for the straight law lecture, the lecture in which the professor stands before the class and dictates rules of law, illustrating the rule with an example before moving forward. Hornbook method takes its name from the hornbook, particularly the form of treatise aiming to present the simplest statements of the black letter law for the benefit of students. Hornbook teaching was largely supplanted by case method teaching in the early twentieth century, but its use, in varying names, is becoming again common in the twenty-first century as a result of student pressure for easier and less stressful work, the rise of student evaluations as a surrogate for peer review, and the use of computer-generated slide shows in lectures.

**Order of the Coif**   Honorary organization for law school graduates with good grades. The Order of the Coif is an American association recognizing high performance among law school students. The association takes its name from the coif, the soft hat once worn by serjeants, senior barristers in England.

*See also:* coif.

**National Association of Law Placement (NALP)** A clearinghouse for potential employment for law students. The National Association of Law Placement is an association of professionals in the placement and recruitment of law students and lawyers for temporary and permanent employment. NALP maintains directories of legal employers as well as current and archival statistics on legal placement and employment.

**legal system**   An effective system of rules that subjects obey as law. A legal system is a particular idea in jurisprudence of an organization of rules that are created by social institutions sufficient to perform the tasks of resolving conflicts and bringing sufficient order that the people who are seemingly required to act according to the rules generally speaking conform to their requirements. The modern idea of the legal system is associated with H.L.A. Hart's theory of legal positivism, in which he described to broad categories of rule, the primary rule (or rule governing the subject) and secondary rule (or rule governing the official). The secondary rules must include at least rules by which to know what a rule is, how to enforce it, and how to change it. To that we may add a rule to determine who is responsible or authorized to do each of those things. Hart recognized that the rules might not have sufficient authority to be the practical basis of action by citizens or officials, a condition he considered the pathology of the legal system.

A legal system as a matter of jurisprudence differs from the institutions of the law in any given time or place. Still, the legal institutions of a given state — Congress or Parliament, courts, Departments, or Ministries — inherently act in a manner that creates and enforces rules that are the legal system as jurisprudence describes it. Every legal system has contingent elements in its structure that inform the meaning of the general depiction of the legal system as a system of rules.

*See also:* rule; jurisprudence, legal positivism (positivism).

**adversarial system (adversary system)**   A process of advocates disputing evidence before an arbiter. The adversary system is an institutional process of determining historical facts and legal obligations that are associated with the Anglo–American legal system of criminal and civil trials, although it most differs from other legal systems in its criminal adjudication. The adversary system divides the prosecutorial from the adjudicatory roles, placing the state in a theoretically equal role to the defense, rather than merging the functions of examiner and arbiter into a single inquisitorial role as is common in civilian European systems.

More generally, the adversary legal system is a method of resolving legal controversies predicated on two opponents presenting evidence to a dispassionate fact finder who then determines the truth of the matter. Origins of the system are sometimes said to be in early combat rituals used for dispute resolution but are as likely to be in scholastic forms of argument rooted in the Roman and Greek philosophical traditions. Proponents hold that truth is most likely to be discovered through competing parties discovering and proffering relevant evidence to the fact finder in an effort to win the case. The adversary system is used in the United States and most common law jurisdictions (as opposed to the inquisitorial system used in most civil law jurisdictions). Prominent features include: trial by jury, evidence limited to material of a particular relevance, cross–examination of witnesses and an emphasis on fairness and procedural due process during the litigation process rather than maintaining equity between the parties. Critics of the adversary system argue that the skill of a litigant's attorney in manipulating evidence or fact finder, a skill that usually correlates to the litigant's wealth, influences the outcome of a case more than the actual truth of the matter.

**inquisitorial legal system**   A process of inquiry by fact finders. The inquisitorial system is an institutional process of determining historical facts and legal obligations that is associated, mainly by U.S. lawyers, with the civilian, or continental, legal system of criminal and civil trials, although it most differs from other legal systems in its criminal adjudication. The inquisitorial system is usually seen as employing judges who are active in investigation and in the examination of evidence but who also rule on its final legal significance. The inquisitorial system does not employ a jury but usually relies on magistrates to both investigate and determine the facts and their legal significance. Although these impressions are true, at times, they are quite general and often untrue depictions of the operation of courts in, for example, Germany or

Spain, yet they remain a tool of comparison by which U.S. lawyers define the adversarial system.

**letter of the law**   The exact requirements of the law. The letter of the law is a metaphor for the comprehensive technical requirements of the law. The phrase particularly occurs in statements that either extol the virtues of careful compliance with the law or that warn of the dangers of pursuing technical perfection at the expense of general purpose. Note: sometimes "the letter of the law" is invoked to mean no more than the text of a source of law, such as the words of a statute or regulation.

*See also:* interpretation, strict construction.

**martial law**   Law controlled by the military. Martial law has several senses, but the ordinary sense is the combination of statutes, regulations, and orders that govern the members of the military services as law. In this sense, martial law is military law. The most significant source of martial law in the United States is the Uniform Code of Military Justice, which is augmented by the Manual for Courts Martial and by the orders of military commanders.

Martial law in its ordinary and customary sense has no jurisdiction over civilians, although certain regulations govern civilians on military bases and reservations. Even so, the recent increase in the use of civilian contractors in military roles has led to ambiguity that may allow some enhanced jurisdiction in martial law over such contractors.

Martial law arises in truly extraordinary circumstances in the United States, when the courts of the military serve as the civilian legal system. This may occur in an area in which the Article III courts are not open and civilian government is suspended, either by act of Congress or by a circumstances such as a military occupation, insurrection, or invasion, when martial law may be asserted by the military commander of a given area — with jurisdiction over civilians as well as military personnel — until Congress suspends such authority or until the crisis has in fact passed. The limits of martial law in such a circumstance are prescribed in part by the Constitutional limits on the power of the executive and in part by Congressional enactment, notably the Posse Comitatus Act, 18 U.S.C. § 1835 (2009).

An abiding suspicion of martial law over civilian populations persists in Western civilization, arising from two essential concerns, among others. The first is the recurrent link between military control of social conduct and the collapse of democratic and constitutional government into military oligarchies or fascist dictatorships. The other is the concern that martial law is too frequently unjust, particularly because military priorities and policy may trump both individual rights and the truth of the matter in a given case.

**natural law**   *See:* jurisprudence, natural law (jure naturae or lex naturale).

**operation of law**   The means of an obligation, power, or effect that would not exist but by the law. Operation of law is a phrase that describes the change in human affairs created by the dictate of law, such as a prohibition created by statute, or a license to operate a business granted by an agency, or the right of a person to take property as the successor to a decedent created by a judicial interpretation of the law of decedent's estates. In each case, the effect of what a person may do or not do, what right or interest a person or entity has, is created by operation of law.

**organic law**   The law that defines the state and its powers over law. Organic law is the law that establishes the power of the institutions that create, enforce, and adjudicate the laws. Organic law might be thought of as the the the most important laws about laws, some of the constitution, some of the most essential statutes, decisions, principles, and customs, in an amalgam of rules that is required for the legal system to function, for the state to be a law–creating and law–enforcing entity. Thus, organic law by its very nature is unlikely to be fixed merely at the dawn of a state, although much of it may be first crafted then. Organic law is the law followed by officials, whether or not citizens have recourse to coerce obedience through the courts. Yet, organic law is still predicated essentially on acceptance by the people, or at least their tolerance, because of the de facto if not implied authority of the people to alter their organic law.

In the United States, the organic law includes the Constitution and its amendments, but certain of the most important provisions are more obviously organic than other provisions. Certain doctrines at best obliquely mentioned in the texts, such as separation of powers and state sovereignty, came to prominence later but became organic law. Other ideas, such as judicial review and equal dignity of each citizen pre–existing the texts arose later but either led to new understandings of the texts or the creation of new texts, or both. Thus, one can argue that the Declaration of Independence is a part of the organic law of the United States, just as one can argue the Preamble of the Constitution is, regardless of their enforceability in a court of law.

**procedural law**   The laws specifying how to use the law in each case. Procedural law includes the laws, doctrines, rules and customs by which the substantive law is applied to any action, question, or dispute, as opposed to the substantive laws that determine the extent of rights, duties, obligations, and privileges that are to be applied according to the procedural law. In other words, procedural law is the law that determines how laws work in legal institutions, while substantive law determines what the law requires or protects in the daily life of individuals and entities. The line between these two is fuzzy, and many substantive laws have procedural implications, and vice versa, such as the procedural law of the statutes of limitations that gives rise to the substantive laws of prescription, adverse possession, and immunity from prosecution. Broad areas of procedural law include the rules of procedure, jurisdiction, and evidence. The distinction between substantive and procedural law is particularly important in cases of federal jurisdiction arising in admiralty and in diversity, in which the Erie rule requires that federal procedural law applies in the action, but state substantive law applies as well.

**real law**  A law as perceived by someone subject to its authority. Real law is a way of describing the law, and specific laws, according to what the law governing some conduct is: a rule is what allows or what forbids what may be done. This approach contrasts with the many rules as seen by lawyers, of liability rules, jurisdiction, procedure, and remedy, each of which are a component of the rule of what may be done. The idea has been promoted by the legal theorist Tony Honoré, who argued that law as seen by the person outside the legal system was really about what behavior would be required, allowed, or forbidden, which requires an answer in a different way from the way lawyers see it. The answer is to individuate laws not by source, age, topic, or institution, but by the sum of their effects on a given question or action. Honoré was likely influenced in this model by LLewellyn's notion of real rules.

*See also:* rules, real rule.

**remedial law (curative law)**  A law that remedies an error, mistake, or abusive aspect of the prior law. Remedial law includes a statute, judicial doctrine or order, executive order or regulation, or other form of law that is promulgated to remedy a defect in the former law that was identified as unjust, contrary to good policy or right reason, or the basis of the abuse of individual rights or interests. Thus, laws that end some form of discrimination, that simplify a procedure, that provide relief for some form of social ill or injustice, or that correct mistakes or defects in early promulgations of the law are remedial. The remedial nature of a law, particularly a statute, usually entitles it to liberal interpretation and to application in close cases.

Remedial law as a matter of judicial practice may refer to the very unusual remedy that requires a supervisory role of the court over a person or entity (but usually a public institution like a school system or a prison) in order to ensure that a complicated remedy is implemented in fact.

*See also:* statute, remedial statute.

**Roman law**  *See:* Roman law.

**Rule of Law**  No one is above the law, and every act of government must be done through laws. The Rule of Law has many controversial aspects, but its core requires fair laws that apply to all persons in a state, that are enacted for the benefit of the citizens, and that are fairly and impartially applied without regard to the status of the persons to whom they are applied, by officials who are themselves bound by the laws in every aspect of their duties.

*See also:* law, law of the land (lex terrae); morality, inner morality of law.

**rules of law**  A set of the principles of the law. One of the rules of law is a specific, individuated law that arises from the law in a given place. A rule of law is,

to some extent, redundant: a rule of law is also a law.

**substantive law**  The laws that specify what one may do or not do. The substantive laws include all of the constitutional law, statutes, regulations, case precedents, policies, rules, and customs that determine the rights, duties, status, interests, and obligations of persons and entities. The substantive law is the law that determines what one may or may not do without penalty or loss, and what others may or may not do, too. Substantive law, or what the law governing some claim is, ordinarily is contrasted with procedural law, or how the law is applied in a given proceeding. In admiralty and in diversity, federal courts apply state substantive law, yet apply federal procedural law. The line between substance and procedure can be quite difficult to discern in some cases.

**epistemology of law**  What law appears to us to be. Legal epistemology is the branch of jurisprudence that describes the law, focusing not on what it really is or might be (which is legal ontology) but on the methods by which we know what law is. This is trickier than it may first appear, because law is the sum of so many different things, and to perceive law at once as a complicated enterprise and also as a host of ideas isn't all that easy. Thus, there are many statements of legal epistemology, but no one perfect, agreed theory of how we know what law is. Among the theories, one of the most important is H.L.A. Hart's view that the law is best understood by looking at the same moment at law both from an internal point of view (that of a lawyer, essentially) and an external point of view (that of a crook).

**ontology of law (legal ontology)**  What the law truly is. The ontology of law is what the law in fact is, regardless of what it is believed to be by lawyers or others. There are many theories of legal ontology that are fiercely argued among scholars. Positivists argue law is a system of rules. Interpretivists argue law is a system of interpretative arguments. Naturalists argue law is an apparatus for reflecting moral norms in legal rules. Realists and sociologists argue that law is a system of behaviors carried on by officials and influencing cultural behaviors. One theory that synthesizes these approaches is that law is a combination of an archive and a culture: an archive in which rules were once articulated and statements made in the past regarding the law have been recorded, and a professional legal culture in which consultation of the archive is performed according to current understandings and expectations of the appropriate means for doing so, appropriate values to be promoted, and appropriate integration of the expectations for law held by the polity into the culture of legal regulation of social action.

**bad-man concept of law (bad man theory)**  Law is nothing more than what officials enforce. The "bad man" concept of law is a viewpoint that allows a useful description of a set of laws that effectively govern the actions of citizens, it was first presented in Justice Holmes speech dedicating a wing of Boston University Law School. By this viewpoint, the law is what makes a person do something, through its coercive power and not through moral or ideal guidance. This viewpoint focuses only on that part of the law that resembles what positivists would call primary rules, as well as the realist notion of law as what officials do in fact: both theories were influenced by the "bad man" idea. Holmes's concept, however, was never meant to be a comprehensive definition of the law. It is merely a concept by an outsider that illuminates a view of the law besides the perception of the insider, the person, like a judge or legislator or lawyer, who knows how the law works and what its goals are.

**uniform law**   Statutes enacted in identical language in each of the various jurisdictions. The uniform laws are model statutes, in nearly all cases drafted by the Uniform Laws Commissioners as model legislation for consideration by and legislative enactment in the various states. Uniform laws include the Uniform Commercial Code as well as the Model Penal Code.

Uniform laws are to legislation somewhat like the Restatements of the Law are to judicial common law. Both are national law reform projects, yet the uniform laws are drafted for the purpose of creating a common body of statutory law among the states, while the restatements are more likely to influence the rulings of judges in the state and federal courts, creating greater national uniformity by providing a national template for the agreement of laws in each jurisdiction.

**unwritten law (lex non scripta or lex non scripta regni angliae)**   Law derived from practice, legal culture, and custom. The unwritten law is the result in law derived from the practice of lawyers and officials, the general understanding and oral tradition of the lawyers and officials, and the customs of the those whose behavior is considered by officials and citizens to be an acceptable example of obedience to the law. When the common law was considered to be a judicial recognition of the customs already adopted by the people, the term properly described the common law, although in an era in which this understanding of the common law is less certain and in which a great many judicial opinions are written, "unwritten law" is less frequently used as to depict common law.

Much of the practice and culture of the law, and much more of the standards of law, remains unwritten. Although very rarely acknowledged in the United States, the effect of customs, of unwritten policies and practices, and of cultural expectation among the participants inform not only the procedures but the substance and interpretation of law in practically every courthouse and hearing room in the land. These practices form an official culture that is as essential to the law and defining of law as is the written law in its archive.

*See also:* law.

**written law (lex scripta)**   The law written in a recognized source of law. The written law is law written in a constitution, treaty, statute, case opinion, regulation, order, or other writing from a source recognized by the law as an appropriate source of law. Written law is often juxtaposed with the unwritten law. Or, as considered in this book, written law represents an archive of the law that is made meaningful in people's lives through interpretation according to the professional culture, which is the province of unwritten law.

*See also:* law.

**lawbook**   Any text related to the law that would be read by a professional or scholarly lawyer. Lawbook is a very general term including books that contain specific written sources of law, such as constitutions, statutes, case reporters, and rulebooks, but also legal treatises and commentaries, legal dictionaries and encyclopedias, form books and pattern jury instruction, bibliographic tool such as digests and citators, and even legal biographies. The most important lawbooks for students have long been hornbooks and casebooks.

In the early twenty–first century, the meaning of lawbook is in transition. As electronic platforms for books develop, the idea of the lawbook is evolving. The term "lawbook" may become more an archaic description of older texts, or, it may be revived to describe distinct units of text in a more porous textual environment.

**abridgment**   A book summarizing cases or elements of a longer work. Abridgments, as lawbooks, were collections of summaries from cases and arguments, rather like the modern digest. Abridgments in this form are now rare.

The sense of abridgment as a text from which text is edited or redacted to present a shorter (or less provocative) text is a more general idea of abridgment, and the two ideas are sometimes confused with one another.

**casebook**   A student text including case opinions and scholarly comments on a given legal topic. The casebook is the dominant form of lawbook used in classroom teaching in U.S. law schools. The casebook in its modern form arose from the bound case collections of the nineteenth century, refined by Christopher Columbus Langdell and James Barr Ames. The casebook as usually employed in the early twentieth century is a collection of cases arranged by topic, with editorial introductions to the topic and with the cases followed by questions intended to spur students to understand the principals of the case in new circumstances, as well as by annotations of other cases and excerpts from articles. The casebook is essential to the case method of instruction.

The audience for casebooks are students. Surveys suggest that most students mistake the purpose of the casebook as being only to locate a holding in each case, treating it as a rule, and they may see the casebook as an unnecessarily difficult rulebook. The intended purpose of the casebook is to encourage the student to examine the facts of the case and the reasoning in the various arguments that arose from those facts, to understand how and why the court ruled as it did, consider alternatives, and to judge among the alternatives which was the best outcome or best methodology of decision and how best would be assessed in a given situation. This purpose is rarely explained by the teachers and even more rarely pursued by the students.

*See also:* law, law school, legal pedagogy, case method (casebook method or socratic method).

**hornbook** A student treatise. A hornbook is a treatise that is written with a particular focus on the explanation of basic questions of the law, for the use of law students. Many contemporary hornbooks are actually student editions of longer treatises, although the traditional approach to a hornbook was not merely to chop up a more sophisticated work but to address the essential areas of a field with great clarity.

**Institute** A summary of the law. An Institute, or a volume of Institutes, is a customary name for a summary of a body of knowledge, and an institute in law is customary name for a summary or foundational depiction of the essential principles of Law. When no other context is given, a reference to the Institutes usually refers to the Institutes of Justinian, the summary volume of the Corpus Juris, written in the early sixth century.

*See also:* Roman law, corpus juris civilis.

**pocket part** An insert into a book that updates its content. A pocket part is a booklet that is written to incorporate new matter, usually citations and ideas from new cases, statutes, and scholarship, that affects the statements of law in a lawbook, or otherwise updates a reference book. The pocket part is usually published by the publisher of the original book and distributed as a subscription service to the buyers of the original book. This practice is becoming less prevalent in the age of digital references.

**reporter (case reports or case reporter or report)** A collection of judicial opinions from specific courts. A reporter is a lawbook containing the opinions issued by the judges or justices of a particular court or courts, printed and bound, usually in chronological order. The Federal Reports are actually one book of many volumes, a case reporter, or series of reports. Reporters are either official or unofficial, or sometimes both. A reporter authorized by the Court or published by the government is official. A reporter that is privately published is unofficial. Some courts and governments have authorized private publishers to act as the official reporter for a court of a jurisdiction. In general, reports from either official or unofficial reports are accepted as authoritative by courts. An increasing trend of state courts is not to publish opinions in reporters but to publish the opinions on-line, although unofficial reporters may continue to publish the opinions. A case opinion not published in a reporter is an unpublished opinion.

**treatise (commentary)** A thorough analysis of a field of the law. A treatise presents a field of the law, detailing its principles and rules, illustrating the application of those principles and rules to specific factual disputes and problems, and raising difficulties or arguments among different problems within the field while resolving these problems, along with a rationale justifying the resolutions endorsed. A treatise may take many names, usually either a commentary, treatise, or sometimes and institute. Treatises were once monographs, single volumes, which were written by a single author, who selected matters from within the field for analysis. Contemporary treatises may comprise many volumes in an effort to be thorough and to present many perspectives on each disputed question.

Treatises are usually treated in the United States as secondary materials, a source of ideas of the law without a special authority over an official. Even so, judges and officials frequently rely on treatises as a sources of ideas and as a basis for selecting among competing ideas in the law. In international law and in the laws of many other countries, treatises are considered an appropriate source of law without such reservations.

Note: the learned treatise rule, or the learned treatise exception to the hearsay rule, applies to any statement made by an authoritative author or source in any published material, including articles and books other than what would be, technically, a treatise.

*See also:* hearsay, hearsay exception, hearsay allowed regardless of witness availability, learned treatise.

**lawful dependent or legal dependent** *See:* dependent (lawful dependent or legal dependent).

**lawfulness (lawful or unlawfulness or unlawful)** Anything not forbidden by the law. Lawfulness describes any activity or status that is not prohibited by the law. Though in the United States, it is rarely acknowledged, the nature of the prohibition may vary in the degree to which it is express or specific. There are three logical forms that lawfulness can take, which vary according to the legal culture:

Lawfulness may include all of the actions that are expressly and specifically permitted, all that is not addressed in the written law being unlawful. In this case, unless there is a clear license to do something, it is presumptively unlawful. This approach places a greater value on order than on liberty, creating a great power in the state to selectively enforce the prohibitions and a great potential for anxiety among the citizens as to when such enforcement will occur.

Lawfulness may include all that is not expressly and specifically forbidden, with only those actions or statuses that are specifically prohibited in the written law being unlawful. In this case, unless there is a clear edict forbidding something, it is presumptively lawful. This approach places a greater value on liberty than on order, creating a risk among the people that novel, dangerous or outrageous behavior will be immune from prosecution or prohibition.

Lawfulness may include all actions or statuses that are not expressly forbidden, but the actions or statuses that are prohibited may be described in the written law in more general terms; these terms must be sufficiently specific that the terms of a prohibition limit the power of officials to employ the prohibition without notice but that license all unprohibited conduct. This approach balances liberty with order, although it still creates a risk that either the individual or the official will not share a common meaning of the general terms of prohibition. The efforts to create such common meaning are inherently context-dependent, varying from factual setting to factual setting, and these are the province of the legal culture and often managed by customs and other sources of unwritten law. Examples of this management include standards of reasonableness, foreseeability, commercial necessity, and ordinary care, all of which require application and interpretation in the light of the facts in which often unwritten, cultural standards must be applied.

Thus, in any legal system there is a gap, a fuzzy space of indeterminate meaning, between what is lawful and what is unlawful, a logical space in which a given action is ambiguous. Some conduct is clearly unlawful and some is clearly lawful, and in the middle is a small arena of indeterminacy in which actions are not known to be perfectly lawful or unlawful. In different legal systems the gap may be greater or lesser, or vary according to the field of law. In the United States, this gap is theoretically greater in areas of civil liability than in criminal liability, because the rule of lenity requires (or is supposed to require) that in this gap, a person accused of a crime is entitled to a defense that the unlawfulness of the conduct is not apparent.

It should be noted that lawfulness in the United States is a matter of both criminal and civil law, with what is lawful being both what is not a criminal action and also what would not expose the actor to civil liability. In general, lawfulness in the U.S. is more a matter of not violating the criminal law. The legal cultures of other countries do not consider the idea of lawfulness in the same way, and in many, what is unlawful is more a matter of private liability, as opposed to penal liability or criminal liability.

*See also:* gap; lenity (rule of lenity); outlaw (outlawry); legal (legality).

**lawsuit**   *See:* suit (lawsuit).

**lawyer**   A licensed professional who is learned in the law. A lawyer is a member of the legal profession. Although the meaning of lawyer overlaps the meanings of legal counselor and attorney at law, each has a distinct emphasis, and lawyer is the broadest of the three terms. A person who has been licensed as a member of the bar of a jurisdiction is a lawyer and thus a member of the profession. As a result of the person's being a lawyer, the person is authorized to act as an attorney at law, that is to be the agent to represent another person's legal interests. A person might be a lawyer and never act as an attorney, but no one is authorized to be an attorney at law who is not a lawyer (though an attorney in fact is usually not a lawyer but is an agent). A legal counselor or counselor at law is a lawyer who renders legal advice to another person, and once again a lawyer (and only a lawyer) is authorized to act as a legal counselor.

*See also:* representation, legal representation (representation by counsel); attorney (attorney at law or attorney-at-law or attorneys at law); counsellor (counselor); serjeant (serjeant at law or serjeant-counter).

**lawyer malpractice**   *See:* practice, malpractice, lawyer malpractice.

**lawyer misconduct**   *See:* misconduct, attorney misconduct (lawyer misconduct).

*let's kill all the lawyers*   The first act of a tyrant will be to dispose of the lawyers. "First thing we do, let's kill all the lawyers" is a line from William Shakespeare's history play, Henry VI, Part Two, in which Shakespeare invents a dialogue between Jack Cade, whom Shakespeare depicted as a vicious, petty demagogue planning to become tyrant over England, and his henchman Dick the Butcher. Dick suggests the first act of Cade's reign must be to kill the lawyers, not only because they would struggle to unseat an illegitimate king but also because they represent learning in the acts of the state.

The line is often quoted out of context by those unfamiliar with the play, who employ the line in an attempt at humor.

**lawyer-witness**   *See:* witness, attorney-witness (lawyer-witness).

**lawyer-witness rule**   *See:* witness, attorney-witness (lawyer-witness).

**lawyer's trust account**   *See:* trust, client trust account (lawyer's trust account).

**advocate as Scots lawyer**   An attorney who is a member of the Faculty of Advocates and called to the bar of the Courts of Scotland. An advocate is a member of the College of the Faculty of Advocates, who has been admitted to practice as an advocate before the Courts of Scotland. Only an advocate may argue before Scotland's superior courts. An advocate differs from a Scots solicitor in that a solicitor generally advises clients and may represent them in the inferior courts of Scotland, while advocates are retained by solicitors to argue before all courts on a client's behalf. In this way, the Scottish advocate is similar to the British barrister. With the exception of a summons, an advocate must sign all documents filed with the court in litigation. Although advocates may not argue before English courts without being licensed in England to do so, advocates may appear before the British House of Lords, Privy Council and Parliamentary Committees.

The College of the Faculty of Advocates is similar to a state bar in the United States but is more involved in training, certification, and management of the bar. Training requirements to become an advocate are rigorous, and involve a person first completing legal curriculum sufficient to become a Scots solicitor (analogous to completing law school in the United States). A person seeking to become an advocate must complete a course of legal education and then a period of professional skills training called devilling, under a devil-master, an advocate instructor before passing a standardized test proctored by the Faculty of Advocates and completing other character and fitness requirements.

See also: lawyer, barrister.

**ambulance chaser**   A derogatory term for a lawyer, especially one who represents plaintiffs. The term "ambulance chaser" invokes an image of a lawyer actually pursuing an emergency vehicle to the hospital in order to procure the patient's business. The term's derogatory flavor suggests that ambulance chasers value their fees over the well-being of their clients and the law. The term has evolved to describe lawyers rather than their runners, and although some urban plaintiffs' lawyers did once pay runners to recruit clients from among victims of accidents, this practice is now considered a violation of professional ethics.

See also: lawyer, shyster; access to justice (access to the courts).

**barrister**   A lawyer qualified to argue in court in England and Wales. A barrister is a lawyer, particularly in England, who is authorized to argue before a court. In England and Wales, lawyers are either barristers or solicitors. Barristers are members of the Inns of Court and are those authorized to appear and argue before the court; solicitors engage in work that transactional lawyers engage in the United States and in the preparation of cases for trial. Barristers, unlike solicitors, have little to no contact with the client, and are only approached by solicitors who instruct the barrister on behalf of the client.

See also: lawyer; lawyer, advocate as Scots lawyer.

**common-law lawyer (common lawyer or admiralty lawyer or canon lawyer or civilian lawyer)**   A lawyer schooled in the tradition of the common law. A common-law lawyer is a lawyer whose professional culture is that of a bar that practices before common-law courts. In most usages, the common-law lawyer is either a term of emphasis, by which the writer seeks to remind the reader that a given idea or approach arises from a specific professional culture, technique, or aesthetic. Thus, common-law lawyers are often contrasted with the lawyers primarily trained in the law of and appearing before the bars of other courts, with different laws, methodologies, and cultures, such as the admiralty bar, the canon courts, courts martial, or the civilians (the admiralty lawyers, the canon lawyers, the military lawyers, or the civilian lawyers). Though quite localized, the practice extends to lawyers who routinely appear in specialized regulatory tribunals, especially to tax lawyers, immigration lawyers, patent lawyers, FERC lawyers, and other even more arcane bars. Such lawyers are only considered common-law lawyers at the most general and international of levels.

**junkyard dog lawyer (cowboy lawyer or Rambo lawyer)**   A lawyer whose work is unprofessional and often counterproductive. The junkyard-dog metaphor is frequently used to describe a lawyer who engages in needlessly undisciplined conduct, particularly a lawyer who employs antagonistic or unduly aggressive argument or behavior toward other attorneys, opposing parties, or witnesses. Such conduct may not only violate an attorney's obligations under the bar's disciplinary rules or the court's powers over attorneys but also expose the client to sanctions, given that the attorney is acting as the client's agent. The term "Rambo lawyer," which was once current and based on a cinematic hero who used violence to write wrongs, has long had many variant expressions for this idea.

See also: civility.

**law firm**   A business entity of lawyers to practice law. A law firm is partnership or other entity owned by lawyers that provides legal services to clients as a single entity, not merely as individual attorneys engaged in counsel and representation. Generally, no person who is not an attorney may have an ownership interest or supervisory authority over attorneys or client matters in a law firm. Law firms may employ non-lawyers, as well as lawyers on full-time or part-time bases, although the conduct of all owners and employees is relevant to the firm's interests and representation of every client. Although law firms in the United States have traditionally been partnerships and governed by partnership laws, some firms are corporations, especially limited-liability companies; many solo practitioners are, in effect, law firms as sole proprietorships.

See also: company, limited-liability company (L.L.C. or LLC).

**boutique law firm**   A law firm focused in a specialized field of law. A boutique law firm specializes in a particular arena of legal practice, rather than building a general practice providing services in nearly every field of law. The boutique firm usually focuses on niche arenas of practice that require an unusual expertise, such as patent law, or practice before a particular agency, such as the Federal Energy Regulatory Commission. Boutique firms tend to be smaller than their general counterparts, and general firms may associate boutique firms for matters in the boutique expertise, just as boutique firms may associate general firms to manage legal issues for a client beyond the boutique's expertise.

Note: although some firms consider general litigation to be a boutique practice, this is not a widely accepted usage, although it may be when limited to litigation for a particular category of clientele.

**associate**   A junior lawyer employed by a law firm or solo practitioner. An associate is a lawyer who is employed by a law firm or another lawyer, and who is designated by the employer by such a title. Not all lawyers employed by other lawyers are associates, and in most cases to designate an attorney as an associate is to offer an opportunity to pursue, eventually, a partnership with the employing firm or lawyer. Lawyers who are not considered eligible for eventual consideration for partnership are often referred to as contract lawyers, of counsel, or some similar designation.

Note: to associate a lawyer with a firm or another lawyer usually does not suggest the associated lawyer is employed by the other attorney. Rather, to associate another lawyer is to enter a joint venture with that lawyer on a given project, case, or representation.

**summer associate (summer clerk)** A law student employed in the summer by a law firm. A summer associate is a law student employed by a law firm, often in part to be considered for long-term employment and in part to perform work that might otherwise be done by young associates in the firm, under the supervision of a practicing attorney.

**counsel (of counsel or special counsel)** A lawyer with a substantial, part-time practice in a law firm. A lawyer of counsel to a law firm has an ongoing relationship with the firm but is not a member of the regular partnership. A lawyer of counsel is usually a part-time employee but is usually accorded a higher status within the firm than an associate or other employee. Taking advantage of this ambiguity, some law firms use the term "of counsel" or a variant for recently recruited attorneys, particularly those subject to some probationary aspect in their hiring. Although the particular significance of a title such as "of counsel" depends upon the employment arrangement between the attorney and the firm, unless there are indicia to the contrary, a client represented by a person of counsel to the firm may justifiably believe the client is represented by the firm itself.

**law partner** A permanent member of a law firm. A partner is a senior member of a law firm, a person who is a partner within the firm's partnership or who has an equity interest in it according to the firm's organization. A partner's interest in the firm is defined by the partnership agreement and state law as well as by the rules of professional responsibility or other laws regulating lawyers and law firms that apply to that firm. Some partners have greater managerial and supervisory responsibility than others, but in most cases, each partner is liable for claims upon the other partners in the firm. Managerial partners may be distinguished by title, such as managing partner or CEO, or by membership on a management committee or some similar body. Such partners determine firm policy and, increasingly, determine the compensation received by each partner from the firm's profits.

**rainmaker** A partner who acquires lucrative clients for the firm. A rainmaker is a person, particularly a partner, who makes the initial contact with potential clients of the firm, manages the relationship between the firm and the client, and is responsible for the client's satisfaction. Rainmakers usually enjoy significant influence within a firm.

**lawyer advertising** The advertisement of legal services directly to potential clients. Lawyer advertising includes all forms of media by which a lawyer, law firm, or legal corporation advertises itself to the general public, particularly in a manner that could be reasonably calculated to make the advertising lawyer attractive to a consumer of legal services. Lawyer advertising may be regulated by the state bars, although such regulation must be limited to the restriction of false or misleading advertisement.

**lawyer discipline (attorney discipline)** The regulation of lawyers and punishment for their misconduct. Lawyer discipline is the sum of the standards and actions of a variety of courts, bar associations, and commissions that collectively oversee the performance of lawyers in each jurisdiction, assessing complaints and levying penalties against lawyers who do not comply with the professional standards of the bar. Each court has an inherent power to discipline the attorneys who appear before it and to discipline lawyers according to the oath each takes as an officer of the court. Discipline by a court may include a sanction within a cause of action, a refusal to allow an attorney to appear, conditions on appearance, an order of civil contempt of court, or a referral for prosecution for contempt of court. Each state has a body of attorney discipline, under the jurisdiction of the state's highest court or the state's bar, which investigates and examines complaints against the conduct of individual lawyers. Discipline by such a body may include private or public warning, reprimand, or censure; suspension from the practice of law, or permanent revocation of the license to practice.

**disciplinary rule** A written standard of attorney conduct that may lead to a penalty if it is violated. A disciplinary rule is a specific statement of professional responsibility putting attorneys on notice that a failure to comply may be the basis for a disciplinary penalty. Not all discipline is based on violation of disciplinary rules, but discipline may also be based on a violation of the lawyer's oath, on rules of court and on standards of professional reasonableness. Although most states had adopted the 1908 Canons of Professional Ethics, and later adopted 1969 Model Code of Professional Responsibility, in 1983 the ABA adopted Model Rules of Professional Conduct as a successor the Model Code. As of 2011, over forty states have adopted the Model Rules of Professional Conduct in whole or in large part.

**canons of ethics (code of professional responsibility)** The basic principles of the Model Code of Professional Responsibility. The canons of ethics are the broad statement of professional requirement in the ABA Model Code of

Professional Responsibility, as it was adopted in 1969 and sometimes amended. The ABA code developed from 32 canons adopted by that association in 1908, although it was superseded in 1983 and has been replaced in many states. In those in which it remains in force, a lawyer who violates a canon of ethics is liable for discipline before the supervisory authority for lawyer in that jurisdiction, usually the state bar.

**oath as basis of discipline** The oath places every attorney on notice of the rules and general duties of office. The oath of an attorney serves not only as notice that the attorney will be held to the more specific rules of conduct required to practice law but also as the attorney's personal commitment to carry out the office of attorney, including the obligations of fidelity that this office entails. A violation of the oath, by any specific failure of the general duty owed to an attorney's client, to a court, to another attorney, or to a member of the public is sufficient basis for a court or bar to sanction the attorney as appropriate. The authority to wield such sanctions cannot be used, however, merely to bar an attorney from presenting unpopular arguments or from challenging the status quo, which are protected by the constitutional rights of speech and due process of law.

*See also:* oath, oath of attorney (attorney oath).

**rules of professional conduct** The ABA Model Rules of Professional Conduct is a code of fifty-one rules of the minimum standards of conduct for a lawyer. The MRPC was promulgated by the ABA in 1983 and has been adopted by most states as the stated basis for attorney discipline.

**disbarment (debar disbar)** Involuntary loss of the privilege of practicing law. Disbarment is a disciplinary action in which an attorney loses the license to practice law, usually as the result of a breach of ethics. All disbarments are presumed to be final, although the the rules of a given jurisdiction may allow a disbarred attorney to petition for readmission after a period of time has elapsed.

A judge may refuse to admit a lawyer to practice before a particular court or withdraw admission, and as long as the lawyer is admitted by the courts of a state, the lawyer is not considered disbarred. Further, a suspension for a limited time is not considered disbarment, even though a disbarred attorney may petition the bar or a state's highest court for reinstatement. In some jurisdictions, an attorney facing a disciplinary proceeding may surrender the license to practice law, which also is not considered a disbarment, although it has the same practical effect.

**letter of censure** The mildest discipline imposed for attorney misconduct. A letter of censure is a penalty that may be issued by the disciplinary body of a state's bar. The letter has no further penalty than serving to shame the attorney, although it is likely that the issuance of a letter of censure will influence for the worse any later complaints against the same lawyer. A letter of censure may be public or confidential, according to the rules governing a bar's disciplinary procedures and the choice of the disciplinary body.

**surrender of law license** A voluntary renunciation of the license to practice law. The surrender of a law license is a means by which a lawyer may volunteer to accept a sanction for a serious misdeed rather than to be disbarred. An offer to surrender one's license may be refused for good cause. A surrender of one's license is absolute, and there is no presumption or assurance that the license to practice will ever be restored. Still, as a practical matter, if a lawyer has acted badly the acceptance of responsibility manifest in voluntary surrender of the license is preferable to an order of disbarment and is more likely to lead eventually to a restoration of the license to practice.

**suspension** A penalty for lawyer's misconduct by barring practice for a period of time. A suspension from the practice of law is a sanction that may be imposed by a bar's disciplinary body for an attorney's misconduct, according to which the attorney is forbidden to engage in the practice of law for a period of time. An attorney who engages in the practice of law while suspended separately and distinctly engages in misconduct and is liable for a new penalty. A period of suspension may end with the lawyer's restoration of privileges or with a requirement that the lawyer petition for reinstatement, sometimes following the successful completion of an ethics exam or other condition on restoration to practice.

*See also:* suspension (suspend).

**lawyer up (lawyering up or lawyered up)** To engage legal counsel. To lawyer up is a slang expression for the preparation to retain or the actual retention of an attorney or legal team by an individual or entity, particularly in the expectation of a criminal investigation or indictment or intense civil litigation, or sometimes other inquiries.

**legal advice (advice of counsel)** A lawyer's opinion to a client regarding the law or a legal obligation. Legal advice is advice given by a lawyer to any person who is likely to rely upon it regarding the law or an obligation under the law. A lawyer giving legal advice has a duty of good faith and reasonable investigation to conduct such research and investigation as to justify reliance on the lawyer's opinion. Legal advice does not depend upon receipt of compensation, and a lawyer giving legal advice pro bono has the same responsibility in giving such advice as a lawyer who has been retained for the purpose. A person who relies on legal advice is not excused from liability in the event the advice is wrong, although such reliance may negate an intent to violate the law in the act committed in reliance on the advice.

In general, the advice given by a lawyer to a client is legal advice. As a matter of usage, the advice relied upon by the client is usually termed "advice of counsel," but there is otherwise no difference.

*See also:* lawyer, legal opinion (opinion of counsel).

**advice-of-counsel defense** A defendant lacks unlawful intent acting in reliance on prior legal advice. The advice-of-counsel-defense is an affirmative defense to certain criminal charges and administrative claims, as well as to claims of willful conduct in some civil actions, according to which a defendant argues that the defendant only engaged in the acts complained of after receiving legal advice that the acts were lawful or harmless, and accordingly the defendant had no intent to perform an unlawful or harmful act. A defendant may only claim reliance of advice of counsel when the reliance is made reasonably and in good faith, which is not possible if the advice is patently false or unreliable. One effect of asserting a defense of advice of counsel is that the defendant waives attorney-client privilege on all communications related to that advice.

Advice of counsel is similar to entrapment by estoppel, but still quite different. Advice of counsel arises from reliance on one's own lawyer; entrapment by estoppel arises from reliance on a government official who is not one's private lawyer.

*See also:* ignorance, ignorance of law (ignorance of the law); entrapment, entrapment by estoppel (EBE or E.B.E.).

**legal aid** An attorney provided at little or no cost to an indigent person. Legal aid is a broad term for a variety of public and charitable means for providing legal services to economically disadvantaged individuals who require an attorney, particularly for criminal defense. Legal aid in its narrowest sense refers to charitable assistance by lawyers who work for a non-profit, private, partially government-funded entity, the most famous of which is The Legal Aid Society in New York. Less technically, the use of the term legal aid may include counsel by a public defender, legal assistance from pro bono attorneys, from legal resource centers, from law school clinics, and minimally compensated, court-appointed counsel from the bar.

**Legal Services Corporation (LSC)** A federal agency to assist indigents seeking justice in civil litigation. The Legal Services Corporation is a federal agency that funds a variety of programs to provide legal assistance in civil litigation and related matters to the economically disadvantaged individuals. Though conceived of as an agency that would assist individuals to seek equal access to justice regardless of poverty, the agency's mission has been limited from some representation, including limitations of actions on behalf of immigrants, in class actions, and for the reform of public institutions or regulation.

**public defender** A state criminal defense attorney who defends indigents. A public defender is an attorney employed by the state to represent any economically disadvantaged individual who is accused of a crime but has no lawyer and cannot afford one. A public defender is roughly the equivalent for defense (at least for the poor) of the public prosecutor.

*See also:* public.

**legal opinion (opinion of counsel)** A lawyer's statement of legal advice. A legal opinion is the analysis provided by a lawyer with the expectation that others will rely upon it, usually in a written form and presented from a lawyer to a client, from a firm to a client, or from a government agency to a person or entity regulated or affected by the regulations of that agency.

*See also:* lawyer, legal advice (advice of counsel).

**legal practice (practice of law)** Legal advice or representation intended for the reliance of others. Legal practice, or the practice of law, includes all of the activities customarily associated with work of a professional lawyer. In the United States, this work includes advising clients regarding transactions, the legal status of their various affairs; the creation of instruments such as contracts, trusts, deeds, and wills; the negotiation for and representation of clients in private matters; representation of clients in civil and criminal litigation; the execution of professional responsibilities of self-education and training; public service; development of the profession; and promotion and protection of the ideals of the law and the legal profession. Essential to understanding legal practice in the United States is that the bar is not divided between a group of advisers and litigators, even though many lawyers specialize in one or another arena of practice. Legal practice also includes the managerial and practical support required to provide services to clients and to manage the office in conformity to the law.

Note: practice was once a term confined to the appearance of a lawyer in court, embracing fields now thought of as pre-trial practice, trial practice, and appellate practice, as well as civil and criminal procedure, federal courts or jurisdiction, conflicts of law, evidence, remedies, equity, and professional responsibility.

**sharp practice** Conduct at the edge of the law or legal ethics. Sharp practice is conduct, by anyone but particularly by an attorney, that borders on what is forbidden. Examples include, but are not limited to, the filing of complaints and of answers that lack merit, failing to produce evidence properly sought in discovery, failing to assist the court in the discovery of witnesses and evidence, performing needless work to bill one's clients and annoy one's opponents, allowing the secretion of assets to avoid judgment, bullying witnesses and opposing counsel, and generally behaving without regard for the requirements of justice. Sharp practice may or may not be misconduct, and the term is usually not employed for conduct that breaks the law outright, but it is improper and contrary to the interests of the law and the profession. Attorneys should refrain from such practices and should not condone the actions of attorneys who engage in them.

**mouthpiece**   A slang term for a lawyer. Mouthpiece is a vulgar term for a lawyer, implying that the lawyer presents the thoughts and words of the client to others.

**newbie (baby lawyer or greenhorn)**   A lawyer who has recently joined a practice or passed the bar. Newbies, or baby lawyers, like many recent members of a profession, are often the butt of considerable humor in law offices. Many suffer from the belief that they possess greater skill and knowledge than can be observed by others. The baby lawyer is often alluded to with the reference, the ink isn't dry on the law license. Despite their inexperience, newbies are presumed to be able to perform all of the functions of a lawyer not requiring specific and additional licensure. However, a court may determine sua sponte that a lawyer certain lacking certain experience may not engage in some representation without jeopardizing the rights of the client or, in criminal matters, violating the due process of law. This is particularly the case in criminal matters involving a potential sentence of death or in fiduciary relationships involving the management of funds or life-altering decisions.

**shyster**   A lawyer who takes advantage of the client. A shyster is a dishonest lawyer, particularly a lawyer who promotes the lawyer's interests over the client's interests.

**solicitor**   A lawyer whose primary task is to advise clients rather than appear in court. A solicitor, in legal systems on the British models, is a lawyer with a practice devoted to the management of clients' affairs, including the planning and drafting of contracts, wills, partnerships, corporate charters and documents, trusts, and other instruments, as well as in managing client affairs. A solicitor is not, however, usually required to appear in court to argue a cause for a client, that being the function of a barrister. In England and Wales, the training, selection, and qualification of solicitors is the province of the Law Society.

**unauthorized practice of law (unlicensed practitioner)**   The practice of law by a person who is not a lawyer licensed to do so. The unauthorized practice of law is the performance of acts or duties that are restricted to members of the legal profession. It is a crime, as well as a basis for contempt of court and a basis for civil action by a person who unknowingly relies on legal advice or representation by someone unqualified to give it. Unauthorized practice includes, first, the provision of legal advice to a person with an expectation that the person will rely on it, second, the representation of another person in a court of law or equity, and, third, the provision of any service that requires specialized skill or knowledge in the law that is customarily performed by lawyers. There are, however, exceptions to these definitions in most jurisdictions. The provision of legal services on which another may rely is forbidden in some states only if the unlicensed adviser receives or expects in return for the advice to receive money or any thing of value. The representation of another is usually allowed for a person pro se who represents a minor family member in the same cause. And, certain services may be allowed by specialists who are independently licensed to perform such services according to statutes.

**lay (layperson or layman or laymen)**   A person who is not a member of a profession or holder of expertise. A layperson is a person who is of lay skills, that is of ordinary qualifications and skills, rather than a holder of special qualification, expertise, or professional standing. The term comes from the term for any person not in holy orders, those in orders being members of the clergy of the church and all others being members of the laity, or lay members. In older U.S. legal writings, the laymen are the jurors or the citizenry.

In contemporary usage, whomever is considered lay is a person who lacks a particular professional or expert relationship to the matter at hand. A lay witness is not an expert witness. In court a layperson is not a lawyer. In any given context regarding a profession, a layperson is not a member of that profession.

*See also:* jury (juror).

**lay a foundation or laying a foundation or foundation for evidence**   *See:* foundation (lay a foundation or laying a foundation or foundation for evidence).

**lay judge**   *See:* judge, lay judge.

**lay opinion**   *See:* opinion, lay opinion.

**lay witness**   *See:* witness, lay witness.

**laity**   Members of a church who are not the clergy. The laity, or the lay people, are the members of a Christian church who are not ordained as members of the clergy. The laity were excluded from the jurisdiction of church courts on many matters, which remains the case except in matters solely of significance in the church. An individual is presumed to be a layperson, unless the person has been ordained or otherwise received as a member of a church's ministerial rank. In the common law, a layperson was not entitled to benefit of clergy.

In the more general sense of a layperson not being a member of any group with arcane knowledge or profession, the use of "laity" includes all non-members.

*See also:* clergy, benefit of clergy.

**LBO** *See:* buyout, corporate buyout, leveraged buyout (LBO).

**LC or L.C.** *See:* credit, letter of credit (LC or L.C.).

**LDF** *See:* civil rights, civil rights organization, National Association for the Advancement of Colored People, NAACP Legal Defence Fund (LDF).

**lead (pb)** A toxic metal that often contaminates water, air, and other substances. Lead is the metallic element with an atomic number of 82, which is used in many materials owing to its density, malleability, appearance, chemical properties, and electrical properties. It is toxic and produces many harmful effects in the human body. It may be carried by air, water, or solids, including concentrations absorbed in meat and vegetative foods. It is a criteria pollutant under the Clean Water Act.

*See also:* pollution, air pollution, criteria pollutants, lead.

**leading case** *See:* precedent, leading case.

**leading case or landmark opinion or landmark decision** *See:* precedent, landmark case (leading case or landmark opinion or landmark decision).

**leading question** *See:* question, leading question.

**league (international league)** An agreement and the states that have entered it. A league, as a matter of international law, is both an agreement to act in concert toward some end — such as a treaty or covenant establishing an organization, alliance, or trading bloc — and the states party to it. The League of Nations of the early twentieth centuries, the Hanseatic League of the middle ages, and the Peloponnesian League of ancient Greece are examples. From this sense, all sorts of leagues, including sports leagues, arise.

**leapfrog development** *See:* development, leapfrog development.

**Learned Hand test or Hand rule** *See:* negligence, Hand formula (Learned Hand test or Hand rule).

**learned treatise** *See:* hearsay, hearsay exception, hearsay allowed regardless of witness availability, learned treatise.

**lease** An agreement to rent property. A lease is a contract by which one party who owns some specific property allows another party to possess it for a time, usually in return for the payment of rents or performance of services, until the end of the time of the lease, when the party owning the property retakes its possession. A lease may be of an interest in real or personal property. A lease may be of a portion of land, including only a mineral interest or even a portion of a mineral interest. A lease creates both a privity of contract and privity of estate between the landlord (or lessor) and the tenant (or lessee).

*See also:* tenancy; tenant, tenant as lessee; rent, abatement of rent (rent abatement).

**lease term** *See:* term, term of estate (lease term).

**assignable lease (non-assignable lease or unassignable lease)** A lease that has no clause barring assignment. An assignable lease is a lease that may be freely assigned to another party, who will then stand fully in the shoes of the assigning party, holding the whole of the benefits and duties under the lease for the remainder of its time in force. A leasehold is presumed to be assignable, and unless the contract between the parties prohibits assignment, either the tenant or the landlord may assign that party's interest in the lease. If the lease contract bars assignment to both parties, the lease is non-assignable.

Although in most cases, the question of assignability is in fact the question of whether the tenant may assign a lease, the same is true of landlords, and a lease is an assignable lease if it may be assigned by the landlord as well as if it may be assigned by a tenant. Some jurisdictions require that a covenant allowing one party to a contract be reciprocal and will imply a power of assignment to a tenant if the landlord has reserved a power of assignment.

*See also:* assignment, assignment as assignment of rights and duties.

**assignment of lease** A lessee's transfer of rights and duties to a successor lessee. An assignment of a lease is the assignment by a tenant of all of the rights and duties of a lease to a new tenant. The new tenant takes the lease as it was for the old, with no change in terms, and holds it until the end of the lease, with the same rights then as the original tenant would have had. Although the lease can provide that there is no assignment or that the tenant can freely assign, an assignment is presumptively made only with the consent of the landlord. Once an assignment is given consent by the landlord and the transfer of the lease effected, the old tenant ceases to have any rights or duties in the assigned lease. Note: an assignment differs from a sublease in that the subtenant has duties only to the tenant and not to the landlord, while an assignee has duties directly to the landlord.

*See also:* lease, sublease (sublessee or subtenant).

**commercial lease** A lease of property as a place for commerce by the tenant. A commercial lease permits the tenant to use the leased property for a commercial purpose, such as as an office facility, restaurant, retail store or supply-chain facility, manufacturing facility, or transport management facility. By its nature, a commercial lease may require greater specificity for the use of property than would a residential or agricultural lease.

**durable lease** A very long-term lease. A durable lease is a lease of real property for a period from twenty to ninety-nine years. In some jurisdictions, leases for longer periods are enforceable, and a lease of a century or more is certainly a durable lease. The rents for a durable lease are usually paid annually.

Note: a lease of durable goods is not a durable lease; a durable lease is a lease in realty.

**duty to provide security**  A landlord may be bound to a promise to provide security over a leasehold. A landlord is not considered to have a distinct obligation to provide security as a part of the property interests created in a lease. Even so, a contract that specifies or implies that the landlord will provide security is enforceable. Further, under conditions in which a recurrent failure to provide security amounts to a breach of a covenant of quiet enjoyment or to constructive eviction, then the failure to provide security may be actionable for those reasons (not as a duty distinct from the duties not to evict or to allow quiet enjoyment).

**ground lease**  A lease of lands on which the tenant holds or erects a building. A ground lease is a lease of lands on which the tenant has or constructs improvements, all of which revert to the landlord at the expiration of the lease. A ground lease is usually for a period of years, and if the lease includes a term of at least fifteen years, as well as rights in the tenant to purchase the land and of assignment, the rents may be deductible in the manner that mortgage payments are deductible.

**lease covenant**

**covenant for quiet enjoyment**  Landlord must ensure the tenant may use the property without interference. The covenant for quiet enjoyment in a lease is an assurance that the landlord will protect the tenant from superior claimants to title who might attempt to oust the landlord and so oust the tenant. As the courts of most jurisdictions have construed the covenant, the covenant includes an assurance by the landlord that neither the landlord nor other tenants will interfere with the tenant's actual use and quiet enjoyment of the leasehold. A failure of the landlord to ensure that the structure itself and the uses of the structure or grounds by the landlord or other tenants that sufficiently interferes with the use of the tenant that the tenant is effectively unable to use the premises as contemplated in the lease thus breaches this covenant, giving rise to an action of constructive eviction. The covenant for quiet enjoyment is similar to the much more narrowly interpreted covenant for quiet enjoyment in a warranty deed, although the deed does not reach the conduct of the landlord or other tenants.

*See also:* covenant, covenant of title, covenant of quiet enjoyment (covenant for quiet enjoyment or warranty of quiet enjoyment or general warranty); eviction, constructive eviction.

**covenant of habitability**  *See:* habitability (warranty of habitability or implied covenant of habitability).

**lease–purchase agreement**  An agreement to lease with an option or commitment of the tenant to purchase. A lease–purchase agreement is a lease that amounts also to a contract to purchase the property leased. A lease–purchase may be made regarding real property or chattels. Lease–purchase agreements include a variety of structures, some closely resembling installment purchase agreements, the difference being that in an installment purchase agreement, the buyer is the owner from the start of possession (though the seller may have a lien on the property until the debt is finally paid), but in a lease–purchase agreement, the seller is the owner of the property from the start of possession, with the buyer having a tenancy (or in the case of a chattel, a license). Although a contract for lease including an option to purchase after some number of payments may be described as a lease–purchase agreement, more technically it is a lease with an option to buy because the tenant has not committed to the purchase, and under most circumstances, the seller may not consider the purchase as an accounting asset until the option is exercised.

**leasehold (non-freehold estate or nonfreehold estate)**  The property rights of a lease in lands. A leasehold is a property estate created by a lease. The lease creates both contractual interests and a property interest, or leasehold. Certain aspects of the leasehold may be limited by contract, but the presumption in the law is that the interests of the lessee and lessor in the leasehold are protected unless the contract clearly and unambiguously alters them. And, the language of lease agreements ordinarily incorporates not only the definitions of leaseholds but also the conditions that distinguish the leasehold created in a given lease — a tenancy at will, a periodic tenancy (such as from day to day, week to week, month to month, or year to year), or a tenancy for a term of years (including a durable tenancy).

In the classifications of property, a leasehold is a possessory, nonfreehold estate, which is sometimes considered a chattel real. The thing owned is a right in lands that exists for the life of the lease, rather than ownership of the lands themselves.

*See also:* rent (renter); tenement.

**American rule of leasehold**  The lease transfers only a right to possession, not possession. The American rule of a leasehold provides a landlord gives a right to enter the property that is unencumbered by any claim superior to the landlord. This means that the landlord has no duty to ensure the tenant will be able to take possession of the premises, if squatters, holdover tenants, or other third parties interfere with possession. Under the American rule, the tenant must evict third parties interfering with the tenant's possession. This is the minority approach among U.S. jurisdictions.

**English rule of leasehold**  The landlord must give the tenant actual possession of the leased premises. The English rule as to leaseholds requires the landlord to give the tenant actual possession, not merely a right to possess the leased premises. Thus, under the English rule, the landlord is obligated to evict third parties, including holdover tenants, squatters, or trespassers from the property subject to lease. The rule is dates at least from Coe v. Clay, 5 Bing. 440, 130 Eng. Rep. 1131 (1829), although it is probably much older.

**leasehold interest**   A property interest in a leasehold, compensable in the event of a taking. A leasehold interest is either a leasehold or a portion of a leasehold, which is a property interest in the tenant for the purposes of the takings clause. Thus, if a government takes a leasehold for a public purpose, the value of the leasehold must be compensated to the tenant. The landlord would be entitled to compensation owing to the taking of the ownership interest, even if it is only reversionary during the life of the leasehold.

**periodic tenancy**   A leasehold for a period of time that repeats until terminated. A periodic tenancy runs for an indefinite time according to periods. Each period—a week, a month, a quarter, a year, or some other recurring period of time—establishes the term of the leasehold. Thus, for example, a month–to–month lease has a period of one month. Each lease is extended by another period if the lease is not terminated by notice. Notice is effective, at common law, at the end of the complete period following notice being given, although this period of notice has been abbreviated in many jurisdictions by statute.

*See also:* period (periodic).

**month-to-month tenancy (monthly lease or month to month lease)**   A leasehold for a month, followed by a month, and so on until terminated. A month–to–month tenancy is a periodic tenancy that runs for an indefinite time according to periods, so that each period of a month establishes the term of the leasehold, which each month is extended by another month if the lease is not terminated by notice. Unless a date is specified in the lease, the month commences on the date the leasehold comes into existence, so a month in a lease commencing on March 15 runs through April 14. Notice is effective, at common law, at the end of the complete month following notice being given. Thus, under the common-law rule, for a month-to-month leasehold commencing on March 15, a notice given on April 20 would end the lease at the end of the day on June 14 (not in May because a whole term would not have run from the time of notice). This period of notice has been abbreviated in many jurisdictions by statute to allow a month-to-month lease to terminate at various times, ranging from thirty days prior to the end of the next

period to two weeks prior. Thus, if either the landlord or the tenant attempts to end a lease, each must give the other notice of that intent prior to the time of notice, or the lease continues for another full period or until the statutory time for notice has run.

**quarter-to-quarter tenancy (quarterly lease)**   A leasehold for three months, followed by another three months, and so on, until terminated. A quarter–to–quarter tenancy is a periodic tenancy that runs for an indefinite time according to quarters of the year, so that each period of three months establishes the term of the leasehold, which each quarter is extended by another quarter if the lease is not terminated by notice. Unless a date is specified in the lease, the quarter commences on the date the leasehold comes into existence, so a lease commencing on March 15 runs through the end of June 14 of the same year. Notice is effective, at common law, at the end of the complete quarter following notice being given, although this period of notice has been abbreviated in many jurisdictions by statute to allow a quarterly lease to terminate at various times, usually with one month's notice.

**week-to-week tenancy**   A leasehold for one week, followed by another week, and so on, until terminated. A week–to–week tenancy is a periodic tenancy that runs for an indefinite time according to weeks, so that each period of seven days establishes the term of the leasehold, which each week is extended by another week if the lease is not terminated by notice. Unless a day of the week is specified in the lease, the week commences on Sunday, although rents due on a weekly basis may also establish the day on which the week begins or ends; in all cases a week is of seven days (not five). Notice is effective, at common law, at the end of the complete week following notice being given. Thus for a weekly lease that begins on a Sunday, a notice on a Monday is effective at the end of the following week, at the end of Sunday the thirteenth day following notice. Although this period of notice has been altered in many jurisdictions by statute, and in some cases specified at seven days or ten days.

**year-to-year tenancy (yearly lease or annual lease or year to year tenancy)**   A leasehold for a year, followed by a year, and so on, until terminated. A year–to–year tenancy is a periodic tenancy that runs for an indefinite time according to periods, so that each period of a year establishes the term of the leasehold, which each year is extended by another year if the lease is not terminated by notice. Unless a date is specified in the lease, the year commences on the date the leasehold comes into existence, so a lease commencing on March 15 runs through the following year's March 14. Notice is effective, at common law, at the end of the complete year following notice being given, although this period of notice has been abbreviated in many jurisdictions by statute to allow a year-to-year lease to terminate at various times, ranging from six months prior to the end of the next period to sixty days prior. Thus, if either the landlord or the tenant attempts to end a lease, each must give the other notice of that intent prior to the time of notice, or the lease continues for another full year or until the statutory time for notice has run.

**tenancy at sufferance**   A tenancy unprotected by law and subject to eviction. A tenancy by sufferance is a leasehold that is created not by agreement of the parties in a lease but by the unilateral act of the tenant, nearly always in holding over in possession of the property after the termination of a prior leasehold. Not all possession amounts to a tenancy at sufferance, and a mere trespasser or squatter does not amount to a tenant at sufferance; the difference is that the tenant at sufferance must have come into possession by lawful means but not lawfully retain possession. The landlord may elect to treat a tenant at sufferance either as a tenant for a new term or as a trespasser. The landlord's failure to act at all allows the tenant by sufferance to continue. The landlord's first acceptance of new rent or action in any manner that would create a reasonable understanding that the tenant will be treated as a tenant in the future gives rise to a new periodic tenancy. The landlord's notice of intent to evict or action in self-help for eviction amounts to election to treat as a trespasser. Once any action that amounts to election is made by the landlord, the landlord is usually estopped from altering that treatment of the tenant without the tenant's consent.

*See also:* remedies, election of remedies (election of plaintiff or election of actions or several-remedies rule); tenancy; eviction (evict).

**tenancy at will (at-will tenancy)**   A leasehold that may be terminated at any time. A tenancy at will is a leasehold established between the landlord and the tenant with no fixed period or structure of periods, which may be terminated by either the tenant or the landlord at any time. A tenancy at will does not imply an absence of an obligation by either the landlord or tenant to abide by the customary obligations of a tenancy, including the payment of rents for the time that the lease is in force. Though at common law a tenancy at will required no notice to terminate, most jurisdictions now require a minimal notice, usually of at least a week if the tenancy has been of a month or more prior to termination.

A tenancy at will arises by operation of law from lease for a term of years or a lease by a periodic tenancy that is invalid for any reason, yet according to which a tenant still takes or retains possession of the premises. A lease that specifies that it may be terminated at will (or without notice) by only one party and not the other will be interpreted to be terminable at will by both parties. Note: this requirement of mutual powers to terminate a tenancy at will is not to be confused with the unilateral right of a landlord to evict a tenant for breach of the lease or the unilateral right or a tenant to vacate owing to breach of the covenant of quiet enjoyment or some similar obligation by the landlord.

*See also:* tenancy; will, at will.

**tenancy of years (tenancy for years or tenancy for a definite term or term of years or term for years)**   A leasehold for a specific period of time, which ends at that time. A tenancy for years is any tenancy that runs for a time certain from the commencement of the leasehold, whether the time is designated by a date in the future or by the lapse of a specific period from its commencement. At common law, no notice is required to terminate such a tenancy because the notice is implied in the initial duration. Many jurisdictions have altered the tenancy for years, if longer than a year, to allow it to be terminated by notice given a specified time or more, prior to the original end of the term. A tenant who holds over at the end of the period was treated by the landlord either as entering a new tenancy for a period (equal either to the original term of years or the periods defined by payments of rents) or as a tenant by sufferance.

**let (letting)**   To lease a property. To let is to lease a property, whether as landlord or as tenant. The distinction between the letting of realty and the hiring of chattels was once common in the United States but is now rare. It persists in British usage.

**mineral lease (hydrocarbon lease or oil lease or gas lease)**   A lease of the subsurface minerals in a parcel of land. A mineral lease is a leasehold in the mineral assets of a parcel of land, which separates the mineral estate from the freehold of the surface estate. For the time that the leasehold is in force, the mineral lessee has the right to exploit the minerals as well as an easement over the surface estate to gain access to the minerals. A mineral lease may be unrestricted as to the mineral, in which case it includes all minerals and may be accessed by well or by mine. Most mineral leases are specific as to the mineral and the means of access, such as a gas lease, gas or oil lease, or mineral lease with an easement to mine. Generally, a mineral lease's terms of termination, notice, and renewal are the same as an ordinary tenancy, although the royalty or payment made for a mineral lease is likely to vary according to the value of the minerals found or extracted.

**re-let (relet or re-letting or re-leasing)** To lease premises vacated by one tenant to a new tenant. To re-let, or relet, premises is the act of a landlord in leasing premises that had been previously leased, leasing them to a new tenant. Re-letting premises is a means of the landlord's mitigation of damages in the event of a tenant's surrender of property prior to the termination of a lease. Whether a landlord has a duty to re-lease, or to take reasonable steps to re-lease premises, or merely the authority to do so, depends in part on the terms of the lease and in part on the opportunities to do so, but absent an affirmative duty in the lease, most courts are reluctant to force a landlord to re-let.

**sublease (sublessee or subtenant)** A lessee's delegation of right to a subordinate lessee. A sublease is a lease of a lease, by the lessee to a sublessee. The sublease amounts to a lease as between the lessee and the sublessee. The lessee may lease no more than the lessee has leased, but the lessee may lease any portion of what the lessee has leased. A defining element of the sublease is that the lessee does not change the underlying relationship between the lessee and the lessor; the lessee remains responsible for rents, for avoiding waste, and for any other covenants of the lease. The sublessee's duty is to the lessee, and the lessee' duty is to the lessor. At common law, a lessee could freely sublease, but the terms of many contemporary leases limit a lessee from subleasing, either forbidding them entirely or allowing a sublease only with the lessor's consent. Statutes and ordinances have sometimes regulated subleases, such as limiting a landlord's denial of consent to a sublease only to situations of reasonable denial. Note: there is no difference between a subtenancy and a sublease. There is, however, a great difference between a sublease and an assignment of a lease. A lessee who assigns a lease places the new lessee in the old lessee's position. The old lessee assigns not only rights but also duties to the new lessee who accepts the duties and renders them directly to the lessor. The old lessee is then free of further duties under the lease. In contrast, a sublease requires the lessee to continue to ensure the duties are performed until the end of the lease.

*See also:* lease, assignment of lease; lease, sublease (sublessee or subtenant).

**leave of court** *See:* permission, leave of court (leave of the court).

**lecture method** *See:* law, law school, legal pedagogy, lecture method (hornbook method).

**ledger** The record of transactions. A ledger is any record of accounts or transactions. In its most customary form, a ledger is an account book, but it may be also a particular form of electronic record, and in either case it is a basis for accounting for debts and assets customarily that have been written by book-keepers into a ledger. More generally, a ledger may be any record of payments, inventory, or events, or the book and any matter written into a printed manuscript, book, database, or other record of a style once used for ledgers.

*See also:* account; book, book as business record (books).

**legacy (legatee or legator)** A bequest of a personal property through a will. A legacy is, in its most technical sense, the grant by a decedent of a gift of goods or chattels through a valid last will and testament. A legacy is created by a testator, who is the legator, and it is conferred on a legatee. When a testator employs the word legacy to depict a grant by testament that is properly a devise, courts will consider the grant to be valid nonetheless. Legacy is used loosely to speak of anything received from one's ancestor or predecessor, but this usage has no real legal significance.

*See also:* inheritance (inherit).

*devise* Legacy applies to personalty, devise to realty. At common law, legacy designated the grant by will of a chattel, and it was the more general term between legacy and devise (though a bequest is a more general term and may be either of real or personal property). After the enactment of the Uniform Probate Code, devise has become more general than legacy.

**abatement of a legacy** Reduction of general bequests to pay debts on specific bequests. The abatement of a legacy is the reduction in value of a general legacy, such as a residuary legacy, in order to pay debts associated with property given in specific legacies. Thus, a mortgage on a property that is given in a specific bequest or devise must be paid from assets in the estate as a whole, even though this will reduce the value of the inheritance of the residuary legatee to the benefit of the recipient of the specific bequest of the property subject to the mortgage.

*See also:* devise | devise and legacy; devise, abatement of a devise.

**absolute legacy** A legacy conferred immediately upon death and with no limitation. An absolute legacy is a legacy that is intended and drafted into a last will and testament to become effective immediately upon the testator's death, without limitations or potential for interference. At the moment of the testator's death, an absolute legacy gives rise to a constructive trust in the res of the legacy to the benefit of the legatee.

*See also:* absolute.

**accumulated legacy** A legacy to be granted after a delay following death. An accumulated legacy is a bequest that is structured to be transferred to the legatee only after a time has elapsed or an event has occurred, so that the proceeds that accumulate in the meantime will be transferred at one time. An accumulated legacy differs from a cumulative legacy, in that the cumulative legacy is subsequent, not delayed.

**conditional legacy (contingent legacy)** A legacy effective if a prior condition is met. A conditional legacy is a legacy that depends for its full vesting in the legatee upon the satisfaction of a condition that might or might not occur. As long as the conditional legacy is granted directly to the legatee, though upon condition, the legacy is not technically a future interest, because there is no prior present interest as the proceeds of the legacy are held by the executor or some other trustee. If, however, a conditional legacy is granted first to one party and then on condition to another party, it is a future interest, either an executory interest or a contingent remainder. Only if the contingent legacy is left to a person unascertained at the death of the testator would the Rule Against Perpetuities apply. A grant of a conditional legacy that never vests—either because of the death of the legatee while the condition remains unfulfilled or because the time passes within which the condition must be satisfied—becomes a part of the testator's residuary legacy or residuary estate.

*See also:* devise, conditional devise.

**demonstrative legacy** A legacy of a given fund, or the estate generally. A demonstrative legacy is a legacy that is specified to be of a given object or from a given fund, but unlike specific legacies that would be void if the designated gift were alienated or destroyed inter vivos, a demonstrative legacy that has insufficient value at the time of distribution is to be satisfied from the general funds of the estate.

**failed legacy** *See:* bequest, lapsed bequest (lapsed legacy or lapse of devise or lapse of legacy).

**general legacy** A bequest to be paid from the estate's general assets. A general legacy, in the common law, is a grant by the testator to a legatee of money or money substitutes such as stocks or bonds that are to be paid not from a specific fund or with a designated asset, but from the assets generally within the estate.

In civil law, a general legacy is a fraction of the estate that has not been given in specific bequests.

**particular legacy (legacy under particular title)** A bequest of specific things in an estate. A particular legacy, in the civil law, is a grant of particular objects or categories of assets to a legatee, expressing the grant not as a grant of everything such as a general or universal legacy, and not as a fraction or proportion of everything, but as a grant of things with a particular form or category otherwise. Thus the particular legacy is analogous to a specific legacy in the common law, although the particular legacy can be broad or vague to a degree unusual in the common-law specific legacy.

**pecuniary legacy** A bequest of money. A pecuniary legacy is a legacy of money, either as a specific amount or as a share of an account or other asset valued in money.

**residuary legacy (residuary estate or residuary legatee)** The estate remaining after all specific legacies. A residuary estate is the remaining portion of an estate of a decedent after all charges, debts, and costs have been settled, and after all specific bequests, legacies, and devises have been honored. The residuary legacy includes all aspects otherwise not distributed, which is the residue of the estate and includes otherwise undesignated post–mortem acquisitions by the estate. The residuary estate may be signaled by various phrases, including "all the rest and residue of my estate." The person to whom the residuary legacy is bequeathed, or each of the persons among whom it is bequeathed, is a residuary legatee.

*See also:* residue (residual or residuary or residuum or rest); legatee, residuary legatee (residuary devisee).

**specific legacy** *See:* bequest, specific bequest (specific legacy or special legacy).

**trust legacy** A legacy placed into trust. A trust legacy is a legacy that becomes the corpus of a trust. This occurs when the executor transfers the assets of the legacy to a trustee or executes an instrument creating the trust, even if it names the executor as the trustee.

**universal legacy (legacy under universal title)** The residuum bequest after particular legacies. A universal legacy, in the civil law, is a bequest of the estate that remains after all particular legacies are paid or distributed. A universal legacy may be granted to one or more people in set proportions or shares, but it may only contain assets that are not by law restricted from transfer by will. The universal legacy is analogous to the residuary legacy in the common law.

*See also:* legatee, universal legatee (universal successor).

**vested legacy** A legacy contingent on an event that has occurred. A vested legacy is a legacy that was initially contingent, but the contingency has been satisfied; the legatee's right to the legacy is now vested.

**void legacy** An impossible testamentary gift. A void legacy is a legacy written into a last will and testament by a testator, but at the time of the writing, the grant is impossible and cannot later become possible. Thus, a legacy granted to a person who is dead at the time the will is executed is void. A legacy to a fictitious person that is not an entity is void. A void legacy differs from a lapsed legacy in the timing: a legacy lapses if a legatee dies following the drafting of the will but before the death of the testator, but a legacy is void if it is impossible at the time of its making, because it is contrary to public policy or is practically impossible and cannot be made possible, as in the case of a grant made to a person already dead.

*See also:* bequest, lapsed bequest (lapsed legacy or lapse of devise or lapse of legacy).

**legal (legality)** By law, especially allowed or required by law. Legal has many senses, but all represent a relationship to the law. In general, a legal anything refers to a thing that is related to the institutions, rules, or practice of law. A legal obligation is one that is enforceable according to law, more often than not, one that is enforced according to the criminal law (as a reflection on the antonym, illegal, usually signals conduct that is prohibited by the criminal law). The gap between what is legal and illegal is similar to the gap between what is lawful and unlawful.

*See also:* lawfulness (lawful or unlawfulness or unlawful).

**legal accountability** *See:* accountability (legal accountability).

**legal advice** *See:* lawyer, legal advice (advice of counsel).

**legal age** *See:* adult, full age (legal age); adult, age of majority (legal age).

**legal aid** *See:* lawyer, legal aid.

**legal anthropology** *See:* law, anthropology of law (legal anthropology).

**legal argument** *See:* argument, legal argument.

**legal authority** *See:* authority, legal authority.

**legal capacity** *See:* capacity, legal capacity.

**legal citation** *See:* citation, legal citation (cite).

**legal citology** *See:* citation, legal citation, legal citology.

**legal classification** *See:* class, legal classification (governmental classification).

**legal conclusion** *See:* ruling, conclusion of law (legal conclusion).

**legal cruelty** *See:* cruelty, legal cruelty (cruel treatment or extreme cruelty).

**legal custody** *See:* custody, legal custody.

**legal disability** *See:* disability (legal disability).

**legal education** *See:* law, law school (legal education).

**legal efficacy** *See:* forgery, legal efficacy; efficacy, legal efficacy.

**legal entity** *See:* entity (legal entity).

**legal ethics** *See:* ethics, legal ethics.

**legal fact** *See:* fact, legal fact.

**legal father** *See:* family, father, legal father.

**legal fiction** *See:* fiction, legal fiction (fiction of law).

**legal formalism** *See:* jurisprudence, legal formalism (formalist).

**legal indeterminacy** *See:* indeterminacy, legal indeterminacy.

**legal injury** *See:* injury, legal injury.

**legal injury rule** *See:* limitation, limitation of actions, statute of limitations, legal injury rule (legal–injury rule).

**legal innocence** *See:* innocence, legal innocence (legal insufficiency).

**legal insufficiency** *See:* innocence, legal innocence (legal insufficiency).

**legal jargon** *See:* jargon, legal jargon (legalese or legalism).

**legal malpractice** *See:* malpractice, legal malpractice.

**legal normativism** *See:* jurisprudence, normativism (legal normativism).

**legal official** *See:* official, legal official.

**legal ontology** *See:* law, theories of law, ontology of law (legal ontology).

**legal opinion** *See:* lawyer, legal opinion (opinion of counsel).

**legal paper or legal pad** *See:* paper, legal size paper (legal paper or legal pad).

**legal pedagogy** *See:* law, law school, legal pedagogy.

**legal perfectionism** *See:* jurisprudence, perfectionism (legal perfectionism).

**legal–personal representative** *See:* representative, legal representative (legal–personal representative).

**legal personality** *See:* person, artificial person (legal personality).

**legal philosophy or legal theory or legal science** *See:* jurisprudence (legal philosophy or legal theory or legal science).

**legal pluralism** *See:* jurisprudence, legal pluralism.

**legal positivism** *See:* jurisprudence, legal positivism (positivism).

**legal practice** *See:* lawyer, legal practice, sharp practice; lawyer, legal practice (practice of law).

**legal pragmatism** *See:* jurisprudence, pragmatism (legal pragmatism).

**legal prejudice** *See:* prejudice, legal prejudice, with prejudice (without prejudice); prejudice, legal prejudice, undue prejudice; prejudice, legal prejudice.

**legal proceeding** *See:* proceeding, legal proceeding.

**legal process** *See:* process, legal process.

**legal realism** *See:* jurisprudence, legal realism.

**legal representative** *See:* representative, legal representative (legal–personal representative).

**legal rescission** *See:* rescission, legal rescission (rescision at law).

**legal research** *See:* research, legal research.

**legal right** *See:* right, legal right.

**legal rule** *See:* rule, legal rule, secondary rule; rule, legal rule, rule–scepticism (rule skepticism); rule, legal rule, primary rule; rule, legal rule (law as a system of rules).

**legal semiotics** *See:* jurisprudence, legal semiotics (semiotics).

**Legal Services Corporation** *See:* lawyer, legal aid, Legal Services Corporation (LSC).

**legal servitude** *See:* servitude, legal servitude.

**legal size paper** *See:* paper, legal size paper (legal paper or legal pad).

**legal system** *See:* law, legal system.

**legal tender** *See:* tender, legal tender.

**legal voluntarism** *See:* jurisprudence, legal voluntarism.

**legalese or legalism** *See:* jargon, legal jargon (legalese or legalism).

**legality principle or principle of legality** *See:* nullum, nullum crimen sine lege (legality principle or principle of legality).

**legatee** A person who receives any form of legacy. A legatee is a person who receives a legacy in a will. As a matter of usage, a legatee is any person who is entitled to receive the legacy as it was designated in a will at the time of the testator's death, even if the legatee does not receive the legacy as a matter of fact owing to exhaustion of assets, predecession or some other cause. Generally, however, a person who would have taken under a void or lapsed legacy is not a legatee.
*See also:* death, wrongful death, wrongful death beneficiaries (wrongful death estate); legacy (legatee or legator).

*devisee and legatee* In common-law usage, a legatee takes personalty or the estate as a whole, though a devisee takes realty. Following the adoption of the Uniform Probate Code, the more generic and inclusive term is less likely to be legatee but devisee.
*See also:* heir | devisee or legatee and heir (heir by devise).

**general legatee** One who receives a general legacy. A general legatee is a legatee whose interest in the estate is a general legacy. A person may be a general legatee and still receive other forms of legacy, such as a special legacy or residuary legacy.

**residuary legatee (residuary devisee)** One who receives a residuary legacy. A residuary legatee is a beneficiary of a last will and testament who receives all or a portion of the residue of the estate, regardless of whether that person receives other bequests in the will. A residuary legatee ordinarily is designated as the recipient of after-acquired assets. There is no essential difference between a residuary devisee or a residuary legatee.
*See also:* legacy, residuary legacy (residuary estate or residuary legatee).

**specific legatee** One who receives a specific legacy.
*See also:* bequest, specific bequest (specific legacy or special legacy).

**universal legatee (universal successor)** One who succeeds to all or a share of all of an estate. A universal legatee in the civil law is a person who is given by will either all of the estate of a decedent or an equal share in all of the estate of a decedent. Because the universal legatee may take an estate for which particular legacies are also validly assigned, the universal legatee is functionally similar to the residuary legatee in the common-law system. A universal legatee generally has the rights an obligations of an heir or of a legatee under universal title. A universal legatee is given the whole of an estate (less particular legacies), and so the universal legatee is one form of universal successor, as are the heir and the general legatee. A universal successor succeeds to all of the rights and charges of the decedent, except for those transferred to others as an element of particular title.

**legation** A diplomatic mission and its personnel. A legation is a diplomatic mission, sometimes seen as lesser in status than an embassy. Under the Vienna Convention on Diplomatic Affairs, there is no difference between an embassy and a legation, and both are entitled to immunity.

**legislation (legislate)** The creation of laws by legislative enactment, and the laws made. Legislation is both the process of creating law and the law created, particularly through the operation of legislature, an assembly of people who participate in the drafting and approval of a text that becomes law owing to its generation in this process. In the United States, legislation includes the statutes enacted by the Congress, the statutes or acts enacted by the legislatures of each state, and (less frequently) the ordinances enacted by local governmental councils. Each must be enacted according to procedures established in the Constitution of the United States or the procedures of each state's constitution or through the rules of procedure for the local government, each procedure conforming to the limits of the procedures of the constitution above it. Law created through other means is usually not included in the term legislation.

Although the common law includes much law that was originated or altered as legislation, and legislation often adopts rules developed in the common law, legislation is generally considered distinct from the common law.
*See also:* statute (statutory law); ordinance.

**amendment from the floor (floor amendment)** An amendment to a bill presented in the chamber of a house. An amendment from the floor is an amendment offered by a member of a legislative chamber while the the bill is under debate before that body. The amendment must be offered in accordance with the rules, which do not always allow amendment, which may limit the subject matter and timing of the motion to amend. An amendment is adopted by vote of the membership of the chamber.

**amendment to a bill** A change adopted to a bill while the bill is pending adoption. An amendment to a bill is an alteration that is proposed to a bill pending in a legislative body, whether a house or committee. Amendments are passed according to the rules of the legislative chamber, which may provide various vote requirements according to the nature of the bill to be amended, the agenda on which it is considered, and the timing of the amendment.

**amendment to a statute**  A change to an existing statute. Amendments are alterations of existing statutes, either by addition or subtraction or substitution of new text, which is incorporated into a new bill that is adopted by the legislative body that enacted the initial statute. Ordinarily, there is no difference in procedures in the rules for passage of an amendment to a statute and the passage of a statute that does not amend an earlier law. Not all amendments to existing statutes are described in the text of the bill as an amendment, but a prior statute may be amended by the effect or operation of a later statute.

**author of legislation**  A legislator responsible for the creation of a bill. The author of a bill is presumed to be the legislator who deposits it for initial consideration in the chamber, but the author is effectively the member who takes responsibility for authorship. The actual drafters of legislation usually do not receive credit as the author of a piece of legislation. Legislation is usually drafted by members of committee staffs, office staffs, and lobbyists rather than one or more members of the House or Senate in which the bill is introduced receives recognition as the author by introducing it.

**House Bill (H.B. or HB)**  A bill originating in a House of Representatives. A House Bill is a bill that was originated in the House of Representatives of a legislature, a designation the bill retains until as long as it is on the legislative docket. In the United States Congress, House Bills are numbered by the congressional session followed by the sequential number for the order in which the bill was placed in the hopper of the house chamber.

**markup of a bill**  A process of informal amendment of a bill in committee. The markup of a bill is the process of amendment possible when the bill is being considered by a committee or subcomittee, during which it may be amended by committee action, which may be much faster and less formal than the procedures used on the floor.

**Senate Bill (S.B. or SB)**  A bill originating in the senate of a legislature. A Senate Bill is a bill that was originated in the senate of a legislature, a designation the bill retains until as long as it is on the legislative docket. In the United States Congress, Senate Bills are numbered by the congressional session followed by the sequential number for the order in which the bill was placed in the hopper of the senate chamber.

**legislative history**  The record of the drafting, amendment, and debate of a bill. Legislative history is the textual, political, and archival record of a statute or bill as it moves from idea to draft to bill, then through the process of introduction or sponsorship, committee review, debate, amendment, voting, passage to the other chamber for a similar process,

reconciliation if needed, executive treatment and, if needed, legislative response. The legislative history of Congressional bills is relatively well archived, and the legislative history of some states is archived, though usually only for formal and public events such as voting records.

Legislative history is consulted to determine the issues before the legislature when a statute was created. The history sometimes gives evidence of legislative purpose, the broad goals that at least some legislators believed would be promoted by the statute, and the legislative intent as to the meaning of specific language in the resulting statute.

*See also:* interpretation, statutory interpretation | legislative history.

**journal entry (entry in a legislative journal)**  A recording of a legislative action. A journal entry (in the context of a legislative record) is the recording of a vote, transmittal, report, or other action related to a particular legislative body or to a given piece of legislation. Journal entries are often the primary source of official legislative history. Generally, the courts have no power to require alteration or publication of an entry in a legislative journal, owing to the limits of separation of powers.

**logrolling**  The combination of unrelated measures in one bill to compromise between the supporters of each. Logrolling has two senses that affect legislation. The first is political, in which legislators trade the support of one initiative for support of another. The second sense is legal, in which the supporters of a bill incorporate a variety of unrelated measures into the bill in order to gain support, or sometimes opposition, to a given bill among other legislators. In many states, this second, internal, sense of logrolling violates constitutional limits on the subject matter of legislation being limited to matters of one object of public concern. In the United States Congress, internal logrolling is not uncommon.

**omnibus legislation (omnibus bill)**  A bill containing a variety of provisions. An omnibus bill is one bill that includes a variety of provisions. In states that have a constitutional limit of legislation to one object or purpose, such omnibus bills must either be a budget or tax bill or be limited to a variety of matters that reasonably amount still to one essential purpose. Omnibus bills are frequently the home of unusual amendments, riders, and authorizations that are sponsored by individual legislators who rely on the essential nature of the core matters of a bill to ensure passage of these more obscure projects through the legislative process.

*See also:* omnibus.

**savings clause**  A division of the remainder of a statute if one part is unconstitutional. A savings clause in a statute is a provision attempting to guide judicial interpretation of the statute, to preserve the force and effect of each element of a statute that would remain if one portion is found to be unconstitutional.

**Session Laws (S.L. or SL)** The statutes of a single legislative session. Session laws are the compilations of acts or statutes enacted in each session of a legislature. Most states print the acts in the order in which they are finally made law, usually by gubernatorial authorization. Session laws are usually integrated into a state code or statutory compilation, which gives rise to potential ambiguity in the event of omission or variation between the two publications. In many states, the text of a particular statute as enrolled and published in the session laws takes precedence over the text of that statute as it is printed following its placement in the code. Even so, a session law that is incompletely rendered into a statutory collection or code may not give notice of a law that would be provided by the code.

**sunset provision (repealer clause or sunset clause)** A self-repealing clause in a a a statute. A sunset clause is a provision in a statute providing for the statute's expiration at a specific time after enactment, unless the legislature enacting it reauthorizes or sufficiently amends the statute.

**legislator** An individual member of a body that holds the legislative powers of a government. A legislator, generally, is any person who participates in the creation of laws. Specifically in the United States, a legislator is a member of a legislative body, such as the Congress of the United States, a state legislature, a county council or its equivalent, or a city council or its equivalent.

Note: although the members of all of these bodies are legislators, generically, it is rare that legislator is a title or a proper means of address. More often, the legislator is addressed as Senator, Representative, or Councilor.

**legislature (legislative branch)** The body empowered to create laws in a jurisdiction. A legislature is the repository of the general duty of legislative authority and the specific obligations of regulating a variety of subjects under the constitution according to which the legislature is created. The Congress of the United States is a legislature, and each state has an independent legislature. The legislative branch of a government includes both the legislature and all offices and agencies that report to the legislature as a body, to one house or another, or to the legislature's officers on its behalf.

**legislative branch** See: legislature (legislative branch).

**legislative court** See: court, U.S. court, legislative court.

**legislative history** See: legislation, legislative history.

**legislative immunity** See: immunity, official immunity, legislative immunity (congressional immunity).

**legislative inaction** See: inaction, legislative inaction (legislative re-enactment).

**legislative intent** See: intent, legislative intent (statutory intent).

**legislative jurisdiction** See: jurisdiction, legislative jurisdiction.

**legislative privilege** See: privilege, evidentiary privilege, legislative privilege.

**legislative purpose** See: interpretation, statutory interpretation, legislative purpose.

**legislative re-enactment** See: inaction, legislative inaction (legislative re-enactment).

**bicameral legislature (bicameralism)** A legislature of two chambers. A bicameral legislature has two separate bodies, which must agree on legislation in order for it to become law. Most legislatures have a small upper house, each of whose members represent a high proportion of citizens or large area of the jurisdiction, and a larger lower house, each of whose members represent a smaller proportion of citizens or a smaller area of the jurisdiction. Bicameralism represents the arguments for a requirement that a given matter be passed by two independent houses.

**unicameral legislature** A legislature composed of one chamber. A unicameral legislature has one deliberative body, which passes legislation without consultation with another legislative institution. In the United States, only Nebraska has a unicameral state legislature, although most municipal legislative bodies are unicameral.

See also: legislature, bicameral legislature (bicameralism).

**legisprudence** The study of legislation. Legisprudence is the study of legislation, its purposes, forms, and best manner of interpretation and application. As of 2011, it is not a well developed discipline.

**legist** A pedantic or overly technical lawyer. The term legist may mean a lawyer particularly interested in the technical rules of law, but it more often is used as a term of derision for a lawyer who is so preoccupied with the narrowest reading of a statute or smallest technical points that the lawyer fails to see or pursue the larger purposes of the law manifest in the statutes, cases, or other materials in issue.

**legitimacy (legitimate or legit)** Lawfulness, justification, or authenticity. Legitimacy is the quality of anything or any person being justified in law and fact or doing something lawfully or correctly. The term is used in a variety of specific tests in law, each ascertaining that the thing tested is legally sufficient or factually appropriate for the purpose to which it is put. The once-most-common use of the term was as the determination that a child is legally entitled to an inheritance from a parent by being born during marriage, although this meaning of the term is now obsolete. Terms requiring legal definition include the legitimate purpose of a law and the legitimate holder of an office. In many senses, legitimacy refers to a factual inquiry, usually whether an object is authentic or that it is in fact what it appears to be. In contrast, for example, a forgery not a legitimate document.

As a matter of jurisprudence and, at times, of constitutional law, legitimacy is a synonym for justification. In other words, a legitimate purpose is one that is not only authorized by some law but is morally and culturally acceptable.

Note: the adjectival form is legitimate, and so is the verb form. Their pronunciations differ. The adjective stresses pronunciation of the second syllable and uses a soft "e" sound for the "a" of the last syllable. The verb stresses the last syllable and has a long "a." Legit is a very informal synonym, which is essentially an abbreviated variant on legitimate.

**legitimate child** *See:* child, legitimate child.

**legitimate child or nonmarital child or bastard or legitimacy or illegitimacy** *See:* child, illegitimate child (legitimate child or nonmarital child or bastard or legitimacy or illegitimacy).

**legitimate governmental purpose** *See:* interest, state interest, legimate state interest (legitimate governmental purpose).

**legitimus** Permitted or required by the law. Legitimus, the basis for the English legitimate, is Latin for a lawful requirement.
*See also:* illegitimus.

**lemon** A defective automobile. A lemon may depict any defective product but is most usually applied to an automobile that does function consistently well, particularly if the automobile was defective at the time of purchase and the defect was not fully disclosed by the seller. To accuse someone other than a fruit dealer of selling a lemon suggests either a deceptive or a negligent act.
*See also:* product, defective product.

**lemon test** *See:* religion, freedom of religion, lemon test.

**lemon law** Statutes defining and allowing suit for defective automobiles. Lemon laws in most states provide a civil action for the enforcement of express or implied warranties for the fitness of an automobile, when the maker or seller will not cure a defect in the car. Most lemon laws allow recovery of the value of the car or the defect or repair, as well as a multiple of that amount in damages. Some lemon laws include criminal penalties for knowing or willful sale of a vehicle with a known and dangerous defect.
*See also:* liability, product liability (products liability).

**lender** A person or entity who lends money or property to another. A lender is the person or entity who loans money or property to another for a period of time. Lenders are either private or commercial, the difference being whether a loan is made in part owing to a business by the lender of making such loans, in which case the lender is commercial. Commercial lenders are regulated by both state and federal law. Private lenders are also regulated, though less comprehensively, and the conduct of private lenders is subject to limitations in the enforceability of contract.
*See also:* usury (usurious).

**payday lender (pay-day lender)** A lender specializing in short-term, high-interest loans. A payday lender is a person, entity, or agent who makes short-term, high-interest loans, regardless of the length of time in which such loans are retired.

**lending or lend** *See:* loan (lending or lend).

**lenity (rule of lenity)** An ambiguous criminal statute is read in favor of a defendant. The rule of lenity is a rule of statutory construction, according to which a criminal statute that is sufficiently ambiguous that it cannot be said exactly what conduct is barred must be read in the light more favorable to the defendant. Or, as Justice Scalia has recently said, when two readings are possible of a criminal prohibition, in the event of a tie, the defendant wins. The rule of lenity is based in part on the requirements of due process of law that a criminal law be clear and not vague in giving notice of what conduct the law prohibits, and it is also based on a common-law interpretation of statutes.

Note: lenity differs from lenience, which is either to ignore and not punish an offense otherwise deserving of punishment or to punish the offense but to do so lightly.
*See also:* vagueness, vagueness doctrine (void for vagueness doctrine); lawfulness (lawful or unlawfulness or unlawful).

**lesser included offense** *See:* offense, lesser included offense, schmuck test; offense, lesser included offense.

**lessor** *See:* landlord (lessor).

**let** *See:* lease, let (letting).

**lethal (lethality)** Deadly. Anything lethal causes death or has the potential to cause death.

**lethal injection** *See:* punishment, death penalty, lethal injection.

**letter** A document intended to transmit information from one person to another. A letter is a piece of written correspondence, either private or official, either personal or public. Private and personal correspondence is customarily a letter written onto sheets of paper, sealed, and sent by mail or messenger to the recipient. Official correspondence is a letter sent to record a decision or matter of information required to be sent to the recipient. Public correspondence is not sealed but created for the purpose of announcing a governmental policy, position, or appointment, and it is usually given to the recipient in a manner to be publicized upon receipt. In an age of electronic mail, the written letter remains a model and metaphor for the structure of much electronic correspondence.

**letter brief**   *See:* brief, letter brief.

**letter of censure**   *See:* lawyer, lawyer discipline, sanctions, letter of censure.

**letter of credit**   *See:* credit, letter of credit (LC or L.C.).

**letter of recall**   *See:* diplomat, recall (letter of recall).

**letter of request or rogatory letter**   *See:* rogatory, letters rogatory (letter of request or rogatory letter).

**letter of the law**   *See:* law, letter of the law.

**letter of undertaking**   *See:* undertaking, letter of undertaking.

**letters of administration**   *See:* probate, letters testamentary (letters of administration).

**letters patent**   *See:* patent, letters patent.

**letters rogatory**   *See:* rogatory, letters rogatory (letter of request or rogatory letter).

**letters testamentary**   *See:* probate, letters testamentary (letters of administration).

**thirty-day letter (30-day letter)**   A notice sent following a unresolved tax examination. The thirty-day letter is a form letter sent by the Internal Revenue Service to a taxpayer following an examination, which states and explains the basis of the examiner's proposed determination and informs the taxpayer of his or her appeal rights if the taxpayer disagrees with the proposed determination.

**letting**   *See:* lease, let (letting).

**leverage (leveraged, leveraging)**   The ratio of debt to value in an enterprise. Leverage, in commercial activity, is the process and the percentage by which an enterprise is financed with debt.

In general usage, leverage is a metaphor for coercion or influence.

*See also:* debt, debt calculation, debt ratio; debt, debt calculation, debt-to-equity ratio.

**leveraged buyout**   *See:* buyout, corporate buyout, leveraged buyout (LBO).

**leveraging**   *See:* leverage (leveraged, leveraging).

**levy**   A seizure of proptery to satisfy a debt, especially a tax owed. A levy is a seizure of property, which may be made in execution of a judgment, particularly a tax deficiency judgment, either by administrative action or under judicial order.

**lewdness (lewd)**   Evocative of particular sexual interest or a specific sex act. Lewdness is an aspect of conduct or appearance which provokes (or reasonably would be expected to provoke) the actor or an observer strongly to associate the conduct or appearance with an action of sexual gratification. Lewdness is more than sexiness or even lasciviousness: it is a matter of degree, but lewdness is direct and evocative of particular conduct, a suggestion of one or more specific acts of sex. Still,

lewdness is not the same as explicitness, and an act may be quite lewd but still subtle or metaphorical, as long as the suggestion implied in the act is of a particular sex act or form of sex act.

*See also:* lasciviousness (lascivious or lasciviously).

**lex**   The law, or the specific laws. Lex is Latin for law, particularly in the most specific senses of the law as applied to a case or enacted in a legislature. Lex is usually contrasted with jus, or right. The idea of Law in the United States is a combination of the ideas of jus and lex, or the law and the laws.

**lex communis**   *See:* law, common law (lex communis).

**lex domicilii**   *See:* choice, choice of law, lex domicilii.

**lex fori**   *See:* choice, choice of law, lex fori.

**lex loci**   *See:* choice, choice of law, lex loci (lex situs or lex rei sitae or lex loci delicti or etc.).

**lex loci contractus**   *See:* locus, locus contractus (lex loci contractus).

**lex loci delicti**   *See:* locus, locus delicti (lex loci delicti).

**lex mercatoria**   *See:* merchant, law merchant (lex mercatoria).

**lex non scripta or lex non scripta regni angliae**   *See:* law, unwritten law (lex non scripta or lex non scripta regni angliae).

**lex patriae**   *See:* choice, choice of law, lex patriae.

**lex scripta**   *See:* law, written law (lex scripta).

**lex situs or lex rei sitae or lex loci delicti or etc.**   *See:* choice, choice of law, lex loci (lex situs or lex rei sitae or lex loci delicti or etc.).

**lex talionis**   *See:* retaliation, lex talionis.

**lex terrae**   *See:* terra, lex terrae; law, law of the land (lex terrae).

**lex domicilii**   The law of one's domicile. Lex domicilii is the law that governs a person's permanent residence or domicile. It is usually the law that governs all questions of that person's status and disputes regarding the person's interests after death, particularly the decedent's movable or personal assets.

*See also:* domicile (domicil or domiciliary).

**lex fori**   The law of the forum. Lex fori is the law applied in the normal course by a court in which a dispute is heard. Lex fori in conflicts of law among states, or private international law, is generally the national law that applies in a forum. In all regards it includes the rules of procedure that a court will apply regardless of the substantive rules that might be required as a matter of conflicts of law.

*See also:* forum.

**lex loci (lex loci delicti or lex loci contractus or lex loci rei sitae or lex situs)**   The law of the place or of the object of a dispute. The lex loci is the law of the place relevant to the thing or act in dispute.

It takes many forms, and has a few variations. Lex loci delecti is the law of the place of the wrong, or the law of the jurisdiction in which a harm occurred. Lex loci contractus is the law of the place in which a contract is made. The lex loci rei sitae is the law of the place where the thing is, and it is often stated by the abbreviated lex situs, both of which mean the law of the jurisdiction in which the property in dispute is situated. In a conflict over ownership or a contract for the transfer of property between the lex loci contractus and the lex situs, the lex situs prevails as to goods, and the lex loci usually prevails as to realty.

Other lex loci include: Lex loci actus, the law of the place of the act, like a contract signature or deed transfer; Lex loci celebrationis, the place where a marriage is celebrated; and Lex loci solutionis, the place where payment or performance occurs. There are variant formulae for writing each phrase.

**lex loci contractus**   The law of the place of the contract. The lex loci contractus is the law of the jurisdiction in which a contract is made. If a written contract specifies a location for its making, this location is presumptively the place of the contract.

*See also:* locus, locus contractus (lex loci contractus).

**lex non curat de minimis (de minimus non curat lex)**   The law does not care about inconsequential matters. Lex non curat de minimus means, literally, that the law will not remedy trivial injuries. It is a maxim as well as a way of life. As a maxim, it is raised as a defense to a claim, by which the defendant argues that the harm suffered by the plaintiff or the wrongdoing alleged to have been done by the defendant are so insignificant that no action should be brought. As a defense to a criminal charge, the maxim is a common law defense and underlies statutory defenses to some offenses but not all.

*See also:* trifle (trifling); de, de minimis.

**lex patriae**   The law of one's own country. Lex patriae is the law of the country of a person's nationality, which is nearly always foreign from the place of a dispute, the law of that place being the lex situs. Lex Domicilii is closely related, in that it is the law of the state in which a litigant is permanently domiciled.

**ley**   Law.
*See also:* law.

**li (li ki)**   The basic rules of state and society in classical Chinese law. Li is the customary basis in classical Chinese philosophy for the social norms that are reflected in law. Li establishes not only the social hierarchy but the duties of each person to others.

*See also:* fa (lu).

**liability (liable)**   A responsibility to do something or to make good not doing so. Liability is the responsibility that may be enforced under the law for ensuring the performance of some duty of action or omission, or for making good the injury of those harmed or threatened by not doing so. Liability is usually spoken of as civil, or private liability, for a violation of a contract, the commission of a tort, or the failure of an equitable duty such as the duty of a trustee. Criminal liability arises independently of civil liability from conduct in violation of a criminal prohibition. Liability in both senses depends upon enforceability, and if there is no person or entity that may enforce a duty against a person who fails in it, there is no liability (despite the failure of duty).

*See also:* fault.

**liability bond**   *See:* bond, liability bond.

**liability insurance**   *See:* insurance, category of insurance, liability insurance, homeowner; insurance, category of insurance, liability insurance, commercial general liability (C.G.L. CGL); insurance, category of insurance, liability insurance (third–party insurance).

**liability phase trial**   *See:* trial, bifurcated trial, guilt phase trial (liability phase trial).

**liability to other on the land**   *See:* land, liability to other on the land, trespasser; land, liability to other on the land, licensee; land, liability to other on the land, invitee; land, liability to other on the land, guest; land, liability to other on the land.

**accomplice liability**   An accomplice is as criminally liable as the principal. Accomplice liability in the United States is a theory by which an accomplice is effectively treated as if the accomplice is the principal. The offense of aiding and abetting amounts effectively to a joint criminal liability for the offense committed by the person aided or abetted.

**apportionment of liability**   The means of ascertaining a degree of liability. Apportionment of liability is the method of division of liability among the parties or others who are responsible for an injury. Liability is to be allocated to each who is responsible for the injury according to the degree to which each is ultimately responsible for the injury that occurred. When perfect assessment is impossible in the light of the evidence, a reasonable approximation must suffice. Apportionment is the means by which the share of contribution is assessed among individual defendants who are jointly and severally liable.

Apportionment is particularly significant in claims of negligence when the parties allege fault by more than one actor. It is an element required in determining the applicability of the defense of contributory negligence, in that the apportionment of responsibility to the plaintiff may bar or limit the plaintiff's recovery from the defendant. Distinctly, apportionment in cases of comparative negligence requires the assessment of the degree to which responsibility for damages is the responsibility of the plaintiff. In such cases, as with matters of joint and several liability generally, the trier of fact is to consider the significance of each party's role in causing the damage and assign a proportion of liability accordingly.

*See also:* liability, joint liability; liability, joint and several liability; negligence, contributory negligence; negligence, comparative negligence, modified comparative negligence (hybrid comparative negligence).

**market-share liability**  Manufacturer liability for a product based on its share of the market. Market share liability is a means of apportioning a manufacturer's liability for harm caused by a product based on the manufacturer's share of the product's overall market. Market share liability is usually available to a plaintiff only when there is proof of an injury by a product but no other means of apportioning liability among its makers in that case.

**civil liability**  Non-criminal liability for a remedy in law or equity. Civil liability is responsibility for a remedy owed to any party, including a state or government, that does not arise from violation of a criminal law.

**comparative liability (comparative fault or comparative responsibility)**  Liability apportioned among parties according to conduct. Comparative liability is a division or responsibility for making whole an injury among the parties found to have been in part responsible for the injury. The original function of comparative liability was a mitigation for the harsh effects of contributory liability, which acted as an absolute bar to recovery for a plaintiff at all responsible for the plaintiff's injury; comparative liability diminished the plaintiff's recovery by the percentage of the plaintiff's own responsibility but allowed a claim against others for their own responsibility.

Comparative liability is also used to allocate responsibility among defendants who are held jointly and severally liable to determine the portion of a recovery paid by one that may be collected from another co-defendant. Thus, if A sues B, C, and D, recovering against all jointly and severally, A may collect the entire award from B, who may recover a pro-rata share based on comparative liability from each of C and D.

*See also:* fault; negligence, comparative negligence.

**contingent liability**  A risk that may ripen into a liability. A contingent liability is a condition or arrangement of conditions that might or might not lead to a liability, depending on events in the future.

*See also:* contingency (contingent).

**joint and several liability**  Shared and independent full liability of each defendant who caused a portion of the plaintiff injury. Joint and several liability is a formula for holding liable each person or entity who participated in causing a harm for the entire harm, along with all other persons or entities who did so. Each is severally and fully responsible for the harm, even though all are jointly responsible for it. A plaintiff may recover a full recovery from any of them, because each is legally responsible for making the plaintiff whole. Or, the plaintiff may recover from all

of them, in proportion to their responsibility in fact. But, if one defendant pays more than a comparative share of the liability ultimately apportioned between them, that defendant may seek a contribution from the others for the amount paid in compensation beyond that defendant's proportion of the responsibility in fact for the plaintiff's harm.

*See also:* liability, joint liability; liability, several liability.

**joint liability**  Shared full liability of each defendant who caused a portion of the plaintiff injury. Joint liability is the liability of several defendants, each accountable for the whole damage caused by the cumulative effect of the breach of duty by each (though any one who pays all of the plaintiff's damages is entitled to contribution from the others, if it can be reached). Joint liability was initially the liability of joint tortfeasors for the damages that the collective of the defendants had caused the plaintiff, the damages being the responsibility of each in full, so that the plaintiff could be made whole by any one of them, who would then seek a pro rata contribution from the others. Courts increased the scope by which plaintiffs were allowed to join defendants whose independent actions added to the plaintiffs' injuries who would otherwise have been seperately liable, an expansion that gave rise to a norm of joint and several liablity for related actions of different defendants that cumulatively caused an injury to the plaintiff.

*See also:* liability, several liability; liability, joint and several liability.

**general average**  Joint liability and contribution for a loss at sea. The rule of general average applies when a vessel suffers a partial loss, either because a portion of the ship or the cargo is jettisoned or lost owing to a peril of the sea, after which the owner of the property lost or sacrificed may recover an average share of the loss form other owners with cargo or ownership interests in the vessel at the time.

**York-Antwerp Rules**  Customary rules for computing the general average. The York–Antwerp Rules are specific rules for computing the general average to be paid by those less injured by a loss at sea to those more injured in the same loss. The Rules were first drafted in 1864 in York then revised in Antwerp in 1877, and periodically revised, most recently in 1994.

The first seven rules, lettered alphabetically, enumerate the general principles of recovering for loss at sea, and, according to the language of the rules themselves, take precedent over the next 22 rules. The next 22 rules, indicated by Roman numerals, discuss particular losses and the coverage for them. The Rules are not laws in thesmelves but have acquired a customary strength and are often adopted by reference in shipping contracts and in the rules of maritime and admiralty organizations.

**personal liability**  Liability of a person regardless of other liabilities. A personal liability is a liability held by a person, regardless of any liability that might be held by a corporation or other entity to which a person might be related or employed and regardless of any other satisfaction that might be available to the claimant. Thus a personal liability is distinct from a corporate liability, and a personal liability might persist after a secured liability is satisfied.

**product liability (products liability)**  The liability of a manufacturer or seller for harm caused by a defective product. Product liability is the civil liability of a designer, manufacturer, seller, or other person or entity engaged in the creation and supply of a product to the ultimate user of that product, for injuries or harm caused by a defect in its design or manufacture. Product liability may be based on a theory of negligence, in which case, the defect must be shown to be the result of unreasonable design or manufacture, or it may be in violation of a duty of care, and that the defect was the cause in fact of injury to the plaintiff. Other theories, particularly of implied warranty, allow a plaintiff to prevail if the product is unfit for the use for which it was intended. In either case, an action may be brought by a person not in direct contractual privity with the manufacturer or an agent, as long as the plaintiff is a foreseeable consumer of the product.

*See also:* redhibition (redhibitory action); lemon, lemon law; product, defective product.

**automobile product liability (automotive product liability)**  A design or manufacture defect in a vehicle creates strict liability for its maker, seller, and middlemen. Automobile product liability is a form of strict product liability, yet the cases and theories arising from alleged defects in automobiles have given rise to several lines of liability specific to vehicle failures and to automobile collisions.

**crashworthiness doctrine**  A vehicle must reasonably protect occupants in a crash. The crashworthiness doctrine in products liability requires that a vehicle be designed and fabricated to make it reasonably likely to prevent or at least not to cause an injury to an occupant during a collision, or the failure of such a design or manufacture is a basis for liability for one injured as a result. Evidence of injury or survival of others in substantially similar accidents involving the same make and model of vehicle is relevant in establishing crashworthiness or a failure of crashworthiness of a given vehicle.

**intended-use doctrine**  A product should be fit for its intended use. The intended-use doctrine establishes a scope of the use of a product within which the consumer has an expectation that the problem should be capable of safe use to perform the use reasonably expected. The scope includes not only the uses advertised or marketed but the uses reasonably foreseeable as intended by the consumer, including reasonable and unintentional misuse.

**unintended use**  A use neither intended nor foreseeable. An unintended use of a product is a use that is neither intended by the manufacturer or seller nor reasonably foreseeable at the time of the manufacture or sale. The doctrine of intended use does not extend to unintended uses, and so product liability that does not rise from an inherent but latent danger does not reach a product that is unfit or dangerous when put to an unintended use. Whether a given use is intended or unintended is inherently a question of fact.

**misuse of product defense**  A consumer who uses a product wrongly may not recover damages from the wrongful use. Misuse of the product is a defense to a product liability action if the misuse by the consumer was intentional or negligent, and the misuse is the sole and proximate cause of the plaintiff's injury. Proof of misuse alone is not, however, sufficient for the defense, as the misuse must be one that is not expected of an ordinary and prudent consumer or other user of the product. Clear labeling of a risk posed by misuse may affect the weight of evidence of misuse as lacking prudence. Likewise, misuse is not a perfect defense if the product is subject to strict liability and a defect was at least in part a cause of the plaintiff's injury.

*See also:* negligence, last clear chance (last-clear–chance doctrine).

**product defect (defective product)**  A harmful fault in a product's design, manufacture, labeling, or instruction. A product defect is any fault in a product that causes the product either to fail to perform according to its ordinary and intended use or to cause unintended injury or harm to persons or property. Product defects take an infinite variety of forms, but they are usually caused by a defective design of the product, by a defective manufacture of the product, or a defect in the manner of labeling, instruction, or marketing of the product.

The existence of a defect in a product may be inferred from the failure or some other incident involving the product, particularly if the failure or incident is one that ordinarily or likely resulted from such a defect. Evidence of another cause of the failure or incident may, of course, rebut the inference of a defect.

A defect that makes a product unreasonably dangerous creates strict liability for the manufacturer, seller, or other commercial provider of the product to a foreseeable consumer.

**consumer expectation test**  A product is defective if it will not perform as a reasonable ordinary consumer expects. Consumer expectation is an objective measure of an allegation of a defect in a given product, by which the product is defective if it will not perform in the manner and with the level of safety that an ordinary and reasonable consumer would expect of such a product. Consumer expectation is available in some jurisdictions to prove a product defect in lieu of the risk benefit standard.

*See also:* consumer.

**failure to warn (marketing defect)** A dangerous aspect of a product about which the consumer is given no notice. Failure to warn is a basis of liability in a product, which arises when there is a latent aspect of the product that is not the subject of a design or manufacturing defect but that presents a danger to the consumer or others when the product is misused. This aspect of the product is a defect unless the customer is given reasonable notice of the danger of the latent defect and of the appropriate means of averting the danger during the product's use.

*See also:* failure (fail); label, warning label.

**reasonable alternative design** A design by which the product can be produced without its defect. A reasonably alternative design is a design that may be employed in substitution for the design of a product that contains a defect in issue, the reasonably alternative design being sufficient to produce a substantially similar product at a substantially similar cost of production (not considering the cost of implementation or retooling of machinery). In jurisdictions that require proof of a reasonably alternative design, the effect may be to require the plaintiff to prove by the existence of the alternative that the selection of the design employed was negligent.

**risk–utility analysis (risk/utility)** A balance of the benefits of a product to society against the risk of harm through its use. Risk–utility analysis is a form of cost–benefit analysis applied to a product that causes harm either because it is defective or because it is unavoidably unsafe. In the event of a defective product, the defect must render it unreasonably dangerous, which is the result of a determination that the benefits of the product as designed, manufactured, or labeled do not outweigh its risks as designed, manufactured, or labeled. Risk–utility takes several forms of analysis. When a dangerous product may be compared to a safe product, the most common analysis is to compare the advantages and risks of the dangerous form of product with the advantages risks of the safe product. When no safe product exists for comparison, the measure is more general, comparing the benefits of the product to society as a whole to the risks it poses.

*See also:* value, cost-benefit analysis (CBA).

**unavoidably unsafe product (dangerous product or unreasonably dangerous product)** A product that is inherently dangerous. An unavoidably unsafe product is a product that, in light of the current state of human knowledge, science, and engineering, cannot be designed or manufactured in a manner that would make the product safe in its intended, ordinary use. No matter what, use of the product poses a risk of harm to the user or others.

An unreasonably dangerous product is either an unavoidably unsafe product or a product that has a defect rendering it dangerous, in either case if the risk of harm the product poses is not outweighed by some benefit to the public in its use or benefit. A manufacturer of an unreasonably dangerous product is liable for injuries it causes if there was a feature or element that might have made it safe that was not incorporated into its design or manufacture.

**theories of product liability** Liability for a product defect arises mainly from warranty and negligence. Product liability may arise from tort, or contract, or both, in a given jurisdiction related to a given claim. The maker of a product may be found liable for its defect if the design or manufacture is negligent, in that a reasonable duty of care was not employed to determine a reasonably foreseeable defect. When such negligence is proven by a theory of res ipsa loquitur, the standard amounts to a form of strict liability. An independent theory of tort liability exists for strict liability for the makers of products that are unreasonably dangerous.

Product liability may also be based on warranty, whether an express warranty that is contradicted by the specific defect that is found to exist, or an implied warranty of merchantability or fitness for a particular use, that is contradicted because the defect rendered the product unmerchantable or unfit. Some jurisdictions rely on one or both approaches to liability, and in all jurisdictions, the proof of liability for a defective product must satisfy the theoretical requirements for a theory that is valid in that jurisdiction.

Other theories of liability for a product include control, in which a manufacturer or other party is liable for control over the product, particularly for its maintenance or repair.

*See also:* negligence (negligent).

**several liability** Independent liability for each defendant who caused a portion of the plaintiff injury. Several liability is independent liability for each defendant whose breach of duty gave rise to a harm to the plaintiff. At common law, several liability was enforced through separate civil actions against each defendant, each being held responsible for the extent of the injury each caused. The burden was considerable on the plaintiff to bring a variety of actions against each of several defendants, particularly when they had engaged in related actions that had cumulatively caused the plaintiff's injury. It also led to each defendant arguing the greater cause was a non–party, so that no party might appear responsible in any given case. Several liability came then to be pled in actions brought against the defendants jointly, and also the availability of joint liability was increased in the early twentieth century to allow joint liability and several liability for independent actions by defendants that combined by natural and direct causes to produce a single injury not rationally apportioned to the cause of one defendant's conduct or another.

*See also:* liability, joint and several liability; liability, joint liability; several.

**strict liability**   Liability for injury regardless of intent or wrongdoing. Strict liability in tort creates liability for a party engaged in certain activities, particularly abnormally dangerous activities, so that the party is liable for all harms caused by the activity, no matter how careful or thorough the party was in minimizing the risk of harm to others.

Strict liability in criminal law is an offense for which there is no mens rea requirement, and thus it may be committed by accident.

*See also:* fault; negligence, negligence per se.

**criminal strict liability (offence of strict liability)** An unintentional criminal offense. Criminal strict liability, or an offense of strict liability, is a crime defined in such a manner that is is committed regardless of any intent or even knowledge by the person committing it, such as unknowing possession of a controlled substance. Courts require a legislature to be very clear in reaching conduct with no mens rea, but such criminal prohibitions are generally upheld.

**vicarious liability**   The liability of one person for the actions of another. Vicarious liability is a specific form of liability by one person for the actions of another, when the person liable is in a position of responsibility for the person creating the liability. Though there are exceptions and limitations, vicarious liability makes a principal liable for an agent, a parent for a child, and an employer for an employee.

**course of employment (scope of employment)** Vicarious liability extends only to acts required in or essential to an employee's work. Vicarious liability for an employee is limited to acts in the course of employment. It may sometimes be difficult to establish what act is genuinely within that scope and what act is beyond it. In general, if the action is one directed to be done by a supervisor, expected as a matter of routine in such jobs, within the scope of a job description, or done within the scope of apparent authority on behalf of the employer, then the employer is vicariously liable.

**libel (libelous)**   A defamation published by writing or in an image. A libel is a false statement that defames a living person that is published (in the sense that it is distributed to a person other than the person defamed) in a written, printed, or electronic form in words or images. The defamatory nature of a libel is described variously in different jurisdictions, but it generally includes a sense by which a person would ordinarily be expected to suffer a diminished regard or respect by others if the others believed the defamatory statement about that person to be true.

*See also:* tort, dignitary tort; torts, economic tort; slander (slanderer); press, freedom of the press (liberty of the press); privacy, invasion of privacy, false light; defamation.

**criminal libel (criminal defamation)**   Publication of a deliberate falsehood to disturb the peace or defame a private person. Criminal libel is the crime of defamation in writing of a private person or of using writings for the intended purpose of disturbing the peace. Criminal libel is limited by the dictates of the First Amendment, and matters of public concern, including the criticism of the government or government officers is not criminal libel.

**food libel**   The disparagement of food. Food libel is a disparaging or negative statement not based on a reasonable and reliable scientific foundation about the health or safety of a given item of food. Actions against statements made regarding food in an attempt to influence public debate, however, may be barred under the First Amendment.

*See also:* disparagement (disparaging goods or disparaging title or trade libel).

**group libel**   A libel of a group of twenty-five or more. Group libel depicts a libel of a group of people too large to be libeled in the manner the law of defamation considers libel, as a loss of personal reputation. As a rule of thumb, a libel of a group of twenty-five or more is a group libel, and it is not actionable, whether by a member of the group or the group as an entity.

**libel as complaint in admiralty**   The initial pleading in an admiralty action. A libel is a petition or allegation for relief, brought by a plaintiff against a defendant in admiralty. Libels were once pled in the common-law courts, but that function is now performed by the use of a complaint. The term and form continue to be used in admiralty to initiate process for the seizure of a vessel.

**libel per quod**   Libel arising from a text in a context. Libel per quod is libel that is not inherent in the terms expressed in the text in issue but that is apparent as a result of interpretation of that text in the context in which it was written or read. An apparently innocent statement or description may be libellous per quod if it uses innuendo, sarcasm, or suggestion to cause a reader to infer libellous claims are made as fact. Unlike libel per se, the plaintiff in an action for libel per quod must prove special damages.

*See also:* slander, slander per quod; defamation, defamation per quod (double entendre); per, per quod.

**libel per se**   A written statement that is inherently defamatory. Libel per se is the publicized writing or printing of a statement that is asserted as a fact about a person that would harm a person's reputation in that person's community, in any context and without requiring interpretation or an interpretation of innuendo. Four recognized categories of statements amount to libel per se: an assertion that a person has committed an infamous crime; an assertion the person has an infectious disease; an assertion that would tend to subject a person to hatred, distrust, ridicule, contempt, or disgrace; and an assertion that tends to injure a person's reputation in that person's trade or profession. Damages are presumed in a case of libel per se, and there is no need to show damages for such an action, as there would be a requirement to prove damages for libel per quod. The primary difference between libel per se and slander per se is the medium of expression, in that libel is written while slander is spoken.

*See also:* slander, slander per se; per, per se.

**seditious libel**  False claims made against the government or an official. Seditious libel is a crime, as well as a tort, of making false claims with the intent of diminishing the loyalty of others to the state or the government, with the ultimate aim of encouraging the state to fail. At common law, the defendant could not assert the truth as a defense, but in the United States, truth has long been a defense. Seditious libel is not a crime in current U.S. law, because to make such speech criminal is generally considered to violate the First Amendment.

*See also:* constitution, U.S. Constitution, amendment 1 (amendment I or first amendment); press, freedom of the press (liberty of the press).

**trade libel**  *See:* libel, food libel; disparagement (disparaging goods or disparaging title or trade libel).

**liberalism**  *See:* jurisprudence, liberalism (liberal).

**libertarianism or libertarian jurisprudence**  *See:* jurisprudence, libertarian legal theory (libertarianism or libertarian jurisprudence).

**libertas (liberam or liberata or libertates)**  Liberty. Libertas is the Latin term for the broad idea of liberty, manifest particularly in the Goddess Libertas. It also represented a status of a free people not under the domination of another state, and, in Roman law, represented specific licenses or exemptions, most importantly libertas directa, an act that amounts to manumission, or the freeing of a slave. Libertas is the root of a term in medieval English for a freehold, or liberum tenentum, as well as a variety of writs in the common law. A number of forms had special meanings in the common or civil laws: Libera may be a form of libertas, or it may be the form that became livery, or delivery. Libertinus was a freedman or manumitted slave. Libertates are franchises, particularly crown grants.

*See also:* livery; liberty.

**liberty**  Freedom from personal restraints created by government or society. Liberty is the state of living in a free society, with the power to do what one chooses without restraints created by other people. Liberty implies, however, a responsibility that is a natural constraint to act with due regard of others and the good of all; liberty is not license. As liberty is usually understood today, it is synonymous with freedom, but as a matter of historical context, liberty is best understood by its most

historically significant antithesis — tyranny — as opposed to slavery, the antithesis of freedom.

**liberty clause**  *See:* constitution, U.S. Constitution, clauses, liberty clause.

**liberty interest**  *See:* due process of law, liberty interest.

**liberty of contract**  *See:* contract, liberty of contract | three-part test; contract, liberty of contract (impairment of contract or freedom of contract or obligations of contract).

**liberty of the press**  *See:* press, freedom of the press (liberty of the press).

**religious liberty**  The freedom of religion. Religious liberty is the liberty to pursue one's own understanding of one's religious beliefs and obligations, without interference or support from the state. In the United States, one limit to such liberty is that its exercise may not violate laws of general application, that is to say laws that are not intended to burden religion but prohibit acts for other reasons that happen to be practiced as an act of faith.

*See also:* religion, freedom of religion.

**license (licensed or licensor or licensee)**  Authorization, or proof thereof. A license is an authorization to do something, without which one ordinarily could not do what one is licensed to do. Licenses can be either public or private.

A public license includes such licenses as professional licenses, automobile driver's licenses, and business licenses. A private license includes the right to enter a fence and use land without trespassing, or the right to use the licensed intellectual property of another. A license is valid whether or not the licensor is compensated by the licensee.

**driver license (driver's license)**  A form demonstrating a valid entitlement to drive a motor vehicle. A driver license, or driver's license, is both the permission of the state or other jurisdiction entitling an individual to operate a motor vehicle on the public roads within the jurisdiction and the form issued by the jurisdiction as evidence of that permission. That form, usually a permanent plastic card or temporary paper form, is also used as a form of proof of the bearer's identification. U.S. jurisdictions recognize the driver's licenses of non-residents issued by other U.S. jurisdictions but require licensure within the jurisdiction by their own residents who drive. A valid driver's license incorporating a photograph of the person to whom it is issued is considered government-issued identification for most regulatory purposes, though, it does not serve as a passport or proof of national citizenship. A driver must carry a valid driver's license in a motor vehicle while operating it on a public way and must surrender the license for inspection to a police officer who requests it in a lawful stop or search. Operation of a vehicle without possession of a driver's license is an offense, usually a misdemeanor or administrative driving offense, but operation of a vehicle without having been issued a then-valid driver's license in most jurisdictions is a more serious offense.

*See also:* stop, police stop, investigative detention (stop and frisk or terry stop); offense, traffic offense; stop, police stop, roadblock.

**license to enter land** Permission to enter land without trespass. A license is oral or written permission given by the licensor, the occupant of land, to the licensee, allowing the licensee to do some act on the land that otherwise would amount to trespass. A defining feature of a license, distinguishing it from an easement or covenant, is that a license may be unilaterally revoked by the licensor, with no advance notice to the licensee (although under certain circumstances, a licensor may be estopped from revocation).

*See also:* invitation (invite or invited); invitee (business guest); trespasser.

*Revocability* The revocability or a license defines it. However, a license upon which a licensee relies, in circumstances the licensee knows the licensor is aware of the reliance, and in which the licensee expends significant money or effort in reliance on the continuation of the license, may become irrevocable because the licensee seek estoppel of the revocation. An irrevocable license to enter land is usually an easement.

**license to marry** *See:* marriage, marriage license (license to marry).

**license to practice medicine or licensed doctor or licensed nurse** *See:* medicine, medical license (license to practice medicine or licensed doctor or licensed nurse).

**licensed** *See:* licentiate (licensed).

**licensee** One with a license to do something otherwise forbidden. The licensee is the person granted a license, which may vary in its significance owing to the nature of the license. Although in no case can a licensee acquire greater rights in the property than those of the licensor, a licensee may benefit from additional duties owed by the licensor to the licensee. In cases in which a license is extended to a licensee by contract, the contract both describes and limits the license.

In the use of land, a licensee is likely to be a social guest. The common law has long distinguished a licensee from others who are the land as an invitee or as a trespasser. An invitee is present on the land for professional or commercial purposes — the customer shopping in a store or the plumber working in a house, for example. A licensee is present, even if expressly invited, for non-commercial reasons; the presumed difference is that the licensee is present for the licensee's own benefit and not for the licensor's benefit.

The difference between a licensee and an invitee is that, under the common law, the occupant of the land has a duty to the invitee but not to the licensee to warn of all dangers known to the occupant, as long as such dangers should be reasonable foreseeable by the licensee.

*See also:* land, liability to other on the land, licensee; invitee (business guest).

**licensee by invitation (licensee by permission)** A licensee who is expressly invited or allowed on the land. A licensee by invitation usually has the same benefits and obligations as any other licensee, even though the licensee is expressly invited or given permission to enter by the occupant of the land to enter the land. An invitation only places the person invited in the role of an invitee if the invitation is "for mutual advantage." That is, an invitation for commercial purposes or for the purpose of carrying out some work or to engage in speculation related to a contract (like shopping) results in the person invited entering as an invitee. All other persons on the lands with the permission of the occupant are licensees, even if they are expressly invited. An invitation to enter property as a licensee may be express or implied from circumstances in which invitation by implication would ordinarily arise.

**licensure** The regulation process to a trade or profession. Licensure is a process by the state of regulating those who would perform a trade or profession. Licensure may serve the interests of the state in the collection of revenue, but its primary function is to ensure that standards for the safe and effective performance of the trade or profession are identified and required of each member, who gives some evidence of ability to perform according to such standards in order to receive a license, and who does not violate such standards in order to retain it.

**licentiate (licensed)** A person licensed to perform a trade or profession. A licentiate is the holder of a license to perform some occupation or engage as a member of a licensed profession.

**licentiousness** The abuse of license or liberty. Licentiousness is conduct ungoverned by any sense of propriety or awareness of the effects of that conduct on others, the abuse of liberty or license. Although licentious conduct is by definition allowed, its performance is by its nature abusive of the purposes of the allowance. For example, a person who claims a right to speak in the name of freedom of speech and does so in order to prevent others from speaking is licentious. Licentiousness is sometimes confused with mere offensiveness, because offensive but lawful conduct is licentious, but licentiousness implies a broader range of burdens upon others, including a risk to the justification of the liberty licentiously abused.

**licit (licet)** Lawful, or permitted. Licit is is a corruption of licet, Latin for anything permitted or lawful.

**illicit** Unlawful. Anything illicit is unlawful or, at least, not permitted. Illicit is more common in contemporary usage than its root, licit. Illicit is best understood as being the contrary of licit, which is what is lawful or permitted. A contract barring illicit activities precludes such activities that violate the criminal law of the jurisdictions in which the contract is made or performed. An insurance contract that excludes coverage for illicit trade or transportation will bar coverage for an incident that occurs while an insured vehicle or person is engaged in conduct that violates the criminal law, though a violation of a traffic law is not within the exclusion as illicit in this sense.

**lie (action will lie)**   Will pass the tests required. To lie, in legal procedure, is to be proper or appropriate in its intended application and will be admitted in court, as in "this action will lie" or "no action will lie."

To lie in this sense has nothing to do with making a false statement; the term is very old in the common law, being derived from the same sense of lie or lay as in a ship's officer being ordered to "lay in a course."

**lie detector**   See: polygraph (lie detector).

**lien (lienholder)**   A bar on the sale of property until an obligation is performed. A lien is a servitude on a specific piece of property, which allows its possession by another until a debt of the property's owner is paid or another obligation of the owner to the lienholder is satisfied, the effect being in most cases to prevent the sale or transfer of the property until the lien is vacated. A lien operates whether the property itself is in the possession of the owner or the lien holder. A lien is routinely used to ensure that a debtor pays those who extend credit to acquire realty, goods, or services. A lien may act to secure property for the payment of a future claim for damages. A lien may be imposed by agreement, by custom, by statute, or as a result of a court order.

A lien is not itself a debt but a security for the satisfaction of a debt or assurance of an opportunity to satisfy a pending debt. A lien is a security against a whole property, although the lien may secure a debt of a greater or lesser amount. If a lien becomes extinguished prior to the payment of a debt, as can happen for various reasons as, for example, expiration of a claim to a lien under a statute of limitations or failure to satisfy a procedural requirement, the debt survives.

See also: lien, abatement of a lien; pilot, pilotage (pilot boat or pilotage ground); judgment, enforcement of judgment, judgment roll; security, security interest; mortgage, mortgage theory (intermediate theory or lien theory or title theory).

**abatement of a lien**   The release of property from a lien. An abatement of a lien is the release of property from under the lien. It contrasts with the abatement of an assessment subject to a lien, which is the forgiveness or all or part of the debt.

See also: lien (lienholder).

**attachment lien**   A lien on property that may be attached as a remedy. An attachment lien is a lien against property that is or may be attached as a remedy in civil litigation. The lien may be filed at the commencement of the suit, but it is perfected only once the suit has concluded with judgment for the lienholder. In most cases, a third party may take possession of the property subject to the lien while it is unperfected.

**circularity of liens (circular priority)**   Multiple liens that are not in a clear priority. A circularity of liens is created when various parties with claims against one property or its owner have acquired liens in an order or manner that creates a loop rather than a hierarchy. (A's interest is superior to B's, and B's is superior to C's but C's is superior to A's). Priority among circular liens is often resolved by resort to equitable principles.

**judgment lien**   A claim on a judgment debtor's property until the judgment is paid. A judgment lien is a lien created by implication from a judgment against a defendant rendered by a court. The judgment may be enrolled in the judgment roll of a court in which the defendant holds property, acting as a lien upon that property until the lien is released. A judgment lien has priority over all subsequent liens but not over prior bona fide liens, such as an existing materialman's lien. The property is subject to attachment and sale to satisfy the lien, but the property holder may satisfy the judgment following enrollment by payment of the amount owed.

**judicial lien**   Any lien ordered by a court or resulting from a judgment. A judicial lien is a lien that arises by operation of a judgment or any other order of a court, usually as a remedy granted to satisfy a judgment in law or in equity. Most judicial liens are judgment liens.

**lienholder**   Any person holding a lien in the property of another. A lienholder is a person with rights in the property of another resulting from a lien, whether the lien is perfected or not, or even known to the lienholder or not. A lienholder ceases to be a lienholder at the extinction of the lien, whether or not the underlying debt giving rise to the lien is satisfied.

**lis pendens**   Pending litigation, or a lien to secure a potential remedy. Lis pendens, literally, is pending litigation. More specifically, lis pendens (or more properly, a notice of lis pendens) is a notice of a potential claim against property that is filed by a plaintiff against a defendant's property, creating a security interest in the property that would allow it to secure a remedy if the plaintiff succeeds in the claims against the defendant.

The procedures for a lis pendens vary from jurisdiction to jurisdiction, in some being determined by statute or court rule and in others being customary. A plaintiff files a notice of lis pendens as to specific property, not merely against the defendant or against some or all of the defendant's assets. In many jurisdictions, the notice may be filed against a party who either served as a defendant in a civil action or is believed in good faith by a plaintiff to soon be served and made a defendant. In such cases, the notice of lis pendens must be timely dismissed if the defendant is not served in a reasonable time.

**mechanic's lien**   A lien implied by law in the materials and work provided to another. A mechanic's lien is the general term for a lien implied by law in the goods sold by a supplier and the work done by a contractor in the structure, goods, vehicle, or other machine or thing in or on which the goods are used or the work is performed. The lien is effective from the time the work is completed, though most jurisdictions require a notice of the lien to be filed in order to perfect the lien against later claimants to the property. The perfected lien persists until the debt is paid in full or until the limitation on the enforcement of liens has run, although an unperfected lien is usually destroyed if the property is sold or at the end of the statute of limitations on the collection of the debt.

At common law, there was a distinct form of materialman's lien for the supplier and mechanic's lien for the artisan or contractor. This distinction in form is now quite rare in the United States, and other than title, each is treated in a manner like the other, although the mechanic's lien may encompass the value of material but a materialman's lien may not encompass the value of labor.

**satisfaction of lien**   The payment of a debt secured by a lien. Satisfaction of a lien is the payment of the debt that the lien secures. A lien that has been satisfied may be released by filing a statement of the lienholder that the debt has been satisfied, and so the lien has been satisfied. Either language is sufficient in most jurisdictions to operate as a release.

**tax lien**   A lien on property to secure unpaid taxes. A tax lien is a lien on the property of a taxpayer who is delinquent in payment of the taxes owed, or whom the taxing authority claims is delinquent. The lien attaches to all property held or acquired by the taxpayer until the lien is released.

**life**   The period of independent and functional existence. Life is the state between the beginning and the end of an organism's active existence. Many definitions of life depend on an organism's ability to function, particularly whether the organism can sustain the operation of its vital organs without assistance, to grow cells, to ingest and process food and water, to circulate blood, and to allow activity in its brain. For humans, a separate concern is recognized in the ability to form thoughts and emotions.

The moment at which life commences and the moment at which it ends are both highly controversial, and there are many tests proposed for each. The solution described by Bouvier in 1853 is useful, that life is different from civil existence, so that life may begin at conception but civil recognition and legal protection as an individual may commence at birth. Likewise, life might persist in a coma or other terminal medical incapacity, but civil independence have ceased.

*See also:* birth; death.

**life estate**   *See:* estate, interest, life estate (life interest).

**life estate pur autre vie**   *See:* estate, interest, life estate pur autre vie.

**life imprisonment**   *See:* incarceration, imprisonment, life imprisonment, life without parole (LWOP or

L.W.O.P.); incarceration, imprisonment, life imprisonment (life sentence or life).

**life in being**   *See:* perpetuity, rule against perpetuities, life in being (measuring life or validating life).

**life insurance**   *See:* insurance, category of insurance, life insurance, whole life insurance (straght life insurance or ordinary life insurance); insurance, category of insurance, life insurance, universal life insurance; insurance, category of insurance, life insurance, term life insurance (term assurance); insurance, category of insurance, life insurance.

**life interest**   *See:* estate, interest, life estate (life interest); due process of law, life interest.

**life sentence or life**   *See:* incarceration, imprisonment, life imprisonment (life sentence or life).

**life tenant**   *See:* tenant, life tenant.

**life without parole**   *See:* incarceration, imprisonment, life imprisonment, life without parole (LWOP or L.W.O.P.).

**brain life**   *See:* death, moment of death, brain death (brain life).

**lifetime learning credit**   A tax credit to aid the pursuance of higher education.

**quality of life**   The physical and material means for the enjoyment of life. Quality of life is a measure of the means by which one may enjoy one's life, whether physical, psychological, or financial.

Quality of life is an important measure in medicine. The quality of life that a person would have owing to pain and disability may be sufficiently degraded from a humane expectation that a diminished quality of life may justify a person's decision to refuse medical care.

Quality of life is also a measure of support, particularly in determining spousal support, in which the quality of life of a person with less money is presumed to be worse than the quality of life of a person with more. Quality of life may be assessed by activities one engages in and the conditions of one's habitation and environment, such that a degradation of quality of life can be determined by the reduction in the forms or frequency of activities or the luxury of one's environment.

*See also:* damages, classes of damages, hedonic damages (loss of enjoyment of life); hedonism.

**useful life**   The expected functional life of an asset. The useful life of an asset is the reasonably expected period of the business use of the asset. Depreciation of the value of the asset is determined by allocating the diminution of the value of the asset over that time.

*See also:* depreciation.

**ligan**   *See:* salvage, ligan (lagan).

**light**

**ancient lights (easement for light and air)**   A right to preserve a view unobstructed for twenty years or more. Ancient lights is a common–law doctrine allowing an easement over lands of a neighbor to ensure that sufficient light and air reach windows that have existed for at least twenty years. Although this doctrine has been rejected in the United States, an easement for light and air may be established when the use of adjoining land in blocking light and air amounts to a private nuisance. Nuisance may be all the more readily found when the neighboring use interferes with the conversion of solar energy to electricity.

*See also:* easement, light and air easement (air and light easement or air easement or light easement or view easement); solar access.

**light-duty work**   *See:* work, light–duty work (light duty work).

**limit**   A boundary that may not be exceeded or diminished. A limit is an extent for any activity or condition that may not be exceeded, either as a practical matter or as a matter of law. A legal limit may be established by statute, contract, or public policy, and there are innumerable kinds: An insurance limit is the extent of coverage, the greatest amount that may be paid in indemnity. A limit on a sentence for a given offense is the longest time that a person may be required to serve for that offense. A blood alcohol limit is the highest saturation of alcohol in the blood that is allowed without legal sanctions for certain activities, such as driving.

**limitation**   A technical limit on some interest or claim. A limitation is any limit on the existence or enforcement of a right, claim, or interest. Limitations on substantive rights may arise from the definition of the right or the interference with the rights of others.

A limitation, in procedure, is a prohibition on a particular action on the basis of a policy independent of the merits of the action. The most common limitations are those arising from time, barring an action that is too stale.

**conditional limitation**   A limitation that is contingent upon a later occurence. A conditional limitation is a limitation that will be either made effective or made void according to a change in a condition in the future. Thus, any limitation on a right or interest made subject to possession or to loss, if an event occurs or if an ongoing condition ends, is a conditional limitation.

*See also:* contingency (contingent).

**limitation of action (limitations of actions)**   A bar to an action for being brought too late in time. Limitations on actions prohibit the late filing of a civil or criminal action, according to the subject matter and the claim, which must be brought within a specific time. Limitations for criminal actions are determined by the appropriate statute of limitations. Limitations for civil matters under law arise under civil statutes of limitations. Claims for the enforcement of contracts may be limited by dispute resolution clauses in the contract, if such clauses are deemed enforceable as a matter of law. Claims in equity are limited by laches.

*See also:* time; time, time immemorial (time of memory or immemorial possession).

**laches**   The limitation of actions by time in equity. Laches is the defense in equity that summarizes the maxim that "equity aids the vigilant and not those who slumber on their rights." A plaintiff who delays too long in bringing an action for relief in equity is essential negligent in waiting so long and will have no relief. The measurement of time is based not on an absolute running of a clock, but is the time after which others are prejudiced by the delay.

**statute of limitations**   Statutory bars to criminal and civil claims based on the passage of time. A statute of limitations is a time limit established by legislation designating the longest time after which an action occurs that a claim may be brought under the law. Statutes of limitations bar private actions for redress as well as criminal prosecutions.

The bases for statutes of limitations, as with all doctrines of repose, are both in fairness and practicality. There is a sense that matters of significance must be brought or lost owing to the unfairness of waiting an unreasonable time, during which evidence is lost and witnesses' memories fade, or they otherwise become unable to testify. Moreover, past a certain lapse of time, parties to disputes are entitled to quietude and confidence that the matter in question will remain undisputed. Hence, the purpose of such statutes is to provide finality and closure and to extinguish actions that become difficult to prove due to the passage of time. Such policies are balanced against the significance of the claims involved, leading to various limits on different claims. Claims that tend to be minor or based on unusually transient evidence tend to have short limitations periods. Claims that may take longer to discover or to prepare an action for, on the other hand, are usually given a longer period. Claims of great seriousness may have no period at all, and in most jurisdictions there is no statute of limitations on a criminal charge of murder.

A statute of limitations may not run from the moment of the action that gives rise to a claim. The statute may be tolled, or the calculation of time suspended, for a variety of reasons.

*See also:* offense, continuing offense; accrual (accrue); equity, equitable pleading, equitable recoupment.

**legal injury rule (legal-injury rule)**   The statute runs from the time a person may bring an action. The legal injury rule establishes the moment at which the statute of limitations for a civil action at law begins to run at the time when a cause of action may be brought. This is the moment of legal injury, as opposed to factual injury.

*See also:* injury, legal injury.

**occurrence rule**  The statute runs when an occurrence is complete. The occurrence rule requires that a statute of limitations will begin to run when an occurrence, or event, that gives rise to a cause of action is complete. A single event that has several component actions only gives rise to a cause of action at the time of the last related action. Thus, the statute only begins to run against a person harmed by the event when the last component action is complete. The statute's time will be later measured back to the last action, not the first. When an occurrence rule is specified in a statute, the discovery rule will usually not toll the running of the statute, unless a deliberate attempt is made to hide or disguise the occurrence.

*See also:* occurrence (incident).

**running of the statute of limitations**  The passing of time during which a claim may be brought. The running of a statute of limitations is a metaphor for the passage of time during which a claim may be brought, the increasing proximity to the time when the statute of limitations will bar the claim. When the statute has run, the time for the claim has passed and it may no longer be brought. The running of the statute is "tolled" when the period is interrupted.

**tolling (toll)**  An interruption in the time a limitations period runs. Tolling interrupts the time of a period for the limitations of action under a statute of limitations, effectively adding on time to commence an action after the moment when the statute would otherwise have barred an action. Tolling may result from many causes, and it may take place at moment of conduct from which a cause of action would have accrued or at some time later. Tolling persists as long as the cause of the tolling persists, and when that cause ends, the calculation of time under the statute commences again.

**continuing violation doctrine**  Tolling for conduct that persists until it ends. The continuing violation doctrine tolls the running of the statute of limitations that would have arisen from actionable conduct because the conduct initially did not rise to a level that a reasonable person would have considered to cause an actionable injury or offense, yet through repetition or continuousness, the injury or offense later became apparent. A claim may be brought any time within the limitations period from an instance of the ongoing pattern of conduct, and the claim may reach back to the earliest conduct that is part and parcel of the same repetitive or continuous pattern.

*See also:* discrimination, employment discrimination, doctrine of continuing violation; harassment, continuing violation.

**continuous-treatment doctrine**  Tolling until a course of medical treatment is concluded. The continuous treatment doctrine tolls a statute of limitations that would have commenced at the moment of a wrongful act during a medical procedure, tolling the running of the statute until the completion of the course of treatment resulting from the wrongful act.

**discovery rule**  Tolling until the discovery of the cause of action. The discovery rule tolls the period of time allowed to commence action until the claimant learns of the facts of the conditions that give rise to the cause of action or until events occur that would give a reasonable person notice of the conditions giving rise to the action.

*See also:* limitation, limitation of actions, statute of limitations, occurrence rule.

**year and a day rule**  An injury resulting in death more than a year and a day later is not homicide. The year and a day rule is a common-law limit on the definition of murder, which operates as a criminal limitation of actions. Following an assault, if the victim dies within a year and a day from the injuries sustained, the assailant may be charged with the death, but if death occurs later than a year and a day, the assailant is only responsible for the injuries prior to death. Most jurisdictions have abandoned this rule in favor of a rule of proximate causation.

**statute of repose**  A statute barring actions of a given form earlier than a given event. A statute of repose terminates rights of action of a given form regardless of the time elapsed since the cause accrued, basing its time from the moment of an event, rather than from the time a cause of action arising from the event becomes known. Unlike limitations, an action cut off by a statute of repose is usually incapable of revival, and the period by which the statute takes effect is usually (though not always) not subject to tolling. Some statutes of repose cut short all claims of a given form, known or unknown, older than a given date. Root of title statutes are a form of statute of repose.

*See also:* repose; title, root of title.

**limitation of estate**  Any condition or contingency that might limit an estate. A limitation, or language of limitation, creates a possibility of defeasance in an estate. Any language that makes an estate's continued possession or ownership dependent upon the occurrence or failure of a condition is a limitation. The limitation creates a future interest in the party who would take the estate in the event the limitation is satisfied and must satisfy the rule against perpetuities and other doctrines affecting limitations.

*See also:* estate, future interest; defeasibility (defeasible or indefeasibility or indefeasible or indefeasibly).

# limited

**limited admissibility**  *See:* admissibility, limited admissibility.

**limited-fund rationale** *See:* class, class action, class action remedy, limited-fund rationale.

**limited appearance** *See:* jurisdiction, in personam jurisdiction, voluntary jurisdiction, special appearance (limited appearance); appearance, limited appearance.

**limited jurisdiction** *See:* jurisdiction, limited jurisdiction.

**limited-liability company** *See:* company, limited-liability company (L.L.C. or LLC).

**limited-liability corporation** *See:* corporation, corporations, limited-liability corporation.

**limited-liability limited partnership** *See:* partnership, limited partnership, limited-liability limited partnership (LLLP or L.L.L.P.).

**limited-liability partnership** *See:* partnership, limited-liability partnership (LLP or L.L.P.).

**limited partner** *See:* partnership, limited partnership (limited partner).

**limited partnership** *See:* partnership, limited partnership, limited-liability limited partnership (LLLP or L.L.L.P.); partnership, limited partnership (limited partner).

**limited power of appointment** *See:* power, power of appointment, limited power of appointment (non-general power of appointment).

**limited public forum** *See:* speech, freedom of speech, forum, public forum, limited public forum.

**limited-purpose public figure** *See:* defamation, defamation of a public figure, limited-purpose public figure.

**Lincoln's Law** *See:* fraud, False Claims Act (Lincoln's Law).

**line** *See:* descent, descendant, lineal descendent, line.

**line of credit** *See:* credit, line of credit.

**line-item veto** *See:* veto, line-item veto (line item veto).

**lineage (lineal)** The serial relationship from parent to child. Lineage is the relationship of direct ancestors to children, in a line from parent to child to that child's child, and so forth. To use lineage as a means of description implies that the analysis involved does not take into account legal changes of relationship, such as adoption or guardianship.

**lineal consanguinity** *See:* consanguinity, lineal consanguinity.

**lineal descendent** *See:* descent, descendant, lineal descendent, line.

**lineal heir** *See:* heir, heir of the blood (lineal heir).

**link in chain** *See:* incrimination, self-incrimination, link in chain (link-in-chain principle).

**lipstick on a pig** *See:* pig, lipstick on a pig.

**liquid asset** *See:* liquidity, liquid asset (liquid assets).

**liquidation (unliquidated liquidate or liquidated)** The determination of the value of a thing, especially by its sale. Liquidation is a process of both ascertaining a fixed value for a thing of otherwise uncertain value and of converting the unknown value thing into its final value, as when a business is wrapped up or an estate's assets are sold or dispersed.

*See also:* priority, claim priority, absolute priority rule; abandonment, abandonment by debtor.

**liquidation of damages** *See:* damages, contract damages, liquidated damages (liquidation of damages).

**liquidation value** *See:* value, liquidation value.

**liquidation of a claim (debt liquidation)** The finite determination of the value of a debt or claim. A liquidated debt or claim is a debt or claim that is known to be in an amount certain, as opposed to an unliquidated debt or claim that is not ascertained in a specific amount.

*See also:* damages, contract damages, liquidated damages (liquidation of damages).

**liquidity** The ability sell an asset quickly or without causing a drop in its value. Liquidity is ease with which an entity can raise money or with which an asset can be bough or sold. A common measure of liquidity is the ratio of cash or similarly convertible assets to an entity's debts and potential requirements. An entity with higher liquidity has a greater ability to meet unforeseen obligations. Market liquidity is the capacity of a market to allow the sale of purchase of an asset without the purchase affecting its price,

**liquid asset (liquid assets)** Assets easily and quickly convertible to cash. Liquid assets are those that are available for use in a brief time by their owner, including cash on hand, cash on bank deposit, and bonds or shares or other instruments of value that may be converted into cash quickly. Particular regulation of various enterprises may define and limit the categories of assets that are included for the purposes of assessing an entity's liquidity.

**lis (litem or lite)** Lawsuit. Lis represents an action in court, even if it is yet to be filed, as in some uses of a lis pendens.

**lis pendens** *See:* lien, lis pendens; equity, equitable procedure, lis pendens.

**lite pendente** *See:* pendente lite (lite pendente).

**litem or lite** *See:* lis (litem or lite).

**literal meaning** *See:* meaning, literal meaning.

**litigation (litigate or litigiously)** The process of any criminal or civil action. Litigation refers to the entire process of an action, or all actions, including civil and criminal actions. In most cases, however, litigation refers to civil litigation, private actions between private parties; criminal litigation is usually more specifically identified. To litigate a matter is to prepare it and argue it in court, and to act litigiously is to act in a manner that presumes the action will be assessed or determined in court.

**litigation privilege**  *See:* privilege, litigation privilege (witness privilege or party privilege).

**litigation sanction**  *See:* sanction, litigation sanction, rule eleven (Rule 11).

**litigant**  A person engaged in litigation. A litigant is a person engaged in a civil or criminal action, or who was at some relevant time. Although a prosecutor or defense counsel might litigate an issue in a criminal case, the term litigant in a criminal case refers to the criminal defendant and not, usually, to the state or the people in whose name a prosecution is brought.

**litigiousness (litigious)**  Having a propensity to resort to suit. Litigiousness is an attitude or preference by which a party is prone to resort to suit in order to resolve a dispute. A litigious person or entity is less likely than average to resolve a dispute or question through negotiation or abandonment.

**litigator**  An attorney representing another in court. A litigator is an attorney who represents a litigant in litigation, whether the representation is in court or in another setting related to the litigation. A litigator is particularly responsible to the court as one of its officers as well as to the client to ensure zealous representation of the client's interest within the bounds of the law.

**little board**  *See:* security, securities, securities exchange, American Stock Exchange, little board.

**littoral area**  *See:* shore, littoral area (foreshore or littoral rights or litorral interests).

**livery**  Delivery of possession of any form of property. Livery is a French word for transfer, and so delivery is derived from "de livery."
*See also:* libertas (liberam or liberata or libertates); delivery, delivery of possession; delivery.

**livery of seisin**  *See:* seisin, livery of seisin.

**livery as stables**  A place for the care of horses. A livery in the sense of horse management, is a facility including stables for the boarding, care, outfitting, sale, and hiring of horses.

**livestock**  Animals raised for human consumption or use. Livestock, or stock animals, are animals that are raised in quantity for profit. Most livestock are raised for human consumption, such as cattle or pigs; for the extract products for human, such as chickens for eggs; or for other commercial use, such as horses or other draft animals, or sheep or other animals raised for fibers. Even so, statutes often define livestock narrowly, so chickens or farmed fish are not included.

**living modified organism or G.M.O. or GMO or L.M.O. or LMO**  *See:* gene, genetically modified organism (living modified organism or G.M.O. or GMO or L.M.O. or LMO).

**living separate and apart**  *See:* divorce, separation, living separate and apart.

**living trust**  *See:* trust, living trust; trust, inter vivos trust (living trust).

**living wage**  *See:* wage, living wage.

**living will**  *See:* will, living will; death, living will (advance directive).

**LL.B. or LLB**  *See:* degree, academic degree, law degree, bachelor of laws (LL.B. or LLB).

**LL.D. or LLD**  *See:* degree, academic degree, law degree, doctor of laws (LL.D. or LLD).

**LL.M. or LLM**  *See:* degree, academic degree, law degree, master of laws (LL.M. or LLM).

**LLLP or L.L.L.P.**  *See:* partnership, limited partnership, limited–liability limited partnership (LLLP or L.L.L.P.).

**Lloyd's of London**  *See:* insurer, insurers, Lloyd's of London (Lloyd's policy).

**loan (lending or lend)**  A grant of money or property to be repaid or returned. A loan is an act by which a person or entity grants money or property to another for a period of time, with the agreement that the property or money lent will be returned to the lender. A loan of property creates a bailment, and a loan of money creates a debt. A loan of money may be made subject to a duty of the borrower to pay interest. A loan made by a banking or commercial establishment or by any person who charges interest is subject to regulation.
*See also:* credit.

**loan packing**  *See:* pack, loan packing.

**amortized loan**  A loan with interest amortized over a repayment period. An amortized loan is a loan structured to be repaid in increments over a fixed period, each increment repaying a structured amount of the amortized interest and principal.
*See also:* amortization (amortize).

**bridge loan**  A short–term loan. A bridge loan is a loan structured to be repaid in eighteen months or less, paid in installments that pay interest only, until the principal is repaid in a lump sum on or before a date due.

**commercial loan**  A loan to a commercial enterprise or for a commercial purpose. A commercial loan is any loan that made to a business or for a business purpose. Put otherwise, a commercial law is any loan made neither to a government nor to a consumer for personal, household, or other non-commercial purposes.

**delinquent loan**   A loan past due thirty days or more. A delinquent loan, in general, is any loan with a payment not paid thirty days after its due date. Specific loan agreements may define a different period of time for the treatment of a late payment as a delinquent payment or a loan with late payments as delinquent. The terms of a loan may specify a fee for late payments, a different fee for delinquent payments, and a different term for the collection of payments on delinquent loans, including the ability, with notice to call the loan and demand repayment in full. Delinquent loans must usually be separately reported and accounted on a lender's books.

**home equity loan**   A loan secured by equity in the borrower's home. A home equity loan is a loan secured against the equity in a home above the debt outstanding in existing mortgages. It is, in effect, a form of mortgage.

**installment loan**   A debt paid by installments that each repay principal and interest. An installment loan is a loan of money that is repaid through installment payments, that are either equal in amount or nearly so, each of which includes a portion of the principal and a portion of the entire interest to be charged on the lent money over the life of the loan. To be considered an installment loan, the terms of repayment are specified at the time of the loan's origination, including the rate of interest, the number and amount and frequency of payments, the allocation of each payment toward principal and interest, and the terms under which the debtor may repay in full in advance (if the debtor may do so).

**loan commitment**   A promise to lend an amount of money at specified terms. A loan commitment is a pledge by a lender to make a specific loan to the borrower at some date in the future, according to the rates and terms specified in the commitment. A loan commitment is not a binding contract requiring the borrower enter a loan agreement on those terms, but it is a promise that is enforceable through reliance if the borrower does so.

**loansharking (extortionate credit transaction or loan shark)**   The unlawful loan of money at unconscionable rates. Loansharking is an unregulated practice of lending money, in which the lender charges an unconscionable rate of interest that would not be enforceable in law, sometimes greater than the limit of usury. Loansharking takes many forms, some of which are more apparently legitimate than others, such as taking an inordinate security interest in the borrower's property with the intent of seizing the property. Some are patently illegal amounting to racketeering, such as the use of violence and threats to secure repayment. Loansharking is a crime when a loan is the basis of an act of extortion.

**mortgage loan**   A loan secured by an interest in realty. A mortgage loan is any loan that has as a security for repayment an interest in real property. A mortgage loan may be secured by a deed of trust, an actual mortgage, by a lien, or by any other instrument recording the security interest.
   *See also:* mortgage.

**non-performing loan (nonperforming loan)**   A loan with payments ninety days or more behind schedule. A nonperforming loan is a loan that is delinquent in payment for ninety days or more.

**non-recourse loan (nonrecourse loan or non-recourse debt or nonrecourse debt)**   A loan secured only by interests in collateral. A non-recourse loan is secured only by collateral, often in the assets acquired from the loan, without any recourse to an individual or entity other than the borrower for payment in the event of a default in which the value of the collateral is less than the then amount owed. The individual or entity borrowing the funds of the loan is solely responsible for their repayment, but this responsibility ends in the event of a default or other event calling the loan, and the value of the collateral is all that is available to make good the outstanding debt. The tax effects of a non-recourse loan differs significantly from a recourse loan.
   *See also:* loan, recourse loan (recourse debt).

**recourse loan**   A loan with recourse to a borrower's personal assets in the event of a default. A recourse loan is a loan that is secured by a promise of the borrower to repay the loan in full beyond the value of any collateral or other security interest that may have been given and regardless of any surety by a third party. Thus in the event of a default by the borrower, a lender may pursue the borrower personally, including collection through the attachment of property not subject to a security interest to the benefit of the lender and through garnishment or wages or other payments owed to the borrower. The contrast, of course, is to a non-recourse loan, in which the lender is limited in its ability to recover value in the event of a default only to such property in which the lender has a security interest for the loan.
   *See also:* surety (suretyship); indorsement, co-signature (co-signer or cosign or cosigner); loan, non-recourse loan (nonrecourse loan or non-recourse debt or nonrecourse debt).

**recourse loan (recourse debt)**   A loan secured by the personal liability of an individual, partnership, or business. A recourse loan is a loan for which the debt is secured by the personal commitment of an individual, partnership, or corporation, rather than through only a security interest in assets purchased with the loan amount. In certain situations, a recourse loan is secured by the personal liability of an individual or entity for a loan to another party, particularly when a debt is entered by a partnership or business, for which at least one individual, or the individual members of the partnership, may be held personally liable to pay the debt in the event of a default by the partnership or business.
   *See also:* recourse.

**secured loan (unsecured loan)** A loan that is subject to a security interest in property. A secured loan is a loan in which the debt is secured by the creation of a security interest in some property that persists as long as the debt persists. In the event of a default, the property may be sold to satisfy the outstanding debt or some percentage of it (with the remainder of the debt still owed by the borrower). An unsecured loan is not subject to such a security interest but is an obligation of the borrower.

**sub-prime loan** A loan at terms worse than the prime lending rate. A sub-prime loan is a loan to a person or entity with a sufficiently poor credit rating that the terms of the loan are below the prime rate, which is extended to preferred borrowers. The interest and fees charged on sub-prime loans are higher than for prime rates, and the potential that the debtor will default on the loan is presumed to be higher, as well.

**Truth in Lending Act (T.I.L.A. or TILA)** Federal law requiring disclosure of loan's terms and interest. The Truth in Lending Act was enacted as Title I of the Consumer Credit Protection Act, codified at 15 U.S.C. § 1601, requiring the Board of Governors of the Federal Reserve System to promulgate regulations and exemptions of consumer credit contracts, which are known as Regulation Z, at 12 C.F.R. Part 226 (2009). In general, the TILA requires creditors to disclose the annual percentage rate of interest as well as the terms of payment and collection prior to entry of the contract. The TILA also allows certain defenses against a lien on realty for personal debts, regulates credit cards in some degree, and provides for arbitration of credit disputes.

**lobby (lobbyist or lobbying)** A process to influence legislation and regulation. A lobby is an enterprise designed to influence legislators or regulators to alter the laws in order to promote the interests of a particular interest group or individual. A lobbyist is a person engaged in lobbying toward such an end. Lobbyists in most jurisdictions are required to register their status, and lobbyists seeking to influence members of Congress must record most gifts or services provided to members, their family, staff, or surrogates.

**political action committee (PAC or P.A.C.)** An organization to raise money to promote a candidate or cause. A political action committee is an organization that is not a political party that raises money to fund political campaigns or otherwise to influence political decision-making. A committee that receives or spends more than one thousand dollars is subject to the records requirements and regulations of the Federal Election Campaign Act, including limits on the value of contributions that may be made to candidates for federal office, to political parties, and to other committees.

**loc. cit.** *See:* loco citato (loc. cit.).

**local rule** *See:* rule, local rule.

**Lochner Court** *See:* court, U.S. court, U.S. Supreme Court, Lochner Court.

**Lochnerism** A dismissive label for a constitutional argument. A Lochnerism is a criticism of a legal argument, particularly a constitutional argument, that implies the argument is rigid, anti-progressive, plutocratic, or illegitimate. The term, from Lochner v. New York, suggests form should always take precedence over reform.

**loci** *See:* locus (loci).

**lock-box** *See:* rent, lock-box (lockbox arrangement).

**lockbox arrangement** *See:* rent, lock-box (lockbox arrangement).

**lockdown** The restriction of personnel to designated areas. A lockdown is a security condition imposed in an institution, especially a prison or other detention facility, in order to maintain order or provide for the safety of members, inmates, and staff. Different institutions may define lockdown in differing ways: in some prisons or jails, a lockdown requires all inmates to be confined to their cells or quarters. In others, a lockdown requires all inmates to be confined to a building or designated area. A lockdown interferes with ordinary services, including sometimes with meal service.

Informally, lockdown is used in many public and private institutions to describe a security alert in which personnel in the institution are restricted in their movements.

**lockout (lock out)** An employer's refusal of work to its employees. A lockout is the refusal of work by an employer to its employees in an effort to gain an advantage in labor relations, particularly during the negotiation of a collective bargaining agreement or contract, during a period of organization, or in response to a threatened job action by workers or their union. A lockout may amount to an unfair labor practice under the National Labor Relations Act.

*See also:* union, labor union, unfair labor practice (ULP).

**loco citato (loc. cit.)** At the place cited. Loco citato, nearly always noted by abbreviation as loc. cit., is a signal that refers to an earlier citation, noting not only the earlier reference but the earlier location in the reference. It is not favored in modern legal writing, which tends to rely on supra or id. for the same purpose.

*See also:* supra; idem (id.); passim.

**locus (loci)** The place. A locus is place, and in most usage refers to a specific geographic place. In that sense, the term may refer to the forum or a jurisdiction of that place rather than to its physical setting. Loci is its plural form.

*See also:* standing in court, locus standi in judicio (locus standi).

**locus standi**  *See:* standing in court, locus standi in judicio (locus standi).

**locus standi in judicio**  *See:* standing in court, locus standi in judicio (locus standi).

**locum tenens**  A substitute for someone else. A person locum tenens holds the place of another, a deputy or a substitute.

**locus contractus (lex loci contractus)**  The place of the contract. The place in which a contract is created or executed. The term is usually part of the lex loci contractus, or law of the place of the contract. As a matter of contract drafting the parties may designate the place in which a contract as made as the law that will govern interpretation and enforcement of the contract. As a matter of conflicts of law, most jurisdictions follow this rule as a matter of presumption. The place is usually defined as the place where the last act required to make the contract occurs, unless the contract specifies expressly where is it is constructively executed.
*See also:* lex, lex loci contractus.

**locus criminis**  The place of the crime. The locus criminis is the place at which a crime is committed, and jurisdiction over the offense is presumptively in that place. There may be more than one such place for a crime, and each jurisdiction may be considered one of the loci crimini, although by custom the forum in which the crime is most associated is designated as the locus. In more general usage, the locus criminis is the crime scene itself.

**locus delicti (lex loci delicti)**  The place where a tort occured. The locus delicti, or the place of the wrong, is the geographic place at which an injury occurred or a wrong was done. The place in which the last act was performed from which an injury resulted is the forum of the lex locus delecti, and the law of that jurisdiction is ordinarily to govern in any action on the tort.

**locus in quo**  The place under discussion. The locus in quo, or the place in which something occurred, is the place under discussion or in dispute, the place relevant to the narrative in which the phrase appears. It translates more easily as the place in question, and it often refers to the scene of a crime, the property in issue, or the place of an accident.
*See also:* in, in situ.

**locus poenitentiae**  The moment to withdraw from an enterprise without penalty. Locus poenitentiae is the opportunity to abandon some scheme, project, or contract before a penalty for entering it would attach. The term literally in Latin means the place of repentance, though as a logical place it has come to mean a time as well, the time to undo what was started without penalty or harm. Thus, the locus poenitentiae of a criminal is the decision to abandon a criminal enterprise before committing a criminal act (or in a conspiracy before any conspirator commits a criminal act). The locus poenitentiae of a contracting party is before the other party relies upon the contract and would suffer a damage as a result of the withdrawal.

**locus rei sitae**  The place where the thing is located. The locus rei sitae is the place where some property is located, particularly land. The lex locus, or lex locus rei sitae, is the law of the jurisdiction in which the property is, and that law presumptively governs any dispute over its ownership or use.

**locus sigilli (L.S.)**  A mark in lieu of a seal on a document. Locus sigilli, which is usually abbreviated "L.S." was once printed or inscribed on instruments required to be under seal, the inscription taking the place of a waxen seal.

**lodestar amount**  *See:* fee, fee for services, attorney's fee, fee shifting, lodestar amount (lode–star or lodestar method).

**log book**  The record of events aboard a ship, or elsewhere. The log book is the official record of each event that occurs while aboard a vessel, including changes of watch, transfers of persons and cargo, encounters with land or other vessels, and events observed by the watch and officers. A log book is admissible as a business record, although a given entry may amount to hearsay.

A log book may be maintained in a variety of circumstances, including taxi records, trucking records, inventory, and the security records of entrance and exit by persons to a building.

**logging**  The cutting of trees for timber or clearance. Logging is the removal of trees from the land. Logging may be clear–cut or selective.

**logrolling**  *See:* legislation, logrolling.

**loi**  A statutory law. Loi in French law means the specific law passed by the legislature or assembly and enacted into the code. Loi is said to fix the principles of droix, or right, into practical rules of law.
*See also:* droit.

**loitering (loiterer or loiter)**  The crime of hanging around. To loiter is to linger in one place, or idle, for no apparent purpose. Loitering is a crime, usually a misdemeanor, of a person's remaining in a place without a purpose for being there for such an unreasonable length of time as to give rise in a reasonable observer a belief that the person intends criminal mischief. As of 2011, many municipalities and states prohibit loitering in language similar to Chicago's law that was declared unconstitutionally vague in 1999.
*See also:* lurking (lurk); vagueness, vagueness doctrine (void for vagueness doctrine).

**gang loitering**  Loitering in support of gang control of a street or area. Gang loitering is loitering in such a place and manner that a reasonable observer would believe that the loiterer is aiding in the assertion of control over a street, neighborhood, or area, on behalf of a criminal gang. Chicago's model gang loitering ordinance was rewritten to avoid vagueness, although it remains controversial.

*See also:* gang.

**long-arm statute**   *See:* jurisdiction, in personam jurisdiction, long-arm statute (long-arm jurisdiction).

**long-dormant claim**   *See:* claim, dormant claim (long-dormant claim).

**long-term holding period or short-term holding period**   *See:* hold, holding as possession, holding period (long-term holding period or short-term holding period).

**longshoreman**   A port worker who loads and unloads ships. Longshoreman are workers based at a port who assist in the loading and unloading of cargo and stores from vessels moored or anchored in the port. A longshoreman may conduct some of the work from land, including quays, docks, and wharfs, or, at times, from the deck or holds of the vessel itself.

The term longshoremen once was distinct from stevedore but now may include them. Prior to containerized shipping, longshoremen worked primarily on land, and stevedores worked primarily aboard the vessel, and though each might be contracted by the same agent, each belonged to a distinct union.

Longshoremen and stevedores suffer a high level of work-related injury and are subject to the federal Longshore & Harbor Worker Compensation Act.

*See also:* stevedore; seaman (sailor).

**lookout**

**proper lookout**   A motorist's duty constantly to look for hazards and danger. A proper lookout is the standard of a vehicle driver's reasonable observation of the road and its proximity to be aware of hazards and dangers so as to avoid them and minimize risks to others. Certain conduct while driving may prevent a driver from performing this duty, causing liability for injury or harm caused by a collision.

**loop-back procedures**   *See:* negotiation, negotiation technique, loop-back procedures.

**loophole**   An exception or omission in a law that frustrates its purpose. A loophole is a aspect of a rule, usually an omission, ambiguity, or exception, that prevents operation of the rule in a specific circumstance. Loopholes may be intended or unintended by the drafters of a rule in which one is found, but the implication from the use of the term is that the loophole is unintended, and while allowance of conduct unreached by the law owing to the loophole may be unavoidable, the allowance is counter to the general purpose of the law. The term loophole is derived in this sense from the breaches in the walls of frontier stockades that were intended for the defenders to shoot from, but which also allowed attackers to shoot in.

*See also:* shelter, tax shelter; recovery, common recovery (common vouchee or recoverer).

**loot (looting)**   Trespass and theft during a period of social instability. Looting describes a variety of forms of theft, the oldest being the war crime of the seizure by soldiers of the goods of civilians during time of war. Looting is also the civilian crime of trespass and thievery of goods during a time of social instability, such as during a hurricane, riot, or electrical failure. From these prohibitions comes the more general and informal understanding of looting as any theft from a fund or property under one's control. To loot such assets or goods may amount not only to theft but also to a breach of fiduciary duty.

**loot or swag or fruit of the crime**   *See:* crime, fruits of a crime (loot or swag or fruit of the crime).

**lord (lady or lordship or ladyship)**   A British title of honour, bestowed on senior judges. A lordship or a ladyship is an office and a title of honour in the United Kingdom and elsewhere. A person who is conferred a lordship by the monarch is either bestowed it by grace or recognized by custom and right as a result of lineage. There are no lords in the United States, where titles of honor are forbidden under the Constitution.

Certain judges and justices of England and Scotland are entitled Lord as a matter of custom or statute. In England, the Lord Chancellor, the President of the Supreme Court, the Deputy President and the Justices of the Supreme Court, the Judges of the Court of Appeal, and Judges of the High Court are lords. In Scotland, the Lord President, the Lord Justice Clerk, the Judges of the Court of Session (or Senators of the College of Justice) are lords. In Northern Ireland, the Chief Justice and judges of the Court of Appeal are lords. Certain other officers, such as the Scottish Lord Advocate, are also titled as a matter of courtesy. Lords are addressed as "Your Lordship" and ladies are addressed as "Your Ladyship."

**Lord Chancellor**   *See:* judge, English judge, Lord Chancellor (Lord High Chancellor or Lord Keeper of the Great Seal).

**Lord High Chancellor or Lord Keeper of the Great Seal**   *See:* judge, English judge, Lord Chancellor (Lord High Chancellor or Lord Keeper of the Great Seal).

**loss (lost)**   A harm to finances or property. A loss is a reduction in wealth, caused by a particular harm or by the nature of the operation of an enterprise. An injury to property resulting in its reduction in value is a loss, as is the sum of expenses exceeding the sum of revenues for an enterprise over a given time.

In admiralty and maritime insurance, a loss may be either of cargo or of a vessel, if either are lost at sea or to other harm. For insurance generally, a loss is an injury or occurrence under which an assured may make a claim.

**lost chance**   *See:* damages, malpractice damages, loss-of-chance doctrine (lost chance).

**lost earning capacity**  *See:* loss, lost earning capacity (loss of earning capacity or L.E.C. or LEC).

**loss of bargain rule**  *See:* damages, contract damages, loss-of-bargain rule (loss of bargain rule).

**loss-of-chance doctrine**  *See:* damages, malpractice damages, loss-of-chance doctrine (lost chance).

**loss of consortium**  *See:* consortium, loss of consortium.

**loss of enjoyment of life**  *See:* damages, classes of damages, hedonic damages (loss of enjoyment of life).

**lost profit**  *See:* profit, lost profit (lost profits).

**lost profits**  *See:* profit, lost profit (lost profits); damages, contract damages, lost profits.

**lost property**  *See:* property, found property, lost property.

**lost value in real property**  *See:* damages, measure of damages, diminution damages (lost value in real property).

**loss-volume**  *See:* damages, contract damages, loss-volume.

**lost will**  *See:* will, last will and testament, lost will (destroyed will).

**actual loss**  Financial or physical loss actually suffered by an assured or a crime victim. In insurance, an actual loss is the value of damage realized in property held by an assured that is subject to indemnity.

Aa a matter of criminal restitution, an actual loss is the reasonably foreseeable loss suffered by a victim of a criminal offense.

**capital loss**  Loss resulting from the sale or trade of a capital asset. A capital loss is the opposite of a capital gain, a loss realized in the sale, exchange, or appraisal of a capital asset. If the capital asset is acquired at a given price and sold at a lower price, the difference is a capital loss. For most purposes, capital losses may include the cost of maintenance in the cost basis.

*See also:* gain, capital gain; asset, capital asset.

**consequential loss**  Untypical losses that caused by a breach of duty. Consequential losses are losses caused by unusual events that, while not necessarily foreseeable or predictable in the circumstances, were either known to the breaching party as a likely result of the breach of duty or were an unavoidable consequence of the breach. Consequential losses may be recovered as consequential or special damages.

*See also:* damages, classes of damages, consequential damages.

**direct loss**  Actual present loss to the taxpayer. A direct loss, as a matter of tax accounting, is one that is an actual present loss to the taxpayer's aggregate amount of assets, as distinguished from a bookkeeping loss.

In legal drafting other than in taxation, a direct loss is a loss that occurs as a direct result of some harm, without any intervening agency.

**insurance loss (loss insured)**  Injury, harm, or a claim against an insured within the scope of insurance coverage. An insurance loss is a loss suffered by policy-holder, additional assured, or claimant against the policy-holder or assured that is within the scope of the coverage of the insurance policy. In other words, an insurance loss is a loss that an insurer must cover, at least to the lesser amount of the value of the loss or the value of the extent of the policy limit. The language of most policies describe a loss as an accident, occurrence, or event. A loss insured in a policy is a loss within the scope of coverage and not subject to a limitation in the policy.

**known loss (known-loss rule)**  A loss known for certain before insurance coverage comes into force. A known loss is a loss to an assured that is not contingent on events but is known to occur prior to the entry into force of an insurance policy. A known loss may occur prior to the policy or be the inevitable result of actions that take place prior to the activation of the policy, although the death of an assured that occurs after a policy comes into force is never considered a known loss, it's inevitability notwithstanding.

**lost earning capacity (loss of earning capacity or L.E.C. or LEC)**  A person's reduced ability to earn money from injury or condition. Lost earning capacity is the reduction in pay a person may suffer as a result of a disability or incapacity. Lost earning capacity is determined by comparing the difference between the amount that the injured person was capable of earning before an injury or disability and the amount the person is capable of earning thereafter. Actual earnings may be a benchmark for prior earnings, but a reasonable estimate of earnings from jobs available to the person is required for present or future earnings (although this may be approximated by the job a person performs in fact). In either case, the earnings are based on the ability of the person to perform and the compensation the person would receive from a regular work week for a person in that trade or profession.

**net operating loss**  Excess of deductions over gross income. A net operating loss is the excess of a taxpayer's deductions over gross income.

**ordinary loss**  Loss from the sale or exchange of a non-capital asset. An ordinary loss is any loss realized in the sale or exchange of property that is not a capital asset.

**lot**  A single parcel of land as surveyed and recorded. A lot is a single unit of land, particularly in a municipal subdivision. Lots vary considerably in size, from a unit in a building to land from an eighth of an acre to five acres or more.

**lot line**  The boundary of a lot. The lot line is the surveyed line delineating the boundary of a lot of land.

**lottery**  *See:* gaming, lottery (gift enterprise or raffle).

**love (natural affection or love and affection or object of affection)** The affection and care of one person for another. Love is an emotional state of deep affection and personal commitment of caring by one person toward another. Love is a basis for many acts in the law, including the basis of a duty of care toward members of one's family or household. Love is generally not considered valid consideration in a contract that may be enforced under the law, though it may justify the making of gifts, whether inter vivos or by will.

In the law, love is usually a matter between persons, although as a matter of speech, people refer to love toward an object or an abstraction.

**Love Canal** The site of a signal environmental disaster and cleanup. Love Canal is a neighborhood in Niagara Falls, New York, in which a massive underground chemical dump created by a plant owned by Hooker Chemical began to leach toxic waste into the soil, and on which the town built a school, knowing the waste pit was below it. The chemicals leached above ground and into the water, causing widespread damage to the health of residents that led to an emergency and federal clean-up in 1978, which was one of the principal causes for the enactment of the Comprehensive Environmental Response, Compensation, and Liability Act of 1980.

**low water mark** *See:* shore, low water mark (mean low watermark or MLW).

**low-value speech** *See:* speech, freedom of speech, low-value speech.

**lower chamber** *See:* chamber, lower chamber.

**lower-of-cost-or-market method** *See:* inventory, inventory accounting, lower-of-cost-or-market method.

**loyalty oath** *See:* oath, loyalty oath.

**LSC** *See:* lawyer, legal aid, legal services corporation (LSC).

**lu** *See:* fa (lu).

**lump sum payment** *See:* payment, lump sum payment.

**lunatic** *See:* insanity, lunatic.

**lurking (lurk)** Loitering with the intent to commit an offense. Lurking, in general, is to lie hidden with some sinister potential or purpose. Thus do hidden issues lurk in legal arguments, and hidden dangers lurk in lands and buildings.

In criminal law, lurking is an offense committed by staying in a public place or private place not one's own, for an unreasonable time, preparing to committing a crime at or from that place. Thus, lying in wait and preparing an ambush are inherently also lurking. Loitering with the intent of committing an assault or theft from a person, even one unknown who might chance by, is lurking.

Note: a lurking ordinance or statute must be sufficiently definite in the conduct prohibited that it meets the requirements of due process of law.

*See also:* loitering (loiterer or loiter); lying, lying in wait; ambush.

**luxury tax** *See:* tax, luxury tax.

**LWOP or L.W.O.P.** *See:* incarceration, imprisonment, life imprisonment, life without parole (LWOP or L.W.O.P.).

**lying**

**lying behind the log or unfair gamesmanship** *See:* sandbagging (lying behind the log or unfair gamesmanship).

**lying in wait** Premeditation of an assault from a place of concealment. Lying in wait, which is the predicate act for committing ambush, is both a form of the offense of attempt and an enhancement to a murder or battery, in either case arising from the preparation to assault another person. A person who deliberately finds a place of concealment from an intended victim and waits there with the intent of eventually assaulting or injuring the victim is lying in wait. Besides being an offense unto itself in most jurisdictions, lying in wait is evidence of the premeditation of an assault or a murder that follows.

Lying in wait is also a form of hunting, and a person lying in wait for wildlife is considered to be actively hunting such animals.

*See also:* lurking (lurk).

**lynching (lynch, lynch-law)** Violence, injury, death, or threat by a mob or other group. Lynching is a broad term for the use of violence, threats, injury, or death by a mob or group animated by some anger or fear toward a group or individual. Lynching is especially associated with the murder by hanging and other injuries of African Americans who sought equal rights during the era of Jim Crow laws. Though the danger of lynching is both older and more universal than this, and lynching and other manifestations of mob rule are always risks when the rule of law is replaced by the force of the people without the moderation of laws.

*See also:* Jim Crow law (race laws).

It is one of the surest indexes of mature and developed
jurisprudence not to make a fortress out of the dictionary.

Cabell v. Markham, 148 F.2d 737, 739 (2d Cir. 1945) (L. Hand, J.), *quoted in* Brian A. Garner,
*The Oxford Law Dictionary*, in –, *Garner on Language and Writing* 335 (ABA 2009).

# M

**m**   The thirteenth letter of the modern English alphabet. "M" serves a variety of functions as a symbol. It is translated into "Mike" for radio signals and NATO military transmissions, into "Mary" for some police radio traffic, and into dash, dash in Morse Code.

**m as a Roman numeral**   The Latin symbol for one thousand (1,000). M is 1,000 when used as a numeral. In the Roman system of numeralization, the addition of an M to the right of another Roman numeral adds 1,000 to the numerical value. The addition of an M to the left of another Roman numeral subtracts 1,000 from the numerical value.

**m as an abbreviation**   A word commencing with the letter M. When used as the first letter of an abbreviation, M often stands for madras, magistrate, Maine, male, mandamus, Manitoba, manual, marine, maritime, married, Maryland, Massachusetts, Medicaid, medicine, Memphis, mercantile, metropolitan, Michigan, military, ministry, Minnesota, miscellaneous, Mississippi, Missouri, modern, modified, Montana, mortgage, multiple, and mutual. It may also stand for the first letter of the abbreviation of an author or case reporter, such as M'Naghten, Maddock, Marshall, Martin, Mary (Queen), Maude, McAllister, McArthur, Menzie, Miles, Miller, Montagu, Moore, and Murphy.

**m as a criminal label**   A brand for manslaughter. M was a medieval brand, which was placed on the thumb of a person convicted of manslaughter and eligible for the more lenient treatment of a first-time offender granted to those who could claim benefit of clergy. The M apparently represented "manslayer." A person who received such a brand could not claim benefit of clergy a second time.

**M.B.E. or MBE**   *See:* bar, admission to the bar, Multistate Bar Examination (M.B.E. or MBE).

**M.E.E. or MEE**   *See:* bar, admission to the bar, Multistate Essay Exam (M.E.E. or MEE).

**M.O.U. or MOU**   *See:* memorandum, memorandum of understanding (M.O.U. or MOU).

**M.P.R.E. or MPRE**   *See:* bar, admission to the bar, Multistate Professional Responsibility Exam (M.P.R.E. or MPRE).

**M.P.T. or MPT**   *See:* bar, admission to the bar, Multistate Performance Test (M.P.T. or MPT).

**M.S.W.L.F.   MSWLF**   *See:* municipality, municipal solid waste landfill (M.S.W.L.F. or MSWLF).

**M.S.W.L.F. or MSWLF**   *See:* landfill, municipal solid waste landfill (M.S.W.L.F. or MSWLF).

**machination**   Unseemly planning. Machination is a term for a scheme that signals an unlawful, unethical, or unprofessional element of the scheme that renders the scheme itself inappropriate.

**madam**   *See:* prostitution, pimp (madam).

**madh'hab**   The way, and the associated disciplines of Islamic law. Madh'hab, or Al–Madhaahib al–'Arba', is a collective of the methodological schools of Islamic jurisprudence, including the four Sunni schools — Hanafi, Shafi'I, Maliki and Hanbali — and the Shii Jafari school. Today, the Sunni schools also include the modern schools of the Ikhwan al–Muslimeen (the Islamic Brotherhood), which adopts the position of the Jamhoor or majority of the scholars, and the Salafi or Wahhabi school, which is an offshoot of the Hanbali school and accepts ahad and daif hadith and athaar as evidence over qiyas.

**madrasah**   A Muslim school or seminary. Madrasah is derived from d r s, to learn, and describes a place of learning. Although the scholarly sense of madrasah refers to higher education, the word may also refer to elementary and high schools, as long as the school provides religious education. Islamic parochial schools in the United States are often referred to as madrasah.

**Mafia**   *See:* racketeering, organized crime, Mafia (La Cosa Nostra).

**magister**   Master. Magister, the Latin for master, may stand for several terms in English. It is the origin of magistrate.
   *See also:* master; judge, magistrate, magistrate–judge (magistrate judge).

**magistrate**   *See:* judge, magistrate.

**magistrate judge**   *See:* judge, magistrate, magistrate–judge (magistrate judge).

**magna (magnum or magnus)**   Large. Magnum means great or large, both in a physical and in a metaphorical sense. There is no difference in translation into English between magnum and magna, which are both forms of the same Latin word, magnus, and which varies according to the noun the adjective modifies.

*See also:* constitution, English Constitution, Magna Carta (Magna Charta or Great Charter).

**Magna Carta** *See:* constitution, English Constitution, Magna Carta (Magna Charta or Great Charter).

**Magna Charta or Great Charter** *See:* constitution, English Constitution, Magna Carta (Magna Charta or Great Charter).

**magna culpa** A big mistake. The phrase magna culpa can be translated from Latin into English in a variety of ways but is most often used as a statement of contrition, the speaker confessing to having committed a mistake of great magnitude. Despite this use of culpa to express a sin of commission, the term becomes a sin of omission in the Roman maxim, "Magna culpa dolus est" which is translated to mean "great neglect is the same as fraud."

**mail (postal service or post)** The correspondence delivery service of the government. The mail, or the mail service of United States Postal Service, is the official means of transmitting correspondence, owing to its control by the national government and participation in the international network of postal services, which is the Universal Postal Union. The federal government is tasked with the creation of a mail service under the Post Offices Clause of the Constitution.

Mail may be sent in a variety of categories depending upon handling, record manifests, and cost, such as first-class, second-class, registered, certified, or express. The rules for process usually require mail to be sent as registered mail or certified mail in order for the mail to satisfy the rules.

**mail fraud** *See:* fraud, mail fraud.

**electronic mail (e-mail)** A person-to-person message sent from computer to computer. Electronic mail is an electronic message sent through a network for the distribution of messages to computers for humans to read, including systems integrated into web pages and social networking sites that generate messages transmitted via an intranet or internet. E-mail also describes a group of such messages. Individuals may contract or license communications between themselves by electronic mail as sufficient both to satisfy notice requirements and to serve as a valid offer or a binding acceptance. Rules and statutes requiring service by mail, notice by mail, or other use of the mail are presumptively not satisfied by the use of electronic mail. Following the service of the complaint (or other initial pleading), however, service of documents is allowed in most courts according to specific court procedures, as long as either the serving party has confirmation that the receiving party in fact receives the document or the serving party has no evidence that the receiving party did not receiving the document.

*See also:* internet (web or world wide web).

**mailbox rule** A mailed letter is presumptively received. The mailbox rule is one of several rules related to mailboxes, and in its most generic sense is a presumption that a document or other material that is properly and timely mailed is received by the addressee within a reasonable and customary time. This presumption can be rebutted by evidence, but in the absence of such evidence, delivery of the mail is presumed.

The mailbox rules for the transmission of offers, acceptance, and payment are not presumptions of receipts but rules of effectiveness, such that these events are considered to have occurred at the time the offers, acceptances, or payments are committed irreversibly to the United States mail. Even so, the effect of the rule in such cases may be rebutted by evidence of the receiving parties' prior and controlling intention to use the time of receipt to rather than the time of transmission in determining the effectiveness of the communication.

*1. electronic communication* The mailbox rule applies to e-mail in many courts, but not all courts and not all agencies, such that e-mail is presumed to have been received if sent. Thus, if A sent an electronic communication to B via a reliable means, and there is no reason of evidence to believe that B did not receive the communication, then presumptively B received it. B can rebut the presumption by demonstrating that no such communication was received or bypass the presumption by arguing that the presumption should not apply in a given case.

*2. fax* Proof of a sent fax might establish a presumption of receipt if the evidence is very strong that the fax was sent and if the evidence is corroborated in some manner. Still, many courts have limited the use of the mailbox rule when a document is sent only by telephone facsimile, either refusing to apply the rule at all or only doing so when receipt of the fax can be confirmed, such as by a confirmation telephone call or a fax receipt confirmation message.

*3. private carrier* The mailbox rule generally applies to letters consigned to private carriers. Although the presumption of delivery is allowed when there is sufficient evidence that a document is consigned to a private carrier, such as Federal Express or UPS, a rule expressly requiring use of the U.S. mails for its application does not apply to private carriers.

*See also:* See: acceptance, acceptance as acceptance of an offer, mailbox rule.

**prison mailbox rule** Prisoners' mail is effectively mailed when given to the prison staff. The prisoner's mailbox rule provides a presumption that delivery is received once the prisoner delivers any outgoing mail to an appropriate corrections official for the purpose of processing and mailing.

**maim**

**maim as injure (maiming)** To injure a body part, rendering it useless. To maim a person is to harm a body part or an organ to such an extent that this portion of the body is rendered incapable of meaningful use or of the performance of its function. A maimed person is one who has suffered such a maiming.

*See also:* mayhem (maim).

**mainprise (mainpernor or mainprize)**  A form of bail with surety held by a third party. Mainprise, or mainprize, was a form of release on bail given by a surety for the appearance of another person in the medieval common law. Mainprise differs from bailment, in that bailment was a pledge by the defendant while mainprise was a pledge made by a third party either for the defendant to appear at a hearing or to make good on the debt. It is a precursor to the modern sense of releasing a prisoner on bail posted by another party.

**mainstreaming**  Integrating special needs students into the classrooms of their peers. Mainstreaming is the practice of educating disabled and other special needs students in the same room and environment as students with no special needs or apparent disabilities, the goals being to enhance the social integration of the students, to minimize the stigma of the needs or disabilities, and to ensure that all students cover the curriculum of the general course. The individual education plan of a mainstreamed student must ensure that the student's unique educational requirements are met via a combination of services provided in the mainstreamed class and services provided in out-of-classroom therapy or instruction.

**maintainors**  *See:* maintenance, maintenance in litigation, maintainors.

**maintenance (maintain)**  To support another person, property, or activity. Maintenance is the keeping or supporting of anything or anyone, especially by regular assistance.

**maintenance bond**  *See:* bond, maintenance bond.

**maintenance call**  *See:* margin, buying on margin, margin call (maintenance call).

**maintenance in gross**  *See:* alimony, separate maintenance, maintenance in gross.

**maintenance of a seaman**  *See:* seaman, maintenance of a seaman (cure and maintenance).

**maintenance in litigation**  Providing unjustified assistance to a party to civil litigation. Maintenance, in the context of civil litigation, is the crime of unjustified or unreasonable assistance of a party (or a potential party) to a civil action, whether the assistance is given in funds, advice, or assistance in providing counsel. There is no clear line between justified and unjustified assistance, but maintenance is likely to be found if an unrelated person or entity provides assistance to a litigant when the assisting person or entity has no interest at all in the case or any relationship to the party, when the party provides assistance for a reason contrary to public policy, when the party seeks to induce litigation for the private ends of the unrelated person or entity, when the assisting party creates a burden for the plaintiff that would otherwise not exist, or when the assisting party appears to be acting deliberately to vex the defendant.

Many forms of support for litigation are not maintenance. The decision by a person or entity to assist a litigant who is a member of the same family or who is a neighbor or other person with a prior relationship is not maintenance, nor is a charitable action with no direct benefit to the assisting party. Similarly, agreements of representation in which the attorney bears the risk of litigation and bears certain expenses and fees as an investment against payment by a contingent fee is not maintenance.

An attorney is not immune from maintenance and may not pay a fee to a client. A contract that amounts to an agreement to provide maintenance is unenforceable as a matter of public policy.

*See also:* champerty (champertous); barratry (barrator).

**maintainors**  One who maintains an action between others. A maintainor is a person, especially an attorney, who engages in maintenance, supporting a cause by one person against another.

**maintenance of a dependent**  The provision of food, needs, and care to another as required by law. Maintenance is the support of another person by the provision of food, shelter, clothing, and physical needs in compliance with a legal obligation to provide such support on the basis of a family relationship, a guardianship, or another relationship. Although maintenance traditionally described the support of a bread-winning parent for the other spouse as well as any children the couple had, the contemporary trend is to use support in reference to children and maintenance in reference to a spouse.

**major**  An adult. As a noun in law, a major is a person who has reached the age of majority. As an adjective, major is comparative, usually being compared to something denoted as minor, and suggests the older or more important between the two people or things compared.

*See also:* juvenile; minor.

**major federal action**  *See:* environment, National Environmental Policy Act, major federal project (major federal action).

**major federal project**  *See:* environment, National Environmental Policy Act, major federal project (major federal action).

**major life activity**  *See:* disability, major life activity; activity, major life activity.

**majority**  The greater number, or more important segment. Majority has a variety of senses important to law, the most important being the greater number among a group of people divided into groups for some reason, such as by the vote cast on an issue or any other aspect of identity or behavior, such as the number who live in a city in a given neighborhood. Though the sense of numerical superiority is important in law, majority in law also connotes other, older senses of majority as superiority or sufficiency. Thus, majority in age represents the age sufficient to engage fully in legal and political life. Majority in a partnership may mean the greater share in proportion to the shares of other partners. The adjectival form, major, makes clear that majority is as often a mark of significance or importance as it is a mark of the larger or more numerous.

When majority represents the larger number of people who have voted, the majority is usually subject to additional rules affecting the vote. These include rules that might require the vote to be taken from a quorum of those eligible to vote and others that would specify whether an abstention counts toward or against a resolution or candidate. In the absence of a specified meaning to the contrary, a majority in any group is one person more than half, or one person more than 50 percent of those eligible, sometimes stated as 50%+1.

**age of majority** *See:* majority, age of majority; adult, age of majority (legal age).

**majority opinion** *See:* opinion, judicial opinion, majority opinion.

**majority rule** *See:* rule, majority rule (minority rule).

**majority rule or mobocracy or mob rule** *See:* government, forms of government, ochlocracy (majority rule or mobocracy or mob rule).

**make book** *See:* bookie (make book).

**make-whole relief** *See:* status, status quo ante (make-whole relief).

**maker** The promissor of a note. The maker of a note is the person who signs it or otherwise authorizes the note by undertaking the promise to pay it. A maker may by signed by more than one person, the signers then being co-makers.

Co-makers are presumed to be jointly and severally liable to the holder even if the instrument does not express such terms (although an express agreement to the contrary made between the co-makers may enforce indemnity or contribution between themselves). If, however, one maker is not a maker but only an accommodation maker (a party who signs an instrument to benefit another and who receives not benefit from doing so), the accommodation maker has recourse against the maker.

**accommodation maker (accommodated party or accomodation party)** A maker of an instrument for the benefit of another party and not for the party's own benefit. An accommodation maker of an instrument is a person who endorses an instrument in order to accommodate the borrower, lender, or another maker of the instrument and not in order to realize any direct benefit to the accommodation maker. The borrower, lender, or maker in such circumstances is the accommodated party, and the accommodation maker is the accommodation party. The

accommodation party may be required by the holder to honor the instrument, but the accommodation party has recourse against the accommodated party. The accommodated party has no recourse against the accommodating party.

**makruh** Something that is good to avoid. Makruh, derived from k r h, means something to be hated or detested. It is one of the five Hukm Shari', the omission of which is commendable, and the commission of which is detestable but not sinful.

**mala** *See:* malum (malus or mala or malo or male or mal–).

**mala fides** *See:* malum, mala fides; faith, bad faith (mala fides).

**mala in se** *See:* malum, malum in se (mala in se).

**mala prohibita** *See:* malum, malum prohibitum (mala prohibita).

**maleficium** A civil theft, or any wrongful act. Maleficium is a general term for a wrongful act and includes the abuse of office and the destruction of property, including the taking of property rights. At common law, maleficium is the tort of theft or conversion. In a civil law jurisdiction, maleficium is the act of waste regarding a property when one has no right to commit waste.

**maleficio** *See:* trustee, trustee ex malefico (maleficio).

**malfeasance** *See:* feasance, malfeasance (mal feasance or mal–feasance).

**malice (malicious, maliciousness)** The intent to harm, or knowing indifference to the harm one might cause. Malice is a state of mind in which a person acts in a manner intended to cause harm to someone or something or acts in a manner as a person would who intends harm but does so with no regard for the risk of harm being created, and has no valid justification or excuse for doing so. Malice may be established by a person's recollection of their thoughts at the time of an action, or it may be presumed from the person's conduct in the light of that person's knowledge at the time of the act. Malice is the mental state required for the commission of some crimes, and it is an alternative mental state to intentionality that is required for other crimes. Malice is also a mental state that may be pled in many jurisdictions to raise claims of a serious breach of duty, one greater than mere negligence though not rising to a level of intent. In such civil actions, malice may require more specific evidence than recklessness, though the mental states are similar. When malice is an element of a tort, it is usually proved by clear and convincing evidence, a more difficult burden for the plaintiff to prove than the usual proof by a preponderance of the evidence.

**actual malice** Knowledge or recklessness that a libelous statement one makes is false. Actual malice is the standard used for the defamation or libel of a public figure. It requires the victim to show that the author (or publisher) of the libel wrote something the author knew was false, knowingly put the victim in a false light, or acted with disregard for the truth of the matter. Actual malice became a constitutional protection of the freedom of speech and the press against suits of actions for defamation, following New York Times Co. v. Sullivan, 376 U.S. 254 (1964).

Malice in other contexts may be termed "actual malice" as a matter of emphasis, in which case the malice implied is usually express malice — deliberate or intentional intent to harm a person's reputation, rather than recklessness.

*See also:* defamation, defamation of a public figure; recklessness, reckless disregard for the truth (knowing disregard for the truth); malice, express malice.

**express malice** An intention to cause a wrongful result by one's action. Express malice is a specific intent to cause a specific wrongful harm. Express malice is malice arising from an intent and not from recklessness or callous disregard for the results that might flow from one's actions. Express malice in torts is sufficient to warrant punitive damages even for tortious conduct that otherwise would give rise only to actual damages.

In actions for libel or defamation, express malice is the intent that an individual's reputation in fact be harmed through the association of a false claim or story with that individual. Evidence of express malice is necessary to overcome a privilege that would otherwise bar discovery or production of the libelous or defamatory text. Actual malice is sometimes used interchangeably with this sense of express malice.

*See also:* expression (explicit or express); malice, actual malice.

**general malice (universal malice)** An unfocused intent to do harmful things or allow harmful events. General malice is an intent to do something harmful and unjustified without specificity as to the act itself. General malice is similar to the common law idea of a depraved heart or to extreme or depraved indifference, the attitude of a person who acts without care toward others, with knowledge that harm is likely to result from the action, or with an intent that such harms will result but without an intent to harm a particular victim.

Universal malice is a form of general malice adopted in some jurisdictions to define first-degree murder.

*See also:* murder, extreme-indifference murder (depraved-heart murder or depraved mind murder).

**implied malice** Malice implied from events. Implied malice is a construction of a person's state of mind derived not from the person's statements or evidence before or during an act but is construed from the act itself in light of the evidence of the person's knowledge at the time of the action.

**malice aforethought** Premeditation of a wrongful act. Malice aforethought is the existence of an intent to commit some harmful act that a person has prior to acting on that intention. Malice aforethought need

not be specific to a particular harm that results, as it is a general intention to commit the act rather than an intention to cause a specific result. Malice aforethought is still used to describe premeditation in some jurisdictions for indictments for intentional or premeditated crimes. It was famously the mental state required under the common law to commit murder.

*See also:* premeditation (premeditate).

**malicious arrest** *See:* arrest, malicious arrest.

**malicious defense** *See:* defense, malicious defense.

**malicious mischief** *See:* mischief, criminal mischief (malicious mischief).

**malicious prosecution** *See:* prosecution, malicious prosecution.

**malo animo** *See:* malum, malo animo.

**malpractice** Harm caused by a professional's wrongful or unskillful act or omission. Malpractice describes any action, omission, or series of actions by a member of a profession or trade that harms the interests of the person served by the professional (or, in some cases, threatens the interests of persons served by the profession) and that does not conform to the generally accepted standards for such actions in the profession or trade. Malpractice was once commonly regulated as a crime, and while this is still occasionally true, the more important effect in criminal law is to bar the use of a defense that might be raised to a criminal charge for which professional practice might otherwise be a defense.

Malpractice is generally a basis for civil liability, both as the basis for a claim in negligence and, in the case of members of certain professions, a claim of breach of fiduciary duty. To be a basis for a civil claim, the malpractice must have been a proximate cause of demonstrable harm to the plaintiff. Malpractice in some professions and trades is regulated by professional boards, such as the state bar or a cosmetology board. Although various codes or rules may establish minimum standards of performance for the practice of a trade or profession, these codes or rules are not the measure of malpractice, which depends upon the generally accepted standards for such actions in the profession or trade. The standard for the knowledge and skill expected of a practitioner of a profession or trade will therefore vary according to the state of the practice. The standards of malpractice are not intended to bar innovation or progress, and the mere fact that an experimental procedure is not received by the leaders of a profession or trade as generally accepted does not mean that the procedure constitutes malpractice, but a failure both to test properly and fully such a procedure by means that are generally accepted and to use the utmost care to avoid harm from such a procedure to the person the practitioner serves may amount to malpractice. Note: Bouvier considers this to be a Latin expression, but it is an Anglicized hybrid of Latin and Greek.

*See also:* practice, malpractice, lawyer malpractice; ethics, legal ethics, malpractice.

**malpractice damages** *See:* damages, malpractice damages, loss–of–chance doctrine (lost chance).

**legal malpractice** A careless or unskillful act or omission committed by an attorney at law. Legal malpractice is an attorney's failure to perform the office and services of an attorney with the degree of skill and care generally accepted as the standard required by an ordinary member of the bar that injures a client or person who similarly would have been served by the attorney or who foreseeably would have been injured by an injury to the client or person served. The failure to perform may occur either by failing to do something that a competent and careful lawyer would do or by doing something in a manner that a competent and careful lawyer would not do. Legal malpractice is the basis for a cause of action against an attorney by a client who is injured as a result of that attorney's malpractice. Owing to the frequency with which attorneys practice as members of partnerships, the liability of one partner for malpractice ordinarily results in the liability of the entire partnership. Regardless of any civil action that may be brought for an incident of legal malpractice, it is also the basis for the discipline of an attorney by the bar or other licensing authority according to which the attorney is (or would be) licensed to practice law, as well as by any court or administrative body before which the attorney practices in which practice the attorney commits malpractice.

**medical malpractice (med. mal. or med/mal)** A careless or unskillful act or omission committed by a medical professional. Medical malpractice is the failure by a doctor, hospital or other provider of medical services to provide that service with the degree of skill and care generally accepted among providers of such services as the standard required in providing it that either injures a person who would have been served by the provider or risks injury to a person in the position of that person. A civil action in medical malpractice may arise for an injury or harm sustained as a result of malpractice in tort, particularly as a claim in negligence. A civil action in medical malpractice may arise in contract both for an injury and for a failure to provide services contracted, and in certain circumstances in which fiduciary reliance exists, a civil action may arise from medical malpractice for breach of fiduciary duty. Medical malpractice is also the basis for discipline by a medical licensing board or by the accrediting agency of an institution, such as a hospital, in which malpractice occurs. Medical malpractice may occur either by failing to do something that a competent and careful medical services provider would do in a given circumstance or by doing something in a manner that a competent and careful medical services provider would not do.

**captain of the ship doctrine (doctrine of the captain of the ship)** A team leader's vicarious liability for negligence by medical staff. Under the captain of the ship doctrine, a doctor is potentially liable for any negligent care provided by members of a medical staff reporting to that doctor. It is another term for vicarious liability for medical malpractice.
*See also:* liability, vicarious liability.

**professional malpractice** A careless or unskillful act or omission by a member of a profession or trade. Professional malpractice is the failure of any member of a profession or trade that harms the interests of the person served by the professional or tradesperson (or in some cases threatens the interests of persons served by such people) and that varies from the generally accepted standards for such actions in the profession or trade.

Professional malpractice may occur by the principal or any agent or employee of the principal in the profession or trade, and the liability for professional malpractice is generally to be ascribed to the principal, to the agent or employee, and to any firm or entity that employs or associates the principal for the provision of such services to others.

The determination of what endeavors amount to a profession is straightforward in certain lines of work customarily known as professions or designated as professions in the common law, such as lawyers and doctors. Yet what amounts to a profession is broader than that and includes many practices that customarily have been thought to be both trades and practices, such as banking, accounting, and financial counseling, as well as practices that have become regulated, such as cosmetology, barbering, and realty. The defining elements of what amounts to a profession are whether it is performed according to common body of knowledge and skill known to its practitioners but not generally to members of the public, and whether there is a customary or mandated process for a person to acquire and to demonstrate a minimal competence in that body of knowledge and skill that is required prior to the commencement of practice in the field.
*See also:* profession.

**malum (malus or mala or malo or male or mal-)** Evil, wicked, or wrong. Malum is a form of malus, the ancient designation for anything wrong, whether as a manifestation of evil or as a matter of inconvenience or prohibition. From malus come many phrases incorporating a variant of the word as well as words derived from it in whole, such as malice, and words with a derivation as a prefix, such as malpractice.

**mala fides** Bad faith. Mala fides is bad faith, or an action made with an intent to mislead or to harm. Though it is the opposite of good faith, because both terms are matters of intent, the absence of good faith, by itself, is not enough to amount bad faith.
*See also:* fiduciary, fiduciary duty, duty of good faith.

**malo animo** Malice or evil intention. Malo animo, literally Latin for a wicked purpose, is malice implied from any deliberate or cruel act intended to hurt or do harm to another person.

**malum in se (mala in se)**   Evil in itself. Malum in se is a designation for a criminal act that is inherently wrong, not merely wrong owing to the act's designation as wrongful by the law. There can be no excuse based on ignorance of the law regarding an act that is malum in se.

*See also:* malum, malum prohibitum (mala prohibita); ignorance, ignorance of law (ignorance of the law); jurisprudence, natural law (jure naturae or lex naturale); mischief (mischevious).

**malum prohibitum (mala prohibita)**   A regulatory wrong. Malum prohibitum designates something as wrongful owing to regulatory choice rather than to its inherent wrongfulness. There is nothing, for instance, inherently evil in driving one's car in the left lane or the right lane, but once a regulatory decision has been made that all traffic should be to the left, a person driving on a lonely road on the right with no notice of the decision made and no intent to cause harm violates the law only because of its regulation, not because of an inherent truth or moral foundation. Note: there is no difference between the phrase in the masculine or in the feminine. The classically adept writer would choose the form matching the gender of the noun for the regulated conduct being described.

*See also:* malum, malum in se (mala in se).

**man bote**   *See:* bote, man bote (manbote or man-bote).

**man of straw argument**   *See:* fallacy, straw argument (man of straw argument).

**management**   Method of and personnel leading an entity. Management is both the technique and the responsibility of managing the affairs and people in an organization, as well as the group of people who are tasked with doing so. The actual and constructive knowledge of management-level personnel is the basis for most corporate liability, particularly for contracts, employment discrimination, and labor law. In U.S. labor law, the role of management contrasts with the role of labor both in the performance of tasks and the negotiation of collective bargaining agreements.

**management buyout**   *See:* buyout, management buyout (MBO).

**executive**   An officer, director, or senior manager of an entity. An executive is a person with the power to execute and direct others in executing the laws, rules, powers, policies or mission of an entity, and usually includes the chief executive of the entity and those who have responsibility in a partnership or corporation for making rules, policy, or decisions that are binding on the entity or its personnel, or who are tasked with the regular supervision of one or more of the significant units of personnel within the entity. Rule-making or policy-making ability is one of the defining aspects of an executive, though there are other functional definitions of executive, including those members of a company whose contracts include a golden parachute and other benefits afforded only to executives. Executives have a fiduciary obligation to the entity in which they are executives. Typically, the chief executive officer, chief operating officer, chief financial officer, chief compliance officer, managing partner, members of a management or executive committee, president, vice presidents, and executive directors are executives.

Executive in the context of government is specific to the chief executive and those who report to the chief executive. The executive in government excludes those with legislative or judicial duties or the employees of such departments.

**management rights**   The authority to manage property, employees, business operations, or other activities. Management rights include a broad array of powers, sometimes general and sometimes specific and limited, that vest in a party the authority to make decisions in the future regarding the management of property, employees, corporate activities, or any other endeavor. Management rights often arise in a collective bargaining agreement, in which a corporation vests certain aspects of employee management in the union whose members are to be managed. Management rights may describe the right of a co-tenant in a property to manage the property, depending on the nature of the tenancy or an agreement between the tenants to the exclusion of management by the other tenant but to the benefit of the other. Management rights are sometimes one aspect of the lease of a corporation or other going concern.

**manciple**   A servant who buys provisions. A manciple was a senior servant, particularly in an Inn of Court, college, monastery, or manor, who was responsible for the acquisition of supplies.

*See also:* reeve; pardoner; summoner.

**mandamus**   A judicial order to a court or official to perform a ministerial duty. A writ of mandamus is an order by the court compelling a judge, public official, or corporation to perform a ministerial duty required by law or custom. Mandamus cannot be used to order a particular outcome from the use of discretion, but it may be used to order a decision in one manner or another that results from discretion, such that an appeals court may order that a trial motion be ruled on but may not determine for whom the decision should be rendered. The writ of mandamus is an extraordinary action, available only when no other remedy is sufficient.

**mandate (mandatory)**   A command or commission. Mandate is both a noun and a verb and in law usually refers to a command. Thus, the mandate of a court opinion is the operative language ordering a party to do something or to refrain from doing something, with an implied or express threat of being in contempt of court if the mandate is not carried out. Note, though, the sense of mandate in an opinion for the purposes of the mandate rule is broader than this, encompassing all findings of fact and conclusions of law. Any entity or official with authority over others may issue a mandate, or mandate some conduct. Thus, the law mandates conduct of officials and citizens alike. Any action that is mandated in this sense of command is mandatory.

In popular usage, especially political usage, mandate is used more in the context of a contract or a commission, in which a candidate runs for office claiming an intent to enact a given proposal, if elected, and claims a mandate of the people to enact the proposal.

*See also:* res, res judicata, law of the case, mandate rule.

**mandate rule**   *See:* res, res judicata, law of the case, mandate rule.

**mandatory abstention**   *See:* abstention, abstention in bankruptcy, mandatory abstention.

**mandatory commitment**   *See:* commitment, civil commitment, involuntary commitment (mandatory commitment).

**mandatory disclosure**   *See:* disclosure, discovery disclosure, automatic disclosure (mandatory disclosure).

**mandatory instruction**   *See:* instruction, jury instruction, peremptory instruction (mandatory instruction).

**mandatory presumption**   *See:* presumption, permissive presumption (mandatory presumption).

**mandate as contract**   A contract creating an agency in another person. A mandate is a contract of agency in civil law. In the law of Louisiana, a mandate is any act by which one party (the principal) gives another party (the mandatary) the power to transact one or more affairs for the principal. A contract of mandate is created when the mandatary accepts the mandate. The principal has the burden of proving a contract of mandate exists between the principal and the mandatary. The mandate may be oral or written, and the mandatary may accept the mandate either in that same manner or by acting in accord with the mandate. The mandate may be general and confer a power to manage all of the principal's affairs, or it may be special and limited to one or more specific affairs. An express mandate is necessary if the mandate is to sell or perform another act of ownership. The contract of mandate terminates when the purpose for which the power was created is accomplished or when the object of the power is disposed of by the principal.

**unfunded mandate**   A state or agency's obligation without provided funds. An unfunded mandate is an obligation that a government or agency perform some task that is required by a superior government or legislature but for which funding is not provided. An unfunded mandate upon local governments in some states is ineffective and therefore voluntary, while in other jurisdictions a court may enjoin the state to provide funding or declare the mandate void.

A federal mandate is either intergovernmental or a private–sector mandate if it is an obligation to do or perform some act that is not a condition to a grant of federal money. A federal intergovernmental or private–sector mandate is a mandate that is not an enforcement of individual rights or social security, a requirement for audit or emergency, or an element of defense or foreign policy, that is not funded by a bill that requires it must have specific reporting in Congress of this fact before enactment. Otherwise, an unfunded mandate is constitutional as long as it meets the requirements of federalism and congressional authority.

**mandub**   *See:* mustahab (mandub).

**manhunt**   *See:* search, manhunt, be on the lookout (all–points bulletin or BOLO or APB).

**manifest (manifestation)**   Obvious and apparent to an observer. Anything manifest is clear and apparent, to the point of being inescapably known to a competent observer who uses an ordinary and reasonable degree of care in the observation of the thing under the relevant circumstances.

To manifest, as a verb, is to display or to develop in a manner that would become visible. A manifestation is such a development, in which certain conditions combine, or develop, until they reach some meaningful conclusion.

**manifest error**   *See:* review, standards of review, manifest error.

**manifest injustice**   *See:* injustice, manifest injustice.

**manifest weight of the evidence**   *See:* proof, burden of proof, manifest weight of the evidence.

**manifestation of mutual assent**   *See:* contract, agreement, meeting of the minds (manifestation of mutual assent).

**cargo manifest**   A standardized listing of cargo aboard a transport vessel. A cargo manifest is an inventory of goods transported aboard a given vessel, car, truck, airplane, or train car. Different forms include the Inward Cargo Manifest for Vessel under Five Tons, Ferry, Train, Car, Vehicle, Etc., the Ocean Cargo Manifest, and the Air Cargo Manifest. Goods are recorded at terminals and ports of entry in the U.S. Customs Automated Manifest Systems data system.

**manifesto**   A declaration of principles or reasons justifying some act. A manifesto is a document intended for public understanding that declares an unusual public action to be justified according to the listed reasons. A declaration of war was once called a manifesto, as were other pronouncements of states that incorporated a rationale. But in the last century or so the term has been more often associated with revolutionary rhetoric and literature. In corporate parlance, manifesto may signal a strategic plan.

**mankind (humankind or man)**   All human beings. Humankind, or as it is written in older works, "mankind," or "man," is a collective noun for all the people of the Earth. Depending upon context, it may mean those of a given moment or all there have been or will be. A person is a member of humankind. When "mankind" or "man" is used in this generic sense, it has no gender implied and includes all people regardless of gender.

**Mann Act** *See:* prostitution, Mann Act (interstate transportation).

**manor (manorial)** A house and the outbuildings and grounds associated with it by custom or plat. A manor is a house and its accompanying property, which is generally transferred intact from one owner to the next. In English law, a manor was a specific estate of land usually, though not always, with a house as its seat, which may have included one or more villages within it. The lord of the manor, or owner of the manor, held a variety of manorial rights and obligations toward the vassals on the manorial lands, who were subject to customary manorial law.

**manprice or weregild** *See:* wergild (manprice or weregild).

**Mansfield Rule** *See:* child, illegitimate child, Mansfield Rule.

**manslaughter (manslaughterer)** Unlawfully killing a person without the fullest level of responsibility. Manslaughter is the act of causing the death of another person without a legal justification or excuse for one's actions, in a circumstance that does not justify the gravest levels of responsibility. Manslaughter is a residual offense for unjustified and unexcused actions causing death that do not meet the definitions of murder. Manslaughter is divided into voluntary or involuntary manslaughter according to the form and degree of the defendant's intent in committing the acts that resulted in the victim's death. Thus, homicide that results from a reckless or negligent act that the actor commenced without any intent to cause death is involuntary manslaughter. Homicide that results from actions intending to harm or even kill another but that are made while the actor is in a condition of temporary insanity or incapacity in which reason would be impaired or the action otherwise would be excused amounts to voluntary homicide.

**crime of passion (heat of passion or sudden passion)** The killing of a person committed when the killer momentarily lacks capacity owing to an emotion that prevents reason. A crime of passion, or a crime committed in the heat of passion, describes a defense of lack of capacity to a murder or felony homicide, based on a temporary lack of capacity or reason, which resulted from the defendant's having learned of something that so provoked the defendant's emotions or passions that the death caused by the defendant was not fully the defendant's responsibility. Typical crimes of passion result from the sudden or recent knowledge or belief that the victim had harmed

or threatened a loved one or that the victim had committed adultery to the harm of the defendant. Crime of passion is not an absolute defense but may justify a reduction in the charge from murder to manslaughter. Note: the heat of passion describes the condition of lack of responsibility caused by emotion sufficient to overcome reason and will; this differs from the crime of passion, which is the crime committed while in the heat of passion. In some cases, generally older cases, a defense of temporary insanity is based on the heat of passion. The difference between the two is that insanity would operate as a defense to the crimes of murder and manslaughter for complete lack of responsibility, while heat of passion operates usually only to limit the charge to manslaughter.

*See also:* insanity, temporary insanity.

**involuntary manslaughter** The unintended killing of another resulting from an intended action. Involuntary manslaughter is a homicide that is the unintended result of an act performed during unlawful conduct, such as battery or reckless behavior. Involuntary manslaughter therefore includes every unintended killing of a person that neither is the more serious crime of murder or voluntary manslaughter, nor is justified by law or excused under the facts. Involuntary manslaughter may result from two broad categories of conduct — either an unlawful act from which death accidentally results or from a lawful but negligent or reckless act from which death results.

Involuntary manslaughter is a crime of intent, but the intent is to commit the act or series of actions from which death results, not an intent to cause the death in itself. Thus, an intent to commit a misdemeanor during which a death results is involuntary manslaughter because the act amounting to a misdemeanor was intended, though the death was not. (Any death resulting from an act that amounts to a felony is felony murder.) Further, an act that is intended, but that in its performance is so reckless or grossly negligent as to cause and yet to disregard an apparent risk to the lives or persons of others, amounts to involuntary manslaughter if someone dies as a result of that act. (Death resulting from mere negligence is negligent homicide; the difference is whether the defendant knew or at least should have known of the risk, in which case the crime is involuntary manslaughter, negligent manslaughter being more appropriate in cases in which the risk was unknown and unapparent.)

*See also:* homicide, negligent homicide.

**voluntary manslaughter** The intended killing of another in conditions of diminished responsibility. Voluntary manslaughter is a category of killing another person that is neither murder nor involuntary homicide, unless it is justified by law or excused under the facts. The most common form of voluntary manslaughter is manslaughter in the heat of passion. Voluntary manslaughter may result from several broad types of conduct under certain circumstances, in which the defendant acts with an intent to kill the victim but forms the intent to do so either in a reasonable circumstance of reduced capacity, such as under an extreme or sudden emotional impulse as in a crime of passion, or due to a reasonable mistake, such as the reasonable but mistaken belief that a third person's life is in danger from the victim in such a way that the defendant would be justified in causing the victim's death in defense of the third party, when in fact the victim posed no such threat to the third party.

**Manu (Menu)**  The customary author of an ancient Hindi code of law. Manu is the father of humankind in the ancient Hindu cosmogony, and the authorship of an ancient book of legal duties is attributed to him. The book, the Ordinances of Menu or the Menusmrti, is a basis of both traditional Hindi courts and of the British colonial legal administration during the British administration of India.

**manual tradition**  *See:* service of process, personal service, manual tradition; delivery, delivery of possession, actual delivery, manual tradition.

**manufacturing defect**  *See:* product, defective product, manufacturing defect (defective manufacture).

**manumission**  A slave's grant of freedom by the slave's former owner. Manumission is a slaveholder's act of freeing a person the slaverholder had held in slavery, as well as the name of the document by which such freedom is declared.
*See also:* emancipation.

**manuscript**  Anything written by hand or that is yet unpublished. Manuscript, in general, is handwriting. In its simplest form a manuscript is anything that is written by hand, or the same as a holograph. More commonly, though, a manuscript is a writing that is intended for publication either through printing and publishing as an article, book, or similar writing, that is not yet edited or laid out for publication or printing, or as a matter of copyright, actually published and distributed to third parties.
*See also:* holograph (holographic).

**mapping**  *See:* jurisprudence, critical legal studies, mapping.

**margin (in the margin)**  The edge, particularly notes in an opinion, brief, or book. The margin of a sheet of paper is the edge of white space between the text and the sheet edge. Customarily, notes and references are glossed in the margin around the text, initially in the vertical margins, and in the bottom margins.

To write in a given text that some issue is dealt with "in the margin," or some references are relegated to the margin, is to say that the issue or references are addressed in the notes accompanying the text. These notes, in contemporary printing, are likely to be footnotes or endnotes.
*See also:* gloss (glossation or glossator); footnote.

**margin of safety**  *See:* safety, margin of safety.

**buying on margin**  Investing with borrowed money. Buying on margin is the practice of purchasing shares, futures contracts, or other investments with money borrowed for that purpose, and often secured against cash or other equity in an investment account, with the intention of selling the investment after its price rises. The risk, however, is that the price will fall to a point at which the equity of the investment is less than the debt acquired in order to purchase it.

**margin call (maintenance call)**  A demand for equity from an investor to cover losses on margin. A margin call is a demand made by the broker who manages the account of an investor to the investor to place more equity in the investor's brokerage account because the equity in the account is less than the broker requires to cover potential claims against the account. A margin call can be answered by an increase in the cash in the account, either by selling an investment or placing more money into the account from an outside source.

**gross margin (net margin)**  Basic profit. Gross margin is the raw profit realized from a given transaction, expressed as the price to sell a good minus the price to purchase or produce it. Net margin is the actual profit that can be realized from the transaction once the sum of all of the overhead and incidental transaction costs are deducted from the gross margin.

**marginal analysis**  The study of the degree to which a gain is offset by a burden. Marginal analysis is the study of marginal costs and benefits, specifically the likelihood that some increased cost will yield a given benefit or the degree of benefit that will be realized according to the additional cost needed for its realization. The usual goal is to increase costs only to the degree that each incremental increase yields the greatest benefit and not to increase a cost beyond its most efficient cost/benefit ratio.

**marginal note (note in the margin)**  A note in the margin alongside the text. A marginal note is an annotation to a text. The term comes from the ancient practice of writing in the side margins of the page. Notes in the margin may function in the same manner as footnotes or endnotes, as annotations of references or authority or as commentary on the text. Marginal notes, however, are likely also to serve as page references to earlier printings, and as headings and finding aids of the present text. Notes at the bottom of the page (footnotes) and the top (which is usually a header) are generally not considered marginal notes. Though marginal notes may contain interpretative data, the uncertain provenance of most notes usually makes such notes weak interpretative tools for later officials.
*See also:* endnote; footnote.

**marginal tax rate**  *See:* tax, tax rate, marginal tax rate.

**marginalization (marginalized group)**  The exclusion of a person or group from social participation in a community. Marginalization is a process of limiting the participation of a person or members of a group from the social interaction in a community that is the most central to the identity of the members of that community. To marginalize someone is to shun or ignore that person and to exclude the person from socially valuable activities or to allow participation only in a less valued manner. For example, the Jim Crow laws marginalized African Americans, and the limits on women's suffrage marginalized women.

*See also:* Jim Crow law (race laws); vote, suffrage (suffragette).

**marime**   Impurity. In the legal tradition and culture of the Gypsies, marime can mean a defiling act or the resulting status of being defiled.

*See also:* krisnitorya (krisnitori).

**marine**   Having to do with the sea. Anything marine has something to do with the sea. Although it is similar to maritime in general use, "marine" has kept a more general understanding, such as marine insurance, marine work, marine shipping.

*See also:* maritime (maritime law).

**marine insurance**   *See:* insurance, category of insurance, marine insurance.

**marine pollution**   *See:* pollution, marine polution.

**marital**   *See:* marriage (marital).

**marital agreement**   *See:* marriage, marital agreement (contract between spouses).

**marital annulment**   *See:* annulment, marital annulment (declaration of invalidity of marriage).

**marital capacity**   *See:* capacity, defendant capacity, marital capacity.

**marital deduction**   *See:* tax, tax deduction, marital deduction.

**marital estate**   *See:* estate, worth, marital estate.

**marital estate or marital asset**   *See:* marriage, marital property (marital estate or marital asset).

**marital exemption**   *See:* rape, rape as sexual assault, spousal rape, marital exemption (spousal defense or marital immunity from rape).

**marital privilege or husband-and-wife privilege**   *See:* privilege, spousal privilege (marital privilege or husband-and-wife privilege).

**marital property**   *See:* marriage, marital property (marital estate or marital asset).

**marital rape**   *See:* rape, rape as sexual assault, spousal rape (marital rape).

**marital right**   *See:* right, legal right, conjugal rights (marital right).

**marital separation or legal separation or judicial separation**   *See:* divorce, separation (marital separation or legal separation or judicial separation).

**marital union**   *See:* union, marital union.

**maritime (maritime law)**   Pertaining to the sea or its regulation by states. Maritime is a general adjective pertaining to anything at sea, and maritime law, for that reason, is essentially the same as admiralty. When the two are distinguished, admiralty is the private law of vessels, seamen, shipping, voyage, cargo, and loss as developed within the jurisdiction of admiralty courts in England and within the admiralty jurisdiction of early federal U.S. courts. The terms are often used interchangeably in international practice, but in the U.S., admiralty is the narrower. Maritime law reaches beyond traditional admiralty to include the obligations of nations, ships, and owners to ensure such matters as the safe navigation of vessels, their safe construction and equipage, and the safety and care of mariners.

**maritime nexus**   *See:* admiralty, maritime nexus.

**mark**   *See:* trademark, mark, service mark (servicemark); trademark, mark, generic mark, genericide (proprietary eponym); trademark, mark, generic mark (genericism); signature, mark (x as mark).

**mark to market**   *See:* inventory, inventory accounting, mark to market (mark-to-market rule).

**market (law of the market)**   The place or activity of buying and selling anything. The market is both a specific place of exchange and the general opportunity to engage in exchange. Historically, a market was a specific place at which vendors gathered and displayed their wares for selection and purchase by passing buyers. This usage continues in both the context of stores and occasional markets, such as street markets or farmer's markets. As markets developed for the exchange of shares of stock, commodities futures, insurance risk, or other investment vehicles, such markets initially were physical places in which transactions occurred by auction or on-site bid and acceptance, usually placed by brokers on behalf of absent principals. Such markets are now managed through a combination of local and distant trading through telecommunications and computer-managed trading systems.

The market, in the abstract, is the opportunity to buy or to sell a given thing, as well as the price that might be given for such a thing at a given time and place. The market is understood by economists to represent a host of behaviors of buyers and sellers, and the law of the market, or the law of supply and demand, is considered in this sense not to be a legal enterprise but an economic description of social practice.

*See also:* security, securities, securities exchange.

**market value**   *See:* value, market value, fair market value (FMV); value, market value (market value rule).

**black market (underground economy or underground market)**   An unlawful market for goods or services. The black market is an informal term for the buying and selling of goods or services that are illegal either because the law prohibits the sale of such goods or such services, or because the sale itself does not conform to the regulation of such transactions. Thus the sale of contraband — such as illegal drugs or weapons or the sale of stolen goods — is a black-market sale. The sale of illegal services — such as battery, homicide, forgery, or illegal prostitution — is a black-market service. The sale of goods or services that might otherwise be lawful but that is not because it is sold without required authorization, records, or taxes — such as the sale of untaxed alcohol or smuggled foreign goods, or the unlicensed sale of pharmaceuticals, or the purchase of rationed goods in excess of one's ration — are black-market sales.

A failure to report income from black-market sales is income tax evasion.

*See also:* smuggling (smuggle or smuggler).

**market dominance** A position in a market with no effective competition. Market dominance is the market power of a buyer or of a seller in a market that is so strong that there is no effective competition to be taken into consideration when the buyer determines a purchase price or the seller considers a sale price.

*See also:* monopoly (monopolize or monopolizer or monopolist); market, market power.

**market failure** The inefficient or undesirable allocation of goods or services. A market failure is a situation in which the ordinary transactions of the market do not (or cannot) ensure that the goods being transacted are allocated safely and efficiently, with the result that certain valuable social goals are not realized or that the market itself cannot operate properly. Market failure describes a variety of outcomes, including the difficulties of achieving desirable long-term goals that do not maximize the short-term opportunities of those in the market, the collapse of exchange when a market condition becomes inefficient, and the difficulties of achieving social goals that are not easily susceptible to the generation of profit while securing the underlying social purpose, such as the enforcement of criminal law.

*See also:* failure (fail).

**market power** A firm's ability to command better-than-market prices. Market power is the ability of a firm to charge a price for its product that is above the competitive market price for similar products. This pricing power may result from the ability to reduce production relative to the market or from the ability to demand a premium based on existing demand. Sufficient market power amounts to market dominance, which may result in the firm's having created a monopoly or otherwise having violated antitrust laws.

*See also:* market, market dominance; monopoly (monopolize or monopolizer or monopolist).

**market share** A seller's percentage of all sales of a given product. Market share is the portion of the market for a given product (or type of product) that is controlled by a given firm, either through its direct sales or sales of its products by others according to its terms. Market share is used to allocate legal responsibility and liability in distinct forms in different arenas of the law. In product liability, market share is a basis both for establishing and for apportioning liability for a defective product supplied or manufactured by several entities. In antitrust, market share is the primary measure of monopoly power in the relevant market.

*See also:* market, market size.

**market size** The quantity or value sold of a given product. Market size describes the actual sales of a given product (or type of product) during a selected period of time, whether measured by the money received for the sales price or by the unit quantity of the products sold. Market share is a portion of market size.

*See also:* market, market share.

**market-share liability** *See:* liability, apportionment of liability, market-share liability.

**marketability (marketable)** The ability in law and in fact to sell a property without encumbrance. Marketability is the capacity of a property to be sold or transferred lawfully to another person for value. In its most common usage, marketability is effectively the same thing as being in a condition fit for sale, and the term "marketable goods" is sometimes used in contracts in this sense. As a matter of property and of sale, marketability is the condition of property that is free of liens, claims, or encumbrances that would interfere with a buyer taking title free of the interests of others in its ownership or possession. To sell property usually implies a warranty that the title is marketable, although under some conditions an interest in unmarketable property may still be sold or transferred if the condition limiting marketability is disclosed and does not itself void the transaction, as in a quit claim.

*See also:* title, marketable title (clear title or merchantable title).

**Marketable Record Title Act** *See:* title, marketable title, Marketable Title Act (Marketable Record Title Act).

**marketable title** *See:* title, marketable title, Marketable Title Act (Marketable Record Title Act); title, marketable title (clear title or merchantable title).

**Marketable Title Act** *See:* title, marketable title, Marketable Title Act (Marketable Record Title Act).

**marketing defect** *See:* liability, product liability, product defect, failure to warn (marketing defect).

**Marks rule** *See:* precedent, Marks rule.

**markup of a bill** *See:* legislation, bill, markup of a bill.

**marque and reprisal** A commission for a privateer to seize foreign vessels at war. Marque and reprisal were the two powers conferred on the captain of a privateer by issuance of a Letter of Marque and a Letter of Reprisal, allowing the private vessel to act in the name of the state issuing the letters and to seize vessels on the high seas in violation of the law of nations. In practice this allowed the privateer to seize a vessel belonging to states at war with the issuing state as a prize. Although the U.S. Constitution forbids states from issuing letters of marque and reprisal, the Congress is effectively limited from doing so by the modern custom of international law.

*See also:* privateer.

**Marque and Reprisal Clauses** *See:* constitution, U.S. Constitution, clauses, Marque and Reprisal Clauses.

**marriage (marital)** A legal commitment between two persons to create a family. A marriage is a union between two individuals that amounts to a contract, a partnership, and a legal status in property in which each agrees to share with the other their joys and burdens in life in the management of a family of themselves and, potentially, of others. Marriage creates and presumes a duty of support from each spouse to the other.

A marriage may only be created between two people of sufficient age as established in that jurisdiction, who are competent to enter into a contract, who are then unmarried, who are not related by blood to a degree closer than that allowed in the jurisdiction, who have the capacity to enter into a mature sexual relationship with another person, and who freely and knowingly intend to do so. A marriage may be created under common law if the parties live together and hold themselves out to the public as husband and wife for seven years, although many states have abolished the creation of new marriages at common law and require a solemnization of the marriage following the acquisition by both spouses of a license from the state to enter a marriage.

A child born to a wife is presumed to be the child of the wife's husband at that time, and each person is presumed at law to enjoy a monopoly over the other's sexual attention to other people. A marital partner who engages in sexual relations with someone other than the partner's spouse engages in adultery.

At common law, a marriage was presumed to be between one man and one woman, and an attempt by a person already married to marry another person is void as bigamy. The implied restriction of marriage to people of different genders has been made explicit in some states by statute. In other jurisdictions, the restriction has been altered by statute or by constitutional interpretation of the obligations of equal protection of the law to allow marriage between any two competent individuals, regardless of gender.

Marriage creates legal interests of each spouse in the property of the other. Most marital property is defined according to the jurisdiction in which the family is domiciled at the time the property is acquired, the primary difference being between common-law jurisdictions and community-property jurisdictions. In all cases, a spouse has an interest in the property of the other spouse at death that may supersede the

designation of property by will. Marriage also creates opportunities in property that may not be held otherwise, as in the community property of some states or the tenancy by the entireties of others.

*See also:* marriage, polygamy, bigamy (bigamous); annulment, marital annulment (declaration of invalidity of marriage); incest (incestuous or incestuousness); divorce (dissolution of marriage); nuptial (nuptials).

**marriage penalty** *See:* tax, tax filing, tax filing status, married filing jointly, marriage penalty.

**ceremonial marriage (solemnized marriage)** A marriage performed by an authority in a public wedding. A ceremonial marriage is a wedding held in a customary manner and presided over, or solemnized, by a religious leader or civil official authorized by the jurisdiction to perform a marriage. In most jurisdictions, a ceremonial marriage is of no effect unless it is conducted between two people already possessing a valid license to marry, and in no case is a marriage valid if one of the parties is barred from marriage at that time.

*See also:* solemnity (solemn or solemnize or solemnization).

**civil marriage (secular marriage)** A marriage officiated by a civil official rather than a religious leader. A civil marriage is a marriage solemnized by a civil official rather than a religious leader. Most jurisdictions specify by statute who may officiate a wedding, and although the list varies from state to state, most include judges, the chief executive of a state or a municipality, and the clerks of certain courts.

**civil union (domestic partnership)** A commitment equivalent to marriage but not so named. A civil union, or a domestic partnership, is a partnership made in lieu of a marriage by persons who either choose not to marry or are barred from marriage, usually being barred because the partners are of the same gender.

A state that recognizes a distinct status in a civil union or a domestic partnership requires treatment of the members of such a partnership or union in a manner similar to husband and wife, although not all privileges of a spouse, such as the elective share, may be conferred. Further, not all states require private entities, such as insurers or hospitals, to extend similar treatment to partners in a civil union. A civil union may be terminated as a partnership is terminated rather than requiring the procedure of divorce.

Civil unions have been recognized in the United States in some jurisdictions but not others, Vermont being the first state to do so in Baker v. State, 170 Vt. 194 (1999), a result legislative codified the following year. Other states that recognize civil unions as of 2011 are Connecticut, New Jersey, New Hampshire, and Hawaii; domestic partnerships are recognized in California, Oregon, District of Columbia, Washington, and Nevada. Domestic partnerships with limited rights are recognized in Maine, Maryland, New Jersey, and Wisconsin, and similar agreements are enforceable in Colorado.

**common-law marriage** Marriage in equity for purposes of property distribution. When two people have lived together as husband and wife without officially marrying one another and their relationship ends, common–law marriage ensures that their property is treated as community property for the sake of wrapping up affairs. The conditions by which common–law marriage have varied somewhat from jurisdiction to jurisdiction but generally require each party to be competent to marry and then to live in notorious cohabitation, holding themselves out to the world as husband and wife, for a period of seven years. As of 2011, only ten states allowed the creation of new common law marriages, though many more recognize a common–law marriage if it was created prior to legislative abolition in favor of solemnized marriage.

**consummation of marriage** The first sexual experience after marriage. Consummation of a marriage occurs when the spouses complete an act of sexual intercourse following the marriage ceremony. A marriage in which this act has not occurred between the spouses is unconsummated, and an unconsummated marriage is grounds for annulment in jurisdictions that grant annulment as well as for divorce.

*See also:* cohabitation (co-habitation).

**covenant marriage** A marriage with limited options for divorce. A covenant marriage is a marrage between parties who agree in advance to limit the bases for and increase the difficulty of divorce. A covenant marriage requires proof of intent to enter such a marriage as well as a valid agreement between the parties to do so, in which case the parties limit the potential grounds for divorce only to the most clear or outrageous bases and, in some jurisdictions, limit themselves to divorce only after they complete marital counseling.

**Defense of Marriage Act (DOMA or D.O.M.A.)** U.S. statute defining marriage to be between a male and a female. The Defense of Marriage Act, Pub.L. 104–199, §2(a), Sept. 21, 1996, 110 Stat. 2419, is codified at 1 U.S.C. §7, defines marriage for federal purposes to be a legal union between one man and one woman and 28 U.S.C. §1738C states that a state need not give full faith and credit to a marriage made in another state that does not meet the first state's gendered definition of marriage.

*See also:* marriage, same–sex marriage (same sex marriage or gay marriage or marriage by homosexuals).

**impediment to marriage** A disability that bars the entry into marriage in general or to a given person. An impediment to marriage is a personal disability that bars a person's entry into a valid marriage and is prescribed by the law of the state in which the marriage is to occur. Canon law, both historically and in its modern governance of Western churches, has its own distinct law of marriage and set of impediments.

The primary impediments to marriage under the law of most states are that no person may marry while under age, while lacking the mental capacity requisite to enter marriage, or while married to another person. Further, no person may marry another who is closer in lineage than allowed by law.

Canon impediments are divided into two forms: diriment impediments, which void a marriage entered in form despite the impediment; and diriment impediments, which do not void a marriage but still violate canon law.

**marital agreement (contract between spouses)** A contract between spouses. A marital agreement is a contract between spouses, on any matter or affecting any subject matter. Marital agreements are subject to the same rules of formation and interpretation as are any other contracts, with a few exceptions. In general, courts are wary of the potential of undue influence or mutual mistake in the creation of marital agreements. In particular a marital agreement may not harm the rights or interests of a child to receive the support of either parent or guardian.

**marital property (marital estate or marital asset)** Property acquired by spouses during marriage. Marital property, generally, means the topic of property held by people who are married. As a matter of law, marital property is property that is held by a husband and a wife and subject to division at the time of divorce or to marital interests at the death of one spouse. In this sense, marital property is distinct from sole property or separate property, which is owned by one spouse alone. Marital property has historically been treated differently in community-property states and common–law states.

More specifically, marital property is a designation in the Uniform Marital Property Act to describe the property subject to the marital estate designation in states that have adopted the act. The marital estate is the sum of the property subject to distribution at the divorce of a marriage in a common–law jurisdiction, including assets earned by either spouse during the marriage, as well as the proceeds of those assets, but excludes separate property (such as the property of each prior to marriage or gifts made to one spouse alone). A marital asset is an asset that is part of the marital estate, and the marital estate is divided equitably between the spouses upon divorce.

*See also:* marriage, marital property, community property.

**tenancy by the entireties** *See:* tenancy, co-tenancy, tenancy by the entireties (entirety or tenancy by the entirety or tenants by the entireties).

**community property** Property acquired during a marriage in a community–property jurisdiction. Community property is the sum of property held by the marital community, which is a quasi–partnership of husband and wife if they live in a community–property state. It includes all of the assets obtained by either spouse during the tenure of their matrimony, but does not include any assets that were given during marriage as a gift clearly intended for one spouse alone. Each spouse holds an undivided half interest in the whole of the community. In the event of a death of one spouse, the decedent spouse may leave one half of the community to others, including the suriving spouse. Similarly, in the event of divorce or annulment, all assets of the community are divided equally between the spouses, though different jurisdictions employ different processes for the actual division.

Community property only exists in states that recognize community property, either because it is an aspect of the civil law that is (or once was) prevalent in that jurisdiction or because it has been adopted by legislation. These states are Arizona, California, Idaho, Louisiana, Nevada, New Mexico, Texas, Washington and Wisconsin. Alaska allows the deliberate creation of community property by spouses, but in the other nine states, property acquired during marriage is inherently community property. The common–law jurisdiction idea of equitable distribution of marital property is strongly influenced by the idea of community property.

*See also:* marriage, marital property (marital estate or marital asset).

**separate property** Property acquired by one spouse alone. Separate property of a spouse is the property held by the spouse that is not marital property, or, in a community–property state, community property. Separate property includes all real and personal property acquired by the spouse before marriage; any property acquired by one spouse though any devises, descents, or gifts to that spouse alone during the course of the marriage; or any acquired after separation or divorce. Each of these bases by which property is separate from marital property may be the subject of controversy, not the least being over when property is acquired as a matter of law and whether a gift was intended by the donor to be to the receipt of one spouse alone or of both spouses.

The fruits of separate property, such as interest earned or appreciation in value, remain separate property, although the gain in value that separate property may accrue through the active investment management of a spouse may be marital or community property. In any event, separate property that is commingled with marital or community property ceases to be separate property and becomes marital or communal.

*See also:* severalty; commingling (comingling or co-mingling).

**marriage certificate** A written decree that a husband and wife were married on a given date. A marriage certificate is a written instrument that is generated by the state and authenticated by the officiant and witnesses that attests to the solemnization of a wedding between two people on the date designated.

A marriage certificate is no assurance that the marriage was valid, only that it was performed. Nor is it proof of a marriage at a later time, which may have been dissolved by annulment or divorce.

**marriage license (license to marry)** A written state authorization for two people to wed. A marriage license is a certificate issued by the state to two people contemplating marriage, which is required to enter into a valid, solemnized marriage in most states. The application generally requires the bride and bridegroom to offer proof of age, to verify the absence of an overly proximate family relationship, and to verify their eligibility otherwise. A very few states and the District of Columbia still require applicants to submit to a blood test to disclose the presence of sexually transmitted disease. In some states, though notoriously not in Nevada, the applicants must have been local residents for a stated period, often at least sixty days. Upon satisfaction of the requirements in that jurisdiction and payment of a small fee, the license is issued and the marriage may lawfully occur. The license expires upon issuance of a marriage certificate or between a month and a year after issuance.

**marriage of convenience (sham marriage)** A marriage for purposes other than to wed for life. A marriage of convenience, or a sham marriage, is a marriage in which one or both parties enters the marriage for a purpose other than to form a permanent marriage as spouses. Though there is no technical difference between the two terms, a sham marriage is more likely to be used to describe a situation in which at least one spouse enters the marriage for a purpose contrary to public policy, usually to allow a person of one citizenship to obtain citizenship in the country of the spouse. A marriage of convenience is usually used to describe a more benign purpose, in which the spouses do not intend to act in private as husband and wife but wish to be considered publicly as spouses.

*See also:* sham.

**matrimony (matrimonial)** The state of marriage. Matrimony, in law, is the same as marriage. A ceremony of matrimony is a marriage or a wedding. Anything matrimonial is related to a ceremony or condition of marriage. A matrimonial action is an action related to divorce, annulment, property settlement, alimony, child custody or support, or any other concern related to the dissolution or validity of a marriage.

**polygamy (plural marriage or polygamous)** Being married to more than one spouse at a time. Polygamy is the attempt to marry more than one person. As explained below, a polygamous marriage is void, so the term applies to a solemnization of marriage or common–law marriage that would be polygamous if it were valid.

Although polygamy was once restricted in law to marriage by one person to three or more spouses (marriage to two spouses being merely bigamy), many jurisdictions consider all plural marriage (including bigamy) to be incidents of polygamy. Polygamy is outlawed in over half of the United States, but under the common law and by statute in most states, no marriage is valid between spouses if either is already married to another person, and still married, at the time of the marriage. Thus, a polygamous marriage is void by definition under law, and the crime of polygamy amounts to conduct of polygamous cohabitation or polygamous cohabitation under the guise of marriage.

Polygamy includes bigamy, polyandry and polygany. All of the terms are neologisms derived from ancient Greek, polys meaning many, bi signifying two, aner meaning husband, gyne meaning wife, and gamos meaning marriage.

**bigamy (bigamous)**  Being married to two spouses at a time. Bigamy is the state of simultaneously having two spouses, and usually refers to a man having multiple wives. Because a bigamous marriage is void under the common law and most statutes, the later marriage is only an apparent marriage and is, thus, legally invalid, unless it was entered into in a state that recognizes bigamous unions and carried on in a state that does not disallow such marriages or consider them a crime. Bigamy is a crime in most U.S. jurisdictions, although it is criminal only for the person married at the time of a subsequent marriage, and then a crime only if the married partner enters the second marriage knowing that a valid marriage persists.

Note: bigamy is a form of polygamy, the primary difference being that a prohibition on a bigamous union voids a second marriage to a person already married, and many statutory prohibitions of bigamy as a crime are written as prohibitions of polygamy.

*See also:* divorce (dissolution of marriage); marriage, polygamy, polyandry; marriage (marital).

**polyandry**  Being married to more than one man at a time. Polyandry is the customary and linguistic term for one person's having attempted to marry more than one male as a husband. Under the statutes of a majority of states and according to the common law, all marriages entered while an earlier marriage persists are void, thus in the United States, the attempted marriages number two and higher would be void. Although there is a grammatical and etymological distinction between polyandry, which is the status of multiple husbands, and polygamy, which is the status of multiple spouses, this is a pedantic distinction, and statutes barring polygamy bar polyandry as well as polygyny, the status of multiple wives. Polyandry is lawful in other countries, and in the United States, a family lawfully wed in such jurisdictions may be recognized, at least in states that do not forbid polygamy.

*See also:* marriage, polygamy, bigamy (bigamous).

**polygyny**  Being married to more than one woman at a time. Polygyny is the customary and linguistic term for one person's having attempted to marry more than one female as a wife. Under the statutes of a majority of states and according to the common law, all marriages entered while an earlier marriage persists are void, thus in the United States, the attempted marriages numbered two and higher would be void. Although there is a grammatical and etymological distinction between polygyny, which is the status of multiple wives, and polygamy, which is the status of multiple spouses, this is a pedantic distinction, and statutes barring polygamy bar polygany as well as polyandry, the status of multiple husbands. Polygany is lawful in other countries, and in the United States, a family lawfully wed in such jurisdictions may be recognized, at least in states that do not forbid polygamy.

*See also:* marriage, polygamy, polyandry.

**premarital agreement (ante-nuptial agreement or prenuptial agreement or prenup or pre-nuptial agreement or pre-nuptial contract or prenuptial contract or marriage settlement)**  A premarital agreement allocating property in case of death or divorce. A prenuptial agreement is an agreement between two people made in contemplation of their imminent marriage and in which they allocate their interests in property, child custody, support, and other interests that would require partition or division in the event of divorce or the death of one of the spouses. Prenuptial agreements are subject to the usual rules of contract formation, interpretation, and enforcement, albeit with a greater attention, at times, to the potential of undue influence or bargaining power by one of the two parties. A prenuptial agreement will generally not be binding on matters of child custody or child support, which must be determined based on findings of the best interest of the child at the time the question arises, although the prenuptial agreement is often followed in determining other matters regarding property or spousal support.

The settlement agreement was once commonly used to both settle property from one spouse upon the other prior to marriage and commit to certain distributions in the event of death. Settlement agreements of this form are generally rare, having been replaced by pre-nuptial agreements for this purpose.

*See also:* nuptial (nuptials).

**breach of promise of marriage (breach of promise to marry)**  An action for breach of a promise to marry is barred in most states. A breach of a promise to marry was the basis for a civil action in the common law and in most U.S. jurisdictions well into the twentieth century. The remedy was either injunctive or, more usually damages for injuries to the plaintiff. It has since been abolished, however, in many jurisdictions and elsewhere subject to a short limitations period or a single year. Where the action is still recognized, enforcement of a promise in which marriage is a consideration to a contract is subject to the statute of frauds. Even so, an action to recover property given in contemplation of a marriage that does not occur remains available under many state laws, although there are different views of whether an engagement ring may be recovered in such an action.

**proxy marriage**  A marriage performed with a stand-in for the bride or groom. A proxy marriage is a marriage solemnized with an agent or surrogate present as the proxy for one of the would-be spouses. As long as the absent bride or groom is eligible to marry, has in fact consented to marry, is licensed to marry, and has accepted the proxy to serve as the agent for this purpose most states will declare the marriage ceremony to be valid. Many jurisdictions do not recognize marriage by proxy as valid, although the U.S. State Department recognizes proxy marriages that were valid at the time and place of their solemnization as valid for the purpose of issuing visas, if the marriage was later consummated.
*See also:* proxy (proxies).

**same-sex marriage (same sex marriage or gay marriage or marriage by homosexuals)**  Marriage between two adults of the same gender. Same-sex marriage is the recognition under law of a marriage between two people of the same gender: the marriage of a man to a man or a woman to a woman. As with all issues of gender identity, this topic has proved very controversial.

Beginning with Massachusetts in 2003, several states have found the right to marry is available to lesbians and gays under their state constitutional laws. Some legislatures have acted to create civil unions available to same-sex couples that have the legal significance of marriage but not the same name or status. This approach, however, was declared insufficient in Massachusetts and California. The Supreme Court of California declared in 2008 that marriage, regardless of gender, is a fundamental right under its state constitution, and any burden on access to matrimony must be justified under strict scrutiny, though it discontinued recognition of new marriages in November of that year following a popularly voted state constitutional amendment. Some states, notably New York in 2011, have authorized same-sex marriage by statute.
*See also:* marriage, Defense of Marriage Act (DOMA or D.O.M.A.).

**wedlock (wed)**  The formal state of marriage. Wedlock is the state of marriage, with an emphasis on its contractual nature and legal formality. The term wed was a medieval pledge, so that wedlock is a covenant of mutual pledges.

**married filing jointly**  *See:* tax, tax filing, tax filing status, married filing jointly (joint return).

**marshal**  A law enforcement officer charged with assisting the court. A marshal is a law enforcement officer who is charged with assisting in the execution of orders of the courts. Although many states provide more focused or more general authority, marshals are customarily charged to execute process or judgments on behalf of certain courts, to provide court and judicial

security, to apprehend wanted individuals, to protect witnesses, to transport and manage prisoners, and to seize and manage assets subject to forfeiture. The United States Marshal is appointed in every federal judicial district by the President, and deputy marshals work under the Marshal's supervision as members of the United States Marshals Service.
*See also:* police, police organization, United States Marshals Service.

**Marshall Court**  *See:* court, U.S. Court, U.S. Supreme Court, Marshall Court.

**martial law**  *See:* law, martial law.

**Mary Carter Agreement**  *See:* settlement, Mary Carter Agreement (Gallagher Agreement).

**Mason (Perry Mason)**  A fictional character who was a model criminal defense lawyer. Perry Mason is a character in the novels of California trial attorney Erle Stanley Gardner, which were developed into radio and television shows, movies, and most notably a television show of the same name in the 1960s in which Mason was played by the actor Raymond Burr. Other characters from the dramas included Mason's secretary Della Street, the investigator Paul Drake, and the competent but luckless prosecutor Hamilton Burger. The character Perry Mason was an extremely able criminal defense lawyer with strong professional ethics and character (at least as portrayed by Burr). "Perry Mason" remains a metaphor for a highly skilled and thorough trial lawyer.
*See also:* metaphor; Finch (Atticus Finch).

**mass**

**mass accident**  *See:* tort, mass tort (mass accident).

**mass action**  *See:* class, class action, mass action.

**mass action theory**  *See:* union, mass action theory.

**mass tort**  *See:* tort, mass tort (mass accident).

**mass tort class action**  *See:* class, class action, mass tort class action.

**master**  A person with superior skills or authority. Master refers to a person with a particular type of authority, the meaning of which varies considerably from context to context. A master in a trade is a person who has achieved the highest level of skill in that trade and who is capable of supervising and training others. The master of a servant or apprentice is the person who supervises the other and is both responsible for the other's actions and charged with the other's care. The master of a slave was the owner of that person.

A thing may also be considered a master to another thing, such as a master plan or master agreement, when subordinate things are defined by it or dependent on it.
*See also:* ship, captain of a vessel, master; magister; ship, captain of a vessel (sea captain or ship captain).

**Master of Laws**  *See:* degree, academic degree, law degree, Master of Laws (LL.M. or LLM).

**Master of the Rolls** *See:* judge, English judge, Master of the Rolls.

**master plan** *See:* zoning, master plan (master planning).

**master planning** *See:* zoning, master plan (master planning).

**master and servant** The relationship between a principal and an employee–agent. Master and servant was the categorical label of the common law for the law governing the varied relationships between servants and their employers, including duties of masters and factors toward servants, an early form of employment law, and the liability of masters for the actions of servants, which amounted both to a form or agency and to a standard of liability by the master for the actions of a servant, particularly those actions within a scope of apparent agency.

The modern usage of master and servant is usually limited to the question of liability owing to respondeat superior of the employer for the actions of the employee. A person is considered a servant, rather than a contractor, if the employer controls (or has the right to control) the physical conduct of the employee in providing the services required for the job. If the job is merely to provide an end result, it is a contractor's job, and there is no liability on the part of the employer. If the job is to perform work in the manner dictated or directed, then the job is a servant's job, and there is liability under respondeat superior.

**master in chancery** An assistant to a chancellor or judge sitting in equity. A master in chancery is an officer of the court of equity and appointed by the chancellor or other senior judge of the court to assess pleadings and motions, ruling on many in the first instance, as well as to make initial reports of findings of fact and recommendations for a remedy in certain complex cases. A master in equity may be a permanent appointment or pro tem. The special master on the modern federal court performs many of these functions, particularly for an action in the federal court seeking equitable relief.

*See also:* master, special master; chancellor.

**Special Master** A person appointed to investigate a matter and report to a court. A Special Master is a person who is appointed by a judge to investigate a matter by reviewing the evidence provided by the parties as well as conducting further investigation as allowed under the rules of evidence and procedure, after which the master will make a report and recommendation to the court, a report of findings of fact, and a recommendation as to orders to be issued. The parties may object to the report and recommendation, but the master is given wide discretion in the types of procedures used and the evidence reviewed. A Special Master may be a magistrate judge in the federal system but is often an attorney with particular expertise in the subject matter of a dispute. Special Masters are in many ways a modern form of the Extraordinary Master in Chancery.

*See also:* master, master in chancery; judge, magistrate, magistrate–judge (magistrate judge).

**mater (maternal)** Mother, or related to a mother or motherhood. Mater is Latin for mother, and maternal means something related to motherhood. In law, a maternal interest is the interest of a mother in raising, caring for, or supporting a child. A maternal line is a descent from a mother as opposed to a father.

*See also:* pater (paternal).

**materiality (material or immateriality or immaterial)** Likely to influence a person's acts or beliefs of a given matter. Materiality is a measure of the importance of an issue, question, fact, statement, or any other thing, in the context of some conduct or question, in that the thing must either influence someone in fact or be sufficiently likely to influence someone to the degree that the person would be reasonable in forming an opinion or deciding to act or not to act as a result of knowledge of the thing. Thus, a material fact to an issue at law is both relevant to that issue and of sufficient potential influence that the fact is likely to affect the outcome of that issue. A material omission or mistatement in a corporate proxy statement is material if it is sufficiently influential that either shareholders in fact rely upon the omission or statement or would be reasonable in doing so.

For some purposes, particularly in evidence, materiality is a limitation on issues, evidence, or facts that may be raised in court to those that are relevant to the case at hand. In such instances, an immaterial fact or other thing would be potentially relevant but unlikely to influence the outcome of the case. In other circumstances, the fact or other thing might be irrelevant but still potentially influential if it were allowed. In both instances, the issue, evidence, or fact is immaterial.

Anything immaterial is not sufficiently material to the purpose at hand or the question in issue to be relevant and also either likely to influence a decision or in fact did influence a decision or action that was in fact made by a person in reliance upon it. The defining element is the degree of relevance and influence to make something material; if it is less relevant or influential, it is immaterial.

**material alteration** *See:* alteration, material alteration.

**material breach** *See:* breach, breach of contract, material breach (immaterial breach).

**material evidence** *See:* evidence, material evidence.

**material fact** *See:* fact, material fact, genuine issue of material fact; fact, material fact.

**material issue** *See:* issue, issue before the court, material issue (immaterial issue).

**material man or materialmen** *See:* materialman (material man or materialmen).

**material or immateriality or immaterial** *See:* materiality (material or immateriality or immaterial).

**material representation** *See:* representation, material representation.

**material support**   *See:* terrorism, material support.

**material witness**   *See:* witness, material witness.

**materially conflicting term**   *See:* acceptance, acceptance as acceptance of an offer, materially conflicting term.

**materialman (material man or materialmen)**   A supplier of goods for the construction or repair of structures or vessels. A materialman is a supplier of components for the construction or repair of buildings, ships, or other vessels. The goods supplied by materialmen are subject to a materialman's lien until the goods are paid in full. The test of whether a person or entity is a materialman, and therefore with the benefit of a lien over the materials supplied, or a sub-contractor, and therefore with recourse limited to the contractor, is whether the materialman does more than deliver the materials as specified. A materialman does not have a substantial, integrated relationship with the contractor, take a significant part of the original construction contract, or perform work on site. Even though the materialman might fabricate goods in its own facilities, its role tends to end upon delivery.

**materials**   Goods for the construction or assembly of other things. Materials are the components from which other things are made. A party to a contract that specifies materials to be used in construction has a right to the use of such materials and not mere substitutes of the same quality, although the remedy, if the material is not visible in the final product, for a failure of the contractor to do so is only the difference in value between the material requested and the material used.

**matriarchy**   *See:* government, forms of government, matriarchy (matriarchate or gynocracy).

**matricide**   *See:* homicide, parricide, matricide.

**matrilineal descendant**   *See:* descent, descendant, matrilineal descendant (patrilineal descendent).

**matrimony**   *See:* marriage, matrimony (matrimonial or matrimonial).

**matter**   The substance in a thing, or the essence of a dispute. The matter is the substance of which anything is composed, and from this sense comes the idea of matter being different from its form.

The matter in law is the substance of any question or dispute, and so when a judge speaks of the matter before the court, it is the essence of the case then pending.

**new matter**   A factual or legal claim not raised in earlier pleadings. New matter is a new allegation of fact or a new claim of law that is raised at some relatively advanced stage in the argument and pleading of a case that had not been raised before. In general, new matter is not to be raised in an action to the prejudice of the other party without good cause and leave of the court. New matter on appeal is usually barred outright.

**maturity (mature or matures)**   The full development of a debt, bond, claim, person, or thing. Maturity is the successive state of development or, for a person, the developmental stage of adolescence. In law, maturity represents the time when some process reaches its fulfillment. For example, when a debt matures, it is due, and when a bond matures, it is payable at its full value. When a claim matures, it is ripe for filing and adjudication. When a person matures, the person has full capacity to perform all legal actions.

*See also:* adult.

**maven (mavin)**   An expert in a particular subject. A maven is an expert, one who has not only knowledge but wisdom in a given field that makes the opinions of the maven especially reliable.

**maxim**   A principle that serves as a source of decision in an action. A maxim is a statement of a principle of equity or the law that may be used as authority for a decision in an action, without further reference to its precedent or origin. Maxims are prone to acquire considerable lore and interpretation through precedent as well as through scholarly development. Although precedent provides authority for the interpretation of a maxim, its limits, or its application, the general concept of a maxim is that it applies directly to an issue from the self-evident persuasiveness of its statement of the principle. Maxims are especially important as the source for decisions in cases arising in equity and in the interpretation of texts, particularly contracts, trusts, wills, and statutes.

*See also:* axiom (axiomatic); brocard.

**equitable maxim**   Principles for decision of actions in equity. Equitable maxims are statements of principle that are to be applied in equity as rules of decision, including in the determination of the existence of a claim, defenses to the claim, adjudication of the claim, and application of remedies. Maxims in equity are interpreted by precedent, yet a precedent that is contrary to the purpose or customary understanding of a maxim may well be less influential than the maxim itself.

**maximin principle**   Justified inequality most benefits the least advantaged. The maximin principle is part of Rawls's description of the just distribution of social goods and resources, in which giving an advantage to some people in society in the distribution of social and economic goods is only justified to the degree that it ensures the greatest possible benefit to the people in society who are the least advantaged.

Maximin has a different usage in economics and game theory, as it represents the minimization of the maximum possible loss that can result in a situation.

*See also:* justice, Rawlsian justice, difference principle (second principle of justice).

**may** What is within a person's discretion to do or not to do. May is a verb or adverb by which a person is either described as having or is thereby granted a power, authority, or permission. As used in language of a grant, "may" is a term of permission, not requirement. A statute or contract that specifies a person or entity may do something does not, without more, create an obligation that the something in fact be done. It is often said that may is permissive, though shall is mandatory.

Even so, may is sometimes mandatory. When a permissive opportunity is made to an official that would be to the benefit of the public good, or permission is given to a fiduciary that would be to the benefit of the beneficiary to exercise, may could be interpreted as must. The person must perform the permitted task or be in breach of the underlying duty of office or fiduciary responsibility.

**mayhem (maim)** The crime of maiming a person. Mayhem is the crime of one person injuring another person, or maiming that person. Various states have differing statutes that have evolved from the Coventry Act in England, and nearly all accept any physical injury to any part of the body. The common law required that the maiming result from a violent act, and while today there are varying levels of intent or mens rea, most states now require the contact that results in a person's being maimed to have been intentional.

*See also:* battery, criminal battery.

**Coventry Act** The statute that extended mayhem to include most injuries. The Coventry Act, 22 & 23 Car. II c. 1 (1670), expanded the definition of mayhem to include any intentional assault that harmed a limb or member of the body. The earlier definition had limited the felony to injury that would prevent a person from engaging in a fight.

**MBO or M.B.O.** *See:* buyout, management buyout (MBO).

**McCarran-Ferguson Act** *See:* insurance, insurance regulation, McCarran–Ferguson Act.

**me too clause or most favored nation clause** *See:* contract, contracts clause, most favored nation clause (me too clause or most favored nation clause).

**mea culpa** *See:* meus, mea culpa.

**mean high water mark or MHW** *See:* shoreline, high water mark (mean high water mark or MHW).

**mean low water mark or MLW** *See:* shore, low water mark (mean low water mark or MLW).

**meander line** *See:* boundary, meander line.

**meaning** An observer's understanding of something's significance. Meaning is an understanding formed by an observer of the significance of the thing observed. In evidence, meaning is the sum of inferences drawn from the evidence that support a conclusion. In the interpretation of a text, it is the reader's understanding of what the text signifies. There is considerable argument over the degree to which a text has meaning per se, but for any meaningful application of the ideas, instructions, or commands of a text, the readers and others who later encounter the text must have their own understanding of its meaning in order to act. The study of meaning is a rich and complicated field, involving sociology, linguistics, semiotics, and philosophy.

*See also:* contract, contract interpretation (contract construction); interpretation (construction or interpret or construe); interpretation, statutory interpretation (construction of a statute or statutory construction); interpretation, plain meaning (plain language rule); objective (objective standard or objectivity); subjective (subjectivity or subjective standard); hermeneutics.

**core meaning (central case)** The most clear illustration or necessary meaning of a word or concept. The core meaning is the fundamental meaning of an idea, word, or rule when considered from all perspectives. Though the terms are used generally in different veins of the literature, there is little difference between the core meaning and the central case.

The central case represents the general meanings of a word or a concept, the illustrations that fully enshrine the most defining aspects of the word or concept. The central case contrasts with the peripheral or penumbral case, in which illustrations only slightly manifest the defining aspects of the word or concept, and all illustrations of the word or concept occur in some relationship in or between one of these two cases.

*See also:* meaning, penumbra.

**literal meaning** The exact and specific meaning of the language employed. The literal meaning of a text is the meaning given by a later reader to the language of the text without context and with no interpretative comparison to the purpose or intent of the drafters of the text. Literal meaning differs from plain meaning in that literal meaning has no reference to the context of the time and place in which a text was created, while plain meaning requires such context in interpreting the text.

**penumbra** The vague edge of a word, idea, or rule. A penumbra is the whole array of meanings or applications that are potentially but not certainly represented by every word, idea, or rule. The term comes from astronomy and art, in which it describes the zone where light blends with shade at the border between an object of light in a dark area or an object of darkness in light. In law, it has long been used to describe those situations in which a word or law might or might not apply. In such instances, the official interpreting the law or word must use discretion in selecting from the customary principles of interpretation in order to determine whether a word or law is indeed to be applied in a given situation.

A penumbral meaning contrasts with the core meaning, in the same manner that a penumbral case, or the peripheral case, contrasts with the central case. That is, there are certain fundamental meanings of a word or applications of a rule that are not reasonably open to debate, but there are less certain meanings of a word or clear applications of a rule that are more reasonably open to debate and must be ascertained through practice or analysis.

*See also:* meaning, core meaning (central case).

**penumbral meaning** Any application of a term outside the core meaning. A potential but not certain meaning that may be associated with an idea, word, or rule. Every idea, word, or rule has an array of penumbral meanings. There is no clear edge to meanings, and an application of a penumbral meaning is rarely a matter of being within or without the meaning, only of being more or less within it.

**means (ends)** A method of pursuing or achieving a result. A means is a method or process that makes possible some act or result. Means are usually contrasted with ends, the result sought by a given means. Note: although the term means is often encountered in legal writing, care should be taken not to confuse it with homonyms; means has specialized meanings in electrical engineering, manufacture, architecture, automotive engineering, and mathematics.

Means is also a synonym for wealth or earnings.

**ends justify the means (end justifies the means)** A good purpose justifies a bad method of pursuing it. Constitutional law, criminal law, and legal philosophy frequently provoke the question of when the use of illegal means may be justified or excused by its claimed use toward a legitimate or important purpose. Great justices have argued both that the ends justify the means and that the ends should never justify the means.

In general, the long-term constitutional answer has depended on a balance of the importance of the end with the problems caused by the means. Thus, such balances have led to the strata of constitutional analysis for laws burdening rights and for laws burdening interstate commerce. Certain questions, such as whether conduct by government officials violates the criminal law, are usually analyzed discretely, and the purpose for which the law was violated is usually not a defense.

**measure** The components of the quantity and quality of anything. Measure is the quantification of any attribute or aspect of a material, such as time, size, density, value, hardness, or any other relationship among the quantity or quality that may be ascertained in a thing. There is one federal, standard measure of most quantifications as a matter of law, although there may be many private or customary standards for the same quantifications. The creation of measures for most purposes is the responsibility of the National Institute of Standards and Technology.

**measurable damages** *See:* damages, classes of damages, measurable damages (ascertainable damages).

**measure of damages** *See:* damages, measure of

**measure of land** *See:* land, measure of

**measuring life or validating life** *See:* perpetuity, rule against perpetuities, life in being (measuring life or validating life).

**mechanic** *See:* lien, mechanic's lien.

**mechanistic jurisprudence** *See:* jurisprudence, mechanistic jurisprudence.

**med. mal. or med/mal** *See:* malpractice, medical malpractice (med. mal. or med/mal).

**media (press)** Those who communicate news or opinions with the public. The media, which is synonymous for constitutional purposes with the press, is the sum of all of those persons and entities who create and distribute to the public information, including news and opinion. The media includes newspapers, magazines, publishers, pamphleteers, television and radio broadcasters, film-makers and distributors, as well as those who maintain web sites and web blogs available to the public.

The media, as the press, is accorded Constitutional protection from government interference under the Press Clause of the First Amendment. States may define the media and the press for the purposes of interpretation of state law and state constitutions, conferring particular rights upon the media or press in state law that are not accorded under federal constitutional law. Likewise, federal agencies or the Congress may extend by statute any privileges to the media or members of the media beyond the limits of constitutional rights conferred on the press. Otherwise, the media enjoy no privilege under the First Amendment in access to information or in the secrecy of information beyond that of any citizen.

Media is a plural noun, and so a given entity within the media is a media company, media outlet, or member of the media. Likewise, a member of the press, press outlet, or representative of the press is a single person or entity within the press.

*See also:* press (member of the press).

**mediate cause** *See:* causation, mediate cause.

**mediation** Negotiation with the aid of a third party. Mediation is a procedure of negotiation between two or more parties with generally adverse interests, who rely on the changed dynamic of the negotiation by the presence of a neutral third party, the mediator, whose role is to assist the parties in communicating their positions and rationale, in an effort to find common ground and to reach an agreement. Mediation is a form of alternative dispute resolution, but it is also a means for the negotiation of contracts and treaties. Mediation is usually voluntary, although parties to a dispute may be required to engage in mediation, either by court order, executive order, or statute. Note: students may confuse mediation with arbitration, which is different. A mediator negotiates between two parties to seek agreement, while an arbitrator hears the arguments of parties to decide which argument is better supported by the evidence and law.

*See also:* arbitration (arbitrament).

**court-annexed mediation**   Court-ordered mediation of an action pending before it. Court-annexed mediation is mediation of any adversary action pending in a court, which is ordered by the court on its own motion or following the motion of any interested party. The court appoints a mediator from a list of qualified mediators, and the parties are required to participate in the mediation in good faith or risk having the matter at issue decided against the party that balks at mediation.

**intermediation (intermediator or intermediatory)**   Mediation. Intermediation is, effectively, mediation. There is no real difference between the two terms to represent the practice of a third party who seeks to reconcile the positions of two or more parties to a dispute.

**labor mediation**   Mediation between labor and management. Labor mediation is the mediation of any dispute or agreement between labor, which is usually represented by a union, and management. Labor mediation is usually performed by mediators of the Federal Mediation and Conciliation Service. Mediation is often employed to avert a work stoppage caused by either side owing to a conflict or the absence of a workable collective bargaining agreement.

**private caucus**   A private discussion between a mediator and one party. A private caucus is a tool of mediation, in which the mediator confers with only one side or one party. During a caucus, the mediator may learn conditions of that party's position that party would not reveal before an adversary and help the party assess the strengths and weaknesses of its position. These caucuses are kept confidential, so that no information from these meetings can be revealed to the other side.

*See also:* negotiation (negotiable, negotiated), negotiation as resolution.

**mediator (intermediary)**   One who mediates a dispute or agreement. A mediator is a neutral party who assists two or more parties with conflicting positions in a negotiation or dispute to reach an agreement. A mediator may be required by law in certain situations, and the professional mediators of various offices and agencies, such as the National Mediation Board and the Federal Mediation and Conciliation Service, may be required to mediate certain forms of dispute. Most states have a network of mediators who are certified to perform specific forms of court-ordered or mandatory mediation, with different training and qualifications for civil mediation per se, domestic relations mediation, probate mediation, and juvenile mediation.

**certified mediator**   A person certified by the state to provide a form of mediation. A certified mediator is a person who has been licensed by a jurisdiction to perform mediation in a particular form or for a given type of dispute or negotiation. A certification usually requires initial experience or education followed by the successful completion of a course that is specific to the form of mediation to be certified. Certified mediators are required in many jurisdictions with court-ordered mediation, although voluntary mediation is often performed by certified mediators as well.

**Federal Mediation and Conciliation Service (F.M.C.S. or FMCS)**   The labor mediators of the U.S. government. The Federal Mediation and Conciliation Service is an independent agency of the federal government that provides professional, independent mediators to assist in labor negotiation and workplace conflict resolution through mediation. The FMCS may enter a labor-management dispute as described by the 1947 Labor-Management Relations Act, whether the parties seek its intervention or not.

## medicine (heating arts or medical or medico-)

The diagnosis and treatment of disease, injury, or similar conditions in the human body. Medicine, in general, includes both the practice of those skills and techniques that are related to the diagnosis and treatment of ill-health in the body of a human being, and the use of such skills and techniques to encourage health and long life. The profession of medicine, in its narrowest sense, is that of the medical doctor—the physician and surgeon—in which case it is restricted to practitioners who have qualified as a doctor of medicine or of a similar degree and who have been qualified by a professional board of practitioners that is accredited by a state for that purpose. Such a narrow definition has sometimes been used to restrict competition for the provision of medical services from professions trained as osteopaths, and most jurisdictions now either recognize osteopaths as professionals in medicine or regulate medicine more broadly, particularly as one of the healing arts, a category including osteopathy. Doctors of medicine or osteopathy may be further qualified according to a variety of specialties, such as surgery, psychiatry, pediatric care, obstetrics, or oncology, and within these are many sub-specialties, such as cardiothoraic surgery, the branch of surgeons who operate on the heart, lungs, and related structures.

Medicine, as a matter of law, includes a group of professions and some trades, most or all of which are regulated by the jurisdiction in which they are practiced, including medical doctors, osteopaths, and nurses. For certain purposes, especially for statutes regulating the unauthorized practice of medicine, some jurisdictions define medicine to include only these professions. For other purposes, such as statutes regulating access to health care, medical insurance, and regulation of medicine in general, medicine may include allied professions, such as dentistry, as well as certain trades and customary skill providers, such as midwifery, chiropractic, physical therapy, occupational therapy, and acupuncture. Some fields of study related to human health include both medical and non-medical services. For example, eye care includes ophthalmology, which is a doctor's specialty; and optometry, which is a specialized profession for the diagnosis and correction of problems with vision not requiring a physician or surgeon; and optical services, which is a trade in which opticians create and dispense corrective lenses according to a prescription.

Medicine includes a variety of specialties that include both professions and trades, including emergency medicine, which is not only treatment by emergency-care physicians but also includes treatment by emergency-care personnel, such as emergency medical technicians and ambulance drivers. Likewise, medicine includes pathology and forensic medicine, which are the study of the conditions of a dead body, including analysis for the causes of death or evidence of illness or criminal conduct. Veterinary medicine is distinct, being related to the health care of animals other than human beings.

Note: medicine may also mean the pharmaceuticals or other drugs or therapies used for a person's medical care.

**medical abandonment** *See:* abandonment, medical abandonment (abandonment of a patient).

**medical abuse** *See:* abuse, medical abuse.

**medical association** *See:* medicine, medical association, American Medical Association (A.M.A. or AMA).

**medical battery** *See:* battery, medical battery (healing arts battery).

**medical device** *See:* medicine, medical device.

**medical examination** *See:* examination, medical examination, independent medical examination (IME).

**medical examiner or pathologist or forensic pathologist or medical legal investigator or MLI** *See:* coroner (medical examiner or pathologist or forensic pathologist or medical legal investigator or MLI).

**medically necessary abortion** *See:* abortion, medically necessary abortion.

**medical jurisprudence (medico-legal jurisprudence or medical-legal jurisprudence)** The study of the legal significance of medical evidence. Medical jurisprudence is a field of study in law dealing with the significance of medical findings as the basis for not only evidence, but also the problems of cause, effect, damage, and remedy in civil procedure, criminal law, criminal procedure, health law, torts, and remedies. Medical jurisprudence extends beyond scientific evidence and evidence of best practices in medical procedures to include the legal and ethical significance of various procedures performed in medical institutions.

**medical license** *See:* medicine, medical license (license to practice medicine or licensed doctor or licensed nurse).

**medical malpractice** *See:* malpractice, medical malpractice (med. mal. or med/mal); malpractice,

medical malpractice, captain of the ship doctrine (doctrine of the captain of the ship).

**medical power of attorney** *See:* attorney, attorney in fact, power of attorney, medical power of attorney.

**medical privacy** *See:* privacy, medical privacy | Health Insurance Portablility and Accountability Act.

**medical records** *See:* record, medical records (health information).

**medical statement** *See:* hearsay, hearsay exception, hearsay allowed regardless of witness availability, medical statement (medical treatment or medical complaint).

**medical treatment or medical complaint** *See:* hearsay, hearsay exception, hearsay allowed regardless of witness availability, medical statement (medical treatment or medical complaint).

**reasonable medical probability (reasonable medical certainty)** The likelihood of a medical result. Reasonable medical probability is a measure of the likelihood that a particular result was to some degree caused by a person's medical condition. It is also a standard of proof for an opinion offered by an expert witness to substantiate the methodology by which the opinion is justified. Other than occurring in the context of examining cause and effect as a matter of human health, there is no essential difference between reasonable medical probability and any other condition of reasonable likelihood or probability, as assessed by comparison to the accepted procedures or analyses of a given field.

Reasonable medical probability may be established either by identifying a pattern in which one or more conditions are likely to lead to a result or by identifying a conclusion remaining after all other reasonable hypotheses have been disproved. In either case, whether the pattern discerned or the means for disproving hypotheses, the concluding opinion must be reached by means that are appropriate for an expert in the field of medicine relevant to the opinion being offered.

**access to medical care** *See also:* health, health care.

**Medicaid** A federally funded medical insurance program for the poor. Medicaid is a state-managed, federally funded system of insurance that provides basic health care and emergency aid to the poor or needy. Medicaid payments are a federal entitlement, although each state sets specific eligibility requirements for the members of the categorically needy, medically needy, and special groups.

**Medicare** A federally funded medical insurance program for the elderly and disabled. Medicaid is a national, federally funded system of insurance that provides hospital insurance, medical care insurance, and pharmaceutical insurance to those over age sixty-five, to people with certain disabilities, and to those with kidney failure. As of 2011, those with disabilities who are eligible for Medicare include those with Lou Gerhrig's disease and those who are eligible for disability payments from Social Security or as a Railroad Retirement Benefit.

**Medicare fraud** *See:* fraud, Medicare fraud (upcoding).

**Emergency Medical Treatment and Labor Act (E.M.T.A.L.A. or EMTALA or Patient Dumping Act)** Hospitals must treat emergency cases even if the patient cannot pay. The Emergency Medical Treatment & Labor Act (EMTALA), codified at 42 U.S.C. § 1395dd (2009), requires hospitals and ambulance services receiving Medicaid or Medicare funds to provide emergency services to an individual requiring emergency care, regardless of the individual's ability to pay. EMTALA requires Medicare-contracting hospitals to provide an individual seeking emergency service with an appropriate medical screening examination (MSE). If an emergency medical condition (EMC) exists, the hospital must stabilize the patient before discharging the patient or transferring the patient to another facility. An individual who seeks care from a covered facility and who is denied may bring suit against the facility, regardless of the motive of the providers in the facility who fail to provide services.

**American Medical Association (A.M.A. or AMA)** A private professional organization of and for doctors. The American Medical Association is a private organization of health care professionals in the United States of America. Its goal is to serve the interests of doctors and to promote the interests of the medical profession in the law and in society, as well as to promote the interests of patients. The AMA publishes the Journal of the American Medical Association (JAMA).

**medical device** Any tool other than drugs used in the medical treatment of humans or animals. A medical device is any device that is on a list of medical devices, for use in the diagnosis of a medical condition or its treatment, that does not primarily work as a chemical metabolized in the body.

**medical license (license to practice medicine or licensed doctor or licensed nurse)** A state license to practice medicine. A medical license is a certificate issued by a state medical board or its equivalent in a given jurisdiction, following a process of study, examination, and qualification by the licensee, which remains valid as long as the licensee keeps current with educational and professional requirements. Medical licenses include licenses for physicians, surgeons, dentists, and other medical specialists, as well as for nurse practitioners, licensed practical nurses, and other medical assistants.

**medico-legal jurisprudence or medical-legal jurisprudence** *See:* medical jurisprudence (medico-legal jurisprudence or medical-legal jurisprudence).

**unauthorized medical practice (unauthorized practice of medicine)** The practice of medicine without a valid license. The unauthorized practice of medicine is the performance of any action that is within a jurisdiction's definition of medicine, or the presentation of oneself to the public as having a qualification to practice medicine, when one has no current and valid license in that jurisdiction to engage in the form of medicine performed or represented.

*See also:* medicine, medical license (license to practice medicine or licensed doctor or licensed nurse).

**meeting of the minds** *See:* contract, agreement, meeting of the minds (manifestation of mutual assent).

**Megan's Law** *See:* sex, sex offender, Megan's Law (sex offender registration or sex offender registry).

**meliorating waste or ameliorating waste** *See:* waste, doctrine of waste, ameliorative waste (meliorating waste or ameliorating waste).

**mem.** *See:* opinion, judicial opinion, memorandum opinion (mem.).

**member** A person who belongs to a group, or a part of the body. Member has two distinct meanings, each being a part of a larger body. The first is a part of the body itself, particularly an appendage. The second is a person within a group or corporate body, however informal. The quality of membership is that it defines the body of which all are members as much as it defines each person or component as a member in itself.

*See also:* corporation, member (corporator); ex, ex officio.

**member of congress** *See:* congress, member of congress (congressman or congresswoman or congressperson or M.C.).

**member of the clergy or cleric or clergyman** *See:* clergy (member of the clergy or cleric or clergyman).

**member of the press** *See:* press (member of the press).

**memento mori** A reminder of mortality. Memento mori, Latin for "remember you are mortal," or "remember you shall die," is a reminder that each person is finite and, metaphorically, a statement that all that is shall one day pass.

**memorandum (memo)** Anything written as a record or an informal statement. A memorandum is a written record of anything to be recorded or preserved for later reference. In most instances, a memorandum is written in a more utilitarian form than that of a letter or more fully developed correspondence or publication. Thus, a memorandum of authorities follows a simpler form and a less formal presentation than a full, printed brief. A memorandum or note is any writing memorializing a contract that is sufficient to satisfy the statute of frauds, and such a memorandum may be quite minimal.

**memorandum brief** *See:* brief, memorandum brief.

**memorandum opinion**  *See:* opinion, judicial opinion, memorandum opinion (mem.).

**memorandum or note**  *See:* fraud, statute of frauds, writing (memorandum or note).

**memorandum of understanding (M.O.U. or MOU)**  A preliminary agreement, or a contract with a public agency. Memorandum of understanding is a generic label for an agreement between two or more parties, particularly when there are limits to the powers of one or more of the parties to enter into an agreement that is titled a contract, compact, or treaty. An MOU usually has the effects of such instruments, and although the selection of the MOU label may signal the expectation of the parties not to enforce the agreement in the courts, this does not mean that an instrument with that label does not, by reason of the label alone, give rise to a judicially enforceable agreement. An MOU may be a broad agreement in principle that is entered in unenforceable language to structure relations between parties. It may be an agreement in principle to negotiate a more enforceable agreement. It may be an agreement between divisions of an entity that have no independent contracting authority, or between one division of a public agency with another. MOUs are especially common labels for the contract enshrining a plea agreement in a criminal case.

**memory**  The recollection of past events. Memory, in contemporary usage, is a person's recall of events and impressions that occurred in the past and that the person once observed or understood and later recollects. Memory, as it is usually understood, is a continuous memory, in which a person is able to recall specific impressions and events with minimal prompting. A repressed memory is a memory that cannot be recalled without great effort or therapy, and these memories recalled following certain conditions of therapy risk a later influence by the person recalling them. Generally, most testimony is a recitation of memory.

Memory, in legal history, may mean a general mental capacity or ability to engage the mental faculties.

*See also:* mind (sound mind or unsound mind).

**time of memory**  *See:* time, time immemorial (time of memory or immemorial possession).

**menace (menaces)**  A threat to a person or to society as a whole. A menace is a threat to cause some harm, and to menace someone is to threaten that person, particularly by gestures or action. Menace includes assault, but a menace is usually not as immediate in its threatened manifestation of harm as is an assault. The causing of a menace is a crime. A person who is a menace is a person who poses a great likelihood of causing some violence or harm to others. Being a menace is not itself a crime, although the conditions by which a person is genuinely a menace may serve either as an enhancement in sentencing for an offense or justify institutionalization.

*See also:* threat, terrorist threat (terroristic threatening); threat (threaten or threatener).

**mens**  The mind. Mens is the mind in all its operation and capacity. In law, mens often represents a person's understanding and intention to bring that person's will to bear on an action.

*See also:* mind (sound mind or unsound mind).

**mens rea (mental state)**  The mind of the person. Mens rea is the mental state of the person under discussion at a given time, particularly the person's beliefs, purpose, and expectations that are relevant to some legally significant action or inaction by that person. Each criminal offense requires an actus reus and a particular mens rea, which varies among purposeful, deliberate, intentional, knowing, negligent, or (in rare cases) none, as in the case for strict liability crimes. The mens rea for a particular crime is set out in either the relevant statute or at common law.

Mens rea is usually translated "guilty mind," "criminal mind" or "evil mind," but these are confusing in most contexts. Literally, mens rea is the "mind of the person" and is the whole category of the many possible states of mind (including innocence and ignorance), as well as the state of mind stated in the offense (such as knowing or intentional), as well as the state of mind a person has in fact in a given moment.

*capacity and mens rea*  A lack of capacity may bar mens rea. Mens rea differs from criminal capacity, however, in that mens rea is the state of mind of a person at a given moment, while capacity is the general ability that persists over time or briefly in some manner that bars the individual from forming the mens rea specified for a particular action to be an offense. Sufficient criminal capacity is a precondition of the formation of a given mens rea.

*intoxication*  Intoxication may be sufficient to interfere with a person's capacity, but if a person has capacity to form the requisite understanding of the consequence of an action, mens rea is generally not a defense when predicated on the intent or purpose being formed in a mental state altered by intoxication.

**automatism**  The involuntariness of a physical action beyond one's control. Automatism is any conduct the actor is unable to control. The lack of control may stem from a state of unconsciousness, such as hypnotism or sleepwalking, or from a reflex or convulsion, such as a spasm or seizure. The person has no control over automatic actions and, indeed, may not be aware of committing them. Automatism is an affirmative defense negating mens rea in most criminal actions in the majority of jurisdictions. A crime of strict liability is not, however, affected by a defense of automatism.

**unintentional act (inadvertent act or unintended act)**  Conduct performed with neither will nor knowledge. An unintentional act is one which is performed by a person or entity, usually voluntarily, though not by the will of the actor. Accidents, mistakes, reflexes, and involuntary movements all may result in unintentional acts. In criminal and tort law, unintentional acts usually relieve the actor of liability. Note: there is no difference in law between an inadvertent act, an unintended act, and an unintentional act.

*See also:* mens, mens rea (mental state).

**mensa et thoro or divorce from bed and board**
*See:* divorce, divorce a mensa et thoro (mensa et thoro or divorce from bed and board).

**mental**

**mental capacity**   *See:* capacity, mental capacity.

**mental cruelty**   *See:* cruelty, mental cruelty.

**mental defect as incapacity**   *See:* capacity, criminal capacity, incapacity to commit a crime, mental defect as incapacity (idiocy or imbecility or idiot or imbecile or idiotic).

**mental distress**   *See:* distress, mental distress.

**mental examination**   *See:* discovery, witness discovery, mental examination.

**mental state**   *See:* mens, mens rea (mental state).

**Menu**   *See:* Manu (Menu).

**merchandise (wares)**   All goods sold by a merchant. Merchandise includes all goods sold or advertised for sale by a merchant to other merchants or to members of the public. In a general, merchandise includes anything for sale, even (in a metaphorical sense) the person, as in a contract for the performance of services, but it may be subject to a variety of categorical limitations, such that it may not include stocks or commercial paper. At common law, merchandise was limited to chattels, whether fungible or non-fungible, and did not include foods or other perishable goods, although that distinction is now quite rare.

Merchandise is subject to particular regulations and taxation, particularly when it is imported, and its sale usually constitutes a commercial transaction.

*See also:* goods.

**merchant**   One whose business is to buy and sell goods or services. A merchant is a person or entity that sells, leases, or offers for sale or lease to the public or to other merchants any goods or services as a routine basis for business. A merchant whose business is to buy and sell a particular form of merchandise is presumed to have an expertise in such merchandise, and a customer may justifiably rely on such apparent expertise, even in the absence of an explicit claim to such expertise by the merchant, giving rise to a claim of negligence if the merchant fails to provide a reasonable level of such expertise. Note: under the Uniform Commercial Code, a merchant is a seller and buyer of goods or someone with the skills of an expert in a given category of goods. But most jurisdictions regulate merchants as a larger category, including those who sell or provide services.

**law merchant (lex mercatoria)**   The customary law among merchants. The law merchant is the commercial law of medieval and early modern Europe that was developed internationally from the customs among merchants and which served as the basis for most American commercial law until the mid-nineteenth century. Note: law merchant is pronounced as in French, with the accent on the second syllable and rhyming with "bear haunt."

**merchantability (merchantable)**   Fit for sale. Merchantability is the attribute of merchandise, or goods that might be merchandise, that renders them fit for sale, including, most importantly, that the goods are reasonably fit for use in the ordinary manner for which they are ordinarily employed. As an aspect of the warranty of merchantability, merchantability represents a standard at which a buyer of ordinary skill and care would accept without complaint the goods and expect to pay for them at their market value.

**merchantable goods**   *See:* merchantability, merchantable goods.

**mercy (throwing oneself on the mercy of the court or in mercy)**   Leniency in sentencing. The mercy of the court is the disposition of the judge to sentence a person convicted of a crime to a light punishment. The term was initially used not to describe a use of discretion to be lenient but the scope of discretion itself. It was, however, common in the early twentieth century for state statutes to vest juries in a capital case with the power to require in the verdict — or in some states, to recommend — the mercy of the court, by which it was understood that if the jury brought in a verdict of guilt, the defendant would not be sentenced to death. The term persists as a general plea for the court to exercise its discretion and to be lenient.

**mere evidence rule**   *See:* seizure, unreasonable seizure, mere evidence rule.

**mere possession**   *See:* possession, naked possession (mere possession).

**merger**   A combination of two things into one thing. A merger is the combination of two things into one, whether one is integrated into the other or both are effectively synthesized into a new entity. The result of a merger is often to alter the interests associated with the two previously independent entities. Thus, when two property interests are merged, such as a dominant estate and a servient estate of an easement, the easement appurtenant to the servient estate is destroyed by the merger. Likewise, when two corporations merge, one or both cease to exist as a separate legal entity, being succeeded by the surviving or new corporation.

*See also:* easement, merger of estates (merger of easement or merger of tenements); res, res judicata, merger and bar; offense, merger of offenses.

**merger and bar**   *See:* res, res judicata, merger and bar.

**merger of easement or merger of tenements**  *See:* easement, merger of estates (merger of easement or merger of tenements).

**merger of estates**  *See:* estate, interest, merger of estates; easement, merger of estates (merger of easement or merger of tenements).

**merger of offenses**  *See:* offense, merger of offenses.

**corporate merger**  A business transaction in which two entities agree to become one entity. A corporate merger is the combination of two corporations by agreement of the shareholders, members, or directors of both corporations, the result of which is that one of the corporations ceases to exist, having been combined with the other. A merger requires a merger plan that details the manner by which the merger will take place, describes the consequences for both entities, and has been approved by the owners of both firms prior to the conclusion of the transaction. Although mergers are generally authorized by state law and carried out by the mechanisms required by state law, mergers that raise a potential for the violation of an anti-trust law or other federal rule, such as the FCC rules on the ownership of media outlets, may require approval from the relevant federal agency before concluding the merger.

*See also:* acquisition, corporate acquisition (business acquisition); reorganization, corporate reorganization.

**plan of merger (merger plan)**  The scheme of a pending merger to be first approved by both corporate boards. A plan of merger is a document approved by the directors of both entities to be merged, providing details of the consolidation of debts and assets, of management and operations, and the other terms and liabilities of the deal. The plan may be subject to regulatory oversight in order to approve the merger, when such an approval is required. The details of the plan are to be reflected in the articles of merger.

**vertical merger**  The merger of a supplier with a vendor. A vertical merger is the combination of two entities, one of which is the supplier of goods or services to the other. The inherent risk in a vertical merger is that the resulting entity may have an unfair advantage against competitors, either in acquiring the goods or services or in reaching the market of the resulting product.

**merger clause (integration clause)**  A contract clause limiting the contract to its written form. A merger clause, or integration clause, in a written contract is a provision according to which all aspects of the agreements between or among the parties to the contract that are related to the contract at issue were merged into the one document with the clause, the effect of which is to bar claims by either party that there was in fact a prior agreement to terms that differed from the terms of the written contract. A merger clause is akin to a private Statute of Frauds, barring the reliance on oral agreements and limiting the use of parol evidence to interpret the contract. Even so, a merger clause is not conclusive in such matters and is subject to the usual scrutiny of potential boilerplate clauses when it is raised as a defense in a contract action.

*See also:* contract, contract formation, form contract, boilerplate contract.

**merger of deed and contract (deed merger or merger of deed and contract)**  Terms of a land purchase agreement are satisfied or persist in the deed at closing. The doctrine of merger of contract and deed implies the appropriate terms of a contract for the purchase and sale of land in the terms of the deed, in that the covenants and obligations of a buy/sell agreement for land are satisfied and consolidated into the deed when the buyer accepts a deed for the land from the seller. Whatever obligations persist between the buyer and the seller are then expressed according to the terms of the deed, particularly the seller's warranties in the deed, if there are any, or the acceptance by the buyer of the property without warranty. Merger usually forecloses arguments of mistake in description or quantity of land asserted as a claim against or defense to the contract. Merger, in this case, is no bar to defenses against fraud in either the making or the performance of the underlying contract, nor does it bar claims on a deed, even a quitclaim deed, arising from collateral promises between the buyer and the seller.

**merits (on the merits)**  The substance of a dispute in law or in fact before a court. The merits are the bases for the substantive arguments of the legal significance of evidence presented by each claimant or defendant in a legal dispute (as opposed to questions of procedure, evidence, or other technical questions of law). Thus, a hearing on the merits is a hearing on the issues of fact and law raised by the pleadings, rather than on technical questions of procedure. A ruling on the merits is a ruling on the substantive claims of a plaintiff's case and the defendant's defenses. A judgment on the merits is final for all of the claims and defenses adjudicated, and it is the basis both for appeal and for res judicata.

**mesne**  Intermediate. Mesne is a feudal term for middle or middling. Mesne was frequently used in feudal law to depict the role of a person or interest subordinate to one person's role or interest but superior to another's. Thus, to refer to someone as the mesne was to refer to someone as a tenant, but not the tenant in chief or the under-tenant. Mesne also refers to an intermediate holder of property or rights, so the holder of title in a chain of title between one grantor and a much later grantee is a mesne grantee, and that person's interest was a mesne conveyance. Mesne profits, on the other hand, were the profits held by a person wrongfully on the land, that is between two rightful owners in possession.

The word is pronounced "meen," with a silent "s."

*See also:* conveyance, mesne conveyance; trespass, trespass for mesne profits.

**mesne conveyance** *See:* conveyance, mesne conveyance.

**mesne lord** *See:* landlord, mesne lord.

**mesothelioma** *See:* cancer, mesothelioma.

**messuage** The homestead. The messuage in the common law is the house in which a person or family lives. The grant of a messuage implied the grant of the buildings and grounds customarily associated with it. Metaphorically, it is any person's residence.

*See also:* homestead; residence (residency or reside).

**metaphor** The use of one idea to describe another. A metaphor is the depiction of an unstated idea or thing through the description of something else. Metaphor takes many forms, and classical rhetoric used to categorize these forms according to the nature of the relationship between the statement and the idea represented by the statement, such as the depiction of a container to describe the thing contained. There are a wide variety of forms of metaphor, some of which, such as stereotype, are quite dangerous in legal rhetoric.

Note: the famous distinction between metaphor and simile in grammar is that the metaphor uses one thing fully to represent the other, while a simile uses one thing to describe the other (and not as a substitute for it). This difference when one or the other is applied in legal argument is of interest, but there is little concern for the difference between metaphor and simile in, say, the evaluation of a closing argument before the jury.

*See also:* Mason (Perry Mason); umpire; rhetoric; pig, blind pig (blind hog); stereotype (gender stereotype or racial stereotype or stereotypical).

**eyes of the law (in the eye of the law)** An ideal legal perspective on affairs in the world. The eye of the law is a metaphor for the legal consideration of any question from an ideal, disinterested, and objective point of view, according to which each person is equal before the law. Wealth and poverty, knowledge or need make no differences, and the careful distinctions of law are applied but moderated when injustice would result in unjust, unintended consequences from the slavish application of a rule.

**mouth of the law (bouche de la loi)** Judges or a judge. The mouth of the law refers to the judge, who speaks the law that originates elsewhere. The author of the phrase appears to have been the Baron de Montesquieu, but the metaphor has developed from its original sense as a limit on the discretion of the judge to suggest a wider scope of discretion. This phrase may be the origin of the slang term for lawyer, the mouthpiece.

**seamless web** Once, the interconnectedness of law; now, its comprehensiveness. Law as a seamless web once metaphorically described law as a great and interconnected enterprise in which a change in one legal rule affected all of the others. In this sense, the phrase was coined by the great historian Frederic William Maitland in 1898. In recent years, however, the metaphor has come unmoored from its origin and is more likely to mean a web that is so thorough and comprehensive that it seemingly regulates everything and catches everyone.

The web is a much older metaphor for law, and it was long identified in many countries with the spider's web that catches a fly but lets the large animals break through it. That metaphor itself is a transition from the metaphor of using a fishing net rather than a web, known at least to Plutarch and attributed to the time of the ancient Greek jurist Solon.

**metes and bounds (butts and bounds)** A description of a property by its measured boundaries. A metes and bounds description of real property is a detailed list of the angles and distances of its boundaries relative to a benchmark. A description by metes and bounds is used in certain areas of the country by custom and elsewhere when the parcel is of irregular shape. Various theories have been put forward as to what, traditionally, the mete signified and what the bound signified, but it appears that metes described physical marks, such roads, ditches, rivers, trees, and buildings, that marked boundaries, while bounds were the jurisdictional or legal effects of the boundaries. There is no difference between metes and bounds and butts and bounds.

**meum et tuum** *See:* meus, meum et tuum.

**meus** Mine, or of mine. Meus is a possessive form of the first person pronoun: my, mine, or of mine.

**mea culpa** An apology. Mea culpa, Latin for "my fault," is the label for an apology. The formula from the Latin prayer of confession, "mea maxima culpa," can be read either as "my grave sin" or, more colloquially, "it is all my fault." In either sense, the statement is both an acceptance of responsibility and an implied plea for forgiveness.

*See also:* culpa.

**meum et tuum** The property one owns. Meum et tuum is Latin for "mine and yours." In law meum et tuum represents property, because the division of ownership is the hallmark of property.

**mezzanine capital** *See:* capital, commercial capital, mezzanine capital (mezzanine equity or mezzanine loan or mezzanine debt or mezzanine financing or mezzanine investment fund).

**Michaelmas term** *See:* court, English Court, terms of court, Michaelmas term.

**mid-level scrutiny** *See:* middle-level scrutiny (mid-level scrutiny).

**middot** *See:* midot (middot).

**mide-oraita (de-oraita)** The law of the Torah. Mide-oraita is the law derived from the written Torah and is thus foundational law in the Jewish tradition.

**mide-rabanan (de-rabanan or de-rabbanan)**
Laws as interpretated by the Rabbinical courts. Mide-
rabanan is the law derived from interpretation of the
laws, particularly in the Rabinnical courts as an aspect
of safeguarding the Torah.

**midot (middot)**   The central principles of interpreting
the Torah. The midot are hermeneutical principles used
to understand the Torah, the "measures" adopted as traditional bases for interpreting the scripture, especially
that the text is the unified and consistent statement of
the word of God.
   *See also:* hermeneutics.

**midwife (midwifery)**   A non–doctor who assists a
woman in the delivery of her baby. A midwife is a person
other than a medical doctor who regularly assists in the
delivery of a child. In most states, midwifes are licensed
by the state through a state–recognized professional
association of midwives.
   Midwife is also a metaphor that represents any
person, institution, or entity that assists in the creation
or generation of an idea or thing. In this sense, any
human who acts as a catalyst or assistant to a creation
is a midwife.

**migration (migrate or migratory)**   The movement
of a quantity of people or things. A migration is any
movement of people, animals, or things from one
place to another. A migration of people may be
voluntary by the individuals who migrate or forced by
external pressures. Though a migration may be of any
movement of a number of people, animals or things,
including a unique movement that does not recur, the
term most often depicts movement according to a cycle
or routine.
   There are many illustrations of migration that are
regulated or affected by law. Animals migrate from
hunting to spawning grounds and from winter feeding
to summer feeding areas. A migration between entities
or suppliers may describe the transfer of inventory, contracts, personnel, or customers from one entity or supplier to another. The migration of chemicals (particularly
oil or distillates) is the movement from one property to
another or through a given property, soil, or aquifer. The
migration of agricultural inputs or seeds is the movement from one field to another.

   **migrant worker**   *See:* worker, migrant worker (seasonal agricultural worker).

   **migration of oil**   *See:* oil, migration of oil (oil
   migration).

**military**   Related to the armed forces. Military refers to
anything of, done by, or associated with the organized
armed forces of a state. The military forces of the United
States are the Army, Navy, Marine Corps, Coast Guard,
Air Force, and their reserves. Members of the military are
regulated by the Uniform Code of Military Justice as well
as the international law of war and sometimes, according
to various status of forces agreements, the law of states in
which such personnel are assigned.

The constitutional principle of civilian leadership
requires Congress to establish regulations for the military, which is under the President's civilian command at
all times.

   **military desertion**   *See:* desertion, military desertion.

   **military discharge**   *See:* discharge, military discharge.

   **military mine**   *See:* mine, military mine, naval mine;
   mine, military mine, landmine; mine, military mine.

   **military officer**   *See:* officer, military officer.

   **military police**   *See:* police, police organization,
   military police, shore patrol (SP or S.P.); police, police
   organization, military police (MP or M.P.).

   **military prison**   *See:* prison, military prison, Guantanamo Bay (Camp Delta or Camp X–Ray).

   **Military Regulation Clause**   *See:* constitution, U.S.
   Constitution, clauses, Regulation of Forces Clause
   (Military Regulation Clause).

   **military tenure**   *See:* tenure, feudal tenure, military
   tenure, knight's tenure, shield money (scutage); tenure, feudal tenure, military tenure, knight's service
   (escuage); tenure, feudal tenure, military tenure.

   **active service (active duty)**   Full–time military service under orders. Active duty in the military means
   that a service member is under orders to perform full-
   time active service in a uniformed branch, or is on
   assignment for such a branch.

   **military law**   The laws governing the military services and their personnel. Military law is the whole
   of the Constitution, statutes, regulations, and orders
   that govern the branches of the military services in
   the United States and the personnel serving in those
   branches. The authority to create military law resides
   in the Congress, tasked in Article I with creating such
   laws, although some measure of subordinate authority to regulate the military resides also in the President
   as Commander in Chief. The primary form of military
   law in the United States is the Uniform Code of
   Military Justice, augmented by the Manual for Courts
   Martial and the decisions of the courts, especially the
   U.S. Court of Appeals for the Armed Forces, and the
   orders of various commands, particularly the Judge
   Advocates General for each service. The purposes of
   military law are to ensure good morale, order, and discipline of service members, and the capacity of the
   members and their units to fulfill their missions and
   carry out such orders as are lawfully assigned to them.
      Each nation–state has a distinct body of military
   law, although there are bodies of shared law owing
   to a strong supranational culture of military training
   and shared value in training. Further, military law is in
   some regard integrated with the law of war, and the
   rules and principles of the law of war are integrated
   into military law to ensure training and conduct
   compatible with the customs and treaties that bind
   states, as well as individuals, to the law of war.
      *See also:* war, law of war (law of armed conflict or
   LOW or LOAC).

**articles of war**   The military law of a given state to regulate its forces. "Articles of war" is the customary term for the regulations of a state's military forces. The Articles of War governed the conduct of both land and naval forces (and eventually the air force) and applied in peace and in war. Sixty-nine Articles of War adopted by the Continental Congress in 1777 were superseded by the one hundred and one articles adopted by Congress in 1806, pursuant to the Regulation of Forces Clause of the Constitution. The articles were replaced in 1951 with the the adoption of the Uniform Code of Military Justice, which incorporated many of their requirements.

**Uniform Code of Military Justice (U.C.M.J. or UCMJ)**   The primary regulation of the conduct of U.S. military personnel. The Uniform Code of Military Justice, 10 U.S.C. § 800, et seq., is the code of law passed by Congress for the regulation or military personnel and the adjudication of offenses by such personnel. The UCMJ is the successor to the Articles of War, and it reflects both military custom, the military policies of the United States, and the international law of war. The courts martial created according to the UCMJ function according to regulations found in the Manual for Courts Martial.

**militia**   The National Guard in each state. The militia, in international law, is a paramilitary force that is presumably under the command and control of its national military forces when it is mobilized, but whose members, when it is not mobilized, are effectively civilians. Militia had the same meaning in the United States in the eighteenth century. Under the Constitution, authority over militia is shared between the individual states and the central government, Congress having the ultimate authority to federalize the militia in specified times of emergency, with the President having authority over the militia as commander in chief. At least one purpose of the Second Amendment was to provide arms for members of the militia in this sense.

Following the Spanish–American War, Congress reorganized the state militia in the Militia Act of 1903, 32 Stat. 775, into the National Guard, more fully integrating units of the state national guard into the structure of the regular army, in a manner similar to the units of the reserves. The governors of the states are the commanders of the national guard units in their respective states unless the unit is ordered into national service.

**Militia Clauses**   *See:* constitution, U.S. Constitution, clauses, Militia Clauses.

**Miller standard**   *See:* obscenity, Miller test (Miller standard).

**Miller test**   *See:* obscenity, Miller test, contemporary community standards of obscenity (community standards of obscenity); obscenity, Miller test (Miller standard).

**million gallons per day**   *See:* gallon, million gallons per day, billion gallons per day (or M.G.D. or MGD or B.G.D. or BGD).

**mind (sound mind or unsound mind)**   A person's perception, analysis, understanding, and memory. Mind, in general, is the broad term for all of a person's mental faculties. In law, it has long stood for the ability in fact of a person to perceive the state of affairs in the world around that person, to make at least some basic analysis of causes and effects in it, to understand the significance of certain causes or effects on other people, and to have sufficient recall of the facts or events that are relevant to a particular situation. A sound mind is capable of each of these tasks of perception, analysis, understanding, and memory, but an unsound mind is not. A person with an unsound mind is therefore unable to understand the significance of certain actions as endangering or harming others, to describe in broad terms the property the person possesses, to describe who the person's living relatives or dependents are, or to recall significant actions the person has already made or not yet made relative to the event in issue. A person with an unsound mind lacks capacity to perform most tasks that have legal significance.

*See also:* mens; memory; capacity, criminal capacity.

**mine**   A facility for the extraction of minerals from the ground. A mine is the passage into the earth from which is extracted a mineral, metal, or other solid, and which includes the shafts, pits, galleries, cuts or other ways into or across the earth that have been dug as a part of the mining operation, as well as the lands, roads, and structures built or used above ground as part of the same activity. Although mine is defined under the Federal Mine Safety and Health Act of 1977, for various other purposes state definitions of mines may be variably inclusive, and some states may include what under federal law might be considered wells.

*See also:* mine, surface mine (open–pit mine or open pit mine or open-pit mining or strip mine or strip mining); mine, shaft mine (shaft mining).

**military mine**   An explosive device used on land or in the sea. A military mine is an explosive device deployed for the purpose of denying an opposing force access to an area. Mines are either landmines or nautical mines and have a host of varying forms of control, detonation, and effect.

**landmine**   An explosive implanted in the ground to harm personnel or vehicles. A landmine, which is often referred to simply as a mine, is an explosive device that is placed on or in the ground by the members of one military force to be discharged when opposing military forces are near it. Landmines may be triggered by a signal from an observer, by pressure from movement on the ground, by the use of a tripwire, by sensing metal, motion, sound, or electrical activity, or by other means. Thus, a constant difficulty is the danger landmines pose to noncombatant populations, particularly after the cessation of hostilities.

Landmines are usually categorized into those intended as anti-personnel mines, those intended as anti-vehicle mines, and those intended as anti-tank mines. Larger mines may have subsidiary explosive devices, such as anti-handling devices, that are intended to cause injury during mine removal operations.

Mines, especially anti-personnel mines, may be distributed in great numbers by air, making their exact location difficult to assess, even by the deploying force. The Ottawa Convention of 1997 bans the use of anti-personnel landmines by signatory states, and all types of landmines are heavily restricted in their use under the 1996 protocol to the Convention on Prohibitions or Restrictions on the Use of Certain Conventional Weapons Which May Be Deemed to Be Excessively Injurious or to Have Indiscriminate Effects.

Mines not created as mass produced weapons for use by regular military forces are improvised explosive devices, or IEDs.

**naval mine** An explosive deployed in a navigable water to harm vessels. A naval mine, which often is referred to as simply a mine, is an explosive device that is deployed either to drift freely in the water or to be moored in a given location and is detonated either by a remote signal from the deploying force or by sensing metal, motion, sound, pressure, or electrical activity. Most mines use a conventional explosive, although some nuclear mines have been developed for naval use.

As a matter of international law and the law of war, any state that lays mines or that has knowledge of mines in its waters is under an obligation to warn the vessels of all states of the presence of those mines. The laying of mines in the waters of another state or in the high seas in a location that hinders the navigation of another state is a use of force that may violate the UN Charter.

**mining** The extraction of a mineral from the earth. Mining is the process of removing a mineral from the earth. In some contexts, mining is understood to be only the removal of minerals underground in their solid state, including the extraction of solids using water, other liquids, steam, or other gases. In other contexts, mining includes all forms of the extraction of materials defined as minerals by law, including oil and gas.

**mining claim** The mineral interest in public lands. A mining claim is the the right to prospect, mine, and process the minerals (as defined by federal law) on a parcel of public land. The mining claim is limited in its use, is distinct from a claim to title, and does not, without more, ripen to title or a right to a land patent.

*See also:* patent, land patent.

**shaft mine (shaft mining)** An underground tunnel or cavern from which minerals are removed. A shaft mine is a hole or pit in the earth that extends under the ground through tunnels, caverns, galleries, or other gaps found or created in the earth, in order to reach the rock or mineral to be extracted. Generally, shafts are vertical, drifts are horizontal, and slopes are angled passages, while galleries are wide horizontal areas, and all of these may have pillars of unextracted matter for support.

*See also:* mine.

**surface mine (open-pit mine or open pit mine or open-pit mining or strip mine or strip mining)** The removal of everything above the rock or mineral sought. Surface mining is the removal of the overburden — trees and vegetation, soil and water, rock and contour that occurs above the mineral or rock to be extracted — from an area, after which the substance desired may be dug from above the ground and removed for processing or use. Surface mines include strip mines, which are comparatively shallow but much longer or wider; open-pit mines, which are deeper; and mountain-top removal operations, which remove the tops of mountains.

Under the Surface Mining Control and Reclamation Act of 1977, 30 U.S.C. §§1234–1328 (2009), an entity that creates or operates a surface mine must seek and receive a permit specifying environmental performance standards for operation and for reclamation when the mine is closed. A bond to assure the cost reclamation is required before operation, and a severance fee is required, which in part funds the cleanup of abandoned mine lands.

*See also:* mine.

**mineral** A substance naturally on the planet extracted from a mine. A mineral, in general usage, is a solid created in the planet's composition that has a definite and consistent chemical combination and structure in the form of crystals, as opposed to the irregular chemistry and forms of rocks, which may include crystals. As a matter of law, a mineral is a substance, other than water, that is extracted from the ground through mines, quarries, or wells for commercial use. The legal designation of mineral is related to, but distinct from, its general chemical or mineralogical definition, in that the law in many jurisdictions includes not only true minerals but also mineral fuels, such as coal, gas, and oil; and some rocks and aggregates of minerals, such as sand and clay. Thus mineral rights usually include the right to extract oil or gas. Mineral interests in real property are subject both to property law in their ownership and transfer and to state and federal regulation relating to their extraction.

**mineral acre** *See:* land, measure of land, acre, mineral acre.

**mineral ferae naturae** *See:* ferae, ferae naturae, mineral ferae naturae.

**mineral interest (mineral rights)** Rights to oil, gas, or mineral deposits in land. A mineral interest refers to the rights to possess and control oil, gas, or mineral deposits in place in the land. A mineral interest is a real property interest, and it may be severed from the surface rights in the land by any owner of both the surface rights and the mineral interests. A holder of a mineral interest in fee may lease the interest to another or alienate it to another without notice to the surface right holder. A mineral interest holder has an easement for access over the surface to extract the minerals. The simultaneous holding of both the once-severed mineral interests and surface rights by the same owner will merge them into a common holding.

*See also:* possession, adverse possession, adverse possession of mineral rights (mineral rights adversely possessed).

**mineral lease**   *See:* lease, mineral lease (hydrocarbon lease or oil lease or gas lease).

**mineral rights adversely possessed**   *See:* possession, adverse possession, adverse possession of mineral rights (mineral rights adversely possessed)

**Ming code**   *See:* Chinese law, Ming code.

**minhag (minhagim)**   Custom. Minhag, in Jewish law, means custom or tradition as the basis of law, particularly custom as a binding source of halakhah. Minhagim is the plural of minhag.

*See also:* custom (customary); halakhah.

**mini-trial**   *See:* arbitration, mini-trial.

**minimal state**   *See:* state, night-watchman state (minimal state); state, minimal state.

**minimum contacts**   *See:* jurisdiction, in personam jurisdiction, minimum contacts, fair play and substantial justice; jurisdiction, in personam jurisdiction, minimum contacts.

**minimum wage**   *See:* wage, minimum wage.

**mining**   *See:* mine, mining.

**mining claim**   *See:* mine, mining, mining claim.

**ministerial act**   *See:* immunity, official immunity, ministerial act.

**minor**   A person under the age of majority. A minor is any person who is not an adult under the law; that is, a person who has not reached the age of majority or been removed of the disability of minority by judicial order. For many purposes, the age of majority is eighteen, though for some it is nineteen, twenty, or twenty-one, and for some reasons of the support of children or dependents it may be older.

*See also:* adult, age of majority (legal age).

**contributing to the delinquency of a minor (corruption of a minor)**   Sexual acts with or the giving of pornography to a minor. Corruption of a minor includes all conduct that encourages a minor child to engage in sexual acts. The act of an adult who engages in sex with a person below the age of consent is always corruption of a minor. In some jurisdictions, the act of an adult who is a teacher who has sex with a student who is under twenty-one years of age but who is subject to that teacher's authority is corruption of a minor. Corruption of a minor is usually a crime and thus must be defined with specificity by statute, which in many cases is a statutory rape statute. Corruption is also, however, a basis for the loss of custody by a parent or guardian as well as a tort. In these senses, corruption bars the encouragement of sexual acts and knowledge given to one culturally deemed too young.

*See also:* adult, age of consent.

**emancipation of a minor (relief from the disabilities of minority or emancipated minor)**   The independence as a matter of law of a person under the age of majority. The emancipation of a minor is the legal recognition of a person physically under the age of majority as independent, either for the purpose of relieving that person of the burdens of minority so that the person may enter contracts, hold property, or perform adult employment or for the purpose of ending the benefit to that person of the obligation of a parent or guardian for the minor's support. Emancipation may result from a lawful wedding, and a person who has entered into a lawful marriage under the law of the jurisdiction in which the marriage occurs is considered under the common law to be emancipated. Otherwise, emancipation requires a petition to a court either by the minor or by a parent or guardian.

A petition of emancipation by a minor is, in many jurisdictions, a petition to be relieved of the burdens of minority. The authority for such a petition is usually the common law of that jurisdiction, although statutory bases may also exist. A petition of emancipation by a parent or guardian is, in many jurisdictions, a petition to decree the independence of the minor from further parental support, and the authority for such a petition is usually statutory. In both cases, the decision to grant the petition rests in the discretion of the family court judge, chancellor, or trial judge, based upon the evidence presented that the minor is already independent, demonstrates sufficient maturity, judgment, and life skills to be emancipated as a matter of fact, and, particularly for statutory emancipation, is already economically self-sufficient.

**minority (minority group)**   A group defined by the ideology or identity of its members, who differ from the majority in society. In general, minority is the condition of a person, group, or thing, that is lesser (or minor) in comparison to a person, group, or thing that is greater (or major). Thus a child is in a state of minority, and an adult is in a state of majority. A group of people holding two opinions may have a majority that holds one and a minority, the lesser number, who hold the other.

Indeed, in any population, a group — however defined — that is less than the majority is a minority. Thus, a minority is any classification that is not that of a majority. Yet the sense of minority in this sense is more than strictly numerical, and in most uses, the sense of minority used implies a lack of political and cultural authority or access. It may be numerically appropriate to speak of billionaires as a minority, yet the billionaires do not fit most senses of minority owing to the cultural or political access that ordinarily accompanies such economic opportunity.

Legal usage similarly incorporates several distinct senses of minority within and among groups, in a manner similar to classification but emphasizing the diminished number or influence of the class. In some senses, a minority is a mathematical or functional question. Thus, a minority shareholder is a person who does not hold or control a majority of shares, and a minority interest is less than a controlling interest. A minority opinion is one not assented by the majority of judges, and so on.

In other senses in law, a minority is a group that differs in some important way from the majority of the population and is in some manner vulnerable as a result of its reduced political or social influence. Some minorities are formed on ideological grounds, as when members become a group because they share an unpopular idea. Other forms of minority may be more essential to a person's identity and less prone to change, though such a group may be as related to ideology as one that is not based on identity. One of the earliest minorities to be recognized in this manner is a group that holds religious beliefs or requires religious practices that differ from the majority's beliefs or practices. Other minority groups eventually recognized in various laws include groups identified by race, color, parentage, national origin, language, military service, physical disability, mental disability, gender, family status, and sexual orientation. Those minorities whose membership is generally fixed and unchangeable and who are not usually significant in their political participation are discrete and insular minorities forming a discrete and insular class. Given that some of these groups are numerically larger than half of the population, like women in the United States, some minorities may be majority-minorities, in which historical obstacles to political and social authority establish the status of diminished influence characteristic of a minority, regardless of a numerical majority.

Federal law and state law protect members of minorities from discrimination in the workplace, in housing, in access to a variety of public services by private providers in commerce, and to public services. The federal government identifies protected minorities by race, color, religion, sex and national origin. Certain groups are defined by Executive Order 11246 (Sept. 24, 1965) as a protected minority, including American Indian or Alaskan Native, Asian or Pacific Islander, Black, and Hispanic.

**minority rule**   *See:* rule, majority rule (minority rule).

**minority business enterprise**   *See:* business, business enterprise, minority business enterprise.

**discrete and insular minority**   An identifiable group that is separate from the majority. A discrete and insular minority is a group of people in a larger community whose members are clearly within the group (or any person about whom it is thought to be reasonably

clear that the person is or is not a member of the group) and whose membership as a whole somehow stays apart from, is kept apart from, or is treated differently by the community as a whole. Chief Justice Stone recognized in footnote four of the Carolene Products opinion, United States v. Carolene Products Co., 304 U. S. 144 (1938), that such groups are in danger of exclusion from the democratic process and stated that laws that create a particular burden on such a group might require more careful judicial review than laws that are more general in their definitions or effects.

*See also:* scrutiny, standards of scrutiny, strict scrutiny, footnote four (footnote four or the footnote).

**under-represented    minority    (underrepresented minority)**   A minority group in a community, whose members are rare in an activity. An under-represented minority is a group that is a minority in terms of race, gender, religion, nationality, or other salient characteristic in the community or population as a whole, whose members are significantly less represented in a sub-population or activity than its proportion in the community or population as a whole. For example, if a community that is 40 percent African American and 60 percent European American has a police force that is only 20 percent African American, then African Americans are an under-represented minority with respect to the police force. Ascertaining the degree of difference required between the percentage of minority members in the community or population and the percentage in the relevant sub-population or activity is controversial when determining whether a minority group is under-represented, yet clear and obvious cases still abound.

**Miranda rule (Miranda warning or Miranda rights)**   A person in custody must be given notice of rights to silence and to representation by counsel. The Miranda rule is the constitutional requirement that a person who is detained or taken into custody by any law enforcement officer must be advised of his or her constitutional right to remain silent and to representation by an attorney before any questioning or prior to making any statement. Any statement made in such circumstances without such warnings is presumptively inadmissible in a prosecution's case in chief against the person who makes it. The rule, from Miranda v. Arizona, 384 U.S. 436 (1966), generally requires "Miranda warnings" to be administered by the police and effectively understood by the person before questioning. The rule was instituted after concerns were raised over the potential psychological pressures that were placed on a suspect when interrogated while in police custody, such that one could waive a constitutional privilege without understanding the consequences of such a decision. The police may continue to question a suspect who does not invoke a right to silence, and an answer to such questioning is considered an implied waiver of the right.

The fundamental purpose of the rule is to ensure that the police advise a person in custody of the right not to speak, as well as the right to terminate questioning. Even so, the right to terminate interrogations has yet to be widely incorporated into the Miranda warnings offered by police.

*waiver of Miranda rights* An accused may waive Miranda rights to silence and representation and give a valid confession that otherwise would be excluded from the prosecution's case in chief at trial. The waiver may be express or implied, and the implication may arise from the confession or statement alone, as long as it follows a Miranda warning. The waiver cannot, however, extend to the notice of Miranda rights; a person may not waive the right to be given notice of rights unless clear evidence is given that the person already understands those rights.

**public-safety exception (exception for public safety to Miranda)** A narrow exception to the traditional requirement for Miranda warnings. The public safety exception to the Miranda rule allows answers to questions or other statements to be used from a person in custody, even if the Miranda warnings were not first given to the person, as long as the officers reasonably believed at the time of the questioning that the suspect's reliance on the underlying constitutional rights to avoid answering a question would endanger the surrounding public. The public safety exception was first carved into the Miranda rule in New York v. Quarles, 467 U.S. 649 (1984).

**mirror-image rule** *See:* acceptance, acceptance as acceptance of an offer, mirror-image rule (mirror image rule).

**misadventure** An accident causing injury that arises during the course of lawful conduct. Misadventure is a common-law term for an accident that results in some harm or injury during an otherwise lawful activity or conduct. Misadventure by one person that results in harm to another person is accidental and not wrongful, so death by misadventure is neither criminal homicide nor manslaughter.

*See:* misappropriation (misappropriate).

**misappropriation (misappropriate)** An unauthorized or improper use of money or property. Misappropriation is any wrongful or mistaken use or allocation of money or property. Thus an allocation of public funds for a purpose for which the funds are not authorized is a misappropriation, as is the taking of property of another person without a license to do so. Misappropriation is therefore sometimes used to depict the theft of tangible property or the wrongful use of intellectual property, particularly trade secrets, trademarks, trade dress, or service marks.

**misbranding** To wrongly label or market a food or drug. Misbranding is the false or misleading presentation of information related to a food or drug, including in the text or labels on its container. The misbranding of food or drugs subject to the Federal Food, Drug, and Cosmetic Act is criminal if it is done with intent. Under

some state laws, misbranding is a misdemeanor if done recklessly, although a separate offense is committed each day a violation continues.

*See also:* adulteration (adulterate or adulterant).

**miscegenation (anti-miscegenation law)** The mixing of races. Miscegenation is the mixing of people who are identified as being of different races, particularly through sexual relations and the birth of children. The term was apparently coined in a book with that title in 1864, and though the book praised racial intermarriage as essential to humanity, the term was taken up in state anti-miscegenation laws banning marriages between persons of different races. These laws were found unconstitutional in 1967 in Loving v. Virginia, 388 U.S. 1. Note: anti-miscegenation should not be confused with misogyny, which is the hatred of women.

**mischief (mischevious)** The wrongful result of malice or circumstance. Mischief is used in the law to describe any conduct or action that is bad or harmful; the mischief being an aspect of the undesirable result. Though mischief implies a sense of deliberate action, the term applies to unintended consequences as well. There are several persistent nuances in its legal usage: legislation is frequently analyzed through the lens of some mischief that the statute in question seeks to abate and the mischief of a petty offender is the wrongful nature of the offending act, as well as its consequence, but usually the term is not used to emphasize the technical fact of its violation of the law.

*See also:* interpretation, statutory interpretation, legislative purpose; malum, malum in se (mala in se).

**criminal mischief (malicious mischief)** The crime of willful injury to property. Criminal mischief, or malicious mischief, is the crime of causing destruction or injury to a person or to property. Though the common-law understanding of criminal mischief included not only deliberate but also reckless conduct and included not only harm to property but also harm to persons, the modern offense is usually brought for acts of vandalism, which is the willful and knowing destruction or damage of personal or public property.

Various statutes specify different elements for defining the offense, though most statutes require that the act be knowing and the damaging result be intended. Most statutes vary the severity of the offense in proportion to the loss caused by the act, and in most states the value of the loss must be pled in the charge, information, or indictment. In some states the harm to the property must be without the effective consent of the owner, which also must be pled. Note: other than as a matter of statutory choice, there is little difference between the offense of criminal mischief and the offense of vandalism.

*See also:* vandalism (vandal).

**misconduct** Behavior contrary to law, to duty of office, or to another norm. Misconduct is a general label for wrongful conduct, particularly conduct in violation of a rule or an obligation arising from a position of duty or trust. An official act based on misconduct is usually subject to being made void, such as a jury verdict rendered when a juror has been bribed, a judicial ruling made despite the judge's conflict of interest, or a trustee's sale when the trustee participates in self-dealing.

**misconduct by employee** *See:* unemployment, unemployment compensation, employee misconduct (misconduct by employee).

**attorney misconduct (lawyer misconduct)** A failure of an attorney to comport with the rules and accepted professional customs of the bar. Attorney misconduct includes any act or omission of duty by an attorney that fails to perform appropriately the office of an attorney as an officer of the court, as a counselor and fiduciary of a client, or as a member of the legal profession. The scope of attorney misconduct includes breaches of the rules of professional responsibility that apply in the jurisdiction in which an attorney is licensed or in which an attorney's conduct has an effect. The scope of attorney misconduct, however, reaches also to conduct of attorneys that is harmful to the pursuit of justice or that is harmful to the appropriate reliance of the citizenry upon the law and the legal profession. Attorney misconduct includes actions or omissions that enable others to cause harm, not just harm caused directly by the attorney.

Not all attorney misconduct is subject to remedy or to sanctions, although a variety of forms of each exist. Misconduct may always be the basis for a client to fire an attorney, as is any other cause for the client's loss of trust in a lawyer. Misconduct may be the basis for attorney discipline by the bar in which the attorney is licensed or by the courts in which the attorney is authorized to practice. Misconduct may be the basis for sanctions by the court against the attorney or the attorney's client in an action then before the court. Misconduct may be the basis for a civil action or a private claim against an attorney for malpractice, professional negligence, breach of contract, breach of fiduciary duty, and other claims, brought by a client, or another person with a right to rely on or right to be free from harm by the attorney.

Attorney misconduct may be the basis for a variety of exceptions to rules of procedure and evidence. Particularly, attorney–client privilege and work–product immunity are limited to allow disclosure of certain materials that would otherwise be protected if they are the result of or evidence of misconduct.

*See also:* lawyer, lawyer discipline, disciplinary rules, rules of professional conduct; ethics, legal ethics.

**miscreant** A person with no sense of moral restraint. A miscreant, in English law, was an apostate, or one who had disavowed the Christian religion and was thus considered to feel free to commit such wrongs as the concept of sin forbade. In contemporary usage, a miscreant has no particular legal significance, but is generally a wrongdoer, a person who engages in wanton, illegal, or improper conduct, often to the harm of others.

*See also:* wrong, wrongdoer (wrong–doer).

**misdemeanor** A criminal offense of less severity than a felony. A misdemeanor is a crime that is less serious than a felony, either because the conduct is defined to be a misdemeanor by statute or because the punishment assessed for the conduct is less than that for a felony. Usually, an offense that is not punishable by death or by imprisonment for a year or longer is a misdemeanor. Misdemeanors tend to be crimes in which the nature of the perceived wrongdoing of the offense is less than that of a felony. Most states distinguish between degrees of misdemeanor, using different language to divide them and assign to each lesser degree a diminished severity of the penalty to be assessed. Some jurisdictions distinguish gross misdemeanors both from misdemeanors and from minor misdemeanors, though minor misdemeanors have at times been treated as a distinct category from other misdemeanors. Some jurisdictions have first-degree through fifth-degree misdemeanors, and some have class A though class D misdemeanors. Note: the U.S. Constitution specifies that the President may be impeached for "High Crimes and Misdemeanors," and similar language is found in state constitutions. It seems clear that the term in this setting is used in its sense as misconduct and not as a category of petty offense.

**gross misdemeanor** An intermediate class of crime below felony and above misdemeanor. A gross misdemeanor is a crime for which a person may be sentenced to a term longer than that assigned to a misdemeanor but still less than a year. Although definitions of offenses vary greatly among jurisdictions, examples include being responsible for reporting suspected child abuse but not doing so, attempt to commit a low-category felony, minor theft, minor sex offense, minor drug possession offense, conducting illegal gambling operations, driving while impaired, and repeated offenses of a misdemeanor.

**misfeasance** *See:* feasance, misfeasance (misfeasance).

**Mishnah** Jewish law codified around 200 C.E. The Mishnah is a code of legal rules codified from oral tradition around 200 C.E. and organized into six tractates on various topics.

**Mishneh Torah** *See:* Torah, Mishneh Torah.

**mishpatim** Jewish laws based on reason rather than authority alone. The mishpatim is the Jewish civil laws, the laws that are attributable to a rational reason for their obedience. Mishpatim are usually contrasted to hukim, which are binding owing to authority alone and not to reason.

*See also:* hukim (chukim chukkim).

**misjoinder** *See:* joinder, misjoinder.

**mislaid property** *See:* property, found property, mislaid property.

**misnomer (misnomer rule)**   A misstatement of the name of a person or entity. Misnomer is the incorrect designation of the name of a person or entity, especially in a pleading or process. A misnomer is a mistake only in labeling the party intended, not in mistakenly selecting the wrong party.

Under the misnomer rule in procedure, a party served by a pleading the party's name with an error is deemed to have been validly served and before the court. The misnomer rule in wills and contracts will allow a grant or an obligation to be binding if the person misnamed can be ascertained with reasonable certainty.

*See also:* idem, idem sonans.

**misogyny (misogynist)**   The hatred of women. Misogyny is the fundamental dislike, resentment, or fear of women, whether in general or in a given employment or role, manifested by speech or conduct. A misogynist is a person who thinks of women, or acts toward a woman, misogynistically. Though there is some controversy regarding the subject, there is no inherent reason why a woman cannot be a misogynist.

**misprision (misprision of a felony)**   The concealment of a crime. Misprision is the concealment of a crime, particularly the failure to report a crime, the reporting of false information, or the reporting of selective information intended to mislead the government, the result of which is that the government was in a worse position than it would have been otherwise. When used by itself, misprision now nearly always refers to a misprision of felony. Misprision is a distinct crime from being an accessory or accomplice, and a person may be guilty of misprision whether or not the person was a conspirator, planner, or actor in the criminal scheme. Misprision in some states is limited only to a public official who has knowledge and fails to reveal it.

*See also:* treason, misprision of treason.

**misprision of treason**   *See:* treason, misprision of treason.

**misrepresentation**   *See:* representation, misrepresentation, intentional misrepresentation (fraudulent misrepresentation); representation, misrepresentation | concealment of facts; representation, misrepresentation.

**negligent misrepresentation**   The provision of false information without due care. Negligent misrepresentation is the provision, for gain or employment, of incorrect information to others with the knowledge that the recipients will rely upon it, without exercising reasonable care or competence either in the acquisition of the information or in the act and means of its transmission. Not every jurisdiction recognizes an action for negligent misrepresentation, and many jurisdictions allow it only in narrow circumstances, such as a fiduciary or employment relationship.

**missing movement**   The avoidable failure of a service member to be present with a unit when it moves. Missing movement is an offense under the Uniform Code of Military Justice (UCMJ) and occurs when a servicemember negligently or intentionally is not present with a unit, vessel, or craft when the unit relocates from one place to another and the servicemember is under orders or assignment to be present. Note: a member need not be absent without leave to miss the movement of a unit.

*See also:* absence, absence without leave (A.W.O.L. or AWOL).

**mistake**   An error in belief, action, or communication. Mistake is a belief contrary to the facts or a statement or action contrary to its maker's intention. Mistaken beliefs arise from a difference between some state of affairs in the world and a person's understanding of that state of affairs, such as a person's belief that the revenues of a company are a certain amount when in fact they are a different amount. Mistaken actions arise from a difference between what a person intends to do or the results intended to be done by some action and the physical act actually performed or the results caused by that action, such as a person's intent to turn a switch on when in fact the person turns the switch off. Mistaken statements arise from a difference between what is intended to be communicated and what is in fact communicated, as when the drafter of a contract intends to set one date for performance but in fact writes another.

The law of mistake is of particular concern in contract law, as mistakes or claims of mistakes in the formation of a contract frequently form the bases of arguments for a party to be relieved of the obligation to perform or to change the nature of the performance required. In general, the mistake of one party to a contract regarding a material fact may make the contract voidable by the party that did not know of the mistake and was not specially charged with the risk for the fact on which the mistake was made. This can happen when one party is relied upon by the other to provide a fact or is responsible for investigating such facts by either the practice between the parties or the customs of the trade in which they are engaged. A mutual mistake, which is one made by all of the parties to the contract, may be avoided by all.

Mistake in the drafting of wills, trusts, legislation, regulation, or other instruments is the subject of significant efforts in interpretation, which would correct the mistake generally to read as the drafter intended the instrument to read.

Mistake in criminal law may be the basis for excuse from criminal liability when it arises from conduct committed by the defendant in circumstances that the defendant misperceives, and if the circumstances had been as the defendant believed them to be, the defendant's action would have been lawful, though because the circumstances were what they were in fact, the defendant's action was unlawful. In other words, if the defendant had been correct the action would not have been criminal. For example, if Smith believes (wrongly) that Jones is holding a loaded gun and preparing to shoot Smith, Smith may shoot Jones, even if Jones was holding a wrench, not holding a loaded gun, and could not have shot Smith. Smith is not guilty of battery, even though Smith did not have a defense of justification from self-defense, because Smith may assert mistake as a defense in excuse. Mistake can excuse crimes that are not of strict liability, though in some jurisdictions the mistake must be reasonable, and in all jurisdictions the mistake must be made in good faith.

Similarly, mistake may be a defense in tort to liability for crimes of intent, although the nature of the mistake and the circumstances in which it is made may in fact be an element of negligence.

**honest mistake (bona fide error in judgment or good faith error in judgment)** A genuine mistake not intended to cause harm. An honest mistake, or a good faith error in judgment, is a mistake made in good faith despite well intended efforts in the task in which the mistake occurs. In most instances, to argue that a mistake is honest or made in good faith is not, however, to argue that it is reasonable to make. Even so, in extreme cases a condition of patent unreasonableness, a violation of a stated workplace rule or law, or circumstances that would put the person on notice that the decision would cause unacceptable consequences could prevent a successful argument that the mistake was indeed made in good faith.

A good faith error in judgment may have varying effects as a defense or rebuttal. As a defense to a claim of negligence, it may be insufficient, though as a defense to a charge of misconduct, it may be successful. A standard of care that depends on the mental state of the actor is usually not violated by a good faith error in judgment, but a standard of care based on professional standards or expectations depends on reasonable and informed decisions made in good faith, and an argument of good faith alone is insufficient for most defenses.

**mistake of law** A mistake regarding the legal effect of a fact. A mistake of law is a mistake concerning the legal consequences, including civil and criminal liability, of a given fact or set of facts. Mistake of law may be the basis for mutual mistake and rescission of contracts, and it may be the basis for a claim of good faith immunity from suit by a police officer or public official. Mistake of law is usually a defense to a criminal charge only when the defendant's mistake was based on the reasonable reliance of a statement made by an appropriate public official to the defendant.

*See also:* ignorance, ignorance of law (ignorance of the law).

**mutual mistake** A mistake as to the same fact made by all parties to a contract. Mutual mistake is a mistake regarding the same putative fact that is independently made by each of the parties to a contract at the time of its formation or at the time of the negotiation or preparation of the contract and not discovered by any of the parties until after the contract is formed. In most instances, a contract with a mutual mistake as to a material term is voidable by the parties, and either rescission or reformation are the usual remedies. As long as the mistake is mutual, no damages are generally allowed as a remedy for partial performance,

although some form of restitution may be required for a party who performs or partly performs if the contract is later rescinded in whole or in part.

It does not matter for most purposes if the mistake is first made by one party and then relied upon by the others, as long as all parties believed in good faith in the same mistaken idea. However, if the party that initially presents a mistaken idea to the others is under a special duty regarding the particular fact and the other parties had a right to rely on the first party (and in the contract had a right to rely on that party) for the idea's accuracy, then the mistake may be a unilateral mistake.

*See also:* rescission.

**reasonable mistake** A mistake that a reasonable person might make. A reasonable mistake is a mistake that might have been made by any reasonable person of the same duty or profession in the same circumstances. A reasonable mistake, by definition, is one that an agent is not already on notice to avoid or that would not be made on casual or typical preparation or investigation.

The primary distinction among forms of mistake is that between reasonableness and good faith. The difference is in the manner in which the circumstances of the mistake are evaluated, reasonableness being an assessment of the objective conditions under which the actor made the mistake in question, while good faith is the assessment of the intent or purpose the actor had at the time, or the degree to which the actor is truthful regarding the actor's genuine motives or purposes at the time of the mistake. Thus, the reasonableness of the mistake is an assessment that is made by comparing the circumstances surrounding the actor's mistake to determine whether the mistake might also have been made by a hypothetical person who acted properly according to the appropriate duty of care, in which case the mistake is a reasonable mistake. Reasonableness does not, therefore, determine whether the duty of care required in many circumstances was breached or satisfied. The question in many instances is whether a mistake was reckless, in that no care for one's duties or toward others was involved in the making of the mistake; negligent, in that some care toward one's duties or toward others was demonstrated, but the care was insufficient under the circumstances; or faultless, in that the care toward one's duties or toward others required under the circumstances was demonstrated, yet a mistake was still made.

*See also:* reasonable (reasonableness).

**unilateral mistake** A mistake by one party as to a material fact made during the formation or performance of a contract. A unilateral mistake is made by only one party to a contract, such that the mistaken party believes some condition or state of the world to be true that is not true. By definition, the other party or parties to the contract do not share the mistaken belief.

A unilateral mistake is not inherently grounds for the avoidance of a contract, but it may be sufficient, in limited circumstances, in some jurisdictions. If the non–mistaken party has reason to know of the mistaken party's mistake at the time of the contract but does not act to correct the mistake and instead relies upon the mistake, then unless the mistaken party has a duty of investigation or otherwise is specially charged with the risk of the mistake, and the mistake is of a material term that would place the mistaken party at a genuine harm in going forward under the contract, then enforcement of the contract may be considered unconscionable.

**mistrial**   A jury trial that ends prematurely owing to a serious error or a hung jury. A mistrial is an adjournment of a trial either because the jury failed to reach a verdict or because of the determination by the judge that some error during the trial is so prejudicial to one or all of the parties that a judgment based on the proceedings would be unconstitutional, unreliable, or unjust. Though a party may move for a mistrial, the decision to grant a mistrial is at the discretion of the trial judge, and the judge will ordinarily be reluctant to use such a remedy for a breach of procedure or courtroom protocol unless the error in the court so prejudices the proceedings that no other remedy will suffice to do justice under the law. The effect of a mistrial is to allow the parties to commence their cases from the start before a new jury.

**misuse of product defense**   *See:* liability, product liability, misuse of product defense.

**mitigation (mitigate or mitigating)**   To make less burdensome. Mitigation is any act that diminishes the harms of an injurious act or condition. Mitigation takes many forms in the law. For example: Mitigation of damages is the action by a plaintiff that diminishes the damages that the plaintiff would suffer as a result of the defendant's conduct. Mitigating criminal evidence is evidence of good conduct or diminished responsibility that might offset the culpability of a wrongdoer. Mitigation of an environmental harm is the reduction or correction of the harm in the physical environment.
   *See also:* debt, abatement of a debt.

   **mitigating circumstance**   *See:* circumstance, mitigating circumstance (mitigating factors).

   **mitigation of damages**   *See:* damages, contract damages, mitigation of damages; damages, calculation of damages, mitigation of damages (avoidable consequences).

   **mitigating evidence**   *See:* sentence, mitigation of sentence (mitigating evidence).

   **mitigating factors**   *See:* circumstance, mitigating circumstance (mitigating factors).

   **mitigation of sentence**   *See:* sentence, mitigation of sentence (mitigating evidence).

   **environmental mitigation**   Man–made changes to diminish harm to an ecosystem. Mitigation as a matter of environmental law includes all human activity intended to reduce the harmful effects of a past, present, or future project in a given ecosystem. Mitigation includes avoiding or reducing a harm that is planned before it occurs, as well as minimizing harms in projects that are ongoing or planned as well as correcting environmental harms or hazards that have occurred. Although more generally, mitigation can include actions to diminish natural events that degrade an ecosystem, such as the effect of erosion on banks, the term in application of the National Environmental Policy Act and other statutes is usually limited to the reduction in harms from human activity.
   *See also:* mitigation, environmental mitigation, mitigation bank.

   **mitigation bank**   A site creating environmental benefits to offset harms to the environment elsewhere. A mitigation bank is a physical area of natural habitat that is given some environmentally advantageous input, such as forestation, wetlands restoration, erosion management, water–filtering plants, artificial reefs, or other improvements intended to offset an environmental harm created somewhere else. The accounting for the form, quality, and quantity of units of credit and debit for such banks is somewhat controversial.
   *See also:* mitigation, environmental mitigation.

**mitzvah (mitsvah or mitsvot or mitzvoth)**   A command to be carried out in daily life, particularly to commit acts of kindness. A mitzvah is, technically, one of the 613 commands to do or refrain from some conduct that are stated in the Torah or by the rabbis, all of which are based on the will of God. In contemporary usage, the mitzvah is likely to mean any act of kindness toward others. The plural forms of mitzvah are mitsvot or mitzvoth.

**mixed government**   *See:* government, forms of government, mixed government.

**mixed nuisance**   *See:* nuisance, mixed nuisance.

**mixed property**   *See:* property, mixed property.

**mixed question or issue of law and fact**   *See:* issue, issue before the court, mixed issue of fact and law (mixed question or issue of law and fact).

**mob**   A group of people acting together in committing a crime. A mob is a group of people acting in concert in committing a crime. Mob has two distinct senses, the first and older being an assembly of people, regardless of the purpose for which they are initially assembled, whose presence and support provides an environment that causes or condones an act of violence committed by an individual within the group, including vandalism, assault, murder, and lynching. A municipality is responsible for the dispersion of mobs and may be liable for damage caused by mob violence under state statute. Under the Ku Klux Klan Act, if an official charged with protecting others fails to act when there is knowledge of impending danger, the individual may be liable for the violation of the civil rights of those whose protection was denied.

The second sense of mob is as a slang term for any criminal organization, most notably the Sicilian mafia in the United States.

*See also:* riot; civil rights, Civil Rights Act, Civil Rights Act of 1871 (Ku Klux Klan Act); racketeering, organized crime, Mafia (La Cosa Nostra).

**mobile source**   *See:* pollution, air pollution, mobile source.

**mock jury**   *See:* jury, mock jury (shadow jury).

**modality**   A method for understanding or argument. A modality, in general, is a particular form for understanding or for argument. A modality is one among other methods for talking or thinking about a thing. There are many modes of understanding the nature of law and justice. Six forms of modality are especially central to legal argument: textual, doctrinal, historical, ethical, structural, and prudential.

**model instruction**   *See:* instruction, jury instruction, model instruction (pattern instruction or standard instruction or suggested instruction or uniform instruction).

**modicum**   Small in quantity or size. Modicum refers to relative smallness or scarcity in number. Thus, a modicum of punishment is a small punishment, and a modicum of evidence is a slight quantity of evidence. Note: in English, modicum is a measure in itself, like a gallon, not an adjective, like light or small. Thus, the word usually is followed by the preposition of followed by the thing quantified, such as a modicum of reserve.

*See also:* proof, burden of proof, modicum of evidence (some evidence or any evidence or no evidence).

**modicum of evidence**   *See:* proof, burden of proof, modicum of evidence (some evidence or any evidence or no evidence); evidence, modicum of evidence.

**modification**   The changing of an existing plan, document, or thing. A modification is an alteration, some change to whatever is in issue. Thus, a modification to a purchase order or a work order amounts to a new term in the contract the order represents. A modification to real property is any alteration of its conditions other than through natural processes. A modification of an order is a variance in any of the terms decreed within it.

**modified comparative negligence**   *See:* negligence, comparative negligence, modified comparative negligence (hybrid comparative negligence).

**modified per stirpes**   *See:* distribution, distribution of estate, per capita, per capita with representation (modified per stirpes).

**modus**   The means or the manner in which something is done. Modus is a Latin term with two distinct senses in English. It is nearly always encountered in law as the label of a manner or process by which something is done. For example, the way in which a crime is committed is the modus of the crime. It is also a measure, particularly a method of measurement, and in this sense it is the root of the English word "moderate."

**modus operandi (signature facts or MO or M.O.)**   A way in which a person performs some task. Modus operandi, literally the manner in which which something is done or the means of operating, depicts the particular steps by which a person performs some task, as well as the style or nuance in which it is done. Modus operandi particularly refers to those elements of performing a task that are the result of habit, so that a person might be identified by the pattern the person employs in the task.

In a criminal trial, evidence of a person's modus operandi in the commission of previous crimes may be introduced to identify that person as having committed the offense. To present such evidence, the prosecution must usually show that the earlier crime was indeed committed by the later defendant, that the particular conduct at issue is sufficiently rare or unusual to demonstrate a person's identity in its performance, and that there is sufficient similarity between the method of the defendant in the earlier crime and the method employed in the later crime that there is a reasonable basis to believe the method suggests a unique actor. Care is required to ensure that such "signature evidence" is not introduced merely to demonstrate that the defendant has a propensity to commit such crimes, which use of the evidence is forbidden. Even so, many courts have winked at such a risk, in violation of the rules of evidence.

*See also:* inference, forbidden inference.

**modus ponendo ponens**   *See:* argument, modus ponens (modus ponendo ponens).

**modus ponens**   *See:* argument, modus ponens (modus ponendo ponens).

**modus tollendo ponens**   *See:* argument, modus tollens (modus tollendo ponens).

**modus tollens**   *See:* argument, modus tollens (modus tollendo ponens).

**modus vivendi**   The settlement of a past conflict. Modus vivendi describes an agreement or pattern of action that resolves a prior conflict between the parties to the agreement or the participants in the action. Literally meaning "a way of living," a modus vivendi might be more appropriately translated in the vernacular as a way of getting along. Thus, modus vivendi may label a settlement agreement or arbitral judgment among private parties or between states.

Modus vivendi in jurisprudence represents a compromise between the particular interests of the parties and not an integration of interests into a common pursuit. Though this definition and the desirability of its underlying means of social organization are controversial, John Rawls contrasted his more robust claim of overlapping consensus, which is based on shared notions of morality, with a depiction of a mere modus vivendi, which is based on compromises among self-interests.

**moiety (moieties)**   One half. A moiety is a half, and the moieties are the two halves of anything, especially of an estate or inheritance. To hold an estate by the moieties is to have an undivided half interest in the whole, which, like a modern co-tenancy, does not grant 50 perecnt of the land, but 50 perecnt of the whole value of the undivided lands. Note: in pharmacology, and thus in the contemporary regulation of drugs and medicine, a moiety is a half of a molecule, or any portion of a molecule of sufficient size and structure to contain a portion of the functional group.

*See also:* half.

**molestation (molest or molester)**   Interference, particularly through unsought or illegal sexual conduct. Molestation is a form of interference with a person's rights, property, or person, and, in general, to molest someone is to aggravate or injure that person. To molest an animal is to aggravate it or to disturb its habitat, and to molest a police officer or soldier is to bother or insult the person to the distraction of the person's duty. Unless defined by statute otherwise, molestation does not require physical contact, so the facts that amount to molestation depend greatly on their context.

In contemporary U.S. law, molestation has acquired the particular sense of engaging in sexual conduct that is inappropriate or unwanted. In particular, molestation is used to describe the prohibitions of sexualized physical contact either with a child or with another person who cannot consent to sexual acts.

*See also:* rape.

**child molestation (molestation of a child or child molester)**   Sexual contact with a child. Child molestation is the crime by an adult or much older child of knowingly or purposefully fondling or sexually touching a child, or causing a child to touch another person in a manner that is for the sexual gratification of the older person. By no means is all contact between an adult and a child molestation, and the customary contact between a parent and child or between older siblings and children that is innocent of sexual purpose cannot amount to molestation.

*See also:* pederasty (pederast).

**moment of death**   *See:* death, moment of death.

**monarchy**   *See:* government, forms of government, monarchy (kingdom or monarch).

**money**   Any system of value used to pay for goods and services. Money is a system of exchange by which value for a physical good, a service, a promise, or a debt is transferred according to relative increments in the value of the system. Money is a more sophisticated system than barter, in that in barter systems, one good (like an apple) or service (like painting a wall) is traded for another good or another service. In money systems, on the other hand, a system of money is first created with a relative value, according to which a good may be valued or a service may be valued, so that the good need not be transferred for another good. The good may be paid for in money, and the money that is received is used to pay for other goods or services. Generally, money systems are managed by the government of a state, which decrees certain forms of money to be legal tender and forbids or discourages the use of other forms. Many systems of money go by other names, such as scrip.

*See also:* tender, legal tender; scrip; currency.

**monetary fee**   *See:* fee, fee for services, monetary fee.

**monetary relief**   *See:* relief, monetary relief.

**monetization or dollarization**   *See:* value, commodification (monetization or dollarization).

**money judgment**   *See:* judgment, money judgment.

**earnest money**   A down payment. Earnest money is a deposit made as a partial payment of a contract. If the contract is not performed, the earnest money is forfeit to the recipient, unless the contract is not performed because of a failure of a condition specified in the contract or because the recipient of the earnest money fails to perform.

*See also:* deposit; payment, down payment.

**laundering of monetary instruments (money laundering or money launderer)**   A transaction performed with assets unlawfully gained. Money laundering is the crime of knowingly engaging in a financial transaction or property transfer using the proceeds of illegal activity, with the result being that money, property, or proceeds from a crime are converted to assets that are otherwise lawfully acquired. Money laundering is a federal offense as well as a crime under most state laws, and it is an aggravating factor in the sentencing of a person convicted of a related offense.

**soft money (soft-money donations)**   Money used by a party not to advertise a candidate but to promote a broader political agenda. Soft money is money outside the limits on campaign expenditures by national political parties that may be used to fund overhead costs, fund raising, voter drives, and issue ads.

**specie**   Coin, or money generally. Specie is now any form of lawful money in cash. Traditionally, specie was money created by public authority out of metal. In ancient states, specie was the sole lawful currency and public tender, though this is no longer the case, and both paper currency and coin are legal tender. The term "specie" or "in specie" in maxims and phrases often usually means money or with money in its generic sense as cash or value in cash.

**monism**

**monism in a legal system (monist or monistic)**   Law is a single intellectual system. Monism represents any single structure for the understanding of ideas, and thus contrasts with pluralism. Monism in international law is therefore the idea that the international legal system is a single system of law incorporating domestic and multi-national institutions. Legal monism in jurisprudence means that the entirety of law and its concepts are within a single intellectual structure. Monism is sometimes also used to describe systems of justice in which all claims of justice are inter-related into a single hierarchy or derived from a single source. From these two notions of monism, an even broader concept of monism is the intregration of law and justice into a single intellectual structure, and, in this, it contrasts with positivism.

**monopoly (monopolize or monopolizer or monopolist)**   The control of a market for goods or services by a single supplier or owner. A monopoly is the control of the sale or potential for sale of a commodity or type of goods by a single supplier, owner, or coordinated group. The common law was hostile to monopolies and would not enforce a contract in furtherance of a business or merchant who sought a monopoly that was not chartered by the crown or licensed by Parliament. Most states prohibit monopolies unless a state statute makes an exception, as it may do for utilities. Monopolies in restraint of trade are prohibited by federal law under Section 2 of the Sherman Antitrust Act, along with attempts to create a monopoly and conspiracy in furtherance of a monopoly. However, not all monopolies are forbidden, and monopolies are lawful that do not restrain trade or that result from regulation or license. In this sense, intellectual property creates a monopoly for the holder of a patent, trademark, or copyright.

A monopoly may be unlawfully created through otherwise lawful acts, but if their intended effect or actual effect is to gain such a share of the market of a good or commodity that the monopolizing individual, entity, or group is capable of suppressing competition, controlling the price of the market for the good or commodity, or harming the public through unilateral action, then an unlawful monopoly results unless it is specifically authorized by other legislation.

*See also:* antitrust, Sherman Antitrust Act (Sherman Act); market, market dominance; market, market share.

**monopoly leveraging**   The use of a monopoly in one market to gain control of another. Monopoly leveraging is the use of the market power a monopolist gains in the market for one good or commodity to gain an advantage or monopoly in the market for a different good or commodity. Although tying agreements do not amount to monopoly leveraging, tying is one method used after a monopoly is established to leverage that market strength to other markets.

*See also:* tying (tied products or tying agreement or tying arrangement).

**natural monopoly**   A market most efficiently served by only one provider. A natural monopoly within a market is a monopoly resulting from a limitation in the scope of the market, as a result of which the most efficient producer is likely to be a sole producer.

This usually results from the criteria of an economy of scale and a high infrastructure cost within a market of sufficiently small scale that the benefits of competition are outweighed by the costs of duplication of the infrastructure.

**month**   One of twelve units of time in the terrestrial year. A month is a customary unit of time equalling roughly one twelfth of the year. For most purposes, a month is not a period of a fixed number of days but is the period that is measured from one day of a month to the same numbered day of the following month (such as from the tenth of the month to the tenth day of the following month), regardless of whether that would, for a given month, include twenty-eight, twenty-nine, thirty, or thirty-one days.

**month-to-month tenancy**   *See:* lease, leasehold, tenancy, periodic tenancy, month-to-month tenancy (monthly lease or month-to-month lease).

**monthly lease or month-to-month lease**   *See:* lease, leasehold, tenancy, periodic tenancy, month-to-month tenancy (monthly lease or month-to-month lease).

**moonshine**   Illegally made or distributed drink of distilled spirits. Moonshine is a colloquial name for distilled spirits that are not produced under a state license, have not been subject to tax, have not been certified to meet health and labeling standards, and have not been produced by workers subject to employment and labor law protections, such as worker's compensation. Contrary to popular belief, there is a great variety of recipes for moonshine, which may be based on nearly any fruit or grain.

**mooring (anchorage or moor or unmooring)**   The place or the act of securing a ship to land. Mooring is the process of a ship or boat as it approaches a port or facility, maneuvers to its final position, and is secured by mooring or anchor lines to a quay, buoy, or other mooring device. When used as a general term in maritime policy, mooring includes entering an anchorage and being secured to the bottom or bed of the body of water, although mariners usually distinguish this process as anchorage. Both mooring and anchorage are also the locations where such processes occur and where the vessel remains moored or anchored.

**moot (mootable)**   Argument, and sometimes only arguable. A moot is a discussion, particularly the interchange of argument typical of legal or legislative debate. The word arose in very early English, and gemot and other terms for assembly or council incorporate it. It is related to the old French word for "word."

In the medieval English Inns of Court, arguments between students on set legal issues were called moots. From this came the contemporary sense of moot court. Yet it also gave rise to the sense of moot as strictly academic, an argument that is irrelevant to practical affairs in the world, and from this comes the sense of mootness as staleness, in which a cause that might have been argued in law is now too late for a ruling to make any difference.

**moot court**   *See:* simulation, moot court; court, moot court.

**mootness (moot)**   *See:* justiciability, mootness.

**morality (moral)**   The duties a good person performs in society. Morality is the sum of what good people would do within a community in general or in specific situations. There are many understandings of both the source and the extent of moral duties. From different perspectives, morality is the sum of the principles for human thought and action based on equality of treatment for all persons, of the genuine care for all persons, of the virtues, of right and wrong, of good and its absence, of happiness or unhappiness, or of wealth and its efficient movement, as well as the sum of all of these approaches. Morality is an inherent aspect of justice, as every argument for justice provides a critique of law based on some notion of morality, either the moral obligations of the citizen that the law ought to promote, or the moral obligations of the officials who ought to use law in a particular manner, or both.

Morality is highly contested, with many competing views. One of the greatest subjects of debate is whether moral ideas exist independently of humanity or social discourse. Moral realists argue that morality is true regardless of our understanding of it, whether that understanding is true or false. A thinner argument of this sort is naturalism, the doctrine that moral ideas may be true and even unchanging for humans owing to their nature or the nature of community. Moral relativists, on the other hand, argue that morality is culturally dependent and that each community forms its own moral ideas, which are as true for them as other ideas are for other communities.

Some writers believe that morality is understood solely as a matter of reason or rationality. Others argue that reason is secondary to moral instincts, emotions, or sympathies. Still others argue that morality is discovered in the natural order, which is understood through observation and then reason or sympathy. Each of these approaches is subject to the many critiques of morality, including moral nihilism, the idea that morality is non-existent — a myth — or, at best, an invention intended to constrain people from their own preferences.

Morality is closely related to ethics, and sometimes there is no real difference between them, but some people distinguish ethics as duties a person has in general from morality, which is what is owed by a person to others.
*See also:* ethics (ethical); justice.

**moral duty to obey the law**   *See:* obedience, moral duty to obey the law (duty to obey the law or obligation to obey the law).

**moral turpitude**   *See:* turpitude (moral turpitude).

**inner morality of law**   Procedural fairness is essential to the law. The inner morality of law is one of several arguments that the law must be inherently moral, claiming that there is an inherent minimum obligation of procedures. The expression was coined by Lon Fuller, who argued that laws must meet the following criteria or they are not law at all: (1) law expressed as rules rather than mere ad hoc adjudications; (2) public statements of law rather than secret laws unknown to those who must obey them; (3) clear laws that are capable of being understood and obeyed; (4) prospective laws, rather than retroactive laws that punish conduct already performed; (5) coherent laws rather than contradictory laws that cannot each be obeyed; (6) practical laws that are within the abilities or powers of those who must obey them; (7) stable laws, rather than frequently changing obligations; and (8) laws consistently applied rather than laws that are adjudicated by different standards than those legislated.

Though few would argue that they are not elements of justice, the rule of law, or other critiques of law, these views are contested as a matter of the definition of law. Positivists argue that unjust laws are still laws, and laws that are enacted in violation of these rules but which conform to other laws for the making of laws are still law by definition.
*See also:* law, rule of law.

**moral hazard**   Any condition that insulates someone from the risk of or responsibility for an action. A moral hazard is any condition or circumstance that either creates an incentive for someone to act inefficiently, as economists would evaluate the act, or removes the usual system of risks or hazards that would accompany inefficient acts. Moral hazard arises from any form of immunity to responses to one's actions, including insurance, legal immunity, and agency. This idea of moral hazard has been employed to criticize acts of charity and assistance or any other sense of responsibility for others. The moral hazard of agency is present in the immunity of legal officials and poor oversight of corporate officials, so that neither is likely to be held accountable for their mistakes or misdeeds.

**moral luck**   Some bases for responsibility are beyond a person's control. Moral luck is the recognition that certain aspects of a person's judgment and character, and certain elements of the ability of a person to respond to a particular opportunity or event, are not within that person's control. Rather, moral luck describes the nearly random sequences of events that constrain individual action or judgment at moments in which responsibility, fault, and blame must be assessed. Moral luck is, to some extent, reflected in the legal doctrines of capacity, justification, and excuse, just as it is also an aspect of fiduciary principles and standards of care and culpability.
*See also:* necessity.

**moral wrong theory**   *See:* ignorance, moral wrong theory (moral-wrong doctrine).

**moratorium**   A postponement of a given activity. A moratorium is an order to postpone some activity, whether by officials or others, usually for an indefinite time. A moratorium may include conditions under which the activity will be resumed, which is typically once the authority that issues the moratorium is satisfied the conditions have been attained. As the authority to issue a moratorium is usually discretionary in the office of the person who issues it, in many instances there is no claim or right to be relieved of a moratorium on such a showing of attainment.

**morbidity (morbidity rate)**  The percentage of a population with a disease or damage to health. Morbidity is a measure of the incidence of disease or other damage to the health of a person in a community, or an animal or plant in a given population. In statistics, morbidity is the measure of damage to health in a population while mortality is used to measure deaths.

*See also:* mortality (mortal or mortality rate).

**Morgan IV rule**  *See:* review, judicial review, judicial review of administrative acts, Morgan rule of administrative judicial review (Morgan IV rule).

**Morgan rule of civil procedure**  *See:* judgment, summary judgment, Morgan rule of civil procedure.

**mort d'ancestor**  An action to recover property following an ancestor's death. The writ known as the assize of mort d'ancestor was used to eject a third party from an estate when a descendant of the deceased prior lawful owner claimed the estate as heir of the lawful decedent. The action in the United States in such cases is that of ejectment, but the writ was significant in the development of the law of estates.

**mortality (mortal or mortality rate)**  Death or the percentage of a population that dies. Mortality, in general, is the incidence of death or liability to die. Anything mortal is fatal, that is to say that it causes death.

A mortality rate is the rate at which death occurs, usually in a particular context, such as within a population over a given time. In environmental law, it is the portion of a population of people, or of the animals or plants of a given species, that die within a given population or distribution over a given time, usually from a specific cause.

*See also:* morbidity (morbidity rate).

**mortgage**  A security interest and debt in real property. A mortgage is a security interest in property that is transferred from a debtor to a creditor as assurance for the payment of the debt between them, according to its terms. The mortgage is given by the debtor, who is thus the mortgagor, to the creditor, who is thus the mortgagee. In the event the debtor defaults on the payment of the debt underlying the mortgage, the creditor has the right of foreclosure, or to take possession of the property subject to the mortgage in order to satisfy the debt. The debtor, however, retains an equity of redemption in the property following such a seizure, and the debtor is entitled to a return of the value realized from the property that exceeds the amount owed at the time of the default, less the costs associated with its seizure and sale. The value of a mortgagor (the debtor) in property subject to mortgage is called equity, even though the the debt may never default and the property never be seized.

In every state, mortgage foreclosures that are followed by a sale of the property are subject to regulation in the method of the advertisement and conduct of the sale. Mortgaged property that is foreclosed is subject to redemption by the mortgagee, in various states by payment of the debtor to the creditor of the amount owed, or by payment of an amount fixed by statute, or if the foreclosing mortgagee has sold the property to a third party, by payment of the purchase price to the third party within a statutory time limit.

In most states, an alternative to common-law mortgage is available by which the debtor provides a deed of trust to the creditor, making the creditor the legal owner of the property in trust to the benefit of the debtor for the life of the debt. When the debt is satisfied, the deed of trust is canceled and legal ownership is transferred to the former debtor. A deed of trust is subject to equity, but a foreclosure under a deed of trust is more streamlined and, in most states, is limited in its rights of redemption.

*See also:* trustee, quasi-trustee; equity, equitable value, equity of redemption (mortgage equity or property equity); redemption, statutory right of redemption; loan, mortgage loan; foreclosure.

**mortgage-backed security**  *See:* security, securities, collateralized debt obligation, mortgage-backed security.

**mortgage equity or property equity**  *See:* equity, equitable value, equity of redemption (mortgage equity or property equity).

**mortgage indemnity guaranty**  *See:* insurance, category of insurance, mortgage insurance (mortgage indemnity guaranty).

**mortgage insurance**  *See:* insurance, category of insurance, mortgage insurance (mortgage indemnity guaranty).

**mortgage loan**  *See:* loan, mortgage loan.

*deed of trust*  The deed of trust is a common vehicle for creating a security interest in land subject to a mortgage, without requiring the formal process of a judicial foreclosure in the event of a default. The mortgagor executes a deed of trust to the mortgagee, who holds the land to the benefit of the mortgagor. When the underlying debt is satisfied, the lender, cancels the loan and dissolves the trust by deeding over its interest to the debtor. In the event of default, however, the lender, the mortgagee, is also the trustee, and may act under the terms of the trust to enter the land and sell the property, returning any equity realized over the debt and expenses to the borrower.

*See also:* foreclosure, non-judicial foreclosure (nonjudicial foreclosure).

**action to foreclose mortgage**  *See:* foreclosure.

**adjustable-rate mortgage (A.R.M. or ARM)**  A mortgage securing a debt with an interest rate that fluctuates with the market. An adjustable rate mortgage, commonly referred to as an ARM, is a mortgage that secures a debt with an interest rate that is linked to an economic index. As the index rises or falls, the interest rate of the debt varies, as does the amount of the payments owed on the debt. Some ARMs are limited in the maximum interest that may be charged, the minimum interest that may be charged, and the range of the adjustments that may occur within a given time period.

*See also:* rate, interest rate, floating rate (adjustable rate or variable rate).

**assumption of mortgage**   The taking on by a third party of a debt secured by real property. The assumption of a mortgage is the acceptance of an existing mortgage by a new owner of the mortgaged property. Assumption of a mortgage requires the transfer of the mortgage on a property from one owner of the property to the subsequent owner, to whom the old owner assigns an existing mortgage securing a debt, which was initially made by the creditor to the seller, and which will now be assumed by the buyer of the property. Many mortgages cannot be assumed, but those that can invariably reserve a right for the creditor to consent to the assignment.

**deed of trust**   A deed for lands subject to a mortgage trust. A deed of trust is a deed filed by a trustee for the benefit of the beneficiary that results from most mortgages. The borrower transfers the realty to the trustee, who holds it in trust for the borrower subject to the borrower's satisfaction of the mortgage debt. The trustee then files the deed of trust, which is succeeded by a title deed, transferring the land from the trustee to the beneficiary when the mortgage is satisfied.

*See also:* mortgage; foreclosure, non-judicial foreclosure (nonjudicial foreclosure).

**land contract (contract for deed)**   The sale of land in installments paid to the seller. A land contract, also called a contract for deed, is an agreement for the sale of land between a seller and a buyer, in which the seller retains legal ownership of the land and the buyer pays in regular installments and does not receive legal title until the terms of the contract are fulfilled by the full payment of the contract. Though a land contract is similar in its payment structure to a mortgage, the retention of the title by the seller distinguishes the land contract from a mortgage or deed of trust. The land contract is financed by the seller, and thus there is no third party financing the transaction. Land contracts create an equitable ownership interest in the buyer prior to the final execution of the contract by the tender of the last payment. The buyer is usually responsible for the payment of taxes, maintenance of insurance, and liability to third parties on the land. If a buyer defaults on a land contract, the amount paid is not forfeit, but the amount remaining on the loan is owed to the seller, and the buyer has the right to redeem the property by payment of the lien amount.

**mortgage theory (intermediate theory or lien theory or title theory)**   One of various state legal techniques for creating a security interest in property. Each state chooses, usually by statute, the mechanism by which a mortgage will be created and enforced in its jurisdiction. The choices are the title theory, by which the mortgagee has title to the property for the benefit of the mortgagor though the mortgagor retains possession; the lien theory, by which the mortgagee has a lien on the property and the mortgagor retains both title and possession; and an intermediate view, by which the mortgagee has a right to take possession and charge rents in the event of default. Though the common law employed the title theory, most states have adopted the lien theory. The three theories vary somewhat in the rights that are technically accorded the mortgagee, or creditor, but in practice are usually similar. Note: the deed of trust relies on none of these legal theories but does rely on the legal recognition of equitable duties in trusts.

*See also:* lien (lienholder).

**purchase money mortgage (owner-financed mortgage or seller financing)**   A mortgage financed in whole or in part by the seller. A purchase money mortgage is a mortgage in which the mortgagor gives the mortgage to the seller, who finances the mortgage, at least in part. Some purchase money mortgages are also financed in part by a bank or traditional mortgage lender. Like a mortgage held by a traditional third-party bank or other lender, the seller/mortgagee of a purchase money mortgage must give appropriate credit for an equity of redemption in the event of a default.

**rights of redemption of mortgage**   A mortgage may be redeemed before or after its foreclosure. The rights of redemption in mortgage consist of the equitable right of redemption and the legal right of redemption. The equitable right of redemption attaches from the time of the notice of default and persists until the moment of foreclosure, requiring payment of all amounts owed to the creditors holding the loan in default. The legal right of redemption, also called the statutory right of redemption, attaches at the time of sale and persists as long as specified by statute. This right is sometimes defined by a statute specific to the redemption of mortgages after a foreclosure sale and sometimes defined by a statute of general redemption following the execution of a sale of property to satisfy a secured debt. In most jurisdictions, it requires payment of the amount paid by the buyer at sale as well as costs and fees, and in some jurisdictions also requires the payment of the underlying, defaulted debt.

*See also:* mortgage, rights of redemption of mortgage, equitable right of redemption; redemption, statutory right of redemption.

**equitable right of redemption**   The right to redeem mortgaged property prior to foreclosure. The equitable right of redemption is the power of a mortgagor, usually the property holder, to redeem the property following a default on the payment of the mortgage up to the moment of the foreclosure of the equity of redemption by a foreclosure sale, even though a notice of default has been made. To redeem the property, however, the mortgagor must pay the mortgagee not only the amount in arrears but the entire value of the principal outstanding on the loan as well as the unpaid accrued interest.

See also: equity, equitable value, equity of redemption (mortgage equity or property equity); redemption, statutory right of redemption; mortgage, rights of redemption of mortgage.

**ship mortgage**   The interest of a money lender in a ship created by a mortgage deed. A ship mortgage is a mortgage in a vessel and varies in substantial aspects from a traditional mortgage in realty, because the vessel will leave the jurisdiction, is susceptible to loss or destruction, and is subject to liens of a higher priority than the mortgage, such as salvage liens. A ship mortgage in the United States may be registered with the Maritime Administration and must be for a U.S.-documented vessel.

**sub-prime mortgage**   See: loan, sub-prime loan.

**mortgagee**   The creditor who has the security interest in mortgaged property. The mortgagee is the lender, or the lender's assign, who holds a property under a deed of trust, owns the property subject to mortgage, or has a mortgage lien in the property. The mortgagee is the party to whom payments are made under the debt secured by the mortgage and who forecloses in the event of default by the mortgagor.

**mortgagor**   The debtor who has assigned the security interest in mortgaged property. The mortgagor is the borrower who holds property under a deed of trust, occupies the property subject to mortgage, or owns the property subject to the mortgage lien. The mortgagor is the party who makes payments on the debt secured by the mortgage and whose interests are at risk in the event of foreclosure by the mortgagee. The mortgagor has equity in the property and, in some states, equitable title.

**mortmain (mortmain statute)**   Lands held by charities and used only for their support. Mortmain literally means "the dead hand" and describes the transfer of previously productive lands or other property to the use of charities, where it will presumably be less productive. The term comes from the assumption that most gifts to charity come in moments when the donor is near death, when, traditionally, the donor cared more for the fate of the donor's everlasting soul than for the fate of the donor's survivors, community, or economy. Statutes in England and the U.S. forbidding or limiting gifts to charities, especially religious charities, were common from the thirteenth to the twentieth centuries but have all been repealed. The concept remains of interest, though, as an illustration of the mistrust of charitable asset management and of the whims of grants in extremis.

See also: in, in extremis.

**in mortua manu**   The dead hand. In mortua manu is the Latin tag for mortmain, which is itself French.

**Morton's fork**   See: argument, Morton's fork.

**most efficient cost avoider**   See: cost, best cost avoider (most efficient cost avoider).

**most favored nation**   See: nation, most favored nation.

**most favored nation as a settlement sub-class**   See: nation, most favored nation, most favored nation as a settlement sub-class (reverse most favored nation).

**most favored nation clause**   See: contract, contracts clause, most favored nation clause (me too clause or most favored nation clause).

**most favoured nation principle**   See: nation, most favored nation, most favored nation principle (most favoured nation principle).

**mother**   See: family, mother, mother in law (mother-in-law); family, mother.

**mother in law**   See: family, mother, mother in law (mother-in-law).

**motion (movant or move)**   A request for a formal decision or order. A motion, in any proceeding, is a request by a party to the proceeding that the authority over it answer a question or order some action be taken. Thus, a motion in a meeting may be directed to the membership present or to the chair, according to the rules of the meeting and the nature of the motion, in either case seeking a decision, action, or order of some form to be considered and either granted or denied.

In court, a motion is generally presented to a judge, though in certain instances a motion may be presented to a clerk of court (especially when such a motion is granted as a matter of course). Motions were once presumptively made in person by spoken plea but now the practice is that the motion be written and submitted for consideration along with a memorandum brief in support of the motion that provides legal authority for its support. Federal rules of civil procedure and the state rules that follow them require written motions to be signed by the attorney or a party, and this signature is intended to warrant the propriety of the motion's purpose as well as the accuracy of the claims in the motion, subject to sanction otherwise.

A motion is presented to a court in a pending action by one party, the movant, who moves some matter for consideration, either by filing a written motion with the clerk and presenting it to opposing counsel and the judge or by moving in a hearing or trial in a manner that the motion is recorded in the record of the proceedings. The opposing party may choose to object to the motion, by which the party opposes the granting of the motion, either offering reasons and argument or not doing so. The judge may entertain argument on the motion, and if the motion is made during a jury trial, the court will often excuse the jury or hear the argument in chambers or the side bar, out of the jury's hearing. The judge may grant the motion, grant it in part, deny it, deny it in part, or hold the motion under advisement, with the expectation that the motion will either be ruled upon later or become moot.

The right to bring certain motions is limited to particular moments before, during, or after trial. A motion not made at the proper time is deemed to be waived and usually will not be allowed; for a few of such motions, a late motion may be allowed if there is a preliminary motion to allow the motion out of time, and the preliminary motion is supported with grounds to excuse its delay.

*See also:* nihil, nihil dicit (nihil dicit judgment); day, motion day; objection (object or objectionable).

**12(b)(6) motion or motion to dismiss for failure to state a claim motion**   *See:* dismissal, grounds for dismissal, failure to state a claim upon which relief can be granted (Rule 12(b)(6) motion or 12(b)(6)).

**motion day**   *See:* day, motion day.

**motion for more definite statement**   *See:* pleading, motion for more definite statement.

**motion for summary judgment**   *See:* judgment, summary judgment.

**motion for new trial**   *See:* trial, new trial (motion for new trial).

**motion for reconsideration or motion to reconsider**   *See:* reconsideration (motion for reconsideration or motion to reconsider).

**motion for retrial**   *See:* trial, retrial (motion for retrial).

**motion hearing**   *See:* hearing, motion hearing.

**motion to alter judgment or motion to amend judgment**   *See:* judgment, amendment of judgment (motion to alter judgment or motion to amend judgment).

**motion to sever**   *See:* trial, severance of trial (motion to sever).

**motion to strike or strike motion**   *See:* strike, strike from the record (motion to strike or strike motion).

**cross motion (cross-motion)**   A motion similar to a motion filed earlier by another party. A cross motion is a motion for some ruling or order filed by a party to an action that is similar in its request to another motion already pending. Thus, a motion by one party for summary judgment might be followed by another motion for summary judgement, this time by the opposing party. Note: a cross motion must seek the same order or similar relief or ruling as a prior motion, with the cross-motion seeking an order or rule to the benefit of the cross-movant, while the original movant sought the original order for its own benefit.

**dispositive motion**   A motion seeking a ruling on the merits of a claim. Dispositive motions allow the court to dispose of an issue or a claim through an order in response to the motion. Thus, a dispositive motion seeks a dispositive order, the grant or denial of which would give relief to one party or the other. The motion to dismiss, motion for summary judgment, motion for nonsuit, and motion for judgment are examples of dispositive motions.

**ex parte motion (ex parte application)**   A motion argued by only one party. An ex parte motion is a motion by one party, made under circumstances in which the other party or parties are not given notice of the motion or an opportunity to object to it. The court ruling on such a motion is an ex parte ruling.

*See also:* ex, ex parte; order, court order, ex parte order.

**motion in limine**   A motion at the start of trial on a matter of evidence or procedure. A motion in limine is a motion filed with the court in advance of trial or raised at the commencement of a trial, in which the movant seeks rulings in advance on matters of evidence or procedure. The most common motions in limine are motions to suppress evidence or to bar witnesses from testimony on certain questions, but all forms of pre-trial motions can be made as motions in limine, including motions to strike claims, to dismiss a cause, or to grant judgment.

**notice of motion**   Notice to an opposing counsel or party of a motion filed in court. A notice of motion is a written notice or notice of record given by one party to an action to the other parties of a motion that has been filed with the court. Some jurisdictions require proof of a notice of motion to be filed with the motion, and it is the responsibility of the party filing the motion to make actual service of the notice to the opposing parties or counsels.

**post-trial motion**   Any motion following the trial's end, in the court in which the trial is held. A post-trial motion is any motion that is properly made following a trial, including motions related to a verdict, such as a motion to poll the jury; motions related to the trial, such as a motion for new trial; and motions related to the judgment, such as a motion for judgment notwithstanding the verdict, a motion to set aside judgment, a motion to alter or amend a judgment, or motions for additur or for remittitur. Motions to dismiss or for other relief that depend on jurisdiction, process, or other initial defenses are usually barred post-trial, unless they are based on new information that could not have been reasonably known before trial or they are renewals of motions timely made pre-trial.

*See also:* jury, jury poll; judgment, judgment notwithstanding the verdict (J.N.O.V. or JNOV or judgment as a matter of law or JML or JMOL or judgment non obstante veredicto); judgment, amendment of judgment (motion to alter judgment or motion to amend judgment).

**pre-trial motion (pretrial motion)**   A motion made prior to trial, especially regarding the pleadings, the court, the parties, the discovery, the evidence, or the trial. A pre-trial motion is a motion that is properly made at any time prior to the trial. Pre-trial motions include the greater portion of all motions made outside of the trial itself. Pretrial motions include all motions to submit, oppose, reform, submit, or otherwise test the pleadings; to test the powers of the court and their technical application in the case; the inclusion or exclusion of parties; the process, timing, and scope of discovery; the validity and use of specific evidence; and the scope, location, timing, and procedures of the trial. In both civil and criminal actions, some pretrial motions are dispositive, in that they would dispose of the matter, such as the motion to quash an indictment in a criminal action, or the motion to dismiss or motion for summary judgment in a civil action. All other motions are non-dispositive.

Specific motions include motions for pre-judgment relief, such as a motion for pre-judgment attachment; motions concerning service of process or jurisdiction, such as a motion to dismiss for want of service; motions regarding the pleadings, such as a motion to dismiss for failure to state a cause of action, a motion for more definite statement, or a motion to dismiss an indictment; in criminal trials, a motion regarding the assurance of the prisoner's appearance or regarding conditions of confinement, such as a motion to grant or to cancel bail; a motion regarding discovery, such as a motion to quash a subpoena or a motion to compel appearance; a motion regarding the trial, such as a motion for change of venue; or a motion regarding the evidence, such as a motion for exclusion or for a protective order. The rules of procedure provide an outline of the motions available to litigants in each forum, yet by custom, a party may raise nearly any concern related to the proper functioning of the trial by motion prior to its commencement.

**motive**  A reason, interest, or cause to do something. Motive is the purpose, reason, interest, condition, or belief that does or might be a cause for a person or entity to commit some action. In its most general sense, motive is sometimes used as a synonym for purpose, as in a legislature's motive in enacting a statute.

The actor's motive is usually important in determining the moral significance of an action, and the liability of the actor for the action and its results often turns upon the motive with which it is made. Thus, many crimes are defined by the mental state of the actor, and many of the mental states of motive amount to a mens rea. Motive is also essential in the evidence of criminal actions in determining the likelihood of guilt by circumstantial evidence and may also be essential in determining the nature of a claim or of a defense, such as an official's qualified immunity from suit for official acts.

There are two very different senses of the concept of motive. The first is subjective, in which the inquiry is exactly what sense the actor had of some reason, impulse, or cause for committing some action prior to doing so. The second is objective, in which the inquiry is what interest, reason or reasons, perceived benefit, or other cause an actor might have had for committing some action prior to its commission. Evidence of one sense of motive might or might not be instructive in understanding the other.

**dual motive**  Two or more reasons to commit the same action. Dual motive describes the causes for any action that is alleged to have resulted from more than one motivating factor. This is particularly the case when an employer is sued for an allegedly unlawful job practice that may be for a discriminatory reason but may also be for a lawful reason.

Dual motive arguments are based on one of two different forms. One follows from contrary claims by the parties as to the motive in fact for a decision, and each side presents evidence of a different motive. The finder of fact may be convinced that both are correct, and that the actor was motivated by both motives. The second form is one in which the evidence thoroughly suggests and, indeed, the actor may agree, that the decision was based on two or more motives. In either case, the finder of fact may determine that both motives were equally important in the decision or that one was predominate. The standards of liability and opportunities for defense vary according to the cause of action, but in general, in a determination that a decision was made in significant part as a result of an unlawful motive, the fact to some degree the action was the result of a lawful motive does not serve as a defense.

**motor vehicle**  *See:* vehicle (motor vehicle).

**motor vehicle emission standards**  *See:* pollution, air pollution, emission, motor vehicle emission standards.

**motorist**  The driver of a motor vehicle. A motorist is a person who operates a motor vehicle, whether or not the person is its owner. A person who is a passenger of a vehicle is not its motorist, even if that person is otherwise capable and licensed to operate it. Motorists must be licensed in every state to drive the particular category of vehicles they operate.

**uninsured motorist**  A motorist without valid insurance for the vehicle driven. An uninsured motorist is a motorist who operates a motor vehicle without insurance then in force covering the vehicle driven. Many states require every driver to carry insurance that includes not only automotive coverage for that driver's vehicle but also uninsured motorist coverage to provide coverage in the event of collision with an uninsured motorist. Uninsured motorists are important in the car insurance context because most standard car insurance policies provide for protection against uninsured motorists in the event the insured is involved in an accident with someone without insurance.

**mouth of the law**  *See:* metaphor, metaphor of law, mouth of the law (bouche de la loi).

**mouthpiece**  *See:* lawyer, mouthpiece.

**movables**  *See:* property, immovable property (immovables or movable property or movables).

**movant (non-movant or cross-movant)** The party bringing forward a motion. The movant is the party who presents a motion for consideration. Several parties may join in a motion, in which case each becomes a movant. If another party seeks a different result from that sought by the movant, but the other party wishes a similar motion to be heard, that party files a cross-motion and is the cross-movant. All other parties who do not join in the motion are non-movant parties as to that motion. A party who objects to a motion is a non-movant, as well as being an objecting party.

**MP or M.P.** *See:* police, police organization, military police (MP or M.P.).

**Mr. or Ms. or Miss or Mrs. or Hon. or Excellency** *See:* title, title as form of address (Mr. or Ms. or Miss or Mrs. or Hon. or Excellency).

**Mr. X or Mrs. X or Ms. X or Miss X** *See:* X, X as in hypotheticals (Mr. X or Mrs. X or Ms. X or Miss X).

**mufti** A jurist in Islamic law. A mufti is a scholar who is recognized as sufficiently learned to issue important opinions. The term comes from the same root as the word Fatwa, meaning a person who is competent to excercise Ijtihad and issue a Fatwa.
*See also:* Fatwa (Fatawa).

**mulct** A fine imposed as a penalty, or a fee. A mulct was a fine for a minor offense, usually paid in goods or animals. Mulct later came to mean a fee like a tariff. Note: mulct was sometimes also a verb, as a judge might fine someone, so then did a judge mulct someone.

**mullah** The religious leader of a Shia Muslim community. A mullah is the religious leader in a community of Shi'ite Muslims, a person of knowledge.

**multi-door courthouse** *See:* courthouse, multi-door courthouse (multidoor courthouse).

**multi-step dispute resolution clause** *See:* alternative dispute resolution, multi-step dispute resolution clause.

**multifariousness (multifarious)** Containing too many charges, goals, or ideas. Multifariousness, in general, is a diversity of actions or ideas in a single thing. Multifariousness was the basis in equity for a demurrer, or petition to dismiss the bill that commenced an action, on the basis that the bill had included too many unrelated objects or bases for the action. The term has other legal connotations, particularly in that some state constitutions or legislative rules prohibit multifarious legislation or legislation that includes or confuses two unrelated matters. Note: some speakers confuse multifarious with nefarious, but many actions are quite properly multifarious, and this confusion should be avoided.

**multiple causes** *See:* causation, multiple causes.

**multiple evidence** *See:* evidence, multiple evidence.

**multiple insurance coverage** *See:* insurance, insurance coverage, multiple insurance coverage, pro rata clause; insurance, insurance coverage, multiple insurance coverage, escape clause (other insurance clause).

**Multistate Bar Examination** *See:* bar, admission to the bar, Multistate Bar Examination (M.B.E. or MBE).

**Multistate Essay Exam** *See:* bar, admission to the bar, Multistate Essay Exam (M.E.E. or MEE).

**Multistate Performance Test** *See:* bar, admission to the bar, Multistate Performance Test (M.P.T. or MPT).

**Multistate Professional Responsibility Exam** *See:* bar, admission to the bar, Multistate Professional Responsibility Exam (M.P.R.E. or MPRE).

**municipality (municipal corporation)** A corporation for local government. A municipality is a city, town, village, or any other community that is incorporated as a municipal corporation by the state in which it exists. The powers of a municipality are dictated and limited by the state constitution and statutes as well as by the charter and ordinances of each municipality. For the purposes of federal constitutional law, a municipality as an entity is distinct from the state and does not enjoy immunity recognized in the Eleventh Amendment, but it is still subject to the federal constitutional requirements of conduct that apply to the states.
*See also:* state; alderman (aldermen).

**muni** *See:* bond, municipal bond (muni).

**municipal bond** *See:* bond, municipal bond (muni).

**municipal corporation** *See:* municipality (municipal corporation).

**municipal court** *See:* court, U.S. court, municipal court.

**municipal solid waste landfill** *See:* landfill, municipal solid waste landfill (M.S.W.L.F. or MSWLF).

**home rule** The power of self-government in a municipal or county government. Home rule is a broad term for the delegation of a variety of powers to a local government that otherwise might be retained and exercised on its behalf by the state. Most importantly, home rule allows the municipality or county to determine its form of government, including the balance of responsibilities among its executive, legislative, and administrative arms. Home rule usually enlarges the scope in which the municipality may legislate matters under the state's police powers over health, safety, morals, and welfare, and it allows the municipality to more easily acquire and manage lands.

**urban renewal (urban redevelopment)** The redevelopment of areas with empty or dangerous buildings. Urban renewal is a plan for the rehabilitation and retasking of property in distressed areas of municipalities. Urban renewal in the 1960s was associated with the replacement of neighborhoods of small apartments or houses with large housing projects, which increasingly acquired dangerous residents with little regard for the property. Urban renewal later incorporated a growing sense of ownership by residents and a more humane scale of building. The purpose of urban renewal remains a valid basis for takings and, when the renewal is of areas seized or condemned as posing a danger to public safety or health, a valid basis for uncompensated use of the police power.

**murder (murderer)**  Willful homicide. Murder is the the killing of another person under such circumstances that the killer is fully responsible for the death. This responsibility is determined by different formulae in different jurisdictions. In many jurisdictions, it is measured by premeditated intent, which is the same as malice aforethought. In others, which follow the Model Penal Code, this responsibility is determined by any of three conditions: The killer commits a voluntary act by which the killer has the purpose of causing death. The killer commits a voluntary act that the killer knew in advance would cause death. The killer commits a voluntary act that is so reckless or indifferent to the danger of death that the act poses to others that death resulting from it is the responsibility of the actor. Murder can only be committed by a legally competent adult. The term "murder" was derived from the Latin murdrum, and it has long been reserved for particularly wicked forms of homicide, particularly killing done in secret.

*See also:* murder, aberemurder (aberemurther or eberemoth or eberemors or ebere–murder); manslaughter (manslaughterer).

*cold blood*  A premeditated killing or attempt to murder. Cold blood is a colloquial phrase for a murder that was premeditated, and thus carried out according to plan in "cold blood." This contrasts with, and is probably derived from, the notion that a killing in the heat of passion is performed hot bloodedly.

**aberemurder (aberemurther or eberemoth or eberemors or ebere–murder)**  A willful murder, in early medieval English law. Aberemurder was traditionally an open, apparent, plain, or downright murder, rather than an accidental murder. Forbidden under this name under the laws of Canute, it is an early form of the modern status of first-degree murder.

**aggravated murder**  Murder committed under aggravating circumstances. Aggravated murder is a murder committed under circumstances in which the killer's culpability is greater even than that of murder would ordinarily be. Bases for aggravation vary from state to state but commonly they include the following: murder for hire (whether the defendant is the buyer or the seller); killing a prison guard, police officer, or judge; premeditated murder; the murder of a child; or the murder of more than one person at a time.

**capital murder**  Murder eligible for the death penalty. Capital murder is murder for which death is a potential sentence. In general, capital murder is similar to aggravated murder in the forms of conduct within its scope, the main differences being statutory definition and death penalty eligibility. An indictment for capital murder is inherently an indictment under which the defendant is eligible for the death penalty, unless a statement to the contrary is on the face of the the indictment or a later undertaking by the prosecution is docketed in the court file.

**first-degree murder (murder in the first degree or murder-one or murder-1)**  Murder committed in the most culpable of circumstances. First-degree murder is murder of the most serious form in most jurisdictions, and while the specific lists of circumstances that amount to murder in the first degree vary, in all cases it includes murder that is willful, intended, or premeditated by the murderer, sometimes specifically including murder by trap, poison, or explosive device. The murder of a police officer or public official is usually first-degree murder, as is the intentional murder of a child or person under one's care. Murder committed during the commission of the most serious or dangerous crimes is usually included in statutory inventories of such crimes, usually include rape and sexual assault, kidnapping, burglary, escape, and torture.

*See also:* homicide, criminal homicide (culpable homicide or felonious homicide); premeditation (premeditate).

**second-degree murder (murder in the second degree or murder-two or murder-2)**  An intentional murder committed in less than fully culpable circumstances. Second–degree murder is the crime of intentionally killing another person in circumstances that are less culpable than those of first-degree murder. Although the specific lists of circumstances that amount to murder in the second degree vary, in most cases it includes murder caused by negligence or without any premeditation or prior intent to kill. Second–degree murder may result from a mistaken belief by the killer, which, if true, would have caused the killing to be justified, or it may result from circumstances that give rise to a sudden or irrational passion, anger, or provocation. It may also result from murder committed in the course of a felony that does not inherently endanger others. Second–degree murder is a lesser included offense to first-degree murder.

*See also:* excuse (excusable or excused); homicide, negligent homicide; provocation (provocateur or provoke).

**third-degree murder (murder in the third degree or murder-three or murder-3)**  An unintended murder in the least culpable degree. Third–degree murder is murder of a less culpable form than first-degree murder or second–degree murder. In most states, murder in the third degree is defined as murder that is not intended and that is not found to meet the definitions of first- or second-degree murder.

**extreme-indifference murder (depraved-heart murder or depraved mind murder)**   A brutal or indifferent act causing unintended death. Extreme-indifference murder and its variants, depraved-heart murder or depraved-mind murder, are the offense of murder caused not by an intent by the offender to bring about the death of a specific individual but caused by the actions of the offender in a circumstance in which the offender was so indifferent to the risk to human life that the resulting death was as great a fault as if it were intended. The function of the crime as a matter of the criminal law is to ensure that a person who deliberately acts in such a manner as to cause death without regard for the consequences does not escape punishment for an absence of the specific intent to cause the death or injury of a particular victim.

*See also:* depravity; indifference; indifference, extreme indifference (depraved indifference); malice, general malice (universal malice).

**felony murder (felony-murder rule)**   A death resulting from the commission of a felony. Felony murder is the crime of committing a felony as a direct consequence of which a person dies, whether as a result of an action of the felon, an accomplice, or another person connected to the felony, such as a victim or witness, and regardless of whether death or injury is intended. In many jurisdictions, felony murder is equivalent to murder in the second degree. Others distinguish between degrees of felony murder, each being equivalent to a higher degree of murder. In jurisdictions with the death penalty, felony murder may be the basis for a capital indictment.

Different jurisdictions vary in the scope of the felony in which a resulting death can trigger felony murder, with some states applying the rule to death resulting from all felonies and others applying the rule only to specified types of felony. Most states include death caused by accomplices and third parties within the scope of felony murder, but some states do not. Most states include deaths of which the act during the felony is a contributing, rather than sole, cause, while some states limit felony murder to acts during the commission of the felony that are the sole cause of death.

*Arson*   At the common law, death resulting from arson may be prosecuted as a felony murder.

**first-degree felony murder**   Death caused by a felon during a serious felony. First-degree felony murder is a murder committed during the commission of certain felonies designated as the basis for first-degree felony murder in those jurisdictions that distinguish degrees of felony murder. Different jurisdictions have quite varied lists of such offenses, but in general they are offenses that pose an inherent danger of death or injury, such as murder (of a person not the victim of the felony murder) robbery, kidnapping, and offenses committed with a deadly weapon.

**second-degree felony murder**   Death caused during the commission of less dangerous crimes. Second-degree felony murder is murder either by causing the death of a person while perpetrating a felony that is not designated as the basis for first-degree felony murder, or by causing the death of a person while perpetrating a felony although the person who specifically causes the death is not the perpetrator of the felony. In those jurisdictions that recognize it, second-degree felony murder is a lesser included offense to first-degree felony murder.

**involuntary murder**   Murder that was not intended and is not felony murder. Involuntary murder is murder committed without any intent to cause death, and without meeting the conditions of felony murder. In some statutes, involuntary murder is third-degree murder.

**murdrum (murthrum or murther)**   The ancient crime of murder in secret. Murdrum was the crime of secret killing, a murder in which the killer took care to prevent the discovery of the death or the killer's identity. A fine for murdrum persisted long after the particular offense was consolidated into the more general concept of murder, being the penalty for less culpable forms of homicide.

**mustahab (mandub)**   Preferred or preferable. Mustahab is what is to be preferred in Islamic law. It is often misunderstood as merely what is good, but it more literally means what is beloved, from the root word hibb. One of the five Hukm Sharia, mustahab is also known as mandub. To commit a mustahab is rewardable, but to omit it is not sinful.

**mutagen (mutagenic)**   A chemical, exposure to which causes genetic changes. A mutagen is a chemical that causes genetic matter to alter its genetic information when the genetic matter and the mutagenic chemical are in contact.

**mutah (nikah mut'ah)**   Temporary marriage practiced only in Shiite Islam. Mut'ah is temporary marriage, a form of marriage permitted under Shia Islam but forbidden as haram under Sunni Islam. In Mut'ah, a man contracts with a woman for marriage for a set time and for a set mahr. Mahr is not a dowry, because it is given to the wife rather than to the husband as part of the marriage contract.

Mutah is temporary, and while the woman has all the rights of a wife for the duration of the contract, after that period neither she nor he have marital rights. This practice, according to Sunni readings of the hadith, was abolished and made haram by the Prophet, but the Shia claim it was not abolished, and quite a few still practice it. Mut'ah houses exist in some Gulf states.

**mutatis mutandis**   Making all of the necessary changes. Mutatis mutandis signals that changes have been made or read into a text in order to correspond with another correction or alteration. Loosely, it translates to "those things being changed that ought to be changed."

**mutilation**  A serious and disfiguring injury. Mutilation is a near destruction of a person, part of the body, or thing. To mutilate a person is to cause the loss or failure of a part of the body or a serious disfigurement of the person. To mutilate an object is to batter or sever it so that it either loses its value in some manner or ceases to perform its function. The mutilation of evidence is to treat it in some manner that is intended or likely to reduce its value as a source of information of legal significance.

*See also:* punishment, cruel and unusual punishment.

**genital mutilation (female circumcision)**  The alteration or removal of a genital organ. Genital mutilation is the alteration or detachment of any part of the genitals for any purpose other than the medical correction of a condition that threatens the life or health of the subject. Genital mutilation of the male includes physical castration (the removal of the testicles alone, testicles and penis, or of the penis and testicles) as well as circumcision, although male circumcision is accepted by custom and believed to provide health benefits to the subject. Female genital mutilation include female circumcision (the removal of the clitoris or parts of the body related to the clitoris), labiectomy (the removal of the labia in whole or in part), and infibulation (the closure of the labia). Chemical interruption of genital activity, such as by chemical castration of the male or the use of chemicals to prevent conception, is usually not considered mutilation. Piercing or other cosmetic alteration may amount to mutilation depending upon the circumstances of the case.

Genital mutilation of another person under the age of consent for reasons other than the protection or preservation of that person's health is a crime, either as assault or as a specific offense. Genital mutilation of a woman under the age of eighteen is a federal crime, and there is no defense based on consent or parental rights.

**mutiny (mutineer or mutinous)**  A rebellion against lawful authority. Mutiny is the attempt to resist or overthrow the lawful authority of the officers or commander of a vessel, a military unit, a prison, a colony, or other population under special command. Mutiny is sometimes used in a more general sense to describe a rebellion, implying the tumult and chaos that is associated with its legal meaning. Mutiny does not require success, so that acts or omissions of duty in furtherance of mutiny are mutinous in and of themselves. Incitement to mutiny is a distinct felony.

**mutuality (mutual)**  Reciprocity in a shared undertaking. Mutuality is the integration of interests that arises when the relevant acts of each party to an enterprise affect the others in a relatively direct manner. In other words, it is the nature of the quid pro quo such that what each party does has a reciprocal benefit or detriment to the others. A mutual activity is reciprocal and contemporaneous, done equally by each at the same time, rather than done once by one in hope of the other's doing.

*See also:* will, last will and testament, joint and mutual will (mutual will); obligation, mutuality of obligation.

**mutual account**  *See:* account, mutual account (mutual running account).

**mutual agreement**  *See:* contract, specific contracts, reciprocal contract (mutual agreement).

**mutual assent**  *See:* assent, mutual assent.

**mutual conditions**  *See:* condition, concurrent conditions (mutual conditions).

**mutual fund**  *See:* security, securities, mutual fund.

**mutual mistake**  *See:* mistake, mutual mistake.

**mutuality of obligation**  *See:* obligation, mutuality of obligation.

**mutual promise or mutually dependent promise**  *See:* promise, dependent promises (mutual promise or mutually dependent promise).

**mutual running account**  *See:* account, mutual account (mutual running account).

**mutual will**  *See:* will, last will and testament, joint and mutual will (mutual will).

**mystic (mystery)**  Anything that is secret, hidden, or mysterious. A mystic is a person with the power to know what is hidden from other people, and in this sense is used as a metaphor to describe any person of such arcane achievements that he or she is beyond the understanding of the ordinary mortal. As an adjective, mystic originally represented anything secret or hidden, from its origin in religion as one who understands the secrets of a faith.

In most senses, mystery relates to the same idea of hidden meanings, particularly those derived from religious faith. In the middle ages, however, the religious or mystery plays gave rise to the relationship between mystery and a form of unfolding drama, from which mystery came to mean the story of a puzzle that must be solved. Mystic lacks this connotation of mystery.

*See also:* profession.

**mystic testament**  *See:* will, last will and testament, mystic will (mystic testament).

# N

**n**   The fourteenth letter of the modern English alphabet. "N" serves a variety of functions as a symbol. It is translated into November for radio signals and NATO military transmissions, into Nora for some police radio traffic, and into dash dot in Morse Code.

**n as a Latin abbreviation**   The Novels of Justinian. In citations to Roman Law, N refers to the Novellae, the Novels of Justinian, though in other Latin contexts it is likely to stand for nota.

**n as an abbreviation**   A word commencing in N. When used as an abbreviation, N often stands for national. It may also stand for footnote, Nagpur, narcotics, native, natural, naval, Nebraska, negligence, net, Netherlands, Nevada, new, Newfoundland, Nigeria, no, north, northern, Norwegian, and note. It may also stand for the first letter of an author's name or case reporter, such as Nasmith, Nevile, Newberry, New York Supplement, Nicholls, Nolan, North Carolina Reports, North Eastern Reporter, Northern Ireland Law, North Western Reporter, and Nott.

**N.A.A.C.P. or NAACP**   *See:* civil rights, civil rights organization, National Association for the Advancement of Colored People (N.A.A.C.P. or NAACP).

**N.A.A.C.P. or NAACP Legal Defense Fund**   *See:* civil rights, civil rights organization, National Association for the Advancement of Colored People, NAACP Legal Defense Fund (LDF).

**N.A.A.Q.S. or NAAQS**   *See:* pollution, air pollution, National Ambient Air Quality Standards (NAAQS).

**N.A.F.T.A. or NAFTA**   *See:* trade, international trade, North American Free Trade Agreement (NAFTA).

**N.A.L.P. or NALP**   *See:* law, law school, placement, National Association of Law Placement (NALP).

**N.B.**   *See:* nota bene (N.B.).

**N.E.P.A. or NEPA**   *See:* environment, National Environmental Policy Act (N.E.P.A. or NEPA).

**N.I.E.D. or NIED**   *See:* distress, emotional distress, negligent infliction of emotional distress (N.I.E.D. or NIED).

**N.L.R.A. or NLRA or Wagner Act**   *See:* union, labor union, labor law, National Labor Relations Act (N.L.R.A. or NLRA or Wagner Act).

**N.S.F. or NSF or NSF check or hot check or bad check or bounced check**   *See:* check, check with insufficient funds (N.S.F. or NSF or NSF check or hot check or bad check or bounced check).

**N.Y.S.E. or NYSE**   *See:* security, securities, securities exchange, New York Stock Exchange (N.Y.S.E. NYSE).

**nail and mail**   *See:* service, service of process, nail and mail.

**nakedness (naked)**   Incomplete, unsupported, or uncovered. Nakedness as a matter of general usage means uncovered or unclothed, and a person who is naked in this sense may be indecent as a matter of law.

More specifically in law, nakedness is a condition of incompleteness, of insufficient support, commitment, or evidence. Thus, the assertion of naked authority by an agent is without rights conferred by the principal. A naked contract, or nudum pactum, either lacks consideration at the time of formation, or at some time later the consideration promised is withdrawn.

**naked confession**   *See:* confession, naked confession.

**naked possession**   *See:* possession, naked possession (mere possession).

**naked trust**   *See:* trust, naked trust (simple trust or naked trustee or bare trust or bare trustee).

**namaz salah**   *See:* salat (namaz salah).

**name**

**alias**   An alternative name for a person. An alias is a nickname, a fictitious name that a person adopts or accepts in lieu of the name the person otherwise holds under the law. When a person is identified by both a legal name and an alias, the alias is usually preceded by a/k/a, for also known as. An example of an alias is the generic name applied when a person is either unknown or not identified for any reason, either by letters, as in A. v. B. or Baby M, or by customary names, such as John Doe, Jane Doe, or Richard Roe. Alias comes from the Law Latin alias dictus, or otherwise called.

*See also:* sub, sub nomine (sub.nom.).

**corporate alias (d/b/a or f/d/b/a or a/k/a or trade name)**   An alternative name for a corporation. Alias is occasionally used in the context of corporations to describe any arrangement by which a company operates under an alternative name, which is often denoted by the abbreviation for "doing business as" or d/b/a. Alias is also applied when a company changes its name and is designated as "formerly doing business as" or f/d/b/a. Other aliases are represented by an alternatively named subdivision, which may be called the company's alter ego or by an alternatively named holding company, which may be called a shell corporation. Although the more generic designation of "also known as," or a/k/a, is customarily applied to an individual alias, it is sometimes encountered to signal the label of a corporate alias, too. For the purposes of an indictment or service of a civil suit, a corporation may be designated as by what name is known as well as by an alias "John Doe Corporation."

A trade name is subject to protection as a trademark, only if it is registered as a trademark. An unregistered trade name may be protected from infringement as a matter of the restriction of unfair competition. A trade name may infringe on a trademark or on another trade name.

**pseudonym (brush name or nom de pinceau or nom de plum or pen name)** An individual's alias used in a particular field of art or craft. A pseudonym is an alias that is usually adopted by an individual for use in a given field or to identify the individual's work as a writer or artist without revealing the legal identification of the individual. Although not a preferred practice, a contract with an individual who entered by an alias may be sufficient to bind the individual, as long as there is no ambiguity as to the individual who has entered the contract and neither the contract itself nor the terms of an offer or its acceptance preclude the use of a pseudonym.

**change of name (corporate name change or personal name change)** The designation of a new label for a person or entity. Change of name is a process by which a person or entity adopts a new name. The process by which this is done as a matter of law varies slightly from jurisdiction to jurisdiction. In most states, a corporate change of name is made by filing a change of name certificate or by filing an amended corporate charter with the state officer responsible for corporate records, such as the state division of corporations or the secretary of state. In most states, a personal change of name is made by filing an ex parte proceeding or petition with a local court of general jurisdiction or by making a statement of change of name at the time a marriage license is issued. A separate notification to the federal government is required by federal law to the Social Security Administration and the Internal Revenue Service for individuals and to the Internal Revenue Service for corporations with an employer identification number. An informal process for changing corporate names is available, allowing a corporation to adopt a trade name or business name and to be addressed in legal matters by its legal name d/ b/a/ its trade name. Personal changes of name may be adopted informally by the adoption of an alias.

**fictitious name** A false name. A fictitious name for a person is an alias used for the purpose of avoiding identification by the person's true name. A fictitious name may be employed for fraudulent or misleading reasons but can also be used in pleading either to identify a party to a case while protecting a person's identity for the sake of that person's legitimate concern for privacy or to designate a person who is material to a case but whose identity is yet unknown.

For corporations or other business entities, a fictitious name is a trade name that is not registered with the appropriate jurisdiction or that is not lawfully capable of being registered.

**Baby Doe (Baby M)** A name to designate an unidentified infant. Baby Doe or the designation of a baby followed by one or two initials is used to designate a baby or infant in a pleading or administrative proceeding. This is commonly done in proceedings for child neglect or abuse, proceedings for medical services, domestic relations cases, and other cases in which a child is a party. The use of initials alone, rather than names, is also required under court rules for materials in which a child's name appears on filings, whether or not the child is a party.

*See also:* name, fictitious name, John Doe (Richard Roe or Jane Doe).

**John Doe (Richard Roe or Jane Doe)** A name used to represent an anonymous or unknown party in a pleading. Fictitious names for parties are used in pleadings when the party is unknown or has a justifiable desire to remain anonymous. Pleadings by the party's initial(s), such as "S" or "J.S." for a person named John Smith, are also used for anonymity. Lawyers drafting pleadings may use fictitious names with leave of the court when there is good cause to protect a party's identity, but otherwise the defendant ought not to be given a fictitious name if the defendant can be identified with reasonable care by the plaintiff.

John Doe and Richard Roe are the most commonly used fictitious names for individuals, but custom has made John Doe the most popular. From this usage, John Doe has become widely used as the designation for any unidentified person, as in the search for an unknown person or as the identity of a person or body in custody whose name is unknown, who has no memory, whose statements are unreliable, who is unconscious, or who is dead.

*See also:* name, fictitious name, Baby Doe (Baby M).

**Titius (Aulus Agerius or Numerius Negidiusor Seius or Stichus)** A hypothetical party in the legal disputes hypothesized in Roman law. Titius and his friends were hypothetical characters in the cases illustrated in the Institutes of Justinian.

**named insured**   *See:* insured, named insured.

**nanny state**   *See:* state, nanny state.

**nanny tax**   *See:* tax, payroll tax, household employment tax (nanny tax).

**narrative**   The use of storytelling to illustrate the law and justice. A narrative is a story told by a narrator to an audience. In legal studies, especially Feminist Jurisprudence and Race Critical Theory, narrative is used to illuminate the nature of the law, its effects on individual lives, and the role played in law by power, gender, race, poverty and other aspects of the lives of members of marginalized groups. Though this practice has been criticized for lacking objectivity and accuracy, it remains a popular means of developing attractive hypotheticals to explore and challenge points of view.

More generally, the legal practice is rich in narrative, and many aspects of law and jurisprudence are understood as narrative and depicted in narrative. The converse is also true, and the narrative of song, stories, fiction, and film is often borrowed by the law.

**Nash equilibrium**   *See:* game, game theory, Nash equilibrium; equilibrium, Nash equilibrium.

**nation (national or nationalism or nationality)**   A group of people who share a strong cultural bond. A nation is a body of people with a shared experience which is often manifested in the single political entity of a state. The word has evolved from the seventeenth century, when it was akin to a clan or race and represented a group descended from common stock or ancestry, to a common use as a term that is synonymous with the political unit of a sovereign state. Thus, a nation in contemporary usage may represent what in international law is meant either by a state or by a people.

This tension between the organic and political senses of nation persists in several usages, as in North American Indian nations, such as the Six Nations (the Seneca, Cayuga, Onondaga, Oneida, Mohawk, and Tuscarora Nations) or the Cherokee Nation, the designation of autonomous groups of native Americans related by common descent, a distinct social organization, and a shared language and history. Although the Indian nations are not wholly and independent sovereign states, they function in many ways as both organic groups and as governing entities.

Despite this tension, the modern and general sense of nation represents the single people within a state. The nation is the group of people with presumably shared history and culture who are the people of the state. Nationalism is the patriotism or dedication a single person or the whole people of the nation have to its identity and independence, thought it may also describe the phenomenon of such groups having such loyalty to their organic or political units. Thus, a national anthem is a hymn to the nation, and there is usually very little to distinguish state from nation in such usage.

As a matter of international law, something international is effectively any matter between states. A national matter is a matter affecting a state. Nationality is the condition of being a citizen or subject of a given state, and so a national is a citizen or subject of that particular state. A foreign national is a person who is a citizen or subject of a state other than the state in which the person is described.

*See also:* state; people.

**most favored nation**   A state to which another state accords its most favorable trade policy. Most favored nation is a designation by one state of another state, according to which the designated state receives the most favorable tariffs and trade regulations the designating state accords to any other states. Employed by the United States in referring to France in 1803, most favored nation required the treatment of French vessels and cargo given to U.S. ships and cargo. Still, the term does not require treatment of the favored nation's goods as a state does its own, only that the favored nation is treated better or as well as goods from all other states.

More broadly, the term refers to the state, legal entity, or goods that are accorded preferential treatment by a party to litigation or other entity.

**most favored nation principle (most favoured nation principle)**   A state's obligation to extend to all trade pact signatory states any preference it gives only to one state. The most favored nation principle is a requirement in several treaties that are the foundation of the World Trade Organization, by which a state must accord all members of a trade treaty conditions for trade that are as favorable as it accords to any other state. In essence, this requires each state to treat all member states of the trading organization as if each member state is the state it most favors. Every agreement allows specific exceptions from this general principle.

*See also:* trade, international trade, World Trade Organization (WTO or W.T.O.).

**nationality (national)**   Membership in a state or nation. Nationality is the obligation of allegiance by a person to a state and of protection by the state for the person, an affiliation between person and state by which the state accepts legal responsibility for the person and the person is subject to the legislative jurisdiction of the state regardless of where the person is physically. Nationality is usually acquired at birth according to the law of nationality in that state, either because the person is born of parents of the nationality or is born on the soil of that nation, although many people acquire nationality later in life through naturalization or decree of the state. In the United States, there is little difference between nationality and citizenship. The standard of international law for one state to recognize the nationality asserted over an individual by another state requires that the state asserting nationality have a dominant and effective relationship with the national, or, at the very least, that the individual have a genuine link of actual connections in fact to establish a bond of connection to the state.

In the United States a national is either a citizen of the United States, whether by birth or by naturalization, or a person who owes permanent allegiance to the United States. This second category generally means members of the armed forces of the United States who are not citizens.

*See also:* citizen, citizenship.

**National Ambient Air Quality Standards**   *See:* pollution, air pollution, National Ambient Air Quality Standards (NAAQS).

**National Association for the Advancement of Colored People**   *See:* civil rights, civil rights organization, National Association for the Advancement of Colored People (N.A.A.C.P. or NAACP).

**National Association of Law Placement**   *See:* law, law school, placement, National Association of Law Placement (NALP).

**National Conference of Commissioners on Uniform State Laws**   *See:* reform, law reform, National Conference of Commissioners on Uniform State Laws (Uniform Law Commission or NCCUSL).

**national defense**   *See:* defense, national defense.

**National Environmental Policy Act**   *See:* environment, National Environmental Policy Act (N.E.P.A. or NEPA).

**National Labor Relations Act**   *See:* union, labor union, labor law, National Labor Relations Act (N.L.R.A. or NLRA or Wagner Act).

**National Labor Relations Board**   *See:* union, labor union, National Labor Relations Board (NLRB).

**National Marine Fisheries Service**   *See:* fishery, National Marine Fisheries Service (NMFS).

**national origin discrimination**   *See:* discrimination, national origin discrimination.

**national pollutant discharge elimination system**   *See:* pollution, water pollution, national pollutant discharge elimination system (NPDES).

**national security privilege**   *See:* privilege, evidentiary privilege, state secrets privilege (national security privilege).

**national waters**   *See:* sea, law of the sea, national waters, territorial waters (territorial sea); sea, law of the sea, national waters, exclusive economic zone (EEZ); sea, law of the sea, national waters, continental shelf (outer continental shelf); sea, law of the sea, national waters, contiguous zone (customs zone or customs enforcement zone).

**nationalization**   The making of any matter an object of national concern. Nationalization is a broad term for the conversion of any matter or property to a matter of the nation–state. In general, a nationalized practice, market, or enterprise is one that affects the nation as a whole rather than a community or region within it. In law, matters that were once committed to local or state regulation may become nationalized and thus subject to national regulation. To say a person who is nationalized is the same as to say the person is naturalized, or made a citizen or subject of a given nation. To designate property as nationalized is to subject it to national ownership or control.

*See also:* naturalization.

**nationalization of property (expropriation or expropriate or nationalize)**   The taking of private property by a nation–state. The nationalization of property, or state expropriation of property, is the assertion by the government of a state that some property or activity is a matter for the nation and so it is subject to the ownership or control of the state. International law does not forbid nationalization, although it does forbid an act of nationalization that discriminates against aliens, including the aliens of a particular state; that is not for a public purpose; or that is not compensated by prompt, adequate, and effective means. Note: in U.S. Constitutional law, nationalization is an exercise of eminent domain as well as a taking, whether the taking is compensated (and constitutional) or uncompensated (and unconstitutional). Though similar, the standards of public use and just compensation in U.S. law are not necessarily the same as those of international law.

*See also:* taking (takings or taking of private property without just compensation).

**Hull formula**   Payment for nationalized property must be prompt, adequate, and effective. The Hull formula was articulated by Secretary of State Cordell Hull in a letter regarding the expropriation of the property of U.S. nationals by Mexico in 1942, in which he argued compensation must be prompt, adequate, and effective. Though not fully integrated into customary international law, this formula has been adopted in most bilateral investment treaties.

*See also:* compensation, just compensation.

**native**   Belonging to a place by birth, longevity, or ancestry. A native is a person who is born in a place or, metaphorically, born of a place. In its narrowest connotation, a native of some place is a person who was in fact born there. More generally, a native is a person who lives in a place, the presumption of long tenure and established residence being implied by the term. A native in this context is thus different from an immigrant.

A native people is therefore a people on the land prior to the entry of others. Native Americans, Native Hawai'ians, and other native groups are the people indigenous to those lands prior to the arrival of European or other settlers.

A native species is a species present in an ecosystem and a part of its equilibria, prior to the introduction of an invasive species.

*See also:* citizen, natural–born citizen (natural born citizen).

**Native American Indian** *See:* Indian, Native American Indian (Native American or American Indian).

**Native American or American Indian** *See:* Indian, Native American Indian (Native American or American Indian).

**natural**

> **natural affection or love and affection or object of affection** *See:* love (natural affection or love and affection or object of affection).

> **natural born citizen** *See:* citizen, natural–born citizen (natural born citizen).

> **Natural Born Citizen Clause** *See:* constitution, U.S. Constitution, clauses, Natural Born Citizen Clause.

> **naturalistic fallacy** *See:* fallacy, naturalistic fallacy.

> **natural father** *See:* family, father, natural father (biological father).

> **natural law** *See:* law, natural law; jurisprudence, natural law (jure naturae or lex naturale).

> **natural monopoly** *See:* monopoly, natural monopoly.

> **natural resources** *See:* resource, natural resource (natural resources).

> **natural right** *See:* right, natural right.

**naturalization** The conferral of citizenship on an alien. Naturalization is the act by which a person who was not a citizen or subject of a state from birth becomes its citizen or subject. Most nation–states specify requirements and procedures to be satisfied before applying for naturalization: permanent residence within the state for a certain number of years; compliance with the law, including the tax laws; maintaining employment or other bases of self-sufficiency; and, in some cases, renouncing allegiance to the alien's former nation–state.

In the United States, there are several processes of naturalization. Generally, a person must be eighteen years old to apply, or the application must be made for the person by a parent or guardian, and the person must be lawfully a permanent resident for five years, demonstrate good moral character, show an attachment to the U.S. Constitution, be skilled in the English language, know the fundamentals of U.S. history and government, and take an oath of allegiance. Eligible alien members of the United States military may be naturalized after one year of service or while serving during a period of military conflict. There is no process of naturalization among states in the United States. A citizen of one state becomes a citizen of another state through residence and intent alone.

*See also:* citizen, citizenship; oath, oath of allegiance (naturalization oath); citizen, naturalized citizen (naturalization).

**Naturalization Clause** *See:* constitution, U.S. Constitution, clauses, Citizenship Clause (Naturalization Clause).

**naturalization oath** *See:* oath, oath of allegiance (Naturalization Oath).

**naturalized citizen** *See:* citizenship, naturalized citizen, Child Citizenship Act; citizen, naturalized citizen (naturalization).

**Naval Clause** *See:* constitution, U.S. Constitution, clauses, Navy Clause (Naval Clause).

**naval mine** *See:* mine, military mine, naval mine.

**navigation (navigable or navigational)** Travel across a body of water. Navigation is both the general act of travel on the water and the specific acts required to ascertain the position of a vessel, to plot its course, and to maneuver it during that travel. Navigation of intrastate waters is a matter for regulation by each state of the union, which has plenary jurisdiction over its waters so long as that regulation does not unduly interfere with interstate commerce nor conflict with federal regulation. Navigation of interstate and international waters is subject to federal regulation, even if the particular vessel engaged in navigation does not leave a state. Navigation of U.S. flagged vessels on the high seas or in the waters of other states is subject to U.S. federal regulation. Note: two adjectives are based on navigation: Navigable refers to the waters that a vessel can navigate; and navigational refers to the human acts, processes, and rules by which the vessel is navigated.

*See also:* sea, law of the sea (sea laws).

> **navigable waters** *See:* waters, navigable waters.

> **aid to navigation (ATON)** Any beacon, buoy, sign, signal, or radio signal for the navigation of vessels. An aid to navigation is any navigational signal placed for the benefit of boats or vessels navigating a waterway. Federal aids to navigation are part of the international system of ATONS, which is administered in the United States by the U.S. Coast Guard. Other aids are placed and maintained by private or state entities. Interference with any aid to navigation is both a crime and a basis of liability in admiralty law.

> **Collision Regulations (COLREGS or Navigation Rules)** The rules of the road for navigation. The Collision Regulations, or the Navigation Rules, enacted as both federal law in the United States and as international law by treaty, specify the rules of navigation for all navigable waterways, including the marking and lighting of vessels, rules of priority and right of way, and general rules for navigation.

**Navy Clause** *See:* constitution, U.S. Constitution, clauses, Navy Clause (Naval Clause).

**ne** Not, or a negative of a statement. Ne is a word that creates a negative in a statement in either law French or

Latin, and it may stand for no, not, never, or other negative adverbs, adjectives, conjunctions, or interjections. The term is most often encountered in French in writs or orders received from the common law, such as a ne exeat order restricting someone from leaving the jurisdiction. In Latin, it is commonly incorporated into civilian maxims, such as ne bis in idem, or not again for the same thing, a civil-law statement of the prohibition on ex post facto prosecution.

**ne bis in idem** *See:* non, non bis in idem (ne bis in idem).

**ne exeat (ne exeat republica or writ of ne exeat)** An order restraining a party from leaving a jurisdiction. A writ of ne exeat is a court order restraining a party from leaving or removing certain assets or property from the jurisdiction. The phrase is from the ancient writ commencing with these words, which mean, "you are not to leave." A writ of ne exeat may also be used to prevent a custodial parent from removing a child from a jurisdiction wherein a non-custodial parent has visitation rights.

**nebbish (nebbishy or nebbishistic)** Someone lacking confidence or willpower. A nebbish is a Yiddish term for a person, usually male, who apparently lacks the mettle needed to be assertive among confident or authoritative people yet seeks to worm through somehow to success. A nebbish may, indeed, be a person of unusual talent or skill. Like many terms of abuse, it has a wider and less informed use, especially as a more general description of someone with a craven manner or annoying passive aggression or just an annoying person.
*See also:* Yiddish.

**necessary (necessaries)** Those goods and services essential to life. Necessaries are those things that are required for the survival of a person in reasonable health, fitness, and basic enjoyment of life in contemporary culture, including food, medicine, clothing, shelter, personal services, and education for the young. A minor may enter into a valid contract for the purchase of necessaries. An adult who is responsible for the care of a child may be held liable for their provision in either a child custody or a fitness hearing.

**Necessary and Proper Clause** *See:* constitution, U.S. Constitution, clauses, Necessary and Proper Clause (Elastic Clause or Basket Clause or Coefficient Clause or Sweeping Clause).

**necessary party** *See:* party, party to an action, necessary party.

**necessity** The defense to a claim or action that no alternative was available. Necessity is a justification for any action based on its unavoidability, which may be determined by an obligation to do something and a lack of alternative means to do it. As Bouvier defined it, something is necessary when it is impossible to do the contrary, but necessity need not be absolute. Necessity can arise from the situation and from the performance of a lawful privilege, right, or obligation, as in the use of force to prevent injury to another from a person using force, or, as in a grantee's use of the grantor's land to reach an otherwise landlocked parcel.

Necessity is a defense to all claims, actions, or crimes that require intent or will. Necessity is thus a defense to trespass both in its civil and criminal senses. Necessity is sometimes a component of other defenses, for example as the underlying concept of self-defense. Because of this relationship to other justifications, necessity is often confused with the excuse of coercion.

In legal philosophy, necessity is a limitation upon the will, one of the elements of moral luck.
*See also:* morality, moral luck; coercion.

**emergency** A time or event requiring assistance to prevent immediate harm. Emergency is both a noun and an adjective, describing an event in which some crisis emerges in a brief time. Emergency is not itself a doctrine of law, but it is the essential element in the defense of necessity to trespass.

An entry to land or use of property that would ordinarily amount to a trespass is justified under the defense of necessity if the entry or use is reasonably believed in good faith, by a person whose life or property is in peril or who is a rescuer, to be reasonably necessary to abate the peril and save the life or property from greater harm. In some jurisdictions an additional element is whether the entry or use would not forseeably cause more harm than the emergency being abated would otherwise cause.

**private necessity (private way of necessity)** A necessity for a private person. Private necessity is a necessity for one person or party, rather than a necessity in general or for the whole public. At its most basic, private necessity distinguishes arguments of necessity into those of necessity to achieve a matter of public interest or to abate a general harm and those of necessity to a matter of private interest or to abate a harm to one party. Private necessity is sometimes used to describe the defense of necessity in criminal law. It is also the basis of both the defense and the claim in property for a way of private necessity and in tort against trespass and other intentional torts.

When used to establish an easement over the lands of the other, private necessity results in two distinct theories. One is that the common-law implied easement, in which an implied easement that arises from a grant of one of two parcels with unity of title when the granted parcel has no access, is held to exist over a grantor's land from the time of the grant from the grantor of a parcel adjoining the grantor's that has no other access. The other theory underlies a statutorily created action to recognize a private way of necessity, which does not require the unity of title essential to the implied easement of necessity. In both theories, different jurisdictions follow different rules in determining the severity of events required to satisfy the private necessity essential for declaring a private way of necessity, the differences being expressed as strict or reasonable necessity.

**reasonable necessity**  All alternatives are costly or grievous. Reasonable necessity is a standard for the assessment of private necessity, particularly whether there are grounds to recognize an easement in a private way of necessity over the adjoining lands of one landowner to the benefit of the lands of another that is reasonably necessary if there are either no alternatives for entry to the other's parcel or if the potential alternatives would be unreasonably expensive or difficult to develop for use or to use on a routine basis.

**strict necessity**  When there are no practical alternatives. Strict necessity is a standard for the assessment of private necessity, particularly whether there are grounds to recognize an easement in a private way of necessity over the adjoining lands of one landowner to the benefit of the lands of the other that is strictly necessary because there are no reasonably practicable alternatives for entry to the other's parcel. For the purposes of strict necessity, access by water is still considered not to be an alternative for access.

**public necessity**  The remedy to danger of public interest. Public necessity, generally, is a remedy essential to abating some harmful condition affecting the public interest. More narrowly, a public necessity is the only reasonable means of abating some harm to the public as a whole that, as a matter of fact, is immediately pending or ongoing. A public necessity may justify the use of the police power to take property without compensation, when compensation would be required if the property had been taken for some other use. A public necessity may justify burdens on constitutional rights that otherwise would be forbidden. Care must be taken both to assess a claim of public necessity and to determine the least burdensome means of implementing the abatement chosen by public officials.
*See also:* public.

**necropsy**  *See:* autopsy (necropsy).

**Needful Rules Clause**  *See:* constitution, U.S. Constitution, clauses, Property Clause (Needful Rules Clause).

**needs theory**  *See:* hierarchy, needs theory (hierarchy of human needs).

**negative**  To contradict. A negative is a vote or statement against a proposition, and to negative something is to contradict it or, if one has the authority to rule on a matter, to refuse it.

A negative report or test is a report or test in which something measured or assessed is found to be absent or below expectations.

**negative act**  *See:* act, act of omission (negative act).

**Negative Commerce Clause**  *See:* constitution, U.S. Constitution, clauses, Commerce Clause, Dormant Commerce Clause (Negative Commerce Clause).

**negative condition**  *See:* condition, negative condition.

**negative easement**  *See:* easement, negative easement.

**negative equity**  *See:* equity, equitable value, equity of redemption, negative equity (under water or underwater).

**negative evidence**  *See:* proof, forms of proof, negative proof (negative evidence).

**negative externality or positive externality**  *See:* externality (negative externality or positive externality).

**negative proof**  *See:* proof, forms of proof, negative proof (negative evidence).

**neglect**  A failure to perform one's obligation. Neglect is a form of omission of duty, in which something is not done that ought to be done; for example, a task that ought to be performed is not, a person or structure that ought to be maintained is not, or a situation that ought to be remedied is not. There are many specific crimes and torts, as well as breaches of contract, administrative obligations, fiduciary obligations, professional obligations, family obligations, and others that constitute neglect of duty.

The tort of negligence incorporates a form of neglect in its definition. As the general tort for a breach of the duty of reasonable care, negligence is probed by evidence that a person neglected to perform some act, or committed some act, in violation of that duty.

Neglect may arise from omission rather than from action, and it need not be an intentional act. A child who is neglected has suffered from neglect by the child's parent or guardian, which may result from nonfeasance or from misfeasance. Neglect is a wrong that may be proved by evidence that amounts to res ipsa loquitur.
*See also:* negligence, res ipsa loquitur; negligence (negligent).

**neglect of duty**  *See:* civil rights, neglect of duty (section 1986).

**child neglect**  A failure to properly care for a child. Child neglect is the failure of a parent or guardian to ensure that a child receives all of the necessary goods and services needed for a child of that age and capacity. Neglect arises if a child does not routinely receive adequate and appropriate food, shelter, clothing, hygiene, medicine, services for disabilities, and education. These are objective measures of support, so that a parent's subjective view that one or another necessity is not required for a child is usually not a defense to claims of neglect, although some states allow religious exemptions from education for the children of religious devotees.

**negligence (negligent)**  A breach of a legal duty that harms another. Negligence is the tort of failing to perform a legal duty, which causes a distinct injury to another person, or to another person's property, or to another person's legal interests. The legal duty may be the general duty not to act in an unreasonable or careless manner or a special duty created by one's office or employment, or one's actions or representations and the reliance of others upon them. Negligence may be committed by an act or an omission, which is the failure to act when a reasonable person would do so. The injury is an element of the wrong, and a mere risk of injury is insufficient to amount to a tort, unless the risk is continuing and the likelihood of immediate or future injury is clearly demonstrable. Though the scope of the injury that is sufficient to give rise to an action in tort varies from jurisdiction to jurisdiction, the essence of the injury required is either a physical injury to a person, to property or a discrete loss in financial positions or legal claims.

Negligence is divided into ordinary negligence and gross negligence. Ordinary negligence is analogous to carelessness or inattentiveness in a circumstance in which harm is foreseeable, but gross negligence is analogous to deliberate risk–taking in which harm is a likely outcome of the conduct, but the actor is reckless or indifferent to the danger the actor causes.

*See also:* diligence.

*foreseeability* The foreseeability of harm to someone like the plaintiff from the defendant's action is an element of a negligence. Foreseeability does not require that the defendant did foresee a risk or the specific harm, rather foreseeability applies if a reasonable person would have foreseen the risk or the specific harm. Nor does foreseeability require foresight of the risk to a specific person, such that a reasonable understanding that someone would be harmed in a manner similar to the manner by which the plaintiff was harmed by the defendant's conduct will suffice.

**negligent entrustment of child or negligent entrustment to a child** *See:* negligence, child negligence (negligent entrustment of child or negligent entrustment to a child).

**negligent homicide** *See:* homicide, negligent homicide.

**negligent infliction of emotional distress** *See:* distress, emotional distress, negligent infliction of emotional distress, zone–of–danger rule; distress, emotional distress, negligent infliction of emotional distress, impact rule; distress, emotional distress, negligent infliction of emotional distress (N.I.E.D. or NIED).

**negligent misrepresentation** *See:* misrepresentation, negligent misrepresentation.

**negligent tort** *See:* tort, negligent tort.

**child negligence (negligent entrustment of child or negligent entrustment to a child)** A child's negligence may be imputed to a parent. Child negligence arises from two theories. The first is a standard of child negligence, recognized in some states as a child's failure to act according to the standards of reasonable conduct imputed to a child of the age of the child who commits some unintended harm. As a result,

the child's parent is held accountable for the injury caused on a standard of strict liability. The second theory of liability is based on one or another standard of parental negligence, which includes both direct liability for parental negligence in supervision of the child and indirect liability, or parental liability for the child's negligence, which arises when the parent negligently entrusts the child to engage in some activity that has some risk to others that should have been reasonably foreseen by the parent.

**collateral negligence** The breach of a duty to perform special or unusual tasks. Collateral negligence is a breach of duty in the performance of some task that is unusual or out of the ordinary from the routine for which risks are regularly assessed and managed by the actor who commits the harm. A contractor or employer might be held responsible for the acts of a subcontractor or an employee that are direct and within the scope of the routine performed and risks routinely managed, but in jurisdictions that recognize a doctrine of collateral negligence, the contractor or employer may have a defense to liability for the collateral negligence of the sub–contractor or the employee.

**comparative negligence** A plaintiff may recover a comparative portion of damages from a negligent harm. Comparative negligence allocates shares of damages that resulted from negligent acts, reducing the award to the plaintiff according to the degree to which the plaintiff was responsible for the events leading to the plaintiff's harms. Comparative negligence is an implied rejection and reform of the older standard of contributory negligence, which barred recovery by the plaintiff if the plaintiff was at all responsible for the negligent event. Some standards of comparative negligence, however, have been hybridized between comparative and contributory standards, barring all recovery by a plaintiff found to be more than 50 (or some other) percent responsible for the harm.

*See also:* negligence, comparative negligence, modified comparative negligence (hybrid comparative negligence); comparative; negligence, last clear chance (last–clear–chance doctrine); liability, comparative liability (comparative fault or comparative responsibility); risk, assumption of risk (assumption of the risk); risk, assumption of risk, implied assumption of risk, secondary implied assumption of risk.

**modified comparative negligence (hybrid comparative negligence)** A defendant is not liable if the plaintiff is significantly at fault. Modified comparative negligence, or hybrid comparative negligence, is a compromise approach to the recovery that may be allowed to a plaintiff who is responsible for a portion of the plaintiff's own injury, in that the plaintiff may be limited to certain forms of damages or any recovery at all, if the plaintiff is responsible for more than fifty per cent of the plaintiff's injury. States have taken different approaches to the effect of substantial plaintiff fault, with some limiting the plaintiff only to economic damages, others barring any recovery, and others limiting recovery only to direct apportionment and not allowing joint and several liability. A further limitation on the doctrine is that most states will yet hold a defendant responsible for gross negligence, or willful and wanton acts causing some percentage of the plaintiff's injury, regardless of the remaining degree of the plaintiff's fault, either because such actions are brought not as negligence or because of a limitation on the comparative negligence formula.

*See also:* negligence, comparative negligence.

**pure comparative negligence**   The defendant is liable for its share of damages. Pure comparative negligence requires each party to be responsible for its share of the responsibility for the injury of the plaintiff, so that a defendant is liable for its portion regardless of the size of the plaintiff's portion. Pure comparative negligence contrasts with modified or hybrid comparative schemes, which bar any recovery from a defendant partly at fault for a plaintiff who is responsible for more than a threshold percentage of the plaintiff's own injury.

*See also:* negligence, comparative negligence, modified comparative negligence (hybrid comparative negligence); negligence, comparative negligence.

**contributory negligence**   A plaintiff at all responsible for an injury may recover nothing for it. Contributory negligence is a defense to a claim of negligence that bars any recovery for a plaintiff who is to a degree responsible for the injury the plaintiff suffered. The degree of responsibility varies among jurisdictions, some allowing the defense if the plaintiff's responsibility is "more than slight," others allowing it if the plaintiff's responsibility is greater than zero. Some jurisdictions retain a rebuttal to the defense of contributory negligence, which is not to bar a plaintiff's recovery if the defendant had the last clear chance to avoid the plaintiff's injury, regardless of any responsibility that may be attributed to the plaintiff. For example, some jurisdictions require a passenger in a moving auto to keep a lookout for dangers on the road. In such a jurisdiction, a passenger injured in a collision caused by the driver may be held partially at fault for a failure to keep a lookout and to warn the driver of the impending danger. Under a strict contributory standard, the passenger could recover nothing from the driver for injuries sustained. Under last clear chance, the passenger could recover only if the driver also saw the danger and could avoid it. Under a comparative standard, the passenger could recover from the driver the extent of damages suffered from the collision, minus the amount apportioned to the passenger's responsibility for the collision caused by not keeping a good lookout.

*See also:* negligence, last clear chance (last–clear–chance doctrine).

**gross negligence (culpable negligence)**   An excessive risk or unusual disregard of duty causing harm. Gross negligence is the extraordinary form of negligence in which a person not only fails in the ordinary duty of care but does so either in a manner that exhibits such disregard of care that a reasonable observer would foresee that an injury would be likely to occur, or in circumstances when the person should know that a failure of care risks an injury of unusual magnitude. Gross negligence is the form of negligence that a jury may deem so culpable and of such clear responsibility that an award of punitive damages is appropriate as a public response to the defendant's conduct.

*See also:* gross.

**Hand formula (Learned Hand test or Hand rule)**   One who could avert a danger more cheaply than its likely costs is negligent and liable for the injuries of another. The Hand formula, developed by Judge Learned Hand in United States v. Carroll Towing Co., 159 F.2d 169, 173–74 (2d Cir. 1947), may be used in the absence of an established custom or a known expectation or reliance by others to determine whether a person is liable in negligence for the harm caused by an arguably negligent act. The Hand formula compares three variables: (1) P, the probability that a potentially harmful event will occur (as that probability could have been understood before the event); (2) L, the gravity of the injury or harm that does in fact result, when the event in fact occurs; and (3) B, the cost to the defendant of taking adequate precautions against the occurrence of the harmful event. The formula is a simple comparison of P and L to B. If B is less than L multiplied by P, the defendant is liable for the harm in negligence. In other words, in the absence of a legal duty, a relevant custom, or some form of reliance, if B is less than P*L, the defendant is liable, but if B is more than P*L, the defendant is not liable.

**last clear chance (last-clear-chance doctrine)**   A defense to negligence that the plaintiff was the last person who could have avoided an injury. The last clear chance is a rebuttal to a defense of contributory negligence (or hybrid comparative negligence) raised if the defendant had the last clear chance to act so as to avoid the accident or other cause of the plaintiff's own harm, regardless of any contribution of responsibility for that harm may be attributed to the plaintiff. If the defendant could have reasonably acted to avoid injury, then even if the injury was otherwise caused in part by the plaintiff, the defendant may not assert contributory negligence or a similar defense to bar all liability. Last clear chance has sometimes been asserted as a technique of assessing plaintiff's conduct under theories of contributory or comparative negligence.

Most jurisdictions have abolished the last clear chance as a doctrine, although its rationale persists, both as an aspect of arguments about proximate cause and as a means of considering apportionment of responsibility under the doctrine of comparative negligence.

See also: negligence, comparative negligence; negligence, contributory negligence; peril (perilous).

**negligence per se** Harm resulting from an act in violation of a regulated duty of care. Negligence per se is harm that results from a breach of a duty of care that is enshrined in a statute, ordinance, or regulation binding the defendant, a violation of which is sufficient to prove a breach of the duty of care and responsibility for injuries that result from the unlawful act. A claim for negligence per se does not depend upon a governmental citation of the defendant for violation of the law, although the plaintiff must plead both the law that the defendant is alleged to have violated and the proof of the violation.

See also: liability, strict liability.

**res ipsa loquitur** Negligence may be presumed from the circumstances. Res ipsa loquitur, Latin for the "thing speaks for itself," is a doctrine of evidence and a rule of pleading that allow the plaintiff to assert an inference that the defendant was negligent in some manner so as to cause the plaintiff's injury, the inference arising from circumstances in which the defendant's negligence is the most likely cause of the events leading to the plaintiff's harm. A plaintiff who pleads res ipsa loquitur must establish sufficient facts showing a substantial likelihood that the defendant was responsible for the plaintiff's injury and acted negligently. Thus, an injury from poor facilities management in a place in which the defendant exercised sole control and management of the facilities is presumably the responsibility of the defendant. For example, a cannery is presumed to be responsible for what is in a can it produces, and additional matter in one of its cans may be inferred as evidence of the cannery's negligence in allowing the matter to be there. Even so, the finder of fact is not bound to the inference that the plaintiff suggests.

As a rule of evidence, rather than a legal presumption, the failure of the defendant to rebut the inference does not alone establish liability. Rather, the finder of fact must still determine that negligence occurred as a matter of fact.

See also: neglect.

**standard of care** The minimum forms of behavior required in particular circumstances. The standard of care is the care that would be expected of a reasonable person with those responsibilities of the actor in the given situation and role in which the actor's harmful conduct is assessed following the harm. This standard varies according to the situation in which the harm is caused. Members of professions or trades are held to the care that a reasonable member of that profession or trade would provide. Thus, the measure of the actor's duty at any given time varies with the actor's responsibility, based on the actor's particular skills or on the form of reliance that must be placed upon them by others.

There are two major departures from the ordinary standard of care. First, some forms of activity, such as operating a common carrier, are subjected to a heightened standard of care, according to which evidence is to be heard of whether the conduct in question met a standard of diligence that exceeds the merely reasonable. Second, the members of certain professions or trades are held to a standard of reasonable care by a person in that position. Thus, the person who designs a street, or provides medical care, legal advice, or financial planning assistance is held to the standard of care for street designers, doctors, lawyers, or financial advisers. The person on the street who knocks a fellow pedestrian into traffic, however, is held to the ordinary care of a pedestrian. Note: there is no meaningful difference between a standard of care and a particular duty of care.

See also: care, duty of care.

## negotiability (negotiable or non-negotiable or nonnegotiable)
Ownership that is assignable with a transfer of title, endorsement, and delivery. Negotiability is the quality of a contract or instrument that allows any person who acquires it in good faith and for value to transfer it for value by assignment. More specifically, negotiability of an instrument is the quality of the instrument allowing it to be transferred from one party to another by assignment, particularly by sale, endorsement by signature, and delivery to another party, without concern for defenses that might otherwise arise to payment. A negotiable instrument is an instrument that is capable of such transfer. A non-negotiable instrument is an instrument that is not assignable under the same conditions.

See also: instrument, negotiable instrument.

**negotiable** See: negotiation (negotiable, negotiated), negotiation as resolution.

**negotiable instrument** See: instrument, negotiable instrument.

**negotiable or non-negotiable or nonnegotiable** See: negotiability (negotiable or non-negotiable or nonnegotiable).

## negotiation (negotiable or negotiated)

**adversarial negotiation (assertive negotiation or hardball tactics or hard-ball tactics)** The uncompromising pursuit of one's position. Adversarial negotiation, or assertiveness in negotiation or hardball tactics, is the promotion of one's position without regard for either the opponent's position or the fairness of one's own. Adversarial negotiatiors work from a zero-sum model of the discussions, in which each gain for one party is seen as a loss for the other. When adversarial negotiation succeeds, it does so usually owing to the fatigue or poverty of the opponent.

See also: negotiation, collaborative negotiation (accommodation in negotiation).

**best alternative to a negotiated agreement (BATNA)** The benchmark of a negotiation. The best alternative to a negotiated agreement, or BATNA, is the hypothetical likely recourse that each party to a negotiation would have if the negotiation failed and there was no negotiated agreement. The BATNA thus serves as a benchmark by which the negotiation is assessed by the negotiators, and according to which all offers are likely to be judged. An optimal result of a negotiation is one in which each party achieves a result through the negotiation that is markedly better for that party than would be the best alternative. Such a result is the most likely to succeed through later compliance.

**collaborative negotiation (accommodation in negotiation)** Showing empathy toward an adversary. Collaborative negotiation, or accommodation during negotiation, is the joint pursuit of a resolution based on each party's demonstration of empathy or understanding of the opponent's position or needs. Collaborative negotiation is based on a win–win perception of the procedure, in which a gain for one side need not be a loss for the other. An accommodating style of negotiating may help to build trust between the opposing parties and lead to concessions by both parties but particularly by the non–accommodating party. Accommodation contrasts with assertiveness in negotiating style.

*See also:* negotiation, adversarial negotiation (assertive negotiation or hardball tactics or hardball tactics).

**loop-back procedures** Shifts in negotiation to remind parties of their interests. Loop–back procedures are intervals in a negotiation between parties that are designed to remind each party of its interests in reaching a conclusion that promotes the party's interests rather than just asserting its rights. Loop–back procedures include mediation windows in the midst of negotiations, mini–trials, and summary jury trial proceedings that are intended not only to remind the parties of the risks of allowing a third party to adjudicate their rights but also to demonstrate the strength of the argument that is available to the other party.

**rejection-then-retreat tactic (door in the face)** An excessive demand to be followed by a reasonable demand. Rejection then retreat is a form of over–reaching in negotiation in which the offeror makes an unreasonable or high demand in the first offer, which is intended to be rejected and followed by a second, more reasonable offer of a lower demand. The tactic depends on the appearance of the acceptance of the first rejection and a conciliatory or compromising second offer, in order to take advantage of the offeree's sense of reciprocity and encourage acceptance of the second offer.

**negotiation as resolution** A discussion to resolve differences between parties. Negotiation is a process of communication between parties with opposing goals related to some matter, with the intent to resolve their conflict through agreement, compromise, or surrender of some of the goals of each party. Negotiation is a crucial part of alternative dispute resolution, and comprises a major part of a lawyer's professional duties.

*See also:* mediation, private caucus.

**Neil standard** *See:* identification, identification procedure, Neil standard.

**nem. con.** *See:* nemo, nemine contradicente (nem. con.).

**nemine contradicente** *See:* nemo, nemine contradicente (nem. con.).

**nemo** No one. Nemo is Latin for nobody, or no person. It is often encountered in prohibitions, such as "nemo tenetur seipsum accusare," or no one is bound to accuse oneself of a crime.

**nemine contradicente (nem. con.)** Done without objection. Nemine contradicente, literally "with no one objecting," is a tag for any decision reached unanimously. A decision by acclamation is nem. con. It is sometimes used to describe either a ruling made without objection or a question in which all evidence is in support of a single outcome.

**NEPA** *See:* environment, National Environmental Policy Act (NEPA), functional equivalence; environment, National Environmental Policy Act (NEPA), environmental impact statement (EIS).

**nepotism** Favoritism toward a member of one's family. Nepotism is the granting of an advantage or position to a person because of a family relationship between the grantor and the grantee. To the degree that such a decision is based on merit and not on the family relationship, however, such a grant is not nepotistic. A public official who provides or secures employment for a member of the official's family, whether by blood or marriage, is presumed to engage in nepotism. Although the merit or qualifications of the applicant may be sufficiently patent that the applicant would be awarded the job regardless of the family connection, the potential for nepotism raises the appearance of possible impropriety. Most states and the federal civil service therefore generally forbid an official or civil servant from any participation in the hiring or supervision of a family member in a position over which the official has influence. Nepotism may take innumerable forms, however, and any use of discretion on behalf of a member of an official's family raises the question of nepotism. Nepotism in political office and political appointments is generally not unlawful. Nepotism in corporations is subject not to legal limitation but to corporate work rules, although a nepotistic hire may amount to a breach of a fiduciary duty or other obligation of best efforts.

**net** A mesh, or a final sum. Net has two distinct senses in law. The older is its ancient sense as a web or rope device in which to capture fish or other animals or to hold cargo and the like. This comes from the same Latin root as knot.

The more common in finance and taxation is the sense of a sum that remains when deductions are complete, the money remaining when the debts are paid or costs are deducted. This sense comes from the French sense of clean or neat.

**net asset value**   See: value, book value (net asset value).

**net asset value or net current assets**   See: assets, net assets (net asset value or net current assets).

**net assets**   See: assets, net assets (net asset value or net current assets).

**net capital gain**   See: gain, capital gain, net capital gain.

**net income**   See: income, net income.

**net margin**   See: margin, gross margin (net margin).

**net operating loss**   See: loss, net operating loss.

**net profit**   See: profit, net profit (net profits or net loss).

**net profits or net loss**   See: profit, net profit (net profits or net loss).

**drift net**   Large fishing nets that float with the currents. Drift nets are large nets that hang from floats on the water's surface down to weights far below, stretching sometimes across miles of a sea or lake and capturing nearly all of the marine life in their paths. Drift nets are usually gill nets and may drown animals caught in the net before they are harvested, leading to the death and destruction of much sea life in order to harvest the commercial fishing target sought. Sea turtles are a common victim of drift nets, although turtle exclusion devices may somewhat abate this risk.

**neutral forum**   See: forum, neutral forum.

**neutrality (neutral principles)**   Fairness in judgment based on the generality of the issues involved. Neutrality is the independence of judgment in a dispute or controversy that arises from a commitment to a fair and principled decision. Neutrality requires a decision-maker to pursue a principled basis for the evaluation of arguments and evidence regardless of the party who presents them. Neutrality does not mean that an arbiter or judge must remain aloof from proceedings, lack sympathy for the parties, or lack empathy or understanding of the situation, but it does require that the person in such a role treat all parties in the same manner and set aside sympathies in reaching a decision. Among other requirements of neutrality in a legal decision, the most important may be scrupulous attention to the sufficiency and quality of evidence in every case to reach each decision in a manner that is least likely to be factually in error.

A particular argument based on neutral principals was raised in an influential twentieth-century book by Herbert Wechsler, who argued for neutral principles of decision in constitutional cases. In such cases, he argued for outcomes that are based not on the particular result of the dispute (which might favor one party or the other) but that best fit with the fundamental principles of law in the long run. In the assessment of rules and principles, neutral principles require that the decisions of private individuals and other officials be disturbed only when a fundamental proposition of law is in issue.

**neutrality in war (neutral state)**   A state's independence of all belligerents in war. Neutrality in international law is a condition of a state being isolated from hostilities during a war which is both declared by a state and true in fact. A neutral state claims the right to engage in peaceful trade with all belligerent states, as long as it does not provide war material to any party and remains non-participatory in the conflict and impartial in fact between the belligerent states. A neutral state claims the right to keep its vessels, land, and people immune from capture or destruction by the warring parties. The principle of neutrality was long promoted by the United States and was confirmed in the Hague Convention of 1907. Though some commentators have argued that neutrality is no longer a principle of international law, being replaced by the regime of the United Nations Charter, many states, such as Switzerland and Costa Rica, assert neutrality in the event of any armed conflict and claim the rights of neutrality, and this assertion has routinely been accepted by other states in the absence of support for a belligerent state.

**new (newness or novel or novelty)**   Known, done, made, or extant for the first time. Anything new is the first of its kind, at least within a relevant context, as context is essential to understanding the requirement of novelty. For instance, to claim that a device is new in applying for a patent requires the assertion that the device is original, thus it has never before existed in this form or been created or designed before. To assert that some matter in trial is new, on the other hand, requires the assertion that the subject of that matter has not been presented as evidence or made in argument before in that trial, but it need not have been unknown to the parties or their counsel beforehand. Since newness, like novelty, is a matter of degree, most questions in law are resolved into a question of whether the matter is new or not, which is to say whether the matter in question, as a whole, is sufficiently new to be designated as "new" in the appropriate context.

See also: novelty (novel).

**new and independent cause**   See: causation, independent cause (new and independent cause).

**New Deal Court**   See: court, U.S. court, U.S. Supreme Court, Hughes Court (New Deal Court).

**new matter**   See: matter, new matter.

**new party**   See: party, party to an action, new party.

**new source**   See: pollution, pollution source, new source.

**new trial**   *See:* trial, new trial (motion for new trial).

**New York Stock Exchange**   *See:* security, securities, securities exchange, New York Stock Exchange (N.Y.S.E. or NYSE).

**newbie**   *See:* lawyer, newbie (baby lawyer, greenhorn).

**newly discovered evidence**   *See:* evidence, newly discovered evidence.

**next friend**   *See:* party, party to an action, next friend; guardian, guardian ad litem, next friend.

**next of kin**   *See:* kin, next of kin.

**nexum (nexus)**   A relationship or connection. Nexus describes a range of connections between persons, places, or things, such as one activity and another, one person and another, a person to a thing, a vessel to a jurisdiction, etc. Nexus implies a sufficient relationship that some legal burden on the one person, place, or thing might be reasonably related to the other.

Nexus in Roman law was more akin to the common law idea of privity, as in privity of estate or privity of contract. This degree of relationship is probably one of greater engagement and involvement than is required in the modern usage of nexus.

*See also:* taking, essential nexus; taking, regulatory taking, conditional use, double–nexus analysis (double nexus test).

**nickah (nikah)**   Marriage. Nickah, also called zawaj, is a contract that is proof of marriage in Islamic law.

**night-watchman state**   *See:* state, night–watchman state (minimal state).

**nihil (nil)**   Nothing. Nihil, Latin for "nothing," was frequently used in writs, returns, and orders. There is no real difference in meaning between nihil and nil.

*See also:* non.

**nihil dicit (nihil dicit judgment)**   A default judgment. Nihil dicit, Latin for "he says nothing," was the name of the common law judgment for the plaintiff granted if the defendant did not reply to the claim. It was the precursor to the default judgment against the defendant. The motion and order by this name are still used in a few jurisdictions, notably Texas, where it is used in circumstances in which the defendant has appeared but has not effectively responded to the claims made by the plaintiff.

*See also:* answer, answer as pleading; motion (movant or move); judgment, default judgment.

**nihil habet (nihil est or nil est or nil habet )**   Service of process has failed. Nihil habet, for "he has nothing to return," or nihil est, for "there is nothing," were routine statements made by an official charged to serve process under the common–law writ system who was unable to do so, usually owing to an inability to locate the person to be served. The designation "nil" or "nihil" was an abbreviation of one of these returns. With the adoption of the service requirements of the rules of civil procedure, this reply is effectively obsolete.

**nikah**   *See:* nickah (nikah).

**nikah mut'ah**   *See:* mutah (nikah mut'ah).

**nil**   *See:* nihil (nil).

**nimbyism (not in my backyard or NIMBY)**   Opposition to an undesirable landuse nearby. NIMBY is the acronym from the slogan "not in my backyard," which echoes the position of landholders, residents, or voters who fight against the location of jails, prisons, rehab centers, cement plants, cattle yards, big–box stores, wetland restorations, predator reintroduction, highways, and other unpopular land uses and projects near their property. The mindset of such opposing persons is nimbyism.

**nine points of the law**   *See:* possession, nine points of the law (nine–tenths of the law).

**nine-tenths of the law**   *See:* possession, nine points of the law (nine–tenths of the law).

**nisi prius court**   *See:* court, English court, nisi prius court.

**nitrogen dioxide**   *See:* pollution, air pollution, criteria pollutants, nitrogen dioxide (NO2).

**NL**   *See:* non, non liquet (NL).

**NLRB**   *See:* union, labor union, National Labor Relations Board (NLRB).

**NMFS**   *See:* fishery, National Marine Fisheries Service (NMFS).

**no action clause**   *See:* insurance, insurance policy, no action clause.

**no bill**   *See:* jury, grand jury, no bill (no true bill).

**no contest or nolo or non vult contendere**   *See:* plea, criminal plea, nolo contendere (no contest or nolo or non vult contendere).

**no objection**   *See:* objection, no objection.

**no true bill**   *See:* jury, grand jury, no bill (no true bill).

**no verdict**   *See:* verdict, no verdict (hung jury or deadlocked jury).

**no-citation rule**   *See:* opinion, judicial opinion, unpublished opinion (no–citation rule).

**no-fault insurance**   *See:* insurance, category of insurance, automobile insurance, no-fault insurance.

**no-knock search**   *See:* search, no-knock search.

**no-knock search warrant**   *See:* warrant, search warrant, no-knock search warrant.

**NO₂**   *See:* pollution, air pollution, criteria pollutants, nitrogen dioxide (NO₂).

**nobility (peerage)**   Title and privilege above the common person. Nobility is a status recognized by the customs or laws of a state that confer privileges and titles that are superior in some form to those available to the common subject or citizen of the state. Titles of peers are hierarchical, the topmost status being that of a monarch. In England, peers include the king or queen, prince or princess, duke or duchess, marquis (or marquess) or marchioness, earl or countess, viscount or viscountess, and baron or baroness. Continental peerages vary somewhat. The nobility in England are peers of the realm created either by inheritance from peers, the hereditary peers who all were once entitled to sit in the House of Lords, though this institution has been altered significantly at the end of the twentieth and beginning of the twenty-first centuries, or created by the monarch on the recommendation of the government.

Titles of nobility are forbidden to citizens of the United States, although foreign states may confer honors of the same title though not the same legal significance on an American citizen. A person holding a title of nobility who takes the oath of citizenship in the United States must renounce the title. Note: a title of honor is not a title of nobility, and none of this affects the use of esquire, honorable, excellency, etc.

*See also:* title, title as form of address (Mr. or Ms. or Miss or Mrs. or Hon. or excellency).

**Noerr–Pennington doctrine**   *See:* petition, right to petition, Noerr–Pennington doctrine.

**nolle**   To be unwilling. Nolle designates an order or return in which the official entering the record will be registering a negative answer in some manner.

> **nolle prosequi (nolle pros. or null pros. or non prosequitur or non pros.)**   An entry by which a case is closed by a prosecutor or court. Nolle prosequi, used more often in its abbreviated form "nolle pros.," is an entry on a record in a criminal case file that the prosecutor or court has discontinued the case. In some jurisdictions, an order of nolle prosequi is specifically made with or without leave to reopen the case, though in most jurisdictions, a nolle prossed case may be reopened by a new indictment or information as long as the new charges are entered and served within the statute of limitations period.
>
> Although the same process was once employed by a plaintiff, this usage is now effectively obsolete, having been replaced by the voluntary dismissal or the nonsuit.

**nolo contendere**   *See:* plea, criminal plea, nolo contendere, Alford plea; plea, criminal plea, nolo contendere (no contest or nolo or non vult contendere).

**nominal**   In name only rather than in substance. Nominal means something, such as an interest, fee, or damage award, of a slight amount. The reason for this is inherent in the fuller meaning of nominality.

Something nominal is done by name, which implies it is not done by interest of fuller commitment. Thus, a nominal plaintiff is present to allow the plaintiff's name to be used, but another party is the real party in interest. Nominal damages are token damages awarded in order to justify the designation of damages but not to compensate a party for damage suffered. A nominal bequest is a token amount given for the purpose of naming the recipient in the will more than to transfer a share of the estate. A nominal fee is a fee that is assessed for the purpose of having a fee rather than actually to support the activity requiring the fee through fee-generated revenues.

> **nominal damages**   *See:* damages, classes of damages, nominal damages.
>
> **nominal party**   *See:* party, party to an action, nominal party.

**nomination (nominate)**   The naming of a person for later consideration. Nomination is a process of designating a person who is to be considered for selection for an appointment, office, or award. Nomination is inherently a step toward selection and is thus not the selection itself, but the selection is then made from among the nominees, whether by election, designation, or competition. Thus, a political party will nominate a person to be a candidate for office in a general election, but the vote of the electorate will lead to the installation of the person in the office. A person may be nominated to a judgeship, ambassadorship, commission, or board, but only once the nomination is ratified does the nomination become an appointment.

*See also:* appointment (appoint); election (elective).

> **nominate reports or named reports**   *See:* reports, case reports, nominative reports (nominate reports or named reports).
>
> **nominate tort**   *See:* tort, nominate tort.
>
> **nominee**   Anyone nominated for an office, award, or responsibility. The nominee is the person or entity who is proposed for a given role. In general, a nominee is presumed to accept a nomination but is free to decline it, at which time the nomination is void.

**nominative reports**   *See:* reports, case reports, nominative reports (nominate reports or named reports).

**non**   No. Non is the Latin adverb that establishes the negative implication of the verb or adjective it modifies. It may mean no, none, not, and other variants of negation.

*See also:* nihil (nil).

> **non-actionable**   *See:* actionable (non-actionable).

**non-age** *See:* child, non-age (not of age).

**non-appearance** *See:* appearance, non-appearance, failure to appear (bail-jumping or bail jumping or jump bail); appearance, non-appearance (nonappearance or failure to appear).

**non-assignable lease or unassignable lease** *See:* lease, assignable lease (non-assignable lease or unassignable lease).

**non-assignable right** *See:* rights, legal right, assignable right (non-assignable right).

**non-attainment zone** *See:* pollution, air pollution, non-attainment zone (nonattainment).

**non-capital crime** *See:* capital, capital crime, non-capital crime (noncapital crime).

**non-claim** *See:* claim, non-claim (nonclaim).

**non-combatant** *See:* combatant, non-combatant (noncombatant).

**non-competition covenant** *See:* covenant, contract covenant, no-competition covenant (non-competition clause or non-compete clause or non-compete clause).

**non compos mentis** *See:* capacity, legal capacity, incapacity, non compos mentis (non compotes mentis or non compos).

**non-conforming goods** *See:* goods, non-conforming goods (nonconforming goods).

**non-conforming use** *See:* zoning, land use, non-conforming use (nonconforming use or prior non-conforming use or pre-existing non-conforming use).

**non-delegable duty** *See:* delegation, non-delegable duty (nondelegable duty).

**non-delegation doctrine or nondelegation doctrine** *See:* delegation, delegation doctrine (non-delegation doctrine or nondelegation doctrine).

**non-disclosure** *See:* disclosure, non-disclosure (nondisclosure).

**non-economic damages** *See:* damages, classes of damages, non-economic damages.

**nonfeasance or non-feasance or non feasance** *See:* feasance, nonfeasance (non-feasance or non feasance).

**non-freehold estate or nonfreehold estate** *See:* lease, leasehold (non-freehold estate or nonfreehold estate).

**non-friable asbestos** *See:* asbestos, non-friable asbestos (nonfriable asbestos).

**non-fundamental** *See:* fundamental (non-fundamental).

**non-general power of appointment** *See:* power, power of appointment, limited power of appointment (non-general power of appointment).

**non-itemized deduction** *See:* tax, tax deduction, above-the-line deduction (non-itemized deduction).

**non-joinder** *See:* joinder, non-joinder (nonjoinder).

**non-judicial foreclosure** *See:* foreclosure, non-judicial foreclosure (nonjudicial foreclosure).

**non-justiciable** *See:* justiciable, non-justiciable (nonjusticiable).

**non-movant or cross-movant** *See:* movant (non-movant or cross-movant).

**non-party witness** *See:* witness, party-witness (non-party witness).

**non-passive income** *See:* income, passive income, non-passive income.

**non-performance** *See:* performance, contract performance, non-performance (nonperformance).

**non-performing loan** *See:* loan, non-performing loan (nonperforming loan).

**non-possessory interest** *See:* estate, interest, non-possessory interest (nonpossessory interest).

**non-probate asset** *See:* probate, non-probate asset (nonprobate).

**nonprofit or non-profit corporation or not-for-profit corporation** *See:* corporation, corporations, nonprofit corporation (non-profit corporation or not-for-profit corporation).

**non-public forum** *See:* speech, freedom of speech, forum, non-public forum (nonpublic forum).

**non-recourse debt** *See:* recourse, non-recourse debt (nonrecourse debt).

**non-recourse loan** *See:* loan, non-recourse loan (nonrecourse loan or non-recourse debt or nonrecourse debt).

**non-refoulement or refoulement** *See:* refouler (non-refoulement or refoulement).

**non-self-executing treaty** *See:* treaty, self-executing treaty (non-self-executing treaty).

**non sequitur** *See:* fallacy, non sequitur.

**non sui juris** *See:* sui, sui juris (non sui juris); capacity, legal capacity, incapacity, non sui juris.

**nonsuit** *See:* dismissal, nonsuit, involuntary nonsuit; dismissal, nonsuit, compulsory nonsuit; dismissal, nonsuit.

**non-suspect class** *See:* class, legal classification, non-suspect class (nonsuspect class or ordinary class).

**non-union** *See:* union, labor union, non-union, scab; union, labor union, non-union (nonunion).

**nonviable or viable**  *See:* viability (nonviable or viable).

**non assumpsit**  A defense to an action for assumpsit. Non assumpsit describes the defense against an argument for assumpsit that is based on no duty having been undertaken. As assumpsit is a claim of breach of duty, the defense that there was no duty is, if proved, conclusive. The old defense of non assumpsit infra sex annos was a claim that the limitations period had run because any duty the defendant accepted was not accepted within the last six years.
*See also:* assumpsit.

**non bis in idem (ne bis in idem)**  A bar on double jeopardy. Non bis in idem, Latin for "not twice for the same thing," is the principle forbidding double jeopardy. Civilian and international criminal courts apply this doctrine, barring a second trial for an offense for which a person has already been tried.
*See also:* jeopardy, double jeopardy.

**non est inventus**  Not to be found. Non est inventus is a return of service on an arrest warrant, in which the party to be served is "not to be found."

**non liquet (NL)**  Unclear, whether in the proof or as a legal issue. Non liquet describes a matter in which there is not a clear legal answer, particularly in civil law or international law. A court announcing a judgment non liquet refuses to rule on the question presented.
In Roman law, non liquet was written on tablets, abbreviated in Latin as NL, and raised as a vote in the comitia, or courts of popular assembly, as a finding that the case was too unclear for the voter to vote to condemn (D for damno) or to free (L for libero) the accused.
*See also:* d, d as a Latin abbreviation; l, l as a Latin abbreviation.

**non obstante**  Notwithstanding. Non obstante is Latin for notwithstanding. It was used by the English king in the exercise of the dispensing power. Non obstante also designates exceptions, exclusions, and grants of authority or discretion in legislation and private instruments.
In its most common contemporary usage in law, however, non obstante is an abbreviated form of non obstante veredicto, or a judgment entered by a judge, notwithstanding the verdict of the jury.
*See also:* judgment, judgment notwithstanding the verdict (J.N.O.V. or JNOV or judgment as a matter of law or JML or JMOL or judgment non obstante veredicto).

**non prosequitur (non pros)**  Not moving forward the suit. Non prosequitur was a judgment entered against a claimant who had failed to meet court deadlines in the civil prosecution of an action.
*See also:* judgment, judgment non prosequitur (non pros); nolle, nolle prosequi (nolle pros. or null pros. or non prosequitur or non pros).

**non sequitur**  A random comment or illogical conclusion. Non sequitur, Latin for "it does not follow," is a label for any statement that is illogical or unconnected to the preceding conversation or argument.
*See also:* fallacy, non sequitur.

**norm**  A standard of behavior accepted as correct. At its most general, a norm is any idea of how a person should behave that is understood within a community as an obligation of the individual. At its most abstract, norms include all such obligations, regardless of their origin in law, morality, community, or family that individuals accept as the source of what they are obligated to do. Laws are a type of norm, as are manners and customs.
*See also:* precept.

**basic norm (grundnorm)**  The idea that is the foundation for all laws in a legal system. The basic norm, grundnorm in German, is a central element of Kelsen's theory of positivism, in which the basic norm is the basis from which the whole legal system acquires its moral imperative and normative legitimacy. To some degree, the norm is both an idea in itself as well as the reflection of some acts by the creators of the state or the legal system. Thus, every change of the laws in the legal system alters the meaning of the basic norm. The basic norm is not created by an act of law but by an act prior to law, and its legitimacy is never questioned by legal officials.

**hierarchy of norms**  Some norms are created and justified according to higher norms. Norms are often derived from the operation of other norms. This derivation can take place institutionally and formally, as when a statute dictates how a rule is made, or it can take place customarily and informally, as when the acceptance of new ideas about treating people with equal dignity gave rise to new standards for polite speech in referring to people by race and gender.
*See also:* rule, legal rule, secondary rule.

**normativism**  *See:* jurisprudence, normativism (legal normativism).

**Norris-Laguardia Act**  *See:* union, labor union, labor laws, Anti-Injunction Bill (Norris–Laguardia Act).

**North American Free Trade Agreement**  *See:* trade, international trade, North American Free Trade Agreement (NAFTA).

**not guilty**  *See:* verdict, not guilty ( verdict of not guilty or not–guilty verdict); plea, criminal plea, not guilty.

**not guilty by reason of insanity**  *See:* plea, criminal plea, not guilty by reason of insanity; insanity, not guilty by reason of insanity.

**not in my backyard or NIMBY**  *See:* nimbyism (not in my backyard or NIMBY).

**not of age** *See:* child, non-age (not of age).

**nota bene (N.B.)** Pay particular attention to what follows. Nota bene, Latin for "note well," is a customary signal by an author to the reader to pay close attention to the information that follows the signal. From this, the phrase is used occasionally as a label for important rules or principles. It is often abbreviated N.B.

**notary (notary public)** An official who attests instruments. A notary, which in the United States is usually called a notary public, is a person appointed by the state to hear and take oaths and to attest to the identity of a person offering to sign a document and to validate the signature of that person on the instrument signed. Notaries customarily place a seal on notarized instruments, although an electronic seal is now used for electronic instruments. Notaries in some jurisdictions are required to maintain a calendar or log of all uses of the notarial seal in the event of later questions regarding the authenticity of a notarized instrument. In most jurisdictions, various offices, including the clerks of court, are designated as a notary by operation of law, while other persons may apply to be appointed a notary by a state office, usually the state's secretary of state.

In civil law jurisdictions, the office of notary is that of an attorney with responsibility for non-adversarial law, particularly matters of property and estate planning, corporations, partnerships, commercial law and contract. A notary in these jurisdictions is a member of the bar.

*See also:* witness; seal; public.

**note (notes)** A summary written record. Notes, in general, are notations, the written evidence of something that occurs, including the thoughts or impressions of their maker. Notes take several distinct forms in law, including notes of transactions or value that are commercial paper, such as bank notes; notes that serve as memorials of contracts; notes as an attorney's record of research or analysis; notes as records of proceedings or meetings; and notes as annotations on a form, instrument, or text. A note may be either a single such record or written communication of a type less than the most formal available, such as a diplomatic note. As a verb, to note, or to take note, is to allude to some event.

**note in the margin** *See:* margin, marginal note (note in the margin).

**bank note (bank bill)** Paper money issued by a bank and used as currency. A bank note is a negotiable instrument issued by a bank that is payable on demand and treated as currency. The form of paper money in the U.S. as of 2008 is the Federal Reserve Note, which has replaced privately issued bank notes in the U.S. as legal tender. In many countries, bank notes are still issued by both public and private banks with a privilege to do so, such as in Scotland.

*See also:* currency.

**footnote** *See:* footnote; scrutiny, standards of scrutiny, strict scrutiny, footnote four (footnote four or the footnote).

**promissory note (promissary note)** A written promise to pay a sum of money in the future. A promissory note is a written promise to pay a certain sum of money, at a future time, with no conditions that must be satisfied prior to the payment. A promissory note must be signed by or on behalf of the maker, noting the amount to be paid and to whom, with words that either identify the note as a promissory note or that amount to the making of a promise. (A note that does not signify a promise is not a promissory note but only an acknowledgment of a debt, such as an IOU.) It is given by a maker to a promissee, and it is good whether or not it specifies the date by which the payment is to be made. A promissory note is commercial paper, and uttering a forged promissory note is a distinct offense. Note: Although the more common spelling is "promissory," many banks and lawyers write the term with an "a." There is no difference in meaning between promissory and promissary.

*See also:* maker; instrument, negotiable instrument.

**notice** Information or knowledge. Notice is knowledge of a specific fact or idea, whether the knowledge is actually had, is imputed from a condition providing information that would lead a reasonable observer to such knowledge, or is charged as a matter of legal responsibility. Notice is therefore actual, implied, or constructive.

Notice varies in its operation when the notice is of broad and general liability, such as notice of a criminal liability or regulatory liability; is of a general duty to private parties, such as the general duty underlying negligence; or is of a private obligation arising from a contract or special duty in performing a service.

Notice as a matter of pleading and service of process is specific to the rules of service.

*See also:* diligence, due diligence; disclaimer.

**notice for trial** *See:* trial, notice for trial (notice of trial).

**notice inquiry** *See:* inquiry, notice inquiry, red flag.

**notice-of-alibi rule** *See:* alibi, notice-of-alibi rule.

**notice of appeal** *See:* appeal, notice of appeal.

**notice of motion** *See:* motion, notice of motion.

**notice of removal** *See:* removal, removal to federal court, notice of removal.

**notice of trial** *See:* trial, notice for trial (notice of trial).

**notice pleading** *See:* pleading, pleading theories, notice pleading, plausible on its face (Twombly standard or Iqbal test or facial plausibility); pleading, pleading theories, notice pleading.

**notice recording act** *See:* title, recordation of title, recording act, notice recording act (notice state or notice act or notice jurisdiction).

**notice state or notice act or notice jurisdiction** *See:* title, recordation of title, recording act, notice recording act (notice state or notice act or notice jurisdiction).

**actual notice**   Specific knowledge held in fact by the party charged with knowing it. Actual notice is information that either is in fact provided to the person or entity to be charged with its information or is in fact known to the person to be charged, regardless of how the person or entity came to have that information. Actual notice of a corporation or other entity arises when any officer or agent with responsibility for that information has actual notice, or when the information with which the entity is to be charged is or was held in its archives or business records.

**constructive notice (record notice)**   Notice construed as a matter of law. Constructive notice is charged to a person or entity as a matter of law, regardless of whether or not the person or entity has actual notice of the information. It is information provided according to some means for which the person or entity is responsible for recognizing, such as official records. Notice of material in a public record, such as a deed or other instrument recorded in the appropriate public office gives rise to record notice, which is a form of constructive notice.

Constructive notice differs from implied notice, in that constructive notice is effective by operation of law, but implied notice is that which as a matter of fact would be understood by a reasonable person from another fact. Even so, constructive notice is often used to mean implied notice, or notice of a given bit of information that a reasonable person would have construed by implication from some other information. The difference is not germane to most questions, however, because in most cases the effect of either implied notice or constructive notice is not to excuse the party claiming not to have had notice from liability for such notice.

*See also:* notice, actual notice.

**fair notice doctrine**   A statute must give adequate notice of what it prohibits. The fair notice doctrine is an element of the due process of law that requires a criminal prohibition or other regulatory limitation on conduct to be sufficiently clear from the face of the statute or regulation, such that a person of the relevant expertise would be on notice of the conduct required or forbidden.

*See also:* vagueness, vagueness doctrine (void for vagueness doctrine).

**implied notice**   Notice reasonably arising from other information. Implied notice is notice that is implied from information of which a party has actual notice or, in some cases, constructive notice. For example, actual notice to a person that mail is delivered to and sent from a given address that the person believes to be empty gives implied notice that the property is in fact occupied by another person. Implied notice differs from constructive notice, in that implied notice is a fact that would be understood by a reasonable person from another fact, while constructive notice is effective by operation of law (such as notice of ownership construed from a deed on file at a courthouse).

*See also:* notice, constructive notice (record notice).

**imputed notice**   Notice charged to one party from notice to another party. Imputed notice is notice to which one party is held, owing to notice having been given to another party, whose relationship with the party charged with imputed notice is such that it is reasonable to impute the notice of one to the other. Imputed notice is a form of constructive notice, as when, for instance, a lead counsel is given notice, and co-counsel are imputed with that notice.

*See also:* notice, constructive notice (record notice).

**inquiry notice**   Notice that should have been discovered by reasonable inquiry. Inquiry notice is a form of implied notice in which a party is charged with notice of information that would have been discovered had the party reasonably investigated further from information of which the party had actual notice. Inquiry notice is not unlimited, but in a situation in which a party has a duty of due diligence or investigation, or a context in which information would be perceived by a reasonable observer to give rise to concerns or questions that could be satisfied with reasonable further investigation, the party will not be excused from ignorance for a failure to investigate further. For example, a buyer's actual notice of a sink and taps in a house may be the basis for inquiry notice of a water utility easement on the land. Inquiry notice is a legal form that reflects the maxim in equity that equity regards as done that which ought to be done.

**judicial notice (judicially noticed fact)**   An acknowledgment by the court of a fact not in question. Judicial notice is the recognition by a court of a fact that is widely known and not subject to any reasonable dispute. Judicial notice is governed by the Federal Rules of Evidence 201 and the corresponding state rule in state rules of evidence, which limit notice to such facts as are generally known within the territorial jurisdiction of the court or capable of determination by resort to sources whose accuracy cannot reasonably be questioned. The mere fact of an objection to a determination by a court to take judicial notice of any fact is no proof of reasonable dispute, though the absence of an objection is no proof that the presumed fact, though widely known, is in fact an accurate statement of the conditions or events it depicts. The court is ultimately responsible for the accuracy of a fact it accepts as a matter of notice. The court in its discretion may entertain a suggestion or motion from either litigant that the court take judicial notice, or the judge may take notice sua sponte.

*See also:* notoriety (notorious); fact; fact, historical fact; knowledge, common knowledge (public knowledge).

**notice of orders or judgments**   Delivery of notice from the court to a party. Notice of an order or judgment is sent from the clerk of court to a party by regular mail. Notice is constructively provided by the docketing of the order or judgment in the court.

In ordinary circumstances, no time is added to a period for filing a motion of reconsideration or notice of appeal to account for the time required for delivery of notice.

**publication notice (notice by publication)** Notice through advertisement to the public. Publication notice is a form of constructive notice in which notice for certain purposes is sufficient when it is made available through publication to the general population, particularly through newspaper advertisements and physical postings in a public place. A party with a duty to serve notice to all who have an adverse interest may give sufficient notice by publication alone if the party in good faith is not aware of any person or entity with a potentially adverse interest. In instances when a party cannot be located, service of process or a summons may be made by publication, usually with leave of the court. Some actions or proceedings, such as an action to quiet title or a sheriff's auction, require notice by publication. Statutes specify the minimum requirements of public notice, but the customary requirements are that a copy of the notice be placed in the legal notices section of a paper of common distribution throughout the jurisdiction, that it be posted at the courthouse, and that it be posted visibly on any realty affected.

**notification (notify)** The effective transfer of information to a recipient. Notification is an act or process that is intended to give an intended recipient some information. Notification may be verbal or written and may be accomplished indirectly through the labeling of a product so as to notify the user of something regarding the product. The degree to which a notification requirement is satisfied by anything less than an acknowledgment of the notice by the recipient varies according to the requirement and the context in which the requirement is enforced or unsatisfied. In certain contexts only proof of actual notification is sufficient, but in others reasonable steps to notify the public or to notify a person with a known interest are sufficient.

**parental notification** Notice to a parent or guardian regarding a child. Parental notification is the act of presenting information to a parent regarding a child, a condition involving a child, or a process involving a child. In general, parental notification is considered effective only when the notifying authority confirms receipt of the notice, such as by the signature of the parent on a notification form. Some states require parental notification for certain educational purposes, and parental notification may be required before a child undergoes certain health procedures, including abortion in some jurisdictions, but such notification procedures may not unduly burden the rights of the child.

**spousal notification** Notice to a spouse regarding the other spouse. Spousal notification is the act of presenting information to a spouse regarding the other spouse, a condition involving the other spouse, or a process involving the other spouse. Spousal notification is required in some states prior to a woman's receiving an abortion, although such requirements may not burden the rights of the wife.

**notoriety (notorious)** Someone or something that is widely known. Notoriety, in general, is a condition of knowledge, whether of a person, fact, or idea, that is widespread in a relevant community. A notorious idea is, in law, something so well known that a court may take judicial notice of it without further evidence. In commercial law prior to the Uniform Commercial Code, a person's notorious insolvency would be sufficient for a holder of a debt or a contractual interest to demand a surety on performance or payment. A narrower understanding of notoriety requires only that the notorious act, conduct, or thing be apparent to the public. Thus, a notorious action is an action in public rather than in private or secret.

Notoriety of possession or use is a requirement of adverse possession or prescription of a use, in which a possessor's possession or use of another's land must be notorious, as well as open, adverse, and hostile, for the continuous period of time required by statute. Notorious in this context need not require that the knowledge of the use or possession actually be widespread among members of the community, as the requirement of notoriety is generally satisfied if the possession and use is open as well as of a sufficient form that others are reasonably likely to know of it.

*See also:* notice, judicial notice (judicially noticed fact); possession, adverse possession, notorious possession; possession, adverse possession, notorious possession.

**notorious possession** *See:* possession, notorious possession; possession, adverse possession, notorious possession.

**novation** A new obligation that is substituted for an old one. A novation is the substitution of a new debt or other obligation for a prior debt or earlier obligation. The novation of a contract is the entry into a new contract that is intended by the parties to an earlier contract to supersede and replace the earlier contract. The novation need not require all of the original parties to be obligated by the new contract, and a new debt may be among new parties as well. In all cases, an effective novation requires that all of the original parties must be satisfied and that they each consent to the novation as sufficient performance or satisfaction of the earlier agreement. The novation of a debt is a new debt usually, though not necessarily, with different terms than the initial debt. Novation involving the substitution of a party for one or more earlier parties is a delegation.

Novation is a defense to enforcing a contract, collecting a debt, or foreclosing on security for a debt, by which the debtor pleads the contract has been extinguished or the debt has been satisfied by a novation. Novation for this purpose requires evidence that the earlier agreement was extinguished by some act that signaled the parties' intent to extinguish the agreement, to which all of the parties consented. A novation may be by express agreement or implied from the conduct of the parties.

**novelty (novel)**   Recently invented and previously unknown. Novelty is a measure of the attribute of newness that applies to any thing or idea that is recently created and sufficiently unusual. Novelty is a matter of degree; the more unusual and distinct a thing or an idea is perceived to be, the more novel it is. As with other aspects of newness, context is essential to the evaluation of novelty. For example, a new device with only slight variations from its predecessors might be thought to lack novelty. Yet, if these slight variations allow a new application of the device, like allowing it to be retasked from space exploration to medical surgery, the new device would be novel when compared to its predecessors. On the other hand, if the new device was in fact very much like devices already used in medical surgery, the novelty of the device would nonetheless be limited.

*See also:* new (newness or novel or novelty).

**novel disseisin**   *See:* disseisin, novel disseisin.

**noxious**   Causing an adverse effect to the body or environment. Anything noxious is harmful. The term once had the connotation of a legal harm, but in recent usage has become more associated with harms to a human being or to the environment caused by harmful chemical interactions or any other invasion into an ecosystem, as in noxious plants or animals.

*See also:* obnoxious (obnoxiousness).

**NPDES**   *See:* pollution, water pollution, National Pollutant Discharge Elimination System (NPDES).

**NPDES permit**   *See:* pollution, water pollution, National Pollutant Discharge Elimination System, NPDES permit.

**nuclear energy**

**Nuclear Regulatory Commission**   The U.S. regulator of civilian nuclear energy. The Nuclear Regulatory Commission is the primary agency for the regulation of nuclear energy for civilian purposes in the United States. Nuclear materials used for military purposes are regulated by the Department of Energy and the Department of Defense.

**nuclear waste**   *See:* waste, waste material, nuclear waste, Nuclear Waste Policy Act; waste, waste material, nuclear waste (radioactive waste).

**nudity (public nudity or nudeness or nude or nakedness or naked)**   A person's condition when not wearing any clothing. Nudity is the state of a person who is without clothes on the body as they are customarily worn, although the term may apply to various, specific stages of undress, particularly when there are no clothes at all or when there are such few clothes that the genitalia are uncovered. Nudity by a person alone in a private place is no concern of the law's, but nudity visible in a public place may be subject to criminal prohibitions as a regulation of a nuisance or of an act contrary to public morals, so long as the prohibition does not go so far as to create an undue burden on expressive speech. Nudity may be an element in acts of sexual harassment, sexual assault, contributing to the delinquency of a minor, prostitution, and other criminal or tortious acts. Nudity is the condition of being nude; a nude is a noun, and nude is an adjective.

**nude contract**   *See:* contract, specific contracts, nude contract (nudum pactum).

**nudum pactum**   *See:* pactum, nudum pactum; contract, specific contracts, nude contract (nudum pactum).

**nugatory**   Misleadingly trivial. Anything nugatory is worthless or nearly so, and use of the term usually implies that the nugatory value is likely the result of a trick or sharp practice. The law will not enforce a nugatory contract.

**nugatory contract**   *See:* contract, specific contracts, nugatory contract.

**nuisance**   The use of one property to the injury of another. Although anything inconvenient is a nuisance, the term in law refers to the tort of the use of property in such a manner that another property is harmed or its owner or occupant is injured or hindered in its use. A nuisance may be public, such that it causes an injury to a right held in common by the people or by a government on their behalf, or it may be private, constituting an injury to the interests of a private individual or entity holding private property. In either case, the injury itself must be caused by the use of property, either in itself or through some activity on the property. Although the same conduct that results in a nuisance may also cause a trespass, the nuisance is distinct and its cause of action does not depend on an entry on the harmed property by a person, animal, or object. Noise, light, smell, effect on value, or other interference with the enjoyment of nearby property is essential to the action, and the cause of the harm must be either unlawful or unusual for property in proximity to the nuisance property. Nuisance may be brought by any person with a property that is affected by the nuisance, and such property need not be adjoining the nuisance property.

*See also:* trespass, indirect trespass; dilapidation; smell (odor); nuisance, abatement of a nuisance; nuisance, mixed nuisance.

**nuisance animal**   *See:* animal, nuisance animal.

**abatement of a nuisance**   The removal of a public or private nuisance. Abatement of a nuisance is the elimination of the activity or its effects that interfere with the use of the property or lands of someone else. So, for instance, a property lawfully used but that is so ugly in its use as to interfere with the use of nearby property could be shielded by a fence, thus abating the aesthetic nuisance (assuming the fence does not amount to a new nuisance in itself).

*See also:* nuisance.

**animal nuisance** A public or private nuisance caused by an animal. An animal nuisance is a nuisance caused by the behavior or one or more animals kept either as a domesticated animal, a pet, or otherwise under human care or captivity. An animal nuisance may arise through the behavior of a specific animal, such as when a dog barks unceasingly at night, or through the effects of maintaining an animal or animal population, such as noise, smell, or the risk of disease. Animal nuisance is a distinct form of nuisance in some jurisdictions, and it is pled as either public or private nuisance in others. Nuisance is not, of course, the extent of owner liability for animals under their control, which include not only regulatory offense such as leash and license laws but also negligence and, in rare cases, strict liability for unusually dangerous animals. Note: a nuisance animal is not the same.

*See also:* animal, nuisance animal.

**attractive nuisance (turntable doctrine)** A dangerous object on a property that will draw potential victims to it. An attractive nuisance is any feature on a property that poses a risk to children, owing to the nature of the feature being so alluring to a child that the child is likely to trespass onto the property, while at the same time being so hazardous that a risk of injury or death would attend the child's being on the property. The classic attractive nuisance was the railroad turntable, and the earliest cases recognizing a particular duty to guard such features were said to apply the "turntable doctrine." The category of attractive nuisances has grown to include swimming pools, heavy machinery, carnival rides, and unspecified dangers that meet the criteria of both attractiveness and danger. Under the modern doctrine, a landowner on whose property is found an attractive nuisance and who can reasonably foresee that a child would trespass onto the property must take the reasonable steps of ordinary care to abate the risk of harm to a trespassing child, if that risk would not be apparent to a child.

**coming to the nuisance** A nuisance that predates the plaintiff's acquiring the property. Coming to the nuisance is a defense to an action in nuisance that bars a claim of nuisance if the conduct asserted as a nuisance predated the acquisition of property by the party who complains of it, or a significant improvement to that property. At common law, coming to the nuisance was a bar to most actions for nuisance. The modern doctrine, followed now in most states, allows a balance of the nature of the complained-of conduct, the character and use of nearby lands, and length of time during which the use has interfered with the plaintiff's use and enjoyment. When the doctrine does not operate as a complete defense or a barrier to an injunction, it may affect the award of damages.

*See also:* risk, assumption of risk (assumption of the risk).

**mixed nuisance** A nuisance affecting both public rights and private property. A mixed nuisance is a use of property that amounts both to a private nuisance and to a public nuisance. An action brought under either theory may be considered under the other and, if the claim is supported by the evidence, either theory may justify a remedy that accords with both theories of nuisance.

*See also:* nuisance.

**nuisance per se** A property use that is always and everywhere a nuisance. Nuisance per se is a use of property that inherently causes a significant injury to a right of the public or to nearby properties, and that results from such use regardless of its location. The most common basis for a nuisance per se is conduct in violation of the criminal law, but conduct in violation of any law protecting the health, safety, welfare, morals, or convenience of the public that has an effect on other property may amount to nuisance per se.

**permanent nuisance** A nuisance that is and has been ongoing with no likely end. A permanent nuisance is a use of land that interferes with others' use and enjoyment of their land but has done so for longer than the statute of limitations period for nuisance. Thus, no claim for nuisance can be brought against a permanent nuisance, unless the use amounting to a nuisance was in fact interrupted or abated for a significant time, after which it was renewed to the new detriment of the adjoining property.

**private nuisance** A nuisance affecting a person upon private land. Private nuisance is the use of one's property in a manner that creates a significant harm in another's use or enjoyment of private lands. A private nuisance need not amount to a violation of a zoning rule, a criminal law, or an ordinance, but the use of the land must be unusual or not customary for lands in the area. A person who owns or lawfully occupies the land, a tenant or lessee, an easement holder, or a person with a future interest in the property may bring an action to abate the nuisance.

**public nuisance** A nuisance affecting the community or government property. A public nuisance is a continuing interference with a common right among members of the public that causes a significant harm to the public as a whole or harms the use of members of the public in their own lands or in government lands, or in a right secured to the people by law. Public nuisance includes not only unlawful conduct on private property but also a continuing use of property for unlawful or unreasonable acts with public consequences as well as persistent conduct that is not associated with real property but can still create a harm or risk of harm to the public health, safety, or convenience. The nuisance laws of some states limit standing to complain of a public nuisance only to a government, or to a person whose interests or property are significantly harmed in a manner distinct from members of the public generally.

*See also:* public.

**drug house (crack house or meth house)**   A house used for drug sales. A drug house is a residence used as a location to manufacture or sell controlled drugs like, in the case of a crack house, crack cocaine. Similarly, meth houses are used for the sale of methamphetamines. Such houses attract buyers, sellers, and competitors, all of whom are engaged in illegal practices and many of whom engage in acts of violence and theft. A crack house is a public nuisance, as are all dwellings or buildings used for the sale or group consumption of illegal drugs. Maintaining or supporting a drug house is a crime in many jurisdictions independent of the property's status as a nuisance.

See also: drug (drugs).

**sic utere tuo ut alienum non laedas**   Use your lands so as not to injure your neighbor's. Sic utere tuo, ut alienum non laedas is the maxim that defines the obligation underlying common-law nuisance, so that if one uses one's lands in such a manner that a neighbor's use of land is harmed, the interfering use is a nuisance. More than a mere basis of trespass, the maxim is essential for an understanding of the common law in the United States throughout the nineteenth and early twentieth centuries, summarized by the colloquial maxim, "live, and let live." This approach is directly challenged by the Coase theorem, which would give no premium to the use that was prior in time or to the non-intruding use of the land.

See also: Coase theorem.

**temporary nuisance**   A non-continuous nuisance. A temporary nuisance is a use of property that interferes with the use or enjoyment of another's property, though only for a time or intermittently. A temporary nuisance may be abated, its future use may be enjoined, and damages may be collected for past injuries.

**nul**   No, or none. Nul is a law French term that makes negative whatever it modifies. Nul signifies that there is none of something.

**nulle poene sine legis**   See: nullum, nullum poene sine legis (nulle poene sine legis).

**nullification**   To ignore a law or obligation. Nullification is the treatment of an obligation or condition as if it were not worthy of obedience or recognition. It is treating a law, contract, or another obligation with complete disregard rather than with compliance. Note: annulment and nullification are similar but differ in that annulment is an act made with authority over an obligation to consider it void ab initio. Nullification is ordinarily not committed by one with authority to repeal or release the obligation.

See also: annulment, marital annulment (declaration of invalidity of marriage).

**nullity**   Something that does not exist. A nullity is nonexistent, being anything that is impossible as a matter of law when its creation is attempted, or that has become impossible to exist or maintain as a matter of law. A nullity includes any obligation that has become void, such that once the obligation is satisfied or extinguished, it is then a nullity.

See also: void (voidability, voidable).

**null (null and void)**   Having no legal effect. Anything that is null in the law is nonexistent as a matter of law. An obligation that is null is one that does not exist. Note: an obligation that is void may have once existed but does no longer, so to say some duty is null and void is technically contradictory or redundant (depending on the circumstances. Nevertheless, its resonance is still quite satisfying to many drafters, so it is often used to describe a situation in which there is no obligation or liability.

## nullum

**nullum crimen sine lege (legality principle or principle of legality)**   No act is criminal unless it was prohibited by law. Nullum crimen sine lege, Latin for "no crime without law," is the civil law prohibition on the retroactive criminalization of prior conduct. In effect, the maxim amounts to a prohibition on ex post facto laws.

See also: ex, ex post facto (ex post facto law).

**nullum poene sine legis (nulle poene sine legis)**   No act can be punished unless it was prohibited by law. Nulle poene sine legis, Latin for "no punishment without law," is a civilian maxim barring punishment for acts that were not criminal as a matter of statute at the time of their commission. The maxim differs from "nulle crimen" in its emphasis on punishment rather than on prohibition or declaration.

**nullum tempus**   Statutes of limitations do not bar civil claims brought by the state. Nullum tempus is an abbreviation of the Latin maxim nullum tempus occurit regis (which means "no time runs against the king"), according to which the statute of limitations does not run against the sovereign. This maxim underlies the doctrine that one cannot acquire property by adverse possession over lands held by a government.

**numbers running**   See: gaming, running the numbers (numbers running).

**numerosity**   See: class, class action, class, numerosity.

**numquamdebitatus**   See: assumpsit, indebitatus assumpsit (numquamdebitatus).

**nunc pro tunc**   To give retroactive effect to an order, judgment, or instrument. Nunc pro tunc designates the backdating of an instrument or order for the purpose of giving it retroactive effect. A judgment entered nunc pro tunc is presumed to have been already in effect from some earlier time when it ought to have been entered. The phrase, Latin for "now for then," ought to be reserved for a later ministerial entry that reflects an earlier action, rather than an attempt at a completely retroactive action.

**nuncupative will**   *See:* will, last will and testament, nuncupative will (oral will or noncupative will).

**nuptial (nuptials)**   Related to the act of marriage. Nuptial is a term for the attributes of marriage, and nuptials refers to the acts committed during a marriage ceremony.

*See also:* marriage (marital).

**post nuptial (ante-nuptial or pre-nuptial or post-nuptial or postnuptial)**   Occurring after (or before) matrimony. Post-nuptial refers to anything that occurs following the moment of marriage. Likewise, pre-nuptial or ante-nuptial refers to anything done prior to the moment of marriage.

A post-nuptial agreement is any agreement between a husband and wife entered into during or after a marriage, often referring to a property settlement reached in contemplation of divorce or during its process. On the other hand, an ante-nuptial agreement is made between the parties prior to wedlock.

**Nuremburg defense or good sergeant defense or lawful order defense**   *See:* war, law of war, war crime, superior order (Nuremburg defense or good sergeant defense or lawful order defense).

**Nuremburg Trials or IMT or IMTN**   *See:* court, international court, international military tribunal, international military tribunal, Nuremberg (Nuremburg Trials or IMT or IMTN).

**nurse (nursing)**   A person licensed to provide nursing or medical care. A nurse is a person licensed by the state to provide the medical care expected of a nurse or nurse–practitioner. Nurses manage patients and a variety of aspects of medical practice, and nurse–practioners are licensed to provide a variety of medical examinations and services in a nursing environment, which is usually centered on patient care.

*See also:* medicine (healing arts).

**nursing home (convalescent home)**   A facility for the long-term care of patients. A nursing home is a state–licensed facility for the long-term care of patients under a long-term program of medical care, observation, and assistance. Nursing homes may provide a range of care, from acute, active care attended by nurses and physicians to monitored, reactive care attended by non–medical staff.

**nurture (nurturing)**   The care and education of a child. To nurture anything or anyone is to provide care during its initial years. The legal conditions for parental fitness require that the parent or guardian nurture the child, providing care, emotional, material, and financial support, and education appropriate to the child's age and needs. The parent with custody is presumed to nurture the child over whom the parent has custody, regardless of what other children may also be nurtured by the parent. A custodial parent who does not provide adequate nurturing may lose custody for this reason alone.

*See also:* neglect, child neglect.

**nutrition**   The effects of food on the body. Nutrition is the sum of the effects of food (or an absence of food) in the development, maintenance, performance, physical health, mental health, and pathologies of an organism. Nutrition is particularly concerned with elements of food, such as vitamins, minerals, fiber, fats, carbohydrates, and calories as all of these affect the body of the consumer. Though the term is usually applied to human beings, animal nutrition and plant nutrition are correlative assessments of the inputs of food on the body of the animal or parts of the plant.

> Probably you will find as I do, that ideas are not difficult,
> that the trouble is in the words in which they are expressed.
>
> Oliver Wendell Holmes, Jr., Letter to Dr. John Wu (May 14, 1923),
> in *Justice Holmes to Dr. Wu: An Intimate Correspondence, 1921-1932* 11
> (Central Book Co., 1947).

# O

**o** The fifteenth letter of the modern English alphabet. "O" signifies a variety of functions as a symbol and as a designation of status. It is translated into Oscar for radio signals and NATO military transmissions, into Ocean for some police radio traffic, and into dash, dash, dash in Morse Code.

**o as an abbreviation** A word commencing in O. When used as an abbreviation, O often stands for Ohio. It may also stand for occupational, office, officer, official, oil, Oklahoma, old, omnibus, Ontario, opinion, order, orders, ordinance, Oregon, organization, overdose, and overrulled. When used as the first letter of an author's name or case reporter, it may stand for O'Brien, Ohio Reports, Olliver, Ollivier, Ontario Reports, Oregon Reports, Orlando, and Otto.

**o as in hypotheticals** The owner. O often stands for the owner, usually the true owner, of property in the story of a legal hypothetical. In property stories, O is often the first character and A is usually the second character, receiving property from O (as in "O to A for life then B"). More than likely, O here is traditionally not an English O but a Greek omicron, though there is no difference in appearance.

**O₃** *See:* pollution, air pollution, criteria pollutants, ozone ($O_3$).

**OASDI** *See:* Social Security, Old Age Survivors and Disability Insurance (OASDI).

**oath** A solemn, public acceptance of a public duty. An oath is the basis of a public obligation that arises from two aspects of its making, in that an oath is both a personal acceptance of a duty and a solemn promise made in public (or at least before a witness) to perform it in good faith. Oaths are required by law and are enforced, in part, by law. No person may offer testimony in court or take a public legal office, including the office of attorney at law, without first taking an oath of office.

Oaths once universally incorporated an invocation to God as surety of the oath, in that the omniscient divinity would know of a violation of the oath, even if the violation were a secret to all others, and would punish the violation, whether during life or after death. In the United States, such language is now usually omitted from oaths required by law, and its use in admission to public office may violate the Religious Tests Clause. Both the United States and the several states allow an individual required to take an oath to take instead an affirmation, which amounts to the same declaration and promises but with no residual implication of religious obligation.

Oaths are rarely subject to enforcement beyond the determination of the oath-taker to interpret the obligations of the oath and to abide by them. Even so, oaths are subject to enforcement as a matter of law. The violation of a testimonial oath is subject to punishment as perjury. Oaths of office, with or without reliance on interpretation or extrapolation through additional rules of conduct, may be the basis for enforcement by disciplinary panels within the legal profession as well as by courts and legislatures.

*See also:* solemnity (solemn or solemnize or solemnization); oath, oath of attorney (attorney oath); pledge; discretion, judicial discretion (discretion of the court or sound discretion); oath, uplifted hand (hand uplifted or raised hand); term, term of office.

**administration** Oaths are administered by a person empowered to do so by law according to the jurisdiction for which the oath is administered. Unless specified by statute, an oath cannot be self-administered. Those empowered to administer oaths include judges and justices, chief executives, members of a legislature for matters within that legislature, a commissioned officer for matters affecting the military, and, for most purposes, a notary public, clerk of court, bailiff, or court reporter.

**oath as basis of discipline** *See:* lawyer, lawyer discipline, disciplinary rules, oath as basis of discipline.

**oath of attorney** *See:* bar, admission to the bar, oath of attorney.

**Oath or Affirmation Clause** *See:* constitution, U.S. Constitution, clauses, Oath or Affirmation Clause (Oath Clause or Affirmation Clause or Oath of Office Clause).

**loyalty oath** A statement of loyalty to a state, association, or cause. A loyalty oath is any statement that includes a promise of loyalty and a promise not to harm or attempt to overthrow a nation, state, association, or other entity. The forms of loyalty oaths vary widely, and many have statements of reverence for values or symbols associated with the object of the loyalty being promised.

In the United States, public and private employers have required loyalty oaths as a condition of commencing or retaining employment in certain positions or occupations. Such oaths are usually promises not to engage in the overthrow of the government by violent means, not to incite or encourage others to do so, and not to associate with organizations that promote such actions. Some oaths require more, including promises to engage in active resistance to such efforts at overthrow by others and the renunciation of affiliations with the Communist party or other groups. The use of such oaths by public employers is constitutional, as long as the oath is neither overbroad nor overly vague as to what is promised nor an unjustifiable burden on the freedoms of speech or association. Private employers may employ such oaths without regard to the First Amendment.

*See also:* association, freedom of association | 4. loyalty oaths.

**Oath of Allegiance (naturalization oath)** The oath of a naturalized U.S. citizen. The Oath of Allegiance is required of all adult immigrants at the time U.S. citizenship is conferred. The oath must be administered in a public ceremony, unless a court orders an expedited ceremony for good cause, or unless the Attorney General excuses the oath owing to the youth, disability, or impairment of the individual. At the time of the oath, a person holding a title of nobility from a foreign sovereign must renounce the title.

In general, an oath of allegiance may be taken by any person to demonstrate allegiance to any sovereign. Not all such oaths require the expression of repudiation of a former allegiance, and when such dual allegiance is allowed by each sovereign, no implied renunciation occurs by the taking of such an oath.

*See also:* naturalization.

**oath of attorney (attorney oath)** A solemn pledge required for admission to the bar. An attorney's oath is the fundamental condition of any person to be admitted to the practice of law. The specific requirements of this oath vary from court to court and jurisdiction to jurisdiction. The oath creates both moral and legal obligations, and its enforcement is left to the inherent power of the courts and the bar as well as to the attorney's conscience.

*See also:* oath; lawyer, lawyer discipline, disciplinary rules, oath as basis of discipline.

**statement under oath (sworn statement or unsworn statement)** Testimony in a trial or deposition, or an affidavit or sworn statement. A statement under oath is a statement made following the writer's or before a speaker's subscription of an oath that swears or affirms the truth of the statement. Such statements are usually made in testimony at trial or in a hearing of record in court, in testimony in a deposition, in an affidavit, or in a sworn statement made as a matter of record and submitted to a public agency. The knowing presentation of false information in a statement under oath is perjury.

An unsworn statement is any statement not made under oath, whether in a proceeding in which an oath might be expected or in some other context. Although perjury does not usually apply to a knowing mistruth in an unsworn statement, such a statement given to the police or a public officer may constitute a distinct offense.

**swearing (swear out or sworn)** To take or to administer an oath. Swearing is the process of taking an oath, and the same word is used to depict the administration of an oath. Owing to the requirement that many pleadings and warrants be made according to an oath that their contents are true, the creation of such instruments is also known by the shorthand of "swearing out," as a police officer might swear out a warrant or a victim swears out a criminal information. Interestingly, an official who administers an oath, particularly to a witness or officer, "swears in" the oath-taker. A person who has taken such an oath is then said to be sworn.

**uplifted hand (hand uplifted or raised hand)** By custom, a person taking an oath raises one hand. The customary posture while taking an oath is to raise one's hand, usually the right hand, in front and to the side of the body. There are several theories as to how this customary procedure arose, with Bouvier claiming that it had been copied from the early form of defendant identification, and others suggesting that it is a reference to the divine. Depictions of oaths in classical culture, however, suggest that the posture predates these rationales. The practice may have originated from a signal of solemnity or allegiance, but it persists mainly as the customary signal of oath taking.

*See also:* oath.

**obedience (disobedience)** Compliance with an order or rule. Obedience is compliance with a requirement for action or inaction from an authority. Obedience takes two general forms: obedience to an order and obedience to a rule. Obedience to an order is the compliance with an order that is given to the obedient person by an individual in authority over that person, whether the order is general and directed to all persons in a community, including the obedient person, or the order is specifically directed toward and delivered to that person. Obedience to a rule requires compliance with the rules, usually without regard to whether the compliant aspect of the behavior is intended or unintended. Obedience demands that a required act be done or a forbidden act not be done, and no motive of compliance with the rule is usually required.

The interpretation of both orders and rules is, at least potentially, a matter of ambiguity. In the case of orders, either the authority issuing the order or an intermediary is usually capable of interpreting the order as needed to apply it to a specific case, but when that is not so, some degree of latitude is required for the person obeying to interpret the order or to determine how to comply with it. In the case of obedience to a rule, such interpretative discretion is usually vested more in officials than in the person obeying them, leaving the person obeying the officials (or attempting to do so) at the mercy of the discretion of the rule-interpreting official.

A perennial difficulty of compliance is to ascertain the mental state of the complying party. Some theorists argue that obedience requires knowing and willful conformity, while others claim that it requires no more than consonant behavior. Obedience does not, per se, require that the compliance with an order or rule be voluntary. The compliant behavior may, indeed, be coerced or at least manipulated and still be obedience. Therefore, obedience might or might not be a question answered by a single step between obedience and disobedience. Rather, there are degrees of obedience that turn on the voluntariness, independence of motive, speed of compliance, and sufficiency of compliance that allow a continuum of more or less obedience.

Disobedience is a failure of obedience, which is best understood as a degree of obedience that is insufficient in light of the circumstances. In many cases disobedience is clear, because the conduct of the person who would be obedient is so contrary to the order or rule that no further consideration is needed. Yet many cases are ambiguous, the clarity of an initial order being muddied by the problems of interpretation, application to specific circumstances, avoidance of patently unintended consequences, delay in compliance, etc.

*See also:* discretion; compliance (comply).

**civil disobedience**   A breach of the law to demonstrate its injustice. Civil disobedience is the purposeful violation of a law in order to invite punishment that will demonstrate the inequity or injustice in the legal prohibition that is violated. By definition, civil disobedience is non-violent and is directed against laws that are so unfair, unjust, or inequitable that the enforcement of these laws against peaceful resistors will provoke a moral repugnance among observers. Civil disobedience is therefore not a defense to a criminal charge or a means of avoiding punishment, as the whole point of civil disobedience is to invite the punishment in order to demonstrate its injustice. Henry David Thoreau argued that civil disobedience is a moral duty to disobey unjust laws, an argument promoted in the work of Mahatma Gandhi and Dr. Martin Luther King.

**moral duty to obey the law (duty to obey the law or obligation to obey the law)**   Each person has a moral obligation to obey the law. The moral duty to obey the law, as a matter of legal theory and moral philosophy, is a moral obligation to comply with the rule of law and to support the officials of the legal system in the performance of their duties. Socrates and Thomas Hobbes are associated with an absolute view, that the citizen has an obligation to support the law regardless of its errors or immorality: the duty exists without regard to the morality of the law's requirements or the conduct of the officials. Legal theorists debate this argument, but the consensus now is that the person subject to the law has a moral obligation to obey the law but only when the law meets certain moral criteria, such as the claim that the law provides greater support and protection for the individual than would exist otherwise. Different forms of this view are associated with St. Thomas Aquinas and John Locke. From that perspective, there is no absolute duty to obey the laws, but there is a prima facie obligation

to obey the laws, which is only rebutted when the laws are in some general way unjust, or they do not promote the freedom, equality, or dignity of the subjects as a whole. Specific and limited instances of injustice, repression, inequality, or degradation, however, do not rebut the presumption in favor of a duty to obey the law.

The general obligation to obey the law is sometimes contrasted with the obligation of civil disobedience, that the citizen might have a moral obligation to disobey a law that is unjust, especially to bring notice of its injustice to others to cause officials to change it. These two approaches can be reconciled by recognizing that the law may be obeyed generally but disobeyed specifically and by arguing that the law is more likely to be obeyed in general if its unjust aspects are cured.

*See also:* ethics (ethical); morality (moral); obedience, civil disobedience.

**willful disobedience**   The intentional defiance of an order, regulation, or rule. Willful disobedience is an action or deliberate inaction known by the actor to be contrary to an order or rule. Willful disobedience requires the specific intent to disobey a lawful order, regulation, or rule, so the rule must have existed before the action or inaction, it must have been known to the defendant, and the defendant must have been capable of obedience.

**obesity**   Excess body weight that harms a person's health. Obesity is the condition of accumulated body fat in a proportion to the body that is sufficiently great to cause additional harm to the person's health. Social Security regulations have sometimes listed obesity as an impairment justifying supplemental relief, but more recently consider obesity to be only one factor in a multiple impairment analysis. The Social Security definition relies on a height-to-weight ratio that determines obesity per se, which is a disability if further conditions compound the danger posed by the weight of the person alone. Some insurers consider obesity to be a pre-existing medical condition.

**obiter dictum or dicta**   *See:* opinion, judicial opinion, dictum (obiter dictum or dicta).

**objection (object or objectionable)**   A complaint that an error is or will be made. An objection is a challenge filed by a counsel or a party to some aspect of the proceedings of the court or to a motion or other action by the opposing counsel or party. A properly made objection states the aspect of the proceeding or motion, etc., to which the objection is made, as well as stating the grounds for the objection — the legal authority for claiming that the proceedings, motion, etc., are proceeding (or are about to proceed) in a manner that is contrary to justice, to the law, to the court rules, or a prior order of the court.

After a party objects to an action, the court will usually hear the argument of the objecting party, then hear the argument of the responding party, and then sometimes hear the reply of the objecting party. The arguments may be dispensed with during trial when the nature of the objection and its arguments are clear to the judge and to counsel. In either case, the objection is either granted or denied. If the objection is granted, the court may require some remedy for an error already made or merely prevent the error from occurring. Whether the objection is granted or denied, the party whose argument loses may move to record an exception to the ruling, which preserves the issue underlying the motion for appeal by that party.

In most instances, an objection must be made at the time of the purported error. If an objection is not timely raised, the court is denied the opportunity to correct any error that occurs, and so the objection is deemed (on most matters) to be waived. Only on fundamental errors may the non-objecting party raise an appeal on a matter that was waived in a lower court. Thus, a party must object to every order, decision, or event in the case (whether it occurs before, during, or after trial) that the party believes is in error and has caused harm to its interest or to justice. If the party fails to object, most issues are presumed to be waived and not later subject to appeal or cross-appeal. Even so, counsel should take care, as courts may discipline lawyers who raise frivolous or needlessly repetitive or trivial objections, particularly during the testimony of a witness, in order to distract the witness or the finder of fact or to vex opposing counsel.

Note: in this sense, the verb "object" is pronounced with the emphasis on the second syllable and with the initial "o" sounded in a softer sound nearer to the "uh" sound. When object is pronounced with a full soft "o" and with the accent on the first syllable, the word is the noun meaning a focus or a thing.

*See also:* motion (movant or move); exception, exception as record of objection.

**continuing objection (durable objection or running objection or standing objection)** An objection made to an act in trial that is meant to extend to a similar subsequent act. A continuing objection is an objection stated at one point in a trial as both an objection to the aspect of the trial then at hand and a new objection to each time such an aspect of the trial is repeated. For instance, if counsel objects to the opposing counsel's introduction of a statement from a deposition, and it appears that more statements from the deposition are to be introduced, the objecting counsel may enter a continuing objection, preserving an exception to alleged error with every statement yet to be made. This saves the court's time and allows the objecting counsel to preserve the exception without having to make a new objection on the same grounds for each new but similar statement from the same deposition. A continuing objection is only in order if the evidence or proceeding objected to is substantially the same in each later instance as the subject of the initial objection, and the grounds of the objection to each later instance are the same. A party raising a continuing objection does not have a right to such an objection, and it is in

the court's discretion to allow or deny a continuing objection. In the absence of a continuing objection on the record, counsel must renew its objection with every new iteration of the initially objected procedure.

**no objection** An express waiver of an objection. No objection is a statement made by a party or counsel at a moment in a trial, hearing, deposition, or other proceeding at which an objection might ordinarily be made, but at which time the party or counsel determines not to raise an objection. If the party expressly waives an objection, only a fundamental error will allow the issue to be reviewed at a later stage.

*See also:* waiver, express waiver.

**renewal of objection** *See:* renewal (renew or renewability or renewable or renewed or non-renewable).

**topical objection (topic objection)** An objection to all evidence on a given topic. A topical objection is an objection to all evidence on a given topic, regardless of the source. For example, a topical objection made regarding the use of tangible evidence to prove a point on a given topic would apply to the later introduction of other tangible evidence or to witness testimony that would attempt to prove the same point. A topical objection is similar to a continuing objection, and it will create an exception in the record only when the court in its discretion allows the party to make a topical objection. Topical objections made in a pretrial conference or similar venue are generally in order.

*See also:* objection, continuing objection (durable objection or running objection or standing objection).

**vexatious objection (baseless objection or frivolous objection)** A meritless objection made to distract the court or the opponent. A vexatious objection is an objection made for the purpose of annoying the opposing counsel or party, the witness, the jury, or the court. There may be tactical, though improper, reasons for counsel to pursue such an apparently self-defeating course, not the least being to disrupt and obscure the evidence. Such motions may be grounds for contempt of court.

A frivolous motion differs from a vexatious motion, in that a frivolous motion is baseless or trivial but not apparently animated by the desire to burden the court or an opponent. A baseless objection is an objection for which there is no valid argument under the law.

**objective (objective standard or objectivity)** Evaluated from an impersonal point of view. Anything objective is understood from the view of an impersonal observer who weighs all of the considerations and data that could be considered evidence, without prior opinion or bias. Objectivity, with its emphasis on the object perceived, is a standard of evaluating a situation, action, text, or anything else to determine its significance without reference to the knowledge or beliefs that a single observer might have in considering it. Objectivity is the basis for reasonableness generally, and although a reasonable person would be expected to act on information or beliefs that person actually holds, a reasonable assessment of that action in light of the information and belief requires an objective evaluation of it.

There are many questions of law in which consideration by an objective approach requires evidence of an objective nature, evidence that could be used for an objective evaluation, which includes nearly everything except a person's opinion or individual conclusions or assessment of data. Objective evidence of a person's understanding or expectation is evidence of that person's conduct or of physical events in the world that would have been manifest to observers, as opposed to evidence of a subjective understanding or expectation, which would be manifest in recorded expressions or later testimony of memories of what the person knew, believed, or felt at the relevant time. Objectivity is a requirement in a variety of other questions of law beyond evidence. For example, an objective assessment or review is one in which the person, entity, or group by assessed by performance toward a goal that is evaluated by means over which the people evaluated have no control.

*See also:* contract, contract interpretation, objective theory of contracts; reasonable (reasonableness); subjective (subjectivity or subjective standard).

**objective interpretation of contracts**  *See:* contract, contract interpretation, plain meaning (objective interpretation of contracts).

**objective theory of contracts**  *See:* contract, contract interpretation, objective theory of contracts.

**oblation**  A donation to the church. An oblation is a donation to the church of money, property, or, more generally, service. Money given in an offertory is an oblation as are rents received from church lands, because they are inherently the fruits of a former donation.

**obligation (oblige or obligator or obligee or obligor)**  A duty to do or refrain from any course of conduct. An obligation is a duty to do something or not to do anything, whether the duty arises from a promise or a circumstance, and whether the justification for the duty is found in norms arising from the following: local culture, such as a particular courtesy like tipping one's hat; society generally, such as an obligation in a community, like waiting one's turn in a queue or line; morality or ethics, like a swimmer's duty to rescue a drowning person; or from the law alone, such as the obligation not to sell Washington state sweet cherries measuring on average less than 61/64 of an inch. Obligations may or may not be enforceable by third parties, although, in general, all legal obligations are enforceable in equity or in law.

More specifically in law, obligation is synonymous with most duties arising from contracts, from the general duties against the creation of torts, from property covenants and conveyances, from criminal and civil procedure, from professional and fiduciary responsibilities, and, in some cases, for officials from administrative,

constitutional, and international law. An obligation in any commercial or contractual sense is usually a requirement to pay money or perform a service. An obligation is also the name for several particular forms of debt that are memorialized in commercial paper, and these obligations are dealt with more fully as securities and negotiable instruments. An obligation regarding a debt manifests the obligation of the debtor to pay, and so a note is from the obligor (or the debtor) to the obligee (or the creditor or the creditor's assignee, at least initially).

*See also:* duty.

**obligation of contracts**  *See:* contract, obligation of contracts.

**obligation to disclose adverse authority**  *See:* ethics, legal ethics, obligation to disclose adverse authority (ethical duty of candor).

**mutuality of obligation**  Something given or offered by each party to a contract. Mutuality of obligation is the this-for-that character of the promises made by each party to a valid contract, the condition by which the consideration offered by each is sufficient for the consideration offered by the other.

*See also:* mutuality (mutual).

**oblique**  An indirect reference. An oblique reference is a reference that, literally, does not lead directly to the idea the reference is meant to represent or evoke. An oblique reference may be a euphemism, an incomplete reference, a vague expression, a metaphor that is loosely drawn, or some other means of evocative but indirect reference to an idea.

**obloquy**  Condemnation or censure. Obloquy is a social charge of wrong or evil, a censure of a person or entity for perceived foul conduct that can be public or private. Obloquy is a form of damage, and a person who suffers obloquy as a result of defamation has suffered harm.

**obnoxious (obnoxiousness)**  Irritating, distracting, and potentially harmful. Obnoxiousness is a characteristic of a person, thing, or condition that causes harm, irritation, or distraction to a person, entity, the environment, or some other thing. The term represents a continuum of inconvenience, which ranges from a mere distraction, such as a buzzing insect, to a great danger, such as a poisonous gas. Though this range may apply to any obnoxious agency, certain usages are common in the law. An obnoxious person is probably bothersome, rude, and irritating but is only harmful to an individual's reputation if the person is the individual's friend or colleague. Obnoxious conditions of property are the stuff of nuisance, interfering with another's use of property, particularly through a strong smell or toxic emission. Obnoxious chemicals or smells are effectively indistinguishable from noxious chemicals or smells. Obnoxious animals are pests or vermin. Note: the term "obnoxious" has evolved and earlier meanings are commonly found in legal materials, particularly in quotations from common-law sources, in which the term initially meant a tendency to be harmed (or the condition of being harmed), and then came to mean having a tendency to cause harm (or the person or thing causing a relatively serious harm).

*See also:* noxious.

**obscenity (obscene)**   Sexualized speech or conduct that offends or harms without sufficient justification. Obscenity is a characteristic of speech or conduct that involves sex or the body of one or more humans or animals; that disgusts, shocks, or offends the sensibilities of those who might encounter it in a community; that appeals (or is intended to appeal) to a person's visceral sexual interest; and that lacks any justification arising from a political, literary, artistic, or scientific value of the speech or conduct. This understanding, from Miller v. California, 413 U.S. 15 (1973), is a constitutional limit within which states and the federal government may regulate obscene speech or conduct. There are many areas of controversy within this definition, including the scope and membership of a community.

Within the constitutional limit of obscenity, the government may more narrowly define conduct that is prohibited or regulated as obscene, including the display of parts of the body in public, the performance or depiction of sexual acts in public, and the performance or depiction of sexual acts in view of children or non-consenting adults for any purpose related to the sexual interests of those involved.

A recurrent argument regarding the scope of obscenity is the requirement that obscene matter be related to sexual or bodily functions. The term has a more general meaning synonymous with disgust, particularly the disgust that arises from waste or excess. As a basis for the regulation of speech and conduct, gratuitous acts or depictions of violence carried out for the amusement of participants or onlookers may be considered obscene, though this view is controversial.

*See also:* pornography (erotica or porn or porno); speech, freedom of speech | 2. Indecency v. Obscenity; lasciviousness (lascivious or lasciviously); speech, freedom of speech (right of free speech or liberty of speech); speech, freedom of speech, low-value speech.

*obscenity and offensiveness*   An act or image may be offensive but not obscene. Obscenity is an aspect of speech, action, or images that is unjustified, harmful or offensive, relates to sex or the body, and appeals to a visceral sexual interest. Thus an act, speech, or image might be offensive and might arise from conduct relating to sex or the body but still not be obscene because the conduct does not appeal to a visceral sexual interest or impulse. Rude gestures and epithets, for instance, may invoke the body or sexuality but have no element of sexual attraction at all, which makes them offensive but not obscene. Even so, offensive speech, actions, and images may be regulable or actionable within carefully defined limits that protect free speech and due process, regardless of their potential for being obscene.

**Comstock law**   Statutes banning immoral publications and materials. A Comstock law is a federal statute or any state law modeled after the Comstock Act, also known as An Act for the Suppression of Trade in, and Circulation of, Obscene Literature and Articles of Immoral Use, 17 Stat. 598 (March 3, 1873). It made the creating, selling, lending, or using of items "of an immoral nature" a federal crime with the punishment of a fine and imprisonment of up to five years at hard labor. Mailing any "obscene, lewd or lascivious" materials or anything of "an indecent or immoral use of nature" could result in a fine and ten years at hard labor. These definitions included contraceptives and information related to abortion. The statute was popularly named for Anthony Comstock, the postal inspector who created the New York Society for the Prevention of Vice. Other state laws followed that barred the sale and possession of such material.

In general, the prohibition of the sale of obscene material or immoral devices, particularly devices intended for sexual gratification, remains constitutional. There are problems in some statutes of vagueness, and the statutes may not reach strictly private, non-commercial, consensual sexual conduct between adults.

*See also:* prostitution, Mann Act (interstate transportation).

**Miller test (Miller standard)**   The three-step assessment of speech that is regulable as obscene. The Miller test is the three-part test articulated by the U.S. Supreme Court in Miller v. California, 413 U.S. 15, 24–25 (1973), for assessing speech as a constitutional matter to determine if it is obscene and thus unprotected by the First Amendment. The first step of the test is whether the average person, applying contemporaneous community standards, would find that the work taken as a whole appeals to a prurient interest. The second step is whether the work as a whole or the speech under consideration depicts acts, objects, or parts of the body in a patently offensive manner and whether those acts, objects, or parts are defined by law in the relevant jurisdiction to be obscene. The final step is whether the work, taken as a whole, lacks serious artistic, literary, scientific or political value.

The community that is relevant is left to the finder of fact to determine, and is thus not inherently a geographic area as a matter of federal law. The second step is really two tests, whether the things depicted are forbidden by law and whether they are depicted in a manner that is apparently and objectively likely to offend. By examining the speech in a work taken as a whole, the Court made clear that even works which may depict some material considered by some to be obscene or offensive in nature were still worthy of First Amendment protection.

The Miller test has been incorporated into many state statutes regulating or prohibiting obscene material.

*See also:* prurience (prurient interest).

**contemporary community standards of obscenity (community standards of obscenity)**   The community considered relevant by the finder of fact in a given obscenity case. The Miller test requires that in order for allegedly obscene matter to be considered obscene, it must be considered so according to a community standard. The community is not, however, a single village, city, or region. Rather, the community is an abstraction imagined by the finder of fact that varies according to the nature of the matter in issue and its means of dissemination. For matter that is nationally distributed, the nation may be the community that matters, and for matter displayed on a single billboard in a rural town with only local roads, some sense of that community and those who might travel through it is appropriate. Yet in neither case is the community a discernible locale whose residents may be surveyed or somehow consulted, because that is not the purpose of the test. The function of the concept of community is for the finder of fact to assess the allegedly obscene matter from a relatively objective point of view, not from the point of view the finder of fact might personally take. A relatively objective view is not one of pure reasonableness or utter objectivity, but is instead a view that attempts to aggregate the likely view of others within a single cultural framework, which is hypothesized by the finder of fact.

**observance (observe as of a duty)**　To comply knowingly with a law or obligation. Observance, in the sense of a duty, is to perform the duty and to do so knowingly, rather than as a matter of coincidence. Thus one observes an obligation whether it is created by law, custom, courtesy, religion, or special arrangement in a deliberate or routine manner according to the obligation, not merely as a coincidence. In this sense, a holiday or ceremony, such as a moment of silence, is observed by an act made with the intent to comply with its significance or at least the conformity of others, such that a person quiet in such a moment because the person is asleep would not be thought to observe the ceremonial silence. Note: observation is sometimes used as a synonym for observance, an unfortunate confusion derived from both words having "observe" as their verb forms.

*See also:* compliance (comply).

**observation (observe as witness)**　The perception of an event or condition. Observation is the recognition of something observed, and this concept takes several distinct forms that are expressed in the term "observed." A person's act of perceiving an event, a person's thought by which a condition or idea is understood, or a person's statement of the understanding of the condition or idea are each observations. Thus a witness may observe a defendant sitting in a courtroom by perceiving the witness. The prosecutor may observe to herself that the witness has a startled reaction by forming a memory of that event and her interpretation of it. The prosecutor may observe to the jury that the witness acted as if the witness recognized the defendant by recounting that memory and interpretation aloud to the jury.

Note: observation was once used in the sense of observance. This usage is now less common, and though "observe" may be used in either sense, the phrase "observance of a duty arising from a custom or law" is less confusing to most readers than would be "observation of the custom or law."

*See also:* witness, eyewitness (eye witness); observance (observe as of a duty).

**obsolescence (obsolete)**　Unsuitability due to being out of date. Obsolescence is the disuse or diminished value of any thing that arises from its age or from differences with subsequently created things of similar or related functions. There are innumerable illustrations in general usage. For example, a product like the slide rule, which is replaced by or incompatible with later products, is obsolete for most purposes. An idea like phrenology, that is superseded by other ideas, is obsolete, as is a style like disco, that is superseded by other styles. In all of these cases, obsolescence is reflected in market valuation. Still, obsolescence may be impermanent, and old products, ideas, and techniques are frequently revived from obsolescence.

As a matter of law, property that is obsolete is less valuable that non-obsolete property and is subject to diminished taxation. Obsolescence may be established by functional obsolescence, in which the property is inherently unusable or less functional owing to age, wear, or decay, or it may be established by economic or external obsolescence, in which the market for the property declines, and so its value diminishes.

A law may itself be obsolete in several ways. A statute may depend for its enforcement or significance on other statutes that are repealed, a statute may depend upon events of a date that has passed, or a statute may be drafted to be enforced by an agency that is later abolished and not replaced. These are constructively lapsed statutes and generally unenforceable. More fundamentally, the purpose of some statutes or common-law principles may have been lost over time, such that enforcement of the statute or principle would serve no rational contemporary purpose and would violate the due process of law.

**obstruction**　An interference with any process or activity. Obstruction is the act of interfering with an activity of any form, as well as any thing that has the effect of obstructing such activities. For example, an obstruction in a roadway or navigable channel restricts or prevents traffic, and an obstruction in a part of the body inhibits or prevents the flow of fluids or gases through that part of the body.

**obstruction of justice**　Interfering with the administration of the courts, police, or a regulatory agency. Obstruction of justice is a broad term for conduct that interferes with any aspect of the system of justice, including any act that interferes with or endeavors to interfere with: an investigation, prosecution, administrative process, or trial; the police, agencies, prosecutors, or courts; their personnel or offices; or the witnesses, parties, or evidence that may be relevant to such proceedings. Examples include tampering with evidence, intimidation of a witness, interference with the service of a warrant, failure to obey a lawful order, and knowingly providing false information to a police officer. As of 2009, Chapter 73 of title 18 in the United States Code contained eighteen sections defining specific crimes of obstruction, including attempting to influence a juror or officer of the court; tampering with a witness, victim, or informant; obstructing a federal criminal investigation; obstructing state or local law enforcement in a gambling law enforcement action; the destruction of records or evidence; obstructing investigations or audits; threatening or retaliating against a witness, victim, or informant; assaulting a process server; and recording a grand jury proceeding.

**road obstruction (obstructing a public way)**  Any thing or conduct that limits traffic on a road or public way. An obstruction of a public way, or the obstruction of a road, is anything or any activity that limits the use of the road or the way for travel. A physical encroachment, such as a parked vehicle, left object, or barrier is an obstruction. An activity such as a pedestrian march, a crowd of people, or a single person refusing to move is also an obstruction. Note: an obstruction differs from a distraction.

*See also:* pedestrian, pedestrian offense (jaywalking).

**obvious danger**  *See:* danger, patent danger (obvious danger).

**occupant (occupation or occupy or occupies or occupancy or occupier)**  The person who in fact is present on or using some property. The occupant is the person or entity who in fact makes use of some property and may or may not be an owner. In law, occupant has two distinct meanings.

A mere occupant of some premises is a person who is present upon them with no claim of ownership or possession beyond a license, invitation, or trespass. Thus, a public room may be certified to hold no more than a stated number of occupants, that number being likely to safely exit the room in the event of an emergency.

An occupant who occupies property in the sense of the law of property is a person or entity who is in actual possession of the land. Occupation of the property over time is, for instance, essential for a trespasser to establish a claim to title by adverse possession. On the other hand, occupation of private property by a governmental entity is a taking of private property governed by the takings clauses.

*See also:* possessor.

**occupation**  The use or working of any position or property. Occupation is the engagement of a person or entity with some property so that the property is used. From this sense occupation means not only the possession by a person of land but also the engagement in a job or profession as well as the military investment of a region or city.

**occupation of property**  The possession in fact of property. The occupation of property is the possession of property in fact, whether by an owner, a tenant, or a trespasser. Occupation is one of the conditions required for adverse possession.

**occupational hazard**  *See:* hazard, occupational hazard.

**Occupational Safety and Health Act**  *See:* labor, Occupational Safety And Health Act (OSHA).

**occurrence (incident)**  An event that gives rise to a liability. An occurrence is any event that gives rise to liability for the assured under an insurance contract. The occurrence includes all of the logically related actions and events that result from the initial occurrence, as well as the damages that result. An occurrence in an insurance contract is usually distinct from the claim, and policies are often structured to insure either occurrences or claims made during the time the policy is in force. A given policy may limit covered occurrences to events or causes that are specified in the contract, or it may limit covered occurrences by excluding certain types of occurrences or certain types of damages. In general, there is no difference between occurrence and incident when used in this context.

*See also:* limitation, limitation of actions, statute of limitations, occurrence rule.

**occurrence rule**  *See:* limitation, limitation of actions, statute of limitations, occurrence rule.

**ochlocracy**  *See:* government, forms of government, ochlocracy (majority rule or mobocracy or mob rule).

**Ockham's razor**  *See:* interpretation, Ockham's razor.

**odor**  *See:* smell (odor).

**of age**  *See:* age (of age).

**of counsel or special counsel**  *See:* lawyer, law firm, lawyers, counsel (of counsel or special counsel).

**of course**  *See:* course, of course.

**of record**  *See:* record, of record.

**of the UN Charter**  *See:* United Nations, United Nations Charter, Article 2(4) of the UN Charter.

**off calendar**  *See:* calendar, off calendar.

**offence**  *See:* offense (offence).

**offender**  A person who violates the law. An offender, in general, is one who commits an offense, particularly a person who is found guilty or pleads guilty to an offense under the criminal law. More specific definitions of offender are employed in statutes or contexts that limit the use of the term to offenses of specified crimes, usually of particular seriousness, or to crimes related to the subject of the statute. Thus an offender registry law may be limited to those persons who have been convicted or pled guilty to specific crimes, and an offender in this context may not include a person who has been convicted or pled guilty to a different crime.

**repeat offender**   *See:* recidivism (recidivist).

**youthful offender (juvenile offender or juvy)**   A child who is found to have committed an offense under the criminal law. A youthful offender is a person who is adjudicated as having committed an act amounting to a violation of the criminal law, but which is not considered a felony or misdemeanor because the person was under the age of criminal capacity at the time the offense was committed and has not been found fit to be tried as an adult. In most jurisdictions, a person found to have violated the criminal law while under the age of capacity is declared either a youthful offender or a juvenile delinquent, and there is no great difference between the two labels.

*See also:* delinquent, juvenile delinquent (delinquent child or juvenile delinquency).

**offense (offence)**   Any violation of the law but especially criminal law. An offense is an act that violates a duty under the criminal law, a regulation, a statute, or other statement of law creating an obligation that may be enforced by a penalty sought by the state. Although offense, generally, may refer to any violation of a regulation or criminal law, the term is sometimes used to distinguish minor offenses, such as traffic offenses or regulatory violations, from felonies and misdemeanors. In any sense, an offense may give rise to a private action as well, such as negligence per se.

**classification of offenses (graded offense or classified offense)**   The hierarchy among criminal offenses and sentences. The classification of offenses is a scale of offenses in which the most serious offenses are grouped together and deemed worthy of the most serious punishments, the next most serious offenses are similarly grouped and associated with a less serious punishment, and so on, until the least significant offenses are described and their punishments established. The most basic classification is between those offenses that are felonies and those that are misdemeanors, but more detailed systems of classification are also used.

**cognate offense**   An offense defined by the same prohibited acts as another offense. Cognate offenses are two different crimes defined by statute to reach similar conduct. The most common cognates, a lesser included offense and the related greater offense are cognates of one another. All other cognate offenses are defined by the common application of the offense to the same conduct. Cognate offenses include all offenses that might be charged for substantially the same conduct, whether they are by definition lesser included offenses or not. Thus, a defendant accused of several cognate offenses arising from the same acts may be convicted only of one offense, though several cognate offenses could be charged for distinct actions that are not otherwise essential to another offense charged.

*See also:* offense, lesser included offense.

**continuing offense**   An offense that takes place over a period of time. A continuing offense is an offense that continues from the time between the first act related to the offense until its conclusion. Continuing offenses do not commence the running of a statute of limitations until their conclusion, and if the offense takes place in several jurisdictions between its commencement and conclusion, the crime is considered to have occurred in every jurisdiction. Examples include robbery, kidnapping, criminal use of the mails, racketeering, and smuggling. Most crimes take place at the moment of the conclusion of the actus reus, and the presumption is that a given offense is not a continuing offense.

*See also:* limitation, limitation of actions, statute of limitations.

**inchoate offense**   An uncompleted crime. An inchoate offense is a crime that has been commenced but not yet completed. In other words, at least one action essential to the plan to commit a crime must have been taken and more must be planned, but from the moment of the predicate acts to the completion of the offense itself, the offense is inchoate. Inchoate offenses include the crimes of attempt to commit a specified crime, conspiracy to commit a specified crime, and solicitation of another to commit a specified crime, all of which require evidence of a specific intent to cause the crime to occur. Other inchoate offenses require only knowledge or recklessness, such as facilitation, participation in a racketeering organization, or acts that are innocent but for their knowledge that might lead to crime, such as possession of burglar tools or possession of illegal drug precursors. Affirmative defenses of particular significance to a charge of an inchoate offense include abandonment and impossibility.

*Attempt*   Attempt is an inchoate offense. In most cases, the actor must manifest the necessary mental state to complete the crime being attempted but must either fail to achieve the requisite unlawful results or be arrested prior to achieving them. Attempt is usually limited to those crimes that require specific intent for the unlawful outcome.

*See also:* attempt, criminal attempt.

**index offense**   The offense for which a person is first convicted and enters the criminal justice system. The index offense is the offense committed by a person that results in a particular cycle of punishment. It is the conviction that put a defendant into the system, differentiating the offense for which a person is initially subject to the supervision of the penal system from both later offenses committed within the penal system and earlier offenses that are not the basis of the punishment or supervision at issue. The index offense is used for statistical management of data regarding offenses and offenders.

**lesser included offense**   A less severely punished crime of similar conduct to a more serious crime. A lesser included offense is a crime defined by substantially the same conduct as another offense, but which is considered less culpable and which is assigned a lesser punishment than the other. If a major and a lesser offense could be committed by the same conduct, and the lesser offense does not require proof of a distinct substantive act or condition not required to prove the major offense, the lesser offense is a lesser included offense.

In most jurisdictions and for most offenses, courts and juries are empowered to find a defendant who is charged with a major offense to be guilty only of a lesser included offense. In some jurisdictions, a jury must be instructed on its capacity to find guilt for a lesser included offense, or the defendant must be specifically charged with both the major and lesser offenses (though a verdict and judgment are allowed only for one level for each act). In most jurisdictions, lesser included offenses are cognate offenses of their major offenses.

*See also:* offense, cognate offense.

**Schmuck test**  The elements test for instructions on a lesser included offense. The Schmuck test is a rule for the inclusion of a criminal jury instruction for a lesser included offense if there exists a lesser offense, all the elements of which are also elements of the offense charged. The term is derived from U.S. v. Schmuck, 489 U.S. 705 (1989).

**merger of offenses**  The incorporation of one offense into a more serious offense. Merger of offenses is a doctrine in which one logically necessary offense is considered a component of another offense, so that the prosecution for the more general offense precludes a separate prosecution for the component offense. Lesser included offenses are generally merged into the general offense into which they are included. To be merged, the offenses must arise from the same conduct and be effectively proven from the same evidence.

*See also:* merger.

**primary offense**  The most serious among several offenses. Primary offense has several meanings in the context of criminal procedure, as well as a particular meaning in traffic law. In general, a primary offense is the most serious offense among several that are at issue, either in the manner of an index offense or major offense when compared to lesser included offenses, or the offense for which a sentence is determined primarily and then adjusted for lesser, earlier, or related offenses. In legal drafting, the phrase may be used more generally to denote the offense that is most important to the analysis, that was the earliest committed, or for which an arrest or indictment is first made.

**status offense (status offender or juvenile status offense or juvenile status offender)**  An offense because the offender belongs to a regulated class. A status offense is a violation of the law that arises not from conduct alone but from conduct by a person of a given status. The most common form is an offense that arises from conduct that is generally lawful but is an offense because it is committed by a child, such as a minor in possession of alcohol. A juvenile status offense is any offense that cannot be committed by an adult as a matter of definition, such as truancy, an offense possible only to a child in the years of mandatory schooling. A finding of delinquency is not a determination that a child has committed a status offense, because delinquency is a status not an offense, yet an act by a delinquent may be treated differently than the same act by a non–delinquent. A status offense is usually not a criminal offense but is a civil or regulatory offense, according to which the offender is subject to regulatory supervision.

A crime or legal liability that is based on having a status or being a person with a particular status that is not rationally identified violates due process of law or equal protection of the laws. Thus, a criminal prohibition that facially appears to create criminal liability for specified conduct but that in fact creates an offense of having a given status likely violates due process of law or equal protection of the laws. By one or the other limit on status offenses, some vagrancy statutes create an offense of having a status and are thus unconstitutional.

**traffic offense**  A violation of a traffic safety law. A traffic offense is an infraction of a traffic safety law, whether the infraction is committed on or near a public roadway or in a vehicle on private lands. Many jurisdictions consider specified traffic offenses to be civil infractions rather than criminal infractions, while some jurisdictions consider some traffic offenses to be misdemeanors or unspecified criminal offenses. In all jurisdictions, however, some serious traffic offenses are also violations of criminal law. For states that use a point system for the retention of the privilege of driving, a determination of liability for a traffic offense usually requires the assessment of points against the license.

**primary offense as traffic offense (secondary offense)**  A traffic offense for which a car may be stopped. A primary offense under the traffic laws of many jurisdictions is a violation of the transportation safety laws for which a police officer is justified in stopping a vehicle to issue a citation. In the course of the stop, the usual procedures apply, and the police officer is justified in assessing the vehicle, driver, and passengers within the limits of due process during the traffic stop. During this assessment, the police officer may observe evidence of other infractions of the transportation safety laws and issue a citation for these infractions as well.

A secondary offense is a traffic offense that is not authorized as the basis for a stop of the vehicle but is authorized only when the violation is discovered during a lawful stop of the vehicle that has already occured.

**offensive words**  *See:* speech, freedom of speech, clear and present danger test (offensive words).

**offer**  Anything presented from one person to another. An offer, generally, is anything that is brought before another person for that person to have, to accept, to rule upon, or to do something. An offer may be limited or conditional, or it may be unlimited or unconditional, which is to say with or without limits or contingencies established by the offeror or by law. An offer is, by definition, made to the offeree with the understanding that the offeree may accept or reject it.

*See also:* gift (gift over or give); proffer (proffer of evidence or proffered evidence or evidence proffered).

**offer of compromise** *See:* compromise, offer of compromise.

**offer of judgment** *See:* judgment, offer of judgment.

**offer of performance** *See:* performance, contract performance, offer of performance (tender of performance).

**offer of proof** *See:* proof, offer of proof.

**contract offer** A promise that may be accepted and bind the promisor to a contract. An offer is a promise, or an action or statement that implies a promise, that will become legally enforceable as a contract if it is accepted. The offer must be sufficiently detailed to allow acceptance without further terms, although most terms may be implied by law. An offer is only valid if it is made by someone competent to enter a contract who is not patently lacking an intent to make an offer that might be accepted. An offer may, ordinarily, be withdrawn any time prior to acceptance, although a firm offer may not be withdrawn until the period established for it to remain open has run.

*See also:* acceptance, acceptance as acceptance of an offer.

*1. definiteness and indefiniteness* A offer must be sufficiently definite in its terms as to be the basis for a contract that may be performed by the offeror. The law may imply most terms that are not specified, but the offer must sufficiently define its terms so as to be objective evidence that the whole of the communication is intended to be an offer and to sufficiently form the basis of enforcement. In general, an offer to enter a contract regarding land must be definite as to the land involved, and a contract regarding the sale of goods must be definite as to quantity.

*2. death or incapacity of offeror* An offer is void if the offeror dies or becomes incapacitated.

*3. advertisement as offer* An advertisement is usually an invitation to receive offers that is disseminated to the public and is only binding insofar as it may not be fraudulent. Even so, the more the language in the advertisement reflects contract terms and principles (like an offer, conditions under which acceptance is to be proffered, and express consideration), the more likely an advertisement is to be deemed an offer.

**bona fide offer** An offer that creates a binding contract upon acceptance. A bona fide offer, or a valid offer made in good faith, is an offer that is sufficient to bind both parties if it is accepted. A bona fide offer must be made in good faith with the intent that it be honored if accepted, be made in clear and unambiguous terms by a party ready, willing, and able to perform its promise in a timely manner, offering appropriate value in its offer for the promise sought from the offeree, and without conditions of duress, fraud, or misrepresentation.

*See also:* bona, bona fide (bona fides).

**counter-offer (counteroffer)** An offer made in response to an earlier offer. A counter-offer is an offer made by a party who had earlier received an offer from another party and whose new offer, which is the counter-offer, seeks different terms from the contract that might have been formed by the first offer. A counter-offer must be related in its subject matter to an offer earlier made by the counter-offeree to the counter-offeror. The effect of the counter-offer is a rejection of the earlier offer, whether or not the counter-offer is accepted by the counter-offeree (who is the original offeror and whose offer is rejected). If the counter-offer is accepted, the contract that is formed usually refers to the counter-offer as the offer and the acceptance of the counter-offer as the acceptance forming the contract.

**cross-offer** Offers made by two parties to one another at the same time. Cross-offers are offers made by two or more parties to one another prior to their reception of the offer or offers made by the other offerors. Unlike a counter-offer, each cross-offer remains a valid offer with no offer being rejected by the making of the other offer, because no offer had been received prior to the issuance of the cross-offer. In most cases, unless there is genuine mutual mistake giving rise to a voidable contract, the party who accepts another's cross-offer accepts according to the terms of the other's cross-offer and not according to the accepting party's terms.

**irrevocable offer (firm offer)** An offer that cannot be revoked by the offeror. An irrevocable offer is an offer that remains open and cannot be revoked by the offeror until either a specific time has elapsed, a reasonable time has elapsed, or a condition has failed or been satisfied. Under the UCC, such offers, called firm offers, are binding if they are made by a merchant in a writing that specifies the terms under which the offer will remain open or expire. For offers that are not governed by the UCC, an offer is made irrevocable if it is the understanding of the parties that the offer is irrevocable and the offeree either timely relies upon the irrevocability or provides even minimal consideration to transform the offer into an option contract.

*See also:* contract, option contract.

**open offer** An offer that may yet be accepted. An open offer is a valid offer that has been made by the offeror and may be accepted by the offeree. An offer that must remain open for a period of time is a firm offer.

An offer remains open until the power of the offeree to accept the offer is terminated. Termination of the power to accept results from the rejection of the offer by the offeree (a counter-offer being such a rejection); by the lapse of time (whether the amount of time is specified in the offer or the amount of time is implied as a reasonable time for such an offer to remain open); by revocation of the offer by the offeror; or by the death or incapacity of the offeror prior to the offer's acceptance. A valid acceptance, however, also terminates the offer in so far as the offer is now a promise of the contract and is no longer revocable.

See also: offer, contract offer, irrevocable offer (firm offer); offer, contract offer, firm offer.

**rejection of offer**   The refusal to accept an offer. The rejection of an offer arises from any statement or conduct that manifests an offeree's intent to reject an offer. The rejection of an offer both terminates the offer and terminates the power of acceptance by the offeree. A counter-offer by the initial offeree is both a rejection of the initial offer and the making of a new offer. An acceptance of an offer that is conditioned upon the agreement to a new term is not necessarily a rejection, as long as the new term is not contrary to a term expressed or implied in the original offer.

See also: acceptance, acceptance as acceptance of an offer; offer, contract offer; rejection (reject or rejected).

**purchase order**   A form offer to purchase specified goods. A purchase order is a form communication from a buyer to a seller that constitutes an offer to buy the quantity and quality of the goods specified by the terms incorporated into the form, which then may be accepted or rejected solely by the seller.

**offering**   A solicitation for offers. An offering is a solicitation for offers to buy certain property, securities, or goods or to perform a certain service. An offering may set a variety of terms according to which offers either conform or fail to conform. In certain circumstances related to a public offering, all conforming offers must be accepted, subject only to limitations of price or quantity.

See also: share, share as stock, offering, public offering, initial public offering (IPO or I.P.O.); share, share as stock, offering, public offering (registered offering).

**initial public offering**   See: share, share as stock, offering, public offering, initial public offering (IPO or I.P.O.).

**public offering**   See: share, share as stock, offering, public offering (registered offering).

**office**   The performance of a service, and the authority to do so. Office, historically, is what was performed in a given service, and from that idea it is currently understood to be the authority to perform certain services, especially services of a particular scope or duty within a government or legal system, corporation or commercial entity, church or religious foundation, or other organization. A person who holds an office is an official and an officer; there is no inherent difference.

An officer is obligated to perform the duties of office, and the scope of the authority of the officer is limited to those duties. The obligations of performing the office, however, create sufficient discretion in the holder of the office to carry out the duties of office within the limits of laws and policies.

See also: duty; discretion; ex, ex officio.

**Office of Information and Regulatory Affairs**   See: president, White House, Office of Management and Budget, Office of Information and Regulatory Affairs (OIRA).

**Office of Management and Budget**   See: president, White House, Office Of Management and Budget, Office of Information and Regulatory Affairs (OIRA); president, White House, Office of Management and Budget (OMB).

**abuse of office (abuse of the public trust or abuse of official trust)**   The tortious use of a public office for private gain. Abuse of the public trust is a tort committed by public officials who employ the powers of office for personal gain or interest. In some jurisdictions it is one form of the tort of outrage. In particular, it includes the acceptance of bribes or benefits from someone who might benefit from the official's influence, the personal appropriation or diversion of public property, the private use of information gained through one's office, and the use of office to abuse the rights and privacy of others. As a basis for pleading outrage, such conduct must be more than reprehensible; it must be outrageous.

See also: public.

**color of office**   The scope of authority, or pretense of authority of office. Color of office is the scope of the duties of office, the extent of the discretion and authority vested in an official who occupies it. An official's act under the color of office is presumed to be valid.

Even so, color of office also includes asserted or putative authority that the official wrongly claims is derived from the authority of office. Acts that are committed under color of office in this sense are not valid, and the liability for these acts may be ascribed not only to the official but also to the entity in which the office is created, the government, or the corporation or other body for whom the official purports to act.

See also: law, color of law.

**lame duck (lame-duck term or lame-duck congress)**   Any holder of an office after a successor has been chosen but not installed. A lame duck is an office holder whose replacement has been designated but not installed, leaving the lame duck to hold the position in the meantime. In such instances, human nature suggests that many significant tasks will be delayed and the authority of the position diminished. A session of Congress following the election prior to the seating of the next Congress is considered a lame duck session, even if most of its members have been re-elected to serve in the next Congress.

**removal from office** The legally authorized act of depriving a person of an office. Removal from office is an action by an officer of the government who is required to — or has the lawful discretion to — act to terminate the services of an individual holding an office within the legal system, whose actions dispossess the official from the office, ending all of the official's authority in the office and pay, benefits, or other emoluments from continued service in that office. Removal may occur expressly, as when a person is notified of termination in the office, or it may be implied, as when a new official is installed or inaugurated in the office in lieu of the previous official.

There is some variation and ambiguity in the rules and statutes that define removal from office as to how long the removal must persist. An official removed is dispossessed from that office only for the remainder of what would be that term of office. Dispossession is not the same as disqualification, and a removal that is not independently a disqualification does not forbid the removed official from seeking a return to the office through later election or appointment.

*See also:* disqualification (disqualify); deposition (depose).

**officer** A person invested with an office. An officer is the holder of an office, being invested by some other authority with a particular responsibility attached to that office, and with such powers and obligations as define the office.

*See also:* official; ex, ex officio.

**executive officer of a corporation** An officer empowered to make policy for a corporation. An executive officer in a corporation is an officer whose position is dictated as an executive position by the corporation's charter, by-laws, or similar instruments, or who is vested with the authority to make policy on behalf of the corporation. Titles of executive officers vary widely from company to company and according to style, but they usually include a chief executive officer, a chief financial officer, a president, vice presidents, and general counsel, as well as executive directors. In many corporations, there is no meaningful distinction between an "executive officer" and an "officer," "executive," or "member of management," except that "executive" used as an adjective usually signals a more senior position than titles without it.

**executive compensation** The pay and benefits given to an executive of a corporation. Executive compensation takes a variety of forms, including salary, benefits (including insurance and retirement contributions), short-term performance bonuses, long-term performance bonuses, perquisites (or perks, including a corporate car and driver, club memberships, free parking, etc.), and compensation protection. There is no standard definition of executive compensation as a matter of law, and different corporations use various forms of compensation and choose to disclose or not to disclose the value of all forms used. No state or federal authority regulates the overall level of executive compensation as of 2011, although certain aspects of it, like the tax implications of certain pay or benefits, are often regulated. The level of compensation, which is usually set by the compensation committee of the corporate board of directors, is often a matter of controversy among shareholders and corporate observers.

*See also:* compensation, employment compensation.

**executive compensation, golden parachute (compensation protection or assured compensation or parachute payment)** Payment to an officer who is fired or whose company is taken over. A golden parachute is a payment or other benefit (such as stock transfers or options) that is contractually assured to an executive officer in the event the officer is fired or the corporation employing the officer is taken over by another corporation. Such parachute payments are not subject to a corporate tax deduction as is regular employee compensation.

**executive compensation, perquisite (perk or perks)** Money and support in kind beyond compensation and benefits. Perquisites are profits or gains associated with an office other than direct compensation, bonuses, or benefits. Historically, perquisites were the rents, profits, and incidental privileges owed by tenants to the lord of a manor. In their modern form as an element of employment compensation, perquisites include travel expenses (especially those beyond the minimum expense essential for the task), entertainment expenses, cars and drivers, aircraft and pilots, membership in clubs, accounts for office decor, personal staff, and assistance with tasks usually born as a matter of personal expense.

*See also:* prerequisite.

**responsible corporate officer doctrine** One who acts for a business is responsible for such acts. The responsible corporate officer doctrine creates administrative and criminal liability for each person within a business entity whose decision in making a policy or executing an act as an officer of the corporation causes the business entity to violate the law.

**federal officer**

**inferior officer** An executive appointee whose appointment does not require Senate Confirmation. An inferior officer is an executive officer whose work is subordinate to others and whose position does not require the advice and consent of the Senate.

**principal officer** An executive appointee whose appointment is subject to the advice and consent of the Senate. A principal officer is an executive officer who must be appointed by the President and confirmed by the Senate. This includes heads of executive agencies and others whose position is created by Congress as principal officers. Although a principal officer's entry into office requires advice and consent, the officer serves at the pleasure of the President, who need not consult further with the Senate to terminate such an appointment.

**military officer**  A person commissioned or warranted to lead military personnel. An officer in the military is a person who is commissioned in the name of the President of the United States or who holds a warrant issued in the name of the secretary of a military department in a military service. An officer is entitled to respect and obedience by all personnel of a lower rank or rating, and officers who hold rank by commission or warrant are entitled to a hand salute by military personnel of lesser rank or rating.

An enlisted member of the service holding a rating as a petty officer or sergeant is generally not considered an officer but may be subject to certain laws, orders, treaties, or instructions that apply to officers with supervisory duties, particularly to enlisted personnel responsible for an independent command, such as an officer-in-charge.

**official**  Related to an office or to public business. An official is a person who occupies an office, and anything official is an aspect of something done by officials in public office. As a depiction of the holder of an office, there is little difference in general between official and officer, although there is a customary understanding that officer is the more responsible title. Note: in the United Kingdom and other states, officials are civil servants whose functions are subordinate to ministers.

Anything that is official is related to an act of office or to the broad domain of public or governmental action. Thus, the official use of a thing is a use authorized by law as an appropriate use of that thing. Similarly, official business is business related to or within the scope of a public employee's duties.

*See also:* office; officer; ex, ex officio.

**official bond**  *See:* bond, government position bond (official bond).

**official capacity**  *See:* capacity, defendant capacity, official capacity (representative capacity as defendant).

**official immunity**  *See:* immunity, official immunity.

**official record**  *See:* record, official record; discovery, document discovery, official record.

**official secret**  *See:* secret, state secret (official secret).

**legal official**  A person who makes, enforces, or adjudicates the law. A legal official is a person with an office defined by law who has the power to make, apply, or enforce the law or the power to give orders so that others are subject to those orders under the authority of the law. Officials are legal subjects when not acting in their official capacity. Under the rule of law, officials may only carry out their duties and exercise their discretion according to the procedures and substantive powers established by law.

**quis custodiet ipsos custodes (who will watch the watchers?)**  Who will police the police? Quis custodiet ipsos custodes is a Latin phrase that was first written by Juvenal in the Satires but alluded to a line from Plato. It translates literally to "who will watch the watchers," but figuratively raises the question of oversight: who will ensure that those with power use it for the ends it is given them, and not for their own ends?

**state official**  A person holding an office created by state law. A state official is a person who holds an office created by the law of a given state or political unit equivalent to a state, such as the District of Columbia. Who is a state official de jure is defined by the specific laws of the state, but there is also a functional analysis whereby those with the ability to make law or policy on behalf of the state are de facto state officials. A state official acting within the scope of office or otherwise under color of state law in a manner that violates the constitutional rights of another person is liable to that person under 42 U.S.C. § 1983, and a suit can be brought against the state official in a personal capacity or an official capacity. A suit against a state official in an official capacity, under section 1983 or other grounds, is usually considered a suit against the state and subject to the defense of state sovereign immunity or to its exceptions.

**officious intermeddler or volunteer or stranger**  *See:* intermeddler (officious intermeddler or volunteer or stranger).

**offset**  *See:* setoff (offset).

**offset or right of setoff or set-off**  *See:* damages, calculation of damages, setoff (offset or right of setoff or set-off).

**oil (petroleum)**  Liquid hydrocarbon used as fuel. Oil is a liquid hydrocarbon that occurs naturally in the crust of the Earth, from which it is extracted primarily through wells. Unextracted oil is a mineral as a matter of mineral interests and property rights. Oil is presently considered to be a finite resource subject to depletion. Oil may be refined, cracked, or fractioned to create a number of fuels and lubricants, including gasoline. There is no inherent difference between unrefined oil and liquid petroleum, although petroleum may also include solids and gases.

*See also:* fungibility (fungible).

**fingerprint of the oil (oil fingerprinting)**  The method of identifying the particular source of oil. An oil fingerprint is the particular combination of trace elements and ratios of distinct forms of hydrocarbon in an oil sample that identifies the source of the oil in the sample by comparing it to the composition of oil in various sources and fields. Oil fingerprinting is thus the process by which sources of oil are identified and individual samples and cargoes traced.

**migration of oil (oil migration)**   The movement of oil other than by a human agency. The migration of oil generally occurs when the oil moves under natural pressure or gravity from one place to another in its natural reservoir. Thus oil may migrate to a pump in one tract from other tracts sharing the same mineral formation.

The migration of oil may also describe the movement, as with any other contaminant, from the soil or aquifer of one parcel of land to another, which may amount to a trespass on the second parcel.

**oil spill**   The discharge of oil in water or on land. An oil spill is the discharge of oil into the environment, whether the spill is on land or into a sea, river, lake, or other body of water. In the United States, oil spills on land are usually under the jurisdiction of the Environmental Protection Agency, and oil spills into navigable waters or the high seas are under the jurisdiction of the U.S. Coast Guard. The person or entity responsible for the vessel or facility from which oil is spilled is responsible for the harms caused by the oil and its containment and removal.

**Oil Pollution Control Act (OPCA)**   Statutes governing liability for oil spills. Oil pollution acts are federal and state statutes that govern liability for oil spills and the expenses related to cleaning up oil spills. The acts usually assign liability to the parties responsible for a particular vessel or facility from which a spill occurs. The federal statute, the Oil Pollution Act of 1990, 33 U.S.C. 2701–2761 (2011), makes polluters liable for the costs of cleanup, including natural resource damages and authorizes emergency clean-up to be paid initially from the federal Oil Spill Liability Trust Fund.

*See also:* pollution, Superfund (Comprehensive Environmental Response Compensation and Liability Act or C.E.R.C.L.A. or CERCLA).

**OIRA**   *See:* president, White House, Office of Management and Budget, Office of Information and Regulatory Affairs (OIRA).

**Old Age Survivors and Disability Insurance**   *See:* Social Security, Old Age Survivors and Disability Insurance (OASDI).

**oligarchy**   *See:* government, forms of government, oligarchy.

**oligopoly**   A market controlled by a few producers. An oligopoly is a market for a good or service that is controlled by a small number of producers or sellers. There is a greater risk of restraint of trade from the behavior of the producer or seller in an oligopolistic market than in a perfect market.

**OMB**   *See:* president, White House, Office of Management and Budget (OMB).

**ombudsman (ombudsperson)**   An officer who investigates complaints. An ombudsman is an officer, or an office, that is independent of the administration of an entity such as a government, agency, or corporation and that is given the task of investigating complaints against the entity's administration. The office was first created by the Swedish Parliament in 1809 to investigate any potential abuse of power or office by ministers or civil servants.

*See also:* inspector, inspector general.

**omerta (silence code or code of silence or blue wall of silence)**   Conspiratorial silence. Omertà in Italian, or omerta in English, depicts the unwillingness of members of a conspiracy or of certain associations to divulge information about their activities or the activities of others that are related to the conspiracy or association. As the "blue wall of silence" or "honor among cops" it describes the reluctance of police officers to divulge wrongdoing by other police officers. Note: though the informal English pronunciation stresses the second syllable, the Italian pronunciation stresses the final syllable.

*See also:* racketeering, organized crime, Mafia (La Cosa Nostra).

**omission (omit or omitted)**   Language left out of a text, or a duty not performed. An omission is something left out or not done. There are several distinct usages of omission in law, as in a term or phrase left out of a text, or as a duty that is not performed. In either case, the omission is a matter of what is left out as against some expectation. An omission may be either accidental or intentional.

An unintended omission in a text may be considered a scrivener's error, and if a later reader or interpreter may, with a high level of likelihood, determine the terms omitted, then they may be supplied. An omission that is deliberate, however, means that the text must be considered as it is, although the effect of the omission may render the text vague.

An omission of the performance of a duty is the failure to do something a reasonable person in the place of the person with the duty would do. An omission in the performance of legal services or other professional services may amount to malpractice.

**omission as a failure of duty**   The failure to perform a task required by an office or duty. Omission of duty, or neglect of duty, is a failure to perform a task or a failure to perform it fully, when an affirmative obligation to do so exists as a matter of contract, of commitment and reliance, of law, or of standards of professional or fiduciary conduct. A person who is harmed by another's omission of a duty owed to that person may bring an action for the omission that an action in contract, tort, or equity depending on the legal basis for the duty. Certain crimes, such as that of being an accessory, may be committed through an omission of a duty, such as the duty to report a crime or disclose the location of a wanted person.

**omnibus** All–encompassing. Omnibus means everything or all of the things relevant in a given context. An omnibus bill or law includes a host of provisions, seemingly all of the law on a given topic or field of law.
*See also:* clause, omnibus clause; legislation, omnibus legislation (omnibus bill).

**omnibus bill** *See:* legislation, omnibus legislation (omnibus bill).

**omnibus clause** *See:* clause, omnibus clause.

**omnibus legislation** *See:* legislation, omnibus legislation (omnibus bill).

**on the merits** *See:* merits (on the merits).

**one man one vote** *See:* vote, vote in public election, one person one vote (one man one vote).

**one person one vote** *See:* vote, vote in public election, one person one vote (one man one vote).

**one-hundred mile bulge** *See:* jurisdiction, territorial jurisdiction, one-hundred mile bulge.

**onerous (onerousness)** Burdensome. Onerousness is the quality of being a burden or a hindrance, particularly a hardship caused by a continuing duty. The term, closely related to onus, was once applied to a load one carried. Thus, something that is a burden or hardship, particularly a duty or task that is unwanted, expensive, difficult, or risky, is onerous. In the civil law, an onerousness represents consideration, and so an onerous title is one title that is paid for with good consideration, which may include work or skill as in the spouse's ownership in community property.
*See also:* onus.

**ontology of law** *See:* law, theories of law, ontology of law, bad-man concept of law (bad man theory); law, theories of law, ontology of law (legal ontology).

**onus** The burden, especially the burden of persuasion. The onus is a classical reference to a burden, and in a legal argument it usually refers to the burden of persuasion or the burden of proof, although it can refer to any obligation at law.
*See also:* burden; onerous (onerousness).

**op. cit.** *See:* opus, opus citato (op. cit.).

**OPCA** *See:* oil, oil spill, Oil Pollution Control Act (OPCA).

**open account** *See:* account, open account.

**open bid** *See:* bid, open bid.

**open court** *See:* court, open court (public court).

**Open Meetings Law** *See:* Sunshine Law (Open Meetings Law).

**open mine doctrine** *See:* waste, doctrine of waste, open mine doctrine.

**open offer** *See:* offer, contract offer, open offer.

**open possession** *See:* possession, adverse possession, open possession.

**open shop** *See:* union, labor union, shop, open shop, right to work law (right to work state); union, labor union, shop, open shop.

**open texture of rules** *See:* rules, open texture of rules.

**open-pit mine or open pit mine or open-pit mining or strip mine or strip mining** *See:* mine, surface mine (open-pit mine or open pit mine or open-pit mining or strip mine or strip mining).

**opening statement** *See:* trial, argument at trial, opening statement.

**opera** *See:* opus (opera).

**operating a vehicle while intoxicated or driving while impaired or D.W.I. or DWI** *See:* driving, driving while intoxicated (operating a vehicle while intoxicated or driving while impaired or D.W.I. or DWI).

**operating profit** *See:* profit, operating profit.

**operation of law** *See:* law, operation of law.

**opinio juris** *See:* custom, international custom, opinio juris (opinio juris sive necessitatis).

**opinion** A belief or statement of belief. An opinion is what a person believes, and a statement of opinion is a statement of subjective belief. An opinion may or may not be derived from the scrutiny of evidence, and a high correlation of a given opinion with the evidence available does not alter the status of the opinion to make it a fact (although it may make the opinion more credible or authoritative). A statement of opinion given in good faith is inherently true, in that it is what is believed, regardless of the accuracy of the opinion or the truth or falsity of the opinion as a statement regarding events in the world. Conversely a false opinion is a statement of opinion that the person who states it does not in fact believe, regardless of whether the opinion accurately reflects events in the world.
*See also:* evidence, opinion evidence.

**opinion evidence** *See:* evidence, opinion evidence.

**opinion of counsel** *See:* lawyer, legal opinion (opinion of counsel).

**judicial opinion** A judicial statement of reasons in support of a ruling. A judicial opinion is the recitation by a judge of the reasons for which a ruling is or ought to be entered in a matter pending before the court. By judicial custom, an opinion recites the facts of the case relevant to the pending matter, states the issues that must be resolved and the sources of law selected for application, and then combines the facts to the requirements of the sources in an analysis by which a determination is reached that is manifest in a ruling.

A judicial opinion might be by a judge sitting alone, as in most trial courts, in which case the opinion is likely to explain the judge's review of the evidence or claims, the legal analysis, and the order manifesting the ruling. A judicial opinion in a court of more than one judge, as in most appellate courts, may take a variety of forms: the opinion of the court (or majority opinion), which explains the ruling entered by the court; an opinion per curiam, which explains the rationale of the court's ruling but is not attributed to a single judge; a plurality opinion, which explains the ruling and offers the rationale most widely accepted in that court at the time; a concurring opinion, which explains the rationale preferred by a judge who agrees with the ruling but supports it for reasons distinct from the majority opinion; and a dissenting opinion, which explains the rationale of a judge who disagrees with the ruling.

See also: reports, case reports (reporter or rpts. or rptr.); rescript.

**advisory opinion** A court's opinion on the requirements or meaning of the law. An advisory opinion is a judicial opinion on a matter submitted to a court for consideration in the abstract or hypothetical rather than for the determination of a case being actively litigated between contesting parties. Most states allow advisory opinions to be issued, usually by the state's highest court upon the request of a legislator, governor, attorney general, or other state officer. The federal courts do not issue advisory opinions, although federal agencies may do so.

See also: judgment, declaratory judgment (declaratory relief or declaration).

*declaratory judgment and advisory opinion* A declaratory judgment differs from an advisory opinion, because a declaratory judgment is issued only once a party or parties are able to demonstrate that there is an adverse relationship that would be affected by a declaration of their respective rights or duties. The mere absence of a further remedy in a declaratory judgment issued by a court does not render the judgment non-binding upon either the parties or the courts.

**bench opinion** An opinion delivered orally by the judge from the bench. A bench opinion is an opinion delivered aloud by the judge in open court and recorded in the transcript of the trial. A notation of the bench opinion is usually docketed in the case file in a manner similar to that for a memorandum opinion.

See also: opinion, judicial opinion, memorandum opinion (mem.).

**dictum (obiter dictum or dicta)** A judge's comments in an opinion that are inessential to its ruling. Dictum is an abbreviation for obiter dictum, Latin for "things said in passing," and it is used to characterize statements in an opinion that are not utterly essential to the justification of the mandate required by the opinion. Thus, obiter dicta are statements in an opinion other than ratio decidendi, or the reasoning required for the decision.

What amounts to dicta is not fully determined by the judge who authors the opinion, and the distinction of dicta from the core reasoning, is made by each later reader. So a later lawyer or judge reading earlier cases may consider a given comment less significant to the analysis of the opinion's author than the author might have thought it. As a matter of the doctrine of precedent, a statement that is dictum is less influential upon later judges than is a statement that is clearly part of a decision's rationale, although the dividing line is imprecise. Indeed, this seeming precision in the use of cases within the doctrine has been criticized as overly weighting the significance of one opinion rather than the weight of the precedent.

See also: opinion, judicial opinion, ratio decidendi.

**dissenting opinion (dissent)** A judge's reasons for rejecting a court's ruling. A dissenting opinion is an opinion by a judge (or justice) who sits on a court that is hearing a case before more than one judge, in which the judge presents the judge's reasons for disagreeing with the majority opinion of the court and the ruling it supports. The legal reasoning expressed in a dissenting opinion is not considered legal authority because it cannot bind lower courts or serve as precedent for future opinions of the same court. Even so, other judges might consider the rationale of the dissent to be persuasive and could use it to form an appropriate basis for later decision.

Note: a judge may dissent without filing a dissenting opinion, either by joining the dissent of another judge or by requesting the clerk of the court to note the dissent in the record. A dissent may be from the majority's ruling, both the ruling and the opinion, or a portion of the opinion.

See also: opinion, judicial opinion, majority opinion.

**majority opinion** An opinion to which most of the court's judges assent. A majority opinion is an opinion of a court of more than one judge (or justice) that is not unanimous but is nonetheless supported by a majority of the judges hearing that case. A majority opinion will nearly always be the opinion of the court. Note: the practices of dissent and concurrence are so common in courts with a large bench that a unanimous opinion is sometimes erroneously described as a majority opinion.

See also: opinion, judicial opinion, dissenting opinion (dissent).

**memorandum opinion (mem.)** A trial court's written opinion, or an unsigned appellate opinion. A memorandum opinion is an opinion of the judge that is written in full. The memorandum opinion usually sets out the issues before the court, the evidence and arguments presented by counsel, the judge's analysis of the evidence and arguments in light of the legal materials, a rationale for judgment, and a ruling on each issue. A memorandum opinion may also incorporate an order that decrees the court's decisions in response to the issue.

Some courts describe an unsigned or unpublished opinion as a memorandum opinion. Such opinions, usually by appellate courts, may be designated as "mem." and reported, if they are reported, in a table according to their decision, namely as affirmances or reversals.

*See also:* opinion, judicial opinion, bench opinion.

**opinion of the court** The opinion that resolves issues pending before a court. The opinion of the court is the opinion that represents the decision of the court, the official ruling of the court on the issues before it, and the opinion from which the mandate in the case is taken. The opinion of the court with one judge is a bench opinion, memorandum opinion, or other opinion issued by that judge. The opinion of the court with more than one judge is a unanimous opinion, majority opinion, or plurality opinion. In most courts, the opinion of the court is designated by that title or something similar.

Note: there is another use of the term that is broader and includes all of the opinions issued in a case. Context is essential in distinguishing between these uses, but usually this more general sense is reflected by using the plural "opinions of the court."

**per curiam opinion** An unsigned opinion by the court. A per curiam opinion is an opinion of the court that is issued "by the court," which is to say that it is not issued under the name of a judge as its primary author. A per curiam opinion is often issued by an appellate court in a ruling that the judges believe is not of particular significance, but the precedential value of a per curium opinion is not less than any other opinion of the court; it merely lacks the additional authority that might be thought to attach to an opinion signed by a respected jurist.

**plurality opinion** An opinion of the largest group of judges but not a majority. A plurality opinion is an opinion of a court of more than one judge (or justice) that presents a rationale in support of the ruling agreed by a majority of the court, even though some of the judges who agree with the ruling do not support the rationale, with the result being that no opinion enjoys a majority of support. In such instances, the plurality opinion cannot represent a rationale supported by a majority of the court; rather its rationale is supported only by the largest group of judges to agree to a single opinion in support of the ruling. The other judges usually issue opinions dissenting or concurring with the plurality opinion.

*See also:* plurality.

**ratio decidendi** The principle of a case. The ratio decidendi is the core significance of a case as precedent, the factual and legal arguments necessary to reach the decision upon which relief was granted or denied in a given dispute before the court. This term, and the argument for limiting the precedential effect of an opinion on it, are less common now than they once were.

*See also:* opinion, judicial opinion, dictum (obiter dictum or dicta).

**seriatim opinion** One of several opinions given one after another. A seriatim opinion is one in a series of opinions, or seriatim, given from the bench in which each judge (or justice) announces that judge's opinion in open court, after which the next does so, and then the next, until each judge has given an opinion. As a result, seriatim opinions were not issued as written by the judge but were reported by courtroom reporters, whose notes of the opinions expressed formed the basis of the written reports. This practice has been generally, but not universally, replaced by the issuance of written opinions.

**slip opinion** An opinion released prior to official publication. A slip opinion is an opinion released by a reporter of opinions or a clerk's office that is unofficial pending its publication in the official reports. Lawyers often rely on slip opinions in arguments, although the rules of courts vary. U.S. Supreme Court slip opinions may be cited as would any published opinion, but some other courts are more cautious regarding slip opinions, as they may be changed before publication. The slip opinions of some courts are never published and remain unpublished opinions.

**unpublished opinion (no-citation rule)** A judicial opinion that is not printed in the official reports. An unpublished opinion is an opinion that is not designated by the judge for publication in the official series of reports. In some courts, an unpublished opinion is neither selected by the judge for publication nor published by the editors of an unofficial reporter.

Courts vary in the degree to which they will allow the citation of unpublished opinions (either their own or those from other courts). Some courts forbid them through no-citation rules; some allow them only in cases related to the parties; some have restrictions that are ignored; and some courts have no restrictions at all on unpublished opinions. The clear trend, however, is to allow attorneys to cite past opinions whether they are published or unpublished. All federal appellate opinions issued after 2007 may be cited without regard to their publication or non-publication.

*See also:* lawbook, reporter (case reports or case reporter or report); opinion, judicial opinion, slip opinion.

**lay opinion**  An opinion based on observation and not on expertise. Lay opinion is the testimony of a matter of opinion based on personal observation and perception, whether at an instant or over time and whether of what one observes or what is reported within a community, that is not based on knowledge or analysis derived from technical, professional, scientific, or similar expertise. Thus, a witness who gives an opinion of another person's reputation in the witness's community is giving a lay opinion, but a pollster reporting the results of a poll regarding the same person's opinion is giving an expert opinion.

Lay opinion, generally, is popular opinion. Popular opinion is an aggregate of the individual opinions in a group. The creation, administration, and assessment of polls is a refined study in political science.

**opponent**  *See:* proponent (opponent).

**opportunity cost**  *See:* cost, opportunity cost.

**oppression (oppress or oppressor)**  The unfair use of power or authority. Oppression is the unfair exploitation of power. Oppression may arise in many contexts, using various forms of power or authority. Examples include market power; bargaining power; the power that arises from personal dependence; the authority of the legal official over a person subject to the law; the authority of an employer, supervisor, or officer over subordinates. Such power or authority is not inherently oppressive, and its use may be fully justified by a mission, by a purpose, or by its use for the benefit of those who may be burdened by it. Or power and authority may be unfairly exploited through innumerable means, the hallmark of which is its use to cause a harm, loss, or fear in the subject or subordinate beyond what that required to achieve a lawful goal related to the power-relationship or situation of authority. Oppression is not a crime or tort in itself, but oppressive tactics or behavior are significant evidence in the proof of a variety of doctrines arising from offenses and civil actions, such as abuse of process, anti-trust, unconscionability of contract, menacing, due process of law, and equal protection of the laws.

**opprobrium**  Public scandal or shame. Opprobrium is condemnation by others for something shameful one has done, or is thought to have done, or for some condition. The public reaction to a person with a disease currently feared by the public, the revulsion individuals feel toward someone accused of a terrible crime, the sense of fear or anger toward someone who abuses the trust of others are all examples of opprobrium.

*See also:* scandal.

**optimality (optimal)**  The most efficient number, allocation, or distribution. Optimality is the condition in which nothing can be improved without making something else worse. Anything optimal is incapable of improvement; it is as good as it gets.

**Pareto optimality**  A market trading at optimal efficiency. Pareto optimality, named for Vilfred Pareto, is an equilibrium in the market in which all goods are traded at their greatest efficiency for all traders, and there is no change that would benefit one trader but not make the other traders worse off. A Pareto optimal outcome cannot be made better without at least one trader being worse off to a greater extent than the gain of the trader who benefits.

**option (opt)**  Choice, or the freedom to choose. Option, in general, is the ability to choose among two or more selections when considering what to do, what not to do, what to acquire, whom to select, or in any other action. In this sense, option is synonymous with election, as in election of remedies. A legal option may describe nearly any choice, particularly to do or to refrain from doing something. Thus, an option in contracts is a right to accept or not to accept an offer that is kept open for a specified period of time. Note: "option" is both the noun of election and the noun of the thing that might be elected; the verb for making such an election is "to opt." The verb "to option" is to preserve a choice for a later time, as in an option contract.

In jurisprudence, a morally significant option requires that the person with the option have as great a liberty to choose one option as any other; the deck cannot be stacked so that one option is impossible or the person is coerced in making the selection. Further, the choice must usually be among meaningfully competing options, either similarly good or similarly bad potential selections.

**opt in**  *See:* option, opt in; class, class action, class, opt in.

**opt out**  *See:* option, opt out; class, class action, class, opt out.

**option bond or tob or multimaturity bond or put bond or put option bond**  *See:* bond, option tender bond (option bond or TOB or multimaturity bond or put bond or put option bond).

**option contract**  *See:* contract, option contract, option contract to purchase land | rule against perpetuities and options; contract, option contract, option contract to purchase land; contract, option contract.

**option contract to purchase land**  *See:* contract, option contract, option contract to purchase land | rule against perpetuities and options; contract, option contract, option contract to purchase land.

**option tender bond**  *See:* bond, option tender bond (option bond or TOB or multimaturity bond or put bond or put option bond).

**opt in** Any signal of an intent to join a plan or common action. To opt in is to signal one's decision to participate in a plan, project, or action. Opting in implies that one will become a part of a common enterprise, usually forgoing an independent course.

**opt out** Any signal to reject a plan or common action. To opt out is to signal one's decision to forgo participation in a plan, project, or action. Opting out usually implies a rejection of a common enterprise in order to take an independent course.

**call option (option call or call)** The right to buy securities at a given price before a given date. A call option is a securities option to buy from the entity that issues the option an agreed upon number of shares of the security at a specified price on or before a specified date.

**put option (put)** The right to sell securities at a given price before a given date. A put option is a securities option to sell to the entity that issues the option an agreed number of shares of the security, at a specified price, on or before a specified date.

**OPTN** *See:* gift, anatomical gift, organ procurement and transportation network (OPTN).

**opus (opera)** A work produced by one's labors, particularly a written work. An opus is a work or composition, usually a work of art, music, writing, architecture, or any other effort of skill or labor. In legal writing, an opus is usually a book, opinion, or article. In intellectual property, an opus is a thing written or invented. Note: the Latin plural of opus is opera.

**opus citato (op. cit.)** The work previously cited. Opus citato, or op. cit., is a citation signal for a work cited in full elsewhere. Unlike ibidem, the work fully cited may be some distance away in the text.

**or** Alternatively. Or is a disjunctive conjunction, meaning that it signals a division between two or more things that are being compared.

As the suffix –or, the term converts a verb to the noun form of the person who does or commits the action of the verb.

*See also:* and.

**oral (orality)** Spoken aloud. Oral relates to the mouth, and anything oral is done by or to the mouth. An oral examination can thus describe two very different situations: the first is a person being examined by questions spoken aloud and answering aloud in return; the other is a person's mouth being examined by a medical specialist.

In law, the term is used to describe several kinds of actions, such as: oral evidence, which is spoken evidence given in person and in the witness's own voice; an oral contract, which consists of the words spoken between the parties; and an oral argument, which is given aloud in person before the court. In general, there is no difference between something "oral," something "verbal," or something "parol" in the law. But if a person communicates directly, for instance by technology in the event of a health concern that prevents speech, the statement is verbal though not oral.

*See also:* verbal.

**oral argument** *See:* argument, oral argument.

**oral contract or verbal contract** *See:* contract, contract interpretation, parol contract (oral contract or verbal contract).

**oral will or noncupative will** *See:* will, last will and testament, nuncupative will (oral will or noncupative will).

**orator** A public speaker. An orator is a person skilled in public speaking. Although the term is rarely used today, the art of rhetoric and the ability to persuade the listener remain essential skills for the contemporary lawyer. Though the styles of effective rhetoric vary, the obligation to develop such skills and employ them for one's client persist.

**ordeal (trial by ordeal or judicium dei)** A trial seeking supernatural mercy to prove innocence. The ordeal is an ancient method of legal proof in which a person accused of a crime was challenged with an event that would usually cause pain or death and found innocent in the event that pain or death did not result, the idea being that God would not allow the innocent to suffer. In a world in which God was understood to be ever-present and an interventionist, this process, like trial by combat, was a submission of the case to divine judgment. Judicium Dei (although humans sometime helped by, for instance, letting the scalding water sit a while before the torment was to begin). This process has been replaced by trial by evidence.

**order** A system of arrangement, or a command to bring one about. Order, generally, is the system by which anything or group of things is arranged. The term has come to mean not only a particular group within other groups, such as an association within society or a group of living things in a taxonomy, but also a command issued to maintain order, which is to say that it has become the basis for an order issued from one person to another. A military or court order is thus a requirement that someone or something act to further the goals of the larger organization, such as the legal order.

**order instrument** *See:* instrument, negotiable instrument, order instrument (payable to order or pay to the order of).

**order of performance** *See:* performance, order of performance.

**order of the coif** *See:* law, law school, order of the coif.

**administrative order** An order by an agency enforcing its regulations. An administrative order is any final order from an official in a government agency, bureau, or department with the authority to enforce its regulations or enabling laws, that requires any conduct on the part of the recipient, that grants or denies relief to any party, or that assesses any penalty against the recipient. Administrative orders are subject to review within the agency and to judicial review. An administrative order may not be issued that fails to comply with the agency's regulations, underlying legislation, and the constitution, including the requirements of due process of law. Note: although the Administrative Procedure Act (APA) only uses the term to describe final orders, subsequent statutes and agency regulations use the term for numerous pre-penalty decrees or requirements to a party, the most common being the administrative compliance order, which may be used in a manner more akin to a show-cause order than a final adjudication.

**administrative compliance order (A.C.O. or ACO)** A demand by an agency that a person or entity obey the law. An administrative compliance order directs an individual or entity to take action, or refrain from action, in order to comply with that agency's regulations. The agency may issue the order as a result of a self-reported infraction, an agency citation, an investigation, or a hearing. In each case, however, the order must be based on a valid regulation, a determination that the person or entity served with the order is subject to the regulation and has violated it, and the person or entity has or will have notice of the impending order and an opportunity to be heard in opposition to the order. The order is subject to administrative review, but is usually prior to a penalty order and considered a preliminary order and not subject to direct judicial review. If, however, the compliance order is a final order, then it is also subject to judicial review following the exhaustion of administrative remedies. Note: the law governing some agencies, notably directives of Congress in the Clean Air Act and Clean Water Act to the Environmental Protection Agency, distinguishes administrative compliance orders from penalty orders and civil enforcement actions. The difference is between a penalty and a warning.

*See also:* order, administrative order, administrative penalty order (APO or A.P.O. or penalty order).

**administrative penalty order (APO or A.P.O. or penalty order)** An agency order penalizing a failure to obey the law. An administrative penalty order directs an individual or entity to pay a sum of money or take some other action as a penalty for a violation of an agency's regulations. The agency may issue the order as a result of a self-reported infraction, an agency citation, an investigation, or a hearing. In each case, however, the order must be based on a valid regulation, a determination that the person or entity served with the order is subject to the regulation and has violated the regulation, and the person or entity has or will have notice of the impending order and an

opportunity to be heard in opposition to the order. The order is subject to judicial review following the exhaustion of administrative remedies.

Note: the law governing some agencies, notably directives of Congress in the Clean Air Act and Clean Water Act to the Environmental Protection Agency, distinguishes administrative penalty orders from administrative compliance orders and from civil enforcement actions. The difference is between a penalty and a warning.

*See also:* order, administrative order, administrative compliance order (A.C.O. or ACO).

**citation order (citations order)** An order penalizing a failure to comply with an earlier citation. A citation order is an order from a court or an administrative agency that demands a penalty for the failure to comply with an earlier citation. Typically, a citation is issued, followed by a short period of time in which the person or entity cited has the chance to comply with the conditions of the citation. If the cited party fails to comply within the stated time period, a citation order may be issued. A recipient of a citation order is usually ordered to a show cause hearing before the citation order is made final.

*See also:* showing, show cause (show-cause proceeding or show-cause order or order to show cause).

**court order** Any directive issued by a court to a party or to counsel. A court order is a decree of a court directed to a specific party in an action before it, to counsel appearing before it, or to the public or any others subject to its jurisdiction, setting forth a requirement for action or inaction. Court orders may be made during the proceedings related to a given action, or they may be general or instructive, as in the promulgation of court rules. Court orders issued in an action are generally interlocutory or final.

**appealable order (appealable decision)** An appealable interlocutory order, or a final order. An appealable order is an order that may be the subject of appeal from the court that enters that order to a higher court, where the order will be reviewed. In general, all final orders in a civil action are appealable, whether the order is a dismissal or a judgment for the plaintiff. In a criminal action, a dismissal, a quashing of the indictment, or any other final order for the defendant prior to an acquittal on the merits is appealable, but an acquittal or verdict of innocence is not subject to appeal. On the other hand, a judgment or sentence rendered on a guilty verdict or plea is usually appealable. In either civil or criminal actions, an interlocutory order is rarely appealable, with the exception of the few such orders that may be appealed by right or with leave of the court. Even so, an otherwise non-appealable decision may be appealed in the same appeal as the appeal of an appealable order, if the appeal of the appealable order cannot justly and completely be heard otherwise.

*See also:* order, court order, interlocutory orders (interlocutory decision).

**collateral-order doctrine** An interlocutory order is appealable if it is important but unreviewable in a final order. The collateral order doctrine allows the appeal as of right of an interlocutory order despite the order's failure to be the final order in the cause of action, if each of four conditions is met. The interlocutory order conclusively determines a matter that is disputed between the parties. The order and its subject matter are completely separable from the merits of the action. The decision would be otherwise unreviewable on appeal from a final order or judgment. The subject matter in issue is sufficiently important that its resolution would affect other actions or parties than those in the case at hand. These four conditions are to be carefully weighed and the doctrine narrowly construed. Interlocutory orders that do not satisfy these requirements may be appealed only by permission or under other doctrines. Note: opinions regularly inventory these as three conditions, owing to the listing of the issue's importance and separability as one issue.

*See also:* order, final order, final order rule.

**ex parte order** An order not argued by all of the parties in an action. An ex parte order is any order that does not follow a contested hearing. An order in the usual process of the court requires that the parties interested in the order had notice of the hearing and an opportunity to be heard; when this is not done, the order resulting is ex parte (Latin for regarding only one party). Although an ex parte order is usually issued on the motion of a party acting alone or at the behest of a governmental agency such as the police or child protective services, an ex parte order can be issued by the court sua sponte. In all cases in which no notice is given to an adverse or affected party, ex parte orders are extraordinary, and they are usually limited in time until a hearing with notice to the parties may be scheduled. Furthermore, some states provide a direct appeal of an ex parte order for an adverse party without notice. Even so, an ex parte order may be extended for cause or made permanent.

*See also:* motion, ex parte motion (ex parte application); ex, ex parte.

**interlocutory orders (interlocutory decision)** An order entered prior to the final order in an action. An interlocutory order is an order entered by the court in any action that does not finally resolve the case before that court. The order need not have the word order in its title, but rather it may be titled a ruling, decision, sentence, judgment, decree, or decision of nearly any form or title. Interlocutory orders include orders regarding the initial pleadings, such as motions to dismiss a civil complaint or quash an indictment or information, motions for civil pre-trial relief motions or regarding bail, regarding parties and trial, motions regarding discovery, motions for judgment, motions regarding evidence, motions regarding instructions, and motions regarding a criminal sentence or a civil remedy.

In general, interlocutory orders are not subject to appeal. An interlocutory appeal may, however, be taken of an order that requires an interpretation of a contested issue of law, particularly when the outcome of such an appeal is likely to increase judicial economy by eliminating a subsequent appeal, remand, or retrial. Particular interest is sometimes paid to an interlocutory appeal of an order denying a party's dismissal on certain grounds, especially on a claim of immunity. Appeals on these grounds to a federal appellate court must be certified by the district court and permitted by the court of appeals. Certain narrow grounds for appeal of an interlocutory order are allowed by right, particularly in cases dealing with receivers and injunctions.

*See also:* order, court order, appealable order (appealable decision).

**restraining order** An order barring someone from activities or places that risk violating the law. A restraining order is an order that creates an unusual legal restraint upon a person or entity, forbidding the defendant from certain listed actions that the court has determined pose a risk of unlawful conduct. In particular, a restraining order is used to limit a person with a propensity for threatening or harming another person from contact, communications, or proximity with that person. Thus, restraining orders are used in cases of domestic violence, threats of domestic violence, child molestation, harassment, outrageous conduct, and other criminal or tortious conduct, not only as a remedy to prevent the perpetrator from continued unlawful actions but also as a pre-emptive tool to restrain conduct that is ruled by the court to present a likelihood of such harm in the future. A restraining order may be issued in an ex parte proceeding, in which case a subsequent hearing with notice and an opportunity of the defendant to be heard is essential for the order to remain valid and in force. A restraining order should be limited in its scope only to prohibit the conduct and the travel to or presence in a location that is determined by the court to lead to a reasonable likelihood that the alleged harm may occur.

Some orders fulfill the purpose of a restraining order but are called by other names, such as protective orders, preventive orders, or prevention orders. In addition, an injunction can be crafted to perform the same functions as a restraining order, although an injunction is subject to the same review as a restraining order.

A restraining order may be enforced in most jurisdictions through the criminal law. In all jurisdictions, a violation of a restraining order may be treated as a criminal act of contempt of court.

**scheduling order**   An order setting a schedule for each stage of a case. A scheduling order is a judicial order entered early on in a case that establishes a calendar for the case, including the time limits for joining additional parties, amending the pleadings, completing discovery, and filing all motions. It may also set the date for the pre-trial conference and adjust the limits on discovery and what material is privileged from discovery.

*See also:* schedule.

**executive order (E.O. or EO or Ex. Ord.)**   A directive by a chief executive to executive personnel. An executive order is a written directive issued by a president, governor, or mayor to the employees of the executive and administrative branches or to the public, declaring an interpretation or an application of the law. Executive orders that purport to alter the rights or obligations of others are subject to judicial review in the same manner as other executive actions, and the legislature may alter the legislation conferring the relevant authority for the executive order.

**Executive Order 12866 (economic analysis of rule-making)**   Every proposed regulation requires a cost–benefit assessment. Executive Order 12,866 was issued by President Bill Clinton in 1993, adopting and extending the requirement from President Reagan's Order 12,291 that every agency perform a cost–benefit analysis for each new regulation. Although Order 12,866 has been amended several times, it remains the platform for agency review by the Office of Information and Regulatory Affairs.

*See also:* value, cost-benefit analysis (CBA).

**final order**   The last decision required in a case. A final order, whether in an administrative action or an action in court, is the last order in the action, the decision after which there is nothing more for the administrative law judge or the judge in the court to do before closing the file or transferring the file upon receiving a notice of appeal. Note: a need to enforce a judgment, once a judgment is final, does not interfere with the finality of the judgment itself, all of the difficulty and controversy that attend judgment enforcement actions notwithstanding.

*See also:* appeal, notice of appeal.

**final order rule**   A final order is subject to appeal as of right. The final order rule, whether in administrative law or in an action before a court, allows an appeal as of right of a final order but usually bars an appeal of any order that is not the final order in the action. There are exceptions to the final order rule, including the collateral order doctrine and the rare statutory exceptions, but the final order rule does not affect permissive appeals or appeals by leave of the court.

*See also:* order, court order, appealable order, collateral–order doctrine.

**order nisi (judgment nisi or common order)**   An order contingent on the parties' appearance or notice. An order nisi is a judgment entered by a court that is contingent upon the parties' conduct for a period of time, after which the judgment becomes final. It is often used in cases of settlement, in which the parties are given a period of time to object to the settlement before it becomes final, thus allowing each to see if the other performs before allowing the case to close. For this reason, a judgment nisi is preferred in some jurisdictions for the judgment of a divorce settlement. A judgment nisi is also used for some default judgments, to be vacated if the defaulting party appears in time. A judgment nisi must specify the conditions under which it will not be made final and the period of time within which such conditions would bar the judgment's becoming final.

*See also:* nisi.

**protective order**   An order limiting discovery, or a restraining order. Protective orders perform two very different functions. In evidence, a protective order is used to protect certain evidence or witnesses from production, testimony, or use in a hearing or trial.

The term is also used in some jurisdictions to designate restraining orders, particularly restraining orders entered to prevent a person with a history of family violence from harassing or threatening past or potential victims.

*See also:* order, court order, restraining order.

**turnover order**   An order to disgorge assets. A turnover order requires a person who is under a judgment or other order to to pay or deliver property to do so or be in contempt of court. In bankruptcy, a turnover order is used to require a bankrupt debtor deliver money or property to the bankruptcy trustee.

**ordered liberty**   *See:* due process of law, ordered liberty.

**ordinance**   An article of municipal legislation. An ordinance, generally, is a law ordained by a lawmaker, which in the modern context is usually a legislative body. The contemporary usage of ordinance typically describes the legislation of a local government, city, county, township, or the like. The label alone, however, does not alter the scope of the authority with which local legislation is invested, so that a law created by a legislative authority is neither enlarged nor limited in scope when it is titled an "ordinance" as opposed to a "law" or a "regulation." In all cases, the scope of the law enacted depends on its own terms, its enabling legislation, and the underlying charter or constitution according to which the enacting body operates.

*See also:* legislation (legislate).

**ordinariness (ordinary as routine or ordinarily)**
The usual course of events. Ordinariness is the expected course of events, which requires the routine forms of effort. The ordinary course of business, ordinary wear, ordinary expectations, and ordinary risks are all such things as are routine when there is no unusual or extraordinary occurrence or information, and when there is no evidence of conduct done in anticipation of

a change of circumstances or routine, such as an unusual act done with the knowledge of an unusual liability or done in anticipation of litigation.

*See also:* buyer, buyer in ordinary course of business (BOCB); ordinariness, extraordinariness (extraordinary or extraordinarily).

**extraordinariness (extraordinary or extraordinarily)** Abnormal, particularly in an unusually demanding way. Extraordinariness is the rare event in the course of normal events that requires unusual care or effort. Extraordinary remedies, extraordinary damages, and extraordinary care all arise from some event that is different in kind or quality from the run-of-the-mill, a departure from the usual or routine.

*See also:* circumstance, extraordinary circumstances; damages, forms of damages, extraordinary damages (extraordinary remedy); expense, extraordinary expense; interrogation, enhanced interrogation (extraordinary interrogation techniques); repair, extraordinary repair.

**ordinary** Jurisdiction that is direct and not delegated. Ordinary, as a matter of legal history and judicial assignment, has a very particular meaning, being the authority of a judge to hear particular causes of action without having the jurisdiction to hear the cause granted by a particular commission or writ. The term distinguished the role of a lord of appeal or other judge from a judge who heard a particular form of case only for the duration of a particular commission, such as the commission of gaol delivery. Thus the Lords of Appeal in Ordinary heard causes based on their commissions as lords of appeal with no further commission required.

Similarly in civil and canon law, ordinary connotes the authority to hear an ecclesiastic dispute or action. In some states of the United States, an ordinary was either designated from among inferior judges or court clerks to serve as probate court judges and special trustees over lands. Ordinary is now rare in this sense.

**ordinary as routine or ordinarily** *See:* ordinariness (ordinary as routine or ordinarily).

**ordinary and necessary expenses** *See:* expense, business expenses, ordinary and necessary expenses.

**ordinary gain** *See:* gain, ordinary gain.

**ordinary income** *See:* income, ordinary income.

**ordinary loss** *See:* loss, ordinary loss.

**ordinary wear and tear** *See:* waste, ordinary wear and tear (wear and tear).

**organ procurement and transportation network** *See:* gift, anatomical gift, organ procurement and transportation network (OPTN).

**organic food** *See:* food, organic food.

**organic law** *See:* law, organic law.

**organization (organize)** A system for designating relationships among persons or things. Organization, in general, is a tool for creating a system among persons, things, processes, ideas, or any combination of things in order to achieve one or more purposes. An organization is the whole system by which such people and things are organized.

In law, an organization may include any entity of individual members, including not only non-legal entities, such as unincorporated voluntary associations but also legal entities, such as corporations, labor unions, and governments. To create an organization is to organize its members and to establish its identity as a practical matter of fact and as a legally recognized entity according to the procedures in that jurisdiction that apply to that organization.

**organizational client** *See:* representation, legal representation, entity representation (organizational client).

**organizational standing** *See:* standing in court, third-party standing, associational standing (organizational standing).

**organized crime** *See:* racketeering, organized crime, Yakuza; racketeering, organized crime, Mafia (La Cosa Nostra); racketeering, organized crime.

**original (originality)** The authentic or first manifestation of something. An original is either an authentic version or the first iteration of anything. Thus an original deed is the authentic version of the deed, the version initially printed, signed, and delivered; in the case of a deed it is likely also to be the first instrument, regardless of the number of copies that are made. Yet some originals are not the only iteration, as in an original casting, which might be one of any number of the authentic castings taken from the original mould by its caster. Context is essential to ascertain whether a given usage of "original" is used in one or the other senses of initial or authentic.

Originality is the quality of something that is an original. Originality can, in general, express either sense of original, but in law it is used practically to describe the initial iteration of a thing. Thus an original idea was the idea first had by the person who thought it. In intellectual property, however, originality has a specific understanding that is not necessarily that of the very first iteration of any idea or thing, but means that the creator of the putatively original idea or thing did not copy it from anywhere else and added at least one new element that demonstrates creativity.

*See also:* court, court of original jurisdiction; justice, Rawlsian justice, original position; jurisdiction, original jurisdiction; title, aboriginal title; work, copyrightable work.

**original intent** *See:* interpretation, intent of the drafter, originalism (original intent).

**original jurisdiction** *See:* jurisdiction, original jurisdiction.

**original position** *See:* justice, Rawlsian justice, original position.

**originalism** *See:* interpretation, intent of the drafter, originalism (original intent).

**Origination Clause** *See:* constitution, U.S. Constitution, clauses, Origination Clause.

**origination fee** *See:* fee, fee for services, financing fee, origination fee.

**orverrule sub silentio** *See:* overrule, orverrule sub silentio (overruled by implication or effectively overruled).

**OSCAR** *See:* clerk, law clerk, OSCAR.

**OSHA** *See:* labor, Occupational Safety and Health Act (OSHA).

**ostrich instruction** *See:* instruction, jury instruction, ostrich instruction (conscious avoidance).

**other insurance clause** *See:* insurance, insurance coverage, multiple insurance coverage, escape clause (other insurance clause).

**oubliette** A cell entered only through the roof, intended as a form of torturous long–term incarceration. The oubliette, from the French for "forgetting," was a cell designed for the permanent or seemingly permanent incarceration of prisoners. It persists as a metaphor for long–term incarceration, such as that of political prisoners or uncharged detention.

**ought** Under some form of obligation. Ought is a verb that represents a requirement to do or to refrain from doing something. It is a generic term for all sorts of obligations, whether the obligation of a moment arises from law, from ethics or morality, from custom, or from status or promise. What one is under an obligation to do is what one ought to do. Ought is often compared in maxims to can and is, such that ought implies can. What is the case cannot be derived from what ought to be the case, and sometimes vice versa. These maxims suggest that no obligation can be valid if it is impossible to perform, and one cannot prove an obligation to do something merely because someone is doing it. There are counter–examples for both maxims, but the basic ideas are deeply rooted in legal thought. Ought is usually a verb ("he ought"), although it is sometimes rather messily used as a noun ("the duty is an ought"), in which case it represents the obligation itself.

*See also:* may.

*ought implies can* A duty to do something exists only if it can be physically done by the person with the duty. If a person physically cannot do something, then that person cannot be under a duty to do it. This is usually seen as a limit on moral duties, but it applies as well to the law under the doctrine of excuse.

*See also:* ought.

**ought and is (is–ought or ought/is)** What ought to be cannot prove what is, and what is cannot prove what ought to be. The ought–is distinction is a general rule of moral and legal philosophy that what is the case cannot prove what ought to be the case, and vice versa. The distinction is sometimes called the Humean maxim owing to its argument by the lawyer-philosopher David Hume, whose basic notion was that we cannot truly claim that a moral imperative comes from observing the accepted state of the real world; otherwise there would be no end to injustice. Rather, moral ideas are derived from thinking about moral notions to begin with. This distinction does not hold up perfectly, because modern understandings of what is moral and what is practical are less than distinct, but the basic notion—that ought cannot be derived from is—might be thought of now as a rebuttable presumption.

**ouster (oust)** To exclude a party in possession from the land. Ouster is the act of turning out a person or entity who is in actual possession of land and otherwise entitled to that possession. The term may apply to anyone who bars a lawful owner (or sometimes a tenant) from possession, but it is most commonly used now to describe the exclusion by one co–tenant of the other co–tenant from the premises held by the co–tenancy and to describe the loss of possession to a trespasser or, in time, to an adverse possessor. The evidence required to demonstrate ouster is usually very context specific, depending on the requirement to prove not only a temporary interference with possession but an interference that is complete and intended to be permanent.

**ouster doctrine** *See:* arbitration, ouster doctrine.

**out of court** *See:* court, out of court (out–of–court).

**outcome–determinative test** *See:* choice, choice of law, Erie doctrine, outcome–determinative test.

**outer continental shelf** *See:* sea, law of the sea, national waters, continental shelf (outer continental shelf).

**outlaw (outlawry)** A person decreed outside the law. An outlaw was a person in England or in the early United States who was declared to be beyond the protection of the law. By a decree of outlawry, any person could take an outlaw prisoner, or harm or kill the outlaw, with no legal action possible on behalf of the outlaw against whomever took such action. The term persists without its legal significance as a description of a person, entity, or group that frequently violates the law or behaves as if the law has no application to that person, entity, or group.

As a verb, to outlaw was to declare a person subject to outlawry. In contemporary usage, to outlaw any practice is to declare it unlawful.

*See also:* lawfulness (lawful or unlawfulness or unlawful).

**output contract**  *See:* contract, specific contracts, supply contract, output contract (outputs contract).

**outrage**  Willful, extreme conduct that harms another. Outrage is a tort that results when a person or entity engages intentionally or recklessly in extreme and outrageous conduct that causes severe emotional distress to another. The person or entity who commits such conduct is liable for the harm caused, including both emotional distress and bodily harm, if bodily harm to the other results from it. The person or entity who commits such conduct is liable to a person against whom such conduct is directed and to members of that person's immediate family for any bodily harm or emotional injury suffered by any of them, as well as being liable to any third person present at the time of the conduct for any bodily harm or emotional injury suffered if that person suffers a bodily injury.

The quality of outrageousness — whether the conduct proved is outrageous or not — is a matter of fact for the jury, but the preliminary question of law depends on whether the conduct is of a form that can be found outrageous. This means that the conduct must demonstrate an obvious risk of harm that would be likely to cause distress to someone who perceives it. The nature of the conduct need not be rare or unusual in every circumstance — in some subcultures and geographic districts, assault and gunfire remain all too common — yet the conduct must be of a form that would likely cause anger, fright, trauma, or another strong and harmful emotion to a reasonable person who observes it.

Outrage is an intentional tort, and in most jurisdictions, a person harmed is entitled not only to compensation for bodily injury and emotional distress but also to punitive or demonstrative damages. Note: there are a variety of approaches to the recognition of an action for outrage. Some jurisdictions recognize the closely related torts of negligent or intentional infliction of emotional distress. Outrage is recognized in some jurisdictions that require proof of physical harm from the outrageous act. Others require no special forms of pleading or proof of damage beyond damages pled with specificity.

*See also:* distress, emotional distress, negligent infliction of emotional distress (N.I.E.D. or NIED); distress, emotional distress, intentional infliction of emotional distress (I.I.E.D. or IIED or outrage).

**outrageous conduct**  *See:* conduct, outrageous conduct.

**outstanding**  Unpaid. Outstanding, in the context of commercial law, is a designation for the balance of a debt owed, unpaid, or uncollected.

**overage**  An amount in excess of an amount required. Overage is any amount over a requirement, whether it is an amount of money, goods, cargo, or any other commodity. There are many forms, for instance: if an invoice is paid in excess of the amount owed, the difference is overage; if a shipment is received in excess of the amount ordered, the difference is overage; and if a fishing vessel takes ships in excess of its license, the difference is overage.

*See also:* surplus, surplusage as overpayment.

**overbreadth (overbreadth doctrine or overbroad statute)**  A law that reaches conduct beyond that intended. Overbreadth is a problem in the application of a statute, regulation, or ordinance that prohibits conduct that is beyond the stated or intended scope of the law or its purpose. An overbroad law that reaches constitutionally protected conduct, even if its intended purpose does not burden constitutionally protected activity, may be found to violate the Due Process Clause.

**overcitation**  *See:* citation, legal citation, cititis (overcitation).

**overdraft**  *See:* draft, draft as negotiable instrument, bank draft, overdraft (overdraw or overdrawn).

**overdraw or overdrawn**  *See:* draft, draft as negotiable instrument, bank draft, overdraft (overdraw or overdrawn).

**overdue**  Anything not done when a time required has passed. Anything overdue is late. A payment to be made by a date certain is overdue once the business hours of that date have passed.

Negotiable instruments have an implied period at which they become overdue if they have not been presented. Instruments that are not paid on installments or paid by a date certain are overdue on the day following a day on which demand for payment is made, if the demand is properly made. Other instruments or obligations are overdue after a reasonable time for demand for payment has passed. A check is overdue for presentment after ninety days have passed from the time it was drawn. Instruments to be paid by a date certain are overdue on the day following the due date. Instruments to be paid in installments are overdue on the date a payment is due but not paid and either the instrument is in default or the principal then owed is not paid. Instruments on which the due date is accelerated are overdue on the day after the accelerated due date.

*See also:* default.

**overhead**  The indirect costs of the operation of an enterprise. Overhead refers to the costs an enterprise incurs to maintain the enterprise as a going concern. Overhead includes costs that are incidental but essential to the enterprise, not including the costs of material and labor that the enterprise must also incur in order to perform any given service or to create any given product. A portion of overhead consists of fixed costs, such as the depreciation of a building or the salary of permanent workers, and a portion of overhead consists of variable costs, such as the cost of utilities and sub-contractors. Overhead is an indirect expense related to all of the work the enterprise performs, and it may be billed to contracts that allow overhead as a cost, either as a portion of the overall performance or accounted as a pro-rata share of the overhead compared to each invoice issued for a given billing period.

*See also:* expense, business expenses, ordinary and necessary expenses.

**overinclusiveness or underinclusiveness** *See:* scrutiny, standards of scrutiny, inclusiveness (overinclusiveness or underinclusiveness).

**overlapping consensus** *See:* justification, overlapping consensus.

**overnight familial visit** *See:* prisoner, conjugal visit (overnight familial visit).

**override of a veto** *See:* veto, override of a veto (veto override).

**overrule (overruling)** To reject or make void. To overrule something is to reject it or to make its effect meaningless. A motion that is overruled is rejected (although an exception to the overruling may be made for the record for review or appeal). A precedent is overruled when it is rendered void by a later court with the authority to do so, whether through an express declaration that the earlier opinion is overruled or by implication through the adoption of a later opinion that materially contradicts the earlier opinion.

**overrule sub silentio (overruled by implication or effectively overruled)** To overrule a precedent by implication. An overruling sub silentio is a decision by a court that contradicts a precedent but fails to expressly state that the precedent is overruled. The later opinion may be written in such a manner to suggest it could be distinguished from the earlier opinion because of some variation in the facts, which would be considered a limitation of the earlier opinion rather than its overruling. When the later opinion appears, however, to be logically inconsistent with the reasoning of the earlier opinion, the earlier opinion is impliedly overruled, or overruled sub silentio.

**overt** Explicit. Anything overt is done in a manner that is both apparent to others and that discloses the intent or purpose of the person doing it. Overt in this sense is the opposite of covert, which is something done in secret or with disguised intent. An overt act related to an enterprise is an act that is observed by others and that manifests a particular intent in the larger enterprise.

*See also:* covert, covert mission (covert operation or covert means or secret mission or black operations or black ops).

**owelty** *See:* partition, owelty.

**owing (owe or owed or owes)** An unsatisfied debt or obligation. What is owing is the amount of a debt, or the debt generally, including obligations to be paid in money as well as obligations that are lawfully bound to be performed to the benefit of a specific person or entity. To owe is to be indebted but not necessarily to be subject to immediate demand, unless what is owed is also what is due.

*See also:* due.

**ownership (owner or own)** Title to exclusive dominion over property. Ownership is a relationship of a person or entity to a given piece of property that is protected in law as having no superior claimant (other than a claim by the state, which may be manifest in the limited circumstances of eminent domain, police powers occupation, escheat, or the enforcement of a security interest). Ownership provides a right of exclusive use or monopoly over the property owned.

An owner may do nearly anything or use the property in nearly any manner. The owner has a strong presumptive right to alienate the property owned, either to sell it or to give it away, and few things cannot be alienated. Likewise, an owner has a presumptive right to leave any property at death through will or intestacy.

*See also:* property.

**owner-financed mortgage or seller financing** *See:* mortgage, purchase money mortgage (owner-financed mortgage or seller financing).

**ownership claim** *See:* claim, property claim, ownership claim.

**ownership of body parts** *See:* body, body part, ownership of body parts.

**adjoining owner (adjacent landowner)** The owner of property bordering the land in question. An adjoining property interest shares a border with the property in question. Adjoining lands differ from adjacent lands, in that the adjacent land must be reasonably proximate to the property in question but need not share a border or actually touch, such as when a public road separates two properties. Adjoining owners are therefore owners who share a common boundary with one another.

**beneficial ownership (beneficial owner)** The person or entity who owns a security. A beneficial owner is a person or entity who has an interest in a property that is distinct from the title ownership, the title holder of the property maintaining it for the ultimate benefit of the beneficial owner. A trust divides beneficial ownership from legal ownership, so that the legal owner, the trustee, owns, possesses and controls the property subject to trust to the benefit of the beneficial owner, or beneficiary. There are other forms of beneficial ownership, however, particularly the ownership of an interest managed by an agent, broker, licensee, or fiduciary. Thus, a beneficial ownership in a security is the ultimate stake in the stock share, bond, or other security that is held on behalf of the beneficial owner by a brokerage, trader, bank, or other party. The beneficial ownership of a copyright is the holder of the copyright who has licensed a use of the copyright to another. The beneficial owner of rented realty is the landlord.

*See also:* trustee; trust.

**concurrent ownership (co-owner or co-tenant)**
Simultaneous title of more than one person in the same property. Concurrent ownership is the same as co-tenancy or co-ownership, meaning that two or more persons or entities each hold an undivided share of the whole property, each enjoying the right to occupy and use the entire property, as long as the occupation does not oust the other owner.

Concurrent ownership in real estate in the common law takes four basic forms: tenancy in common, joint tenancy with rights of survivorship, tenancy by the entireties, and co-tenancies in a trust held by a trustee. Concurrent ownership of other properties arises through gift or contract or through the acquisition of interests jointly, as when two people open a joint bank account or an insurance policy has several named beneficiaries of the same priority. While concurrent ownership is also created through partnership and equitable shares in a corporation or other entity, this scenario is not generally analyzed as concurrent property interests but through the more particular ownership rules of business organizations.

*See also:* undivided; ownership, part ownership (part owners).

**ownership in indivision**   Concurrent ownership in civil law. Ownership in indivision is the civilian concept of ownership of an undivided share in the same thing. The shares are presumed to be equal, although by agreement or other means this presumption may be rebutted.

**incidents of ownership**   The rights to economic benefits of property owned. Incidents of ownership are the indirect benefits or economic result of property ownership in addition to the benefits of use and trading. Examples include incidental rights in a contract, such as an insured's right to alter a beneficiary or a purchaser's right to assign delivery of the thing purchased to a donee, or the rights in an equity account to receive income generated or dividends paid. These are the modern analogues to the feudal incidents, those rights over the people of an estate accorded to the lord as a result of the ownership of its lands.

*See also:* feud, feudal incidents; incident, incident as incidental.

**landowner**   The owner of a specific parcel of real property. A landowner is the person or entity with title to exclusive dominion over a given parcel of land. The term is sometimes used more broadly to include tenants as owners for the purposes of

describing or assessing a government act against the title, such as in emminent domain.

**part ownership (part owners)**   Co-tenants, or quasi-partners. Part ownership describes a portion of an ownership interest in any thing and is one of a variety of legal states of interest held by more than one person at a time in the same property. Part ownership may be as a co-tenant, either as a joint tenant, tenant in common, or tenant by the entireties; as a member of a quasi-partnership, when persons pool resources to acquire a common property on behalf of the whole; or as a shareholder in a partnership or a corporation, usually a small corporation but necessarily with more than one shareholder. Other than the fact that it is not the entire ownership, no legal significance attaches to part ownership, and the law describing the rights and obligations depends on the form the part ownerships take.

*See also:* ownership, concurrent ownership (co-owner or co-tenant).

**oyer**   A hearing, or a prayer to the court to be heard. Oyer is a law French term meaning to hear that was used customarily in pleadings as an aspect of a prayer for proof of the claims against the pleader. In general, it depicts a hearing of any sort.

*See also:* court, oyer and terminer.

**oyer and terminer**   *See:* court, oyer and terminer.

**oyez**   *See:* court, court cry, oyez.

**ozone**   An air pollutant essential in the atmosphere. Ozone is a gas made of three oxygen atoms that is generated in many processes, not least being the passage of lightning through the air, though far more is created by human industrial production and chemical use. In concentrations near the planet's surface, ozone is a pollutant that harms the lungs and diminishes human respiratory capacity. For this purpose, ozone is a criterion pollutant under the Clean Air Act.

Ozone is also a greenhouse gas, contributing to the warming of the earth's surface by diminishing heat radiation from the surface. In the upper atmosphere, however, it is essential in the atmosphere to filter solar radiation that might otherwise damage plant and animal life on the surface. The ozone layer that performs this function is decaying due to contact with other air pollutants.

*See also:* pollution, air pollution, criteria pollutants, ozone ($O_3$).

> If an attorney did not know the meaning of such terms so frequently used in the law and in business transactions, he would hardly be expected to advertise his inexcusable ignorance . . .
>
> Capps v. Capps, 110 Utah 468, 175 P.2d 470 (Utah, 1946) (McDonough, J.).

# P

**p** The sixteenth letter of the modern English alphabet. "P" signifies a variety of functions as a symbol. It is translated into "Papa" for radio signals and NATO military transmissions, into "Paul" for some police radio traffic, and into dot, dash, dash, dot in Morse Code.

**p&s** *See:* damages, measure of damages, pain and suffering (p&s) | per diem; damages, measure of damages, pain and suffering (p&s).

**p as an abbreviation** A word commencing in P. When used as an abbreviation, P often stands for Court of Probate (England), Easter (Paschal) Term, Pace, Pacific, page, Pakistan, panel, Parliamentary, part, particles, passive, patent, paying, penal, Pennsylvania, pension, Persian, Philippine, philosophy, Pittsburgh, placiditum, plaintiff, planning, pleas, policy, postal, postmaster, power, practice, precedent, presiding, price, prince, private, private trust, privy, pro, probate, procedure, product, professional, proof, provincial, publisher, and Punjab. It may also stand for the first letter of an author's last name or reporter, such as Pacific Reporter, Page, Paige, Paine, Paley, Palmer, Parker, Parsons, Paterson, Patton, Peabody, Peake, Pearson, Peckwell, Peeples, Pennypacker, Penrose, Perry, Peter, Pickering, Pike, Plowden, Pollock, Price, and Pugsley.

**p as in hypotheticals** The plaintiff. "P" often stands for the plaintiff in a civil proceeding in the story of a law school hypothetical. It can also stand for a promisor, a promisee, or a payee. Traditionally, when p is used for the plaintiff, it is invoked with a Greek pi, π.

**P.A.C. or PAC** *See:* lobby, political action committee (PAC or P.A.C.).

**P.A.C.E.R. or PACER** *See:* record, court records, public access to court electronic records (P.A.C.E.R. or PACER).

**P.C. or PC** *See:* corporation, professional corporation (P.C. or PC).

**P.C.I.J or PCIJ** *See:* court, international court, Permanent Court of International Justice (P.C.I.J. or PCIJ).

**P.I. or PI** *See:* injury, personal injury (P.I. or PI); injunction, preliminary injunction (P.I. or PI).

**P.L. or PL** *See:* statute, public law (P.L. or PL).

**P.R.P. or PRP** *See:* pollution, Superfund, potentially responsible party (P.R.P. or PRP).

**P/E or PE ratio** *See:* share, share as stock, shareholder value, price to earnings ratio (P/E or PE Ratio).

**pack** The improper selection of legal officials with a bias toward a person or an idea. To pack is to place individuals in a jury, court, office, or agency owing to their presumed loyalty to the person who places the individuals in office or to some shared ideology or agenda. Thus, to pack a court or pack a jury is to place loyalists or biased members on the court or the jury. Jury tampering is a criminal offense, although the selection of judges on the basis of politics or ideology is not.

More generally, to pack individuals is to place them in an unusual concentration into some space or category, such as packing voters into a district.

**court-packing plan (Judiciary Reorganization Bill of 1937 or switch in time that saved nine)** Franklin Roosevelt's plan to enlarge the Supreme Court. A court-packing plan is any effort, especially by a chief executive or a political party, to enlarge a court or to place allies on it to alter the philosophy of the court in a particular manner. Courts may be packed at all levels, and the attempts of the Federalists to fill the federal courts after the election of 1800 amounted to a court-packing effort.

The most famous court-packing plan arose from the opposition in the 1930s of a majority of the U.S. Supreme Court to President Franklin Roosevelt's New Deal legislation, which frustrated both him and his allies as statute after statute was declared unconstitutional. Following Roosevelt's 1936 election, he proposed the Judiciary Reorganization Bill of 1937, which would have allowed the President to appoint an additional justice to the Court for every sitting member over the age of seventy years and six months, up to a maximum of six new appointees. Opposition to the bill in Congress was considerable, but the bill became effectively moot when soon after the bill was introduced, the Supreme Court upheld a state minimum wage law in West Coast Hotel Co. v. Parrish, 300 U.S. 379 (1937), with Justice Roberts voting to uphold the law (though he had earlier opposed such laws). Justice Roberts's vote was viewed in the press as a response to the pressure of Roosevelt's bill, although Justice Roberts apparently had decided his vote in the case before the bill was introduced.

**loan packing** Unjustified increase of the principal of the loan after the debt is initiated. Loan packing is a technique used by commercial lenders to increase the principal of a debt by adding to the principal any debt or fee from other services, usually without the borrower's informed consent. Loan packing may violate the terms of the loan or, if allowed by the loan's written terms, violate the banking laws or public policy.

*See also:* credit.

**pact**   A treaty, or a contract. A pact is a treaty between states or a contract among private parties. In international affairs, an agreement among states that gives rise to a working relationship may be informally termed a pact, even if the agreement itself does not use the term, such as informal use of the "NATO pact" to depict either the treaty or the alliance. Pact is the English term derived from the Latin term for agreement, pactum.

*See also:* treaty.

**pactum (pacta)**   A contract, treaty, or other agreement. Pactum is Latin for the making of an agreement, and it refers in modern legal formulations both to the formation of a contact, treaty, or other instrument, and to the instrument itself. The usage from the action of making the agrement is seen, for instance, in "fraud in the pactum," and the agreement itself is apparent in other usages, as in "pacta sunt servanda."

**nudum pactum**   An apparent contract but one that lacks consideration and is unenforceable. A nudum pactum, or naked agreement, is the legal metaphor of an offer that lacks the clothing of consideration and therefore cannot go to court, which is to say that an agreement that seems to be enforceable for other reasons but that lacks consideration will not give rise to an action for its enforcement as a contract. This is not to say that a promise in a nudum pactum can never be enforced, as such a promise could give rise to detrimental reliance.

**pacta sunt servanda**   The custom of international law that treaties are to be honored. Pacta sunt servanda, Latin for "the agreement shall be observed," is the maxim expressing the custom of international law that requires officials of states that enter into a treaty to honor the obligations of the treaty. The customary law is manifest in treaties themselves but independent of the treaties that are made. The principle of treaty compliance logically must precede the commitments of any given treaty, and this custom is a principle of jus cogens.

*See also:* treaty.

**paddling**   *See:* punishment, corporal punishment (paddling or spanking or torture).

**paid or to pay**   *See:* payment (paid or to pay).

**paid-up insurance**   *See:* insurance, insurance premium, paid-up insurance.

**pain and suffering**   *See:* damages, measure of damages, pain and suffering (p&s).

**pais (in pais or pays)**   By a jury. Pais is law French for country, and a trial by the country was once a common law term for a jury trial, thus a trial in pais was a trial by jury.

*See also:* jury (juror).

**pakiv**   Respect. Pakiv refers to a display of deference and consideration for other Romani, usually as individuals, and usually with regards to their morality and purity.

**palimony**   *See:* alimony, palimony.

**palming off**   *See:* trademark, infringement of trademark, palming off (reverse palming off).

**Palsgraf rule**   *See:* foreseeability, Palsgraf rule.

**panderer (pandering or pander)**   A recruiter of prostitutes or similar criminal actors. Pandering, in general, is the encouragement of the baser instincts of another person, sometimes through flattery. In law, pandering is effectively the same as pimping, though there is a distinction between the two that is often lost in statute and precedents: a panderer is a person who recruits a person to commit the unlawful act. Usually, the panderer recruits a person to serve as a sex worker and to perform an act for a client. A pimp is a person other than the sex worker who arranges a client for the sex worker, or who takes money from a sex worker earned through sexual services, manages the finances or other affairs of a sex worker, or who manages a house of prostitution. Thus a pimp is likely to engage in pandering. In Nevada, pandering is the detention of a person in a house of prostitution in order to collect a debt created there. There are other forms of pandering besides the pandering of prostitution; pandering is also the recruiting of a person to consume child pornography or obscene matter.

*See also:* procurer.

**pandering of child pornography**   *See:* pornography, child pornography, pandering of child pornography (pandering obscenity involving a minor or promotion of child pornography).

**panel**   A group of people engaged in a single enquiry or endeavor. A panel is a term for a group of people who are each authorized by law to serve jointly on a single enterprise. Thus, a group of jurors selected for service on a jury is a panel, as is a venire of people summoned for jury service but not yet selected or excused; context is essential to know which is meant in a given statement, though the use of panel to denote the jurors selected from the venire is the presumed meaning. A judicial panel is a bench of more than one judge or justice, and an administrative panel is a group of administrators or administrative judges sitting in a single review of a decision or issue.

**panel attorney**   *See:* attorney, panel attorney (court-appointed attorney).

**paper**

**chattel paper**   *See:* chattel, chattel paper.

**legal sized paper (legal paper or legal pad)** Paper fourteen inches long. Legal sized paper, as a matter of custom, is eight and a half inches wide and fourteen inches long. Some lawyers persist in creating documents on legal paper, and it remains popular for certain contracts and wills owing to the greater amount of content that can be printed on one page (especially when each page is initialed by the document's signator). Even so, most state courts have followed the change to the federal rules and now require all papers to be filed to be printed on eleven–inch–long paper. (The Supreme Court of the United States requires briefs to be in a six-and-an-eighth-inch by nine-and-a-quarter-inch booklet but other documents to be on eleven-inch paper.)

The legal pad, now usually yellow, was originally white and then more often green. Its pages are usually bound and serrated at the top and either fourteen inches long or eleven inches long, but in all cases with a one–and–a–half–inch marginal line.

**par (parity or disparity)** Equal in treatment or value. Par represents equal measure, and to treat someone or something as par is to treat them in the same manner as any other person or thing would be treated. Par value of a stock is a base value for all such shares. To treat one company on par with another is to treat the one as the other is treated. Par is the root of parity, for equality of treatment, and of disparity, for inequality of treatment.

**par value** *See:* value, par value.

**parade of horribles** The undesirable consequences of a legal decision. A parade of horribles is a slang phrase that is used to describe a series of bad events that will occur if a particular course of action is taken. The use of this device relies on the severe emotional impact that is made by the series of events, even though the likelihood of their occurrence may be actually slim. The parade of horribles is similar to the fallacy of the slippery slope; the difference is that the fallacy presents a series of precedential effects to be created by a given decision, yet these effects each depend on the exercise of discretion to further extend the effect of the decision then being taken. A carefully made parade-of-horribles argument does not inventory future legal decisions in other questions of law influenced by the case under consideration but presents future applications of the same doctrine under consideration in that case demonstrating undesirable outcomes.

**paradigm (paradigmatic)** A pattern in a group, or the most illustrative case in the group. A paradigm is a pattern, attribute, or process that is repeated or demonstrated through a number of cases or elements in a set or population of events, people, or things. It is also the event, person, or thing that best represents the pattern, attribute, or process, so a paradigmatic case is the case that best illustrates the thing in common among the group.

**paradigm shift** A change in the fundamental assumptions of a field of thought. A paradigm shift is a change in the basic understandings essential to a variety of acts and thoughts. The term, coined by Thomas Kuhn, is based on his observations of the history of science that led him to see many small advances culminate in occasional great discoveries, which alter forever how many areas of science are understood. Thus, the discovery of a principle of gravity, or heliocentric solar system, altered how much was understood in science as well as in daily life. The term is overused in the social sciences, often applied to any seemingly novel context for thought.

Note: the change of a paradigm for the production of evidence in trial, as in the move of a burden of proof in discrimination cases, is very different from the paradigm shift in social science.

**paradox** A statement containing two assertions that are logically inconsistent. A paradox is an argument that is self-contradicting, in that it rests on at least two statements which cannot both be true because the truth of the statement of one requires that the other statement be not true. Many statements are described as a paradox because the statement is logically self-defeating or impossible. Two independent arguments are, however, not logically a paradox though they are logically inconsistent, because one (or both) may be found to be false.

**paralegal (paralegalism)** A non–lawyer trained to perform specific legal tasks. A paralegal is a non–lawyer who is trained to perform certain tasks related to the practice of law, either in the assistance of a lawyer or judge in practice, such as the collection and management of evidence, or in the independent performance of specific tasks, such as the study of records of title to lands. Paralegals may be certified in some jurisdictions following the completion of courses of training or following a process of examination, and there are academic degrees in paralegalism.

**parallel behavior** *See:* antitrust, Sherman Antitrust Act, parallel conduct (parallel behavior).

**parallel citation** *See:* citation, legal citation, parallel citation.

**parallel conduct** *See:* antitrust, Sherman Antitrust Act, parallel conduct (parallel behavior).

**paramount provision** *See:* bill, bill of lading, COGSA provision (paramount provision).

**paramount title** *See:* title, paramount title (superior title).

**parcener** *See:* heir, parcener (coparcency or co–parcener or coparceners or parcenary).

**pardon** An executive order excusing a criminal or convict from guilt or punishment. A pardon is an executive action that exempts a person who is accused of a crime, may be accused of a crime, or has been convicted of a crime, from either a finding of guilt, from criminal punishment, or from continuing disabilities as a result of a conviction. A pardon may be issued in such a manner that it absolves or exonerates the person of all legal claims, or it may be limited only to a pardon from a given punishment. The President of the United States may pardon any person for crimes against the United States, but governors must pardon crimes against each state, though a governor may not pardon an offense under the jurisdiction of, or conviction entered in, another state. In many states, the governor's pardon results not from gubernatorial discretion alone but from a recommendation of a board of pardons or parole. A pardon is not the same as an expungement of the record, and a person pardoned who commits another offense may be tried in most jurisdictions in light of the record of the earlier offense.

*See also:* commutation (commutative or commute); execution, execution of a sentence of death (execution); clemency.

**Pardon Clause** *See:* constitution, U.S. Constitution, clauses, Pardon Clause.

**pardoner** A person who dispenses a pardon or clemency for a crime or sin. A pardoner is anyone, whether a chief executive or other person, who issues or delivers a pardon or clemency. The term is rarely used for a contemporary giver of pardons, as it more often invokes a medieval church official, usually a priest but sometimes a clerk in lesser orders, who dispensed indulgences. The pardoner was memorialized in Chaucer's Canterbury Tales.

*See also:* summoner; reeve; manciple.

**parens patriae** The state is as a parent to its members. Parens patrie, Latin for parent of the people, is a doctrine in which a state or court has a paternal relationship over, and a protective role toward, the citizens or others subject to its jurisdiction. Universities, colleges, and schools are sometimes said to be in a parens patriae relationship toward their students.

In the law of standing, the doctrine of parens patriae is a form of third-party standing, allowing a state to pursue claims that might be brought by its citizens according to its quasi-sovereign interests for the well-being of its citizens despite being a state entity. Some actions, such as the power of a state to enforce a charitable trust, are equitable or legal. Others are created by statute, such as a state's attorney general may bring a federal action for treble damages against entities that injure the citizens of that state in violation of the Sherman Anti-Trust Act.

Note: parens patriae also denotes the rights and duties of a parent over children. This sense is now rare in the United States, and indeed the obligation of a state to protect children within its jurisdiction is an important aspect of the doctrine of parens patriae, and this doctrine requires the state to terminate parental rights for an unfit or abusive parent.

*See also:* parent, surrogate parent.

**parent** The direct ancestor of a child, whether by nature or legal decree. A parent is a person who is the lawful mother or father of a child, whether the relationship is established by biology because the child is born to the mother and is the offspring of the father, or because the child is legally recognized by judicial decree as the child of the parent through adoption. A guardian has all of the responsibilities of a minor child that a parent has, yet those responsibilities end when the child reaches the age of majority for that purpose in that jurisdiction. Further, a parent is heir to a child and a child is heir to a parent, neither of which is true for a guardian. In most circumstances, a foster parent is a guardian rather than a parent as parenthood is understood in the common law, although a foster parent may adopt a foster child and become an adoptive parent. A person may take on the responsibilities de facto of a parent, acting in loco parentis for a minor child, with limited legal authorities but with a responsibility of care and security over the child.

*See also:* family, mother; family, father.

**parent corporation** *See:* corporation, corporations, conglomerate, parent corporation.

**parental alienation** *See:* alienation, parental alienation (alienation of affections of a child).

**parental immunity** *See:* immunity, civil immunity, parental immunity.

**parental kidnapping** *See:* kidnapping, parental kidnapping (international parental kidnapping).

**parental notification** *See:* notification, parental notification.

**fitness of parent (parental fitness)** The skill, means, and effort required to raise a child well. The fitness of a parent is the measure of a person's ability to provide the reasonably necessary goods and services required for a child, including adequate food, clothing, shelter, health care, and education; to provide a safe and supportive environment for the child in the home; and to ensure that the child receives appropriate supervision and instruction as the child matures. In a divorce or custody determination, the fitness of each parent is a matter of inquiry prior to making a determination, and the more fit parent is presumably the parent to whom custody will be awarded, although most states now bar a presumption that a mother is more fit as a parent than is a father. A person deemed unfit as a parent may lose custody of a child to the state. Parents are presumed to be fit, although that presumption is reversed in many jurisdictions if a parent has a history of neglect or abuse, has been found unfit in the past, has been convicted of certain crimes, or failed for a length of time to care for a child.

**foster parent** An adult caring for a child placed in the adult's care by the state. A foster parent is a person who raises a child — other than the parent's biological or adoptive child — who is placed with the parent by a state agency to be raised according to a foster parenting order or agreement. The duties of the foster parent are those of a legal guardian, and the expectation of law is that the parent will raise the foster child as if it were a natural child of the foster parent. Different states have varying systems for the certification of adults as foster parents and the placement or award of foster children to them for care. A foster parent is not the same as an adoptive parent unless a formal order of adoption is entered, and the foster parent does not ordinarily acquire an interest as heir to the child, nor does a child usually acquire an interest as heir to the foster parent.

*See also:* child, foster child.

**in loco parentis**  In the role of a parent. A person in loco parentis to a minor child is a person acting as the de facto parent, someone providing parental care and support of a child other than a biological parent, adoptive parent, or foster parent. A person who is a parent in all but name for a child is in loco parentis to that child. A person in loco parentis and the child may become natural objects of each others' affections, and a reference to a father or mother in a will or holograph may lawfully refer to one who has been in loco parentis, although there is no other lawful sign of parental relationship, as long as there is evidence that this is the testator's intent.

Schools, colleges, and other institutions with a supervisory role over minors have long been said to stand in loco parentis to their students. This doctrine allows the institutions to provide security and care, to set certain standards for moral instruction, including discipline. This doctrine persists as to schools in many jurisdictions, but it has been replaced with a fiduciary model for colleges in most instances.

**parental rights**  The rights of a parent to have, raise, and nurture a child. Parental rights include a variety of rights in the decisions involved in the final stages of reproduction, in the care of a child, in the management of a child's life and provision of welfare — including the child's location, discipline, and education — and in the companionship and custody of the child until the child reaches adulthood. Parental rights are individual in each parent even if they are exercised jointly by two parents in a household. Parental rights are contingent, however, on parental exercise of parental responsibilities of adequate care, security, and support. They are a constitutionally protected liberty interest, which may not be forfeit without due process of law.

Although a parental right to custody may be forfeit for cause or voluntarily surrendered, some parental rights may persist. Thus a parent who surrenders custody at the time of divorce retains an interest in the parent's child, which is at least sufficient to establish standing in later proceedings related to the child's welfare. Certain parental rights following a custody decree may persist as a matter of the decree, such as a right to determine religious indoctrination or education.

**intentional interference with parental rights (causing a minor child to leave or not to return home)**  The tort of causing a child to be separated from a parent. Intentional interference with parental rights is the broad tort including child abduction, enticement, and harboring a child from a parent. To commit intentional interference with parental rights, the tortfeasor must actively commit some act to separate a child from a parent, induce the child to leave or remain away from a parent, or keep a child from a parent, knowing or constructively knowing that the child is separated or kept from the parent without the parent's consent, though the parent has a right to custody. The right of action is in the parent whose rights have been harmed. Like the more narrow action for child abduction, this cause of action is a tool of divorced parents seeking access to a child pursuant to a custody decree, though enforcement of the decree may be brought as a matter of contempt of court.

*See also:* abduction, child abduction (abduction of a child); child, child custody.

**patria potestas**  Paternal authority over a child. Patria potestas, which is sometimes written as parens potestas, is Latin for the authority and responsibility of a parent over a child. It includes the right of visitation when another parent has custody and patria potestas is still held by a noncustodial parent. It also includes duties to provide affection, care, support, education, and management for the child.

In Roman Law and early civil law, patria potestas is the authority of the paterfamilias, the Roman citizen who was head of the extended family, although this authority was to be exercised through consultation with the family consilium, or committee.

*See also:* parens patriae.

**parental rights hearing**  *See:* child, child custody, child dependency hearing (parental rights hearing).

**parental-liability statute**  Statute making a parent or guardian liable for a minor's conduct. A parental-liability statute creates legal liability for the custodial parents or guardians for the wrongdoing of a child in the adult's custody. The most common allows the victim of a harmful action by a minor child to bring an action in tort against the child's parents, seeking compensation for the harm done. Other statutes create criminal or administrative liability for the adult for criminal conduct by the child, particularly for an adolescent. These statutes reverse the common law, which usually found no parental liability for the actions of a minor owing to a lack of agency (and gave no relief in an action against a minor, who owned no property). The new approach presumes parental responsibility for supervision and moral education of a minor, although most civil actions are limited to negligence and intentional torts, with a damages limit. Most criminal sanctions are fines.

**surrogate parent**  One who assumes the role of a parent for a time. A surrogate parent is an adult who accepts a quasi-parental relationship to a minor child who is not the adult's biological child, adoptive child, or foster child. Such a relationship may develop in fact, in the same manner (and meaning the same thing) as the common-law adult in loco parentis, especially with an adult member of the child's extended family. It may also result from a teacher–student relationship in which the teacher must act in the place of an absent parent, as in the agreement to an IEP for a learning disabled child, or in any other formal relationship created as a matter of law, such as a custodian or temporary guardian might have.

Note: a surrogate parent in this context differs from a surrogate mother, whose role is contemplated to end soon after the child's birth.

*See also:* parens patriae; family, family planning, assisted reproduction, gestational surrogacy (surrogate mother).

**parenthetical**   *See:* citation, legal citation, parenthetical (parentheticals).

**Pareto optimality**   *See:* optimality, pareto optimality; efficiency, Pareto optimality (Pareto efficiency or Pareto superiority).

**pari materia**   *See:* interpretation, in pari materia (pari materia).

**parish**   *See:* county, parish, police jury; county, parish.

**parliament**   The legislature of Great Britain, or of other ministerial states. Parliament, in the United States, usually refers to the British Parliament, which sits in the Palace of Westminster in London and is the legislative body for the United Kingdom. Even so, there are many parliaments, and states — such as Canada and Australia — whose governments are patterned on the Westminster model, denote their chief legislative body a parliament. Parliaments are usually bicameral, with an upper house and a lower house, and in most cases legislation originates in the lower house. The political party with the majority of seats, or whose affiliations control the majority of seats, in the parliament is usually empowered to form a government, which means that whichever party controls the lower house of parliament usually also controls the executive branch of government.

The British Parliament originated in the gemots of the Anglo-Saxons. After the Norman Conquest, the merger of the native council with the feudal practice of the monarch summoning his counselors evolved into the English Parliament, which was considered a court of the King. The High Court of Parliament was summoned by royal decree from the peerage and church, who sat in its House of Lords, and (from 1265 onward) the representatives of counties and towns, who sat in its House of Commons. In time, senior judges were also summoned to sit with the Lords. The custom was established that the King could raise certain forms of tax only through the levy of Parliament, and certain forms of law only through its decree. Members were sent to the English Parliament from Wales beginning in 1534, from Scotland after union to the new British Parliament in 1707, and from Ireland in 1801, or Northern Ireland after 1927. Though parliaments were recreated in Wales, Scotland, and Northern Ireland in the 1990s, the British Parliament retains a legislative role in each kingdom.

The House of Lords held a judicial function as a court of law, which was largely performed by the judges sitting in it, the Law Lords. In 2009, the Law Lords left Parliament, sitting as an independent Supreme Court of the United Kingdom. Likewise, the influence of the hereditary peerage and the bishopric of the Church of England in the House of Lords has steadily declined, and most seats are now held by peers for life, individuals designated by the crown on the recommendation of the government.

**parliamentary vote**   *See:* vote, parliamentary vote, voice vote.

**Witanagemot (Witangemot or witena-gemot)**   The assembly of counselors to the Anglo-Saxon kings. The Witanagemot, or witena-gemot, was the assembly of the king's witan, or royal advisers, whom he would call to ratify laws, to attest grants of land, to advise him, and to enforce edicts on matters of war, peace, treason, and order. It lasted until Harold's defeat to William of Normandy in 1066 and is sometimes seen as a spiritual predecessor to Parliament, which did not arise for two centuries more, in the reign of Edward I.

**Parmenides' fallacy**   *See:* fallacy, Parmenides' fallacy.

**parody (satire or spoof)**   A comical representation of something else. Parody is a distorted imitation of a person, group, practice, or other thing or idea, that is intended to mock the person or thing imitated. Essential to a parody is an effect intended to entertain or engage the observer by association or humor that is at the expense of the person or thing imitated. A parody of copyrighted matter is fair use, outside the scope of the matter's original copyright. A parody of a public figure is constitutionally protected speech, even if the statements or representations would otherwise be defamatory. The line between defamatory and protected parody is whether a reasonable person would likely understand that the parodic representation is untrue, whether the falsity of the depiction arises from fiction or exaggeration of real characteristics of the person or thing parodied.

Note: though there is no essential difference between parody and satire in general, copyright cases have distinguished satire from parody. Satire, in the law, is imitation that is instrumental in a broader or more general use in which the humor or associations that are found to be satirical are not, as a matter of fact, effectively references intended to evoke a response to the person or thing imitated. Satire is not protected but a violation of a copyright. Parody is protected and not a violation of copyright. A spoof may be either satire or parody.

*See also:* copyright.

**parol**   Spoken aloud, or informal. Parol signifies something spoken, and as a result it also is used to represent something done without all of the formalities the law might require in a writing. Thus a parol contract is an oral contract, yet some contracts are written but still parol because they are subject to the statute of frauds because of their subject matter but do not fully comply with the statute because essential terms are missing from the writing. Parol evidence is evidence from outside the writing of a written contract, and that evidence is usually oral testimony of one or more of the parties or their negotiators, but some of the parol evidence may itself be written, because all evidence of the meaning of a written contract that might be used to interpret its terms is parol.

Note: parol and parole are both derived from the idea of spoken statements but differ in contemporary meaning. Parole is a pledge to appear or to do something, while anything parol is oral or informal.

*See also:* verbal.

**parol contract** *See:* contract, contract interpretation, parol contract (oral contract or verbal contract).

**parol evidence** *See:* evidence, parol evidence (parol evidence rule or parol-evidence rule).

**parole (parolee)** A promise to do something in lieu of detention, especially to appear in court. Parole is a pledge to do or refrain from some conduct made by a person in return for release from detention. Parole is used as the basis for the pretrial release of a criminal defendant, allowing to the defendant liberty to leave detention in return of a pledge to return to court and appear from a hearing or trial at a specified future time. The promise of parole for a pre-trial defendant may be secured by bail or by a bond: money that is forfeit if the defendant does not appear as required without good cause. Most parole orders set both a condition of appearance and a series of behavioral conditions that the parolee must satisfy to remain free of detention.

Parole is also a conditional release for those sentenced to incarceration as a punishment for a crime. Parole eligibility is usually based on a statutory proportion of the time of sentence served, although parole is only granted to those eligible upon a finding by an appropriate administrator or board that parole would be in the public interest, including a determination that the defendant does not pose a danger to the community following release. Even so, parole is often used in state prison systems as a means of alleviating overcrowded prisons, and the inmates subject to parole in such conditions are often not as carefully evaluated before their release. In any case, parolees are subject to a variety of conditions of parole, usually including supervision by a parole officer, restrictions on travel, prohibitions on the use of weapons, and requirements to obey the law.

Parole was once required of officers, soldiers, or sailors who were captured in war, to promise not to take up arms against the captor state or military forces in return for a release or repatriation. This practice is now rare.

*See also:* probation.

**parole revocation hearing** A review of a parole violation charge to determine whether to revoke parole. A parole revocation hearing is conducted in most jurisdictions by a parole board, to consider evidence that a parolee has violated a significant condition of parole and whether the parole should be revoked, which would result in the parolee's return to detention, or a less serious sanction should be implemented. The standards of evidence and procedure for a parole revocation hearing are administrative and not subject to the rights accorded in a criminal trial, although the strictures of procedural due process usually apply.

**Parratt–Hudson doctrine** *See:* due process of law, procedural due process, Parratt–Hudson doctrine.

**parricide** Causing the death of a member of one's own family. Parricide is the homicide of any member of one's family. Parricide is therefore sometimes used in lieu of patricide to refer to the particular crime of the murder of one's father, but the term is broader in its scope to include taking the life of a child, sibling, parent, or a grandchild or grandparent.

*See also:* homicide, parricide, patricide; homicide, parricide, matricide; homicide, parricide, fratricide.

**part (partial)**

**part owners** *See:* ownership, part ownership (part owners).

**part performance doctrine** *See:* fraud, statute of frauds, partial performance doctrine (part performance doctrine).

**partial account** *See:* account, partial account.

**partial birth abortion** *See:* abortion, partial birth abortion (dilation and evacuation procedure or d&e).

**partial breach** *See:* breach, breach of contract, partial breach.

**partial certification** *See:* class, class action, class, partial certification.

**partial disability** *See:* disability, personal disability, total disability (partial disability).

**partial eviction** *See:* eviction, partial eviction.

**partial performance** *See:* performance, partial performance.

**partial performance doctrine** *See:* fraud, statute of frauds, partial performance doctrine (part performance doctrine).

**partial summary judgment** *See:* judgment, summary judgment, partial summary judgment.

**partially disclosed principal** *See:* principal, principal of agent, partially disclosed principal.

**particular act** *See:* act, special act (particular act).

**particular legacy** *See:* legacy, particular legacy (legacy under particular title).

**particulate matter**   *See:* pollution, air pollution, criteria pollutants, particulate matter (particulates or PM or P.M.).

**partition**   The division of co-owned property into separate assets for each owner. Partition is a judicial proceeding, traditionally in equity but also in law, by which one or more co-owners of property request that the property interests be divided so that each has an independent property interest that is no longer intermingled with the others' interests. Partition is used to divide the assets of co-tenants—including tenants in common, joint tenants, and tenants by the entirety—as well as of partnerships.

Partition may be in kind or by sale. Partition in kind is an allocation of portions of the property to each owner in turn, seeking a balance of value rather than quantity among each and all, so that each receives a value commensurate with the ownership stake each had prior to partition. Owners, such as joint tenants, with an equal stake should receive equal value, or as nearly equal a value as can be made without waste to the property. Owners with unequal stakes, such as tenants in common with varying shares, receive property reflecting the pro rata value of their ownership, or as nearly as that share can be established by division of the property into parcels. Partition by sale is the sale of the assets partitioned, after which the net proceeds are divided among the owners according to their shares of ownership. The common law gave a preference to partition in kind, resorting to sale only when partition in kind was impossible. This preference is now less significant in most jurisdictions.

**equitable partition**   Division of property in common among its owners. Equitable partition is the division of a common asset held among several owners or beneficiaries. In usage, equitable partition is sometimes used to refer to partition in kind, the allocation to each owner of specific holdings from the once-common parcel. Even so, equitable partition as a proceeding allows partition by sale as well, followed by a distribution of the proceeds among the owners, such as the sale or liquidation of the res of a trust held to the benefit of several beneficiaries. As with partition in law, there is a presumption of equality in apportionment, unless ownership shares require a different allocation. The primary difference in equitable partition is a greater flexibility in the procedure than that required in statutory partition allowances, which often allow equitable decrees of partition to offset the value of one part of the formerly common property against another in order to achieve equity among the parties.

**owelty**   Money paid by one co-owner to another at partition. Owelty is money required in a partition in kind when the property partitioned cannot be divided into portions of equal value without harming the use or value of the property, in which case the party who receives property of greater value compensates the party who receives less by a payment of money in owelty. Thus, owelty is a payment that is charged from one co-owner to be paid to the other because the charged co-owner received greater value in kind. The owelty is the value in money of the greater value the charged co-owner received than the value received by the other co-owner or co-owners.

Thus, if co-tenants A and B own Blackacre, which has a manor on one corner of the land, and A and B seek partition in kind, the portion with the manor may be to A, but that portion being worth more than the portion awarded to B the court requires A to pay B owelty for the difference in value. Owelty is thus a means of assuring equality in a partition in kind without diminishing the value of the property through a division of the property only to achieve equality of value in its parts.

**partition by sale**   The sale and distribution of assets from a single property among multiple owners. Partition by sale is the partition of property held in co-ownership, or a benefit to co-beneficiaries, in which the property is sold or liquidated and the proceeds are distributed pro rata among the owners or beneficiaries. When a partition is sought, partition by sale is available either by consent of the distributees or when partition in kind is impractical.

**partition in kind**   The division into separate parcels of a single property held by multiple owners. Partition in kind is the partition of property held in co-ownership, or a benefit to co-beneficiaries, in which the property is sub-divided, and distinct portions are allocated to the various owners or beneficiaries. Among owners with an equal share, the division of the property is made such that each acquires as nearly equal value as possible. Among owners with unequal shares, varying in their extent of the ownership or benefit in the property, the division is made such that each acquires as nearly as possible a portion of a value equivalent to the pro rata stake of ownership or benefit. Partition in kind is usually preferred over partition by sale.

**voluntary partition**   Partition through voluntary transfers of interests. A voluntary partition is a partition created by the parties without resort to the courts, in which individual co-owners buy, sell, donate, or aggregate the shares of the various co-owners. Voluntary partition may not be possible when one co-owner is incompetent and lacks a disinterested guardian or when one co-owner objects.

**partner (partners)**   An owner of an interest in a partnership. A partner is a member of a partnership, a person with an equitable share of ownership in the assets, liabilities, and activities of the whole partnership and an agency of and fiduciary relationship to the other partners. A partner's interest in the partnership is determined according to the partnership agreement, and a partner may have an equal or an unequal share of the equity. Thus a person who has no equity at all, with the commensurate failure to have liability or rights to profits, is not a partner in the sense of partnership but an employee with that title. A partner may be a natural person, an organization, a business entity, another partnership, or any other person as a matter of law. At common law, minors could be partners, though a partnership agreement might be voidable at the time of majority. Because partners are inherently agents of one another, jurisdictions that bar a minor from appointing an agent owing to the minor's lack of capacity may not become partners.

Note: "partner" may be used in its informal senses to represent any person who works closely with another and shares a common enterprise, such as contracting parties, criminal accomplices, and married persons.

*See also:* partnership.

**copartner (co-partner)** The partner of another in a general partnership. A copartner is the partner of another partner. Under the traditional view of a general partnership, a copartnership is effectively the same as a partnership, but following the development of partnerships with limited liability, partners who have no share in a partnership's liability are not copartners with those who do.

**junior partner** A partner with less than a full, voting ownership. The designation junior partner may represent a person with an interest in a partnership that is less than a full share of portion of equity, usually with limited managerial authority and less than a full share in profits. In most cases, a junior partner on such terms is liable pro rata for liabilities of the partnership.

The term "junior partner" may also designate the employee of a partnership who is not a partner in fact but who is given some privileges of partnership but no equity in the partnership, being paid instead by salary or other means than a share of the partnership's profits. The partnership agreement, employment agreement, or history of communications between the partnership and the junior partner determines the form of the junior partnership created, the stake in the equity of the partnership, the right to a portion of profits, and the liability for debts or claims against the partnership.

**secret partner** A partner whose stake in a partnership is not revealed to the public. A secret partner is a person with a partner's equity in a partnership whose identity is not known to the public. A secret partner is, however, a person liable for claims against the partnership, complicating efforts to satisfy such claims.

**silent partner** A person who is not active in managing the partnership. A silent partner is a partner who takes no part in the management or activities of the partnership, leaving such affairs to other partners. Silent partners remain liable for claims and debts as are other partners. Note: a silent partner is sometimes also a secret partner, whose identity is not revealed to the public.

**partnership** One entity formed by two or more parties sharing liabilities and liabilities to carry on a business or trade. A partnership is the entity created by an agreement between two or more persons (whether natural persons, corporations, or other entities) to carry on a business for profit, as co-owners of the entity, sharing proportionately in its profits and losses. The partnership is a distinct entity from the partners, but under the traditional structure of a partnership, the partners are each agents of one another and empowered to act on behalf of the partnership, with each individually liable for losses or debts of the partnership if the partnership's assets are exhausted.

The early common law did not recognize partnership but considered liability of each person in a joint enterprise to be liable for that person's action, though the law then recognized the societas, which allowed agency liability among its members for other members' actions, and from this evolved the common-law partnership. Statutes in England and in some of the United States, beginning in 1890, allowed shared liability among the members of partnerships, and more recent statutes allow partnerships to be formed with partners of limited liability, as long as one partner remains generally liable, as well as partnerships that function in varying degrees like a corporation. U.S. states now regulate partnerships under the Uniform Partnership Act (1914) (UPA), the Revised Uniform Partnership Act (1994) (RUPA), or variations on one of these two statutory systems. The primary difference is the UPA defined a partnership under an aggregate theory, in which the partnership was not a legal entity distinct from its members. This approach has generally been replaced by the RUPA's entity approach, in which the partnership is a distinct legal person, independent from the individual partners (though partner's personal liability for the partnership as a whole persists, and partners still have individual responsibility for certain aspects of partnership liability, such as for taxes).

*See also:* jurisdiction, equitable jurisdiction | partnership; partner (partners); partner (partners).

**dissolution of partnership (to disolve a partnership)** The liquidation of a partnership and distribution of its assets. The dissolution of a partnership is its destruction or termination, whether it is voluntary or involuntary, whether it is structured through the planned or negotiated disaggregation of assets and liabilities to each partner, or it is structured through a contested action of partition. After a partnership is dissolved, no ownership interests in it persist, and the pro rata share is transferred to each partner of any property that remains after the settling of debts and claims.

*See also:* partition.

**partnership for a term of years** A partnership that persists until a date specified at its creation. A partnership for a term of years is a partnership created to persist until a certain date, at which time it is to be dissolved or continued. A partnership for a term of years protects each partner in an investment in the partnership from a premature dissolution or removal of investment by the other partners.

**partnership for an undertaking** A partnership that is not terminable until an undertaking is finished. A partnership for a particular undertaking may be created to persist until the conclusion or failure of a particular endeavor. The partnership remains committed until that time, such that it is not terminated by the act of one partner, although the partners may terminate such a partnership early by unanimous consent.

**family partnership**  A partnership among members of the same family. A family partnership is a partnership under the law, in which each partner is a member of the same family. Each partner must, however, have joined the partnership in good faith to conduct a business and have acquired their capital, if capital is essential, through bona fide transactions rather than as conditional gifts or other means by which the equitable ownership is not fully and independently vested in each member of the partnership. A family partnership is a means of allocating revenue of a business enterprise among family members to avoid gift or estate taxes, though each partner remains individually subject to tax.

**general partnership (general partner)**  A partnership among partners without limits on individual liability for partnership debts. A general partnership is a partnership at common law, the basic form of partnership in which each partner is an agent of the others, each has an equitable share of ownership, each is to benefit from the partnership's profits, and each is liable for the losses, claims, and debts of the partnership. General partners may have varying shares of equity, with those who contribute more capital (of whatever form) receiving a greater ownership interest. Still, in the absence of an agreement among the general partners establishing a variable ownership interest, each partner is presumed to have an equal share of the partnership.

A general partnership may also represent a class of partners within a limited partnership, which is established by the partnership agreement to have general partners and limited partners. In such cases, the general partners are agents of the limited partners, have the liability for the whole partnership, and may exercise managerial authority that is not vested in the limited partners.

**limited partnership (limited partner)**  A share in a partnership with restricted liability. A limited partnership is a partnership including limited partners and at least one general partner. A limited partnership is created by the filing of a limited partnership agreement with the state under which laws it is to be recognized. A limited partner has a limited liability, as well as a limited equitable stake in the partnership.

A limited partnership must have at least one general partner, whose liabilities for the partnership remains unlimited. This obligation on a partnership to have at least one general partner is sufficient to change a limited partner to a general partner, if no general partners are designated in the partnership agreement. Although a limited partner usually exercises no managerial authority, this limitation depends both on the partnership agreement and on circumstance, and some limited partners are active in partnership management.

Note: unless there is a clear reason to read the term "partnerships" in a regulation or law to mean only general partnerships, "partnerships" in a regulation or law would include both general and limited partnerships.

*See also:* societe en commendite.

**limited–liability limited partnership (LLLP or L.L.L.P.)**  A partnership with limited partners that also has limited liability in the partnership. A limited–liability limited partnership is a limited–liability partnership formed by a limited partnership. Thus, the partnership is structured with limited partners and general partners, though the general partners also have a limited liability. In some jurisdictions, the partnership would be designated merely a limited–liability partnership, though the additional designation serves to provide fuller notice to other entities of the liability allocation within the partnership.

*See also:* partnership, limited–liability partnership (LLP or L.L.P.).

**limited–liability partnership (LLP or L.L.P.)**  A limited–liability entity structured as a partnership. A limited–liability partnership is a partnership that is authorized by the state in which it is registered to do business with a limit to the liability of its owners, similar to that extended to owners of the equity of corporations: an owner has no liability for a debt of the entity that is greater than the owner's investment. (This limitation is subject to a variety of exceptions in various jurisdictions, however, and in many states partners remain liable for some claims against the partnership.) By limiting the liability of partners, the contributions to capital that are required from partners may also be reduced, but also the ability of partners to enforce the capital requirement of other partners is reduced. Either a partnership (sometimes thought of as a general partnership) or a limited partnership may become an LLP, although in some jurisdictions a limited–liability partnership formed by a limited partnership will be designated as a limited–liability limited partnership (LLLP).

*See also:* partnership, limited partnership, limited liability limited partnership (LLLP or L.L.L.P.).

**partnership agreement (articles of partnership)**  The contract according to which a partnership is created. A partnership agreement, or articles of partnership, is the contract among the would–be partners that creates a partnership and governs the relationships among the partners. Although a partnership agreement is usually a written instrument specifying these relationships, a partnership may be created by conduct and oral understanding, and the contract among the partners is thus an oral agreement, with its essential terms implied if not expressed. A partnership agreement is read with a presumption of equal equity and liability and a fiduciary obligation among the partners, without a right or assignment of a partnership without the consent of the other partners. The agreement may structure the partnership otherwise, but it must do so in clear and unambiguous language.

**partnership at will (indefinite partnership)** A partnership that may be dissolved by a partner at any time. A partnership at will is a partnership that lasts only so long as each partner consents to the partnership, and it may be dissolved with the withdrawal of one or more partners at any time, according to the partnership agreement. Also, a partnership at will may be indefinite, presumed to continue until the death of one partner. This form of partnership is treated as a partnership at will, because a partner will not be compelled to participate in a partnership or owe an obligation to do so unless there is a more specific time or enterprise as the object of the partnership.

**theory of partnership** The law of partnership reflects varying theories of what a partnership is. The two primary views of partnerships are the entity and the aggregate theories. The difference between them is one of emphasis: whether a partnership is a group of members or is better seen as members who act as a group. The entity theory sees the group as an entity formed by the group, with a distinct existence like a corporation. The aggregate theory sees the group as a collective of individually responsible actors who share agency, resources, and liability among one another. Though the law of partnership is rife with principles that reflect a tension between these theories, the legal implications of each approach are reflected in the traditional partnership model of the common law, which more represents an aggregate model, and the limited liability partnership which more represents the entity model. In general, states that have enacted the Uniform Partnership Act of 1914 or its variations follow the aggregate theory. States that have adopted the Revised Uniform Partnership Act in any of its forms since 1992 are likely to follow the entity theory.

The difference between the statutory adoption of one theory or the other has practical effects on both the partnership and their (or its) legal affairs. For example, process may be filed against an aggregate-theory general partner anywhere the partner is amenable to suit, but entity-theory partnerships may only be sued in their principle place of business or where a general partner is present for the conduct of partnership business.

**aggregate theory of partnership** The traditional view of a partnership as the sum of the partners' actions. The aggregate theory of partnership is based on a view of the partnership as a collective, in which each individual is an agent of the others, but there is no independent entity and no liability of the partnership other than that created by each partner. Although the law of partnership has included other views, the aggregate theory of the partnership remains influential in the law.

*See also:* aggregation (aggregate or aggregated or aggregable).

**entity theory of partnership** A view of partnership as a legal person distinct from its members. The entity theory of partnership is an interpretive framework that views a commercial partnership as a business entity distinct from its individual members. The entity theory allows partners to enter and leave the partnership more easily without fundamentally recreating the partnership. The entity theory is not entirely novel, yet its influence is more pronounced in modern partnership statutes and in the limited-liability partnership.

*See also:* entity (legal entity).

**parts per billion** *See:* solution, chemical solution, parts per billion (PPB).

**parts per million** *See:* solution, chemical solution, parts per million (PPM).

**parts per thousand** *See:* solution, chemical solution, parts per thousand (PPT).

**partus sequitur ventrem** The young belong to the mother. Partus sequitur ventrem, or the young belong to the mother, is a maxim by which the owner of the female animal owns its offspring. It also narrates matrilineal descent rules in the civil law and among various peoples, particularly some American Indian tribes.

**party** One person or entity among several in an action, contract, or relationship. A party is one of the direct participants in some activity, one with a particular interest that is distinct from the others. It is this sense in which "party" is derived from the French "partie," or thing divided (or parted).

In law, there are many senses of party, each of which has slightly distinct aspects of definition: The parties to a given action are the plaintiffs and defendants. The parties to a contract are the individuals or entities that participate in its performance. The parties to a negotiable instrument are the maker, drawer, bearer, etc. To be a party to a criminal action or activity is to participate in it, in other words, to be principal or an accomplice.

**party to be charged** *See:* signature, party to be charged; charge, party to be charged.

**party wall** *See:* wall, party wall.

**charging party** An employee who charges an employer with discrimination or retaliation. A charging party is an employee or former employee who has filed formal charges that the employer has engaged in discriminatory employment practices or has retaliated against the employee for exercising lawfully protected rights.

**innocent party** The party who did not commit some wrongdoing. An innocent party is a party who has not committed the particular wrong in a consideration that is then before the court or relevant to some administrative examination. Though an innocent party is often identified with criminal wrongdoing, the condition of innocence of one party among several who are liable is also a matter of civil liability and administrative responsibility. To designate one party among several as innocent regarding one form of wrong or error does not, of course, suggest innocence in other arenas of conduct.

**interested party**   A person or entity whose interests would be affected by a decision or act. An interested party is a party with an interest in a decision, action, contract, procedure, or other act. The scope or form of the interest may be defined by a given rule more narrowly to allow what otherwise would be a conflict of interest; an interest includes any potential financial benefit, interest in reputation, or interest in employment.

Note: an interested party is not inherently a party to an action or other proceeding or to a contract or other relationship. Conversely, an interested person is likely to be a party under local rules requiring a filing of a Certificate of Interested Persons.

**party to a contract**   A person or entity who enters a contract with another. The parties to a contract are the persons who enter the contract and are responsible for its performance. To become a party to a contract, a person must have legal capacity or be represented by an agent who has the legal ability to represent the party's interests as well as the capacity to enter a contract on the party's behalf.

In older usage, the parties were identified as party of the first part, party of the second part, third part, and so on, in order to allow printed forms to be used without constant insertion of the parties' names. This practice led to frequent errors and thus has generally been replaced by referring to the parties either by name or by function, such as buyer, seller, offeror, payor, lessor, shipper, etc.

Not all persons interested in a contract are parties. A contract may affect a non-party, as in the case of a third-party beneficiary.

*See also:* disability (legal disability); defendant, codefendant (co-defendant); contract (K).

**party to action**   A person or entity before the court in a civil action. A party in a civil action is any person or entity who appears in court, voluntarily or involuntarily, as plaintiff, defendant, intervenor or in any other capacity that would be potentially affected by a ruling in the action. A witness is not a party as a result of giving evidence alone. A party may appear either in person or through counsel, although counsel for a party must enter an appearance as counsel on the party's behalf. All parties are entitled to service of documents filed with the court and subject to service on any party.

*See also:* plaintiff.

**adverse party**   Party taking a contrary position to another party on any given issue in a case. An adverse party is a party that has a contrary interest to another party on a given issue in a case in which they are both parties. In most instances, adverse parties oppose one another on all of the issues contested in a matter, such as the plaintiff and the defendant, or the appellant and the appellee. Even so, to be adverse, parties need not be opposed to one another in the case overall, such as when co-defendants are adverse as to contribution between one another in the event of their liability to the plaintiff.

**co-party (co-parties or coparty)**   A party with the same interests as another party in the outcome of an action. A co-party is a party on the same side as another party in a civil action. Thus, co-plaintiffs are co-parties of one another, as is a co-defendant a co-party of another co-defendant. Yet parties of varying titles may also be co-parties, so that a plaintiff-intervenor is a co-party of the plaintiff, and so forth.

**defect of parties (defect in parties)**   A failure to serve or to join required parties in an action. A defect of parties is a condition in a civil action in which a necessary party or proper party is not before the court. A defect of parties does not require dismissal of other parties properly before the court, unless the defect is not cured in a timely manner. An objection or motion to dismiss for defect of parties is waived if it is not itself timely made.

**indispensable party**   A party so essential to an action, it is dismissed unless the party is joined. An indispensable party is a person or entity with an interest in the subject matter that is so engaged with the interests of the other parties or with the controversy itself that, in equity and good conscience, no final decree could be rendered affecting the other parties that would not be likely to harm the interests of the indispensable party or leave the controversy unresolved even as to the other parties. In other words, when a potential party is not present in an action but is found to be a necessary party and yet still cannot be joined to it, the action must be dismissed if the court finds the potential party to be indispensable. Thus, an indispensable party is a necessary party to an action and meets the criteria of necessity, but still cannot be joined, and is so essential that the cause must be therefore dismissed.

There is no definitive test for the indispensability of parties, but courts in various jurisdictions have suggested several factors in assessing the indispensability of an absent but necessary party: whether the interest is inseparable from the parties before the court, whether a full judgment can be rendered between the parties before the court in the absence of the party, whether the interests of the absent party will be harmed by a judgment, whether a judgment without the absent party risks inconsistent decisions among courts, whether the parties before the court might be harassed by duplicative litigation, and whether the determination of the issues before the court can be concluded in good conscience with full justice without the absent party. Even so, every decision of indispensability must be made in the light of the unique facts of each case. An action must be dismissed if the court finds an indispensable party has not and will not be joined.

Note: an indispensable party is also a necessary party, but an action may continue if a necessary party is not joined.

*See also:* joinder, joinder of parties | required party or indispensable party or necessary party; party, party to an action, necessary party.

**necessary party** A party whose presence is essential to justice among other parties to an action. A necessary party is a person or entity with an interest in the subject matter that is so engaged with the interests of the other parties or with the controversy itself that, in equity and good conscience, no final decree could be rendered affecting the other parties that would not be likely to harm the interests of the indispensable party or leave the controversy unresolved even as to the other parties. A necessary party who is not present in an action must usually be joined to the case, in order for it to continue to judgment. If, however, the necessary party cannot be joined to the case, the case need not be dismissed. An action must be dismissed if, in the unique context of that action, the court finds that the interests of the parties before the court can not be sufficiently segregated from the necessary party that the party is not indispensable. On the other hand, if the necessary party is indispensable and still not joined to the case, it must be dismissed.

*See also:* party, party to an action, indispensable party.

**new party** A party newly joined or entered into an action. A new party is a party not present earlier in an action. A party that is a successor in interest to a party in a prior action or a party that has already appeared in an action is not a new party. Neither is a party who had earlier appeared through a representative or as an alter ego.

**next friend** A party who represents a party lacking capacity to carry forward the litigation. A next friend is a representative party, present in the action on behalf of another named party who cannot maintain the legal action personally, usually owing to minority or mental incapacity. A next friend may appear though a filing or by leave of the court when the real party in interest has no conservator or guardian. A next friend is often a member of the family of the real party in interest. A guardian ad litem is a distinct office, appointed to ensure the interests of a person lacking capacity, either as a representative litigant or as a separate party, but not as next friend.

**nominal party** A party whose interests will not be altered by the outcome of an action. A nominal party is a party present in an action only for

technical reasons, such as a trustee or employer who is present in order to allow an effective judgment against a beneficiary or employee, or a party present when in fact the party's interest has been entirely assigned to another.

**party opponent** A party in the same action whose interests are opposed to the movant. As a matter of evidence, a party opponent is a party whose interests are opposed to the movant who seeks to introduce evidence that might be hearsay. An admission by a party opponent is admissible, even though it would not be admissible if the statement were made by other persons.

A party opponent, generally, is an adverse party, although the significance of the term "party opponent" is generally limited to hearsay in evidence, and adversity of the parties is a matter of procedure. A party opponent is, however, the party opposing the moving party as a matter of the action as a whole, and not merely on a given issue.

**proper party (improper party)** A party appropriate under the rules and laws to represent a given position in an action. A proper party is a person or entity who has a direct or immediate stake in the outcome of a cause of action, in that the grant or denial of a remedy will affect the party's rights, finances, or other legal interests. A proper party may include a party representing a real party in interest who is a proper party, as when a next friend represents a minor who would be a proper party. In contrast, an improper party is intermeddling in a dispute properly between others.

*See also:* standing in court.

**real party in interest** The party whose rights or interests are ultimately in issue in an action. A real party in interest is the party whose rights or interests are at stake in the judgment sought by the various parties to an action. Thus, an insurer may be the real party in interest when an action is brought for a claim that has been assigned from the assured to the insurer because the judgment will either benefit or fail to benefit the insurer, with no direct influence on the assured regardless of the outcome. A real party in interest is the party represented when another party is present in a representative capacity. Thus, a government is the real party in interest in an action brought by an official in that official's representative capacity.

**political party** An association formed to promote the election of its members to public office. A political party is an association formed for the purpose of selecting candidates for office and then promoting their election, as well as raising funds and engaging in marketing for its office holders and to wield greater influence and authority in government.

**party-witness** *See:* witness, party-witness (nonparty witness).

**pass-through**   The transfer of a cost or benefit to a consumer or supplier. A pass-through mechanism is the allowance of a direct charge or deduction to a purchaser or a supplier, allowing a merchant or supplier to pass a tax or other charge to the purchaser as a surcharge or requiring a merchant or supplier to pass a price reduction or abatement to the purchaser as a discount. Other forms of pass-through are from a corporation to a shareholder, from one government to another, etc.

**passage**   A way of travel. Passage, as a matter of shipping, navigation, or other forms of movement or transport, is a generic term for a variety of means of movement, including the route a vessel or vehicle may take, the right of the vessel or vehicle to travel the route, the right to travel on such a vessel or vehicle, including a contract for personal carriage.

**free passage (innocent passage over land)**   The travel of persons and goods from one state over the lands of another. Free passage, or innocent passage over land, is the movement of private persons and goods from one state over the lands of another state, or at least through a frontier or border. Free passage is not a right established universally in international law but the result of treaties or custom in specific cases. Even so, some arguments have been advanced in support of a right of free passage by landlocked states to the nearest sea or to rivers for the movement of people and goods. The scope of free passage varies according to circumstance in every case, and in some cases it extends to the peaceful movement of police or military personnel.

**innocent passage (innocent passage at sea)**   Peaceful movement through the territorial sea of another state. Innocent passage is the movement of a ship or aircraft through the territorial sea of another state. All vessels have a right of innocent passage through a territorial sea to a port to which the craft may call or in order to reach international waters. During passage, a vessel must travel continuously unless barred from movement by force majeure; may not engage in military maneuvers, fire weapons or launch aircraft; engage in threatening behavior or violate the law; fish or harvest mineral or animal resources; map, survey, or conduct scientific experiments; or deviate from channels marked for such passage. The coastwise state must allow innocent passage but is entitled to enforce its laws as they related to navigation, peace, and order over the vessel.

**transit passage**   The peaceful movement of ships or aircraft through an international strait. Transit passage is the transit of a vessel or aircraft through an international strait. When the strait is otherwise through the waters of a coastal state, the transiting vessel is subject to restrictions similar to those of a vessel in innocent passage.

*See also:* sea, law of the sea, international waters, international strait (international waterway).

**passenger**   A person transported in a vehicle, vessel, or other craft. A passenger is a person who is transported by a vehicle, vessel, aircraft, or other means and who is neither the operator, navigator, or other member of the crew of the craft but is present with the operator's consent. A stowaway is not a passenger.

The passenger of a vehicle has a privacy interest that is distinct from the interest of the driver.

**passim**   In various places in the text. Passim is a general reference to the unspecified locations in a text from which a quotation or idea is collected, used because the locations are of a quantity and distribution throughout the whole that it is more efficient for most readers to be directed to the text generally than to be sent to each location specifically. The signal is rarely used, and its use is becoming obsolete.

*See also:* infra; supra; loco citato (loc. cit.).

**passive income**   *See:* income, passive income, non-passive income; income, passive income (passive activity).

**passport (e-passport)**   A document identifying the name and nationality of a traveler. A passport is a physical document, usually a small book or a card, that is issued by the government of a state to an individual, whom the document identifies and whose nationality the document asserts. A passport is used at the international frontier — the border, crossing, port, or entry — into a state to identify travelers into the state and to determine their national allegiance. A passport ordinarily contains a photograph of its holder, comments identifying the holder (including name, address, and date of birth), an assertion of the holder's nationality, and a request for assistance to the holder by officials and others. The passport book contains pages for visas issued by states allowing the holder entry to the visa-issuing state, as well as immigration control marks.

The United States issues e-passports, electronic passports with personal identification recorded in a computer-readable chip. Books are issued in various colors according to purpose, the general passport being blue, the diplomatic passport being black, and the official passport being dark red. Passport cards with an RFID chip are issued in lieu of books to U.S. residents near the borders with Mexico and Canada.

*See also:* visa.

**past recollection recorded**   *See:* hearsay, hearsay exception, hearsay allowed regardless of witness availability, recorded recollection (past recollection recorded).

**pat down or pat-down search**   *See:* search, bodily search, frisk (pat down or pat-down search).

**patency (patent)**   A quality or condition that is reasonably apparent by inspection alone. Patency is a quality of anything that is visible or obvious to reasonable observation or inspection. Thus, an object with a patent strength or failing would be perceived by most observers or inspectors accurately. A patent defect of a product is a defect that is reasonably discoverable by a buyer or consumer of ordinary acumen. A patent defect in a title or instrument is an ambiguity or irrationality that is apparent in the text. From this sense of information available from the text comes the sense of patent as a land title and patent as a letter conveying a monopoly or privilege. Patent (the apparent) is often contrasted with latent (the hidden).

*See also:* latency (latent); title, title defect, patent defect.

**patent**   A monopoly to produce an invention granted by the state to the inventor. A patent is the right to the exclusive use, production, and sale or importation of a process, machine, thing, design, or plant that is newly invented, which is given to the inventor by the government of a state such as the United States, protecting the inventor's rights for twenty years. A patent is issued only after the inventor files an application with the patent office of a state, which in the United States is the U.S. Patent and Trademark Office. The invention must be novel, non-obvious, unknown, unpatented, and unpublished prior to its application in the United States, and not subject to an earlier abandonment of a patentee. A patent holder may bring suit against an infringement of the patent, seeking both damages for lost market share and an injunction against future infringement, and prosecutors may pursue criminal charges against certain forms of patent abuse. Patents issued in the United States may be filed and enforced in other countries, particularly those states that are members of the World Intellectual Property Organization, which has harmonized patent designations.

*See also:* intellectual property (I.P. or IP); patency (patent); invention; copyright; trademark.

**patent ambiguity**   *See:* contract, contract interpretation, contract ambiguity, patent ambiguity.

**patent danger**   *See:* danger, patent danger (obvious danger).

**patent defect**   *See:* title, title defect, patent defect.

**patent deposit**   *See:* deposit, patent deposit.

**abandonment of a patent**   The conversion of a patent to public use. Abandonment of a patent is the express or constructive renunciation of a right to a patent by an inventor, whether by expressly abandoning the patent or by constructively abandoning it by failing to comply with patent law (such as by disclosing the invention in violation of a patent office order, by wrongly filing for patent protection in a foreign country, or by failing to pay fees required to maintain the patent). Note: the abandonment of a patent application is not the same as the abandonment of a patent; the timely abandonment of an uncompleted application results in no patent being issued and does not place the process or device in the public domain but leaves it in the control of its owner.

**constructive abandonment of a patent (statutory forfeiture or prior public use bar)**   Publication of an invention without a patent. Constructive

abandonment of a patent occurs when an inventor or other person describes or depicts or patents the process or invention in a foreign country, or describes or depicts it in the United States more than a year prior to the application for a patent. Constructive abandonment results in the intellectual property entering the public domain. Constructive abandonment is a presumption arising that may be overcome by a showing of a lack of intent to abandon by the inventor.

**express abandonment (formal abandonment)**   A formal release of intellectual property to the public domain or repudiation of an application. Express abandonment is the deliberate and intentional act of abandoning intellectual property that has been perfected and recognized — such as a patent, trademark, or copyright — which places the rights to such property in the public domain. However, express abandonment of an application for protection, mainly by application for a patent, does not place the property in the public domain. Indeed, a process that is withdrawn from a patent application may continue to be protected as a trade secret. Express abandonment of a patent or patent application is made by filing a letter or form with the patent office, which becomes effective only when the office acts on the request.

**business method patent (business model patent)**   A patent on a machine or process for a business transaction. A business method patent is a patent on a machine or on a patent-eligible process that includes at least some method of doing or conducting business. Though there is no precise definition of a business patent, it is generally a machine or process of doing business that is novel or invented; that is not an abstract idea or a mathematical formula or formulae; that is not a natural process or otherwise outside the scope of patentability, such as attempting to patent something obvious or already in use by the public, and that can be fully and completely described. The idea that a patent may be granted for a general method of engaging in business transactions is controversial, and though in general it was allowed by the Supreme Court in 2010, that court found the process before it to be unpatentable as being too abstract. Note: though as a matter of grammar, one might wish for a hyphen in business-method patent, it seems not to have yet evolved.

*See also:* secret, trade secret.

**infringement of patent (patent infringement or infringer)**   Unlawful creation, possession, or other use of a patented device. The infringement of a patent is the violation by the creation, possession, importation, sale, or other use of a devise, process, or plant that is substantially the same as one subject to the patent, by a person other than the patent holder or an assignee of the patent holder. A patent holder or assign may bring a civil action for infringement against the infringer, seeking damages that may include lost profits but in no event will be less than a reasonable royalty. In some cases, a patent holder may recover attorneys' fees from the infringer.

*See also:* piracy, piracy of copyright or patent (software piracy or anti-piracy).

**land patent**   A sovereign's grant of lands to private party. A patent is a grant of lands by a government to a private entity. It is inscribed and recorded in the same manner as a deed. A patent serves as a root of title or origin of title in title searches.

*See also:* charter, charter as deed; mine, mining, mining claim.

**fee patent**   Tribal land ownership granted to American Indians. A fee patent is a particular form of land patent by which the United States government allotted reservation lands to individuals in 1934 under the Indian Reorganization Act.

**letters patent**   An instrument conveying an interest from the government. Letters patent is an instrument by which a right conferred by the state is memorialized, as when an office is conferred by the crown in England. In the United States, the most common form of letters patent is the instrument by which a land patent is memorialized.

**patent pending**   A notice that an application for a patent has been filed. Patent pending is a customary mark applied to various objects that are not in fact subject to patent but for which a patent has been applied (or which the party who applies the mark thereby asserts a patent has been applied). The notice "patent pending" provides no more protection against infringement than the existence of the object itself.

**patentee**   A patent holder. A patentee is an inventor to whom a patent has been issued and has an exclusive right to create, use, sell, or import the thing patented. The patentee may assign the patent or license its use in an exclusive or non–exclusive manner, and the patentee or an assign may bring an action to enforce the patent against an infringer.

**pater (paternal)**   A father, fatherly, or related to fatherhood. Pater is Latin for father, and from it are derived paternal, for a father's interest, duty, or attitude, and patriotism, for a devotion to one's fatherland. A paternal line is a descent from the father rather than the mother.

*See also:* mater (maternal).

**paterfamilias**   The male head of household in Rome and medieval England. The paterfamilias in Roman law is the head of the family, which in the extended family of ancient Rome, was usually the head of a family including several generations and several smaller family units. The term was used in the common law to denote any male who was not under the domicile or family authority of a father. This use is now rare, having been supplanted by a sense of the paterfamilias as the provider and head of household.

**paternalism**   *See:* jurisprudence, paternalism (paternalist law).

**paternity (paternity test or paternity suit)**   Fatherhood. Paternity is the biological relationship of a father to that father's child, which is a fundamental basis of paternal responsibility as a matter of law. A man's paternity is presumed for the child conceived or born to his wife, although that presumption can be rebutted by proof of the paternity of another man or by proof of impossibility. Paternity may be established by unrebutted acknowledgment by the father. Or it may be established through a clinical analysis in a paternity test. Paternity must be established during the life of the putative father, or the matter is generally estopped.

A paternity test is often based on a comparison of blood types in a Human Leukocyte Antigen Test, which could eliminate some individuals from paternity and establish a statistical likelihood of paternity but could not confirm paternity. A more accurate determination of paternity is available in DNA comparisons through polymerase chain reaction (PCR) or restriction fragment length polymorphism, which can determine with great certainty whether a given child is a direct descendant of a given male.

**avowal action**   A father's civil–law action to acknowledge an illegitimate child. An avowal action is a proceeding in Louisiana for a father to establish his paternity over a child who was born when the child's father and mother were not married. The child is deemed the child of the father in the action and becomes an heir.

**paternity suit**   A civil action to determine if the defendant is the father of a specific child. A paternity suit is a civil proceeding brought against a man who has not acknowledged a child as his biological offspring to determine whether the child is his own, and if so, to declare his paternity and liability for child support. A paternity suit may be brought by the mother, by the child, or by the state. As a means of acquiring evidence, the court may order the putative father to submit to a medical examination, including the submission of evidence for use in blood tests and DNA analyses.

**pathogen**   An agent that causes disease in a plant or animal. A pathogen is a germ, bacterium, or virus that causes disease. In most instances in law, pathogen refers to those specific microscopic germs and animals that may cause infection or disease in human beings.

**patient**   A person under the care of a medical professional. A patient is a person who in any manner is under the care, supervision, analysis, or treatment of a medical professional or medical institution, whether the patient is a recurrent client of a family doctor or the admitted inpatient of a hospital.

*See also:* abandonment, medical abandonment (abandonment of a patient).

**Patient Protection and Affordable Care Act**   *See:* health, health care, Patient Protection and Affordable Care Act (Affordable Case Act or Obamacare or PPACA).

**dumping of patients (patient dumping)** Private hospitals transferring poor patients to public hospitals. "Patient dumping" is a slang term referring to the practice by private hospitals of refusing to treat indigent and uninsured patients. The indigent or uninsured patients are forced to seek treatment at a public hospital.

**patria potestas** *See:* parent, parental rights, patria potestas.

**patriarch or papacy** *See:* pope (patriarch or papacy).

**patriarchy** *See:* government, forms of government, patriarchy (patriachate or phallocracy).

**patricide** *See:* homicide, parricide, patricide.

**patrilineal descendent** *See:* descent, descendant, matrilineal descendant (patrilineal descendent).

**patrimony** Inheritance from father, or one's property generally. Patrimony represents those things related to a father or, more generally, one's ancestry or obligations as a father or head of household. The term is still occasionally found to represent parental responsibility to care for a child.

In the common law, patrimony is a phrase for one's inheritance, whether by law or by will—those things that one receives from one's ancestors. Heirlooms are part of one's patrimony.

In civil law, patrimony is sum of all of the property and debts one has that may be valued; the sum of a person's financial worth.

**patron** A customer, benefactor, or sponsor. A patron is a person who supports others, and the term has several quite distinct meanings in general usage and law, though all are derived from the Roman notion of the protector and advocate who supports his clients or wards. A patron in the commercial sense is a customer—a person who provides money or trade to a merchant or other purveyor of goods or services in return for the goods or the service. A patron in the charitable sense is a benefactor—a donor of money, property, or services to a person, institution, or cause in order to support some endeavor and not as consideration for something of value in return. Patron is still used in many contexts, particularly in employment, and in its older sense as a sponsor—a person who acts as a mentor, advocate, or surrogate father–protector.

**patronage** The power to appoint a person to an office, position, or job. Patronage is the discretion of one official to select and appoint a person to hold an office, position, or employment, especially in a governmental role or when the appointment is not subject to the review or consent of others. More broadly, patronage is the effective ability to designate the holder of a public office.

Though patronage is an ancient prerogative of office, U.S. law has limited the opportunities for patronage, particularly through the regulation of appointments to jobs in the executive branch to selection based on criteria intended to determine merit and qualifications, through the Pendleton Act, of the Civil Service Act of 1883, 5 U.S.C. 1101, et seq. (2011), which has been amended many times, particularly through the Civil Service Reform Act, which increased presidential influence over senior executive employees. Patronage is still an important basis for the appointment of certain federal executive positions, particularly Schedule–C positions, cabinet positions, ambassadorial appointments, and other positions of direct presidential appointment. Legislators often have patronage, sometimes to appoint their own staff and other times to influence executive appointments, such as the senatorial courtesy by which the federal senior senator of the president's party usually designates the nominee to federal courts in that senator's state. Patronage in state and local governments remains common, despite state civil service laws, anti–nepotism laws, and conflict–of–interest rules.

**pattern and practice** Repeated behavior that gives rise to an implied rule or a law. A pattern and practice of behavior is a practice in an office or corporation or by a police department or other governmental agency, which becomes sufficiently established through repetition and the expectation of those engaged in it that the behavior becomes the functional equivalent of a business practice, rule, or law.

A practice that exists in a community, workplace, or public agency that is manifest in a recurrent and common pattern is a form of culture that may amount to a rule or operating procedure or, in the case of a law enforcement agency, a policy amounting to a rule or law. Such practices are common and in most cases essential to the coordination or operation of a group: they are accepted as appropriate by those in authority and asserted as allowed against those who would prefer not to comply with them. When, however, such practices are unlawful, such as unjustifiably discriminatory on the basis of illegal criteria, the practice may be sufficient to give rise to an action as if a formal policy or law were the basis of any harm caused by it.

*See also:* custom (customary).

**pattern bargaining** *See:* bargain, pattern bargaining.

**pattern instruction or standard instruction or suggested instruction or uniform instruction** *See:* instruction, jury instruction, model instruction (pattern instruction or standard instruction or suggested instruction or uniform instruction).

**pauper** A poor person who may be supported by public funds. A pauper is a person sufficiently impoverished that the person may be supported by public funds. A pauper is entitled to a waiver of fees and costs in court.

*See also:* poverty.

**pawn** To borrow money secured by a bailment of goods. To pawn is to pledge goods as the security for a loan of money, and to pawn the goods is to leave them in pledge, to be returned to the borrower when the debt (including its interest) is repaid or to be forfeit then to the lender if the loan is not repaid by a date certain, after which the lender may sell them. Not all securities in goods amount to a pawn, only those in which the goods are transferred in bail to the lender. The lender, a pawn broker or pawnshop, has a duty as bailee to secure and maintain the goods until they are either returned or forfeit.

*See also:* bailment.

### pawn-broker (pawnbroker or pawn shop or pawnee)
A person or entity in the business of lending money upon pawn. A pawnbroker is a person or entity in the trade of lending money to be repaid with interest, secured by a bailment of goods in pawn. Pawn-brokers are usually registered and licensed by the state, are subject to limitations on the terms and interest that may be applied to loans and to the time after the loan or default on a loan after which goods may be sold. Some jurisdiction require pawn-brokers to maintain a register of goods presented or received in pawn, which are to be available for police inspection.

Note: in older cases, the pawnbroker is referred to as the pawnee, and the borrower is the pawnor.

*See also:* pledge, pledge as assurance (pledgee or pledger).

**Paxton's case** *See:* warrant, general warrant, writ of assistance (Paxton's case).

**pay (paycheck)** Compensation for employment, or to make a payment. Pay, as a noun, is the money received in return for services rendered on a contract for employment, particularly the gross receipt or salary including wages, commissions, bonuses, or other forms of compensation that do not include benefits (such as health, pension, or insurance) or allowances (such as a housing allowance or travel allowance). Pay, as a verb, refers to the making of any payment for goods, services, debts, or other purposes. Informally and generally, pay encompasses the sense of what one deserves for things done, as in the sense that crime does not pay, but virtue is its own reward.

Pay as money or value for employment is accounted on a payroll by the employer. Pay may take many forms, including base pay and additional allocations such as overtime pay, premium pay, hazard pay, holiday pay, or special pay. Pay may be for regular employment or pay for services rendered earlier or in lieu of a later commitment, such as retirement pay or severance pay. Pay is thus a signal of employment, and to be in one's pay is to be an employee of that person.

*See also:* wage (wages); compensation, employment compensation.

**back pay (backpay)** Money owed to an employee for prior work. Back pay is unpaid compensation that is paid to an employee after it has accrued. Back pay may be pay not distributed owing to the inaccessability of an employee, or it may be unpaid wages, salary, or other compensation that would have been paid but for an error in its calculation or award. Thus,

an employee wrongfully denied a promotion may be later awarded back pay in the amount of the higher salary that would have been paid from the time the promotion was wrongfully denied.

**base pay** The pay allocated to basic work by an employee in a given position. Base pay is the amount of wages or salary allocated for ordinarily scheduled work in an ordinary week; overtime, premium pay, holiday pay, and other adjusted levels of pay are calculated as a percentage of base pay. Base pay also represents the basis for most income tax withholding and other benefit calculations, such as retirement fund contributions. Each employer may calculate base pay according to its own means, whether as the pay an employee receives, as the pay an employee would receive working the maximum number of base hours, or another formula.

**call-in pay** Special wage paid to work an unexpected shift. Call-in pay is a compensation specified in collective bargaining agreements that is awarded to workers who are suddenly assigned to work a shift that was not regularly or previously unassigned.

**equal pay (fair pay)** Pay that does not vary according to an employee's gender, race, or other prohibited characteristics. Equal pay, or fair pay, is pay that is awarded on grounds that do not discriminate between or among employees on the basis of race, color, religion, sex, older age, or national origin. Under state law, the equal pay concept may also bar discrimination on the basis of familial status, gender preference, and other characteristics. Thus, an employer who pays female employees less than male employees of similar rank, time in service, training, skill, and performance, denies to the female employee equal pay.

**pay day** A day in each pay period on which pay is disbursed. Pay day is a day regularly designated by an employer for the disbursement of pay to employees. Pay days are regulated in some states, which require employees under contracts in certain trades or in certain positions to be paid a minimum of twice monthly.

**severance pay** Pay to an employee whose employment is terminated. Severance pay is pay to employee at the time the employee is severed from employment, usually when the employee is fired for reasons other than employee misconduct. Severance pay is a form of compensation paid, which may be a requirement of an employment contract, collective bargaining agreement, or a requirement of law in specified circumstances, such as a mass layoff.

**pay-day lender** *See:* lender, payday lender (payday lender).

**payable** Subject to payment. Payable designates any obligation that may be paid, or paid in a given manner. Although the designation of a debt or payment as payable implies discretion on the part of the payor, that implication does not excuse a failure to pay according to the terms of the obligation generally.

**payable to bearer** *See:* instrument, negotiable instrument, bearer instrument (payable to bearer).

**payable to order or pay to the order of** *See:* instrument, negotiable instrument, order instrument (payable to order or pay to the order of).

**payment (paid or to pay)** The satisfaction of a promise, especially by the transfer of money. Payment, from the Latin and French for peace, is the satisfaction of an obligation or debt, particularly in contemporary usage, through the transfer of money. Payment is accomplished when an obligation is fulfilled, and there is no bar to payment that it may be made by a person or entity other than the party to a contract or other initial obligee.

Payment, when payment is required in money, must be made in a legal form, either in cash or as specified for the purposes of the payment, such as by check, note, or order. A party has the right to refuse payment when it is made in a manner intended to vex the payee, such as a payment of a large debt in pennies.

**payment bond** *See:* bond, payment bond.

**payment warrant** *See:* warrant, warrant as commercial paper (payment warrant).

**back-loaded payment** More benefits are dispensed at the contract term's end. To back load a contract is to offer a proportionally greater compensation or value at or near the end of the contractual period.

**balloon payment** Payment significantly larger than regular payments. A balloon payment is a large, lump sum payment made either at specific intervals, or most commonly, at the end of a long-term balloon loan. They are most commonly found on morgages, but can also be found on auto and personal loans.

**down payment** An initial payment as part performance on a contract. A down payment is a payment of a portion of a purchase price paid by a purchaser to a seller, made at the time of the contract both as partial performance and as security for full performance when owed. The down payment is forfeit if performance is not forthcoming as required, although a breach of a condition that would make the contract voidable or void may require return of the down payment. There is little difference between a down payment and earnest money.
*See also:* money, earnest money.

**lump sum payment** A single payment made in lieu of multiple payments. A lump sum payment is a single payment that is made in satisfaction of an obligation that might otherwise be satisfied through payments in installments. A lump sum payment usually avoids the interest that would be owed with installment payments of the underlying obligation, though a lump sum (when paid according to an existing installment agreement) may be subject to a specified charge as liquidated interest, which compensates the payee

for interest lost owing to the diminished period of repayment.

**payola** Inducements paid to a broadcaster to market music or other media. Payola is a form of commercial inducement paid by record producers, recording corporations, or others to broadcasters and radio announcers in order to secure air time for commercial records. Broadcast of such subsidized material is forbidden unless it is made with an acknowledgment of a sponsor.

**payor bank** *See:* bank, payor bank (drawee bank).

**payroll tax** *See:* tax, payroll tax, household employment tax (nanny tax); tax, payroll tax, Federal Insurance Contributions Act (F.I.C.A. tax or FICA tax); tax, payroll tax.

**payroll tax withholding** *See:* tax, income tax, payroll tax withholding.

**Pb** *See:* lead (Pb).

**peace** The tranquility and good order of the community. The peace, as a matter of legal usage, is the quiet and orderly life of a community in which individuals may engage in their daily lives and commerce free of interference or disorder or the fear of harm from others. In this sense, all criminal conduct was, according to the common law, a breach of the King's peace, and this sense continues in crimes and conduct that are a breach of the peace or disturb the peace.

Peace as a matter of international law is a condition of stability between states among whom there is no armed conflict or threat of imminent armed conflict.
*See also:* peace, disturbing the peace (breach of the peace ).

**peace bond** *See:* bond, peace bond (bond to keep the peace or surety of the peace).

**peace warrant** *See:* warrant, peace warrant (warrant to keep the peace).

**disturbing the peace (breach of the peace)** Any conduct that disturbs or threatens persons nearby. Disturbing the peace, or causing a breach of the peace, includes any act that disturbs or disrupts the public right to quiet enjoyment of public places in peace and tranquility. There are a host of vague statements attempting to define this: a breach of the peace may involve any act that violates a law intended to keep public order, that offends public decorum, that violates generally agreed-upon social norms and values, or that involves conduct that is dangerous or violent, or conduct that provokes others to violence or further breaches of the peace. A definition of the offense and evidence that is generally found sufficient to sustain an arrest and not to be unconstitutionally vague usually amounts to this: conduct that is itself unlawful—such as a fight, or an assault, or speech creating an unlicensed assembly in a public place, or a public performance of music loud enough to be a nuisance, that either disturbs or creates a fear of harm in other people nearby.

*See also:* disorder, disorderly conduct (disorderly person).

**peaceable possession**   *See:* possession, peaceable possession.

**peculation (peculate or peculative)**   The appropriation of funds entrusted to one's care. Peculation is the unlawful conversion of money entrusted to one's care for one's own use. Peculation was once limited to the taking of public funds, which is one of two distinctions between this term and embezzlement, the other being that embezzlement includes the conversion of property other than money. The limit of peculation to the taking of public funds is now rare in usage, so that peculation is a rarely used synonym for the embezzlement of money.

*See also:* embezzlement.

**pecuniary (pecunious or impecunious)**   Related to money. Pecuniary represents something done with money or wealth, or something defined by money or wealth, or the interests essential to the creation or maintenance of wealth. Thus a pecuniary interest is a financial interest, and to be pecunious is to have money, or to be impecunious is to be poor. "Pecuniary" distinguishes actions that must be done with money from those that might be done through conduct, and so a pecuniary remedy is a remedy to be paid in money.

**pecuniary bias**   *See:* bias, pecuniary bias.

**pecuniary legacy**   *See:* legacy, pecuniary legacy.

**pecunious or impecunious**   *See:* pecuniary (pecunious or impecunious).

**pedal possession**   *See:* possession, pedal possession.

**pederasty (pederast)**   The sexual abuse of a child. Pederasty, generally, is contact by an adult with a child for the purposes of the sexual gratification of the adult. As a historical matter, it depicts sexualized conduct between an adult man and a boy. Pederasty is inherently criminal, usually under the specific crimes of sexual assault, child molestation, or child abuse.

Owing to some confusion among lawyers regarding the meaning of pederasty and other forms of sexual activity, pederasty is sometimes used in statutes and by judges to mean anal intercourse. (See, e.g., U.S. v. Strand Art Theatre Corp., 325 F. Supp. 256 (D.C. Mo. 1970), Simpson v. Spice, 390 F. Supp. 1271, 1274 (D.C. Wis. 1975)). Thus, "pederasty" in some contexts of legal usage means penetration of the anus. Unless used in this limited context, pederasty is not committed between adults or between children.

*See also:* molestation, child molestation (molestation of a child or child molester).

**pedestrian**   A person who travels on foot or by similar means. In general, a pedestrian is a person who is engaged in walking or standing as an aspect of travel by foot. As a matter of traffic regulation, a person on a road, path, or other way who is traveling on foot, by wheelchair. Similar means of assisted self-propulsion, such as a motorized walker, may be used by a pedestrian, though a bicycle rider is not a pedestrian, any more than is the rider of a horse or mule. A pedestrian on a roadway is subject to regulation as traffic. Unless a jurisdiction forbids crossing a road other than in a crosswalk, a pedestrian in a road is usually presumed to have a right of way as a matter of public safety. Note: the adjective "pedestrian" has a quite different meaning, referring to anything plain or common in taste or manner, the connection being that those who go on foot rather than horseback were assumed to be commoners.

**pedestrian offense (jaywalking)**   The unlawful use of a roadway by a pedestrian. A pedestrian offense is any one of several unlawful uses of a roadway by a pedestrian, including interference with vehicle passage, playing in traffic, and most famously jaywalking, or entering a street other than in a crosswalk. Pedestrian offenses are usually defined by state law or by local ordinances and are treated as traffic offenses or as administrative offenses. Nonetheless, a police office may approach and stop a pedestrian under reasonable suspicion of the pedestrian's having committed a traffic offense, which is treated as a Terry stop as a matter of criminal procedure and constitutional law.

*See also:* stop, police stop, investigative detention (stop and frisk or Terry stop).

**pedophile (pedophilia)**   An adult attracted to children as objects of sexual gratification. A pedophile is an adult with a persistent attraction to children as a source of sexual gratification, whether or not the adult acts on the attraction. Evidence of pedophilia may be used to support a case for probable cause to investigate a claim of specific molestation, but it is generally not admissible to prove an individual molested an individual child.

*See also:* molestation, child molestation (molestation of a child or child molester); pederasty (pederast).

**peeping Tom**   *See:* voyeurism, peeping Tom.

**peer review**   Review of a paper or scholarly finding by experts in the relevant field. Peer review is a process of examination by members of an academic or professional field, by which an experimental process, observation, finding, or scholarly argument is reviewed and tested against the standards of knowledge and practice in the field. Peer review is often presumed from publication in a peer-reviewed journal, and review in such circumstances is widely varied in its depth, objectivity, and skill.

**peerage**   *See:* nobility (peerage).

**peine forte et dure**   *See:* torture, peine forte et dure.

**pen register**   *See:* surveillance, electronic surveillance, pen register.

**penal (penal law)**   Related to crime, punishment, or penalty under law. Penal is an adjective that relates to the law and institutions of punishment, especially the criminal law and the means of assessing criminal wrong, but occasionally referring also to restitutionary and civil punitive remedies. Penal law, as a category, generally refers to the criminal law, the designation of conduct worthy of criminal sanction and the sanction appropriate for it. Penal law has various other senses, and context and the intent of the writer or speaker might include criminal law in the sense of the word but focus more on the regulation of prisons, on the selection or management of criminal penalties, on the methods and limits of criminal procedure, or on the methods and limits of criminal investigation. Note: penal is derived from the Latin poena, for punishment.

*See also:* penal, penal code; law, criminal law; crime; penology; punishment (punish).

**penal custody**   *See:* custody, penal custody (physical custody).

**penal interest**   *See:* admission, evidentiary admission, admission against penal interest (penal interest).

**penal sum**   *See:* surety, penal sum (penal sum limit).

**penal sum limit**   *See:* surety, penal sum (penal sum limit).

**penal code**   The system of statutes defining crimes in a jurisdiction. A penal code is a legislative declaration of the criminal law in the jurisdiction, organized to define all conduct and circumstance that are subject to a criminal penalty, forms and severity of penalty that are to be applied, and the justifications, excuses, and mitigations that might affect the definition of a crime or the determination of its punishment in a given case. Although "penal code" may refer to any set of criminal prohibitions by statute, it is usually reserved for an integrated system of statutes, organized into a general part, which establishes basic principles of criminal liability, and a special part, which applies those principles to specific crimes, for each of which the elements of the crime are detailed and punishment is specifically assigned. A penal code is therefore to be interpreted as a whole, in which a particular statute is read in the light of the whole and not in isolation. The most significant penal code in the United States is the Model Penal Code, which has influenced the law in every state.

*See also:* code (codification or codify); crime; penal (penal law).

**penalty (penalize or penalized or penalizing)**   A punishment. A penalty is a fine, incarceration, or other loss imposed on a person or entity in retribution for an illegal action or condition for which the person or entity penalized is held to account. A penalty is intended to condemn the person or entity who receives it, designating the penalized recipient as a wrongdoer, not only to encourage remorse and to discourage the wrongdoer from repetition of the wrongful act, but also to serve as an example to others to discourage such actions in them.

A penalty differs from a fee, tax, compensation, or restitution. A penalty is intended to punish in a manner that exceeds the obligations that fall upon all citizens or subjects of the law; the penalty is created in response to the need for a public response sufficient to deter the offender or would-be offender, to compensate the public, and, for some, to exact punishment for wrong-doing. It is not merely a toll or price.

*See also:* fine, fine as penalty; fine; punishment (punish).

**penalty clause**   *See:* damages, contract damages, penalty clause.

**penalty phase**   *See:* trial, bifurcated trial, penalty phase (punishment phase or remedy phase).

**civil penalty (civil sanction)**   Non-criminal remedy for illegal conduct. A civil penalty is a a civil remedy sought by a government, or occasionally by a private plaintiff in the shoes of the government, from a person or entity who has violated a statute or regulation. In many instances, a statute creating regulatory liability may allow for criminal enforcement or civil enforcement, and in such cases, as civil enforcement is required under the law or chosen by the government's representative as a matter of discretion, the penalty sought is a civil penalty rather than a criminal penalty. By definition, civil penalties do not include incarceration or a criminal fine, though they do include an assessment of money as a civil penalty, restitution, damages, and forfeiture.

An action seeking a civil penalty is brought on the civil docket and under the rules of civil procedure, not the rules of criminal procedure. More significantly in most cases, the burden of proof is a civil burden — of proof by a preponderance of the evidence or proof by clear and convincing evidence — rather than the criminal burden of proof beyond a reasonable doubt, which is more difficult for the government to prove.

**prepayment penalty**   A charge to pay off an installment debt before its term is run. A prepayment penalty is a sum of money that is charged by a lender to a borrower who has entered an installment loan for a period of time, the charge being assessed if the borrower attempts to pay the debt in full prior to the loan's maturity at the end of its term. Although the charge appears to borrowers to be a windfall demanded by the bank in an adhesive contract, various theories have been suggested to justify the lenders' contracts requiring such charges, including a compensation to the lender for the risk of settling at the time of an unfavorable interest rate, an amount (or proportion of outstanding debt) in liquidated damages to compensate for diminished interest, or a compensation for a settlement of a debt that would have been collateralised on the assumption of its continuation.

**statutory penalty**   A remedy for a civil wrong or a crime assigned by statute. A statutory penalty may be either a civil or a criminal penalty, in either case being the penalty for wrongdoing that is specified by statute. A statutory penalty for a civil wrong may be specified as a formula for a specific amount in damages or a multiple of other forms of damages, such as treble damages. A statutory penalty for a crime is the range of punishment assigned to the crime, which is an element of the crime's definition.

**tax penalty**  Punishment for non-compliance with a tax law. A tax penalty is a fee charged to a taxpayer by the taxing authority of a government as a punishment for taxpayer's failure to timely pay a tax or other assessment for which the taxpayer is liable or to file a form or report timely and accurately. A tax penalty may be assessed in addition to an amount owed by a taxpayer and to any interest on that amount that accrues between the date it is owed and the date it is paid. If the underlying tax liability is discharged in bankruptcy or excused after being found not to be owed, the penalty is ordinarily discharged or excused, too. A tax penalty is a civil penalty, though serious offenses under the tax code may be charged as a crime for which a fine is assessed.

**pendent jurisdiction**  See: jurisdiction, pendent jurisdiction.

**pendent-party jurisdiction**  See: jurisdiction, pendent-party jurisdiction.

**pendente lite (lite pendente)**  During litigation. Pendente lite, Latin for during the litigation, describes any obligation or office that persists or is stayed while a suit is pending. Thus, an administrator pendente lite is an administrator only for so long as the relevant litigation is in issue; once the litigation is resolved, the administration is terminated. Likewise, a debt stayed pendente lite is not subject to collection or payment until the resolution of the relevant litigation; if the debt persists after the litigation, the unpaid principal and initial interest (including interest accrued during the litigation) is then to be paid according to the same periodic schedule as before.

**penetration or physical penetration**  See: rape, rape as sexual assault, bodily intrusion (penetration or physical penetration).

**penitentiary or reformatory**  See: prison (penitentiary or reformatory).

**Penn Central test**  See: taking, regulatory taking, Penn Central test.

**Pennoyer rule**  See: service, service of process, Pennoyer rule.

**penny stock**  See: share, share as stock, penny share (penny stock).

**penology**  The study of punishment. Penology is both the study and practice of the punishment for criminal behavior. Penology includes the study and criticism of the rationales of punishment—particularly deterrence but also retribution, isolation, and other justifications, such as ritual protection of the community—as well as the study and evaluation of individuals exposed to punishment, the response of society to such exposure, including the efficacy of punishment in manifesting these goals, both to a specific offender and to other potential offenders. Despite such theoretical and historical breadth, the object and scope of penology is largely driven by contemporary means of punishment, today being mainly incarceration and supervision through parole. Penology includes not only the basic forms of punishment but also the techniques of their administration. Note: the word is derived from the Latin (and Greek) poena, for the suffering of punishment. Poena was the Roman god of vengeance.

*See also:* punishment (punish); criminology; penal (penal law).

**pension**  Money paid by or for an employer to its retirees. A pension is a scheme of deferred wages accrued during employment that are paid to a worker following retirement, including a promise made by an employer to an employee to pay a pension, the sequestration or management of funds during employment to ensure payment later, the determination of qualification for payment, and the payment or payments of such funds when owed. The pension may be managed by the employer itself, which maintains such funds as have accrued for the purpose, or the funds may be contributed to a pension fund that accepts both the funds and the liability to pay the pension, and then invests and manages such funds to pay current and future pension obligations. In the United States, a pension, from the French term for a payment from a benefice or endowment, was originally a payment or allowance by the government to old soldiers and sailors or their survivors, but the benefit didn't become a widely offered (and sought) employment benefit until the twentieth century. Most pensions are regulated under the federal Employee Retirement Income Security Act.

*See also:* employment, employee benefit plan, retirement plan, Employee Retirement Income Security Act (E.R.I.S.A. or ERISA); retirement, retirement plan.

**individual retirement account (I.R.A. or IRA)**  A defined-contribution pension account. An individual retirement account, or IRA, is a simplified employee pension plan that establishes a trust account into which an employer and, usually, the employee pays or contributes funds that are invested according to a scheme of investment that is usually selected or approved by the employee, and that is structured to pay benefits to the employee at retirement. To qualify as an IRA, the trust must be created or organized in the United States for the exclusive benefit of an employee or the employee's beneficiaries, and established in a writing that provides: (1) Contributions must be rolled over from another fund or in cash. (2) The trustee is a bank or approved institution. (3) The account is not invested in a life insurance contract. (4) The employee's interest in the balance in his account is nonforfeitable. (5) The assets will not be commingled with other property except in a common trust fund or common investment fund. (6) The distribution is subject to federal rules.

*See also:* employment, employee benefit plan, retirement plan, Employee Retirement Income Security Act (E.R.I.S.A. or ERISA); retirement.

**Pentateuch** The first five books of the Jewish and Christian Bible. The Pentateuch, or the law in five parts, is the collective term for the first five books of the Tanakh and the Christian Bible (or the Old Testament): Genesis, Exodus, Leviticus, Numbers, and Deuteronomy. These texts collate the laws of ancient Israel, remain an essential basis of Jewish law and an influence on canon law, and are indirectly influential on many Islamic scholars. Tradition ascribes the authorship of all five books to Moses, though this tradition has grown weaker since the early modern criticism of Benedict Spinoza.

*See also:* Torah (Pentateuch).

**penumbra** *See:* meaning, penumbra, penumbral meaning; meaning, penumbra.

**penumbra theory** *See:* privacy, right to privacy, penumbra theory (penumbral right).

**penumbral meaning** *See:* meaning, penumbra, penumbral meaning.

**penumbral right** *See:* privacy, right to privacy, penumbra theory (penumbral right).

**peonage** *See:* slavery, involuntary servitude, peonage (debt bondage).

**people** The state itself or a nation that has no state. The people, in the domestic constitutional sense in the United States of America as a whole, a single corporate entity comprising each individual citizen. The people are the sovereign in the United States and in each state. The people are represented by the state, and so a criminal action in many jurisdictions is brought in the name of the people of the state.

In international law, a people is a group associated by culture, language, lineage, or history who are not geographically distributed in a single state. A people might or might not have any state in which the state recognizes or values its language or heritage. In this sense "a people" is used in a sense in which "a nation" is also sometimes used, not as a nation-state but as a national group with a source of coherence and communal identity distinct from the identity of a state.

*See also:* nation (national or nationalism or nationality).

**sovereign people** The official sovereign in a state governed by popular rule. A sovereign people describes the role of the polity as a whole as the superior over the state. Although the theory is that of government of the people, by the people, and for the people, in practice, the fundamental significance of a sovereign people is that no individual or group smaller than the people as a whole may be sovereign.

*See also:* sovereign (sovereignty).

**per** By, of, or through. Per is a useful preposition in Latin, representing a relationship of transit, process, or change, which in English might be represented as "by," "of," or "through."

**per autre vie** *See:* vie, per autre vie (pur autre vie).

**per capita** *See:* distribution, distribution of estate, per capita, per capita with representation (modified per stirpes); distribution, distribution of estate, per capita.

**per capita with representation** *See:* distribution, distribution of estate, per capita, per capita with representation (modified per stirpes).

**per curiam opinion** *See:* opinion, judicial opinion, per curiam opinion.

**per my et per tout** *See:* tenancy, co-tenancy, joint tenancy, per my et per tout (per tout).

**per stirpes** *See:* distribution, distribution of estate, per stirpes (in stirpes or rule of representation).

**per tout** *See:* tenancy, co-tenancy, joint tenancy, per my et per tout (per tout).

**per annum** Per year. Per annum, Latin for by the year or in each year, is a designation for anything that occurs or is measured by a year of 365 days or, in a leap year, of 366 days, whether the year is an annual year from January through December, a year from one day until the same day in the year following or preceding, or an accounting year.

**per capita** Per person. Per capita, or per person, is a Latin term meaning "by heads," and in English is used to denote an individualistic apportionment of given data, an assessment divided by the number of people in a relevant group or an assessment made by assessing each person relevant to the assessment. A distribution of an inheritance made per capita gives all eligible heirs an equal share, as opposed to a distribution per stirpes, which would give shares of varying size to a spouse and to the children. In social or economic statistics, it is a measure of an aggregate sum divided by the number of people in the population for which the sum is relevant. A statistic reported per capita divides the sum found by the people among whom it is found, so a GDP per capita divides a national gross domestic product by the presumed number of people in the nation.

**per contra** On the contrary. Per contra, Latin for on the contrary or on the other hand, labels an argument or proof in opposition to an argument earlier advanced, whether by the speaker or by another speaker. The label may precede the proof in opposition or be used to refer to the argument by reference. There is a subtle difference in usage between per contra and vice versa.

*See also:* vice, vice versa.

**per diem**   Per day. Per diem is Latin for by the day, or per day. Per diem may describe anything that is calculated on a daily basis, including profits, losses, expenses, damages, income, or any other ongoing obligation or activity. Context is essential to know the thing tallied by day. When "per diem" is used alone (rather than to modify a noun like allocations per diem), it usually refers to an employee's allowance for reimbursable travel expenses, which are calculated on a fixed sum per day (often not counting specific expenses, such as lodging and transport ticket fares, which are accounted separately), regardless of the expenses the employee in fact incurs.

**per quod**   Something specific to the circumstances. Per quod, Latin for "by which" has several distinct senses in law. A damage suffered per quod is a special damage that arises in the circumstances, and the damage may not be presumed but must be pled and proven. In this sense, a claim for defamation per quod must allege and demonstrate actual damages.

A claim brought per quod is one derivative of another person's claim, as when a spouse claims for loss of consortium from the injury or death of the other spouse. In the common law, such derivative actions were specific: an action per quod consortium amisit, or "by which he lost her companionship," was for the injury or loss of a spouse; an action per quod servitum amisit, or "by which he lost the services," was for injuries to someone under the plaintiff's employment or supervision, such as injury to a child or servant.

*See also:* libel, libel per quod; slander, slander per quod.

**per se**   In and of itself. Per se, Latin for in itself, depicts something generalized, something considered in its most essential and generic character, without considering irrelevant or idiosyncratic descriptions. Anything considered per se is seen without context, innuendo, or unnecessary specificity. For example, to refer to law per se is to refer to the essential aspects of law, rather than any given law or even national set of laws. Any law that applies to an act per se applies to all such acts, and it does not distinguish among acts according to context. Conversely any law that is unconstitutional per se violates the constitution inherently and may not be applied to any situation in a constitutionally acceptable manner.

**percolation (soil percolation or water percolation)**   Water that passes through soils and other matter in the Earth. Percolating water is water that migrates through soil, rock, and the strata below the ground. Percolation is a means of a liquid moving among tiny channels and gaps among the particulate that comprise the soil and strata. Percolating waters differ from streams and channels whether on the surface or below. Soil is considered to percolate or not to percolate according to the speed by which water may percolate through it. Generally, soils with a higher content of fine clay percolate less. Strata of hard rock, such as granite, do not generally percolate except at rock seams, while soft and porous rock, such as sandstone, may percolate.

**peremptory (peremptorily)**   By absolute right. Anything peremptory is done by authority that is not subject to refusal, debate, justification, or exception but done as a matter of right in the discretion of the person who does it. Thus, a peremptory challenge is a challenge to a juror that requires no reason or justification. A peremptory motion is not subject to argument or denial. Even so, a peremptory act is inherently limited, and the peremptory nature of a motion, action, or order does not preclude its review to determine that the conditions required to make such a motion, commit such an action, or issue such an order, were satisfied before and in the doing. Likewise, the authority to act in a peremptory manner in one regard does not abrogate other obligations; thus, the license to strike a person from the jury list through peremptory challenges does not allow an attorney to pick a jury based on race.

**peremptory challenge**   *See:* jury, jury selection, juror challenge, peremptory challenge, Batson challenge (racial challenge or gender challenge or Batson motion); jury, jury selection, juror challenge, peremptory challenge.

**peremptory instruction**   *See:* instruction, jury instruction, peremptory instruction (mandatory instruction).

**perfect competition**   *See:* competition, perfect competition.

**perfected security interest**   *See:* security, security interest, perfected security interest.

**perfection (imperfection or perfect or imperfect)**   Complete and legally enforceable. To perfect something is to finish it so that no further change is required to complete or improve it. In law, to perfect an interest or document is to do all that is required to make it final, complete, and legally enforceable. Thus, to perfect an instrument is to complete all of its requirements for legal status. To perfect a claim is to make it enforceable and defensible, and to perfect commercial paper is properly to endorse, present, or transfer it. To perfect a will is to sign it and have it appropriately witnessed. To perfect a claim is to file a notice of a claim that may be enforced in an action against third parties.

Therefore, a perfected interest or a perfect interest is one that is subject to such action, or one that is complete as a matter of law. Thus, a perfect defense to a claim will bar the claim utterly.

Perfection is often contrasted with imperfection, and an imperfect claim may not ordinarily be enforced at all in the law. A moral right was once considered an imperfect right because it could not be enforced at law, as could a perfect right. This dichotomy is not always true, though, and, for instance, an imperfect defense in a criminal case usually allows a mitigation of a penalty (though a perfect defense required dismissal of the charges).

Note: there is a difference of stress in the pronunciation of perfect as a noun and as a verb or adjective. A perfect right is said with an emphasis on the first syllable, PERfect. To perfect a right is said with the emphasis on the second syllable, perFECT. A perfected right, however, is akin to the verb and said with emphasis on the middle syllable, perFECted.

**perfection of title**  *See:* title, perfection of title (imperfect title).

**perfectionism**  *See:* jurisprudence, perfectionism (legal perfectionism).

**perfidy (perfidious or perfidiously)**  A breach of good faith. Perfidy is unprofessional conduct, particularly a breach of an obligation of good faith by an act of commission. Perfidy may occur whether the breached duty of good faith had been express or implied.
*See also:* faith, good faith (bona fide).

**performance (perform)**  A thing done, or the means and manner by which it is done. Performance is the act of doing something, such as carrying out one's promise in a contract. It is also an assessment of the degree of success or quality in the doing of it. Complicating these two senses, performance is also the end a term for the end result of such an act. The fact of performance is therefore important during the time it is carried out and at all times after. To carry out one's promise under a contract is to perform the contract.

Performance is the essential aspect of the satisfaction of duty, promise, and obligation. The duty, promise, or obligation is legally enforceable if a legal action will lie against the obligated person who fails to perform the duty, promise, or obligation in an adequate and timely fashion.

**performance bond**  *See:* bond, surety bond (performance bond); bond, performance bond.

**performance in more than one year**  *See:* fraud, statute of frauds, performance in more than one year.

**contract performance**

**alternative performance**  Performance of one of several interchangeable obligations. Alternative performance is a form of contract performance that is available when the contract is structured so that a party can perform fully its obligations in more than one manner, and that party does perform its obligations by electing to perform in one or another of the manners it may choose. If, for instance, A promises to sell a widget to B, and B promises either to buy the widget or secure another buyer to purchase the widget from A, then B may perform fully through persuading C, who would not otherwise have bought the widget from A, to do so. B's alternative performance satisfies the contract, and the contingent obligation to complete the alternative performance, to buy the widget, lapses. Yet, alternative performance is not available as a defense to a claim of breach unless the contract is structured to do so. If the contract between A and B merely had a promise by B to purchase, and B had

not purchased but offered a promise by C to purchase, B would still be in breach of its promise (though A's damages might be mitigated).

**best efforts**  A heightened duty to perform an obligation under a contract. Best efforts is a standard of performance and a duty of care. A duty to use best efforts is expressly required in many contracts but implied by law in outputs and requirements contracts, although this implication can be rebutted by specific language in the agreement. Best efforts is more than reasonable efforts, and although best efforts does not require a contractor to perform this duty ahead of all other tasks, it means at least performing the duties required under this duty as well or better than performing duties for others to whom the contractor is not similarly bound. Courts have held best efforts to require reasonable foresight and contingency plans to overcome obstacles to performance, such as force majeure.
*See also:* contract, specific contracts, supply contract, output contract (outputs contract); contract, specific contracts, supply contract, requirements contract.

**course of performance**  Routine conduct related to past contract performance that parties may expect in future performance. The course of performance depicts the routine performance of duties required under a contract or actions that are essential to perform duties under a contract, when one party engages in this routine and the other is or should be aware of it and acknowledges or at least does not object to the routine. A course of performance can be incorporated into later contracts by explicit reference or by implication based on the parties' reasonable expectations.

**non-performance (nonperformance)**  The unjustified failure to perform an obligation. Non-performance is the failure of a party to perform its obligation when the obligation is in force and no basis for excusing or abating the obligation exists. Not all failures to perform an obligation amount to non-performance. For example, performance that becomes impossible or was in fact impossible at the time of the contract is not non-performance because the contract is voidable or void. More commonly, the failure of one party to perform an obligation is not non-performance if its obligation was alleviated by the other party's prior breach of its own obligations under the contract from which the obligations arise.

**offer of performance (tender of performance)**  A good-faith statement that a party is ready and willing to perform. An offer of performance, or a tender of a performance, is an overt statement or demonstration by one party that it is prepared to perform its obligation under a contract, which is made in good faith to the other party. An offer of performance is usually required by the non-breaching party when the other party manifests an anticipatory breach of a contract. Even so, an offer of performance is not required if the other party so clearly manifests its intent to breach that the offer would have only ceremonial benefit.

**simultaneous performances**  Performance by two or more parties at the same time. Simultaneous performance is the performance at the same time by two or more parties to a contract of some contractually obligated conduct. Though simultaneous performance may occur as a matter of happenstance, a contract may specify that its parties shall perform some required action under the agreement at the same time. A contract that requires simultaneous performance, whether expressly or by implication, must be performed simultaneously. Though simultaneous performance is often accomplished by payment at the time of transfer of goods, it may be accomplished through many means, including the use of escrow agents, so that the parties prepare to perform at various times, but their performance is executed, in effect, by the agents for each at once.

**time of performance (time is of the essence or time of essence)**  A failure to perform in time amounts to a breach. The time of performance is a time expressed or implied under a contract for the performance of obligations. In the absence of an express time for performance, a reasonable time is implied. When one party does not fully perform within the time expressed or within a reasonable time, that party has breached the contract if time is of the essence of the contract. Time is of the essence in any contract that has a clause to this effect. For some transactions, it may be that time is of the essence of the contract, such as contracts for the sale of land, for the delivery of perishables, or for the purchase of goods that the seller knows to be needed on a given date. If time is not of the essence, then an unreasonable delay in performance that operates to the harm of the other party who is ready, willing, and able to perform will also amount to breach.

**cost of performance**  The expenses accounted for the performance of a business or duty. Generally, the cost of performance is the expense incurred in the performance of an obligation under a contract or in any other endeavor, including the ordinary performance of business transactions or production. Cost of performance is generally based on accounting principles by which the expenses of performance are assessed within the broader activities of the performing individual or entity, so that performance would include indirect costs, such as a share of overhead and the depreciation of deployed assets. Even so, the term has several specialized applications that are broader or narrower than this basic premise.

The cost of performance is a measure of restitution for breach of contract, by which a plaintiff may recover not only the benefit of the plaintiff's performance that is realized by a breaching defendant but also the expenses of performance that were actually borne by the plaintiff.

The cost of performance is an accounting measure to determine where an activity took place, particularly in what jurisdiction an activity is performed. The cost of performance is allocated for a given task among the various places where part performance occurred, locating a performance in any place according to the formula applied to the costs incurred.

**election of performance**  Freedom of a contracting party to choose a method of performance. Election of performance is a right of a party to an alternative contract who may select among several methods to perform the obligation under the contract, either because the contract is silent as to the means of performance or because several are contemplated and the choice among them is expressly dedicated to that party. The choice of means of performance is the election, although the performance itself may serve as the election.

**future performance**  Performance at a time later than a promise is made or a condition is satisfied. Future performance is a performance yet to occur when it is promised, assessed, or estimated for the purpose of reliance by others. To some degree, most promises are commitments to future performance, and the term is ordinarily used to describe a promise to perform an obligation after the other party has partly or fully performed, or after a contingency is satisfied. Thus, many promises of future performance amount to a warranty in the sense that the promise is a commitment to do something in the event of future requirement.

Future performance may be the basis for prior reliance giving rise to estoppel, in that a pattern of performance may give rise to an expectation that the person or entity performing will continue to perform in the same manner. Such reliance must be reasonable, known to the performer prior to or at the time of reliance, and either accepted or at least not rejected.

*See also:* warranty.

**order of performance**  Which party shall perform, or does perform, before or after others. The order of performance is the order according to which each party will carry out specific obligations under a contract, particularly when one party's action is a precondition to action by another party. If the order of performance is immaterial to a contract and time is not of the essence, a party's failure to perform, alone, may not excuse the other's breach or non-performance.

Note: although order of performance usually refers to the order of performance contemplated by the parties in the making of the contract, context is essential in reading the term in later correspondence or litigation, as "order of performance" may also refer to the order in which the parties did in fact perform.

**ready, willing, and able**  The desire and capacity of a party to perform a task. To be ready, willing, and able is the condition of a party that is capable of performing a given service, obligation, or responsibility and that will, in fact, do so if any conditions requiring or allowing such performance are satisfied. Thus, a party ready, willing, and able to enter a contract would accept an offer to such a contract if it was made. A party, ready, willing, and able to perform a contract will perform it if a precondition to its performance is satisfied. A party, ready, willing, and able to convey land holds title to the land and is ready to transfer it when called upon to do so.

The existence of a party ready, willing, and able to perform may be a condition of other obligations. For example, a party under an obligation to cover following a breach by another party to a contract must do so if an alternate party is ready, willing, and able to enter an appropriate contract for the goods. Yet if the party with the obligation to cover makes a reasonable effort to discover an alternative party with which to cover, and finds no party ready, willing, and able to do so, its obligation to cover may be considered either satisfied or excused.

**specific performance** An equitable remedy compelling performance of a stated action. Specific performance is an equitable remedy, which compels the defendant to perform the specified actions in order to do equity, especially to perform some conduct that was promised yet not performed, resulting in a breach of contract. The decision of whether to compel performance rests within the court's discretion according to the balance of the equities. Owing in part to the equitable maxims, specific performance is not available to a plaintiff who could be made whole by damages or another judgment in law.

*equitable principles* Specific performance is an equitable remedy and not to be ordered unless it is appropriate under the standards of equity. Thus, specific performance is not appropriate if a remedy at law would make the plaintiff whole, if the defendant has unclean hands, or if in the balance of the equities, it is not appropriate for the court to exercise its powers of equity in this manner as between these parties.
*See also:* equity (equitable).

**substantial performance** The performance of essential if not all obligations. Substantial performance is the performance of the most essential obligations in a contract, even if every detail of every obligation is not concluded. The measure of substantial performance is from the promissee's reasonable expectations under the agreement; if the promissee has received what is effectively all of the benefit the promissee contemplated in the agreement, the promissor has substantially performed.

A party to a contract in which the performance by each party is a condition of the performance of the other may not complain of the other party's breach unless the complaining party has substantially performed its obligations under the contract. This requirement of substantial performance in order to complain of breach by the other party in a mutual agreement is the substantial performance doctrine.

**peril (perilous)** The cause of an accidental injury or loss. A peril is the accidental cause of a loss to property or injury to a person. Owing to the more general sense of a peril as a danger or risk of injury as the result of a peril, lawyers and judges sometimes use peril to mean the potential for a harm rather than its more traditional (and still common) sense as the cause of the harm. Thus, to be in peril is to be at risk of harm, whether or not the harm is manifest. Some jurisdictions distinguish peril for the purposes of defenses, as well as the rebuttal doctrine of last clear chance. This distinction contrasts voluntary peril (in which a person places oneself at risk of a peril knowingly and in control of the risk) with inadvertant peril (in which a person is negligently unaware of a peril until it causes harm), and helpless peril (in which a person's own negligence creates a risk to an additional peril).

*See also:* negligence, last clear chance (last–clear–chance doctrine); risk.

**period (periodic)** A specified length of time. A period is an interval of time, which may be defined in many ways. A period may exist from one time to another, from one event to another, for a specific amount of time that elapses from one moment, day, or event. In law, a period of time for a given action may be express or implied, but the time implied may vary according to the purpose of the period.

Many interests are tied to time in law, and the time for such interests to be protected or to be forfeit is often expressed according to a period. The period for performance of a contract is either expressed in a contract or a reasonable period for performance is implied. On the other hand, the period for the compliance of a court order is either expressed or is implied to be as soon as practicable. To say that a condition or obligation is periodic is to suggest it is to be performed over one or more periods, implying that the condition or obligation may continue into successive periods. In property or contracts, a periodic obligation is presumed to repeat into later periods unless there is express language in an agreement or evidence from conduct of the parties to rebut the presumption.

*See also:* lease, leasehold, tenancy, periodic tenancy.

**periodic tenancy** *See:* lease, lease, leasehold, tenancy, periodic tenancy.

**grace period** A period during which a delay in performance or action is excused. A grace period is a period during which an action or other performance that is otherwise late may still be carried out without barrier or significant penalty; the late act is treated as if it was made on time.

**perjury (perjure)** A false statement made knowingly while under oath. Perjury is the crime of making any statement under oath that the speaker knows to be false. Perjury does not depend on whether the false statement is one of fact, belief, or opinion or whether the falsehood is obvious or not. In some jurisdictions a statement is not criminally perjurious unless it relates to a matter that is material to the cause of action for which the testimony of the speaker is sought. Although perjury in some jurisdictions requires the false statement to be made willfully, if a witness is legally competent and under no coercion beyond the obligation to appear and to tell the truth, willfulness may be found in the voluntary nature of the statement made when there is evidence that proves beyond a reasonable doubt that the witness knows the statement to be false. Even so, perjury committed in significant part owing to the inducement of the state or a party opponent, as in a perjury trap, may not be willful.

Perjury may occur through the making of any false statement under oath, whether written or spoken. Thus, perjury may occur in an affidavit, in a deposition, or in any statement made under oath in a matter of legal record.

*See also:* fabrication (fabricate or fabricated or fabricated testimony); truth, whole truth and nothing but the truth; exculpation, exculpatory evidence, Giglio material (Giglio evidence); oath, statement under oath (sworn statement or unsworn statement); statement, false statement; ethics, legal ethics | 1. false testimony.

**perjury trap**   The inducement of a witness to commit perjury. A perjury trap is the use by an attorney or investigator of questions to a witness under oath for the purpose of eliciting perjurious answers rather than for the purpose of developing evidence of factual information. Perjury traps often employ questions that are not material to the purpose of an inquiry, that are ambiguous or confusing and easily misunderstood or misanswered, or that are not essential to the purpose of the testimony sought but that have a peculiar likelihood of untruthful answers, such as questions dealing with irrelevant wrongdoing or with personal or private affairs. By definition the use of a perjury trap is potentially an abuse of process by a private attorney, and it is usually a defense to a criminal charge of perjury because it diminishes the willfulness of the witness in making the false statement or the materiality of the statement as a basis for the charge.

**subornation of perjury**   Inciting a witness to commit perjury. Subornation of perjury is the procurement of a witness to give testimony under oath that the witness knows at the time of the testimony to be false. A person's efforts to persuade another person to give false testimony in a potential civil or criminal proceeding amounts to subornation, if the person later commits perjury. It is not a defense to perjury that the perjurer would have lied anyway.

Attempted subornation is both attempted perjury and conspiracy to commit perjury. A person commits subornation by attempting to persuade a potential witness to give false testimony, regardless or whether the witness tells the truth under oath or whether the witness ever testifies.

*See also:* subornation (suborn or suborned).

**testilying**   False testimony given by a police officer. Testilying is a slang phrase used in wry description of the giving of police testimony intended either to hide police misconduct or to convict an accused, regardless of the truth or falsity of the testimony.

**perk or perks**   *See:* officer, corporate officer, executive officer, executive compensation, perquisite (perk or perks).

**Permanent Court of International Justice**   *See:* court, international court, Permanent Court of International Justice (P.C.I.J. or PCIJ).

**permanent disability**   *See:* disability, personal disability, permanent disability (temporary disability).

**permanent injunction**   *See:* injunction, permanent injunction.

**permanent nuisance**   *See:* nuisance, permanent nuisance.

**permanent resident card**   *See:* immigration, green card (permanent resident card).

**permission (permissive)**   Consent to do something that would otherwise be forbidden. Permission is a license granted by an entity or person that allows another to do something that could not be done absent the license without violating the law or the rights or authority of the person or entity granting permission. Permission may be express or implied, though implied permission must be based on a good faith and reasonable perception of any statements or circumstances on which the implied permission is based. The law will not imply permission to do anything for which express permission would be invalid, such as permission to commit an otherwise criminal act.

Permission usually has a scope in which the permission is valid, beyond which the permitted conduct is unlawful or actionable. Permission to enter land may be bounded by area, use, and time, and in the absence of an expression of such boundaries, limits may be implied.

In varying contexts, a permit, sufferance, license, and invitation amount to permission.

Note: permissive may mean that conduct is subject to permission, yet it also suggests a laxity of regulation, as in the sense of permissive parents who give permission readily, or too readily, to their children.

*See also:* permit (permitted).

**permission to search**   *See:* search, permission to search, common–authority rule (common authority rule).

**permissive abstention**   *See:* abstention, abstention in bankruptcy, permissive abstention.

**permissive counterclaim**   *See:* claim, counterclaim, permissive counterclaim.

**permissive intervention**   *See:* intervention, permissive intervention.

**permissive joinder**   *See:* joinder, joinder of parties, permissive joinder.

**permissive presumption**   *See:* presumption, permissive presumption (mandatory presumption).

**permissive waste** *See:* waste, doctrine of waste, permissive waste.

**leave of court (leave of the court)** Permission to do something in an action or hearing before a court that is not allowed by right, custom, or court rules. Leave of the court is the customary term for the permission of the court, whether given by a justice, judge, or clerk, to do or perform some act that the person receiving the permission has no right to do otherwise. Leave of the court is usually given within the discretion of the court official granting it, and this discretion is not without limits.

**permit (permitted)** Permission granted by a government to do something that is regulated. A permit is a license by a government to engage in some conduct or activity that is allowed only according to the conditions of such a permit. Business and participation in regulated professions, hunting and the extraction of natural resources, polluting and the production of dangerous materials, construction and the development of land in cities, and countless other activities subject to local, state, and federal regulation may be conducted only following the application for and receipt of a permit to engage in such activities, and then only according to the conditions of the permit and the regulations governing its use. Engaging in activities subject to a permit, or failure to comply with the terms of a permit or the regulations of permitted activities may result in civil and criminal penalties.

Note: to permit something may connote either an activity subject to a permit in the sense of a government permit or some activity permitted in the sense that a private party may consent to it; only context can provide a basis for that distinction.

*See also:* pollution, pollution permit.

**perpetrator (perp or perpetrate)** Whoever carries out a criminal act. A perpetrator is a person or entity who executes or carries out a criminal act. At common law, a perpetrator was a principal in a felony. Contemporary usage, particularly in police slang, considers as a perpetrator any person who has criminal liability from that person's own conduct, as opposed to a person who is only an accessory to the criminal acts of another person. The practice of describing a person as a perpetrator, or a perp, on the basis of a suspicion or of arrest alone is in derogation of the presumption of innocence.

**perp walk** The public display of an arrested suspect. The "perp walk" is a police method of publicly displaying an arrested suspect before the press, especially if that person is accused of committing a highly publicized crime. Police justify the practice by claiming it deters potential criminals or that it reassures the public that a criminal is restrained, but the practice may harm the presumption of innocence and burden the court's later efforts to provide the displayed suspect with a fair trial with an unbiased jury. Simply put, the arrest does not assure that the arrestee is the perpetrator of the crime. An arrestee may have a diminished privacy interest, but the perp walk may violate Fourth Amendment rights.

**perpetual (in perpetuity)** Unending. Perpetual is an adjective that applies to any legal power, authority, or right, designating that interest as being without limitation or end in time. In general, anything that is perpetual is both unconditional and irrevocable. Even so, something perpetual that is personal or a claim or power related to a individual is conditioned upon the person's life, and an interest like a perpetual care policy is intended to lapse at the death of its recipient. An interest in property that is perpetual but not vested is a perpetuity, and it may violate the rule against perpetuities. There is no difference between something perpetual and something to exist or continue in perpetuity.

*See also:* perpetuity, rule against perpetuities (rap or rule against remoteness).

**perpetual rents** *See:* rent, quit rents (perpetual rents).

**perpetuity** A future interest that might not vest within two generations. A perpetuity is any limitation or condition that restricts the use or commerce of property for a time that amounts to at least two generations, or — as the formula for this period has become — for a period longer than a relevant life in being at the time of the limitation plus twenty-one years. Because an option to purchase land restricts its transfer to anyone other than the option holder, an option contract to buy land amounts to a perpetuity, as do future interests in land. Most other forms of perpetuity have become obsolete. At common law, all perpetuities were void under the rule against perpetuities or the prohibition on restraints on alienation. The contemporary practice, followed in many jurisdictions, is to allow a grant or option subject to a perpetuity to persist for the length of time by which it is determined to vest or fail or for ninety years, whichever is less.

**in perpetuam (perpetuam)** Without end. In perpetuam is a Latin designation for something intended to be or created as perpetual.

*See also:* perpetuity.

**perpetuity in land (perpetuities)** A grant of land that might last too long without vesting or failing. A perpetuity in land is a particular form of grant that may exist in perpetuity, or at least effectively in perpetuity, without vesting in a specific grantee and without failing and becoming void. A perpetuity may be void under the rule against perpetuities, in which case the instrument that purported to grant the interest is reformed, and either the grant is transferred to the next vested interest or the best efforts of the courts are employed to determine the likely intent of the grantor and to reform the instrument to most nearly approximate that intent without violating the law.

**rule against perpetuities (RAP or rule against remoteness)** All grants in land must vest or fail within two generations. The rule against perpetuities limits grants of interests in land that are not definite in identifying the grantee, so that the interest in land must either vest in a specific grantee or fail to vest within a time that amounts to two generations. The measure of those generations is the longest of the lives of the individuals relevant to the grant of the interest, to which is added the time it takes a child to reach majority, a formula known as the measuring lives plus twenty-one years. (The measuring lives are sometimes called the lives in being, which include the grantor, any potential grantees who are alive or conceived at the moment of the grant, and any person essential to identifying a grantee who is alive at the moment of the grant.) If a future interest is created so that it is possible that it will be neither vested nor destroyed within that time, the interest creates a perpetuity and violates the rule.

For example, a grant by A to the "firstborn male child of B if he shall join the army" depends on whether B has a boy alive at the time of the grant. Assuming B has a male child alive at the time of the grant, the measuring lives are A, B, and the son. Because the boy is alive and must join or not join the army within his own lifetime, the grant is good. But assuming that, at the time of the grant, B has no live male child, the measuring lives are only A and B. In that case, the rule requires an analysis of what might happen to A and to B. A might die before B has a male child. B might well have a male child then die, and the boy (who is not a measuring life) might later enter the army, doing so more than twenty-one years later than A's death and B's death, and so this grant violates the rule.

The problem would be that no one would know at the time of the grant whether B's firstborn male child will ever take or not take the property and could not tell for certain that B's firstborn male would or would not take it until, effectively, the death of B's firstborn male child, or the time B's firstborn male child enters the army, or the date of B's death if B had no living firstborn male child, or the date of the death of B's firstborn male child, if one was born. This indeterminacy in ownership would be hard on the people who own the land waiting to see if they lose it to B's son. They could not sell the land without limiting it by the chance it would be lost, one day, nor can they invest in it or use it themselves without the risk of such loss. The perpetuity limits the land from commerce and in its own use, and the common law voided it.

The common law considered the future interest to have been void from its inception, and the instrument that granted the future interest was to be reformed. In general, the grant subject to the interest that voided the rule would descend to the next vested interest, either to a vested or rule-compatible contingent future interest that would have followed the rule-violating interest or to the implied reversionary interest of the grantor. The contemporary approach in jurisdictions that apply the common law rule often uses a tool in equity, cy pres, by which a court attempts to discern the intent of the grantor and reform the instrument as a whole to give the greatest degree of effect to the instrument, allocating the void interest in the manner that best respects that inferred intent.

Yet not all jurisdictions follow the common-law rule, and not all interests that violate the rule are inherently void. In jurisdictions that have adopted a wait-and-see approach, usually by statute, the perpetuity may be good if it in fact vests or fails within the time created by the measuring lives and the twenty-first year after the last person who is a measuring life does die. Or, some jurisdictions cut the time off at ninety years. At the end of the time, if the interest has yet to vest, it is void, and the instrument creating it is reformed, using either the common-law approach or cy pres.

*See also:* fee, estate in fee, fee simple determinable | rule against perpetuities; interest, executory interest | rule against perpetuities; perpetuity; Shelley's case (rule in Shelley's case); title, doctrine of worthier title (doctrine of reversions); alienability, restraint on alienation; remainder, contingent remainder | 2. rule against perpetuities; remote (remoteness or remotely).

**contingent remainder** The rule applies to a contingent remainder.

**executory interest** The rule against perpetuities applies to executory interests. Under the common law, an executory interest which might not take effect until after the death of all of the lives in being and twenty-one years and ten months, is void.

**option to purchase land** At common law, an option to purchase land is subject to the rule against perpetuities. Under the common law, an option in land that might persist and neither lapse nor be exercised within the time of the lives in being plus twenty-one years is void. Contemporary U.S. practice has limited the rule in several ways. In some jurisdictions, the rule no longer applies to option contracts. In others, the rule does not apply to options that originate in a lease and amount to a contingent right to renew an ongoing lease. In others, the rule still applies to options to purchase an interest in lands. In all cases, some care must be used to distinguish an option contract for services or use provided by a holder of lands and an option to acquire an equitable or legal interest in the land itself.

*See also:* contract, option contract.

**dead hand (the dead hand)** The control of property by the decisions of owners long past. The dead hand is a metaphor for the limitations on use or designation of ownership set in place by owners long ago, which continue to limit the use or ownership of property long into the future. Though present owners may like such effects, the risk to property in general is that it will be tied up by these "dead hands" so that subsequent generations will not enjoy the liberty of property of their predecessors, the individuals selected for the ownership or management of property will not be wisely selected, and the property itself will not be used to its highest and best purpose.

*See also:* metaphor.

**life in being (measuring life or validating life)** A person whose life may measure a non-vested interest under the rule against perpetuities. A life in being, which is the same as a measuring life or a validating life, identifies any person whose relationship to a grant might invalidate that grant under the rule against perpetuities, so that person's lifespan may be a measurement for the allowed time in which the grant must vest or fail in order for the grant to be valid. Measuring lives include the grantor, the grantee (if the grantee is alive at the time of the grant), a person who is essential to the identity of the grantee (if this person is also alive at the time of the grant), such as A, if the grant is to A's child; or a person who is logically necessary for the interest to grant (if this person is alive at the time of the grant), such as B, if the grant was first to B for life, then C if a condition precedent occurred during B's life. A measuring life must be a natural human being, not an entity or non-human animal or plant.

**wait-and-see test (wait-and-see approach)** An interest that might violate the rule is not void unless it eventually violates the rule in fact. The wait-and-see test is the general approach to the rule against perpetuities that does not void a grant that might violate the rule, instead presuming the grant to be valid until sufficient time elapses to determine whether the grant in fact vests or fails within twenty-one years of the end of a measuring life. There are two forms of wait-and-see test, one of which requires the interest to vest or fail within a set number of years, the other of which runs the clock out until twenty-one years have passed from the last measuring life. The Uniform Statutory Rule Against Perpetuities takes the first approach, determining interests after waiting ninety years from the grant.

*See also:* perpetuity, rule against perpetuities, what-might-happen test (what-might-happen approach).

**Uniform Statutory Rule Against Perpetuities (USRAP)** Statute voiding interests under the rule after ninety years. The Uniform Statutory Rule Against Perpetuities takes a wait-and-see approach to interests that are subject to the rule, voiding the interest only if it does not in fact vest or fail within ninety years of the time of the grant. An interest that has neither failed nor vested at the end of ninety years is then declared void and grant is reformed so that the interests that would have been thereby granted are transferred to the next vested interest.

**what-might-happen test (what-might-happen approach)** An interest that might somehow violate the rule is void. The what-might-happen test is the approach to perpetuities analysis of the common law in which a grant is utterly void, void ab initio, if there is a circumstance by which an interest might fail to vest within the required period of time, no matter how unlikely the circumstance may be. The what-might-happen test is the domain of hypothetical after-born widows and octogenarian mothers.

**afterborn widow (unborn widow)** The widow of a grantee born after the death of a grantor. The afterborn widow is a metaphor for the many complications in the rule against perpetuities that must be considered when analyzing the logical chances for a grant to vest or fail in time under the rule. The afterborn widow, who is sometimes called the unborn widow, is a person who marries a grantee or someone else relevant to a grant, even though the widow was born and the widow's spouse died after the time of the grant itself. This might arise in a grant from a grandparent to a grandchild and then to that child's children. It is quite possible that the grandchild might have a spouse who is born after the grant, and the grandchild-grantee might die before the grant vests, leaving behind an afterborn surviving spouse, or afterborn widow. The afterborn widow reminds anyone analyzing a grant that a person is always presumed capable of gaining or losing a spouse or children.

Note: the term "unborn widow" is meant to suggest the same condition, but seems more paradoxical, though the person was merely unborn at the time of the grant, being born, of course, later. This term is needlessly confusing and probably should be avoided.

*See also:* perpetuity, rule against perpetuity, what-might-happen test, fertile octogenarian.

**fertile octogenarian** A person aged eighty or more who may have a child. The fertile octogenarian is a metaphor for the unlikely events that must be accounted for when considering the logical possibilities that might require a grant to vest or fail in time under the rule or that might create an uncertainty as to whether that will happen, which would violate the rule. The fertile octogenarian is simply a person of advanced years who might still have a child, particularly a woman who would once have been effectively unable to conceive. Given the advances in geriatric medicine and the medical, pharmaceutical, and bioengineering responses to diminished human fertility, the potential of such events is greater in contemporary times. Even so, the potential truth of the fertile octogenarian has existed for many years owing to the possibility of adoption.

**perquisite** *See:* officer, corporate officer, executive officer, executive compensation, perquisite (perk or perks).

**Perry Mason** *See:* Mason (Perry Mason).

**persistent vegetative state or PVS** *See:* death, vegetative state (persistent vegetative state or PVS).

**person (personality)**   A human being, or an entity that is treated in law like one. A person is an entity with significance as an actor in law or in equity. A person may be a natural or artificial.

A natural person is a human being, and each human being is a natural person. Person includes each human being, regardless of gender or age. The term is thus used as a generic pronoun to include men, women, children, boys, girls, citizens, aliens, voters, non-voters, felons, police officers — each and every human being. Civil rights are vested in each natural person.

An artificial person is an entity recognized in law as having a capacity to act in the law, such as a state, corporation, partnership, or other entity with a legal power similar to that of a human being. Artificial person includes all entities that are created by humans that are invested by the legal system with obligations, powers, and rights in a manner similar to those held by natural persons. Artificial persons, however, are not considered to hold civil rights, although they do hold such rights as are specifically vested in them by law (for example, a corporation cannot vote in an election). When "person" is used in a statute or other law, it is presumed, however, to mean to apply to natural persons. If the text or context suggests otherwise, however, it may apply to both. To regulate all persons, then, is to regulate both all human beings (or natural persons) and all governments, corporations, and partnerships (or artificial persons).

Personality, as a matter of law, is the aspect of a human or entity that makes it a person. Anyone or anything with legal personality has an independent significance and the potential to commit to have a legal capacity.

*See also:* capacity, legal capacity.

**person in need of supervision**   *See:* delinquent, juvenile delinquent, person in need of supervision (PINS or CHINS or JINS).

**artificial person (legal personality)**   An entity created by natural persons that is treated by law as if it is a single person. An artificial person is a corporation or a partnership (which is sometimes called a quasi-artificial person), or other entity of legal personality that is created by individuals according to law, often receiving a charter to do so from a government. The personhood of the entity is a long-standing metaphor, in that the artificial person is subject to sovereign power in the same manner a natural person is; the artificial person may be arrested, sued, taxed, and its property impounded, and within certain limits set by law, the artificial person has certain powers and even rights that are exercised through its officers and agents. Even so, the artificial person, as has often been said, has no soul; it lacks the natural and civil significance of a natural person.

*See also:* corporation (corporate or incorporate).

**emotionally disturbed person (EDP or E.D.P.)**   A person in an unhealthy mental state. An emotionally disturbed person is a person whom the police encounter and whose behavior appears to the police to indicate a mental state that is disturbed, requiring an officer to assess the risk of harm posed by the EDP to self or to others, or a professional assessment by a mental health professional to determine the need for protective custody or involuntary commitment to a mental health facility.

**persona non grata (persona non grata letter)**   An unwelcome person. Persona non grata is a designation for a person whose presence in a state, jurisdiction, institution, or property is unwelcome, such that any license that the person had to be present is revoked. A persona non grata letter is a communication to the person by a property owner or institutional agent to the person that the person is to leave the property or institution or is barred from presence there in the future. When a persona non grata letter is issued by a state institution, the letter must be based on at least a demonstrably legitimate basis, and if the letter or bar from entry burdens a vested right, the letter from a governmental agent may require notice and hearing.

*See also:* diplomat, recall, persona non grata.

**personal**   Belonging to the person, or relating to a natural person. Personal designates property, rights, or interests that belong to a natural person. In general, the term is used to signal the interests of a single person from those of a larger group, but the term is frequently used in law in several distinct senses, one of which is to distinguish a person's relation to a legal action between a personal capacity and an official or corporate capacity. Based on an older, now obsolete distinction between property one can own and property one might only hold in fee, an important residual meaning of personal is as personalty, the distinction between personal property, or chattels, and real property, or lands.

*See also:* in, in personam.

**personal capacity**   *See:* capacity, defendant capacity, individual capacity (personal capacity).

**personal chattel**   *See:* chattel, personal chattel (chattel personal).

**personal deterrence**   *See:* deterrence, specific deterrence (personal deterrence).

**personal disability**   *See:* disability, personal disability (handicap or mental disability or physical disability).

**personal effects**   *See:* effects, personal effects; chattel, personal effects.

**personal exemption**   *See:* tax, tax exemption, personal exemption (spousal exemption).

**personal expense**   *See:* expense, personal expense.

**personal history**   *See:* hearsay, hearsay exception, exception only when declarant is unavailable, family history (personal history).

**personal injury**   *See:* injury, personal injury (P.I. or PI).

**personal jurisdiction**   *See:* jurisdiction, personal jurisdiction; jurisdiction, in personam jurisdiction (personal jurisdiction).

**personal liability**   *See:* liability, personal liability.

**personal property**   *See:* property, personal property, tangible personal property; property, personal property (personalty).

**personal recognizance**   *See:* bail, personal recognizance (personal recognizance bond or release on recognizance or ROR or R.O.R.).

**personal representative**   *See:* representative, personal representative.

**personal service**   *See:* service, service of process, personal service; contract, specific contracts, personal services contract (personal service).

**personal service on corporate officer**   *See:* service of process, personal service on corporate officer.

**personal services contract**   *See:* contract, specific contracts, personal services contract (personal service).

**personalty**   *See:* property, personal property (personalty).

**personalty adversely possessed**   *See:* possession, adverse possession, chattels subject to adverse possession (personalty adversely possessed).

**persuasion (persuade or persuader)**   The use of argument to convince a person to do or believe something. Persuasion is the act of inducing another to believe an idea or to do anything through the use of language, reason, or sentiment. A persuasive argument need not appeal to reason but to any basis for agreement or acceptance, including assertions based on sentiment and emotion; yet to be persuasive, the assertions must influence the person to accept the result of the argument as correct or true or influence the person to an action the person commits with at least some modicum of intent or will.

All inducement is not persuasion; for instance, coercion, fraud, and bribery may result in a person's being induced to do something or to assert a belief, yet these are not persuasion, even if the person induced forms a belief as a result. Enticement is a particular form of inducement that is not persuasion, but luring or seduction, particularly when it is attempted through a trick or by a means that interferes with the individual's will or intent.

To persuade a person to commit a crime is to be an accessory to the crime the person commits. Such persuasion must be deliberate and knowing to amount to a crime in itself, although the intent may be satisfied if the persuader intends that someone will be persuaded; the intent need not be limited to persuade a given person, though it must be intended that those who are persuaded would be within the foreseeable category of people who would be persuaded.

**persuasive authority**   *See:* authority, legal authority, persuasive authority.

**pertinent trait of character**   *See:* propensity (pertinent trait of character).

**perverse incentive**   *See:* incentive, perverse incentive.

**pesha**   A rebellion against God. Pesha, in Jewish law, is a sin against God that constitutes a rebellion against God or God's dominion over mankind and the world.

**pest**   An organism that endangers other living things. A pest is an animal or plant that harms or risks harm to human beings, to the equilibrium in an ecosystem, or to domesticated plants or animals, usually crops or livestock. Animal pests are defined for specific purposes in statutes and regulations, and usually include insects, rodents, and other vermin, especially organisms that carry and transmit disease. Animal pests include invasive species that threaten native species.

Plant pests include weeds, plants carrying disease, and invasive plants that threaten native species or ecosystem stability. Pest control is the management of pests through eradication, isolation, or relocation.

**pesticide**   A chemical or other agent intended to kill or control pests. Pesticide, generally, is the killing of pests, but the term has long been used in law and the chemical industry to refer to a chemical intended for use to kill, repel, or control any animal or plant that is a pest. Pesticides include herbicides, insecticides, rodenticides, fungicides, and bactericides. As biological means of pest control have become more common, the term pesticide has sometimes been extended to include media that encourage fungal or other parasitic growths or genetic alteration to reduce the population of a given pest.

**The Federal Insecticide, Fungicide, and Rodenticide Act (FIFRA or F.I.F.R.A.)**   A federal statute regulating pesticides. The Federal Insecticide, Fungicide, and Rodenticide Act (FIFRA) is the comprehensive federal act regulating pesticides. FIFRA requires the registration of pesticides prior to their distribution, sale, and use. FIFRA also contains stringent labeling requirements designed to protect the end user. FIFRA does not, however, preempt the local regulation of pesticides or of pest control companies.
*See also:* fungicide.

**pesticide residue (residue from pesticide)**   Any substance in food from a pesticide. Pesticide residue includes any substance in food, agricultural commodities, or animal feed that results from the use of a pesticide, regardless of the form of pesticide or where the pesticide was employed in the supply chain. Residue includes the active chemicals of the pesticide itself as well as its derivatives and products altered as a result of interactions with it.

**petard (hoist by your own petard)**   A self-defeating ploy or argument. A petard was a French bomb, or underground explosive mine, and to be hoist by one's own petard evokes the danger to sappers or engineers being thrown into the air by the explosion they hope to bring to their enemies. Thus, the Shakespearean echo, to "be hoist by your own petard" is a metaphor for a self-defeating argument or strategem, which is popular among lawyers and especially a certain stripe of judge while watching lawyerly maneuvers.

Note: It is better to say "they were hoist" than they were "hoisted."

**petit**    Small. Petit means small, and the term, inherited from law French, is used when one of several institutions or objects is smaller than the other. The most famous illustration is the petit jury, the trial jury, which has fewer members than the grand (or big) jury. Likewise, petit larceny and other petit crimes are of smaller amounts, smaller offense, and — usually — smaller punishment than grand larceny and other larger crimes.

Note: petit is pronounced like petty; the second "t" is silent.

*See also:* jury, petit jury (trial jury); larceny, petty larceny (petit larceny or small larceny); grand (graund).

**petit jury**    *See:* jury, petit jury (trial jury).

**petit larceny or small larceny**    *See:* larceny, petty larceny (petit larceny or small larceny).

**petitio principii**    *See:* fallacy, petitio principii (begging the question or to beg the question).

**petition**    A request that an official grant extraordinary legal relief or executive grace. A petition is a plea for relief, presented to a judge or other official with the power to grant such relief under law in extraordinary circumstances or with the power to grant such relief as a matter of the grace of the state conferred on the official in the discretion of office. The primary difference in contemporary legal usage between a petition and a pleading, such as a complaint or a motion, is one of custom; many petitions, such as a petition in bankruptcy, are more stringently governed by the standards of law than would be a discretionary petition, such as a petition for clemency. Petitions are used, however, in one highly discretionary proceeding in law — the petition for certiorari.

*See also:* certiorari, petition for a writ of certiorari.

**Petition Clause**    *See:* constitution, U.S. Constitution, clauses, Petition Clause.

**petition for a writ of certiorari**    *See:* certiorari, petition for a writ of certiorari.

**Petition of Right of 1628**    *See:* constitution, English constitution, Petition of Right of 1628.

**petition of right**    A pleading in chancery seeking relief from the wrongful retention of a right by the monarch. A petition of right was one of two forms of claim against the monarch seeking to have the monarch to release some claim made or property held in contravention of the law. The petition of right by Parliament was a statutory instrument asking the monarch to redress wrongs or to defend claims under the law, and the Petition of 1628 is the most

famous of these. The petition of right in chancery was a private action brought seeking the crown to be brought into chancery to answer the petition, which — if the crown did not agree to grant the petition — could be adjudged by the chancery (which in such cases often applied the common law).

*See also:* constitution, English constitution, Petition of Right of 1628.

**right to petition**    An individual has the right to petition the government or a court or agency. The right to petition the government for redress of grievances is assured to the people in the First Amendment. The right provides a fundamental protection to a citizen or person subject to federal jurisdiction to send a communication to the President, a member of Congress, an agency, a court, or any other officer or department of the federal government. Similar provisions allow for similar petitions to states in state constitutions. The right is not absolute, however, and it is subject to limits in the event the petition contains defamatory statements as defined under New York Times v. Sullivan, 376 U.S. 254 (1964), or harmful statements made knowingly or in reckless disregard of the truth. Further, the right may be limited in support of a compelling governmental interest provided any limits constitute the narrowest possible means to effect the governmental interests.

**Noerr-Pennington doctrine**    A petition to restrain competition is not an anti-trust violation. The Noerr-Pennington Doctrine arises from Eastern Railroad Presidents Conference v. Noerr Motor Freight, Inc. (Noerr), 365 U.S. 127 (1961), and United Mine Workers of America v. Pennington, (Pennington), 381 U.S. 657 (1965), which established that any attempt by two or more persons or entities to petition the government or some officer, branch, or agency, even an attempt that would restrict competition if it were successful, does not violate the Sherman Act or otherwise amount to an anti-trust violation. The Noerr-Pennington doctrine does not amount to an absolute immunity for statements made to government officials, nor does it apply to statements made to parties other than a government official.

**petitioner**    One who files a petition. A petitioner is a person or entity who files a petition, which in those actions that are initiated by petition, such as bankruptcy, would place the petitioner in the same situation as a plaintiff. In actions for appellate review that are commenced by a petition, such as a petition for certiorari, the petitioner is in the same situation as the appellant. A party who must reply to a petition in an adversarial proceeding is a respondent.

*See also:* respondent.

**petroleum**    *See:* oil (petroleum).

**petty larceny**    *See:* larceny, petty larceny (petit larceny or small larceny).

**phallocracy** *See:* government, forms of government, patriarchy (patriarchate or phallocracy).

**phobia** Fear of an object or situation. A phobia is an anxiety disorder wherein a person has a genuine fear of an object or situation that is not at that moment a basis for a reasonable fear of injury or harm. A phobia resulting from a trauma is not uncommon, and the results of a phobia may be the basis for pain and suffering in a claim arising from the traumatic event. More colloquially, a prejudice caused by ignorance is also described as a phobia.

**phonorecord (digital phonorecord delivery)** The medium in which a sound is recorded and subject to patent. A phonorecord is the physical object (other than a film) in or on which sound is recorded and from which it may be reproduced, and its production, reproduction, and possession is subject to the copyright governing the sounds contained within it. Phonorecords include vinyl records, tapes, compact discs, and other media.

Though some questions regarding digital forms of phonorecords are far from settled in 2011, a phonorecord delivery includes a computer record or file created for the purpose of reproducing and delivering sound (despite computer programs being separately defined as a matter of patent). Thus a file holding a ring tone for a cell phone is a phonorecord.

**physical**

> **physical custody** *See:* custody, penal custody (physical custody); child, child custody, physical custody.

> **physical examination** *See:* discovery, witness discovery, physical examination.

> **physical force** *See:* force, physical force.

> **physical occupation** *See:* taking, regulatory taking, physical occupation.

> **physical restraint** *See:* restraint, physical restraint, shackles (fetters or legcuffs or leg irons or shackling); restraint, physical restraint, handcuff (handcuffs).

> **physical-facts rule** *See:* testimony, physical-facts rule.

> **physical-proximity test** *See:* search, search warrant, physical-proximity test.

**physician** A person who is lawfully engaged in the practice of medicine. A physician is one who is licensed and lawfully engaged in the practice of medicine. This is typically a person who is qualified as a doctor of medicine, has received the requisite degrees, and has been licensed to practice medicine or osteopathic medicine. In England and elsewhere, the term physician refers to a specialist in internal medicine and diagnosis and is distinguished from a surgeon. This distinction, however, is rare in the United States.

*See also:* doctor, doctor of medicine (Dr. or M.D. or physician); medicine (healing arts).

**physician-patient privilege or patient-physician privilege** *See:* privilege, evidentiary privilege, doctor-patient privilege (physician-patient privilege or patient-physician privilege).

**picket (picketers or picketing or picket line)** A protest in which people are arrayed like the pickets of a fence. Picket has many meanings, originally being military senses for a series of pointed stakes erected by infantry to deter cavalry in combat, then a series of sentries guarding a larger military force. In civilian use, it was first associated with a regular series of slats in a fence — the picket fence — and then from this image the term evolved to label protesters or other groups assembled in public who stand or walk in a line to carry signs and to block passage, like the pickets of a fence.

As a matter of labor law and of free speech, to picket is to engage in such a demonstration, whether the participants are one or many, whether they are in a line or a cluster, and whether they have signs or not. A ban on picketing is a violation of the picketers' rights of free speech and assembly, though a municipality is entitled reasonably to regulate the time, place, and manner of picketing, as well as to charge a reasonable and non-prohibitory fee for services required to support and protect it. A private property holder is not required to allow picketing on the property the property is a public forum, unless there is an affirmative duty created by contract. Public property that is a public forum or an appropriate quasi-public forum is required to allow picketing.

> **consumer picket** Consumer protest of a place based on its business practices. Consumer picketing is the maintenance of a picket line by consumers, protesting the goods, services, or practices of the enterprise being picketed or a prohibition or an allowance of such practices under the law.

**piercing the corporate veil or pierce the corporate veil** *See:* veil, corporate veil (piercing the corporate veil or pierce the corporate veil).

**pig**

> **blind pig (blind hog)** The star in "Even a blind pig finds an acorn now and then." The "blind pig" metaphor is a lawyer's proverb sometimes used by judges in evaluating the sufficiency and propriety of filings, particularly search warrants, to discount the lucky catch made on a generalized fishing expedition. When applied by a court to itself, the metaphor refers to its own research of a case or issue, even when that case or issue wasn't discussed by the briefs of counsel.
> *See also:* metaphor.

> **blind pig as bar** Illegal tavern. A blind pig is an illegal saloon. The term originated in the late 1800s, when the owners of bars and taverns would charge money for customers to see an attraction and then offer a complimentary drink, thereby circumventing the laws against alcohol then on the

book. Illicit bars continued under this name during Prohibition.

*See also:* prohibition, prohibition of alcohol.

**lipstick on a pig**   A foolish attempt to make something appear as something else. Lipstick on a pig is a shorthand for a phrase much used by some trial lawyers to depict a sham argument. It is based on a phrase popularized by Anne Richards, a governor of Texas, "You can put lipstick on a hog and call it Monique, but it is still a pig."

**pig in a poke**   Something on offer that cannot be inspected by the buyer. A pig in a poke is a metaphor for anything offered for sale or acceptance that cannot be inspected or proven to be indeed what is offered before the sale is consummated or the transaction completed. The phrase comes from the purported former practice of selling a pig in a blanket or sack. (A poke is a cloth sack.)

**Pigovian efficiency**   *See:* efficiency, Pigovian efficiency.

**Pike test**   *See:* commerce, regulation of commerce, dormant commerce power, Pike test (balancing test).

**pilferage (pilfer)**   Petty larceny. Pilgerage is the theft of chattels or goods of modest value. Pilferage, however, is often a label for the cumulative effect of many such acts of larceny, and if such acts are committed as a sequence of thefts by one thief against one victim, as in an employee against an employer, pilferage may amount to grand larceny. Even so, such a basis for indictment for grand larceny must be based on the acts of the defendant alone. Pilferage also describes the cumulative acts of petty larceny of customers, employees, contractors, and licensees, in which it amounts to a means of describing a rate or quantity of loss in inventory.

**pillage (pillaging or pillager)**   The seizure of private property by members of an invading or occupying military force. Pillage is the taking by force of private property by the members or affiliates of a military force that invades, enters, or occupies land. There is no distinction between pillage done under orders or with the acknowledgment of the chain of command governing the pillagers, or pillage done independently. Pillage is prohibited under the laws of war.

**pillory**   *See:* punishment, shaming punishment, stocks (pillory).

**pilot**   A person who navigates a craft. A pilot is a person who determines the course and speed of a ship, boat, aircraft, spaceship, or similar vessel. A pilot may be an officer of that title assigned to the vessel permanently or for a voyage, an officer or other person aboard the vessel who is assigned that task, or a local expert hired by the vessel for a particular transit or leg of a longer journey. Local vessel pilots are usually experts in the navigation of local waters and waterways.

**pilotage (pilot boat or pilotage ground)**   The profession of a vessel pilot, and the pilot's fee. Pilotage, in general, is the profession of the pilots of vessels, particularly local pilots for seagoing vessels.

In admiralty, pilotage is the compensation paid to a pilot, which may give rise to a lien over the vessel until it is paid. In the United States, pilotage is generally fixed by state law.

The pilot boat is a small ship that awaits ships at a pilotage ground, located seaward of a passage requiring a pilot. Ships approaching the passage from sea collect their pilot from the pilot boat, and ships leaving the passage for sea deposit their pilot there.

*See also:* lien (lienholder).

**pimp**   *See:* prostitution, pimp (madam).

**Pinkerton doctrine or Pinkerton instruction**   *See:* conspiracy, conspirator, Pinkerton rule (Pinkerton doctrine or Pinkerton instruction).

**pinpoint citation**   *See:* citation, legal citation, pinpoint citation (pinpoint cite).

**PINS or CHINS or JINS**   *See:* delinquent, juvenile delinquent, person in need of supervision (PINS or CHINS or JINS).

**Pinto case**   Punitive damages are available for deadly product defects. The Pinto case, Grimshaw v. Ford Motor Co., 174 Cal. Rptr. 348, 359 (Cal. Ct. App. 1981), is a celebrated example of high punitive damages and of corporate callousness, in which a jury found Ford Motor Company to have calculated the cost of repair to a defect in its Pinto line of automobiles as being greater than the cost of defending the wrongful death suits that would result from the explosions the defect caused.

**pious use**   *See:* use, use of property, charitable use (pious use).

**piracy (pirate or piratical or piratically)**   The seizure of a vessel for private gain, or a related crime. Piracy is the violation of the peace or security of a vessel, whether a boat, ship, or aircraft, for the personal gain of those who do so, rather than to advance the military or policy interests of a state. Thus, the seizure or boarding of a vessel by a military or state vessel in accord with state policy is not piracy but an act of state. Though private vessels were once authorized by a letter of marque to engage in such activities, the letters of marque and reprisal are no longer recognized under international law. Piracy is a crime of universal jurisdiction, and any state's vessels may seize a pirate vessel on the high seas regardless of its nationality. Under customary international law, pirates may well be pursued into territorial seas and boarded there.

U.S. law has defined the crime according to the law of nations, as well as designating as crimes of piracy or related to piracy: a sailor's mutiny against a captain defending a vessel or cargo, a captain's conversion or surrender of a vessel or cargo for personal gain, assisting or recruiting pirates from sailors, plundering a distressed vessel or luring it to danger, plundering or attempting to plunder a vessel, robbing ashore from a pirate vessel, or receiving pirate property. The law of nations has long defined piracy as the boarding or attempt to take a vessel for the profit of the pirates, as well as murder, theft, or other crimes associated with the endeavors of the pirates, including the plunder of goods ashore. The United Nations Convention on the Law of the Sea has coalesced a single definition of piracy of some utility, including as piracy any illegal act of violence, detention, or depredation, for private ends on a private vessel or aircraft outside its national jurisdiction or on the high seas, or any knowing and voluntary assistance to a pirate or the operation of a pirate vessel. Public vessels and craft can also be the target of piracy.

Note: to claim in a criminal charge that some act is piratical or done piratically is to charge the act is an act of piracy.

*See also:* copyright, infringement of copyright (copyright piracy or copyright infringement).

**air piracy (aircraft piracy or skyjacking)** Taking control of an aircraft by force, threat, or trick. Air piracy is piracy aboard an aircraft or, potentially, a space craft. Air piracy includes all attempts or acts intended to gain control of an aircraft, including its seizure or destruction, by force, violence, threats, or intimidation. Fraud or trick are the basis of air piracy if the pirate or accomplices of the pirate maintain the control of the craft despite a demand by anyone lawfully enabled to restore its control to another.

**piracy of copyright or patent (software piracy or anti-piracy)** The infringement of a copyright or patent through duplication. Piracy is a generic term for the infringement of a copyright or patent through counterfeiting or duplication. Minor variations or alterations of name or label do not bar a finding of piracy. Software piracy is the duplication of a sufficient quantity of copyrighted code in a computer program to amount to an infringement, even if the entire program from which the code is duplicated is not fully reproduced.

*See also:* patent, infringement of patent (patent infringement or infringer).

**place of abode** *See:* abode (place of abode).

**place of business** *See:* business, place of business.

**place of habitation** *See:* habitation, place of habitations.

**place of worship** *See:* religion, place of worship, damage to a place of worship (church bombing); religion, place of worship.

**placement** *See:* law, law school, placement, National Association of Law Placement (NALP).

**plagiarism (plagiarize)** The wrongful appropriation of the ideas or words of another. Plagiarism is the use of the thought, ideas, speech, or writing of another person in any manner that has a reasonable potential to create the impression in a reader or hearer that the material used is the work of the party using it rather than the party who had created it. There is no hard-and-fast rule for how similar the use of an idea must be or how many words in which sequences are required to amount to plagiarism. Such inquiries are inherently contextual, depending on the degree of borrowing under the circumstances. Still, a single clause quoted without attribution or a single idea paraphrased may be sufficient.

Plagiarism is related to, but distinct from, copyright infringement, not least in that a person may plagiarize materials in the public domain, as well as materials not subject to copyright. Even so, plagiarism usually provokes strong professional and moral condemnation, often with legal implications. Plagiarism is a violation of the codes of conduct or professional standards of most educational institutions, whether committed by a student, teacher, or professor. It may be a violation of contract for a professional writer or writer for hire.

Interestingly, borrowing in legal drafting is often acceptable as a matter of custom in situations that otherwise might amount to plagiarism. Examples include lawyers' use of forms, model instructions, and other materials created with the intent that the materials be the basis for duplication by others, and their use of legal arguments and pleading standards that need not be cited to specific sources. Care and professional expertise are required, however, to determine which unattributed use of an earlier argument or form is borrowing that is accepted as a matter of professional custom and which is plagiarism or copyright infringement.

**plain**

**plain error** *See:* review, standards of review, plain error.

**plain language rule** *See:* interpretation, plain meaning (plain language rule).

**plain meaning** *See:* interpretation, plain meaning (plain language rule); contract, contract interpretation, plain meaning (objective interpretation of contracts).

**plain view** *See:* search, warrantless search, plain view, immediate appearance (immediately apparent); search, warrantless search, plain view (plain-view doctrine).

**plaint** A claim for relief in an action in equity or law. A plaint is a written claim for relief. It was once the common term for the formal text through which the plaintiff presented the allegations of fact that supported an action at law and that the plaintiff claimed was the basis for a writ granting a remedy. The plaint is the origin for the modern complaint as well as the identity of the plaintiff, the party who submitted a plaint.

*See also:* complaint; querela.

**plaintiff**   One who claims to have been wronged and seeks a remedy in a civil action. The plaintiff is the party, whether a person, government, or other entity, who seeks a remedy for an injury or wrong through a civil proceeding in a court of law or in equity. The plaintiff is often the party who initiates the action, although a defendant or third party who brings forward a claim for a remedy becomes a plaintiff as to that claim, either a counter-plaintiff or cross-plaintiff. Although the plaintiff is often the party who is so designated in the court pleadings, that designation may not be dispositive if a procedural right depends upon the plaintiff's performance of a given role, in which case the party whose claim for a remedy is the essential focus of a given action may be considered the plaintiff, regardless of title, for such purposes. The term is derived from plaint, the early English word for lament or grievance, from which now the plaintiff asserts as the basis for the complaint.

*See also:* party, party to action.

**plaintiff in error**   *See:* error, writ of error, plaintiff in error (defendant in error).

**co-plaintiff (coplaintiff)**   One of several plaintiffs in one civil action. A co-plaintiff is any one of several plaintiffs in the same civil action.

*See also:* plaintiff.

**egg-shell plaintiff (abnormally sensitive plaintiff or glass-jaw plaintiff or eggshell-skull rule or thin skull rule)**   A plaintiff whose tort damages were exacerbated by an unusual prior condition. An egg-shell plaintiff is any person who is injured, or who alleges injury, owing to the tortious conduct of another party, but whose injuries occurred or were worsened owing to an unusual condition that afflicted the plaintiff before the tort. The condition is often a physical infirmity or weakness, which might or might not have been known to the plaintiff prior to the injury. The rule generally is that if the defendant's acts were in violation of some duty, the defendant is responsible for the proximate consequences of those acts, even if they were exacerbated by a prior condition of the plaintiff. This rule does not, of course, excuse a plaintiff from taking reasonable steps to limit the plaintiff's injuries or excuse a plaintiff to commit an act that intentionally worsens or exacerbates the plaintiff's harm in the hope of accruing a greater claim against the defendant. Rather, it requires the defendant to make good the injuries actually suffered by the plaintiff rather than be limited to some average damages that a fictional, reasonably anticipated plaintiff might have suffered from the same tort.

**third-party plaintiff**   A defendant who brings a claim against a new party to the action. A third-party plaintiff is an original defendant in a civil action who brings a third-party claim against a person or entity not previously a party, claiming that the person or entity is or may be liable for all or part of the claim brought by the original plaintiff against the defendant. Thus, the new person or entity is called a third-party defendant, and the original defendant is called a third-party plaintiff.

The third-party plaintiff must initiate its claim against the third-party defendant by regular summons and process, which is by right within fourteen days of filing the original answer or by leave of the court if filed thereafter.

**unforeseeable plaintiff**   A person whose injuries were unforeseeable. An unforeseeable plaintiff is a plaintiff whose injuries could not reasonably have been foreseen prior to the negligent acts that resulted in the injuries. Such a plaintiff may not recover for such injuries in negligence in a jurisdiction that defines the scope of actionable negligence by foreseeability. Even so, such injuries are actionable if the injury gives rise to an action of strict liability. In many cases, the question is whether a given plaintiff was unforeseeable; in others the unforeseeable plaintiff is hypothetical and represents a line beyond which claims of negligence would not lie.

*See also:* foreseeability (foreseeable); liability, strict liability.

**plan of merger**   *See:* merger, corporate merger, plan of merger (merger plan).

**Planned Parenthood v. Casey**   Planned Parenthood v. Casey held an informed consent requirement in the abortion context is valid.

*See also:* abortion | 4. Planned Parenthood v. Casey.

**planned unit development**   *See:* zoning, planned unit development (PUD).

**plat (plat map)**   A map demarcating parcels of property and essential infrastructure. A plat, or plat map, is a map of the distinct parcels of land subject to separate ownership or regulation in a given area. Plats usually display the boundaries of each specific lot, plot, or parcel of land, its designation according to a survey or plan, and its file index number, along with such other features of infrastructure and landmarks as are required by local or state law. A subdivider will usually be required to create a subdivision plat designating the boundaries of each parcel divided from the original, and a consolidator will usually be required to create a consolidation plat designating new boundaries of parcels joined into a single consolidated parcel. A plat may be of a municipality, especially at the time of its incorporation or at the time of its annexation of lands platted, or of a township, or of a parcel subject to zoning, planning, or development, as well as for the specific plans of land use.

*See also:* survey (surveyor or surveying).

**plato o plomo**   *See:* corruption, silver or lead (plato o plomo).

**plausible on its face**   *See:* pleading, pleading theories, notice pleading, plausible on its face (Twombly standard or Iqbal test or facial plausibility).

**playing the race card**   *See:* race, race as social category, race card (playing the race card).

**plea (plead)**   An answer to a charge in civil or criminal court, or an argument or claim for other relief. The plea has several distinct senses in law, most significantly as a formal statement by the defense in response to a civil complaint or criminal charge. Some answers and other responsive pleadings in civil cases still contain pleas, though the civil plea in defense is less common and less technical in most jurisdictions than before the move toward rule-based civil procedure. The plea in the sense of the defendant's response to a charge is still a central feature of contemporary pre-trial practice in criminal procedure.

More broadly, a plea is an argument, the means used to plead for specific relief related to a motion or a remedy or to plead one's case in general.

Note: a plea is the statement or argument, which is pleaded or, less felicitously, is pled. Thus, in a criminal case, the judge will ask the defendant how the defendant pleads, after which the defendant will enter a plea.

**plea in avoidance**   *See:* defense, defense in pleading, affirmative defense (plea in avoidance).

**criminal plea**   The defendant's answer to criminal charges. A criminal plea is a plea entered in a criminal action by the defendant in response to the charges presented, which as to each charge must be guilty, not guilty, or no contest (which is the same as nolo contendere), or some variations of these three, such as guilty but insane, not guilty by reason of insanity, or seeking the mercy of the court.

A plea of guilty or nolo contendere must usually be accompanied by a plea colloquy, in which the judge establishes that the defendant is aware of the nature of the charges, the effect of the plea, and is satisfied that the defendant is acting voluntarily and with a sufficient understanding of the rights available during the process. A defendant who does not enter a plea will be considered to plea not guilty.

A plea is normally entered in person at an arraignment in open court, although certain exceptions are provided in most jurisdictions for a guilty plea to minor offenses. A plea once entered becomes a matter of record, but it may be withdrawn with leave of the court; a guilty or nolo plea is usually eligible for withdrawal prior to sentencing, and a plea of not guilty may usually be withdrawn at any time prior to a verdict.

*See also:* arraignment; colloquy (colloquium or plea colloquy).

**blind plea (plead blind)**   A defendant's guilty plea not knowing the potential sentence. A blind plea is a guilty plea in a criminal case, entered by a defendant before the defendant becomes aware of the likely sentence or range of sentences to be imposed. A blind plea may result from a charge bargain form of plea bargain, and there are benefits a prosecutor may offer in a plea bargain to a defendant who enters a blind plea. Even so, a blind plea entered at the advice of counsel with no explanation from counsel of the limits of punishment available may be evidence suggesting ineffective assistance of counsel.

**conditional plea**   A plea contingent on the unsuccessful appeal of a motion that had been denied. A conditional plea is a plea of guilt or of nolo contendere, which is entered contingent only on the failure of an appeal of some motion that the defendant had lost in the trial court. If the appeal is successful, then the defendant is entitled to withdraw the plea. A conditional plea requires the consent of the court, the consent of the prosecutor, and a written statement of the motion that had been ruled against the defendant that is to be appealed. The requirement of the written statement may be relaxed in limited circumstances, particularly when the issue under appeal would be dispositive, when the record could prove the matter subject to appeal, or when the government acquiesces in the appeal. Nevertheless, in some state courts, the appellate court lacks jurisdiction over the appeal if the statement is not filed in writing, in which case the plea must stand unless it is vacated by the trial court.

**false plea (take the fall)**   A guilty plea entered by a person who did not commit the offense charged. A false plea, particularly a false guilty plea, is a plea of guilty that is entered by a person who did not commit the crimes charged to which the person pleads guilt. One purpose of the colloquy required in most jurisdictions to accept a guilty plea is to diminish the likelihood of the court's accepting a false plea, which would amount to the conviction of a person innocent of the crime (regardless of that person's intention to be convicted) as well as to the potential escape from responsibility of the person who committed it.

*See also:* colloquy (colloquium or plea colloquy).

**guilty plea**   Confession of guilt by an accused. A guilty plea is a formal acknowledgment by an accused of the performance or omission of specified acts required by law. Once the accused enters a guilty plea, the judge must determine to accept or reject the plea, which is usually done on the basis of a colloquy by which the judge determines on the record that the defendant knowingly and intentionally pleads, with an understanding of its consequences, and (in most jurisdictions) establishing the likely validity of the foundation of the plea. Once a plea is accepted, the process remaining involves no further assessment of the facts of the case or guilt of the defendant but only the defendant's judgment and sentencing.

**guilty but mentally ill (guilty but insane or GBMI or G.B.M.I.)**   A plea of guilt seeking mental treatment for the defendant. Guilty but mentally ill (or guilty but insane) is a criminal plea by which a defendant admits to the charges brought but pleads mental illness at the time of the offense as a basis for sentencing. The finding of mental illness will depend on clinical standards of mental illness rather than the legal standard for criminal responsibility, and so the guilty but insane verdict differs from not guilty by reason of insanity.

In some jurisdictions, guilty but mentally ill is available only by plea, and in others it is available as a verdict that may be reached by a jury regardless of plea. A defendant found to be guilty but insane or guilty but mentally ill is, in most jurisdictions, remanded to a prison psychiatric ward to serve the length of the sentence, which is otherwise unmitigated or unreduced.

**nolo contendere (no contest or nolo or non vult contendere)** A plea not contesting the charge but seeking mercy in sentencing. Nolo contendere, or no contest, is a criminal plea in which the defendant does not argue innocence but impliedly accepts as true the charges and seeks a sentence without an express finding of guilt, in the hopes of a lighter sentence than might be levied if the defendant were convicted after contesting the charge or charges, but also in the expectation that some measure of civil liability or other consequence of a guilty verdict might be avoided. A defendant does not generally have a right to plead nolo, but the court may allow a defendant to plead in its discretion, which in some federal jurisdictions will not be exercised unless there is some public benefit in allowing the plea. Not every state allows a plea of no contest or of nolo contendere, though states that do not usually recognize such a plea entered in other jurisdictions and treat it as akin to a guilty plea.

*See also:* nolle, nolle prosequi (nolle pros. or null pros. or non prosequitur or non pros.).

**Alford plea** A plea accepting sentence but rejecting guilt for the crime charged. An Alford plea, allowed in North Carolina v. Alford, 400 U.S. 25, 37 (1970), is a form of nolo plea in which the defendant specifically rejects guilt for the crime charged but accepts the imposition of punishment for it. Unlike a regular plea of nolo contendere, in which the defendant takes no position on the defendant's guilt, the Alford plea contests guilt, though like the nolo plea, accepts liability for punishment.

**not guilty** A plea denying guilt for the crimes charged. A not-guilty plea is a criminal plea in which the defendant denies guilt for the crimes charged in a criminal action. The plea of not guilty may be based on a claim of factual innocence, a defense, a defect or constitutional infirmity in the law on which the charge is brought, on a right to require the state to prove guilt, or any other ground. The decision to plead not guilty is the defendant's alone, and the court may not deny a defendant the right to plead not guilty. Once a not-guilty plea is entered by an accused, the process of the criminal court continues until a trial court renders a verdict, which may accept as its verdict the plea of not guilty, or any other verdict supported by the

evidence. A plea bargain, however, often follows an initial plea of not guilty.

*See also:* verdict; jury (juror).

**not guilty by reason of insanity** A plea of not guilty based on a lack of criminal capacity. Not guilty by reason of insanity is a criminal plea essentially admitting the defendant committed the act of the offense yet denying responsibility because the defendant lacked the capacity to act with criminal intent at the time. A defendant may enter such a plea, which may be accepted by the court, or the defendant may have an instruction on such a plea submitted to a jury, which may render it as its verdict. In the federal courts and most state courts, a judgment of not guilty by reason of insanity requires a commitment to a mental institution for an unspecified time for treatment. A finding of not guilty by reason of insanity operates as a final verdict, and jeopardy attaches to it for the purposes of later criminal charges from the same conduct.

**plea bargain (plea deal or plea agreement)** A defendant and prosecutor agree the defendant will plead guilty to a limited charge or for a reduced sentence. A plea bargain, or plea agreement, is a contract between the defendant and the prosecutor in a case based on charges that have been or are liable to be brought against the defendant, in which the defendant agrees to plead guilty to a particular charge rather than be tried for more serious charges or plead guilty in the expectation of receiving a particular sentence rather than be tried and risk a harsher punishment. A plea bargain is not, however, usually binding on the court until the court accepts it and enters judgment based on the plea. A court may refuse a plea bargain and require a matter to be tried. Plea bargains are more common in most jurisdiction than are trials.

*See also:* plea, criminal plea, plea bargain, charge bargain.

**charge bargain** Plea agreed to one criminal charge to dismiss or reduce other charges. A charge bargain is a plea agreement in which the criminal defendant pleads guilty to one charge in exchange for the prosecution's dismissal of other possible charges (usually more serious charges), rather than a plea agreement regarding the sentence to be served or recommended. A plea agreement is usually a sentence agreement, but it may be a charge bargain, or both.

**plea in abeyance** A plea accepted subject to conditions to be performed prior to sentencing. A plea in abeyance is a plea that has been accepted by a court subject to specific conditions agreed upon in advance between the defense and the prosecutor. The defendant and prosecution enter an agreement, after which the defendant enters a conditional plea of guilt or nolo contendere, according to which the defendant's plea is subject to a motion by the defense and prosecution to hold the plea in abeyance, which the court grants. Judgment and sentence are then delayed until the defendant performs or is found to have failed to perform the conditions of the agreement. After the defendant performs the requirement to the satisfaction of the prosecution and court, the court enters the sentence initially agreed.

*See also:* abeyance.

**jurisdictional plea**    A plea based on lack of jurisdiction. A jurisdictional plea seeks to dismiss an action owing to a court's lack of jurisdiction over at least one of the parties or over the grounds alleged in the petition or complaint.

**plea in abatement (abatement of action)**    Pleading by the plaintiff seeking to terminate an action without prejudice. A plea in abatement is, traditionally, a pleading by the plaintiff that seeks to dismiss the action voluntarily and allow its later refiling. In this it is similar to a voluntary non-suit or a voluntary dismissal, although a plea in abatement is usually available later in a proceeding, and the plea in abatement is usually based on specific failings to bring suit in a proper capacity or against the real party in interest. More recently, it is a constructive aspect of some motions that have the effect of staying or suspending proceedings, such as a motion for arbitration.

**plea in equity**    A plea in an equitable matter, contesting jurisdiction, party, or bar to suit. A plea in equity is an answer to a bill or, in modern practice, a complaint raising equitable claims or seeking an equitable remedy, in which a defense is raised related to the court's jurisdiction, the fitness of the plaintiff to seek the remedy, or the claim of a bar to suit.

**plea roll (plea rolls or pleas rolls)**    A record of court pleadings, handwritten on long parchment stored rolled up. The plea rolls are great strips of parchment on which clerks copy the pleadings in various cases. The parchment was rolled up, making it into a heavy tube. A great collection of these tubes remain as the records of the court dockets of the English courts from the eleventh century to the seventeenth. The cases and their pleadings are indexed in calendars. Both the rolls and the calendars have been transcribed at least in part by the Selden Society.

**rolled-up plea**    A plea of several related arguments. A rolled-up plea is a plea with multiple arguments, whether the arguments are essentially related yet distinct, or are in the alternative, but which, for one reason or the other, are allowed despite the general rule that a plea should present a single argument. The most common form in which the "rolled-up plea" is still found in an age of code pleading is the alternative arguments in defense to defamation: the allegedly defamatory statements were true but if they were not susceptible to truth, they were fair comment.

**verified plea (verification of pleading)**    A plea with a statement that the pleader is willing to verify the facts therein. A verified plea is a plea containing factual allegations, which must be verified by a statement by the pleader that the pleader (either the party or the counsel signing the plea) is willing to verify the statements made in the plea. In jurisdictions following the federal rules of civil procedure, the verification requirement has been largely replaced by the signature requirements of Federal Rule of Civil Procedure 11.

*See also:* complaint, verified complaint; verification (verify).

**pleader**    A person who pleads, or the pleading itself. A pleader, in U.S. practice, is one who enters a plea, or who pleads a motion or a case. In the context of a motion, the pleader is the party or counsel who presents a specific argument or defense. The pleader, in general, is the person who presents a whole case, and to use pleader without a clear reference to a plea in answer is not to suggest a defendant only, but pleader in this broad sense suggests a party or the party's counsel bringing the cause of action. Note: in English practice, pleader refers not to the person but to the pleading and the manner by which the pleading is drafted.

**pleading**    A written presentation of a claim or defense filed in a civil or criminal action. A pleading is an instrument in writing that is served on the parties to a lawsuit and becomes part of the court record for that action. In the Federal Rules of Civil Procedure, those instruments that are considered pleadings are limited to complaints and answers. Thus a judgment on the pleadings under the federal rules is limited to the legal significance of the statements in the complaints and answers, with whatever exhibits are incorporated into them by reference. The scope of pleadings in state court vary somewhat and may include written motions and notices.

Pleadings in criminal procedure are the prosecution's indictment or information, the defendant's demurrer (if one of these now rare pleadings is filed), and the defendant's plea (if the plea is filed as an instrument rather than made orally).

A pleading must be organized according to rule and to custom, with the caption of the case, court and docket information, a clear designation of the form of pleading, and clear statements stating the facts, claims, or defenses in issue. A pleading may incorporate exhibits and other matter by reference, although both the length of the pleading and the number and length of such exhibits may be limited by the court by rule or order. A pleading must be signed by a party or by counsel and must be based on a good faith investigation of the law and facts underlying all statements and averments within it. A pleading is subject to amendment, and in most cases, a pleading must be amended, substituted, or withdrawn if the party who files it becomes aware of materially false statements made in the pleading, though such changes made long after filing must usually be made only with leave of the court.

Note: in general, to plead is also to file a pleading or to articulate an argument in a pleading. Yet plead has a variety of other meanings, not the least being for a defendant to enter a plea in a criminal case, which may be done orally rather than in a pleading filed on the record.

**accusatory pleading**  A criminal complaint, information, or indictment. An accusatory pleading is a pleading filed in a criminal action stating criminal charges brought against a defendant. The accusatory pleading does not initiate the criminal file, however, which may be based on arrest alone, but when a person is arrested and no accusatory pleading is filed, the arrestee may usually petition to have the record of arrest expunged.

**alternative pleading (pleading in the alternative or pled in the alternative)**  The pleading of several mutually exclusive theories or remedies. Alternative pleading is the presentation of two or more theories of the case, each in the alternative, or a prayer for several remedies, each in the alternative, when the pleader knows that the theories or remedies are mutually exclusive and that no more than one will be proven or will be granted by the court. To plead in the alternative allows the pleader to seek relief with imperfect knowledge of the evidence that will be developed during the course of an action, as well as to present several alternative explanations of the evidence to the finder of fact. The plaintiff may plead both theories of the case and remedies in the alternative, and the defendant may plead both theories of the case and defenses in the alternative.

*See also:* remedies, election of remedies (election of plaintiff or election of actions or several-remedies rule).

**amended pleading**  A revised pleading. An amended pleading is a revision of a pleading already filed in an action, and once the amended pleading is filed, either by right or by leave of the court, the amended pleading takes the place of the earlier pleading for all substantive purposes.

Note: if an amendment's sole function is to incorporate or respond to events occurring after the pleading was filed, the new pleading is supplemental rather than amended.

*See also:* amendment, amendment to a pleading; pleading, supplemental pleading.

**amendment of pleading (amended pleading or amendment to a pleading)**  The later filing of an altered pleading earlier filed. Amendments are allowed for pleadings in civil and criminal matters in all jurisdictions. An amended pleading may be filed, usually as a matter of right before a response is made and by leave of the court thereafter or, if no response is required, the amendment is usually made by motion, with leave of the court to be allowed in the court's discretion. A significant delay in amendment that has no particular excuse is usually a barrier to amendment, unless the amendment would not be unfair to an opponent. Amendment in a criminal matter is generally more restricted.

**face of the pleadings**  The allegations the parties state in the pleadings. The face of the pleadings is a traditional euphemism for what is written in the text of the pleadings in a civil or criminal action. The face of the pleadings technically includes the texts of all of the pleadings filed. Still, the term as it ordinarily is used means only the pleadings in which the primary claims, jurisdictional statements, and defenses are pled. In criminal actions, the pleadings include the information or indictment, as well as responsive pleading documents. In civil actions, they include the statements of the complaint and answer or other responsive pleadings. In all cases, to look to the face of the pleadings is to consider only the statements and arguments actually made in writing and not to include inferences or derivative arguments that might be later implied.

**impertinent matter in a pleading**  Irrelevant matter in a pleading. Impertinent matter in a civil pleading is matter raising an issue that is neither a claim or a defense in the action nor practically related to a claim or defense. Though great effort has been expended to determine the difference between matter that is impertinent and matter that is irrelevant or immaterial, there really isn't a significant difference. Thus, potential relevance of evidence is a useful tool for the discrimination of impertinent matter: if any textual matter does not present or relate to evidence that might be admissible to prove an issue that might appropriately be before the court, then that text is impertinent.

**motion for more definite statement**  A motion to add clarity to a pleading. A motion for a more definite statement is a request to the court to require greater specificity in a pleading filed by an opposing party. A motion for a more definite statement may be brought by a party obligated to file a responsive pleading, if the pleading or an issue in the pleading to which that party must respond is too vague or ambiguous to file a reasonable response. The court may grant the motion in its discretion, thus requiring the original pleader to file an amended pleading or an answer to the motion. The amended pleading or response should make sufficiently clear the factual and legal basis of the issue in question that the movant can reasonably respond. In the federal rules, the court may strike the pleading if the pleader fails timely to respond to the motion.

**pleading standards**

**code pleading (fact pleading)**  Pleading based on the ultimate facts of the case. Code pleading, based on the legislative codes of civil procedure, such as David Dudley Field's Code of 1848, requires fewer forms of pleading than the common law. The primary focus of code pleading is for each side to assert its view of the ultimate facts in issue, incorporating into the pleadings the allegations of fact and claims in law to present the entire case on the face of the complaints, answers, and replies. Code pleading is used in a minority of states, the others using notice pleading. The Federal Rules of Civil Procedure use notice pleading.

Despite the greater flexibility that code pleading offered in comparison to the writ system, code pleading's emphasis on the recitation of facts to be proved required the plaintiff to argue facts in the pleadings that would ultimately be proved in court. This requirement of factual detail in the pleadings contrasts with the greater flexibility of notice pleading, which allows the plaintiff to develop facts in discovery sufficient to prove one or another theory of the case, as long as the plaintiff pleads sufficient facts to put a defendant on notice as to the nature of the bases for relief.

**issue pleading**   The pleadings must present a definite issue to adjudicate. Issue pleading is a frame by which to consider pleading under the rules of civil procedure, in which the pleadings must present issues for adjudication and not merely notice of a claim. Issue pleading places a greater emphasis on the sufficiency of facts to establish the legal issues articulated, which are likely to be or are in genuine dispute between the parties rather than the general basis for one or more claims for relief.

*See also:* issue, issue before the court (question before the court or contested issue or disputed issue or issue in dispute); pleading, pleading theories, notice pleading, plausible on its face (Twombly standard or Iqbal test or facial plausibility).

**notice pleading**   Pleading designed to put the opponent on notice of the claims, defenses, and their bases. Notice pleading is the form of pleading adopted in the Federal Rules of Civil Procedure, in that the pleader need not set out all of the facts pertaining to most claims or defenses but only a short and plain statement of the claim including the most elemental assertions of fact required to give the other party notice of the basis of the claim for relief and to establish a plausible basis for that relief. (Even in notice pleading, there are exceptions requiring more factual detail, such as claims for fraud or for racketeering.) Notice pleading uses a complaint, answer, or reply rather than the array of specific forms of pleading associated with the common law forms for pleading arguments of law or pleading arguments of fact. Notice pleading is thus less detailed than code pleading and less legally formal in the construction of the pleadings than common-law pleading.

**plausible on its face (Twombly standard or Iqbal test or facial plausibility)**   Pleading required to present facts sufficient to justify the legal theory remedy requested. Plausibility on its face, or facial plausibility, is a requirement for pleading articulated in an anti-trust action, Bell Atlantic Corp. v. Twombly, 550 U.S. 544 (2007) and applied generally in Ashcroft v. Iqbal, 129 S. Ct. 1937 (2009), requiring a claimant in a pleading to present facts in the pleading that are plausible and sufficient to support the legal theory argued for the relief the pleading seeks. On this basis, a plaintiff must know sufficient facts prior to

pleading and prior to discovery to sustain the action. Though it is less a matter thus far considered by the courts, a logical extension must also be that the defendant must also know sufficient facts prior to pleading and prior to discovery to sustain any defense. This approach has been very strongly criticized as a misinterpretation of Federal Rule of Civil Procedure 8 and contrary to the purpose of notice pleading. As of 2011, it remains the standard for civil pleading in federal courts, although Congress is considering bills to reinvigorate notice pleading.

*See also:* dismissal, grounds for dismissal, failure to state a claim upon which relief can be granted, Twombly test (Twombly standard).

**responsive pleading**   A pleading that responds to an earlier pleading. A responsive pleading is a pleading that is required under the rules of procedure in response to a pleading filed by another party, at the risk of otherwise being barred from contesting the statements or claims of the earlier pleading. The two primary forms of responsive pleading are an answer and a reply. The time for filing a responsive pleading is limited, under the Federal Rules of Civil Procedure to twenty-one days (or sixty days for an answer, if the time for answer is extended by a waiver of service or for the United States to answer as a defendant, or ninety days for a foreign defendant). The time for filing a responsive pleading may be extended by the court in its discretion on motion from the responding party if the responding party demonstrates a good cause for the delay.

*See also:* answer; reply.

**scandalous matter in a pleading**   Unnecessary and inappropriate matter in a pleading. Scandalous matter in a civil pleading is an unnecessary statement or statements that would reasonably be expected to shock, offend, or cause a party, a person, or the court. Scandal is a matter of greater and lesser offense, and though there is no perfect boundary as to what level of offense or harm is scandal and what is not, certain benchmarks suggest the matter is scandalous: scandalous matter includes matter that would reasonably be expected to shock, offend, or cause a person to have a diminished reputation in the community in which the person lives or works; or that would diminish the value of a corporation; or that would be sufficiently outrageous to the dignity of the court that such a statement in open court would be subject to sanctions by the court. Scandalous matter may be stricken from a pleading by the court on motion or sua sponte. It is essential, however, that such matter be unnecessary to the pleading or action, and such matter that is related to a claim or defense raised in an action will not ordinarily be stricken from the pleading.

*See also:* scandal.

**sham pleading**   A false pleading. A sham pleading presents claims of fact or law that are not true. The fact that a party believes them to be true when they are filed cannot absolve a party from having filed a sham pleading. A sham pleading filed for the real purpose of delay is a dilatory pleading.

**shotgun pleading (shotgun complaint or shotgun answer)** A pleading of too many claims, none well focused on the facts. A shotgun pleading, particularly a shotgun complaint or a shotgun answer, raises a host of claims or defenses, usually with redundant statements of fact repeated in support of nearly every legal theory. A shotgun pleading not only defeats the purpose of notice pleading to put the opponent on fair notice of the claim or defense against it, but also strains the attention of the court in considering which arguments have merit, if any, because these arguments are veiled in the haze of unlikely arguments raised — often — in an unlearned attempt to gamble on a remote argument rather than to state persuasively the arguments well supported in law and fact.

**special pleading** The pleading of specific matters that are not typical in a claim or defense. Special pleading in civil procedure is the pleading of special matter that must be specifically alleged in a pleading in order to be later subject to proof, such as special damages (as opposed to general damages) or special defenses, such as the statute of limitations as a bar to a claim. Once an action has been subject to a responsive pleading, certain new allegations must also be raised by special pleading. Special pleading is now often referred to as specific allegation or separate allegation.

Special pleading as a matter of the law of civil procedure differs from other senses with which it is easily confused. More generally, "special pleading" is an argumentative fallacy in which the speaker falsely implies or claims entitlement to an exception from general standards or proofs. For instance, a statement like "I can drive my car like this because jet pilots do" attempts to exempt the speaker from general traffic laws and basic reason by alluding to a false claim (perhaps two false claims): jet pilots are not subject to special rules of automobile driving, nor is it all clear that the speaker would be entitled to the benefit of such an exception if it did exist, as there is no statement that the speaker is, in fact, a jet pilot. The statement is a fallacy.

*See also:* special; fallacy, fallacy of division.

**supplemental pleading** A pleading relating events known only after an earlier pleading. A supplemental pleading is a pleading that augments a pleading already filed in an action, incorporating into the new pleading a statement of events that occurred after the first pleading was filed. A supplemental pleading is distinct from an amended pleading, both in presenting matter that occurred after the earlier pleading and in that a supplemental pleading is allowed even if there was a defect in the earlier pleading.

*See also:* amendment, amendment to a pleading; pleading, amended pleading.

**plebiscite or direct legislation** *See:* referendum (plebiscite or direct legislation).

**pledge** A promise made with great solemnity and apparent sincerity. A pledge is the statement by an individual of a particular commitment or promise, made to another person, to a group, or to an entity. A pledge may be to support the statement, promise, or obligation of another, with or without an undertaking to perform in the other's stead. In the medieval common law, pledges were required to secure a suit, and this sense persists in the law of secured transactions and bailment. Yet the more general sense of pledge includes a pledge of less tangible but still essential commitments, such as a pledge of love or of support, or in the matrimonial sense to pledge one's troth or in the patriotic sense to pledge one's allegiance. Such pledges are enforceable in any context in which a promise becomes enforceable in law or in equity. In general, the pledge in such senses is similar to the sense of oath, the primary differences being customary.

*See also:* oath.

**pledge as assurance (pledgee or pledger)** To secure another's obligations, or the security of a deposit. A pledge in the common law is a promise to fulfill the promise or obligation of another person, in the manner of a surety or a bailment. In this sense, the pledger is the maker of the promise and the pledgee is the recipient of the pledge.

In the civil law and in Article 9 of the Uniform Commercial Code, a pledge is a security for the performance of an obligation or promise, such as the money or valuable objects deposited with the promissee as a bailment to be kept until the promise is performed, after which they will be returned or, if the promise is not performed, they will be forfeit to the promissee.

*See also:* pawn, pawn-broker (pawnbroker or pawn shop or pawnee).

**Pledge of Allegiance** A pledge demonstrating allegiance to the United States. The Pledge of Allegiance, as currently designated by federal statute, is: "I pledge allegiance to the Flag of the United States of America, and to the Republic for which it stands, one Nation under God, indivisible, with liberty and justice for all." Written in 1892 for a youth rally, "under God" was added in 1954. The statute specifies decorum during the pledge but does not require its recitation by any individual. Schoolchildren may not be compelled to recite the pledge, a recognition that a requirement to recite the pledge would violate the First Amendment.

*See also:* religion, freedom of religion | 3. pledge of allegiance and religious freedom.

**plenary**

**plenary power** *See:* power, plenary power.

**plenary as full** Complete and unlimited. Plenary depicts anything full and complete, of the greatest breadth and comprehensiveness. Thus plenary jurisdiction is full jurisdiction, and the one government among several with plenary authority has a presumptive authority to regulate anything, without regard to what the others must do (though the regulations of the others must be compatible with the acts of the legislature with plenary jurisdiction).

**plenary review**  The fullest scope of review. Plenary review is full review, a complete consideration or reconsideration of the matter before the court. On appeal, there is no difference between plenary review and review de novo. Note: in some appellate courts, plenary review is used to describe a case heard en banc, that is review given by the full court, but this usage is less common than that of full review in the sense of de novo review the matters in an action.
*See also:* de, de novo.

**plenipotentiary**  A person or entity possessing full powers. A plenipotentiary has full powers to enter diplomatic agreements or, otherwise, the fullest extent of authority possible. A plenipotentiary committee, delegation, or representative of a larger institution has the power to act for the whole of the institution. An ambassador or envoy plenipotentiary has full powers to enter into treaties on behalf of the country represented by the ambassador or envoy.

**plot**  A small landholding, or the marks on a map or chart, or an organization. A plot is a particular parcel of land, usually not of great size, such as a garden or yard for a small house or a single property in a sub-division (which is more commonly now called a lot). Plot is also a customary designation for lands dedicated to a specific burial in a cemetery. The term is derived from "plat" and may also mean the general plan of a city or town, as well as its map. The term has come to represent a variety of organizations created out of specific components, such as the drawing of tracklines on maps and courses on charts as well as the devising of a dramatic scheme or a complex (and perhaps criminal) endeavor.
*See also:* plat (plat map).

**plunder**  Theft of property by a public enemy. Plunder is a form of theft, either a seizure of goods at sea by a military vessel or privateer (when these were lawful) from a neutral vessel, or by a pirate from land or sea. The plunder of goods results in their spoliation.
*See also:* pillage (pillaging or pillager); spoliation (spoliator).

**plural marriage or polygamous**  *See:* marriage, polygamy (plural marriage or polygamous).

**pluralism**  *See:* jurisprudence, legal pluralism.

**plurality**  The greatest number when there is no majority. A plurality is a number larger than another, and it is often used to designate the largest quantity that remains less than a majority. Thus a plurality opinion is the opinion that receives the most votes when no opinion receives a majority.
*See also:* opinion, judicial opinion, plurality opinion.

**plurality opinion**  *See:* opinion, judicial opinion, plurality opinion.

**pluribus**  Many. Pluribus is a derivation from the Latin adjective multus, or many, peculiarly representing both concrete and abstract aggregates by the same word. It is a component of the phrase "e pluribus unum."

**plutocracy**  *See:* government, forms of government, plutocracy (timocracy).

**pocket immunity**  *See:* immunity, witness immunity, informal immunity (pocket immunity).

**pocket part**  *See:* lawbook, pocket part.

**pocket veto**  *See:* veto, pocket veto (absolute veto or silent veto).

**point**  A single statement or argument, often one in a series. A point, in legal rhetoric, is a single argument or claim, including both a conclusion and its rationale. A point may be disputed or be conclusively proven.
*See also:* possession, nine points of the law (nine-tenths of the law).

**point system**  Any scheme by which factors in a decision are given relative weights. A point system is any means by which a series of activities or components are singly evaluated and then consolidated into a decision. Point systems are often used in administration and regulation, by which a program or application is evaluated according to points. A point system in assessment is a means of allocating a single decision among a variety of scaled assessments: a set of criteria is defined, and each criterion is allocated a portion of varying weight within a maximum point range. When a given conduct or project is assessed, each criterion is separately examined by further assessment criteria relevant to that criterion and assessed a portion of the points available within that criterion. The cumulative score for the points awarded after review of each criterion is summed to make the final score in points for the thing assessed. The things assessed can then be placed in a rank order according to their points awarded.

Point systems in some administrative and military regulation are designed to allow points to be assigned to infractions or misconduct, and if sufficient points are accrued during a period of time, a punishment is assessed or qualification or permit is revoked. Thus, many states use a point system for recording traffic citations, and if a driver accrues sufficient points in a given year or several years, the driver's license may be suspended or revoked.

**poison pill**  *See:* takeover, corporate takeover, poison pill.

**pole tax**  *See:* tax, sin tax, pole tax (sexually oriented business tax or sob tax).

**police**   The regulation of public order and the officials responsible for doing so. Police has several distinct meanings in law: the power of officials to regulate the safety, health, welfare, and morals of the people through law; the definition, identification, and punishment of crimes against such regulations; and the legal officials tasked with criminal enforcement. Its oldest and most important sense is represented by the police power, the authority of the state to regulate the affairs of every person in the polis. This authority is understood in police regulations and actions, in which the legal officials are required to respond to some threat to the body politic. (A classic illustration is the need to destroy a building to stop the spread of a fire or to cut and burn a tree to stop the spread of a blight; such actions are police actions and not, for instance, subject to the ordinary analysis of a taking of private property for a public good.) Yet it is most well-known in the sense of the police forces, the many departments of law enforcement officers who are particularly tasked with the maintenance of public safety and order, particularly in the enforcement of the criminal law.

**police animal**   *See:* animal, police animal.

**police jury**   *See:* county, parish, police jury.

**police lineup**   *See:* identification, identification procedure, police lineup (array or identification parade or line up or line-up or photo array or show up or showup or show-up).

**police profiling or criminal profiling**   *See:* profile (police profiling or criminal profiling).

**police stop**   *See:* stop, police stop (investigative stop or traffic stop).

**enquête de police**   Police investigation. Enquête de police is French for an official inquiry conducted, usually, by the French police under the supervision or delegated authority of an investigating magistrate. It may be commenced, however, by a judicial police officer who observes evidence of a crime in progress.

**police agent (government agent or federal agent)**   A law enforcement officer or person acting at one's request or direction. A police agent is either a police officer or a person who is acting at the request or under the direction of a police officer in carrying out a police function. Particularly, a private individual may become a police agent if a police officer recruits or otherwise directs the individual to observe and report on the activities of a suspect or the activities of a given place or organization in gathering evidence of criminal activity. The direction must be sufficiently specific as to amount to direction generally to do what the agent later does do that is material to some investigation or prosecution, and a request must be sufficient in creating the agency such that use later made of the agent's actions or information provided would be within the scope of the request. An informant may or may not be a police agent; if the informant acts out of the independent will of the informant to gather the information provided to police, with no prior request

or direction to do so, the informant was not acting as a police agent at the time the information was gathered. On the other hand, an informant may become a police agent for the purposes of gathering further information.

A police agent's search is subject to the Fourth Amendment. However, an interrogation by a police agent that is made in circumstances in which the suspect is not in custody and is unaware the interrogator is a police agent may not be subject to the Fifth Amendment or the Miranda Rule.

**informant (informer or confidential informant or ci or canary or pigeon or rat or snitch or stool pigeon)**   A person who provides information to the police. An informant is an individual who provides information to a police agency regarding activities that may amount to criminal conduct. Informants may be police employees, whether a professional police officer or not, but the term is usually reserved for informants who are not employed by the police as a career. Paid informants are private citizens who receive money for serving as informants, and professional criminal informants are paid informants.

A warrant based on evidence provided by an informant must be based on sufficient evidence that the informant is reliable that the evidence itself may be considered to determine its sufficiency to demonstrate probable cause. A jury is entitled to determine for itself the reliability of an informant's evidence, and material related to an informant's reliability, interest, independence, and credibility, is always relevant.

**police brutality (excessive force or unjustified force)**   The use of force without justification by a police officer or agent. Police brutality is a general expression for the use of excessive force by a police officer, prison guard, or other law enforcement official, whether in the course of the official's duties or otherwise. Police brutality is, by definition, an excessive use of force, which is inherently more force than is reasonably required by the circumstances.

Police brutality, or the use of excessive force by a police officer, is an act or series of acts by one or more police officers or agents that result in physical harm to a person during arrest or while in custody, when the acts are in excess of a reasonable level of force required for the safety of the police or other persons or another lawful purpose. The level of force that amounts to excessive force will always vary according to the context of the incident in which force is used and the nature of the legal inquiry that follows.

Acts of police brutality violate the constitutional right to be free from interference with life and liberty without due process of law, and they are violations of one's civil rights when carried out under the color of law, even when it is a matter of practice, custom, or improper training or supervision. A claim for excessive force, which is the nature of police brutality, may be brought under state laws, under departmental complaint procedures, and in federal actions, such as a Bivens action or a Section 1983 complaint for the deprivation of civil rights. These actions depend in part on whom the complaint is brought against, and a complaint against the officer's agency or department will depend on evidence that the department either required or condoned the conduct or failed adequately to train or to supervise the agents. In all cases, claims will depend on the use of force being in excess of that allowed either under departmental rules for the use of force, under the Fourth Amendment, or under the Fifth or Fourteenth Amendment. The officer may also be liable for suit for the torts of assault, battery, or the use of excessive force. The officer may also be liable for criminal assault or homicide if death results to the victim. The police officer will generally have a qualified immunity, which requires that the officer not violate a right clearly established at the time of the act. States, though not municipalities, are entitled to Eleventh Amendment immunity from such claims.

*See also:* brutality (brutal); force, physical force, excessive force.

**chokehold (choke-hold or choke hold or sleeper hold)** Restraint of a suspect by holding the neck from behind. A chokehold is a means of restraint of a suspect or other person being detained, which is intended quickly to provide the police or security officer maximum control over the suspect. It is accomplished by placing the suspect's neck against a baton, night stick, the officer's bent arm, and pulling the suspect backward against the police officer's shoulder or chest, thus both placing the suspect off balance and allowing the officer to block blood flow to the brain, while creating an apparent risk to the suspect of choking if the suspect moves. The dangers, of course, are that the hold will be overused so that suspects who pose no danger of assault or flight are exposed to excessive force and that the hold will be badly managed and the suspect will be injured or killed. Use of the hold, which was once widely taught in police training, has been banned in most police departments.

**police officer (law enforcement officer or peace officer)** An official sworn or deputized to enforce the laws of a jurisdiction. A police officer is an individual who is sworn, commissioned, or deputized to enforce the law in a given jurisdiction by an official authorized to take such oaths or make such commissions or deputations in that jurisdiction. This sense of police officer includes both individuals employed by police departments as uniformed or plain clothes officers of various ranks, including a chief of police, as well as other law enforcement officers, such as sheriffs, deputies, state troopers, and (in Texas) rangers. Various jurisdictions differ somewhat in their designations and the scope of that designation. Some states use a broad or generic term, such as peace officer or law enforcement officer for certain purposes, reserving police officer for use by municipal or state police departments, but including other law enforcement

personnel, such as sheriffs and deputies, in the broader term.

States often define police officer distinctly for different purposes. Thus, a broad definition of police officer is used, or a broader term such as peace officer is used to determine in whom shall be vested the authority to make an arrest in the name of the state or a subdivision of the state, or who shall be immune from civil liability for certain actions in enforcing the law. A narrower definition is often employed in determining who is entitled to workers' compensation as a police officer, to organize a police union or to enjoy other benefits of employment in that designation.

**undercover agent** A police officer posing as a civilian to gather evidence. An undercover agent poses as a person not in law enforcement for the purpose of gathering evidence. Undercover agents are under the same restrictions as identified law enforcement officers regarding searches, but they may enter premises by invitation or, in prisons, by assignment. An undercover agent is not an informant.

**police organization**

**Drug Enforcement Administration (D.E.A. or DEA)** An agency of the Department of Justice that enforces drug laws. The Drug Enforcement Administration, or DEA, is an agency or the U.S. Department of Justice for the domestic and international enforcement of laws restraining the criminal flow of drugs.

**Federal Bureau of Alcohol, Tobacco Firearms, and Explosives** Federal agency to police and ensure taxes from regulated substances. The Federal Bureau of Alcohol, Tobacco, Firearms, and Explosives is tasked with both regulating and collecting taxes on the four substances with which it has special expertise, including the regulation and enforcement of laws dealing with (a) the manufacture and importation of arms, ammunition, and military munitions; (b) explosives; (c) tobacco and tobacco products; and (d) the federal regulation of alcohol production and commerce. The ATF is the successor to early attempts to enforce domestic tax laws, including prohibition, originally by the Department of the Treasury, but transferred to the Department of Justice in 2003.

**Federal Bureau of Investigation (F.B.I. or FBI)** The principal federal agency for the enforcement of federal criminal law. The Federal Bureau of Investigation is the principal law enforcement agency of the United States government. A division of the Department of Justice, the bureau is charged with investigating violations of U.S. criminal law, investigating threats to U.S. security from terrorists and foreign intelligence agencies, investigating cases of peculiar likelihood of federal interest or interstate transportation, such as cases of kidnapping, child abduction, and bank robbery, and providing assistance and coordination to state and local law enforcement organizations.

**International Criminal Police Organization (INTER-POL)** Global body of national police services to coordinate law enforcement. INTERPOL, or more fully the International Criminal Police Organization, is an international association of the police services of member nations, which assists in the location and arrest of criminal suspects across national borders, manages a secure international communications system, develops and provides training in counter-terrorism and the suppression of transnational crime, manages access to national databases and provides emergency operational support to police operations in the field. The General Secretariat is in Lyon, France.

**military police (MP or M.P.)** Uniformed law enforcement units of the military forces. Military police is the specific designation for units constituted and personnel trained to serve as the law enforcement organizations for the U.S. Army, operating as a police force on land subject to army jurisdiction, usually under the operational command of a provost marshal. It is also the generic term for such units and personnel in all of the military services, although they vary considerably in the scope of their jurisdiction: the Air Force Security Forces being the most similar, but every service having a senior investigative arm.

**shore patrol (SP or S.P.)** A naval detail to ensure order among military personnel ashore. A shore patrol is established by every naval command for the insurance of order among service members on liberty. Although not a law enforcement service generally, the shore patrol may carry out its lawful orders in enforcing military discipline and laws applicable to service personnel, including the coordination of the delivery of incarcerated personnel from civilian authorities to their host commands for appropriate discipline. Law enforcement for more serious criminal laws within the Department of the Navy is committed to the Naval Criminal Investigative Service, or NCIS.

**United States Marshals Service** The security and law enforcement service of the federal courts. The United States Marshals Service provides court security in federal courthouses and courtrooms, assures judicial security, locates and arrests fugitives from federal jurisdiction, manages the federal witness security program, transports prisoners, manages courthouse detention, and supervises federal asset forfeitures. The deputy marshals, inspectors, and courtroom security officers of the USMS operate under the supervision of a federal marshal who is a presidential appointee in every judicial district.
*See also:* marshal.

**U.S. Secret Service** A federal service to enforce currency laws and protect national leaders. The U.S. Secret Service is a federal police service, tasked with detecting and prosecuting counterfeiters of U.S. currency and providing security to the president and senior officials. The service was created during the American Civil War to detect and prosecute counterfeiters of U.S. currency, a role it continues to perform. Following the assassination of President Lincoln, it was tasked with the protection of the life of the president, and it now provides security and protection for senior government officials and presidential candidates, as well as for designated events. Authorized by Congress in 1865 as a branch of the Department of the Treasury, since 2003 the service has been an arm of the Department of Homeland Security.
*See also:* counterfeiting (counterfeit or counterfeitor or counterfeitable); assassination (assassin).

**police power (powers of police)** The authority of government to regulate health, safety, welfare, and morals. The police power is the fundamental authority of the state over the people within it. The term is derived from the Greek polis, the city-state and its people, and though the power is variously formulated, it is generally the authority to regulate all conditions and actions required to promote the good health, safety, welfare, and morals of its people. Though the regulation of morals is often criticized in this context, it includes such fundamental moral expressions of law as the prohibitions on murder and on unequal treatment by state officials.

In the United States, the individual states are said to have a reserved plenary police power, which is limited only by constitutional protections of individual rights and delegations of power to the sole authority of the federal government. The federal government is said not to have a general police power though it exercises police powers through its specific delegated powers, particularly through the regulation of interstate and foreign commerce.
*See also:* taking | police powers and takings.

**policing** The means and ends of police operations. Policing includes the tactics and strategy of police operations, including patrol, neighborhood and community supervision, surveillance, investigation, arrest, and detention of suspects as well as the public policy to be promoted or hindered by various means approaches.

**broken windows policing (quality of life policing or neighborhood order policing)** The strict enforcement of lesser laws to deter violation of major laws. Broken-windows policing is the strict enforcement of minor criminal laws against vandalism, abandonment of property, and public misbehavior in an attempt to deter more serious crimes such as gang-related violence, burglary, arson, and homicide. This approach has been controversial but instigated proactive assignment of police patrols, including foot patrols to municipal areas with higher short-term crime rates, leading in some cases to demonstrable rates of diminished criminal activity.
*See also:* disorder, civil disorder.

**policy**   The sum purpose that a legal rule or institution is intended to achieve. Policy, in the grand sense, is the purpose for which law is created or enforced. The policy underlying a statute is the set of ends that are to be pursued by officials applying the statute, and when an application by rote of the language of the statute would be contrary to those ends, the application is absurd. In its broadest sense, policy includes both the rational and moral justifications for law as well as the various justifications of each and every specific law. In this sense, policy depends more on the effects created by such laws in the society that they govern than it depends on any purpose or intent with which the rules are made.

In a more specific sense, policy may refer to any written order or evidence of a contract, such as an insurance policy. This sense is derived not from the Greek polis, as in the sense of policy of law, but from the older French word police, for a contract.

**policy exclusion**   *See:* insurance, insurance policy, policy exclusion, exception to the exclusion; insurance, insurance policy, policy exclusion.

**policy limit**   *See:* insurance, insurance policy, policy limit.

**policy rider**   *See:* insurance, insurance policy, policy rider.

**public policy**   What is right, just, and promotes the public good. Public policy takes several forms, legislatively as the calculus for what legislative goals should be promoted through statutes or regulation, and judicially as a basis for determining when the courts should exercise or stay the use of judicial power. As a legislative calculus, public policy includes the prudent, pragmatic, and political as well as the economically efficient, humanitarian good, and moral right. As a basis for judicial authority, public policy incorporates certain aspects of justice with the goals, purposes, and reasons for laws and the delegation of legal and equitable powers to provide an unspecified limitation on the actions to enforce a right or protect an interest that is not in the interest of the public as a whole. Public policy may thus guide the retention or rejection of precedent, but it is an independent element of many rules of law, most notably that a contract contrary to public policy is voidable or unenforceable.

**politics (political)**   The patterns and methods by which people influence government and laws. Politics is both the practice of individuals and groups and the processes by which they seek the ability to exercise authority through the offices of government and of the law. The political process is the competition or coordination of such individuals and groups as they seek to acquire or retain such authority or to remove others from it. The term is derived from the Greek for "matters of state" which Aristotle entitled his great book on the subject.

Every citizen has a right of political participation, and a burden on that right within a jurisdiction in which a person is a citizen or domiciliary is examined with strict scrutiny. Yet political rights are not unlimited, and the rights of a person to engage in the politics of a jurisdiction of which the person is neither a citizen nor a domiciliary may be limited on any rational basis.

Note: Bouvier describes a sense of politics and political science that is still found in older cases, that of a rational exercise of a science of government. The modern sense of political science is generally more concerned with the promotion of particular interests by groups, especially that of the political parties. Still, the difference between the two senses is not a stark division but one of emphasis.

**political action committee**   *See:* lobby, political action committee (PAC or P.A.C.).

**political campaign spending**   *See:* speech, freedom of speech, political speech, political campaign spending.

**political offense**   *See:* refugee, political refugee, political offense.

**political opinion**   *See:* refugee, political refugee (political opinion).

**political party**   *See:* party, political party.

**political question**   *See:* justiciability, political question.

**political refugee**   *See:* refugee, political refugee, political offense; refugee, political refugee (political opinion).

**political speech**   *See:* speech, freedom of speech, political speech, political campaign spending.

**political trial**   *See:* trial, show trial (political trial).

**political union**   *See:* union, political union.

**polity**   The whole people within a jurisdiction, or its organization. The polity is the whole of the people within the relevant group, whether it is the whole of the species of human beings, of the members of a nation or state, of the members of a church or association, or any other group of people.

In ecclesiastical law, some churches are governed by a polity, which is both the rules of organization and the standards regarding who is a member of the organization and what rights or authority various members enjoy.

*See also:* church, church autonomy doctrine.

**poll**   An election or survey, or anything affecting each person in a group. Poll, in general, is something of the person, so that anything done by poll is similar to anything done per capita; it is done according to each person in the relevant group. Thus, an election poll is a vote to be taken one ballot per person. A jury poll is an inquiry of each person on the jury. A poll tax is a tax on each person in the jurisdiction (rather than, say, each person owning property). A labor poll is a vote either of the membership of a local or union or of the workers of a given employer or site. A poll need not be exhaustive or a population, but it must be done person by person;

thus, an opinion poll is a survey of individual opinions among those selected to participate.

**poll tax** *See:* tax, poll tax (head tax or capitation tax).

**poll, jury poll** *See:* jury, jury poll.

**polling place** *See:* vote, vote in public election, polling place (polls or voting station).

**polls or voting station** *See:* vote, vote in public election, polling place (polls or voting station).

**pollution** The discharge of a substance that harms the environment. Pollution is anything that corrupts or harms the environment in which it is found. Pollution has several nuanced meanings in environmental law, particularly as it is used in pollution exclusion clauses in insurance policies and in various statutes. However, when it is not more specifically defined, pollution is either any substance, or the process of discharging any substance, introduced by human activity into the natural or artificial environment in a form and quantity that may harm people, animals, plants, or the environmental cycles of the area or the Earth. The term in a general sense has long depicted the corruption of a place or person, usually by the commission of an act or the presence of a substance that is unclean under the law.

*See also:* environment (environmental).

**pollution control technology** *See:* technology, control technology (pollution control technology).

**air pollution** Gases and particulates in the air that harm humans or the environment. Air pollution includes all forms of gas or solid particulates that are mixed or suspended in the air that have a harmful effect on humans, animals, or plants, or on the built or natural environment. Air pollution is regulated primarily by the federal Clean Air Act, which requires permits for the release of criteria pollutants into the atmosphere.

Note: although noise pollution is transmitted in most cases through the air, and though water pollution may be caused by air pollution, both are considered to be distinct forms of pollution in the law.

**acid rain** Precipitation contaminated with sulfur or nitrogen. Acid rain includes all forms of precipitation containing acids from fossil fuel combustion, particularly sulfuric acid. Acid rain causes the lowering of the pH in streams and lakes, which affect sensitive organisms at the lower levels of the food chain all the way through the predator level of the food chain. Acids deposited by acid rain onto plants cause the degradation of the cuticle of plant tissue in higher order plants, which allows the plant to hold in moisture and prevent it from transpiring too rapidly. Acid rain also causes an increase in the rate of weathering of man-made structures, affecting the rate of oxidation of iron and other metals, as well as the weathering of stonework and many synthetic materials.

**Air Quality Index (Air Pollution Index or API or Pollutant Standard Index or PSI)** A color-coded, numerical index of air pollution levels. The Air Quality Index that assesses the health risk of varying levels of pollutants in a given location. Ground level ozone and particulate matter 2.5 are the primary pollutant among five pollutants measured in air-quality indices. The index in 2011 was accessible online at http://www.airnow.gov.

**Clean Air Act (C.A.A. or CAA)** The primary federal statute regulating air emissions. The Clean Air Act (84 Stat. 1676, Public Law 91–604, codified at 42 U.S.C. §7401, et seq.) amended the the Air Quality Act of 1967 to require the U.S. Environmental Protection Agency to establish a national system for monitoring air quality and to require permits for significant sources of air pollution. It was amended in 1990 to encourage the use of market-based principles in regulating air pollution. The CAA has led to the use of air pollution models such as point-source and roadway-dispersion models.

**implementation plan (F.I.P. or FIP or S.I.P. or SIP)** A plan for air pollution emissions permits and enforcement actions. An implementation plan under the Clean Air Act is a management plan for a given jurisdiction to establish and maintain specific local air quality standards and enforcement procedures. Each state may create a State Implementation Plan, which establishes the methods of implementing the National Ambient Air Quality Standards in that state, using a system of permits and enforcement. Such plans are subject to approval by the U.S. Environmental Protection Agency (U.S. EPA). A state that does not create such a plan or that does not receive approval will be subject to a plan for that state created by the U.S. EPA, or a Federal Implementation Plan.

**criteria pollutant** The six pollutants measured and controlled under the Clean Air Act. Criteria pollutants or contaminants are presently the six for which the Clean Air Act requires measurement and abatement: ozone, carbon monoxide, suspended particulates, sulfur dioxide, lead, and nitrogen dioxide. Two pollutants, PM2.5. and ground-level ozone, are important in establishing the air quality index. As of 2011, the Environmental Protection Agency had begun a process that may lead to the listing of one or more greenhouse gasses as an additional criteria pollutant.

**carbon monoxide (CO)** A poisonous and asphyxiating gas that pollutes the air. Carbon monoxide, or CO, is derived most commonly from the burning of fossil fuels, particularly coal or gasoline. CO is a a toxic asphyxient, and CO detectors are now widely used in homes and businesses.

**lead** A polluting heavy metal that becomes airborne from burning coal and other processes.

Lead, or Pb, is a heavy metal that is capable of transmission through air as a component of particulates and of gases. In 1991, the Secretary to the Department of Health and Safety designated lead as the number one environmental health risk to children in the United States. Lead can be found in air, drinking water, food, contaminated soil, deteriorating paint, and dust. Airborne lead enters the body when an individual breathes or swallows lead particles or dust. Before it was known how harmful lead could be, it was used in paint, gasoline, water pipes, and many other products. Lead levels at or above 80 micrograms per deciliter of blood can cause convulsions, coma, and even death. Lower levels of lead can cause adverse health effects on the central nervous system, kidney, and blood cells. Blood lead levels as low as 10 micrograms per deciliter can impair mental and physical development.

**nitrogen dioxide (NO$_2$)** A toxic gas. Nitrogen dioxide, or NO$_2$, is a poisonous gas at room temperature, as well as a basis for nitric acid. It is a component of automotive exhaust fumes and a common basis for smog, though in isolation it is a red–brown gas or yellow liquid that becomes a colorless solid at −11.2°C.

**ozone (O$_3$)** A gas pollutant affecting respiration. Ozone, or O$_3$, is a highly reactive gas that affects human and animal respiration and is considered a ground–level pollutant, although it is also a critical element in the upper atmosphere, where it acts as a chemical photobarrier to diminish the passage of harmful solar radiation to the surface of the Earth. It is a primary air pollutant measured in Air Quality Indices because its presence in sufficient proportion causes asthma and other breathing difficulties.

**particulate matter (particulates or PM or P.M.)** Tiny particles of solids and sometimes liquids suspended in air or water. Particulate is the generic term for all sorts of tiny, often invisible, lumps of solids (and sometimes liquids) suspended in a gas in or solids suspended in a liquid. In environmental monitoring, particulates in air include the solids from dust, smoke, industrial production, engine exhaust, agribusiness, and natural activities, while particulates in water include soil runoff and underground leaching, content from point discharges, and the natural results of water erosion.

Air particulates are monitored by the size of the particulate. In EPA regulations under the Clean Air Act, these are coarse but inhalable (larger than 2.5 to 10 micrometers), fine (0.1 to 2.5 micrometers), or ultrafine (less than 10 micrometers). (A micrometer, or micron, is a millionth of a meter.) An acceptably low load of particulates at each size is one criterion of air quality attainment.

**particulate matter, total suspended particles (TSP)** An average mass of particulate matter in the air. Total suspended particles, or TSP, is one measure of the particulate matter in air, considering the weight in a given volume of air. This measurement of the aggregate of particulates has been superseded in the National Ambient Air Quality Standards by measurements of particulate at specific microvolumes, to PM–10, and since 1997, to PM2.5.

**sulfur dioxide (SO$_2$)** A gas pollutant that contributes to acid rain. Sulfur dioxide, or SO$_2$, is a primary contributor to the formation of acid rain, which is associated with acidification of soils, lakes, and streams, and accelerated corrosion of buildings and monuments. In addition, sulfur dioxide can become particulate matter. Emissions of SO$_2$ can be chemically transformed into ammonium sulfates, which are very tiny particles that can be carried hundreds of miles by wind. Sulfur dioxide levels have decreased in the last twenty years, owing to advances in technology, such as coal–fired power plant scrubbers and reduced sulfur content in coal. SO$_2$ is still a primary air pollutant, however.

*See also:* sulfur oxides (sulfur dioxide or SO$_2$).

**emission (emit)** To discharge from a given place. Emission is the action of putting anything out into the world, and the term was once used mainly to depict the issuance of money or other legal instruments intended to circulate with no direct or indirect intended recipient. In environmental law, emission refers to the generation of anything into the environment, particularly radiation, gasses, noise, leachate, liquids, and solid particulates into the atmosphere. Most particularly, emissions are the gasses and particulate matter put out into the atmosphere that are the components of air pollution. Vehicular emissions and fixed–source emissions are both subject to regulation under the Clean Air Act.

*See also:* emission (emit or bodily emission).

**motor vehicle emission standards** Limits on the amount of pollution vehicles can emit. Emissions standards are limits set out by the Environmental Protection Agency (EPA), as well as state and local authorities on the amount of pollution vehicles can emit into the atmosphere. These standards limit the amount of carbon monoxide, sulfur oxides, nitrogen oxide, and other pollutants that can be released into the atmosphere by the vehicle and may vary according to the vehicle's size, weight, or use. California was the first state to set stricter levels of limits on motor vehicle emissions than the levels set by the U.S. EPA.

*See also:* vehicle (motor vehicle).

**tailpipe emissions (exhaust)** Gasses and solids released from a vehicle's exhaust system by design. Tailpipe emissions are the products of the combustion of fuel in the vehicle's engine that are piped from the engine to the vehicle's exhaust system. The major pollutants emitted include unburned or partially burned fuel, nitrogen oxides ($NO_x$), carbon monoxide (CO), carbon dioxide, and water. Not all vehicle emissions are tailpipe emissions; evaporative emissions are released from the fuel intake and other elements of the fuel system, and microleaks and other sources of emissions are common, particularly in aging vehicles.

*See also:* emission (emit or bolidy emission).

**greenhouse gas (GHG or G.H.G.)**  Any gas that increases the atmosphere's retention of heat near the Earth. Greenhouse gases include all gases that increase the insulating effect of the atmosphere so that heat is less quickly expended from the Earth into space, owing to the effect of the gas. The primary forms of greenhouse gas are carbon dioxide ($CO_2$), methane ($CH_4$), nitrous oxide ($N_2O$), hydrofluorocarbons (HFCs), perfluorocarbons (PFCs), and sulfur hexafluoride ($SF_6$). Practically all greenhouse gases exist naturally, but in the nineteenth and twentieth centuries, concentrations increased owing to human activity, particularly the combustion of fuels that produce such gases and the use of gases in products and processes in great quantity. In 2009, the Environmental Protection Agency found greenhouse gasses threaten public health.

**mobile source**  Any means of transportation that emits air pollution. Mobile sources include all non-stationary sources of pollution, particularly motor vehicles, boats and ships, trains, airplanes, and portable engines within machinery, such as generators. The most significant source is from motor vehicles.

**National Ambient Air Quality Standards (NAAQS)**  The national system of air-pollution standards. The National Ambient Air Quality Standards (NAAQS) were established in by Congress in the Clean Air Act amendments of 1990. Primary standards set limits on six criteria contaminants to protect public health, including the health of sensitive populations such as asthmatics, children, and the elderly. Secondary standards set limits to protect public welfare, including protection against decreased visibility, damage to animals, crops, vegetation, and buildings. The standards of the NAAQS are enforced in the attainment zones in each state through State Implementation Plans. The NAAQS can be viewed at www.epa.gov/air/criteria.html.

**attainment zone**  A zone for testing whether air quality meets national standards. An "attainment zone" is a geographic area in the United States subject to separate evaluation of its air quality according to the National Ambient Air Quality Standards, which determines the load limits for regulated pollutants that are available for air emissions permits within the zone.

**non-attainment zone (nonattainment)**  Air quality falling below allowed levels in a particular measurement zone. A non-attainment zone is an area of land that does not meet national air-quality standards pursuant to the Clean Air Act. In most cases, the limits for emissions under new permits and renewed permits are restricted in non-attainment zones, in accord with state implementation plans or Environmental Protection Agency rules.

**scrubber**  A device that reduces the discharge of pollution from a vent or stack. A scrubber is any of a variety of devices using various technologies that are attached to the exhaust of smoke stacks to reduce air pollution. Scrubbers use water or chemical sprays, dry agent reactions, filters, and other traps to collect particulates and gasses that would otherwise be emitted.

**cap and trade**  A pollution valuation and trading scheme. Cap and trade regulations set a limit on the emission or production of specific wastes, set a value on each unit of waste, and create a market for the trading of units of the waste. A party that exceeds its allocation of the cap must purchase units from those whose demand is below their allocations, creating a market incentive for producers to diminish their wastes as well as a market commitment from those who do not. For example, if smelters could not emit smoke that contained more than 100 tons of sulfur, and smelter A produces only 50 tons of sulfur, but smelter B produces 150 tons of sulfur, A could profit by selling a refinery the right to emit 50 tons of sulfur, which B could purchase to continue producing without violating the regulation.

*See also:* pollution, cap and trade, emissions cap.

**emissions cap**  A maximum load of air pollution allowed in a given region. Emissions caps are ceilings set to establish a maximum production of emissions in an area over period of time, in effect, considering air as an "airshed" as water is considered a "watershed." Contributions to pollution in the particular airshed can then be "traded" among polluters.

*See also:* pollution, cap and trade.

**emissions trading**  Transfer of rights to pollute the air. Emissions trading creates a market for selling unused units of emission from an allocation for a maximum level of emission allowed under an emissions cap. Emissions trading depends on a governmental or other systemic designation of a quantitative emissions cap, a valuation of each unit of emissions (whether it is acquired through reduction or otherwise), and a market and means of transferring the units created.

**degradation (anti-degradation or non-degredation or antidegredation or nondegradation)**  Standards prohibiting harm to environmental quality. Degradation of the environment represents an increase in the quantity of pollution present in an ecosystem or, less commonly, an increase in the danger environmental risks pose to human health or a decrease in the ability of an ecosystem to support native plants and animals. Anti-degradation standards apply to waters or areas of the atmosphere that have relatively high pollutant levels, and forbid actions that would degrade such waters further. Though the Environmental Protection Agency prefers non-degradation to depict its policy to prevent any lowering of existing environmental quality, and anti-degradation clauses to refer to such contractual commitments in non-attainment areas, the policy underlying both terms is the same.

**interstate pollution**  Pollution that travels from one state into another. Interstate pollution is pollution that migrates through air, water, or the ground from a generator, point source, or non-point source in one state into another state. Specifically, a generator of interstate pollution is a stationary source of air pollution that may significantly contribute to levels of air pollution that exceed the national ambient air quality standards in a state other than the state where of the source's location. Federal law requires interstate pollution abatement implementation plans, according to which state officials my require the interstate pollution generator to notify nearby states whose air quality will be affected by proposed or modified sources of pollution and stationary sources that may also degrade their air quality. Interstate pollution was an early focus of federal legislation. Not only the nature of air and water pollution, which are generally migratory, but also the market for solid and hazardous waste managment, which is not only interstate but global, suggest that there is a strong case for all pollution having an inherently interstate nature.

**Trail Smelter arbitration**  An international arbitration establishing state responsibility for harms from interstate pollution. In the Trail Smelter case, 3 R.I.A.A. 1905, the United States sought arbitration to determine the responsibility of Canada for damages to the U.S. environment caused by acid rain from a large smelter in Trail, British Columbia, near the U.S. boundary. The arbitral award determined Canadian liability for the U.S. damage, ultimately awarding over $420,000 in damages.

**marine pollution**  Pollution of the waters of the seas. Marine pollution is pollution of the seas, including any discharge or emission of an artificially created or refined substance directly into the waters of an ocean or sea, as well as the indirect effect of chemicals or altered riverine chemistry in waters flowing into the seas from rivers and lakes.

In its most common usage in law, marine pollution is narrower in its scope and connotes any discharge of oil, other chemicals, or waste from a vessel or facility into the sea. Marine pollution from vessels and facilities may be regulated by states through the regulation of flag vessels or through regulation of activities in their exclusive economic zones and ports.

**pollution permit**  Authorization to emit or discharge a pollutant under an environmental regulation. A pollution permit is an authorization, license, or equivalent control document issued by a governmental agency to implement an environmental regulation. A common example of an action requiring a pollution permit is a wastewater discharge permit issued to the operator of a municipal wastewater treatment facility. A permit does not amount to a license to trespass or otherwise violate the law, and a permit-holder is subject not only to governmental enforcement of the permit but also (in some cases) to citizen suits for permit enforcement. Common-law actions for private claims are often available regardless of the permitted nature of the harm that amounts to a tort under the common law.

*See also:* permit (permitted).

**new source**  A source of pollution created after a regulation comes into force. A new source, in the context of pollution regulation, is a source of pollution that is constructed, whether as a new facility or as new construction in an existing facility, after the effective date of a statute or regulation of the pollution that the facility will emit into the air or water. The new source must use the best available demonstrated control technology for discharges of water pollution or receive a pre-construction permit for air emissions. This definition, owing to statutory exemption and separate regulation, may not apply to mobile sources of pollution, such as automobiles.

**Superfund (Comprehensive Environmental Response Compensation and Liability Act or C.E.R.C.L.A. or CERCLA)**  Federal law requiring private or governmental cleanup of polluted sites. Superfund, or the Comprehensive Environmental Response Cleanup Liability Act of 1980 and its 1982 amendments, established a federal Hazardous Waste Cleanup Fund to reclaim and restore the environment in the most seriously polluted sites in the country. Under the statute, the federal Environmental Protection Agency, working with state agencies, located and assessed sites across the country with hazardous wastes contaminating the environment, and established a National Priorities List of the sites of greatest contamination and greatest risks to human health. Sites from this list were subject to removal actions or to approved cleanup plans, allowing the responsible parties to clean up the site subject to federal oversight or requiring the federal government to clean up the site, enforcing financial responsibility for the clean up onto responsible parties. Superfund is administered in the states by state environmental protection agencies and nationally by the EPA's Office of Solid Waste and Emergency Response.

*See also:* oil, oil spill, Oil Pollution Control Act (OPCA); waste, waste material, Resource Conservation and Recovery Act (RCRA).

**de micromis party**  A party responsible for less than one percent of a Superfund site. A de micromis party is a party whose responsibility for a Superfund site is tiny even when compared to the standard of de minimus responsibility. The Environmental Protection Agency may allow discounted settlement of claims for the cleanup of a site by a party found to be responsible but only for a share de micromis.

**potentially responsible party (P.R.P. or PRP)** A party that may be responsible for the cleanup of a Superfund site. A potentially responsible party, or PRP, under the federal Superfund program is a party whose conduct related to the contamination of a site with hazardous waste or to the site itself makes the party potentially responsible for the performance or cost of its remediation. PRPs include the owner of a site at the time the site is designated on the National Priority List, the operator of a facility or other activity on the site at the time it is listed, an owner or operator of the site at any time when hazardous wastes were disposed there, any person who arranged for the disposal or treatment of hazardous waste at the site, and any transporter of hazardous waste to the site. A PRP is subject to strict liability for the damage caused by hazardous wastes at a Superfund site, and neither non-negligence nor good faith is a defense. The Environmental Protection Agency will usually allow the PRPs to remediate a site before activating a federal remediation, and a PRP that does remediate a site may claim contributions toward its costs from other PRPs. Not all PRPs are liable, however, and statutory defenses such as those based on a very small contribution of waste, on a status as a homeowner or municipal solid waste agency, and an act of God may limit liability. Liable PRPs are jointly and severally liable for the entire cost of cleanup.

Note: many state standards of liability for the cleanup of state-designated polluted sites rely on the same definitions as the federal standard, though nomenclature may vary. Some states designate such parties as liable parties or responsible parties rather than potentially responsible parties.

**remedial investigation/feasibility study (RI/FS)** The initial inventory of hazardous material in a Superfund site. The remedial investigation and feasibility study, or RI/FS, is a preliminary assessment of the contamination in a site being evaluated for potential inclusion on the national priority list, the assessment following a routine to determine the type and extent of harzardous contamination in the site, as well as the potential threat to the environment posed by the contamination.

**Time-Weighted Average (TWA)** Measurement of contamination over time. The Time-Weighted Average, or TWA, measures exposure of a substance, particularly of pollutant or potential contaminant, over a period of time that is a means of accounting for variations caused by changes in temperature and human activity on a daily cycle.

**water pollution** Chemical or physical inputs from human activity that harm organisms or limit uses in a body of water. Water pollution is the generic term for chemicals, runoff, sewerage, sediment, heat, or other byproducts of human activity that enter the lakes, streams, and oceans that have an individual or cumulative effect that harms animals or plants in the aquatic environment or limits the use of the body of water or its component waters for human endeavors. The forms of water pollution include chemicals such as fertilizers, petroleum, toxins, solid wastes, and biological wastes as well as soil runoff from fields and chemical runoff from residential and commercial lands. It includes the introduction of hot or cold water from industrial use. Biological effects in the water body from such inputs may be inextricably linked with the water pollution, though the effects are not themselves pollution, the most important example being the hypoxic affect of reduced oxygen from algae that bloom in fertilizer-rich waters. Indeed, water pollution does not encompass all harmful human interaction with waters; for instance, pollution does not ordinarily include the introduction of foreign invasive species of plant or animal, the diversion of waters to diminish water flow or water level, or the loss of erosion-mitigating wetlands.

*See also:* sewer.

**Clean Water Act (CWA)** The principal federal regulation of water quality and pollution. The Clean Water Act was initially passed in 1972, enlarging on earlier laws, particularly the Federal Water Pollution Control Act, primarily to create a national system of federal and state regulation of waters that limits the pollution in every stream and watershed though a system of water quality analysis and discharge permits. Other portions of the act set standards and provide grants for wastewater management and regulate dredging and filling that would diminish wetlands. The Environmental Protection Agency is tasked by Congress in the act with developing a national standard for water quality that is applied to specific waters, to determine the maximum levels of pollution that may be introduced to each body of water without degrading its quality. Any person or entity that discharges any effluent into the water must do so under the conditions of a permit, which limits the pollutants that may be discharged on a daily basis.

**Federal Water Pollution Control Act (F.W.P.C.A. FWPCA)** The predecessor to the Clean Water Act. The Federal Water Pollution Control Act was initially passed in 1948 and remained in force through many amendments, particularly the 1972 Amendments which created the National Pollution Discharge Elimination System, which is now the hallmark of the federal law of water quality, and the 1977 Amendments, which formalized the popular name for the Act, i.e., the Clean Water Act. The whole of the FWPCA is now within the CWA.

**National Pollutant Discharge Elimination System (NPDES)** The national system of permits for point-source discharges of pollutants. The National

Pollutant Discharge Elimination System, or NPDES, was established under the federal Clean Water Act as a national program to eliminate pollution from America's waterways by regulating every point at which pollution is discharged into federal waters. The NPDES permit structure limits the contaminants that may be discharged from any point source to a permit load that is determined by the load that may be carried in a watershed. It also sets standards and permit requirements for stormwater discharge, concentrated animal feeding operations, and specialized operational regulations for discharges from oil and gas facilities, industrial facilities, and mining facilities. The NPDES also requires permits for any construction project that disturbs earth of an acre or more to be permitted to ensure adequate erosion control and pollution prevention measures in the project design and execution.

**NPDES permit** A permit required for a discharge or project subject to the NPDES. An NPDES permit is required for every facility or activity that has a fixed point of discharge of a pollutant or water carrying a pollutant into any federal water, whether the discharge is through a pipe, ditch, vent, or other means. Although construction permits and stormwater permits are also required under the NPDES, an NPDES permit usually refers to a point discharge permit, which specifies the pollutants that may be discharged and the average total maximum daily load that may be discharged in various seasons. A permit holder must collect accurate and verifiable records of the discharge quantities and maintain accurate records of discharges for inspection. Most NPDES permits are issued by state agencies subject to Environmental Protection Agency standards.

**total maximum daily load (TMDL)** The pollutant amount dischargeable daily into a federal waterway. The total maximum daily load, or TMDL, is both the amount that may be carried by a specific waterway daily without degradation and the permitted amount that a point pollution source subject to a NPDES permit may discharge in a given period of twenty-four hours. Both are expressed as a total quantity of a given pollutant, regardless of its proportion or saturation in waters carrying the pollutant that is being added to the waterway. The TMDL may be averaged over a given period, and as a practical matter represents an average of ratios of the pollutant in water sampled at given times, multiplied by the amount of discharge. TMDLs are established for a given source by a proportion of the TMDL from all sources for a given pollutant that is considered ecologically acceptable, or nondegrading, for a given stream or watershed.

**pollution source**

**publicly owned treatment works (POTW)** Government owned wastewater treatment facility. A publicly owned treatment works, or a POTW, is a wastewater treatment facility that is owned by a municipality or other government entity, and that is permitted as a POTW by the state or the Environmental Protection Agency under the national pollutant discharge elimination system (NPDES). Wastes of other entities that are transferred to a POTW are subject to the contract requirements between the entities and the POTW and are not otherwise subject to an NPDES permit.
See also: sewage (sewerage).

**polyandry** See: marriage, polygamy, polyandry.

**polygamy** See: marriage, polygamy (plural marriage or polygamous).

**polygraph (lie detector)** A device measuring changes in body functions that might indicate false statements. A polygraph is a machine that assesses a subject's perspiration, pulse, blood pressure, and breathing over a period of time. When a subject is asked a series of questions, an observer may note a variation in these assessments that might indicate a change in stress, which may indicate a false statement made in answer to a question. Polygraphs are controversial, as are other mechanical devices that are used to assess the veracity of a subject. The results of such tests are generally inadmissible in court. Contemporary research into the use of brain imagery through PET and CAT scans may prove more reliable as an indicator of honesty or dishonesty in speech, though this research is undeveloped. The Employee Polygraph Protection Act of 1988, 29 U.S.C. § 2001, et seq., forbids nearly all private employers from requiring an employee to take a polygraph.

**polygyny** See: marriage, polygamy, polygyny.

**Pomerene bill of lading** See: bill, bill of lading, Pomerene bill of lading.

**pomo** See: jurisprudence, postmodern legal theory (pomo).

**Ponzi scheme** See: fraud, confidence game, Ponzi scheme (Ponzi game).

**Pope (patriarch or papacy)** The chief of the Catholic religion. Pope is the title of a bishop who is the leader of a Christian church, which in the United States usually refers to the Pope of Rome, who is also the head of state of the Vatican City State and the leader of the Roman Catholic Church, exercising his authority through the Roman Curia and the Holy See.

As a title, pope is equivalent to patriarch, both terms meaning father of the church. The Pope of Rome is first among equals of the leaders of the churches that were established by the end of the Roman Empire, including those who are now the Orthodox Ecumenical Patriarch of Constantinople, Coptic Orthodox Pope of Alexandria, Patriarch of Antioch, and Patriarch of Jerusalem, as well as the medieval patriarchs of Bulgaria, Georgia, Serbia, Moscow, and Romania, and the eastern patriarchs of Kiev and Moscow.

**pornography (erotica or porn or porno)**  Sexually explicit words or pictures. Pornography has famously been subject to a range of definitions, which at least include words, symbols, or graphics that represent or evoke the human body in a manner that depicts its sexual nature. Many definitions include not only a sexually focused depiction but also a potentially sexually arousing effect upon a person who perceives it. Pornography need not be explicit in depicting an act of sexual conduct or even the sexual organs, although the more such depiction occurs the more surely the depiction is pornographic.

More important, under U.S. law, defining pornography is defining that aspect of pornography that is obscene. Pornography that is not obscene is lawful for adults to create, possess, sell, or disseminate through any means other than by unsolicited mailing or means that are likely to reach children. Yet some pornography is obscene, because it offends or harms without sufficient justification.

The private viewing and commercial dissemination of pornography are protected under the First Amendment's guarantee of freedom of speech, but this guarantee is not unlimited. Public depictions of pornography may be regulated. Imagery that is potentially pornographic but in fact obscene is not protected speech. Pornography involving children is not constitutionally protected in any manner, and its creation, distribution, or possession is generally a criminal offense.

*See also:* obscenity (obscene); pornography, child pornography.

**child pornography**  A sexually explicit picture of a child. Child pornography is the graphic depiction of a child in a sexualized manner or posed in a sexually explicit manner. The mere depiction of a nude child is not child pornography, though a depiction of a child may amount to child pornography though the child is clothed. Child pornography includes pornographic images of computer-simulated children. Child pornography may vary with the apparent age of the child, being eighteen or younger under federal law but only as old as fourteen under some state laws. Child pornography is not protected speech under the First Amendment, and the knowing possession of child pornography is a criminal offense. Child, for the purposes of this offense, is defined by the statute in which the offense is prosecuted, the most common age being eighteen years, although more serious offenses are sometimes defined by creating a pornographic image of a child under twelve.

*See also:* pornography (erotica or porn or porno).

**pandering of child pornography (pandering obscenity involving a minor or promotion of child pornography)**  Creation, advertising, marketing, or encouraging the purchase of child pornography. Pandering child pornography is any act that makes likely a person's acquiring such material, including the creation, publication, reprinting, or publishing of child pornography, or its marketing, display, sale, or distribution. The federal statute criminalizes only possession or distribution if the defendant both knows of the participation of a child (or virtual child) and has an intent to sell, distribute, or view the material.

**posek**  A rabbi who may adjudge disputes. A posek is a rabbi with the the authority power to resolve disputes over the meaning of Jewish law and its application to a specific circumstance.

**positive proof**  *See:* proof, forms of proof, affirmative proof (positive proof).

**positivism**  *See:* jurisprudence, legal positivism (positivism).

**posse**  Potential, or power. Posse is a Latin word with two distinct meanings in law, both taken from "possum" in classical Latin, which meant the ability or power to do something. Thus, posse means both the potential to do something and the power or authority to do it. This has led to different meanings in the common law, illustrated in the terms in posse, or something that is potential, and posse comitatus, the power of the county. Thus, a posse may be a sheriff's patrol, but to a person in posse is a fetus.

*See also:* posse, posse comitatus (sheriff).

**posse or covenant for a thing in posse**  *See:* in, in posse (posse or covenant for a thing in posse).

**posse comitatus (sheriff's posse)**  Civilians called or sworn to aid a sheriff in enforcing the law. A posse, or posse comitatus, is a group of civilians called out by a sheriff or sheriff's deputy to aid in the enforcement of the law. In the early common law, the posse arose as a result of the hue and cry, which was to be raised by any person discovering a felony, but the later common law reserved to the sheriff or a deputy the power to raise a group of citizens to search for a fleeing felon, guard a courthouse, or take other steps under the sheriff's direction to enforce the law or keep the peace.

In contemporary usage, some jurisdictions retain the common law authority of a sheriff to summon a posse in an emergency. Others have augmented that power to include a power of the sheriff to call a standing volunteer force of citizens sworn or deputized as law enforcement officers that acts as reserve police officers. In some jurisdictions, a sheriff's posse is not a law enforcement organization but a volunteer service organization that does good works in the community. The distinction among these organizations is both functional and dependent on the powers conferred on the members by statute and the acts and directions of the sheriff.

*See also:* posse.

**Posse Comitatus Act** U.S. statute barring the military from use of civilian law enforcement. The Posse Comitatus Act, 18 U.S.C. § 1385, bars the assignment or recruitment of military personnel to perform an act of civilian law enforcement, unless Congress has approved that dedication of personnel to that specific purpose. The Posse Comitatus Act, however, does not restrict military police or investigators from performing within the scope of their statutory authority, nor does it forbid the use of military resources in support of civilian criminal investigations when Congress authorizes such coordination.

**possession (possess or possessory)** Control over a thing, or the thing possessed. Possession is a state of control in fact over tangible property. Possession is a property interest in the thing possessed, and possession is primarily significant in contrast to title, which is the lawful right of possession regardless of whether one with title can exercise it. Possession creates a property interest, but that interest may be subject to a superior interest arising from title. It is possible to have possession and title, or possession without title, or title without possession. Thus, a trespasser and a thief each have possession but lack title. Possession is only possible of tangible things, whether chattel or real property or things that may not be property, such as a body part.

Though lawyers may speak of possessing a right, possession of a right is a quasi-possession under the common law, and rights, liberties or claims that one may have, particularly a chose in action, are property held by a particular individual, though there is no thing to possess. Like incorporeal hereditaments, there is a property interest but nothing possessed.

Possession may be actual or constructive, that is possession may be a matter of direct control or indirect control over the property, as when a person possesses the keys to a safe; the possession of the keys amounts to constructive possession of the safe and to its contents.

At common law, possession must be actual, knowing, and intentional, which is to say that the control must be effective, as when a person actually holds an object or occupies some land, but it must also be intentional, which is to say that the control may not be possession if it was accidental or unintended. As a matter of property, these conditions are generally still valid.

Possession as an element of a criminal offense, such as possession of contraband, may be shown by actual or constructive possession, and no intent to possess the contraband is required under some statutes, although nearly all statutory prohibitions of possession require knowing possession of the thing prohibited (though knowledge of the prohibition or of a character may not be required) or at least of the thing that gives constructive possession, such as a car that contains a controlled substance.

*See also:* property; title.

**actual possession (possession in fact)** Physical control over the thing. Actual possession, or possession in fact, is the state of real and exclusive control over the thing possessed. Actual possession does not depend on legal right or claim, on construction or inference but on the state of affairs being as they are. The person or entity in possession may in fact do what it likes with the thing possessed (though it may do so in violation of the claims or rights of others).

**adverse possession** The acquisition of title through long and obvious possession. Adverse possession is a process by which title in property is acquired not through grant of the property but through actual use of that property over a sufficient period of time and in such circumstances that the law will not interfere with the user's right to continue to do so. Adverse possession is both the use, or occupation, of the property under such conditions, and the ripening of title so that it can no longer be taken by the true owner. The conditions required are written in slightly different ways in different jurisdictions, but generally the occupant must hold the property as if it is the occupant's own, in an actual, continuous, open, notorious, exclusive and hostile manner, or under a claim or a legal right to hold it, for a period of time that varies by statute. Once the property is held in such manners for the appropriate length of time, the occupant acquires title by adverse possession.

Put another way, adverse possession is the logical result of the statute of limitations for ejectment. Once a squatter is on an owner's lands in an open and notorious manner, the owner is on constructive notice that there is a squatter and may bring an action to eject the squatter from the land. The statute of limitations then begins to run, and once it has run out, the owner may no longer eject the squatter, the squatter's possession has ripened into title, and the owner has lost title in the property. If the squatter claims to hold the land under a color of right, that is if the squatter asserts a right to the land under a deed or other basis for legal title, many states will not require as detailed a proof of improvement, enclosure, or notoriety or as long an occupation, although they will expect conduct consistent with the claim, such as the payment of taxes.

There is great variation in the time required for title to ripen through adverse possession. Most states require possession for the twenty years required by the common law or the more modern ten years for the statute to run, though some statutes require as long as thirty, such as Louisiana, and some as short as five (under color of right), as in California.

*See also:* prescription, prescription of property (prescriptible); property; nullum, nullum tempus; squatter (squat or squatting).

*adversity of co-tenants* If multiple parties share title to a property, adverse possession for one requires ouster of the others. When property is owned by co-tenants, if one or more of them wishes to obtain the title of the other co-tenants through adverse possession, the adverse possessors must pay particular attention to the elements of open and adverse possession. Because any of the co-tenants are entitled to exclusive enjoyment of the property, such enjoyment does not satisfy the elements, and there must be an expression of intent to dispossess the others. Only then will the statute begin to run.

*effects on future interests* A person with a future interest in property cannot lose that interest through adverse possession until it has vested. A remainderman or other holder of a future interest may not usually bring an action for ouster or ejectment until the future interest becomes possessory. Thus, the holder of the future interest cannot lose the future interest to adverse possession until the number of statutory years following the interest's becoming possessory. For instance, assume John gives Blackacre to Jane for life then Ralph, but then Sam enters Blackacre and lives there openly, notoriously, continuously, with hostility, etc. for twenty years, the length of the statute in that state. If John and Jane are still alive then, Sam has acquired Jane's life estate through adverse possession but Ralph's remainder is untouched and could not be lost to adverse possession until twenty years after Jane died.

**actual possession** Control and use by the possessor or an assignee. Actual possession is dominion over property through use or occupation of the land in fact by the possessor or a licensee or agent. The use and occupation must be actual, and merely holding a property for speculation or as an investment and failing to work it is not enough. Still, the occupation and use need not be by the possesor alone; it may be through another person, such as an agent, tenant, or family member.
*See also:* possession, pedal possession.

**adverse possession of mineral rights (mineral rights adversely possessed)** Mineral rights are subject to adverse possession. Mineral rights can be acquired via adverse possession, but possession of the minerals does not result in the adverse possession of the surface. Likewise, if the mineral estate is severed from the surface rights, an adverse possessor of the mineral rights must satisfy each of the elements for the mineral rights themselves and not just for the property in the surface rights above them.
*See also:* mineral interest (mineral rights).

**chattels subject to adverse possession (personalty adversely possessed)** Title to chattels may ripen through adverse possession. Chattels are subject to adverse possession in the manner as is realty, through operation of the statute of limitations for conversion. Even so, there is an ambiguous line between adverse possession and theft when the property is mobile. In the case of real property, a true owner has many opportunities to dispute the adverse possessor's claim or have the adverse possessor removed as a trespasser if the true owner is paying attention. It is more difficult for the true owner of chattels to assess open and notorious possession or some other means of showing that a

person possesses the property in such a manner as to ripen to title. Various jurisdictions have various rules, based less on the manner of possession than on when the statute would fairly have begun to run against the true owner.
*See also:* chattel.

**claim of right** An assertion of intent to dispossess any other claimant. A claim of right is a claim to possession that is asserted against all others, including the true owner. When an adverse possessor asserts a claim of right, it is a notification of a resolve to challenge the true owner's interest in the property.

**constructive adverse possession** Ownership of a whole parcel can be obtained by adverse possession of a part. Constructive adverse possession exploits an inference that title to one portion of a tract gained successfully through adverse possession gives title to the entire tract. Constructive adverse possession requires that the tract be understood throughout the community as a single defined lot or parcel, and it is usually only available when the possessor holds the tract under color of title, satisfying all of the conditions for adversity in that jurisdiction under that theory.

**continuous possession** Uninterrupted possession and control. Continuous possession is possession without interruption by others claiming a right to possess and with a continuity of use and control by the possessor that is appropriate and reasonable occupation or use for land of that location and character. Continuous possession does not mean continual occupation, and the possessor remains in possession when coming and going from the property in a manner that would be normal for an owner of such property. Farmland can be left fallow for planting in the ordinary patterns of farming, and a vacation home can be empty but for the vacation season, and both could still be considered in continuous possession so long as they are occupied when one would expect them to be. Continuity of possession is possible by several possessors by tacking.

**seasonal possession** Cyclical occupation in accord with the custom for such property. Seasonal possession is possession of property in a given time of the year, on a regular basis year after year. Continuous possession may be seasonal for property of a form that is routinely used only seasonally. When property only has utility for certain periods of time in a yearly cycle, continuity of possession will be measured by control or use of the property during the viable periods of use.

**contra non valentum (contra non valentem)** Land cannot be prescribed if owner cannot protect it in court. Contra non valentum is a defense against an action to obtain title through adverse possession, which bars prescription or adverse possession against an owner who could not bring an action to eject the plaintiff. The defense may lie if the court would not have had jurisdiction to bar the plaintiff's possession during the adverse use or occupation, if the defendant true owner could not bring an action owing to a legal or contractual relationship, or if either the plaintiff had prevented the defendant owner from discovering the use or occupation or it could not reasonably have been discovered.

**exclusive possession**   Possession subject to one's sole control. Exclusive possession is a restrictive use and enjoyment of the property, so that no other use or possession is tolerated except under a license or invitation of the possessor. The possessor can allow others onto the property, if the possessor acts as the licensor for their use. Brief attempts to challenge the possessor's dominion and brief visits or lapses do not defeat the exclusivity of possession, as long as the possessor responds to such deviations from exclusive possession as an owner would do.

**hostile possession (adversity of possession)** Property held without permission of the true owner. Hostile possession is possession without permission or license to be present on the land or in possession of it. A license by the true owner to occupy the land defeats the adversity or hostility of possession, unless such a license has patently expired and the licensee is present in a hostile manner following the expiry.

Possession under a claim or right or color of title is usually construed to be hostile, in that the possessor claims the title or right as against the world.

**notorious possession**   Property use that could be known in a community. Notorious possession of land is use and enjoyment that is known widely in the community. The measures of notoriety are whether the land is used as it would ordinarily be used by the true owner in possession of it, so that an owner of reasonable diligence would be likely to become actually aware of the possession (whether or not the true owner acquires such knowledge in a given case). Evidence would include routine receipt of the mails by the possessor on the property, the hookup and payment of utilities and other services there in the possessor's name, and entertainment of others on the land.

*See also:* notoriety (notorious); possession, adverse possession, open possession.

**open possession**   Property use that be easily seen by the public. Open possession is possession and use of land in such a manner that the possession is apparent to other people in the area. Evidence of secrecy or subterfuge in the possession or use may defeat an argument of open possession. In most instances, sufficiently open possession is also notorious possession.

*See also:* possession, adverse possession, notorious possession.

**tacking**   Control by several persons in privity one from another can be sufficient continuity for adverse possession. Tacking is the cumulation of successive periods of occupation by different adverse possessors, whose total time of occupation is asserted as sufficient continuous occupation to establish title by adverse possession to a property in the last person. Tacking requires each successor to be in privity of estate with the predecessor, which requires there to have been no lapse of time between one's abandonment of the property and the next person's entry.

*See also:* tacking (tack).

**constructive possession**   Possession of a thing ascribed to a person owing to some circumstance. Constructive possession is possession ascribed to a person as a matter of law owing to some circumstance. This arises typically in three circumstances: the person has possession of one thing that entails the possession of another; or the person has effective and exclusive control of a place, car, or premises that entails constructive possession of the things within; or the person has a relationship with a second person or entity whose possession is ascribed to the first. The person may or may not have knowledge of the existence of the thing constructively possessed or intend to possess it, but has knowledge of the circumstances from which possession is construed. There is an interesting tension in the law of constructive possession, in that the person attempting to assert a property claim over some thing may seek to establish constructive possession of it, but a person attempting to defend against a claim of unlawful possession may seek to deny it.

**constructive possession in property**   Possession construed from a right to possess or an indirect possession. Constructive possession of property is established both to determine rights of the possessor in the property and to determine the priority of the rights of others to it. In general, constructive possession is established as a matter of law in a thing to which one has a right of possession, even though the thing is in the possession of another (and this constructive possession may be protected through the imposition of a constructive trust over the thing).

The circumstances by which the right in the constructive possessor arises despite the physical possession in another party both illustrate and manifest this general view. When delivery of property is effected by constructive or symbolic delivery, so the recipient does not have actual possession, the property is constructively possessed. When delivery of goods is agreed between buyer and seller to be accomplished through an agent, or by a delivery to a third party, or by a mere record of the transaction, and the agreed means of delivery is performed by the seller though the buyer has not received the goods, the buyer has constructive possession.

*See also:* delivery, delivery of possession, constructive delivery (constructive–receipt doctrine).

**constructive possession of goods later stolen**  A store employee possesses constructively goods in the store for purposes of the robbery law. Constructive possession by an agent of the legal owner requires little evidence of exclusive control over goods, money, or objects later stolen. For the purposes of burglary, robbery, or other crimes of theft, the victim may be established as a store employee even if there is little proof of the special relationship between the person in constructive possession and the goods that are possessed. All that may be required is evidence that a store employee was the agent of the owner who had possession for the goods to be possessed by the employee.

*See also:* robbery (rob).

**constructive unlawful possession (accessorial possession)**  Knowing possession through control of premises or control by an accomplice. Constructive unlawful possession arises under circumstances that are broader than constructive possession as a basis for the possessor's property interests. Notably, possession of a thing for the purpose of establishing unlawful possession may be construed from the mere control of an occupied space in which the thing is found or from the control of the thing by an accomplice. Constructive unlawful possession is nearly always proved by circumstantial evidence. Even so, knowledge of the the existence of the thing, either in the place or in the accessory's possession, is essential to a charge of its possession, and there must be evidence from which a jury may infer that the defendant had that knowledge.

Constructive possession by possession of an occupied space includes the control of living quarters, offices, cars, or other spaces in which a person would live or work and that would be subject to one person's exclusive control. Besides proof of such control (including proof of sufficient exclusivity as to disprove the likelihood another placed the thing there), proof of constructive possession of a thing in the space requires evidence that a person in control of such a space would have knowledge of the thing that is there. Evidence in these cases is inherently unique and fact–specific.

Constructive possession by one accomplice is sufficient to establish possession by a second accomplice, if the second accomplice knew of the possession and the thing possessed was either essential to their common enterprise or unavoidable in some way according to the understanding of the first accomplice of the second's plans. Constructive possession by an accomplice is sometimes analyzed as accomplice liability rather than as constructive possession by an agent. Such an analysis is accessorial possession.

**equal access rule (equal-access rule)**  Constructive possession is barred when several people have equal access to the possessed goods. The equal access rule bars a determination of constructive possession of contraband by one person on the basis of ownership of a car or place, when several people had equal access to the contraband. Thus, a defendant may not be convicted for illegal possession of an item when the only evidence of possession is that the material was found in the defendant's car, if other people had access to the car that was equal to the defendant's access. Likewise, a theory of joint possession may not be used against one accused possessor if the other accused possessor is not charged.

**immediate possession**  Right to possession without delay or intermediaries. Immediate possession takes two forms, actual and constructive. Actual immediate possession is possession in fact at the time relevant by the person or entity whose possession is relevant, rather than by another as agent or constructive trustee. Constructive immediate possession is possession inferred by law from the circumstances in which the right to possess is a right of possession without delay or any condition that must be satisfied prior to possession.

**immemorial possession**  *See:* time, time immemorial (time of memory or immemorial possession).

**naked possession (mere possession)**  Possession of premises with no claim of title or right. Naked possession of property is possession as a trespasser or by sufferance, or otherwise with no claim at all to right or title to the land or thing possessed. Naked possession is the same as mere possession.

**nine points of the law (nine-tenths of the law)**  Possession creates a presumption of ownership. The venerable tag "possession is nine points of the law" is a metaphor for the legal presumption arising from possession, that the possession suggests a right to possess, and so the possessor is presumed to be an owner when ownership is contested. By the seventeenth century there were ten points over all.

This popular maxim is not conclusive, and is, like all presumptions, open for rebuttal. Though the phrase customarily employs points, there is no difference in the meaning of the less artful "nine-tenths of the law."

*See also:* point.

**peaceable possession**  Possession undisturbed by an action to eject the possessor. Peaceable possession is possession of property for a period of time during which no action in law or equity has been brought against the possessor seeking to oust or eject the possessor from the property or to prove a claim of title to the property that is superior to the possessor's.

**pedal possession**  Actual occupation of the specific lands on which the possessor walks. Pedal possession is actual possession, which, when applied to lands, implies possession of so much of a parcel as is actually worked, or used, or regularly walked by the possessor.

*See also:* possession, adverse possession, actual possession.

**possessory action**  A civil action to gain or regain possession of a thing. A possessory action is one of several forms of civil action to gain possession of property held by another person. At common law, a possessory action was a technical procedure by which a demandant sought to recover property to which the demandant held title, but this action is obsolete, having been replaced by ejectment and other actions. In civil law, particularly Louisana law, a possessory action is a civil action similar to a quiet title action or ejectment in the common law, in which the possessor of immovable property who has been disturbed in possession or enjoyment, seeks to be maintained in the possession. In general, however, lawyers speak of any action to gain possession of property from another as a form of possessory action, including ejectment, garnishment, replevin, recovery of a bailment, etc. Such actions depend on a right to possess, which may or may not amount to the right of ownership, though an owner with a right to possess may bring a possessory action just as a bailee or tenant.

**quasi-possession**   The equivalent of possession for a thing that cannot be possessed. Quasi-possession is recognition of a possession-like interest in an incorporeal right or property interest that, owing to its nature, is incapable of being possessed. Instead the property interest is treated, asserted, or claimed by the quasi-possessor in the manner that would amount to possession if possession were possible. Thus, a chose in action is held or transferred as if it is possessed, though it is not a tangible property and so incapable of possession. A servitude may be exercised as if it is possessed, but it cannot be possessed—only asserted through use of the land over which its burdens run or asserted in its defense. Either amounts to quasi-possession. In this sense, to be in possession of a right or liberty is to be in quasi-possession of it. Although this concept was once widely used in the common law, it is now more frequently used in Louisiana law.

*See also:* property, forms of property, incorporeal property (intangible property or intangibles); ownership, corporeal ownership (incorporeal ownership); hereditament, incorporeal hereditament.

**unlawful possession (criminal possession)**   The crime of being in possession of a contraband thing. Unlawful possession is the crime of possession of a prohibited substance or item by a person not lawfully allowed to possess it by a license or justification. Unlawful possession requires scienter; some offenses require knowledge of the unlawful characteristic of the thing possessed, but in others, knowledge may be required only of the possession. Unlawful possession is often designated as "possession of" the prohibited substance or item, as well as by the nature of the person to whom possession is forbidden. The possession of many things amounts to a crime in itself. These include, for example, illegal drugs, precursor chemicals for making drugs, unregistered firearms, unlicensed explosives, burglar tools, stolen goods, or the identification or identity of another person.

Unlawful possession may be defined not as possession of the contraband object by any person but defined in a way that is limited to possession of the contraband by any person of a certain category or characteristic, or it may be limited from a person who lacks a certain qualification. Thus, the unlawful possession of a controlled substance is inherently limited, so that certain persons may be authorized to possess it, i.e., a doctor, pharmacy, research facility, or patient with a lawful prescription would not be in unlawful possession. Some offenses are defined by the status of the offender in possession, such as a felon in possession of a firearm, or an election official in possession of alcoholic beverages. Such a definition does not amount to a status offense, as the offense is further defined by the act of possession.

*See also:* contraband.

**possessor**   One who holds property. A possessor is a person who holds, detains, or enjoys a thing that the possessor intends to possess. A possessor of lands may take several forms in law: A person who possess lands is the person who is usually the occupant of the land, such as an owner on the lands or a tenant in possession, as long as the occupant manifests an intent to control it. A person who is entitled to immediate occupation of the land is also considered to possess it, if no other person is in possession. Once a person has occupied land, that occupation is assumed to continue until another person occupies it while manifesting an intent to control it.

A possessor of a chattel is any person who is in physical possession of the object, including its possession by virtue of location in a space otherwise controlled by the possessor.

A possessor may possess through actual or constructive possession, directly or indirectly through an agent. A common example of possession through an agent would be a personal investment account held by a securities dealer for a client.

*See also:* occupant (occupation or occupy or occupies or occupancy or occupier).

**possessory action**   *See:* possession, possessory action.

**possessory estate or present estate**   *See:* estate, interest, present possessory interest (possessory estate or present estate).

**possibility**   What might or might not happen, especially an uncertain future interest in property. A possibility, in general usage, is the contingency of an event that might happen, though it is not likely to happen. In property law, a possibility is a particular form of contingent future interest that depends on a failure of the condition of another person's grant, often by that person's death.

Under the common law, possibilities in property are divided among near and distant possibilities; those coupled to an interest may be validly transferred as opposed to a naked possibility or mere possibility. These distinctions among property interests are now somewhat rare, and a general presumption of the assignment of a property interest has made the differences somewhat obsolete for most purposes, though the distinction is still significant in determining who has standing to challenge the actions of a trustee or executor.

*See also:* reversion, reverter, possibility of reverter (possibility of a reverter).

**possibility of a reverter** *See:* reversion, reverter, possibility of reverter (possibility of a reverter).

**post** After, or following. Post, in Latin, is a designation for something after something else. It is both a word that stands alone and a common prefix, as in post–trial motion, for a motion made after a trial. When used with a reference, it may be the equivalent of the term "infra" to mean something after the reference in the text.
*See also:* ante.

**post-conviction relief or postconviction relief** *See:* appeal, post–conviction relief (postconviction relief).

**post-conviction remedy** *See:* remedy, post–conviction remedy.

**post date or post-date or postdate** *See:* date, post date (post–date or postdate).

**post hoc ergo propter hoc** *See:* fallacy, post hoc ergo propter hoc.

**post nuptial** *See:* nuptial, post nuptial (ante–nuptial or pre–nuptial or post–nuptial or postnuptial).

**Post Offices Clause** *See:* constitution, U.S. Constitution, clauses, Post Offices Clause (Post Road Clause).

**Post Road Clause** *See:* constitution, U.S. Constitution, clauses, Post Offices Clause (Post Road Clause).

**post-trial motion** *See:* motion, post–trial motion.

**postal service or post** *See:* mail (postal service or post).

**posthumous heir** *See:* heir, posthumous heir (after-born child or posthumous child or quasi–posthumous child or afterborn heir).

**postmodern legal theory** *See:* jurisprudence, post-modern legal theory (pomo).

**postremogeniture** *See:* ultimogeniture (postremo-geniture).

**post facto** After the fact. Post facto, Latin for after the fact, refers to anything known or done after another event.

**post hoc** After the event. Post hoc depicts anything done or understood after an event. To understand something post hoc is to understand the event in the light of the causes that in fact took place, or at least to have an opportunity to do so. Post hoc runs risks of mistaken attribution of a necessary outcome, in that what took place may appear as inevitable, when different causes might have led to different results. Thus, post hoc propter hoc, or what followed that was caused by that, confuses correlation with causation: that one thing is followed by a second thing does not prove that the one thing caused the second thing.

**post mortem** Anything done after death, especially an autopsy. Post mortem, Latin for after death, describes any thing or any time following a person's death. An examination post mortem is an autopsy, the medical examination of a dead body, which is often conducted to establish a cause of death or to reveal forensic evidence related to the person's identity, medical history, and events at or after death.

A post–mortem punishment is a punishment meted out following the death of the defendant, including abuse of the corpse, but also including attainder or other punishment on the defendant's surviving family. Such punishments are barred in the United States as cruel and unusual punishment.

**post-mortem annulment** *See:* annulment, marital annulment, post–mortem annulment.

**postea** The record of a case heard nisi prius. The postea, Latin for afterwards, was the judge's endorsement and record of the proceedings in a case heard nisi prius, i.e., a local trial in lieu of a trial in London. It was the predecessor of the modern judgment and order.

**potentially responsible party** *See:* pollution, Superfund, potentially responsible party (P.R.P. or PRP).

**potestas** Power or authority, including jurisdiction. Potestas is Latin for power, and it is used in a variety of common–law formulations to represent not only various forms of authority but also jurisdiction by officials and courts. In the civil law, patria potestas or parens potestas are the rights and authority of a parent over a child.
*See also:* power.

**potlatch** A system of ceremonial gift giving among northwest nations. Potlatch is a system of giving gifts at ceremonial occasions among the nations and tribes of the Pacific northwest. The exact significance of the gifts, which may be of great value, is argued among social scientists, though both natives and their students seemingly agree that potlatch is a means of transferring value as well as establishing social standing; property of the people who engage in potlatch is both transferred by and subject to its discipline. Potlatch feasts were once banned by Canadian and U.S. laws, but have returned to contemporary practice with ceremonial festivals.

**POTUS** *See:* president, President of the United States of America (POTUS).

**POTW** *See:* pollution, water pollution, pollution source, publicly owned treatment works (POTW).

**pourover trust** *See:* trust, pourover trust.

**pourover will** *See:* will, last will and testament, pourover will.

**poursuivant** *See:* pursuivant (poursuivant).

**poverty** Having less money than the cost of basic needs. Poverty is the condition of being poor, of not having or receiving the money needed to purchase the necessities of contemporary life, such as food, safe and adequate housing, clothing, and medical care. The federal government assigns a threshold income as the definition of poverty for each family unit, which in 2011 was an annual income of $10,890 for a single person, or $22,350 for a family with one adult and three minor children.

*See also:* pauper.

**POW or P.O.W.** *See:* war, prisoner of war (POW or P.O.W.).

**power** The ability to do something. Power is the whole range of attributes required for a person or entity to cause something to occur or not to occur. Power may be exercised through the direct action of a person on property, such as a person's physical delivery of a chattel, or through the direct action of a person on another person, such as when the person with the power causes another person to do or to refrain from some action. Power may also be exercised indirectly, by causing a person, entity, or thing to do something that then causes something else to be done. Power is often thought of as absolute and unmitigated. Yet moderate forms of power exist as well, in which the person subject to the person in power may choose not to do the that person's bidding, but nonetheless acts on the powerful person's initiative to do the thing requested. Such moderated and shared forms of power are common in negotiated circumstances.

Power may be a public authority or a private right or license. Broadly understood, many forms of power are recognized by law, such as authority, power, right, license, claim, privilege, or immunity. Among these is the specific concept of a power.

In the common law, a power is the lawful authority delegated from one person or entity to another to do something specific, which is both defining of the power and a limit upon it. For example, a power of appointment is a power of the grantor that is delegated to a grantee to appoint a person to do something that the grantor could have done, but the power of appointment is not in itself the power to do the thing to be done. Similarly a power of termination is the power of a grantor to terminate a use in violation of a limit on such uses of land the grantor had granted to a second grantee to exercise, conferring the grantor's former authority to terminate a fee under certain circumstances (in which case the structure is a limit on the power: the power is not the termination of the fee simple but only the ability to act to terminate the free simple, which must be exercised by an affirmative act in order to be carried out).

An important way of understanding a power in law is that described by Professor Wesley Hohfeld in 1919, that a power is the capacity in a party to change a legal relationship between that party and another party or parties. Thus, an offeror gives to the offeree a power, which is the power to accept the offer and thus to alter the legal relationship between them.

**power of attorney** *See:* attorney, attorney in fact, power of attorney, medical power of attorney; attorney, attorney in fact, power of attorney, general power of attorney (general agent); attorney, attorney in fact, power of attorney, durable power of attorney; attorney, attorney in fact, power of attorney.

**power of revocation** *See:* revocation, power of revocation.

**power of the purse** *See:* spending, spending power (power of the purse); purse, power of the purse.

**concurrent power** A power that exists with another's power to do the same thing. A concurrent power is a form of shared power, although it may be exercised unilaterally by one of the holders of the power. A co-tenant has a form of concurrent power over the property held by the tenants, in that each tenant is entitled to the occupancy of the whole, without the approval or agreement of the other co-tenants (though occupation that amounts to dispossession of the others gives rise to an action).

The most significant concurrent powers in the United States are the concurrent powers of the federal and of state governments to regulate the commercial and police affairs of the nation. These powers are usually spoken of as concurrent powers rather than as a unitary power that is shared or divided because the source, nature, and scope of each government's powers vary according to their constitutions. Still, the effect of their collective authority on an individual who must conform to both sets of laws, which in most cases may be enforced by officials of either government, may appear undifferentiated. Despite the concurrence of these authorities, except in the few state matters reserved for state sovereignty, the federal power is supreme in any conflict.

A similar concurrence of powers exists in state and local regulation. Depending on how the state's constitution and statutes design its allocations of state police powers, the state, county, and municipalities (and sometimes regional boards or commissions) have concurrent powers over local matters, whether public or private.

**implied power** A power unstated in a grant but required to effect a power expressly conferred. An implied power is a power that is inferred to have been implied by the donor or other author of a document granting express powers because the implied power is logically or practically essential for the donee to exercise one of the powers that was expressly given. Famously, the U.S. Constitution has a variety of implied powers that were not mentioned in the constitutional text but that are necessary and proper in order for Congress or some other agency to fulfill the duties or exercise the powers that are expressly conferred.

**plenary power** The most unlimited possible power. Plenary power is the broadest discretion in a public official or public body that is possible in a given context. Within the limits of that discretion, the exercise of that power is generally beyond the review of other officials, though other officials may be required to review such decisions to ensure they are within that discretion and not an abuse of it. A conflict among rules or orders issued by several other bodies or officials would be resolved in favor of the entity with plenary power.

In general, state legislatures are said to have plenary power over police matters. The federal Congress, president, or courts are often said to have plenary power over limited subjects committed to that branch as an element of its dedicated powers, such as the Congress's plenary authority over immigration policy. The broader understanding of plenary power, however, must take into account the coordinated nature of the checks and balances in the exercise of this authority, which divides the plenary power of the government among the three branches.

*See also:* discretion.

**power of appointment (general power of appointment)** The power to dispose of property that is not one's own. A power of appointment is the power to appoint, grant, give, or otherwise dispose of property that is not owned by the power's donee, who is the holder of the power (the power of appointment is inherent in ownership and so merged into the ownership interests otherwise). The power is conferred by the donor, the owner of the property or a prior owner, to the donee. The definition of the power is functional more than formal, and a power of appointment may be found in various instruments, including a power of attorney or a delegation of agency. The donee is not an owner, in law or equity, of the property, and the owner's interests in the property are then subject to the donee's exercise of the power.

Powers of appointment may be general, limited, special, or limited and special. A general power of appointment is unlimited, i.e. places no limits on the person to whom the property may be granted and the means to be used; the donee or holder of the power may confer the property upon himself or herself or on anyone else. A special power of appointment is created with binding instructions designating the class or categories of people who may be the recipients. A limited power of appointment limits the power so the donee may not also be the person or entity to whom the property is eventually granted.

Note: when the donee of a general power appoints the new holders of the property, the appointment is taxable, but when the donee of a limited power or a special power appoints the new holders of the property, the appointment is generally not taxable.

**limited power of appointment (non-general power of appointment)** A power of appointment that may not benefit the holder. A limited power of appointment is a power of appointment that is limited by the donor of the power so that the donee of the power may not appoint the donee as the recipient of the property. The limitation extends not only to the donee but also to the donee's estate, creditors, or estate's creditors.

Note: though many courts equate the limited power of appointment with the special power of appointment, and in some cases a power is both, the difference is a limited power of appointment excludes the donee from ultimate receipt of the property while a special power of appointment includes only a class of receipients, which may or may not include the donee.

**special power of appointment** A power of appointment with special instructions. A special power of appointment is a power of appointment that is given from the donor to the donee with limitations as to whom the donee may appoint to take the property subject to the power. Any limitation (other than a bar on the donee or power holder alone) or any specification of whom the donee may select among creates a special power.

Note: although some statutes and courts merge the common-law categories of special and limited powers, in jurisdictions that retain the difference, a special power need not be a limited power, and in those jurisdictions it is possible for the donor to create a class of grantees from whom the donee may appoint, in which the donee could be included. Even in jurisdictions in which the division is blurred, if the intention of the donor is clear that the donee may appoint the donee as well as others, the clearly expressed intent of the donor should govern.

*See also:* special.

**testamentary power of appointment** A power of appointment created in a will. A testamentary power of appointment is a power of appointment that is designated by the testator in a last will and testament. The testamentary power has been interpreted in Arizona according to Section 101 of the Uniform Nonprobate Transfers on Death Act (1991) actually to be nontestamentary in effect, and is effective at the death of the testator and donor, if the power is in a will that is not probated. This approach may (or may not) become a national rule. In either event, if there is evidence of the intent of the Testator to the contrary, or if the will is probated, the power becomes effectively donated once the will is given effect, usually by judicial order or in a probate decree.

**power to borrow** The authority to issue debt, particularly for a state. The power to borrow is the lawful capacity to give out debt on behalf of another entity, which creates the indebtedness of the entity to those who accept the debt. The power to borrow for debt to be satisfied on the faith of the United States is in the Congress, which authorizes the President to issue such debt, which is done through the Department of the Treasury.

**power to tax (taxing power or taxation power)** The lawful authority to levy a tax on a person or entity. The power to tax is the constitutional authority to levy a tax that is to be paid by a given person or entity. In the federal system, the federal Congress has the power to lay and collect taxes, imposts, excises, and duties on goods, as well as on the income of individuals, though not on the operations of state government. Each state has the power to tax its own citizens, property holders, those who extract materials from its resources, and those who perform transactions within its borders, although the operations of the federal government are immune from state taxation. Depending on the state's constitution, municipalities, counties, and regional entities also have a taxing power. American Indian tribes have the power to tax their members and those on their reservations.

A tax must in fact be created for a constitutionally lawful purpose, the taxing power alone is insufficient for that purpose unless the only purpose of the tax is to raise revenue. Thus, a tax created primarily in order to burden a constitutional right is unlikely to pass the strict scrutiny such taxes receive.

**reserved power**　A power not delegated along with other powers; a state constitutional power. A reserved power is a power that a person or entity retains rather than transferring or delegating it when other powers (or bases of powers) are assigned to another person or entity. For example, if a grantor gives Blackacre in a grant subject to a power of appointment in the grantor, the grantee takes a fee simple subject to an executory interest, and the grantor has a reserved power of appointment.

The most famous reserved powers in the United States are the state powers that were impliedly retained by the states when the states enacted and ratified the U.S. Constitution. Powers of the new federal government were (and are) considered delegated powers, and the powers retained by the states were said to be reserved powers.

**statutory power**　A power vested in an office or agency by statute. Statutory power is the authority of an individual, official, or agency that is created by legislative decree, specifying that the person or entity (or those in such circumstances) has the authority to do something that otherwise the person or entity may not be able to do. Statutory power is power delegated from the legislature to the individual or entity from the legislative power, and an attempt to make an overbroad delegation by providing a power to an agency but failing to limit or reasonably constrain the recipient's means or ends may amount to an unlawful delegation.

**PPB**　*See:* solution, chemical solution, parts per billion (PPB).

**PPM**　*See:* solution, chemical solution, parts per million (PPM).

**PPT**　*See:* solution, chemical solution, parts per thousand (PPT).

**practical reason**　*See:* reason, practical reason.

**practice**　The routine or technique associated with any endeavor. Practice has several related senses, all of them being the manner in which things are accomplished, most broadly the way in which any form of work is done. In all cases, however, a practice becomes a matter of habit or custom. When a practice is established within a subculture, it becomes so much a habit or custom that an expectation arises: it becomes so much a habit or custom that it is done without thinking and becomes the basis of expectations so that its absence or contradiction is considered an error.

A practice related to a specific act is the manner in which the act is performed when done repetitively. Within the professions, a practice has two distinct senses, one relating the scope of work associated with the profession and the expectation of its members as to how the work is to be performed, the other depicting the clientele of a given professional and the work required to service their needs.

**lawyer malpractice**　*See:* malpractice, legal malpractice.

**practice of law**　*See:* lawyer, legal practice (practice of law).

**praecipe (precipe)**　A filing an attorney gives the court clerk, with details for a writ or order. A praecipe is a paper on which an attorney writes the form of writ being requested, along with the details essential to the drafting of the writ, which is then supplied to the clerk of the court for the writ to be drafted. Many U.S. jurisdictions still require a praecipe to accompany a motion for a subpoena or order. A contemporary praecipe to enforce a judgment may be quite lengthy, though at the common law the praecipe was usually just a small slip of paper.

*See also:* motion (movant or move).

**praemunire (premunire or praemunire facias or praemonere)**　The English crime of supporting Catholic jurisdiction in England. Praemunire was the generic term in England for the unlawful promotion of the Roman Catholic religion, especially by seeking legal recourse in Rome for a matter affecting England or English law (such as who controlled the income and positions over church property in England), and extending after the schism of Henry VIII to include supporting priests and failing to take an oath to support the monarch. The term arises from the opening language of writ, which summoned the accused to appear. Praemunire came to be commonly used to describe the anti–Catholic statutes, each of the various offenses that amounted to promoting Catholicism, and to the writ itself.

**pragmatism**　*See:* jurisprudence, pragmatism (legal pragmatism).

**prayer (pray)**　A solemn and earnest request. The prayer is the customary close of a pleading that seeks the court to do or not to do something, the prayer being the part in which the party filing the pleading asks for the court to do the specific thing that is the object of the pleading. In a complaint or other pleading seeking a remedy, this is the prayer for relief. The prayer should be specific in seeking the exact remedy to which the party claims entitlement and seeks to be granted, although the prayer may also include a prayer for general relief, "such other relief as the court shall find" the party to be entitled.

Note: in general use, prayer is well known as a communication intended from a person to the divine being, though this sense is not directly significant in pleading and other technical legal usage. A prayer, in general, is a request, a plea for assistance, and neither the prayer nor the acting of praying in law has a direct religious connotation; it is more akin to begging.

**prayer for relief**   *See:* relief, prayer for relief.

**preamble**   An introductory statement that precedes a document. A preamble is a preface, an introduction to the instrument that follows, usually setting forth its purposes, history, or rationale. A contract or statute may be preceded by a preamble, as are many public acts, most famously the United States Constitution. A preamble is rarely enforceable in itself, although it is a useful basis for interpretation of the document it introduces.

**precariousness (precarious)**   Having an unpredictable risk. Precariousness implies having some risk that is difficult to assess but that may lead to the loss of position, property or other gain. In the seventeenth century, a precarious position was one that was dependent on the grace or favor of another person. From this sense of favor granted by petition, we have the current understanding of riskiness.

**precatory trust**   *See:* trust, precatory trust.

**precatory words**   Language in an instrument that requests some conduct rather than commanding it. Precatory words in a will, deed of gift, trust, or other instrument serve to instruct or request a person who receives the instrument to do something (or to do something in a given manner), but do not require the person to do it. Thus, for instance, the testator of a will may request a trustee to allow legatees to select chattels from the estate in a particular order, or may request a devisee of land to keep the land in the family rather than to sell it on the open market. Such entreaties may be made when the maker of the instrument prefers to give guidance rather than make requirements for reasons of courtesy or convenience, or they may be made when the law would not enforce a requirement. In either case, the language is unenforceable in the law, and unless the object of the request or the means of request are inherently unlawful, the decision to comply with such instructions is left to the discretion of the person to whom the request is directed. There is often considerable argument over whether some language is precatory or mandatory. Interpretation may turn on the choice of words, and

language more inviting of the use of discretion is more likely to be precatory. Or the interpretation may be functional, and language that appears more to amount to a specific and lawful condition on the grant of identifiable property subject to grant will be seen as mandatory, but vague language (particularly in the description of the conduct or the property to which it relates) is likely to be construed as precatory.

*See also:* trust, precatory trust.

**precautionary principle**   A policy to err on the side of safety in pollution standards. The precautionary principle is a policy underlying a variety of federal statutes regulating the allowable contamination of air, water, soil, food, and other substances, which requires that standards set for a chemical in the absence of perfect information regarding the hazards the chemical might pose to human health or the environment be set to minimize the potential risks the chemical might pose.

**precedent (doctrine of precedent)**   An earlier, similar case and its influence on a later case. Precedent, in the sense of a legal precedent, is a decision by an institutional official, such as a judge, that resolves a legal question and that may serve as a reason to resolve similar legal questions in the same way at a later date. In essence, every decision made in a court of law is a precedent.

There is a more narrow sense of precedent in which some past decisions are considered a source of strong reasons for future decisions, other past decisions are either criticized or rejected by later officials or judges as bases for later decisions, and others are rarely if ever considered or followed. In this sense, precedent is used to refer to the degree to which later officials believe themselves justified in following the earlier decision, a belief expressed by describing the earlier decision as good precedent or bad precedent. Sometimes this sense will be used in saying an influential precedent is precedent and a rejected or ignored precedent is no precedent at all.

The term "precedent" in law almost always refers to judicial precedents. Even so, it also may be used for executive and legislative actions. In international law, constitutional law, and administrative law, precedent from the non-judicial branches is often quite influential in establishing custom or patterns and practices.

Precedent is at the heart of the common law, in that the principles and rules of the common law are to be found in precedents, in past decisions already enforced upon those subject to the law. This relationship of principle to rule takes two primary forms: in one, the body of cases, their results, and their rationales form a source of principles and rules; and in the other, every single case or official action under law gives rise to a precedent that is to be copied in later, similar circumstances. Neither of these forms is practicable in itself, and the doctrine of precedent, that new cases are to be resolved by following rules from old cases, lies somewhere in between these two ideas.

That the decision in a case or some other official act is precedent does not inherently make it a good precedent, and careful examination of a precedent is essential to determine the degree of its validity as a basis for later decisions emulating its result. A precedent is only proper authority for later decisions when the initial decision was properly made according to the procedures for its issuance, when it was seen as a valid exercise of authority at the time, and when its rationale and its conclusion are reasonable, fitting with the related rules of law, and just as to the parties involved in the later case.

Determining the scope of a precedent can be difficult, and various tools cause more difficulties than they solve. The division of a judicial precedent into ratio decidendi and obiter dictum, by which statements that are essential to the decision are more important for later reliance than other statements, is notoriously fuzzy. More pertinently, a decision is stronger precedent when the questions it is thought later to answer were clearly argued in the earlier case, and the prior doctrines and precedents were apparently considered.

In the United States, the decision of a court of more than one judge is sometimes considered only to stronger precedent according to the number of justices who agree with it. Thus a unanimous decision is the strongest precedent, a decision without dissent is still quite strong despite concurrences, and a decision that is agreed by a majority of justices is still stronger than a decision that is agreed by only a plurality less than a majority. When a majority of judges disagrees with the holding, some judges consider the decision to lack precedential value. Such consideration are influential on later judges, but the influence of the opinions is often poorly explained by such mathematical strictures. In many instances, the strength of the reasoning in the opinions is later considered more significant. Still, in the absence of a majority, later attorneys and judges may attempt to synthesize an opinion from among the concurrences and plurality that represent the rule that has the logically narrowest application to later cases.

Efforts by a judge or official at the moment of a decision to limit the precedential effect of a decision are immaterial to the precedential nature of the decision. The decision was made as a matter of law, and it will be considered a good precedent and emulated in the future according to the judgment of a later judge or official. Indeed, there are risks in imagining a legal decision that cannot be a precedent, which are to be avoided.

**all fours**   A precedential case that is very strongly similar to the case at hand. All fours is a metaphor for a case's being effectively indistinguishable from a later case.

*See also:* analogy.

**binding precedent**   An earlier court opinion so similar to the later case that it must be followed. Binding precedent is a earlier decision arising from a case of such similar facts and from a court of such authority relative to a later case that the judge hearing the later case would expect and be expected to apply the decision of the earlier case in resolving the question in the later case. The binding nature of a precedent is a

matter of degree. Various factors increase or decrease the degree to which a later judge would be thought to have an obligation to apply the earlier opinion. A precedent is more likely to be thought binding if (a) the earlier decision was handed down by a higher court to which the later court's decisions are appealed, or (b) the earlier decision was made by the same court hearing the later case; (c) the earlier decision arose under the same doctrine of law, or the same statute with little or no relevant intervening amendments; (d) the decision in the earlier case that might be applied in the later case was essential to the outcome of the case as it was seen at the time; and (e) the facts of the earlier case are similar to the facts of the later case. Though these relationships of the earlier case to the later case are important in considering the weight of precedent, the precedent may not be thought binding unless the later judges consider it good law both at the time of the initial decision and the time of the later decision. If the earlier case was not a widely accepted precedent, being subject to criticism by scholars or by the judges of other courts, it appears less binding when the same question is raised later on similar facts. If the earlier case has been cited often with approval by scholars, by judges on the same or superior courts, or by judges of other courts, the precedential effect appears greater. Still, if the later court considers social circumstances to have altered so that the underlying rationale for the earlier case is no longer a compelling justification for the later decision, the earlier decision is less likely to be seen as binding.

Note: there is no difference between a binding precedent and a controlling precedent.

*See also:* stare decisis.

**case of first impression**   A case without precedent. A case of first impression is an action raising an issue of law that has not been raised before in the jurisdiction in which the action arises. Some cases of first impression raise an issue of law that has never been decided in any jurisdiction. The resolution of such a case usually depends on the degree to which the attorney for the plaintiff can demonstrate that the general principals of law, the constitution or statutes, or analogous rules of law support the plaintiff's theory of the case. The defendant will usually seek to demonstrate that a case of first impression is improvident, either because there is no principal of law to support the claim argued by the plaintiff, and there should not be one, or because if there is such a principal of law, it would be unfair to apply it to the defendant at the time of its first recognition, such an application being inherently retroactive.

**landmark case (leading case or landmark opinion or landmark decision)**   A case that greatly alters the law, creating a new doctrine. A landmark decision is an opinion of unusual significance because over time it influences a great number of later decisions. A landmark decision usually creates or refines a doctrine that is often applied in the later cases, which may refer to the landmark case for the authority to apply the doctrine in later disputes. Examples of landmark cases include Marbury v. Madison, 5 U.S. (1 Cranch) 137 (1803) (Marshall, C.J.), which established the Supreme Court's judicial review over federal legislation, and MacPherson v. Buick, 217 N.Y. 382, 111 N.E. 1050 (1916) (Cardozo, J.), which established vendor liability for defective goods to the ultimate consumer, rather than limiting it to those in privity of contract.

No difference between a landmark case and other precedents affects the later analysis of the precedential effect of a landmark case in its application to a later dispute. Even so, there may be a greater reluctance by later judges to disregard a landmark case and a much greater reluctance to overrule one. A landmark case is also a leading case.

*See also:* precedent, leading case.

**leading case**   A case that established a basic principle of law. A leading case is a precedent that articulated, announced, or refined a particular rule of law, which has been applied, but also developed and detailed, in later opinions that have been written by judges who perceived their cases to be governed by the leading case. The later cases that apply, develop, and provide detail to the leading case, are sometimes called the progeny (or offspring) of the leading case.

*See also:* precedent, landmark case (leading case or landmark opinion or landmark decision).

**Marks rule**   The rationales of the narrowest supporting opinions best explain a non-majority ruling. In Marks v. United States, 430 U.S. 188, 193 (1977), Justice Powell writing for the Court instructed, "When a fragmented Court decides a case and no single rationale explaining the result enjoys the assent of five Justices, the holding of the Court may be viewed as that position taken by those Members who concurred in the judgments on the narrowest grounds." This approach to reading the Court's opinions is hard to do, but at the least it means that the narrowest related rationales that support the mandate of the court are the most reliable in explaining that rationale. This analysis is not limited solely to those opinions labeled "concurring" but includes all opinions that argue in some manner for the result reflected in the mandate of the court.

**progeny case**   A later case that applies or develops the precedent of an earlier leading case. Progeny, in general, is a child, or the children and descendants of a progenitor, which is to say a parent or an ancestor generally. In the writing of judicial opinions, progeny is popular as a metaphor for a case that applies a specific precedent, particularly using progeny to depict a later case that developed or detailed the effects of the earlier landmark case it applied. The idea of intellectual progeny is wider in scope than its legal usage in describing precedent, and the concept is used (if rarely in American law) to depict literature or art influenced by a given piece, as well as the students or disciples of a teacher or intellectual leader.

Note: progeny is a collective noun, and it may represent one or represent more descendants. In legal use, however, it is nearly always collective,

representing a line of cases extending from the leading case, such as "Chevron and its progeny establish . . ."

*See also:* precedent, leading case; progeny.

**precept**   A command, rule, or norm to be followed. A precept is a principle to be followed either in performing a specific task or in living one's life in general. The term is derived from the language of command in the medieval writ, praecipimus, which might be followed by any number of royal orders to be carried out by a sheriff. In contemporary usage, authors have ascribed various specific meanings to precept that are specific to their own writings, but the term generally represents a variety of statements or understandings of authority that guide individual conduct, including rules, principles, commands, and customs. In this sense it is similar to the broad meaning of norm.

*See also:* norm.

**precipe**   *See:* praecipe (precipe).

**preconception injury**   *See:* injury, pre-conception injury (preconception injury).

**predatory pricing**   *See:* price, predatory pricing (excessively low pricing).

**predecessor**   *See:* succession (successor or predecessor).

**predial servitude**   *See:* servitude, predial servitude.

**predisposition (predisposed)**   A personal bias to do or to believe something before a critical event. A predisposition, in general, is a person's willingness to do something or believe something which the person has before an event that is later considered significant in evaluating the person's behavior. Thus, a person may be predisposed to dislike, to mistrust, or to believe other people on the basis of individual appearance, or a person may be predisposed to certain conduct before an opportunity to engage in that conduct becomes apparent.

Predisposition is an essential element in disproving the criminal defense that the defendant was entrapped by a government agent, and but for the entrapment the defendant would not have committed a criminal act. But defendant who is ready to commit an act and willing to do so when the opportunity is presented is predisposed to committing that act. Evidence of a predisposition includes proof that the defendant had committed similar acts prior to the new opportunity and had planned to commit or had at least considered committing similar acts prior to the new opportunity. Though evidence of predisposition should generally be of the defendant's knowledge or conduct prior to a government-created opportunity, proof of the defendant's quick or unconsidered acceptance of an opportunity may amount to proof of predisposition. Not all evidence of predisposition is sufficient to rebut a claim of entrapment: if the government creates or significantly encourages the defendant's predisposition prior to creating the opportunity, the encouragement of the defendant's interest in committing unlawful acts may prove entrapment rather than predisposition. The question of predisposition, like the question of entrapment generally is a matter of fact, though what evidence may logically prove predisposition is a matter of law.

*See also:* entrapment.

**preembryo** *See:* zygote, embryo, pre–embryo (pre–embryo).

**preemption (preempt or preemptive or pre-emption or pre-empt or pre-emptive)** Taking precedence or assuming priority over the powers or actions of another. Preemption is the assertion of a priority or superiority of authority or preference in action, such as when a person exercises an option or makes an early offer to purchase a good before another buyer's offer is considered. This may occur among parties of equal status or authority, for instance in the sense that to preempt an argument is to rebut it before it is made. More often, however, preemption occurs between powers of differing authority, as when a government preempts claims of one party for another, or when a superior authority preempts the authority of a junior. In either case, to preempt is to take precedence, to be first in priority or in order, or to be the only person or entity deemed eligible to perform the thing in question.

Note: Preemption, which is done by action or potential action, should not be confused with presumption, which is done by knowledge or belief.

**constitutional preemption** A superior government's preemption of the laws of a subordinate government. Constitutional preemption is the preemption of one authority by a superior authority, as a matter of the constitutional relationships between those governments. In the United States, constitutional preemption may refer to federal preemption of state law or state preemption of local law. Preemption takes several forms, particularly federal preemption of state law. The most essential form of preemption occurs when Congress enacts a statute regulating an arena of activity and expressly preempting state laws that would regulate the same field of activity, such as air traffic control. Preemption in such a case is express preemption owing to the declaration in the text of the statute. Preemption may also be implied from the subject matter, structure and breadth of the statute, and potential for inconsistency if multiple sovereigns regulate the same field. Preemption may be total, barring any regulation by the state, or partial and so barring only regulation that is in conflict with the federal regulations.

**federal preemption of state law (congressional preemption or express preemption or implied pre-emption)** Priority of federal authority barring enforcement of state laws. Federal preemption of state law occurs when a federal law conflicts with a state law, whether directly or indirectly, rendering the state law void. The general basis for preemption is the doctrine of supremacy, as enshrined in the Supremacy Clause, which states that federal laws and treaties are "the supreme Law of the Land; . . . any Thing in the Constitution or Laws of any State to the Contrary notwithstanding." There is, however, a strong constitutional presumption against preemption because the different governments are presumed to work together rather than to conflict with one another. The presumption can only be overcome with clear evidence of the intent of Congress to preempt state law or of a logical conflict between state and federal law that cannot be resolved through interpretation.

Preemption, in its most direct form, is said to occur when a federal and state law regarding the same matter are in logical conflict, requiring different conduct of the person or entity regulated or different actions by state officials, or setting different and incompatible standards for regulated conduct. A mere difference in standards is insufficient to find a conflict; rather, the difference must be of a kind requiring full compliance with the federal law. More difficult questions arise not when the state law is in direct conflict with a federal law, but when a matter regulated by state law falls logically within a category of federal regulation. Then there may be concurrent regulation, or the state regulation may be preempted, leaving only the federal regulation, or (in very rare circumstances) the federal law may be subject to reverse preemption.

Federal preemption of regulation affecting a whole arena of human conduct is sometimes labeled categorical preemption or field preemption, because the whole category of action or field of regulation is occupied by federal law. It arises in potential concurrent regulation in either express preemption or implied preemption.

Express preemption occurs when Congress expresses its intention to occupy a field with federal regulation to the exclusion of state regulation by saying so clearly in the text of a statute. The words must be clear, and the intent of Congress to preempt state law should be clear from the text alone.

Implied preemption is inferred by the courts through analysis of the structure and requirements of a statute or statutes, to determine that Congress intended to preempt state law in the field of human action that is the subject of the federal law. Evidence of such an intent can be found in the subject matter's being inherently federal, interstate, or international in character; in the comprehensiveness of the federal law; in the difficulty of creating additional laws that do not alter policy balances and decisions enshrined in the federal law; and in the structure of enforcement required of the federal law. Implied preemption is sometimes also called field preemption, though field preemption is more properly applied to categorical preemption.

State preemption by federal law includes preemption of the regulation of the same subject matter by municipal, county, and other local laws.

**reverse preemption (reversely preempt)** A preemption of federal law by state law or state law by local law. Reverse preemption is the rare circumstance in which the law of the junior jurisdiction preempts the senior, as when federal law requires that state law preempt other federal law. While areas of local privilege from state laws or state privilege from federal laws are not uncommon, the recognition of priority for these local privileges is not usually thought of as preemption, but preemption may occur when the federal law reserves an arena of concurrent jurisdiction for state regulation, giving the state regulation priority over contrary federal regulation. The U.S. McCarran-Ferguson Act, 15 U.S.C. § 1012(b), for example, requires state insurance law to trump contrary federal general statutes, unless the federal statute is clearly intended to regulate insurance or insurance obligations.

**state preemption of local law (state-local preemption)** Priority of state authority barring enforcement of municipal or county laws. State preemption of municipal or local law requires either the categorical prohibition of local regulation on a given subject or the specific incompatibility of any local regulation with any state regulation on the same matter. Many state constitutions and local government statutes, including home-rule laws, allocate certain matters to the exclusive province of local authority, but specifically preempt local laws on all other subjects.

Note: local laws may also be preempted by federal preemption.

**right of preemption (preemptive right or preemption right or right of pre-emption)** A right to acquire property before another person. A right of preemption is the power of its holder related to a given piece of property to acquire by purchase the property from the property's owner before another person may do so. A right of preemption may take various forms, including an option to buy, a right of first refusal, and a conditional grant. A preemptive right may amount to a conditional future interest, and options are subject to the rule against perpetuities for this reason. Even so, a preemptive right is not inherently an assurance of possession because its exercise is a right to purchase, not a right to possess. The terms of purchase may be fixed at the time of the right's creation or implied by law, particularly from terms by which the property owner agrees to sell the property to a third party.

A valid right of preemption is not perpetual but lasts only until an event on which it is conditioned, such as a lapse of time or as an attempt by the owner to sell the property to another. An attempt by the owner to transfer the property inter vivos will usually give rise to the right of preemption (although some rights of preemption, such as an option open for a period of time, may survive some types of assignment of the property and bind the assign). A failure to exercise a preemptive right in a reasonable time after a condition precedent is fulfilled may cause the right to lapse.

*See also:* contract, option contract.

**first refusal (right of first refusal)** A potential buyer's right to preempt a sale of a property to another. The right of first refusal is a form of right of preemption in that the holder of the right of first refusal has a claim against the owner of some property, and if the owner offers to sell or transfer the property to anyone, the owner must first offer to sell the property to the holder of the right of first refusal, who then has the power to purchase the property and to preempt all other purchases or transfers. If the right of first refusal is not exercised, it lapses, so that once the holder of a right of first refusal is offered the property for sale and fails to exercise the right, the right is destroyed. A right of first refusal may be structured in a variety of ways, in the valuation of the offer, in the structure of the offer, and in other conditions, such as whether the right runs with the land to bind an assign. Presumptively, a right of first refusal requires the owner to offer the property at a reasonable price in the market, which will be the price at which the owner will offer the property if the right is not exercised. Further, the presumptions in a right of first refusal are that the owner is the offeror, and the right or refusal is a personal right in the holder binding only the owner, which is destroyed at the death of either. These presumptions may be altered by the creation of a contract or other means, including a signed instrument that creates a servitude on land subject to such a right.

*See also:* refusal (refuse).

**preexisting duty rule** *See:* consideration, preexisting duty rule (pre-existing duty rule).

**preference**

**bankruptcy, preference** *See:* bankruptcy, preference (prefer).

**preferential rule** *See:* rule, preferential rule.

**preferred share or preference share** *See:* share, share as stock, preferred stock (preferred share or preference share).

**preferred stock** *See:* share, share as stock, preferred stock (preferred share or preference share).

**pregnancy (quick with child or pregnant woman)** The condition from which a woman may give birth. Pregnancy is the physical and medical condition of a woman who is developing a fertilized egg, embryo, or fetus. Pregnancy exists when it is ongoing, and it is independent of whether the pregnancy results in a successful birth. Because pregnancy is a biological condition of the woman whose body contains the developing fetus, a woman whose egg has been removed for fertilization is not at that moment pregnant. Pregnancy creates a range of physical changes in the body of the pregnant woman and may cause, especially in its later stages, temporary disability. An employer must make reasonable accommodations for a pregnant employee, but an employer who discriminates on the basis of pregnancy or the basis of fetal safety is presumptively engaging in gender discrimination.

Note: statutes that apply to a woman who is quick with child apply to a pregnant woman. The medical specialty that particularly cares for pregnant women is obstetrics.

*See also:* pregnancy, trimester.

**trimester**   One third of the term, or three months of a human pregnancy. The trimester is a division of a pregnancy into thirds of its term, or roughly, into three periods of about 12 weeks. The first trimester is estimated as 12 weeks following conception, or 14 weeks following the last menstrual period. An average pregnancy lasts approximately 38 weeks from the time of conception or, as more commonly measured, 40 weeks from the beginning of the woman's last menstrual period. Under both methods there may be more than a two-week deviation either way. Because of the approximate nature of these measurements, there is no certain method of delineating trimesters. Using current medical technology, a fetus becomes viable when a woman enters the third trimester.

*See also:* pregnancy (quick with child or pregnant woman); abortion (abort).

**wrongful pregnancy (wrongful conception)**   Claim arising from pregnancy after a medical procedure that should have precluded it. Wrongful pregnancy is a form of action for medical malpractice, or potentially for product liability, brought for damages by a person who became pregnant or causes a person to become pregnant following a medical procedure that should have made such pregnancy impossible, such as sterilization and abortion. Wrongful pregnancy also includes similar actions for product liability arising from failures of contraceptive devices or pharmaceuticals.

*See also:* birth, wrongful birth (wrongful life).

**pregnant**   Rich with implied meaning. Pregnant, in legal writing, has had a variety of meanings, and its sense should be considered in connection with the period in which the term was employed. Pregnant once meant that an argument was fully convincing. By Bouvier's time, it suggested a writing in a pleading that intentionally or unintentionally presented information favoring the party against whom the pleading was filed. In the late twentieth century, it is likely to have its more general meaning in prose, that a matter is either very important or the writing is especially meaningful, particularly with a meaning implied that is more important than the words employed.

**prehearing conference**   *See:* hearing, prehearing conference.

**prejudice**   Prejudgment or bias. Prejudice is a mental state of conclusion before an argument in which a person

relies (whether knowingly or unknowingly) on supposition or bias, stereotype or presumption, to reach a decision before considering the evidence in detail that would otherwise have been the basis for decision.

Prejudice takes many forms, but to speak of prejudice in the context of civil rights is to invoke an expectation of the social relationships attributed to race or gender, limiting individuals to roles and conduct considered appropriate for people of a particular race or gender. Until the 1950s in the United States, this was most manifest in an expectation that women and non-white people were expected not to challenge the social or legal authority of white men.

*See also:* bias; stereotype (gender stereotype or racial stereotype or stereotypical).

**legal prejudice**   A barrier to hearing a legal claim or action. Legal prejudice is a prejudgment or other hindrance that acts as if a claim, action, or other legal interest has been adjudged, so that it may no longer be asserted or maintained. Judicial decisions that create no legal prejudice against a claim are no bar to its later prosecution. Prejudice, however, arises when any interest is foreclosed, not only when a claim is barred, and thus procedural and evidentiary rulings give rise to prejudice when a litigant may no longer seek a favorable procedure, introduce helpful evidence, or exclude evidence contrary to the litigant's case.

**undue prejudice**   A decision based on improper grounds or reaching improper ends. Undue prejudice arises from a ruling or decision that either is predicated on improper evidence or insufficient law such that an argument or evidence is wrongfully barred or allowed in a hearing or trial, to the substantial harm of a party before the court. Undue prejudice may arise from a ruling or decision that is likely to result in a burden on the party whose interests are foreclosed, and the burden is greater than the basis for the ruling or decision would require or support. A common form of undue prejudice is the introduction of inadmissible evidence that might suggest liability or fault to the finder of fact, an error that might not be curable.

**with prejudice (without prejudice)**   The degree to which a decision forecloses reargument. Prejudice attaching to a decision is finality, the attribute of the decision that forecloses its underlying arguments from being brought by these same parties later in law for another consideration. A dismissal or other decree in an action made with prejudice bars the parties in that action from bringing another case on the same grounds, in that forum or another (although this foreclosure does not affect appeal of the decree). Similarly, a dismissal or other decree that is without prejudice does not foreclose the same arguments being brought again (although a new case to bring such arguments again might be foreclosed for other reasons).

**prejudicial error**   *See:* error, reversible error (prejudicial error).

**pre-judgment remedy**   *See:* remedy, pre-judgment remedy (pre-trial relief).

**preliminary**   Done prior to something else. Preliminary designates something done in advance of something else or to initiate a process. A preliminary order is an order in advance of a final order, which gives the authority issuing the order time to consider the basis and effect of the order before issuing an order intended to be permanent. Likewise, a preliminary injunction is an injunction issued while a court determines whether there are grounds for a permanent injunction.

    **preliminary hearing**   *See:* hearing, preliminary hearing (first appearance or preliminary examination).

    **preliminary injunction**   *See:* injunction, preliminary injunction (P.I. or PI).

**premarital agreement**   *See:* marriage, premarital agreement (ante-nuptial agreement or prenuptial agreement or prenup or pre-nuptial agreement or pre-nuptial contract or prenuptial contract or marriage settlement).

**prematurity or unripe of premature**   *See:* justiciability, ripeness, unripeness (prematurity or unripe of premature).

**premeditation (premeditate)**   The consideration or decision to do a thing before doing it. Premeditation is either the possession of knowledge that a person will engage in some conduct or the making of a decision to engage in that conduct, in either case considered by the person some time sufficiently prior to the person's performing the conduct that the person's possession, knowledge, or act of decision were distinct and separate in time from the person's conduct itself. Premeditation is usually a concern in determining the mens rea of a person who commits a criminal act. A criminal act that is premeditated is both knowing and, in most cases, intentional. Premeditation may be proven through circumstantial evidence.

*See also:* murder, degrees of murder, first-degree murder (murder in the first degree or murder-one or murder-1).

**premises (premise)**   The first propositions in an argument, or particular realty and its buildings. Premises, as a matter of property, refers to the lands and structures that comprise a parcel of property. Yet premises are also the statements from which an argument is made and a conclusion is drawn.

Both senses have a common origin, because premise, from the medieval Latin premissa, was the proposition set before, just as the description of lands usually was set first in a conveyance, in that part of the deed that, technically was the premise of the transfer. Thus, the lands were the premises.

Note: when referring to lands or buildings, even a single tiny parcel is said to be the premises. In discussing the elements of an argument, each proposition from which an argument is to be drawn is a premise, and collectively they are premises.

**premises considered clause or whererfore paragraph**   *See:* wherefore, wherefore clause (premises considered clause or whererfore paragraph).

**premium**   A reward or payment. Premium was once a term for the profits realized from the sale of ill-gotten gains, a meaning now rare, having been supplanted by several distinct meanings in law. As a general term, it is a profit or surcharge, particularly one that is derived from a sale or contract, although insurers do not consider the premium of an insurance contract to be profit so much as an allocative share of risk. As a term in the labeling of food and other goods, premium denotes a high quality.

    **insurance premium**   Payment on behalf of an insured in consideration of an insurance contract. An insurance premium is an amount of money paid to an insurance company or other insurance carrier by or on behalf of the insured as consideration in an insurance contract; this is in return for assurance that the insurer will protect the insured in the event the insured suffers a loss covered by the insurance contract. The premium is owed by a date certain, although the premiums of a contract may be structured in various ways for payment, such as prepayment of the premium in its entirety or payments made in periodic installments for as long as the contract stays in force. In the event of periodic payments, a failure of the payor to make a timely payment as defined in the contract may be grounds for the insurer to give notice of termination of the contract before completion of its term, after which the insurer may cancel the contract (a process usually governed by state insurance regulations).

    *See also:* deductible, deductible as insurance claim offset.

**premunire or praemunire facias or praemonere**   *See:* praemunire (premunire or praemunire facias or praemonere).

**prenatal injury**   *See:* injury, prenatal injury.

**prenuptial will**   *See:* will, last will and testament, prenuptial will (prenuptial will).

**prepayment penalty**   *See:* penalty, prepayment penalty.

**preponderance (preponderate)**   More than less. A preponderance has greater weight than something else, either literally or, more commonly, figuratively. Thus, an argument that is more persuasive than another, even if it is only barely more persuasive, preponderates. Preponderance is a relative and not an absolute term; its only significance is in comparing one thing to another, though in matters of proof this may be whether an argument is to be believed or not.

    **preponderance of the evidence**   *See:* proof, burden of proof, preponderance of the evidence.

**prerequisite**   A condition precedent to an occurrence or action. A prerequisite is something that must happen or be done before something else. It is a condition precedent to another event or condition. Prerequisite is not to be confused with perquisite.

*See also:* officer, corporate officer, executive officer, executive compensation, perquisite (perk or perks).

**prerogative**   The scope of one's discretion. A prerogative is the power or privilege of one person to do or have something done without the approval of others. More technically, a prerogative is the privilege to precede another in action, authority, or any other thing. Prerogative is usually limited in scope as to the action, conduct, or property interests to which it relates, as well as to those over whom it may be exercised. A sovereign prerogative, however, has no superior at all, and so it is synonymous with the power of the state. Thus, prerogative in early U.S. cases referred to state power or to legislative authority. In contemporary usage, it is any privilege that might not be interfered with by another, such as the powers of a landholder or of an offeree to accept a valid and open offer.

*See also:* discretion.

**royal prerogative**   The customary power of the monarch. The royal prerogative is the power of the monarch to act in a given context or regarding a certain subject, without regard to the will of Parliament or the limits of the common law. The prerogative includes duties and rights but also proprietary interests, such as those in royal beasts. Although the monarchs of England have recognized or acceded to many limitations on the scope of the royal prerogative — most significantly in the constitutional instruments such as Magna Carta, the Petition of Right of 1628, the Bill of Rights of 1789, and the Act of Settlement of 1701, as well as by custom performing acts of prerogative according to the recommendation of the ministers of government — the scope of the prerogative that remains in the monarch's hands to be exercised regardless of the preference of the government is inherently unknown until it is tested.

**prescribed fee**   *See:* fee, fee for services, prescribed fee.

**prescriptible**   *See:* prescription,   prescription of property (prescriptible).

**prescription (prescribable or prescriptive or prescribe)**   A written requirement or order. Prescription has several contemporary senses, each derived from the various Latin meanings for a written instruction to do something, and several of these have a distinct use in law. In general, a law is said to prescribe some conduct, which is to say that the law requires it. This sense of prescription is, however, now less related to the idea of a writing, and a prescription of the law need not be written down in a single, explicit written statement. On the other hand, an injunction is prescriptive, in that it is a written requirement. From these senses of prescription is the broad sense of prescription as merely a form of command or decree, which need not be written.

Several distinct senses of prescription in law involve the curtailment or destruction of rights. Prescription in these senses arise from the operation of time to terminate an interest that may be secured in litigation, so that an action that is stale owing to laches, a statute of limitations, or other doctrine is prescribed. From this sense an interest acquired through adverse use or possession does so because the action to bar the use or possession is prescribed. Lands or property acquired through adverse possession are acquired by prescription because the action to oust the possessor is prescribed. Similarly, a non-possessory interest can be prescribed, and so an easement may be acquired in the lands of another through prescription.

There are more senses of prescription as a written instruction. In medicine and pharmacy, prescription is a written medical instruction, from which prescription has acquired a rhetorical sense to mean any plan or path that might be followed. These senses of prescription as a requirement to do something all arise from one sense of a writing before something. Another sense of prescription applies to the idea of what happens before the writing, in particular what happens before a deed, which is the sense of prescription of an interest in property. Note: prescription is generally an obligation to do something; proscription is generally a prohibition from doing something. Note also: prescription is both a noun and a verb. What is prescribed is done by prescription, resulting in a prescription that prescribes it.

*See also:* proscription (proscribe or proscribed).

**prescription of property (prescriptible)**   The acquisition of title to property through long possession. Prescription is the acquisition of title arising from possession for a period of time that no action may be brought because the period of time specified in the statute of limitations that would have applied to a claim that the possession was wrongful has lapsed. Prescription describes title acquired by such long possession regardless of whether the prescription cut off an earlier claim to title, even by someone who was the true owner, or prescription merely settled title when there had been no prior claimant or title holder. The most well known form of prescription is prescription through adverse possession.

Prescription describes any form of title through possession, including the prescription of incorporeal interests, which cannot be possessed. Thus, an easement may be prescribed just as title in fee may be. Not all property is prescriptable, however, and just as the property of the monarch could not be lost to prescription, neither can property of a government.

Possession alone is rarely sufficient to ripen into a prescriptive title. Rather, possession coupled with use in an ordinary, open manner that would allow others to be aware of the possession and use is essential in order for the statute of limitations fairly to run to exclude the claims the others might bring. The possession must be made in a manner like that of a true owner, not under a claim of permission, license, or permission. The possession must continue without lapse for the whole time of the statute for the statute to extinguish claims. From these conditions come the various formulae for adverse possession, such as open, notorious, hostile, adverse, and continuous.

Note: prescription in this sense arises from the same origin as prescription as a written instruction to be later carried out, but this is a sense in which title is based on what happened before the writing, and it reflects customary title, which in modern property law is merged with prescriptive title.

*See also:* right, legal right, prescriptive right.

*continuous-adverse-use principle* Prescription, in any form that extinguishes the right of another in property (including adverse possession) requires that the possessor use the property in an open manner that is not hidden or sly, continuously for the period of the statute of limitations.

**prescriptive easement** *See:* easement, prescriptive easement, tacking; easement, prescriptive easement.

**prescriptive right** *See:* right, legal right, prescriptive right.

**present covenant** *See:* covenant, covenant of title, present covenant.

**pre-sentence report or PSR or P.S.R.** *See:* sentence, presentence-investigation report (pre-sentence report or PSR or P.S.R.).

**present possessory interest** *See:* estate, interest, present possessory interest (possessory estate or present estate).

**present sale** *See:* sale, present sale.

**present sense impression** *See:* hearsay, hearsay exception, hearsay allowed regardless of witness availability, present sense impression.

**present value** *See:* value, present value, actuarial value; value, present value (future value).

**presentation of a check** *See:* instrument, negotiable instrument, presentment of a negotiable instrument (presentation of a check).

**presentence-investigation report** *See:* sentence, presentence-investigation report (pre-sentence report or PSR or P.S.R.).

**presenting bank** *See:* bank, presenting bank.

**presentment** The formal presentation of a person or thing to a person for an action of legal significance. Presentment is the formal act of giving a writing, person, or thing into the custody of its intended recipient, particularly when a legal duty is to be performed by the recipient. The presentment of the medieval grand jury was the act of the jury's giving over to the sheriff or the court its written report of crimes committed, which the jury itself had discovered. The presentment of a negotiable instrument is its physical transfer to the party on whom the paper is drawn. The presentment of a legislative bill is the delivery of the bill to the governor or president for signature or other disposition. In each illustration, the presentment includes both a physical delivery and the creation or alteration of a legal power or obligation.

Any thing or person may be subject to a presentment. For instance, the presentment for initial appearance of a person arrested for a crime is the delivery of the detainee to the court for the colloquy of the initial appearance. Or, a claim or issue may be presented to an administrative body.

**presentment for initial appearance** *See:* appearance, initial appearance (presentment for initial appearance).

**presentment of a negotiable instrument** *See:* instrument, negotiable instrument, presentment of a negotiable instrument (presentation of a check).

**presentment of the grand jury** *See:* jury, grand jury, presentment of the grand jury.

**presents (know by these presents)** The words of a writing. Presents in the sense of a document or instrument are the terms of the writing itself. The presents are what are subject to presentment when the instrument is tendered to another person for some purpose.

**preservation of error** *See:* error, preservation of error.

**preside** Formally and actively to chair a group or meeting. To preside is to manage in fact the activities of a session of court or of a legislature or any other formal activity among people. A person who is nominally a president of an organization need not be the same person who in fact presides. The Vice President's duties as President of the U.S. Senate are often performed by a junior senator, who presides by delegation, although the actual selection of the person to act as president pro tempore may be made by the Senate Majority Leader or Minority Leader. Among a panel of judges, one is usually designated to preside or is determined by custom (owing usually to seniority) as the presiding judge.

**president** The leader of an organization. A president is an officer of an organization who directs the manner in which business is to be transacted. In a corporation, the president might or might not be the chief operating officer, and although the president in some corporations presides over meetings of the directors, in others there is a distinct office of chair of the board of directors.

Among nation-states, a president is a head of state. Most presidents are not also head of government, a post usually held by a prime minister. The President of the United States is both head of state and head of government.

**President of the United States of America (POTUS)** The head of state and head of government of the United States of America. The President of the United

States of America is the person in whom the executive power of the United States is vested. The presidency is described in the U.S. Constitution, and the authority of the office is largely set out in Article Two. Besides ensuring the defense of the Constitution, the president is to ensure that the laws are faithfully executed, to serve as commander in chief, and to direct the foreign affairs of the nation. The president appoints executive officers, ambassadors, and judges, though all but lower level executive officers must be confirmed by vote of the Senate. There are many other constitutional, statutory, and customary duties of the office. The official residence is the White House, which was initially known as the Executive Mansion.

The president must be a natural-born citizen, fourteen years a resident of the United States, and at least thirty-five years old. The president is elected by the Electoral College following a popular vote in November of every leap year. The president is required to take a specific oath of office prior to assuming the duties of the presidency. If the President resigns, dies, becomes incapacitated or is impeached, according to the Twentieth and Twenty-Fifth Amendments, the Vice President would become President. A line of succession in the event of multiple vacancies was established by Congress in the Presidential Succession Law of 1947, which works as follows: after the Vice President comes the Speaker of the House of Representatives, then the President pro Tempore of the Senate, then members of the Cabinet in this order: Secretary of State, Secretary of the Treasury, Secretary of Defense, Attorney General, Secretary of the Interior, Secretary of Agriculture, Secretary of Commerce, Secretary of Labor, Secretary of Health & Human Services, Secretary of Housing & Urban Development, Secretary of Transportation, Secretary of Energy, Secretary of Education, Secretary of Veterans' Affairs, and Secretary of Homeland Security.

**Electoral College (presidential elector)** The 535 individuals who elect the President and Vice-President. The Electoral College is a group of individual electors, each appointed by the legislature of a state according to the number of members of Congress from both houses who are allocated to that state. The presidential electors meet approximately a month after a Presidential election and cast the votes that elect the President and Vice-President. Every state selects electors according to the popular election held within that state on the day of the national presidential election. Potential electors in each state are designated to vote for a presidential candidate who is selected according to which presidential candidate receives the most votes, or a certain percentage of votes, in the election in that state. Thus citizens voting for a presidential candidate are in fact voting to designate the electors in their jurisdiction who are designated to vote in the electoral college for that candidate. States vary in the detail of their instructions to the state's electors, and it is not constitutionally certain the degree to which a state may demand an elector cast a vote

in accordance with the outcome of the popular vote.

**unitary executive (unitary theory or unitary presidency)** The degree to which the president may act alone. The theory of the unitary executive is a controversial theory regarding the scope of presidential authority, which became influential in the late twentieth century. As asserted by some presidents, notably President George W. Bush, the doctrine would justify presidential interpretations of any executive power or action arising from a statute, treaty, or constitutional power, without oversight by Congress or the Courts. This broad power was defended by some as essential to the office of president, particularly a president during war, but it was widely rejected by scholars and judges. The theory is sometimes anachronistically rooted in the decision of the framers to have one person as president rather than a triumvirate or other power-sharing group. In its much more widely accepted form, the unitary executive stands merely for the idea that the president maintains authority over all executive agencies and presidential powers.

*See also:* government, forms of government, tyranny (tyrant).

**White House (Executive Office of the President)** The administrative office of the President of the United States. The White House is both the official residence and physical office of the President of the United States and the seat of the administration of the executive branch of the federal government. The White House is administered by the Executive Office of the President, which in turn is administered by the Chief of Staff. Its address is The White House, 1600 Pennsylvania Avenue NW, Washington, D.C. 20500.

Other agencies that report directly to the President, rather than being created as an independent agency or department, are said to be White House agencies and are within the Executive Office of the President. Such offices are created by statute or executive order and are moved or recreated with some frequency. In 2011, they include the Council of Economic Advisers, Council on Environmental Quality, Domestic Policy Council, National Economic Council, National Security Council, Office of Administration, Office of Management and Budget, Office of National Drug Control Policy, Office of Science and Technology Policy, Office of the United States Trade Representative, President's Economic Recovery Advisory Board, President's Intelligence Advisory Board and Intelligence Oversight Board, White House Military Office, and White House Office. Other offices of the White House include staff offices in support of policy and operations.

**Office of Management and Budget (OMB)** A White House agency that manages spending in other agencies and departments. The Office of Management and Budget (OMB) is an executive agency in the White House that assists the president in the creation of the budget and its submission to

Congress, and coordinates executive policies regarding spending, budget, and policy, among the various other agencies of the executive branch. The OMB includes the Office of Information and Regulatory Affairs.

**Office of Information and Regulatory Affairs (OIRA)** The White House office that approves all federal regulations. The Office of Information and Regulatory Affairs, or OIRA, is a White House office within the Office of Management and Budget (OMB) that reviews and approves all of the regulations to be promulgated by executive agencies in the federal government. Besides ensuring that the regulations accord with the acts of Congress and executive orders that govern them, OIRA provides coordination of executive policies that are manifest in agency discretion.

*See also:* value, cost–benefit analysis (CBA).

**presidential immunity** *See:* immunity, official immunity, presidential immunity.

**press (member of the press)** One who publishes news and opinions to the public. The press are the individuals and entities who gather, report, and publish news and opinions for the benefit of the public or some segment of the public as a whole. Although the customary model of the press would be those who wrote in and published pamphlets and newspapers in the late eighteenth century, the boundary of the press as a matter of law is very imprecise. To start, the scope of what amounts to news or to opinion is difficult to specify, generally including all facts and perceptions regarding people, things, places, and events. Although the manner, extent, frequency and means of such publication influence the idea of what person or entity is within the press and not, there are no standards that establish absolutely a defining boundary. Various entities and offices establish differing criteria regarding those to whom they will issue press credentials, which are a pass allowing those holding them access to areas or events, yet these are a matter of the policy of the entity or agency that issues them rather than a matter of law.

The freedom of the press is assured in the United States by the First Amendment, which limits prior restraints on publication by the press, limits the liability of members of the press and press organizations for claims of libel, defamation, or similar torts, although it provides no privilege of access to government or private information that is not assured to members of the public as a whole.

*See also:* media (press).

**freedom of the press (liberty of the press)** The government may not interfere with the press without very good cause. The freedom of the press limits the federal and state governments from unjustified prior restraint of the press and restricts regulation and litigation that would interfere with the operation of the press. Claims and litigation arising from past publication in the press are not barred by freedom of the press, but the press enjoys some immunity from such claims and judgments by virtue of the protection of the freedoms of speech and other liberties. Freedom of the press does not, in itself, give a right of access to information, although statutes, such as the Freedom of Information Act may give such access to the public, which cannot be then denied to the press.

*See also:* information, Freedom of Information Act (F.O.I.A. or FOIA or Foiable); libel (libelous); libel, seditious libel.

**shield laws** Laws allowing reporters to conceal a source's identity. Shield laws are statutory privileges enacted in some states, allowing reporters to protect the identity of a person who reveals information to the reporter. Statutes vary with the scope of this privilege, but it is usually applied for information in the public interest when the source fears retaliation for the disclosure. State shield laws are not usually a privilege against disclosure in federal court, and some state shield laws do not bar disclosure to law enforcement personnel.

**presumption (presume or presumed or presumptive)** A conclusion inferred from sufficient but inconclusive evidence. A presumption is a finding of fact derived from evidence that would not otherwise be sufficient to demonstrate the finding conclusively, but which reaches a threshold of sufficiency to be accepted as a fact. Presumptions in the law are routinely described as of two sorts, presumptions of fact and presumptions of law, though presumptions of law are now quite rare. Presumptions of fact fall mainly into two categories: first, when a statutory or customary presumption arises related to a given question or from certain forms of evidence; and second, when a prima facie case is made, in which a sufficient level of evidence is presented to make likely a given conclusion on a wide variety of causal theories. The most famous presumption in criminal law is that the defendant is innocent of the crime, a presumption that can only be rebutted by proof beyond a reasonable doubt. The most famous presumption in civil actions is res ipsa loquitur—that something which could not have occurred but for negligence by a given actor did occur, thus giving rise to a presumption of that actor's negligence.

Presumptions may be (1) permissive, which is to say that in the absence of evidence contradicting the presumptive conclusion, the finder of fact may be allowed to accept the presumed conclusion as true or to reject it, or (2) mandatory, requiring the finder of fact to accept it unless sufficient evidence disproves it. In the Federal Rules of Evidence, presumptions created by federal law are permissive, because the burden of proof does not shift to the rebutting party.

Presumptions are either absolute and cannot be rebutted (which is rare) or rebuttable (which is usually the case). A rebuttable presumption may be rebutted by sufficient evidence that contradicts the premise or the conclusion drawn from the initial evidence. After a presumption is rebutted, the question of fact must be determined according to the persuasive value of the evidence regarding each theory of the case. The sufficiency of the evidence may vary with the presumption and the standard of proof required in the cause of action.

See also: evidence, presumptive evidence (presumption).

**presumed damages** See: damages, classes of damages, general damages (presumed damages).

**presumed father** See: family, father, presumed father (presumed paternity).

**presumed intent** See: intent, constructive intent (presumed intent).

**presumed knowledge** See: knowledge, constructive knowledge (presumed knowledge, presumptive knowledge).

**presumed paternity** See: family, father, presumed father (presumed paternity).

**presumption of death** See: death, presumption of death.

**presumption of innocence** See: innocence, presumption of innocence.

**presumptive evidence** See: evidence, presumptive evidence (presumption).

**presumptive knowledge** See: knowledge, constructive knowledge (presumed knowledge, presumptive knowledge).

**bursting-bubble theory (Thayerian rule)** A presumption dispelled by any credible evidence to the contrary. The bursting–bubble theory is a type of factual presumption in which the presumption is established by the party seeking to establish a fact presumed from predicate evidence of other facts from which an inference may support the fact presumed. If the other party introduces any credible evidence to the contrary, regarding either the presumed fact or the credibility of the predicate evidence, then the presumption is no longer established, and the parties must each prove their case as well as they can from the evidence. In other words, the bubble created by the presumptive evidence is burst.

**conflicting presumptions (competing presumptions)** Presumptions requiring opposing conclusions in the same issue. Conflicting presumptions arise in a single action when distinct facts or claims give rise to several distinct presumptions of fact, and at least one presumption would suggest a conclusion of fact contrary to that suggested by another presumption, so that the presumptions were in conflict. In such a case, if one presumption is based on a policy or legal doctrine more fundamental than the other, that presumption should prevail. Thus, an evidentiary presumption in a criminal trial that would conflict with the presumption of innocence is not to be applied in the case. If both doctrines are effectively equivalent in the significance of their underlying policies, and there is no logical means of reconciling the presumption in the case, then usually neither presumption is conclusive, and the finder

of fact would have to determine which theory of the case is the more fully proved by the evidence without regard to either presumption.

**permissive presumption (mandatory presumption)** A presumption that a finder of fact may accept as true but is not obligated to accept as true. A permissive presumption is a presumption that the finder of fact may choose to accept or reject as the basis for a finding of fact in the light of the evidence, even in the absence of any evidence rebutting the presumption. In contrast, a mandatory presumption is binding on the finder of fact, and once the predicate required to establish the presumption applies in a case, unless sufficient evidence is presented that rebuts the presumption, the finder of fact has no option but to find the fact that is presumed. In criminal trials, the presumption of innocence is mandatory, but all other presumptions are permissive, and an attempt to establish by a mandatory presumption any fact that establishes guilt is an unconstitutional conflict with the presumption of innocence.

**rebuttable presumption** A presumption that may be rebutted by sufficient contrary evidence. A rebuttable presumption is a presumption that is conclusive until evidence sufficient to rebut its conclusion is introduced, at which time the presumption ceases to provide any weight beyond the weight inherent in the evidence from which the presumption first arose. For example, if a plaintiff introduces evidence of damage to a bailment, the evidence gives rise to a presumption by inference that the bailee was negligent in its care. If the bailee introduces evidence that the bailment was damaged at the time of the bailor's transfer of the property to the bailee, the presumption is rebutted, and the question goes forward as a dispute of fact as to the cause (or timing of the cause) of the damage, with no presumption favoring one theory or the other. A presumption based on a prima facie case may likewise be rebutted by evidence contradicting the prima facie evidence.

**irrebuttable presumption (conclusive presumption)** A presumption that may not be rebutted. An irrebuttable presumption is an inference that, as a matter of law, can never be rebutted. Many presumptions in the common law that could not be rebutted have been overturned, such as a presumption of consent to intercourse by one spouse toward another, which is no longer accepted as a lawful presumption. Many more are now understood in ways other than as a presumption, such as the presumption that a child lacks criminal capacity, which is more often thought to be an aspect of the substantive law of capacity than of presumption.

An irrebuttable presumption in a criminal action may amount to a violation of due process. The defendant has the right to force the state to prove its case, and the use of an irrebutable presumption, at least as to proof of the crime, would allow proof of one fact by the prosecution would have the effect of proving a second fact by inference, with no opportunity for the defense to disprove the second fact. Such an effect would both reduce the burden of proof and compromise the right of the defendant to present a defense.

**statutory presumption**  A presumption established in a statute or its interpretation. A statutory presumption is a presumption that is required by statute, by which an agency or court is to presume some condition to be true or false or some fact to establish another fact, unless there is evidence to the contrary sufficient to defeat the presumption and require a conclusion to be drawn from the proof available (which might, or might not, agree with the presumed conclusion). A statutory presumption may be expressed in the text of the statute or arise through its interpretation.

**pretermission**  The deliberate disregard of something or someone. Pretermission is an intentional disregard of something that might otherwise be the object of particular attetion. In procedure, a pretermission is an argument, claim, or defense in an action that is omitted or expressly disregarded in favor of a different position. A court may pretermit an argument owing to a logically prior argument that would resolve the pretermitted argument, and a litigant may ask the court to pretermit one or more aspects of an opponent's action on such a basis. The most well known form of pretermission, however, is the deliberate omission of a child from one's last will and testament, the omitted person being a pretermitted heir or pretermitted child.

**pretermitted child**  *See:* heir, pretermitted heir (pretermitted child).

**pretermitted heir**  *See:* heir, pretermitted heir (pretermitted child).

**pretext (pretextual)**  A false reason for an action intended to distract from its true cause. A pretext is a reason falsely asserted as the justification for, or cause of, some action, particularly in order to obscure the real cause or purpose for which the action was performed or in order to obscure the absence of any real cause or purpose. Derived from Latin for what comes first, a pretext is a facade, a false purpose.

**pretextual arrest**  *See:* arrest, pretextual arrest (pretextual stop).

**pretextual justification**  *See:* discrimination, pretextual reason (pretextual justification).

**pretextual reason**  *See:* discrimination, pretextual reason (pretextual justification).

**pretextual stop**  *See:* arrest, pretextual arrest (pretextual stop).

**pretrial (pretrial practice or pre-trial)**  Motions, hearings, and negotiations prior to trial. Pretrial is the period between the filing of the initial pleading and the commencement of the trial in any action, and pretrial practice describes the legal work required to manage the

case during this time. The major components of pretrial include motions practice, discovery, and trial preparation. The goal of pretrial as a matter of procedure is to ensure that an action that reaches trial is a real dispute of law based on genuine questions of material fact, which can be effectively presented, that the evidence is efficiently presented and considered, and that a verdict is effectively reached.

Many actions conclude during pre-trial. The careful practitioner will attempt to win the action on motion, if possible, or via a favorable settlement or plea agreement, if possible, while managing the tactics of motions and discovery and while preparing comprehensively for trial.

Note: pre-trial is both a noun and an adjective. The term pretrial, when used as a noun alone (as in "we'll take care of that at pre-trial"), usually refers to a pretrial conference.

**pretrial attachment or pre-trial attachment**  *See:* attachment (pretrial attachment or pre-trial attachment).

**pretrial conference (pretrial memorandum or pretrial conference)**  A meeting to plan the trial and resolve open issues. A pretrial conference is a conference held prior to trial by the judge with the counsel for all parties in order to discuss and negotiate the specific components of the trial. The function varies somewhat for a pretrial conference before a criminal trial from that before a civil trial. Yet in each, the lawyers are likely to present their witness lists, a round of objections to particular witnesses or testimony, their evidence lists, a round of objections to particular evidence or its intended use, and proposed jury instructions. The conference must be attended by at least one lawyer for each party to the trial. The agenda of the pretrial conference is usually set by the judge according to the rules of procedure and local rules. The recurrent purpose of such meetings, however, is to encourage settlement discussions in civil actions or plea discussions in criminal actions, and in the absence of such a resolution, to promote as many stipulated facts and agreed questions of law as possible between the parties.

In the federal system and most state systems, each attorney for a party must file a pretrial memorandum at some time prior the pretrial conference (which is usually set in a scheduling order). Although contents vary from court to court, the contents are usually specified by local rules or court order, mostly requiring the memorandum to set out the party's theory of the case, including a memorandum of law that is submitted with the pretrial memorandum or under separate cover, the claims or defenses that are to be litigated according to it, the evidence to be offered, and outstanding motions requiring judicial attention. After the pretrial conference, the judge will issue a pretrial order setting forth the issues to be proved and integrating the proof to be presented by each side, as established at the conference.

Note: when a lawyer or judge says something was done at pretrial or is to be done at pretrial, such phrases usually refer to the pretrial conference.

Note, too: there is no difference between the hyphenated or unhyphenated form of the term.

**pretrial detention**   *See:* detention, pretrial detention.

**pretrial disclosure**   *See:* disclosure, discovery disclosure, pretrial disclosure.

**pretrial diversion or pre-trial diversion**   *See:* diversion (pretrial diversion or pre-trial diversion).

**pretrial motion**   *See:* motion, pre-trial motion (pre-trial motion).

**pretrial order**   An order setting the agenda for a trial. A pretrial order is an order entered prior to trial to prepare the court and the parties to present their theories and evidence efficiently. The order varies according to its character as criminal or civil. A pretrial order in a criminal case usually specifies the discovery and motions to be completed prior to a pretrial conference, and requires specific preparation by counsel for the conference. A civil pretrial order will usually set the agenda for the trial itself, including (1) the issues to be tried; (2) the issues that are stipulated or admitted; (3) the evidence to be presented, including the specific witnesses, exhibits and their intended function in support of each party's theory of the case; (4) the expected time each party will require for the presentation of their evidence, and (5) the remedy each seeks.

**pre-trial relief**   *See:* remedy, pre-judgment remedy (pre-trial relief).

**prevail (prevailing party)**   To gain relief from a civil action. To prevail is to be the stronger party, and to be the prevailing party in a civil action is to be the party who wins the action, either through settlement or judgment and order. Determining who wins may be difficult, however, particularly in the event of a compromise or in a complex case in which many issues are raised, and in such cases, a party may prevail on one issue but not others. Thus, it is possible that for an action as a whole, several opposing parties may each prevail, at least for one or another element of the action.

In actions that allow attorney fee shifting, the prevailing party may be entitle to attorney's fees from the losing party. In such instances, the questions by which a party is said to prevail are whether the party received a judgment to the party's benefit, either by order based on a settlement or on a motion or trial, and whether the order materially alters the party's legal relationship, either to the other party or in a manner sought through the litigation.

**prevarication (prevaricate)**   To evade the truth of the matter in issue. Prevarication is the act of hiding the truth in speech or writing. Prevarication might be done though a bald-faced lie, or by subtle omission, by true statements creating a false impression, or by any number of means by which the truth of the matter at hand is deliberately obscured.

*See also:* perjury (perjure).

**preventive detention**   *See:* detention, preventive detention (confinement after acquittal on grounds of insanity).

**price (sale price)**   The value of consideration given for a purchase. Price is the value of consideration in money or other property that is given from the buyer to the seller for the purchase of a thing. Although not specifically property, assuming a liability of a seller is also treated as providing consideration in connection with a purchase.

Metaphorically, a price describes any quid pro quo, anything given in expectation of a return, such as a duty or opportunity that one forgoes or impliedly trades in return for a preferment or opportunity.

Note: there is no difference between price and sale price.

**price to earnings ratio**   *See:* share, share as stock, shareholder value, price to earnings ratio (P/E or PE ratio).

**Consumer Price Index (CPI)**   An average price of common goods and services. The Consumer Price Index is a measure of an average price paid by consumers in the United States for staples and basic needs, which is measured by a basket of goods and services common to most consumers in attempt to ascertain and report the changes in prices paid by consumers for goods and services. Milk is a typical item that is included in the Consumer Price Index (CPI). Movement in the CPI is a gauge of inflation or deflation.

**discriminatory price (discriminatory pricing)**   Two different prices for the same goods or services offered to competing buyers. A discriminatory price is a price that varies according to the buyer, i.e., a price that is set not by the value of the goods or services sold but by the identity of the purchaser, as opposed to others. Discriminatory pricing is not illegal in itself, although it may be used as part of an illegal scheme to create a monopoly or to further other illegal anti-competitive practices.

**escalating price (laddering or escalator clause)**   A price that varies in time or according to change in a benchmark outside the contract. An escalating price is a price that rises or falls according to an escalator clause in a contract — typically, though not necessarily, a lease, services, or commodities contract — which provides the price to be paid to the seller or lessor will rise over time, either by a fixed amount or percentage per unit of time or by reference with an external benchmark. Examples of such benchmarks include the Consumer Price Index, a regulated level of increase set by law, or a benchmark price for a commodity or security on a given exchange. When securities are offered for sale only in a series of purchases at escalating prices, this is laddering and a discriminatory pricing practice.

**excessive pricing (gouging or price gouging)** Setting an price unreasonably high for the value of the good or service. Excessive pricing, or setting a price for a good or service unreasonably high when compared to its value or cost may violate anti-competition law and other regulations in the European Union, while in the United States, it may be a factor indicating the existence of a predatory or monopolistic practice forbidden by U.S. anti-trust law. For regulated industries or sales, an excessive price may be directly forbidden by state regulation or federal law.

Note: informally, excessive pricing is known as price gouging, particularly when the excessive price is set during a period of sudden scarcity during an emergency.

**predatory pricing (excessively low pricing)** Discriminatory or below-cost price intended to harm a competitor. Predatory pricing is the setting of the price of a good or category of goods either below the seller's cost or at a discriminatory price, usually one below the price offered to the buyer's competitor in a limited market, so that the seller not only captures market share but also causes the competitor to compete by lowering prices to a level that ensures it operates at a loss, so that its business will be harmed or fail. This allows a well capitalized predatory business to price below the market for a time, capture the market, then establish a local monopoly and raise prices above the market. Predatory pricing violates anti-trust rules under the Robinson–Patman Act, 15 U.S.C. § 13(a) (2010), as well as the laws regulating trade in many states.

Predatory pricing does not, however, bar all pricing below cost, and the pricing of some goods for sale below cost as "loss-leaders" to attract customers is not predatory. So long as the price of the average of goods likely to be purchased is not below cost or there is no evidence of intent to harm the business potential of competitors, the pricing is not predatory.

**horizontal price fixing** An agreement among competitors to fix the prices of goods or services in the same market. Horizontal price fixing includes any means by which two or more entities who otherwise are competitors to provide goods or service to the market agree, expressly or impliedly, on a price range in which the goods or service will be provided, either as a means of restricting competition or as a means of establishing a monopoly. Horizontal price fixing is a classic violation of anti-trust law.

**price war** Price competition between sellers or between buyers. A price war is a competition for market share between two or more sellers of the same commodities, who reflexively drop their prices to undercut their rivals, each attempting to lure buyers from the other. Price wars may lead to sales below cost by all sides, a condition that will likely prove unsustainable for any length of time. A price war is not inherently illegal, although when one party with greater capital or access to capital participates in a price war in a predatory manner, its conduct may violate antitrust rules.

**price-fixing** Agreement by competitors or suppliers that sets the retail prices. Price-fixing is an arrangement by which the prices to be charged to buyers or consumers of particular goods or services are set by arrangements between the seller and either competing sellers or vendors to the seller. Price fixing, with rare exception, violates antitrust rules, notably Section 1 of the Sherman Act.

**vertical price-fixing (resale price maintenance)** A supplier's requiring vendors to sell its goods at a specified price. Vertical price-fixing, or a resale price maintenance scheme, is a pattern of contracts by the supplier of a particular good or commodity that require all of the vendors or distributors whom it supplies to agree to a specified price or price range for the good or commodity. The specification is usually contractual, and usually enforced by the threat that the supplier will withdraw or withhold its supply of the good or commodity to a vendor or distributor who does not agree to, and abide by, the scheme.

A vertical price-fixing arrangement is not illegal per se under the anti-trust law but subject to the rule of reason. If the price-fixing arrangement is no more than the seller maintaining its price, it is reasonable. But, if the arrangement is intended to create a monopoly for its goods, or restrict competition or fix prices among competitors amounting to horizontal price-fixing, then the arrangement is ureasonable and illegal.

*See also:* agreement, vertical agreement.

**support price (price support)** Government action sustaining a market price. Price supports are a range of governmental actions by which the price for a given commodity is maintained within a range of values or above or below a particular price point. Price supports include government purchases, subsidies, and insurance, as well as mandated prices below or above which a purchase is either unenforceable or illegal. A support price is the price at which a given program becomes operable, such as the price of a good below which an insurance claim may be made, or the price above which a contract is void.

*See also:* subsidy (subsidize).

**transfer price (transfer pricing)** The price charged for goods moved between related corporate entities. The transfer price is the value assessed for goods, services, or intangibles that are moved from the inventory of one corporation, division, or subsidiary, into the inventory of a related entity within the same corporate group. Transfer prices are particularly essential for taxation when salable interests move from one tax jurisdiction into another. Regulators attempt to ensure that all transfer pricing is in approximate accord with the market value of the interests priced.

**priest-penitent privilege**   See: privilege, evidentiary privilege, priest-penitent privilege (clerical privilege or minister's privilege).

**prima (primo)**   First. Prima, or primo, is Latin for the first, whether the the first in time, precedence, or order, or in a more metaphorical sense, at the beginning or at a preliminary stage to something else, such as a primary.

> **prima facie case of discrimination**   See: discrimination, employment discrimination, prima facie case of discrimination.

> **prima facie evidence**   See: evidence, prima facie evidence.

> **prima facie tort**   See: tort, prima facie tort.

> **prima facie**   On first consideration. Prima facie is Latin and is customarily translated as "at first blush," "at first sight," "on first appearance," or "on the face of it." Prima facie describes the initial presentation of evidence or argument. Depending on context, prima facie usually demonstrates either that sufficient evidence exists to support an action or that sufficient evidence for a particular claim or defense is presented to create a presumption. If so, then if evidence is not presented that rebuts the prima facie evidence, either the action is successful or the presumption is accepted as fact.
> See also: prima, prima facie, prima facie case.

> **prima facie case**   The introduction of credible evidence to prove every element of a claim or defense. A prima facie case is evidence required to satisfy every element of a cause of action or every element of an affirmative defense. The evidence offered must appear sufficient to satisfy the burden of proof required to sustain the action, defense, or case as a whole. Once a party establishes a prima facie case in a civil action, that party will win its claim or defense unless the other party introduces evidence to rebut the first party's case through a contradiction of evidence, a defense of fact or of law, or the impeachment of the credibility of the evidence. In a criminal action, no prima facie case can establish the defendant's guilt owing to the presumption of innocence.
> See also: prima, prima facie; flagrante delicto (in flagrante delicto or red handed).

**primary (primarily)**   First, most basic, or most important. Primary is a relative designation for something that occurs first, or has a greater significance, priority, or precedence than other similar things. There is an inherent ambiguity in the sense of primary as between (1) something that is first in order among several ordered things, (2) something that is a foundation or fundamental in relation to other things, (3) something that is first among equals, and (4) something of overwhelming significance. Primary is used in law in all of these senses.

A primary election, for instance, is first in order because it precedes a general election (allowing parties to nominate their candidates to run in the general races).

A primary school occurs in order before a secondary school, though the sense of primary in this sense also includes primary's sense as fundamental.

The primary reason or primary offense among several is the reason of greatest significance or salience among the reasons or offenses. It need not represent the majority or greatest part of the motivation of a person or group, but it must represent the largest or most animating motivation.

There are many cases of a dichotomy between something primary that is overwhelming or defining, and the other illustrations that are so defined. For example, the primary authority of an agent determines the scope of the agent's authority, while the mediate authority includes the incidental powers that need not be designated but by implication in the dedication of primary authority.

Primary authority in law represents materials in which law is created or applied, such as constitutions, statutes, case opinions, and contracts. Secondary authority is derived from such materials, such as treatises and commentaries. This hierarchy is not perfect, and secondary authority may be a persuasive source of law, even when it is to the contrary of primary authority.
See also: diplomat, diplomatic precedence (diplomatic rank or diplomatic staff).

> **primary good or fundamental good**   See: good, basic good (primary good or fundamental good).

> **primary implied assumption of risk**   See: risk, assumption of risk, implied assumption of risk, primary implied assumption of risk.

> **primary offense**   See: offense, primary offense.

> **primary offense as traffic offense**   See: offense, traffic offense, primary offense as traffic offense (secondary offense).

> **primary rule**   See: rule, legal rule, primary rule; jurisprudence, legal positivism, primary rule.

**prime rate**   See: rate, interest rate, prime rate.

**primo**   See: prima (primo).

**primogeniture**   The descent of a whole estate to the first born. Primogeniture is the system by which a family's estate would descend at the death of a parent to the first-born child, usually the first-born son, who was responsible for the maintenance of the other members of the family. If the first-born son died before his father, the next son would be the sole heir, and if the two eldest sons had died then a third might take the estate, but if no sons survived the father, then the estate passed to the eldest daughter or, if she were dead, to a younger sister. This system maintained large estates, preserving them from fragmentation at the transition from one generation to the next, while ensuring that the land was held by a male, who was presumed capable of rendering military service as well as furnishing additional men for military service from those working on his lands. It also perpetuated a hierarchy within families in which women and younger siblings remained dependent on the oldest male of each generation. Primogeture was abolished in the United States at the time of the American Revolution. It became increasingly rare in England after the Statute of Wills (1540), but did not disappear entirely until 1925.

*See also:* will, Statute of Wills (Wills Act).

**primogenitus (primogenita)**  The first-born child. The primogenitus is a person's first-born son, or more generally the first-born child. The primogenita is the first-born daughter. Primogenitus refers also to the birthright or inheritance ascribed to the first born.

**principal**  A fundamental element, or a leading person. Principal denotes a variety of things and persons in the law, though each is primary either in status or authority or in order or development. Thus, a person who is a principal is a person with the highest level of responsibility, whether an institutional officer (such as the principal who is the head of a school), the superior to an agent, or the most liable person in a criminal act. Principal in finance is the core value of an asset from which interest or derivatives are created or computed. Principal as a relative depiction marks someone in charge or in a position of responsibility; or something fundamental, earlier in time, or primary relative to other derivative or later things.

Note: principal (the leader or the fundamental) is often confused with principle (the moral rule, or undeniable argument); in an age of nearly universal education, the phrase "principled principal" meaning a head teacher with sound morals, may help.

*See also:* principle (principled); principle (principled).

**principal officer**  *See:* officer, federal officer, principal officer.

**principal place of business**  *See:* business, place of business, principal place of business (corporate domicile).

**co-principals (coprincipal)**  Two or more who share authority and liability as principal. Co-principals are individuals or entities who are each jointly principal for whatever purpose one is a principal. As to an agency, co-principals each have authority to instruct the agent and each are represented and liable for the agent's actions. As to a criminal act, each are actors in the criminal act, and each is a co-principal of the other and as fully liable for the conduct of the other co-principals as if each had committed the same acts.

**criminal principal**  The person who performs or causes a criminal act. A principal, in the criminal law, is the actor who causes the violation of the criminal law, as opposed to an accessory who merely assists the principal. A principal may physically participate in the criminal act, may induce others to commit the crime, or may perform one act among several that are in sum the crime.

The common law distinguished between principals in the first and second degree. Principals in the first degree committed the act, and principals in the second degree directly aided or abetted the act. Most jurisdictions now treat principals in the second degree as accomplices or accessories.

**partially disclosed principal**  A principal who is known to exist but unidentified. A partially disclosed principal is a principal whose existence, but not identity, is known by other parties negotiating or entering a transaction with the principal's agent.

**undisclosed principal**  Principal whose existence and identity are unknown. An undisclosed principal is one whose existence and identity are unknown to a party to a transaction with the principal's agent. This arrangement is problematic for agents because agents are held liable for transactions entered into on behalf of an undisclosed principal.

**principle (principled)**  An argument that is so apparently true it is practically beyond dispute. A principle is an idea that is understood to be true, particularly an idea that reflects a moral or ethical idea of right or good conduct that is not open to rational objection. Principle, in law, has come to mean some moral or logical basis for decision, which may be applied with consistency, particularly in isolating rules from the legal materials. Thus, a principled distinction or principled decision is one that is based on a rationale that is capable of consistent, repetitive use in later decisions on related questions, as opposed to an arbitrary rationale that is deployed to justify a preferred result.

*See also:* principal.

**principle of right**  *See:* justice, rawlsian justice, principle of right (first principle of justice).

**prior**  Before. Prior means before, or earlier. The term has a particular significance in law because prior also means superior in any instance when the first in time prevails. For instance, a prior lien on a piece of real estate is superior to a later lien, i.e., the prior lien will be paid first (and likely will be the only lien repaid).

*See also:* a, a posteriori (a postiori).

**prior appropriation doctrine**  *See:* river, riparian, riparian ownership, prior appropriation doctrine.

**prior consistent statement**  *See:* hearsay, hearsay exclusion, prior statement by witness, prior consistent statement.

**prior inconsistent statement**  *See:* hearsay, hearsay exclusion, prior statement by witness, prior inconsistent statement.

**prior restraint**  *See:* restraint, prior restraint.

**prior restraint of speech**  *See:* speech, regulation of speech, prior restraint of speech.

**prior statement by witness**  *See:* hearsay, hearsay exclusion, prior statement by witness, prior inconsistent statement; hearsay, hearsay exclusion, prior statement by witness, prior consistent statement;

hearsay, hearsay exclusion, prior statement by witness.

**priority**  An order of precedence. Priority is the precedence of one thing or person before another, an order of significance: something that has priority over another is the more significant. Debts or claims of higher priority are to be satisfied before those of lower priority. Priority among heirs at law requires all heirs of the first degree alive at the death of an intestate to inherit the estate of an intestate, excluding all heirs of a lesser degree.

*See also:* subordination (equitable subordination or subordination agreement).

**priority claim**  *See:* bankruptcy, bankruptcy claim, priority claim.

**claim priority (priority of claims)**  The order in which claims against a bankrupt are to be satisfied before other claims. Claim priority, or the priority of claims in bankruptcy, is the statutory order of classifications of claims, by which unsecured claims within a given class of claims or expense that are pending against a bankrupt are to be fully paid from the bankruptcy estate before classes of lesser unsecured claims are to be paid. Under the Bankruptcy Code in 2010, the claims for domestic support are first, followed by administrative expenses of the bankruptcy, then unsecured claims for debts or damages, then for business debts to employees, then for employee pensions, then certain farmer's debts, then rents or services, then for back taxes, then for banking capital obligations, then for damages for personal injury or death from impaired operation or a vehicle or vessel.

**absolute priority rule**  Claims in each priority are fully paid before lesser claims. The absolute priority rule ensures that creditors in each category of priority will be paid before claims of the next priority. If the assets of the debtor are insufficient to pay all of the claims and expenses owed, the claims and expenses will be paid in each category, in full if possible, before paying any claims of lower priority.

**super priority**  A priority above others. Super priority is the priority assigned to a claim incurred by a trustee in bankruptcy in order to secure credit with which to operate the debtor's business. In such a case, the trustee may treat the claim as an administrative expense, or receive court permission to give the security a priority over secured liens on property, the result being that the priority of the new claim is higher than the highest priority claim that existed before.

**prison (penitentiary or reformatory)**  A facility for the long-term incarceration of criminal convicts. A prison is a facility for the long-term service of a sentence of penal servitude. As a practical matter, a prison is usually a facility owned, managed, or under the supervision of the federal or a state government. A jail, on the other hand, is usually owned, managed, or supervised by a county, parish, or municipal government. As a matter of design, prisons usually have a greater size and array of facilities for rehabilitation, prisoner recreation, prisoner counseling, and health care. Prisons are usually the location for the service of a sentence for a number of years, with shorter sentences served in a jail. Though the penitentiary was originally conceived of as an institution more fully dedicated to the reform, or penitence, of the convict than is a prison, this distinction is now largely obsolete, and there is rarely more than a customary difference in name between a prison and a penitentiary. A person who is convicted of a crime and sentenced to imprisonment may usually be committed to either a prison or a penitentiary, and in many jurisdictions, to a jail that is qualified to receive such prisoners.

Note: although the usage has varied over time and among jurisdictions, in contemporary usage, a reformatory is usually a place for the detention of minors or, in Ohio, of adult women.

*See also:* incarceration, imprisonment, imprisonment as criminal punishment.

**prison cell**  *See:* cell, prison cell (jail cell).

**prison mailbox rule**  *See:* mail, mailbox rule, prison mailbox rule.

**military prison**

**Guantanamo Bay (Camp Delta or Camp X-Ray)**  The U.S. naval station in Cuba holding detainees from 2001 onwards. Naval Station Guantanamo Bay is the home of the U.S. Joint Task Force that maintained, from 2001 to at least 2010, a detention facility to house prisoners transferred from Iraq, Afghanistan, and elsewhere, some of whom were believed to have committed crimes and some of whom were believed to have useful intelligence. A scandal involving the abuse of prisoners developed when intelligence officers and contractors there were accused of using techniques on detainees that were developed to train U.S. service members captured abroad to inure them to the effects of abuse and torture.

**private prison**  A prison owned or operated by a private entity. A private prison may or may not be owned by a government, but in either case it is operated by a corporation or other entity that enters into a contract with a government either to manage a facility or to house its prisoners for a fee. Private prisons are not immune from suit, and state-contracted prisons may be sued for deprivations of rights under color of state law under 42 U.S.C. §1983. Bivens actions and other claims that would ordinarily be brought against prison employees as governmental agents are usually unavailable against private guards, although state claims for negligence or intentional torts are usually available.

*See also:* civil rights, civil rights enforcement action, Bivens action; civil rights, civil rights enforcement action, 1983 action.

**prisoner (inmate)**  A person subject to detention by another. A prisoner is any person who is confined by the state or confined by another person against that prisoner's will. A prisoner may be illegally detained or confined, as is a victim of kidnapping or wrongful imprisonment. In most legal usage, however, a prisoner (or inmate) is lawfully detained, being in detention, jail, or prison, by a lawful arrest or court order. A person who is convicted of a criminal offense and sentenced to penal servitude becomes a prisoner in a jail or prison to serve out the sentence. A prisoner is denied or limited in most of the privileges and liberties of citizenship, such as the freedom of speech and the right to travel, but a prisoner retains fundamental rights, particularly the right to be free from cruel and unusual punishment.

*See also:* inmate; detention (detain or detainee).

**prisoner escape** *See:* escape, prisoner escape (escape from custody).

**prisoner of war** *See:* war, prisoner of war (POW or P.O.W.).

**prisoner retaliation action** *See:* retaliation, prisoner retaliation action.

**prisoner's dilemma** *See:* game, game theory, prisoner's dilemma.

**conjugal visit (overnight familial visit)** An authorized, intimate visit with an institutionalized person. A conjugal visit to an adult committed to an institution is an opportunity allowed by the institution for that person to have sufficient time and privacy to engage in sexual intimacy with a spouse or other adult. A conjugal visit is a form of family visit, which may include members of the institutionalized person's family other than a spouse, for which the institution provides a measure of privacy and time.

Conjugal visits with a spouse have been allowed in many state prison systems to prisoners who meet certain regulatory standards. Such visits are officially sanctioned either by administrative or judicial order, and the prisoner is usually transferred to a part of the facility designed to ensure the security of the guest and the privacy of both. There is no right of an inmate to such visitation, either under the prohibition against cruel and unusual punishment in the Eighth Amendment, the right of association, or due process of law. There is some controversy over whether incarceration amounts to a loss of the right to reproduce — temporarily for a person sentenced to a period of incarceration or in perpetuity for a person sentenced to life. The allowance of the conjugal visit is sometimes used as evidence in both sides of this debate.

Conjugal visits with an adult who is committed to an institution for the mentally or physically disabled, or for the elderly, have been declared by many states to a right of the adult, which the institution is required reasonably to respect and to facilitate.

*See also:* conjugal (conjugacy).

**prisoner at the bar (prisoner in the dock)** The criminal defendant in court during the trial. The prisoner at the bar is the defendant in a criminal trial. The term is particularly used to describe the statement of a defendant who has been convicted and who is afforded the right to make a statement to the court prior to sentencing. The phrase is loosely used to describe a criminal defendant throughout the trial. However, the phrase may be technically inaccurate, as many defendants are out on bail during trial and not actually prisoners, and it may be seen as prejudicial to the defense, summoning in the minds of the jurors the image of bars of a jail rather than the bar of the courtroom. In any event, the defendant is not usually at the bar but inside it, sitting at counsel's table. The phrase is probably an adaptation of the English phrase of the "prisoner in the dock" owing to English courtrooms that have a specific booth, called the dock, in which a defendant sits during a trial. American courtrooms usually lack this furnishing.

**trustee (trusty or trusties)** A prisoner accorded special privileges or duties. A trustee is a prisoner who has been evaluated by supervisors in the jail or prison as posing no threat of harm or escape and, consequently, has been accorded unusual privileges, such as the license to leave the facility unsupervised, or duties, such as the responsibility for performing support tasks in the jail or courthouse. Trustees are employed in part to reward model prisoner behavior, in part to perform services that otherwise would require more highly paid personnel, and in part to reduce facility overcrowding.

Note: different jurisdictions and facilities spell the term trusty or trustee, but there appears to be no functional difference in the role by either spelling; the plural of trusty is trusties.

*See also:* trustee.

**privacy** A person's liberty from intrusion or publicity. Privacy is a condition in which a person is free from the observation and knowledge of others, including governmental agents, in the person's place, actions, relations, thought, and speech. Privacy need not be absolute to exist, and one person may share private thoughts or spaces with a limited number of others without destroying the private nature of the thought or space, yet at some point that varies according to context, sufficient intrusion into the person's privacy has occurred that the privacy no longer persists.

Privacy is significant in several distinct senses in law. Privacy denotes what is not public, in that a private enterprise is not a public enterprise or that a private use of lands is not a public use of lands. Privacy is a designation of a variety of liberty interests, both in general as a barrier to regulation, and in particular as a barrier to certain police intrusions. Privacy is an interest protected by the common law from tortious invasion.

*See also:* trash (garbage); family, family planning, birth control.

**privacy interest** *See:* interest, privacy interest, abandonment of a privacy interest.

**invasion of privacy** The wrongful disturbance of a person's private life. Invasion of privacy is the intentional tort of unreasonable interference or intrusion into the private affairs of another person. Invasion may take many forms, including the physical intrusion or observation of a person engaged in conduct that is private as a matter of custom; the use of another person's name, appearance, or identity; unreasonable publicity of another person's private life or affairs; or the creation of publicity that places a person's actions or reputation in a false light before the public. Unjustified invasion of privacy is also a limitation on the conduct of police or government officials.

*See also:* voyeurism (voyeur).

**appropriation of likeness**  The unconsented use of a person's image for gain. Appropriation of likeness is a form of invasion of privacy, recognized in most jurisdictions as an independent tort, arising from a person's (a) use of an image, graphic, or representation that resembles another person; (b) for the user's advantage, whether for commercial gain or otherwise; (c) without the victim's consent; (d) in a manner that harms the victim. The plaintiff must prove a lack of consent. The outrage of the victim may be sufficient to demonstrate harm, although such dignitary interests are subordinate to the property interest that defines the tort.

**appropriation of name**  The use of a person's name for gain without consent. Appropriation of name is a form of invasion of privacy, recognized in most jurisdictions as an independent tort, arising from one person's use of an another person's name or identity; for the user's advantage, whether for commercial gain or otherwise; without the victim's consent; in a manner that harms the victim. The plaintiff must prove a lack of consent. The outrage of the victim may be sufficient to demonstrate harm, although such dignitary interests are subordinate to the property interest that defines the tort.

**false light**  Publicizing some matter to create a false and harmful impression. False light is both a theory of invasion of privacy and, in some jurisdictions, an independent cause of action, arising when a person (1) gives publicity to a matter concerning another person that places the victim before the public in a false light; (2) that would be highly offensive to a reasonable person; (3) when the person giving the publicity either had knowledge of the false light that would result or acted in reckless disregard of the falsity of the publicized matter or the false light in which the other would be placed.

*See also:* libel (libelous); slander (slanderer).

**intrusion upon solitude (intrusion upon seclusion)**  Tort of entry or spying on a person in private. Intrusion upon solitude is both a tort recognized independently in some jurisdictions and a form of invasion of privacy, caused by a person's entry or other intrusion into another person's private space, activities, or concerns, in a manner that a reasonable person would consider offensive. The form of intrusion may vary widely, including trespass, recording, broadcasting, electronic eavesdropping,

physical eavesdropping, the reading of apparently private papers by a person not authorized, the use of subterfuge for entry, and the exploitation of a license to enter premises for one reason used to gain information or to intrude into otherwise private areas. The intrusion's offensiveness may arise from a combination of factors, including illegality of the intrusion, the form of the intrusion, the degree to which the victim has sought to evade such intrusions, breach of confidence or trust by the intruder, and the nature of the private interests that are compromised.

**public disclosure of private facts**  Offensive disclosure of private information to the public without consent. Public disclosure of private facts is a form of the tort of invasion of privacy, recognized in a few jurisdictions as an independent tort, arising from a person's (a) public dissemination of information or matters concerning the private life of another; (b) done without the victim's consent; (c) if either the publication or the subject matter would be highly offensive to a reasonable person of ordinary sensibilities; and (d) the subject matter is not of legitimate public concern. The plaintiff must prove a lack of consent. The outrage of the victim may be sufficient to demonstrate harm, although such dignitary interests are subordinate to the property interest that defines the tort.

*Health Insurance Portablility and Accountability Act*  Healthcare providers and insurers may not usually disclose patient information. The Health Insurance Portability and Accountability Act (HIPPA) forbids a covered entity from disclosing protected health information to an entity other than the government or as required by law or authorized by the patient or needed for the patient's care, diagnosis, or treatment, or to facilitate billing and payment. Protected health information includes health status, treatment, and history, as well as payment information.

**right to privacy (right of privacy or privacy rights)**  The liberty from unjustified interference by the government or by other persons in one's personal affairs. The right to privacy is a liberty of the person to be free from unwanted scrutiny and interference from both the government and from private individuals. It is protected by constitutional law and by the common law of tort, and sometimes by statute.

The constitutional right to privacy is the right of the individual to be free from both government regulation of personal conduct and government intrusion—including surveillance and search of the person and areas in which reasonable persons would expect their privacy to be respected, unless there is a sufficient justification for the government's intrusion. A person's interests in privacy may be diminished or lost as the person participates in the public sphere—by becoming a public figure, for example, or engaging in acts or speech of public interest, in which case the privacy protection for acts related to such matters of interest may be diminished. The text of the U.S. Constitution does not refer directly to a right of privacy. The right has been interpreted as the collective sense, or penumbral meaning, of a variety of other rights that work to protect the privacy of the individual from state interference.

The right to privacy in the common law is protected by a variety of actions in tort from invasion, including the tort of invasion of privacy as well as the forms of action for public disclosure of private information, intrusion on solitude, intrusion into private affairs, false light publicity, appropriation of identity, and appropriation of likeness. Context is essential to distinguish the role privacy plays in such actions, as the scope of privacy that is protected in one context might not be the same as in others.

**expectation of privacy**   A person's reasonable and genuine belief in some space as private. An expectation of privacy is the basis for a person's privilege in a given space from unjustified governmental search or surveillance, which arises when the person has an actual, genuine expectation that the space would be private, and so shielded from public knowledge or view. This expectation must be reasonable and consonant with what members in the community would expect to be private. The privacy interest is personal, related to the person's expectations for a space, not the nature of the space in itself. The reasonableness aspect of the definition makes likely such an expectation will be protected, as Justice Harlan has said, in a home but not in a field.

**penumbra theory (penumbral right)**   Privacy arises from the periphery of enumerated rights. A penumbra is the periphery around a core, like the sun's corona. The penumbra of a right is the application of that right to protect conduct that is not principally the function of the right but a reasonable extension of the core function, which may indeed be necessary to achieve the purpose of the right. In Griswold v. Connecticut, 381 U.S. 479, 481–482 (1965), Justice Douglass argued that a right of privacy arises within the penumbras of the rights of the First Amendment, as the fundamental idea within the penumbras of rights within the First, Third, Fourth, Fifth, and Ninth Amendments. The right of privacy and any other concept of such rights are thus "penumbral rights."

**zone of privacy**   The constitutional extent of the right to privacy. The zone of privacy is a metaphor that is used to describe the extent of personal interests in which the right of privacy is protected from unjustified governmental interference. The zone is both physical, describing the extent of the home, car, or other place in which a person's privacy is to be recognized, and functional, describing the extent of the conduct, decision-making, or thought in which the privacy is to be recognized.

**private**   Neither public nor general. Private, in general, is the adjective signally an interest in privacy or

something cloaked in privacy. In law, however, private may have a particular significance as something specific to one person and not general, such as a private bill or private act in a legislature, or a private wrong, which is a tort rather than a public wrong. Private may designate non-public ownership, such as private property, a private road, or private house. And, private may designate something not open to public consumption or public subscription, such as a private transport carrier or a private bank.

**private act**   *See:* statute, private act (private law or private bill).

**private attorney general theory**   *See:* citizen, citizen suit, private attorney general theory.

**private carrier**   *See:* carrier (private carrier).

**private caucus**   *See:* mediation, private caucus.

**private international law**   *See:* conflict, conflicts of laws (private international law).

**private law as legislation**   *See:* law, private law as legislation.

**private law or private bill**   *See:* statute, private act (private law or private bill).

**private necessity**   *See:* necessity, private necessity, strict necessity; necessity, private necessity, reasonable necessity; necessity, private necessity (private way of necessity).

**private nuisance**   *See:* nuisance, private nuisance.

**private prison**   *See:* prison, private prison.

**private property**   *See:* property, private property.

**private trust**   *See:* trust, private trust.

**private way of necessity**   *See:* necessity, private necessity (private way of necessity).

**privateer**   A private vessel licensed by a state to seize the vessels of other states. A privateer is both a vessel and a captain, officer, or crewman of such a vessel, that is privately owned and commanded but that operates as a military vessel under the license and flag of a state, which authorizes the privateer to engage in military action against the vessels of other states and to seize them as prizes. The practice was widespread at the time of American independence, and the continental government authorized privateers in the absence of a significant American naval force. The U.S. Constitution gives the sole power to authorize privateers to the Congress, which may authorize privateers through the issuance of letters of marque and reprisal. Privateers at sea are now no longer lawful, having been banned under Hague Convention VII of 1907, the Convention Relating to the Conversion of Merchant Ships into War.

*See also:* prize, prize as captured vessel (prize vessel or law of prize); marque and reprisal.

**privation**   To lack the necessities of life. Privation in its narrowest sense is the condition of having something valued taken away, but it is more generally used to express the lack or denial of adequate food, drink, clothing, shelter, or human support and comfort, particularly for a child. Privation is the result of deprivation.

**privatization (privatize)** The transfer of government property or duties to private property or duties. Privatization is the conversion of property or a role or duty from the ownership or performance by a government to the ownership or performance by a private party. The conversion of a job or mission once performed by government personnel to performance by an entity under government contract is to privatize that job. The privatization of government work is considered by some to increase competitiveness and thus to spur efficiency and innovation, but it is considered by others to divert public funds for private profit and to risk public control over public assets or authority.

**privies** *See:* privy (privies).

**privilege** The legal assurance one may act or abstain without interference. A privilege is the legal power of an individual to do or to refrain from some action without any interference by a government or by another person. A privilege is personal, and in many instances a cause of action accrues to the person with a privilege against a person or entity that interferes with its exercise. Although a privilege is personal, it arises in most circumstances by a person's participation in a category of behavior to which a privilege is accorded by custom, although some privileges are extended universally by statute or constitutional fiat. Some privileges include: (a) constitutional privileges, available to all persons, such as the privilege against self-incrimination; (b) privileges of citizenship, such as the right to vote when a person is of age; (c) Privileges of public office, such as the congressional frank and immunity from suit; (d) privileges arising from litigation, such as the privilege of parties and witnesses to be free from defamation for statements under oath; and (e) privileges against giving evidence, such as the privileges asserted by spouses, clergy, lawyers, and others on behalf of their confidants.
*See also:* bar, admission to the bar, diploma privilege (diplomate privilege); discovery, discovery immunity (discovery privilege); privilege, evidentiary privilege, executive privilege; frank (congressional frank or frank privilege); immunity, discovery immunity, work-product immunity (work product immunity or work-product rule or work product privilege).

#### privilege against self-incrimination or right to silence
*See:* incrimination, self-incrimination (privilege against self-incrimination or right to silence).

**absolute privilege** A privilege without qualification or exception. An absolute privilege protects individuals in certain roles, making certain statements, or engaged in certain acts, from liability for defamation, negligence, or any other private cause of action, without qualification or exception. The absolute privilege extends to acts and statements made by legislators in the process of legislation; by judges,

litigants, and witnesses in the process of litigation; by governmental officers in the execution of their duties; and by military officers in the conduct of military affairs. The privilege is limited only to acts related to the purpose for which the privilege is extended in each case. The mere fact that a person is a judge or an official does not privilege every act or statement.
*See also:* privilege, litigation privilege (witness privilege or party privilege); privilege, conditional privilege.

**abuse of privilege (abuse of privileges)** The claim of a privilege for an improper purpose. Abuse of privilege is the attempt to do something according to a privilege for reasons or under circumstances that are improper, especially if the use of the privilege is contrary to the purpose for which the privilege exists, or the privilege is used to an extent that is not compatible with its purpose. Thus, a person with a privilege to use the property of another who uses that property for the sole purpose of vexing the owner abuses the privilege.
Abuse of privilege is grounds for denying a petition to appear in court in forma pauperis, because the petitioner has brought a great number of petitions already, all of them generally lacking merit.
Abuse of privileges is a ground for a citation within the prison system, given to an inmate who takes advantage of a privilege in some manner that is inconsistent with the nature of the privilege or the good order of the facility.
*See also:* indigency, in forma pauperis (I.F.P. or IFP).

**conditional privilege** A privilege that is forfeit if conditions are not met. A conditional privilege is a privilege that is not absolute under either of two circumstances, either a condition must be met in order for a person to enjoy the privilege, or the privilege applies or entity but may be lost in the event a condition is not fulfilled. Many privileges are conditional, such as the privilege of driving, which is conditioned upon satisfactory proof of age and fitness and completion of a driver's exam to commence, but which may be forfeit for unsafe driving.
Note: a conditional privilege differs from a qualified privilege, in that the satisfaction or non-satisfaction of its conditions determines whether or not a person or entity enjoys a privilege; a qualified privilege determines whether a privilege that does exist applies in a given situation. In many instances, though, particularly in the case law regarding privileged communications, this difference is immaterial. An absolute privilege is neither conditioned nor qualified.
*See also:* privilege, absolute privilege; qualification, qualification as condition (qualified right or qualified interest); condition (unconditional or conditional or defeasance).

**evidentiary privilege** A privilege to bar certain evidence from being required of oneself or another. An evidentiary privilege is the lawful power to refuse to give evidence or to require a court to prevent another person from giving evidence because the information sought as evidence, or the conditions affecting the person from which it is sought, require the privilege as a matter of the constitution, the common law, or sound policy of evidence. Privileged information is only admitted if the person who holds the privilege waives its exercise. There are a variety of such privileges, including customary privileges such as those arising from the immunity of a foreign head of state, constitutional privileges such as the privilege against self-incrimination, and common-law privileges such as those created by the drafting of legally required reports, and those allowed in communications between lawyer and client, doctor and patient, therapist and patient, husband and wife, and clergyman and believer. Other privileges relate to one's vote in an election, to trade secrets, to secrets of state and to executive information. Not every jurisdiction recognizes every privilege.

**accountant–client privilege**  A client's privilege to bar evidence given to the client's accountant. The accountant–client privilege bars evidence provided by a client to an accountant in the preparation of reports or books from discovery or admission in civil actions. The privilege is the client's, which the client may waive. The privilege is only recognized in some states and not in the federal courts, although it may be applied in federal court in diversity actions. The privilege does not extend to the preparation of federal tax filings.

*See also:* accountant (accountancy).

**attorney–client privilege**  A client's privilege to bar introduction or evidence given to the client's attorney. The attorney–client privilege bars introduction or evidence provided by a client to an attorney in the attorney's performance of legal services for the client. Services eligible for the privilege include counseling, preparation, or the representation (or preparation for the representation) of the the client in litigation, administrative matters, negotiations with other parties, or related matters. In some states, the privilege extends also to the attorney's communications with the client, although in other states such communications are only privileged when they reflect the client's own statements or information. The privilege is the client's, who may waive it, though it is of no application in a dispute between the client and the attorney. The privilege extends to communications with the attorney's agents, including paralegals and secretaries, but applies only to information provided to the attorney or the attorney's agents that is related to the representation of the client. The privilege is qualified, and an attorney is not barred by the privilege from disclosing information required: (a) to avert reasonably certain death or injury to the client, to the lawyer, or other others; (b) to prevent, mitigate, or rectify a serious crime or fraud by the client; (c) to secure advice about the extent of the privilege; (d) to defend the attorney from charges or claims arising from the representation; or (e) to comply with a court order. The privilege is to be narrowly construed, and doubts as to its applicability are to be resolved in favor of disclosure.

*government attorney*  A government attorney must disclose evidence of criminal conduct. The unusual role of the government attorney precludes the assertion of an attorney–client privilege in a manner that would prevent discovery of evidence that might reasonably be evidence of a criminal act by a government official. The client of the government attorney is the constitution itself and not an official, and in any event, no government official could lawfully fail to allow such information to be produced.

**work-product immunity and attorney client privilege**  *See:* immunity, discovery immunity, work-product immunity | attorney–client privilege and work product.

**crime-fraud exception**  An attorney must divulge information from a client to avert a serious crime or fraud. The crime–fraud exception to the attorney–client privilege requires an attorney to divulge information that arises in circumstances that otherwise would be privileged, but that is in furtherance of a crime or fraud by the client and is essential to the attorney's prevention, mitigation, or reparation of the client's wrongful act. Different jurisdictions have a narrower, and others a more expansive, definition.

**joint-defense privilege**  A privilege by one party to bar statements made to a joint defendant's attorney. The joint-defense privilege is a form of the attorney–client privilege that protects communications between an individual and the attorney representing another party, when the communications are made in conjunction with the development of a common or joint defense of the two parties to a single action or closely related actions. The privilege applies to statements by either party to counsel and not to statements between parties without counsel present, and it applies only to statements related to the defense or theories of defense made in support of the attorney's representation.

**counselor-patient privilege (psychotherapist privilege or therapist-patient privilege or psychiatrist privilege)**  A patient's privilege to bar use in evidence of information given to the client's licensed psychotherapist. The counselor–patient privilege bars the use in evidence of information provided by a patient to a psychiatrist, psychologist, or licensed psychological counselor, therapist, family counselor, or social worker, in the course of evaluation, counseling, or treatment. (Different jurisdictions include various professions within this scope.) The privilege is the patient's, who may waive it, though in circumstances in which the patient is a child, the waiver would be by a parent or guardian. The privilege applies to all information in disputes between the counselor and patient unless the information is itself relevant to the dispute.

**doctor-patient privilege (physician-patient privilege or patient-physician privilege)** A patient's privilege to bar the use in evidence of information given to the client's medical professional. The doctor–patient privilege bars the use in evidence of information provided by a patient to a doctor, nurse, medical practitioner, medical technician, or other medical professional, in the course of evaluation, counseling, or treatment. (Different jurisdictions include various professions within this scope.) The privilege is the patient's, who may waive it, though in circumstances in which the patient is a child, the waiver would be by a parent or guardian. The privilege applies to all information in disputes between the doctor and patient unless the information is itself relevant to the dispute. It is not absolute, and the doctor may release information in order to prevent harm to the patient or to others; statutory exceptions to the privilege require the reporting of certain information, such as infections endangering the public, evidence of the abuse of a child, or injuries from weapons.

**executive privilege** The president's or governor's qualified privilege against producing evidence. Executive privilege is a qualified privilege in the office of the President and of some governors to withhold information the executive deems likely to inhibit the candid functioning of executive advisers or harm the national security or functioning of the state. The privilege is not absolute but qualified: its relevance and significance in a particular instance must be demonstrated to the satisfaction of the court. It is strongest in matters of national defense and security, but it cannot impede the introduction of evidence in a criminal matter. Many states do not recognize a state executive privilege, and it may be of no avail in federal court.
*See also:* privilege.

**legislative privilege** Legislator's privilege not to divulge information regarding acts in the preparation of legislation. Legislative privilege is the evidentiary equivalent to legislative immunity: the legislator cannot be compelled to give evidence related to acts done in preparation of legislation. This privilege is personal to the legislator and may only be waived by the legislator. The privilege is limited in most jurisdiction to evidence related to acts in office, and in many it is limited to the standard of congressional immunity, applying only to the legislator's acts and statements made in relationship to the research, drafting, debate or discussion, or negotiation related to a specific piece of legislation.
*See also:* immunity, official immunity, legislative immunity (congressional immunity).

**priest-penitent privilege (clerical privilege or minister's privilege)** A believer's privilege to bar the use in evidence of information given to a religious adviser. The priest–penitent privilege bars the use in evidence of information provided by a person who is a member or believer in a religion to a minister, priest, rabbi, imam, cleric, or similar leader of a religious organization, if the information is given as part of the process of personal or religious counseling or confession. The privilege is the member's, which the member may waive. There is no difference in the privilege based upon the religion of the member and leader, but the religion must be an established and recognized faith in which the member in fact believes. The religious leader must be a person responsible for the care or counseling of members of that religion. The privilege, under various names, is recognized in federal and state courts.

**state secrets privilege (national security privilege)** A government privilege to bar the use in evidence of information that in fact poses a reasonable danger to the country's national or military interests. The state secrets privilege bars the introduction of evidence in court of information that would, if disclosed, harm the national or military interests of the United States. To assert the privilege, the U.S. government must identify the information as having the potential to harm those interests, and the court must find a reasonable basis for believing that harm reasonably may follow from its disclosure. The court must determine whether circumstances are appropriate for the claim of privilege, but the government need not usually disclose the evidence in the process of that determination. The privilege is the government's, not a single officer's, although it may be raised by the government counsel for any member of the executive in charge of the department that is responsible for such evidence.
*See also:* secret, state secret (official secret).

**waiver of privilege** Surrender of a privilege by one it protects. Waiver of an evidentiary privilege is the voluntary surrender of that privilege, thus allowing the information that had been privileged to be eligible for discovery or introduction into evidence, unless it is barred on other grounds. A waiver of a privilege is irrevocable, and a waiver for one purpose is a waiver for all. A waiver may be express or implied from conduct that is contrary to the maintenance of the privilege, most often by the sharing of privileged information with people beyond the scope of the confidence allowed by the privilege. The privilege may be extinguished by means other than by waiver, not the least by incidental publicity by third parties.

**litigation privilege (witness privilege or party privilege)** Statements made in litigation are not actionable. The litigation privilege bars all civil suits for statements made in pleadings or testimony in litigation. The privilege extends in most jurisdictions to all statements spoken or written in the course of the proceeding, by parties, counsel, and witnesses.

The privilege does not, however, bar claims based on the litigation itself, such as abuse of process, nor does it bar criminal actions, such as for perjury.

*See also:* privilege, absolute privilege.

**privileged communications (privileged material)** Information that is subject to an evidentiary privilege or other privilege barring public discourse. Privileged communications include all forms of information passing to people between whom an evidentiary privilege exists, or forms of information created or held in such a manner or by such a person as to subject that information to a privilege from involuntary disclosure, whether an immunity from process or an evidentiary privilege. Such material is generally considered confidential for all purposes until either a waiver occurs, expressly or through implication from conduct, or the material is disclosed by a third party. Once such a waiver or disclosure occurs, the material is then considered discoverable and appropriate for use as evidence. Exceptions to this approach are often made on an ad hoc basis and turn on the circumstances of waiver and disclosure, efforts by the party with the privilege to prevent dissemination, and the nature of the harm that may be caused by further dissemination.

**privileges and immunities** The basic conditions of citizenship, including travel, commerce, and employment. The privileges and immunities described in Article Four of the U.S. Constitution are not fully defined but include the fundamental liberties associated with a free citizen, including the privilege to travel unhindered from state to state, the privilege to engage in commerce in trade, the privilege of engaging in a local trade or profession, and, when qualified under local laws, to vote in elections. A state may infringe a privilege, but only if it does not discriminate between its own citizens and the citizens of other states, unless there is a sufficient justification for the discrimination in treatment that is substantial and related to the form and extent of the discriminatory action.

**qualified privilege** A privilege that depends on the good faith of its exercise. A qualified privilege is a privilege that is available to an individual who has satisfied the conditions under which the person may be privileged, but which is qualified by the conduct, motive, or understanding of the individual claiming the privilege at the time of the potentially privileged act. Thus, a qualified privilege in the use of privileged communications is available to a person who acts in good faith and uses the information at the proper time and in the proper manner with the proper parties and no others.

**reporter's privilege** A reporter's privilege not to disclose a source of news. The reporter's privilege is a reporter's exemption from the duty to disclose the identity of a source or content of information provided by others to the reporter, in order to protect the confidentiality of informants and to encourage public cooperation with the press. The reporter's privilege exists in the law of most states, either under their constitutions or shield laws enacted by statute. Still, freedom of the press under the U.S. Constitution does not clearly establish such a privilege, which has been recognized in some federal courts of appeals but not all. Even so, it may be an application recognized under the rules of evidence, preserved under Federal Rule of Evidence 501, of the common-law privilege protecting confidential communications, which itself treats confidential communications in a quasi-fiduciary manner.

The locus of the reporter's privilege is significant; it is not a personal privilege in the reporter, but either a privilege of the person who is the source of the information that is asserted on that person's behalf by the reporter, or it is a public privilege asserted on behalf of the people by the reporter. This ambiguity in the source of the privilege exacerbates problems in its scope, which are difficult to assess when the privilege conflicts with a defendant's right to fair trial or with the state's obligation to pursue crime. Likewise, who may claim the privilege is a matter in transition as the nature of news reporting shifts from the twentieth-century model of professional journalism to include amateur and informal reporting. Most such questions are best resolved by in camera review of the evidence, seeking a balance that prefers the protection of the interests of the public and the source in confidentiality but recognizes that unusual cases require limited use of such information to ensure the justice of criminal trials.

**spousal privilege (marital privilege or husband-and-wife privilege)** A spouse's privilege not to give testimony, or to bar testimony by the other spouse. The spousal privilege bars the introduction of the evidence of one spouse in a proceeding involving the other spouse. The privilege is broad, encompassing all matters known by the one regarding the other.

Jurisdictions vary as to which spouse possesses the privilege. The privilege in the federal courts is held by the spouse who testifies, who may choose to testify or refrain from testifying without regard to the waiver or assertion of the privilege by the other spouse. Most states provide the privilege to both, in which jurisdictions the assertion by either is sufficient to bar the testimony of the other, and the waiver by both is usually required.

*See also:* spouse.

**Privileges and Immunities Clause** *See:* constitution, U.S. Constitution, clauses, Privileges And Immunities Clause (Comity Clause).

**privity** Legal connection or relationship between two parties. Privity refers to any of several forms of specific relationship shared between the parties to a transaction that are of significance in the law. Privity, from the French for alliance, suggests a mutuality or shared interest, even one transferred from one to another party, which is briefly held by both. Thus, privity of contract occurs between two parties to the same contract. Privity of estate arises when two parties share an interest in the same parcel, even through the transfer of one to another. Likewise privity of possession requires that the second possessor takes the thing possessed from first possessor immediately, with no interval between the possessors. Privity of blood is shared ancestry. Though less common now than standing doctrines or interest analysis, privity is sometimes required by specific doctrines in the law in order to determine the category of parties interested in some matter, allowing one party to proceed against the other or one to stand for the other in an action against a third party.

**privity of blood (privity of blood)**  The relationship between ancestors and descendants or between siblings. Privity of blood is the privity arising from the shared bonds of family, recognized at the common law between parent and child, between grandparent and grandchild (and so on), and between siblings, mainly for the purpose of binding all as privies to any dispute affecting family lands. Privity of blood was recognized for other functions, however — in the assertion of the right to stand as next friend to a child, for example. The effect of res judicata on members of a family is usually based now on questions of notice and interest than on the mere fact of privity of blood.

*See also:* blood.

**privity of contract**  The relationship among contracting parties. Privity of contract is the mutual relationship between or among the parties to a contract. Privity is required in many instances in order to have standing to complain of breach of the contract. Privity of contract was once a bar to actions for a breach of warranty if the party injured by the failure of warranty lacked privity, a condition common in products liability, when the manufacturer was unlikely to have a contract with a consumer. The privity requirement was surmounted in the U.S. in McPherson v. Buick, 217 N.Y. 382 (1916) and in England in Donoghue v. Stevenson [1932] AC 562, by allowing such claims to proceed in tort under a theory of negligence. Privity of contract remains significant, as to other theories of contract enforcement, with the additional exception of relaxed rules for a third-party beneficiary to enforce the aspects of the contract that creates a benefit to the third party.

**privity of estate**  The relation between a landlord and tenant or between successive owners in fee. Privity of estate describes the shared interests in the legal ownership of lands that arises from either mutual or successive interests. Thus, a mutual interest arises between landlord and tenant (though not between landlord and sub-tenant) as well as between co-tenants. A successive interest arises between the grantor and the grantee of the land. Privity of estate from succession can be broken in the event, for instance an intermediary gains title. A delay in transfer owing to death and probate is not considered a loss of privity of estate. Two adverse possessors in privity of estate (owing to deeds transferring such interests as they have) may tack their possession to allow their cumulative possession as the basis for satisfying the limitations period.

**horizontal privity of estate**  Privity between the parties who create a covenant on the land. Horizontal privity is a privity between equals, and actually exists in many forms, not the least as between co-tenants. Horizontal privity of estate also arises between the two parties who create a covenant on the land, the party owning the burdened land and either the party who owns the benefited land or party receiving the covenant in gross. Horizontal privity is required in many jurisdictions to create a covenant on the land that runs with the land.

**vertical privity of estate**  The privity between successors in interest. Vertical privity of estate is the privity between grantor and grantee, those who take an interest already created from one who created it or a successor.

Note: vertical privity of contract relates to the contracts of a supply chain, the sale of a product from maker to distributor to wholesaler to retailer to consumer is a series of contracts in vertical privity.

**privity of possession**  The relationship between successors in unbroken possession of a single thing. Privity of possession is the relationship that comes from shared possession arising when one person possessing land or some object transfers it to a successor, or the successor takes it from the previous possessor, as long as there is no meaningful interruption in possession. In most jurisdictions, privity of possession is sufficient to allow tacking for the calculation of time to satisfy the statute for adverse possession.

**privy (privies)**  One with a personal interest. Privy, in general, connotes a person or thing of a strong personal interest or relation to the person or matter at hand. Privy is related to the sense of alliance that is the core notion of privity.

Privy has several distinct senses in law:

A person or entity may be a privy to an action if the privy has a relationship with a party to the action that creates an interest or stake in the outcome of the action, even though the privy does not make an appearance in the case. The privy is said to partake in the case regardless of making an appearance. Thus, a third-party beneficiary of a contract whose interest is asserted by the contracting party is a privy of that party, and a spouse is privy with the other spouse who is a party to an action related to marital property. A privy has an interest in filing an appeal of an action, because a privy is bound by its result through res judicata.

A privy is a confidante, and to be privy to information is to be shared with it, particularly when the information is considered confidential otherwise.

In English law, privy designates an office, role, or seal that is personal to the monarch. Thus the privy seal is the royal seal. The privy council is the council of the monarch, and privy councilors are her (or his) councilors. A privy audience is a personal audience before the monarch.

**privy seal**   *See:* seal, privy seal.

**prize**   A reward, particularly the value of an enemy vessel taken in war. A prize, in general, is a reward given for some achievement, especially in a competition. Its award is generally governed either by contract or by regulation. A prize in international law is a vessel captured in war.

*See also:* ransom.

**prize as captured vessel (prize vessel or law of prize)**
An enemy vessel captured for its value. A prize is a ship or other vessel captured during war, which at the time of the capture was either flying the flag of an enemy state or carrying contraband goods to the benefit of an enemy state. The vessel, cargo, and goods are each elements of the prize, the maritime equivalent to booty on land. The value of the prize was divided among the capturing state, the capturing fleet, captain, and crew, although the status of a vessel as a lawful prize and the valuation and sale of the vessel, cargo, and goods were supervised by a prize court, which in the U.S. is still the prize commissioners appointed (as needed) by the U.S. district court for the port in which the prize is brought. Flag vessels or privateers could once take prizes, although privateers are now banned, and the concept of the prize is now discredited in international law.

*See also:* booty; privateer.

**pro**   For, on, or otherwise in favor of. Pro is a Latin preposition that represents a variety of English concepts, most often "for," but also "on behalf of" or "before" or "for the sake of." In English, the word may be an informal abbreviation for "professional."

*See also:* contra.

**pro rata clause**   *See:* insurance, insurance coverage, multiple insurance coverage, pro rata clause.

**pro bono publico (pro bono service or pro bono lawyer)**   For the good of the people. Pro bono publico describes anything that exists or is done for the public good and not for private gain or reward. In law, prono bono publico, or just "pro bono" describes services provided without compensation by lawyers as a matter of public service, whether the service is representation or counseling of indigent clients, charitable causes, or the government. A pro bono lawyer is, thus, a lawyer providing legal services without compensation. Each lawyer has a professional obligation to render some service pro bono each year, and state bar authorities are increasingly enshrining this duty, which was once understood as a customary obligation attendant on the privilege of practice, as a rule of licensure.

*See also:* indigency, in forma pauperis (I.F.P. or IFP).

**pro forma**   For the sake of form, not substance. Pro forma designates anything done or required for the purpose of satisfying a rule or expectation in the ordinary course of business. In law, pro forma usually designates that what is done or required is a procedural requirement rather than one of great significance or likely controversy. A pro forma pleading is a pleading that satisfies a requirement there be a pleading, not one in which the substantive argument is material.

Pro forma has a distinct, technical sense in accountancy, and different senses in trade business. Pro forma accounting of transactions and balances is a projection or statement that excludes unique or unusual events to depict routine and annual business. Pro forma financial statements are estimates of the results of a transaction's expenses, savings, and revenues. A pro forma invoice is a commitment to buy and to sell goods, subject to price fluctuations.

**pro hac vice**   A temporary appointment limited to a particular case or issue. Pro hac vice, or for this matter, is a term of limitation used for an appointment or admission of someone to a particular office. Now mainly used to describe the admission of a foreign lawyer to practice in a court in which the attorney is not generally admitted, the term was historically used to describe any appointment of a person to a role for a particular cause. The appointment of special masters and judges was pro hac, and while judges pro hac vice were usually official appointments, the designation of an arbitrator chosen by the parties to a dispute was also a judge pro hac vice. The term has been superseded in these contexts by, among others: guardian ad litem, special master, special justice, justice by designation, arbitrator, de facto agent, constructive owner, constructive agent.

*See also:* bar, admission to the bar, admission pro hac vice (admission pro hoc vice).

**pro rata**   Proportionally, according to the appropriate share. Pro rata means by proportion, frequently according to the share or contribution that each has made to the whole. One person's pro rata share of joint savings account would be the portion of the account's value that represents the percentage of deposits that person made. Similarly, a pro rata distribution by a partnership would yield the portion for each partner equal to that partner's ownership interest.

*See also:* proportionality (disproportional or proportional or proportionate).

**pro se (in propria persona or in pro. per.)**   In one's own person. Both "pro se" and "in propria persona" designate the appearance in court without legal counsel of a natural person who is a party to a civil or criminal action, that person representing the person's own interests. There is no significant difference between the two terms.

A litigant appearing pro se cannot represent a class in a class action or otherwise represent the case of another person. A corporation cannot appear pro se. In criminal cases, a defendant must petition the court to appear in pro. per. or pro se, and the defendant must make a clear and unequivocal demand to do so, which may only be granted if the court is satisfied the defendant is mentally competent to do so. Most jurisdictions have particular standards allowing for error by litigants pro se, but also have statutes specifically forbidding litigants pro se from filling repetitive motions and claims.

**pro tanto**   For so much. Pro tanto is a Latin phrase that relates an action to a quantity. In English it translates as "for so much," "for the amount of," or "for this amount that." Thus, a judgment pro tanto following a verdict is a judgment entered for the amount of the verdict.

**pro tempore (pro tem)**   For the time being. Pro tempore is Latin for "for the time being," usually for the length of a term of office, court session, or legislative session, or as needed. Thus, a president pro tempore (usually abbreviated to "pro tem") is the person who acts as president during the absences of the president.

*See also:* trustee, interim trustee (temporary trustee or trustee ad litem or trustee pro tem); ex, ex officio.

**probability**   The likelihood of an event or a condition being true. Probability is the range of potential according to which anything is true or not, ranging from impossible to certain. Probability can be expressed rhetorically, such as by saying something is "more likely than not," or using a ratio of conditions or odds, like "a chance of six out of ten" or "odds of three to five."

Probability in itself is sometimes confused with what is probable, and care in the use of "probability" and "probable" is essential to distinguish the concept of the range of probability from what is itself probably true. The probable is merely a range within the scale of probability, something akin to what is more likely than not or of odds between sixty and ninety-nine percent.

*See also:* probable; proof, burden of proof (standard of proof).

**probable**   Likely to be true. Probable describes something that is likely to be true, which a prudent person would consider a sufficient basis for confidence, e.g., that an investment is likely to yield its anticipated return. More generally, probable represents a level of confidence at which a reasonable person would be willing to base most decisions, although not perhaps the most serious. Probable is not the same as certain, and it is not so low as possible or potential. What is probable is what is likely, at least more likely than not. Probable is a rhetorical statement of probability, a word-based assessment of the degree of probability appropriate to some prediction, risk assessment, or evaluation of evidence. Probable is the basis for a variety of legal standards demanding a level of confidence in the probability that an assessment is accurate, particularly probable cause but also probable injury and probable consequence.

*See also:* probability.

**probable cause**   *See:* cause, probable cause, fellow-officer rule (fellow officer rule or collective knowledge doctrine); cause, probable cause, Darden hearing (informant tip suppression hearing); cause, probable cause.

**probable-desistance test**   *See:* attempt, criminal attempt, probable-desistance test.

**substantially probable (substantial probability)**   Very likely. Substantial probability is a level of confidence markedly greater than probability, but not yet at a level of convincing certainty; it is very likely.

**probate**   To prove something as genuine or true. Probate is a means of ascertaining the truth of something in doubt. The medieval sense of probo as a judgment of fitness is the reason the term is used both as the root of probate, as in proving a will, and probation, as in proving an offender is ready to return to society. Another variant is the jurisdiction that became administratively convenient for the court probating wills, which now includes matters once in the court of wards governing orphans, delinquents, and child abuse or neglect, as well as the mentally incompetent and infirm. Similarly, probation has come to mean many forms of cautionary punishment.

*See also:* executor (executrix).

**probate court**   *See:* court, court of limited jurisdiction, probate court.

**probate homestead**   *See:* homestead, probate homestead.

**informal probate**   Probate for uncomplicated testamentary estates. Informal probate is a method by which a person who has a legally cognizable interest in the estate of a decedent may move for appointment as personal representative and seek an inexpensive and relatively fast probate of a will. It is available in most jurisdictions if the decedent has been dead for at least one hundred and twenty hours but not more than three years, if there is one valid and original testamentary instrument, and if there is no known challenge to the instrument. In most jurisdictions there is no statutory limit on the value of an estate that may be managed through informal probate, although the technical demands of a larger estate may suggest formal probate is more appropriate.

**letters testamentary (letters of administration)**   The judicial grant of authority to administer the estate of a decedent. Letters testamentary denominate the order from a court to an executor, appointing the person as executor or personal representative and investing the executor or representative with the authority to represent the decedent's estate and to inventory, take possession of, and dispose of property, including bank accounts, and to do all that is required to probate the will, to pay claims and taxes, and to distribute assets of the estate to its rightful devisees and legatees.

Letters of administration serve the same purpose, the difference in title reflecting the appointment of an administrator rather than an executor, which is appropriate either in the absence of an apparently valid will or in the management of assets for an estate probated in another jurisdiction.

**non-probate asset (nonprobate)** An asset related to the estate but not subject to probate. Nonprobate assets are properties or accounts that the decedent owned or has some interest in while alive, which are not property owned after death and so not within the scope of the probate estate. Remainders and reversions following the life of the decedent, trust interests that pass at death, bank accounts that are payable to another party at death, and insurance policies for the life of the decedent are examples of non-probate assets.

**probate code** The statutes governing probate in a given jurisdiction. A probate code is a set of related statutes adopted to govern probate jurisdiction, probate affairs, and the procedure of probate, usually including not only the probate of wills and administration of intestate succession but also the affairs of minors, missing persons, and the mentally incapacitated. The Uniform Probate Code is a model code adopted in many states. In many jurisdictions, the courts or a rules committee have promulgated regulations implementing the state's probate code providing further guidance and forms for the regulation of proceedings in probate.

**probate estate** The entity that represents the estate and its property. A probate estate is the entity that is created by the appointment of a personal representative, executor, or administrator to probate the estate of the decedent. The probate estate also describes the scope and content of all property that is subject to probate, which is to say all property in which the decedent had a claim or ownership while alive, except what property became a non-probate asset through transfer as a matter of law, estate, contract, or assignment at the time of death. The personal representative, executor, or administrator both represents the estate as a legal entity and is responsible for the management of its assets as a fiduciary to the devisees, legatees, and heirs.

**probate of a will** Process to prove a will and settle an estate. The probate of a will, under equity or the common law, is the procedure for proving and establishing a will before an appropriate court of law. Statutes in many states have enlarged the scope of probate to include the process, in the absence of a valid will, to determine the disposition by law and to administer the estate of a decedent. The probate process involves (a) a legal recognition of the death of the testator or intestate decedent, (b) the determination of validity of a will, (c) the inventory of assets of the estate, (d) the inventory of claims against the estate, (e) the clearing of title to land owned by the decedent, (f) the liquidation of such property as is required to settle claims, and (g) the settlement of claims, (h) to make distributions that are not made in kind, the distribution of property to devisees, legatees, or heirs, (i) the accounting of the estate and its closure.

Probate was once the province of courts of equity and then, in jurisdictions in which equity and law were merged, in the common law courts of general jurisdiction. Specialized courts of probate now hear causes in many jurisdictions, sometimes also being designated to hear related causes arising from trusts or family law.

**will contest** Action to deny a will's admission to probate. A will contest occurs when a person institutes an action to deny a will's admission to probate. A contest asserts that the will is invalid, either as a forgery or fraud, as having been revoked by the testator or superseded by another will, or as being invalid owing to the testator's lack of capacity, action under undue influence or for some other reason.

> **caveat to the probate of a will (caveator)** A pleading initiating a will contest. A caveat to the probate of a last will and testament is a pleading requiring a caveat proceeding, which is the phrase describing a contest to a will in some jurisdictions. The contestant to the will is then designated the caveator.

**probation** Supervised release instead of incarceration. Probation is a period as well as a status, during which a person convicted of a criminal offense is subject to regulation and supervision by probation enforcement officials. Probation serves both as a less serious form of punishment through its restrictions from unfettered liberty and as a means of testing the fitness of the probationer to determine if the person is prepared for full liberty to be restored as a law-abiding member of the community. A person who violates the conditions of probation may be incarcerated. Probation, in some jurisdictions, is the same as parole, and in others parole is a distinct system used prior to a conviction, probation being the system or punishment employed, other than incarceration, after conviction.

Probation is managed by probation officers, and a person on probation is subject to a variety of conditions, some of which are imposed as a condition of probation generally, and some of which are ordered by the court in the light of the offense for which punishment is required and the probationer's history and abilities, which are usually researched and presented to the court prior to sentence (in the federal courts, being done by officers in the district probation office).

*See also:* parole (parolee).

> **probation officer** Officer who manages the probation of individual convicts. A probation officer is an officer of the court working for the probation office or probation service, who advises the court prior to a person's sentence, regarding the person's history and conditions, and who supervises, counsels, and reports on individuals who are on probation.

**probativeness (probative)** Tending to prove something. Probativeness is the potential for one thing to prove another. Probative is likely a corruption of the French a prover, to prove, owing to the similar pronunciation of b and v, the French was in turn derived from Latin. The term was used earlier in Scots law than in English or U.S. law.

**probative evidence**  *See:* evidence, probative evidence.

**probative fact**  *See:* fact, probative fact.

**procedendo**  *See:* remand, procedendo (writ of procedendo).

**procedure**  The statutes, rules, and customs by which legal work is performed. Procedure is the method by which any work is performed within the legal system. There are procedures in legislatures; procedures for voting in elections; procedures for making rules; for filing complaints before tribunals; for managing the flow of pleadings motions, and documents in court; for presenting evidence, hearing objections to evidence, and ruling on whether to allow it or bar it from court; for taking pleas in criminal cases; for impaneling juries, for instructing juries and rendering verdicts; and for bringing appeals. In short, there is a procedure for doing anything that is to be done in a legal system, whether it is done by a private party of done by a legal official.

The purposes of procedure are many but include (a) the need to make decisions as a matter of law according to rules that are themselves law and subject to the oversight of lawmakers; (b) the need to allocate responsibilities for tasks required in making a decision; (c) the goal of giving interested parties notice of what they must do, how they must do it, and when they must act in order to be heard prior to any legal decisions; (d) the goal of ensuring decisions are made with oversight by officials other than those who make them; and (e) the need to balance the interests of various parties who might be burdened or benefited by any given procedure. Laws creating procedures are usually created by the legislature in the first instance and then developed by rules, regulations, or precedents by the institution in which the procedure is followed.

**procedural due process**  *See:* due process of law, procedural due process.

**procedural error**  *See:* error, procedural error.

**procedural law**  *See:* law, procedural law.

**procedural right**  *See:* right, legal right, procedural right.

**procedural-default doctrine**  *See:* habeas corpus, procedural-default doctrine.

**appellate procedure**  The process for raising and objecting to an appeal. Appellate procedure is the whole process by which an appeal is brought, is contested, and is decided. Appellate procedure in most jurisdiction is an amalgam of constitutional provisions, statutes, and the rules of the appellate court, although certain reqirements for the commencement of the appeal may be contained in the rules of criminal procedure or civil procedure or local rules in the trial court.

**civil procedure**  The rules and customs governing the parties in civil actions. Civil procedure includes all of the statutes, precedents, and court rules governing the conduct of the parties and counsel in private proceedings at law or in equity that are not subject to special rules of equity, admiralty, or other special courts. Civil procedure usually governs questions pleading, the identity of parties, the jurisdiction of courts, the management of discovery and trial, and some forms of remedy. Rules of civil procedure ought to encourage fairness among the parties, as well as judicial economy and efficiency.

**criminal procedure**  Laws governing official steps to the identify, process, and prosecute persons accused of crime. Criminal procedure is an amalgam of constitutional principles, statutes, administrative rules, court rules, and customs, that regulate official conduct at every stage of the process related to a criminal act, from the observation of a potential criminal suspect or investigation of a crime to the conviction of a criminal defendant. The United States has adopted the Federal Rules of Criminal Procedure, which are followed in many jurisdictions.

**proceeding**  A gathering that moves toward a goal. A proceeding is any hearing, trial, assembly, or other meeting that follows an agenda, such as a pretrial order or rules of order, such as the rules of evidence and rules of procedure, in order to achieve some end among a set of predesignated outcomes. The term is from the Latin for going forward, and to proceed is to go forward or go ahead.

**collateral proceeding**  A proceeding indirectly related to another proceeding. A collateral proceeding is related to another proceeding, which might or might not be held at the same time, but the relationship is indirect. An appeal of a trial verdict is not collateral to the trial, but a habeas proceeding is collateral to a criminal trial.

*See also:* res, res judicata, collateral attack on a judgment (collateral action).

**legal proceeding**  Any proceeding required to assert or defend an interest created or protected by law. A legal proceeding is any proceeding in which a law requires the proceeding in order to alter or protect a right, interest, duty, status, or obligation of legal significance. Though judicial proceedings are the most well known legal proceedings, there are many forms, including administrative proceedings and legislative proceedings. In legal writing, the significance intended may vary, and the term often means only legal proceedings of record, which usually are those in a court of law.

**summary proceeding**  A proceeding with limited argument and evidence and abbreviated procedures. A summary proceeding is a hearing or, sometimes, a trial, in which procedures are restricted in order to ensure a speedy determination of the question before the proceeding. Limitations on such proceedings may include truncation of the procedures required or allowed prior to the proceeding, the quantity and form of evidence presented, time allowed for argument, and the scope of what may be argued. Summary proceedings are usually provided for in statutes and rules, and in many instances, are employed to reach only a temporary judgment or resolution, followed by the opportunity of the parties affected to demand a full proceeding when time is less pressing.

**proceeds**  Revenue received. Proceeds are the money or value received from the sale, exchange, collection or other disposition of property, services, or claims.

**procès-verbal**  A record of statements made in an official setting. Le procès-verbal is the record of statements made in any proceeding, such as the statements made to a public official, the statements of parties to a negotiation of a contract, or the statements of delegates negotiating a treaty. In the case of treaty negotiation, it may also serve as the recording of minor changes by informal agreement of the parties, even after the treaty is in force, as long the changes are technical or scrivener's alterations rather than material to the state's parties' obligations.

**process**  A method of doing anything, including a legal action. A process is a means of doing or performing any task. A process as a matter of patent is a particular routine that, when followed, allows the production of a particular device or thing.

Process, as a matter of procedure, is an abbreviation of legal process.

*See also:* process, legal process.

**process agent**  *See:* agent, process agent.

**process server**  *See:* service, service of process, process server.

**abuse of process**  A tort claim for harm from the misuse of a legitimate legal process. Abuse of process is a claim that can be brought in a civil action when a pleading or procedure is wrongly employed for the purpose of harassing or injuring the opposing litigant. Examples include filing a vexatious suit or a false denial or answer, filing a false affidavit, making false claims, introducing fraudulent evidence, intentionally delaying procedures, or refusing on spurious grounds to produce evidence to which the other party is entitled. In raising a claim of abuse of process, the movant must be very specific regarding the wrongdoing alleged, and such claims are usually subject to a high burden of proof, such as by clear and convincing evidence. Pleading the tort of abuse of process requires the movant to prove three elements: that a legal process had been initiated properly and with probable cause, the process was subsequently perverted to accomplish an ulterior purpose for which the process was not originally designed, and that perversion caused harm.

*See also:* prosecution, malicious prosecution; defense, malicious defense.

**legal process**  The means by which a defendant is brought into court. Legal process is both the procedure and the paper according to which a defendant is brought into court for a civil or a criminal action.

Although the specifics vary from jurisdiction to jurisdiction and according to the nature of the action, the signal aspect of process is to put the defendant on notice that an action has been brought, the reasons for the action, and the extent of the defendant's potential liability. The process in civil actions is a summons to appear in court, which may be accompanied by a complaint or a motion. The process in criminal actions may be physical arrest followed by an appearance, or it may be a warrant for arrest or summons to appear in court, which is the process. The service of process may also include a copy of the information or indictment in a criminal action, or the complaint in a civil action, at its most narrow, the process that must be served is the notice of the required appearance. To be effective, process must be served upon the defendant, either through personal service, service on an agent, or service by publication. A failure of process is grounds for any judgment entered in the action to be vacated.

*See also:* process; service, service of process.

**proclamation**  A formal announcement. A proclamation is both the method and the result of an announcement made by an official in a public manner. Proclamations may serve as a form of notice, such that an interested party has constructive notice of what is proclaimed. Policy may be announced by proclamation.

**proctor (procurator)**  An agent who carries out an official task, particularly to give examinations or evaluations of evidence. A proctor, or procurator, is an agent for a more senior official, who is responsible for some form of investigation or evaluation, or the administration of evaluations. In England, proctors were often assigned to assist a judge. In this sense, the office is rare in the United States, such work usually being done either by a special master, by a magistrate, or by a police service. In both the U.K. and the U.S., a proctor is likely to be an examiner, the administrator of either an academic examination or an examination for students or apprentices for a license to practice a trade.

**procurement**  Acquisition, especially of things for government use. Procurement, generally, is the arrangement of some circumstance, and it has come most often to mean the acquisition of goods or arrangement of services. More specifically, procurement is the method by which a government contract to provide property, goods or services is established between a government and a private concern or another government. Historically, procurement generally meant the acquisition of goods and stores for government use, especially for use by the military. Procurement for the federal government is a process of acquiring property or services, beginning with the process for determining a need for property or services and ending with contract completion and closeout.

*See also:* procurer.

**procurer**  One who acquires, arranges, or supplies goods or services. A procurer is a person who acquires something, usually but not always as an agent or representative of someone else. Procurer has quite varied senses in the law. In admiralty, a procurer is an agent of a vessel, or the owner of the vessel, who arranges the purchase of necessary goods and services from suppliers in ports of call. In commercial law, a procurer is a person who designated the acquiring party of a negotiable instrument. In insurance, the procurer is the person or entity who negotiates the policy on behalf of the insured. In criminal law, the procurer is a panderer, the person who recruits other persons to engage in an unlawful act, particularly to engage in acts of commercial or otherwise unlawful sex.

*See also:* procurement.

**product**   Any real or tangible good sold for the use of others. A product is a tangible thing, either chattel or real, that is sold or distributed as part of a commercial enterprise. The manufacture or preparation of a product for distribution and sale serves as a metaphor for all other goods sold to determine whether, in a given context, the goods are a product. Thus, for instance, a house is a product of its builder, and gas is a product not only of the well owner but also of the subsequent distributors and utilities.

**product defect**   *See:* liability, product liability, product defect, failure to warn (marketing defect); liability, product liability, product defect, consumer expectation test; liability, product liability, product defect (defective product).

**product liability**   *See:* liability, product liability (products liability).

**defective product**   A product having a flaw that prevents it from operating as intended. A defective product is a product with a flaw that prevents the product from operating in its normal or intended fashion. Such a flaw is legally significant when it prevents or hinders the product's ability to work for its intended purpose, or it creates a threat to the health, safety, or welfare of the user or passersby. A defect may be present in individual products, or may be inherent in the product's design, and can expose a manufacturer to liability for her failure to correct the error. A defect may be patent, or apparent to a reasonable consumer, or may be latent, or hidden from a reasonable consumer.

*See also:* warranty; manufacture, manufacturing defect; lemon.

**design defect (defective design)**   A shortcoming inherent in a product's design. A design defect is a shortcoming in the intended form or function of a product that causes a risk of injury or interferes with its intended use. A defective design differs from defective production, in which the shortcoming results form a flaw in the product's manufacture. Although the product may in fact be ideal from the producer's perspective, the producer will be liable if the product's design causes injury in its proper use or fails to perform as it is claimed to perform. In order for a producer to be liable for injuries proximately caused by the design

defect, in many jurisdictions the plaintiff must show that a reasonable alternative design was available to the producer. This alternative will be considered reasonable by the fact-finder if the plaintiff shows that, accounting for the alternative's potential benefit as well as the burden, its use would place on the producer, the alternative design should have been used in place of the actual, injurious design. The plaintiff can demonstrate that the actual design was defective, regardless of the existence of a reasonable alternative design, by means of the consumer–expectation test, under which the fact-finder is presented with evidence that the injurious product did not perform in accordance with general market assumptions as to its safety, risk, etc. As with manufacturing defects, a producer will be held strictly liable for injuries caused by a defectively designed product.

*See also:* product, defective product, manufacturing defect (defective manufacture); negligence (negligent).

**latent product defect (inherent vice)**   A product defect that is not easily discovered. A latent product defect is not readily apparent, even upon a reasonable inspection. A buyer cannot consent to accept a product with a latent defect unless the seller expressly discloses the defect prior to delivery. More, a seller and others in a supply chain cannot usually ascertain a latent defect in the product. A manufacturer has a duty to warn buyers and ultimate consumers of latent defects, and a failure to do so gives rise to strict liability of the manufacturer for injuries, loss, or harm in most instances. On the other hand, in the absence of actual knowledge, sellers and others in the supply chain are usually not liable for latent defects.

*See also:* latency (latent).

**manufacturing defect (defective manufacture)**   A shortcoming that results from the production, but not the design, of a consumer product. A manufacturing defect is a shortcoming that results from the production or distribution of a product, as opposed to a shortcoming owing to a flaw in the product's design. Thus, the design or form that the producer intended for the product would not have been harmful, but due to the manufacturing defect, the product departed from this design and became dangerous to consumers. In order for a producer to be liable for injuries proximately caused by the manufacturing defect, the product must have been defective when last in the producer's control. If a plaintiff can prove there is a link between control and defect, the plaintiff does not need to prove the producer was negligent when producing the product; the producer will be strictly liable for harm caused by the defect.

*See also:* product, defective product, design defect (defective design); negligence (negligent).

**risk-utility test**   A product is defective if a reasonable alternative would have been safer. The risk–utility test of products liability balances the determination of defectiveness of a product that causes harm by whether a reasonable alternative design would, at reasonable cost, have reduced the foreseeable risks of harm posed by the product as made. The test also requires the omission of the alternative design to render the product not reasonably safe. As of 2010, the risk–utility test is not widely adopted as the primary standard of liability, though it may be used in some jurisdictions when a manufacturer asserts as a defense that no safer alternative design existed at the time of the manufacturing of the product in question.

**product recall**    A request or order to return an unsafe product to its source. A product recall is a request by the maker or seller of a product, or an order from a government, for sellers and consumers of a product that has been found likely to have a dangerous defect, to return the product for replacement, repair, or refund. Product recalls may be made by a manufacturer only to distributors or to sellers or made directly to consumers. Product recalls may be voluntary by a manufacturer, distributor, or seller; or they may be ordered by a government agency with the authority to issue them, in particular the Consumer Product Safety Commission, the National Highway Transportation Safety Administration, the Food and Drug Administration, the Department of Agriculture, the Environmental Protection Agency, and the U.S. Coast Guard, each with jurisdiction over different products.

**production request or request to produce or inspect documents**    See: discovery, documentary discovery, request for production (production request or request to produce or inspect documents).

**product liability**    See: liability, product liability (products liability).

**profession**    A vocation of complex skills acquired through mentored performance. A profession in its oldest sense is a statement of principle, something that a person professes. From this arose its more widely used sense, in which a profession is an order of practitioners of a vocation that requires adherence to certain principles and practice by its members. The law is a profession, as are medicine, military service, religious ministry, teaching, architecture, accountancy, and engineering, among others. There are subdivisions among most professions that are essential to their education and regulation, as well as the coordination among members of related professions; so there are differing professions in medicine, now including doctors of medicine and of osteopathy, dentists, nurses, pharmacists, and administrators, each of which may be considered a distinct profession.

The hallmarks of a profession are a distinct set of principles and skills that are associated with its performance, from which are derived the rubrics of preliminary education or training, followed by some demonstration or examination of these principles and skills in order to qualify for entry into the profession. Members of a profession ordinarily are regulated according to law, usually by a commission appointed from among the senior members of the profession within a jurisdiction.

See also: trade.

**professional corporation**    See: corporation, professional corporation (P.C. or PC).

**professional malpractice**    See: malpractice, professional malpractice.

**professional rescuer doctrine**    See: rescue, professional rescuer doctrine (firefighter's rule).

**professional services insurance or lawyer**    See: insurance, category of insurance, errors and omissions insurance (e&o) (professional services insurance or lawyer).

**professionalism**    The care, effort, preparation, and decorum required of each member by the others in a profession. Professionalism is the sum of the ethics required by a profession to enter into the profession and maintain the respect of its membership. In law, professionalism requires knowledge of the law in its generalities and in its specific requirements; respect for the fundamental principles of the law as the basis for a fair social order; a devotion to the best interests of each client, subject only to requirements of law; service to the law, to the profession, and to the society and state it serves; and civility toward both other members of the profession and members of the public.

See also: civility.

**proffer (proffer of evidence or proffered evidence or evidence proffered)**    An offer to produce or do something. Proffer is an offer to produce evidence, make an argument, or proceed with any other aspect of a case, usually offered immediately prior to seeking a ruling on the admissibility of the thing offered. Proffer may be either a verb or a noun, the proffer being the thing offered as well as the act of offering it. Testimony or objects presented in a proffer are the proffered evidence.

Note: a proffer was once a payment or payment made as well as the return made by a sheriff or process server. These usages are now rare.

See also: offer; proof, offer of proof.

**profile (police profiling or criminal profiling)**    The selection of whom to observe or investigate by appearance or trait. A profile of an individual is the inventory of various characteristics of the person's identity and action (such as gender, age, psychology, education, putative race, nationality, skills, physical attributes, interests, etc.). To create a criminal profile of the suspect whose identity is unknown in the investigation of a crime is to deduce from such evidence as is known what characteristics are apparent and from such patterns as are observed in prior, similar crimes, what various individual characteristics are statistically likely to relate to the perpetrator of the crime. Such analysis, when based on sufficient data and used with sufficient skill and caution, has been used successfully to predict the profile of a suspect later proven to be the perpetrator in fact. To create a profile as a matter of crime prevention is to assume the characteristics that are sufficiently likely to be essential to a likely perpetrator of a crime that they may identify a suspect before the crime might be committed.

Though of potential utility, each of these forms of profile is inherently subject to inaccuracy and inefficiency in its use. The more that a profile depends on statistical likelihood from past or cumulative actions by a variety of people, the greater the danger will be of over-reliance upon it. Experience with racial profiling by police in the United States has been very controversial, leading not only to selective enforcement of laws but violations of equal protection of the law and other individual rights.

*See also:* stereotype (gender stereotype or racial stereotype or stereotypical).

**drug courier profile (durg courier indicators)** Aspects of behavior or appearance that may indicate a person carries contraband. A drug courier profile is a set of behaviors and characteristics of appearance that have been identified by law enforcement as indicative of a person who is transporting contraband, particularly transporting illegal drugs. Examples include erratic or nervous behavior at security checkpoints, unusual acts that seem intended to evade identification, such as paying for tickets or items with large amounts of cash, and particular travel patterns, such as visits to cities known as sources of drugs for brief stays. Similar profile information is used in the detection of other potential criminal conduct, including terrorist acts. Police agencies may use such profiles to determine subjects of special interest or more deliberate scrutiny but may not base arrests or invasive searches without a warrant on a profile alone, which itself does not amount to probable cause. See Florida v. Royer, 460 U.S. 491 (1983) (White, J.).

**racial profiling** The selection of whom to observe or investigate by apparent race. Racial profiling is the use of assumptions regarding a person's race as a basis for determining to observe, investigate, interrogate, search, or arrest an individual, or not to do so, whether for a specific offense or to determine whether an unknown offense may be committed. The use of racial profiling, even when buttressed by surrogates for racial characteristics, such as presence in a given neighborhood, is a violation of equal protection of the law. Only bona fide and reasonable suspicions arising from considerations other than race alone, regarding a particular individual, support such police actions. Profiling according to national origin, ethnicity, and other characteristics are sometimes called "racial profiling," the term sometimes being little more than a synonym for judging people according to stereotypes when making investigatory or administrative decisions.

*See also:* stereotype (gender stereotype or racial stereotype or stereotypical).

**driving while black (DWB)** A traffic stop made for no cause other than the race of the driver. "Driving while black" is an ironic play on the phrase "driving while intoxicated." It refers to profiling, selective arrest, and discrimination when traffic police stop a car driven by a person of color solely because of that person's race.

**profit (profits)** The value of income minus expenses. Profit is the sum value that is realized from any endeavor over a period of time for a going concern, which is the remainder of the income received or accounted minus the costs and expenses paid or accounted. There are a variety of measures of profit, with different costs and expenses included or excluded. Note: there is no real difference between profit and profits in this context.
*See also:* gain.

**profit and loss statement or pandl** *See:* income, income statement (profit and loss statement or pandl).

**gross profit (gross profits or gross loss)** Value of sales receipts minus direct expenses for a given project. Gross profit is the profit for a project or venture, considering only revenues generated by a project less its direct costs, without incorporating the project's share of overhead expenses and taxes of the venture as a whole. If this number is negative, there is negative gross profit, which is the same as a gross loss.

**lost profit (lost profits)** The profits that were likely had a project been completed. Lost profits is a reasonable estimate of the profits that would have been realized on a specific project had it been completed, a measure of the loss an enterprise may realize when for any reason it is not able to complete a project. Most often, lost profit is a measure of damages for breach of contract, when the breach is by a supplier or other party whose goods or services are essential to the other party's completion of some project. Lost profit is usually available as a measure of damages only if either the loss of the profits was foreseeable to the non-breaching party at the time of the contract or if the breaching party is on notice of the anticipated use by the non-breaching party at the time of the contract. In either case, the estimate of lost profits must be reasonable and the profits must be ascertainable to a level of reasonable certainty.

**net profit (net profits or net loss)** Value of sales receipts minus both direct expenses and overhead. Net profit is the profit of a project or venture, considering the revenues generated by the project less its direct and indirect costs, thus incorporating the project's share of overhead expenses and taxes of the venture as a whole. Net profit also describes the whole profit for an enterprise for a given period of time, incorporating all of its revenues, and all of its expenses. If this number is negative, there is negative net profit, which is the same as a net loss.

**operating profit** Value of receipts minus direct costs and overhead costs other than taxes and interest. Operating profit is the profit of a venture, considering the revenues generated less its direct and indirect costs other than tax and interest payments, thus incorporating the deductions from profit for overhead from salaries, property, and insurance but not incorporating the deductions for debt service and taxes.

**profit a prendre (profits a prendre)**  The right to a natural or agricultural resource from another person's land. A profit a prendre is an incorporeal property interest in the lands owned by another, specifically being the privileges to enter the other's land and to sever and retain specific natural or physical substances from it. A profit a prendre is specific to the resource and the lands, such as the rights to take fish from a given pond, or to plant and harvest corn in specified fields, or to hunt in a given wood or field or on the tract as a whole. A profit a prendre may be appurtenant, its benefit running with the land, or it may be in gross, held by an owner regardless of the land the owner holds. A profit a prendre in gross is alienable and heritable. Profits are now rare, but many cases of easements, covenants, and scope rely on precedent arising in cases about profits a prendre.

**progeny**  Direct descendants. Progeny are offspring and descendants, the child or children of a given parent or parents, as well as the children of their children and so on. In animal law, progeny include all of the descendants from a given sire or dam or group of them, such as a herd. In botany, any transgenic plant created from a given plant's DNA is progeny of that plant. In all cases, progeny are designated by biological descent, regardless of direct reproduction, adoption, or acknowledgment.

Metaphorically, progeny represent anything descended from something specific, including intellectual progeny as students carry forth the ideas of their teachers.

*See also:* child (children).

**progeny case**  *See:* precedent, progeny case.

**progressive tax**  *See:* tax, tax burden, progressive tax (progressivity).

**prohibition (prohibit)**  A legal command forbidding some conduct. A prohibition is a law, order, or other source of legal rule that either forbids a specific person or entity from some conduct, or forbids all persons or entities from such conduct. A frequent form of prohibition is the designation of certain goods as contraband, possession of which is forbidden. A prohibition occurs when any conduct is forbidden, by whatever label given to the order or rule. So it is not improper to speak of any bar to conduct as a prohibition; the homicide law is a prohibition on the unjustified taking of a human life. More commonly, certain forms of order or rule are customarily termed as a prohibition, which is no different from any other designation forbidding the decreed conduct or possession.

**prohibition of alcohol**  A ban on the possession of alcohol for drink. The prohibition of alcohol is the legal restriction of its manufacture, import, export, possession, and of the consumption of alcohol as drink. Although prohibition implies a complete ban, most forms of legal alcohol prohibition have incorporated exceptions of one form or another subject to regulation. To speak of Prohibition in American legal history is to speak of the national prohibition of alcohol following the ratification of the Eighteenth Amendment to the Constitution in 1918. Federal efforts to combat smuggling, sale, and possession were dwarfed by widespread disobedience, which led to an increase in the wealth and organization of criminal enterprises. Prohibition came to an end with the ratification of the Twenty-First Amendment in 1933, after which the states were free to regulate the transportation, sale, and consumption of alcohol, subject only to other constitutional limits.

*See also:* pig, blind pig, blind pig as bar.

**Volstead Act**  Statute enforcing Prohibition. The Volstead Act is the popular name for the statute creating federal enforcement of Prohibition, barring the making and possession of drink of more than one half of one percent alcohol (with exceptions for sacramental wine and non-potable spirits), tasking the Commissioner of Internal Revenue and United States Attorneys to enforce it, and creating federal jurisdiction over criminal actions. Its formal name is the National Prohibition Act, Public Law 66-66, ch. 85, 66 Cong., sess. 1 § 26, 41 Stat. 305, 315-16 (1919) (repealed 1935).

**writ of prohibition**  A writ to bar a court or official from an unlawful use of office. The writ of prohibition is an ancient remedy that is still in use in both federal and state courts, which orders an official subject to the jurisdiction of the issuing court to refrain from some conduct that is or would be in violation of the law. The writ of prohibition is an extraordinary remedy, and although it is similar to an equitable injunction, this legal remedy is issued in quite limited situations, by an appellate or supervisory court to the judge of a court subject to its appeal or supervision or by any court to an executive officer subject to the court's jurisdiction. A prohibition will usually lie if a court or official is exercising an apparent authority arising from that office, in a manner or to a result that is not allowed by rules of procedure, jurisdiction, statute, or precedent or the customary evolution of the law, that will cause irreparable harm to the person or entity against whom the authority is used. In a sense, prohibition is the corollary writ to mandamus.

*See also:* mandamus; remedy, extraordinary remedy (extraordinary relief).

**prolixity (prolix)**  Saying too much. Prolixity is the use of too many words in writing or speech. An argument should be presented in the fewest words that allow the detail of facts, the nuance of law, and the emphasis among the good and the bad in the arguments in issue; to use more words is prolix. Judges tend to be harsh critics of lawyers' writing, and the best style to appease them is the most direct. Lawyers, and judges, should avoid prolixity.

Many court rules bar prolix arguments by assigning page limits to pleadings and briefs. These limits are exceeded only with leave of the court, which should only be sought for good cause and rarely. A court confronted with a filing that violates the rule may excuse the violation in its discretion, strike the filing (without or with leave to refile), or strike only so much as exceed the rule. Yet, a dismissal of an action or the striking of a defense on such grounds alone is an abuse of discretion.

**prolonged detention** *See:* incarceration, prolonged incarceration (prolonged detention); detention, prolonged detention.

**prolonged incarceration** *See:* incarceration, prolonged incarceration (prolonged detention).

**promise** A statement that encourages another to rely upon the statement as a commitment. A promise is a statement (or some conduct) by one person in such a form that the person to whom it is made is likely to rely upon the statement as a commitment by the person making the statement or performing the conduct. In general usage, a promise can relate to some future conduct by the speaker, or it can relate the speaker's belief that some past, present, or future condition is (or will be) true or false. For instance, "I will build a wall here" is a promise of future conduct, and "this bridge is safe" is a promise relating a speaker's knowledge or belief. Not all such statements amount to promises, which are limited only to statements on which there is some basis for reasonable reliance, usually because the statement is made in such a manner that a reasonable person who hears it would rely on it as a commitment of the speaker, or because the speaker knows the hearer in fact will likely rely on it. A promise may be expressed in words, implied by the speaker in words (or inferred by the hearer), or construed from conduct. A statement may depend on another event to be true, and so a promise may be conditional or unconditional. The speaker of the promise is the promissor, and the person to whom a promise is made is the promisee. If someone other than the promisee is to receive the benefit of the promise, that person is the beneficary.

A promise, if it does not concern something unlawful, may become legally binding on the promissor and enforceable by the promisee in several ways. Statements of future conduct may give rise to contracts to perform the conduct if the content of the promise is negotiated between the promissor and promisee before the promise is made, either the promisee makes a sufficient promise in return, or the promisee otherwise gives adequate consideration in exchange for the promise. A promise of belief is usually not enforceable, though in some circumstances it gives rise to a warranty. A promise may give rise to a quasi-contract through the detrimental reliance of the promisee or the beneficiary. In all of these circumstances, essential further conditions are usually required, which is the focus the law of contract, as well as some questions of property, tort, and equity.

*See also:* offer, contract offer; acceptance, acceptance as acceptance of an offer | 7. promise as acceptance; promisor; promisee.

**promise of marriage** *See:* marriage, promise of marriage, breach of promise of marriage (breach of promise to marry).

**promise to make a gift** *See:* gift, promise to make a gift.

**alternative promises** Multiple promises, only one of which may be accepted. Alternative promises are multiple promises made so the promisee will perform either one or another but does not intend to perform both or all of the promises. More technically, each alternative promise is contingent on the non-performance of the other by the promisor. The promisor must do one thing promised, or failing that, do the other, but if either is done, the promises are both satisfied. A promise to deliver either pineapples or to deliver coconuts is in fact two alternative promises.

Another form of alternative promises arise in the offer as an election to be made by the offeree, where they are multiple promises each of which are contingent on non-selection by the promissee, which is the case in some contingent offers. As a matter of contract, either sense of alternative promise is possible, and context essential to know which sense is meant in a usage.

As a matter of the theory of contracts, alternative promises mirror Oliver Wendell Holmes, Jr.'s theory that all contractual promises are alternative promises, in that the contracting party promises to perform the contract or promises to pay damages, and either is sufficient.

*See also:* alternative (alternate); contract, specific contracts, alternative contract.

**binding promise** A promise that is legally enforceable by the promisee. A binding promise is an enforceable promise, which arises if the promise is made for consideration amounting to an option, if the promise is made as an offer that is accepted, or if the promise is made in such a manner that the beneficiary may rely upon it, does rely upon it, and the promissor would be estopped from failing to perform owing to detrimental reliance.

**conditional promise** A promise that is not binding unless a condition is satisfied. A conditional promise is a promise subject to condition, so that the promisee cannot demand performance unless the condition is satisfied. A condition may affect either the power of a promisee to accept or the conditions under which duty must be performed once the promise is binding. The most essential aspect of conditional promise is that a promise is not binding until a condition is satisfied in its acceptance or reliance. A condition that depends upon future action or inaction by the promisor does not give rise to an enforceable conditional promise, unless the condition is actually another promise amounting to an alternative promise, the promise conditioned on conduct of the promisor is usually not an unenforceable promise.

Questions of conditional promises arise in considering the duty to perform a promise that is otherwise binding but that is subject to an express or implied condition in its performance. Thus, a contract to provide a service in a new building may be conditioned upon the completion of the building, and if the new building is not complete the promisor may not be bound to perform. Determining what implied conditions limit a promise can be very difficult, regardless of whether the promise is in writing. For instance, some personal promises are impliedly conditioned on the life of the promisor, and if the promisor dies prior to the performance of such promises, the promise is void (though further debts incurred from reliance on the promise by the promisee might persist).

**counterpromise** A promise that is adequate as consideration for other promises. A counterpromise is a promise made as consideration for another promise, the quid pro quo. Once a promise is considered adequate consideration, the common-law rule is that the promise is adequate as consideration for any number of promises. Even so, the sum of the value of the consideration of all counterpromises compared to all promises must satisfy the doctrine of consideration within the jurisdiction.

**dependent promises (mutual promise or mutually dependent promise)** A promise conditioned on prior performance by the other party. A dependent promise is a promise conditioned on another promise, such that the promisor of the dependent promise is not bound to perform unless the promisee has completed performance or has performed so much of the mutual promise that the condition of the dependency is satisfied. A dependent promise is effectively the same as a mutual promise, as expressed in the term "mutually dependent promises." Careful understanding of a contract with such promises is required to determine whether a given promise by one party is dependent only on one among several promises of the other or upon full performance of all promises under the contract. Despite the accurate depictions of the promisor's mutual promises and dependent promises being sufficient consideration for all of the counterpromises of the promisee, this need not be the case depending on the structure of the contract, and some promises of a contract may be mutually dependent only on the other party's performance of the same promise or a related promise.

**gratuitous promise** A promise for which no consideration is given. A gratuitous promise is a promise made as a gift, one for which no consideration is given by the promisee or sought by the promisor. A gratuitous promise cannot give rise to a contract, although it can become enforceable under the circumstances of detrimental reliance or promissory estoppel.

*See also:* reliance, detrimental reliance; gratis.

**illusory promise** An apparent promise that would make no commitment. An illusory promise is a statement that is the form of a promise but that does not include in its substance a definite undertaking or commitment that could be enforced if the promise were binding. An illusory promise promises nothing to the promisee or to a beneficiary whom the promisee would intend to benefit. A promise, for example, that is so dependent on conditions to be performed that performance will not occur is illusory.

**implied promise** A promise arising from conduct or implication. An implied promise arises from circumstance, either from the conduct of the promisor or by statements that imply a promise but do not make a promise expressly. The determinative question is whether the conduct or statements manifest an intent by the promisor to make a promise. In most cases, the inquiry is whether a promisee was reasonable in infering that a promisor had implied a promise.

**independent promises** A promise not conditioned on prior performance by the promissee. An independent promise is a promise that is not conditioned on the performance of a different promise by the other party. A promise is independent relative to each specific promise by the other party, so that a promise may be independent of one promise but dependent on another.

**promissory estoppel** *See:* estoppel (estop or estopped).

**unconditional promise** Promise not subject to condition for performance. An unconditional promise is a promise that is not subject to a specified condition, such as a mutual promise or a specific condition to performance. In a contract, however, a promise is always subject to the implied condition of performance by the other party.

*See also:* promise, conditional promise.

**promisee** The party to whom a promisor makes a promise. A promisee is a person or entity to whom a promise has been made. The promisee may or may not also be the beneficiary of the promise.

*See also:* promise; promisor; beneficiary.

**promisor** The party who makes a promise to a promisee. A promisor is a person or entity who makes a promise. There is no reason a promisor is not also a promisee, as in a contract of mutual promises, in which both parties are promisors and both are promisees of the others. During a negotiation, a promisor remains a promisor until the promise is rejected, and thus, if A promises X to B, B rejects A's offer but offers Y, and A accepts B's offer of Y, B is now considered the promisor.

*See also:* promise.

**promissary note** *See:* note, promissory note (promissary note).

**promissory estoppel**   See: estoppel, promissory estoppel.

**promissory note**   See: note, promissory note (promissary note).

**promoter or incorporator**   See: incorporation, corporate incorporation (promoter or incorporator).

**promoting prostitution**   See: prostitution, promoting prostitution (advancing prostitution).

**promulgation (promulgate)**   The act of making something publicly known. Promulgation is the act of making public something, especially the publication under order of a law or regulation, although the act of promulgation is not the same as ordering that the law or regulation come into force. Various rules and legislation have varying means of promulgation, usually including publication in an official journal or record. Promulgation gives constructive notice of the rule or order to all who are or will be bound by it.

**prong**   A line of an argument or one doctrine among several. A prong, physically, is a projection, usually one among several such as one of the tines of a fork. From this, legal analysis has adopted the prong as a metaphor for one element in a larger analytical pattern: a three-part test might be described as an analysis with three prongs (though each could as easily be called an element or an argument or a test). Further, when a general doctrine has a particular extension or element subject to independent application, that element is also called a prong, such as the equal protection prong of due process.

**pronotary**   See: clerk, clerk of court, prothonotary (pronotary).

**pronoun**   A general term used instead of a specific noun. A pronoun is a part of speech used instead of a noun. Pronouns are frequently used to refer to proper nouns rather than repeating the whole name of a person or whole of a place. Pronouns may also serve to avoid redundancy in prose and to ensure accuracy, such as when a pronoun in a clause signals the noun that the clause modifies.

In drafting, care must be taken to avoid unclear reference in a pronoun, so that each pronoun used has one and only one meaning. In interpretation, nineteenth-century rules of construction to determine an objective meaning for an ambiguous pronoun tend to be difficult to apply and inconclusive in result, and the best efforts of a reader to divine the writer's intent, which is nearly always a matter of fact, may not lead to a conclusive result.

**proof (provable or prove)**   The evidence that demonstrates the truth or falsity of a claim. Proof is a demonstration of the truth of falsity of some argument or claim, based upon evidence and argument. In law, proof is the test of an asserted fact or legal claim that leads an observer, such as a judge or a jury, to believe the assertion or claim is true or false, or at least believe that the assertion of claim is true or false to some level of confidence in that belief. Proof takes many forms, but generally, proof of an argument of some state of affairs in the law depends on sufficient evidence that the claimed state of affairs exists in fact as well as an argument that the demonstrated state of affairs has a particular significance in the law. Thus, customarily legal proof (or judicial proof) requires proof of facts as well as application of those facts to law. As a matter of shorthand, though, proof is often considered to be proof of facts alone.

Proof in law is rarely perfect, and the law does not require evidence sufficient to support most findings of fact by incontrovertible evidence. Rather a system of presumptions and burdens allow facts to be proven to a particular level of confidence at which time the fact is accepted as proven. So to prove a fact is to present evidence sufficient to demonstrate the fact, to the required burden of proof for the action in which fact is in issue.

See also: evidence (evidentiary).

**proof of claim**   See: claim, proof of claim.

**proof of damages**   See: damages, proof of damages.

**burden of persuasion**   A duty to prove a fact in issue, assigned to one or another party. The burden of persuasion is the determination of who must prove a fact in issue, which is allocated according to express or implied presumptions that must be overcome by the party with the burden to persuade the finder of fact. The presumption of innocence must be rebutted by the prosecutor, so the prosecutor bears the burden of persuasion on all matters affecting the basis of guilt, which must be proven according to the burden of proof beyond a reasonable doubt. The burden of persuasion does not shift, even if the burden of production may shift. A plaintiff bears the burden of persuasion on all elements of a claim in a civil action, and if the plaintiff fails sufficiently to prove the case, then the defendant is entitled to the verdict. Yet once the plaintiff has established a prima facie case, while the burden of persuasion remains with the plaintiff, the burden of producing evidence (which had been the plaintiff's) shifts to the defendant in order to disprove the plaintiff's case, and if the defendant fails to do so, the plaintiff has met the burden of persuasion. Throughout, however, whomever has the burden of persuasion must still meet the appropriate burden of proof, which for most claims in a civil action is by a preponderance of the evidence.

See also: proof, burden of proof | burden of persuasion and burden of production and burden of proof; proof, burden of production (burden of going forward).

**burden of production (burden of going forward)**   The obligation to offer evidence in support of a defense or a claim. The burden of production is a requirement on a party to introduce evidence to support an issue in a civil or criminal action. The burden of production is, in the first instance, on the plaintiff in a civil action and on the government in a criminal action.

In a criminal action, if the defendant raises an affirmative defense, the defendant may be required to produce evidence in support of the defense, or the jury will not be instructed it may find the defense was satisfied. Even if the defendant has a burden of production, the government retains the burden of persuasion as to all elements of the crime, including proving that the defense is not proven. The burden of production may shift, but the burden of persuasion, which must be satisfied to the level of the burden of proof, remained unchanged.

In a civil case, a plaintiff may establish a prima facie case, shifting the burden of production to the defendant, and if the defendant cannot produce evidence to rebut the plaintiff's case, the plaintiff has satisfied the burden of persuasion.

The burden of production is effectively the same as the burden of going forward.

*See also:* proof, burden of proof | burden of persuasion and burden of production and burden of proof.

**burden of proof (standard of proof)** The level of confidence with which a fact must be proven in a given action. The burden of proof, or standard of proof, is the degree of certitude that must be engendered by the evidence and argument to prove the truth of any fact that is in dispute in a particular cause of action. If the moving party on a particular issue, or the party with the burden of persuasion, does not meet the burden of proof on that issue, the non-moving party on the issue wins, owing to the effect of the presumptions of lawful conduct, innocence, or good faith.

The burden of proof required to prove a fact will vary according to the nature of the action and the nature of the claim that would be proven by the fact. Consequently, to prove an issue requires the party who seeks to prove the facts underlying that issue must meet a specific burden of proof. These vary from a minor burden, such as a scintilla of evidence, required to win certain motions at a hearing, to proof beyond a reasonable doubt, which is required to convict a person of a crime.

*burden of persuasion and burden of production and burden of proof* The burden of persuasion determines who must prove a case, but the burden of proof is how well the case must be proved. These two burdens are further complicated by the burden of production, which is who must present evidence regarding a fact in issue at a particular stage in the proceedings.

*See also:* proof, burden of persuasion; proof, burden of production (burden of going forward).

**beyond a reasonable doubt (proof beyond a reasonable doubt)** Proof that is convincing to the finder of fact of the truth of a fact in dispute. Proof beyond a reasonable doubt is the highest burden of proof presently required in the U.S. legal system. Proof beyond a reasonable doubt is

proof sufficiently convincing of some matter of fact that the finder of fact is convinced the matter is true, and therefore the finder of fact has no doubt that arises from the evidence, either that the matter is proved in general or that the evidence was sufficient and reliable as to each distinct question essential to the matter.

The reasonable–doubt element of this formulation is a doubt that would be held by a reasonable person based on the evidence or lack of evidence. Reasonable implies both the objective nature of the doubt and that it would be held by reasonable people, as well as the rejection of certain bases of doubt such as hypothetical, conjectural, theological, or other sources of doubt that do not depend on the evidence.

Despite the relative strictness of proof beyond a reasonable doubt, the instruction was created as a means of lowering the threshold of confidence in order to allow easier convictions. The earlier instruction had required the prosecution to convince the finder of fact of the defendant's guilt, and if the jury was not convinced, it did not convict. Some jurisdictions have gone farther, defining "reasonable doubt" as doubt for which a reason can be given. This formulation is not reasonable doubt, because a reasonable person may have a genuine doubt but not be able to reduce that doubt to words. A doubt for which a reason can be given is articulable doubt. The articulable–doubt standard places the defendant in the position of having to prove that a doubt has a rationale, which effectively reverses the burden of persuasion, and it amounts to an unconstitutional shift of the burden of proof onto the defendant.

**clear and convincing evidence (proof by clear and convincing evidence)** Sufficient evidence to make highly likely the truth of the matter proposed. Proof by clear and convincing evidence is a high standard but not the most stringent burden of proof in the U.S. legal system. Variously labeled in different jurisdictions, the functional role of the standard is to require more evidence than a proof by a preponderance of the evidence but not quite so much as proof beyond a reasonable doubt. The finder of fact must be convinced by evidence that clearly supports a given assertion or claim as true, although the finder of fact may still harbor doubts of unlikely bases for the claim or assertion's falsity. Stated another way, a clear and convincing standard requires proof sufficient for the finder of fact to believe that it is highly probable that the claim or allegation is true. Clear and convincing evidence should create in the mind of the trier of a fact an abiding conviction matter it supports is highly probable. The clear and convincing standard is required in civil actions when a liberty interest is in issue, such as a civil commitment for mental illness, and when a presumption of legality exists, in a claim against a patent or for breach of fiduciary duty.

**clear and positive proof**  Clear and convincing evidence. Clear and positive proof is variation on and alternative form of clear and convincing evidence.

**irrefragable proof (irrefutable proof)**  Proof that cannot be disproved. Irrefragable proof, or irrefutable proof, is proof to the highest possible level of confidence. Irrefragable is a synonym of irrefutable. The presumption of the good faith of government officials is sometimes said to be so strong it is rebutted only with well nigh irrefragable proof.

"Well nigh irrefragable" is a diminution of the standard of irrefragability, yet it is still very high, and it is usually equated with a standard of proof by clear and convincing evidence. Without such moderation, this often-quoted standard of proof contradicts public policy.

**manifest weight of the evidence**  A threshold standard for obtaining a new trial after verdict. The manifest weight of the evidence is a standard of confidence in the evidence somewhere between a preponderance of the evidence and clear and convincing evidence. The manifest weight of the evidence is the standard used in some jurisdictions for a litigant to demonstrate the falsity of a verdict in order to obtain a new trial after a verdict has been rendered. The litigant is entitled to a new trial only if it is shown that the verdict rendered was against the "manifest weight of the evidence."

**modicum of evidence (some evidence or any evidence or no evidence)**  Any amount of credible evidence that is more than none to support a conclusion. A modicum of evidence is a small amount of evidence, and though this quantity is probably more than a scintilla, is is not enough to persuade every reasonable observer to a conclusion. A "modicum of evidence" is the same as "some evidence" or "any evidence" in support of a decision or conclusion. An administrative decision that is subject to judicial review for abuse of discretion or a similarly low standard of review will be upheld if there is a modicum of evidence in the record before the administrative decision-maker that would support the decision made. The modicum standard is higher than a standard require no evidence at all, and it is less than a standard requiring evidence in the record sufficient as a matter of law to meet a civil or criminal standard of proof required for a finding of liability or guilt.

**preponderance of the evidence**  Proof that an issue is more likely true than not. A preponderance of the evidence is the lowest burden of proof, used in civil actions for damages in connection with claims not involving deliberate wrongdoing or breach of fiduciary duty and not seeking punitive damages. In such cases, the finder of fact must be persuaded that there is more evidence in favor of a given claim or assertion than there is against it. This is sometimes framed as 50%+1, in which the preponderance is satisfied if the party with the burden of persuasion has demonstrated its claims to a level of confidence that is at least barely more than a perfect balance of the evidence.

**scintilla of evidence**  Very little evidence, but evidence nonetheless. A scintilla of evidence, or a spark of evidence, is the least quantum of evidence possible in support of a given fact in issue. A scintilla of evidence is the requirement when there is an implied legal bias toward a given result; the result is had if there is only a faint showing of evidence in its favor, as in the degree to which evidence is required to sustain a jury verdict on appeal. The appellate scintilla of evidence may be described as equal inferences, when there is sufficient evidence to infer either outcome in an action. A scintilla of evidence may also be sufficient to shift the burden of production on certain claims or defenses.

*See also:* scintilla.

### forms of proof

**affirmative proof (positive proof)**  Proof that demonstrates the truth of a claim. Affirmative proof is evidence that affirms a specific claim of fact, usually by demonstrating either the fact in issue or by demonstrating a fact that must be true as one of several component facts in the issue being proved. To prove a person was present at a place at a given time, a photograph taken of the person there at that time is affirmative proof. Affirmative proof is usually contrasted with rebuttal proof or circumstantial proof.

Note: there appears to be no difference between positive proof and affirmative proof. In each usage, the question is whether the claimant puts forward proof that demonstrates the claim, rather than relying only on evidence that refutes the claim's denial.

*See also:* affirmative.

**epidemiological proof (epidemiological evidence)**  Proof of a likely medical cause. Epidemiological proof is proof of likely causation of an effect on the health or vitality of a person (or on plants or other animals) that is derived by large-scale analysis of cause and effects from disease or other conditions affecting health. Epidemiological evidence may demonstrate the potential of a person's exposure to a particular risk factor to manifest a particular resulting health condition.

**negative proof (negative evidence)**  Proof of a claim by disproving the rejection of the claim. Negative proof is evidence that contradicts a specific claim of fact, by demonstrating that a logically reverse claim or assertion is false. A demonstration that something is true by offering affirmative evidence to demonstrate it amounts to a demonstration that the logically opposed claim must be false. For example, proving that a person is in one place at one time is negative evidence of the opposing claim that the person was at a different place at the same time. Negative evidence includes rebuttal evidence and alibis.

**offer of proof**   A record of evidence to be entered in court. An offer of proof is a statement by counsel of evidence available to the court that the party moves be admitted, which describes the testimony or exhibit offered, relates the significance of the testimony or exhibit to the party's theory of the case, and provides the foundation for its admissibility. An offer of proof is essentially the same as a proffer of evidence, prior to the court's ruling on its admission, though it may be made after the court denies its admission as a record for appeal.

*See also:* proffer (proffer of evidence or proffered evidence or evidence proffered).

**proof as measure of alcohol**   Twice the percentage of a liquid that is alcohol. Proof is a measure of the alcoholic content of a liquid. Pure, denatured alcohol is full-proof, or 200 proof, which is difficult to maintain. Most spirits are between 70 and 110 proof, or between 35 percent and 55 percent alcohol. Most wines are between 6 and 25 proof, or 3 percent to 12.5 percent alcohol, and most beers are lower proof than most wines.

**proof as tested (proving)**   Having a demonstrated ability or tolerance. A proof of someone or something, or the proving of a person or thing, is to test it for a particular ability, or to assess its ability to perform under a particular condition. Thus, a person's mettle, bravery, or honesty may be proof against challenge, and a rope or metal sheet may be proof against strain.

**statistical proof (statistical evidence)**   Proof of likely causation from the study of many causes and many effects. Statistical proof is evidence from a statistical assessment of any group of events. Most often, it is an assessment of a cause relative to a potential effect, or an effect relative to a potential cause, among a population of people affected by a cause or demonstrating an effect. Thus, statistics may be used to determine whether a cause is likely or unlikely to manifest an effect in among a group of people. Statistics can never prove a particular effect followed from a single cause in a single instance or case, although statistics can determine the probability of the result from a given cause. Statistical evidence is accepted in a variety of cases, such as mass tort, indeed required in certain cases, such as employment discrimination proven by disparate impact.

**propensity (pertinent trait of character)**   A likelihood of behavior. A propensity is a pertinent trait of character, the likelihood or inclination that a person or animal has to engage in certain forms of behavior. Evidence of past acts is not admissible in a trial to determine whether a person has committed a later similar act or to demonstrate a propensity to commit the specific act in question (although it is allowed for other purposes, such as identification). Evidence of a lack or propensity toward such acts may, however, be admitted by a defendant, and rebuttal evidence based on similar past acts is then allowed. Regarding domestic animals, knowledge of propensity toward a given behavior is sufficient to put an owner on notice the animal may behave in that manner.

*See also:* inference, forbidden inference.

**proper**   Appropriate to the task according to custom. Proper designates the scope of conduct, actions, or projects that are appropriate for a given task, according to the rules and precedents that would be customary for the person carrying out the task to respect.

Famously, the Necessary and Proper Clause allows to Congress the powers necessary and proper to carry out its enumerated powers. As interpreted by Chief Justice Marshall in McCulloch v. Maryland, 17 U.S. 4 Wheat. 316 316 (1819), the extent of the power depends on necessity as judged by the purposes for which Congress was delegated its powers.

**proper law**   *See:* choice, choice of law, proper law.

**proper lookout**   *See:* lookout, proper lookout.

**proper party**   *See:* party, party to an action, proper party (improper party).

**property**   What may be owned and the relationship of owning and using it. Property is a system of legal relationships between an owner or owners, the thing owned, third parties, and the state. Property is also the label for each specific thing that is subject to such ownership relationships. The relations of owner to property include a broad array of rights, duties, and interests, including the legal allowance of an owner to use the thing and to control its use, to exclude others from its use, to divide or apportion it, to transfer it to others, to exist in a market in which value is transferred among individuals, and to serve as the basis for the creation, aggregation, and distribution of wealth in society.

*See also:* ownership (owner or own).

**property claim**   *See:* claim, property claim.

**property clause**   *See:* constitution, U.S. Constitution, clauses, Property Clause (Needful Rules Clause).

**property insurance**   *See:* insurance, category of insurance, property insurance.

**property interest**   *See:* due process of law, property interest.

**property right**   *See:* right, property right, correlative rights; right, property right.

**property settlement**   *See:* divorce, property settlement | community property.

**property tax**   *See:* tax, property tax.

**property waste**   *See:* waste, doctrine of waste (property waste).

**after-acquired property**   Property obtained after a date or event. After-acquired property includes any interest or ownership in any property following a specific date or event, such as a bankruptcy, perfection of a security interest, or death. There is no limit on after acquisition of property of a decedent's estate caused by the close of probate. The property so acquired is transmitted directly to the specified devisees, legatees, or heirs.

**air rights**   Property interests in the air above the land. Air rights are the vested interest of the owner of lands in the space directly above the land. Air rights are usually considered in two forms, the first being the ability to build up from the land, the second being the right to control activity in the air above the land. Air rights for development and construction may be regulated like any other land use. Although air rights are now not unlimited, they allow a property owner to control interference with the property from aircraft or other objects traveling directly above the ground at a level low enough to interfere with uses on the ground. Air rights do not extend to the upper reaches of the atmosphere. Air rights are subject to compensated condemnation when required, for instance, for the approach lanes of airport runways.

*See also:* coelum (coelo).

**bundle of rights metaphor (bundle of sticks)**   Ownership is the sum of a bundle of rights. The bundle of rights is a pervasive metaphor for the ideas of ownership and of property itself. Ownership is depicted as the sum of all of the interests owned relative to some thing, which may be pulled like a straw from a bundle, dividing component elements of the thing, as well as privileges in each or all, and also ownership divided among one or several and divided between present and future. This model is useful but limiting, as it does little to explain when or how each such interest will be recognized by the law or protected from intrusion by someone else.

**forms of property**

**corporeal property (tangible property)**   Property that exists in physical form. Corporeal property is property capable of being possessed in a physical form as a solid, liquid, or gas, which can be touched and seen, or at least detected by physical means. Corporeal property is tangible, and tangible property is in effect synonymous with corporeal property. Land, chattels, structures, animals, commodities, oil, water, and waste are all corporeal property.

The primary difference between corporeal and incorporeal is the ability to be physically in one's possession, the hallmark of corporeal interests, and the right to do or to use some other property, which is the hallmark of incorporeal interests. Certain interests, such as severed mineral rights are considered corporeal in some jurisdictions and incorporeal in others.

**incorporeal property (intangible property or intangibles)**   Non-physical rights from physical property. Incorporeal property is property that has no corpus, no physical existence, but is a right, claim, or defensible interest that is protected as property, and most of which arise from a relationship to some corporal property. Incorporeal property is intangible, and the two terms are effectively interchangeable. Incorporeal property includes patents, copyrights, trademarks, and other intellectual property; easements, and interests in another's land such as profits; options and certain future interests in land; corporate good will; some forms of corporate shares, partnership shares, bonds, and other forms of debt; bank accounts, insurance benefits, retirement benefits, and annuities; intangibles represented by negotiable instruments (including cash); and choses in action.

**found property (finds or law of finds or law of finders)**   Property mislaid, lost, or abandoned and found by someone not its true owner. Found property includes all chattels and accounts that were once possessed but then were mislaid, lost, or abandoned, later to be found in circumstances making the determination of the true owner immaterial or impracticable. Such property is analyzed according to the property rules known as the law of finders, which characterizes the property according to the manner of its being separated from its owner, and so abandoned, lost, and mislaid property is subject to varying rules of ownership when they are later discovered.

In general, a finder of mislaid property does not acquire an ownership interest in mislaid property but in most jurisdictions has a claim to the property that ripens to ownership over a period of time if no owner can be found. A finder of lost property has an ownership interest that is good against everyone except the true owner. A finder of abandoned property in a public place acquires an ownership interest. In all three cases, however, the owner of the place where the property is found will have a superior claim to the property if the property is in any way connected to the land (though there is an additional exception for a treasure trove, which is again given to the finder). The common law rules have been frequently changed by statute to create public accounts and depositories, and to better manage abandoned accounts, gift cards, and buying cards, which now more quickly escheat to the state.

*See also:* find (finder or finders); escheat.

**abandoned property**   Property relinquished but to no one. Abandoned property is any property with no owner, in which the immediate past owner of the property intentionally relinquished any claim, possession, right, and title to ownership of the property without ensuring there would be a subsequent owner. It may also be inferred that property has been abandoned if it has been lost and unclaimed for a significant amount of time. Abandoned chattel property found in public may be claimed as owned by the finder, but abandoned property found embedded in private realty is, like lost property, ordinarily the property of the owner of that realty. If abandoned property is not claimed by a person with a lawful right to do so, it may escheat to the state. Abandoned accounts are disbursed to known successors in interest or allowed to escheat. Abandoned property may be searched without a warrant, because there is no privacy interest remaining in it.

*See also:* property, found property, lost property.

**lost property**  Property that has been left by mistake. Lost property is property that has been unknowingly and accidentally discarded, and the true owner still intends or desires to recover it. Lost property is neither mislaid nor abandoned. The general rule is that the finder of lost property has an ownership interest in it, which is good as against any other claimant but the true owner. The finder has a duty to take reasonable steps to locate the true owner, but failing the discovery of the true owner or the claim for the lost property within the time of the statute of limitations, the ownership is absolute in the finder. Lost property found that is in any manner embedded in the land is, however, owned by the owner of the land.

See also: property, found property, abandoned property.

**mislaid property**  Property deliberately placed but forgotten. Mislaid property is property that an owner left in a place with an intention to return to the property but then failed to do so. A finder acquires no ownership interest in mislaid property, which is considered a bailment of the owner of the locus in quo, the place in which the misplaced property is found. The owner of the locus in quo then acquires a duty to use reasonable efforts to seek the true owner. After the time in which the statute of limitations has run, the property owner as bailee may take title to it. In some jurisdictions, statutes have modified this rule to create a claim of the finder that may be asserted against the state, to which the property is entrusted until the claim of the finder ripens or until the true owner is located.

**treasure trove (trove)**  Objects of unusual value once lost or hidden and later found. A trove is something that was lost for a time and is later found. Treasure trove is treasure that was lost or hidden for some period of time and that is later found. The content of the treasure is a defining aspect of its treatment in law, and it may include money and objects of unusual value such as gold, silver, jewels, valuable commercial papers, or antiquities that were of value when lost or hidden. Treasure trove need not be buried but must be hidden, for some long time, perhaps at least for a generation. Treasure trove found on land is considered the property of the finder as against all but the true owner or the true owner's successors, and the finder must take reasonable steps to locate the owner or successors, the title ripening to full ownership after the statute of limitations has run. Treasure found at sea is subject to the rights of salvage and sovereignty.

See also: property, found property (finds or law of finds or law of finders).

**immovable property (immovables or movable property or movables)**  The civil division between property that is movable and property that is not. Immovable and movable property is a categorical difference in the treatment of property in the civil law.

Immovable property includes land and buildings, whether the buildings are fully fixed onto the land or not, crops, natural resources, and other things closely associated with the land. Immovables are roughly equivalent to the common-law category of realty. Immovables are subject to distinct property law, particularly in the interests of spouses and children.

Movables include all forms or property that are inherently capable of movement. Movables are roughly equivalent to the common-law category of chattels.

**interest in property (property interest)**  An ownership interest in property, whether real or chattel. A property interest is an ownership interest in property, whether real or chattel, tangible or intangible. Property interests are protected under the Due Process Clause of the Constitution, and neither a state nor the United States may infringe on a property interest without due process of law. This breadth of interest is distinct from an interest in real property that is subject to the protection of the Just Compensation Clause, which applies only to property taken for the public benefit and not property incidentally injured or occupied as a matter of the police protection of public health or safety.

Property interests as a matter of the common law are divided into present possessory interests and future interests.

See also: due process of law; taking (takings or taking of private property without just compensation).

**future interest**  See: estate, future interest.

**terminable interest**  Property interest that will end with the lapse of time or a fulfillment of a contingency. A terminable interest is an interest in property that will terminate based solely upon the lapse of time or upon the occurrence of a specified event or contingency. Life estates are a common terminable interest. Terminable interests are particularly important in calculating the taxable estate of a decedent, because the Code provides that terminable interests do not qualify for the marital deduction under IRC § 2056.

**mixed property**  Two or more forms of property combined. Mixed property arises from several distinctions in property when property of two categories is combined, such as: (a) when personal property is combined with real property, (b) when marital property is combined with separate property, (c) when property of a marital community is combined with separate property, (d) when property subject to a security interest is combined with other property (whether the other property is unsecured or subject to a security interest held by a different party), or (e) when property of a partnership is combined with the separate property of a partner.

**personal property (personalty)**  A person's property that is not realty. Personal property includes all rights and interests in all forms of property that are not themselves real property. Personal property includes tangible and intangible property, even property that is related to or incidental to an ownership in real property. Personal property includes ownership in all of the physically manifest property of movable objects and chattels, as well as intangible property such as securities, and accounts receivable, claims and actions, and intellectual property. Money in the form of currency or coin, that is, cash, is personal property, and when it is on deposit in a bank or other institution, it is intangible personal property. Personal property, or at least tangible personal property and cash are subject to the tort of conversion.

Personal property is subject to many narrower definitions by statutes that define personal property for certain uses or purposes, such as for taxation of ownership, for taxation at severance, or taxation at sale. Personal property is sometimes particularly defined for a conversion statute or for the protection of personal property sold as trade goods. Certain items of personal property are particularly listed in non-exclusive lists for the purposes of guiding partition as in divorce. In some jurisdictions, an allowance for personal property is given to a debtor to free it from attachment by creditors or from being assets of a bankruptcy estate. This allowance may be set as a dollar amount or as a percentage of the value of assets held.

Note: there is no great difference between personal property and personalty, though the term "Personalty" is often used, when it is still used, for tangible personal property.

**tangible personal property**  Physically manifested personal property. Tangible personal property is property other than realty that has a physical presence or a discernible, measurable effect in the physical world. Tangible physical property has a reality of form in matter or energy; it does not exist merely as a record or idea of itself. Chattels (or movables) are tangible real property, and tangible real property is subject to theft and to the tort of conversion.

Tangible physical property does not include either real property or intangible property or incorporeal rights, such as an account receivable or intellectual property. Thus, papers, books, account records, films, and photographs are tangible physical property, though the rights to control the ideas and images or the information and claims reflected within them are intangible, as are the debts or claims in commercial paper and the equity or claims in securities. Tangible personal property includes materials consumed, including electricity, water, and gas, as well as materials only slightly discernible, such as broadcast radio or computer signals. Still, the most common forms of tangible property are patently physical objects that are owned by an individual: personal effects, such as clothes and jewels; furniture and art; automobiles, boats, and airplanes; tools; books, records, discs, computers, and such other objects as people may own or possess.

Tangible personal property may be specifically defined in each jurisdiction for the purpose of its tax on personal property, which is often assessed annually. Tangible personal property is subject to taxation by the state in which it is located, no matter where the owner is domiciled. In many instances, the general definition of personal property above resonates with the statutory use of "tangible personal property" or "personal property." Yet a distinct and narrower definition of personal property may be used to determine those forms of property that are subject to a sales tax.

*See also:* chattel.

**private property**  Property a private person holds exclusively, subject only to limited state interference. Private property is a concept of ownership that allows a person to hold property that is exclusive of the rights of others, with the rights to use, take, exploit according to the will of the owner. Private property may be granted, sold, inherited or retained at the will of the private owner. Private property is subject only to certain limitations necessary for the continuation of the property, including restrictions on the use of property in a manner that does not harm the use of other property and maintenance of the state's right to intrude for reasonable enforcement of the law. This intrusion might include the collection of a property tax, the service of an arrest warrant, or inspection of a dangerous structure, all of which must be done within the limits of the Constitution and the laws.

**property right (property rights)**  Ownership, use, or claim in land, things, or ideas protected by law. Property rights is a broad, collective term for the powers to do or to use or to affect some interest that are protected by law from at least some forms of interference. As a matter of the law of property, property rights are the rights of ownership, possession, and use of lands, things, and ideas, including intellectual property. As a matter of constitutional law, property rights include the privilege of a person to acquire and hold property; the right to own, possess, and use property without its taking by the government for a public use without compensation; and the right to be free in the use of one's property from unreasonable and unwarranted searches.

*See also:* right, legal right.

**quasi-property right**  An interest protected by law as if it were property though it is not. A quasi-property right is an interest of some form that is not a property interest—such as an interest in one's removed tissues or body parts, an interest in the dead body of a family member, an interest in child rearing or education—that is nonetheless a status between the person and the thing or service that is worthy of recognition and protection by law. A quasi-property right may provide support for standing in a lawsuit, injunctive relief, unjust enrichment, and damages for emotional distress, even though the thing or service itself is not given a value as a matter of policy and is therefore not subject to damages for its loss per se.

*See also:* corpse (cadaver or dead body).

**surface right**   A right to the use of the surface of the land, but not its mineral interests. A surface right, or surface estate, is the ownership and right to use the surface of a parcel, which is independent of the mineral rights in the same parcel. A single owner might hold both, in which case the estates are merged, but if they are separate, the holder of the surface estate holds the surface rights, which are subject to an easement in the mineral-rights holder.

**public property**   Property owned by a government. Public property includes all property owned by a government, usually but not always meaning public lands. For the purposes of determining jurisdiction, a public way over private land is usually considered public property, at least as to a person lawfully using the way.

Public property is not inherently open to use by the public, but it is regulated by the governmental entity that owns it. Thus, the determination of the scope of public entrance and any purpose that limits that scope may alter the character of the public property for certain constitutional purposes. Public property that is generally open to the public for all uses may amount to a public forum, in which public speech or assembly may be limited only as truly needed to support a compelling governmental interest. Public property open to the public only for a limited purpose and in limited scope is a quasi-public or designated public forum, is open to regulation as to time, place, manner. Public property that is not open to the public without meeting the usual constraints of an invitee or licensee is not a public forum and subject to any content-neutral regulation that is reasonable.

**real property (realty or property in land)**   Permanent, alienable, and heritable property, especially land. Real property is the category of property that is permanent and that is potentially subject to alienation or inheritance, the most common form of which is the ownership of land or any interest in lands. Real property therefore includes the corporeal ownership of the thing that may be owned, such as the land itself, as well as the incorporeal ownership of distinct rights that may exist in the thing, such as an easement over the land or a non-possessory future interest in the land. Real property generally may be alienated but only by deed. All property that is not real property is personal property.

*See also:* property, real property, real estate.

**cujus est solum ejus est usque ad coelum (center of the earth to the roof of the sky)**   Who owns the land owns it from the underworld to the heavens. Cujus est Solum Ejus Est Usque ad Coelum is a maxim from the common law that describes an absolute sense of ownership in real property, that the owner of the land owned all above and below it, including both its rights to be free from overhanging impediment and its rights to the minerals below. The maxim is essentially poetic, and various translations represent the interest as from from the depths of the Earth to the roof of the sky, or from the center of the Earth to the heavens. In all, the idea remained the same.

In an age of pooled mineral interests and aircraft overflights, this maxim has been largely abandoned. As a matter of federal law, ownership creates no basis for a claim against aircraft, although if an aircraft creates specific and individual harm on a parcel of land, liability would be based on an ultrahazardous activity rather than on trespass.

**real estate**   All land and interests in land subject to sale, lease, or tax. Real estate is the whole of the property in land or related to land that is subject to commercial transaction or to taxation, including ownership interests, leaseholds, easements, covenants, mineral interests, development rights, air rights, and severance rights in lands or structures on the land.

*See also:* property, real property (realty or property in land).

**realtor**   A realty broker or agent. A realtor is any person licensed to represent the buyer or the seller of real property, including a broker, an agent, or a sales associate employed by either a broker or agent. A realtor represents a buyer or a seller in the negotation and closing of a transaction involving real estate, including the creation of a lease, when the realtor might represent the landlord or the tenant.

**stolen property**   *See:* goods, stolen goods, receiver of stolen goods (receiving stolen property); goods, stolen goods (stolen poperty).

**wasting property (wasting asset)**   Property with a commercial value that depletes over time to nothing. A wasting property is a real, personal, or incorporeal property that has a commercial use or natural source of income that is finite or that otherwise deteriorates over time, either through human use, exploitation, or owing to natural degradation. An ore mine or oil well are wasting properties, but a forest, which may be renewed, is not.

**prophylactic**   Preventative. A prophylactic is a thing or idea that is intended to prevent something from occurring. A prophylactic law is, therefore, a law intended to prevent the occurrence of some harmful occurrence, rather than to respond only after it has occurred. All laws with a deterrent effect are, to that extent, prophylactic, but the term is more appropriately used not for a response by state officials but for an active prevention of harm before harm occurs, such as the Miranda warning as a means of avoiding uninstructed confession, or the Clean Water permit system as a means of avoiding pollution spills into a river.

Prophylactic is both an adjective and a noun. When used as a noun without other context, it likely refers to a prophylactic device, such as a condom, intended to limit pregnancy and disease transmission during sex.

**prophylactic instruction** *See:* instruction, jury instruction, cautionary jury instruction (prophylactic instruction).

**propinquity** Proximity, or a family relationship. Propinquity is closeness or nearness. It was once used primarily in the law to denote a family relationship, but it is now more commonly used in the sense of physical nearness. A police officer cannot search or arrest a person for no more probable cause than the person's propinquity to another person taken under arrest, though that proximity may be one among several bases for probable cause to believe the person has committed a crime or poses a danger to the officer or others.

*See also:* proximity.

**proponent (opponent)** One arguing in favor of an issue. The proponent is the party who propounds a given argument, who proposes a given judgment, who moves for a given order, or who supports the argument of the party who does so. The proponent, in each instance, propounds, or argues for the purpose of seeing the desired result occur. The party who opposes that result is the opponent.

**proportionality (disproportional or proportional or proportionate)** Balance among people, and between crime and punishment. Proportionality is a fundamental concept in law and justice, requiring that the law be balanced in allocating powers and benefits, as well as burdens and sanctions, among all people. Proportionality is similar to utilitarianism, one school of which seeks method to establish what a proportional outcome would be in specific circumstances. Anything that lacks proportionality is disproportionate.

Proportionality takes several important, recurrent forms, though it pervades nearly every principle and rule in the legal system. Some of its major legal applications are:

Proportional punishment. The punishment for a crime should be proportionate to the harm committed by the criminal. Thus, crimes of similar harm should have similar punishment.

Proportional remedies. Proportionality is a fundamental doctrine in many remedial theories. In general, the compensatory formula is intended to assure a level of compensation that is equal to the harm caused. As among defendants, however, the level of compensation owed is to be proportioned according to the responsibility each bears for the harm that caused the plaintiff's injuries.

Proportional representation. Representative bodies should be proportionally representative of the people whom they represent. This takes a variety of forms, depending on what aspects of the people represented are considered most important. The most fundamental sense is that each representative should represent nearly the same number of people, so that each person represented has approximately the same level of representation, as expressed as a portion of a representative's vote. When categorical ideas of the person are seen as important in making decisions, such as race, gender, religion, or wealth, proportional representation would require that the group of representatives have, in sum, a proportion by category of each race, or each gender, etc. that reflects the community at large.

Proportional hiring. When employment is allocated by a proportional means, then the number of people hired should be selected so that the proportion of those hired in each relevant category reflect approximately the proportion of the population as a whole. Likewise, proportional promotion requires that the group of people promoted in a job reflects within it an approximation of the relevant category of the workforce from which they were promoted.

*See also:* pro, pro rata; punishment, cruel and unusual punishment, proportionality review; retaliation, lex talionis; taking, regulatory taking, conditional use, rough proportionality.

**proportionality review** *See:* punishment, cruel and unusual punishment, proportionality review.

**proposal (propose)** A formal offer, recommendation, or plan. A proposal is a formal presentation by one party to another party for the second party's consideration or acceptance. A proposal may be an offer, including a bid for a contract for which requests for bids have been made, that might be accepted to form a contract or that might be the basis for negotiation toward that end. A proposal might also be a plan submitted for notice, review, or approval by a regulatory agency, or a draft or precis of such a plan.

**proposition** An offer of work, of an idea, or of a law. A proposition is any idea or offer put forth for the acceptance of another. An offer to do business or enter a contract is a business proposition. From this sense, the term became synonymous with the solicitation by a prostitute to a client. A proposition in an electoral sense is a proposed law that is put before the voters in a referendum.

In formal argument, the proposition is the first statement, the initial premise of the argument or the major premise of a syllogism. From this a less technical sense has developed, and a proposition may now mean any distinct argument in support of some result.

**proprietary** To own things, or to be owned. Proprietary demonstrates a relationship to a proprietor, or owner, and so proprietary may mean either that something is owned, such as a proprietary secret or a proprietary relationship, or that one owns something, such as a proprietary interest. In nineteenth-century usage, a proprietary was also a noun, a synonym for proprietor.

*See also:* proprietor.

**proprietary eponym** *See:* trademark, mark, generic mark, genericide (proprietary eponym).

**proprietary interest** Ownership. Proprietary interest is the interest an owner has in something, such as a shareholder in a corporation, a farmer in a crop, or a storekeeper in the store inventory. The interest of a consumer or contractor or creditor in a concern is not a proprietary interest, which turns on an ownership or equitable interest like ownership.

**proprietor**   An owner. A proprietor is the owner of anything, but there are several historical and customary uses.

A proprietor is an owner of a trade or business enterprise, in which the selection of proprietor rather than owner communicates an expectation that a proprietor will take an active role as owner in the endeavors of the enterprise. This usage generally implies a natural person, not an artificial person, and that the nature of the ownership is not highly diffuse among many owners. Thus, a shareholder of a large publicly held corporation rarely is spoken of as a proprietor, although, interestingly, shareholders are considered proprietors of a corporation in the event of its insolvency.

A proprietor of land has an ownership interest in the land, including a co-tenancy, but usually some form of freehold interest, and not including a leasehold or easement.

A proprietor is the owner of a venue in which copyrighted works of music or drama are to be performed.

A proprietor is the owner and keeper of a hotel, motel or guest house.

A proprietor was the holder of a charter granting lands in the English colonies, with the power to grant ownership in those lands to others.

**proprietorship**

**sole proprietorship**   A business owned by one person. A sole proprietorship is a business owned entirely by an individual, and there is no legal difference between the business and the owner. A sole proprietorship contrasts with business corporations (which ordinarily have more than one director and usually have more than one co-owner or shareholder) and partnerships (which by definition have more than one owner).

*See also:* corporation (corporate or incorporate); partnership.

**proration (prorate)**   To allocate an amount or share proportionally. A proration is an allocation of a cost, benefit, fee, service, or any other thing according to a proportion, whether of a fee for a service owed or shares among distributees or costs among those severally liable. Frequently, a fee for service over time is prorated to reduce the fee for a fixed term for time during the term in which the service is not provided. Interest, rents, or other payments that are computed by terms may be similarly prorated when a complete term is inappropriate for a payment. Proration occurs in the allocation of shares among wells in common pools of oil, and the income from a partnership is prorated among the partners who hold varying shares in it.

*See also:* pro, pro rata; proportionality (disproportional or proportional or proportionate).

**prorogation (prorogue)**   The recess of a proceeding or activity until a later time. Prorogation is the suspending or delaying of a duty for some time in the future, though its original meaning was to continue a duty into the future, like an extension. Today it is now more like a recess from the duty.

The term is most often used to describe a brief recess of Parliament, as opposed to its adjournment or dissolution. Yet the term is applied by lawyers to any proceeding or task that is prorogued for an interval, or even suspended until recalled at some unspecified later time.

*See also:* forum, forum selection clause, prorogation clause (prorogated jurisdiction); parliament.

> **prorogated jurisdiction**   *See:* forum, forum selection clause, prorogation clause (prorogated jurisdiction).

> **prorogation clause**   *See:* forum, forum selection clause, prorogation clause (prorogated jurisdiction).

**proscription (proscribe or proscribed)**   A written decree prohibiting some person or conduct. A proscription is a writing, particularly a decree, order, or statute, that gives notice that some conduct is forbidden or that orders some person to be punished. Thus, a person may be proscribed, which ordinarily would have meant banishment or a decree of outlawry. A course of conduct may also be proscribed, and this is the more common sense of the term now.

Note: proscription is often confused with prescription, but to proscribe conduct is to prohibit it and to prescribe conduct is to require it.

*See also:* prescription (prescribable or prescriptive or prescribe).

**prosecution (prosecute)**   The means by which one is accused of a crime and tried by a public official. Prosecution is the procedure by which a person or entity is accused of a crime as a matter of record, and whose case is prepared and tried by the attorney for the government in whose name the accusation is made, seeking to determine whether there is evidence sufficient for a jury to convict the accused and for the judge to pass sentence for the crime. Although prosecutions were once brought by private persons in the name of the state, prosecutions for crimes are now brought exclusively by prosecutors who are officials of the state or federal executives. The prosecution is subject to the rules of criminal procedure in its jurisdiction, and if the prosecution is in state court, to the constitutional procedural and substantive rights afforded by both the federal and state constitutions and to state statutes. Federal prosecutions are conducted according to the Federal Rules of Criminal Procedure, federal statutes, and the United States Constitution.

Note: in its most general sense, to prosecute is to to pursue some person, project, or effort, and it is still said that a private litigant may prosecute a claim or defense, and dilatory procedures in a civil action are called a failure to prosecute. This usage does not signal a criminal action.

*See also:* defendant, criminal defendant (criminal defense).

**malicious prosecution** A remedy for an acquitted criminal defendant whose accuser lacked probable cause. Malicious prosecution is a tort claim by a plaintiff against whom a criminal prosecution was brought by a defendant, who initiated or procured the criminal prosecution for an improper purpose and without probable cause when the plaintiff was innocent and was acquitted or otherwise received an affirmative result in the criminal proceedings. Although efforts have been made to create a general federal action for malicious prosecution under 42 U.S.C. § 1983, the tort remains a state–law action, although denials of the due process of law or other federal constitutional rights may be independently asserted in some cases of malicious prosecution.

*See also:* tort, dignitary tort.

**selective prosecution** Prosecutorial discrimination in charging certain defendants. Selective prosecution is the determination by a prosecutor to charge one or more defendants in a manner that discriminates against the defendant or defendants in violation of the equal protection of the law. The defendant may raise a defense of selective prosecution if, either in its effect and its purpose, the prosecution discriminated against the defendant on grounds forbidden by the Equal Protection Clause. To substantiate this claim the defendant must demonstrate either discriminatory purpose or discriminatory effect. The defendant must have evidence of motive to demonstrate the prosecution had a purpose of prosecuting individuals of the defendant's race, gender, or other qualified characteristic. The defendant may, alternatively, demonstrate effect by proving that the prosecution had failed to prosecute others who are not in defendant's protected class who were liable to prosecution, but had prosecuted those in defendant's protected class in sufficient numbers to demonstrate discriminatory effect.

**want of prosecution** *See:* prosecution, want of prosecution.

**prosecutor** A government official who prosecutes criminal actions. A prosecutor is an official of the United States, a state, or a municipality, who is responsible for reviewing evidence and assisting in the investigation of allegations of criminal wrongdoing, determining who is to be prosecuted for sufficiently substantiated allegations of criminal wrongdoing, for initiating a criminal judicial proceeding and overseeing the prosecution according to the constitutions, statutes, precedents, and rules that apply. This would include moving to dismiss a prosecution, negotiating a plea, or trying an action according to the evidence available. A prosecutor may be a full-time employee, a part-time employee, or a special appointee for a given cause, but in all cases the prosecutor represents the state, or the people, of the jurisdiction. The prosecutor's highest duty is to seek the truth of the matter and justice in each cause; it is not merely to seek convictions or sentences.

**independent counsel** An independent federal prosecutor who investigates senior federal officials. An independent counsel is a federal investigating attorney. Presently, such attorneys are appointed by the Attorney General under the inherent powers of that office. Most famously, a special counsel was an attorney appointed by a panel of the Circuit Court of Appeals for the District of Columbia at the request of the U.S. Attorney General to investigate allegations of potentially criminal wrongdoing by the President, senior officials of the executive branch or Congress or a political party, or other individuals whose investigation might be a conflict of interest for the department. The IC reports to the Court, not to the Attorney General. Independent Counsels are created under a statute different from that of Special Attorneys, who report to the Attorney General, rather than to the court, as do Independent Counsels. The Independent Counsel statute was upheld as a constitutional exercise of the powers of the three branches in Morrison v. Olson, 487 U.S. 654 (1988). In 1999, Congress replaced the Office of the Independent Counsel with a new Office of Special Councel.

*See also:* prosecutor, special attorney.

**prosecutorial discretion** Prosecutor's personal judgment as to whether to bring a criminal charge. Prosecutorial discretion is the authority of a supervising prosecutor to determine whether or not to bring a criminal charge against a person or entity who has been accused of criminal conduct. The decision is subject to little meaningful review, primarily to administrative review by more senior prosecutors and, in very rare circumstances, the possibility that the jurisdiction's attorney general will appoint a special prosecutor or attorney. Even so, because the decision of one prosecutor not to prosecute is no bar to another prosecutor with jurisdiction over the same offense, prosecutorial discretion is limited in its scope. Prosecutorial discretion is sometimes said to extend to the plea negotiation process, but because the acceptance of a plea is subject to judicial oversight, the discretion of the prosecutor is in negotiating a plea is more limited.

**prosecutorial misconduct** A criminal defense based on wrongdoing by the prosecution. Prosecutorial misconduct includes every error or wrongful act committed by a prosecutor or agent of the prosecutor that materially violates the laws or rules of a criminal investigation or criminal trial or otherwise interferes with the fair investigation or trial of a person suspected or accused of a crime. Misconduct may occur without intent or even knowledge by the prosecutor or agent, nor need it be related to a plan to interfere with the acquittal or a person suspected or accused of a crime. The prosecutor might not know that the act is wrongful, because it is the result of negligence of malfeasance by others upon whom the prosecutor relies, but, if the effect upon the defendant's case is to deny due process or a fair trial, the act is still misconduct. Misconduct includes, at least, the introduction into court of false testimony or fraudulent evidence; the suppression or destruction of evidence that might suggest the defendant's innocence or the guilt of another; abetting police misconduct such as entrapment; jury tampering, prejudicing the proceedings through out-of-court publicity; failing to produce evidence as required by a statute, rule, or order; making misleading and inappropriate comments during the trial; and failing to comply with any court order. Selective prosecution and the use of prosecution for personal gain or interest are also misconduct, although particular questions of proof and limits on the defense arise in such cases.

Not all errors affecting the conduct of a criminal action are considered misconduct. Indictment after the statute of limitations has run, a defective indictment, error before the grand jury, denial of a speedy trial, and improper remarks by the prosecutor before the jury are usually examined to determine if the error may be cured or if dismissal or a new trial is required without regard to misconduct.

Prosecutorial misconduct is a defense in a criminal action that may be raised by a defendant who is prejudiced by any wrongful conduct committed or abetted by the prosecution. Most misconduct, however, is not the basis for a successful defense but requires the court to cure defects in the trial caused by the misconduct, for instance by barring tainted evidence or by admonishing counsel and giving a curative instruction to the jury. Serious misconduct is the basis for a mistrial or new trial or the final dismissal of an indictment. Prosecutorial misconduct is only the basis for a reversal of a conviction if the misconduct was so prejudicial that a fair trial would not have been possible or otherwise amounted to prejudicial error. Serious misconduct that amounts to an independent constitutional tort may give rise to a constitutional civil action. Knowing and intentional misconduct may even give rise to a criminal action against the prosecutor for specific crimes, such as jury tampering or obstruction of justice.

**special attorney**   An attorney assigned to conduct a special investigation. A special attorney is a lawyer appointed by the U.S. Attorney General or other representative of the Department of Justice to investigate any matter, usually outside the ordinary chain of command. These attorneys are informally known as special prosecutors, although they may report on a matter under investigation without summoning a grand jury or initiating a criminal investigation.

*See also:* prosecutor, independent counsel.

**special counsel**   An attorney appointed to manage or prosecute a public cause. A special counsel is an attorney appointed by a judge, district attorney, attorney general, or U.S. attorney, to act as a prosecutor or attorney to investigate, advise, report, or litigate for a time or in a specific matter, usually of public importance. A prosecutor pro tem. is a special counsel.

**special prosecutor**   An ad hoc prosecutor appointed to manage a specific case or cases. A special prosecutor is an attorney, often an experienced prosecutor in

retirement or seconded from another position, who is appointed to investigate a particular matter, to determine whether to bring forward a criminal prosecution based on that matter, and if so, to manage the prosecution of the case. States vary in the procedures and roles of special prosecutors, who is appointed in some states by the state attorney general or Chief State Attorney, in others by the governor, and in others by a court or local prosecutor. Special prosecutors may be appointed for a variety of reasons but are most often employed when allegations of criminal misconduct are raised against public officials or police officers, or when the circumstances of an event raise such a possibility.

The federal Ethics in Government Act of 1978, Pub. L. 95–521, titles I–V, Oct. 26, 1978, 92 Stat. 1824–1867, codified the practice of the appointment of federal special prosecutors, the most famous of whom, Archibald Cox, had been dismissed on the orders of President Richard Nixon, and for such purposes the office was renamed the office of independent counsel. Special counsels, appointed by the U.S. Attorney General, also perform many functions carried out by state special prosecutors.

*See also:* special.

**United States Attorney**   The chief federal litigator in a United States judicial district. The United States Attorney is appointed by the President of the United States with the advice and consent of the Senate to serve as the chief law enforcement officer, prosecutor, civil litigator, and claims collector of the United States in the judicial district in which the U.S. Attorney serves. The U.S. Attorney is assisted by a staff of permanent Assistant U.S. Attorneys.

**prospectivity (prospective)**   Having an effect or taking place in the future. Something of prospective application has meaning or is intended to occur or take its status in the future. Although prospective application is usually contrasted with retrospective application, to make something prospective does not make it only prospective unless that limitation is made expressly. The mere fact that a rule, law, or agreement is prospective does not inherently bar its immediate application or its retrospective application, and care in drafting is essential to ensure that what is said is what is intended.

*See also:* retrospective.

**prospectus (485 filing)**   An overview, particularly of a project or a security. A prospectus is any summary or overview of a project, corporation, equity, mutual fund or similar activity or writing. An entity that issues a security subject to federal regulation as a registered public offering is required to file a prospectus as Part I of its registration statement with the Securities and Exchange Commission that describes the entity's business operation, finances, and management. An entity that sells shares in a mutual fund is required to file a prospectus, or 485 filing, summarizing the fund assets and financial details. The prospectus, along with other required and optional corporate and fund filings must be filed in an electronic form suitable for management in the EDGAR online database of the SEC.

Note: The plural of prospectus in Latin, prospecti, is now quite rare, and the convention of using an English suffix has superseded it: prospectuses.

**prostitute** *See:* prostitution, prostitute (sex worker or hooker or rent boy or call girl).

**prostitution** The trade of a sexual act for money or things of value. Prostitution is the commerce of sex, a transaction in which an act of sex is traded for money or things or conditions of value. Prostitution is committed by both females and males, and the participation in an act of prostitution, whether as buyer or seller, is now a crime in nearly every jurisdiction in the United States. In those jurisdictions in which it is not an offense, it is regulated: places of prostitution must be licensed, the fees that may be collected from prostitutes are regulated, prostitute standards of health are regulated, and the whole process is subject to tax.

*See also:* sex, sexual act (sexual conduct or sex act); prostitution, brothel (bawdy-house or bordello or house of ill fame or house of ill repute or house of prostitution); prostitution, Mann Act (interstate transportation).

**brothel (bawdy-house or bordello or house of ill fame or house of ill repute or house of prostitution)** A building primarily used in support of prostitution. A brothel is any building that is used or maintained substantially for the purpose of sheltering acts of prostitution. A brothel need not be used solely for prostitution, nor must the sex workers there engage in a single business enterprise. A brothel may, but need not, be a place of residence for sex workers. A hotel in which prostitution occurs but which is predominately a place for transient lodging and not commercial sex is not, thereby, a brothel. Brothels are inherently disorderly houses or houses of ill fame under the law, and they are considered public nuisances nearly everywhere in the United States and may be restrained by public or private action. There is no legal difference among brothel, bawdy house, bordello, or house of ill fame.

*See also:* prostitution.

**ill fame** Immoral conduct but especially prostitution. Ill fame is bad reputation, generally, but it is usually a polite label for a person, place, or act of sex for hire. A house of ill fame is a brothel.

*See also:* prostitution, brothel (bawdy-house or bordello or house of ill fame or house of ill repute or house of prostitution).

**John** The client of a prostitute. John is police slang for a person who patronizes a sex worker. The term is usually applied to males seeking or receiving such services.

**Mann Act (interstate transportation)** A federal ban on the transportation of persons for immoral conduct. The Mann Act was the popular name for an Act to Further Regulate Interstate and Foreign Commerce by Prohibiting the Transportation Therein for Immoral Purposes of Women and Girls, and for Other Purposes, 36 Stat. 825, ch 395, and named for Illinois Congressman James Robert Mann. The act banned the transportation of any woman or girl "with the intent and purpose to induce, entice, or compel such woman or girl to become a prostitute or to give herself up to debauchery, or to engage in any other immoral practice . . ." was to be fined and sentenced to up to five years in prison, ten if the victim was under eighteen years of age. The statute as amended remains in force, codified at 18 U.S.C. § 2421–2424.

*See also:* obscenity, Comstock Law; Sabbath, blue law (Sunday law or Sunday closing law); prostitution.

**pimp (madam)** A manager of prostitutes. A pimp is a male who engages in the management of prostitutes. A pimp's primary function is to arrange client meetings for prostitutes in return for a percentage of the prostitute's earnings. In many jurisdictions, receiving money from a prostitute is a criminal offense, as is furthering prostitution, both offenses intended to define pimping. A madam is a term for a female manager of prostitutes.

**promoting prostitution (advancing prostitution)** Facilitating, managing, profiting, or assisting in prostitution. The crime of promoting prostitution makes unlawful all acts that a person knowingly commits that manage, facilitate, or aid in any way an act or enterprise of prostitution. This includes both pandering and pimping, and in most statutes includes receiving money from prostitutes or their clients by anyone other than a prostitute. More serious levels of the offense include the use of threats or violence and the recruitment or facilitation of prostitution by anyone under the age of eighteen.

*See also:* solicitation (solicit or solicted or soliciting).

**prostitute (sex worker or hooker or rent boy or call girl)** A commercial sex worker. A prostitute is a person who engages in sexual activity for hire. A prostitute may be male or female. There is no offense of being a prostitute. However, most jurisdictions consider an act of prostitution, the provision of an act of sex in return for money, to be a criminal offense. Note: in the nineteenth century, some legal commentators distinguished a prostitute from a common prostitute. A prostitute was a person (nearly always a woman) who frequently engaged in sexual activity with various partners, but a common prostitute was a commercial sex worker. This distinction is now obsolete, though it is still found occasionally in older cases.

**protection (protective)** To guard from injury, disturbance, or legal process. Protection is the act of keeping something from harm, whether the harm is specific and immediate or general and prospective or only potential at some time in the future. The word, from the Latin for covering, has several distinct meanings in law.

In general, the function of the law is to keep from harm the people governed by officials acting under law. In this sense, law is an assurance that the officials will act timely and effectively to prevent wrongs and to correct them when they occur. More specifically, protection is a privilege from legal process, and a protective order or protective motion is intended to save a person or party from the inconvenience of answering a legal order, summons, or other command. Protection in its non–legal senses is frequently in issue in law, as in lawfully provided security services or insurance, or as in unlawful acts of racketeering in which money is demanded for protection from the demandant.

**protected class**  *See:* class, legal classification, protected class.

**protectionism**  *See:* trade, protectionism.

**protective custody**  *See:* custody, protective custody, witness security (witness protection).

**protective custody of a prisoner**  *See:* custody, protective custody of a prisoner.

**protective order**  *See:* order, protective order; discovery, discovery order, protective order.

**protective search**  *See:* search, protective search.

**protective sweep**  *See:* search, incident to arrest, protective sweep.

**protective tariff**  *See:* tariff, tariff as tax, protective tariff.

**prothonotary**  *See:* clerk, clerk of court, prothonotary (pronotary).

**protocol**  The written record of an official act, and the customs by which they are made. Protocol has two distinct senses with a common origin. The oldest sense of it is the written record of a transaction. From that sense derived the later meaning in international diplomacy, that being the custom and practices governing the conduct of diplomacy. A breach of protocol by a representative of one state to another is an act that violates the expected customs of diplomacy, which may be thought by the other state as a deliberate provocation.
*See also:* diplomat, diplomacy.

**provable or prove**  *See:* proof (provable or prove).

**province**  A geographic jurisdiction or a matter under some authority. A province is a state or other political jurisdiction that is subordinate to a higher authority.

In legal usage, it is a figure of speech with a meaning similar to an exclusive domain, in that it delineates the area in which a person, rule, or institution has authority or responsibility. This is especially true of the term "province of the jury," which describes the constitutional and customary dedication of questions of fact to the determination by a jury rather than a court.
*See also:* domain.

**province of the jury**  *See:* jury, province of the jury.

**proving**  *See:* proof, proof as tested (proving).

**proviso**  A condition or other clause in a statute or instrument. A proviso is a specific provision in a statute, contract, deed, or other instrument, that creates a condition, covenant, or general obligation. Depending upon the language of the proviso, the proviso applies either in general or to the clause that precedes it.

**provocation (provocateur or provoke)**  Inciting another to perform an act. A provocation is the cause of some result, and in the law it usually depicts an act, statement, or conduct that incites, or is reasonably expected to incite, another person to perform some act in retaliation. Provocation is not in itself criminal, although some criminal acts, such as battery, are provocative. Thus, a provocative act that is not criminal per se and does not present a continuing danger of harm that would justify self–defense is no defense to a criminal charge for the retaliation.
*See also:* murder, degrees of murder, second–degree murder (murder in the second degree or murder–two or murder–2); speech, freedom of speech, clear and present danger test (offensive words).

**proximity**  A close and direct relationship between one thing and another. Proximity depicts a close relationship, which is direct and not subject to an intermediating influence. In general, proximity is the result of a short physical distance between two things or two people. Proximity in the common law may mean either a family relationship between two people or a close relationship between a cause and effect.
*See also:* search, search warrant, physical–proximity test; propinquity.

**proximate cause**  *See:* causation, specific causation.

**proxy (proxies)**  A person appointed to represent another. A proxy is a person appointed to represent another person, especially in carrying out an office or duty. Although some offices are a form of representation that is inherently one of proxy, such as a diplomat for a head of state, the most important role of many proxies is to cast a vote, thus a vote cast by one person in the place of a person eligible to cast the vote is a vote by proxy, or a proxy vote. Proxy voting is common among the shareholders of public corporations, though it is used in many private elective contexts.

**proxy marriage**  *See:* marriage, proxy marriage.

**prudence (imprudent or prudent)**  Wise and careful thought and action. Prudence is the art of applied wisdom, the commission of each decision and action with knowledge, skill, and reasonable foresight to select the best result available in a circumstance and achieve it. A fiduciary owes a duty of prudence toward a person relying on the fiduciary. Every legal official has a duty of prudence implied in the nature of the office as a trust for the benefit of the people the office serves, and that duty is often expressed, but always implied in its oath.

Every act that is not prudent risks being imprudent, but the logical range may invite a more subtle range than this. There are decisions that are clearly prudent, even if they prove over time to be less advantageous than reasonably hoped, because the decision was carefully, skillfully, and reasonably made with all the foresight then available. There are decisions that are clearly imprudent — decisions that are self-serving rather than intended to benefit those to whom the duty is owed, that are ill-informed, prejudiced, whimsical, and careless both of the broad purposes for which the duty is bestowed and mindless of future consequence; some such decisions may prove fruitful by accident yet there were still imprudent. And there are many decisions that are lacking in some degree in prudence. To determine whether a person has succeeded or failed in the duty of prudence the person's conduct must be assessed both in each decision, action, and omission and in the sum of all such conduct over time.

*See also:* fiduciary; oath.

**Prudent-Investor Rule** *See:* trustee, Prudent-Investor Rule.

**prurience (prurient interest)** A shameful or morbid interest in nudity, sex, or excretion. Prurience is an unhealthy interest in sex or sexy things, which extends beyond the healthy interest in sex and sexy things that is a part of an adult life. Prurience also includes an excessive interest in excretion or other subjects that suggest a morbid or unhealthy approach to living one's life. Although morbidity and health as factors in this context are highly controversial, there seems to be sufficient consensus that such concepts are meaningful in this regard. Materials that appeal to a prurient interest are potentially obscene, because one of the essential tests of obscenity is whether the materials appeal to a prurient interest in potential consumers of the media.

*See also:* sex, sexual act (sexual conduct or sex act); obscenity (obscene); lasciviousness (lascivious or lasciviously); obscenity, Miller test (Miller standard).

**pseudonym** *See:* name, alias, pseudonym (brush name or nom de pinceau or nom de plum or pen name).

**psychotherapist privilege or therapist-patient privilege or psychiatrist privilege** *See:* privilege, evidentiary privilege, counselor-patient privilege (psychotherapist privilege or therapist-patient privilege or psychiatrist privilege).

**public** Beyond the private sphere, and particularly affecting the people as a whole. Public refers not only to the whole of the people but also to anything affecting them; it has a number of specific senses in law. Public has historically been most understood as relating to the interests in common among many people: public space, public building, and public interest all evoke a common undertaking, in which the government might or might not have a defining role. As the state came to be defined less by the medieval ideas of royal interests and more by the modern idea of interests common to the people, it became more common to associate state and government with the public good, and in the U.S., it is common to refer to buildings, lands, and policies of the government as public. Laws of general application are public laws, which contrast with laws that apply only to one person or a limited group, in which case they are private laws.

An important contrast in the law is between the public and the private. Spaces owned by individuals, not visible or open to access to others are private; while spaces privately owned but accessible to others without special invitation are public, like a public house or tavern. Hauling and transport done for a sole client is private, but when available to all comers is public. What concerns only an individual or a small and intimate group is private; what concerns the state or the commonality of people is public. This division can be very difficult to determine, as when abusive or harmful acts take place between two people in a private place; the character of the action is considered to violate a public interest and to have a public consequence, and so it leads to a public interest in criminal prosecution. Yet the public/private distinction is much farther ranging, including the difference in such diverse contexts as the public use and private intended use of land subject to takings, the carriers who provide public service and private service, speech on a matter of public concern and private concern, public purpose and private purpose or a statute, and so on.

*See also:* trust, abuse of public or private trust; act, act as a public act; defamation, defamation of a public figure; international law (law of nations or public international law); notary (notary public); office, abuse of office (abuse of the public trust or abuse of official trust).

**public access to court electronic records** *See:* record, court records, public access to court electronic records (P.A.C.E.R. or PACER).

**public accommodation** *See:* accommodation, public accommodation.

**public administrator** *See:* administrator, administrator of estate, public administrator (government probate).

**public authority** *See:* authority, public authority.

**public authority or government corporation or public-benefit corporation** *See:* corporation, public corporation (public authority or government corporation or public-benefit corporation).

**public comment** *See:* rulemaking, public comment (public comment period).

**public comment period** *See:* rulemaking, public comment (public comment period).

**public concern** *See:* concern, public concern.

**public corporation** *See:* corporation, public corporation (public authority or government corporation or public-benefit corporation).

**public court** *See:* court, open court (public court).

**public defender** *See:* lawyer, legal aid, public defender.

**public disclosure of private facts** *See:* privacy, invasion of privacy, public disclosure of private facts.

**public domain** *See:* domain, public domain.

**public domain land** *See:* land, public lands, public domain land.

**public drunkenness** *See:* intoxication, public intoxication (public drunkenness).

**public easement** *See:* easement, public easement.

**public employee** *See:* employment, employee, public employee.

**public forum** *See:* speech, freedom of speech, forum, public forum, limited public forum; speech, freedom of speech, forum, public forum, designated public forum; speech, freedom of speech, forum, public forum (traditional public forum).

**public health** *See:* health, public health.

**public housing** *See:* housing, public housing, public housing authority; housing, public housing.

**public housing authority** *See:* housing, public housing, public housing authority.

**public indecency** *See:* indecency, indecent exposure (public indecency).

**public interest exception** *See:* justiciability, mootness, public interest exception.

**public intoxication** *See:* intoxication, public intoxication (public drunkenness).

**public knowledge** *See:* knowledge, common knowledge (public knowledge).

**public lands** *See:* land, public lands, U.S. department of Interior, Bureau of Land Management; land, public lands, public domain land; land, public lands (land on public domain or sovereign lands).

**public law** *See:* statute, public law (P.L. or PL).

**public necessity** *See:* necessity, public necessity.

**public notice of proposed rule** *See:* rulemaking, public notice of proposed rule (advanced notice of proposed rulemaking).

**public nudity or nudeness or nude or nakedness or naked** *See:* nudity (public nudity or nudeness or nude or nakedness or naked).

**public nuisance** *See:* nuisance, public nuisance, drug house (crack house or meth house); nuisance, public nuisance.

**public offering** *See:* share, share as stock, offering, public offering, initial public offering (IPO or I.P.O.); share, share as stock, offering, public offering (registered offering); offering, public offering.

**public policy** *See:* policy, public policy.

**public property** *See:* property, public property.

**public purpose** *See:* takings, public use (public purpose).

**public reason** *See:* reason, public reason.

**public record** *See:* record, public record; hearsay, hearsay exception, hearsay allowed regardless of witness availability, public record (public records or public reports).

**public records or public reports** *See:* hearsay, hearsay exception, hearsay allowed regardless of witness availability, public record (public records or public reports).

**public trial** *See:* trial, public trial (right to public trial).

**public trust** *See:* trust, public trust, public trust doctrine; trust, public trust.

**public trust doctrine** *See:* trust, public trust, public trust doctrine.

**public-safety exception** *See:* Miranda rule, public-safety exception (exception for public safety to Miranda).

**public-service corporation** *See:* corporation, public-service corporation.

**public use** *See:* use, use of property, public use; takings, public use (public purpose).

**public utility** *See:* utility, public utility.

**publicly assisted housing** *See:* housing, publicly assisted housing.

**publicly owned treatment works** *See:* pollution, water pollution, pollution source, publicly owned treatment works (POTW).

**public-private distinction (public/private)** A classic boundary between the sphere of regulation and freedom. The public–private distinction is a characterization of an interest, conduct, speech, or any other concept of human endeavor that determines whether there is a public or communal aspect that predominates in the endeavor or a private or individual aspect that predominates in the endeavor. The difference is that a public aspect is appropriate for the regulation of the endeavor by law but a solely private aspect is appropriately free of such regulation because it is the proper domain of freedom of the individual. Ascertaining whether a given act is truly public or private is seen by some as a matter of reason and by others as culturally contingent. It might be both when, for example, a person's choice of religion is usually now thought a private matter, but in U.S. colonial history, it was a public matter and regulated by law.

The distinction between public and private is significant in considering the constitutional limits on regulation, both as a matter of due process and the interests of privacy. Matters of state action are inherently public, and matters of individual action with public effects are presumably public, but determining what is a public effect can be difficult to assess, as in the debates over the public ramifications of of acts by or between consenting adults.

**public sector**  Administered by, or a component of, a government. The public sector is the sum of the governmental operations, staffing, or responsibilities, including the economic effects of government. An entity of the public sector is a governmental unit or agency, and public-sector employees are governmental employees or contractors.

**publication**  The act of making public any thing. Publication is the act by which a thing is made public, whether the thing is an idea, a concept or a specific text, such as a book, article, web page, image, design, or law. The extent of distribution varies with the context of the publication, but as a general matter, publication may be made to all the world or only to one person.

The forms of publication relevant to distinct legal issues vary considerably in their form and scope of distribution. For example, publication of a confidence, such that a privilege over that confidence is destroyed, occurs when the confidence is published to any person not subject to the privilege. Likewise, publication of defamatory matter occurs when the defamer speaks of that matter to a third party. On the other hand, publication as the subject of a book publishing contract occurs when the book is duplicated and distributed according to the contractual terms. Publication of a legal notice occurs when it is distributed according to the applicable law, which usually includes a posting at the local courthouse and on the property affected and the printing of a paid advertisement in a local newspaper of record. Publication of a law occurs when the rule is printed according to the constitution or law in that jurisdiction, in an official set of session laws or on an official web site. Publication of a federal statute, for instance, occurs when it is issued as a slip law and then again when it is issued in the U.S. Statutes at Large. Publication of a federal rule occurs when it is entered into the Federal Register at http://www.gpoaccess.gov/fr/.

See also: defamation, publication of a defamatory statement.

**publication notice**  See: notice, publication notice (notice by publication).

**publication of a defamatory statement**  See: defamation, publication of a defamatory statement.

**publicity (publicize)**  Making a thing known to members of the public. Publicity is an act that encourages knowledge of anything by members at large of the public, who otherwise might not know of the thing publicized. Closely related to publication, publicity may be seen as the creation of the opportunity for public knowledge. For example, an act in open court is given publicity, even if it is hardly known beyond the few litigants, counsel, and court staff. In addition, it may be seen as the extent to which the knowledge of the thing is common among the members of the community, such as an opinion held in common knowledge.

So publicity may include the media by which information is distributed, the effort or opportunity for such distribution, and the effect of such distribution.

See also: publication; defamation, defamation of a public figure.

**PUD**  See: zoning, planned unit development (PUD).

**puff or puffing**  See: deceit, false advertising, puffery (puff or puffing).

**puffer**

**puffer in an auction**  A shill who falsely bids up an auction price on behalf of the seller or auctioner.

See also: auction; sale, conditions of sale.

**puffery**  See: deceit, false advertising, puffery (puff or puffing).

**Pullman abstention**  See: abstention, abstention doctrine, Pullman abstention.

**punishment (punish)**  Penalty ordered by a court of law. Punishment includes any form of penalty required when a person or entity breaks a public law, particularly a law that forbids criminal conduct, as well as harmful conduct in that harms a private party that is not just damaging but that is demonstrably wrongful. The laws specify a range of forms of punishment, in categories including execution, or the death of the criminal; incarceration, the loss of all freedom by the criminal; parole and other regulation out of prison, or the loss of equal privileges (such as the right to live near children, own a weapon, drive a car, or vote); hard labor or civic works, or free labor by the criminal; shame and a loss of status, in specific penalties as well as in the process as a whole; and fines and forfeitures, or financial losses in the form of penalties or restitution; and ceremonial demotion in a capitalist society. Criminals who are not citizens may be exiled, or expelled from the territory. Although more complex and sophisticated punishments exist, including training and education—the most common forms of punishment remain fine, incarceration, and the loss of social privileges.

In the United States, punishments are limited by the U.S. Constitution and, if the punishment is enacted by a state, the state constitution. No punishment may be cruel or unusual, as understood both at the time of the framing of the Bill of Rights and as understood through evolving sentiment in civilized society. Further, no punishment in the United States may be required by an ex post facto law, or law that creates a penalty for an act after the act is concluded. No punishment may be inflicted on a person other than by an appropriate, lawful process that accords with the requirements of due process of law. At a minimum, due process requires notice of the liability and the right to be heard in one's defense by a neutral arbiter. Due process in a criminal proceeding that may lead to the fullest penalties imposes a plethora of requirements. No penalty be imposed unless the accused either confesses and accepts the penalty in a process overseen by a judge or the accused receives a trial by jury that includes: the right to hear the charges against the accused and all evidence in support of them, the right to cross examine witnesses and challenge evidence with the assistance of legal counsel, a privilege against self-incrimination that allows the defendant not to testify, a right to acquittal unless the jury finds guilt beyond a reasonable doubt, a penalty that is judicially ratified or a verdict on which a judge imposes penalty, either of which are subject to review on appeal.

The moral authority of the state to require punishments has been often argued, and Bouvier accepts the view that it arises from an implied contract among people and between individuals and the state, that each of us gives the state the power to punish in return for the state giving back order and security from wrongful conduct. There are sometimes great arguments over what conduct by individuals is sufficient to justify the use of such power against them. Immanuel Kant and others have argued that the state has a moral obligation to punish when a person commits a crime, not owed to other people but owed to the criminal, because the state must treat each person with so much dignity that it respects their power to transgress and to accept the consequences. Jeremy Bentham and others have argued the state's moral claim to authority depends on its use of its power to create more happiness, so it must punish actions that cause pain, but do so in a manner that does not cause more pain than it abates. Michel Foucault has argued that to define punishable crimes is to create deviance, that deviance flows from the law, not that the law responds to deviance. Ancient and modern justifications for punishment include the requirement of isolation of the criminal from the community in order to protect the community from further danger; the requirement of punishment as a ceremonial, religious, or social purge of the antisocial, evil, or wrongful act from the community; the requirement of harm to a wrongdoer as a means of education of right and wrong as well as deterrence of others; and the education, training, or rehabilitation of a criminal to provide lawful alternative ways of law to a wrongdoer, as well as incentives to pursue them.

*See also:* penalty (penalize or penalized or penalizing); penal (penal law); penology; sentence.

**punishment phase or remedy phase** *See:* trial, bifurcated trial, penalty phase (punishment phase or remedy phase).

**corporal punishment (paddling or spanking or torture)** Punishment inflicted painfully on the human body. Corporal punishment is the intentional infliction of bodily pain upon a person as a penalty. Corporal punishment employed as a legal punishment for criminal behavior in many legal systems, but in the United States, the use of physical pain as a criminal punishment, in most instances, violates the ban on cruel and unusual punishment. Punishment is, however, allowed in administrative and educational contexts.

In the United States, corporal punishment often refers to the use of a paddle to spank disobedient school children. This punishment is generally regulated by state law, and it not unconstitutional under federal standards.

History has provided many examples of corporal punishment as a penalty for criminal wrongdoing, including some forms of torture, caning, lashing, cutting, branding, amputation, stress positions, restrained and cramped positions, the use of electricity, weights, physical invasions of the body, and exposure to excessive heat, cold, sound, or light. The use of starvation, dehydration, and infusion are sometimes treated as corporal punishment. These punishments are generally forbidden as cruel and unusual.

**cruel and unusual punishment** Punishment that is contrary to the practice of civilized society. Cruel and unusual punishment is any punishment for a crime or other treatment of a criminal that is contrary to the practices of civilized states and violates both the Eighth Amendment and international law. Excessive punishments are forbidden under this clause as well as the Excessive Fines Clause, although the determination of excessiveness is controversial. All forms of torture are forbidden, as are punishments for the benefit of guards or the amusement of others. There is a continuing controversy in the United States as to whether the execution of an adult is cruel. There are also questions of whether punishments intended to create personal shame or public disgrace are now cruel and unusual, although measures to publish the identity of those convicted of crimes do not violate this limit.

*See also:* usual (unusual); mutilation.

**proportionality review** A criminal sentence may not be grossly disproportionate. Proportionality review is a process of assuring the constitutionality of a criminal sentence under the Eighth Amendment's prohibition of cruel and unusual punishment, according to which no punishment is allowed to be grossly disproportionate to the crime for which the defendant is sentenced. Exact proportionality is not required, although extreme and grossly disproportionate sentences are to forbidden.

The balance of the harm of a crime to its sentence is neither exact nor fixed for all time. The values and the objective factors by which the harm of the crime a person is found to have committed are to be assessed are understood to evolve over time.

*See also:* proportionality (disproportional or proportional or proportionate).

**death penalty (capital punishment or execution)** Execution of an individual as punishment. The death penalty, or capital punishment, is a sentence of death, according to which an official of the state may be ordered to cause the death of the person sentenced. The death penalty is a lawful penalty in the United States only for acts committed by an adult who has criminal capacity sufficient to be responsible at the time of the offense. As of 2011, it is a sentence in the courts of the United States, as well as in Alabama, Arizona, Arkansas,

California, Colorado, Connecticut, Delaware, Florida, Georgia, Idaho, Indiana, Kansas, Kentucky, Louisiana, Maryland, Mississippi, Missouri, Montana, Nebraska, Nevada, New Hampshire, North Carolina, South Dakota, Ohio, Oklahoma, Oregon, Pennsylvania, South Carolina, South Dakota, Tennessee, Texas, Utah, Virginia, Washington, and Wyoming. In all states, aggravated murder is eligible for the death penalty, but some states add other offenses, including air piracy, kidnapping, train wrecking, and treason.

A person may not be sentenced to death unless a jury has ruled that there is proof beyond a reasonable doubt that the person has committed a crime eligible for death, and a jury must pronounce that death is an appropriate sentence in the light of such aggravating and mitigating evidence as is submitted for the sentencing phase of the proceedings. In some states, a judge must render an additional judgment not only that the defendant is eligible for the death penalty but also that the evidence supports both the finding of guilt and the sentence of death.

The means of inflicting the death sentence in the United States is subject to the limits of the Cruel and Unusual Punishment Clause of the Constitution. Means of execution allowed by law in various jurisdictions include electrocution, the gas chamber, hanging, and shooting by a firing squad, although lethal injection is the most common means and an alternative means in most other jurisdictions.

Controversies persist regarding all phases of capital sentencing. In Baez v. Rees, 128 S.Ct. 1520 (2008), the U.S. Supreme Court upheld the most common form of lethal injection, although the effect of the drugs remains controversial, as does the use of non-medical personnel as executioners.

*See also:* execution, execution of a sentence of death (execution).

**lethal injection**  Execution by the injection of chemicals into the body. Lethal injection is the means of execution used in most jurisdictions that employ the death penalty. Lethal injection is administered by prison employees who are not medical doctors. Most states follow the example upheld by the U.S. Supreme Court in 2008, using a combination of the drugs sodium thiopental, pancuronium bromide, and potassium chloride, although the effects and the risks of this procedure remain highly controversial. Several states allow a condemned prisoner to opt for death by other means.

**deterrent punishment (exemplary punishment or deterrent theory or exemplary theory)**  The punishment of criminals for past acts to deter others from future acts. Deterrent punishment is a theory of justification for criminal law and punishment, asserting that the punishment of a person who has committed a prohibited act is justified by the effect upon others who therefore will not commit such an act. This is the idea that punishing a criminal makes an example of the criminal for the rest of society. The effect of the

example may be argued as rooted in a utilitarian or hedonistic calculus that a person would prefer to avoid the pain, or it may be a perfectionist claim that the law therefore demonstrates what is immoral so the person who desires to be good knows to avoid it. Deterrence contrasts with retribution, which, following Kant, should punish the wrongdoer for the wrong done, and not in order to influence or affect others, which would be an unethical treatment of the wrongdoer.

**draw and quarter (quartering or to be drawn and quartered)**  To be dragged by horses into four pieces, or to be severely punished. To be drawn and quartered was a gruesome punishment for a defendant found guilty of treason or other grave felonies, although the punishment was carried out, at least in English law, upon the dead body of the defendant immediately after hanging, beheading, or other execution. The body was dragged by horses and then pulled into four parts, the reins of four horses tethered to the arms and legs of the body before the horses were whipped. The mutilation had significance for the potential of Christian burial as well as serving as a spectacle to the crowd. Sir James Stephen suggested that English law never performed this act on a living person, though it was done so in continental Europe.

To be drawn and quartered is a metaphor for a severe trial or punishment.

*See also:* punishment, cruel and unusual punishment.

**rajm (stoning)**  The punishment of stoning. Rajm is to stone someone, as a punishment in classical Shari'ah. Generally it is considered to be the punishment for Zina, or adulterous sexual intercourse committed by a married person. Zina includes both adultery and fornication, though two types forms of sex out of marriage have the same term in Arabic — Zina. Rajm is the form of punishment for an adulterer, whether male or female. It is not prescribed in the Qur'an but believed to be required by a hadith attributed to Umar Ibn al-Khattab, the 2nd Khalif al-Rashidun, through the narrator, Ibn Musayyab.

**rehabilitative punishment (reformation of criminals)**  Punishment intended to improve the offender. Rehabilitative punishment is intended to change the thoughts, conduct, and habits of the offender, to provide the offender with vocational and social skills, and to prepare the offender to reenter society and not to continue to commit criminal acts.

**retributive punishment**  A harm inflicted on a wrongdoer as punishment for a crime. Retributive punishment is punishment intended to harm the wrongdoer as a response to the wrongfulness of the criminal act. Retribution is seen as a moral obligation of the state from two different perspectives. The first emphasizes the relationship between the criminal and the state, the state exacts punishment equal to the violation of the moral obligation of the criminal. The second emphasizes the state as standing in the shoes of the non-criminals who are owed vengeance not only for the wrong done to them but also vindication for their obedience. Not all retributive theories accept each of these bases for justification.

*See also:* justice, retributive justice (retributivism); retribution.

**shaming punishment (shame as punishment)** *See:* reprimand; shame.

**scarlet letter** Punishment or designation intended to create shame. A scarlet letter depicts any public punishment that has the effect of shaming the person sentenced or causing that person to be to be ostracized in the community. The maintenance of lists of sex offenders and other registries, though primarily justified as a preventative regulation, is widely perceived to have a shaming function, and such laws are sometimes described as scarlet-letter laws.

*See also:* a, a as criminal label.

**stocks (pillory)** Penal device for constraining a prisoner for public ridicule. The stocks and the pillory were large wooden devices in a public square, market, or other central place in the community, in which a prisoner convicted of certain misdemeanors was sentenced to be locked for a period of time, the aim being to expose the prisoner to public ridicule both to shame the prisoner and to serve as an example to others. The stocks were a low bench or seat behind wooden beams with holes for prisoner's hands or hands and head. The pillory was a taller machine behind which the prisoner stood, again with head and hands restrained in holes between two wooden beams.

The punishments are now long abandoned but the terms survive. To pillory someone is to hold the person up to public ridicule. To put someone in the stocks is to put the person in an uncomfortable or difficult situation.

**punitive damages** *See:* damages, classes of damages, punitive damages (exemplary damages or punis or punitives).

**pur** By or for. Pur is a law French preposition that translates into English as "by" or "for."

**pur autre vie** *See:* vie, per autre vie (pur autre vie).

**purchase** The acquisition of property, usually from sale. Purchase refers both to the act of acquiring property and to the property that is thus acquired. The modern usage of purchase refers almost invariably to acquisition through a contract of sale, by which the purchaser gives money or other value in return for the property purchased.

Apart from its current usage, purchase has an older and broader meaning as the acquisition of property by any means other than by descent to an heir at death. Thus, technically, purchase includes acquisition by conquest in war, by prescription, and, according to Bouvier, even by legacy or devise in a last will and testament. As a result, purchase usually now means a sale, or a purchase

made in return for value. The formulae "purchase for value" and "purchaser for value" make clear the form of the purchase as one by sale.

*See also:* buyer (buy); seller (sell); descent (descender).

**purchase money mortgage** *See:* mortgage, purchase money mortgage (owner-financed mortgage or seller financing).

**purchase order** *See:* offer, purchase order.

**closing statement of purchase** Final statement of all details concerning the transaction. An instrument prepared for a title company or other institution at the time a financed purchase of land is closed, that discloses the costs that have been paid that were associated with the purchase, including the parties to whom each cost has been or is to be paid. The statement is not intended to benefit the seller or the purchaser but to limit liability for the title company. The lender must be satisfied that the property is not subject to claims from either the seller or third parties, such as surveyors or realtors, and so the payments to such claimants are made directly from the lender or the closing agent. Yet some payments are the responsibility of the seller, and some are the responsibility of the buyer, and the closing statement allocates which fees, taxes, costs, or expenses are deducted from the purchase price — and so deducted from the payment to be made to the seller — and which are added to the costs of the buyer.

**purchase agreement** Executory agreement to sell and to purchase anything. A purchase agreement is a executory contract agreed between a buyer and a seller specifying material terms of the transaction negotiated between the parties, as well as many boilerplate contractual provisions dealing with the interpretation and application of the agreement to the parties. A purchase agreement is a contract, although it may have specified contingencies relieving one party or the other from performance. A purchase agreement regarding lands is usually called a buy-sell agreement in many jurisdictions.

*See also:* sale, land sale, buy-sell agreement (buy/sell agreement).

**purchaser** A buyer. A purchaser is the person or entity who purchases a given property, the same as a buyer or vendee.

*See also:* buyer (buy); vendor (vend or vendee).

**bona fide purchaser (bona fide purchaser for value or B.F.P. or B.F.P.V. or BFP or BFPV)** A buyer in good faith. A bona fide purchaser is a person or entity who pays value for property, with no notice or grounds to suspect any irregularity in the transaction, in particular lacking any reason to suspect that the seller does not have right or title to sell the property. By definition, a person cannot be a bona fide purchaser if prior to or during the purchase, the purchaser has actual knowledge the seller has no right or title to sell, or the purchaser has a basis for constructive notice, or the purchaser has a reasonable basis from which an ordinary purchaser would make further inquiries that are not in fact made. A bona fide purchaser may be protected from the subsequent invalidation of the transaction in the event the seller lacked title or right to sell.

Note: as a purchaser must give value in order to purchase (as opposed to receiving a gift), the addition of "for value" to a bona fide purchaser is somewhat redundant, though it creates an emphasis.

See also: holder, bona fide holder for value (holder in good faith); bona, bona fide (bona fides); fides (fide).

**shelter rule (shelter doctrine)** An owner or holder is sheltered by a predecessor's privilege. The shelter rule the allows a transferee who is not a bona fide purchaser but who takes an interest in property from a transferor who is bona fide purchaser to have the benefit of the transferor's protected status. Thus the rule transfers the status of a bona fide purchaser that is once held by a seller to a buyer, or by a donor to a donee, protecting the transferee who is not a bona fide purchaser as if the transferee is one, owing to the status of the transferor. The shelter rule in commercial law follows from the shelter doctrine, that whomever has acquired property from a holder in due course succeeds to the holder's rights.

See also: shelter.

**pure (purity or purely)** Without dilution, impairment, or condition. Pure has a variety of senses, but in law, its customary usage is to mean something without conditions: a pure obligation is undiluted, simple, and unconditional. In some usages, to be pure in some way signals a specific absence of some other way, or that only one cause, purpose, or effect is present, as in a purely legal title (such as a fee simple absolute) versus a purely equitable title (such as a trust benefit). In this sense, Hans Kelsen argued for a pure theory of law, that was undiluted by sources of law other than the law itself.

Purity in the sense of pure food or drugs is the degree to which the food or drug is free of adulteration.

See also: adulteration (adulterate or adulterant).

**pure comparative negligence** See: negligence, comparative negligence, pure comparative negligence.

**pure race act or pure race jurisdiction** See: title, recordation of title, recording act, race recording act (pure race act or pure race jurisdiction).

**purged taint exception** See: search, exclusionary rule, purged taint exception.

**purpose** The objective of a plan or course of conduct. A purpose is the primary reason for doing anything, a specific goal that a person or entity seeks to fulfill when engaging in a project, whether it is action or speech. To speak of the purpose of underlying some action is be to speak of the goal of the person who acts, or the decision-makers of the entity, in carrying out the project. In a meaningful sense, a purpose must be identified prior to the actual carrying out of the

project. A reason identified only after the project cannot be the project's purpose, though it could be a rationalization after the fact if, on reflection, those involved in a project considered a purpose to be insufficient or impolitic. There may be several purposes for any given project.

In law, there are numerous instances when an act is allowed for one purpose but not another. For example: evidence may often be admitted for one purpose but not another. Purpose is closely related to the concept of mens rea. A government action is often assessed by its purpose, and the purpose may determine the level of judicial scrutiny the action receives.

See also: business, business purpose doctrine (business-purpose); charity, charitable purpose; discrimination, discriminatory purpose (discriminatory intent or purposeful discrimination).

**conditional purpose** A purpose to be pursued only if a precondition is satisfied. A conditional purpose is a purpose for doing something, the intent to do the something being subject to a prior condition. For example, if A plans to steal a jewel by force in the event a planned fraud were to fail, A has a conditional purpose of stealing the jewel by force.

A person's purpose for an act is a significant reason that person has to carry out that act, which is identified before the action, and so to determine a conditional purpose exists, both the purpose and the condition that might alter the purpose would usually have been known to the person and have been bases for action prior to the act. Even so, the role knowledge plays in evaluating an actor's purpose can be very complicated, especially when a person acts at the moment of acquiring some knowledge. Thus it is possible that a conditional purpose is known only to have been satisfied because the condition was only known to be satisfied after the action.

See also: condition (unconditional or conditional or defeasance).

**purse**

**power of the purse** The legislative power to fund government operations, or not to. The power of the purse is the authority to fund or not to fund the specific operations of an entity. In American government and politics, the legislatures enjoy the power of the purse, and the discretion of the Congress to fund or not to fund any project or executive action is nearly without limit. This power accords to the legislator not only the direct responsibility for the actions of the executive but considerable influence in policy that must be compromised by the executive to retain preferred elements of the budget.

**pursuant** What is in order to carry out a given task. Pursuance is what is done to pursue a goal or to completed a task. An act "in pursuance" of a given purpose is an act that will assist in accomplishing that purpose. "Pursuant to" is synonymous with both the phrase "in accordance with" as well as "in order to carry out."

## pursuit

**pursuit of happiness** *See:* constitution, U.S. Constitution, ideals, pursuit of happiness.

**hot pursuit (fresh suit)** The uninterrupted pursuit of a fleeing suspect. Hot pursuit is the continued pursuit of a person, vehicle, vessel, or craft, having lawfully commenced to stop, board, seize arrest, or inspect the person or craft, who flees, after which pursuit has continued without losing contact (by sight or by monitoring through radar or other technological means). The effect of hot pursuit is to continue effective jurisdiction, established at the commencement of the pursuit and continued by the pursuit even out of the physical jurisdiction in which it was established. A law enforcement officer or a several officers in succession may maintain hot pursuit, and thus jurisdiction, just as pursuit may last through several geographic jurisdictions. Further, an arresting officer who commences a pursuit in circumstances that would allow arrest or search without a warrant does not lose such jurisdiction and its allowance for arrest or search without warrant if the arrestee flees, and the officer or the officer with other police eventually arrest the suspect as a result of uninterrupted hot pursuit. This is an exigent circumstance to the warrant requirements.

**pursuivant (poursuivant)** Initially, a royal messenger but later a spy to enforce some privilege or law. Pursuivants were agents who traveled the countryside seeking violators of various laws or prohibitions, capturing the miscreants, and delivering them to their authorities for a fee. Initially a royal messenger, the office was extended to support a variety of functions, including municipalities and ecclesiastical courts. The actions of pursuivants, both as the finders of witches and heretics and as the enforcers of commercial monopolies, led to considerable resentment. The Commons complained to the king of the actions of pursuivants in 1610. The memory of their powers of investigation without a warrant may have been one basis for the warrant requirements of the Fourth Amendment.
*See also:* warrant.

**purveyor** A seller or provider of goods or services; a promoter. A purveyor is a provider, a person or entity who sells or provides goods or services to others, whether for a price, fee, or otherwise. The term "purveyor" implies more than seller, in that a purveyor usually is associated with the provision of a particular good or service and is thus also associated with the marketing of that good or service.
*See also:* seller (sell).

**purview** The scope of potential jurisdiction or of a given subject matter. Purview is the scope of what is or may be done regarding a given subject or by a given person or institutional body. Purview is derived from the law French term for the various provisos that made up the operable portion of a statute. Thus, the purview of the statute is the scope of what the statute requires, while the purview of the legislature is the scope of the subject matter over which the legislature might issue statutes. In an agency context, purview generally refers to the authority of a particular agency with respect to certain actions. More broadly, a purview is an area for thought or study, any arena of dedication or expertise for any person and field of study.
*See also:* discretion; jurisdiction (legislative jurisdiction or executive jurisdiction or judicial jurisdiction); authority.

**put option** *See:* option, securities option, put option (put).

**putative (putative class or putative debtor)** False but believed, or possible but unproven, or maybe. Putative, in careful legal usage, refers to anything that is widely believed to be true that is not necessarily the case. Specific usages may vary somewhat, though. A "putative father" refers to a person believed to be a child's biological father and performing that role but who is not yet determined to be the child's biological father, which is to suggest that the reputation might prove correct.

Putative has acquired a strange meaning of "maybe" or "possibly" in legal usage, which is distinct both from its general use and from its customary use in law. Owing to the use in situations like a putative father in which the father is believed to be the father but not proven to be, the putative has been reinterpreted to mean alleged, potential, or suggested but not finally established or done by law. Thus, it is now common to refer to a claim that is not proved as a putative claim, a class that is not certified as a putative class, or a plaintiff whose claim is not proved as a putative plaintiff, and a putative debtor is a debtor who is not eligible to be a debtor in bankruptcy. In each of these cases, the condition might become true, or it might not.
*See also:* allegation (allege or alleged).

**putative father** *See:* family, father, putative father.

**putz** A jerk. Putz is a derogatory term for an offensive person, yet it is itself an offensive term used in the context, derived from the Yiddish for penis. Putz is also a verb for puttering about, or fiddling with something.
*See also:* Yiddish.

# Q

**q** The seventeenth letter of the modern English alphabet. "Q" signifies a variety of functions as a symbol. It is translated into Quebec for radio signals and NATO military transmissions, into Queen for some police radio traffic, and into dash, dash, dot, dash in Morse Code.

**q as an abbreviation** A word commencing in q. When used as the sole letter of an abbreviation, Q often stands for qua, quare, quarter, quarterly, Quebec, queen, Queensland, question, qui, quod, and quorum. It may also stand for the initial of an author or case reporter, such as Quin or Quincy. In the transcript of a trial or deposition, "q" designates a question.

**Q.D.R.O. or QDRO** *See:* employment, employee benefit plan, qualified domestic–relations order (Q.D.R.O. or QDRO).

**Q.E.D. or QED** *See:* quod, quod erat demonstrandum (Q.E.D. or QED).

**q.v.** *See:* quod, quod vide (q.v.).

**qadi (cadi or kadi)** An Islamic judge. A qadi is a judge in the Islamic legal system. The word is derived from Qada'a, meaning justice or balance. The authority of the Islamic judiciary is theoretically independent from that of any temporal sovereign, having been bestowed directly by the ultimate sovereign, Allah. Commentators, Muslim and non–Muslim alike, complain that some qadis apply the "discretion of their bellies" rather than the legislation of the Qur'an and precedent of the Prophet.

**qiya (qiyas)** An opinion in Islamic law reached by analogical reasoning. Quiya is analogical reasoning, one of the methods employed in Usul al Fiqh to deal with issues that are not expressly discussed in the text of the Qur'an or in in the Sunnah. It differs from opinion. Not all analogy is quiya. Ra'y is Zunni or speculation, generally not permitted in most madhahib.
*See also:* sharia, sources, qur'an.

**QTIP** *See:* trust, qualified–terminable–interest property trust (QTIP).

**qua** As. Qua means as, or in the manner of. In this sense, it establishes a particular role. For instance "judge qua supervisor" depicts the judge as the administrator over law clerks and administrative staff, but "judge qua judge" depicts the judge as the official who manages the legal aspects and judgment of a trial.

**quack** *See:* doctor, doctor of medicine, quack.

**quaere** Inquiry. Quaere is a Latin word for judicial inquiry or any other official investigation, from which many writs are made, each demanding that an investigation be conducted as a result of some sort of suspicion. Quaere in English has led to both query and inquiry.
*See also:* quaere.

**qualification (qualify or qualified)** A quality required of a person, thing, statement, or idea. Qualification has several distinct senses—all of which are derived from the same source as quality—which is to assess a condition for some position, office, job, or personal commendation, or to serve as criteria for the suitability of a thing, or assess the sufficiency for some purpose of a statement or idea. Thus, a qualification for a position is a criterion that an applicant must satisfy to be considered for or appointed to that position. A person meeting the requisite criteria is qualified for the position. The qualifications of a person or thing, in general, are the sum of the required relevant criteria by which each is considered. A slightly different sense of qualification arises when it is used to modify or condition a statement, as in to qualify an idea, which requires that the idea be understood with a particular criterion as a limitation upon it.

**qualified domestic-relations order** *See:* employment, employee benefit plan, qualified domestic-relations order (Q.D.R.O. or QDRO).

**qualified immunity** *See:* immunity, official immunity, qualified immunity.

**qualified privilege** *See:* privilege, qualified privilege.

**qualified retirement plan** *See:* retirement, retirement plan, qualified retirement plan.

**qualified right or qualified interest** *See:* qualification, qualification as condition (qualified right or qualified interest).

**qualified-terminable-interest property trust** *See:* trust, qualified–terminable–interest property trust (QTIP).

**qualification as condition (qualified right or qualified interest)** A condition upon a right, authority, or statement. Qualified is a signal that something under consideration is not universal or unlimited but is subject to conditions in its understanding or exercise. A qualified right may be exercised only when the qualifications on that right, its conditions, are satisfied. A qualified statement is true only in the context according to which it is qualified.

*See also:* privilege, conditional privilege.

**qualification as requirement**  A required characteristic. A qualification is a condition that a person or entity must manifest in order to be eligible for consideration for a position, office, contract, or other qualified activity.

**quality (qualitative)**  An attribute distinguishing one thing from another, or varying grades of value. A quality is an attribute of any thing that distinguishes it from other examples of the same kind of thing. Quality in this sense is an aspect of the one rather than a characteristic of the type.

Quality is also an indication of the relative value or desirability of one thing among others. Thus, a high-quality example of a trade good is likely to be more valuable than a low-quality example of the same good. Fungible commodities may vary in grade, but within a given grade they have the same quality. In a contract, the omission of a quality may be implied from a reasonable understanding of the quality of the good or goods likely to have been intended by the parties.

Qualitative evidence is evidence of quality.

*See also:* fungibility (fungible); quantity (quantitative).

**quality of life**  *See:* life, quality of life.

**quality of life policing or neighborhood order policing**  *See:* police, policing, broken windows policing (quality of life policing or neighborhood order policing).

**quantity (quantitative)**  The number, weight, volume, size, or other measure of a thing. Quantity is a measure of content without regard to quality. Depending on the thing measured, quantity may be a matter of count or number; of weight or mass; of volume occupied or volume required; of height, width, or depth; of multiples such as grosses or tons; or of standard containers such as a tea chest or truckload. The term may be used in a vague manner to express the presence of an unknown or irrelevant quantity, but quantity is more carefully used to describe a measure that is ascertained with some specificity, especially in determining a quantity of goods to be sold.

A contract subject to the statute of frauds may have any term implied as a matter of reasonableness, with the exception of quantity; the quantity of the thing sold must be in the writing. A quantity of land is satisfied by the description of the land or even by an address. A quantity of goods, on the other hand, must be sufficiently described according to the customs related to the trade of such goods as to be unambiguous among traders of those goods.

Quantity is essential to the definition of some crimes based on the possession of contraband, particularly the possession of a controlled substance. In other instances, such as for the crime of distribution, the quantity of the contraband involved is not essential in defining the elements of the crime but is determinative of the range of the sentence. When a quantity is a defining element of a crime, the quantity must be proven with evidence supporting proof beyond a reasonable doubt. But when a quantity is only an aspect of sentencing, it must be proven with evidence supporting a finding by a preponderance of the evidence.

Quantitative evidence is evidence of quantity.

*See also:* term, contract term; quality (qualitative).

**quantum**  A measure or standard, especially a small measure. Quantum, in general, is any measure or standard for measure. Once a measure is determined, a single unit of that measure is a quantum. For example, the quantum of evidence required for proof in a criminal case is proof beyond a reasonable doubt. At times, quantum is used to suggest the least quantum, or the slightest amount that has significance. Thus a quantum of doubt in a criminal case is the slightest possible reasonable doubt.

**quantum meruit**  *See:* damages, contract damages, quantum meruit (quantum valebant).

**quantum valebant**  *See:* damages, contract damages, quantum meruit (quantum valebant).

**quarantine**  Isolation. Quarantine is an order and a practice by which a thing, animal, person, vessel, place, state, or nation is kept isolated from contact with others. Quarantine in a military sense is an isolation that is maintained by a blockade, siege, or embargo. Quarantine as a matter of public health is isolation in order to avoid the spread of a disease, infection, or other threat to health.

Note: quarantine is both a verb and a noun.

**quare**  Why, how, or wherefore? Quare is a general interrogatory in Latin for why or for what reason, or how or by what means. Quare is a common term for the commencement of a writ. Note: quare is not to be confused with quaere, which means to question or interrogate in a legal proceeding.

*See also:* quaere.

**quare clausum fregit**  *See:* trespass, trespass clausum fregit (quare clausum fregit).

**quarrel**  Dispute. A quarrel is a disagreement with a party, a statement, or a state of affairs. A quarrel as a matter of law may represent a claim that is adverse to another's claim, whether the two parties have disputed their claims formally or informally. A quarrel more generally may represent a grudge, dispute, or fight.

**quarry**

**quarry as mine**  A source of rock or minerals in the Earth. A quarry is a place in the ground from which stone, sand, gravel, or other rocks or minerals are extracted.

**quarry as prey**  The object of a search or hunt. A quarry is the object sought by some endeavor, such as an animal that is being tracked or hunted, or an escaped prisoner who is being sought for recapture.

**quarter** The acceptance of a surrender. Quarter is a customary term for the acceptance of the surrender of an enemy. The term may come from the idea of quarters, in that accepting a surrender required giving the surrendered enemy lodging, or quarters. The law of war requires soldiers, even in combat, to give quarter when surrender is offered.

*See also:* surrender.

**quarter-to-quarter tenancy** *See:* lease, leasehold, tenancy, periodic tenancy, quarter-to-quarter tenancy (quarterly lease).

**quartering or to be drawn and quartered** *See:* punishment, draw and quarter (quartering or to be drawn and quartered).

**quarterly lease** *See:* lease, leasehold, tenancy, periodic tenancy, quarter-to-quarter tenancy (quarterly lease).

**quartermaster (storekeeper)** Treasurer. A quartermaster is an official charged with maintaining finances. In modern discourse, it is usually only seen in two contexts in the military. In the land services, a quartermaster is responsible for pay and supply. In the sea services, a quartermaster is responsible for navigation, and the functions of pay and supply are performed by a storekeeper.

**quarters** Housing, particularly for military personnel. Quarters is housing. In military law, it is a unit of lodging for a member of the military, or a military unit, on a permanent or temporary basis. The term may come from the more general sense of quarter as a portion of a town or city.

> **quartering of soldiers** To assign military personnel a place for food and lodging. Quartering is the act of assignment to quarters, and to quarter soldiers is to assign them to a location usually in a barracks, for lodging and food. The U.S. Constitution forbids the quartering of soldiers in a private house in peacetime without the consent of the owner or in wartime according to regulations, which usually require government compensation to the dispossessed homeowner.

**quash** The annulment of a motion, order, or proceeding. To quash something is to render it void. Motions, subpoenas, proceedings, indictments, and other orders from proceedings are to be quashed if they are defective in their procedure, substance, or form.

*See also:* void (voidability, voidable).

**quasi** Almost alike but not perfectly alike. Quasi is an adjective or prefix that signifies some measure of similarity yet with a critical degree of incompleteness or inexactitude in the noun that follows. Thus, a quasi-contract is nearly but not fully a contract (though it may yet be enforceable). A quasi-something is not an entirely accurate example of the something, but it is so close that it might as well be, though it would lack the technical benefits of being the real something.

> **quasi contract** *See:* contract, contract formation, quasi contract (contract implied in law or implied-in-law-contract or quasi-contract or quasi contractus).

> **quasi-corporation** *See:* corporation, quasi-corporation.

> **quasi-delict or delictual** *See:* delict (quasi-delict or delictual).

> **quasi in rem** *See:* in, in rem, quasi in rem.

> **quasi in rem jurisdiction** *See:* jurisdiction, in rem jurisdiction, quasi in rem jurisdiction.

> **quasi-possession** *See:* possession, quasi-possession.

> **quasi-property right** *See:* property, property right, quasi-property right.

> **quasi-suspect class** *See:* class, legal classification, quasi-suspect classification (quasi-suspect class).

> **quasi-suspect classification** *See:* class, legal classification, quasi-suspect classification (quasi-suspect class).

> **quasi-trustee** *See:* trustee, quasi-trustee.

**quay (key)** A wharf for the loading and unloading of cargo to vessels. A quay is a concrete, stone, or, very rarely, wooden wharf for the transit of stores and cargo onto a vessel. The term comes from the nearly obsolete term for the lands in a port between the buildings and the water, over which a public easement runs. The term is pronounced (and sometimes spelled) "key."

**queen** *See:* government, forms of government, monarchy, queen.

**Queen's Counsel** *See:* counsel, Queen's Counsel (King's Counsel or Q.C. or K.C.).

**queer legal theory** *See:* jurisprudence, queer legal theory.

**querela** A medieval civil action commenced by plaint. A querela was the term for a complainant's action in the early common law brought. Then, the querens, who would later be called a plaintiff, filed a plaint to initiate a civil dispute for seeking a remedy. The whole of the argument reflected in the complaint, including the claims of the querens, the theory of law they relied on, and the facts asserted amount to the querela, which today might be thought of as merely the plaintiff's case. The term comes from the Latin word for sad sounds, such as those made by ill persons or dark instruments like the oboe.

*See also:* plaint.

**query**   A question, or to question. Query is a very near synonym of question. There is a sense in which query is a more formal and technical word than question, query usually describing a sole question submitted to a person or entity; in contrast, questions often come in great number. Owing to increased popularity from the use of query in computer research, this distinction is probably fading away.

Query also depicts a search inquiry in a database.

*See also:* quaere.

**question**   Inquiry, or interrogation. A question is an interrogatory, a statement that seeks to evoke an answer from the person to whom it is made. To question a person is to present such interrogatories in an examination or interrogation. To question a statement is to ask questions that test its premise, logic, and conclusion.

In legal practice, a question is a particular issue presented to the court in every civil and criminal action that is considered either a question of law, a question of fact, or a mixed question of law and of fact.

*See also:* issue, issue before the court (question before the court or contested issue or disputed issue or issue in dispute).

**question before the court or contested issue or disputed issue or issue in dispute**   *See:* issue, issue before the court (question before the court or contested issue or disputed issue or issue in dispute).

**question of fact or factual issue**   *See:* issue, issue before the court, issue of fact (question of fact or factual issue).

**question of law or legal issue**   *See:* issue, issue before the court, issue of law (question of law or legal issue).

**question presented for review**   *See:* issue, issue before the court, issue on appeal (question presented for review).

**hypothetical question**   A question asked in the abstract. A hypothetical question is a question that relates to a hypothesis or a theoretical question, the answer to which does not directly affect a concrete matter at hand. A hypothetical question differs from a rhetorical question, in that a hypothetical question is posed with the intention of eliciting a response, usually in order to examine the answerer's approach to the answer. In contrast, a rhetorical question is used to suggest a question or an answer and achieves its intended result by the asking; no answer is needed. Law school hypotheticals employ a number of customary forms, including the use of Blackacre and similar lands and the use of certain abbreviations, notably a, b, c, d, h, k, l, o, p, s, t, v, w, and x. All are defined throughout this dictionary.

*See also:* question, rhetorical question.

**leading question**   A question that includes or indicates the answer. A leading question suggests its own correct answer or at least the answer to be avoided. An attorney may not ask a leading question of a witness at trial or in a deposition, unless the witness is hostile or the question is in cross-examination of previous testimony.

**rhetorical question**   A question asked for the sake of asking it rather than to solicit an answer. A rhetorical question is a statement disguised as question, usually intended to provoke the hearer to consider or utter an answer that the speaker intends. The rhetorical function of such a question, with the speaker's hope that encouraging a listener to answer the question in a given manner will encourage the listener to accept the preferred answer as true (or at least be more likely than if the speaker had suggested the answer to the listener). In argument, lawyers may use rhetorical questions, though care must be taken not to improperly suggest material that is not in issue or in evidence, and in closing arguments rhetorical questions must be used with care to avoid confusing the issues or the burdens of persuasion or proof.

*See also:* question, hypothetical question.

**vexed question**   An unsettled point of law. A vexed question is a point of law on which there is no settled answer among the sources of law and the customary understanding of the bench and bar.

**qui (quo)**   By what? Qui, and its various forms including quo, is a Latin interrogatory usually representing "how?" or "by what?" or, sometimes, "where?"

**qui tam**   *See:* whistleblower, qui tam (action qui tam or qui tam action).

**quia**   Because. Quia is a conjunction demonstrating causation: because of x, y.

**quia timet (bill quia timet or writ quia timet)**   An obsolete order for the security of an imperiled interest. Quia timet is the title of a variety of orders that were once available in law and in equity to prevent a variety of wrongful harms of which the plaintiff had a reasonable fear. Quia temet is Latin for "because he fears." The writ quia temet was a remedy at law to compel the possessor of some personal property to give a security against its loss to a person who claims to be the true owner and who alleges a basis for belief that the property might be destroyed. Qui temet also described a class of orders in equity intended to prevent some harm to a legal interest that could not otherwise be protected in law, or harm to an equitable interest that had no other order for its security. These writs and orders have generally been succeeded by bond or by injunction.

*See also:* injunction (injunctive relief).

**quibble (quibbling)**   A trivial argument, or to raise one. A quibble is a complaint or argument that is so minor that it is highly unlikely to alter the outcome of a larger dispute or to affect any practical matter. Quibble is both a noun and a verb, and to quibble, or quibbling, is to raise a quibble.

*See also:* scintilla.

**quick condemnation**  *See:* condemnation, quick condemnation (quick–take proceeding).

**quick ratio**  *See:* ratio, quick ratio.

**quick with child or pregnant woman**  *See:* pregnancy (quick with child or pregnant woman).

**quick-take proceeding**  *See:* condemnation, quick condemnation (quick–take proceeding).

**quid**  What? Quid is a term of general interrogation, particularly for what? how? or by what right? In maxims, the term may be presented in a statement, along the lines of "the question is what is the question," which is not actually a question at all.

**quid pro quo**  This for that. Quid pro quo, literally, is Latin for "what for what." In English, this idea is often seen in various colloquial phrases as "this for that" or "tit for tat" or "one good turn deserves another" In one sense, quid pro quo implies a bargain or trade, the mutual consideration of a contract, a favor done for a favor owed. In another sense, it implies retaliation, in which one wrong deserves another.
*See also:* harassment, quid pro quo harassment.

**quid pro quo harassment**  *See:* harassment, quid pro quo harassment.

**quidam**  Someone unknown. Quidam is a Latin pronoun for a person, and it is used to denote a person or persons unknown.

**quiet title**  *See:* title, action to quiet title (quiet title).

**quis custodiet ipsos custodes**  *See:* official, legal official, quis custodiet ipsos custodes (who will watch the watchers?).

**quit**  To be free of any endeavor. To quit is to become free of some burden or obligation, or to cease from engaging in an activity. Thus, one may quit a claim or interest as well as quit an employment or position. To quit some action is to cease performing it. To quit a job is to resign from it. To quit a claim is to waive its further pursuit or potential for pursuit.
*See also:* rent, quit rents (perpetual rents).

**quit rents**  *See:* rent, quit rents (perpetual rents).

**quitclaim deed**  *See:* deed, quitclaim deed.

**quittance**  The surrender of interests and waiver of claims. Quittance is an act or record of being quit of a legal interest, claim, or right, giving repose to any whose interests might have been affected, particularly any who might have been dispossessed by the party who quits. A quittance was once routinely memorialized in a document of the same name, which, for instance, was often filed in a court record to record the terms agreed during divorce. A quittance may operate in a

variety of ways, according to what is quit, such as a waiver of rights, disclaimer, or a release from liability.

**quo**  *See:* qui (quo).

**quo warranto (writ of quo warranto)**  By what authority. Quo warranto, or "by what authority," is an action that is still in use in the United States to challenge the authority by which a person holds an office or has committed an act of office in either a public or corporate capacity. A quo warranto proceeding is the basis for challenging the apparent or declared results of a public election in some jurisdictions. A petition for a writ of quo warranto is available in most jurisdictions to challenge an act of a corporate official, corporation, trustee, or fiduciary, by asserting that the action was beyond the scope of the respondent's (or defendant's) authority. Such a petition must usually be proved by the petitioner (or plaintiff) by clear and convincing evidence.
*See also:* remedy, extraordinary remedy (extraordinary relief).

**quod**

**quod erat demonstrandum (Q.E.D. or QED)**  Thus it is proven. Q.E.D., or quod erat demonstratum, is a Latin term of logical rhetoric that asserts that an argument has been proven or, more specifically, that the premises already offered demonstrate a single conclusion that follows. The use of the phrase adds nothing to the force of an argument; it is a rhetorical flourish.
*See also:* therefore (therefor).

**quod vide (q.v.)**  See there the specific reference listed here. Quod vide, or q.v., is a signal in a citation or general reference to a source that alerts the reader to look for some matter by the name according to which it is cited. The term literally translates from Latin as "which see," and in a citation to a dictionary entry it suggests that looking up the term itself is the best way to the source, rather than a page number or other reference.

**quondam**  At the time, or for that moment. Quondam is a Latin term specifying a given time in the future, present, or past that something happens, an event transpires, a status is held, and so forth. It is used figuratively to refer to a status that is likely to be temporary or one in the past that has come to an end. Thus, a quandam partner might be either a partner at a time in question though no longer a partner or a partner in a partnership now that is not likely to persist.

**quorum**  The number of attendees required to conduct business. A quorum is the minimum number of participants in a meeting for business to be conducted or a vote to be taken. A quorum is counted as the number present, not the number who choose to vote. A quorum is specified in an entity's by-laws or charter as either a number of the persons or entities who are members or as a percentage of the membership. In the absence of a number specified in such a governing document, a customary requirement is to have at least a majority of members present. If a body meets without a sufficient quorum, it is inquorate, and the only legitimate business that may be conducted includes actions necessary to establish that no quorum exists and to seek to establish a quorum at that time or a future meeting. Corporate shareholder meetings often must have a specific number of persons or entities represented in attendance before actions may be taken that lawfully bind other members of the organization.

**quorum court** *See:* court, U.S. state court, county court (quorum court).

**quota** A required percentage or amount. A quota is the amount of anything that is required according to a percentage of the whole or a specified amount. A quota in an employment context refers to a proportion of individuals who are hired, promoted, or otherwise subject to some job action and who share some characteristic, usually of race or gender. Such hiring quotas by businesses subject to anti-discrimination laws are presumptively discriminatory and illegal.

*affirmative action* Quotas are generally disallowed as a means of affirmative action, and a raw number or percentage of positions or promotions allocated by race, gender, or some other criterion will ordinarily not survive scrutiny under anti-discrimination laws or the constitutional doctrine of equal protection. Factors such as race, gender, age, disability, and similar criteria may be used to prefer one individual over another as among similarly qualified people when needed to achieve a broader goal of social and institutional significance, but applicant quotas and population targets may not be directly pursued.

**quotient verdict** *See:* verdict, quotient verdict.

**Qur'an** *See:* Sharia, sources, Qur'an.

> [W]ords are chameleons, which reflect
> the color of their environment.
>
> Commissioner of Internal Revenue v. National Carbide Co.,
> 167 F.2d 304, 306 (1948) (Hand, J.).

# R

**r** The eighteenth letter of the modern English alphabet. "R" signifies a variety of functions as a symbol. It is translated into Romeo for radio signals and NATO military transmissions, into Robert for some police radio traffic, and into dot, dash, dot in Morse Code.

**R as trademark symbol** ® *See:* trademark, trademark symbol, R as trademark symbol ®.

**r as an abbreviation** A word commencing in r. When used as the sole letter of an abbreviation, R often stands for race, radical, railroad, railway, range, rating, real, record, registered, registration, Regna (Queen), regulation, repeal, repealed, repealing, reports, republicana, rescinded, research, resolved, response, revised, revision, revolved, Rex (King), Richard (King), rolls, rule, and Russian. It may also stand for the initial of an author or case reporter, such as the Kentucky Law Reporter (1880–1908), Raff, Ramsay, Randall, Rawle, Raymond, Rettie, Robinson, Roscoe, Russell, and The Reports (Coke's King's Bench). When used in Shepard's Citations, R means reversed, revoked, or rescinded. In the transcript of a trial or deposition, "r" designates the response to a question or statement.
*See also:* rex (regina or regis or regnal).

**R.O.E. or ROE or right of re-entry or power of termination** *See:* entry, right of entry (R.O.E. or ROE or right of re-entry or power of termination).

**race**

**critical race theory** *See:* jurisprudence, critical race theory (critical-race theory or C.R.T. or CRT).

**racial challenge or gender challenge or Batson motion** *See:* jury, jury selection, juror challenge, peremptory challenge, Batson challenge (racial challenge or gender challenge or Batson motion).

**racial covenant** *See:* covenant, real covenant, restrictive covenant, racial covenant (racially restrictive covenant).

**racial discrimination** *See:* discrimination, racial discrimination, benign discrimination (benign use of racial classifications); discrimination, racial discrimination.

**racial profiling** *See:* profile, racial profiling, driving while black (DWB); profile, racial profiling.

**racial segregation or segregation by gender** *See:* segregation (racial segregation or segregation by gender).

**racially restrictive covenant** *See:* covenant, real covenant, restrictive covenant, racial covenant (racially restrictive covenant).

**cross-race identification theory (C.R.I.T. or CRT or CRIT)** Theory that racial differences may deter accurate personal identification. Cross-race theory suggests that individuals who identify themselves as members of a particular race may have difficulty in identifying the differences and identities of specific individuals who have the features associated with another race. Though the theory is controversial, it has been raised in court to contest lineup identifications, particularly by majority-race witnesses attempting to distinguish among otherwise anonymous persons of color. Note: cross-race theory is a theory of bias in identification. It is related to but different from critical race theory, which is the examination of the effects of law and race on one another.
*See also:* jurisprudence, critical race theory (critical-race theory or C.R.T. or CRT).

**race as social category** A vague category of people based on differences among ancestry. Race, as a matter of law, has a particular meaning in the United States, which arises from the historical use of race in the maltreatment of people perceived as racially inferior to others. Race was once defined by blood or lineage from people of a particular national origin reflecting differences in appearance or culture. Owing to the use of race in the definition of slavery in the United States and in the de jure prohibitions and social barriers that were revived during and after Reconstruction, especially in Jim Crow laws but more pervasively in social segregation, race has long been essential in determining individual rights in the U.S.

Race is increasingly considered by popular understanding to be a matter of social construction, and is therefore left increasingly to personal definition. Race in the United States has long been associated with skin color, though very few people are in fact the color assigned to them as a racial label. Even so, it is now defined largely by the origins of oneself or one's family from a few large places that are specifically identified with a race, such as an origin in sub-Saharan Africa for an African American or an origin in Europe for a white or "Caucasian" person.

An essential legal definition of race, however, is the use of race in the nineteenth century statutes passed during Reconstruction to implement the Thirteenth, Fourteenth, and Fifteenth Amendments. Race, as it was understood then, was less broadly defined and included aspects that would now be considered as color, national origin, perhaps even religious subculture, and alienage. These definitions continue in antidiscrimination laws.

**race card (playing the race card)**   To assign race as a cause for an act or condition. To play the race card is to interject race into a situation or argument as a basis for criticism or for action. In its rhetorical form, the race card is a claim, made expressly or by implication, that a given state of affairs is the result of racial discrimination, stereotypical assumptions regarding race, or otherwise caused by the historical and current implications of race. In its practical form, it is a claim that a person is relying upon that person's race or the race of others in seeking some advantage or is placing another person at a disadvantage by claiming a license or privilege on the basis of the race of one or another of the participants.

There is a limit and a subtlety to the extent of the race card in both speech and action, such that not all arguments that a situation is explained by race amount to playing the race card. When race is clearly an existing, motivating factor of discriminatory behavior, to describe that behavior in terms of race is considered either not to play the race card or to play it but to do so fairly.

In all events, the race card is controversial and engenders high emotions, all the more so in certain circumstances and forms by which it may be employed. Perhaps most controversially, it may be raised as a form of backlash, in which a person of a majority race suggests a person of color has played the race card as a passive-aggressive means of characterizing an argument on other issues as being based on the sub-text of an undeserved claim for privilege based on race. The phrase "the race card" may be deliberately used to label a case of genuine discrimination in a manner so as to undermine the credibility of the underlying evidence.

**race laws**   See: Jim Crow law (race laws).

**race to the bottom**   See: game, game theory, race to the bottom (race for the bottom).

**race to the courthouse**   The attempt to gain from a rule favoring the first to file a legal notice among competing claimants. The race to the courthouse is a metaphor describing the efforts of claimants to be the first to file in any proceeding that gives priority to the earliest-filed claim, as well as the legal benefits that accrue to the first claimant who does. Several procedures encourage the race to the courthouse, not the least being laws conferring ownership between two or more parties who each have a claim to own the same land, which in some jurisdictions are governed by recording acts that prefer the claimant who wins the race or the claimant who wins the race without violating the rules of notice. These recording acts give priority to the first party to record title for a given parcel of land. The priority of some creditors who file first in bankruptcy, and the priority of

claimants in equity among whom the equities are equal, may also be based on the first filing. Many judges have taken notice of the inefficiency and the potential for abuse from a race to the courthouse and have avoided payment and claims rules that encourage it.

**race-notice**   See: title, recordation of title, recording act, race notice recording act (race-notice).

**race notice recording act**   See: title, recordation of title, recording act, race notice recording act (race-notice).

**race recording act**   See: title, recordation of title, recording act, race recording act (pure race act or pure race jurisdiction).

**racketeering (racket)**   A fraud or other crime, particularly when it is part of a larger scheme. Racketeering is the participation in a racket, which in the law is a fraud, criminal act, or criminal enterprise carried out by a group of people. Confidence games and other criminal conspiracies are within the definition of some racketeering statutes, but racketeering tends to be defined according to specific, serious forms of already criminal conduct. The most significant federal statute defining racketeering is the Racketeer Influence Criminal Organization statute, or RICO. Racketeering activity as identified in the RICO statute includes bribery, sports bribery, counterfeiting, embezzlement of union funds, mail fraud, wire fraud, money laundering, obstruction of justice, murder for hire, drug trafficking, prostitution, sexual exploitation of children, alien smuggling, trafficking in counterfeit goods, theft from interstate shipment, interstate transportation of stolen property, as well as state crimes of murder, kidnapping, gambling, arson, robbery, bribery, extortion, drug distribution and related offenses.

See also: fraud, confidence game (scam or swindle or swindling or con game or con artist or con man); trafficking, drug trafficking, continuing criminal enterprise (CCE).

**organized crime**   Any hierarchy of groups or individuals structured to obtain money from criminal activities. Organized crime is the sum of criminal organizations operating in the United States and around the globe. Organized crime is defined for the purposes of law-enforcement policy as, effectively, large organizations with established structures and hierarchies, sometimes among component organizations. Organized crime includes both domestic and international organizations and is the particular concern of national law enforcement agencies, such as the FBI and DEA, as well as international organizations, such as INTERPOL. Although some gangs are large enough to be considered organized crime, as a matter of policy most local gangs are the object of investigation by municipal and state police.

Both federal and state law provide special procedures for the investigation of organized crime, allowing an unusually broad scope to wiretaps and surveillance that might otherwise amount to a search, provided the law enforcement agency has demonstrated to a judge that there is probable cause to believe that a criminal organization is in operation. Expert witnesses in organized crime exist who may testify as to the methods and culture of criminal organizations but not as to the guilt or participation of individuals.

As a matter of criminal law, the activities of organized crime are prosecuted either as racketeering; or, if the racket involves drug trafficking, as participation in a Continuing Criminal Enterprise (CCE); or as the specific criminal acts, such as murder, smuggling, fraud, or other acts from which the organization realizes a profit or by which it supports, protects, and maintains its operations.

See also: gang; trafficking, drug trafficking, continuing criminal enterprise (CCE); syndicate, criminal syndicate.

**Mafia (La Cosa Nostra)**   A network of criminal organizations originating in Sicily. The Mafia is a network of criminal gangs active in Italy and in the United States, which has been a criminal influence in the U.S. throughout the twentieth century and remains a focus of law enforcement as of 2011. The mafia is a paradigmatic criminal organization, and the attempt by government agents to interfere with mafia smuggling, criminal enterprises, sale of contraband liquor and drugs, money laundering and tax evasion, and fostering of public corruption have been the basis for numerous statutes, including the Racketeer Influenced Corrupt Organizations Act. As a result of its influence, "mafia" in popular speech has come to mean any group of confederates engaged in a common purpose, with a common identity or origin, even if the purpose might be legitimate.

**Yakuza**   A Japanese network of criminal organizations. The Yakuza are the largest network of criminal organizations in China, with allied organizations in most Western countries. In Japan, they are not secretive; members wear distinctive tatoos, and local offices often have signs advertising their purpose. In the United States and other countries, the Yakuza are secretive and are usually treated as another form of organized crime.

**Racketeer Influenced and Corrupt Organizations Act (RICO or R.I.C.O.)**   Laws allowing civil and criminal prosecution of organizations that engage in a pattern of illegal acts. The Racketeer Influenced and Corrupt Organizations Act, codified at 18 U.S.C. §1962 and known universally as RICO, is a federal law that has been emulated in many states that provides for the criminal prosecution of a person who creates or employs an organization that engages in a pattern or enterprise of illegal activities, and allows civil suits by a party directly harmed by such activities.

To violate the act, an organization must engage in predicate criminal acts. The organization must have a structure, although it need not be a business-like structure, as long as it is ascertainable and, effectively, has some allocation of duties among its participants. Predicate acts include any activities listed in the statute as racketeering. Civil actions under RICO allow for treble damages and attorneys' fees and are subject to a four-year statute of limitations.

See also: tort, intentional tort.

**radioactive waste**   See: waste, waste material, nuclear waste (radioactive waste).

**radon**   A radioactive gas emitted from the soil. Radon is an element (Rn) that is usually found as a naturally occurring, radioactive but chemically inert gas that is emitted from the soil as a result of the decay of naturally radioactive rocks and soil. Radon may enter houses where, in sufficient quantity, it may cause lung cancer and other risks to health.

**rainmaker**   See: lawyer, law firm, lawyers, law partner, rainmaker.

**raised check**   See: check, raised check (altered check).

**rajm**   See: punishment, rajm (stoning).

**rake**

**rake as commission (rake off or take or vigorish or vig)**   The percentage of a bet retained by a broker or bookie. A rake is a percentage of a transaction retained by the broker who places a sale, trade, bet, or similar transaction, or who performs purchases as an agent or provides services for hire and retains a portion of the price as compensation for the service performed. Although the term is often used to describe an undisclosed commission, which is usually a theft or a fraud, the term and its analogues are also used when the commission is fully disclosed. The Yiddish term vig, or vigorish, is used in the same manner, particularly in the placing of bets and in the sale of stocks and other financial instruments in the market.

See also: commission, commission as fee.

**rank**   The order of precedence among military, diplomatic, and private titles. Rank is an order of priority or hierarchy, and in the military, the diplomatic community, the corporate world, and other hierarchies, rank is both the system of hierarchy and the individual levels of hierarchy.

In the United States military, only officers technically hold a rank, while enlisted personnel hold a rating. In both cases, all personnel are required to obey a lawful order given by an officer of superior rank. Although a superior order was once a justification for any illegal act committed according to orders, the law now holds every officer and member individually accountable for their actions, although a failure to obey a lawful order is a court-martial offense.

In the diplomatic community, rank and the time in place at that rank, determines order of precedence as a matter of protocol.

**rank and file**   The workers in an organization. The rank and file are the workers, sometimes including the lowest levels of supervisory workers, whose attitudes toward the workplace would be more sympathetic to the workers than to the highest echelons of the organization. Rank and file is a metaphor for a formation of enlisted troops in a military unit.

**ransom**   Money or conduct traded for the freedom of a person or vessel. Ransom is what is paid to free a person or vessel from custody, either as a victim of kidnapping or piracy or, as a matter of legal history, for the release of a prize vessel captured at sea. By far, the most common usage is what is paid to free a victim of a kidnapping. Although ransom is usually a payment in money, the term has sometimes been applied to conduct in lieu of payment, such as the release of other prisoners.

The crime of kidnapping is defined, in part, as an unlawful custody with the potential intention of collecting ransom or other reward, but the crime's definition does not make such a purpose exclusive. The ransom element may be satisfied by any demand of money or conduct by another, regardless of the relationship of the other person to the kidnapped victim, and regardless of whether what is demanded was otherwise a preexisting obligation.

*See also:* kidnapping (kidnapper or kidnap); prize.

**RAP or rule against remoteness**   *See:* perpetuity, rule against perpetuities (RAP or rule against remoteness).

**rape**   The crime of causing a sexual act with another person without that person's consent. Rape is the crime of perpetrating a sexual act with another person without that person's consent, either because the victim, being of sufficient age and capacity to consent, does not consent or because the victim is too young or lacks the capacity to give consent. Rape is a category of crimes of sexual assault, and the offense requires an act of penetration of the body of the victim as well as some evidence that the rapist used force, a threat of force, or a condition in which consent was impossible, such as age, incapacity, sleep, unconsciousness, or the influence of drugs or alcohol sufficient to interrupt the victim's awareness. A sexual act with a minor is also called statutory rape.

Rape is a violent crime for the purposes of classification, although many states will examine the conditions in which statutory rape occurs or refuse to classify it as violent. Rape is a crime of general intent, and it is a separate offense for each act, rather than a crime that applies but once to a course of conduct. Many jurisdictions have several gradations of rape. Some follow the Model Penal Code approach and define less serious forms of sexual assault by other titles, such as gross sexual imposition.

The definition of rape has changed markedly in the last fifty years. The Model Penal Code defines rape as a crime committed only by a male against a female, that is committed (other than against a minor less than ten years of age, or against an unconscious victim or one impaired through drugs or intoxicants the rapist administered) by force or threats of a very grave nature, including a threat of "imminent death, grievous bodily harm, [or]

extreme pain of kidnapping," though no evidence of resistance is required under the Code. Since the adoption of the Code, many states have redefined rape with gender–neutral language and have adopted a standard of non–consent rather than force, and those states that had required proof of resistance by the victim have moved toward only requiring evidence of a reasonable degree of resistance to the assault.

At common law, rape was not possible within marriage. Most states have altered the marital immunity, some abolishing it outright, others suspending it if the couple are separated, and others finding exceptions according to the facts.

*See also:* molestation (molest or molester); ravishment (ravish).

**gross sexual imposition**   A sexual act with a minor accomplished by deceit or threats. Gross sexual imposition is a lesser form of sexual assault than rape used in states that follow the Model Penal Code, and in these jurisdictions it is both an offense and a lesser included offense in a rape instruction. The offense is committed by a person who compels another to have sexual contact through force or a threat of force, or who administers an intoxicant for the purpose of diminishing judgment or control, or who knows of the other person's impairment of judgment from other causes. The offense may be committed by any person if that person engages in a sexual act with a person who has not reached a statutory age that varies from jurisdiction to jurisdiction between ten and thirteen.

**bodily intrusion (penetration or physical penetration)**   A physical insertion of any part of the body of one person into the body of another. A bodily intrusion, or physical penetration, is any entry caused by one person using a part of the human body or an object controlled by that person to enter into a human body through any orifice or the skin, entering no matter how slightly. The intrusion or penetration amounts to rape or sexual assault if it occurs without the lawful consent of the person whose body is penetrated, and if the intrusion is performed by any means on the genitals or anus of the victim, or by the mouth by means of the mouth of genitals of the assailant. If any portion of the bodily organ or object enters the body or organ of the victim, intrusion or penetration occurs, regardless of whether the intrusion might have been more thorough. Intrusion or penetration by a penis occurs regardless of whether any emission occurs. If an unconsented intrusion or penetration is committed on another portion of the victim's body, it is an assault.

*See also:* injury, bodily injury (bodily harm); seduction (seduce).

**criminal sexual conduct (sexual conduct)**   The illegal penetration of one person's body by another person. Sexual conduct is the involuntary sexual penetration of the body of another. Sexual penetration may occur in any manner into the victim's body, by any body part or instrument of the perpetrator, such that any entry into the victim's body is sufficient. Some states categorize the offense. First-degree sexual conduct includes all penetrative acts with a child or involuntary penetrative acts with an adult.

**date rape (acquaintance rape)** Rape by a social acquaintance or friend. Date rape is a colloquial expression for an act of unconsented sex, in which the victim is a social acquaintance of the rapist and consents to a visit with the rapist that leads to sex without the victim's consent, either because the victim lacks the capacity to consent owing to the influence of alcohol or drugs or because the rapist uses force or a threat of force. As of 2011, date rape is not a specific category of crime but is prosecuted according to the definition of rape, sexual misconduct, or sexual assault appropriate to the jurisdiction.

Note: drugs intended to produce unconsciousness or diminished capacity or judgment, notably sedatives like ketamine hydrochloride and gamma hydroxybutyrate or their analogs, used to facilitate a date rape, are regulated, and the intentional distribution of such a drug to a victim for the intention of subsequent unconsented sex is both an assault and a distinct offense in many jurisdictions.

**rape by instrumentation (rape by instrument)** The use of a device or thing to commit a rape. Rape by instrumentation is the insertion of an object other than a sexual organ of the human body into the anus or vagina of another person without that person's consent. In Oklahoma, marital immunity from prosecution for rape is specifically waived for this offense.

**rape of a child (child rape or carnal knowledge of a juvenile)** A sexual act with a child below the statutory age, usually thirteen. The rape of a child is the least euphemistic and most specific of the variety of labels for a sexual act with a child. Rape of a child, or an act that in any way includes penetration of the victim's body in a manner that would be otherwise sexual in nature, is a class A felony. In many jurisdictions, it is one form of gross sexual misconduct, sexual assault, or aggravated statutory rape. The highest age of the victim varies from state to state, being as low as ten or as high as thirteen; a victim who is older being within the range governed by statutory rape. In Louisiana, this crime is referred to as felony carnal knowledge of a juvenile.

See also: rape, statutory rape (sexual abuse of a minor).

**spousal rape (marital rape)** A rape committed by one spouse against another. Spousal rape, or marital rape, is a rape as otherwise defined by statute that takes place between two married people. At common law, legal and social barriers prevented the prosecution of a husband for the rape of his wife, but contemporary criminal law requires every sexual act to be consensual. Although there are still social barriers to overcome in prosecuting such cases, the fact of marriage is no defense to a charge of rape or assault against either spouse.

**marital exemption (spousal defense or marital immunity from rape)** A defense to sexual assault or rape that the victim was the perpetrator's spouse. The spousal exemption to rape, or marital immunity from prosecution for sexual assault, was a common-law affirmative defense to a charge of rape or assault that was available to a husband. Most states have abrogated this defense, at least in situations in which the spouses are separated or in which the victim alleges an assault in which force or a threat of force against the victim or another are used to coerce the spousal victim. Spousal rape is now recognized as a particular form of rape, although it is not defined as a separate offense.

**rape trauma syndrome (child abuse syndrome)** Patterns of behavioral response to the trauma of a rape. Rape trauma syndrome is a category of patterns of behavior that have been routinely observed by individuals suffering from trauma as a result of a sexual assault. The symptoms are varied but may include difficulties in communication regarding the person of the victim and of the assailant and the events of the assault, as well as delay in recognition or response to the events. Expert evidence of rape trauma syndrome is controversial, and although it has generally been admitted in trials, it is not admissible to prove that a defendant committed an assault, though it may be admitted in order to explain certain aspects of the evidence or to disprove defense narratives attempting to explain omissions in a victim's testimony or a delay in reporting an offense. The qualifications of the expert and the limitation on the use of the evidence to matters that are more probative than prejudicial are essential to ensuring such evidence does not invade the province of the jury or interfere with a fair trial.

Child abuse syndrome may be admissible in similar circumstances.

See also: witness, expert (expert witness).

**statutory rape (sexual abuse of a minor)** Sexual conduct with a person who has not reached the statutory age of consent. Statutory rape is any act of sex in violation of the statutory presumptions of the age of consent. The once-common rule was that all sexual acts by a person over the age of eighteen with a person under the age of eighteen amounted to statutory rape. Following the Model Penal Code, the offense is defined as a sexual act by a person four years or older than the victim, if the victim is sixteen or younger. Different jurisdictions have enacted different age limits and different age ranges. In all cases, a sexual act with a minor below a lower threshold range, usually twelve but ranging from ten to thirteen, is considered the rape of a child or an analog offense.

See also: ravishment (ravish); rape, rape as sexual assault, rape of a child (child rape or carnal knowledge of a juvenile).

**illicit sexual activity**   Sexual activity with a person under the age of eighteen. Illicit sexual activity is the federal offense of an adult engaging in sexual activity with a person under the age of eighteen years in any manner that involves more than one state jurisdiction or any foreign jurisdiction, such as transporting the victim across state lines, enticing the victim to cross state lines, traveling abroad, or enticing the victim to go abroad. It is the equivalent of federal statutory rape.

**rascality test**   *See:* deceit, deceptive practices, rascality test.

**rat**   A traitor or whistleblower. Metaphorically, a rat is either a person who betrays a confederate or a person who discloses information regarding the wrongdoing of others. To rat is to engage in such activities, especially in providing testimony or information to the police.

**ratable (ratably or rateable)**   Calculable by an appropriate share of what is owed or owing. Ratable means capable of being assessed at a proper rate or proportion. One among several debts, one tax among several taxes, and one claim among several claims are each ratable because it is possible to determine what is owed relative to the other amounts that are owed. In other words, when a debt is to be calculated by a formula, such as an equal share of the assets available divided among all claimants of a given class, the debt is ratable, in that its rate is ascertained once the variables of the amount of money available and the number of claimants equally sharing from it are known. Ratable is not the same as equal, although equal shares are often allocated among each claim in a class of debt, and within that class all of the claims are ratable, thus they are equal and ratable.

Note: the preferred American spelling has no "e" after the "t," though the English spelling does.

**rate**   The applicable level of taxation, interest, or other calculation. The rate is the ratio at which some monetary function is calculated, especially the percentage of value at which tax is assessed (whether on a sales transaction, on property holdings, on income, or on some other basis) or the percentage of capital at which interest shall be charged or paid. There are, however, myriad forms of rate, including inflation, temperature change, building completion, and, indeed, anything that is measured or estimated as a portion of something or as data over time.

**rate of exchange or exchange rate or security exchange**   *See:* conversion, conversion rate for currency exchange (rate of exchange or exchange rate or security exchange).

**interest rate (rate of interest)**   The compensation paid for the use of money for a period of time. An interest rate is a charge made for the use of money for a period of time, the rate itself being a designated percentage of the principal owed, calculated by the means by which the percentage is assessed and the means by which the interest is itself added to the principal as it is assessed, and the rate at which interest is either billed or added to the principal. An interest rate may be straight or compound, in which interest is charged on interest, and the compound rate may be compounded at various intervals, including annually, quarterly, monthly, weekly, or daily. To compare, a 1% base interest rate as a straight annual interest on $1,000 would amount to $10 of interest in a year, so the amount owed at the end of one year would be $1,010. But, the interest on $1,000 for a 1% base interest rate as a compound monthly interest would amount to $126.80, so the amount owed would be $1,126.80.

**floating rate (adjustable rate or variable rate)**   A rate of interest that varies according to changes in a benchmark rate. A floating rate of interest is a rate that is not fixed for the period of a loan but is changed at specific intervals to reflect changes in a benchmark economic statistic, such as the Federal Reserve's discount rate or some other easily ascertained economic indicator. A floating rate may have a floor rate or ceiling rate, which are parameters the rate may not exceed, and may have a limit on the scale of increase by which the rate may be adjusted in any single time period. Although the rate of any transaction may be calculated according to a specific benchmark or interval, there is no inherent difference among rates that are designated adjustable, changeable, floating, or variable.

*See also:* mortgage, adjustable-rate mortgage (A.R.M. or ARM).

**prime rate**   A short-term interest rate extended to preferred borrowers. The prime rate is an interest rate given by lenders to their most credit-worthy customers. A national prime rate is calculated daily by the Wall Street Journal as an average of the prime rates offered by major lenders. Even so, the most significant influence on the prime rate is the designation of the federal funds target rate made every six weeks at the Federal Open Market Committee of the Federal Reserve. As a rule of thumb, the prime rate is three percent above the federal funds target rate.

**rate lock (rate-lock)**   A commitment to provide a loan at a specified rate of interest. A rate lock is a statement made by a lender with the intent that a borrower will rely upon it to commit to a loan at a specified rate of interest within a given time. A rate lock may be integral to an option contract, the basis of a rate-lock agreement, or a statement made with the intent that another rely upon it. A rate lock in an option or agreement is enforceable according to its terms, but a rate lock otherwise is enforceable only in the limited circumstance of detrimental reliance. Rate locks are common among mortgage lenders.

**ratification (ratify or ratified or ratifiable)**   The later affirmation of an act already once made. Ratification is an act by which an earlier act is affirmed, particularly when the earlier act was by an agent and the ratification is by a principal, or when the earlier act was voidable and the ratification is a final commitment. Ratification may be required in certain circumstances in order to give effect to an earlier act, as when a contract or treaty specifies ratification in order to bring the instrument fully into force. In such cases, the means or form of ratification may be specified, and a failure of the party that must ratify to carry out ratification by such means or form may be ineffective.

Ratification in private law arises most often in three cases, as ratification by a principal of an act by an agent, as ratification by a corporation or an act of an agent or officer, and as ratification by a guardian of a voidable commitment or contract by a minor (or by an adult of a commitment or contract made earlier by the adult while the adult was still a minor). In all of these cases, ratification may occur expressly or by conduct, as long as the conduct is by the ratifying party and manifests a later awareness of the initial undertaking and a later intent to be bound to it. Ratification of public acts, however, particularly treaties and public contracts, may require express and formal ratification.

**ratification of a contract**  See: contract, specific contracts, voidable contract, ratification of a contract.

**ratification of a treaty**  See: treaty, ratification of a treaty, instrument of ratification.

**ratification of treaty**  See: treaty, ratification of treaty (treaty ratification).

**ratio**  An analytical relationship between two elements that supports a conclusion. A ratio is both a mathematical relationship between two quantities that yields a conclusion and also a line of reasoning that supports a conclusion or judgment.

As a mathematical property, a ratio is a proportion, such as two to three. People in the general populace tend to forget how such ratios relate to sums, as in the example above, which would suggest that whatever is the lesser is forty percent (or two-fifths) of a whole, but the lesser is actually sixty-six and two-thirds of the larger when the two are compared without summing them.

As a property of reasoning or of justification, the ratio is the reasoning, the basis for a conclusion or, literally, its rationale. In this sense, the ratio of a decision is the synthesis between the facts and the law that is essential for the court to support an order mandating some action regarding the parties before it.

**ratio decidendi**  See: opinion, judicial opinion, ratio decidendi.

**quick ratio**  Cash plus receivables divided by payables. A quick ratio is an elementary function of the finances of a business or organization by comparing its debts to its assets and expected revenue.

**rational**  See: rationality (rational).

**rationale**  The relationship between reasons and a conclusion or action. A rationale is the reasoning that explains or justifies a decision, understanding, or action. A rationale that would explain or justify an understanding usually incorporates an observation of fact with a principle of interpretation, according to which a conclusion is reached. In general, a rationale that would justify a decision or action incorporates a premise that includes a statement of a purpose or goal, as well as a premise that is a condition that must be satisfied to accomplish the purpose or goal, and a conclusion that the pursuit of the satisfaction of the condition was required in order to pursue the purpose of the goal. There are countless variations on this theme, and there are usually many component arguments required to sustain such a rationale. The mere existence of a rationale is not proof that the rationale is sufficient explanation or justification. Every rationale is open to criticism, both as to the sufficiency of its premises and the logic of the analyses.

A rationale that is made prior to an act or decision is a rationale ex ante, which may also be used to describe a later assessment of a rationale that, given the evidence then available, could have been made prior to an act or decision, even if it was not. A rationale ex post is made after an act or decision, taking into account whatever additional information becomes available.

**rationale ex ante**  Reasoning before the fact, or based on information knowable prior to an event. Rationale ex ante is reasoning before the fact. A rationale ex ante is a reason for action that is known to a person before an act takes place or a decision is made, rather than the rationale ex post, which is a justification that is considered only after an action is committed or decision is reached. Rationale ex ante emphasizes foresight and foreseeability, not requiring or expecting an accurate prediction of the future but a reasonable assessment of practical likelihoods in the future that is made in the light of past events.

See also: ex, ex ante; rationale, rationale ex post.

**rationale ex post**  Reasoning after the fact, or based on information knowable after an event. A rationale ex post is reasoning after the fact. A rationale ex post is useful in determining an actual result from specific causes, but there is a high likelihood of skew in the assessment of the foreseeability of a given event. Reliance on a rationale ex post to describe why a person or institution did something risks mischaracterizing its purpose in the light of later events unknown to the person or institutional agents at the time of their decisions or actions.

**rationality (rational)**  A legal model of awareness, or an economic model of selfishness. Rationality, in general, is the capacity of making accurate assessments of oneself in one's surroundings and of using the tools of reason to make the best decisions possible in a given situation. Rationality is used by writers within and among academic disciplines in very different ways. Rationality has many different meanings, particularly differing in the law and in economics.

Summarizing the descriptions of the rational person from judicial opinions, a rational person is a reasonable person who is aware of that person's surroundings, including the practical likelihoods of cause and effect among physical objects and human agents, and whose decisions and actions incorporate such knowledge in a reasonable manner to live a life of constructive projects that respects the interests of all persons affected by a decision, both in the short term or the long term. This approach reflects, to some degree, all four of the ideal types of rationality described by the social theorist Max Weber, which are (roughly) action manifesting the pursuit of a selected purpose, the adherence to understood concepts of morality or value in life, emotion or sentiment, and habit or custom.

In economics, or at least neo-classical economics, a rational actor is meant as a hypothetical actor who seeks to maximize the actor's own welfare in every choice. An essential difference between the economic and legal conceptions of rationality is that it is legally rational to respect the interests of others without a personal cost imposed for not doing so, though, in the neo-classical sense, it is not economically rational to do so.

In philosophy, rationality often is used to distinguish emotionality or sentimentality in making decisions. Even so some philosophers, notably David Hume, would think such a distinction is meaningless.

See also: reasonable (reasonableness).

**rational relationship test**   See: scrutiny, standards of scrutiny, rational-basis review (rational relationship test).

**rational-basis review**   See: scrutiny, standards of scrutiny, rational-basis review (rational relationship test).

**bounded rationality**   Rationality cannot exceed cognitive and environmental limits. Bounded rationality depicts several different limits on the use of reason or the extent of reason that may be used by an individual or humans generally. In its most accepted forms, theories of bounded rationality argue that rationality cannot overcome limits on human understanding that result either from the limits of human cognition or from human understanding of and from the environment. Thus, a lack of relevant information leads to a reduced level of rationality. In more controversial forms, bounded rationality incorporates emotional and sentimental bases of decision that do not reflect purely rational motives or understanding. Bounded rationality thus becomes a tool for assessing such limits on rational decision-making to incorporate realistic assumptions that limit rational choice.

**ratione**   A justification for a right or interest in the law. Ratione is a Latin term indicating the application of a rationale, or ratio, from a given source that provides justification for a right or interest in the law. Thus, ratione imperii is "on account of the command."

**ratione personae**   By reason of identity. Ratione personae, or requirements ratione personae, is the basis for jurisdiction over the person on the basis of the person's identity, status, or actions. To have jurisdiction ratione personae is to have personal jurisdiction over an individual or entity, including the power to compel appearance.

**ratione soli**   By reason of the land. Ratione soli describes the common law right in lands to possess all of the natural and wild elements of them, including the right to hunt or take all animals and trees on the property, whether they are cultivated or wild. The right was not, of course, absolute, and royal animals or animals patently domesticated and owned by another were not considered within the scope of the right.

See also: jus, jus as right of citizenship, jus soli.

**ravishment (ravish)**   An unlawful sexual act. Ravishment is a euphemism for a sexual act outside of marriage, particularly one that is unlawful because it is either an act of fornication, an act of statutory rape or indecency with a minor, or it is forcible rape. At common law, ravishment included the marriage of a ward without the guardian's consent.

See also: fornication; rape; rape, statutory rape (sexual abuse of a minor).

**Rawlsian justice**   See: justice, Rawlsian justice.

**RCRA**   See: waste, waste material, Resource Conservation and Recovery Act (RCRA).

**re (in re)**   In the matter of . . . In re is a customary form in the title of a case for "in the matter of" or "concerning." Derived from Latin, it is a shorthand for "in the matter of" or "as to the cause regarding."

**re-cross or recross-examination**   See: examination, examination of a witness, recross examination (re-cross or recross-examination).

**re-examination or re-direct examination**   See: examination, examination of a witness, redirect examination (re-examination or re-direct examination).

**re-insurance or reinsure**   See: insurance, reinsurance (re-insurance or reinsure).

**re-let**   See: lease, re-let (relet or re-letting or re-leasing).

**read the riot act**   See: riot, riot act (read the riot act).

**ready**   See: performance, ready, willing and able.

**real**   Related to land, or certain and tangible. Real, in legal usage, usually refers to an interest in land. There are some instances, however, such as considering an injury or a potential for harm, when real is used in its more general sense to suggest something tangible, measurable, and extant, rather than something fanciful or hypothetical, such as real or concrete harm. Real may also mean that a term or amount is of a practical significance rather than a theoretical result, such as real laws or real impact.

Real generally refers to land, as in realty, not because of its tangible nature but because of the history of the word itself: "real" in medieval English meant royal, like regal. Owing to the feudal common law structure of royal overlordship, the monarch was the ultimate owner of all estates in land, and so interests in land, which were heritable as tenancies, were all subject to royal interests. Thus, all interests in land were real interests.

**real chattel**   *See:* chattel, real chattel (chattel real).

**real covenant**   *See:* covenant, real covenant (covenant in land or covenant real).

**real estate**   *See:* property, real property, real estate.

**real law**   *See:* law, real law.

**real party in interest**   *See:* party, party to an action, real party in interest.

**real property**   *See:* property, real property (realty or property in land).

**real rule**   *See:* rules, real rule.

**real thing**   *See:* thing, real thing.

**realism**   *See:* jurisprudence, legal realism.

**realm**   A kingdom, jurisdiction, or intellectual domain. A realm is the extent of the lands that are ruled by a monarch. Realm is still used metaphysically to describe a jurisdiction or any domain in which a given idea, institution, or law has either primacy or particular significance.

**realtor**   *See:* property, real property, real estate, realtor.

**realty or property in land**   *See:* property, real property (realty or property in land).

**reapportionment re-apportionment**   *See:* apportionment, apportionment as allocation of voters (reapportionment re-apportionment).

**reason (reasons or reasoning)**   The power of thought and understanding, or a given cause for understanding or action. Reason, in general, is the power associated with the mind or the brain of considering information perceived, comparing information, and forming understandings from it, including the ability to discern truth from falsehood, right from wrong, and practical conclusions to problems. The nature and extent of reason is highly controversial among philosophers, neuroscientists, and psychiatrists.

In law, reason is accepted as a human capacity that is not fully formed until a person reaches an age of legal maturity and legal capacity. A person may not fully develop the tools of reason or may lose the faculty of reason owing to incapacitation from alcohol or drugs or as the result of advanced age, illness, or trauma.

The common law reflects a particular sense of reason, so much so that reason was often held up as a synonym for the law. Some of the practical aspects of reason, as reflected in this view of law, remain influential in modern law: Each individual is responsible for that individual's actions. The person responsible for a harm is the person who causes it. The specific conditions of a grant govern the grant, unless the provision was beyond the power of the grantor. Each person is entitled to rely on the promise of another, when the promise is made with sufficient seriousness as to invite reliance. The law must treat each person with equality.

A reason is different from reason, per se. Reason, or the capability of reasoning, may or may not yield a distinct, articulable basis for every conclusion that is reached using a reasoned approach. A reason is a distinct, specific basis for believing something or doing something. That there is a reason to believe something, however, does not assure its truth, as the reason may be unnecessary, insufficient, false, or subject to a countervailing reason.

Reasoning, particularly legal reasoning, may refer not only to the method by which a legal official reaches a conclusion of law, but also to a formal means of posing premises derived from the legal materials, comparing these premises to premises derived from facts, and reaching conclusions as to the legal significance of a given situation. This form of legal reasoning is the basis of legal argument.

A reason in an opinion is a basis for a conclusion, from which a judgment may be reached. A reason may arise from a source of law, from a fact derived from evidence, from evidence to support a fact, from public policy, or from a combination of all these things.

*See also:* argument, legal argument; argument, legal argument, CRAC (conclusion rule application conclusion or conclusion rule analysis conclusion or C.R.A.C.); sevara; rationale; rationality (rational); reasonable (reasonableness).

**reason in antitrust**   *See:* antitrust, Sherman Antitrust Act, rule of reason (reason in antitrust).

**reason to know**   *See:* knowledge, constructive knowledge, reason to know.

**analogical reasoning**   *See:* argument, analogical reasoning.

**deductive reasoning**   *See:* argument, deductive reasoning.

**inductive reasoning**   *See:* argument, inductive reasoning.

**practical reason**   A reason that is sufficient for a person to act. Practical reason is both the sense of reason in which a person determines what to do or not to do in daily life and the sense of a reason that forms a reason for action, a reason to do something or not to do something. There is a wide scope in jurisprudence for practical reason: some views having it more purposive, teleological, or ends-driven, such that practical reason is a means for achieving a pre-selected end. Other views consider practical reasoning as the more causal view, while deontology is more concerned with the conditions in which an action is right or wrong. From this view, practical reason is an analysis of a situation that leads to an action required by the right way of doing things in such a situation.

**public reason**   A reason for law or policy that can be understood by everybody. A public reason is a reason for a legal, political, or social action or status that can be understood by each person affected by it. This requires that the reason be based on a justification that is sensible and persuasive to each person in the society. As formulated by some theorists, notably John Rawls, a public reason may not be based on religion or other views of social good that are not universally accepted in society.

*See also:* public.

**reasonable (reasonableness)**   The practical judgment of a person of ordinary awareness and good will. Reasonableness is the understanding that people endowed with ordinary reason and knowledge have of what is appropriate to do in a given situation. A reasonable action is what most rational and fair-minded people could be expected to do in a given situation.

Reasonableness differs from but is related to the idea of the right thing to do, or the moral duty to do what is right. As an aspect of reasonableness, that duty is moderated by the practical affairs of each person and the competing duties and interests that would affect any action at a given moment. Reasonableness moderates the purity of right or reason with the practical limits of human behavior. Reasonableness is not the same as logic, morality, duty, prudence, courage, knowledge, skill, or judgment, but neither is reasonableness an excuse for a person to avoid such attributes of human understanding and conduct as a person of good will would ordinarily do.

*See also:* usage; objective (objective standard or objectivity); rationality (rational); mistake, reasonable mistake; time, reasonable time.

**reasonable accommodation**   *See:* accomodation, reasonable accommodation (disability accomodation).

**reasonable alternative design**   *See:* liability, product liability, strict product liability, reasonable alternative design.

**reasonable attorneys fees**   *See:* fee, fee for services, attorney's fees, reasonable attorney's fees.

**reasonable care**   *See:* care, duty of care, reasonable care.

**reasonable doubt**   *See:* doubt, reasonable doubt.

**reasonable inference**   *See:* judgment, summary judgment, reasonable–inference rule (reasonable inference).

**reasonable-inference rule**   *See:* judgment, summary judgment, reasonable-inference rule (reasonable inference).

**reasonable medical certainty**   *See:* medical, reasonable medical probability (reasonable medical certainty).

**reasonable medical probability**   *See:* medical, reasonable medical probability (reasonable medical certainty).

**reasonable mistake**   *See:* mistake, reasonable mistake.

**reasonable necessity**   *See:* necessity, private necessity, reasonable necessity.

**reasonable time**   *See:* time, reasonable time.

**reasonable use**   *See:* use, use of property, reasonable use (reasonable–use theory).

**reasonable-use theory**   *See:* use, use of property, reasonable use (reasonable–use theory).

**commercially reasonable (commercial reasonableness)**   Customary for the form of trade and type of goods. Commercial reasonableness is a requirement upon a creditor who holds a security interest in any property that has secured a debt that went into default, so the creditor, as secured party, has taken possession of the collateral and elects to dispose of the collateral. Because either the debtor is entitled to any value of the collateral in excess of the debt and costs of collection, or the debtor is liable to the secured creditor for the amount of the debt in excess of the amount realized from the sale of the collateral, the creditor has an obligation to the debtor to dispose of the collateral in a commercially reasonable manner.

A commercially reasonable manner will vary according to the form of goods or property that form the collateral, but, in general, if the property is disposed of in a manner by which such property is generally sold, using reasonable pricing, advertising, and negotiation, or at least such methods as are typical of the market or trade for such property, the disposal is likely to be commercially reasonable. Sale of the collateral in an existing market for such property or at the price then current for such property is commercially reasonable, but the mere fact that a better price might have been had at another time or in another market does not demonstrate unreasonableness.

*See also:* commerce (commercial).

**reasonable person (reasonable man or reasonable woman)**   A standard of behavior based on the likely conduct of a typical, but thoughtful person. The reasonable person is a hypothetical person who is conjured up by attorneys for the comparison of the harmful conduct of a defendant in litigation, to determine whether the defendant's conduct met or failed to meet the standard that society would expect from another person in the defendant's situation, if that hypothetical person was of average awareness and understanding, though sufficiently thoughtful and reasonable. The primary function of the reasonable person is to attempt to assess the actual conduct of a party who is accused of negligence, or a breach of duty or foresight, by comparing what the person did in fact to what a different person, who would not be negligent or knowingly in breach of a duty, would have done. If such a reasonable person would have done what the defendant did (or something similar to it or less than was in fact done), the defendant was not negligent, and the harm was not the defendant's fault. But if a reasonable person would not have done what the defendant did (or would not have done anything similar to it), then the harm caused by the defendant was caused by the defendant's negligence or by some other breach of duty.

**rebate**   A discount from the asking price. A rebate is a discount as against the asking price for the sale of goods or services, whether by a fixed amount or a percentage of the price, which is customarily paid in cash back to the buyer. A rebate may allow a discount in purchase price to be excepted from the amount of a financed purchase, amounting to a loan of cash in the form of the rebate with that amount financed and subject to repayment according to the terms of the financing agreement. A rebate may be conditioned upon further conduct by the buyer after the sale is otherwise complete, but once such conduct is performed, the rebate becomes a debt owed by the seller to the buyer.

*See also:* discount; refund.

**rebuttal (rebut or rebuttable or rebutter)**   An argument in response to an argument against one's position. A rebuttal is an argument that contradicts an argument already made. Rebuttal takes many forms, but primarily it is the response to an initial claim in the presentation of arguments and evidence. Thus, a prima facie case establishes a fact or a claim as a matter of law unless it is rebutted by sufficient evidence to present a genuine dispute of fact or law to be argued on its merits. A rebuttal argument is made in trial or on appeal to contradict or present a counter-narrative to the argument made initially, the direct argument. Rebuttal testimony is testimonial evidence introduced to demonstrate the falsity or other weakness of evidence earlier testified to by another witness. Owing to each party's ability to present its own evidence when presenting its case, evidence (and argument) in rebuttal is limited in scope to rejection, criticism, contradiction, or otherwise responding to the argument already made.

The term rebuttal was originally a French term for a thrust or jab in response to an attack, something like a riposte. The term metaphorically shifted to include an argument in response to an argument made against one's position.

The common-law pleading of the rebutter is a civil defendant's argument made as to facts in response to the plaintiff's allegations, or the factual argument of a plaintiff made in response to a defendant's rejoinder. Thus, the rebutter was similar in rejecting an argument on factual grounds to the demurrer's rejection on legal grounds. This use is now very rare, and a rebutter is now more likely to mean any party that rebuts the argument of the other.

*See also:* evidence, rebuttal evidence (rebutting evidence).

**rebuttable presumption**   *See:* presumption, rebuttable presumption, irrebuttable presumption (conclusive presumption); presumption, rebuttable presumption.

**rebutting evidence**   *See:* evidence, rebuttal evidence (rebutting evidence).

**surrebuttal (surrebutter)**   An argument or evidence in response to a rebuttal. Surrebuttal is an argument presented after the rebuttal, in a trial often presenting additional evidence. Thus, if a plaintiff argues a case in chief, the defendant answers it, the plaintiff rebuts the answer, and the defendant surrebuts the rebuttal. There is usually not a right to a surrebuttal, and the question of when a defendant may present an argument or additional evidence in surrebuttal is usually left to the discretion of the trial court. Even so, when the rebuttal case presents sufficiently new evidence that it would be unfair not to allow evidence in contradiction of it, many jurisdictions either allow a surrebuttal as a matter or right or examine a denial of such evidence carefully for any abuse of discretion.

In the presentation of evidence, the role of surrebuttal is limited to contradiction of evidence and argument raised in the reply.

If a rebutter is filed in court, the response arguing facts to contradict it is a surrebutter.

**recall**   *See:* diplomat, recall, persona non grata; diplomat, recall (letter of recall); product, product recall.

**recall of product (food recall or product recall)**   A request to return a consumer product or food owing to a defect or danger. A recall is a request by a manufacturer, packager, integrator, or other producer of consumer products, foods, or other material for sale, which is made both to the end consumer and to merchants and distributors in a supply chain, to return the product or food, because a defect in a product or adulteration in the food poses a risk to the consumer. Recalls are usually accompanied with an offer of refund or replacement. A recall may be mandatory, ordered either by a government agency, such as the Department of Agriculture or the Consumer Product Safety Commission, or by a court as a remedy in a recall proceeding, or it may be voluntary, issued by the producer in response to its own internal safety guidelines.

**representative recall (election recall or recall election or recall referendum)**   A popular election to repeal a law or to unseat an elected official. Recall is a process established by statute in many states, by which citizens vote on the continuation of an elected official in office until the end of the present term, or on the continuation of a law or tax in force. A recall may result in the official's removal from office or the repeal of the law or tax. A recall is usually initiated by a petition, which must be signed by a statutory percentage of registered voters within a designated period of time.

**recantation (recant or recants or recanted)**   To renounce a statement earlier made. A recantation is a retraction and repudiation of a statement or other communication made earlier by the party recanting. The effect of a recantation varies considerably. A witness in a criminal trial who recants testimony after a verdict and judgment of sentence is not considered inherently to affect the enforceability of the verdict or sentence. The general rule is that only if the evidence of the witness's recantation is heard by a court in reconsideration or collateral review is it material, and only then if the jury was likely to have reached a different outcome without the testimony of the witness. Yet, the more practical question is why the witness gave the initial testimony and then recanted. The witness may offer good cause to reopen the initial investigation or to initiate a new investigation as to the original crime.

When a defendant recants a confession prior to an entry of a plea, the plea based on the confession cannot be entered. However, if the confession is recanted after the acceptance of the plea and entry of a sentence, the evidence is in the same limbo as the evidence of a recanting juror. If a juror recants regarding the juror's vote, and the time for reconsideration is not past, the recantation could be the basis for a mistrial or new trial or, in quite unusual cases, a different verdict, in the discretion of the judge.

**recapitalization** See: capital, commercial capital, recapitalization (recapitalize).

**recapture** Repayment or payment back on other grounds, after funds are disbursed. Recapture, as a matter of sales, entitlements, or other systems of payment, amounts to any means by which the payee is required to return some or all of the money received. Recapture includes any attempt by the payor to require the payee to pay the payor money for some reason, even though the money is at best collateral or unrelated to the first payment, but which will practically offset the effect of the first payment in whole or in part. Recapture of taxes is the method by which wrongfully collected or retained tax revenues are returned to the taxpayers.

Recapture as a matter of international law is the taking of a vessel, position, or person of one's own forces, after the vessel, position, or person had been captured by a hostile force.

Recapture as a matter of criminal and police procedure is the apprehension of a person who has broken custody.

**recapture of chattel** See: chattel, recapture of chattel (self-help).

**receipt (receive or recipient)** The act of receiving, and a record acknowledging what was received. Receipt is both the act of receiving anything and the status of having done so. Receipt results in possession of the thing received, if only momentarily and only constructively. Receipt is the corollary to delivery, and a delivery is not effective unless there is receipt of the thing delivered. Correspondingly, receipt may be effective by any means of delivery, including symbolic and constructive delivery. To receive is to knowingly accept a thing that has been delivered to the recipient by another party.

A receipt is a written acknowledgment by the recipient that the thing received was indeed received. A receipt is either signed by the recipient or an agent of the recipient or acknowledged in print by the entity receiving the thing. A receipt does not require any specific formalities or details to be valid or effective beyond a reference to the thing received, although the more specific the information regarding the date, time, and location of the receipt's issue, and the description and number of goods, their price and terms, and the identity of the receiving agent, the more useful the receipt is as later evidence.

See also: delivery.

**receivable** Any right or claim on which payment is required to be made. A receivable is any right of payment from others. There are many forms of receivable, and as to a given party, a receivable is any form of claim, right, contract, or other obligation held by that party that forms a reasonable expectation that there is a legal or equitable duty by another party to pay money.

Note: although an account receivable is one form of receivable, receivable itself is a broader category, and unlike an account receivable, other forms of receivable need not have been billed or invoiced to be accounted.

See also: account, account receivable (accounts receivable).

**receiver (receivership)** A court-appointed manager of assets in dispute. A receiver is a person or entity appointed by a court to hold property that is subject to a dispute, whether the dispute concerns ownership or rights in the property or claims against the property's owner that might be satisfied from the property. A receiver has the obligation to manage the property, to conserve it, and to prevent its waste, as well as the powers to receive rents and other income from it, to collect debts, to bring or defend actions related to it, and to receive a fee for doing so. A receiver is under the supervision of the court and responsible to the court for carrying out all orders regarding the property. A receivership may be established by a court on motion for the preservation of property for the duration of an action. Although an order of receivership was originally equitable, courts of general jurisdiction are usually given such powers by statute or rule.

In a metaphorical sense, to be in receivership represents any system or plan that has failed and must be supervised by a caretaker.

See also: accounting, accounting as a remedy (equitable accounting); remedy, pre-judgment remedy (pretrial relief).

**receiver of stolen goods** See: goods, stolen goods, receiver of stolen goods (receiving stolen property).

**receiving stolen property** See: goods, stolen goods, receiver of stolen goods (receiving stolen property).

**reception** A process of receiving anything or anyone. Reception is the act or process of receiving and of being received. Reception has several, quite distinct meanings in law, including its senses as a synonym for receipt of goods or property delivered; the receipt of information or broadcast signals, the recognition of a diplomat, and the incorporation of law from another jurisdiction.

**reception of foreign law** The application of law from a foreign legal system. The reception of foreign law is a process by a court in acknowledging that an issue before the court may be best resolved by a process that includes consideration of the obligations of the parties arising from foreign law, in considering sources of foreign law, in considering the rules or principles arising from foreign law that may affect the obligations of the parties before the court, and in determining the weight to give such rules or principles in reaching the court's judgment of the dispute between them.

**reception of the common law (reception statutes)** Reliance on the English common law in the colonies and early states. The reception of the common law is a process that commenced with the establishment of the first English colonies and persisted after independence in every British colonial legal system, by which the English common law was either decreed or understood to be the primary source of law in the colony or in the new state, until such time as a new law by the state replaced it. In the United States, reception was varied in the different colonies and in the different states, although most states following independence enacted reception statutes that accepted the common law of England as the law of that state unless or until the common law was modified by constitution, statute, or judicial decision of the state or of the United States. The works of Sir Edward Coke, Matthew Hale, and Sir William Blackstone are frequently considered by contemporary courts as a basis for determining the state of the common law at reception. To this would be wisely added the manuals of justices of the peace of Burn, Sheppard, Dalton or Jacob; Charles Viner's Abridgment of the Laws; and the law dictionaries of Giles Jacob (1739) or Timothy Cunningham (1765).

**recess** A period during which formal business is suspended. Recess is a period during which a court or legislature is not in session and not formally conducting official business. To be in recess implies that the court or legislature will return to session at an appointed or customary time. A recess may be as brief as a few moments, or it may last for several months. A judge who orders a break in the proceedings of a trial to take a rest or to provide one to the parties orders the court to be in recess.
*See also:* sine, sine die (without day); adjournment (adjourn).

**recess appointment** *See:* appointment, recess appointment (vacancy appointment).

**recess appointments clause** *See:* constitution, U.S. Constitution, clauses, appointments clauses (recess appointments clause).

**recht** The fundamental principles of German law. Recht depicts the law in general, the fundamental concepts of law or spirit of the law rather than one or another specific rule. Recht is equivalent to the Law as in the Due Process of Law Clause, law in its grandest sense. Recht is often contrasted with Gesetz, the more specific idea of a legal rule or statute. Recht is more like droit in French law or diritto in Italian.
*See also:* recto; gesetz.

**recidivism (recidivist)** A person who falls back into criminal behavior after arrest. Recidivism, in general, is the tendency to relapse into past behavior. In criminal law, it is the repetition of criminal conduct by a person who had been earlier arrested and punished for such conduct. Thus, a recidivist is one who commits a crime and commits it again, particularly after having been punished for an earlier commission. Although statutes vary, most jurisdictions require a heavier sentence for repeat offenses, not under a theory of duplicate punishments for the prior offense but with the ideas either that the repeat offense is a greater threat to the public than a first offense or that the recidivist requires heavier punishment to curb the criminal behavior. Note: the term is derived from the Latin for falling back, or returning to one's past.
*See also:* offender, repeat offender.

**three–strikes law (anti-recidivist law or three strikes law)** A statute declaring an offense by a recidivist to be a distinct, more serious offense. A three–strikes law is a popular name for an anti-recidivist law, which either creates a distinct and serious crime of committing multiple offenses or requires a significant minimum sentence for an offender with past offenses. The procedure of a three–strikes law is to assess a person accused of committing a felony to determine if there is proof of two prior felonies, whether committed as an adult or a minor, in which case the accused is to be charged as a recidivist and subject to a mandatory prison term. A person charged under such an indictment must have the prior offenses proved beyond a reasonable doubt to the jury in the later case. Such laws are distinct from sentencing guidelines or discretion, in which a judge may take into account past offenses when setting the sentence for the crime of which the defendant is then convicted.

**reciprocity (reciprocal)** Treatment of one party as it treats the other party. Reciprocity is the equality of respect and treatment between or among different parties. What one allows the other, the other is expected to allow to it. Reciprocity is an implied justification for the performance of contracts, as well as of the whole of the implied social contract that is presumed to justify the constitution, regulations, and criminal laws. Thus, as we each expect others to behave so must we behave, and the government is the guarantor of such reciprocal expectations. Reciprocity is the essential basis for customary international law.
*See also:* bar, admission to the bar, admission by reciprocity.

**reciprocal contract**  *See:* contract, specific contracts, reciprocal contract (mutual agreement).

**reciprocal dealing**  *See:* consideration, reciprocal dealing.

**reciprocal negative easement**  *See:* servitude, equitable servitude (reciprocal negative easement).

**reciprocity or the golden rule**  *See:* ethics, categorical imperative (reciprocity or the golden rule).

**recital**  The quotation of an instrument or record in a later instrument. A recital is prefatory language at the beginning of an instrument or pleading. It is often a statement of the preliminary events or preceding instruments. The recitals may include the repetition of the terms or language of an earlier instrument, record, law, or other writing in a later writing or speech. Pleadings incorporate recitals that may not be exact quotations but that are narrations of events. A recital of text from an earlier written instrument should be exact in its rendering of the earlier text, although immaterial omissions or scrivener's errors will not be a cause to strike a recital from a pleading. A recital of an earlier record is not the best evidence of that record but may serve as prima facie evidence of the record. A last will and testament, trust, or contract may incorporate recitals that are intended to guide the interpretation of terms in the event of a later dispute.
*See also:* whereas.

**recklessness (reckless)**  Lacking in care for the harm one knows one might cause. Recklessness describes the behavior of a person whose actions create a significant risk of harm to others but who is either aware of the risk and makes no effort to abate it or who is indifferent to the risk. It is an extreme departure from the duty of ordinary care, amounting to more than negligence. Harms caused as a result of reckless behavior are actionable in tort, either as a separate standard of liability or as the basis for gross negligence, and in either case, a plaintiff may seek punitive damages. Recklessness is also the basis for the crimes of reckless endangerment and criminal recklessness.

**recklessness as state of mind**  An awareness of a risk but a willingness to disregard it. Recklessness is a mental state comprising two elements at the same time: first, an awareness of a condition or consequence of an action that on even the least consideration or reflection would be apparent to a reasonable person that it amounts to a risk of harm to a person or to property; and second, a willful disregard of that risk. Recklessness is sometimes defined to include a third element that there is no lawful requirement or justification for the act that is committed recklessly. This condition is implied even when it is not an element of a definition.
*See also:* mens, mens rea (mental state).

**reckless disregard**  Apathy regarding the harm likely caused to others or to their rights. Reckless disregard is recklessness manifested toward other people or their rights or some other value, in which the reckless person acts in such a way to risk harm but with no apparent care to avoid the harm or to mitigate it. An action for gross negligence may describe the defendant's conduct, as in reckless disregard of the danger posed to the plaintiff's person (or the plaintiff's safety, the plaintiff's rights, or so on).
*See also:* recklessness, reckless disregard for the truth (knowing disregard for the truth).

**reckless disregard for the truth (knowing disregard for the truth)**  A statement made without regard to whether it communicates the truth. Reckless disregard for the truth characterizes a statement that either states events or conditions that are not true or that omits information necessary to create a true impression of a significant aspect of the statement, without regard for the degree to which the statement creates an accurate impression of the actual or historical truth of the matter. A statement made with reckless disregard of the truth is akin to a knowing falsehood, being a statement that is deliberately false or creates an impression that the person knows to be a likely and untrue impression. Nonetheless, the standard of reckless disregard is used to avoid the difficult evidentiary goal of proving that a person knew he or she lied when making the statement.

A knowing or reckless disregard for the truth is the constitutional standard of care of actual malice required to sustain an action for libel against a public figure under New York Times Co. v. Sullivan, 376 U.S. 254 (1964). The standard makes libelous speech actionable only if the author and publisher know the story to be false or act with reckless disregard for the truth, which is to say that the usual forms of research or confirmation of the truth that would be employed by a responsible person have not been reasonably pursued. Reckless disregard of the truth regarding a material fact in a statement made by a police officer in a request for a warrant violates the officer's duty of good faith in the application and may be sufficient to remove the qualified immunity of the officer from civil liability for false arrest or other violations of civil rights.
*See also:* recklessness, reckless disregard; malice, actual malice.

**reckless endangerment**  The crime of knowingly and carelessly causing a risk of serious harm to another. Reckless endangerment is an act of knowing and intentional conduct that poses a substantial risk of immediate and serious harm to another person, and the potential for harm is either known to the person who commits the act or is knowable and the person acts with deliberate indifference to the risk. Reckless endangerment is a crime, which is committed whether or not a harm results from the reckless action. Reckless endangerment is a lesser included offense for assault. Depending upon the results of such conduct, reckless endangerment may give rise to a variety of civil actions in tort, including gross negligence, battery, assault, outrage, and wrongful death.

**recognizance**  Acceptance of an obligation. Recognizance is a recognition of one's obligation through a new commitment to perform it. Recognizance, or one's own recognizance, is a promise to do something that one was obligated to do, such as to appear for a hearing. Thus, a person released on his own recognizance is released on his pledge to appear.

*See also:* cognizance, cognizable (cognisable).

## recognition (recognize or recognized)

**recognized gain**   *See:* gain, recognized gain (Section 1231 gain or gain under Section 1231).

**recognized tribe**   *See:* tribe, recognized tribe (federally recognized tribe).

**recollection (recollect)**  Memory, or to recount events or knowledge from memory. Recollection is the act of remembering, the means by which a person later recalls the person's impressions and thoughts formed at a time in the past. Present recollection of a past event for many people is a difficult and vague enterprise, and details are more difficult for most people to recall the longer the interval between the event and the recollection. Recollection may therefore be aided by later reference to notes or other evidence of the time, and yet the more the witness refers to such material, the greater is the likelihood that the recollection is derived not so much from the events themselves but from the material used to recover memory. An unduly refreshed recollection may be a newly imagined recollection, but the assessment of the degree to which the witness is genuinely recollecting the past or is presently embellishing it is a matter for the finder of fact.

*See also:* testimony (testify); hearsay, hearsay exception, hearsay allowed regardless of witness availability, recorded recollection (past recollection recorded).

**recompense**  Compensation, restitution, or reward. Recompense is a broad term for a reward for services rendered or performed or goods or property lost or surrendered. It includes the payment of any lawfully required compensation or reimbursement for employment or other services that are not wholly gratuitous, as well as a gratuitous payment the recipient might choose to make for gratuitous service. It includes payment for goods used or consumed or property given, whether for a time or in fee. Recompense also includes restitution for costs incurred in performing a service or providing goods that would otherwise amount to unjust enrichment by the beneficiary.

**reconciliation (reconcile)**  Acceptance of differences and agreement among those once divided. Reconciliation is a process of the renewal of trust between those who were once united but then divided. Reconciliation takes many forms, including among business partners, among contracting parties, among members of communities, and so on; but its most fundamental sense and most common usage is its sense in the reconciliation of spouses following an argument, separation, or divorce. Reconciliation of spouses who were separated or divorced is the recommitment of the spouses to their marriage, which in law is demonstrated by the renewal of cohabitation.

Reconciliation is also a process of the synthesis of arguments, documents, analysis or computations. In each the sense of elements that are reconciled is an analysis that finds agreement and commonality of meaning in the disparate elements among the things analyzed.

*See also:* rights, human rights, human rights tribunal, truth and reconciliation commission.

**congressional reconciliation (reconciliation bill or reconciliation instruction or reconciliation process)**  Conforming two bills in conference, or amending a law to conform to the budget. Reconciliation in Congress has two very distinct meanings. The older is the process of amending two related bills in conference; the younger is the process of altering laws to conform to the current budget.

Reconciliation of conflicting bills occurs when two related bills pass their respective houses but do not conform with one another. To become law, a bill must be passed in the same form by each house, and so when one house incorporates changes the other house did not, the two non-conforming bills are sent to a conference committee of members of both the Senate and the House, which drafts a reconciled bill, or a single compromise bill, that is sent back to both houses for adoption or rejection. If the reconciled bill is passed by both houses, it is presented to the President.

A reconciliation bill is different, arising from the process of budget reconciliation. Congress may enact a bill under special rules for the purpose of amending existing laws to conform to the budget passed in a specific year. A bill establishing the budget, such as a Congressional Omnibus Budget Reconciliation Act (or COBRA) may alter any law that depends on federal appropriations or taxes. These enormous bills often contain numerous amendments altering federal standards on a variety of activities.

*See also:* budget; budget, budget of the United States government.

**reconsideration (motion for reconsideration or motion to reconsider)**  The review and potential alteration of an earlier ruling. Reconsideration is the reexamination of a ruling, order, or judgment, in which a court, agency, or other entity reviews the request or motion made, the arguments and evidence presented, the basis for its decision, the decision made, and the instrument in which it was written or language in which it was expressed. Reconsideration might, but might not, result in a change in the ruling, order, or judgment. Reconsideration may be granted in the form of the review, though the usage varies, and some judges may in fact reconsider a decision but then deny the motion because the result of the reconsideration is to determine that the initial ruling, order, or judgment was correct and will not be altered.

In pre-trial proceedings, trials, post-trial proceedings, and appeals, rules of procedure often denote the option of a party to move for reconsideration of a ruling, and for some motions specify a time within which such a motion is to be brought forward. In the absence of such a rule, a motion for reconsideration is available by custom and is to be presented within a reasonable time. In most instances, the effect of a motion to reconsider is to stay the effect of the ruling, order, or judgment, until the motion is granted or denied. Even so, the time for filing an appeal is rarely tolled or enlarged by a motion to reconsider a civil judgment.

## Reconstruction

**Reconstruction as an American era** The period following the American Civil War. Reconstruction was the period and the process for the re-integration of the former Confederate states into the United States, as well as for the abolition of slavery and the first serious attempt to move former slaves into citizenship and equal participation and protection in the legal system. It was also a period of military occupation of the Southern states, martial law, unrest, and — in the short term — the failure of many of the goals that animated the Union cause during the war itself. Reconstruction is given various dates, but the most influential writer on the period has designated it to be from 1863 to 1877.

**Reconstruction Acts** Statutes regulating the former Confederate states. The Reconstruction Acts were a series of laws passed by Congress after the Civil War that regulated the constitutional, criminal, economic, and social life of the former Confederacy. The four acts most often described as Reconstruction Acts are those of March 2, 1867 (39 Cong. Ch. 153 14 Stat. 428), March 23, 1867 (40 Cong. Ch. 6 15 Stat. 2), July 19, 1867 (40 Cong. Ch. 30 15 Stat. 14), and March 11, 1868 (ch. 25, 15 Stat. 25). The acts created five military districts in the seceded states, other than Tennessee, required congressional approval for new state constitutions, and required all states formerly in rebellion to grant universal male suffrage and ratify the Fourteenth Amendment as a condition of readmittance to the union.

**Reconstruction Amendments** The constitutional amendments passed following the American Civil War. The Reconstruction Amendments are the Thirteenth, Fourteenth, and Fifteenth Amendments. The effect of these amendments was to alter the balance of federalism, creating a federal power to abolish slavery, establish a national basis for citizenship, ensure equality under the law and due process of law, and to ensure fair access to voting in all public elections, regardless of the preference of the states.

## record

**record expungement** *See:* expungement (record expungement).

**record notice** *See:* notice, constructive notice (record notice).

**record of religious organization** *See:* hearsay, hearsay exception, hearsay allowed regardless of witness availability, record of religious organization.

**record title** *See:* title, record title.

**appellate record (trial record or record on appeal)** The trial pleadings, papers, exhibits, transcript, and docket sheet. The appellate record is the record filed by the appellant in the appellate court in support of an appeal, which must include a certified copy of the trial court docket sheet, a copy of the material filed in the court (including pleadings, motions, and orders), exhibits accepted in court, and the trial transcript or, if there is no transcript, a summary or statement of record. The appellant bears the cost of production of the appellate record, although in a criminal appeal brought in forma pauperis, the costs may be borne by the government.
*See also:* error, evidentiary error.

**defective record** A record missing essential components. A defective record is a record that was either not compiled effectively or that has not been maintained appropriately so that it has omissions. A defective appellate record is a record that is missing essential documents from the trial court, such as a pleading, docket sheet, motion, transcript, or order. The appellant is responsible for submitting a sufficient record. In the event of a defective record, the appellee is not entitled to strike unless there is evidence of deliberate or gross neglect or the defendant can make a clear showing of harm or prejudice. In all other cases, indeed in practically all cases, the remedy is for the appellant to supplement the record, including any lost material through description and affidavit.

**arrest record (criminal history record or rap sheet)** A record of an individual's arrests and convictions. An arrest record is an official record of the arrests of one individual, usually providing the arrests, and sometimes the contacts not leading to any arrests, the date of each arrest, and the possible charges for each arrest, as well as the ultimate disposition for each arrest. Arrest records are usually maintained by individual police agencies, but an arrest record is also an aggregation of all such records.
*See also:* expungement (record expungement).

**Sandoval hearing** A pre-trial hearing on evidence of a defendant's past misconduct. A Sandoval hearing, from New York v. Sandoval, 34 N.Y.2d 371 (1974), is a pre-trial criminal hearing to determine the extent to which a defendant's past crimes or misconduct may be admitted on cross-examination of the defendant, in the event the defendant testifies. The hearing is required in New York state criminal procedure, and analogous hearings have been adopted in other states.

**business record** *See:* hearsay, hearsay exception, hearsay allowed regardless of witness availability, business record (regularly conducted activity or business-records).

## court record

**Public Access to Court Electronic Records (P.A.C.E.R. or PACER)** The internet access to federal court filings and records. The Public Access to Court Electronic Records Service, or "PACER," is an electronic public access service that allows users to obtain case and docket information from the federal courts, including the bankruptcy courts. Registered users may read public filings for active cases and some inactive cases in all participating federal courts.

**medical record (health information)** Any information recorded as part of a medical diagnosis or treatment. Medical records include any document, electronic file, or other information storage system that contain health information related to a single, identifiable person that was collected as a part of the medical examination, diagnosis, or treatment of that person. The release of health information is governed by the Health Insurance Portability and Accountability Act of 1996, Pub.L. No. 104-191, §§ 261-264, 110 Stat.1936 (Aug. 21, 1996), or HIPAA, which allows the release of health information in accord with court orders, although such information is limited in its lawful use to the litigation from which the order originated. State laws further regulate medical records and health information.

Medical records are considered business records as an exception to the hearsay rule, although a proper foundation is required for their admission in court.

*See also:* hearsay, hearsay exception, hearsay allowed regardless of witness availability, business record (regularly conducted activity or business-records).

**of record** Having been recorded, or maintaining a record as a matter of course. Anything of record is recorded. The forms that something of record takes are generally customary according to the form of information that is to be recorded. A title or lien is of record only after it is properly recorded in the appropriate office and record. An attorney is of record only after making an appearance and causing it to be recorded on the docket sheet or appearance book of the court.

A court is said to be of record when it maintains a record of its proceedings, and only a court of record has the authority to order the incarceration of a person convicted of a criminal offense.

*See also:* court, court of record.

**official record** The record maintained by a public agency. An official record is any record maintained as a matter of course by a public agency, usually by an administrator, clerk, archivist, or other head of an office tasked by law with the maintenance of such records. Official records include the information collected by officers and employees of the agency as well as information provided to the agency by others who are required by law to file or deposit such information with the agency.

Official records may be public records, which is to say that the record is available to a member of the public on request, but official records may also be non-public records, maintained only for official use. Non-public official records are subject to discovery and subpoena but are also subject to various privileges against disclosure.

**public record** The legally required record maintained by a public agency for access by the public. A public record is an official record maintained by a public agency or official as a part of the duties of office, which is required to be maintained by law for the dissemination of the information recorded to the public. A public record may comprise information gathered or created by public officials or gathered or recorded by others and provided to the agency or official by a person with a legal requirement or license to do so. A public record may be in any form of media, including documents, texts, electronic files, sound or visual recordings, or any other storable media. Not all official records are public records.

*See also:* record, official record.

**sealed record (sealing of records or record under seal)** Record restricted from public access by law or order. A sealed record is a record that is subject to a law or an order forbidding access by members of the public, or by any person, or by any person who does not meet criteria designated in the law or the order sealing the record. An order sealing the record in a judicial proceeding is binding on the parties and on the court personnel, and all such records are accessible afterwards only according to the terms of the order or by leave of the court. However, an order sealing a record does not, in itself, imply or amount to a gag order, or an order forbidding discussion of material in the record; such an order restraining speech must be clearly expressed and justified. Note, the record in an action in court is spoken of as a single record, though it usually contains many specific records within it. There is no difference in a sense of sealed records and that of a sealed record.

*See also:* seal.

**service record** A record of an employee's service. A service record is a business record maintained by an employer with statements of fact regarding an employee's training, job assignments, work performance, work quality, and attitude. The service records of public employees are subject to greater protection from requests under the freedom of information acts of most states, though harmful false statements in a service record may be the basis for a claim of defamation.

## recordation

**recordation of defective instrument** *See:* title, recordation of title, recordation of defective instrument (defective deed).

**recordation of title** *See:* title, recordation of title.

## recording (recorded)

**recording act**  *See:* title, recordation of title, recording act.

**recorded contract**  *See:* contract, recorded contract (unrecorded contract).

**recorded recollection**  *See:* hearsay, hearsay exception, hearsay allowed regardless of witness availability, recorded recollection (past recollection recorded).

**recording system**  *See:* title, recordation of title (recording system).

**recoupment (recoup)**  The recovery of lost assets, or the offset of moneys owed. Recoupment is the collection of value or money that either reduces or offsets an expenditure of money or value already made or a claim for money owed. Although recoupment in its narrowest sense is to be had from the party to whom money was paid or to whom money is owed, recoupment may often be had from third parties either acting as sureties or indemnitors for that party, or having a joint liability with that party, or even holding a similar position in the market as that party. In other words, payment by an insurer on behalf of an insured may be recouped by a claim from the insurer to the actor who caused the insured's injury, or a tax bill overpaid to the government could be recouped by an allowed reduction in the next payment owed. To recoup one's losses, then, is broadly to pursue any means of restoring funds or gaining new funds to restore a balance sheet or revenue stream.

**recourse**  The right to payment from an instrument's makers, not just its payor. Recourse, in general, is the movement to assistance, shelter, advice, or support from a person, thing, or institution. It is a move made to avoid a difficulty or adversity, especially as a means of protecting one's interests, including recourse to the courts in civil litigation or recourse to the police for assistance with criminal matters.

Recourse takes several specific forms in contracts. In banking or contracts, recourse is a surety or guaranty that provides the lender or contracting party with a means of assurance in the event of a failure of performance by the debtor or the contracting party. In commercial law, recourse is a particular right to seek payment for a negotiable instrument not only from the payor of the instrument but also from the drawer and the indorser of the instrument, unless the instrument or the indorsement is qualified as being without recourse.

*See also:* loan, recourse loan (recourse debt).

**recourse debt**  *See:* loan, recourse loan (recourse debt).

**recourse loan**  *See:* loan, recourse loan (recourse debt); loan, recourse loan.

**non-recourse debt (nonrecourse debt)**  *See:* loan, non-recourse loan (nonrecourse loan or non-recourse debt or nonrecourse debt).

**without recourse (sans recours or with recourse)**  Without an obligation to pay by the party disclaiming recourse. Without recourse is a signal on an instrument that whomever placed the signal on it will not stand behind the instrument to pay any claim made related to it. This is possible, in that the drawer of a non-recourse instrument to be paid by a bank requires the bank to pay the instrument, even though the drawer makes the instrument without recourse and so does not agree to stand behind the note to make good if the bank does not. The drawee of the instrument is on notice that the only payment will come on the instrument, if it comes, from the bank. An indorsement may be made without recourse, in which the indorser disavows an obligation to make good the instrument. Many commercial entities will not accept a note or other instrument without recourse, because the entity wants to pursue as many parties as possible to cover the note.

An instrument is presumed to be an instrument with recourse to the drawer and any indorsing party. Thus, any negotiable instrument that is not expressly marked or endorsed "without recourse" is with recourse.

*See also:* indorsement (endorsement, endorse, indorse).

**recovery (recover)**  A remedy, particularly the vindication of a right denied. A recovery, broadly, is any remedy that reflects compensation for damages or loss or any other theory of restitution or restoration for the violation of one's rights or interests. Recovery is often defined in contracts, statutes or regulations to include or exclude specific remedies, but in the absence of such technical modifications, a recovery includes any judgment in which a party is vindicated in any claim, including a declaration or injunction, as long as the judgment is predicated on the recognition and protection of a right in the plaintiff or a duty by the defendant toward the plaintiff.

**common recovery (common vouchee or recoverer)**  A collusive legal action once used in lieu of a conveyance. A common recovery was a classic lawyer's trick that evolved to allow the transfer of land that was entailed or otherwise legally capable of transfer by its owner. More specifically, the recovery was a lawsuit that allowed for the conveyance of land. The common recovery was a fictitious action in law, a fake lawsuit, brought by the parties to the sale who colluded to sue for the land on a trumped-up claim and to win title to it by default.

A common recovery was a bit complicated, with particular roles among the litigants: The party who would receive the land in the end was the demandant. The party who held the land to start with was the tenant. They recruited a third party who would play a part in the fictitious suit, called the common vouchee. The order of the suit then played out: the demandant brings suit against the tenant, seeking a writ of praecipe (after which the tenant is called the tenant of the praecipe). The tenant appears in court, usually by counsel. The tenant does not, however, defend the title but calls on a third party to do so, a third party who allegedly warranted the title to the tenant (or the tenant's predecessor). This third party, the common vouchee, had done no such thing, and indeed the part was usually played (for a very small fee) by the court crier. Even so, the common vouchee is then called to defend the title by warranty or to give lands of equal value if no defense is made. The tenant impleads the vouchee as a party. The tenant then desires leave of the court to confer with the vouchee in private, which the court grants as a matter of course. The demandant then returns into court and seeks relief from the vouchee. The vouchee now disappears or takes default, and the court then finds that — quite to everybody's surprise — the vouchee must not have had title to the lands after all, because the vouchee does not defend them. The court now enters judgment by default for the demandant, who is from that point called the recoverer. The recoverer is given judgment to recover the lands from the tenant. The tenant is given a judgment against the vouchee to recover the lands warranted or lands of equal value in recompense for those so warranted by the vouchee and lost by default, although this was a nominal recovery. The recoverer then seeks a writ of habere facias, directed to the sheriff of the county including the lands, and on the execution and return of the writ, the recovery is completed. Depending on the complexity of the title, tail, or parties, this process might be performed not just once but many times. In the end, the recoverer received the land, free not only of claims by descendants of the grantor in tail but also of the reversionary claim of the grantor and the grantor's heirs.

The process, loony as it now seems, was designed not only to disentail property but also to allow monasteries and other institutions barred from receiving property subject to mortmain to take title to property through a means other than conveyance. Of course, the owner was paid, just as the tenant in tail was paid. And, of course, the lawyers were paid.

The common recovery has been rendered obsolete, first by the exceptions to mortmain and then by its repeal, as well as the advent of the power of the tenant to disentail by through an inter vivos grant. Still, the process of common recovery remains an essential lesson in the history of legal loopholes.

*See also:* loophole.

**recovery of natural resource (species recovery or habitat recovery)** The restoration of a species population or habitat to sustainablity. Recovery, in the sense that a species or habitat is subject to recovery, is a process by which a species formerly rare, threatened, or endangered becomes stable in its numbers and in the quality of the habitat and environment in which the species occurs. Similarly, the restoration of a habitat, such as a forest restoration or stream restoration, is a process by which the defining elements of the habitat are made stable, so that the habitat is capable of supporting the physical, hydrological, and biological demands of maintaining equilibrium among native plants and animals. The process of recovery may be artificial as well as natural, and a recovery project includes all actions and methods reasonably believed to be required to bring about the restoration.

**recrimination** A counter-accusation. A recrimination is an accusation made by one in response to an accusation from another; it is an accusation raised by a person who has been otherwise accused of wrongdoing and who brings a new accusation against the original accuser. Recrimination in equity occurs in raising defenses like unclean hands. In traditional divorce actions for cause, an accusation of adultery raised and proved by the defendant could lead to the dismissal of a plaintiff's claim for divorce, though this doctrine has been rendered largely obsolete both by the rise of non-adversarial divorce proceedings and by changes in the defenses of divorce for cause. Recrimination in criminal law may affect sentencing but not the guilt of the accused.

Note: recrimination's technical sense is often ignored or unknown to those who use recrimination to mean mere accusation or criticism.

*See also:* accusation (accuse or accusatory).

**recross examination** *See:* examination, examination of a witness, recross examination (re-cross or recross-examination).

**recruit (gang recruitment or recruiting)** A person who has just joined the military, or any other endeavor. A recruit is a person newly joined to an institution, particularly a newly enlisted soldier, sailor, or airman. The term is also applied to any newly committed member of an association or entity, whether the new recruit is a member or client.

To recruit is to attract and cause such a person to become enlisted. The term is widely used for the attraction of new employees to a legitimate employment position, which is lawful, as well as the attraction of new members to organizations, including new members of gangs or criminal enterprises, in which case the recruiting is a crime in itself. The term is also used for the marketing of services to contract new clients to law firms and to other professional services entities.

*See also:* solicitation (solicit or solicted or soliciting); gang.

**recruiting on campus (Solomon Amendment)** Colleges receiving federal funds must allow military recruitment on campus. The Solomon Amendment, codified at 10 U.S.C. § 983(b) (2010), requires all institutions of higher learning and their constituent colleges, schools, or divisions that receive federal funds, including money from federal student aid, to allow recruiters from the military services and the

Department of Homeland Security to recruit on the campuses in the same degree to which any other employer might recruit. Schools and universities that bar recruiters who discriminate against homosexual applicants or others in violation of their anti-discrimination policy may not bar the military or DHS recruiters on that basis, if other employers are allowed to recruit, without losing their access to federal funds.

*See also:* discrimination.

**rectification (rectify)**   The correction of a wrong or mistake. Rectification is the act of making right a wrong done to someone or in some way. To rectify a mistake is to correct it and to reverse any damage done as a result of it. Rectification of a contract, last will and testament, trust instrument, or other document is to alter its mistaken terms to correspond with the drafters' intent, particularly to correct a scrivener's error. A court order rectifying an instrument is a remedy.

To rectify a wrong is both to undo remediable damage or give compensation or restitution and to seek to avert a repetition of the wrongful act or event. Mitigation of some harm that is full and complete is rectification of that harm.

**recto**   Right. Recto is Latin for right, in both senses of being the right thing to do and of being a legally protected right. Recto is the origin of Recht in German as well as right in English.

*See also:* recht.

**recusal (recuse or recusation)**   Abstention by a judge or official from a decision or proceeding. Recusal is the decision of a judge or other official to refuse to take part in a proceeding owing to a potential for the appearance of bias or interest in the proceeding. A judge or official with the authority or discretion to grant or deny some legal claim should recuse themselves from participation in a legal or administrative proceeding if there is a basis for perceiving a financial interest or significant personal interest of the judge or a family member of the judge that might be affected by the case. Although most cases are clear in the potential for a person to have an interest or to lack an interest in a case, there is a large and murky range between which some parties would see an obvious basis for interest or bias but others would see none. This problem is compounded by the belief that is common to many people that they are capable of ignoring a bias or interest to act fairly, even in circumstances that they themselves would question if done by another. There are many variations of the test for recusal, but all are based on the perception of a reasonable observer: if most thoughtful observers would believe that there is a reasonable basis in the particular facts and circumstances of a case to doubt the impartiality of the judge or official, or to believe that the judge or official did not or will not base the decision on the merits of the case in the facts and law alone, then the judge or official should recuse himself or herself from the proceeding and allow another person to take that place for that action.

In most cases, the decision to recuse is left to the discretion of the judge or official, but that decision will be reversed if the judge or official fails to recuse in a circumstance that appears to be an abuse of that discretion. There is a constitutional right to a fair and impartial judge, and if a judge or administrator whose interest in the case or potential to favor one party or another is apparent to a reasonable observer, then a failure to recuse may violate the due process clauses of the Constitution. The exception to this review is in the Supreme Court, in which there is no review of a justice's decision not to recuse.

**red circle rate**   *See:* wage, red–circle wages (red circle rate).

**red flag**   *See:* inquiry, notice inquiry, red flag.

**red herring**   *See:* fallacy, red herring.

**redaction (redact or redacted or redacted document)**   To excise or omit material when reproducing an earlier writing. Redaction is the process of removing text, whether words or phrases or whole passages, from a writing that is being reproduced. Redaction may be used to remove confidential or secret information; to remove redundant, irrelevant, or mistaken information; or to emphasize certain or the most essential information in a summary of the original. In law, it is essential that text redacted from a text be noted, either with signals in the redacted text, such as elipses and brackets, or in a notice noting the means and purpose of the redaction. In general, care must be taken not to alter the meaning or purpose of an instrument through its redaction.

**redemise**   *See:* mortgage, redemise.

**redemption (redeem)**   The repurchase of property forfeited or sold to a lawful holder. Redemption is the reacquisition of property lost to forfeiture, execution, foreclosure, or any other means by which the property was forcibly but legally removed from ownership. The former owner may redeem the property by satisfying a statutory process, which usually involves paying the purchase price to anyone who had purchased the property at an official sale, as well as satisfying the underlying unmet obligation that had itself led to the forced sale.

**statutory right of redemption**   The legal right to redeem property after a sale following foreclosure or execution. The statutory right of redemption is the power of a secured debtor to recover the property that secured a debt and was seized and sold to satisfy the debt. Its most well known form is the right of a mortgagor to recover mortgaged property sold at foreclosure, allowing the mortgagor (who is the debtor) to redeem the property and to regain title and possession after the foreclosure sale. The statutory right is also extended in most jurisdictions to judgment debtors and other secured debtors whose property is taken and sold in an execution of judgment. The right is conferred in every state by statute, and it persists for various lengths of time, depending on the terms of the statute, ranging from a few months to several years. In some jurisdictions and in some cases, the right is extinguished on the lapse of the redemption period, and in others it is extinguished following an order foreclosing the right of redemption, which is available on motion and hearing after a lapse of time. The amount to be paid is usually the amount paid by the buyer of the property, as well as costs and fees, although in some jurisdictions the redemption also requires payment of the original underlying debt. Note: the statutory right of redemption differs from the equitable right of redemption, which is available only for mortgages and similar security interests in lands and which terminates at foreclosure and sale.

*See also:* mortgage, rights of redemption of mortgage, equitable right of redemption; mortgage; mortgage, rights of redemption of mortgage.

**redhibition (redhibitory action)** The avoidance of a contract to purchase goods found to be defective. Redhibition is a private act allowed in the civil law by which a buyer refuses to accept goods that are defective and unusable for the purpose for which they were purchased. A redhibitory action is a private cause of action brought by the purchaser to annul a sale agreement and to recover the cost paid for goods that later proved to have been defective.

*See also:* liability, product liability (products liability); liability, product liability, theories of product liability.

**redirect examination** *See:* examination, examination of a witness, redirect examination (re-examination or re-direct examination).

**redlining (redline)** The designation of neighborhoods in which insurance will not be underwritten. Redlining, in general, is a process of designation on a map or in a text. In housing law, redlining is a slang term for the designation by insurers of neighborhoods in which the insurer will underwrite no insurance, particularly homeowner's insurance. The process is controversial because its burdens often fall disproportionately on members of minority racial categories, and the practice risks violating not only federal and state anti-discrimination laws in general but also federal fair housing laws.

**redress (redressability)** Satisfaction for some wrong, or some harm suffered. Redress is a remedy for any form of loss suffered as the result of another's conduct. The term is sometimes used for any sort of restitution or compensation, but its core meaning is closer to reparations for a harm suffered as the result of wrongdoing. A harm capable of being redressed is redressable, and some forms of harm are irredressable.

Note: redress is both a noun and a verb.

*See also:* remedy (remediable or remedied or remedies); reparation (reparations).

**reductio ad absurdam** *See:* fallacy, reductio ad absurdam.

**reduction of sentence** *See:* sentence, reduction of sentence, good behavior (good time).

**reductionism (reductionist)** A criticism that someone is stereotyping the critic's argument. Reductionism is a pattern of argument in which the thing described is reduced to its least still-recognizable elements. In most instances, reductionism amounts to characterizing the thing described in a stereotypical manner. As a result, reductionism is more often heard as a criticism of an argument, such as "you are being reductionist," than it is heard being deliberately asserted as a means for understanding what is argued.

**redundancy (redundant)** More than is needed. Redundancy is the effect created by any quantity of a thing beyond what can be usefully done with it. In law, redundancy characterizes argument, evidence, testimony, pleading, or anything else that is offered in greater quantity than is needed to make the point for which it is offered. An unneeded duplication is inherently redundant.

Redundancy once had a technical meaning in pleading, to represent arguments or information in an answer that was outside the proper scope of an answer because it raised new matter beyond the matters of the complaint, but this meaning is now quite rare, particularly owing to the common practice of incorporating a counterclaim with an answer. Redundancy is also a term sometimes heard in the U.S., but more often used in the U.K., to describe the termination of an employee during a reduction in force.

**reeve** One of several local officers of law. A reeve was initially the representative of the monarch in a county who was ultimately responsible for keeping the king's peace and raising the king's taxes. The position was later memorialized as the reeve of the shire, or "sheriff." The term was eventually used for a variety of ecclesiastical and judicial offices of a significance that diminished over time.

*See also:* manciple; pardoner; sheriff.

**referee** A neutral assessor of conduct against rules. Referee has a variety of subtle implications, but its essential role is as a neutral assessor of the claims and conduct of opponents in a dispute or contest. Thus, a referee is an official supervising play in a variety of contested sports, whose role is to assess the form of play against the laws or rules of the game and to govern the relations between teams accordingly.

In law, a referee may be an arbitrator or mediator selected by the parties, an arbitrator or mediator appointed by a judge or administrator, or a reviewing official of an application or claim. A referee may in fact be an official of a different title, who is functionally acting as judge of the rules of engagement or the merits of an argument between disputants in another context. Note: referee is both a noun and a verb.

**referendum (plebiscite or direct legislation)**
Any law enacted by the people directly. A referendum as to a law is the enactment of a law as a result of a direct, popular election (rather than adoption as legislation by a legislature). A referendum may be used to adopt a law that was initiated by petition or proposed first as legislation and passed with a requirement of adoption by referendum before the law comes into force. Most amendments to state constitutions require adoption by referendum.

A plebiscite, a neologism for law enacted by the plebians, refers to any manner of direct democracy, including any election in which all of the people, or at least all free adults, may vote. It is often used in a somewhat derogatory manner for describing the enactment or attempt to enact laws by initiative or referendum.

**reflective equilibrium** *See:* equilibrium, reflective equilibrium.

**reform (reformation)** Improvement, correction, or restoration. Reform is a process by which a person, idea, document, institution or anything else is made better, or by which its defects are diminished. Reform has a particular sense in which the person or thing improved is corrected and brought closer to its former or natural condition. Law reform and other arenas of institutional reform suggest the improvement of the efficiency and effectiveness with which legal institutions and legal rules give effect to the goals of the law, as those goals are understood by the reformers of that time and place.

Note: reform is both a noun and a verb. An additional noun form is derived from reform's verb form, reformation, which is the process and the result of being reformed. When reformation is capitalized and preceded by a definite article — The Reformation — it is usually intended to refer to the process of criticism, reform, and schism in the Western Church in the sixteenth century. Other than customary usage, there is no essential difference between reformation and reform in law.

Reformation in law has a variety of specific senses and may refer to the correction or improvement of an instrument, such as the reformation of contract; or an institution, such as the reformation of a corporation; or a person, such as the reformation of the criminal convict.

**law reform** The changing of legal rules and institutions to better serve those who are bound to obey the law. Law reform is a wide term that includes all efforts to improve the nature of the law and legal institutions. It includes such massive institutional efforts as the restatements of the law and the uniform laws projects, as well as the improvement of standards required for the practice of law. Many projects to improve the law, including scholarly synthesis and criticism, as well as popular movements for change, such as the recognition of the rights and interests of victims of crime, have been influential in the law both in the United States and across the globe.

**American Law Institute (A.L.I. or ALI)** An organization of lawyers, judges, and teachers devoted to improvement of the law. The American Law Institute is a nationwide organization with international members of judges, lawyers, and law professors, who promote a national core of essential legal principles and best practices. The ALI, founded in 1923, is the source of the Restatements of Law and, with the Uniform Law Commissioners, the Uniform Commercial Code and the Model Penal Code. Membership is limited to 3,000 members, and an effort is made to recruit members from every state with significant professional achievement and a demonstrated interest in improvement of the law.

*See also:* restatement (restatement of law).

**National Conference of Commissioners on Uniform State Laws (Uniform Law Commission or NCCUSL)** A national organization that promulgates uniform state statutes. The National Conference of Commissioners on Uniform State Laws, which is also known as the Uniform Law Commission, is one of the oldest law reform associations still operating in the United States. Its volunteer commissioners from every state draft model legislation for adoption in state legislatures, bringing national uniformity to American legal rules. Its model uniform acts cover dozens of subjects, such as the rule against perpetuities and marketable title. In conjunction with the American Law Institute, the NCCUSL promulgated and maintains the the Uniform Commercial Code.

**reformation of a writing (reformation of contract or reformation of an instrument)** A judicial remedy interpreting a written instrument. Reformation of a writing — such as the reformation of a contract, a negotiable instrument, a will, a deed, a trust instrument or any other writing that creates or dedicates a legal or equitable interest — is a judicial remedy decreed upon sufficient evidence that the instrument before the court is ambiguous and cannot be applied with confidence in only one manner as opposed to another, or violates in some manner the law or public policy, or requires some action or condition that is effectively not possible. In such cases, the court may reform the instrument to accord as well as possible with what is knowable from the evidence of the intent of the instrument's drafter or makers, to be lawful and appropriate for judicial recognition and enforcement, and to be practically capable of being given effect.

It should be noted that there is a strong judicial policy against the reformation of a written instrument. If the language of the instrument is susceptible to a clear, lawful, and practicable meaning, most courts will interpret the instrument so, even if the result is somewhat less than obvious to a casual reader. Courts are particularly reluctant to reform a will, and only a minority of jurisdictions will do so in the event the will does not manifest the intent of the testator according to clear evidence of the testator's intent at the time the will was executed.

**tort reform** The pursuit of defenses to limit or bar liability for harms once compensable in tort. Tort reform labels a series of policies to limit the number and scale of civil actions that may be brought in tort, especially by limiting actions for products liability and for negligence by manufacturers, medical services providers, environmental polluters, and other corporate defendants and their insurers. The most common arguments for tort reform are that plaintiffs bring claims that do not arise in their own injuries in fact, that they seek punitive damages as a windfall, that their claims are too often for injuries or harms they should absorb themselves, and that regardless of harm suffered, their claims are a drain on the more important and economically essential businesses that they sue. The most common arguments against tort reform are that the defendants have negligently, knowingly, or intentionally caused harms, usually doing so by employing a process that was selected in order to save money at the expense of the health, safety, or risk to others, and the corporations that cause such harms are both morally responsible and economically better placed to bear the costs of their actions.

The most common forms of tort reform are shorter statutes of limitations; the return to joint liability; the limitation or abolition of several liability; the return to some form of contributory negligence that bars actions in which the plaintiff was responsible for a portion of the plaintiff's injuries (ranging from 1% to 75% plaintiff fault, in which the plaintiff can bring no case for the remainder of the responsibility); the elimination or reduction of the availability of punitive damages; the limitation of actual damages for future or continuing injury to a restrictive formula for future damages; immunity for new classes of defendant; requirements for specific forms of evidence; increased burdens of proof; elimination of the jury from certain classes of action; and the shifting of legal fees onto a losing party in at least some torts lawsuits.

**reformation of criminals**  *See:* punishment, rehabilitative punishment (reformation of criminals).

**refouler (non-refoulement or refoulement)**  The return of a person to the person's native state. Refouler, among several senses, is the process of expulsion of an alien from one country or the repatriation of an alien to the state of citizenship or nationality. The noun form is refoulement. Non-refoulement is the right of a refugee not to be returned to a state from which the refugee has fled, particularly if the refugee would face persecution on return. The right of non-foulement is effectively the right of asylum.
*See also:* extradition; asylum; refugee (asylum seeker).

**refugee (asylum seeker)**  A person who cannot return to a home country without fear of persecution. A refugee in U.S. law is a person who has left the state of that person's nationality or citizenship and is barred from returning by a genuine and well-founded fear of persecution based on race, religion, nationality, membership in a particular social group or speech expressing a political opinion contrary to the established government.

Under the principle of non-refoulement, refugees are generally given asylum in another country and not forced to return home. A refugee is distinct from an economic migrant or one who immigrates for other reasons.

An asylum seeker is a person who seeks asylum and claims the status of a refugee, though this status will usually not be granted unless the asylum seeker can offer proof that repatriation is reasonably likely to result in acts of persecution.
*See also:* refouler (non-refoulement or refoulement); displacement, displaced person.

**political refugee (political opinion)**  A person seeking asylum from political persecution. A political refugee is a person who has a well-founded fear of persecution on the basis of the refugee's political opinion or political actions, particularly a person who has been charged with a political crime.

**political offense**  A crime of political opposition to a foreign government. A political offense is a crime against a government, other than the United States or a state of the union, by a crime that can be committed only against a government, such as treason; or that is prosecuted solely for the government's political benefit, such as sedition or a sham crime; or that is a crime of ordinary definition but that is committed during an uprising or rebellion, such as assault during an anti-government protest. A person in the United States who might be extradited to a foreign state and punished for a political offense there may not be extradited under most treaties.

The political offense exception to extradition reflects the history of the United States as having been born in civil war, and it respects the rights associated with popular struggle for self-determination. Even so, the doctrine will not protect individuals who engage in acts of brutality or violence that are not within the scope of customary opposition to a government in power, taking place within a broader movement of opposition or rebellion within the place of that rebellion. Acts of terrorism or exported violence are not within the doctrine. Further, the defendant's commission of serious non-political crimes may outweigh the shelter to be given from prosecution for political crimes.

Political offense is a basis in international law for the provision of asylum and for the recognition of status as a political refugee.

**well-founded fear of persecution**  Fear of persecution that is more likely than not. Well-founded fear of persecution is the test for a refugee's petition for asylum, which requires that the asylee have a subjective, good faith fear of persecution, and the evidence suggests that the potential for such persecution is more likely than not to occur.

**refund**  A repayment of some or all of the money a party has paid. A refund is a repayment of the whole or a portion of an amount of money a party had earlier paid, from the party (or an agent of the party) to whom the money had been paid. A refund may be required because the payment was made by mistake, because the payment made was in excess of the amount that was owed, because the amount that was due was recalculated and diminished, or a refund may be made not because it is required but because the payee voluntarily renounces receipt of the payment.

Note: refund is both a noun and a verb.

*See also:* rebate.

**refusal (refuse)**  The rejection of a delivery or request. A refusal is the act of denial of anything that might be requested, conferred, transferred, delivered, or given. To refuse a delivery of a gift or object subject to sale prevents the effective transfer of title. To refuse an offer not only prevents the formation of a contract based on the offer, but also makes the offer void. Some things are binding and incapable of refusal: an acceptance of a valid offer cannot be refused. To refuse a claim or demand is presumptively to reject the obligation to pay on the claim or demand, and though the validity of the claim or demand may be expressly admitted, the payment may be rejected on other grounds.

*See also:* disclaimer, disclaimer as refusal to accept estate; preemption, right of preemption, first refusal (right of first refusal).

> **wrongful refusal by insurer**  *See:* insurance, insurance claim, denial of claim, bad faith denial (denial in bad faith or wrongful refusal or tortious denial of benefits).

**refutation (refute)**  Proof that an argument is false. Refutation is an argument, proof, or evidence that demonstrates the falsity of an earlier statement or argument. Refutation is more than rejection or disagreement, because it requires either persuasive criticism of the validity or sufficiency of the evidence asserted in the earlier argument, or of the validity of a premise or sufficiency of the reasoning supporting a conclusion. Refutation may also take the form of a counter-argument based on new evidence to support a competing narrative or argument describing the events or claims asserted in the original argument.

**regency or regnant**  *See:* rex, regent (regency or regnant).

**regent**  *See:* rex, regent (regency or regnant).

**regicide**  *See:* homicide, regicide (tyrannicide).

**regina**  *See:* rex (regina or regis or regnal).

**regis**  *See:* rex (regina or regis or regnal).

**register (registry)**  A public record of events that are entered as they occur. A register, or registry, is any record in which specific events or transactions are recorded more or less at the time they occur. A public register may also be the person who enters materials into the register (though this is usually a registrar), as well as

the office in which such records are kept (though this is usually a registry). The effect of the registrar recording an action in an official or public register or registry (especially if the action recorded is a transaction or record of events) is to assign public significance and recognition of the act as of the date of recordation or registration. Such acts as the registry of title for an automobile or the registry of a marriage certificate, or the registry of a sex offender or parolee alter the legal responsibilities of the parties who may be affected by the underlying transaction, occurrence, or status. Many registers may be maintained by a single public official, such as a clerk of court, recorder, or keeper of a hall of records. With a proper foundation, a public register or entry from a public register is admissible in court as a public record, without regard to the potential for hearsay.

*See also:* registrar (register or register of deeds or register of probate).

> **register or register of deeds or register of probate**  *See:* registrar (register or register of deeds or register of probate).

> **registered broker or stock broker or initiating broker of future commodities merchant**  *See:* broker, securities broker (registered broker or stock broker or initiating broker of future commodities merchant).

> **registered corporation**  *See:* corporation, registered corporation.

> **registered offering**  *See:* share, share as stock, offering, public offering (registered offering); offering, registered offering.

**registrar (register or register of deeds or register of probate)**  A person or office tasked with the maintenance of a register or registry. A registrar is the keeper of a registry, register, or sometimes a roll or other public record. A registrar may be both an individual and an office with a staff, perhaps a staff of some size, who receive, authenticate, record, and retrieve the records maintained. In many states, the state secretary of state acts as the registrar for many functions, including the registry of automotive titles and the registry of secured interests. A voting or electoral registrar maintains voters' rolls. A registrar in fact may have a variety of titles, such as a clerk of court, who may maintain judgment rolls.

**registration of title**  *See:* title, registration of title (Torrens System).

**regnal year**  *See:* year, regnal year.

**regressive tax**  *See:* tax, tax burden, regressive tax (regressivity).

**regressivity**  *See:* tax, tax burden, regressive tax (regressivity).

**regula (regulae or regula generalis or reg. gen.)**  A maxim of law, a rule of law, or a general rule. Regula is Latin for a rule, in law, particularly a maxim or general principle that is intended by the official who announces it to apply not only to those to whom it is announced but to apply generally to all in a similar situation. In English practice through the nineteenth century, rules of court were pronounced in decrees of regula generalis. An obsolete rule, or dead rule, was referred to as a regula mortis. Regula was the translation for the rule of a monastic order, such as the Regula Benedicti.

*See also:* regulation (regulate or reg.).

**regularly conducted activity** *See:* hearsay, hearsay exception, hearsay allowed regardless of witness availability, regularly conducted activity.

**regulation (regulate or reg.)** The rules issued by agencies, or the rules governing any conduct. Regulation, in the United States, usually refers to the issuance of rules by the agencies of the executive branch, according to the legislative power delegated to those agencies by a legislature. In the federal government, such power is delegated by the Congress, which has established broad legislative guidelines to be interpreted by the President and the department or agency to which authority is delegated. The legal sufficiency, authority, and applicability of such regulations is the field of administrative law. Administrative regulations must be published or otherwise distributed in such a manner that the public or those regulated have notice of them, a process in the federal system that is done through publication in the Federal Register and the Code of Federal Regulations and that is subject to review under the Administrative Procedures Act. State regulations are usually published in a state regulatory code. Increasingly, such regulations are distributed and published only via the Internet. A valid federal regulation has the force of law and is subject to the supremacy of federal law over contrary state law. A valid state regulation must accord with the constitution of its state as well as the federal constitution.

Regulation, particularly governing the rules affecting attorneys and parties to judicial proceedings, may be created by courts through the promulgation of court rules, including the rules of procedure, the rules of evidence, and local rules.

More broadly, regulation as a matter of jurisprudence signifies the creation and enforcement of rules by the legal system governing all conduct, regardless of the rules' source within the legal system. Thus, it is sensible to speak of the regulation of interstate commerce by statute, the regulation of state conduct by the constitution, the regulation of trade by the World Trade Organization, or even the regulation of criminal conduct by law.

*See also:* law, administrative law; law, administrative law, Administrative Procedure Act (APA); regula (regulae or regula generalis or reg. gen.).

**regulation of abortion** *See:* abortion, regulation of abortion.

**regulation of commerce** *See:* commerce, regulation of commerce.

**regulation of forces clause** *See:* constitution, U.S. Constitution, clauses, Regulation of Forces Clause (Military Regulation Clause).

**regulation of speech** *See:* speech, regulation of speech, prior restraint of speech; speech, regulation of speech, gag order.

**regulatory causation** *See:* causation, regulatory causation.

**regulatory taking** *See:* taking (inverse condemnation or regulatory takings).

**Code of Federal Regulations (C.F.R. or CFR)** The codified publication of federal regulations of general application. The Code of Federal Regulations (CFR) is a publication of the Government Printing Office that organizes the permanent and general regulations issued by the President of the United States through Executive Order, as well as the regulations issued by the departments, bureaus, and agencies of the federal government that remain in force. The CFR is updated in print each year and supplemented by a quarterly electronic supplemental issue. Rules yet to be entered into the CFR are promulgated in the Federal Register.

*See also:* regulation, federal register.

**Federal Register** Daily publication for federal regulations and general orders. The Federal Register is the official daily publication for rules, proposed rules, and notices of federal agencies and organizations, as well as executive orders and other documents from the executive branch of the United States government. Rules published in the Federal Register of general application and intended for permanent application are later codified in the Code of Federal Regulations.

*See also:* regulation, Code of Federal Regulations (C.F.R. or CFR).

**rehabilitation (rehabilitate)** To cure a person, or mitigate the harm of some malady or injury. Rehabilitation has several, quite different meanings in the law. In the nineteenth century, its common usage in law was the rehabilitation of a person subject to legal disability in the sense of the loss of civil or legal rights owing to a criminal conviction or similar act of law. Rehabilitation through pardon, legislative decree, or judicial order retains this sense.

Rehabilitation as a matter of criminal law and penology is the educational and moral development of a criminal offender, after which the offender will participate in society as a full and productive member, without violating the criminal law.

Rehabilitation as a matter of health and medicine is the recovery of the person's physical and mental health following an injury, disease, or similar medical condition diminishing the person's capacity for healthy activity. From this sense of rehabilitation comes the idea of rehabilitation of a person disabled by a mental or physical condition, in which the effects of that condition interfering with normal daily functioning in life will be mitigated or ameliorated. Such rehabilitation includes therapies of many forms, including pharmaceutical regimes, occupational and physical therapy, speech therapy, and cognitive therapy, as well as the use of prosthetic and therapeutic devices.

Rehabilitation of the site of an environmental harm is the mitigation of that harm and the restoration of the ecosystem in which it occurs so that the site will be capable of sustaining the indigenous plant and animal population and support prior and future human uses.

Rehabilitation of a witness is the use of examination, particularly re–direct examination, to restore confidence of the finder of fact in the credibility of a witness whose testimony had been tested in cross–examination.

> **rehabilitative punishment**  See: punishment, rehabilitative punishment (reformation of criminals).

**rehearing**  See: hearing, rehearing.

**Rehnquist Court**  See: court, U.S. court, U.S. Supreme Court, Rehnquist Court.

**reinsurance**  See: insurance, reinsurance (reinsurance or reinsure).

**rejection (reject or rejected)**  To refuse or return something without accepting it. Rejection is the act of refusing something, particularly an offer to enter into a contract, a delivery of property, or the performance of an obligation under a contract. Rejection may be express or it may be implied in action, such as by the return of the offer, property delivered, or goods or other things or service owed under the contract. A rejection is effective under the same conditions by which an offer is effective, usually once its recipient has actual or constructive knowledge of it, and once a rejection is effective, the rejecting party has no further power of acceptance of the thing offered, delivered, or performed.

See also: offer, contract offer, rejection of offer.

> **rejection of goods**  See: goods, rejection of goods.

> **rejection of offer**  See: offer, contract offer, rejection of offer.

> **rejection–then–retreat tactic**  See: negotiation, negotiation technique, rejection–then–retreat tactic (door in the face).

**rejoinder**  An answer, reply, or rebuttal to an argument. Rejoinder was once the title for a technical pleading in a civil action, being the defendant's answer to a replication filed by the plaintiff, which is to say that it would be the second pleading filed by the defendant in the chain of complaint, answer, replication, rejoinder. That specific usage is now less common, and in many systems of civil procedure, the rejoinder describes any response of the defendant to a pleading of the plaintiff, if the response raises or contests a triable issue.

Generally, a rejoinder is a rhetorically sound answer to an argument, particularly a response or rebuttal to the argument of an opponent.

See also: answer, answer as pleading.

**relation back**  See: amendment, amendment to a pleading, relation back (relation back doctrine).

**relativity of title**  See: title, relativity of title.

**relator (relatrix)**  An informant on a public matter, or an applicant for extraordinary review or relief. A relator is a person, in general, whose claim or story is the basis for a particular legal action. Usually, a relator has a relationship to the action that is beneficial to the relator, but the action is brought either by a government or on behalf of the government by the relator. In its most common usages in this sense, the relator is in the role of the plaintiff in an action for an extraordinary remedy, such as an action qui tam, quo warranto, or for a writ of mandamus.

In criminal actions and investigations, a relator usually is an informant. In Louisiana, relator is used in several contexts in which the common law would use petitioner, particularly for a criminal convict seeking habeas corpus or a person seeking judicial review of an administrative decision, such as a clerk's entry or zoning order.

Note: though relator now includes all persons regardless of gender, older cases use the feminine form for females in the role of a relator, a relatrix.

See also: ex relatione (ex rel.).

**release**  The end of some restraint, such as the surrender of a right, claim, or interest. A release, in general, is an action by which someone or something is unbound from a restraint. Release has many senses in law, but the most common usage is the release of an obligation. In this sense, a release is the act or the instrument by which a person surrenders or transfers a legal or equitable right, claim, or interest in any thing to another person. While an abandonment is a form of release of one's interest, "release" is generally used to describe a release in favor of a given party rather than to all the world. A release may also signal the discharge of a specific debt or obligation or all debts or obligations owed or potentially owed to the releasor (who was the obligee) by the releasee (the obligor).

At common law, the release of a claim against one tortfeasor operated as a release of all joint or contributing tortfeasors. This rule has been rejected in most jurisdictions in the United States, either by statute or court ruling, in order to allow settlement of claims with individual parties.

Other senses of release that are significant to the law include the release of pollution, such as the release of radiation, the release of contaminating liquids into the ground or water, or the release of contaminants into the air. The release of information may include a press release. A release to a publisher of the creator's rights of copyright or a human model's right in the personal image may be demanded in order to publish a text or an image of that model. The release of a lawful prisoner must be intentional or intended by the officer with custody, or it amounts to escape.

See also: discharge; claim, surrender of claim (release).

**contaminate release (release of contaminate)** The release of any pollutant into the air, water, or ground. A contaminate release is any discharge or emission into the immediate environment of a machine or storage facility of a solid, liquid, or gas pollutant, whether the release is knowingly caused, negligently caused, or the result of natural or physical forces. Although some insurance policies may employ release to mean a release onto the property of another, the nature of a release is one in which the pollutant has combined with or entered into a substance other than that in which it was stored or used, so that a release occurs once the pollutant has become migratory, not when it reaches a given destination.

*See also:* discharge, discharge as emission.

**deliberate release** The intentional discharge of a contaminant into the air, water, or soil. A deliberate release is an intentional act that causes pollution, in which, as a result of a deliberate act, contaminated and untreated water is discharged into waters or onto or into the ground, in which contaminated solids are placed on or in the grounds or waters other than in an appropriate waste facility, or in which contaminating gasses, solids, or liquids are dispersed into the air.

**custodial release (discharge or release from custody)** To be discharged from supervision in a jail, hospital, or other facility. Custodial release is the discharge of a person who had been held in custody, whether as a matter of penal servitude or criminal detention or as a means of supervision for mental or physical care. The releasing authority is responsible for determining that the person is entitled to release and for the timely release of each person in custody under such conditions as are required by law.

*See also:* discharge.

**conditional release** A custodial release subject to conditions that require the return to custody for violation. The conditional release of a person in custody is a release subject to conditions, which may require the return of the person to custody if the conditions are violated. Conditions may include routine contact with parole or police officers, lawful behavior, the absence of contact with known or suspected felons, the absence of contact with children, the avoidance of weapons, drugs, or alcohol, and limitations on movement, among others. Parole is a form of conditional release.

**release in full (full and final release)** An unconditional release of all debts and obligations owed to the releasor. A release in full is a statement or instrument by which the releasing party releases the released party from all obligations, debts, or claims that it was or may have been owed and discharges the party from further payment to it, without any condition or qualification. A release in full is usually a signal that a debt has been paid in full or that the debt is found to have been wrongfully asserted.

**relet or re-letting or re-leasing** *See:* lease, re-let (relet or re-letting or re-leasing).

**relevance (relevancy or relevant)** Potential for use in resolving the matter in issue. Relevance is the likelihood that some evidence or issue applies to the questions that must be answered in a given case. Although relevance is always a matter of degree — some evidence is potentially more or less relevant to a given issue, courts tend to evade this problem by asking whether evidence is relevant. The question thus becomes whether the evidence is sufficiently relevant to be admitted in the case. Evidence that might reasonably assist a finder of fact in answering a question in the case is inherently relevant to the case.

As with evidence, so are issues more relevant or less relevant to a dispute. An issue that does not have a relationship to any facts or allegations in a dispute between the parties or to any legal issues directly based on those facts or allegations, is irrelevant to them.

Relevance and irrelevance are not perfectly divided categories, binary so that an issue or evidence is clearly one or the other. Rather, relevance and irrelevance are ends of a scale, and matters must be assessed to determine how relevant they are, or how irrelevant they are, to the matters in issue.

*See also:* evidence, relevant evidence (relevance); fallacy, false dichotomy (false binarism).

**relevant evidence** *See:* evidence, relevant evidence, irrelevant evidence (irrelevance); evidence, relevant evidence (relevance).

**reliance (justifiable reliance or reasonable reliance or rely)** To depend on a person, thing, or idea. Reliance is a relationship between one person, thing, or idea and another, in which the relying person, thing, or idea depends for some essential element on the person, thing, or idea relied upon. A person might base a decision, action, or idea on the advice or authority of another person, a perceived condition, or a source of authority, trusting in the person, condition, or source to be adequate for the person's purpose. As a matter of speech, ideas and authority rely on component or predicate ideas and authority, and objects are said to rely on one another, as each link in a chain relies on the rest. Yet, the most significant form of reliance in law is that of a person relying upon some statement or action of another person in deciding to act or in acting in some manner.

Reliance is a matter of fact, although in many cases reliance may be inferred or construed from circumstances. Reliance in fact requires that a person know of the other person's statement, condition, or conduct (whether committed, ongoing, or planned) and then make a plan or decide to act in some manner that is affected by that knowledge. The effect may be to do something that would not have been done but for that knowledge, to forebear from doing something that otherwise would have been done, or to alter a plan or method so that some portion of the plan or method will then succeed or fail depending on the truth of that knowledge.

Constructive reliance is reliance that may be presumed in a given case from certain acts or statements that are made in a circumstance that invites reliance by other parties. Constructive reliance is sometimes confused with reasonable reliance.

Reasonable reliance is a condition both on constructive reliance and on reliance in fact, in which the relying party may only have the legal benefit of the reliance on the relied-on party if the reliance occurred in circumstances in which a reasonable person would have similarly relied on another's statement or conduct. In other words, if the relying party was on notice of a condition so that it would be unreasonable to rely on the relied-on party's statement or conduct, then the relying party may not assert reliance as a basis for a duty or breach of duty in law or equity. For instance, if the relying party sees the relied-on party at a party, speaking with slurred speech and blurry eyes, and trailing an empty rum bottle, and the relied-on party says, "yes, I'm sober," the relying party might not reasonably rely on the statement. Reasonable reliance is effectively the same as justifiable reliance. A person is justified in relying on statements or conduct on which it is reasonable so to rely.

*See also:* justification (justify or justified or justifiable); reasonable (reasonableness).

**reliance damages**  *See:* damages, contract damages, reliance damages.

**detrimental reliance**  Harm to one who depends on the assurance of another, who reneges. Detrimental reliance is a theory under which a claim may be brought without relying on a contract to enforce an assurance given by one party to another, when the assuring party is aware of the harm that would be done to the relying party if the assurance is not carried out in fact. Detrimental reliance requires that the plaintiff show a statement or conduct by the defendant: (a) that the defendant made to the plaintiff or knew was known to the plaintiff, and that the plaintiff had a right to rely upon, (b) that the plaintiff does in fact rely on when changing his or her position or commitments, (c) that the defendant knows or should know of plaintiff's reliance and yet the defendant does not persist in the conduct or satisfy the conditions assured, and (d) and that has caused the plaintiff to suffer demonstrable injury. Detrimental reliance is a means of enforcing promises and similar statements, including plea offers by a prosecutor. Detrimental reliance may give rise to a claim for a variety of remedies, including estoppel, injunction, constructive trust, restitution, and damages.

*See also:* reliance, unbargained-for reliance (induced reliance); promise, gratuitous promise; culpa, culpa in contrahendo (C in C).

**essential reliance**  Reliance on the other party in performing contractual duties. Essential reliance is the reliance by one party upon the obligations of the other party under a contract, when the first party prepares for its performance and the

performance by the other party, as well as the first party's own performance of its obligations under the contract.

**unbargained-for reliance (induced reliance)**  Reliance encouraged by the non-relying party, without negotiation. Unbargained-for reliance includes all instances of the reliance on a promise that was not the result of negotiation, exchange, consideration, or the other predicates of a contract. Rather, unbargained-for reliance occurs when the promissee's reliance was not expressly invited by the promissor but followed the promise without any demand or bargain other than the inducement of the promise itself. The effect of unbargained-for reliance is to remove the enforcement of the promise from the doctrines of contract and to place it in the domain of either promissory estoppel or detrimental reliance.

*See also:* reliance, detrimental reliance; estoppel, promissory estoppel.

**relief**  The assistance of a court to a litigant who proves harm from the unlawful or inequitable conduct of another. Relief, in general, is assistance in alleviating some harmful condition or injury suffered. In law it is the action that is sought to be ordered or required by a court in response to sufficient proof of a legally cognizable injury the plaintiff has or is likely to suffer. Relief may be given to a plaintiff or to a defendant, but only in response to a claim for relief, which incorporates a prayer for relief setting forth in general or specific terms the relief sought, and either upon a showing of proof in court or before an administrative agency that the relief is deserved or upon a default by the other party. The relief must take the form of a remedy within the powers of the court or agency to confer.

*See also:* remedy (remediable or remedied or remedies); damages; restitution (writ of restitution); equity, equitable remedy (equitable relief).

**relief from judgment**  *See:* judgment, relief from judgment.

**relief from the disabilities of minority or emancipated minor**  *See:* minor, minority, emancipation of a minor (relief from the disabilities of minority or emancipated minor).

**adequate relief (inadequate relief)**  Relief sufficient to cure a harm but not to cause a windfall. Adequate relief is relief sufficient in form and quantity to cure the past, present, and future damage suffered as a result of the defendant's actionable conduct and to prevent future damage either by an ongoing or imminent action by the defendant. If possible, the relief must be sufficient to place the plaintiff in as good a position as the plaintiff was in, both as a matter of present condition and future prospect, immediately prior to suffering the damage. Adequacy includes an aspect of sufficiency and promptness, so that relief delayed requires additional relief. Relief is inadequate if it is not prompt, full, and as complete as the practical administration of justice will allow, including the substitution of impracticable remedy for a remedy that is within the ability of the court to administer and the defendant to satisfy.

**affirmative relief**   The relief sought to remedy a claim for relief. Affirmative relief is the primary form or forms of relief requested in a claim for relief. Affirmative relief is inherently the relief sought in a complaint as the basis for the remedy of the damage suffered by the plaintiff, and any relief sought merely for the purpose of securing or assisting in the provision of that relief is ancillary. An answer or responsive pleading does not in itself allow for a claim for affirmative relief, although a counter-claim, cross-complaint, or other pleading in which a new claim for relief may be asserted does so allow.

**ancillary relief**   Remedies distinct but related to the affirmative relief that is primarily sought in an action. Ancillary relief is relief that is granted by the court, or at least requested by a party who has been successful on at least one claim in a civil action, that is necessary or beneficial in ensuring that the affirmative relief ordered as a result of the claim is efficiently and effectively secured for the benefit of the successful party. Some forms of ancillary relief include orders securing assets required to satisfy judgment, orders for costs, orders for the payment of the opponent's attorneys' fees, and equitable orders governing conduct of the parties required to assure the performance of affirmative relief.

**claim for relief**   The specific demands the plaintiff seeks to prove that the court will order of the defendant. The claim for relief is the plaintiff's asser-tion of the court's jurisdiction, the factual and legal bases of the claim, and a demand for relief that states exactly what the plaintiff seeks the court to order the defendant to do, even if it is an unspecified request for general relief. The claim for relief is the ultimate focus of every complaint, counterclaim, cross-claim, or any pleading that seeks an order from the court, to specify what order is requested at the end of the action and to give clear legal reasons why it is justified.

Note: the prayer for relief is the statement of the remedy sought, while the claim for relief is the more general statement of the whole claim upon which the prayer is predicated.

**declaratory relief**   See: judgment, declaratory judg-ment (declaratory relief or declaration).

**monetary relief**   Any remedy payable in money. Monetary relief is relief that is wholly payable in money from the defendant or other liable party to the plaintiff or other successful claimant. Damages and restitution (other than restitution in kind) are monetary relief. Monetary relief may be incidental to non-monetary relief, particularly when there is no practicable manner to order or perform non-monetary relief (such as specific performance) that would otherwise be due.

See also: restitution (writ of restitution); damages.

**prayer for relief**   The pleading of a claim for relief that states the remedy sought. A prayer for relief is the request for a remedy or remedies, made as a part of a claim for relief, and stating both the specific or general remedies that the plaintiff (or counter-claimant, cross-claimant, co-plaintiff, etc.) asserts are appropriate remedies for the claim presented. A prayer may assert remedies that are mutually exclusive without electing between the remedies, as long as they are presented in the alternative. A remedy that might later be perceived as appropriate to a claim is barred if it is not sought either expressly in a prayer for special relief or impliedly in a prayer for general or unspecified relief.

See also: complaint.

**relief as public assistance (disaster relief or poor relief)**   Funds or services provided to aid a person or entity in distress. Relief is a generic term for the funds, supplies, or services including health care, transport, or housing, which are provided to an individual, family, entity, or category of animals, enti-ties, or persons who are either endemically or tempo-rarily in distress. Relief may be provided by a private or public entity, using private or public funds. The relief of the poor is a charitable activity.

**religion**   Any communal system for understanding creation and performing obligations related to that understanding. Religion is an activity protected by the Constitution. In the Establishment Clause and Free Exercise Clause, and under the Equal Protection Clause and statutes based upon it, discrimination on the basis of religion is forbidden by the government and by most employers. Religious organizations are entitled to pref-erential treatment in the tax laws of the United States and most states. Yet religion is itself difficult to define. Most enquiries are directed to determining whether a religious position is advanced in good faith. Though U.S. officials sometimes attempt to define religion in the light of one religion alone, this is not sufficient in the light of the Establishment Clause. Religion, in general, is an amalgam of ideas regarding the meaning of life and creation; the idea of a creator or creators of existence; the role of humankind and each individual in the cosmos; obliga-tions of conduct toward a deity, toward creation, and toward one another; the sources of such knowledge; the veneration of these ideas and their sources; various practices recognizing these ideas and acting in accord with them, particularly in specialized places and at des-ignated times. As a general matter, religion includes not only recognized faiths — such as Christianity, Islam, Buddhism, and Indigenous religions — but also new conceptions of religion that lack a considerable historical predicate, occasionally even conceptions of religion that have as yet only one adherent. For the purposes of pro-tection under the Equal Protection Clause, immigration laws, tax laws, etc., participation in an organized religion with shared ideas and practices among others establishes what amounts to a rebuttable presumption that a belief derived from such a religion is protected as religious. Whether a belief is religious or not requires the belief be held in good faith, that the belief be related to an understanding of a divinity or the nature of the cosmos, that either it be related to a community of people that shares that understanding and engages in practices related to that understanding, or it be related to or derived from a tradition in which that understanding has been promoted or developed. Such a relation or derivation may be in the form of criticism, reform, or rejection as well as application or revival.

*See also:* God (supreme being or creator); religion, freedom of religion.

**religious discrimination**   *See:* discrimination, employment discrimination, religious discrimination.

**Religious Freedom Restoration Act**   *See:* religion, freedom of religion, Religious Freedom Restoration Act (RFRA).

**Religious Land Use and Institutionalized Persons Act**   *See:* religion, freedom of religion, Religious Land Use and Institutionalized Persons Act (RLUIPA).

**religious liberty**   *See:* liberty, religious liberty.

**religious tenure**   *See:* tenure, feudal tenure, frankalmoign (religious tenure).

**Religious Test Clause**   *See:* constitution, U.S. Constitution, clauses, Religious Test Clause.

**freedom of religion**   The freedom to practice or change one's own religion or not to believe in or practice a religion at all. Freedom of religion is the constitutional principle underlying both the Free Exercise Clause and the Establishment Clause. In general, these clauses both require consonant action from the state in maintaining what Thomas Jefferson described a "wall of separation between church and state" in which the state does not become an avenue of religious indoctrination, leaving the freedom to choose one's religious principles to the individual. Even so, there is some tension between these approaches, noticeable most when a religious impulse moves from the private sphere to the public sphere, and within the arena of that tension, some laws and policy may be neither required by the Free Exercise Clause nor forbidden by the Establishment Clause.

*See also:* liberty, religious liberty; religion.

*1. health care for child*   The religious belief of a parent or a child cannot be the basis for the parent's endangerment of the child through the denial of health care.

*2. establishment and free exercise*   There is a tension between the two clauses, but the appropriate tests tend to resolve any such conflicts. The Establishment Clause prohibits state actions that promote a particular religion, and the Free Exercise Clause requires the government to refrain from interfering in an individual's religious expression, which leads to a potential conflict when an individual's religious observance requires the use of a government space or public space attributable to the establishment of a church. The general principles of government neutrality among religions may be insufficient to separate or prioritize between the assurance of private religious

observance and limitation on public religious establishment. The inherent limits on establishment articulated in the Lemon Test are the dominant balance between the interests by limiting government from religious purposes, effects, or entanglement.

*See also:* religion, freedom of religion, Lemon test.

*3. pledge of allegiance and religious freedom*   The Pledge of Allegiance now includes the phrase "under God," which does not, in itself, establish a religion in the United States. However, public officials, including teachers and school officials, may not require that any person, including a student, recite the Pledge in violation of a personal adherence to a religious conviction associated with that person's faith.

*See also:* pledge, pledge of allegiance.

**establishment of religion (separation of church and state)**   The government may neither endorse nor intrude on religion. The establishment of religion is forbidden to the United States and to each state. This prohibition is an aspect of the requirement that no government interfere with the free exercise of religion, as endorsing one idea of religion would necessarily interfere with another. The Framers were familiar with the dangers of religious civil war, and the purposes of the separation of church and state is two-fold, to protect religion from government and to protect the government from religion. The prohibition on establishment does not forbid the U.S. or states from allowing or denying religious institutions privileges or benefits allowed to similar non-religious institutions, but it does forbid the governments to create any preference, endorsement, or prohibition that is contingent upon the ideology of the religious institution (as opposed to the conduct of members of that institution). Under the Free Exercise Clause, a law that burdens religious practice need not be justified by a compelling governmental interest if it is neutral and of general applicability. However, where such a law is not neutral or not of general application, it must undergo the most rigorous of scrutiny: it must be justified by a compelling governmental interest, and must be narrowly tailored to advance that interest. Neutrality and general applicability are interrelated, and failure to satisfy one requirement is a likely indication that the other has not been satisfied.

*See also:* constitution, U.S. Constitution, amendment 1, freedom of religion.

*1. celebration of holidays*   The prohibition on the establishment of religion does not forbid a government or public agency from recognizing religious holidays, but the recognition may not amount to the endorsement of religion or any one religious tradition.

*2. moment of silence*   A moment of silence in a public school or otherwise at the government's behest is presumptively constitutional because it lacks the elements of endorsement or entanglement typical of vocal prayers. Even so, if a moment of silence is patently a surrogate for a prayer or encouragement of prayer, the moment of silence favors prayer and so violates the Establishment Clause.

**3. public instruction** Public instruction on matters of religious significance must remain neutral among the beliefs of different religions. This admonition does not treat science as a religion, nor does it require neutrality between religious views on a matter of scientific inquiry and the views of scientific research. Thus, a view of evolutionary biology need not be contrasted with views of the divine creation (or even of the rejection of evolutionary biology and its evidence in favor of skepticism or of unknown origins for life), and efforts to require the teaching of such views are usually both an endorsement of a religious view and an entanglement of the state in religion.

**4. religious displays on state property** A government may allow a religious display, such as a creche or a tablet of the Ten Commandments, on public property without violating the Establishment Clause, if there is a predominately secular purpose to the display.

*See:* religion, freedom of religion, establishment of religion, Endorsement test, creche.

**ceremonial deism** Religious references in public ceremonies without religious content. Ceremonial deism labels all symbols and references that are used in public ceremonies as a matter of solemnity and tradition and without a religious purpose or effect. Coined in 1962 by Eugene Rostow, the term refers to references to the divine made on symbols and in federal and state institutions that do not offend the Establishment Clause, because they are historically rooted and ubiquitous in usage, invoke no aspect of worship or prayer, do not favor any sect or religion, and have a minimal religious content.

*See also:* God (supreme being or creator).

**Endorsement Test** An act of the government that endorses a religion violates the Establishment Clause. The Endorsement Test is a test of government action to determine whether it violates the Establishment Clause, by which a government acton that endorses or favors a given religion is unconstitutional. This is sometimes seen as an alternative to the three-pronged Lemon Test, and at other times seen as a refinement of the effects prong of the Lemon Test. It may be that the Endorsement Test is a preliminary analysis, and a governmental act that passes it is then to be considered under the Lemon Test. As of 2008, the Court had yet to adopt the test in a majority opinion.

*See also:* religion, freedom of religion, Lemon Test.

**creche** A display depicting the infant Jesus and family. A creche is a physical depiction of the customary scene of the birth of Jesus of Nazareth, usually in a barn with Mary, Joseph, and attendants. The installation of a creche, or nativity scene, on public property has been an object of frequent litigation under the First Amendment. There is usually no Constitutional claim against the installation of a creche on private property, which would be an exercise of the right to religious expression. Still, such installations are subject to the same land use laws that would govern all activities. Note: "creche" is derived from the French for "manger," which itself derived from the same Latin term that was the basis for the English "crib." In English, creche has several meanings that are unrelated to a nativity scene, though they are similarly derived, including nursery school, orphanage, foundling hospital, and group of young animals.

**three-plastic-animals rule** Secular symbols must be included in a government-sponsored creche to offset any religious message. The three-plastic-animals rule is a metaphorical assessment of a religious symbol on public property, especially a creche, nativity scene, or other presentation related to a Christian holiday placed on civic property near that holiday. The assessment, suggested by Judge Michael McConnell (who was then a law professor) is based on the constitutional requirement that religious symbolism be mitigated to some degree by secular symbolism.

**free exercise of religion** The government shall tolerate all religious beliefs. The free exercise of religion is the constitutional liberty of each person to believe in any (or no) conception of the divine and to participate in worship in any (or by no) means the individual should choose, without any hindrance or liability from the government. This freedom is limited, however, in that any action that a person or group takes that is forbidden by law or creates a liability under law is not made lawful or immune because it is religious. As long as a legal prohibition or liability has no basis in religion or faith or in opposition to a religion or faith, then the exercise of religion is not a privilege to violate the law. The freedom of free exercise of religion is both implemented by and limited by the prohibition on the establishment of religion, in that no faith may become the church of the state, even if the religious beliefs of some individuals or faiths require that their faith be the one religion of the state. The Constitution further protects free exercise by forbidding a religious test for office.

**1. life-saving medical treatment** Although an individual may reject medical treatment on the basis of a religious belief, the individual may not do so for a child, even if a parent desires to do so for a child. Constitutionally protected rights, such as the freedom to exercise religious beliefs, can be regulated to protect a compelling state interest. The protection of children is a compelling state interest, thus the state can intervene when parents refuse medical treatment for their children.

**2. *polygamy and free exercise*** Polygamy is not a constitutionally protected interest under the Free Exercise Clause. The police powers authority of the state in regulating the family is sufficient to justify regulation of marriage to forbid a single adult from a polygamous marriage.

**3. *prisoner religious exercise*** A prisoner is entitled to exercise private religious beliefs and not to be discriminated against as a result of prison policy or guard conduct that is specifically based on the prisoner's religion. Even so, the prisoner may not exercise a religious belief contrary to a generally applicable policy that promotes a compelling governmental interest by the least restrictive means. A prisoner must demonstrate that a constitutional right to a religious exercise is clearly established in law at the time that the conduct of prison officials burdens its exercise, and the burden on that exercise must be significant and not a mere isolated incident.

*See also:* religion, freedom of religion, Religious Land Use and Institutionalized Persons Act (RLUIPA).

**4. *sabbath accommodation*** An employee is entitled to exercise a sincere personal religious belief in limited activity on the sabbath as it is defined in the employee's religious tradition. An employer who fails to provide reasonable accommodation of an employee's sabbatarian obligations violates Title VII, and a state that denies unemployment insurance or similar services for a termination based on job action resulting from a sabbath observance violates the Free Exercise Clause.

*See also:* sabbath (shabat or yaum al-jumua or sabbatarian or sabbatarianism).

**5. *sacrifice of animals*** Although a government may regulate animal cruelty under ordinances and statutes of general applicability, a law that is enacted with the purpose of forbidding the sacrifice of animals in a bona fide and traditional religious custom and belief is an unconstitutional suppression of a religious practice.

**Lemon Test** Government action violates the Establishment Clause if it has a religious purpose, fosters or inhibits religion, or excessively entangles the government in religion. The Lemon Test is a three-pronged analysis of Establishment Clause claims pronounced in Lemon v. Kurtzman, 403 U.S. 602 (1971), measuring purpose, effects, and entanglement. A government action that primarily has a religious purpose, or that has effects that inhibit or promote religion, or that excessively entangles the government in a religion violates the Establishment Clause.

*See also:* religion, freedom of religion | 2. establishment and free exercise; religion, freedom of religion, establishment of religion, endorsement test.

**Religious Freedom Restoration Act (RFRA)** A statute purporting to require strict scrutiny of burdens on religion. The Religious Freedom Restoration Act, 42 U.S.C. §2000bb (2010), bars Congress from passing laws that prohibit the free exercise of religion, including laws that burden religion as an incident to laws that are generally applicable to all citizens, unless the law serves a compelling governmental interest. The Constitutional standard allowing burdens on religion incidental to general laws remains the limit on state and local law, language extending RFRA to local laws being found unconstitutional in City of Boerne v. Flores, 521 U.S. 507 (1997). Amendments to RFRA in 1994 specifically exempt American Indians' use of peyote from federal penalties or discrimination.

**Religious Land Use and Institutionalized Persons Act (RLUIPA)** A government regulating religious land use or prisoner religious observance must narrowly pursue a compelling state interest. The Religious Land Use and Institutionalized Persons Act of 2000, Pub. L 106–274, codified at 42 U.S.C. §2000cc (2010), prohibits a government from regulating the lands of religious entities or creating a burden on the exercise of a prisoner's clearly established, bona fide religious observance, without a compelling governmental interest that is pursued by the least burdensome means.

*See also:* religion, freedom of religion, free exercise of religion | 3. prisoner religious exercise.

**Virginia Statute for Religious Freedom** Virginia law establishing religious freedom in the commonwealth. The Virginia Statute for Religious Freedom was passed by the Virginia General Assembly on January 16, 1786, having been proposed by Thomas Jefferson in 1779 and drafted by him. It was an important benchmark during the Constitutional ratification debates, underscoring the argument that the U.S. Constitution should have a similar requirement in a Bill of Rights. It influenced the adoption of the two clauses respecting religion in the First Amendment — the Establishment Clause and the Free Exercise Clause.

**place of worship** *See:* church.

**damage to a place of worship (church bombing)** The damage or destruction of a place of religious worship is a federal crime. The Freedom of Access to Clinic Entrances Act, 18 U.S.C. §248, forbids intentional destruction or damage to a place of church, temple, mosque, or other place of religious worship or its property.

**rem** Thing. Rem is the accusative form of the Latin word "res," for thing. It is therefore the form used to follow a preposition, such as "in rem" or "against the thing."

*See also:* in, in rem; res.

**remainder** A grantee's future interest following a definitely limited possessory estate. A remainder is a future interest created when a life estate, a fee tail, or another fee limited by a definite occurrence is followed by a grant to another grantee, rather than a reversion to the grantor. Remainders may be vested at the time the grant is made, or they may be contingent on events occurring or failing to occur between the time of the grant and the termination of the preceding estate.

Remainder has a more generic sense in probate and in trusts, as the portion of the decedent's estate or the res of the trust that is not given in specific grants. In this sense, a remainder in the estate is distributable as a specific devise, usually to a residuary legatee or residuary devisee, or it will pass as an asset to the heirs at law. A remainder in a trust may be created in a grant to a specific remainder trust, distributed according to the settlor's instructions at a future date, or distributed pro rata to the beneficiaries when the trust is dissolved.

*See also:* estate, interest, life estate (life interest); fee, estate in fee, fee tail; estate, future interest, remainder; remainder, contingent remainder.

*1. reversion and remainder* A reversion is an interest retained by the grantor, but a remainder is given to a grantee. The remainder must be specified by the grantor, and anything not clearly intended to be granted to a grantee in remainder is not within the grant. On the other hand, all property transferred to grantees by a grant in a limited fee create an implied reversion. There is no remainder in general that arises by implication.

*2. executory interest and remainder* An executory interest cuts short a preceding interest, but a remainder follows the inherent conclusion of the preceding interest. An executory interest is similar to a contingent remainder, but the executory interest arises only when a preceding vested right to possession is terminated as the result of an event's occurrence or the termination of a condition, at which time the preceding right of possession is terminated, or cut short, and the interest which was executory (or contingent) until then becomes possessory. In contrast, a remainder follows an interest that is certain to occur and does occur as the result of an interest by which it is inherently ended, at which time the remainder (which may have been vested or contingent until then) becomes possessory.

*3. valuation of remainder* The remainder following a life estate may be given a present value, whether the remainder is vested or contingent. In either case the present value of the land must be divided by the actuarially computed likely period until the death of the prior possessing life tenant.

**alternative remainder** One of several contingent remainders, one or the other of which will vest. An alternative remainder is a form of contingent remainder created when the grantor establishes two or more contingent remainders, one of which will necessarily vest. Thus, one remainder is the alternative to the other.

**contingent remainder** A remainder that might or might not ever become possessory. A contingent remainder is a remainder that is not vested or certain to become possessory. Rather, a contingent remainder depends upon a condition being satisfied either before it can become possessory or when it would become possessory, and if the condition is not satisfied by the time that it would become possessory, the remainder fails. A remainder given to any person who

is not identifiable at the time of the grant is a remainder to an unascertained grantee, making it a contingent remainder.

For example, A grants Blackacre to B for life then to C if C has by then become a lawyer (and at the time of the grant C is not a lawyer). This would create a contingent remainder in C. The contingency cannot be known to be satisfied until C becomes a lawyer but it cannot be known to have failed until B's death (if C had not by then become a lawyer). In other words, if C becomes a lawyer while B is alive, C will take Blackacre when B dies, but if B dies and C is not a lawyer, then C does not take Blackacre, and from what little we know, Blackacre reverts automatically to A under a reversion implied by law, even though it was unstated.

A contingent remainder is not a vested interest for the purposes of the rule against perpetuities. So, in order to be valid under the common law, a contingent remainder had to be created so that it must vest or must fail within twenty-one years of the death of any person whose live could serve as a measuring life. Under the modern rules, in most U.S. jurisdictions, a contingent remainder that violates the rule is not void but must still vest in time under the statute, which may take nearly a century.

*See also:* remainder; vesting (vest or vested); perpetuity, rule against perpetuities (RAP or rule against remoteness).

*1. condition subsequent or condition precedent* A contingent remainder is subject to a condition that, usually, is a condition subsequent to the making of the grant but that is always a condition precedent to taking possession of the property granted. If the condition is not satisfied before or when the property would otherwise become possessory in the person holding the contingent remainder, the remainder lapses and the property passes to the next holder of a then-vested interest.

*2. rule against perpetuities* A contingent remainder is subject to the rule against perpetuities.

*See also:* perpetuity, rule against perpetuities (RAP or rule against remoteness).

*3. vested remainder and contingent remainder* A vested remainder is created under such conditions that there is no doubt at the time of the grant that the remainder will one day become possessory either in the grantee or the grantee's successors. A contingent remainder is in doubt over whether it will become possessory, but at the time the doubt is erased, the remainder is either destroyed or vested, even if this happens long before the property becomes possessory.

**acceleration of the remainder (acceleration of estate or accelerated remainder)** A remainder created to follow an interest that cannot itself become possessory. Acceleration of the remainder occurs when a preceding tenancy becomes vacant for some reason not contemplated in the grant of the tenancy, so the remainder vests as possessory without waiting until the intended completion of the prior estate. This might happen because a life tenant renounces the interest, such as when a devisee renounces an interest that is granted by a testamentary will. It might also happen if the remainder follows an interest that is void as a matter of law, such as a contingent remainder that violates the Rule against Perpetuities. In such cases, the will would be interpreted so as to most closely approximate the intent of the testator, and the remainder that succeeded the interest that could not be given effect would be accelerated to commence at the time the earlier interest would have become possessory.

### Rule of the Destructibility of Contingent Remainders (Destructibility Rule)

Contingent remainders cannot outlast the prior interest. The Rule of the Destructibility of Contingent Remainders required that a contingent remainder could not persist beyond the existence of the estate prior to its remainder. Thus, if a life estate was followed by a contingent remainder, the remainder must have become vested while the life tenant lived, and if it had not become vested at the life tenant's death, the contingent remainder was destroyed. The Destructibility Rule is no longer a rule of law in most states, although it occasionally arises as a basis for interpretation. It does, however, persist in Florida, a haven of probate.

*See also:* Shelley's Case (Rule in Shelley's Case).

### cross remainder (cross-remainder)

One of several remainders shared among several holders. A cross remainder arises when a grantor grants either two or more people a co-tenancy for life, or grants two or more people individual life interests in different properties, and grants the remainders the grantees as well, either granting each a remainder in all the property, or granting the last survivor of them all a remainder in all the property. For example, A grants Blackacre to B, C, and D as tenants in common for the life of each, with cross remainders. If B dies, C and D each possess one-half of B's interest, doing so only for their lives. If C dies, then D takes all of C's interest, merging into D's, so D possesses all of Blackacre. The difference between a cross-remainder and a remainder without modification or further instruction is that using a conventional remainder, when B dies, C and D would each have taken one-half of B's interest in fee simple absolute, and so when C died, D would have been left only with five sixths of Blackacre (D's original third, plus one-sixth from B plus C's original third), the other sixth going to C's heirs or devisees. To avoid this sort of confusion, a court may interpret a last will and testament according to the intent of the grantor to find cross-remainders when the testator failed to identify them or describe them, as long as it appears the testator intended such a result.

Granting a cross-remainder amounts to granting a remainder for life that incorporates a remainder that follows another remainder for life and that is followed by a remainder in favor of the remainder for life for which it has the remainder. Cross remainders are created of two or more remainders to the same prior interest in a manner that either expresses or implies a shared interest in a remainder among several parties. Each then has a remainder for life, its remainder (in the remainder) to the other remainderholders. Though rarely said this way, the cross remainder is somewhat like a joint tenancy with a right of survivorship.

### defeasible remainder (remainder subject to defeasance)

A remainder that may be cut short by an executory interest, possibility of reverter, or right of entry. A defeasible remainder is a remainder in a fee simple determinable or fee simple subject to a condition subsequent or fee simple subject to an executory interest, so that the remainder is itself subject to loss owing to a failure of condition. The defeasible remainder is also called a remainder subject to defeasance, a remainder determinable, a remainder subject to a condition subsequent, and a remainder subject to an executory interest. All of these terms signal the same interest as a defeasible remainder, and if the remainder becomes possessory, it becomes a fee subject to same limitation and destruction, in favor of the grantor or of the holder of an executory interest.

*See also:* defeasibility (defeasible or indefeasibility or indefeasible or indefeasibly).

### indefeasibly vested remainder

A remainder that is not subject to defeasance. An indefeasibly vested remainder is a remainder vested in its holder, usually by language granting a remainder to "X, her heirs and assigns" and in a context in which no interest is reserved to the grantor or assigned to a third party that could cut short the remainder. In such case, the remainder descends to devisees or heirs if the remainderholder dies before the remainder becomes possessory.

### vested remainder subject to complete defeasance

A remainder vested and certain in its holder but still subject to loss on failure of a condition subsequent. A vested remainder subject to complete defeasance has no condition precedent to its vesting, and so it is not contingent. Even so, there is a condition subsequent to its continued right to ultimate possession, and in the event that condition subsequent fails, the vested remainder is subject to loss to the grantor as a possibility of reverter or right of entry, or to a grantee as an executory interest.

*See also:* defeasibility (defeasible or indefeasibility or indefeasible or indefeasibly).

### remainder subject to open

A remainder in a class whose membership is not yet final. A remainder subject to open is a grant of a remainder to a class that is not ascertained until an event in the future, usually the termination of the estate that precedes the remainder. For example, a grant to "A for life then to my grandchildren then living" creates a remainder subject to open in the grandchildren of the grantor; the class is subject to open so long as A is alive or until the last child or the grantor dies, at either time the class is fully ascertained. The remainder is contingent in this case, because a grand-child must survive A. A grant to "A for life then to my grandchildren who are then or have ever been born alive" would vest as soon as a grandchild of the grantor is born, although the class would not be fully ascertained until the last child of the grantor dies or until A dies.

*See also:* class, class of descendants, class gift rule (rule of convenience).

**remainderman (remainder holder or remainderer)** The person or entity who holds a remainder. The remainderman, or remainder-man, is the customary term for the holder of the remainder of an estate. Modern usage resists terms specific to a gender, and so remainderholder or the older term, remainderer, may be substituted.

**vested remainder** A remainder given with no condition precedent to its possession at the end of the preceding estate. A vested remainder is not contingent or conditioned on any event prior to its becoming possessory, other than that the preceding estate is terminated. For example, a grant to "A for life, then to B" creates a vested remainder in B, which will necessarily become possessory by B or B's successors at the end of A's life. A vested remainder does not cease to have been vested because it is subject to later divestment or defeasance, or loss owing to the failure of a condition subsequent.

*See also:* vesting (vest or vested).

**remand** The recommitment to an institution of a person or cause. Remand is an order by a court sending back or recommitting a person or a cause of action to the institution from which the person or cause has come before the court. Remand takes several forms.

On appeal, it is a return of an action to the court or agency from which the action was appealed. In this sense, remand restores jurisdiction to the court or agency that had been lost on appeal, allowing the court or agency to proceed with the action in the light of the opinion or instruction of the appellate body.

On removal, a federal court may remand an action that has been removed to it from a state court. Remand is required if the court lacks jurisdiction, but it may also be ordered if the court finds that prudence dictates the return of the action to state court.

In a criminal proceeding, a person in custody who is called before the court may be transferred to the court's custody. At the conclusion of the proceeding, the person is remanded to the institution of original custody. Like-wise, a person on parole or released on bail who is returned to custody for cause is remanded. As a conse-quence, remand is sometimes used as the signal for transfer into custody when a person is transferred to the custody of a prison agency, even if the person had not been in the custody of that agency previously.

**procedendo (writ of procedendo)** A writ remanding a case to a court from which it was taken. A writ of procedendo, or order of procedendo, is an order by

a court reviewing an action, either on appeal or by collateral review, to remand the action to the court from which it was drawn. The basis at common law for procedendo was that the grounds given to the reviewing court establishing its authority for review were not satisfied, although contemporary practice includes procedendo at the conclusion of appellate disposition. Some jurisdictions remand an action from an appellate court back to the trial court by pro-cedendo. Once the reviewing court has issued proce-dendo, it will withdraw the procedendo only under extraordinary circumstances.

**remediation** *See:* remedy, remediation (remedial).

**remedies**

**election of remedies (election of plaintiff or election of actions or several-remedies rule)** The ability and duty of a plaintiff to select one among alternate remedies. The doctrine of election of remedies requires the plaintiff, rather than the defendant, to select which among the remedies available for a cause of action is to be pursued. Election is a choice among mutually exclusive remedies, such as between damages or restitution for the same injury, or between eviction or rents for future occupation from the same holdover tenant for the same time. Election is not required among remedies for injuries distinct in time or kind, such as damages for past harm and an injunction against future harm, or damages for an auto collision for both a personal injury and for prop-erty damage.

To elect a remedy is to waive the remedies that are not elected. A plaintiff who elects one remedy and waives others, even if the plaintiff is unaware of the nature of the election but merely seeks one and not the others, waives the other remedies as against that defendant for that cause of action, and the waiver is final barring later causes of action under the other theories of remedy as a matter of res judicata.

Election may be avoided in the initial pleadings by seeking several remedies that are mutually exclusive, but by seeking them in the alternative. This process allows the election to be postponed until the conclu-sion of discovery or even trial, in which case the elec-tion may be avoided and the jury or judge requested to grant one of the available modes of relief. In some cases, however, the burden on the defense in defend-ing against a variety of remedies is sufficient that the plaintiff may be required to elect prior to the close of the case. Even so, contemporary practice is more likely to allow a plaintiff to avoid election and submit a claim for remedy in the alternative or in a claim for general relief.

*See also:* pleading, alternative pleading (pleading in the alternative or pled in the alternative); res, res judicata, claim preclusion.

**remedy (remediable or remedied or remedies)** What may be done to enforce a right or redress an injury. A remedy, generally, is a cure for a malady or relief for some form of trouble. In law, a remedy is any of the many actions that might be done by a party or ordered by a court or agency to do any thing allowed by law or equity and required to protect or to vindicate the interests of a party who successfully brings a claim for relief. A remedy may be used to declare the interests of the parties, to prevent or undo a harm, to compensate for its damage, to prevent its recurrence, or to punish the harm's maker. There are several ways to categorize remedies, the most common being to consider monetary, injunctive, declaratory, ancillary, and extraordinary remedies.

Note: remedy is both a noun and a verb: a remedy that is sought to remedy the trespass. A remediable condition is one that may be improved by a remedy, just as an irremediable condition is beyond remedy, and a condition that was in some manner unsatisfactory but that is now corrected is remedied. In all of these senses, there is an ambiguity like that concerning damage (which may mean the harm or the legal claim for the harm), in that the term may mean the cure as a matter of fact for some harm, or it may mean the response ordered by law to effect such a cure. For example, a wrongful death action may be remediable as a matter of law through the payment of damages, though clearly the underlying damage can never be fully remediated.

*See also:* relief; redress (redressability); damages, contract damages; damages; reparation (reparations).

**remedial investigation/feasibility study**   *See:* pollution, superfund, remedial investigation/feasibility study (RI/FS).

**remedial law**   *See:* law, remedial law (curative law).

**remedial statute**   *See:* statute, remedial statute.

**equitable remedy**   *See:* equity, equitable remedy.

**extraordinary remedy (extraordinary relief)**   A remedy available only in rare cases to vindicate a right otherwise at risk. An extraordinary remedy is a judicial remedy that is within the discretion of the court to be issued in unusual circumstances, when the remedies of law are inadequate to ensure the protection of a right or interest. In many cases, extraordinary remedies are remedies available in courts of law, appeal, or general jurisdiction that were initially available only in equity. Each petition for an extraordinary remedy must demonstrate that there is a right or interest recognized in law or equity that is at risk of loss or impairment that cannot be remedied by the ordinary remedies available to the petitioner, and that the remedy sought is essential to avoiding the loss or impairment. The most common forms of extraordinary remedy are injunction, relief from judgment, mandamus, prohibition, quo warranto, and certiorari.

With the merger of law and equity, the growth of constitutional remedies rooted in the federal courts' equitable powers, and the decline of specialized knowledge of equity among members of the bar, the injunction has become a generic form of remedy. Courts may use an injunction to achieve a variety of ends by ordering a party to act or refrain from action with great specificity. Although earlier courts might have used writs that were intended to serve in some of these same situations, and those writs are still available in many courts, the contemporary practice is more likely to craft injunctions to fulfill these needs.

*See also:* judgment, relief from judgment; mandamus; prohibition, writ of prohibition; quo, quo warranto (writ of quo warranto).

**post-conviction remedy**   Any remedy that alters or vacates a criminal conviction or sentence. A post-conviction remedy is any of several forms of remedy by which a criminal conviction, judgment, or sentence may be vacated or amended. Post-conviction remedies include remedies that may be ordered by the criminal court that entered the conviction, on appeal of that conviction or its sentence, or by collateral review in a civil proceeding (although many jurisdictions consider an action for collateral review to be distinct from post-conviction remedies, which are governed by a rule for review by the issuing court or by statute for a separate cause of action).

Post conviction remedies through collateral review include proceedings on a petition for a writ of audita querela, coram nobis, coram vobis, or habeas corpus. In many states, a rule or statute providing for a post-conviction remedy has supplanted these earlier remedies of equity or the common law. Even so, the potential for a federal review even of a state conviction and sentence remains open in a constitutional review by a petition for habeas corpus. The federal All Writs Act may permit such remedies when there is a gap in the habeas statute or no more general relief is sufficient. The exhaustion of state post-conviction remedies is a precondition to the pursuit of federal review by habeas corpus.

In some jurisdictions, a right to post-conviction remedies, and in all jurisdictions a right of federal review by habeas corpus, cannot be waived in a plea agreement or otherwise.

*See also:* audita querela (writ of audita querela); coram, coram nobis (coram vobis).

**pre-judgment remedy (pre-trial relief)**   An initial order to control a defendant's assets that may be needed to satisfy a final judgment. A prejudgment remedy is a form of preliminary relief, by which the court orders some property of the defendant to be secured, either in the possession of the defendant, of the plaintiff, of the sheriff or marshal, of the court, or of a third-party receiver, in order to ensure that the property is available if needed to satisfy a judgment against the defendant at the close of the proceeding.

Federal Rule of Civil Procedure 64 requires plaintiffs to use state pre-judgment remedies, which are defined as a matter of state law. Among the various states, the scope of these remedies varies. At its broadest, pre-judgment remedies include equitable orders such as the pre-judgment injunction, preliminary injunction, or temporary restraining order. As used in some states, however, pre-judgment remedy usually includes only legal remedies. In either case, unless the context clearly includes more, the use of pre–judgment remedy implies an order regarding assets, such as orders for attachment, receivership, replevin, garnishment, and sequestration, as well as injunctive remedies limited to the control of assets. Unless the plaintiff is the government, the plaintiff is usually required to post a bond as security for repayment to the defendant of damages that the defendant will suffer by the loss of access, control, or possession of the assets, damages that the defendant need not have suffered in the event the plaintiff is unsuccessful in the action or the assets are in excess of the requirements for the judgment.

*See also:* replevin (writ of replevin or replevy or repleviable); receiver (receivership).

**remediation (remedial)** Affording a remedy for damage or hardship. Remediation is the process of implementation of a remedy, and any action that is a component of or related to a process of remediation is remedial. Remediation may relate to a condition subject to a judicial order decreeing a remedy as a result of a civil action, but it may also arise from an administrative order or by voluntary compliance with a law or through a process voluntarily initiated by the remediating person or entity. Remediation takes many forms, such as the mitigation of an environmental hazard, therapy for a student who is developmentally disabled, or reconstruction of a property that has suffered damage.

**remission (remitter of bail or remitter of debt)** Reduction or rebate of an obligation. Remission, generally, is a form of forgiveness, particularly one invoking a pardon or reduction in a penalty or hardship. Thus, remission is now used in medicine to describe the reduction of symptoms of a disease or condition toward a benign state. In law, remission is a release or reduction of a debt owed, particularly in the whole or partial return of a payment already made as a security or payment. This takes several distinct forms.

A remission of a debt is either the reduction in the amount of the debt in whole or the amount outstanding to be paid. In either case, a remission presumes a reduction of principal as well as a corresponding reduction in the value of the interest owed, though not the interest rate.

A remission of bail is an order to the clerk of court, sheriff, or other custodian of funds paid as bail for a person to appear in court. An order of remission is also termed an order of remitter of bail. The funds are returned to the the individual or entity who deposited them, not otherwise to the person whose appearance was subject to bail.

A remission of judgment, or a remission of sentence, is a reduction of sentence, particularly the reduction of a period of incarceration or supervised release, or a reduction in the severity or hardship of the conditions of incarceration or release.

Note: all of these terms are homonyms with variant forms of "remission" in the generic sense of payment, and care is required to distinguish among them.

*See also:* remittance (remitter or remittee).

**remit** To give, to give back, or to annul. Remit is an ambiguous word at the intersection of several senses of remission and remittance. According to context, it is the verb form of remission (to give back, forgive, annul, or reduce) or remittance (to give, pay, or transfer). Yet, it may also be a noun for what is given, particularly to emphasize the scope of duties or obligations conferred by some grant. In that sense, remit is often found as the test of what duties are within or beyond the remit of a person, office, or agency.

**remittance (remitter or remittee)** A generic term for the transfer of funds. A remittance is a payment of funds or value to a bank, government, merchant, or (potentially but not usually) an individual, whether in cash, transfer, or via a negotiable instrument or other object of value. Use of the term remittance signals that the transfer of value is made but does not specify whether the transfer is intended to be a deposit, payment against future liabilities, security, or payment on a debt or obligation. Remittance is generic among the reasons for which a transfer of funds might be made. The person or entity who makes a remittance is the remitter, and the recipient is the remittee.

Note: remittance is not only the act or fact of the payment but also the payment itself (both the physical cash, check, or note and the value represented in it), both of these senses being nouns. "To remit" is the verb for remittance, although remit has other meanings as a noun. All of these terms are homonyms with variant forms of "remission" in the sense of the excuse of forfeiture or debt, and care is required to distinguish among them.

*See also:* remission (remitter of bail or remitter of debt).

**remitter of bail or remitter of debt** *See:* remission (remitter of bail or remitter of debt).

**remittitur** A judicial order reducing damages or granting a new trial. Remittitur is an order entered by a court following a jury verdict awarding the defendant to pay damages to the plaintiff, in which the judge finds the award excessive in comparison to the evidence and orders the plaintiff to accept a lesser award, which the plaintiff must do or the judge will order a new trial. Remittitur is not a post–trial settlement but an order made either on motion or sua sponte.

*See also:* additur.

**remonstrance (remonstrant or remonstrator)** A petition seeking a governmental agency not to do something. A remonstrance is a form of petition to the government, in which the petitioners seek the government, or a court or agency of the government, not to do something the petitioners have cause to believe the recipient is doing or would otherwise do. A party who would block an annexation or zoning decree, or the granting of a permit in some jurisdictions, files a remonstrance as the instrument of objection to the official action in question. A party who files a remonstrance is a remonstrator or a remonstrant.

The Grand Remonstrance was a petition of the English Parliament to Charles I, transmitted in 1641, seeking the king to change many policies affecting the law, revenues, Irish lands, and the Church of England. Charles's half-hearted response was one of the greivances leading to the English Civil War.

**remorse**   A sense of regret. Remorse is the sense of responsibility and regret that comes of the recognition that one has done harm or wrong. It is the sentiment that must be truly felt by a person to make an apology that is authentic as opposed to a mere formality. In the sentencing of criminals, the prisoner's true remorse is a traditional basis for the reduction of a sentence, while an absence of remorse has been at times considered a basis for a harsher sentence. Statutory schemes tend to be less prone to consider remorse than are judges in their discretion.

*See also:* teshuvah.

**remote (remoteness or remotely)**   Distant, diminished, rare, or unlikely. Remoteness is a relatively greater distance than something else nearer, and remote used as a matter of property describes a physical distance from something else. Remoteness in terms of consanguinity is a matter of degree of relationship, at least of one skipped generation and one degree of filiation (a grandfather or cousin to the person in question or more distant in relation than that). Remoteness as a matter of future interests is a measure of the time that must elapse and conditions that must occur before a future interest vests, and if the last condition might or might not be satisfied until three generations have run from the gift, the grant is too remote to survive the rule against perpetuities.

Judges considering early cases of causation often examined a chain of causation, in which one thing causes a second thing that causes a third thing that causes a damage — the question being whether the damage was too remote from the first thing (or the first thing was too remote from the damage) for the person who was responsible for causing the first thing to be liable for the ultimate damage. This sense of remoteness, or distance, from a result underlies the idea of a remote cause, or a remote damage, and of remote damages. There is no defining aspect of the remoteness in each circumstance: it is an assessment as a matter of fact derived from a function of the degree of causation combined with the foreseeability of the ultimate result prior to the cause. To label a cause or damage or damages remote is to diminish or destroy the legal responsibility or liability that might otherwise attach to it. The factual finding is often little more than a justification for a prior, unacknowledged decision to excuse the defendant from liability.

A similar but distinct idea underlies the sense of a remote possibility or remote chance of an event, in which the event that is considered would only occur in the event a variety of circumstances were to coincide. Thus, a remote possibility is unlikely to occur.

*See also:* causation, remote cause; perpetuity, rule against perpetuities (RAP or rule against remoteness).

**remote cause**   *See:* causation, remote cause.

**remote vesting**   *See:* vesting, remote vesting.

**removal (remove)**   To take something or someone from a setting, place, or role. Removal is the action by which a person, thing, or idea is taken from a location, office, or some other relationship. Removal is both a term of art and an essential aspect of other terms of art in the law. For example: removal from a place or from a person's control is the central factual element of the asportation of property in defining an act of larceny, theft, or burglary. Taking an action from the jurisdiction of a state court is the central aspect of removal of a civil action to federal court. Taking a person's power to exercise the authority associated with some office is the essential part of removal from office, or the removal of a trustee, or the removal of an executor.

**removal of survey mark**   *See:* survey, removal of survey mark (benchmark tampering).

**removal from office**   *See:* office, removal from office.

**removal to federal court (removal jurisdiction)**   A defendant's taking of a civil action from state court to federal court. Removal, in the sense of removal of an action to federal court, is the act of a defendant in a civil action initially filed in a state court to take the action to the federal district court with jurisdiction over the same area as the state court, because the action is appropriate to federal jurisdiction as it is either one that raises a federal question or one brought between diverse parties. Removal allows a defendant access to federal jurisdiction for a civil action, regardless of the choice between federal or state jurisdiction initially made by the plaintiff (though one should notice that there is no correlative choice of the defendant to take to state court a civil action initially filed by the plaintiff in federal court). The mere fact of removal does not assure the action will go forward in the federal court; the plaintiff may argue the removal was wrongful, or the court on its own motion may determine the removal was wrongful, in either case the court ordering the case remanded to the court from which it was removed.

An action in state court that is fit for removal to federal court is removable.

Removal jurisdiction is the jurisdiction of a federal court over an action once it has been removed. Removal jurisdiction may be broader than the court's jurisdiction otherwise, as it necessarily extends not only to actions that have been properly removed but also to actions that have been wrongly removed, in order to evaluate the jurisdiction and the bases of removal and then to remand the action to state court.

*See also:* remand; jurisdiction, diversity jurisdiction (diversity of citizenship); jurisdiction, federal-question jurisdiction (federal question jurisdiction).

**notice of removal**   A filing in federal court that commences a removed action there. The notice of removal is the form that is filed by a defendant who removes an action from state to federal court. The notice must be signed by the party or counsel for the party as required by Federal Rule of Procedure 11, and contain a short, plain statement of the grounds on which the action is removed. This statement must state the exact basis of the federal jurisdiction according to which the action could lawfully have been first filed in federal court, making clear the basis for federal question or the diversity of the parties, according to the basis for the federal jurisdiction asserted. If the action is removed on the basis of diversity of citizenship, the underlying facts asserted in the notice must make clear that the amount in controversy is greater than the statutory minimum. The notice should have attached to it a copy of all process, pleadings, and orders served on the defendant in the state action prior to removal.

**remuneration (remunerative)**  Reimbursement, pay, or salary. Remuneration, technically, is reimbursement, but it has come to be more widely used to represent any compensation for the performance of employment or a service. Pay, salary, commission, tips, and the like are all remuneration. Work that generates remuneration is remunerative.

*See also:* compensation (compensable or compensate or compensatory).

**rendition (render)**  The yielding of a person or a thing from some situation or process. Rendition, and its verb to render, have a variety of senses, each from the ideas of yielding or returning. In its most common sense, to render something is to deliver it to someone, to give it, to provide it, or to yield one's control to another, such as in rendering payment, rendering assistance, or rendering a service. In this sense, a judge renders judgment or renders sentence.

As a matter of rhetoric, to say that one idea renders another in some manner is to describe the effect of the first idea upon the other, such as one idea rendering the other moot or meaningful or meaningless, that being the yield of the two ideas. In this sense, render may also depict reduction, separation, or disjunction, as in rendering stock from bones or rendering an animal is the separation of its parts.

Rendition as a matter of intellectual property is repetition, publication, or distribution of the property, as in the rendition of an image, an argument, or a song.

In criminal and police matters, to render a person is to transfer that person from the facility or person with custody over to the person in another facility or jurisdiction. When the rendering of a person takes place between two jurisdictions, the process of rendition is usually done by extradition. A warrant seeking the arrest of a person in one jurisdiction in order to transfer custody of that person to another jurisdiction is a rendition warrant. Note: render is an element of surrender, to give oneself up to an enemy.

**rendition warrant**  *See:* warrant, rendition warrant (warrant of rendition); warrant, extradition warrant (rendition warrant).

**extraordinary rendition (irregular rendition)**  The transfer of a detainee to another jurisdiction other than by ordinary extradition. Extraordinary rendition is a process of prisoner transfer from one jurisdiction to another, in a manner or for a purpose that for some reason does not comply with the usual judicial procedures or with the law of one or both jurisdictions. Extraordinary rendition initially meant the capture by American agents of a person on foreign soil who is wanted in the United States and who is brought to the United States for detention, interrogation, or trial. It has come to mean the transfer, by a means other than extradition, of a person already in U.S. custody to the custody of another power, particularly for some purpose that is apparently unlawful. Allegations persist that extraordinary rendition was used as a policy of the United States between 2001 and 2008 to transfer detainees to states for interrogation by means that would be unlawful if performed by U.S. agents.

*See also:* torture; extradition.

**renewal (renew or renewability or renewable or renewed or non-renewable)**  An act of continuation of a condition, statement, or license. Renewal is the substitution of a new thing for something old that performs the same function, and for which the new thing serves as either a continuation or revival. In law, renewal is an action by which a person or entity acts or allows the revival or continuation of a contract, lease, note, license, or other legal interest, according to either the original terms or revised terms. A status, such as a license, or a contractual relationship, such as a lease, may be renewed according to its terms, or it may be allowed to lapse or be non-renewed. Any status or relationship that is capable of being renewed without an inherent requirement of new negotiation (such as a lease that may be renewed merely by notice to the other party or a failure of notice of non-renewal) is renewable. Renewability is the condition of a status or relationship that makes it renewable.

A government-issued license or permit may be renewed according to the regulations governing the license or permit. In general, there is no constitutional interest presumed in the terms of a permit beyond the permit's term, and new or differing terms may be required at the time of renewal without raising the same concerns related to taking of property, interference with contracts, or due process of law, that might affect an alteration of a permit or license during its term.

A renewal of a motion is to reassert a motion earlier made, whether the motion was granted or denied. A renewal of a motion may be required to preserve a record on appeal, such as the need to renew a denied objection to the introduction of certain evidence that is not sufficiently related to the introduction of additional evidence to give notice to the court of the nature of the objection to the additional evidence.

**renewal of objection**  *See:* objection, renewal of objection.

**renounce or renounced or renounceable** *See:* renunciation (renounce or renounced or renounceable).

**rent (renter)** Money or value paid in exchange for a lease of property. Rent has several distinct senses, but its primary sense in law is that of the value paid from a lessee to a lessor in exchange for the property leased during the time the lease persists. Rent may be money paid in cash, value given by property in kind, or value provided in services. Rent may be paid, owed, or collected from the lease of realty or personalty, and it is subject to taxation. A failure without justification to pay rents owed under a lease is a violation of the covenant of rents and a material violation of the lease. The lease being violated by the tenant, the tenant becomes a tenant by sufferance, and the landlord may elect to eject the tenant or to hold the tenant to the terms of the lease. Note: rent is both a noun and a verb, the amount to be paid as well as the action of allowing the use of the property in return for rents. A renter is one who rents, particularly one who rents housing.

At common law, rents included all profits from the use of the land, including all value realized from the use of land or tenements, whether the value was in money, goods, labor, or chattels. From this idea developed the economic notion of rent as any profit one realizes from one's exploitation of capital. In the early common law, rent was a fine paid, or an indictment or accusation. *See also:* lease, leasehold (non–freehold estate or non–freehold estate).

**abatement of rent (rent abatement)** Reduction in the amount owed in rent. An abatement of rent relieves a tenant of the duty to pay all or part of the rent owed to a landlord. Abatement may be based on contractual or equitable grounds, such as a landlord's failure to maintain the property as described in the rental contract or restitution of the tenant's out–of–pocket expenditures for property maintenance. *See also:* lease; landlord (lessor); landlord, landlord–tenant relationship.

**acceleration of rent (rent acceleration)** Upon tenant's default, all rent for the entire lease term is due. Rent acceleration is a demand by a landlord for the payment at one time of all rent due under a lease for the whole of its term. Rent acceleration may be a condition of the lease, which is also known as the payment of pre–paid rents, or it may be a provision in the lease allowing the landlord to elect, or requiring the tenant to pay, accelerated rents in the event of the tenant's default of the covenant of rents. Acceleration of rents must, however, be specified in a lease or specifically agreed to between landlord and tenant, as it is not a common law remedy for breach of the covenant of rents. *See also:* acceleration (accelerate or accelerated).

**economic rent (rentiers)** The surplus profits generated by any activity. Economic rent is a term used by economists to describe the unearned premium that some products or services command in the market, allowing them to fetch a higher price than their costs of production. This sense of rent differs from the rent paid for the use of land or buildings.

From an economic standpoint, economic rent is greater than the profit that would be reasonably necessary to generate the investment needed to sustain the profitable activity. It is excess to the value required to provide sufficient incentive to generate the activity. Thus, economic rent is similar to economic waste. A person who charges or receives such rents is a rentier and engages in rent seeking.

**rent seeking (rent seeker or rent-seeking)** Profits sought through market exploitation. Rent seeking is a term in economics for the pursuit of rent (in the general sense of profits and income, not just payments on a lease) through market exploitation, rather than through the production of goods and services or through trading. Examples of rent seeking that are often discussed are the exploitation of monopolies, free–rider opportunities, and the pursuit of preferential regulation and taxation. Rent seeking may also describe the deliberate generation of negative externalities.

**lock-box (lockbox arrangement)** A lease with rents paid to an agent to pay the landlord's debts. A lockbox arrangement is a structure of the payment of rents owed under a lease that ensures the payment of rents to a creditor of the landlord. The tenant pays an escrow agent or bank, which deducts the value from rents paid that equals the landlord's debt or debts, then credits the landlord's debt due to the landlord's account with the creditor, transferring only the remainder to the landlord. Such an arrangement is sometimes a condition of financing for leased properties.

**quit rents (perpetual rents)** Rents once paid in lieu of incidents and of all further rents. Quit rents were rents paid by tenants in England and the English colonies that exonerated the tenant from any further rent or service to the landlord. They were, in effect, very much like a purchase price, intended to be paid once and for all, representing the present value of the future annual payments that the landlord would otherwise receive. Even so, unless the landlord released the tenancy, a small, nominal rent would usually be owed annually. *See also:* quit.

**rent control law** Laws regulating the terms of leases. A rent control law is any federal, state, or municipal regulation of the terms of leases, particularly the rents for rental housing that may be charged or the rate at which rents may rise from one period to the next during the term of a lease or from one term to the next when a lease is renewed by the same tenant in the same leasehold. Although rent control laws are sometimes controversial, limiting the profit that a landlord may realize from the ownership of a building or property, challenges to such laws as being a taking of a property interest or an interference with contract have usually failed in the face of the state interest in the protection of the welfare of the citizenry in its need for housing.

**withholding of rent (rent withholding)**   The refusal of a tenant to pay rents to a landlord during a lease. The withholding of rent, generally, is the failure of a tenant to pay a landlord rents owed at the time they are owing. More specifically, the withholding of rent usually is intended as the denial of rents in response to the landlord's toleration of unsafe conditions or conditions that render the premises leased unfit for the use for which they are rented or unfit for human habitation. In many jurisdictions, statutes and ordinances have established a process for rent withholding. In some, the tenant may not withhold rent until a finding by a housing or building inspector qualifies the premises for withholding, and in some, the rent withheld must be paid either into a designated state agency or into an escrow account. In some jurisdictions, rent withholding is allowed under a repair–and–deduct rule allowing the withholding of rents to make essential repairs, and in other jurisdictions, rent withholding is only allowed when the landlord's conduct or inaction has resulted in constructive eviction or a violation of an implied covenant of habitability.

**rent strike**   An organized denial of rents by various tenants of one landlord. A rent strike is a collective refusal to pay rents to a landlord, usually by residential tenants. A rent strike that amounts to a communal withholding of rents in response to a violation of the leases of each by the landlord, resulting from a failure of the covenant of quiet enjoyment as to each is not actionable by the landlord in most jurisdictions. Likewise, a collective decision of tenants to deny rents to a landlord under a rent withholding law cannot lawfully give rise to an eviction or other response by the landlord. However, a rent strike in which some tenants encourage others to violate their leases may amount to tortious interference with a contract.

**repair and deduct**   A tenant's retention of rent to pay for repairs made to a tenancy. Repair and deduct is the action of a tenant in possession of leased premises with a material defect, which in some jurisdictions must be a defect that makes the premises uninhabitable, who repairs or pays for repairs to the premises and then deducts the actual cost of the repairs from rents paid to the landlord. The common law provided no basis for repair–and–deduct adjustments to rent, though in some jurisdictions the implied warranty of habitability has been judicially construed to include repair and deduct as an appropriate remedy, allowing any reasonable expense necessary to make the premises habitable. In some jursdictions, such deductions are possible either according to an express allowance in the lease or according to statute or ordinance in the jurisdiction of the premises. Some laws specify that tenant repair may only be made with prior written notice of the defects given to the landlord, followed by a period in which the landlord fails to remedy the defect. Some jurisdictions require notice to a public agency, and others specify that the deduction is limited in amount to a particular sum or the value of the rent for a given term.

**rental**   A place or thing that is rented, or anything related to it. Rental is a noun or an adjective related to the renting of a place or thing. Examples are many: the property rented is both rental and a rental, as in a rental car, which is also called "a rental." A rental agreement establishes a rental, which is usually a short hand term for a rental price, though it may also refer to a time period for the rental or any other term. A rental agent arranges a rental agreement, often collecting rental payments during the life of the rental.

**renunciation   (renounce   or   renounced   or renounceable)**   To make public one's rejection or abandonment of a right, interest, or position. Renunciation, the act of renouncing something, is a declaration to the world that a person rejects or abandons a claim, right, interest, or position. A renunciation must be knowing and intentional, which requires that a renunciation be made only by a person with legal capacity at the time of the renunciation. A renunciation is not temporary but permanent, and although in some circumstances a renunciation may itself be later repudiated, in most cases such an attempt is void, because once a right or interest is renounced, like an interest abandoned, it may only be reclaimed both if the renouncing party has not acted in a manner to forbid the revival of the renounced interest and if the interest had not been otherwise compromised so that it cannot be revived. Thus, for example, a renounced interest in a will may not be revived after the will has been probated.

A waiver or failure to exercise a right or interest does not amount to its renunciation. For example, a citizen may fail to assert or exercise a privilege from search without a warrant through the act of inviting a police officer to search a house, but such a failure to rely on a right is limited to the one invitation and cannot be inferred to have been a renunciation of the rights of the Fourth Amendment generally.

Renunciation may be inferred from language or conduct that clearly or unequivocally signals renunciation or that requires renunciation as a predicate to the conduct. Thus, a person who enjoys a title of nobility in a foreign state who takes an oath of citizenship thereby renounces that title as a matter of U.S. law.

Although most interests protected or created by law may be renounced, some are inalienable and incapable of renunciation. Thus, one may renounce one's citizenship, one's interests under a last will and testament, one's beneficial interest in a trust, one's third party benefit in a contract to which one is not a party, and in abandoning property, or quit claiming it to another, one renounces all ownership in it. One may renounce certain interests but not others, and no one may renounce, for instance one's interest not to be murdered.

Note: renunciation is sometimes confused with denunciation, which is quite different (though there is a relationship between the two actions). To renounce something is to give up something one has or might have; to denounce something is to repudiate it or criticize it. While one might denounce something and also renounce it, the two actions are independent unless context makes clear an implication that the denunciation amounts to renunciation (though history has many actions of public denunciation of privileges that continued to be quietly enjoyed).

### reorganization (reorg)
The creation of a new organizational structure. A reorganization has several senses. Most commonly, it is a process of reallocating personnel, assets, liabilities, or facilities in a given enterprise. In law, the two major forms of reorganization are a reorganization in bankruptcy and a corporate reorganization. The reorganization in bankruptcy, or Chapter 11 bankruptcy, is dealt with under that heading.

A corporate reorganization is more often a corporate transition intended to protect assets from claims against the corporation. In this sense, a reorganization is the creation of a new corporation by the old corporation, or, in any event, the transfer of some or all of the old company's assets to another company that has joint control or interlocking officers or directors with the old company, the transfer being only of assets and not of liabilities or claims. Thus, this form of reorganization leaves creditors or claimants against the old company with fewer assets to pursue to collect a judgment. Note: a common slang term for reorganization is its abbreviated form, reorg.

#### reorganization in bankruptcy or chapter eleven filing
*See:* bankruptcy, Chapter 11 filing (reorganization in bankruptcy or Chapter Eleven filing).

#### corporate reorganization
Material change of a corporation, especially of its ownership. A corporate reorganization as a matter of law differs from a managerial reorganization (which alters the structure of reporting among employees, divisions and offices, and officers) in that it alters some significant aspect of the company's form of ownership, assets, capital, location, identity, or form, the reporting of which would be of significance as a matter of tax reporting and structure. Corporate reorganizations identified under the Internal Revenue Code are denominated as A through G reorganizations.

The A reorganization is a statutory merger or consolidation in which one entity merges or consolidates with another, and there is a continuity of interest in the resulting entity from the prior entities, which requires at least 40% of the consideration to be stock in the resulting entity.

The B reorganization is a stock-for-stock exchange, an acquisition by one corporation in exchange solely for all or a part of its voting stock, of at least 80% of the voting stock and at least 80% of the total number of shares of all other classes of stock of another corporation.

The C reorganization is the acquisition by one corporation in exchange solely for all or part of its voting stock, of substantially all the properties of another corporation. In determining whether the exchange is solely for voting stock, the assumption by the acquiring corporation of a liability of the other, or the fact that property acquired is subject to a liability, shall be disregarded. The measure of substantially all assets is 90% of net assets or 70% of gross assets.

The D reorganization is a transfer by the acquiring corporation of all or a part of its assets to the target corporation. The measure of a D reorganization is that, immediately after the transfer, the transferor entity (or its shareholders, or both the company and its shareholders) has control of the transferee corporation.

An E reorganization is a recapitalization, which may occur many ways, including the issuance of preferred stock in exchange for bonds or outstanding shares of common stock; the issuance of new common stock in exchange for shares of outstanding preferred stock and dividends owed to stockholders; the exchange of old stock for new stock of the same class (such as old common stock for new common stock); the exchange of old bonds for new bonds with the same principal amount; and the issuance of stock in exchange for long-term bonds qualifying as a tax security.

An F reorganization does not involve a change of ownership or acquisition but is a mere change in identity, form, or place of organization, however the change is brought about.

A G reorganization is a transfer of some or all of an entity's assets to another entity, which is possible only in specific cases and by a qualified transaction.

*See also:* merger, corporate merger.

### repair (covenant of repair)
The condition of premises or a thing, or their improvement. Repair has several distinct meanings, the oldest being to return to some place, but more relevant to the law are two that relate to property: to make ready for use or that state of readiness for use. Thus, a property in good repair is ready for its intended use, and a property in bad repair is not. Repair, or a repair, is also the work needed to restore something that is no longer in good repair. There is no difference in the nouns repair and repairs in the sense of work done to restore a thing or premises.

A covenant of repair is a covenant to maintain premises in good repair. The covenant requires the use of ordinary care in the use of the premises, including ordinary cleaning and maintenance of premises and repair any defects that arise. Unless there is express language to the contrary, a convenant of repair is a covenant to maintain premises rather than to restore premises. In other words, the covenant obligates the covenantee to commit such repairs as are essential to keep the premises and structures in the condition in which the covenantee acquired possession, not to restore them to a better condition than when they were taken into the possession of covenantee.

#### repair and deduct
*See:* rent, withholding of rent, repair and deduct.

#### extraordinary repair
Unforeseen repairs required by an unusual occurrence. An extraordinary repair is any

form of repair other than the ordinary maintenance required of property, that is required because of an unusual event or circumstance that renders a building or fixture less fit for the use it was intended for at the time of the lease or sale, but which does not utterly destroy the building or fixture. Examples include damage from a fire, or damage to short-lived equipment installed in a long-used structure. Unless a lease specifies otherwise, a tenant is responsible for ordinary repairs during a tenancy, but the landlord is responsible for extraordinary repairs.

*See also:* ordinariness, extraordinariness (extraordinary or extraordinarily).

**repairs (subsequent remedial measure)** The restoration of a place or thing to its proper use. Repairs, or repair in this sense, include all forms of construction, replacement, or other work engaged in or required to restore the appearance and function of any form of thing, building, fixture, or land. A contract for repair of a broken or non-functioning chattel that does not specify the precise means is presumed to encompass the restoration of a thing to a reasonable state of operation, use, or appearance.

Repairs to premises or chattels are not generally admissible to demonstrate that the premises or chattels were once defective. Repairs may, however, be admissible under Federal Rule of Evidence 407 to prove the possibility of repair or ownership of the thing repaired (though not to prove negligence, defect, or culpability). The common law of evidence excluded such evidence because repair or improvement of a thing or condition does not always prove negligence in the thing's or location's prior construction or maintenance. As noted in the history of Rule 407, Baron Bramwell defended the rule saying, "because the world gets wiser as it gets older, therefore it was foolish before." Hart v. Lancashire & Yorkshire Railway Co., 21 L.T.R. N.S. 261, 263 (1869). Further, the rule prevents the possible use of repair evidence as an excuse from repairing a dangerous condition.

**reparation (reparations)** A remedy for a harm, especially as a means of reconciliation. Reparation is a generic term for a remedy for a harm. Reparation is often used as a term in lieu of damages to denote monetary relief that is not the result of the usual system of fault designation in litigation. For instance, states with no-fault insurance laws may use reparation to designate a payment made for a covered injury or damage. Some administrative awards of payment from one party to another are reparation orders.

Reparations are used specifically to denote any actions or payments intended as redress for an injury and as a means of reconciliation between a party or group that was injured and the party or group who injured them. Reparations are sometimes payments of money or transfers of supplies given by the state that initiates armed hostilities against another state, though these are usually a requirement of a peace treaty or surrender and are rarely a voluntary admission of responsibility by the state that makes them. Reparations are sometimes made to a group

that has been mistreated as a matter of government policy, as in the payments authorized by the U.S. Congress as reparations to American citizens of Japanese descent who were interned during World War II.

*See also:* redress (redressability); remedy (remediable or remedied or remedies).

**repatriation** To restore a person or thing to its place of origin. Repatriation is the restoration of a person or thing to its place or state of origin. Repatriation is often used to describe the transport of a person to that person's native state. Repatriation may also be used to describe the return of art or culturally significant objects from a state in which they are housed to their state of origin.

The federal Native American Graves Protection and Repatriation Act, P.L. 101–601, 104 Stat. 3048, (1991), codified at 25 U.S.C. § 3005 (2010), requires the repatriation to contemporary Indian tribes or nations of artifacts significant to the tribe's culture or religion, or human remains taken from the gravesites associated with the tribe or nation and now housed in a federal agency or museum.

**repeal** The revocation of a statute or rule by a later, similar enactment. Repeal is the revocation of a statute or other rule created by a form of enactment, that is revoked by the same body or entity that enacted it, using similar means. Repeal is usually of legislation, such as a statute or ordinance duly enacted that is revoked by the passage of a later statute or ordinance. The most common form of repeal by far is a statute or bill of repeal that is passed by a legislature that expressly repeals a statute passed earlier by the same body. Constitutional provisions may be repealed by amendment or by the passage of a new constitution. By custom, administrative orders are not repealed but withdrawn, rescinded, canceled, or revoked, though the effect of annulling the application of their effects is similar. A statute that is repealed is not annulled, and the repeal does operate retroactively to rescind any orders made under the repealed statute or law while it was in force, unless there is language or other clear evidence in the repealing legislation to the contrary. Repeal may be express or implied, which is to say that the later legislation may expressly state in words that the earlier legislation is repealed, but it might be silent as to its repealing effect though it still operates to repeal the earlier law.

**express repeal** A law stating that an earlier law is repealed. Express repeal is the revocation of an earlier law by means of a later law passed by the same body or by the same procedure as the earlier law, when the later law states in clear language that the earlier law is repealed, revoked, or otherwise no longer in force owing to the passage of the later law.

*See also:* expression (explicit or express).

**implied repeal (repeal by implication)** Unexpressed statutory repeal by a later, inconsistent statute. Implied repeal, or an appeal by implication, is the effect on one statute from a later statute that does not expressly repeal the earlier statute but that contains requirements that are inconsistent or contrary to the requirements of the earlier statute. Repeals by implication are not favored, which is to say that any interpretation of either or both statutes that would reach a different result is to be preferred to a determination of repeal by implication. Repeal by implication is to be found only when there is clear and manifest intent of the legislature in passing the later statute that it intended the earlier statute to be repealed. Otherwise, the later statute is to be construed as a continuation of the earlier statute, rather than as a substitute for it, and the first statute will continue in force, so that the two acts apply as if the first act was only amended and continues to apply from the time of its enactment. Thus, when two statutes regulate the same subject matter, both should be given effect if there is a reasonable and rational way to do so.

Implied repeal usually arises from either of two circumstances: First, if there are two acts regulating the same subject and the regulations present an irreconcilable conflict, the later statute prevails over the earlier, and — to the extent of the conflict — the later statute constitutes an implied repeal of the earlier one. Second, if the later act regulates the whole subject that is the focus of the earlier statute, and the later statute is clearly intended to substitute for the earlier statute or to create a comprehensive regulatory scheme in which the earlier requirement would be irrational, the later statutes will operate to repeal the earlier act.

An interesting question recurrently arises when a statute that impliedly repealed an earlier statute is itself repealed by a later statute: does statute 3's repeal of statute 2 (which impliedly repealed statute 1) effectively revive statute 1? The general rule is that if statute 2 indeed repealed statute 1, statute 1 is not revived unless there is clear language in statute 3 that does revive it.

**repealer clause or sunset clause**  See: legislation, sunset provision (repealer clause or sunset clause).

**repeat offender**  See: offender, repeat offender.

**replacement cost**  See: cost, replacement cost, replacement value; cost, replacement cost.

**replevin (writ of replevin or replevy or repleviable)**  An action to recover personal property wrongly held by the defendant. Replevin is an action at law for the permanent recovery of goods that are unlawfully in the possession of the defendant. It is also a pre-trial remedy that allows a plaintiff to take possession of goods before a suit to reclaim title or possession of the goods. Replevin is not a suitable remedy for the taking of goods to satisfy a judgment in general, which is done by attachment. Rather, replevin is used solely for the recovery of possession of goods, chattels, or movables, to which the plaintiff has a right of possession but that are nevertheless in the possession of the defendant.

Some jurisdictions have provided for replevin by having the plaintiff act upon a summary proceeding in which the magistrate, clerk, or judge authorizes the replevy of the defendant's goods without notice and without a hearing before a neutral magistrate with the discretion to grant or deny the order. Such procedures fail to provide sufficient assurance of the due process of law, and the use of such procedures without sufficient notice or hearing violates the rights of the defendant.

*See also:* repossession (repo or repossess); bond, replevin bond (claim–property bond or redelivery bond); remedy, pre–judgment remedy (pre–trial relief).

**replevin bond**  See: bond, replevin bond (claim–property bond or redelivery bond).

**replication (repliant)**  The plaintiff's reply in common–law pleading. A replication was a pleading under the common law prior to the adoption of modern rules of civil procedure, that was made by the plaintiff in reply to the defendant's answer. The party who files a replication is the repliant, although that party is also, in most cases, a plaintiff as well. The term is now more often encountered in its sense as a synonym for duplication, or the making of replicas, which, in environmental law, may mean the creation of a habitat similar to another habitat.

**reply**  A movant's pleading or argument made after the non–movant's response. A reply is the the response to the response to a motion, claim, or other petition to a court. That is, the reply is the usually the third argument or pleading to be submitted by two parties in an action, appeal, argument on motion, or any other adversary process.

The reply takes a variety of specific forms: In a civil action, the reply is the plaintiff's pleading filed in response to the defendant's answer, although this may be allowed only on a court order requiring its filing. In a criminal action, the reply is the government's pleading filed after the defendant's statement. In a motion filed with briefs, such as a motion for summary judgment, the reply is the brief filed by the movant after the non–movant has filed a response brief. Likewise, on appeal, the appellant or petitioner may ordinarily file a very short reply brief after the response brief is filed by the appellee or respondent.

*See also:* pleading, responsive pleading.

**repo**  See: security, securities, repo, reverse repo; security, securities, repo (repo sale).

**repo man**  See: repossession, repossession agent (repo man).

**repo or repossess**  See: repossession (repo or repossess).

**repo sale**  See: security, securities, repo (repo sale).

**reporter**

**reporter**  See: lawbook, reporter (case reports or case reporter or report).

**reporter or rpts. or rptr.**  See: reports, case reports (reporter or rpts. or rptr.).

**court reporter**  The person who transcribes the events at trial. The court reporter records the statements, motions, records of exhibits, testimony, and other events of record at a trial and transcribes the trial transcript, as well as recording and transcribing an official record of depositions, hearings and other matters that are officially recorded. In many states, court reporters are examined and licensed as Certified Court Reporters. Reporters are now often trained in vocational schools or colleges, and in 2008, the National Court Reporters Association (NCRA) had certified about 20 programs. The minimum standard of proficiency for certification by the NCRA is 225 words per minute.

**reporter of decisions**  The individual who reports judicial opinions of a given court. The reporter of decisions is an individual who collects, transcribes, reports, and summarizes judicial opinions. English reports and early U.S. reports were transcribed by the reporter, who often sat in the courtroom and wrote notes while the judges gave their spoken, unwritten opinions from the bench. Early reporters in England included Sir James Dyer, Sir Edmund Plowden, and, perhaps most notably, Sir Edward Coke and Sir James Burrow. Coke and Burrow successively developed the form of reports in a manner that greatly influenced the form and structure of the judge's own opinions. Unofficial reports were common in the American colonies and in the early United States, and reports were made by lawyers both for publication and, like their English antecedents, for the attorney's own use. Both Thomas Jefferson and James Madison wrote case reports. Unlike the English practice, soon after independence, states in the United States began appointing official reporters of decisions, whose reports would be a matter of public record.

Early official reporters in the U.S. included James Kent in New York, Alexander Dallas in Pennsylvania, Ephraim Kirby in Connecticut, and Ephraim Williams in Massachusetts. The U.S. Supreme Court appointed Dallas its first Reporter, more or less by default as the Court then sat in Philadelphia. His reports suffered from delay, omission, and error, as did those of the second Reporter, William Cranch. The Court's first professional Reporter was Henry Wheaton, whose collaboration with Justice Joseph Story established a routine of careful collection, transcription and summary that persists to the present. Today, most judges issue written opinions, which simplifies the process of reporting. The title "Reporter of Decisions" has been used in the U.S. Supreme Court since 1953.

*See also:* reports, case reports, nominative reports (nominate reports or named reports).

**reporter's privilege**  *See:* privilege, reporter's privilege.

## reports

**case reports (reporter or rpts. or rptr.)**  Published collections of judicial opinions ruling on motions, trials, and appeals. Case reports are the volumes of printed opinions of justices, judges, and magistrates issued in the resolution of disputes on appeal, at trial, and following motions and hearings. Case reports are either official or unofficial, though in most instances the unofficial reports are authoritative and may be cited as a valid source for the opinion.

In 1853, John Bouvier noted that the number of reports had by then increased to an inconvenient extent and warned of the serious evil their continued growth might portend. This increase did indeed occur, and a reasonably full set of case reports at the end of the twentieth century would include all of the volumes in two official and one unofficial reports of opinions of the U.S. Supreme Court, three series of reports of federal courts of appeals, two series of reports of opinions of lower federal courts, several series of reports from most U.S. jurisdictions, and the regional state reports of the West Company, as well as the reports of several foreign jurisdictions, conservatively requiring storage of 100,000 volumes, not counting digests and citators that are helpful in their use. This scale provoked two responses, the first being the increasingly draconian fight against unpublished opinions, the second being the growing practice of electronic publication. As of 2010, the United States Supreme Court and a near majority of states publish official and citable opinions online.

*See also:* opinion, judicial opinion.

**headnote**  A preliminary summary of a point of law. A headnote is a brief summary of a point of law expressed in a case report, which is usually written by the reporter or an editor rather than the judge. The headnotes of an opinion, like the syllabus, are not parts of the opinion per se and are not to be cited as authority.

**nominative reports (nominate reports or named reports)**  Reports known by the name of their reporters. Nominative reports are reports of judicial decisions that are known by the name of the reporter. From the 1500s until the advent of official reports or the continuity of long-published private reports, most reports were nominative. English reports by Coke and Burrow were particularly influential in the development of reporting style, but reports by U.S. reporters such as Thomas Jefferson became highly prized owing to the later significance of their service. In their early years, most states had nominative reports, some of which have been renumbered into an official report series. Note: there is no difference between a reference to a nominative reporter, nominate reporter, or named reporter, other than a few preferences among publishers and reporters over time.

The most famous nominative reports in the United States are those of the U.S. Supreme Court, which were titled and numbered by the name of the official Reporter until the late nineteenth century. A table for the conversion of these citations to citations in the United States Reports follows:

Black. Jeremiah Sullivan Black (1861–1862) (1–2 Black = 66–67 U.S.)

1 Black 66 U.S.

2 Black 67 U.S.

Cranch. William Cranch (1801–1815)
(1–9 Cranch= 5–13 U.S.)
 1 Cranch 5 U.S.
 2 Cranch 6 U.S.
 3 Cranch 7 U.S.
 4 Cranch 8 U.S.
 5 Cranch 9 U.S.
 6 Cranch 10 U.S.
 7 Cranch 11 U.S.
 8 Cranch 12 U.S.
 9 Cranch 13 U.S.
Dallas. Alexander J. Dallas (1790–1800)
(1–4 Dallas= 1–4 U.S.)
 1 Dallas 1 U.S.
 2 Dallas 2 U.S.
 3 Dallas 3 U.S.
Howard. Benjamin Chew Howard (1843–1860)
(1–24 Howard = 42–65 U.S.)
 1 Howard 42 U.S.
 2 Howard 43 U.S.
 3 Howard 44 U.S.
 4 Howard 45 U.S.
 5 Howard 46 U.S.
 6 Howard 47 U.S.
 7 Howard 48 U.S.
 8 Howard 49 U.S.
 9 Howard 50 U.S.
 10 Howard 51 U.S.
 11 Howard 52 U.S.
 12 Howard 53 U.S.
 13 Howard 54 U.S.
 14 Howard 55 U.S.
 15 Howard 56 U.S.
 16 Howard 57 U.S.
 17 Howard 58 U.S.
 18 Howard 59 U.S.
 19 Howard 60 U.S.
 20 Howard 61 U.S.
 21 Howard 62 U.S.
 22 Howard 63 U.S.
 23 Howard 64 U.S.
 24 Howard 65 U.S.
Peters. Richard Peters (1828–1842)
(1–16 Peters = 26–41 U.S.)
 1 Peters 26 U.S.
 2 Peters 27 U.S.
 3 Peters 28 U.S.
 4 Peters 29 U.S.
 5 Peters 30 U.S.
 6 Peters 31 U.S.
 7 Peters 32 U.S.
 8 Peters 33 U.S.
 9 Peters 34 U.S.
 10 Peters 35 U.S.
 11 Peters 36 U.S.
 12 Peters 37 U.S.
 13 Peters 38 U.S.
 14 Peters 39 U.S.
 15 Peters 40 U.S.
 16 Peters 41 U.S.
Wallace. John William Wallace (1863–1874)
(1–23 Wall. = 68–90 U.S.)

 1 Wallace 68 U.S.
 2 Wall. 69 U.S.
 3 Wall. 70 U.S.
 4 Wall. 71 U.S.
 5 Wall. 72 U.S.
 6 Wall. 73 U.S.
 7 Wall. 74 U.S.
 8 Wall. 75 U.S.
 9 Wall. 76 U.S.
 10 Wall. 77 U.S.
 11 Wall. 78 U.S.
 12 Wall. 79 U.S.
 13 Wall. 80 U.S.
 14 Wall. 81 U.S.
 15 Wall. 82 U.S.
 16 Wall. 83 U.S.
 17 Wall. 84 U.S.
 18 Wall. 85 U.S.
 19 Wall. 86 U.S.
 20 Wall. 87 U.S.
 21 Wall. 88 U.S.
 22 Wall. 89 U.S.
 23 Wall. 90 U.S.
Wheaton. Henry Wheaton (1816–1827)
(1–12 Wheat. = 14–25 U.S.)
 1 Wheat. 14 U.S.
 2 Wheat. 15 U.S.
 3 Wheat. 16 U.S.
 4 Wheat. 17 U.S.
 5 Wheat. 18 U.S.
 6 Wheat. 19 U.S.
 7 Wheat. 20 U.S.
 8 Wheat. 21 U.S.
 9 Wheat. 22 U.S.
 10 Wheat. 23 U.S.
 11 Wheat. 24 U.S.
*See also:* reporter, reporter of decisions.

**repose**   Rest, or a time when an action or claim is no longer active. Repose is rest, a time or state of relief and quietude. In law, repose is the laying to rest of an action or claim, usually at a given time or after a period has elapsed. In its broadest sense, there are various doctrines of repose, which include not only the doctrines of limitations and statutes of limitations but also the equitable doctrine of laches, marketable title and root of title statutes, and the constitutional and jurisprudential restraint on ex post facto laws.

*See also:* time, time immemorial (time of memory or immemorial possession); time; limitation, limitation of actions, statute of repose.

**repossession (repo or repossess)**   The creditor's seizure of a debtor's collateral securing a debt in default. Repossession is the private action of a creditor or, more often, an agent employed by a creditor, to take possession of a chattel that is subject to a security interest as collateral for a debt owed to the creditor on which the debtor has defaulted. Repossession is also used by lessors or lessors' agents to regain possession of leased property when the lessee has defaulted on the lease or the lease is terminated and the leased goods are not returned. In either case, repossession is usually a matter of self-help by the owner or creditor, without the benefit of a court order (such as claim and delivery, replevin, or attachment). Most states by statute require a party or agent engaging in repossession to notify the sheriff or local police to assure there is no breach of the peace during the repossession.

The repossession is lawful under the security agreement or lease, which effectively transfers title to the repossessor and (in most cases) confers a right to enter the premises of the debtor to recover the secured or leased goods. Even so, a repossessing party or agent may not commit a breach of the peace or other crime while engaging in the seizure, and a battery, assault, trespass beyond the scope of license, or other tort is also actionable.

*See also:* replevin (writ of replevin or replevy or repleviable); self, self help (self-help).

**claim and delivery**  A prejudgment seizure of disputed goods to secure them against a final judgment. Claim and delivery is a statutory procedure for a hearing to allow the prejudgment seizure of goods whose ownership is claimed by the plaintiff, though the goods are in the possession of the defendant. Claim and possession is a successor proceeding to replevin, but unlike most replevin procedures, which did not require a hearing prior to allowing the plaintiff to seize property under a claim of superior title, claim and delivery requires a judicial proceeding prior to an order to take custody of the goods.

*See also:* repossession (repo or repossess); replevin (writ of replevin or replevy or repleviable).

**debtor's rights**  The rights of a debtor against the creditor in repossession. A debtor's rights include any assurances that are agreed between the debtor and creditor at the time the security interest is created. The Uniform Commercial Code provides further rights, regardless of their statement in agreement. The debtor may demand that the creditor act with due care to preserve the collateral and to be notified before the creditor disposes of the collateral. Regardless of demand, the debtor is entitled to a remittance of any surplus over the amount of the indebtedness that the creditor receives from the sale of the collateral, and the debtor is entitled to damages for the creditor's failure to comply with any provisions of the UCC.

**repossession agent (repo man)**  A person or entity who seizes collateral for a debt in default. A repossession agent, or a repo man, is a person or entity that engages in a repossession on behalf of a landlord, creditor, or other party with a lawful claim to title of the property held without license by another. A repossession agent is usually required to register with the state and to maintain a bond against wrongful or mistaken repossession. In most jurisdictions, repossession agents are required to notify local sheriffs or other law enforcement prior to a repossession in order to allow police notice to maintain the peace and to avoid a mistaken claim of robbery or theft against the repossession agent. In all jurisdictions,

repossession agents are forbidden to use force or a threat of force against individuals, and a repossession agent is not immune generally from other criminal laws or civil claims that might arise from a breach of the peace caused by the repossession.

**representation (represent or representative)**
To present an argument or information for oneself or for others. Representation is a broad term for the presentation of something to others on one's behalf or on behalf of another party, whether the thing presented is a petition, argument, claim, statement of fact, or depiction.

Representation may be of an idea reduced to words, as in oratory or rhetoric. In this sense, every legal argument is a representation of a position. A representation may be an image, as in a painting or sculpture. Or, a representation may be a presentation of data, such as a statistical sample of a broader set of data.

Representation is often a form of agency. In such cases, a representation suggests an integration of the position of the representative with that of the parties represented. For example, a representative may make a representation on the representative's own behalf, as a statement representing the truth in some matter or as a statement of the representative's own position or argument, integrated with that made as an agent for another, such as lawyer representing a client or a Senator representing a constituent, or an executor representing a decedent's estate.

Representation may be made in a deliberate form of agency, such as a legislator's representation of the members of a constituency. Or, it may arise owing to an alignment of interests between parties, as when a parent's role in litigation is deemed by a court to be sufficient to represent the interests of the parent's child, who is not present before the court.

**representation of multiple parties**  *See:* conflict, conflict of interest, representation of multiple parties.

**representation as statement of fact**  To produce a thing, or to describe a thing or condition. A representation is a statement that some condition or state of affairs is true. A representation may be made orally or in writing, and it may be made expressly or by implication, just as it may be made affirmatively or negatively. An express representation is a statement that asserts something to be the case, to be a true and accurate depiction of the condition or state of affairs at the time relative to the statement. A representation by implication arises when a person makes a statement in such conditions that the only logical, or at least a reasonable and likely, significance of the statement is the representation, such as when an affirmative term is given in answer to a question, the affirmation is taken as a representation adopting the implication of the question as uttered. An affirmative representation is to represent something as true, while a negative representation is to represent something as false.

*See also:* statement.

**false representation**  A misrepresentation offered as a fact. A false representation is the representation of any condition or situation that is not in fact true. A false representation may be innocent or knowing, though in general, the term is used in the sense of a knowing false representation. An innocent false representation is a representation made in good faith by a person who relies on information that is false, misunderstood, or insufficient. A knowing false representation is made either with an intent to mislead or a disregard for whether the hearer or reader is mislead, when the person making the representation knows, or has sufficient related knowledge that the person reasonably should know, is not true in fact. A false representation is a deliberate misrepresentation.

A material false representation, whether innocent or knowing, that is made to a party with which one is negotiating a contract that is relied upon by the other party in drafting or accepting a draft of the contract is sufficient to void the contract. To make knowing false representation to a police officer on a matter of police concern is both an offense in itself in many jurisdictions or the offense of obstruction of justice.

**legal representation (representation by counsel)**  A client's statement or action made by an attorney as its agent. Legal representation is the agency by which an attorney at law acts in any way on behalf of a client. Legal representation, and the identity of the client, depends on whom the lawyer represents, not necessarily on the party who engages the lawyer or who reimburses the lawyer, as these may be quite distinct. Legal representation may occur regardless of whether the client is present at the place in which the lawyer is acting for the client, and the action or statement by a client does not terminate the ongoing representation of the lawyer for the client in an appearance, negotiation, proceeding, or other circumstance. Legal representation is deliberate, and the relationship of representation must be commenced knowingly and intentionally by both the lawyer and the client or an agent of the client. Legal representation may be distinct from acts of an attorney, such as legal counsel or advice. Legal representation may be limited to a given cause, issue, or proceeding, and it may terminate at a given time, although certain obligations of the attorney persist, such as the duty to maintain client confidences or to avoid a conflict of interest.

*See also:* attorney (attorney at law or attorney-at-law or attorneys at law); lawyer.

**entity representation (organizational client)**  A lawyer representing an entity represents the the whole organization and not just an officer. Entity representation is legal representation of an organization, whether it is a partnership, corporation, or unincorporated association. A corporation or other entity may not appear in court except through a lawyer. A lawyer engaged in entity representation does not represent the officers or members directly, and when their interests and the entity's interests are potentially adverse, the lawyer may not represent the individual but must represent the entity unless both parties waive the conflict, and the conflict is not one that is so significant that it cannot be waived.

*See also:* entity (legal entity).

**joint representation (concurrent representation or multiple representation)**  One lawyer's representation of two or more parties in the same action. Joint representation is the representation of more than one party in a single cause of action, whether the cause is civil or criminal. Joint representation is the same as concurrent multiple representation, in that the same lawyer represents multiple parties concurrently. In a civil action, the lawyer has a duty to avoid any conflict of interest that would prevent the attorney from adequate and full representation of all parties and to disclose to all represented parties any potential conflict of interest, allowing the parties to waive the potential conflict or to limit the representation so as to abate the potential conflict. In a criminal action, the potential for a conflict requires the court to inquire into the attorney's representation and the propriety of the joint representation in order to ensure that each criminal defendant is assured constitutionally adequate and independent representation.

*See also:* conflict, conflict of interest.

**scope of representation**  Limits to a representation by subject, proceeding, time, tactics, or goals. The scope of representation is the extent of representation agreed between the lawyer and the client or inherent in a given representation. The scope of representation is best agreed between the lawyer and client at the start of a relationship, although it may change of necessity as the needs of the client change or are better understood by the lawyer. The scope may be limited by the subject matter for which the lawyer is retained as representative of the client, by the forum in which the lawyer is expected to represent the client, by the time during which representation will occur, by the tactics that the lawyer will pursue or assist the client in pursuing, or by the client's goals in seeking the representation. The scope of representation is inherently limited by the law and by the ethical and professional obligations of the lawyer.

**successive representation**  Representation of a new defendant after representing a co-defendant or witness. Successive representation is the representation of a party to an action in court, having earlier represented a party with distinct or adverse interests or a witness who might be called to give evidence before or during trial. There is a potential of conflict of interest in the later representation because of the potential that the lawyer might not be as zealous in examining a witness whom the lawyer had once represented or might be foreclosed from asking certain questions owing to a duty to protect the former client's confidences.

Successive representation in criminal trials raises a potential of a conflict of interest when the attorney for a criminal defendant has previously represented a co-defendant or a witness whose testimony might be called at trial. Rules of professional conduct limit such representation, and in the event of such representation, if the circumstances suggest that there is indeed a conflict, the court must examine the potential of that conflict to ensure the defendant is provided with adequate representation. *See also:* conflict, conflict of interest.

**material representation**   A representation on which the hearer is likely to rely. A material representation is a representation on a matter, the subject of which or the form of representation of which render a hearer or reader of the representation likely to rely on the representation. Materiality in this context depends not only on the goals or interests of the speaker and hearer but also on the nature of the representation itself, which might change the prior goals or interests of the hearer. In a negotiation, any representation of fact essential to an understanding of one of the objects of the negotiation is inherently material.

**misrepresentation**   The presentation of false information on which another is bound to rely. Misrepresentation is the communication of information that is inaccurate or incomplete to a recipient so that the recipient is likely to form a false understanding of some circumstance relevant to the relationship between the communicator and the recipient. Misrepresentation is an element of several crimes, including fraud, as well as of private actions in tort and a basis for avoiding a contract.

Misrepresentation in tort may be either intentional or negligent. An intentional misrepresentation results when the communicator knows the information provided is false but provides it with the intent that the recipient will rely upon it, which the recipient does to the recipient's harm or loss. Intentional misrepresentation is the basis for the action for deceit. A negligent misrepresentation results when the communicator provides information upon which the recipient relies to the recipient's detriment, when the information was false and the communicator was negligent in ascertaining its truth or falsity. Not every jurisdiction recognizes an action for negligent misrepresentation, though all do for intentional misrepresentation. In federal law, misrepresentation is an exception under the Federal Tort Claims Act, and no recovery may be had either for express misrepresentation by a federal officer or for negligent or intentional misrepresentation of government information.

Misrepresentation in the inducement of a person to enter a contract is a basis for the person induced to avoid the contract. The party that knowingly misrepresented some material fact may not, however, avoid the contract on that basis. Misrepresentation is also a basis for rejecting performance as insufficient and asserting that the misrepresenting party is in breach, the damages for which are the difference between the performance that was bargained for and the performance that occurred in fact.

*concealment of facts*   Misrepresentation may occur through the omission of information as well as by the commission of false speech, if the defendant has a duty of speech, either arising from a transaction, such as an obligation to disclose information like latent defects in property known to a seller, or from a relationship, such as a confidential relationship or position of trust. A duty to disclose one datum may arise from the disclosure of others, as when a party discloses one defect, leading to a reasonable inference that there are not any others.

**intentional misrepresentation (fraudulent misrepresentation)**   The communication of information one knows to be false with the intent to make another rely on it. Intentional misrepresentation, or fraudulent misrepresentation, is an intentional tort in which a communicator provides information known to the communicating person or entity to be false, with the intent that the recipient rely upon the false information, which the recipient does to the harm or loss of the recipient. The nature of the information communicated must, in the nature of the claim, be information that is susceptible to truth or falsity, and the reliance of the recipient must be genuine and harmful. The recipient may recover the damages suffered as well as punitive or exemplary damages from the communicator.

**representation by entity**   A representation by an officer, director, or agent. A representation by an entity is a representation by any officer, director, agent, or designated representative made within the scope of the office or agency, both as to a given statement and as to a course of dealing or business. An entity acts only through its individuals, and an entity is held to the representations made on its behalf by individuals authorized, or apparently authorized, to act for it. A representation by an agent of an entity in a given place may render that place a place of the entity's business.

**virtual representation**   The judicially presumed agency of a party in an action for a non-party. Virtual representation, in civil procedure, is a metaphor for the relationship of a party before the court in a civil action for another party who is not present in the action, such that the party who was not present but presumed to have been represented in the first action by the other party is precluded from bringing a later action in its own right, whether the bar is a matter of collateral estoppel or res judicata. To support a finding of virtual representation, the later court ordinarily must find that a party in the earlier action was in some sense a proper agent for the party seeking to bring the later action, so as to support preclusion of the later claim. This agency may arise because the party seeking to bring a later action was a dependent, assignee, or successor in interest to a party in the first action or the party in the second action was represented, such as a member of a class who was given notice of a class action by the class-representative party.

The idea of virtual representation arose first not in law but in politics. The British Parliament was said to virtually represent the colonies in 1766, although no colonist was a member of the Parliament.

*See also:* res, res judicata (res adjudicata); res, res judicata, collateral estoppel.

**representative**   A person who serves in place of another person or people. A representative is a person who represents another person, a group of persons, or an entity. The sense of representative is one of greater independence and wider discretion than that of most forms of agency, and though a representative must act always to the benefit and in the interest of those represented, the representative is presumed to be capable of acting in the best interests of the represented without regard to the represented's consent or instruction. There are a variety of forms of representative.

A representative in an elected office is a person who represents the citizens in the jurisdiction or electoral region from which the representative is elected. Although in a generic sense, all elected officials are said to represent the will of the people, the specific offices of Representative are held by the members of the more populous house in the legislatures of most states, and a Member of Congress is a Representative, being a member of the House of Representatives.

A personal representative is a person appointed to manage the affairs required in the estate of a decedent. Although some states employ the term personal representative instead of the customary terms of executor or administrator, the functions of the personal representative by any of the three titles are similar, in liquidating the estate, settling claims of creditors and taxes, and distributing the assets to devisees, legatees, and heirs.

A representative by succession in interest is a successor in interest who stands in the shoes of a predecessor. Thus, an heir or assign may be the representative of a decedent or assignor, and a successor corporation may be the representative of a predecessor entity.

**representative capacity**   *See:* capacity, capacity as agency, capacity as agent (representative capacity).

**representative capacity as defendant**   *See:* capacity, defendant capacity, official capacity (representative capacity as defendant).

**representative recall**   *See:* recall, representative recall (election recall or recall election or recall referendum).

**accredited representative**   A person accorded credentials to represent a nation, a union, or another organization. An accredited representative is a representative of a nation-state, a labor union, a charitable organization, or any other group who has been accorded credentials required to engage in that representation. There are many forms, for example: An ambassador or other diplomatic or consular agent is an accredited representative of a state; a union's chairman or designee is an accredited representative of a union; a representative of a charitable or other organization who is designated by that organization and recognized by the Board of Immigration Appeals is an accredited representative of an immigrant client.

**legal representative (legal-personal representative)**   An agent in a legal capacity, such as a lawyer, guardian, or executor. Legal representative has a variety of meanings, which may only be understood by context. In general, a legal representative is an attorney at law who acts as an agent with powers of negotiation as well as a legal counsel to the principal when representing the principal to third parties. A legal representative, however, is a generic term for any agent in a capacity affecting legal interests, such as an agent in fact with legal authority to act on the principal's behalf, as in the legal authority to receive service of process against the principal. When used in a last will and testament, a statement that some person or entity shall act as the testator's legal representative is usually a statement of designation that the legal representative shall serve as the executor or personal representative of the estate in probate.

**personal representative**   The person charged with probating a will or administering an estate. A personal representative is the individual who is appointed by a court either to probate a last will and testament or to administer the estate of a decedent. It is the generic term for both executors and administrators, and it is the term employed in states that have adopted the Uniform Probate Code. The personal representative is responsible for proving the will (if there is one), inventorying the assets of the estate, settling claims against it and taxes owed by it, distributing all bequests, devises, legacies, and inheritances, making a final accounting, and closing the estate.

*See also:* administrator, administrator of estate (administratrix or administrator for the estate); executor (executrix); representative, legal representative (legal-personal representative).

**reprieve**   A delay in the execution of a criminal sentence. A reprieve is a suspension of a criminal sentence, a delay during which the effect of the sentence is withheld. A reprieve is inherently in place only for a time, after which the sentence will commence or recommence, this being the difference between a reprieve and a pardon or commutation. A reprieve can, however, be extended. A reprieve is usually issued by the executive, and in most state laws it is either an express power given to the governor or implied in the power of pardon. A stay of sentence or delay in execution ordered by a court may not technically be called a reprieve but can have that effect.

At common law, the reprieve took three forms, the reprieve ex mandato regis, or by order of the Crown, which is the antecedent to the modern executive reprieve; the reprieve ex arbitrio judicis, or by the discretion of the court, which is the antecedent to the modern stay; and the reprieve ex necessitate legis, or as required by law, which is the antecedent to the modern administrative and executive decrees granted when a condition of law requires it to be, such as in the event of loss of capacity or a medical emergency.

*See also:* stay.

**reprimand**    A chastising statement to a person who acted wrongfully. A reprimand is a rebuke, a statement declaring a person to have acted wrongly, to act as a punishment for the wrongdoing and to deter similar conduct in the future. The reprimand may be intended as a warning that wrongdoing has been noticed and will be more severely punished in the future. It is also a punishment for officials whose loss of reputation is thought to be sufficient for the wrong committed.

The reprimand of an attorney may be made by a judge, the judges of a court, a bar in which an attorney is licensed, or a disciplinary committee. In general, a reprimand is a less serious punishment than a suspension or disbarment, though some jurisdictions have orders of censure that are less significant. In most jurisdictions, reprimands are usually issued as a matter of public notice, though in some cases a reprimand is made confidentially.

*See also:* punishment, shaming punishment (shame as punishment); shame.

**reprisal**    A harm inflicted in retaliation for a perceived offense. A reprisal is a response intended to punish a person, entity, or state for conduct against the party engaged in the reprisal. Reprisal is usually argued to be a form of self-help intended both to restore a sense of aggrieved honor or sovereignty and to deter future aggression or harm. In most cases, however, reprisal begets reprisal, and international law now condemns the use of force in reprisal, although lesser sanctions in reprisal are allowed within the limits of retorsion. Reprisal, or an act borne of a desire for vengeance, is no defense to a crime or an intentional tort.

Reprisal in an employment context is a job action in response to some conduct believed to be by the employee. Reprisal is forbidden against an employee who engages in conduct protected by law, such as the disclosure of a hazardous condition or unlawful practice protected by a whistleblower law, or who organizes a union in a manner protected by law. Likewise, reprisal is forbidden against an employee who does not tolerate unlawful conduct, such as sexual harassment or discrimination on the basis of protected characteristics.

*See also:* retorsion (retorsive or retortion).

**republic**    *See:* government, forms of government, republic.

**Republican Form of Government Clause**    *See:* constitution, U.S. Constitution, clauses, Republican Form of Government Clause (Guarantee Clause).

**republicanism**    *See:* government, forms of government, republicanism.

**repudiation (repudiate)**    The rejection of a claim, interest, right, or relationship. Repudiation is the act of renouncing something, including a refusal to accept its benefit or to perform its duties, or abandoning any benefits or claims derived from it in the past. Repudiation takes many forms in law: a repudiation of a contract or agreement is the rejection of the performance of duties required by it, and so a repudiation of an engagement to marry is to withdraw the promise to marry. A repudiation of testimony is a rejection of the testimony as true. A repudiation of a last will and testament is the refusal of a court to probate a will owing to a defect in its creation. A repudiation of a trust is the denial by a trustee that property held by the trustee is subject to trust.

**anticipatory repudiation**    Rejection of a contract prior to the time of performance. Anticipatory repudiation is the more accurate term for anticipatory breach, an act or statement by one party to a contract that demonstrates to the other party that the first party will not perform obligations under the contract at the time required. The repudiator may renounce its performance of the contract expressly, amounting to express anticipatory repudiation. The repudiator might also engage in conduct from which the other party may reasonably infer repudiation, including conduct that makes performance impossible or unusually difficult (such as closing a factory from which performance would be rendered or entering into insolvency). This is implied anticipatory repudiation.

In the event the repudiatee acquires knowledge of conditions suggesting implied anticipatory repudiation the repudiatee may require further assurances. In the event sufficient further assurances are not provided by the putative repudiator, the repudiatee is entitled to treat the repudiatee as in anticipatory breach.

In the event of express repudiation or a refusal of sufficient further assurances, a repudiatee may elect among several options. Under the Uniform Commercial Code the repudiatee may treat the other party as if it is in breach of the contract, even though the time of the performance required has not yet been reached. The repudiatee may then seek damages or, in some circumstances, specific performance. Or, the repudiatee may elect to await performance by the repudiator and then sue for damages. Or, the repudiator may seek to abandon or to rescind the contract.

*See also:* breach, breach of contract, anticipatory breach; assurances (further assurances or adequate assurance of performance); renunciation (renounce or renounced or renounceable).

*insolvency as anticipatory repudiation*    If a party becomes insolvent, it is reasonable for the other party to infer that the insolvent party lacks the financial ability necessary to continue doing business on the basis contracted. Financial instability means not only that the party lacks funds presently, but also that it will not be able to obtain credit either. Under these circumstances, the party on the other side is entitled to assume that the contract has been anticipatorily repudiated.

**repudiatee** A party to a contract that the other party has repudiated. A repudiatee is a contracting party on notice of acts by another party that constitute either an express or implied repudiation of the contract. A repudiatee must act within a reasonable time from learning of the conditions of repudiation to mitigate losses from the repudiation and non–performance of the contract, but the repudiatee may recover damages reasonably suffered from the repudiator.

**repugnancy (repugnant)** Inconsistent terms or contradictory requirements. A repugnancy is an inconsistency or contradiction. It is still occasionally used in the interpretation of contracts but is more often used to describe statutes. As a matter of contracts, wills, trusts, deeds, and other instruments, a repugnant clause or language is inconsistent with the rest of the instrument. As far as possible, the repugnant language should be interpreted to be consistent with the whole instrument while still giving the repugnant language meaning and effect. In a written contract, the interpretation must be based on the writing alone in an attempt to understand the parties' intent, and it is presumed the parties did not intend the inconsistent clause to have no meaning.

Famous as a result of its use in Marbury v. Madison, repugnancy is a conclusion of interpretation of statutes. As between two texts or laws, if the later law is incompatible with the earlier law, the later law is repugnant to the earlier law. As between statutes, the result is that the earlier law is impliedly appealed (if there is no other interpretative compromise that may reconcile them, in which case the later statute was not truly repugnant to the first). As between a constitutional text or principle and a statute or other law, the statute is repugnant if it cannot be interpreted consistently with the requirements of the constitution, in which case the statute is void.

**reputation** An opinion about any thing that is widely held among members of a community. Reputation is an opinion held by various people in a community about a person or entity, about a condition or a fact, about an institution or state. The specific aspects of reputation may include various details of fact or putative fact. Reputation may be a matter of degree regarding particular qualities, such as to matters of character, honesty, or trustworthiness, which might not admit to perfect judgment but to estimates or percentages. Reputation is generally most significant within a community in which the object of reputation is known or an object of common knowledge or discussion, though this community may or may not be geographically defined.

The reputation or "good name" of an individual, institution, family, or state has value that is to be protected by law, whether the sense of reputation at issue in a given dispute of law is understood as an interest in property, dignity, or honor. Acts that wrongly injure any aspect of reputation by presenting false information or claims or putting the person, group, or state in a false light may amount to defamation or a delict.

*See also:* hearsay, hearsay exception, hearsay allowed regardless of witness availability, reputation; hearsay, hearsay exception, hearsay allowed regardless of witness availability, reputation, reputation as to character.

**reputation as to character** *See:* hearsay, hearsay exception, hearsay allowed regardless of witness availability, reputation, reputation as to character.

**request for admissions** *See:* discovery, request for admissions; admission, request for admissions.

**request for production** *See:* discovery, documentary discovery, request for production (production request or request to produce or inspect documents).

**request to inspect property** *See:* discovery, discovery of physical evidence, request to inspect property.

**requirements contract** *See:* contract, specific contracts, supply contract, requirements contract.

**requisition** A request made, according to a right that it be honored. A requisition is a statement of what is required, a claim for personnel, equipment, property, or money, made within a context in which the claimant has a right to demand the provision of the people or things required. A government requisition is a compensable taking of property. A requisition within an entity is an order for such supplies to be delivered from the entity's stores or stock. A prisoner requisition is a request from one executive to another to extradite a prisoner between states. Note: requisition is both a noun and a verb.

**res** The thing. Res is Latin for the thing, a generic pronoun that may serve as English does for the following: it, that, the thing, all of it, the thingamajig, a doohickey, or a whatsit. In law, res is a particularly helpful pronoun, as it may refer to the whole of the things in a particular category, such as the res of a trust, as well as a particular object or property even when that object is unidentified, or for any matter, even if it is abstract or metaphysical, such as an issue or claim of a lawsuit, as in res judicata. *See also:* rem.

**res gestae witness** *See:* witness, res gestae witness.

**res ipsa loquitur** *See:* negligence, res ipsa loquitur.

**res judicata** *See:* dismissal, grounds for dismissal, res judicata.

**res as trust corpus** The whole property of the trust. The res, when speaking of a trust, is the entire property subject to the trust, including all of the property (including cash and intangibles) initially given or taken into trust, as well as all assets generated from that property whether by appreciation, investment, sale, or other conversions or commingling. Note: there is no great difference between the res of a trust or the corpus of the trust.

**res gestae (res gesta)** The matter in question. Res gestae, Latin for the deed (or, the thing that was done), is used in law to describe the whole of a particular action or course of conduct. The relevant facts underlying a dispute are the res gestae of the cause of action.

In criminal law, res gestae is the extent of the felonious act for the purposes of defining the felony of a felony murder. Res gestae extends before and after the moment of a felony to include the chain of events so essential to the crime that they are a part of it. For instance, a homicide connected to a robbery would be felony murder if it took place after the robbery but while the robber was attempting to flee, a condition that would persist until the robber reaches some hiatus or shelter from further pursuit.

In the law of evidence prior to the modern codes of evidence, the doctrine of res gestae was an exception to the common-law hearsay rule, in which words or statements made at the time of the event were admissible if they were part of a physical action, were a spontaneous utterance, or were evidence of a state of mind. These purposes are now incorporated into the exceptions to hearsay in its code definition.

**res judicata (res adjudicata)**   A matter finally adjudicated is not to be relitigated. Res judicata, Latin for the thing adjudged, is, technically, the final determination of a civil action, including all appeals and rehearings. More famously, res judicata is a doctrine creating finality by limiting the litigation of civil actions, so that once a final determination has been reached to resolve a dispute between parties, the parties and their surrogates may not bring into any court any legal issues that arose or might have arisen from the underlying factual dispute. Res judicata applied both to bar a later action by the parties and those for whom they speak over a specific claim between them, whether the initial civil action was ultimately adjudicated or settled. Res judicata is a judicial doctrine of the common law, a limitation in the statutes and rules of procedure in many jurisdictions, and a constitutional doctrine under the Seventh Amendment, although the constitutional limitation does not apply to motions in the same action or to its appeals.

Res judicata applies at the conclusion of all direct review and appeals, when the mandate of the court or another form of final judgment is entered in the case, whether the final determination is as to one claim or all claims, and whether it is to the benefit of the defendant or the plaintiff. Res judicata takes two essential forms, claim preclusion and issue preclusion. Claim preclusion bars claims already litigated from being raised again, and it is often said to incorporate two older doctrines: merger and bar. Merger occurs when the judgment favors the plaintiff and the claim is merged into the judgment, so that all aspects of the claim are extinguished by the judgment, the plaintiff may bring no further charges on the same claim, and the defendant may not further contest the judgment. Bar occurs when the judgment favors the defendant, and the plaintiff is estopped from pursuing any further satisfaction on any aspect of the claim that was the basis of the litigation. Regardless of the party favored in the judgment, issue preclusion bars both parties from raising again any issue that was litigated between them.

There are exceptions to res judicata, and an action is not entitled to the effects of res judicata in a few, very limited circumstances, for example: If the parties, particularly the defendant, have agreed that the plaintiff may bring several actions with distinct claims; if the court reserves the plaintiff's right to bring a later, distinct action; if the court was barred from hearing a theory of the case or granting a remedy owing to the limits of its jurisdiction (in which case only that theory or right to that remedy may be later litigated); if the claim arises under a constitutional or statutory scheme that allows claims to be split for litigation; if the plaintiff has sought only relief for past or for present or for future harm, saving such other claims for a separate action; or if some violation of constitutional right, equity, or good conscience by the judgment require it to be disturbed.

*See also:* representation, virtual representation; res, res judicata, collateral estoppel; judgment, judgment on the merits.

**claim preclusion**   A party may bring no claim that could have been brought in an earlier action. Claim preclusion is a doctrine of res judicata that provides that once a final judgment has been rendered in a court of competent jurisdiction, it will be treated as granting the full relief to which both parties in the same cause of action are entitled. Claim preclusion only applies to judgments of courts and not to administrative rulings. Claim preclusion is broader than the doctrines of merger and bar but operates to bring about the same results: whatever was claimed in the complaint, counterclaims, or defenses, was merged into the judgment and extinguished from later litigation.

*See also:* res, res judicata, merger and bar; remedies, election of remedies (election of plaintiff or election of actions or several-remedies rule).

**collateral attack on a judgment (collateral action)**   An attempt to void or evade a judgment in a different proceeding. A collateral attack, or a collateral action, on a judgment is an argument that the judgment is defective, void, or unenforceable, that is brought not in a direct action, such as by a post-judgment motion in the same action on its appeal, but which is brought in a collateral proceeding, a new action, or a distinct action. A collateral action may be brought as a new action in the same court as the original judgment was filed, but it is more likely to be brought in a different court with jurisdiction over the parties, as when a state judgment of law is attacked by an action to enjoin its enforcement in a court of equity, in the court of another state, or in a federal court. Not all collateral attacks are on civil judgments; a proceeding for habeas corpus is a collateral attack on a criminal judgment.

*See also:* proceeding, collateral proceeding.

**collateral estoppel**   A fact adjudged between two parties is not to be relitigated. Collateral estoppel, which is also called issue preclusion, bars litigation between two parties of a factual matter that has already been litigated between them and is either the subject of a final judgment or a binding settlement. Collateral estoppel only applies as between the same parties who were initially in litigation and does not bar a new party from raising some claims, although that party may be otherwise procedurally barred. Collateral estoppel is the technical operation in double jeopardy that prevents the state from bringing a new indictment on grounds for which a defendant was acquitted, and it is grounds for dismissal of a redundant civil action brought by a dissatisfied litigant on a matter once lost. Collateral estoppel in a civil matter applies in any forum in which the same parties might appear, although it only applies in a new forum in criminal matters if the same government brings new charges on the same facts for which there was an acquittal.

*See also:* representation, virtual representation; res, res judicata, issue preclusion; res, res judicata (res adjudicata); jeopardy, double jeopardy.

**issue preclusion**  A party may not litigate an issue against another that was resolved in an earlier action between them. Issue preclusion is an aspect of res judicata that bars a party (or those in privity with a party) from bringing forward an issue with another party that has already been resolved in litigation between the parties in an earlier civil action. Issue preclusion applies regardless of whether the issue was decided in favor of the plaintiff or the defendant, though it does not apply if the issue was dismissed solely on procedural grounds and the substance was never litigated. Note: issue preclusion is effectively the same as collateral estoppel, the only difference being one of emphasis: the party precluded from raising an issue is estopped from raising it in a collateral action.

*See also:* res, res judicata, collateral estoppel.

**law of the case**  A final legal ruling governs the parties throughout the action in which it is made. The law of the case is a doctrine of repose, according to which a decision finally reached by a court in a dispute between two parties is binding on those parties for the remainder of the action, unless some extraordinary circumstance would justify a court in altering that decision as a matter of prudence. Put another way, each party to an action is bound by a decision of a court that is final, and once it is final the party is barred from attempting to relitigate that issue at another stage of the litigation.

A decision of a court becomes law of the case as to the parties before it at the time of the decision. A party added later or removed earlier is not bound to the decision under this doctrine.

A decision of a court becomes law of the case when it is final as between the parties. Thus, a decision in the trial court that is accepted by the parties becomes law of the case: a partial summary judgment or other pre-trial order, a jury instruction, an order, or a judgment — to which the parties do not timely object — becomes final and

is not subject to relitigation. Likewise, a decision reached by a court on appeal is final and binding on the parties, both on remand and on any later appeal, if the decision is not subject to further appeal. Prudential values that might justify departure from the law of the case depend on extraordinary circumstances. Examples include the change of a rule of law that was essential to the earlier rule, the discovery of substantially new evidence that could not be found earlier (or was not found despite diligent investigation), misconduct by a party that affected the other party's ability to present its case, and evidence of clear error or manifest injustice in the earlier decision.

**mandate rule**  The law of the case applies to past findings and rulings. The mandate rule is a particular application of law of the case, which requires a trial court with an action on remand following an appeal to apply the appellate court's mandate in its later considerations of the action. As with all applications of the law of the case, the mandate rule is subject to prudential considerations that arise in extraordinary circumstances, especially in the event of the discovery of significant new evidence or the change of a rule of law that was essential to the appellate decision.

*See also:* mandate (mandatory).

**merger and bar**  Claims in an action are merged into the judgment and barred from later actions. The doctrines of merger and bar are essential to the claims preclusion of res judicata. Though the doctrines work together, they are customarily treated as disinct.

The doctrine of merger provides that when a final judgment favors the plaintiff, all of the claims, counterclaims, and defenses that might then have been brought by the parties arising from the facts underlying the cause of action are merged into the judgment. Thus, the plaintiff cannot later maintain an action on any part of the adjudged claim, except to enforce its judgment. So, too, the defendant cannot later raise a defense against enforcement of the judgment or in collateral attack of the judgment, whether it was raised in the action or not.

The doctrine of bar provides that a valid and final personal judgment rendered in favor of the defendant bars another action by the plaintiff on the same claim.

*See also:* merger; res, res judicata, claim preclusion.

**res nullius**  A thing belonging to no one. Res nullius, Latin for "thing of no person," is a thing that has no owner. Abandoned property is res nullius. Wild animals on public lands that are not restricted from hunting are res nullius. The doctrine originated in Roman law, allowing any person who occupied or possessed the property to own it by virtue of possession in fact.

*See also:* terra, terra nullius (terrae nullius).

**resale (resell or right to resell)**  The seller's resale of goods not accepted by the buyer. Resale is the buyer's sale of goods that had been sold to a buyer who wrong-fully refuses to accept the goods, repudiates the contract, or fails to pay. The seller's right to resell goods is an option to the seller, according to which the seller sells the goods to another party and recovers damages from the buyer, offset by the benefits of the sale, so that the damages are the difference between the original contract price and the resale contract price, plus the expenses of the resale.

*See also:* cover; cure, cure as mitigation of damages.

**resale price maintenance** *See:* price, price–fixing, vertical price–fixing (resale price maintenance).

**rescission** The annulment of a contract. Rescission is an equitable remedy that treats a contract as if it were never entered, canceling it utterly and restoring the parties to a position as if the contract had never been made. Rescission is only possible if there is no remedy at law that would be sufficient to cure a breach of duty under the contract or a related wrong by one party and if the party seeking rescission is not in breach. The breach by the other party must be substantial and so affect the subject matter of the contract as to render it non-performable.

*See also:* remedy, equitable remedy, rescission.

**equitable rescission** Avoidance ab initio of an agreement or instrument awarded as a remedy in equity. Equitable rescission is a remedy available to a party to a contract or is the maker of a unilateral instrument who has equitable grounds for the rescission of the instrument and who is granted rescission as a remedy by court in equity. The grounds for rescission as a remedy include a failure of a condition according to which the agreement or instrument is first created. An order of equitable rescission will be sought when the plaintiff seeks to restore the parties to their condition as if the contract or other instrument had not been created.

In contracts, equitable rescission may be appropriate if the contract was the result of a mutual mistake, fraud, incapacity, or failure of consideration. In no case, however, is rescission available unless the plaintiff can meet the pleading standards of equity, including being able to demonstrate that rescission is appropriate in the balance of the equities and being able to withstand defenses that an adequate legal remedy exists, that the plaintiff does not come with clean hands, and so forth.

**legal rescission (rescission at law)** Termination by the parties of a contract ab initio. Legal rescission is action by the parties to an agreement, or the maker of a unilateral instrument, to void the agreement or instrument. Rescission is performed by the return of benefits received already under the agreement or tender of the agreement itself, in such a manner as to communicate the intent to rescind. The effect of rescission is to void an instrument or agreement ab initio, or to restore the party or parties to their positions as they would have been if no such instrument or agreement had ever been made. Effects of the

parties that have meaning only from that time forward (for instance, in keeping benefits already received) amount to either cancellation or avoidance.

Legal rescission is not, in itself, a judicial act, although a party or parties may seek judicial recognition that private action amounted to rescission. Rescission granted by a court under circumstances proven by a party for which rescission is relief is a matter of equity.

*See also:* rescission, equitable rescission; void, void ab initio.

**rescript** A judicial instruction, or brief opinion. A rescript is something written in response. Specifically, it is a summary statement entered after the resolution of an appeal, stating the grounds and reasons for the decision on appeal. The rescript is mostly used in north-eastern states.

The rescript was, originally, a form of receipt, a short copy of a longer instrument that served as a receipt and proof of the longer instrument, such as the counterpart of an indenture. It was also, in the civil law, an instruction sent by a monarch to a magistrate or agent or one who sought instructions, and from this became a note of instruction from a judge to a clerk of an order from a superior court to an inferior court regarding a cause pending before it. The term is still in use in some courts, particularly appellate courts, to describe short opinions of the court.

*See also:* opinion, judicial opinion.

**rescue (rescuer)** Aiding a person, animal, or entity in danger. Rescue has two very distinct senses in law, both of which arise from the same idea of rescue as aid to a person in peril or confinement. The earlier notion of rescue is that of aiding a prisoner in custody, or jail-breaking. The more contemporary sense is in bringing some material aid to a person, animal, or an entity that is in danger or distress.

Rescue as assistance rendered to someone in distress is a broad concept, and it includes a person in immediate peril of death, injury, or property damage, as well as assistance in a condition in which such a peril may arise. Rescue may be from natural forces or from human agency or from a danger caused by the combination of the two. Rescue is not affected by the victim's having caused the victim's own danger. An act of rescue may occur despite the victim's claim that there is no danger or the victim's desire not to be rescued, if there is an objective basis for believing that the victim is in fact in immediate danger of death or injury and the rescuer acts in good faith in attempting to remove the victim from the condition of danger.

Rescue is also used in a more general sense for the shelter and care of animals and people in distress.

**duty to rescue** An obligation to rescue a person in danger or distress. The duty to rescue is an obligation upon an individual at a given moment to use that individual's reasonable efforts to give aid to a person in danger or distress. There was no general duty to rescue in the common law, and a person who observes another in danger of death or injury who does not give aid to that person does not commit a tort as a result of the omission of aid. Even so, a person who does give such aid may be immune from liability for any mistake or negligence in rendering it, under a Good Samaritan rule. There may, however, be a special duty to rescue arising from the relationship between the person in danger and the potential rescuer. A contractual obligation as by a professional rescuer, such as a fireman, police officer, emergency medical technician, or lifeguard; or a contractual relationship, such as a bus driver or airline steward to a passenger; or a family relationship such as a parent to a child, any of these can give rise to a duty to offer some form of aid or assistance. Note: the absence of a duty to rescue is distinct from any obligation in the criminal law to render information or aid to law enforcement officers.

Although the common law had no general duty, the civil law of most European states and the statutes of some U.S. jurisdictions do now require rescue when a person has knowledge of the exposure of another to grave physical harm and the opportunity of rendering reasonable assistance without personal risk. In most instances, a person acting under such a duty is immune from personal liability under a Good Samaritan rule. A failure to perform a rescue when there is a duty to do so may give rise to both criminal and private liability in a jurisdiction in which the duty is statutory.

The absence of a general duty in U.S. law to rescue is a perennial distinction between moral obligations and legal obligations, because most people believe in a moral obligation of a healthy and competent adult to rescue or aid a person in danger if such aid can be given with little or no risk to the rescuer.

*See also:* Samaritan, bad Samaritan; Samaritan, good Samaritan statute (good Samaritan law or good Samaritan doctrine).

**professional rescuer doctrine (firefighter's rule)** Professional rescuers may not recover from a victim whose negligence causes them injuries. The professional rescuer doctrine is distinct from the rescue doctrine, applying only to an individual whose employment requires that person to engage in the rescue of others. A professional rescuer who is injured while engaged in a rescue within the scope of the rescuers' employment may not bring an action against the victim being rescued if the victim's own negligence causes the rescuer's injury. Although there is some variation, most jurisdictions do not apply the professional rescuer doctrine to bar an action against parties other than the victim whose intentional or negligent acts during a rescue cause the rescuer injury.

*See also:* risk, assumption of risk (assumption of the risk).

**rescue as release from custody** The release of a person in custody or property seized by the state. The crime of rescue is the use of force or stealth either to release a prisoner from government custody or to remove property that has been lawfully seized by the government, whether the property is in the possession of the government, a court, or a private party. The rescue of an individual is more frequently treated as the crime of escape or of being an accomplice to escape or jail-breaking.

**rescue doctrine** An injured rescuer may sue the person who imperiled the victim rescued. The rescue doctrine is a doctrine of standing that allows a party who rescues a person placed in peril by the negligence or intentional tort of a third party to bring an action against the third party to recover injuries or costs that the rescuer sustained in the rescue. The rescue doctrine also bars the third party whose acts required the rescue from raising a defense based on any negligence by the rescuer, unless acts in the rescue were unreasonably reckless as a matter of fact.

## research

**legal research** The location and organization of sources of law on a given topic. Legal research is the method and practice of locating documents and portions of documents that frame or describe or pronounce the law on a given question or interest, seeking them in the archive of legal sources — the constitutions, statutes, legislative histories, case reports, briefs of counsel, rules, administrative materials, forms, scholarly essays, articles, books, and general histories and technical references — and organizing the texts according to customary significance and authority. There is an art to locating the most essential of such sources and using the sources found, along with finding aids such as computers and digests, to locating further sources until all of the sources essential to the question in a given jurisdiction or affecting its law have been located. The resulting materials are synthesized to present and to defend statements of what the law is or is not on a given topic. The most useful means of this organization generally is to consider a series of potential outcomes and then compare the relative strength and weakness of such outcomes in the light of the legal materials applied.

**Computer Assisted Legal Research (C.A.L.R. or CALR)** The search for legal materials in computer databases. Computer Assisted Legal Research, or CALR, is the use of databases to locate, sort, select, and store sources of law, using computerized algorithms to search legal materials that have been digitized and stored as records in the databases. The practice commenced in 1970 with the Lexis proprietary service, which is now one of several, including Loislaw and Westlaw. As of 2011, CALR is often performed using open-source and public databases, particularly those created by public agencies, such as THOMAS and the web sites of the various courts.

*See also:* law, law school, legal pedagogy, Computer Assisted Legal Instruction (C.A.L.I. or CALI).

**resell or right to resell**   *See:* resale (resell or right to resell).

**reservation**   Any property or rights reserved from a transaction. A reservation, in general, is something set aside for a specific purpose or to avoid its being used in general. In law, there are many forms of reservation, each usually limiting something — such as a right, power, claim, property, or authority — for the use of a specified party or use toward a specified end. There are many illustrations of a reservation of a power, obligation, or property from a transaction in which it would otherwise have been conveyed, required, or restricted. Thus, a reservation in a deed is the retention by the grantor of some land or some portion of a property such as a covenant or easement that is not transferred to the grantee, though it otherwise would have been under the general terms and descriptions of the deed. A reservation of lands by a state is a restriction of those lands for a specific use rather than their use according to the general laws. A reservation in a contract is a limitation of some right, interest, or condition that would otherwise have potentially been subject to the contract according to its general terms. A reservation to a treaty is a limitation on its meaning or requirements that is withheld as a condition of a state's signature or ratification, despite the terms in the treaty itself.

**reservation of easement**   *See:* easement, reservation of easement (reserved easement).

**reserved power**   *See:* power, reserved power.

**treaty reservation (reservation to a treaty)**   A statement by one party to a treaty limiting its obligations under a treaty. A treaty reservation is a statement made at the time of a signature, ratification, accession, or other moment in which the state might be bound to the terms of a treaty, by which the state reserves certain powers from the obligations it accepts under the treaty. Reservations may attempt to limit the meaning of a treaty to a particular interpretation; they may attempt to limit a state's obligation to comply with a treaty from certain actions, including actions forbidden by its organic or constitutional law or by other treaties; they may attempt to limit a state's obligations only to certain circumstances depending on the conduct of the other states parties to the treaty. Or, they may otherwise limit the state's participation or obligation under the treaty in any manner and to any extent. Not all reservations are valid, and a reservation that is barred by the text of a treaty itself, or that contradicts a fundamental concept of the treaty, or that is objected to by another state party, may have the effects either of voiding the reservation or of voiding the signature or other acceptance of the treaty.

*See also:* treaty.

**tribal reservation (Indian reservation)**   Lands set aside by the U.S. for the use of tribal Indians. A tribal reservation is land set aside by the federal government for the use of a specific American Indian tribe or nation, and which is governed by that tribe or nation. The term arises owing to the original sense in which tribal lands were reservations, having been reserved by the tribe when it granted a concession in its lands to the United States. These lands remain described in this manner under U.S. law, whether the grant was voluntary or forced upon the tribe or nation with great hardship and suffering.

**Assimilative Crimes Act**   Federal courts may prosecute state crimes on federal lands and reservations. The Assimilative Crimes Act, codified at 18 U.S.C. § 13, assigns federal law enforcement and judicial authority the authority and jurisdiction to enforce laws under state law that are committed on a federal enclave, or a federal reservation, facility, or installation, including federally protected Indian reservations. The state law is the law of the state on which the enclave is located.

**residence (residency or reside)**   A place where a person resides from time to time. A residence is a place where a person lives and conducts the daily affairs of life, though not necessarily exclusively or permanently. A person may have several residences at once. A residence is contrasted with a domicile, which is a principal residence, the place where a person is considered exclusively and permanently to be a domiciliary, though the permanence of such an arrangement is a matter of expectation at a given time and not a limitation on the ability to change domiciles. Thus, a resident is the inhabitant of a residence, although a resident may be a resident of several places. A person with one residence is a resident and domiciliary of the same place.

The mere maintenance of a residence is not usually sufficient to acquire nationality by a person who is not a citizen or subject of the place of residence. However, residence for a specified period may be a condition on the application for naturalization. Likewise, residence for a time is often a precondition to register to vote or to hold office or to engage in other civic and legal obligations, such as jury duty.

*See also:* domicile (domicil or domiciliary); homestead; resident.

**resident**   A person with a physical presence in a residence. A resident is a person who has a physical presence in a residence, whether the residence is temporary or one of many, or the residence is the sole residence and domicile of the resident. A resident may have an intent to continue living in a given residence, which is under the control of another person, and still be a resident there. More generally, a resident is a person who resides in a place, a community, a jurisdiction, or a state.

Note: resident is both a noun and an adjective. As an adjective, resident suggests not a person in a residence but a person assigned to or occupying voluntarily a local role, such as a resident expert or resident physician. Both senses may be incorporated into an adjective, though, as in the title of British judges assigned to Northern Ireland and elsewhere as Resident Magistrates, a nineteenth-century practice only ending in 2008.

*See also:* residence (residency or reside).

**resident alien**   *See:* alien, resident alien.

**residential cooperative**   *See:* cooperative, residential cooperative (co-operative tenancy or co-operative ownership or coop or co-op).

**residue (residual or residuary or residuum or rest)**   The things that remain after a process is complete. Residue is what remains after an event, whether physical, metaphorical or financial. Thus, the residue from a chemical reaction includes the chemicals that are left over or thrown off from the reaction, usually as debris. Residue in the estate of a decedent is the amount of money and all property remaining after expenses are paid and all of the specific bequests are paid or distributed.

*See also:* legacy, residuary legacy (residuary estate or residuary legatee).

**residual beneficiary**   *See:* beneficiary, residuary beneficiary (residual beneficiary).

**residual exception**   *See:* hearsay, hearsay exception, residual exception (catchall exception).

**residual or residuary or residuum or rest**   *See:* residue (residual or residuary or residuum or rest).

**residual value or scrap value**   *See:* value, salvage value (residual value or scrap value).

**residuary beneficiary**   *See:* beneficiary, residuary beneficiary (residual beneficiary).

**residuary devisee**   *See:* legatee, residuary legatee (residuary devisee).

**residuary estate or residuary legatee**   *See:* legacy, residuary legacy (residuary estate or residuary legatee).

**residuary legacy**   *See:* legacy, residuary legacy (residuary estate or residuary legatee).

**residuary legatee**   *See:* legatee, residuary legatee (residuary devisee).

**residue from pesticide**   *See:* pesticide, pesticide residue (residue from pesticide).

**resignation**   The act of renouncing an office or position. A resignation is an act by which a person renounces the further occupation of an office, job, position, or any employment. A resignation may be expressed in words or implied in conduct. For instance, to take up a new position or office that is incompatible with the position or office then held may amount to a resignation. A written resignation is invalid unless it is signed. The conditions of resignation for some positions of employment are governed by the employment contract, or for positions of public employment by statutes, which may provide for automatic resignation, or an implication of resignation upon the commission of certain acts. The termination of an employee is not a resignation, but benefits that are denied to an employee who voluntarily resigns may be granted to an employee who is effectively terminated through automatic resignation. The resignation of a position that is held by the

will of both the holder and another, such as an office held at the pleasure of the President, may be ineffective unless it is accepted, although enforcement of the continued performance of an employment or office is impossible under the law.

*See also:* abdication; retirement.

**resistance (resist)**   The hindrance of an objective or action. Resistance is any force that opposes a force. In law, resistance is human conduct that hinders a person or entity seeking to accomplish some action or achieve or maintain some condition. The hindrance may be effected or only intended, because the resistance is assessed by what is done to resist, not the effectiveness of the resistance. Although resistance may include the use of force against force, resistance may be non-violent and non-forceful; the hallmark of resistance is the potential to interfere with the accomplishment of the action or condition sought by the other person or entity.

**resisting arrest**   *See:* arrest, resisting arrest.

**resolution**   A statement, particularly the solution to a problem, question, or dispute. A resolution, in general, is a statement of position by a person, group, or entity, which in many instances is an answer to a question. Resolution is a broad term and has many senses and applications. In law, it includes the statement of a legislative body, the statement of a judge offered as a solution to a legal dispute, and the statement of an arbitrator or conduct of the parties in mediation or negotiation in solving a dispute between them.

**congressional resolution**   An enactment by Congress that does not result in a statute. A Congressional resolution is a specific form of action taken by one or both houses of Congress that does not start as a bill or result in an act or statute, but that expresses the will of the Congress. Although a resolution does not become a statute, it may become law. There are three forms of resolution: A simple resolution might be passed by only one chamber or by both chambers regarding a matter of internal procedure or a matter on which the chamber or chambers are expressing an opinion. A concurrent resolution is similar but is introduced into both chambers at the start with the intention it be passed by both. Neither a simple nor a concurrent resolution become law, although they may be signed by the President. In contrast, a joint resolution is passed by both chambers and presented to the President for signature, veto, or enactment as law without signature in the same manner as a bill. A joint resolution becomes federal law, even though it is not technically a statute. By custom, a constitutional amendment is passed by Congress as a joint resolution, though it is not presented to the President but to the states for ratification.

**joint resolution**   A law passed by Congress that is not a statute. A joint resolution is a resolution introduced simultaneously in identical form in the House and the Senate, which is approved in the same language by both houses and becomes law by the signature of the president or the override of a presidential veto. The budget and other laws that are not statutes are passed in this manner. Joint resolutions are designated H.J.Res. or S.J.Res.

**resort (last resort)**   A place or act where one seeks relief, especially the courts. Resort is a place to which one retreats for assistance, or an action one takes in order to find relief or assistance in some task. In law, resort is both something one does for one's own relief, as in self-help, as well as something one seeks from others, particularly in requesting relief in the jurisdiction of the courts. The court in a legal system beyond which there is no appeal is a court of last resort.

**resource**

**Resource Conservation and Recovery Act**   See: waste, waste material, resource conservation and recovery act (RCRA).

**natural resource (natural resources)**   All the substances of the Earth and space used by humankind. Natural resources, in general, is the broad concept for all of the material in the planet and other bodies that is or may be of use in sustaining life for human beings, including: land; soil for farming; minerals, including oil and gas; water; air; animals; plants; solar radiation; wind and sea power; and the cycles of energy. As used in law, natural resources is often a jurisdictional term, allocating authority over the exploitation and conservation of certain resources to a given agency. As a matter of property, an owner of property in fee simple is, at common law, the owner of all of the natural resources that occur on it, over it, or under it, although the exploitation of such resources may not create a nuisance to others.

**respondeat**   Let the person answer. Respondeat is Latin for "let the person answer." It is a command found in common law writs, but it is also a signal of responsibility, because the person responsible for answering a legal charge or complaint is responsible for the matter of the action. Note: in nearly every instance in use in the United States, respondeat used alone is an abbreviated reference to the doctrine of respondeat superior.

**respondeat superior**   The liability of a principal for the wrongdoing of an agent. Respondeat superior, Latin for "let the master answer," is the maxim underlying the law of agency; it labels the many doctrines of liability that require a principal to make good a loss to a third party that was caused by the principal's agent. Employer liability for the wrongful acts of an employee within the scope and course of the employee's actual employment is usually referred to as respondeat superior, unless a more specific statute governs the conditions in which the employer will be liable. Thus, not all employers are subject to respondeat superior; for example, a municipality is not subject to respondeat liability under the federal civil rights acts (though liability for the acts of officials

and employees may arise otherwise). Although the doctrine of respondeat superior is usually invoked in tort, it is a general maxim of agency and is used, for instance, to describe the responsibility of a shipper for the representations of an agent, or an insurer for the actions of its agent.

*See also:* union, mass action theory.

**respondent**   The party who responds to a petition. A respondent is a person or entity who, as a party, responds directly in opposition to a petition filed in an adversarial proceeding or, in some cases, to an administrative complaint. Not all actions that are initiated by petition have a respondent. In an action that is effectively administrative, no person or entity is likely to respond. In an action, such as bankruptcy, that is initiated by petition but that is not opposed, the other parties appear under other titles, such as creditor. However, in actions in which the respondent replies to the petition to argue against its grant, the respondent is in the effective position of a defendant in other actions. In actions for appellate review that are commenced by a petition, such as a petition for certiorari, the respondent is in the same situation as an appellee.

*See also:* petitioner.

**responsibility (responsible)**   Accountability for something, or capacity for that duty. Responsibility denotes the accountability of a person or entity (and within an entity, the accountability of specific individuals) for ensuring that some action occurs or some condition is satisfied. Responsibility takes many forms in the law. Most often it is a synonym for legal liability, because one is liable for acts or omissions for which one is responsible. More generally, responsibility for one's actions is a matter of legal capacity, the ability to be held legally accountable for one's actions and one's faculties necessary for one's actions to have legal significance. Likewise, responsibility in criminal law is a matter of individual capacity to be held responsible, or accountable, for one's actions as a matter of criminal liability. Responsibility as a matter of agency is the degree to which one person or entity must answer for the actions of another. Responsibility in tort, contract, environmental law, and other broad arenas of liability is the degree to which a given condition or event is attributable to one's actions or duties.

**diminished responsibility (capacity diminished or diminished capacity)**   A defense of lack of restraint or control. Diminished responsibility owing to a lack of capacity or a lack of restraint is a defense to intentional crimes in some jurisdictions, though not all. The defense depends on the same forms of proof as irresistible impulse, in that the defendant must demonstrate a mental inability to control the actions that amounted to the criminal act.

*See also:* insanity, irresistible impulse (insane impulse or policeman at the elbow test).

**responsible corporate officer doctrine**   See: officer, corporate officer, responsible corporate officer doctrine.

**responsive pleading** *See:* pleading, responsive pleading.

**Restatement (Restatement of Law)** A reformed summary of the rules of practice in a given field of law. A Restatement is a collection of rules of law in a given subject area organized into a coherent exposition of the law of that subject. Restatements are each drafted by one or a few reporters, who are expert in the field and who collate significant judicial opinions, statutes, and scholarship. From these the reporters draft rules that express the best resolution of the many controversies attending each rule, which are then subject to study and debate among members of the American Law Institute, after which a final version is adopted as a Restatement of the law of that field. The Restatements are then considered by lawyers and judges, many of whom rely on a Restatement in resolving a disputed point of law.

*See also:* reform, law reform, American Law Institute (A.L.I. or ALI).

**restitution (writ of restitution)** The return of property, value, or privileges, wrongfully taken or kept. Restitution is a remedy by which a person or entity in possession of property or value that was wrongfully acquired or retained is required to restore it to a party with a right to its possession. Restitution was initially an equitable remedy, required particularly in cases of unjust enrichment. There is also a legal remedy of restitution, required in cases of conversion or of breach of contract when the return of gains is more appropriate than an award of damages. Restitution is a means for the recovery of the benefits of part performance by a non-breaching party, which would be retained by a party that breaches a contract, who would otherwise be required only to make good the plaintiff's actual loss. The hallmark of restitution as a civil remedy is the requirement that the defendant restore to the plaintiff all of the defendant's gains relevant to the action. The measure is not the plaintiff's loss but the reward of the defendant, all of which must be disgorged to the plaintiff.

Restitution in a criminal proceeding is a judicial order made as an element of a criminal sentence or as a condition of release or parole, requiring the person convicted of a crime to pay compensation of one or more victim of the criminal's action.

*See also:* unjust enrichment; relief; intermeddler (officious intermeddler or volunteer or stranger); relief, monetary relief.

**criminal restitution (victim compensation)** Payment from a criminal to a victim of the crime. Criminal restitution is a payment by a criminal to a victim of the criminal's crime, which is ordered either by the sentencing court or as an administrative condition of parole or release. Although restitution differs from a fine in that it is paid directly to the victim, it is not a debt that is dischargeable in bankruptcy. Criminal restitution is also referred to as victim compensation, although victim compensation is a broader term, encompassing payments from a public fund as well as private, charitable relief.

**restraint (restrain or restraining)** The prevention of an occurrence or action. Restraint, in general, is any cause that prevents a person or entity from doing something that it might otherwise do or any condition from altering in a way to give rise to a particular occurrence. Thus, a physical restraint includes both ropes that tie down cargo and one person's hand grasping the arm of another person. Yet restraint is broader, including a person's own knowledge, thoughts, or emotions that prevent the person from some action.

Restraint created by law is usually the result of either a duty or an order forbidding a person or entity from some conduct, whether by a general duty, like the standard of negligence, or a specific order, such as an injunction or writ of prohibition. Restraints created by private parties take many forms, including economic disincentives and conditions on grants or gifts, and contract conditions barring or requiring certain practices that may amount not only to a restraint on the party to a contract but also upon third parties who might otherwise trade or contract with them.

*See also:* judge, judicial activism (judicial restraint).

**restraining order** *See:* order, court order, restraining order.

**restraint of trade** *See:* trade, restraint of trade.

**restraint on alienation** *See:* alienability, restraint on alienation.

**physical restraint**

**handcuff (handcuffs)** A restraint placed on the wrists. Though there are simpler devices, as a matter of law enforcement use generally, handcuffs are two connected restraints that are placed upon a persons wrists in order to diminish the mobility of the hands and arms of the person who wears them. Though handcuffs are designed to be worn on the two wrists of one person, one of the two restraints may be attached to another person or to an object. Handcuffs may be tied with chains to other restraining devices. By definition, for a police official to place a person in handcuffs amounts to arrest. The manner in which a person is placed into handcuffs is subject to considerable scrutiny in the risk of the use of excessive force. Handcuffs used by police should be designed in such a manner as to prevent a cuff from being tightened after it is placed on a person's wrist, in order to avoid overly constricting the wrist and injuring the wearer. As noted above, handcuffs may be simpler devices, such as Plasticuffs of Flexcuffs, brands of locking plastic ties sold for use as handcuffs during the speedy intake of large numbers of people, though such materials are subject to easier escape. Note: handcuff is a noun as well as a verb, and to handcuff, or cuff, a suspect is to place handcuffs on one or both of a suspect's wrists. This usage differs from the older use of the word "cuff" for a physical battery.

**shackles (fetters or legcuffs or leg irons or shackling)** Leg restraints or, generally, a burden. Shackles are a form of physical restraint applied to the body of a person, usually as a form of temporary and portable detention. Though a shackle includes any type of metal or other device that can encircle a limb of the body, in modern usage, shackles more often refer to leg restraints, or leg irons. Leg shackles used by contemporary law enforcement are similar to hand cuffs in their design and safety apparatus, though of larger diameter and with longer connecting chains or rods. Shackles are often linked to a belt and handcuffs for prisoner transportation.

Historically, shackles have been used for many purposes of restraint, and earlier forms were often heavy iron fixtures used to incapacitate a prisoner or a slave. To shackle a person or a group remains a metaphorical term for an unjust restraint or prohibition. Note: fetters is another term for leg shackles, the device initially having been used to keep horses from running away.

**prior restraint**   A restraint of conduct or speech before it occurs. Prior restraint is the restraint of a person or entity from doing something planned that is created or imposed before doing it. In a sense, most restraints are prior restraints, particularly those that seek to avert a harm from a wrongful act. Yet a prior restraint emphasizes the advance nature of a prohibition and contrasts it with a retrospective effort of punishment or compensation, basing the restraint only on the potential of harm and failing to allow the person restrained to do something that might not, in fact, be harmful.

The most famous sense of prior restraint is a prior restraint of speech. A law or order that would prevent a person from speech or create in advance a penalty or threat that would be manifest if a person were to exercise a right of speech is a prior restraint of speech.

**unlawful restraint (unlawful detention)**   The crime of detaining a person without lawful authority to do so. Unlawful restraint is the restriction of a person's movement or conduct, against that person's will, without lawful authority to do so. A private citizen who holds a person against the person's will with no license to do so engages in unlawful restraint, which may also amount to kidnapping or false imprisonment, for which unlawful restraint is, in many jurisdictions, a lesser included offense. A police officer who detains an individual with no lawful cause or license do so engages in unlawful restraint. Unlawful detention is a crime of moral turpitude for the purposes of sentencing.

*See also:* trespass, trespass vi et armis.

## restriction (restrict or restricted or restrictive)

**restricted appeal**   *See:* error, writ of error (restricted appeal).

**restrictive covenant**   *See:* covenant, real covenant, restrictive covenant.

**restructuring (restructure)**   A change to a structure, as of ownership, organization, or finances. Restructuring is the act of changing the structure of any array of people or things that are managed or exist in a structure. In law, restructure is often a synonym for alteration or reorganization. For example, restructuring is a generic description of a reorganization of a person's or an entity's debt or finances, particularly a conversion of some debt for equity or other forms of debt. The restructure of a debt is the substitution of new terms for old terms to vary the rate or frequency of repayment or the allocation of payments to principal. A company may be restructured, or reorganized, either in its ownership or equity structure or in its employee organization. A contract or other business relationship may be restructured to alter the obligations or benefits between the parties.

**resulting trust**   *See:* trust, resulting trust.

**resumption (resume or reassumption)**   To recommence an action or condition that had ceased. Resumption is the starting anew of some condition, action, status, or practice that had been the case in the past but then stopped. The performance of work at a site that had ceased but then recommenced is said to have resumed. Resumption may be a matter only of restarting the former practice, or it may require new initiation. For example, a debt that had been canceled or subject to default will ordinarily require a new promise to pay for its resumption.

Resumption may be accomplished in fact or through operation of law, particularly through notice. Resumption of a name may occur by a person using a name as a matter of personal practice or by registration or judicial order.

Resumption of title occurs when a party has either physically or constructively entered a property that the party had surrendered, abandoned, or even left unprotected. The title may be resumed, as long as both any abandonment of title had not become effective and title has not vested in another through adverse possession. Because of these two conditions, resumption of title is most often accomplished by a sovereign.

When resumption may be unilaterally accomplished varies according to doctrine, but, in general, a resumption of some duty after the other party has been affected requires consent by the other party to be effective resumption. Thus, a contracting party who ceased to perform on a contract may resume unilaterally unless the cessation amounted to a material breach, but otherwise, the other party must elect to treat the breach as curable. Similarly, after a marital separation, a separation agreement may be made void if both parties resume living as spouses.

**retail (retailer)**   The selling of goods to consumers. Retail is the sale of goods to consumers, as opposed to wholesale, which is the sale of goods to merchants. Retail sales are sales of goods made to consumers, not including sales made between merchants. Although rules vary from jurisdiction to jurisdiction, sales tax is usually collected only from retail sales. A retail area, or a zone for land use regulation designated for retail use, is an area for stores selling to the public. A retailer is liable for a defect in goods sold and may be strictly liable for dangerous latent defects, as a matter of warranty in the sale and of reliance by the consumer on the retailer's marketing and implied warranty of merchantability.

*See also:* tax, sales tax (sales and use tax).

**retainer (retain or retaining fee)** A contract for services of a professional, particularly a lawyer. A retainer is an arrangement to engage a person or entity to provide services on an ongoing basis, especially through payment of a fee in advance of the services. The term is derived from the relationship between the person retained and the client being somewhat in the same manner as the retainers of the English monarch, who were and are the sovereign's personal advisers and entourage.

In the U.S., to retain an individual is to engage the services of that individual, especially in a temporary or professional capacity. A client who engages a lawyer for advice or representation is said to retain that lawyer.

The retention of a lawyer is best done according to a retention agreement or representation agreement, in which the attorney describes the professional services to be performed by the lawyer and discloses all fees and costs, and the client consents to pay the fees and costs and to carry out such commitments as are required by the client in furtherance of the representation. The client usually tenders a retainer or a retaining fee, which the lawyer deposits in a trust account for the client's benefit, for the satisfaction of later fees incurred in representation or by the duration of the retention.

*See also:* trust, client trust account (lawyer's trust account).

**retainer fee** *See:* fee, fee for services, attorney's fee, retainer fee (retainer or on retainer).

**retaliation (retaliate or retaliatory)** An act in reprisal for any act, offense or harm. Retaliation is a response by one person, entity, or state to another, whom the first believes has caused it offense or harm. Retaliation is itself neither lawful nor unlawful, although there are forms of retaliation that are both. In international law, a retaliatory act that is lawful is retorsive, but a retaliatory act that violates international law is a reprisal. In torts, property, and criminal law, retaliation is no justification for an act that is otherwise criminal or tortious, although self-help in the recovery of property or the detention of an assailant is not considered retaliation. Self-defense is distinct from retaliation, in that self-defense is an immediate act required to prevent imminent injury or death, while retaliation follows after an interval in time and is not in fact essential to stop an assault or other injury that has by then either occurred or not.

*See also:* eviction, retaliatory eviction; retorsion (retorsive or retortion).

**anti-retaliation law** *See:* whistleblower, Whistleblower Protection Act (WPA).

**retaliatory discharge** *See:* discharge, employment discharge, retaliatory discharge.

**retaliatory eviction** *See:* eviction, retaliatory eviction.

**employment retaliation** Retribution for complaints of wrongdoing by an employee. Employment retaliation, which is sometimes called actionable retaliation, is a specific act, series of acts, or statement by an employer or supervisor that threatens or harms an employee who has or may reveal tortious or criminal actions by the employer, as a means of punishment for the revelation or a means of deterring it. Retaliation is not limited to retaliatory discharge or other job actions but may take forms that do not affect the conditions of employment.

*See also:* discharge, employment discharge, retaliatory discharge.

**lex talionis** The law of retaliation, based on proportionality. Lex talionis, the law of retaliation, is the ancient view that the proper criminal punishment is to visit the crime committed upon the criminal, but it is also a recognition that the punishment should be proportionate to the offense and no worse than the offense committed. The principle is evident in the Code of Hammurabi and well known in modern Western culture owing to its use in very early Jewish law, as well as its influence on Immanuel Kant. In Roman law, the talio was an act of private vengeance rather than public penalty.

*See also:* proportionality (disproportional or proportional or proportionate); retribution; justice, retributive justice (retributivism).

**prisoner retaliation action** A prisoner is free from retaliation for protected speech or conduct. A prisoner retaliation action is a civil rights action brought under Bivens or section 1983, against police or prison officials who retaliate against a prisoner solely for the exercise of constitutionally protected rights, such as the rights of speech or petition. To prevail and recover either damages or an injunction, the prisoner must demonstrate that the defendant police officer, prison official, or other governmental agent took an adverse action against the plaintiff prisoner, that was caused by or causally related to speech or conduct by the prisoner that is protected under the Constitution, as it is limited in the context of a prisoner in confinement. For example, a prisoner who is beaten by a guard for complaining to the warden that the guard beats prisoners may succeed in a prisoner retaliation action.

*See also:* whistleblower (whistle-blower).

**retention of benefits** *See:* benefit, retention of benefits.

**retirement** The termination of employment at a given age or time in service. Retirement is the termination of a person's employment or occupation owing to the age the person has reached or the number of years a person has been employed by a given employer, at which time, according to the employment contract or to law, the employee is eligible to receive retirement benefits, such as a pension from the employer or old-age benefits from the government, or both.

*See also:* pension, individual retirement account (I.R.A. or IRA); resignation.

**retirement plan** A trust arrangement to collect payments, invest them, and pay pensions. A retirement plan is any arrangement by which an employer, employee, union, or other third party commits to pay funds toward an employee's pension at retirement. Most plans are funded during an employee's working years and are regulated under the federal Employee Retirement Security Act, which divides qualifying retirement plans into defined contribution plans (also known as individual account plans, like an IRA) and defined benefit plans (a more traditional pension fund intended to support a defined payout).

*See also:* pension; employment, employee benefit plan, retirement plan, Employee Retirement Income Security Act (E.R.I.S.A. or ERISA).

**qualified retirement plan** A tax deductible plan for investment toward retirement. A qualified retirement plan is an employee retirement plan that qualifies under the federal Employee Retirement Income Security Act and under the tax code for deduction of contributions from current earnings for the purpose of using the accumulated funds for support and maintenance when a certain age is reached. Payments from the fund are then taxed at what will, presumably, be a lower rate owing to the reduced income that customarily follows retirement. Qualified retirement plans include an individual retirement account (IRA), the Roth IRA, a 401(k) plan, and a Keogh plan, for each of which an individual contributes a specified amount of monies to the account each year and receives a tax deduction up to a certain amount of that contribution.

*See also:* employment, employee benefit plan, retirement plan, Employee Retirement Income Security Act (E.R.I.S.A. or ERISA).

**retorsion (retorsive or retortion)** A state's lawful but inconvenient act in response to an offense by another state. Retorsion is an act by one state in retaliation against an offensive, though not necessarily illegal, act by another state, intended both as punishment and as encouragement of the other state to act with greater care toward the retorsive state. Retorsion may not be unlawful. If state A refuses to import certain goods from state B, state B's refusal to import similar goods, or goods of equal value, from state A is retorsion. (And, if state B is not a member of the World Trade Organization and does not have a similar treaty commitment, it may refuse to import all goods from state A.) If, however, state B resorts to armed force, this is illegal as a violation of customary international law forbidding the use of force except in self defense and of the United Nations Charter, and it is not retorsion. Note: a retorsive act is an act of retorsion, or retortion.

*See also:* reprisal; retaliation (retaliate or retaliatory).

**retraction (retract or retracted)** The renunciation of an earlier statement or action. A retraction is a pulling back or withdrawal. In law, a retraction is a rejection of a statement or publication earlier made by the person or entity retracting it. To retract a statement or claim is to disclaim its validity or reliability while seeking to annul any effects it might have, as if the statement or claim had never been made. A retraction of a slanderous or libelous statement might mitigate the damages or moot a claim for injunction, but otherwise retraction is no defense against the claim in the common law, although it is by statute in some jurisdictions. Even so, a demand for retraction is a precondition to suit for defamation in some jurisdictions. For example, in Wisconsin, a timely retraction or correction is a defense, and in California, it limits a plaintiff to special damages, if the retraction is as prominent as was the libel.

**retreat** *See:* defense, self-defense, retreat (duty to retreat or retreat rule or rule of retreat).

**retrial** *See:* trial, retrial (motion for retrial).

**retribution** A harm given as punishment for a misdeed. Retribution is now understood as a harmful act inflicted as punishment for a harm committed, although its earlier understanding was more general, as compensation for what one does, whether beneficial or detrimental. Thus, in earlier cases, retribution is synonymous with compensation, pay, or rent.

Retribution, limited by proportionality, as a basis for criminal punishment is retributive justice, and the instinct to retaliate in a like manner for a harm or unjust act toward oneself or one's community is retributivism.

*See also:* deterrence, deterrence theory; punishment, retributive punishment; justice, retributive justice (retributivism); retaliation, lex talionis.

**retributive justice** *See:* justice, retributive justice (retributivism).

**retributive punishment** *See:* punishment, retributive punishment.

**retro (retroanalysis or retrocaculation)** Looking backward. Retro is both an adjective and a prefix applied to any word or concept to demonstrate its root in a past time. To make a retrocalculation, retroanalysis, or other retroadjustment is to recalculate some figures or factors from a past time, creating in the present a new conclusion that ought to have applied in the past.

**retroactivity (retroactive effect)** Applicability to an occurrence or thing in the past. Retroactivity is the applicability of anything to past conduct, events, or things; the idea that something happening in the present relates back and alters the significance of something that happened in the past. Laws that have retroactive application are, generally, disfavored because one of the fundamental notions of the law is that it guides the behavior of the people bound by them, which is rarely possible when a person does something allowed that is then disallowed. There is no blanket rule against retroactive law, however.

Retroactive effect of a law is a much narrower concept than retroactivity generally. There are a variety of rules on determining when a given statute, case opinion, constitutional interpretation, statutory interpretation, or rule change has a retroactive effect, and there are additional rules on when such effects are acceptable or unacceptable under doctrines such as the prohibition of ex post facto laws, which applies only in criminal law, and the requirements of due process of law, which apply to all laws in the United States. The most important questions in determining retroactive effect are whether the new law alters or extinguishes a legal right or interest that had already vested in the person or entity in question, or whether the new law creates a duty, burden, disability, or obligation that affects a transaction or event that had already concluded or passed. Note: the opposite of retroactive is proactive, which has acquired a different sense; thus in legal usage a law that is intended not to have retroactive effect is usually referred to as having only prospective application.

See also: ex, ex post facto (ex post facto law); retrospective.

**retroactive effect** See: retroactivity (retroactive effect).

**retroactive statute or retroactive rule or retroactive interpretation** See: retroactivity, retroactive law (retroactive statute or retroactive rule or retroactive interpretation).

**retroactive law (retroactive statute or retroactive rule or retroactive interpretation)** A law that has a retroactive effect. A retroactive law is any law that has a retroactive effect by altering or extinguishing a legal right or interest that had already vested in the person or entity in question, or by creating a duty, burden, disability, or obligation that affects a transaction or event that had already concluded or passed. Any law may have a retroactive effect, whether the law is a constitutional amendment, an interpretation of a constitutional doctrine, a treaty, a statute, a judicial interpretation of a statute, a judicial opinion, a judicial rule, an administrative regulation, an administrative rule, an ordinance, or another source of law. Although the Ex Post Facto Clause bars the retroactive declaration of past acts as current crimes, civil laws with retroactive effects are examined not under that clause but under the principles of due process of law.

Not all retroactive laws are barred. The federal courts are responsible for federal principles of retroactivity that apply to the interpretation of statutes, as well as for constitutional doctrines of retroactivity as a matter of due process and ex post facto limits. State law, however, is the province of state constitutional law, statutes, and judicial construction. Constitutionally, a law that affects procedural rights in a proceeding that is not final, a law that has a retroactive effect for which there was sufficient notice to the citizen as to amount to fair warning that the effect would likely occur, a law that does not disturb a vested substantive right or create a new obligation on a completed prior transaction, are each acceptable as matters of due process of law. This can be a difficult arena for prediction, not only because of the problems of determining when a new interpretation of a law relates back to the original law but also because of the perennial difficulties of determining the difference between substantive and procedural rights, completed and continuing acts, and vested or non-vested interests, among others.

See also: ex, ex post facto (ex post facto law).

**retrospective** A look at things in the past. A retrospective is an examination of things past, and to have retrospective consideration is to consider something done before, in the past. Retrospective is a rough synonym to retroactive, the primary difference being the emphasis in retrospectivity of a consideration of something before while the emphasis in retroactivity is to affect or change the meaning of something done before. A law of retrospective application is analyzed in the same manner as a law of retroactive application.

See also: retroactivity (retroactive effect).

**return** Any person or thing sent or brought back to a place of origin. To return is to go back to a place one has left, or to carry or send back something that was once dispatched to the place of its dispatch. In law, return has a variety of senses. Regarding people, return denotes both the ordinary transport of a person to a place the person once was, such as the return to a jurisdiction from which the person had fled, and the international sense of repatriation of a person who has left a native state or family homeland.

Regarding goods, to return goods is to send or transport them back to their point of origin or to another location in lieu of their point of origin. Whether goods are effectively returned depends on whether they are received by the original party who caused them initially to be shipped, or by a valid agent for that party.

Regarding notice or paperwork, a return is a form that is completed to demonstrate that some act or some filing is completed. Thus, a return is a report by a process server noting the service of process and the state and condition of its service. A tax return is a completed filing required to determine one's tax status. Note: return is both a verb and a noun, a return being a both the noun for an act of returning and a noun for the thing returned.

See also: receipt (receive or recipient).

**reus** Guilty, or related to an act for which one is responsible. Reus, the adjective in both mens rea and actus reus, has many senses in Latin, but the most central to these terms is fairly equivalent to a sense of responsibility for a wrongful act, or guilty. Reus is sometimes used in older cases in the sense that Bouvier depicted in 1853, as a party to the suit or to a contract, or otherwise someone with a responsibility to carry out.

*See also:* mens, mens rea (mental state); actus, actus reus.

**revenue**   Income, particularly income derived from the activities of others. Revenue includes all income realized from all sources by a public or private party, including all funds collected or realized from a person's employment, investments, or gifts or from a business's ordinary activities. Private revenue is usually distinguished between gross revenue (the funds received) and net revenue (funds received less expenses incurred). The term once had a stronger sense of emphasizing funds realized from unearned income, like rent or taxes or excises, or the proceeds of the sale of assets.

Public revenues, or government revenue are all funds raised by taxation, royalties, and fees. A revenue measure in Congress is a bill that, if it becomes law, will affect the income received by the Treasury. Internal revenue includes all public revenues from taxes other than customs, tariffs, or imposts.

*See also:* taxes, ways and means (ways and means committee).

**revenue bill**   *See:* bill, bill as legislation, revenue bill.

**revenue bond**   *See:* bond, revenue bond (improvement bond).

**Internal Revenue Bulletin (I.R.B. or IRB)**   An official announcement of recent substantive rulings of the IRS. The Internal Revenue Bulletin (IRB) is the method the IRS uses to announce all substantive rulings that the service deems are necessary to promote a uniform application of tax law, usually making announcements of decisions affecting income tax, employee plans, exempt organizations, and specific taxes. The IRB used to be distributed in paper, but it is now predominately an electronic service, accessible in 2010 at http://www.irs.gov/irb/.

**Internal Revenue Code (Tax Code or IRC)**   The statutes creating and regulating federal taxation of individuals and entities. The Internal Revenue Code is the core of federal tax law. Various statutes codified into Title 26 of the United States Code, the IRC provides for the taxation of all types of businesses and individuals. As of 2010, the most recent significant revisions of the Internal Revenue Code had occurred in 1986. Minor changes to the Code are made by Congress every year, and the interpretations of the Code by the IRS and the courts grow and alter constantly.

**Internal Revenue Service (I.R.S. or IRS)**   The Treasury bureau that collects federal taxes and administers tax law. The U.S. Internal Revenue Service creates tax regulations interpreting and applying the Tax Code, collects taxes from individuals and entities, and manages the federal revenue collection system, including the enforcement of tax laws and the regulatory adjudication of tax disputes. Enforcement of currency laws generally is the province of the Secret Service.

*See also:* police, police organizations, Secret Service.

**revenue ruling**   A published IRS ruling on a tax question. A revenue ruling is an official interpretation of a tax statute or regulation issued in answer to a question or dispute and published for the guidance of officials, taxpayers, and others. Notices of revenue rulings are published in the Internal Revenue Bulletin. Revenue rulings apply retroactively unless they are specifically designated as only of prospective application.

**unearned revenue**   Money received before sending a good or service. Unearned revenue is revenue received in advance of the dispatch of goods or the provision of services for which the revenue is payment. A lawyer's retainer prior to the rendering of legal services is unearned income. Unearned income is both income and an obligation.

**reversal (reverse or reversed or reversing)**   The annulment and contradiction of an earlier or subordinate decision. A reversal, generally, is a change about, a switch in position. In law, a reversal is a decision by a court or other tribunal to annul the effect of an earlier pronouncement or decision and to substitute a new pronouncement or decision for the old one. The reversal of a decision may be made only by a court or other body with the jurisdiction and authority to do so, either a court with supervisory or appellate authority over the court or agency that made the older ruling, or a body reversing a decision made earlier by the same body, whether in the same or a different dispute. The new ruling need not be perfectly and logically opposed to the older ruling, nor need the reversal be announced or declared using the word "reverse." A reversal may be express or implied, an express reversal stating that the former opinion or decision is reversed or otherwise that it is no longer of any effect. An implied reversal occurs when the result of the new decision is logically incompatible with the result of the earlier decision, or when a critical element of the reasoning or authority of the new decision is so incompatible with the earlier decision that the older decision must be of no further effect. Determining when an earlier decision is impliedly reversed can be a difficult and controversial process.

**reverse most favored nation**   *See:* nation, most favored nation, most favored nation as a settlement sub-class (reverse most favored nation).

**reverse or reversed or reversing**   *See:* reversal (reverse or reversed or reversing).

**reverse palming off**   *See:* trademark, infringement of trademark, palming off (reverse palming off).

**reverse preemption**   *See:* preemption, constitutional preemption, reverse preemption (reversely preempt).

**reverse repo**   *See:* security, securities, repo, reverse repo.

**reverse spot zoning** *See:* zoning, spot zoning (reverse spot zoning).

**reversely preempt** *See:* preemption, constitutional preemption, reverse preemption (reversely preempt).

**reversible error** *See:* error, reversible error (prejudicial error).

**reversion** The grantor's future interest following a life estate, fee tail, or leasehold. A reversion is a future interest that is kept by the grantor and that becomes possessory when one of several specific present possessory interests given to a grantee by the grantor expires. Like all future interests, a reversion is created by the owner of a property who divides the ownership interest in the property between a present possessory interest and a future interest (or more than one). Also, like all future interests, certain future interests are inherently the interests that follow certain defeasible present interests, and a reversion designates the grantor's interest retained when the grantor creates a life estate without a remainder, creates a fee tail without a remainder, or creates a leasehold or other non-freehold tenancy. Put another way, a reversion is created whenever the grantor gives a fee for life, or a fee good until failure of issue, or a nonfreehold for a period of time or upon a condition, unless the grantor grants every aspect of the future interests created by any of those grants to a grantee or grantees. Any interest or portion of an interest that follows these present possessory grants that is not fully given to a grantee creates a reversion.

Whether the grantor specifies the existence of a reversion, a reversion is the result of the creation of any of the three limited grants without granting away the subsequent interests. Thus, a grant of a life estate alone creates an implied reversion. Similarly, when a grantor creates a life estate, fee tail, or tenancy, and also grants contingent remainders, unless every contingency is accounted for by the logical possibilities of each condition, any situation that is unaccounted for gives rise to an implied reversion. Thus, a grant of Blackacre "from O to A for life" creates a reversion in O. So, too, does a grant of Blackacre "from O to A for life, and upon A's death O shall have reversion." The two are effectively the same, although the second example is an express reservation of the reversion and the first example has an implied reversion.

Although a grant of a fee simple subject to an executory interest is usually followed by the executory interest, a reversion may be implied if the executory interest is qualified in any manner so that — should the condition that cuts short the fee occur — the interest might not be posessory. Thus, a grant of Blackacre "from O to A for as long as Blackacre shall be used for the cultivation of llamas, if not then to B if B has, at that time, completed a bachelor's degree" creates a fee simple subject to an executory limitation in A, creates an executory limitation in B, but creates an implied reversion in O.

*See also:* estate, future interest, reversion.

*possibility of reverter and reversion* Reversion and possibility of reverter are similar future interests, in that each is an interest that may be held only by a grantor (or the grantor's successor in interest). They differ in that they arise as the successive interest to two different types of present possessory interest. A reversion arises or follows a present interest that is certain to terminate, either at the end of a person's life or the end of a period or periods of time; thus a reversion follows a life estate or a lease, both of which are bound to end one day. A possibility of reverter only follows a contingent event that might or might not happen; thus the possibility of reverter follows a fee simple determinable, which might never end.

*remainder and reversion* A remainder differs from a reversion in that a remainder is in a grantee (or the grantee's successor) while a reversion is in the grantor (or the grantor's successor). Certain limited fees give rise either to a remainder or a reversion. Thus, a life estate is followed by one or the other: a life estate followed by an interest in a grantee is followed by a remainder, but a life estate followed by an interest in the grantor is followed by a reversion.

**reversioner** A person who is entitled to reversion. A reversioner is a person with a vested interest in property owing to the present holding of the future interest. A reversioner is either the grantor or the grantor's successor in interest by grant, assignment, devise, legacy, or inheritance.

**possibility of reverter (possibility of a reverter)** The grantor's future interest that accompanies a fee simple determinable. A possibility of reverter is a future interest in land that is vested in the grantor by the operation of law when the grantor conveys a fee simple determinable in property to a grantee. Because a fee simple determinable, by definition, will end if a condition necessary to the continuation of the fee were to fail, then if that condition were to fail the fee would be destroyed and the possibility of reverter would become possessory as a fee simple absolute in the grantor (or the grantor's heirs or assigns). Unlike other future interests, the possibility of reverter is not technically an estate in land but a possibility of an estate, though many writers describe it as an estate. On the failure of a condition to a fee simple determinable, the reverter becomes possessory without a decree of a court, although enforcement of that interest may require judicial assistance. A possibility of reverter is vested in the grantor at its creation and not subject to the rule against perpetuities.

*See also:* entry, right of entry (R.O.E. or ROE or right of re-entry or power of termination); reverter (revert); possibility.

**reverter (revert)** A form of reversion. Reverter is a form of reversion, or return, by which any property once granted may return to the grantor. As a matter of usage and custom in law, reverter may refer to any reversionary interest, or interest that returns to its grantor. Reverter is used primarily in cases of the particular hybrid that combine a contingency, or possibility, with the reversionary interest, thus forming the future interest of a possibility of reverter.

*See also:* reversion; reversion | possibility of reverter and reversion; reversion, reverter, possibility of reverter (possibility of a reverter).

**review**  Consideration, or assessment. Review is, literally, a second consideration, and the term is sometimes used in the law to mean a reconsideration of a matter, particularly by a different body from the first to consider it. A strong custom in the legal usage of review is as assessment or careful examination.

Review in law often incorporates both senses — both a second consideration and a close examination — as in judicial review, administrative review, or constitutional review. Each review is an examination that follows an earlier examination and decision, but the later review is not only a reconsideration of the substantive result but also a careful examination of that decision. In other words, later review requires scrutinizing not only the subject matter in the earlier decision itself (which is likely a subsequent review) but also the means, bases, and authority for the earlier decision (which is likely an initial review).

**review of judgment**  *See:* judgment, review of judgment, collateral attack.

**administrative review**  Appellate review of an order within an agency, or above it. Administrative review has two distinct but related senses, and context is essential to distinguish them. Administrative review within an agency is the consideration of a complaint or appeal of an administrative order or ruling by an administrator, administrative law judge, board, administrative court, or appeals body within the agency that is empowered to examine such orders and to alter, reverse, or uphold them. Administrative review of an agency's order is a judicial review of the final decision of an administrative agency, and in this sense administrative review and judicial review of the administrative action are the same. In the federal system, exhaustion of administrative review and appeals available within the agency is required before seeking judicial review. Many states have a single system of administrative review of state agency decisions, with certiorari or a similar system for the review of municipal administrative decisions.

*See also:* adjudication, administrative adjudication.

**appellate review**  *See:* appeal (appealable or appellate).

**discretionary review**  Review in the discretion of the reviewing body, not by right of those who seek it. Discretionary review includes any process by which the review is not a right of the party seeking review but in the discretion of those from whom it is sought. Certiorari and most appeals to the highest court of a state after a hearing in a court of appeal are discretionary. Interlocutory appeal is, in most cases, discretionary.

**judicial review**  The judicial assessment of the constitutionality of a statute or administrative act. Judicial review is the judicial examination of an action by the legislative or executive branch to determine whether it conforms with or violates the constitutional law of the jurisdiction. Judicial review is an inherent power of each court, which must ultimately determine whether it is constitutionally allowed to enforce or not to enforce each law and to allow or to forbid each executive action that affects a citizen or subject of the laws.

Judicial review was a feature of English colonial law prior to the creation of the United States, being, in one form or another, at least as old as the judicial review of administrative and delegated actions and the interpretation of acts under statutes of Parliament from the time of Sir Edward Coke in the early 1600s. Developed more thoroughly in the United States after 1800, judicial review has been adopted by most of the world's constitutions.

*See also:* sober second thoughts.

**countermajoritarian difficulty**  The need to justify judicial review in a democracy. The countermajoritarian difficulty describes the problem with the idea in a democracy that the courts may have the last word on the meaning of laws and the powers allowed to the state by laws. The term captures the conflict between two great concepts of the state: on the one hand are the popular justifications for the state and law based upon majority rule, and on the other hand are the legal justifications arising from the protection of minority rights and fundamental principles of justice, the recognition of traditions and customs, and the requirements to employ expertise and manage complex questions not suited to popular decision, among other bases for law.

*See also:* review, judicial review.

**judicial review of administrative action (administrative judicial review)**  Review by the courts of a final administrative decision. Judicial review of an administrative action is the review by the courts of either an administrative order, citation, ruling, or other decision affecting a single party, or of an administrative rule or regulation that has been challenged as unlawful or unconstitutional. Judicial review in the federal courts is generally governed by the Administrative Procedures Act, 5 U.S.C. § 500, et seq., which requires the court to set aside an administrative decision if it is arbitrary or capricious, an abuse of discretion, or not in accordance with the law, which usually means that it is not a reasonable interpretation of the statute the agency believes authorized the agency to act as it did, with some deference given by the courts to the agency's interpretation of a statute on which it has special expertise. Congress may alter the standard of review except for claims that the agency's action or its enabling legislation violate the Constitution. State judicial review is governed by similar state statutes, though these statutes set a range of levels of deference, many of which are less deferential to the agency.

*See also:* adjudication, administrative adjudication.

**Morgan Rule of Administrative Judicial Review (Morgan IV Rule)** Administrative review is limited to the record unless there is bad faith or no record. The Morgan IV Rule is a limitation of the review of federal administrative decisions, particularly in the making of rules, so that the court will consider only such material as is in the record unless the record is patently insufficient to review or unless there is a strong showing of bad faith or improper behavior. The rule is from a 1941 opinion by Justice Frankfurter in United States v. Morgan, 307 U.S. 183.

**law review (L.J. or LJ or law journal or review or l. rev. or LR)** A scholarly legal journal of articles, commentary, and case notes. A law review or law journal is, in most instances, a student–edited periodical that publishes articles, commentaries, and notes related to developments in law, legal theory, and legal history. Some few of these (which are usually among those denominated as journals) are peer–reviewed and peer–edited, which is to say that the articles are selected or edited by professional scholars with a specialty related to the subject matter of the journal. Law review articles are influential sources of law and legal analysis, but the strength of their authority varies not only according to the fame of the author, the comprehensiveness of the research, and the insight and coherence of the writing, but also with the degree to which the reading judges or lawyers believe the article advances an argument that seems to them to be a compelling depiction of the law as it is or should be.

**plenary review** *See:* plenary, plenary review.

**standard of review** The degree of deference to be given to the author of the ruling under review. A standard of review is a rhetorical measure of the degree of deference to which a judge or other official who is reviewing a decision should accord to the judge or other official who rendered the decision under review. The corollary to the degree of deference required by a standard is the degree to which (or the causes for which) the reviewing judge or official should feel free to second-guess, criticize, or substitute for the judge or official whose decision is under review. Standards of review range from standards that demonstrate a very high level of deference to those that grant no deference at all. Standards vary according to the type of decision, the subject matter under consideration in the decision, the decision-maker, and the reviewer. There are two distinct hierarchies of standards of review in the federal system, one for appellate review, the other for judicial review.

The least deferential appellate review is review de novo, in which the reviewing official or court considers the entire matter as if it had never been decided before. There is no presumption regarding the outcome, either that the decision under review will be upheld or that it will be reversed. Questions of law on appeal are considered de novo. Certain matters appealed in agencies from an officer to a reviewing board, and certain matters appealed from a state court of limited jurisdiction to the first court of general jurisdiction are heard de novo. Judicial review of an arbitrator's decision is usually de novo.

A variety of intermediate standards of appellate review limit the discretion of the reviewing official or judge but still require a careful examination of the record and a thorough review of the decision in order to uphold it. These include the plain error rule and the clearly erroneous standard, under which the decision is reviewed to determine if there was a plain or clear error of law or of factual conclusion. This standard is sometimes used in the review of findings of fact made by a judge or magistrate hearing an action without a jury. Under these standards, the decision under review is presumed to be upheld.

Among the most deferential standards of appellate review are also the standards for review of a jury verdict on a question of fact (applied both by the trial court and on appeal): unless there is evidence of jury tampering or other wrongdoing, is not to be disturbed unless no rational jury could have reached the same conclusion. Decisions left to the sound discretion of the trial court are likewise to be overturned only in the event they are found arbitrary or capricious, are based on a clear error of law, or (in most states) demonstrate manifest injustice or a miscarriage of justice. Under these standards, the decision under review is strongly presumed to be upheld.

Standards of review for judicial review of legislation or administrative actions sometimes use similar language to that of appellate review. For instance, the judicial review of an administrative decision requires the decision to be upheld unless it was arbitrary or capricious, or the product of manifest error.

The hierarchy of standards of review of legislation, at least in the federal courts establishes two (or maybe three) levels of review. Legislation is always presumed to be constitutional. The most deferential standard is applied to the regulation of economic matters that does not create a burden on a constitutionally protected right, does not burden a suspect class, and does not apparently offend procedural or substantive notions of the due process of law. Such legislation is upheld if it is rationally related to a legitimate governmental purpose. An intermediate standard is applied to legislation that creates a burden on a quasi-fundamental right or a quasi-suspect class, such that the law must be substantially related to an important government interest. The least deferential standard is applied to laws that burden a fundamental constitutional right or create a burden on a suspect class, or to state laws intended to create a burden on interstate commerce. Such laws are presumed unconstitutional and are upheld only if the government proves the law pursues a compelling governmental interest by the least burdensome, or more narrowly tailored, means.

*See also:* discretion, abuse of discretion as standard in judicial review of administrative decision; appeal (appealable or appellate).

**appeal de novo (de novo review)**  *See:* de, de novo.

**arbitrary and capricious**  A decision should be reversed only if evidence has been ignored or badly used. Arbitrary and capricious is a standard of review of an administrative decision by an appellate review board or a court in judicial review, or of a trial court's decision by an appellate court. The reviewing body works from a presumption that the lower decision was proper and is only to be reversed if review of the decisions leads the reviewing body to believe the first decision was made in an arbitrary or capricious manner. Evidence of arbitrariness or caprice includes evidence that the judge or officer who made the first decision failed to consider all of the evidence, to hear the relevant arguments, to consider reasonable alternative conclusions, to give a reasonable explanation for the decision reached, or to reach an answer that logically relates to the evidence and to the arguments made. Evidence of bias, vindictiveness, personal animosity, conflict of interest, or incapacity may also demonstrate capriciousness.

*See also:* arbitrariness (arbitrary); capriciousness (capricious or capriciously or caprice); discretion, abuse of discretion as standard in judicial review of administrative decision.

**clearly erroneous**  A decision should be reversed if the evidence in its entirety refutes it. Clearly erroneous is a standard of review for a finding of fact made by a judge sitting without a jury. A finding of fact or similar decision should be upheld if there is sufficient evidence to support the conclusion that reasonable minds might differ on the outcome, but the decision should be overturned, even if there is some evidence in support of the decision, if the evidence considered in its entirety would leave a reasonable observer with the firm belief that a mistake had been made.

*See also:* discretion, abuse of discretion as standard in judicial review of administrative decision.

**clear error**  *See:* error, clear error (clearly erroneous or manifest error or obvious error or plain error or clearly wrong).

**de novo**  *See:* de, de novo.

**manifest error**  *See:* error, clear error (clearly erroneous or manifest error or obvious error or plain error or clearly wrong).

**plain error**  *See:* error, clear error (clearly erroneous or manifest error or obvious error or plain error or clearly wrong).

**substantial evidence**  *See:* evidence, substantial evidence.

**unreviewable**  A decision that is not subject to review by another official or judge. An unreviewable decision in the law is a decision that is not capable of meaningful review by any judge or official other than the person who first decides it. There is a strong bias in the modern legal system and in most systems of justice against an unreviewable decision, not only because of the likelihood that any error will remain uncorrected but also because of the risk of tyranny in the decider whose decisions are not subject to review. This is the meaning of Lord Acton's famous line that absolute power tends to corrupt absolutely.

**revival (revive)**  The restored effectiveness of an instrument or right that had lapsed. Revival, in law, is the renewed effect of a right, claim, instrument, pleading, or other power or instrument that had lapsed or been determined to be ineffective because of some defect or other reason. When the reason for its lapse is abated, or its defect is cured, or otherwise the ineffective thing is given renewed authority or effectiveness, it is said to be revived. A will, judgment, action, motion, claim, appeal, or demand may all be tolled or abated or renounced but then revived by various means.

**revocation (revocability or revocation or revoke)**  The annulment of an instrument or any interest or power earlier conferred. Revocation is the cancellation or annulment of anything that had been granted or conferred that remains subject to the license or discretion of the person or entity that revokes it. Any grant of property or power that is subject to revocation may be revoked, whether the power of revocation is express or implied by law. A public license or privilege that is conditioned on certain qualifications or performance by its holder, such as a driver's license or corporate charter, is inherently revocable if the terms of the license or privilege are not satisfied. A private grant may be revocable either by the grantor or a party in whom the power of revocation was vested by the grantor. Thus, a revocable license may be revoked by the grantor, or the grantor may give the power of revocation to a third party. Certain interests or actions are inherently revocable, such as a will, which may be revoked by the testator as long as the testator lives (although a contract or other grant conditioned on the existence of the will could be breached, the will may still be revoked and the contract or grant breached).

*See also:* trust, inter vivos trust, revocable trust (irrevocable trust).

**revocable trust**  *See:* trust, inter vivos trust, revocable trust (irrevocable trust).

**revocation of acceptance**  *See:* acceptance, acceptance of goods, revocation of acceptance.

**irrevocability (irrevocable)**  Lacking any means of revocation, or any unilateral means of doing so. Irrevocability is the incapacity by design of the maker of a legal commitment to revoke that commitment. An irrevocable trust may not be destroyed by the settlor who created the trust. An irrevocable assignment cannot be withdrawn by the assignor.

Many irrevocable instruments or grants are only irrevocable by the party who entered or made them. Thus, a contract that is irrevocable may legally be revoked, though it may not be so done by one party acting unilaterally, because all of the parties to the agreement may yet revoke it by a new agreement.

Certain assignments and delegations may not be made irrevocably. The assignment of a proxy to vote in a corporation may not be made without a power of timely revocation. So, too, is a power of attorney or appointment of attorney inherently revocable (although certain acts by one's agent or attorney may be irrevocable owing to the reliance on those acts by a third party).

**power of revocation**  The authority to revoke an agency or other revocable delegation or grant. A power of revocation is the ability to revoke or to terminate any delegation of authority or revocable interest or grant. A power of revocation may itself be delegated or assigned to a third party, although such delegation must usually be in writing, particularly when the initial authority, interest, or grant is in writing. The power of revocation by a principal over most forms of agency is absolute and cannot be alienated by a delegation of the power, and so such a delegation does not result in a loss of the power of a principle to revoke, but a non-exclusive delegation results in the third party.

**revolving fund**  *See:* funds, revolving fund.

**rex (regina or regis or regnal)**  The monarch. Rex is Latin for "the king," and regina is Latin for "the queen." Reges is sometimes used for the king and queen collectively. The monarch is a significant designation of royal institutions, which are often denominated "regis," the genitive possessive form of "rex." Criminal actions in Great Britain are brought in the name of the monarch, as "R. v. [The Name of the Defendant]." The adjective form is regnal, and a regnal year is the year of a monarch's reign.
*See also:* curia, curia regis (aula regis); R, R as an abbreviation; year, regnal year.

**regent (regency or regnant)**  Having the authority to govern. A regent has the authority to govern, particularly as one who exercises authority on behalf of another, such as a ruler acting for an absent or indisposed monarch. A prince regent is a prince who is the acknowledged ruler in fact of a monarchy in which a king reigns in absentia. Regent may also be used, and in education is often used, as the title of the chief executive or a member of a board of trustees.

Note: regnant depicts the exercise of monarchical authority, and it is not properly used to describe the conduct of a regent who is not the monarch. Regency describes the scope of authority of a regent.

**rezoning**  *See:* zoning, rezoning (rezone).

**RFRA**  *See:* religion, freedom of religion, Religious Freedom Restoration Act (RFRA).

**rhetoric**  The art of persuasion or influence through the use of words. Rhetoric is the art of communication, the means and tools by which the words one speaks or writes create the effect one intends. Rhetoric is similar to oratory, but rhetoric is the study and practice of the structures and effects of words, statements, and arguments rather than their presentation. Metaphorically, rhetoric is more about the script, while oratory is more about the actor who presents it, though there is much overlap between the two concepts. Rhetoric was once a central focus of legal education, and it remains so, though submerged into courses on legal writing or oral advocacy.

It is the custom of the bar in at least one state, Indiana, to distinguish rhetorical paragraphs from legal paragraphs in its pleadings. Rhetorical paragraphs mainly present arguments of facts, and legal paragraphs mainly present claims or defenses in law.
*See also:* law, law school (legal education); metaphor.

**rhetorical question**  *See:* question, rhetorical question.

**RI/FS**  *See:* pollution, Superfund, remedial investigation/feasibility study (RI/FS).

**riba**  Interest, particularly interest charged for the use of money that is excessive in Islamic law. Riba is a charge for the use of money, or interest charged for money lent, which is forbidden by shariah. Although an excessive rate of interest is barred as riba under all views of shariah, some schools consider only a usurious rate of interest to be forbidden.
*See also:* usury (usurious).

**Richard Roe or Jane Doe**  *See:* name, fictitious name, John Doe (Richard Roe or Jane Doe).

**RICO or R.I.C.O.**  *See:* racketeering, racketeer influenced and corrupt organizations act (RICO or R.I.C.O.).

**rider**  A brief amendment to an instrument or legislation. A rider is a short, separate, written addition to a written document usually, though not always, added while the document is in a draft form. A rider to legislation is an amendment making a small addition to the bill. A rider to an insurance policy is usually the addition of further coverage or exception from stated coverage in the agreement, with a concomitant change in the premium. A rider to a contract is usually the addition of a term, such as the date of delivery or a late-calculated price or quantity. At common law, a rider to the jury verdict might state damages awarded.
*See also:* amendment (amend).

**riding the circuit**  *See:* court, circuit court (riding the circuit).

**right**  A liberty, claim, or power to be respected by the government or by private parties. Right, in its broadest sense, is what a person should do, or is obligated to do, according to law, morality, ethics, or any other source of a valid obligation. From this comes the sense of a right, which is the lawful privilege to do something without interference from others. Rights in this sense may be private rights, such as those that arise in tort as to the duty of others, from contract as to other contracting parties, or from property as to those others who might use it. Rights may also be public rights, such as constitutional rights or human rights, that give rise to a claim of immunity from governmental interference or to a claim for assistance in realizing such rights through governmental intervention.

Right has many senses in the law. A great category of rights are considered to be held by individuals and entities, including constitutional rights, private legal rights, contractual rights, property rights, substantive rights, procedural rights, and other forms of right. Right has important and distinct senses in which the right is the basis for understanding one's rational duty, the thing that one ought to do in a given situation, the right or correct thing. In this sense, it is also a verb by which wrongs are corrected.

There are many rights that are most specific to certain conduct, interests, or a specific status. The terminology and substantive limits of rights vary considerably among jurisdictions. Some forms of privilege or claim are considered rights under the law of one jurisdiction or claims, entitlements, or privileges, under another, or deemed not to exist at all.

*right and duty* As between private parties, it is often said that to assert a right in one is to assert a duty in another. This form of symmetry is often present, and though some theorists consider it to define a right, for others, this symmetry is not a defining element in the law. A party may have a right as against the world, as in ownership, but another person may be able to overcome that right owing to a justification, such as necessity or emergency, and therefore have no duty as against the owner. Purists might say, then, that the right of the owner is limited so that there is no right against the party with a justification at the moment of emergency or necessity. Others would say that at this point, the right becomes subject to sufficient qualification that the right/duty distinction is unhelpful in defining the right or the duty. Wesley Hohfeld divided rights among several forms, that which corresponded to duty being "claim-rights," with other rights corresponding with liberty, power, or immunity.

**right of entry** *See:* estate, future interest, right of entry; entry, right of entry (R.O.E. or ROE or right of re-entry or power of termination).

**right of first refusal** *See:* preemption, right of preemption, first refusal (right of first refusal).

**right of free speech or liberty of speech** *See:* speech, freedom of speech (right of free speech or liberty of speech).

**right of preemption** *See:* preemption, right of preemption (preemptive right or preemption right or right of pre-emption).

**right of privacy or privacy rights** *See:* privacy, right to privacy (right of privacy or privacy rights).

**right of sepulchre** *See:* sepulchre, right of sepulchre (burial rights).

**right of support** *See:* support, support of property (right of support).

**right of survivorship** *See:* survivor, right of survivorship.

**right of way** *See:* way, right of way (right-of-way).

**right to a jury** *See:* jury, right to trial by jury (right to a jury).

**right to a speedy trial or speedy trial clock** *See:* trial, speedy trial (right to a speedy trial or speedy trial clock).

**right to choose** *See:* abortion, right to choose.

**right to civil counsel** *See:* counselor, right to counsel, right to civil counsel (civil gideon).

**right to counsel** *See:* counselor, right to counsel.

**right to die** *See:* death, right to die.

**right to interstate travel** *See:* travel (right to interstate travel).

**right to petition** *See:* petition, right to petition, Noerr–Pennington doctrine; petition, right to petition.

**right to privacy** *See:* privacy, right to privacy (right of privacy or privacy rights).

**right to public trial** *See:* trial, public trial (right to public trial).

**right to resist unlawful arrest** *See:* arrest, unlawful arrest, right to resist unlawful arrest.

**right to sue letter** *See:* exhaustion, exhaustion of remedies, right to sue letter.

**right to trial by jury** *See:* jury, right to trial by jury (right to a jury).

**right to work law** *See:* union, labor union, shop, open shop, right to work law (right to work state).

**right to work state** *See:* union, labor union, shop, open shop, right to work law (right to work state).

**rights arbitration** *See:* arbitration, grievance arbitration (rights arbitration).

**rights of criminal defendants** *See:* trial, fair trial (rights of criminal defendants).

**rights of redemption of mortgage** *See:* mortgage, rights of redemption of mortgage.

**right as correct** Accurate in the application of information or use of things. Right has a distinct sense related to accuracy or correctness. In this sense, what is right is the accurate application of information to a task, the sense of the right answer to a school quiz, rather than the wrong one. This is usually the sense of right in deciding rightly.

**right as proper** Morally appropriate or required. Right has a distinct sense within righteousness, that of the morally or inherently proper thing to do. The right, in this sense, incorporates any concept of a moral duty according to which a person ought to act. This is the sense of right in acting rightly.

**absolute right (right absolute)** A right with no condition or qualification on its exercise. An absolute right is a right that the right-holder may exercise without first seeking permission or meeting preconditions or other criteria. An absolute right may, however, be waived expressly or be waived impliedly, particularly if it is not exercised in a timely manner. A right that is dependent for its exercise upon the conduct of another party, upon the permission of another party (including the court), or upon a qualification or certification having been first gained by the rights-holder is not absolute.

**animal rights** An argument that animals other than people have rights as a matter of law. Animal rights is an argument based on equality, both rejecting the idea that there is an inherent difference between humans and other species and claiming that each animal has an equal claim to survival, resources, habitat, and an appropriate quality of life. Thus, animals should be free from exploitation, particularly use by humans for food, for sport, for production by industrial farming, by habitat destruction, and by experimentation. This is a controversial position that has not been accepted as the law. Critics argue that there is a difference in kind between humans and other species sufficient to justify the position that equality does not extend beyond humans. Moreover, the same goals may be as easily accomplished if humans are considered to have duties toward animals, indeed toward animals, plants, and habitats, that may be enforced by other humans.

> **speciesism** The human exploitation of other species. Speciesism is a critical label of the animal rights movement to identify human activities that exploit other animal species, and to identify legal distinctions between humans and animals that are not tenable to the animal rights movements, like human rights that do not include animal rights.
> *See also:* species (speciation).

**assignable right (non-assignable right)** A right that may be transferred to another person and remain valid. An assignable right is capable of assignment to another person. A non-assignable right must be enjoyed only by the original party who holds it; any attempt to assign the right is either void or destroys the right. An inalienable right is non-assignable.
> *See also:* assignment, assignment as assignment of rights and duties.

**civil right** *See:* civil rights (civil liberties).

**constitutional right (civil right)** A right protected under the Constitution. Constitutional right may be the most important contemporary sense of right. Constitutional rights in the United States arise under the U.S. Constitution as well as under the constitutions of each state. Although the courts are careful to base all federal constitutional rights on the U.S. Constitution as enacted in 1787 and as amended, by tradition, certain ideas regarding those rights are understood to have arisen from the period of the Framing, reaching back to the Declaration of Independence. Other ideas arose not only from amendments but also from the interpretations of the textual rights that became apparent as the Constitution was understood in the light of succeeding generations' experience with them. The enforcement of constitutional rights is a matter not only for the courts but also for all of the branches of government.

Constitutional rights take four major forms:

First is a liberty, or negative right, the constitutionally protected ability to engage in certain conduct or to hold a certain status and in doing so to be protected from interference by police or other agents of the government, unless that interference is very well justified. The freedom of speech and right to privacy are examples.

Second is a privilege, or positive right (sometimes called a claim-right), the constitutionally protected ability to call upon agents of the government to assist in performing certain conduct or to hold a certain status and in doing so to be protected from interference by other government agents and by private parties as well as, in some instances, to be provided resources. The rights to habeas corpus and, where it is a right, to education, are examples.

Third is a procedural right, the constitutional requirement enforceable by the citizen that the agents of government act only in certain ways, according to certain rules, and in consultation and agreement with one another. The rights to laws made according to specified procedures, to trial by jury, and to be free from torture are examples.

Fundamental to all of these rights is a constitutional right in each individual that the agents of the government will abide by the constitution and do nothing through the power of the state that is not allowed to them to do by the constitution. The right not to be taxed for an unlawful purpose is an example.

There is a customary difference in emphasis when one refers to such rights as constitutional rights or as civil rights. The term constitutional right implies a greater emphasis on the idea that the right is conferred upon the person by the constitution, and without a constitution the person would have no rights; thus if the constitution were suspended or abrogated the rights it creates would be annulled. The term civil right implies a greater emphasis on the idea that the right is inherent in a person's being or in the person's citizenship. Thus a suspension of the constitution cannot limit a civil right that exists before and will exist after a constitution. The structure of the U.S. Constitution and its Bill of Rights suggests that the Framers of these instruments applied ideas in balancing these differences in emphasis in this way: the rights they considered in the Constitution were inherent in each person, existed before the Constitution, and are only recognized in the Constitution rather than being conferred there, but the

Constitution creates obligations on all officials whose offices are derived from or limited by the Constitution, and the Constitution added obligations upon them to respect and enforce these rights.

Despite this sense of rights as an inherent aspect of humanity or citizenship, civil rights as a matter of law, however, incorporate a broader range of legal rights than just constitutional rights, including rights that are created by statutes, treaties, and other sources of law.

Constitutional rights are categorized in various ways that run through the various divisions depicted above, including the four major forms of negative rights, claim right, procedural rights, and rights to official restraint. One of these is the division between substance and procedure in the recognition and enforcement of rights (even rights to official conduct according to procedures). A person may have a substantive right against interference by officials through law, yet must also have a procedural right to enforce the substantive right.

**bill of rights** *See:* constitution, Bill of Rights (bills of rights).

**English Bill of Rights (Bill of Rights of 1689)** The crown must abide by the rights of Parliament and of the people of England. The Bill of Rights of 1689 was a condition of Parliamentary acceptance and ratification of the rule of William of Orange as king of England. It reaffirmed many of the obligations of the crown enshrined in Magna Carta in 1215 and the Petition of Right in 1628. It also strongly influenced the framers of the U.S. Constitution and the U.S. Bill of Rights.

**correlative rights** The rights of owners in a common pool or resource held in common. Correlative rights are rights of each owner of a resource in common among all, which each may take, such as the rights of several surface owners through whose property percolates a single pool of groundwater, oil, or gas. Applying the correlative rights, each has a right in the common pool, and so each owner's right is limited by the other owners' rights. In practice, this means each is entitled to reasonable use or reasonable extraction but not to extract so much as to exploit the common resource as a monopoly or to unreasonably harm the other owners.

**fundamental constitutional right (fundamental right)** A right rooted in the national tradition and essential to ordered liberty. A fundamental right under the U.S. Constitution is an individual right that is given the highest levels of judicial protection from interference by legislation or executive action. Fundamental rights include the rights to free speech on political matters, religious belief and practice, privacy, marriage, procreation, interstate travel, rights specifically expressed in the constitutional text, and rights both implicit in the concept of ordered liberty and deeply rooted in the Nation's tradition. A fundamental right may not be burdened or abridged by a law or action by government officials unless the law or action is in furtherance of a compelling governmental interest that is pursued by the means narrowly tailored to least burden the fundamental right.

*See also:* due process of law, ordered liberty.

**Miranda rights** *See:* Miranda Rule (Miranda warning or Miranda rights).

**procedural right** A right to participate in or benefit from specific legal processes. Procedural right includes both the right to be accorded access to certain procedures and the right to require others to follow certain procedures before any interest may be impaired according to law. Procedural rights arise under the constitution, statutes, judicial doctrines, and rules of procedure. The due process of law requires certain procedures to be followed before any interest may be taken, the most important of which are effective notice and an opportunity to be heard. Constitutional procedural rights include rights to specific procedures in criminal proceedings, such as a right to learn the charges filed against one, and in civil proceedings, such as a right to a federal civil jury.

Procedural rights arise whenever a legal procedure is created that is not available to all. The deprivation of some people of a process allowed to others must be rational, and those denied are entitled to a review of the rationality of the limitation, both in general and as it would apply to their case.

*See also:* due process of law.

**substantive right** A right to do or to refrain from some conduct without interference. A substantive right is a right in every sense that is not a matter of procedure, a right to do or receive something or to refrain from doing something. A substantive right may be a constitutional right that arises from an inherent understanding of the person or citizenship, but it must be recognized in some manner by the courts, legislature, or executive. Otherwise, all substantive rights are conferred by the operation of law or contract, and any interest that a person has in doing or refraining from any conduct; in having a given status or achieving it; or in having, receiving, or granting a thing, which is protected by law, is a substantive right. The distinction between substantive and procedural rights is very important in the federal system, as it determines the rules that are applied in ascertaining or enforcing that right in diversity cases in federal court.

**unenumerated right (unnamed rights)** A right interpreted from the Constitution or inherent in the people. An unenumerated right is a right that is not enumerated, or expressed in exact terms, in the text of the U.S. Constitution or its amendments, but that is integrated into the Constitution other than by the text directly. Some rights are essential to the due process of law, some rights are implicit in its promise of ordered liberty, some are established as a matter of custom in the national tradition of respect for certain other rights, and some rights are reserved to the people, having never been delegated to a government.

It is more textually appropriate, but still resisted by some members of the Supreme Court, to consider unenumerated rights as an aspect of the Ninth Amendment's assurance that the "enumeration in the Constitution, of certain rights, shall not be construed to deny or disparage others retained by the people."

*See also:* constitution, U.S. Constitution, Amendment 9 (Amendment IX or Ninth Amendment).

**Hohfeldian right (Hohfeldian duty)**   Every right held by one implies a duty by another. A Hohfeldian right is a right as analyzed by Professor Wesley Hohfeld in his 1913 article on fundamamental legal conceptions. He describes eight conceptions, four affirmative (right, privilege, power, and immunity) and four negative (duty, no–right, liability, and disability), and drew relations of opposition and correlation between them. The most famous of these relationships is that a Hohfeldian right is a correlative of a Hohfeldian duty, and so to validly say someone has a legal right requires that it be true that someone else has a correlative duty toward the right holder to allow the right holder to exercise that right. Thus, not everything lawyers call a right is a right; many are privileges or immunities.

*See also:* correlative.

**human right (human rights)**   A right inherent in each person. A human right is a right held by every human being, regardless of its recognition at a given moment by a state that has jurisdiction over a given person. Human right is closely related to the concept of constitutional right, or civil right, although it shares its origins with natural right. Human right is seen by most as a right inherent in the person that cannot be abrogated by law. A human right is a right that each person has that is not only a right that may be asserted against a government or government agent but that is enforceable by all governments, which have an obligation to ensure that each government respects it. Examples include freedom from arbitrary harm and detention, as well as access to food, shelter, and medical care, but also the right to one's nationality and to political expression. The history of modern human government is a history of the recognition of specific human rights by individual states and the ultimate recognition and protection of human rights as universal laws by international law.

**Universal Declaration of Human Rights**   The UN General Assembly list of human rights. The Universal Declaration of Human Rights (UDHR), adopted on December 10, 1948 by the United Nations General Assembly, consists of 30 articles describing rights to which all human beings are inherently entitled. Although the declaration is considered aspirational rather than a binding treaty, it is a catalyst to the formation of custom, in that many countries have adopted or have been influenced by the language in the document,

and it has served as a foundation for future international treaties and national laws dealing with human rights.

**human rights tribunal**   A court for the enforcement of human rights through mediation or adjudication. Human rights tribunals include all formal schemes of adjudication, mediation, and reconciliation involving the definition, recognition, protection, and vindication of human rights. Some human rights tribunals are created by a state or government, either within the court system or as an executive agency. Others are created by treaty or operation of the United Nations or a similar organization. Some have legal authority, including the powers of subpoena, arrest, prosecution, and punishment. Others are mediation or reconciliation bodies that have no authority to require appearance or punishment.

**European Court of Human Rights**   The supranational court to hear cases under the European Convention on Human Rights. The European Court of Human Rights was created by the European Convention on Human Rights, to which all member states of the Council of Europe subscribe, providing jurisdiction to the court of both states and citizens to enforce state obligations under the Convention, including human rights to be assured gurantees of life, fair hearing in legal proceedings, freedom of expression and religion, and a right to participate in elections, as well as prohibitions of torture, slavery, arbitrary detention, discrimination, and forced exile, among other rights. The Court has been based in Strasbourg since 1959.

*See also:* Europe, Council of Europe.

**Truth and Reconciliation Commission**   A body to investigate, hear testimony, and accept apologies for a violation of human rights and to recommend future measures to heal a community and prevent recurrence. A truth and reconciliation commission is an entity created by a government, an international organization, or a democratic or grass–roots organization, which is tasked with the investigation of a particular event in contravention of human rights, with a particular role for encouraging the testimony of victims and the apology of wrongdoers in determining an objective narrative of the event. Various commissions are tasked with requiring or recommending sanctions under criminal law, though many are not. Commissions tasked to investigate large–scale events often incorporate a host of local commissions.

*See also:* reconciliation (reconcile).

**Gacaca court**   The judicial–communal justice system investigating genocidal acts in Rwanda. The Gacaca courts of Rwanda are community-based quasi–judicial tribunals that hear evidence against and statements from those accused of participating in the genocide and dispossession of

Rwandans in 1994. Defendants accused of the most serious crimes are referred to traditional law courts for prosecution.

**Greensboro Truth and Reconciliation Commission** A commission to examine the events of a deadly 1979 riot in North Carolina. The Greensboro Truth and Reconciliation Commission is the first truth and reconciliation process in the United States, a private organization whose members were elected in Greensboro, North Carolina, to investigate, hear testimony, and to examine the context, causes, sequence, and consequences of a Ku Klux Klan rally and anti-Klan rally on November 3, 1979, in which five anti-Klan demonstrators were killed. Two trials of alleged assailants by all-white jurors resulted in acquittals of all defendants, despite videographic evidence of the attacks. The Commission released a report in 2006 and closed.

**inalienable right (inalienable rights or unalienable right or unalienable rights)** A right that cannot be transferred or lost. An inalienable right is one that must endure to the benefit of the holder regardless of any attempt to take it away or of the holder to surrender it.

**legal right** A right that may be enforced in a court of law. Legal right is a claim one person has against another that is enforceable in law. A legal right ordinarily results from a duty that another person has toward the person who holds the right. Though some theories of legal rights focus on whether the duty or the right exists prior to the other, not all theories of legal rights do so. A legal right arises either through the operation of law in a given situation (including the incorporated powers of equity) or from obligations arising in contract.

A property right arises from a property interest, which by definition establishes an array of legally enforceable relationships between the holder of the interest and the thing in which the interest exists. An essential example is the right to hold property without the interference of others, which is related to duties not to trespass, not to steal, and not to use one's own property so as to harm another's use (which is nuisance).

See also: contract, contract right (contractual right); property, property right (property rights).

**by right (as of right)** Done by legal entitlement rather than permission or grace. Anything done by right, or done as of right, is something one is entitled to do, because the law requires that the thing done, in this circumstance, be allowed. Likewise, anything sought by right, or sought as of right, is something to which one is entitled, because the law requires, in this circumstance, that the thing sought be granted. "By right" in this sense is the opposite of "by permission."

**color of right (claim of right or colour of right)** A good faith belief that what is done is justified in law.

Color of right, or claim of right, is a mental state in which a person who engages in some conduct or asserts some interest does so believing that the conduct or interest is justified in the law, even if that belief is founded on a mistaken impression. Thus, a person who believes that person has full title and interest to a piece of property and uses it as an owner would, engages in that use under color of right. As far as the action is done under color of right, it does not matter whether the person is right or wrong about being the true owner, because the person has a genuine belief the person owns it.

See also: color (colorable or colour or colourable); title, color of title.

**conjugal rights (marital right)** The emotional, financial, social, and physical rights of companionship of a spouse. Conjugal rights are the rights of spousal relationship, the whole range of support that one spouse gives to another, including society, companionship, love, affection, aid, services, support, sexual relations and comfort. When used in its least form, conjugal rights refers to the lawful capacity of spouses to enjoy voluntary sexual relations with one another. Conjugal rights do not, however, imply a right of one spouse to sexual relations with the other in the absence of consent by the other, nor do they imply a power of attorney, although an implied agency may arise from the conduct of the spouses, nor is there a right of one spouse to enter any place where the other spouse lives.

**enumerated right** An individual right expressed in a text. An enumerated right is a right expressed in a writing, whether a contract or a statute. In this sense, a valid written contract granting a party a right to enforce it creates an enumerated right of enforcement.

Constitutionally enumerated rights are those rights that are enumerated in the text of the U.S. Constitution as adopted in 1787 and its amendments, particularly the Bill of Rights and the Fourteenth Amendment. The term arises from the Ninth Amendment's description of the rights described. Note: enumerated rights are all fundamental rights, though they have not all been incorporated into the Due Process Clause.

**prescriptive right** A right acquired through long exercise. A prescriptive right is a right that is enforceable as a result of the right-holder's having engaged in the conduct in question for so long that a custom has arisen not only by the right-holder's conduct, but also by the acceptance and conformity of others. Prescription generally occurs when a statute of limitations has run or a doctrine of repose has expired, or when sufficient time has run that enforcement of an interest would be so unjust as to bar equitable relief. A party may never prescribe a right to engage in criminal or harmful conduct (although harm to a property interest is not considered a barrier). For this reason and owing to the nature of sovereignty, no prescriptive rights are generally available against the government.

*See also:* prescription, prescription of property (prescriptible).

**natural right**  A right inherent in a person or state or in relations with society. A natural right is a right that exists, or is believed to exist, independently of the state or the legal system, providing a fundamental moral right for an individual, or perhaps a state, to do or refrain from some conduct, that ought to be respected and enforced by the legal system. Historically, the idea of natural right was a consequence of understanding humanity as a creation by a divine creator who also created natural right, or as a result of the natural principles of order in which humans find themselves. The natural origin of rights in each person may be understood as the enduring and repetitively reasonable and right answer to recurrent questions in society, or it may follow from the nature of the reciprocal dependence of each person on others for survival. An alternative, modern conception of natural right relies on the same foundations as human right, which is that there is no power or right in another person, not even an official in a state, that can be superior to it.

*See also:* jurisprudence, natural law (jure naturae or lex naturale).

**property right**  *See:* property, property right (property rights).

**rigor mortis**  *See:* death, indications of death, rigor mortis.

**rimless wheel conspiracy**  *See:* conspiracy, wheel conspiracy (rimless wheel conspiracy).

**riot**  A public disturbance caused by three or more people. Riot is a crime committed by each member of a group of people who assemble in some public place, where they commit a breach of the peace that risks causing harm to other people or to property. The number of individuals needed to amount to a riot varies from three, the number of the common law, to at least ten, the necessary number for riot in New York. Federal law defines a riot as consisting of three or more perpetrators.

Many states still use the formula of the common law, which defines a riot as a tumultuous disturbance of the peace by three persons or more assembling together of their own authority with an intent to mutually assist each other against any who shall oppose them in the execution of some enterprise of a private nature, and afterwords actually executing the same in a violent and turbulent manner to the terror of the people, whether the act intended was of itself lawful or unlawful. At common law, riot was distinguished from affray, the latter being used to charge a lawful assembly that became unruly. This distinction seems inappropriate in light of the contemporary understanding of the constitutional freedom of assembly, by which most public assemblies are lawful in their origin. Thus, whether an occurrence is a riot now requires that a public assembly is both a disturbance in itself and that it reasonably poses a danger of harm to property or persons.

*See also:* disorder, civil disorder; mob.

**aggravated riot**  A riot commenced with the intent to commit a further crime. Aggravated riot is the crime of creating or sustaining a riot in some manner that is more egregious than the riot per se, such as initiating the riot for the purpose of committing a different felony, such as for the purpose of violence against another person; or in a manner that makes the danger of the riot greater, such as while possessing a firearm or knowing others possess a firearm.

*See also:* aggravation (aggravated or aggravating).

**incitement to riot**  Instigating or recruiting a person to engage in a riot. Incitement to riot is the crime of encouraging another person to engage in a riot, through specific acts that are intended to urge the person to violate the law. Incitement requires more than the advocacy of ideas or assertions of a belief that riot would be right or justified. There must be conduct that provokes, instigates, or recruits a person to engage in a riot. It is not, however, necessary that a riot occur to commit this offense. Federal law makes criminal any interstate travel or interstate communication as a means of incitement to riot.

**Riot Act (read the riot act)**  A charge warning rioters to disperse or be arrested. The Riot Act was initially a British statute, passed in 1714 and in force until 1973, which created the additional crime of failing to disperse and eased the questions attendant on who was a rioter and who was a bystander in prosecutions under the common-law crime of riot, which was a separate offense. The statute provided that any persons at a riot who did not disburse after an officer required them to do, in language like that of the statute, would be liable for arrest. The whole statute was not read aloud, but the officer dispersing the crown read only a charge from it:

"Our sovereign Lord the King chargeth and commandeth all persons, being assembled, immediately to disperse themselves, and peaceably to depart to their habitations, or to their lawful business, upon the pains contained in the act made in the first year of King George, for preventing tumults and riotous assemblies. God save the King."

A similar statute remains in many state statutes and in the U.S. Code, adopted in the Militia Act of 1792, codified at 10 U.S.C. § 334 (2010).

**riparian**  *See:* river, riparian, riparian ownership, prior appropriation doctrine; river, riparian, riparian ownership (riparian rights); river, riparian.

**riparian erosion or littoral erosion**  *See:* erosion, erosion as decrease of a shore (riparian erosion or littoral erosion).

**riparian habitat**  *See:* habitat, riparian habitat.

**riparian ownership**  *See:* river, riparian, riparian ownership, prior appropriation doctrine; river, riparian, riparian ownership (riparian rights).

**riparian rights**  *See:* river, riparian, riparian ownership (riparian rights).

**ripeness**  *See:* justiciability, ripeness (unripeness or ripe or unripe claim).

**risk**  Something harmful that may occur, or the potential that it will occur. Risk in law is a danger, the potential of a peril — a harm to a person, property, or enterprise. This sense of risk incorporates into a single term the possibility that the event that might happen and the consequences if it does happen. Thus, once there is an understood potential for the loss of a vessel at sea, the loss is a risk, and the full value of the risk is not only the value of the lost lives, lost vessel, and lost cargo but also the damages that would flow from those losses for breached contracts and other forms of reliance.

In law, the idea of risk is a concept of the peril itself and its consequences, much more than the degree of probability of the risk becoming manifest, which is an assessment or evaluation of the risk. In law, the risk is either sufficiently possible that the risk should be allocated or managed, or it is not. This legal sense of risk contrasts with the more general sense of risk, which is a matter of probability, the potential that the peril, or harm to a person, property, or enterprise will occur. Although each, in some contexts, incorporates the other, the differences between risk in these senses is significant.

Risk is significant in many arenas of the law, particularly in policies for insurance, in contracts for the sale of goods, in torts, and in transportation or shipping tariffs and agreements. Each is a form of risk allocation, a means by which one party assumes or accepts responsibility for a given risk, transfers the risk to another party, or receives the risk from another party. When the agreements or tariffs are silent, the risk is allocated according to background rules in law, which designate some risk allocations but otherwise create liability for the party holding the risk.

Risk in the legal sense underlies the idea of assumption of risk. In the manner of an implied allocation of risk, a person who voluntarily engages in some conduct assumes all of the risks of that conduct, which may bar that person from complaining of the harm committed by others if their harm was a risk that was reasonably apparent and therefore constructively assumed.

Risk in the general sense is also an element of every non-intentional tort, as well as of crimes of recklessness. The risk of harm, that is the probability of harm, is a component of the assessment of the reasonableness of conduct. All other variables being equal, the higher the risk, the less reasonable the conduct usually is.

Risk in the general sense is used in law as a means of assessing the likelihood of an offender's recidivism in the event of release. A high risk factor is considered a basis for a longer sentence of incarceration.

*See also:* peril (perilous).

**allocation of risk (allocable risk or risk allocation)**  Designation by agreement of the party liable for a risk of loss. Allocation of risk includes any method by which parties to a contract or otherwise engaged in a joint enterprise may apportion among them risk of loss. An essential form of allocation of risk is an insurance contract, by which a risk is allocated from the assured to the insurer, defined according to the policy definitions, less exclusions and less exceptions. Insurers may allocate risks further by entering reinsurance policies.

Most contracts for the sale of goods allocate risk of loss of the goods through a term establishing when the seller's risk of loss terminates and the buyer's risk commences, that being the extent of the insurance each party is likely to carry over the goods in transit. Most leases, construction agreements, joint venture agreements, and other specialized contracts allocate the various risks to personnel, property, and enterprise, sometimes by allocating duties among contracting parties, sometimes by limiting liability, and sometimes by requiring insurance by one party favoring the other, indemnity of one party for the other, and an assurance by one party to hold the other harmless. Contracts that omit such arrangements leave the parties liable according to statutory and common-law rules of liability.

Not all risk is allocable. Some risk is simply inherent in the party assuming it and not transferable or insurable. Moreover, statutes may limit the parties' ability to allocate risk or indemnify another for intentional acts, criminal acts, or certain forms of negligence that threaten the public welfare.

**assumption of risk (assumption of the risk)**  The willful exposure to a danger inherent in an activity. Assumption of risk is a defense to a claim for injuries for negligence in a given activity that would bar a recovery by a plaintiff who expressly or impliedly agreed to accept the danger and bear the consequences of a certain activity before engaging in that activity. Assumption of risk was once an absolute defense, and the plaintiff was barred under the common law from any recovery for injuries of which the plaintiff had assumed the risk, an especially harsh rule when the doctrine was triggered by assumption as a condition of employment or through the doctrines of implied assumption or constructive assumption of risk for injuries a worker received on the job. The modern doctrine of assumption of risk requires the plaintiff to have known in fact the nature of the risks in order for the doctrine to apply to express, or some implied, forms of assumption and to have either expressly assumed the risk or impliedly assumed the risks reasonably known to be associated with an activity the plaintiff knows to be risky.

Assumption of risk has generally been integrated into the doctrine of comparative negligence, and in all jurisdictions assumption of risk is limited to knowing and reasonable assumptions. In certain fields, assumption of risk has been rendered obsolete, as in employment injuries, for which assumption of risk has been abrogated in favor of workers compensation. Assumption of risk persists in most jurisdictions as a bar to claims for most forms of express assumption and for implied assumption in inherently and obviously risk-prone activities, such as contact sports and other activities in which the risks of injury are patent and assumption of risk is implied.

Assumption of risk in many jurisdictions is divided into three categories: express, primary implied, and secondary implied. Express assumption is a deliberate statement assuming a specific risk, usually made by the plaintiff to the defendant. Primary implied risk arises when the plaintiff engages in conduct facilitated in some manner by the defendant, but the defendant has no duty to guard the plaintiff against any risk, and the plaintiff accepts the risk anyway. Secondary implied risk arises when the plaintiff engages in conduct facilitated in some manner by the defendant, the defendant has some duty to guard the plaintiff from risk but breaches that duty, and the plaintiff knowingly encounters and accepts a risk arising as a result of the breach of duty.

See also: negligence, comparative negligence; compensation, employment compensation; insurance, category of insurance, worker; nuisance, coming to the nuisance; rescue, professional rescuer doctrine (firefighter's rule).

**express assumption of risk**   An informed, stated choice to be exposed to a danger. Express assumption of risk is the spoken or written assumption of risk, by which the plaintiff states a desire to voluntarily risk the dangers depicted in the expression that might result from the actions the plaintiff thereafter performed or participated in. Express assumption of risk requires that the plaintiff have the capacity to make a binding legal act, particularly the ability to understand the implications of the assumption and the nature of the danger. An express agreement to run a given risk may include all risks routinely and inherently associated with it, but this is not an element of the express assumption of risk though it is a form of implied assumption.

In a jurisdiction that allows a defense of express assumption of risk, the jurisdiction might not allow express assumption of risk to perform criminal or deliberately and unjustifiably harmful acts, finding the assumption of risk of this form to be contrary to public policy even if the assumption is a matter of contract. Further, some express assumption of the risk of another's future negligence in the performance of a duty may be barred by public policy; even when it is not, such agreements are subject to scrutiny for adequacy of consideration and for adhesive character.

See also: expression (explicit or express); exculpation, exculpatory clause.

**implied assumption of risk**   The knowing acceptance of risks associated with an activity deliberately performed. Implied assumption of risk is an assumption of risk that is logically a facet of a decision to engage in some conduct giving rise to the risk. If the plaintiff knows the risk is derivative of the conduct, or if the risk is apparent in the conduct, the plaintiff impliedly assumes the risk when the plaintiff engages in the conduct.

Implied assumption of risk in some jurisdictions takes two forms, which operate differently as defenses. Primary implied assumption of risk occurs when the plaintiff knows the defendant owes no duty to the plaintiff to protect the plaintiff from a particular risk. Primary implied assumption of risk operates in most jurisdictions as a complete bar to recovery for damages in negligence. Secondary implied assumption of risk occurs when the defendant owes the plaintiff a duty to protect the plaintiff against a risk but breaches that duty, after which a risk arises as a result of the breach, and the plaintiff knowingly encounters the risk. Secondary implied assumption of risk gives rise to a defense of comparative fault, and the finder of fact is to apportion the plaintiff's damages between the parties according to their ultimate responsibility for the plaintiff's injury.

See also: risk, assumption of risk, implied assumption of risk, primary implied assumption of risk; risk, assumption of risk, implied assumption of risk, secondary implied assumption of risk.

**primary implied assumption of risk**   Knowledge by the plaintiff that the defendant owed no duty to guard the plaintiff from risk. Primary implied assumption of risk occurs when the plaintiff engages in some conduct that incorporates certain risks the plaintiff knows or should know to exist as an element of the conduct the plaintiff elects, and when the plaintiff knows the defendant has no duty to guard or protect the plaintiff from a particular risk. Primary implied assumption of risk operates in some jurisdictions as a complete bar to recovery for damages in negligence.

See also: risk, assumption of risk, implied assumption of risk.

**secondary implied assumption of risk**   A basis for comparative negligence when the plaintiff assumes a risk arising from a defendant's breach of duty. Secondary implied assumption of risk is risk accepted by a plaintiff despite some unusual circumstance in the plaintiff's acceptance of it. The doctrine is defined in different ways in different jurisdictions.

In its strongest sense, secondary implied assumption of risk arises when the plaintiff engages in some conduct that incorporates certain risks, and the defendant has a duty to guard the plaintiff against such risks, or at least some of the risks, but the defendant breaches that duty, after which a risk arises as a result of the breach, and the plaintiff knowingly encounters the risk and engages in conduct knowing of the risk. Secondary implied assumption of risk is the basis for a defense of comparative fault, and the finder of fact is to apportion the plaintiff's damages between the parties according to their ultimate responsibility for the plaintiff's injury.

Secondary implied assumption of risk in some states arises when the plaintiff encounters a risk of such severity that no potential benefit would have justified its acceptance. This formula of the defense of assumption of risk is intended to avoid liability for the defendant according to a calculus of comparative negligence. This sense has not been adopted in many states or retained in all that have used it.

*See also:* negligence, comparative negligence.

**knowledge of risk (knowing assumption)** A risk perceived in fact or construed from its obviousness. Knowledge of risk arises from actual knowledge of the potential for a specific harm or injury from some conduct or condition, but knowledge also arises constructively from the obviousness of a specific risk to a person before commencing the conduct or accepting or persisting in the condition giving rise to the risk. The risk must be foreseeable, and knowledge of the risk cannot be construed from actual or apparent knowledge gained after the person has commenced the conduct or persisted in a given condition.

*See also:* knowledge (know or knowing or knowingly); knowledge, constructive knowledge (presumed knowledge, presumptive knowledge); knowledge, constructive knowledge, willful blindness (conscious avoidance or willful ignorance or deliberate ignorance).

**beta coefficient** The measure of risk posed by stock or other securities. Beta is a measure of the degree to which an investment's value changes according to changes in the broader markets. Positive beta values indicate an investment that gains value as a given market rises in value, and a negative beta value indicates a loss in value as the market rises. Beta is particularly important in measuring risk in a portfolio, and a beta value that is too high may indicate an insufficiently diversified investment strategy, which may be an element in evaluating the management of trust and business assets.

**force-majeure clause** *See:* force, force majeure.

**risk assessment** Any evaluation of criteria to predict a risk becoming manifest as harm. A risk assessment is a process by which the potential is assessed for some risk occurring in fact, as well as the circumstances that would make such an occurrence more likely or less likely in the future. The analysis required for a risk assessment varies, but in general, the analysis reflects lessons learned from previous occurrences in which the harm occurred, using hindsight to compare circumstances and conditions that were either causal or indicative of the harm's occurrence. The analysis then compares the circumstances and conditions of the later risk to assess the apparent likelihood of a similar harmful occurrence.

Risk assessments are common in both legal procedures and in private procedures in regulated businesses. For example: risk assessments are used in parole hearings to determine the likelihood that a person convicted of a crime will commit the crime again. Risk assessments are used to consider the forms of emergency preparedness and response required for industrial sites and potentially environmentally damaging facilities. Risk assessments are used to determine whether a person poses a danger to others, particularly whether a parent poses a danger to a child or a spouse poses a danger to the other spouse. Risk assessments are used to determine the safety of consumer products and the allowable dosage of pharmaceuticals. Risk assessments are also used by insurers to determine the structure of policies and the amount of premiums.

**environmental risk assessment** An inventory of risks arising from an enterprise and the potential for their manifestation. An environmental risk assessment is both a process of inventorying the risks of a given operation or facility and the report that is produced by that process. The assessment lists each of the risks attendant in the operation or facility and the potential of the risk becoming manifest, means by which the potential of the risk may be diminished, means required by law to ensure compliance of regulations affecting the risk, and the effectiveness of the implementation of such means to date.

Environmental risk assessments particularly determine the risk posed by each chemical, process, and activity at a facility or in an entity's operations (including waste management and transportation) to determine the potential risk not only to property, persons, or the enterprise but also to the environment including water quality, air quality, and potential affects on animal and plant species. Risk assessments in the late twentieth century were often limited to risks to the enterprise that did not include environmental risks. Risk assessment in the twenty-first century increasingly incorporates environmental risk assessment with other forms of risk management.

**risk aversion (risk averse)** Dislike for risk, particularly physical or financial. Risk aversion is an attitude that seeks to avoid risks. The term is used in legal prose with a variety of limited senses, and a party that is risk averse may be seeking to limit its physical risks, or economic risks, or risks of liability, etc.

**risk management** The minimization of liability and management of liability claims against an entity. Risk management is a process of both reducing potential liability and managing liability claims arising from the operation of an entity. The minimization of claims includes a risk inventory to ascertain every significant risk to persons, to property, to enterprise performance, to the environment, or to regulatory compliance that might arise from the entity's operations; as well as the development of work rules and business techniques that minimize the risks inventoried; training and supervision of personnel to ensure such rules and techniques are followed routinely; and monitoring of operations to ensure compliance. Underlying this process is the management of effective means of allocating risks, including the maintenance of appropriate levels of insurance. The management of claims includes the investigation of events in which risks are manifest and the mitigation of harms from such events; the identification of claimants injured or harmed in such events and the rendering of appropriate aid; the reliance on insurance or risk–allocation partners for indemnity when appropriate; the defense of the entity against spurious claims of liability; and the resort to insurance for defense or indemnity as appropriate.

**risk of loss**  The risk that goods subject to purchase will be lost or damaged prior to delivery. Risk of loss is the potential for goods to be damaged in transit between the seller and the buyer, through no breach of duty by the seller or the buyer but by accident or negligence by the transporter of the goods. Risk of loss is usually allocated in the contract, often through the use of shipping terms.

**risk retention (risk retention group)**  Allocating risk to oneself: self–insurance. Risk retention is the failure to allocate risk of an enterprise to others, either through contracts, insurance, bonds, or other forms of risk pooling or risk transfer to a second or third party. Risk retention is not allowed for certain regulated transactions or enterprises, such as banking, without meeting regulatory standards of capitalization and capital reserves as risk assurance.

A risk retention group is an association of several persons or entities who pool risk and resources among themselves. Thus, the members of the group make a very limited allocation of risk in return for accepting the allocation of some risk from the other parties, while each entity still retains a share of its own risk.

*See also:* insurance, self insurance.

**risk/utility**  *See:* liability, product liability, strict product liability, risk–utility analysis (risk/utility).

**risk–utility analysis**  *See:* liability, product liability, strict product liability, risk–utility analysis (risk/utility).

**risk–utility test**  *See:* product, defective product, risk–utility test.

**river**  A body of water flowing from a source toward the sea. A river is a natural watercourse through which waters flow from inland sources toward the sea or toward their dissipation. A river may include any number of named bodies of water, including rivers, streams, creeks, runs, kills, rills, and small lakes as well as mouths and estuaries, or a section, portion, or tributaries of an estuary. In general, there is no difference as a matter of the legal designation of a river that it is customary or jurisdictionally known as a creek, stream, or other form of watercourse. A body of water that meets these definitional elements other than having been created through the natural hydrologic activity on land but is created artificially is usually a canal.

At common law, a river that is navigable by the smallest commercial vessels is a public river, and rivers that are not navigable by such vessels are private rivers. The riparian owner of lands adjoining a private river also owns half or all of the river bottom, according to whether one or both banks are owned by the same party, and such rivers could be closed to traffic. Public riverbottoms were owned by the sovereign, a state owning intrastate rivers and the United States owning interstate rivers, which could not be closed. This system is still followed in some jurisdictions, though it has been modified in many with the increased acceptance of the public trust doctrine as applied to rivers, with the channelization and federalization of many rivers, and with the advent of riverine parks, including the U.S. Wild and Scenic River system.

A boundary in a river that divides two parcels with riparian ownership of the channel, or two jurisdictions, particularly two states, is determined by local custom or by treaty, but otherwise is allocated by either a thalweg or a centerline method at the time a boundary is established. The boundary changes with later movements of the banks or channels through accretion, but the boundary remains unchanged if the channel or banks should move by avulsion.

*See also:* river, riparian, riparian ownership (riparian rights); accretion, accretion as increase of a shore; avulsion; erosion (erode); erosion, erosion as decrease of a shore (riparian erosion or littoral erosion).

**riparian**  Pertaining to the banks of a river, or the parcel of land that includes one. Riparian designates anything that is the boundary of a river or stream. Thus, riparian lands are lands that include one or both of the banks of a river or stream, and riparian ownership is an ownership interest in the river or stream arising from ownership of one of the banks. Many inland American states incorporate littoral interests into riparian interests, ascribing the same rights in a lake to a littoral landholder that would be the rights in a river ascribed to a riparian landholder. Western states in the U.S. tend to limit riparian rights, and eastern states tend to give a fuller slate of rights from the common–law riparian–rights doctrines.

*See also:* shore, littoral area (foreshore or littoral rights or litorral interests).

**riparian ownership (riparian rights)**  Ownership interest in a river or stream derived from ownership of one of the banks. Riparian ownership is ownership in lands that reach the banks of a river or stream. As a result of ownership of at least one bank, the riparian owner acquires a riparian interest in the river or stream itself, owning the land under the river or stream to its center (if the watercourse is not navigable) but acquiring a right of entry, use, and reasonable consumption of waters whether it is navigable or not. In some jurisdictions, a riparian owner of both banks has not only the right to take water from the stream but also the right to set dams and weirs upon it and the right to exclude transit across it. These extensive rights have been moderated for navigable streams in all jurisdictions, and states now vary in the extent of these rights afforded to riparian owners.

*See also:* river.

**prior appropriation doctrine**  Whoever appropriates water for a reasonable use has priority over later appropriators. The prior appropriation doctrine assures those who first appropriate water from a watercourse for a reasonable use that this appropriation will have priority as against a later appropriation for a different use by a different appropriator. The reasonableness of the use by the first appropriator is essential to establish and to maintain the benefit of the doctrine, but the reasonableness of the intended use by the later appropriator does not affect its application.

**riverbank or banks**  *See:* bank, bank as shore (riverbank or banks).

**RLUIPA**  *See:* religion, freedom of religion, Religious Land Use and Institutionalized Persons Act (RLUIPA).

**road**  A route of travel over land, or a waterway. A road is the generic term for all forms of way, street, highway, avenue, or any other way that is designated for travel over the ground. A road implies access to property, but only if the party in possession of the property has a license to use it, either because the road is a public road or because it is a private road over which the property holder enjoys an easement. Road has distinct meanings for transportation otherwise. A road may mean a railway. For vessels, road has two meanings, as a way by which vessels navigate on rivers, lakes, channels, and the sea, and as an anchorage giving shelter from the sea.

**road obstruction**  *See:* obstruction, road obstruction (obstructing a public way).

**roadblock**  *See:* stop, police stop, roadblock.

**robber**  A person who attempts or commits a robbery. A robber is a person who attempts or who commits a robbery. As a matter of general usage, the term attaches to a person who is believed to have done so prior to arrest or conviction, but as a matter of law, no person may be referred to as a robber in a legal proceeding until that person has been convicted of robbery. Note: a matter of legal slang, robber is often equated with thief, both being a generic term for a person who commits any form of larceny.

*See also:* burglary (burglar or burgle or burglarize or burglarious or burglariously); thief; robbery (rob).

**robbery (rob)**  Theft of personal property by violence, force, or threat. Robbery is the use of violence, force, a weapon, or threat to take personal property from the control of another person. Robbery requires a specific intent to take the property of another, and a would-be robbery does not occur if the would-be robber acts from a good-faith belief that the property is in fact owned by the robber or some other party for which the property is being lawfully recovered. The violence, force, or threat may be implied by circumstances created or exploited by the robber, and a threat may be implied rather than express, though the threat of harm must be of serious bodily injury.

There is some variation among jurisdictions in the definition of robbery as being a taking by force or threat or being the use of force or threat to take property. The difference is when the crime of robbery is complete, as opposed to being an attempted robbery. In jurisdictions making the use or threat of force the crime, a robbery may be complete once the force or threat of force is employed with the intent to commit a theft, whether or not the theft is complete and the robber is successful in acquiring the property. In other jurisdictions, the robbery is not complete until the property is taken from the control of the victim.

*See also:* burglary (burglar or burgle or burglarize or burglarious or burglariously); kleptomaniac (kleptomania); embezzlement; larceny (larcenous); theft; robber; possession, constructive possession, constructive possession of goods later stolen.

**armed robbery**  Robbery committed by a person carrying a weapon. Armed robbery is a robbery committed by a person while the person is carrying a deadly weapon or a device simulated to resemble a deadly weapon. A firearm, knife, pipe, bomb, or other weapon capable of a mortal injury is sufficient. In some jurisdictions, armed robbery is a form of robbery in the first degree.

**grave robbing (grave robbery)**  The unauthorized removal of anything from a grave or tomb. At common law, grave robbing is the act of removing a body, body part, or other object interred with a body from a grave, tomb, or burial site. Grave robbing is now generally dealt with as the statutory offense of interference with or abuse of a corpse, desecration of a grave, or desecration of a venerated object.

*See also:* sepulchre (cemetery or mausoleum).

**strong arm robbery**  Robbery without the use of a weapon. Strong arm robbery is robbery by violence or by putting a person in fear of violence, using only the robber's physical force as the means of injury or threat.

**Roberts Court**  *See:* court, U.S. court, U.S. Supreme Court, Roberts Court.

**robosignature  or  robo-signer**  *See:* signature, robosigner (robosignature or robo-signer).

**rogatory**

**letters rogatory (letter of request or rogatory letter)**  A request for evidence from officials in another country. A letter rogatory, or more often letters rogatory, is an instrument issued in the court of one state and directed to officials in another legal institution or in an another state, seeking their cooperation in the location and transfer of evidence for use in the requesting court. A letter rogatory is the usual means by which to request a deposition in a foreign country.

In some jurisdictions, a letter of request is issued by one court seeking the assistance of another. The Hague Convention on Taking of Evidence Abroad in Civil or Commercial Matters, to which the U.S. is a party, codifies the practice, although the convention designates the instrument as a "letter of request." Customary international law still recognizes the term as "letters rogatory," and the U.S. Department of State assists in the submission of letters rogatory to states that are not signatories to the Hague Convention. Letters of request or letter rogatory are to be written in the language of the receiving state.

**roll**  A record, particularly of cases, parties, or transactions. A roll is a record, or index, of official transactions. There are many forms, but the most common is the judgment roll, still used in many U.S. jurisdictions, which has the official record of each action up to and including the judgment entered. The word is derived from the old habit of rolling the records up into a great tube for storage.

A roll is also a list, an index of the participants or members of a group, like a muster roll, roll of members in a legislative chamber, or class roll. Roll–call is the actual calling of each name on a roll to determine the presence, vote, or status of the person whose name appears on the roll.

Roll is also a verb, which in commercial transactions may mean either to incorporate one fund into another or to transfer funds into a given account. In this, roll comes figuratively from its sense of movement rather than from its sense in the common law.

**roll call vote**  See: vote, parliamentary vote, yeas and nays (roll call vote).

**rolled–up plea**  See: plea, rolled–up plea.

**Roman law**  The records and books of the legal system of the ancient Roman empires. Roman law is a highly developed system of law that evolved over the thousand years of Roman civilization, and which is recorded in books and records that still influence our understanding of the nature of law and specific rules of law. Roman law has had a direct influence on the civil law of continental Europe and an indirect influence on the common law.

The earliest materials in Roman law that are usually studied are the Twelve Tables, a written collection of laws from both earlier writings and custom, recorded by ten citizens and organized by topics, which was promulgated in 450 and 449 B.C.E. while Rome was a republic. Otherwise, the law of the Republic, from 508 B.C.E. to 27 B.C.E., is largely studied through the writings of jurists such as Flavius and Scaevola and the arguments of lawyers such as Cicero. The law of the early empire, from 27 B.C.E. to the mid 200s C.E., is usually studied through the writings of the jurists Paulus, Ulpian, and Papinian, although statutes and decrees during this period are of increasing importance, as are judicial decisions. The height of Roman law came not from Rome itself but from Constantinople and the eastern empire, with the publication of a new code of law under Theodosius in 438 C.E. and the compilation of the great materials of the Corpus Juris Civilis in the time of Justinian, around 530 C.E.

Roman law was unusual in its scope, in the detail of its rules, in the accessibility of its organization, and in the degree to which its rules were modeled to fit the customs of both the citizens of Rome and those of other peoples who dealt with Romans. It was particularly clear and balanced in its regulation of commercial transactions, and it has continued to influence commercial law as a result.

*See also:* law, Roman law.

**Corpus Juris Civilis**  The laws collected in the time of Justinian. The Corpus Juris Civilis, or body of the civil law, is the collective title for the laws collected, summarized, and promulgated in 535 C.E. by decree of the Emperor Justinian, including the Institutes, Pandects, Code, Novels, and Edicts. The Corpus Juris remains an important, if indirect, influence upon civil law.

**Institutes of Justinian (Justinian's Institutes)**  A student's overview of Roman law. The Institutes of Justinian is a summary of the late imperial Roman law, distilled from the whole of the Corpus Juris and issued as a part of that great project. It is a short, easily read condensation of the basic sources and principles of Roman law, which was intended for the use of students first encountering the law, and which also serves as a means of understanding the whole body of the larger work. It is largely modeled on the work of Gaius, an earlier jurist, and it has been copied in many lawbooks, institutes, and treatises in the centuries since.

**romaniya (romanija)**  Gypsy law. Romaniya is the body of the historical social customs, beliefs, and values that constitute the code of the Romani people, the Gypsies.

**Rooker–Feldman doctrine**  See: jurisdiction, appellate jurisdiction, Rooker–Feldman doctrine.

**root of title**  See: title, root of title.

**rough proportionality**  See: taking, regulatory taking, conditional use, rough proportionality.

**royal prerogative**  See: prerogative, royal prerogative.

**royalty (royalties)**  A fee for a license in a mine, well, or intellectual property. A royalty is a payment in money or in kind by the licensee of property other than land in fee to the owner or former owner of the property. Royalties are paid to authors, inventors, and others who hold intellectual property and license it for duplication, publication, or use. By custom, the term royalty is still used for payments when the ownership is transferred to the grantee of the use rather than retained by the former owner, if the duty to compensate the grantor of the rights persists in the grantee. The lessee of a mineral interest or other right to take natural resources in land is usually responsible not for rents but for royalties to the lessor.

A royalty may be based on a percentage of the value realized by the sale of the products derived from intellectual property, or as a percentage of the value or a fixed fee per unit according to the volume of such products made or on the quantity of minerals, timber, oil, or gas extracted. The apportioning of payment to use or to value extracted distinguishes royalties from rents, which are usually a fixed value per quantum of time.

**rubric**   A subject title, or a form to be followed. A rubric is a guide or form that is to be followed, and it also means the general label under which something is to be done or a rule is to be found. The term lives on in law from the habit of copyists and printers of prayer books and service materials for churches, who printed in red, or rubio, the instructions to be carried out during a service. The term was then applied to the red titles of statutes and laws in law books, so that it now has both senses: a title that signals a division of one subject from others, as well as a form according to which something is to be done or written, such as a model jury instruction.

**rule**   A statement of legal duty written or drawn from the law. In the law generally, a rule is a statement of what one may do or not do according to law. The statement is sometimes derived exactly from a writing called a rule, such as the rules of civil procedure, but it is usually derived from a host of writings from legislative, regulatory, judicial, and academic sources that are interpreted into a single statement of what is to be done or not done by an individual or an official. There is a continuing argument among legal philosophers over the extent to which a rule has a genuine form, a reality that has authority over officials independent of their choices, or whether a rule is a metaphor for the sum of the written and customary law that is interpreted by officials to be the basis for finding an obligation. Bouvier, it should be noted, took the metaphorical understanding of rule to be accurate.

A rule has a narrower meaning in the specific sense found in the writings of legal materials, such as the rules of procedure, the nautical rules of the road, or the disciplinary rules of professional conduct. In these settings, the rule is part of a larger code of obligations that regulate a specialized activity, rather like one rule among the rules of a game that bind only those who play it.

*See also:* law, legal system.

**Rule 10b-5**   *See:* security, securities, securities fraud (Rule 10b-5).

**Rule 11**   *See:* sanction, litigation sanction, Rule Eleven (Rule 11).

**Rule 12**   *See:* dismissal, grounds for dismissal, failure to state a claim upon which relief can be granted (Rule 12(b)(6) motion or 12(b)(6)).

**Rule 30**   *See:* deposition, Rule 30(b)(6) deposition (corporate deposition).

**Rule Against Perpetuities**   *See:* perpetuity, Rule Against Perpetuities (RAP or rule against remoteness).

**rule against perpetuity**   *See:* perpetutity, rule against perpetuity, what-might-happen test, fertile octogenarian.

**Rule Eleven**   *See:* sanction, litigation sanction, Rule Eleven (Rule 11).

**Rule in Shelley's Case**   *See:* Shelley's Case (Rule in Shelley's Case).

**rule of capture**   *See:* capture, rule of capture.

**rule of convenience**   *See:* class, class of descendants, class gift rule (rule of convenience).

**rule of four**   *See:* certiorari, rule of four.

**rule of law**   *See:* law, rule of law, rules of law; law, rule of law.

**rule of lenity**   *See:* lenity (rule of lenity).

**rule of reason**   *See:* antitrust, Sherman Antitrust Act, rule of reason (reason in antitrust).

**rule of reason in interpretation**   *See:* interpretation, statutory interpretation, rule of reason in interpretation.

**rule of the destructibility of contingent remainders**   *See:* remainder, contingent remainder, rule of the destructibility of contingent remainders (destructibility rule).

**rule of the road**   *See:* navigation, rules of the road (rule of the road).

**rule or the rule of separation of witnesses**   *See:* witness, sequestration of witness (rule or or the rule of separation of witnesses).

**interpretative rule**   A rule intended to give guidance in applying or understanding a rule or statute. An interpretative rule does not create obligations or privileges in itself but provides elaboration, application, and guidance in the interpretation of a regulation, statute, or other law. An interpretative rule is sometimes applied quite strictly as a rule of construction, but in general, as a rule of interpretation it is not considered a source of law in itself and is applied with greater flexibility.

**legal rule (law as a system of rules)**   A legal system is made of rules, with different functions. A rule, as the term is used in legal theory, is a law. A rule is the form that law takes as a basis for action by officials or by citizens. For ease in distinguishing a law as a rule, rule in this sense may be called a legal rule.

The most enduring taxonomy of legal rules is that of H.L.A. Hart in his classic text, The Concept of Law. In this text, he identifies two major forms of rule: primary rules, which prescribe the day-to-day conduct of the subject or citizen; and secondary rules, which prescribe the duties, powers, and conduct of officials. There are various forms of secondary rule, which account for rules specific to essential functions in a legal system: rules of recognition determine whether some rule has been enacted by an appropriate procedure and is a valid law; rules of adjudication determine how the rules shall be applied to specific factual cases; and rules of change allow officials to change rules over time. These three were identified by Hart, but he imagined there must be more, and a fourth may be a rule of role, in which a rule determines who holds what authority to recognize law, adjudicate law, or to change law.

**primary rule**   The laws that regulate the daily lives of ordinary individuals. A primary rule is a law that governs the conduct of persons who are subject to the law, not as officials but as ordinary persons. In legal positivism, the law is the union of primary and secondary rules, in which primary laws regulate the affairs of all individuals in society, and secondary laws regulate the affairs of legal officials when they create or enforce laws. Roughly, one can think of primary rules as akin to rules of tort, property, and criminal law, with contract being somewhat more complicated.

Contract law is a system of laws that allow the person to create law, performing tasks usually performed by officials according to secondary rules. Thus, the primary rules of the legal system are also secondary rules, in which they recognize acts of private parties as making laws that bind them.

*See also:* rule, legal rule, secondary rule.

**rule-scepticism (rule skepticism)**   Systemic doubt that legal officials base actions on rules. Rule skepticism, or rule-scepticism, includes a variety of approaches, which each reject the notion that officials act according to the requirements of rules, regardless of the official's acceptance of or agreement with the rules. Rule skepticism takes many forms, including the realist position that the officials in fact make the rules through the process by which they appear to apply them, and rule nihilism, which rejects the existence of rules.

*See also:* jurisprudence, legal realism.

**secondary rule**   A law regulating how officials make, change, and enforce laws. A secondary rule is a law that allocates legal authority to officials to manage the legal system as a whole, particularly to designate a rule as law, to adjudicate disputes under that rule, and to change that rule. In legal positivism, the law is the union of primary and secondary rules, in which primary laws regulate the affairs of all individuals in society, and secondary laws regulate the affairs of legal officials when they create or enforce laws. In a sense, one can think of secondary rules as akin to rules of constitutional law, administrative law, criminal procedure, and civil procedure, with contract being somewhat more complicated. The inventory of secondary rules first articulated by H.L.A. Hart included three: rules of recognition, adjudication, and change, though there are many others.

*See also:* norm, hierarchy of norms.

**local rule**   A rule or procedure or evidence adopted in a single court. A local rule is a rule, no matter in what form, adopted by a judge or court, which applies to all matters and counsel heard in that court. Local rules often extend and adapt more general rules of procedure and evidence, as well as give guidance on the performance of counsel. A violation of a local rule may be treated by that court as contempt, although custom usually dictates moderation in the enforcement of such rules.

**majority rule (minority rule)**   A rule followed in a majority of jurisdictions. A majority rule, as a designation between rules of law, is the rule followed in a majority of jurisdictions. In some instances, it may be the most subscribed rule among many rules, none of which in fact is adopted by a majority of jurisdictions. (Though such a rule would be more properly considered a plurality rule.)

A minority rule is, therefore, a rule followed in a minority of jurisdictions.

Note: these phrases are easily distinguished by context from the sense of government by the majority or by a minority, though the phrases are the same.

**preferential rule**   A rule establishing a presumption in favor of a given outcome to a specific question. A preferential rule establishes a preference that is to be accorded some weight as a matter of policy when considering a dispute or question for which the rule is relevant. The preferential rule creates a presumption that, all other factors being equal, the outcome that favors the preference is, as a matter of judicial policy, the preferred outcome. Rules may establish a preference like a bias within the rule, for instance, toward intent over form in interpreting a trust instrument, or toward allowing relevant evidence.

It is often said that the best evidence rule is not an exclusionary rule but a preferential rule; in other words, the rule creates a presumption that, for instance, an original photograph is to be introduced, but it does not exclude a duplicate if no original is available and there are other bases of determining the authenticity of the copy.

**rule of court (court rule)**   A rule of procedure or administration for proceedings in a given court. A rule of court is a rule of procedure or administration that applies in a given court. There are many forms, including general rules that may apply to all courts in a jurisdiction, which may include general rules on court operation as well as specific rules of procedure in certain types of matters, such as the rules of bankruptcy courts, rules of family courts, rules of probate, or rules of civil procedure or rules of criminal procedure. Some general rules govern certain procedures common to all actions, such as rules of evidence or rules affecting remedies. Besides general rules, most courts have local rules, which govern actions pending in that court alone.

The rules are intended to establish a reasonable basis for fair proceedings between parties and sufficient process for matter ex parte. The courts may enforce the rules through sanctions of counsel, parties, and those within the confines of the court for other reasons. Yet the courts also have discretion to interpret or apply the rules to do justice as to the parties before them. That said, lower courts are bound to the interpretation and application of general rules by the courts superior to them, and the rules of court overall must be appropriate exercises of the judicial power of that jurisdiction and compatible with the governing constitutions, laws, and statutes.

**rulemaking**   The process by which an administrative agency issues a rule as law. Rulemaking is the procedure that is followed by an agency as it makes, changes, or revokes a rule. Rulemaking is governed in the federal system both by the specific instructions of Congress in statutes delegating legislative power to the agency for further rulemaking, as well as the Administrative Procedures Act, which requires rules to be made only after sufficient notice of the pending rule is provided to those likely to be interested in it, an opportunity to be heard is accorded to interested parties, the agency has reviewed such comments as it receives, and the rule is made available for review by the Office of the President. Rules must be made public, which is usually done by publication, as in the Federal Register and Code of Federal Regulations. Similar state laws govern the issuance of rules by state and local administrative agencies.

**formal rulemaking**   Rulemaking made on the record using formal rulemaking procedures. Formal rulemaking occurs when an agency is creating rules according to the express dictates of Congress in the agency's organic statute, the statute that establishes the agency or vests it with specific jurisdiction and the delegation of Congressional authority, if that statute requires the agency to engage in formal rulemaking, including the use of a hearing and discussion in the drafting and development of the rule that take place on a record prior to the promulgation of the rule.

**informal rulemaking**   Agency creation of internal or administrative rules without formal public hearings. Informal rulemaking is rulemaking that occurs using less public procedures for matters that are less likely to affect the public. It is allowed when an agency creates rules within its administrative jurisdiction (including certain regulations or tariff) or prepares to issue an order that does not have a broad public effect. The agency is required to allow interested persons to submit data or arguments and is required to respond to such comments before making a final rule, but the agency is not required to hold hearings to receive oral comments or to use any one of the many forms of informal consultation, including hearings on or off the record, consultation with interest groups, negotiation with regulated parties, and the review of written submissions.

**public comment (public comment period)**   Objections and information offered while a rule or permit is under review before issuance. Public comment includes all statements made by members of the public, whether acting in a personal or representative capacity, in criticism, support, or query of a proposed rule, regulation, or permit to be issued by an agency.

Public comment may generally be made during a designated period, and includes both oral statements made at a public hearing for which notice is given and written statements are provided to the agency. Under the Administrative Procedures Act, a party who does not make a comment raising a particular concern is estopped from challenging the regulation through judicial review on that ground, unless the rule has been specifically applied to create a burden for that party.

**public notice of proposed rule (advanced notice of proposed rulemaking)**   Notice of a rule under agency consideration for adoption. Public notice of a proposed rule is required under the Administrative Procedures Act to give citizens an opportunity to raise objections, questions, or concerns and to allow the agency to respond to the matters raised before promulgating a final rule. Notice must take place according to regulations, which vary according to the nature of the regulation, permit, or other action made by the rule, but in all cases, notice must be completed before the start of the public comment period, and the notice must give specific instructions on effects of the proposed rule and the method by which comment must be made.

**Rules of Decision Act**   *See:* choice, choice of law, Rules of Decision Act.

**rules of law**   *See:* law, rule of law, rules of law.

**rules of professional conduct**   *See:* lawyer, lawyer discipline, disciplinary rules, rules of professional conduct.

**rules of the road**   *See:* navigation, rules of the road (rule of the road).

**open texture of rules**   Rules have a degree of vagueness that depends on discretionary application. Open texture is a model of rules in which every rule is inherently bound to some degree of interpretation in order to determine a close call or its application to a novel situation. More specifically open texture refers to the penumbral aspect of every rule, beyond its core meaning in which ambiguity is at its least, in which officials, especially judges, must exercise discretion to apply the rule.

**real rule**   The commands actually issued by courts rather than the rules by which they are justified. A real rule is the command or requirement that actually issues from a court, rather than the rules that appear to be followed by the judge. Karl Llewellyn proposed the distinction between real rules and paper rules to explain "realistically" that the judge will behave in a given, often unpredictable manner, rather than through the predictable application of the rules written on paper. Paper rules are mainly used, according to Llewellyn's approach, to give a justification post hoc to the judge's actions.

*See also:* law, real law.

**ruling**   A decision that applies a rule or a law to a question of fact. A ruling, generally, is a decision, an adjudication of some matter in dispute. More specifically, a ruling is a decision by a judge or an official that applies a rule or law in a given situation, thus interpreting or clarifying the rule. Many forms of decision, opinion, and order are rulings though not identified by that term.

*See also:* rule; opinion; mandate (mandatory).

**conclusion of law (legal conclusion)**  The application of laws to a specific circumstance. A conclusion of law is the statement of the laws that generally apply in a given case, dispute, or question, followed by the factual parameters within which the laws must yield a specific rule that can be satisfied or not satisfied by the comparison of facts to the rule. The statement of such a rule, or several of them, is the refinement of the general law to the needs of the moment, and it amounts to the conclusions of law in a matter.

*See also:* ruling, finding of fact (fact finding or fact finder or finder of fact).

**finding of fact (fact finding or fact finder or finder of fact)**  A fact determined as a matter of legal record. A finding of fact is a conclusion of facts stated by a court or administrative agency, nearly always by a judge, magistrate, or administrative judge following a review of the evidence in the record. A finding of fact may be the enrolled findings of fact or special verdict rendered by a jury. A finding of fact may also be a judicial determination reached following a review of the evidence in a trial or hearing without a jury.

Findings of fact are a matter of record. They must be both reasonably supported by the evidence in the record and sufficient to establish the factual predicate for conclusions of law that depend upon them.

*See also:* ruling, conclusion of law (legal conclusion); fact, finding of fact (findings of fact or conclusion of fact or factual conclusion).

## run (running)

**run with the land (running with the land)**  To apply to the successor in title or possession of the land. For an interest to run with the land is for that interest to apply to whomever has title or possession of the land. A benefit or a burden will run with the land, and an easement, covenant, or servitude may run with the land. In all cases, to run with the land requires that the interest first be inherent in the property itself and not personal to an owner of the property.

Under a covenant, a burden will run with the land or bind successors to the owner of the land who first accepts the burden, if the parties were initially in privity with one another by contract or estate, if they initially intended the burden to run, and if the burden is in writing, the burden touches and concerns the land, and the successor owner has privity with the predecessor owner. Under a covenant, a benefit runs more readily, but under the same conditions. An easement runs with the land for both the dominant and servient estates if it is appurtenant rather than in gross.

*See also:* covenant, real covenant, burden of the covenant (running of the burden).

**running of the burden**  *See:* covenant, real covenant, burden of the covenant (running of the burden).

**running of the statute of limitations**  *See:* limitation, limitation of actions, statute of limitations, running of the statute of limitations.

**running the numbers**  *See:* gaming, running the numbers (numbers running).

**runoff**  *See:* water, groundwater, runoff.

**rural**  Related to any area that is not urban. A rural area, as a matter of federal law, is any area that is not near or in a town of 50,000 or more people. Some state laws consider communities or areas rural if there are only 10,000 people in a municipality not near another municipality in the area.

*See also:* urban.

**Rutledge Court**  *See:* court, U.S. court, U.S. Supreme Court, Rutledge Court.

> [W]ith words we govern men.
>
> Benjamin Disraeli, *1 Contarini Fleming: A Psychological Autobiography* 85 (Harper, 1832).

# S

**s**  The nineteenth letter of the modern English alphabet. "S" signifies a variety of functions as a symbol. It is translated into Sierra for radio signals and NATO military transmissions, into Sam for some police radio traffic, and into dot, dot, dot in Morse Code.

**s as an abbreviation**  A word commencing in S. When used as the sole letter of an abbreviation, S often stands for saint, sales, Saskatchewan, Scotland, Scottish, section, see, selected, Senate, service, session, social, society, solicitor, South, Spanish, special, standard, state, statute, strategic, and supervised. It may also stand for the initial of an author or case reporter, such as Sadler, Sadley, Sandels, Sandford, Saunders, Searle, Shaw, Shearman, Smale, Smedes, Smith, Smythe, Southern, Southwestern, Stone, and Supreme. When used in Shepard's Citations, S means superseded.

**s as in hypotheticals**  Son. S may stand for a son in a law school hypothetical, as in A to S and D, for a transfer from character A to son and to daughter. When referring to something served, "s" likely stands for subpoena.

**S-corporation**  *See:* corporation, small-business corporation (S-corporation).

**s. or SS. or scil.**  *See:* scilicet (S. or SS. or scil.).

**S.B. or SB**  *See:* legislation, bill, senate bill (S.B. SB).

**S.E.C. or SEC**  *See:* security, securities, securities regulation, Securities and Exchange Commission (S.E.C. or SEC).

**S.L. or SL**  *See:* legislation, session laws (S.L. SL).

**sabbath (shabat or yaum al-jumua or sabbatarian or sabbatarianism)**  Holy day of rest and religious devotion. The sabbath is a day of the week designated by a religious custom to be set aside for rest or religious observance. Many Christian churches in the United States observed Sunday as the sabbath day, and its observance was once mandated by law.

The Jewish shabbat or shabbos is on Saturday, as is the recognition of sabbath by some Christian churches. The Muslim yaum al-jumu'a is on Friday.

No federal law provides a worker with a right to enjoy the sabbath. However, an employer may not discriminate against a religiously observant employee who seeks to do so. Therefore employers subject to the regulations of Title VII of the Civil Rights Act, 42 U.S.C. § 2000e, et seq., must accommodate workers' observance of the sabbath required by their religions, unless to do so would cause the employer undue hardship.

*See also:* religion, freedom of religion, free exercise of religion | 4. sabbath accommodation.

**blue law (Sunday law or Sunday closing law)**  A statute prohibiting commercial activity on Sundays. Blue laws once enforced the Christian sabbath, as observed in then-dominant churches, although such mandated prohibitions on commerce have been overturned under the Establishment Clause.

**sabotage (saboteur)**  Harm to property intended to obstruct its use in some function or production. Sabotage is the act of the destruction, damage, or contamination of a facility, building, roadway, railway, or any other property for the intended purpose of creating difficulties or inefficiency in the use of that property for some purpose expected by the saboteur. Generally, sabotage is a lawful act in wartime when committed by uniformed members of a state's armed forces against a lawful target of a state with which it is at war. Military sabotage, or sabotage of national-defense material or premises, includes sabotage of both public and private property, if the property is to be used in a manner to support a military or defense activity. Sabotage committed by civilians is a crime, and the U.S. criminal statute for sabotage has no exception or defense expressed for enemy military personnel, although such a defense may be implied by international law.

Industrial sabotage, or private sabotage may also be committed against private property used for non-military purposes. Sabotage that is not against war material or premises or national-defense material or premises is a distinct crime in many jurisdictions. Otherwise, it amounts to a variety of criminal offenses.

Note: as a matter of general usage, sabotage includes acts far less dangerous than the destruction of property, and any statement or act that would frustrate an endeavor or argument is said to be sabotage.

**sac and soc, toll and team**  The ancient privileges of a manor. Sac and soc, toll and team describe the legal powers of the manor lord over his tenants. Sac and soc (the power to hold court and to collect and retain fines assessed there), toll — the right of tollage (customary collections like a tax), and team (the right to hold court over a stranger, at least as a warrantor), were the jurisdictional prerequisites of a manor. Indeed a recitation of these powers in a grant defined the lands in the grant as a manor.

**sachem**  A particularly important American Indian chief. A sachem was a great chief among some nations and tribes in the Northeast, and the term has an added significance of wisdom.

**sacrifice** *See:* religion, freedom of religion, free exercise of religion | 5. sacrifice of animals.

**sacrilege** The deliberate misuse of a place or object sacred to a religious organization. Sacrilege was once a crime, and though it is no longer, it is a recurrent element of the regulation of conduct, to forbid the taking of objects from temples or churches or other places dedicated to the veneration of a divine being or to worship by members of a religious organization, or the misuse of such objects or places in a manner that is reasonably likely to cause offense to members of the religious organization. The term has been used for a wider scope of conduct, and like desecration, it risks vagueness through incomplete definition: to forbid "sacrilege" is insufficient definition for a legal standard. Sacrilege is an ancient term for the "law of holy things," and its many meanings and applications over the millennia are too varied to employ the label alone.

*See also:* desecration (desecrate).

**safety (safe)** Free from threat or harm. To be safe is to be in a condition of safety, a condition in which no harm or threat of harm to a person or other object of concern exists or will arise in the foreseeable future. Safety varies according to context. For example, a safe employment setting, a safe food, and a safe children's consumer product must each be free of the particular dangers or potentials for harm attendant to each object.

**margin of safety** The gap between a standard and the danger the standard prevents. A margin of safety is the difference between a regulatory standard, such as the level of contamination allowed in a substance for human consumption, and the quantity at which the risk the standard seeks to prevent will become manifest. Thus, if a rope would break lifting 1,000 pounds and it is rated to lift only 750 pounds, there is a 250-pound margin of safety.

**safe harbor** Diminished punishment for mitigating behavior when a statute or regulation is broken. In admiralty, a safe harbor is a harbor that provides a sheltered anchorage and, perhaps, a fortification that can protect a vessel from attach. From this is derived the regulatory sense of a safe-harbor provision in a statute or regulation, which provides individuals or entities that it governs a diminished or waived punishment in return for conduct that mitigates the harm the statute or regulation seeks to prevent.

For example, a "safe-harbor" aspect to the rule providing sanctions for an attorney's or party's failure to investigate facts or the law in litigation, allows a time-period within to correct or withdraw inaccuracy. Rule 11(c)(1)(A), Fed. R. Civ. P. But see bankruptcy, in which such safe-harbor may not be available. Rule 9011(c)(1)(A), Fed. R. Bankr. P. In the jurisdictional setting, a "safe-harbor" provision excepts at least a portion of an employee-benefits cause of action from federal preemption, reserving that kind of action, instead, for state-law determination. Such safe-harbor provisions become compellingly important to the parties when a federal cause of action severely limits a plaintiff's right to sue, and when a state-law cause of action contains no such restriction. For example, the preemptive force of the Employment Retirement Income and Security Act (ERISA) is sweeping and broad, and its procedural consequences seriously constrain the federal judiciary's willingness to review an insurance-company's denial of an employee's health benefits. Such limitations do not, however, apply under state law. ERISA's safe-harbor provision exempts benefits if the employer performs ministerial duties, only, and if the benefits-plan otherwise originates from, and profits, the insurance companies. In such cases, where the employer is only the intermediary, the safe-harbor provision permits an employee to sue the insurance companies in state court on broad state-law contract theories. Consequently, a "safe-harbored" plaintiff is free from discovery, as well as from standard-of-review strictures that are imposed in federal ERISA review, though not under state contract law.

*See also:* court, court of limited jurisdiction; court, court of original jurisdiction; jurisdiction, subject matter jurisdiction.

**sailor** *See:* seaman (sailor).

**salability** *See:* sale, salability (salable).

**salary** Fixed annual or periodic compensation for services. A salary is a fixed annual or periodic payment made by an employer to an employee for services rendered, depending upon the expectations of the position and the lapse of time, and not upon the amount or quality of the services rendered.

**salat (namaz salah)** Prayer, one of the five Pillars of Islam. Salat is the prayers to be offered five times daily, a term that literally is derived from the Arabic salala, or complete peace. Salat is one of the five pillars of Islam, and is a fard, or obligation.

**sale (exchange or sale)** An exchange of property for money or anything of value. Sale is a form of contract in which title to some goods pass from the seller to a buyer, who gives to the seller either money or other things of value in return. For a sale to occur, the parties to the sale must be legally competent to contract. The thing to be sold must be capable of transfer, and it must be lawful to do so. There must be mutual assent to the sale, which must be a transfer of the thing in return for money, value, or a promise of future payment of money or value.

In the common law, sales are inherently made in exchange for a certain sum of money, and the overwhelming number of sale agreements still are. Transactions not made for money are exchanges. By statute, however, many jurisdictions have collapsed the distinction with exchange for the purposes of ensuring taxes on sales reach barter and other transactions that amount to a transfer of property for value. There is no difference as to the sale in the seller being titled a seller, vendor, merchant, or purchasee, and there is no difference as to the sale in the buyer being titled buyer, purchaser, vendee, or merchant; the roles are functional rather than formal.

*See also:* transfer.

**sale price**   *See:* price (sale price).

**bulk sale**   A sale liquidating half or more of the seller's business. A bulk sale is a sale, or a series of sales, of a quantity of goods that is significantly beyond the seller's usual transaction. Under the Uniform Commercial Code, a bulk sale is one that is not only out of the ordinary course of the seller's business but also part of the liquidation of a business that is being wound up, or a sale of half or more of the value of the seller's inventory at the time. Note: do not confuse bulk sale with bulk load.

**conditions of sale**   The terms setting for the duties of the buyer and the seller. The conditions of sale are a series of terms that may be express or implied in any sale agreement. As long as there is sufficient evidence of a contract to enforce, the law will imply any omitted terms. The express terms include all terms that were specifically negotiated and agreed upon by the parties, or, in the case of a written agreement, such terms as are written in the instrument. Usual terms include the description of the property sold, as well as its quantity, price, date of delivery, responsibility for delivery, allocations of risk of harm to the property prior to its delivery, date of payment, form of payment, covenants for use, conditions for return, and other terms that may be agreed, some of which might be form or boilerplate terms in a written sale agreement, such as an arbitration clause, forum selection clause, choice of law clause, locus of the agreement, and designation of parties. Some sale agreements incorporate an express warranty as a condition of sale, and some treat a warranty as a separate contract.

*See also:* auction; puffer, puffer in an auction.

**land sale (sale of land or sale of lands or sale of property or real estate transaction)**   A sale of an interest in real property. A land sale is any sale of a legal or equitable interest in real property. A land sale is subject to the Statute of Frauds and must be memorialized in a writing that sufficiently describes the land, whether by metes and bounds, by tract and parcel, by address, or by some other means sufficient to ensure that the object of the sale is a unique and unambiguous parcel of land and that the quantity of land is established. The writing must be signed by the party to be bound, as a minimum criterion of the statute. As a matter of common practice, land sales are often contingent sales agreements, in which the seller accords the buyer a license to enter the land for inspections, and the buyer reserves a variety of conditions in the sale agreement that must be satisfied prior to closing on the sale agreement, until which time, the land sale remains executory.

*See also:* sale, land sale, buy–sell agreement (buy/sell agreement).

**buy-sell agreement (buy/sell agreement)**   A conditional contract for the sale of property. A buy-sell agreement is an executory contract to transfer property. A buy–sell agreement establishes certain rights and expectations between the would-be seller and would-be buyer, but it remains void as to transfer of the property until and unless one or more specified conditions are met, which usually occurs at a closing, at which time ownership and payment are exchanged as contemplated in the buy-sell. In a typical executory agreement, title transfers to a buyer of property at the execution of the contract, but in a buy–sell agreement, title does not transfer until the prerequisite is satisfied. A buy-sell agreement is a form of purchase agreement.

*See also:* purchase, purchase agreement; sale, land sale (sale of land or sale of lands or sale of property or real estate transaction).

**closing and settlement (closing)**   The final transfer of value for title in a land sale. The closing and settlement are the actions that execute most land sale agreements, at which time the buyer releases any remaining conditions on the sale of the land, the seller transfers title, and the buyer, or a lender on the buyer's behalf, transfers payment to the seller (or to lienholders or mortgagees on the seller's behalf, with any surplus tendered to the seller). The closing of the sale executes the contract, and all contract terms are considered merged into the deed.

*See also:* sale, sale closing.

**equitable conversion (equitable owner)**   A sale agreement creates a trust in the property to the buyer's benefit. Equitable conversion is a doctrine in equity that has been long accepted in the common law, by which a trust is implied over realty upon the entrance of a buy-sell agreement. The trust requires the property held by the seller to be held to the benefit of the buyer, limiting the seller from waste and creating a fiduciary relationship regarding the assets by the seller toward the buyer. The obligations of the trust cease at closing, when the legal title and equitable benefit merge in the buyer, destroying the trust through merger. Thus, a buyer is an equitable owner prior to closing.

*See also:* title, equitable title.

**lease-purchase agreement**   *See:* lease, lease–purchase agreement.

**present sale**   A sale of goods accomplished at the making of the contract. A present sale is a sale of goods that occurs when the bargain is made, whether or not the goods are delivered at that time or a different time. One form of contract for sale under the U.C.C., it differs from a contract to sell goods at a future time.

**salability (salable)**   Legally and practicably capable of being sold for a reasonable price. Salability is the legal and physical condition of goods, lands, or other products that render it capable of being sold as a matter of law and reasonably likely to be bought by a purchaser of reasonable discernment, at a price reasonable in comparison with other similar products for sale. Property subject to a lien is not salable, nor is a product damaged beyond ordinary use. Salability is a matter of degree, and property may be more or less salable according to circumstance.

**sale closing**   Satisfaction of a contract for sale. Closing in a contract, generally, is the final performance of the last actions that were contemplated in the contract. The closing is the moment at which a contract is executed, and prior to that moment, the contract is executory. The most common usage of closing is in the transaction that concludes a buy–sell agreement for the purchase of land.

*See also:* sale, land sale, closing and settlement (closing); day, law day (lage dayum).

   **short sale of mortgaged property**   Sale of property for less than the outstanding mortgage. A short sale of mortgaged property occurs when property subject to mortgage is sold for an amount less than the outstanding debt secured by the mortgage. The seller remains responsible for the remaining amount of the debt. A short sale is only possible with the consent of the mortgagee or lender, which usually allows the buyer to assume the mortgage while still holding the seller accountable for any arrearage, which must usually be satisfied prior to the transfer.

**true sale**   A sale in which risk and benefit are transferred from seller to buyer. A true sale of financial assets occurs when the parties both intend a sale rather than some lesser interest, surety, or insurance stake, intending that all of the benefits and risks attendant with ownership are transferred from the seller to the buyer. A true sale implies a transaction for fair value made at arm's length.

**sales tax**   *See:* tax, sales tax (sales and use tax).

**sales warranty**   *See:* warranty, sales warranty, warranty of merchantability (consumer warranty or manufacturer's warranty).

**Salic law**   *See:* feud, fedualism, Carolingian law (Salic law).

**salmonella**   Bacteria that sicken humans found in foods exposed to animal wastes. Salmonella is a group of bacteria that cause diarrhea, sickness, and death in humans exposed to it, the bacteria being found in some foods that have been exposed to animal or human wastes.

*See also:* contaminant, contamination.

**salvage**   The recovery and claim of goods that are abandoned or lost, especially at sea. Salvage is recovery, and to salvage something generally is to take possession of it from a state of abandonment or distress and to restore it to use.

In admiralty and maritime law, salvage is the arena of law governing title, possession, and claims in vessels, cargo, and equipment that are found after a vessel has been in distress or wrecked. In general, a salvor may keep all that is recovered from a wreck abondoned in fact and in title, but as against a wreck over which title is still asserted, the salvor may take only a customary salvor's fee.

*See also:* abandonment, abandonee.

**salvage value**   *See:* value, salvage value (residual value or scrap value).

**salvage as reclaimed waste**   To retask or reuse property abandoned from its initial use. Salvage, in its senses other than in admiralty, is the process of either designating property to be taken from use, service or inventory or reclaiming such property and refitting or retasking it for reuse, either in the same function it was once used or in a different function. Salvage is one form of recycling.

**flotsam**   Goods that float away from a ship or shipwreck. Flotsam are goods that float on the seas after a ship has been damaged, wrecked, or sunk. Flotsam differ from jetsam, which are goods deliberately jettisoned in order to lighten the ship. The critical aspect of flotsam is not that it floats or sinks but that it left the confinement of the vessel through natural actions of the wind, sea, and gravity rather than by the deliberate action of the crew. Both flotsam and jetsam have a metaphorical significance as anything or anyone left to the mercy of circumstances.

*See also:* salvage, jetsam (jettison).

**jetsam (jettison)**   Materials cast overboard from a vessel in distress at sea. Jetsam is whatever is deliberately jettisoned from a vessel as the result of a seaman-like decision to lighten the vessel while it is in distress. Jetsam may include cargo, equipment, personal effects, or any other thing carried on board. Jetsam is distinct from ligan, because jetsam floats away and ligan is subject to a marker or buoy. (Bouvier noted that jetsam often sinks, and often it does. One reason jetsam sinks more than flotsam is that heavier objects are usually chosen for jettison in an effort to lighten a ship. Sinking is still not a defining aspect of jetsam.) Both ligan and jetsam, as well as flotsam, are now generally considered part of the wreck.

Jetsam, usually in the phrase "flotsam and jetsam," is metaphorically used to describe people who are economically or socially marginalized.

*See also:* salvage, flotsam; salvage, ligan (lagan).

**ligan (lagan)**   Goods cast overboard but that have sunk to the sea floor. Ligan, or lagan, are goods, usually cargo but sometimes also fittings and equipment of the vessel, that are deliberately jettisoned from a vessel and allowed to sink to the seafloor, after which a marker buoy is placed to allow later recovery. Ligan is part of the wreck and subject to the laws of salvage.

*See also:* salvage, flotsam; salvage, jetsam (jettison).

**salvor**  A person who voluntarily preserves a ship or cargo from loss. A salvor is a person or entity who saves a ship in distress with the master's assent, or a derelict ship, or abandoned cargo, who have no pre-existing contract or direct obligation to do so. A salvor has immediate possession of the salvage and a salvor's lien on all of it until salvage charges are paid, though the salvor also has a duty of good faith and of reasonable diligence in the protection of the salvage until it is restored, if it is to be restored, to its true owner.

**shipwreck (wreck of a vessel)**  The remains of a vessel and its goods after it is wrecked at sea. A shipwreck, or wreck, in U.S. law includes both the remains of the vessel and the goods and cargo that are found on or near it. This contrasts with the common law definition of the wreck as only the goods cast up on shore. The rights to vessels and goods on the ocean floor varies according to whether the vessel is found in the high seas or in the territorial sea. A vessel on the floor of the territorial sea is property of the sovereign; in the U.S. the United States has delegated its rights to the coastal states, who have individual rules for preservation and salvage. A vessel on the floor of the high seas, however, is the salvor's subject to the claim of the true owner if title has not been abandoned.

## Samaritan

**bad Samaritan**  One who will not go to the rescue of a stranger. The bad Samaritan, a neologism from the idea of the good Samaritan who renders assistance to strangers, is a person who fails to aid a stranger in distress, a person who could render aid to another but fails to do so. It is also sometimes used to depict a stranger who intervenes in the life of another for an improper purpose. The term arises most often in debating the duties involved in abortion.

*See also:* rescue, duty to rescue.

**Good Samaritan Statute (Good Samaritan Law or Good Samaritan Doctrine)**  A person who renders aid to a stranger. A Samaritan is a person who renders aid to a stranger, particularly a person who rescues someone in peril from another person, from a natural disaster, or from a medical or other crisis. The term is metaphorically derived from the Christian parable. In law, a "Good Samaritan" is a person who assists a person in need of assistance, especially when there is no legal duty to do so.

Good Samaritan laws are of two forms. The first are laws that provide some level of immunity from suit for negligence by a Good Samaritan, holding the rescuer harmless from a claim that might be brought by the person rescued or another for any injury or damages brought about by the rescue effort. At common law, a rescuer is liable if the rescuer fails to exercise reasonable care and if the person rescued relies on the rescuer, suffering a harm that would not otherwise have occurred. Good Samaritan statutes limit such liability for negligent acts to either gross negligence or a professional standard for professionals involved.

The second form of laws are the relatively rare laws that either enact a duty to rescue a person in peril if one may reasonably do so or enact a duty to assist a person in danger if one may do so without risk to oneself. These laws create liability for injuries sustained by the person in distress, when a potential rescuer fails to make a good-faith effort to rescue or assist in a rescue.

*See also:* rescue, duty to rescue.

**same-sex marriage**  *See:* marriage, same-sex marriage (same sex marriage or gay marriage or marriage by homosexuals).

**sanction (sanctions)**  A decree that authorizes some conduct, or penalizes it. A sanction is a decree or order that has two nearly opposite meanings: it is an authorization of conduct, but it is a statement of a penalty for engaging in conduct. Though the earliest forms of both sense vary in that the penalty was initially a noun (decree of sanctions) and the authorization a verb (we sanction this expedition) both senses are now used as both nouns and verbs. Thus, a legislature may sanction a once forbidden practice, which allows people to engage in that practice without penalty. On the other hand, to sanction a person who engages in forbidden conduct is to order a penalty against that person. The primary difference in usage is not a reliable guide, but the tendency is still that a person sanctioned is punished but conduct sanctioned is permitted. "To have the sanction of the court," or any other other authority, must be understood as either license or penalty according to small variations in usage and, of course, context. Both senses of the word come from the Latin sanctio, meaning a law or decree.

**sanction as approval**  An allowance or permission to do something. Sanction, particularly to sanction, is the particular allowance or permission for an activity or conduct, particularly in a circumstance in which such a license would be required or at least helpful to demonstrate that the activity or conduct is not forbidden. Although a common usage of sanction in this sense is as an order or notice given directly to a person or entity (the CEO sanctioned this operation at the meeting), the term is often used in a general sense as an allowance expressed or implied in a rule or law (this move is sanctioned under the rules). Note: clearly, sanction of an act differs from sanction as punishment for an act. Context is essential in distinguishing these Janus-terms. Sanction in this sense is both a noun and a verb.

**discovery sanction**  Penalties for a party's failure to permit discovery or to obey a discovery order. Discovery sanctions are penalties ordered by a trial court against a party or a party's attorney for failing to perform requested discovery or failing to obey a discovery order. The trial judge has broad discretion in awarding or in withholding sanctions, although sanctions are mandated for parties that fail to offer admissions or disclosures of information that they are later found to have had. Discovery sanctions may include the award of attorneys' fees, the directing of a finding of fact, the striking of pleadings, the dismissal of claims or of defenses, staying the action, rendering a judgment, and contempt of court. The severity of the sanctions may depend upon the wrong-doing party's apparent intent to impede the action or to hide evidence, the harm to the other parties, the inconvenience to the court, and the party's past conduct.

*See also:* ethics, legal ethics, discovery abuse.

**Rule Eleven (Rule 11)** Every court writing must be reasonably researched and honestly presented, or its signer is subject to sanction. Rule 11 of the Federal Rules of Civil Procedure requires every pleading, motion, and other writing filed in court to be signed by an attorney or party, who is thereby held to have engaged in a reasonable and good faith investigation into the subject of the writing, established that the writing or pleading is not filed for a vexatious or improper reason, claimed that there is good evidence or likely to be good evidence to support the statements of fact made and good law to support the claims or defenses of law. A failure of the attorney or the pro se litigant to sign a pleading or other writing filed with the court requires the court to strike it from the record unless the failure is timely cured. More fundamentally, a signator whose pleading or writing fails to satisfy the standards of Rule 11 may be sanctioned by the court, including payment to the opposing party, striking of the filing, and judgment for the opponent. Rule 11 applies equally to the defense as to the plaintiff, and either party who files an argument, motion, claim or defense, or other writing in violation of the rule is subject to its penalties. Note: Rule 11 is not exhaustive of the remedies for a false civil filing, as the inherent powers of the court over members of its bar and those appearing before it is more extensive than the rule.

*See also:* ethics, legal ethics, obligation to disclose adverse authority (ethical duty of candor).

**sanctions of attorneys** *See:* lawyer, lawyer discipline, sanctions.

**sanctity of contract** *See:* contract, contract interpretation, sanctity of contract.

**sanctuary** A shelter for a criminal from the law or an animal from humans. Sanctuary in the common law, was a place of refuge in which a person who was accused of a crime, indeed a person who had confessed to a crime, could find asylum, at least for a time, without fear of arrest or prosecution. Churches were the primary place of sanctuary, though civil sanctuaries existed as well. This practice was abolished by statute in the seventeenth century. The idea of sanctuary has persisted, however, in notion of privacy, particularly in the domain of the home or other areas free from police intrusion without probable cause or a warrant. In drafting, sanctuary is used metaphorically to mean a legal privilege, excuse, or justification that would give a person who commits some act either immunity or near-immunity for it, but this is to refer to the effect of legal doctrines providing refuge or sanctuary, not the doctrines themselves.

The modern sanctuary is usually a preserve for natural resources, particularly for wildlife. Federal and state law designates wildlife sanctuaries under the National Forest Policy Act with a greater protection for individual species than that offered in a wildlife reserve.

**sandbagging (lying behind the log or unfair gamesmanship)** Delay to improve one's strategic or tactical position. Sandbagging is the act of delaying a procedure in order to gain some benefit from the delay or prejudice to one's opponent. The tactic is known by many names (in Texas, it is "lying behind the log"). Although sandbagging is usually a fault of the defense, either party may be guilty of dragging out a process in order to increase its cost, hinder witnesses or parties, forestall a recovery, or maintain the process to the inconvenience of the opponent or the benefit of the sandbagger. Even so, not every form of delay is forbidden, and small delays that allow a reasonable and fair trial strategy are not barred. One example of excusable delay is a delay in presenting a legal argument or piece of evidence until one's opponent has taken a position that would otherwise have been altered. As long as the delaying party has provided sufficient notice of the claims or defenses and their basis to the opposing party and has not delayed so long as to cause waste of the other party's time or unfair surprise, such a tactical delay may be excused.

*See also:* stonewalling (stonewall).

**Sandoval Hearing** *See:* record, arrest record, Sandoval Hearing.

**Sanhedrin** The highest Jewish court during the time of the Temple in Jerusalem. The Sanhedrin was the highest court of Jewish law during the time of the Temple in Jerusalem. It was also the name of a lesser court in each Jewish city in ancient Israel. The Great Sanhedrin was responsible for both legislation and judgment of the law, until it was disbanded in the fifth century CE owing to increased Roman persecution. The trial of Jesus depicted in the Christian gospels is before the Sanhedrin of Jerusalem, though that account is controversial.

**sanitary** Beneficial to good health. Sanitary means encouraging of good health. The term is a general term including, at times, conditions that encourage good mental health and good physical health. Even so, the term has narrowed in its usage and now is often used to mean clean, disinfected, or relatively free of pathogens such as bacteria. In many engineering situations, a sanitary facility or sanitary equipment is related to the evacuation of human waste, from toilets to a waste treatment facility.

**sanitary sewer overflow or CSO or SSO** *See:* sewerage, combined sewer overflow (sanitary sewer overflow or CSO or SSO).

**sans recours or with recourse** *See:* recourse, without recourse (sans recours or with recourse).

**Sarbanes-Oxley claim** *See:* whistleblower, Sarbanes-Oxley claim (SOX Act claim).

**satire or spoof** *See:* parody (satire or spoof).

**satisfaction (satisfy)** The full performance of a duty. Satisfaction is the fulfillment of an obligation, whether it is a duty of performance under a contract, the payment of a debt, the provision of a reason, or any other thing that one ought to do under a requirement of law, equity, or morality. In all cases, the doing of what one ought to do satisfies the requirement. Thus a payment in full satisfies a debt. A full and truthful explanation is a satisfactory explanation. The full performance of the contract satisfies the contract. The full inventory and consolidation of the estate, payment of creditors, distribution of bequests, and filing of a final accounting with the court satisfies the executor's duty, and so on.

Note: there are two senses of satisfaction when a contract specifies performance by one party to the other party's satisfaction. The satisfaction of the other party is, by definition, manifest when the first party fully performs. On the other hand, the satisfaction of the party implies a subjective level of discretion in determining whether the sufficiency and quality of performance merit acceptance. Unless the contract further defines the non-performing party's satisfaction, this power is limited to a reasonable interpretation of the contract and may not be unreasonably withheld.

> **satisfaction of judgment** *See:* judgment, enforcement of judgment, satisfaction of judgment.

> **satisfaction of lien** *See:* lien, satisfaction of lien.

**savings bond** *See:* bond, savings bond (government bond or government security).

**savings clause** *See:* severability of statute, savings clause (saving clause); legislation, savings clause.

**sawm** Fasting in the month of Ramadan. Sawm is fasting, the fourth pillar of Islam, is fard — obligatory during the month of Ramadan, for all who are able.

**scab** *See:* union, labor union, non-union, scab.

**scam or swindle or swindling or con game or con artist or con man** *See:* fraud, confidence game (scam or swindle or swindling or con game or con artist or con man).

**scandal** The harm of public notice of a wrongful act. Scandal is the public discussion of a wrongful and embarrassing act, whether the act is committed by or attributed to a private individual, a public figure, or officers or employees of a business entity or public institution. Scandal includes not only matters of fascination to the national media, but also the publication of information within a smaller community, spread by word of mouth like gossip or the publication of such matter through court documents.

A claim that a person has engaged in a scandalous act gives rise to a scandal. The act need not be illegal, but it is an act that a reasonable person would believe to be disgraceful or shameful; wrong to have been done by the person who did it, either violating a duty of law, office, responsibility, or morality.

Scandal is the public effect of a claim of a wrongful act, as well as the nature of the act itself. Though there is a distinct difference in causation, so that a scandal is the result of public knowledge coupled with either the allegation of or the commitment of the scandalous act, only a scandalous act or false allegation of a scandalous act may produce a scandal.

The common law recognized a distinct action in tort for scandal. A party harmed by a false claim of a scandalous act that gives rise to a scandal could bring an action for trespass on the case for scandal for damage. This eventually became an action for scandal. This action has generally been superseded by actions for defamation, libel, slander, outrage, and (depending on the circumstances) negligence and blackmail.

One theory of negligence arises from the commission of a scandalous act to the harm of a corporation or of another party. The question in determining liability is whether specific harm from a public scandal could reasonably be foreseen as a result of a scandalous act, presuming such an act would become public knowledge. (One cannot presume secrecy for a wrongful act.) A scandalous act that reasonably foreseeably will give rise to a scandal to the foreseeable specific harm of another amounts to negligence.

Scandal, unlike defamation, need not be true or false, and indeed some scandals are disseminated more widely owing to curiosity as to the truth of the allegation of wrongdoing. A scandal that arises from a false allegation of a scandalous act gives rise to an action for defamation, libel, or slander, although such actions are subject to the limits of claims that are brought against public figures under the New York Times test.

Two residual aspects of the old action for scandal remain in courtroom procedure. In some jurisdictions, the discussion of scandalous matter, particularly salacious details regarding immoral conduct, is a basis for the courtroom to be cleared of minors. As a matter of federal and state pleading practice, pleadings are to be free of scandalous matter, which is particularly defined as any unnecessary statement that amounts to a scandal upon the court, such as unnecessarily impugning the character of a judge, lawyer, witness, party, third party, or institution.

Scandalous subject matter, particularly immoral or obscene matter or, presumably, matter that defames a person, is not subject to trademark.

*See also:* slander (slanderer); negligence (negligent); pleading, scandalous matter in a pleading; trademark, scandalous matter in a trademark; opprobrium.

**scandalous matter in a pleading**  *See:* pleading, scandalous matter in a pleading.

**scandalous matter in a trademark**  *See:* trademark, scandalous matter in a trademark.

**scarlet letter**  *See:* punishment, shaming punishment, scarlet letter.

**schedule**  A list of people, things, acts, or times. A schedule, most often, is a list of tasks to be performed (or that have been performed) organized by time. The term is broader though, from the Latin for scrap of paper, and includes all types of list, including lists of accounts, lists of income, lists of evidence, lists of proceedings, lists of people and duties, etc.
*See also:* order, court order, scheduling order.

**Schedule B Number**  *See:* export, Schedule B Number (Schedule B System).

**Schedule I or Schedule II or Schedule III or Schedule IV or Schedule V**  *See:* drug, controlled substance, drug schedule (Schedule I or Schedule II or Schedule III or Schedule IV or Schedule V).

**Scheduling Order**  *See:* Order, Court Order, Scheduling Order.

**schlemiel**  A person who brings bad fortune on himself. A schlemiel is Yiddish for a person with chronic bad luck, but whose bad luck is the result of the schlemiel's own bungling or schemes.
*See also:* Yiddish.

**schlock**  Shoddy merchandise or work. Schlock, a Yiddish term for cheap goods, is used by lawyers and others to describe work of mediocrity, particularly poor legal argument or research.

**schmooze**  A charming discussion. Schmooze is Yiddish for a pleasant discussion that leaves each participant pleased with the others. Note: schmooze is both a noun and a verb.

**schmuck**  Term of abuse for an offensive or foolish person. Schmuck, a Yiddish term for a fool or oaf widely used among lawyers, is a term that should not be used in formal prose.

**Schmuck Test**  *See:* offense, lesser included offense, Schmuck Test.

**schnook**  A pathetic but lovable fool. Schnook is a Yiddish term for a person easily taken advantage of by others, someone like the comic-strip character of Charlie Brown, though without the wisdom.
*See also:* Yiddish.

**school**  An institution for teaching, or a tradition of study or thought. School has two distinct senses. The more common sense of school is an institution for the instruction of students in any general or specialized field of knowledge, profession, or craft. A school may have just one teacher or it may have a great many, but the function of a school is to teach. Though the distinction between a school and a college has been lost to most contemporary usage, the once-signal difference is that a school is the place of instruction and the college is the community of faculty.

A school is also a tradition or framework for thought, study, or scholarship using a particular method or organized to a particular purpose. Thus, a school of thought.

**school trust land**  *See:* land, school trust land (sixteenth section land).

**school voucher or education voucher**  *See:* voucher, tuition voucher (school voucher or education voucher).

**school zone**  The geography near a school. A school zone is the land near a school, which is variously defined according to the purpose for which it is designated. Under federal law, for certain forms of conduct, it is all grounds of the school and a buffer of a thousand feet. As a matter of traffic law, it extends to roads that support a significant density of pedestrian traffic going to and from the school, or as marked by proper authority.

**schtick (shtick)**  A performance. In Yiddish, a schtick is a signature tune or performance that is closely identified with a particular entertainer. It is used by lawyers to describe an area of legal practice, particularly a specialized from of representation. It also describes the modus operandi or frequently employed technique or frequently attempted endeavor of a client, opponent, or person accused of a crime.

**scienter**  Knowledge. Scienter is the state of knowing something, whether the thing known is general or specific to some purpose. Many criminal statutes include an element of scienter that must be proved. As the 1853 edition notes, a person who passes a counterfeit coin and does not know that it is counterfeit is innocent of passing counterfeit money. The element of scienter in a crime may be of a condition or of a result or of an intended result. Scienter may be inferred or presumed from circumstances in which the person must have known a predicate fact to do something the person did or have known a fact to know another fact of which the persons' knowledge is proved. Note: it would be clearer for most speakers for legislators to use "knowingly" or "with knowledge" rather than the language of scienter.

**scilicet (S. or SS. or scil.)**  That is to say. Scilicet, or more often its abbreviations, is used in older lawbooks to introduce an example or an appositive, rather in the way that modern writers still use either i.e., for id est, or e.g., for exempli gratia.
*See also:* videlicet (viz.).

**scintilla**  A very small amount. Scintilla is Latin for spark, and it represents a trace or minute amount of anything—the equivalent of what material is needed to make a spark. In law, a scintilla is the least possible amount of something to be given legal recognition, as in a scintilla of cause or a scintilla of evidence. This to say that there is not much cause or evidence. An action based on no more than a scintilla of cause may be unreasonable, and a scintilla of evidence, alone, is usually insufficient to support a verdict. Still, a scintilla is something, and an unrebutted scintilla of cause may be enough to support a claim of good faith, and a scintilla of evidence may be enough to sustain a complaint.

*See also:* proof, burden of proof, scintilla of evidence; quibble (quibbling).

**scintilla of evidence** *See:* proof, burden of proof, scintilla of evidence.

**scire** Knowledge or understanding. Scire is a form of scio, Latin for knowledge or understanding.

**scire facias** A show cause order used to enforce a matter of record. A scire facias is a writ issued requiring its recipient to show cause why a judgment or other matter of record should not be enforced. It is equivalent to an order granting a motion for judgment or an order granting an award based on an enrolled judgment.

*See also:* judgment, enforcement of judgment (execution of judgment).

**scope of discovery** *See:* discovery, scope of discovery.

**scope of employment** *See:* liability, vicarious liability, course of employment (scope of employment).

**scope of representation** *See:* representation, legal representation, scope of representation.

**SCOTUS** *See:* court, U.S. court, U.S. Supreme Court (SCOTUS).

**scrip** A money substitute. Scrip is a form of money that is used in lieu of the legal tender authorized by the state for monetary transactions and the payment of debts. The scrip has a predesignated value and is traded among holders of scrip as well as between those who receive scrip in return for goods or services. Gift certificates are a form of scrip. Scrip may be created and distributed by a government or by a private individual, merchant, employer, or group. Scrip has at times been used for pay both by private employers and the U.S. government.

*See also:* money.

**scrip issue or share split or bonus issue or capitalization issue** *See:* share, share as stock, stock split (scrip issue or share split or bonus issue or capitalization issue).

**scrivener** A professional drafter who puts an instrument into final form. A scrivener is a person who prepares documents or writings for another, usually professionally or commercially. A scrivener usually works from a written rough copy, placing it in final form, which distinguishes the role of scrivener from that of an amanuensis, who transcribes dictation. Even so, both roles are included in the legal sense of the scrivener as the person who drafts the document under consideration.

*See also:* amanuensis.

**scrivener's error** *See:* error, scrivener's error.

**scrubber** *See:* pollution, air pollution, scrubber.

**scrutiny** Investigation. Scrutiny is investigation, whether by the examination of evidence in some place and the interrogation of witnesses or by close observation, analysis, and interpretation of some evidence or text. A scrutiny in English law may mean a variety of examinations, particularly of an election result or candidacy to stand for an office.

**standards of scrutiny** Constitutional standards are strict scrutiny, intermediate scrutiny, or the rational relationship. The standards of scrutiny are applied in judicial review of state or federal laws or actions that are alleged to burden a fundamental right or violate equal protection or due process. Depending on the right, interest, or classification burdened, the standards are of strict scrutiny, intermediate scrutiny, or rational relationship. Strict scrutiny is applied when an action to enforce the equal protection of the laws arises from a difference of treatment based upon a suspect classification, such as race; it is applied as a matter of due process of law when an action burdens a fundamental right that is essential to ordered liberty, such as the freedom of speech, and it is applied to laws that intentionally burden other constitutional interests, such as a state law deliberately barring commerce from other states. All regulations that do not burden such rights or interests are subject to a rational relationship review, but burdens on certain interests that are recognized as significant but not as prone to abuse as a suspect classification, such as burdens on one gender, are subject to intermediate scrutiny.

Note: though the three-tiered system of review has persisted for fifty years, there are many arguments that each standard is deeply flawed and that the system is too easy on economic regulation and too hard on regulation that affects matters of race or gender in various constructive ways. There are also arguments that a more generalized balancing test or a greater distribution of bright line tests would be better.

**disproportionate burden** A law is valid unless it disproportionately burdens free speech. The disproportionate burden test has been suggested by Justice Stephen Breyer as an alternative to strict scrutiny or rational-basis review of laws that burden constitutional rights, namely the freedom of speech but potentially other rights of great significance. The disproportionate burden test would invalidate a law that creates a burden on speech disproportionately greater than the interests the state's officials sought to achieve by the law.

**inclusiveness (overinclusiveness or underinclusiveness)** The scope of a legal category, prohibition or license. Inclusiveness is the effect of a statute, rule, or other law in creating a category within which some conduct is allowed or forbidden. The manner by which the law includes or excludes may vary according to any aspect of the definition of a person, place, or thing, so that the law may bar or allow some conduct according to who does it, what it is, some aspect of what it is, where it is done, or when it is done. Because laws should have a point to them, a purpose or reason to create a burden or benefit in society, the extent to which the law includes conduct or fails to include conduct in its scope should fit the rationale for the law.

An overinclusive law is a law that is written or applied in such a manner as to forbid conduct outside the scope of the conduct that would fit the rationale of the law. An overinclusive law includes people (or conduct) within its burden or benefit who are either not intended by the drafters of the law or whose inclusion is not justified by the purposes underlying the law. The problem of overinclusion is patent, the justification for the law does not justify the burden created upon the overly included group.

An underinclusive law is a law written or applied in such a manner as to allow conduct within the scope of the conduct that must fit the rationale of the law. An underinclusive law omits people (or conduct) within its burden or benefit who were either intended by the drafters of the law or whose inclusion is essential to the justification of the purposes underlying the law. The problem of underinclusion is the patent unfairness either conferring a benefit on some but not all of the people whose status or conduct deserves some benefit, or of burdening some but not all of those whose conduct is fit for prohibition by law.

Some degree of overinclusion or underinclusion may be unavoidable in the drafting or application of laws, yet when such problems in definition lead to irrational distinctions or counterproductive laws, or when the law creates a burden on a constitutional right, or creates a burden on a suspect or quasi-suspect class, the law does not assure the due process of law and is unconstitutional.

**intermediate scrutiny** A legal burden on a quasi-suspect class must substantially serve an important governmental objective. Intermediate scrutiny is a test under the Equal Protection Clause of the 14th Amendment to review laws that create a burden that falls upon a group that the courts have recognized as quasi-suspect (which currently means laws burdening people owing to gender, illegitimate birth, or being a lawful resident alien). Such laws will only be upheld if the use of that classification to define the burden is not created for an invidious purpose and does in fact serve an important governmental objective, and the burden is substantially related to achievement of that objective.

*See also:* class, legal classification, quasi-suspect classification (quasi-suspect class).

**rational-basis review (rational relationship test)** All laws must at least be rationally related to a legitimate purpose of government. Rational-basis review is the standard for determining whether a law is constitutional that is the most deferential to Congress or to the states. A law that neither burdens a fundamental constitutional right nor creates a burden on a suspect or quasi-suspect class of people is to be upheld unless there is no rational basis for the law. Rational-basis review presumes strongly that the law is a valid exercise of constitutional power and will be upheld unless the party who challenges it demonstrates that there is either no legitimate governmental purpose at all or that the means chosen to implement that purpose are in fact not justified by that purpose because the means do not in fact support or reasonably achieve that purpose. In practice, such arguments are usually based on a more affirmative argument, that the law in fact promotes a purpose that is not a legitimate exercise of governmental authority or the means that are essential to the law are unrelated or are not rationally related to the stated purpose or any reasonable set of alternatives. The fit between purpose and means may be quite loose and still reasonable, including some margin of overinclusion and of underinclusion. Thus, nearly every law passes this standard.

*See also:* interest, state interest, legimate state interest (legitimate governmental purpose).

**strict scrutiny** A burden on a suspect class or fundamental right must promote a compelling interest by the least burdensome means. Strict scrutiny is the standard of judicial review of any law that potentially either violates equal protection of the laws because the law creates a burden on a suspect class or infringes on a fundamental individual right. Strict scrutiny requires the court to examine the purpose for which the law in fact was adopted or enforced to determine whether the law promoted a compelling governmental purpose. If it does, the court must then examine the means chosen to implement the law to determine that the law is narrowly tailored to promote the compelling governmental purpose by the means that least burdens the interest (for a fundamental right protected by due process) or the class (for equal protection) from among all means possible to promote the compelling governmental purpose.

*See also:* interest, state interest, compelling state interest (compelling governmental purpose).

**footnote four (footnote four or the footnote)** The origin of strict scrutiny review. Footnote four of the Carolene Products (United States v. Carolene Products Co., 304 U.S. 144 (1938)) opinion, in which Justice Harlan Fiske Stone questioned whether the courts should presume that a statute is constitutional if (1) it is within a specific prohibition of the Constitution such as those in the Bill of Rights or Fourteenth Amendment, (2) it restricts a political process (3) is subject to more serious concern under the Fourteenth Amendment, (4) is directed against a religious minority, (5) is directed against a national minority, (6) is directed against a racial minority, or (7) generally reflects a prejudice against a discrete or insular minority. Particularly in the last case, Justice Stone's note suggests that the courts must inquire more deeply into a statute's constitutionality than they would ordinarily because of the potential for a limit on the political process that would not sufficiently protect minorities in the population.

*See also:* minority, minority group, discrete and insular minority; footnote.

**strict in scrutiny fatal in fact**   The fallacy that no law may survive strict scrutiny. The tag line that strict scrutiny is only strict in theory but it is fatal in fact was suggested initially by Professor Gerald Gunther, to mean that in the 1960's, the Court's aggressive judicial review of laws that burdened race and other suspect classes pre-determined that laws based on race would not be upheld under equal protection. That suggestion has long been understood not to describe the Court's view of all race-burdening laws, which upholds certain laws, particularly laws that are carefully tailored to remediate clear and demonstrable past injustice.

**scutage**   *See:* tenure, feudal tenure, military tenure, knight's tenure, shield money (scutage).

**se**   The person or thing. Se is a Latin pronoun that may stand in for a person or a thing in the third person. Context and custom help make clear when se refers to a person or thing. Thus, pro se is for himself or on his own behalf; per se is in its own regard or considering the thing in itself.

**sea**   The oceans and other waters that ebb and flow with the tide. The sea includes all the oceans and great bodies of water, both collectively and individually. Certain bodies entitled seas are actually quite removed from the sea, and components of the sea, such as gulfs and bays, are clearly portions of the sea. The sea includes both the high seas and the territorial seas and other waters dedicated to the control of one nation or another.

**sea captain or ship captain**   *See:* ship, captain of a vessel (sea captain or ship captain).

**law of the sea (sea laws)**   International law of waters, vessels, and resources in the sea. The law of the sea is an international body of law that governs the boundaries between international and national controls of the sea, the conduct and use of vessels at sea in peace and in war, and the use of natural resources in the sea. The law of the sea is manifest in the domestic law of each nation with a littoral, or seaward, boundary. Although the law of the sea developed mainly as a matter of customary international law, which persists as an important source of the law of the sea, many of its principles are now reflected in conventions that have extended those principles, particularly the United Nations Conventions on the Law of the Sea of 1958 and 1982. Other multilateral conventions address a variety of questions of the law of the sea, including treaties on navigation and collision, navigation and rescue, the protection of marine life and responsibility for fisheries, the construction of ships and certification of vessels, as well as numerous bilateral and regional treaties.

*See also:* international law, customary international law; treaty; navigation (navigable or navigational).

**high seas (freedom of the seas)**   The sea beyond the national seas. The high seas, as a matter of customary international law, are those waters beyond the territorial sea, or all waters more than 12 miles from shore. Under the U.N. Convention on the Law of the Sea of 1982, coastal states are entitled to additional measures of control for law enforcement over an additional band of another 12 nautical miles and to the exclusive use of the waters extending out 200 miles from shore for economic exploitation and, in some places, farther on the sea floor on a continental shelf and among the islands of archipelagic states. All waters beyond national control for a given purpose are the high seas under that convention.

All states, both coastal and land-locked, enjoy freedom of the seas, the right to use the high seas by vessels flying the flag of that state. Freedom of the high seas includes the freedom of navigation, overflight; installation of undersea cables, pipelines, and artificial islands; freedom to fish and take resources; and freedom of scientific exploration. These freedoms are limited in various extents by the law of the sea and the requirement of respect for the interests of other states.

**international strait (international waterway)**   A narrows connecting two seas. A strait is a narrow but navigable sea or channel between two much larger bodies of water, usually between two seas or oceans. International straits connect two bodies of water containing high seas. Straits are usually treated as high seas for the purposes of navigation, although they traverse national waters, and the right of transit passage is protected in straits.

**contiguous zone (customs zone or customs enforcement zone)**   The twelve miles under coastal control beyond the territorial sea. The contiguous zone is the internationally recognized area for law enforcement by a coastal state that extends twelve miles beyond the territorial sea. A coastal state must exercise its right to claim the contiguous zone. In the United States, the contiguous zone is effectively the same as its customs enforcement zone. In the contiguous zone, the coastal state may stop a vessel and inspect it and to enforce its laws as they affect the coastal state, although the rights of innocent passage and transit passage are not otherwise limited.

**continental shelf (outer continental shelf)** The seabed near shore above the deep sea. The continental shelf is the sea floor from the shore extending to submarine slopes and cliffs reaching to the deep seabed floor. The contours of the sea floor vary, and in some areas, the continental shelf extends from shore much greater distances than elsewhere. The law of the sea gives a coastal state exclusive rights to exploit minerals and sea life on the continental shelf near its shore, extending outward in places beyond an exclusive economic zone, or for states that have not declared an exclusive economic zone, giving similar functional rights. In no case can a state assert rights over its continental shelf out beyond 350 nautical miles or more than 100 nautical miles beyond a sea depth of 2500 meters.

**exclusive economic zone (EEZ)** A 200–mile band of sea whose resources are controlled by the coastal state. The exclusive economic zone (EEZ) is an area of the sea bordering a coastal state in which the coastal state has exclusive rights to control exploration, exploitation, conservation, and management of the natural resources in the water, on the seafloor, and its subsoil, including the use of the sea for the production of energy from the water, currents, and winds. The coastal state has jurisdiction in the EEZ over the establishment and use of artificial islands, installations, and structures; marine scientific research; and the protection and preservation of the marine environment. For the purposes of navigation, the EEZ has no effect, and the navigation of vessels is considered that of the high seas, without even the need to resort to the rights of innocent passage or transit passage.

**territorial waters (territorial sea)** The 12–mile strip of sea bordering the land of a coastal state. The territorial sea, or territorial waters, of a state is a band of the sea reaching 12 miles from land (measured from the baseline of the mean low water mark). The state has complete sovereignty of the waters, subsoil, and airspace of the territorial sea.

Some states of the United States have defined their territorial waters to include inland waters, or waters distinct from the sea and inland from the coast. This is not the principle by which the United States defines the territorial sea, as opposed to other federal waters.

The United States, generally, considers inland waters to be distinct from the territorial sea or territorial waters, though they, like the land, are part of the territory of the United States. There have been a few convoluted readings of statutes conferring jurisdiction for law enforcement for vessels or aircraft on or over the territorial sea to include inland waters, though these readings are, at best, unpersuasive for other purposes.

*See also:* shore (shoreline).

**seal** A sign authenticating an original instrument. A seal is a mark, usually made by impression into a paper or into a wax disk or piece of foil that is affixed to a paper that proves an instrument written on the paper is an original writing or a formal instrument, such as a license, deed, will, contract, or other public or private instrument of legal significance. Some instruments employ a seal described in the text and only manifest in the word "seal" printed or written on the instrument. The doctrine of seal used to provide a form of self-authentication to documents under seal, and certain private instruments were once void unless a seal is affixed. In contemporary practice, some instruments are void if not under seal, including not only public instruments such as warrants and commissions of office, judgments in civil actions, letters testamentary, and diplomas, but also private instruments such as deeds, promissory notes, and contracts, or any instrument that in its text declares the instrument to be invalid unless a seal has been affixed. Although many jurisdictions have abolished the law of seal, some still establish a presumption of validity for sealed documents and a specific Statute of Limitations for bringing an action that depends upon the challenge to the validity of the instrument. Note: the use by a notary public of a seal to authenticate an instrument indicates the instrument has been notarized, but this is not what is meant by a document under seal in the general sense.

A seal is used to secure an instrument or thing from being read, in that the only apparent means of viewing the instrument requires the seal to be broken. So, to say that a paper, file or file cabinet is sealed is to say that access to the information therein is restricted. A court may order any record sealed according to its rules, although files and records that are sealed are usually subject to review of their status on motion.

*See also:* notary (notary public); record, sealed record (sealing of records or record under seal).

**corporate seal (common seal)** A sign or impression placed on corporate documents. A corporate seal, or a common seal, is an impression made in a paper document, or now, placed electronically in a transmission. The seal's use is generally authorized for certain documents, such as a charter, or such contracts or instruments that are authorized to bind the corporation.

**Privy Seal** The personal seal of the monarch. The Privy Seal was by custom the personal seal of the monarch, affixed to royal warrants or to instruments sent from the monarch to be sealed under the Great Seal. It is now affixed by The Lord Keeper of the Privy Seal, or Lord Privy Seal, to all Royal Charters, Royal Warrants, Orders in Council, Letters Patent, judgments, decrees, orders, rules, regulations, schemes, by-laws, awards, contracts and other agreements, memoranda and articles of association, certificates, deeds and other documents issued in the name of the monarch. The Keeper is a member of the cabinet responsible, in 2010, for anti-discrimination laws.

*See also:* judge, English judge, Lord Chancellor (Lord High Chancellor or Lord Keeper of the Great Seal).

**sealed bid**   *See:* bid, sealed bid (sealed-bid process or sealed-bid system or closed bid or closed-bid process).

**sealed-bid process or sealed-bid system or closed bid or closed-bid process**   *See:* bid, sealed bid (sealed-bid process or sealed-bid system or closed bid or closed-bid process).

**sealed record**   *See:* record, sealed record (sealing of records or record under seal).

**sealing of records or record under seal**   *See:* record, sealed record (sealing of records or record under seal).

**sigillum**   A seal. Sigillum is Latin for seal (though it was initially the term for the wee figures engraved in the seal). The word is sometimes placed on an instrument to serve as the seal itself.

**seaman (sailor)**   A person employed in a connection to a vessel in navigation. A seaman, in admiralty, is either each of the personnel employed aboard a vessel of the members of the crew other than the officers. In the United States, there are several statutory regimes that define who is a seaman within the meaning of the statute, including the Jones Act, the Longshore Harbor Worker Compensation Act (LHWC) and the Fair Labor Standards Act (FLSA). A sailor under the Jones Act and the LHWC is broadly defined, including any person who is employed in connection with a vessel in navigation. A sailor for the purposes of exclusion from the overtime wages protection of the FLSA is narrowly defined, so that a sailor is either the master of a vessel or someone under a master's direction substantially engaged in work in support of the operation of the vessel. Note: the designation "sailor" in various forms in the U.S. Navy and U.S. Coast Guard comprises three military ratings, from E-1 to E-3; these are specific to their functions as pay grades and ratings and differs from other senses of the term. Likewise, the Ordinary Sailor in the U.S. Merchant Marine is likely a sailor aboard a vessel, because of the function the sailor performs and not solely as a result of title.

*See also:* longshoreman; stevedore.

**maintenance of a seaman (cure and maintenance)**   Shipowner's duty to care for an injured seaman. Maintenance is the right of a seaman under the common law of admiralty to support from the shipowner on whose vessel the seaman becomes injured or ill. The right of maintenance is a quasi-contractual right and may not be bargained away by the shipowner, nor may an individual seaman's right be superseded by a union's collective bargaining agreement.

**seamless web**   *See:* metaphor, metaphor of law, seamless web.

**search**   A state inspection of matter a party reasonably considers to be private. A search is any activity by governmental officials or agents that intrudes upon the reasonable expectation of privacy of a person or entity, for the purposes of investigation, or the discovery of contraband, or the security of the state agents or others, or the acquisition of evidence of a crime or administrative offense. Every search is governed by the Fourth Amendment limit on unreasonable searches, and those conducted pursuant to a warrant are limited to the scope in time, place, and purpose of the warrant.

*See also:* search, search and seizure.

**search warrant**   *See:* warrant, search warrant, no-knock search warrant; warrant, search warrant, hot pursuit exception; warrant, search warrant, automobile exception; warrant, search warrant | oath or affirmation; warrant, search warrant.

**bodily search**   Any search of a living suspect's body. A bodily search, or a bodily examination, is a search of the person of a suspect in any manner beyond visible examination of the fully clothed suspect. A search of the person is inherently a violation of the person's privacy and must be justified by consent, probable cause, or a warrant. Bodily searches include a Terry stop (or stop and frisk), a frisk incident to arrest, a strip search, a bodily intrusion (including the involuntary sampling of fluids or tissues), and a body cavity search. The involuntary collection of a urine sample, hair sample, or breath test is a form of bodily search but usually analyzed according to more discrete questions. Not all bodily searches, of course, are unconsented.

*See also:* search, bodily search, strip search.

**bodily intrusion**   An unconsented search within a suspect's body. A bodily intrusion is search performed on an individual that requires any entry into the individual's body, through an orifice or the skin, the entry being a search no matter how slight, without the consent of the person whose body it is. When the intrusion is performed by a police officer or other state actor searching for evidence or seizing samples as evidence, as in a body cavity search or forced blood sampling, the intrusion is subject to the limits of the Fourth Amendment. Urine tests and voice tests are not bodily intrusions. Such a search performed by consent is not an intrusion but a consented search.

**frisk (pat down or pat-down search)**   A physical search of a clothed suspect. A frisk is a brief pat down of the subject's outer clothing. A frisk may include rolling cloth and feeling specifically over pockets and folds of material over every part of the body but does not include the removal of any of the suspect's clothes. The object of most frisks is to determine whether the suspect is carrying a weapon that might endanger the officer. A frisk may also be used to determine whether there is probable cause for detention and a more intrusive search.

**strip search**   A search of the body requiring the removal of all the suspect's clothing. A strip search is a search of the human subject's body that requires the removal of all clothing and the inspection of all folds of skin and exterior parts of the body in which an object may be carried without immediate detection. The search may be visual, tactile, by machine, or some combination thereof. As some jurisdictions define a strip search, the search may include a body cavity search. The potential for abuse by police officials in a strip search is patent, as is the indignity to the person being searched. The justification for a strip search must be specific to a risk or suspicion justifying a strip search and not a search in general.

See also: search, bodily search.

**exclusionary rule**   Evidence unconstitutionally obtained by the government may not be admitted into court. The exclusionary rule is a constitutional remedy for violation of constitutional limits on the collection of evidence, particularly the the Fourth, Fifth, or Sixth Amendments, that forbids the government from using of evidence gathered in violation of an individual's rights in a proceeding in court against that individual. Generally, such evidence is inadmissible if it would not have been obtained but for the constitutional violation. The exclusionary rule is as much a remedy for the public as for the person against whom the evidence would be used, because the rule removes the incentive for police to violate the Constitution in gathering evidence. The rule is not absolute but bars the use of evidence that is the direct result of a constitutional deprivation in an action that is closely connected to the investigation in which the violation occurred. Yet if the purposes of the rule would not be furthered by the exclusion, as when a constitutional violation resulted from a genuine mistake or accident or when police officers engage in unconstitutional activity in mistaken, but good-faith belief that they were acting lawfully—then evidence may be held admissible. The exclusionary rule is often said to be prophylactic; that is, it is a common-law mechanism intended to protect constitutional rights, rather than a constitutional right in itself. Yet the exclusionary rule is also said to flow directly from the Constitution, such as the Fifth Amendment prohibition of self-incrimination.

Although the principles of the exclusionary rule are found in English common law, the United States Supreme Court first excluded evidence obtained in violation of the Fourth and Fifth Amendments in Boyd v. United States, 116 U.S. 616 (1886), and the contemporary exclusionary rule was established in Weeks v. United States, 232 U.S. 383 (1914) and extended to the states through incorporation into the Due Process Clause in Mapp v. Ohio, 367 U.S. 643 (1961) (Clark, J.).

See also: exclusion (exclude); evidence, illegally obtained evidence (unlawfully obtained evidence).

**attenuation doctrine**   Unconstitutional evidence is admissible for a use but slightly related to the constitutional breach. The attenuation doctrine is a limit to the exclusionary rule, allowing evidence that is sufficiently removed from the illegality of its acquisition. In other words, the attenuation doctrine allows evidence to be admitted even though the evidence was either obtained in circumstances that violate the Constitution or is fruit of the poisonous tree, if a court finds that there is not a sufficient causal link between the constitutional violation and the use for which the evidence will be admitted. The rationale for the rule is that the deterrent purposes of the rule would likely not be served if the utility of the evidence was not apparent to law enforcement officials at the time of the constitutional violation that made the evidence available. This is controversial.

**independent-source doctrine (independent source)**   A warrant based on illegal evidence is valid if it was also based on sufficient legal evidence. The independent-source doctrine is a limit on the exclusionary rule that allows evidence acquired under a search warrant that was based on unconstitutionally gathered evidence, if the warrant was also based on sufficient independent evidence. The measure of sufficiency is twofold. The first measure is whether the police decision to seek the warrant was in fact caused by consideration of the unconstitutional evidence. The second is whether a pragmatic magistrate would have been influenced by the unconstitutional evidence to issue the warrant. Thus, if the police would have sought the warrant anyway, and the magistrate would have issued the warrant anyway, that the police presented unconstitutional evidence did not affect the constitutionality of the warrant.

See also: warrant, search warrant; search, exclusionary rule, exception to the exclusionary rule, inevitable-discovery doctrine (inevitable discovery).

**inevitable-discovery doctrine (inevitable discovery)**   Fruits of an unlawful search that would have been found lawfully are admissible. The inevitable-discovery doctrine is a limit to the exclusionary rule (and the fruit of the poisonous tree doctrine) that allows the admission of evidence that was acquired by the police in unconstitutional circumstances, allowing admission if the evidence would have been certain to have been found regardless of police employment or reliance on the unconstitutional circumstance. The inevitable-discovery doctrine is related to the independent-source rule, but there is a critical difference: the evidence serving as an independent source must have been in police hands at the time of the warrant's issue, while the circumstances that demonstrate the inevitability of the evidence's discovery might only become known later. (That said, the chain of events leading to that inevitability must have been initiated independently of the evidence's discovery).

See also: search, exclusionary rule, exception to the exclusionary rule, independent-source doctrine (independent source).

**fruit of the poisonous tree** Evidence acquired from unconstitutionally obtained information is inadmissible. The "fruit of the poisonous tree" doctrine bars the use of evidence that was obtained as a result of the governmental exploitation of unconstitutionally obtained information. Like the core meaning of the exclusionary rule, police and their agents may not use an initial constitutional violation to gather further information, without it amounting to conduct akin to a continuing violation of the constitution. The tree, it is said, having been poisonous, the fruits of the tree are likewise. The doctrine is not unlimited, however, and evidence that is too attenuated from the unconstitutional conduct, that is available from an independent source, or that would have been inevitably discovered is not barred.

**good-faith exception (good faith exception or Leon exception or reasonable error exception)** Evidence seized under a faulty warrant is admissible if taken in good faith. The good-faith exception allows the admission of evidence at trial that was seized under a warrant that was invalid, as long as the police officers who obtained the evidence did so in reasonable and objective reliance in good faith upon the search warrant, believing it to be valid. This belief in the warrant's validity must be objectively reasonable, and the evidence must sustain the requirement of good faith, that the officer relying on the warrant did genuinely believe that it was lawfully requested and lawfully issued in the light of the law and the facts as they were then known or could reasonably have been known.

**purged taint exception** Presumably excludable evidence is admissible if it is found by a means free of the taint of unconstitutional conduct. The purged taint exception allows evidence to be admitted in a criminal trial, even though the evidence could not have been discovered except for a prior unconstitutional search, investigation, or seizure, as long as the evidence that is later identified was both discovered not as a result of exploiting the illegality of the first action and discovered as a result of an investigation or effort truly distinct from the first, illegal action.

**suppression hearing (Dunaway hearing or Franks hearing or Huntley hearing or Mapp hearing)** A proceeding to determine whether evidence was obtained unconstitutionally, and its admissibility.

A suppression hearing, sometimes referred to as an exclusionary hearing, is a pre-trial hearing in a criminal action to determine whether evidence is inadmissible because it was discovered or seized in violation of the Fourth, Fifth, or Sixth Amendments. A suppression hearing often follows a motion in limine to suppress evidence. There are various forms of suppression hearing, named for cases in which rules have evolved for suppression or admission on specific grounds. For instance, a Dunaway hearing considers evidence collected following to an illegal arrest. A Franks hearing considers evidence from a search warrant challenged on the facts presented or omitted from the warrant. A Huntley hearing considers evidence collected after illegal interrogation. A Mapp hearing considers evidence collected after an illegal search. A Wade hearing considers evidence from an improper line-up.

See also: evidence, admissibility, exclusionary hearing.

**Dunaway hearing** A hearing on evidence seized after an unconstitutional arrest. A Dunaway hearing is a judicial motion hearing to determine whether evidence should be excluded from use at trial because it was obtained pursuant to an arrest in violation of the Fourth Amendment. In Dunaway v. New York, 442 U.S. 200 (1979), the Supreme Court held a suspect's confession obtained subsequent to his unconstitutional arrest was inadmissible despite a prior Miranda warning. More loosely, a Dunaway hearing is occasionally used to refer to suppression hearings generally.

**incident to arrest (search incident to arrest)** The search of a detainee and area at the time of arrest. A search incident to arrest is a search conducted at or soon after the arrest of a person of the person's body and of the area from which the person was arrested. The search must be limited to the area that was under the control of the detainee at the time of the arrest, the extent of the control being a functional question of what the arrestee would be reasonably likely to do rather than a matter of constructive legal control, such as by ownership. The extent of the search and its limits must be reasonable in the light of the events prior to the arrest and the circumstances at the time of the arrest and prior to the search. The arrest may not be a ruse to avoid the constitutional requirements of a warrant and reasonable search.

**protective sweep** A quick, limited, wide-spread search incident to arrest. A "protective sweep" is a form of search incident to an arrest that is wider in its scope than a search of the area subject to the detainee's control, by which police officers identify each person in or near the premises and manage their presence during the arrest and search incident to the arrest of the detainee. The functions of the protective sweep are to ensure the safety of the police officers and to diminish the likelihood of the spoliation of evidence. This search can be conducted solely on the basis of the arrest, but the police must have a reasonable suspicion that such a search could reveal other persons. This sweep is also only limited to areas in which a person could reasonably be expected to be found.

**inventory search** A search of property already seized. An inventory search is the search of property lawfully seized and detained by a police agency; inventory searches of personal effects in the possession of a person arrested are performed when a person is processed into a detention facility, and other inventory searches are performed as property seized is processed into storage, impoundment, or a facility for evaluation. The purposes of the search are to accurately list the materials to be returned to the owner once the legitimate needs for law enforcement are completed; to ensure that the property is harmless; to secure dangerous property; to impound contraband property; to secure valuable items; and to protect against false claims for loss or damage.

*See also:* inventory.

**knock-and-announce rule** Police must identify themselves before entering private property. The knock-and-announce rule is a requirement of a reasonable search under the Fourth Amendment, that, unless doing so would be unreasonable, police officers must knock and announce their presence and identity prior to entering private property. A failure to do so would allow a home-owner or resident a right of reasonable defense against the intrusion, at least until the intruder is identified. This rule has been moderated to allow a "no-knock" entry if there is a reasonable suspicion that an announced entry would be dangerous to the officers or others, destructive to the purposes of the investigation, or generally futile. The extent of the "no-knock allowance" has been widely criticized as encouraging unnecessary but dangerous entries by police.

**useless-gesture exception** A police door knock and request to enter is unneeded if it would be a useless gesture. The useless-gesture exception allows the police to dispense with the knock and announce requirement under the Fourth Amendment when the police have an objectively reasonable and good faith belief that the purposes of the Fourth Amendment would not be served by knocking on the door, announcing their presence and purpose, and requesting admission. Some states require the officer to be almost certain, given the facts the officer knows, that the person in the room or building already knows the officer's purpose. See Commonwealth of Massachusetts v. Lewin (No. 1), 407 Mass. 617 (1990) (Greaney, J.).

**be on the lookout (all-points bulletin or BOLO or APB)** Bulletin to police units identifying a person to detain. The BOLO alert is one of several abbreviated alerts sent as either radio or computer text bulletins from a dispatcher to police units, or by teletype or other alert systems among police agencies, identifying a person of interest to be detained either as a suspect, witness, or missing person. Different departments and states have varying protocols for the use of these alerts, which are variously BOLO or BOL for "be on the lookout," ATL for "attempt to locate," or the once common APB for "all points bulletin."

**no-knock search** *See:* warrant, search warrant, no-knock search warrant.

**permissive search (consented search or search subject to permission)** A search made with the assent of the person to be searched or whose premises will be searched. A permissive search of a person or place is made with the consent of the person who is to be searched or who is in control of the premises to be searched, and who waives the person's Fourth Amendment privileges from unwarranted or unreasonable search by giving such consent. Permission for a search may only be given by a person competent to act in law, and so permission to search premises may not be given by a minor not apparently competent and in control of the premises. Permission is only effective if it is required, and it is therefore only pertinent as to property over which the person has a genuine, legitimate, and reasonable expectation of privacy. Any person who owns or controls a given property may give consent to its search, and the permission given to a police officer by an owner, tenant, resident, bailee, or other person in control of some property and with a privacy interest in it is sufficient to allow the officer to search, even if the search would disclose evidence affecting another person whose privacy interests were affected and who does not give such consent.

**common-authority rule (common authority rule)** Presumption that people with a joint interest in property have joint control over the property. The common-authority rule occurs when two or more people each have an ownership interest or right to possess a property, but only one exercises that control at a given time, that one may consent to its search without consultation or interference by the others. The common-authority rule is usually invoked in search and seizure cases where the one party grants police access to a property for a search, and the other party contests the lawfulness of that consent as a basis for a reasonable search of the second party's property.

**search and seizure** Governmental intrusion into one's privacy and control of one's property or liberty. Search and seizure is the depiction in the Fourth Amendment of government activities that are limited from unreasonable intrusion on the security of the people in their persons, houses, papers, and effects. A search includes the intrusion into any of these areas by a government official who examines one or another area in which a person has a constitutionally protected privacy interest. A seizure is the arrest of the person or any property, such as the taking into custody of the person or any possession, whether it is real, chattel, or intangible. Any search or seizure is allowed only in circumstances that are not unreasonable. A search or seizure made pursuant to a valid warrant properly attained is inherently reasonable, because the warrant must be obtained only upon a demonstration to the magistrate who issues the warrant that there is probable cause to believe there is evidence of a crime for a search or seizure or that a person has committed a crime for a seizure by arrest. The warrant must specifically describe the place to be searched or describe the persons or things to be seized. A warrantless search may be reasonable, but only under circumstances that justify the failure of the police or other government official to obtain a warrant.

*See also:* arrest; seizure (seize); constitution, U.S. Constitution, Amendment 4 (Amendment IV or Fourth Amendment).

**physical-proximity test** A search may include places and things near the locus of the warrant. The physical-proximity test is a basis for determining the scope of the search authorized under a search warrant, allowing a search not only of the premises or place designated, but also things and places physically proximate to them, as reasonably needed to give effect to the purposes of the warrant. The test is not unlimited but allows the search of plausible locations where the things being sought in the search warrant could be expected to be found in an area connected to or closely related to the premises designated for their search. The test does not, however, extend to property in the clothing or on the person of a person not listed in the search warrant or arrested. The physical-proximity standard has been criticized as allowing a suspect to grab an object to keep it from seizure.

*See also:* proximity.

**unreasonable search** A search not reasonably justified under the Constitution. An unreasonable search is an unconstitutional search, one not based on a valid warrant properly obtained, one that exceeds the scope of a warrant without justification, or one not based on probable cause or another recognized exception to the presumption in favor of a warrant to search. In general, an unreasonable search is a search in which the evidence known to the police or prosecution prior to the search cannot justify the intrusion into the privacy of the persons affected by the search. The greater the degree of privacy at stake and the greater the intrusion, the greater the requirement for a well-justified and specific reason for the intrusion. Such a justification must be based on evidence of a crime or of potential for harm as well as on the likelihood that evidence will be found in the place or on the person searched.

**warranted search** A search conducted pursuant to a search warrant. A warranted search is a search conducted following service of a valid search warrant upon the owner or occupant of the place designated in the warrant for search. The search under a warrant is limited to the scope and purpose detailed in the warrant, with such additional searches as are necessary to ensure the safety of the officers performing the search.

**warrantless search** A search conducted without a search warrant. A warrantless search is any search conducted other than following service of a valid search warrant on the owner or occupant of the place or thing searched. A warrantless search is constitutional as long as it is reasonable. Reasonable warrantless searches include those that occur on the basis of probable cause or in circumstances that amount to an exception to the requirements of warrant or probable cause, such as a checkpoint stop, border stop, special needs search, automobile search, or exigent circumstances generally. Such searches are, however, limited in scope by the conditions that make them exceptional.

**administrative search** A search to determine compliance with administrative regulations. An administrative search is an inspection of a place, vessel, or, in some jurisdictions, a vehicle that is subject to specific regulations in order to determine that the place is operated and maintained according to the regulations. An administrative search may be conducted by police officers or agents, or administrative staff of the state or local government, or even by governmental contractors. An administrative search is defined not by who performs it but by the purposes of the search, and a purpose to ensure compliance with administrative rules, with the owner or operator of the premises liable predominately for administrative penalties is an administrative search. An administrative search may be conducted without the consent of the owner, occupant, or operator of the place but still be conducted without a warrant or probable cause. The discretion of the searching official is expected to be inherently limited by the bureaucratic requirements of the inspection.

**automobile exception (vehicle exception)** The cursory search of a vehicle. The automobile exception allows a limited search of the portions of a vehicle that are in plain sight of an officer outside the vehicle, and if from such a search evidence is found that gives rise to probable cause to believe there is further evidence of a crime hidden in the vehicle, the exception allows a further search into portions of the vehicle that are not open to view from outside the vehicle. The rationales for an exception from the presumption of a warrant requirement for automobiles are their inherent mobility allowing them to be moved from the jurisdiction in the time required to obtain a warrant, their public nature, and their status as a highly regulated instrumentality. Note: the automobile exception applies to all vehicles for human transport on roads, including trucks and cycles.

*See also:* automobile.

**consent search (consented search)** A search conducted with permission of the person whose person or place is searched. A consent search is a search to which a person has consented for the search of that person's body, or of property that person owns, occupies, or controls. A police officer may conduct a search with consent even if there is no warrant for the search or probable cause to do so. Such permission must be voluntary, and the question of voluntariness is determined from all the circumstances, not the least being a presumption that a person is not voluntarily giving consent while in custody.

**exigent circumstances** An emergency that excuses the need for a search warrant. Exigent circumstances are conditions at a specific place and time in which a police officer must act swiftly in order to prevent danger to persons or to property or to secure evidence that is likely to be lost if it is not sought or impounded immediately. Exigent circumstances may excuse the general requirement that police officers secure a search warrant, and therefore the police officer may not willfully bring about the exigency by intentionally provoking an urgent circumstance in order to conduct a warrantless search. Even so, there is no perfect legal test for the degree of urgency or immediacy that amounts to an exigency, and the evaluation of the circumstances must be made in the light of facts known to the officer at the time, and the officer must have had a reasonable and good faith belief in the urgency of the situation that required the search in order to secure the safety of people, property, or evidence.

*See also:* exigency (exigencies or exigent).

**plain view (plain-view doctrine)** Evidence in open view is observed with no need of a search. The plain-view doctrine allows for the seizure of evidence perceived by a police officer in a place where the officer is justified in being, while the evidence is a place visible to a passerby or to the public at large, as long as the officer has probable cause to believe the evidence is in fact evidence of a crime or otherwise subject to seizure. The rationale is an owner or possessor has no legitimate expectation of privacy in property put on public view. Moreover, no search is needed to discover the property, and so there is no constitutional limit on the search that discovers it because there was in fact no search. Even so, a constitutional limit on its seizure exists, in that the property must be reasonably seized.

**immediate appearance (immediately apparent)** Incriminating aspect of evidence is known and visible. Immediate appearance is an essential condition of evidence that may be searched or seized because it is in plain view. Evidence in plain view is immediately apparent, and vice versa. Immediate appearance requires the searching official to be able to perceive without moving objects or altering the conditions of the scene of the search either the evidence itself or thing so associated with a crime or some aspect of criminal conduct that it is overwhelmingly likely to signal presence of evidence of a crime, such as a container unique to the evidence. Thus, a handgun, burglar tools, or a bag that appears to hold illegal drugs that are in plain view are immediately apparent owing to their likely evidentiary relationship to a crime. Likewise, a holster, a ski mask on a warm day, or powdered baggies with a scale might be immediately apparent owing to their relationship to criminal evidence.

**special needs exception** A category of search excused from a warrant owing to the reasonable needs of administration. A special needs exception to the search warrant requirement arises when the person or premises to be searched are in an environment, location, or circumstances that give rise to special needs that would limit a reasonable expectation of privacy while also increasing the justification for the form of search performed. Special needs environments include prisons and jails, schools and educational institutions, building inspections, certain forms of government service or employment, employment in transportation or other fields responsible for public safety, and administrative searches. That a search is conducted in a special needs environment does not ensure it is reasonable; a search lacking a warrant must still be justified in advance in some manner sufficient to justify the form and extent of police intrusion on the world of the suspect or controller of the property to be searched.

**seasonable** Timely. Seasonable suggests that something is done at a reasonable, customary, proper, or agreed time.

*See also:* time.

**seasonal agricultural worker** *See:* worker, migrant worker (seasonal agricultural worker).

**seasonal possession** *See:* possession, adverse possession, continuous possession, seasonal possession.

**seat the jury or select the jury or jury return or return of a jury** *See:* jury, impanel a jury (seat the jury or select the jury or jury return or return of a jury).

**second degree murder** *See:* murder, degrees of murder, second degree murder (murder in the second degree or murder-two or murder-2).

**second principle of justice** *See:* justice, Rawlsian justice, difference principle (second principle of justice).

**second-degree felony murder** *See:* murder, felony murder, second-degree felony murder.

**second-story man**  *See:* burglary, cat burglar (second-story man).

**secondary boycott**  *See:* boycott, secondary boycott.

**secondary implied assumption of risk**  *See:* risk, assumption of risk, implied assumption of risk, secondary implied assumption of risk.

**secondary offense**  *See:* offense, traffic offense, primary offense as traffic offense (secondary offense).

**secondary rule**  *See:* rule, legal rule, secondary rule; jurisprudence, legal positivism, secondary rule.

**secret (secrete)**  A thing kept hidden. A secret is a an idea, information, or thing that is kept hidden from all the world, or at least kept hidden from selected parties. A secret is only a secret as long as it is successfully kept from the world at large or at least contained from the knowledge of those whose ignorance was the purpose of its hiding.

To secrete something is physically to hide it, placing it in a place where it is unlikely to be found. Of course, secrete is also the verb for secretion, or the emission or extrusion of a substance from an organism. Context should clarify which opposing sense of this Janus word, secrete, is meant.

**secret partner**  *See:* partner, secret partner.

**Secret Service**  *See:* police, police organizations, Secret Service.

**state secret (official secret)**  Information affecting the state a private citizen may not disclose. A state secret is any information not disclosed already to the public or to significant non-governmental recipients, that should be kept hidden from public disclosure in order to avoid actual or likely harm to a military operation or capability of the United States, to an intelligence-gathering operation or capability, or to diplomatic relations with foreign governments. There is no privilege to protect government officials from embarrassment or from the disclosure of wrongdoing, misfeasance, error, or neglect. The mere classification of information as secret does not prove such information is a state secret within the meaning of any legal doctrine (although it is sufficient for the control of such information among government personnel).

The government may constitutionally order a prior restraint on the public dissemination of a state secret in some material, if the order is narrowly tailored to protect the secret information. The government may move to bar evidence containing state secrets from submission in court or to control its use in court to protect its secret. Even so, in either case, the government must prove the information involved is worthy of being treated as a secret and of sufficient significance as to warrant the burden of the constitutional rights of speech or fair trial. In court, the state-secret, or official-secret, privilege belongs to the Government and must be asserted by the head of the department which has control over the matter, and then only after actual, personal consideration by that officer. A private party cannot invoke or waive it.

*See also:* privilege, evidentiary privilege, state secrets privilege (national security privilege).

**trade secret**  A secret with commercial value. A trade secret is a secret held by a person or entity that either has a potential value to others that may be commercially realized by them or that has a value to its holder that may be commercially realized and that would be less valuable to the holder if it were disclosed. The appropriation of a trade secret by a person or entity that is not if its holder is a specialized form of conversion and may be the basis for an action in theft. In many jurisdictions, theft of a trade secret is both a crime and a tort. Disclosure of a trade secret by a person with access to it who is not its owner is a tort in most jurisdictions, although it is not if it the trade secret protected information that should be disclosed in the public interest, such as a recipe requiring unsafe ingredients in food. In no case is there an action for disclosure or theft of a trade secret that is not maintained effectively as a secret, its details unknown to the public.

*See also:* patent, business method patent (business model patent).

**Section 1031 exchange**  *See:* tax, tax deferred transaction, Section 1031 exchange.

**Section 1231 gain or gain under Section 1231**  *See:* gain, recognized gain (Section 1231 gain or gain under Section 1231).

**Section 1981**  *See:* civil rights, Civil Rights Act, Civil Rights Act of 1866 (Section 1981).

**Section 1985**  *See:* conspiracy, conspiracy to interfere with civil rights (Section 1985); civil rights, Civil Rights Act, conspiracy to interfere with civil rights (Section 1985).

**Section 1986**  *See:* civil rights, civil rights, neglect of duty (Section 1986).

**secular marriage**  *See:* marriage, civil marriage (secular marriage).

**secure (secured)**  To acquire, protect, or insure. To secure is to invoke some security in a thing or state of affairs, and in law to secure some thing may mean either to acquire a security interest in the thing, such as a lien or a bond or a judgment or to acquire some assurance of the thing such as insurance. To secure something may mean to acquire ownership in the thing or otherwise to settle it as a state of affairs (in this sense, the Framers of the Constitution desired to secure certain conditions for themselves and their posterity). In its non-legal sense, to secure something is to anchor it securely, as with ropes or anchors. Context is essential in distinguishing these senses.

**secured claim**  *See:* claim, secured claim.

**secured debt** *See:* debt, secured debt, unsecured debt; debt, secured debt.

**secured loan** *See:* loan, secured loan (unsecured loan).

**secured transaction** *See:* transaction, secured transaction (security agreement).

**securities** *See:* security, securities.

**Securities Act of 1933** *See:* security, securities, securities regulation, Securities Act of 1933 (Securities Act).

**Securities and Exchange Commission** *See:* security, securities, securities regulation, Securities and Exchange Commission (S.E.C. or SEC).

**securities broker** *See:* broker, securities broker (registered broker or stock broker or initiating broker of future commodities merchant).

**Securities Exchange** *See:* security, securities, Securities Exchange, American Stock Exchange (A.M.E.X. AMEX).

**securities fraud** *See:* securities, securities fraud (Rule 10b–5).

**Securities Investor Protection Corporation** *See:* security, securities, securities regulation, Securities Investor Protection Corporation (SIPC).

**securities option** *See:* option, securities option, put option (put); option, securities option, call option (option call or call).

**securities regulation** *See:* security, securities, securities regulation.

**securities valuation** *See:* security, securities, securities valuation, capital asset pricing model (CAPM).

**securities warrant** *See:* security, securities, securities warrant (stock purchase warrant).

**securitization** *See:* security, securities, securitization.

**security** Anything providing assurance or confidence. Security is a general term for a variety of forms of protection of the interests of an individual, family, entity, or state. Security includes all of those acts and procedures that make them safe from harm. Myriad forms of security exist, including forms specific to interests in one's safety and personal protection from harm; interests in financial expectation, investments, and obligations; and interests in national interest and defense. Security is one of the fundamental purposes of the law.

In legal usage, a security may be a financial instrument representing a share of equity or an obligation or a debt. A security may also be a surety, a person, promise, or collateral to ensure the performance of some action.

Security represents an aspect of risk management in insurance and in property law. Security is also a private service or public duty in protecting individuals and property from harm. Security is also the protection of a nation from harm or threat to its people, properties and interests.

*See also:* surety (suretyship).

**security agreement** *See:* transaction, secured transaction (security agreement).

**security deposit** *See:* deposit, security deposit (damage deposit).

**security as personal and physical protection** To guard a person or property from harm. Security in the sense of the security of a person or of property is the physical protection of the person from interference, assault, or injury and the physical protection of the property from trespass, theft, or harm. The state has a police power to ensure the security of the personal integrity and property of the citizenry. A private provider of security may enter into a contract to provide such security, but unless the recipient of the service has an obligation to provide the security of a third party, the private provider does not acquire an obligation to provide security to the third party. Even so, a store or other enterprise may have an obligation to provide security to its invitees to take reasonable steps to provide security to protect invitees from harm.

**securities** All forms of debt or equity that may be traded on a public exchange. Securities is the generic and inclusive term for all forms of security that may be traded for profit or held as an investment. In this sense, securities include debt securities such as bonds, equity securities, shares, and derivative contracts based on debt or equity obligations. The whole list of securities might appear infinite, particularly owing to the novelties possible in the creation of new derivatives. The Securities Act of 1933, 48 Stat. 74, codified at 15 U.S.C. § 77b(1), remains an essential point of reference, however, including in its thirty-seven forms of security not only stocks, bonds, and futures but also any interest or instrument commonly called a security and any right to purchase one.

**American depositary receipt (ADR)** A locally created share of equitable ownership in a foreign company. An American depositary receipt, or ADR, is a security issued in the United States by a U.S. bank. It represents an equitable ownership in shares of a foreign company on deposit in a custodial bank in the company's home jurisdiction, which becomes an agent of the U.S. depositary bank. An ADR is issued in shares that equate to a share of the company held, the whole of the purchase being the ADR, each share being an American Depositary Share, or ADS.

*See also:* depositary (depository or repository).

**collateralized debt obligation (collateralized loan obligation or CLO or CDO)** A security representing a pool of income from debt. A collateralized debt obligation, commonly called a CDO, is a security that is backed by a pool of debt obligations. The pools of debt that back the security are commonly aggregated from pools of bonds, commercial loans, and personal loans with varying maturity dates, organized into tranches. CDO's are often insured by credit-default swaps, or CDS's. Unwinding an individual CDO to assess its actual book value or the value of the underlying debt is complex, making the true valuation of CDO's dependent in part on their CDS's but otherwise difficult to assess when debtors have increased risks of default on the payment of the underlying indebtedness.

*See also:* tranch (tranche).

**mortgage-backed security** A security representing a pool of income from mortgages. A mortgage-backed security is a form of collateralized debt obligation based on pools of debt created from mortgages. The mortgages may be residential or commercial or both.

**exchange traded fund (ETF or E.T.F.)** A fund of stocks listed on an exchange. An exchange traded fund, or ETF, is a fund holding shares of stocks traded on a given exchange. Each share of an ETF represents an indirect ownership in the corporations listed on the exchange, so the return of the fund as a whole, less the management fee of the fund, is reflected in the performance of the ETF share.

**high-yield security (junk bond)** A bond with a low rating but high rate of payment. A high-yield security is a bond or other debt-based security that has greater risk than an investment-grade security and so pays a higher yield — or regular, structured payment — in order to induce a buyer to acquire it. In other words the underlying payee on the debt pays more but has a potential of default that is high relative to other debt-security issuers.

**investment security** A security held by a bank as a capital investment. An investment security is a security purchased and held by a bank or banking institution as an investment for the purposes of maintaining and developing its own capital, rather than for resale to consumers. In this sense, investment securities are highly regulated and usually are required to have a limited exposure to equities. The term may be used, loosely, to describe any security.

**mutual fund** An investment fund owning securities and other property. A mutual fund is a professionally managed fund registered with the Securities and Exchange Commission, in which shares are sold as a security, that holds property in various forms of investment property, particularly debt and equity securities, commodities, and other property. Purchases of shares in a mutual fund are made from the entity that manages the fund rather than other holders of shares, and, unlike securities traded among buyers and sellers on exchanges, the value of the fund varies not according to the share price at which a party agrees to buy into the fund from another owner but according to the value of the fund's assets at the end of the trading day.

**repo (repo sale)** A sale of securities subject to an agreed repurchase. A repo is a sale of securities in which the selling agent requires the buyer to accept a condition on the sale that requires the seller or seller's agent to repurchase the securities. A repo is not a conditional sale because the repurchase is not conditioned. The repurchase is a requirement, usually at a fixed price. A repo may amount, in effect, to a loan of the purchase money from the initial buyer/later seller to the initial seller/later buyer. Note: repo is also a slang term for the repossession of goods by self-help, which has nothing to do with a securities repo.

**reverse repo** A purchase of securities subject to an agreed sell-back. A reverse repo is a sale of securities in which the securities are bought subject to a condition that they will be sold back to the initial seller. A reverse repo is to the initial buyer what a repo is to the initial seller.

### Securities Exchange

**American Stock Exchange (A.M.E.X. or AMEX)** A floor-based exchange and securities market. The American Stock Exhange (AMEX) is a floor-based exchange auction market, located in New York City, that specializes in stocks, bonds, and exchange-traded funds (ETFs). AMEX lists primarily small and midsized companies and newer issues, and it is the United States' second-largest options exchange. It is now a component of NYSE Euronext.

*See also:* market (law of the market); share, share as stock, common stock (common share).

**Little Board** The American Stock Exchange. The "Little Board" is an appellation given to the American Stock Exchange, as opposed to its rival, the New York Stock Exchange, which has long been known as the "Big Board."

*See also:* security, securities, Securities Exchange, American Stock Exchange (A.M.E.X. AMEX).

**Big Board** The New York Stock Exchange. The "Big Board" refers to the New York Stock Exchange. The term is derived from the large electronic board located on the stock exchange floor, which displays stock quotations during the trading day.

**New York Stock Exchange (N.Y.S.E. or NYSE)** The largest U.S. public exchange for stocks. The New York Stock Exchange, or NYSE, is a component of an international network of equity exchanges. The U.S. branch is the largest equity market in the country.

**securities fraud (Rule 10b-5)** A fraud related to the sale or management of securities. Securities fraud is the crime of misrepresentation, deception, or wrongful acquisition of property in connection with the purchase or sale of securities. A federal private action for recovery of a loss due to securities fraud may be brought under the Private Securities Litigation Reform Act of 1995. The primary regulatory definition of securities fraud is SEC Rule 10b-5, which makes unlawful any person's use of "a device, scheme, or artifice to defraud;" untrue or misleading statement or omission of a material fact; or an "act, practice, or course of business which operates or would operate as a fraud or deceit upon any person, in connection with the purchase or sale of any security."

See also: fraud, consumer fraud.

**blue-sky law** Legislation governing the exchange of securities. A blue-sky law is a state securities regulation, delineating standards for buying and selling of securities, particularly when the security is not listed on an exchange. The term comes from the propensity of corporate developers to promise the blue sky to investors. Blue-sky laws vary among jurisdictions, but they usually provide both criminal and regulatory limits on certain frauds and misrepresentations regarding securities, and they create private actions for recovery of losses under covered transactions.

See also: share, share as stock, stock offering.

**churning** The management of a client's account to increase the manager's fees. Churning is a practice of some investment managers of frequent buying and selling of securities for the purpose of generating or justifying fees for the manager rather than optimizing returns for the investor. Churning by an investment broker or manager who exercises control over a client's account, occurs when trades are excessive in the light of the client's investment goals, and who acts in willful disregard for the investor's interests or an intent to defraud the investor.

**securities regulation** The laws and rules governing the nature, issuance, sale, trading, holding, and redemption of securities. Securities regulation is a complex system of federal law, state law, industry rules, and customs that both define and regulate every facet of a security from its creation and issuance, through its trading and management, to its redemption or cancellation. Securities regulation includes federal law derived primarily from a dozen or so statutes based on Congress's power to regulate interstate commerce; state laws regulating corporations, securities, and securities trading, particularly blue sky laws; the regulation of exchanges over their members, particularly the rules of the Financial Industry Regulatory Authority; and the related federal and state regulations of banking and, to a lesser degree, insurance entities. Though securities regulation is usually thought of as the province of statutes and rules, the creation, use, and trading of securities is also subject to the judicial oversight of trading contracts and standards of care arising both from contract and tort law and fiduciary law. Increasingly, a corporation is subject to the regulation of its securities in more than one nation, just as a corporation in one U.S. state is often subject to regulation by several states in which it is considered to be actively subject to investment and ownership.

The purposes of securities regulation include the assurance of transparency in that what is sold as a security represents what it appears to do (particularly in assessing the risks posed by a given security); fairness in that each buyer in a market has an equal access to information; and stability, in that the securities market is managed in such a way that the fundamental economic capacity of the investors and entities relying on the market is not harmed by it.

**Commodity Futures Trading Commission** The agency that regulates the commodities exchanges. The Commodity Futures Trading Commission, or CFTC, is an independent federal agency tasked with the regulation of the markets for commodities futures, commodities future contracts, and commodities options in the United States. Much of the hedging in commodities conducted by hedge funds and other investment entities is subject to regulation by the CFTC. The commission promulgates regulations to implement statutes governing the issuance, sale, and exercise of commodities options and derivatives, notably provisions of the Dodd–Frank Wall Street Reform and Consumer Protection Act, Pub.L. 111–203 (2010), that regulate the swap market, or exchange of securities for other securities rather than for money. The CFTC may bring administrative complaints against regulated entities before its own Administrative Law Judges, or it may bring civil actions in federal court or refer criminal matters to the Department of Justice for prosecution.

**Financial Industry Regulatory Authority (FINRA NASD)** The private, self-regulating agency of securities dealers. The Financial Industry Regulatory Authority, or FINRA, is an independent regulator for securities firms doing business in the United States. FINRA is the successor entity to the National Association of Securities Dealers, and it incorporated the regulation of members as well as most enforcement and arbitration functions of the New York Stock Exchange.

**Securities and Exchange Commission (S.E.C. or SEC)** The public agency that regulates securities and securities trading. The U.S. Securities and Exchange Commission is a federal agency created by Congress in the Securities Exchange Act of 1934, tasked with the interpretation of securities laws, the protection of investors, and the maintenance of fair, orderly, and efficient markets that facilitate capital formation. The SEC issues regulations and brings enforcement actions.

*See also:* share, share as stock, stock offering.

**EDGAR** The SEC's electronic system for corporate filings. EDGAR, the SEC's Electronic Data Gathering, Analysis, and Retrieval system, is the e-filing system for all filings by corporations required to file registration statements, periodic reports, or other forms with the Securities and Exchange Commission. The system allows public access and searches at http://www.sec.gov/edgar/searchedgar/webusers.htm.

**Securities Investor Protection Corporation (SIPC)** An entity to recover investor funds from financially troubled securities dealers. The Securities Investor Protection Corporation, or SIPC, is a non-profit organization created by Congress in the Securities Investor Protection Act, codified at 15 U.S.C. § 78aaa, et seq. (2010), to facilitate the recovery of funds for investors from bankrupt and insolvent brokerage firms. The SIPC is not a government agency but a nonprofit, membership corporation, funded by its securities broker and dealers.

**securities valuation**

**capital asset pricing model (CAPM)** A theoretical estimate of a reasonable rate of return on an asset. The capital asset pricing model is a formula for estimating the likely return on a single asset as a single component of a diversified portfolio, by accounting for the expected growth of the market for the asset and its risk to generate a ratio of risk to return.

**securities warrant (stock purchase warrant)** A corporate instrument authorizing future stock purchases. A warrant is an instrument issued by a corporation that allows its holder to purchase equities, particularly shares of stock in the issuing corporation, at or after a given time, and for a given amount or according to a set formula for determining the price. A warrant is similar to an option to purchase the equity. A warrant is itself an equity.

*See also:* share, share as stock, stock option (warrant for stock or stock warrant or securities option or share option).

**securitization** The conversion of debts into new securities. Securitization is a process of converting obligations such as debts into new securities. The securitizing agency acquires rights in a range of debts then uses the debts as collateral upon which to issue a new range of securities. The securities may be bonds, equities in a fund with the debts as all or part of its assets, or a similar vehicle secured by the debt. In theory, the new securities have a diminished level of risk owing to the spread of risk from the individual obligations, although the risk from securitized debt is no less than for such debts as a whole.

**short sale (sell short)** A short-term acquisition of a security to sell after it falls in value. A short sale is an arrangement by which an investor borrows a security from a broker and sells it subject to its being bought back at a later date, when the investor expects it to be at a lower price. Thus, the investor accurately forecasting the price decline can profit from the falling price of the security. For example, if an investor plans to short a stock, the investor may borrow them by instructing the investor's broker to borrow the stock (for a fee); the investor sells the borrowed stock at the current market price, then later covers the short position by buying them back. As long as the price fell in the interim, the investor can return the shares and realize a profit. If the price rises, however, the investor must still cover the short but will be required to buy replacement shares at a loss.

**security interest** An interest in property that secures the performance of an obligation. A security interest is an interest held by a creditor, or more generally a person or entity owed some obligation, in property owned by a debtor, or the person or entity owing the obligation, which allows the creditor (or obligee) to take possession or sell the property in compensation if the debt is not repaid or the obligation not performed. Security interests take many forms, particularly liens. The security interest may be in property of greater or lesser value than the debt or obligation. If property less valuable is taken, the remaining portion of the debt or value of the obligation is not extinguished. If property more valuable is taken, the creditor (or obligee) is responsible for return of the excess value to the debtor or obligor, minus expenses incurred in the process. A transaction in which at least one promise or obligation is secured by the acquisition of a security interest is a secured transaction.

*See also:* lien (lienholder); transaction, secured transaction (security agreement).

**collateral security** *See:* collateral.

**due-on-sale clause** Security agreement that the debt is due if the collateral is sold. A due-on-sale clause is a portion of a written security agreement that binds the debtor to pay the debt in full if and when the property that secures the debt is sold by the debtor. It is frequently placed in a mortgage agreement or other instrument creating a security interest in land, accelerating the debt if the debtor sells all or a portion of the land without the prior written approval of the creditor.

**perfected security interest** A security interest recorded in the appropriate public office. A perfected security interest is a recorded security interest. To perfect the interest, the holder of the interest in the property must file a notice of the interest in the appropriate office of public records for the jurisdiction in which the property subject to the interest is located, or in which the owner of the property is domiciled, or both.

A perfected security interest is not proof the interest will be honored, not the least as it is subordinate to earlier perfected interests in the same property and because a security interest may be subordinate to the claims of others such as the government, a spouse or child, or a purchase for value. Yet with such exceptions, a perfected security interest has priority over unperfected interests as well as interests that are later perfected.

**sediment**   Particles from rocks and soil suspended in, or deposited by, water. Sediment is both the particulate carried in river, lake, and ocean water and the deposits that result from it. Sediments in freshwater are created primarily by runoff from rain, snowmelt, and irrigation, which carry topsoil and eroded minerals into watersheds, although sediment also occurs from erosion by the waters themselves as they travel across their beds and banks. Sediments in saltwater result both from the deposit of sediment from rivers and from the erosion of minerals, shells, corals, and other biological and mineral matter on the seabed and from the chemical activity of seawater. Sedimentary deposits on banks, shores, and islands that gradually enlarge the landmass alter both the landward and seaward boundaries affected by accretion.

**sedition**   The advocacy of violent overthrow of the government. Sedition is the advocacy of insurrection, the argument or promotion of the destruction of the government of the United States or a state within it by force, violence, or assassination. Sedition is a federal crime under the Smith Act, 18 U.S.C. § 2385, which preempts state crimes on similar grounds. Sedition was first prosecuted under the Sedition Act of 1789, and although the scope of such prosecution is limited by the First Amendment, both the practice of sedition and membership in a group devoted to sedition are illegal.

*See also:* syndicalism; immigration, Alien and Sedition Acts (Smith Act); alien, Alien and Sedition Acts (Alien Act or Sedition Act ).

**seditious conspiracy**   *See:* conspiracy, seditious conspiracy.

**seditious libel**   *See:* libel, seditious libel.

**subversive organization (subversion or overthrow of the government or subvert)**   To overturn an organization or overthrow a state of government. Subversion is the destruction or overthrow of any enterprise or purpose. To subvert a person, entity, or state is to ruin it or overthrow its organization. As a crime, it is action the purpose of which is to overthrow the government of the United States or a state by unlawful means, particularly by violence.

A subversive organization is an organization whose conduct or purpose is subversive. A variety of state laws outlaw such organizations and make membership in such organizations criminal, although such laws are probably preempted by federal law. Prosecution under any prohibition of subversion or membership in a subversive organization cannot reach protected exercises of speech or organization, and thus cannot reach actions that do not, in fact, practice violence, support terrorism, or advocate the overthrow of the government by force, violence, or assassination. Historically, labor unions and civil rights organizations were prosecuted as subversive organizations, and use of subversive activities as a basis for investigation or arrest remains a constitutionally dubious proposition.

*See also:* sedition.

**seduction (seduce)**   A dignitary law of inducing another to have unlawful sexual intercourse. Seduction was once the crime of a man's inducing a woman to have sex in violation of the law. More commonly, seduction was a common-law action that could be brought by a parent against a male who engaged in sexual intercourse with the parent's daughter, having induced her to do so through any means other than trickery or force. That tort has been enlarged in some jurisdictions to include any inducement to sexual intercourse brought about by misrepresentation or false promises. This cause of action, in one formulation or another, was recognized by the common law and enacted by statute in many states, although most have repealed their seduction statutes in the repeal of heart balm actions. Some have been found to violate equal protection either by limiting the action to a father or by limiting the defendant to a class of males. In some states, the action may persist.

*See also:* tort, dignitary tort, heart balm tort (amatory tort or Heart Balm Act); rape, rape as sexual assault, bodily intrusion (penetration or physical penetration).

**see**   *See:* citation, citation signal, see.

**see also**   *See:* citation, citation signal, see also.

**seeing eye dog**   *See:* dog, seeing eye dog; animal, service animal (seeing eye dog).

**segregation (racial segregation or segregation by gender)**   Public discrimination between races, genders, or groups. Segregation is separation of members of one category from members of another, or of one person or thing from the rest. Thus, when a prisoner is segregated from a prison population, that prisoner is separated and isolated from the others.

In U.S. legal history, segregation of races in access to public facilities and to public resources was the legal doctrine of the federal and state governments as well as a dominant aspect of social and political structures in much of the United States. Justified by the constitutional doctrine that races could be provided separate but equal public facilities, accepted under the 14th Amendment despite its purpose to require equal and fair treatment of all citizens in denying African Americans a right to travel in the comfort given to Whites in Plessy v. Ferguson, 163 U.S. 537 (1896), applied to public schools in

Cumming v. Richmond County Board of Education, 175 U.S. 528 (1899), and to colleges in Berea College v. Kentucky, 211 U.S. 45 (1908). Segregation in the southern states was enforced through "Jim Crow laws" effectively barring most African Americans from voting or serving on juries. The Supreme Court, in Sweatt v. Painter, 339 U.S. 629 (1950), and finally in Brown v. Board of Education, 347 U.S. 483 (1954), finally rejected the separate-but–equal doctrine, eventually dismantling all legal segregation in public services and access. Legal segregation, or de jure segregation, both resulted and supported social segregation, or de facto segregation. De facto segregation in social behavior, institutional behavior, and in the intersection between society and law, is still common in many communities in the U.S.

Gender segregation is the division of activities between men and women. Until recently, transgendered persons were not considered distinctly but were lumped into one category or another. Segregation by gender barred women from holding property, voting, education, serving as jurors, holding public office, holding most forms of employment, and having access to many public services. Such segregation now violates the Nineteenth Amendment as well as contemporary interpretations of equal protection of the law. Gender segregation is still prevalent, however, in circumstances dealing with certain public facilities, sports teams, and education of the young, in which separate facilities are made available reflecting either bona fide physical differences or a public benefit in restricting access between young people of different genders.

*See also:* discrimination.

**desegregation (integration)** The end of segregation. Desegregation is the end of a program of segregation. Particularly, when used without other modifiers, segregation usually refers to the practices and to the era from the 1940s to the 1980s in which segregated facilities for education, transportation, and services were burdened with Jim Crow laws and associated customs in the United States. Desegregation in public schools and universities was a complicated series of judicially required acts, voluntary acts, and institutional resistance. Desegregation is the ending of forced or legal segregation, which often did not lead to integration but new patterns of voluntary segregation.

**with all deliberate speed** The institutional speed of desegregation. All deliberate speed is the ambiguous pace required by Chief Justice Earl Warren in instructing courts to oversee the desegregation of public institutions that had been subject to segregation under law. The requirement followed admonitions that the courts must give weight to public and private considerations favoring resistance to desegregation but still require a "prompt and reasonable" start to compliance leading to "good faith compliance at the earliest practicable date."

**seisin (seizin or seisin in law or seised of seized of)** Possession of a freehold in fee simple. Seisin is the legal possession of land in fee simple, the medieval form of title nearest to modern ownership. Seisin at common law was one of several forms of lawful possession, seisin usually being contrasted with villenage. Seisin was transferable by death or, eventually, by sale, grant, or gift by will. In contemporary usage, seisin is equivalent to ownership. To be seised of a given property is to own it and to have a right of possession in it. Likewise for a person to die seised of some tract means the person owned the property at the time of death.

*See also:* covenant, covenant of title, Covenant of Seisin (Covenant for Title).

**livery of seisin** The ceremony of transfer of lawful possession of land. Livery of seisin was a medieval ceremony marking the transfer of seisin to the new holder of a freehold in land. Although the ceremony was performed when an heir took land by descent from the prior possessor's death, the ceremony was more significant in recognizing a grant from a grantor to a grantee. In this case, the grantor would hand to the grantee something symbolic of the particular estate — a key, a branch or flower from a well-known tree, or some other symbol of the place. The ceremony would be performed before witnesses and ensured continuity of management of the freehold estate, although a written grant of feoffment was also transferred. The modern term "delivery" is a corruption of this phrase.

*See also:* delivery.

**seizin** Seisin. Seizin is a variant spelling of seisin. This spelling is especially found in states that were once French or Spanish colonies; there is no difference in meaning that turns on the spelling. Both originate in the Law French seisine, for possession of land, yet the unvoiced pronunciation of the second s as a "z" sound led to the curious typology, even in the Louisiana Code.

**seizure (seize)** To take possession of a person or thing. Seizure is the act of arrest, the taking of physical custody by an agent of the state of a person, place, or thing, regardless of the agreement of the person or willingness of the person otherwise in control, possession, or ownership of the place or thing. A seizure may be temporary or permanent. A police officer's brief assertion of physical authority over a person or property is sufficient to amount to a seizure, even if the assertion is quickly ended.

A seizure must be within the limits of the Fourth Amendment of the Constitution, made either according to a valid warrant or made reasonably and according to the law in the light of the circumstances of the seizure.

*See also:* search, search and seizure; detainer.

**unreasonable seizure** An arrest unjustified in its cause or manner. An unreasonable seizure is a violation of the Fourth Amendment of the U.S. Constitution, arising either from the seizure of a person or thing without a valid warrant or sufficiently reasonable cause, or from the means employed in a seizure that might otherwise be reasonable but that is conducted in a manner that causes unjustified and unreasonable harm to the person or thing. The test of such reasonableness is whether the harm to the person or thing, or the nature and quality of the intrusion on the individual's Fourth Amendment interests, outweighs the importance of the governmental interests alleged to have justified that intrusion. An arrest employing unreasonable or excessive force in the light of the circumstances at the time is an unreasonable seizure.

> **mere evidence rule** Former rule forbidding the seizure of certain evidence without a warrant. The mere evidence rule, abandoned in 1967, forbade police seizure of "mere evidence," or information or papers that was intended only to be used as evidence of a crime (as opposed to the instrumentalities of the crime itself), as inherently unreasonable under the Fourth Amendment.

**selective enforcement** *See:* enforcement, law enforcement, selective enforcement.

**selective incorporation** *See:* constitution, U.S. Constitution, Bill of Rights, incorporation of rights, selective incorporation.

**selective prosecution** *See:* prosecution, selective prosecution.

**self** A reference to one's own person, independent of others. The self is the identity of each person, a reflexive identification according to which anything perceived by a person about that person is perceived about the self. The self represents a boundary between the individual and others, the limit of the self is the limit of the individual.

Although self, generally, applies only to natural persons, in the law the term can apply to artificial persons, too. Thus, a company may engage in self-help to recover an asset wrongly held by another party. A company may engage in self-criticism in reviewing its operating procedures. There are limits, however, to this concept of the self, and it is quite impossible for a company to act with force in self-defense (although individual officers of a company can do so).

Many aspects of law turn on the role of the individual alone, and these are defined by the self. Self-support, self-defense, self-criticism, self-censorship, self-interest, self-reporting, self-insurance, self-referral, self-dealing, self-service, self-employment, self-propelled, self-injury, self-dealing, and so on – each phrase meaning that the person or entity was the actor as well as the object of the action.

> **self-authenticating will** *See:* will, last will and testament, self-proved will (self-authenticating will).

> **self dealing** *See:* conflict, conflict of interest, self-dealing (self dealing).

> **self defense** *See:* defense, self defense, castle doctrine; defense, self defense, Battered-Woman Syndrome (Battered Woman Syndrome); defense, self defense (self-defense or defense of others or defense of property).

> **self-executing** *See:* execution, self-executing; clause, execution clause (self-executing).

> **self-executing treaty** *See:* treaty, self-executing treaty (non–self-executing treaty).

> **self-incrimination** *See:* incrimination, self-incrimination, link in chain (link-in-chain principle); incrimination, self-incrimination, collective entity doctrine; incrimination, self-incrimination (privilege against self-incrimination or right to silence).

> **Self-Incrimination Clause** *See:* constitution, U.S. Constitution, clauses, Self-Incrimination Clause.

> **self insurance** *See:* insurance, self insurance.

> **self-proved will** *See:* will, last will and testament, self-proved will (self-authenticating will).

> **self-settled trust** *See:* trust, self-settled trust.

> **self help (self-help)** Acting on one's behalf to protect or restore one's lawful right. Self help is the lawful use of one's own initiative, without a court order, to do what one may legally do to protect one's interests under the law. It includes the entry on lands one owns that are held unlawfully by another, the recovery of chattels wrongly held by another, and cover and other mitigation of damages in contract. Self help may not be used in many jurisdictions for eviction of a tenant in a residential lease, even if the tenant is a holdover tenant or tenant by sufferance. Self help is not the same as self defense, and self help may not be exercised in circumstances that might reasonably be expected to lead to violence or a breach of the peace.
>
> *See also:* chattel, recapture of chattel (self-help); repossession (repo or repossess).

**seller (sell)** The one who provides the property or service in a contract. The seller is the party in a sale who brings the goods or service to the transaction. The seller sells the goods or service to the buyer, and the transaction results in the transfer of the goods or services from the seller to the buyer or the recipient the buyer designates. In many contracts, more than one party is a seller. To sell refers to the action or conduct of a seller. Note: there is no required relationship between being the seller and being the offeror; an offer may be made by the buyer and often is, but when the offer is made by the seller, the seller is also the offeror.

*See also:* buyer (buy); purveyor.

> **sell short** *See:* security, securities, short sale (sell short).

**semantics** The study of the meaning, or a dismissive label for a technical argument. Semantics is a study of meaning, particularly the meaning communicated in language. It is closely related to semiotics and is usually thought of as a branch of linguistics. In this sense, semantics has much to give jurisprudence, for instance, in the study of criteria for meaning and the structure of relationships among related words.

Lawyers use semantics in a pejorative sense that loosely relates to its technical meaning as a field of study, though not directly. As often used in legal argument, "semantics" is used to label arguments arising from distinctions in meaning in a contract or statute. The label "semantic" suggests the argument presents overly fine shades of difference among the meanings of words or about the appropriate word to represent a concept. It is a dismissive trope, and sometimes unfairly or mistakenly used.

*See also:* jurisprudence, legal semiotics (semiotics).

**semiotics**  *See:* jurisprudence, legal semiotics (semiotics).

**semper**  Always. Semper is Latin for a time that never ends, always or forever.

**senate**  *See:* congress, senate.

**senate bill**  *See:* legislation, bill, senate bill (S.B. or SB).

**senator**  *See:* congress, senate, senator.

**senatorial courtesy**  *See:* congress, senate, senator, senatorial courtesy.

**senior**  The elder, earlier, or more important. Senior signifies greater age, authority, or significance relative to someone or something else. In its most customary form, a senior is the older of people or things, according to some criterion, which may be physical age or may be determined by entrance into an employment, organization, or placement. By custom, people of the same name in a family are distinguished by the elder being designated senior or accepting a numeric title at the end of the name.

A senior is also a person with greater authority, as an officer has over an employee in a corporation. A senior within a category of office is within the elevated category of offices, as in the military, which distinguish senior officers from junior officers, or faculties that distinguish senior faculty from junior faculty, or corporations that distinguish senior officers or executives from junior officers or executives.

Senior may imply an earlier placement of a thing, as in a senior debt or senior obligation, which is given priority over junior debt, or later debt, of the same class. (Although secured debt is still given priority over senior unsecured debt relative to the property in which there is security.)

**senior judge**  *See:* judge, senior judge (senior status or judge on senior status).

**senior status or judge on senior status**  *See:* judge, senior judge (senior status or judge on senior status).

**seniority**  The relative length of time for an employee's service. Seniority is an employment characteristic that, in general, is a measure of an employee's length of continuous service since the employee was hired by the employing entity or its direct predecessor entities. Seniority is a relative measure, and a person employed longer than another person has seniority over that person.

Seniority may vary in its calculation under different contracts or in different positions of employment. It is sometimes demarcated by seniority in a given rank or a given category of position, so that a person with seniority as an employee in one division may lose that seniority if the person transfers to another division.

More generally, seniority is the quality of being senior. Thus, a senior debt has seniority over a junior debt, and an officer has seniority over an employee.

**sentence**  A judgment, as of a criminal punishment. A sentence is a final determination in an action in a court of law. Although the term has been applied to judgments in civil cases, its contemporary use is primarily as a judgment of punishment in a criminal action. A sentence may include any lawful form of punishment, usually including fine, community service, shaming penalties, probation, imprisonment, hard labor, or death, as well as costs and victim restitution. Certain conditions may be imposed as a component of a sentence, including restrictions on certain employment, loss of state privileges such as a driving license, requirements for counseling or treatment, and conformity with registries as for sex offenders. The sentence available or required for specific offenses, including a separate range or requirement for offenses committed by recidivists, is established by the legislature for an offense in a given state or the Congress for federal offense. Most sentences are not a specific punishment but a range of punishments varying in severity, and the judge is left with discretion to assign a sentence within that range. The federal courts and some states use sentencing guidelines that detail specific aggravating and mitigating factors that should be weighed in calculating the sentence, although judges may disregard the guidelines for good cause.

The sentence in a minor criminal cause may be rendered by a judge at the time of a finding or verdict of guilt, but the sentence in most actions for serious crimes is usually in a separate proceeding before the judge alone, held after the jury has rendered its verdict and been discharged, after post–verdict motions have been heard, and after a pre–sentence report has been completed by the appropriate probation office or police agency. In capital cases, a jury will give a recommendation of sentence, though sentence is still imposed by the judge.

*See also:* fine; punishment (punish); incarceration, imprisonment, imprisonment as criminal punishment; instruction, jury instruction, sentencing instruction.

**death sentence**  *See:* punishment, death penalty (capital punishment, execution).

**mitigation of sentence (mitigating evidence)** A milder sentence based on reduced culpability. Mitigation of a sentence is the reduction of a sentence from the punishment that would otherwise be required or mandated, in the light of evidence that demonstrates a reduced level of culpability by the person to be sentenced. Mitigation, at its broadest, includes evidence that supports a defense of justification or excuse, yet mitigating evidence is usually introduced to reduce a sentence rather than to avoid liability. Mitigating evidence may always be introduced in a criminal trial in which the sentence is potentially an issue. In a capital case, a defendant has a constitutional right to introduce not only evidence required to be allowed by statute, but any mitigating evidence that would be relevant to the consideration of the sentence.

**presentence-investigation report (pre-sentence report or PSR or P.S.R.)** A report of mitigating and aggravating factors affecting sentencing. A presentence-investigation report, or PSR, is a report prepared prior to sentencing in the United States courts by the local federal probation office, summarizing evidence from the criminal action for which a convict has been found guilty and collecting further evidence that might mitigate or aggravate the defendant's guilt, including a complete report of the defendant's background, including police, medical, work, school, military, penal, and other records. The investigator is usually required to interview the defendant, conduct an independent investigation, evaluate its results in the light of applicable regulations, and recommend a sentence. The PSR is submitted to the sentencing magistrate or judge in advance of sentencing, and counsel for defense may move for alterations in its findings. The report is also used by the Bureau of Prisons in categorizing the convict if incarceration is ordered. Similar reports are submitted in many state courts prior to sentencing, and in these the report is also used in parole hearings.

**reduction of sentence, good behavior (good time)** Lawful conduct justifying early release. Good behavior is conduct that conforms to the rules that govern the person in question. Good behavior is therefore different for a person incarcerated in a penitentiary from a person who is not: each must comply with the laws governing behavior, but the prisoner must comply more strictly with many more rules, particularly affirmative obligations to do certain things, while the free person must comply more broadly with fewer rules, which are particularly likely to be negative obligations, such as an obligation not to harm or to interfere with another person. Good behavior in a prison over a period of time will, in most jurisdictions, allow a reduction in the prisoner's sentence or an earlier parole. Good behavior when especially required by a bond, parole term, or other particular source of duty for a person free from jail, is a condition of that person's bond forfeiture, continued liberty, or liability for violating the duty.

**sentencing**

**sentencing instruction** *See:* instruction, jury instruction, sentencing instruction.

**Sentencing Guidelines** A manual for computing a sentence for each specific offender. Sentencing Guidelines are judicial rules specifying the means by which a sentence may be calculated for a given offender found guilty of a given offense. The guidelines account for the effect of past offenses and sentences, mitigating evidence, and aggravating evidence. In jurisdictions that follow a sentencing guideline, a sentencing judge may depart from the guidelines if facts not accounted for in the guidelines are present, but a sentence within the guidelines that accurately accounts for evidence in the record is accorded a higher level of deference on appeal.

The U.S. Sentencing Guidelines are issued by the U.S. Sentencing Commission and amended yearly. The federal guidelines contemplate departure from their recommendations for a variety of causes when appropriate as determined by the sentencing judge.

**separation (separate or separability)**

**separability thesis** *See:* jurisprudence, legal positivism, separability thesis.

**separate-but-equal doctrine** *See:* equality, separate-but-equal doctrine (separate but equal).

**separate caucus** *See:* caucus, caucus as in negotiation (separate caucus).

**separate estate** *See:* estate, separate estate.

**separate maintenance** *See:* alimony, separate maintenance (spousal maintenance).

**separate property** *See:* marriage, marital property, separate property.

**separation** *See:* divorce, separation (marital separation or legal separation or judicial separation).

**separation of church and state** *See:* religion, freedom of religion, establishment of religion (separation of church and state).

**separation of powers** *See:* U.S. Constitution, ideals, separation of powers.

**trial separation** An informal separation between husband and wife. A trial separation is an informal separation, very rarely commenced pursuant to a judicial order, during which the spouses have time to consider their positions before attempting to reconcile or committing to the dissolution of the marriage. Many trial separations are managed with the assistance of marriage counselors.

**sepulchre (cemetery or mausoleum)** A tomb. A sepulchre is the place for the final internment of a dead body or, in some instances, the ashes or other remains thereof. A tomb, vault, grave, or other place for reception of the body is a sepulchre, though the casket, box, shroud or other device by which the body is placed into the sepulchre is usually considered a distinct entity. In the United States, a sepulchre is usually considered the place for a single body or a small number of bodies placed together, such as a family. A place housing the sepulchres of more people is a cemetery or, if under cover, a mortuary. Cemeteries are usually regulated by statutes and local ordinances, and land held as a cemetery may be subject to particular zoning protections and health regulations. Interference with a cemetery is usually a specific offense as trespass or vandalism.

See also: robbery, grave robbing (grave robbery).

**right of sepulchre (burial rights)**   The rights to possess, bury, and protect the body of a dead family member. The right of sepulchre is a common-law right recognized in most jurisdictions in which a next of kin may take possession of a dead body, enter into a contract for its burial, enforce rights over the body, the burial, and its internment or other permanent disposition, and bring an action for damages, injunction, or specific performance to both secure these rights and recover for emotional injury when they have been violated.

See also: corpse (cadaver or dead body).

**sequestration (sequester)**   To isolate a person, group, or property; or to renounce a claim to property. Sequestration is the action of isolating or separating a person or property from someone or something else. In law, it has had several distinct senses with many applications.

Sequestration of property is its separation from a larger whole or from its owner. Sequestration may mean the separation of funds or property for accounting, such as funds deposited for a specific purpose into a common account being diverted to a specific account for their separate management and accounting.

Sequestration was once a common means of placing property in dispute into custody. It may be voluntary or by order of the court. This was once also an order or writ once used to take custody of property under sequestrators, who were officers of the court like trustees, who would manage it for a time, usually until the conclusion of litigation over its ownership or for which it would be likely required to pay relief. This is still done in England, and it is still potentially available in some American jurisdictions, although deposition, replevin, attachment, or claim and delivery are more likely used for this purpose. Sequestration was once also a statement of renunciation to a claim in property, particularly a statement by a spouse renouncing an interest in a will, by which the spouse sequestered her interest.

The sequestration of persons is their isolation, although the significance of the sequestration varies by context. The jury may be sequestered, which removes them from the public. Witnesses (other than a party) may be sequestered, which removes them from the courtroom.

See also: equity, equitable remedies, sequestration.

**sequestered jury**   See: jury, sequestration of the jury (sequestered jury).

**sequestration of the jury**   See: jury, sequestration of the jury (sequestered jury).

**sequestration of witness**   See: witness, sequestration of witness (the rule of separation of witnesses).

**serfdom (serf)**   A feudal status of being tied to the land in quasi-slavery. Serfdom was the status of the unfree, serfs who possessed no rights or lands but were bound to an estate for service. Serf is a corruption of the Latin for slave, and was a common Anglo-Saxon condition both before and after conquest. The common law did not recognize serfdom, the lowest estates being those of villeinage.

See also: tenure; villein (villeinage).

**sergeant (serjeant)**   A representative, a servant, or a non-commissioned officer. Sergeant, an old French term for servant, has a variety of differing senses, the most common of which in contemporary usage is as a non-commissioned officer in the army, air force, or marines, equivalent in rating to a senior or chief petty officer in the naval services. A sergeant is both a servant and champion of some other principal, a sense retained not only in its military usage but also in the use to designate senior members of the medieval English bar and in its continuing use for sergeants at arms.

See also: tenure, feudal tenure, serjeanty (sergeantry).

**sergeant at arms (sergeant-at-arms or serjeant at arms)**   An officer to enforce order and security. A sergeant at arms is an officer of an organization or a legislative chamber who enforces rules of the organization or chamber. In some entities, the sergeant at arms provides security and logistics for the entity's operations or meetings.

**sergeantry**   See: tenure, feudal tenure, serjeanty (sergeantry).

**seriatim opinion**   See: opinion, judicial opinion, seriatim opinion.

**serjeant (serjeant at law or serjeant-counter)**   A senior member of the English bar, until 1921. A serjeant was a senior barrister, holding the title by a writ under the great seal, and a member of the Order of the Coif. Serjeants were once expected to render service to the crown, but the title was later merely a designation of high status. Serjeants were the highest order of common-law lawyer, both entitled to wear the coif and to belong to Serjeant's Inn, and, at one time, exclusively entitled to appear before the Court of Common Pleas. The last serjeant died in 1921, the title having been phased out in favor of Queen's Counsel or King's Counsel.

See also: lawyer; coif; counsel, Queen's Counsel (King's Counsel or Q.C. or K.C.).

**serjeanty**   See: tenure, feudal tenure, serjeanty (sergeantry).

**servant** An employee or agent. Servant, in general, is a person in the employ of another. The law of agency was once widely known as the law of master and servant, and servant is still found as a term for an agent, whether or not the person or entity in the role of the servant is also an employee of the principal. Even so, in most contexts the servant is an employee, whether a personal or household servant or an employee of a corporation. As with an employee, a contractor or temporary laborer is not a servant.

See also: employment (employ or employed or employee or employer).

**service**

**service animal** See: animal, service animal (seeing eye dog).

**service mark** See: trademark, mark, service mark (servicemark).

**feudal service (tenant services)** The work for a lord required of a feudal tenant. Feudal service included all of the duties owed by a tenant to the lord from whom the land was held. If the lord was the monarch, the services were serjeanty. Services were divided among a great number of categories, including personal and real, certain and uncertain, free and base, secular and temporal, and many others. The duties included nearly all of the work in the feudal world, and the more common forms include military service, such as knight's service; spiritual service, such as frankalmoign; agricultural and customary, and menial services. With the rise of the fee simple, services have been replaced by purchase, and only some few services persist as incorporeal hereditaments.

See also: tenure, feudal tenure, serjeanty (sergeantry).

**service of process** Presentation of court documents establishing jurisdiction over a person or thing. Service of process is the formal presentation, delivery, or publication of instruments of record initiating a civil or criminal action against a person or a civil action against some property. Service of process must be made within the constitutional limits of jurisdiction and according to the particular rules governing the procedures of a given court. In most instances, service of process must be by personal service upon the defendant by delivery of the complaint and summons, or of the warrant, writ, petition or other instrument initiating the action. Rules may require the service to be in person or at a person's domicile, delivered by an officer of the court or a person appointed by the court for that purpose.

Substituted service is allowed in some circumstances, in which service through an agent or at a domicile in lieu of personal service. In cases in which the defendant is unknown or unlocatable, service by publication is allowed, in which service is accomplished through advertisement and public notice in the courthouse and, if relevant, on affected realty. If a defendant elects to waive service of process, waiver amounts to an acceptance of service and jurisdiction.

**affidavit of service** An oath that service has been accomplished. An affidavit of service attests under oath that service has in fact been given on the defendant. An affidavit of service raises a rebuttable presumption that service was proper.

**certificate of service** A record of process served filed with the court. A certificate of service is a written statement made under oath by an attorney or party setting forth the names and addresses of individuals upon whom process of a document was served, as well as the means by which service was affected. The certificate of service is required for all pleadings under the applicable rules of procedure.

**nail and mail** Service left at the defendant's property and mailed to the defendant's residence. Nail and mail is a slang term for service of process by physical location of a summons on the property of the defendant or property at which the defendant works. Nail and mail is common in New York state courts, but it is only available after the process server has exercised due diligence in attempting personal service but failed to succeed in it.

**Pennoyer rule** Former rule requiring in-state personal service of a foreign defendant. The Pennoyer rule, from Pennoyer v. Neff, 95 U.S. 714 (1878), provided that a United States court has no personal jurisdiction over a defendant in a civil action, unless the defendant is served with process while physically within the state. In Shaffer v. Heitner, 433 U.S. 186 (1977), the Penoyer rule was replaced by the minimum contacts rule announced in International Shoe Co. v. Washington (326 U.S. 310 (1945)).

**personal service** Actual service upon the individual served. Personal service, in its traditional sense, is service upon the individual defendant, witness, or other person upon whom service is required, by which the process server places the instrument served into the hands of the defendant. Even so, under under most rules personal service now includes not only bodily personal service but also substituted service upon the defendant's domicile or with a competent person at that domicile.

**personal service on corporate officer** Personal service on a corporate officer is service on the corporation. Personal service on a corporate officer is actual or direct delivery of the summons, or an appropriate copy of the summons, to a person who is authorized to receive it on behalf of the corporation, or to a person authorized to receive process on behalf of that person. Authorization may be express or implied by virtue of office, as in the case of the CEO.

**process server** A person who is appointed to serve process for a court. A process server is a person appointed by the court to serve process in various civil actions filed in that court's jurisdiction. A process server may be a person employed by a private service, a constable, a deputy, or a person employed by a sheriff or police agency.

**service record**   *See:* record, service record.

**servient**   Land subject to the service of other lands. Servient property is subject to a servitude to the benefit of other property.
*See also:* easement, servient estate (servient tenement).

**servient estate**   *See:* easement, servient estate (servient tenement).

**servient tenement**   *See:* tenement, servient tenement; easement, servient estate (servient tenement).

**servitude**   Service to another, particularly a service required in land. Servitude, in general, is the obligation of service from one person to another. A person in a position of servitude is a servant or employee, and in the United States, all servitude must be voluntary or the result of a legal conviction for a crime.

A servitude is also the obligation of a landholder to allow lands to be used to the benefit of another person, particularly the holder of another parcel of land. A legal servitude may arise as a matter of a covenant, or by operation of law through the dedication of an easement or limitation of a use. An equitable servitude may arise from circumstances that allow such a servitude to be enforced in equity by the party who benefits from it.
*See also:* employment (employ or employed or employee or employer); easement; covenant; in, in gross.

**equitable servitude (reciprocal negative easement)**   A servitude implied over a grantor's lands from restrictions on a grantee's. A servitude implied by equity on the lands of a grantor and the grantor's successors, because the grantor restricted lands granted to others in a common scheme that would be inequitable were the same restrictions not also implied upon the lands then held by the grantor. An equitable servitude runs with the land to bind the successive holders of the grantor's lands that were part of the common scheme, as long as there is sufficient notice, usually constructive notice, of the burden to the successors.

In its most common form, a subdivider of lands sells parcels to buyers, burdening each parcel with covenants limiting certain uses from the land or requiring certain acts upon it or by its owners. The creation of such a scheme and its acceptance by the initial grantees is sufficient to require that the grantor abide by the same covenants in the other tracts in the subdivision, and so not only the grantor but subsequent grantees of these tracts will be bound to the same covenants.
*See also:* easement; covenant, real covenant (covenant in land or covenant real).

*condemnation*   Governmental entities can take an equitable servitude through eminent domain, however the servitude must be specifically condemned or it may persist over the lands otherwise condemned.

**abandonment of an equitable servitude**   Conduct which extinguishes rights to benefit from the property of another. Abandonment of a servitude occurs when a party is entitled to some benefit from another's property and manifests by an affirmative act that this benefit has been given up forever. Failure to enforce a covenant is rarely sufficient to prove its abandonment, which is usually best demonstrated by a writing, such as a letter or a notice of abandonment. Conduct by the covenant beneficiary that is incompatible with reliance on the servitude created by the covenant or benefit to the beneficiary is usually sufficient to prove either abandonment or estoppel from enforcement.
*See also:* abdication; covenant.

**legal servitude**   A servitude arising from a covenant, easement, or zoning rule. A legal servitude, in general, is a servitude on property that is enforceable in law and not in equity, arising generally from an easement, license, covenant, or zoning law. A legal servitude may, but usually does not, have a relationship to an equitable servitude. In most cases, a legal servitude is not enforced as a servitude but as an easement, license, or the legal vehicle from which the servitude arises. In civil law, a legal easement is an easement that arises from law rather than a conventional servitude.

**predial servitude**   A servitude for the benefit of other lands, rather than the benefit of a person. A predial servitude is one of the two categories of servitude in the civil law, the predial being a servitude on a burdened estate that operates to the benefit of the dominant estate, i.e. it benefits the land itself rather than a person. Thus, the predial servitude contrasts with the personal servitude. A servitude in the common law that would be an appurtenant easement would be, in the civil law, predial servitude.

**session**   One business period of a legislature or court. A session is a time during which a legislature or court holds itself open for the transaction of official business, which must generally be concluded within that session, be specifically held over to the next session, or (in legislative sessions) be rendered void. The schedule of business for a session is generally governed by a calendar set according to the rules of the court or the legislative bodies.
*See also:* calendar.

**session laws**   *See:* legislation, session laws (S.L. SL).

**session of court**   *See:* term, court term (session of court).

**set back**   *See:* boundary, building line (set back); zoning, setback.

**setoff (offset)**   A sum or practice that is used to balance another. A setoff is anything used to balance something else, an accounting of the setoff against a sum or value previously ascertained, so the setoff will alter the balance to the positive or to the negative or to reach closer to an equivalence. A setoff may be an amount of money used to balance another sum of money, such as a reserve used to setoff a loss. A setoff may be a pollution reduction in one operation used to balance a pollution generation in another.

A setoff is effectively the same as an offset, although the term "setoff" is used particularly for money used to balance money (particularly money owed against money owed), and offset is more often used to describe balances affecting land, pollution, construction, and other actions in the physical world. There is no requirement that an offset be of the same kind as the thing it is set against, and in contractual relationships, the value of a duty to be performed is often used to offset a debt owed. Setoff and offset may be used both as nouns and as verbs.

*See also:* damages, calculation of damages, setoff (offset or right of setoff or set-off).

**settlement (settle)** The reconciliation of a bill, claim, or dispute. Settlement is the process of concluding an agreement that satisfies a bill or obligation that is owed by one party to another, or that compromises or concludes a claim or dispute between several parties. Thus, to settle an account is either for the debtor to pay the debt or the creditor to excuse or void it. To settle a dispute is finally to resolve the arguments or claims of the parties through performance, payment, abandonment of the claim, or compromise.

**settlement of class action** *See:* class, class action, settlement of class action (Girsh factors).

**Mary Carter agreement (Gallagher agreement)** Dispute settlement between the plaintiff and selected defendants. A Mary Carter agreement is a confidential settlement agreement in multi-party litigation between the plaintiff and one or some (but not all) of the defendants. Under this agreement, the settling defendant remains a party to the lawsuit and guarantees the plaintiff a set payout, regardless of the trial outcome. However, the defendant's payment may be partially or completely offset by any award the plaintiff may receive from the defendants as a whole. These agreements are controversial because the settling defendant has a financial interest in ensuring that the plaintiff recovers. Many courts have declared such agreements void as against public policy. The agreement is effectively the same whether it is named for the agreement in Booth v. Mary Carter Paint Co., 202 So. 2d 8 (Fla. Dist. Ct. App. 1967), or in City of Tuscon v. Gallagher, 493 P.2d 1197 (Ariz. 1972).

**settlor** *See:* trust, settlor (trustor or truster).

**sevara** Jewish law derived from reason. Sevara is law that is based solely on logical inference. "A person may act through an agent," or "a person who wishes to prove something has the burden of proof to do so" are both sevara. Their legal validity is inherent and does not require validation in the legal sources of Jewish law.

*See also:* reason (reasons or reasoning).

**severability (severable)**

**severable contract** *See:* contract, specific contracts, severable contract.

**severability of statute** *See:* statute, severability of statute (severance of statute).

**savings clause (saving clause)** *See:* legislation, savings clause.

**several** A state of being in more than one component. Several is the nature of separation or partition between or among distinct units or components of a whole. Anything in the law that is several is divisible so that a distinction may be drawn in the manner it is performed or the result that is reached. Thus, for example, several liability is liability among defendants that is independent of each from the rest.

*See also:* liability, several liability.

**several liability** *See:* liability, several liability.

**severalty** Property held by one party and not jointly. Severalty is separate property – the property of one party that is distinct from other property that is subject to co-ownership. For example, spouses may have property that is subject to a community or that is held by a tenancy by the entireties, and severalty is property distinctly held by one spouse in which the other spouse has no ownership. Property is severalty if it is given not with other property that is given to a class or community or group, but it is given particularly to one member of such a class, community, or group.

*See also:* marriage, marital property, separate property.

**severance** *See:* contracts, contract interpretation, severance (doctrine of severance or severability of clauses or blue pencil rule).

**severance of statute** *See:* statute, severability of statute (severance of statute).

**severance of trial** *See:* trial, severance of trial (motion to sever).

**severance pay** *See:* pay, severance pay.

**sewage (sewerage)** Wastes from houses, businesses and surface drains in the sewers. Sewage is the combination of wastes that enter sewers including human, animal, and other wastes plumbed from installations in houses and businesses into the sewer system (which is the sanitary sewer system), as well as surface water and other runoff collected from surface drains (which is the stormwater sewer system). The sewage system is the whole system for the collection, treatment, and disposal of both forms of wastewater. Many older sewage systems combine stormwater sewerage with sanitary sewerage systems. Most sewerage systems direct the flow through pipes either by gravity or by means of lifts stations (or pump stations) to a permitted wastewater treatment works, where the water is treated before being discharged into natural waters. Note: the older term is sewerage, and there is no difference between it and sewage.

*See also:* effluent (discharge or wastewater); sewer.

**sewer**  A drain for disposing of water or waste. A sewer is a system of drains for the removal of water or waste from an area and for its disposal, hopefully, in a lawfully permitted water treatment facility or in a permitted or excluded discharge system. Sewers are either sanitary sewers, for the carriage of human and other wastes; storm sewers, for the carriage of storm water runoff; or combined sewers, for the carriage of both.

A sewer was initially a drain, particularly the great trenches and canals by which swamps were drained and made into agricultural fields. As cities grew, urban sewers were dug underground and covered over to remove human waste from city centers.

*See also:* pollution, water pollution; sewage (sewerage).

**combined sewer overflow (sanitary sewer overflow or CSO or SSO)**  The diversion of wastewater from treatment systems into public waters. An overflow is the intentional or negligent allowance of wastewater from a sewerage transport system into the environment without first being properly treated in a licensed treatment works. Overflows vary in form depending on whether the sewer system is a sanitary system, in which the sewer is not designed to incorporate surfacewater drainage, or a combined system, in which the sewer transports both sanitary waste from commercial and residential human-waste disposal systems and surfacewater from storm drains. Combined sewer overflow (CSO) frequently results by design when a system is incapable of carrying the flow during periods of significant rainfall or snowmelt. A sanitary sewer overflow (SSO) is similar, resulting usually from a loss of system integrity from leaks or cracks in pipes, drains, and pumps, which allow rainwater, surfacewater, and subsurface water to enter a sanitary sewer during a period of heavy precipitation or snowmelt. CSOs and SSOs inherently violate the Clean Water Act.

**floatable (floatables)**  Litter and objects discharged from sewers that float in water. Floatables are the litter and other debris in sewerage that is discharged into open waters and floats on the surface. Wastewater collection systems and management plans are required to control floatables, which may be trapped during overflows or skimmed following release.

**sex**  Gender, or some form of sexual act. Sex, in the law generally, has no particularized sense different from its meanings in the culture. Sex therefore is often used as a synonym for gender. In this sense, sex discrimination is discrimination on the basis of a person's sex, or gender. Sexual equality, likewise, is equality among women and men, generally, and increasingly among women, men, and the transgendered.

Sex is also used to signify a sexual act, although that use is not common in legal materials, which are more likely to describe the act more specifically or to describe it as a "sexual act." In this sense, however, sex is a broad term describing more than actual intercourse to include all acts of a sexual nature and their implications, as in "sex offender" or "sex crime."

*See also:* gender (sex as identity).

**sex abuse**  *See:* abuse, sexual abuse (sex abuse).

**sex as identity**  *See:* gender (sex as identity).

**sex discrimination**  *See:* discrimination, sex discrimination (gender discrimination).

**sex worker or hooker or rent boy or call girl**  *See:* prostitution, prostitute (sex worker or hooker or rent boy or call girl).

**sexual abuse of a minor**  *See:* rape, statutory rape (sexual abuse of a minor).

**sexual assault**  *See:* assault, sexual assault (indecent assault).

**sexual battery**  *See:* battery, sexual battery (criminal sexual battery or CSC).

**sexual conduct**  *See:* rape, rape as sexual assault, criminal sexual conduct (sexual conduct).

**sexual harassment**  *See:* harassment, sexual harassment.

**sexual orientation discrimination**  *See:* discrimination, sexual orientation discrimination.

**sex offender (sex crime or sex offense)**  A person convicted of a sex crime. A sex offender, or sometimes a sexual offender, is a person who has been convicted of any offense that is by nature an offense with a sexualized aspect or an offense on a list of such offenses in force in a given jurisdiction. Many jurisdictions have a sex offender registry, and sex offenders are subject to limitations in the location of residence and work to avoid contact with children.

Sex crimes include rape, sexual assault, child molestation or child sexual abuse, statutory rape (or sex with a minor), sodomy, prostitution, promoting prostitution, and the possession or creation of pornography involving children. The breadth of some definitions of sex offender, including old convictions for consensual acts of sodomy and some convictions for statutory rape, raise problems of overinclusion; yet the general principle remains that the regulation of sex offenders is not in itself punishment.

**Megan's Law (sex offender registration or sex offender registry)**  Statutory public access to sex-offender information. "Megan's Law" refers to several federal and state statutes requiring authorities to give public access to information concerning registered sex offenders in the various neighborhoods of the jurisdiction. These laws require sex offenders to register with the appropriate authorities prior to moving into a particular area, and require reregistration when the offenders move to a different location. Information including the identity and record of each offender is disseminated through websites, pamphlets, newspapers, or other appropriate literature.

**sexual act (sexual conduct or sex act)** Contact between the genitals, anus, mouth, or hands for sexual gratification. A sexual act is a form of sexual conduct that requires physical contact between two people, in which one places a hand, mouth, anus, or genitals on the hand, mouth, anus, or genitals of the other, or makes a similar bodily contact for the purpose of the sexual arousal of either party. Sexual acts are generally lawful when they are consensual but are unlawful when they are non-consensual, with consent deemed to be impossible by a person under the age of consent or otherwise lacking the power of consent.

Sexual conduct is a broader category than a sexual act. Sexual conduct includes speech, written communication, public displays, bodily movement, double entendre, and other acts that would communicate — intentionally or in some cases unintentionally — to an observer a personal interest by the actor in the sexual nature of the actor, the observer, or of other persons.

Note: in common parlance, a sexual act is often referred to as "having sex" or just "sex." That sense is rarely used in legal materials except in the recording of evidence from witnesses.

*See also:* prostitution.

**sexuality** The characteristics of a person related to gender and sexual interests. Sexuality is those aspects of a person that reflect that person's nature as a sexual being, including appearance, behavior, and attitudes that others perceive as related to the person's sexual preference and sexual behavior. Sexuality is also an internal aspect of a person's identity, including thoughts, impressions, instincts, and emotions caused by sexual identity, preference, and desire both for personal expression and for expression by others.

*See also:* gender (sex as identity).

**sexually oriented business tax or SOB tax** *See:* tax, sin tax, pole tax (sexually oriented business tax or SOB tax).

**shabat or yaum al-jumua or sabbatarian or sabbatarianism** *See:* sabbath (shabat or yaum al-jumua or sabbatarian or sabbatarianism).

**shackles** *See:* restraint, physical restraint, shackles (fetters or legcuffs or leg irons or shackling).

**shadow jury** *See:* jury, mock jury (shadow jury).

**shaft mine** *See:* mine, shaft mine (shaft mining).

**shaft mining** *See:* mine, shaft mine (shaft mining).

**shaikh or shaykh** *See:* sheikh (shaikh or shaykh).

**sham** Something presented as other than it is. A sham is a trick or a fraud, particularly something presented as genuine or bona fide when it is not, or a person presented as if in good faith when the person is up to no good. A sham will is a fake will. Sham merchandise is either counterfeit or a lure for a bait and switch. A sham injury is feigned, and a sham witness is offering false or misleading evidence. A sham juror is not unbiased but introduced to the jury to favor one party. Note: sham is both a noun and a verb.

*See also:* answer, sham answer (false answer or sham); marriage, marriage of convenience (sham marriage); will, last will and testament, sham will.

**sham answer** *See:* answer, sham answer (false answer or sham).

**sham consideration** *See:* consideration, sham consideration.

**sham marriage** *See:* marriage, marriage of convenience (sham marriage).

**sham pleading** *See:* pleading, sham pleading.

**sham will** *See:* will, last will and testament, sham will.

**shame** A very strong sense of embarrassment. Shame is an emotion arising from a sense of disgrace, regret, or guilt at one's not being as good a person as one should be, or belonging to a group that is less human or good than it should be. A person may feel shame as a result of conduct directed toward that person by another, or as a result of other conditions over which the person has no control, and a sense of shame arising from events beyond one's control may have a psychological pathology. Shame is distinct from humiliation, which is a sense of shame reflected in the apparent opinion of others, although humiliation may be an essential cause of a sense of shame.

Shame is a consideration in several forms in the law. Improper conduct that causes shame in another person is a basis in the common law for a finding of aggravation of assault, battery, or another tort or crime. A genuine sense of shame arising from one's crimes is a basis for the reduction of a criminal sentence, in contrast with a failure of remorse or shame for one's offense, which may be a basis for an enhancement of sentence. Criminal sentences that are intended to cause shame are both punitive and deterrent, although the Supreme Court has ruled that an offender registry is, by itself, not a punishment but a regulation.

*See also:* reprimand; punishment, shaming punishment (shame as punishment).

**share** A portion of a larger whole. A share is a piece of a larger thing, a part that is distinct and that may be held as a component of ownership or a component taken from the larger thing. In other words, a share may be a portion that is segregated and removed from a thing, like a slice of pie, or it may be a portion that is mingled with others' shares in an undivided whole, like a ride with another in a car. Thus, for example, a share in an inheritance or a share in a cash legacy to a class are each portions that will be segregated. On the other hand, a share in a cotenancy, in a partnership, or in a corporation represent a portion of ownership in the whole.

Shares are presumably of equal proportion among one another, but a share need not be equal in proportion to others. With a few exceptions, a grantor can give shares in varying percentages of a thing to grantees of most forms of property.

**share as stock**   A single unit of ownership. A share is a single unit of ownership in a corporation, partnership or other entity that is owned by shareholders. Each share is subject to the rights of ownership assigned to that share as within a category of shares issued. All of the shares issued may have the same ownership rights, or different categories of share may have varying categories of rights. Rights include the degree to which a holder of a share is entitled to receive dividends declared from profits as well as the right to participate in managerial decisions through votes of shareholders.

*See also:* broker, securities broker (registered broker or stock broker or initiating broker of future commodities merchant).

**common stock (common share)**   Shares in a corporation with voting rights. The common share, or common stock, is the basic form of share in a corporation, with voting rights in all issues of management (except, potentially, the voting rights of common stocks) and the rights to receive income. The corporation's charter and by-laws define common stock and the rights of common stock, which may be divided into various classes with various rights, and which may be subordinate in some regards to preferred or special stock. Even so, the common share has the residual interests in the corporation, and upon liquidation of the corporation, following satisfaction of debts and the satisfaction of preferred share rights, all that remains is allocated among the common shares.

*See also:* security, securities, Securities Exchange, American Stock Exchange (A.M.E.X. or AMEX); share, share as stock, preferred stock (preferred share or preference share).

**fractional share**   Less than a whole share in a corporation. A fractional share is an ownership interest in a corporation of less than one whole share. A fractional share allows a receipt of dividends and capital at liquidation in proportion to the percentage of the share and the value allocated to one share. A corporation might or might not provide for a proportional voting power to a fractional share.

*See also:* fraction (fractional).

**offering**

**public offering (registered offering)**   A sale of shares to the public through an exchange. A public offering of shares is the sale of a designated number of shares in a corporation by offering them for sale to the public through an exchange. A public offering may be an initial public offering, the first public offering of an entity, or it may be an offering made by a corporation that is already listed.

A public offering must be registered with the Securities and Exchange Commission, which must first approve the corporation's registration statement containing the company's current financial information, the price at which the shares will be offered to the public, the value and recipients of any commissions that have been paid to underwriters, and any options to purchase that will have already been issued. The company must issue a written prospectus that discloses the company's financial status and liabilities as well as all facts material to a potential investor's assessment of the risks and benefits of investment.

*See also:* offering; public.

**initial public offering (IPO or I.P.O.)**   The first issuance of shares to the public by a corporation. An initial public offering (IPO) is the first offering of a corporation's shares to be made on a public exchange. A close corporation that is taken public usually does so through an IPO. An IPO must meet all of the requirements of a public offering, including registration and the issuance of a prospectus.

**penny share (penny stock)**   A share traded over the counter for a low price. A penny stock is a relatively inexpensive equity security that is not traded on a major stock exchange but on an over-the-counter trading system, such as a bulletin board. As of 2010, penny stocks are defined to trade for less than five dollars per share.

**preferred stock (preferred share or preference share)**   A stock with rights prior to common stock. The preferred share, or preferred stock, is the share with rights that must be satisfied prior to the rights of common shares. Dividends must be awarded to preferred shares before being awarded to common shares, and in the event of liquidation of the corporation, capital remaining after the liquidation of debts is allocated to preferred shares before common shares. As with common shares, there may be classes of preferred share. There is no essential basis to define a share as preferred; the definition is made according to the corporation's charter and by-laws. Some shares are defined as preferred because they were those existing before a given offering of common shares, or those of a category of shareholders, or those of a group of buyers in a merger, or for any other reason determined by the corporation. Many preferred shares have no voting rights associated with them, such rights being reserved to common shares. Shares may be exchanged from preferred to common or common to preferred as provided for by the corporation.

*See also:* share, share as stock, common stock (common share).

### shareholder value

**earnings per share (EPS)**  Revenue divided by outstanding shares. Earnings per share, or EPS, is the quotient that results from dividing a corporation's total earnings by the number of its outstanding shares of stock. EPS is a significant calculation of the shareholder value.

**price to earnings ratio (P/E or PE ratio)**  A ratio of share price to corporate earnings. A corporation's price to earnings ratio, or P/E, is used to determine the value of a share in a corporation relative to the earnings of the corporation as a profit-seeking entity. The measure compares the cost of a single share per dollar of current earnings per share. In other words, it is the ratio of price per share divided by annual earnings per share. A P/E ratio for a stock that is higher than stock in comparable companies is acceptable for a corporation expecting unusual growth in its earnings, but it indicates a less valuable investment for a corporation that is expecting more modest performance.

**stock offering**  An offer to sell shares in a corporation. A stock offering is an offering of stock for sale. Usually, a stock offering is a sale by the corporation itself as authorized by its directors, whether the offering is as a private offering or placement or as a public offering through a public exchange. Even so, a shareholder may also offer shares, whether in a close transaction or in a public offering. An offering by the corporation and some large offerings by certain shareholders must be first registered with the Securities and Exchange Commission. All offerings are subject either to regulation by the SEC or to the blue sky laws of the states in which they are made. Note: a tender is an offer to buy shares, either as a buyback by the corporation as a portion of acquisition of a minority or controlling share by a shareholder or another entity.

*See also:* security, securities, securities regulation, Securities and Exchange Commission (S.E.C. or SEC); security, securities, securities fraud, blue-sky law.

**stock option (warrant for stock or stock warrant or securities option or share option)**  An option contract to purchase a share at a fixed price in the future. A share option, or stock option or stock warrant, is an option for the purchase or sale of a share (or a specified number of shares), of a specified corporation at a set price (or striking price), on or before an expiration date in the future. Option contracts have both a buyer's side and a seller's side, giving rise to two types of options — call options and put options.

In a call option, the option lies with the buyer, and the seller (or writer) is obligated, at the buyer's option, to sell the underlying stock to the buyer at the buyer's request at any time during the life of the option.

In a put option, the option lies with the seller (or writer), and the buyer is obligated, at the seller's option, to buy the underlying stock from the seller at the seller's request at any time during the life of the option.

An option contract to purchase a share from the corporation itself is not ordinarily an option. It is a warrant. Typically a corporation will issue a warrant to purchase shares at a designated price on a specified date in the future, or in a band of time in the future. Warrants may be issued by the corporation according to its charter and by-laws and are used for many purposes, including the compensation for officers and employees, as well as increasing value of the corporation in the event of a merger or acquisition.

*See also:* security, securities, securities warrant (stock purchase warrant); contract, option contract.

**stock split (scrip issue or share split or bonus issue or capitalization issue)**  A corporate conversion of a share into more than one share. A stock split is a change made by a corporation of the number of shares of ownership that are represented by a single outstanding share prior to the split. A split, as it is generally thought of, is a forward split, in which one existing share is replaced by two or more shares. The value of the former share is thus allocated among the successor shares according to the ratio of the split. A forward one-to-two split of a share worth $10 results in two shares worth $5 each. A forward one-to-three split of a share worth $10 results in three shares of $3.33 1/3 each. The benefit of a forward split is to reduce the cost to new buyers of a corporation's share price, which is thus done without diminishing the value held by any existing shareholder.

A reverse split is the conversion of shares outstanding into a lesser number of shares. A reverse two-to-one split of two shares worth $10 results in one share worth $20. A reverse one-to-three split of three shares of $3 each results in one share of $9. Depending on the manner in which the reverse split is made, fractional shares may be merged upward or downward, sometimes being destroyed or bought out. Note: the use of profits to fund an allocation of additional shares of a corporation to existing shareholders is not the same as a stock split but is a dividend.

**warrant**  *See:* share, share as stock, stock option (warrant for stock or stock warrant or securities option or share option).

**shareholder (stockholder)**  The owner of a share in an entity. A shareholder, or stockholder, is a person or entity who owns a share of equity in an entity in which ownership is allocated by shares, such as a corporation or partnership. All shares are not alike in the rights and obligations of ownership they confer. In a corporation, a shareholder has the rights of a holder of the share of the given class of share in the management and equity of the corporation. In a partnership, a shareholder may have the rights and obligations of a general or a limited partner. In all cases, however, officers, directors, or managers of an entity that has shareholders have a fiduciary obligation to all classes of shareholders in the management of the entity and the treatment of the shareholders' rights.

*See also:* corporation, member (corporator); corporation (corporate or incorporate).

**freeze out (squeeze out or squeeze-out or freeze-out)** Any action to force the sale of a minority shareholder's stake. A freeze out describes any action by the officers or a majority shareholder in an entity to cause a minority shareholder to surrender or lose that shareholder's stake in the entity. The most common freeze-out strategy is for a majority shareholder to authorize a reverse stock split, leaving the minority shareholder with only fractional shares of the company, and at the same time authorizing an amendment to the corporation's bylaws mandating that all fractional shares of stock must be sold to the company. A freeze-out merger is a merger in which the merger plan results in the class of shares or the portion of shares of the minority shareholder being liquidated as part of the acquisition.

**shareholder equity (stockholder equity)** The capital and retained earnings of an entity. Shareholder equity is the value of the entity's assets minus its liabilities. Particularly of a corporation, shareholder equity is the present value of the initial capital paid into the corporation and value it has retained from earnings, less its costs.

**shareholder litigation** Litigation against a corporation or those against whom it has a claim. Shareholder litigation takes several forms. In a direct action, a shareholder brings an action for injury to the shareholder, as in an action against the corporation or a group of other shareholders for a violation of the shareholder's rights. Direct action may be individual or brought as a class action. Any recovery in a direct action benefits the plaintiff shareholders directly. In a derivative action, the shareholder brings a claim against a third party that the corporation would have had a right to bring but chose not to bring. Any recovery benefits the corporation.

**direct action** A shareholder action for a personal complaint against the corporation. A direct action is an action by a shareholder, which may be brought by a shareholder against either the company or other shareholders for injuries suffered directly by the shareholder from actions taken that affect the shareholder's rights or interests. A direct action may be an individual complaint or a class action, and any recovery is paid to the plaintiffs rather than the corporation.

**shareholder derivative suit** An action brought by a shareholder to enforce a corporate right. A derivative shareholder suit is a civil action on behalf of a corporation by one of its shareholders, against a person or entity against whom the plaintiff believes the corporation has a valid claim and from whom the corporation ought to recover. A derivative suit may be brought against a corporate officer or any other party whom the plaintiff has good reason to believe has committed an actionable wrong or breach of duty that would be the basis for an action by the corporation, if its officers had chosen to bring such an action. A recovery from a derivative suit benefits the corporation rather than directly benefiting the plaintiff. The derivative suit is a suit in equity and subject to equitable pleading and principles and, in most jurisdictions, special rules for ascertaining the nature of the claim and the sufficiency of the action. Among other requirements, a plaintiff must be a shareholder and retain ownership of the shares throughout the litigation; the plaintiff must have made a demand on the board of directors to bring the action or a similar action, which was denied or effectively ignored, before the suit was filed; and any settlement of a derivative suit is subject to judicial approval.

*See also:* derivative.

**sharia (shari'a)** Islamic sacred law. Sharia, from the Arabic shra'a, for the path or the way, is the Law of Islam. Sharia was given by the Lawgiver, Allah, through his Prophet Muhammad, and contained in the the Qur'an and the authentic Sunnah. Understandings of sharia vary according to traditions of interpretation of the Qur'an and Sunnah, that are associated with particular schools of interpretation, which themselves are associated with different communities of traditional Islam, particularly the Shia Ja'fari schools, the Sunni Mdahhab schools—Hanafi, Shafi'i, Maliki, and Hanbali. The Ja'faris schools of Usuli (prominent in Iran and Shiite communities), emphasizes reasoned argument, and of Akbbari (prominent in parts of Iraq and Barhrain) emphasizes customary understanding. The Hanafi school (prominent in Egypt, Sudan, Syria, and Asia) emphasize reason and interpretation. The Shafi'i school (prominent in Syria, Egypt, the Middle East, Eastern Asia, and the Pacific) emphasizes the application of earlier reasoning and the customs built upon early jurisprudence. The Maliki school (prominent in the Muslim communities in north and west African and Mediterranean states) emphasizes the scriptural bases of the practices of early Muslims in Medina, applied with reason to modern questions. And the Hanbali school (prominent in Saudi Arabia) is particularly conservative and emphasizes customary understanding.

**fiqh** Human understanding of divine law in shari'a. Fiqh are the practical rules of Islamic law, derived from the sources of Islamic legislation – the Qur'an and Sunnah. It includes legislation, as well as the interpretation by the scholars.

**Usul al-Fiqh (Usul al'fiqh, usool al-fiqh)** The principles of Islamic jurisprudence. Usul al-Fiqh, or the sciences of fiqh, could be translated as the letter of the law, but it is more often thought of as the root of law. The fiqh is rendered through it into the regulations and codes derived from the sources of the law.

### sources of shari'a

**Hadith (Ahadith)** Traditions regarding the Prophet's life. The Hadith are collections of observations of the life of the Prophet Mohammad, written in the generations after his death. The Hadith are second in authority as a source of law only to the Qur'an itself.

**ijma** Law arising from consensus among jurists. Ijma is a juristic consensus on a legal issue that was not explicitly addressed in the quran and the Sunna. Considered the third most authoritative source of Islamic law, ijma is of particular importance in Sunni Islam.

**Qur'an (Koran or Quran)** Holy Scripture. Qur'an comes from qara'a, to read, and literally means the reader. The classic definition is that the Qur'an is the word of God, sent through the Archangel Gabriel to the Prophet Muhammad, and passed down by Mutawwatir, or broadcast widely beginning with Surah al-Fatiha and ending with Surah an-Nas. In Sunni Islam, the Qur'an is believed to predate creation and to be the actual Speech of God. Most Shia and Sunnis use the same text, but some Shia groups support differing tafsir and wording. Note: The transliteration from Arabic into English is often "Koran," which is not preferred by scholars who consider it a legacy of occidentalist thought.
*See also:* qiya (qiyas).

**Sunnah** The sayings and intellectual legacy of the Prophet Muhammad. The Sunnah is the legacy of the Prophet in his collected sayings, acts, and tacit approvals. Many of the Hadith are Sunnah.

**Tafsir** Interpretative literature derived from the Qur'an. Tafsir, from the Arabic, fa sa ra — to interpret — is a short form of tafsir al-Qur'an — the interpretation of the Qur'an. There are numerous Tafasir including Tafsir Ibn Kathir, in English as The Meaning of the Qur'an by Maulana Mawdudi, and In the Shade of Qur'an by Sayed Qutb.

**sharp** Unethical, raising suspicion of fraud. Sharp has many meanings in general, not the least being a state of particular attention and awareness. In law, sharpness or a sharp aspect of a person's practice or conduct implies a deceptive aspect, some unethical or illegal aspect, such as in self-dealing, deception, or fraud. Yet sharpness further implies an abuse of procedures or privileges that seeks to avoid, just barely, criminal or civil liability yet still gain an unfair advantage. A series of sharp practices, however, which each alone might not be actionable, may amount to fraud, deceit, or a breach of duty.

**sharp practice** *See:* lawyer, legal practice, sharp practice.

**sheikh (shaikh or shaykh)** A social and religious leader in an Islamic community. A sheikh, the Arabic literally meaning an old man, is a respected leader of a Muslim community. A sheikh might not have particular religious knowledge, but is still an alim, or knowledgable person, in whom others feel confident to consult on religious matters.

**shell corporation** *See:* corporation, shell corporation.

**Shelley's Case (Rule in Shelley's Case)** A grant of a life estate and remainder to the heirs of the same person grants a fee simple. The Rule in Shelley's Case is a common-law rule that alters a grant as a matter of law, so that a grant in a single instrument of a life estate to one grantee and the remainder in the heirs of the same grantee (or the heirs of the body of the same grantee) converts the remainder to a remainder in fee simple. This conversion then triggers the doctrine of merger, so that the grant of the life estate and remainder in fee are merged into a single fee simple in the grantee. The Rule in Shelley's Case was once an important means of encouraging the alienability of land and has always been enjoyed by bar examiners, though it has been repealed by statute in most states.
*See also:* remainder, contingent remainder, rule of the destructibility of contingent remainders (destructibility rule); perpetuity, Rule Against Perpetuities (RAP or Rule Against Remoteness); title, Doctrine of Worthier Title (Doctrine of Reversions).

**shelter** A place of refuge, or a doctrine giving unusual relief. Shelter is a place of physical refuge for a person, animal, or thing. Shelter in its general sense for human beings is a condition in which the person is in a place that is not exposed to weather and in which the basic needs of human existence can be safely met. International law recognizes shelter as a basic human right. Shelter is not considered a constitutional right in the United States, but it is the basis for many government entitlement programs.

A shelter may be an institution providing lodging and social services for people in distress, or it may be an institution rescuing animals. A shelter may also be merely a place for protection of persons or things from the elements, such as a bus shelter.

Legal doctrines of shelter are rules or interpretations of rules that provide some immunity from a liability that would otherwise apply to the harm of a person's interests. Thus, the shelter doctrine and shelter rule allow a person to be treated as a bona fide purchaser who is not one. A tax shelter allows a person to keep property from taxation that would otherwise be demanded.
*See also:* purchaser, bona fide purchaser, shelter rule (shelter doctrine).

**shelter doctrine** *See:* purchaser, bona fide purchaser, shelter rule (shelter doctrine).

**shelter rule** *See:* purchaser, bona fide purchaser, shelter rule (shelter doctrine).

**tax shelter** An activity qualifying for reduced taxation. A tax shelter is an activity — whether it is a form of business, investment, purchase, accounting, or actual conduct by a taxpayer — that allows money or property held by or used for that activity to be subject to a reduced tax liability. The tax shelter may result either from an express statement in a rule or statutory provision, or in the absence of such a statement or rule.

By definition, a tax shelter is lawful and allowed under the tax laws and regulations. It is presumed that the use of a tax shelter is in fact desired by the authors of the tax laws, or they would have changed the tax laws to eliminate it.

*See also:* tax, tax burden; loophole.

**shenpanyuan** The Chinese term for judge. Shenpanyuan, a Mandarin term literally translated as adjudication official, is the modern Chinese term for judge.

*See also:* judge (judicial).

**Shepardizing or key-citing** *See:* citation, cite-checking (Shepardizing or key-citing).

**sheriff** The chief law enforcement officer of a county. A sheriff, in the United States, is a state or county official who is the official responsible for the enforcement of state law and county ordinance throughout the jurisdiction. The sheriff in most states is responsible not only for leading and managing the sheriff's office, which is responsible for law enforcement throughout the county, but also for court security, for the management of prisoners and jails, for the enforcement of judicial orders and judgments, for the seizure and disposal of property according to judgments, and for traffic safety. In some states, the sheriff has additional administrative duties including responsibility for the courthouse maintenance. As of 2010, there are sheriffs in all of the U.S. states but Alaska, Connecticut, and Hawai'i. In most states, the sheriff is directly elected by the people of the county in which the sheriff serves, although sheriffs in some jurisdictions are appointed to their office. In some municipalities that have effectively merged with their county governments, the sheriff is also the chief of the municipal police. In the City of New York, there is only one sheriff for the five counties within the city. The statutes of many states give unusual powers of investigation and authority to the sheriff.

*See also:* deputy; posse, posse comitatus (sheriff; reeve; shire.

**sheriff's sale (foreclosure sale or courthouse auction)** An auction of property by the sheriff. A sheriff's sale is an auction, sometimes literally held on the courthouse steps, in which property that has been seized in an execution of judgment or in a foreclosure is put up for auction. The county or sheriff receives a fee, after which the amount owed is paid to the judgment creditor or mortgatee, and if there is any money remaining, it is paid to the judgment

debtor, mortgagor, or otherwise the party from whom the property was taken.

*See also:* foreclosure; judgment, enforcement of judgment (execution of judgment).

**Sherman Act** *See:* antitrust, Sherman Antitrust Act (Sherman Act).

**Sherman Antitrust Act** *See:* antitrust, Sherman Antitrust Act, rule of reason (reason in antitrust); antitrust, Sherman Antitrust Act, parallel conduct (parallel behavior); antitrust, Sherman Antitrust Act (Sherman Act).

**Sherman-Sorrells doctrine** *See:* entrapment, Sherman-Sorrells doctrine (subjective approach).

**shield laws** *See:* press, freedom of the press, shield laws.

**shield money** *See:* tenure, feudal tenure, military tenure, knight's tenure, shield money (scutage).

**shifting executory interest** *See:* interest, executory interest, shifting executory interest.

**Shiism** *See:* Islam, Shiism (Shi'ah Islam or Shi'a Islam).

**ship** A large vessel for transit over water. A ship is a large water-going vessel, built and used as a means for the transportation of people and things on bodies of water, including rivers, inland lakes and seas, and the oceans. Many customary rules of thumb distinguish a boat from a ship, such as: a ship is a vessel that may carry a boat; a ship has a watertight deck running fore and aft; a ship displaces 500 tons; a ship has three masts and a bowsprit; a ship is over sixty-five feet in length, etc. The essential difference is that ships are big and not of a form by custom called a boat. All submarines are boats, for example, and some submarines are well over five hundred feet long. Note: the verb to ship does not imply shipping by ship but shipping by any means.

**ship charter** *See:* charter, charter-party (ship charter).

**ship mortgage** *See:* mortgage, ship mortgage.

**shipment contract** *See:* contract, specific contracts, shipment contract.

**captain of a vessel (sea captain or ship captain)** Officer in charge on a ship or boat. The captain is the master or commander on board the vessel. The captain has command over every person on a vessel. While there may be several officers who may stand watch or be responsible for the navigation or maneuvering of a vessel, the captain is always responsible for what occurs on board. A captain is so-called at the time the person assumes command of the vessel and acts as the person in charge of it, regardless of whatever assignment, rank, or qualification the person has otherwise.

*See also:* master.

**master**   The person in overall command of a vessel. The master of a ship is the person who captains the vessel. Although certain shipping companies may distinguish a captain from a master for purposes of pay or assignment, there is no difference in law.

*See also:* master.

**derelict vessel**   A vessel abandoned at sea. A derelict vessel is a vessel at sea that has been abandoned by her captain and crew. Not every evacuation of a seaborne vessel amounts to dereliction, and a brief evacuation made to acquire supplies, prepare for repair, allow decontamination, or the like, after which the captain and crew have a reasonable expectation of immediate return does not amount to dereliction of the vessel. But evacuation without the intention of immediate return amounts to dereliction, rendering the vessel eligible for salvage.

*See also:* derelict, derelict as outcast person; derelict (derelicto).

## shipping

**shipping term (terms of shipping)**   Any term in a contract for sale related to shipping, insurance, or payment through a carrier. A shipping term is a clause or designation in an agreement for the sale of goods that specifies how the goods will be carried, the time or place of delivery, the liability for loss during carriage, or the means of payment when made through the carrier. When no shipping terms are specified, the contract is a shipment contract under the U.C.C., and the risk of loss is transferred to the buyer at the time the goods are delivered by the seller to the carrier.

*See also:* term, contract term; risk, risk of loss.

**cash on delivery (C.O.D.)**   Buyer must pay the purchase price of goods at the time of delivery from a carrier. Cash on delivery (COD) is the delivery of goods purchased, which requires payment of the price for the purchase of the goods to the carrier, who collects the payment and remits it to the seller.

**freight on board (F.O.B. or FOB)**   The buyer is responsible for shipping and insurance. Freight on board, or FOB ____, is a domestic shipping term, not an international term, which requires the buyer to take delivery of goods at the seller's place of shipment, and the seller has no liability for freight or insurance. Freight on board employs the same initials as Free on Board, which is a shipping term under the Uniform Commercial Code and international shipping practice, which is quite different.

*See also:* shipping, shipping term, incoterm, free on board (F.O.B. or FOB); shipping, shipping term, incoterm, free alongside ship (F.A.S. or FAS).

**incoterm (shipping term)**   The list of shipping terms establishing instructions for payment and responsibility. Incoterms are internationally accepted commercial terms, the shipping terms standardized by the International Chamber of Commerce (ICC). Most of the terms pre-exist the copyrighted and standardized language by which the ICC defines them. Incoterms allocate responsibility for payment, delivery, and insurance for goods shipped, and they sometimes designate the location of the transfer of that responsibility. The terms are grouped into categories according to the extent to which the buyer or the seller are responsible for payment of shipping. Within each category, further distinctions determine who is responsible for the expense and responsibility of transport, taxes of the exporting state, loading, landing, insurance, custom clearance and duties, and taxes at the importing state.

**cost of insurance and freight (C.I.F. or CIF)**   Seller pays shipping and insurance to a port or terminal. Cost of Insurance and Freight ____, or CIF, is a shipping term used in the international sale or transport of goods, that requires the buyer to take responsibility for the goods sold at the port designated but requires the seller to pay for transport of the goods as well as for the insurance coverage necessary up to the designated port or freight terminal.

**free alongside ship (F.A.S. or FAS)**   The seller must deliver goods to the vessel specified. Free Alongside Ship ____ is a shipping term requiring the seller to deliver to a particular vessel in a given port, or cause the goods to be delivered there, and in either case to bear the risk of loss of goods until they are delivered. The designation must include the vessel's name and port, as specified at the time by the buyer, such as "FAS, The M/V Malaga, Portsmouth."

**free on board (F.O.B. or FOB)**   Seller is responsible for cost of delivery. Free on board, or F.O.B. ____, is a shipping term in the international sale or transport of goods that requires the seller to take responsibility for the goods sold only until they are loaded onto a designated vessel or onto a vessel, train, or ship at a designated port or loading facility. The buyer then pays for their international shipment and carriage to delivery.

Note: F.O.B. meaning "freight on board" in the Uniform Commercial Code and in domestic shipping has a different meaning from free on board. The term freight on board requires the buyer to take responsibility for placing the goods as soon as they leave the seller's premises. The Incoterm closest to the U.S. domestic F.O.B. is Free Carrier, or F.C.A.

*See also:* shipping, shipping term, freight on board (F.O.B. or FOB).

**shipwreck**   *See:* salvage, shipwreck (wreck of a vessel).

**shire**   An old English land district. A shire was an Anglo-Saxon district of land that was the prior form of what became the county following the Norman invasion. The term sheriff is derived from being the reeve, or manager, of the shire.

*See also:* county; sheriff.

**Shi'ah Islam or Shi'a Islam**   *See:* Islam, Shiism (Shi'ah Islam or Shi'a Islam).

**shop**   *See:* union, labor union, shop.

**shoplifting (shrinkage or shoplift or shoplifted)**
A theft of goods from a retail store. Shoplifting is taking goods from a store without paying for them in full. As usually defined by statute, it is the unlawful removal of goods on display or for sale in a store, whether the person removing the goods is a customer or an employee; whether or not the goods are falsely accounted, sold or destroyed, and whether a partial price is paid or not, unless an authorized rebate or discount is applied to the sale. Goods lost to shoplifting, whether to theft by customers or by employees, is known to retailers as store inventory shrinkage, or shrink.

*See also:* theft.

**shore (shoreline)**   The land that adjoins a body of water. The shore is that part of the land that is in contact with a body of water. In this sense, every watercourse and waterbody has a shore. Riparian rights of rivers give ownership in non-navigable rivers to the owner of property with a shore, or bank, on the river, or to the low-water mark on the shore of a navigable river. A shoreline is the line that marks the edge of the shore and the start of the water. The shoreline of a state on an international water establishes the baseline for its seaward boundary, which runs from the mean low-water mark, or the average of locations at which the sea ends at low tide. In U.S. law, some states hold lands between the low and high water marks, the foreshore, in public trust.

*See also:* bank, bank as shore (riverbank or banks); trust, public trust, public trust doctrine.

**shore patrol**   *See:* police, police organization, military police, shore patrol (SP or S.P.).

**littoral area (foreshore or littoral rights or litorral interests)**   The shore of a lake or of the sea. A littoral area or region is the shoreline of a body of water other than a river or a stream and the lands immediately abutting it. Littoral rights and interests are the rights and interests of landowners and the state adjoining the waters, the private interests of which may be subject to claims of the state under the public trust doctrine.

*See also:* trust, public trust, public trust doctrine.

**high water mark (mean high water mark or MHW)**
The average of the water's edge at high tide. The high water mark, or more accurately the mean high water mark, is the annual average of the height on the shore reached by the water at its highest flood each day. Bays, lakes, seas, and other waters affected by tide have a daily variance from which the mark is averaged, although non-tidal waters do not. The

foreshore, or littoral zone, is below the high water mark and above the low water mark. When these are laterally quite distant from one another, the area includes tidelands.

**low water mark (mean low watermark or MLW)**   The average of the water's edge at low tide. The low water mark, or more accurately the mean low water mark, is the annual average of the height on the shore reached by the water at its lowest ebb each day. Bays, lakes, seas, and other waters affected by tide have a daily variance from which the mark is averaged, although non-tidal waters do not. Boundaries are taken from the low water mark unless custom, treaty, statute, or deed dictate otherwise.

**short sale**   *See:* security, securities, short sale (sell short); sale, short sale, short sale of mortgaged property.

**shotgun pleading**   *See:* pleading, shotgun pleading (shotgun complaint or shotgun answer).

**showing (show)**   Demonstration, or proof of some claim. In legal usage, a showing is a demonstration of evidence and construction of argument from the legal materials that demonstrate a particular argument, fact, or claim. To show is to prove, or at least to provide a reasonable substantiation for, some claim. A sufficient showing is the presentation of enough evidence to meet some standard of proof.

**show trial**   *See:* trial, show trial (political trial).

**show cause (show-cause proceeding or show-cause order or order to show cause)**   A hearing to defend against a pending adverse ruling. Show cause, or more properly a motion for an order to show cause and an order to show cause, are predicates to hearing to show cause, which is a hearing by the court to determine whether to grant a different motion or petition. A show-cause hearing may be ordered by the court on motion or sua sponte. Show-cause hearings often precede an order for sanctions or for contempt of court, giving the party one last chance to comply with a rule or order prior to the imposition of a punitive measure.

**shrinkage or shoplift or shoplifted**   *See:* shoplifting (shrinkage or shoplift or shoplifted).

**shrinkwrap agreement**   *See:* contract, specific contracts, shrinkwrap agreement (shrink wrap contract).

**shtick**   *See:* schtick (shtick).

**shyster**   *See:* lawyer, shyster.

**sibling**   *See:* family, sibling, half-brother (half-sister); family, sibling, brother in law (brother-in-law or sister in law or sister-in-law); family, sibling, brother (sister).

**sic**   Thus, or as it was written then. Sic is a Latin adverb that generally demonstrates the conclusion from a premise, argument, or cause, as in "thus," "so," "therefore," or "to that degree."

Sic was classically used to designate a text or matter as it stood at the time of its creation. Sic is still used in this sense in English, primarily to designate text that appears to be in error as accurately transcribed from its original. In this use, sic is often placed within parentheses or brackets. For example, a typographical error in a deed that is restated in a pleading might read, "thence 40 (sic) feet" when the text should have read "140 feet" but was originally written as 40 in error. Sic in this sense is sometimes used to bring attention to poor grammar, spelling, or speech employed by the person being quoted, whether to allay the reader's suspicion the error was by the later writer or to cast a particular light upon the earlier writer or speaker.

*See also:* error, scrivener's error.

**sic utere tuo ut alienum non laedas** *See:* nuisance, sic utere tuo ut alienum non laedas.

**sickness (sick)** Illness, malady, or disease. Sickness is an illness, disease, or any cause of poor physical health other than physical injury, although one may lead to the other.

**side bar** *See:* trial, argument at trial, side bar (bench conference or side-bar or sidebar conference).

**sight draft** *See:* draft, draft as negotiable instrument, sight draft.

**sigillum** *See:* seal, sigillum.

**sign** Anything that represents information. A sign is anything that signifies an idea, concept, or information. The nature of communication is through signs, the result being always an interpretation of the sign to determine the thing signified. The nature of investigation is to observe signs and to interpret them, as a diagnostician interprets symptoms to diagnose a disease.

Words, phrases, and language are nothing but signs, with more or less agreed signification for what each mean in isolation and again in various groups. The law uses such signs to communicate legal concepts through statutes, regulations, court opinions, and constitutions. To a degree, the law also communicates through non-verbal signs, such as the conduct (or absence of conduct) of legal officials.

A sign, as in a road sign, communicates information to a driver or others on the road, usually by means of symbols, words, and numbers. The very shape of a sign communicates information, as in the use in the U.S. of the octagon for a stop sign. A sign that is an authorized traffic control device creates standards for the performance of drivers or for the liability of drivers within an area that is subject to instructions on the sign. This area is implied by the location of the sign.

As a verb, to sign has various senses, not the least being to communicate by sign language. In law, to sign is usually to affix a signature to an instrument.

*See also:* signature; signature, mark (X as mark).

**signature** A sign one uses to indicate one's name. A signature is any sign, mark, or words that identify a particular individual, affixed by that individual as a sign of the person's identity, particularly to identify the person in an act of receipt, assent, or acknowledgement. Its most common form is that person's handwritten engrossment of that person's name onto a document.

Any sign that represents the person is a signature if it is used regularly by that person for the purpose of signing. By custom a person who, owing to incapacity or an inability to write, cannot sign his or her full name in letters may make a mark, such as a cross or an X. Initials may serve as a signature.

A signature can also be an electronic emblem of a person's name, if it is entered into an electronic document with the intent that it serve the customary purposes of signature. To affix or engross a signature is to sign the thing on which it appears.

All pleadings filed with a court in a civil action must be signed, by counsel or a party, and a signature is the predicate act by which the signer affirms conformity with the duties of good-faith investigation and pleading. Since the Statute of Frauds in 1677, contracts for the sale of an interest in land must be signed, or at least must be signed by a person who is being held to account for the contract. Prior to the widespread use of signatures and their eventual requirement in the Statute of Frauds, the use of ceremonies and transfers of physical objects, as in the livery of seisin, were used to assure the validity of the act of the transferor of lands.

Many instruments must bear a signature or are not legally valid. A last will and testament must be signed by the testator, unless it is an oral will, which is allowed only in quite limited circumstances. Trust instruments must be signed by the settlor or the settlor's agent, and powers of attorney must be signed by the principal.

Many legal instruments require the signature of the party making the instrument to be witnessed. Indeed, one of the primary functions of the notary public is to witness a signature and to be available later to authenticate a signature.

Signature has a more general meaning than the affixing of one's name. A manner of performing some act or creating some thing that so identifies the performer or creator is considered a signature. Certain forms of criminal conduct are sufficiently idiosyncratic that the pattern of conduct, the modus operandi, is considered a signature of a given criminal who is associated with that pattern of conduct.

*See also:* indorsement, co-signature (co-signer or cosign or cosigner); name; crime, signature crime (common scheme evidence); seisin, livery of seisin.

**signature crime** *See:* crime, signature crime (common scheme evidence).

**signature facts or MO or M.O.** *See:* modus, modus operandi (signature facts or MO or M.O.).

**signature of pleading** *See:* pleading, signature of pleading.

**conditional signature**   A signature that is valid only on satisfaction of a condition subsequent. A conditional signature on an instrument or document signals assent or authorization that is only valid upon the satisfaction of a condition, that is either expressed in a notation on the instrument or document or that is implied by the circumstances in a manner that would make it known to other parties or holders of the signed matter.

**countersignature (countersign)**   A signature added to a document already signed. A countersignature is a signature added by a witness, party to a contract, or other interested party to an instrument that has already been signed by a principal. The purpose of a countersignature is later to ensure that the signed copy was indeed the copy signed and not an alteration made by the principal and re-signed. The countersign also provides assurance that the principal has met any conditions required for signature.

*See also:* indorsement (endorsement, endorse, indorse).

**digital signature**   Any electronically stored symbol that serves for legal purposes as a personal signature. An electronic signature is any electronic signal, including a sound, graphic symbol, or process, that is attached to or logically associated with a file, document, or transmission, if the signal was created by a person represented by that signal or was adopted by that person to be that person's representation, and the signal was then attached or associated with the document by that person or under that person's authority with the intent that the signal would operate in the manner that a signature would operate had the document been a paper writing.

*See also:* commerce, e-commerce.

**in witness whereof**   Language that prefaces a signature. "In Witness Whereof" is a customary phrase that once introduced the prefatory clause before the signature of a will or a trust instrument or the signatures of a contract. The language is not a signal that the signatures that follow are of witnesses or are only of witnesses. The language remains in frequent use, though it adds little to the text except in the most archaic and formal instruments, such as a university degree.

**mark (X as mark)**   An X, cross, or other sign placed as a signature. A mark is a substitute for a signature, employed by a person who is infirm and lacks the motor skills required to sign an instrument or a person who is illiterate or a person who for other reasons chooses to use a particular mark as a means of assenting to or accepting a document. A person who is illiterate and also lacks the skills required to make a signature may validly sign a document with a mark, but in many contexts, there must be some evidence that this person was aware of the meaning of the document that was thereby endorsed.

**party to be charged**   The party who must sign a written contract under the Statute of Frauds. The party to be charged is the party against whom an action might be brought to enforce a contract. Contracts subject to the Statute of Frauds must be signed, but the signature requirement does not require all parties to sign, only the party whose accession to the contract is in doubt, the party to be charged. Recent editions of the U.C.C. Statute of Frauds (which applies only to the sale of goods) have replaced this language with "the party against whom enforcement is sought or by his authorized agent or broker."

**robosigner (robosignature or robo-signer)**   A person who signs many instruments without sufficient review. A robosigner is a person required to authorize or review a document who processes and signs so many such documents that the person does not, or cannot, review them sufficiently to determine the document is in fact fit for authorization. The term became popular in 2010 when bank foreclosures were processed in such bulk that documents were signed without review.

**signature card**   A bank's physical record of the signature of a depositor. A signature card is a physical record of the signature of each person who is authorized to make a withdrawal from the account to which the card is assigned. Signature cards are increasingly, as of 2011, electronic records of digitized images of a signature. The function of the card is to allow the bank to authenticate a signature before honoring a check bearing a signature purporting to be that of an account holder.

**undersigned**   Those who sign an instrument. The undersigned are, literally, those who sign below such a reference. Unless the instrument specifically designates only one party, or otherwise defines the undersigned other than as the actual signer (such as a non-signing principal rather than a signing agent), all persons who signed are included in the term, "undersigned."

**X as signature (cross as signature)**   A mark in lieu of a full signature. A cross, an "X," or a similar mark can be a valid signature as long as it is intended by its marker to serve in this capacity. Though presumptively valid, such a mark is clearly acceptable for a person who lacks the capacity to sign the person's name in full.

**silence (silent)**   The absence of communication. Silence, in general, is the absence of sound, but in law it is the absence of relevant communication, whether in spoken or written speech. Silence may result from inability, from a deliberate act, or from omission in the course of other speech.

In the interpretation of a constitutional provision, legislation, or regulation, or of a contract, will, trust, or other instrument, silence is the omission of any text on a given point. Text relative to the point that is incomplete or unclear is not silence but ambiguous text.

Silence following receipt of an offer to enter a contract is generally not regarded as acceptance. Still, silence regarding a specific term in an offer that is accepted generally is generally regarded as assent to that term.

Silence by a criminal defendant, or by a person interrogated or interviewed by agents of the police is the refusal to discuss matters relevant to the police inquiry. The privilege against self-incrimination is a right to silence, which may be waived by speech on the matter in issue after which the right may be reasserted, but speech on other matters does not affect or amount to waiver of the right. Although a person's silence may not be raised as evidence of guilt in a criminal proceeding, the police may use silence as a basis for considering a person a suspect or as a component of evidence for the purpose of establishing probable cause sufficient to seek a warrant.

### silence code or code of silence or blue wall of silence
*See:* omerta (silence code or code of silence or blue wall of silence).

### silent partner   *See:* partner, silent partner.

### silence as acceptance of offer   In general, silence is not acceptance. Silence by the offeree is generally not acceptance of the offer. Even if the offeror couches the offer in terms that would require the offeree to opt-out of the offer, the offeree's silence does not amount to acceptance. There are, however, exceptions to the general rule: when the offeree accepts or takes the benefit of the offer in a circumstance that would reasonably be the basis of compensation for the benefit; when the offeror had already given the offeree reason to know that silence or inaction would amount to assent and also when the offeree intends silence to manifest acceptance; and when the past dealings between the offeror and the offeree support a reasonable inference that the offeree silently accepts.

*See also:* acceptance, acceptance as acceptance of an offer | 10. silence as acceptance (failure to respond); acceptance, acceptance as acceptance of an offer.

### silence implies consent (tacit consent or tacit agreement)   Silence implies assent only when there is a duty to speak. Silence implies consent, or silence condones an action, is a maxim of the common law and of equity that applies when a person has a duty to speak or object but does not do so, amounting to tacit assent to the conduct or condition to which the speaker failed to object. The maxim in law arises when a person creates a condition (or, sometimes, when a person becomes aware of a condition) in which a second person will form a false impression and this misapprehension will cause harm to the second person unless the first person warns the second person of the danger of the misapprehension; if that harm works to the advantage of the first person or to a confederate of the first person, the silence amounts to fraud. The maxim in equity is the nub of equitable estoppel: when a person is aware of another's conduct to which the first person has a right to object, and fails to object while the second person commits resources to the conduct, relying on the silence as permission, the first person may be estopped from later objection to the second person's unnecessary harm. Modern examples are hardly scarce: Silence by a manager in a governmental or corporate setting may amount to a condonation of misconduct by employees, and indeed may even serve as evidence of a workplace environment or workplace rule or policy. Silence by members of a class action, who have a duty to participate in their claim if they wish their preferences known, is assent to a settlement or to other decisions in the case.

Even so, in the law, silence only amounts to consent when there is a duty to speak. Silence when there is discretion not to speak and when no duty arises from circumstance does not amount to consent or condonation.

Thus, the rule in contracts is that an offer is not accepted by silence. The rare exception to this rule is the most unusual circumstance of an established pattern of renewed or repeated transactions between two parties, in which the parties are presumed to have opted in to a transaction unless one party opts out.

### silver or lead   *See:* corruption, silver or lead (plato o plomo).

### simony   The purchase of religious offices or blessings. Simony is the the sale or purchase of a church office, order, blessing, or other preferment. It is most associated with the purchase of indulgences. Although the most technical understanding of simony is only the purchase of the ecclesiastical benefit, simony became more widely associated with both buying and selling church offices in early modern England.

### simple battery   *See:* battery, criminal battery, simple battery.

### simple larceny   *See:* larceny, simple larceny.

### simple trust or naked trustee or bare trust or bare trustee   *See:* trust, naked trust (simple trust or naked trustee or bare trust or bare trustee).

### simpliciter   Summarily. Simpliciter is Latin for plain and simple, and in contemporary writing it may mean summarily or without elaboration, explanation, or limitation.
*See also:* fallacy, dicto simpliciter.

### simulation (simulate)   An invented depiction of an event as if it were real. A simulation creates the appearance of the place, people and events simulated. Simulations are used to recreate accidents and other events for the purpose of assessing theories that would explain cause and effect in the original events. A simulation may be created with small-scale models, with human actors, with computer-driven graphics, or by other means.

Simulations are also used in training and education to develop professional tools for use in specific situations. Moot court, practice negotiation, trial competition, and client counseling practice are simulations of this form.

### moot court   A simulated argument before a court of law. Moot court is a custom of long standing in the professional education of law students, by which

two students argue a legal proposition in a hypothetical case before a bench of lawyers, professors, judges, or other students. The function of the moot court is not only to develop the advocacy skills of the students, but to expose the students to the customs and techniques of argument in court. Although moot court has traditionally been engaged in appellate argument, trial practice competitions and other simulated judicial arguments provide a wider range of experience. Moot courts in the United States are usually held among students within a law school's student body, although there are many inter-school competitions. One moot court competition, named for Philip C. Jessup, is devoted to international legal argument and is modeled on the procedures of the International Court of Justice.

**simultaneous death**   *See:* death, simultaneous death, Uniform Simultaneous Death Act.

**simultaneous performances**   *See:* performance, contract performance, simultaneous performances.

**sin tax**   *See:* tax, sin tax, pole tax (sexually oriented business tax or SOB tax); tax, sin tax.

**sine**   Without. Sine is Latin for being without, or lacking something. Note: sine in Latin is pronounced as see-nay, not like sign.

**sine damno**   Without injury. Sine damno is Latin for harmless, or lacking a legally cognizable damage or injury.
   *See also:* absque injuria (absque iniuria).

**sine die (without day)**   Indefinitely. Sine die, Latin for "without a day specified," is a designation for any order that has an effect on the future but does not specify the date on which the effect might occur. This has varying implications according to the order. An adjournment sine die of a legislature is the final adjournment, because the legislature is not adjourned to a definite time of its own choosing but adjourned until it is called; bills then pending in the legislature are usually considered dead when the legislature is recalled. A judicial hearing, motion, or action that is stayed sine die is postponed without a date for hearing, and so it may be kept pending indefinitely. At times, as in a corporate board or a law firm, an adjournment sine die suggests the adjournment is permanent. Note: there are a range of customary pronunciations that vary from place to place and among forums; the more accepted is seenay deeay, though many locales say sigh-nee dye.

**sine qua non**   Something required or essential. Sine qua non, literally the Latin for "without this there is nothing" represents an essential element, component, or condition of something else. The death of a person is, for instance, a sine qua non of the crime of murder.

**single-employer rule**   *See:* veil, corporate veil, single-employer rule (single-entity test or integrated enterprise standard).

**single-entity test or integrated enterprise standard**   *See:* veil, corporate veil, single-employer rule (single-entity test or integrated enterprise standard).

**single-juror instruction**   *See:* instruction, jury instruction, single-juror instruction (unanimity instruction).

**sinking fund**   *See:* funds, sinking fund.

**SIPC**   *See:* security, securities, securities regulation, Securities Investor Protection Corporation (SIPC).

**sister**   *See:* family, sibling, brother (sister).

**situs**   The place. Situs is Latin for the location of a thing. The situs of land determines the jurisdiction that governs it.
   *See also:* venue; forum.

**sixteenth section land**   *See:* land, school trust land (sixteenth section land).

**skimmer device**   *See:* theft, identity theft, skimmer device.

**skip person or GST**   *See:* tax, estate tax, generation-skipping transfer tax (skip person or GST).

**skirting the issue or straw argument**   *See:* fallacy, ignoratio elenchi (skirting the issue or straw argument).

**slander (slanderer)**   A defamation published by being spoken aloud. Slander is a false statement defaming a living person that is communicated orally to a third party. While the defamatory element of slander is defined differently between jurisdictions, it generally includes situations in which the victim would ordinarily be expected to suffer a diminished regard or respect by others if the others believed the defamatory statement to be true. One who commits a slander is a slanderer.

**slander per quod**   Slander arising from a statement in context. Slander per quod is slander that is not inherent in the terms expressed in statement in issue but that is apparent as a result of interpretation of the words of the statement in the context in which they were spoken or heard. An apparently innocent statement or description may be slanderous per quod if it uses innuendo, sarcasm, or suggestion to cause a hearer to infer slanderous claims are made as fact. Unlike slander per se, the plaintiff in an action for slander per quod must prove special damages.
   *See also:* defamation, defamation per quod (double entendre); libel, libel per quod; per, per quod.

**slander per se**   A spoken statement that is inherently defamatory. Slander per se is the publicized making aloud of a statement that is asserted as a fact about a person that would harm a person's reputation in that person's community, in any context and without requiring interpretation or an interpretation of innuendo. Four recognized categories of statements amount to slander per se: an assertion that a person has committed an infamous crime; an assertion the person has an infectious disease; an assertion that would tend to subject a person to hatred, distrust, ridicule, contempt, or disgrace; and an assertion that tends to injure a person's reputation in that person's trade or profession. Damages are presumed in a case of slander per se, and there is no need to show damages for such an action, as there would be a requirement to prove damages for slander per quod. The primary difference between slander per se and libel per se is the medium of expression, in that slander is spoken while libel is written.

*See also:* slander, slander per quod; libel, libel per se; per, per se.

**slavery (slave)**  A person owned as if property by another person or an entity. A slave is a person with no liberty, who is held in a state of captivity or restraint by another person or an entity as if the slave is property. The condition of slavery is universally condemned as immoral and intolerable under modern standards of civilized law.

Slavery was a persistent aspect of life in Europe from the time of ancient Greece and Persia. Rome, Africa, Asia, and the Americas all seem to have had ancient cultures that practiced slavery, primarily by enslaving people conquered in war and sometimes enslaving people in payment of debts. Slaves brought from Africa by Europeans to work in American plantations and mines led to an otherwise unusual cultural relationship between perceived race and eligibility for slavery, an association that persisted in the United States long into its history as a nation. Slavery was abolished in many cultures in the seventeenth and eighteenth and nineteenth century. The law in the United States recognized slavery and protected it under the Constitution, until slavery was abolished by the passage of the Thirteenth Amendment in 1865.

Slavery persists in parts of the world. To hold or transport a slave is considered to be a crime of universal jurisdiction, punishable by any nation on earth.

**abolition of slavery**  *See:* abolition, abolition of slavery.

**slave wage**  *See:* wage, slave wage.

**badge of slavery**  A persistent condition that evokes the past burden of slavery. A badge of slavery is any burden or disability, whether it originates in law or social custom, that was associated or persists to limit the freedom of a person whose ancestors were in slavery. Before passage of the Thirteenth Amendment, the term was applied to dark color of a person's skin, but since then has included the aspects of discrimination associated with slavery, Jim Crow, and the categorical restraints of African Americans from full integration into American law, society, and business.

*See also:* Jim Crow law (race laws).

**forced labor**  Involuntary labor. Forced labor is any labor, service, or employment which is extracted from any person through the use of violence, restraint or threat to that person or another, for which that person would not otherwise have volunteered. Forced labor may or may not be given compensation; its defining attribute is that it is given involuntarily. Forced labor is involuntary servitude in the United States, and it is only allowed of persons convicted under law of an offense for which labor is a lawful punishment. Forced labor in all other contexts that as a lawful criminal sentence is a federal crime, punishable by imprisonment of up to twenty years, and if kidnapping is involved, the punishment is up to life.

**involuntary servitude**  Employment that is physically or legally coerced. Involuntary servitude occurs when a victim is forced to work for a person or entity by the use or threat of physical restraint or physical injury, including the use or threat of coercion through law or the legal process, or the use of fear of such means. Determining whether a person engages in a particular job, work, or employment involuntarily may include consideration of the absence or miserliness of compensation, of other means of coercion, of poor working conditions, or of the victim's special vulnerabilities; any of which may corroborate disputed evidence regarding the use or threatened use of physical or legal coercion.

The requirement of involuntary servitude from another is a crime in the United States, unless the requirement is pursuant to a lawful sentence of the person for a crime for which such service is a legal punishment. The federal offense allows imprisonment for life if the servitude involves kidnapping or the death of the victim.

**peonage (debt bondage)**  Service in bondage to satisfy a debt. Peonage is labor in service to another as a means of repayment or satisfaction of a debt by the laborer, required by the creditor or an agent of the creditor under an actual or implied threat of legal action or violence. Peonage is illegal, barred as a form of involuntary servitude by the Thirteenth Amendment, and by federal statute. The term is derived from the Spanish peon, for an agricultural laborer tied to the land, like a serf.

**wage slave**  An employee dependent on income from work to survive. Wage slave in the contemporary capitalist society is a slang term for a person dependent upon income from wages to survive, lacking savings or other assets for income and having no means of generating income other than by employment. A wage slave is not a slave in any legal sense.

Wage slave also describes the compelled employees who found themselves in "wage slavery" when an employer encouraged employees to build debts to the employer through low wages and accessible credit for basic goods such as food and housing. Such employees in company towns owed the company store enough that their continued employment was a matter of compulsion.

**slip opinion** *See:* opinion, judicial opinion, slip opinion.

**slip-and-fall case (slip and fall)** An action by a person injured by falling on another's property. A slip and fall case is either a tort action in negligence or a property action, in either case brought by a plaintiff who is injured by slipping and falling on the premises for an owner's or tenant's failure to maintain the premises according to the duty of care owed to the plaintiff. If a plaintiff slips and falls, suffering some injury in the fall, and if the fall occurred, at least in part, because of some defect in the walks, grounds, stairs, or other surface on the property, which is a defect that the owner or tenant knew or should have known of and that presented an unreasonable risk of injury, the failure of the owner or tenant to cure the defect gives rise to liability.

*See also:* negligence (negligent).

**slippery slope** *See:* fallacy, slippery slope (thin edge of the wedge or camel's nose argument).

**sludge (activated sludge)** The residue of a waste treatment process. Sludge is the gunk at the bottom or in the filters in any process of waste treatment or particulate removal. In waste water treatment plants, sludge is divided between active sludge (or bio-active sludge) and inactive sludge. Sludge from waste water treatment plants is usually removed, pressed or dried, and then disposed of as fuel, fertilizer, or solid waste.

Activated sludge contains bacteria, protozoa, and other microbial life that digests organic content in sewage. The part of the sludge with concentrations of the nibbling microbes is called "floc," separating through a process of flocculation. Activated sludge usually requires some form of aeration for its maintenance.

**slum** *See:* zoning, slum.

**small-business corporation** *See:* corporation, small-business corporation (S-corporation).

**small-claims court** *See:* court, U.S. court, small-claims court.

**smell (odor)** The detection of chemicals in the air by the nose or mouth. Smell is the means by which animals recognize odor, and the two terms are effectively interchangeable. The sense of smell may detect small quantities of particulate, gas, or suspended liquids in the air. People may use smell to detect a variety of odors, though dogs and other animals do so with smaller chemical quantities of wider variety and may be trained to alert humans of their presence.

Smell may be used as the basis for probable cause to search for a substance indicated by its odor. Smell may also be evidence of activity used in trial.

Smell, particularly strong smell, may be both proof of a trespass of chemicals over the property of another and the basis for nuisance. If the use of one property continuingly creates such odor on another property as to interfere with its use, the odor is a nuisance.

*See also:* dog, sniffer dog (cadaver dog or detection dog); nuisance.

**smelter** A facility for separating metals from ores. A smelter is an operation that segregates metals from ores mined from the Earth or in recycling products already made. Smelting usually requires large amounts of heat and chemicals. The emissions of a smelter are inherently air pollution.

**Smith Act** *See:* immigration, Alien and Sedition Acts (Smith Act).

**smoking gun** *See:* evidence, direct evidence, smoking gun.

**smuggling (smuggle or smuggler)** The unlawful movement of goods, money, or people. Smuggling is the act of knowingly transporting money, goods, or people whose transport in general, or whose transport in that instance, is against the law. Interstate smuggling is the smuggling of goods and people into a state, or between states, when such transport is unlawful. International smuggling is the same act from one state to another. Smuggling requires only the knowing carriage of goods or of a person in a context that renders the carriage illegal; it does not require concealment. In the United States, knowingly or willfully bringing any merchandise into the United States that is not properly invoiced is smuggling, as is knowingly bringing an alien into the country without a visa and without proper processing by immigration officials, as is knowingly bringing a firearm into the U.S. with the intent to use it for a drug offense or crime of violence.

**smuggling and trafficking** *See:* trafficking | trafficking and smuggling.

**sniffer dog** *See:* dog, sniffer dog (cadaver dog or detection dog).

**snitch** *See:* informant, snitch (canary or stool pigeon or pigeon).

**SO₂** *See:* pollution, air pollution, criteria pollutants, sulfur dioxide ($SO_2$).

**sobriety (sober)** A person not significantly affected by alcohol or drugs. Sobriety is the condition of being unintoxicated, that is not having consumed alcohol or drugs of a form or quantity to impair one's reasoning, reactions, abilities, or actions. Sobriety, in its general legal sense, does not require complete abstinence from alcohol or lawful pharmaceuticals. Sobriety in a regulatory scheme with no tolerance for any consumption of alcohol or drugs has, however, a specific requirement that these substances not have been consumed at all in the relative time prior to and during participation in conduct governed by such a scheme.

*See also:* driving, driving under the influence (D.U.I. or DUI or operating a vehicle under the influence or O.V.U.I. or OVUI); driving, driving while intoxicated (operating a vehicle while intoxicated or driving while impaired or D.W.I. or DWI); intoxication (drunkenness or alcoholic impairment).

**sobriety checkpoint** *See:* stop, police stop, checkpoint stop, sobriety checkpoint.

**sober second thoughts** A metaphor for careful constitutional governance. Sober second thoughts represents a considered opinion, as opposed to rash first thoughts. Sober second thoughts has long been a justification and thence a metaphor for a constitutional method to assure a careful decision. Apparently, the phrase was first used by Fisher Ames to justify Congressional elections every two years. It has also been used to justify a bicameral legislature. Its most prominent contemporary use is to justify judicial review of legislation, echoing its use by Harlan Fiske Stone.
*See also:* review, judicial review.

**field sobriety test** An assessment to screen for mental impairment, made at or near a stop. A field sobriety test is any objectively reliable means for assessing a person's mental impairment that may be administered by a police officer at or near the place of a stop, in order to determine the likelihood a person is influenced by alcohol or drugs. An appropriately administered battery of field sobriety tests may provide probable cause to arrest a person for operating under the influence, or for arrest into custody for the purpose of more accurate testing, such as testing for blood alcohol content to be performed at the police station.
*See also:* stop, police stop, checkpoint stop, sobriety checkpoint; blood, blood alcohol level (blood alchohol content or B.A.C. or BAC).

**socage** *See:* tenure, feudal tenure, socage, villein socage (villeinage socage); tenure, feudal tenure, socage, free and common socage; tenure, feudal tenure, socage.

**social contract (contractarianism)** A grand, implied contract justifies laws. The social contract is a metaphor for the relationship between the people governed by the state and the state that governs them. Many writers have argued that the best way to understand the laws, the government, or the state, is to see them as the result of a contract, either a contract negotiated among the people or one negotiated between the people and the rulers. The idea has sometimes been argued as if such a contract literally is enacted. The contractarian idea, especially as developed by Thomas Hobbes and criticised by John Locke and Jean-Jacques Rousseau, is seen by some authors, especially Hobbes, to justify a sovereign above the law, and by others, notably Locke, to set definite limits not only to the law but to its exercise. This restrictive view of the social contract influenced the drafting of the Declaration of Independence and the U.S. Constitution. It has been the object of renewed study and debate following the theory of justice of John Rawls.

**Social Security (Social Security Act)** A federal system of insurance to support retirement or disability. Social Security, in general, is the provision by the state of economic assistance to those unable to acquire the basic necessities of life, particularly owing to age. In the United States, social security denominates two major programs: the federal retirement insurance program and the federal disability payments program. The retirement insurance program was created in the Social Security Act of 1932, ch. 531, 49 Stat. 620, codified at 42 U.S.C. § 301, et seq (2010), and the Federal Insurance Contributions Act (FICA) of 1935, codified at 26 U.S.C. ch. 21 (2010), which is the taxing authority for both Social Security and Medicare, as well as later amendments. The disability payments program is Supplemental Social Security, or SSI, which is funded from the general revenues rather than the FICA insurance fund. It is the successor to several state and federal disability programs for the blind, the disabled, and the elderly poor, consolidated in the Social Security Amendments of 1972.

The Social Security Administration, created under the 1932 act, collects payments from active workers over their working lives and then provides payments to workers who reach an age of retirement or who become disabled and are no longer capable of full-time or part-time employment. It also administers SSI.

**Federal Insurance Contibutions Act (FICA)** The federal tax on employers and employers to support Social Security and Medicare. The Federal Insurance Contributions Act (FICA), is the statutory authority for the payroll deduction of federal insurance payments to support Social Security and Medicare. The statute is in chapter 21 of the Internal Revenue Code, requires payroll withholding by employers for the employee contribution, and payment by employers of an employer contribution. Under a 1954 amendment, individuals who are self-employed or partners in a partnership must pay their own contributions as both employer and employee. In 2011, the employee withholding requirement for 2010 for Social Security was 4.2 percent on wages up to $106,800, and for Medicare was 1.45 percent on all wages. The employer tax for Social Security was 6.2 percent and for Medicare was 1.45 percent.
*See also:* tax, income tax, payroll tax withholding.

**Old Age Survivors and Disability Insurance (OASDI)** Federal benefits paid to the retired, disabled, and their dependents. Old Age Survivors and Disability Insurance refers to benefits provided to the retired, disabled, and their dependents, as provided by Title II of the Social Security Act, 42 U.S.C. §401 et seq. OASDI is paid by workers through a payroll deduction.
*See also:* tax, payroll tax, Federal Insurance Contributions Act (F.I.C.A. tax or FICA tax).

**societe en commendite (societe en commandite)** The limited partnership, in French law. La société en commandite is a legal structure for partnership recognized by the French Code de Commerce (1807), which was the basis for the recognition of the limited partnership in U.S. law, beginning in 1822. The structure is created by a contract, by which one person or partnership agrees to furnish another person or partnership a certain amount, either in property or money, to be employed by the person or partnership to whom it is furnished, in his or their own name or firm, on condition of receiving a share in the profits, in the proportion determined by the contract, and of being liable to losses and expenses to the amount furnished and no more.

*See also:* partnership, limited partnership (limited partner).

**sociological jurisprudence** *See:* jurisprudence, sociological jurisprudence (sociology of law).

**sodality (sodalities)** A small association or close-knit group. A sodality is a small organization whose members are particularly committed to the support of one another. It is often a unit within a larger organization.

*See also:* association (associate).

**sodomy (sodomize or sodomite)** Sex in a manner that is prohibited by law. Sodomy is either any act of sexual penetration with one's penis or mouth of the mouth or anus of another person, or any act of sex with an animal other than a human being. Although sodomy has sometimes been distinguished from buggery, both terms have been used interchangeably for centuries, as has the "crime against nature."

Sodomy between two consenting adults that is not in public or in a commercial transaction is constitutionally protected within the right of privacy. Sodomy that is not consensual, that is in public, that is committed with a partner under the age of consent, or that is committed for money are still criminal in most jurisdictions under these titles, and in others such acts are indicted as sodomy or as sexual assault, child molestation, or a similar offense. Sodomy with animals is likewise prosecutable either as sodomy or as animal abuse and is not a matter of privacy. A person who commits sodomy is a sodomite or a sodomizer. The victim is sodomized.

*See also:* buggery (bugger or buggerer).

**crime against nature (unnatural act)** A legal euphemism for sodomy. The "infamous crime against nature, not fit to be named among Christians" was once widely considered sufficient notice to the average Joe that if he had sex with another average Joe or sex in an improper manner with the average Jane (or in any way with an animal), he was facing twenty years at hard labor or, in an earlier age, death. That is to say this phrase was the customary statutory name of—and description for—the crime of sodomy. (The problem was even greater for states that used the Latin phrase, as did William Blackstone in his otherwise English–language book: peccatum horribile, inter christianos non nominandum, which was the basis for prosecutions in the United States in the early nineteenth century). The phrase "crime against nature" persists in many states into the twentieth–first century.

*See also:* sodomy (sodomize or sodomite); buggery (bugger or buggerer).

**soft money** *See:* money, soft money (soft–money donations).

**software piracy or anti-piracy** *See:* piracy, piracy of copyright or patent (software piracy or anti-piracy).

**soil** The ground, or the upper surface of the Earth, in which grow plants. Soil is often used in law to describe so much of the ground and its subsurface as are in a tract of property in land. Sometimes, a distinction is made between soil and minerals, but generally, both are used interchangeably for property below the surface of the ground.

As a matter of environmental law, agriculture, food law, and natural resources, soil is a distinct substance found in a band of variable width on the surface of the Earth everywhere but in places of solid rock, solid ice or deep water, in which plants are capable of nutrition and growth. Soil is also the mixture of substances of which the soil is made.

**soil percolation or water percolation** *See:* percolation (soil percolation or water percolation).

**soil erosion** The loss of soil from an area through contact with wind, water, or animals. Soil erosion is the loss of soil from the ground. Soil moves as a result of wind, water, biological action, and geological forces. Soil that is displaced from the land by contact with water, air, or animal activity is eroded. Soil erosion provokes a considerable loss of topsoil and significant degradation of water quality and, sometimes, air quality.

**solar access** A land use regulation assuring access to sunlight. A solar access requirement in land use regulation prohibits development or construction that would shade adjoining property to the exclusion of the nearby property's generating electricity by solar energy conversion.

*See also:* light, ancient lights (easement for light and air).

**solar easement** *See:* easement, solar easement.

**sole** Only, or single. Sole is an adjective designating only one, particularly for a party that might otherwise be one of a group, such as a co-tenant, partner, or spouse. To designate an action by or against a person in that person's sole capacity is to distinguish the claims, liabilities, privilege, or immunities of the person from those in a governmental, official, corporate, or other capacity. Sole might also designate a person or entity as having but one component, as in a sole corporation or sole proprietorship. The feme sole, or single woman, was a component of a regime of property held by women or men that is now obsolete.

**sole cause** *See:* causation, sole cause.

**sole custody** *See:* child, child custody, sole custody.

**sole proprietorship**   *See:* proprietorship, sole proprietorship.

**solemnity (solemn or solemnize or solemnization)**   Formality. Solemnity, in general, is that aspect of something done by ceremony in a careful and customary manner. In the law, solemnity is the formality by which a thing is done, in accord with rules and customs required by the law for such a thing. A hearing is performed with solemnity when it is held in a courtroom or hearing room, when the court is summoned, and when the judge, counsel, and parties are in their accustomed places and then the proceedings go forward according to form. A marriage is solemnized when it is performed in a ceremony officiated by a person authorized to do so. A formal will is made solemnly before appropriate witnesses. Taking an oath is always a solemn act.

Solemnization has several distinct but related requirements that underlie the effects of solemn acts in law upon the people who participate. In nearly every instance, solemn acts require witnesses. Solemn acts require some degree of preparation. Solemn acts are done with an acceptance of a customary form rather than as one might choose to act on one's own. As a result, solemn acts may be made only after the actor has spent at least a bit of time between deciding to do something and doing it; the act is at least that much a considered undertaking subject to second thoughts and reconsideration before it is committed. A solemn act is usually public, so that it is known by others and can be described by others, both to remind the actor it was done and to validate it for official purposes. With all that, a solemn act is usually done only for important things, and the solemn nature of an act makes more likely that the actor accepts a responsibility to act in the future in accordance with the oath or other solemn commitment.

*See also:* oath; marriage, ceremonial marriage (solemnized marriage).

**solemnized marriage**   *See:* marriage, ceremonial marriage (solemnized marriage).

**solicitation (solicit or solicted or soliciting)**   Requesting or petitioning the recipient to do something. Solicitation is a general term for the making of a request by one party to another, often to enter a contract or to make a gift but potentially for any purpose. A solicitation may be an offer or a request for an offer, like an advertisement. Context is essential to determine whether an affirmative response to a solicitation that might result in a contract amounts to an acceptance or to an offer.

Solicitation may take nearly infinite forms, some of them subject to particular laws. For instance, solicitation of donations for political or charitable causes is subject to regulation, as is solicitation to join a union.

Solicitation in criminal law is recruitment or attempt to recruit a person to engage in unlawful activity. In a common form, solicitation is solicitation to engage in an act of prostitution.

*See also:* recruit (gang recruitment or recruiting).

**solicitor**   *See:* lawyer, solicitor.

**solid waste**   *See:* waste, waste material, solid waste.

**solitary confinement**   *See:* incarceration, imprisonment, solitary confinement (solitary imprisonment or solitary incarceration or isolation cell).

**Solomon Amendment**   *See:* recruit, recruiting on campus (Solomon Amendment).

**solution**

**chemical solution (chemical suspension)**   A mixture of substances. A solution is a mixture of substances in which the two have physically become indistinctly distributed among one another. A solution contrasts with a suspension, in which one substance is immersed in the other, even in particles, and the two substances remain distinct. Usually, a liquid in a liquid yields a solution, and a gas in a gas yields a solution, but a liquid in a gas yields a suspension, and a solid in a liquid or a gas yields a suspension. This difference is rough and a matter more of degree than definition in some instances.

**parts per billion (PPB)**   The number of units of one substance in a billion units of another. Parts per billion, or ppb, is a measure for very tiny amounts of a chemical in a sample substance. If a sample of air has one ppb of a chemical, then on average, for every 1,000,000,000 molecules of the sample, one molecule is of the test chemical.

**parts per million (PPM)**   The number of units of one substance in a million units of another. Parts per million, or ppm, is a measure for small amounts of a chemical in a sample substance. If a sample of water has one ppm of a chemical, then on average, for every 1,000,000 molecules of the sample, one molecule is of the test chemical.

**parts per thousand (PPT)**   The number of units of one substance in a thousand units of another. Parts per thousand, or ppt, is a measure for large amounts of a chemical in a sample substance. If a sample of animal tissue air has one ppt of a chemical, then on average, for every 1,000 molecules of the sample, one molecule is of the test chemical.

**solubility**   The likelihood a substance will dissolve into a solution. Solubility is the degree to which one substance will form a solution when in contact with another substance. The measure of solubility is the amount of mass of the compound that will dissolve into a unit of the other compound.

**solvency or insolvent or solvent**   *See:* insolvency (solvency or insolvent or solvent).

**some evidence or any evidence or no evidence**   *See:* proof, burden of proof, modicum of evidence (some evidence or any evidence or no evidence).

**son in law**   *See:* family, child, son in law (son-in-law).

**sound mind or unsound mind** *See:* mind (sound mind or unsound mind).

**Southern Poverty Law Center** *See:* civil rights, civil rights organization, Southern Poverty Law Center (SPLC).

**sovereign (sovereignty)** The supreme power and authority in a state or legal system. Sovereignty is the source of power in the state and of the law. The word is derived from the French soverain, meaning either above or excellent, and it initially connoted the person of the monarch, then the legal powers of the monarch, and then the legal powers of the state. To a degree, the idea of sovereignty is a practical aspect of the ability to issue and enforce laws that act as genuine authority for the conduct of officials and people in a state, and to a degree, the idea of sovereignty represents a nearly mythical understanding of the justifications for law and the state in a society. Note: sovereign is both a noun and an adjective. Sovereignty is the capacity and power of the sovereign.

*See also:* people, sovereign people; government, forms of government, monarchy (kingdom or monarch); government.

> **sovereign immunity** *See:* immunity, sovereign immunity.

> **sovereign people** *See:* people, sovereign people.

**sovereignty** The highest legal authority. Sovereignty identifies the authority to employ the power of the state, including the authorities of law, above which there is no higher authority. The term is derived from the Law French souvereaigne, meaning superior or what is above, and for one thing or person to be sovereign over another initially meant merely for the one to be above the other, the Sovereign Paramount meaning the sovereignty of a monarch or state, or supremacy. The relative sense of sovereignty is now rare, and sovereignty is now used nearly always in the sense of the power and authority of a state, both over its subjects and lands and relative to the similar powers of other states.

*See also:* supremacy (supreme).

> **state sovereignty** The supremacy of a state over non–federal matters. State sovereignty is a doctrine depicting the continuing vitality of each state's power to regulate matters affecting the state itself and local affairs, in which it is not subordinate to the government of the United States. The federal balance has been struck to leave some matters in the control of the states and free from federal regulation or interference. The Tenth Amendment and particularly the Supreme Court's anachronistic reading of state sovereign immunity into the Eleventh Amendment have sometimes been offered as textual sources for sovereign immunity, but the balance is best seen in the structure and text of the Constitution as ratified, which delegated powers to the central government, in which it was supreme, but reserved powers to the states. This balance was altered by the Civil War and the Reconstruction Amendments to the Constitution, as well as by judicial recognition of changes in meaning to the regulation of interstate and foreign commerce by the federal government. As a result of these changes, the scope of state sovereignty has been reduced over the centuries. Its boundaries remain controversial.

> *See also:* immunity, sovereign immunity, state sovereign immunity (Eleventh Amendment Immunity); federalism.

>> **equal footing doctrine (equal-footing doctrine)** New states possess the same sovereignty as older states. The equal footing doctrine is a constitutional principle emanating from the Statehood Clause, which requires the federal government, in admitting new states to the Union, to grant to the new state sovereign powers neither more, nor less, nor different from the powers held by the states already admitted.

**SOX Act claim** *See:* whistleblower, Sarbanes–Oxley claim (SOX Act claim).

**SP or S.P.** *See:* police, police organization, military police, shore patrol (SP or S.P.).

**special** Specific, rather than general. Special, in legal usage, signals some function that is a relationship to an individual or specific state of affairs, rather than a general or typical state of affairs. There are many examples. A special administrator is appointed for a particular motion or time. Special damages are unusual and pled distinctly in a cause of action in which they might not otherwise be apparent. Special rules apply to a particular type of action or even to a particular action. A special verdict is a ruling on a particular fact in dispute rather than the general verdict on liability as a whole.

*See also:* administration, administration of estate, special administration; bequest, specific bequest (specific legacy or special legacy); damages, classes of damages, special damages; defamation, special harm; extradition, specialty; guardian, guardian ad litem (special guardian); interrogatory, jury instruction, special interrogatory (jury interrogatory); jurisdiction, in personam jurisdiction, voluntary jurisdiction, special appearance (limited appearance); power, power of appointment, special power of appointment; prosecutor, special prosecutor; venire, special venire.

> **special act** *See:* act, special act (particular act).

> **special administration** *See:* administrator, administrator of estate, special administrator (special administration); administration, administration of estate, special administration.

> **special administrator** *See:* administrator, administrator of estate, special administrator (special administration).

**special agent**  *See:* agent, special agent.

**special appearance**  *See:* jurisdiction, in personam jurisdiction, voluntary jurisdiction, special appearance (limited appearance); appearance, special appearance.

**special attorney**  *See:* prosecutor, special attorney.

**special counsel**  *See:* prosecutor, special counsel; counsellor, special counsel.

**special covenant against encumbrances**  *See:* covenant, covenant of title, special covenant against encumbrances.

**special damages**  *See:* damages, classes of damages, special damages.

**special deposit**  *See:* deposit, special deposit.

**special executor**  *See:* executor, special executor.

**special guardian**  *See:* guardian, guardian ad litem (special guardian).

**special harm**  *See:* defamation, special harm.

**special interrogatory**  *See:* interrogatory, jury instruction, special interrogatory (jury interrogatory).

**special master**  *See:* master, special master.

**special needs exception**  *See:* search, warrantless search, special needs exception.

**special pleading**  *See:* pleading, special pleading.

**special power of appointment**  *See:* power, power of appointment, special power of appointment.

**special prosecutor**  *See:* prosecutor, special prosecutor.

**special use zoning**  *See:* zoning, special use zoning (conditional use permit or special permit zoning or special use permit).

**special venire**  *See:* venire, special venire.

**special verdict**  *See:* verdict, special verdict.

**special warranty deed**  *See:* deed, warranty deed, special warranty deed.

**specialty**  *See:* extradition, specialty.

**specialty bar associations**  *See:* bar, bar organization, specialty bar associations.

**specie**  *See:* money, specie.

**species (speciation)**  A distinct life form that reproduces others of its own kind. A species is a category within the classification of the domain of living things, particularly within animals and plants, being the specific category within which the animals or the plants share all salient characteristics so that all members of the species that reproduce, if they reproduce, produce offspring that share all of the same characteristics. In other words, members of a species interbreed and produce new members of the same species. As used in the law governing endangered species, each subspecies and each distinct population segment of a species of vertebrate fish or wildlife are treated as a species. The technique of identifying the categorical definition of a species is speciation.

**species recovery or habitat recovery**  *See:* recovery, recovery of natural resource (species recovery or habitat recovery).

**alien species (exotic species)**  A species of animal or plant not native to an area. An alien species, or an exotic species, is a plant or animal that has been introduced into an ecosystem that is not native to it. An alien species may either fail to adapt and perish, or, lacking suitable predators, it will adapt very well, potentially threatening native species or altering the habitat. Zebra mussels in the Great Lakes and kudzu in the American south are classic alien species.

**endangered species**  A species that that may soon become extinct, whether as a whole or in a given range. An endangered species is a species of animal or plant that has been recognized by the United States or another state as being in danger of extinction, whether it is at risk in only one range or over the Earth as a whole. Endangered species, as defined in the Endangered Species Act, does not include any species of insect that the U.S. Secretary of Commerce determines is a pest whose protection would present an overwhelming and overriding risk to man. In the United States, it is a crime to take an example of an endangered species from the wild, including interfering with its habitat, unless the taking is pursuant to a permit or within a very few statutory exceptions. The transportation of examples of an endangered species or a part of an endangered animal or plant is strictly controlled under the Convention on International Trade in Endangered Species, which coordinates a licensing system among its member states.
*See also:* habitat.

**Convention on the International Trade in Endangered Species (C.I.T.E.S. or CITES)**  A legal regime to prevent the loss of species through international trade. The Convention on the International Trade in Endangered Species of Flora and Fauna, or CITES, is an international convention of 175 states, as of 2010, that maintains a global registry of endangered and threatened animals and plants, seeking through its member states to prevent trade in whole specimens or their parts that would increase the likelihood of the extinction of the species. CITES is also an international agency maintaining the international network into which efforts to enforce the U.S. Endangered Species Act is integrated.
*See also:* species, Endangered Species, Endangered Species Act (E.S.A. or ESA).

**Endangered Species Act (E.S.A. or ESA)**  The primary federal law protecting biodiversity. The Endangered Species Act of 1973, Pub. L. 93–205, codified at 7 U.S.C. §136, and 16 U.S.C. §1531 et seq., requires federal protection of animals and plants that are sufficiently scarce that their continued survival is threatened or endangered. The Act requires the identification of endangered and threatened species, which, after a process of evaluation, are listed on the federal lists of endangered or threatened species. Listed species are protected by restricting loss or harm to habitat critical to the survival of the species, by a prohibition against the taking of any animal or plant of a listed species, and by the implementation of a recovery plan by which affirmative steps are taken to improve the chances for the species's survival. The federal ESA list and ESA enforcement are coordinated with enforcement of the Convention on International Trade in Endangered Species of Wild Fauna and Flora ("CITES"), and the ESA is the statutory enactment in compliance with the CITES treaty.

*See also:* species, endangered species, Convention on the International Trade in Endangered Species (C.I.T.E.S. or CITES).

**critical habitat** Habitat that is essential to conserve a species of animal or plant. Critical habitat is habitat that is essential to the conservation of a species of plant or animal that is listed according to the Endangered Species Act. Critical habitat may include habitat that is not inside the range of an animal or plant, but is still essential to its survival, as, for instance, a source of food or a sufficient habitat to sustain habitat within its range.

**take prohibition** No animal or plant may be taken from its habitat without a permit. The take prohibition is the criminal bar in the Endangered Species Act, at 16 U.S.C. § 1538(a)(1)(B) (2010), forbidding any person from taking an endangered species of fish or wildlife within the United States or its territorial sea. Taking includes any means to harass, harm, pursue, hunt, shoot, wound, kill, trap, capture, or collect, as well as attempts to do so. 16 U.S.C. § 1532(19). Harass has been further defined by the U.S. Fish and Wildlife Service, at 50 C.F.R. § 17.3, (2010) to mean acts likely to injure wildlife by annoying it so that its normal behavioral patterns like breeding, feeding, or sheltering are significantly disrupted. Interference with critical habitat also amounts to a taking. Taking is allowed, however, under circumstances permitted in the Act, which are approved by the appropriate agency as beneficial to the species' survival.

**focal species** One of several indicator species chosen for assessment of an ecosystem. A focal species is a species selected by a government agency for particular study as a means of monitoring the health of an ecosystem or of a wider array of species. Although a focal species is used as an indicator species, the criteria for selection of a given species for intensive study as a focal species may differ from the particular interrelationships with other species and similarity or differences of environmental

sensitivities and tolerances to other species that are the scientific basis for selection as an indicator species. Though such biological or environmental criteria may be used to designate a focal species, so too are political criteria, such as interest to politically active groups, and practical criteria, such as prior study of a given species.

*See also:* species, indicator species (canary in the coal mine).

**indicator species (canary in the coal mine)** A species whose population or health signals ecological conditions. An indicator species is a species of plant or animal that is used to assess a particular condition or the overall health of a particular ecosystem. An indicator species must be present in the ecosystem and responsive to the environmental conditions selected for study, the response occurring by changes in behavior, health, or mortality for an individual member of the species or by changes in population, range, or behavior for all or many of the members of the species in the ecosystem being studied. The observation of an indicator species may indicate stress or harm to a variety of other animals and plants in the ecosystem without a full census of their populations or health. Changes to an indicator species may also suggest changes in an ecosystem before they are more widely manifest. An artificial example of an indicator species, which is often used metaphorically to represent a means of warning, is the old miners' practice of placing canaries in cages in coal mines, the canary succumbing to the presence of methane before the miners could detect it otherwise.

*See also:* species, keystone species.

**keystone species** A species causing a significant effect in a given ecosystem. A keystone species is a species that has a greater effect upon a particular ecosystem than would be accounted by its biomass alone, primarily through its effect on the animals and plants it consumes. A keystone species is sometimes used informally to define the boundaries of an ecosystem, such as an herbivore of a range that indicates the extent of salient plant species or a carnivore that defines by range a particular mixture and density of prey. Note: a keystone species may happen to be an indicator species, but the function of each role is independent of the other.

*See also:* species, indicator species (canary in the coal mine).

**threatened species** A species likely soon to become endangered. A threatened species is a species that is declining in numbers or is threatened with habitat loss likely to make its numbers decline, so that it is likely to become endangered in the foreseeable future.

*See also:* species, endangered species.

**speciesism** *See:* right, animal rights, speciesism.

**specificity (specific or specification)** The designation of the unique or particular rather than the general or vague. Specificity is the degree to which a thing is described according to its attributes that distinguish it from other things. A specific description relates to the unique thing, or form of thing described, or to one person rather than to a type of person. Derived from the same sense of the Latin word for something seen from which comes the word species, specification is the act of describing the one rather than the many, the unique rather than the general, the exact rather than the vague.

Specificity is required in many legal standards, such as the designation of a legal claim made from an alleged harm, as the basis for a departure from a general standard, and as the argument for unusual relief. Further, some legal arguments that are specific give rise to particular obligations, such as the pleading rule that specific defenses must be pled when general defenses need not be. Note: although it is a mistake in the law to require unnecessary specificity, sufficient specificity to make clear the legal issues in a given matter is always welcome. As a practical matter, the more specific a legal argument is, the more likely it is to persuade.

**specific bequest** *See:* bequest, specific bequest (specific legacy or special legacy).

**specific causation** *See:* causation, specific causation.

**specific defense** *See:* defense, specific defense.

**specific deterrence** *See:* deterrence, specific deterrence (personal deterrence).

**specific devise** *See:* devise, specific devise.

**specific intent** *See:* intent, specific intent.

**specific legacy** *See:* legacy, specific legacy.

**specific legacy or special legacy** *See:* bequest, specific bequest (specific legacy or special legacy).

**specific legatee** *See:* legatee, specific legatee.

**specific performance** *See:* performance, specific performance | equitable principles; performance, specific performance; equity, equitable remedies, specific performance.

**specific pleading** *See:* defense, specific pleading, XYY chromosome defense; defense, specific pleading, entrapment (inducement).

**speculation (speculate or speculator or speculative)** The assessment of something unknown, such as investment. Speculation is guessing, the use of whatever evidence one has to estimate what one does not know. At some level of fit between the evidence and the question, speculation becomes more like forecasting or estimation, and the differences among these are a matter of degree.

Speculation in investment is the purchase of a position in some property or security in the hope of making a profit. Speculators are investors who speculate in this manner.

*See also:* derivative, financial derivative.

**speech** The expression of an idea or concept, especially by voice or sign. Speech, in general, is the

human capacity to generate communication of words by voice, or any activity similar to it, such as the use of sign language. As speech by words, the person must be able to make audible sounds that are intelligible as words to a speaker of the same language and be made with a measure of efficiency. The inability to engage in speech is a basis for disability.

In this sense, too, a speech is any spoken or signed presentation of ideas to the public. A speech, such as a lecture or an address, is eligible for copyright protection by the speaker, in its spoken, audiophonic form as well as in its written or transcribed form.

In constitutional law, speech is protected as the basis for one of the freedoms most fundamental to American civic life. Speech in this context has a broader connotation that includes not only speech that is spoken or immediately communicated but also written or published speech and speech that is expressed through conduct and performance, such as by art, music, or dance. Speech may be uttered by an individual or the agents of a corporation. Speech may be public or private, and the protections of speech apply to any governmental action made on the basis of speech. All speech is not equivalent in this sense, however, and burdens on speech may be more extensive for speech of constitutionally less value. Thus, obscenity and incitements to violence have no protected constitutional value, and political speech regarding the issues pertinent to governance has a very high constitutional value, so that the government must have a much greater justification for interfering with political speech than it would need to interfere with obscene speech.

Not all speech in law is assessed by the boundaries of speech accorded constitutional protection. Slanderous speech includes defamatory speech that is published as little as to one person other than the speaker and victim, and other than its defamatory aspect, its aspects as speech turn more on the more general notion of words expressed by voice.

**Speech and Debate Clause or Speech Clause** *See:* constitution, U.S. Constitution, clauses, Speech or Debate Clause (Speech and Debate Clause or Speech Clause).

**commercial speech** Advertisement and marketing information. Commercial speech is any speech for the purpose of trade or to induce the sale of any goods or services.

*See also:* speech, freedom of speech, corporate speech; speech, freedom of speech, low–value speech.

**expressive conduct** Actions that amount to speech for constitutional purposes. Expressive conduct is speech created when a person engages in actions that express an idea or concept that is in any manner intelligible to another person who observes it. The concept or idea expressed need not be articulable in words; as long as there is artistic expression of an aesthetic sensibility, some expression is taking place.

*See also:* expression, freedom of expression.

**forum** The space or place of speech. The forum is the place in which speech occurs, and there are a variety of forum types. In the analysis of permissible limits on speech under the First Amendment, the type of forum often determines the degree to which the government may regulate the speech. Although Latin would never countenance a plural such as "forums," the word in English may be made plural in that manner with less confusion than by using fora or fori.

**fighting words** Words that provoke immediate violence. Fighting words describe statements that are rude, obscene, or threatening, and that are reasonably likely to incite the person to whom they are addressed or a bystander to commit an act of violence. Fighting words are not speech protected under the First Amendment.

*See also:* speech, freedom of speech, clear and present danger test (offensive words); speech, freedom of speech, low-value speech.

**freedom of speech (right of free speech or liberty of speech)** Neither Congress nor a state shall abridge the freedom of speech. Freedom of speech is the individual liberty of speaking, writing, and spreading ideas through symbols or conduct without censorship, unreasonable restrictions, or the fear of punishment from the government; it is one of the most fundamental liberties in the Constitution. The federal government and the states are forbidden from regulating speech according to its content without a compelling reason for the government to do so, and they may only regulate the time, place, and manner of speech by creating rational limits that are content-neutral and allow other avenues of speech, such as the regulation of highway billboards. The government may not restrain speech prior to its delivery or based on its content without a compelling interest, though such interests have been found in speech advocating imminent lawless activity and in obscene speech.

*See also:* obscenity (obscene).

*1. content-based restriction (viewpoint neutrality)* The regulation of speech must be neutral to the content of the speech regulated. Laws regulating speech based on its content must promote a compelling governmental interest and must be the least restrictive way to do so. Thus, any law that restricts speech in any way on the basis of its content is subject to this high level of scrutiny. Put another way, restrictions on speech that are content neutral, or laws that affect speech but that have content neutrality, are more easily justified.

*2. indecency v. obscenity* Indecent speech is protected, but obscene speech is not.

*See also:* obscenity, Miller test (Miller standard); obscenity (obscene).

**clear and present danger test (offensive words)** Speech that promotes imminent lawlessness or force or violence to others is not protected. The clear and present danger test, articulated by Justice Holmes in Schenck v. U.S., 249 U.S. 47 (1919), subjects speech that poses a clear and present danger of illegal wrongdoing to prohibition without violating the First Amendment. The "clear and dangerous" tag has been supplanted by other statements, such as a true threat or an incitement to imminent lawlessness, but the core idea has remained largely the same. Thus, words that incite imminent violence are not protected under the First Amendment, although words that merely offend are.

*See also:* provocation (provocateur or provoke); speech, fighting words.

**corporate speech** Expression on behalf of a corporation is protected under the First Amendment. The freedom of speech has been extended to include speech made not by a natural person but on behalf of a corporation. This speech may, at least in some circumstances, include the expenditure of money, at least when the expenditure is a component of advertising, lobbying, or other means of disseminating information. Corporate speech is any speech on behalf of a corporation, and it need not be commercial speech.

*See also:* speech, commercial speech.

**non-public forum (nonpublic forum)** A forum created by the state for a limited use. A non-public forum is a forum created by the government in a medium or place that is under the government's control that the government opens for the purposes of speech limited to a governmental message or a message by governmental officials. Such a non-public forum is allowed, as long as there is no evidence of the suppression of speech contrary to the interests of officials.

**public forum (traditional public forum)** A place or medium customarily employed for public speech. A traditional public forum exists wherever people traditionally or commonly engage in public speech. When the term public forum is used without any other qualification, it likely means a traditional public forum. A speaker's corner in a public park, certain pavilions in a city, and a bulletin board for public use may all be established by custom as a public forum. Access to a traditional forum cannot be denied because of the subject matter of the speech, although it may be limited by reasonable regulations of time, place, and matter.

**designated public forum** A governmental forum created for specified public use. A designated public forum is a limited forum created by the government on public property or in a medium otherwise controlled by the government, that is dedicated to a particular speaker or class of speakers. Not all governmentally designated forums are public, and the government may create a non-public forum if its purpose and effect in creating a forum is limited to a particular governmental message. The government has the power to create such a forum as a public forum and still to limit access to it, but such limits will be analyzed as any other regulation of speech.

**limited public forum**　A temporary forum. A limited public forum is a space opened temporarily for the discussion of a given topic. Its use may be limited to that time and purpose, but access during that time for that purpose may not be restricted according to the viewpoint of a potential speaker.

**hate speech (intimidation)**　An expression of bigotry, prejudice, or disdain is protected unless it amounts to a threat of harm. Hate speech is not ordinarily subject to prior restraint because, as speech alone, it is subject to protection under the First Amendment. Yet, if the speech amounts to intimidation or threats, it is regulable and punishable after the fact.

**heckler's veto**　The risk that an opponent to a speaker may cause a disturbance to chill speech. The heckler's veto describes the problem of an opponent to a law-abiding speaker, whose efforts to disturb the speech might lead to police interference with the speaker in order to preserve the peace. Early free speech doctrines allowed the arrest of a speaker to avoid the danger of a disturbance in response, as in Feiner v. New York, 340 U.S. 315, (1951). Later caselaw recognized the risks these doctrines posed to free speech by allowing a heckler to veto the speech of others, recruiting the state to chill speech the heckler seeks to prevent. The term was coined by free speech scholar Harry Kalven, and the heckler's veto was rejected, allowing a law-abiding speaker police protection even against social disturbance, in 1966. See Brown v. Louisiana, 383 U.S. 131 (1966) (Fortas, J.).

**low-value speech**　Speech subject to low constitutional protection. Low-value speech is speech that lacks the significance or importance to enjoy the highest levels of constitutional protection and is therefore subject to reasonable regulation by the federal and state government. Speech is of a constitutionally low value when it falls into a category recognized as having low value, such as threats, statements made in criminal acts, false statements of fact, fighting words, express incitement of unlawful conduct, obscenity, and commercial advertising; or when it fails to fall into a category recognized as having a high value (such as political speech, or speech of artistic, cultural, or literary merit). Otherwise, low-value speech may be determined on a case-by-case basis if the speech does not advance a political cause or argument, if it does not advance a given viewpoint or position in politics or society (especially a viewpoint that is disfavored by the majority or the elite in society), if the speech is predominately not likely to appeal to a rational response or reaction in reasoned discourse but is more likely to appeal to an instinctive, non-cognitive and emotional response, and if the form of speech is one that has been historically subject to regulation or prohibition by law.

See also: speech, fighting words; obscenity (obscene); speech, commercial speech.

**political campaign spending**　Spending money on political campaigns is protected speech. The spending of money to influence an election is a form of political speech and protected by the First Amendment. This protection is understood both to apply to individuals who would give money toward a candidate or party, and the candidate or party who would spend it.

**inflammatory speech (incendiary speech)**　Speech intended and likely to rouse its hearers to unlawful conduct. Inflammatory speech, or incendiary speech, is speech that may be regulated under the First Amendment if it is intended to provoke its hearers to commit immediate violations of the law, and it is likely to succeed in doing so. By definition, speech that is intended to provoke but fails utterly to do so is not really inflammatory. Likewise, speech that incites its hearers to consider illegal conduct as conduct in the future is not inflammatory. Finally, the action being provoked must be illegal, not merely potentially illegal.

See also: incendiary (accelerant).

**gag order**　Any prohibition on speech directed to an individual or group. A gag order is any regulation, judicial decree, statute, or other mandate by an official that forbids a person or member of a group from making a statement or other act that related to a given topic. A gag order is a prior restraint on speech, and it will be subject to strict scrutiny under judicial review. The designation of military or governmental information by a security classification to prevent its dissemination is not considered a gag order.

**prior restraint of speech**　A law or order that would suppress speech in advance of its making. A prior restraint is a restraint prior to speech. The restraint may take the form of a prohibition on speech by a person or member of an entity, or regarding a given subject matter. The restraint may occur as a result of a statute, an ordinance, a regulation, a judicial order, or an administrative order. The speech may be vocal, transmitted, written, or printed, by words or other expression. Thus, an injunction to prevent a person from publishing a book or giving a speech not yet given is a prior restraint, as a law making a crime of speaking on a given topic or in a given place. The First Amendment does not forbid a prior restraint of speech, though it does require that all prior restraints of speech satisfy the stringent test of strict scrutiny to determine that the restraint is narrowly tailored and the least burdensome means to protect a compelling state interest.

**speedy trial**　See: trial, speedy trial (right to a speedy trial or speedy trial clock).

## spending

**spending power (power of the purse)** The power of Congress to control the allocation and use of federal money. The spending power of the United States is dedicated to the Congress, which alone may appropriate funds from the federal Treasury. The executive agencies, states, and other recipients have such discretion as Congress allows in the uses to which funds may be directed. The authority to remove or to limit the use of federal funds by an executive agency is one of the checks and balances of separation of powers. The authority to grant money to states is one of the influences on federalism.

Congress may condition the use of federal money on certain conduct by the recipient, including conditions that must be met not by spending a given appropriation in one way or another but through action independent of that expenditure. This authority is limited, however, in that there must be at least a reasonable relationship between the condition and the purpose of the appropriation, and the condition may not itself require conduct that violates the constitution when performed by the recipient.

**spendthrift** One who spends money too freely to maintain the person's obligations. A spendthrift is a person, or occasionally an entity, who spends money recklessly, making unnecessary purchases or engaging in obligations that cannot be met from any reasonably expected income. To suggest a person is a spendthrift is to imply irresponsibility and not mere poverty.

**spendthrift trust** *See:* trust, spendthrift trust (asset protection trust).

**SPLC** *See:* civil rights, civil rights organization, Southern Poverty Law Center (SPLC).

**split gift** *See:* gift, split gift.

**spoliation (spoliator)** Destruction. Spoliation is the destruction of a thing of value, particularly a thing of value in the legal process. Although the notion of spoliation was once limited to the utter destruction of a thing, it may include its ill use sufficient to make it unfit for its purpose.

Commonly, the destruction of a last will and testament is spoliation. So, too, is the destruction of evidence or, in some jurisdictions, it is the same as evidence tampering, that is an alteration sufficient to render the evidence misleading or inadmissible.

**spoliation of evidence** *See:* evidence, spoliation of evidence; dismissal, grounds for dismissal, spoliation of evidence.

**spoliation of a will** The intentional destruction or alteration of another person's last will and testament. Spoliation of a will is its destruction by someone other than the testator or the testator's agent acting under the testator's instructions. Spoliation includes partial spoliation, which is an alteration in language of the will through any form of removal, addition, or substitution of the language written or executed by the testator. Spoliation of a will is a tort as well as a crime, often defined by statute or otherwise as a species of fraud.

**spoliation of evidence** The destruction of evidence through intent or neglect. Spoliation of evidence is the treatment of any tangible evidence or potential in such a manner that it becomes unfit for use as evidence. Spoliation may be intentional, in which a person deliberately alters or destroys evidence, or it may be accidental, in which the evidence is allowed to decay or be destroyed. Willful spoliation of evidence that might affect a criminal matter is itself a crime. Willful spoliation of evidence affecting a civil matter may be a crime, depending on the circumstances and the jurisdiction. Negligent spoliation of evidence in the control of an attorney is malpractice. Negligent spoliation of evidence is a particular tort brought by a litigant or would-be litigant harmed by the spoliation of evidence in someone's possession who actually knows it is likely to be evidence in a pending or likely civil action; who has a contractual, fiduciary, or other duty to maintain the evidence; which is essential to demonstrate a claim or a defense; and the loss of which will very likely alter that outcome of the action to the damage of one party. The party or would-be party harmed may bring the tort claim against the spoliator in most jurisdictions. Spoliation by a party in active litigation is subject to sanctions by the court.

*See also:* tampering (tamper).

*dismissal* A court finding a party has destroyed evidence may dismiss the party's claim or defense as a sanction.

**spontaneous declaration or spontaneous exclamation** *See:* hearsay, hearsay exception, hearsay allowed regardless of witness availability, excited utterance (spontaneous declaration or spontaneous exclamation).

**spot contract** *See:* contract, spot contract; contract, specific contracts, forward contract (spot contract).

**spot zoning** *See:* zoning, spot zoning (reverse spot zoning).

**spouse** One who is married. A spouse is a person to whom another person is lawfully married, regardless of whether the spouses are cohabiting or separated. At common law, a spouse was either a husband or a wife. In an age in which marriage is possible between members of the same gender, a spouse would also include a partner in marriage.

*See also:* family, spouse, wife; family, spouse, husband; family, spouse; privilege, spousal privilege (marital privilege or husband–and–wife privilege).

**spousal defense or marital immunity from rape** *See:* rape, rape as sexual assault, spousal rape, marital exemption (spousal defense or marital immunity from rape).

**spousal exemption**  *See:* tax, tax exemption, personal exemption (spousal exemption).

**spousal immunity**  *See:* immunity, spousal immunity (husband–wife immunity or interspousal immunity).

**spousal maintenance**  *See:* alimony, separate maintenance (spousal maintenance).

**spousal notification**  *See:* notification, spousal notification.

**spousal privilege**  *See:* privilege, spousal privilege (marital privilege or husband-and-wife privilege).

**spousal rape**  *See:* rape, rape as sexual assault, spousal rape, marital exemption (spousal defense or marital immunity from rape); rape, rape as sexual assault, spousal rape (marital rape).

**surviving spouse (widow or widower)**  The person who lives after the death of the person's spouse. A surviving spouse is the living spouse following the other spouse's death. A wife who survives her husband is a widow. A husband who survives his wife is a widower.

>**widow (widower)**  The surviving spouse of a dead husband. A widow is a woman whose husband has died during their marriage. The term is still essential in some few benefits designated as "widow's benefits" in insurance. The equivalent term for a male whose wife had died during their marriage is a widower. The distinction in law turned in part on a widow taking dower but a widower taking only curtesy. Both widow and widower are generally now subsumed in the law under the term "surviving spouse" although both remain in common use. At common law, the status of a widow or widower ceased if the survivor remarried, though in contemporary non-legal usage, this convention is now rare.
>
>*See also:* spouse, surviving spouse's interest, curtesy (courtesy).

>**curtesy (courtesy)**  A husband's interest in his wife's estate. Curtesy is a common law interest of a surviving husband in a decedent wife's estate, creating a life estate in the husband in each piece of realty held by his wife at her death, as long as the couple had given birth to a child during the marriage. Few states still allow for a curtesy, and though some still use the term, each has modified the interest by statute, and most have abandoned curtesy or incorporated it into dower or have adopted the spousal elective share instead. Like all spousal interests, if curtesy is available a spouse must elect to take by will or to assert the right to curtesy.
>
>*See also:* spouse, surviving spouse's interest, elective share; spouse, surviving spouse, widow (widower).

>**dower**  A widow's life estate in one-third of her deceased husband's estate. Dower is an interest created by law for a widow in the assets of a husband after his death, thus protecting her interests in widowhood. The traditional common law approach gave a widow a one-third interest in the husband's estate. It is the correlative of curtesy, a widower's life estate after the death of his wife (if they had issue) in her realty. Both interests have been abolished in many states in favor of the elective share.
>
>*See also:* spouse, surviving spouse's interest, elective share; spouse, surviving spouse's interest, curtesy (courtesy); spouse, surviving spouse, widow (widower).

>>**dowress**  A widow who is entitled to receive dower. A dowress is a widow who has not yet received—but who is entitled to receive—dower. More broadly, it is a widow who has received dower. Both senses are now rare in usage.

>**elective share**  A portion of the estate a surviving spouse may take in lieu of a will. An elective share is the right of a surviving spouse to take from the augmented estate of the decedent spouse, instead of accepting the legacies or devises bequeathed by the decedent spouse in a last will and testament. An alternative calculation is used by states that have adopted the Uniform Probate Code, in which the surviving spouse may take under the will and still enjoy a value of the elective share in excess of what is taken according to the will until the value of the elected share of the augmented estate is reached. The augmented estate includes gifts made by the decedent in the last year of life, all interests that paid on the death of the decedent, and insurance. The definition and calculation of the augmented estate vary from state to state, as does the percentage of its value that amounts to the elective share, which is often 30 percent. Note: an elective share is not to be confused with the inheritance a spouse would take in the absence of a will.
>
>*See also:* dower; spouse, surviving spouse's interest, curtesy (courtesy).

**spring gun**  *See:* gun, spring gun (trap gun or man trap).

**springing executory interest**  *See:* interest, executory interest, springing executory interest.

**spurious**  False, fraudulent, or counterfeit. Spuriousness depicts something that is not as it seems, particularly a description or claim that is false and is made by a person who knows it to be false. The term once described illegitimacy of a child, though that sense was supplanted by the sense of fraud while still used in ancient Rome. Many instruments or claims are spurious, and a person who believes in good faith that a lien or instrument is spurious may seek a declaration that it is and be relieved of its burden.

*See also:* class, class action, spurious class action; class, class action, spurious class action.

>**spurious class action**  *See:* class, class action, spurious class action.

**squatter (squat or squatting)**   One who lives or settles the land without authority to possess it. A squatter is a trespasser for residential purposes, a person who lives on a tract or who settles on the lands of another without legal authority. A squatter who persists on private lands as long as the Statute of Limitations for ejectment takes title through adverse possession, though only in certain jurisdictions and not in those that require color of title or claim of right for prescription. Squatters on public lands once acquired a right to a patent, but this doctrine has been abandoned in favor of claim and purchase.

*See also:* trespass (trespass to land).

**squeeze out or squeeze-out or freeze-out**   *See:* shareholder, freeze out (squeeze out or squeeze-out or freeze-out).

**staffing meeting**   *See:* court, drug court, staffing meeting.

**stag hunt**   *See:* game, game theory, stag hunt (trust dilemma or assurance game).

**staleness (stale)**   Being too long delayed. Staleness is the attribute of any action, cause, or complaint that has been kept too long from use. A stale claim is too old to be fairly heard. As with laches, staleness is not susceptible to a perfect measure in days or years, but staleness is measured by the difficulty a court would have in finding facts longer in the past, by the lack of witnesses, evidence, or tools to assess their reliability, and by the surprise or injustice that raising such a claim so late would cause the defendant or the opposing party. Staleness may be the basis for denying certain evidence into the record, for denying certain motions, and even for barring claims or defenses. More commonly, staleness is a basis for denying a search warrant or arrest warrant based on evidence that is stale at the time of the warrant application.

*See also:* repose; limitation, limitation of action (limitations of actions); desuetude.

**stale check**   *See:* check, stale check (stale-dated check).

**stale claim**   *See:* claim, stale claim.

**stale-dated check**   *See:* check, stale check (stale-dated check).

**stalking (stalk or stalker)**   Persistent observation of a person that poses a threat or harassment. Stalking is a crime committed by a person whose conduct — which may include communications, visits, attempts to visit, attempts to observe or be seen, or positioning near to another whether seen or not — is not desired or encouraged by the person to whom it is directed, and whose conduct would cause a reasonable person to feel harassed, frightened, intimidated, or threatened, and whose conduct does cause the person to whom it is directed to feel harassed, frightened, intimidated, or threatened. Definitions vary widely among jurisdictions, but a common denominator is that the crime is not one

of intent to cause such a condition in the victim or knowledge that the conduct would do so.

*See also:* harassment.

**stamp**

**Bates stamp**   A numbered stamp on paper, produced in sequence by a machine. A Bates stamp is any inked mark from a stamping device for dating or numbering each article stamped with a given day, or a number that changes with each impression. Offices often mark correspondence with these devices, and prudent lawyers mark each page of discovery with them to ensure pages do not later go missing. The term increasingly includes computer generated tags created for the same purposes of document inventory and control. The term is an eponym derived from a company making a popular mechanical hand stamp of this type, the Bates Automatic Numbering Machines.

**standard deduction**   *See:* tax, tax deduction, standard deduction.

**standard of care**   *See:* negligence, standard of care.

**standard of proof**   *See:* proof, burden of proof (standard of proof).

**standards of review**   *See:* review, standards of review.

**standards of scrutiny**   *See:* scrutiny, standards of scrutiny.

**standing**   *See:* dismissal, grounds for dismissal, standing.

**Standing Appellate Body**   *See:* trade, international trade, World Trade Organization, Standing Appellate Body (AB).

**standing in court**   The sufficiency of the plaintiff's interest in a claim to be heard by the court. Standing is a relationship between a plaintiff and each claim presented in an action, in which the plaintiff can demonstrate a legally or equitably sufficient interest in the resolution of that claim. The interest underlying the plaintiff's standing has several senses in time and may take a variety of forms. In time, standing may arise from an already manifest harm to an interest or from an imminent harm that is likely to occur without judicial intervention. In form, among others, the interest may arise from an interference with the plaintiff's personal or corporate exercise of a right under the law; from a failure of duty owed to the plaintiff by the defendant that has or may result in harm; from harm, limitation, or taking of an interest in property owned by the plaintiff; or from the loss of a benefit or interest subject to equitable enforcement. A plaintiff lacks standing if the plaintiff cannot demonstrate an interest sufficient for standing, either in the plaintiff's personal or corporate interests or in the rare circumstances in which the plaintiff may invoke the interests of third parties who would themselves have standing.

To determine the sufficiency of an interest in the law of standing can be remarkably discretionary, which leads to the doctrine's recurrent criticism as little more than a sly means for a judge or court to rule for the defense by avoiding a hearing on the merits. This perception is compounded when judges consider the questions of fact related to standing to be a matter of law: a tension sometimes arises from the demand that a plaintiff prove standing from factual allegations but that the proof be treated as an argument of law, to be determined in the discretion of the judge (or judges on appeal). As a result, both of this tension and of the underlying problem that standing inherently closes the courthouse door to allegations of wrongdoing, the rejection of a case on the basis of standing creates the impression that the courts have ignored a potentially valid case and claim, preferring the veil of standing to a more visible relief of an otherwise liable defendant. The same risk attends all dismissals on the bases of justiciability, though the factual assertions related to standing may place the potential for justice denied in higher relief.

Federal standing is both constitutional and prudential. A plaintiff's claim must demonstrate an interest sufficient to satisfy the case and controversy clause, by which the plaintiff has suffered or is in imminent danger of suffering an injury in fact. A plaintiff's claim must also demonstrate prudential standing, in which the nature of the claim, its subject matter, and its remedy are deemed appropriate by the court to be heard. Prudential standing is a form of justiciability per se.

Standing in the federal courts is distinct from standing in state courts. The state courts are free to have more liberal rules allowing a wider scope of standing, or a more constrained rule allowing less standing than would the federal courts. Most allow states a wider range of parties to have standing than do the federal courts.

Standing in both the federal courts and the state courts is distinct, according to whether the claim is a claim of law, or equity, or of admiralty. Each domain of law is specific in its pleading requirements, and it is error to apply the standard of one subject area to others.

*See also:* justiciability (justiciable or non-justiciable or non-justiciability or unjusticiable or prudential rules); interest.

### locus standi in judicio (locus standi)

The standing of the person before the court. Locus standi is the place of person to appear in court, which is to say it is the specific application of the general law of standing that applies in a jurisdiction. Locus standi includes not only the general problem of capacity to appear, but also the specific relationship of the plaintiff to the cause of action and the remedy sought. Although the phrase is used in U.S. courts as a synonym for standing, the term invokes the civilian and equitable requirements of standing, which are quite different from many common-law requirements and include a doctrine of clean hands.

*See also:* locus (loci).

### taxpayer standing (citizen standing or double-nexus test)

Standing to constrain an unconstitutional expenditure or causing a harm specific to the plaintiff. Taxpayer standing, or citizen standing, is a very rare exception to the general prohibition on suits by citizens who disagree with a policy of the Congress or President and seek to enjoin operation of the policy in court. Taxpayer standing is limited to the rare instance in which a taxpayer seeks to enjoin an expenditure specifically authorized by the Congress on the grounds that the expenditure related to the taxing and spending power violates the Constitution and in which the taxpayer can demonstrate a logical link between the plaintiff's argument of harm and the unconstitutionality of the expenditure.

Put another way, taxpayer standing must satisfy the famed "double nexus test": a nexus between between the plaintiff's status and the type of legislative enactment attacked, which is usually a use of the taxing and spending power, and a nexus between that status and the precise nature of the constitutional infringement alleged.

The arena in which such cases have been the most successful has been to enjoin an expenditure that would itself violate the Establishment Clause.

### third-party standing (jus tertii or vendor standing or agency standing)

The standing of one person to assert the claim of another. Third-party standing is the allowance of one person to argue the claims or case of another, not as an agent or next friend but owing to a secondary effect upon the party seeking standing from the primary effect upon the person not in court. Thus, the party who achieves standing is said to "stand in the shoes" of the party whose injury is the basis of that party's argument. At common law, the person who claims standing asserts jus tertii, the right of a third party. Some relationship is usually required between the person injured and the third party who would present a claim based on the other's injury, such as the vendor of a product whose purchase is banned by a vendee. The vendor may argue the rights of the vendee, claiming jus tertii from the relationship. Associations have a form of jus tertii when the association represents the interests of its members.

#### associational standing (organizational standing)

The ability of an association to argue the claims of its members in court. Associational standing is the power of an association to present claims on behalf of its members. Standing in federal court is restricted to situations in which the association can prove three elements: if its members would have otherwise had standing to sue, each in their own right; if the interests the association seeks to protect are germane to the association's purpose; and if neither the claim asserted by the association nor the relief it requests requires the participation of individual members in the lawsuit. Standing for associations in state courts is usually less restrictive. An association, even in federal court, need not be incorporated.

**autre droit (auter droit or en autre droit)** A party with standing to assert the rights of another. A party autre droit is a representative of another, whether as a plaintiff or as a defendant. Thus, an executor or an agent may be in an action as a representative of a real party in interest, such as the estate or the principal.

**zone of interests (zone-of-interests test)** The public and private interests to be protected by a law. The zone-of-interests test is an element of standing to challenge an administrative ruling through judicial review, by which the plaintiff must assert an interest that is within the scope of the interests that the statute or constitutional provision underlying the administrative rule is intended to protect. Therefore the zone of interests is roughly equivalent to the legislative purpose of constitutional policy, in that the zone of interests is the purpose to be carried out by the administrative rule. The plaintiff must have an interest that would have been furthered or affected by that purpose in order to complain of a rule or regulation. The zone-of-interests test is not exhaustive of the bases of standing, and traditional claims of direct and unique harms are sufficient even if the harm was not to an interest affected by an underlying purpose of the statute or constitution.

**Star Chamber** *See:* court, English court, Star Chamber (Court of Star Chamber).

**stare decisis** New cases should be compatible with old cases. Stare decisis is a maxim of precedent that requires judges to apply the reasoning from earlier decisions so that later cases reach the same result as earlier cases with similar facts. Latin for "let the decision stand," the primary rationale for the maxim is to ensure fairness among similar litigants, but it also increases predictability in the common law. On the other hand, stare decisis can lead to an overly rigid view of law that does not evolve to reflect new social circumstances and new views of justice. Further, it encourages the application of general rulings in specific factual circumstances that distort the original rationale.

Thus, the general understanding of stare decisis is that the rationale of an earlier case arising under a given doctrine of law is to be applied in a later case on similar facts arising under the same doctrine. Even so, the general understanding is not to be followed if (a) the older case was based on flawed reasoning or application of the precedents even as seen in the context of its time; (b) the application of the older reasoning would work some injustice in the circumstances of the later case; or (c) if application of the older reasoning in the later case would reach an absurd or unreasonable result in the light of a change in circumstance brought about by time.

*See also:* precedent, binding precedent.

**state** The political unit that is capable of making and enforcing laws. The state is the political unit that has no superior as a matter of governance. Sovereignty is assigned to some entity within the state at the level of the state, and laws are made by and for the state as a corporate action. In international law, the state is the basic unit of legal personality. The United States, in this context, is one state.

In the United States and other federations, the state may describe sub-national subdivisions that hold a lesser degree of authority but operate in a similar way while still subordinate to a larger state. A state of the U.S. may have further subdivisions, such as counties, municipalities, or regional boards, which derive their authority from the state.

*See also:* county; municipality (municipal corporation); nation (national or nationalism or nationality).

**state actor** *See:* civil rights, Civil Rights Act, state actor (governmental actor).

**state agency or federal agency** *See:* agency, agency as government authority (state agency or federal agency).

**state bar association** *See:* bar, bar organization, state bar association.

**state constitution** *See:* constitution, state constitution.

**state court** *See:* court, U.S. court, state court.

**state criminal appellate court** *See:* court, U.S. court, court of criminal appeals (state criminal appellate court).

**state interest** *See:* interest, state interest, substantial state interest; interest, state interest, legimate state interest (legitimate governmental purpose); interest, state interest, important governmental objective; interest, state interest, compelling state interest (compelling governmental purpose); interest, state interest (governmental interest or govermental purpose).

**state official** *See:* official, state official.

**state preemption of local law** *See:* preemption, constitutional preemption, state preemption of local law (state-local preemption).

**state residence requirement** *See:* bar, admission to the bar, state residence requirement.

**state secret** *See:* secret, state secret (official secret).

**state secrets privilege** *See:* privilege, evidentiary privilege, state secrets privilege (national security privilege).

**state sovereign immunity** *See:* immunity, sovereign immunity, state sovereign immunity | 2. cities and counties; immunity, sovereign immunity, state sovereign immunity | 1. exceptions; immunity, sovereign immunity, state sovereign immunity (eleventh amendment immunity).

**state sovereignty** *See:* sovereignty, state sovereignty, equal footing doctrine (equal-footing doctrine); sovereignty, state sovereignty.

**Act of State Doctrine** Rule requiring judicial abstension from adjudication of official acts by foreign governments. The Act of State Doctrine is a judicial policy by which a U.S. court cannot hear a claim or resolve a dispute that involves an adjudication of the lawfulness of an act by a foreign government, even if that government is not a party to the case. Any case that requires a decision of whether a foreign state or department of a foreign state acting within its sovereignty violated the law should be avoided as a prudential matter by the U.S. courts. Act of State is often confused with sovereign immunity, and the primary difference is that the foreign government is not a party to the claim in which Act of State arises; the government is usually a defendant pleading sovereign immunity in a case in which that doctrine arises. Act of State is a prudential rule of abstention that may be abrogated by the court or by the Congress, as in the Second Hickenlooper Amendment.

**Bernstein letter**  An executive letter disclaiming act of state in a given action. A Bernstein letter is a letter issued by a responsible official in the U.S. Department of State for the purpose of disclaiming any interest by the executive branch in the courts avoiding a particular action under the act of state doctrine, because the action might require a judgment that an act by a foreign sovereign is in violation of international law, and the United States has no foreign policy that would conflict with such a determination. The issuance of such letters is not, as of 2010, a current practice by the Department of State, although a related but quite different practice, of issuing a letter requesting court abstention in such cases has arisen under the same name. A court may consider a Bernstein letter in its decision, yet the court is not bound by it. On the other hand, the absence of a Bernstein letter in an action means nothing. The original Bernstein letter was issued by State Department Acting Legal Advisor Jack Tate in Bernstein v. N. V. Nederlandsche-Amerikaansche, Stoomvaart-Maatschappij, 210 F.2d 375, 376 (2d Cir. 1954). Note: Tate letters are letters invoked in actions in which sovereign immunity is raised as a defense, all of them based on the Tate letter announcing U.S. adoption of a restrictive view of immunity; Tate letters should not be confused with Bernstein letters, which are directed toward act of state defenses.

See also: immunity, sovereign immunity, foreign sovereign immunity, Tate letter.

**flag state**  See: vessel, flag vessel (flag state or flag ship).

**head of state (head of government)**  The leader of a state, or its government, or both. A head of state is the leader of the state, the person (or sometimes a group) who is vested with the power and authority of the state, and who either leads the government as well or has powers on behalf of the state that are superior to those of the government. The head of government is the leader of the government, the chief executive who is personally responsible for the administration of the state. In parliamentary systems, the head of government is also the head of the parliament.

Most states of the Earth have divided the role of the head of state from the head of government. The United States has a single chief executive in the presidency, who is both head of state and head of government. More commonly, the offices are divided, and a head of state is selected by a distinct means from the head of government. A monarch is usually selected by descent from a prior monarch. A president is often head of state and is usually elected, often by a different means and with a distinct electoral. A prime minister is usually a head of government and is usually elected from a parliament or assembly or selected by the head of state.

Under international law, both heads of state and heads of government are absolutely immune from criminal and civil process while in office. Attempts to serve process on a head of state or a head of government may only succeed if the recipient waives immunity.

**minimal state**  The state and laws that least regulate the individual. The minimal state is a libertarian ideal of government that promotes radical individualism, leaving the state and the laws no role in society other than to secure protection against violence and fraud, thus leaving the state no police powers to regulate most matters of health, safety, welfare, or morals or to provide basic elements of social welfare, such as education. In the minimal state, such matters are provided by individuals for themselves, acquiring their fruits by trade, or by voluntarily forming associations.

See also: jurisprudence, libertarian legal theory (libertarianism or libertarian jurisprudence).

**nanny state**  A derisive term for a paternalistic and regulatory state. The nanny state is a derogatory term for the regulatory state, in its paternalist rules, such as seat-belt laws; in its safety-net social services, such as last-resort medical care, old age insurance, and anti-disability regulation; and in its regulation of the market through such tools as property zoning, environmental laws, product safety laws, anti-trust laws, and banking regulations. With rare and ironic exception, the term has a strong political bias, and it is rarely used to label similar supports for financial and tax incentives for industry and agriculture or to describe protective tariffs or trade laws.

**night-watchman state (minimal state)**  The state least able to intrude in personal lives. The night-watchman state is a metaphor for the minimal state, which reflects an approach promoting radical individualism, leaving the state and the laws no role in society other than to secure the minimum protection against violence and fraud. Thus, the state should have no police powers to regulate most matters of health, safety, welfare, or morals and do not ensure or provide basic elements of social welfare, such as education.

**U.S. state**  One of the states and commonwealths comprising the United States. A state of the United

States is one of the fifty states and commonwealths that are the components of the United States. Of these, forty six are states and four — Kentucky, Massachusetts, Pennsylvania, and Virginia, are commonwealths. There is no constitutional difference among them, and these states are represented in the United States Senate and the United States House of Representative with a vote. For most purposes, to say "state" implies these fifty jurisdictions as well as the District of Columbia. These fifty-one jurisdictions have votes in the presidential electoral college.

For other purposes, state includes all insular possessions, including the fifty states and commonwealths and D.C., as well as the insular jurisdictions, such the commonwealths of Puerto Rico and the Northern Mariana Islands, American Samoa, Guam, the U.S. Virgin Islands, the Trust Territory of the Pacific Islands, and the Federated States of Micronesia.

### state action (governmental actor or state actor)

An action by, for, with, or under the protection of state law or officials. State action is an action that deprives a person of a federally protected right because of some relationship between the action and the state. The element of state responsibility or involvement or authorization of the act makes the act state action. In the absence of a state relationship to an act that harms a person, the person might have a private cause of action but no constitutional claim, because the Constitution, or at least the Fourteenth Amendment, has been interpreted to apply to state action and not to private, or non-state, action.

The forms that state relationship to an act may take are numerous. Some are direct, including all sovereign acts of the state, such as the passage of a state constitution, statute, or regulation, or the act of a state official within the scope of the official's duties. Some are indirect, such as the property relationship of leasing from the state, or acting as a surrogate or agent for the state. Some are matters of state license, as when a person acts under color of state law, to do something that benefits that person but does so under an allowance reasonably claimed under state laws.

*See also:* law, color of law.

### state-local preemption *See:* preemption, constitutional preemption, state preemption of local law (state-local preemption).

### state-of-mind exception *See:* hearsay, hearsay exception, hearsay allowed regardless of witness availability, then-existing condition (state-of-mind exception).

### Statehood Clause *See:* constitution, U.S. Constitution, clauses, Statehood Clause.

### statement

A declaration made aloud or in writing. A statement is any position made in words, whether the words are written or spoken aloud. A statement may be made in a pleading, affidavit, deposition, or testimony. A statement may be made before a witness or reporter. A statement may be voluntarily made in the speaker's own words, or it may be coerced or subscribed by the speaker by assenting to responsibility for written and presented by a drafter. In general, the law presumes a statement is voluntary and made in the words of the speaker.

A statement may also be a bill or account.

*See also:* declarant; representation, representation as statement of fact; hearsay, statement (hearsay statement).

### statement against interest *See:* hearsay, hearsay exception, hearsay exception declarant is unavailable, statement against interest (admission against interest or declaration against interest).

### Statement and Accounts Clause *See:* constitution, U.S. Constitution, clauses, Statement and Accounts Clause.

### statement under oath *See:* oath, statement under oath (sworn statement or unsworn statement).

### false statement

Deliberate act of false speech or omission to an official. A false statement is the act of making a written or oral statement to a government official, including a police officer, that the speaker or writer knows to be false or misleading with the intention that the reader or hearer will form a false impression of a fact that is material to the purpose of the official's investigation, examination, analysis, or review. Making a false statement is a felony. Making a false statement under oath is perjury.

Making a false statement is closely related to many offenses, some of which may be lesser included offenses. Giving an official or state agent a false name or alias is, in many jurisdictions, a distinct misdemeanor, while the falsification of a government-issued identification is a different offense and may be either a felony or a misdemeanor.

*See also:* perjury (perjure).

### incriminating statement

A statement by a defendant or witness tending to demonstrate a person has committed a crime. An incriminating statement is any statement that tends to identify a specific person as having performed a criminal act or having criminal responsibility. An incriminating statement may be a self-incriminating statement, a statement that inculpates the speaker, suggesting the person speaking has committed a crime of some sort. Yet incriminating statement also includes a statement that exculpates the speaker, as is the case when a person's statement tends to demonstrate a different person committed a crime. A rule of thumb for identifying an incriminating statement is whether a prosecutor would be reasonably likely to attempt to introduce the statement at trial.

*See also:* incrimination (incriminate or incriminating).

### voluntary statement

A statement freely made by the speaker. A voluntary statement is a statement made by a person competent to act and make such a statement, made as result of the speaker's rational and free will and without coercion, violence, threats, or intimidation to the speaker or to another person or thing causing the speaker to do so.

*See also:* voluntariness (voluntary or volunteer).

## statistic

**statistical evidence**   *See:* proof, statistical proof (statistical evidence).

**statistical proof**   *See:* proof, statistical proof (statistical evidence).

**vital statistics**   The collected data on births, deaths, marriages, and divorce. Vital statistics are the records that affect the overall growth or decline of a human population in a given area, which are usually collected from official records or from customary records, such as a birth certificate or death certificate, of general reliability, such as a hospital record or church record. Statistics collected include each live birth, each still birth or abortion, each death (usually including the cause of death, each marriage, and each divorce. The statistical analysis of such information is essential to many modern activities, including the prevention of disease and the planning for future needs of the labor force and retirees. Vital statistics are collected by each state in the United States and coordinated by the National Vital Statistics System of the Centers for Disease Control.

*See also:* hearsay, hearsay exception, hearsay allowed regardless of witness availability, vital statistics.

**status**   A person's condition, especially within a hierarchy. Status is the condition of a thing or a person, a measure of its utility or significance, wealth or value. A person's status depends on the criteria that are then relevant, such as whether a person is a suspect or not, a convict or not, a parolee or not.

In the feudal common law, status was largely a matter of the tenancy one controlled. The primary forms of status were the monarch, tenant in chief, mesne tenant, lord of a manor, freeman, villein, and serf.

In modern law, status is highly context-dependent, and a person at any moment may be thought of as having a variety of distinct forms of status. A person may be an adult as opposed to a minor, a person competent as opposed to legally incompetent, and so on. Nearly every category of legal relationship or classification leads to some form of status, such as an owner, a landlord, an adverse possessor, a licensee, a tenant, a trespasser; or a fugitive or a police officer.

A status offense, which is generally unconstitutional, is a criminal offense defined by a person's condition, such as being homeless.

*See also:* condition, condition as status; crime, status crime; offense, status offense (status offender or juvenile status offense or juvenile status offender).

**status crime**   *See:* crime, status crime.

**status offender or juvenile status offense or juvenile status offender**   *See:* offense, status offense (status offender or juvenile status offense or juvenile status offender).

**status offense**   *See:* offense, status offense (status offender or juvenile status offense or juvenile status offender).

**status quo**   The way things are. Status quo is Latin for the way the situation is now. The phrase has entered English to mean not only the present state of affairs, but to imply a certain equilibrium (or, occasionally, advantage or disadvantage) in various forces or interests that exist for the time being.

**status quo ante (make-whole relief)**   The way things were before. Status quo ante, Latin for "the way things were before" (impliedly, before some event in question occurred), is a measure of remedy, which is the amount of money or the tasks required to restore some relevant conditions to their condition before the defendant's action had brought the plaintiff harm. The status quo ante is sometimes called make-whole relief, as it requires either an order enjoining the defendant to do what is required to reverse the effects of an unlawful action or an assessment of damages sufficient to reflect the entire costs of the injury to the plaintiff.

**statute (statutory law)**   A law written by a legislature and enacted by a constitutional process. A statute is a law passed by the legislature of a state or the Congress of the United States and then enacted into law according to the procedures specified for the enactment of legislation. A statute may be a public bill or a private bill, and it may provide for any law within the legislative power to create. The procedure for enactment usually is signature by the chief executive, although it may also result from a legislative vote to override the executive's refusal to assent to a proposed statute. A statute becomes effective, or enters into force, on the date of its enactment or on the date specified within its text.

*See also:* legislation (legislate).

**Statute de Donis Conditionalibus**   *See:* de, de Donis (Statute de Donis Conditionalibus).

**Statute of Descent**   *See:* descent, Statute of Descent.

**Statute of Frauds**   *See:* fraud, Statute of Frauds.

**Statute of Limitations**   *See:* limitation of actions, Statute of Limitations.

**Statute of Repose**   *See:* limitation, limitation of actions, Statute of Repose.

**Statute of Uses**   *See:* use, doctrine of uses, Statute of Uses.

**Statute of Wills**   *See:* will, Statute of Wills (Wills Act).

**statutory displacement of the common law**   *See:* displacement, statutory displacement of the common law.

**statutory forfeiture or prior public use bar**   *See:* patent, abandonment of a patent, constructive abandonment of a patent (statutory forfeiture or prior public use bar).

**statutory heir** *See:* heir, forced heir (statutory heir).

**statutory homestead** *See:* homestead, statutory homestead.

**statutory intent** *See:* intent, legislative intent (statutory intent).

**statutory interpretation** *See:* interpretation, statutory interpretation, rule of reason in interpretation; interpretation, statutory interpretation, legislative purpose, Yick Wo case (Yick Wo rule or Yick Wo doctrine); interpretation, statutory interpretation, legislative purpose; interpretation, statutory interpretation, canon of construction; interpretation, statutory interpretation | legislative history; interpretation, statutory interpretation (construction of a statute or statutory construction).

**statutory law** *See:* statute (statutory law).

**statutory penalty** *See:* penalty, statutory penalty.

**statutory power** *See:* power, statutory power.

**statutory presumption** *See:* presumption, statutory presumption.

**statutory rape** *See:* rape, statutory rape, illicit sexual activity; rape, statutory rape (sexual abuse of a minor).

**statutory right of redemption** *See:* redemption, statutory right of redemption.

**creature of statute** Any entity or legal doctrine created by legislation. A creature of statute is something created by the passage of a statute, particularly an entity such as a corporation, or a doctrine, such as workers' compensation, that originates in the law through legislative creation. Creatures of statute are peculiarly limited by the courts to the attributes created by the legislature, although judicial interpretation and construction of those attributes is inevitable.

**private act (private law or private bill)** An act that does not regulate general conduct but only a private concern. A private law — also known as a private act, or special law — is an act passed as a private bill within a legislature's powers but relating only to a specific matter between one or a small number of individuals or entities. Many private laws are allocations of funds to reimburse a particular cost or expense or to make an ex gratia payment or settlement for a wrong done by the government.

**public law (P.L. or PL)** A law of universal application. A public law is a law that has the potential to affect any and all members of the public. It contrasts with a private law, which is passed for the relief of an individual, entity, or group.

**remedial statute** A statute that reforms the existing law in some manner. A remedial statute is a statute that reforms the law in some way, other than a penal statute or other statute creating a burden or criminal liability for an individual. Remedial statutes are customarily interpreted with liberality, to apply to situations in which application is possible but not inevitable. Contrastingly, penal statutes are narrowly construed. A single statute may, however, be both penal and remedial, so that it is applied more liberally in situations in which its remedial effects are the more significant in the application of the statute to the case at hand.

*See also:* law, remedial law (curative law).

**severability of statute (severance of statute)** Legislation may be modified by excising unenforceable clauses. Severance of a statute, or the general principle that the statute's provisions are severable, allow the statute to be interpreted in components, so that if a provision is found to be unconstitutional and unenforceable, that portion may be voided, but the remainder of the statute may still be enforced. This might not be possible if an essential provision of some statute is void, but in a complex code, one portion that is improper may be elided leaving the rest fairly intact.

*See also:* contracts, contract interpretation, severance (doctrine of severance or severability of clauses or blue pencil rule).

**stay** A halt to proceedings for a time or until a further order. A stay is a legal obligation to stop some action or proceeding for a set time, or until an event occurs, or until an order is issued by a competent authority that lifts the stay. A stay may be ordered by a court or may occur by operation of law, automatically upon some condition, such as a filing in bankruptcy.

*See also:* reprieve.

**stay pending appeal** *See:* supersedeas (stay pending appeal).

**automatic stay** Statutory injunction against debt collection from a debtor in a bankruptcy proceeding. The automatic stay bars creditors from attempting or continuing to collect debts after a debtor has filed for bankruptcy, except under rare circumstances when a motion for relief is granted by the bankruptcy court. The stay has numerous exceptions, but applies to most commercial and private unsecured debts, and it ordinarily continues to apply to all property subject to the bankruptcy estate after the debtor is discharged.

**stealing (steal or stolen)** Taking the property of another and intending to keep it illegally. To steal is to take the property of another, whether in violation of the law or not. This general term is usually not the basis of a criminal prohibition, which usually employs the more technical terms of theft, larceny, burglary, embezzlement, trespass, and the like. However, property acquired by any such methods is stolen property, and the intentional or knowing receipt, possession, or sale of stolen property is a separate offense.

*See also:* burglary (burglar or burgle or burglarize or burglarious or burglariously); theft; kleptomaniac (kleptomania); larceny (larcenous); embezzlement; trespass (trespass to land).

**stem cell**   *See:* biotechnology, stem cell.

**stereotype (gender stereotype or racial stereotype or stereotypical)**   A preconception regarding one or all members of a group. A stereotype is an assertion that some attribute or characteristic is to be found in most or all of the members of a group or class of people or any category of thing. A stereotype is a generalization, and in some instances the stereotypical expectation may have a high likelihood of accurate depiction of a given person or thing.

The law forbids the use of stereotypes in regulating some aspects of human activity. For example, in employment law, personnel decisions that affect an individual that are based on stereotypical assumptions regarding race, gender, ethnicity, or other regulated classifications are generally barred under Title VII. The creation of categorical regulation affecting individuals that are based on stereotypical assumptions are unlikely to pass even the lowest levels of scrutiny under the due process of law. The application of general regulations or exercise of regulatory discretion according to stereotype also violates due process, as in the forbidden forms of racial profiling in arrest or detention of suspects.

An assertion of some aspect of a person within a category that is in fact defining of the category, such as the assertion that only females become pregnant, is not a stereotype because it is both factually correct and qualified so as not to define the whole group. Yet an assumption or observation that is not inherently true for each member of a group or class, or an assertion derived from something else, particularly when applied to a specific person based only on the assumption of the aggregate, is a stereotype, such as the assertion that a particular woman will be a poor employee because she will become pregnant. This is a stereotypical observation because there is no basis for it to be true, and it is an assertion about a specific person derived from a categorical stereotype.

*See also:* prejudice; discrimination, employment discrimination, bona fide occupational qualification (B.F.O.Q. or BFOQ); metaphor; discrimination; profile, racial profiling; profile (police profiling or criminal profiling).

**stet**   Do not alter. Stet is an editorial mark, Latin for "let it stand," which is commonly written when a change or deletion is suggested, to countermand the suggestion and leave the text as it was before the change or deletion. The effect is the same whether the author marks stet to an edit or an editor marks stet to an author's change, the text and corrections prior to the edit or change is to be printed. Stet is so commonly used, the word is also treated as a verb, as to stet, or, "Did she stet that?"

**stevedore**   A person who loads or unloads a vessel in port. A stevedore is a specialized form of a dockworker, the person who is responsible for loading and unloading cargo into a vessel, as well as for maintenance and repair of the cargo and its containers in the vessel or on the pier or in the facility in which it is stored on land. As the work of dockworkers has become more specialized, and the provinces of distinct unions, a stevedore is likely to be an operator of a crane or loader or a cargo handler, in contrast to longshoremen, who conduct more general work. Similar work may be done by members of the crew, who do not thereby become stevedores but are seamen or sailors.

*See also:* longshoreman; seaman (sailor).

**still born child**   *See:* child, dead–born child (still born child).

**stipulation (stipulate)**   A formal agreement, especially of a fact in evidence. A stipulation is an agreement between parties. In contracts, a stipulation was once an agreement concluded with specific formalities in a ceremony in which the parties asked and answered questions. In contemporary usage, a stipulation is fact or promise agreed between the two parties in a larger contract. Any provision within a contract or an agreement may be referred to as a stipulation.

In evidence and in trial practice, a stipulation is an agreement between the parties in the action as to a specific fact that might otherwise be contested, or to a jury instruction or other point of law that might be contested. A stipulation may not ordinarily be the basis for an appeal unless the party that challenges it can prove a fraud or mistake based on later discovered evidence.

**stock**   *See:* share.

**stock as equity security**   *See:* share, share as stock.

**stock offering**   *See:* share, share as stock, stock offering.

**stock option**   *See:* share, share as stock, stock option (warrant for stock or stock warrant or securities option or share option).

**stock purchase warrant**   *See:* security, securities, securities warrant (stock purchase warrant).

**stock split**   *See:* share, share as stock, stock split (scrip issue or share split or bonus issue or capitalization issue).

**stockholder**   *See:* shareholder (stockholder).

**stockholder equity**   *See:* shareholder, shareholder equity (stockholder equity).

**stocks**   *See:* punishment, shaming punishment, stocks (pillory).

**stolen**   *See:* stealing.

**stolen property**   *See:* goods, stolen goods (stolen property); property, stolen property.

**Stone Court**   *See:* court, U.S. court, U.S. Supreme Court, Stone Court.

**stonewalling (stonewall)**   Refusal to disclose information or to engage in a process to which another party is entitled. Stonewalling is the refusal to disclose information, or to engage in some process, despite a legal obligation of the stonewalling party. The term "stonewall" is a reference to the Confederate General Andrew Jackson, whose soldiers held their line against a fierce Union advance at the first battle of Manassas, or Bull Run. The analogy, made popular during the Nixon administration, suggests that the stonewalling party will be assailed to release the required information or to engage in the negotiation or legal proceeding but will not give in.

Despite the illustrous name, a lawyer should neither bar nor delay the disclosure of information that is required in law or equity to be disclosed to the requesting party. When such a request for information is made under court rules or a court order, to fail to provide it is sanctionable as contempt. Further, a refusal to participate in a mandated legal process is the basis both for sanctions under the rules and contempt of court.

*See also:* sandbagging (lying behind the log or unfair gamesmanship).

**stoning**   *See:* punishment, rajm (stoning).

**stop**

**police stop (investigative stop or traffic stop)**   A stop of a vehicle or pedestrian by police officers. A police stop is the stop of a pedestrian or of a vehicle, in order to cite the pedestrian for a law affecting public decency or behavior, or to cite the driver for an infraction of the traffic laws, or as a part of a checkpoint or other safety or law enforcement exercise.

A police stop, particularly a traffic stop, is a seizure within the meaning of the Fourth Amendment, which does not require a warrant owing to its inherently limited and specific purpose. The stop should be limited and brief, unless the officer reasonably develops probable cause to believe an offense has been committed by an occupant of the vehicle, or there is evidence of a crime in the vehicle. In either case, any attenuated search then commenced by the officer must be conducted within the limits of an allowed search conducted by observation of such of the vehicle and passengers as are in plain view and review of the license and registration. The limits to traffic stops are constitutional, and the government responsible for the officer is required to train police officers to respect them. Even so, the danger that a police stop can be a pretext for a more general search must be considered in examining the validity of an arrest or a search that is initiated by the stop.

*See also:* pretext (pretextual); arrest, pretextual arrest (pretextual stop).

**checkpoint stop**   A police stop of all passing vehicles on a road. A checkpoint is a police stop and limited search of all vehicles passing on a road, for a specific purpose of law enforcement. A checkpoint stop is a search in the meaning of the Fourth Amendment, but it is allowed despite the lack of individualized suspicion or probable cause as to any vehicle, driver, or passenger prior to the stop.

The stop is allowed owing to the balance of the needs of law enforcement compared to the light burden to privacy. A checkpoint must be carried out toward some appropriate purpose of law enforcement, which cannot be a dragnet to see what criminal conduct can be found. Stops limited in their purpose and performance to such purposes as are allowed, such as a search for illegal aliens near the border, a search for drunken drivers, or a search for an escaped prisoner or dangerous person known to be in an area, or to seek information from the public about a recent hit-and-run accident.

**sobriety checkpoint**   A traffic checkpoint intended to ensure unimpaired driving. A checkpoint whose intended and primary purpose is to assess the condition of the drivers of the vehicle checked, in order to determine that each is in a sober condition to drive safely and not posing a danger owing to the influence of a drug or alcohol. If evidence of a crime is determined related to the driver's consumption of drugs or alcohol, the driver may be subject to arrest, and if there is evidence in plain sight giving probable cause another crime has occurred, the search of the vehicle may be expanded beyond that purpose.

*See also:* sobriety, field sobriety test.

**investigative detention (stop and frisk or Terry stop)**   A stop and brief search based on probable cause. An investigative detention, which is a "Terry stop" or a stop and frisk, is a stop and cursory search of a suspect reaching no farther than the suspect's outer clothing, based either on the suspect's consent or on the police officer's already established reason to believe the person is involved in criminal activity; or the officer's belief from observation of the individual that criminal activity is in progress and that the individual may be armed and dangerous; or the police officer's knowledge of information obtained from another source such as citizen witness, reliable informant or official report indicating that the subject is involved in criminal activity. Such unwarranted stops and frisks were declared constitutional in Terry v. Ohio, 392 U.S. 1 (1968).

*See also:* stop, police stop, roadblock; search, warrantless search.

**roadblock**   A systematic operation stop and check of some or all vehicles passing a given location. A roadblock, generally, is any device or police operation that stops traffic from proceeding on a road or past a checkpoint. Roadblocks are used to close roads to all traffic, to close roads to unauthorized traffic, or to inspect traffic and search vehicles.

A police roadblock is an operation using police officers and equipment to evaluate systematically all vehicles passing the operation, employing some routing for further investigation of some or all vehicles, drivers, passengers, or cargo in furtherance of some legitimate police goal. Ensuring conformity with driver safety laws and laws against contraband, searching for a wanted or missing person, and license inspection are all legitimate police goals, although searches that may proceed beyond the minimal invasion of public inspection of the vehicle from outside, question of the driver and passengers, and reviewing license and registration are subject to the standards of warrant or probable cause and/or constitutionally reasonable search. A roadblock that allows too much discretion to the police officers managing it, or that is unreasonable, violates the Fourth Amendment ban on unreasonable searches. Still, a roadblock managed according to standards that are neutral as to any vehicle or person and that are objectively applied to achieve a valid aim of law enforcement is appropriate, and its stops are not unconstitutional.

*See also:* stop, police stop, investigative detention (stop and frisk or Terry stop).

**stop-loss insurance** *See:* insurance, insurance coverage, stop–loss insurance.

**storekeeper** *See:* quartermaster (storekeeper).

**straight life insurance or ordinary life insurance** *See:* insurance, category of insurance, life insurance, whole life insurance (straight life insurance or ordinary life insurance).

**straight-line method interest** *See:* interest, interest for money, straight-line method interest ( add–on or precomputed interest or straight–line interest or rule of 78s).

**stranger** A non–party, or a non–citizen. A stranger, in general, is a person who is unknown to the parties relevant in some conversation. In most contemporary legal usage, a stranger is a person or entity who is not a party, either to a judicial proceeding or to a contract, negotiation, or some other legal or social relationship. Thus, for example: a stranger to a proceeding is neither a party nor a person or entity having a sufficient relationship to a party as to be bound to its judgment or outcome as a matter of stare decisis. A stranger to a contract is neither a party to the contract nor an intended beneficiary. A stranger for purposes of child custody is a person who is neither a parent nor a close family member.

*See also:* intermeddler (officious intermeddler or volunteer or stranger).

**stranger picketing** *See:* union, labor union, labor dispute, labor picket (stranger picketing).

**stranger to the deed** *See:* deed, stranger to the deed.

**straw (strawman or straw man or straw person)** A third party who holds property solely to transfer it to another. A straw, or a straw man, is a third party to whom a grantor transfers land strictly for some technical reason, after which the straw obligingly transfers the land back to the grantor or on to the intended grantee. A straw was once popular as the person to whom the owner of lands in tail would grant the land, thus disentailing the land, after which the straw would regrant the lands to the original grantor who would subsequently hold them not in fee tail but in fee simple. The practice is still used in some jurisdictions to create a joint tenancy or a trust. Any transaction in which a party represents another in a purchase, to whom the purchase will later be transferred, is a straw transaction.

*See also:* fee, estate in fee, fee tail, bar of entail (barring of entail).

**straw argument** *See:* fallacy, straw argument (man of straw argument).

**Strickland test** *See:* counselor, right to counsel, ineffective assistance of counsel, Strickland test.

**strict construction** *See:* interpretation, strict construction.

**strict in scrutiny fatal in fact** *See:* scrutiny, standards of scrutiny, strict scrutiny, strict in scrutiny fatal in fact.

**strict liability** *See:* liability, strict liability.

**strict necessity** *See:* necessity, private necessity, strict necessity.

**strict product liability** *See:* liability, product liability, strict product liability.

**strict scrutiny** *See:* scrutiny, standards of scrutiny, strict scrutiny, strict in scrutiny fatal in fact; scrutiny, standards of scrutiny, strict scrutiny, footnote four (footnote four or the footnote); scrutiny, standards of scrutiny, strict scrutiny.

**strike (struck or strike off or struck off)** To write through or to remove. To strike, as an exercise of judicial authority is to remove something or someone from a list, record, or writing. The term, from the old English for making a stroke with with a pen, is used when a person is removed from a list, language is removed from a pleading or filing, or an act or statement in the courtroom is removed from the record. Thus, a witness who is struck is not to be called to testify.

**strike from the record (motion to Strike or Strike Motion)** An order to remove a statement or occurrence from the record of proceedings. An order to strike from the record is an order, ruling, or judgment that requires a word, phrase, sentence, passage of testimony, or a pleading, an exhibit or other document, to be marked as removed from the record of a proceeding. Any matter that is introduced into the record in violation of the law, the rules of court, or a valid court order matter may be struck for cause from the record, unless it has become final and the period for modification of the record has passed. Likewise, any improper matter may be struck from a pleading or filing in court. Once struck from the record, the matter that has been excised may not be the subject of reliance by any party, except for the purpose of arguing the validity of the order to strike.

In a trial, hearing, or other proceeding, an order to strike is a requirement that some statement or occurrence was not allowed under the rules or customs of the court, and it is to be disregarded from all further proceedings. In most cases, the court reporter does not actually excise the matter, but makes a note that it is struck. Further reference to matter struck from the record is forbidden, except for such limited purposes as claiming that striking is insufficient or improper.

*See also:* mistrial.

**strip mine**   *See:* mine, strip mine.

**strip search**   *See:* search, bodily search, strip search.

**strong arm robbery**   *See:* robbery, strong arm robbery.

**structural error**   *See:* error, structural error.

**structuralism**   Human thought and action are products of the structures of society. Structuralism is a way of understanding law and the effect of law on individuals. It arose in linguistics, psychology, anthropology, and sociology, becoming a tool not only of legal sociology but a strong influence on critical legal scholars and their successors, as well as upon communitarians. In law, it was presaged by Sir Henry Maine and Freidrich von Savigny, whose studies of custom as a source for national understandings of law resonates with this approach.

**student intern or internship or clerkship**   *See:* clerk, law clerk (student intern or internship or clerkship).

**student lawyer rules**   *See:* clinic, clinical legal education, student lawyer rules.

**sua sponte**   At one's own instigation, or on one's own motion. Sua sponte is Latin for of one's own will, and in law, it refers to an act by a court that might have been made at the request or motion of a party but is instead done at the court's instigation. An order sua sponte is an order for which no party cast a motion.

**sub**   Under, or beneath. Sub is Latin for below, under, underneath, or any sense in which something is in a physical or rhetorical place lesser than something else.

**subclass**   *See:* class, class action, subclass.

**subcontract**   *See:* contract, subcontract.

**subcontractor**   *See:* contract, contractor, sub-contractor (subcontractor).

**sub judice**   Before the court. Sub judice is a Latin tag that is used to describe an issue, party, claim, or other element of the case that is then before the court for consideration.

*See also:* case, case at bar (instant case or case at issue).

**sub-prime loan**   *See:* loan, sub-prime loan.

**sub-prime mortgage**   *See:* mortgage, sub-prime mortgage.

**sub-tenant**   *See:* tenant, tenant as lessee, sub-tenant (undertenant or sub-lessee).

**sub nomine (sub. nom.)**   Under that name. Sub nomine is a Latin term for "under the name of" something specifed. A person acting under an alias "John Doe" is sub nomine John Doe. To use the term more generally is to describe a particular label for some concept, as in "England has long had no judicial review sub nomine" which means the name wasn't used, though the concept might possibly be found under another name.

*See also:* name, alias.

**sub rosa**   Secret. Sub Rosa, Latin for under the rose, describes any process that is off the record or done in secrecy. The term has many sources in antiquity and the middle ages, when the rose was widely accepted as a symbol of secrecy. A sub-rosa hearing is kept secret from the jury, usually being held in chambers with its participants admonished not to reveal contents of the discussion in court. Intelligence services are sometimes said to be sub rosa.

**subdivision (subdivide)**   The division of a portion, as in dividing a parcel of land. Subdivision is the process as well as the result of dividing a thing divided into smaller portions. The most common use of the term is the subdivision of a parcel of land with a single owner into smaller parcels of land for sale to different owners.

A subdivision, in many jurisdictions, requires a particular hearing before the land-use authority or zoning board following a specific process. In many jurisdictions, a subdivision must be approved following the submission of a map of the proposed new tracts, including such easements, and infrastructure such as roads, sewers, water, and power will be required, as well as a covenant that such infrastructure will be constructed before the sale of any property.

Other contexts at law require subdivision as process of dividing a portion, such as an inheritance among the survivors or an heir. The process for subdivision in most cases is specified in equity or law. For instance, the subdivision among surviving heirs may be per stirpes or per capita.

**subinfeudation**   *See:* feud, feudalism, subinfeudation.

**subjacent support**   *See:* support, support of land, subjacent support.

**subject**   Any person required to obey the law. Subject has a variety of distinct senses, the most fundamental to the law being a person who is required to obey the law and is liable to sanction under the orders of legal officials. This sense is most visible in the technical description of subjects in a monarchy, the ordinary person subject to the authority of the crown. Such a person is the effective equivalent within the legal system to a citizen in a democracy. Yet in a jurisprudential sense, a subject includes not only subjects of the crown in England or citizens of the United States in the U.S., but any person or entity that is subject to the law of those states at a given moment. Thus, an alien is a subject while in the jurisdiction of either legal system. Note: subject is both a noun and a verb, a subject is a person whom the state subjects to certain requirements by law.

**subject matter jurisdiction**    *See:* jurisdiction, subject matter jurisdiction.

**subject as experimental object**    A person, animal, plant, sample, or other thing, on which is made an experiment, procedure, or observation. The subject of any technical operation, experiment, observation, or other activity is the person, animal, plant, sample, device, or other thing on which it is performed or from which observations are made. A human or vertebrate animal subject to experimentation that is federally funded requires that the experimentation be conducted according to a protocol approved by an institutional review board.

**subject as national**    A member of a nation-state without citizens. A subject is a person who is a member of a nation-state who owes allegiance to its monarch or other head of state. There is a great similarity between the meaning of subject in such states and the meaning of citizen in others. Both subjects and citizens are nationals of their respective states.

*See also:* citizen; citizen, citizenship; nationality (national).

**subject as subject matter**    The thing in issue. The subject is whatever is the object of a law, contract, complaint, indictment, action, or any other thing. Subject matter is a redundant but customary phrase for the subject of any law or proceeding.

The subject, or subject matter, of a contract includes all of the purposes of the contracting parties, both those patent in the contract and the understandings of the parties.

The subject matter of a civil action is an element of the jurisdiction of the court over the action. The subject matter must fall within the scope of the subject matter allowed to the court, or the court lacks the jurisdiction to hear the matter. Subject matter is usually by the nature of the dispute that gives rise to the action, such as a contract dispute or a family law dispute. However, for certain purposes, the subject matter is defined as much by the sources of law that are proposed as the basis for the resolution of the dispute or by the dominant remedy sought. It is unexceptional that certain matters are not heard before certain courts, such as a criminal proceeding not being brought in a court of equity to determine guilt (although a court of equity might hear an action to enjoin a criminal proceeding). The greatest source of controversy tends to be the federal division of subject matter by those matters in federal competence because the action presents a federal question, which

may be defined by any of the three forms of subject matter: topic, source, and remedy.

**subjective (subjectivity or subjective standard)**    Evaluated from one person's actual point of view. Anything subjective is understood from the view actually held of an actual observer at a given event, including secrets, beliefs, emotions, and mistakes in impressions that go to make up the understanding a person has in fact at some time in question. Subjectivity, with its emphasis on the subject forming the impression, is the standard for evaluating a person's motives, beliefs, satisfaction, or mental state. Subjective understanding and knowledge is the basis for good faith, bad faith, mens rea, mistake, intention, willfulness, and a variety of other standards in the law that depend on state of mind.

Evidence of a subjective understanding held by a person at some time past is usually developed from that person's testimony. Yet the danger of self-serving testimony in such cases is often great, and collateral evidence of an objective nature may be useful in assessing a past subjective understanding.

*See also:* faith, good faith (bona fide); objective (objective standard or objectivity).

**subjective approach**    *See:* entrapment, Sherman-Sorrells doctrine (subjective approach).

**subjective theory of contract**    *See:* contract, contract interpretation, subjective theory of contract.

**sublease**    *See:* lease, sublease (sublessee or subtenant).

**subordination (equitable subordination or subordination agreement)**    The placing of one obligation in a lower priority than another. Subordination is an aspect of the reorganization of obligations or debts, by which obligations are given varying levels of priority, and those given less priority are subordinated to those with higher priority. Subordination may occur as a result of a subordination agreement, by which a debtor and lienholders agree to subordinate an existing debt to a newer debt. When the priority of an obligation is lowered owing to misconduct or a failure of duty by the obligee, the lowering is equitable subordination.

*See also:* priority.

**subornation (suborn or suborned)**    To instigate another's wrongdoing, especially to engage in deceit. Subornation is the act of encouraging another person to commit a deceitful act, or otherwise to breach some duty. To suborn a witness is to encourage perjury; to suborn a juror or official to encourage favoritism. The manner in which a person is suborned is immaterial to the fact of subonation, whether it is accomplished by enticement, persuasion, threats, or violence.

*See also:* perjury, subornation of perjury.

**subornation of perjury**    *See:* perjury, subornation of perjury.

**subpoena**    An order to appear before the court to provide evidence. A subpoena is a summons issued to a witness or other party who might give evidence or assist the court to appear in court. A subpoena is usually served on a witness as a means of notice of a procedure at which the witness is desired and assuring the witness will appear, at a trial, hearing, or discovery. Failure to appear makes the witness liable for contempt of court or whichever body issued the subpoena. Legislative assemblies, grand juries, courts, and similar bodies have the authority to issue a subpoena, which is the subpoena power and implies the lawful ability to enforce the subpoena with a contempt power. The term, from the opening words of the common–law writ in Latin, is "under penalty," the warning of the potential for punishment if the order is not obeyed by the recipient. Note: a subpoena differs from a summons, in that a subpoena requires a person to appear to give evidence or for some similar purpose, while a summons is used to hale a party into court as a defendant.

*See also:* contempt of court; summons (summon or summoned).

**subpoena duces tecum** A subpoena ordering a witness to bring documents. A subpoena duces tecum, which is sometimes now issued as a subpoena ordering the production of documents, is a subpoena that requires not only that the witness appear at the time and place stated but to produce documents, books, papers, or other evidence under the control of the witness. The extent of control for which a witness may be required to produce is sometimes heavily argued, but if the witness has a legal ability to gain access to the documents, the subpoena may require their production.

**subrogation** The substitution of one creditor for another. Subrogation is the substitution of one claimant by another claimant for the same claim, brought about when the new claimant pays the earlier claimant's claim in a circumstance in which the earlier claimant then assigns the claim to the later claimant. The most common form of subrogation occurs when an insurer pays an insured for an injury caused by a third party, and the insured assigns the insured's underlying claim to the insurer, who then pursues the third party on the subrogated claim. Subrogation thus requires both payment to the original claimant and assignment by that claimant. Assignment may occur as a result of the insurance agreement or as a result of an assignment particular to the settlement of the claim.

*See also:* insurance, insurance claim, subrogation (subrogation clause).

**subrogation clause** *See:* insurance, insurance claim, subrogation (subrogation clause).

**subscribing witness** *See:* witness, attesting witness (subscribing witness).

**subsequent agreement** *See:* agreement, subsequent agreement.

**subsequent condition** *See:* condition, condition subsequent (subsequent condition).

**subsequent remedial measure** *See:* repair, repairs (subsequent remedial measure).

**subsidence (subside)** The settlement of property lower into the ground. Subsidence is the lowering of a property or structure compared to the surrounding land. A portion of a building may settle, slide, shift, fall, or slip; and soil may sink, seep, or ooze owing to subsidence. Subsidence may be caused through the natural movements of the earth, or it may result from human activity, including excavation, construction, and the extraction of water or other substances from wells. Note: "subsidence" is pronounced with a long "i".

*See also:* support, support of property (right of support); support, support of land, subjacent support; support, support of land, lateral support.

**subsidiary corporation** *See:* corporation, corporations, conglomerate, subsidiary corporation.

**subsidy (subsidize)** Money given in aid of an activity. A subsidy is a grant of aid, usually though not always a grant of money, to a person or entity in order to assist in the performance of some activity. A subsidy may be made by any person or entity to another. In particular, however, subsidy is a practice of governments in giving funds or aid to manufacturers, planters, miners, or others to diminish the costs of production or of doing business generally.

In international law, one state's subsidy of its producers may violate international trade treaties that prevent one state from artificially supporting the trade from its producers in another state. The effect of a subsidy allows a producer who receives it to lower the price of goods and remain profitable. Not all subsidies are forbidden, however, and the forms, purposes, and scale of subsidies that are allowed or forbidden is subject to frequent change. Note: subsidy is both the practice in general (which is also subsidization) and the specific grant provided to a given recipient. The verb for such practices is subsidize.

*See also:* price, support price (price support).

**substantial (substantially)** Solid, and clearly enough to serve a given purpose. Substantial is a measure of sufficiency, which is applied, in general discourse, to depict a number of properties, such as the solid construction of a building or the impressive extent of a person's riches. In these and other general senses, substantial usually means more than enough or more than required. In law, substantial is usually a measure by which some standard is met, a substantial purpose or substantial evidence. These senses in particular tests of law each have subtle differences, yet their sense in common differs from the general meaning.

In law, substantial has both the older sense of being solid or meaningful as well as the comparative sense of being sufficient for a given purpose but not necessarily all that is possible. In its sense as solidity, it is found in a substantial right or a substantial duty (as opposed to being hypothetical or speculative).

In its comparative legal sense, substantial is more than the least but not so much as perfection. A substantial showing is a reasonably sufficient showing. A substantial purpose is more than legitimate but not as much as compelling. A substantial cause is significant but not all. Substantiality in law is enough to be real, enough on which to rely for most purposes but not so much as to be unquestionable.

**substantial advancement of a legitimate interest** *See:* taking, regulatory taking, substantial advancement of a legitimate interest (substantially–advances test).

**substantial cause** *See:* causation, substantial cause (substantial factor).

**substantial compliance** *See:* compliance, substantial compliance.

**substantial evidence** *See:* review, standards of review, substantial evidence; evidence, substantial evidence.

**substantial factor** *See:* causation, substantial cause (substantial factor).

**substantial performance** *See:* performance, substantial performance.

**substantial probability** *See:* probable, substantially probable (substantial probability).

**substantial similarity** *See:* copyright, infringment of copyright, substantial similarity.

**substantial state interest** *See:* interest, state interest, substantial state interest.

**substantially probable** *See:* probable, substantially probable (substantial probability).

**substantially-advances test** *See:* taking, regulatory taking, substantial advancement of a legitimate interest (substantially–advances test).

**substantiation (substantiate)** Substantial proof, or its provision. Substantiation is the process of, and the evidence for, the proof of a thing in issue by sufficient evidence for the process in which the thing is considered. Substantial evidence is not perfect evidence but evidence that is enough to prove the claim, defense, tax deduction, allegation, or other issue in the proceeding in which it is considered. What amounts to substantial is often defined by statute or regulation. A tax deduction is substantiated by a valid receipt for the deductible expenditure. An allegation of abuse is substantiated when all of the evidence available indicates that an act of abuse as defined by law has occurred.

**substantive due process** *See:* due process of law, substantive due process.

**substantive law** *See:* law, substantive law.

**substantive right** *See:* right, legal right, substantive right.

**substitution (substitute)** The replacement of one with another. Substitution, in general, is the replacement of one thing by another. In law, substitution is the alternation by one party for another in any legal role. The party placed into the role is the substitute; both parties are substituted, one for the other.

Substitution of parties in litigation occurs when one party succeeds to the claims of another, say through subrogation, assignment, or inheritance, the successor party is substituted for the first party. Substituted as to the party against whom a claim may be made may take place with less formal requirements than for substitution of a party, for, generally, the same reasons.

Substitution in the legal powers takes many forms, including that of an agent who may stand in the place of a principal and that of an estate that stands in the place of a decedent.

*See also:* subrogation.

**substitution of parties** *See:* appearance, substitution of parties.

**subterfuge** A plan or scheme to deceive. A subterfuge is a plan, scheme, or activity of any form that is intended to evade the truth or to deceive an observer in any manner. Subterfuge may be an element of fraud or other specific crimes, such as forgery.

Subterfuge is not, however, inherently illegal. Acts of misdirection, camouflage, confusion, false impression, or advertising that do not violate a duty or amount to fraud are lawful. Subterfuge by a witness under oath, however, is perjury.

**subversion or overthrow of the government or subvert** *See:* sedition, subversive organization (subversion or overthrow of the government or subvert).

**succession (successor or predecessor)** The transmission of a right or obligation from one to another. Succession is the process by which rights and obligations in one person or entity are transferred to another. In law, succession takes myriad forms, particularly the process of an heir, devisee, or legatee succeeding to an interest on the death of its holder. A future interest holder succeeds to the interest at the termination of the prior possessory interest. When a duty or right is assigned, the assignee succeeds to the obligation or benefit conferred by the assignor. When one corporation acquires another, the acquiring company succeeds to such rights and interests as it acquires as well as to what debts and obligations it acquires from the acquired corporation. When one state succeeds another, acquiring the property and population of the prior state, along with its compatible or accepted legal duties and obligations. A person elected or appointed in the place of the holder of public office or corporate office succeeds the present holder in a process of succession. (In the case of the President of the United States, the process in preparation for succession is transition, and the succession is accomplished by inauguration.) Note: the successor is the one who succeeds, and the predecessor is the one who is succeeded.

*See also:* assignment, assignment as succession to property (assign); heir, haeres (heres or haeredes proximi or natus or legitimus or remotiores or factus).

**successive confession** *See:* confession, successive confession.

**successive representation** *See:* representation, legal representation, successive representation.

**successor or predecessor** *See:* succession (successor or predecessor).

**successor trustee** *See:* trustee, fiduciary law, successor trustee.

**sue (countersue)** To commence or to continue a lawsuit. To sue is to act as a claimant in a civil action in law or equity. Whomever is the claimant sues those against whom the claim is brought; so the plaintiff sues the defendant. A counterclaim is said to be countersued, so the defendant countersues the plaintiff.

*See also:* suit (lawsuit); claim, counterclaim.

**suffrage** *See:* vote, suffrage (suffragette).

**suggestion of bankruptcy** *See:* bankruptcy, suggestion of bankruptcy.

**suggestion of death** *See:* death, suggestion of death.

**sui** Of himself, herself, or itself. Sui is a common root for words and phrases that refer to something done to oneself or aspects that affect a thing in itself or person in the doing. It is the root of suicide.

**sui generis** One of a kind. Anything sui generis is an example of its type, often implying it is the only one of its kind. In this latter sense, the implication might be that whatever is referred to is unusual because of its rarity or its recent creation, or it might be a token of such excellence, such as in a person's performance, that the performance is in a class of achievement above all others. There is a more linguistically informed sense in which the implication is that the entity under discussion is simply of a different form from the other compared entities, which is to say that it is of its own kind. In this sense, a delict according to law is neither a tort alone nor a crime alone in a common law system (though the conduct underlying the delict might be either), but a delict is a breached obligation in the civil system. It is sui generis of delicts.

**sui juris (non sui juris)** Legal capacity to act independently under the law. Any person or entity sui juris has a full and independent capacity to act in a manner that the law will bind that person or entity to valid contracts or other obligations entered and likewise bind others to them. A person over the age of majority who is not under an order of conservatorship or guardianship or is patently under some incapacity is presumed to be sui juris.

*See also:* capacity; capacity, legal capacity, incapacity (lack of contractual capacity or lack of capacity).

**suicide (felo de se)** Self-homicide. Suicide is the intentional taking of one's own life. At common law, suicide, or felo de se, was a felony if it was made by a person of sound mind, otherwise it was the act of a person insane and not a crime at all. Such distinctions have been eliminated in U.S. jurisdictions, in which suicide is not a crime by the victim. Some states have criminalized attempted suicide, although none do as of 2010.

Many states have interpreted murder statutes to include the provision of assistance to a suicide or provided for a distinct offense for providing material assistance to a person contemplating suicide, if the victim does commit the suicide. Note: a suicide has several senses as a noun, including both the act causing death, the resulting death, and the person who commits it.

**assisted suicide (aiding a suicide)** The crime of assisting another in committing suicide. Assisted suicide is the knowing provision of material aid to a person who intends to commit suicide, with the intent of assisting that person in the successful ending of that person's own life, and that person then commits suicide within a time relevant to the assistance or using such assistance provided. The specific elements of the offense vary slightly from jurisdiction to jurisdiction. In general, physicians who provide pain relief for a person in chronic pain have not, as a matter of fact, been found to have assisted in suicide.

*See also:* death, right to die.

**suit (lawsuit)** Any proceeding in a court of justice. Suit, broadly, is any action in court, although contemporary usage is more likely than in Bouvier's day to restrict the use to civil actions. In civil actions at law there is no difference in meaning between suit and lawsuit, although it would be only appropriate to use suit to describe a cause in admiralty or equity, rather than lawsuit.

Suit bears a similar origin as both the action heard in court and the clothes worn there, in that the law French suitte for the attendance of the court officials gave rise also to siwte, for the officials' uniforms, from which emerged both suit as attendance in court and suit as the clothes one wears there.

*See also:* sue (countersue).

**suitor** A party to a civil action. A suitor is any party to a lawsuit. It is a more general term than merely one who sues, which is generally the role of the plaintiff or claimant. A party who brings suit or defends one is a suitor.

In medieval English law, a suitor was a person bound to attend the county court or the court of the hundred.

In its more general sense, a suitor is a person who seeks to persuade another person to become that person's spouse, or at least to favor the first person with special attention. From this sense comes the sense of a suitor as any party seeking a special relationship with another, selected party, such as a target for a negotiated merger or other voluntary acquisition, or a supplier seeking a contract with a merchant.

**sulfur oxides (sulfur dioxide or SO₂)** A product of burning sulfur. Sulfur oxides are a group of chemicals formed by the combustion or oxidation of sulfur. Sulfur oxides are released by any combustion for energy production in which the fuel contains sulfur. Sulfur dioxide is a common form of sulfur oxide that is used as a criterion contaminant for the measurement of sulfur oxides generally.

Sulfur oxides form acids when combined with water. Acid rain is usually produced by the interaction of atmospheric sulfur oxides, as well as nitrogen oxides, with water in the air. The contact of sulfur oxides with water bodies may increase the acidity of the water directly.

See also: pollution, air pollution, criteria pollutants, sulfur dioxide ($SO_2$).

**sum (sum certain)** An amount. A sum, in U.S. law, is an amount of money, usually the amount that a debtor owes a creditor or the amount to be paid on a contract. The term is derived from the addition of component values to reach a total, or a sum, that is owed. A sum certain is an amount that is unchanging, but that is fixed at a precise number, at least for the given time it is to be paid.

**Sumerian law**

**Code of Hammurabi** The earliest extant collection of laws. The Code of Hammurabi is the modern title for a collection of 282 laws from Babylonia, or Sumer, created under the auspices of King Hammurabi, around 1780 B.C.E., and carved into a great stone stele. Though there were earlier laws, and there is indirect evidence of much earlier legal systems, this is the oldest and most complete compilation of early laws known as of the beginning of the twenty-first century. Discovered in 1901, it is now located in the Louvre.

**summary** A recitation of the essential elements of something longer or detailed. A summary is the presentation of the high points of a proceeding, instrument, pleading, book, argument, or any other thing or process of greater length of detail. A summary is, generally, considered less authoritative than is the full narrative from which it is drawn. The term is the Anglicized version of summa; some lawbooks are entitled summae, and others are summaries.

**summary eviction** See: eviction, summary eviction (disposess proceeding).

**summary judgment** See: judgment, summary judgment, reasonable-inference rule (reasonable inference); judgment, summary judgment, partial summary judgment; judgment, summary judgment, Morgan Rule of Civil Procedure; judgment, summary judgment, Celotex standard; judgment, summary judgment.

**summary proceeding** See: proceeding, summary proceeding.

**summation or closing statement at trial** See: trial, argument at trial, closing argument (summation or closing statement at trial).

**summer associate** See: lawyer, law firm, lawyers, associate, summer associate (summer clerk).

**summon or summoned** See: summons (summon or summoned).

**summoner** A person who summons others to appear in court. A summoner is a minor officer of the court who summons individuals to appear in court as witnesses, as defendants or others who must answer a subpoena, or as jurors. The role is performed in contemporary U.S. courts by bailiffs, constables, deputies, and other police officers. In some civil-law countries, the office is still common. The role was immortalized in Chaucer's Canterbury Tales, in which the summoner was an officer of an English ecclesiastical court.

See also: manciple; pardoner; summons (summon or summoned).

**summons (summon or summoned)** An order of the court that a defendant appear before it. A summons is an order issued by a court in a civil or criminal action that orders the defendant to appear in court to defend the complaint or to suffer a default judgment or not doing so (in a civil action) or a penalty for not doing so (in a criminal action). The summons is part of service of process, delivered with the complaint in a civil action. It may be used in lieu of an arrest warrant in a criminal action. In either case, the summons must be served on the defendant.

In federal court, the civil summons is actually written by the attorney for the plaintiff, signed by the clerk of court, and served by a U.S. marshal or appointed process server. In cases not against the government, the defendant must appear, usually within 21 days of service of the summons and complaint, or the plaintiff may move for default judgment. A criminal summons is prepared by the prosecutor, specifying a date and time for the defendant to appear. A magistrate or judge must sign it, and it is served either by a U.S. marshal or police officer. If the defendant does not appear, the judicial officer will issue a warrant for failure to appear. Note: a summons differs from a subpoena, in that a subpoena requires a person to appear to give evidence or for some similar purpose, while a summons is used to hale a party into court as a defendant. Note also: to summon a party is both to issue a summons and to have it served.

See also: subpoena; warrant, arrest warrant; hale into court (hale to court or hail into court).

**Sunday law or Sunday closing law** See: sabbath, blue law (Sunday law or Sunday closing law).

**Sunnah** See: sharia, sources, Sunnah.

**Sunni Islam** Followers of the Sunna, a branch of Islam. Sunni Islam was founded by those who felt that the leadership after the death of the Prophet Muhammad should be determined by consensus of the community from among the Quraish tribe.

**sunset provision**  *See:* legislation, sunset provision (repealer clause or sunset clause).

**sunshine law (open meetings law)**  A law requiring most meetings of public agencies be public. A sunshine law, or open meetings law, is both a requirement that most meetings of public bodies and hearings by public agencies be open to the public and a prohibition on private meetings by members of such bodies or agencies to discuss the work of the group. Exceptions in such laws allow for executive session, or private discussion, for matters of personnel appointment, promotion, discipline, or discharge; matters affecting trade secrets; matters affecting national security or criminal investigations; or financial matters that would affect trade in securities. In some jurisdictions matters related to decisions affecting the management of litigation are excepted. The structure of open meetings laws vary from state to state.

*See also:* information, feedom of information, sunshine law.

**super**  Upon, on, above, ahead, or more important than something else. Super, in English, is a word of relationship depicting something more than ordinary, often something more important, more authoritative, more powerful, or simply larger or better. It is both a word and a prefix in Latin and law French (which used sur in the same sense), in which it is much more likely to represent a relationship in space, usually above, or in time, usually to be moved ahead or to be before something else, or in number or size, usually more than another or more than required, from this arose its sense in law Latin of upon as a matter of time, as in "upon receiving this writ." From this physical sense metaphorically comes the sense of superiority as a matter of authority or responsibility. Thus, a court is sometimes said, but is generally unwilling to be, a super–legislature or a super–administrator.

**supercargo**  *See:* cargo, supercargo.

**superceding cause**  *See:* causation, superseding cause (superceding cause).

**Superfund**  *See:* pollution, Superfund (Comprehensive Environmental Response Compensation and Liability Act or C.E.R.C.L.A. or CERCLA).

**super priority**  *See:* priority, claim priority, super priority.

**superior**  The more important or more authoritative. Anything superior is above something else, something inferior. Superiority is a standard of one person, thing, or idea relative to another. In law generally, something superior is a person or institution that has an authority over another, as, for instance, a superior court has authority over an inferior court. In employment, a superior has a responsibility and authority to supervise an employee. Likewise, in military law, a superior has authority over a subordinate. In commercial law, a superior obligation is an obligation that must be satisfied before an inferior or subordinate obligation. In property, superior title is better and provides a right of ownership greater than inferior title.

**superior order**  *See:* war, law of war, war crime, superior order (Nuremburg defense or good sergeant defense or lawful order defense).

**superior title**  *See:* title, paramount title (superior title).

**supersede**  *See:* supersedeas, supersede.

**supersedeas (stay pending appeal)**  A stay of the enforcement of a judgment pending appeal. Supersedeas is the term for the writ ordering a stay pending appeal, which is the stay of enforcement of a judgment rendered in a trial court while the party bound by the judgment pursues its appeal. The usual condition to take an appeal that a bond be posted as assurance that the judgment will be satisfied if the appeal is lost is thus known as a supersedeas bond (although not all jurisdictions still use this term). As a result, supersedeas is now more likely to be a shorthand description of the bond than of the stay itself.

*See also:* bond, supersedeas bond.

**supersedeas bond**  *See:* bond, supersedeas bond.

**supersede**  To stay an action pending appeal. The verb form of supersedeas is supersede, which in law means to stay a judgment pending appeal (whether or not a security is posted to secure the stay).

Supersede is easily confused both in meaning and in its spelling. The sense in which it is used in general, non–legal usage is to replace something or someone that is obsolete or decrepit with a newer or superior thing or person. Yet supersedeas is not a substitution or an alteration of the judgment, and so to supersede in the sense does not lead to the replacement of anything unless the judgment is reversed or vacated on appeal, which in any event would occur owing to a different order. The other manner in which supersede might be confused is that it really is not to be spelled with a "c."

**superseding cause**  *See:* causation, superseding cause (superceding cause).

**supervening condition**  *See:* condition, supervening condition (supervene).

**supervening illegality**  *See:* illegality, supervening illegality.

**supervisor**  A person who oversees or manages another person or a place. A supervisor is a person who literally watches over something or someone. As a matter of employment, a supervisor is a person who is responsible for the assignment of tasks of another person.

In many counties, the legislators of the county are supervisors.

**supervising attorney**  *See:* clinic, clinical legal education, supervising attorney.

**supplement (supplemental)**  Anything added to something else to complete or update it. A supplement is an addition, a thing added to another thing as an extension and not as a substitution. For example, a supplemental brief is a brief in addition to a brief filed before, not a substitution for it.

**supplemental disclosure**  *See:* disclosure, discovery disclosure, supplemental disclosure.

**supplemental jurisdiction**  *See:* jurisdiction, supplemental jurisdiction, common nucleus of facts (common question); jurisdiction, supplemental jurisdiction.

**supplemental pleading**  *See:* pleading, supplemental pleading.

**suppliant**  Petitioner or movant for discretionary relief. A suppliant is, in effect, a supplicant, a party who humbly petitions or seeks a remedy or some other relief, impliedly suggesting that the remedy is not clearly justified or the relief clearly owed, but seeking the exercise of the authority of the court as a matter of discretion or grace.

**supply contract**  *See:* contract, specific contracts, supply contract, take or pay clause; contract, specific contracts, supply contract, requirements contract; contract, specific contracts, supply contract, output contract (outputs contract); contract, specific contracts, supply contract.

**support**

**support price**  *See:* price, support price (price support).

**support of property (right of support)**  The support of a structure or the land itself. The support of property is the physical requirement of the property to rest on and against other property to avoid collapse. A right of support is inherent in all real property, unless it has been specifically conveyed away by covenant. The right of support in buildings creates an easement over each of several adjoining buildings that each must be maintained sufficiently so as not to cause damage to the others. The right of support in lands requires that no use of one's land cause the subsidence of another's. The right of support in land is a right both to lateral and to subjacent support.
*See also:* subsidence (subside).

**lateral support**  The support of the lands beside it. Lateral support of land is the support of land by soil and rock in the land nearby the land in question. A right of lateral support in a parcel, for example, includes a right to bar a quarry from digging beside the parcel in any manner that might cause the upper lands to subside or collapse. Lateral support may sometimes also require subjacent support. Lateral support is also required of adjoining buildings, especially of buildings sharing a party wall. The right of lateral support creates an easement over surrounding parcels that must be maintained to ensure support of the dominant parcel.
*See also:* subsidence (subside); support, support of land, subjacent support.

**subjacent support**  The support of land by lands below it. Subjacent support of land is the support of land by soil and rock in the land below the land in question. A right of subjacent support in a parcel, for example, includes a right to bar a mine from digging below the parcel in any manner that might cause the upper lands to subside or collapse. Subjacent support may sometimes also require lateral support. The right of subjacent support creates an easement over surrounding parcels that must be maintained to ensure support of the dominant parcel.
*See also:* subsidence (subside); support, support of land, lateral support.

**suppression (suppress)**  The restriction of a person's action or speech. Suppression, politically, is the restriction of the activities of a person or group, to harass, scare, or diminish the potential for greater political or cultural power. It has also generally been considered as the prohibition of circulation of publication of written material, such as pamphlets, books, or newspapers.

In trial, to suppress some evidence or testimony is to bar its introduction. Evidence collected or offered in violation of the law may be barred by an order following hearing on a motion to suppress.

**suppression hearing**  *See:* search, exclusionary rule, suppression hearing, Dunaway hearing; search, exclusionary rule, suppression hearing (Dunaway hearing or Franks hearing or Huntley hearing or Mapp hearing).

**supra**  Above, higher, or preceding in a text. Supra represents anything that is above or preceding something else. Supra when used in a note or citation signals a reference that is prior to that point in the text; the citation referred to will be found before this reference to it.
*See also:* infra; loco citato (loc. cit.); passim.

**supremacy (supreme)**  Being subject to no higher authority. Supremacy is the aspect of sovereignty that allows no authority above it. A supreme power is the highest power, and a supreme court is the highest court.

The Supremacy Clause notes federal law "shall be the supreme Law of the Land; and the Judges in every State shall be bound thereby" regardless of state laws to the contrary. Thus, federal law is more authoritative than state law, and when there is a conflict between them, the state law must be given no force but avoided in order to enforce the federal law.

*See also:* preemption, constitutional preemption, federal preemption of state law (congressional preemption or express preemption or implied preemption); sovereignty.

**Supremacy and Oaths Article**  *See:* constitution, U.S. Constitution, Article 6 (Article VI or Article Six or Obligations, Supremacy and Oaths Article).

**Supremacy Clause**  *See:* constitution, U.S. Constitution, clauses, Supremacy Clause.

**supreme being or creator**  *See:* God (supreme being or creator).

**supreme court**  *See:* court, supreme court.

**surcharge**  An additional or premium charge applied to a debt. A surcharge is, literally, a charge on top of what would otherwise be owed. A surcharge is a fee, tax, service charge, or other amount that is added to a debt, bill, or claim that would otherwise be owed, that is added owing to an additional service or expense incurred by the creditor beyond the services or expenses subject to a standing agreement. That said, a surcharge may be a fee that is added by a creditor or seller without the buyer's consent or other legal justification, in which case it is an overcharge. Note: as with "charge," the word "surcharge" is both a noun and a verb, and to surcharge a party is to add a surcharge to that party's bill or debt.

A surcharge is the remedy assessed against a trustee or other fiduciary for breaching a duty by failure to exercise common prudence in managing the assets of which the fiduciary had charge, to the harm of the trust or other principal of the fiduciary. The surcharge is calculated according to the amount of the loss attributed to the fiduciary's breach of duty.

Surcharge has a more general sense, in which it is the addition of any load to a space, vessel, or device already given a load.

**surety (suretyship)**  A person who promises to pay another person's debt. A surety is a person or entity that agrees to pay the debt of another, who is the principal. Although a surety may stand ready to make good on the promise by the principal that is the subject of the suretyship, most sureties are created as an assurance that a debt or obligation in money will be paid. A suretyship is similar to a guaranty, and at times the terms are used interchangeably. Even so, a creditor may ordinarily make a demand on a surety after the creditor has made a demand and attempted to enforce payment of the debt from the principal debtor (while a creditor may make a demand from a guarantor upon the initial default of payment by the debtor).

**surety bond**  *See:* bond, surety bond (performance bond).

**penal sum (penal sum limit)**  The liability ceiling for a surety. The penal sum is the amount that a surety may be penalized in the event of a default on the obligation assured. In other words, the penal sum is the maximum liability the surety accepts, and therefore the extent of all claims that may be made against the surety, on the surety obligation, whether that obligation was to assure performance or to assure payment on another obligation, regardless of the value of the other obligation.

**surface bargaining**  *See:* bargain, surface bargaining (bad faith bargaining).

**surface mine**  *See:* mine, surface mine (open–pit mine or open pit mine or open–pit mining or strip mine or strip mining).

**surface right**  *See:* property, property right, surface right.

**surgeon general**  *See:* health, health care, surgeon general.

**surplus (surplusage)**  Anything more than needed. Surplus is what is more than was expected or is required in any activity; it is what is left over when a purpose is accomplished or requirement satisfied. What is surplus is always a matter of fact in a given context. Surplus money is more than is budgeted. Surplus goods are more than are contracted or more than are needed. Note: surplus is a noun, a verb, and an adjective. Customarily, surplus was written with no article because it was more often used has an adjective, as in "the money was surplus to requirements." Surplusage was the associated noun. As surplusage has faded in use, the once less–common nominative use of surplus has become more frequent, and it sometimes requires an article and sometimes not: "we are in surplus," or "we have a surplus."

**surplusage as irrelevant language**  Language that is irrelevant to a text. Surplusage in a writing is language beyond what is needed or proper to the form of that writing or to the purpose as it was intended or later understood. Words that are truly surplus to a text are read out of it; they are treated as if they are not there. Yet such a drastic interpretation is not to be employed if there is any meaning or appropriate use that may be assigned to the words. Thus, in pleadings, surplusage may be struck from a pleading by the court if the party can prove the surplus language can serve no useful purpose within the scope of the rules. Yet, if such language is useful to the party opposing its submission, the party may take advantage of the language to show what it will of the weakness of the submitting party's case.

Surplusage in a statute, will, trust, contract, or other instrument is to be given no effect, yet there is a presumption against finding that language is surplus, and it should not be avoided unless no reasonable use for the language may serve as the basis for its interpretation. Likewise, an interpretation of a text, such as a contract or a statute that incorporates the entire text and leaves no surplus is to be preferred over an interpretation that would leave surplusage.

*See also:* hortatory.

**surplusage as overpayment** An amount paid greater than that owed. A surplusage, in the sense of accountancy, is an overpayment, an amount paid from one party to another that is above the amount that was due and owing. A surplusage remains the property of the payor, though it is in the possession of the payee. The payee may, with the agreement of the payor, apply the surplusage to other existing or future debts of the payor to the payee, or the surplusage is to be repaid.

*See also:* overage.

**surprise** Something without warning or notice. A surprise, generally, is something that occurs when those materially affected by it do not expect it to occur. Surprise in the law occurs when something happens without proper and sufficient notice, whether the notice was actual, implied, or constructive. A surprise witness, for instance, is a witness introduced at trial, without having been disclosed during discovery. That the counsel producing the witness might have notified opposing counsel the night before that the witness exists and they will call the witness does not alter the legal significance of the surprise. Surprise is the basis for a reformation of judgment.

Surprise arising from unknown or late–discovered information is also a customary basis for mistake in the reformation of a contract. An instrument drafted as a result of a mistake arising from surprise, or information unknown or known too late to be properly accounted in the drafting, may be reformed. Note: surprise is both a noun and a verb.

**surprise witness** *See:* witness, surprise witness.

**surrebuttal** *See:* rebuttal, surrebuttal (surrebutter).

**surrender** To give up. Surrender, in law, is the act of yielding an interest to another party. To surrender a property interest to another is to transfer the interest to the other, such that the other accepts it. A grant of title is the surrender of title from the grantor to the grantee. A surrender of a lease is the tender of possession and rights in the leasehold from the tenant back to the landlord.

Surrender in military law is the act of a unit, command, or state, in ending armed combat and submitting to the control of an opposing force. International law requires a unit or state to accept surrender when it is offered.

*See also:* quarter.

**surrender of claim** *See:* consideration, surrender of claim; claim, surrender of claim (release).

**surrender of law license** *See:* lawyer, lawyer discipline, sanctions, surrender of law license.

**surrogate** An agent who substitutes for another person or official. A surrogate is a person who is designated to act in the place of another person, either as a deputy or as a replacement. Note: a person designated as surrogate is the surrogate for someone else, such as

a surrogate bishop, who is the bishop's deputy, or a surrogate parent, who takes the place of an absent parent. In New Jersey, the Surrogate's Court is a probate court, and the Surrogate is the probate judge, with jurisdiction over minors and guardianships as well as probate and administration.

**surrogate mother** *See:* family, family planning, assisted reproduction, gestational surrogacy (surrogate mother).

**surrogate parent** *See:* parent, surrogate parent.

**surrogate's court** *See:* court, court of limited jurisdiction, family court, surrogate's court.

**surrounding circumstances** *See:* circumstance, surrounding circumstances.

**surtax** *See:* tax, surtax.

**surveillance** The persistent observation of some object. Surveillance is the practice of watching, listening, or otherwise sensing the presence or actions of a person, place, or thing, in a manner that intrudes upon the privacy of a person observed as the object of surveillance or in the presence of the place or thing observed. Surveillance conducted by police agents from a public space, observing only so much activity as would be available to a passing observer, is not a search. Surveillance is a search if it intrudes upon a reasonable expectation of privacy, such as by an uninvited presence in a residence or car or through electronic surveillance placed in an area of privacy.

**electronic surveillance** Technological observation of an individual or place. Electronic surveillance is any method of observing, covertly or overtly, the actions and conversations of an individual using electronic technology. It includes the use of wiretaps, pen registers, covert listening, transcribing, or recording devices, directional microphones, videographic surveillance, thermal imaging devices, and satellite tracking technology. The Fourth Amendment applies to electronic surveillance just as it does to physical searches. The use of electronic surveillance by agents of the police to intercept and record communications and actions by individuals is a search, unless the surveillance is of activity in which there is no reasonable expectation of privacy. In this respect surveillance is not a search if it amounts to no more than a collection of information in public that might be seen or overheard by passersby.

**covert listening device (bug or wire or hidden microphone)** A device for eavesdropping and recording conversations and other sounds. A covert listening device is a machine for hearing sounds and recording them or transmitting them to a distant receiver, allowing a person to eavesdrop on sounds and conversation elsewhere without being observed. In general, a device placed in a building, place, or another device is called a bug. A device worn on a person's body is called a wire.

A device placed on a phone line is a wiretap or tap. The use of all such devices by the government is subject to the limits of the Fourth Amendment. The use of such devices by private parties is subject to federal and state eavesdropping laws.

**pen register**   A means of recording the number or address of communications. A pen register is a program or machine that detects, decodes, and records information from telephone calls, emails, or other communications, and that stores information regarding the number, address, and identity of the parties communicating. As a matter of statute, a pen register does not collect or record the substance of the communications. A device that records the substance of communications is a wiretap.

**thermal imager**   A sensor depicting heat from people, animals, or buildings. A thermal imager is a form of camera that detects heat rather than light, allowing the user to create a high resolution image of humans, animals, machinery, buildings, and other things or places with variations in the heat emitted. A thermal imager allows its user to detect and observe people at night, in the dark, and in buildings. The use of a thermal imager may amount to a search.

**wiretap (wiretapping)**   Eavesdropping on electronic communications. A wiretap is a device or process by which a person or entity may intercept a communication through a system for the transmission of telephone, telegraph, or other electronic or electric transmission, to listen or record the transmission. A wiretap may be made with the knowledge and permission of one of the parties to the communication, or not. A wiretap by police officers is a search under the Fourth Amendment, and when performed by a private party a wiretap may amount to an invasion of privacy under state law.

**survey (surveyor or surveying)**   The measurement of land and determination of its boundaries. A survey is an assessment of the quantity of land within a tract or parcel as well as the boundaries of the tract, established at the corners and lines running between corners to determine an exact line demarcating the tract from adjoining tracts. The survey creates or confirms the description of property in a deed or conveyance.

A survey must be performed according to the customary methods employed by professional surveyors at the time of the survey, and these customs evolve according to changes in technology. The modern survey is correlated to global positioning satellites, a technique not possible when George Washington surveyed the colony of Virginia. Contemporary surveyors are licensed by the state, and many are bonded. Public lands require a government survey, which is performed by government surveyors.

See also: deed; tract; boundary, boundary line.

**removal of survey mark (benchmark tampering)**   The movement or alteration of a survey mark. The removal, change, or disguise of a survey stake, pin,

benchmark, flag, or other mark by a person without a lawful right to do so is a crime. It is a federal crime to make such alterations of a government-placed surveyor's mark. A person with a lawful right to remove, move, or change a surveyor's mark is a later surveyor who is licensed by the appropriate authority to do so.

**survivor (survive or survival or surviving)**   A person who lives after the death of another, or after a time of danger. A survivor, generally, is a person who survives some dangerous event, such as a storm at sea or personal illness. In law, though, a survivor is a person who lives after the death of another person. A member of the family of a person who dies is a survivor of that person, as is the heir of a decedent. By definition, all heirs are survivors, because one must be alive at the moment of the decedent's death to be the decedent's heir.

A survivor does not necessarily hold a right of survivorship, which exists only for a survivor who is a joint tenant or tenant by the entireties. A surviving trustee of several joint trustees succeeds to the authority of the deceased trustee.

In the event of simultaneous death of two people who would be otherwise heirs, devisees, legatees, or hold other mutual interests such as a tenancy by the entireties, the Uniform Simultaneous Death Act, which is enacted in 20 states, allows persons who die within 120 hours of one another to each be treated as if the other had predeceased, thus allowing the estate of each to descend to heirs or beneficiaries without double taxation or the confounding of wills.

**surviving spouse**   See: spouse, surviving spouse, widow (widower); spouse, surviving spouse (widow or widower).

**surviving spouse's interest**   See: spouse, surviving spouse's interest.

**right of survivorship**   A joint tenant's right to the whole tenancy if the other tenant dies. The right of survivorship is the right in a joint tenant or a tenant by the entireties to ownership of the whole interest in the property subject to the co-tenancy, a right that persists when the right of the co-tenants is destroyed by death. The right exists as a corollary to the defining element in both the joint tenancy and the tenancy by the entireties, by which each tenancy persists only as long as the tenant is alive; when the tenant dies the tenancy interest is destroyed, leaving the other tenant (or tenants) with interests enlarged by the destruction of that tenancy. Thus, of two joint tenants or of the tenants by the entireties, when one tenant dies, the other tenant holds the whole of the property in sole fee, which is the meaning of the right of survivorship.

See also: tenancy, co-tenancy, tenancy by the entireties (entirety or tenancy by the entirety or tenants by the entireties); tenancy, co-tenancy, joint tenancy (joint tenants or joint estate); tenancy, co-tenancy, joint tenancy | right of survivorship.

**survival statute**   A statute preserving a claim after the plaintiff's death. A survival statute preserves a claim that could have been brought by a person while alive so that it may be brought by another person after the person's death. The most common form of survival statute allows an executor or administrator to bring an action on behalf of the decedent (as opposed to the decedent's wrongful death estate or survivors) for compensation for the wrongful death, including damages suffered by the decedent's death. General survival statutes allow all claims in tort to be brought by the executor of the decedent for damages suffered by the decedent prior to death. Both are distinct from statutory wrongful death actions that allow an executor, administrator, next of kin, or interested person to bring an action on behalf of the decedent's wrongful-death estate or survivors for compensation for the wrongful death.

**suspect or reasonable suspicion**   *See:* suspicion (suspect or reasonable suspicion).

**suspect classification**   *See:* class, legal classification, suspect classification (suspect class).

**suspension (suspend)**   A temporary halt to any status, activity, or requirement. A suspension is a stop for a time of anything that would otherwise continue. Thus, to suspend a hearing is to postpone its continuation for an unspecified time. To toll a limitations period suspends its running. A suspension from employment is a temporary halt in employment. To suspend the operation of a rule or a law is to bar its enforcement for a time, without repealing it. The term comes from the word in Latin for hanging up, or, literally, suspending something briefly from the ceiling.
*See also:* constitution, U.S. Constitution, clauses, Habeas Corpus Clause.

**suspension**   *See:* lawyer, lawyer discipline, sanctions, suspension.

**Suspension Clause**   *See:* constitution, U.S. Constitution, clauses, Suspension Clause.

**suspicion (suspect or reasonable suspicion)**   A thought or imagining something is true. A suspicion is a belief that is based on less than complete proof, and it is often a belief that something bad has occurred or that someone has done something wrong or illegal. A suspicion may be based on any quantum of evidence, including a mere possibility.

As a matter of criminal procedure, a suspicion may be the basis of investigation without more, although suspicion may not be the basis of police action in derogation of someone's rights, such as for an investigatory stop or detention, unless it is a reasonable suspicion. Reasonable suspicion requires an articulable basis for a specific suspicion, a belief derived from or justified by evidence that is consonant with the suspicion regarding a specific person or entity and at least a specific category of criminal activity. Reasonable suspicion does not require the level of confidence in the evidence required for probable cause, but it must be based on evidence that

a reasonable investigator would consider sufficient to believe the person suspected of a crime might well have committed it.

Suspect is a derivation of suspicion. To have a suspicion regarding a thing is to suspect the thing. A person who is suspected of committing a crime is therefore a suspect.

**sustainability**   The conditions for a system to persist. Sustainability is the ability of an organism or an ecosystem, a human or a community, a species or a civilization to continue to exist within the conditions that are to be created or found in the future. A given practice, action, or process is sustainable if it is compatible with sustainability overall. Actions that consume more resources than are sustainable when such actions are repeated throughout the population are unsustainable.

Sustainability has become a goal of environmental conservation and protection, the management of the human and natural environments so that they are sustaining and capable of persistence without intervention. Practically every aspect of human activity may be assessed by its degree of sustainability.

**suzeraignty (suzerain suzerainship)**   Sovereignty, particularly by an overlord. Suzeraignty is the capacity to rule over the ruler of others, as when an overlord rules over a lord, a caliph rules over a sultan, or an emperor rules over a prince. This sense is now usually incorporated into the word sovereignty.

**swap (swap agreement)**   An exchange of one thing for another. A swap is an agreement between two or more parties to exchange any things of value for one another, but not to exchange something of value for money alone. All acts of barter are swaps. A thing of value in this sense includes a promise, obligation, option, future obligation, derivative obligation, or collateral obligation. A swap related to a security is not a security but is regulable under the rules governing securities dealers.

Swaps take myriad forms in the exchange of securities and other investments:

An interest swap, or interest-rate swap, allows two parties to make interest payments to one another on a notional principal amount, in order to trade the benefit of rising or falling interest rates without actually making or taking a loan or principal.

A swap agreement includes any contract or transaction that trades a security, debt, commodity, currency, future, option, access to an interest rate, access to a currency rate, benefit or detriment from weather, or any collateral or derivative obligation or claim arising from such things for another quantum of such things. Security-based swap agreements may be swaps of securities or information derived or related to a security or securities. The rest are non-security-based swap agreements. Swap agreements are regulated according to the Commodity Futures Modernization Act and the Dodd–Frank Act by the U.S. Securities and Exchange Commission and the U.S. Commodity Futures Trading Commission.

Note: swap is pronounced "swop."

*See also:* barter; credit, credit default swap (CDS); security, securities, securities regulation, Securities and Exchange Commission (S.E.C. or SEC); security, securities, securities regulation, Commodity Futures Trading Commission.

**swear out or sworn**   *See:* oath, swearing (swear out or sworn).

**sweat equity**   *See:* equity, equitable value, sweat equity.

**sweatshop**   Dangerous, unpleasant, and low-paying work site. A sweatshop is a plant, factory, or other work site in which the workers are routinely worked long hours in dangerous or unpleasant conditions for the least compensation that market will bear. In the U.S. in the early twentieth century, the sweatshop was widely associated with textile plants such as the infamous Triangle Shirtwaist factory, which burned in 1911, killing 146 young garment workers in New York. Although still applied to dangerous workplaces, the force of the term has diminished, and it is now used colloquially to describe any employer that overworks its employees.

**sworn statement or unsworn statement**   *See:* oath, statement under oath (sworn statement or unsworn statement).

**syllogism**   *See:* argument, syllogism (false syllogism).

**symbol (symbolic)**   Anything that depicts or represents something else. A symbol is a sign or anything that represents something else. The symbol may be a physical thing, a person, a person's conduct, a graphic, words that are written or spoken, a sound, or any combination of such things. Words are all symbols, being signs that represent concepts, and their function being to convey to the person who reads or hears them the concepts represented by the words and phrases.

The law employs countless symbols besides words alone. Symbolic delivery is a representation of delivery. Consideration is a representation of intent to be bound to a contract. A badge represents the authority of a law enforcement agent. Physical signs are used to designate the applicability of traffic laws and navigational rules of the road. There are countless others.

The study of symbols, their operation, and their interaction is semiotics.

*See also:* jurisprudence, legal semiotics (semiotics); trademark.

**symbolic delivery**   *See:* delivery, delivery of possession, symbolic delivery | constructive delivery and symbolic delivery; delivery, delivery of possession, symbolic delivery.

**symbolic transfer**   *See:* transfer, symbolic transfer.

**sympathy strike**   *See:* union, labor union, labor dispute, labor strike, sympathy strike.

**syndic**   A civilian fiduciary, like a corporate director or bankruptcy trustee. A syndic is civilian term for a fiduciary agent, the two most common forms being the directors of a corporation, especially a non-profit corporation like the Cambridge University Press, or the assignee of the estates of a bankrupt, something akin to the bankruptcy trustee in U.S. bankruptcy law.

*See also:* trustee.

**syndicalism**   Violence or agitation to overthrow the government. Syndicalism is a term in considerable use in the early twentieth century to depict the advocacy of violence to overthrow the government, particularly on the basis of injustice to workers or support by the government of employers. Criminal syndicalism included not only acts of violence or obstruction but also acts of advocacy for change of the government and, in many jurisdictions, organization of labor into unions. Most state syndicalism laws were rendered void by the Supreme Court in its consideration of the Ohio syndicalism law in Brandenburg v. Ohio, 395 U.S. 444 (1969).

*See also:* sedition; anarchy (criminal anarchy or anarchist).

**syndicate (syndication)**   An affiliation of individuals for a business deal. A syndicate is an aggregation of individuals that is formed in order to enter and perform some particular business transaction. A syndicate may take the form of a business entity such as a corporation or partnership, or it might not, being merely a group who coordinate their participation. A syndicate allows each individual to participate in the transaction, dispersing the risk among the members along with the potential for reward or opportunity. Interests in a syndicate need not be allocated in fair or equal shares among its members, and the shares of a corporate syndicate may be unevenly allocated, just as a partnership syndicate may be general or limited. A syndicate may be long lived or temporary. There are many examples, such as the use of a syndicate to create, fund, and acquire assets for a real estate trust, which then makes a public offering of shares. Syndication is the creation of a syndicate, which is usually done by entry into a syndicate agreement or a syndication agreement.

*See also:* corporation (corporate or incorporate).

**criminal syndicate**   People collaborating over time in criminal acts. A criminal syndicate is a form of criminal organization, being a group of individuals who collaborate in the commission of crimes over time. Different states have slightly varying definitions, some requiring an intent to affiliate with the others to commit any felony, while others limit the crimes to those customarily associated with organized crime, namely extortion, prostitution, theft, gaming offenses, and smuggling contraband.

*See also:* racketeering, organized crime; trafficking, drug trafficking, continuing criminal enterprise (CCE).

**syndrome**   A group of symptoms that may be a disorder or disease. A syndrome is a group of symptoms that are recognizable and identifiable and that are suggestive of a common cause among different people manifesting sufficient symptoms from the group. A syndrome may be a disorder, a disease, or several diseases, or it may be a coincidence of symptoms with various, unrelated causes. In general, however, use of the label "syndrome" suggests that the pathology involved is either unknown or incompletely understood.

**systemic discrimination**   *See:* discrimination, employment discrimination, systemic discrimination.

> The language so far as it affects the present case is pretty sweeping,
> but like all language it has to be interpreted in the light of the tacit
> assumptions upon which it is reasonable to suppose that the
> language was used.
>
> Ohio v. Agler, 280 U.S. 379, 383 (1930) (Holmes, J.).

# T

**t** The twentieth letter of the modern English alphabet. "T" signifies a variety of functions as a symbol. It is translated into Tango for radio signals and NATO military transmissions, into Tom for some police radio traffic, and into dash in Morse Code.

**t as an abbreviation** A word commencing in T. When used as the sole letter of an abbreviation, T may stand for tariff, Tanzania, Tasmanian, tax, taxes, technical, telegraph, telephone, temporarily, temporary, tempore, Tennessee, territory, term, testament, Texas, time, Times, the, title, to, tobacco, top, tort, total, town, trade, trading, traffic, training, trainer, traite, transit, transnational, transport, transportation, treaty, trial, tribunal, trinity, trust, truth, Tulane, Turkey, or Turkish. T&T is usually Trinidad and Tobago, and TNT is trinitrotolulene (an explosive). It may also stand for the initial of the name of an author or case reporter, such as Tappan's Common Pleas Reports, Thompson & Cooke, or Tobacco Tax Ruling.

**t as criminal label** A brand for conviction under benefit of clergy. The letter T branded on the thumb was used to mark those who had been convicted under benefit of clergy of a felony less than murder.
*See also:* f, f as criminal label.

**t as in hypotheticals** Testator, trespasser, tenant, or trustee. T often stands for the testator, the maker of the last will and testament that is in issue in the story of a law school hypothetical. T might also stand for the tenant, or occasionally a trustee or (in torts) a trespasser. When used broadly, as when it is an abbreviation opposed to K, T is likely to mean "tort." More than likely, the T for tenant was traditionally not an English t but a Greek tau, though that distinction is now largely lost.

**T.C. memo** *See:* tax, tax decision, tax court memo decision (T.C. memo).

**T.I.L.A. or TILA** *See:* loan, Truth in Lending Act (T.I.L.A. or TILA).

**T.I.T.S. or TITS** *See:* tenancy, co-tenancy, joint tenancy, unities, four unities (T.I.T.S. or TITS).

**T.R.O. or TRO** *See:* injunction, temporary restraining order (T.R.O. or TRO).

**table**

**table of authorities** *See:* brief, table of authorities (argument list or index of authorities).

**to table (tabled)** To postpone discussion of some matter for an indefinite time. To table a topic, discussion, agenda item, or other discussion of any form of business in a meeting, is to declare the topic "tabled" and so move on to other business or, if there is no business, to move to adjourn. Tabling a matter once was accomplished by a motion "to lay on the table" but now is ordinarily accomplished by a motion "to table." A matter may be tabled for a specified period (until a designated meeting, for example) or, if no period is specified, indefinitely. A motion to table must usually pass by a majority vote. A matter tabled indefinitely may be later placed on the agenda by the secretary or removed from the table by motion voted up by a majority.

**tableau of distribution** *See:* creditor, tableau of distribution.

**tabula rasa** A blank slate. Tabula rasa, in Latin literally translating a smooth table, is a metaphor for either an unknowing person or a project at its start with no commitments yet made.

**tacit (tacitly)** An implied or understood meaning. Anything tacit happens in silence, which in law means that it is known through implication. A meaning that is construed or interpreted in a text that does not have such a meaning on its face is tacitly within the text. A legal circumstance, such as an acceptance of an obligation, that is not expressed in words but is implied by law from circumstances is tacit. A tacit admission is an admission that is a necessary implication of a statement of some other form.

**tacit admission** *See:* admission, evidentiary admission, implied admission, adoptive admission, tacit admission (admission by silence).

**tacit consent or tacit agreement** *See:* silence, silence implies consent (tacit consent or tacit agreement).

**tacking (tack)** Joining several components into a whole. Tacking is the joining of distinct elements into a single legal entity. In law, there are a variety of forms of tacking, such as when a contract provision is tacked onto a draft contract, or several holding periods for a security are combined, or the time of several holders of land is combined for one measure in instances of adverse possession.

In each case, conditions are required in order for the components to be tacked. In order for the components of the contract to be tacked, the contract may not have been finally agreed between the parties, and the insertion must be intended by both parties to be included. Tacking in the holding of a security for the purposes of satisfying a holding period under Rule 144 is only possible in certain instances when the security of a predecessor company is exchanged for a holding company that holds it. In order for tacking to occur between adverse possessors of land, there must be either privity of estate or privity of possession between successive possessors of the land, and for tacking to occur between owners of the land being adversely possessed, there must have been privity of estate.

*See also:* easement, prescriptive easement, tacking; possession, adverse possession, tacking.

**tafsir**   *See:* Shari'a, sources, tafsir.

**Taft Court**   *See:* court, U.S. court, U.S. Supreme Court, Taft Court.

**Taft-Hartley Act**   *See:* union, labor union, labor law, Labor-Management Relations Act (Taft-Hartley Act).

**tail**   An estate tail, or fee tail. Tail is the limitation on an entailed estate, requiring that the interest of the owner be destroyed if there is a failure of issue, in other words if the owner of the estate dies leaving no living child. Tail comes from the French word for prune, as in pruning trees.

*See also:* fee, estate in fee, fee tail.

**tailpipe emissions**   *See:* pollution, air pollution, emission, motor vehicle emission standards, tailpipe emissions (exhaust).

**taint**   Contamination. Taint is corruption through association or intermixing. Originally from the same source as tint or dye added to a material to alter its appearance, taint is both a thing added to a substance or a resulting characteristic of the substance. Taint has a variety of non-legal senses, such as the sulfurous chemical added to natural gas to allow the odorless fuel to be detected by smell.

Though taint is not a term of art in law, it is recurrently used to describe a person or thing that has become less fit for some purpose through a relationship with someone else or something else that is unfit. A person's reputation is tainted through associating with disreputable people. An account is tainted if deposits from an unlawful source are made into it. A witness is tainted if the witness is given false evidence or encouraged to believe false memories. Taint, in this sense, is a component of "attainder."

**takanah (takkanah, takanot [pl.])**   Later Rabbinic legislation. A takanah is an enactment by Rabbinical authorities for the well-being of society, intended to deal with situations not adequately covered in existing halakhah. The takanot were created from the earliest periods, some being ascribed to Moses, to the Geonic period.

**take (took or taken or taking)**   To seize, or to have an entitlement. Take has a general sense in law that is the same as its ancient sense in general usage, to acquire control or possession of something. In this sense, to take—or take control or take possession—is a central act in many actions of legal significance: in all forms of theft and larceny, in conversion and trespass, in acceptance of delivery, in salvage, in entry onto the land, in constitutional takings of property, in the harming of an endangered animal, and in taking custody of a person or evidence.

Take has a distinct sense in property and wills, to mean the entitlement of a person to a grant or share from an estate under a will or from a decedent's intestate estate.

*See also:* taking (takings or taking of private property without just compensation).

**take or pay clause**   *See:* contract, specific contracts, supply contract, take or pay clause.

**take-nothing judgment**   *See:* judgment, take-nothing judgment.

**take prohibition**   *See:* species, endangered species, Endangered Species Act, take prohibition.

**take the fall**   *See:* plea, criminal plea, false plea (take the fall).

**constructive taking (constructively take)**   A taking that is inferred from circumstances without proof of intent. A constructive taking is a taking, whether by a private actor or a government official, that is not determined by proof of a deliberate, intentional act but that is determined by a result in which a taking of some form in fact has taken place. Thus, a person who is in possession of something taken from another person is said, by virtue of the possession alone, to have constructively taken the something. Likewise, a regulation that in a given situation has effectively appropriated so much of the use or benefit or investment in a particular parcel of land that it has become public property has effected a constructive taking, and it is considered inverse condemnation.

**takeover**   The acquisition of a controlling interest in an entity. A takeover is an act, really a series of actions by an individual or entity to acquire control of another entity, either through acquiring a controlling share of voting equity or though acquiring a right to manage the entity and direct its operations. Most takeovers are a result of a process of purchasing a stake in the entity, either through a payment in cash for shares of voting stock, through a swap of equity in the acquiring entity for equity in the takeover target, through an acquisition or assurance of the takeover target's outstanding debt, or some combination of these. Different jurisdictions variously define the portion of equity shares outstanding that amount to a takeover bid, but an offer to acquire five percent or more may be enough to be considered a takeover effort.

**poison pill** Deterrent to a hostile takeover built into the corporate share structure. A poison pill is a provision or amendment to a corporation's bylaws enabling the board of directors to alter shareholder rights in order to prevent a hostile corporate acquisition. There are numerous methods, though one of the most popular remains the preferred share purchase rights plan, by which an acquisition attempt by a single buyer to capture a designated percentage of ownership leads to a dilution of shares, thwarting the takeover. Shareholders can sometimes defeat or assist such plans by forcing a vote on a precatory rights plan, which would attempt to influence the directors to specified actions in response to acts by a potentially acquiring entity. The term "poison pill" seems to have been coined by New York attorney Martin Lipton in 1982.

**tender offer** An offer to purchase outstanding shares of a corporation. A tender offer is a solicitation to the shareholders of a corporation to tender their shares to the offeror for purchase. A tender offer may be made for many reasons, including a corporate buyback of shares outstanding, but the tender offer is a common device for a party seeking to engage in a corporate takeover. What type of offer or announcement constitutes a tender offer has never been fully defined, leaving a deliberately vague definition that requires all tender offerors to comply with securities regulations of such offers. These require disclosure of the real party making the tender and the setting of a public price that persists until the offer is terminated, and they bar price discrimination by which the offeror favors some shareholders over others.

**best price rule** Each shareholder accepting a tender offer is given the best price. The best price rule is a requirement of statute and the rules of the Securities and Exchange Commission that the offeror of a tender offer who varies the terms of price while the offer is open must pay the highest price offered to every shareholder who tenders shares while the offer is open. The rule is intended to prevent price discrimination by the offeror among shareholders.

See also: price (sale price).

**taker** A recipient. A taker is a recipient of a legal or equitable interest, whether the interest is assigned by contract, will, gift, or operation of law. A taker may be considered a taker as soon as an interest is vested or contingently assigned, even if the interest is non-possessory future interest or a contingent interest, in which case the taker is a contingent taker. Not all takers are takers of a lawful interest: a thief is also a taker.

**taker in default** A taker whose benefit depends on another's default. A taker in default is a taker under an instrument, such as a last will and testament or a trust instrument, who receives a grant or benefit only in the event of a failure of condition or failure of a grant or benefit in another taker with a higher priority. Thus, a residuary legatee or residuary beneficiary is a taker in default.

See also: default.

**taking (takings or taking of private property without just compensation)** A government acquisition or control of land requiring compensation to its owner. To take something is to acquire control over it, not necessarily to take possession of it. This broad sense of taking is essential to the idea of taking in the Fifth Amendment prohibition on the taking of private property for a public use without due compensation.

A taking of private property for a public use is an act by a government, or by a private entity to which the power of eminent domain has been delegated, in either of two forms. If the government or entity either takes title to the land by condemnation through eminent domain or if it regulates the use of the land in such a manner that the effect is like taking title in an interest, then the land owner or user is entitled to just compensation for the lost value in the land under the Takings Clause and Due Process Clause.

Not every act of government that intrudes upon the land is a taking. An ancient distinction divides state use of the property for public purposes and state use of the property as an aspect of other police power obligations. Thus, the requirement that a landowner allow the entry of police, medical, fire, and social services officials on the land is not a taking. The destruction of a building or of timber to control the spread of a fire, is not a taking, even if the building or trees destroyed were not then aflame. The prohibition of the use of property in a manner that encourages the spread of disease or that encourages criminal conduct is a police exercise that does not amount to a taking.

The line between exercise of the police power and takings is sometimes difficult to draw because of the breadth of the police powers, the state power to regulate health, safety, welfare, and morals, and indeed the power to take lands is really an aspect of the police power. Yet the difference is one not of power but when that power gives rise to a duty of the state to compensate the landowner or possessor for the loss of the property or its use. Thus, the two general principles in federal takings jurisprudence that divide compensable takings from regulation and police exercise: if the government takes real or effective title to the property, or if the government so thoroughly regulates the property that the regulation goes too far. Some state takings jurisprudence goes farther, to compensate landowners for regulations that in fact diminish the market value of property.

Note: the Takings Clause of the Fifth Amendment is plural owing to its prohibition of all takings of private property for a public use without compensation. Thus, the plural form of taking is properly used for an analysis, claim, or case, such as "a takings case." This does not mean that one action upon a property should be a takings; it might be a taking but not a takings (though quite well educated people do talk that way).

*See also:* use, use of property, public use; property, interest in property (property interest); take (took or taken or taking).

***police powers and takings*** A regulation or order by the United States or a state that burdens a property owner's interest strictly in pursuit of a traditional police interest in protecting health, safety, welfare, or morals, that is not intended generally to transfer a private benefit to the public use is not a taking as understood in the Takings Clause. Thus, an order to destroy infected trees that risk an orchard, a nuisance abatement order, the destruction of a building to stop the spread of a fire, the destruction of a door or wall for a police entry in service of a warrant and similar measures in furtherance of a police goal that have an incidental harm to property are not takings. A government may choose to order a payment ex gratia for such losses, but the losses are not subject to just compensation as if the property were condemned to build a park.

**Takings Clause** *See:* constitution, U.S. Constitution, clauses, Takings Clause.

**ad hoc taking** A regulatory taking that does not result in physical presence on the land. An ad hoc taking is a taking by means other than through regular appropriation or condemnation. A regulatory taking that does not result in a permanent, physical occupation of the land is an ad hoc taking. The term is taken from Justice Brennan's summary of regulatory takings analysis in the Penn Central case, Penn Cent. Transp. Co. v. City of New York, 438 U.S. 104 (1978). The determination of an ad hoc taking requires a balance between the extent a regulation amounts to something more like a physical intrusion or more like mere interference by governmental action in the balance of benefits and burdens in economic life for the common good. This approach has been refined in later formulae but remains essentially valid in 2011.

*See also:* taking, de facto taking (inverse condemnation); ad, ad hoc; taking, regulatory taking (inverse condemnation or regulatory takings).

**de facto taking (inverse condemnation)** A taking in fact rather than through a legal process. A de facto taking is a taking that occurs as a matter of fact though there has been no condemnation or other proceeding. A de facto taking may arise as a result of the occupation or appropriation of land without payment or process by either a government or a private entity with a delegated power of eminent domain, such as a utility. Examples include an occupation of private land as a result of government operations, such as dumping great piles of earth or creating flooding; or the erection of a high-capacity utility line without first condemning the easement to do so.

De facto taking under the law of some states includes the diminished value of property owing to governmental action, such as the lost value to one parcel of land owing to a change of zoning nearby.

De facto taking is sometimes used to describe a regulatory taking or the denial of a use by a governmental entity, such as in an inverse condemnation. A de facto taking is a taking, and it gives rise to an action for compensation, either as a temporary or permanent taking.

Note: de facto taking is easily confused with ad hoc taking, and there is a considerable overlap, though the terms are not the same. An ad hoc taking is the category of regulatory taking that does not result in physical occupation, so some ad hoc takings are de facto takings. Some de facto takings, as when a utility builds a service line or pipe without process, are not ad hoc takings.

**essential nexus** A relationship between a taking and a legitimate state interest. An essential nexus is a logical or functional relationship between the appropriation or regulation and a legitimate state interest. An essential nexus is required for a constitutionally valid taking, whether as an appropriation or as a regulation.

*See also:* nexum (nexus).

**public use (public purpose)** The right of use or benefit to the public in any form. Public use, within the meaning of the Takings Clause, is a land use that will benefit the government as a corporate enterprise or the public in any manner. Public use includes not only the use of land for the provision of public services, like parks, schools, police stations, and other public buildings; roads and highways; and easements for utility pipes and lines; but also generally for economic development.

*See also:* public.

**regulatory taking (inverse condemnation or regulatory takings)** The taking of a profitable use of private property through regulation. A regulatory taking is the imposition of governmental regulations or restrictions that effectively limit all profitable use of the land, amounting to a taking of the property in all but title. It is also referred to as inverse condemnation. The property owner will often argue that the regulation (regardless of the extent of the uses infringed) does not serve a legitimate state purpose. Therefore, a regulatory taking arises from a regulation of land use that permanently denies all economically viable uses of a whole parcel for purposes that are not a legitimate state or governmental interest, from a physical invasion required by regulation, or by an unconstitutional condition on a land use. An action for inverse condemnation may either enjoin the application of the regulation or seek damages for the value of the lost use of the property.

*See also:* condemnation (condemn).

***limitation of police powers*** A regulation of land use or structures that is a valid exercise of a police power over health, safety, welfare, or morals is not a compensable taking under the Fifth Amendment. There are three theories for this limit: First, the framers would never have imagined paying the keeper of a public nuisance or hazard to abate it. Second, a use contrary to good health, safety, welfare, or morals is not a property interest worthy of federal or judicial protection. Third, the property presumably does not lose value by being made safer or more wholesome.

*parcel as a whole*  A regulatory taking does not occur if only a portion of a parcel is affected by a regulation. The regulation must affect the parcel as a whole. That said, the effect on the whole parcel is then the measure of the regulatory effect.

**amortization of a land use**  A use of the land may be regulated without taking over time through amortization. Amortization of an investment in property allows a government to regulate a use of land without a liability for taking private property for public use, so long as the regulation is effective far enough in the future to allow the present owner to realize a reasonable return on any investment-backed expectations in the property that would be limited or extinguished by the regulation. The minimum time required to reasonably amortize expectations is not a set period, but spans as brief as seven years have been found sufficient.

*See also:* zoning (land-use zone).

**categorical taking (denial of economically viable use or wipe out of use)**  A regulation that denies all economically reasonable uses of land. A categorical taking results from a land use regulation that creates a permanent interference with land use so that the owner or possessor is barred from all economically viable uses of the land. A regulation that allows at least some use of the property that may generate income is not a categorical taking. A regulation that allows some revenue to be generated from the land is only a taking if, in the light of all of the circumstances, the regulation destroys investment-backed expectations with an insufficient benefit to the owner.

**conditional use**  Use allowed under land use laws only if a condition is met. A conditional use is a use of property allowed under a local zoning ordinance or other land-use regulation, that requires a condition or conditions to be met before specific uses are allowed on specific lands. For example, some lands may only be used for commercial purposes if sufficient access is provided.

*See also:* zoning, conditional zoning.

**double-nexus analysis (double nexus test)**  A state condition imposed on the use of land must be related and proportionate to the use. The double-nexus test is a combination of the essential nexus required between a government condition imposed as a quid pro quo for the approval of a land use application, and the requirement of proportionality, by which the government's condition must be reasonable in scope when compared to the land use. A municipality or other government that attempts to condition any grant of permission to use land on compliance with other requirements by the landholder, such as giving up an easement to the benefit of the public, must satisfy both conditions or risk violating the Takings Clause.

Otherwise, a double-nexus may describe any test that requires proof of two distinct conceptual relationships to justify a result.

*See also:* nexum (nexus).

**rough proportionality**  The burden of a land-use regulation on the landowner must not be unreasonable compared to the use. Rough proportionality is a relative measure of the burden on the landowner and the benefit of the landowner's use that must be satisfied by a regulatory condition upon the use. A regulatory burden that is not roughly proportional may amount to a taking.

*See also:* proportionality (disproportional or proportional or proportionate).

**investment-backed expectations**  A distinct and reasonable plan on which money is spent before notice of a regulation limiting it. Distinct and reasonable investment-backed expectations are a particular element of private interests in property that are not to be unfairly or unduly the subject of interference by regulation, or the Takings Clause requires the investor be compensated for the interference. The inquiry of the form and extent of interference in the expectation is independent of other elements of takings analysis, which are the extent of the economic impact and the character of the governmental action.

A reasonable, distinct investment-backed expectation in a given use requires that the property owner or user have intended a particular use that cannot be carried out in the manner intended owing only to the regulation; the regulation must require a significant change of plans, and the new plans must be likely to be significantly less profitable in their implementation than the plans thwarted by regulation. The plan must have existed prior to notice of the regulation or the likelihood of such a regulation. A significant and distinct investment of money must have been made toward the implementation of that plan. The investment must not be merely proposed or have been made as a general investment in a development that would yield a variety of plans or a plan unformulated at the time of the investment. The plan must be reasonable, lawful, realizable, and likely have yielded a reasonable return on the investment had the regulation not interfered with it. The plan must not have created or enhanced a danger to the public, including to the landowner or occupants of the land in dispute, nor could it create what would amount to a nuisance to the public or other properties.

An interference with an investment-backed expectation is not enough to find a taking. The interference must be of sufficient unfairness and extent to amount to a compensable taking.

*See also:* investment (invest).

**Penn Central test**  A finding of a regulatory taking requires a fact-specific balance of interests. The

Penn Central test is the primary test for a regulatory taking that does not destroy all viable economic use, create a permanent physical occupation, or fail to promote a legitimate governmental purpose, the test being announced in Penn Central Transportation Co. v. City of New York, 438 U.S. 104 (1978). Under the test, a plaintiff land user must demonstrate not only that the regulation in question is confiscatory, inordinately burdensome, or denies at least one economically viable use of his property, but also that the character of the governmental action, its economic impact and its interference with reasonable investment-backed expectations is sufficiently great that in this case, a taking has occurred. Every case is a matter of its own facts, and no one condition is sufficient to determine the question. The greater the state rationale, the greater the denial must be in order to find a taking. The greater the economic loss of investment backed expectations, the greater the governmental justification must be, and the more that the loss is suffered by one land user or a small group of land users as opposed to the community as a whole, the easier it is to find a taking has occurred.

**physical occupation** A regulation effecting a permanent physical presence on land is a taking. Physical occupation of land required by a regulation amounts to a taking under the Takings Clause. Even so, the measurement of the compensation required for such a taking is the difference in value in the land before the taking and after. If the land is more valuable following with the physical presence, no payment in compensation is required.

**substantial advancement of a legitimate interest (substantially-advances test)** The focus of a land-use regulation on a police interest. Substantial advancement of a legitimate interest is one element in a two-part test of the validity of a land-use regulation. A regulation meeting this element may not amount to a taking of private property that it regulates under the test, which distinguishes regulations that promote a customary or state purpose from regulations of economic convenience or mere public services. A regulation that furthers the health, safety, or morals of the community, such as one preventing the loss of property and life through floods, advances a legitimate state interest.

**temporary taking** A regulation or state interference with land for a period of time. A temporary taking is a taking that comes to an end, requiring the owner of the land to suffer a state interference for a period of time but leaving the owner in possession with no interference at the conclusion. A temporary taking is subject to analysis as a taking, either as a physical occupation or under the Penn Central balancing test, and if a taking is found to occur, the remedy is equivalent not to the lost use but to a rent for the time of the use lost.

**takkanah** *See:* takanah (takkanah, takanot [pl.]).

**talaq (khulu)** The dissolution of marriage. Talaq is divorce. Although in Arabic the term means, literally, to separate, talaq is a divorce effected by the husband. Divorce by the wife is khulu'a.
*See also:* divorce (dissolution of marriage).

**Talmud (Talmudic)** An authoritative collection of law derived from the classical oral tradition. The Talmud is a summary of Jewish oral law, comprising the Mishnah and the Gemara. The Talmud is organized in successive layers of commentary on the central texts of Jewish law. There is not one Talmud but two, one arising in Jerusalem and one in Bablyon, each with an array of important rabbinic commentary. Talmudic is a reference to the critical scope, depth, and comprehensiveness of the commentaries, and a reference to Talmudic wisdom is a suggestion of a thought very well informed and wise.

**tampering (tamper)** Harmful meddling. Tampering is any form of interference that harms or corrupts a person, thing, or procedure, whether the interference is a physical alteration or destruction of a thing or an attempt to influence, threaten, or bribe a person. Specific crimes forbid, for example, tampering with the mails; with witnesses; with juries or jurors; with evidence; with a last will and testament; with a security device or safe; and with a player, team, or sports official in a sports game or broadcast game show.
*See also:* spoliation, spoliation of evidence.

**tampering with the jury or embracer or jury tampering or juror bribery** *See:* jury, embracery (tampering with the jury or embracer or jury tampering or juror bribery).

**Tanakh** The central texts of the Jewish Bible. The Tanakh is the Hebrew Bible, an acronym for Torah, Neviim, Ketuvim, i.e., Torah, Prophets, and Writings, the books are the same as those in the Protestant Old Testament, though in a different order and, of course, either untranslated or translated in a rabbinic tradition into a vernacular tongue. The Tanakh is the most authoritative basis for the law in Judaism.

**Taney Court** *See:* court, U.S. court, U.S. Supreme Court, Taney Court.

**Tang Code** The seventh-century exposition of Confucian-inspired Chinese law. The Tang Code of Perpetual Splendor, the legal code of the Tang Dynasty in China, was issued in 624 CE, and integrated Confucian principles into older Chinese laws. The 500 sections of the code were issued in twelve volumes, organized by Tang Minister Fan Xuanling. The criminal sections of the code enshrine a sophisticated system of criminal responsibility and lenity.

**tangible** Touchable, real and with substance. Tangible means capable of being touched, and in general, anything tangible exists in time and space as an object, whether it is solid, liquid, or gas, as long as it is physically detectable. As a metaphor, anything measurable in money, including profits or success, can be said to be tangible.

**tangible asset**   *See:* asset, tangible asset.

**tangible personal property**   *See:* property, personal property, tangible personal property.

**tangible property**   *See:* property, forms of property, corporeal property (tangible property).

**taqlid**   Obedience to precedents and commandments. Taqlid, or qa la dam, is the principle of unquestioned following that is found amongst the Shia and also in the Hanafi fiqh of southern Asia. The principle is that a muqallid, or follower, must follow the rulings of the school or madhab the mugallid follows.

**tariff (impost or customs duty or import fee or rate tariff)**   A tax on imported goods. A tariff, generally, is a rate set as a part of a table of rates. The term is descended from the Arabic ta'rif, or list of fees. There are two categories of tariff in contemporary law.

A tariff is a tax, and in the United States, its use is a tax placed on imported goods that is collected by the central government. No state may collect a tariff on goods from other states. Note: a tax on imports is usually referred to as an impost in the constitutional text, as a tariff in nineteenth-century tax law, and as a tariff, import fee, or customs duty in contemporary usage.

Tariff has another meaning, as a regulated contract rate. When state tariffs, gas tariffs, or transportation tariffs are discussed, this sense of tariff is practically always meant.

**tariff as fee**   A fee for service, particularly transport. A tariff as a fee is a cost for the purchase of services according to a schedule. Tariffs are particularly common in regulated transport services, such as trucking haulage routes regulated by a state or interstate commission, rail services, and gas pipelines. The schedule of tariffs for each transportation provider is approved by a regulator, sometimes with fees for particular routes or lines, sometimes with fees for particular shipments or carriage requirements. The shippers are then free to contract with the transporter at the published tariff schedule that applies. Beside price, the tariff may set terms and conditions of the transport contract, including limitations of liability.

**Harmonized Tariff System (Tariff System of the United States or TSUS or HTS)**   The international classification and rates system for all imported goods. The Harmonized Tariff Schedule (or, HTS) is an international index of categories of goods that are shipped in international trade. Each category is assigned a six-digit number as its HTS number. National tariff numbers of up to four additional digits are added to the HTS number, which allow greater detail and specification of commonly shipped or received products in each nation. The Tariff Schedules of the United States (or, TSUS)

were an independent system that was converted into the U.S. Harmonized Tariff Schedule. Tariff codes are used for imports. Export Codes, or "Schedule B codes", are used for exported goods.

**protective tariff**   A tariff meant to protect the domestic economy. A protective tariff is a tariff created not for the purpose of raising revenue generally but for the purpose of protecting a domestic production or supply of the commodity whose foreign imports are subject to the tariff. Protective tariffs were once common but are now strictly regulated and limited by the World Trade Organization.

**tarriff duty**   *See:* duties (tarriff duty).

**Tate letter**   *See:* immunity, sovereign immunity, foreign sovereign immunity, Tate letter.

**tautology**   *See:* fallacy, tautology (circular argument or circulus in demonstrando or circularity).

**tax (taxation)**   Money that must be paid to a government. A tax is a contribution to the revenues of the government that is required by law to be paid to support the general operations of the state. There are many bases of taxation, including taxes on nearly all forms of wealth, property, or income, that are levied at times of severance, sale or purchase, on importation or export, on an annual basis, or at death. Although broadly all revenues collected involuntarily are taxes, by law and by custom neither fees for the use of governmental services or fines or administrative charges are considered taxes. Taxes are charged as a percentage of some value or at a flat rate. Taxes may be reduced or offset by deductions, credits, or exemptions created by law and claimed by the taxpayer. Note: tax is a noun and a verb.

Taxation is the act of creating a tax as well as the system of state finance that depends on tax-generated revenue. State revenues generated by fees for service or through the sale of state-owned natural resources support the operations of some governments, but taxation is the most common form of state revenue worldwide.

Taxes may be assessed on nearly every aspect of the human condition, a short list including a tax payable: (a) for the mere fact of living (a capitation or poll tax); (b) on the act or preparation for dying (inheritance tax or estate tax); (c) on ownership (property tax); (d) on giving or receiving gifts (gift tax); (e) on work for wages or salary (income tax); (f) on consumption through the purchase of goods (sales tax); (g) on the consumption of unnecessary goods (special taxes, such as sin tax, luxury tax, restaurant tax); (h) on the profit from the sale of investments (capital gains tax or stock-transfer tax); (i) on the performance of a task like driving (license tag fee or gas tax or road tolls) or like entertainment (admission tax or amusement tax); (j) on having a business (privilege tax or occupation tax or payroll tax); (k) on the manufacture of goods (excise tax); (l) on the making of spirits (stamp tax); (m) on the shipment of goods (duty); (n) on the importation of goods (tariffs); (o) on the exportation of goods (export tax); (p) on the capture of natural resources (severance tax); and (q) on the filing of litigation or court documents (stamp tax or filing fee).

A failure to pay taxes when owed may be a civil offense or a criminal offense or give rise to an action in forfeiture to satisfy the deficiency. A failure to pay taxes on property results in a tax lien on the property and may lead to forfeiture to satisfy a tax deficiency. A knowing and intentional false statement on a tax return is a criminal offense.

In the United States, the individual states have had a plenary power of taxation since their creation, limited by their state constitutions, the federal constitutional limits of due process of law, equal protection of the laws, and the protection of interstate commerce, and the political will of the legislatures and people. The federal government was initially limited only to taxes on imports, state assessments, and similar taxes, receiving a broad power to assess a tax on the incomes of individuals and businesses with the passage of the Sixteenth Amendment in 1913.

Taxes are rarely beloved by their payers, yet the requirement of funds for the government was understood and accepted without reservation by both the leaders of the American Revolution and the Framers of the Constitution. Despite occasional outbursts to the contrary, the payment of taxes is considered one of the basic duties of citizenship.

**tax audit**   *See:* audit, tax audit (examination of tax return).

**tax claim**   *See:* claim, tax claim, claim of right; claim, tax claim.

**tax code or IRC**   *See:* revenue, internal revenue, internal revenue code (tax code or IRC).

**tax court**   *See:* court, U.S. court, tax court (U.S. tax court).

**tax lien**   *See:* lien, tax lien.

**tax penalty**   *See:* penalty, tax penalty.

**tax shelter**   *See:* shelter, tax shelter.

**ad valorem tax**   An annual tax on the property one owns. A tax ad valorem, Latin for "according to value" is an annual tax based on the taxable value of a particular property. It is a generic name for an annual assessment of state or local taxes on personal property or on real estate. Payment of the tax is secured by an implied lien on the property itself.

**business income tax (business privilege tax)**   A tax on the income of an entity registered to do business. A business income tax is a tax levied on the eligible income or profits of any person or entity engaging in the sale of goods or services or revenue from the management of its assets. There are both state and federal business income taxes. Taxes vary particularly from state to state and may be on all of the activities of the person or entity that occur within the jurisdiction of the government that levies the tax, or it may apply only to those sales that are made within the

jurisdiction. The tax is sometimes known as a privilege tax, or a tax upon the privilege of doing business.

**capital-gains tax**   A tax on a profit realized from the sale of capital. Capital-gains tax is a tax collected by the United States and many individual states on net profits realized from the sale of capital. The tax is computed variously, but in general the tax applies to the net of gains from capital sales over losses from capital sales realized in a given year. Various forms of capital sale and capital gain are subject to different tax exemptions and rates. In 2010, the rate applied by the United States varied from 0% to 28%.

*See also:* capital, commercial capital.

**checkoff**   Toll paid per specified unit of produced goods sold. A checkoff is a specialized tax, although it is usually described as a fee, that is paid by businesses that produce certain goods (into a state or federal program that promotes the goods). Checkoffs are particularly common among agribusinesses, which pay the checkoff in increments according to the volume of produce sold.

**death tax**   All forms of tax on the property of the dead or aged. A death tax is a generic term for all taxes on property that apply particularly because the property is transferred post-mortem in probate or administration of a decedent's estate or is transferred inter vivos but in contemplation of death in a transaction intended to diminish a post-mortem estate or in lieu of a grant by will. A death tax may be assessed against the grantor while alive, against the estate after death, or against the grantee before or after the death of the grantor. The primary forms are an estate tax, assessed on the property of the decedent and payable by the decedent's estate, and an inheritance tax, assessed on the legacy, devise, or inheritance and payable by the survivor. Note: death tax is itself a rarely used term. More often the term is used as a rhetorical device by opponents of taxes in general to create the impression that the estate tax is a tax on death itself rather than the transfer of property.

**inheritance tax**   A state tax on an inheritance. An inheritance tax is a tax on the receipt of assets by non-exempt heir, devisee, legatee, or beneficiary from the estate or trust of a person post mortem. Spouses are exempt from inheritance tax, and in most states descendants are exempt as well. An inheritance tax differs from an estate tax in being payable by the recipient of the grant rather than by the donor or the estate. As of 2010, there is no federal inheritance tax, although seven states have an inheritance tax (two of which have both an estate tax and an inheritance tax).

**estate tax**   A federal or state tax on the property of a wealthy decedent. The federal estate tax is a tax on the transfer of assets made after death by individuals with taxable property held by the wealthiest two per cent of American taxpayers. The tax is paid by the estate of the decedent during probate or administration, based not on the gross estate but on a taxable estate including property at death and qualified transfers made while alive, from which are excepted grants to a surviving spouse, gifts to qualified charities, and certain expenses. The tax applies to taxable estates worth, in 2010, more than $1,000,000. Many states have an estate tax as well, most with definitions of the taxable estate that mirror the federal definition.

**generation-skipping transfer tax (skip person or GST)** A tax on transfers that would avoid estate tax. The generation skipping transfer tax, often called the generation skipping tax, or GST, applies to defined transfers of property made by a transferor while alive to a "skip person." A skip person may be any person at least 37.5 years younger than the transferor, but not the transferor's spouse. The usual skip person is a grandchild or later descendant of the transferor. Each skip person is entitled to a GST estate tax credit, which in 2010 is $2,000,000. The value of the sum of all GSTs received by one skip person from one transferor above the GST tax exemption is taxed at a rate that historically has been between 45% and 55%. The tax is assessed at the time of the property transfer, like a gift tax, taxable to the transferor but payable by the skip person or another person.

**gift tax** A federal tax on certain gratuitous transfers. The gift tax is a federal tax on the value of property given from a donor to a non–exempt recipient as a gift, which is to say when the recipient does not give full and fair value in return. If the recipient is the donor's spouse, or a qualified political or charitable organization, or if the gift is given for bona fide medical or educational expenses by the recipient, or if the sum of all of the amounts given from one person to one recipient is less than the annual exemption, then the recipient is exempt. The gift tax is payable by the donor, although the recipient or another person may pay the tax on the donor's behalf.

*See also:* gift (gift over or give).

**annual exclusion** The value of gifts from one person to another in one year not subject to gift tax. The annual exclusion is an amount of the ceiling under which the gifts from one person to another (who is not otherwise exempt from the gift tax, such as a spouse, charity, or otherwise) are not subject to the gift tax. The annual exclusion is cumulative, and all gifts given in a tax year apply to its amount. Gifts of property held by two people given by both to one recipient are subject to a cumulative exclusion. In the 2009, the annual exclusion amount was $12,000, although the amount varies in most years.

**income tax** A tax on income from certain sources. An income tax is a tax on income, as income is defined for the purposes of assessing the tax. In the United States, an income tax is assessed against individuals both by the federal government and by most state governments. There is also a form of income tax assessed by federal and state governments on businesses, although the business tax is a tax on profit rather than revenue, and is in addition to sales taxes, tariffs, and other taxes that are a part of doing business. In most usages, however, income tax is used in the sense of the individual income tax, which may be paid by an individual, by married persons filing jointly, or by a head of household.

The individual income tax applies to all taxable income, which includes wages, tips, payments for contract services, pension payments, interest and dividend payments, and capital gains realized by the sale of capital assets, among other sources (though certain forms of income are exempt and not added to taxable income, such as income from municipal bonds). The tax on the taxable income is calculated either by deducting qualified expenses (such as employee business expenses) from the gross taxable income received during the tax year, as well as standard or adjusted amounts for eligible exemptions (such as a personal exemption for a qualifying dependent) or by taking a standard deduction for each dependent. The net taxable income is then multiplied by the tax rate that applies to that level or income to determine the gross tax liability. From that, any tax credits are deducted, including credit for tax already paid against that year's tax liability. The result is either the amount of taxes owed by the taxpayer to the government or of the refund for overpayment due to the taxpayer from the government.

*See also:* income.

**alternative minimum tax (A.M.T. or AMT)** Federal income tax calculation that overrides deductions. The alternative minimum tax, or AMT, is alternative calculation of individual income tax based on a percentage of income over an exemption amount, that becomes the basis for annual federal tax liability if the tax required under the AMT formulation is higher than the tax required in a standard calculation incorporating deductions.

**estimated tax** Tax paid quarterly in advance in lieu of withholding. Estimated tax is an amount paid in advance of filing a return for federal income tax by individuals whose income is not subject to payroll withholding. Estimated tax is usually computed at 90% of the present year's actual tax liability, or 100% or 110% of the prior year's tax liability, and it is paid quarterly.

**payroll tax withholding** The payment of an employee's income tax by the employer. Payroll tax withholding, often called a withholding tax, is a process by which an employer deducts an estimated amount of tax from each payment of wages. The withholding is not itself a tax but only a means for the collection of the income tax that would otherwise be owed based on an estimate of the taxes likely to be paid by a person with the annual income being paid by the employer in wages, offset by deductions for the number of allowances claimed by the employee. If more tax is withheld than is actually owed when the employee files a return, the difference is refunded by the Internal

Revenue Service. If less tax is withheld than actually owed, the employee must pay the difference to the Internal Revenue Service.

*See also:* Social Security, Federal Insurance Contibutions Act (FICA).

**tax credit** A reduction of tax liability for a qualified expenditure. A tax credit is a specific amount that a taxpayer may claim for a qualified expenditure, which directly reduces the amount of taxes owed in a given period. Tax credits differ from deductions in that deductions reduce taxable income, but credits reduce the tax to be paid. Tax credits are offered for many specific activities, sometimes only by certain classes of taxpayers. Presently, U.S. tax credits are available, for example, to qualified individual taxpayers for energy efficient home improvements, for first-time home purchases, for the adoption of children (especially children with special needs) and to qualified corporations for the provision of low-income housing, for the purchase of certain fuels, for placing electric vehicles in service, and other business decisions. Both individuals and corporations may receive credits for foreign tax payments.

**child and dependent care expenses credit (child care credit)** A tax credit for care of a child or dependent. The child care and dependent care expenses credit is a federal tax credit for the cost a working parent or guardian incurs by paying for the care of a child or dependent in order to work. As of 2009, the credit was available for (a) the care of a child younger than 13, if (b) the parent or guardian had earned income and required the child care in order to work or look for work, and (c) paid a person for child care, not the parent's or guardian's own dependent or spouse, and (d) over $3,000 of the expenses were not reimbursed. The credit in 2009 was up to $3,000 per child, but is reduced according to child-care benefits received from other sources.

**earned income tax credit (E.I.T.C. or EITC)** A refundable tax credit for the relief of lower-wage workers. The earned income tax credit is a refundable federal income tax credit that allows low-income working individuals and families who file a return to receive a credit greater than the taxes owed, which allows poor people to receive a tax refund and provides a source of federal revenue to the poor based upon wages earned. Congress originally approved the tax credit in 1975 in part to offset the burden of Social Security taxes and to provide an incentive to work.

**unearned income of minor children (kiddie tax)** A parent's tax on a child's investment income. The kiddie tax is a slang term for the tax on unearned income of minor children, which is taxed as if it were the parent's income. This tax was created in 1986 to apply to a child (in 2011 a child under 17), to whom investments were given by a parent in order to benefit from the child's lower tax rate. The parent is taxed on all unearned income realized by the child over a deduction amount (in 2011, the deduction was $900). The tax does not apply if the child files a return separately from the parent.

*See also:* child (children).

**luxury tax** A sales or property tax on particularly expensive goods. A luxury tax is a sales tax or property tax that applies only to defined goods or categories of goods or that applies an unusually high tax rate to such goods, when the goods are unusually expensive. Private boats, private planes, cars over a given price, jewelry over a given price, and fur apparel are common objects of luxury tax.

*See also:* tax, tax burden, progressive tax (progressivity).

**payroll tax** A tax paid by an employer for each employee. A payroll tax is any tax payable by an employer based on the payment of wages to an employee, whether as a tax on the employer calculated according to the number and wages of its employees or as a tax on the employee that is collected from the employer. In the U.S. in 2010, payroll taxes include federal payment of employer liability for unemployment insurance collected as FICA payments, as well as employee liability for income tax and FICA, as well as state employer liability and state employee income tax liability. Other payroll taxes, such as municipal income tax, vary from jurisdiction to jurisdiction.

*See also:* tax, payroll tax, Federal Insurance Contributions Act (F.I.C.A. tax or FICA tax).

**Federal Insurance Contributions Act (F.I.C.A. tax or FICA tax)** Social Security payments made by an employer for an employee. A Federal Insurance Contributions Act payment, or FICA payment, is a Social Security payment. Most FICA payments are made by a payroll tax required by the United States as payments on behalf of an employee in the Social Security trust. The self-employed are required to make FICA payments through their individual income tax filings.

*See also:* Social Security, Old Age Survivors And Disability Insurance (OASDI).

**household employment tax (nanny tax)** Taxes paid for a household employee. The household employment taxes, known colloquially as the nanny tax, are paid by a household employer for each regular employee. They include both state and federal taxes, such as Social Security (or FICA) contributions, unemployment insurance, and, in some cases health care insurance, as well as income tax withholding when the employee requests it and the employer agrees. Payment of taxes is not required for all household employees; the Social Security and Medicare wage threshold remained at $1,700 for 2010. The Federal Unemployment Tax threshold is $1,000. A household employer must file a separate form with the annual return.

See also: Social Security, Federal Insurance Contributions Act (FICA).

**poll tax (head tax or capitation tax)** A tax required to vote in a public election. A poll tax is a tax that must be paid as a condition of eligibility to vote in public elections, effectively burdening the poor in their attempts to vote. The poll tax was a prominent feature of Jim Crow legislation in the American South. The poll tax is forbidden as a predicate to federal elections by the Twenty-Fourth Amendment and as a predicate to state elections by the Equal Protection Clause.

A poll tax in England is the same as a capitation tax, or tax on every person regardless of income. The term in this sense is derived not from poll in the sense of an election, but poll in the sense of a person's head, a usage rare in the U.S.

See also: Jim Crow law (race laws); capitation; constitution, U.S. Constitution, Amendment 24 (Amendment XXIV or Twenty-Fourth Amendment).

**property tax** An annual tax on the value of property owned. A property tax is a yearly tax on ownership, which may be a real property tax, a personal property tax, or both. Most states have some form of property tax, which is assessed on specific categories of property and subject to various exemptions. The homestead exemption is the most common exemption from real property taxation, an allowance given for a home up to a given value that is not taxed.

Property taxes are usually assessed on the value of property based on its actual cost amortized over time. The tax required to be paid on an automobile in most states is a property tax, although it is frequently thought of (and sometimes is) a license fee.

**sales tax (sales and use tax)** A tax on sales of goods or services. A sales tax is a consumption tax paid either by the buyer to the seller and then by the seller to the state or paid directly by the buyer to the state. Most states have a sales tax, and most municipalities and local governmental bodies, such as school districts, receive revenues from sales taxes, either collected directly or collected by the state and transmitted to the local entity. The tax applies to all purchases of goods or services that are not exempt from sales tax and that occur within that jurisdiction. Most jurisdictions have some transactions that are, by statute, regulation, or custom exempt from sales tax. In some states, the purchase of medical supplies is exempt by statute or regulation. In most states, as a matter of statute or custom, sales other than that of automobiles or machinery not made by businesses or merchants are not taxed. As of 2010, there is no federal sales tax in the United States.

See also: excise; retail (retailer).

**sin tax** A sales or property tax on goods considered immoral, harmful, or unusually expensive. A sin tax is a slang expression for a sales tax or property tax that applies only to defined goods or categories of goods or that applies an unusually high tax rate to such goods, when the possession or consumption of such goods is considered to be immoral, unusually harmful to the consumer, or unusually harmful to others or unusually expensive. The purposes of such taxes vary considerably, and the purpose may be essential to the tax's validity. Sin taxes are sometimes intended to deter consumption of the goods, sometimes intended to punish the consumer, sometimes intended to regulate consumption by requiring records of the tax payment, sometimes intended to recover costs incurred by the state associated with the consumption, but are often intended to raise revenues from unpopular or unnecessary activities. Sin taxes on bets placed at gaming establishments, on private lottery tickets, and on alcohol sales and tobacco sales are common and are usually valid revenue generating devices. Sin taxes on the possession of illegal drugs and other substances are usually illegal if they have the potential for double jeopardy. Sin taxes on expressive conduct are potentially unconstitutional violations of free speech.

**pole tax (sexually oriented business tax or SOB tax)** A tax on venues for adult entertainment. A pole tax is the slang term for a tax, unique to Texas, which attempted to raise funds for victims of sexual assault by charging a per capita tax on the patrons of clubs licensed to present exhibitions of nude dancing. The Texas appellate court in 2010 declared such a tax an unconstitutional burden on free expression. Note: a tax on utilities may also be a pole tax, or tax per unit of distance or lines or per pole placed on a utility easement.

**surtax** A tax on top of another tax. A surtax is a special tax applied to an activity that is already subject to a general tax, such as an additional income tax on income above a specified amount. The tax is a tool of progressive taxation, and because a surtax is applied on unusually high earnings or revenues, it results in a higher rate than the rate that applies to earnings or revenues of lesser amounts.

**tax abatement** Reduction of taxes. Tax abatement is the reduction of the taxes on an assessed value of a property or, more rarely, on personal incomes. Tax abatements may be temporary or permanent, but they are usually for a period of time.

See also: abatement (abate).

**tax bunching** Timing expenses to maximize tax benefits. Bunching is a tax planning practice of adjusting the timing of activities that are deductible from income taxes, so that deductions are higher in a given tax year and lower in the next. This legitimate practice allows taxpayers to have a higher level of deduction in a year in which there is unusually higher income or revenue, though it may be used for other purposes, such as for a taxpayer whose average year does not have enough itemized deductions to allow itemization, but would prefer to do so.

**tax burden** The sum of what must be paid in tax. The tax burden, at its most narrow, is the liability of an individual or entity to pay a given amount in tax. A tax burden may be shifted, which means only that the taxpayer may arrange to be reimbursed by others for the tax, not that the taxpayer can assign payment directly, as when a manufacturer passes a tax on to a buyer in a higher price or a corporation passes a tax on to shareholders by a lower dividend.

More generally, the tax burden is the measure of the tax required of a nation as well as of an individual or entity within the nation. Thus, a national tax burden is a measure of the amount of a nation's wealth that must be taken for the support of the state and its support of private and public activity. The individual tax burden is a portion of a property or income from an individual or entity that must be taken in order to contribute to the national tax burden. There are myriad schemes to design tax burdens.

Some tax burden schemes are intended to promote behavior by individuals or businesses that officials consider beneficial to the public. By creating taxes that apply to certain activities, the state raises the price of those activities discouraging their performance. By lowering a tax or exempting from tax certain activities among others that are highly taxed, the state lowers the relative price of these activities, encouraging their performance. Thus, a negative tax burden may amount to a subsidy.

One of the most salient distinctions between comprehensive tax policies and one of the most important analyses of specific taxes is whether the tax is progressive or regressive, that is whether the tax allocates more of the national burden to the rich or to the poor.

See also: shelter, tax shelter.

**progressive tax (progressivity)**  A tax that is a greater burden on the wealthy. A progressive tax applies to, or applies more often or with a higher rate to, taxpayers with a higher income. Thus, a progressive tax is structured so that a greater proportion of the income of a high-wage earner is paid in taxes than is paid by a low-wage earner. The theory in support of a progressive tax is the diminishing marginal utility of money, which, loosely, argues that the same quantity of money is more valuable to a person with less than with more. Certain taxes are structured or defined in such a way as to be inherently progressive, like an estate tax on the wealthy or a luxury tax. The U.S. income tax employs several progressive elements in its tax rates, the earned income tax credit, the personal exemption, and the graduated tax rate, increasing the taxable rate of income according to the amount of income. In 2010, the tax rate ranged from 10%, for those earning $8,375 per year, to 35% for those earning $373,650 per year, with four intermediate rates.

See also: tax, luxury tax.

**regressive tax (regressivity)**  A tax that is a greater proportional burden on those with lower incomes. A regressive tax applies to, or applies more often or with a higher rate to, the poor. Thus, a regressive tax is structured so that a greater proportion of the income of a lower-wage earner is paid in taxes

than a higher-wage earner. The theory in support of a regressive tax structure is that there is more public benefit to the acquisition of capital by the rich, whose consumption leads to greater economic growth and employment. This position is controversial. A tax can be structured in a regressive manner by applying only to those with low incomes; being applied only to goods or sales frequented by the poor; or by incorporating deductions or exemptions accessible only to the rich. Many taxes that appear uniform, such as a sales tax on food, in fact fall disproportionately on the poor because the fixed percentage of the price of food is a higher percentage of the income of a poor person than a wealthy person. The U.S. income tax has a host of regressive aspects owing to deductions and credits available only to the wealthy. The Social Security payment, or FICA, is regressive, having a cap on the annual payments of contributing-age workers, so that the wealthy pay the same amount as the middle class, though a much smaller proportion of income. Some state constitutions forbid regressive taxation, thus exempting necessities such as groceries, clothes, and newspapers from state taxation.

**child tax credit (child-and-dependent-care tax credit)**  A tax credit for a taxpayer raising children. The child tax credit is an allowance to a taxpayer who is maintaining a child. In 2008, the federal child tax credit allowed a taxpayer earning less than $55,000 per filer to receive a credit for each eligible child living in the taxpayer's household who was less than 17 years old at the end of the tax year and who was not self-supporting.

See also: dependent (lawful dependent or legal dependent).

**tax crime**  The willful failure to file an honest return amounts to several crimes. Tax crimes include a range of offenses for failure to file a return or report as required, failure to pay taxes required to be collected, failure to make accurate and honest statements, engaging in fraud, and misuse of tax stamps. With the exception of a misdemeanor failure to file a return or maintain records, the statutes require a willful violation of the code or its requirements, which require knowledge of the requirements.

*willfullness*  Willfulness in a tax code violation requires that the taxpayer committed a willful act in violation of a duty under the tax law that the taxpayer knew to exist. A good faith belief that the taxpayer acted lawfully is an absolute bar to a prosecution for a willful violation. Thus, a prosecution of willful violation may be rebutted by proof of good faith belief. Even so, although the standard is subjective belief and not objective reasonableness of the belief, the jury is entitled to consider the reasonableness of the defendant's belief in considering whether the defendant genuinely believed it.

See also: willfulness (willful or wilfully).

**failure to file return**   The offense of failing to file a required return or report. A failure to file a return or report or to supply information when requested to the IRS is a misdemeanor, unless the failure was willful, in which case it is a felony.

*See also:* tax, tax return.

**tax evasion**   Willful avoidance of a tax owed. Tax evasion is the crime of willfully acting in any manner to evade, avoid, or defeat a claim of tax that is lawfully owed. Evasion is not committed by filing a faulty return alone, but in committing any willful act that would unjustifiably diminish or avoid a tax liability, such as moving assets to conceal them, destroying records, altering records, or making a misleading or false statement. The statute of limitations for evasion is six years from the last related act of evasion.

**tax fraud**   Knowingly presenting to the IRS a false statement or document related to taxes. Tax fraud is a broad term for any action in which a person makes a false statement or presents a false document related to taxes or liability to the Internal Revenue Service. Three statutes proscribe various knowing and willful misstatements or false documents, the broadest being 26 U.S.C. § 7206(1). That statute makes it a felony for a taxpayer to willfully make and subscribe any return, statement, or other document, which contains or is verified by a written declaration that it is made under the penalties of perjury, and which the taxpayer does not believe to be true and correct as to every material matter.

**Tax Court Memo Decision (T.C. memo)**   A decision of the Tax Court of limited precedential value. A Tax Court Memorandum Decision, or Memo, is the resolution of a case before the tax court that is rendered by one judge of that court and not subject to the review by other judges that a "regular" decision of the court receive. Tax Court memos were long unpublished, but they are available on-line from the Tax Court and the CCH Tax Research Network. Their precedential effects are growing as their accessibility increases.

**Tax Court Regular Decision**   A Tax Court opinion issued intended to have precedential effect. Tax Court Regular Decisions are issued with a designation by the Chief Judge of the court with the intent that it be a precedent in future tax cases. They are published in the United States Tax Court Reports or its predecessors.

**tax deduction (deduction from taxable income)**   An authorized subtraction from a basis for computing taxes. A tax deduction is a category of expenses, exemptions, or exclusions from the basis from which a given tax will be calculated. A deduction can be created from any tax basis, such as a business's net profits, an individual's income, a property valuation, a capital gain, or a transfer price. The deduction reduces the sum of the basis prior to the calculation of the tax owed. (This differs from a credit, which reduces

the amount of tax calculated as owed.) Federal tax deductions for business revenue taxes and individual income taxes are specified in the Internal Revenue Code and Treasury Regulations, but deductions of other forms, such as tariffs are in their respective sections of the code. State deductions often vary from federal deductions and are creatures of state statute.

*See also:* depreciation; trade.

**above-the-line deduction (non-itemized deduction)**   A deduction that is not itemized and reduces gross income. An above-the-line-deduction from personal federal income tax is not itemized on Schedule A. Instead, it is subtracted from total income on the Form 1040, the result being the adjusted gross income (AGI). Above-the-line deductions are not, therefore, limited by the standard deduction but always reduce taxable income. Moreover, above-the-line deductions are not affected by the AGI, which is used as a limit on many below-the-line deductions.

In 2010, above-the-line deductions included (a) reimbursed employee expenses; (b) certain expenses of performing artists, state officials, teachers, and reservists; (c) losses from the sale of property; (d) expenses from producing rental or royalty income; (e) adjustments for property life tenants and income beneficiaries; (f) retirement plan savings for the self-employed; (g) penalties forfeited through premature withdrawal of funds; (h) alimony payments; (i) reforestation expenses; (j) required repayments of supplemental unemployment compensation; (k) jury duty pay given to one's employer; (l) clean fuel vehicles costs; (m) moving expenses; (n) Archer Medical Savings Accounts; (o) qualified student loan interest; (p) higher education expenses; (q) health savings accounts; and (r) costs from certain discrimination suits or whistleblower suits.

**dividends-received deduction**   A deduction meant to prevent triple taxation on dividends. The deduction for dividends received is intended to prevent triple taxation. When a corporation receives dividends from another corporation, multiple taxation of the same income is eased, or avoided, by allowing the corporate shareholder a dividends received deduction. The deductible percentage of the dividends received deduction depends upon the percentage of ownership that the receiving corporate shareholder holds in the corporation making the dividend distribution. If the corporation owns less than 20% of the corporation making the dividend distribution, it can deduct 70%, between 20% and 80%, it can deduct 80%, more than 80%, it can deduct 100%.

**itemized deduction (below-the-line deduction)**   An itemized deduction from the adjusted gross income. A below-the-line deduction for federal personal income is an itemized deduction that must be itemized on Schedule A. Taxable income is computed by subtracting all itemized deductions (or the standard deduction if it is greater than the sum of itemized deductions) from the adjusted gross income (AGI). Thus, itemized deductions are calculated following the determination of the AGI, and certain itemized deductions are limited by reference to the AGI, such as the medical expenses deduction, which (in 2010) only became deductible if the sum of medical and dental expenses in the year were 7.5% or greater of the AGI. Further, because below-the-line deductions are compared to the standard deduction, they are used only if they exceed the standard deduction.

There are many itemized deductions. In 2010, non-miscellaneous itemized deductions included: (a) qualified interest, including mortgage interest, student loan interest, and investment interest (if more than investment income); (b) qualified state and local taxes; (c) losses to casualty or theft (if over 10% of AGI and over $500); (d) qualified charitable donations (if no more than 30% or 50% of AGI, depending on the donee); (e) medical expenses (over 7.5% of AGI); (f) impairment-related work expenses; (g) estate taxes of decedent; (h) losses from the sale of personal property; (i) restoration of amounts under a claim of right; (j) annuity losses, bond payments, and cooperative housing payments. Deductions that are not within these categories are miscellaneous deductions, the sum of which must be more than 2% of AGI.

**marital deduction**   Deduction from estate and gift tax for gifts to one's spouse. The marital deduction in the federal gift and estate taxes allows one spouse to transfer property to the other spouse with no transfer tax at all, whether the gift is made while the donor is alive or as a matter of the donor's estate.

**standard deduction**   A set deduction that substitutes for itemization. The standard deduction is a minimum deduction available to every federal income taxpayer that serves both to equalize returns between taxpayers who itemize and those who don't and to set a criterion sum below which deductions need not be itemized or proved to be applied. The standard deduction is a fixed amount per person for whom the return applies, which rises with inflation. For the 2009 tax year, the individual standard deduction was $5,700, for heads of households was $8,400, for married couples filing jointly was $11,400, and for non-earning dependents was $850.

**tax deferred transaction (tax-deferred transaction)**   A transaction that is taxed in a later year. A tax-deferred transaction is any transaction that is eligible for a delay in its tax consequences until a later filing period than the period of the transaction. A variety of transactions allows the tax to be deferred, including corporate transfers among subsidiaries, and including individual transfers to a section 1031 exchange through a qualified intermediary, (see 26 U.S.C. § 1031) a transfer to a charitable remainder trust, a transfer to a private annuity trust, a transfer to a deferred sales trust, a purchase by a self-directed individual retirement account of investment property not owned by a family member, and an exchange between co-tenants.

**Section 1031 exchange**   A tax-deferred barter of property for similar property. A Section 1031 exchange is an exchange between investors or businesses of one productive property in return for a property of a similar nature and productivity, which allows each transferee to recognize the gain or the loss from the exchange in a later tax period, when the transferee finally disposes of the acquired property. To preserve the appropriate tax consequences, the transferee retains the original basis in the newly acquired property. Section 1031 of the Internal Revenue Code, 26 U.S.C. § 1031, which authorizes the tax deferral of these trades, excepts a number of transactions from deferred recognition of their tax status, notably, a transaction with a purpose of avoiding tax.

**tax exemption (tax exempt)**   The release of a transaction from tax liability. A tax exemption is a provision in the tax code or regulations of a tax jurisdiction that either allows a deduction for income or business taxes that would otherwise be owed on a specific transaction or excuses the reporting of such a transaction or collection on taxes at its source. Transactions not subject to sales tax are tax exempt. The following, among others, are all subject to tax exemptions under various tax laws: (a) organizations, such as qualified charities; (b) individuals, such as members of the clergy; (c) income, such as income earned and taxed abroad; and (d) property, such as homesteads.

**dependency exemption**   A reduction from taxable income for each dependent. The dependency exemption is a reduction in taxable income provided for each dependent of a taxpayer. Determining dependency requires that the person is qualified as a dependent.

For a person to qualify as a dependent of a taxpayer, the person must meet five dependency tests, as of 2009: The person must be a child or relative of the taxpayer. The person must have an annual gross income of less than $3,650, unless the person is the taxpayer's child and either under age 19 or a full-time student under age 24. The person must have received more than one half of the person's support from the taxpayer. The person cannot file a joint tax return, unless it was filed only as a claim for refund. The person must be a U.S. citizen or national, or U.S. resident, or a citizen or resident of Canada or of Mexico. For determining a dependent relative, a family member includes a child, stepchild, adopted child, grandchild, great-grandchild, son-in-law, daughter-in-law, father-in-law, mother-in-law, brother-in-law, sister-in-law, parent, brother, sister, grandparent, step-parent, step-brother or sister, half–brother or half–sister, as well as an uncle, aunt, niece, or nephew (if related by blood).

**personal exemption (spousal exemption)**  Amount every taxpayer may deduct from taxable income. The personal exemption is an inflation–adjusted amount that every taxpayer is entitled to deduct from taxable income. For tax year 2010, the personal exemption amount was $3,650.

A spousal exemption is a personal exemption for the spouse of the taxpayer filing a return. A taxpayer filing as head of household, or two taxpayers in a joint filling, or a taxpayer in a separate return, may deduct a spouse's personal exemption, as long as the spouse had no gross income, is not filing a different return, and was not the dependent of another taxpayer.

**tax filing status (tax-filing status)**  The personal or family unit represented in a filing. The tax–filing status of a taxpayer is both the form for the federal income tax return to be filed and the nature of the personal or family unit to be represented in the filing. There are five categories of status as of 2009: single; married filing jointly; married filing separately; head of household; and qualifying widow(er) with dependent child.

> **married filling jointly (joint return)**  Two spouses filling a single return. Married filing jointly is the filing status of two spouses who file a single combined return, reporting their combined incomes and combined deductions. Each must use the same accounting period, and each is fully responsible for the tax of both, although each is solely responsible for any errors each makes in the filing.

> **married filling jointly, marriage penalty**  A greater tax liability for a joint return than two separate returns. The marriage penalty in federal individual income tax is the higher effective rate applied to two married filers of similar income who file jointly than the rate would be if they each filed separately. This effect has varied in different tax brackets and different years according to changes in the Tax Code. Even so, the Tax Code allows taxpayers to elect each year to file jointly or separately, and the choice of one year has no bearing on the choice that must be made the next.

**W-2 form (W-2)**  Annual employer report of an employee's income and withholding. IRS form W–2 is documentation filed annually by every employer with the Social Security Administration and provided to the employee, which summarizes taxable wages and earnings and withholding for Social Security (FICA), Medicare, and taxes. The W–2 provided to the employee is filed with state and local tax authorities as well as with the IRS with the employee's tax returns.

*See also:* Social Security, Federal Insurance Contibutions Act (FICA).

**W-4 form (W-4)**  Employee report on withholding given to an employer. IRS form W–4 is documentation an employee completes and submits to an employer to determine the portion of wages and other income that will be withheld from the employee's paycheck and submitted to tax authorities.

**tax haven**  A jurisdiction with low taxes. A tax haven is a jurisdiction with low taxes, particularly a tax code that allows the movement of income or wealth into the jurisdiction for tax purposes in order to encourage avoidance of tax in other jurisdictions. Most tax havens require no physical presence for a taxpayer to proclaim a domicile in the jurisdiction, have laws protecting against financial information disclosures, and have minimal financial reporting requirements.

Tax havens have long existed to lure wealth to smaller, poorer states. Contemporary problems in tracking the funds of criminal organizations and terrorists have brought much greater transparency in the laws of many tax havens, yet tracking transactions in such jurisdictions remains difficult.

**tax rate**  The percentage of value or income that equals the tax liability. A tax rate is a specific multiple of a value, income, profit, or any other basis that results in a tax liability. Determining the tax rate for a given tax may require great specificity. The sales tax rate on a given product may vary by jurisdiction, just as the sales tax rate in a jurisdiction may vary by the category of product. The tax rate for property may vary widely according to the use of the property. The federal individual income tax rate varies according to the taxable income of the filer.

> **effective tax rate**  The ratio of tax paid to actual income. The effective tax rate is an assessment of the burden in fact upon a taxpayer compared to all earnings and income, rather than the official rate applied to income adjusted by exclusions, deductions and the like. There are several formulae for estimating an effective tax rate, whether the estimate is of the rate applied to a person or business or the rate in a jurisdiction or category of filers. In general, each requires the amount actually paid in taxes to be divided by a sum equal to income or value. The formulae vary according to both the definition of value or income and to the scope of the taxes included. The effective tax rate of the poor is, for instance, much higher when sales tax is included.

**flat tax**  A single–rate income tax without deductions. The flat tax is a proposed income tax that replaces all rate schedules, deductions, and exclusions and requires a 19% tax rate on all personal and business income, except for earnings from savings. Business income would be measured by deducting the cost of doing business from gross receipts. As proposed, however, the flat tax would have a personal or family allowance that amounts to a deduction, and certain of the costs of business would amount to deductions as well.

The flat tax is alluring to many critics of the complex taxation system in the United States. It is controversial owing to claims it would unfairly increase the burden on the poor, to arguments that the taxpayer incentives created by tax policy are too valuable to abolish, and to observations that the tax would be more complex and avoidable in practice than it first appears.

**marginal tax rate** The highest rate that applies to a taxpayer. A marginal tax rate is a tax rate that applies to a taxpayer's "last dollar," in other words, the rate that applies to the stratum of a taxpayer's income that represents the highest tax bracket in which the taxpayer's income can be taxed. If, for instance, there are six tax brackets (the range in which a rate applies), and a taxpayer earns enough to be in the fourth tax bracket, the 28% bracket, then this is that taxpayer's marginal rate (income in brackets below the amount in that bracket is taxed at the lower rates). The marginal rate may mean the highest possible rate, the rate that applies only to the wealthiest filers.

**tax bracket** The category of tax rate applicable to a particular level of income or profit. A tax bracket is the level of personal income or business profit by which the taxpayer is determined to be subject to a particular tax rate. For federal personal income taxes, there were, in 2009, six brackets, for a single taxpayer the highest applying a 35% rate to taxable incomes of $335,650 or more; the next highest applying a 33% rate to taxable incomes between $171,850 and $335,650; the next higher applying a 28% rate to taxable incomes between $82,400 and $171,850; the next higher applying a 25% rate to taxable incomes between $34,000 and $82,400; the next higher applying a 15% rate to taxable incomes between and $8,375 and $34,000; and the lowest applying a 10% rate to taxable incomes from $0 to $8,375.

**tax return** A report stating a tax basis and liability. A tax return is a report filed with a taxing authority that discloses the information required by law regarding the sources and amount of income for a taxpayer, as well as the taxpayer's assessment of the taxpayer's liability for such income, and a statement of an amount owed to be paid or to be refunded.
See also: tax, tax crime, failure to file return.

**tax shelter** A business arrangement entered solely to avoid tax. A tax shelter is the use of any assets in a decision, investment, sale, or purchase, including the entry into a partnership, corporation or other entity, that results in reduced or avoided taxation. The use of a tax shelter is not an inherent violation of the Tax Code, as long as there is a bona fide reason for the underlying decision other than tax avoidance and the information provided on the return and any reports related to the shelter is accurate.

**Dutch Sandwich (double Irish)** A transfer of corporate funds among shell companies in different jurisdictions to lower tax liability. The Dutch sandwich is the diversion of profits made in jurisdictions with high tax rates through shell companies in jurisdictions that have low taxes on transfers into jurisdictions with low tax rates, where the profit is booked. The label arises from the frequent resort of corporations to the Netherlands as the pivot state for such transactions in 2010, though many jurisdictions allow such transfers with low or no transfer taxes. Ireland and other states are also employed for this purpose, and so there are a variety of names for it.
See also: price, transfer price (transfer pricing).

**tax year (taxable year)** A fiscal year or calendar year. The tax year, or taxable year, is the time increment of twelve months that is the basis for the taxpayer's reporting of taxes. For a business, the tax year is calculated as the taxpayer selects, whether the taxpayer elects to use a calendar year or a fiscal year. The taxpayer must either continue to use the same year basis for reporting taxes or file an adjusted return for the prior year when changing the basis.
For individuals, the tax year is the calendar year.

**use tax** A tax on goods, especially applied to foreign sales. A use tax is a form of consumption tax, like a sales tax, although use tax may include transactions that are beyond the definition of a sale in the jurisdiction of the taxing authority, both in the form of transaction and in the location of the transaction. Thus, a use tax reaches transactions by a person subject to tax by a given authority even in a location not otherwise subject to tax by that authority. In practice there is little difference between a sales tax and a use tax, and many jurisdictions have a "sales and use tax," and some states use the terms interchangeably.

**value-added tax (V.A.T or VAT or value added tax)** A form of sales tax allocated to each point in a supply chain. A value-added tax, or VAT, is a consumption tax that is allocated at every stage of transfer or services, even between merchants or businesses. VAT is thought of as a tax on value added to goods, but because VAT in practice includes a rebate to the entity that adds value, the effect is to allocate payment of the tax by the ultimate consumer to each stage of the manufacture and service that led to the goods or services the consumer receives. The benefit is a fairer and more comprehensive tax system, which allows the same tax rates on the ultimate consumer but better ensures their collection from intermediaries, producers, and consumers.

**taxable estate** See: estate, worth, taxable estate.

**taxable gift** See: gift, taxable gift, gift to a minor (Uniform Gifts To Minors Act or U.G.M.A. or UGMA or Uniform Transfers To Minors Act or U.T.M.A.); gift, taxable gift.

**taxable income** See: income, taxable income.

**taxation and tax law** See: income, earned income, taxation and tax law.

**taxes**

**ways and means (ways and means committee)**
The methods of taxation and governmental funding. Ways and means to raise revenue is the euphemistic title for the jurisdiction of tax legislation and other laws for the generation of revenue for a state or government. Both the U.S. Senate and the U.S. House of Representatives have committees on ways and means, the House Committee on Ways and Means being the originating committee for all revenue bills. Most state legislatures have similar committees.
*See also:* revenue.

**taxing power or taxation power**   *See:* power, power to tax (taxing power or taxation power).

**taxpayer action or taxpayer suit**   *See:* citizen, citizen suit (taxpayer action or taxpayer suit).

**taxpayer standing**   *See:* standing in court, taxpayer standing (citizen standing or double–nexus test).

**TDR**   *See:* zoning, transferable development right (TDR).

**technical**   Related to the technique of a trade, art, profession, or specialty. Technical, or those things related to a technique, are associated with a particular category of skills, knowledge, vocabulary, custom, and practices that are essential to a specialty of human activity and, by their nature, are less likely to be expressed in general language, as opposed to the technical language of the specialty.

Material written in technical language must be read according to the customs and vocabulary of the specialty, not merely translating words of art but interpreting the whole of the text according to a reasonable and customary understanding that would be appropriate within the specialty. A technical document in evidence may be appropriately interpreted by an expert qualified in the specialty appropriate to that document. Likewise physical evidence or lay testimony requiring technical understanding is appropriately described or interpreted by an expert in the appropriate specialty. In none of these cases, however, may the expert's evidence be so conclusive as to whether negligence or a breach of duty occurred as to invade the province of the jury.
*See also:* expert (expertise).

**technology**   The application of knowledge to a thing made or done by humans. Technology is the application of science, technique, knowledge, or skill to make or to do anything related to a process or system created by human beings. Although technology is often manifest in a thing or device, it includes processes developed from science or knowledge, especially a practice that becomes an accepted standard in a given field of endeavor. Technology is the broadest possible term for the invention or use of devices, the implementation of scientific understanding, and the creation of things and processes from theory. Technology is manifest in every invention that is capable of being patented, but it may

also manifest in generic processes and basic techniques that are unpatentable.
*See also:* biotechnology.

**control technology (pollution control technology)**
Devices, substances, and processes to control any activity. In general, a control technology is a device, system, or process, with components that are mechanical, electrical, chemical, or biological that control any activity. There are control technologies, for instance, to manage the transfer of electronic recordings, to ensure the quality of manufactured goods, and to provide all manner of monitoring, safety, and comfort, ranging from thermostats in buildings to the automatic brakes of trains.

Control technology is commonly used in environmental law to mean pollution control technology. Pollution control technology includes every aspect of transportation, industrial, or commercial process that is intended to control the emission of pollution into the environment, whether directly or indirectly. Control technologies include any process, design element, input or input limitation, extractor, monitoring system, filtration system, operations protocol or any other step done or thing used to reduce, abate, or monitor potential pollutants or elements of pollutants in a process.

Various pollution control laws and permits require differing standards of control technology. All water effluent point discharges since March 31, 1989, require at least the best conventional pollutant control technology (although for the decade earlier, they had required only the best practicable control technology). Point sources that are designated for standards of performance, however, must employ best available demonstrated control technology. Long–permitted facilities generating non–hazardous air pollution must usually demonstrate the use of reasonably available control technology. In contrast, hazardous air pollutant emitters must employ the maximum achievable control technology. For vehicles, verified technology is any form of technology that has been verified for use by the EPA or a state pollution control agency. The hallmark of a technology–driven standard is that compliance alters as the technology alters, thus creating an inherent market for the improvement of technology as well as a legal requirement for the improvement of pollution control devices and systems.
*See also:* pollution, water pollution, Clean Water Act (CWA); pollution, air pollution, Clean Air Act (C.A.A. or CAA).

**teleology**   *See:* jurisprudence, teleology (consequentialism or teleological).

**telephone appearance**   *See:* appearance, telephone appearance.

**temporary**   Something intended not to be permanent. Temporary is a limit by time on any action, conduct, or condition. Any condition that is limited in the time in which it can occur is, by that limitation, a temporary condition. The law may specify a length of time for a temporary condition, such as the twenty-one days of a temporary restraining order, or by stating the fact that a law or order is temporary, may imply that whatever privileges or liabilities created by it are abolished after a stated or reasonable time.

*See also:* ex, ex tempore.

**temporary disability** *See:* disability, personal disability, permanent disability (temporary disability).

**temporary insanity** *See:* insanity, temporary insanity.

**temporary nuisance** *See:* nuisance, temporary nuisance.

**temporary restraining order** *See:* injunction, temporary restraining order (T.R.O. or TRO).

**temporary taking** *See:* taking, temporary taking.

**temporary trustee or trustee ad litem or trustee pro tem** *See:* trustee, interim trustee (temporary trustee or trustee ad litem or trustee pro tem).

**tenancy** The condition of owning or possessing land. A tenancy is a legal interest in land under the common law. The definition of tenancy has been extended by statutes to reach some types of personal property, particularly in the sense of a co-tenancy. Even so, every form of present possessory ownership in land is a form of tenancy.

A tenancy is commonly used in contemporary practice to refer to a leasehold, the non-freehold interest of a tenant. A lease or rental arrangement in lands gives rise to a form of tenancy in the common law. Thus, a landlord who owns a parcel in fee simple is the tenant on the land, but should the landlord lease the land to another party, then the other party is a non-freehold tenant of the fee tenant.

*See also:* lease, leasehold, tenancy, tenancy of years (tenancy for years or tenancy for a definite term or term of years or term for years); lease, leasehold, tenancy, tenancy at will (at-will tenancy); lease, leasehold, tenancy, tenancy at sufferance; lease, leasehold, tenancy, periodic tenancy, year-to-year tenancy (yearly lease or annual lease or year to year tenancy); lease, leasehold, tenancy, periodic tenancy, week-to-week tenancy; lease, leasehold, tenancy, periodic tenancy, quarter-to-quarter tenancy (quarterly lease); lease, leasehold, tenancy, periodic tenancy, month-to-month tenancy (monthly lease or month to month lease); lease, leasehold, tenancy, periodic tenancy; lease.

**tenancy at sufferance** *See:* lease, leasehold, tenancy, tenancy at sufferance.

**tenancy at will** *See:* lease, leasehold, tenancy, tenancy at will (at-will tenancy).

**tenancy for years or tenancy for a definite term or term of years or term for years** *See:* lease, leasehold, tenancy, tenancy of years (tenancy for years or tenancy for a definite term or term of years or term for years).

**tenancy of years** *See:* lease, leasehold, tenancy, tenancy of years (tenancy for years or tenancy for a definite term or term of years or term for years).

**co-tenancy (cotenant or co-tenant or cotenancy)** One of several interests in the same land at the same time. A co-tenancy is an interest in land that is simultaneous with another person's right to use the exact same land. A co-tenancy is a right in every bit of the land, not merely to one part. Co-tenancy can be thought of as one of several ownerships in a house, though not one in which one co-tenant has one room and another the next; both or all co-tenants have interests in all of the rooms, the walls, the floors, the ceilings, and the use of the spaces. Co-tenancy takes several, distinct forms, particularly tenancy in common, joint tenancy, and tenancy by the entireties. There may be any number of co-tenants in a single estate, although if the co-tenancy is by the entireties, there may be only two co-tenants. A co-tenancy may be dissolved involuntarily through an action in partition, brought by one co-tenant against the other.

*See also:* tenancy, co-tenancy, tenancy by the entireties (entirety or tenancy by the entirety or tenants by the entireties); heir, parcener (coparceny or co-parcener or coparceners or parcenary).

***right to exclude co-tenant*** A cotenant has the right to use the whole of the property subject to the cotenancy, as do the other cotenants. A cotenant exercising the right of full occupancy who excludes another cotenant from occupancy violates the other cotenant's right to occupancy. The excluded cotenant has a right of action against the greedy cotenant for damages for past exclusion and injunction against future exclusion.

**joint tenancy (joint tenants or joint estate)** A co-tenancy created with a right of survivorship, not between spouses though. A joint tenancy is a co-tenancy in which both joint tenants have an identical interest in the property jointly held, as well as a right of survivorship that vests the sole ownership in one if the other dies. A joint tenancy must be created by a prior owner, who transfers the property to the joint tenants with language making clear the intent to create the right of survivorship, which is usually done by a grant using the formulaic "as joint tenants with rights of survivorhip and not as tenants in common." The grantor must create the joint tenancy with the four unities intact, which is to say that each must be given an undivided, equal interest of the same form and degree, which is given to each at the same as it is given to the other, to last for the same time. A co-tenancy that does not meet these requirements is not a joint tenancy but a tenancy in common, which has no right of survivorship. A co-tenancy that is created with these four unities and also the unity of marriage between the parties may be a tenancy by the entireties.

A joint tenancy persists only for as long as the identical interests among the co-tenants persist. If one joint tenant sells the share, the new owner of the share is not a joint tenant but a tenant in kind.

See also: tenancy, co-tenancy, tenancy by the entireties (entirety or tenancy by the entirety or tenants by the entireties).

*right of survivorship*   A joint tenancy, like a tenancy by the entireties, has a right of survivorship. If any joint tenant dies, the interest of that tenant is destroyed. The interest is not transferred to the surviving tenants; it just ceases to be, leaving the surviving interests intact. A joint tenancy is not heritable or alienable, although an attempt to alienate it destroys it and creates a tenancy in common, which is heritable and alienable.
See also: survivor, right of survivorship.

**per my et per tout (per tout)**   By every part and by the whole. Per my et per tout is a customary signal that property is to be held in joint tenancy. Even so, property given in joint tenancy in contemporary practice must rebut the presumption that a co-tenancy is in common, not only by establishing the four unities but also by a statement that the tenancy is not in common. A tenancy in common is also, in fact, per my et per tout, though this tag should not be used for it. Note: cases in the U.S. have translated "per my" as by the half, but the common law considered it by the part; the difference becomes important if there are three or more joint tenants.

**unities**

**four unities (T.I.T.S. or TITS)**   Time, interest, title, and seisin. The four unities of a joint tenancy are the four unities between or among the co-tenants that must be established at the time the co-tenancy is created and persist as long as the co-tenancy persists, or the joint tenancy is converted to a tenancy in common, destroying the right of survivorship. Establishing the unities is not enough, and appropriate language to rebut the presumption of individual heritability in the tenancy in common is required. The four unities are time, in that the interests must vest at the same time and last for the same time; interest, in that each must have an equal and undivided interest in the whole; title, in that each must have the same priority of title; and seisin, in that each must receive title at the same time and through the same vehicle.
See also: unity.

**tenancy by the entireties (entirety or tenancy by the entirety or tenants by the entireties)**   A co-tenancy between spouses, with rights of survivorship. A tenancy by the entireties is created when all of the conditions required to create a joint tenancy are satisfied, and the co-tenants are spouses of one another. The language of creation must be specific to vest both as tenants by the entireties with rights of survivorship, in language sufficient to rebut the presumption of a tenancy in common. The five unities of a tenancy by the entirety are time, interest, title, seisin, and matrimony (or marriage). At the

death of one spouse, that spouse's tenancy is then destroyed, leaving the surviving spouse as sole tenant of the property.
See also: tenancy, co-tenancy, joint tenancy (joint tenants or joint estate); tenancy, co-tenancy (co-tenant or co-tenant or cotenancy); survivor, right of survivorship.

**tenancy in common (tenants in common)**   A co-tenant with no right of survivorship. A tenancy in common is the co-tenancy of the most basic form, in which each co-tenant has a unity of possession with other co-tenants. In other words, each co-tenant has a right to possess the whole of the property, but no other unity or formality is required. There may be any number of tenants in common, and they may have different shares of the benefit of ownership, different interests and forms of title, and they need not have acquired seisin in common. Indeed, when a joint tenancy among A, B, and C is broken by C's sale to D, D is a tenant in common for 1/3 interest with the joint tenancy of A and B, which has a 2/3 interest. A tenancy in common is alienable and heritable; it may be given or sold while alive, and at the death of the tenant in common, the tenancy is an asset of the estate in probate or administration.

*right of survivorship*   There is no right of survivorship in a tenancy-in-common. At the death of one tenant-in-common, the interest of the decedent is transferred to devisees or heirs, not to the other tenants unless they are devisees or heirs.

**tenant**   The lessee, or the owner of an estate. A tenant is a lessee. A tenant is also an owner. The much more common use of tenant is, in current U.S. practice, in the sense of lessee.

As a lessee, a tenant is usually both the holder of a non-freehold interest in the property and a contracting party in an agreement with the landlord. In the absence of an agreement, however, the tenant as lessee is still a tenant, albeit a tenant by sufferance. Tenants as lessees are defined according to the interest they have in their leaseholds, i.e., tenancy for years, periodic tenancy (for example, a month-to-month tenancy), tenancy at sufferance, holdover tenancy, etc. These, in turn, give rise to a tenant for years, a periodic tenant (for example, a month-to-month tenant), a tenant at sufferance, a holdover tenant, etc.

As a tenant of an estate in land, the tenant also holds according to the interest, such as a co-tenant (or a tenant in common, joint tenant, or tenant by the entireties), or a tenant in fee. This sense of tenant is by far the less common in usage, but it is still encountered, and context is essential to distinguish the two senses.

**tenant eviction**   See: eviction (evict).

**tenant services**   See: service, feudal service (tenant services).

**tenants in common**   See: tenancy, co-tenancy, tenancy in common (tenants in common).

**life tenant** A holder of a life estate in lands. A life tenant holds a life estate, which is a fee simple in land that persists for the life of the tenant and no longer. A life tenant may transfer an interest, including the fee, to another person, but that interest will become a life estate pur autre vie, and it will expire when the life tenant does. Note: a life tenancy in the benefits of a trust is not ordinarily transferable by the beneficiary, although transferability depends on the terms of the trust.

*See also:* estate, interest, life estate (life interest).

**tenant as lessee** The holder under a lease of a non-freehold interest in land. A tenant, in the sense of a lessee, is a holder of a non-freehold interest in the land, subject to a reversion to the landlord at the termination of the lease. During the period of the lease, the tenant has the right of possession of the land, even, at common law, to the exclusion of the landlord, although contemporary landlord–tenant law and contracts have usually reserved to the landlord a right to enter. A tenant remains the tenant until possession is surrendered, although the status of the tenancy and title of the tenant may change. Thus, a tenant for a term of years becomes a holdover tenant if the tenant remains in possession when the lease expires.

*See also:* lease.

**holdover tenant (hold-over or holding over or hold-over tenant)** A tenant in possession after the lease expires. A holdover tenant is a tenant remaining in possession of leasehold estate after the lease has come to an end. The landlord may elect to eject a holdover, to treat the tenant as a tenant by sufferance or to treat the tenant as entering a periodic tenancy.

*See also:* landlord, landlord–tenant relationship.

**sub-tenant (undertenant or sub-lessee)** The lessee of a lessee. A sub-tenant is the tenant of a tenant, or the lessee of a lessee. The sub-tenant takes as much of the tenant's leasehold as the tenant chooses to lease, which may be all or part of the tenant's own leasehold, placing the tenant in a relationship like a landlord to the sub-tenant, with a reversion as to the sub-tenancy. At common law, a tenant could freely sub-lease, although most leases now require the written consent of the landlord to do so.

A sub-lease does not excuse the obligations of the tenant, even if the sub-lease is of the entire leasehold. Unlike an assignment of the lease, the sub-tenancy does not release the tenant from the covenant of rents, covenant not to waste, or any other duty under the lease. Note: there is no difference between a sub-tenant and a sub-lessee.

*See also:* tenant; lease, assignment of lease; lease, sublease (sublessee or subtenant).

**tenant in chief (tenant-in-chief)** A tenant holding land directly below the crown. A tenant-in-chief was (and to a slight extent still is) the tenant holding land directly from the crown, the tenant whose obligations were directly to the monarch and within whose estates were likely to be several levels of mesne tenancy.

**tenant of the desmesne (tenant in desmesne)** The feudal tenant of a lesser lord. A tenant of the desmesne is a tenant of a mesne lord, that is, a tenant of a lesser member of the nobility who is himself a tenant of a superior.

*See also:* landlord, mesne lord.

**terre-tenant** The owner of land who is seized of it and who possesses it. A terre-tenant, or tenant on the land, is a tenant in fee simple in the common law. The terre-tenant was once particularly the title of the holder of land subject to use by another. The term is still used, particularly to describe the "real owner" or possessor of land subject to a mortgage.

*See also:* use, doctrine of uses, cestui que use.

**tender** An offer, particularly to pay a current debt. A tender, generally, is an offer. There are several specialized senses of tender, mainly in commercial law, contracts for the sale of goods, and evidence.

Tender as a matter of commercial law is also the sense in which it is also most encountered in the common law, as an offer by a debtor to pay the entirety of an outstanding debt in cash. The tender of full payment must be made in cash and without condition, presented to the creditor, who may or may not accept it and need not accept it unless the debt allows for payment in full prior to its maturity. Even so, a tender of payment in full exonerates the debtor in an action for collection brought against the debtor by the creditor.

A tender of performance, particularly a tender of goods in performance of a contract for the sale of goods, is deemed full performance as long as the goods conform to the contract requirement.

A tender of evidence is an offer of evidence, whether in argument or in a motion for admission in court.

To tender of a witness, or the tender of a witness, is for an attorney to yield to another attorney the right to examine the witness then under oath.

**tender of issue** *See:* issue, issue before the court, tender of issue.

**tender of performance** *See:* performance, contract performance, offer of performance (tender of performance).

**tender of the witness** *See:* witness, tender of the witness (tender the witness).

**tender offer** *See:* takeover, tender offer, best price rule; takeover, tender offer.

**tender the witness** *See:* witness, tender of the witness (tender the witness).

**legal tender** The money authorized by law for payment of debts. Legal tender is money, the form of money allowed by law to be offered for the payment of a debt owing, that must by law be accepted in satisfaction of the debt. In the United States, legal tender includes all bills and coins issued in dollars by the Federal Reserve.

*See also:* money.

**tenement**   Any interest in land that is divisible from others. A tenement is any component of ownership of property in land, particularly an interest that is non-freehold such as an easement or a lease, but any component of ownership less than a fee or a full estate, such as a right to rents or profits. Though technically under the common law the tenement is the right to take rents from the lessee of lands, the term has long been applied also to the lease that generates the rents.

Owing to the use of tenement as a leasehold, a tenement is also a term for a leased residence, particularly a poorly maintained or dangerous apartment in a larger building, which is a tenement building. Tenement in this sense is associated with slums and poverty-stricken neighborhoods.

*See also:* lease, leasehold (non-freehold estate or non-freehold estate); lease, leasehold (non-freehold estate or nonfreehold estate).

**dominant   tenement**   *See:* easement,   dominant estate (dominant tenement).

**servient tenement**   *See:* easement, servient estate (servient tenement).

**tenendum clause or habendum et tenendum clause**   *See:* deed, habendum clause (tenendum clause or habendum et tenendum clause).

**tenure**   The form by which one holds a tenancy. Tenure is, generally, the holding of something, particularly for a long time. In its original sense in the common law, tenure is the manner by which one holds a tenancy, whether as tenant-in-chief, so that the tenure is immediate, or as a mesne tenant so the tenure is mediate, or not directly from the crown. This sense of tenure suggests that the manner by which a property interest is held determines the ease with which one may protect that interest or be ousted from the property.

From that sense arises the notion of tenure in employment, by which an employee may be vested with tenure and thus not subject to discharge except on proof of some stated cause for discharge.

*See also:* tenure, feudal tenure, military tenure, knight's service (escuage); serfdom (serf).

**feudal tenure (feudalism or feudal system)**   The system of medieval landholding. Feudal tenure is the structure of interests in land by which all lands were owned by the crown and held by each tenant subject to the rendering of services or payments of rents in a descending hierarchy from the monarch to tenants in chief, to mesne tenants, to the serfs, copyholders, and freemen. Each held an estate of some form, including rights in the estate and its liberties, which were enjoyed so long as the services that were required to be rendered to the lord over that estate were performed.

*See also:* time; feud, feudalism (feudal law).

**base estate (base fee)**   The lowest fee in the feudal hierarchy. The base fee is the fee below which there are no more fee interests, although others may hold a non-fee interest, such as a serf or villein with customary interests or a copyholder. The base fee was usually held by service to a mesne lord.

**copyhold**   The estate in land of a serf or villein on a manor. Copyhold teure was the lowest estate in lands acknowledged by feudal law, usually held by a serf or villein tied to the lands of a manor. The copyholder did not have a deed reflecting the estate or its boundaries, but the interests were recorded on a roll, the copyholder having only a copy of that entry. The estate ceased to be recognized in England in 1922 and 1925, under Lord Birkenhead's property reforms, in which they were converted into either freeholds or leaseholds in which the lord of the manor continued to hold mineral rights and some other franchises.

**copyholder**   A serf or villein on a manor. A copyholder holds lands by virtue of a record in the manor rolls rather than by deed.

*See also:* manor (manorial); feud, feudalism (feudal law).

**frankalmoign (religious tenure)**   Land held by an ecclesiastical body in return for prayers for the soul of the donor. Frankalmoign was a medieval tenure by which a diocese, church, monastery, order, or other ecclesiastical corporation held real property. The land was given with a stipulation or understanding that the donee churchmen would ensure that some unspecified services would be rendered, usually eternal prayers for the soul of the donor or others for whom the donor sought intercession, although this requirement varied with the terms of the grant or the interpretation of the donees. The enforcement of this duty was not a matter for the law courts but left to the donees or, at most, the canon courts. Frankalmoign was not a tenure under the grantor's estate but a freehold treated as a fee simple.

**gavelkind**   Lands in the County of Kent held in fee for farming services given to the lord. Gavelkind is a particular tenure established in Kent, by which the tenant did not render knight's service but gave services as husbandman, or as a farmer tenant, to the lord over the fee. Gavelkind was not subject to primogeniture but descended equally to all of the sons of a tenant or, if there were no sons living at the death of the tenant, then equally to any daughters alive. There were a host of other customs related to the tenure and to land subject to it, which are of interest solely as a matter of history. Gavelkind was abolished in 1925 in England and never used in the United States. It remains beloved, though, of a certain tradition of property professor.

**military tenure**   Tenure in land in return for military service to the monarch directly. Military tenures in land included knight's service, grand serjeanty, and petit serjeanty, each of which originated as personal services owed to the monarch. Knight's service was the most common form of tenancy, and most feudal lands not held by the church were once subject to knight's service. Some few tenancies in England are still subject to grand serjeanty, the holders of which tenures are required to provide sergeants for ceremonies in service to the monarch.

**knight's service (escuage)** Tenure in lands in return for military service or a fee. Knights service, or escuage, was a tenure in lands by which the tenant held the land subject to service to the monarch by providing a fully equipped knight when required for the defense of the realm. Initially the core service of the system of feudal tenures, the requirement of personal service was soon replaced by a requirement of provision, which in many cases was waived in return for a fee, or scutage, which eventually became the norm. Knights service was abolished in 1660.

*See also:* tenure.

**knight's tenure, shield money (scutage)** Rents for land subject to knight's tenure. Shield money was money paid as scutage or in lieu of military service by a tenant in lands held by military tenure. The original obligation to provide the service of a knight complete with equipage suitable for service in the field eventually became a tax on land held according to one of the basic tenures. Scutage was not abolished until 1660.

**serjeanty (sergeantry)** Tenure in return for service owed directly to the monarch. Sergeantry, or serjeanty, was a tenure in Crown lands, which were held directly in return for service directly to the monarch. It was further divided into grand or petit serjeanty. Lands in English colonies held by a proprietor or by Crown grant were sometimes held in petit serjeanty.

*See also:* sergeant (serjeant).

**socage** Tenure in lands for services to the lord. Socage was a medieval form of tenure in lands, held by the tenant in return for either rents or agricultural services rendered to the lord over the socage estate. The tenant, or socager, would always have an obligation of fealty to the lord of the estate regardless of whether rents or services were owed. Some socagers, the villeins, were obligated to provide a specified number of days of labor on the lands of the feudal lord and sometimes to provide other services, such as labor on the roads or otherwise. Free socagers, or freemen, needed only to pay rents to the lord. Free socage was further divided between socage in chief (or socage in capite, in which the tenant held directly from the monarch and, usually, other tenants were beholden to the socager) and common free socage. Following the abolition of rents service for socage, the modern freehold developed from common free socage.

**free and common socage** The estate of the freeman. Free and common socage was a tenure held on the estate of a lord, or in some few cases, immediately from the crown, in which the tenant owed fealty and fixed rent to the lord or king in return for the lands. Such services as were required were honorable, which is to say not menial.

**villein socage (villeinage socage)** Tenure of land in retrun for base agricultural service. Villein socage, or villeinage, was usually the base fee, held in return for services rendered on the lands of the lord over the estate. Villein socage was inferior to free socage, which required only fealty and rents, while villein socage required actual services, usually established by custom. Most villeins' interests were eventually destroyed or were converted to copyhold tenures.

**term** A word or phrase, contract condition, or time. A term, generally, is a unit of language, or of time, or of geography, or of human expectations as in a contract. The word has all these meanings because it comes from terminus, Latin for a limit or boundary, and all these things were at one time used with emphasis on the edges of their application or meaning or requirement. In law, term has nearly all these senses.

Terms in law include words, phrases, and requirements. A legal term is a term of art. The terms of an instrument are the operative specifics that apply in a given situation, whether the terms are in a will, trust, contract, commercial paper, or anything else.

Terms in a contract are more than the words employed in the writing of a written contract, being the requirements of performance by each party specific to that contract, such as performance required, identity of goods, quality of goods, price, location of delivery, etc. The terms of a contract may be expressed but they may also be implied.

Term is used in the law to represent units of time in which something is to be done or performed or during which something may occur after which it may not. The term of a lease, such as a term of years or a periodic lease, is the time within which the lease runs and the tenant has legal right to the leasehold, after which the lease is terminated and the landlord's reversion becomes possessory. The term of a debt, which is the period during which the debt is to be repaid. A term of court is the period of time (or one among several periods of time) when the court is in session. A term of office is the period an office is occupied before a new appointment or election is required. A prison term is the time required of penal servitude as a sentence following criminal conviction.

There are uses of term that are not special to the law but are specialized and used often enough in legal drafting. A person who comes to terms with something or someone has reached an agreement or understanding regarding the thing or person (in the manner that contracting parties come to terms, or agree on terms). A pregnant mother who has come to term has completed the period of pregnancy and is ready to deliver a child. A semester, quarter, or trimester is a school term.

**term assurance** *See:* insurance, category of insurance, life insurance, term life insurance (term assurance).

**term life insurance** *See:* insurance, category of insurance, life insurance, term life insurance (term assurance).

**contract term** A condition specific to a given agreement. A contract term is any condition or requirement that governs the conduct or duties of the parties or the interpretation or enforcement of the contract. In many instances, the sense implied by contractual terms is a more limited set of material or essential terms, the terms that are specific to a given agreement and necessary for each party to perform.

Material or essential terms vary according to the object of the agreement. An agreement to perform services, buy or sell land, or buy or sell goods have different essential terms. Yet, for all agreements, the performance of each party must be specified by terms that make clear what that party is to do. In general, as long as the essential aspect of performance by all parties is expressed, all other terms may be implied according to customary expectation in a trade, the examples of prior dealing between the parties, or principles of reasonableness. The essential terms that cannot be implied are the quantity of goods, the location of land, and the nature of a service. These terms and other material terms that are expressed in an agreement must be expressed with certainty, though this does not mean they must be determined at the time of the contract. A contract may be sufficiently certain as to terms that are designated to be later chosen by the parties or even one party.

*See also:* contract (k); quantity (quantitative).

**court term (session of court)** A period during which a court is routinely in session. A court term is a period during which a court remains in session, sitting on designated days throughout the term. Various courts have sessions of various lengths, between which the court is in vacation. The English crown courts had four terms of court each year. The U.S. Supreme Court has one term, officially running each year from October to the following October, although the Court is unlikely to calendar argument or other public business between June and October. In general, there is no difference between a term and a session of a court.

*See also:* time.

**term of art (words of art)** A term with a meaning particular to a profession or trade. A term of art is a word or phrase that has a particular meaning within a community sharing a specialized vocabulary as a means of carrying on a profession, trade, or specialized activity not performed by or known in detail by the general public. A term of art employed by a member of such a community, especially when communicating with another member of such a community, should be interpreted according to its meaning in the community and not according to its general meaning. Thus, a legal term used by a lawyer should be understood by its senses as a legal term and not as its plain meaning or senses as a general term.

*See also:* jargon, legal jargon (legalese or legalism).

**term of estate (lease term)** The time during which the leasehold persists. The term of an estate is the period in which the estate exists before it is destroyed by a failure of condition. An absolute estate is said either to have no term at all or a perpetual term, as the estate is hypothetically capable of enduring forever. A limited estate has a term measured either by an event certain or a condition. The term of a life estate is indeterminate in amount but certain to end with the life of the life tenant. The term of a fee simple subject to a condition subsequent is indeterminate and wholly contingent on the occurrence of the condition.

The term of a leasehold varies with the form of the lease. A lease for a term of years has a fixed, certain term that ends at the time initially specified. A periodic tenancy has a term that is indefinite but ends at the end of the period following notice (or as specified by statute). A tenancy at will or by sufferance has a term that is indefinite and ends when the contingency of the landlord's will or sufferance ends.

*See also:* lease.

**term of office** How long an official may hold office without reappointment or reelection. A term of office is a period of time specified in the law by which a given official may remain vested in an office, without the requirement of a reappointment or reelection. A term of office is usually defined specifically by a constitutional provision or statute, which specifies the date in a given year or the event in a given term at which the office is commenced and the latest time at which an office-holder must either leave the office or renew the term through a new appointment or election. Most terms of office commence at the moment the person takes an oath of office.

*See also:* oath.

**term limit** A limit on the terms one person may hold an office. A term limit is a cap on the number of terms or portions of a term of office that one person may hold in one official position. Term limits may be cumulative or serial, in that a limit may be a lifetime limitation on the number of terms of one office a person may hold or merely limit the number of terms one person may hold without an intervening term in which the office is held by someone else.

Under the Twenty-Second Amendment, the President of the United States is limited to two full terms, as well as to a period of two years in another term when someone else had initially been elected. Ratified in 1951, it followed the death in office of President Franklin Roosevelt, who died in 1945 during his fourth term.

State constitutions and statutes may limit the terms of state officials. State law cannot, however, limit the terms of federal officials, even those elected to represent a given state.

**terminable interest** *See:* property, interest in property, terminable interest.

**terminal value**   *See:* value, terminal value.

**terms of court**   *See:* court, English court, terms of court, Trinity term; court, English court, terms of court, Michaelmas term; court, English court, terms of court, Hilary term; court, English court, terms of court, Easter term; court, English court, terms of court.

**terms of shipping**   *See:* shipping, shipping term (terms of shipping).

**terra (terrae)**   Lands, both great masses and specific parcels. Terra is Latin for the earth, and in a variety of maxims and doctrines, terra occurs to represent land or lands. Context is essential to distinguish terra from lands in the most abstract to a particular land and its people to a finite parcel of land.

**Lex Terrae**   *See:* law, Law of the Land (Lex Terrae).

**terra nullius (terrae nullius)**   Land belonging to nobody. Terra nullius, Latin for "land of no person," is a territory that has no owner. Newly discovered lands with no humans living on them are res nullius. Under present doctrines, Antarctica, the sea floor, and celestial bodies such as the Moon are each terra nullius. According to customary international law, the first sovereign whose subjects discovered and claimed terra nullius had a superior claim to sovereignty over those lands than other sovereigns. This doctrine has been generally challenged, however, by the doctrine of the common heritage of mankind, which holds such discovered lands in trust for the whole of humankind rather than a monopoly by one state. Moreover, the doctrine as it is now thought to have been understood in the fifteenth through the nineteenth centuries was to consider inhabited lands as terra nullius if the inhabitants were uncivilized by European standards, meaning they lacked organized government, written language, Christian religion, and diplomatic relations, but effectively meaning they lacked the military capacity to withstand conquest. The degree to which the European empires based their conquests on the doctrine of terra nullius is, however, open to some doubt.
*See also:* res, res nullius.

**terre-tenant**   *See:* tenant, terre-tenant.

**territory (territorial)**   A region or jurisdiction. A territory is an area on the land, particularly one that is dedicated to a particular governance or jurisdiction. A territory may be marked out for many reasons, including the natural activity of the animals or plants of a habitat, or the corporate or political management or activity over a given area. For example, a territory represents the practical domain of activities by a given animal, or it may be the range of a given salesperson or franchisee.
    In the United States, to designate lands as a territory is to demarcate them as lands owned by the United States (but not organized as a state or federal district) and administered as a federal territory, either as an organized

territory, incorporated territory, or a territory. Organized territories have an organic act that has been approved by Congress. Incorporated territories are components of the United States rather than a possession, and all provisions of the U.S. Constitution apply in them. As of 2010, the U.S. possesses one incorporated unorganized territory, the Palmyra Atoll in the Pacific Ocean, as well as four organized and twelve unorganized and unincorporated territories.

**territorial jurisdiction**   *See:* jurisdiction, territorial jurisdiction, one-hundred mile bulge; jurisdiction, territorial jurisdiction.

**territorial sea**   *See:* sea, law of the sea, national waters, territorial waters (territorial sea).

**territorial waters**   *See:* sea, law of the sea, national waters, territorial waters (territorial sea).

**terror**   Fear of harm and of future harm. Terror is a state of mind that arises when one is confronted with great harm or fears an apparent danger, immediately or in the future, it is more than ordinary fear or alarm. Terror may exist in one person alone or in a group or community of people. Terror is an element of the crime of causing terror or of terrorist threatening, and it is an element of aggravation in many crimes, such as aggravated kidnapping. In the common law, terror was a long-standing basis for criminal prosecution, for those who cause terror by riot or forcible entry.

**terrorism (terroristic)**   Harm or threats to scare a populace or intimidate a government. Terrorism is an act of violence or harm against a civilian population, members of the public, infrastructure, places, or vehicles that is intended to sow fear within a population or to intimidate a government or retaliate against a government, people or state for past actions. Terrorism may include threats of such harm, but it does not include acts of a state that are within the customary boundaries of military action and governed by the laws of war. The mere fact of a state sponsor does not, however, prevent an act from being terrorism, and state-sponsored terrorism includes terroristic actions committed by private surrogates for a state that funds them.
    Terrorism is a specific crime, although any terroristic act is nearly always a distinct crime as well, such as murder, highjacking, use of a weapon of mass destruction, trespass, or the destruction of public property. The federal crime of terrorism in the U.S. includes an offense that is intended to intimidate a civilian population, influence or affect the conduct of government, or retaliate against government conduct. State offenses of terrorism are distinct and may include a variety of specific offenses intended to cause fear or influence state action.

**terrorist threat**   *See:* threat, terrorist threat (terroristic threatening).

**terroristic threatening**   *See:* threat, terrorist threat (terroristic threatening).

**agriterrorism (agriterrorist)** An attack on a food source or food production as an act of terrorism. Agriterrorism is an attack on the production, supply, processing, or distribution system of crops or livestock of a nation with the intent of causing panic or terror among the populace, or of distracting government and police personnel from other commitments.

**domestic terrorism** An act of terrorism committed in the United States. An act of domestic terrorism is a violent or dangerous criminal act committed in the insular area of the United States, that is intended to coerce or intimidate a state, people, or government in the United States, or to retaliate for some act by the government. Domestic terrorism is both a crime and a factor for the enhancement of a sentence for the commission of underlying offenses.

Note: domestic terrorism (as opposed to international terrorism) is defined by where an offense occurs. This differs from the police terms "domestic terrorist" and "foreign terrorist," which distinguish acts of terrorism by U.S. citizens from acts by non-citizens. The greater number, by far, of acts of domestic terrorism have been committed by domestic terrorists rather than by foreign terrorists.

**international terrorism** An act of terrorism committed outside the United States. An act of international terrorism is a violent or dangerous act that would (if it was in the proper jurisdiction) violate the laws of the United States or a U.S. state, that appears to be committed outside the United States, that is intended to coerce or intimidate a state, people, or government in the United States, or to retaliate for some act by such a government. International terrorism is both a crime under federal law and a factor for the enhancement of a sentence for the commission of underlying offenses

**material support** The crime of giving funds or aid to a terrorist organization. Material support is a particular form of crime under federal law, of knowingly providing material support or resources to a foreign terrorist organization, or attempting or conspiring to do so. The forms of support include any forms of funding, financing, transport, logistics, or training, assistance, advice, or expertise, other than medical or religious aid. Application of the criminal support statute in some cases may violate the First and Fifth Amendment prohibitions on crimes based on guilt by association. See Scales v. U.S., 367 U.S. 203 (1961). The language of the statute does not provide for prosecution for material support of a domestic terrorist organization, although the general statutes for conspiracy and accessories would apply.

**teshuvah** Repentance. Teshuvah, literally return, is a healing response to one's transgression in Jewish law, which may include some elements of genuine remorse, a sense of repentance, a desire to manifest atonement for one's transgressions. The forty days preceding Yom Kippur, and the day itself are days of teshuvah.
*See also:* remorse.

**test** A standard of evidence, proof, or argument. A test, in law, is actually a rule setting forth standards to be met in order to prove or argue some point. A test structures the form of evidence or points of argument that must be made and sets a threshold that the evidence or argument must meet in order to be heard. There are innumerable tests in the law, and many standards and rules are described interchangeably as tests.

The origin of test is not the same as of testimony, although both seek some truth of the matter. Test comes from the testa, the small crucible used to assay gold and silver, from which it has long meant the separation of the true and valuable from the waste.

**testacy (testate)** Status of a decedent with a valid will. Testacy is the status of an individual who has died and has while alive and with testamentary capacity executed some form of valid last will and testament. A person who enjoyed testacy at death died testate.
*See also:* intestacy (intestatable or intestate or intestation or testacy).

**testament** *See:* will, last will and testament (testament).

**testamentary** *See:* will, last will and testament, testamentary.

**testamentary beneficiary** *See:* will, last will and testament, testamentary beneficiary; beneficiary, testamentary beneficiary.

**testamentary capacity** *See:* capacity, testamentary capacity, insane delusion; capacity, testamentary capacity.

**testamentary class** *See:* class, class of descendants (testamentary class).

**testamentary executor** *See:* executor, testamentary executor (executor testamentarius).

**testamentary power of appointment** *See:* power, power of appointment, testamentary power of appointment.

**testamentary trust** *See:* trust, testamentary trust (trust legacy or trust devise).

**testamentary trustee** *See:* trustee, testamentary trustee.

**testation (freedom of testation)** The power to control property after death by testament. Testation is the ability of a decedent to control the distribution of assets and property through a last will and testament that had been executed while alive. Put another way, it is the power of the living to control the actions of others in disposing their property after their deaths through the creation of a will.

Freedom of testation is the ability to exercise the power of testation as one chooses and without limits or requirements in the disposition of one's post-mortem assets. Thus, a testator has the testatory freedom to disinherit a child or parent.

Testation is not unlimited in U.S. law, but is subject to the laws governing debtors' and creditors' rights; the law of wills; the various laws governing the interests of spouses, trusts, charities, taxes, and gifts; and the procedure and substance of probate.

**testator (testatrix)**  The person who creates a valid will, or who created one. The testator is the maker of a valid last will and testament, and in the probate or administration of a will, the decedent and the testator are presumptively the same person. Any person with testamentary capacity may make a will. Even so, a person who attempts to make a will but lacks capacity or fails in some essential criterion for the creation of the form of will attempted is not a testator. A person who has made a will and yet lives is the testator of that will, although the testator retains the power to revoke or amend it so long as the testator retains testamentary capacity. Note: Law Latin distinguished the male and female forms of the term so that the female form was testatrix. This usage is now obsolete, though it is still found in older cases. The contemporary usage is to refer to a person of either gender as the testator.

*See also:* decedent.

**testatrix**  *See:* testator (testatrix).

**testimony (testify)**  A statement made by a witness under oath or affirmation. Testimony is a solemn statement that a witness makes under an oath or having affirmed that the assertions made in the statement are true. Testimony may be given before many legal bodies, including courts and legislatures, or in specific proceedings, such as in depositions and in statements by affidavit, as well as in a trial. A witness may only testify as to matters on which the person has personal knowledge.

To testify falsely, or to give false or misleading testimony, may be perjury, and refusing to testify may be contempt of court (unless the refusal is privileged under the Fifth Amendment, or some similar privilege.)

*See also:* recollection (recollect); deposition (depose); witness.

**testilying**  *See:* perjury, testilying.

**testimonial immunity**  *See:* immunity, witness immunity, testimonial immunity.

**testimonial statement**  *See:* testimony, testimonial statement.

**hypnotically induced testimony (hypnotic testimony or post-hypnotic testimony)**  Testimony during or following hypnosis of the witness. Hypnotically induced testimony includes all testimony that is made under or following a period of hypnosis by a witness, during which the witness spoke or was addressed on any matter related to the subject of the testimony. Hypnotic testimony occurs while the witness is in fact hypnotized; post–hypnotic testimony is testimony following hypnosis. Pre–hypnotic testimony is not actually hypnotically induced but is often essential in evaluating hypnotically induced testimony.

A person in a hypnotic state may be able to recall memories that the person could not recall otherwise,

and hypnosis is sometimes used to accurate effect in assisting victims of trauma in recalling events. On the other hand, a person in a hypnotic state is unusually vulnerable to believing the suggestions of others and may come to accept suggestions of facts as being true, whether the suggestion is true or not. And, witnesses tend to become more confident of memories following hypnosis when that confidence was the result of hypnosis rather than evaluation of the conditions remembered.

The use of hypnotically induced testimony is a question of recurrent controversy. Many states have banned such testimony entirely, although such bans are subject to a constitutional limit that prohibits a ban that would interfere with the confrontation of witnesses. Some states have allowed it subject to a few limitations. Others have allowed testimony that meets tests for procedural safeguards. The approach that has proved more successful in recent years has been to allow some hypnotically induced testimony under a totality of the circumstances test, which evaluates the potential for distortion of memory.

**physical-facts rule**  Testimony that contradicts the physical facts or laws of nature is barred. The physical facts rule bars from court the testimony of a witness that contradicts either the established scientific facts of the natural world or the physical facts established in a given action.

**testimonial statement**  A hearsay statement that is not admissible because it amounts to testimony in violation of the Confrontation Clause. A testimonial statement is a statement made out of court that amounts to testimony regarding the facts material to a case or proceeding. Even though such a statement might be allowed in a civil action under an exception to hearsay, its introduction in a criminal case as evidence of the proof of the matters asserted is forbidden in most instances as a violation of the defendant's rights to confront and cross–examine witnesses. The indicia of testimony are statements of past events made at a time of calm and protection following the events for the purpose of making a record. Statements made at the time of an event are not testimonial statements, but rather they are statements made in an effort to seek help or assistance.

*See also:* hearsay.

**Thalweg**  *See:* boundary, Thalweg (Thalweg doctrine or Rule of the Thalweg).

**Thalweg doctrine or Rule of the Thalweg**  *See:* boundary, Thalweg (Thalweg doctrine or Rule of the Thalweg).

**Thayerian rule**  *See:* presumption, bursting–bubble theory (Thayerian rule).

**The Hague**  *See:* Hague (the Hague, Den Haag).

**theft**  Common stealing. Theft, like larceny, is a general term for the wrongful removal of the property of others, and used that broadly is a synonym for more both minor and serious crimes arising from the removal of property. More specifically, theft is taking the property of another without a license to do so and without the use of force, violence, or trespass into a house by night. Theft at common law was the carrying away of property without a license or justification to do so, and the definition has been expanded by statute in many jurisdictions to include receiving property that has been stolen. Under the model penal code, theft includes acquisition of property through improper threats.

*See also:* goods, stolen goods (stolen property); stealing (steal or stolen); trespass, trespass to chattel; robbery (rob); larceny (larcenous); shoplifting (shrinkage or shoplift or shoplifted).

**identity theft (identity fraud)** The unauthorized use of another's name or identification. Identity theft is the employment of a person's name, image, Social Security number, credit card numbers, voter identification information, address, or any other identifying association without that person's permission. The theft is established through use, although identity fraud may require that some advantage be attained, either through the acquisition of information, money or value, or opportunity as a result of the use of the stolen identity.

**skimmer device** A device for copying credit or debit cards used in legitimate machines. A skimmer device is a recording device designed or adapted to obtain personal identifying information from a credit card, debit card, public benefit card, access card or device, or other card or device that contains personal identifying information. A skimmer devise is hidden by a thief on or in an Automated Teller Machine or other card reading device, in a manner that would allow the thief to capture the data from the card when it is used normally in the machine, allowing the thief to use the captured information.

**then-existing condition** *See:* hearsay, hearsay exception, hearsay allowed regardless of witness availability, then-existing condition (state-of-mind exception).

**theocracy** *See:* government, forms of government, theocracy (theocratic).

**theory (theories or theoretical)**

**theories of law** *See:* law, theories of law, ontology of law, bad-man concept of law (bad man theory); law, theories of law, ontology of law (legal ontology); law, theories of law, epistemology of law.

**theories of product liability** *See:* liability, product liability, theories of product liability.

**theory of partnership** *See:* partnership, theory of partnership, entity theory of partnership; partnership, theory of partnership, aggregate theory of partnership; partnership, theory of partnership.

**theory of the case** *See:* case, case as argument (theory of the case).

**therefore (therefor)** The introduction to the conclusion of an argument. Therefore means for these foregoing reasons, or for the reasons set forth just preceding the word. It signals the conclusion that follows from the statements preceding. Note: "therefore" should not be used unless the premises stated prior to it lead to a logical and sufficient conclusion. A fallacy or incomplete series of observations should not lead to a statement starting "therefore," but a solid argument may do so.

*See also:* argument; quod, quod erat demonstrandum (Q.E.D. or QED).

**Thibodaux abstention** *See:* abstention, abstention doctrine, Thibodaux abstention.

**thief** A person who steals something. A thief is someone who commits a theft or who has committed a theft. Because of the distinctions between theft and larceny, as opposed to robbery (which is dangerous or violent) or various forms of fraud, a thief is generally one who takes things without violence or trickery. Even so, the meaning of larceny and theft are often interchanged, and "thief" is routinely used to depict a person accused or convicted of either.

*See also:* theft; robber.

**thin edge of the wedge or camel's nose argument** *See:* fallacy, slippery slope (thin edge of the wedge or camel's nose argument).

**thing in action or chose en action or chose in suspense** *See:* chose, chose in action (thing in action or chose en action or chose in suspense).

**third**

**third degree murder** *See:* murder, degrees of murder, third degree murder (murder in the third degree or murder-three or murder-3).

**third party (third-party)** A party not directly involved in a transaction or event. A third party is any person or entity not directly participating in the matter in issue. Most notably, a third-party beneficiary of a contract is a third party in comparison to the offeror (the first party) and the offeree (the second party), whose agreement contemplates some benefit to the third-party, thus according the third-party beneficiary standing to enforce the contract.

Third parties are everywhere in law. For example, a third party to a lawsuit is a party with an interest in the case other than the plaintiffs and defendants. Third-party liability arises when one party is liable for the conduct of another, such as a principal responsible for a victim's injury by the principal's agent.

**third-party beneficiary** *See:* beneficiary, third-party beneficiary.

**third-party check** *See:* check, third-party check.

**third-party defendant** *See:* defendant, third-party defendant.

**third party entrapment** *See:* entrapment, derivative entrapment (third party entrapment).

**third-party guilt** *See:* defense, specific defense, third-party guilt (empty chair defense or fellow servant rule or hypothetical person defense or SODDI defense).

**third-party insurance** *See:* insurance, category of insurance, liability insurance (third-party insurance).

**third-party plaintiff** *See:* plaintiff, third-party plaintiff.

**third-party practice or third party practice** *See:* impleader (third-party practice or third party practice).

**third-party standing** *See:* standing in court, third-party standing, autre droit (auter droit or en autre droit); standing in court, third-party standing, associational standing (organizational standing); standing in court, third-party standing (jus tertii or vendor standing or agency standing).

**thirty-day letter** *See:* letter, thirty-day letter (30-day letter).

**thought** The operation of the mind. Thought is the operation of the mind, whether in ideas or reasons or sentiments or instincts, in a manner that the thinker understands or notices or not. Thoughts alone are protected by law from prosecution or criminalization, from private causes of action or interference. Thoughts coupled with action, however, may be the basis for both criminal and civil liability, such as the thoughts that form the basis of mens rea, or the guilty mind, in determining the criminal culpability for an illegal act.

**thought crime** Criminal liability for thoughts without speech or action. Thought crime describes the criminalization of holding a certain idea or an idea from a category of ideas. It is contrary to the idea of freedom of thought, considered a component of both the First Amendment and the Ninth Amendment of the U.S. Constitution.

**threat (threaten or threatener)** A contingent offer of injury or harm. A threat is a statement of some injury or other bad thing that will happen in the future, which is ordinarily not merely a prediction but a claim that is contingent on some state of affairs coming to pass or not coming to pass, the idea of the threatener being that the victim should cause the events to unfold as the threatener desires them. A threat is effectively the same as a menace, though a threat is spoken, while a menace is gestured. More generally, a threat is any danger or condition that may cause harm or distress, as the sea poses a threat to mariners.

A threat is a crime in itself in many jurisdictions, either as an offense of uttering a threat or of menacing.

Terroristic threatening is a threat of harm with the intent of causing terror or panic or the intent either to retaliate against a government for its action or to coerce or induce government action. A threat made with the intent to gain money or property is extortion. Speech that constitutes a threat, or a true threat of physical injury, is not protected under the First Amendment.

*See also:* menace (menaces).

**threat to breach** *See:* breach, breach of contract, threat to breach.

**threatened species** *See:* species, threatened species.

**terrorist threat (terroristic threatening)** A threat of violence intended to cause fear. A terroristic threat is an assault by threat, a statement that violent action will occur that is made with the intent to cause fear in the victim or others. A terroristic threat may also be a threat to commit a violent offense that amounts to terrorism, the use of violence in retaliation for a government action or to coerce or manipulate government policy or action. Terroristic threatening is a crime in many states, and the elements of a threat that amount to a terrorist threat vary somewhat among jurisdictions. As of 2011, the U.S. does not have a federal crime of terrorist threatening, although specific threats are criminal if they relate to a variety of federal interests, such as a threat against a federal official or facility or a threat to use a weapon of mass destruction. A conviction for a crime of terrorist threatening is considered a conviction for a crime of violence only when the underlying threat amounts to a threat of violence.

*See also:* menace (menaces).

**three**

**three wicked sisters** *See:* defense, three wicked sisters (wicked sisters of the common law or unholy trinity).

**three-plastic-animals rule** *See:* religion, freedom of religion, creche, three-plastic-animals rule.

**three-pony rule** *See:* child, child support, three-pony rule.

**three-strikes law** *See:* recidivism, three-strikes law (anti-recidivist law or three strikes law).

**throwing oneself on the mercy of the court or in mercy** *See:* mercy (throwing oneself on the mercy of the court or in mercy).

**tickler calendar** *See:* calendar, tickler calendar.

**tied products or tying agreement or tying arrangement** *See:* tying (tied products or tying agreement or tying arrangement).

**timber** Trees and tree parts with commercial use. Timber is a broad term, including all trees and part of trees that have a commercial application or market.

Timber may not be wasted on property subject to limits on waste.

**clearcutting** The removal of all the trees in a parcel. Clearcutting is a common practice in forest harvesting, urban development and agriculture, in which all of the vegetation on a property is cut or removed. Clearcutting not only removes commercially significant timber but all other trees and shrubs, destroying habitat utterly and removing the natural barriers to erosion.

**time** The span of existence, or a duration. Time is the physical difference between moments in the past, present, and future. Time is experienced as the relationship between one phenomenon and another, and time on Earth is assessed by the passage of intervals demarcated as portions of the rotation of the Earth on its axis or of its rotation about the Sun. Thus, time is measured in law according to a calender marked out in years, quarters, months, weeks, days, hours, and minutes according to custom and to astrophysical standards. Other units of measure, including older measures such as the fortnight and lustrum, and newer measures such as the attosecond, may be employed in contracts, wills, and other instruments before the law but are rarely measures of time in rules of law. Certain measures of time in law are based on events rather than the calendar. Two commonly used events are the end of a person's life, which is used to measure a life estate, and the end of two generations, formulated as the "last measuring life plus twenty-one years," which is used to distinguish valid contingent future interests from invalid perpetuities. Yet most measures of time in law incorporate a span of calendric time, such as three days, twenty days, a year and a day, two years, three years, twenty-one years, and even the ninety years of the uniform statutory rule against perpetuities, all of which the law sets as the limits for certain actions or the extent of certain responsibilities, privileges, or conditions.

Time is essential to the existence of law, especially to specific rules of the law. Because law is a construct of human understanding and cooperation, it is quite difficult to create a law in an instant. A state that issues laws by decree is generally thought to have a less than mature legal system. Instead, the creation of law is usually done in a specified routine for statutes or executive decrees, including both a span required for its creation and an additional span between its enactment and when it comes into force. Law arising from precedent is inherently dependent on time, so that the authority of a later pronouncement is based at least in part on its relationship to an earlier, similar pronouncement. Custom is defined by time, so that proof of a practice that is accepted over time is an essential aspect of its recognition.

Time is the basis for many rules of law, including the principles of limitations of action, laches, and repose. As one result, time is a component of ownership through prescription or adverse possession. Time is an aspect of contracts, and sometimes time is of the essence of the contract, which is to say that the time of performance is a material term so that breach results if performance is late. Officials employ time to balance a variety of moral and practical limits in statutes and regulations, such as the number of hours in a fair work week or the times of day allowed for the service of alcohol. Time is an element of procedure, the passage of time barring various claims, defenses, and tactics, not the least being appeal. In these senses, time is assessed (and has meaning) as the law requires it to be assessed, which is why lawyers may move in court to "enlarge time."

*See also:* desuetude; seasonable; repose; limitation, limitation of action (limitations of actions); custom (customary); fee, fee for services, attorney's fee, billable hour (billable time or billables or hourly fee); tenure, feudal tenure (feudalism or feudal system); term, court term (session of court).

**time is of the essence or time of essence** *See:* performance, contract performance, time of performance (time is of the essence or time of essence).

**time of memory** *See:* memory, time of memory.

**time of performance** *See:* performance, contract performance, time of performance (time is of the essence or time of essence).

**extension of time (enlargement of time)** The addition of time to the period allowed for some action. An extension of time is the tacking on of time to that period allowed for some action. The older term for referring to such an increase in allowed time was to enlarge time, rather like an addition enlarges a building. In most systems of rules, a timetable governs the time that may be allowed for each action, and extensions are ordinarily allowed once as a matter of custom and thereafter only for good cause. Note: as a matter of practice, most extensions in court proceedings are allowed unless the opponent objects. It is considered unprofessional not to allow an opponent one extension without objection of nearly every deadline, yet additional extensions should be the object of consent only if they are not intended for either the tactical advantage of one's opponent or to enable the sloth of opposing counsel.

**good time** *See:* sentence, reduction of sentence, good behavior (good time).

**hour (hours)**

**business hours (close of business or COB)** The customary beginning and end of the business day. Business hours are a matter of custom that vary from place to place and among types of business. Certain retail operations trade at restricted hours, some according to hours restricted by law. The payment of a bill or presentation of a demand or note made before business hours is usually credited to that day's activity, if it is received and processed at all. A payment or presentation made after business hours, unless it is accepted as on that day by special agreement, is considered made the following business day. The business hours of public offices, particularly clerk's offices, are set either by statute, court rule, or the policy of the executive or administrator in charge. A filing made in such an office after business hours may be rejected outright or recorded as filed the following day.

**reasonable time**   A sufficient time, neither too quick or soon nor too late or slow. A reasonable time is the amount of time that is reasonable in the context in which the question arises and according to the situation as it is in fact. What is a reasonable time as to purely legal obligations, such as whether an equitable claim is brought on time, is a question of law and fact appropriately decided as a mixed question by the judge. What is a reasonable time as to the performance of an obligation or exercise of a duty to a private party other than as a matter of procedural obligation is a mixed question of law and fact better decided by a jury.

*See also:* reasonable (reasonableness); reasonable (reasonableness).

**time immemorial (time out of memory or immemorial possession)**   Since a time before living memory, or twenty-one years. Time immemorial is a space of time greater than memory. The three phrases — time out of memory, before the time of memory, and time immemorial — all represent an occurrence or commencement of a practice that either allows repose for any legal responsibility related to the occurrence or establishes the practice with authority owing to its age. Law, or rules of law, established for time immemorial constitute common law. A practice that has been ongoing for time immemorial is customary, and any reliance on it is justified. Possession since time immemorial gives rise to a prescription of any claims to the contrary. In the U.S., a practice that has been established from time immemorial, which was once considered before the memory of any available witness, is now measured by years. A practice is sometimes thought immemorial if it has continued between ten years and more, or sometimes twenty years and more. Indian lands held before European settlement are always considered to have been held from time immemorial.

Edward I's once-famous Statute of Westminster of 1275, among other things, established then time immemorial to be from the reign of Richard I, allowing repose of all claims against those in possession of land from before 1189. That measure was updated in the nineteenth century to be "living memory."

*See also:* limitation, limitation of action (limitations of actions); repose.

**untimeliness (untimely)**   Too late, or too early. Untimeliness afflicts anything that is or is done other than at a proper, expected, or required time. An action that is unripe is untimely in its prematurity; an action that is moot is untimely in its antiquity. An action filed after a statute of repose or limitations has foreclosed its claim is untimely, as is an equitable action that is brought so late that it is barred by laches. A motion that is untimely is likely filed too late under the rules, although in some instances the fault may be cured by motion and a showing of good cause. In general discourse, an untimely death comes to one who dies either younger than the average age of death or through an avoidable cause or human agency.

*See also:* justiciability, mootness; justiciability, ripeness (unripeness or ripe or unripe claim); repose; limitation, limitation of action (limitations of actions).

**time-weighted average**   *See:* pollution, time-weighted average (TWA).

**timocracy**   *See:* government, forms of government, plutocracy (timocracy).

**tipstaff**   A law-court official, like a bailiff. A tipstaff is an official who serves the court in a function similar to that of a bailiff. The office in the United States is rare outside of Pennsylvania.

*See also:* bailiff.

**tithe (tithes or tithing)**   The once legal requirement to pay a tenth of income to the church. The tithe is a tenth, the amount of one's income that was required by law to be paid to the Church in England. Many American churches retain the custom as an ecclesiastical practice and expectation for their members, but the obligation to pay the tithe is no longer a matter of public law. Tithing is the practice of paying tithes.

A tithing was also a medieval English district of ten families, probably ten manors, within a hundred in a county.

**titius**   *See:* name, fictitious name, titius (aulus agerius or numerius negidiusor seius or stichus).

**title**   The right of ownership in property. Title is the right of ownership. Possession is different from title, although whoever has title either has possession or has a right that is superior to the person who has possession (such as the title of the landlord and the possession of the tenant). Title in this sense depends on the means, or how the right was acquired, and as in the case of adverse possession or prescription, title might or might not be reflected in a paper documenting its transfer from someone else.

**title abstract**   *See:* abstract, abstract of title (title abstract).

**title company**   *See:* insurer, insurers, title company; company, title company.

**Title IX**   *See:* civil rights, Civil Rights Act, Title IX (Title Nine or Title 9 or Patsy T. Mink Equal Opportunity in Education Act).

**Title Nine or Title 9 or Patsy T. Mink Equal Opportunity in Education Act**   *See:* civil rights, Civil Rights Act, Title IX (Title Nine or Title 9 or Patsy T. Mink Equal Opportunity in Education Act).

**Title Seven**   *See:* civil rights, Civil Rights Act, Civil Rights Act of 1964, Title VII (Title Seven).

**Title Six** *See:* civil rights, Civil Rights Act, Civil Rights Act of 1964, Title VI (Title Six).

**Title VI** *See:* civil rights, Civil Rights Act, Civil Rights Act of 1964, Title VI (Title Six).

**Title VII** *See:* civil rights, Civil Rights Act, Civil Rights Act of 1964, Title VII, anti-retaliation provision; civil rights, Civil Rights Act, Civil Rights Act of 1964, Title VII (Title Seven).

**Titles of Nobility Clauses** *See:* constitution, U.S. Constitution, clauses, Titles of Nobility Clauses.

**title as document or deed (title deed)** Instrument evidencing ownership in a given property. A title instrument or title deed is a written instrument that states a person has title in a specific and described parcel of land, or an automobile, or other real or tangible property. The title instrument is either issued by the state or by the grantor of title to the present title holder in the title instrument. Title instruments take many forms but, if the instrument is from the grantor, it must be signed by or for the grantor and have a sufficiently specific description of the property to be unique. If the instrument is from the state, it must be completed and authorized as required by that state's law.

**title as form of address (Mr. or Ms. or Miss or Mrs. or Hon. or Excellency)** The terms by which a person is addressed. Titles include not only courtesies required by custom and protocol among diplomats and officials, but also forms of address employed as a matter of etiquette and custom. The Constitution forbids the grant of titles of nobility by a U.S. or state government, and U.S. citizens do not bear a title as a matter of right or law. Titles of courtesy and titles of honor in the United States, however, are not titles of nobility any more than are ranks or ratings in the military. Titles recognized by law or custom in other nations are recognized in the United States for the officials and nationals of those states, as are religious titles.

In most states, an attorney is given the written title of Esquire, though this is only said aloud in the most formal of situations. Some states employ the courtesy title "Honorable" (written as "the honorable Jane Smith" in prose, "The Honorable Jane Smith" as an address, or "Hon. Jane Smith" in abbreviation) in order to avoid the anachronistic connotation of gender in "esquire." Judges and elected officials are usually accorded the courtesy title of "Honorable," as are the heads of commissions and departments of government. Heads of state are often given the title "Excellency," as are foreign ambassadors and the governors of certain U.S. states and possessions, though most are addressed as "Honorable," as are U.S. ambassadors.

Custom in the United States does not distinguish among levels of honor, and there is no equivalent to the "Right Honorable" title in the U.K. which is abbreviated "Rt. Hon." and pronounced "right on." In the U.K., and in present and former British dominions, Right Honorable is applied to certain institutions and to a person who is a member of the Privy Council or the peerage or who holds certain offices, as does the Lord Mayor of London.

For any adult male not addressed by such courtesy titles, etiquette still suggests the use of the abbreviated or spoken Mr. (for which the French is used for a plural abbreviation: Mssrs.) The use of Master for a young boy or unmarried man is now considered archaic.

Customs regarding titles of address for women underwent great change in the later half of the twentieth century. Ms. is appropriate for all women and is not inappropriate for the young. Miss is still considered by many to be more appropriate for unmarried women in their youth, which for this purpose is considered to last well past the commencement of lawful adulthood. Mrs., the abbreviated form of Mistress, is pronounced "missus" and is appropriate for all women who are married and who prefer that title, although it is used nearly always in abbreviation rather than being written in full. The plural, also from French, is Mmes. Convention now requires that when a person's preference among titles of address is known, the speaker or writer should honor that preference.

Difficulty arises when writing to a woman whose marital state or preference of title is not known, in which case contemporary etiquette suggests that Ms. is to be used. Ms. is also preferred for a woman who is married but whose surname differs from that of her husband. There are also regional variations in etiquette, such that Ms. is presumed in the Northeastern and coastal West for women known to be married but whose preference is unknown, while Mrs. is presumed in the West and South in the same circumstances. Modern communications being what they are, the writer to whom such questions are significant is advised to call in advance of writing to ask.

Interestingly, in salutations for correspondence, the use of madam and sir have remained acceptable, indeed preferable, when the name of the addressee is unknown or omitted. When in doubt as to the gender of the recipient for a letter, the writer may employ "Dear Reader."

*See also:* nobility (peerage).

**aboriginal title** A claim of American Indians' rights to land from pre–Columbian occupation. Aboriginal title denotes the claim of right held by the descendants of the people who first inhabited a land. Aboriginal title applies only to lands held by a tribe, people, or individual, when the title is not derived from a government grant or patent but from ancient occupation. If lands held by aboriginal title have been alienated, aboriginal title is the earliest link in a chain of title.

*See also:* original (originality).

**action to quiet title (quiet title)** An action to vest record title in the plaintiff. An action to quiet title is brought by a person claiming title to land against any party known to have an interest or claim and against all the world, seeking to prove a superior title to any claimant and have title vested in the plaintiff. An action to quiet title was once an equitable action, but is brought in most jurisdictions according to statute and following the statutory procedure. This usually requires notice to be published as well as notice to be actually served to any person on the property or known to the plaintiff to have a claim or interest against the property. The plaintiff must prove title in the plaintiff superior to any claimant who appears.

See also: title, cloud on title.

**after-acquired title**  Title obtained after it is transferred, which goes to the transferee. After-acquired property is property acquired by a transferor after it has been already transferred to another. After-acquired title by the transferor creates an equitable and legal title in the transferee. Thus, if a seller without legitimate title at the time of an attempted conveyance attempts to convey property to a buyer, and then after the transfer the seller receives title from the former title-holder, the seller is deemed to convey the title immediately to the buyer as after-acquired title.

Note: occasionally after-acquired title also refers to after-acquired assets of a decedent's estate, that is property that transfers to the estate following the death of its recipient. This is more often considered an after-acquired asset.

**chain of title in intellectual property**  The whole array of assigned or licensed interests in a movie, device or other intellectual property. Chain of title in a given intellectual property is the whole documentation demonstrating that each source of a patented, trademarked, or copyrighted work that is employed in the given property is used according to an appropriate license or assignment.

**chain of title in land**  The succession of title holders to a tract or parcel of land. The chain of title is a list that chronicles the succession of grants, working backward by starting with the grantee in possession (or now claiming title) to that grantee's grantor, to that grantor's prior grantor, and working backward to the root title or to the initial grant, such as a land patent or charter. The chain of title is not in itself a document but is work product, which is usually recorded in an abstract of title. In root-of-title states, the chain of title required to prove good title may be shorter, recording only the most recent 50 or 75 years, or as needed to reach the root of title and no farther.

See also: title, root of title.

**cloud on title**  A claim or encumbrance that affects title to a parcel. A cloud on title is any serious and potential limit to the value of title over a specific parcel. A cloud on title may arise from an encumbrance, including an undisclosed easement or servitude on the land, which would reduce the value of ownership of the land. A cloud may also arise from a defect in any instrument on which title is based, such as a wild deed, or any claim or lien that may yield title in the land to a third party, including tax liens, or any ongoing claim to title by a third party or action by the grantor or a third party that may affect the title. A cloud on title may be relieved by an action to quiet title.

See also: title, action to quiet title (quiet title).

**color of title**  Apparent title from an instrument of title. Color of title is an interest in property arising from an instrument, such as a deed, will, charter, or patent that appears to confer title to a parcel of land, when the claimant has no reason to believe the instrument does not provide a basis for the claimant's title to the land, and when the claimant does in fact claim title based on the instrument. Color of title often becomes an important argument in situations when the instrument is no good, and color of title persists in the claimant who sought title from the instrument even though the claimant cannot receive title from the instrument or the grant it purported to make. Color of title is required in some jurisdictions to assert adverse possession, which may arise in such situations. Even so, color of title is an aspect of title based on an instrument and occurs even if the title conferred by the instrument is not false.

See also: right, legal right, color of right (claim of right or colour of right); title, void title.

**covenants of title**  See: covenant, covenant of title (deed warranty or title covenant).

**doctrine of worthier title (doctrine of reversions)**  Rule that purchaser has greater interest in title than an heir. The doctrine of worthier title is a rule of construction that applies to the grants of property to a first grantee or grantees and then to the heirs of the grantor. The doctrine construes the second grant not to be to the heirs of the grantor but to be a reversion in the grantor. The rule has been abolished in some jurisdictions by statute. Note: some jurisdictions distinguish the doctrine of worthier title, which applies to testamentary transfers, from the doctrine of reversions, which applies to inter vivos transfers (though the effects of the two doctrines are essentially the same).

See also: Shelley's Case (Rule in Shelley's Case); perpetuity, Rule Against Perpetuities (RAP or Rule Against Remoteness).

**inter vivos branch of the doctrine of worthier title**  The living cannot convey interest to heirs. The inter vivos branch of the doctrine of worthier title is an interpretation of the doctrine that operates to void any attempted inter vivos conveyance of land by a person "to my heirs." While the person lives the heirs are impossible to ascertain, and when the person dies the heirs are the heirs at the person's death. Such a grant is void and creates a reversion in the grantor.

See also: inter, inter vivos.

**equitable title**  Title enforceable in equity. Title in equity is an interest in property that is subject to legal title in another party, but is nonetheless an interest protected in equity, which includes a right in the equitable title holder to compel the transfer of legal title. Equitable title takes several forms, including the interest of a buyer between the execution of a buy/sell agreement and closing and the interest of the beneficiary of a trust, particularly the interest of a mortgagor.

*See also:* sale, land sale, equitable conversion (equitable owner); equity, equitable value, equitable interest.

**marketable title (clear title or merchantable title)** Title to land without a significant risk of burden by claims or unknown encumbrances. Marketable title is title to land that is based on a chain of title with nothing significant to be found after a reasonable title search and physical inspection that would put a reasonable buyer on notice that another claimant to the property exists or that there is an unknown encumbrance on the land. Although there are reasons to avoid substitution in the application of the term employed in a given precedent or statute, there is no essential difference in practice between marketable title, merchantable title, and clear title.

*See also:* marketability (marketable).

**marketable title act (marketable record title act)** A claim to land older than the root of title is barred. The marketable title statutes employ the root of title as the basis for determining which interests are valid in lands and which are extinguished. Claims based on an instrument that is older than the root of title are, unless properly and timely preserved or visible on the land, cut off in favor of interests in the chain of title from the root of title. As a practical matter, states with marketable title acts cut off most easements, covenants, and claims to title older than thirty years.

*See also:* title, root of title.

**paramount title (superior title)** A claim stronger than another to the same land. Paramount title is superior title, the better basis for ownership compared to another claimant's basis for ownership in the same parcel of land. Superior title is always relative to other possible bases of title, although paramount title is superior to all the world. If, for instance, A holds Blackacre from a grant by O in 2005, but B claims Blackacre from a grant by O in 2003, then B has paramount title and may oust A (and A has an action against O). Note: between two claimants, paramount title and superior title are the same, though the larger implication of paramount title is that a party with paramount title cannot be divested by another claimant under any theory or claim to title based on past acts (later transfer, prescription, lien, etc., notwithstanding).

**perfection of title (imperfect title)** Title in property that is officially recorded. Perfection of title is the process of recording eligible title in an official system of recordation, so that the world is on notice of the recorder's claim to title, and no claim or lien may be later made with a claim to being superior or earlier in time. Recordation alone is insufficient in most jurisdictions, which require that the title recorded must have been based on a valid instrument received by the recording party from a party with valid title,

and the recording party must have recorded it in good faith, having no notice of a party with a superior title. Perfected title, or perfect title, is therefore recorded, and imperfect title is not.

**record title** *See:* title, recordation of title (recording system).

**recordation of title** The method and act of recording or registering a title to property. Recordation of title is not only the system or means by which title to certain forms of property is recorded in a given jurisdiction, but also the act of recording in such a system any instrument that purports to give or represent title in a specific parcel of property. Most jurisdictions have separate systems of recordation for title in real property (mainly land) and for title in personal property (mainly goods), as well as a distinct system of registration for some personal property (mainly automobiles). Note: recordation of title differs from registration, in that the system of recordation depends on the relationship of each instrument recorded to other instruments recorded, while registration is specific to the property in which title is registered.

**recordation of title (recording system)** The system of recording title instruments. Recordation of title, or the recording system, is the predominate means of determining the owner of an interest in land in the United States. Recordation is based on the recording of each instrument that affects ownership in land, organizing these instruments chronologically and accessing these records through both reference to the tract of the property and the chain of title from grantor forward to grantee or from grantee backward to grantor. Recordation of title in any jurisdiction is based on a recording act, a statute that specifies the means of recordation and the priority among claims that conflict despite having been recorded. Jurisdictions that do not use recordation use registration of title.

**recordation of defective instrument (defective deed)** A recorded but invalid instrument might serve as notice. The recordation of a defective instrument has a significance that varies among jurisdictions. In no jurisdiction does recordation make valid an instrument that is invalid, whether it was forged, created by a person lacking capacity to create the instrument or authority over the property, or otherwise. The question is the degree of notice a recorded but defective instrument creates. Some jurisdictions consider such instruments to give no notice, others to give notice. Even so, a party acting in good faith and on reasonable reliance on a recorded instrument is generally sheltered by recordation from liability for such reliance.

**recording act** A statute setting priority of recorded interests. The recording act in each state is the legislation that sets out the means by which recordation is performed and determines the priority among conflicting claims to title. The means of recordation include not only the definition of instruments that should be recorded, such as deeds, mortgages, easements, covenants, licenses, and wills, but also the techniques for recordation and requirements to present an instrument to be recorded. Interestingly, no two states seem to have recording acts that are exactly like one another.

A significant aspect of recording acts is the various ways established in one act or another to determine which claim of title among several is to have priority, based on recordation. The forms of recording act vary according to the form selected for that priority: notice statutes, race statutes, and race–notice statutes. Although in many cases the same party would have priority, these statutes lead to different result when interests have not been properly recorded in a timely manner, or when several interests are created in a brief period of time. Pure race statutes are rare, but notice and race–notice are roughly equal in the number of states that have adopted them.

In most states, recordation is part of a statewide system under the statute. Interests are usually recorded in the courthouse for the county or parish in which the property in question is located, and minor variations in the procedure of recordation occur from courthouse to courthouse in most jurisdictions. Note: the advent of land title companies and computerized records have diminished such variation, but the young title searcher is always well advised to seek the advice of the local staff.

See also: title, recordation of title, recording act, race recording act (pure race act or pure race jurisdiction); title, recordation of title, recording act, notice recording act (notice state or notice act or notice jurisdiction); title, recordation of title, recording act, race notice recording act (race–notice).

**notice recording act (notice state or notice act or notice jurisdiction)** A bona fide purchaser for value has title superior to all claimants based on prior title. A notice recording act establishes priority of title so that the claimant who holds the property in issue as a bona fide purchaser for value, that is, a title holder who acquired title with neither actual notice of a prior conflicting claim nor constructive notice of such a claim, has priority over the prior conflicting claim. In a notice state, if A purchases Blackacre with no notice of an interest by B and then B records an instrument of title not based on a good faith purchase, made prior to A's purchase, A still has priority over B. In contrast, if A purchases Blackacre knowing of a prior claim that B has (though believing, wrongly that B's claim is no good), A has no priority over B, but B has priority over A. So, had A purchased Blackacre knowing of B's claim but not a claim by C, then A would have priority over C but B would have priority over A. When A, B, or C recorded would establish notice, because each party's recordation would put the others on constructive notice of the claim that party recorded.

But, if none had recorded when each had completed their purchase, then priority would go to the latest in time who had no notice.

**race notice recording act (race-notice)** A bona fide purchaser for value who records first has superior title. A race–notice recording act establishes priority of title so that the claimant who holds the property in issue as the most recent bona fide purchaser for value and who records before others has priority. The first claimant to title who records a basis for title and who has no notice of another claimant has priority over other claimants. On the other hand, a party who records a deed knowing that another party has a claim that would, if true, void the deed, gains no priority over the other party by recording. In a race–notice state, if A purchases Blackacre with no notice of an interest by B, and then B records an older instrument of title based on a good faith purchase made prior to A's purchase, B has priority over A, because B filed first, and B had no notice of A's claim. In contrast, if A purchases Blackacre knowing of a prior claim that B has (though believing, wrongly, that B's claim is no good), and A files then B files, A has no priority over B, because A's filing was invalid as to B because of A's actual notice of B's claim. (A might still have priority over C or D if other filings are later made.)

See also: race, race to the courthouse.

**race recording act (pure race act or pure race jurisdiction)** Who records first has superior title. A race recording act (sometimes called a "pure race" act to distinguish it from a race–notice act) establishes priority of title between two claimants to the same land in the party who is the first to record the instrument on which that party's claim is based. In a race jurisdiction, it does not matter whether the first party to record has notice of the other's claim or not. The statute's preference for certainty creates a bonus for whomever wins the race to the courthouse to record an instrument of title. In a race state, if A purchases Blackacre from O and has actual notice of an earlier — unrecorded — claim of ownership by B, but A records an instrument of title before B, A has priority over B. In contrast, if A purchases Blackacre knowing of a prior claim of ownership by B, and B files B's interest before A files, then B has priority over A. Whether A or B first records is what controls the outcome in any contest between A or B as to title, and no dispute over who knew what when will affect the outcome.

See also: race, race to the courthouse; title, recordation of title, recording act, race recording act (pure race act or pure race jurisdiction).

**registration of title (Torrens system)** A current state certificate proves title. Registration of title is a system for proving title to property based on application to a state–run registrar, which issues a certificate to the present holder of title to a given property. The certificate is proof of title, without regard to earlier grants or the source of title. To obtain a certificate, the present holder must present the certificate from a prior holder signed over to the new holder. The state then issues a new certificate that mirrors the recorded property description in the registry. Registration creates a strong presumption that the registered title holder is the superior title holder, although that presumption can be overcome with a showing of superior title by a claimant or filing in bad faith by the registree. A third party who relies on the registered information in error to that party's loss may be held harmless by other parties or indemnified by the state, depending on the jurisdiction.

The system is often named for Sir Robert Richard Torrens, then governor of South Australia, who introduced a registration system there in 1853 rather than continue a creaky recordation system. Though not the inventor of registration, which has a long history in civilian jurisdictions, for instance as cadastre, Torrens use of the system drew attention to it in the common-law world.

**relativity of title**   Title is not absolute but a priority against another's claim. Relativity of title is a theoretical understanding of title as inherently comparative between two or more different claims of ownership. Title is not considered proof against all possible claims, in part because conditions of ownership change and in part because even when the conditions of ownership do not change, the information available may change. Relativity of title emphasizes that aspect of title that is meaningful in comparison to another claimant to own the property subject to title. The title to a single parcel is either subordinate or superior to another claim of title. The superior title is entitled to occupation or future occupation as against the suboridinate title. Even a finding of title as against all the world, the title made quiet in a single holder, has aspects of relativity, both once the claim is proved (and thus it is superior to all others' claims) and as time goes on, when other, more superior claims may emerge.

*See also:* fee, estate in fee, fee simple absolute (FSA or F.S.A.).

**root of title**   The earliest transaction in a parcel older than thirty years. The root of title is the date at which a parcel's title is established as superior to earlier claims under a state's Marketable Record Title Act. It is calculated according to statute, but it is usually the first sufficient transaction recorded earlier than thirty years from the present. A sale, transfer by death, mortgage, or other recorded interest affecting the ownership of the whole parcel is usually sufficient, though it must of course be recorded. Thus, if one was searching the title of Blackacre in 2005, and there are sales from grantor to grantee in 1998, 1981, and 1956, the recorded sale in 1956 was then the root of title. In 2011, however, the 1981 sale would become the new root of title.

*See also:* title, chain of title, chain of title in land; title, marketable title, Marketable Title Act (Marketable Record Title Act); Blackacre (Whiteacre or Redacre or Greenacre); limitation, limitation of actions, statute of repose; title, title search (examination of title).

**title assurance**   Recordation, covenant, and insurance. Title assurance is often used as a synonym for title insurance, an insurance policy that defends and indemnifies the assured against certain claims to superior title in the property. Even so, the term has a broader meaning to include any measure enforceable in law or equity to assure the title vests and rests in the assured owner. Forms of title assurance include title insurance, as well as recordation or registration, covenants in the warranty deed, and, sometimes, the warranty, bond, and insurance of attorneys or others providing title work on the property.

**title company (title plant)**   An insurer specializing in title insurance. A title company provides insurance for the title to property. The title insurance is usually provided for a single premium at the time of issuance and continues for the period of ownership by the assured. Title insurance companies maintain proprietary records of title transfers, known as the title plant, a title by which the insurer is also sometimes known.

**title defect**   A flaw in the basis of title. A title defect is any basis for determining that title cannot be transferred from the title holder to another in the manner and degree anticipated. Defects include any cloud on title, including any wild deed in the chain of title; a lack of a record title holder, particularly owing to adverse possession or prescription; and undisclosed incumbrances, such as easements or covenants. Each of these conditions may amount to a defect if they are not properly disclosed or anticipated in a given circumstance, yet they might not be either, e.g., when an interest is being quit claimed to another, or when the defect was disclosed prior to a negotiation in which the defect was a factor in the bargain.

**latent defect of title**   A concealed or obscure deficiency in title A latent defect of title arises when the apparent title holder appears to meet all of the conditions to be met by a title holder, and a person engaging in reasonable inquiry and inspection would have no notice that title was defective or cause for further investigation, but the title transferred or to be transferred is defective nonetheless. There are innumerable forms. A common latent defect is an heir of a prior owner who died intestate and whose claim was not satisfied or extinguished in the administration of the estate. A latent defect may have a more limited range of liability than a patent defect for title insurers and land title companies if the defect is not disclosed to a buyer. Moreover, the statute of limitations for injury from a latent defect will normally not begin to run from closing but from when the defect is actually discovered or should have been discovered.

*See also:* latency (latent).

**patent defect**   A reasonably ascertainable defect in title. A patent defect in title is a defect that is capable of discovery through reasonable inquiry and investigation. Not all patent defects are easily discovered. Still, some are, such as the putative title holder's having no ownership interest while the real owner occupies the property. A patent defect creates a wider range of liability than a latent defect for title insurers and land title companies if the defect is not disclosed to a buyer. Moreover, the statute of limitations for injury from a patent defect begins to run from closing.

*See also:* patency (patent).

**title insurance**   Lender's or owner's insurance against some title defects. Title insurance is an insurance policy underwritten either by a general insurance company or a title insurance company, that insures against losses from certain claims against title, from loss of access to the land, and from certain bars to the enforcement of the mortgage lien. Most title insurance is issued to the lender of a debt secured by a mortgage, although policies are also available to owners. Most defects of title within the scope of coverage must have arisen prior to the sale as defects of title at the time of sale. The premium for title insurance is usually prepaid in a lump sum by an owner of property to the benefit of the lender. The beneficiary being the lender and not the owner, the insurer may have no duty to defend the owner against an adverse claim to title unless the claim risks the interests of the lender.

**title search (examination of title)**   An examination of the record title of a given parcel. A title search is an examination of the record of interests recorded for a given property, to assemble a history of the grants of and interests in a property, resulting in an opinion as to who has title in the property at the time of the search and the basis for that title. A title search is not usually a report in itself but a presentation of the basis for the chain of title presented in an abstract of title. A well performed title search will detail every interest filed regarding a single parcel, including those affecting larger parcels of which it was once part and smaller parcels from which it has been constituted, and including all liens, easements, wills, conveyances, deeds, notices, judicial decrees, and other filings. A title search may reach back to the time of the first grant from a sovereign or reach back only to the root of title (in a root-of-title jurisdiction).

*See also:* title, root of title.

**grantor–grantee index (grantor grantee index)**   The record of conveyances indexed by party. The grantor–grantee index is a list of all of the conveyances recorded in a jurisdiction according to the grantor. Likwise, the grantee–grantor index lists all conveyances recorded by grantee. To research a chain of title backward from the current title holder, a researcher takes the following steps. Beginning with the present title holder, who is a grantee, ascertain who was the grantor conveying to that grantee. This is most easily done by looking at the deed granting title, which has the grantor, grantee, and date. Then searching for the grantor as a prior grantee, do the same search to locate the grantor to the prior grantor, and so forth until either

reaching the first grant or passing the root of title if it is relevant in that jurisdiction (the root of title being the most recent grant of title over thirty years). Care must be taken to look for duplicate grants by one grantor, to look for wild deeds whose grantor cannot be ascertained, or other irregularities in compiling the chain of title. Many jurisdictions have automated the indexes, and many have replaced them with plat indexes or parcel indexes by which every interest is recorded by its location; yet, such searches risk locating double grants or grants not recorded appropriately following a subdivision or aggregation.

*See also:* grantee; grantor.

**tract index**   The record of conveyances indexed by tract. The tract index is a record of all instruments that have been recorded that relate to a given tract of land or, usually, to the component tracts that may have been aggregated into the current tract and to the former tracts from which it was subdivided. The tract index in most jurisdictions is a useful tool for correlating the instruments traced through the grantor–grantee and grantee–grantor indexes. The tract index is sometimes the more likely means of locating a wild deed.

*See also:* deed, wild deed; tract.

**void title**   Apparent title of no effect in law or equity. Void title is no title. Title that appears to arise from an instrument that is defective or invalid, even if it might be relied on under color of title, is void at least as to the basis in the defective instrument. (Void title may, under color of title, ripen under circumstances of adverse possession into good title based on the prescription of claims, but this is a new basis of title and not an impossible revival of the void title.)

*See also:* title, color of title.

**voidable title**   Title that may be avoided if its sale is avoided. Voidable title is title acquired through a contract for sale that is voidable, as when a contract is made by one lacking capacity or in circumstances amounting to fraud. In these cases, the person lacking capacity or the victim of fraud may avoid the transaction. If the person who may avoid the sale does so, the title to the property sold is void in the buyer and revests in the seller. Until such time as the person who may avoid the transaction elects to do so, title in the thing sold remains voidable.

*See also:* contract, specific contracts, voidable contract.

**warranty of title**   An assurance by a seller to the buyer that there is no superior title. Warranty of title is an assurance implied or expressed in all contracts for the sale of goods under the U.C.C. and under contracts for sale that do not expressly renounce it, that the seller has the right to sell the thing in issue, and there is no superior title or rightful claimant to the thing sold. A breach of the warranty of title gives rise to an action for indemnity by the buyer against the seller.

*warranty of marketable title and warranty of title*   Warranty of title differs from a warranty of marketable title, in that the warranty of title applies to the sale of chattels as well as to realty and is no more than an assurance that the seller holds the property with no superior claimant to ownership. On the other hand, the warranty of marketable title is a warranty that is usually implied or expressed only as to realty, and it includes a broader assurance–that there is no cloud or encumbrance on title or possession. Thus, a warranty of title may be implied when no warranty of marketable title is implied, and vice versa.

**TMDL** *See:* pollution, water pollution, national pollutant discharge elimination system, total maximum daily load (TMDL).

**tobacco** *See:* police, police organizations, Bureau of Alcohol, Tobacco, Firearms, and Explosives.

**tolerance**

**zero tolerance** A rule enforced regardless of the intent or severity of its breach. Zero tolerance is label for policies of enforcement of rules that require officials to punish every breach regardless of the severity of the breach or other mitigating circumstances. The term is derived from engineering and machine fabrication, in which no deviation from a design is allowed, and is applied in contracts requirements, a usage that persists despite the term's more popular use in environmental law, criminal law, and educational policy. Zero tolerance is both a limit on the discretion of officials and a form of strict liability for those who must comply with the rule.

*See also:* liability, strict liability.

**toll (tolling)** To pause a span of time, or to destroy an interest. Toll, in its oldest sense, is to break something into pieces or destroy it, and tolling in law occurs when the time to exercise an interest or claim is broken into portions and paused. The time that is lost may be considered to be added to the end of the time that otherwise would have been allowed (or one may consider the time remaining in the period when the tolling commenced to remain yet to run and to start when the tolling ceases). In general, any period running for a set period or until a date certain, in which some interest may be asserted, some right protected or discharged, or some obligation performed, may be tolled.

An older sense of tolling is that an interest is destroyed completely, usually though not always by the running of time. Context is essential to distinguish these senses, and a writer should be clear that this less common usage is meant.

**tolling** *See:* limitation, limitation of actions, statute of limitations, tolling (toll); equity, equitable pleading, tolling.

**toll as fee (tolls)** A charge to use some service or thing. A toll is a price paid to authority, originally like a customs or tax payment. Toll, or tolls, are now mainly the term for a fee or fees charged for a service or the use of some property collected in the manner that a state might collect it, particularly for the use of roads or other public resources. A highway use fee is a highway toll. The price for certain private services of a public nature, such as mill grinding for grains, is still termed a toll. More generally, a toll is a price paid for some conduct, though not necessarily in money.

**tonnage** The volume of a vessel, or a weight in tons. Tonnage, as a matter of admiralty and constitutional law, is any of several measures of a maritime vessel, as well as the tax or duty once paid on the ownership or operation of a vessel. Tonnage, used in general shipping, is the volume of cargo the vessel may carry, though deadweight tonnage refers to the vessel's actual displacement or weight including equipment, crew, and cargo.

Tonnage is also short-hand for a duty on tonnage, a tax on shipping that is based on the tonnage of the vessel. The Tonnage Clause limits states and municipals from charging such a tax without Congressional approval.

Tonnage in other senses represents the weight of something, particularly a cargo, in tons.

*See also:* constitution, U.S. Constitution, Tonnage Clause.

**Tonnage Clause** *See:* constitution, U.S. Constitution, Tonnage Clause.

**tontine (tontine trust or tontine fund)** Money pledged for a group that is paid to its last members alive. A tontine is a trust, insurance fund, or other investment scheme that is established to the benefit of a small group of survivors from among a larger group of designated contingent beneficiaries. The funds gather interest over the lives of the participants and are only disbursed to the last survivor. Although the classic and fascinating tontine pays only to the last survivor, variations on the tontine would allow payments to a group of survivors once others have either died or been divested in some other manner.

**took or taken or taking** *See:* take (took or taken or taking).

**topical objection** *See:* objection, topical objection (topic objection).

**Torah (Pentateuch)** The core texts of the Jewish law. The Torah, literally the Teaching, is the collection of the five books of Moses: Bereshit (Genesis), Shmot (Exodus), Vayikra (Leviticus), Bamidbar (Numbers), and Dvarim (Deuteronomy). It contains the central ethical teachings and the history of the Jewish people.

*See also:* Pentateuch.

**Mishneh Torah** The Torah of Maimonedes. The Mishneh Torah is the organization of the Mishnah and its rabbinic interpretations codified by Moses Maimonides. It is the first widely accepted codification of Jewish law.

**Torrens system**   *See:* title, registration of title (Torrens system).

**tort (tortious)**   A wrongful act giving rise to a civil action. Tort is a very broad term for the wrongful acts or omissions that cause harm, when that harm can be stopped or redressed through a private cause of action that does not arise from a specialized category in law or equity such as contract, trust, or criminal law. The wrongfulness of the act is often expressed as a duty of care that is violated. The most general of these is the duty to act toward others as a reasonable person would be expected to act, and an unreasonable act that causes foreseeable harm is a tort.

Torts are often grouped by various levels of intent to cause harm — intentional torts, negligence, and torts of strict liability. That an act may be a tort or given rise to an action in tort does not preclude its being actionable under another doctrine in law, including contracts, fiduciary duty, or criminal law. Torts may arise as a breach of constitutional duty. And conduct in violation of a statutory regulation of some enterprise that results in harm may be tortious, although the statute may limit a recovery only to its express remedies.

In general, the remedy for an ongoing tort is an injunction, and the remedy for a past tort is compensatory damages. If, however, the nature of the wrongdoing is deliberate, excessive, or outrageous, the tort may be considered gross or otherwise worthy of a punitive remedy in addition to a compensatory remedy. Some tort actions give rise not to damages but restitution.

*See also:* delict (quasi-delict or delictual).

**tort damages**   *See:* damages, tort damages, economic loss rule (economic-loss rule); damages, tort damages, collateral-source rule; damages, tort damages.

**tort reform**   *See:* reform, tort reform.

**alien tort**

> **Alien Tort Claims Act (alien torts)**   Statute providing original jurisdiction in federal district court over tort suits by aliens. The Alien Torts Claims Act, 28 U.S.C. § 1350, provides jurisdiction in federal court to hear claims, brought by aliens, for torts in violation of the law of nations or a treaty of the United States. A foreign national may thus bring an action against individuals or entities in the United States or any other jurisdiction for any common-law tort that violates the "law of nations" or international law.
>
> The Alien Tort Statute was passed by the first Congress in 1789, and remained unused for almost nearly two centuries until in Filartiga v. Pena-Irala, 630 F.2d 876 (2d Cir. 1980), plaintiffs invoked its jurisdiction to sue a former Paraguayan police inspector-general for torture and wrongful death in violation of the law of nations. The act has been interpreted to be limited, granting jurisdiction only for claims arising from acts that would have been recognized by the common law in 1789.
>
> *See also:* international law (law of nations or public international law).

**dignitary tort**   An intentional tort that harms the victim's dignity. A dignitary tort is an intentional tort that ordinarily results in an offense to the dignity of the victim, whether or not it also causes a physical injury. (Though in some jurisdictions, a tort causing a physical injury is considered as an intentional, non-dignitary tort or as negligence.) The assessment of damages in dignitary torts is intended to include the harm to the victim's dignity, which is distinct from any physical injury, and which is sometimes included in the compensation for emotional distress. Even so, dignitary torts are subject to exemplary and punitive damages.

At common law, many of the dignitary torts were forms of injury for which the victim could recover in trespass, particularly for battery, assault, or false imprisonment. This is the element in battery requiring no more than an "offensive touching" as the basis for an action, even if no injury results. Other harms that might be heard as trespass on the case or in distinct actions, such as libel and defamation, are now considered secondary dignitary torts, including defamation, libel, slander, false light, intentional infliction of emotional distress (and, in some jurisdictions, negligent infliction of emotional distress), malicious prosecution, invasion of privacy, and alienation of affections.

*See also:* tort, dignitary tort, heart balm tort (amatory tort or Heart Balm Act); libel (libelous); slander (slanderer); prosecution, malicious prosecution.

**heart balm tort (amatory tort or Heart Balm Act)**   Tort claims for intervention in the marital relations of others. The heart balm torts are dignitary torts that arise from the interference with a relationship between spouses or fiances: seduction, alienation of affections, and criminal conversation. Although breach of contract to marry is often listed, this mention here is only in its tortious sense, not in its contractual sense. These actions have been abolished in most U.S. jurisdictions, in many through legislation known within the state as a Heart Balm Statute or Heart Balm Act.

*See also:* conversation, criminal conversation; seduction (seduce); tort, dignitary tort.

**economic tort**   An intentional tort that harms another's fiscal interests. An economic tort is an intentional tort that breaches a duty and harms an economic interest, without directly causing a bodily injury. The law of torts does not recognize a cause of action for causing another party to suffer an economic loss. However, economic torts are those actions for a breach of a duty or failure to comply with a standard of care related to another's business or economic activities, which result in the other's financial loss or lost opportunity. The remedy for such torts is the whole of the foreseeable and proximate losses sustained or foregone by the victim of the breach of duty. There are few consistent pleading requirements that apply solely because a cause of action is an economic tort. The pleading requirements for each cause of action tend to be quite specific. There is no taxonomic boundary in torts that would separate one form of tort perfectly from others, and some economic torts are also, for instance, dignitary torts.

Forms of economic tort include tortious breach of contract and bad faith denial of a claim of insurance; interference with economic or business relationships; interference with a contract; restraint of trade, wrongful monopoly, and anti-competitive behavior; invasions of privacy, conversion, violations of trademark, copyright, or patent, including infringement and passing off; and libel of goods or products. Some quite traditional torts may be considered economic torts, particularly trespass, trespass to chattels, and conversion. Many of these actions are statutory, either under state legislation, federal legislation, or both.

*See also:* deceit, deceptive practices; trespass, trespass on the case (case); libel (libelous); slander (slanderer); trade, restraint of trade.

**Federal Tort Claims Act (F.T.C.A. or FTCA)** Law allowing certain tort actions against the federal government. The Federal Tort Claims Act (FTCA), codified at 28 U.S.C. § 2680, waives federal sovereign immunity in some civil actions against the United States that arise from an allegation of negligence and certain other torts by a federal employee. The statute permits negligence suits, but it specifically excludes claims for enumerated intentional torts, such as battery (unless the allegation arises from an act in law enforcement). The FTCA is not the only means by which a tort action may be brought. Claims of violations of federal rights by employees may be brought against them as Bivens actions (actions against the individual employee for violating a federal right), and actions by government employees are more likely brought under the Federal Employees' Compensation Act (FECA).

*See also:* immunity, sovereign immunity; immunity, sovereign immunity, abrogation of sovereign immunity; civil rights, civil rights enforcement action, Bivens action.

**intentional tort** A tort causing a harm intended by the tortfeasor. An intentional tort is a wrong giving rise to a private civil action in tort, in which the tortfeasor intended to cause the harm that resulted from the wrongful conduct. The long-standing policy of the common law, reflected universally in statutes, is both to compensate victims of intentional torts and to punish the tortfeasors, which is the basis for punitive damages in law. Most intentional torts are also criminal acts, but in the common law, the private cause of action in tort and the public, criminal action are independent. A penalty in one action does not diminish or limit a penalty in the other (with the rare exception of victim compensation or restitution awarded in a criminal action). Intentional torts at common law include assault, battery, conversion, defamation, false imprisonment, intentional infliction of emotional distress, libel, slander, trespass to land, and trespass to chattels. Many statutes have created additional intentional torts, such as intentional wrongful death, and other statutes have created means for actions for intentional torts unknown to the common law, such as a civil action for racketeering.

*See also:* racketeering, Racketeer Influenced and Corrupt Organizations Act (RICO or R.I.C.O.).

**mass tort (mass accident)** A single event or process harming a great number of people. A mass tort is an event, a process, or a defect in a product that causes injury or damage to a great number of people. Iconic examples include the leakage of toxic chemicals from the Hooker Chemical plant in Love Canal in New York; the explosion of the Union Carbide pesticide plant in Bhopal, India; the oil spill from the Exxon Valdez; the exposure of personnel in Vietnam to Agent Orange; and the inhalation and sickness of workers exposed to friable asbestos.

**negligent tort** A wrongful act resulting in an unintended harm. A negligent tort is a tort that results from a breach of a duty of care and that causes a harm that was not intended by the tortfeasor. (Although some discussions of negligence include acts arising from conduct subject to strict liability, most do not, and strict liability is generally considered distinct from negligent torts.) Negligent torts include the tort of negligence as well as a variety of torts that would be wrongful if caused deliberately but remain actionable if caused through a failure of reasonable care and attention to one's actions or responsibilities. Many of these incorporate negligent into the name of the cause of action. Examples include negligent infliction of emotional distress and negligent wrongful death. In some jurisdictions, these actions are considered species of negligence, in others they are more related to the specific nature or the harm. The standards of liability and proof required in both cases arise from both sources, so there is little significant difference between approaches.

*See also:* negligence (negligent).

**nominate tort** A cause of action recognized in tort. A nominate tort is a named tort, one for which a cause of action is recognized in the law of a given jurisdiction, with pleading standards and remedies understood.

*See also:* tort, prima facie tort.

**prima facie tort** The performance of a lawful act solely to cause harm. A prima facie tort is an intentional tort that is not a nominate tort, but that is committed by a party who performs an act that is not unlawful but that is primarily intended to cause harm to another party. A cause of action for a prima facie tort requires proof that the defendant committed an intentional, lawful act; that the defendant's purpose or intent was primarily to injure the plaintiff; that the plaintiff was in fact injured by the defendant's act; and that there is insufficient justification for defendant's act. If a plaintiff can demonstrate these four elements of the case, then the court must balance the likelihood that the defendant acted out of malice toward the plaintiff against any justification that the defendant offers to excuse the action.

*See also:* tort, nominate tort.

**tortious act (tortious liability)** Conduct that amounts to a tort. A tortious act is any harmful act that could result in civil litigation in tort against the actor. A tortious act may also be criminal, but tortiousness depends solely on the scope of civil liability, whether the theory of tort liability is intentional, negligent, or strict.

**tortious breach of contract** *See:* breach, breach of contract, bad-faith breach (tortious breach of contract).

**tortious breach of duty** *See:* breach, tortious breach of duty.

**tortious conversion** *See:* conversion, tortious conversion, conversion of intangibles; conversion, tortious conversion (civil theft).

**tortious interference with contract** *See:* interference, tortious interference with contract (interference with a right of contract).

**tortfeasor (tort-feasor)** A person who commits a tort. Primarily, a tortfeasor is a person or entity whose conduct amounts to a tort, whether the tort is intentional, negligent, or strict. Secondarily, a tortfeasor may be responsible for a tort as a result of liability arising vicariously from the actions of another tortfeasor. No person is a tortfeasor unless that person was bound by a duty of care recognized in the law that was breached to the harm of another. Unless some duty existed, the person is not a tortfeasor. Even so, every person is bound by general duties.
*See also:* feasance; wrong, wrongdoer (wrong–doer).

**joint tortfeasor (active tortfeasor or passive tortfeasor or concurrent tortfeasor)** Two or more parties who are liable for a tort. Joint tortfeasors are parties who share liability for a civil wrong in tort. This shared liability may arise because the parties act in concert to commit the wrong, because they are each responsible for one event in a sequence of events that amounts to a tort, or because one party causes a tort and the other or others are responsible for the actions of the party causing it. When there are joint tortfeasors in negligence, one or the other may be active or passive, the difference being whether the actions or omissions of the tortfeasor cause the harm giving rise to an action (the active tortfeasor). On the other hand, the liability of the tortfeasor may be only vicarious, arising from the action or omission of the active tortfeasor (the passive tortfeasor). A passive tortfeasor who is held liable to a plaintiff may seek full indemnity from the active tortfeasor.
*See also:* liability, joint liability; liability, several liability; liability, joint and several liability.

**torture** The intentional abuse of a prisoner. Torture is a crime under the law of the United States as well as under international law. It consists of any serious mental or physical abuse of a prisoner by an official, guard, or agent in any way under the control of a government that has custody of the prisoner. A person who commits torture may be imprisoned for up to twenty years,

although if the torture victim dies, the torturer may be sentenced to death or to life imprisonment.

Torture has long been prohibited under customary international law, which was reflected in the 1984 Convention against Torture. It may also be considered a war crime and a crime against humanity.

Treatment that would amount to torture may also constitute both the crime of battery and the tort of battery. Some U.S. jurisdictions have defined a crime of torture to include the serious harm of any person by any person with physical custody or control of the victim, whether the person with custody has acquired it as a result of authority or office or not. Under either theory, torture is a basis for a claim under the Alien Tort Claims Act.

**evidence from torture** Evidence acquired through torture is inadmissible in a court of law. Torture evidence is barred from admission in a court of law in the United States for purposes other than to establish the fact of the torture.
*See also:* treaty.

**peine forte et dure** Torture in lieu of pleading in a criminal action under the common law. Peine forte et dure, or punishment hard and long, was a process of torture inflicted on a person accused of a felony who refused to plead. The torture was usually carried out by pressing, the piling of crushing weights onto a large board on the defendant's chest. A person who died rather than plead was, however, not subject to attainder, which some preferred to execution after which the defendant's family was left destitute.
*See also:* interrogation (examination of a suspect).

**total** *See:* insurance, insurance claim, total loss (total).

**total breach** *See:* breach, breach of contract, total breach.

**total disability** *See:* disability, personal disability, total disability (partial disability).

**total incorporation** *See:* constitution, U.S. Constitution, Bill of Rights, incorporation of rights, total incorporation.

**total loss** *See:* insurance, insurance claim, total loss (total).

**total maximum daily load** *See:* pollution, water pollution, national pollutant discharge elimination system, total maximum daily load (TMDL).

**total suspended particles** *See:* pollution, air pollution, criteria pollutants, particulate matter, total suspended particles (TSP).

**totality** The whole sum or quantity. A totality is the entirety, the whole of whatever is in consideration. When a sum is offered in total, it is the whole amount rather than a component or portion.

Several tests for judgment require a consideration of the data in its totality. The totality of the evidence is the consideration of all evidence without omitting or discounting any evidence from consideration. The totality of circumstances considers all relevant circumstances, even those that seem initially to be remote or insignificant. Totality does not, however, require that every facet of a consideration be given equal weight, rather it means that all be considered.

**totality of the circumstances** *See:* circumstance, totality of the circumstances (totality of the circumstances test).

**totality of the evidence** *See:* evidence, totality of the evidence.

**Totten trust** *See:* trust, Totten trust.

**touch and concern** *See:* concern, touch and concern.

**touming** Transparency, especially in village affairs in Chinese law.

**toxin (toxic chemical or toxicant or toxic material or toxic substance)** A substance that poisons animals or plants. Toxin is a broad term for a chemical or material that causes injury or death to an organism that comes into contact with it through any chemical disruption of a biological process, whether the contact is through ingestion, respiration, or absorption. Generally, a toxin is poisonous, although the means by which a toxin may cause harm vary widely. Not every harmful substance is toxic; asphyxiants, for instance, are not usually toxic. As a matter of definition, for purposes of some regulations, toxins do not include radioactive material, although for other purposes toxic radioactive material is included. Toxic substances are regulated under state law and by the federal Toxic Substances Control Act, codified at 15 U.S.C. § 2601 (2010), et seq.

**toxic chemical or toxicant or toxic material or toxic substance** *See:* toxin (toxic chemical or toxicant or toxic material or toxic substance).

**toxic waste** *See:* waste, waste material, hazardous waste, toxic waste.

**toxicity (acute toxicity or chronic toxicity)** The degree to which a substance can harm humans or animals. Toxicity is the function of the toxic characteristics of a chemical in a substance, with its concentration in the substance, and with the substance's form, which determine in sum the rate of intake and toxic reaction a person will experience from the substance. Many toxins are retained in the tissue of an animal or plant, and the result of exposure to a toxin over a period of time is an increase in residual contamination of the tissue. Chronic toxicity results from continued exposure, which may impede any means by which the organism would otherwise diminish the effects of exposure either by wasting the toxin from the tissue, altering its chemical effect, or isolating it from cells it might damage. Acute toxicity and lethal toxicity are concentrations of the toxin in an organism, or in an organ within the organism, sufficient to destroy the organ or kill the organism.

**trace (tracing)** Locating something from a pattern or path. A trace is the act of following a path, or a series of acts, in order to locate or uncover either the process or identity of the path–maker or some thing related to one of the acts. A trace is also an indication or evidence that might be followed in such a task.

Thus, to trace a phone transmission is to locate its source through its switching and routing between callers. A trace of such a call is the action of locating it, as well as a record of the call having been made. Tracing funds is the collection of information regarding every transaction and every subsequent transactions related to the funds. Tracing title is the collection of information as to each grant or other recorded interest to determine the path of ownership in the titled property.

**tract** All contiguous property with a common owner. A tract is a geographic unit of lands that are connected, with a continuous boundary and a common owner. The unit may have been assembled from individual parcels or tracts, but once a common owner holds lands that are contiguous to one another, they form a common tract. A tract is usually assessed for taxable value as a single unit with all of the improvements on the tract affecting the entire quantity of land within it. That a road owned by a government in fee may divide what was once a common tract is, in some jurisdictions, sufficient to make two tracts, though in others a single tract persists.

*See also:* survey (surveyor or surveying).

**tract index** *See:* title, title search, tract index.

**trade** The transactions of commerce, or the craft of skilled service or manufacture. Trade is a quite broad term synonymous generally with business. The term, probably adopted from the old English term for walking, or treading, initially comes from the traveling salesman, who would purchase goods here to sell them there and yon. From this, the term has several related but distinct meanings.

Trade is the actual exchange or sale of a service or product. A person or entity that trades or is a trader thus engages in such transactions. A trade of goods or services for goods or services (rather than money) is either a sale or barter. Trades of all form in these senses are commerce.

Trade is often used in a sense that means international trade, or the trade among all of the entities in one nation with all of the entities in another nation. (There is no distinction in this sense of trade between a transaction in which the state itself buys or sells goods and a transaction between private entities.) The regulation of that trade is both a matter for the domestic law of the two states in question and a subject of international law, which provides both a framework for bilateral relations and certain limits on the domestic laws. In this sense, international trade includes not only trade between two states but trade among all states.

A trade is a particular category of skilled service or manufacture that produces goods or services for trade. Trade unions (or trades unions or labor unions), therefore, are unions that represent members of specific trades to their employers or, sometimes, their contractors. A trade in this sense was once largely a group engaged in a narrow category of labor or craft, such as carpenter, shoemaker, glaziers, bricklayers, or teamsters, which was often distinguished from other trades by the particular training required of an apprentice within that trade. There was once a strong customary division between trades, which primarily produce goods, and professions, which largely perform services, though this division often masked a mere division in social status. Contemporary usage is often more general and less rigorous as to the definition of a trade or the members of a given trade.

The trade of an individual, usually referred to as "trade or business" is the endeavor by which a taxpayer seeks to earn money or engage in commerce to make a profit. Qualified expenses that are incurred in the engagement of a taxpayer's trade or business are deductible as business expenses.

*See also:* tax, tax deduction (deduction from taxable income); profession; union, labor union (labor organization); commerce (commercial).

> **trade dress** *See:* trademark, trade dress.

> **trade fixture** *See:* fixture, trade fixture.

> **trade libel** *See:* libel, trade libel.

> **trade secret** *See:* secret, trade secret.

> **trade usage** *See:* usage, trade usage.

**international trade** Commerce among the states of the world. International trade is the export and import of capital, goods, and services among and between the entities of one country and the entities of other countries. The performance of services in one state for the benefit of an entity in another is international trade, as is the movement of a person into the other state to perform the same service. Foreign direct investment is also international trade, and any direction of money or instruments of value from one states into an entity in another state or subject only to the laws or jurisdiction of another state is also international trade.

> **anti-dumping laws (anti-dumping duties)** Limits on foreign sales below a fair market price. Anti-dumping laws are domestic laws and international treaties that proscribe the unfair pricing of exported products so that the products will sell in their market country at an unfairly low price. The usual measure of dumping is whether the entity that exported the product sells it below the price it would charge, on average, in its home market (not counting variations attributable only to taxes or regulations).

A state whose entities dump goods in another state is itself dumping in the other state. Though the lower price of the imports benefits consumers in the target state, and presumably benefits the entities in the dumping state by allowing them to maintain production that otherwise would be lost, the effect of the dumping is anti-competitive for the competing manufacturers and sellers in the target state. Thus, the target state is usually allowed to retaliate against a dumping state by charging anti-dumping duties against the dumping state, sometimes raising the tariff on the dumped goods and sometimes raising tariffs on other goods from the dumping state.

**balance of trade (trade balance)** The difference in value between the goods exported and imported between two countries. The balance of trade is the amount exchanged in goods between countries. In 2008, most trade-balance data continues to omit the value of services exchanged, although this data has an increasing significance in world trade. Balance of trade may also represent the balance between a country and all of its trading partners.

**General Agreement on Tariffs and Trade (GATT)** A global treaty of international trade regulation. The General Agreement on Tariffs and Trade, or GATT, is the name for a series of treaties that have been the primary body of international law governing international trade regulation and taxation since 1947. The purpose of the GATT is to provide a global conference to negotiate reduced barriers to international trade by making rules governing international trade more consistent and more efficient; by reducing and limiting the role of tariffs and customs duties; and by establishing a means for dispute resolution. Prior to the widespread acceptance of GATT rules, nations would engage in "trade wars" by limiting or barring imports from states, which encouraged those states to retaliate, which led to lost trade and economic harms that could be long-lived, and which also, sometimes, led to armed conflict. Such trade conflicts are now mediated and arbitrated by the World Trade Organization, or WTO, an entity created in 1994 under the GATT treaty regimes.

The GATT has developed through a succession of treaties, each negotiated in a long-running conference, or round. The first, which established a provisional GATT, was in 1947, negotiated in part in Geneva, Switzerland, and in part in Havana, Cuba, leading to an agreement on tariff reduction among twenty-three states. The following rounds, mainly on tariffs and dumping, were in 1949 (Annecy, France), 1951 (Torquay, England), 1956 (Geneva), 1960-1961 (Geneva, called the Dillon Round), 1964-1967 (Geneva, called the Kennedy Round), 1973-1979 (Tokyo, Japan, etc.), 1986-1994 (Punta del Este, Uruguay, etc.), and the Doha, Qatar, Round, which in 2010 is still under way. From the Tokyo Round forward, the negotiations have been far-reaching, including non–tariff regulations, the protection of intellectual property, dispute resolution mechanisms, and the WTO structure itself. There are now one hundred and ten states party to the GATT system, which is now managed under the WTO.

*See also:* trade, international trade, World Trade Organization (WTO or W.T.O.).

**International Trade Commission** Federal agency to investigate and regulate international trade in the U.S. The United States International Trade Commission (ITC) is an independent, quasi–judicial federal agency that investigates allegations of dumped and subsidized imports and their effects on domestic industries. The ITC adjudicates specific charges of unlawful trade practices. The agency also collects data on trade and reports to the President and Congress, thus helping to formulate United States trade policy.

**North American Free Trade Agreement (NAFTA)** A customs union of Canada, Mexico, and the United States. The North American Free Trade Agreement, or NAFTA, creates a single market in North America for most forms of international trade. Since coming into force in 1994, NAFTA has eliminated most tariffs that once applied to trade between any of the three states, and it has created a schedule for the reduction of those that remain. NAFTA has reduced barriers to the movement of goods, services, and capital, although it does not directly affect the movement of labor or immigration policy.

**World Trade Organization (WTO or W.T.O.)** The global treaty and dispute resolution agency for international trade. The World Trade Organization is a permanent body established under the General Agreement on Tariff and Trade in 1994, which now has over one hundred and fifty members, which have agreed to the WTO's rules on tariffs and trade regulations, and who submit disputes with other members to the WTO for resolution. The WTO has a permanent staff but works through biennial meetings of its Council of Ministers to make policy and through ongoing meetings of the national diplomatic representatives in its General Council to interpret and implement policy, hear and review disputes, and review national trade policies.

*See also:* trade, international trade, General Agreement on Tariffs and Trade (GATT).

**Dispute Settlement Body (DSB)** An international trade arbitration body in the WTO. The Dispute Settlement Body, or DSB, comprises all states in the WTO which are represented by the national representatives to the General Council. The DSB sits as panels created for each dispute, the findings of which may be reviewed by the seven–member Appellate Body. The entire process is subject to strict deadlines imposed during the Uruguay Round and is completed in less than a year and a half. As with many dispute resolution systems, the parties may reach an agreement outside of the panel and appellate system and then withdraw their dispute.

**Standing Appellate Body (AB)** The multinational body for appellate review or a trade arbitration. The Standing Appellate Body of the World Trade Organization is a permanent group of seven jurists who hear appeals from the Dispute Settlement Body.

**protectionism** The protection of local business from foreign competition through tariffs, subsidies, or other trade barriers. Protectionism is the use of tariffs, import controls, or other import regulations, or the use of subsidies in some forms, to limit foreign competition in a domestic market for goods or services. Protectionist laws and policies are subject to international regulation according to treaty, including both bilateral agreements between states and the multilateral apparatus of the General Agreements on Tariffs and Trade administered by the World Trade Organization.

**restraint of trade** A contract or action intended to reduce the custom or trade of another. A restraint of trade is an action by one party that lessens the ability of another party to engage in commerce, including the interference with the contract of other parties, interference with a trade or commercial possibility, trade libel, monopoly, and behavior that diminishes the scale or effectiveness of competition in a given market. Restraint of trade is not inherently unlawful, though acts in unreasonable restraint of trade give rise to civil actions in tort, and some restraints amount to violations of regulations over a given arena of commerce or to violations of the criminal law.

A contract in unreasonable restraint of trade is unenforceable as contrary to public policy, with a few exceptions. A non–compete clause related to the sale of a business or property is valid, unless it is in furtherance of a monopoly, and an exclusive trading arrangement, such as an outputs contract, is valid. A non–competition clause in an employment agreement of services contract is valid, as long as the conditions related to time and geography are reasonable.

*See also:* monopoly (monopolize or monopolizer or monopolist).

**trade association** A marketing and lobby association for a trade, business, or industry. A trade association is an organization composed of members of a given trade or business segment, such as the manufacturers of a given product, providers of a given service, or growers of a given crop. A trade association may perform a variety of services for its members, including marketing of its products, lobbying the government for favorable regulation and taxation, and developing standards for best practices and product quality. A trade association may be organized so that it may sue or be sued on behalf of its members. Some trade associations have been integral in developing private standards of reasonable or best practices that have been adopted as legislation as well as standards of care for private liability. The American Bar Association is a trade association. A trade association, however, also risks trading information and coordinating practices in restraint of trade that may amount to a trust in violation of anti-trust law.

*See also:* usage, trade usage.

**trademark**   A sign identifying the unique source of products. A trademark is any symbol that is used to identify and distinguish the goods of the trademark's owner, that sold in interstate or international commerce, from the goods made, sold, or owned by competitors. The symbol employed as a trademark may be a word, phrase, name, symbol, ticket, color, sound, motion, aroma, image, or hologram, device, or any combination of them. The symbol must be affixed in some manner to goods in commerce, and it must be distinctive and unique within the particular trade within which it is employed. The mark must be established through use in commerce, and in order to be protected by an enforcement action, it must be registered with the U.S. Patent and Trademark Office. The protection of trademarks from infringement or dilution through use by others is a matter of federal law in the United States, under the Lanham Act, codified at 15 U.S.C. §1051, et seq., as well as of the domestic law in other states and international law. A trademark that has been registered is to be designated with the ® symbol, and an unregistered trademark whose owner seeks to protect it through use is designated with the superscripted "TM" symbol.

*See also:* symbol (symbolic); intellectual property (I.P. or IP).

**dilution of trademark (trademark dilution)**   Competitor or consumer acts that weaken a trademark. Dilution of a trademark is either the reduction of the unique perception of the trademark owing to the use of similar labeling or marketing by competitors or the association by consumers of the trademark with other goods or entities than the owner's entity or goods. Dilution may occur through confusion owing to similarity between the trademark being protected and the diluting mark or through tarnishment owing to both similarity and a harmful association with the similar mark. The use of a product description or mark that is sufficiently similar to another's trademark may be enjoined as dilution.

*See also:* dilution (dilute or diluted).

**infringement of trademark (trademark infringement)**   The unlicensed use of another's registered trademark. Trademark infringement is the unauthorized or unjustified use of another's trademark. An action for infringement under the Lanham Act may only be brought by a person to protect a trademark registered with the U.S. Patent and Trademark Office. Infringement requires use in commerce of a reproduction or imitation of a trademark that is related to a product that might cause confusion between the source of a legitimately trademarked product and the source of a product bearing the similar or duplicated mark, or otherwise cause confusion, mistake, or deception amounting to unfair competition or business fraud.

An action for trademark infringement may seek the profits realized by the infringer, as well as the damages of the victim and costs.

**palming off (reverse palming off)**   Passing off goods as if they were made by one who did not make them. Palming off goods is the act of presenting goods as if they were made by a person or entity that did not make them. In general, palming off is a synonym for passing counterfeit goods. The Lanham Act governing trademarks prohibits as false description any palming off of goods one has made or caused to be made as if they were made by another maker.

Reverse palming off is the converse deception, in which a person or entity presents the goods of another maker as if they are made by the person or entity presenting them.

**generic mark (genericism)**   A mark too common to distinguish a source of goods. A generic mark is a symbol that is used to identify a source of goods as if it were a trademark, but the mark is too common or generic to be a distinctive mark, unique to the sole producer of goods in that category or categories of goods. A word or phrase or image that is already in use for a product without regard to its maker, source, or seller cannot be trademarked for that product. A trademark might be unique when registered and become generic, or a mark may be used that is initially generic but becomes unique as the generic sense becomes obsolete.

**genericide (proprietary eponym)**   The conversion of a trademark to generic use. Genericide is a slang term for the acceptance of a trademarked name or phrase as a generic representation not only of the products for which the trademark was created but for all forms of product in a related category. The trademark becomes generic, an eponym by which all such products are known, and it ceases to be enforceable. Aspirin, Coke, Kleenex, and Heroin were all once subject to trademark protection but are now generic terms for such goods.

**service mark (servicemark)**   A unique mark identifying the producer of a service. A service mark is effectively the analogue of a trademark, registered and protected for use by a provider of services to the public. The requirements that the mark be distinctive and unique to the particular category of services are essentially the same as the requirement for trademarks. The mark is placed on advertising, vehicles, stationery, and other representations of the entity providing the service. The mark is made with the superscripted "SM".

**scandalous matter in a trademark**   Matter sufficiently vulgar or offensive as not to be trademarked. Scandalous matter that may not be incorporated into a trademark includes any word, phrase, image, or other sign that is vulgar or that is considered by the general public to be offensive. Both vulgarity and offensiveness are objective criteria that may be established either by references or by survey of public attitudes. The mere fact that some individuals are not offended by some image, word or phrase or find it not to be vulgar is no proof that it is not. Such matters are questions decided neither by the majority nor a vocal minority or individual; the basic questions are whether the matter would offend a person of average sensibilities in the national polity, or whether such a person would consider the matter inappropriate in a federally-sanctioned and legally protected trademark.

*See also:* scandal.

**trade dress**   The impression or image overall of a product. Trade dress is the appearance overall of a product, including the sum of its size, shape, color, and labels and the impression created in the consumer who views it. Trade dress consists of strictly non-functional aspects of a product and does not reach the functional design, but includes packaging and appearance.

Trade dress is related to a trademark but not the trademark itself. Trade dress may be registered but need not be in order to be the basis for an infringement action, although for an infringement action, the plaintiff must prove that the aspect of the trade dress in issue is a non-functional component of the product.

*See also:* label.

**R as trademark symbol ®**   The registration mark for a trademark. An R enclosed in a circle is the trademark symbol. The effect of a registration mark near a registered trademark is to provide notice to anyone who would copy it that the mark is trademarked. If such a mark is not present on the goods subject to trademark registry, the mark holder who attempts to enforce it must prove actual notice of registration by the copier in order to pursue damages for any infringement. The symbol is to be used only once a mark is in fact registered and not before, even if an application to register a mark has been filed.

*See also:* c, c as copyright symbol ©.

**tradition**   A custom of long standing, or a value placed on such a custom. Tradition, in general, is a manner of doing things for a long time, especially a value placed on certain practices or behavior that are of long standing within a relevant community. Tradition is analogous to custom.

Tradition has long been understood as a basis for the justification of law, not only because the benefits of stability and reliance but also because of the role traditions, including legal traditions, play in defining community and personal identity as a member of a community. Liberty is a tradition. On the other hand, tradition may also be a means of justifying inequitable and unjust treatment. Slavery was a tradition until its abolition. When a tradition is in issue as the justification either for conduct that might be legally prohibited or for a legal principle, great controversy is likely in identifying the nature of the tradition that is in fact in issue. Such controversy is likely to depend in part on the level of abstraction with which the conduct in issue is depicted and related to a tradition subject to social commendation, practice, toleration, or prohibition. Other bases of controversy may turn on class distinctions in tradition, particularly recognition by the state or by social elites or only by one or another ethnic, demographic, economic, or geographic sub-culture.

Although now nearly obsolete, tradition in the civil law is the equivalent of the common-law doctrine of delivery, the means by which something is transferred manually in order to vest ownership through posession.

*See also:* delivery; custom (customary).

**traditional public forum**   *See:* speech, freedom of speech, forum, public forum (traditional public forum).

**traffic (traffick or trafficking)**   The movement of goods or people in commerce. Traffic, or trafficking, was once a synonym for trade or commerce, and it remains primarily the movement of goods or people for the purpose of commerce, as well as any given transaction of commerce. Thus, a single transfer of a chattel from one person to another is trafficking, as is the shipment of millions of goods in a complex supply chain. Traffic has a variety of senses, though, not the least being the people, goods, and vessels or vehicles in transit, and from that sense, information broadcast or carried in a given channel of communication.

Despite the long-standing sense of traffic as commerce, traffic has acquired a sense of the movement or sale of contraband. This sense is often the sense implied in the use of the term alone, and it arises from the tendency to describe the commercial but illegal transfer or transport of drugs, people, or contraband goods as trafficking: drug trafficking, trafficking in human beings, weapons trafficking, trafficking in endangered species, and so on. Note: both traffic and trafficking are nouns and verbs.

*trafficking and smuggling*   Trafficking, in contrast to smuggling, is always commercial or coercive. Trafficking is a distinct offense from smuggling, though the two offenses may overlap in many instances. The differences for the smuggling of a person are that human smuggling is non-coercive, but human trafficking is the movement of someone who has not willed to be moved, owing to coercion, fraud, trickery, or minority so that no consent can be formed (when the person moving the child is not a parent or guardian). The differences between smuggling and trafficking goods are that the trafficking of goods is the movement and sale, while smuggling is movement alone.

**traffic offense**   *See:* offense, traffic offense, primary offense as traffic offense (secondary offense); offense, traffic offense.

**careless interference with traffic**   *See:* pedestrian, pedestrian offense (jaywalking).

**trafficking**

**drug trafficking**   Illegal sale, transport, or possession of drugs. Drug trafficking is the sale or transport, or the possession with the intent to sell or to transport illegal drugs. Drug trafficking is both an offense and also a category of offenses that include nearly all possession, manufacture, and distribution offenses, which are the basis for enhanced sentencing upon conviction.

**continuing criminal enterprise (CCE)** An organization to make, transport, or sell illegal drugs. A continuing criminal enterprise, or CCE, is a racketeering organization that generates revenue or resources from any criminal activity related to illegal drugs. A CCE exists when six or more people are in a relationship in which one is an organizer, supervisor, or manager of the others, and the organization generates substantial income or resources from any activity forbidden under the federal laws regarding drug abuse prevention and control in Chapter 13 of Title 21 of the U.S. Code, whether subchapter I, dealing with manufacturing, transportation, and sale generally, or subchapter II, dealing with importing and exporting drug–related materials in the customs territory of the United States. A person convicted of being a manager, organizer, or supervisor of a CCE involved in significant quantities of illegal substances shall be sentenced to life in prison, and a person subject to prosecution as a CCE participant who kills or attempts to kill or have killed a law enforcement officer is subject to the death penalty.

*See also:* racketeering (racket); drug, controlled substance; racketeering, organized crime; syndicate, criminal syndicate.

**human trafficking** The transport of a person for an illegal purpose. Human trafficking is the transportation of any person or group of people for an illegal purpose, whether or not the person or people transported consent to their movement. Examples of human trafficking include (a) the movement of a person in order to engage in illegal prostitution; (b) the movement of children or adults abducted or kidnapped and held for sale or ransom; (c) the movement of a person to allow the person to enter a state without a visa or lawful basis for entry; and (d) the movement of a person to engage in labor or secure the labor of others in violation of labor laws.

**trafficking animals or plants (animal trafficking or plant trafficking)** The movement of restricted animals or plants. The trafficking of animals or trafficking of plants is the taking, possession, sale, or transport of listed animals or plants that are barred from transport, including any part or organ of such animals or plants, without governmental authorization. In the United States, trafficking includes transport in violation of the Endangered Species Act, 16 U.S.C. 1531 (2010), the Convention on International Trade in Endangered Species of Wild Fauna and Flora, T.I.A.S. 8249 (1973) the Convention on Nature Protection and Wildlife Preservation in the Western Hemisphere, 50 Stat. 1354 (1940), or quarantine orders under the Plant Protection Act of 2000, codified at 7 U.S.C. § 1505 (2010).

**tragedy of the commons** The notion that public goods are destroyed by individuals. The tragedy of the commons is a metaphor derived in game theory from the public grazing field open to all of the neighborhood; each neighbor is said to have an incentive to graze more animals than other neighbors, which would lead to overgrazing and the destruction of the pasture. The game theory answers to the dilemma are either to privatize or, less popularly, to regulate the use. This metaphor has been widely criticized as failing to account for collaborative behavior and the role of community reputation, and it has been defended with historical analogues, being used both to argue for the privitization of all public goods and to argue for regulation and government ownership.

**tragic choice** *See:* choice, tragic choice.

**Trail Smelter arbitration** *See:* pollution, interstate pollution, Trail Smelter arbitration.

**traitor** *See:* treason (traitor).

**tranch (tranche)** A slice of a large group of claims, bonds, debts, or other legal interests. A tranch, or tranche, is a group within a larger set of groups. It comes from tranche, the French for slice, as in a slice of a fish, and it is now a popular way of describing the organization of categories, as well as a single category within it. In particular, a tranch may represent one class of bonds among all of the bonds a company issues or it may represent one group of claims among all of the claims associated with complex litigation. Thus, an entity may have five tranches of debts, or share, or claims. Tranches are usually classified in an order according to the seniority of the rating of the assets within each tranche. The tranche with the least risk assessed in its assets is usually the highest category tranche. A single financing arrangement may have two, three, five, or more tranches; the relationship among them, and the order in which obligations in each tranche will be serviced is determined by the financing agreement or indenture. Though each tranch has a different status or priority relative to the other tranches, unless the financing agreement specifies otherwise, all debts, shares, or claims within a tranche are treated equally.

*See also:* security, securities, collateralized debt obligation (collateralized loan obligation or CLO or CDO).

**transaction (transact)** An agreement between parties, especially a sale. A transaction is a final agreement between or among parties, as opposed to a negotiation or predicate to the agreement and not including a unilateral act. Though the term may mean any contract or agreement, it is most often associated with a sale, or an agreement resulting in the transfer of goods or services.

**transaction cost** *See:* cost, transaction cost.

**secured transaction (security agreement)** A transaction contingent on a security interest in collateral. A secured transaction is an agreement of any form, in which the agreement is related to and contingent on the creation of a security agreement, in which the debtor grants a security interest in some collateral to a creditor. The usual secured transaction is a sale of goods, such as a car, in which the buyer finances the purchase and so assigns a security interest in the car to the third-party who provides the proceeds of the loan to the seller. The car is the collateral for the buyer's commitment to repay the loan. The third party has a right to take possession of the car in the event of a default on the repayment of the car note. In order to have priority in the collection of a debt that is secured with collateral, however, the third-party creditor must perfect the security interest by filing a notice of the interest in the depository appropriate to that jurisdiction, usually an office or contract of the state secretary of state.

*See also:* security, security interest.

**transactional immunity** *See:* immunity, witness immunity, transactional immunity.

**transcript (transcribe or transcription)**  A writing of written or spoken words. A transcript is a recording of the words written in an instrument or spoken at a proceeding or event. A transcript of a conversation or testimony is a rendering of spoken words into a written record. A transcript of an instrument is the copying or duplication into a new writing and, in contemporary practice, conversion into an electronic file format. The record created at a trial or hearing on the record by a court reporter is produced as a transcript.

*See also:* reporter, court reporter; deposition (depose).

**verbatim**  Word by word. Verbatim is a shortened form of an old scrivener's entry of verbatim et literatum, word for word and letter for letter, an assurance (or promise) that a copy would be made exactly and with not even the least error or omission. In its modern sense, to record something verbatim is to record it word for word, as a transcript is to be when made by a court reporter. Small errors or omissions are bound to occur, however, and court rules generally accept a transcript as verbatim as long as no material or substantial omission or error has been made.

**transfer**  Movement from one place or status to another. Transfer is the movement of a thing, person, or interest from one place or ownership to another. Transfer is an essential aspect of delivery, in which the physical or constructive possession of a thing is relocated from the owner to a successor with the intent to transfer ownership along with the thing itself. Transfer may be accomplished by constructive delivery through endorsement of a title or instrument demonstrating ownership, such as a bill of lading. It can occur through symbolic delivery, such as by the transfer of keys or other symbols of the thing transferred. It can occur through the operation of law, when title to something formerly in one party is decreed to be in another party.

A variety of legal relations depend on transfer. For example, transfer is essential to the completion or execution of a sale, in that the thing sold must be transferred from seller to buyer, and until that time a contract for sale remains executory. And, transfer is essential to delivery to complete a gift.

In judicial procedure, an action validly before a court may be transferred. Although there is a procedure for motion and order of transfer of a matter, transfer may happen either expressly by order of transfer or effectively, such as by an order granting appeal or removal. Similarly, prisoners may be transferred from the custody of one institution or jurisdiction to another.

More generally, a transfer involves any change or shift of activity or location, assessed by the effect of the shift rather than any purpose in it. Thus, transferred intent recognizes that an action begun with one intent that is manifest in a different result transferred the intent from the intended goal to the realized act.

*See also:* delivery; sale (exchange or sale).

**transfer price**  *See:* price, transfer price (transfer pricing).

**transfer pricing**  *See:* price, transfer price (transfer pricing).

**transfer to a more convenient forum**  *See:* jurisdiction, forum non conveniens (transfer to a more convenient forum).

**transferable development right**  *See:* zoning, transferable development right (TDR).

**transferred intent**  *See:* intent, transferred intent; assault, transferred intent.

**symbolic transfer**  *See:* delivery, delivery of possession, symbolic delivery.

**transgenic**  A cell, organ, or organism into which a new gene is transplanted.

**transgression**  The violation of a duty or rule. A transgression is a violation of a duty, particularly a duty arising from a rule, the law, an oath, custom, morality, or religious precept.

*See also:* violation (violate or violative).

**transience (transient or transient person)**  Temporary, especially a person passing through. Transience is a condition of temporary presence that implies the condition will cease or its cause will leave. Thus, a transient condition is brief.

A transient is a person who is not a resident of the place in question but is a person in transit, a person who is present in a given place only for a time, there with the intent of moving on to another place in the near future. A transient may be a recurrent visitor, even a frequent visitor, but the transient does not maintain a domicile or principal residence in the place in question.

Although all travelers are transient by definition, the word has long been associated in legal drafting with drifters, vagabonds, and the image of the potentially law-breaking poor person. The regulation of housing intended for renters, time-share owners and other transients, such as hotel and motel guests, does not, however, have this connotation.

*See also:* resident; domicile (domicil or domiciliary).

**transit passage**   *See:* passage, transit passage.

**transitory (transit)**   Fleeting in time or fragmented in places. Transitory implies movement in time or space, and a transitory effect exists, or a transitory fact is true, only for a time. A transitory action or operation either moves from place to place or occurs in stages located in different places.

**transitory action**   *See:* action, transitory action.

**translation (translator)**   A conversion from one language to another. Translation is the act of rendering the ideas and words presented in the forms of one language into the form and words of another language, so that the ideas are rendered accurately in the second language. Translation may be required from all sorts of languages into a language useful to parties or a court, including the private language, short-hand, or code used by an individual, a language spoken by a distinct linguistic community, a jargon specific to a trade or sub-culture, or a code or language used in the arts, science, or technology.

A person who does not speak English who is accused of a crime or an administrative or immigration violation is entitled to have a translator in order to understand the proceedings generally and in particular to hear and respond to questions. Translations should be provided by a qualified interpreter.

*See also:* interpreter.

**trap gun or man trap**   *See:* gun, spring gun (trap gun or man trap).

**trash (garbage)**   Dry solid waste material. Trash is refuse, garbage, the dry solid waste cast off by individuals and entities to be destroyed, disposed of, or, potentially, recycled. The collection, disposal, or regulation of trash is one of the customary police powers of state and local government, and the movement of trash in interstate commerce is subject to both regulation and limits to that regulation under the dormant commerce clause.

The trash a person, family, or entity places in a waste stream for collection and disposal has a limited privacy interest while it remains within the dwelling or structure of the person or entity disposing of it. Yet, once trash is placed outside the curtilage of a house or into a commercial waste stream it is abandoned and any privacy interest that would affect its search is destroyed.

*See also:* privacy; warrant, search warrant.

**trashing**   *See:* jurisprudence, critical legal studies, trashing.

**travaux préparatoires**   *See:* treaty, travaux préparatoires.

**travel (right to interstate travel)**   The movement of a person or thing from place to place. Travel is

movement, and in most usages in law, travel is the movement of people, vehicles, or vessels from one place to another. Travel that crosses a state line within the United States is interstate travel, and travel that crosses an international frontier, or the boundary between two countries, is international travel.

The Constitution assures to every person in the United States a right to interstate travel unless the person is subject to a judicial order restraining the person to a jurisdiction or is a member of the military subject to orders, or in some other legal exclusion. The source of the right to interstate travel is various, including the inherent structure of the Constitution as enacted in 1789, the Ninth Amendment, the structure of article one of the Fourteenth Amendment, the right to travel to petition the government, the federal privileges or immunities, the right to engage in interstate commerce, and the right to due process; but the right is firmly established whatever its source.

**traverse (traverser)**   The denial of an allegation in a complaint. A traverse was once a common term in common law pleading in civil actions, the pleading by which a defendant denies an allegation made by another party in an earlier pleading. It is equivalent to an answer containing denials under the federal rules.

In criminal pleading, a traverse was a motion to contest an allegation or rebut an indictment. In criminal actions, the motion to hold over a criminal action until the next term of court was also called a traverse.

**treason (traitor)**   Waging war against one's country or aiding an enemy at war against it. Treason is the act of waging war against a state to which one owes allegiance, or the act of providing aid and comfort, which is some material benefit to an enemy at war against one's country. In the United States, treason may be committed by a citizen, resident alien, resident of an insular possession, or member of the U.S. Armed Forces. Under the Treason Clauses, conviction of treason requires either two witnesses to the same overt act of treason or a voluntary confession by the defendant in open court. Treason is a capital offense, punishable by death or imprisonment and fine, and any traitor is barred from holding office under the United States.

*See also:* insurrection.

**Treason Clauses**   *See:* constitution, U.S. Constitution, clauses, Treason Clauses.

**misprision of treason**   The failure to report treason. Misprision of treason is the specific crime of knowing of an act or planned act of treason and failing to make a timely report of the treasonous conduct to a judge, a state or a representative of an executive officer, such as a police officer. The crime is both a federal offense and a state offense. As with misprision of felony, an action for treason against the traitor is not required to bring an action for misprision against a person with knowledge of a traitorous scheme.

*See also:* misprision (misprision of a felony).

**treasure trove** *See:* property, found property, treasure trove (trove).

**treasury** The department responsible for overseeing money and finance laws. The treasury, literally, is the place where money or treasure is kept, and in law, the treasury refers to the agency responsible for creating and managing the money, debt, assets, and taxes, of the government. In the United States government, the U.S. Department of the Treasury performs that function, in coordination with autonomous agencies including the Securities and Exchange Commission and the Governors of the Federal Reserve.

**treatise** *See:* lawbook, treatise (commentary).

**treaty** An agreement between one or more nations. A treaty is an international agreement concluded between States in a written form and governed by international law. A treaty may be embodied in a single instrument or in two or more related instruments. A treaty may have any title or no title, some of these titles being: treaty, convention, pact, accord, agreement, concordat, peace, armistice, and charter. A protocol or annexe is generally not a treaty, but each is an extension incorporated into another treaty.

Treaties in U.S. law are federal law and supreme over state law to the contrary. A formal treaty is entered by or on behalf of the President and ratified following the advice and consent to the treaty by the Senate. Informal treaties are made by executive agreement.

*See also:* sea, law of the sea (sea laws); pactum, pacta sunt servanda; torture, evidence from torture; pact.

**Treaty Clause** *See:* constitution, U.S. Constitution, clauses, Treaty Clause.

**treaty reservation** *See:* reservation, treaty reservation (reservation to a treaty).

**full powers** The authorization to represent a state in negotiation, signature, or ratification of a treaty. Full powers represent the authority of a state in an individual representative to enter into negotiations on behalf of the state that might result in a treaty with another state or international person, or to sign or to ratify the treaty. Heads of state and heads of government inherently have full powers, as have ministers of foreign relations or secretaries of state. Ambassadors have full powers as to the state to which they are credentialed. Other diplomatic representatives are granted full powers through assignment by an instrument issued by the head of government or an appropriate minister.

*See also:* diplomat, full powers.

**ratification of a treaty (treaty ratification)** A formal national acceptance of a treaty made by a national representative. Ratification is one process of acceptance of a treaty as binding on a state as a matter of international law. The terms of a given treaty may specify that it is fully binding on its state's party at signature, at the time of exchange of instruments, or at a later time of accession, approval, or ratification. Ratification occurs according to the terms of the treaty itself, or by custom, with the transmission by the ratifying state of a notice of ratification, either to the other signatory states or states party or to a depository, such as an international agency like the Secretariat of the United Nations.

In the United States, it has become common to refer to the process of advice and consent to a treaty by the United States Senate as "ratification." Under the U.S. Constitution, the President may enter a treaty, which must be given the advice and consent of the Senate by a two-thirds vote. This process is referred to as "ratification" in the United States, but is distinct from ratification as a matter of international law. Presidents have interpreted the two forms of ratification to require certain treaties to be accorded consent by the Senate before the President causes the treaty to be ratified. Yet, as a matter of international law, ratification is still done by the executive, when an instrument of ratification is deposited according to the terms of the treaty or international custom. Note: if the President acts under the inherent authority of executive power to enter into an executive agreement or under delegated powers according to a statute, the process of advice and consent usually does not apply, and the agreement may come into force without further legislative consultation.

*See also:* ratification (ratify or ratified or ratifiable).

**instrument of ratification** An acceptance of a treaty signed by an official empowered to do so. An instrument of ratification is a unilateral instrument, a document, signed by the head of state or government or by a diplomat or agent of that person, which is then dispatched to the parties specified in the treaty, usually the other signatory states or to an agreed or customary depository, such as the Secretariat of the United Nations. The instrument of ratification may contain or incorporate reservations to the treaty.

*See also:* ratification (ratify or ratified or ratifiable); instrument.

**self-executing treaty (non-self-executing treaty)** A treaty that becomes U.S. law without further legislation. A self-executing treaty, in the law of the United States and some other nation-states, is a treaty that becomes domestic law, binding on officials and other persons in the country, as soon as it is ratified and without further implementing legislation or interpretation. Thus a self-executing treaty that is – ratified by the U.S. Senate becomes federal law the moment it comes into force. A self-executing treaty in the U.S. is federal law and pre-empts state law that contradicts it. The opposite is a non-self-executing treaty, a treaty that is written in such a manner that has no effect on domestic law until additional legislation or regulations are adopted that are based upon its requirements. Certain other treaties, such as those that create no individually enforceable rights, are also considered non-self-executing. Whether a treaty is self-executing or not depends on its language and structure more than any label or pronouncement in its text. Thus, a treaty that requires legislation to have domestic effect or that dictates that states a party shall endeavor to do something by appropriate means is not self-executing. But, a treaty that declares a boundary at a given point, or bans certain importations, or declares some conduct to be illegal is structured in a self-executing manner. Presumptively, treaties are self-executing.

*See also:* execution, self-executing.

**travaux préparatoires**   The record of negotiation of a treaty. The travaux préparatoires of a treaty or convention is the formal record of negotiation and drafting that is kept during the process from initial discussion to the preparation of a treaty for signature, usually including the specific proposals, drafts, and supplementary materials offered by all parties, including parties to the drafting who do not ultimately become states party to the treaty. The travaux are the most significant source of what would be legislative history were the treaty created in a process of domestic legislation.

**treble damages**   *See:* damages, calculation of damages, treble damages (double damages or double or multiple damages or trebles).

**trespass (trespass to land)**   Any unlawful act that injures another, particularly another's interest in land. Trespass, generally, is an unlawful action by one party that causes harm to another party. At common law, a great family of writs in trespass was available for remedies for harms caused through an act of commission or duty breached by action, as opposed to writs of debt that were available for acts of omission or duty not performed. The most significant writs for trespass were trespass vi et armis, for an injury committed by force, trespas de bonis asportatis, for an injury committed by the taking of property, trespass on the case, for injury unaccompanied by force or injury delayed from the time of the trespass, and trespass quare clausum fregit, which was for injury from an entry onto one's lands. The first three of these actions have generally been supplanted by other actions, such as assault, conversion, and breach of contract; but the last form has persisted and is the basis for the contemporary actions for injury to an interest in property.

Trespass to land occurs when a person physically enters the lands of another without an invitation, license, or warrant of law to do so and there causes any damage to the lands or to the title in the lands. As a practical matter presence alone is sufficient. There are defenses to trespass, particularly necessity, in which a person requires refuge in an emergency.

Trespass by chattel occurs by the intrusion of a person's chattel onto the lands of another. A horse, goat, or other animal on the premises of another is a trespass, as is the sending of objects, such as bullets, arrows, sludge, waters, or smoke over the other's lands. In most jurisdictions a property owner who alters the property so that waters from that property flood the lands of its neighbor commits a trespass by chattel. A party who builds a structure on another's lands commits trespass in the construction by sending people on the land although the building itself amounts to trespass by chattel.

Both trespass to land and trespass by chattel are torts that are subject to an action for damages. If the trespass persists, it is a continuing trespass, which is subject to injunction. Trespass is usually subject to the statute of limitations for actions in land, although limitations for a continuing trespass do not begin to run until the trespass abates.

Trespass is also a crime. Criminal trespass is an offense of a person's being present in or on the property of another without a license or invitation to be there. Criminal trespass requires intent to be present on the premises, and mistake is a defense to a criminal trespass although it is no defense to civil trespass.

*See also:* stealing (steal or stolen); squatter (squat or squatting).

**indirect trespass**   Trespass proven by its effects rather than by entry. Indirect trespass is a theory for the proof of trespass by chattel, which is recognized as a distinct cause of action in some jurisdictions for the movement of chemical or particulates through air or water into the property of another, which is proven by the effects of the substances on the property. The damage to property on which the substance settles or through which it passes is evidence towards the proof of harm as well as, in some cases, proof of entry.

*See also:* nuisance.

**trespass clausum fregit (quare clausum fregit)**   A common law action for trespass to real property. Trespass clausum fregit is the common-law action for trespass to land. The Latin clausum fregis, or "he broke the close," is often translated as breaking the close, or intruding on the close. The close is the land itself, and the law presumed an enclosure. Thus, from a very early time the writ was used whether there was a wall, hedge, or fence not around the perimeter of the land on which the trespass was alleged. Trespass quare clausum fregit includes every unlawful intrusion upon the land of another, whether by direct bodily entry, by chattel, or by indirect eminent entry. Thus, standing upon one's own land and throwing stones at one's neighbor's house constitutes trespass quare clausum fregit, as would lofting particulate matter from one's factory's smoke stack over one's neighbor's lands.

**trespass for mesne profits**   Damages arising in trespass from wrongful possession. Mesne profits are the damages suffered by the rightful owner of property as a result of the trespass and possession of the property by another, and trespass for mesne profits is a claim that is collateral to an action for ejectment. Mesne profits generally include the value of the use of the property for the time the true owner is dispossessed, which is usually measured in the rental value of the property during that period as well as any value actually realized from the crops or minerals severed from the land during the period, offset by the value of any reasonable improvements made. An action for mesne profits may be brought even if the trespasser voluntarily surrenders the land, but the action is subject to the same limitations period.

*See also:* ejectment (eject or ejection); mesne.

**trespass on the case (case)** An unlawful act that results in injury to another, committed without force. Trespass on the case was a writ for trespass when an unlawful act caused injury to another though the act had not been accompanied by force, or the injury had not been a direct and immediate result of the wrongful act. In general, case was a means of vindicating legal rights when the injury against them was not one that fit the pleading requirements for a breach of covenant in debt or a trespass by force. A great variety of claims were brought under the theory of trespass on the case, including actions for the enforcement of contracts, economic torts, negligence, and restitution.

*See also:* torts, economic tort.

**trespass to chattel** Damage from taking or using another's chattel. Trespass to chattel is an intentional tort that includes not only the dispossession of control by the owner of a chattel but also the use of another's chattel in a manner that denies the owner use of it for a substantial time, impairs its value or use, or risks harm to the owner. Title, license, and necessity are defenses to a claim for trespass to chattel. Thus, a repossession of a chattel for repayment of a debt in default is not a trespass to chattel if the owner had granted a prior lien and license to take possession in the event of such a default. Trespass to chattel is similar to but broader than conversion.

*See also:* chattel; theft.

**trespass vi et armis** Trespass by force and arms. Trespass vi et armis is the common-law action of trespass committed in an act accompanied by a use of force. Battery, assault, false imprisonment, wrongful death, and other intentional torts accomplished by force were pled under the writ of trespass vi et armis. Although generally supplanted by more specific causes of action, trespass vi et armis is still recognized in some jurisdictions, both as a cause in general and as the basis for certain actions, sometimes by statute and sometimes in the state's common law.

*See also:* entry, forcible entry.

**trespasser** One who commits a trespass. A trespasser is a party who commits a trespass, whether the trespass is committed by the trespasser in person as an intrusion on the land of the plaintiff, or by chattel by allowing or causing chattel to enter the plaintiff's land, or against chattel by the person committing a trespass against the plaintiff's chattel. An entity whose agent enters the property of another is a trespasser by respondeat superior. A trespasser is a trespasser as a result of the presence on the land of another, and a lack of intent to trespass is no defense.

*See also:* invitee (business guest); land, liability to other on the land, trespasser.

**duty to trespassers** A lawful occupant has a limited duty to a trespasser. The duty to trespassers of the owner or occupant of land is limited, in that in general, the owner is not liable for injuries suffered by a trespasser from conditions of the premises. Even so, an owner or occupant is liable for injuries suffered by a trespassing child who enters the property to reach an attractive nuisance; for wanton, reckless, or intentional conduct that injures a trespasser; and for injuries resulting from unusually dangerous activities by the owner or occupant. The classic violation of such duties is an owner's placement of spring guns or man traps so as to deliberately injure a trespasser.

*See also:* eviction self-help.

**trial** A court proceeding to review evidence in order to find facts and apply law to adjudge claims and defenses. A trial, in contemporary U.S. law, is a judicial proceeding in a court of law or of equity, in which the party or parties to the action produce witnesses and tangible evidence for consideration of a judge or jury, whose findings of facts and applications of law are the basis for judgment for one party or another by the judge, who must have authority over the action according to law. Trials of a given legal action take several forms that reflect their subject matter and the jurisdiction appropriate to the cause of action. Criminal trials, civil trials, and trials in equity or admiralty each occur under somewhat different rules of procedure. In particular, trials before a judge and jury differ somewhat from trials before a judge alone; although the rules of evidence and procedure are the same, in a bench trial without a jury, there is no need for instruction of the jury or for a jury verdict. Although most trials are adversarial, certain trials are ex parte, and the court tests the sufficiency of the evidence presented by only one side, in the absence of an opponent.

*See also:* trial, trial by battle (battel or judicial duel or trial by combat or wager of battle).

**trial brief** *See:* brief, trial brief.

**trial by ordeal or judicium dei** *See:* ordeal (trial by ordeal or judicium dei).

**trial court** *See:* court, trial court (court of first instance).

**trial jury** *See:* jury, petit jury (trial jury).

**trial record or record on appeal** *See:* record, appellate record (trial record or record on appeal).

**trial separation** *See:* separation, trial separation.

**argument at trial (trial argument)** The moments in a trial when counsel argue the merits of the case. Argument at trial is a specialized procedure that provides counsel for each party in a trial an opportunity to present an argument of the facts that should be derived from the evidence and the legal conclusions that should be derived from the facts. (If a party is not represented by counsel, the party pro se presents the argument.) Each side is confined in actual argument to the opening and closing arguments. In theory, all other procedures are confined to the specific tasks of selecting the jury or developing the evidence for the finder of fact to assess. In practice, crafty lawyers use every stage of the trial as means to present certain aspects of the case as they hope the finder of fact will perceive it, but if such presentations stray too far from the purpose of the trial at that stage, the court is required to restrain counsel to the task at hand.

**closing argument (summation or closing statement at trial)**  A party's final summary of the evidence and the law. Closing argument, or closing statement, is the last argument of counsel regarding the meaning of the evidence and the application of the law, as that counsel's side would seek the finder of fact to understand it. The closing argument is a party's last opportunity to persuade the trier of fact. A party may waive closing argument, and though this waiver is rare, a plaintiff or prosecutor who waives closing argument may also waive it for the defendant. Closing arguments before a jury are particularly limited. A closing argument in a jury trial may not be used to inflame the jury's sympathy for one party or against another, to raise matters not in issue, to raise evidence that has not been introduced into the record, or to make inflammatory arguments that seek the jury to rule on a basis other than the evidence in the record, and the judge's instructions of the law and of the role of the juror. A closing argument may compare the theories of the parties in the light of the evidence and argue for certain inferences to be drawn from the evidence, and it may state the verdict sought by that party and its rationale from the evidence overall. In criminal cases, the closing argument of the prosecution is usually the more constrained, for instance in that it should not criticize counsel for the defense or trial tactics.

**opening statement**  A party's road map of what the evidence will be at trial and what it will mean. An opening argument, or opening statement, is a review of the claims and defenses in the case, as seen through a preliminary review of the evidence that counsel anticipates will be presented, along with the factual meaning the counsel hopes will be ascribed to that evidence by the finder of fact. Opening argument before a jury is usually more elaborate and specific than would be expected before a judge in a bench trial, who is (or should be) already familiar with the evidence to be presented. Opening argument before a jury may not raise claims that are not intended in good faith to be argued, may not introduce matter not relevant to the case, may not attempt to inflame the passions of the jury for or against any party, and should not attempt to rebut evidence of the other party's case in chief that has yet to be introduced or to impeach witnesses who have not yet testified in the action.

**side bar (bench conference or side-bar or sidebar conference)**  A quiet discussion among counsel and the judge. A side-bar conference, or bench conference, is a discussion between the judge and the counsel for both parties, or otherwise a private conference at the bench during open court. The judge calls such a conference by ordering counsel to approach the bench or to meet at the side bar, which is on the side of the bench away from the jury box. The argument of counsel there may be heard by the judge out of the hearing of the jury without the jury being excused. In some but not all courts, such conferences are recorded and a matter of record. There is risk in such conferences happening off the record that inappropriate argument or communication will be made by counsel. An argument longer or more complicated may require the court to order the jury to retire to the jury room or for the court to be adjourned for a conference in chambers.

*See also:* camera, in camera.

**bench trial**  A trial without a jury, held before a judge or panel of judges. A bench trial is a trial in which a judge or judges sit as finder of fact as well as judge of the law. Bench trials are available in civil actions in state court for which no jury is available or sought, particularly when the parties agree to a bench trial. Bench trials are available in federal court in civil actions for which a jury trial is not demanded and for actions arising not in law but in equity, admiralty, or other specialized jurisdictions. Criminal trials may be held as bench trials if the defendant waives a right to a jury or if the offense risks a penalty so minor that there is no right to a jury.

*See also:* trial, jury trial (trial by jury).

**bifurcated trial (bifurcation or bifurcate or bifurcated)**  A trial held in a liability phase and a penalty phase. Bifurcation is the separation of one thing or process into two. Bifurcation in the comparative sense of the common law depicts the distinct roles of the finder of fact and the finder of law.

A bifurcated trial, as a matter of procedure is the splitting of a trial or hearing into two components, such as a guilt and an innocence phase in a criminal action or a liability and a remedy phase for a civil action. A bifurcated trial might therefore be heard in two phases, one that concludes with a jury verdict and one that concludes with a judge's order. Or, it could be heard in two phases that both lead to a jury verdict. The distinction is in the two trials, each performing a different function, rather than on the different role of the judge or jury. The benefits of a bifurcated trial are, in the criminal action, to allow the jury to hear evidence of the crime without being unduly influenced in its verdict by the passion that may be aroused by sympathy for the victim or by a sense of mercy that may arise from the potential of a harsh verdict. In a civil trial, divorcing evidence of the culpability of a defendant from the nature of the damages may allow the jury to focus on the nature of the duty and breach alleged. Further, the bifurcation allows the parties to consider their positions after the first verdict and reach a settlement.

*See also:* complaint.

**guilt phase trial (liability phase trial)** The trial to determine the defendant's liability, preceding the sentencing phase. In a bifurcated criminal trial, the guilt phase is a trial to consider only questions of whether a crime occurred and the defendant is guilty of its commission. No evidence is to be introduced that would relate solely or mainly to victim impact or to the mitigation or enhancement of a sentence.

Likewise, in a bifurcated civil trial, the liability phase is a trial to consider only questions arising from the cause of action and defenses, without evidence of the plaintiff's damages or defendant's gains subject to restitution, unless such evidence is essential to plead the cause of action and has not been stipulated.

*See also:* guilt (guilty).

**penalty phase (punishment phase or remedy phase)** A trial to determine the defendant's punishment or the plaintiff's remedy. In a bifurcated criminal trial, the penalty phase, or punishment phase, is a trial held only after a verdict has been reached in the guilt phase in which the jury finds that a crime occurred and the defendant committed it. In the penalty phase, evidence is introduced to demonstrate the effects of the crime on specific victims or their survivors as well as to society; evidence is also introduced regarding the defendant that is to be considered by the jury in mitigation or enhancement of a sentence.

Likewise, in a bifurcated civil trial, the liability phase in the trial only takes place after a jury has found the defendant liable for some or all of the claims made against it by the plaintiff. The remedy phase allows the introduction of evidence on the appropriate scale and scope of a remedy, including the damages of the plaintiff or gains of the defendant subject to restitution. If punitive damages are potentially to be awarded, most jurisdictions allow evidence of the income and potential effect of an award upon the defendant.

**de novo trial (trial de novo)** A new trial repeating a claim already heard between the same parties. A trial de novo is a new trial, one usually held after a trial has already been held but that will be conducted without regard to the earlier disposition. A trial de novo may occur when an action is appealed from a court of limited jurisdiction to a court of general jurisdiction, when an action is appealed and a new trial is granted, or when a new trial is ordered by a court owing to some mistake or error in a trial.

*See also:* de, de novo.

**disposition without trial** An action resolved on motion or by agreement. A disposition without trial arises either because the action is disposed of by dismissal or judgment without trial, as by summary judgment or judgment as a matter of law, or because the parties settle the action or otherwise resolve it, leading to an agreed settlement, withdrawal, voluntary dismissal, or nonsuit. A disposition without trial, other than a judgment on the merits, has less significance as a basis for res judicata than does a judgment following trial.

**ex parte trial (trial in absentia)** A trial with only one party present. An ex parte trial is a trial in which only one side appears, either because the defendant fails to appear or the state or the plaintiff fails to appear. When notice of a trial has been properly minuted, and the parties have been given notice of the trial date and time under the rules, a court may hold the trial in the absence of the absent party, particularly in the absence of the defendant in a civil action, to determine whether there is sufficient evidence for the plaintiff to meet the standard of proof for the claims in the case as to both liability and remedy, in which case the court may enter a judgment against the defendant. Certain quite rare actions, usually derived from equity or heard in equity, such as an action to be relieved of minority, are heard ex parte, whether as a hearing or trial, because there is no opposing party to the action.

*See also:* ex, ex parte.

**fair trial (rights of criminal defendants)** A fair, impartial trial for which the party may fully prepare. A fair trial is a constitutional requirement for all trials. A fair trial requires a competent and impartial magistrate and (if summoned) an impartial jury, to hear an action according to rules of court that are fair to all parties and appropriate to the matter involved, so that the truth of the matter regarding all questions of facts is made more likely to be known, and the laws that apply to them are presented in the light most favorable to both sides and then carefully applied.

A fair criminal trial includes not only the general requirements above but also a pre-trial and trial process that meet constitutional requirements for specific rights and procedural due process of law. The pre-trial rights of an accused are often best protected in the trial, and a conviction based on a trial relying on evidence taken in violation of constitutional rights is likely to be overturned. Pre-trial rights include a right to effective counsel before and at questioning, a right to speedy trial, a right to be free from double jeopardy, a right to be free from an ex post facto law, a right to be free from an unconstitutional burden on a constitutional right (such as to speech or the exercise of religion), a right to arraignment and knowledge of the charges brought, as well as a right to knowledge of the identity of the accuser or accusers, and of all exculpatory evidence known to the prosecution. Trial rights include a right to a public trial, in which the defendant is represented by effective counsel who have had an opportunity to investigate the events alleged and to prepare a reasonable defense, who may question accusers in open court, may challenge all evidence and arguments of guilt, and may present an argument of innocence.

Fairness is the opportunity to present all relevant arguments and evidence. The impartiality of the finders of fact and judge may be the essence of the fair trial.

*See also:* trial, speedy trial (right to a speedy trial or speedy trial clock); counselor, right to counsel, effective assistance of counsel; confrontation; arraignment.

**jury trial (trial by jury)**  A trial in which a jury sits as trier of facts. A jury trial is a trial before a jury, in which the jury sits as finder of facts, subject to the management of the court by the judge, including the instruction of the jury by the judge, and either the acceptance of the jury's verdict or of the separate determination of a judgment of law based on the jury's findings.

*See also:* trial, bench trial; jury (juror); instruction, jury instruction (charge to the jury or to charge the jury or jury charge or instruction to the jury).

**new trial (motion for new trial)**  A trial held to correct errors in an earlier trial of a criminal action. A new trial is a trial in a criminal action set following the conclusion of a trial in which an error occurred, material evidence was unavailable, or the judge otherwise concludes that a new trial is in the interest of justice. A motion for new trial under the federal rules is to be made within 14 days of a verdict, unless it is based on new evidence, when it must be made within three years.

New trial and retrial are used by many courts as if they are the same. Indeed, many states provide for a retrial in a criminal action in a manner similar to that provided for retrial of a civil action. In the federal rules, however, a civil action is not given a new trial but retried, per Federal Rule of Civil Procedure 59.

**notice for trial (notice of trial)**  A notice of a trial date sent to all parties. A notice for trial, or notice of trial, is a notice that a trial in a given action has been set for a specific place, at a specific date and time. The notice is sent according to the appropriate rules of procedure and local rules, usually by the clerk of court to all parties who have entered an appearance on the docket. In some jurisdictions, no notice is individually sent to parties, and notice is considered effective when a date is posted on the court calendar.

**public trial (right to public trial)**  A trial open to observation by the public. A public trial is a trial, whether civil or criminal, that is open to members of the public throughout the time that court is in session for the trial. The purpose of the trial is to allow publicity and notice to serve as a form of guaranty of fairness in the proceeding. The Sixth Amendment, incorporated into the Fourteenth Amendment, requires all federal or state criminal trials to be held in public.

**retrial (motion for retrial)**  A trial held to correct errors in an earlier trial of a civil action. A retrial is a new trial of a civil action, which was sufficiently flawed owing either to error in the trial or the unavailability of material evidence which later becomes available, that the court in which the trial was held, or a court on direct review or collateral review, orders

a new trial. Under the federal rules, a motion for retrial by a party must provide specific grounds for the retrial and be entered within 28 days of the entry of judgment. A court may grant a new trial sua sponte.

Retrial and new trial are used by many courts as if they are the same. Indeed, many states provide for a retrial in a criminal action in a manner similar to that provided for retrial. In the federal rules, however, a criminal action is not retried but given a new trial, per Federal Rule of Criminal Procedure 33.

**severance of trial (motion to sever)**  Division of an action against two or more defendants into two or more trials. Severance of trial is the separation of a single action with multiple defendants, into multiple trials or at least into independent hearings. The severance is made so that all or a portion of the trial against one defendant that raises proof or evidence of distinct claims against the other defendants may be heard independently. Severance of a criminal trial is required if a joint trial would prejudice the right of at least one defendant to a fair trial.

**show trial (political trial)**  A trial used to legitimatize a politically ordained judgment. A show trial is a trial used to justify a politically determined persecution of a person, group, or cause, through a procedure orchestrated to present a veneer of fairness and independent judgment arising from the assessment of fairly acquired evidence and neutral law. Show trials are often used for political purposes, when a government uses the legal system to persecute its enemies, to frighten others who might oppose it, and to justify its actions by discrediting its opponents. Show trials are also used to create the impression of effective law enforcement by producing convictions without regard to the genuine innocence or guilt of those convicted.

**speedy trial (right to a speedy trial or speedy trial clock)**  The obligation to try the accused in a criminal case without delay after arrest. A speedy trial is a trial brought without unnecessary or unjustified delay, and in all cases without too much delay. The Sixth Amendment ensures a speedy trial, but there is no constitutional clock for enforcement. Instead, each jurisdiction establishes its rules, and there is a constitutional balance that may not be exceeded. The Federal Speedy Trial Act, for instance, requires a trial within seventy days of arraignment or indictment, although that period may be tolled for specific reasons, particularly for preparation of the defense. Most states have standards for trial preparation and a latest scheduled time for criminal cases.

The Sixth Amendment guaranty is to be construed according to a balance among four factors: (1) length of the delay, (2) the reason for the delay, (3) whether the defendant has asserted the right to a speedy trial, and (4) the nature and degree of the prejudice suffered by the defendant. Thus, a defendant who has been held in custody for a year and a half awaiting trial, mainly for reasons of court scheduling and the convenience of the prosecution, and who has asserted the right to speedy trial, has a strong argument for trial or release.

*See also:* trial, fair trial (rights of criminal defendants).

**trial by battle (battel or judicial duel or trial by combat or wager of battle)**  Physical combat as proof in a legal dispute. Trial by battle was an ancient mode of trial by single combat, which had various names, including wager of battel and judicial duel. Combat was available in matters now considered both criminal and civil, the underlying philosophy in either case being that God would intervene to spare the innocent and punish the wicked, although a good sword arm seems to have encouraged divine favor. Increasingly rare following Papal condemnations throughout the Middle Ages, battel was finally abolished in England in 1820 and has never been accepted in the United States as a lawful means of dispute settlement. Dueling is closely related to battel, but private duels were unsanctioned by courts of law and had no significance as proof in a legal dispute.

*See also:* trial.

**tribe**  A political and social unit of native people. A tribe is a group of American Indians or Alaskan natives, who are organized by heredity, shared history and culture into a group that has a shared leadership and customary identity. The identity of a tribe may be based on a shared and coherent history, language, arts, and family relationships among clans. Some tribes are autonomous as a nation, and others are organized as a band that is a part of a larger nation, but mostly, the terms band, tribe, and nation are effectively synonymous.

*See also:* Indian.

**tribal jurisdiction**  *See:* jurisdiction, tribal jurisdiction.

**tribal reservation**  *See:* reservation, tribal reservation, Assimilative Crimes Act; reservation, tribal reservation (Indian reservation).

**recognized tribe (federally recognized tribe)**  A tribe listed by the U.S. or a state as self-governing. A recognized tribe is an Indian tribe or Alaskan native entity that is recognized by the federal government or a state, which then treats the tribe as a government and negotiates with it as a unit. Although some states have recognized tribes that are not recognized by the U.S. Bureau of Indian Affairs, most recognized tribes are federally recognized tribes.

A federally recognized tribe is an American Indian or Alaska Native tribal entity that is recognized by the government of the United States as having a direct relationship between the United States government and the tribal government. Recognized tribes are acknowledged to have tribal sovereignty, including an inherent right of self-government. They are vested under federal laws with certain responsibilities, powers, limitations, and obligations, and they are eligible for funding and services from the Bureau of Indian Affairs. Recognition occurs through treaties, acts of Congress, presidential executive orders or other federal administrative actions, or federal court decisions. As of 2009, the BIA recognized 564 tribal entities, including native Alaskan and Indian tribes and villages.

**tribunal**  A court, or anyone who sits in judgment of others. A tribunal is a seat of judgment, and in its use, it refers to the judge or judges who hear a cause and adjudicate it. In contemporary usage, a tribunal is the institution of a court, including both the person of the judge or judges and the other officials and procedures by which the adjudication is prepared and performed. There is no inherent difference in a court called a tribunal and one called a court, although there is a tendency for military courts and other courts established by executive fiat or international decree to be called tribunals.

*See also:* court.

**trifle (trifling)**  Something trivial. A trifle is a matter that is too insignificant to warrant the attention of the law. It is the object of the phrase, de minimis non curat lex, or the law does not concern itself with trifles.

*See also:* triviality (trivial); lex, lex non curat de minimis (de minimus non curat lex).

**trimester**  *See:* pregnancy, trimester.

**Trinity term**  *See:* court, English court, terms of court, Trinity term.

**triviality (trivial)**  A matter of small importance. A triviality is a commonplace matter of no importance. Triviality and trifle are near synonyms. The difference is that trivial suggests the ordinariness of a thing, while a trifle suggests a matter of insignificance, i.e., a mere distraction of the idle.

*See also:* trifle (trifling).

**trove**  *See:* property, found property, treasure trove (trove).

**trover**  An action for damages for converted chattels. Trover is an action for damages suffered by the conversion of chattels, brought either by the true owner or a party with a right to possess them superior to the person who holds them as a result of conversion. The measure of damages is the market value of the chattel as of the time of the conversion. By electing to bring an action for trover rather than compel restitution for the conversion by replevin, the plaintiff waives the right to compel their return.

*See also:* replevin (writ of replevin or replevy or repleviable).

**troy weight**  *See:* weight, troy weight.

**truancy (truant)**  A child's absence from school without justification. Truancy is a child's failure to attend school without a justification or excuse for the absence being communicated to school authorities. Such a child is truant while absent. Most states require attendance for all children in school between the years of kindergarten and at least the eighth grade. Students engaged in qualified home schooling are exempted from attendance. Otherwise, failure to attend school may be an administrative offense for the child and a misdemeanor for the parent or guardian.

*See also:* delinquent, juvenile delinquent (delinquent child or juvenile delinquency).

**true bill indictment**   *See:* indictment, true bill indictment (billa vera or no bill or no true bill or not found or ignoramus).

**true or truthful**   *See:* truth (true or truthful).

**true sale**   *See:* sale, true sale.

**trust**   A division of property between ownership and benefit. A trust is a form of property holding in which the owner of the property holds the property for the benefit of another. A defining element of a trust is that the holder of title, or trustee, must be a different party from the holder of the benefit, the beneficiary. If the benefit and title were conveyed to one party, the trust would be dissolved. A trust is created by a settlor, who conveys the corpus of the trust to the trustee subject to trust and who conveys the benefit of the trust to the beneficiary. The beneficiary is said to have equitable title in the corpus of the trust, and the trustee is duty-bound not to commit waste of the trust assets, except as required to use or convey property by the settlor in the creation of the trust.

The settlor may be the beneficiary, or the settlor may be the trustee. As the defining element of a trust is the division of title from benefit, the settlor may retain one interest and transfer the other, effectively creating the trust. The trustee has a fiduciary responsibility to the beneficiary to use the assets of the trust to the benefit of the beneficiary, according to the intent of the settlor.

Note: trust in general is an unusual level of confidence or reliance by one person in another or in an entity. A party acting in the knowledge of another's trust is usually for that reason alone a fiduciary to that party in matters affecting that person's reliance.

**trust administration**   *See:* administration, trust administration.

**trust beneficiary**   *See:* beneficiary, trust beneficiary.

**trust company**   *See:* company, trust company; bank, trust company.

**trust dilemma or assurance game**   *See:* game, game theory, stag hunt (trust dilemma or assurance game).

**trust legacy**   *See:* legacy, trust legacy.

**abuse of public or private trust (abuse-of-trust enhancement)**   An enhanced sentence for a criminal whose offense violated a position of trust. Abuse of public or private trust is a sentencing enhancement under the federal sentencing guidelines, reflecting a customary recognition that a crime is made more severe when one element of it is the corruption of trust others place in the criminal. Any position of

unusual reliance — lawyer, bank teller, police officer, store manager, guard — can be the basis for private trust, and any appointment in or office of government at any level can be the basis for public trust. Abuse is demonstrated either by an act in facilitation or concealment of the crime. Whether the position is one of trust depends on the perception of the victim, not the criminal, and it may also depend on whether the victim placed the criminal into the position of trust.

*See also:* public.

**blind trust (business trust)**   A trust whose beneficiary knows nothing of its holdings. A blind trust, or a business trust, is a trust organized in a manner that gives the trustee full discretion to manage, buy, and sell assets of the trust, while denying the beneficiary knowledge of the identity of assets held or management used by the trust. A blind trust may be used to allow a person to sequester investments that might otherwise risk or cause the beneficiary a conflict of interest. A blind trust is often organized by the beneficiary who, as settlor, conveys investments to the trustee for management as a blind trust for a period or until the occurrence of a specified event.

Note: blind trust in its non-technical sense means unquestioning faith in someone or something.

**cestui que trust**   The beneficiary of an estate held in trust. The cestui que trust is the person for whom another holds property subject to trust, i.e., the beneficiary. This phrase is still common in some states, although its use is diminishing as lawyers increasingly call the cestui que trust the beneficiary.

**charitable remainder trust (unitrust or charitable remainder unitrust or CRUT)**   A trust benefiting a person or persons for life with its remainder to a charity. A charitable remainder trust, or unitrust, is a trust created with a benefit to a person or persons for life, or for a period of time up to twenty years, after which the trust is dissolved and the res is granted to a charitable enterprise. The trust operates by annually paying a fixed portion of its assets to the beneficiary (or beneficiaries) for the lifetime of the trust, with its remainder being distributed to a legally defined charity. Often, the beneficiary for life is the settlor, or the beneficiaries for their joint lives are the settlor and the settlor's spouse, and upon the death of the latter to die, the trust is dissolved and its assets passed by the trustee to one or more charities designated when the trust was established. The valid creation of a unitrust allows the settlor to treat the present value of the remainder as a charitable contribution in the tax year the unitrust is created.

*See also:* remainder.

**charitable trust**   A trust established to support a charity. A charitable trust is a public or private trust created to the benefit of a charitable entity or entities. A charitable trust is usually an operating foundation, being a charitable organization only if it is organized as a non-profit organization for charitable purposes. As a foundation, though, all contributions from the charitable trust to a bona fide charity are tax deductible.

**client trust account (lawyer's trust account)**  A lawyer must maintain a separate account for client funds in trust. A client trust account is a distinct account in which an attorney maintains client funds or the funds of third persons that are in the lawyer's possession. The attorney should not commingle funds of the attorney's personal or firm accounts with those of the trust account.

*See also:* funds, comingled funds (commingling of funds); retainer (retain or retaining fee).

**interest on client trust account (interest on lawyer's trust account or IOLTA)**  A client trust account for small client fund deposits. A client trust account managed in a state IOLTA program is used to generate public assistance for access to justice from the small deposits or short–lived deposits by attorneys that would ordinarily generate a very small return for the client, usually a return less than the cost of opening or maintaining the account. The IOLTA account protects the principal of the deposit for withdrawal by the attorney for use by or for the client, while capturing the small amount of interest generated and pooling it with other amounts from other deposits to create a fund for the support of access to justice by the poor.

**constructive trust**  A trust equity implies over assets of another that one wrongly holds. A constructive trust is not a trust created in the usual manner by the action of a settlor, but a trust implied in equity over property that was acquired through a breach of duty or over property that otherwise is wrongfully held or was wrongfully held before transfer. In other words, a constructive trust arises over property held by a person or entity who—in good conscience—should not keep the property. Property subject to a constructive trust retains its character as trust property even when transferred to another, and assets realized from a sale of trust property become trust property. A constructive trust persists until the property subject to it is transferred to the party with superior title or to a party who will properly use it for the benefit of those whom it is to benefit. The difference between a constructive trust and a resulting trust is that a constructive trust arises from a wrongful act, while a resulting trust arises from mistake. Some jurisdictions no longer recognize this difference and use the terms interchangeably.

A constructive trust arises over property stolen or converted, property wrongfully or mistakenly delivered, property taken by embezzlement or self–dealing from an entity, or property wrongfully converted to personal benefit by a fiduciary, such as a partner or trustee. A constructive trust will give rise to an action for accounting, injunction, restitution, disgorgement of profits, or damages.

*See also:* trust, implied trust; trustee, trustee ex malefico (maleficio).

**destructible trust (indestructible trust)**  A trust that may be dissolved. A destructible trust is a trust established by the settlor according to terms that allow the trust to be destroyed under specified circumstances, either at the occurrence of a specified event or at the demand of the beneficiary. By contrast, an indestructible trust cannot be terminated by an act of a beneficiary but persists until the object of the trust is fulfilled.

**implied trust**  A trust implied in equity from events. An implied trust is created by the operation of equity under one of three circumstances, each depending on the actions of an owner (or owner's agent), who transfers the property owned in some manner that implies a trust in the property. First, the owner or agent transfers property to another (intentionally or unintentionally) that is not intended to benefit the party who receives it but intended to benefit another. A mistaken delivery of goods to an unintended recipient is a common illustration. This is a form of resulting trust. Second, the owner or agent transfers an equitable interest in property through sale or representation and reliance to another party. This is another form of resulting trust. Third, the owner or agent acquires an interest in property through a breach of duty. This is a constructive trust. Note: an implied trust is generally like a constructive trust, its creation in the first two illustrations depends on the act of the prior, true owner of the property rather than on the act of the holder of the property. It is not deliberately created through the conscious act of a settlor who intends to create a trust but is created through the conduct of the settlor or the settlor's agent.

*See also:* trust, constructive trust.

**insurance trust**  Trust formed solely to hold insurance policies. An insurance trust is an agreement between a person whose life is insured and a trustee, usually a trust company, whereby the proceeds of the insurance policy are paid directly to the trustee for their investment and distribution to designated beneficiaries in any manner or at any time as the trust directs.

**inter vivos trust (living trust)**  A trust created by a settlor while alive, usually to benefit the settlor. An inter vivos trust, generally, is any trust created by an individual settlor during the settlor's lifetime. In this general sense, an inter vivos trust includes all trusts created by an individual other than a testamentary trust.

As the term is often used, an inter vivos trust, or living trust, means a trust created by a settlor that transfers property to a trustee to be used for the benefit of the settlor while the settlor is alive, and upon the settlor's death, the trust will either benefit another designated beneficiary or be dissolved so that the assets are given to a designated recipient. Charitable remainder trusts are a form of living trust.

**revocable trust (irrevocable trust)**  A trust that may be revoked by the settlor. A revocable trust is an inter vivos trust that persists only for the time the settlor desires it to persist. At the time the trust is created, the settlor reserves the right to terminate the trust, recover the corpus of the trust and any assets it has generated. When a revocable trust specifies the means by which it may be revoked or the conditions under which it may be revoked, revocation is only allowed by such means or under such conditions.

An irrevocable trust cannot be revoked or dissolved by an act of the settlor after the trust is created.

See also: revocation (revocability or revocation or revoke).

**land trust**   A trust over lands. A land trust, in general, is a trust which has a principal asset of land. More specifically, a land trust is a trust holding lands either for the benefit of a particular beneficiary or a public trust holding lands for a particular use. In the case of trusts held for a particular beneficiary, the lands are presumptively used for their highest and best use. Yet a public trust is held for the benefit of the public through a specific use, often as the location of preserve for the habitat of animals and plants or for other purposes of environmental management.

**living trust**   A trust to the benefit of the settlor who creates it. A living trust is a trust created by its own beneficiary, which persists for as long as the beneficiary lives. The settlor must transfer ownership of the settlor's property to the trustee, creating a benefit in the property in the interests of the settlor. A living trust usually provides a remainder that would transfer the benefit to another at the settlor's death, otherwise the trust is dissolved at the settlor's death, the assets becoming a part of the settlor's estate (though there are considerable tax benefits in most instances of the benefit going directly to the remainderman).

**naked trust (simple trust or naked trustee or bare trust or bare trustee)**   A trust to deliver the corpus to a third party. A naked trust, or a bare trust, is created for the purpose of delivering property to a third party. The naked trustee holds the property for the benefit of the settlor or for the recipient, depending upon the intent of the settlor. A naked trust implies no duty on the trustee's part to manage the property. The trust is dissolved upon delivery.

**pourover trust**   A trust that receives assets by the settlor's will. A pourover trust is an inter vivos or testamentary trust that is intended to receive testamentary assets. In its more common form, the trust is created during the life of the settlor, and the settlor designates further assets to be assigned to the trust after death. A testamentary trust can create a pourover trust, by requiring the executor to establish a trust into which assets are poured after some prior purpose is accomplished.

**precatory trust**   A trust created by language in the grant framed as a request rather than a command. A precatory trust is a trust created by a grant of property accompanied by precatory words that suggest that the grant should be used for the benefit of a party other than the grantee, which are interpreted not merely as an expression of hope but as the manifestation of the intent of the grantor to confer the property for the purpose of benefiting the other party, thus making the grantor a settlor, the grantee a trustee, and the third party a beneficiary.

See also: precatory words.

**private trust**   A trust to the benefit of private individuals. A private trust is a trust created to the benefit of one or more designated, private individuals. A private trust is any trust other than a public trust or a charitable trust. To create a private trust, the settlor transfers to a trustee the property subject to trust with express or implied terms for its management, then designating the beneficiary or beneficiaries of the trust, thus dividing the legal ownership from the equitable ownership of the property. The trustee pays taxes on the property according to the tax liability of the beneficiary.

**public trust**   A trust whose beneficiaries are members of the public. A public trust is a trust created by the conveyance of assets to a person or entity for use to the benefit of the public as a whole or to some category of the public or for a specific use that benefits the public. A public trust is created when the settlor conveys property to a party who accepts it subject to its designation by the settlor for a use that is of a public nature or with a designation that the property be used for the benefit of the public, the citizens of some area, or the people of some area. A trust created to the benefit of an indeterminate class of beneficiaries is a public trust. A public trust may be a charitable trust but might not be, as in a trust to the benefit of the members of a political party.

A trustee of a public trust is subject to the same fiduciary responsibilities as is the trustee of a private trust. The primary difference is that the obligation to enforce a public trust in the event of wrongdoing by the trustee is primarily in the government of the public whose benefit is in issue. The settlor may enforce the trust if the settlor reserved such enforcement powers. In some circumstances, members of the group of beneficiaries who have a particularized interest in the performance of the trust may enforce it.

See also: standing in court.

**public trust doctrine**   Certain resources are subject to protection by the government for the benefit of the people. The public trust doctrine is distinct from a public trust in the usual sense in trust law, being a basis for governmental protection of certain natural resources from destruction or harm and from interference with public use by private citizens. Rivers, riverbanks, tidal areas, and certain natural resources are subject to the public trust doctrine.

See also: shore, littoral area (foreshore or littoral rights or litorral interests); shore (shoreline).

**qualified-terminable-interest property trust (QTIP)**
A trust giving income for life to a surviving spouse. A qualified terminable interest property trust is a trust created to provide for a surviving spouse for life, with the remainder to the beneficiaries designated by the settlor of the trust. The interest passed to the surviving spouse must be the complete and whole income from whatever property is subject to the trust, and there is no power to divide or dilute its share to the surviving spouse. At the death of the surviving spouse, the trust is dissolved, with its corpus distributed to those designated by the settlor. QTIPS are commonly established as testamentary dispositions and are not uncommon when the testator has children by a spouse other than the spouse likely to survive, so that the beneficiary of the QTIP is the surviving spouse but the beneficiaries of the remainder on dissolution include the children born of another spouse.

**resulting trust** An equitable trust arising from circumstances. A resulting trust is another term for equitable title, which is the relationship of a party to property in a circumstance when equity would enforce the transfer of title to another. The most common example arises after a landowner agrees to sell the land to another. A contract for sale creates a resulting trust in the property sold to the benefit of the buyer, which persists until the property is delivered. A wrongful or mistaken delivery of goods creates a resulting trust in the recipient to the benefit of the shipper, with alternative beneficiary being the intended recipient, which persists until the goods are collected or a reasonable time to do so has passed. A resulting trust is a form of implied trust, as is a constructive trust, but no wrongdoing by the trustee caused the trust to be implied.

*See also:* title, equitable title; trust, constructive trust; trust, implied trust.

**self-settled trust** A trust benefiting a person who causes its creation. A self-settled trust is a trust whose beneficiary is the person who causes to be created, or (in some circumstances) the spouse of that person. The settlor, or the person who creates the trust, must transfer (or cause to be transferred) the assets of the trust to another party, reserving the benefit of the trust to be for the person creating it. The self-settled trust is a valid trust, although certain conditions expressed at the creation of a trust, particularly efforts to shelter assets from taxation or creditors, may fail owing to its character as self-settled.

**settlor (trustor or truster)** The maker of a trust. A settlor is the person who gives property to another subject to trust. Thus, the settlor is the creator of the trust. The settlor may designate any person either as beneficiary or as trustee and owner of the trust, though the same person may not be both (or there is no trust). Thus, the settlor may designate the settlor as trustee, or the settlor may designate the settlor as beneficiary: neither is implausible in trusts.

There is no difference between a settlor and a trustor, which may be derived from the Scots law term "truster" for the maker of a trust. Settlor does, however, remain the preferred term in the United States.

**spendthrift trust (asset protection trust)** A trust beyond the reach of a beneficiary's creditors. A spendthrift trust, or an asset protection trust, is a trust created by the settlor so that the trustee must make regular distributions to the beneficiary, but has no discretion to make further payment or assignment from the corpus of the trust to the beneficiary, and the trust is specifically structured to forbid an assignment of assets or a lien against assets to secure a debt or for any other purpose than to manage the assets themselves. Although a creditor may not attach the assets of a spendthrift trust, in most jurisdictions the payment from a spendthrift trust is subject to garnishment. Self-settled spendthrift trusts, that is a spendthrift trust created by the beneficiary, are generally not immune from creditors.

The spendthrift trust has been abolished in England, and in the United States, many jurisdictions have allowed the trust to be reached if needed to pay support for a spouse or child, if needed to supply necessary support, or to pay claims brought by government or by a judgment creditor in tort.

*See also:* spendthrift.

**testamentary trust (trust legacy or trust devise)** A trust created by will and established by the executor. A testamentary trust, which is sometimes called a trust legacy or trust devise, is a trust created in a decedent's last will and testament, which designates assets to be conveyed to a trustee for the benefit of some named or designated individual, individuals, or entity. Although the testamentary disposition authorizes the trust, and the decedent is customarily thought of as the settlor, the executor or personal respresentative is responsible for creating the trust during probate.

*See also:* trustee, testamentary trustee.

**Tontine trust** *See:* Tontine (Tontine trust or Tontine fund).

**Totten trust** A bank account in the depositor's name as trustee for another. A Totten trust, named for the New York case, In re Totten, 71 N.E. 748, 752 (N.Y. 1904), is a revocable trust created by the structure of a bank account by a depositor as the depositor's account to the benefit of a named beneficiary. Every deposit is a placement of assets into trust, and every withdrawal is to that extent a revocation of the trust over that much of its corpus. At death, however, the trust is either considered irrevocable or dissolved, and the balance in the account becomes the beneficiary's.

*See also:* account, bank account (account in bank).

**trust account (trust fund)** An account held in trust for a named beneficiary. A trust account, or trust fund, is an account, investment, or other holding by a banking or investment institution that is segregated so it may be managed or held for the benefit of a beneficiary. An account in which the institution itself is an executor, trustee, personal representative, guardian, or other form of fiduciary is a trust account. An account held for an executor, an attorney, guardian, agent, or other fiduciary for the benefit of another is a trust fund. A fund deposited by a settlor in trust in an institution to the benefit of a designated party is a trust account, even if the trust is a self-settled trust.

**trustee**   A party holding property subject to trust. A trustee is a person or entity holding property subject to trust, whether the trust is express or implied, and whether the trust itself is public or private. A trustee is a fiduciary of the beneficiary. The assets of a trustee as trustee must be kept segregated from the trustee's personal assets, and commingling of assets may in itself violate the the trustee's fiduciary duty to the beneficiary. The assets of the trust as well as its income are, however, also distinct from the trustee's assets for tax purposes, and taxes are to be paid by the trustee from the trust. In many instances, a trustee is entitled to receive a fee for the management of a trust.

*See also:* syndic; prisoner, trustee (trusty or trusties).

**trustee in bankruptcy**   *See:* bankruptcy, trustee in bankruptcy (bankruptcy trustee).

**corporate trustee**   A business entity that serves as a trustee. A corporate trustee is a bank, corporation, or in some instances, a business partnership that serves as trustee over a trust. Unless there is an agreement between the settlor and the trustee, a settlor who vests property subject to trust in a corporate trustee may not have a power of appointment or the right to designate the individual managers of the trust.

**interim trustee (temporary trustee or trustee ad litem or trustee pro tem)**   A trustee appointed only for a time. An interim trustee holds property in trust only for a period of time, usually until the appointment of a permanent trustee or a resolution of a dispute affecting the trust already pending. An interim trustee may be appointed by a trustee, or designated by a settlor as a contingent trustee at the time of the trust's creation, or appointed by a court with jurisdiction over a trust. There is no difference between an interim trustee and a temporary trustee or trustee pro tem. A trustee appointed by a court solely to hold property in trust during litigation regarding the trust or an interest in it is a trustee ad litem.

*See also:* ad, ad litem; pro, pro tempore (pro tem).

**joint trustees (co-trustees)**   Trustees who must act together in managing a trust. Joint trustees, or co-trustees, are individuals appointed as trustee along with others to serve as trustee at the same time. Joint trustees are effectively a single trustee, each holding the property subject to trust as a joint tenant. Joint trustees must each concur in the action of the other in every act that affects the trust. An act by a single joint trustee without the concurrence of the other joint trustee or trustees is presumptively void. Note: a joint trustee serves simultaneously with other joint trustees, this being the difference from successive trustees, who follow one another in time.

**prudent-investor rule**   A duty of a trustee to manage investment property subject to trust as a prudent investor. The prudent-investor rule is a central duty of the trustee of assets that are invested, or that are susceptible to investment, if the trustee is charged with management of the corpus for profit rather than for use or conservation. The prudent-investment rule requires the trustee to select investments of a form, risk, structure, and liquidity that are appropriate to the purposes of and demands upon the trust assets; to use reasonable care, skill, and caution; and to manage the whole portfolio of assets reasonably. The trustee is therefore to be expected to balance reasonably the investments of the trust across the whole portfolio, and one asset or class of assets is not to be considered in isolation of the whole res.

**quasi-trustee**   A mortgagee in possession of mortgaged property. A person who acts as if the person is trustee over some property the person holds or controls for the benefit of another, although the person has no formal title or designation as a trustee. Former partners in possession of partnership assets are quasi-trustees to other partners. A quasi-trust is a form of constructive trust. For example, a common form of quasi-trustee is a party who has given a mortgage over property the party occupies. The occupant holds the legal title with a beneficial interest in the property in the mortgagee, and the quasi-trust that results creates an obligation of the quasi-trustee to the mortgagee to maintain the property, which is the corpus of the quasi-trust.

*See also:* mortgage.

**successor trustee**   Trustee who takes ownership in trust from a trustee. A successor trustee is a trustee who accepts the ownership of property subject to trust from a prior trustee. The prior trustee assigns all of the power and responsibility of the trust to the successor. In general, the successor trustee is charged with the knowledge regarding the trust held by the prior trustee. A successor trustee may be designated by the settlor at the time the trust is created, or the power to select a successor may be exercised by a trustee, in which case the prior trustee has a fiduciary obligation to select a trustee of sufficient care and competence.

**testamentary trustee**   A trustee of a trust created by will. A testamentary trustee is given property in fee as a result of the probate of a last will and testament, the property to be held in trust for the beneficiary or beneficiaries of the testamentary trust established in the will.

*See also:* executor, testamentary executor (executor testamentarius).

**trustee de son tort**   A constructive trustee created by possession or management of the property of another. A trustee de son tort is a constructive trustee, a person who takes on the role of a trustee by intermeddling in the assets of a trust or taking possession of trust property but is not in fact appointed to be a trustee. A trustee de son tort is not entitled to compensation.

**trustee ex malefico (maleficio)**   The holder of a constructive trust resulting from a breach of a fiduciary duty. A trustee ex malifico is a constructive trustee over assets that were taken wrongfully as a result of a failure to perform a fiduciary duty. A trustee ex malifico is subject to an action for the recognition of a constructive trust, to an action for unjust enrichment, for restitution and, potentially, for conversion. A trustee ex malifico may also have committed the crimes of fraud, theft, or embezzlement.

*See also:* trust, constructive trust.

**trusty or trusties**   *See:* prisoner, trustee (trusty or trusties).

**United States Trustee**   The federal trustee in bankruptcy. The United States Trustee is a federal official empowered to take title to assets in bankruptcy and to manage the assets and dispose of such assets as needed to liquidate a bankrupt estate or otherwise manage a bankrupt estate or private trust committed to its management.

**truth (true or truthful)**   The state of things as they are or were. The truth is the most honest, complete, and objective understanding of any thing. In the law, the truth usually refers to the most accurate possible depiction of historical events. Witnesses are asked to describe their observations of events truthfully, swearing to (or affirming they will) tell the truth, the whole truth, and nothing but the truth, which is to say that they are to say what they know or what they can recall as fully, accurately, and honestly as they can, without embroidering or enhancing their best recollection of events. Thus, to speak truthfully is to state what one knows of some matter, as fully as is reasonably likely to be needed to relate the matter without any intended alteration, omission, or addition of detail, and with an effort to avoid error or the presentation of a mistaken impression or false recollection.

The truth–telling role for witnesses differs from the sense in which we speak of truth as it has meaning for the jury or other finders of fact. These truth–finders must use inference, interpretation, reason, and instinct to find the truth of the matter from the sum of all the evidence available. Such a construct of truth is a depiction of the events using the best analytical tools available to the finder of fact. Judges and lawyers must similarly find the truth of what the law is by interpretation and analysis of the legal materials according to the customs of the law and the values of society.

As a matter of jurisprudence, truth is a very controversial idea. Reflecting the problems of truth in philosophy generally, legal philosophy has not agreed on a meaning for truth, and there is a significant gap between understandings of truth in an ontological sense (the way something really is) and the epistemological or linguistic senses (the ways it is perceived or related). Despite occasional arguments by nihilists, however, there is little scope in law for arguments that truth has no meaning or existence as a means of understanding or criticising an event, a concept, or a representation.

**truth and reconciliation commission**   *See:* rights, human right, Human Rights Tribunal, Truth and Reconciliation Commission.

**Truth In Lending Act**   *See:* loan, Truth In Lending Act (T.I.L.A. or TILA).

**whole truth and nothing but the truth**   The promise of truth in a witness's oath. The formula of the oath or affirmation administered to witnesses varies from jurisdiction to jurisdiction, but the common denominator is a statement required of the witness that the testimony the witness will give will be "the truth, the whole truth, and nothing but the truth." This customary definition of a witness's truth evolved in the early common law as a means of barring incomplete truths, half truths, and truths intended or likely to mislead. Thus, a witness may commit perjury by telling the truth, if a material omission from what is said made the testimony less than the whole truth, in sum creating a false impression.

*See also:* perjury (perjure); oath, statement under oath (sworn statement or unsworn statement).

**TSP**   *See:* pollution, air pollution, criteria pollutants, particulate matter, total suspended particles (TSP).

**tuition voucher**   *See:* voucher, tuition voucher (school voucher or education voucher).

**turbidity**   The degree of muddiness or haziness. Turbidity is the degree to which air or water lack clarity owing to particles and chemicals suspended or mixed in them. From the Latin word for the mixing of dirt into muddy water, turbidity measures the loss of clarity in air or water caused by the presence of pollutants or debris. Turbidity is thus a direct measure of light penetration. In water, turbidity is an indicator of the loads of silt, particulate, oil, runoff, or other inputs that are both harmful in themselves and affect the species of plants and animals that may be sustained in the body of water. In air, turbidity not only measures the loss of sunlight reaching the ground but also indicates the particulate level, which may in turn affect air quality for breathing.

**turnover order**   *See:* order, turnover order.

**turntable doctrine**   *See:* nuisance, attractive nuisance (turntable doctrine).

**turpitude (moral turpitude)**   Anything demonstrating an immoral or unethical nature. Turpitude is a base or corrupt act or condition that would cause others to shun the person who commits such an act or suffers from such a condition. The law frequently denominates certain acts and offenses as acts and offenses demonstrating moral turpitude.

Moral turpitude is a condition of an act or omission that is unjust, dishonest, or immoral. Moral turpitude includes both action and inaction that violates a trust or amounts to dishonesty; conduct that demonstrates a disregard for the safety and interests of others; and both conduct and inaction that amounts to a failure of duty by a fiduciary or public official who is responsible for the safety or security of others and who fails to make a good faith effort to provide such security.

**TWA**   *See:* pollution, time–weighted average (TWA).

**two–witness rule**   *See:* witness, two–witness rule.

**Twombly standard**   *See:* dismissal, grounds for dismissal, failure to state a claim upon which relief can be granted, Twombly test (Twombly standard).

**tying (tied products or tying agreement or tying arrangement)**   A condition of purchase requiring the buyer to purchase another product. Tying is a practice of sellers in which a seller offers a product for purchase on the condition that any buyer also acquire a separate product, an arrangement that is intended to use the market share of the first product to promote the market for the second. The buyer need not acquire the second product to constitute a tying in buying the first; a commitment to buy the second only from the vendor of the first is sufficient. A tying arrangement or contract is usually illegal and unenforceable as a violation of antitrust laws because it is generally considered to be an unfair restriction on trade. All bundled products are not tied, however. One of the hallmarks of untied bundled products is the opportunity of the consumer to choose to acquire the bundled products individually.
   *See also:* monopoly, monopoly leveraging.

**tyrannicide**   *See:* homicide, regicide (tyrannicide).

**tyranny**   *See:* government, forms of government, tyranny (tyrant).

> [A]lthough the spirit of an instrument, especially of a constitution, is to be respected not less than its letter, yet the spirit is to be collected chiefly from the letter.
>
> Joseph Story, 1 *Commentaries on the Constitution of the United States* 326 (§ 427)(5th ed.) (Melvin Bigelow, ed.)(Little, Brown, 1891).

# U

**u**   The twenty–first letter of the modern English alpha–bet. "U" signifies a variety of functions as a symbol and as a designation of status, as in "unfit." It is translated into Uniform for radio signals and NATO military transmis–sions, into Union for some police radio traffic, and into dot, dot, dash in Morse Code. Until the use of the letter "u" became common in the seventeenth century, its function was often performed by a "v."

**u as an abbreviation**   A word commencing in U. When used as the sole letter of an abbreviation, U often stands for university or universities. In Latin abbreviations, it is likely to stand for ut, though it might be ubi. It may also represent under, underwriters, unemployment, unfair, unified, uniform, union, united, Ukraine, unpublished, upper, and Utah. It may also stand for the initial of the name of an author or case reporter, such as Underwood, Udal, or Utah Reports.

**U.C.C. battle of the forms or UCC battle of the forms**   *See:* acceptance, acceptance as acceptance of an offer, battle of the forms (U.C.C. battle of the forms or UCC battle of the forms).

**U.C.M.J. or UCMJ**   *See:* military, military law, Uniform Code of Military Justice (U.C.M.J. or UCMJ).

**U.F.C.A. or UFCA**   *See:* conveyance, fraudulent con–veyance, Uniform Fraudulent Conveyances Act (U.F.C.A. or UFCA).

**U.S. Constitution**   *See:* constitution, U.S. Constitu–tion (United States Constitution).

**U.S. court**   *See:* court, U.S. court.

**U.S. Court of Appeals**   *See:* court, U.S. court, U.S. court of appeals, law of the circuit (circuit law); court, U.S. court, U.S. Court of Appeals (circuit court).

**U.S. Court of Appeals for the Armed Forces**   *See:* court, U.S. court, court–martial, U.S. Court of Appeals for the Armed Forces.

**U.S. Customs and Border Protection**   *See:* customs, U.S. Customs and Border Protection.

**U.S. Department of Interior**   *See:* land, public lands, U.S. Department of Interior, Bureau of Land Man–agement.

**U.S. District Court**   *See:* court, U.S. court, U.S. District Court.

**U.S. Immigration and Customs Enforcement**   *See:* customs, U.S. Immigration and Customs Enforce–ment (I.C.E. or ICE).

**U.S. state**   *See:* state, U.S. state.

**U.S. state court**   *See:* court, U.S. state court.

**U.S. Supreme Court**   *See:* court, U.S. court, U.S. Supreme Court.

**U.S. Tax Court**   *See:* court, U.S. court, tax court (U.S. Tax Court).

**UCC Article Nine**   *See:* contracts, Uniform Commer–cial Code, Article 9 of the UCC (UCC Article Nine).

**UCC Article Three**   *See:* contracts, Uniform Com–mer–Cial Code, article 3 of the UCC (UCC Article Three).

**UCC Article Two**   *See:* contracts, Uniform Com–mercial Code, article 2 of the UCC (UCC Article Two).

**UCC or U.C.C.**   *See:* contracts, Uniform Commercial Code (UCC or U.C.C.).

**UEFJA**   *See:* judgment, enforcement of judgment, Uniform Enforcement of Foreign Judgments Act (UEFJA).

**UL**   *See:* laboratory, Underwriters Laboratories (UL).

**Ulema (Ulama, alim)**   The community of religious scholars. The Ulema are the community of religious scholars, whose conference on questions of Islamic law has great authority. The word Ulema is the pural of the word alim, meaning one who has religious knowledge or a scholar of shari'a.

**ullage**   The void above the cargo in a tank, cask, or barrel. Ullage is the volume in a container of a liquid cargo that is empty, i.e., in a barrel, cask, or vessel such as a tanker. Determining the ullage in the hold of a tanker requires measurement and calculation according to the specific ullage holes or sensors and the specific tables created for that vessel. Some ullage is essential for the safe handling of most liquids to account for expansion owing to changes in temperature.

**ulma** *See:* alim (ulma or ulema).

**ULP** *See:* union, labor union, unfair labor practice (ULP).

**ultimate fact** *See:* fact, ultimate fact.

**ultimatum** A final offer or demand. An ultimatum is, literally, a final proposition, the last position that will be taken by one side in a negotiation, either because the party taking it will take no more positions or because an agreement is reached based on that proposition. In its contemporary usage, an ultimatum is strictly an offer presented to a negotiating opponent that is a take–it–or–leave–it proposition, often made with an express or implied threat of some coercive or harmful action if the proposition is not accepted.

*See also:* union, labor union, collective bargaining, Boulwarism; negotiability (negotiable or non–negotiable or nonnegotiable).

**ultimogeniture (postremogeniture)** Priority of the youngest child in the succession of heirs. Ultimogeniture is the settling of the estate of a parent on the youngest child. The practice is followed in several parts of the world, having been followed for certain lands held in the English borough of Nottingham, apparently, from the Saxon governance of the area until 1925.

*See also:* primogeniture.

**ultra vires** Exceeding a given scope of authority. Ultra vires, Latin for beyond the powers, designates acts that are outside the scope of the powers, jurisdiction, or authority of a person, office, or entity. An act by a legal official beyond the scope of the official's duties, an act by a court outside of its jurisdiction, an act by a corporation beyond the powers conferred in its corporate charter, and an act by an agent beyond the scope of the agency are all ultra vires. An act ultra vires is, depending on the act, authority, and context, either void or voidable.

*See also:* intra, intra vires.

**ultra–hazardous activity** *See:* hazard, ultra–hazardous activity.

**umpire** The tie–breaker among arbitrators, or judge of a sporting game. An umpire judges among competitors. The term, from the Old French for "odd rather than even" was initially used, and is still used, to describe the final arbiter who is selected by two arbitrators and is to cast a deciding vote if they disagree. From this sense has come the office of chief referee in sporting games.

The sporting umpire has been used as a metaphor for all forms of judging and judgment, the casual sense being that an umpire in baseball is required to make only objective assessments of matters of fact. Yet the metaphor is richer in that umpires must use discretion to apply rules that are inherently dependent on interpretation to events that have a significance that can vary according to perspective. Note: umpire, and its slang abbreviation "ump" are each a noun and a verb.

*See also:* metaphor.

**UN** *See:* United Nations (UN).

**unalienable or inalienable** *See:* alienability, inalienability (unalienable or inalienable).

**unanimity (unanimous vote)** Agreement among every participant in a decision. Unanimity is the effect of every person engaged in a vote, discussion, or operation agreeing with a decision or action. Latin for being of one spirit, the unanimous act is the collective act without dissent. In most cases, unanimity within a group requires an affirmative commitment by each person in the group; silence or abstention thwarts unanimity. The verdict of the jury at common law was required to be unanimous, and in most jurisdictions, a unanimous verdict is still required, although some allow a majority or supermajority verdict.

**unanimity instruction** *See:* instruction, jury instruction, single–juror instruction (unanimity instruction).

**unauthorized practice of law** *See:* lawyer, unauthorized practice of law (unlicensed practitioner).

**unauthorized practice of medicine** *See:* medicine, unauthorized medical practice (unauthorized practice of medicine).

**unavailability** *See:* hearsay, hearsay exception, exception only when declarant is unavailable (unavailability).

**unavailable witness** *See:* witness, unavailable witness.

**unavoidable accident** *See:* accident, unavoidable accident (accidental harm or inevitable accident).

**unavoidably unsafe product** *See:* liability, product liability, strict product liability, unavoidably unsafe product (dangerous product or unreasonably dangerous product).

**unbargained–for reliance** *See:* reliance, unbargained–for reliance (induced reliance).

**unborn widow** *See:* perpetuity, rule against perpetuities, what–might–happen test, afterborn widow (unborn widow).

**unclean hands doctrine** *See:* equity, equitable defense, unclean hands doctrine (clean–hands doctrine).

**unconditional or conditional or defeasance** *See:* condition (unconditional or conditional or defeasance).

**unconditional promise** *See:* promise, unconditional promise.

**unconscionability (unconscionable or unconscionably)** A defense to a contact when enforcement cannot be ordered in good conscience. Unconscionability is an aspect of any act, statement, or agreement that is contrary to good conscience. As a general matter, it is contrary to the public policy of the courts of the United States to enforce a claim based on an unconscionable action or arising from an unconscionable arrangement, when the enforcement recognition and enforcement of the unconscionable act or arrangement.

Unconscionability is most often argued as a defense to a claim to enforce a contract or the security arrangement related to a contract. In such cases, unconscionability is an equitable and legal defense to a claim for breach or contract or default on the debt, the defense arguing that the contract's terms strongly favored one party at the time the contract was entered, and the other party had no meaningful choice in its acceptance of the terms at the time. An unconscionable agreement is not enforceable in a court.

A person who acts unconscionably toward another does not, without more, commit a tort. But, if the person who commits the unconscionable act causes a harm to the person and the unconscionable aspect of the act is found to be unreasonable, the act may amount to a variety of torts, including negligence, outrage, and infliction of emotional distress. If a fiduciary acts unconscionably toward a person to whom fiduciary owes a fiduciary obligation and does so to the person's harm, the fiduciary is liable either for damages or for restitution.

**unconscionable bargain** See: unconscionability, unconscionable contract (unconscionable bargain).

**unconscionable contract (unconscionable bargain)** An unfair, one-sided contract. An unconscionable contract is so lopsided in the benefits and burdens allocated in the agreement that neither a sensible person who is not under a delusion or improper influence would accept it, nor would a fair and honest person attempt to enforce it. Unconscionability is assessed by either procedural unconscionability or substantive unconscionability. Procedural unconscionability requires assessment of the process by which the contract was entered, to determine whether it was procured by the drafting party through a process of significant unfairness, as through the use of high-pressure sales tactics; undisclosed, poorly disclosed, or unnecessarily opaque terms; misrepresentation or other evidence of unfair advantage in the negotiation and entry. Substantive unconscionability requires assessment of the terms of the agreement to determine whether they are so one-sided that they are not conscionable under the circumstances at the time the contract was entered. An unconscionable contract may be rescinded as void.

**unconstitutional** See: constitutional, unconstitutional.

**under water or underwater** See: equity, equitable value, equity of redemption, negative equity (under water or underwater).

**undercover agent** See: police, police officer, undercover agent.

**underemployment** See: employment, unemployment, underemployment (under-employed).

**underground economy or underground market** See: market, black market (underground economy or underground market).

**underived good** See: good, underived good (Finnisian goods).

**under-represented minority** See: minority, minority group, under-represented minority (underrepresented minority).

**undersigned** See: signature, undersigned.

**understanding** Agreement among several people in a common idea. Understanding, in its most general sense, is knowledge. In law, understanding is frequently used to describe a person's opinion or belief as to some fact, which is often essential to an analysis of motive or intent or to consider the effectiveness of notice or an instruction.

"An understanding" is a general term that refers to a shared belief or idea, held in common among two or more parties. A contract may be called an understanding, and an understanding may be a contract, if and only if the other requisites of a contract, such as intent to form a contract and mutuality of consideration are present in the understanding. Often a contract among public entities is entitled a "memorandum of understanding" or MOU.

**undertaking (undertook or undertakes)** A promise, commitment, or assumption of a duty. An undertaking, in general, is any project or activity to which one is committed sufficiently that others may rely upon the commitment and that its completion becomes a duty. In law, this takes several forms. In torts, an undertaking is an action providing a service, such as protection or a rescue, that a person may commence and having done so accepts a duty to perform the service with reasonable care. In contracts, an undertaking is the promise of one party to a contract, the commitment that forms one party's consideration. In contracts also, an undertaking is an assumption of the debt, whether for oneself or another, whether as a surety, assignee, or otherwise, in a manner on which the creditor may rely.

In New York, an undertaking is a payment by a plaintiff in security for damages that may be suffered by a defendant restrained by a temporary restraining order issued on the plaintiff's motion. The undertaking is discharged if the plaintiff is later found entitled to injunctive relief.

**undertenant or sub-lessee** See: tenant, tenant as lessee, sub-tenant (undertenant or sub-lessee).

**underwriter (underwrite or underwriting)** A seller of securities or insurer of an insurance risk. An underwriter is a party who either sells securities of an issuer or insures the risk in an insurance policy. Both senses of the term arise from the once–customary practice of the underwriter's signing at the bottom of the relevant instrument of issuance, usually one among many subscribers to it.

A securities underwriter is any party who purchases a security from its issuer with the intent to sell it to others. A security underwriter is regulated as a seller of securities.

An insurance underwriter is an insurer, the party who accepts the risk in an insurance policy in return for the payment of premiums, and who must stand ready to honor a valid claim under the policy. An insurance underwriter may be represented by an agent or broker in the entry of the policy.

**Underwriters Laboratories** *See:* laboratory, Underwriters Laboratories (UL).

**undisclosed principal** *See:* principal, principal of agent, undisclosed principal.

**undivided** All there is is held by all. Undivided, or an undivided interest, signals that more than one person has an interest in a property, but all who have such an interest share in the totality of the property, rather than having a claim to a particular parcel or slice. An undivided interest is a share in the right to the whole, which must be shared with all others with a similar interest; it is not a right to a portion from which the others may be excluded.

*See also:* ownership, concurrent ownership (co–owner or co–tenant).

**undocumented worker** *See:* worker, undocumented worker; alien, undocumented alien (undocumented worker).

**undue (undue influence or undue hardship or unduly)** Unusual and improper. Anything undue is contrary to what is due. Something undue is not what should be expected or done in a given situation, either because it is worse in form or a violation of some duty. Thus, undue hardship is hardship that is unexpected in its form or unusual in its severity in a given situation. Undue influence is influence greater in its persuasiveness than ordinarily exerted and often involves a quasi–fiduciary influence directed to the benefit of the person exerting the influence, rather than to the intent of the person on whom it is exercised.

**undue prejudice** *See:* prejudice, legal prejudice, undue prejudice.

**unearned income** *See:* income, unearned income.

**unearned income of minor children** *See:* tax, income tax, unearned income of minor children (kiddie tax).

**unearned revenue** *See:* revenue, unearned revenue.

**unemployment**

**unemployment benefits or unemployment insurance** *See:* employment, unemployment, unemployment compensation (unemployment benefits or unemployment insurance).

**unemployment compensation** *See:* employment, unemployment, unemployment compensation (unemployment benefits or unemployment insurance).

**employee misconduct (misconduct by employee)** A breach of duty toward the employer sufficient to bar unemployment insurance benefits. Employee misconduct is an employer's defense to a dismissed employee's claim for benefits under an unemployment insurance program, in which the employer must demonstrate that the termination followed actions by the employee that exhibit a willful and deliberate disregard of the standards of behavior that an employer may reasonably expect from an employee or that demonstrate an intentional and substantial disregard of the employer's interests or the employee's duties and obligations to the employer. Thus, an honest mistake or good faith error in judgment is not misconduct.

**unenumerated right** *See:* right, constitutional right, unenumerated right (unnamed rights).

**unethical conduct** *See:* ethics, legal ethics, unethical conduct.

**unfair competition** *See:* competition, unfair competition.

**unfair labor practice** *See:* union, labor union, unfair labor practice (ULP).

**unfit** *See:* fitness (unfit).

**unforeseeable plaintiff** *See:* plaintiff, unforeseeable plaintiff.

**unforseeability** *See:* forseeability, unforseeability (unforseen).

**unfunded mandate** *See:* mandate, unfunded mandate.

**unicameral legislature** *See:* legislature, unicameral legislature.

**unified bar** *See:* bar, integrated bar (unified bar).

**Uniform Code of Military Justice** *See:* military, military law, Uniform Code of Military Justice (U.C.M.J. or UCMJ).

**uniform law** *See:* law, uniform law.

**Uniform Commercial Code** *See:* contracts, Uniform Commercial Code (UCC or U.C.C.).

**Uniform Determination of Death Act** *See:* death, moment of death, Uniform Determination of Death Act.

**Uniform Enforcement of Foreign Judgments Act** *See:* judgment, enforcement of judgment, Uniform Enforcement of Foreign Judgments Act (UEFJA).

**Uniform Fraudulent Conveyances Act** *See:* conveyance, fraudulent conveyance, Uniform Fraudulent Conveyances Act (U.F.C.A. or UFCA).

**Uniform Gifts to Minors Act or U.G.M.A. or UGMA or Uniform Transfers to Minors Act or U.T.M.A.** *See:* gift, taxable gift, gift to a minor (Uniform Gifts to Minors Act or U.G.M.A. or UGMA or Uniform Transfers to Minors Act or U.T.M.A.).

**Uniform Law Commission or NCCUSL** *See:* reform, law reform, National Conference of Commissioners on Uniform State Laws (Uniform Law Commission or NCCUSL).

**Uniform Simultaneous Death Act** *See:* death, simultaneous death, Uniform Simultaneous Death Act.

**Uniform Statutory Rule Against Perpetuities** *See:* perpetuity, Rule Against Perpetuities, wait-and-see test, Uniform Statutory Rule Against Perpetuities (USRAP).

**unilateral contract** *See:* contract, specific contracts, unilateral contract.

**unilateral mistake** *See:* mistake, unilateral mistake.

**unimproved land** *See:* land, improved land (unimproved land).

**unindicted co-conspirator** *See:* conspiracy, unindicted co-conspirator.

**uninsured motorist** *See:* motorist, uninsured motorist.

**unintended use** *See:* liability, product liability, intended-use doctrine, unintended use.

**unintentional act** *See:* mens, mens rea, unintentional act (inadvertent act or unintended act).

**union** Combination or collaboration. A union is anything that is formed of two or more parts. The United States was considered a union from its very beginning, an idea that is central to its once-popular Latin description on the Great Seal, e pluribus unum, and that was the common identity of the Northern states and the military forces of the United States while fighting in the American Civil War.

Many arrangements and contracts are referred to as a union, though the term is most often to describe a marriage. Although many entities are sometimes described as a union, such as a partnership, a conglomerate, or a joint venture, when used casually, the term usually refers to a labor organization or worker's union.

**labor union (labor organization)** An association representing workers to management. A labor union, or labor organization, is an organization with members who are the employees of one or more entities, for whom the organization serves as an agent or representative to the entities to present and resolve grievances, labor disputes, wage issues, rates of pay, hours of employment, or conditions of work. The right to form a labor union is an element of freedom of association and cannot be made illegal. The degree to which an employer may interfere or must facilitate the formation of a labor union is regulated by federal and state laws.

*See also:* trade; union, labor union, labor organization, authorization card.

**collective bargaining** A union's negotiation on employees' behalf with their employer or employers. Collective bargaining is negotiation between the employer and the union rather than individual bargaining between the employer and each employee. The process of collective bargaining occurs not only as negotiation and discussion prior to the creation of a labor agreement, but also during and after its negotiation and creation. Collective bargaining occurs under federal law even if there is only one employee, as long as the bargaining is done on behalf of all of the unionized employees or all employees by a union representative.

> **bargaining impasse** A deadlock in collective bargaining, allowing the employer to set the terms of the contract. A bargaining impasse is reached when the union and employer representatives are negotiating in vain, with no remaining method by which the parties will reach an accord. At this point, the law allows the employer unilaterally to determine the terms of the agreement. Even so, there is no assurance that the union membership will approve the agreement.

> **bargaining unit** The positions or jobs represented by the union. A bargaining unit is the set of jobs or positions whose holders are represented by the union in collective bargaining. The union is authorized to negotiate the pay and conditions that are offered to the holders of those positions, not to negotiate the pay and conditions of individual employees.

> **Boulwarism** An employer's non-negotiable offer to a union. A Boulwarism is an ultimatum given by an employer, stating the terms of the only agreement the employer will accept, rather than participating in a meaningful bargaining discussion with representatives of a union. The eponym is for Lemuel Boulware, a former vice president of General Electric who famously employed the tactic in the 1940s and 50s.
> *See also:* ultimatum.

**coalition bargaining** Labor negotiation with multiple employers. Coalition bargaining is bargaining between a union and two or more employers, so that the resulting agreement applies to the employees of all of the employers. An agreement reached through coalition bargaining may require separate approval by each union bargaining unit represented.

**collective bargaining agreement (C.B.A. CBA)** The collectively bargained employment contract. A collective bargaining agreement is an employment contract between the union on behalf of the bargaining unit or units and the employer or employers for whom the employees in the union work. The CBA governs an entire, evolving labor-management relationship, including the means for the certification and decertification of unions, the bargaining obligations of unions and employers, the responsibilities of the employer in the event of the sale or transfer of the employment operations, and the procedures for the resolution of workplace disputes.

**labor dispute** Any disagreement between the union and management. A labor dispute is a disagreement between union and management over the pay, terms, tenure or seniority, or conditions of employment; or over the association or representation of employees or other persons in negotiating, fixing, maintaining, or seeking to arrange terms or conditions of employment. Statutes are quite specific as to the scope of disagreements between the parties that qualify as disputes, such that some matters are recognized as labor disputes generally, but railway and certain transportation labor disputes are regulated separately. A strike or other labor action resulting from a recognized labor dispute may not be subject to an injunction or other judicial or legal interference.

**cooling-off period** A period in which neither union nor employer may take action. A cooling-off period, in general, is a period of inactivity during a legal process that is required by rules, court order, or administrative order, during which the parties are barred from activity that will affect the process. The purpose of the time is to allow the parties both to reconsider their positions and to engage in alternative dispute resolution.

During a labor dispute, a cooling-off period may be ordered by a labor arbitrator or court, designating a time during which neither side of a labor dispute may resort to measures to change their positions, allowing both more time for mediation and negotiation without strikes, lockouts, or other severe changes in the labor-management relationship.

*See also:* wait, waiting period (cooling off period).

**corporate campaign** Union tactics other than a strike used to influence an employer. A union corporate campaign is a coordinated effort by a union to influence an employer to change work practices, safety standards, pay, or working conditions, using a variety of means but not a strike. The union seeks to use public relations, marketing, investigation, and whistle-blowing to create an environment in which the employer cannot force compliance with its work rules, working conditions, or bargaining demands.

**labor picket (stranger picketing)** Picketing of the employer by employees and sympathizers. A labor picket line is a picket line composed of members of the bargaining unit of a union, their friends, and supporters, who picket at least one place of employment of the bargaining unit. The line may not physically bar a street or public way, but members of the line may banter with others passing it as the others enter the place of employment. Members of other unions without a common interest with the striking employees may sometimes honor the picket line in a sympathy strike. Members of unions with no direct common interests may sometimes honor the picket line through stranger picketing.

**labor strike (walkout)** A stoppage of work by an entities' employees. A labor strike is the refusal to work by employees as a means to coerce their employer to agree to a workers' demand related to labor dispute. A labor strike may be an action of two or more employees, all of the members of a union, or some or all of the employees of an entity. The strike may involve a picket line, in which the striking employees seek to prevent non-striking employees from entering the place of employment. A union must give an employer in certain circumstance, such as a health care provider, ten days notice prior to any strike, picketing, or concerted refusal to work, and a union that contemplates a strike upon the expiration of a current collective bargaining agreement must give any employer covered by the statutory requirement of sixty days notice. The corollary of a strike is a lockout, when an employer bars employees from working.

*See also:* union, labor union, labor law, National Labor Relations Act (N.L.R.A. or NLRA or Wagner Act).

**sympathy strike** A strike by one bargaining unit in sympathy with another's strike. A sympathy strike is a strike by a bargaining unit in support of an ongoing strike by a different bargaining unit. A sympathy strike is lawful under section 7 of the National Labor Relations Act. Not all strikes by one union in support of another are protected, however. There must be some commonality of interest shared between the two and related to the employer.

**wildcat strike**  A strike not authorized by the union. A wildcat strike is a work stoppage by employees who strike individually or as a group, which is not authorized by their union and that may be in violation of either the collective bargaining agreement or union rules or orders.

### labor law

**Anti-Injunction Bill (Norris-Laguardia Act)**  Law barring federal courts from enjoining lawful union activities. The Anti-Injunction Bill of 1934, codified at 29 U.S.C. §§104 and 105, or the Norris-LaGuardia Act, bars federal injunctions of lawful organizing activities by unions or other labor organizations, as well as outlawing any agreement not to join a union as a condition of employment. Nonetheless, the union is exempt from injunction under the anti-trust acts only as long as the union is acting in its own interests and not in combination with other unions or entities.
*See also:* union, labor union, union organization, yellow-dog contract (yellow dog).

**Labor-Management Relations Act (Taft-Hartley Act)**  Federal limits on unions, including limits on the form of lawful strike. The Labor-Management Relations Act, 80 Pub. L. 101; 61 Stat. 136, amended the National Labor Relations Act, enlarged the meaning of unfair labor practices to include practices by unions and other labor organizations, barred unions from contributing money directly to political campaigns, allowed states to bar union-only or closed shops, and barred jurisdictional strikes, wildcat strikes, solidarity or political strikes, secondary boycotts, and "common situs" picketing.

**National Labor Relations Act (N.L.R.A. or NLRA or Wagner Act)**  Federal law barring employers from interfering with unions or punishing employees for lawful union activity. The National Labor Relations Act of 1935, codified at 9 U.S.C. §§ 151-169 (2009), prohibits a variety of unfair labor practices by employers and, as amended, by unions, as well as creating the National Labor Relations Board. The act forbids employers from firing or threatening to fire employees for participating in lawful union activities, from interfering with union elections and activities, from discrimination against union members in hiring and promotion, from discrimination against employees who attempt to enforce the act, and from refusing to bargain collectively with union representatives.

### labor organization

**authorization card**  A card for the purpose of union voting. An authorization card is a ballot according to which employees may vote to authorize the union to perform some act on their behalf. If authorization cards stating no specific purpose are cast, the collected signatures should only be used to call an election.
*See also:* union, labor union (labor organization).

**bargaining order**  Order for collective bargaining regardless of union election results. A bargaining order may be issued by an arbitrator or court, requiring an employer to engage in collective bargaining with a union regardless of the outcome of an organization vote, because the employer engaged in practices that were so likely to undermine the organization vote that the union election was impeded. A bargaining order may give the union the right to represent both member and non-member employees.

**card check election**  An absentee system of union balloting. A card check election allows workers who vote to be represented by a union to sign authorization cards, which are usually made available outside the place of employment in places the workers might frequent, such as churches and grocery stores, rather than holding an election in person on the worksite.

**certification bar**  Time constraint on unionization elections. A certification bar is a maximum time, usually one year, after a union has been certified as the exclusive representative of the workers in a given workplace, during which no petitions to replace or remove the union will be entertained. The bar is intended to allow a union a reasonable time to negotiate a new contract without the distraction of defending its position.

**decertification**  A vote to end a union's representation of employees. Decertification is the process by which employees terminate a union's representation of them to their employer. The process requires a petition, followed by a vote held in a manner like a certification election.

**yellow-dog contract (yellow dog)**  Employment agreement surrendering right to remain in or join a union. A yellow-dog contract is an employment agreement that stipulates the employee will not join a union or other labor association, or remain in one, as a condition of employment. Yellow-dog contracts were banned with the passage of the Norris-LaGuardia Act.
*See also:* union, labor union, labor laws, Anti-Injunction Bill (Norris-Laguardia Act).

**National Labor Relations Board (NLRB)**  The federal agency that implements the national labor laws. The National Labor Relations Board ("NLRB") is a five-member board that manages a staff to carry out duties assigned by Congress in the National Labor Relations Act, primarily to regulate the organization of labor associations. It enforces the Act in most industries and investigates complaints of unfair employment practices by employers or unions. Note: the NLRB does not manage most labor arbitrations, a task usually performed by the Federal Mediation and Conciliation Service.

*See also:* mediator, Federal Mediation and Conciliation Service (F.M.C.S. or FMCS).

**non-union (nonunion)** An employee, shop, or employer who is not unionized. Non-union designates an employee who is not a member of a union, a shop that has not authorized a union to represent it, an employer of a shop that has no union representation, or another person or entity not affiliated with a union. In more general terms, it may also represent goods or work done by a non-union shop.

**scab** A worker who replaces a striking worker. A scab is a slang term for a non-union worker, particularly a non-union worker who continues to provide work to an employer during a labor strike. A scab may also refer to outside workers hired during a strike to replace striking workers. Scabs have sometimes been personally mistreated by union workers.

**shop**

**agency shop** Workplace allowing but not requiring union membership. An agency shop is a workplace in which some workers are represented in a collective bargaining agreement, and each worker may opt in or opt out of union membership. A worker opting out of membership may still be required to pay union dues but will not be subject to union discipline.

**closed shop (union shop)** Workplace requiring union membership. A closed shop is a workplace in which all workers are represented in one or more collective bargaining agreements, and each worker is required to be a member of the authorized union in order to commence or retain employment in jobs of the employer within the bargaining unit. Union members in a closed shop are subject to union dues and union discipline as a condition of employment.

**double-breasted operation** An employer with union and nonunion subsidiaries. A double-breasted operation is a single entity comprising component entities, at least one of which is a union shop and one of which is an agency or open shop. In some industries, the double-breasted operation has flexibility in bidding on contract work not available to a closed or an open shop. A double-breasted operation may be treated as a single entity for labor law enforcement under the single-employer test.

*See also:* veil, corporate veil, single-employer rule (single-entity test or integrated enterprise standard).

**open shop** Workplace without required union membership. An open shop is a workplace in which no workers are subject to collective bargaining or union representation recognized by management, and hiring is, as a matter of law, not influenced by whether a job candidate is a member of a union or not. As a matter of practice, some union members whose membership is known to the management of an open shop may find difficulties in employment there.

**right to work law (right to work state)** A state law banning closed shops. A right-to-work-state is a state with a right-to-work law, a statute that makes unenforceable any contract or collective bargaining agreement so far as it requires an employee to become or be a member of a union as a condition of employment. As of 2011, there are twenty-two right-to-work states.

**unfair labor practice (ULP)** An employer's punishment of a worker or union's interference with an employer. An unfair labor practice is a violation of the National Labor Relations Act, as amended, committed by an employer or by a union, either of which may be enjoined or fined by the National Labor Relations Board or a court for the violation. Unfair labor practices by the employer are acts intended to chill union membership or organiza-tion, including firing or threatening to fire a worker for joining or voting to join a union, threatening to close a workplace if it is unionized, and questioning or harassing its employees to ascertain their views of unionization. Unfair practices by a union include threatening employees with job losses or other harm for non-support of the union, fining employees for resigning from the union, or preferring some over others in a union hiring hall on the basis of union activities or race.

*See also:* lockout (lock out).

**union dues**

**Beck rights** Non-union employee consent is required for fees to be used beyond collective bargaining. Beck rights are the rights of employees who do not join a union but pay agency fees for collective bargaining to limit the use of their payments only to the costs of collective bargaining or activities to which they do not object.

**checkoff** Payment of union dues through paycheck. A checkoff is a scheme by which a union member may pay union dues through a payroll deduction. Checkoff programs, by definition, must be administered by employers and not by the union or the employees.

**marital union** Marriage. A marital union is a marriage, although the term is sometimes used for a wedding, to signal the ceremony or the solemnization of matrimony.

**mass action theory** Union liability for members' acts not approved by the union. Mass action is a theory under which a labor union or its officers may be liable for harm to an employer caused by unlawful acts by a group of the employers' employees who are the union's members, where there is no proof the union ordered its members to undertake an unlawful strike or other acts.

Mass action was initially associated with Communists and revolutionary groups seeking to overthrow the government by violence. The phrase appears to have been appropriated to labor law by Judge Goldsborough in United States v. International Union, United Mine Workers, 77 F. Supp. 563 (D. D.C., 1948).

*See also:* class, class action; respondeat, respondeat superior; class, class action, mass action.

**political union**   Individual states united in or under one state. The Union usually refers to the United States of America, which is a single entity of separate states. In its broader, political sense, union can refer to any collection of states that retain some degree of autonomy while being governed by or through a single sovereign body.

**unitary executive**   *See:* president, President of the United States of America, unitary executive (unitary theory or unitary presidency).

**United Nations (UN or U.N.)**   The international organization composed of nearly all of the world's states. The United Nations is an organization of state members, created in 1945 as an international center for the maintenance of international peace and security; for the development of law, justice, and human rights; and for the coordination of the actions of states in the promotion of peace, justice, and prosperity. The organization has four main bodies, the Secretariat, Security Council, General Assembly, and the International Court of Justice, as well as many agencies, such as the World Health Organization and World Maritime Organization. The UN is not a government and has no powers other than those conferred on it by its states members. Yet as a coordinating body, it has the power to request its members to take all necessary measures to protect the peace and secure other goals of the U.N. Charter.

**United Nations Charter (Charter of the United Nations)**   The organization treaty of the UN and a source of international law. The United Nations Charter, signed by fifty-one nations in 1945 and now by nearly two hundred, is a treaty binding every signatory to its purposes and requirements as a matter of international law. Under the principles of the Charter, every state renounces war as a means of policy, reserving only the right to use armed force in self-defense. Each state agrees to the peaceful resolution of disputes, to promote justice and equality, and to participate in international discussion. All signatories of the Charter must also come under the Statute of the International Court of Justice. The United States, a principal drafter of the Charter, is a party to it and bound to the Charter as a matter of international law and the Constitution.

**United Nations Convention on Contracts for the International Sale of Goods**   *See:* contracts, contract for the sale of goods, United Nations Convention on Contracts for the International Sale of Goods (CISG).

**Article 2(4) of the UN Charter**   Provision barring UN Members from using or threatening force against other nations. Article Two, paragraph four, of the Charter of the United Nations provides: "All Members shall refrain in their international relations from the threat or use of force against the territorial integrity or political independence of any state, or in any other manner inconsistent with the Purposes of the United Nations." U.N. Charter, art. 2(4) (1945).

*See also:* war, law of war, jus ad bellum.

**Article 51 of the UN Charter**   Provision allowing UN Members to use force in individual or collective self defense. Article Fifty–One of the Charter of the United Nations provides: "Nothing in the present Charter shall impair the inherent right of individual or collective self–defence if an armed attack occurs against a Member of the United Nations, until the Security Council has taken measures necessary to maintain international peace and security. Measures taken by Members in the exercise of this right of self–defence shall be immediately reported to the Security Council and shall not in any way affect the authority and responsibility of the Security Council under the present Charter to take at any time such action as it deems necessary in order to maintain or restore international peace and security."

**United States Armed Forces**   *See:* armed forces, United States Armed Forces.

**United States Attorney**   *See:* prosecutor, United States Attorney.

**United States Constitution**   *See:* constitution, U.S. Constitution (United States Constitution).

**United States Marshals Service**   *See:* police, police organization, United States Marshals Service.

**United States Trustee**   *See:* trustee, United States Trustee.

**unities**   *See:* tenancy, co–tenancy, joint tenancy, unities, four unities (T.I.T.S. or TITS).

**unitrust or charitable remainder unitrust or CRUT**   *See:* trust, charitable remainder trust (unitrust or charitable remainder unitrust or CRUT).

**unity**   A coincidence or simultaneous agreement. A unity is an act of coincidence, in the sense of simultaneous agreement rather than the sense of chance, in which the interests of two or more parties coincide such that each has the same degree and form of an interest as the others in the same thing at the same time. The degree, form and duration of an interest take may vary, but as to the parties in unity, they must vary exactly in the same manner for each. Thus, in an estate held by a co-tenancy, the co-tenants may have differing interests at different times. But if the parties are conferred precisely the same form and degree of an interest, at precisely the same time, to persist the same for each as long as either has it, then there is a unity in that interest. In a tenancy in common, there is only one unity, that of possession, in that each is entitled to a possession of the whole, regardless of the size or portion each has in the whole. In a joint tenancy, the grantor must not only expressly rebut the presumption of a tenancy in common, but the grant must be made with four interests in unity, or four unities — the unity of possession, the unity of time, the unity of title, and the unity of interest. Thus, each joint tenant must have exactly the same right of possession (not that one may occupy the whole but the other occupy only half); for exactly the same time frame (not that one takes title later than the others); with the same quality and extent of title (not with one as landlord and one as tenant), and with the same degree or limitation of interest (not one taking a fee simple absolute and the other a life tenancy). A couple holding by the entireties must have five unities from the creation of the estate, satisfying the four unities of a joint tenancy and a fifth unity, that of matrimony.

## universal

**universal declaration of human rights**　See: rights, human right, universal declaration of human rights.

**universal legacy**　See: legacy, universal legacy (legacy under universal title).

**universal legatee**　See: legatee, universal legatee (universal successor).

**universal life insurance**　See: insurance, category of insurance, life insurance, universal life insurance.

**universal malice**　See: malice, general malice (universal malice).

**universal successor**　See: legatee, universal legatee (universal successor).

**university**　An institution of higher learning comprising colleges or schools. A university is a public or private entity dedicated to the post-secondary instruction and scholarly research, often with a commitment to public service and the application of new knowledge to the world. A university is usually composed of colleges or schools that, in America, are usually organized by academic discipline. A college or school may be independent of a university and performing the same functions as a university. Universities, colleges, schools, and departments, as well as individual degree programs are subject to accreditation programs as a matter of state and federal law. Successful maintenance of accreditation is usually required in order to receive federal and state funds, as well as to place students in employment or further education, or to receive recognition of the degree awarded by other institutions.

**academic freedom**　The liberty of free inquiry and expression by scholars and in institutions. Academic freedom is a customary principle protecting research, inquiry, expression, and teaching by scholars and institutions devoted to higher learning, which is protected by the First Amendment's freedom of expression. Owing to the greater license of private institutions not bound to the First Amendment as are public institutions, the academic freedom of individual scholars in private institutions is a matter of contract, state law, and of such statutory protections as apply through accreditation and other regulations of the institution.

**college**　An association among colleagues. A college is an association among equals, such as the faculty of a school, the electors of the Electoral College, or a college of professionals. A college may be an institution of higher learning, either a component of a university or a free-standing institution performing similar tasks.

**unjust**　See: justice, just (unjust); justice, injustice (unjust).

**unjust enrichment**　One's gain at another's expense as a result of one's unjust action. Unjust enrichment is a basis of liability that arises when one party acts in an unjust manner, in violation of a duty in law or in equity, and realizes a gain of some form at the expense of another party. A party who unjustifiably retains a thing or funds that are owned by another commits unjust enrichment. Thus, a bailee who retains the bailment and refuses to return it to the bailor; a trustee who converts assets from the trust corporation to a corporation owned by the trustee; a landlord who retains a damage deposit when a tenant leaves without having damaged the property all commit unjust enrichment. Even so, unjust enrichment turns upon the specific facts of every case, and a party seeking to recover for unjust enrichment must demonstrate that the defendant has acted unjustly to the harm of the plaintiff and to the benefit of the defendant, in which case the court has an equitable power to order restitution by the defendant to the plaintiff.
See also: restitution (writ of restitution); influence.

## unlawful

**unlawful arrest**　See: arrest, unlawful arrest, right to resist unlawful arrest; arrest, unlawful arrest (wrongful arrest).

**unlawful combatant**　See: combatant, unlawful combatant (unlawful enemy combatant).

**unlawful detention**　See: restraint, unlawful restraint (unlawful detention).

**unlawful eavesdropping**　See: eavesdropping, unlawful eavesdropping.

**unlawful enemy combatant**　See: combatant, unlawful combatant (unlawful enemy combatant).

**unlawful possession**  *See:* possession, unlawful possession (criminal possession).

**unlawful restraint**  *See:* restraint, unlawful restraint (unlawful detention).

**unlawfully obtained evidence**  *See:* evidence, illegally obtained evidence (unlawfully obtained evidence).

**unlicensed practitioner**  *See:* lawyer, unauthorized practice of law (unlicensed practitioner).

**unliquidated claim**  *See:* debt, unliquidated debt (unliquidated claim).

**unliquidated   liquidate   or   liquidated**  *See:* liquidation (unliquidated liquidate or liquidated).

**unnamed rights**  *See:* right, constitutional right, unenumerated right (unnamed rights).

**unnatural act**  *See:* sodomy, crime against nature (unnatural act).

**unnecessary hardship**  *See:* zoning, zoning variance, unnecessary hardship.

**unpublished opinion**  *See:* opinion, judicial opinion, unpublished opinion (no–citation rule).

**unrealized receivable**  *See:* receivable, unrealized receivable.

**unreasonable search**  *See:* search, unreasonable search.

**unreasonable seizure**  *See:* seizure, unreasonable seizure.

**unrecorded contract**  *See:* contract, recorded contract (unrecorded contract).

**unreviewable**  *See:* review, unreviewable.

**unripeness**  *See:* justiciability, ripeness, unripeness (prematurity or unripe of premature).

**unsecured claim**  *See:* claim, bankruptcy claim, unsecured claim.

**unsecured debt**  *See:* debt, secured debt, unsecured debt.

**unsecured loan**  *See:* loan, secured loan (unsecured loan).

**untimeliness**  *See:* time, untimeliness (untimely).

**unum**  One. Unum is a form of the Latin noun unus, which represents an aggregate, or a single entity, as in the expression, e pluribus unum.

**unusual**  *See:* usual (unusual).

**unwritten law**  *See:* law, unwritten law (lex non scripta or lex non scripta regni angliae).

**upcoding**  *See:* fraud, Medicare fraud (upcoding).

**uplifted hand**  *See:* oath, uplifted hand (hand uplifted or raised hand).

**upper chamber**  *See:* chamber, upper chamber.

**urban**  Related to a city or metropolitan area. An urban area, as a matter of federal law, is any city or metropolitan area that has a population of 50,000 or more. Urban relates to a city, and the concept of the urban in law is one of people in a dense community with a considerable division of labor among trades, professions, and livelihoods, as well as one in which crime, policing, and public services are concentrated in their scope and function. Some laws that would be unreasonable in a rural area become essential in an urban area, and vice versa.

*See also:* rural.

**urban blight**  *See:* blight, urban blight.

**urban redevelopment**  *See:* municipality, urban renewal (urban redevelopment).

**urban renewal**  *See:* municipality, urban renewal (urban redevelopment).

**urf**  A social custom that is considered a source of law. Urf is custom in Islamic law. In Usul al–Fiqh, it is one of the sources of law when a thing or action is not expressly regulated in the Qur'an, the Sunnah, or other more preferred sources; urf is used in Muamalaat or business transactions.

*See also:* custom (customary).

**usage**  Long practice that has grown into custom. Usage in law is a practice or custom of language or action within a relevant community of individuals and entities with shared practices. Usages vary in the scope of the community in which they exist, and a given usage may be common across a culture, within a whole trade or commercial sector, within a profession, among people in a given geography, or among a small group of people in communication among themselves. Within that community, a usage may give rise to an expectation like a custom, such that a person or entity would be reasonably expected to employ the usage by another person or entity in a community, or, more often, the significance of a usage by a member of the community would be reasonably expected by another member of the community to be in keeping with the shared meaning and practice of the custom in the community.

Usages as language are very common. Thus, a legal usage is a particular meaning or definitional significance common to a word or phrase among lawyers. A trade usage is a phrase with a particular meaning in the contracts employed within a trade. There are, for instance, usages specific to insurance contracts, and to construction contracts, and to professional representation contracts. A regional usage is a usage common among speakers or writers in an area, whether within a sub-subculture of a profession or a trade or more generally. Thus, certain legal usages may be specific to the lawyers of one or a few states, such as the practice of some states of referring to members of the bar as "the honorable" in lieu of being titled "esquire," and a practice may be represented by such a phrase.

Usages are also practices and actions that become commonly expected, which may reach a point of expectation that amounts to custom. Usage may determine a standard of liability even if the usage is not to the level of custom, when a usage demonstrates the course of ordinary prudence or reasonable conduct.

*See also:* reasonable (reasonableness).

**trade usage**   A practice, method, or jargon unique to a specific trade. Trade usage is the language and custom of the sub-culture formed within a specialized trade. Trade in this sense may be variably defined but is to some degree recognizable by the very existence of such a sub-culture, with a vocabulary and practices that are widely shared within it, specialized to tasks performed or commodities employed by it, and distinct from the talk and custom of the broader community. Contract terms that employ trade usage, such as the identity of goods or practices, are to be understood according to the accepted practices and meanings of the trade. Standards of reasonable conduct by members of trades are usually determined by reference to trade usage.

*See also:* trade, trade association.

**USCG**   *See:* coast, Coast Guard (USCG).

**use**   The employment of, or benefit from, a thing. Use has several categories of meaning in law, all derived from the general idea of the function or employment to which something is put, as in the use of a tool or the use of the land. Law has general senses of use in that context as well as specific senses of a use in the law of property and equity.

In its most general sense, a use is the function for which some property is employed. A house, for instance, may be used as a residence, or a commercial business, or a place of unlawful activity. Each function is a use of that structure.

One sense of use is as the consumption or exploitation of a thing, perhaps for a given purpose, though not necessarily. For example, to use coal or gas to generate electricity is to consume those fuels for the purpose of power generation. To use people in this sense is to treat the persons involved as means to an end.

Use in its more specific legal sense as the employment of some property signals either a right of ownership, right to possess, or right to do something related to the property. Thus an owner and a tenant may have a right to use property, but so may a person with an easement or license, depending on the nature of the easement or license. Not every license or easement gives a right of

use; a covenant not to build on a property given by the owner of Blackacre to the owner of Whiteacre does not give a right to use Blackacre.

The contemporary sense of the use of property is more general and is distinct from the use in property that was recognized in the common law and equity. That use was a benefit in property that was segregated from its actual ownership. This is the sense of the cestui que use, the person who enjoys the benefit of the use possessed by the feofee of property subject to use. It was protected by the doctrine of uses, manifested in a host of statutes and common-law rules. This sense of use has generally been supplanted by the modern doctrines of the trust. That sense of use is explored further below in doctrine of uses.

**use immunity**   *See:* immunity, witness immunity, use immunity.

**use tax**   *See:* tax, use tax.

**doctrine of uses (equitable use or beneficial use)**   Property in a thing may be divided into ownership and use. The doctrine of uses is a common law doctrine, altered by the English Statute of Uses but still viable even after it was largely superseded by the law of trusts, that allows a tenant to enfeoff a new tenant subject to the use of another, so that the tenant holds the property and manages it but transfers the benefits and profits from the property to the third party. The holder in fee, the terre-tenant, could be directed in the use of the property by the party with the right to the use of the property, who is the cestui que use.

**cestui que use**   The beneficiary of the use in another's property. A cestui que use is a person to whose use another party, the terre-tenant, is holding lands. The cestui que use is the recipient of rents or profits, or any other benefits segregated from the property, and the cestui que use ordinarily held a power to direct the terre-tenant in the management of the property and the handling of income or assets generated by the property. The cestui que use could descend through inheritance.

**statute of uses**   Ownership and a use could be united into a single ownership in fee simple. The Statute of Uses (1535) attempted to restrict the employment of the use, a forerunner of the trust, so that the use could neither be employed to cut out the heirs of a landowner nor be employed to deny fees to the crown. The statute was very technical and did not apply to all uses. For example, one limitation was that only estates in esse subject to a use that were neither copyholds nor a use on a use were subject to the act. The act was not easy to enforce and resulted largely in the restructuring of uses to fall within statutory exceptions or exclusions to allow conveyances, particularly for bargain and sale.

**use of property (use and occupation)**   An employment, function, or purpose to which property is put. A use of property is its enjoyment, occupation, or otherwise the manner in which a person or entity engages with and exercises control over the property. A use of property may vary in its designation by both the use and the user, so that there is a difference understood between public use and private use, as well as exclusive use or common use, all of which turn on the identity of the user. Likewise, commercial use, private use, appurtenant use, reasonable use, limited use, and other functional definitions of use describe not only the use itself but also limits of license or legal balances of property interests.

**beneficial use**  Common resources may be taken for a beneficial use. A beneficial use is a use of a natural resource to which the owner of a parcel has a right in common with others, when the use is not wasteful and is related to the use of the land. The beneficial use is a limit on the taking of resources by one owner when the resources are owned (or have rights of access) by several owners. The most common disputes arise over water, like the water of a river subject to numerous riparian holders. Other resources are subject to similar limits when one of several landholders occupy or take the resource. Some jurisdictions employ a functional test for beneficial use, in that the use must be enjoyed by the landholder and may not place a commercial purpose not related to the land above an interest related to the land.

*See also:* water, water rights.

**charitable use (pious use)**  Use of property for the support of a charity. A charitable use is the use of property by, or for the support of, a non–profit corporation or charity. Care must be taken because while nearly all contemporary use of this term refers to the actual ownership or use of lands or other assets by or for a charity, the term could be used to signify the use or a trust. A charitable use for the benefit of a religious foundation, such as a church or religious non–profit corporation, is a pious use.

**conditional use**  *See:* zoning, conditional zoning; taking, regulatory taking, conditional use.

**entire use**  The control exercised by a spouse who holds as a tenant by the entirety. Entire use is the control that either husband or wife may exercise over a property they hold as tenants by the entireties. As each is seized *per tout*, neither has the right to alienate any portion of the property without the consent of the other; but as neither are seized *per my*, neither has the right to alienate, give, or devise their interest in the land. Tenancy by the entirety is also characterized by the right of survivorship, in which the surviving spouse will inherit the whole of the estate in fee simple.

**exclusive use**  Use limited to specific users or specific purposes. Exclusive use of property has three distinct senses. One is a customary aspect of ownership, which is the right to exclude others from the use of property, a right that may be licensed to others, as in a lease. The second is a scope of license that may be transferred, so that an interest in a property is limited only to the use of the recipient, such as the exclusive use of the licensee of a copyrighted song. The third is a limitation on use according to purpose of function, either in a grant, or by regulation, or by voluntary limitation as in a covenant, so that the holder of property has limited the use of some property only to its exclusive use.

*See also:* exclusion (exclude).

**highest and best use**  The most valuable use of property. The highest and best use is the use of property that is the most valuable use. This is the use according to which property is valued for the purposes of determining a fair value when it is condemned through eminent domain proceedings. Thus, undeveloped property being held for development may be priced at its highest best use as if it were purchased for development rather than priced as mere empty land. Even so, land is presumed to be used for its highest, best use.

**public use**  The use of property by the state or the general public. Public use signifies several different uses of land. Foremost is ownership of property by a government, whether the government is a municipality, state, the United States, or a subdivision of any of them. Thus, the taking of private property for a public use, as described in the Takings Clause, contemplates the taking of the land in condemnation to be held by the government in fee. Public use also signifies a regulatory interest in private land, such that a limitation of a use by regulation constitutes the intrusion of the regulatory power into the fee of the land, thus creating a public use. Public use may also describe the right of the public to enter and use property, and an easement to the benefit of the public creates a public use, even if no government is the holder of the easement on the public's behalf.

*See also:* taking (takings or taking of private property without just compensation).

**reasonable use (reasonable-use theory)**  A use of land or water that is not too harmful or unusual. A reasonable use of land or natural resources is a use that is in keeping with the customary uses by other land holders in the region. A reasonable use does not create an unusual level of harm to others with lands or use of the same resource, and any harm created is similar to that usually suffered by those in the same community of landholders and resource users. A use of land or water that creates a significantly greater harm than that customarily inflicted by a member of the community of landholders or resource users, or that has a harmful quality or effect that is unusual in the community, is not reasonable.

**usefulness**  Having a private or commercial benefit. Usefulness in an object is its capacity to be put to gainful use. This contrasts with objects that are obsolete or non-functioning for the purpose for which they are designed. Thus, a useful life is the expected time over which a product may be expected to function as intended, after which the product may continue in fact to be useful, although its value or cost may have already been amortized to nothing.

*See also:* utility, functional utility.

**useful life**   *See:* life, useful life.

**useless-gesture exception**   *See:* search, knock-and-announce rule, useless-gesture exception.

**USRAP**   *See:* perpetuity, rule against perpetuities, wait-and-see test, uniform statutory rule against perpetuities (USRAP).

**usual (unusual)**   Customary or ordinary under the circumstances. Usual depicts the customary practice or behavior under certain circumstances. By its very nature, "usual" incorporates a tension between the long-standing nature of custom and the evolutionary nature of custom. Unusual is anything that is not usual or is contrary to the usual; it need only conflict with custom rather than reject it.

*See also:* punishment, cruel and unusual punishment.

**usufruct**   The right to the benefits of the property of another. Usufruct is the benefit one may have in another's property, literally in Latin, to take the fruits of another's property. A civil law concept in use in Louisiana, it is similar to a servitude or profits a prendre in the common law. An example of usufruct is for a grantor to grant ownership of a property to one member of a family while granting the usufruct to all members of the family, thus dividing the interests in the land and ensuring that the family as a whole has such profits as come from it, while the responsibility of management remains with one member. Usufruct may also be used to divide other interests, such as the life-time usufruct, which is similar to the common-law life estates.

**usul al-fiqh**   *See:* shari'a, fiqh, usul al-fiqh (usul al'fiqh, usool al-fiqh).

**usurpation (usurp or usurper)**   To displace the rightful holder of an office or property. Usurpation is the act of unauthorized replacement of a person, group, or system of authority from its office, property or power with another. A usurpation of government is a rebellion or revolution, although a political usurpation may be accomplished with lawful authority if done through the regularly constituted process of election. A person who usurps the office or authority of another is a usurper.

**usurpation of property**   Unlicensed entry or use of the property of another. Usurpation of property is an unlicensed and uninvited use by one party of the property owned by another. Usurpation of realty is a trespass, and usurpation of a chattel is either a conversion or a trespass to chattel. Usurpation for the period of limitations may, however, ripen into adverse possession or prescription.

**usury (usurious)**   Interest so excessive that it violates the law. Usury is interest charged by a lender of money to a borrower at a rate of interest over the lawful ceiling on such charges. It is also the act of making a loan at such a rate of interest. Loans of money for the purpose of usury include the extension of credit implied in an option to purchase and in a repurchase agreement. Usury was prohibited under canon law and remains prohibited under Islamic law, as well as the law of most states. The federal government, however, has no usury law, and most federally chartered financial institutions are exempt from state usury limits. Even so, state laws govern private loans and loans by other institutions and private lenders, and such loans may not be usurious. The state limits on interest that define usury vary widely, from 8 percent to 45 percent, with some defining usury as the sum of a federal funds rate plus some additive amount. Loans made at a usurious rate of interest are usually considered void and unenforceable, although the act of usury is a crime in many jurisdictions, often known by its slang term, "loan sharking."

*See also:* RIBA; interest, interest for money, annual percentage rate (APR); interest, interest for money; lender.

**uterus (utero or in utero)**   The womb of the female. The uterus is the organ of the female body in which the fetus is conceived and develops, in ordinary pregnancies, where it stays until the moment of birth. A fetus in utero is in place within the body of the mother.

*See also:* abortion (abort); fetus (fetal, foetus or unborn child); in, in vitro.

**utility**   The sum of a thing's potential for happiness, or its value. Utility, as a matter of legal theory or economics, is a measure of the value of an action, law, rule, or any thing. In economics, utility is the expected utility, or the preference given to an unknown return. In utilitarian jurisprudence, utility is the sum of the happiness created less the happiness destroyed by the thing in question.

Note: the colloquial, contemporary understanding of utility is now merely functional utility, or usefulness. The usage as a matter of legal philosophy is distinct and remains the balance of pain versus pleasure caused by an action or by a law, in any of the analogs of this comparison.

*See also:* jurisprudence, utilitarianism.

**functional utility**   Having a capability for use. Utility, when used in a sense other than as a theoretical tool of utilitarianism or as a public source of power, light, and waste management, generally means functionality. To describe a thing's utility is to describe the bases of its usefulness.

*See also:* usefulness.

**public utility**   A source of public services such as power, water, and sewerage. A public utility is a provider of a public service for a fee, particularly an entity that provides electricity or natural gas, water, sewer services, waste disposal services, and telecommunications services. Which providers are considered utilities as a matter of law varies from jurisdiction to jurisdiction. Most public utilities are related owing to the cost reductions of allowing a natural monopoly in the services provided by a utility, so that services are not duplicated. In theory, the potential for monopolistic behavior and pricing that arises from allowing such a monopoly is offset by regulation of rates and the conditions of service.

**utter (utterly)**   The most extreme example. Utter as an adjective comes from the same idea, that is the utmost or outer sense of any word or statement. Thus, an utter refusal is as complete a refusal as possible, and an utter scoundrel is a severe example of a scoundrel. As an adverb, it is utterly, as in utterly scandalous. Note: utter in this sense should not be confused with utter as a verb, which is different.

*See also:* utter, uttering.

**uttering**   To make something public, or to put something into circulation. Uttering is to make a statement, to publish a libel, or to issue or to pass an instrument, or otherwise to cause some thing, statement, or idea to move from one's own control into the control of another or of the public. From the old English for outside, the term implies either making something public or putting it into public circulation. Note: the verb, to utter, should not be confused with utter the adjective.

*See also:* utter (utterly).

**uxor (ux.)**   A wife. Uxor was a customary term for wife, usually one's own wife or the wife of a husband pleading in an action, but uxor, like feme covert, once represented any married woman. It is now obsolete but still commonly found in older pleadings.

**et uxor (et ux.)**   And spouse. Et ux., the abbreviation of et uxor, was once frequently used to designate a pleading by a husband and wife, naming the husband and adding the wife designation. It is possible for uxor to stand for either spouse, yet women were overwhelmingly more likely to be so designated. Although it was once an aspect of representation through a spouse when women lacked standing, it persists as a signal of marital interests in property. When the phrase occurs as part of vir et uxor it means man and wife.

> If the words express the meaning of the parties plainly, distinctly, and perfectly, there ought to be no other means of interpretation; but if the words are obscure, or ambiguous, or imperfect, recourse must be had to other means of interpretation, and in these three cases, we must collect the meaning from the words, or from probable or rational conjectures, or from both.
>
> Ware v. Hylton, 3 U.S. (3 Dall.) 199, 239–40 (1796) (Chase, C.J.).

# V

**v** The twenty-second letter of the modern English alphabet. "V" signifies a variety of functions as a symbol and as a designation of status. It is translated into Victor for radio signals and NATO military transmissions, into Victor for some police radio traffic, and into dot, dot, dot, dash in Morse Code. The use of the letter "v" in Latin descended from the Upsilon (Y or u) in Greek, but it became was common as "v" in Latin and Romance Languages. Nonetheless, the use of "v" was rather unsettled in medieval printing as well as in pronunciation, and some senses of "v" shifted to "u" (and vice versa), and sometimes "w" was formed by two typeset "v"s between 1500 and the 1650s.

**v as a roman numeral** Latin symbol for five (5). V is five when used as a numeral. In the Roman system of numeralization, the addition of a V to the right of another Roman numeral adds 5 to the numerical value. The addition of a V to the left of another Roman numeral subtracts 5 from the numerical value.

**v as an abbreviation** A word commencing in V. When used as the sole letter of an abbreviation, V usually stands for versus. In Shepardization, it means vacated or, sometimes, void. It also often stands for vagrant, Valparaiso, variable, various, vehicle, vehicular, Venezuela, verb, verba, version, veteran's, vice, victim, Victoria, vide, Villanova, voce, voci, and volume. V.I. is Virgin Islands. It may also stand for the initial of the name of an author or case reporter, such as Vernon's, Vermont, and Virginia.

**v as in hypotheticals** Victim. V often stands for victim in criminal in law school hypothetical questions or law enforcement training and documentation.

**v. or contra or c.** *See:* versus (v. or contra or c.).

**V.A.T or VAT or value added tax** *See:* tax, value-added tax (V.A.T or VAT or value added tax).

**vacancy (vacant)** Anything that is empty or unoccupied. Vacancy is the condition of being without an occupant or contents. A legal or public office is vacant when there is no incumbent person validly assigned to perform the duties of that office. Property is vacant when it is unoccupied or unused in any meaningful or profitable manner.

**vacancy appointment** *See:* appointment, recess appointment (vacancy appointment).

**vacation** A period when court is not regularly in session. Vacation is the period between terms of court. In most jurisdictions, a judge retains authority over cases filed in the court and may hear new matters on an emergency basis; in rare instances, a judge in vacation may summon a grand jury, but usually juries are not summoned by the court out of term.

Vacation is also used in lieu of vacatur to describe the action of vacating an order or other ruling.

**vacatur (vacate)** The annulment of a court ruling, or a remedy to do so. To vacate a ruling is to annul it, treating it as if it had not been issued. As a case moves forward in the court system, a court may, on its own motion, vacate its own opinion within its discretion if doing so would correct an error or provide for more efficient disposition of a case. On appeal, an appellate court may vacate an earlier ruling or order, rather than reverse it, particularly if the court determines that the earlier order was entered without jurisdiction, or was entered in an action that was unripe, moot, or unjusticiable, or the appellate opinion substitutes for the vacated opinion.

Vacatur, the noun for the act of vacating an order, is a designation for a remedy by which a party or parties to an action seek to vacate an order in that action or an earlier proceeding. Though both parties may join in the motion, vacatur is usually sought by a defendant who settles an action following an adverse ruling, and seeks to bar the use of that ruling by other plaintiffs with similar claims. Vacatur limits the precedential effect of the ruling, and in cases in which the vacated order or opinion has not been published, a vacated opinion may become unavailable to third parties.

The remedy of vacatur is disfavored in the courts as a matter of policy. Not only does vacatur encourage the wasting of judicial resources but also the use of a remedy to favor one party that denies knowledge to litigants situated similarly to the other party distorts the legal process. A court may enter vacatur under Rule 60, however, for specific reasons that demonstrate cause or that the interests of justice outweigh the presumption against it.

**vagabond** An itinerant vagrant. A vagabond is a person of no fixed residence who in one place or another engages in vagrancy from time to time; a traveling homeless person. The law once designated a person as a vagabond, which was a status offense. Contemporary standards of due process forbid the use of a status offense.

**vagrant (vagrancy)** A homeless person. A vagrant, at common law, was a person of no known address, who was to give an account of the person's means and purpose or be arrested under the laws for the regulation of the poor. Similar laws persisted in the U.S. until 1972, when vagrancy laws were declared unconstitutionally vague. The term persists as a term describing a homeless person, especially one who commits a crime.

*See also:* loitering (loiterer or loiter); offense, status offense (status offender or juvenile status offense or juvenile status offender).

**vagueness (vague)** An uncertain meaning in a text or statement. Vagueness is an imprecision in any communication that causes meaning to become unclear and uncertain. Vagueness in language arises when a single concept or statement has a range of possible meanings, which is sufficiently wide to provoke confusion as to which meanings are intended or included and which are not. Vagueness in law includes not only this sense, but also the sense of ambiguity, in which some words or concepts may signal two or more different meanings.

A law or order affecting the rights, obligations, or powers of the people that is sufficiently vague that an ordinary person would not be given sufficient notice of what was required or forbidden violates due process of law. Such laws may be unconstitutional generally or as applied, if the application is not reasonably predictable from the terms of the law.

A vague and material term in a contract will necessitate its interpretation by a court of law, which may read according to collateral evidence of the parties' intent, or read the term against the interests of the party drafting it or the party with the greater economic power and sophistication in the negotiation. A term so vague or a contract of such form that such interpretation is not possible may be void.

A complaint or other pleading initiating an action that is so vague that it fails to put the other party on notice of the grounds of the action brought may be dismissed, or it may be the basis for an order for a more sufficient statement.

Determining when a law is vague can be difficult, because lawyers and others who are used to a specialized meaning or customary understanding of a term may find that a term's meaning is clear, though the term remains unintelligible, ambiguous, or imprecise to others. Vagueness thus must be assessed according to the community that must interpret the law, and if the law is reasonably susceptible to more than one meaning within that community, or if the scope of the law would be unknown, the law is vague. As a matter of jurisprudence, vagueness has been argued over at least since ancient Greeks debated how many grains of rice make a heap and how few hairs mean a man is bald. One answer is the law of excluded middle, to define every

idea by whether it is fully met or not met at all. This bivalent approach (everything is either in or out, one or not–one with the definition of the word) has been challenged by the use of ordinary language and multivalence, which thrive on the ambiguity in every concept, testing each application to see if it is more or less in the concept, not in or out of it. In this vein, seeing words, rules, or concepts as having a central case and peripheral cases is an application of vagueness.

*See also:* rhetoric.

**vagueness doctrine (void for vagueness doctrine)** Every legal requirement the state enforces must be clear in what is required. The vagueness doctrine is a constitutional requirement within due process of law, which demands that every criminal liability, and every regulation enforced by the federal or state government that burdens a constitutional right, must be clear in the obligations placed upon the citizen, so that the citizen can determine what conduct will comply and what conduct will not comply with the law, and so that the official enforcing the law is able to do so according to fair and consistent standards without arbitrary or ad hoc interpretation. Therefore, vagueness bars the enforcement of a law that creates a criminal liability or regulatory burden on a right either if the law fails to provide the kind of notice that will enable ordinary people to understand what conduct it prohibits; or if the law authorizes arbitrary and discriminatory enforcement.

Due process requires every criminal and regulatory law to be clear or to lack vagueness. Even so, purely economic regulations are held to a broader standard that is more tolerant of some imprecision than laws that burden rights or create a criminal penalty.

*See also:* lenity (rule of lenity); notice, fair notice doctrine.

**validity (invalidity or invalid or invalidation or valid or validation or validate)** In full force as a matter of law, or true as a matter of fact and reason. Validity has two distinct senses in law. The first is the aspect of a rule, statute, or law, or an agreement, contract, will, or trust in which it is in force. A valid law, doctrine, or instrument is effective, having been passed or created by sufficient and authorized means and being strong enough as a source of obligation that it should be respected by those bound to it and given effect by the legal institution. The second sense of validity used in law is closer to its more general sense as a measure of the observation of logic that underlies all reasoning, that a statement is supported by the facts or by logic. A valid observation, argument, or claim has strong evidence and reason to sustain it.

**value (valuation)** The worth of a person or thing, or test of merit. Value is merit, and in certain senses related to people, ideas, and things, value is the sum of the merit or goodness contained. Thus, a value held by a person is a moral preference, a measure by which certain actions, ideas, or things are esteemed by that person. In this sense, value is equivalent to virtue, and some observers believe that value in this sense is an objective measure, and so values are incommensurable: there is no way to trade one value for another. Yet when value represents what a person will trade for a thing, a service, or an idea, value is a measure of what one person will exchange for something else, its worth relative to other things of value. That concept of relative worth is both a matter of the moment when it is made and a matter then that estimates the future worth that the person trading or others might assess.

For most purposes in law, value is what a thing is worth, whether the thing is a tangible property, service, or any other thing. When no other aspect of value is specified, the presumptive value is equivalent to market value. Market value is what a willing, informed buyer would pay to a willing, informed seller, if there is no pressure on the sale from time, finance, or other extrinsic forces than competition to purchase the one thing from other buyers or to sell similar things by other sellers. Market value might or might not be equal to a price offered by the seller alone, although price is a substitute for market value when comparable sales at the asking price are common. There are many other aspects of value, though, including depreciated value, replacement value, insured value, tax value, each assessed using a specific methodology. Both value and valuation are used as a noun and as a verb, though as a noun, a thing's value is the same as its valuation. As a verb, valuation is the means of ascertaining how much one values the thing.

*See also:* price (sale price).

**valuable consideration** *See:* consideration, valuable consideration.

**book value (net asset value)** The value of the material assets of a business less its liabilities. Book value is the worth of a business, measured by its tangible assets minus its liabilities, both of which are accounted by means of a standard asset–liability balance sheet. Intangible assets, particularly good will, are not included in book value. Therefore, book value is usually less than fair value or real value, and is a useful approximation of net asset value.

**commodification (monetization or dollarization)** Valuation of anything only by its trading value in commerce. Commodification, is a theoretical process for quantifying the value of something that is not a traded commodity, usually by comparison to a market or by analogy to something else that is a traded commodity, in order to assess the value it would have if it were a commodity. Thus, a value may be estimated of things that do not have a legal market, such as a human life or an endangered animal, by estimation or comparison to the worth people will trade for it, without regard to its moral or intrinsic worth. When the result is expressed as money, the process is terms monetization or as dollarization.

**cost-benefit analysis (CBA)** A comparison of the benefit to the costs of a specific action or rule. A cost-benefit analysis is an analysis of the sum of the effects of an action, particularly of a regulation, rule, or law, to determine its reasonableness by examining whether it will ultimately add value or diminish value in the economy. Cost–benefit analysis requires the monetization of all benefits as well as of all costs for their comparison.

Every federal agency must complete a cost–benefit analysis of new regulations before the regulation is promulgated, which must demonstrate that the benefits to society outweigh the costs that the regulation will impose. The CBA of a pollution control rule would, for instance, require the agency to monetize the statistically likely benefit to human health and the environment from reduced pollution, minus the costs of compliance to be borne by the polluters. The rule is reasonable if the cost of compliance is less than the benefits of reduced pollution. (The process by which this is routinely done, however, accounts for all acts of compliance as costs alone rather than as benefits, even though the cost to the regulated entity is often a benefit to society because it is a profit to a vendor to the regulated entity. That profit is usually omitted from the federal cost–benefit analysis.)

*See also:* president, White House, Office of Management and Budget, Office of Information and Regulatory Affairs (OIRA); order, executive order, Executive Order 12866 (Economic Analysis of Rulemaking).

**economic life** The period of a thing's profitability, or the economy as a whole. Economic life is a metaphor with at least two distinct senses. More commonly, it is the period of profitable use that may be expected or that has been exhausted by a thing, whether it is a person (especially an employee), a product, a machine or assembly line, a patent or other intellectual property, or anything else that may be used to generate a profit. The depreciation of a capital asset is calculated using an estimate of the asset's economic life.

The other sense of economic life is non-technical, which is as a synonym for economy, the interaction of people in economic terms in a community, nation, or other grouping.

**enterprise value** The value a buyer would pay for a whole enterprise. Enterprise value is the fair market value for a business or enterprise, an estimate of what a willing, reasonable, and knowledgeable buyer would be willing to pay using ordinary financing to acquire the whole of a given enterprise on a designated day.

**free cash flow** The money that can be taken from an enterprise without hurting operations. Free cash flow is the greatest amount of money in an enterprise at a given moment that could be removed from the enterprise without impairing operations. Free cash flow is the limit of funds available to pay the holders of long-term debt or of equity, which is to say that free cash flow must service bonds and other debt and also forms the basis of dividend payments to shareholders.

**going-concern value (value as a going concern)** Value of an enterprise as an operating business. Going–concern value is the value of an enterprise as a business, including not only its capital and material assets but also its good will, market share, and other intangible assets, the sum of which is presumed to exceed the value of its net capital value, the amount that could be realized in liquidation.

**hedonic valuation**  The value of the enjoyment people derive from life, from others, or from any thing. Hedonic valuation is an estimation of the worth of the enjoyment or happiness realized by an individual or people generally from any thing. Hedonic valuation of a person's life would be based not on income or earnings but upon the sum of happiness realized by that person from everything in that person's life (including those things bought by wealth) as well as the net happiness others realize as a result of their knowledge or contact with the person. Net happiness is the sum of hypothetical quanta of happiness minus unhappiness.

Monetizing hedonic valuation is inherently controversial. A popular means is to survey a group of individuals to ask how much money, or what portion of their money, would they pay to realize in their lives some opportunity for happiness (or pay to avoid some opportunity for unhappiness).

**liquidation value**  The likely value of assets if they are forced into a sale. Liquidation value is an estimate of the value of property, either a particular thing or the sum of assets of an enterprise, discounted below market value by the presumed effect of the conditions required to sell the property quickly under the compulsion of liquidation. The liquidation value of an enterprise is discounted from book value rather than from value as a going concern, since the concern would no longer be going.

**market value (market value rule)**  The price a thing would be reasonably likely to receive in the market at a given moment. Market value is a reasonable estimate of the value of a thing according to the price prevailing for comparable things in a public market for the thing in issue at a specific day or time and in an appropriate locale. Market value cannot be measured only by a price offered or accepted for the thing, because of the many variables that might affect both the buyer's decisions to make a single purchase at a given price and the seller's decisions to sell and to accept a given price. Rather, market value is assessed by comparison to similar sales at the same time in the most analogous market available for things of a comparable type. The relevant market for comparison should be the market that would otherwise be resorted to by the parties: goods that would be replaced by a party at a wholesale market should be valued in a wholesale market, but goods that would be replaced by a party in a resale market should be priced in a resale market. And, the market should be in the place or reflect prices in the place where replacement would be made.

The market value rule requires damages for lost goods or cargo to be assessed according to market value, unless a more accurate means of assessing value is available.

**fair market value (FMV)**  What a willing buyer would pay in cash to a willing seller for property at a given time. Fair market value is the measure of value or property assessed for most governmental purposes, including for the computation of taxable value. Fair market value is the amount the government must pay in compensation for the taking of private property for a public use under eminent domain or regulatory takings.

The measure of fair market value is a reasonable estimate of what a willing buyer, who is reasonable and knowledgeable, would pay in cash for the property at the time of the taking to a willing seller, who is also willing and reasonable. No adjustment is made to fair market value to account for an increase or decrease in the value of the property that would be caused by the governmental use of the property or nearby properties used or condemned by the government for the same project.

Fair market value in other contexts is effectively the same as market value generally.

**par value**  Lowest value for which a security may be sold. Par value is the lowest price at which a security may be sold. Par value is often a somewhat arbitrary amount asserted as the basis of nominal worth when issuing securities and is generally only used to calculate franchise tax liability for businesses. Par value has only an accidental relationship to market value.

**present value (future value)**  The current measure of future worth. Present value is a means of estimating the value in the present of an asset that will not be realized or disbursed until a time or a period of time in the future. It is a function of future value, the rate of return anticipated on investment, and time. Thus, future value is also a function of present value. To compute present value from future value, one must know or estimate both the rate of return and time frame by which the future is defined. Present value then equals future value, divided by the result of the rate return +1 to the power of the number of years. This is $PV = FV/(r+1)y$.

Future value is the estimated value of a given investment over a given period of time at an estimated or known rate of return. Future value is computed in the same manner as compound interest. To compute future value from present value, one must know or estimate both the rate of return and the time frame by which the future is defined. Future value then equals present value times the rate of return +1 to the power of the number of years. This is $FV-PV(r+1)y$ (assuming the return is compounded only once annually).

**actuarial value**  The present value of a pension plan compared to expected mortality of its members. Actuarial value is the calculation of the present value of a pension plan, computed to determine the value of assets as against the statistically likely claims that may be made on the assets by members between retirement and death.

*See also:* actuary.

**salvage value (residual value or scrap value)**  Value remaining after its full depreciation. Salvage value is the value of an asset or property at the end of its useful life. Salvage value is estimated by calculating the value of the property's use after it has been fully depreciated or by estimating the worth that is reasonably likely to be received if the property is sold. Salvage value may be nothing if the property is incapable of sale, and it may be negative if greater cost will be incurred in disposal than the value that is likely to be realized by it. Under the Uniform Commercial Code, a seller whose buyer breaches a contract for finished goods that are unfinished at the time of the breach may mitigate damages, either by finishing and selling the goods or selling them for their salvage value.

**terminal value**  Estimated present value that a thing will have in the future. Terminal value is a means of estimating the present value that a security or company will have at a future time. Terminal value is a means, for instance of estimating a future enterprise value. Terminal value is assessed using either of two methods, the perpetuity growth model, which is used to consider an enterprise value assuming continuing cash flow, and the exit multiple approach, which is used more often to estimate the future value of a business enterprise that will then be sold. Using either method, terminal value creates an anticipated value of a future value that might be paid for an enterprise by a purchaser at that time. Terminal value may also be used to mean salvage value.

See also: value, salvage value (residual value or scrap value).

**value-added tax**  See: tax, value-added tax (V.A.T or VAT or value added tax).

**vandalism (vandal)**  The unjustified and deliberate injury of another's property. Vandalism is the willful or deliberate destruction of or harm to property owned by another person without a legal justification for doing so. Vandalism is a crime by that name in some jurisdictions and considered within the offense of criminal mischief or malicious mischief in others.

Vandalism is of particular interest in insurance law, because insurance contracts may provide coverage or exclude coverage for damage suffered by the insured by acts of vandalism by others. Several courts have found the term vandalism in policies to be ambiguous as to certain losses caused by the acts of others, and so the term has been interpreted against the interests of the insurer. When the damage has been to real and to personal property, caused by arson, or caused by squatters as well as by other trespassers and passersby to realty the term has been found to be unambiguous.

Vandalism is a crime of moral turpitude under California law, for the purposes of impeachment evidence and, probably, sentencing.

See also: mischief, criminal mischief (malicious mischief).

**variance**  A difference between a specific instance and a general plan, or between two standards or data. Variance is difference in any significant degree. In law, variance is used in a variety of senses. In contemporary usage, a variance is often an allowance or permission, granted by a government agency to a person or entity it regulates, allowing the person or entity to be excepted from a general regulation, whether the exception is for a time or in perpetuity. This is its meaning as a zoning variance, but administrative variances of many kinds are common, each being allowed when the variance is in keeping with the overall plan of regulation.

Variance takes many forms in specific arenas of law, each being a difference that is of sufficient scale to be legally relevant. In pleading or evidence, it is a difference between a declaration in one pleading proffer and the corresponding declaration in another. Variance in construction law and in contracts generally is a distinction between the work ordered and the work performed, or the goods bought and the goods delivered. A variance in a plat is a deviation between what is described or drawn on a map and the physical characteristics on the ground.

See also: zoning, zoning variance (variance from zoning regulation).

**variance from zoning regulation**  See: zoning, zoning variance (variance from zoning regulation).

**varying acceptance**  See: acceptance, acceptance as acceptance of an offer, varying acceptance (acceptance at variance to an offer).

**VC or risk capital or start-up capital**  See: capital, commercial capital, venture capital (VC or risk capital or start-up capital).

**vector**  See: carrier, carrier of disease (vector).

**vegetative state**  See: death, vegetative state (persistent vegetative state or PVS).

**vehicle (motor vehicle)**  A machine for transporting people on land. A vehicle is a man-made device for the carriage over land of people, or people and goods. Vehicle includes both motor vehicle (or self-propelled or motorized vehicle) as well as non-motorized vehicles that are propelled by human energy or muscle. Although statutes may be specific in including or excluding examples in any definition, vehicle does not usually include machines for the carriage of people in or over water or in the air. The meaning of the term "vehicle" is especially sensitive to context to determine whether it includes only motor vehicles or only vehicles that might be driven on roads. Without such limitations, vehicle includes railroad engines and cars, tractors, graders, asphalt spreaders, riding lawn mowers, combines, automobiles, trucks, motorcycles, bicycles, tricycles, scooters, and all manner of specialized machines that carry one or more persons, including Zambonis.

The term "motor vehicle" is more specific than vehicle and includes only such machines as are self-propelled that have as their primary function the transport of people and goods or the performance of specific tasks that take place on roadways, or for which travel on roadways is essential. A motor vehicle may not be operated on the roads without a license from at least one jurisdiction to do so.

*See also:* pollution, air pollution, emission, motor vehicle emission standards.

**910 vehicle**  A vehicle purchased by a bankrupt within 910 days of the petition. A 910 vehicle is a vehicle purchased by a debtor on a date 910 days or less than the date the debtor later petitions for bankruptcy. Debts secured by a 910 vehicle may not be crammed down in the manner a vehicle owned for a longer period might be.

**vehicle exception**  *See:* search, warrantless search, automobile exception (vehicle exception).

**vehicular accident**  *See:* accident, vehicular accident (automobile accident or car accident).

**vehicular homicide**  *See:* homicide, vehicular homicide.

## veil (burqa or burqua or burka or niqab or purdah)

A face covering, or anything that cloaks its wearer or content. A veil is a cloth that hangs down over all or most of the face to conceal the wearer's features. Thus, the veil is common in legal drafting as a metaphor, whether as a noun or as a verb, for anything that cloaks or protects its wearer, as in the "corporate veil" or "veil of administrative secrecy."

The veil is of particular significance in some Muslim cultures, in which women customarily wear a veil, which takes one of two primary forms. The niqab (or nikab, or in Persian, purdah) covers the face alone. The burqa (or burka) covers the head and body. Western legal systems have wrestled with the conflict between religious freedoms on the one hand and concerns for both the need to identify individuals rapidly for security reasons and the sense that women so burdened by a culture are denied equal rights on the other. Such few U.S. precedents as exist suggest that the religious interest will be outweighed by a state interest in identification. Note: the custom of wearing a veil is distinct from that of the headscarf, or hijab.

*See also:* hijab.

**veil of ignorance**  *See:* justice, Rawlsian justice, veil of ignorance.

**corporate veil (piercing the corporate veil or pierce the corporate veil)**  Shareholder immunity for corporate liability may be breached. The corporate veil is a metaphor for the customary and statutory limitations against corporate shareholders, which makes them usually immune from personal actions brought to recover for actions committed by the corporation. The extent of the shareholder's ordinary liability is the loss that may be suffered by the corporation that is payable from its assets, which in turn reduces the shareholder's equity in the corporation.

The corporate veil may be pierced, allowing a direct action against a shareholder, in unusual circumstances that are evaluated on a case-by-case basis but that include the domination of the corporation by one or a small group of owners so that the corporation is effectively only an alter ego of its owner or owners, the failure to abide by the forms of incorporation and corporate practice, including a demonstration of reasonable independence in the action of the corporation from the owners themselves.

**alter-ego rule (instrumentality rule)**  Sufficient control of an alter ego may justify piercing a corporate veil. The alter-ego rule, or instrumentality rule, allows a claimant to pierce the corporate veil between two entities and to hold the parent entity, joint-stock entity, holding company, or other related enterprise liable for claims upon a subsidiary or other owned entity that amounts to no more than an instrumentality of the parent. A claimant who relies on this approach must demonstrate that the parent has control over the subsidiary not only in ownership or finances but also in directing policy and business practices related to the transaction in issue; that the control by the parent was used in an illegal manner, in a fraudulent manner, or to harm the claimant's rights that would be enforceable under the criminal or private law; and the plaintiff suffered harm as a result of the parent's direction of its subsidiary or the subsidiary's employees or operations. This stringent test for reaching one entity through another is used mainly in the enforcement of private interests, such as in contract or tort, and it is not the only test for holding one entity accountable for the conduct of its related entities.

**single-employer rule (single-entity test or integrated enterprise standard)**  A parent and a subsidiary may be one employer for federal regulatory analysis. The single employer rule requires separate business entities to be considered sometimes in the aggregate for determining the application of laws and regulations. The rule, also called the integrated enterprise test, allows a parent enterprise to be considered as one unit with a subsidiary, and also allows several subsidiaries or related enterprises to be considered one entity, both for the purpose of determining its number of employees and for the purpose of determining liability of the parent entity for the subsidiary. The rule applies if traditional conditions are present for piercing the corporate veil of the parent, such as the alter ego test; or if the enterprises had once been a common entity with a larger number of employees that was divided to avoid liability under the law; or if the parent corporation might have directed the discriminatory act of which the employee of the subsidiary complains.

*See also:* worker, Worker Adjustment and Retraining Notification Act (WARN Act); union, labor union, shop, double-breasted operation.

**vel**   Or. Vel is a conjunction that represents choice.

**vel non**   Or not. Vel non indicates a choice between one result or its opposite — it either is or it isn't — with an implication that there is no third choice or contingent outcome available. In this sense, vel non implies a duty to make a decision. As with the old proceeding to prove a will by devasavit vel non, in which a proffered testament either is the valid will or it is not, the state that something has an aspect vel non means that it either has or lacks that aspect. So, to say a court must find an employment practice discriminatory vel non is to say that the court must make a finding of whether or not the practice is discriminatory, and the court may not somehow evade the decision.

**vendor (vend or vendee)**   The seller. The vendor is the seller of property or services, and the vendee is the buyer. The difference between seller and vendor is one of emphasis: a vendor is usually not making a unique or one-time sale but tends to provide a service or sales to a vendee on a continuing basis or to provide commercial sales or services to the public. A vendor is usually required to have a license from its domiciliary state and to pay a sales tax.

**veniality (venial)**   Pardonable, or open to forgiveness or excuse. Veniality is the condition of an error or wrong that suggests it might be forgiven or excused. A slight offense or minor wrong that do not suggest a greater danger are venial.
   *See also:* trifle (trifling).

**venire (venire member or venireman or venire person)**   The jury pool. A venire, in contemporary practice, is the jury pool, the group of citizens summoned to serve on one or more juries during a period of time or for a particular jury. The members of the venire are usually selected at random from a jury wheel or from the voter rolls, or, more commonly now, from a computer program into which the names of adult residents are entered from either a census, tax roll, or voter roll. Once summoned, a venire is often maintained for a period of days or weeks in order to provide jurors as needed when a jury is required during that time. Practices in this regard vary from jurisdiction to jurisdiction.

   A member of the venire was once called a venireman, as all members of juries were male. Of the contemporary terms in replacement, venire member is less inelegant that venireperson.

   The term venire is a residual label from the common-law writ by which the sheriff was directed to summon the jury, the venire facias juratores. There were many venire writs, most of which were similar to a modern summons.
   *See also:* jury, jury selection (voir dire of the jury).

**special venire**   A jury pool for a specific trial or to supplement a jury. A special venire is summoned to provide a jury for a trial when no jury is already empaneled. The special venire allows a court to increase the available pool of jurors when the jury summoned as a matter of routine for a given period is either insufficient in size to hear all the actions that are to be tried or has had more members than expected excused from service. It is also used to provide a pool of qualified jurors to supplement a jury already seated in a given cause, and it is used to provide a jury for a trial when a venire is not already summoned as a matter of course.
   *See also:* special.

**venture (venturer)**   A business enterprise of some risk. A venture is any discrete business enterprise with an unusual level of risk for the backers or participants, usually an effort to establish a new business or develop an existing business into a new market. Venture itself is a corruption of the word "adventure." A venturer is a participant in a venture.

**venture capital**   *See:* capital, commercial capital, venture capital (VC or risk capital or start-up capital).

**joint venture (co-venturer or coventurer)**   An enterprise shared between two or more entities. A joint venture is a business entity created by two or more business entities, which enter into an agreement to share funding, profits or losses, and control over the new entity. A joint venture is a common device for businesses in different countries to partner in developing a new project, business, or market, particularly in a state with laws that limit foreign investment or foreign ownership of local businesses.

   There are many business reasons for such ventures. Joint ventures may involve technology transfers or the licensing of other intellectual property. They often provide a means for a company in one country to develop markets in other countries for its products through means other than sale or supply to other unrelated entities.

   A joint venture may be created by the venturers as an independent corporation; it may result from one company taking a significant equity stake and control in another; or it may result from a debt or equity restructuring. Only a separately incorporated joint venture may limit the liability for the venture to itself rather than passing liability through to the venturers.

   A co-venturer is a fiduciary of other co-venturers. No venturer may act to benefit solely from the joint venture but must act to the benefit of the venture a whole and in the best interests of all of the venturers.

**venue**   The jurisdiction within which is located a court. Venue is the extent of the geographic location of the jurisdiction for a court. It is the place where an action arises or a place to which jurisdiction over an action is created or taken. Venue is a legal idea that attaches to a specific region of geography because of the laws of jurisdiction and conflict of law. The scope of the geography that amounts to venue varies according to the law of the jurisdiction. In federal courts, venue is divided among the federal districts for the various U.S. District Courts. In state courts, it is usually the county or (in Louisiana) the parish.

Every action brought in a court of law or equity must be brought in the proper forum for a given venue, but the venue must itself be proper for the cause of action. In other words, the cause of action must arise in the venue or be an appropriate jurisdiction for parties to bring an action. If venue is improper in the place in which an action is brought, the action may be dismissed without prejudice and brought in a proper venue. More, the action may be moved by an order changing venue, which requires the transfer of the action to an appropriate court in the proper venue.

*See also:* situs.

**change of venue**  The transfer of an action, or a component from one court to another. Change of venue is the transfer of an action, or one phase of an action from one venue to another, so the court in which the action was pending transfers it to another court. Change of venue may be made for a variety of reasons, including the convenience of the parties, the convenience of the witnesses, proximity to potential evidence, the security of proceedings, the avoidance of publicity or interference with proceedings, and the fundamental rules of venue, though there is a strong presumption in favor of the plaintiff's choice of forum if venue there is proper. A change of venue in a state court may be from one court to another within the same county or from one county to another, or from one state to another state. Change of venue in a federal court may be from one division to another within a district, from one district to another within a state, from one district to another in another state. In the event jurisdiction was initially properly established with venue in the first court, if change of venue results in the action being transferred to another state, the law of the initial forum, from which the action was transferred, remains the substantive law applied in the proceeding.

**improper venue**  A court in which an action has been filed lacking the requirements of venue. Improper venue occurs when an action is filed in a court in which there is no venue for the action. In federal court venue is usually improper, for example, for an action brought in a district in which no defendant resides and in which there is no contested property or facts from which the action arose. Improper venue is a defense to an action and a basis for transfer, but it is waived if not timely raised by the defense or by the court sua sponte.

*improper venue and forum non conveniens*  Jurisdictional basis for a motion to dismiss. Improper venue is a defense to the action, while forum non conveniens presumes the action will be heard elsewhere. In deciding a motion to dismiss on the basis of improper venue, the court must determine that the cause of action did not arise or is not properly asserted within the venue over which it has jurisdiction. If so, the court may dismiss the action even if it might not be filed elsewhere, or transfer it. The motion for dismissal on the basis of forum non conveniens requires the court to determine a more appropriate forum does exist where the action may be heard, and the motion based on convenience may be granted even if the action could have been heard in that court.

**veracity (veracious)**  Truthfulness. Veracity is the habit of telling the truth, as well as the truthful content of a given statement. A false statement lacks veracity. Under Federal Rule of Evidence 608, character evidence in support or attack of a witness is barred, unless the evidence is of truthful character, which is to say, veracious. Though veracity is sometimes thought to mean trustworthy, and the two are related, they are not the same. Trust is reliance by one person that another will be truthful. Note: veracious means truthful; voracious means over-consuming.

**verbal**  Something done through direct speech. A verbal act is usually a spoken act, but technically it is something done through direct communication rather than in writing. In general, there is no difference between oral and verbal communication, though a person who relies upon a device other than the human mouth to speak communicates verbally but not orally.

*See also:* oral (orality); parol.

**verbal act**  *See:* act, verbal act.

**verbatim**  *See:* transcript, verbatim.

**verdict**  A statement of what the finder of fact believes is the truth in a case. A verdict is a statement by a jury of what it believes is the truth established by the evidence before it as to questions or issues that have been submitted to it for decision. The most common form of verdict is the jury verdict.

At common law, a jury could act only through a unanimous decision, and although in some jurisdictions unanimity is no longer required, the verdict is still a single statement of the whole, rendered to the judge on the jury's behalf by the foreperson. A jury's verdict answers a question or issue presented to it, which usually has at least two components and one presumption. The presumption establishes the burden of persuasion, so that one party must prove its case sufficiently for the jury to find a verdict in its favor; otherwise the party without the burden is to be awarded the verdict. The two components are a substantive question and the burden of proof. Unless the jury finds that the substantive issue submitted to it is proved to the level of proof required, the jury is instructed to render a verdict for the party without the burden of persuasion. So a jury may be asked to determine whether there is sufficient evidence to find a defendant guilty of larceny, in which case, the jury must believe that the prosecution has proved beyond a reasonable doubt that the defendant committed the larceny charged, in which case, it finds a verdict of guilt, or if it does not find that the prosecution has proved beyond a reasonable doubt that the defendant committed larceny, it finds a verdict of not guilty.

Verdict is derived from French, and before that Latin, from veredictum, which is as much a phrase as a word for, "you speak the truth," the same phrase in French from persists as voir dire.

Note: in the United States, a verdict is nearly always made by a jury, and the term "verdict" in a legal reference, without more, is highly likely to refer to the verdict of a jury. There are other forms of verdict, most notably the coroner's verdict, which may be issued by a coroner as an act of office, but is more usually the statement of a coroner's jury following an inquest. In more general parlance, a verdict is any judgment, including a slang reference to an election result, at least as to any one candidate's campaign. A judge or chancellor who sits as the finder of fact in an action does not, however, issue a verdict but renders findings of fact or a judgment.

*See also:* voir dire; plea, criminal plea, not guilty.

**compromise verdict (jury pardon or jury mercy)**  A verdict splitting the difference between strongly held views. A compromise verdict is a verdict reached by jurors who are at an impasse in reaching an agreed verdict, and rather than either negotiating until there is consensus or failing to reach a verdict, the members agree to a verdict that was not actually believed by the jury, but was a middling position between the two verdicts in which one faction or the other did believe. A compromise verdict in such circumstances is invalid. For example, a verdict to find a defendant guilty of a lesser included offense would be valid if the jurors supporting the verdict believe the evidence supports the truth of that verdict. Yet it would be invalid if the jury did not believe the evidence supported the truth of a lesser offense, but that some believed the evidence proved a more serious offense, and that others believed the evidence did not support the truth of any offense at all. A compromise verdict tends to moderate a criminal sentence as well as a plaintiff's award of damages from a defendant. A compromise verdict is sometimes referred to as jury mercy or a jury pardon (although a jury pardon is more properly applied to a verdict of not guilty).

*See also:* jury, jury nullification (jury lenity or jury annulment or jury pardon power or jury mercy-dispensing power).

**coroner's verdict**  A coroner's statement of the cause of death and the way in which it occurred. A coroner's verdict is a determination of the cause of death of a person found to have died or located after death within a jurisdiction. The scope of the findings varies slightly from state to state, but the verdict generally is required to find whether death was by natural causes, homicide, suicide, accident, or undetermined causes. In some states, the circumstances of death are also rendered. In general a coroner's verdict is rendered by a coroner's jury following an inquest. Some jurisdictions have altered the procedures of inquest to rely on forensic examination by a medical examiner, although the report of the coroner is still called a verdict. A verdict is usually not admissible as evidence in a criminal trial to determine the guilt of a person accused of the homicide reported in a verdict, although it is presumptively admissible for other purposes, including proof of death and cause of death.

**directed verdict**  A verdict found by the judge rather than the jury. A directed verdict is a verdict entered by the court in an action before a jury, but found by the court in lieu of referral of an issue or action to a jury, on the basis of evidence in favor of the verdict so persuasive that no rational jury could find for the other side.

Although a directed verdict is used in criminal actions in state courts, the Federal Rules of Criminal Procedure adopted judgment of acquittal in lieu of a directed verdict in 1944. In older federal cases or in state cases, a judge may grant a directed verdict to a criminal defendant, but not to the government, because a prosecutor must always prove the case to the jury.

*See also:* judgment, judgment notwithstanding the verdict (J.N.O.V. or JNOV or judgment as a matter of law or JML or JMOL or judgment non obstante veredicto).

**general verdict**  A single verdict on the basic issue of an action. A general verdict is a verdict on the underlying issue of an action rather than a series of answers to specific questions. A general verdict in a criminal action will be one that finds the defendant either guilty or not guilty of the offense charged. A general verdict in a civil action will either find the defendant liable or not liable or do so and, if the defendant is liable, specify an amount of damages suffered. A judge may poll the jury to ensure the verdict is supported by all of the members, or a sufficient number of them, and this polling does not alter the nature of the general verdict or make it a special verdict.

**general-verdict rule**  A general verdict is upheld if there is sufficient evidence for any count or claim. The general verdict rule requires that a general verdict is presumed to represent a verdict as to each claim and defense instructed and is upheld if there is any claim for which there is evidence sufficient to meet the burden of proof. (If the parties had preferred a verdict on each claim or defense, they should have moved instead for special verdicts.)

**guilty (guilty verdict or verdict of guilt)**  A verdict finding the government has proved the charge against a criminal defendant. A verdict of guilt is a finding of the jury delivered to the judge in open court that the jury believes beyond a reasonable doubt that the defendant has in fact committed the charge, or charges, of which the defendant was accused and tried. A verdict may be a general verdict, in which case it is presumed to find guilt on all charges in the indictment or information laid against the defendant in that court and subject to that trial. Or, it may be limited to one charge or another.

A verdict of guilt is not a judgment of guilt, and it does not have legal significance for the defendant until the judge accepts the verdict and enrolls it, or enters judgment upon it, or passes a sentence on it, or enters a similar order. At that time, the jeopardy of the verdict attaches, and the defendant may not be tried again for the same offense.

**inadequate verdict** A verdict awarding a remedy clearly less than the liability found. An inadequate verdict has an improperly low award of damages, restitution, or other remedial award in comparison to the determination of liability and the basis for that liability that was logically necessary to find the defendant liable. Although an inadequate verdict is related to an inconsistent verdict (in which there is inconsistency between substantive findings of liability), they differ in both form and effect. An objection to a verdict on the basis of inconsistency must be raised, in most jurisdictions, before the jury is discharged. An objection based on inadequacy may be dealt with later in a motion for new trial or in a motion for additur, just as an objection based on surplus may be dealt with by remittitur.

*See also:* additur.

**no verdict (hung jury or deadlocked jury)** A jury that is unable to reach a verdict. A failure to reach a verdict, which is known universally as a "hung jury," results when the jurors cannot agree on a unanimous verdict in the case of a criminal trial, or the requisite majority number in a civil trial cannot agree on a single verdict. This result may occur despite exhortations by the judge in the case and despite being sequestered or being required to deliberate under increasingly stressful conditions. A hung jury results in a mistrial, which in the case of a criminal proceeding allows the prosecution to try the case again.

*See also:* mistrial.

**not guilty (verdict of not guilty or not-guilty verdict)** A verdict finding the government has not proved the charge against a criminal defendant. A not-guilty verdict is a jury verdict finding the the prosecution has not proved a charge, or all charges, against a criminal defendant sufficiently to meet the prosecution's burden of proof and overcome the defendant's presumption of innocence. A verdict of not guilty is not proof of innocence, and an action for civil liability for the same conduct on which a criminal charge was brought is not estopped because of a verdict of not guilty. A verdict of not guilty is a basis for the attachment of jeopardy, and a further action for the same offense or for a different charge arising from the same conduct is barred. Note: although a jury is sometimes said to acquit a defendant by means of a verdict of not guilty, in general, the acquittal is the judgment of the court rendered on the verdict, rather than the verdict itself.

*See also:* jeopardy, double jeopardy; acquittal (acquit).

**quotient verdict** a verdict averaged among the preferred outcomes of each juror. A quotient verdict is a verdict in which each juror expresses a preference for a verdict, particularly a quantified verdict such as the amount of damages due to the plaintiff. The jurors then average the preferences rather than negotiate toward a consensus. A quotient verdict is usually invalid in the same manner as a verdict by lot or a compromise verdict.

**special verdict** A jury ruling on a specific contested fact in a trial. A special verdict is an answer by a jury to a special interrogatory, a question regarding a particular fact in dispute or mixed question of fact and law, which does not in itself amount to the existence or absence of guilt or liability. The special verdict is usually requested along with a general verdict, which answers the summary question of whether the defendant is guilty of a count or each count charged in a criminal action, or whether the defendant is liable for each claim in a civil action.

If an answer to a jury interrogatory, the special verdict, is inconsistent with the general verdict, in most cases in a criminal case, the remedy is usually a new trial. In a civil case, the judge may enter a judgment notwithstanding the verdict or order a new trial.

*See also:* interrogatory, jury instruction, special interrogatory (jury interrogatory).

**verdict by lot (chance verdict)** A verdict decided by gambling among the jurors. A verdict by lot, or a chance verdict, is a verdict reached by throwing dice, tossing a coin, or any other means of chance, rather than a careful examination of the evidence and discussion until a consensus emerges among the jurors. A verdict by lot is unlawful, and the court should not enter judgment on such a verdict, or if judgment is entered after which evidence suggests the verdict was by lot, the judgment should be vacated.

**verification (verify)** Proven true according to evidence or testimony, or an uncontradicted assertion that something is true. Verification is both the process of proving something true and a statement that it is true. Verification often takes the form of a written statement appended to a document by which a party or attorney for a party verifies that document, or asserts under oath and penalty of perjury, or as required by rule or law that the statements made in the document are true. The signature requirement of Fed. R. Civ. P. 11 is a form of verification, and many state courts require pleadings to be verified. The process of verification is not one of independent assessment of the truth of the speaker but one of requiring the speaker to make a solemn declaration with an implication of liability for error. The most common form of verification is the oath before a notary public or, sometimes, a clerk of court, in which the party making the statement submits the statement and a signature below as an acceptance of responsibility for the accuracy of the statement to the notary who accepts the oath and attests to the signature. (The oath or swearing in the notary's formulaic attestation is usually a matter of implied ceremony; it is rare for a notary or clerk to require the statement of the oath aloud.)

More generally, what is called verification is often an act of validation, an act of comparison between something and an authoritative list, as when a license is verified against a registry, or an identification is verified against some form of identity characteristics index.

*See also:* plea, verified plea (verification of pleading).

**verification of pleading**  *See:* plea, verified plea (verification of pleading).

**verified complaint**  *See:* complaint, verified complaint.

**verified plea**  *See:* plea, verified plea (verification of pleading).

**veritas**  The truth. Veritas is Latin for the truth, and it represents not only the sense of accuracy in depiction but faithfulness to the meaning of something depicted. Veritas is often used in lieu of truth to signal a particular depth of commitment to truth in an enduring sense.
*See also:* fides (fide).

**versus (v. or contra or c.)**  Against, the signal of one party opposed to another. Versus is Latin for against, and it is used to describe the relation of opposing parties in an action, whether the action is criminal or civil. The same notion is reflected in the use of "contra" in other legal systems, which is abbreviated "c". Note: in writing other than in case captions, "versus" may be used in the sense of "against," as in "Jets versus Sharks," but it may be better translated "as opposed to," as in "state court versus federal court."

**vertical**  Entities above and below one another in a hierarchy or series. Anything in a vertical organization is in a system in which there is a definite hierarchy, such as a vertical organization, as when all management of a system is in a central office that governs all other operations directly, or a definite order of procedures, such as a vertically integrated production line, which flows from raw materials through stages to finished goods. States are sometimes said to be vertically organized toward their subjects and citizens, and horizontally organized toward one another.

**vertical agreement**  *See:* agreement, vertical agreement.

**vertical merger**  *See:* merger, corporate merger, vertical merger.

**vertical price-fixing**  *See:* price, price-fixing, vertical price-fixing (resale price maintenance).

**vertical privity of estate**  *See:* privity, privity of estate, vertical privity of estate.

**vessel (boat or ship)**  Any form of craft or device used for transport in or on water. A vessel, as a matter of law, includes any craft or contrivance that is used or may be used for the transport of people or cargo under, in, on, or intermittently above the water. A vessel need not be created for the purpose of waterborne transport or have that purpose as its primary use, as long as it is sometimes usable as a vessel. U.S. vessels are required to be registered by either the United States or a particular state or jurisdiction. A vessel is subject to the laws of the jurisdictions in which it operates, as well as the jurisdictions in which it is registered.

A ship and a boat are both vessels. By custom, a ship is any surface vessel of over sixty-five feet in length, and a boat is any vessel of a lesser length. A ship's boat is a vessel ordinarily carried on and launched from a ship. A submarine is considered a boat regardless of its length. Statutes use the terms boat, ship, and vessel with surprising indiscriminancy, and care is required in interpreting a statutory use of such terms to determine if the use of one form of vessel is intended to exclude others or to include them.

**abandonment of a vessel**  Surrender of title to a vessel. Abandonment occurs when the owner relinquishes all property rights to the vessel. This may be the result of the owner's express renunciation of title or it may be inferred from the facts. At this point the vessel, usually a shipwreck, is subject to salvage.

**flag vessel (flag state or flag ship)**  A vessel of a given nationality, signaled by the ensign it flies. A flag vessel is a vessel registered, documented, or otherwise subject to the laws of a particular state, entitling that vessel to fly the national ensign of that state. As to a vessel, the state in which it is registered and whose ensign it may fly is the flag state. Flag vessels include both vessels owned and crewed by nationals of the state in which it is registered and vessels owned or crewed or both by nationals of a state other than the flag state. Ships in this second category, which have no meaningful relationship with the flag state than payment of taxes and fees, registration, documentation, and (in theory) inspection, and compliance with the law, are ships considered to fly a flag of convenience. A flag state always has jurisdiction over its flag vessel. Although the question of flag vessels is usually a question arising over merchant vessels or other private vessels, as a matter of categorization, the military vessels and other state vessels of a given state are also flag vessels of that state. Note: "flag ship" as a synonym for "flag vessel" should not be confused with flagship, the vessel in a naval formation carrying the senior admiral or formation commander.

**flag of convenience**  A registration of a vessel in a state in which it is not owned. A flag of convenience denotes the registration of a vessel in a state in which it has no owner domiciled. A flag of convenience extends the jurisdiction of the flag state over the vessel, regardless of the state's relationship with the vessel otherwise. For a state to flag a foreign vessel creates a flag of convenience. Flagging a foreign vessel allows the vessel to claim protection by the flag state, although it also limits national inspections and legal compliance to the flag state and to states in which the vessel calls and is subject to inspection.

**vesting (vest or vested)**  Having an unconditional and immediate interest or right. Vesting, in general, is to put on clothes, and as an intellectual legacy of the conferral of status by bestowing clothes with a badge of office or token of allegiance, the sense remains that to vest someone with something is to confer it, rather like clothing the person in it. In law, vesting is the creation of some right, estate, claim, or other legal or equitable interest that from that moment is settled and established; it is not dependent upon a condition to be satisfied or an event to occur in order for the party in whom it is vested to enforce it. An interest may vest in degrees, however, as an estate in land may vest as a possessory estate or as a future interest; the future interest vesting in the owner of it does not confer a right of immediate possession but an immediate right to protect or enforce the interest as well as the right to transfer or devise it (within the scope of the interest). Note: A person does not vest an interest; the interest vests in the person, or is vested in the person, by operation of an instrument or of the law.

See also: legacy, vested legacy; remainder, vested remainder; remainder, contingent remainder.

**vested legacy**   See: legacy, vested legacy.

**vested remainder**   See: remainder, vested remainder.

**vested remainder subject to complete defeasance** See: remainder, defeasible remainder, vested remainder subject to complete defeasance.

**remote vesting**   Vesting that might not occur until a time long in the future. Remote vesting describes a future interest that might or might not vest until an event occurs or a condition fails or is satisfied, which might not happen for a significant time. Remote vesting is a synonym for a perpetuity subject to analysis under the rule against perpetuities.

See also: perpetuity, rule against perpetuities (rap or rule against remoteness).

**veteran**   A person with great experience, or who served in the military. A veteran, in general, is a person who has developed an unusual level of experience in an occupation or role. Thus a veteran lawyer, teacher, police officer, carpenter, or other specialist is a person who has worked in such a trade or profession for sufficient time to be considered to have expertise in that field.

As a matter of military law, a veteran is a person who has served but ended service in one of the uniformed military services. There is no more specific definition of veteran in U.S. law, although there are varying definitions of veteran eligibility for veteran's benefits and privileges, including preference in hiring for specified police and civilian employment by the federal and state governments. Thus, although for purposes of the rights and benefits of a veteran, a person must have served and have been discharged in a status other than dishonorable, for other purposes, such as insurance, service for a period of a whole enlistment or service in combat may be sufficient for a person to be labeled a veteran. Even so, a general or dishonorable discharge of a service member found then to have been insane may not bar the award of veteran's benefits.

**veto**   To forbid some action, particularly to bar the enactment of a law. A veto is a prohibition on something proposed to be done. The term is Latin for "I forbid" and generally refers to the act of any person who exercises some form of authority to prevent an activity from taking place or a law being made. As a matter of custom, veto describes the act of the President of the United States when the president refuses to sign a bill presented for signature but returns the bill with reasons not to sign it. Likewise, the refusal of a governor to sign a bill as a matter of state law is usually referred to as a veto, whether the term is used in the state constitution or not.

**Veto Clause**   See: constitution, U.S. Constitution, clauses, Veto Clause.

**line-item veto (line item veto)**   An executive veto of a single provision in a bill. A line-item veto is a veto not of a whole bill but of a single provision in a bill. It is used by governors with the authority to modify bills (especially spending bills) prior to signature, granted to them under their state constitution. The President of the United States is limited to the bill as presented by the Congress and must either sign it, not sign it, or veto it whole.

**override of a veto (veto override)**   A legislative rejection of an executive veto. The override of a veto is a vote by a legislature to enact a vetoed bill as law, the veto of the chief executive notwithstanding. By a vote, required in both houses and by a supermajority, the legislative branch rejects the veto by the executive that the executive had entered to prevent a bill presented to the executive from becoming law; with that rejection the bill is enrolled as law without the executive's assent. The U.S. Constitution provides Congress may override a veto of the President only if two-thirds of the members of each house vote to do so.

**pocket veto (absolute veto or silent veto)**   A president's failure to sign a bill at the end of term. A pocket veto is a de facto veto that results from a president's failure to sign a bill that has been presented for signature within ten days of the adjournment of Congress. Article I, section 7 of the Constitution provides that an unsigned bill becomes law within ten days (not counting Sundays), unless Congress adjourns during that ten days, "in which case it shall not be a Law." Because Congress has no recourse to override a pocket veto, it is sometimes referred to as an absolute veto.

**vexation**   The damage suffered as the result of harassment or trickery. Vexation is the result of being vexed, being tricked or harassed. Vexation is the traditional description and measure of damages suffered by deliberate wrongdoing leading to one's inconvenience, particularly as a result of vexatious suit.

**vexatious   objection**   See: objection, vexatious objection (baseless objection or frivolous objection).

**vexed question**   See: question, vexed question.

**vexatious suit (vexatious prosecution or vexatious litigation)**   A suit brought to harass the defendant. A vexatious suit is a cause of action lacking merit in law or equity that is brought for the purpose of harassing, intimidating, inconveniencing, or causing expense or unwarranted delay for the defendant. A vexatious suit may be a civil action or a criminal proceeding. It may have some foundation but lack merit in the specifics that are intended to trouble the defendant. A vexatious civil suit that is terminated in the defendant's favor gives rise to a cause of action for vexatious litigation.

*See also:* process, abuse of process.

**vi et armis**    Done with the use of force or a weapon. Vi et armis is Latin for "with force and arms" or "by force and arms," which translate more appropriately as "done with force or while armed." A wrong vi et armis included any intentional wrong accomplished with force. A trespass vi et armis included what today would be considered as a battery, abduction, or forcible ejectment. A person assailed vi et armis was justified in using force in self-defense, but the greater significance of an action against a wrong committed vi et armis was that the allegation of force brought the action within the jurisdiction of the royal courts.

**viability (nonviable or viable)**    Capable of independent life. Viability is the capability of living independently of the support of others. A child who is viable is a child who has been delivered and is capable of developing to a point at which the child will be capable of life independent of life support or immediate medical care. As a matter of law in some jurisdictions, this is the point at which rights and interests are vested in a child who later dies. A child who was nonviable from the moment of delivery was never vested with rights and interests.

A fetus is viable though undelivered, if it is capable of life outside the womb, with or without medical assistance for life support. At the point of fetal viability, the state interest in protecting the fetus increases to a point at which some regulation over the decision and operation of a potential abortion is constitutional. The mother's interest is stronger than the state's interest in a nonviable fetus, and until the moment when the fetus becomes viable, the mother's interest in choosing whether to terminate the pregnancy is protected from regulation other than for compelling reasons.

More generally, viability designates an idea or project, such as a business enterprise, argument, or claim, that is likely to survive the obstacles or counters that would interfere with its success. Thus, a viable business plan has a reasonable likelihood of profitability; a viable argument is sufficiently well grounded to survive its attempted rebuttal; a viable plan is likely to achieve its practical goals.

**vicariousness (vicarious or vicariously)**    To be in the place of another person. Vicariousness is substitution, the treatment of one person or thing as a surrogate for another. Thus, vicarious liability is substituted liability, allowing the liability of one to be substituted for another, as when a parent is liable for the acts of a child, an employer is liable for the acts of an employee, or a principal is liable for the acts of an agent.

*See also:* liability, vicarious liability.

**vicarious liability**    *See:* liability, vicarious liability.

**vice**    A crime demonstrating moral corruption, or any imperfection. Vice, in law, includes all forms of moral or physical corruption. In a person a vice is an imperfection of motive, of conduct, or of the body that is likely to lead to further degradation. In a thing, particularly in the civil law, a vice is any aspect of the thing that renders it unfit for its purpose or use.

Specifically, vice describes a category of offenses against public morality. This category has been significantly redefined over the twentieth century. Vice once included fraud, petty theft, and other minor offenses against others. Contemporary use includes crimes that are said to be "victimless", including prostitution, unlicensed gambling, and illegal drug or alcohol consumption. Note: the claim that vice crimes are without a victim is controversial.

**vice as deputy**    A deputy prepared to act in the place of a superior. Vice as a preposition or prefix demonstrates that the person in that office is a deputy who is prepared to occupy the more senior office that the deputy serves and who may represent the senior official as a matter of office. Thus a vice president is prepared to serve in lieu of the president or represent the president, but otherwise assists the president in the performance of executive functions.

**vice versa**    Switching the argument the other way. Vice versa suggests the reverse of an argument just made. Latin for "turning to the reverse argument," an argument vice versa does not require the rejection of the preceding argument. Instead to claim a point vice versa is to claim that if premises were reversed, the conclusion would be reversed also. Thus, to say, "if Adam strikes Bob first, Adam is liable for all of Bob's injury in the fight, and vice versa" is to say that if Bob strikes Adam first, Bob is liable for all of Adam's injury in the fight. Vice versa may also denote the reverse of any statement. So in transportation, it is the reverse of the route described or traveled. Thus to say a tariff covers carriage from Pittsburgh to Cincinnati and vice versa is to say that the tariff also covers carriage from Cincinnati to Pittsburgh. Note: both vice versa and per contra represent, generally, a contrary argument, but there are subtle if important differences. Vice versa is usually thought of as the exact reversal to the argument in issue, and per contra the more general negative argument in opposition to the argument in issue. Thus an argument per contra is usually offered as a refutation of an argument, and an argument vice versa is offered to suggest that if a condition or premise were to be reversed, a conclusion would be reversed as well. Thus, an argument vice versa is not a comprehensive rejection of the earlier argument; indeed the second argument accepts the methodology of the first argument and applies it to the second, reaching the opposite conclusion only if the methodology was used to analyze opposite data.

**vicinage (vicenage)**    The neighborhood affected by a crime. A vicinage is a neighborhood, an area in which neighbors know one another and are likely to be aware of one another's affairs. In early criminal jury trials, the jury was summoned to try a matter arising from within its vicinage, in the main because the jury was expected to know something of the facts prior to the trial. As the role of the jury shifted from being self-informed to being informed by evidence and witnesses, the common-law requirement that a jury be drawn from the neighborhood of the offense grew less significant. The idea lives on in the requirement in the Sixth Amendment that a jury be drawn from the "State and district wherin the crime shall have been committed" and similar rules in state law, which usually require a trial to be held in the county in which the crime is committed unless the interests of justice require another venue. In some states, notably New Jersey, a vicinage is a judicial district.

*See also:* district; venue.

**victim**   A person who has suffered harm as a result of a particular cause or event. A victim is the person who has been the object of some harmful event or action. A victim of crime is a person who was the recipient of harm caused by another person's act in violation of the criminal law, whether the criminal actor specifically directed the harm toward the victim or intended harm to the victim or not. A person may be the victim of harm caused by human or non-human forces, such as the victim of a crime, a tort, a regulatory offense, or a natural disaster or a disease. By definition, a person is not the victim of that person's own conduct; acts that harm oneself do not make oneself one's victim.

> **victim compensation**   *See:* restitution, criminal restitution (victim compensation).

> **victim-impact statement**   A record of the effect of a crime on its victims used in sentencing the criminal. A victim-impact statement is a record prepared in some jurisdictions as a part of the presentence investigation, that identifies the specific victims of the defendant's crimes, determines the nature, scope, and expense of the harm suffered by the victims, as well as the changes to the family or welfare of the victims caused by the criminal act, and such other information gathered from the victims or about harm to the victims that the court requests. Note: A victim statement is a statement made by a victim, while a victim-impact statement is a report that may incorporate such statements but that is made by a government official.

> **victimless crime**   *See:* crime, victimless crime.

> **victim's shoes argument**   *See:* argument, golden-rule argument (victim's shoes argument).

**videlicet (viz.)**   For example. Videlicit, or viz., is a signal that the text that follows illustrates or exemplifies the text before. Thus, if a general definition is followed by "viz.," the text that follows it ought to be a specific example of the concept just defined. Viz. is roughly equivalent to "namely," "for example," "e.g.," or "i.e."

*See also:* exempli gratia (e.g. or eg); id est (i.e.); scilicet (S. or SS. or scil.); citation, citation signal, e.g.

**vie**

> **per autre vie (pur autre vie)**   The life of another person. Autre vie, literally translated into French,

means other life. Conveyances in property may sometimes be conditioned pur autre vie, that is, on the lifespan of a person other than than the grantee.

**vigilance**   The required intensity of awareness of care, when it is required. Vigilance is watchfulness, the type of attentiveness ascribed to a good sentry or to the night watch. In law, vigilance is the attentiveness required in specific activity, a part of the general duty of care or the special duty of care that may attend certain activities. The driver of a car has a duty of vigilance, including the duty to maintain a lookout, for pedestrians, other vehicles, and dangers.

**vigilante**   A private person who presumes to enforce public order. A vigilante is a person who seeks to prevent or punish individuals whom that person believes are a threat to public order or decency, yet who has no public authority or office to do so. A vigilante generally does not assist or support the institutions of the legal system, and is not limited by either the definitions of a crime or the system of criminal law enforcement, and the majority are a greater threat to the peace and order of the community than the people they seek to restrain or to punish.

**villein (villeinage)**   A peasant required to live and labor on a manor, whose children would also be villeins. A villein was a member of the lowest orders in feudal society. Villeins were allowed a parcel of land on a manor, which the villein could work half the week, the other half providing services on the lord's estate. Villeins lacked freedom in any legal sense and had practically no rights against their lords other than what custom and expedience required the owner to provide. Villeins were tied to the manor, laboring on the lord's lands and supplying goods with no ownership or interest in them. That said, a villein did have some limited rights as against people other than the villein's lord or overlords.

*See also:* serfdom (serf).

> **villein socage**   *See:* tenure, feudal tenure, socage, villein socage (villeinage socage).

**Vinson Court**   *See:* court, U.S. court, U.S. Supreme Court, Vinson Court.

**violation (violate or violative)**   An act forbidden or a failure to act as required, by a law, rule, or contract. A violation is failure of a duty, whether the duty is established by law, regulation, rule, contract, or any other source, and whether the duty requires a party to engage in some action or to refrain from some action. The idea of violation is that the source of the duty is itself injured by the failure of the duty, and so a marginal or trivial failure, such as some form of minor incompleteness is not a violation, unless the duty in question is one that is either technical, like a speed limit, or fundamental, like the homicide law, such that the least omission or departure from duty would be a comprehensive contradiction of the duty.

*See also:* transgression.

**violence (violent or violently)** Unreasonable or overwhelmingly dangerous force. Violence, in general, is the uncontrolled, overwhelming, or unreasonable use of force. In the common law, violence was an element in pleading that was essential to certain offenses, and so it acquired a technical meaning to include not only the use of force to create injury or damage without rational control to achieve a lawful purpose or goal, but also the use of the potential of such force to achieve an unlawful goal. Thus, the use of force in a battery is violence, though the use of force limited in scope only to avert the battery is not violence. Thus, at common law, the threat of force in aid of a robbery is also an act of violence. Statutes and contemporary law tend to distinguish violence from threats of violence, and in most contemporary usage, violence includes only acts that are violent rather than threats.

**violent crime** *See:* crime, violent crime.

**vir** Man. Vir is Latin for man, and though it may represent humankind, as "homo" often does, it is more often found in Latin maxims to represent the masculine as opposed to the feminine.
*See also:* homo.

**Virginia Statute for Religious Freedom** *See:* religion, freedom of religion, Virginia Statute for Religious Freedom.

**virtual representation** *See:* representation, virtual representation.

**virtue** The truly right and moral aspects of human character and conduct. A virtue is an ideal, and the virtues represent different concepts of the best behaviors of human beings. The four natural virtues were prudence, temperance, fortitude and justice, which have been promoted at least since Socrates, and charity, which has been promoted by Christian philosophers and articulated as the basis of justice by Gottfried Liebniz.

**virus**

**human immunodeficiency virus (H.I.V. or HIV)** The virus that leads to AIDS. Human Immunodeficiency Virus ("HIV") attacks the human body's T-lymphocyte cells, which are a critical part of the body's immune system, resulting in Acquired Immune Deficiency Syndrome, or AIDS.
The deliberate infection of another person with HIV is an assault, and the negligent infection of a person with HIV is negligence.
*See also:* acquired immune deficiency syndrome (A.I.D.S. or AIDS).

**vis** Force, or violence. Vis is Latin for force, whether exercised against a person or property, directly or by threat. Vis includes both violent and non-violent force, and it is sometimes translated as violence, as in Sir Edward Coke's maxim at 3 Institutes 176, vis legibus est inimica, or violence is inimical to the law. Note, vis

in this sense is Latin, and it should not be confused with its sense from French, in which vis is face, as in vis-à-vis.
*See also:* vis-à-vis (vis a vis); violence (violent or violently).

**vis major** The cause of an inevitable accident. Vis major is overwhelming force, the law Latin form of the law French term force majeur. The common law recognized vis major as an unstoppable force that led to an unavoidable harm or accident.
*See also:* force, force majeure.

**vis-à-vis (vis a vis)** As one thing relates to another. Vis-à-vis is French for face to face, but it is more properly understood as a matter of relationship between two people or things in issue. It emphasizes a particular relationship between the two things or people, as in "the bankruptcy was a success in keeping the employer afloat but a disaster vis-à-vis the secondary creditor."

**visa** An authorization for a foreign national to enter a state. A visa is the authorization of a state to an individual who is the subject of another state, allowing the individual to enter and setting restrictions on the length of stay, forms of activity allowed, and, sometimes, locations within the state to which the visa-holder may travel. Not all states require visas of all entrants, and many states no longer require visas from the entrants of specific states. A visa may be issued as a stamp or insert in a passport or in an independent identification card or book.
The forms of visa issued by the United States vary from time to time. As of 2010, non-immigrant visas include over seventy categories designating forms of occupation, purpose of travel, family status, or other salient characteristics, including ambassadorial visas (A-1), tourist visas for business (B-1) or pleasure (B-2), student visas (F-1), temporary worker of a specialized occupation (H-1B), and fiance of US citizen (K-1); immigrant visas include distinct catagories for applicants sponsored by employers, sponsored by family members, or falling into special categories such as states that have few U.S. immigrants. The procedures for processing requests for asylum are independent of the ordinary visa system.
*See also:* refugee (asylum seeker); passport (e-passport).

**visitation rights** *See:* custody, child custody, visitation rights (visitation order).

**vital statistics** *See:* statistic, vital statistics; hearsay, hearsay exception, hearsay allowed regardless of witness availability, vital statistics.

**vitiation (vitiate)** Harm, or destruction. Vitiation is the corruption, harm, or degradation of any thing, up to its complete destruction or abolition. The vitiation of a rule is either its repeal or rejection in general or a bar to its application in a given action. The vitiation of a contract is to void it completely or the avoidance of certain requirements under it. Note: In its broadest sense, the opposite of vitiation is mitigation.
*See also:* void (voidability, voidable).

**viva voce**  By spoken word. Viva voce, Latin for by living voice, designates actions done by a living person speaking aloud. Live testimony is testimony viva voce, and oral instructions are instructions viva voce.

**viz.**  *See:* videlicet (viz.).

**voice of the law**  *See:* vox, vox legis (voice of the law).

**voice vote**  *See:* vote, parliamentary vote, voice vote.

**void (voidability, voidable)**  Empty of any meaning or force. Void is an attribute of a legal obligation or its source, such as a contract, statute, trust instrument, will, agency, or any other written or oral basis for the duty, by which the obligation and its source are of no effect; whatever obligation the source purported to create is either terminated or is found never to have been created. Anything void is unenforceable.

Something voidable, however, is not inherently unenforceable, but its enforcement is contingent on the election of the person with the power to void it. A voidable contract, claim, or other interest may be declared void by a party but is not inherently void. Thus, in nearly every circumstance, an otherwise valid contract entered by a party who is too young to have legal capacity is voidable, not void, and when the party reaches majority (or if the party is represented by a guardian) the party may still enforce the contract.

*See also:* contract, specific contracts, void contract; contract, specific contracts, voidable contract; title, void title; nullity.

**void contract**  *See:* contract, specific contracts, void contract.

**void for vagueness doctrine**  *See:* vagueness, vagueness doctrine (void for vagueness doctrine).

**void legacy**  *See:* legacy, void legacy.

**void title**  *See:* title, void title.

**voidable contract**  *See:* contract, specific contracts, voidable contract.

**voidable title**  *See:* title, voidable title.

**void ab initio**  Void from the very start. Void ab initio is voidness in an instrument, writing, claim, or other apparent source of an obligation, that reaches back to the source's creation, declaring the source and all of its intended effects to have been void all along, that whatever effects that had followed from it were unjustified by it, and potentially giving rise to an action for restitution or rescission or other remedy to restore the parties affected by it to the position they would have been in without it. Voidness ab initio affects any instrument or doctrine that was improperly created or created without proper authority. Thus, a statute that is found unconstitutional is void ab initio; a contract that was procured by fraud is void ab initio, as is a marriage by a bigamist.

**voir**  True. Voir is French for truth, particularly in some sense of the truth, or accuracy and fidelity in a statement. Note: there are variations among the custom of American lawyers in the pronunciation of voir, some saying vwhah, some saying voher, and others saying voyer. As the term entered English legal pronunciation several hundred years ago, contemporary French pronunciation is not controlling; it is probably best to allow regional variations.

**voir dire**  Preliminary judicial evaluation of a juror or of evidence. Voir dire is a process of evaluation by which the court evaluates potential jurors to assess the likelihood that the juror will act truthfully in carrying out the duties of a juror. The term is also used in the preliminary review of evidence — especially testimony — to ensure that it is properly authenticated and appropriate for the task at trial for which it is proffered. The term, French for "to speak the truth," arises from the preparation of a person to take an oath.

*See also:* jury, jury selection (voir dire of the jury); evidence, authentication of evidence (voir dire of evidence); verdict.

**voir dire of evidence**  *See:* evidence, authentication of evidence (voir dire of evidence).

**voir dire of the jury**  *See:* jury, jury selection (voir dire of the jury).

**volenti non fit injuria**  No legal injury is done to a volunteer. Volenti non fit injuria, is a Latin maxim that excludes legally significant harm to a person who has willingly accepted its risk. It was a common-law basis for the early principle of assumption of risk.

*See also:* risk, assumption of risk (assumption of the risk).

**volition (volitional)**  Free will. Volition is will, or the power of one's will. For a person to act of that person's own volition is for that person to have been free of the influence, manipulation, or coercion of others or, in some senses, of circumstance. A volitional act is a voluntary act.

**Volstead Act**  *See:* prohibition, prohibition of alcohol, Volstead Act.

**voluntariness (voluntary or volunteer)**  Willingness. Voluntariness is a condition of acting from one's free will, a knowing and willful act, without coercion or manipulation, and free from the influence of another person. The voluntariness of an act, at least as some see it, is not lost by the actor's belief that the act is a moral or legal requirement, or that there are benefits to acting or detriments to refraining from the given act. Though there are philosophical doubts as to the existence of free will, the law presumes it to exist, and voluntariness is presumed in considering any action, unless there is evidence of influence, coercion, deception, or the like, by another person or of ignorance or mistake that affected the decision to act.

*See also:* statement, voluntary statement.

**voluntariness of a confession** *See:* confession, voluntary confession (voluntariness of a confession).

**voluntarism** *See:* jurisprudence, legal voluntarism.

**voluntary commitment** *See:* commitment, civil commitment, voluntary commitment.

**voluntary confession** *See:* confession, voluntary confession (voluntariness of a confession).

**voluntary dismissal** *See:* dismissal, voluntary dismissal.

**voluntary ignorance** *See:* ignorance, voluntary ignorance (willful ignorance).

**voluntary intoxication** *See:* intoxication, voluntary intoxication.

**voluntary jurisdiction** *See:* jurisdiction, in personam jurisdiction, voluntary jurisdiction, special appearance (limited appearance); jurisdiction, in personam jurisdiction, voluntary jurisdiction, general appearance; jurisdiction, in personam jurisdiction, voluntary jurisdiction (consent jurisdiction).

**voluntary manslaughter** *See:* manslaughter, voluntary manslaughter.

**voluntary or volunteer** *See:* voluntariness (voluntary or volunteer).

**voluntary partition** *See:* partition, voluntary partition.

**voluntary statement** *See:* statement, voluntary statement.

**voluntary waste** *See:* waste, doctrine of waste, commissive waste (voluntary waste).

**involuntary** Done without free will. An involuntary action is done either without knowledge or the independent will to act. Thus, any act in which the actor is aware of a choice and may freely choose otherwise is voluntary, but any act in circumstances in which one condition of voluntariness is not satisfied is involuntary. An act by a person without the capacity to act voluntarily is involuntary. An act based on the orders, coercion, influence, or manipulation of others is involuntary.

The law divides all knowing actions of a person between the voluntary and the involuntary, resolving the great many doubts and ambiguities of this division by a general presumption that all knowing actions are either involuntary or they are presumed voluntary. Acts of which the person had no knowledge are, by definition, involuntary.

**vote (voting)** One choice in a process of cumulating choices into a corporate choice. A vote is both the choice and the process of making a single corporate choice through the accumulation of a variety of individual choices. For example, when an electorate votes for the new holder of an elective office, each elector casts a vote, or votes for one or more among the candidates for the office. The votes are counted, tabulated, and the candidate for whom the most votes have been cast wins the vote, thus winning election to the office. The term, vote, comes from the Latin word for a votive, or solemn offering to the gods. Note: vote is both a noun and a verb.

**parliamentary vote**

**voice vote** A vote made aloud rather than by roll call or ballot. A voice vote is a vote in which all of the electors voice their answer in response to a call for votes, all those answering yea at once, and all those answering nay at once, the chair then determining from the appearance of the electors during the vote and from the volume heard during each vote, which side had the more votes. A voice vote is not capable in most instances of being recorded by the number of votes cast.

**yeas and nays (roll call vote)** A voice vote recording those in favor of a measure and those opposed. A vote by yeas and nays, or a roll call vote, is a vote taken by calling the name of each person who may vote and recording whether the person votes "yea," to support, or "nay," to oppose the measure on the floor. Both houses of congress must record the yeas and neas of all roll call votes.

**casting vote (deciding vote or tie-breaking vote)** A vote cast by a chair or president to break a tie. A casting vote is a vote assigned by the rules of a legislative body to the chair or to the presiding officer of the body, to be cast in the event a vote is evenly split between the votes cast in favor and those cast opposed to the proposition on the floor. The person with the authority of a casting vote is usually otherwise forbidden to vote. The Vice President of the United States, as President of the Senate, has the casting vote in that body.

*See also:* vote (voting); ballot.

**suffrage (suffragette)** The right to vote, or the act of voting. Suffrage is the right to vote or the vote itself. The term is derived from the Latin word for the ballot. A suffragette was a woman who advocated the right of women to vote in the nineteenth and twentieth centuries.

*See also:* marginalization (marginalized group).

**vote in public election**

**one person one vote (one man one vote)** Election districts must be equal in populations. One Person, One Vote, was stated as the fundamental test of fair electoral districts in Gray v. Sanders, 372, U.S. 368, 381 (1963). The maxim, following the principles in Baker v. Carr, 369 U.S. 186 (1962), is the hallmark of the constitutional requirement that different electoral districts for the election of members to a single governmental body must be equal in population, or as equal as they may practicably be made. The idea of one person, one vote as a basis for fair participation in collective action is obviously older.

**polling place (polls or voting station)** The place for voters to cast their votes in an election. A polling place is a location under the supervision of an election commission or other appointed supervisor of public elections in a state, at which qualified voters cast their votes during an election. States may regulate the conduct in and near polling places in order to balance the interests of electors and election workers with the interests of candidates and their supporters, but such regulation must be narrowly tailored to minimize the burdens on the speech of the candidates. A prohibition on campaign speech within seventy-five feet of a polling place is permissible.

**voter (elector)** A person entitled to cast a vote in a decision of a body, or in a public election. A voter is a person who is entitled to vote. A full member of a legislative body is a voter in that body. In most senses, there is no difference between a voter and an elector. Not all citizens are voters in public elections, because a citizen must register to vote. A person who is a citizen of the United States, over the age of eighteen, and not disenfranchised as a result of a felony, may register, after which that person is a registered voter.

*See also:* president, President of the United States of America, Electoral College (presidential elector).

**Voting Rights Act of 1965 (Voting Rights Act)** A federal protection of the right to vote. The Voting Rights Act of 1965, codified at 42 U.S.C. §1973, et seq., enforced the requirement of equal access to voting established in the Fifteenth Amendment, making a federal crime of interfering with a voter's access to the vote, outlawing practices among the states that discouraged citizens of color and other disenfranchised groups from registration or voting, and requiring the approval of changes to voting laws and districts in states or counties that were then known to have engaged in willful voter discrimination.

**voucher** A record of payments made or to be made. A voucher is an account or record of account that is used either to demonstrate payments that have been made, to substantiate payments to be requested, or to authorize payments to be made. A voucher is particularly used in authorizing payments or services given by a third party to a recipient designated by the voucher's holder. The term comes from the early French term meaning to call upon another, either as a summons or as a source of proof.

**tuition voucher (school voucher or education voucher)** A payment from public funds to attend private school. A tuition voucher is a right to the payment of a certain amount of tuition on behalf of an individual student. Payment for the voucher is allocated from public funds, which are ultimately allocated either to the pupil's family or, more commonly, to the school in which that student is enrolled. Vouchers are used both to allocate public money for students enrolling in private schools and in public schools, according to different voucher program structures.

Publicly funded school vouchers are controversial, seen by some both as a weakening of the system of public education and, in the case of religious schools, either a grant to religious institutions or a denial of access to them. On the other hand, vouchers are seen as a means of encouraging choice among families and competition among schools to improve their educational capacity.

**vox** Voice.

**vox legis (voice of the law)** The voice of the law. The vox legis was a term used to describe the Roman Praetor, the voice of the law, but it has later been used to describe any judge or judges.

**vox populi** The voice of the people. The vox populi is the metaphor for any expression of the will of the people, whether that will is expressed in a ballot box during an election or referendum, is asserted through actions such as demonstrations, polling results, or petitions, or is claimed by a populist or demagogue who would speak on the people's behalf.

**voyeurism (voyeur)** The deliberate observation of acts customarily private. Voyeurism is an invasion of privacy by the intentional observation of another person engaged in conduct that is by custom private. Voyeurism is treated as a crime, usually as an example of disorderly conduct or loitering, although it may occur in circumstances that amount also to trespass or stalking. Although the observed person may give permission to another in such circumstances, permission for such observation is not presumed.

*See also:* stalking (stalk or stalker); trespass (trespass to land); voyeurism, Peeping Tom; privacy, invasion of privacy.

**Peeping Tom** A person who intentionally observes individuals in moments of privacy. A Peeping Tom is voyeur, especially a person who intentionally observes others in their homes or other places of privacy in an attempt to see the person nude or in other situations of unusual privacy. A Peeping Tom may violate specific local ordinances or statutes, some of which specifically condemn the "Peeping Tom" and some of which bar voyeurism. Such conduct may also violate laws against trespass, invasion of privacy, disorderly conduct, or breach of the peace. Delaware law allows the commitment of a Peeping Tom to psychiatric care.

Note: The in judicial opinions and legal writing, the P in peeping seems nearly always to be capitalized, and though the style books would have it otherwise, legal usage prefers Peeping Tom.

*See also:* voyeurism (voyeur).

**vujo** Purity. Vujo connotes purity or cleanliness among the Romani, something appropriate for a person to use or be associated with.

**vulnerable zone** An area with air polluted enough to near non-attainment.

> What is it that the judicial expositor seeks to ascertain — is it the meaning of the words or the meaning of the writer? . . . We answer, neither. Not the meaning of the words alone, nor the meaning of the writer alone, but the meaning of the words as used by the writer.
>
> Charles A. Graves, *Extrinsic Evidence in Respect to Written Instruments*, 28 Am. L. Rev. 321, 323 (1854).

# W

**w** The twenty-third letter of the modern English alphabet. "W" signifies a variety of functions as a symbol and as a designation of status, as in "withdrawn." It is translated into Whiskey for radio signals and NATO military transmissions, into William for some police radio traffic, and into dot, dash, dash in Morse Code. W was not a letter in classical Latin, which used a u, often doubled, to denote the w sound, as in equus. The French made more standard the use of the double–u, which evolved in appearance with the development of some u's into v's in the 1500s, when the modern w became more common in English.

**w as an abbreviation** A word commencing in W. When used as the sole letter of an abbreviation, W often stands for west, western, as well as wake, wage, warehouse, warden, warrant, Washburn, week, weekly, white, Whittier, will, wireless, withholding, without, woman, women, women's, worker, workman, workmen, world. W&L is Washington and Lee, and W&M is William and Mary. It may also stand for the name of an author or case reporter, such as Wales, Washington, Water, Watt, Wendell, Wheaton, William, Wilson, Wisconsin, Wood, Wright, Wyoming, and Wythe.

**w as in hypotheticals** Will, Wife, Widow, or Witness. W often stands for a will, or last will and testament, in the story of a law school hypothetical. It might also stand for wife, widow, or widower, or for a witness.

**W-2** *See:* tax, tax form, W–2 form (W–2).

**W-2 form** *See:* tax, tax form, W–2 form (W–2).

**W-4** *See:* tax, tax form, W–4 form (W–4).

**W-4 form** *See:* tax, tax form, W–4 form (W–4).

**Wade hearing** *See:* identification, identification procedure, Wade hearing.

**wage (wages)** Periodic payments made to an employee, servant, or contractor for work performed. A wage is the amount of money, or the money itself, earned by an employee for services performed for an employer over a specified period of time. A wage may be measured by the hours of work performed, as in the minimum wage, or by payment over any other quantum of time, the rate of pay daily, weekly, biweekly, monthly, yearly, or at other intervals. The longer the interval — and in any case in which the compensation is calculated by the year — the more likely the wage will be referred to as a salary.

The term "wage" originates as the idea of pledge or security, which is how its root is near to the modern wager. There is now no practical difference between the meaning of the term in the singular or the plural, and so wages and wage are now interchangeable except for specific uses in contracts and statutes. This does, however, explain what to modern ears is a problem of noun–verb agreement in the seventeenth century translation, "the wages of sin is death." Romans 6:23 (KJV). Today, one may say "the wage is" or "the wages are" with equal meaning, but the Biblical combination of forms would seem affected.

*See also:* pay (paycheck); salary.

**wage slave** *See:* slavery, wage slave.

**living wage** A wage at least comparable to the standard of living. A living wage is a level of compensation for work that is equivalent to the standard of living above poverty, an income for full-time work that is sufficient to meet the basic needs of an employee and a customary number of dependents. The standard is not a subjective view of each individual employee's needs, but a general look at the prices of shelter, transportation, and food in a geographic location.

**minimum wage** The lowest amount of money an employer can pay by the hour under the law. Minimum wage is the least rate of pay an employer subject to wage and hour laws can legally offer an employee, according to federal or state law and any applicable collective bargaining agreement. In 2009, employers subject to the Fair Labor Standards Act had to pay most workers at least $7.25 per hour, and $10.86 per hour for each hour worked over forty hours per week. States may set a higher minimum wage, and, in 2009, twenty–seven states were higher, the state of Washington then being the highest, at $8.55 per hour. States may also apply a minimum wage to workers who are exempt from the federal minimum wage.

*See also:* minimum wage.

**red-circle wages (red circle rate)** A protected, preferential wage based on longevity of employment. A red–circle wage or rate, which is paid to a red–circle person, is a relatively high pay rate that is assured in a collective bargaining agreement to certain employees in an entity as a result of their long-standing employment. Even if a red–circle employee is shifted to less valuable work, the employee continues to receive the red–circle wage at its former rate.

**slave wage** A slang term for wages that make a worker dependent on others for support. Slave wage is a slang term of dubious utility, used to depict wages too low for a person to survive without some other income, or too low for a person to support a family and survive without some other income. The comparison, however, is inapt, as slaves were and are paid no wages.

**wage scale**  A schedule of wages paid to workers in different categories. A wage scale is a list created by or for an employer that specifies the wages and benefits to be paid per hour or per pay period to workers in specific categories of employment. In most private corporations, management and executive pay is not subject to a wage scale.

**wager**  A commitment contingent on a future event with an uncertain outcome. A wager is a commitment made upon some form of future risk. Often, a wager is a bet, the taking of a stake against others in a contest or game of chance. In this sense, a wager is a form of gambling that amounts to a contract, which in some jurisdictions is unenforceable as a matter of public policy. Although the common law would not enforce a wager or gambling contract, in a private agreement, a wager in some jurisdictions is enforceable if the terms have sufficient specificity to disclose the risk to the party incurring the risk as well as the usual requirements for an enforceable contract of offer, acceptance, and sufficient consideration by both parties. In most jurisdictions, however, various forms of wagers are allowed by statute within the limits of public regulation or of private action not for commercial profit. Lotteries and other state-owned or state-licensed wagering opportunities are required by statute both to honor terms of contests and to honor bona fide claims.

The idea of wagering is a broader concept than of betting in games of chance. At law, the wager of battle was a commitment to prove one's cause through the outcome of combat in a judicial duel of arms. The investment of money in various exchanges of securities is a wager that the instruments purchased will increase in value. The wager that is inherent in the sale of a futures contract was once a barrier to its enforcement, though contemporary contracts law allows such agreements. Note: wager of law was quite different from wager of battle, in that wager of law was a defendant's disavowal of a debt, proved by a dozen oathtakers; wager of battle was the one with swords.

*See also:* gaming (gambling or gamble); bet (betting or bettor or numbers).

**wait**

**wait-and-see test**  *See:* perpetuity, rule against perpetuities, wait-and-see test, Uniform Statutory Rule Against Perpetuities (USRAP); perpetuity, rule against perpetuities, wait-and-see test (wait-and-see approach).

**waiting period (cooling off period)**  A period of time that must elapse before an action or change of status. A waiting period is a period of time that must elapse

before some event may take place, before some status is bestowed, some application may be effectively approved, some interest may vest or any other event that is contingent upon a specified lapse of time. There are many forms: Waiting periods are required by some employers before an employee's employment benefits vest; in many jurisdictions before a new resident may register to vote; and before resident aliens under most visas may apply for citizenship.

A time that amounts to a waiting period for the purpose of allowing a party or parties to reconsider their actions or seek a different resolution of their problems is known as a cooling-off period, as is the waiting period before action on a filing for divorce in some states. Examples of other cooling-off periods include: limiting access of someone who commits domestic battery from returning to the domestic residence; limiting strikes and job actions while union-management negotiations progress; and delaying a criminal trial to allow abatement of the effects of pre-trial publicity.

**Waite Court**  *See:* court, U.S. court, U.S. Supreme Court, Waite Court.

**waiver (waive)**  The giving up of a right or other privilege in law. Waiver is an act by which a person or entity holding a right, privilege, claim, or any other interest in law or equity that may be asserted or defended in any forum elects not to assert it or defend it, electing not to do so in some manner that makes the election final. Nearly any interest can be waived, though the waiver in most instances becomes final once another person reasonably relies on the waiver. Waiver is possible, even of some constitutional rights, although the policy of protecting constitutional rights is strong, and there must be clear evidence of the waiver of such a right, and the waiver is narrowly construed. Waiver must be intentional, voluntary, and knowing.

Waiver may be express or implied. An express waiver is a statement by the party holding the interest, or by an authorized agent for that party such as an attorney, that communicates to another interested party or into a public record the exact interest and the scope of that interest being waived. A waiver affecting an interest in land is likely to require a writing, owing to the Statute of Frauds. An implied waiver is a waiver construed from conduct, in that the party holding the interest has acted in such a manner that the interest must have been waived, because the action either is impossible if the interest is not waived or is contrary to or inconsistent with the interest in question. Even so, an implied waiver must still be intentional and knowing, and evidence that a party holding the interest acted in a manner contrary to the interest but with no knowledge of the interest or the conflict is a bar to the implication of waiver.

It is well to bear in mind that a waiver is voluntary, and unless the waiver is either a consideration or performance of a contract or the basis for another party's reasonable reliance, a waiver can be withdrawn. Thus, doubts as to the capacity, knowledge, intentionality, or voluntariness of a party at the moment of a purported waiver are usually to be resolved in the favor of the party with the interest, because that party is free (unless there is a contract or reliance) later to renounce or reaffirm the waiver. The circumstances of a waiver as an element of a contract or as the basis of reliance must be considered in the light of their specific facts.

The effect of waiver varies according to the interest waived and the context of its waiver. Some rights or interests may be waived only for a time, that is abrogated for a specific purpose but still asserted by their holder at a later time or in relationship to a different party. Some rights or interests are waived finally and forever once they are waived. The difference in the contexts of waiver as abrogation of a right or of final abandonment usually depends both on the nature of the right or interest and the reasonableness with which other parties are likely to (or in fact) rely upon the waiver.

**waiver of counsel** *See:* counselor, right to counsel, waiver of counsel (waiver of right to counsel).

**waiver of privilege** *See:* privilege, evidentiary privilege, waiver of privilege.

**waiver of right to counsel** *See:* counselor, right to counsel, waiver of counsel (waiver of right to counsel).

**express waiver** A waiver stated clearly and unambiguously. An express waiver is a waiver by which the party holding the interest waived clearly and unambiguously expresses the waiver in words, whether the words are written or oral. The waiver must be clear as to the interest waived, and the intent to waive the interest must be unambiguously manifest in the statement made. Any ambiguity as to intent or lack of clarity in the interest waived and its scope would make unreasonable any reliance by another party upon the statement as a waiver of the interest.

*See also:* objection, no objection; expression (explicit or express).

**implied waiver** A waiver implied from the conduct of the party holding the interest otherwise. An implied waiver is a waiver that is not made in words by the party holding the interest but is inferred by others to have been implied by the party through conduct. Conduct that may imply a waiver is conduct that is contradictory to the existence of the right, interest, claim, defense, or other interest in issue, or that destroys the interest, or is logically possible only if the interest has been waived. Because the question of implied waiver usually arises only when another party seeks to charge the party with the interest as having waived it and when the party with the interest seeks not to be held to a waiver, most courts are skeptical of claims of an implied waiver. In some jurisdictions, implied waiver is only to be found in circumstances that otherwise justify equitable estoppel. In any case, a waiver must be knowing and voluntary, and conduct that is said to imply a waiver of a right that the party holding the right did not then know exists is ordinarily insufficient to support a claim of implied waiver,

although later reliance by a second party on a good faith belief of implied waiver, which reliance and belief are known to the party holding the right, is sufficient to justify estoppel, regardless of whether waiver is found.

*See also:* estoppel (estop or estopped).

**waiver of term** An offeror may surrender any term expressed or implied in the offer. A waiver of a term in an offer may be expressed or implied by the conduct of the offeror, and a waiver of a term in an acceptance may be expressed or implied by the conduct of the offeree. Nearly any term may be waived, including a right to communication of the acceptance, a specific acceptance date, terms of delivery, and so on. A waiver of acceptance is a deliberate surrender of the ordinary right of the offeror to receive the acceptance in order to be bound by the contract. A waiver of acceptance may be essential in an offer that the offeror expects to be accepted by the offeree's performance. A waiver may be express, or it may be implied from other terms or from the conduct of the offeror.

**wajib** An important duty. Wajib means obligatory, an aspect of duty that is like a command in Islamic law. In most schools, the term is synonymous with Fard, except in the Hanafi school where it has a peculiar Usul al–Fiqh meaning as something between Fard and Mustahab, a sort of fard in the second degree. To omit a wajib or fard is haraam, a serious violation of the law and a sin. To perform a wajib is commendable.

*See also:* fard; haraam (haram).

**walkout** *See:* union, labor union, labor dispute, labor strike (walkout).

**wall** A physical, metaphorical, or virtual structure of separation. A wall, of course, is a structure for separation of spaces, whether on open land or in a building, when it may also serve as a load–bearing structure for the support of upper floors or a roof. In contemporary usage, a wall implies a complete separation between activities, such as a Chinese Wall, a policy forbidding the transfer of information between two groups or divisions of employees within the same enterprise, or a computer structure or program that prevents data in one system from reaching another, such as a firewall. Yet, as Shakespeare reminds us, all that is needed to communicate through a wall is a very small hole.

*See also:* conflict, conflict of interest, Chinese Wall (ethical wall).

**party wall** A wall shared by two different properties. A party wall is a wall on the border of two properties with different owners. Such a wall may be built jointly and subject to the responsibility of each, or built by one alone, the other having an implied or express easement for its proper maintenance. In the absence of an agreement or evidence to the contrary, most jurisdictions presume a party wall to be property in common and of joint responsibility between the owners.

**want of jurisdiction**   *See:* jurisdiction, want of jurisdiction (lack of jurisdiction or beyond the jurisdiction).

**want of prosecution;**   *See:* prosecution, want of prosecution.

**wantonness (wanton)**   Offensively or dangerously careless conduct. Wantonness depicts an unusual lack of care in one's conduct that manifests a failure of regard for one's duties toward others or the rights or interests of others, with the knowledge or willful disregard of the knowledge that some harm or injury to another is a likely result of the conduct. Although "wanton" has acquired a particular sense of sexual promiscuity or lewdness, it is broader and applies to acts that are offensively or dangerously careless.

**war (warfare)**   A condition of armed hostility between states. War is a condition that exists between two or more states, either as a result of a formal declaration of war or as a result of the prolonged engagement in or significant commitment to armed conflict. In international law, the legal significance of war has been largely though not fully replaced by the concept of "armed conflict." In U.S. law, war is a condition established as a matter of law, either by a formal declaration of the United States Congress or as a matter de facto that is recognized by the courts, and that establishes certain conditions in law that are dependent on the United States being at war, such as contingencies in a contract.

"War" is also used in the United States to designate a policy that is not war at all but a large-scale commitment of resources, such as the war on drugs or the war on poverty. This leads to ambiguity when a President declares a war as a matter of policy that also involves the commitment of military forces in an arena of armed hostility, as in the Global War on Terror, a policy that included a variety of military operations, particularly in Afghanistan and Iraq, each of which would meet the technical sense of a war de facto.

**War Clause**   *See:* constitution, U.S. Constitution, clauses, Declaration of War Clause (War Clause).

**armed conflict**   War in fact. Armed conflict is the prolonged use of armed forces in combat between states or within a state, regardless of whether a formal state of war exists or could exist between the parties or of whether the parties each have political or organized structure, or whether one party seeks to use organized violent force to achieve a policy change or personnel change in the political structure. Armed conflict is the situation in fact that amounts to combat or warfare. A brief incident involving military personnel is not an armed conflict, although the period of combat or military engagement has no minimum time. The forms of armed conflicts are international armed conflicts, internal armed conflicts, and internationalized internal armed conflicts. The law of armed conflicts applies to all armed conflicts regardless of the form, although varying duties arise for other states according to the form of the conflict.

*See also:* arms, arms as weaponry (arm).

**declaration of war**   A joint resolution of Congress designating a state of war between the U.S. and another state. A declaration of war, in general, is an official statement by the executive or legislature of a state that declares another state an enemy, and altering the juridical relationships between the states to a belligerent state. A declaration of war creates a state of war between the declarant state and the object state, regardless of whether a war de facto commences. In the United States, the Congress has the sole power to declare war, although the President has the power to commit military forces to a theater in which war might be possible, a tension sometimes resolved by a Congressional authorization to use force, which does not amount to a declaration of war.

**law of war (law of armed conflict or LOW or LOAC)**   The law that governs states and individuals in armed conflict. The law of war is both a part of international law that regulates the conduct of armed hostilities and a part of the law of the United States and of other nation-states that binds those individuals within its jurisdiction to comply. The law of war includes all international law for the conduct of hostilities binding on the United States or its individual citizens, including treaties and international agreements to which the United States is a party, and applicable customary international law. The law of armed conflict is another name for the law of war, the principles and rules of the two being the same, the difference being only the emphasis in the law of armed conflict extending to a conflict that is not formally denominated as a war.

The law of war has two primary components: the law that governs when states may engage in armed conflict, known as the jus ad bellum, and the law that governs the conduct of states, their military components, and their individual personnel during a conflict, which is the jus in bello.

*See also:* military, military law.

**casus belli**   Act of war, or, more precisely, cause of war. An act of war, or a casus belli, is an action by a state or an agent for a state that is a sufficient cause for another state to demand satisfaction and, if no satisfaction is to be had, to declare war. The doctrine of casus belli is now considered obsolete, having been superseded by the universal obligation of states to pursue peaceful means to resolve disputes. Even so, an act of war amounting to armed attack against a state is sufficient to allow a state to resort to individual or collective self-defense.

*See also:* casus; cause, cause of action.

**Geneva Conventions**   Treaties governing the treatment of individuals affected by armed conflict. A Geneva Convention is one of the many multilateral treaties concluded in Geneva Switzerland, and to speak of a Geneva Convention requires context to identify it. The first to deal with the law of war is the Red Cross Convention of 1864. The Geneva Conventions of 1928, regulating gas warfare, and 1929 regulating the treatment of prisoners, had come into force before World War II. In contemporary usage, the Geneva Conventions are four international agreements concluded in 1949 and later amended, which set out rules for the treatment of individuals affected by war. The First Geneva Convention deals with wounded persons on the battlefield, protecting both wounded and sick personnel and civilians engaged in assisting those persons. This Second Geneva Convention protects wounded and stranded personnel at sea. The Third Geneva Convention sets minimum international standards for the treatment of prisoners. The Fourth Convention deals with the treatment of civilians during armed conflict. The United States has ratified all four conventions. Protocols added to these conventions in 1977 and 2005 address specific issues not resolved in the initial conventions. Note: the law of war, including restrictions on the use of force, has developed both through customary law and through many treaties and conventions. Many instruments of the law of war are in force other than the Geneva Conventions and are easily confused with them. Many protections accorded to prisoners of war, for instance, are in part the result of the Fourth Hague Convention of 1907.

**common article**   One of the first three articles of the Geneva Conventions of 1949. The common articles of the Geneva Conventions of 1949 are the first three articles, which are stated verbatim in each convention, setting forth commitments from the party states that each will adhere to the convention in all armed conflict and in peacetime, as well as during occupations, and each will recognize and assure the minimum standards for treatment of each non-combatant, each prisoner, and each person who is wounded, sick, or shipwrecked, regardless of the convention under which the person is considered. The minimum standards of treatment forbid "(a) violence to life and person, in particular murder of all kinds, mutilation, cruel treatment and torture; (b) taking of hostages; (c) outrages upon personal dignity, in particular, humiliating and degrading treatment; (d) the passing of sentences and the carrying out of executions without previous judgment pronounced by a regularly constituted court, affording all the judicial guarantees which are recognized as indispensable by civilized peoples."

**Hague Conventions (Hague Convention)**   Several treaties on the law of war and child protection. A Hague Convention is one of the many international conventions negotiated in The Hague, in the Netherlands. When no other context is available, a reference to the Hague Conventions probably relates to the conventions on the law of peace and war of 1899 and 1907. The major areas of the conventions are much broader:

Hague Conference on Private International Law began work in 1893, having now over sixty member states, which have enacted a series of conventions on civil procedure, remedies, trusts, and contracts.

The Hague Conventions of 1899 and 1907 codified numerous elements of the modern law of war and of war crimes, requiring international arbitration in lieu of war, codifying laws and customs of the law of war on land, on sea, and in balloons, and outlawing certain weapons such as the exploding bullet.

The International Opium Convention of 1912 sought to control the manufacture, sale, and traffic of morphine and cocaine.

Hague Convention on the Civil Aspects of International Child Abduction of 1980, as well as a further conventions on adoption in 1993 and parental responsiblity in 1996.

The Hague Convention for the Protection of Cultural Property in the Event of Armed Conflict established a regime for marking and protecting culturally sensitive sites during combat, which would be recognized and protected by signatory troops.

**jus ad bellum**   The law of war governing the entry into conflict. Jus ad bellum is the law of war as it applies to the conduct of states and non-state actors in the decision to use force and the use of force in war. Jus ad bellum includes both the justifications for the use of force, such as those inherent in the right of individual and collective self-defense and the responsibilities of states to act upon the requests of the United Nations Security Council, as well as limits on the use of force in lieu of non-violent means of dispute resolution and on the use of force for the aggrandizement of the state, government, or entity. Violations of the jus ad bellum are violations of the customary law prohibiting crimes against the peace as well as violations of the Charter of the United Nations and other instruments.

*See also:* United Nations, United Nations Charter, Article 2(4) of the UN Charter.

**jus in bello**   The law of war in battle. Jus in bello is a modern designation for the law of war as it applies to the conduct of combatants and military force as it is deployed in battle and, by extension in occupation and in all other manners by which the law of war relates to the conduct of individuals and units toward both combatants, non-combatants, property, and the environment. Violations of the jus in bello are war crimes under the customary law of war as well as violations of the United Nations Charter, the Hague and Geneva conventions and other instruments.

**war crime**   A violation of the law or war committed by an individual, group, or state. A war crime is a violation of the law of war, particularly a violation committed by an individual for which the individual may be held to account in a criminal tribunal, whether in a military court, national civilian court, or international court or tribunal. In U.S. law, a war crime as defined by certain treaties gives rise to an individual civil action under the Alien Tort Claims Act that may be brought by a person harmed by the war crime. A war crime is established either by a grave violation of a convention establishing the law of war, such as the Geneva or Hague Conventions, or by a violation of the customs of war on land or on the sea, as established by the doctrines and practices of professional military services.

**crime against humanity** An inhumane act contrary to the universal principles of international criminal law. A crime against humanity is an act of murder, extermination, enslavement, deportation, forcible transfer, torture, rape, or other inhumane acts committed against any civilian population, before or during a period of armed combat; or a persecution against an individual or group on political, racial or religious grounds. A crime against humanity is a crime of universal jurisdiction, punishable in any domestic or international tribunal regardless of its legality or illegality under the domestic law of the country where it is perpetrated. In U.S. law, a crime against humanity also gives rise to a civil action on behalf of a person harmed by it, under the Alien Tort Claims Act.

*See also:* war, law of war, war crime; tort, alien tort, Alien Tort Claims Act (alien torts).

**genocide** A harm to a group or member of a group with the intent to destroy the group. Genocide is the crime of homicide or other injury to one or more members of a national, ethnic, racial, or religious group, with the intent to destroy the group in part or in whole. Genocide is a crime under international law and the laws of nearly every state, and it is a crime of universal jurisdiction. Genocide was prosecuted in the Nuremberg tribunals as one of the crimes against humanity.

*See also:* tort, alien tort, Alien Tort Claims Act (alien torts).

**superior order (Nuremburg defense or good sergeant defense or lawful order defense)** A mitigation of a war crime but not a defense. Superior orders is a claim that may be raised by a military service member or government officer accused of a war crime, that the accused was acting under orders by a senior officer or official and had no discretion to disobey. Superior orders are not a defense to a war crime, and a person ordered to commit a violation of the law of war, a crime against humanity, an act of genocide, or a crime of aggression and who does so remains responsible for doing so. However, a person who indeed acts solely out of orders may be entitled to mitigation of a sentence for a crime committed as a result of that compliance. The defense is sometimes called the "good sergeant" defense owing to its use by German soldiers accused of war crimes for acts done under orders during World War II.

*See also:* sentence, mitigation of sentence (mitigating evidence).

**prisoner of war (POW or P.O.W.)** A member of an organized military unit who is in the custody of an enemy military force. A prisoner of war is a member of the regular or irregular military units of a state engaged in an armed conflict, who has surrendered to, been captured by, or been given into the custody of an enemy military force, or who has otherwise fallen into the power of the enemy. A prisoner of war is entitled to the protections assured by the Third Geneva Convention of 1949. The obligations to protect prisoners of war from harm, to provide food, shelter, and medical care, not to hold them as hostage, and to respect the dignity of prisoners are matters also of the customary law of war. A person who has been taken prisoner by a military force or an occupying power who is not a prisoner of war is still entitled to the protections of common article three of the Geneva Conventions.

**war powers** The power to control the military and to commit it to an operation. War powers include the powers of the Commander in Chief as well as the power to regulate the armed forces and to declare war. Under the U.S. Constitution, the war powers are divided between the President and the Congress.

**War-Powers Resolution (War Powers Act)** The President must advise Congress when committing military forces into hostile circumstances. The War Powers Resolution of 1973, codified at 50 U.S.C. § 1541, et seq., balances the war powers of the President and of the Congress to recognize that the President must defend the nation from attack and commit troops, sometimes, to hostilities without Congressional authorization, but also to recognize a Congressional role of authorization, which must be made for the President's commitment to be maintained.

**ward** A person under guardianship, or anyone or anywhere specially protected. A ward is a child committed to the care and protection of a guardian. The guardian has the capacity to act for the ward that a parent would have to act for the parent's child. A wardship is a status and estate of a ward, and a guardian is responsible for the prudent management of the assets of a wardship, drawing such income as is required for the reasonable maintenance of the ward and, in some instances, taking from it a fee. There are various distinctions among wards. A child who has been taken from the custody of a parent or guardian and is awaiting a resolution of parental fitness or guardianship is a ward of the court. A child in the custody of the state and committed to an institution or to foster care is a ward of the state.

More generally, a ward is any place or thing that is subject to protection or special guard. From this sense, a ward is also a subdivision of a municipality, once having been an area subject to a single police patrol.

**wardship** The estate of a ward, whether as an individual or a people. Wardship is the estate of a ward, which takes several different forms. In U.S. law, wardship is not only the condition of being a ward but also the estate of the ward subject to a guardianship, and a guardian must act as a fiduciary in managing the assets of the wardship.

More generally, the relationship of the American Indian tribes and nations to the United States of America is described as one of wardship, in which the United States acts as guardian of Indian property and rights. This status, and the powers it accords the respective parties, is controversial.

At common law, wardship occurred when a tenant by knight's service died, leaving a child as heir, in which case the lord to whom the tenant owed service became the guardian of the child, and the child's estates were in wardship, subject to the will of the lord until the child became of age.

**warden**  A keeper or guardian of an institution, especially a prison. A warden is a guardian, a person responsible for the management and protection of a particular institution. Commonly, the title is accorded to the senior officer responsible for the security and management of a prison. The title is also used for the senior administrator of certain churches and colleges.

**warehouse**  A building for the storage of goods. A warehouse is, literally, a building used to house wares, or goods. A warehouse may be purpose-built or not. Zoning laws distinguish between warehouses of different sizes, transportation and storage facilities, and the capacity to store goods of varying hazard and pollution.

**wares**  *See:* merchandise (wares).

**WARN Act**  *See:* worker, Worker Adjustment and Retraining Notification Act (WARN Act).

**warning**  Notice of some danger to a person at risk from it. A warning is a notice, whether it is made to a specific person, vessel, or entity or made to all the world, of some danger. To be a sufficient warning, the notice should be clear as to the danger posed, the conditions under which the risk of the danger may be manifest, and the means by which those receiving the notice may mitigate their risk to it. A warning may take many forms, among them a label on a dangerous device or substance, a verbal statement, a public notice, a sign on a building or lands, or written correspondence.
*See also:* label, warning label.

**warning label**  *See:* label, warning label, heeding presumption; label, warning label.

**adequate warning**  Warning sufficient and timely so a reasonable hearer could mitigate the risk. Adequate warning is a standard of the sufficiency of a warning. An adequate warning must be clear in its communication of the particular danger in issue, the source of cause of the danger, the form by which the danger may be manifest, and its potential consequences, as well as the means by which the hearer may mitigate such dangers. The measure of such adequacy is whether it would put a reasonably prudent observer

on notice to the risk, so that the observer would have time and knowledge sufficient to act to avoid its danger.

**duty to warn**  The obligation to warn another person of a hidden danger. A duty to warn is an obligation on a party with particular knowledge of a dangerous condition who knows or should know of the exposure of others to the danger of that condition, particularly as a result of the inducement of the duty-holding party to the other party to become exposed to that danger, or the reasonable reliance of the other on the duty-holding party to disclose such dangers. A products manufacturer to a consumer or user, a landlord to a tenant, a property owner to an invitee, a fiduciary to a client, all have a duty to warn the other of a hidden danger. A fiduciary has a further duty, to warn not only of hidden dangers but also of some apparent dangers, if there is reason to believe the client is unaware of them.

**fair warning (fair notice)**  Sufficient notice of what conduct is criminal prior to engaging in the conduct. Fair warning is a standard of constitutional law limiting the process by which criminal laws are enacted, that requires a law to put a person on sufficient notice of the conduct that will be made criminal and to provide that notice prior to the person's commission of such conduct. A failure of fair notice is both a failure of due process of law and, in most instances, the creation of an ex post facto law. Fair warning may fail either because a law is enacted after an act it makes criminal or because the law was expressed in terms sufficiently obscure that it would not have been clear to a reasonable observer that the conduct in question was forbidden.
*See also:* vagueness, vagueness doctrine (void for vagueness doctrine); ex, ex post facto (ex post facto law).

**warrant**  Assurance and authorization. A warrant is both an assurance that something is proper or of a given quality and an authorization to do something. Both senses are apparent in the warrant as a writ or order of the court to an official or other person competent to carry out an order of the court, in which case the person is to carry out the order and be generally immune from damages (although the common-law immunity from action or damages for conduct pursuant to a warrant will not bar all claims for damages arising from an unconstitutional or invalid warrant.) Most warrants are directives to officials to seize a person or property, usually for criminal process though not always, as in orders to restore a person to premises or otherwise to enforce a judgment.

Warrants for private purposes exist, particularly a warrant as an issuance of stock or equity in a corporation, or a warrant authorizing payment of a debt.
*See also:* share, share as stock, warrant; pursuivant (poursuivant).

**warrant for stock or stock warrant or securities option or share option**  *See:* share, share as stock, stock option (warrant for stock or stock warrant or securities option or share option).

**warrant as commercial paper (payment warrant)** An order authorizing one person to pay money on another's behalf. A warrant is a form of commercial paper, not unlike a check, in which a drawer authorizes one person to pay the drawee a sum of money. Warrants are often used by public agencies.

**warrant as justification** To be sufficiently justified as to act. To warrant is to state an assurance or justification that some action is appropriate, or some conclusion is true. This sense of warrant is often applied to evidence or to pleadings in describing the justification for an order, finding or other determination. Thus, a judge may find the evidence warrants a given finding.

**arrest warrant** A judicial order requiring peace officers to bring a person into custody to be charged with a specific offense. An arrest warrant is an official instrument that authorizes police officers to take a named individual into custody. More specifically, it is usually a judicial warrant issued by a judge, magistrate, or other authorized judicial officer, who upon either an indictment or a review of a petition that demonstrates the basis for a finding that there is probable cause to believe one or more specific individuals have committed one or more specific criminal offenses, directs a police official to arrest the named individual or individuals and present them before the court to be charged with that specific crime or crimes. An arrest warrant must be dated and signed by the judicial officer.

The requirement that a person be arrested only pursuant to a valid arrest warrant is limited under the Fourth Amendment. The Constitution states only that a seizure of the person is not to be unreasonable. This has been interpreted to mean police officers must obtain a warrant to enter a private place such as a home or other place where a person has an expectation of privacy to arrest a suspect there. The Constitution does not require a warrant for arrest in a public place, and not if police officers who make an arrest themselves have independent probable cause to believe the suspect has committed an offense, such as by observing the conduct on which the arrest is based. Even so, statutes may further determine the scope of arrests that may be made without a warrant.
*See also:* summons (summon or summoned).

**bench warrant** A warrant issued sua sponte to compel a person to appear in court. A bench warrant is an order from a magistrate or judge to a police officer requiring that a named individual be brought before the court. A bench warrant is typically issued for a failure of a person who had been summoned to court to make an appearance as required.
*See also:* summons (summon or summoned).

**death warrant** An order to a prison official to carry out a death sentence. A death warrant is an order either from an executive, usually a governor, or a court directed to a prison warden or corrections official, to require the execution of sentence upon an inmate convicted of a capital crime and sentenced to die. Upon the completion of the sentence, the return

of the warrant is made to the judge or official who issued it.

**escape warrant (fugitive warrant)** An arrest warrant for a fugitive from justice. A fugitive warrant is a warrant for the arrest of a person who has been determined to be a fugitive from justice, because the person has been charged with an offense after which the person left the jurisdiction or took steps to avoid being located and served with process. An escape warrant is similar, being issued for a fugitive who has escaped from custody.

**extradition warrant (rendition warrant)** An administrative warrant seeking extradition of the designee from another state. An extradition warrant is a form of arrest warrant issued by the governor of the requesting state, that is the state that seeks to extradite a person from another state. A rendition warrant is executed by the governor of the asylum state, that is the state in which the person is to be found, ordering the person be taken into custody and extradited under an extradition order to the requesting state.
*See also:* extradition.

**general warrant** A warrant for the search of an unspecified place or arrest of an unspecified person. A general warrant is a blank warrant, a warrant that does not specify the person or place to be affected by it. A warrant that lacks particularity regarding either the person to be arrested and the charge against that person or the place to be searched and for what does not satisfy the requirements of the Fourth Amendment and is invalid.

**writ of assistance (Paxton's Case)** A general warrant allowing colonial customs officials to search for smuggled goods. A writ of assistance was a general search warrant issued by the colonial superior court to a customs official, empowering the official to search in any place and to command the assistance of any person in searching for goods imported without the payment of the appropriate tax, as well as contraband imports. The legality of the general warrant was upheld in Paxton's Case (1761), despite the powerful argument of James Otis against the use of a general warrant. The case influenced John Adams, James Madison, and other framers, who later drafted the Fourth Amendment to forbid the practice in the United States.

**John Doe warrant** An arrest warrant which does not specifically name a person. A John Doe warrant is an arrest warrant that does not name the person to be arrested but only gives information about the physical appearance of such a person. It is used when police are authorized to arrest a specific individual, but the subject's name is unknown. Aside from missing a name, the warrant still must meet all the requirements of an arrest warrant.
*See also:* name, fictitious name.

**peace warrant (warrant to keep the peace)** A warrant to arrest a party for a peace bond hearing. A peace warrant is a form of arrest warrant, limited to require the appearance of a person whom a court on hearing has found to present a threat to the peace. Following the hearing, the court may require the person to enter into a peace bond, and if the person later violates the peace bond, the person may be committed to jail.

**rendition warrant (warrant of rendition)** An arrest warrant for the purpose of extraditing the person arrested. A rendition warrant is an arrest warrant, issued by a court or by an executive official seeking the arrest of a person in the jurisdiction in which the warrant is valid, not for the prosecution of the person there but to establish custody for the purpose of extraditing the person to custody in another jurisdiction. The arrestee is entitled to a hearing prior to the extradition.

**search warrant** A judicial order that peace officers may enter a specific location and search for specified evidence of a crime. A search warrant is an official instrument that authorizes police officers to enter a specific location or otherwise to invade a private activity, and thus to search for specified forms of evidence related to specific behavior in violation of the criminal law. A search warrant must be dated and signed by the judge or magistrate who enters it, and it is subject to the limits of the Fourth Amendment, so that a search warrant must be based on probable cause, which is to say that the magistrate or judge who issues the warrant must have done so only after finding there is probable cause to believe that the premises to be searched will contain evidence of a crime.

*See also:* search, exclusionary rule, exception to the exclusionary rule, independent-source doctrine (independent source).

*oath or affirmation* A sworn or affirmed affidavit is required for all search or arrest warrants.

**automobile exception** A warrant is not required to search a vehicle. The automobile exception to the warrant requirement allows a reasonable search of a vehicle without first obtaining a warrant for the search, as long as the search itself is based upon and within the limits of probable cause. The exception arises from the exigencies inherent in waiting for a warrant to search a location that is inherently mobile.

**hot pursuit exception** A warrant is not needed to enter a house pursuing a person from the scene of a crime. The hot pursuit exception to the warrant requirement allows the entrance into a building that would otherwise require a warrant if the officer entering the building does so in hot pursuit of a person fleeing the scene of a crime. The pursuit need not have been long or at high speed, but it must be uninterrupted and contact between at least one pursuer and the person pursued must have been effectively continuous.

**no-knock search warrant** Warrant allowing entry into a residence without knocking. A no-knock search warrant contains language authorizing law enforcement officers to enter the residence that is the target of the warrant without knocking or alerting the occupants inside that a search is about to be conducted. A no-knock warrant is issued if the judge finds probable cause that notice in service of the warrant would endanger police officers or another party or alert occupants sufficiently to allow the destruction of evidence.

**warranted search** *See:* search, warranted search.

**warrantee** *See:* warranty, warrantor (warrantee).

**warrantless search** *See:* search, warrantless search, special needs exception; search, warrantless search, plain view, immediate appearance (immediately apparent); search, warrantless search, plain view (plain-view doctrine); search, warrantless search, exigent circumstances; search, warrantless search, consent search (consented search); search, warrantless search, automobile exception (vehicle exception); search, warrantless search, administrative search; search, warrantless search.

**warrantless arrest** *See:* arrest, warrantless arrest.

**warranty** A promise assuring a statement of fact or future performance. A warranty is a generic term for a promise that is inherently subject to enforcement by those to whom it is made or those who are entitled to rely upon it. A warranty may be expressed, implied, or construed by law. In the event of a breach, warranty is usually enforced in tort law if the warranty amounts to a representation and enforced in contract law if the warranty amounts to a promise to do or to refrain from some conduct.

The primary forms of warranty are warranties affecting the transfer of land, including the general or special warranties of title and the warranty of habitability; warranties in documents of title, including the warranty on negotiation or transfer; warranties in negotiable instruments, including the warranty on presentment and transfer, the warranty of customer and collecting banks, and the warranty of title; warranties affecting sales, including warranty of title, warranty of fitness for purpose, warranty of merchantability, and warranty against infringement of intellectual property; warranties specific to the sale of consumer products, such as full warranty and limited warranty; and warranties associated with insurance.

The word "warranty" comes from the same origins as "guaranty," and the differences between them are mainly the specific forms that such a promise takes as a matter of custom. At common law, guaranty was the narrower in meaning, referring to a promise to pay the debt of another, while warranty meant any assurance of a statement of the warrantor as to the truth of some matter or of a promise to do or refrain from some conduct.

*See also:* guaranty | guaranty and insurance and letter of credit and surety and warranty; disclaimer; guaranty; performance, future performance.

*privity of contract*   A contractual basis for warranty does not automatically bar an action for breach of warranty if the plaintiff is not in privity of contract. If the plaintiff is a party reasonably intended to benefit from an express warranty, in most jurisdictions, privity is no bar to the action. A lack of privity is more often a bar for an action arising from an implied warranty.

**warranty against encumbrances**   *See:* covenant, covenant of title, covenant against encumbrances (warranty against encumbrances).

**warranty deed**   *See:* deed, warranty deed, special warranty deed; deed, warranty deed.

**warranty of further assurances**   *See:* covenant, covenant of title, covenant of further assurances (warranty of further assurances).

**warranty of habitability or implied covenant of habitability**   *See:* habitability (warranty of habitability or implied covenant of habitability).

**warranty of title**   *See:* title, warranty of title | warranty of marketable title and warranty of title; title, warranty of title.

**breach of warranty**   A failure to perform a warranted task or a misrepresentation of a warranted statement. Breach of warranty is a failure of the warrantor to provide the assurance warranted, a failure that generally takes one of two forms: a misrepresentation of a fact or condition warranted to be true, or a failure to do or refrain from some conduct warranted to be done. Breach of warranty by misrepresentation may be brought in tort for damages in an action for misrepresentation or in contract, if the representation was made as an inducement or in performance of a contract. Breach of warranty to do or refrain from some action is usually brought as a breach of contract action, for damages, rescission, or for specific performance.

**disclaimer of warranty**   A statement refusing to be bound by a warranty. A disclaimer of warranty is a statement made by a party whose conduct might give rise to an implied warranty—such as a seller of goods, a landlord letting a habitation, a transferor of a negotiable instrument, an insurance company, or seller of goods—rejecting any intent to provide a warranty in that transaction. Not all warranties may be diclaimed, and some statutes forbid a disclaimer of a warranty of habitability, for instance, by a commercial housing provider. In other instances, a warranty may be disclaimed, although the disclaimer must be made prior to the transaction in a manner that puts the implied warrantee on actual notice of the disclaimer. A valid disclaimer of warranty bars the warranty from being implied in the transaction.
*See also:* disclaimer.

**general warranty (general warranty of property)**   A covenant of quiet enjoyment in a warranty deed. A general warranty is another name for a covenant of quiet enjoyment.

*See also:* covenant, covenant of title, covenant of quiet enjoyment (covenant for quiet enjoyment or warranty of quiet enjoyment or general warranty).

**warranty of merchantability (consumer warranty or manufacturer's warranty)**   An implied warranty that a product is fit for its ordinary use. The warranty of merchantability is a warranty implied in the sale from a manufacturer to a merchant, from a merchant to a merchant, and from a merchant to a consumer, that the product sold is fit for its intended use and ordinary purpose. A defect in the product, whether as a result of defective design, defective manufacture, or defective labeling, such that the product is unsafe for ordinary use or fails to perform reasonably in its purpose, is a violation of the warranty. The Uniform Commercial Code enshrines an implied warranty of merchantability and usage for trade in section 2–314.
*See also:* liability, product liability (products liability).

**warrantor (warrantee)**   A warrantor makes a warranty to or for a warrantee. A warrantor is the party who makes a warranty, and the warrantee is the party to whom a warranty is made or the party who is intended to be the beneficiary of the warranty.

**Warren Court**   *See:* court, U.S. court, U.S. Supreme Court, Warren Court.

**waste**   Any resource that is not or cannot be used productively. Waste has several distinct senses in law. Its most significant contemporary sense in U.S. law is as waste materials, items which have been discarded from use, whether they are reclaimed, stored, dumped in a landfill or discharged into the environment.

Waste in the common law remains an important, technical aspect of property law, in which some valuable aspect of real property is consumed, neglected, or destroyed in such a manner that its value cannot be replaced or restored without further investment.

Other forms of waste in law include waste as empty and unused ground and waste by a trustee or fiduciary, which occurs when the assets of the trust are not managed in a prudent fashion and decline in value. Legal drafters frequently employ waste in its more general sense to indicate when some resource is neglected or consumed in an inefficient manner, a resource or person is destroyed, or a resource or person decays into uselessness or nothingness. Note: waste is both a noun and a verb.
*See also:* depletion.

**doctrine of waste (property waste)**   The neglect, destruction, or consumption of physical resources in land. The doctrine of waste makes the possessor of a limited interest in land liable to the holders of future interests for the loss of any fixed asset in land that is consumed, neglected, or destroyed in a manner that its value cannot be replaced or restored without further investment. Waste at common law was a matter of the destruction of the assets, not merely a diminution in value, and waste can occur under the common law even if the market value of the property rises as a result of the waste. Under contemporary U.S. law, waste is only actionable when the value of the property is reduced.

Waste may be committed by the owner of the fee simple absolute in land without limit. Yet when the person in possession of the land has a limited interest, as a tenant to a landlord, as a present possessor when there is a holder of a remainder or reversion, when there is a vested spousal right, or when the land is held subject to a mortgage, then the possessor's waste is actionable by the person holding the non-possessory interest. The most common actions are by a landlord against a tenant, by a mortgagee against a mortgagor, and by a future interest holder against a present possessor.

The alteration of physical structures, including the breaking down of a building, the removal of walls or roads, the cutting of trees, the removal of minerals and ore, the loss of a well are all waste. The allowance of a property to decline in value through routine maintenance; the neglect of a fault in the property, such as a damaged roof, drain, or water pipe, that causes greater damage; or the willful destruction of a structure are waste.

Waste takes several forms, which divide between those that are subject to an injunction and those that are not. Those that may be enjoined include voluntary or commissive waste, the loss of property through the intentional act of the occupant resulting in a loss of value to the property overall; and permissive waste, the loss of property through neglect that results in a loss of value to the property overall. Waste that may not be subject to injunction includes ameliorating waste, in which the value to the property is increased; and authorized waste, in which the future interest holder permits the waste. Waste may also give rise to damages at the time the future interest holder takes possession.

**affirmative waste**  Waste from deliberate or intentional acts by the possessor. Affirmative waste is intentional waste committed by acts. Although affirmative waste may be actionable, not all affirmative waste is. Such waste as is considered prudent management of the land, such as the separation of crops or the routine harvesting of trees in a managed forest, is not actionable. Further, affirmative waste that was part and parcel of the use of the land when or before the possessor entered and the future interests were created is not actionable.

**ameliorative waste (meliorating waste or ameliorating waste)**  Affirmative waste that changes a property's character without a loss in value. Ameliorative waste is affirmative waste that alters a structure or fixture on a property, or alters the property in some manner, but still improves the property and does not diminish its market value. Ameliorative waste is not subject to injunction unless it is in violation of the express terms of a lease or condition upon the tenancy.

**commissive waste (voluntary waste)**  Affirmative waste that diminishes the value of the property. Commissive waste, or voluntary waste, is a direct injury to the property committed by the possessor, or allowed by the possessor to be committed by others, which results in a loss of marketable value in the property. Commissive waste is subject to injunction during the possession and to damages for unremediated waste upon the entry of the future interest holder.

**equitable waste**  Imprudent use, particularly the destruction of buildings soil, or trees. Equitable waste is affirmative waste that so clearly violates the duty to protect the property owed by the present possessor to a future-interest holder that equity will enjoin it. Examples are usually destruction of assets of the land, such as the destruction of buildings, cutting of timber, removal of soil, and the destruction of trees and shrubs.

**impeachment of waste**  An action for waste, for injunction or damages. Impeachment of waste is an action under the doctrine of waste, either to enjoin a present possessor from further waste or to seek damages from the prior possessor for waste suffered on the property, sought when the future interest holder takes possession. A tenant holding "without impeachment for waste" is not liable for affirmative waste unless the waste is wanton or malicious.

**open mine doctrine**  A life tenant may take royalties from a pre-existing mineral lease. The open mine doctrine is an exception to the bar on waste by a life tenant, which would usually prevent the life tenant from severing minerals from the estate, but would allow the life tenant to take royalties or minerals from a lease established by the grantor prior to the entry of the life tenant on the land.

**permissive waste**  Waste arising from neglect or a failure of duty. Permissive waste is injury to the property that results from the failure of the present possessor to provide the ordinary maintenance and care that ownership entails of real property. Permissive waste includes all forms of negligence — such as the failure to make repairs as needed, failure to perform maintenance routinely, or failure to avert patent risks to the property, or failure of proper storage and care of flammable or toxic materials, that results in a loss of value to the property.

**economic waste**  *See:* damages, contract damages, expectation damages, economic waste.

**ordinary wear and tear (wear and tear)**  Minor, typical degradation of property is not waste. Ordinary wear and tear is the minor loss of value to property through ordinary use that accompanies age, fatigue of materials, erosion through use, and the typical consequences of use, cleaning, and operation of any building, machinery, or other thing. Ordinary wear and tear is not waste, and unless a tenant enters a special covenant at the outset of the lease to commit maintenance and repair, the tenant is not responsible to the landlord for losses owing to ordinary wear and tear.

*See also:* deposit, security deposit (damage deposit); lease, leasehold (non–freehold estate or nonfreehold estate).

**waste material**  Any material that has been discarded from use and considered effectively useless. Waste includes material of all forms, solid, liquid, gas, and combinations of each, that has no planned use and that is treated as trash, refuse, or excess to requirements, to be destroyed, stored, or abandoned according to ease and expense.

**hazardous waste**  Waste matter with a potential hazard to human health or the environment. Hazardous waste is any solid, liquid, gas, or combination that is either danger or potentially harmful to human health or to the environment. Hazardous wastes as regulated under the Resource Conservation and Recovery Act, codified at 42 U.S.C. § 6901, et seq., include only solid wastes that are hazardous or mixtures of solid wastes that are hazardous as combined. A hazard includes any attribute that may cause, or significantly contribute to an increase in human mortality, or cause or contribute to an increase in serious irreversible, or incapacitating illness; or pose a substantial present or potential hazard to human health or the environment. Hazardous wastes include characteristic wastes (that ignite, corrode, react, or are toxic), listed wastes (that are specific chemicals), universal wastes (that are pesticides, batteries, light bulbs, and mercury), and mixed wastes.

Hazardous solid wastes are regulated by the EPA under the authority of the RCRA, to require generators, transporters, storers, and disposers of hazardous waste to track the movement of such wastes by manifests and to ensure that no hazardous wastes are managed by unpermitted operations, in order to insure such materials are not lost or disposed of in a manner that is not consistent with the danger the materials pose to human health or the environment. The RCRA Federal Hazardous and Solid Waste Amendments (1984) require the minimization of waste and the gradual decommissioning of land disposal of hazardous wastes.

**hazardous waste manifest**  A record of hazardous waste being transported. A hazardous waste manifest is a document used to document and track the movement of hazardous waste and to ensure that it is ultimately disposed of in a proper, permitted facility. No person may ship, nor may a transporter or facility receive, any hazardous waste without a manifest declaring the content and quantity of the waste as well as its origin.

**toxic waste**  A waste material that is harmful or fatal in the human body. A toxic waste is a characteristic form of hazardous waste that

causes harm or death if it is ingested or absorbed into the human body.

**nuclear waste (radioactive waste)**  Any waste that is radioactive. Nuclear waste includes all forms of waste that are radioactive or are contaminated by radiation, whether the waste is a byproduct of nuclear materials or waste from material exposed to nuclear materials, or waste that has been exposed to nuclear radiation. Regulated nuclear waste includes low–level waste (LLW), or clothing, tools, filters, lab equipment or other things contaminated with radiation; waste incidental to reprocessing (WIR), or waste byproducts from reprocessing spent nuclear fuel; high–level waste (HLW), or spent nuclear reactor fuel; and uranium mill tailings, the residue from uranium and thorium mining.

**Resource Conservation and Recovery Act (RCRA)**  The primary federal statute for solid and hazardous wastes. The Resource Conservation and Recovery Act of 1976 (RCRA), codified at 42 U.S.C. § 6901, et seq., established federal regulation of the solid wastes generated in the United States, including federal–state regulation of solid waste disposal facilities and regulation from generation to disposal of hazardous wastes. Both are subject to state regulation and federal oversight or regulation by the EPA.

**solid waste**  Non–liquid waste materials, including sewer sludge. Solid waste includes all forms of non–liquid, non–soluble waste material, including those containing complex and hazardous substances and those that don't. Solid waste as defined by the Resource Conservation and Recovery Act specifically includes sewage sludge, agricultural refuse, demolition wastes, mining residues, and containers of liquids and gases.

**waste generator**  A producer of waste or the emitter of waste into the environment. A waste generator is the person or entity that creates waste or that releases it into the environment. A waste generator that creates a waste product regulated under the Resource Conservation and Recovery Act, 42 U.S.C. §§ 6301, et seq., is responsible for its proper storage, transfer, or disposal, until such time as the waste is transferred to a properly permitted recipient.

**wasting asset**  *See:* property, wasting property (wasting asset).

**wasting property**  *See:* property, wasting property (wasting asset).

**watch**  *See also:* lookout.

**watchdog**  An office charged with the oversight of others. Watchdog is a metaphor based on the canine watchdog, but it is used in the sense of a person or agency, whether public or private that oversees the activities of others in order to ensure that they act according to the law and the common good or, sometimes, according to more narrow standards.

**water**   The chemical basis both of drink and of the waters of the earth. Water is the chemical that sustains life as the basis for hydration in plants and animals, and it is the medium for the rivers, the seas, the rains and snows, and in some degree all habitable environments. Water comprises one basic form of two atoms of hydrogen and one of oxygen, although isotopes exist and are used in nuclear energy. When pure, water is clear, colorless, and odorless. Water both reflects and refracts light. Potable water is water fit for human consumption. Navigable water is water capable for use in commercial transportation by boats or ships.

**water pollution**   *See:* pollution, water pollution.

**groundwater**   Water under ground. Groundwater is water in any form in the ground, including water seeping in soil and rock formations and naturally-occurring subsurface bodies of water.
*See also:* well.

**runoff**   Surface water not in a stream or lake. Runoff is surface water from precipitation, snow melt, or irrigation that traverses the surface of the land before reaching a stream. Runoff may collect a variety of pollutants, including agricultural inputs and commercial, urban, and petroleum wastes from urban areas, roads, and parking surfaces. Runoff eventually seeps into the water table or runs into streams.

**water rights**   A property interest in a watercourse or water body. Water rights are the rights to use water in or from a watercourse or body of water and include the right to divert or separate water from its source, within the limits of law, custom, and use. Water rights are either inherent in the ownership of land that adjoins or contains the watercourse or waterbody, or they arise from a license or conveyance of rights from a landowner. Water rights are either public or private.
*See also:* use, use of property, beneficial use.

*artificial use*   The right to divert water for artificial use. In many jurisdictions, water rights do not inherently include the right to divert water for artificial use, that is, for the profit or comfort of the rights holder. In some jurisdictions, the water taken for artificial use is limited to reasonable use or to use that does not degrade the ability of downstream users. In other jurisdictions, the distinction among uses is less essential than the quantity or proportion of flow that may be taken.

*natural use*   The right to the natural use of water. Water rights in land inherently include the right to the natural use of water, or such uses as are essential to the necessities of life. In some jurisdictions, this distinction is not made.

**watercourse**   A stream, river, canal, or other regularly flowing body of water. A watercourse is a river, creek, canal, or other body of water through which water regularly flows. Whether a given course or channel amounts to a watercourse is a matter of fact, and the division between a watercourse, which may be occasionally dry, and a dry channel, which may be occasionally wet, can be difficult to discern. The primary difference is that a watercourse should at least have standing or flowing water in some discernable measure most years, that come from a source other than local rainfall and associated light and dark runoff. A navigable watercourse is owned by the state in which it occurs, in trust for the benefit of its people. A non-navigable watercourse is owned by the riparian landholders, or the owners of land that touches the watercourse at its banks.

**wetlands**   Land recurrently saturated with water at its surface. Wetlands are areas of land that has soils that are recurrently saturated with water, so that the presence of the water on or in the soil is the dominant factor in the soil chemistry and biology, and the types of plant and animal living in it or on it. Wetlands include not only coastal marshes, shallows, tidal swamps, and flats but also inland riparian wetlands, marshes, swamps, potholes, and the margins of lakes and ponds. Wetlands need not be unceasingly wet but may be recurrently saturated, such as vernal bogs. Wetlands are not limited only to the results of natural activity, but may be created by artificial activity as well, such as quarrying, dredging, and mining. Wetlands are essential for the survival of many animal and plant species, are essential for the migration of waterfowl, are components of the hydrologic systems from which many municipal water systems ultimately draw their water, and provide ecological stability and terrestrial buffers against storms.

Wetlands may be a component of the waters of the United States, and the discharge of fill into federal wetlands without a federal permit or exception under section 404 of the Clean Water Act is an offense.

**fill**   Dirt, rock and other materials dumped into wetlands. Fill includes all solid matter dumped into wetlands to create dry land, dumped on or in the earth to stabilize the foundation of a structure, or dumped as debris from dredging or digging other than mining. (Mining fill is called "tailings.") Fill may be natural or artificial. Fill materials may not be introduced into the water of the United States, including wetlands, in violation of section 404 of the Clean Water Act.
*See also:* pollution, water pollution, Clean Water Act (CWA).

**waters**

**federal waters (waters of the United States)**   Waters that are interstate or affect interstate commerce, and their tributaries and wetlands. The definition of federal waters has two forms, one for the regulation of vessels, and the other for the regulation of the environment. The extent of federal waters subject to environmental regulation is more extensive.

Federal waters for the regulation of vessels include all navigable interstate and international waterways, including the territorial sea, the contiguous zone, and the high seas for limited purposes.

Federal waters for the regulation of the environment are waters of the United States and include the territorial sea and such of the high seas as over which the United States has jurisdiction for that purpose and international lakes, rivers, and other waters. They include all waterways that are interstate or that do, have, or might affect interstate commerce, as well as their tributary waterways and wetlands. Wetlands that are interstate are federal waters, and wetlands that are intrastate are federal waters as long as the wetland is either connected continuously on the surface or has a significant hydrological nexus to a federal water. In the cases of waters or wetlands, federal waters must in fact be waters, which may include intermittent streams and other bodies of water that have an annual and recurrent presence that is more than sporadic runoff, flooding, or drainage.

**navigable waters**  Waters that are designated by law for navigation or are navigable in fact. Navigable waters include the coastal waters of the sea as well as all watercourses, that are either designated by law as navigable or are in fact navigable by a commercial vessel. Navigable waters that are interstate are federal waters, and to the degree they are within a state, state waters. Navigable waters that are solely intrastate are state waters. The extent of navigable waters is controversial, though navigable water has never implied that every league of the watercourse or body is itself open to navigation. Wetlands and other waters designated by law as navigable waters owing to their relationship to navigable water need only have a relationship to the navigable portion of the waters that is relevant to the purpose of the designation by law. Thus, a protection of sources of water for a navigable waterway may include within the definition the tributary waterways needed to sustain the navigable level of flow, even though the tributaries are themselves non-navigable. Likewise, waters that are not navigable or connected to the navigable channel by flow but that are hydrologically or ecologically related to the body of water that is navigable may be navigable waters for the purpose of its environmental protection.

**way**  Any route by which one has a license to travel over another's land. A way is the area over land that is encumbered by the license of someone, who is not the owner or tenant of the land, to cross the land. The way is neither the right of way, which is the license itself, nor the land in which the way runs. The way is separate from the fee simple in the land, and separate again from the rights to use it, which may be held by the government or the public, by one or more individuals, by specific landholders, or by a group in common. The way is the idea of the road, rather than the land or surface of the road, but the way is not the license to use the road, which is the right of way that may be held by one or more people, or by the state or by the public.

**right of way (right-of-way)**  A right to travel over a way on land or sea, or to maintain the way. A right of way has three distinct senses: the right to travel over a way on the land, the extent of the easement required for such a way over land, or the privilege to pass before another vehicle or vessel.

As a right to travel over land, a right of way arises either from a right in the public or the state that is protected by the state for the use of the individual or from an individual right arising from an easement in the way. An easement is limited in its scope, if it arises in a covenant to the scope expressed or implied in it, or if it arises from prescription or necessity the scope of the use by which the easement was prescribed or required.

As an extent of land subject to an easement, a right of way is a designation of public land, either owned by a government in fee or subject to an easement or to a dedication of use. The right of way in this sense is a matter of conveyance, statute, or regulation and may extend wider than the roadway or way itself.

As a privilege relative to other vehicles or vessels, the right of way is governed by the relative rules of the road. For vehicles, for instance, if two vehicles reaching an unsignalled four-way intersection at the same time, one of which would turn left and the other that would go straight, the vehicle that would cross the other's path, the left-turning vehicle, yields the right of way to other. For vessels in a river, if there is no controlling local custom, the vessel approaching from downstream gives way to the vessel from upstream, because the upstream vessel is more difficult to control, though for vessels at sea, the concept of right of way is only applied obliquely, the vessel approaching another on its starboard bow being required to give way, while the vessel approaching another on its port bow being expected to stand on, unless the vessels send and receive signals to the contrary.

**ways and means**  *See:* taxes, ways and means (ways and means committee).

**weapon**  A device designed to injure another person, or used as if to injure another person. A weapon, in general, is a device that is intended for use to injure or kill a person, is customarily used to injure or kill a person, or is a device created for no injurious purpose but employed as a matter of opportunity to threaten or cause injury or death. A device that has as its primary use the injury or incapacity of a person is a weapon; thus, tazers, stun guns, bazookas, and handguns with no sporting significance are inherently weapons. A device that is customarily used by one person to cause injury to another person, whether in defense or assault, regardless of whether the primary purpose of the device is to cause injury, is also a weapon; thus, a firearm used for hunting, knife, spear, slingshot, bow and arrow, atlatl, boomerang, and reinforced flashlight, which all have primary uses other than human injury, are weapons. A device that is not ordinarily considered a weapon may be a weapon when used to threaten, injure, or kill another, such as a car, scissors, power tool, saw, or pencil. A device need not be complex or machined in order to be a weapon; in an appropriate context, a rock is a weapon. A device used to create the threat of a weapon need not be a real weapon but a facsimile, and in context, a toy used in the manner of a weapon to threaten another person and create the impression it is a weapon, is a weapon.

Whether a device amounts to a weapon for specific purposes in law depends on specific contexts. The definition of weapon for the crime of possession of a weapon or possession of a concealed weapon must be narrowly construed to avoid both vagueness and overbreadth. The definition of weapon for a crime involving the use of a weapon involves intent, and so weapon may be more broadly construed.

*See also:* gun; gun, firearm (arm or arms).

**concealed weapon**   A weapon hidden from view. A concealed weapon is a weapon that is stored or carried in such a manner that is not visible, or not apparently visible to a reasonable, casual observer, being obscured fully or partially by clothing or a container not ordinarily associated with the carriage of a weapon. A weapon in this sense is either a device intended for use to kill or injure another person or customarily used for that purpose.

**weapon of mass destruction (WMD)**   A device intended to injure many by the use of chemical, biological, or radioactive matter. A weapon of mass destruction is a weapon, delivery system, or device intended to cause injury to a significant number of individuals targeted indiscriminately at a specific location, through the release of biological contamination, toxic or poisonous chemicals, or radioactive material, or by an explosion caused by a nuclear device. The federal crime of the use of weapons of mass destruction includes the use of destructive devices such as bombs, rockets, mines, or large bore guns, as well as a single rocket with an explosive of over a quarter ounce or a firearm of any form except a shotgun with a barrel over a half inch in diameter.

In the context of international weapons inspection and arms control, weapons of mass destruction are generally weapons that have the potential to harm a population through chemical, biological, nuclear, or radiological means. Note: although advanced conventional military weapons, such as cluster bombs, flachette rounds, high–explosive bombs, and thermobaric munitions are intended to have a mass effect, they are not considered weapons of mass destruction when used by a national military service within the laws of war.

*See also:* destruction.

**wear and tear**   *See:* waste, ordinary wear and tear (wear and tear).

**weasel word**   *See:* word, weasel word.

**web or world wide web**   *See:* internet (web or world wide web).

**wedlock**   *See:* marriage, wedlock (wed).

**week**   A period of seven days, by custom commencing on Sunday. A week is a period of seven days, and any seven days is one week's time. By custom a week in the Western calendar commences at 12:01 AM on Sunday morning and concludes at midnight the following Saturday night. Although a "work week" commences on a Monday, this period of five days is not presumed when the term "week" is used alone, but it is still the case that when an obligation ordinarily performed in a business or bank is to be performed on the first day of a week, that day is presumably Monday.

**week-to-week tenancy**   *See:* lease, leasehold, tenancy, periodic tenancy, week–to–week tenancy.

**weight**   The effect of gravity on the mass of an object on the surface of the Earth. Weight, as a matter of physics, is the effect of gravity on any matter, which varies according to the mass of the object containing the matter. Weight is relative to the gravity exerted (unlike mass), so the weight of an object diminishes the farther it is from a source of gravity.

Weight, for all purposes of law, is the weight of an object wherever it is measured on the surface of the Earth. There are various standards of weight, in the United States varying according to the form of the object being weighed and the standards of units of measure. English or customary weights, are either avoirdupois weight, which is used for most things, or troy weight, which is used for precious metals such as gold and silver; metric weight is used in lieu of either and is common in chemical, scientific, and pharmaceutical measure, as well as for international shipment.

Weight in transport is reported according to whether the object weighed includes its packaging and container. Gross weight is the total weight of the object and packaging or container. Net weight is the weight of the object alone. Tare weight is the weight of the packaging and container alone.

**avoirdupois (avdp)**   A system of weight used in the United States for most goods. Avoirdupois measures of weight is the basic system of measures for weight in the United States, which accepted it from England, where it was used until the adoption of the metric system. Most goods and objects are weighed in avoirdupois measures, but medicine, black powder, precious metals, and gems are not. The avoirdupois pound has sixteen avoirdupois ounces, the Troy pound is twelve Troy ounces. A Troy ounce weighs more than an avoirdupois ounce, so an avoirdupois pound is heavier than a Troy pound. The avoirdupois pound is divided into sixteen ounces each of which is divided into sixteen drams. An avoiduprois pound has 7,000 grains, as opposed to a Troy pound, which has 5,760 grains. (The weight of a grain is common to both systems of measure, being 0.0649 metric grams.)

**Troy weight**  A system of weight used in the United States for precious metals, stones, and black powder. Troy measures of weight is a rare system of measures for weight in the United States, which accepted it from England, where it was used until the adoption of the metric system. Most goods and objects are weighed in avoirdupois measures, but medicine, black powder, precious metals, and gems are measured by troy weight. The Troy pound is lighter than an avoirdupois pound. Troy pound is twelve Troy ounces, and the avoirdupois pound has sixteen avoirdupois ounces. A Troy ounce weighs more than an avoirdupois ounce, so an avoirdupois pound is heavier than a Troy pound. A Troy ounce is further divided into twenty pennnyweights, and a pennyweight is divided into twenty-four grains. For comparison, a Troy pound has 5,760 grains, while an avoirdupois pound has 7,000 grains. (The weight of a grain is common to both systems of measure, being 0.0649 metric grams.)

**welfare (general welfare or public welfare)**  Happiness or prosperity, or support for the poor. Welfare has two distinct senses in law, the more general being the sense of well-being, happiness, and material prosperity of an individual, community or state; the more specific being the financial, material, and developmental support of poor people in a community, state, or nation. The two senses are related, and often both senses are intended in one use of the word, particularly in the phrase "public welfare."

**welfare state**  The state as guarantor or provider of basic needs for all individuals. The term welfare state, usually employed as a term of abuse for social programs, describes the idea of a state that ensures to each person in the state a series of goods, including housing, food, health care, and education, as well as (in some arguments) meaningful employment and recreation. Critics decry the costs of such programs as well as their potential to limit ambition and reward bad habits, but proponents argue both a moral imperative and greater social opportunity demand such programs.

**well**  A source of liquids from under the ground. A well is a place of access to liquids that are otherwise under the ground, such as water, oil, and gas. Although its customary use in some property descriptions includes natural springs and other natural apertures, its contemporary use is generally confined to artificial structures of pipes that allow the liquid to be extracted, either under natural pressure, as in an artesian well, or artificial pressure from a pump. An oil well may extract oil or oil and gas, and may be located on the ground or in a body of water. A water well extracts water primarily, although gas and minerals are commonly released with it.

The owner of property in fee simple holds the mineral estates in the property, unless the mineral estates were reserved or otherwise severed in the past. When the interests are severed, the mineral interest holder has an easement over the property in order to dig and service a well to reach the minerals.

In some jurisdictions in the United States, there is a common-law interest in a water well that establishes an easement over other properties sharing an aquifer that bars the diminution of flow from the well through the extraction of water for an unreasonable use. In most jurisdictions, interjection of a pollutant under the ground that migrates into the well of another is a trespass on the estate of the other. In most jurisdictions, the placement of wells for the extraction of oil and gas is subject to federal or state licensing and regulation.

*See also:* trespass (trespass to land).

**well-founded fear of persecution**  *See:* refugee, well-founded fear of persecution.

**well-pleaded complaint**  *See:* complaint, well-pleaded complaint.

**wergild (manprice or weregild)**  A payment made in private reparation for homicide or serious offense. Weregild was a payment made in reparation for wrongful death or homicide, from the killer or killer's family to the family of the victim, in lieu of a criminal prosecution, the amount to be paid varying according to the legal and social status of the victim. It was a continental practice used among Saxons and others in Britain.

*See also:* deodand; reparation (reparations).

**wetlands**  *See:* water, wetlands, fill; water, wetlands.

**Wharton's rule**  *See:* conspiracy, concert-of-action rule (Wharton's rule).

**what-might-happen test**  *See:* perpetuity, rule against perpetuities, what-might-happen test (what-might-happen approach).

**wheel conspiracy**  *See:* conspiracy, wheel conspiracy (rimless wheel conspiracy).

**when**  At a given time, or under what conditions. When, literally, represents a specific moment or period of time. Figuratively, "when" represents a condition that must be or has been satisfied. Thus, a will that became valid when signed becomes valid on the date of the signature, but a grant in it that is to a grantee "when she graduates from college" signals a contingency.

*See also:* time.

**whence**  From where. Whence is a preposition in formal English used to denote where the object of the preposition is from. It is a term of location and not time. Note: grammarians understand that whence is a preposition, so "from whence" is redundant, but it is a popular redundancy.

*See also:* where (wherever or wheresoever).

**where (wherever or wheresoever)**  At a given location. Where is a pronoun representing a place. Because the idea of place can be literal—such as a town or street corner or chair, or figurative—such as point in an argument or twist in a plot—"where" has been much abused as an all-purpose pronoun and conjunction, often meaning little or nothing but serving as a place holder in a roundabout clause that suggests causation or time or some other relationship that might otherwise have been expressed with "that" or "which." It is usually preferable, then, to reserve "where" to describe a place, and to use "because" or similar words for causation, and "when" or similar words to describe time. Note: where, wherever, and wheresoever are very close synonyms, the difference between where and the others being that where is a restrictive pronoun (identifying a specific place or places) and the others are non-restrictive (leaving unidentified the place or places intended). Still, the reason for some selection by drafters seems to be that longer words convey more emphasis, the longest being the most grand.

**whereas** Because, or on the contrary. Whereas is a formal term often used in instruments and resolutions to introduce prefatory clauses stating facts, conditions, or reasons, usually leading to the wherefore clause. In other contexts, particularly in interpreting older instruments, it is important to know that whereas has a Janus aspect, so while its most common legal sense is "because," it has also frequently been used in senses that have a reversed meaning, such as "on the contrary" or "although." Context is essential to understanding which sense was intended by the drafter.

*See also:* recital; wherefore (wherefor).

**wherefore (wherefor)** Why, or because. Wherefore is a splendid term for resolutions and formal instruments that adds that touch of formality that is missing when "why" or "because" (or sometimes, then, there, or therefore) are used instead.

*See also:* whereas.

**wherefore clause (premises considered clause or whererfore paragraph)** The conclusion of an argument, especially the request for a remedy in a pleading. A wherefore clause is a clause in an instrument that reaches a conclusion drawn from the premises that went before it. In pleadings, a wherefore clause is the same as a prayer for relief, a paragraph that states the remedy sought; there may be more than one. Each is usually a separate paragraph, the first paragraph still sometimes initiated with the customary phrase, "Wherefore, premises considered," and then listing the remedies the plaintiff asserts are justified by the preceding allegations. The answer or other responsive pleading that must respond to allegations need not respond to a wherefore paragraph, although most defendants deny it.

**whistleblower (whistle-blower)** Informant against one's employer. A whistleblower is an employee who knows of some wrongdoing occurring in a corporate or governmental enterprise and who notifies a senior supervisor, public authority, or the public press of the wrongful activity. When the whistleblower discloses evidence of criminal activity to law enforcement, the whistleblower performs not only an important public service but avoids further liability as an accomplice. Even so, many corporations require non-disclosure of information harmful to the corporate image, and will engage in retaliatory job actions against a whistleblower. Governmental offices

will scrupulously employ rules on the disclosure of classified information as the basis of retaliation. Retaliation for whistleblowing by a private employer may be lawful, despite increased statutory protections for whistleblowers in both public and private employment.

*See also:* retaliation, prisoner retaliation action.

**qui tam (action qui tam or qui tam action)** A private action to collect moneys from fraud on the government. A qui tam action is a private civil action brought against a person or entity, particularly a contractor that has committed fraud against the U.S. government. Qui tam is an abbreviation for the maxim qui tam pro domino rege quam pro se ipso in hac parte sequitur, or "who pursues this action does so on the behalf of our Lord the King as well as on his own behalf."

In a federal qui tam action, the plaintiff, or relator, is a private party with access to information not otherwise known to the public, who brings an action qui tam in the name of the United States, under the federal False Claims Act, 31 U.S.C. §3730(b)(2010), against the parties engaged in the fraud. The government may then intervene and manage the suit or allow it to proceed by the relator. If government intervenes and the action is successful, the relator may recover up to one-quarter of the value recovered, or if the relator maintains the suit without the government, up to thirty per cent, and attorneys' fees. If the government does not proceed and the claim fails, the defendant may recover attorneys' fees.

State actions in qui tam follow various rules, in some states providing for a state reward for information that leads to a recovery. In other states the basis being moved under whistleblowing laws, particularly related to the payment of Medicaid funds.

*See also:* whistleblower (whistle-blower); fraud, False Claims Act (Lincoln's Law); tort, Federal Tort Claims Act (F.T.C.A. or FTCA).

**Sarbanes-Oxley claim (SOX Act claim)** A corporate whistleblower may bring a retaliation claim within ninety days. The Sarbanes-Oxley Act of 2002, codified at 18 U.S.C. §1514A (2010), provides a cause of action to employees in publicly traded companies who disclose information to a supervisor, regulator or police official, member of Congress, supervisor, or the Securities and Exchange Commission, related to fraud or a violation of rules of the SEC, for certain job actions by the company, if the employee files the complaint within ninety days.

**Whistleblower Protection Act (WPA)** Law safeguarding against termination of informants against the company for whom they work. A whistleblower protection act offers legal protection against certain forms of retaliation by either public or private employers who report certain illegal, dangerous, fraudulent, or improper activity to a public body. The scope of such acts varies widely among the jurisdictions that have enacted them. A federal whistleblower protection law enacted in 1989, (Pub. L. 101-12, 103 Stat. 16), provides rather limited protection to federal employees who report misconduct by an agency, which gives some protection to federal employees in the absence of First Amendment protection for statements made in the course of their employment, a state of affairs that followed the ruling in Garcetti v. Ceballos, 547 U.S. 410 (2006), which has been subject to discussion in Congress that, as of 2009 may lead to further developments.

**White Court**   *See:* court, U.S. court, U.S. Supreme Court, White Court.

**White House**   *See:* president, White House (Executive Office of the President).

**white-collar crime**   *See:* crime, white-collar crime (white collar crime).

**Whiteacre or Redacre or Greenacre**   *See:* Blackacre (Whiteacre or Redacre or Greenacre).

**who will watch the watchers?**   *See:* official, legal official, quis custodiet ipsos custodes (who will watch the watchers?).

**whole life insurance**   *See:* insurance, category of insurance, life insurance, whole life insurance (straght life insurance or ordinary life insurance).

**whole truth and nothing but the truth**   *See:* truth, whole truth and nothing but the truth.

**wholesale (wholesaler)**   The selling of goods to retailers or suppliers to retailers. Wholesale is the sale of goods to suppliers or retailers, as opposed to retail, which is the sale of goods to consumers. Although rules vary from jurisdiction to jurisdiction, wholesale transactions are not usually subject to sales tax, although there may be a transfer tax or value added tax when such regimes apply. A wholesaler is liable for defects in goods sold, though the liability under the common law was limited to those in privity of contract, and it is sometimes still limited to parties within privity, although within a chain of privity, though this is not so when the product defect is pursued under a claim of negligence or some bases of strict liability.
   *See also:* retail (retailer).

**whorehouse**   *See:* prostitution, brothel (bawdy-house or bordello or house of ill fame or house of ill repute or house of prostitution).

**wicked sisters of the common law or unholy trinity**   *See:* defense, three wicked sisters (wicked sisters of the common law or unholy trinity).

**widget**   A hypothetical fungible, marketable object. The widget is a thing, one that has been manufactured by the millions upon millions for law school hypotheticals. They are sold among merchants, heaved into cargo holds, insured and lost at sea in admiralty and insurance, bought and sold on arcane markets in commercial law, while in property various widgets, some of them heirlooms, are owned (solely or jointly, in marital estates or by unmarried lovers), abandoned, given as gifts, left in wills, and found in attics. Widgets even show up in constitutional law as the object of privacy and property interests. Widgets are everywhere. Unless the storyteller says otherwise, however, all widgets are the same, a perfectly fungible commodity.
   *See also:* fungibility (fungible); res.

**widow or widower**   *See:* spouse, surviving spouse (widow or widower).

**wife**   *See:* family, spouse, wife.

**wild animal**   *See:* animal, wild animal, ferae naturae; animal, wild animal.

**wild deed**   *See:* deed, wild deed.

**wildcat strike**   *See:* union, labor union, labor dispute, labor strike, wildcat strike.

**will (human will)**   The mental power that leads to thought and action. Will is the aspect of the individual that allows the formation of desire and thought and their translation into action. An act that is willful is the result of an exercise of the human will, rather than an accident or unintended consequence of some other act. Will is similar to intention, but will includes both intent and action in the same concept, and the intentionality of will might not require an individuated reason to act. What will excludes are involuntary actions – actions that are accidental and actions that are spasmodic or uncontrolled.

   Will, in the law, is distinct from philosophical ideas of human will generally, and is synonymous with the will in willfulness. In this sense, law does not include acts that are the result of coercion. (More general senses of the human will would consider will to be possible in action responding to coercion.)

   Will is also thought of, both in the law and more generally, as both an individual and collective act. A group who collaborate and act together act through their collective will, or their corporate will. In this sense the national will is the basis for the survival of the constitution and legal system.

   Will may be construed from circumstance, later inferred from the action in context. The formulations of some philosophers to the contrary, the law does not require an articulable reason as the basis of an intent prior to a willful act, but a willful act may be the result of passion, emotion, or instinctive reaction.

**will contest**   *See:* probate, will contest, caveat to the probate of a will (caveator); probate, will contest.

**at will**   Without specified duration. At will signals that a person or entity engages in an activity out of free will, continuing to do so only so long as that will continues, and not according to a set term or commitment of time. An at-will employee may quit or be fired with only the most minimal notice required by law for all employees, and for no particular reason at all. Even so, even at-will employees are protected from abusive or discriminatory treatment barred by statute.

**last will and testament (testament)** A declaration made while living of the disposition of one's property at death. A last will and testament is a declaration made by an individual while alive that makes a variety of arrangements for the disposition of the property that the individual will own at the time of the individual's death. A will is valid once it is made, as long as it is made according to the laws governing the particular form in which the will is made, but it is not effective until its maker's death. A will may be revoked, revived, or amended as long as its maker is alive and has the capacity required to do so. Although the term will is sufficient, the customary name of Last Will and Testament is still commonly in use. Regardless of which name is assigned to the instrument, the maker of a will is known as the testator.

A will made in the ordinary course of life is to be formal and witnessed. Wills made in circumstances precluding such formalities are either a holographic will, which is written by hand by the testator, or an oral will, which is spoken aloud by the testator to a reliable witness.

In most circumstances, a will is not automatically put into effect by the death of the testator. Rather, it is submitted to probate by an interested party, an estate is created, an executor or personal representative is appointed, the will is proved, the estate is liquidated, the debts of the estate are settled, and the various devises and legacies created are distributed, an accounting is filed with the court, and the estate is closed. If there is reason to believe the will is invalid, a challenge to the will may be brought and heard in the probate court, which will either uphold the will and require its execution, accept another will in its stead as proved and require the execution of the other will, or void the will and require the estate to be administered as if the decedent had died intestate, or with no will at all.

*See also:* probate.

**living will** *See:* death, living will (advance directive).

**will contest** *See:* probate, will contest.

**antilapse statute** A statute providing cures for flaws in a will after death. An antilapse statute provides a scheme for bequests and devises that might lapse in a will, owing either to a predeceasing legatee, or to a difficulty with the definition of a class or to flaws in the language. Antilapse statutes cannot cure a necessary violation of the rule against perpetuities, but they may allow a redefinition of a gift or class to avoid the violation.

**codicil** An amendment to a will. A codicil is an addition or supplement to a will, which amends a last will and testament, if it is executed in the same manner that the will was originally executed: a witnessed will must have a witnessed codicil, but a holograph may have a valid holographic amendment. A codicil is thus read into a will and

considered valid as long as the will it modifies is valid. Codicils are not required for a revocation of the will or in the event a substitute will is issued.

**holographic will (holograph)** A will written by hand. A holographic will, or holograph, is a last will and testament written in the handwriting of the testator and signed by the testator, rather than being typed or printed as is usually the case for a formal will. A holograph may be witnessed, but by definition, it need not be. The entire instrument need not be in the testator's hand, but all material portions of the will must be written by hand for the instrument to qualify as a holograph, unless it meets all of the conditions of formality of an executed will. Not all jurisdictions recognize a holograph, and some of those that do, allow the use of a holograph only for the disposition of small estates or small portions of a larger estate.

In jurisdictions that allow it, a holographic will is an exception to the requirement of execution of a will. Even so, the testator must meet all of the extrinsic requirements, in that the testator must have testamentary capacity, and the will must clearly manifest the intent of the testator to leave property at death to the designated legatees and devisees, and there may be no evidence of later renunciation or revocation.

**joint and mutual will (mutual will)** Two wills created according to a common plan. A joint and mutual will, also called a conjoint will or a mutual will, is a will that is related to another will, the two wills being created according to a common plan for the disposition of the assets of both testators. A joint and mutual will may exist in a single instrument or in two instruments, though in either case the effect is the same as creating two wills. The wills are likely to be reciprocal, although this is not a necessary element of their mutuality. The wills may contain clauses declaring one not to be revocable unless the other is also or to be irrevocable, and while such clauses are generally void as a matter of the construction of wills, a breach of such a clause may amount to a breach of a contract implied in the making of the wills.

Each will comes into force with the death of the testator of that will. The death of one joint testator does not affect the validity of the will of the other.

*See also:* mutuality (mutual).

**lost will (destroyed will)** A valid will believed to exist but not to be found. A lost will is a last will and testament that is believed to exist and to be valid but that cannot be located after the death of the testator. If a copy of the will is available, in many jurisdictions, the will may be presented for formal probate.

A destroyed will is a last will and testament known to have been destroyed and so not to be available for introduction into probate. Even so, a destroyed will may be probated like a lost will, as long as the destruction of the will had not been the result of the intent of the testator in an act of revocation.

The existence and content of either a lost will or a destroyed will may be established by parol evidence. The proponent of the lost or destroyed will must usually present clear and convincing evidence of the will's former existence and sufficient evidence to overcome a presumption that the will that was lost or destroyed was revoked.

**mystic will (mystic testament)**  A will made in secret and sealed until probate. The mystic will is a form of last will and testament that is recognized in Louisiana under the Louisiana Code, in which the testator writes a will in secrecy, signs it, places it into an envelope and seals it, and then presents the sealed envelope containing the will to a notary and to three witnesses, declaring the instrument within to be the person's will, after which the testator, the notary, and the witnesses sign a superscription. The envelope is not to be opened until probate unless the testator contacts the notary to revoke the will. Thus can the testator preserve the mystery, or secrecy, of the testament, even from the witnesses, for as long as the testator lives.

**nuncupative will (oral will or noncupative will)**  A will vocally expressed by a testator near unto death. A nuncupative will is a last will and testament that is orally expressed to witnesses rather than made in writing. The law disfavors oral testaments, and a nuncupative will is only valid if the will not only is made in extremis, or in the testator's belief that death is imminent, but also the testator dies soon thereafter. The policy underlying the requirement of death is obvious; if the testator recovers there would be time to write and execute a valid will. To prove a nuncupative will of any value, the statement must have been made before witnesses, and a requirement of three witnesses to the same act is not unusual, although this requirement is customarily relaxed in the case of a soldier or sailor.

*See also:* in, in extremis.

**pourover will**  A will funding a pourover trust. A pourover will is a last will and testament that includes a provision dedicating funds to be transferred to a trust established either by the testator while alive, in the will itself, or to be established by the executor and used to some other end before being transferred to the trust. For purposes of considering who has an interest in the will, the trustee of the trust is the devisee or legatee of the provision, and the beneficiary of the trust has an interest in it.

**pre-nuptial will (prenuptial will)**  A will executed before the testator's marriage. A pre-nuptial will is a will that was executed by the testator prior to the marriage of the testator to the spouse who is married to the testator at the time of the testator's death. A pre-nuptial will that does not make a provision for a surviving spouse is presumed to be modified or revoked, at least as to the spouse's share, unless there is clear evidence that the testator intended to omit any interest to the spouse.

Note: a pre-nuptial agreement may be sufficient to indicate an intent by the testator to omit the pretermitted spouse, although this must be the clear and unambiguous intent of the decedent spouse.

**self-proved will (self-authenticating will)**  A will that need not be proved by witnesses. A self-proved will is allowed in states that follow the Uniform Probate Code approach, which provides that a formal last will and testament that is properly executed by the testator, with the usual witnesses, all of whom sign before a notary or other official authorized to administer oaths, does not require the witnesses to prove the will during probate. That a will is self proved is no bar to a contest and does not affect a codicil, amendment or revocation, any of which are effective if they are done in the usual manner, without a notary.

**sham will**  A will executed without the intent to be valid at death. A sham will is an instrument that appears to be a last will and testament that is created by the testator for some purpose other than to serve as the disposition of the testator's estate after death. A sham will is void, even if all of the formalities of execution have been otherwise satisfied.

*See also:* sham.

**testamentary**  Having to do with a last will and testament. Anything testamentary arose from or is related to a last will and testament. A testamentary disposition is a grant made in the will. Letters testamentary are the written appointment and authority from a probate judge to an executor, authorizing the executor to probate the estate.

**testamentary beneficiary**  Any party who is to receive anything under a will. A testamentary beneficiary is any party designated as the recipient of a legacy, devise, trust benefit, trusteeship, or any other gift of value in any form of last will and testament. As a general rule, the executor cannot be a testamentary beneficiary, although in most states a surviving spouse may be an executor and also a beneficiary. Otherwise, a testamentary beneficiary may renounce the gift under the will and then serve as executor. Note: there is a critical difference between a beneficiary of a testamentary trust and a testamentary beneficiary. The class of testamentary beneficiaries includes any who take under a will either directly through devise or indirectly through being named the beneficiary of a trust created in the will, such a party being a beneficiary of the testamentary trust. A beneficiary of a testamentary trust is thus also a testamentary beneficiary.

A testamentary beneficiary may have a cause of action under a third–party beneficiary theory of the attorney–client contract between the testator and an attorney who prepares the will, for harm from negligent assistance of counsel given to the testator, if the testator had clearly expressed an intent that the will would directly benefit the beneficiary and the beneficiary was harmed by the negligence of the testator's counsel.

**Statute of Wills (Wills Act)**   An owner may choose the grantees of property at death. The Statute of Wills, 32 Hen. 8 c. 1 (1540), created the power of each free land holder to bequeath the land to whomever the landholder chooses, through testamentary devise. Prior to the statute, land either descended to surviving relatives through primogeniture according to consanguinity, or it escheated to the crown. The Wills Act of 1837, 1 Vict. c.26, superseded the statute.

*See also:* primogeniture.

**willfulness (willful or wilfully)**   The intention to cause some result through a given action. Willfulness is the application of a person's will to achieve some result, that is to intend some action to achieve some intended purpose, when both the intention and the action are voluntary and committed by a person with legal capacity, and the action is not the result of coercion or deception. An actor performing a willful act is usually liable for the effects of that act, including effects arising as unintended consequences. Willfulness in the definition of a criminal prohibition was read in the nineteenth century as ill will or bad faith, an intent to commit the evil that the criminal statute was enacted to prevent; this sense of willfulness persists in many jurisdictions, although it is more often merged now with specific intent.

*See also:* tax, tax crime willfullness; mens, mens rea (mental state).

**willful blindness**   *See:* knowledge, constructive knowledge, willful blindness (conscious avoidance or willful ignorance or deliberate ignorance).

**willful disobedience**   *See:* obedience, willful disobedience.

**willful ignorance**   *See:* ignorance, voluntary ignorance (willful ignorance).

**willing and able**   *See:* performance, ready, willing and able.

**winding up (wrap up or wind up)**   The settlement of obligations and distribution of assets. Winding up is the process of ending an enterprise, in which creditors and debtors are put on notice of the termination of the enterprise in order to complete outstanding business; payments owed to the enterprise are collected or written off; debts owed are paid or otherwise settled; the assets of the enterprise are liquidated or distributed in kind to those with legal or equitable interests in the enterprise, according to the quantity and kind of their interest; and the government in the jurisdiction that incorporates, recognizes, or charters the entity is given notice. Business entities, such as corporations, partnerships, and sole proprietorships, are wrapped up, as are entities for a time, such as trusts, estates and administrations.

**wiretap**   *See:* surveillance, electronic surveillance, wiretap (wiretapping).

**wit (to wit)**   That is to say. Wit is mental acumen, particularly the ability to combine thoughts and observations with novelty and elegance. The phrase "to wit" introduces a summary of what has been said, implying a helpful or pithy restatement. One could substitute "that is to say" or "in other words," though these are longer and more likely to interrupt the flow of the language.

*See also:* scilicet (S. or SS. or scil.).

**Witanagemot**   *See:* parliament, Witanagemot (Witangemot or Witena–Gemot).

**with all deliberate speed**   *See:* segregation, desegregation, with all deliberate speed.

**with prejudice**   *See:* prejudice, legal prejudice, with prejudice (without prejudice).

**withdrawal of counsel**   *See:* counsellor, counsel, withdrawal of counsel.

**withholding of rent**   *See:* rent, withholding of rent (rent withholding).

**without**   Not with, or outside. Without, initially, was a synonym of "outside," a sense it has in early cases. The more common contemporary sense is as the opposite of "with." Thus, to describe a person's action as without due attention care is roughly the same as to describe the person's action as lacking due attention or as done not with due attention.

**without day**   *See:* sine, sine die (without day).

**without prejudice**   *See:* prejudice, legal prejudice, with prejudice (without prejudice).

**without recourse**   *See:* recourse, without recourse (sans recours or with recourse).

**witness**   One with knowledge, as an observer or expert. A witness has information of use to legal officials who are examining the state of affairs in the world for some purpose. Witness, from old English, means a person with knowledge, and the kinds of knowledge the witness may have is as extensive as the scope of human understanding, limited only by the needs of a particular inquiry and the manner in which the knowledge was gained. Witnesses may exist who are unknown to legal officials, or they may be consulted informally.

In general, the law is concerned with witnesses in legislative, administrative, judicial, and private proceedings. Legislative witnesses are individuals called by a legislative body to give testimony for whatever purpose the body deems appropriate. Administrative witnesses are present in either a quasi-judicial or a quasi-legislative proceeding and are accorded the rights and privileges required under the relevant regulations.

Witnesses in judicial proceedings are individuals who provide evidence, either as a lay witness (sometimes called an "eye witness"), one who gives lay testimony, or as an expert witness, one who gives expert testimony. The qualifications of such witnesses, the scope of appropriate testimony, and the means by which that testimony may be elicited by counsel, are subject to the rules of evidence as well as the rules of procedure. That a witness gives evidence does not require the court to accept the evidence as true, and the jury or the judge sitting as the finder of fact is entitled to assess the credibility of the witness.

Certain proceedings require witnesses of certain forms or qualifications, or of a given number. For example, the probate of a will requires the testimony of witnesses to the will, if available, and an action for treason may not be brought unless there are two witnesses who testify to the same overt act of treason by the defendant.

Witnesses in private proceedings, such as arbitrations or mediations, are usually present only as volunteers and are accorded such privileges as decorum requires. In some private proceedings, a consent to be a witness implies consent to be a witness in a later judicial forum. Thus a witness to the execution of a will impliedly consents to providing relevant evidence when the will is submitted to probate.

Several constitutional limits and privileges apply to the questioning of witnesses, depending on the forum in which the witness appears. The Fifth Amendment privilege against self-incrimination applies in every forum, while the right to the assistance of counsel applies only to witnesses who are, or are likely to be, accused of a crime. Freedom of speech does not apply to witnesses in most instances, and a witness is not privileged to engage in self-expression beyond the scope of an inquiry to which the witness is summoned. Though a witness is inherently free to answer a question or to make a relevant statement of the witness's choice, a failure to provide a truthful statement exposes the witness to liability for the crimes of perjury or, in some instance, obstruction of justice.

The qualifications of a witness are always a relevant question. A person must be thought to have sufficient capacity to have accurately perceived a relevant circumstance, sufficient memory to recall it, and sufficient narrative skill to describe it. A lay witness must have had some exposure to the relevant information that would lead to a reliable perception of it. An expert witness must have some basis of expertise in knowledge, skill, training, education, or experience, as well as a sufficient basis in the review of information relevant to the proceeding on which a credible opinion might be based. The question arises in rare instances as to the qualifications of a non-human to serve as a witness, such as when a dog or other animal is known to have observed some event. In this case, an examination of an animal is sometimes allowed in court, though as evidence rather than as testimony. Similarly, machines are not considered witnesses but evidence.

Note: witness is both a noun and a verb. As a noun, a witness is the person who observed and who recalls some event. As a verb, witness has two meanings: one is the act of observing it and the other is testifying or relating what was first observed.

*See also:* notary (notary public); testimony (testify); deposition, deponent.

**witness discovery**   *See:* discovery, witness discovery.

**witness immunity**   *See:* immunity, witness immunity.

**witness privilege or party privilege**   *See:* privilege, litigation privilege (witness privilege or party privilege).

**witness protection**   *See:* custody, protective custody, witness security (witness protection).

**witness statement**   *See:* discovery, witness discovery, witness statement.

**absent witness**   One who does not appear to testify. An absent witness is one not present on the stand. Absent witnesses may appear through the presentation of evidence from depositions or affidavits, in which case the evidence is subjected to objections for hearsay when there is an absent witness. If a prosecution witness is known to have exculpatory evidence relevant to a criminal trial and is not called by the prosecutor, the effect of the absent witness may be a reversible error.

**accomplice witness**   A witness who was an accomplice of a criminal defendant. An accomplice witness in a criminal action is a person who admits to having committed a crime and testifies to having been an accomplice of the defendant in doing so. The fact of the criminal confession may be weighed by the jury in considering the credibility of the witness, as may any consideration the prosecution or state may offer the witness, but neither bars the witness from testifying. At common law, the uncorroborated testimony of one accomplice was sufficient to sustain the conviction of another accomplice. In many jurisdictions, statutes now require at least some independent, corroborating evidence besides the testimony of an accomplice who would otherwise be liable for the same offense as the defendant.

*See also:* accomplice.

**attesting witness (subscribing witness)**   A person who signed a document, testifying to its authenticity An attesting witness, or a subscribing witness, is a witness to the execution of an instrument. There are many legal forms — such as the creation of certain contracts, deeds, grants, and other instruments — in which a witness attests to an event, and an attesting witness not only attests to its occurrence or subscribes to the instrument but stands ready to testify to that occurrence and to incidents relevant to that occurrence, such as the apparent capacity and independence of judgment of the testator, contractor, donor or other party or parties executing the instrument witnessed. An attesting witness must have legal capacity at the time of the event witnessed.

An attesting witness to a last will and testament must ordinarily have no interest in the will, and when a person is given a legacy or devise in a will for which that person was an attesting witness, the legacy or devise may be void. If, however, there were sufficient other witnesses for the will to be valid without that witness, the attesting witness would be considered a nullity as a witness.

**attorney-witness (lawyer-witness)**   An attorney who testifies in an action, particularly when representing a party to it. An attorney–witness, or lawyer–witness, is an attorney who is called to give evidence in an action, whether a criminal or civil action, and whether at trial or in a deposition. There is a fundamental conflict of roles in an attorney serving as an advocate for a party and providing evidence in an action between that party and another. An attorney who is likely to be called as a witness in an action may be disqualified by the court from serving as counsel for a party in that action. Yet, the opposing party may not seek to call an attorney for its opponent for the purpose of disqualification, nor is disqualification a matter of right with an opposing party.

**character witness**  A witness who testifies as to the character of a party or another witness. A character witness is a witness called primarily to give character evidence regarding a party or another witness. Character witnesses under the federal rules are not allowed to give evidence of any aspect of character other than a reputation for truthfulness or untruthfulness, and evidence in support of a witness's truthfulness is admissible only after the witness's veracity has been attacked. The same person may be both an eye witness and a character witness.

*See also:* evidence, character evidence.

**competent witness (incompetent witness)**  The legal fitness of a person to testify under oath. A competent witness is a person with the capacity to testify under oath, having sufficient awareness and reason and not being disqualified owing to the subject matter. Every person is presumed competent, and incompetence must be alleged and proved. Under contemporary standards, a witness is usually competent to testify if the witness is capable of distinguishing truth from falsity, and thus capable of testifying truthfully (whether or not the witness does so is a matter of credibility, not competency). An otherwise competent witnesses might not be qualified as a witness, such as a person sitting as a judge or juror in the same action or a person who is a beneficiary of a will to be witnessed. Constitutional questions arise when a criminal defendant is deemed incompetent, and the Fifth and Sixth Amendments trump any rule of competency that restrict a criminal defendant from testifying, although evidence of incompetence relevant to the likelihood of the testimony's accuracy is then usually admissible.

**credible witness**  A competent and believable witness. A credible witness is both competent and believable. Although the credibility of a witness is a matter for the finder of fact, the court may take the apparent credibility of a witness or relative credibility of several witnesses in evaluating the sufficiency of evidence.

*See also:* credibility.

**disinterested witness (interested witness)**  A witness with no interest in the relevant matter. A disinterested witness is a witness with no stake in the outcome of the matter at hand. The fundamental ideal of disinterest by a witness is that neither the witness nor a family member, business acquaintance, or social ally may realize any benefit or detriment of any form through the witness's testifying or failing to testify. Narrower questions of interest apply in specific contexts, in which an interested witness is defined by a particular interest or interests; this is not to say that a person who is without such an interest is disinterested, but the person is not barred as interested: an interested witness to a will is a person for whom a grant of a devise or legacy is made in the will. An interested witness in a criminal case has a familial, business, or personal relationship with the defendant, or has a potential for a benefit or detriment from offering or failing to offer testimony in the action. An interested witness in a civil action has a financial relationship to any of the parties or in some property subject to the dispute. Only in the case of serving as an attesting witness to a will does interest disqualify a witness. In other cases, interest is a basis for diminished credibility, and disinterestedness a basis for increased credibility.

**earwitness (ear witness)**  A person who testifies to things heard. An earwitness is a lay witness who testifies to sounds or speech the witness heard at a time relevant to a legal action, including comparisons of speech or sound to known speech or sounds as a basis of identification of a speaker, device, or event heard.

**expert (expert witness)**  A witness providing expert narrative or analysis. An expert assists the finder of fact in understanding the meaning or significance of evidence otherwise before the court. An expert may give an opinion on any relevant matter, although the expert's opinion is never conclusive, and expert evidence is not to invade the province of the jury as the final arbiter of questions of fact in a jury trial.

An expert must be qualified in some scientific, professional, technical, or other specialized knowledge that is distinct from the knowledge that the average juror would be expected to have achieved or that is intended to dispel a misconception regarding the facts that the average juror might be expected to hold. There is no definite inventory of the fields in which expert evidence may be given.

An expert's qualification in the field in which the expert is to testify must be demonstrable, although the basis of that qualification may be from education, training, experience, knowledge, or skill. The court must be satisfied that the expert's qualifications are bona fide and sufficient to provide the evidence required, although there are few if any formal criteria that must be satisfied in lieu of other criteria, in any category of qualification. Still, the qualification of an expert requires expertise before the fact. A person whose sole expertise arises from the evaluation of the evidence in an action is not an expert.

An expert may offer an opinion based on the analysis of evidence alone, or by comparison of the evidence to a basis of evaluation by a method of analysis employed among the community of those with similar expertise. If the basis of evaluation is comparison to some analysis, the method of analysis must be disclosed and is open to examination for its sufficiency and acceptability in order for the expert to be qualified to testify.

An expert is not allowed to testify as to whether a defendant is liable. As a general rule, the expert may explain the evidence but may not draw conclusions as to what the evidence means related to the responsibility of one party or another. This can be a very difficult rule to follow, and there are countless exceptions as well as overlaps that make impossible a clear division between the meaning of evidence and responsibility for action. When an expert goes too far in presenting evidence of guilt or liability, so that there is a risk the jury will rely on the expert's opinion or belief rather than forming an independent assessment, the expert is said to have invaded the province of the jury. Such a risk is greater when there is only one expert on a given matter. When an expert does render opinions on guilt, liability, or responsibility, a curative instruction may be sufficient, but a mistrial may also be the only practical remedy.

*See also:* rape, Rape Trauma Syndrome (Child Abuse Syndrome); expert (expertise); evidence, opinion evidence; jury, province of the jury.

**Daubert test**   An expert's analysis is qualified if it is tested, published, quantified, or accepted. The Daubert test, announced in Daubert v. Merrell Dow Pharmaceuticals, Inc., 509 U.S. 579 (1993), interprets Federal Rule of Evidence 702 with a liberal qualification for expert witnesses, allowing an otherwise qualified witness to testify employing an analytic methodology that is to be allowed if it satisfies a four-factor test. The methodology employed by the expert is qualified according to the four factors, which are to be applied by the court in some manner though not necessarily by requiring satisfaction of all four factors, by being objectively tested, by being subjected to peer review and publication, by having a known or potential rate of error, given standards used for the analysis, and by having been generally accepted by the scientific community. The methodology of the expert is usually disclosed at the time the expert is designated as a possible or likely witness at trial, and the pre-trial qualification of the expert usually incorporates an examination of the methodology.

**eyewitness (fact witness or eye witness)**   A person who testifies to things the person has perceived. An eyewitness is a lay witness who testifies to events and conditions the witness saw, heard, felt, smelled, or otherwise perceived at a time relevant to a legal action. Eyewitness testimony may include identifications of a person, including comparisons of a person's appearance to specific, identified individuals as a basis for identification of a person present at a place the witness observed.

*See also:* observation (observe as witness).

**grand-jury witness**   A witness before the grand jury. A grand-jury witness is any person who is called to give evidence before a grand jury. A person who has been accused or suspected of committing a crime may be a grand-jury witness, but unless an indictment, charge, information, or arrest has been made, the person is not entitled to the assistance of counsel before the grand jury. Although the evidence introduced before a grand jury is secret and not to be revealed, a grand-jury witness cannot be barred from later discussing that witness's own testimony.

*See also:* jury, grand jury.

**hostile witness**   A witness who intends not to assist the lawyer while testifying. A hostile witness is a witness whose purpose is not to provide a full, open, and neutral testimony in response to the questions asked by the attorney during the witness's testimony. Hostile witnesses include two groups. First are individuals who are inherently or automatically presumed to be hostile to the lawyer or party who has called them to the stand for questioning: individuals with an interest adverse to the lawyer's client, such as the opposing party; officers, employees and agents of an entity that is an opposing party, or an individual with a personal or professional relationship to the opposing party. Second are individuals who are not inherently hostile as a result of opposing interests but whose behavior, attitude, or statements demonstrate to the court that the witness is indeed unwilling to fully, fairly, and neutrally provide evidence in response to questions by the lawyer eliciting testimony.

In either case, the lawyer may employ leading questions in the questioning of the witness. In the case of an adverse party or other inherently hostile witness, the lawyer may lead the witness as a matter of right. In other cases, the lawyer may employ leading questions by order of the court on motion by the lawyer.

**judge as witness**   A judge who testifies in an action, particularly an action before the judge. A judge acting as a witness is usually disqualified from acting as judge in the same cause. Although the rule varies somewhat among jurisdictions as to scope and its basis as a statute, rule of judicial conduct, or rule of witness qualification, the general principle is that a judge cannot be perceived as an independent arbiter in a cause in which the judge has a personal involvement, even as a neutral witness. In some jurisdictions, the requirement of judicial qualification applies once there is an apparent likelihood the judge may be called in any capacity as a witness. In others, it attaches only when either the judge is called or subpoenaed or if the judge is a material witness.

**lay witness**   A person testifying from personal knowledge rather than expertise. A witness who testifies to what the witness observes or knows as a matter of observation or the knowledge gained through the use of ordinary reasoning applied in daily life, rather than a particular understanding or knowledge based on a scientific, technical, or professional expertise.

A lay witness may give an opinion on a matter of reputation or other matter of common knowledge, and may offer certain limited opinions as to a perception based on an observation but is usually barred from offering an opinion as to the legal significance of the matter observed, which is an opinion reserved to the jurors to form.

See also: opinion, lay opinion.

**material witness** A person whom prosecutors believe has evidence of a material fact in a criminal investigation. A material witness is a witness who can, or whom the prosecutor believes can, provide testimony that would be material in a criminal proceeding. If a police officer or prosecutor files an affidavit alleging that a person is a material witness, and showing that it may become impracticable to secure the presence of the person in court by subpoena, a judge or magistrate may order the arrest and detention or bail of the person, at least until the person is deposed.

A material witness who has been deposed is to be released, although there are numerous instances in which the witness was detained until trial. Detention of a material witness may not be in a manner that amounts to or is similar to detention ordered as a punishment for a person convicted of a crime. The detention of a person as a material witness for the purposes of investigation as a possible criminal defendant or for interrogation is a violation of the statute and the warrant of probable cause requirements of the Fourth Amendment.

**party-witness (non-party witness)** A party who testifies in a civil action. A party-witness is a witness who is also a party to the action. A non-party witness is a witness who is not a party to the action in which the witness gives testimony. Unlike non-party witnesses, a party-witness is not sequestered from the courtroom or deposition room if the rule for the sequestration of witnesses is invoked.

See also: witness, sequestration of witness (the rule of separation of witnesses).

**res gestae witness** A witness to some portion of a crime. A res gestae witness is a lay witness who observed or heard some action, circumstance, or event that is alleged to have been part of a criminal transaction, and whose testimony is believed by the prosecutor to aid in developing a full narrative of the facts relevant to the charged offense.

See also: res, res gestae (res gesta).

**sequestration of witness (the rule of separation of witnesses)** The isolation of witnesses from the trial. The sequestration of witnesses is the removal of witnesses from the courtroom during the trial to prevent a witness from being influenced by the argument or evidence presented before the witness testifies. Sequestration is sometimes authorized by statute or rule, but it is within the inherent power of the judge to manage the trial. A party may not be sequestered, whether or not the party may be called as a witness.

See also: sequestration (sequester).

**surprise witness** A witness called without prior notice to the opposing side. A surprise witness is a witness called by a party to testify at trial, though that party had not given notice to opposing counsel that the witness would testify, or was likely to testify, or was a witness. Thus, a surprise witness was not listed on a pre-trial witness list or otherwise identified to opposing counsel prior to trial. There is no right of a party to call a surprise witness, and the trial court has the discretion to qualify or deny the witness, which the court should base on a balance between the degree to which the evidence the witness may offer appears probative of a material element of the case and the degree to which the opposing party had no means to prepare for the cross-examination of the witness.

**tender of the witness (tender the witness)** To present a witness for questioning under oath. To tender a witness is to present a witness for questioning, particularly when an attorney concludes the questions that attorney asks of a witness, presenting the witness for examination by opposing counsel. The term is also used, though much more rarely, for the general listing of a witness on a witness list or by an attorney's first call of a witness to the stand to testify.

See also: tender.

**two-witness rule** Two witnesses must testify to perjury or treason. The two-witness rule requires two witnesses to testify to a single event in an action for treason, perjury, or subornation of perjury. In such cases, the prosecution must present either two competent witnesses to the same overt act by the defendant or one witness who testifies to the criminal act and another who can corroborate the evidence of the first. The two-witness rule is Constitutional as to treason but statutory as to perjury, having once been a common-law doctrine in capital cases.

**unavailable witness** A witness who is unable to testify in a given proceeding. An unavailable witness is a witness who cannot or will not give testimony in a given proceeding. An unavailable witness might but might not be absent from the courtroom; the unavailability is a matter of a given subject of testimony not merely physical presence.

The unavailability of a witness is an essential element in allowing as evidence certain hearsay statements by an unavailable witness. Hearsay from an unavailable witness is allowed under Fed. R. Evid. 804(b) if the witness is exempted from testifying on a matter of privilege, refuses to testify despite a court order to do so, testifies to a lack of memory on a matter, is dead or physically or mentally incapable of testimony, or is absent though the proponent made a reasonable and good faith effort to procure the witness's attendance at the proceeding. A declarant is not unavailable under the rules if the proponent of the hearsay caused the witness's unavailability.

See also: hearsay.

**witness as Jehovah's Witness** See: church, church, Jehovah.

**Witness Security Program (Witness Protection Program or Witness Protection Act)** Federal program to conceal witness identity. The United States Witness Security Program was established as the Federal Witness Protection Program under Title V of the Organized Crime Control Act of 1970 and is administered by the U.S. Department of Justice and the U.S. Attorney General. Its role is to protect witnesses who may be threatened by criminal defendants or others by relocating the witness and providing the witness a new identity.

**zealous witness** A witness more keen to support one side than to tell the truth. A zealous witness is loyal to one side or another in an action to a sufficient extent that the witness's accuracy is likely to be compromised.

**WMD** *See:* weapon, weapon of mass destruction (WMD).

**word** The basic unit of language. A word, the cluster of letters and syllables that is the smallest unit that is separated from other such clusters in writing or language, is the representation of an idea. The idea is usually one that has many manifestations, and the idea represented is said to have a core meaning that is clearly within what is represented and is manifest, perhaps, in many similar but distinct examples, as well as countless peripheral examples that are only somewhat represented by the word. This complexity is made more difficult by the many ideas that a word may represent, including literal or technical and figurative or metaphorical meanings.

In law, words often have a technical meaning that is specific to the context within which the word is used. Despite many efforts to purge the law of technique and specialization of vocabulary, legal language persists with countless technical words and phrases, whose meaning is often obscure to the observer unschooled in the technical meaning. Words without a technical meaning in law that are written in legal instruments or pronounced in a legal forum are presumed to have their ordinary meaning within the culture of speakers of that language generally, understood within the context in which the word is used. Even so, a technical legal word used in a technical context in a legal instrument such as a statute, contract, will, or trust is presumed to have its technical meaning.

**precatory words** *See:* precatory words.

**weasel word** A word qualifying a statement to avoid the reader actually relying on it. A weasel word is an adverb, clause, or other modifier on what otherwise would be a simple statement, intended to limit a statement to a narrow field and to absolve the writer if the statement happens not to be true. In law, general statements of law across the United States are usually hedged with weasel words owing to the variations in law among the many jurisdictions, the speed with which it changes, and the unlikelihood that the writer would find the research needed to be absolute in such a statement to be worth the effort. Still, when specificity and exactitude are possible, a weasel word should be avoided.

**words of art** *See:* term, term of art (words of art).

**work**

**work as employment** One's job, or one's place of employment. Work, in general, is both a person's form of employment including its tasks and responsibilities and a person's place of employment—the workplace.

**copyrightable work** A work of a form that may be copyrighted. A copyrightable work is a work that may be given copyright protection, whether such protection attaches or is renounced by the person or entity entitled to copyright it. The copyright in the work protects its manifestation or form, not its concept or idea, and a copyright in a work does not extend to any idea, procedure, process, system, method of operation, concept, principle, or discovery. Under the Copyright Act, a copyrightable work is an original work of authorship fixed in any tangible medium of expression, now known or later developed, from which the work can be perceived, reproduced, or otherwise communicated, either directly or with the aid of a machine or a device. Works of authorship include literary works; musical works, including any accompanying words; dramatic works, including any accompanying music; pantomimes and choreographic works; pictorial, graphic, and sculptural works; motion pictures and other audiovisual works; sound recordings; and architectural works.
*See also:* original (originality); copyright.

**composite work** A work of distinct parts, open to copyright. A composite work is a work that is not itself an original work that is copyrightable by one author or creator but that contains distinct parts, at least some of which are separately copyrightable.

**work for hire (work made for hire)** A work created by an employee or by commission. A work for hire is a copyrightable work that is either created by one or more employees of a company working within the scope of their employment or created by a person or entity as a result of a commission, order, or contract as a component of a larger work or of for other specific functions, if the parties agree in writing that the work that results is a work for hire. The employer or commissioning entity owns the copyright of a work for hire.

**light-duty work (light duty work)** Less demanding tasks assigned to a disabled employee. Light-duty work is a specialized set of tasks that are selected in order to accommodate the disability of an employee, whether the disability is temporary or permanent. Light duty may include assignment to a different role or job, particularly if the employee's regular employment requires physical or mental activity that is either not possible without pain or risk or potentially dangerous or hazardous owing to the employee's disability.

**work-product immunity**   *See:* immunity, discovery immunity, work-product immunity (work product immunity or work-product rule or work product privilege).

**work-related or employment related**   *See:* job, job-relatedness (work-related or employment related).

**worker**   One who works for others. A worker, in general, is a person who does work. "Worker" includes a broad category of forms of work taken by individuals, and unless the regulation or statute in issue specifically and expressly limits it, the word includes both the self-employed, employees, contractors, and a contractor's employees, and a contractor's contractors. Despite such breadth of scope, in some contexts, worker does not ordinarily include owners, directors, management, or managerial workers.

*See also:* insurance, category of insurance, worker; employment (employ or employed or employee or employer); laborer.

**migrant worker (seasonal agricultural worker)**   An alien worker who provides temporary labor. A migrant worker, or a seasonal agricultural worker, is a foreign national who provides labor, particularly agricultural labor, for the period of a season or some days in the year when labor is needed by a farm, factory, or similar employer. A migrant worker must be away from the worker's permanent residence overnight in order to perform the work, while a seasonal agricultural worker is not. Both are protected by the Migrant and Seasonal Agricultural Workers Protection Act, 29 U.S.C. § 1823 (2010).

**Worker Adjustment and Retraining Notification Act (WARN Act)**   Law requiring notice be given to employees of mass lay-offs or closings. The Worker Adjustment and Retraining Notification Act, codified at 29 U.S.C. § 2101, et seq. (2010), also known as the "WARN Act," requires an employer of one hundred or more employees to give notice to its employees at least sixty calendar days before a plant closing, mass layoff, or one of a series of reductions in force over ninety days that would amount to a mass layoff if done at one time. If an employer is integrated into another enterprise, the single employer rule determines the nature and identity of the employer liable to the employees. The notice is intended to give workers time to plan for relocation and adjustment. A company may give pay in lieu of notice, equal to back pay and benefits for the notice period.

**World Trade Organization**   *See:* trade, international trade, World Trade Organization, Standing Appellate Body (AB); trade, international trade, World Trade Organization, Dispute Settlement Body (DSB); trade, international trade, World Trade Organization (WTO or W.T.O.).

**worth**   *See:* estate, worth, taxable estate; estate, worth, marital estate; estate, worth, bankruptcy estate.

**WPA**   *See:* whistleblower, Whistleblower Protection Act (WPA).

**wrap up or wind up**   *See:* winding up (wrap up or wind up).

**wreck**   *See:* ship, wreck, derelict vessel.

**wreck as collision**   *See:* collision (collide).

**wreck of a vessel**   *See:* salvage, shipwreck (wreck of a vessel).

**writ (brevia)**   A written order that by law must be obeyed. A writ is an order, a writing from an official, usually though not always a judge, that mandates the official or other person to whom it is issued do or refrain from the conduct written in the order. Writ, or brevia in Latin, meant "the thing written." Writs in England were used for many procedures, including the summons of members of Parliament. At common law, most writs were directed to the sheriff or a similar executive officer to execute, which the officer would either do or fail to do, in either case returning the writ with a report. Writs were used to both order a final remedy and most other acts of a party, juror, surety or other third party, or witness that were required for the administration of an action.

English law had two fundamental categories of writ: the prerogative writ used for the administration of justice, such as certiorari, procedendo, mandamus, prohibition, and habeas corpus; and the writ of right, which was largely used to vindicate rights in property or the person. The writ of right was either issued by the Exchequer as an original writ, or issued by the court as a judicial writ.

Over the centuries, the writs became increasingly specialized until there were hundreds of distinct forms of writ, each requiring the demonstration of specific proofs in order to be granted, and the task of the attorney for the plaintiff came to be discerning which writ would be satisfied by the evidence, while the attorney for the defense sought to demonstrate that the writ was in error, requiring some proof that was not available in the case. The writs system was often more about the form of the pleading than the substance of the complaint. This approach in the United States has been largely, though not entirely replaced by code pleading, in which a very few, generic pleadings are used.

Writs in the United States are available in federal courts under the All Writs Act, and in state courts according to state law, rules, and custom. Many jurisdictions, for instance, still use the writ of summons.

**writ of assistance**   *See:* warrant, general warrant, writ of assistance (Paxton's case).

**writ of audita querela**   *See:* audita querela (writ of audita querela).

**writ of certiorari in equity**   *See:* certiorari, bill of certiorari (writ of certiorari in equity).

**writ of error**   *See:* error, writ of error, plaintiff in error (defendant in error); error, writ of error (restricted appeal).

**writ of mandamus**   *See:* mandamus.

**writ of procedendo**   *See:* remand, procedendo (writ of procedendo).

**writ of prohibition**   *See:* prohibition, writ of prohibition.

**writ of quo warranto**   *See:* quo, quo warranto (writ of quo warranto).

**writ of replevin or replevy or repleviable**   *See:* replevin (writ of replevin or replevy or repleviable).

**writ of restitution**   *See:* restitution (writ of restitution).

**All Writs Act**   Federal courts may issue any common-law writ to protect their jurisdiction and powers. The All Writs Act was originally enacted, in part, as § 14 of the Judiciary Act of 1789. The purpose and function of the All Writs Act is to supply the courts with the instruments needed to perform their duty, as pre-scribed by the Congress and the Constitution. The All Writs Act creates no appellate powers, but grants an auxiliary power in aid of and to protect the appel-late jurisdiction conferred upon the court of appeals by other provisions of law, and to permit review by mandamus of unappealable orders which the court believes should be immediately reviewable in the interest of justice.

   *remedy against agencies*   The All Writs Act applies to federal agencies as well as to the courts, and a person or entity may bring a writ against an agency, using mandamus and other orders to review both the intermediate orders of agencies and the failure of agen-cies to act when there is a lawful duty to do so.

**fieri facias (fi fa or fi. fa.)**   A writ of execution allow-ing garnishment of personal property to satisfy a civil or administrative judgment. A writ of fieri facias is an order directing a police officer or other state peace officer to take custody and to sell some specified personal property of a defendant in order to satisfy a judgment. The writ is often known by its abbrevia-tion: "fi. fa." A fi. fa. may be issued to collect on either a civil judgment or a tax judgment, although the fi. fa. must be issued by a court.

**writing (write or written)**   The physical recording of words or numbers. Writing has several related senses. A writing is a thing on or in which are recorded words or numbers that signify specific ideas. Writing as a course of conduct is not only the means by which a writing is created but also the art by which writing is performed and criticized. A writing may be made on any surface or in any medium, including with an elec-tronic device in which the writing only appears on a screen, otherwise being stored as a record in electronic or other memory.

   A writing, in the law of contracts, is required for a con-tract to satisfy the Statute of Frauds, and in this context, a thing amounts to a writing if it includes the material terms of the contract expressed in words and numbers in a manner sufficient to be clear as to what it is and is signed or marked by the party whose agreement or per-formance is in issue and who is to be bound to the agree-ment by an action enforcing it.

   Note: writing is both a noun and a verb.

   *See also:* fraud, statute of frauds, writing (memoran-dum or note).

**written confirmation of oral agreement**   *See:* contract, confirmation of contract, written confirma-tion of oral agreement.

**written law**   *See:* law, written law (lex scripta).

**writing**   *See:* fraud, statute of frauds, writing (mem-orandum or note).

## wrong (wrongfulness or wrondoing or wrongful)

An injury caused by the violation of a duty. A wrong is a harm caused as a result of unjustified conduct. Wrong-fulness is an aspect of something done or not done in violation of a duty, whether the duty is a moral duty or a legal duty. Thus, a wrong is any harm or injury that results from a violation of a duty recognized by law or social understandings of morality.

   The law employs both legal and moral bases of duty in a host of laws that remedy, forbid, or punish wrongs, wrongdoing, or wrongful conduct. The context of the specific law involved is essential to relating the sense of wrongdoing to the form of duty in question.

   A public wrong is a wrong against the public as a whole or the government or state, rather than a wrong committed against an individual or private property. Public wrongs include crimes, and a criminal act is based on a wrongful motive. The wrongfulness in both of these senses of wrong is both moral and legal, but the definitions of law are usually specific in the particular wrong underlying a criminal definition, depending on the failure of regard for the rights and interests of others. Further, a sense of wrongdoing is a prerequisite to criminal capacity, and this sense is a moral sense or understanding of what actions would be condemned in ordinary society as wrongful. Public wrongs that are not criminal are usually subject to administrative rem-edies, such as the violation of a regulation, or to private action, such as an action for public nuisance.

   The adjective "wrongful" is used to distinguish actions which give rise to a private cause of action in one context from actions that are allowed in a different context. Thus, an employer who discharges an employee on a discrim-inatory basis forbidden by Title VII engages in a wrong-ful discharge, and a person whose tortious conduct results in the death of another causes a wrongful death. Most of these usages reflect both the violation of a legal right and of a moral duty enforced by the pro-tection of the law.

   Even so, there are senses in which a wrong results from an injury in breach of legal obligations that have no parallel moral obligations, as when a party to a con-tract breaches the contract but stands ready to pay damages or restore the non–breaching party.

   *See also:* delict (quasi–delict or delictual).

**wrongdoer rule**   *See:* damages, calculation of damages, wrongdoer rule.

**wrongful arrest**   *See:* arrest, unlawful arrest (wrongful arrest).

**wrongful birth**   *See:* birth, wrongful birth (wrongful life).

**wrongful conception**   *See:* pregnancy, wrongful pregnancy (wrongful conception).

**wrongful conviction**   *See:* conviction, wrongful conviction.

**wrongful death**   *See:* death, wrongful death.

**wrongful denial of benefits**   *See:* insurance, insurance claim, denial of claim, wrongful denial of benefits.

**wrongful discharge**   *See:* discharge, employment discharge, wrongful discharge.

**wrongful life**   *See:* birth, wrongful birth (wrongful life).

**wrongful pregnancy**   *See:* pregnancy, wrongful pregnancy (wrongful conception).

**double–effect test (double effects test)**   An act that can be justified by a good purpose, though there are bad consequences. The double–effect test of wrong-doing is a justification of an act based on the rightness of its principal goal or purpose. Under this rationale, if an act will have more than one effect, and if the primary intended effect is morally justified, then the act is morally justified, even if other effects would not be justified independently. The double–effects test is often linked to Aquinas's argument in Summa Theologica II–II, question 64, art. 7, which allows the killing of an unjust aggressor.

**wrongdoer (wrong-doer)**   A tortfeasor, or criminal. A wrongdoer is a person or entity who commits a wrong. The term is sometimes used in law to describe the violator of some legal duty, particularly an individual who or entity that commits a crime or tort.

   *See also:* tortfeasor (tort-feasor); criminal (criminality or criminalization or decriminalization); miscreant.

**WTO or W.T.O.**   *See:* trade, international trade, World Trade Organization (WTO or W.T.O.).

> Exactness in the use of words is the basis of all serious thinking.
> You will get nowhere without it.
>
> Felix Frankfurter, *Some Reflections on the Reading of Statutes: Benjamin N. Cardozo Lecture,*
> Association of the Bar of the City of New York, March 18, 1947.

# X

**x**  The twenty-fourth letter of the modern English alphabet. "X" signifies a variety of functions as a symbol and as a designation of status, as in X–rated. It is translated into X–Ray (or Xray) for radio signals and NATO military transmissions, into X–ray for some police radio traffic, and into dash, dot, dot, dash in Morse Code. X was the last letter of the Latin alphabet.

**x as mark**  *See:* signature, mark (x as mark).

**x as signature**  *See:* signature, x as signature (cross as signature).

**x as a latin abbreviation**  The Extra of Gregory's Decretals. X was an abbreviation for the Extra, a portion of the Decretals of Gregory.
  *See also:* canon, canon law, decretals (Decretals of Gratian or decretum gratiani).

**x as a roman numeral**  Latin symbol for ten (10). X is ten when used as a numeral. In the Roman system of numeralization, the addition of an X to the right of another Roman numeral adds 10 to the numerical value. The addition of an X to the left of another Roman numeral subtracts 10 from the numerical value.

**x as an abbreviation**  A word commencing in X. When used as the sole letter of an abbreviation, X usually stands for ex, as in former or without, or cross, as in cross-walk. Though not an abbreviation, an X alone is also a mark in lieu of a signature.
  *See also:* signature, mark (X as mark).

**x as cross**  An abbreviation for the word, cross. In some instances, "X" stands for "cross." For example, X–Ref is a common abbreviation for cross–reference.

**x as ex**  Abbreviation for ex as former. X is increasingly used as an abbreviation for ex, not only in the customary sense of without such as ex–quay, but also in the sense of former, as in ex–spouse.

**x as in hypotheticals (Mr. X or Mrs. X or Ms. X or Miss X)**  A character in a hypo. When used as the sole letter of an abbreviation, X often stands for a person in the story of a law school hypothetical. Usually, if X is used as a character, there is a non-person entity being represented by the earlier letters.

**x as variable**  An amount or substance with no known or relevant designation. X is commonly used as a pronoun that represents either a number or a noun that is unknown or unspecified. The law, like algebra, geometry, and statistics, frequently uses X in a hypothetical that employs from one to three variables — x, y, and z — whether the variables represent quantity, people, location, or any other thing.

**xenophobia (xenophobic)**  Fear of difference, especially of a person from abroad. Xenophobia, literally, is a fear of difference, but it usually describes a person's fear of people whom the person perceives to be different, particularly if the people are from a different nation or culture. Immigration is often opposed by those with xenophobic attitudes.

**xing**  Criminal laws and punishments. Xing is an ancient term for punishment in Mandarin Chinese. In contemporary usage, it refers broadly to criminal and penal laws, both to prohibitions and punishments.

**XYY Chromosome Defense**  *See:* defense, specific pleading, XYY Chromosome Defense.

Definitions are difficult and sometimes dangerous
to the correct understanding of a subject . . .

Harlan Fiske Stone, *Law and Its Administration* 2 (Columbia University Press, 1915).

# Y

**y**   The twenty–fifth letter of the modern English alphabet. "Y" signifies a variety of functions as a symbol. It is translated into Yankee for radio signals and NATO military transmissions, into Young for some police radio traffic, and into dash, dot, dash, dash in Morse Code. Y and y were used in early English law books in place of the Anglo–Saxon letter thorn, or Þ. Other than in ecclesiastical writing, by the time of American independence, the use of the thorn Þ was unknown and this use of y was archaic, both being supplanted by th. (The conversion from thorn to y may explain some of the evolution and distinctions between you and thou as well as ye and the.) Thus, in early lawbooks, one might find words such as "yis" which is pronounced "this."

**y as an abbreviation**   A word commencing in Y. When used as an abbreviation, Y almost always stands for year or yearly, as well as Yale, yearbook, York, young, Yugoslavia, and Yukon. YTD is year–to–date. It may also stand for the initial of the name of an author or case reporter, like Yeates or Yates.

**Yakuza**   *See:* racketeering, organized crime, Yakuza.

**ye**   Once the or thee but now you. Ye in contemporary usage is an anachronistic form for "you," used in both the plural and the singular, as in "hear ye" for "each and all of you, hear this." In older documents, particularly deeds, ye represents either "the" as the definite article or "thee" as the form of you. Indeed, the y is not really the letter y in the modern alphabet but the letter thorn, which has been so forgotten that the word is now routinely pronounced with a letter y sound as it has in yellow, rather than the th sound it had when its use was commonplace.

**year**   The time of Earth's orbit of its Sun. A year is a very common frame of time for the measurement of legal obligations, powers, and duties, measured by custom according to the Gregorian calendar of four–year cycles that incorporated one additional day in February to the otherwise 365–day year. Years are measured in U.S. law from the date of the Christian calendar, now labeled more often as the Common Era or C.E. the slightly longer than 365 and one–fourth days. A year from a given date is the the number of days in that and the succeeding year required to reach the eve of the same date the following year according to this system. A year and a day ends on the same date on which the period commences.

The calendar year is not the only year in law, and accounting years, tax years, fiscal years, academic years, and other measures commencing at specific dates are often designated in contracts or other instruments. Unless the context or a designation presumes otherwise,

however, a year is presumed to commence on January 1, or upon the date an instrument is signed or comes into force.

*See also:* limitation, limitation of actions, statute of limitations, year and a day rule.

**year and a day rule**   *See:* limitation, limitation of actions, statute of limitations, year and a day rule.

**annual**   Yearly. Annual designates a year–long period or cycle. Thus, an annual is also a book or journal issued only once yearly. A specification that some event or requirement is annual, or yearly, does not assure that the event is to take on the precise date each year but within a reasonable and flexible period near the date of the first event or required performance, in each succeeding year.

*See also:* tax, gift tax, annual exclusion; interest, interest for money, annual percentage rate (APR).

**fiscal year (FY)**   A year for the purpose of budgeting, set from any date. A fiscal year is a budget year, which may be set to commence on any date in the calendar year. The fiscal year for the United States government commences on October 1 and ends on September 30, being denominated by the year in which it ends. Thus, FY2010 begins on September 30, 2009.

**regnal year**   The years of English law, by the year of each monarch's reign. A regnal year is the year measured according to the year of the reign of the monarch or monarchs then on the throne. English legal materials (and some colonial materials) are dated not by years in the common era but by regnal years. Each year commences on the anniversary of the coronation or official date of accession. Converting these years requires knowing the year in which the monarch attained the throne and the number of years following the dated event took place, or working back from the date the number of years prior to the coronation of the monarch then reigning. An abbreviated table follows:

1 Wil. 1 (William I) Dec. 25, 1066
1 Wil. 2 (William II [Rufus]) Sep. 26, 1087
1 Hen. 1 (Henry I) Aug. 5, 1100
1 Steph. (Stephen) Dec. 22, 1135
1 Hen. 2 (Henry II) Dec. 19, 1154
1 Ric. 1 (Richard I) Sep. 3, 1189
1 John (John) May 27, 1199
1 Hen. 3 (Henry III) Oct. 28, 1216
1 Edw. 1 (Edward I) Nov. 20, 1272
1 Edw. 2 (Edward II) July 8, 1307
1 Edw. 3 (Edward III) Jan. 25, 1327
1 Ric. 2 (Richard II) June 22, 1377

1 Hen. 4 (Henry IV) Sep. 30, 1399
1 Hen. 5 (Henry V) March 21, 1413
1 Hen. 6 (Henry VI ) Sep. 1, 1422
1 Edw. 4 (Edward IV) March 4, 1461
1 Edw. 5 (Edward V) April 9, 1483
1 Ric. 3 (Richard III) June 26, 1483
1 Hen. 7 (Henry VII) Aug. 21, 1485
1 Hen. 8 (Henry VIII) Apr. 22, 1509
1 Edw. 6 (Edward VI) Jan. 28, 1547
1 Jane (Jane) July 6, 1553
1 Mar. (Mary) July 19, 1553
1&2 P.&M. (Philip and Mary ) July 25, 1554
1 Eliz. 1 (Elizabeth I) Nov. 17, 1558
1 Jac. 1 (James I) March 24, 1603
1 Caro. 1 (Charles I) March 27, 1625
Commonwealth/Protectorate
(Interregnum 30 Jan 1648/9 – 29 May 1660)
Oliver Cromwell, Lord Protector, 1653
Richard Cromwell, Lord Protector, 1658
(Restoration)
1 Car. 2 (Charles II) 29 May 1660
1 Jac. 2 (James II) 6 Feb 1685
Glorious Revolution
(Interregnum 12 Dec 1688 – 12 Feb 1689)
1 W&M (William & Mary) 13 Feb 1689 – 27 Dec 1694
1 W3 (William III) 28 Dec 1694
1 Anne (Anne) 8 Mar 1702
1 Geo. 1 (George I) 1 Aug 1714
1 Geo. 2 ( George II) 11 Jun 1727
1 Geo. 3 (George III) 25 Oct 1760
1 Geo. 4 (George IV) 29 Jan 1820
1 W.4 (William IV) 29 Jun 1830
1 Vict. (Victoria) 20 Jun 1837
1 Edw. 7 (Edward VII) 22 Jan 1901
1 Geo. 5 (George V) 6 May 1910
1 Edw. 8 (Edward VIII) 20 Jan 1936
1 Geo. 6 (George VI) 11 Dec 1936
1 Eliz. 2 (Elizabeth II) 6 Feb 1952
*See also:* government, forms of government, monarchy, queen; government, forms of government, monarchy, king; rex (regina or regis or regnal).

**year-to-year tenancy** *See:* lease, leasehold, tenancy, periodic tenancy, year-to-year tenancy (yearly lease or annual lease or year to year tenancy).

**yeas and nays** *See:* vote, parliamentary vote, yeas and nays (roll call vote).

**yellow-dog contract** *See:* union, labor union, union organization, yellow-dog contract (yellow dog).

**yeshivah** Jewish school teaching the Talmud. A yeshivah is an institution of higher learning dedicated to instruction and study of the Talmud.

**Yick Wo case** *See:* interpretation, statutory interpretation, legislative purpose, Yick Wo case (Yick Wo rule or Yick Wo doctrine).

**Yiddish** A Jewish vernacular, popular among lawyers. Yiddish is a Hebrew–German hybrid language spoken by Jews of the diaspora around the world. During the twentieth century, Yiddish was ever more frequently employed both by Jewish and non-Jewish lawyers and judges, until many terms from Yiddish have become common in legal slang.
*See also:* putz; schlemiel; schnook; nebbish (nebbishy or nebbishistic).

**yield** To surrender, although with a potential qualification. To yield is to concede or surrender, although perhaps with some reservation. In law the term has a variety of specific meanings. To yield in combat is to surrender oneself or one's command to the enemy, although such a surrender may be made according to terms. Likewise, for a person to yield to a police officer is to surrender to the officer's jurisdiction, which has certain boundaries.
To yield a point in a dispute is to concede to one's opponent the futility of further argument, albeit not necessarily because the point is disproved. To yield a witness is to surrender the witness to opposing counsel for questioning, with an understood opportunity of rebuttal. To yield in traffic is to surrender the way to the priority of other vehicles or vessels, though not necessarily to stop. To yield the floor or to yield time in a parliamentary, congressional, or other formal proceeding is to surrender one's privilege to speak to another person, though not without a sense of having such a privilege again.

**yield as profit** What is paid for efforts or returned from an investment. Yield, in its earliest forms in English, represents pay or value, both as a noun and a verb with similar meanings. In this sense a crop yield is the gain in value from land in crops, just as a bond yield is the rate of interest paid to the bond holder. Lands yield taxes as well as crops. Not all yield is profit; a particular investment may yield a loss or yield nothing.
From this sense of yield is derived the sense of yield in which a line of inquiry or investigation results in information or conclusions. A test may yield such results.

**York-Antwerp rules** *See:* liability, joint liability, York–Antwerp rules.

**Younger abstention** *See:* abstention, abstention doctrine, Younger abstention.

**your honor** *See:* honor, your honor (her honor or his honor or their honors or hizzoner).

**youth as incapacity** *See:* capacity, criminal capacity, incapacity to commit a crime, youth as incapacity (infancy).

**youthful offender** *See:* offender, youthful offender (juvenile offender or juvy).

By thy words shalt thou be justified, and by thy words
thou shalt be condemned.

Jesus of Nazareth, *Matthew* 12:37.

# Z

**z**   The twenty-sixth letter of the modern English alphabet. "Z" signifies a variety of functions as a symbol and as a designation of status, as in the last category. Z was sometimes used in place of "y" in medieval manuscript and early printing. Z is translated into Zulu for radio signals and NATO military transmissions, into Zebra for some police radio traffic, and into dash, dash, dot, dot in Morse Code.

**z as an abbreviation**   A word commencing in Z. When used as the sole letter of an abbreviation, Z often stands for sleep, and it abbreviates Zambia, zenith, zeitschrift, zeitung, Zimbabwe, zoll, zoning, Zulu (time, or GMT), and zygote. It may also stand for the initial of an author or case reporter, such as Zabriskie, Zane, Zanzibar, Zinn, and Zouche.

**zakat**   The obligation of giving alms. Zakat literally means to purify, in this case to purify one's earnings and money by giving at least 2.5 percent of one's total wealth in charity, among eight classes of deserving people such as the poor, or orphans, or travelers. Zakat is one of the five pillars of Islam, and it is Fard on all those who have more than a certain amount of money (in the early twenty-first century, about $750 in the United States).

**zealous advocacy**   *See:* advocacy, zealous advocacy (zealous advocate).

**zealous witness**   *See:* witness, zealous witness.

**zero coupon bond**   *See:* bond, zero coupon bond.

**zero tolerance**   *See:* tolerance, zero tolerance.

**zero-sum game**   *See:* game, game theory, zero-sum game.

**zhimmi**   *See:* dhimmi (zhimmi).

**zoning (land-use zone)**   Local regulation of lands by zones restricted to particular uses. Zoning is a comprehensive regulation of the land in a jurisdiction, setting forth a general plan to control and direct the use and development of property to promote the greater good and stabilize community development, by minimizing neighboring conflicting uses and by limiting not only the load on municipal infrastructure but also the environmental and social impacts of specific uses of land. The plan may limit the forms and density of uses of property, heights of buildings, aesthetics, greenery, lawns, trees, water drainage, and access.
*See also:* taking, regulatory taking, amortization of a land use.

**zone-of-danger rule**   *See:* distress, emotional distress, negligent infliction of emotional distress, zone-of-danger rule.

**zone of interests**   *See:* standing in court, zone of interests (zone-of-interests test).

**zone of privacy**   *See:* privacy, zone of privacy.

**aesthetic zoning**   Regulations of the appearance of land and buildings. Aesthetic zoning is the regulation of the appearance of real property, buildings, or other uses of land. Zoning authorities have a legitimate public purpose in creating a harmonious appearance throughout a community, but this purpose is limited in that the regulations may not be so extensive as to amount to a taking of the property or to a limitation on the freedom of speech by its owners.

**conditional zoning**   A rezoning conditioned upon the petitioner's granting of specified benefits to the community. Conditional zoning is a form of rezoning in which the petition to rezone a given parcel is granted only if the person or entity that seeks the rezoning agrees to a condition, such as the dedication of land or an easement to the public, limitations on use or the grant of a covenant to the government of the zoning authority. A condition required as a matter of rezoning must be reasonably related to the purpose to which the land would be rezoned or otherwise to the effect of the land or the use itself, or the denial of the rezoning based on the requirement or even the failure of the condition may amount to a regulatory taking.
*See also:* taking, regulatory taking, conditional use.

**incentive zoning**   High-density zoning conditioned on the creation of public amenities. Incentive zoning is a form of conditional zoning, in which a tract owner is allowed an unusually profitable zoning designation, such as a high-density zoning designation, in return for commitments either to use the land in a specific manner to the benefit of the public or to provide specified public amenities as a part of the development of the tract. Incentive zoning may require, for instance, low-income housing development, parks, museums, schools, public art, or other developments that are not usually required as part of a zoning or development approval, such as basic infrastructure like roads or utilities.

**Euclidean zoning**   Customary zoning by dividing an area into use districts. Euclidean zoning is the customary means of zoning according to a plan defining various zones, each limiting the land use within it to a few closely related uses, and defining specific districts that are assigned a specific zone. The term is derived from Euclid, Illinois, the appellant in the great zoning case of 1926, Euclid v. Ambler Realty, 272 U.S. 365 (1926), in which such a scheme was upheld against a complaint that it violates the taking clause (although the term is likely popular among lawyers for the near pun of its resemblance to the much more venerable Euclidean geometry).

**floating zone**  A zoning use allowed throughout an area regardless of zone. A floating zone is created in the text of a zoning ordinance to allow a particular use of land under specified conditions in any parcel regardless of its other zoning characteristics, or in specific zones regardless of other conflicts with uses in that zone. An allowance of a particular use on a parcel that would otherwise amount to spot zoning owing to a conflict with the other allowed land uses in that zone is allowed if it conforms to the conditions required for a floating zone.

**historic district**  Planning or zoning area regulated to protect historic features. A historic district is a geographically defined area possessing a significant concentration, linkage, or continuity of sites or of structures that are related by their history or appearance, within which the structures and land use is regulated to preserve or restore the historic character of the buildings and grounds. Historic districts often include collections of houses or public buildings of specific architectural periods. More generally, historic district may describe a neighborhood of relatively greater age within an urban area, which is not thereby specially regulated.

**non-conforming use (nonconforming use or prior non-conforming use or pre-existing non-conforming use)**  A land use that conflicts with a land-use regulation. A non-conforming use is any land use that is not permitted according to the zoning laws, land use regulation generally, or (in some cases) not permitted according to private land use limitations such as deed restrictions, easements, or covenants. Still, the most common usage is a use that is not permitted by zoning. A non-conforming use may be a prior non-conforming use, in which case the use existed prior to the regulatory prohibition.

**master plan (master planning)**  The overall plan for the regulation of land use in a jurisdiction. A master plan is a comprehensive plan for the regulation of specific uses of land, particularly by defining zones and designating zoning areas, and setting standards for roads and ways, utility infrastructure, and other requirements for the development of lands for agricultural, industrial, commercial, residential, public and other uses throughout a jurisdiction. The master plan is usually a narrative of rules that applies both to all lands and to the lands in specific zones, usually accompanied by a map of the land in the jurisdiction to which zones are assigned. The master plan is adopted by the city council, county supervisors, or other legislative entity governing the locality, after which it becomes the standard by which all future decisions, including exceptions and variations, are to be considered.

Master planning in some contexts is related to a master plan but distinct. Master planning is a comprehensive approach to municipal development and marketing that reaches beyond the map of present and future land use planning to consider social, commercial, industrial, residential, and governmental opportunities and challenges for development.

**planned unit development (PUD)**  A single zoning unit incorporating a variety of integrated land uses. A planned unit development, or PUD, is a development on a given tract of land that includes a variety of land uses, which ordinarily would not be permitted in a single zone, but that are sufficiently integrated into a single plan for the development of the tract that there is no inherent incompatibility among the uses. A PUD is regulated in a zoning master plan just as a conditional use might be, with requirements for infrastructure and integration with other tracts that must be accounted for in planning and design in order for a PUD to be approved.

**rezoning (rezone)**  The change in designation of the zoned land use of a parcel. Rezoning is a process of redesignating the uses allowed of property after a prior use has been designated in a master plan. Rezoning may occur over whole zones or for a single parcel, and it is required from time to time, not only to update the plan to reflect events on the ground but also to account for changes in zoning policy. Although used for both senses of zoning change, the term "rezoning" is more often used to depict the change of zoning for a single parcel or tract, made at the request of an owner, developer, or other person or entity with an interest in the land. When rezoning of a parcel or tract is allowed in a manner inconsistent with the zoning authority's master plan or with the land use of nearby lands, rezoning may be barred as "spot zoning."

*See also:* zoning, spot zoning (reverse spot zoning); zoning, spot zoning (reverse spot zoning).

**slum**  An area of unsafe housing. A slum is an area in which residential housing has become unsafe owing to the deterioration of the structures, the substandard provision of infrastructure or services, overcrowding or, conversely an absence of public or civic life, or persistently recurrent events of violence or criminal activity. A slum presents a danger to its inhabitants and a potential danger to the city in which it occurs. Further, a slum may indicate a need for sustainable low-income housing in an area that is not otherwise met. Cities may use their police powers to control land use to prevent or abate slums.

*See also:* zoning (land–use zone).

**special use zoning (conditional use permit or special permit zoning or special use permit)**  Use of land allowed by permission rather than as a matter of entitlement. Special use zoning, also called "conditional use zoning" or "special permit zoning," is zoning both in specific areas and throughout a master plan, in which a variety of specified uses or categories of uses are not allowed as a matter or right or entitlement but are only allowed upon landowner's successful application for a permit to engage in the particular use on a specific parcel.

**spot zoning (reverse spot zoning)** Zoning one parcel contrary to nearby lands and the zoning plan. Spot zoning is a zoning designation of one parcel of land to allow a zoning use that is incompatible both with the zoning of most of the lands nearby and with the zoning master plan, to accommodate a preferred use by an owner or other person with an interest or putative interest in the parcel. Spot zoning is forbidden under most state planning and zoning laws, amounting to an arbitrary or capricious decision rather than a considered application of zoning law supported by the evidence.

Spot zoning may occur either by changes to the texts of a zoning designation or by amendments to the master plan or by the alteration of the map and zone of a given parcel, or it may occur through variance or use permits; the defining elements are the benefit to a small parcel that is not in harmony with adjacent and nearby land uses or that does not reflect the policies of the master plan. A mere change to a use of a single lot or parcel is not enough to prove spot zoning. The new use must amount to a conflicting use with the nearby lands as well as being contrary to the policies of the zoning master plan. A determination that a zoning change for a single parcel is spot zoning is a matter of fact that depends on the facts of each zoning decision. Many zoning changes of a small parcel, even to a zoning allowance that is rare or unique in a given area are appropriate exercises of zoning authority, either because the changes further the overall policies of the master zoning plan or because the resulting zoning is still compatible with the zoning of the surrounding lands.

A zoning change of a given parcel, or a refusal of a zoning change, that prohibits the parcel's owner from a contemplated zoning use may amount to reverse spot zoning, which is also forbidden in most states.

**transferable development right (TDR)** Unused regulatory capacity to use land, allocated to other land. A transferable development right, or TDR, is a right to alienate a particular land use allowed under zoning or other land use regulations, taking it from the land to which it is allocated to another parcel of land. Thus, if zoning rules allow each building on a street to be no more than one hundred feet but allow TDRs among the parcels, an owner of two parcels may be allowed to transfer the right to develop one parcel to the other, resulting in a park on one parcel but a two-hundred-foot-tall building on the other. The great case discussing the validity of TDRs is Penn Central Transportation Co. v. New York City, 438 U.S. 104 (1978).

**zoning variance (variance from zoning regulation)** A parcel's use allowed despite its zoning. A zoning variance is an allowance for a use that otherwise would not conform to the zoning of a parcel, the allowance being granted by the zoning authority because the differing use would not substantially affect the policies reflected in the authority's comprehensive zoning plan, and because the strict enforcement of the plan would amount to an unusual hardship for the owner of the parcel in question. Variances, like rezoning decisions, are essential to allow flexibility in a zoning plan and to allow for changes in fact in the manner in which land is used, but a variance that is not compatible with the master plan or with the surrounding land uses may amount to spot zoning.

*See also:* zoning, rezoning (rezone); zoning, spot zoning (reverse spot zoning).

**unnecessary hardship** A zoning burden on a parcel different from other parcels in the same zone. An unnecessary hardship is one of the essential requirements to justify a variance under most comprehensive zoning plans, which requires a parcel subject to a petition for a zoning variance to be burdened by the zoning regulations because of a unique (or at least rare) relationship of the land use in question and the zoning requirements. The demonstration of an unnecessary hardship is usually insufficient in itself for a variance; the party seeking the variance must usually show the variance would not substantially violate the policies of the comprehensive zoning plan.

**zygote** A fertilized egg. A zygote results from the combination of the reproductive cells of two animals; it is the cell that results when an egg is fertilized by a sperm cell. The zygote has only one cell, ceasing to be a zygote as soon as the cells divide.

*See also:* in, in vitro; family, family planning, assisted reproduction.

**embryo** A former zygote with an inner cell mass. An embryo is the development from a fertilized egg that is capable, under some circumstances, of developing into a fetus. Medical or biological definitions of embryo are not always controlling in legal meaning, and embryo is used in state and federal law with a variety of senses. All of these meanings are subject to changes in their significance in the twenty-first century, owing to changes in the regulation of human fertilization technology, stem-cell research, and abortion.

At its most general, some states define an embryo to include all fertilized eggs from the moment of fertilization through to the development of a mature embryo at eight weeks, without regard to whether the fertilization occurs in utero or ex utero in a laboratory. In other states, an embryo, by definition, is a more developed form than the fertilized egg cell or the zygote, and the embryo must be in a uterus or in an environment in which it may develop; these states tend to label a frozen conceptus as a pre-embryo.

**pre-embryo (preembryo)** The developing result of a fertilized egg out of a uterus. A pre-embryo is a developed fertilized cell that has progressed beyond the stage of being a zygote but that is not in a uterus or otherwise in an environment in which it may continue to develop. In effect, in law an embryo that is not implanted in a uterus is considered a pre-embryo, and thus subject to greater control by the individuals whose egg and sperm were combined in its creation. This distinction between pre-embryo and embryo is not without criticism, particularly from those who believe that life begins at the moment of fertilization, but also by biologists and medical specialists who believe the term is confusing with a stage of biological development of the conceptus. The term pre-embryo is derived from the botanical term, pro-embryo, which describes the fertilized cells of a plant.

# The Declaration of Independence and the United States Constitution

## The Declaration of Independence

**In Congress, July 4, 1776.**

**The Unanimous Declaration of the Thirteen United States of America.**

When in the Course of human events, it becomes necessary for one people to dissolve the political bands which have connected them with another, and to assume among the powers of the earth, the separate and equal station to which the Laws of Nature and of Nature's God entitle them, a decent respect to the opinions of mankind requires that they should declare the causes which impel them to the separation.

We hold these truths to be self-evident, that all men are created equal, that they are endowed by their Creator with certain unalienable Rights, that among these are Life, Liberty and the pursuit of Happiness. — That to secure these rights, Governments are instituted among Men, deriving their just powers from the consent of the governed, — That whenever any Form of Government becomes destructive of these ends, it is the Right of the People to alter or to abolish it, and to institute new Government, laying its foundation on such principles and organizing its powers in such form, as to them shall seem most likely to effect their Safety and Happiness. Prudence, indeed, will dictate that Governments long established should not be changed for light and transient causes; and accordingly all experience hath shewn, that mankind are more disposed to suffer, while evils are sufferable, than to right themselves by abolishing the forms to which they are accustomed. But when a long train of abuses and usurpations, pursuing invariably the same Object evinces a design to reduce them under absolute Despotism, it is their right, it is their duty, to throw off such Government, and to provide new Guards for their future security. — Such has been the patient sufferance of these Colonies; and such is now the necessity which constrains them to alter their former Systems of Government. The history of the present King of Great Britain is a history of repeated injuries and usurpations, all having in direct object the establishment of an absolute Tyranny over these States. To prove this, let Facts be submitted to a candid world.

He has refused his Assent to Laws, the most wholesome and necessary for the public good.

He has forbidden his Governors to pass Laws of immediate and pressing importance, unless suspended in their operation till his Assent should be obtained; and when so suspended, he has utterly neglected to attend to them.

He has refused to pass other Laws for the accommodation of large districts of people, unless those people would relinquish the right of Representation in the Legislature, a right inestimable to them and formidable to tyrants only.

He has called together legislative bodies at places unusual, uncomfortable, and distant from the depository of their public Records, for the sole purpose of fatiguing them into compliance with his measures.

He has dissolved Representative Houses repeatedly, for opposing with manly firmness his invasions on the rights of the people.

He has refused for a long time, after such dissolutions, to cause others to be elected; whereby the Legislative powers, incapable of Annihilation, have returned to the People at large for their exercise; the State remaining in the mean time exposed to all the dangers of invasion from without, and convulsions within.

He has endeavoured to prevent the population of these States; for that purpose obstructing the Laws for Naturalization of Foreigners; refusing to pass others to encourage their migrations hither, and raising the conditions of new Appropriations of Lands.

He has obstructed the Administration of Justice, by refusing his Assent to Laws for establishing Judiciary powers.

He has made Judges dependent on his Will alone, for the tenure of their offices, and the amount and payment of their salaries.

He has erected a multitude of New Offices, and sent hither swarms of Officers to harrass our people, and eat out their substance.

He has kept among us, in times of peace, Standing Armies without the Consent of our legislatures.

He has affected to render the Military independent of and superior to the Civil power.

He has combined with others to subject us to a jurisdiction foreign to our constitution, and unacknowledged by our laws; giving his Assent to their Acts of pretended Legislation:

For Quartering large bodies of armed troops among us:

For protecting them, by a mock Trial, from punishment for any Murders which they should commit on the Inhabitants of these States:

For cutting off our Trade with all parts of the world:

For imposing Taxes on us without our Consent:

For depriving us in many cases, of the benefits of Trial by Jury:

For transporting us beyond Seas to be tried for pretended offences

For abolishing the free System of English Laws in a neighbouring Province, establishing therein an Arbitrary government, and enlarging its Boundaries so as to render it at once an example and fit instrument for introducing the same absolute rule into these Colonies:

For taking away our Charters, abolishing our most valuable Laws, and altering fundamentally the Forms of our Governments:

For suspending our own Legislatures, and declaring themselves invested with power to legislate for us in all cases whatsoever.

He has abdicated Government here, by declaring us out of his Protection and waging War against us.

He has plundered our seas, ravaged our Coasts, burnt our towns, and destroyed the lives of our people.

He is at this time transporting large Armies of foreign Mercenaries to compleat the works of death, desolation and tyranny, already begun with circumstances of Cruelty & perfidy scarcely paralleled in the most barbarous ages, and totally unworthy the Head of a civilized nation.

He has constrained our fellow Citizens taken Captive on the high Seas to bear Arms against their Country, to become the executioners of their friends and Brethren, or to fall themselves by their Hands.

He has excited domestic insurrections amongst us, and has endeavoured to bring on the inhabitants of our frontiers, the merciless Indian Savages, whose known rule of warfare, is an undistinguished destruction of all ages, sexes and conditions.

In every stage of these Oppressions We have Petitioned for Redress in the most humble terms: Our repeated Petitions have been answered only by repeated injury. A Prince whose character is thus marked by every act which may define a Tyrant, is unfit to be the ruler of a free people.

Nor have We been wanting in attentions to our Brittish brethren. We have warned them from time to time of attempts by their legislature to extend an unwarrantable jurisdiction over us. We have reminded them of the circumstances of our emigration and settlement here. We have appealed to their native justice and magnanimity, and we have conjured them by the ties of our common kindred to disavow these usurpations, which, would inevitably interrupt our connections and correspondence. They too have been deaf to the voice of justice and of consanguinity. We must, therefore, acquiesce in the necessity, which denounces our Separation, and hold them, as we hold the rest of mankind, Enemies in War, in Peace Friends.

We, therefore, the Representatives of the united States of America, in General Congress, Assembled, appealing to the Supreme Judge of the world for the rectitude of our intentions, do, in the Name, and by Authority of the good People of these Colonies, solemnly publish and declare, That these United Colonies are, and of Right ought to be Free and Independent States; that they are Absolved from all Allegiance to the British Crown, and that all political connection between them and the State of Great Britain, is and ought to be totally dissolved; and that as Free and Independent States, they have full Power to levy War, conclude Peace, contract Alliances, establish Commerce, and to do all other Acts and Things which Independent States may of right do. And for the support of this Declaration, with a firm reliance on the protection of divine Providence, we mutually pledge to each other our Lives, our Fortunes and our sacred Honor.

# The Constitution of the United States of America, The Bill of Rights, and Subsequent Amendments

**We the People** of the United States, in Order to form a more perfect Union, establish Justice, insure domestic Tranquility, provide for the common defence, promote the general Welfare, and secure the Blessings of Liberty to ourselves and our Posterity, do ordain and establish this Constitution for the United States of America.

### Article I.

**Section 1.** All legislative Powers herein granted shall be vested in a Congress of the United States, which shall consist of a Senate and House of Representatives.

**Section 2.** The House of Representatives shall be composed of Members chosen every second Year by the People of the several States, and the Electors in each State shall have the Qualifications requisite for Electors of the most numerous Branch of the State Legislature.

No Person shall be a Representative who shall not have attained to the Age of twenty five Years, and been seven Years a Citizen of the United States, and who shall not, when elected, be an Inhabitant of that State in which he shall be chosen.

*Representatives and direct Taxes shall be apportioned among the several States which may be included within this Union, according to their respective Numbers, which shall be determined by adding to the whole Number of free Persons, including those bound to Service for a Term of Years, and excluding Indians not taxed, three fifths of all other Persons.* [Modified by Amdt. XIV.] The actual Enumeration shall be made within three Years after the first Meeting of the Congress of the United States, and within every subsequent Term of ten Years, in such Manner as they shall by Law direct. The Number of Representatives shall not exceed one for every thirty Thousand, but each State shall have at Least one Representative; and until such enumeration shall be made, the State of New Hampshire shall be entitled to chuse three, Massachusetts eight, Rhode Island and Providence Plantations one, Connecticut five, New York six, New Jersey four, Pennsylvania eight, Delaware one, Maryland six, Virginia ten, North Carolina five, South Carolina five, and Georgia three.

When vacancies happen in the Representation from any State, the Executive Authority thereof shall issue Writs of Election to fill such Vacancies.

The House of Representatives shall chuse their Speaker and other Officers; and shall have the sole Power of Impeachment.

**Section 3.** The Senate of the United States shall be composed of two Senators from each State, *chosen by the Legislature* [Modified by Amdt. XVII] thereof for six Years; and each Senator shall have one Vote.

Immediately after they shall be assembled in Consequence of the first Election, they shall be divided as equally as may be into three Classes. The Seats of the Senators of the first Class shall be vacated at the Expiration of the second Year, of the second Class at the Expiration of the fourth Year, and of the third Class at the Expiration of the sixth Year, so that one third may be chosen every second Year; *and if Vacancies happen by Resignation, or otherwise, during the Recess of the Legislature of any State, the Executive thereof may make temporary Appointments until the next Meeting of the Legislature, which shall then fill such Vacancies.* [Modified by Amdt. XVII.]

No Person shall be a Senator who shall not have attained to the Age of thirty Years, and been nine Years a Citizen of the United States, and who shall not, when elected, be an Inhabitant of that State for which he shall be chosen.

The Vice President of the United States shall be President of the Senate, but shall have no Vote, unless they be equally divided.

The Senate shall chuse their other Officers, and also a President pro tempore, in the Absence of the Vice President, or when he shall exercise the Office of President of the United States.

The Senate shall have the sole Power to try all Impeachments. When sitting for that Purpose, they shall be on Oath or Affirmation. When the President of the United States is tried, the Chief Justice shall preside: And no Person shall be convicted without the Concurrence of two thirds of the Members present.

Judgment in Cases of Impeachment shall not extend further than to removal from Office, and disqualification to hold and enjoy any Office of honor, Trust or Profit under the United States: but the Party convicted shall nevertheless be liable and subject to Indictment, Trial, Judgment and Punishment, according to Law.

**Section 4.** The Times, Places and Manner of holding Elections for Senators and Representatives, shall be prescribed in each State by the Legislature thereof; but the Congress may at any time by Law make or alter such Regulations, except as to the Places of chusing Senators.

The Congress shall assemble at least once in every Year, *and such Meeting shall be on the first Monday in December,* * [Modified by Amdt. XX] unless they shall by Law appoint a different Day.

**Section 5.** Each House shall be the Judge of the Elections, Returns and Qualifications of its own Members, and a Majority of each shall constitute a Quorum to do Business; but a smaller Number may adjourn from day to day, and may be authorized to compel the Attendance of absent Members, in such Manner, and under such Penalties as each House may provide.

Each House may determine the Rules of its Proceedings, punish its Members for disorderly Behaviour, and, with the Concurrence of two thirds, expel a Member.

Each House shall keep a Journal of its Proceedings, and from time to time publish the same, excepting such Parts as may in their Judgment require Secrecy; and the Yeas and Nays of the Members of either House on any question shall, at the Desire of one fifth of those Present, be entered on the Journal.

Neither House, during the Session of Congress, shall, without the Consent of the other, adjourn for more than three days, nor to any other Place than that in which the two Houses shall be sitting.

**Section 6.** The Senators and Representatives shall receive a Compensation for their Services, to be ascertained by Law, and paid out of the Treasury of the United States. They shall in all Cases, except Treason, Felony and Breach of the Peace, be privileged from Arrest during their Attendance at the Session of their respective Houses, and in going to and returning from the same; and for any Speech or Debate in either House, they shall not be questioned in any other Place.

No Senator or Representative shall, during the Time for which he was elected, be appointed to any civil Office under the Authority of the United States, which shall have been created, or the Emoluments whereof shall have been encreased during such time; and no Person holding any Office under the United States, shall be a Member of either House during his Continuance in Office.

**Section 7.** All Bills for raising Revenue shall originate in the House of Representatives; but the Senate may propose or concur with Amendments as on other Bills.

Every Bill which shall have passed the House of Representatives and the Senate, shall, before it become a Law, be presented to the President of the United States: If he approve he shall sign it, but if not he shall return it, with his Objections to that House in which it shall have originated, who shall enter the Objections at large on their Journal, and proceed to reconsider it. If after such Reconsideration two thirds of that House shall agree to pass the Bill, it shall be sent, together with the Objections, to the other House, by which it shall likewise be reconsidered, and if approved by two thirds of that House, it shall become a Law. But in all such Cases the Votes of both Houses shall be determined by yeas and Nays, and the Names of the Persons voting for and against the Bill shall be entered on the Journal of each House respectively. If any Bill shall not be returned by the President within ten Days (Sundays excepted) after it shall have been presented to him, the Same shall be a Law, in like Manner as if he had signed it, unless the Congress by their Adjournment prevent its Return, in which Case it shall not be a Law.

Every Order, Resolution, or Vote to which the Concurrence of the Senate and House of Representatives may be necessary (except on a question of Adjournment) shall be presented to the President of the United States; and before the Same shall take Effect, shall be approved by him, or being disapproved by him, shall be repassed by two thirds of the Senate and House of Representatives,

according to the Rules and Limitations prescribed in the Case of a Bill.

**Section 8.** The Congress shall have Power To lay and collect Taxes, Duties, Imposts and Excises, to pay the Debts and provide for the common Defence and general Welfare of the United States; but all Duties, Imposts and Excises shall be uniform throughout the United States;

To borrow Money on the credit of the United States;

To regulate Commerce with foreign Nations, and among the several States, and with the Indian Tribes;

To establish an uniform Rule of Naturalization, and uniform Laws on the subject of Bankruptcies throughout the United States;

To coin Money, regulate the Value thereof, and of foreign Coin, and fix the Standard of Weights and Measures;

To provide for the Punishment of counterfeiting the Securities and current Coin of the United States;

To establish Post Offices and post Roads;

To promote the Progress of Science and useful Arts, by securing for limited Times to Authors and Inventors the exclusive Right to their respective Writings and Discoveries;

To constitute Tribunals inferior to the supreme Court;

To define and punish Piracies and Felonies committed on the high Seas, and Offences against the Law of Nations;

To declare War, grant Letters of Marque and Reprisal, and make Rules concerning Captures on Land and Water;

To raise and support Armies, but no Appropriation of Money to that Use shall be for a longer Term than two Years;

To provide and maintain a Navy;

To make Rules for the Government and Regulation of the land and naval Forces;

To provide for calling forth the Militia to execute the Laws of the Union, suppress Insurrections and repel Invasions;

To provide for organizing, arming, and disciplining, the Militia, and for governing such Part of them as may be employed in the Service of the United States, reserving to the States respectively, the Appointment of the Officers, and the Authority of training the Militia according to the discipline prescribed by Congress;

To exercise exclusive Legislation in all Cases whatsoever, over such District (not exceeding ten Miles square) as may, by Cession of particular States, and the Acceptance of Congress, become the Seat of the Government of the United States, and to exercise like Authority over all Places purchased by the Consent of the Legislature of the State in which the Same shall be, for the Erection of Forts, Magazines, Arsenals, dock-Yards, and other needful Buildings; — And

To make all Laws which shall be necessary and proper for carrying into Execution the foregoing Powers, and all other Powers vested by this Constitution in the Government of the United States, or in any Department or Officer thereof.

**Section 9.** The Migration or Importation of such Persons as any of the States now existing shall think proper to admit, shall not be prohibited by the Congress prior to the Year one thousand eight hundred and eight, but a Tax or duty may be imposed on such Importation, not exceeding ten dollars for each Person.

The Privilege of the Writ of Habeas Corpus shall not be suspended, unless when in Cases of Rebellion or Invasion the public Safety may require it.

No Bill of Attainder or ex post facto Law shall be passed.

No Capitation, or other direct, Tax shall be laid, *unless in Proportion to the Census or enumeration herein before directed to be taken.* [Modified by Amdt. XVI.]

No Tax or Duty shall be laid on Articles exported from any State.

No Preference shall be given by any Regulation of Commerce or Revenue to the Ports of one State over those of another; nor shall Vessels bound to, or from, one State, be obliged to enter, clear, or pay Duties in another.

No Money shall be drawn from the Treasury, but in Consequence of Appropriations made by Law; and a regular Statement and Account of the Receipts and Expenditures of all public Money shall be published from time to time.

No Title of Nobility shall be granted by the United States: And no Person holding any Office of Profit or Trust under them, shall, without the Consent of the Congress, accept of any present, Emolument, Office, or Title, of any kind whatever, from any King, Prince, or foreign State.

**Section 10.** No State shall enter into any Treaty, Alliance, or Confederation; grant Letters of Marque and Reprisal; coin Money; emit Bills of Credit; make any Thing but gold and silver Coin a Tender in Payment of Debts; pass any Bill of Attainder, ex post facto Law, or Law impairing the Obligation of Contracts, or grant any Title of Nobility.

No State shall, without the Consent of the Congress, lay any Imposts or Duties on Imports or Exports, except what may be absolutely necessary for executing it's inspection Laws: and the net Produce of all Duties and Imposts, laid by any State on Imports or Exports, shall be for the Use of the Treasury of the United States; and all such Laws shall be subject to the Revision and Controul of the Congress.

No State shall, without the Consent of Congress, lay any Duty of Tonnage, keep Troops, or Ships of War in time of Peace, enter into any Agreement or Compact with another State, or with a foreign Power, or engage in War, unless actually invaded, or in such imminent Danger as will not admit of delay.

## Article II.

**Section 1.** The executive Power shall be vested in a President of the United States of America. He shall hold his Office during the Term of four Years, and, together with the Vice President, chosen for the same Term, be elected, as follows:

Each State shall appoint, in such Manner as the Legislature thereof may direct, a Number of Electors, equal to the whole Number of Senators and Representatives to which the State may be entitled in the Congress: but no Senator or Representative, or Person holding an Office of Trust or Profit under the United States, shall be appointed an Elector.

*The Electors shall meet in their respective States, and vote by Ballot for two Persons, of whom one at least shall not be an Inhabitant of the same State with themselves. And they shall make a List of all the Persons voted for, and of the Number of Votes for each; which List they shall sign and certify, and transmit sealed to the Seat of the Government of the United States, directed to the President of the Senate. The President of the Senate shall, in the Presence of the Senate and House of Representatives, open all the Certificates, and the Votes shall then be counted. The Person having the greatest Number of Votes shall be the President, if such Number be a Majority of the whole Number of Electors appointed; and if there be more than one who have such Majority, and have an equal Number of Votes, then the House of Representatives shall immediately chuse by Ballot one of them for President; and if no Person have a Majority, then from the five highest on the List the said House shall in like Manner chuse the President. But in chusing the President, the Votes shall be taken by States, the Representation from each State having one Vote; A quorum for this purpose shall consist of a Member or Members from two thirds of the States, and a Majority of all the States shall be necessary to a Choice. In every Case, after the Choice of the President, the Person having the greatest Number of Votes of the Electors shall be the Vice President. But if there should remain two or more who have equal Votes, the Senate shall chuse from them by Ballot the Vice President.* [Modified by Amdt. XXI.]

The Congress may determine the Time of chusing the Electors, and the Day on which they shall give their Votes; which Day shall be the same throughout the United States.

No Person except a natural born Citizen, or a Citizen of the United States, at the time of the Adoption of this Constitution, shall be eligible to the Office of President; neither shall any Person be eligible to that Office who shall not have attained to the Age of thirty five Years, and been fourteen Years a Resident within the United States.

*In Case of the Removal of the President from Office, or of his Death, Resignation, or Inability to discharge the Powers and Duties of the said Office, the Same shall devolve on the Vice President, and the Congress may by Law provide for the Case of Removal, Death, Resignation or Inability, both of the President and Vice President, declaring what Officer shall then act as President, and such Officer shall act accordingly, until the Disability be removed, or a President shall be elected.* [Modified by Amdt. XXV.]

The President shall, at stated Times, receive for his Services, a Compensation, which shall neither be increased nor diminished during the Period for which he shall have been elected, and he shall not receive within that Period any other Emolument from the United States, or any of them.

Before he enter on the Execution of his Office, he shall take the following Oath or Affirmation: — "I do solemnly swear (or affirm) that I will faithfully execute the Office of President of the United States, and will to the best of my Ability, preserve, protect and defend the Constitution of the United States."

**Section 2.** The President shall be Commander in Chief of the Army and Navy of the United States, and of the Militia of the several States, when called into the actual Service of the United States; he may require the Opinion, in writing, of the principal Officer in each of the executive Departments, upon any Subject relating to the Duties of their respective Offices, and he shall have Power to grant Reprieves and Pardons for Offences against the United States, except in Cases of Impeachment.

He shall have Power, by and with the Advice and Consent of the Senate, to make Treaties, provided two thirds of the Senators present concur; and he shall nominate, and by and with the Advice and Consent of the Senate, shall appoint Ambassadors, other public Ministers and Consuls, Judges of the supreme Court, and all other Officers of the United States, whose Appointments are not herein otherwise provided for, and which shall be established by Law: but the Congress may by Law vest the Appointment of such inferior Officers, as they think proper, in the President alone, in the Courts of Law, or in the Heads of Departments.

The President shall have Power to fill up all Vacancies that may happen during the Recess of the Senate, by granting Commissions which shall expire at the End of their next Session.

**Section 3.** He shall from time to time give to the Congress Information of the State of the Union, and recommend to their Consideration such Measures as he shall judge necessary and expedient; he may, on extraordinary Occasions, convene both Houses, or either of them, and in Case of Disagreement between them, with Respect to the Time of Adjournment, he may adjourn them to such Time as he shall think proper; he shall receive Ambassadors and other public Ministers; he shall take Care that the Laws be faithfully executed, and shall Commission all the Officers of the United States.

**Section 4.** The President, Vice President and all civil Officers of the United States, shall be removed from Office on Impeachment for, and Conviction of, Treason, Bribery, or other high Crimes and Misdemeanors.

### Article III.

**Section 1.** The judicial Power of the United States shall be vested in one supreme Court, and in such inferior Courts as the Congress may from time to time ordain and establish. The Judges, both of the supreme and inferior Courts, shall hold their Offices during good Behaviour, and shall, at stated Times, receive for their Services a Compensation, which shall not be diminished during their Continuance in Office.

**Section 2.** The judicial Power shall extend to all Cases, in Law and Equity, arising under this Constitution, the Laws of the United States, and Treaties made, or which shall be made, under their Authority; — to all Cases affecting Ambassadors, other public Ministers and Consuls; — to all Cases of admiralty and maritime Jurisdiction; — to Controversies to which the United States shall be a Party; — to Controversies between two or more States; — *between a State and Citizens of another State,* [Modified by Amdt. XI] — between Citizens of different States, — between Citizens of the same State claiming Lands under Grants of different States, and between a State, or the Citizens thereof, and foreign States, Citizens or Subjects.

In all Cases affecting Ambassadors, other public Ministers and Consuls, and those in which a State shall be Party, the supreme Court shall have original Jurisdiction. In all the other Cases before mentioned, the supreme Court shall have appellate Jurisdiction, both as to Law and Fact, with such Exceptions, and under such Regulations as the Congress shall make.

The Trial of all Crimes, except in Cases of Impeachment, shall be by Jury; and such Trial shall be held in the State where the said Crimes shall have been committed; but when not committed within any State, the Trial shall be at such Place or Places as the Congress may by Law have directed.

**Section 3.** Treason against the United States, shall consist only in levying War against them, or in adhering to their Enemies, giving them Aid and Comfort. No Person shall be convicted of Treason unless on the Testimony of two Witnesses to the same overt Act, or on Confession in open Court.

The Congress shall have Power to declare the Punishment of Treason, but no Attainder of Treason shall work Corruption of Blood, or Forfeiture except during the Life of the Person attainted.

### Article IV.

**Section 1.** Full Faith and Credit shall be given in each State to the public Acts, Records, and judicial Proceedings of every other State. And the Congress may by general Laws prescribe the Manner in which such Acts, Records and Proceedings shall be proved, and the Effect thereof.

**Section 2.** The Citizens of each State shall be entitled to all Privileges and Immunities of Citizens in the several States.

A Person charged in any State with Treason, Felony, or other Crime, who shall flee from Justice, and be found in another State, shall on Demand of the executive Authority of the State from which he fled, be delivered up, to be removed to the State having Jurisdiction of the Crime.

*No Person held to Service or Labour in one State, under the Laws thereof, escaping into another, shall, in Consequence of any Law or Regulation therein, be discharged from such Service or Labour, but shall be delivered up on Claim of the Party to whom such Service or Labour may be due.* [Repealed by Amdt. XIII.]

**Section 3.** New States may be admitted by the Congress into this Union; but no new State shall be formed or erected within the Jurisdiction of any other State; nor any State be formed by the Junction of two or more States, or Parts of States, without the Consent of the Legislatures of the States concerned as well as of the Congress.

The Congress shall have Power to dispose of and make all needful Rules and Regulations respecting the Territory or other Property belonging to the United States; and nothing in this Constitution shall be so construed as to Prejudice any Claims of the United States, or of any particular State.

**Section 4.** The United States shall guarantee to every State in this Union a Republican Form of Government, and shall protect each of them against Invasion; and on Application of the Legislature, or of the Executive (when the Legislature cannot be convened), against domestic Violence.

### Article V.

The Congress, whenever two thirds of both Houses shall deem it necessary, shall propose Amendments to this Constitution, or, on the Application of the Legislatures of two thirds of the several States, shall call a Convention for proposing Amendments, which, in either Case, shall be valid to all Intents and Purposes, as Part of this Constitution, when ratified by the Legislatures of three fourths of the several States, or by Conventions in three fourths thereof, as the one or the other Mode of Ratification may be proposed by the Congress; Provided

that no Amendment which may be made prior to the Year One thousand eight hundred and eight shall in any Manner affect the first and fourth Clauses in the Ninth Section of the first Article; and that no State, without its Consent, shall be deprived of its equal Suffrage in the Senate.

### Article VI.

All Debts contracted and Engagements entered into, before the Adoption of this Constitution, shall be as valid against the United States under this Constitution, as under the Confederation.

This Constitution, and the Laws of the United States which shall be made in Pursuance thereof; and all Treaties made, or which shall be made, under the Authority of the United States, shall be the supreme Law of the Land; and the Judges in every State shall be bound thereby, any Thing in the Constitution or Laws of any State to the Contrary notwithstanding.

The Senators and Representatives before mentioned, and the Members of the several State Legislatures, and all executive and judicial Officers, both of the United States and of the several States, shall be bound by Oath or Affirmation, to support this Constitution; but no religious Test shall ever be required as a Qualification to any Office or public Trust under the United States.

### Article VII.

The Ratification of the Conventions of nine States, shall be sufficient for the Establishment of this Constitution between the States so ratifying the Same.

[D]one in Convention by the Unanimous Consent of the States present the Seventeenth Day of September in the Year of our Lord one thousand seven hundred and Eighty seven and of the Independence of the United States of America the Twelfth In witness whereof We have hereunto subscribed our Names . . .

# The Bill of Rights

[The First Congress proposed twelve amendments, of which ten were ratified on December 15, 1791. These are the first ten Amendments to the Constitution of the United States and are known as the Bill of Rights. Amendment 27 was also then proposed but was not ratified until 1992. The Preamble of the Bill of Rights is not Considered a part of the Constitutional text but is included here for reference.]

### The Preamble to the Bill of Rights

Congress of the United States, begun and held at the City of New York, on, Wednesday the fourth of March, one thousand seven hundred and eighty nine.

The Conventions of a number of the States, having at the time of their adopting the Constitution, expressed a desire, in order to prevent misconstruction or abuse of its powers, that further declaratory and restrictive clauses should be added: And as extending the ground of public confidence in the Government, will best ensure the beneficent ends of its institution.

Resolved by the Senate and House of Representatives of the United States of America, in Congress assembled, two thirds of both Houses concurring, that the following Articles be proposed to the Legislatures of the several States, as Amendments to the Constitution of the United States, all, or any of which Articles, when ratified by three fourths of the said Legislatures, to be valid to all intents and purposes, as part of the said Constitution; viz.

Articles in addition to, and Amendment of the Constitution of the United States of America, proposed by Congress, and ratified by the Legislatures of the several States, pursuant to the fifth Article of the original Constitution.

### Amendment I

Congress shall make no law respecting an establishment of religion, or prohibiting the free exercise thereof; or abridging the freedom of speech, or of the press; or the right of the people peaceably to assemble, and to petition the Government for a redress of grievances.

### Amendment II

A well regulated Militia, being necessary to the security of a free State, the right of the people to keep and bear Arms, shall not be infringed.

### Amendment III

No Soldier shall, in time of peace be quartered in any house, without the consent of the Owner, nor in time of war, but in a manner to be prescribed by law.

### Amendment IV

The right of the people to be secure in their persons, houses, papers, and effects, against unreasonable searches and seizures, shall not be violated, and no Warrants shall issue, but upon probable cause, supported by Oath or affirmation, and particularly describing the place to be searched, and the persons or things to be seized.

### Amendment V

No person shall be held to answer for a capital, or otherwise infamous crime, unless on a presentment or indictment of a Grand Jury, except in cases arising in the land or naval forces, or in the Militia, when in actual service in time of War or public danger; nor shall any person be subject for the same offence to be twice put in jeopardy of life or limb; nor shall be compelled in any criminal case to be a witness against himself, nor be deprived of life, liberty, or property, without due process of law; nor shall private property be taken for public use, without just compensation.

### Amendment VI

In all criminal prosecutions, the accused shall enjoy the right to a speedy and public trial, by an impartial jury of the State and district wherein the crime shall have been committed, which district shall have been previously ascertained by law, and to be informed of the nature and cause of the accusation; to be confronted with the witnesses against him; to have compulsory process for obtaining witnesses in his favor, and to have the Assistance of Counsel for his defence.

### Amendment VII

In Suits at common law, where the value in controversy shall exceed twenty dollars, the right of trial by jury shall be preserved, and no fact tried by a jury, shall be otherwise re-examined in any Court of the United States, than according to the rules of the common law.

### Amendment VIII

Excessive bail shall not be required, nor excessive fines imposed, nor cruel and unusual punishments inflicted.

### Amendment IX

The enumeration in the Constitution, of certain rights, shall not be construed to deny or disparage others retained by the people.

### Amendment X

The powers not delegated to the United States by the Constitution, nor prohibited by it to the States, are reserved to the States respectively, or to the people.

### Amendment XI

The Judicial power of the United States shall not be construed to extend to any suit in law or equity, commenced or prosecuted against one of the United States by Citizens of another State, or by Citizens or Subjects of any Foreign State. *Passed by Congress March 4, 1794. Ratified February 7, 1795.*

### Amendment XII

The Electors shall meet in their respective states and vote by ballot for President and Vice-President, one of whom, at least, shall not be an inhabitant of the same state with themselves; they shall name in their ballots the person voted for as President, and in distinct ballots the person voted for as Vice-President, and they shall make distinct lists of all persons voted for as President, and of all persons voted for as Vice-President, and of the number of votes for each, which lists they shall sign and certify, and transmit sealed to the seat of the government of the United States, directed to the President of the Senate; — the President of the Senate shall, in the presence of the Senate and House of Representatives, open all the certificates and the votes shall then be counted; — The person having the greatest number of votes for President, shall be the President, if such number be a majority of the whole number of Electors appointed; and if no person have such majority, then from the persons having the highest numbers not exceeding three on the list of those voted for as President, the House of Representatives shall choose immediately, by ballot, the President. But in choosing the President, the votes shall be taken by states, the representation from each state having one vote; a quorum for this purpose shall consist of a member or members from two-thirds of the states, and a majority of all the states shall be necessary to a choice. *And if the House of Representatives shall not choose a President whenever the right of choice shall devolve upon them, before the fourth day of March next following, then the Vice-President shall act as President, as in case of the death or other constitutional disability of the President * [Modified by Amdt. XX.] The person having the greatest number of votes as Vice-President, shall be the Vice-President, if such number be a majority of the whole number of Electors appointed, and if no person have a majority, then from the two highest numbers on the list, the Senate shall choose the Vice-President; a quorum for the purpose shall consist of two-thirds of the whole number of Senators, and a majority of the whole number shall be necessary to a choice. But no person constitutionally ineligible to the office of President shall be eligible to that of Vice-President of the United States. *Passed by Congress December 9, 1803. Ratified June 15, 1804.*

### Amendment XIII

**Section 1.** Neither slavery nor involuntary servitude, except as a punishment for crime whereof the party shall have been duly convicted, shall exist within the United States, or any place subject to their jurisdiction.

**Section 2.** Congress shall have power to enforce this article by appropriate legislation. *Passed by Congress January 31, 1865. Ratified December 6, 1865.*

### Amendment XIV

**Section 1.** All persons born or naturalized in the United States, and subject to the jurisdiction thereof, are citizens of the United States and of the State wherein they reside. No State shall make or enforce any law which shall abridge the privileges or immunities of citizens of the United States; nor shall any State deprive any person of life, liberty, or property, without due process of law; nor deny to any person within its jurisdiction the equal protection of the laws.

**Section 2.** Representatives shall be apportioned among the several States according to their respective numbers, counting the whole number of persons in each State, excluding Indians not taxed. But when the right to vote at any election for the choice of electors for President and Vice-President of the United States, Representatives in Congress, the Executive and Judicial officers of a State, or the members of the Legislature thereof, is denied to any of the male inhabitants of such State,* being twenty-one years of age,* [Modified by Amdt. XXVI] and citizens of the United States, or in any way abridged, except for participation in rebellion, or other crime, the basis of representation therein shall be reduced in the proportion which the number of such male citizens shall bear to the whole number of male citizens twenty-one years of age in such State.

**Section 3.** No person shall be a Senator or Representative in Congress, or elector of President and Vice-President, or hold any office, civil or military, under the United States, or under any State, who, having previously taken an oath, as a member of Congress, or as an officer of the United States, or as a member of any State legislature, or as an executive or judicial officer of any State, to support the Constitution of the United States, shall have engaged in insurrection or rebellion against the same, or given aid or comfort to the enemies thereof. But Congress may by a vote of two-thirds of each House, remove such disability.

**Section 4.** The validity of the public debt of the United States, authorized by law, including debts incurred for payment of pensions and bounties for services in suppressing insurrection or rebellion, shall not be questioned. But neither the United States nor any State shall assume or pay any debt or obligation incurred in aid of insurrection or rebellion against the United States, or any claim for the loss or emancipation of any slave; but all such debts, obligations and claims shall be held illegal and void.

**Section 5.** The Congress shall have the power to enforce, by appropriate legislation, the provisions of this article. *Passed by Congress June 13, 1866. Ratified July 9, 1868.*

### Amendment XV

**Section 1.** The right of citizens of the United States to vote shall not be denied or abridged by the United States or by any State on account of race, color, or previous condition of servitude —

**Section 2.** The Congress shall have the power to enforce this article by appropriate legislation. *Passed by Congress February 26, 1869. Ratified February 3, 1870.*

### Amendment XVI

The Congress shall have power to lay and collect taxes on incomes, from whatever source derived, without apportionment among the several States, and without regard to any census or enumeration. *Passed by Congress July 2, 1909. Ratified February 3, 1913.*

## Amendment XVII

The Senate of the United States shall be composed of two Senators from each State, elected by the people thereof, for six years; and each Senator shall have one vote. The electors in each State shall have the qualifications requisite for electors of the most numerous branch of the State legislatures.

When vacancies happen in the representation of any State in the Senate, the executive authority of such State shall issue writs of election to fill such vacancies: Provided, That the legislature of any State may empower the executive thereof to make temporary appointments until the people fill the vacancies by election as the legislature may direct.

This Amendment shall not be so construed as to affect the election or term of any Senator chosen before it becomes valid as part of the Constitution. *Passed by Congress May 13, 1912. Ratified April 8, 1913.*

## Amendment XVIII

**Section 1.** After one year from the ratification of this article the manufacture, sale, or transportation of intoxicating liquors within, the importation thereof into, or the exportation thereof from the United States and all territory subject to the jurisdiction thereof for beverage purposes is hereby prohibited.

**Section 2.** The Congress and the several States shall have concurrent power to enforce this article by appropriate legislation.

**Section 3.** This article shall be inoperative unless it shall have been ratified as an Amendment to the Constitution by the legislatures of the several States, as provided in the Constitution, within seven years from the date of the submission hereof to the States by the Congress. *Passed by Congress December 18, 1917. Ratified January 16, 1919. Repealed by Amendment XXI.*

## Amendment XIX

The right of citizens of the United States to vote shall not be denied or abridged by the United States or by any State on account of sex.

Congress shall have power to enforce this article by appropriate legislation. *Passed by Congress June 4, 1919. Ratified August 18, 1920.*

## Amendment XX

**Section 1.** The terms of the President and the Vice President shall end at noon on the 20th day of January, and the terms of Senators and Representatives at noon on the 3d day of January, of the years in which such terms would have ended if this article had not been ratified; and the terms of their successors shall then begin.

**Section 2.** The Congress shall assemble at least once in every year, and such meeting shall begin at noon on the 3d day of January, unless they shall by law appoint a different day.

**Section 3.** If, at the time fixed for the beginning of the term of the President, the President elect shall have died, the Vice President elect shall become President. If a President shall not have been chosen before the time fixed for the beginning of his term, or if the President elect shall have failed to qualify, then the Vice President elect shall act as President until a President shall have qualified; and the Congress may by law provide for the case wherein neither a President elect nor a Vice President elect shall have qualified, declaring who shall then act as President, or the manner in which one who is to act shall be selected, and such person shall act accordingly until a President or Vice President shall have qualified.

**Section 4.** The Congress may by law provide for the case of the death of any of the persons from whom the House of Representatives may choose a President whenever the right of choice shall have devolved upon them, and for the case of the death of any of the persons from whom the Senate may choose a Vice President whenever the right of choice shall have devolved upon them.

**Section 5.** Sections 1 and 2 shall take effect on the 15th day of October following the ratification of this article.

**Section 6.** This article shall be inoperative unless it shall have been ratified as an Amendment to the Constitution by the legislatures of three-fourths of the several States within seven years from the date of its submission. *Passed by Congress March 2, 1932. Ratified January 23, 1933.*

## Amendment XXI

**Section 1.** The eighteenth article of Amendment to the Constitution of the United States is hereby repealed.

**Section 2.** The transportation or importation into any State, Territory, or Possession of the United States for delivery or use therein of intoxicating liquors, in violation of the laws thereof, is hereby prohibited.

**Section 3.** This article shall be inoperative unless it shall have been ratified as an Amendment to the Constitution by conventions in the several States, as provided in the Constitution, within seven years from the date of the submission hereof to the States by the Congress. *Passed by Congress February 20, 1933. Ratified December 5, 1933.*

## Amendment XXII

**Section 1.** No person shall be elected to the office of the President more than twice, and no person who has held the office of President, or acted as President, for more than two years of a term to which some other person was elected President shall be elected to the office of President more than once. But this Article shall not apply to any person holding the office of President when this Article was proposed by Congress, and shall not prevent any person who may be holding the office of President, or acting as President, during the term within which this Article becomes operative from holding the office of President or acting as President during the remainder of such term.

**Section 2.** This article shall be inoperative unless it shall have been ratified as an Amendment to the Constitution by the legislatures of three-fourths of the several States within seven years from the date of its submission to the

States by the Congress. *Passed by Congress March 21, 1947. Ratified February 27, 1951.*

## Amendment XXIII

**Section 1.** The District constituting the seat of Government of the United States shall appoint in such manner as Congress may direct:

A number of electors of President and Vice President equal to the whole number of Senators and Representatives in Congress to which the District would be entitled if it were a State, but in no event more than the least populous State; they shall be in addition to those appointed by the States, but they shall be considered, for the purposes of the election of President and Vice President, to be electors appointed by a State; and they shall meet in the District and perform such duties as provided by the twelfth article of Amendment.

**Section 2.** The Congress shall have power to enforce this article by appropriate legislation. *Passed by Congress June 16, 1960. Ratified March 29, 1961.*

## Amendment XXIV

**Section 1.** The right of citizens of the United States to vote in any primary or other election for President or Vice President, for electors for President or Vice President, or for Senator or Representative in Congress, shall not be denied or abridged by the United States or any State by reason of failure to pay poll tax or other tax.

**Section 2.** The Congress shall have power to enforce this article by appropriate legislation. *Passed by Congress August 27, 1962. Ratified January 23, 1964.*

## Amendment XXV

**Section 1.** In case of the removal of the President from office or of his death or resignation, the Vice President shall become President.

**Section 2.** Whenever there is a vacancy in the office of the Vice President, the President shall nominate a Vice President who shall take office upon confirmation by a majority vote of both Houses of Congress.

**Section 3.** Whenever the President transmits to the President pro tempore of the Senate and the Speaker of the House of Representatives his written declaration that he is unable to discharge the powers and duties of his office, and until he transmits to them a written declaration to the contrary, such powers and duties shall be discharged by the Vice President as Acting President.

**Section 4.** Whenever the Vice President and a majority of either the principal officers of the executive departments or of such other body as Congress may by law provide, transmit to the President pro tempore of the Senate and the Speaker of the House of Representatives their written declaration that the President is unable to discharge the powers and duties of his office, the Vice President shall immediately assume the powers and duties of the office as Acting President.

Thereafter, when the President transmits to the President pro tempore of the Senate and the Speaker of the House of Representatives his written declaration that no inability exists, he shall resume the powers and duties of his office unless the Vice President and a majority of either the principal officers of the executive department or of such other body as Congress may by law provide, transmit within four days to the President pro tempore of the Senate and the Speaker of the House of Representatives their written declaration that the President is unable to discharge the powers and duties of his office. Thereupon Congress shall decide the issue, assembling within forty-eight hours for that purpose if not in session. If the Congress, within twenty-one days after receipt of the latter written declaration, or, if Congress is not in session, within twenty-one days after Congress is required to assemble, determines by two-thirds vote of both Houses that the President is unable to discharge the powers and duties of his office, the Vice President shall continue to discharge the same as Acting President; otherwise, the President shall resume the powers and duties of his office. *Passed by Congress July 6, 1965. Ratified February 10, 1967.*

## Amendment XXVI

**Section 1.** The right of citizens of the United States, who are eighteen years of age or older, to vote shall not be denied or abridged by the United States or by any State on account of age.

**Section 2.** The Congress shall have power to enforce this article by appropriate legislation. *Passed by Congress March 23, 1971. Ratified July 1, 1971.*

## Amendment XXVII

No law, varying the compensation for the services of the Senators and Representatives, shall take effect, until an election of representatives shall have intervened. *Proposed Sept. 25, 1789. Ratified May 7, 1992.*

## Second Appendix
# Justices of the United States Supreme Court

Alito **Samuel Alito** (b. 1950) U.S. Supreme Court Justice. After taking his law degree from Yale in 1975, Alito clerked for a year before becoming an assistant U.S. attorney for New Jersey, then worked for the U.S. Solicitor General's Office, then was made deputy assistant attorney general before being appointed U.S. attorney for New Jersey. In 1990, President George H.W. Bush nominated Alito to the Third Circuit, where he worked until 2005, when President George W. Bush nominated him to fill Justice O'Connor's seat on the U.S. Supreme Court. He is considered a conservative who favors corporate interests and executive power. *See:* Samuel A. Alito, Jr., Documents and the Privilege against Self-Incrimination, 48 U. Pitt. L. Rev. 27 (1986).

Baldwin **Henry Baldwin** (1780-1844) U.S. Supreme Court Justice. Graduating from Yale College in 1797, Baldwin studied law and entered the bar in Pennsylvania. In 1816, Baldwin was elected to the U.S. House of Representatives, from which he resigned in 1822 due to deteriorating health. President Jackson nominated Baldwin to the Supreme Court in 1829, where he served for fourteen years. *See:* Henry Baldwin, A General View of the Origin and Nature of the Constitution and Government of the United States (Da Capo Press, 1970) (1837); Flavia M. Taylor, The Political and Civil Career of Henry Baldwin, 24 W. Pa. Hist. Mag. 37 (1941).

Barbour **Philip Barbour** (1783-1841) U.S. Supreme Court Justice. After studying law briefly at the College of William & Mary, Philip Pendleton Barbour opened and successfully ran a private practice in Virginia. In 1812, Barbour made his first foray into politics with his election to the Virginia House of Delegates. An election to the U.S. House of Representatives followed two years later; Barbour served as Speaker from 1821 to 1823. Barbour is most noted for his opinion in *City of New York v. Miln*, 36 U.S. 102 (1837), in which he supports state regulation of corporations. *See:* Joseph Story, Eulogy, U.S. Rep. (15 Peters), v-vii. (1841).

Black **Hugo Black** (1886-1971) Statesman and U.S. Supreme Court Justice. Black was a native of Alabama, graduating from the University of Alabama Law School in 1906. He entered private practice upon completion of law school. On his return to practice after military service in World War I, Black sought election to the U.S. Senate, where he served until his nomination to the high court in 1937 by President Franklin D. Roosevelt. Though often thought liberal owing to his defense of individual rights, he relied more on the text of the Constitution, a copy of which he kept always in his pocket. *See:* Tinsley E. Yarbrough, Mr. Justice Black and His Critics (Duke Univ. Press, 1989); Hugo LaFayette Black, Mr. Justice and Mrs. Black: The Memoirs of Hugo L. Black and Elizabeth Black (Random House, 1986); James F. Simon, The Antagonists: Hugo Black, Felix Frankfurter and Civil Liberties in Modern America (Simon & Schuster, 1989).

Blackmun **Harry Blackmun** (1908-1999) U.S. Supreme Court Justice. A native of Illinois, Blackmun attended Harvard College before taking his degree from Harvard Law School in 1932. Blackmun taught law and practiced privately until nominated by President Eisenhower to the Eighth Circuit in 1959. President Nixon would nominate Blackmun to the U.S. Supreme Court in 1970. Though he authored many significant opinions, particularly extending individual rights and developing the philosophy of affirmative action, he is best known as the author of *Roe v. Wade*, 410 U.S. 113 (1973). *See:* Linda Greenhouse, Becoming Justice Blackmun: Harry Blackmun's Supreme Court Journey (Times Books, 2005).

Blair **John Blair, Jr.** (1732-1800) Statesman and U.S. Supreme Court Justice. Born in Williamsburg to a wealthy Virginia political family, Blair attended the College of William & Mary and studied law in the Middle Temple in London. Blair practiced law in Virginia, sitting on the Virginia Court of Appeals and becoming chancellor, as well as serving as a delegate to the Constitutional Convention. Nominated to the first Supreme Court in 1789 by President Washington, Blair resigned his seat on the high court in 1795.

Blatchford **Samuel Blatchford** (1820-1893) U.S. Supreme Court Justice. Blatchford took his degree from Columbia College before working in politics and later reading for admission to the bar in 1843. Blatchford was nominated to the Supreme Court in 1882 by President Arthur and is known for his opinion in *Chicago, Milwaukee & St. Paul Ry. v. Minnesota*, 134 U.S. 418 (1890), dealing with railroad price structure and regulation. *See:* A. Oakley Hall, Justice Samuel Blatchford, 48 Alb. L. J. 489 (1893).

Bradley **Joseph P. Bradley** (1813-1892) U.S. Supreme Court Justice. A graduate of Rutgers University, Bradley went on to study law, gaining admittance to the New Jersey Bar in 1839. Bradley worked as a private attorney for the next twenty years, and having developed close ties to the political elite, was nominated to the Supreme Court of the United States by President Grant in 1870. Bradley notably wrote the majority opinion in *Civil Rights Cases*, 109 U.S. 3 (1883), greatly restricting the scope of the Fourteenth Amendment. *See:* Charles Bradley, comp., Miscellaneous Writings of the Late Hon. Joseph P. Bradley, Associate Justice of the Supreme Court of the United States (Fred B. Rothman, 1986) (1901); Charles Fairman, The Education of a Justice: Justice Bradley and Some of His Colleagues, 1 Stan. L. Rev. 217 (1949).

Brandeis **Louis Dembitz Brandeis** (1856-1941) U.S. Supreme Court Justice. A native of Kentucky, Brandeis graduated after a stellar career at Harvard Law School and set up a practice in Boston, Massachusetts, developing a career as a lawyer for private clients and social causes. His advocacy for labor in the U.S. Supreme Court was supported by social science data, in arguments soon known as "Brandeis Briefs" for their conclusive density. In 1916, President Wilson nominated Brandeis to the U.S. Supreme Court, where he was a frequent advocate for individual liberty, often joining Justice Holmes in dissent. Among his majority opinions is *Erie Railroad Co. v. Tompkins*, 304 U.S. 64 (1938). *See:* Louis Brandeis, Other People's Money and How Bankers Use It (1914) (Martino, 2009); Melvin I. Urofsky, Louis D. Brandeis: A Life (Pantheon, 2009); Felix Frankfurter, Mr. Justice Brandeis (Da Capo, 1972) (1932); Philippa Strum, Louis D. Brandeis: Justice for the People (Schocken Books, 1984); Melvin I. Urofsky, Louis D. Brandeis and the Progressive Tradition (Brown, 1981).

Brennan **William J. Brennan, Jr.** (1906–1997) U.S. Supreme Court Justice. Brennan worked in private practice after graduating from Harvard Law School in 1931. Upon his return from military service in World War II, he resumed private practice before being appointed to the trial, and then the appellate division, of the New Jersey Superior Court. President Eisenhower nominated Brennan to fill Justice Milton's seat on the high court in 1956. Brennan was a consistent advocate for individual rights and equal protection of the law and argued, often in dissent, for the extension of constitutional protections of the individual against corporate, state, and national power. *See:* William J. Brennan, an Affair with Freedom: A Collection of His Opinions and Speeches Drawn from His First Decade as a United States Supreme Court Justice (Atheneum, 1967); Seth Stern and Stephen Wermiel, Justice Brennan, Liberal Champion (Houghton Mifflin Harcourt 2010); Robert C. Post, Justice William J. Brennan and the Warren Court, 11 Const. Comm. 8 (1991).

Brewer **David Josiah Brewer** (1837–1910) U.S. Supreme Court Justice. Born to missionaries abroad, Brewer would later return to the United States and graduate from Yale University and Albany Law School. Relocating to Kansas, Brewer spent much of his early career sitting on lower courts until he was elected to the Kansas Supreme Court in 1870. President Arthur named Brewer to the Eighth Circuit in 1884, where he served for five years before being nominated by President Harrison to the Supreme Court of the United States. *See:* Joseph Gordon Hylton, David Josiah Brewer: A Conservative Justice Reconsidered, J. of Sp. C. Hist. Soc. 45 (1994).

Breyer **Stephen G. Breyer** (b. 1938) U.S. Supreme Court Justice. A graduate of Harvard Law School, Breyer clerked for Justice Goldberg at the Supreme Court before briefly working in the U.S. Assistant Attorney General's Office, then settling into a professorial role at Harvard Law School. In 1980, President Carter nominated Breyer to the First Circuit. President Bill Clinton nominated him to the high court to fill Justice Blackmun's newly vacated seat in 1994. Breyer is a notable pragmatist who is sensitive to the purpose and

consequence of the law. *See:* Stephen G. Breyer, Making Our Democracy Work: A Judge's View (Knopf, 2010); Stephen Breyer, Active Liberty: Interpreting Our Democratic Constitution (Vintage, 2006); Judge Breyer's Life, The Washington Post, June 26, 1994 at A-1; Breyer: Pragmatic Leader, The Washington Post, June 27, 1994 at A-1.

Brown **Henry Billings Brown** (1836–1913) U.S. Supreme Court Justice. Born in Massachusetts, Brown took his undergraduate degree from Yale before studying law at both Yale and Harvard, though he never took a formal law degree. Brown moved to Detroit shortly after graduation, where he served in local office for a short time before President Grant nominated him to the Federal District Court in 1875. President Harrison later nominated Brown to the Supreme Court, where he is best known for writing *Plessy v. Ferguson*, 163 U.S. 537 (1896), which upheld the separate but equal doctrine. *See:* Robert J. Glennon, Jr., Justice Henry Billings Brown: Values in Tension, 44 U. Colo. L. Rev. 553 (1973).

Burger **Warren E. Burger** (1907–1995) Fifteenth Chief Justice of the United States. Grandson of a Civil War hero from Minnesota, Burger graduated from St. Paul College of Law in 1931, where he then taught law while practicing privately. Burger was appointed assistant attorney general for the claims division in 1953, and in 1955 was appointed to the U.S. Court of Appeals in Washington, D.C. In 1969, President Nixon nominated Burger to the U.S. Supreme Court to fill Justice Warren's seat as Chief Justice. Burger supported many of Warren's civil rights cases, though limiting their reach. In 1974, he wrote the unanimous opinion in *U.S. v. Nixon*, 418 U.S. 683 (1974), which required the president to produce documents for the courts, leading to President Nixon's resignation from office. *See:* Warren E. Burger, It Is So Ordered: A Constitution Unfolds (William Morrow, 1995); Bernard Schwartz, The Ascent of Pragmatism: The Burger Court in Action (Addison-Wesley, 1989); Warren E. Burger, Delivery of Justice (West Publishing Co., 1990); A Tribute to Chief Justice Warren E Burger, 100 Harv. L. Rev. 969 (1987).

Burton **Harold H. Burton** (1888–1964) U.S. Supreme Court Justice. Burton, a 1912 graduate of Harvard Law School, lived for a short time in Ohio before moving on to Utah. After World War I, Burton moved back to Ohio, settling in Cleveland, where he set up a private practice and lectured at Western Reserve Law School. Elected mayor of Cleveland in 1935, Burton mounted a successful Senate campaign in 1941. He served in the U.S. Senate until President Truman nominated him to the U.S. Supreme Court in 1945. *See:* David N. Atkinson, Justice Harold H. Burton and the Work of the Supreme Court, 27 Clev. St. L. Rev. 69 (1987); Edward G. Hudon, The Occasional Papers of Mr. Justice Burton (Bowdoin College, 1969).

Butler **Pierce Butler** (1866–1939) U.S. Supreme Court Justice. A graduate of Carleton College, Butler moved to St. Paul, Minnesota, where he was admitted to the bar in 1888. After a brief stint as the county attorney, Butler committed himself to building a private practice in St. Paul. Through political connections, President Harding would learn of Butler and nominate him to the high court in 1922. Butler is a noted member of the Four Horsemen of the Supreme Court. *See:* Barry Cushman, The Secret Lives of the Four Horsemen, 83 Va. L. Rev. 559 (1997); David Joseph Danelski, A Supreme Court Justice Is Appointed (Greenwood Press, 1980) (1964).

Byrnes **James F. Byrnes** (1882–1972) Statesman and U.S. Supreme Court Justice. Byrnes notably never received a formal education, but rather read for the South Carolina Bar and was admitted in 1903. Quickly becoming enthralled with politics, Byrnes won a House seat in 1910 and moved on to the Senate twenty years later. In 1941, President Franklin D. Roosevelt nominated Byrnes to the high court, where he would serve a remarkably short term before resigning to serve as director of the Office of Economic Stabilization. *See:* Ronald D. Burns, James F. Byrnes (McGraw–Hill, 1961); Robert L. Messer, The End of an Alliance: James F. Byrnes, Roosevelt, Truman, and the Origins of the Cold War (Univ. of N.C. Press, 1982).

Campbell **John Archibald Campbell** (1811–1889) U.S. Supreme Court Justice. A native of Georgia, Campbell moved to Alabama and was admitted to the bar in 1830. Campbell was nominated in 1853 by President Pierce to the Supreme Court of the United States to fill a long-vacant seat. Campbell was noted for his pro-slavery stance and resigned from the high court when Alabama seceded from the Union in 1860. *See:* James P. McPherson, The Career of John Archibald Campbell: A Study in Politics and Law, 19 Ala. L. Rev. 53 (1966).

Cardozo **Benjamin N. Cardozo** (1870–1938) U.S. Supreme Court Justice. Born in New York City, Cardozo graduated from Columbia College but dropped out of Columbia Law School, electing to read for the bar; he entered practice in 1891. Cardozo was appointed to the New York Court of Appeals in 1917, becoming chief judge in 1926. President Hoover nominated Cardozo to the high court in 1932. While his writing style is a challenge for some law students, U.S. law was transformed by such cases as *MacPherson v. Buick Motor Co.*, 217 N.Y. 382, 111 N.E. 1050 (1916), *Jacob & Youngs v. Kent*, 230 N.Y. 239 (1921), *Palsgraf v. Long Island Railroad Co.*, 248 N.Y. 339, 162 N.E. 99 (1928), and *Palko v. Connecticut*, 302 U.S. 319 (1937). *See:* Benjamin N. Cardozo, The Nature of the Judicial Process (1922) (Quid Pro Quo 2010); Richard A. Posner, Cardozo: A Study in Reputation (Univ. of Chi. Press, 1993); Andrew L. Kaufman, Cardozo (Harv. Univ. Press, 2000); Beryl Harold Levy, Cardozo and Frontiers in Legal Thinking (Press of Case Western Reserve Univ., 1969); John Thomas Noonan, Persons and Masks of the Law: Cardozo, Holmes, Jefferson, and Wythe as Makers of the Masks (Farrar, Straus, and Giroux, 1969).

Catron **John Catron** (c.1786–1865) U.S. Supreme Court Justice. While the birth place of Catron is uncertain, it is known that he studied law in Tennessee and was admitted to the bar there in 1815. Soon after, he was elected to the Tennessee Supreme Court of Errors and Appeals in 1824; he would later sit as Tennessee's first

chief justice. President Jackson appointed Catron to the Supreme Court of the United States in 1837, where Catron supported the pro-slavery movement. *See: Dred Scott v. Sandford, 60 U.S.* (19 How.) 393 (1857). Walter Chandler, The Centenary of Associate Justice John Catron of the United States Supreme Court (U.S. Govt. Printing Off., 1937).

Chase **Salmon P. Chase** (1808–1873) Sixth Chief Justice of the United States. Born in New Hampshire, Chase graduated from Dartmouth, taught school, and studied law under William Wirt, being admitted to the bar in 1829. After private practice in Ohio, Chase became a powerful political opponent of slavery. A member of the Free Soil Party, Chase was elected governor of Ohio in 1855 and to the U.S. Senate in 1860, resigning after two days to become Secretary of the Treasury in the Lincoln administration. Appointed Chief Justice by President Lincoln in 1864, he wrote *Texas v. White*, 4 U.S. 700 (1869), which established the constitutional indivisibility of the Union, and presided over the 1868 impeachment trial of President Johnson. *See:* John Niven, Salmon P. Chase: A Biography (Oxford Univ. Press, 1995); Salmon Portland Chase, Inside Lincoln's Cabinet; the Civil War Diaries of Salmon P. Chase (Longmans, Green, 1954).

Chase **Samuel Chase** (1741–1811) Statesman and U.S. Supreme Court Justice. Chase, a Maryland native, read into the bar in 1761 before serving in the Maryland Legislature from 1764 to 1768. Elected to the Continental Congress in 1774, Chase is noted for persuading Maryland officials to vote in favor of independence. After the war, Chase turned to the judiciary, becoming chief judge of the General Court of Maryland in 1791. Chase would hold the position until 1795, when President Washington nominated him to the U.S. Supreme Court. *See:* Trial of Samuel Chase (Da Capo, 1970) (1805); James A. Haw, et al., Stormy Patriot: The Life of Samuel Chase (Md. Hist. Socy., 1980); William H. Rehnquist, Grant Inquests: The Historic Impeachments of Justice Samuel Chase and President Andrew Johnson (Morrow, 1992).

Clark **Tom C. Clark** (1899–1977) U.S. Supreme Court Justice. After graduating the University of Texas School of Law in 1922, Clark set up a private practice in Dallas before joining the Justice Department in 1937. In 1945, President Truman appointed him Attorney General before naming him to the high court in 1949 to replace Frank Murphy. Notably, Clark upset Truman not long into his tenure on the bench by reversing his prior advice as Attorney General. *See: Youngstown Sheet & Tube Co. v. Sawyer*, 343 U.S. 579 (1952). James A. Gazell, Justice Tom C. Clark as Judicial Reformer, 15 Hous. L. Rev 307 (1978).

Clarke **John H. Clarke** (1857–1945) U.S. Supreme Court Justice. Clarke, a native of Ohio, graduated from Western Reserve College before passing the bar in 1878. Clarke maintained a successful private practice and dabbled in politics until his nomination to the Federal Circuit Court for Northern Ohio by President Wilson in 1914. Two years later, when Justice Hughes resigned, President Wilson nominated Clarke to fill his seat; Clarke was confirmed in 1916 to the U.S.

Supreme Court. *See*: David Maurice Levitan, The Jurisprudence of Mr. Justice Clarke, 7 U. Miami L. Rev. 44 (1952).

Clifford **Nathan Clifford** (1803–1881) Statesman and U.S. Supreme Court Justice. Clifford, a New Hampshire native, was deprived of much of his formal education by familial obligations. Studying with a local attorney, Clifford was admitted to the bar in 1827 and settled in Maine. Elected to the U.S. House of Representatives in 1838, Clifford was redistricted out of his seat and was offered the position of Attorney General by President Polk in 1846. President Buchanan nominated Clifford to the Supreme Court in 1858. Notably, Clifford dissented in the *Prize Cases*, 67 U.S. 635 (1863). *See*: Walter Chandler, Nathan Clifford: A Triumph of Untiring Effort, 2 A.B.A. J. 57 (1925).

Curtis **Benjamin Robbins Curtis** (1809–1874) Statesman and U.S. Supreme Court Justice. Born in Massachusetts, Curtis attended Harvard College and later, Harvard Law School. Curtis is known to have taken many high-profile cases at a young age while practicing law, and he was nominated by President Fillmore in 1851 after serving in the Massachusetts House of Representatives. Curtis is the first Supreme Court Justice known to have received a degree as a student from an American law school. A noted dissenter in *Dred Scott v. Sandford*, 60 U.S. (19 How.) 393 (1857), Curtis is said to have resigned from the high court after the decision in protest. *See*: Benjamin Robbins Curtis, ed., A Memoir of Benjamin Robbins Curtis, LL.D., with Some of his Professional and Miscellaneous Writings (Da Capo Press, 1970) (1879).

Cushing **William Cushing** (1732–1810) U.S. Supreme Court Justice. After a graduating from Harvard College and a period of private practice, Cushing took his father's seat on the Massachusetts Superior Court of Judicature in 1772. He played a significant role in the ratification of the U.S. Constitution in Massachusetts, his home state. One of his most significant contributions to law was to preside over the *Quock-Walker Case*, in which the court held that the Massachusetts constitution prohibited slavery in the state, the first time a written constitution was applied to a case as law. Nominated to the first Supreme Court in 1789 by President Washington, Cushing declined nomination to Chief Justice in 1796. Cushing authored an opinion in *Ware v. Hylton*, 3 U.S. (3 Dall.) 199 (1796), which affirmed the legal supremacy of federal treaties over state legislative acts. *See*: Ross E. Davies, William Cushing, Chief Justice of the United States, 37 U. Toledo L. Rev. 597 (2006); Francis R. Jones, William Cushing, 13 Green Bag 415 (1901); F.W. O'Brien, The Pre-Marshall Court and the Role of William Cushing, Mass. L.Q. 43 (Mar., 1958).

Daniel **Peter Vivian Daniel** (1784–1860) U.S. Supreme Court Justice. A Virginian, Daniel studied at the College of New Jersey (later Princeton University) before joining the Virginia Bar in 1808. After serving in the Virginia House of Delegates, Daniel accepted President Jackson's appointment to the U.S. District Court of Virginia in 1836. In 1841, Daniel was nominated to the Supreme Court of the United States by President Van Buren; the nomination was heartily contested and succeeded only narrowly. Early in his career, Daniel wrote on the status of corporations as entities, not citizens. *See*: *Rundle v. Delaware & Raritan Canal Company*, 55 U.S. 80 (1852). John P. Frank, Justice Daniel Dissenting: A Biography of Peter V. Daniel, 1784–1860 (1964).

Davis **David Davis** (1815–1886) U.S. Supreme Court Justice. Davis, a Maryland native, eventually settled in Pekin, Illinois, where he was elected to the Eighth Circuit in 1848. When Lincoln was elected president, he nominated his close friend Davis to fill one of three vacant seats on the Supreme Court. Davis was confirmed in 1862 and is most noted for his writings in *Ex parte Milligan*, 71 U.S. 2 (1866), where he held the president's suspension of habeas corpus for prisoners unconstitutional. *See*: Dennis H. Pope, Personality and Judicial Performance: A Psychobiography of Justice Joseph P. Bradley (Ph.D. diss., Rutgers Univ., 1988); Thomas Dent, David Davis of Illinois: A Sketch, 52 Am. L. Rev. 535 (1919); Willard Leroy King, Lincoln's Manager, David Davis (Harv. Univ. Press, 1960).

Day **William R. Day** (1849–1923) Statesman and U.S. Supreme Court Justice. After receiving an undergraduate degree from the University of Michigan and then studying law there for a year, Day returned to his home state of Ohio, where he practiced privately. A close friend of President McKinley, Day served as Secretary of State in McKinley's administration. President Theodore Roosevelt nominated Day to the U.S. Supreme Court in 1903 to fill the vacancy left by George Shiras. *See*: Joseph E. McLean, William Rufus Day: Supreme Court Justice from Ohio (Johns Hopkins Univ. Press, 1946); James Simon, Independent Journey (Harper & Row, 1980).

Douglas **William O. Douglas** (1898–1980) U.S. Supreme Court Justice. Born in Minnesota, a child in Yakima, Washington, and a student at Whitman College, Douglas took his law degree from Columbia before teaching there; he was later Stirling Professor at Yale Law School. A New Deal administrator, he chaired the Securities and Exchange Commission from 1937 until his nomination in 1939 to the high court by President Franklin D. Roosevelt. Over his forty-three-year tenure, Douglas's opinions stressed the protection of individual rights and natural resources. *See*: William O. Douglas, An Almanac of Liberty (Greenwood, 1973); Bruce Murphy, Wild Bill: The Legend and Life of William O. Douglas (Random House, 2003); Howard Ball and Phillip J. Cooper, Of Power and Right: Hugo Black, William O. Douglas, and America's Constitutional Revolution (Oxford Univ. Press, 1992); James F. Simon, Independent Journey: The Life of William O. Douglas (Harper & Row, 1990).

Duvall **Gabriel Duvall** (1752–1844) Statesman and U.S. Supreme Court Justice. Duvall began his legal studies just as the American Revolution started, and he quickly became entangled in the fight for independence. Duvall was elected to the Maryland House of Representatives nine years before joining the

Maryland judiciary in 1796. Duvall was nominated to the Supreme Court in 1811 by President Monroe and is remembered for his note in *Mima Queen v. Hepburn*, 11 U.S. (7 Cranch) 290 (1834), in which he urged the acceptance of hearsay evidence in an emancipation case. He is considered potentially the least important Supreme Court Justice ever. *See*: David P. Currie, The Most Insignificant Justice: A Preliminary Inquiry, 50 U. Chi. L. Rev. 466 (1983).

Ellsworth **Oliver Ellsworth** (1745–1807) Statesman and third Chief Justice of the United States. Ellsworth, born in Connecticut, graduated from the College of New Jersey (later Princeton University). He studied law privately and was admitted to the bar in 1771. A Connecticut delegate to the Constitutional Convention, Ellsworth was active in a number of committees while simultaneously serving as judge on the Connecticut Superior Court. Ellsworth represented Connecticut in the Senate of the first Congress. Appointed the third Chief Justice of the Supreme Court by President Washington, Ellsworth was confirmed in 1796. After resignation from the bench in 1800, Ellsworth served as special envoy to France. *See*: William R. Casto, The Supreme Court in the Early Republic: The Chief Justiceships of John Jay and Oliver Ellsworth (1995); William Garrott Brown, The Life of Oliver Ellsworth (Da Capo Press, 1970) (1901); Francis R. Jones, Oliver Ellsworth, 13 Green Bag 503 (1901).

Field **Stephen Johnson Field** (1816–1899) U.S. Supreme Court Justice. After studying at Williams College, Field moved to New York, where he read for the bar, gaining admittance in 1841. Relocating to California, Field was elected to the California Supreme Court in 1857 as an associate justice, becoming the state's chief justice a year later. President Lincoln nominated Field to the Supreme Court of the United States in 1863, after the expansion of the high court to ten members created an open seat. Field's best-known opinion is in the *Slaughter-House Cases*, 83 U.S. 36 (1873). *See*: Paul Kens, Justice Stephen Field: Shaping Liberty from the Gold Rush to the Gilded Age (1997); Carl Brent Swisher, Stephen J. Field, Craftsman of the Law (Univ. of Chi. Press, 1969) (1930).

Fortas **Abe Fortas** (1910–1982) U.S. Supreme Court Justice. Fortas graduated from Yale Law School in 1933 before working simultaneously for the Roosevelt administration on the New Deal and teaching law at Yale. Serving briefly as undersecretary of the interior in 1942, Fortas left government work for private practice. After a distinguished private practice career, including the representation of Charles Gideon before the U.S. Supreme Court, Fortas was nominated by President Johnson for the high court, which he joined in 1965. Controversial payments made by businesses to fund his lectures at American University and continuing payments from a retainer received in private practice fueled Republican opposition to Johnson's efforts to promote him to Chief Justice and eventually forced Fortas's resignation in

1969. *See*: John C. Jeffries, Jr., Justice Lewis F. Powell, Jr. (1994); Laura Kalman, Abe Fortas: A Biography (Yale Univ. Press, 1990); Bruce Allen Murphy, Fortas: the Rise and Ruin of a Supreme Court Justice (Morrow, 1988).

Frankfurter **Felix Frankfurter** (1882–1965) U.S. Supreme Court Justice. A native of Austria, Frankfurter studied at Harvard Law School, where he edited the law review. He practiced law and worked for Henry Stimson in the Taft administration before becoming a professor at Harvard Law, eventually joining President Franklin D. Roosevelt's brain trust and helping to draft many of the New Deal reforms. President Roosevelt nominated Frankfurter to the high court in 1939, where he would serve until 1962. Frankfurter was thought liberal but was also a strong advocate of judicial restraint and deference to the elected branches. *See*: Michael E. Parrish, Felix Frankfurter and His Times: The Reform Years (1982); Liva Baker, Felix Frankfurter (Coward–McCann, 1969); James F. Simon, The Antagonists: Hugo Black, Felix Frankfurter and Civil Liberties in Modern America (Simon and Schuster, 1989); Melvin I. Urofsky, Felix Frankfurter: Judicial Restraint and Individual Liberties (Twayne Publishers, 1991).

Fuller **Melville W. Fuller** (1833–1910) Eighth Chief Justice of the United States. Born in Maine, Fuller took his degree from Bowdoin College before attending Harvard Law School for a short period. Fuller relocated to Chicago, where he built a prominent law practice and held office as a state representative. President Cleveland nominated Fuller to the Supreme Court in 1888 as Chief Justice after the death of Morrison Waite. Importantly, Fuller's court held income tax unconstitutional in *Pollock v. Farmer's Loan & Trust Co.*, 157 U.S. 429 (1895). *See*: Willard L. King, Melville Weston Fuller (1950); Howard B. Furer, The Fuller Court, 1888–1910 (Associated Faculty Press, 1986); Willard Leroy King, Melville Weston Fuller, Chief Justice of the United States, 1888–1910 (Univ. of Chi. Press, 1967).

Goldberg **Arthur J. Goldberg** (1908–1990) Statesman and U.S. Supreme Court Justice. Goldberg graduated from Northwestern University Law School magna cum laude in 1930. During World War II, Goldberg worked for the Office of Strategic Services, an intelligence service regarded as the precursor to the CIA. President Kennedy appointed Goldberg to be U.S. Secretary of Labor in 1961 and then nominated him to the Supreme Court in 1962. In 1965, Goldberg resigned his seat on the high court to become the U.S. Ambassador to the United Nations, and he later entered private practice. *See*: Dorothy Goldberg, A Private View of a Public Life (1975); Daniel P. Moynihan, ed., The Defenses of Freedom: Public Papers of Arthur J. Goldberg (Harper & Row, 1966).

Ginsburg **Ruth Bader Ginsburg** (b. 1933) U.S. Supreme Court Justice. A native of Brooklyn, New York, Ginsburg took her undergraduate degree from Cornell University before attending Harvard Law School, eventually transferring to Columbia Law School from which she received an LL.B in 1959. After clerking at a lower federal court, Ginsburg was a research associate at Columbia, where she became a professor of law following a brief stint at Rutgers Law School. In 1980, President Carter nominated Ginsburg to the U.S. Court of Appeals in Washington, D.C., where she would serve until President Clinton's nomination in 1993 to the high court. A strong advocate for the recognition of women's interests, including the right to choose an abortion and the protection of children, Justice Ginsburg is also perceived as a careful analyst. *See:* Deborah L. Markowitz, In Pursuit of Equality: One Woman's Work to Change the Law, 14 Women's Rts. L. Rep. 335 (1992); Ruth Bader Ginsburg: Her Life and Her Law, The Washington Post, July 18–20, at A; Amy Leigh Campbell, Raising the Bar: Ruth Bader Ginsburg and the ACLU Women's Rights Project (Xlibris, 2010).

**Gray** **Horace Gray** (1828–1902) U.S. Supreme Court Justice. Gray, a native of Massachusetts, would attend Harvard as an undergraduate and later as a law student. Shortly after being admitted to the bar in 1851, Gray worked as a clerk at the Massachusetts Supreme Judicial Court. In 1864, Gray was appointed to the state supreme court, assuming the chief justice role in 1873. President Arthur nominated Gray to the U.S. Supreme Court in 1881, where Gray served for twenty-four years. *See:* Stephen R. Mitchell, Mr. Justice Gray (Ph.D. diss., Univ. of Wisconsin, 1961); Robert M. Spector, Legal Historian on the United States Supreme Court: Justice Horace Gray, Jr., and the Historical Method, 12 Am. J. Legal Hist. 181 (1968).

**Grier** **Robert Grier** (1794–1870) U.S. Supreme Court Justice. A Pennsylvanian, Grier was admitted to the bar in 1817 and practiced in Dansville for fifteen years before being appointed to the District Court of Allegheny County in 1833. In 1846, Grier was nominated by President Polk for the Supreme Court of the United States, and the Senate confirmed him in a seat that had been vacant for two years due to political positioning. Grier is most noted for his writings in *Prize Cases*, 67 U.S. 635 (1862), in which he supported the Union blockade of southern ports. *See:* Carl B. Swisher, The Taney Period, 1836–64 (1974); Francis R. Jones, Robert Cooper Grier, 16 Green Bag 221 (1904).

**Harlan** **John Marshall Harlan** (1833–1911) U.S. Supreme Court Justice. A Kentucky native, Harlan studied at Centre College and Transylvania University before being admitted to the bar in 1853. After a long career in private practice and moments of political ambition, Harlan was nominated to the U.S. Supreme Court by President Hayes in 1877. Harlan's grandson of the same name would later sit on the Court. The first Justice Harlan is well remembered for his dissenting opinions in the *Civil Rights Cases*, 109 U.S. 3 (1883), and *Plessy v. Ferguson*, 163 U.S. 537 (1896). *See:* Tinsley E. Yarbrough, Judicial Enigma: The First Justice Harlan (Oxford Univ. Press, 1995).

**Harlan** **John Marshall Harlan** (1899–1971) U.S. Supreme Court Justice. The second Justice Harlan was the son of a prominent Chicago attorney and grandson of the first Justice Harlan, for whom he was named. The namesake studied at Princeton University and Balliol College, Oxford, before taking his law degree from New York Law School in 1924. Before World War II, Harlan practiced privately in New York City, to which he returned after military service in Europe. President Eisenhower appointed Harlan to the Second Circuit in 1954 and soon thereafter nominated him to the U.S. Supreme Court in 1955. Harlan was critical of an expansive view of judicial power but supported an adherence to precedent and a robust interpretation of the Fourteenth Amendment as a direct limit on states, without the need for incorporation. *See:* Tinsley E. Yarbrough, John Marshall Harlan: Great Dissenter of the Warren Court (Oxford Univ. Press, 1992); David L. Shapiro, ed. The Evolution of a Judicial Philosophy: Selected Opinions and Papers of Justice John M. Harlan (Harv. Univ. Press, 1969).

**Holmes** **Oliver Wendell Holmes, Jr.** (1841–1935) U.S. Supreme Court Justice. Born in Boston to a prominent family, Holmes entered Harvard College, left to join the Union Army in 1861, and saw much combat. He finished Harvard in law, married, and practiced law for fifteen years before briefly teaching at Harvard and then joining the Massachusetts Supreme Judicial Court. President Theodore Roosevelt nominated him to the U.S. Supreme Court in 1902, where he served for thirty years, writing famously pithy opinions generally supporting both constitutional rights and legislative authority over anti-democratic applications of the common law. Though he wrote many famous opinions for the high court, such as *Schenck v. United States*, 249 U.S. 47 (1919) defining the "clear and present danger" test, he often dissented, as he did from *Lochner v. New York*, 198 U.S. 45, 76 (1095). Both Holmes's The Common Law of 1881 and his speeches are still widely read. *See:* Albert W. Alschuler, Law Without Values: The Life, Work, and Legacy of Justice Holmes (Univ. of Chi. Press, 2000); Catherine Drinker Bowen, Yankee from Olympus (Little, Brown, 1944); Mark De Wolfe Howe, Justice Oliver Wendell Holmes: The Shaping Years, 1841–1870; The Proving Years 1870–1882 (Belknap Press of Harv. Univ. Press, 1957–1962); Sheldon M. Novick, Honorable Justice: The Life of Oliver Wendell Homes (Dell, 1989).

**Hughes** **Charles Evans Hughes** (1862–1948) Statesman and eleventh Chief Justice of the United States. Hughes, an 1884 graduate of Columbia Law School, was in private practice until 1906, when he was elected governor of New York. Just four years later, President Taft nominated Hughes to the U.S. Supreme Court. In 1916, Hughes stepped down from the high court to try his hand at presidential politics. After failing in his attempt, Hughes was nominated Chief Justice by President Hoover in 1930. *See:* Merlo J. Pusey, Charles Evans Hughes (Garland, 1979) (1951); Betty Glad, Charles Evans Hughes and the Illusions of Innocence: A Study in American Diplomacy (Univ. of Ill. Press, 1966); Charles Evans Hughes, The Autobiographical Notes of Charles Evans Hughes (Harv. Univ. Press, 1973).

Hunt **Ward Hunt** (1810–1866) U.S. Supreme Court Justice. A native of New York, Hunt attended law lectures in Connecticut before joining the New York Bar in 1831 and practicing privately. After the Civil War, Hunt was active in local politics, which eventually led to his nomination to the U.S. Supreme Court in 1872 by President Grant. While on the bench, Hunt was noted for his belief that suffrage was a function of the states, rather than a right bestowed by the Constitution. *See, e.g., Minor v. Happersett*, 88 U.S. 162 (1874). *See:* The Old Judge and the New: Mr. Justice Nelson and his Successor, Ward Hunt, 6 Alb. L.J. 400 (1872).

Iredell **James Iredell** (1751–1799) U.S. Supreme Court Justice. Born in Sussex County, England, Iredell immigrated to North Carolina to hold positions as tax and customs collector for the British Crown. He read law under Samuel Johnston and was appointed crown prosecutor at the age of twenty-three. He sided with the American revolutionaries in 1776 and served as attorney general for the state of North Carolina in 1779. He rose in prominence in the North Carolina judiciary, and attracted the attention of President Washington, who nominated him to the U.S. Supreme Court in 1790. Iredell authored *Calder v. Bull*, 3 U.S. 386 (1798), which found a Connecticut legislative act to be an unconstitutional ex post facto law, based in part on natural law, and he dissented in *Chisholm v. Georgia*, 2 U.S. (2 Dall.) 419 (1793), a case later overturned by the Eleventh Amendment. *See:* Don Higginbotham, ed., The Papers of James Iredell (1976); Christopher T. Graebe, The Federalism of James Iredell in Historical Context, 69 N.C. L. Rev. 251 (1990); Junius Davis, Alfred Moore and James Iredell, Revolutionary Patriots (N.C. Socy. of the Sons of the Revolution, 1899).

Jackson **Howell Edmunds Jackson** (1832–1895) Statesman and U.S. Supreme Court Justice. Jackson, born in Tennessee, graduated from West Tennessee College before taking his law degree from Cumberland University in 1856. On returning to Memphis, Tennessee, Jackson established a successful private practice where he worked until elected to the Tennessee House of Representatives in 1880, and was further elected to U.S. Senate. President Cleveland nominated Jackson to the Sixth Circuit in 1886, where he served until President Harrison nominated him to the high court in 1893. *See:* Terry Calvani, The Early Career of Howell Jackson, 30 Vand. L. Rev. 39 (1977); Henry M. Doak, Howell Edmunds Jackson, 5 Green Bag 209 (1893).

Jackson **Robert H. Jackson** (1892–1954) U.S. Supreme Court Justice. Jackson was the last member of the U.S. Supreme Court to come to the high court by way of reading for the bar, to which he was admitted in 1913 after a brief stint at Albany Law School. Jackson maintained a private practice until, having held a series of public offices, he was appointed U.S. Attorney General in 1940 by President Franklin D. Roosevelt. Shortly thereafter, President Roosevelt nominated Jackson to the U.S. Supreme Court. He took leave in 1945 to serve as Chief Prosecutor for the United States at Nuremburg. *See:* Eugene C. Gerhardt, America's

Advocate, Robert H. Jackson (1958); Charles S. Desmond, et al., Mr. Justice Jackson; Four Lectures in His Honor (Columbia Press, 1969).

Jay **John Jay** (1754–1829) Statesman and first Chief Justice of the United States. The first Chief Justice of the United States, Jay was more a statesman and politician than a legal scholar. Born in New York, Jay attended King's College (now Columbia University), read law, and opened a practice with Robert Livingston. As secretary for the New York Committee of Correspondence, Jay was that state's delegate to the Continental Congress, where he served as president. With Benjamin Franklin and John Adams, Jay negotiated the Treaty of Paris to end the American Revolution, and Jay later served as an envoy to Spain. A Federalist, Jay authored five of the Federalist Papers. Nominated to the Court in 1789 by President Washington, he served until 1795, when he resigned the bench to become governor of New York. Author of an important circuit opinion in *Hayburn's Case*, 2 U.S. 409 (1792), his most notable opinion is found in *Chisholm v. Georgia*, 2 U.S. (2 Dall.) 419 (1793), finding citizens of one state could bring a federal suit against another state, a holding which was superseded by the Eleventh Amendment. *See:* Henry P. Johnston, Correspondence and Public Papers of John Jay (4 vols., 1890–1893); Herbert Alan Johnson, John Jay, Colonial Lawyer (Garland Publishing, 1989); Herbert Alan Johnson, John Jay, 1745–1829 (Office of State History, 1970).

Johnson **Thomas Johnson** (1732–1819) Statesman and U.S. Supreme Court Justice. After a private education, Johnson was admitted to the bar in Maryland in 1753. A delegate to the Continental Congress, Johnson served as governor of Maryland and chief judge of the Maryland General Court. Johnson received a recess appointment to the U.S. Supreme Court in August 1791 and was confirmed to his seat in November that same year. Johnson resigned his seat in 1793, serving the shortest tenure of any U.S. Supreme Court Justice. *See:* Maeva Marcus, ed., The Documentary History of the Supreme Court of the United States, 1789–1800 (1985); Edward S. Delaplaine, The Life of Thomas Johnson: Member of the Continental Congress, First Governor of the State of Maryland, and Associate Justice of the United States Supreme Court (Hitchcock, 1927).

Johnson **William Johnson** (1771–1834) U.S. Supreme Court Justice. Born to a notable family in Charleston, South Carolina, Johnson attended the College of New Jersey (later Princeton University) and studied law under Charles Pinckney. Elected to the South Carolina House of Representatives, Johnson served as speaker from 1789 to 1799. A successful private attorney, Johnson was a judge on the South Carolina Court of Common Pleas from 1799 until he was nominated to the U.S. Supreme Court by President Thomas Jefferson in 1804. *See:* Donald Morgan, Justice William Johnson: The First Dissenter (Univ. of S.C. Press, 1954).

Kagan **Elena Kagan** (b. 1960) U.S. Supreme Court Justice. A graduate of Harvard Law School, Kagan would clerk for both the U.S. Court of Appeals in

Washington, D.C., and in the U.S. Supreme Court under Justice Marshall before joining the University of Chicago to teach law. In 1995, Kagan went to work for President Clinton's administration; in 1999, President Clinton would nominate Kagan to the U.S. Court of Appeals, but no hearing was ever scheduled. Returning to academia, Kagan taught at Harvard Law School before being named dean in 2003. In 2009, Kagan returned to public service as the solicitor general for President Obama. When, in 2010, Justice Stevens announced his retirement, President Obama nominated Kagan to the high court and the Senate confirmed her.

Kennedy **Anthony Kennedy** (b. 1936) U.S. Supreme Court Justice. Kennedy, a native of California, studied at Stanford University before taking his law degree from Harvard Law School in 1961. After returning to California, Kennedy entered private practice and began teaching law in 1965 at McGeorge Law School. In 1975, President Ford nominated Kennedy to the Ninth Circuit, where he would serve until President Reagan nominated him for the high court in 1987. Considered a moderate and careful judge, Kennedy has been in favor of restricting capital punishment during his tenure on the Supreme Court. *See, e.g., Atkins v. Virginia*, 536 U.S. 304 (2002), *Kennedy v. Louisiana*, 554 U.S. __ (2008). *See:* Albert P. Melone, Revisiting the Freshman Effect Hypothesis: The First Two Terms of Justice Anthony Kennedy, 74 Judicature 6 (1990).

Lamar **Joseph R. Lamar** (1857–1916) U.S. Supreme Court Justice. A Georgia cousin of Justice L.Q.C. Lamar, Joseph Rucker Lamar read for the bar in 1878. Lamar maintained a private practice until nominated to the Georgia Supreme Court in 1902. President Taft nominated Lamar to the U.S. Supreme Court in 1908, after the two had become social acquaintances. *See:* S. Price Gilbert, The Lamars of Georgia: L.Q.C., Mirabeau B., and Joseph R. Lamar, 34 A.B.A. J. 1100, 1156 (1948); Clarinda Huntington Lamar, The Life of Joseph Rucker Lamar, 1857–1916 (Putnam, 1926).

Lamar **Lucius Quintus Cincinnatus Lamar (L.Q.C. Lamar)** (1825–1893) Statesman and U.S. Supreme Court Justice. Born in Georgia, Lamar moved to Oxford, Mississippi, where he was elected to the U.S. House of Representatives in 1857. Lamar would return to the House of Representatives in 1873 and was elected to the Senate in 1877. After serving President Cleveland as Secretary of the Interior for two years, Lamar was nominated for the Supreme Court by the president in 1887. *See:* James B. Murphy, L.Q.C. Lamar: Pragmatic Patriot (La. State Univ., 1973).

Livingston **Henry Brockholst Livingston** (1757–1823) U.S. Supreme Court Justice. Educated at the College of New Jersey (later Princeton University), Livingston was a staff officer in the Continental Army and then privately read law, joining the bar in 1783. After serving as John Jay's private secretary, Livingston practiced law in New York for several years. Livingston served as an associate justice of the New York Supreme Court from 1802 until President Jefferson nominated him to the U.S. Supreme Court by recess appointment in 1806. He was seated in 1807 and served until his death. Livingston dissented in *Pierson v. Post*, 3 Cai. R. 175, 2 Am. Dec. 264 (N.Y. 1805), known as "the fox case" in many property textbooks. *See:* Daniel R. Ernst, *Pierson v. Post*, 13 Green Bag 2d 31 (2009); Alexander Gunn, Memoirs of the Rev. John Henry Livingston (Bd. of Publication of the Reformed Protestant Dutch Church, 1856); George Dangerfield, Chancellor Robert R. Livingston of New York (Harcourt, Brace, 1960).

Lurton **Horace Lurton** (1844–1914) U.S. Supreme Court Justice. Lurton graduated Cumberland University's law program in 1867 after twice being captured and released by the Union side during the Civil War. Lurton then returned to Tennessee where he was appointed to the Sixth Chancery Division for a short time before taking to private practice. In 1886, Lurton was elected to the Supreme Court of Tennessee, and later became the chief justice of that court before President Cleveland nominated him to the Sixth Circuit in 1893. Following some sixteen years on the Sixth Circuit, Lurton was nominated to the U.S. Supreme Court in 1909 by President Taft. *See:* Samuel C. Williams, Judge Horace H. Lurton, 18 Tenn. L. Rev. 242 (1944).

Marshall **John Marshall** (1755–1835) Statesman and fourth Chief Justice of the United States. Marshall was born in Virginia, served in the Continental Army, and attended law lectures at the College of William & Mary in 1779. Admitted to the bar in 1780, Marshall then ran a successful law practice. After acting as a delegate to the Constitutional Convention, Marshall was elected to Congress, appointed secretary of state, and confirmed as Chief Justice in 1801. Marshall wrote such landmark cases as *Marbury v. Madison*, 5 U.S. (1 Cranch) 137 (1803), *McColluch v. Maryland*, 17 U.S. (4 Wheat.) 316 (1819), and *Dartmouth College v. Woodward*, 17 U.S. (4 Wheat.) 518 (1819). There is a rich historical and biographical literature on Marshall. *See:* R. Kent Newmyer, John Marshall and the Heroic Age of the Supreme Court (La. State Univ. Press, 2007); The Chief Justiceship of John Marshall, 1801–1835 (Univ. of S.C. Press, 1998); John Stokes Adams, ed., An Autobiographical Sketch by John Marshall (Da Capo Press, 1973) (1937); G. Edward White, The Marshall Court and Cultural Change, 1815–1835 (Oxford Univ. Press, 1991); James Bradley Thayer, John Marshall (Da Capo Press, 1974) (1901).

Marshall **Thurgood Marshall** (1908–1993) U.S. Supreme Court Justice. Marshall graduated first in his class from Howard University School of Law in 1933 before setting up a private practice in Baltimore. A civil rights attorney, Marshall worked with the NAACP, becoming its chief counsel in 1940, and notably arguing *Brown v. Board of Education of Topeka*, 347 U.S. 483 (1954). President Johnson nominated Marshall, the first African American Justice, to the U.S. Supreme Court in 1967, where he served with distinction until 1991. *See:* Randall Walton Bland, Private Pressure on Public Law: the Legal Career of Justice Thurgood Marshall, 1934–1991 (Univ. Press of Am., 1993);

Mark V. Tushnet, Making Civil Rights Law: Thurgood Marshall and the Supreme Court 1936-1961 (Oxford Univ. Press, 1994).

Matthews **Stanley Matthews** (1824-1889) U.S. Supreme Court Justice. Matthews, born in Kentucky, studied in Ohio before being admitted to the Tennessee Bar. Matthews would soon return to Ohio, however, and open a successful private practice. President Hayes nominated his good friend Matthews to the U.S. Supreme Court in 1881, but the appointment was held up in Senate for political reasons. President Garfield resubmitted Matthews's nomination, and he was confirmed in 1881. *See:* Proceedings of the Bench and Bar of the Supreme Court of the United States: In Memoriam Stanley Matthews (G.P.O., 1889).

McKenna **Joseph McKenna** (1843-1926) Statesman and U.S. Supreme Court Justice. McKenna joined the California Bar in 1865 and immediately went into local politics, which led to his appointment in 1892 by President Harrison to the Ninth Circuit. President-elect McKinley named McKenna his attorney general in 1897 and later that same year nominated McKenna to the U.S. Supreme Court. *See:* Matthew McDevitt, Joseph McKenna: Associate Justice of the United States (Da Capo Press, 1974) (1946); Attorney-General McKenna, 9 Green Bag 289 (1897).

McKinley **John McKinley** (1780-1852) Statesman and U.S. Supreme Court Justice. Born in Virginia and raised in Kentucky, McKinley read for the law and in 1800 was admitted to practice. McKinley moved to Alabama in 1810, established a banking practice, and entered politics. He entered the U.S. House of Representatives in 1833 and the Senate in 1836, as an ally of Andrew Jackson. In 1837 President Martin Van Buren nominated him to a newly created seat on the Supreme Court. A supporter of state's rights on the Court, he still supported federal power over immigration. Much of his time was spent riding circuit, and he claimed to travel 10,000 miles in a single year. His most famous opinion protected state rights under the public trust doctrine, *Pollard's Lessee v. Hagan*, 44 U.S. 212 (1845). *See:* Alabama's Forgotten Justices: John McKinley and John A. Campbell, 63 Ala. Law. 236, 237-238 (2002); David Currie, The Most Insignificant Justice: A Preliminary Inquiry, 50 U. Chi. L. Rev. 466 (1983); Frank H. Easterbrook, The Most Insignificant Justice Further Evidence, 50 U. Chi. L. Rev. 481 (1983).

McLean **John McLean** (1785-1861) Statesman and U.S. Supreme Court Justice. Born in New Jersey, McLean was moved to Ohio where he received his formal education. After reading for his law license in 1807, McLean worked in private practice before serving on the state supreme court and being appointed to Postmaster General in 1823. President Jackson nominated McLean to the U.S. Supreme Court in 1829. McLean is best known for his dissent in *Dred Scott v. Sanford* (1857), where he argued that slaves, once freed, were citizens of the United States. *See:* Francis P. Weisenburger, The Life of John McLean, A Politician on the United States Supreme Court (Da Capo Press, 1971) (1937).

McReynolds **James Clark McReynolds** (1862-1946) U.S. Supreme Court Justice. A graduate of Vanderbilt University and the University of Virginia Law School,

McReynolds had a successful practice in Nashville, Tennessee, while also teaching at Vanderbilt Law School. After a term as assistant attorney general under President Theodore Roosevelt, McReynolds moved to New York and set up a private practice. He was once again called to public service by President Wilson, who appointed McReynolds attorney general. In 1914, President Wilson nominated and Senate confirmed McReynolds to the U.S. Supreme Court. McReynolds is a noted member of the Four Horsemen of the Supreme Court. *See:* Barry Cushman, The Secret Lives of the Four Horsemen, 83 Va. L. Rev. 559 (1997); James E. Bond, I Dissent: The Legacy of Chief Justice James Clark McReynolds (George Mason Univ. Press, 1992).

Miller **Samuel Freeman Miller** (1816-1890) U.S. Supreme Court Justice. Miller first trained as a medical doctor and, later in life, became an attorney, having been admitted to the bar in 1847. Born in Kentucky, Miller moved to Iowa in 1850 after disagreements with slavery advocates. As a Justice, Miller was remembered for his strong sense of nationalism during the Civil War. *See, e.g., Ex parte Garland* (1867), *Hepburn v. Griswold* (1870), and *Wabash v. Illinois* (1886). *See:* Charles Fairman, Mr. Justice Miller and the Supreme Court, 1862-1890 (Harv. Univ. Press, 1939).

Minton **Sherman Minton** (1890-1965) Statesman and U.S. Supreme Court Justice. Minton graduated from Indiana University before taking his law degree from Yale. After his return from military service in World War I, Minton worked privately until his election to the U.S. Senate in 1934. In 1941, when Minton failed to win re-election, President Franklin D. Roosevelt nominated him to the Seventh Circuit. In 1949, President Truman nominated Minton to fill Rutledge's seat on the high court, where he would serve until 1956. *See:* Linda C. Gugin, Sherman Minton: Restraint against a Tide of Judicial Activism, 62 Vand. L. Rev. 757 (2009); Harry L. Wallace, Mr. Justice Minton, Hoosier Justice on the Supreme Court, 34 Ind. L.J. 145 (1959).

Moody **William H. Moody** (1853-1917) Statesman and U.S. Supreme Court Justice. Moody, a graduate of Harvard University, attended Harvard Law School for a short period before reading for the bar. Moody started early in politics, and in 1895 was elected to the U.S. House of Representatives. He later served as the Secretary of the Navy and then as the Attorney General. President Theodore Roosevelt nominated Moody to the U.S. Supreme Court in 1906, where he wrote the opinion in *Louisville & Nashville Railroad Co. v. Mottley*, 211 U.S. 149 (1908), which articulated the well-pleaded complaint rule. *See:* Theodore Roosevelt and the Appointment of Mr. Justice Moody, 18 Vand. L. Rev. 545 (1965).

Moore **Alfred Moore** (1755-1810) U.S. Supreme Court Justice. After reading law under his father, Moore served as an officer in the Continental Army and then practiced law in North Carolina. He was that state's attorney general from 1782 to 1791. Following a short period on the North Carolina Superior Court, Moore was nominated to the U.S. Supreme Court by

President Adams in 1799 and was confirmed that same year. In five years on the high court, Moore authored one opinion. He resigned his seat in 1804. *See:* Junius Davis, Alfred Moore and James Iredell, Revolutionary Patriots (N.C. Socy. of the Sons of the Revolution, 1899).

Murphy **Frank Murphy** (1890–1949) U.S. Supreme Court Justice. Having earned his degree from the University of Michigan Law School, Murphy set up a private practice in Detroit, eventually working his way into politics. Elected governor of Michigan in 1936, Murphy served for two years before being appointed as Attorney General of the United States by President Franklin D. Roosevelt. When Justice Butler vacated his seat, President Roosevelt seized the opportunity to nominate Murphy for the high court in 1940. *See:* J. Woodford Howard, Mr. Justice Murphy; A Political Biography (Princeton Univ. Press, 1968).

Nelson **Samuel Nelson** (1792–1873) U.S. Supreme Court Justice. A New York native, Nelson attended school in Vermont, then returned home and sat for the bar in 1817. After successfully running a private practice, Nelson sat on the Sixth Circuit, where he was promoted to associate justice of the New York Supreme Court, and eventually was made Chief Justice in 1837. President Tyler nominated Nelson to the Supreme Court of the United States in 1845, where he was noted for his appreciation of the technical aspects of law. See *Dred Scott v. Sandford*, 60 U.S. (19 How.) 393 (1857). *See:* Biographical Sketch of Justice Samuel Nelson, 1 Cent. L.J. 2 (1874); Edwin Countryman, Samuel Nelson, 19 Green Bag 329 (1907).

O'Connor **Sandra Day O'Connor** (b. 1930) U.S. Supreme Court Justice. Having graduated from Stanford Law School, O'Connor found herself snubbed by California private practice firms for being female. After opening a private practice in Arizona, O'Connor was named assistant attorney general of that state in 1965. Four years later, O'Connor was named to the state Senate, where she served until 1975, when she was elected judge. Three years subsequent to her 1979 appointment to the Arizona Court of Appeals, O'Connor was nominated to the U.S. Supreme Court by President Reagan. The U.S. Senate confirmed her that same year, making her the first woman on the high court. Though a consistent advocate for individual rights and the rights of women, her careful analysis of case arguments and preference for law over ideology gave her great influence as the "swing justice," whose vote could make a majority opinion. *See:* Sandra Day O'Connor, The Majesty of the Law: Reflections of a Supreme Court Justice (Random House, 2004); Joan Biskupic, Sandra Day O'Connor: How the First Woman on the Supreme Court Became Its Most Influential Justice (Harper, 2006).

Paterson **William Paterson** (1745–1806) Statesman and U.S. Supreme Court Justice. After immigrating from Northern Ireland, Paterson attended the College of New Jersey (later Princeton University) before reading for the law under Richard Stockton and joining the bar in 1768. Paterson served in New Jersey's provincial Congress and, from 1776 to 1783, was New Jersey's attorney general. He represented New Jersey in the Constitutional Convention. In 1787, he entered the Senate, and he was later the second governor of New Jersey. Nominated twice to the Supreme Court by President Washington, Paterson was confirmed to the bench in 1793. Paterson presided over the Whisky Rebellion treason trials. *See:* John E. O'Connor, William Paterson: Lawyer and Statesman, 1745–1806 (1979); Daniel A. Degnan, Justice William Paterson: Founder, 16 Seton Hall L. Rev. 313 (1986); Charles F. Hickox III and Andrew C. Laviano, William Paterson, J. Sup. Ct. Hist. (1992) at 53.

Peckham **Rufus Wheeler Peckham** (1838–1909) U.S. Supreme Court Justice. A native of New York, Peckham worked in private practice after reading for the bar in 1859. In 1883, Peckham was nominated to the New York Supreme Court, with help from then Governor Cleveland, and a year later was elected to the Court of Appeals. Peckham stayed on that court until 1895, when President Cleveland nominated Peckham to fill the U.S. Supreme Court seat vacated by Howell Jackson. *See:* A. Oakley Hall, The New Supreme Court Justice, 8 Green Bag 1 (1896).

Pitney **Mahlon Pitney** (1858–1924) Statesman and U.S. Supreme Court Justice. A graduate of the College of New Jersey (later Princeton University), Pitney read for the New Jersey Bar in 1882. Pitney entered politics in 1894 when he was elected to the U.S. House of Representatives and, in 1898, was elected to the U.S. Senate. Pitney then served on the New Jersey Supreme Court before President Taft nominated him to the U.S. Supreme Court in 1912. *See:* David Maurice Levitan, Mahlon Pitney, Labor Judge, 40 Va. L. Rev. 733 (1954).

Powell **Lewis F. Powell, Jr.** (1907–1998) U.S. Supreme Court Justice. Powell took two degrees from Washington and Lee University before seeking a LL.M. from Harvard Law School in 1932. Afterwards, Powell returned to Virginia to set up private practice, and in 1964 was elected president of the American Bar Association. In 1971, President Nixon nominated Powell to fill Justice Black's seat on the high court, where he authored the opinion in *First National Bank of Boston v. Bellotti*, 435 U.S. 765 (1978), overruling Massachusetts's restrictions on corporate campaign contributions. *See:* John C. Jeffries, Jr., Justice Lewis F. Powell, Jr. (C. Scribner, 1994); Paul W. Kahn, The Court, the Community and the Judicial Balance: The Jurisprudence of Justice Powell, 97 Yale L.J. 1 (1987).

Reed **Stanley Forman Reed** (1884–1980) U.S. Supreme Court Justice. Reed studied law at both Virginia and Columbia, but elected not to take a law degree, instead studying in France at the Sorbonne. Upon his return to the United States, and admission to the bar in 1910, Reed practiced privately and held local public office until named solicitor general in 1935. There he further gained favor with President Franklin D. Roosevelt, leading to his nomination to the high court in 1938. Reed was a notable hold-out in *Brown v. Board of Education of Topeka*, 347 U.S. 483 (1954), eventually giving in to the majority for a unanimous decision. *See*: John D. Fassett, The New Deal Justice: The Life of Stanley Reed of Kentucky (Vantage, 1994).

Rehnquist **William Rehnquist** (1924–2005) Sixteenth Chief Justice of the United States. After graduation from Stanford Law School in 1952, Rehnquist clerked for Justice Jackson at the U.S. Supreme Court and later moved to Phoenix, Arizona, where he practiced privately. In 1969, Rehnquist went to work for President Nixon as an assistant attorney general in the Office of Legal Counsel, where he stayed until President Nixon nominated him to the high court in 1971. His first fifteen years were marked by often vitriolic dissents in support of conservative revision of the precedents of the 1960's, though his own use of precedent was not always straightforward. In 1986, President Regan nominated him to serve as Chief Justice. In this role, his opinions were somewhat more moderate, though his concurrence in support of *Bush v. Gore*, 531 U.S. 98 (2000), which overturned the Florida Supreme Court's review of the presidential election in that state, remains highly controversial. Rehnquist notably presided over the impeachment trial of President Clinton. *See*: William H. Rehnquist, The Supreme Court, How It Was; How It Is (William Morrow, 1987); Sue Davis, Justice Rehnquist and the Constitution (Princeton Univ. Press, 1989); Martin H. Belsky, ed., The Rehnquist Court: A Retrospective (Oxford Univ. Press, 2002).

Roberts **John G. Roberts** (b. 1955) Seventeenth Chief Justice of the United States. Roberts, a native of Indiana, took his undergraduate degree from Harvard College before taking his law degree from Harvard, clerking for Justice Rehnquist, and going to work for the U.S. Attorney General's office. President George H. W. Bush named Roberts to the U.S. Court of Appeals for the District of Columbia in 1992, but as President Bush's term expired Roberts would have to wait for a second nomination in 2001, and eventually a third in 2003 by President George W. Bush, before being appointed. During this time, Roberts built a national reputation as an appellate advocate, frequently appearing and winning important cases before the U.S. Supreme Court. President George W. Bush nominated Roberts to fill Chief Justice Rehnquist's seat in 2005. Roberts is considered a conservative who favors executive power, limited regulation, and corporate interests over the expansion of individual rights.

Roberts **Owen Roberts** (1875–1955) U.S. Supreme Court Justice. After graduating from the University of Pennsylvania Law School in 1898, Roberts worked in both the public and private arenas until 1924, when President Coolidge appointed him special U.S. attorney. President Hoover nominated Roberts to the high court in 1930, where Roberts notably ruled against President Franklin D. Roosevelt in *Korematsu v. United States*, 323 U.S. 214 (1944), holding Japanese internment unethical. *See*: Merlo J. Pusey, Justice Roberts's 1937 Turnaround, 1983 Supreme Court Historical Society Yearbook 102 (Sup. Ct. Hist. Socy., 1983); Barry Cushman, Rethinking the New Deal Court: The Structure of a Constitutional Revolution (Oxford Univ. Press, 1998).

Rutledge **John Rutledge** (1739–1800) Statesman and second Chief Justice of the United States. A South Carolina native, John Rutledge practiced law in Charleston after completing legal studies at the Middle Temple. Rutledge was elected governor of South Carolina in 1779. A member of the Continental Congresses and the Constitutional Convention, Rutledge was nominated by President George Washington to serve on the first Supreme Court in 1789. Roberts resigned for ill health and returned home, where he was made chief justice of the South Carolina Court of Common Pleas. Rutledge was reappointed to the U.S. Supreme Court as Chief Justice of the United States in 1795, though he was not confirmed by the Senate and served only six months by recess appointment. *See*: Richard Barry, Mr. Rutledge of South Carolina (1942) (Ayer, 1995). Richard Hayes Barry, Mr. Rutledge of South Carolina (Duell, Sloan and Pearce, 1942).

Rutledge **Wiley Rutledge** (1894–1949) U.S. Supreme Court Justice. A native of Kentucky, Wiley Blount Rutledge was a graduate of the University of Colorado Law School, where he would later join the faculty. An accomplished academic, Rutledge served as dean at both Washington University in St. Louis and the State University of Iowa. Rutledge was named to the high court by President Franklin D. Roosevelt in 1943, where Rutledge was considered a reliable vote on the liberal wing of the Court. *See*: Fowler Vincent Harper, Justice Rutledge and the Bright Constellation (Bobbs–Merrill, 1965); Louis H. Pollak, W.B.R.: Some Reflections, 71 Yale L.J. 1451 (1962).

Sanford **Edward Terry Sanford** (1865–1930) U.S. Supreme Court Justice. Sanford took his A.B. and Ph.B from the University of Tennessee before taking a second A.B. from Harvard University and eventually his LL.B. from Harvard Law School in 1889. President Theodore Roosevelt nominated Sanford in 1908 to sit on the U.S. district court in Tennessee, where he served until President Harding nominated him to the high court in 1922. *See*: Stanley A. Cook, Path to the High Bench: The Pre–Supreme Court Career of Justice Edward Terry Sanford (Ph.D. diss., Univ. of Tenn., 1977); James A. Fowler, Mr. Justice Edward Terry Sanford, 17 A.B.A. J. 229 (1931).

Scalia **Antonin Scalia** (b. 1936) U.S. Supreme Court Justice. A New Jersey native, Scalia took his undergraduate degree from Georgetown University before attending Harvard Law School. Scalia worked in the private realm before teaching law at the University of Virginia, after which he worked in various roles during the Nixon and Ford administrations, returning to teaching during the Carter administration. In 1982, President Ronald Reagan nominated him to the Washington, D.C., Circuit, where he served until 1986, when President Reagan nominated him to the high court. An active and witty inquisitor on the bench, he is particularly known for strict construction of the Constitution and for rule–oriented standards rather than balancing tests. Among his many controversial positions on the Supreme Court is his insistence that the U.S. Constitution be interpreted only according to American law and precedent. *See:* Antonin Scalia, A Matter of Interpretation: Federal Courts and the Law (Princeton Univ. Press, 1998); Joan Biskupic, American Original: The Life and Constitution of Supreme Court Justice Antonin Scalia (Farrar, Straus and Giroux, 2010).

Shiras **George Shiras, Jr.** (1832–1924) U.S. Supreme Court Justice. Having taken his undergraduate degree from Yale, Shiras studied law at Yale briefly before returning to his home in Pittsburg. Admitted to the bar in 1855, Shiras built a phenomenally successful practice before being nominated to the Supreme Court by President Harrison in 1892. Shiras notably stood with the majority in *Plessy v. Ferguson*, 163 U.S. 537 (1896), upholding the separate but equal doctrine. *See:* Winfield Shiras, Justice George Shiras, Jr. of Pittsburgh, Associate justice of the United States Supreme Court, 1892–1903; A Chronicle of His Family, Life and Times (Univ. of Pitts. Press, 1953).

Sotomayor **Sonia Maria Sotomayor** (b. 1954) U.S. Supreme Court Justice. A native of New York City, Sotomayor took her law degree from Yale before going to work as an assistant district attorney for New York County. Sotomayor would then practice privately before being nominated to the U.S. District Court for the Southern District of New York by President George H. W. Bush in 1991, and then to the Second Circuit by President Bill Clinton in 1997. President Barack Obama nominated her to fill Justice Souter's seat in 2009; despite considerable partisan controversy, the Senate ratified her nomination with bipartisan support.

Souter **David Hackett Souter** (b. 1939) U.S. Supreme Court Justice. Souter, a graduate of both Harvard College in 1961 and Harvard Law School in 1966, worked briefly in private practice before taking a role as an assistant attorney general in New Hampshire in 1968. In 1978, Souter was named to the Superior Court of New Hampshire, and then in 1983 was appointed to the New Hampshire Supreme Court. President George H. W. Bush nominated Souter to the high court in 1990 to fill Justice Brennan's seat; Souter resigned in 2009. Though initially perceived as a conservative, he became a centrist, dissenting in *Bush v. Gore*, 531 U.S. 98 (2000), and writing in *Planned Parenthood v. Casey*, 505 U.S. 884 (1992), that *Roe v. Wade*, 410 U.S. 113 (1973), should not be overturned. *See:* Tinsley E. Yarbrough, David Hackett Souter: Traditional Republican on The Rehnquist Court (Oxford Univ. Press, 2005); Margaret Carlson, An 18th Century Man, Time, Aug. 6, 1990 at 19.

Stevens **John Paul Stevens** (b. 1920) U.S. Supreme Court Justice. Stevens took his law degree from the Northwestern University School of Law in 1947, before clerking on the U.S. Supreme Court under Justice Rutledge from 1947 to 1948. After a successful private career, and a brief interlude as an associate counsel in Washington, D.C., Stevens was appointed by President Nixon to the Seventh Circuit in 1970. Five years later, President Ford nominated Stevens to the high court, where Stevens was generally considered to vote consistently in favor of the claims of individuals against corporations and government. *See:* William D. Popkin, A Common Law Lawyer on the Supreme Court: The Opinions of Justice Stevens, 1989 Duke L.J. 1087 (1989); Bill Barnhart and Gene Schlickman, John Paul Stevens: An Independent Life (N. Ill. Univ. Press, 2010).

Stewart **Potter Stewart** (1915–1985) U.S. Supreme Court Justice. Stewart graduated from both Yale University and Yale Law School before serving in World War II. On his return, Stewart moved to Ohio, where he established a private practice. President Eisenhower appointed Stewart to the U.S. Court of Appeals in 1954, and then to the U.S. Supreme Court in 1958. Though known for a bright analytic mind, he is best remembered for observing in *Jacobellis v. Ohio*, 378 U.S. 184 (1964), that pornography is difficult to define but, "I know it when I see it." *See:* Potter Stewart, The Road to *Mapp v. Ohio* and beyond: The Origins, Development and Future of the Exclusionary Rule in Search-and-Seizure Cases, 83 Colum. L. Rev. 1365 (1983); Robert S. Marsel, The Constitutional Jurisprudence of Justice Potter Stewart: Reflections on a Life of Public Service, 55 Tenn. L. Rev. 1 (1987).

Stone **Harlan Fiske Stone** (1872–1946) Twelfth Chief Justice of the United States. Stone took an undergraduate degree from Amherst College before studying at Columbia Law School. On graduation, he turned to private practice briefly before adopting a joint role as practitioner and professor at Columbia Law School. Stone would go on to become dean of Columbia Law School before becoming U.S Attorney General in 1924. He was nominated to the high court by President Coolidge in 1925. A consistent advocate for individual rights, his opinion in *United States v. Carolene Products Co.*, 304 U.S. 144 (1938), set the stage for modern constitutional analysis. In 1941, when Hughes left the high court, President Franklin D. Roosevelt elevated Stone to Chief Justice. *See:* Harlan Fiske Stone, Law and its Administration (1915); Alpheus T. Mason, Harlan Fiske Stone: Pillar of the Law (Archon Books, 1956).

Story **Joseph Story** (1779–1845) U.S. Supreme Court Justice. Born in Massachusetts, Story graduated from Harvard Law School in 1798. After a period of private practice and time in the Massachusetts state legislature, he was nominated to the U.S. Supreme Court by President Madison. Confirmed at the age of thirty-two, he was the architect of much of the early national law the Court established. While on the bench, he became the first Dane Professor of Law at Harvard Law School, teaching each year at the law school while simultaneously serving as Justice. He wrote many of the essential books of U.S. law, including his Commentaries on the Constitution, a classic text. Story's best-known opinion is likely *Martin v. Hunter's Lessee*, 14 U.S. 304 (1816). *See:* R. Kent Newmyer, Supreme Court Justice Joseph Story: Statesman of the Old Republic (Univ. of N.C. Press, 1985); William W. Story, ed., Life and Letters of Joseph Story (Books for Libraries Press, 1971) (1851).

Strong **William Strong** (1808–1895) U.S. Supreme Court Justice. After graduating from Yale College, Strong taught in Connecticut and New Jersey; he attended Yale Law School briefly. Admitted to the Pennsylvania Bar in 1832, Strong moved to Reading, where he practiced privately until being elected to the U.S. House of Representatives in 1846; he was re-elected in 1848, but decided against a third term. Strong was elected to the Pennsylvania Supreme Court, serving there for eleven years before returning to private practice. Nominated by President Ulysses S. Grant, Strong was confirmed to the Supreme Court in 1870, where he immediately began work on post–Civil War law. *See, e.g., The Legal Tender Cases*, 75 U.S. 603 (1870). *See:* Retirement of William J. Strong, 15 Am. L. Rev. 130 (1881); William Strong, The Needs of the Supreme Court, 132 N. Am. Rev. 437 (1881).

Sutherland **George Sutherland** (1862–1942) Statesman and U.S. Supreme Court Justice. Sutherland emigrated from England at the age of two with his family. After graduating from Brigham Young University, Sutherland went on to study law at the University of Michigan before returning to Utah, where he practiced privately. In 1896, Utah was admitted to the Union, and Sutherland sought public office. Following two terms in the U.S. Senate, Sutherland was defeated in a third-term bid. As president of the ABA, he set up practice in Washington, D.C., until President Harding nominated him to fill Justice Clarke's seat on the high court in 1922. Sutherland is a noted member of the Four Horsemen of the Supreme Court. *See:* Barry Cushman, The Secret Lives of the Four Horsemen, 83 Va. L. Rev. 559 (1997).

Swayne **Noah Haynes Swayne** (1804–1884) U.S. Supreme Court Justice. Swayne, born in Virginia, moved to Ohio in 1824 to practice law. For the next seven years, Swayne held various political offices, until President Jackson appointed him U.S. attorney for Ohio. Known for his antislavery beliefs, Swayne was nominated to the high court by President Lincoln in 1862. Swayne is most noted for his political support of President Lincoln. *See, e.g., Prize Cases*, 67 U.S. 635 (1863). *See:* William Gillette, Justices of the United States Supreme Court 1789-1969, vol. 2 (1969), pp. 989–999; C. Peter Magrath, Morrision R. Waite: The Triumph of Character (Macmillan, 1963).

Taft **William Howard Taft** (1857–1930) President and tenth Chief Justice of the United States. Taft studied at Yale University before taking his degree from Cincinnati Law School in 1880. After graduation, Taft immediately became active in politics, serving on the Ohio Supreme Court before sitting on the Sixth Circuit. When President Theodore Roosevelt decided not to run for re-election, Taft mounted a successful campaign for the presidency, easily besting his opponent, William Jennings Bryan. Taft would return to the judiciary after his presidency, with President Harding's nomination to the high court as Chief Justice, in 1921. He was responsible for the creation of the magnificent architecture of a new building for the Supreme Court when it moved from the Capitol Building, and he convinced Congress to alter the high court's jurisdiction to a nearly discretionary basis. *See:* Henry F. Pringle, The Life and Times of William Howard Taft (Easton Press, 1939); Alpheus Thomas Mason, William Howard Taft, Chief Justice (Univ. Press of Am., 1983) (1965).

Taney **Roger B. Taney** (1777–1864) Statesman and fifth Chief Justice of the United States. A graduate of Dickinson College, Taney pursued politics in his home state of Maryland until 1931, when he was appointed Attorney General by President Andrew Jackson. Nominated and confirmed as Chief Justice of the Supreme Court in 1836, he maintained this position until 1864. Taney authored the majority opinion in the infamous case *Dred Scott v. Sandford*, 60 U.S. (19 How.) 393 (1857), which denied a slave freedom by entering a state that did not recognize slavery under state law and also deprived the descendants of African slaves protection under the U.S. Constitution. *See:* R. Kent Newmyer, The Supreme Court Under Marshall and Taney (Harlan Davidson, 1986) (1968); Cal Brent Swisher, Roger B. Taney (Macmillan Company, 1935).

Thomas **Clarence Thomas** (b. 1948) U.S. Supreme Court Justice. A graduate of Yale Law School, Thomas worked as an assistant attorney general in Missouri before entering private practice. In 1979, Thomas began a long course of public service appointments, until President George H. W. Bush nominated him to the U.S. Court of Appeals for the District of Columbia in 1990. President Bush nominated Thomas to the high court in 1991 to replace Justice Marshall. Following a famously contentious Senate hearing, Justice Thomas was confirmed and became the second African American to sit on the U.S. Supreme Court. Notably, Thomas joined the dissent in *Planned Parenthood v. Casey*, 505 U.S. 884 (1992), holding *Roe v. Wade*, 410 U.S. 113 (1973), had been wrongly decided. Justice Thomas is noted for having remained silent in the high court for five years, after having questioned Assistant Deputy Attorney General of South Carolina Donald J. Zelenka about the *Gregory* standard in a death penalty case in 2006. However enigmatic, he is considered a conservative, often favoring corporate, state, police, and executive interests over claims based on individual rights. *See:* Clarence Thomas, My Grandfather's Son: A Memoir (Harper, 2007); Henry Mark Holzer, The Supreme Court Opinions of Clarence Thomas, 1991–2006: A Conservative's Perspective (McFarland, 2010).

Thompson **Smith Thompson** (1768–1843) Statesman and U.S. Supreme Court Justice. Born in Amenia, New York, Thompson studied at Princeton University before starting his three-year legal apprenticeship. After a short stint in the New York State Assembly, Thompson was appointed to the state supreme court in 1802, before being appointed Secretary of the Navy in 1818. Thompson was nominated to the U.S. Supreme Court by President Monroe in 1823. Notably, Thompson wrote a dissent in *Cherokee Nation v. Georgia*, 30 U.S. 1 (1831) in which he argued for the independent sovereignty of the Cherokee Nation. *See:* Donald M. Roper, Mr. Justice Thompson and the Constitution (Garland, 1987) (1963).

Todd  **Thomas Todd** (1765–1826) U.S. Supreme Court Justice. Born and educated in Virginia, Todd served briefly in the Continental Army before attending Liberty Hall Academy (later known as Washington and Lee University), taking his degree in 1783. Todd served as clerk to the Constitutional Conventions in which Kentucky sought entry into the United States. In 1789, Todd became the chief clerk to the newly founded Kentucky Court of Appeals, being appointed justice, then chief justice, of the Kentucky Supreme Court. Todd was nominated to the U.S. Supreme Court in 1807 by President Jefferson; during his tenure on the bench, he drafted few opinions. His most notable opinion, *Watts v. Lindsey's Heirs*, 20 U.S. (7 Wheat.) 158 (1822), related to a land dispute in settled American territory. *See:* Edward C. O'Rear, Justice Thomas Todd, 38 Ky. State Hist. Socy. Reg. 112 (1940); Woodford L. Gardner, Kentucky Justices on the U.S. Supreme Court, 70 Reg. of Ky. Historical Socy. 121 (1972); Frank H. Easterbrook, The Most Insignificant Justice Further Evidence, 50 U. Chi. L. Rev. 481 (1983).

Trimble  **Robert Trimble** (1776–1828) U.S. Supreme Court Justice. After reading for and taking his law license in 1800, Trimble went in to private practice in Paris, Kentucky. Two years later, he sat in the Kentucky House of Representatives and, from 1807 to 1810, served in various roles on the Kentucky Court of Appeals. President Madison appointed Trimble to the federal judiciary in 1817, and in 1826, President Adams nominated him to the U.S. Supreme Court. This was the first elevation of a sitting federal judge to the Supreme Court. *See:* Alan N. Schneider, Robert Trimble: A Kentucky Justice on the Supreme Court, 12 Ky. St. B.J. 21 (1947).

Van Devanter  **Willis Van Devanter** (1859–1941) U.S. Supreme Court Justice. Van Devanter, a graduate of Cincinnati Law School, moved to Wyoming, where he quickly established a powerful and successful private law practice. After a short appointment to a territorial court in Wyoming, and a successful run for the state supreme court, Van Devanter was nominated to the Eighth Circuit in 1903 by President Theodore Roosevelt. In 1910, he was nominated by President Taft to the U.S. Supreme Court. Van Devanter is a noted member of the Four Horsemen of the Supreme Court. *See:* Barry Cushman, The Secret Lives of the Four Horsemen, 83 Va. L. Rev. 559 (1997); M. Paul Holsinger, The Appointment of Supreme Court Justice Van Devanter: A Study of Political Preferment, 12 Am. J. Legal Hist. 324 (1968).

Vinson  **Fred M. Vinson** (1890–1953) Thirteenth Chief Justice of the United States. Vinson, a native of Kentucky, took his law degree from Centre College before admission to the bar in 1911. After returning from World War I, Vinson took an active interest in politics, which resulted in his election to the U.S. House of Representatives. President Franklin D. Roosevelt nominated Vinson to the court of appeals in 1937, where he would serve until his resignation in 1943, when he took over the Office of Economic Stabilization. Vinson then served as Secretary of the Treasury under President

Truman, before being nominated to the high court in 1946. *See:* James Bolner, Mr. Chief Justice Vinson: His Politics and His Constitutional Law (Ph.D. diss., Univ. of Va., 1962); John Paul Frank, Fred Vinson and the Chief Justiceship, 21 U. Chi. L. Rev. 212 (1954).

Waite  **Morrison R. Waite** (1816–1888) Seventh Chief Justice of the United States. The son of a Connecticut supreme court justice, Waite graduated from Yale College and was admitted to the bar in Ohio in 1837. Having experienced some success in private practice and state politics, Waite represented the U.S. in the Alabama Tribunal. After presiding over the Ohio Constitutional Convention in 1874, President Ulysses S. Grant nominated Waite as the seventh Chief Justice. The Senate approved Waite's appointment as the Chief Justice in 1874 after much political wrangling. Waite's tenure on the high court is best remembered as a productive one, having decided roughly 3,470 cases, particularly affecting Reconstruction and the evolving law of American industrialization. *See:* C. Peter Magrath, Morrison R. Waite: The Triumph of Character (Macmillan, 1963).

Warren  **Earl Warren** (1891–1974) Statesman and fourteenth Chief Justice of the United States. Warren took both his undergraduate and law degree from the University of California at Berkeley before serving in World War I. On returning, he moved back to the Bay Area and worked as a deputy city attorney before successfully running for California attorney general in 1938. Not long after, in 1942, Warren would be elected governor of California and serve three successive terms. President Eisenhower nominated Warren to the high court in 1953, and he was confirmed by the Senate in 1954. He was considered an unusually influential Chief Justice, who led the court in the expansion of individual rights, perhaps best remembered for his role in Brown v. Board of Education, 347 U.S. 483 (1954). *See:* G. Edward White, Earl Warren: A Public Life (Oxford Univ. Press, 1982); Earl Warren, The Memoirs of Earl Warren (Doubleday, 1977).

Washington  **Bushrod Washington** (1762–1829) U.S. Supreme Court Justice. A nephew of President George Washington, Bushrod Washington served in the Continental Army. After graduation from the College of William & Mary, Washington studied law and entered private practice. Washington received a recess appointment to the Supreme Court in 1789 by President Adams and was confirmed to his seat later that year. Washington's tenure in the Supreme Court was overshadowed by Chief Justice Marshall, with whom Washington sided in all but three cases during thirty years on the bench. *See:* David L. Annis, Mr. Bushrod Washington (Ph.D. diss., Univ. of Notre Dame, 1974); Lawrence B. Custer, Bushrod Washington and John Marshall: A Preliminary Inquiry, 4 Am. J. Legal Hist. 34 (1960).

Wayne  **James Moore Wayne** (1790–1867) Statesman and U.S. Supreme Court Justice. Wayne, born to British Loyalists, received his formal education at the College of New Jersey, now known as Princeton University. After joining the bar, Wayne held various roles in the Georgia state government before being elected to the United States Congress. A supporter of President Jackson, Wayne was nominated by him to the U.S. Supreme Court in 1835, where Wayne served until his death. Wayne was decidedly pro-slavery, concurring to that effect in *Prigg v. Pennsylvania*, 41 U.S. 539 (1842), and *Dred Scott v. Sandford*, 60 U.S. (19 How.) 393 (1857). *See*: Alexander A. Lawrence, James Moore Wayne: Southern Unionist, 14 Fordham Urb. L.J. 42 (1943).

White   **Byron R. White** (1917–2002) U.S. Supreme Court Justice. White, the first high court Justice from Colorado, graduated from the University of Colorado at Boulder before serving in World War II and taking his law degree from Yale in 1946. After returning to Colorado to practice, White was appointed deputy attorney general under Robert Kennedy in 1960, where he served until he was nominated to fill Justice Whittaker's seat on the high court in 1962 by President Kennedy. *See*: Dennis Hutchinson, The Man Who Once Was Whizzer White: A Portrait of Justice Byron R. White (Free Press, 1998); Byron R. White, Some Current Debates, 73 Judicature 155 (1989).

White   **Edward Douglass White** (1845–1921) Statesman and ninth Chief Justice of the United States. After the Civil War, White returned to his native Louisiana, where he served briefly on the state supreme court and spent time in private practice. Elected to the U.S. Senate in 1891, White served until his nomination by President Cleveland in 1894 to the Supreme Court of the United States, where in 1910 President Taft would elevate him to Chief Justice. This marked the first time a president would successfully elevate a Justice to Chief Justice. *See*: Robert Baker Highsaw, Edward Douglass White: Defender of the Conservative Faith (La. St. Univ. Press, 1981).

Whittaker   **Charles E. Whittaker** (1901–1973) U.S. Supreme Court Justice. Whittaker took his law degree from the Kansas City School of Law (now UMKC) in 1924, and worked in private practice before being appointed to the U.S. District Court in the Western District of Missouri by President Eisenhower in 1954. Just two years later, President Eisenhower appointed Whittaker to the court of appeals and then, in 1957, to the U.S. Supreme Court, marking the first time a Justice served on all three levels of the Federal Judiciary. *See*: Daniel M. Berman, Mr. Justice Whittaker: A Preliminary Appraisal, 24 Mo. L. Rev. 1 (1959); Barbara B. Christensen, Mister Justice Whittaker: The Man on the Right, 19 Santa Clara L. Rev. 1039 (1979); William H. Rehnquist, The Making of a Supreme Court Justice, 29 Harv. L. Rev. 7 (1959).

Wilson   **James Wilson** (1742–1798) Statesman and U.S. Supreme Court Justice. Born in Scotland, Wilson emigrated to the American colonies in 1765. Wilson was a member of the Continental Congress, a signer of the Declaration of Independence, and advocate general for France in America. Wilson practiced law in Philadelphia and lectured at the College of Philadelphia (later incorporated into the University of Pennsylvania). Nominated by President Washington to the Supreme Court in 1789, he served until his death in 1798. Wilson authored an opinion in *Chisholm v. Georgia*, 2 U.S. (2 Dall.) 419 (1793), which abrogated states' sovereign immunity in federal cases. *See*: John Marshall Harlan, James Wilson and the Formation of the Constitution, 34 Am. L. Rev. 481 (1900); Page Smith, James Wilson, Founding Father, 1742–1798 (Greenwood Press, 1973) (1956).

Woodbury   **Levi Woodbury** (1789–1851) Statesman and U.S. Supreme Court Justice. Woodbury took his degree from Dartmouth College before attending the Litchfield School of Law in Connecticut. Shortly after being admitted to the bar in 1817, Woodbury was appointed to the New Hampshire supreme court. Six years later, he was elected governor of New Hampshire. In 1825, Woodbury was elected a U.S. senator; he served in the Senate until 1831. James Polk nominated, and the Senate confirmed, Woodbury to the Supreme Court of the United States in 1846. *See*: William D. Bader, Henry J. Abraham, and James B. Staab, The Jurisprudence of Levi Woodbury, 28 Vt. L. Rev. 261 (1994).

Woods   **William Burnham Woods** (1824–1887) U.S. Supreme Court Justice. Born in Ohio, Woods studied at Yale Law School before earning bar admission. After his military service during the Civil War, Woods settled in Alabama where he took to farming and private practice. In 1869, President Grant appointed Woods to the Fifth Circuit, where he would hear the *Slaughter-House Cases*, 1 Woods 21 (C.C.D. La. 1870). President Hayes nominated Woods to the U.S. Supreme Court in late 1880, and Senate confirmed him shortly thereafter in 1881. *See*: Thomas E. Baynes, A Search for Justice Woods: Yankee from Georgia, Supreme Court Historical Society Yearbook, 1978 (Sup. Ct. Hist. Socy., 1978) at 31.